Savings Certificate

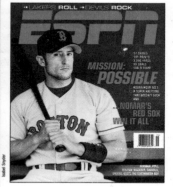

The 2001

ESPn

Information Please®

Sports Almanac

With Year in Review Commentary from
ESPN anchors and analysts:

John Anderson
on the Top 20 Moments

Chris Berman
on Pro Football

Al Bernstein
on Boxing

Jay Bilas
on Women's College Basketball

Ric Bucher
on Pro Basketball

John Clayton
on Pro Football

Linda Cohn
on the Top 20 Personalities

Lee Corso
on College Football

Steve Cyphers
on College Sports

Rece Davis
on Auto Racing

Jack Edwards
on International Sports
and Soccer

Chris Fowler
on College Basketball
and College Football

Hank Goldberg
on Horse Racing

Steve Levy
on Pro Hockey

Sal Paolantonio
on Tennis

Dan Patrick
on the Top 20 Personalities

Karl Ravech
on Golf and Baseball

Robin Roberts
on Summer Olympics

Dave Ryan
on College Baseball

Stuart Scott
on the Top 20 Moments

Bob Stevens
on Business

Dick Vitale
on College Basketball

YEAR IN REVIEW

BASEBALL

COLLEGE FOOTBALL

PRO FOOTBALL

COLLEGE BASKETBALL

PRO BASKETBALL

HOCKEY

COLLEGE SPORTS

HALLS OF FAME AND AWARDS

WHO'S WHO

The Champions of 2000

Auto Racing

NASCAR Circuit
Daytona 500 . . . . .Dale Jarrett
Winston 500 . . . . .Dale Earnhardt
Coca-Cola 600 . . . . .Matt Kenseth
Pepsi Southern 500 . . . . .Bobby Labonte
Winston Cup Points Title . . . . . .Bobby Labonte, 4645 pts
(through Oct. 22)   Dale Earnhardt, 4444 pts

CART Circuit
Michigan 500 . . . . .Juan Montoya
FedEx Championship . . . . .Gil de Ferran, 153 pts
(through Oct. 15)   Adrian Fernandez, 148 pts

Indy Racing League Circuit
Indianapolis 500 . . . . Juan Montoya
Points Championship . . . . .Buddy Lazier

Formula One Circuit
U.S. Grand Prix . . . . .Michael Schumacher
World Driving Champion .Michael Schumacher, 108 pts

Baseball

World Series .N.Y. Yankees def. N.Y. Mets, 4 games to 1
MVP . . . . .Derek Jeter, Yankees, SS
All-Star Game . . . . .AL 6, NL 3 in Atlanta
MVP . . . . .Derek Jeter, Yankees, SS
College World Series . . . . .LSU 6, Stanford 5
MVP . . . . .Trey Hodges, LSU, P

College Basketball

Men's NCAA Final Four
Championship . . . . .Michigan State 89, Florida 76
MVP . . . . .Mateen Cleaves, Michigan St., G
Women's NCAA Final Four
Championship . . . . .Connecticut 71, Tennessee 52
MVP .Shea Ralph, Connecticut, G

Pro Basketball

NBA Finals .L.A. Lakers def. Indiana Pacers, 4 games to 2
MVP . . . . .Shaquille O'Neal, L.A. Lakers, C
Eastern Final . . . . . .Indiana def. New York, 4 games to 2
Western Final . .Los Angeles def. Portland, 4 games to 3
All-Star Game . . . . .West 137, East 126 in Oakland
MVP .Tim Duncan, West, C & Shaquille O'Neal, West, C

Bowling

Men's Major Championships
Tournament of Champions (1999) . . . . .Jason Couch
PBA National . . . . .Norm Duke
ABC Masters .Mika Koivuniemi
BPAA U.S. Open . . . . .Robert Smith
Women's Major Championships
Sam's Town Invitational (1999) . . . . .Wendy Macpherson
WIBC Queens . . . . .Wendy Macpherson
BPAA U.S. Open . . . . .Tennelle Grijalva
AMF Gold Cup (1999) . . . . .Dana Miller-Mackie

College Football (1999)

National Champions
AP . . . . .Florida State (12-0)
ESPN/USA Today Coaches' . . . . .Florida State (12-0)
Major Bowls
Sugar . . . . .Florida St. 46, Virginia Tech 29
Fiesta .Nebraska 31, Tennessee 21
Rose . . . . .Wisconsin 17, Stanford 9
Orange . . . . .Michigan 35, Alabama 34
Heisman Trophy . . . . .Ron Dayne, Wisconsin, RB

Pro Football (1999)

Super Bowl XXXIV . . . . .St. Louis 23, Tennessee 16
MVP .Kurt Warner, St. Louis, QB

AFC Championship . . . . . .Tennessee 33, Jacksonville 14
NFC Championship . . . . .St. Louis 11, Tampa Bay 6
Pro Bowl . . . . .NFC 51, AFC 31
MVP . . . . .Randy Moss, Minnesota, WR
CFL Grey Cup Final . . . . .Hamilton 32, Calgary 21
MVP . . . . .Danny McManus, Hamilton, QB

Golf

Men's Major Championships
Masters . . . . .Vijay Singh
U.S. Open . . . . .Tiger Woods
British Open . . . . .Tiger Woods
PGA Championship . . . . .Tiger Woods
Seniors Major Championships
The Tradition . . . . .Tom Kite
PGA Seniors . . . . .Doug Tewell
U.S. Senior Open . . . . .Hale Irwin
Senior Players Championship . . . . .Ray Floyd
Women's Major Championships
Nabisco Championship . . . . .Karrie Webb
LPGA Championship . . . . .Juli Inkster
U.S. Women's Open . . . . .Karrie Webb
du Maurier Classic . . . . .Meg Mallon
National Team Competition
Solheim Cup . . . . .Europe 14½, United States 11½
President's Cup . .United States 21½, International 10½

Hockey

Stanley Cup . . . . . .New Jersey def. Dallas, 4 games to 2
MVP .Scott Stevens, New Jersey, D
Eastern Final .New Jersey def. Philadelphia, 4 games to 3
Western Final . . . . . .Dallas def. Colorado, 4 games to 3
All-Star Game . . . . .World 9, North America 4 in Toronto
MVP .Pavel Bure, World, RW
NCAA Div. 1 Final . . .North Dakota 4, Boston College 2
MVP .Lee Goren, North Dakota, F

Horse Racing

Triple Crown Champions
Kentucky Derby . . . .Fusaichi Pegasus (Kent Desormeaux)
Preakness .Red Bullet (Jerry Bailey)
Belmont . . . . .Commendable (Pat Day)
Harness Racing
Hambletonian . . . . .Yankee Paco (Trevor Ritchie)
Little Brown Jug . . . . .Astreos (Chris Christoforou)

Soccer

MLS Cup .Kansas City 1, Chicago 0
MVP . . . . .Tony Meola, Kansas City, G

Tennis

Men's Grand Slam Championships
Australian Open . . . . .Andre Agassi
French Open .Gustavo Kuerten
Wimbledon . . . . .Pete Sampras
U.S. Open . . . . .Marat Safin
Women's Grand Slam Championships
Australian Open . . . . .Lindsay Davenport
French Open . . . . .Mary Pierce
Wimbledon . . . . .Venus Williams
U.S. Open . . . . .Venus Williams

Miscellaneous Champions

Little League World Series . . . . .Maracaibo, Venezuela
Tour de France . . . . .Lance Armstrong (USA)
Iditarod . . . . .Doug Swingley

THE 2001
ESPN INFORMATION PLEASE®
SPORTS
ALMANAC

Gerry Brown
Michael Morrison
EDITORS

Information Please
www.infoplease.com
Part of **LEARNING** NETWORK

HYPERION
ESPN
BOOKS

Editors
Gerry Brown, Michael Morrison
Associate Editor
John Gettings
Reporter
Todd Kline
Production Editor
Elaine Rho
Database/Production Manager
Susan Hyde
Graphics
Sean Dessureau, Barbara Pennucci
Technical Support
Karl DeBisschop

Comments and suggestions from readers are invited. Because of the many letters received, however, it is not possible to respond personally to every correspondent. Nevertheless, all letters are welcome and each will be carefully considered. The **2001 ESPN Information Please Sports Almanac** does not rule on bets or wagers. Address all correspondence to: Sports, Information Please, 20 Park Plaza, Boston, MA 02116.
Email: ipsa@infoplease.com.

CONTENTS   5

CONTENTS

As the new century dawned there were a multitude of burning questions to be answered. Here are a few that were answered this year: Can a former stock boy come out of nowhere to lead his team to a Super Bowl championship? Yes. Can anyone beat Tiger Woods? Apparently not. Can Shaq hit enough free throws to earn a ring? Yes. Will Bobby Knight coach at Indiana forever? Umm, guess not.

Despite all the questions that were answered in 2000, plenty more remain unanswered: Who would win in a race, Maurice Greene or Michael Johnson? Who would win in a fight, Mike Tyson or Andrew Golota? Will the Marty McSorley conviction lead to players spending time in the jail cell instead of the penalty box? And, finally, perhaps the most maddening question of all . . . Who let the dogs out?

The completion of the book you're holding in your hands took the dedication and determination of many folks during the year. Thanks go out to Associate Editor John Gettings. John got married this year and we know that if he brings home even half the effort that he brings to the book, his marriage will thrive.

Thanks to reporter Todd Kline. For the second time in three years we had a Maryland alumnus on staff, and despite that, we managed to put together a superior product. Seriously, Todd was a late season call up and quickly he showed us that he's a money player.

Thanks as always to the Information Please production crew, starting with Production Editor Elaine Rho and Database/Production Manager Susan Hyde. Elaine, out in the hinterlands of New Jersey, and Susan, leaning over our shoulders, helped to keep things on track and looking their best.

We are also indebted to many other persons at Infoplease. Graphics expert Barbara Pennucci departed along this year's journey and Sean Dessureau picked up on her high standards without missing a beat. Paul Evenson, Amanda Kudler and Ricco Siasoco worked their magic on the web and, as usual, the technical staff of Boris Goldowsky and Karl DeBisschop kept the lights on and the computers whirring.

Thanks must also go out to our other cohorts at Information Please: Liz Kubik for her continually strong leadership, Borgna Brunner, Pam Greene, Kate Wrigley, Dan Shafto, Jarrett (briznasti) Tolman and Andrew Nyberg for their individual and unique contributions.

There are many people at ESPN and our publisher Hyperion that deserve a big-old slap on the back. At ESPN, former editor of this book John Hassan helped deliver the goods when we really needed it. Director of Research Jim Jenks and his staff were a pleasure to work with and got us all the great Inside The Numbers stuff that appears at the close of the essays. Thanks also go out to all the ESPN essay contributors. For a full roster check out page one. Extra special thanks go to John Walsh and NFL guru Russell Baxter. Thanks also to Judy Murrone and Tricia Reed.

At Hyperion, Gretchen Young, David Lott and Natalie Kaire all were on the ball as usual. Rick Sommers at Command Web was flexible when we needed him to be.

We also relied on the generous support of other individuals while gathering the many components that fill these pages. Rick Campbell and Gary Johnson at the NCAA, Adam Polgreen at Foulpole.com, Barbara Zidovsky at Nielsen Media Research, Bill Magrath at the *Sports Business Daily*, former editor Mike Meserole, Larry Barber of the MEAC, David Beld at the National Academy of Television Arts and Sciences, and the Captain Daryl Dragon and Toni Tennille. And thanks also to Carolyn McMahon at AP and Paul Michinard at Allsport, for helping us get the perfect picture every time.

And perhaps most importantly, thanks to our families and friends especially Gerry's wife Lisa for keeping us fat and happy with a steady stream of delicious baked goods.

Gerry Brown and Michael Morrison
Boston
October 25, 2000

Major League Cities & Teams

As of Oct. 31, 2000, there were 132 major league teams playing or scheduled to play baseball, basketball, NFL football, hockey and soccer in 50 cities in the United States and Canada. Listed below are the cities and the teams that play there.

Anaheim
AL   Angels
NHL   Mighty Ducks of Anaheim

Atlanta
NL   Braves
NBA   Hawks
NFL   Falcons
NHL   Thrashers

Baltimore
AL   Orioles
NFL   Ravens

Boston
AL   Red Sox
NBA   Celtics
NFL   N.E. Patriots (Foxboro)
NHL   Bruins
MLS   N.E. Revolution (Foxboro)

Buffalo
NFL   Bills (Orchard Park)
NHL   Sabres

Calgary
NHL   Flames

Charlotte
NBA   Hornets
NFL   Carolina Panthers

Chicago
AL   White Sox
NL   Cubs
NBA   Bulls
NFL   Bears
NHL   Blackhawks
MLS   Fire

Cincinnati
NL   Reds
NFL   Bengals

Cleveland
AL   Indians
NBA   Cavaliers
NFL   Browns

Columbus
NHL   Blue Jackets
MLS   Crew

Dallas
AL   Texas Rangers (Arlington)
NBA   Mavericks
NFL   Cowboys (Irving)
NHL   Stars
MLS   Burn

Denver
NL   Colorado Rockies
NBA   Nuggets
NFL   Broncos
NHL   Colorado Avalanche
MLS   Colorado Rapids

Detroit
AL   Tigers
NBA   Pistons (Auburn Hills)
NFL   Lions (Pontiac)
NHL   Red Wings

East Rutherford
NBA   New Jersey Nets
NFL   New York Giants
NFL   New York Jets
NHL   New Jersey Devils
MLS   NY/NJ Metrostars

Edmonton
NHL   Oilers

Green Bay
NFL   Packers

Houston
NL   Astros
NBA   Rockets

Indianapolis
NBA   Indiana Pacers
NFL   Colts

Jacksonville
NFL   Jaguars

Kansas City
AL   Royals
NFL   Chiefs
MLS   Wizards

Los Angeles
NL   Dodgers
NBA   Clippers
NBA   Lakers
NHL   Kings
MLS   Galaxy

Miami
NL   Florida Marlins
NBA   Heat
NFL   Dolphins
NHL   Florida Panthers (Sunrise)
MLS   Fusion (Ft. Lauderdale)

Milwaukee
NL   Brewers
NBA   Bucks

Minneapolis
AL   Minn. Twins
NBA   Minn. Timberwolves
NFL   Minn. Vikings

Montreal
NL   Expos
NHL   Canadiens

Nashville
NFL   Tennessee Titans
NHL   Predators

New Orleans
NFL   Saints

New York
AL   Yankees
NL   Mets (Flushing)
NBA   Knicks
NHL   Rangers
NHL   Islanders (Uniondale)

Oakland
AL   Athletics
NBA   Golden St. Warriors
NFL   Raiders

Orlando
NBA   Magic

Ottawa
NHL   Senators (Kanata)

Philadelphia
NL   Phillies
NBA   76ers
NFL   Eagles
NHL   Flyers

Phoenix
NBA   Suns
NFL   Arizona Cardinals (Tempe)
NL   Arizona Diamondbacks
NHL   Coyotes

Pittsburgh
NL   Pirates
NFL   Steelers
NHL   Penguins

Portland
NBA   Trail Blazers

Raleigh
NHL   Carolina Hurricanes

Sacramento
NBA   Kings

St. Louis
NL   Cardinals
NFL   Rams
NHL   Blues

St. Paul
NHL   Minnesota Wild

Salt Lake City
NBA   Utah Jazz

San Antonio
NBA   Spurs

San Diego
NL   Padres
NFL   Chargers

San Francisco
NL   Giants
NFL   49ers

San Jose
NHL   Sharks
MLS   Earthquakes

Seattle
AL   Mariners
NBA   SuperSonics
NFL   Seahawks

Tampa
NFL   T.B. Buccaneers
NHL   T.B. Lightning
AL   T.B. Devil Rays (St. Petersburg)
MLS   T.B. Mutiny

Toronto
AL   Blue Jays
NBA   Raptors
NHL   Maple Leafs

Vancouver
NBA   Grizzlies
NHL   Canucks

Washington
NBA   Wizards
NFL   Redskins (Raljon, Md.)
NHL   Capitals
MLS   D.C. United

Updates

Team captain **Ken Venturi**, center, **Hal Sutton**, left, and **Kirk Triplett** gather around the Presidents Cup following the U.S. team's win over the International team on Oct. 22, 2000.

AP/Wide World Photos

GOLF

2000 Presidents Cup

The 4th Presidents Cup tournament, Oct. 17-22, at Robert Trent Jones Golf Club, Lake Manassas, Virginia

ROSTERS

The Presidents Cup was developed to give the world's best non-European players an opportunity to compete in team international match-play competition. A biennial event played in non-Ryder Cup years, the first Presidents Cup was played Sept. 16-18, 1994, at Robert Trent Jones Golf Club. The United States Team, captained by Hale Irwin, defeated the International Team, captained by David Graham, 20-12.

Members of the 2000 U.S. Team were selected based on official earnings from the start of the 1999 season through the 2000 PGA Championship. International Team players for the 2000 Presidents Cup were chosen on the basis of the Official World Golf Ranking from tournaments played through August 20. International Teams do not include players eligible for the European Ryder Cup Team.

United States: Captain Ken Venturi, Tiger Woods, Phil Mickelson, Hal Sutton, David Duval, Davis Love III, Tom Lehman, Jim Furyk, Notah Begay III, Kirk Triplett, Stewart Cink, Loren Roberts, Paul Azinger.

International: Captain Peter Thomson (Australia), Ernie Els (South Africa), Vijay Singh (Fiji), Nick Price (Zimbabwe), Carlos Franco (Paraguay), Stuart Appleby (Australia), Michael Campbell (New Zealand), Mike Weir (Canada), Shigeki Maruyama (Japan), Greg Norman (Australia), Retief Goosen (South Africa), Robert Allenby (Australia), Steve Elkington (Australia)

First Day
Foursome Match Results

Winner	Score	Loser
Mickelson/Lehman	5&4	Norman/Elkington
Sutton/Furyk	1-up	Allenby/Appleby
Cink/Triplett	3&2	Weir/Goosen
Woods/Begay III	1-up	Singh/Els
Duval/Love III	1-up	Price/Franco

USA wins first day, 5-0

Second Day
Four-Ball Match Results

Winner	Score	Loser
Campbell/Goosen	4&3	Sutton/Azinger
Weir/Elkington	3&2	Lehman/Roberts
Price/Norman	6&5	Furyk/Duval
Maruyama/Franco	3&2	Woods/Begay III
Mickelson/Love III	2&1	Singh/Els

International wins morning, 4-1; (US leads, 6-4)

Foursome Match Results

Winner	Score	Loser
Cink/Triplett	2&1	Allenby/Appleby
Roberts/Azinger	5&4	Franco/Maruyama
Woods/Begay III	6&5	Singh/Els
Sutton/Lehman	4&2	Campbell/Goosen
Price/Weir	6&4	Mickelson/Duval

US wins afternoon, 4-1; (US leads 10-5)

Third Day
Four-Ball Match Results

Winner	Score	Loser
Sutton/Furyk	6&5	Norman/Campbell
Lehman/Mickelson	2&1	Weir/Elkington
Duval/Love III	3&2	Els/Price
Triplett/Cink	1-up	Allenby/Franco
Goosen/Singh	2&1	Woods/Begay III

US wins day, 4-1; (US leads, 14-6)

Fourth Day
Singles Match Results

Winner	Score	Loser
Allenby	2&1	Azinger
Duval	2&1	Price
Roberts	3&2	Appleby
Weir	4&3	Mickelson
Love III	4&3	Els
Elkington	1-up	Lehman
Woods	2&1	Singh
Cink	2&1	Norman
Franco	6&5	Sutton
Furyk	5&4	Maruyama
Triplett	halved	Campbell
Begay III	1-up	Goosen

US wins day, 7½-4½

US wins Presidents Cup, 21½-10½

Overall Records
Team and Individual match play combined

United States

	W-L-H
Stewart Cink	4-0-0
Davis Love III	4-0-0
Kirk Triplett	3-0-1
Jim Furyk	3-1-0
Notah Begay III	3-2-0
David Duval	3-2-0
Tom Lehman	3-2-0
Phil Mickelson	3-2-0
Hal Sutton	3-2-0
Tiger Woods	3-2-0
Loren Roberts	2-1-0
Paul Azinger	1-2-0

International

	W-L-H
Mike Weir	3-2-0
Steve Elkington	2-2-0
Carlos Franco	2-3-0
Retief Goosen	2-3-0
Nick Price	2-3-0
Michael Campbell	1-2-1
Shigeki Maruyama	1-2-0
Robert Allenby	1-3-0
Greg Norman	1-3-0
Vijay Singh	1-4-0
Stuart Appleby	0-3-0
Ernie Els	0-5-0

Late 2000 Tournament Results
PGA Tour

Last Rd	Tournament	Winner	Earnings	Runner-Up
Oct. 22	The Presidents Cup	US (21½)	—	International (10½)
Oct. 22	Tampa Bay Classic..................	John Huston (271)	$432,000	C. Paulson (274)

Remaining Events (9): National Car Rental Classic at Walt Disney World Resort (Oct. 26-29); The Tour Championship (Nov. 2-5); Southern Farm Bureau Classic (Nov. 2-5); World Golf Championships: American Express Championship (Nov. 9-12); Franklin Templeton Shark Shootout (Nov. 17-19); Skins Game (Nov. 25-26); Williams World Challenge (Nov. 30-Dec. 3); World Golf Championships: EMC World Cup (Dec. 7-10); Diners Club Matches (Dec. 11-13).
Note: The American Express Championship (Nov. 9-12) is the final official PGA Tour event of 2000.

European PGA Tour

Last Rd	Tournament	Winner	Earnings	Runner-Up
Oct. 22	Turespana Masters..................	Padraig Harrington (267)	E 166,600	G. Orr (269)

Remaining Events (3): Italian Open (Oct. 26-29) Volvo Masters (Nov. 2-5); World Golf Championships: American Express Championship (Nov. 9-12).

Senior PGA Tour

Last Rd	Tournament	Winner	Earnings	Runner-Up
Oct. 22	EMC Kaanapali Classic	Hale Irwin (198)	$165,000	J. Inman (202)

Remaining Events (5): Pacific Bell Senior Classic (Oct. 27-29); Senior Tour Championship (Nov. 3-5); Senior Match Play (Nov. 10-12); Senior Slam (Dec. 1-3); Diners Club Matches (Dec. 11-12).

LPGA Tour

Last Rd	Tournament	Winner	Earnings	Runner-Up
Oct. 22	AFLAC Champions..................	Karrie Webb (273)*	$122,000	D. Pepper (273)

*Playoff: Webb won on the first hole.
Remaining Events (6): Cisco World Ladies Challenge (Oct. 27-29); Mizuno Classic (Nov. 3-5); Arch Championship (Nov. 16-19); Women's World Cup of Golf (Dec. 1-3); Hyundai Team Matches (Dec. 15-17); Wendy's Three-Tour Challenge (Dec. 23-24).

TENNIS

Late 2000 Tournament Results
Men's Tour

Finals	Tournament	Winner	Earnings	Loser	Score
Oct. 1	Int'l Championship of Sicily	Olivier Rochus	$49,500	D. Nargiso	76 61
Oct. 8	Salem Open at Hong Kong	Nicolas Kiefer	49,500	M. Philippoussis	76 26 62
Oct. 15	Japan Open (Tokyo)	Sjeng Schalken	115,000	N. Lapentti	64 36 61
Oct. 15	CA Tennis Trophy (Vienna)	Tim Henman	130,000	T. Haas	64 64 64
Oct. 22	Adidas Open (Toulouse)	Alex Corretja	54,000	C. Moya	63 62
Oct. 22	Heineken Open (Shanghai)	Magnus Norman	49,500	S. Schalken	64 64 63

Remaining Events (10): Kremlin Cup (Oct. 29); Swiss Indoors (Oct. 29); Tennis Masters-Stuttgart (Nov. 5); Grand Prix of Lyon (Nov. 12); St. Petersburg Open (Nov. 12); Paris Open (Nov. 19); Stockholm Open (Nov. 26); Samsung Open (Nov. 26); Masters Cup-Lisbon (Dec. 3); ATP Tour World Double Championship (Dec. 10)

Women's Tour

Finals	Tournament	Winner	Earnings	Loser	Score
Oct. 1	Seat Open (Luxembourg)	Jennifer Capriati	$27,000	M. Maleeva	46 61 64
Oct. 8	Princess Cup (Tokyo)	Serena Williams	87,000	J. Halard-Decugis	75 61
Oct. 8	Porsche Tennis GP (Filderstadt)........	Martina Hingis	87,000	K. Clijsters	60 63
Oct. 15	Swisscom Challenge (Zurich)	Martina Hingis	166,000	L. Davenport	64 46 75
Oct. 15	Japan Open (Tokyo)	Julie Halard-Decugis	27,000	A. Frazier	57 75 64
Oct. 22	Generali Ladies Open (Linz)...........	Lindsay Davenport	87,000	V. Williams	64 36 62
Oct. 22	Heineken Open (Shanghai)	Meghan Shaughnessy	22,000	I. Tulyaganova	76 75

Remaining Events (9): Kremlin Cup (Oct. 29); Slovak Indoors (Oct. 29); Sparkassen Cup (Nov. 5); Bell Challenge (Nov. 5); Advanta Championships (Nov. 12); Wismilak International (Nov. 12); Chase Championships (Nov. 19); Volvo Women's Open (Nov. 19); Fed Cup Final (Nov. 26).

THOROUGHBRED RACING

Late 2000 Major Stakes Races

Date	Race	Location	Miles	Winner	Jockey	Purse
Sept. 16	Kentucky Cup	Turfway	1⅛	Captain Steve	Shane Sellers	$500,000
Sept. 17	Atto Mile	Woodbine	1 (T)	Riveira	John Velazquez	1,000,000
Sept. 17	Matron Stakes	Belmont	1	Raging Fever	Jerry Bailey	200,000
Sept. 17	Futurity Stakes.............	Belmont	1	Burning Roma	Rick Wilson	200,000
Sept. 23	Mazarine B.C. Stakes.......	Woodbine	1¹⁄₁₆	Salty You	Todd Kabel	200,000
Sept. 23	Vosburgh Stakes...........	Belmont	7 F	Trippi	Jerry Bailey	300,000
Sept. 23	Jerome Handicap...........	Belmont	1	Fusaichi Pegasus	Kent Desormeaux	150,000
Sept. 23	Kentucky Cup Mile..........	Kentucky Downs	1	Glick	Mark Guidry	200,000
Sept. 23	Kentucky Cup Turf	Kentucky Downs	1½ (T)	Down the Aisle	Robby Albarado	300,000

Date	Race	Location	Miles	Winner	Jockey	Purse
Sept. 30	Super Derby XXI............	Louisiana Downs	1¼	Tiznow	Chris McCarron	500,000
Oct. 7	Meadowlands Cup	Meadowlands	1⅛	North East Bound	Jose Velez, Jr.	400,000
Oct. 7	Flower Bowl Handicap	Belmont	1¼ (T)	Colstar	Jean-Luc Samyn	750,000
Oct. 7	Turf Classic Invitational	Belmont	1½	John's Call	Jean-Luc Samyn	750,000
Oct. 7	Shadwell Keeneland					
	Turf Mile	Keeneland	1 (T)	Altibr	Richard Migliore	400,000
Oct. 7	In Reality Stakes............	Calder	1¹⁄₁₆	Express Tour	Julio A. Garcia	450,000
Oct. 7	My Dear Girl	Calder	1¹⁄₁₆	Valid Forbes	Julio A. Garcia	400,000
Oct. 7	Smile Sprint Handicap	Calder	6 F	Forty One Carats	Javier Castellano	300,000
Oct. 7	Yellow Ribbon Stakes	Santa Anita	1¼ (T)	Tranquility Lake	Eddie Delahoussaye	500,000
Oct. 8	Clement L. Hirsch Turf					
	Championship Stakes	Santa Anita	1¼ (T)	Mash One (CHI)	David Flores	300,000
Oct. 8	Oak Leaf Stakes............	Santa Anita	1	Notable Career	David Flores	200,000
Oct. 8	Lane's End Breeders' Futurity					
	Stakes	Keeneland	1¹⁄₁₆	Arabian Light	Shane Sellers	450,000
Oct. 8	QE II Challenge Cup........	Keeneland	1⅛ (T)	Collect the Cash	Shane Sellers	500,000
Oct. 9	Grey Breeder's Cup Stakes ..	Woodbine	1¹⁄₁₆	Macho Uno	Jerry Bailey	200,000
Oct. 13	WinStar Galaxy Stakes......	Keeneland	1³⁄₁₆	Tout Charmant	Chris McCarron	500,000
Oct. 14	Three Chimneys Spinster					
	Stakes	Keeneland	1⅛	Plenty of Light	Garrett Gomez	500,000
Oct. 14	Frizette Stakes.............	Belmont	1¹⁄₁₆	Raging Fever	Jerry Bailey	500,000
Oct. 14	Beldame Stakes	Belmont	1⅛	Riboletta (BRZ)	Chris McCarron	750,000
Oct. 14	Champagne Stakes	Belmont	1¹⁄₁₆	A.P. Valentine	Jorge Chavez	500,000
Oct. 14	Jockey Gold Cup	Belmont	1¼	Albert the Great	Jorge Chavez	1,000,000
Oct. 14	Ancient Title B.C. Handicap .	Santa Anita	6 F	Kona Gold	Alex Solis	200,000
Oct. 14	Oak Tree B.C. Mile	Santa Anita	1 (T)	War Chant	Gary Stevens	250,000
Oct. 15	E.P. Taylor Stakes	Woodbine	1¼ (T)	Fly for Avie	Todd Kabel	500,000
Oct. 15	Canadian International	Woodbine	1½ (T)	Mutafaweq	Frankie Dettori	1,500,000
Oct. 15	Goodwood B.C. Handicap ..	Santa Anita	1⅛	Tiznow	Chris McCarron	400,000
Oct. 21	Oak Tree Derby	Santa Anita	1⅛	Sign of Hope (GB)	Alex Solis	250,000

HARNESS RACING

Late 2000 Major Stakes Races

	Race	Raceway	Winner	Driver	Purse
Oct. 6	Kentucky Futurity	Lexington	Credit Winner	Jim Meittinis	$535,000
Oct. 14	Messenger Stakes	Ladbroke	Ain't No Stopn Him	John Campbell	323,000

BOWLING

2000 Fall Tour Results
PBA

Final	Event	Winner	Earnings	Final	Runner-Up
Sept. 17	Japan Cup	Parker Bohn III	$50,000	235-206	Yasuyuki Sadamatsu
Oct. 10	Track Canandaigua Open........	Walter Ray Williams Jr.	20,000	225-217	Patrick Healey Jr.
Oct. 17	Johnny Petraglia Open..........	Walter Ray Williams Jr.	26,000	215-177	Bob Learn Jr.
Oct. 24	Flagship Open................	Robert Smith	19,000	239-233	Walter Ray Williams Jr.

Remaining Events: See PBA fall schedule on page 759.

Senior PBA

Final	Event	Winner	Earnings	Final	Runner-Up
Oct. 5	Gastonia Classic	Roger Workman	$8,000	266-191	Gary Dickinson
Oct. 13	**PBA National Championship**	Bob Glass	20,000	246-236	Rohn Morton
Oct. 20	Hammond Open	Mike Pullin	8,000	190-171	Roger Workman

Note: The Atlantic City Senior Open, scheduled for Sept 17-21 was postponed indefinitely.

PWBA

Final	Event	Winner	Earnings	Final	Runner-Up
Sept. 7	Greater Orlando Classic	Cara Honeychurch	$11,000	218-184	DeDe Davidson
Sept. 14	Paula Carter Classic	Debbie McMullen	11,000	234-228	Michelle Feldman
Sept. 28	Brunswick World Open	Cara Honeychurch	14,000	179-160	Marianne DiRupo
Oct. 5	N. Myrtle Beach Classic........	Tish Johnson	11,000	229-200	Cara Honeychurch
Oct. 12	Columbia 300 Open	Caroli Gianotti-Block	14,400	211-198	Wendy Macpherson

Remaining Events See PWBA fall schedule on page 759.

AMF Bowling World Cup Final (Oct. 21)

Final	Event	Winner	Earnings	Final	Runner-Up
Men	AMF Bowling World Cup........	Tomas Leandersson, SWE	—	2 games to 1	M. Al-Qubaisi, UAE
Women	AMF Bowling World Cup........	Mel Issacs, WALES	—	2 games to 1	Clara Juliana Guerrero, COL

Personalities

The reign of Indiana coaching legend **Bobby Knight** came crashing down in 2000.

AP/Wide World Photos

Top 20 Sports Personalities of 2000

Dan and Linda take a look back and choose their top newsmakers of the year.

by

Dan Patrick and
Linda Cohn

We'd like to have you believe that there was some kind of logical system put in place to decide whether Dan or Linda got to give their top personalities first. Quite frankly, there isn't. It has nothing to do with the tides, the earth's rotation or the presidential election. There were no friendly wagers to decide, not even rock-paper-scissors. Basically, Dan went second last year so he has honors now. And away we go...

Pedro Martinez

Two years ago we all went appropriately crazy over Mark McGwire and Sammy Sosa. They ushered in the new era of offense in baseball which is still in full swing. That's why Pedro Martinez of the Boston Red Sox is such an amazing pitcher. In this era of the long ball and double digit run totals, Martinez has put together two remarkable seasons in a row. With a 9 to 1 strikeout-to-walk ratio and an ERA that was 1.96 runs below the next best A.L. mark, Martinez has set a new standard for pitching. We really should be making more of a fuss over him.

Marion Jones

It's like Watergate. What did she know and when did she know it? Her husband, American shot putter C.J. Hunter, tested positive for steroids four times. I mean fool me once, shame on you. Fool me twice, shame on me. Fool me four times and you have to make up a new expression.

Dan Patrick and Linda Cohn are anchors of ESPN's *SportsCenter*. Dan also hosts *The Dan Patrick Show* from 1-4 p.m. EST, Monday through Friday on ESPN Radio.

AP/Wide World Photos

Pedro Martinez was his usual dominant self in 2000, whiffing 284 batters and recording the lowest American League ERA (1.74) since Ron Guidry in 1978. It still wasn't quite enough to push the Red Sox into the postseason.

Unfortunately, her husband's problems overshadowed her remarkable five medal winning performance in Sydney. He even ruined this tribute to her, now that I think of it.

Pete Sampras

By winning his seventh Wimbledon and 13th overall Grand Slam title, Pete Sampras passed Roy Emerson as the most accomplished male tennis champion of all time. I don't know how many more he has left in him. Maybe another Wimbledon. He's just not that durable any more. He also married actress Bridgette Wilson this year, something of a grand slam in its own right. Congratulations Pete, on both accounts.

Lennox Lewis

This quiet British boxer, in his own way, has restored a little bit of the old luster to being the heavyweight champion of the world. His dignity and class, his style and substance, make him a fighter we don't have to apologize for. How refreshing.

Daniel Snyder

He came on the scene like the crazy, willful son of Jerry Jones. Just when Jones had settled in as part of the new NFL power structure, a more daring and individualistic owner comes along and shakes things up. In his brashest move to date, Daniel Snyder charged admission to the Redskins' training camp. People paid of

AP/Wide World Photos

If only we could all *fail* like **Marion Jones** does. Jones came up short on her bid to win five golds at Sydney. All she could muster up were three golds and two bronzes. *Pitiful.* Here she celebrates after winning the 100 meters with a time of 10.75 seconds.

course which will only encourage him. Snyder also has some Steinbrenner in him as he put his money on the table to get a winner on the field.

Phil Jackson

Seven rings as a coach. But he'll never get all the credit he deserves. Critics say that in Chicago he had Michael Jordan and Scottie Pippen, two of the greatest players of all time. In Los Angeles, he has Shaquille O'Neal and Kobe Bryant, two of the best players in the game today. And while Jackson handles the stars brilliantly, he does his best work with the role players he brings in. Lots of teams have two superstars. Phil Jackson's genius is in getting the other guys to come through.

Dennis Miller

If you're a sanctimonious, overly serious "football guy," you don't like Dennis Miller in the Monday Night Football booth. But if you have a sense of humor and simply enjoy the game, you welcome him. The guys at ABC know the real deal: if the game is good, people watch. If it's a stinker, people don't watch. Miller wasn't going to change that. By week eight of the 2000 season, the criticism had died down. Dennis Miller was not ruining MNF. What a relief! I think, though, that the early rips he took may make Miller think twice about coming back to the booth.

Ray Lewis

He was found not guilty. We may never know what really happened in Atlanta in the hours following Super Bowl XXXIV. If any good is to come from Lewis' ordeal, it may be that other athletes realize that those people hanging around may not all be friends with their best interests in mind. The shame is that Ray Lewis is one hell of a football player. But most people don't know his name for that reason.

Rulon Gardner

In the failed drug test games of Sydney, where modern pharmaceutical technology was on display, Rulon Gardner was an old-fashioned hero. This American Greco-Roman wrestler defeated Russian Alexandre Kareline in the biggest upset of the Games. He acted with class, unlike a lot of American Olympians, and was easy to root for. Gardner was such a throwback that his defeat of Kareline even summoned up those old Cold War feelings.

Tiger Woods

In 2000, Woods won, among his nine victories (through late Oct.), the U.S. Open, the British Open and the PGA. So if he wins the '01 Masters, he'll be the reigning champion of the four majors. Many would not agree but I'll give him the Grand Slam. As Dennis Miller said, Tiger Woods is the one guy in the world that Michael Jordan is jealous of. But I think he'll end up even bigger than Jordan. Woods is changing people's perception of his sport. He is changing the way the game is played and who plays it.

Now over to you, Linda.

Thanks Dan. And thanks for leaving me some juicy ones too.

Kurt Warner

Just because I cover sports for a living doesn't mean I can't also be a sports fan. And one of the biggest reasons I love sports is that it's never predictable. Just when you think you've got it all figured out, the unexpected comes along. Most people remember coach Dick Vermeil crying after his starter Trent Green went down in preseason and we figured the Rams' season was over. Then along came "Mr. Unexpected." Just two years removed from the Arena Football League, this former grocery store stock boy became just the second player in history to throw 40 TDs in a season and led his team to a stunning Super Bowl win. The story was too good to be true.

Marty McSorley

Every athlete loves to get their name in the paper, but in 2000 Marty McSorley could have done without all the headlines. A bruising NHL enforcer since 1983, McSorley gained respect for becoming a very serviceable hockey player, while still protecting the likes of stars Wayne Gretzky and Mario Lemieux. He may have lost that respect and more on Feb. 21 when he made like a lumberjack and took a two-handed chop at the head of Vancouver tough guy Donald Brashear. The case made even more ripples when it went to the Canadian court system, blurring the line between sports and "the real world." Only time will tell if McSorley can salvage his career and his name.

Venus Williams

Of the two Williams sisters, most "experts" thought the elder Venus would be the one to win the first Grand Slam title. It didn't happen that way and when Serena showed her mettle and prevailed at the 1999 U.S. Open, Venus looked like she wanted to crawl into a hole. There is no doubting the love the sisters have for each other, but amidst all the Serena "hullabaloo" Venus rarely cracked a smile and appeared to reach the depths of her tennis life. The word "retirement" was even thrown around a few times. Venus bounced back in 2000, winning two Grand Slams and gold in Sydney. She was unbeatable through the fall season. In the end, she may have her sister to thank for pushing her to the next level.

Rae Carruth

It's impossible to fathom how anyone, let alone a professional athlete whose life appears so golden and easy, could orchestrate the murder of a woman carrying his child. The Carruth case was the most gruesome in a long list of negative events surrounding the sports world in 1999-00. It seemed like night after night on *SportsCenter*, we'd lead with something tragic — the Ray Lewis incident, the deaths of Cory Erving, Bobby Phills and Malik Sealy — but this one is just unreal.

Mateen Cleaves

It was a classic story of "good guy makes good." With more and more college hoop stars coming out early, Mateen Cleaves followed the lead of Tim Duncan and Peyton Manning and opted to stay for his senior year to graduate and take another shot at the NCAA championship. Unlike the other two, Cleaves led Michigan State to the promised land. He represented everything you look for in a sports hero, a guy you just couldn't help but root for. And after being taken in the NBA draft by his hometown Detroit Pistons, maybe the real story is still to come.

Timo Perez

We hear so much about "fate" and "destiny" playing a major role in the outcome of sporting events. Sometimes it really does seem like it's true. When Mets rightfielder Derek Bell sprained his ankle (after pitcher Mike Hampton didn't get a call on a close two-strike pitch to Barry Bonds) in Game 1 of their playoff series with San Francisco, the unknown Perez took his place. He began the year in A-ball and even most Mets fans had never heard of him, but all he did was provide timely hitting and play the outfield with reckless abandon when his team needed it. Maybe he's just a flash in the pan, but during October of the baseball season, one of sports' most sacred times, he provided the necessary ingredient to get the Mets to the World Series and closer to the pot of gold.

AP/Wide World Photos

Venus Williams laughs as she holds the women's singles trophy on Centre Court at Wimbledon after beating Lindsay Davenport 6-3, 7-6 in the final. She was an unstoppable force in the fall, adding a U.S. Open title and an Olympic gold medal to her growing resume.

Shaquille O'Neal

We knew he was good, but the intangible this year was his maturity. In 2000, Shaq put his ego aside, did whatever coach Phil Jackson told him to do, and never lost sight of his mission — an NBA title. He became a team leader and managed to forge a healthy relationship with fellow star Kobe Bryant on and off the court. He even improved his foul shooting. It's been a long time since an NBA center was so feared around the league. He should have been a unanimous choice for league MVP. Finally, we don't have to listen to his infamous quote that he "won championships at every level — except college and pro."

Karrie Webb

When Tiger was in the middle of his tournament win streak in early 2000, Karrie Webb was doing the same thing on the LPGA Tour, and almost no one noticed. She won the first four tournaments of the year that she entered, narrowly missed out on her fifth with a second place finish at the Standard Register Ping, and then made it five-for-six by winning the Nabisco Championship by a record 10 strokes. It was the first of two major championships for the Australia native in 2000. Like her male counterpart, she played at a different level than the rest of the tour. All the quotes you've heard praising Tiger would still be

AP/Wide World Photos

Center **Shaquille O'Neal**, left, and Kobe Bryant yuk it up on the bench after yet another Lakers win in 2000. "The Combo" (as O'Neal dubbed them) averaged over 52 points per game en route to the Lakers' first title since 1988.

applicable if you removed his name and inserted Webb's.

Bobby Knight

The whole mess not only reached a boiling point in 2000, it spilled over. Knight could no longer contain it because he couldn't contain himself. You just can't choke a player. Period. The evidence was there. It ultimately signaled the end (possibly temporarily) of a coaching career that spanned 35 years and included 763 wins, three national titles and propelled numerous players to the NBA and the college coaching ranks. Unfortunately it was a also a career rife with questionable coaching tactics and accusations of physical abuse.

Lance Armstrong

We're constantly hearing about athletes going through rehab and making recoveries from injuries, but those stories usually involve a hurt shoulder or a knee or an ankle. But cancer? The fact that Armstrong could come back and win the Tour de France once is unreal, but to do it again is even more astounding. With critics devaluing his first win due to drug speculation and the absence of many other top riders, his 2000 win may be even sweeter. And the fact that he was able to celebrate with his newborn son was the icing on the cake. Cycling will never be one of the big-four sports in the United States, but people should never forget this amazing accomplishment by one of our own. ∎

Moments

Vince Carter *leapfrogged 7-foot-2 French center Fred Weis, stunning everyone with his unforgettable Olympic dunk.*

Darren McNamara/Allsport

Top 20 Sports Moments of 2000

Stuart Scott and John Anderson give us their picks for the biggest moments of the year in sports.

by

Stuart Scott and
John Anderson

Y2K and the only thing I can say is...for all the moments that DON'T make the list . . . "I'm sorry" . . . and "Blame Tiger." We could, and maybe should, lump all of his moments into ONE but "A" that would shortchange him and "B" it would make for more work for John and I . . . so we'll include some of his moments, leave some out and leave the readers to argue whether we made the right choices. Since John's the rookie here, I'll take the first 10. It's like him having to carry my duffel bag on road trips. I could be mean and make all 10 moments of mine Tiger moments and not leave him any. But I'm not that mean.

Stuart Scott and John Anderson are anchor/reporters on ESPN's *SportsCenter.*

Rams over Titans in Super Bowl for the Ages

Best Super Bowl ever?? Could be. Some critics say it was the best fourth quarter and that's it. I disagree. The first half was a chess match. Scoring doesn't make a great game, strategy, big hits and emotion do. The Rams went offensive SILLY during the season. Quarterback Kurt Warner went from being a grocery store worker to the Arena League to Super Bowl MVP. His story is one of the best EVER in sports. The irony of all this is that the Rams won the game with a defensive stop. Mike Jones (the only man I know other than me to have a daughter named Taelor and spell her name with an "e" instead of a "y") made a great tackle on Kevin Dyson a yard shy of the end zone as time and the Titans expired.

Jamie Squire/Allsport

Tiger Woods took time out to pose with the employees following his monumental win at the 100th U.S. Open at Pebble Beach in 2000.

Michigan State wins the NCAA hoops title

Mateen Cleaves isn't the fastest point guard or the best shooter or even the most athletic. But he knows how to win, and he channeled every emotion in the book into leading his Spartans to the title 21 years after Magic Johnson did the same. His Flint, Mich. homeboy Morris Peterson provided the offense . . . Cleaves provided the heart . . . Tom Izzo provided the leadership.

Lakers win NBA Championship

New home. New coach. New-found friendship between Shaquille O'Neal and Kobe Bryant. The Lakers won their first NBA title since 1988. Kobe understood he's the number two option . . . except when he NEEDED to be the number one option. Shaq understood he's the best center in the league. He finally got his ring and guess what he did? The same thing Jordan did when he won his first. The 7-1, 320-pound giant cried . . . unashamedly.

Tiger wins the U.S. Open

Nobody finishes 12-under at the U.S. Open. Nobody wins by 15 strokes. Impossible, right? Aannnngg! Wrong answer. Tiger did, Tiger does and Tiger probably will again. On the sacred grounds at Pebble Beach, even with a triple bogey in round three, Tiger made a mockery of the field and the course. He can't be *this* much better than the rest of the world . . . Can he??

In fairness to John, I'll just take one more Tiger moment . . . John can use the other Tiger moments in his list. I won't even take one of Tiger's other majors . . . I'll just take a shot.

Tiger hits an approach on 18 that's sick

It was dark outside. I guess Tiger Woods didn't notice. On the 18th hole of the NEC Invitational, knowing he had to give a clinic the next morning, then fly cross country for a made-for-TV match with Sergio Garcia, Tiger sat about 160 yards away from the green in the nearly pitch-black evening. He stuck it so close you could have blown it in for birdie. He says it might have been one of his best shots, "But I couldn't see it, so I don't know."

Wimbledon: Ladies First

She sulked a little when her little sister, Serena, won the U.S. Open in 1999. As the older sister, Venus Williams was supposed to win the majors first. Well, I beat my big brother, Stephen, in a foot race when I was a sophomore in high school and he was a senior and he never raced me again . . . ever. At least Venus came back. No African-American woman had won Wimbledon since Althea Gibson in 1958. And Gibson didn't have a 128 m.p.h. serve. With flash, skill, smarts, and power, Venus ran through Martina Hingis and Lindsay Davenport and made history.

Pete gets Lucky 13

Grace . . . in that quiet, cool, "aw shucks" way. That's what Pete Sampras exudes. Who said 13 was an unlucky number? With a dignity befitting the tournament, Sampras broke Roy Emerson's record with his 13th career grand slam win. It was pretty cool, especially since Pete's mom and dad, who had never come to Wimbledon to watch their son . . . finally did.

Marion Jones

If her husband wasn't such a large man, and if my wife didn't read the Sports Almanac, I'd have noticed how sexy Marion is in those Nike ads where she's a radio disc jockey and we only see her lips . . . but her husband IS big . . . and my wife DOES read . . . so I didn't notice. I just noticed how classy she was at the Olympics. She has grace, beauty and a smile that models in the *Sports Illustrated* swimsuit issue don't come close to touching. Marion didn't reach her goal of five gold medals. But if three golds and two bronzes is failure, then I don't need to be a sportscaster. Marion smiled and won . . . and did it all while accusations of steriod use by her husband followed her everywhere she went. If Tiger Woods is the sportsman of the year . . . Marion Jones might be the sportsPERSON of the year.

Rocky beats Ivan Drago Part Deux

Alexandre Kareline was the stereotypical Russian in the late 1980's movies. Except he was real. He was also a BAD MAN. As big as his opponents were, Kareline would intimidate most of them even before the match began. As a matter of fact, he hadn't lost a Greco-Roman wrestling match in 13 years. His fourth gold medal at the Olympics was a given . . . until an American named Rulon Gardner, who grew up on a farm wrestling his brothers in a barn, pulled off what is perhaps the second biggest upset in Olympic history (remember Lake Placid). Gardner won gold . . . and the hearts of the country.

Rams-Falcons Week 7

Like with Tiger, the St. Louis Rams could fill up several moments . . . but this one was one of the gazillion records the team broke. The Falcons opened the game by taking the opening kickoff back for a touchdown. You knew what everyone was thinking. Uh-oh . . . the Rams will probably score on their first play from scrimmage . . . like an 80-yard TD pass from Kurt Warner to Isaac Bruce, or Az Hakim, or Marshall Faulk, or Ricky Proehl, or Tony Horne. Well, Horne did score . . . but he didn't wait until the first play from scrimmage. He simply took the Falcons kick . . . and brought that thing back 103 yards for the score. Just one of the long, gaudy TDs the Rams score . . . but it was the first time, EVER an NFL game began with back-to-back kickoff returns for TDs.

OK guys . . . that's my list. See, John, I was nice. I left a lot of moments for you . . . including three or four you could use on Tiger alone.

🐚　　🐚　　🐚

Stu, your kindness overwhelms me. It does not, however, help me. Your generosity in leaving so many fine sporting moments to choose makes my job of selecting just 10 harder than hitting a 6-iron, 216 yards out of a bunker, over a pond fronting the 18th green to a pin on a shelf the size of a manhole. Oh well, if Tiger can pull it off with a one-shot lead on the 72nd hole of the Canadian Open . . . then I

can too. Pick 10 that is, not hit the 6-iron. By the way Stu where do I put this bag? And, after this, I refuse to haul around the video equipment.

Tiger's May Day at the PGA

The U.S. and British Open champ, looking to become the first man since Ben Hogan in 1953 to win three majors in a season, ran into journeyman-pro Bob May and almost got Jack Fleck-ed into the Kentucky Bluegrass. Tied, heading to Valhalla's back nine, May promptly ran off three straight birdies to take a one-shot lead. Woods, perhaps even more impressive than in his Pebble Beach and St. Andrews blowouts, accepted and relished the challenge, finally catching May on the 17th. After May dropped a CPR 12 footer on 18 for birdie . . . Woods matched the four with a downhill six-footer that could drive a deacon to drink. The OT is vintage Tiger. He buried a birdie on the first extra hole then did a half-Fred Astaire, half-Ricky Martin race to the cup to retrieve his ball. Two pars off the cart path later and Woods had won his second straight Wannamaker Trophy, capping the finest season of professional golf ever. EVER. May shot 66, 66 on the weekend and lost the tournament . . . but won a world full of fans.

Lance Armstrong Part Deux

If the hardest thing do to in sports is repeat as champion then what do we make of Lance Armstrong? His first Tour de France victory was so outrageous and courageous that a second straight should earn him a statue somewhere. There has to be a sculptor somewhere in Paris that can start carving. Armstrong was no less a cancer survivor than he was in 1999 and the 2000 Tour didn't get any shorter or easier. Armstrong made his move in the mountains, the Tour's toughest stages, burying the world's best

AP/Wide World Photos

Rulon Gardner was on top of the world after pulling off one of the greatest upsets in Olympic history besting Russian bear Alexandre Kareline, 1-0, in their 130 kg gold medal match.

cyclists on a climb so tough it was off the rating charts. After beating death . . . climbing mountains is down hill.

Bobby Knight Stays . . . Goes

It took nearly 30 years but finally civility won out over victory at Indiana University. How exactly do you fire Bob Knight? Well you don't at first. You scold him. Tell him he needs to reverse three decades of boorish behavior and watch his temper. In May President Myles Brand set down a "zero tolerance" policy for the General. Three NCAA titles, 11 Big Ten titles, more than 700 wins and a superior graduation rate got him one last chance. He never had a chance . . . Knight couldn't conform and was fired four months later in September. Ironically, the final straw was Knight disciplining a freshman student for a lack of manners.

Dan Marino's Last Pass

You could read the NFL record book cover to cover to get the scope of Dan Marino's greatness. Or you could just find any picture of number 13 and look at those eyes. Cold, stone, killer, and aqua. Whose eyes match their uniform? Marino's arm made him famous but it was those eyes that made it possible. Seeing the whole field, every receiver, every confused defensive back, every open inch in which to squeeze in another completion. The greatest passer in the history of football retired after 17 seasons. That's sad. No Super Bowl . . . that's not sad . . . that's not even an issue . . . Marino can come play all-time quarterback in my neighborhood for life.

AP/Wide World Photos

Colorado Avalanche goaltender **Patrick Roy** is carried off the ice by teammates Ray Bourque and Adam Foote after the Avalanche beat the Capitals 4-3 in overtime on Oct. 17. The win gave Roy the all-time NHL record for career victories with 448, surpassing Terry Sawchuk.

Vin-sanity at the All-Star Weekend

In yet another sign of Stu's true benevolence . . . not only does he leave me great moments . . . but two Carolina guys to boot.

The Slam Dunk contest at the All-Star Game means nothing. So why couldn't we stop watching? It was Vince Carter's coronation. A 360-reverse, through the legs after catching a pass from cousin Tracy McGrady? Come on, where are those laws of gravity? A jam that ended with VC hanging from the rim by the crook in his elbow. Where was the trampoline hidden? When Vince went to Australia for the Olympics . . . the kangaroos were jealous. Better than dunks, Carter led his team to the playoffs.

MJ goes to Washington . . . Owns the Wiz

Gone are those days when Wizards players use to beat owner Abe Polian in HORSE. Any takers for one-on-one with Mr. Jordan? Michael Jordan got a share of ownership in Washington and took over all basketball related operations and decisions. The Wiz not only needed this, the NBA needed this. Its highest profile star was back out front. The Wiz are bad . . . but you get the feeling Jordan will not like losing as an owner any more than he did as a player. Clear up some salary cap things and we'll see if his Airness has a flare for front office work.

Subway Series

The Olympics and presidential elections are held every four years . . . but the World Series is so important they have to play it every year. And for the first time in 44 years it was an all-New York affair. A Subway Series. Yankees–Mets. It's a small world after all . . . the team's ballparks are separated by all of eight miles. New York City goes officially off-the-board zany. It was the Fall Classic on steroids. Families split over series loyalties. Families came together as dad regales the kids with long ago stories of the Yanks, Dodgers and Giants. Good for baseball? It is baseball.

Who is that masked man? . . . Patrick Roy

Sports fans require two things from their athletes: Greatness . . . and then sustained greatness. They want superstars with longevity, like Patrick Roy. Roy got his first NHL win by playing a period in relief for the Canadiens back in 1984. It would be eight months before he earned number two. The wins came with greater frequency after that until, finally, on Oct. 17, Roy recorded victory number 448, breaking Terry Sawchuk's NHL record for all-time wins. After beating the Washington Capitals 4-3 in OT, Roy cut down the net . . . a new twist on an old tradition.

Marty McSorley – Crime and Punishment.

Even hockey players winced. And these are guys who spit out teeth like sunflower seeds. Bruins tough guy Marty McSorley clubbed Canucks tough guy Donald Brashear in the head. Brashear dropped, his head crashing to the ice knocking him unconscious. An unconscionable act. McSorley apologized and got suspended for the remainder of the season, a penalty of 23 games. Then it got worse. McSorley was brought up and convicted of criminal charges in Vancouver. Hockey now has new worries. What is assault, what is action? Who polices the sport now . . . the league, coaches, players, prosecutors, the referees, the cops? It was not a great moment in 2000 but a memorable one nonetheless.

In a Tie for 10th

In a cop out of Queen Mary-sized proportions . . . a 10-way tie for 10th. Florida State won the National Championship . . . too tired to celebrate from chasing Virginia Tech's Michael Vick. Tiger's slacks. Devils won Stanley Cup in Texas . . . in June . . . in 95-degree heat. Sean Elliot returned to the Spurs after a kidney transplant. Tiger won British Open. Ken Griffey Jr. was traded to the Reds and the Mariners made the playoffs. Patrick Ewing was traded to Seattle for the Space Needle (Luc Longley). Ray Bourque was traded to the Avs after playing in Boston since the Tea Party. Mike Tyson discussed nutritional value of Lennox Lewis' children . . . Lewis has no kids. Tiger did the impossible . . . he made brown golf shoes look good. ∎

Calendar

Atlanta Braves pitcher **John Rocker** had trouble finding friends and the plate this year.

NOV '99

Sun	Mon	Tue	Wed	Thu	Fri	Sat
	1	2	3	4	5	6
7	8	9	10	11	12	13
14	15	16	17	18	19	20
21	22	23	24	25	26	27
28	29	30				

Quote of the Month

"Charismatic is easily one of the more stunning-looking stallions and we'd like to keep him that way." – DEVON KATZEV, president of the company that manufactures Mane 'n Tail shampoo, which inked a deal with the 1999 Derby and Preakness winner to make him their official "spokesman." It's believed to be the first time a celebrity animal has endorsed a national product.

Like Father, Like Son

A list of the fathers and sons who have won major auto racing series championships (in alphabetical order):

ANDRETTI
CART
Father: Mario Andretti, 1984
Son: Michael Andretti, 1991

HILL
Formula One
Father: Graham Hill, 1962, 68
Son: Damon Hill, 1996

JARRETT
Winston Cup
Father: Ned Jarrett, 1961, 65
Son: Dale Jarrett, 1999

PETTY
Winston Cup
Father: Lee Petty, 1954, 58-59
Son: Richard Petty, 1964, 67, 71-72, 74-75, 79

UNSER
CART
Father: Al Unser, 1983, 85
Son: Al Unser Jr., 1990, 94

1 NFL Hall of Famer Walter Payton, 45, dies of bile duct cancer, which was discovered earlier this year during his treatment for a rare liver disease.

Atlanta hitting coach Don Baylor agrees to a deal to manage the Chicago Cubs.

2 Two-time A.L. MVP Juan Gonzalez is traded from the Texas Rangers to the Detroit Tigers in a nine-player deal.

Seattle star Ken Griffey Jr. rejects an eight-year contract offer from the team and asks to be traded.

Chargers quarterback Ryan Leaf makes headlines again, this time for an obscenity-laced tirade against team management that earns him a four week suspension and loss of one week's pay.

3 Former Cleveland manager Mike Hargrove signs a three-year contract with the Baltimore Orioles.

4 Cleveland lawyer Larry Dolan agrees to buy the Cleveland Indians franchise for $320 million from Richard Jacobs. Dolan's acquisition must be approved by league owners.

San Diego first base coach Davey Lopes is hired to replace Phil Garner as manager of the Milwaukee Brewers.

6 Trainer D. Wayne Lukas's Cat Thief, a 19-1 shot who wore the horse equivalent of a Breathe Right strip across his nose, holds off the field at the $4 million Breeders' Cup Classic at Gulfstream Park.

7 Tiger Woods becomes the first player since Ben Hogan in 1953 to win four consecutive events on the PGA Tour, beating Miguel Angel Jimenez on the first playoff hole to capture the American Express Championship.

Several thousand Chicago Bears fans gather at Soldier Field for a public memorial to Walter Payton.

8 Seattle Seahawks receiver Joey Galloway ends his holdout after eight games and joins his teammates for a meeting and light workout.

The L.A. Dodgers make Shawn Green one of baseball's highest-paid players, agreeing to a six-year, $84 million contract to complete a deal that sends Raul Mondesi to the Toronto Blue Jays.

10 IOC vice president Dick Pound is named chairman of the newly formed World Anti-Doping Agency by the International Olympic Committee. The agency will focus on establishing a universal list of banned substances, developing standards for drug testing, and promoting research.

11 Tampa Bay Devil Rays 3B Wade Boggs announces his retirement and accepts a job in the team's front office.

Fox, NBC, and TBS announce they have won the rights to televise NASCAR events starting in 2001, agreeing to a six-year, $400 million deal with the auto racing circuit.

13 Wisconsin running back Ron Dayne breaks Ricky Williams' all-time college football rushing record in a home victory over Iowa.

14 NASCAR driver Dale Jarrett, knowing he had only to finish eighth or better to clinch his first Winston Cup title, drives to a solid, fifth-place finish at Homestead-Miami Speedway.

Memphis men's basketball coach George "Tic" Price unexpectedly announces his retirement, eight days before the tipoff of his third season with the team.

15 Dallas Mavericks rookie Leon Smith, 19, is admitted to a psychiatric ward after police find him overdosed on aspirin a night earlier.

17 Former L.A. Dodgers catcher Mike Scioscia is hired as the new manager of the Anaheim Angels.

AP/Wide World Photos

Rescuers work to remove logs from a **40-foot-high bonfire stack** that collapsed in a few thunderous seconds on Nov. 18 in College Station, Texas, killing 12 Texas A&M students and injuring 27 others.

18 Tragedy strikes the Texas A&M campus when a 40-foot stack of logs designed for a pep rally bonfire comes tumbling down at 2:30 a.m, trapping more than 30 people underneath.

Texas catcher Ivan Rodriguez upsets Red Sox pitcher Pedro Martinez in the race for the American League's Most Valuable Player Award.

CBS retains the rights to the NCAA men's basketball tournament well into the next millennium after the two sides agree to a $6 billion, 11-year deal.

19 Two top athletic officials at the University of Minnesota resign hours before a report is released by school-hired investigators accusing former men's basketball coach Clem Haskins of lying about "widespread academic misconduct" in his basketball program and telling his players to lie.

20 TCU's LaDainian Tomlinson breaks the NCAA Division I-A single game rushing record, gaining 406 yards and scoring six touchdowns in a 52-24 victory over Texas-El Paso.

Golden State Warriors coach P.J. Carlesimo is left standing at half court after N.Y. Knicks guard Latrell Sprewell chooses to ignore (rather than shake the hand of) his former coach before their first meeting since the 1997 assault.

21 D.C. United captures its third MLS Cup in the league's four-year history after a 2-0 victory over the Los Angeles Galaxy in rainy Foxboro, Mass.

22 The Boston Celtics announce they will replace the parquet floor they have used for 53 years with a new floor that will resemble and contain scraps from the old one.

Oakland Raiders players fire snowballs back at the crowd after being pelted by Broncos fans during, and after, a Monday night loss in Denver.

23 The NFL sends a letter to all 31 teams threatening fines and penalties for player who continues to use a throat slashing gesture as a form of celebration, claiming that the new trend in taunting depicted an unacceptable act of violence.

San Francisco 49ers RB Lawrence Phillips' stormy tenure with the team ends when he is waived by the team while serving a team-imposed three-game suspension.

25 Carolina Panthers WR Rae Carruth is arrested nine days after his wife, Cherica Adams, was critically wounded in a drive-by shooting.

26 A day after an estimated 93,000 fans turned out for a candlelight vigil, host Texas A&M defeats Texas, 20-16, in an emotional game layered with tributes to the 12 students who died in a pep-rally accident on Nov. 18.

Portland forward Scottie Pippen helps the Blazers to a 91-88 victory over Charles Barkley and the Houston Rockets. The former teammates don't speak to each other in their first meeting since Pippen's well-publicized barbs at Barkley last September.

Detroit Red Wings star Steve Yzerman scores his 600th goal in the first period of Detroit's game against Edmonton, becoming the 11th NHL player to reach the milestone.

27 Fred Couples knocks down a 15-foot birdie putt on the 18th hole and wins a $410,000 skin at the Skins Game, bringing his record total to $635,000 for the weekend.

29 Utah Jazz power forward Karl Malone makes an 18-foot jumper from the right side with 9:24 remaining in the first quarter for his sixth point of the game, carrying him past Michael Jordan and into third place on the NBA's career scoring list.

DEC '99

Sun	Mon	Tue	Wed	Thu	Fri	Sat
			1	2	3	4
5	6	7	8	9	10	11
12	13	14	15	16	17	18
19	20	21	22	23	24	25
26	27	28	29	30	31	

Quote of the Month

"How can it be neglect when you call for help? We were just trying to do the right thing. If we were neglecting or abusing them we could have just thrown them over the fence into (neighbor) Wayne Newton's yard."
– **DARRYL FRANCIS**, personal assistant to former heavyweight champion Mike Tyson, answering charges of ferret neglect from animal control officers.

Heisman in the Heartland

College football programs that have won the most Heisman Trophies:

Notre Dame	7
Ohio State	6
USC	4
Army	3
Michigan	3
Oklahoma	3
Nine tied at 2 each	

Arguments of the Century

So who came out on top after all the Athlete of the Century arguments? Here's a sampling of national media and other organizations.

Associated Press	Babe Ruth
Gallup Poll	Michael Jordan
ESPN SportsCentury	Michael Jordan
Scripps Howard News Service	Muhammad Ali
Sports Illustrated	Muhammad Ali
The Sporting News	Muhammad Ali
U.S. Congress	Jim Thorpe
U.S. Olympic Committee	Jim Thorpe
USA Today	Babe Ruth

1 **Top free-agent closer Mike Jackson** agrees to a $3 million deal with the Philadelphia Phillies.

Major league veteran DH Chili Davis is released by the Yankees and then announces his retirement from baseball after 19 seasons.

Dodgers shortstop Mark Grudzielanek is arrested for allegedly punching a bouncer in a Hawaiian bar.

2 **Chicago Blackhawks senior vice president** Bob Pulford returns to the bench as head coach and general manager to help rescue the team after it announces the firing of GM Bob Murray and the demotion of coach Lorne Molleken.

4 **Navy's Brian Madden runs** for a career-high 177 yards, leading the Midshipmen to a 19-9 victory in the 100th edition of the Army-Navy game.

5 **Australia's Mark Philippoussis beats** Cedric Pioline of France in four sets, leading the Australian team to its 27th Davis Cup title and first since 1986.

6 **Major League Baseball and ESPN** settle their lawsuit hours before a jury was set to hear their case, signing a reported six-year, $800 million deal to broadcast baseball games.

Carolina Panthers wide receiver Rae Carruth posts a $3 million bond, nearly 12 days after he was arrested on charges he plotted to kill his pregnant girlfriend. His bond agreement requires him to return to jail if his girlfriend dies.

Pitcher David Cone signs a $12 million contract to pitch for the N.Y. Yankees for one more season.

8 **Houston Rockets forward Charles Barkley,** playing in Philadelphia, the city where his remarkable career began, ruptures a tendon in his knee and tells the media that his 16-year career is over.

9 **Houston Astros 2B Craig Biggio** signs a three-year, $28 million, contract extension that makes him the highest-paid player in club history.

Penguins coach Kevin Constantine is fired and replaced by 1980 U.S. Olympic coach Herb Brooks who hopes to turn things around for the team which is in danger of missing the playoffs for the first time since 1990.

10 **Philadelphia Flyers coach Roger Neilson** announces that he's been diagnosed with bone cancer and expects to undergo three months of chemotherapy plus a bone marrow transplant but doesn't expect to miss any games.

Horse racing legend Laffit Pincay Jr. guides Irish Nip to a two-length victory in the sixth race at Hollywood Park for his 8,834th victory, breaking Bill Shoemaker's 29-year-old record and making him the world's winningest jockey.

11 **Wisconsin running back Ron Dayne** wins the Heisman Trophy in a landslide, becoming the first Badger to win the award since Alan Ameche in 1954.

12 **The International Olympic Committee** approves sweeping reforms, including banning visits to bid cities, in the finale of a historic weekend-long restructuring meeting in Switzerland.

13 **Milwaukee third baseman Jeff Cirillo** and pitchers Rolando Arrojo and Scott Karl are traded to Colorado and third baseman Vinny Castilla is moved to Tampa Bay in a nine-player deal that also includes Oakland and is believed to be baseball's first four-team trade since 1977.

Phoenix Suns coach Danny Ainge abruptly resigns to devote more time to his wife and six children. He is replaced by assistant coach Scott Skiles.

14 **Carolina Panthers wide receiver Rae Carruth** is sought on murder charges after his girlfriend dies of wounds from a shooting last month.

Family and friends of **Laffit Pincay Jr.** (c) gather around legendary jockey Bill Shoemaker, the man Pincay Jr. tied in career victories (8,833) on Dec. 9 at Hollywood Park in Inglewood, Calif. Jockeying for position around the pair are, from left, Pincay's daughter and granddaughter, Lisa and Madelyn Bernstein, fellow jockies, Chris McCarron, David Flores, Corey Nakatani, and Pincay's son Jean-Laffit, who is being held by Isaias Enriquez.

NBC Sports chairman Dick Ebersol announces Marv Albert will return next fall as NBC's lead basketball announcer, two years after he was fired amidst a sex scandal.

15 Fugitive Rae Carruth is apprehended in western Tennessee, where police find him hiding in the trunk of a friend's car a day after he failed to surrender on a murder charge in the shooting death of his girlfriend.

International Olympic Committee president Juan Antonio Samaranch is questioned on Capitol Hill by a House subcommittee investigating the Olympic bribery scandal.

17 Notre Dame is placed on probation for the first time ever, after the NCAA hands down light penalties on the most storied school in college football for an improper relationship with a booster.

18 Xavier's Kevin Frey hits an inside bank shot and then a pair of free throws with 8.9 seconds left as underdog Xavier upsets No. 1 Cincinnati 66-64, setting off a wild on-court celebration.

Phoenix Suns forward Tom Gugliotta is released from a Portland, Ore., hospital and returns to Arizona for further tests to try to determine what caused his seizure on a team bus a night earlier.

Viagra, the popular medication used to treat erectile dysfunction, will be the primary sponsor of a NASCAR racing team in 2000, reports the *Charlotte Observer*.

19 Cleveland Browns tackle Orlando Brown storms back onto the field and shoves referee Jeff Triplette to the ground moments after being seriously injured by a penalty flag thrown by Triplette which inadvertently struck him in the eye.

N.Y. Islanders goalie Felix Potvin and a pair of draft picks are traded to Vancouver for goalie Kevin Weekes and forwards Bill Muckalt and Dave Scatchard.

20 The Pittsburgh Penguins sign an $18 million, 10-year agreement to rename the Civic Arena, Mellon Arena, after the Pittsburgh-based bank.

23 A car belonging to Maria Butyrskaya, a world champion figure skater from Russia, explodes on a Moscow street minutes before she planned to head to the Russian national championships.

26 ESPN selects Michael Jordan athlete of the century, finishing the network's year-long dedication to a list of the top 100 athletes of the century.

Hall of Fame jockey Gary Stevens announces that degenerative arthritis in his right knee is forcing him to end his career, which included six victories in Triple Crown races.

27 Golden State Warriors coach P.J. Carlesimo is fired and replaced by GM Garry St. Jean.

28 Utah Jazz president Frank Layden, 67, retires after 20 memorable, wise-cracking years with team as coach and executive.

Three-time Wimbledon champion Boris Becker steps down as Germany's Davis Cup team chief, citing differences with top player Nicolas Kiefer.

30 Pittsburgh's Jaromir Jagr sets a career high for points in a game, scoring three goals and assisting on four others in the Penguins 9-3 victory over the Islanders.

31 Dallas Stars RW Brett Hull scores his 600th and 601st goals in Dallas' 5-4 victory over Anaheim to become the 12th NHL player to reach the milestone.

JAN '00

Sun	Mon	Tue	Wed	Thu	Fri	Sat
						1
2	3	4	5	6	7	8
9	10	11	12	13	14	15
16	17	18	19	20	21	22
23	24	25	26	27	28	29
30	31					

Quote of the Month

"As I told Trent, it's the first operation I've ever done (that) when I finished I looked up and the patient had skates on." — Doctor **DAVID MULDER**, talking about how the fast actions of everyone involved might have saved the life of Montreal Canadiens center Trent McCleary, 27, who came within minutes of dying after being hit in the throat by a slap shot during a game against Philadelphia on Jan 29.

Winning Isn't Everything

Here are the NCAA Division I football programs with the most all-time wins without winning a national championship.

	Wins
West Virginia	596
North Carolina	594
Miami-OH	591
Navy	578
Virginia Tech	568

Electing Fisk Is No Risk

Where new inductee Carlton Fisk ranks among National Baseball Hall of Fame catchers in career home runs:

Johnny Bench	389
Carlton Fisk	**376**
Yogi Berra	358
Roy Campanella	242
Gabby Hartnett	236
Bill Dickey	202
Ernie Lombardi	190
Mickey Cochrane	119
Buck Ewing	71
Rick Ferrell	28
Roger Bresnahan	26
Ray Schalk	11

Note: Records are incomplete for negro leagues catcher Josh Gibson, who was inducted in 1972.

3 Three NFL coaches exit today. N.Y. Jets coach Bill Parcells announces his resignation and hands the reins to defensive coordinator Bill Belichick; and after identical 8-8 records, Pete Carroll is fired by New England and Ray Rhodes is fired by Green Bay.

Buffalo Bills coach Wade Phillips announces that he'll bench starting quarterback Doug Flutie for this weekend's AFC wildcard game in favor of backup Rob Johnson.

4 Florida State WR Peter Warrick scores three touchdowns, leading the Seminoles to a 46-29 Sugar Bowl victory over Virginia Tech and the school's second national championship.

New York Jets former defensive coordinator Bill Belichick drops a bombshell, telling the media and team ownership he doesn't want the team's head coaching job.

5 New Orleans Saints coach Mike Ditka is fired by the team after three straight losing seasons.

6 Atlanta Braves relief pitcher John Rocker is ordered to undergo psychological testing by Major League Baseball before the league decides his punishment for disparaging remarks he made about New York City and New Yorkers in *Sports Illustrated* last month.

7 Rainbow/PUSH Coalition president Jesse Jackson criticizes the firing of Green Bay Packers coach Ray Rhodes as a setback in the NFL's efforts toward racial equality.

8 Tennessee wide receiver Kevin Dyson speeds 75 yards down the left sideline after a lateral from Frank Wycheck on a kickoff, scoring the winning touchdown with three seconds remaining and lifting the Titans to a 22-16 playoff victory over the stunned Buffalo Bills.

9 PGA golfer Tiger Woods keeps alive golf's longest winning streak in 46 years with a 40-foot birdie putt on the second hole of sudden-death to win the Mercedes Championship, his fifth straight tournament victory.

10 Florida State quarterback Chris Weinke, who'll turn 28 before next football season, announces he'll not enter the NFL draft and instead stay one more year with the team to defend its national title.

11 Cowboys coach Chan Gailey is fired two days after the team was knocked out of the first round of the playoffs.

Philanthropist Robert Wood Johnson IV purchases the New York Jets from the estate of the late Leon Hess for $635 million—the highest price ever for an established team without its own stadium.

Catcher Carlton Fisk and infielder Tony Perez are elected to the National Baseball Hall of Fame.

12 Charlotte Hornets guard Bobby Phills is killed on his way home after a team shoot-around when he loses control of his Porsche and crashes into another car.

Braves reliever John Rocker admits in an interview that his comments about minorities and homosexuals in a magazine article made him sound "like a complete jerk."

15 The Jacksonville Jaguars hammer the Miami Dolphins 62-7 in the second-most lopsided playoff game in NFL history.

St. Louis Rams coach Dick Vermeil is named NFL Coach of the Year by the Associated Press.

16 PGA golfer Paul Azinger cards a bogey-free 5-under-par 65 en route to a victory at the Sony Open in Hawaii. It's his first tour victory since being diagnosed and treated for cancer in 1994.

Miami Dolphins coach Jimmy Johnson retires and is replaced by assistant Dave Wannstedt.

AP/Wide World Photos

Tennessee Titans wide receiver **Kevin Dyson** (87) takes one more peek over his shoulder—and blockers Perry Phenix (35) and Greg Favors (51)—during his game-winning kickoff return in Nashville which eliminated Buffalo from the playoffs and was immediately dubbed "The Music City Miracle."

17 **The Sydney Olympic Organizing Committee** fires three senior managers in the first step toward making up a $65 million budget shortfall.

18 **The U.S. women's soccer team announces** that 1991 World Cup team captain April Heinrichs has been hired as the team's new coach.

Seattle Seahawks offensive coordinator Mike Sherman is hired as the new coach of the Green Bay Packers.

19 **NBA legend Michael Jordan returns** to the league as part-owner and president of basketball operations for the Washington Wizards.

The women's basketball game between Seton Hall and Boston College is postponed due to an early-morning dormitory fire at Seton Hall that kills three students and injures several others.

Baseball owners approve a proposal to give commissioner Bud Selig sweeping new powers, allowing him to block trades and redistribute the wealth in order to restore competitive balance in baseball.

21 **NFL Commissioner Paul Tagliabue rules** that Bill Belichick breached his contract (which has three years remaining) when he resigned as coach of the Jets on Jan. 4 and cannot work for another team this year without the Jets' approval.

23 **K.C. Chiefs All-Pro Derrick Thomas** breaks his back and suffers partial paralysis after he loses control of his SUV on an icy road in Kansas City and crashes. One passenger in the car is killed and another suffers minor injuries.

N.Y. Rangers forward Kevin Stevens is arrested and jailed on misdemeanor charges of soliciting prostitution and possessing drug paraphernalia after police raid his motel room in Collinsville, Ill.

24 **N.Y. Jets assistant coach Al Groh** is promoted to replace Bill Parcells as head coach.

25 **The NCAA adopts a rule change** that allows basketball officials to use instant replay to review last-second baskets.

An unexpectedly strong snowstorm blankets the East Coast, forcing the cancellation of a New York-Washington NBA game, a Phoenix-Carolina NHL game, and several college games.

26 **Dallas Cowboys owner Jerry Jones names** assistant coach Dave Campo head coach.

N.Y. Jets defensive coordinator Bill Belichick drops his antitrust lawsuit against the NFL, a day after a judge refused to free him to negotiate with other teams.

27 **The Bill Belichick saga ends.** The New England Patriots hire him after N.Y. Jets boss Bill Parcells makes a phone call to acquire New England's top pick in this year's draft as compensation.

ABC and the Bowl Championship Series agree on a four-year contract extension worth about $400 million that keeps the college football games on the network through the 2005 season.

29 **Tennis star Lindsay Davenport** holds off Martina Hingis in the finals and never drops a set along the way to her first Australian Open singles title.

Washington Wizards coach Gar Heard is fired, the team's first major move since Michael Jordan became head of basketball operations.

Montreal Canadiens center Trent McCleary undergoes emergency throat surgery to save his life moments after he was struck with a slap shot that fractured his larynx and caused a lung to collapse during a 2-2 tie with the Philadelphia Flyers.

30 **Titans quarterback Steve McNair leads** a valiant second-half comeback that comes up one yard short, as the St. Louis Rams hold off Tennessee to win a thrilling Super Bowl XXXIV, 23-16.

FEB '00

Sun	Mon	Tue	Wed	Thu	Fri	Sat
			1	2	3	4	5
6	7	8	9	10	11	12
13	14	15	16	17	18	19
20	21	22	23	24	25	26
27	28	29				

Quote of the Month

"Some people never forget their first car, but a hockey player never forgets his first centerman." —GORDIE HOWE, Detroit Red Wings legend remembering his first captain and hockey mentor, Sid Abel, who died of heart disease in Farmington Hills, Mich. on Feb. 8 at the age of 81.

No Doubting Thomas

A closer look at which quarterbacks Kansas City Chiefs LB Derrick Thomas most frequently victimized during his career.

Quarterbacks	Times Sacked
John Elway	17
Dave Krieg	15
Jeff George	11
Jim Kelly	6

He's Grrrrreat!

How Tiger Woods' consecutive tournament victories streak ranks in the PGA record book:

Golfer	Year	Wins
Byron Nelson	1945	11
Tiger Woods	1999-2000	6
Ben Hogan	1948	6
Jack Burke Jr.	1952	4

Putting the Goal in Goalie

NHL goalies who've scored goals.

	Opponent	Date
Billy Smith, NYI	Colorado	12/28/79
Ron Hextall, Phi.	Boston	12/8/87
*Ron Hextall, Phi.	Washington	4/11/89
Chris Osgood, Det.	Hartford	3/6/96
*Martin Brodeur, NJ	Montreal	4/17/97
Damian Rhodes, Ott.	New Jersey	1/2/99
Martin Brodeur, NJ	Philadelphia	2/15/00
*Playoff game.		

1 **St. Louis Rams coach Dick Vermeil** announces his retirement two days after winning the Super Bowl, claiming the time was right for him to go out on top.

3 **Renegade forward Dennis Rodman signs** a contract to play with the Dallas Mavericks.

L.A. Clippers coach Chris Ford is fired following humiliating losses to Golden State and Phoenix by a combined 77 points.

Pittsburgh Steelers defensive coordinator Jim Haslett signs a three-year deal to coach the New Orleans Saints.

Pro wrestling mastermind Vince McMahon announces the formation of the XFL, a pro football league set to open in February 2001.

4 **Mets reliever Turk Wendell one-ups** last year's bonus request of 99 cents by signing a $2.05 million contract plus a $13.99 bonus.

Hall of Fame third baseman Mike Schmidt makes his debut on the Senior PGA Tour at the season-opening Royal Caribbean Classic.

The PGA Tour of America reaches a financial agreement with the 1999 Ryder Cup team that will pay each player $200,000—half of which will go to a charity of their choice and half to their alma-maters.

6 **World team all-star Pavel Bure scores** three goals, two set up by little brother Valeri, leading his team to a 9-4 victory over North America at the 50th NHL All-Star Game.

Vikings wide receiver Randy Moss sets records for catches (nine) and receiving yards (212) in the NFC's 51-31 victory over the AFC in the highest-scoring Pro Bowl ever.

7 **Golfer Tiger Woods erases** rookie Matt Gogel's seven-stroke lead with seven holes to play and captures the Pebble Beach National Pro-Am, his sixth straight tournament victory.

8 **Kansas City linebacker Derrick Thomas**, 33, dies of a massive blood clot in a Miami hospital, 16 days after suffering a broken back and partial paralysis in a car accident.

Baseball commissioner Bud Selig rules that the hormone supplement androstenedione, which is banned by the Olympics, NCAA, NFL and men's and women's tennis tours will remain legal for Major League Baseball players.

10 **Seattle Mariners superstar Ken Griffey Jr.** is traded to Cincinnati for four players, settling for less money than Seattle offered for the opportunity to play for his hometown team.

NASCAR driver Dale Earnhardt and owner Richard Childress announce a contract extension that will keep Earnhardt driving through at least 2003.

Buffalo Bills stars Thurman Thomas, Bruce Smith, and Andre Reed are released by the team in an effort to reach the league's salary cap.

11 **NFL free agent quarterback Jeff Blake** signs a deal with the New Orleans Saints.

13 **Golfer Phil Mickelson holds off** Tiger Woods and wins the Buick Invitational by four strokes, ending Woods' tournament-victory streak at six.

Western Conference frontcourt giants Shaquille O'Neal, Tim Duncan, and Kevin Garnett lead the West to a 137-126 victory at the NBA All-Star Game.

14 **Boston University skates to a 4-1 victory** over Boston College, earning the Terriers a record sixth-straight Beanpot Championship.

Baltimore linebacker Ray Lewis, jailed since Jan. 31, is released on $1 million bond and agrees to restrictions (including a 9 p.m. curfew) at a hearing in Atlanta.

AP/Wide World Photos

In this photo taken from television, Boston Bruins defenseman **Marty McSorley** delivers a violent two-handed slash to the temple of Vancouver's **Donald Brashear** during the final minute of their game on Feb. 21. In response, Vancouver police subsequently charged McSorley with assault with a weapon.

Nearly 23,000 fans pay final respects to K.C. linebacker Derrick Thomas, filing past an open casket in the end zone at Arrowhead Stadium.

15 Former Detroit Lions running back Barry Sanders is ordered by an arbitrator to repay one-sixth of the $11 million signing bonus ($1.83 million) he received in 1997 from the team.

L.A. Lakers coach Phil Jackson returns to the United Center in Chicago for the first time as an opposing coach, beating the host Bulls 88-76.

N.J. Devils goalie Martin Brodeur is credited with his second career goal after officials rule he was the last to touch the puck before teammate Sergei Brylin of the Devils forced it loose from Flyers center Daymond Langkow causing it to roll into the empty net in the third period of a 4-2 Devils victory.

Organizers announce a new eight-team professional women's soccer league. The Women's United Soccer Association will start in April 2001.

16 Chicago Bulls forward Toni Kukoc, the last key player from the Bulls dynasty, is the centerpiece of a three-team deal that sends him to the 76ers. The deal also sends Sixers Larry Hughes and Billy Owens to Golden State.

Dallas Mavericks forward Dennis Rodman continues to tally some remarkable numbers: during his second game with the team he records his 23rd career ejection (Feb. 15) and his 12th league suspension (today) for "not leaving the court in a timely manner."

18 Georgia Tech men's basketball coach Bobby Cremins announces that he will retire at the end of the season after missing the NCAA Tournament for the fourth straight year.

NBA Hall of Famer Kareem Abdul-Jabbar is hired as an assistant coach for the L.A. Clippers.

20 Reigning Winston Cup champion Dale Jarrett leads a parade of five Ford cars across the finish line to capture his second career Daytona 500 title.

21 Boston Bruins defenseman Marty McSorley lands a violent and deliberate two-handed slash to the head of Vancouver's Donald Brashear with three seconds left in a 5-2 Vancouver win.

22 Published reports say Yankees outfielder Darryl Strawberry tested positive for cocaine during a routine drug test on Jan. 19.

23 Bruins defenseman Marty McSorley is suspended indefinitely by the NHL for his slash of Donald Brashear.

Former figure skater Tonya Harding is arrested for fourth-degree domestic violence assault, after throwing a hubcap at her live-in boyfriend and repeatedly punching him in the face.

26 The Washington Redskins acquire the No. 3 overall draft pick from San Francisco in exchange for four later picks, giving the Redskins two of the top three selections in April's NFL draft.

27 Toronto Raptors forward Vince Carter scores 51 points in a nationally televised 103-102 victory over the Phoenix Suns.

American League umpire John Hirschbeck is elected as president of the World Umpires Association, the new union formed to represent Major League Baseball's umpires.

28 Yankees outfielder Darryl Strawberry is handed a one-year suspension by baseball commissioner Bud Selig for his failed drug test last month.

29 Atlanta Braves reliever John Rocker, suspended until May 1 for his offensive comments against gays, foreigners, and minorities, agrees to a one-year contract with the team.

MAR '00

Sun	Mon	Tue	Wed	Thu	Fri	Sat
			1	2	3	4
5	6	7	8	9	10	11
12	13	14	15	16	17	18
19	20	21	22	23	24	25
26	27	28	29	30	31	

Quote of the Month

"I have used a lot of different things for motivational purposes. I've always tried to act that part of my coaching is to move you where you're supposed to be. We're not learning to play bridge. We're learning to play basketball." —BOBBY KNIGHT, Indiana University basketball coach, tells a local television station in response to allegations by a former player that Knight choked him during practice.

One Hull of a Start

After two career America's Cup finals, New Zealand skipper Russell Coutts is on his way to becoming the most successful skipper in the event's history.

Skipper	Finals	W-L	Cups
Harold Vanderbilt, USA	1930, 34, 37	12-2	3
Dennis Conner, USA	1980, 83, 87	10-4	3
Russell Coutts, NZE	**1995, 2000**	**10-0**	**2**
Charles Barr, USA	1899, 1901, 03	9-0	3
Bus Mosbacher, USA	1962, 67	8-1	2

Baby Boomers

The Kingdome's demolition on Mar. 26 was the latest in a wave of ballparks and stadiums being razed before their 30th birthday. Here is a list of big-four-sports parks and arenas that have bitten the dust recently.

Age	Stadium	Location	Imploded
24	Kingdome	Seattle	2000
25	The Omni	Atlanta	1997
25	McNichols Arena	Denver	2000
25	Richfield Coliseum	Cleveland	1999
26	Market Sq. Arena	Indianapolis	2000
27	HemisFair Arena	San Antonio	1995
28	Met Center	Bloomington, MN	1995
29	Arlington Stadium	Arlington, Texas	1994

1 **Braves closer John Rocker has his fine** and suspension reduced by an arbitrator, clearing the way for him to report to the team's spring training.

New Zealand skipper Russell Coutts hands over the wheel of Black Magic to Dean Barker who leads the Kiwis to a Race 5 victory and a 5-0 sweep of Italy in the America's Cup finals.

4 **Flyers captain Eric Lindros suffers** his fourth concussion in two years when he is hit in the jaw by Bruin Hal Gill.

6 **Boston Bruins veteran Ray Bourque is traded** to the Colorado Avalanche along with forward Dave Andreychuk for forward Brian Rolston, defenseman Martin Grenier, center Sami Pahlsson and Boston's choice of a first-round pick in either 2000 or 2001.

Detroit Pistons coach Alvin Gentry is fired and replaced by assistant George Irvine after the team starts to lose ground in the race for a playoff spot.

A San Francisco appeals court upholds a 1998 ruling that allows disabled golfer Casey Martin to use a motorized cart in PGA Tour events.

7 **Boston Bruins defenseman Marty McSorley** is formerly charged with assault by a Canadian court and, if convicted, faces a maximum sentence of 18 months in jail for his slash of Donald Brashear on Feb. 21.

8 **Dallas Stars goalie Ed Belfour scuffles** with a security guard at The Mansion on Turtle Creek Hotel during the early hours of the morning and is arrested and charged with misdemeanor assault and resisting arrest.

ABC president Howard Katz fires Monday Night Football analyst Boomer Esiason, 14-year producer Ken Wolfe and 13-year director Craig Janoff, claiming that he wants the show to "try a fresh approach."

Dallas Mavericks forward Dennis Rodman is released by the team after 13 tumultuous games.

9 **Cincinnati men's basketball star** Kenyon Martin breaks his leg during the opening minutes of a first-round Conference USA tournament game and is out for the rest of the season.

Basketball legend Wilt Chamberlain's No. 13 becomes the first number ever retired in the 74-year history of the Harlem Globetrotters.

10 **Baltimore Ravens star Ray Lewis pleads** not guilty in Fulton County (Ga.) Superior Court to murder and assault charges stemming from two stabbing deaths after a Super Bowl party in Atlanta.

Veteran center Doug Gilmour of the Chicago Blackhawks is acquired by the Buffalo Sabres who are hoping to close in on a playoff spot.

11 **Britain's Prince Naseem Hamed** successfully defends his WBO featherweight title against previously undefeated Vuyani Bungu of South Africa, extending his winning streak to 34 matches.

12 **Toronto Maple Leafs defenseman** Bryan Berard suffers a serious injury to his eye after being hit by the stick of Ottawa forward Marian Hossa as he followed through on a shot.

L.A. Dodgers pitcher Carlos Perez is arrested for investigation for drunken driving by Florida police after they find him stopped at a traffic light asleep at the wheel.

LPGA golfer Annika Sorenstam wins the Welch's-Circle K Championship in a playoff and in doing so qualifies for the LPGA Hall of Fame with her 19th career title.

AP/Wide World Photos

He tried every line in the book, but this dejected **N.Y. Mets mascot** knew all along she was way out of his league. The woman (who looks like she is having second thoughts) is on the field inside Japan's Tokyo Dome waiting to present flowers to Mets and Cubs players taking part in the first Opening Day series in baseball history to occur outside of North America.

13 Miami quarterback Dan Marino holds a press conference where he announces his retirement after 17 NFL seasons.

14 San Antonio Spurs forward Sean Elliott returns to the lineup in a game against Atlanta, seven months after receiving a kidney transplant.

Six Boston Red Sox pitchers combine to throw a perfect game in a 5-0 spring training victory over Toronto.

Braves reliever John Rocker gets a standing ovation in his first appearance of spring training.

NBA coaches and the league compromise on a policy for wearing microphones during games, allowing coaches to opt for having a boom mic placed near the bench instead of wearing the wireless mic and thus avoid a fine.

18 The top three seeds in the West Region are eliminated in second round action of the NCAA men's basketball tournament: Arizona, St. John's, and Oklahoma fall to Wisconsin, Gonzaga, and Purdue.

Former 49ers owner Eddie DeBartolo signs over the team to his sister Denise DeBartolo York, ending the siblings' feud over the team's ownership that began when DeBartolo fell into legal trouble in 1997.

19 Tennis starlet Anna Kournikova and her mother reportedly cause a commotion on a flight to the Ericsson Open in Florida after Kournikova allegedly refuses to put her miniature Doberman pinscher in its carrying case, as FAA rules require. The pilot and police are forced to intervene.

21 New Jersey Devils defenseman Scott Niedermayer is suspended for 10 games by the NHL (including one playoff game) for whacking his stick over the head of Florida's Peter Worrell.

23 Angels outfielder Jim Edmonds is traded to the St. Louis Cardinals for pitcher Kent Bottenfield and second baseman Adam Kennedy.

26 Previously snubbed Toronto Raptors guard Vince Carter is added to the U.S. Olympic men's basketball team, replacing the injured Tom Gugliotta.

It takes 17 seconds for the Seattle Kingdome to be imploded, bringing an end to the 24-year-old former home of the Seahawks and Mariners.

27 Philadelphia defenseman Eric Desjardins is named captain of the team after the players vote to replace Eric Lindros who suffered a season-ending concussion earlier in the month and then criticized the team's treatment of it.

28 General manager Neil Smith and coach John Muckler of the New York Rangers are fired with four NHL regular season games remaining, as the Rangers miss the playoffs for the third straight season.

29 In front of a sellout crowd at the Tokyo Dome in Japan the Chicago Cubs beat the N.Y. Mets, 5-3, in the first regular season Major League Baseball game played outside North America.

A van carrying nine members of the Tennessee-Martin baseball team collides with a tractor-trailer around midnight near Memphis, Tenn., injuring the coach and two players critically.

30 University of Houston coach Clyde Drexler ends his two-year stint running the men's basketball program to return to parenting, admitting that he couldn't do both.

Former Dallas Cowboys linebacker Thomas "Hollywood" Henderson surprises lottery officials when he shows up at their headquarters and claims his $10.4 million prize.

APRIL '00

Sun	Mon	Tue	Wed	Thu	Fri	Sat
						1
2	3	4	5	6	7	8
9	10	11	12	13	14	15
16	17	18	19	20	21	22
23/30	24	25	26	27	28	29

Quote of the Month

"You go through streaks like this. It's kind of like the 'Barefoot Bears,' or whatever you call 'em. But you can't panic." —JACK McKEON, Cincinnati Reds manager referring to the movie, "The Bad News Bears" after the Reds struggle to meet expectations and lose three straight games by a combined score of 31-7.

Thanks, but No Thanks

The 1999-2000 St. Louis Blues became the 11th team in the last 15 seasons to win The President's Trophy (awarded to the NHL regular season champion) and not win the Stanley Cup. Here are the only four teams that have won both in the same season.

		W-L-T (Pts)*
1999	Dallas Stars	51-19-12 (114)
1994	New York Rangers	52-24-8 (112)
1989	Calgary Flames	54-17-9 (117)
1987	Edmonton Oilers	50-24-6 (106)

*Final regular season.

Poor Man's Forrest Gump

Baltimore Orioles eight-year veteran relief pitcher **Mike Trombley** has been present at four occasions when someone has joined the 3,000 Hit Club. He was a Minnesota teammate of Dave Winfield (1993) and Paul Molitor (1996). He gave up the milestone hit to Cleveland's Eddie Murray (1995). And he was in the Orioles bullpen when Cal Ripken joined on April 15.

2 **UConn junior Shea Ralph scores** 12 points and teammate Asjha Jones adds 12 more, leading the Huskies to a 71-52 victory over Tennessee in the NCAA Women's Basketball Championship Game.

NASCAR rookie Dale Earnhardt Jr. wins his first Winston Cup race at the DirectTV 500 at Texas Motor Speedway.

3 **Michigan State point guard** Mateen Cleaves guides the Spartans to a 89-76 victory over Florida in the NCAA Men's Basketball Championship Game.

Dallas Stars right wing Brett Hull scores his 610th career goal, tying him with his Hall of Fame father, Bobby, for ninth place on the all-time list.

Atlanta Braves first baseman Andres Galarraga returns to the lineup on Opening Day, after missing all of 1999 due to chemotherapy, and hits a home run to help the Braves beat Colorado 2-0.

6 **Twin Georgia guards Coco and Kelly Miller** win the Sullivan Award, becoming the first duo to win the award in its 70-year history.

8 **North Dakota scores three goals** in the third period to come back and beat Boston College and win the school's seventh NCAA hockey championship, 4-2.

Cowboys quarterback Troy Aikman weds former team public relations staffer Rhonda Worthey at his home in Plano, Texas.

9 **Fiji-born golfer Vijay Singh cards** a final-round 69 and holds off a talented pack of golfers, including Ernie Els, Loren Roberts, and David Duval to win the Masters.

New York Yankees pitching coach Mel Stottlemyre reveals that he will miss four months to receive chemotherapy treatment for a form of blood cancer.

10 **Green Bay Packers tight end Mark Chmura** is arrested after a 17-year-old babysitter accuses him of sexual assault.

Ken Griffey Jr. becomes the youngest player to hit 400 career home runs when he blasts one in the fourth inning off Colorado's Rolando Arrojo.

11 **Calgary Flames GM Al Coates,** coach Brian Sutter, plus an assistant and the director of player personnel are all fired after the Flames miss the playoffs for the fourth straight season.

12 **New York Jets WR Keyshawn Johnson** is traded to the Tampa Bay Buccaneers for two first-round picks, and is signed to an eight-year, $56 million contract.

Brazilian soccer superstar Ronaldo ruptures the patella tendon in his right knee seven minutes into his first game after missing five months due to surgery on the same knee. He is expected to miss 7-8 months.

Philadelphia native Dawn Staley is named women's basketball coach at Temple.

15 **Baltimore Orioles 3B Cal Ripken Jr.'s** third single of the night, in a 6-4 victory over Minnesota, makes him the 24th player in baseball history to reach 3,000 hits.

Penn State defensive end Courtney Brown is selected first overall by the Cleveland Browns at the 2000 NFL amateur draft.

17 **Kenyans Elijah Lagat and** Catherine Ndereba win their first Boston Marathons in the closest men's and women's finishes in race history.

18 **Atlanta Braves closer John Rocker gets** a standing ovation and some scattered boos before pitching a scoreless ninth inning against Philadelphia in his first action after a two-week suspension for his remarks in a *Sports Illustrated* article.

When angry Davis Cup tennis fans from host Chile began tossing fruit, coins, and bottles at Argentine players during a match in Santiago on April 7, the police stepped in with shields to escort players safely off the court. But the **Argentinian fans** weren't as lucky. All they had to protect them from the garbage storm were green plastic chairs.

A hot dog promotion before the third inning of the Angels-Blue Jays game in Toronto goes awry, when fans are splattered with wiener parts after dogs shot from the "Hot Dog Blaster" fall apart in midair. (An extra layer of wrapping was added the following day, and the promotion went off without a hitch.)

19 Houston Rockets forward Charles Barkley returns to the court for the first time since Dec. 8, playing six minutes and recording two points, one rebound, an assist and a blocked shot against Vancouver in his final NBA game.

22 White Sox reliever Keith Foulke needs stitches to mend a cut under his eye that resulted from two bench-clearing brawls during Chicago's 14-6 victory over Detroit in which there were 10 ejections and five players hit by pitches.

23 Hall of Fame pitcher Nolan Ryan undergoes emergency double-bypass heart surgery in Austin, Texas after doctors find a substantial blockage of the left main coronary artery.

N.Y. Yankees switch-hitters Bernie Williams and Jorge Posada each homer right-handed and left-handed in a 10-7 victory over Toronto, marking the first time teammates have done so in a game.

IRL driver Al Unser Jr. ends a five-year winless streak at the Vegas Indy 300 and dedicates the victory to his 13-year-old daughter, Cody, who was paralyzed last year by a rare neurological infection in her spinal cord.

24 The NBA's winningest coach, Lenny Wilkens, resigns as head coach of the Atlanta Hawks after seven seasons with the team.

Wal-Mart heir Stan Kroenke buys the Colorado Avalanche, Denver Nuggets, and the Pepsi Center in Denver from Liberty Media Group for $450 million.

NHL veteran goalie Bill Ranford retires after a 15-year career in which he won two Stanley Cups and a Conn Smythe Trophy.

25 Players and coaches from five major league baseball teams sit out games in recognition of Miami's Cuban-American work stoppage to protest Elian Gonzalez's removal from a relative's home.

San Diego Chargers general manager Bobby Beathard retires after a 37-year front-office career that included four Super Bowl championships.

San Jose Sharks goalie Steve Shields stops 21 shots en route to a 3-1 victory over St. Louis in Game 7 of their first round playoff series, making the Blues the second regular-season points champion in NHL history to get knocked out of the first round.

27 Major League Baseball hands out 82 games worth of suspensions and $21,000 in total fines for the White Sox-Tigers brawl on April 22.

28 The NCAA says it will cancel all events in South Carolina, including the first and second rounds of the 2002 men's basketball tournament, if the Confederate flag is not removed from the statehouse dome.

29 Heavyweight champion Lennox Lewis successfully defends his title after landing a devastating right uppercut that knocks previously unbeaten Michael Grant to the mat with 21 seconds left in the second round.

Sprinter Marion Jones anchors the U.S. women's 800-meter relay team to a world record (1:27.46) at the Penn Relays in Philadelphia.

30 Red Sox pitcher Pedro Martinez is ejected by umpire Tim Tschida in the eighth inning after hitting Indians second baseman Roberto Alomar. Benches empty but no punches are thrown.

MAY '00

Sun	Mon	Tue	Wed	Thu	Fri	Sat
	1	2	3	4	5	6
7	8	9	10	11	12	13
14	15	16	17	18	19	20
21	22	23	24	25	26	27
28	29	30	31			

Quote of the Month

"She has a very strong desire to win. She says to me, 'Grandpa, second sucks.'" —Jim Fisher, grandfather of Sarah Fisher, 19, who became the the third (and youngest) woman to ever qualify for the Indianapolis 500.

Juan for the Record Books

On May 28 Juan Montoya became the seventh rookie to win the Indianapolis 500 and just the second in the last 73 years. Here is how his performance stacks up.

Year	Driver (Start pos.)	MPH	Winnings
1911	Ray Harroun (28)	—	$10,000
1913	Jules Goux (7)	—	20,000
1914	Rene Thomas (15)	—	39,750
1926	Frank Lockhart (20)	95.904	35,600
1927	George Souders (22)	97.545	26,100
1966	Graham Hill (15)	144.317	156,297
2000	Juan Montoya (2)	167.607	1,235,690

Note: MPH records are incomplete for 1911, 1913, and 1914.

A Few of our Favorite Things

Kentucky Derby winner Fusaichi Pegasus became the first favorite to win the first jewel of the Triple Crown since Spectacular Bid in 1979. Despite two decades without a favorite winning, the Derby is still on an even keel with thoroughbred racing's other big paydays.

Race	% Won by Favorites	Last Time
Kentucky Derby	39% (49-126)	Fusaichi Pegasus (2000)
Preakness Stakes	50% (63-126)	Real Quiet (1998)
Belmont Stakes	39% (52-132)	Thunder Gulch (1995)
Breeders' Cup	39% (44-113)	Daylami, Soaring Softly (1999)*

*Daylami won the Turf race and Soaring Softly won the Filly & Mare Turf at Gulfstream Park.

2 NASCAR officials strip driver Jeremy Mayfield of 151 Winston Cup points and fine and suspend his team owner and crew chief in the harshest penalty in circuit history for using an illegal fuel additive.

Cubs pitcher Kerry Wood allows three hits over six innings en route to an 11-1 victory over Houston in his first start since undergoing "Tommy John" surgery on his elbow 13 months earlier.

Jockey Julie Krone becomes the first female jockey elected to the National Museum of Racing's Hall of Fame.

5 Philadelphia's Keith Primeau ends the NHL's longest game in 64 years with a wrist shot past Pittsburgh goalie Ron Tugnutt at 12:01 of the fifth overtime, giving the Flyers a 2-1 victory in Game 4 of their Eastern Conference semifinals series.

6 Fusaichi Pegasus dominates the field at the 126th running of the Kentucky Derby and becomes the first favorite to win since 1979.

9 Los Angeles Lakers center Shaquille O'Neal wins the NBA's Most Valuable Player Award, earning 120 of 121 first-place votes in the most decisive margin since the media began voting in 1980-81.

NHL players are given the OK to compete in the 2002 Winter Games in Salt Lake City, according to an agreement between the NHL, the players association, and the International Ice Hockey Federation.

10 The Olympic torch is lit in Ancient Olympia in Greece, and the event is immediately marred by accusations of nepotism when the second person to carry the torch is the 11-year-old daughter of IOC vice president Kevan Gosper.

11 NBA newcomers Elton Brand of the Chicago Bulls and Steve Francis of the Houston Rockets are named co-winners of the NBA Rookie of the Year Award.

12 NASCAR rookie Adam Petty, 19, is killed during a practice run at New Hampshire International Speedway when his red-and-blue Sprint PCS Chevy slams into a wall in Turn 3 at around 130 mph.

IOC vice president Kevan Gosper apologizes for his "lapse of judgment" in allowing his daughter to replace another girl scheduled to carry the Olympic torch (See May 10) and offers to give up his leg of the relay to the 15-year-old Australian-Greek student his daughter replaced.

15 Indiana University athletic officials announce much-awaited penalties against basketball coach Bobby Knight, including a three-game suspension, fines, and an ultimatum to cool his infamous temper.

Green Bay Packers tight end Mark Chmura is formally charged with third-degree sexual assault by a 17-year-old girl who claims he had sex with her following a high school prom in April.

16 A melee breaks out at Wrigley Field after a fan apparently strikes Dodgers bullpen catcher Chad Kreuter and takes off with his cap, causing as many as six players and coaches to give chase in the stands.

New York Knicks coach Jeff Van Gundy watches his luck go from bad to worse when a few hours after his team loses a playoff game in Miami his 1995 Honda Civic is demolished by the blasting engines of the team's chartered plane.

18 Former Olympic figure skater Tonya Harding pleads guilty to misdemeanor assault and third-degree malicious mischief charges that she punched her boyfriend and threw a hubcap at his head. She is sentenced to three days in jail and community service.

20 Jockey Jerry Bailey rides Red Bullet to a convincing victory over favorite Fusaichi Pegasus at the 125th running of the Preakness Stakes at Pimlico.

Whether she is whacking knees or whacking weeds, former U.S. Olympic figure skater **Tonya Harding** can't seem to avoid the media's relentless, unforgiving eye. On May 23 photographers caught Harding, who pleaded guilty to attacking her boyfriend on May 18, performing part of her court-ordered community service in a cemetery in Camas, Wash.

Tragedy strikes Lowe's Motor Speedway when a pedestrian bridge collapses, injuring more than 100 fans leaving The Winston auto race.

Indy car driver Sarah Fisher, 19, records a four-lap average of 220.237 mph and becomes the third (and youngest) woman to ever qualify for the Indianapolis 500.

Minnesota Timberwolves swingman Malik Sealy, 30, becomes the second active NBA player to die in an auto accident this year when his SUV is hit head-on by a pickup truck traveling the wrong way on a divided highway in Minneapolis.

21 Anaheim's Garret Anderson helps set a Major League Baseball record by becoming the sixth player of the day to hit a grand slam, topping the record of five set last season.

23 Women's tennis great Martina Navratilova makes an impressive return to pro tennis after a 5½-year layoff, teaming up with Mariaan de Swardt to win their opening-round doubles match at the Madrid Open in two sets.

24 Major League Baseball hands down suspensions and fines for 16 Dodgers players and three coaches for charging into the stands at Wrigley Field to confront unruly fans on May 16.

New York Yankees pinch hitter Lance Johnson appears in his first game with the team and becomes the third major leaguer in baseball history to play for the Cubs, White Sox, Mets and Yankees (Charley Smith and Dick Tidrow were the others).

25 The legal defense team for Ray Lewis gets an unexpected boost from Lewis' limousine driver Duane Fassett, who testifies that he saw Lewis raise his hand but did not see him hit the victim.

26 Devils' Patrik Elias scores two goals as New Jersey beats Philadelphia, 2-1, in Game 7, completing one of the greatest comebacks in playoff history by winning three straight games to take the Eastern Conference final series.

28 Defending CART series champion Juan Montoya dazzles the crowd and field at the 84th running of the Indianapolis 500, becoming the first rookie to win the race since Graham Hill in 1966.

N.Y. Yankees pitcher Roger Clemens (5H, 2ER, 13K) and Red Sox ace Pedro Martinez (4H, 0ER, 9K) face off in a classic pitching duel in front of a sellout crowd at Yankee Stadium. Boston wins, 2-0, on a two-out ninth-inning home run by OF Trot Nixon.

Oakland Raiders DB Eric Turner, who earlier this month denied reports he was ill, dies of complications from abdominal cancer at the age of 31.

29 Oakland A's 2B Randy Velarde records the 12th unassisted triple play in Major League Baseball history, and the first in almost six years.

Houston Comets star Sheryl Swoopes becomes the first player in WNBA history to reach the 2,000-point mark with a three-pointer during an 84-68 victory over New York in the season opener.

30 Indiana coach Bobby Knight sits for an hour-long TV interview with ESPN's Roy Firestone and Digger Phelps, where he admits that his "temper is a problem" but offers no further apologies.

Washington Redskins DB Darrell Green, 40, signs a contract extension with the team that will keep him in a Skins uniform for at least five more years.

JUNE '00

Sun	Mon	Tue	Wed	Thu	Fri	Sat
				1	2	3
4	5	6	7	8	9	10
11	12	13	14	15	16	17
18	19	20	21	22	23	24
25	26	27	28	29	30	

Quote of the Month

"I'm numb. I'm just numb right now. I didn't know champagne burned this much when it gets in your eyes." —Kobe Bryant, 21, Los Angeles Lakers forward, after winning his first NBA championship.

Monday Night Service

Veteran broadcaster Al Michaels dodged the broom when ABC cleaned house this winter, meaning he'll be in the booth for his 15th season. The following is a list of the TV personalities to log the most years in the Monday Night Football broadcast booth.

Years

27	Frank Gifford	(1971-97)
15	Al Michaels	(1986-present)
14	Howard Cosell	(1970-83)
12	Dan Dierdorf	(1987-98)
12	Don Meredith	(1970-73, 77-84)

NBA Finals
30-something Club

L.A. Lakers center Shaquille O'Neal added his name to an exclusive list of players to score 30 points or more in each game of the NBA Finals.

Player, Team	Year(s)	Games
Bob Pettit, St. Louis	1960	7
Elgin Baylor, Los Angeles	1962	7
Jerry West, Los Angeles	1962, 69-70	*
K. Abdul-Jabbar, Milwaukee	1974	7
Larry Bird, Boston	1984	7
Hakeem Olajuwon, Houston	1994	7
Shaquille O'Neal, Los Angeles	2000	6

*West did it three times, against Boston in the 1962 (7 games) and 1969 (7) Finals, and New York in 1970 (7).

1 Former NBA player Sidney Lowe is named head coach of the Vancouver Grizzlies, the team's fifth coach in the franchise's five-year history.

2 Hockey legend Wayne Gretzky joins the ownership group of the NHL's Phoenix Coyotes.

Tampa Bay's Fred McGriff becomes the 31st player to hit 400 career home runs with a two-run blast off the Mets' Glendon Rusch.

4 Atlanta Braves reliever John Rocker instigates a confrontation at Turner Field before a game against the N.Y. Yankees and *Sports Illustrated* reporter Jeff Pearlman, whose interview included the disparaging remarks for which Rocker was suspended.

5 Baltimore Ravens LB Ray Lewis accepts a plea bargain that drops his six felony counts provided he pleads guilty to a misdemeanor obstruction of justice charge that will carry one year probation.

Atlanta's John Rocker is demoted and fined $5,000 one day after a confrontation with a reporter. Braves officials say the move is a result of Rocker's control problems on the field, not off it.

Japanese pro golfer Shigeki Maruyama cards a record-breaking 13-under-par 58 during U.S. Open sectional qualifying in Rockville, Md.

All-pro defensive back Deion Sanders signs a seven-year, $56 million contract, with an $8 million signing bonus, to join the Washington Redskins.

Green Bay Packers TE Mark Chmura is released by the team in a move termed "strictly business," despite the fact Chmura is awaiting trial on sexual assault charges.

6 Baltimore Ravens LB Ray Lewis takes the stand for the prosecution in his well-publicized murder trial and testifies against his former co-defendants.

San Francisco WR Jerry Rice signs a restructured five-year, $31 million contract with the 49ers.

7 Chicago Cubs slugger Sammy Sosa and manager Don Baylor trade barbs in the press before a game against Arizona, sparking Sosa trade rumors over the next several weeks.

Edmonton Oilers coach Kevin Lowe announces his resignation after one season with the team.

8 Philadelphia Flyers interim coach Craig Ramsay is named head coach, replacing Roger Neilson, who Ramsay replaced in mid-February, while he underwent cancer treatment.

Quarterback Randall Cunningham, cut by the Vikings, agrees to be Troy Aikman's backup in Dallas.

9 Former Edmonton coach Kevin Lowe, who resigned two days prior, is announced as the team's new general manager.

10 Center Jason Arnott scores at 8:20 of the second overtime of Game 6 to give the N.J. Devils a 2-1 victory over the Dallas Stars and the franchise's second Stanley Cup championship.

Hard-charging Commendable earns trainer D. Wayne Lukas and jockey Pat Day a victory at the 132nd running of the Belmont Stakes.

Australians Mark Woodforde and Todd Woodbridge win the men's doubles competition at the French Open. It's their 58th career doubles title, setting a new tennis record.

11 France's Mary Pierce becomes the first woman since Martina Navratilova (1984) to win French Open singles and doubles crowns in the same year after teaming with Martina Hingis to capture the women's doubles title. Gustavo Kuerten wins his second French Open men's singles title.

12 San Francisco 49ers QB Steve Young, 38, announces his retirement from the NFL.

AP/Wide World Photos

"Our team played so well, we're going to bust up a van," must have been what these rambunctious **Los Angeles Lakers fans** were thinking after they took to the streets during the early morning of June 20 to celebrate the team's 12th NBA championship.

An Atlanta jury acquits the two remaining defendants in the Ray Lewis murder trial.

13 **Toronto Raptors coach Butch Carter** is fired by the team because of off-court distractions despite his success in leading the team to its first playoff appearance last season.

NBA Hall of Famer Julius Erving pleads for the public's help in trying to find his 19-year-old son who has had drug problems in the past and has been missing since May 28.

Former Florida State kicker Sebastian Janikowski is acquitted of charges that he bribed police to get his roommate out of a trespassing charge.

14 **Washington Wizards boss Michael Jordan** hires University of Miami coach Leonard Hamilton to be the team's head coach, signing him to a five-year, $10 million deal.

Colorado Avalanche D Ray Bourque signs a one-year, $5 million contract extension with an option for a second year.

17 **Undefeated boxer "Sugar" Shane Mosley** earns a split decision victory over Oscar De La Hoya, and claims the world welterweight title in front of a sellout crowd at the Staples Center in Los Angeles.

18 **Golfer Tiger Woods finishes** his domination of the field at the 100th U.S. Open, carding his third consecutive round in the 60s en route to a 15-stroke win and his third career major tournament victory.

19 **L.A. Lakers center Shaquille O'Neal** pours in 41 points, leading the Lakers to a 116-111 victory over the Indiana Pacers in Game 6 of the NBA Finals and the franchise's 12th NBA championship.

NHL Hall of Famer Jacques Lemaire is hired to be the first coach of the expansion Minnesota Wild.

20 **Rookie NFL kicker Sebastian Janikowski** is arrested and charged with possession of GHB, a so-called date-rape drug, in Tallahassee, Fla.

21 **NBA coaching legend Lenny Wilkens** agrees to a reported four-year, $20 million deal to coach the Toronto Raptors.

Former Olympic Czech Republic coach Ivan Hlinka is promoted from assistant to head coach the Pittsburgh Penguins.

22 **ABC-TV unveils its new** Monday Night Football broadcast lineup, teaming up veteran Al Michaels with former NFL quarterback Dan Fouts and comedian Dennis Miller.

Assistant coach Craig MacTavish is promoted to replace Kevin Lowe as coach of the Edmonton Oilers.

24 **Boston University goaltender Rick DiPietro** makes history when the N.Y. Islanders make him the first goaltender taken with the first overall pick in the NHL draft since it was modified in 1969.

28 **University of Cincinnati's Kenyon Martin** is picked first overall by the N.J. Nets at the NBA draft.

Outspoken NBA star Jayson Williams, who missed the entire 1999-2000 season with a broken leg, announces his retirement from basketball.

Arbitrator Lawrence Holden sides with the NHL in its arbitration case against Alexei Yashin, a decision that the NHL says binds the star center to the Ottawa Senators for one more season.

29 **Atlanta Braves reliever John Rocker** makes his first appearance in New York and is greeted with mostly boos and jeers, with only a golf ball being thrown in his direction by the fans at Shea Stadium.

30 **North Carolina men's basketball coach** Bill Guthridge steps down and early rumors claim that he will be replaced by another disciple of Dean Smith – Kansas coach Roy Williams.

JULY '00

Sun	Mon	Tue	Wed	Thu	Fri	Sat
						1
2	3	4	5	6	7	8
9	10	11	12	13	14	15
16	17	18	19	20	21	22
23/30	24/31	25	26	27	28	29

Quote of the Month

"Of all the days to come and show your breasts, they picked Family Day." —Brad Fullmer, Blue Jays DH commenting on four topless women who unwittingly chose July 16, "Family Day" at the Skydome, to advertise a local strip club by leaning out of a hotel window and waving at fans.

Built for Fantastic Finishes

Three of the closest finishes in Championship Auto Racing Teams history have occured at Michigan International Speedway in Brooklyn, Mich:

Seconds	Drivers (Year)	Track
0.027	Mark Blundell def. Gil de Ferran (1997)	Portland
0.032	Tony Kanaan def. Juan Montoya (1999)	Michigan
0.040	Juan Montoya def. Michael Andretti (2000)	Michigan
0.043	Al Unser Jr. def. Scott Goodyear (1992)	Indianapolis
0.056	Scott Pruett def. Al Unser Jr. (1995)	Michigan

Grand Slam Sampras

A look at who Pete Sampras defeated in the finals of each of his record 13 career Grand Slam titles.

Wimbledon		Australian	
2000	Patrick Rafter	1997	Carlos Moya
1999	Andre Agassi	1994	Todd Martin
1998	Goran Ivanisevic	**U.S. Open**	
1997	Cedric Pioline	1996	Michael Chang
1995	Boris Becker	1995	Andre Agassi
1994	Goran Ivanisevic	1993	Cedric Pioline
1993	Jim Courier	1990	Andre Agassi

Source: USA Today

3 Jamaican sprinter Merlene Ottey has her two-year ban for steroid use lifted after the IAAF says the lab improperly tested her urine sample.

5 Former Calgary coach Dave King signs a three-year contract to be the first head coach of the NHL expansion Columbus Blue Jackets.

6 Colts running back Fred Lane is shot and killed during a domestic dispute at his home in Charlotte, N.C.

Tennis star Venus Williams defeats her little sister in a rare battle of siblings in the semifinals of a Grand Slam event, taking the Wimbledon match 6-2, 7-6.

Kansas coach Roy Williams ends weeks of speculation by announcing that he has turned down the offer to coach at North Carolina.

Dodgers pitcher Orel Hershiser announces his retirement after 18 seasons in the major leagues.

The 19-year-old son of Dr. J., Cory Erving, is found dead in his car, submerged in eight feet of water in a pond less than a mile from the Erving home.

7 Winston Cup driver Kenny Irwin is killed during a practice run in Turn 3 at New Hampshire International Speedway, eight weeks (to the day) after fellow driver Adam Petty was killed on the same turn.

NBA all-star free agent Grant Hill tells Detroit Pistons' management that he will sign with Orlando on Aug. 1.

8 Twenty-year-old Venus Williams becomes the first female African-American tennis player to win a singles title at Wimbledon in 42 years.

9 Tennis champion Pete Sampras wins the men's singles title at Wimbledon to earn his 13th Grand Slam single's title, surpassing Roy Emerson for the all-time career record.

Twelve people are killed in a soccer stampede in Zimbabwe after police fire tear gas at bottle-throwing fans during a World Cup qualifying game.

N.Y. Mets catcher Mike Piazza, who suffered a slight concussion when he was hit by a Roger Clemens' pitch a night earlier, accuses the Yankees pitcher of intentionally throwing at his head.

Chicago Cubs OF Sammy Sosa reverses his decision and tells the team he does not wish to be traded.

10 Cyclist Lance Armstrong roars from the back of the pack and erases almost all of Spaniard Javier Otxoa's 9-minute, 20-second lead in an amazing turn of events at the Tour de France.

11 Game MVP Derek Jeter goes 3-for-3 with two RBI as the American League goes on to a 6-3 victory over the National League in the 71st Major League Baseball All-Star Game.

Dallas Cowboys WR Michael Irvin announces his retirement after 12 seasons in the NFL.

Notre Dame's Matt Doherty accepts the head men's basketball coaching job at North Carolina, returning to the school he helped take to the 1982 NCAA national championship as a player.

12 Cincinnati pitcher Denny Neagle is shipped to the Yankees along with a minor league outfielder in exchange for four prospects. Hours later, Atlanta counters by obtaining pitcher Andy Ashby from the Phillies for Bruce Chen and a minor league pitcher.

Former Edmonton coach Ron Low is announced as the new coach of the N.Y. Rangers and is reunited with former Oilers president-GM Glen Sather.

13 Hockey all-star Mark Messier returns to captain the N.Y. Rangers, signing a two-year, $11 million deal with the team.

The buzz caused by ABC's new Monday Night Football broadcast team reached a climax on July 31 with the debut of veteran Al Michaels, new analyst Dan Fouts, and comedian **Dennis Miller**, who in this photo looks like (insert obscure reference here) who just (insert obscure reference here).

14 Prized free agent Tracy McGrady announces that he has chosen to leave Toronto and sign with the Orlando Magic on Aug. 1 because he wants to play close to his home in Auburndale, Fla.

15 Boston Red Sox OF Carl Everett goes into hysterics and head-butts plate umpire Ronald Kulpa after a second-inning at-bat. Everett gets ejected and will wait for what is expected to be a hefty suspension.

16 Legally blind runner Marla Runyan becomes the first blind U.S. athlete to qualify for the Olympics after she places third in the 1,500-meter race at the U.S. Track and Field Trials.

Dodgers manager Davey Johnson is hospitalized after experiencing dizziness caused by an irregular heart rhythm.

18 Tennessee Titans RB Eddie George signs a six-year, $42 million contract extension that makes him the NFL's highest-paid rusher.

Basketball great Kareem Abdul-Jabbar is arrested for investigation of driving under the influence of marijuana.

19 Cubs general manager Ed Lynch steps down from the position he's held since 1994, calling himself, "an equal opportunity failure."

Chicago Bears legend Dick Butkus is named head coach of the Chicago team in Vince McMahon's pro football league, the XFL.

20 Red Sox outfielder Carl Everett is suspended 10 games and fined $5,000 for twice bumping an umpire during a game on July 15.

Two men who led the effort to bring the 2002 Winter Games to Salt Lake City are indicted on charges they orchestrated cash bribes and other illegal inducements aimed at luring the Games to Utah.

NBA Hall of Famer Isiah Thomas takes the head coaching job with the Indiana Pacers, the post left open by the resignation of Larry Bird.

23 Cancer survivor Lance Armstrong successfully defends his Tour de France championship, joining Greg LeMond as the only multiple American winners of the race.

Golfer Tiger Woods follows up his dominating U.S. Open victory with a record-breaking 19-under-par performance to win the British Open, making him the youngest player ever to win the career Grand Slam.

Sprinters Michael Johnson and Maurice Greene both pull up lame in qualifying for the 200-meter race at the U.S. Track and Field Trials, meaning each will compete in one event at the Olympics.

Reds shortstop Barry Larkin rejects a trade to the Mets and signs a three-year, $27 million contract extension with Cincinnati.

26 Phillies ace Curt Schilling is traded to Arizona for pitchers Omar Daal, Vincente Padilla and Nelson Figueroa, and 1B Travis Lee.

British Open champ Tiger Woods goes to Canada to break the Screen Actors Guild strike and tape a television commercial for Buick.

29 The Pro Football Hall of Fame is the site of what is reportedly sports' largest gathering of hall of fame members when 111 of the 136 living members gather for the 2000 induction ceremonies in Canton, Ohio.

31 Comedian Dennis Miller makes his much-anticipated debut along with Dan Fouts and Al Michaels in the ABC-TV Monday Night Football broadcast booth at the San Francisco-New England preseason Hall of Fame game.

AUG '00

Sun	Mon	Tue	Wed	Thu	Fri	Sat
		1	2	3	4	5
6	7	8	9	10	11	12
13	14	15	16	17	18	19
20	21	22	23	24	25	26
27	28	29	30	31		

Quote of the Month

"It's a lose-lose situation. If you get a hit, you're supposed to, and if you don't, you're a geek." — **Chipper Jones**, Atlanta Braves third baseman and reigning N.L. MVP who grounded to third off of Colorado catcher Brent Mayne, ending the game in which Mayne became the first position player to earn a victory since 1968.

Flirting with .400

Colorado first baseman Todd Helton became the first player since George Brett in 1980 to reach the .400 mark after the dog days of summer. The following is a look at the latest dates players batted .400 in the past decade

Player, team	Date	Avg. (hits-AB)
Todd Helton, Col.	Aug. 21, 2000	.400 (176-440)
John Olerud, Tor.	Aug. 2, 1993	.400 (146-365)
Nomar Garciaparra, Bos.	July 20, 2000	.403 (112-278)
Larry Walker, Col.	July 17, 1997	.402 (138-343)
Tony Gwynn, SD	July 14, 1997	.402 (143-356)
Andres Galarraga, Col.	July 5, 1993	.400 (102-255)

Elias Sports Bureau contributed to this table.

Record Killer

By shooting an 18-under-par 270 at the PGA Championship from Aug. 17-20, Tiger Woods won his fifth career major golf championship (out of 16 played) and, incredibly, now holds the scoring record in relation to par for all four major tournaments.

Masters	18 under par
U.S. Open	12 under par
British Open	19 under par
PGA Championship	18 under par

1 **Miami Heat coach Pat Riley** revamps the team's roster, swinging a nine-player deal with Charlotte.

2 **Cuban high jump champion** Javier Sotomayor is cleared to compete in the Olympics when track and field's ruling body cuts his suspension for cocaine use in half.

4 **Outfielder Dave Martinez is traded** from Texas to Toronto, tying a major league record by joining his fourth team this baseball season.

7 **L.A. Lakers executive Jerry West** retires after 40 years of service with the team as a player and executive.

Tampa Bay slugger Jose Canseco is claimed in a waiver-wire deal by the N.Y. Yankees, who are loading up for pennant run.

10 **Former Detroit coach Alvin Gentry** is announced as the new coach of the L.A. Clippers.

11 **Philadelphia Flyers' John LeClair wins** the largest arbitration award in NHL history, getting a one-year deal worth $7 million, which is a 92 percent pay hike from the average of his last contract.

Softball pitcher Lisa Fernandez strikes out all 21 batters in a 5-0 U.S. national team victory in St. Louis. It's Fernandez's fifth consecutive perfect game and she has retired the last 111 batters she has faced.

12 **Heavyweight boxer Evander Holyfield** earns a unanimous, but controversial, victory over Johnny Ruiz before a sellout crowd at the ballroom of the Paris Hotel in Las Vegas.

14 **Colorado Avalanche star** Joe Sakic re-signs with the team, agreeing to a one-year, $7.9 million contract.

15 **Top heavyweight contender David Tua** and his representatives agree on a deal to fight Lennox Lewis on Nov. 11 at a site to be determined.

17 **BYU football coach LaVell Edwards** announces that he'll retire after the 2000 season, ending his 29-year tenure as the Cougars' head coach.

Baltimore LB Ray Lewis is fined $250,000 by the NFL for "conduct detrimental to the league" as a result of his double-murder charge that was eventually reduced to a misdemeanor count of obstruction of justice.

Atlanta 3B Chipper Jones agrees to a $90 million, six-year deal to remain with the Braves.

Thoroughbred Zippy Chippy, the losingest horse in racing history (0-86), is beaten by minor league baseball player Jose Herrera in a 40-yard dash before a Rochester (N.Y.) Red Wings game.

18 **Forty-seven women golfers** make history at the ShopKo Great Lakes Classic, playing in the first of two events this year that make up the new Women's Senior Golf Tour for players age 43 and older.

19 **WBO featherweight champ** Prince Naseem Hamed drops Augie Sanchez with a vicious combination in the fourth round at Foxwoods Casino on the Mashantucket Pequot Reservation in Connecticut.

20 **Golfer Tiger Woods birdies** the last two holes in regulation and wins the PGA Championship in a play-off over Bob May to become the first player since Ben Hogan in 1953 to win three majors in one year.

The Earnhardt family gathers at Michigan Speedway for the Pepsi 400 as father Dale, and sons Kerry and Dale Jr., race together for the first time in a Winston Cup event, marking the first father-son-son matchup since Lee Petty and sons Richard and Maurice appeared in a race in 1960.

Orlando kicker David Cool connects on a 19-yard field goal as time expires, leading the Predators to a 41-38 victory over Nashville in the 2000 ArenaBowl in Orlando.

AP/Wide World Photos

For the first time in their careers **Tiger Woods** and **Jack Nicklaus** were paired up in competition Aug. 17-18 during the first two rounds of the 2000 PGA Championship at the Valhalla Golf Club in Louisville, Ky. Woods has a long way to go to catch Nicklaus' record 18 major golf titles, but it sure looks like he has the right idea.

21 **Colorado 1B Todd Helton reaches** .400 with two singles in his first three at-bats, becoming the first player since George Brett (9/4/80) to reach that mark this late in the season.

Miami RB J.J. Johnson is the subject of reports that he will be suspended for the first four games of the NFL season for violating the league's steroid policy.

22 **Cincinnati OF Alex Ochoa** hits baseball's 142nd grand slam of the season, setting a new major-league record.

Colorado catcher Brent Mayne becomes the first position player in 32 years to earn a win by pitching the 12th inning of the Rockies 7-6 victory over Atlanta.

New York City breaks ground on a minor league ballpark in Coney Island, reaffirming its intention to bring professional baseball back to Brooklyn for the first time since the Dodgers left for Los Angeles 43 years ago.

23 **Miami Dolphins legend Dan Marino** is the guest of honor at a three-hour tribute that includes former coach Don Shula and a reunion of the quarterback class of 1983 at Pro Player Stadium.

24 **Deidra Lane, 25, the wife** of NFL running back Fred Lane is ordered held without bond as prosecutors announce that she could be charged with first-degree murder in the shooting death of her husband.

25 **Olympic speedskater Chris Witty** is named to the U.S. cycling team, making it possible for her to become the first American woman to medal in both the Winter and Summer Games.

Golfer Karrie Webb ties the LPGA 18-hole scoring record, firing an 11-under-par 61 at the Oldsmobile Classic in East Lansing, Mich.

26 **The *New Zealand Herald* reports** that detectives in New Zealand have foiled a plot that apparently targeted a nuclear reactor in Sydney during the Olympics.

Houston's Sheryl Swoopes scores 31 points and Cynthia Cooper has 25 in her final game as the duo rallies the Houston Comets to a 79-73 victory over the New York Liberty for their fourth straight WNBA championship.

Tennis star Venus Williams extends her career-high winning streak to four tournaments and 19 matches after disposing of Monica Seles at the Pilot Pen finals in New Haven, Conn.

27 **USC running back Sultan McCullogh** and a tough defense lead the Trojans to a decisive 29-5 victory over Penn State in the Kickoff Classic at East Rutherford, N.J.

28 **Spain's Sergio Garcia birdies** the 16th hole and never looks back in handing Tiger Woods a rare defeat this year, 1-up, at the made-for-TV primetime special "Battle at Bighorn."

Baseball's players' association exercises its option to extend the sport's collective bargaining agreement, assuring MLB will have labor peace through 2001.

30 **Defending Tour de France champion** Lance Armstrong and a teammate suffer various injuries when they are struck by a car while training for the Olympics in Nice, France.

Portland forward Brian Grant and Cleveland's Shawn Kemp highlight a five-player, three-team trade in the NBA that sends Grant to Miami, Kemp to Portland, and three players and a first-round draft pick to Cleveland.

SEPT '00

Sun	Mon	Tue	Wed	Thu	Fri	Sat
					1	2
3	4	5	6	7	8	9
10	11	12	13	14	15	16
17	18	19	20	21	22	23
24	25	26	27	28	29	30

Quote of the Month

"I managed the Dodgers for 20 years and I've had a lot of great moments. But this is the greatest moment of my life, to watch these youngsters beat Cuba." —TOMMY LASORDA, U.S. Olympic baseball coach after his team upset favored Cuba, 4-0, in the gold medal game.

Knick No Longer

The complicated four-team, 12-person trade that sent Patrick Ewing from New York to Seattle means Ewing won't climb any higher on the list of NBA players to play the most games with one team. Active streaks are in **bold**.

Player, Team	Games	Beginning
John Havlicek, Boston	1270	1962-63
John Stockton, Utah	**1258**	**1984-85**
Karl Malone, Utah	**1192**	**1985-86**
Hal Greer, Syra/Phi	1122	1958-59
Hakeem Olajuwon, Hou	**1119**	**1984-85**
Robert Parish, Boston	1106	1980-81
K. Abdul-Jabbar, Los Angeles	1093	1975-76
Dolph Schayes, Syra/Phi	1059	1948-49
Patrick Ewing, New York	1039	1985-86

Hall of Famer Fuhr Sure

A look at some of the impressive numbers that veteran goalie Grant Fuhr, who retired on Sept. 6, put up during his 19-year career in the National Hockey League.

1—	Vezina Trophy (1988).
5—	Stanley Cups (1984, 85, 87, 88, 90).
6—	All-Star Games (1982, 84, 85, 86, 88, 89).
14—	Record for points scored in a season by a goalie (1983-84).
16—	Record (tied) for wins by a goalie in a post-season (1987-88).
25—	Career shutouts.
403—	Career victories

1   **Rogers Communications agrees** to purchase controlling interest in the Toronto Blue Jays from Interbrew SA, a Belgian brewery, for $112 million.

Major League Baseball and the World Umpires Association reach a tentative agreement on a new collective bargaining agreement through 2004.

4   **Former Maple Leafs president** Cliff Fletcher signs a contract to help incoming part-owner Wayne Gretzky run the Phoenix Coyotes.

6   **New NFL owner Bob McNair** announces the nickname of the league's next expansion franchise in Houston will be the Texans.

Calgary Flames goalie Grant Fuhr retires from the NHL after 19 seasons and is named the team's goalie coach.

Princeton hires John Thompson III, son of the former Georgetown basketball coach, to replace Bill Carmody who left for Northwestern.

8   **NBA officials start an** arbitration proceeding charging the Minnesota Timberwolves, player Joe Smith and agent Eric Fleisher with violating salary cap rules.

9   **Wimbledon champ Venus Williams** captures her second straight major championship with a 6-4, 7-5 victory over Lindsay Davenport in the U.S. Open women's singles final.

Ottawa Senators GM Marshall Johnston announces the arbitrator-forced return of Alexei Yashin, ending a holdout that began last summer when Yashin demanded his contract be renegotiated.

Boxing's Roy Jones Jr. retains his light heavyweight title in an unexpectedly hard fight against Eric Harding who doesn't come out for the 11th round because of a torn left biceps.

NASCAR officials announce that they will attempt to control speeds at New Hampshire International Speedway, where two drivers have died this year, by requiring restrictor plates for upcoming events.

10   **Legendary Indiana coach** Bobby Knight is fired by university President Myles Brand after 29 seasons coaching men's basketball at the school because of a "pattern of unacceptable behavior."

Russian Marat Safin hands Pete Sampras his third-ever loss in a major tournament final, winning the U.S. Open crown in three sets, 6-4, 6-3, 6-3.

Olympic organizers announce that North and South Korea will enter the Sydney Games as a unified team under one flag during opening ceremonies, but will compete separately.

11   **The University of Minnesota sues** former basketball coach Clem Haskins, looking to recover its $1.5 million contract buyout and contending he lied about academic cheating.

13   **Fired Indiana coach** Bobby Knight bids farewell to the school and its students at an outdoor speech at Dunn Meadow in Bloomington, Ind.

15   **Australian aborigine Cathy Freeman** lights the Olympic cauldron in front of more than 110,000 people at Sydney's Olympic Stadium, capping off the opening ceremonies of the 2000 Summer Games.

16   **Australian swimmer Ian Thorpe** anchors Australia's 4 x 100 freestyle relay team to a gold medal at the Sydney Games, handing the U.S. its first-ever defeat in the event.

18   **The widow of NFL running back Fred Lane** is held without bail on bank larceny charges after documents in federal court suggest she might have killed her husband to stop him from reporting the theft.

19   **Cleveland tackle Orlando Brown**, whose eye was injured by a thrown penalty flag last December, is released by the team.

Indianapolis Motor Speedway hosted its first Formula One race, the **U.S. Grand Prix**, on Sept. 24. Pole-sitter Michael Schumacher won the race, which was the first in the track's 91-year history to run clockwise.

Officials at Lowe's Motor Speedway announce that a newly developed "soft wall" will be used for the UAW-GM Quality 500 on Oct. 8 to lessen the trauma on drivers when cars hit the retaining wall.

20 Dutch swimmer Pieter van den Hoogenband dazzles the Olympic crowds and becomes the first swimmer since Mark Spitz to win the gold in both the 100- and 200-meter freestyle races.

Montreal Canadiens center Trent McCleary, 28, ends his attempted comeback from a near-fatal larynx injury by announcing his retirement.

The new football scoreboard at the University of Arkansas malfunctions during a test run and creates a sound that stops traffic and sends nearby federal aviation officials (who confuse it with a signal from a downed aircraft) into action.

21 N.Y. Knicks center Patrick Ewing is traded to Seattle amidst a four-team, 12-player deal that also includes Glen Rice.

24 Formula One driver Michael Schumacher avoids crashing during a late-race spin out and cruises to victory in the first F1 Grand Prix race to be held on U.S. soil since 1991.

San Francisco WR Terrell Owens taunts Dallas Cowboys' players and fans by running to midfield and celebrating a touchdown catch on the Cowboys' logo. On a second attempt he is hit by George Teague and a fracas ensues.

25 News reaches Sydney that U.S. shot putter C.J. Hunter tested positive for a banned steriod in July.

Boston Celtics forward Paul Pierce undergoes emergency surgery after suffering multiple stab wounds in an altercation at a nightclub.

NHL enforcer Marty McSorley goes on trial in Vancouver for assault with a weapon for slashing Canucks' Donald Brashear in a game on Feb. 21.

Cincinnati Bengals coach Bruce Coslet resigns after starting the season 0-3 and is replaced by defensive coordinator Dick LeBeau.

27 Pitcher Ben Sheets leads the United States to a 4-0 shutout over Cuba in the gold medal baseball game at Sydney.

U.S. Greco-Roman wrestler Rulon Gardner wins a gold medal by defeating Russian wrestling legend Alexandre Kareline, who had not lost an international match in 13 years.

Tennis phenom Venus Williams follows up her Wimbledon and U.S. Open titles by winning a gold medal in women's singles tennis at Sydney.

Indiana Pacers center Rik Smits announces his retirement from the NBA, citing chronic sore feet which have plagued him the last four seasons.

The LPGA announces the Weetabix Women's British Open will replace the du Maurier Classic as the tour's fourth major tournament.

Baseball signs a new six-year, $2.5 billion deal with FOX that gives the network exclusive rights to broadcast major league postseason games and All-Star Games beginning in 2001.

28 Greece's Konstantinos Kenteris stuns the crowd as he sprints to the gold medal in the 200-meter race in Sydney. He's the first Greek man to win an Olympic running event since 1896.

Tampa Bay LW Gordie Dwyer is suspended by the NHL for 23 games for leaving the penalty box and making contact with an official during an exhibition game Sept. 19.

29 The U.S. Dream Team gets a scare, barely squeezing past Lithuania 85-83 to advance to the gold medal final.

OCT '00

Sun	Mon	Tue	Wed	Thu	Fri	Sat
1	2	3	4	5	6	7
8	9	10	11	12	13	14
15	16	17	18	19	20	21
22	23	24	25	26	27	28
29	30	31				

Quote of the Month

"You can't do well if you're think-ing about anything else. . . . This is the nearest I ever am to being a normal person." — PRESIDENT BILL CLINTON, during an interview for *Golf Digest*, discussing how he likes the fact that golf takes his mind off work.

Out of this World

Venus Williams' amazing 2000 season was punctuated by a 35-match winning streak that was the third-longest in the last 10 years but a ways off from the longest single-season streaks in WTA Tour history.

	Player, Year	Snapped By
74	Martina Navratilova, 1984	H. Sukova
55	Chris Evert, 1974	E. Goolagong
53+	Martina Navratilova, 1986	—
50+	Martina Navratilova, 1983	—
46	Steffi Graf, 1988	P. Shriver
45	Steffi Graf, 1987	M. Navratilova
44	Steffi Graf, 1993	C. Martinez
41	Martina Navratilova, 1982	P. Shriver
37	Martina Hingis, 1997	I. Majoli
	Martina Navratilova, 1978	T. Austin
36	Chris Evert, 1976	V. Wade
	Monica Seles, 1990	Z. Garrison-Jackson
35	Venus Williams, 2000	L. Davenport

+Streak carried over into the following season.

Final Fantastic

Here is how the Yankees' 14-game World Series winning streak stands up to the longest streaks in NBA and NHL finals history.

World Series	14	Yankees (1996-2000)
Stanley Cup Finals	11	Canadiens (1973-78)
NBA Finals	6	Rockets (1994-95)

1 IOC President Juan Antonio Samaranch takes in the closing ceremonies and praises the 2000 Summer Games in Sydney as the "best ever."

Drag racer Gary Scelzi breaks an NHRA record by winning his seventh Top Fuel victory of the season. There have been 12 six-win seasons, including two by Scelzi.

Philadelphia Phillies manager Terry Francona is fired after a 65-97 record, tying the Cubs for baseball's worst.

2 Television ratings released today show the average rating for NBC's coverage of the Olympics was the lowest for any Olympics since 1968.

3 Cardinals pitcher Rick Ankiel becomes the first player in baseball history to throw five wild pitches in an inning, but amazingly his team goes on to win Game 1 of its divisional series against Atlanta, 7-5.

A Romanian film company says gymnast Andreea Raducan, who was stripped of her all-around Olympic gold medal after failing a drug test, has agreed to have a film made of her life.

A lawsuit contending Indiana University violated state law when trustees discussed firing coach Bobby Knight without public notice is filed on behalf of 46 plaintiffs, most of them alumni and fans.

6 A Vancouver judge convicts Boston Bruin Marty McSorley of assault for his slashing of Donald Brashear. The conviction will be expunged from McSorley's record if he completes 18 months of probation.

The Boston Red Sox are put up for sale by the trust that has owned the franchise for 67 years.

Los Angeles Dodgers manager Davey Johnson is fired after failing to make the playoffs in his first two years with the team.

Arizona Diamondbacks manager Buck Showalter, the only manager in team history, is fired.

8 The United States' comeback on the third day of the Solheim Cup isn't enough as Europe holds on for the 14½-11½ victory.

German race car driver Michael Schumacher wins the Japanese Grand Prix and captures his third Formula One season title and Ferrari's first in 21 years.

10 Undefeated featherweight Prince Naseem Hamed gives up the WBO title he's held since 1995 instead of agreeing to fight No. 1 contender Istvan Kovacs on Nov. 4.

Former European Ryder Cup captain Mark James announces that he will undergo treatment for lymphoma.

Toronto Blue Jays manager Jim Fregosi is fired after two seasons of third-place finishes.

12 Duke female place-kicker Heather Mercer is awarded $2 million in punitive damages by a North Carolina jury that agreed that she was discriminated against when she was cut from the football team solely because of her gender.

13 L.A. Lakers star Shaquille O'Neal signs a three-year contract extension that will keep him with the team for a total of six more seasons.

15 K.C. Wizard Miklos Molnar scores in the 12th minute and goalie Tony Meola secures a shutout, powering the Wizards to a 1-0 victory in the MLS Cup.

16 Miami Heat center Alonzo Mourning announces he will miss the entire 2000-01 NBA season due to a kidney disorder.

17 Colorado Avalanche goalie Patrick Roy beats Washington 4-3 in overtime for his 448th victory, becoming hockey's all-time winningest goaltender.

International Olympic Committee President Juan Antonio Samaranch had one request for the closing ceremonies at Olympic Stadium in Sydney: **giant prawns** on mountain bikes. And there they are. It's no wonder he called the 2000 Summer Games the "best ever."

Atlanta Hawks GM Pete Babcock announces that center Dikembe Mutombo will miss two weeks because of a mild case of malaria.

18 The N.Y. Yankees defeat the Mariners in Game 6 of the A.L.C.S. and clinch a trip to the World Series to face the Mets, setting up baseball's first "Subway Series" in 44 years.

22 Mets catcher Mike Piazza and World Series fans are stunned when pitcher Roger Clemens throws the jagged barrel of Piazza's broken bat back towards him during a tense and bizarre confrontation during Game 2 of the World Series.

Vikings kicker Gary Anderson scores 11 points in a 31-27 victory over Buffalo and breaks George Blanda's all-time NFL scoring record by two points.

Bengals RB Corey Dillon rushes for 278 yards in a 31-21 victory over Denver, breaking the NFL single-game rushing record set by Walter Payton in 1977.

U.S. golfer David Love III clinches the Presidents Cup trophy on the 15th hole as the U.S. coasts to victory over the International team 21½–10½.

Colorado goalie Patrick Roy is arrested on investigation of domestic violence charges after police respond to a 911 hangup call at his house.

23 German wrestler Alexander Leipold is stripped of his Olympic gold medal by the IOC for using a banned steroid. United States silver medallist Brandon Slay is awarded the gold.

Arizona Cardinals coach Vince Tobin is fired a day after a 48-7 loss to the Dallas Cowboys.

Former player and hitting coach Lloyd McClendon is hired to manage the Pittsburgh Pirates, becoming the fifth African-American coach in the majors.

St. Louis slugger Mark McGwire has surgery on the sore right knee that turned him into a part-time player this season but is expected to be ready for spring training in February.

24 N.Y. Yankees pitcher Roger Clemens is fined $50,000 for the bat-throwing incident in Game 2 of the World Series.

Outfielder Benny Agbayani doubles home the game-winning run in the eighth inning as the Mets beat the Yankees in Game 3, snapping the Yankees' 14-game World Series winning streak.

The NCAA places the University of Minnesota men's basketball program on probation for four years and cuts an additional scholarship as penalties for academic fraud but does not ban them from another year of postseason play.

St. Louis Rams quarterback Kurt Warner is expected to miss five to six weeks after undergoing surgery to repair the broken little finger on his throwing hand, which he injured in a loss to the Chiefs on Oct. 22.

25 NBA commissioner David Stern comes down hard on the Minnesota Timberwolves for its secret salary agreement with Joe Smith, fining the team $3.5 million and taking away their next five first-round draft picks.

Boston Bruins coach Pat Burns is fired and replaced immediately by NHL coaching veteran Mike Keenan, a coach they passed over when they hired Burns three years ago.

26 N.Y. Yankees 2B Luis Sojo hits a two-out, tie-breaking single off Al Leiter in the ninth inning to decide Game 5 and give the Yankees their record 26th world championship.

Olympics
Winter Games

Year	No.	Host City	Dates
2002	XIX	Salt Lake City, Utah	Feb. 8-24
2006	XX	Turin, Italy	Feb. 4-19

Summer Games

Year	No.	Host City	Dates
2004	XXVIII	Athens, Greece	Aug. 13-29

All-Star Games
Baseball

Year	Site	Date
2001	SAFECO Field, Seattle	July 10
2002	Miller Park, Milwaukee	TBA

NBA Basketball

Year	Site	Date
2001	MCI Center, Washington D.C.	Feb. 11
2002	First Union Center, Philadelphia	Feb. 10

NFL Pro Bowl

Year	Site	Date
2001	Aloha Stadium, Honolulu	Feb. 4
2002	Aloha Stadium, Honolulu	Feb. 3
2003	Aloha Stadium, Honolulu	Feb. 2

NHL Hockey

Year	Site	Date
2001	Pepsi Center, Denver	Feb. 4

Auto Racing

The Daytona 500 stock car race is usually held on the Sunday before the third Monday in February, while the Indianapolis 500 is usually held on the Sunday of Memorial Day weekend in May. The following dates are tentative.

Year	Daytona 500	Indianapolis 500
2001	Feb. 18	May 27
2002	Feb. 17	May 26
2003	Feb. 16	May 25

NCAA Basketball
Men's Final Four

Year	Site	Date
2001	Metrodome, Minneapolis	Mar. 31-Apr. 2
2002	Georgia Dome, Atlanta	Mar. 30-Apr. 1
2003	Louisiana Superdome, New Orleans	April 5-7
2004	Alamodome, San Antonio	April 3-5

Women's Final Four

Year	Site	Date
2001	Kiel Center, St. Louis	Mar. 30-Apr. 1
2002	Alamodome, San Antonio	March 29-31
2003	Georgia Dome, Atlanta	April 4-6
2004	New Orleans Sports Arena	April 2-4

NFL Football
Super Bowl

No.	Site	Date
XXXV	Raymond James Stadium, Tampa	Jan. 28, 2001
XXXVI	Louisiana Superdome, New Orleans	Jan. 27, 2002
XXXVII	Qualcomm Stadium, San Diego	Jan. 26, 2003

Golf
The Masters

Year	Site	Date
2001	Augusta National Ga.	April 5-8
2002	Augusta National Ga.	April 11-14

U.S. Open

Year	Site	Date
2001	Southern Hills, Tulsa, Okla.	June 14-17
2002	Bethpage St. Park (Farmingdale, N.Y.)	June 13-16
2003	Olympia Fields (Ill.) Country Club	June 12-15

U.S. Women's Open

Year	Site	Date
2001	Pine Needles, Southern Pines N.C.	May 31-June 3
2002	Prairie Dunes CC, Hutchinson, Kan.	July 4-7

U.S. Senior Open

Year	Site	Date
2001	Salem CC, Peabody Mass.	June 28-July 1
2002	Caves Valley GC, Owing Mills, Md.	June 27-30

PGA Championship

Year	Site	Date
2001	Atlanta Athletic Club, Duluth, Ga.	TBA
2002	Hazeltine National CC, Chaska, Minn.	TBA
2003	Oak Hill CC, Rochester, N.Y.	TBA

British Open

Year	Site	Date
2001	Royal Lytham, England	July 19-22
2002	Muirfield, Scotland	July 18-21

Ryder Cup

Year	Site	Date
2001	The Belfrey, England	Sept. 28-30
2003	Oakland Hills CC, Bloomfield Hills, Mich.	TBA
2005	Kildare Hotel and CC, Dublin, Ireland	TBA
2007	Valhalla GC, Louisville, Ky.	TBA

Horse Racing
Triple Crown

The Kentucky Derby is always held at Churchill Downs in Louisville on the first Saturday in May, followed two weeks later by the Preakness Stakes at Pimlico Race Course in Baltimore and three weeks after that by the Belmont Stakes at Belmont Park in Elmont, N.Y.

Year	Ky Derby	Preakness	Belmont
2001	May 5	May 19	June 9
2002	May 4	May 18	June 8
2003	May 3	May 17	June 7

Tennis
U.S. Open

Usually held from the last Monday in August through the second Sunday in September, with Labor Day weekend the midway point in the tournament.

Year	Site	Date
2001	Arthur Ashe Stadium, NYC	Aug. 27-Sept. 9
2002	Arthur Ashe Stadium, NYC	Aug. 26-Sept. 8
2003	Arthur Ashe Stadium, NYC	Aug. 25-Sept. 7

Baseball

World Series MVP **Derek Jeter** *gives a high four, signifying the number of titles he's won with the Yankees.*

Triple Crown

Yankees prove they're New York's finest, winning the Subway Series for their third consecutive title.

by

Karl Ravech

It was 11:59 p.m. on Oct. 26, 2000 when the New York Mets' best player, Mike Piazza stood in the batters box against the Yankees' Mariano Rivera in Game 5 of the World Series. There were two outs and a man on second base, the Mets' entire season resting in the capable hands of arguably the greatest offensive catcher baseball has ever seen.

Earlier in the Series, Piazza had been in the middle of one of the most bizarre scenes ever to play out on a baseball field. Now he was the last chance the Mets had against the two-time defending champions. He alone could prolong the first Subway Series in 44 years. With everyone in the park on their feet and an entire city watching on television, the clock struck midnight, his bat struck the ball and it sailed towards the deepest part of the park. It was one of those majes-

Karl Ravech is the host of ESPN's *Baseball Tonight*.

tic drives that seemed to hang in the foggy night for an eternity, providing an opportunity to reflect on just how we all got here.

The 2000 baseball season began as the previous two had, with the mighty Yankees favored to win it all again. Joe Torre's clubs had amassed an amazing record since winning their first of three titles in four years and once again the club returned the core of its roster. If they were to put together a fourth World Series run in five years, surely they would be mentioned in the same breath as the greatest teams ever.

New York's chief American League competition in 2000 came from some rather unlikely foes. In the Central Division, the big surprise was the Chicago White Sox. They had dethroned the Cleveland Indians despite the fact that Cleveland had added the one ingredient which had seemingly been missing from their team for the latter half of the 90's, a solid pitcher with a record of beating the Yankees. Chuck

Mets catcher **Mike Piazza** tries to approach Yankees pitcher **Roger Clemens** after Clemens threw a piece of Piazza's broken bat back at the catcher as he was running up the first base line in the first inning of Game 2 of the World Series. The two players have had a rocky relationship since Clemens beaned Piazza during the regular season.

Finley proved valuable, but the White Sox' combination of power and young pitching proved to be too much for the charging Indians at the end of the season. Chicago won more games than any team in the league and had home-field advantage throughout the American League playoffs, but they couldn't get past the Seattle Mariners in the first round.

The Oakland A's had defied all baseball logic. A low-budget team, relative to the Yankees, their payroll was about one-third what George Steinbrenner was doling out in New York. Oakland had great young pitching and a softball team-like attitude of playing hard both on and off the field. Their tenacity helped them force the Yankees to a fifth and deciding game in the opening round but a six-run first inning for the Yankees was too much to overcome and Oakland was done.

The ALCS was next for New York and Seattle. The Yankees won in six games but their psyche had been dented. With a chance to close out the series at home in five games, the Yankees faltered badly. A 6-2 Mariners win sent the teams 3,000 miles across the country to play one game while New York's hometown rival, the Mets, watched and waited to find out who they'd be playing for the title. The Yankees beat Seattle, barely, 9-7 and warily headed back to New York where a city was braced for a Subway Series.

The Mets' run to the Fall Classic was less predictable than the Yankees'. Once again they had come up short of knocking the Atlanta Braves from the top of the N.L.'s East Division and thus didn't have home-field advantage during the first round of the playoffs. They did, however, have two of the best left-handed starting pitchers in baseball, Al Leiter and Mike Hampton.

San Francisco provided the opposition. With a new ballpark and the same great player in Barry Bonds leading the way, the Giants marched through the regular season, winning a baseball-best 97 games. The series see-sawed back and forth, the highlight being the Giants' three-run pinch-hit home run by J.T. Snow in the bottom of the ninth of Game 3. It tied the game at five and had all the characteristics of Carlton Fisk's wondrous home run in the '75 series against the Reds. A shot down the foul line, a batter waving it fair and a hometown crowd going nuts. But unlike Fisk's blast, this one only tied the game and the Mets prevailed in 10, ultimately winning the series in four games.

Their opponent in the NLCS would be the St. Louis Cardinals, not the hated Braves. St. Louis had taken advantage of poor play by Atlanta to sweep them in three games. It turned out, however, that St. Louis had expended so much of its energy in beating Atlanta, it had nothing left for the Mets. New York won it in five games, outscoring St. Louis 14-6 in the final two.

After a five-day hiatus, both the Mets and Yankees were anxious to get things going. Having heard and read all about the glory days of the 20's, 30's, 40's and 50's when Subway Series were more the rule than the exception, these two clubs were ready to create their own history. They did

Colorado Rockies first baseman **Todd Helton** got his bat on the ball a lot in 2000, flirting with a .400 batting average into September.

not disappoint.

Game 1 wasn't decided until the 12th inning when seldom-used Jose Vizcaino singled in the Yankees' winning run. The sellout crowd of 55,000 at Yankee Stadium went home happy that night, having no idea what was in store when they returned the following evening for Game 2.

On the mound for the Yankees was Roger Clemens, the fireball-throwing right-hander who earlier in the season had drilled Piazza in the head with a fastball. Piazza was knocked silly that July night, and much of the pre-game talk focused on their first meeting since then. Both players tried to downplay the significance of that event, but neither could silence the talk of what was about to happen. Clemens threw a fastball, Piazza swung, the bat splintered and the barrel headed right at Clemens on the mound. He fielded the shrapnel of wood as if it were a ball and fired it in the direction of Piazza who was running down the first base line, not knowing the ball he had hit had gone foul. As Piazza realized that, he also understood that Clemens had just thrown part of his own bat at him. Piazza took the handle of the bat, still in his hand, and walked towards the mound to find out what, if anything, Clemens was thinking about. The two never touched, as the umpires and players from both benches intervened. There was no brawling and no explanation from Clemens, other than he was emotional and did not intentionally throw at Piazza. After the game both sides were incensed, the Mets angry that Clemens was allowed to stay in the game and the Yankees upset at those who suggested Clemens had actually done it on purpose. Lost in the mayhem was an eight-inning, two-hit performance by Clemens, followed by a five-run ninth inning by the Mets which got them within one run of the Yankees but no closer.

No game the two teams played was decided by more than two runs, the first time that had happened since 1915 when the Red Sox played the Phillies and Boston had a guy named Babe Ruth on its roster. With Clemens scheduled to pitch Game 6 back at Yankee Stadium, the Mets had to take care of business in Game 5 and hope they could get to Clemens in Game 6.

As Piazza's ball drifted towards the fence, Yankees manager Joe Torre screamed "Oh no!" Derek Jeter, the Yankees shortstop who had carried this club to a 3-games-to-1 lead and had homered earlier in the game, craned his neck to see if it would land in the glove of Bernie Williams or over the fence. Williams went back,

Piazza had almost reached first base when Williams stopped, looked up and guided the ball into his glove about eight feet short of the wall.

The Yankees had won their third consecutive title, Jeter's fourth in five years at the tender age of 26. The Subway Series, with all its hype, had done exactly what subways had done for 96 years in New York — deliver. ■

The Ten Biggest Stories of the 2000 Baseball Season

10. **St. Louis slugger Mark McGwire** suffers a knee injury and other assorted ailments, reducing him to a pinch hitting role over the second half of the season and taking the air out of any home run record chase like we had seen the past two seasons.

9. **Job security?** For the first time since 1942, no manager is fired during the season.

8. **Colorado's Todd Helton and Boston's Nomar Garciaparra** take aim at one of baseball's most hallowed numbers — .400. Garciaparra was at the mark on July 20 and Helton lasted until late August, but neither could sustain it, each finishing the year at .372.

7. **New state-of-the-art ballparks** open in San Francisco, Detroit and Houston and each draw positive reviews and more fans. San Fran's Pacific Bell Park, with McCovey Cove beyond the right field fence, receives the most attention.

6. **Pedro vs. the Devil Rays.** In one of the wilder games of the year, Pedro Martinez carries a no-hitter into the ninth inning against

Tampa Bay before finally surrendering a hit to catcher John Flaherty. He strikes out 13, but the performance is somewhat overshadowed by bench-clearing brawls that see five Devil Rays players, manager Larry Rothschild and two coaches ejected.

5. **Wild Thing.** In Game 2 of the NLCS, rookie pitcher Rick Ankiel loses control and hits the backstop with five of his first 20 pitches. He comes on in relief in Game 5 and suffers similar problems.

4. Speaking of wild and out of control, **Atlanta reliever John Rocker** makes his long-awaited return to Shea Stadium for the first time since his well-publicized rant about New York City. He is booed mightily but otherwise unharmed.

3. After 11 seasons in Seattle, **Ken Griffey Jr. bolts** the Mariners for the Cincinnati Reds to be closer to his family. In a strange twist, the Reds finish 10 games behind St. Louis in the N.L. Central, while the Mariners make it all the way to the ALCS.

2. In a play that no one, even **Roger Clemens**, could really explain, the Yankees flamethrower picks up a piece of Mike Piazza's splintered bat in Game 2 of the World Series and whips it back towards Piazza. Among other excuses, Clemens later said he thought it was the ball.

1. The Yankees and Mets play baseball's **first Subway Series in 44 years** and the Yankees shine once again, winning their third consecutive championship and their fourth in the last five years. ◼

inside the **numbers**

BRONX BABY BOMBERS

World Series MVP Derek Jeter became the fourth-youngest player in baseball history to win a fourth league title. The three youngsters ahead of Jeter are also former Yankees.

Age		4th Title
24	Joe DiMaggio	1939
24	Mickey Mantle	1956
25	Billy Martin	1953
26	Derek Jeter	2000

NOT-SO WINNING PERCENTAGES

The San Francisco Giants led all major league teams in 2000 with a .599 winning percentage (97-65). Only three other times has the best team in the majors finished with a winning percentage below .600.

2000	.599	San Francisco Giants
1982	.586	Milwaukee Brewers
1958	.597	Milwaukee Braves
1926	.591	New York Yankees

PERM-PENNANT RESIDENTS

Don't be surprised if fans of American League teams complain of deja-vu. That's because only five different teams have represented the A.L. in the World Series since 1987. In that same span the National League has had eight different champions. Here is a list of the five A.L. teams along with their number of appearances.

New York Yankees	4
Oakland A's	3
Cleveland Indians	2
Minnesota Twins	2
Toronto Blue Jays	2
All nine other teams	0

◼

Final Major League Standings

Division champions (*) and Wild Card (†) winners are noted. Number of seasons listed after each manager refers to current tenure with club.

American League

East Division

	W	L	Pct	GB	Home	Road
*New York	87	74	.540	–	44-36	43-38
Boston	85	77	.525	2½	42-39	43-38
Toronto	83	79	.512	4½	45-36	38-43
Baltimore	74	88	.457	13½	44-37	30-51
Tampa Bay	69	92	.429	18	36-44	33-48

2000 Managers: NY– Joe Torre (5th season); **Bos**– Jimy Williams (4th); **Tor**– Jim Fregosi (2nd); **Bal**– Mike Hargrove (1st); **TB**–Larry Rothschild (3rd).
1999 Standings: 1. New York (98-64); 2. Boston (94-68); 3. Toronto (84-78); 4. Baltimore (78-84); 5. Tampa Bay (69-93).

Central Division

	W	L	Pct	GB	Home	Road
*Chicago	95	67	.586	–	46-35	49-32
Cleveland	90	72	.556	5	48-33	42-39
Detroit	79	83	.488	16	43-38	36-45
Kansas City	77	85	.475	18	42-39	35-46
Minnesota	69	93	.426	26	36-45	33-48

2000 Managers: Chi– Jerry Manuel (3rd season); **Cle**– Charlie Manuel (4th); **Det**– Phil Garner (1st); **KC**– Tony Muser (4th); **Min**– Tom Kelly (15th).
1999 Standings: 1. Cleveland (97-65); 2. Chicago (75-86); 3. Detroit (69-92); 4. Kansas City (64-97); 5. Minnesota (63-97).

West Division

	W	L	Pct	GB	Home	Road
*Oakland	91	70	.565	–	47-34	44-36
†Seattle	91	71	.562	½	47-34	44-37
Anaheim	82	80	.506	9½	46-34	36-46
Texas	71	91	.438	20½	42-39	29-52

2000 Managers: Oak– Art Howe (5th season); **Sea**– Lou Piniella (8th); **Ana**– Mike Scioscia (1st); **Tex**– Johnny Oates (6th).
1999 Standings: 1. Texas (95-67); 2. Oakland (87-75); 3. Seattle (79-83); 4. Anaheim (70-92).

National League

East Division

	W	L	Pct	GB	Home	Road
*Atlanta	95	67	.586	–	51-30	44-37
†New York	94	68	.580	1	55-26	39-42
Florida	79	82	.491	15½	43-38	36-44
Montreal	67	95	.414	28	37-44	30-51
Philadelphia	65	97	.401	30	34-47	31-50

2000 Managers: Atl– Bobby Cox (11th season); **NY**– Bobby Valentine (5th); **Fla**– John Boles (2nd); **Mon**– Felipe Alou (9th); **Phi**– Terry Francona (4th).
1999 Standings: 1. Atlanta (103-59); 2. New York (97-66); 3. Philadelphia (77-85); 4. Montreal (68-94); 5. Florida (64-98).

Central Division

	W	L	Pct	GB	Home	Road
*St. Louis	95	67	.586	–	50-31	45-36
Cincinnati	85	77	.525	10	43-38	42-39
Milwaukee	73	89	.451	22	42-39	31-50
Houston	72	90	.444	23	39-42	33-48
Pittsburgh	69	93	.426	26	37-44	32-49
Chicago	65	97	.401	30	38-43	27-54

2000 Managers: St.L– Tony La Russa (5th season); **Cin**– Jack McKeon (4th); **Mil**– Dave Lopes (1st); **Hou**– Larry Dierker (4th); **Pit**– Gene Lamont (4th); **Chi**– Don Baylor (1st).
1999 Standings: 1. Houston (97-65); 2. Cincinnati (96-67); 3. Pittsburgh (78-83); 4. St. Louis (75-86); 5. Milwaukee (74-87); 6. Chicago (67-95).

West Division

	W	L	Pct	GB	Home	Road
*San Francisco	97	65	.599	–	55-26	42-39
Los Angeles	86	76	.531	11	44-37	42-39
Arizona	85	77	.525	12	47-34	38-43
Colorado	82	80	.506	15	48-33	34-47
San Diego	76	86	.469	21	41-40	35-46

2000 Managers: SF– Dusty Baker (8th season); **LA**– Davey Johnson (2nd); **Ari**– Buck Showalter (3rd); **Col**– Buddy Bell (1st); **SD**– Bruce Bochy (6th).
1999 Standings: 1. Arizona (100-62); 2. San Francisco (86-76); 3. Los Angeles (77-85); 4. San Diego (74-88); 5. Colorado (72-90).

Interleague Play Standings

American League

	W-L	Pct		W-L	Pct
Cleveland	13-5	.722	Toronto	9-9	.500
Anaheim	12-6	.667	Tampa Bay	9-9	.500
Chicago	12-6	.667	Kansas City	8-10	.444
New York	11-6	.647	Baltimore	7-11	.389
Oakland	11-7	.611	Minnesota	7-11	.389
Seattle	11-7	.611	Texas	7-11	.389
Detroit	10-8	.556	**Totals**	**136-115**	**.542**
Boston	9-9	.500			

National League

	W-L	Pct		W-L	Pct
Atlanta	11-7	.611	Milwaukee	6-9	.400
San Francisco	8-7	.533	Houston	6-9	.400
Chicago	8-7	.533	Pittsburgh	6-9	.400
New York	9-9	.500	Los Angeles	6-9	.400
Philadelphia	9-9	.500	Arizona	6-9	.400
Colorado	6-6	.500	Montreal	7-11	.389
Florida	8-9	.471	San Diego	5-10	.333
St. Louis	7-8	.467	**Totals**	**115-136**	**.458**
Cincinnati	7-8	.467			

Anaheim Angels
Troy Glaus
Home Runs

Oakland A's
Jason Giambi
OBP, Walks

Toronto Blue Jays
Carlos Delgado
Doubles, Total Bases

Boston Red Sox
Pedro Martinez
ERA, Shutouts, Strikeouts,
Opp. BA

American League Leaders

(*) indicates rookie.

Batting

	Bat	Gm	AB	R	H	Avg	TB	2B	3B	HR	RBI	BB	SO	SB	Slg Pct	OBP
Nomar Garciaparra, Bos.	R	140	529	104	197	.372	317	51	3	21	96	61	50	5	.599	.434
Darin Erstad, Ana	L	157	676	121	240	.355	366	39	6	25	100	64	82	28	.541	.409
Manny Ramirez, Cle	R	118	439	92	154	.351	306	34	2	38	122	86	117	1	.697	.457
Carlos Delgado, Tor	L	162	569	115	196	.344	378	57	1	41	137	123	104	0	.664	.470
Derek Jeter, NY	R	148	593	119	201	.339	285	31	4	15	73	68	99	22	.481	.416
David Segui, Tex-Cle	S	150	574	93	192	.334	293	42	1	19	103	53	84	0	.510	.388
Jason Giambi. Oak	L	152	510	108	170	.333	330	29	1	43	137	137	96	2	.647	.476
Mike Sweeney, KC	R	159	618	105	206	.333	323	30	0	29	144	71	67	8	.523	.407
Frank Thomas, Chi	R	159	582	115	191	.328	364	44	0	43	143	112	94	1	.625	.436
Johnny Damon, KC	L	159	655	136	214	.327	324	42	10	16	88	65	60	46	.495	.382
Edgar Martinez, Sea	R	153	556	100	180	.324	322	31	0	37	145	96	95	3	.579	.423
Travis Fryman, Cle	R	155	574	93	184	.321	296	38	4	22	106	73	111	1	.516	.392
Jermaine Dye, KC	R	157	601	107	193	.321	337	41	2	33	118	69	99	0	.561	.390
Shannon Stewart, Tor	R	136	583	107	186	.319	302	43	5	21	69	37	79	20	.518	.363
Alex Rodriguez, Sea	R	148	554	134	175	.316	336	34	2	41	132	100	121	15	.606	.420

Note: Batters must have 3.1 plate appearances per their team's games played to qualify.

Home Runs

Glaus, Ana	47
Thomas, Chi	43
Ja. Giambi, Oak	43
Justice, Cle-NY	41
Delgado, Tor	41
Rodriguez, Sea	41
Batista, Tor	41
Palmeiro, Tex	39
Ramirez, Cle	38

Triples

Guzman, Min	20
Kennedy*, Ana	11
Damon, KC	10
Durham, Chi	9
Alicea, Tex	8
Nixon, Bos	8
Hunter, Min	7

Four tied with 6 each.

On Base Pct.

Ja. Giambi, Oak	.476
Delgado, Tor	.470
Ramirez, Cle	.457
Thomas, Chi	.436
Garciaparra, Bos	.434
Martinez, Sea	.423
Rodriguez, Sea	.420
Posada, NY	.417

Runs Batted In

Martinez, Sea	145
Sweeney, KC	144
Thomas, Chi	143
Delgado, Tor	137
Ja. Giambi, Oak	137
Rodriguez, Sea	132
Ordonez, Chi	126
Ramirez, Cle	122
Williams, NY	121
Palmeiro, Tex	120

Doubles

Delgado, Tor	57
Garciaparra, Bos	51
Cruz, Det	46
Olerud, Sea	45
Thomas, Chi	44
Higginson, Det	44
Lawton, Min	44

Slugging Pct.

Ramirez, Cle	.697
Delgado, Tor	.664
Ja. Giambi, Oak	.647
Thomas, Chi	.625
Rodriguez, Sea	.606
Glaus, Ana	.604
Garciaparra, Bos	.599

Hits

Erstad, Ana	240
Damon, KC	214
Sweeney, KC	206
Jeter, NY	201
Garciaparra, Bos	197
Delgado, Tor	196
Dye, KC	193
Segui, Tex-Cle	192
Thomas, Chi	191
R. Alomar, Cle	189
Randa, KC	186
Stewart, Tor	186

Runs

Damon, KC	136
Rodriguez, Sea	134
Durham, Chi	121
Erstad, Ana	121
Glaus, Ana	120
Jeter, NY	119
Thomas, Chi	115
Delgado, Tor	115

Walks

Ja. Giambi, Oak	137
Delgado, Tor	123
Thome, Cle	118
Thomas, Chi	112
Glaus, Ana	112

Stolen Bases

	SB	CS
Damon, KC	46	9
R. Alomar, Cle	39	4
DeShields, Bal	37	10
Henderson, Sea	31	9
McLemore, Tex	30	14
Lofton, Cle	30	7
Cairo, TB	28	7
Erstad, Ana	28	8
Guzman, Min	28	10
Durham, Chi	25	13
Cameron, Sea	24	7
Lawton, Min	23	7

Five tied with 22 each.

Total Bases

Delgado, Tor	378
Erstad, Ana	366
Thomas, Chi	364
Glaus, Ana	340
Dye, KC	337
Rodriguez, Sea	336
Anderson, Ana	336
Ja. Giambi, Oak	330
Damon, KC	324
Sweeney, Sea	323
Martinez, Sea	322
Batista, Tor	322

Pitching

	Arm	W	L	ERA	Gm	GS	CG	ShO	Sv	IP	H	R	ER	HR	HB	BB	SO	WP
Pedro Martinez, Bos	R	18	6	**1.74**	29	29	7	4	0	217.0	128	44	42	17	14	32	284	1
Roger Clemens, NY	R	13	8	**3.70**	32	32	1	0	0	204.1	184	96	84	26	10	84	188	2
Mike Mussina, Bal	R	11	15	**3.79**	34	34	6	1	0	237.2	236	105	100	28	3	46	210	3
Mike Sirotka, Chi	L	15	10	**3.79**	32	32	1	0	0	197.0	203	101	83	23	1	69	128	8
Bartolo Colon, Cle	R	15	8	**3.88**	30	30	2	1	0	188.0	163	86	81	21	4	98	212	4
David Wells, Tor	L	20	8	**4.11**	35	35	9	1	0	229.2	266	115	105	23	8	31	166	9
Gil Heredia, Oak	R	15	11	**4.12**	32	32	2	0	0	198.2	214	106	91	24	4	66	101	3
Albie Lopez, TB	R	11	13	**4.13**	45	24	4	1	0	185.1	199	95	85	24	1	70	96	4
Tim Hudson, Oak	R	20	6	**4.14**	32	32	2	2	0	202.1	169	100	93	24	7	82	169	7
Chuck Finley, Cle	L	16	11	**4.17**	34	34	3	0	0	218.0	211	108	101	23	2	101	189	9
Paul Abbott, Sea	R	9	7	**4.22**	35	27	0	0	0	179.0	164	89	84	23	5	80	100	3
Jim Parque, Chi	L	13	6	**4.28**	33	32	0	0	0	187.0	208	105	89	21	11	71	111	2
Jeff Weaver, Det	R	11	15	**4.32**	31	30	2	0	0	200.0	205	102	96	26	15	52	136	3
Makoto Suzuki, KC	R	8	10	**4.34**	32	29	1	1	0	188.2	195	100	91	26	3	94	135	11
Andy Pettitte, NY	L	19	9	**4.35**	32	32	3	1	0	204.2	219	111	99	17	4	80	125	2

Note: Pitchers must have 1 inning pitched per their team's games played to qualify.

Wins

Hudson, Oak 20-6
Wells, Tor 20-8
Pettitte, NY 19-9
P. Martinez, Bos 18-6
Sele, Sea 17-10
Burba, Cle 16-6
Finley, Cle 16-11
Helling, Tex 16-13
Colon, Cle 15-8
Sirotka, Chi 15-10
Heredia, Oak 15-11
Appier, Oak 15-11

Appearances

Wunsch*, Chi 83
Venafro, Tex 77
Wells, Min 76
Trombley, Bal 75
Lowe, Bos 74
Nelson, NY 73
Rhodes, Sea 72
Karsay, Cle 72
Foulke, Chi 72
Tam, Oak 72

Complete Games

Wells, Tor 9
P. Martinez, Bos 7
Mussina, Bal 6
Ponson, Bal 6
Lopez, TB 4
Radke, Min 4

Shutouts

P. Martinez, Bos 4
Sele, Sea 2
Hudson, Oak 2
24 tied with 1 each.

Losses

Radke, Min 12-16
Mays, Min 7-15
Trachsel, TB-Tor 8-15
Escobar, Tor 10-15
Weaver, Det 11-15
Mussina, Bal 11-15
Cone, NY 4-14
Ponson, Bal 9-13
Loaiza, Tex-Tor 10-13
Lopez, TB 11-13
Hernandez, NY 12-13
Rogers, Tex 13-13
Helling, Tex 16-13

Innings

Mussina, Bal 237.2
Wells, Tor 229.2
Rogers, Tex 227.1
Radke, Min 226.2
Ponson, Bal 222.0
Finley, Cle 218.0
P. Martinez, Bos . . .217.0
Helling, Tex 217.0
Suppan, KC 217.0
Sele, Sea 211.2

Saves

	SV	BS
Jones, Det	42	4
Lowe, Bos	42	5
Sasaki*, Sea	37	3
Rivera, NY	36	5
Foulke, Chi	34	5
Wetteland, Tex	34	9
Koch, Tor	33	5
Isringhausen, Oak	.33	7
Hernandez, TB	32	8
Percival, Ana	32	10

Holds

Shuey, Cle 28
Groom, Bal 27
Wunsch*, Chi 25
Rhodes, Sea 24
Zimmerman, Tex 21
Mecir, TB-Oak 21
Brocail, Det 19
Hasegawa, Ana 19
Tam, Oak 19

HRs Given Up

Suppan, KC 36
Milton, Min 35
Baldwin, Chi 34
Hernandez, NY 34
Wakefield, Bos 31
Nomo, Det 31
Carpenter, Tor 30
Ponson, Bal 30

Wild Pitches

Reichert*, KC 18
Grimsley, NY 16
Nomo, Det 16
Carrasco, Min-Bos 14
Cone, NY 11
Mays, Min 11
Suzuki, KC 11

Walks

Appier, Oak 102
Finley, Cle 101
Helling, Tex 99
Colon, Cle 98
Suzuki, KC 94
Burba, Cle 91
Reichert*, KC 91

Strikeouts

P. Martinez, Bos 284
Colon, Cle 212
Mussina, Bal 210
Finley, Cle 189
Clemens, NY 188
Nomo, Det. 181
Burba, Cle 180
Hudson, Oak. 169
Wells, Tor 166
Milton, Min 160
Ponson, Bal 152
Helling, Tex 146
Escobar, Tor 142

Opp. Batting Average

P. Martinez, Bos. 167
Hudson, Oak 227
Colon, Cle 233
Clemens, NY 236
Abbott, Sea 243
Hernandez, NY 247
Helling, Tex 252
Mussina, Bal 255
Finley, Cle. 256
Ponson, Bal 258

SB Allowed

Burba, Cle 21
Suzuki, KC 21
Wakefield, Bos 20
Hudson, Oak. 16
Clemens, NY 15
R. Martinez, Bos 15
Escobar, Tor 14
Castillo, Tor 13
Schoeneweis, Ana 13
Bergman, Min 12

Fielding

Put Outs

Delgado, Tor 1416
McGriff, TB 1300
Olerud, Sea 1271
Vaughn, Ana 1257
Ja. Giambi, Oak 1161
Martinez, NY 1154
Konerko, Chi. 1053
Coomer, Min. 1023
Sweeney, KC. 960
Posada, NY 955

Assists

Tejada, Oak 501
Cruz, Det 482
Valentin, Chi 456
Sanchez, KC 446
Rodriguez, Sea 438
R. Alomar, Cle. 437
Kennedy*, Ana. 425
Durham, Chi 419
Vizquel, Cle. 414
Guzman, Min 413

OF Assists

Higginson, Det 19
Martinez, TB-Tex-Tor . . .15
Ordonez, Chi 12
Hunter, Min 12
Salmon, Ana 12
Dye, KC 11
Everett, Bos 11
Lee, Chi 10
Six tied with 9 each.

Errors

Valentin, Chi 36
Lamb*, Tex. 33
Glaus, Ana 33
Palmer, Det. 25
Jeter, NY. 24
Guzman, Min 22
Guillen*, Sea. 21
Tejada, Oak. 21
Mora, Bal 20

Colorado Rockies
Todd Helton
BA, OBP, SLG, RBI,
Doubles, Hits, TB

Chicago Cubs
Sammy Sosa
Hone Runs

Los Angeles Dodgers
Kevin Brown
ERA, Opp. BA

Arizona Diamondbacks
Randy Johnson
Complete Games, Shutouts,
Strikeouts

National League Leaders

(*) indicates rookie.

Batting

	Bat	Gm	AB	R	H	Avg	TB	2B	3B	HR	RBI	BB	SO	SB	Slg Pct	OBP
Todd Helton, Col L		160	580	138	216	.372	405	59	2	42	147	103	61	5	.698	.463
Moises Alou, Hou .... .R		126	454	82	161	.355	283	28	2	30	114	52	45	3	.623	.416
Vladimir Guerrero, Mon... .R		154	571	101	197	.345	379	28	11	44	123	58	74	9	.664	.410
Jeffrey Hammonds, Col.... .R		122	454	94	152	.335	240	24	2	20	106	44	83	14	.529	.395
Jeff Kent, SF .... .R		159	587	114	196	.334	350	41	7	33	125	90	107	12	.596	.424
Luis Castillo, Fla.........S		136	539	101	180	.334	209	17	3	2	17	78	86	62	.388	.418
Jose Vidro, Mon......... .S		153	606	101	200	.330	327	51	2	24	97	49	69	5	.540	.379
Jeff Cirillo, Col .... .R		157	598	111	195	.326	285	53	2	11	115	67	72	3	.477	.392
Gary Sheffield, LA....... .R		141	501	105	163	.325	322	24	3	43	109	101	71	4	.643	.438
Mike Piazza, NY......... .R		136	482	90	156	.324	296	26	0	38	113	58	69	4	.614	.398
Edgardo Alfonzo, NY.... .R		150	544	109	176	.324	295	40	2	25	94	95	70	3	.542	.425
Sammy Sosa, Chi........ .R		156	604	106	193	.320	383	38	1	50	138	91	168	7	.634	.406
Jason Kendall, Pit........ .R		152	579	112	185	.320	272	33	6	14	58	79	79	22	.470	.412
Bobby Abreu, Phi........ .L		154	576	103	182	.316	319	42	10	25	79	100	116	28	.554	.416
Brian Giles, Pit L		156	559	111	176	.315	332	37	7	35	123	114	69	6	.594	.432

Note: Batters must have 3.1 plate appearances per their team's games played to qualify.

Home Runs

Sosa, Chi 50	
Bonds, SF.............49	
Bagwell, Hou 47	
V. Guerrero, Mon 44	
Hidalgo, Hou.....44	
Sheffield, LA........43	
Edmonds, St.l 42	
Helton, Col.....42	
Griffey, Cin 40	
Piazza, NY 38	

Triples

Womack, Ari..........14	
Perez, Col 11	
V. Guerrero, Mon 11	
Abreu, Phi 10	
Goodwin, Col-LA 9	
Belliard, Mil 9	
Seven tied with 7 each.	

On Base Pct.

Helton, Col..........463	
Bonds, SF 440	
Sheffield, LA..........438	
Giles, Pit 432	
Alfonzo, NY 425	
Bagwell, Hou........424	
Kent, SF 424	
Castillo, Fla 418	

Runs Batted In

Helton, Col 147	
Sosa, Chi.............138	
Bagwell, Hou 132	
Kent, SF 125	
Giles, Pit..........123	
V. Guerrero, Mon 123	
Hidalgo, Hou 122	
Wilson, Fla 121	

Doubles

Helton, Col.............59	
Cirillo, Col 53	
Vidro, Mon..........51	
Gonzalez, Ari 47	
Green, LA..........44	
Abreu, Phi 42	
Hidalgo, Hou..........42	
Grace, Chi..........41	
Kent, SF 41	

Slugging Pct.

Helton, Col..........698	
Bonds, SF 688	
V. Guerrero, Mon ... .664	
Sheffield, LA..........643	
Hidalgo, Hou..........636	
Sosa, Chi..........634	
Alou, Hou..........623	

Hits

Helton, Col 216	
Vidro, Mon 200	
A. Jones, Atl 199	
V. Guerrero, Mon 197	
Kent, SF 196	
Cirillo, Col..........195	
Sosa, Chi..........193	
Gonzalez, Ari 192	
Perez, Col 187	
Kendall, Pit 185	

Runs

Bagwell, Hou 152	
Helton, Col 138	
Bonds, SF..........129	
Edmonds, St.l 129	
A. Jones, Atl 122	
C. Jones, Atl 118	
Hidalgo, Hou 118	

Walks

Bonds, SF..........117	
Giles, Pit..............114	
Bagwell, Hou 107	
Edmonds, St.l 103	
Helton, Col 103	
Sheffield, LA 100	
Abreu, Phi 100	
Burnitz, Mil 99	

Stolen Bases

	SB	CS
Castillo, Fla 62	22	
Goodwin, Col-LA ..55	10	
Young, Chi..........54	7	
Womack, Ari......45	11	
Furcal*, Atl 40	14	
Wilson, Fla 36	14	
Glanville, Phi......31	8	
Owens, SD 29	14	
Reese, Cin 29	3	

Total Bases

Helton, Col 405	
Sosa, Chi..........383	
V. Guerrero, Mon 379	
Bagwell, Hou 363	
A. Jones, Atl 355	
Hidalgo, Hou 355	
Kent, SF 350	
Gonzalez, Ari 336	

Strikeouts

Wilson, Fla 187	
Sosa, Chi..........168	
Edmonds, St.l 167	
Lankford, St.l 148	
Burrell*, Phi..........139	
Rivera, SD 137	
Jenkins, Mil 135	

Pitching

	Arm	W	L	ERA	Gm	GS	CG	ShO	Sv	IP	H	R	ER	HR	HB	BB	SO	WP
Kevin Brown, LA ....R		13	6	2.58	33	33	5	1	0	230.0	181	76	66	21	9	47	216	4
Randy Johnson, Ari L		19	7	2.64	35	35	8	3	0	248.2	202	89	73	23	6	76	347	5
Jeff D'Amico, Mil........R		12	7	2.66	23	23	1	1	0	162.1	143	55	48	14	6	46	101	5
Greg Maddux, Atl........R		19	9	3.00	35	35	6	3	0	249.1	225	91	83	19	10	42	190	1
Mike Hampton, NY L		15	10	3.14	33	33	3	1	0	217.2	194	89	76	10	8	99	151	10
Al Leiter, NY L		16	8	3.20	31	31	2	1	0	208.0	176	84	74	19	11	76	200	4
Chan Ho Park, LA ....R		18	10	3.27	34	34	3	1	0	226.0	173	92	82	21	12	124	217	13
Tom Glavine, Atl.........L		21	9	3.40	35	35	4	2	0	241.0	222	101	91	24	4	65	152	0
Rick Ankiel*, St.L........L		11	7	3.50	31	30	0	0	0	175.0	137	80	68	21	6	90	194	12
Robert Person, Phi ....R		9	7	3.63	28	28	1	1	0	173.1	144	73	70	13	6	95	164	10
Ryan Dempster, Fla ......R		14	10	3.66	33	33	2	1	0	226.1	210	102	92	30	5	97	209	4
Livan Hernandez, SF......R		17	11	3.75	33	33	5	2	0	240.0	254	114	100	22	4	73	165	3
Woody Williams, SD ......R		10	8	3.75	23	23	4	0	0	168.0	152	74	70	23	3	54	111	4
Curt Schilling, Phi-Ari......R		11	12	3.81	29	29	8	2	0	210.1	204	90	89	27	1	45	168	4
Kris Benson, Pit ....R		10	12	3.85	32	32	2	1	0	217.2	206	104	93	24	10	86	184	5

Note: Pitchers must have 1 inning pitched per their team's games played to qualify.

Wins

Glavine, Atl 21-9
Kile, St.L 20-9
Johnson, Ari 19-7
Maddux, Atl 19-9
Park, LA 18-10
Elarton, Hou 17-7
Hernandez, SF......17-11
Leiter, NY 16-8
Stephenson, St.L 16-9

Appearances

Kline, Mon 83
Sullivan, Cin 79
Myers, Col 78
Wendell, NY 77
Benitez, NY 76
Rodriguez, SF 76
Sauerbeck, Pit 75
Heredia, Chi 74

Complete Games

Johnson, Ari 8
Schilling, Phi-Ari........8
Lieber, Chi 6
Maddux, Atl 6
Brown, LA...........5
Hernandez, SF.........5
Kile, St.L 5

Losses

Daal, Ari-Phi 4-19
Clement, SD 13-17
Parris, Cin 12-17
Holt, Hou 8-16
Lima, Hou 7-16
Yoshii, Col.........6-15
Hermanson, Mon ...12-14

Innings

Lieber, Chi 251.0
Maddux, Atl.......249.1
Johnson, Ari......248.2
Glavine, Atl 241.0
Hernandez, SF 240.0
Kile, St.L 232.1
Brown, LA 230.0
Dempster, Fla......226.1
Park, LA 226.0

Shutouts

Johnson, Ari 3
Maddux, Atl.........3
Estes, SF 2
Glavine, Atl 2
Hernandez, SF.........2
Sanchez, Fla 2
Schilling, Phi-Ari.....2
Stephenson, St.L.....2

Saves

	SV	BS
Alfonseca, Fla 45		4
Hoffman, SD 43		7
Benitez, NY 41		5
Nen, SF 41		5
Graves, Cin 30		5
Aguilera, Chi......29		8
Veres, St.L 29		7
Shaw, LA 27		7

Three tied with 24 each.

HRs Given Up

Lima, Hou.............48
Anderson, Ari 38
Lieber, Chi 36
Tapani, Chi 35

Wild Pitches

Clement, SD...........23
Williamson, Cin 21
Dreifort, LA...........17
Park, LA.............13
Ankiel*, St.L..........12
Bell*, Cin 11
Estes, SF.............11

Five tied with 10 each.

Walks

Clement, SD 125
Park, LA 124
Ortiz, SF 112
Estes, SF...........108
Haynes, Mil.........100
Hampton, NY 99
Dempster, Fla.........97
Person, Phi..........95
Ankiel*, St.L..........90
Hentgen, St.L.........89

Strikeouts

Johnson, Ari...........347
Park, LA 217
Brown, LA 216
Dempster, Fla 209
Leiter, NY..........200
Vazquez, Mon 196
Ankiel*, St.L 194
Astacio, Col.........193
Kile, St.L...........192
Lieber, Chi.........192
Maddux, Atl.........190
Benson, Pit.........184
Clement, SD 170
Millwood, Atl 168
Schilling, Phi-Ari 168

Holds

Rodriguez, SF 30
Remlinger, Atl 23
Christiansen, Pit-St.L 22
Sullivan, Cin 22
Franco, NY 20
Walker*, SD 19
White, Cin-Col 19
Looper, Fla 18
Brock, Phi 16
Wendell, NY 16

Opp. Batting Average

Brown, LA.......... .213
Park, LA .... .214
Ankiel*, St.L.......... .219
Johnson, Ari.......... .224
Leiter, NY .... .228
Person, Phi.......... .229
Dreifort, LA.......... .238
Maddux, Atl....... .238
Williams, SD .... .239
Hampton, NY....... .241
Dempster, Fla....... .243
Glavine, Atl .... .244
Kile, St.L .... .247

SB Allowed

Maddux, Atl...........25
Spencer, SD...........18
Dotel, Hou 15
Gagne*, LA...........15
B.J. Jones, NY 15
Ortiz, SF.............15
Witasick, SD 15

Fielding

Put Outs

Helton, Col 1328
Karros, NY 1296
Bagwell, Hou 1264
Zeile, NY...........1205
Snow, SF 1197
Young, Pit 1109
Galarraga, Atl 1105
Lee, Fla 1101
Grace, Chi 1098
Stevens, Mon 1072

Assists

Perez, Col 524
Vidro, Mon 442
Belliard, Mil.........437
Grudzielanek, LA 416
Morris, Pit 414
Aurilia, SF 403
Meares, Pit 401
Young, Chi.........400
Bordick, NY.........398
Kent, SF 394

OF Assists

Bergeron*, Mon 16
Giles, Pit.............14
Kotsay, Fla 14
Abreu, Phi 13
Hollandsworth, LA-Col ..12
Burnitz, Mil 12
V. Guerrero, Mon 12
Jenkins, Mil 12
Walker, Col 11
Benard, SF............11

Errors

Relaford, Phi 31
Renteria, St.L 27
Nevin, SD............26
Jackson, SD 25
C. Jones, Atl.........25
Furcal*, Atl 24
Beltre, LA 23
Aurilia, SF 21
Meares, Pit 20

Team Batting Statistics

American League

Team	Avg	AB	R	H	HR	RBI	SB
Cleveland ...	.288	5683	950	1639	221	889	113
Kansas City..	.288	5709	879	1644	150	831	121
Chicago	.286	5646	978	1615	216	926	119
Texas	.283	5648	848	1601	173	806	69
Anaheim	.280	5628	864	1574	236	837	93
New York ...	.277	5556	871	1541	205	833	99
Detroit	.275	5644	823	1553	177	785	83
Toronto......	.275	5677	861	1562	244	826	89
Baltimore....	.272	5549	794	1508	184	750	126
Minnesota ...	.270	5615	748	1516	116	711	90
Oakland	.270	5560	947	1501	239	908	40
Seattle	.269	5497	907	1481	198	869	122
Boston	.267	5630	792	1503	167	755	43
Tampa Bay ..	.257	5505	733	1414	162	692	90

National League

Team	Avg	AB	R	H	HR	RBI	SB
Colorado	.294	5660	968	1664	161	905	131
S. Francisco .	.278	5519	925	1535	226	889	79
Houston	.278	5570	938	1547	249	900	114
Cincinnati ...	.274	5635	825	1545	200	794	99
Atlanta.......	.271	5489	810	1490	179	758	148
St. Louis.....	.270	5489	887	1481	235	841	87
Pittsburgh....	.267	5643	793	1506	168	749	86
Montreal	.266	5535	738	1475	178	705	58
Arizona	.265	5527	792	1466	179	756	97
New York ...	.263	5486	807	1445	198	761	66
Florida.......	.262	5509	731	1441	160	691	168
Los Angeles..	.257	5481	798	1408	211	756	95
Chicago	.256	5577	764	1426	183	722	93
San Diego...	.254	5560	752	1413	157	714	131
Philadelphia .	.251	5511	708	1386	144	668	102
Milwaukee ..	.246	5563	740	1366	177	708	72

Team Pitching Statistics

American League

	ERA	W	Sv	CG	ShO	HR	BB	SO
Boston	4.23	85	46	7	4	173	499	1121
Seattle	4.49	91	44	4	4	167	634	998
Oakland	4.58	91	43	7	4	158	615	963
Chicago	4.66	95	43	5	2	195	614	1037
Detroit	4.71	79	44	6	1	177	496	978
New York ...	4.76	87	40	9	2	177	577	1040
Cleveland ...	4.84	90	34	6	2	173	666	1213
Tampa Bay ..	4.86	69	38	10	3	198	533	955
Anaheim	5.00	82	46	5	2	228	662	846
Toronto......	5.14	83	37	15	3	195	560	978
Minnesota ...	5.14	69	35	6	2	212	516	1042
Baltimore....	5.37	74	33	14	2	202	665	1017
Kansas City..	5.48	77	29	10	3	239	693	927
Texas	5.52	71	39	3	0	202	661	918

National League

	ERA	W	Sv	CG	ShO	HR	BB	SO
Atlanta......	4.06	95	53	13	6	165	484	1093
Los Angeles.	4.10	86	36	9	3	176	600	1154
New York ...	4.16	94	49	8	2	164	574	1164
S. Francisco .	4.21	97	47	9	4	151	623	1076
Cincinnati ...	4.33	85	42	8	1	190	659	1015
Arizona	4.35	85	38	16	4	190	500	1220
St. Louis.....	4.38	95	37	10	4	196	606	1100
San Diego...	4.52	76	46	5	0	191	649	1071
Florida......	4.56	79	48	5	3	169	650	1051
Milwaukee ..	4.63	73	29	2	1	174	728	967
Philadelphia .	4.77	65	34	8	3	201	640	1123
Pittsburgh....	4.93	69	27	5	2	163	711	1070
Montreal	5.13	67	39	4	2	181	579	1011
Chicago	5.25	65	39	10	1	231	658	1143
Colorado....	5.26	82	33	7	1	221	588	1001
Houston	5.41	71	30	8	1	234	598	1064

Team Fielding Statistics

American League

	Pct	TC	E	PO	A	OFA	DP
Cleveland ...	.988	6066	72	4327	1667	26	147
Seattle	.984	6057	99	4325	1633	20	176
Toronto......	.984	6088	100	4312	1676	28	176
Detroit	.983	6188	105	4330	1753	33	172
Kansas City..	.983	6172	102	4318	1752	33	185
Minnesota ...	.983	5926	102	4298	1526	41	155
Boston	.982	6113	109	4358	1646	34	120
Baltimore....	.981	5992	116	4300	1576	26	151
New York ...	.981	5869	109	4273	1487	18	132
Tampa Bay ..	.981	6227	118	4294	1815	37	169
Anaheim	.978	6222	134	4344	1744	35	182
Chicago	.978	6171	133	4351	1687	24	190
Oakland	.978	6165	134	4306	1725	21	164
Texas	.978	6018	135	4287	1596	32	162

National League

	Pct	TC	E	PO	A	OFA	DP
Colorado....	.985	6112	94	4290	1728	35	176
S. Francisco .	.985	6072	93	4333	1646	31	173
Chicago	.983	6040	100	4364	1576	19	139
Philadelphia .	.983	5908	100	4316	1492	33	136
Arizona	.982	5979	107	4331	1541	29	138
Cincinnati ...	.982	6123	111	4369	1643	38	156
Milwaukee ..	.981	6265	118	4399	1748	37	187
St. Louis.....	.981	5936	111	4301	1524	25	148
Florida......	.980	6128	125	4289	1714	38	144
New York ...	.980	6047	118	4350	1579	27	121
Atlanta......	.979	6183	129	4321	1733	28	138
Pittsburgh....	.979	6306	132	4347	1827	34	169
Houston	.978	6007	133	4313	1561	22	149
Los Angeles..	.978	6189	135	4335	1719	25	151
Montreal	.978	6109	132	4274	1703	47	151
San Diego...	.977	6189	141	4378	1670	33	155

2000 All-Star Game

71st Baseball All-Star Game. **Date:** July 11 at Turner Field, Atlanta, Ga.; **Managers:** Joe Torre, New York (AL) and Bobby Cox, Atlanta (NL); **Most Valuable Player:** SS Derek Jeter, New York (AL): 3-for-3 with a double, a run and 2 RBI.

American League

	AB	R	H	BI	BB	SO	Avg
Roberto Alomar, Cle, 2b	2	0	0	0	1	0	.000
Ray Durham, Chi, 2b	2	1	1	0	0	0	.500
Derek Jeter, NY, ss	3	1	3	2	0	0	1.000
Nomar Garciaparra, Bos, ss	2	1	1	0	0	0	.500
Bernie Williams, NY, cf	3	0	0	0	0	0	.000
Matt Lawton, Min, cf	2	1	1	1	0	0	.500
Jason Giambi, Oak, 1b	2	0	0	0	1	2	.000
Magglio Ordonez, Chi	1	0	1	1	0	0	1.000
Carl Everett, Bos, lf	2	0	0	1	1	0	.000
Darin Erstad, Ana, lf	2	0	0	1	0	0	.000
Ivan Rodriguez, Tex, c	3	0	1	0	0	0	.333
Jorge Posada, NY, c	2	0	0	0	0	1	.000
Jermaine Dye, KC, rf	2	1	0	0	1	1	.000
Fred McGriff, TB, 1b	2	0	0	0	0	1	.000
Travis Fryman, Cle, 3b	2	1	1	0	0	1	.500
Troy Glaus, Ana, 3b	1	0	0	0	0	0	.000
Tony Batista, Tor, ph-3b	1	0	0	0	0	1	.000
David Wells, Tor, sp	0	0	0	0	0	0	.000
Mike Bordick, Bal, ph	1	0	0	0	0	0	.000
Mike Sweeney, KC, ph	1	0	0	0	0	0	.000
Carlos Delgado, Tor, 1b	1	0	1	0	0	0	1.000
Edgar Martinez, Sea, ph	1	0	0	0	0	0	.000
TOTALS	38	6	10	6	4	7	.263

National League

	AB	R	H	BI	BB	SO	Avg
Barry Larkin, Cin, ss	3	0	0	0	0	0	.000
Edgar Renteria, St.L, ss	2	0	0	0	0	0	.000
Chipper Jones, Atl, 3b	3	1	3	1	0	0	1.000
Jeff Cirillo, Col, 3b	1	0	0	0	0	0	.000
Vladimir Guerrero, Mon, lf	2	0	1	0	0	0	.500
Andruw Jones, Atl, cf	2	0	1	1	0	1	.500
Sammy Sosa, Chi, rf	3	0	0	0	0	1	.000
Jose Vidro, Mon, ph-2b	1	0	0	0	0	0	.000
Jeff Kent, SF, 2b	2	0	0	0	0	0	.000
Edgardo Alfonzo, NYM, 2b	2	0	0	0	0	1	.000
Andres Galarraga, Atl, 1b	2	0	1	0	0	0	.500
Todd Helton, Col, pr-1b	2	0	0	0	0	0	.000
Jim Edmonds, St.L, cf	2	0	1	0	0	0	.500
Mike Lieberthal, Phi, c	2	1	1	0	0	0	.500
Jason Kendall, Pit, c	2	0	0	0	0	1	.000
Brian Giles, Pit, rf	2	0	0	0	0	0	.000
Randy Johnson, Ari, sp	0	0	0	0	0	0	.000
Jeffrey Hammonds, Col, ph	1	0	0	0	0	0	.000
Gary Sheffield, LA, lf	1	1	0	0	1	0	.000
Steve Finley, Ari, lf	1	0	1	1	0	0	.000
TOTALS	36	3	9	3	1	4	.250

	1	2	3	4	5	6	7	8	9		R	H	E
American League	0	0	1	2	0	0	0	0	3	–	6	10	2
National League	0	0	1	0	1	0	0	0	1	–	3	9	2

E— Garciaparra 2 (AL), Larkin and Vidro (NL). **LOB**— American 10, National 7. **2B**—Jeter, Delgado, and Ordonez (AL). **HR**—Chipper Jones (NL, off Baldwin). **SB**—Lawton (AL, 2nd base off Hoffman/Lieberthal). **SF**—Ordonez (AL). **GIDP**—Renteria (NL).

AL Pitching

	IP	H	R	ER	BB	SO
David Wells, Tor	2	2	0	0	0	2
James Baldwin, Chi (W)	1	2	1	1	0	0
Aaron Sele, Sea	1	1	0	0	0	0
Jason Isringhausen, Oak	1	2	1	1	1	0
Derek Lowe, Bos	1	0	0	0	0	0
Todd Jones, Det	1	0	0	0	0	1
Tim Hudson, Oak	1	0	0	0	0	1
Mariano Rivera, NY	1	2	1	0	0	0

NL Pitching

	IP	H	R	ER	BB	SO
Randy Johnson, Ari	1	1	0	0	0	1
Danny Graves, Cin	1	0	0	0	0	1
Kevin Brown, LA	1	1	1	1	3	0
Al Leiter, NY (L)	1	2	2	1	1	1
Tom Glavine, Atl	1	0	0	0	0	0
Darryl Kile, St.L	2	2	0	0	0	0
Bob Wickman, Mil	1	0	0	0	0	0
Trevor Hoffman, SD	1	3	3	3	0	2

Umpires—Mike Reilly (plate); Mark Hirschbeck (1b); Wally Bell (2b); Paul Schrieber (3b); Brian Onora (lf); Laz Diaz (rf). **Attendance**—51,323. **Time**—2:56. **TV Rating**—10.1/18 share (ESPN).

Home Run Derby

Results of the All-Star Home Run Derby at Turner Field, Atlanta, Ga. on July 10. **Avg**. refers to the average distance traveled by the home runs, in feet.

First Round

	No.	Long
Sammy Sosa, Chi. Cubs	6	508
Carl Everett, Boston	6	447
Ken Griffey, Cincinnati	6	424
Carlos Delgado, Toronto	5	443
Vladimir Guerrero, Montreal	2	454
Chipper Jones, Atlanta	2	412
Edgar Martinez, Seattle	2	432
Ivan Rodriguez, Texas	1	423

Semifinals

Sosa def. Everett, 11-6
Griffey def. Delgado, 3-1

Finals

Sosa def. Griffey, 9-2

Top 5 Homers by Distance

Sosa, 508 feet
Sosa, 508 feet
Sosa, 496 feet
Sosa, 488 feet
Sosa, 486 feet

AL Team by Team Statistics

At least 135 at bats or 40 innings pitched during the regular season, unless otherwise indicated. Players who competed for more than one AL team are listed with their final club. Players traded from the NL are listed with AL team only if they have 135 AB or 40 IP. Note that (*) indicates rookie and PTBN indicates player to be named.

Anaheim Angels

Batting (150 AB)	Avg	AB	R	H	HR	RBI	SB
Darin Erstad	.355	676	121	240	25	100	28
Orlando Palmeiro	.300	243	38	73	0	25	4
Tim Salmon	.290	568	108	165	34	97	0
Garret Anderson	.286	647	92	185	35	117	7
Troy Glaus	.284	563	120	160	47	102	14
Ben Molina*	.281	473	59	133	14	71	1
Mo Vaughn	.272	614	93	167	36	117	2
Adam Kennedy*	.266	598	82	159	9	72	22
Scott Spiezio	.242	297	47	72	17	49	1
Benji Gil	.239	301	28	72	6	23	10
Kevin Stocker	.219	343	41	75	2	24	1

Traded: P Bottenfield to Phi. for OF Ron Gant (July 30).
Signed: IF Stocker, released by TB (May 30).

Pitching (50 IP)	ERA	W-L	Gm	IP	BB	SO
Mike Fyhrie	2.39	0-0	32	52.2	15	43
Lou Pote*	3.40	1-1	32	50.1	17	44
Shigetoshi Hasegawa	3.57	10-6	66	95.2	38	59
Jarrod Washburn	3.74	7-2	14	84.1	37	49
Al Levine	3.87	3-4	51	95.1	49	42
Mark Petkovsek	4.22	4-2	64	81.0	23	31
Troy Percival	4.50	5-5	54	50.0	30	49
Ramon Ortiz*	5.09	8-6	18	111.1	55	73
Scott Schoeneweis	5.45	7-10	27	170.0	67	78
Seth Etherton*	5.52	5-1	11	60.1	22	32
Kent Bottenfield	5.71	7-8	21	127.2	56	75
Brian Cooper	5.90	4-8	15	87.0	35	36

Saves: Percival (32); Hasegawa (9); Levine and Petkovsek (2); Pote (1). **Complete games:** Ortiz (2); Schoeneweis, Cooper and Belcher (1). **Shutouts:** Schoeneweis and Cooper (1).

Baltimore Orioles

Batting (170 AB)	Avg	AB	R	H	HR	RBI	SB
Brook Fordyce	.301	302	41	91	14	49	0
Will Clark	.301	256	49	77	9	28	4
Mike Bordick	.297	391	70	116	16	59	6
Delino DeShields	.296	561	84	166	10	86	37
B.J. Surhoff	.292	411	56	120	13	57	7
Melvin Mora	.291	199	25	58	2	17	5
Jeff Conine	.284	409	53	116	13	46	4
Albert Belle	.281	559	71	157	23	103	0
Chris Richard	.276	199	38	55	13	36	7
Brady Anderson	.257	506	89	130	19	50	16
Cal Ripken Jr.	.256	309	43	79	15	56	0
Jerry Hairston Jr.	.256	180	27	46	5	19	8
Luis Matos*	.225	182	21	41	1	17	13

Acquired: IF Mora, IF Mike Kinkade, P Pat Gorman and P Lesli Brea from NYM for IF Bordick (July 28); IF Richard and P Mark Nussbech from St.L for P Mike Timlin (July 29); C Fordyce and 3 minor leaguers from ChW for DH Harold Baines and C Charles Johnson (July 30).
Traded: IF Clark and cash to St.L for IF Jose Leon (July 31); OF Surhoff and P Gabe Molina to Atl. for C Fernando Lunar, OF Trenidad Hubbard and P Luis Rivera (July 31).

Pitching (50 IP)	ERA	W-L	Gm	IP	BB	SO
Mike Mussina	3.79	11-15	34	237.2	46	210
Jose Mercedes	4.02	14-7	36	145.2	64	70
Mike Trombley	4.13	4-5	75	72.0	38	72
Chuck McElroy	4.69	3-0	43	63.1	34	50
Sidney Ponson	4.82	9-13	32	222.0	83	152
Buddy Groom	4.85	6-3	70	59.1	21	44
Pat Rapp	5.90	9-12	31	174.0	83	106
Jason Johnson	7.02	1-10	25	107.2	61	79
Scott Erickson	7.87	5-8	16	92.2	48	41

Saves: Ryan Kohlmeier (13); Mike Timlin (11); Trombley and Groom (4); Alan Mills (1). **Complete games:** Mussina and Ponson (6); Erickson and Mercedes (1). **Shutouts:** Mussina and Ponson (1).

Boston Red Sox

Batting (200 AB)	Avg	AB	R	H	HR	RBI	SB
Nomar Garciaparra	.372	529	104	197	21	96	5
Carl Everett	.300	496	82	149	34	108	11
Jeff Frye	.289	239	35	69	1	13	1
Midre Cummings	.277	206	29	57	4	24	0
Trot Nixon	.276	427	66	118	12	60	8
Scott Hatteberg	.265	230	21	61	8	36	0
Troy O'Leary	.261	513	68	134	13	70	0
Jose Offerman	.255	451	73	115	9	41	0
Brian Daubach	.248	495	55	123	21	76	1
Jason Varitek	.248	448	55	111	10	65	1
Darren Lewis	.241	270	44	65	2	17	10

Acquired: P Arrojo, P Rick Croushore and IF Mike Lansing from Col. for P Brian Rose, P John Wasdin, P Jeff Taglienti and IF Jeff Frye (July 27); OF Cummings from Min. for IF Hector De Los Santos (Aug. 31); P Carrasco from Min. for OF Lew Ford (Sept. 10).

Pitching (70 IP)	ERA	W-L	Gm	IP	BB	SO
Pedro Martinez	1.74	18-6	29	217.0	32	284
Derek Lowe	2.56	4-4	74	91.1	22	79
Rich Garces	3.25	8-1	64	74.2	23	69
Hector Carrasco	4.69	5-4	69	78.2	38	64
Jeff Fassero	4.78	8-8	38	130.0	50	97
Rolando Arrojo	5.05	5-2	13	71.1	22	44
Pete Schourek	5.11	3-10	21	107.1	38	63
Tim Wakefield	5.48	6-10	51	159.1	65	102
Ramon Martinez	6.13	10-8	27	127.2	67	89

Saves: Lowe (42); Garces, Pichardo, Florie, Carrasco, Wasdin and Jesus Pena (1). **Complete games:** P. Martinez (7). **Shutouts:** P. Martinez (4).

Chicago White Sox

Batting (170 AB)	Avg	AB	R	H	HR	RBI	SB
Frank Thomas	.328	582	115	191	43	143	1
Magglio Ordonez	.315	588	102	185	32	126	18
Charles Johnson	.304	421	76	128	31	91	2
Herbert Perry	.302	411	71	124	12	62	4
Carlos Lee	.301	572	107	172	24	92	13
Paul Konerko	.298	524	84	156	21	97	1
Ray Durham	.280	614	121	172	17	75	25
Jeff Abbott	.274	215	31	59	3	29	2
Jose Valentin	.273	568	107	155	25	92	19
Harold Baines	.254	283	26	72	11	39	0
Chris Singleton	.254	511	83	130	11	62	22
Greg Norton	.244	201	25	49	6	28	1
Mark Johnson	.225	213	29	48	3	23	3

Acquired: DH Baines and C Johnson from Bal. for C Brook Fordyce and 3 minor leaguers (July 30).
Signed: IF Perry off waivers from TB (Apr. 21); P Hill off waivers from Ana (Aug. 18). **Waived:** P Hill (Aug. 30).

Pitching (60 IP)	ERA	W-L	Gm	IP	BB	SO
Kelly Wunsch	2.93	6-3	83	61.1	29	51
Keith Foulke	2.97	3-1	72	88.0	22	91
Bob Howry	3.17	2-4	65	71.0	29	60
Bill Simas	3.46	2-3	60	67.2	22	49
Mike Sirotka	3.79	15-10	32	197.0	69	128
Jim Parque	4.28	13-6	33	187.0	71	111
Cal Eldred	4.58	10-2	20	112.0	59	97
James Baldwin	4.65	14-7	29	178.0	59	116
Sean Lowe	5.48	4-1	50	70.2	39	53
Kip Wells*	6.02	6-9	20	98.2	58	71
Jon Garland*	6.46	4-8	15	69.2	40	42
Ken Hill	7.16	5-8	18	81.2	59	50

Saves: Foulke (34); Howry (7); Wunsch (1). **Complete games:** Eldred and Baldwin (2); Sirotka (1). **Shutouts:** Eldred and Baldwin (1).

Cleveland Indians

Batting (135 AB)	Avg	AB	R	H	HR	RBI	SB
Manny Ramirez	.351	439	92	154	38	122	1
David Segui	.334	574	93	192	19	103	0
Travis Fryman	.321	574	93	184	22	106	1
Roberto Alomar	.310	610	111	189	19	89	39
Sandy Alomar	.289	356	44	103	7	42	2
Omar Vizquel	.287	613	101	176	7	66	22
Kenny Lofton	.278	543	107	151	15	73	30
Einar Diaz	.272	250	29	68	4	25	4
Jim Thome	.269	557	106	150	37	106	1
Wil Cordero	.264	148	18	39	0	17	0
Richie Sexson	.256	324	45	83	16	44	1
Jolbert Cabrera*	.251	175	27	44	2	15	6
Russ Branyan*	.238	193	32	46	16	38	0

Acquired: IF Segui from Tex. for OF Ricky Ledee (July 28); OF Cordero from Pit. for IF Enrique Wilson and OF Alex Ramirez (July 28); P Woodard, P Bere and P Bob Wickman from Mil. for OF Sexson, P Paul Rigdon, P Kane Davis and PTBN (July 28).

Pitching (40 IP)	ERA	W-L	Gm	IP	BB	SO
Justin Speier	3.29	5-2	47	68.1	28	69
Paul Shuey	3.39	4-2	57	63.2	30	69
Steve Karsay	3.76	5-9	72	76.2	25	66
Bartolo Colon	3.88	15-8	30	188.0	98	212
Chuck Finley	4.17	16-11	34	218.0	101	189
Steve Reed	4.34	2-0	57	56.0	21	39
Dave Burba	4.47	16-6	32	191.1	91	180
Jaret Wright	4.70	3-4	9	51.2	28	36
Jamie Brewington	5.36	3-0	26	45.1	19	34
Steve Woodard	5.67	3-3	13	54.0	11	35
Jim Brower*	6.24	2-3	17	62.0	31	32
Jason Bere	6.63	6-3	11	54.1	26	44
Charles Nagy	8.21	2-7	11	57.0	21	41

Saves: Karsay (20); Wickman (14). **Complete games:** Finley (3); Colon (2); Wright (1). **Shutouts:** Colon and Wright (1).

Detroit Tigers

Batting (135 AB)	Avg	AB	R	H	HR	RBI	SB
Deivi Cruz	.302	583	68	176	10	82	1
Bobby Higginson	.300	597	104	179	30	102	15
Juan Encarnacion	.289	547	75	158	14	72	16
Juan Gonzalez	.289	461	69	133	22	67	1
Gregg Jefferies	.275	142	18	39	2	14	0
Wendell Magee	.274	186	31	51	7	31	1
Tony Clark	.274	208	32	57	13	37	0
Brad Ausmus	.266	523	75	139	7	51	11
Shane Halter	.261	238	26	62	3	27	5
Damion Easley	.259	464	76	120	14	58	13
Dean Palmer	.256	524	73	134	29	102	4
Jose Macias	.254	173	25	44	2	24	2
Robert Fick*	.252	163	18	41	3	22	2
Rich Becker	.242	285	59	69	8	39	2

Signed: OF Becker off waivers from Oak. (May 10).

Pitching (40 IP)	ERA	W-L	Gm	IP	BB	SO
Nelson Cruz	3.07	5-2	27	41.0	13	34
Todd Jones	3.52	2-4	67	64.0	25	67
Danny Patterson	3.97	5-1	58	56.2	14	29
Steve Sparks	4.07	7-5	20	104.0	29	53
Doug Brocail	4.09	5-4	49	50.2	14	41
Jeff Weaver	4.32	11-15	31	200.0	52	136
Brian Moehler	4.50	12-9	29	178.0	40	103
Matt Anderson	4.72	3-2	69	74.1	45	71
Hideo Nomo	4.74	8-12	32	190.0	89	181
Willie Blair	4.88	10-6	47	156.2	35	74
C.J. Nitkowski	5.25	4-9	67	109.2	49	81
Dave Mlicki	5.58	6-11	24	119.1	44	57

Saves: Jones (42); Sparks and Anderson (1). **Complete games:** Weaver and Moehler (2); Sparks and Nomo (1). **Shutouts:** Sparks (1).

Kansas City Royals

Batting (135 AB)	Avg	AB	R	H	HR	RBI	SB
Mike Sweeney	.333	618	105	206	29	144	8
Johnny Damon	.327	655	136	214	16	88	46
Jermaine Dye	.321	601	107	193	33	118	0
Joe Randa	.304	612	88	186	15	106	6
Mark Quinn	.294	500	76	147	20	78	5
Jorge Fabregas	.282	142	13	40	3	17	1
David McCarty	.278	270	34	75	12	53	0
Gregg Zaun	.274	234	36	64	7	33	7
Rey Sanchez	.273	509	68	139	1	38	7
Carlos Febles	.257	339	59	87	2	29	17
Carlos Beltran	.247	372	49	92	7	44	13
Jeff Reboulet	.242	182	29	44	0	14	3
Todd Dunwoody	.208	178	12	37	1	23	3

Acquired: P Batista from Mon. for P Brad Rigby (Apr. 24); P Meadows from SD for P Witasick (July 31). **Waived:** P Spradlin (Aug. 30).

Pitching (40 IP)	ERA	W-L	Gm	IP	BB	SO
Jose Santiago	3.91	8-6	45	69.0	26	44
Makato Suzuki	4.34	8-10	32	188.2	94	135
Blake Stein	4.68	8-5	17	107.2	57	78
Dan Reichert*	4.70	8-10	44	153.1	91	94
Brian Meadows	4.77	6-2	11	71.2	14	26
Ricky Bottalico	4.83	9-6	62	72.2	41	56
Jeff Suppan	4.94	10-9	35	217.0	84	128
Jerry Spradlin	5.52	4-4	50	75.0	27	54
Jay Witasick	5.94	3-8	22	89.1	38	67
Chris Fussell	6.30	5-3	20	70.0	44	46
Miguel Batista	7.74	2-6	14	57.0	34	30
Chad Durbin*	8.21	2-5	16	72.1	43	37

Saves: Bottalico (16); Spradlin (7); Reichert (2); Andy Larkin and Brad Rigby (1). **Complete games:** Suppan (3); Meadows and Witasick (2); Suzuki, Stein and Reichert (1). **Shutouts:** Suzuki, Reichert and Suppan (1).

Minnesota Twins

Batting (135 AB)	Avg	AB	R	H	HR	RBI	SB
Matt Lawton	.305	561	84	171	13	88	23
Corey Koskie	.300	474	79	142	9	65	5
Denny Hocking	.298	373	52	111	4	47	7
Jacque Jones	.285	523	66	149	19	76	7
David Ortiz	.282	415	59	117	10	63	1
Torri Hunter	.280	336	44	94	5	44	4
Ron Coomer	.270	544	64	147	16	82	2
Jay Canizaro	.269	346	43	93	7	40	4
Cristian Guzman	.247	631	89	156	8	54	28
Butch Huskey	.223	215	22	48	5	27	0
Marcus Jensen	.209	139	16	29	3	14	0
Matt LeCroy*	.174	167	18	29	5	17	0

Traded: OF Huskey and IF Todd Walker to Col. for IF Todd Sears and cash (July 16).

Pitching (40 IP)	ERA	W-L	Gm	IP	BB	SO
LaTroy Hawkins	3.39	2-5	66	87.2	32	59
Bob Wells	3.65	0-7	76	86.1	15	76
Travis Miller	3.90	2-3	67	67.0	32	62
Eddie Guardado	3.94	7-4	70	61.2	25	52
Brad Radke	4.45	12-16	34	226.2	51	141
Mark Redman*	4.76	12-9	32	151.1	45	117
Eric Milton	4.86	13-10	33	200.0	44	160
Matt Kinney*	5.10	2-2	8	42.1	25	24
Joe Mays	5.56	7-15	31	160.1	67	102
Johan Santana*	5.50	2-3	30	86.0	54	64
J.C. Romero*	7.02	2-7	12	57.2	30	50
Sean Bergman	9.66	4-5	15	68.0	33	35

Saves: Hawkins (14); Wells (10); Guardado (9); Miller (1). **Complete games:** Radke (4); Mays (2). **Shutouts:** Radke and Mays (1).

New York Yankees

Batting (135 AB)	Avg	AB	R	H	HR	RBI	SB
Derek Jeter	.339	593	119	201	15	73	22
Bernie Williams	.307	537	108	165	30	121	13
Jorge Posada	.287	505	92	145	28	86	2
Dave Justice	.286	524	89	150	41	118	2
Paul O'Neill	.283	566	79	160	18	100	14
Chuck Knoblauch	.283	400	75	113	5	26	15
Shane Spencer	.282	248	33	70	9	40	1
Luis Polonia	.276	344	48	95	7	30	12
Jose Vizcaino	.276	174	23	48	0	10	5
Tino Martinez	.258	569	69	147	16	91	4
Jose Canseco	.252	329	47	83	15	49	2
Scott Brosius	.230	470	45	108	16	64	0
Clay Bellinger*	.207	184	33	38	6	21	5

Acquired: IF Vizcaino from LA for IF Jim Leyritz (June 20); OF Justice from Cle. for OF Ricky Ledee, P Jake Westbrook and P Zach Day (June 28); P Neagle and OF Mike Frank from Cin. for four minor leaguers (July 12).
Signed: OF Polonia off waivers from TB (June 11); OF Polonia off waivers from Det. (Aug. 3); OF Canseco off waivers from TB (Aug. 7).

Pitching (40 IP)	ERA	W-L	Gm	IP	BB	SO
Jeff Nelson	2.45	8-4	73	69.2	45	71
Mariano Rivera	2.85	7-4	66	75.2	25	58
Roger Clemens	3.70	13-8	32	204.1	84	188
Mike Stanton	4.10	2-3	69	68.0	24	75
Ramiro Mendoza	4.25	7-4	14	65.2	20	30
Andy Pettitte	4.35	19-9	32	204.2	80	125
Orlando Hernandez	4.51	12-13	29	195.2	51	141
Dwight Gooden	4.54	6-5	26	101.0	41	54
Jason Grimsley	5.04	3-2	63	96.1	42	53
Denny Neagle	5.81	7-7	16	91.1	31	58
David Cone	6.91	4-14	30	155.0	82	120

Saves: Rivera (36); Gooden (2); Grimsley and Todd Erdos (1).
Complete games: Hernandez and Pettitte (3); Clemens, Mendoza and Neagle (1). **Shutouts:** Mendoza and Pettitte (1).

Oakland Athletics

Batting (135 AB)	Avg	AB	R	H	HR	RBI	SB
Jason Giambi	.333	510	108	170	43	137	2
Olmedo Saenz	.313	214	40	67	9	33	1
Adam Piatt*	.299	157	24	47	5	23	0
Terrence Long*	.288	584	104	168	18	80	5
Ben Grieve	.279	594	92	166	27	104	3
Randy Velarde	.278	485	82	135	12	41	9
Eric Chavez	.277	501	89	139	26	86	2
Miguel Tejada	.275	607	105	167	30	115	6
Frank Menechino*	.255	145	31	37	6	26	1
Jeremy Giambi	.254	260	42	66	10	50	0
Ramon Hernandez	.241	419	52	101	14	62	1
Mike Stanley	.238	282	33	67	14	46	0
Matt Stairs	.227	476	74	108	21	81	5

Acquired: P Mecir and P Todd Belitz from TB for P Jesus Colome and PTBN (July 28).
Signed: IF Stanley off waivers from Bos. (Aug. 4).

Pitching (40 IP)	ERA	W-L	Gm	IP	BB	SO
Jeff Tam	2.63	3-3	72	85.2	23	46
Barry Zito*	2.72	7-4	14	92.2	45	78
Jim Mecir	2.96	10-3	63	85.0	36	70
Jason Isringhausen	3.78	6-4	66	69.0	32	57
Doug Jones	3.93	4-2	54	73.1	18	54
Gil Heredia	4.12	15-11	32	198.2	66	101
Tim Hudson	4.14	20-6	32	202.1	82	169
Kevin Appier	4.52	15-11	31	195.1	102	129
Mark Mulder*	5.44	9-10	27	154.0	69	88
T.J. Mathews	6.03	2-3	50	59.2	25	42
Omar Olivares	6.75	4-8	21	108.0	60	57

Saves: Isringhausen (33); Mecir (5); Tam (3); Jones (2); Scott Service (1). **Complete games:** Heredia and Hudson (2); Zito, Appier and Olivares (1). **Shutouts:** Hudson (2); Zito and Appier (1).

Seattle Mariners

Batting (135 AB)	Avg	AB	R	H	HR	RBI	SB
Edgar Martinez	.324	556	100	180	37	145	3
Alex Rodriguez	.316	554	134	175	41	132	15
John Olerud	.285	565	84	161	14	103	0
Stan Javier	.275	342	61	94	5	40	4
Mike Cameron	.267	543	96	145	19	78	24
Joe Oliver	.265	200	33	53	10	35	5
Carlos Guillen*	.257	288	45	74	7	42	1
Jay Buhner	.253	364	50	92	26	82	0
David Bell	.247	454	57	112	11	47	2
Mark McLemore	.245	481	72	118	3	46	30
Rickey Henderson	.238	324	58	77	4	30	31
Dan Wilson	.235	268	31	63	5	27	1
Raul Ibanez	.229	140	21	32	2	15	2

Signed: OF Henderson off waivers from NYM (May 17).

Pitching (40 IP)	ERA	W-L	Gm	IP	BB	SO
Kazuhiro Sasaki*	3.16	2-5	63	62.2	31	78
Rob Ramsay*	3.40	1-1	37	50.1	40	32
Jose Paniagua	3.47	3-0	69	80.1	38	71
Gil Meche	3.78	4-4	15	85.2	40	60
Freddy Garcia	3.91	9-5	21	124.1	64	79
Paul Abbott	4.22	9-7	35	179.0	80	100
Arthur Rhodes	4.28	5-8	72	69.1	29	77
Aaron Sele	4.51	17-10	34	211.2	74	137
Brett Tomko	4.68	7-5	32	92.1	40	59
John Halama	5.08	14-9	30	166.2	56	87
Jose Mesa	5.36	4-6	66	80.2	41	84
Jamie Moyer	5.49	13-10	26	154.0	53	98
Frank Rodriguez	6.27	2-1	23	47.1	22	19

Saves: Sasaki (37); Paniagua (5); Tomko and Mesa (1). **Complete games:** Sele (2); Meche and Halama (1). **Shutouts:** Sele (2); Meche and Halama (1).

Tampa Bay Devil Rays

Batting (135 AB)	Avg	AB	R	H	HR	RBI	SB
Steve Cox*	.283	318	44	90	11	35	1
Fred McGriff	.277	566	82	157	27	106	2
Bubba Trammell	.275	189	19	52	7	33	3
Gerald Williams	.274	632	87	173	21	89	12
John Flaherty	.261	394	36	103	10	39	0
Miguel Cairo	.261	375	49	98	1	34	28
Russ Johnson	.254	185	28	47	2	17	4
Greg Vaughn	.254	461	83	117	28	74	8
Jose Guillen	.253	316	40	80	10	41	3
Randy Winn	.252	159	28	40	1	16	6
Mike DeFelice	.240	204	23	49	6	19	0
Bobby Smith	.234	175	21	41	6	26	2
Vinny Castilla	.221	331	22	73	6	42	1
Felix Martinez	.214	299	42	64	2	17	9

Acquired: IF Johnson from Hou. for P Marc Valdes (May 27); P Sturtze from ChW for IF Tony Graffanino (May 31); P Wilson and OF Jason Tyner from NYM for OF Trammell and P White (July 28).
Signed: IF Martinez off waivers from Phi. (Apr. 5); IF O. Guillen (Apr. 5).

Pitching (40 IP)	ERA	W-L	Gm	IP	BB	SO
Roberto Hernandez	3.19	4-7	68	73.1	23	61
Paul Wilson	3.35	1-4	11	51.0	16	40
Rick White	3.41	3-6	44	71.1	26	47
Albie Lopez	4.13	11-13	45	185.1	70	96
Bryan Rekar	4.41	7-10	30	173.1	39	95
Doug Creek	4.60	1-3	45	60.2	39	73
Tanyon Sturtze	4.74	5-2	29	68.1	29	44
Cory Lidle	5.03	4-6	31	96.2	29	62
Esteban Yan	6.21	7-8	43	137.2	42	111
Ryan Rupe	6.92	5-6	18	91.0	31	61
Dave Eiland	7.24	2-3	17	54.2	18	17

Saves: Hernandez (32); White and Lopez (2); Creek (1). **Complete games:** Lopez (4); Rekar (2); Travis Harper (1). **Shutouts:** Lopez and Harper (1).

Texas Rangers

Batting (135 AB)

	Avg	AB	R	H	HR	RBI	SB
Ivan Rodriguez	.347	363	66	126	27	83	5
Gabe Kapler	.302	444	59	134	14	66	8
Rusty Greer	.297	394	65	117	8	65	4
Luis Alicea	.294	540	85	159	6	63	1
Ruben Mateo*.......	.291	206	32	60	7	19	6
Frank Catalanotto	.291	282	55	82	10	42	6
Rafael Palmeiro	.288	565	102	163	39	120	2
Mike Lamb*	.278	493	65	137	6	47	0
Bill Hasselman	.275	193	23	53	6	26	0
Chad Curtis	.272	335	48	91	8	48	3
Royce Clayton	.242	513	70	124	14	54	11
Ricky Ledee	.236	467	59	110	13	77	13

Acquired: OF Ledee from Cle. for IF David Segui (July 28).

Pitching (40 IP)

	ERA	W-L	Gm	IP	BB	SO
Mike Venafro	3.83	3-1	77	56.1	21	32
John Wetteland	4.20	6-5	62	60.0	24	53
Rick Helling	4.48	16-13	35	217.0	99	146
Kenny Rogers	4.55	13-13	34	227.1	78	127
Tim Crabtree	5.15	2-7	68	80.1	31	54
Jeff Zimmerman	5.30	4-5	65	69.2	34	74
Francisco Cordero* ..	5.35	1-2	56	77.1	48	49
Doug Davis*	5.38	7-6	30	98.2	58	66
Ryan Glynn	5.58	5-7	16	88.2	41	33
Matt Perisho	7.37	2-7	34	105.0	67	74
Darren Oliver	7.42	2-9	21	108.0	42	49
Mark Clark.........	7.98	3-5	12	44.0	24	16

Saves: Wetteland (34); Crabtree (2); Venafro and Zimmerman (1). **Complete games:** Rogers (2); Davis (1). **Shutouts:** none.

Toronto Blue Jays

Batting (135 AB)

	Avg	AB	R	H	HR	RBI	SB
Carlos Delgado.......	.344	569	115	196	41	137	0
Darrin Fletcher........	.320	416	43	133	20	58	1
Shannon Stewart.....	.319	583	107	186	21	69	20
Brad Fullmer..........	.295	482	76	142	32	104	3
Craig Grebeck........	.295	241	38	71	3	23	0
Dave Martinez.......	.285	403	55	115	5	46	7
Raul Mondesi........	.271	388	78	105	24	67	22
Tony Batista........	.263	620	96	163	41	114	5
Alex Gonzalez	.252	527	68	133	15	69	4
Marty Cordova	.245	200	23	49	4	18	3
Jose Cruz Jr..........	.242	603	91	146	31	76	15
Homer Bush	.215	297	38	64	1	18	9
Alberto Castillo	.211	185	14	39	1	16	0

Acquired: P Loaiza from Tex. for 2 minor leaguers (July 19); P Trachsel and P Guthrie from TB for IF Brent Abernathy (July 31); OF Martinez from Tex. for P Peter Munro (Aug. 4).

Pitching (40 IP)

	ERA	W-L	Gm	IP	BB	SO
Billy Koch	2.63	9-3	68	78.2	18	60
Frank Castillo.........	3.59	10-5	25	138.0	56	104
David Wells	4.11	20-8	35	229.2	31	166
Paul Quantrill........	4.52	2-5	68	83.2	25	47
Esteban Loaiza	4.56	10-13	34	199.1	57	137
Mark Guthrie	4.61	1-3	57	52.2	27	46
Lance Painter	4.73	2-0	42	66.2	22	53
Steve Trachsel	4.80	8-15	34	200.2	74	110
Kelvim Escobar	5.35	10-15	43	180.0	85	142
John Frascatore......	5.42	2-4	60	73.0	33	30
Chris Carpenter......	6.26	10-12	34	175.1	83	113
Pedro Borbon........	6.48	1-1	59	41.2	38	29
Roy Halladay	10.64	4-7	19	67.2	42	44

Saves: Koch (33); Escobar (2); Quantrill, Loaiza and Borbon (1). **Complete games:** Wells (9); Trachsel and Escobar (3); Carpenter (2); Loaiza (1). **Shutouts:** Wells, Loaiza, Trachsel and Escobar (1).

Home Attendance

Overall 2000 regular season attendance in Major League Baseball was a record 72,782,013 in 2,416 games for an average per game crowd of 30,125; numbers in parentheses indicate ranking in 1999; HD indicates home dates; Attendance is based on tickets sold.

American League

	Attendance	HD	Average
1 Cleveland (2)	3,456,278	81	42,670
2 Baltimore (1).......	3,297,031	81	40,704
3 New York (3)	3,227,657	80	40,346
4 Seattle (4)	3,148,317	81	38,868
5 Texas (5)	2,800,075	80	35,001
6 Boston (6)	2,585,895	81	31,925
7 Detroit (9)	2,533,753	81	31,281
8 Anaheim (7)	2,066,982	81	25,518
9 Chicago (13)	1,947,799	80	24,347
10 Toronto (8)........	1,819,919	81	22,468
11 Oakland (12)......	1,728,885	81	21,344
12 Kansas City (11) ..	1,677,915	81	20,715
13 Tampa Bay (10)	1,549,592	80	19,370
14 Minnesota (14)....	1,059,415	81	13,079
TOTALS	32,899,513	1130	29,115

National League

	Attendance	HD	Average
1 Colorado (1).......	3,293,354	81	40,659
2 St. Louis (2)	3,336,493	81	41,191
3 Atlanta (3)........	3,234,304	81	39,930
4 Los Angeles (4).....	3,011,539	81	37,179
5 Arizona (5)........	2,942,251	81	36,324
6 Chicago (6)	2,734,511	79	34,614
7 New York (7)	2,766,160	77	35,924
8 Houston (8)........	3,054,139	81	37,705
9 San Diego (9)......	2,423,142	81	29,915
10 San Francisco (10)..	3,319,340	81	40,980
11 Cincinnati (11)....	2,577,371	81	31,819
12 Philadelphia (12)..	1,612,769	80	20,160
13 Milwaukee (13)	1,573,621	79	19,919
14 Pittsburgh (14)	1,748,908	79	22,138
15 Florida (15).......	1,218,326	80	15,229
16 Montreal (16)......	926,272	81	11,435
TOTALS	39,772,500	1284	30,975

Note: Not included in the above table are the two games played in Japan between the Chicago Cubs and New York Mets. A total of 110,000 fans attended the two games.

NL Team by Team Statistics

At least 135 at bats or 40 innings pitched during the regular season unless otherwise indicated. Players who competed for more than one NL team are listed with their final club. Players traded from the AL are listed with NL team only if they have 135 AB or 40 IP. Note that (*) indicates rookie and PTBN indicates player to be named.

Arizona Diamondbacks

Batting (135 AB)	Avg	AB	R	H	HR	RBI	SB
Craig Counsell	.316	152	23	48	2	11	3
Greg Colbrunn	.313	329	48	103	15	57	0
Luis Gonzalez	.311	618	106	192	31	114	2
Danny Bautista	.285	351	54	100	11	59	6
Steve Finley	.280	539	100	151	35	96	12
Matt Williams	.275	371	43	102	12	47	1
Damian Miller	.275	324	43	89	10	44	2
Tony Womack	.271	617	95	167	7	57	45
Erubiel Durazo	.265	196	35	52	8	33	1
Kelly Stinnett	.217	240	22	52	8	33	0

Acquired: OF Bautista from Fla. for IF Andy Fox (June 9); P Schilling from Phi. for OF Travis Lee, P Omar Daal, P Vicente Padilla and P Nelson Figueroa (July 26).

Pitching (40 IP)	ERA	W-L	Gm	IP	BB	SO
Randy Johnson	2.64	19-7	35	248.2	76	347
Dan Plesac	3.15	5-1	62	40.0	26	45
Greg Swindell	3.20	2-6	64	76.0	20	64
Curt Schilling	3.81	11-12	29	210.1	45	168
Brian Anderson	4.05	11-7	33	213.1	39	104
Byung-Hyun Kim*	4.46	6-6	61	70.2	46	111
Matt Mantei	4.57	1-1	47	45.1	35	53
Mike Morgan	4.87	5-5	60	101.2	40	56
Todd Stottlemyre	4.91	9-6	18	95.1	36	76
Russ Springer	5.08	2-4	52	62.0	34	59
Armando Reynoso	5.27	11-12	31	170.2	52	89
Geraldo Guzman*	5.37	5-4	13	60.1	22	52

Saves: Mantei (17); Kim (14); Morgan (5); Swindell and Darren Holmes (1). **Complete games:** Johnson and Schilling (8); Anderson and Reynoso (2). **Shutouts:** Johnson (3); Schilling (2).

Atlanta Braves

Batting (135 AB)	Avg	AB	R	H	HR	RBI	SB
Chipper Jones	.311	579	118	180	36	111	14
Quilvio Veras	.309	298	56	92	5	37	25
Andruw Jones	.303	656	122	199	36	104	21
Andres Galarraga	.302	494	67	149	28	100	3
Rafael Furcal*	.295	455	87	134	4	37	40
Javy Lopez	.287	481	60	138	24	89	0
Wally Joyner	.281	224	24	63	5	32	0
Keith Lockhart	.265	275	32	73	2	32	4
Brian Jordan	.264	489	71	129	17	77	10
Walt Weiss	.260	192	29	50	0	18	1
Bobby Bonilla	.255	239	23	61	5	28	0
Reggie Sanders	.232	340	43	79	11	37	21
Paul Bako	.226	221	18	50	2	20	0

Acquired: P Ashby from Phi. for P Bruce Chen and P Jim Osting (July 12). **Signed:** C Bako off waivers from Fla. (July 21); P Belinda off waivers from Col. (July 29).

Pitching (40 IP)	ERA	W-L	Gm	IP	BB	SO
John Rocker	2.89	1-2	59	53.0	48	77
Greg Maddux	3.00	19-9	35	249.1	42	190
Tom Glavine	3.40	21-9	35	241.0	65	152
Mike Remlinger	3.47	5-3	71	72.2	37	72
Kerry Ligtenberg	3.61	2-3	59	52.1	24	51
Kevin Millwood	4.66	10-13	36	212.2	62	168
John Burkett	4.89	10-6	31	134.1	51	110
Andy Ashby	4.92	12-13	31	199.1	61	106
Terry Mulholland	5.11	9-9	54	156.2	41	78
Stan Belinda	7.71	1-3	56	46.2	22	51

Saves: Rocker (24); Remlinger and Ligtenberg (12); Rudy Seanez and Scott Kamieniecki (2); Mulholland and Belinda (1). **Complete games:** Maddux (6); Glavine (4); Ashby (3); Mulholland (1). **Shutouts:** Maddux (3); Glavine (2); Ashby (1).

Chicago Cubs

Batting (170 AB)	Avg	AB	R	H	HR	RBI	SB
Sammy Sosa	.320	604	106	193	50	138	7
Rondell White	.311	357	59	111	13	61	5
Eric Young	.297	607	98	180	6	47	54
Mark Grace	.280	510	75	143	11	82	1
Joe Girardi	.278	363	47	101	6	40	1
Ricky Gutierrez	.276	449	73	124	11	56	8
Damon Buford	.251	495	64	124	15	48	4
Shane Andrews	.229	192	25	44	14	39	1
Jeff Reed	.214	229	26	49	4	25	0
Jose Nieves	.212	198	17	42	5	24	1
Willie Greene	.201	299	34	60	10	37	4

Acquired: OF White from Mon. for P Scott Downs (July 31).

Pitching (40 IP)	ERA	W-L	Gm	IP	BB	SO
Tim Worrell	2.47	3-4	54	62.0	24	52
Todd Van Poppel	3.75	4-5	51	86.1	48	77
Steve Rain*	4.35	3-4	37	49.2	27	54
Jon Lieber	4.41	12-11	35	251.0	54	192
Felix Heredia	4.76	7-3	74	58.2	33	52
Kerry Wood	4.80	8-7	23	137.0	87	132
Rick Aguilera	4.91	1-2	54	47.2	18	38
Kevin Tapani	5.01	8-12	30	195.2	47	150
Daniel Garibay*	6.03	2-8	30	74.2	39	46
Kyle Farnsworth	6.43	2-9	46	77.0	50	74
Ruben Quevedo*	7.47	3-10	21	88.0	54	65

Saves: Aguilera (29); Worrell (3); Van Poppel and Heredia (2); Farnsworth, Jamie Arnold and Brian Williams (1). **Complete games:** Lieber (6); Tapani (2); Wood and Quevedo (1). **Shutouts:** Lieber (1).

Cincinnati Reds

Batting (135 AB)	Avg	AB	R	H	HR	RBI	SB
Chris Stynes	.334	380	71	127	12	40	5
Alex Ochoa	.316	244	50	77	13	58	8
Sean Casey	.315	480	69	151	20	85	1
Barry Larkin	.313	396	71	124	11	41	14
Dmitri Young	.303	548	68	166	18	88	0
Dante Bichette	.295	461	67	136	16	76	5
Aaron Boone	.285	291	44	83	12	43	6
Ken Griffey Jr.	.271	520	100	141	40	118	6
Ed Taubensee	.267	266	29	71	6	24	0
Brian L. Hunter	.267	240	47	64	1	14	20
Michael Tucker	.267	270	55	72	15	36	13
Benito Santiago	.262	252	22	66	8	45	2
Pokey Reese	.255	518	76	132	12	46	29
Juan Castro	.241	224	20	54	4	23	0

Acquired: IF Castro from LA for P Kenny Kutz (Apr. 1); OF Hunter from Col. for P Robert Averette (Aug. 6). **Traded:** P Neagle and OF Mike Frank to NYY for four minor leaguers (July 12); OF Bichette to Bos. for P Chris Reitsma and P John Curtice (Aug. 31).

Pitching (40 IP)	ERA	W-L	Gm	IP	BB	SO
Danny Graves	2.56	10-5	66	91.1	42	56
Scott Williamson	3.29	5-8	48	112.0	75	136
Scott Sullivan	3.47	3-6	79	106.1	38	96
Denny Neagle	3.52	8-2	18	117.2	50	88
Osvaldo Fernandez	3.62	4-3	15	79.2	31	36
Elmer Dessens	4.28	11-5	40	147.1	43	85
Dennys Reyes	4.53	2-1	62	43.2	29	36
Pete Harnisch	4.74	8-6	22	131.0	46	71
Steve Parris	4.81	12-17	33	192.2	71	117
Rob Bell*	5.00	7-8	26	140.1	73	112
Ron Villone	5.43	10-10	35	141.0	78	77

Saves: Graves (30); Williamson (6); Sullivan (3); Dessens, Larry Luebbers and John Riedling (1). **Complete games:** Harnisch (3); Villone (2); Fernandez, Dessens and Bell (1). **Shutouts:** Harnisch (1).

Colorado Rockies

Batting (180 AB)

	Avg	AB	R	H	HR	RBI	SB
Todd Helton	.372	580	138	216	42	147	5
Jeffrey Hammonds	.335	454	94	152	20	106	14
Jeff Cirillo	.326	598	111	195	11	115	3
Juan Pierre*	.310	200	26	62	0	20	7
Larry Walker	.309	314	64	97	9	51	5
Brent Mayne	.301	335	36	101	6	64	1
Neifi Perez	.287	651	92	187	10	71	3
Todd Hollandsworth	.269	428	81	115	19	47	18
Terry Shumpert	.259	263	52	68	9	40	8
Mike Lansing	.258	365	62	94	11	47	8

Acquired: P White from Cin. for P Manny Aybar (Apr. 7); IF Walker and OF Butch Huskey from Min. for IF Todd Sears and cash (July 16); P Rose, P John Wasdin, P Jeff Taglienti and IF Jeff Frye from Bos. for P Arrojo, P Rick Croushore and IF Lansing (July 27); OF Hollandsworth, OF Kevin Gibbs and P Randey Dorame from LA for OF Tom Goodwin and cash (July 31).
Traded: P Karl and cash to Ana. for PTBN (Aug. 22).

Pitching (40 IP)

	ERA	W-L	Gm	IP	BB	SO
Mike Myers	1.99	0-1	78	45.1	24	41
Gabe White	2.36	11-2	68	84.0	15	84
Jose Jimenez	3.18	5-2	72	70.2	28	44
Julian Tavarez	4.43	11-5	51	120.0	53	62
Brian Bohanon	4.68	12-10	34	177.0	79	98
Mike DeJean	4.89	4-4	54	53.1	30	34
Pedro Astacio	5.27	12-9	32	196.1	77	193
Brian Rose	5.51	4-5	12	63.2	30	40
Masato Yoshii	5.86	6-15	29	167.1	53	88
Kevin Jarvis	5.95	3-4	24	115.0	33	60
Rolando Arrojo	6.04	5-9	19	101.1	46	80
Scott Karl	7.68	2-3	17	65.2	33	29

Saves: Jimenez (24); White (5); Myers, Tavarez and David Lee (1). **Complete games:** Astacio (3); Bohanon (2); Tavarez and John Wasdin (1). **Shutouts:** Bohanon (1).

Florida Marlins

Batting (200 AB)

	Avg	AB	R	H	HR	RBI	SB
Luis Castillo	.334	539	101	180	2	17	62
Cliff Floyd	.300	420	75	126	22	91	24
Mark Kotsay	.298	530	87	158	12	57	19
Derrek Lee	.281	477	70	134	28	70	0
Mike Lowell	.270	508	73	137	22	91	4
Preston Wilson	.264	605	94	160	31	121	36
Kevin Millar	.259	259	36	67	3	14	0
Henry Rodriguez	.256	367	47	94	20	61	1
Dave Berg	.252	210	23	53	1	21	3
Mike Redmond	.252	210	17	53	0	15	0
Andy Fox	.232	250	29	58	4	20	10
Alex Gonzalez	.200	385	35	77	7	42	7

Acquired: P Smith from Tex. in a 3-player trade that sent Brant Brown from Fla. to ChC and OF Dave Martinez from ChC to Tex. (June 9); IF Fox from Ari. for OF Danny Bautista (June 9); P Aybar from Cin. for P Jorge Cordova (July 26); OF Rodriguez and cash from ChC for OF Ross Gload and P David Noyce (July 31).

Pitching (65 IP)

	ERA	W-L	Gm	IP	BB	SO
Chuck Smith*	3.23	6-6	19	122.2	54	118
Ryan Dempster	3.66	14-10	33	226.1	97	209
Antonio Alfonseca	4.24	5-6	68	70.0	24	47
Manny Aybar	4.31	2-2	54	79.1	35	45
Braden Looper	4.41	5-1	73	67.1	36	29
Ricky Bones	4.54	2-3	56	77.1	27	59
A.J. Burnett*	4.79	3-7	13	82.2	44	57
Brad Penny*	4.81	8-7	23	119.2	60	80
Reid Cornelius	4.82	4-10	22	125.0	50	50
Jesus Sanchez	5.34	9-12	32	182.0	76	123
Vladimir Nunez	7.90	0-6	19	68.1	34	43

Saves: Alfonseca (45); Looper (2); Joe Strong (1). **Complete games:** Dempster and Sanchez (2). **Shutouts:** Sanchez (2); Dempster (1).

Houston Astros

Batting (135 AB)

	Avg	AB	R	H	HR	RBI	SB
Moises Alou	.355	454	82	161	30	114	3
Richard Hidalgo	.314	558	118	175	44	122	13
Jeff Bagwell	.310	590	152	183	47	132	9
Ken Caminiti	.303	208	42	63	15	45	3
Bill Spiers	.301	355	41	107	3	43	7
Mitch Meluskey*	.300	337	47	101	14	69	1
Lance Berkman*	.297	353	76	105	21	67	6
Julio Lugo*	.283	420	78	119	10	40	22
Roger Cedeno	.282	259	54	73	6	26	25
Tony Eusebio	.280	218	24	61	7	33	0
Craig Biggio	.268	377	67	101	8	35	12
Chris Truby*	.260	258	28	67	11	59	2
Daryle Ward	.258	264	36	68	20	47	0
Tim Bogar	.207	304	32	63	7	33	1

Acquired: P Valdes from TB for IF Russ Johnson (May 27).

Pitchers (40 IP)

	ERA	W-L	Gm	IP	BB	SO
Joe Slusarski	4.21	2-7	54	77.0	22	54
Scott Elarton	4.81	17-7	30	192.2	84	131
Marc Valdes	5.08	5-5	53	56.2	25	35
Wade Miller*	5.14	6-6	16	105.0	42	89
Shane Reynolds	5.22	7-8	22	131.0	45	93
Chris Holt	5.35	8-16	34	207.0	75	136
Octavio Dotel	5.40	3-7	50	125.0	61	142
Jose Cabrera	5.92	2-3	52	59.1	17	41
Jose Lima	6.65	7-16	33	196.1	68	124

Saves: Dotel (16); Wagner (6); Slusarski (3); Valdes and Cabrera (2). **Complete games:** Holt (3); Elarton and Miller (2); Tony McKnight (1). **Shutouts:** Holt (1).

Los Angeles Dodgers

Batting (135 AB)

	Avg	AB	R	H	HR	RBI	SB
Gary Sheffield	.325	501	105	163	43	109	4
Adrian Beltre	.290	510	71	148	20	85	12
Todd Hundley	.284	299	49	85	24	70	0
Mark Grudzielanek	.279	617	101	172	7	49	12
Shawn Green	.269	610	98	164	24	99	24
Devon White	.266	158	26	42	4	13	3
Chad Kreuter	.264	212	32	56	6	28	1
Tom Goodwin	.263	528	94	139	6	58	55
Bruce Aven	.250	168	20	42	7	29	2
Eric Karros	.250	584	84	146	31	106	4
Alex Cora*	.238	353	39	84	4	32	4
Kevin Elster	.227	220	29	50	14	32	0
F.P. Santangelo	.197	142	19	28	1	9	5

Acquired: P Valdes from ChC for P Jamie Arnold and OF Jorge Piedra (July 26); OF Goodwin and cash from Col. for OF Todd Hollandsworth, OF Kevin Gibbs and P Randey Dorame (July 31); OF Aven from Pit. for cash or PTBN (Aug. 6).

Pitching (40 IP)

	ERA	W-L	Gm	IP	BB	SO
Kevin Brown	2.58	13-6	33	230.0	47	216
Matt Herges*	3.17	11-3	59	110.2	40	75
Mike Fetters	3.24	6-2	51	50.0	25	40
Chan Ho Park	3.27	18-10	34	226.0	124	217
Terry Adams	3.52	6-9	66	84.1	36	56
Antonio Osuna	3.74	3-6	46	67.1	35	70
Darren Dreifort	4.16	12-9	32	192.2	87	164
Jeff Shaw	4.24	3-4	60	57.1	16	39
Eric Gagne*	5.15	4-6	20	101.1	60	79
Carlos Perez	5.56	5-8	30	144.0	33	64
Ismael Valdes	5.64	2-7	21	107.0	40	74

Saves: Shaw (27); Fetters (5); Adams (2); Herges and Alan Mills (1). **Complete games:** Brown (5); Park (3); Dreifort (1). **Shutouts:** Brown, Park and Dreifort (1).

Milwaukee Brewers

Batting (135 AB)	Avg	AB	R	H	HR	RBI	SB
Geoff Jenkins	.303	512	100	155	34	94	11
Richie Sexson	.296	213	44	63	14	47	1
Mark Loretta	.281	352	49	99	7	40	0
Luis Lopez	.264	201	24	53	6	27	1
Ron Belliard	.263	571	83	150	8	54	7
Charlie Hayes	.251	370	46	93	9	46	1
Tyler Houston	.250	284	30	71	18	43	2
Raul Casanova	.247	231	20	57	6	36	1
Jose Hernandez	.244	446	51	109	11	59	3
Marquis Grissom	.244	595	67	145	14	62	20
Henry Blanco	.236	284	29	67	7	31	0
James Mouton	.233	159	28	37	2	17	13
Jeromy Burnitz	.232	564	91	131	31	98	6

Acquired: OF Sexson, P Rigdon, P Kane Davis and PTBN from Cle for P Woodard, P Bere and P Wickman (July 28).

Pitching (40 IP)	ERA	W-L	Gm	IP	BB	SO
Curtis Leskanic	2.56	9-3	73	77.1	51	75
Jeff D'Amico	2.66	12-7	23	162.1	46	101
Bob Wickman	2.93	2-2	43	46.0	20	44
Dave Weathers	3.07	3-5	69	76.1	32	50
Juan Acevedo	3.81	3-7	62	82.2	31	51
Jamey Wright	4.10	7-9	26	164.2	88	96
Paul Rigdon*	4.52	4-4	12	69.2	26	48
Jason Bere	4.93	6-7	20	115.0	63	98
Valerio de los Santos*	5.13	2-3	66	73.2	33	70
Jimmy Haynes	5.33	12-13	33	199.1	100	88
Everett Stull*	5.82	2-3	20	43.1	30	33
Steve Woodard	5.96	1-7	27	93.2	33	65
John Snyder	6.17	3-10	23	127.0	77	69

Saves: Wickman (16); Leskanic (12); Weathers (1). **Complete games:** D'Amico and Woodard (1). **Shutouts:** D'Amico (1).

Montreal Expos

Batting (135 AB)	Avg	AB	R	H	HR	RBI	SB
Vladimir Guerrero	.345	571	101	197	44	123	9
Jose Vidro	.330	606	101	200	24	97	5
Mike Mordecai	.284	169	20	48	4	16	2
Geoff Blum	.283	343	40	97	11	45	1
Fernando Seguignol	.278	162	22	45	10	22	0
Wilton Guerrero	.267	288	30	77	2	23	8
Lee Stevens	.265	449	60	119	22	75	0
Andy Tracy*	.260	192	29	50	11	32	1
Terry Jones	.250	168	30	42	0	13	7
Peter Bergeron*	.245	518	80	127	5	31	11
Chris Widger	.238	281	31	67	12	34	1
Orlando Cabrera	.237	422	47	100	13	55	4
Milton Bradley*	.221	154	20	34	2	15	2
Michael Barrett	.214	271	28	58	1	22	0

Acquired: P Downs from ChC for OF Rondell White (July 31).
Traded: C Widger to Sea. for 2 PTBN (Aug. 8).

Pitching (40 IP)	ERA	W-L	Gm	IP	BB	SO
Scott Strickland*	3.00	4-3	49	48.0	16	48
Carl Pavano	3.06	8-4	15	97.0	34	64
Steve Kline	3.50	1-5	83	82.1	27	64
Anthony Telford	3.79	5-4	64	78.1	23	68
Javier Vazquez	4.05	11-9	33	217.2	61	196
Tony Armas Jr.*	4.36	7-9	17	95.0	50	59
Dustin Hermanson	4.77	12-14	38	198.0	75	94
Scott Downs	5.29	4-3	19	97.0	40	63
Felipe Lira	5.40	5-8	53	101.2	36	51
Julio Santana	5.67	1-5	36	66.2	33	58
Mike Johnson	6.39	5-6	41	101.1	53	70
Mike Thurman	6.42	4-9	17	88.1	46	52
Hideki Irabu	7.24	2-5	11	54.2	14	42

Saves: Kline (14); Strickland (9); Urbina (8); Hermanson (4); Telford (3); Brad Rigby (1). **Complete games:** Vazquez and Hermanson (2). **Shutouts:** Vazquez and Hermanson (1).

New York Mets

Batting (135 AB)	Avg	AB	R	H	HR	RBI	SB
Mike Piazza	.324	482	90	156	38	113	4
Edgardo Alfonzo	.324	544	109	176	25	94	3
Jay Payton*	.291	488	63	142	17	62	5
Benny Agbayani	.289	350	59	101	15	60	5
Todd Pratt	.275	160	33	44	8	25	0
Todd Zeile	.268	544	67	146	22	79	3
Derek Bell	.266	546	87	145	18	69	8
Melvin Mora	.260	215	35	56	6	30	7
Mike Bordick	.260	192	18	50	4	21	3
Lenny Harris	.260	223	31	58	4	26	13
Robin Ventura	.232	469	61	109	24	84	3
Joe McEwing	.222	153	20	34	2	19	3
Kurt Abbott	.217	157	22	34	6	12	1

Acquired: OF Harris from Ari. for P Bill Pulsipher (June 2); IF Bordick from Bal. for IF Mora, IF Mike Kinkade, P Pat Gorman and P Lesli Brea (July 28).

Pitching (40 IP)	ERA	W-L	Gm	IP	BB	SO
Armando Benitez	2.61	4-4	76	76.0	38	106
Mike Hampton	3.14	15-10	33	217.2	99	151
Al Leiter	3.20	16-8	31	208.0	76	200
John Franco	3.40	5-4	62	55.2	26	56
Turk Wendell	3.59	8-6	77	82.2	41	73
Glendon Rusch	4.01	11-11	31	190.2	44	157
Rick Reed	4.11	11-5	30	184.0	34	121
Bobby J. Jones	5.06	11-6	27	154.2	49	85
Dennis Cook	5.34	6-3	68	59.0	31	53
Pat Mahomes	5.46	5-3	53	94.0	66	76

Saves: Benitez (41); Franco (4); Cook (2); Wendell and Rick White (1). **Complete games:** Hampton (3); Leiter and Rusch (2); Jones (1). **Shutouts:** Hampton and Leiter (1).

Philadelphia Phillies

Batting (135 AB)	Avg	AB	R	H	HR	RBI	SB
Bobby Abreu	.316	576	103	182	25	79	28
Scott Rolen	.298	483	88	144	26	89	8
Mike Lieberthal	.278	389	55	108	15	71	2
Doug Glanville	.275	637	89	175	8	52	31
Pat Burrell*	.260	408	57	106	18	79	0
Ron Gant	.254	343	54	87	20	38	5
Mickey Morandini	.252	302	31	76	0	22	5
Kevin Sefcik	.235	153	15	36	0	10	4
Travis Lee	.235	404	53	95	9	54	8
Marlon Anderson	.228	162	10	37	1	15	2
Tomas Perez	.221	140	17	31	1	13	1
Kevin Jordan	.220	337	30	74	5	36	0
Brian Hunter	.214	140	14	30	8	23	0
Rob Ducey	.197	152	24	30	6	25	1
Alex Arias	.187	155	17	29	2	15	1

Acquired: P Chen and P Jim Osting from Atl. for P Andy Ashby (July 12); OF Lee, P Daal, P Padilla and P Nelson Figueroa from Ari. for P Curt Schilling (July 26); P Bottenfield from Ana. for OF Gant (July 30).
Traded: IF Morandini to Tor. for OF Ducey (Aug. 6).
Signed: OF Hunter off waivers from Atl. (Apr. 21).

Pitchers (40 IP)	ERA	W-L	Gm	IP	BB	SO
Bruce Chen	3.29	7-4	37	134.0	46	112
Robert Person	3.63	9-7	28	173.1	95	164
Cliff Politte	3.66	4-3	12	59.0	27	50
Vicente Padilla*	3.72	4-7	55	65.1	28	51
Chris Brock	4.34	7-8	63	93.1	41	69
Randy Wolf	4.36	11-9	32	206.1	83	160
Wayne Gomes	4.40	4-6	65	73.2	35	49
Kent Bottenfield	4.50	1-2	8	44.0	21	31
Jeff Brantley	5.86	2-7	55	55.1	29	57
Omar Daal	6.14	4-19	32	167.0	72	96
Paul Byrd	6.51	2-9	11	69.0	20	50

Saves: Brantley (23); Gomes (7); Padilla (2); Broack and Tom Jacquez (1). **Complete games:** Person, Wolf and Bottenfield (1). **Shutouts:** Person and Bottenfield (1).

Pittsburgh Pirates

Batting (135 AB)	Avg	AB	R	H	HR	RBI	SB
Jason Kendall	.320	579	112	185	14	58	22
Adrian Brown	.315	308	64	97	4	28	13
Brian Giles	.315	559	111	176	35	123	6
John Vander Wal	.299	384	74	115	24	94	11
Luis Sojo	.284	176	14	50	5	20	1
Wil Cordero	.282	348	46	98	16	51	1
Mike Benjamin	.270	233	28	63	2	19	5
Warren Morris	.259	528	68	137	3	43	7
Kevin Young	.258	496	77	128	20	88	8
Aramis Ramirez	.256	254	19	65	6	35	0
Pat Meares	.240	462	55	111	13	47	1

Acquired: P Serafini from SD for PTBN (June 28).
Traded: OF Cordero to Cle. for IF Enrique Wilson and OF Alex Ramirez (July 28); IF Sojo to NYY for P Chris Spurling (Aug. 7).

Pitching (40 IP)	ERA	W-L	Gm	IP	BB	SO
Josias Manzanillo	3.38	2-2	43	58.2	32	39
Mike Williams	3.50	3-4	72	72.0	40	71
Kris Benson	3.85	10-12	32	217.2	86	184
Scott Sauerbeck	4.04	5-4	75	75.2	61	83
Todd Ritchie	4.81	9-8	31	187.0	51	124
Marc Wilkins	5.07	4-2	52	60.1	43	37
Rich Loiselle	5.10	2-3	40	42.1	30	32
Francisco Cordova	5.21	6-8	18	95.0	38	66
Jimmy Anderson*	5.25	5-11	27	144.0	58	73
Jason Schmidt	5.40	2-5	11	63.1	41	51
Dan Serafini	5.51	2-5	14	65.1	28	35
Jose Silva	5.56	11-9	51	136.0	50	98
Bronson Arroyo	6.40	2-6	20	71.2	36	50

Saves: Williams (24); Sauerbeck and Chris Peters (1). **Complete games:** Benson (2); Ritchie, Anderson and Silva (1). **Shutouts:** Benson and Ritchie (1).

St. Louis Cardinals

Batting (135 AB)	Avg	AB	R	H	HR	RBI	SB
Will Clark	.345	171	29	59	12	42	1
Placido Polanco	.316	323	50	102	5	39	4
Mark McGwire	.305	236	60	72	32	73	1
Eric Davis	.303	254	38	77	6	40	1
Fernando Vina	.300	487	81	146	4	31	10
Jim Edmonds	.295	525	129	155	42	108	10
J.D. Drew	.295	407	73	120	18	57	17
Edgar Renteria	.278	562	94	156	16	76	21
Mike Matheny	.261	417	43	109	6	47	0
Carlos Hernandez	.256	242	23	62	3	35	2
Fernando Tatis	.253	324	59	82	18	64	2
Ray Lankford	.253	392	73	99	26	65	5
Shawon Dunston	.250	216	28	54	12	43	3
Craig Paquette	.245	384	47	94	15	61	4

Acquired: P Christiansen from Pit. for IF Jack Wilson (July 30); IF Clark and cash from Bal. for IF Jose Leon (July 31); C Hernandez and IF Nathan Tebbs from SD for P Heathcliff Slocumb and OF Ben Johnson (July 31).

Pitching (40 IP)	ERA	W-L	Gm	IP	BB	SO
Dave Veres	2.85	3-5	71	75.2	25	67
Britt Reames*	2.88	2-1	8	40.2	23	31
Mike James	3.16	2-2	51	51.1	24	41
Rick Ankiel*	3.50	11-7	31	175.0	90	194
Matt Morris	3.57	3-3	31	53.0	17	34
Darryl Kile	3.91	20-9	34	232.1	58	192
Garrett Stephenson	4.49	16-9	32	200.1	63	123
Pat Hentgen	4.72	15-12	33	194.1	89	118
Andy Benes	4.88	12-9	30	166.0	68	137
Jason Christiansen	5.06	3-8	65	48.0	27	53
Alan Benes	5.67	2-2	30	46.0	23	26

Saves: Veres (29); Morris (4); James (2); Christiansen and Mike Timlin (1). **Complete games:** Kile (5); Stephenson (3); Hentgen and Andy Benes (1). **Shutouts:** Stephenson (2); Kile and Hentgen (1).

San Diego Padres

Batting (135 AB)	Avg	AB	R	H	HR	RBI	SB
Al Martin	.306	346	62	106	11	27	6
Phil Nevin	.303	538	87	163	31	107	2
Eric Owens	.293	583	87	171	6	51	29
Ryan Klesko	.283	494	88	140	26	92	23
Mike Darr*	.268	205	21	55	1	30	9
Ed Sprague	.261	157	19	41	10	27	0
Damian Jackson	.255	470	68	120	6	37	28
Bret Boone	.251	463	61	116	19	74	8
Wiki Gonzalez*	.232	284	25	66	5	30	1
Desi Relaford	.215	410	55	88	5	46	13
Ruben Rivera	.208	423	62	88	17	57	8

Acquired: P Witasick from KC for P Meadows (July 31); P Slocumb and OF Ben Johnson from St.L for C Carlos Hernandez and IF Nathan Tebbs (July 31); IF Relaford off waivers from Phi. for IF David Newhan (Aug. 4).
Traded: IF Sprague to Bos. for 2 minor leaguers (June 30); OF Martin to Sea. for OF John Mabry and P Tom Davey (July 31).
Signed: IF Sprague off waivers from Bos. (Sept. 3).

Pitching (40 IP)	ERA	W-L	Gm	IP	BB	SO
Trevor Hoffman	2.99	4-7	70	72.1	11	85
Stan Spencer	3.26	2-2	8	49.2	19	40
Donne Wall	3.35	5-2	44	53.2	21	29
Brian Tollberg*	3.58	4-5	19	118.0	35	76
Woody Williams	3.75	10-8	23	168.0	54	111
Adam Eaton	4.13	7-4	22	135.0	61	90
Kevin Walker*	4.19	7-1	70	66.2	38	56
Carlos Almanzar	4.39	4-5	62	69.2	25	56
Sterling Hitchcock	4.93	1-6	11	65.2	26	61
Heathcliff Slocumb	4.98	2-4	65	68.2	37	46
Matt Clement	5.14	13-17	34	205.0	125	170
Brian Meadows	5.34	7-8	22	124.2	50	53
Jay Witasick	5.64	3-2	11	60.2	35	54

Saves: Hoffman (43); Wall, Slocumb, Carlos Reyes and Todd Erdos (1). **Complete games:** Williams (4); Tollberg (1). **Shutouts:** none.

San Francisco Giants

Batting (135 AB)	Avg	AB	R	H	HR	RBI	SB
Ellis Burks	.344	393	74	135	24	96	5
Jeff Kent	.334	587	114	196	33	125	12
Barry Bonds	.306	480	129	147	49	106	11
Ramon Martinez	.302	189	30	57	6	25	3
J.T. Snow	.284	530	82	152	19	96	1
Rich Aurilia	.271	509	67	138	20	79	1
Bill Mueller	.268	560	97	150	10	55	4
Armando Rios	.266	233	38	62	10	50	3
Marvin Benard	.263	560	102	147	12	55	22
Russ Davis	.261	180	27	47	9	24	0
Calvin Murray	.242	194	35	47	2	22	9
Bobby Estalella	.234	299	45	70	14	53	3
Doug Mirabelli	.230	230	23	53	6	28	1

Acquired: P Henry from Hou. for P Scot Linebrink (July 30).

Pitching (40 IP)	ERA	W-L	Gm	IP	BB	SO
Robb Nen	1.50	4-3	68	66.0	19	92
Felix Rodriguez	2.64	4-2	76	81.2	42	95
Livan Hernandez	3.75	17-11	33	240.0	73	165
Doug Henry	3.79	4-4	72	78.1	49	62
Kirk Rueter	3.96	11-9	32	184.0	62	71
Mark Gardner	4.05	11-7	30	149.0	42	92
Shawn Estes	4.26	15-6	30	190.1	108	136
Aaron Fultz*	4.67	5-2	58	69.1	28	62
Alan Embree	4.95	3-5	63	60.0	25	49
Russ Ortiz	5.01	14-12	33	195.2	112	167
Joe Nathan	5.21	5-2	20	93.1	63	61
John Johnstone	6.30	3-4	47	50.0	13	57

Saves: Nen (41); Rodriguez (3); Embree (2); Henry and Fultz (1). **Complete games:** Hernandez (5); Estes (4). **Shutouts:** Hernandez and Estes (2).

Players Who Played in Both Leagues in 2000

While all indivdual major league statistics count on career records, players cannot transfer their stats from one league to the other if they are traded during the regular season. Here are the combined stats for batters with 250 at bats and pitchers with 60 innings pitched, who played in both leagues in 2000.

Batters (250 AB)

	Avg	AB	R	H	HR	RBI	SB		Avg	AB	R	H	HR	RBI	SB
Dante Bichette	.294	575	80	169	23	90	5	Dave Martinez	.274	457	60	125	5	47	8
CIN	.295	461	67	136	16	76	5	TB	.260	104	12	27	1	12	1
BOS	.289	114	13	33	7	14	0	CHC	.185	54	5	10	0	1	1
Mike Bordick	.285	583	88	166	20	80	9	TEX	.269	119	14	32	2	12	2
BAL	.297	391	70	116	16	59	6	TOR	.311	180	29	56	2	22	4
NYM	.260	192	18	50	4	21	3	Melvin Mora	.275	414	60	114	8	47	12
Will Clark	.319	427	78	136	21	70	5	NYM	.260	215	35	56	6	30	7
BAL	.301	256	49	77	9	28	4	BAL	.291	199	25	58	2	17	5
ST.L	.345	171	29	59	12	42	1	Mickey Morandini	.257	409	41	105	0	29	6
Wil Cordero	.276	496	64	137	16	68	1	PHI	.252	302	31	76	0	22	5
PIT	.282	348	46	98	16	51	1	TOR	.271	107	10	29	0	7	1
CLE	.264	148	18	39	0	17	0	Richie Sexson	.272	537	89	146	30	91	2
Jeff Frye	.307	326	49	100	1	16	5	CLE	.256	324	45	83	16	44	1
BOS	.289	239	35	69	1	13	1	MIL	.296	213	44	63	14	47	1
COL	.356	87	14	31	0	3	4	Luis Sojo	.286	301	33	86	7	37	2
Ron Gant	.249	425	69	106	26	54	6	PIT	.284	176	14	50	5	20	1
PHI	.254	343	54	87	20	38	5	NYY	.288	125	19	36	2	17	1
ANA	.232	82	15	19	6	16	1	Ed Sprague	.243	268	30	65	12	36	0
Rickey Henderson	.233	420	75	98	4	32	36	SD	.261	157	19	41	10	27	0
NYM	.219	96	17	21	0	2	5	BOS	.216	111	11	24	2	9	0
SEA	.238	324	58	77	4	30	31	B.J. Surhoff	.291	539	69	157	14	68	10
Glenallen Hill	.293	300	45	88	27	58	0	BAL	.292	411	56	120	13	57	7
CHC	.262	168	23	44	11	29	0	ATL	.289	128	13	37	1	11	3
NYY	.333	132	22	44	16	29	0	Jose Vizcaino	.251	267	32	67	0	14	6
Butch Huskey	.261	307	40	80	9	45	1	LA	.204	93	9	19	0	4	1
MIN	.223	215	22	48	5	27	0	NYY	.276	174	23	48	0	10	5
COL	.348	92	18	32	4	18	1	Chris Widger	.233	292	32	68	13	35	1
Mike Lansing	.240	504	72	121	11	60	8	MON	.238	281	31	67	12	34	1
COL	.258	365	62	94	11	47	8	SEA	.091	11	1	1	1	1	0
BOS	.194	139	10	27	0	13	0								
Al Martin	.285	480	81	137	15	36	10								
SD	.306	346	62	106	11	27	6								
SEA	.231	134	19	31	4	9	4								

Pitchers (60 IP)

	ERA	W-L	Gm	IP	BB	SO		ERA	W-L	Gm	IP	BB	SO
Rolando Arrojo	5.63	10-11	32	172.2	68	124	Paul Rigdon	5.15	5-5	17	87.2	35	63
COL	6.04	5-9	19	101.1	46	80	CLE	7.64	1-1	5	17.2	9	15
BOS	5.05	5-2	13	71.1	22	44	MIL	4.52	4-4	12	69.2	26	48
Miguel Batista	8.54	2-7	18	65.1	37	37	Brian Rose	5.79	7-10	27	116.2	51	64
MON	14.04	0-1	4	8.1	3	7	BOS	6.11	3-5	15	53.0	21	24
KC	7.74	2-6	14	57.0	34	30	COL	5.51	4-5	12	63.2	30	40
Jason Bere	5.47	12-10	31	169.1	89	142	Jerry Spradlin	6.00	4-5	58	90.0	32	67
MIL	4.93	6-7	20	115.0	63	98	KC	5.52	4-4	50	75.0	27	54
CLE	6.63	6-3	11	54.1	26	44	CHC	8.40	0-1	8	15.0	5	13
Kent Bottenfield	5.40	8-10	29	171.2	77	106	Mike Timlin	4.18	5-4	62	64.2	35	52
ANA	5.71	7-8	21	127.2	56	75	BAL	4.89	2-3	37	35.0	15	26
PHI	4.50	1-2	8	44.0	21	31	ST.L	3.34	3-1	25	29.2	20	26
Dwight Gooden	4.71	6-5	27	105.0	44	55	John Wasdin	5.38	1-6	39	80.1	24	71
HOU	9.00	0-0	1	4.0	3	1	BOS	5.04	1-3	25	44.2	15	36
TB	6.63	2-3	8	36.2	20	23	COL	5.80	0-3	14	35.2	9	35
NYY	3.36	4-2	18	64.1	21	31	Rick White	3.52	5-9	66	99.2	38	67
Mark Guthrie	4.67	3-6	76	71.1	37	63	TB	3.41	3-6	44	71.1	26	47
CHC	4.82	2-3	19	18.2	10	17	NYM	3.81	2-3	22	28.1	12	20
TB	4.50	1-1	34	32.0	18	26	Bob Wickman	3.10	3-5	69	72.2	32	55
TOR	4.79	0-2	23	20.2	9	20	MIL	2.93	2-2	43	46.0	20	44
Scott Karl	7.42	4-5	23	87.1	45	38	CLE	3.38	1-3	26	26.2	12	11
COL	7.68	2-3	17	65.2	33	29	Jay Witasick	5.82	6-10	33	150.0	73	121
ANA	6.65	2-2	6	21.2	12	9	KC	5.94	3-8	22	89.1	38	67
Brian Meadows	5.13	13-10	33	196.1	64	79	SD	5.64	3-2	11	60.2	35	54
SD	5.34	7-8	22	124.2	50	53	Steve Woodard	5.85	4-10	40	147.2	44	100
KC	4.77	6-2	11	71.2	14	26	MIL	5.96	1-7	27	93.2	33	65
Denny Neagle	4.52	15-9	34	209.0	81	146	CLE	5.67	3-3	13	54.0	11	35
CIN	3.52	8-2	18	117.2	50	88							
NYY	5.81	7-7	16	91.1	31	58							

Divisional Series Summaries
AMERICAN LEAGUE

Yankees, 3-2

Date	Winner	Home Field
Oct. 3	Athletics, 5-3	at Oakland
Oct. 4	Yankees, 4-0	at Oakland
Oct. 6	Yankees, 4-2	at New York
Oct. 7	Athletics, 11-1	at New York
Oct. 8	Yankees, 7-5	at Oakland

Game 1
Tuesday, Oct. 3, at Oakland

	1 2 3	4 5 6	7 8 9	R H E
New York	0 2 0	0 0 1	0 0 0	- 3 7 0
Oakland	0 0 0	0 3 1	0 1 x	- 5 10 2

Win: Isringhausen, Oak. (1-0). **Loss:** Clemens, NY (0-1). **Save:** Isringhausen, Oak. (1).
2B: New York— Sojo, Brosius, Williams; Oakland— R Hernandez. **RBI:** New York— Sojo, Brosius, Martinez; Oakland— R Hernandez 2, Velarde, Chavez. **SB:** Oakland— Ja Giambi (1), Velarde (1).
Attendance: 47,360. **Time:** 3:04.

Game 2
Wednesday, Oct. 4, at Oakland

	1 2 3	4 5 6	7 8 9	R H E
New York	0 0 0	0 0 3	0 0 1	- 4 8 1
Oakland	0 0 0	0 0 0	0 0 0	- 0 6 1

Win: Pettitte, NY (1-0). **Loss:** Appier, Oak. (0-1). **Save:** Rivera, NY (1).
2B: New York— Williams, Sojo, Posada, Bellinger. Oakland— Chavez, R Hernandez, Tejada. **RBI:** New York— Hill, Sojo 2, Bellinger. **CS:** New York— Williams.
Attendance: 47,860. **Time:** 3:15.

Game 3
Friday, Oct. 6, at New York

	1 2 3	4 5 6	7 8 9	R H E
Oakland	0 1 0	0 1 0	0 0 0	- 2 4 2
New York	0 2 0	1 0 0	0 0 1	- 4 6 1

Win: Hernandez, NY (1-0). **Loss:** Hudson, Oak. (0-1). **Save:** Rivera, NY (2).
2B: New York— Williams. **HR:** Oakland— Long (1). **RBI:** Oakland— Je Giambi, Long; New York— Hill, Jeter 2, Sojo **CS:** New York— Jeter.
Attendance: 56,606. **Time:** 3:12.

Game 4
Saturday, Oct. 7, at New York

	1 2 3	4 5 6	7 8 9	R H E
Oakland	3 0 0	0 0 3	0 1 4	-11 11 0
New York	0 0 0	0 0 1	0 0 0	- 1 8 0

Win: Zito, Oak. (1-0). **Loss:** Clemens, NY (0-2).
2B: Oakland— Tejada, Velarde, Chavez. New York— Posada. **HR:** Oakland— Saenz (1). **RBI:** Oakland— Saenz 3, Grieve 2, R Hernandez, Christenson, Chavez 2, Tejada, Porter; New York— Posada. **SB:** Oakland— Tejada.
Attendance: 56,915. **Time:** 3:42.

Game 5
Sunday, Oct. 8, at Oakland

	1 2 3	4 5 6	7 8 9	R H E
New York	6 0 0	1 0 0	0 0 0	- 7 12 0
Oakland	0 2 1	2 0 0	0 0 0	- 5 13 0

Win: Stanton, NY (1-0). **Loss:** Heredia, Oak. (1-1). **Save:** Rivera, NY (3).
2B: New York— Martinez 2, O'Neill; Oakland— Chavez, Stairs. **HR:** New York— Justice (1). **RBI:** New York— Williams, Martinez 3, Sojo, Knoblauch, Justice; Oakland— Velarde 2, Chavez, Ja Giambi, Saenz. **SB:** New York— Knoblauch.
Attendance: 41,170. **Time:** 3:50.

Mariners, 3-0

Date	Winner	Home Field
Oct. 3	Mariners, 7-4 (10 inn.)	at Chicago
Oct. 4	Mariners, 5-2	at Chicago
Oct. 6	Mariners, 2-1	at Seattle

Game 1
Tuesday, Oct. 3, at Chicago

	1 2 3	4 5 6	7 8 9 10	R H E
Seattle	2 1 0	0 0 0	1 0 0 3	- 7 13 0
Chicago	0 2 2	0 0 0	0 0 0	- 4 9 0

Win: Mesa, Sea. (1-0). **Loss:** Foulke, Chi. (0-1). **Save:** Sasaki (1).
2B: Seattle— Da Bell; Chicago— Jose Valentin, Ca Lee. **3B:** Chicago— Singleton, M Ordonez. **HR:** Seattle— J Oliver (1), E Martinez (1), Olerud (1); Chicago— Durham (1). **RBI:** Seattle— A Rodriguez, Olerud 2, J Oliver, Cameron, E Martinez 2; Chicago— Singleton, Durham, M Ordonez. **SB:** Seattle— Cameron (1). Chicago— Jose Valentin (1). **CS:** Seattle— A Rodriguez (1)
Attendance: 45,290. **Time:** 4:12.

Game 2
Wednesday, Oct. 4, at Chicago

	1 2 3	4 5 6	7 8 9	R H E
Seattle	0 2 0	1 1 0	0 0 1	- 5 9 1
Chicago	1 0 1	0 0 0	0 0 0	- 2 5 1

Win: Abbott, Sea. (1-0). **Loss:** Sirotka, Chi. (0-1). **Save:** Sasaki (2).
2B: Seattle— E Martinez; Chicago— Durham, Jose Valentin, H Perry. **HR:** Seattle— Buhner (1). **RBI:** Seattle— Da Bell, D Wilson, Buhner, A Rodriguez, Cameron; Chicago— Jose Valentin, Ca Lee. **SB:** Seattle— Henderson (1); Chicago— Jose Valentin 2 (3), M Ordonez (1).
Attendance: 45,383. **Time:** 3:16.

Game 3
Friday, Oct. 6, at Seattle

	1 2 3	4 5 6	7 8 9	R H E
Chicago	0 1 0	0 0 0	0 0 0	- 1 3 1
Seattle	0 0 0	1 0 0	0 0 1	- 2 6 0

Win: Paniagua, Sea (1-0). **Loss:** Wunsch, Chi. (0-1).
2B: Chicago— Baines. **RBI:** Chicago— H Perry (1); Seattle— Javier (1), C Guillen (1).
Attendance: 48,010. **Time:** 2:40.

NATIONAL LEAGUE

Mets, 3-1

Date	Winner	Home Field
Oct. 4	Giants, 5-1	at S. Francisco
Oct. 5	Mets, 5-4 (10 inn.)	at S. Francisco
Oct. 7	Mets, 3-2 (13 inn.)	at New York
Oct. 8	Mets, 4-0	at New York

Game 1
Wednesday, Oct. 4, at San Francisco

	1 2 3	4 5 6	7 8 9	R H E
New York	0 0 1	0 0 0	0 0 0	- 1 5 0
San Francisco	1 0 4	0 0 0	0 0 x	- 5 10 0

Win: Hernandez, SF (1-0). **Loss:** Hampton, NY (0-1).
2B: New York— Zeile; San Francisco— Mueller, Aurilia. **3B:** San Francisco— Bonds. **HR:** San Francisco— Burks (1). **RBI:** New York— Payton (1); San Francisco— Kent (1), Bonds (1), Burks 3 (3). **SB:** San Francisco— Bonds (1).
Attendance: 40,430. **Time:** 3:06.

Game 2
Thursday, Oct. 5, at San Francisco

	1 2 3	4 5 6	7 8 9 10	R H E
New York	0 2 0	0 0 0	0 0 2 1 -	5 10 0
San Francisco	0 1 0	0 0 0	0 3 0 -	4 8 0

Win: Benitez, NY (1-0). **Loss:** Rodriguez, SF (0-1). **Save:** Franco, NY (1).
2B: New York— Piazza, Hamilton; San Francisco— Burks, Bonds. **HR:** New York— Alfonzo (1); San Francisco— Snow. **RBI:** New York— Perez 2 (2), Alfonzo 2 (2), Payton (2); San Francisco— Burks (4), Snow 3 (3); **SB:** San Francisco— Kent (1).
Attendance: 40,430. **Time:** 3:41.

Game 3
Saturday, Oct. 7, at New York

	1 2 3 4 5 6 7 8 9 10 11 12 13	R H E
S.F.	0 0 0 2 0 0 0 0 0 0 0 0 0 -	2 11 0
N.Y.	0 0 0 0 0 1 0 1 0 0 0 0 1 -	3 9 0

Win: White, NY (1-0). **Loss:** Fultz, SF (0-1).
2B: San Francisco— Mueller; New York— Alfonzo. **HR:** New York— Agbayani (1). **RBI:** New York— Perez (3), Alfonzo (3), Agbayani (1); San Francisco— Estalella (1), Benard (1). **SB:** New York— Harris (1), Payton (1).
Attendance: 56,270. **Time:** 5:22.

Game 4
Sunday, Oct. 8, at New York

	1 2 3	4 5 6	7 8 9	R H E
San Francisco	0 0 0	0 0 0	0 0 0 -	0 1 1
New York	2 0 0	0 2 0	0 0 x -	4 6 0

Win: B.J. Jones, NY (1-0). **Loss:** Gardner, SF (0-1).
2B: San Francisco— Kent; New York— Perez, Alfonso, Agbayani. **HR:** New York— Ventura (1). **RBI:** New York— Ventura 2 (2), Alfonzo 2 (5).
SB: New York— Perez (1). **CS:** Payton (1).
Attendance: 56,245. **Time:** 2:48.

Cardinals, 3-0

Date	Winner	Home Field
Oct. 3	Cardinals, 7-5	at St. Louis
Oct. 5	Cardinals, 10-4	at St. Louis
Oct. 7	Cardinals, 7-1	at Atlanta

American League Championship Series

Yankees, 4-2

Date	Winner	Home Field
Oct. 10	Mariners, 2-0	at New York
Oct. 11	Yankees, 7-1	at New York
Oct. 13	Yankees, 8-2	at Seattle
Oct. 14	Yankees, 5-0	at Seattle
Oct. 15	Mariners, 6-2	at Seattle
Oct. 17	Yankees, 9-7	at New York

Game 1
Tuesday, Oct. 10, at New York

	1 2 3	4 5 6	7 8 9	R H E
Seattle	0 0 0	0 1 1	0 0 0 -	2 5 0
New York	0 0 0	0 0 0	0 0 0 -	0 6 1

Win: Garcia, Sea (1-0). **Loss:** Neagle, NY (0-1).
2B: Seattle— McLemore; New York— Knoblauch. **HR:** Seattle— A. Rodriguez. **RBI:** Seattle— Henderson (1), A Rodriguez (3). **CS:** Seattle— Henderson (1).
Attendance: 54,481. **Time:** 3:45.

Most Valuable Player
Dave Justice, New York, OF

AB	R	H	RBI	AVG	HR
26	4	6	8	.231	2

Game 1
Tuesday, Oct. 3, at St. Louis

	1 2 3	4 5 6	7 8 9	R H E
Atlanta	0 0 4	0 0 0	0 0 1 -	5 8 3
St. Louis	6 0 0	1 0 0	0 0 x -	7 11 1

Win: James, St.L (1-0). **Loss:** Maddux, Atl. (0-1).
2B: Atlanta— Weiss, B Jordan, Joyner. **HR:** St. Louis— Edmonds (1). **RBI:** Atlanta— B Jordan 2 (2), Weiss 2 (2); St. Louis— Edmonds 2 (2), W Clark (1), R Lankford (1), P Polanco 2 (2). **SB:** St. Louis— Edmonds (1), Drew (1). **CS:** Atlanta— Furcal (1), A Jones (1).
Attendance: 52,378. **Time:** 3:34.

Game 2
Thursday, Oct. 5, at St. Louis

	1 2 3	4 5 6	7 8 9	R H E
Atlanta	2 0 0	0 0 0	0 2 0 -	4 7 1
St. Louis	3 1 3	1 0 1	0 1 x -	10 9 0

Win: Kile, St. L. (1-0). **Loss:** Glavine, Atl. (0-1).
2B: Atlanta— Galarraga, C Jones; St. Louis— Edmonds 3, R Lankford; **HR:** Atlanta— A Jones (1); St. Louis— W Clark (1), Ca Hernandez (1), McGwire (1). **RBI:** Atlanta— C Jones (1), B Jordan 2 (4), A Jones (1); St. Louis— W Clark 3 (4), Ca Hernandez (1), E Davis (1), R Lankford 2 (3), Edmonds 2 (4), McGwire (1).
SB: St. Louis— Renteria (1).
Attendance: 52,389. **Time:** 3:02.

Game 3
Saturday, Oct. 7, at Atlanta

	1 2 3	4 5 6	7 8 9	R H E
St. Louis	1 0 2	0 1 3	0 0 0 -	7 8 0
Atlanta	1 0 0	0 0 0	0 0 0 -	1 3 1

Win: Reames, St. L (1-0). **Loss:** Millwood, Atl. (0-1).
2B: St. Louis— Edmonds. **HR:** St. Louis— Vina (1), Edmonds (2). **RBI:** St. Louis— Vina 3 (3), Edmonds 3 (7); P Polanco (3); Atlanta— Galarraga (1). **SB:** St. Louis— Drew (2), Renteria (2); Atlanta— Furcal (1). **CS:** St. Louis— Vina (1); Atlanta— J Lopez (1).
Attendance: 49,898. **Time:** 3:09.

Game 2
Wednesday, Oct. 11, at New York

	1 2 3	4 5 6	7 8 9	R H E
Seattle	0 0 1	0 0 0	0 0 0 -	1 7 1
New York	0 0 0	0 0 0	7 0 x -	7 14 0

Win: Hernandez, NY (2-0). **Loss:** Rhodes, Sea (0-1).
2B: Seattle— A Martin, McLemore, Olerud; New York— Knoblauch, Justice, Vizcaino. **HR:** New York— Jeter (1). **RBI:** Seattle— Javier (1); New York— Williams (2), Posada (2), O'Neill (1), Vizcaino (1) Knoblauch (2), Jeter 2 (4). **SB:** Seattle— Cameron (2); New York— Vizcaino (1). **CS:** New York— Posada (1).
Attendance: 55,317. **Time:** 3:36.

Game 3
Friday, Oct. 13, at Seattle

	1 2 3	4 5 6	7 8 9	R H E
New York	0 2 1	0 0 1	0 0 4 -	8 13 0
Seattle	1 0 0	1 0 0	0 0 0 -	2 10 1

Win: Pettitte, NY (2-0). **Loss:** Sele, Sea (0-1). **Save:** Rivera (4).
2B: New York— Justice; Seattle— Henderson. **HR:** New York— Williams (1), T Martinez (1). **RBI:** New York— Williams 2 (4), T Martinez (5), Justice 3 (4), Knoblauch (3); Seattle— E Martinez (3), Cameron (3). **SB:** New York— Vizcaino (2), A Rodriguez (1). **CS:** New York— Brosius (1).
Attendance: 47,827. **Time:** 3:35.

Game 4
Saturday, Oct. 14, at Seattle

	1 2 3	4 5 6	7 8 9	R	H	E
New York	0 0 0	0 3 0	0 2 0	- 5	5	0
Seattle	0 0 0	0 0 0	0 0 0	- 0	1	0

Win: Clemens, NY (1-2). **Loss:** Abbott, Sea. (1-1).
2B: Seattle— A Martin. **HR:** New York— Jeter (2), Justice (2). **RBI:** New York— Jeter 3 (7), Justice 2 (6). **SB:** New York— Williams (1).
Attendance: 47,803. **Time:** 2:59.

Game 5
Sunday, Oct. 15, at Seattle

	1 2 3	4 5 6	7 8 9	R	H	E
New York	0 0 0	2 0 0	0 0 0	- 2	8	0
Seattle	1 0 0	0 5 0	0 0 x	- 6	8	0

Win: Garcia, Sea (2-0). **Loss:** Neagle, NY (0-2).
2B: New York— T Martinez, Sojo, Williams. **HR:** Seattle—E Martinez (2), Olerud (2). **RBI:** New York— Sojo 2 (7); Seattle— Olerud 2 (4), A Rodriguez 2 (5), E Martinez 2 (5).
SB: Seattle— Olerud (1).
Attendance: 47,802. **Time:** 4:14.

Game 6
Tuesday, Oct. 17, at New York

	1 2 3	4 5 6	7 8 9	R	H	E
Seattle	2 0 0	2 0 0	0 3 0	- 7	10	0
New York	0 0 0	3 0 0	6 0 x	- 9	11	0

Win: Hernandez, NY (3-0). **Loss:** Paniagua, Sea (1-1).
2B: Seattle— A Rodriguez 2, E Martinez, Olerud 2, McLemore; New York— Posada, T Martinez. **HR:** Seattle— Guillen (1), A Rodriguez (2); New York— Justice (3). **RBI:** Seattle— A Rodriguez 2 (7); E Martinez (6); Guillen 2 (3), McLemore 2 (2); New York— Posada 2 (4), O'Neill 3 (5), Justice 3 (9), Vizcaino (2).
SB: New York—Jeter (1). **CS:** Seattle—Guillen (1).
Attendance: 56,598. **Time:** 4:03.

ALCS Composite Box Score
Seattle Mariners

Batting		LCS vs. New York							Overall AL Playoffs						
	Avg	AB	R	H	HR	RBI	BB	SO	Avg	AB	R	H	HR	RBI	BB	SO
Alex Rodriguez	.409	22	4	9	2	5	3	8	.371	35	4	13	2	7	3	10
John Olerud	.350	20	3	7	1	2	2	2	.333	30	5	10	2	4	4	3
Mark McLemore	.250	16	2	4	0	2	2	1	.200	25	3	5	0	2	4	2
Edgar Martinez	.238	21	2	5	1	4	3	5	.281	32	4	9	2	6	5	6
Rickey Henderson	.222	9	2	2	0	1	2	2	.286	14	5	4	0	1	3	2
David Bell	.222	18	0	4	4	0	0	0	.276	29	0	8	0	1	2	2
Carlos Guillen	.200	5	1	1	1	2	2	2	.333	6	1	2	1	3	2	2
Jay Buhner	.182	11	0	2	0	0	1	6	.188	16	1	3	1	1	3	6
Al Martin	.182	11	1	2	0	0	2	3	.167	12	1	2	0	0	2	3
Joe Oliver	.167	6	0	1	0	0	1	1	.200	10	1	2	1	1	1	2
Mike Cameron	.111	18	3	2	0	1	2	7	.167	30	5	5	0	3	2	7
Dan Wilson	.091	11	0	1	0	0	1	5	.071	14	0	1	0	1	2	7
Stan Javier	.071	14	0	1	0	1	0	4	.100	20	0	2	0	2	0	7
Raul Ibanez	.000	9	0	0	0	0	0	2	.176	17	2	3	0	0	0	2
Charles Gipson	—	0	0	0	0	0	0	0	—	0	0	0	0	0	0	0
TOTALS	.215	191	18	41	5	18	21	48	.238	290	32	69	9	32	33	61

Pitching																
	ERA	W-L	SV	Gm	IP	H	BB	SO	ERA	W-L	Sv	Gm	IP	H	BB	SO
Rob Ramsay	0.00	0-0	0	2	1.2	2	0	1	0.00	0-0	0	2	1.2	2	0	1
Kazuhiro Sasaki	0.00	0-0	1	2	2.2	3	1	3	0.00	0-0	3	4	4.2	4	1	8
Freddy Garcia	1.54	2-0	0	2	11.2	10	4	11	3.60	2-0	0	3	15.0	16	7	13
John Halama	2.89	0-0	0	2	9.1	10	5	3	2.89	0-0	0	2	9.1	10	5	3
Jose Paniagua	4.15	0-1	0	5	4.1	4	1	4	2.70	1-1	0	7	6.2	5	3	7
Paul Abbott	5.40	0-1	0	1	5.0	3	3	3	3.38	1-1	0	2	10.2	8	6	4
Aaron Sele	6.00	0-1	0	1	6.0	9	0	4	3.38	0-1	0	2	13.1	12	3	5
Brett Tomko	7.20	0-0	0	2	5.0	3	4	4	4.70	0-0	0	3	7.2	4	5	4
Jose Mesa	12.46	0-0	0	3	4.1	5	3	3	8.53	0-0	0	5	6.1	5	4	5
Arthur Rhodes	31.50	0-1	0	4	2.0	8	1	4	13.50	0-1	0	7	4.2	8	6	7
TOTALS	5.37	2-4	1	6	52.0	57	25	41	4.16	5-4	3	9	80.0	74	40	57

Wild Pitches— LCS (Sasaki, Tomko, Grimsley); OVERALL (Garcia, Sasaki, Tomko 2, Grimsley). **Hit Batters—** LCS (Garcia 2, Sasaki); OVERALL (Abbott, Garcia 2, Sasaki).

New York Yankees

Batting		LCS vs Seattle							Overall AL Playoffs						
	Avg	AB	R	H	HR	RBI	BB	SO	Avg	AB	R	H	HR	RBI	BB	SO
Jose Vizcaino	1.000	2	3	2	0	2	0	0	1.000	2	4	2	0	2	0	0
Bernie Williams	.435	23	5	10	1	3	2	3	.349	43	8	15	1	4	3	7
Tino Martinez	.320	25	5	8	1	1	2	4	.364	44	7	16	1	5	3	7
Derek Jeter	.318	22	6	7	2	5	6	7	.268	41	7	11	2	7	8	10
Luis Sojo	.261	23	1	6	0	2	2	3	.231	39	3	9	0	4	4	4
Chuck Knoblauch	.261	23	3	6	0	2	3	4	.281	32	4	9	0	3	3	6
Paul O'Neill	.250	20	0	5	0	5	1	2	.231	39	4	9	0	5	3	6
David Justice	.231	26	4	6	2	8	2	7	.227	44	6	10	3	9	5	11
Scott Brosius	.222	18	2	4	0	0	3	7	.200	35	2	7	0	1	3	7
Jorge Posada	.158	19	2	3	0	3	5	5	.194	36	4	7	0	4	8	10

Batting		LCS vs Seattle							Overall AL Playoffs						
	Avg	AB	R	H	HR	RBI	BB	SO	Avg	AB	R	H	HR	RBI	BB	SO
Glenallen Hill	.000	2	0	0	0	0	0	2	.071	14	1	1	0	2	1	7
Luis Polonia	.000	1	0	0	0	0	0	1	.500	2	0	1	0	0	0	1
Clay Bellinger	—	0	0	0	0	0	0	0	1.000	1	0	1	0	1	0	0
TOTALS	.279	204	31	57	6	31	25	41	.263	372	50	98	7	50	41	76

Pitching																
	ERA	W-L	Sv	Gm	IP	H	BB	SO	ERA	W-L	Sv	Gm	IP	H	BB	SO
Randy Choate	0.00	0-0	0	1	0.1	0	0	1	5.40	0-0	0	2	1.2	0	1	2
Dwight Gooden	0.00	0-0	0	1	2.1	1	0	1	9.00	0-0	0	2	4.0	5	1	2
Roger Clemens	0.00	1-0	0	1	9.0	1	2	15	4.50	1-2	0	3	20.0	14	10	25
David Cone	0.00	0-0	0	1	1.0	0	0	0	0.00	0-0	0	1	1.0	0	0	0
Jason Grimsley	0.00	0-0	0	2	1.0	2	3	1	0.00	0-0	0	2	1.0	2	3	1
Mariano Rivera	1.93	0-0	1	3	4.2	4	0	1	0.93	0-0	4	6	9.2	6	0	3
Andy Pettitte	2.70	1-0	0	1	6.2	9	1	2	3.50	2-0	0	3	18.0	24	4	9
Orlando Hernandez	4.20	2-0	0	2	15.0	13	8	14	3.63	3-0	0	4	22.1	18	13	19
Denny Neagle	4.50	0-2	0	2	10.0	6	7	7	4.50	0-2	0	2	10.0	6	7	7
Jeff Nelson	9.00	0-0	0	3	3.0	5	0	6	5.40	0-0	0	5	5.0	5	0	8
TOTALS	3.06	4-2	1	6	53.0	41	21	48	3.80	7-4	4	11	97.0	85	40	79

Wild Pitches— LCS (none); OVERALL (Clemens, Stanton). **Hit Batters—**LCS (none); OVERALL (Gooden 2).

Score by Innings

	1	2	3	4	5	6	7	8	9		R	H	E
Seattle	4	0	1	2	7	1	0	3	0	–	18	41	3
New York	0	2	1	5	3	1	6	9	4	–	31	57	1

E: Seattle— McLemore 2, Wilson; New York— Brosius. **DP:** Seattle 4, New York 5. **2B:** Seattle— McLemore 3, Olerud 3, Martin 2, Rodriguez 2, E. Martinez, Posada; New York— Justice 2, Knoblauch 2, T. Martinez, Posada, Sojo, Williams, Vizcaino. **SB:** Seattle— Cameron, Olerud, Rodriguez; New York— Vizcaino 2, Jeter, Williams. **CS:** Seattle— Cameron, New York— Guillen, Brosius, Posada. **S:** Seattle— Cameron, McLemore; New York— Knoblauch. **SF:** Seattle— Olerud; New York— O'Neill, Vizcaino, Williams. **HBP:** by Garcia (Knoblauch, Posada), by Sasaki (Williams).
Umpires: Wally Bell, Gerry Davis, Angel Hernandez, John Hirschbeck, Mark Hirschbeck, Randy Marsh.

National League Championship Series

Mets, 4-1

Date	Winner	Home Field
Oct. 11	Mets, 6-2	at St. Louis
Oct. 12	Mets, 6-5	at St. Louis
Oct. 14	Cardinals, 8-2	at New York
Oct. 15	Mets, 10-6	at New York
Oct. 16	Mets, 7-0	at New York

Game 1
Wednesday, Oct. 11, at St. Louis

	1 2 3	4 5 6	7 8 9	R H E
New York	2 0 0	0 1 0	0 0 3	6 8 3
St. Louis	0 0 0	0 0 0	0 0 2	2 9 0

Win: Hampton, NY (1-1). **Loss:** Kile, St. L (1-1).
2B: New York— Perez, Piazza; St. Louis— Clark, Lankford. **HR:** New York— Zeile (1), Payton (1). **RBI:** New York— Piazza (1), Ventura (3), Alfonzo (6), Zeile (1), Payton 2 (4). **Attendance:** 52,255. **Time:** 3:08.

Game 2
Thursday, Oct. 12, at St. Louis

	1 2 3	4 5 6	7 8 9	R H E
New York	2 0 1	0 0 0	0 2 1	6 9 0
St. Louis	0 1 0	0 2 0	0 2 0	5 10 3

Win: Wendell, NY (1-0). **Loss:** Timlin, St. L (0-1). **Save:** Benitez, NY (1).
2B: New York— Agbayani, Zeile; St. Louis— Dunston, Clark, Renteria, Tatis, Drew. **HR:** New York— Piazza (1). **RBI:** New York— Zeile (2), Agbayani (2), Piazza (2), Alfonzo (7), Payton (5); St. Louis— Marrero (1), Renteria (2), Tatis (1), Drew (1). **SB:** St. Louis— Renteria 3 (5). **Attendance:** 52,250. **Time:** 3:59.

Game 3
Saturday, Oct. 14, at New York

	1 2 3	4 5 6	7 8 9	R H E
St. Louis	2 0 2	1 3 0	0 0 0	8 14 0
New York	1 0 0	1 0 0	0 0 0	2 7 1

Win: Benes, St.L (1-0). **Loss:** Reed, NY (0-1).
2B: St. Louis— Edmonds, Tatis; **RBI:** Edmonds 2, Lankford, Tatis, Renteria 2 (3), Hernandez (2), Vina (4). **Attendance:** 55,693. **Time:** 3:23.

Game 4
Sunday, Oct. 15, at New York

	1 2 3	4 5 6	7 8 9	R H E
St. Louis	2 0 0	1 3 0	0 0 0	6 11 2
New York	4 3 0	1 0 2	0 0 x	10 9 0

Win: Rusch, NY (1-0). **Loss:** Kile, St. L (1-2).
2B: St. Louis—Vina, Davis; New York— Perez, Alfonzo, Piazza, Ventura, Agbayani, Zeile. **HR:** St. Louis— Edmonds (3), Clark (2); New York— Piazza (2). **RBI:** St. Louis— Edmonds 3 (12), Clark (5), Davis (2), Renteria (4); New York— Alfonzo (8), Ventura 3 (6), Agbayani 2 (4), Zeile 2 (5), Piazza 2 (4). **SB:** New York— Perez (2). **CS:** St. Louis— Perez (1). **Attendance:** 55,665. **Time:** 3:14.

Game 5
Monday, Oct. 16, at New York

	1 2 3	4 5 6	7 8 9	R H E
St. Louis	0 0 0	0 0 0	0 0 0	0 3 2
New York	3 0 0	3 0 0	1 0 x	7 10 0

Win: Hampton, NY (2-1). **Loss:** Hentgen, St. L (0-1).
2B: New York— Piazza. **RBI:** New York— Alfonzo. **SB:** New York— Perez (3).
Attendance: 55,695. **Time:** 3:17.

Most Valuable Player

Mike Hampton, New York, P

ERA	W-L	BB	K	IP	H	R	ER
0.00	2-0	4	12	16.0	9	0	0

NLCS Composite Box Score
New York Mets

Batting		LCS vs St. Louis								Overall NL Playoffs						
	Avg	AB	R	H	HR	RBI	BB	SO	Avg	AB	R	H	HR	RBI	BB	SO
Edgardo Alfonzo	.444	18	5	8	0	4	4	1	.361	36	6	13	1	9	5	3
Mike Piazza	.412	17	7	7	2	4	5	0	.323	31	8	10	2	4	9	3
Todd Zeile	.368	19	1	7	1	8	2	4	.242	33	1	8	1	8	6	7
Benny Agbayani	.353	17	0	6	0	3	4	0	.361	36	6	13	1	9	5	3
Timo Perez	.304	23	8	7	0	0	1	3	.300	40	10	12	0	3	1	5
Robin Ventura	.214	14	4	3	0	5	6	0	.179	28	5	5	1	7	10	1
Mike Hampton	.167	6	1	1	0	0	0	1	.250	8	1	2	0	0	0	2
Jay Payton	.158	19	1	3	1	3	2	5	.167	36	2	6	1	5	2	9
Mike Bordick	.077	13	2	1	0	0	3	1	.120	25	5	3	0	0	6	5
Al Leiter	.000	3	0	0	0	0	0	2	.000	7	0	0	0	0	0	4
Darryl Hamilton	.000	2	0	0	0	0	0	1	.333	6	1	2	0	0	1	1
Rick Reed	.000	1	0	0	0	0	0	0	.000	2	0	0	0	0	0	0
Lenny Harris	.000	1	0	0	0	0	0	1	.000	3	1	0	0	0	0	1
Bobby Jones	.000	2	0	0	0	0	0	1	.000	6	1	0	0	0	0	4
Kurt Abbott	.000	3	0	0	0	0	0	2	.000	5	0	0	0	0	0	3
Matt Franco	.000	3	0	0	0	0	0	1	.000	3	0	0	0	0	0	1
Bubba Trammell	.000	3	0	0	0	0	0	2	.000	3	0	0	0	0	0	2
Joe McEwing	—	0	2	0	0	0	0	0	1.000	1	2	1	0	0	0	0
TOTALS	.262	164	31	43	4	27	27	24	.238	307	44	73	7	40	47	54

Pitching																
	ERA	W-L	Sv	Gm	IP	H	BB	SO	ERA	W-L	Sv	Gm	IP	H	BB	SO
Dennis Cook	0.00	0-0	0	1	1.0	1	0	2	0.00	0-0	0	3	2.1	1	2	3
Mike Hampton	0.00	2-0	0	2	16.0	9	4	12	2.11	2-1	0	3	21.1	15	7	14
Turk Wendell	0.00	1-0	0	2	1.1	1	1	2	0.00	1-0	0	4	3.1	1	2	7
Armando Benitez	0.00	0-0	1	3	3.0	3	2	2	3.00	1-0	1	5	6.0	7	3	5
Glendon Rusch	0.00	1-0	0	2	3.2	3	0	3	0.00	1-0	0	3	4.1	3	0	5
Al Leiter	3.86	0-0	0	1	7.0	8	0	9	3.00	0-0	0	2	15.0	13	3	15
John Franco	6.75	0-0	0	3	2.2	3	2	2	3.86	0-0	0	5	4.2	4	2	4
Rick White	9.00	0-0	0	1	3.0	5	1	1	4.76	1-0	0	3	5.2	11	3	5
Rick Reed	10.80	0-1	0	1	3.1	8	1	4	5.79	0-1	0	2	9.1	15	3	10
Bobby Jones	13.50	0-0	0	1	4.0	6	0	2	4.15	1-0	0	2	13.0	7	2	7
TOTALS	3.60	4-1	1	5	45.0	47	11	39	3.07	7-2	2	9	85.0	77	27	75

Wild Pitches— LCS (J. Franco, Hampton); OVERALL (J. Franco, Hampton). **Hit Batters—**LCS (Rusch); OVERALL (Rusch).

St. Louis Cardinals

Batting		LCS vs New York								Overall NL Playoffs						
	Avg	AB	R	H	HR	RBI	BB	SO	Avg	AB	R	H	HR	RBI	BB	SO
Pat Hentgen	1.000	1	0	1	0	0	0	0	1.000	1	0	1	0	0	0	0
Will Clark	.412	17	3	7	1	1	2	1	.345	29	6	10	2	5	3	4
Shawon Dunston	.333	6	1	2	0	0	0	0	.429	7	1	3	0	0	0	0
Andy Benes	.333	3	1	1	0	0	0	2	.333	3	1	1	0	0	0	2
Ray Lankford	.333	12	1	4	0	1	1	5	.273	22	3	6	0	4	3	10
J.D. Drew	.333	12	2	4	0	1	0	3	.278	18	3	5	0	1	2	4
Edgar Renteria	.300	20	4	6	0	4	0	2	.267	30	9	8	0	4	4	3
Fernando Vina	.261	23	3	6	0	1	1	4	.278	36	6	10	1	4	2	5
Carlos Hernandez	.250	16	3	4	0	1	1	1	.259	27	6	7	1	2	2	3
Fernando Tatis	.231	13	1	3	0	2	1	5	.231	13	1	3	0	2	1	5
Jim Edmonds	.227	22	1	5	1	5	1	9	.361	36	6	13	3	12	2	11
Eric Davis	.200	10	1	2	0	1	0	2	.143	14	1	2	0	2	0	4
Placido Polanco	.200	5	0	1	0	0	2	1	.267	15	1	4	0	3	3	1
Craig Paquette	.167	6	0	1	0	0	0	2	.125	8	0	1	0	0	0	2
Mark McGwire	.000	2	0	0	0	0	1	0	.250	4	1	1	1	1	2	0
Darryl Kile	.000	2	0	0	0	0	1	0	.000	5	0	0	0	0	1	1
Rick Wilkins	.000	2	0	0	0	0	0	0	.000	2	0	0	0	0	0	0
Eli Marrero	.000	4	0	0	0	1	0	1	.000	4	0	0	0	1	0	1
Britt Reames	.000	1	0	0	0	0	0	1	.000	2	0	0	0	0	0	1
Mike James	—	0	0	0	0	0	0	0	.000	1	0	0	0	0	0	0
Rick Ankiel	—	0	0	0	0	0	0	0	.000	1	0	0	0	0	0	0
Garrett Stephenson	—	0	0	0	0	0	0	0	.000	1	0	0	0	0	0	0
TOTALS	.266	177	21	47	2	18	11	39	.269	279	45	75	8	41	25	58

Pitching																
	ERA	W-L	Sv	Gm	IP	H	BB	SO	ERA	W-L	Sv	Gm	IP	H	BB	SO
Mike Timlin	0.00	0-1	0	3	3.1	1	2	0	3.60	0-1	0	5	5.0	6	3	2
Dave Veres	0.00	0-0	0	3	2.1	2	0	3	0.00	0-0	1	5	4.1	3	0	7
Jason Christiansen	0.00	0-0	0	2	2.0	0	0	1	0.00	0-0	0	3	2.1	0	0	1
Britt Reames	1.42	0-0	0	2	6.1	5	4	6	0.93	1-0	0	4	9.2	5	7	8
Andy Benes	2.25	1-0	0	2	8.0	6	3	5	4.91	0-0	0	2	3.2	6	3	5
Matt Morris	4.91	0-0	0	2	3.2	3	2	2	3.18	0-0	0	4	5.2	3	3	2

Pitching	ERA	W-L	Sv	Gm	IP	H	BB	SO	ERA	W-L	Sv	Gm	IP	H	BB	SO
Darryl Kile	9.00	0-2	0	2	10.0	13	5	3	6.35	1-2	0	3	17.0	17	7	9
Pat Hentgen	14.73	0-1	0	1	3.2	7	5	2	14.73	0-1	0	1	3.2	7	5	2
Mike James	15.43	0-0	0	4	2.1	5	1	0	5.40	1-0	0	6	6.2	6	2	1
Rick Ankiel	20.25	0-0	0	2	1.1	1	5	2	15.75	0-0	0	3	4.0	5	11	5
TOTALS	5.86	1-4	0	5	43.0	43	27	24	4.76	4-4	1	8	70.0	61	43	44

Wild Pitches— LCS (Ankiel 4, Kile); OVERALL (Ankiel 9, Kile). **Hit Batters—** LCS (Timlin, James, Veres); OVERALL (Timlin, James, Veres 2).

Score by Innings

	1	2	3	4	5	6	7	8	9		R	H	E
New York	12	3	1	5	1	2	1	2	4	–	31	43	4
St. Louis	4	1	2	2	8	0	0	2	2	–	21	47	7

E: New York— Abbott, Agbayani, Perez, Ventura; St. Louis— Clark 2, Tatis 2, Edmonds Hernandez, Vina. **DP:** New York 1, St. Louis 3. **2B:** New York— Piazza 3, Zeile 3, Agbayani 2, Perez 2, Alfonzo, Ventura; St. Louis— Clark 2, Tatis 2, Davis, Drew, Dunston, Edmonds, Lankford, Renteria, Vina. **3B:** New York— Alfonzo. **SB:** New York— Perez 2; St. Louis— Renteria 3. **CS:** New York— Perez. **S:** New York— Agbayani, Hampton, Rusch; St. Louis— Renteria 2, Benes, Dunston. **SF:** New York— Ventura 2, Zeile; St. Louis— Renteria, Tatis. **PB:** St. Louis— Marrero.
Umpires: Dana Demuth, Bruce Froemming, Ed Rapuano, Steve Rippley, Dale Scott and Tim Tschida.

WORLD SERIES

N.Y. Yankees, 4-1

Date	Winner	Home Field
Oct. 21	Yankees, 4-3 (12 inn.)	at Yankees
Oct. 22	Yankees, 6-5	at Yankees
Oct. 24	Mets, 4-2	at Mets
Oct. 25	Yankees, 3-2	at Mets
Oct. 26	Yankees, 4-2	at Mets

Most Valuable Player
Derek Jeter, NY Yankees, SS

AVG	AB	R	H	RBI	HR	TB
.409	22	6	9	2	2	19

Game 1
Saturday, Oct. 21, at Yankee Stadium.

	1	2	3	4	5	6	7	8	9	10	11	12	R	H	E
Mets	0	0	0	0	0	0	3	0	0	0	0	0	– 3	10	0
Yankees	0	0	0	0	0	2	0	0	1	0	0	1	– 4	12	0

Mets	AB	R	H	RBI	BB	SO
Perez, rf	6	0	1	0	0	1
Alfonzo, 2b	6	0	1	1	0	2
Piazza, dh	5	0	1	0	0	1
Zeile, 1b	5	0	2	0	0	1
Ventura, 3b	5	0	0	0	0	1
Agbayani, lf	4	1	2	0	0	1
McEwing, lf	1	0	0	0	0	0
Payton, cf	5	1	1	0	0	0
Pratt, c	2	1	0	0	1	2
Bordick, ss	1	0	1	2	0	0
Trammell, ph	1	0	1	2	0	0
Abbott, ss	2	0	1	0	0	0
TOTALS	43	3	10	3	1	10

Mets	IP	H	ER	BB	SO
Leiter	7	5	2	3	7
J. Franco (H, 1)	1	1	0	0	0
Benitez (BS, 1)	1	2	1	1	1
Cook	0	0	0	2	0
Rusch	1⅔	1	0	2	0
Wendell (L, 0-1)	1	3	1	1	0

Yankees	AB	R	H	RBI	BB	SO
Knoblauch, dh	4	1	0	1	1	1
Jeter, ss	4	1	1	0	2	2
Justice, lf	4	0	1	2	1	0
Bellinger, pr-lf	0	0	0	0	0	0
Hill, ph-lf	1	0	0	0	0	0
Williams, cf	4	0	0	0	2	1
Martinez, 1b	6	1	2	0	0	1
Posada, c	5	0	1	0	1	1
O'Neill, rf	4	1	1	0	2	1
Brosius, 3b	3	0	1	0	0	0
Polonia, ph	1	0	1	0	0	0
Sojo, 3b	2	0	0	0	0	0
Vizcaino, 2b	6	0	4	1	0	1
TOTALS	44	4	12	4	9	8

Yankees	IP	H	ER	BB	SO
Pettitte	6⅔	8	3	1	4
Nelson	1⅓	1	0	0	0
Rivera	2	1	0	0	3
Stanton (W, 1-0)	2	0	0	0	3

2B: Mets— Agbayani, Zeile, Abbott; Yankees— Justice, Posada. **RBI:** Mets— Trammell 2, Alfonzo; Yankees— Justice 2, Knoblauch, Vizcaino. **S:** Mets— Bordick. **CS:** Mets— Piazza; Yankees— Knoblauch.
Attendance: 55,913. **Time:** 4:51.

Game 2
Sunday, Oct. 22, at Yankee Stadium.

	1	2	3	4	5	6	7	8	9	R	H	E
Mets	0	0	0	0	0	0	0	0	5	5	7	3
Yankees	2	1	0	0	1	0	1	1	x	6	12	1

Mets	AB	R	H	RBI	BB	SO
Perez, rf	4	0	0	0	0	1
Alfonzo, 2b	3	1	1	0	0	1
Piazza, c	4	1	1	2	0	0
Ventura, 3b	4	0	1	0	0	1
Zeile, 1b	4	0	2	0	0	0
Agbayani, lf	4	1	1	0	0	2
Harris, dh	4	1	0	0	0	1
Payton, cf	4	1	1	3	0	1
Bordick, ss	2	0	0	0	0	1
Hamilton, ph	1	0	0	0	0	1
Abbott, ss	1	0	0	0	0	1
TOTALS	35	5	7	5	0	10

Yankees	AB	R	H	RBI	BB	SO
Knoblauch, dh	4	0	0	0	1	0
Jeter, ss	5	1	3	0	0	1
Justice, lf	3	1	0	1	1	1
Bellinger, lf	0	0	0	0	0	0
Williams, cf	3	1	0	0	2	0
Martinez, 1b	5	1	3	2	0	0
Posada, c	3	1	2	1	2	0
O'Neill, rf	4	0	3	1	0	1
Brosius, 3b	3	1	1	2	0	1
Vizcaino, 2b	4	0	0	0	0	1
TOTALS	34	6	12	6	6	5

Mets	IP	H	ER	BB	SO
Hampton (L, 0-1)	6	8	4	5	4
Rusch	1/3	2	1	0	0
White	1 1/3	1	1	1	1
Cook	1/3	1	0	0	0

Yankees	IP	H	ER	BB	SO
Clemens (W, 1-0)	8	2	0	0	9
Nelson	0	3	3	0	0
Rivera	1	2	2	0	1

2B: Yankees— Martinez, Jeter 2, O'Neill. **HR:** Mets— Piazza (1), Payton (1); Yankees— Brosius (1). **RBI:** Mets— Piazza 2 (2), Payton 3 (3); Yankees— Martinez 2 (2), Posada (1), Brosius 2 (2), O'Neill (1). **SF:** Yankees— Brosius. **CS:** Yankees— Vizcaino.
Attendance: 51,226. **Time:** 3:30.

Game 3
Tuesday, Oct. 24 at Shea Stadium.

	1	2	3	4	5	6	7	8	9		R	H	E
Yankees	0	0	1	1	0	0	0	0	0	—	2	8	0
Mets	0	1	0	0	0	1	0	2	x	—	4	9	0

Yankees	AB	R	H	RBI	BB	SO
Vizcaino, 2b	4	0	0	0	0	2
Polonia, ph	1	0	0	0	0	0
Jeter, ss	4	1	2	0	1	2
Justice, lf	3	0	1	1	1	0
Williams, cf	4	0	0	0	0	2
Martinez, 1b	3	1	1	0	1	1
Posada, c	4	0	0	0	2	0
O'Neill, rf	4	0	3	1	0	0
Brosius, 3b	2	0	0	0	0	1
Hill, ph	1	0	0	0	0	1
Sojo, 3b	0	0	0	0	0	0
Hernandez, p	2	0	0	0	0	2
Knoblauch, ph	1	0	1	0	0	0
TOTALS	33	2	8	2	3	12

Yankees	IP	H	ER	BB	SO
Hernandez (L, 0-1)	7 1/3	9	4	3	12
Stanton	2/3	0	0	0	1

Mets	AB	R	H	RBI	BB	SO
Perez, rf	3	0	0	0	1	1
Alfonzo, 2b	4	0	0	0	0	2
Piazza, c	4	1	1	0	0	2
Ventura, 3b	3	1	2	1	1	1
Zeile, 1b	4	1	2	1	0	2
Agbayani, lf	3	0	1	1	1	1
McEwing, pr-lf	0	1	0	0	0	0
Payton, cf	4	0	1	0	0	2
Bordick, ss	3	0	1	0	0	1
Harris, ph	0	0	0	1	0	0
Trammell, ph	0	0	0	1	0	0
Benitez, p	0	0	0	0	0	0
Reed, p	1	0	1	0	0	0
Hamilton, ph	1	0	0	0	0	0
Wendell, p	0	0	0	0	0	0
Cook, p	0	0	0	0	0	0
J. Franco, p	0	0	0	0	0	0
Abbott, ph-ss	1	0	0	0	0	1
TOTALS	31	4	9	4	3	13

Mets	IP	H	ER	BB	SO
Reed	6	6	2	1	8
Wendell	2/3	0	0	1	2
Cook	1/3	1	1	1	1
J. Franco (W, 1-0)	1	1	0	0	0
Benitez (S, 1)	1	1	0	0	1

2B: Yankees— O'Neill, Justice; Mets— Ventura, Piazza, Zeile, Agbayani. **3B:** Yankees— O'Neill. **HR:** Mets— Ventura (1). **RBI:** Yankees— Justice (3), O'Neill (2); Mets— Ventura (1), Zeile (1), Agbayani (1), Trammell (3). **S:** Yankees— Hernandez; Mets— Reed. **SF:** Mets—Trammell.
Attendance: 55,299. **Time:** 3:39.

Game 4
Wednesday, Oct. 25, at Shea Stadium.

	1	2	3	4	5	6	7	8	9		R	H	E
Yankees	1	1	1	0	0	0	0	0	0	—	3	8	0
Mets	0	0	2	0	0	0	0	0	0	—	2	6	1

Yankees	AB	R	H	RBI	BB	SO
Jeter, ss	5	2	2	1	0	1
Sojo, 2b	4	0	1	1	1	0
Justice, lf	5	0	0	0	0	0
Bellinger, lf	0	0	0	0	0	0
Williams, cf	4	0	0	0	0	1
Martinez, 1b	4	0	2	0	0	1
O'Neill, rf	4	1	2	0	0	0
Posada, c	3	0	0	0	1	1
Brosius, 3b	1	0	1	1	2	0
Neagle, p	0	0	0	0	0	0
Cone, p	0	0	0	0	0	0
Caneco, ph	1	0	0	0	0	0
Nelson, p	0	0	0	0	0	0
Stanton, p	0	0	0	0	0	0
Rivera, p	1	0	0	0	0	0
TOTALS	34	3	8	3	4	6

Yankees	IP	H	ER	BB	SO
Neagle	4⅔	4	2	2	3
Cone	⅓	0	0	0	0
Nelson (W, 1-0)	⅓	1	0	1	1
Stanton (H, 1)	⅔	0	0	0	2
Rivera (S, 1)	2	1	0	0	2

Mets	AB	R	H	RBI	BB	SO
Perez, rf	3	1	1	0	0	1
Abbott, ph-ss	1	0	0	0	1	0
Alfonzo, 2b	3	0	0	0	1	0
Piazza, c	4	1	1	2	0	1
Zeile, 1b	4	0	2	0	0	0
McEwing, pr	0	0	0	0	0	0
Benitez, p	0	0	0	0	0	0
Ventura, 3b	4	0	0	0	0	0
Agbayani, lf	3	0	0	0	1	1
Payton, cf	4	0	2	0	0	1
Bordick, ss	2	0	0	0	0	0
Harris, ph	0	0	0	0	1	0
J. Franco, p	0	0	0	0	0	0
M. Franco, 1b	1	0	0	0	0	1
B.J. Jones, p	0	0	0	0	0	0
Rusch, p	0	0	0	0	0	0
Hamilton, ph	0	0	0	0	0	0
Trammell, ph-rf	1	0	0	0	0	1
TOTALS	32	2	6	2	3	8

Mets	IP	H	ER	BB	SO
B.J. Jones (L, 0-1)	5	4	3	3	3
Rusch	2	3	0	0	2
J. Franco	1	1	0	0	1
Benitez	1	0	0	1	0

3B: Yankees— O'Neill. **HR:** Yankees— Jeter (1); Mets— Piazza. **RBI:** Yankees— Jeter (1), Brosius (3), Sojo (1); Mets— Piazza 2 (4). **SF:** Yankees—Brosius. **SB:** Yankees— Sojo.
Attendance: 55,290. **Time:** 3:20.

Game 5

Thursday, Oct. 26, at Shea Stadium.

	1	2	3	4	5	6	7	8	9		R	H	E
Yankees	0	1	0	0	0	1	0	0	2	—	4	7	1
Mets	0	2	0	0	0	0	0	0	0	—	2	8	1

Yankees	AB	R	H	RBI	BB	SO
Vizcaino, 2b	3	0	0	0	0	1
Knoblauch, ph	1	0	0	0	0	0
Stanton, p	0	0	0	0	0	0
Hill, ph	1	0	0	0	0	0
Rivera, p	0	0	0	0	0	0
Jeter, ss	4	1	1	1	0	2
Justice, lf	4	0	1	0	0	1
Bellinger, lf	0	0	0	0	0	0
Williams, cf	3	1	2	1	1	1
Martinez, 1b	4	0	0	0	0	1
O'Neill, rf	3	0	0	0	1	2
Posada, c	3	1	1	0	1	0
Brosius, 3b	4	1	1	0	0	0
Pettitte, p	3	0	0	0	0	1
Sojo, p	3	0	0	0	0	1
TOTALS	34	4	7	3	3	9

Yankees	IP	H	ER	BB	SO
Pettitte	7	8	0	3	5
Stanton (W, 2-0)	1	0	0	0	1
Rivera (S, 2)	1	0	0	1	1

Mets	AB	R	H	RBI	BB	SO
Agbayani, lf	4	0	1	1	1	1
Alfonzo, 2b	5	0	1	0	0	0
Piazza, c	5	0	2	0	0	0
Zeile, 1b	3	0	0	0	1	2
Ventura, 2b	4	0	0	0	0	2
Trammell, rf	3	1	1	0	1	0
Perez, rf	0	0	0	0	0	0
Payton, cf	4	1	2	0	0	1
Abbott, ss	3	0	1	0	1	0
Leiter, p	2	0	0	0	0	0
J. Franco, p	0	0	0	0	0	0
Hamilton, ph	1	0	0	0	0	1
TOTALS	34	2	8	1	4	7

Mets	IP	H	ER	BB	SO
Leiter (L, 0-1)	8⅔	7	3	3	9
J. Franco	⅓	0	0	0	0

2B: Mets— Piazza. **HR:** Yankees— Williams (1), Jeter (2). **RBI:** Yankees— Williams (1), Jeter (2), Sojo (2); Mets— Agbayani (2). **S:** Mets— Leiter.
Attendance: 55,292. **Time:** 3:32.

World Series Composite Box Score

New York Mets

	WS vs Yankees							Overall Playoffs						
Batting	Avg	AB	R	H	HR	RBI	BB	SO	Avg	AB	R	H	HR	RBI	BB	SO
Rick Reed	1.000	1	0	1	0	0	0	0	.333	3	0	1	0	0	0	0
Todd Zeile	.400	20	1	8	0	1	1	5	.302	53	2	16	1	9	7	12
Bubba Trammell	.400	5	1	2	0	3	1	1	.250	8	1	2	0	3	1	3
Jay Payton	.333	21	3	7	1	3	0	5	.228	57	5	13	2	8	2	14
Benny Agbayani	.278	18	2	5	0	2	3	6	.320	50	3	16	1	6	10	9
Mike Piazza	.273	22	3	6	2	4	0	4	.302	53	11	16	4	8	9	7
Kurt Abbott	.250	8	0	2	0	0	1	3	.154	13	0	2	0	0	1	6
Robin Ventura	.150	20	1	3	1	1	1	5	.167	48	6	8	2	8	11	6

WS vs Yankees / Overall Playoffs

Batting	Avg	AB	R	H	HR	RBI	BB	SO	Avg	AB	R	H	HR	RBI	BB	SO
Edgardo Alfonzo	.143	21	1	3	0	1	1	5	.281	57	7	16	1	10	6	8
Mike Bordick	.125	8	0	1	0	0	0	3	.121	33	5	4	0	0	6	8
Timo Perez	.125	16	1	2	0	0	1	4	.250	56	11	14	0	3	2	9
Al Leiter	.000	2	0	0	0	0	0	0	.000	9	0	0	0	0	0	4
Daryl Hamilton	.000	3	0	0	0	0	0	2	.222	9	1	2	0	0	1	3
Lenny Harris	.000	4	1	0	0	0	1	0	.000	7	2	0	0	0	1	2
Todd Pratt	.000	2	1	0	0	0	1	2	.000	3	1	0	0	0	1	2
Bobby J. Jones	.000	2	0	0	0	0	0	1	.000	8	1	0	0	0	0	5
Matt Franco	.000	1	0	0	0	0	0	1	.000	4	0	0	0	0	0	2
Joe McEwing	.000	1	1	0	0	0	0	0	.500	2	3	1	0	0	0	0
Mike Hampton	—	0	0	0	0	0	0	0	.250	8	1	2	0	0	0	2
Derek Bell	—	0	0	0	0	0	0	0	.000	1	0	0	0	0	0	0
TOTALS	.229	175	16	40	4	15	11	48	.234	482	60	113	11	55	58	102

Pitching	ERA	W-L	Sv	Gm	IP	H	BB	SO	ERA	W-L	Sv	Gm	IP	H	BB	SO
John Franco	.000	1-0	0	4	3.1	3	0	1	2.25	1-0	1	9	8.0	7	2	5
Dennis Cook	.000	0-0	0	3	0.2	1	3	1	0.00	0-0	0	6	3.0	2	5	4
Glendon Rusch	2.25	0-0	0	3	4.0	6	2	2	1.08	1-0	0	6	8.1	9	2	7
Al Leiter	2.87	0-1	0	2	15.2	12	6	16	2.93	0-1	0	4	30.2	25	9	31
Rick Reed	3.00	0-0	0	1	6.0	6	1	8	4.70	0-1	0	3	15.1	21	4	18
Armando Benitez	3.00	0-0	1	3	3.0	3	2	2	3.00	1-0	2	8	9.0	10	5	7
Turk Wendell	5.40	0-1	0	2	1.2	3	2	2	1.80	1-1	0	6	5.0	4	4	9
Bobby J. Jones	5.40	0-1	0	1	5.0	4	3	3	4.50	1-1	0	3	18.0	11	3	5
Mike Hampton	6.00	0-1	0	1	6.0	8	5	4	2.96	2-2	0	4	27.1	23	12	18
Rick White	6.75	0-0	0	1	1.1	1	1	1	5.14	1-0	0	4	7.0	12	4	6
TOTALS	3.47	1-4	1	5	46.2	47	25	40	3.21	8-6	3	14	131.2	124	52	115

Wild Pitches—WS (Rusch 2); OVERALL (Rusch 2, J. Franco, Hampton). **Hit Batters**—WS (Hampton, Cook, Reed); OVERALL (Hampton, Cook, Reed, Rusch).

New York Yankees

WS vs Mets / Overall Playoffs

Batting	Avg	AB	R	H	HR	RBI	BB	SO	Avg	AB	R	H	HR	RBI	BB	SO
Luis Polonia	.500	2	0	1	0	0	0	0	.500	4	0	2	0	0	0	1
Paul O'Neill	.474	19	2	9	0	2	3	4	.310	58	6	18	0	7	6	10
Derek Jeter	.409	22	6	9	2	2	3	8	.317	63	13	20	4	9	11	18
Tino Martinez	.364	22	3	8	0	2	1	4	.364	66	10	24	1	7	4	11
Scott Brosius	.308	13	2	4	1	3	2	2	.229	48	4	11	1	4	5	9
Luis Sojo	.286	7	0	2	0	2	1	0	.239	46	3	11	0	9	5	4
Jose Vizcaino	.235	17	0	4	0	1	0	5	.316	19	4	6	0	3	0	5
Jorge Posada	.222	18	2	4	0	1	5	4	.204	54	6	11	0	5	13	14
David Justice	.158	19	1	3	0	3	3	2	.206	63	7	13	3	12	8	13
Bernie Williams	.111	18	2	2	1	1	5	5	.279	61	10	17	2	5	8	12
Chuck Knoblauch	.100	10	1	1	0	1	2	1	.238	42	5	10	0	4	5	7
Jose Canseco	.000	1	0	0	0	0	0	0	.000	1	0	0	0	0	0	1
Glenallen Hill	.000	3	0	0	0	0	0	0	.059	17	1	1	0	2	1	7
Denny Neagle	.000	2	0	0	0	0	0	0	.000	2	0	0	0	0	0	0
Andy Pettitte	.000	3	0	0	0	0	0	1	.000	3	0	0	0	0	0	1
Mariano Rivera	.000	1	0	0	0	0	0	0	.000	1	0	0	0	0	0	0
Orlando Hernandez	.000	2	0	0	0	0	0	2	.000	2	0	0	0	0	0	2
TOTALS	.263	179	19	47	4	18	25	40	.263	551	69	145	11	68	66	116

Pitching	ERA	W-L	Sv	Gm	IP	H	BB	SO	ERA	W-L	Sv	Gm	IP	H	BB	SO
Roger Clemens	0.00	1-0	0	1	8.0	2	0	9	3.21	2-2	0	4	28.0	16	10	34
David Cone	0.00	0-0	0	1	0.1	0	0	0	0.00	0-0	0	2	1.1	0	0	0
Mike Stanton	0.00	0-0	0	4	4.1	0	0	7	1.04	3-0	0	7	8.2	5	1	10
Andy Pettitte	1.98	0-0	0	2	13.2	16	4	9	2.84	2-0	0	5	31.2	40	8	18
Mariano Rivera	3.00	0-0	2	4	6.0	4	1	7	1.72	0-0	6	10	15.2	10	1	10
Denny Neagle	3.86	0-0	0	1	4.2	4	2	3	4.30	0-2	0	3	14.2	10	9	10
Orlando Hernandez	4.91	0-1	0	1	7.1	9	3	12	3.94	3-1	0	5	29.2	27	16	31
Jeff Nelson	10.13	1-0	0	3	2.2	5	1	1	7.04	1-0	0	8	7.2	10	1	9
Jason Grimsley	—	0-0	0	0	0.0	0	0	0	0.00	0-0	0	2	1.0	0	3	1
Dwight Gooden	—	0-0	0	0	0.0	0	0	0	9.00	0-0	0	2	4.0	5	1	2
Randy Choate	—	0-0	0	0	0.0	0	0	0	5.40	0-0	0	8	1.2	0	1	2
TOTALS	2.68	4-1	2	5	47.0	40	11	48	3.44	11-5	6	16	144.0	125	51	127

Wild Pitches—WS (Clemens); OVERALL (Clemens 2, Stanton, Grimsley). **Hit Batters**—WS (Clemens); OVERALL (Gooden 2, Clemens).

Score by Innings

	1	2	3	4	5	6	7	8	9	10	11	12		R	H	E
Mets	0	3	2	0	0	1	3	2	5	0	0	0	–	16	40	5
Yankees	3	3	2	1	1	3	1	1	3	0	0	0	–	19	47	2

E: Mets— Payton 2, Bordick, Perez, Trammell; Yankees— Clemens, Pettitte. **DP:** Mets 3; Yankees 1. **LOB:** Mets 36, Yankees 52. **2B:** Mets— Agbayani 2, Piazza 2, Zeile 2, Abbott, Ventura; Yankees— Jeter 2, Justice 2, O'Neill 2, Martinez, Posada. **3B:** Yankees— O'Neill 2, Jeter. **HR:** Mets— Piazza 2, Payton, Ventura; Yankees— Jeter 2, Brosius, Williams. **SB:** Yankees— Sojo. **CS:** Mets— Piazza; Yankees— Knoblauch, Vizcaino. **PO:** Mets— Abbott (by Pettitte); **PB:** Yankees— Posada. **S:** Mets— Bordick, Leiter, Reed; Yankees— Hernandez. **SF:** Mets— Trammell; Yankees— Brosius 2, Knoblauch.

Umpires: Jerry Crawford, Jeffrey Kellogg, Tim McClelland, Ed Montague, Charles Reliford, Tim Welke.

COLLEGE

Final *Baseball America* Top 25

Final 2000 Division I Top 25, voted on by the editors of *Baseball America* and released after the NCAA College World Series. Given are final records (excluding ties) and winning percentage (including all postseason games); records in College World Series and team eliminated by (DNP indicates team did not play in tourney); head coach (career years and Division I record including 2000 postseason); preseason ranking and rank before start of CWS.

		Record	Pct	CWS Recap	Head Coach	Preseason Rank	Rank before CWS
1	Louisiana St.	.52-17	.754	4-0	Skip Bertman (17 yrs: 826-308-2)	8	2
2	Stanford	.50-16	.758	3-1 (LSU)	Mark Marquess (24 yrs: 995-498-5)	1	1
3	Florida St.	.53-19	.736	2-2 (LSU)	Mike Martin (21 yrs: 1132-383-3)	7	5
4	South Carolina	.56-10	.848	DNP	Ray Tanner (13 yrs: 563-248-3)	25	6
5	Southern California	.44-20	.688	1-2 (Fla. St.)	Mike Gillespie (14 yrs: 563-313-2)	11	4
6	Georgia Tech	.50-16	.758	DNP	Danny Hall (13 yrs: 511-253-0)	9	7
7	Clemson	.51-18	.739	1-2 (La.-Laf.)	Jack Leggett (21 yrs: 716-420)	24	3
8	Nebraska	.51-17	.750	DNP	Dave Van Horn (6 yrs: 223-120)	NR	8
9	UL-Lafayette	.49-20	.710	2-2 (Stanford)	Tony Robichaux (13 yrs: 462-289)	NR	11
10	Texas	.46-21	.687	0-2 (Fla. St.)	Augie Garrido (32 yrs: 1284-622-8)	15	9
11	Houston	.48-18	.727	DNP	Rayner Noble (6 yrs: 217-147)	6	10
12	Arizona St.	.44-15	.746	DNP	Pat Murphy (13 yrs: 550-239-1)	22	14
13	Miami-FL	.41-19-1	.683	DNP	Jim Morris (19 yrs: 844-351-2)	5	13
14	Baylor	.45-17	.726	DNP	Steve Smith (6 yrs: 225-129-1)	10	15
15	Mississippi St.	.41-20	.672	DNP	Pat McMahon (8 yrs: 314-150)	NR	16
16	Loyola Marymount	.40-19	.678	DNP	Frank Cruz (4 yrs: 128-109-1)	17	17
17	UCLA	.38-26	.594	DNP	Gary Adams (26 yrs: 866-700-7)	4	18
18	San Jose St.	.41-24	.631	0-2 (La.-Laf.)	Sam Piraro (15 yrs: 454-345-3)	NR	12
19	Penn St.	.45-19	.703	DNP	Joe Hindelang (18 yrs: 438-391-3)	NR	19
20	Florida	.43-23	.652	DNP	Andy Lopez (12 yrs: 483-239-3)	18	20
21	Wake Forest	.41-20	.672	DNP	George Greer (19 yrs: 577-416-6)	21	21
22	CS-Fullerton	.38-21	.644	DNP	George Horton (4 yrs: 174-76-1)	2	22
23	Rutgers	.40-18	.690	DNP	Fred Hill (17 yrs: 540-333-5)	NR	23
24	Alabama	.41-24	.631	DNP	Jim Wells (11 yrs: 480-203)	3	24
25	Auburn	.41-20	.672	DNP	Hal Baird (21 yrs: 779-394)	12	25

College World Series

CWS Participants: LSU (48-17); Clemson (50-16); Florida St. (51-17); Stanford (47-15); USC (43-18); Texas (46-19); Louisiana-Lafayette (47-18); San Jose St. (41-22).

Bracket One

June 9—Clemson 10	San Jose St. 6
June 9—Stanford 6	UL-Lafayette 4
June 11—Stanford 10	Clemson 4
June 11—UL-Lafayette 6	San Jose St. 3 (out)
June 14—UL-Lafayette 5	Clemson 4 (out)
June 15—Stanford 19	UL-Lafayette 9 (out)

Bracket Two

June 10—USC 6	Florida St. 4
June 10—LSU 13	Texas 5
June 12—LSU 10	USC 4
June 12—Florida St. 6	Texas 2 (out)
June 14—Florida St. 3	USC 2 (out)
June 15—LSU 6	Florida St. 3 (out)

CWS Championship Game

Saturday, June 17, at Rosenblatt Stadium in Omaha.

	1	2	3	4	5	6	7	8	9	R	H	E
Stanford	0	0	0	4	0	1	0	0	0	—5	13	0
LSU	0	2	0	0	0	0	3	1	—6	8	0

Win: LSU— Trey Hodges (5-2). **Loss:** STAN— Justin Wayne (15-4). **Save:** None. **Starters:** STAN— Jason Young; LSU— Brian Tallet. **Strikeouts:** STAN—Young 2, Wayne 7; LSU— Tallet 4, Hodges 4.

2B: STAN— Craig Thompson, Arik Van Zandt; LSU— Mike Fontenot, Wally Pontiff. **HR:** STAN— Thompson (12); LSU— Blair Barbier (9), Jeremy Witten (7). **SB:** STAN— Eric Bruntlett (11).

Attendance: 24,282. **Time** 3:42.

Most Outstanding Player

Trey Hodges, LSU, P

IP	H	ER	BB	K	W-L	Svs
10.2	6	2	2	8	2-0	1

All-Tournament Team

C– Beau Craig, USC; **1B**– Craig Thompson, Stanford; **2B**– Mike Fontenot, LSU; **3B**– Blair Barbier, LSU; **SS**– Ryan Theriot, LSU; **OF**– Steven Feehan, UL-Lafayette; Edmund Muth, Stanford; Joe Borchard, Stanford; **DH**– Brad Hawpe, LSU; **P**– Jon McDonald, FSU; Trey Hodges, LSU.

Annual Awards

Chosen by *Baseball America*, *Collegiate Baseball*, National Collegiate Baseball Writers Association and the American Baseball Coaches Association. The Rotary Smith award is chosen by college sports information directors.

Player of the Year

Kip Bouknight, P, South Carolina......Smith, ABCA, *CB*
Mark Teixeira, 3B, Georgia Tech......Dick Howser (*BA*/NCBWA)

Coaches of the Year

Skip Bertman, LSU..........................ABCA, *CB*
Ray Tanner, South Carolina.......................*BA*

Consensus All-America Team

NCAA Division I players cited most frequently by the following four selectors: the American Baseball Coaches Assn. (ABCA), *Baseball America*, *Collegiate Baseball* and the National Collegiate Baseball Writers Assn. (NCBWA).

First Team

Pos		Cl	Avg	HR	RBI
C	Brad Cresse, LSU	Sr.	.399	30	106
1B	Todd Faulkner, Auburn	Jr.	.423	22	103
2B	Chase Utley, UCLA	Jr.	.382	22	69
SS	Tim Hummel, Old Dominion	Jr.	.408	8	68
3B	Mark Teixeira, Ga. Tech	So.	.427	18	80
OF	Bill Scott, UCLA	Jr.	.421	21	76
OF	Mitch Jones, Arizona St.	Sr.	.357	27	92
OF	Michael Campo, Penn St.	Sr.	.425	6	48
UT	Jason Dubois, Va. Comm.	Jr.	.435	19	74

		Cl	W-L	Sv	ERA
P	Kip Bouknight, S. Carolina	Jr.	17-1	0	2.81
P	Lenny DiNardo, Stetson	So.	16-1	0	1.90
P	Justin Wayne, Stanford	Jr.	15-4	0	3.21
P	Shane Komine, Nebraska	So.	11-4	0	2.24
P	Charlie Thames, Texas	Jr.	4-2	19	2.22
P	Cory Scott, E. Carolina	Sr.	5-0	22	1.52

Second Team

Pos		Cl	Avg	HR	RBI
C	Casey Myers, Arizona St.	Jr.	.412	18	97
1B	Philip Hartig, Citadel	Jr.	.393	14	86
2B	Matt Easterday, Ga. Southern	Jr.	.440	16	77
SS	Darren Fenster, Rutgers	Sr.	.433	4	55
3B	Justin Gemoll, USC	Sr.	.374	18	67
OF	Frank Corr, Stetson	Jr.	.431	18	98
OF	Gabe Gross, Auburn	So.	.430	13	86
OF	Joe Inglett, Nevada	Sr.	.435	10	48
UT	Jeff Bajenaru, Oklahoma	Sr.	.342	11	58

		Cl	W-L	Sv	ERA
P	Jason Anderson, Illinois	Jr.	14-3	0	3.15
P	Rik Currier, USC	Jr.	15-3	0	3.31
P	Kyle Crowell, Houston	Jr.	13-3	0	2.86
P	Aaron Heilman, Notre Dame	Jr.	10-2	0	3.04
P	Kenny Baugh, Rice	Jr.	10-2	1	2.22
P	Chad Hawkins, Baylor	Sr.	11-2	0	1.82

NCAA Division I Leaders

Batting

Average

(At least 75 AB)		Cl	Gm	AB	H	Avg
Patrick Hollander, Lehigh		Jr.	42	138	67	.486
Keith Lillash, Cleveland St.		Jr.	55	216	99	.458
Dario Rosa, Alcorn St.		Sr.	29	104	47	.452
Jermaine Harrison, Alab. St.		Jr.	37	129	57	.442
Matt Easterday, Ga. Southern		Jr.	57	243	107	.440
Steve Holm, Oral Roberts		Jr.	64	238	104	.437
Jason Dubois, Va. Comm.		Jr.	57	193	84	.435
Joe Inglett, Nevada		Sr.	57	237	103	.435
Shayne Ridley, Ball St.		Sr.	46	166	72	.434
Darren Fenster, Rutgers		Sr.	58	233	101	.433

Home Runs (per game)

(At least 15 HR)		Cl	Gm	HR	Avg
Mitch Jones, Arizona St.		Sr.	59	27	0.46
Jesse Gutierrez, Tex-Pan Am		Jr.	46	21	0.46
Brad Cresse, LSU		Sr.	69	30	0.43
Aaron Sisk, New Mexico		Jr.	56	24	0.43
Jeff Haase, Cleveland St.		Sr.	56	22	0.39
Brooks Vogel, Dayton		Jr.	54	21	0.39
T.J. Soto, Louisiana Tech		Sr.	55	21	0.38
Dan Johnson, Nebraska		Jr.	55	21	0.38
Lale Esquivel, Miami-FL.		Sr.	53	20	0.38
Chad Smith, Georgia St.		Sr.	56	21	0.38

Runs Batted In (per game)

(At least 50 RBI)		Cl	Gm	RBI	Avg
Chris Cottonham, Grambling		Sr.	50	87	1.74
Todd Faulkner, Auburn		Jr.	61	103	1.69
Casey Myers, Arizona St.		Jr.	59	97	1.64
Mitch Jones, Arizona St.		Sr.	59	92	1.56
Brad Cresse, LSU		Sr.	69	106	1.54
Frank Corr, Stetson		Jr.	64	98	1.53
Frank Fresconi, Bucknell		Sr.	47	70	1.49
Philip Hartig, Citadel		Jr.	59	86	1.46
Aaron Sisk, New Mexico		Jr.	56	81	1.45
Gabe Gross, Auburn		So.	61	86	1.41

Stolen Bases (per game)

(At least 25)		Cl	Gm	SB	SBA	Avg
Dwaine Bacon, Florida A&M		Jr.	48	74	76	1.54
Chris Morris, Citadel		So.	58	84	94	1.45
Alex Smith, Florida A&M		Jr.	41	42	47	1.02
Will Smith, UAB		Sr.	57	55	66	0.96
Stevie Daniel, Tennessee		Jr.	63	58	65	0.92
Chris Burke, Tennessee		So.	63	56	63	0.89
Rich Thompson, J. Madison		Jr.	59	50	58	0.85
John Nelson, Kansas		Jr.	50	42	47	0.84
Josh Edgeworth, C. of Charleston		Jr.	50	40	44	0.80
Adonis Smith, N.C. A&T		So.	48	37	43	0.77

Pitching

Earned Run Avg.

(At least 50 inn.)		Cl	Gm	IP	ERA
Steve Langone, Boston Col.		Sr.	13	76.0	1.54
Jeffrey Hilz, SE Missouri St.		Jr.	28	58.0	1.71
Chad Hawkins, Baylor		Sr.	16	123.1	1.82
John Novinsky, Iona		Jr.	14	82.1	1.86
Jason Fardella, St. Francis		So.	11	72.0	1.88
Lenny DiNardo, Stetson		Fr.	20	132.2	1.90
Conor Brooks, Dartmouth		Sr.	12	87.2	2.05
Trevor Bullock, Nebraska		Sr.	19	71.2	2.13
Dan Jackson, Fla. Atlantic		Sr.	14	83.2	2.15
Riley Stephens, Oral Roberts		Sr.	32	77.1	2.21

Wins

		Cl	Gm	IP	W-L
Kip Bouknight, S. Carolina		Jr.	19	144.0	17-1
Lenny DiNardo, Stetson		Fr.	20	132.2	16-1
Brian Tallet, LSU		Jr.	25	143.1	15-3
Rik Currier, USC		Jr.	22	125.0	15-3
Justin Wayne, Stanford		Jr.	20	143.0	15-4
Darrell Rasner, Nevada		Fr.	18	122.2	14-2
Jason Anderson, Illinois		Jr.	20	134.1	14-3
Peter Bauer, S. Carolina		Jr.	19	124.1	13-2
Kyle Crowell, Houston		Jr.	23	138.1	13-3
Cory Vance, Georgia Tech		Jr.	16	119.0	13-3
Chris Key, San Jose St.		Sr.	22	119.2	13-4
Scott Dohmann, UL-Lafayette		Jr.	19	131.0	13-5

Strikeouts (per 9 inn.)

(At least 50 inn.)	Cl	IP	SO	Avg
Bill White, Jacksonville St..........Jr.	76.2	136	16.0
Rob Henkel, UCLA................Jr.	90.1	136	13.5
Kevin Miller, Long Island ....Sr.	78.2	112	12.8
Dan Valentin, Liberty ....Jr.	71.2	100	12.6
Adam Johnson, CS-Fullerton.......Jr.	119.1	166	12.5
Dan Jackson, Fla. Atlantic ....Sr.	83.2	116	12.5
Chris Flinn, Stony Brook ....So.	82.1	114	12.5
Chad Wells, Ball St. ....Sr.	58.2	79	12.1
Beau Anderson, Samford ....Jr.	65.2	84	11.5
David Ray, Ga. Southern ....So.	89.1	114	11.5

Saves

	Cl	IP	ERA	Saves
Cory Scott, E. Carolina ....Sr.	41.1	1.52	22
Jeff Bajenaru, Oklahoma ....Sr.	48.1	2.61	20
Charlie Thames, Texas...........Jr.	77.0	2.22	19
Ozzie Lugo, Florida Int'l.........Fr.	28.0	4.50	17
Josh Brey, Liberty ....So.	28.0	1.61	16
Zane Carlson, Baylor ....Fr.	43.1	2.28	15
Nick Glaser, Clemson ....Jr.	40.1	2.45	15
Greg Bauer, Wichita St..........Sr.	46.1	2.72	15
Jackson Markert. Oral Roberts...Jr.	28.1	2.86	15
Scott Barber, S. Carolina ....Jr.	106.1	2.96	15

Other College World Series
Participants' final records in parentheses.

NCAA Div. II
at Montgomery, Ala. (May 27-June 3)

Participants: Central Missouri St. (50-13); Fort Hays St., Ks. (54-12); Gardner-Webb, NC (44-21); Indianapolis (42-23); North Florida (49-14); Slippery Rock, Pa. (37-14); Southeastern Oklahoma St. (43-12); St. Rose, NY (32-16-1).
Championship: Southeastern Oklahoma St. def. Fort Hays St., 7-2.

NAIA
at Lewiston, Id. (May 26-June 2)

Participants: Albertson, Id. (49-14); Bellevue, Neb. (49-28); Birmingham-Southern, Al. (46-20); Brewton-Parker, Ga. (61-17); Dallas Baptist, Tex. (43-23-1); Indiana Tech (47-22); Lewis-Clark St., Id. (59-12); The Masters, Calif. (37-15); Shawnee St., Oh. (48-16); St. Thomas, Fla. (43-14).
Championship: Lewis-Clark def. Dallas Baptist, 10-1.

NCAA Div. III
at Appleton, Wisc. (May 26-30)

Participants: Allegheny, Pa. (38-10); Chapman, Calif. (33-12-1); Cortland St., N.Y. (36-9); Emory, Ga. (33-16); Montclair St., N.J. (42-7-1); Southern Maine (35-14); St. Thomas, Minn. (36-14); Wartburg, Iowa (41-9).
Championship: Montclair St. def. St. Thomas, 6-2.

NJCAA Div. I
at Grand Junction, Colo. (May 27-June 3)

Participants: Allen County CC, Kan. (39-25); Briarcliffe, N.Y. (39-18); Dixie, Utah (49-11); Florida CC/Jacksonville (44-20); Grayson County, Tex. (55-11); Meridian CC, Miss. (46-19); Motlow St., Tenn. (56-13); San Jacinto, Tex. (43-17); Seminole St., Okla. (50-16); Triton, Il. (48-17).
Championship: Grayson County def. Motlow St., 14-1.

MLB Amateur Draft

First round selections at the 36th Amateur Draft held June 5-7, 2000 in New York. Clubs select in reverse order of their standing from the preceding season. The worst National League team selects first in even years and the worst American League team goes first in odd years. Leagues then alternate picks throughout the rounds.

First Round

No		Pos
1	Florida......Adrian Gonzalez, Eastlake HS, Bonita, Calif.	1B
2	Minnesota.......Adam Johnson, CS-Fullerton	RHP
3	Chicago-NL....Luis Montanez, Coral Park HS Miami, Fla.	SS
4	Kansas City .Michael Stodolka, Centennial HS Corona, Calif.	LHP
5	Montreal ....Justin Wayne, Stanford	RHP
6	Tampa Bay.Rocco Baldelli, Bishop Hendricken HS, Cumberland, R.I.	CF
7	Colorado .....Matthew Harrington, Palmdale (Calif.) HS	RHP
8	Detroit........Matthew Wheatland, Rancho Bernardo HS, Poway, Calif.	RHP
9	San Diego ..Mark Phillips, Hanover (Pa.) HS	LHP
10	Anaheim ....Joseph Torres, Gateway HS Kissimmee, Fla.	LHP
11	Milwaukee ..David Krynzel, Green Valley HS Henderson, Nev.	CF
12	Chicago-AL ......Joseph Borchard, Stanford	RF
13	St. Louis..............Shaun Boyd, Vista HS Pala, Calif.	2B
14	Baltimore..................Beau Hale, Texas	RHP
15	Philadelphia.............Chase Utley, UCLA	2B

No		Pos
16	a-New York-NL........William Traber, Loyola Marymount	LHP
17	Los Angeles .....Benjamin Diggins, Arizona	RHP
18	Toronto ....Miguel Negron, Manuela Toro HS Caguas, P.R.	CF
19	Pittsburgh ......Sean Burnett, Wellington (Fla.) Community HS	LHP
20	b-Anaheim ....Christopher Bootcheck, Auburn	RHP
21	San Francisco .. John Bonser, Gibbs Senior HS Pinellas Park, Fla.	RHP
22	Boston ......Phillip Dumatrait, Bakersfield Col.	LHP
23	Cincinnati ......David Espinosa, Gulliver Prep Miami, Fla.	SS
24	c-St. Louis.......Blake Williams, SW Texas St.	RHP
25	d-Texas....Scott Heard, Rancho Bernardo HS Poway, Calif.	C
26	Cleveland ..Corey Smith, Piscataway (N.J.) HS	SS
27	Houston ....Robert Stiehl, El Camino JC	C
28	New York-AL........David Parrish, Michigan	C
29	e-Atlanta ..Adam Wainwright, Glynn Academy St. Simons, Ga.	RHP
30	Atlanta ....Scott Thorman, Preston HS Cambridge, Conn.	3B

Acquired picks: a–from Seattle for signing John Olerud; **b**–from Oakland for signing Mike Magnante; **c**–from Texas for signing Darren Oliver; **d**–from NY Mets for signing Todd Zeile; **e**–from Arizona for signing Russ Springer.

Cresse Comes Full Circle

by Dave Ryan

AP/Wide World Photos

LSU's **Brad Cresse** celebrates after hitting the game-winning single at the College World Series.

One of the most memorable moments of my ESPN career is easy to recall. It was an early game in the 1998 College Baseball World Series.

I was sent into the stands of Rosenblatt Stadium in Omaha to interview Mark Cresse, at the time a bullpen coach for the Los Angeles Dodgers. His job on Tommy Lasorda's staff didn't allow for much free time. In fact it was the first time Mark had ever seen his son Brad, the star catcher for LSU, play in person. As he answered my questions, Brad crushed a hanging curve ball deep into the right field stands. The emotional moment was too much for Mark. He was moved to tears as his son circled the bases.

"This is why I came here!" he screamed. ."Unbelievable!"

That moment was still being talked about in Omaha when LSU returned to the College World Series in 2000. Brad approached me at the batting cage early in the week, thanking me again for the coverage from the 1998 event. As he went into the cage for his set of swings, he added, "Let's make a better ending this year!" Little did either of us know how much better it would be for Brad Cresse and the Tigers.

During one of LSU's early games, we interviewed Mark again in the stands. He answered questions about that incredible 1998 moment, and Brad's future as a fifth-round draft pick of the Arizona Diamondbacks. But there was a slight edge to his personality this time around. Brad was struggling mightily at the plate in Omaha. Opposing pitchers were giving him a steady diet of sliders and off-speed stuff away. He was striking out more than he was making contact, some at-bats in three straight pitches. He was taking extra batting practice, getting advice from Mark. Nothing worked. After leading the nation with 30 homers and 106 RBI, being a 1st team All-American selection, and the national catcher of the year, Brad Cresse was ice cold at the College World Series.

Watching from the dugout, I could see the frustrated look in his teammates' eyes. In key at bats, they were hoping their star hitter would come to life. It simply wasn't happening. Shouts of encouragement "C'mon number 22, this is your time!" could be heard in each of his at bats. Still, Cresse's normally lethal bat remained silent.

Despite the struggles of their best hitter, LSU used great pitching and clutch hitting to reach the championship game. Pitching-strong Stanford stood in the Tigers' way, with high draft picks Jason Young and Justin Wayne rested and available. Cresse was overmatched in his first two at bats against Wayne. Six sliders produced two strikeouts, and his nosedive slump reached new depths.

In the bottom of the 9th of a 5-5 game, Cresse had one more chance. With teammate Ryan Theriot at second base, and a national championship on the line, Cresse had one thing in mind.

"I just wanted a better swing than the prior two at bats against his slider. I knew it was coming."

A line drive to left field later, Theriot scampered home with the winning run. All the frustration of his struggles was over. Brad Cresse left the college game as a champion. ∎

Dave Ryan is an in-the-stands reporter for ESPN's college baseball coverage.

Minor League Triple-A Final Standings

Division champions (*) and Wild Card (†) winners are noted. Number of seasons listed after each manager refers to current tenure with club.

International League

North Division	W	L	Pct	GB
*Buffalo (Indians)	86	59	.593	—
†Scranton-WB (Phillies)	85	60	.586	1
Pawtucket (Red Sox)	82	61	.573	3
Syracuse (Blue Jays)	74	66	.529	9½
Rochester (Orioles)	65	79	.451	20½
Ottawa (Expos)	53	88	.376	31

South Division	W	L	Pct	GB
*Durham (Devil Rays)	81	62	.566	—
Charlotte (White Sox)	78	65	.545	3
Norfolk (Mets)	65	79	.451	16½
Richmond (Braves)	51	92	.357	30

West Division	W	L	Pct	GB
*Indianapolis (Brewers)	81	63	.563	—
Columbus (Yankees)	75	69	.521	6
Louisville (Reds)	71	73	.493	10
Toledo (Tigers)	55	86	.390	24½

Playoffs

Division Finals (Best-of-Five)

Scranton-WB 3 . . . . Buffalo 1
Indianapolis 3 . . . . Durham 2

Championship (Best-of-Five)

Scranton-WB vs. Indianapolis

Sept. 11	Scranton-WB, 6-4	at Scranton-WB
Sept. 12	Indianapolis, 6-3	at Scranton-WB
Sept. 13	Indianapolis, 4-3	at Indianapolis
Sept. 14	Scranton-WB, 1-0	at Indianapolis
Sept. 15	Indianapolis, 6-1	at Indianapolis

Indianapolis wins series, 3-2

Pacific Coast League

American Conference

East Division	W	L	Pct	GB
*Memphis (Cardinals)	82	60	.577	—
Oklahoma (Rangers)	69	72	.489	12½
New Orleans (Astros)	67	73	.479	14
Nashville (Pirates)	62	78	.443	19

Central Division	W	L	Pct	GB
*Albuquerque (Dodgers)	85	57	.599	—
Colorado Springs (Rockies)	71	68	.511	12½
Omaha (Royals)	63	78	.447	21½
Iowa (Cubs)	56	86	.394	29

Pacific Conference

West Division	W	L	Pct	GB
*Salt Lake (Twins)	88	53	.624	—
Tacoma (Mariners)	76	65	.539	12
Edmonton (Angels)	62	76	.449	24½
Calgary (Marlins)	58	82	.414	29½

South Division	W	L	Pct	GB
*Sacramento (A's)	89	53	.627	—
Las Vegas (Padres)	71	69	.507	17
Tucson (D'Backs)	67	72	.482	20½
Fresno (Giants)	57	82	.410	30½

Playoffs

Division Finals (Best-of-Five)

Salt Lake 3 . . . . Sacramento 2
Memphis 3 . . . . Albuquerque 2

Championship (Best-of-Five)

Salt Lake vs. Memphis

Sept. 12	Memphis, 12-4	at Salt Lake
Sept. 13	Salt Lake, 8-4	at Salt Lake
Sept. 14	Memphis, 6-4	at Memphis
Sept. 15	Memphis, 4-3 (13 inn.)	at Memphis

Memphis wins series, 3-1

Triple-A World Series

The Triple-A World Series was introduced in 1998 and will continue at least through 2001. Played between the champions of the International and Pacific Coast leagues, it is the first time in history that there is a single Triple-A champion on a continuing basis. All games are played at Cashman Field in Las Vegas.

Indianapolis vs. Memphis

(Best-of-Five)

Sept. 18	Indianapolis, 8-3
Sept. 19	Indianapolis, 3-2
Sept. 20	Memphis, 11-4
Sept. 21	Indianapolis, 9-2

Indianapolis wins series, 3-1
MVP: Santiago Perez, SS, Indianapolis

2000 Minor League All-Star Team

As presented by *Baseball America* and covering all Minor League levels.

Pos.	Name, Team (Major Affiliate)
C	J.R. House, Hickory (Pirates)
1B	Jason Hart, Midland/Sacramento (A's)
2B	Keith Ginter, Round Rock (Astros)
3B	Joe Crede, Birmingham (White Sox)
SS	Jose Ortiz, Sacramento (A's)
OF	Kevin Mench, Charlotte (Rangers)
OF	Chad Mottola, Syracuse (Blue Jays)
OF	Juan Silvestre, Lancaster (Mariners)
DH	Alex Cabrera, Tucson/El Paso (D'Backs)
SP	Roy Oswalt, Kissimmee/Round Rock (Astros)
SP	Christian Parra, Myrtle Beach (Braves)
SP	Jon Rauch*, Winston-Salem/Birm. (White Sox)
SP	Bud Smith, Arkansas/Memphis (Cardinals)
SP	Greg Wooten, New Haven (Mariners)
RP	Maximo Regalado, Vero/S. Antonio (Dodgers)

*Player of the Year

BASEBALL
1876-2000 Through the Years

The World Series

The World Series began in 1903 when Pittsburgh of the older National League (founded in 1876) invited Boston of the American League (founded in 1901) to play a best-of-9 game series to determine which of the two league champions was the best. Boston was the surprise winner, 5 games to 3. The 1904 NL champion New York Giants refused to play Boston the following year, so there was no Series. Giants' owner John T. Brush and his manager John McGraw both despised AL president Ban Johnson and considered the junior circuit to be a minor league. By the following year, however, Brush and Johnson had smoothed out their differences and the Giants agreed to play Philadelphia in a best-of-7 game series. Since then the World Series has been a best-of-7 format, except from 1919-21 when it returned to best-of-9.

After surviving two world wars and an earthquake in 1989, the World Series was cancelled for only the second time in 1994 due to the players' strike.

In the chart below, the National League teams are listed in CAPITAL letters. Also, each World Series champion's wins and losses are noted in parentheses after the Series score in games.

Multiple champions: New York Yankees (26); Philadelphia-Oakland A's and St. Louis Cardinals (9); Brooklyn-Los Angeles Dodgers (6); Boston Red Sox, Cincinnati Reds, New York-San Francisco Giants and Pittsburgh Pirates (5); Detroit Tigers (4); Baltimore Orioles, Boston-Milwaukee-Atlanta Braves and Washington Senators-Minnesota Twins (3); Chicago Cubs, Chicago White Sox, Cleveland Indians, New York Mets and Toronto Blue Jays (2).

Year	Winner	Manager	Series	Loser	Manager
1903	Boston Red Sox	Jimmy Collins	5-3 (LWLLWWWW)	PITTSBURGH	Fred Clarke
1904	Not held				
1905	NY GIANTS	John McGraw	4-1 (WLWWW)	Philadelphia A's	Connie Mack
1906	Chicago White Sox	Fielder Jones	4-2 (WLWLWW)	CHICAGO CUBS	Frank Chance
1907	CHICAGO CUBS	Frank Chance	4-0-1 (TWWWW)	Detroit	Hughie Jennings
1908	CHICAGO CUBS	Frank Chance	4-1 (WWLWW)	Detroit	Hughie Jennings
1909	PITTSBURGH	Fred Clarke	4-3 (WLWLWLW)	Detroit	Hughie Jennings
1910	Philadelphia A's	Connie Mack	4-1 (WWWLW)	CHICAGO CUBS	Frank Chance
1911	Philadelphia A's	Connie Mack	4-2 (LWWWLW)	NY GIANTS	John McGraw
1912	Boston Red Sox	Jake Stahl	4-3-1 (WTLWWLLW)	NY GIANTS	John McGraw
1913	Philadelphia A's	Connie Mack	4-1 (WLWWW)	NY GIANTS	John McGraw
1914	BOSTON BRAVES	George Stallings	4-0	Philadelphia A's	Connie Mack
1915	Boston Red Sox	Bill Carrigan	4-1 (LWWWW)	PHILA. PHILLIES	Pat Moran
1916	Boston Red Sox	Bill Carrigan	4-1 (WWLWW)	BROOKLYN	Wilbert Robinson
1917	Chicago White Sox	Pants Rowland	4-2 (WWLLWW)	NY GIANTS	John McGraw
1918	Boston Red Sox	Ed Barrow	4-2 (WLWWLW)	CHICAGO CUBS	Fred Mitchell
1919	CINCINNATI	Pat Moran	5-3 (WWLWWLLW)	Chicago White Sox	Kid Gleason
1920	Cleveland	Tris Speaker	5-2 (WLLWWWW)	BROOKLYN	Wilbert Robinson
1921	NY GIANTS	John McGraw	5-3 (LLWWLWWW)	NY Yankees	Miller Huggins
1922	NY GIANTS	John McGraw	4-0-1 (WTWWW)	NY Yankees	Miller Huggins
1923	NY Yankees	Miller Huggins	4-2 (LWLWWW)	NY GIANTS	John McGraw
1924	Washington	Bucky Harris	4-3 (LWLWLW)	NY GIANTS	John McGraw
1925	PITTSBURGH	Bill McKechnie	4-3 (LWLLWW)	Washington	Bucky Harris
1926	ST.L. CARDINALS	Rogers Hornsby	4-3 (LWWLLWW)	NY Yankees	Miller Huggins
1927	NY Yankees	Miller Huggins	4-0	PITTSBURGH	Donie Bush
1928	NY Yankees	Miller Huggins	4-0	ST.L. CARDINALS	Bill McKechnie
1929	Philadelphia A's	Connie Mack	4-1 (WWLWW)	CHICAGO CUBS	Joe McCarthy
1930	Philadelphia A's	Connie Mack	4-2 (WWLLWW)	ST.L. CARDINALS	Gabby Street
1931	ST.L. CARDINALS	Gabby Street	4-3 (LWWLWLW)	Philadelphia A's	Connie Mack
1932	NY Yankees	Joe McCarthy	4-0	CHICAGO CUBS	Charlie Grimm
1933	NY GIANTS	Bill Terry	4-1 (WWLWW)	Washington	Joe Cronin
1934	ST.L. CARDINALS	Frankie Frisch	4-3 (WLWLLWW)	Detroit	Mickey Cochrane
1935	Detroit	Mickey Cochrane	4-2 (LWWWLW)	CHICAGO CUBS	Charlie Grimm
1936	NY Yankees	Joe McCarthy	4-2 (LWWWLW)	NY GIANTS	Bill Terry
1937	NY Yankees	Joe McCarthy	4-1 (WWWLW)	NY GIANTS	Bill Terry
1938	NY Yankees	Joe McCarthy	4-0	CHICAGO CUBS	Gabby Hartnett
1939	NY Yankees	Joe McCarthy	4-0	CINCINNATI	Bill McKechnie
1940	CINCINNATI	Bill McKechnie	4-3 (LWLWLWW)	Detroit	Del Baker
1941	NY Yankees	Joe McCarthy	4-1 (WLWWW)	BKLN. DODGERS	Leo Durocher
1942	ST.L. CARDINALS	Billy Southworth	4-1 (LWWWW)	NY Yankees	Joe McCarthy
1943	NY Yankees	Joe McCarthy	4-1 (WLWWW)	ST.L. CARDINALS	Billy Southworth
1944	ST.L. CARDINALS	Billy Southworth	4-2 (LWLWWW)	St. Louis Browns	Luke Sewell

Year	Winner	Manager	Series	Loser	Manager
1945	Detroit	Steve O'Neill	4-3 (LWLWLWLW)	CHICAGO CUBS	Charlie Grimm
1946	ST.L. CARDINALS	Eddie Dyer	4-3 (LWLWLWLW)	Boston Red Sox	Joe Cronin
1947	NY Yankees	Bucky Harris	4-3 (WWLLWLW)	BKLN. DODGERS	Burt Shotton
1948	Cleveland	Lou Boudreau	4-2 (LWWWLW)	BOSTON BRAVES	Billy Southworth
1949	NY Yankees	Casey Stengel	4-1 (WLWWW)	BKLN. DODGERS	Burt Shotton
1950	NY Yankees	Casey Stengel	4-0	PHILA. PHILLIES	Eddie Sawyer
1951	NY Yankees	Casey Stengel	4-2 (LWLWWW)	NY GIANTS	Leo Durocher
1952	NY Yankees	Casey Stengel	4-3 (LWLWLWW)	BKLN. DODGERS	Charlie Dressen
1953	NY Yankees	Casey Stengel	4-2 (WWLLWW)	BKLN. DODGERS	Charlie Dressen
1954	NY GIANTS	Leo Durocher	4-0	Cleveland	Al Lopez
1955	BKLN. DODGERS	Walter Alston	4-3 (LLWWWLW)	NY Yankees	Casey Stengel
1956	NY Yankees	Casey Stengel	4-3 (LLWWWLW)	BKLN. DODGERS	Walter Alston
1957	MILW. BRAVES	Fred Haney	4-3 (LWLWLWW)	NY Yankees	Casey Stengel
1958	NY Yankees	Casey Stengel	4-3 (LWLLWWW)	MILW. BRAVES	Fred Haney
1959	LA DODGERS	Walter Alston	4-2 (LWWWLW)	Chicago White Sox	Al Lopez
1960	PITTSBURGH	Danny Murtaugh	4-3 (WLLWWLW)	NY Yankees	Casey Stengel
1961	NY Yankees	Ralph Houk	4-1 (WLWWW)	CINCINNATI	Fred Hutchinson
1962	NY Yankees	Ralph Houk	4-3 (WLWLWLW)	SF GIANTS	Alvin Dark
1963	LA DODGERS	Walter Alston	4-0	NY Yankees	Ralph Houk
1964	ST.L. CARDINALS	Johnny Keane	4-3 (WLWLWLW)	NY Yankees	Yogi Berra
1965	LA DODGERS	Walter Alston	4-3 (LLWWWLW)	Minnesota	Sam Mele
1966	Baltimore	Hank Bauer	4-0	LA DODGERS	Walter Alston
1967	ST.L. CARDINALS	Red Schoendienst	4-3 (WLWLWLW)	Boston Red Sox	Dick Williams
1968	Detroit	Mayo Smith	4-3 (LWLLWWW)	ST.L. CARDINALS	Red Schoendienst
1969	NY METS	Gil Hodges	4-1 (LWWWW)	Baltimore	Earl Weaver
1970	Baltimore	Earl Weaver	4-1 (WWWLW)	CINCINNATI	Sparky Anderson
1971	PITTSBURGH	Danny Murtaugh	4-3 (LLWWWLW)	Baltimore	Earl Weaver
1972	Oakland A's	Dick Williams	4-3 (WWLWLLW)	CINCINNATI	Sparky Anderson
1973	Oakland A's	Dick Williams	4-3 (WLWLLWW)	NY METS	Yogi Berra
1974	Oakland A's	Alvin Dark	4-1 (WLWWW)	LA DODGERS	Walter Alston
1975	CINCINNATI	Sparky Anderson	4-3 (LWWWLWLW)	Boston Red Sox	Darrell Johnson
1976	CINCINNATI	Sparky Anderson	4-0	NY Yankees	Billy Martin
1977	NY Yankees	Billy Martin	4-2 (WWLWLW)	LA DODGERS	Tommy Lasorda
1978	NY Yankees	Bob Lemon	4-2 (LLWWWW)	LA DODGERS	Tommy Lasorda
1979	PITTSBURGH	Chuck Tanner	4-3 (LWLLWWW)	Baltimore	Earl Weaver
1980	PHILA. PHILLIES	Dallas Green	4-2 (WWLLWW)	Kansas City	Jim Frey
1981	LA DODGERS	Tommy Lasorda	4-2 (LLWWWW)	NY Yankees	Bob Lemon
1982	ST.L. CARDINALS	Whitey Herzog	4-3 (LWWLWLW)	Milwaukee Brewers	Harvey Kuenn
1983	Baltimore	Joe Altobelli	4-1 (LWWWW)	PHILA. PHILLIES	Paul Owens
1984	Detroit	Sparky Anderson	4-1 (WLWWW)	SAN DIEGO	Dick Williams
1985	Kansas City	Dick Howser	4-3 (LLWLWWW)	ST.L. CARDINALS	Whitey Herzog
1986	NY METS	Davey Johnson	4-3 (LLWWLWW)	Boston Red Sox	John McNamara
1987	Minnesota	Tom Kelly	4-3 (WWLLLWW)	ST.L. CARDINALS	Whitey Herzog
1988	LA DODGERS	Tommy Lasorda	4-1 (WWLWW)	Oakland A's	Tony La Russa
1989	Oakland A's	Tony La Russa	4-0	SF GIANTS	Roger Craig
1990	CINCINNATI	Lou Piniella	4-0	Oakland A's	Tony La Russa
1991	Minnesota	Tom Kelly	4-3 (WWLLLWW)	ATLANTA BRAVES	Bobby Cox
1992	Toronto	Cito Gaston	4-2 (LWWWLW)	ATLANTA BRAVES	Bobby Cox
1993	Toronto	Cito Gaston	4-2 (WLWWLW)	PHILA. PHILLIES	Jim Fregosi
1994	Not held				
1995	ATLANTA BRAVES	Bobby Cox	4-2 (WWLWLW)	Cleveland	Mike Hargrove
1996	NY Yankees	Joe Torre	4-2 (LLWWWW)	ATLANTA BRAVES	Bobby Cox
1997	FLORIDA MARLINS	Jim Leyland	4-3 (WLWLWLW)	Cleveland	Mike Hargrove
1998	NY Yankees	Joe Torre	4-0	SAN DIEGO	Bruce Bochy
1999	NY Yankees	Joe Torre	4-0	ATLANTA BRAVES	Bobby Cox
2000	NY Yankees	Joe Torre	4-1 (WWLWW)	NY METS	Bobby Valentine

Most Valuable Players

Currently selected by media panel and World Series official scorers. Presented by *Sport* magazine from 1955-88 and by Major League Baseball since 1989. Winner who did not play for World Series champions is in **bold** type.

Multiple winners: Bob Gibson, Reggie Jackson and Sandy Koufax (2).

Year	Year	Year
1955 Johnny Podres, Bklyn, P	1964 Bob Gibson, St.L., P	1973 Reggie Jackson, Oak., OF
1956 Don Larsen, NY, P	1965 Sandy Koufax, LA, P	1974 Rollie Fingers, Oak., P
1957 Lew Burdette, Mil., P	1966 Frank Robinson, Bal., OF	1975 Pete Rose, Cin., 3B
1958 Bob Turley, NY, P	1967 Bob Gibson, St.L., P	1976 Johnny Bench, Cin., C
1959 Larry Sherry, LA, P	1968 Mickey Lolich, Det., P	1977 Reggie Jackson, NY, OF
1960 **Bobby Richardson**, NY, 2B	1969 Donn Clendenon, NY, 1B	1978 Bucky Dent, NY, SS
1961 Whitey Ford, NY, P	1970 Brooks Robinson, Bal., 3B	1979 Willie Stargell, Pit., 1B
1962 Ralph Terry, NY, P	1971 Roberto Clemente, Pit., OF	1980 Mike Schmidt, Phi., 3B
1963 Sandy Koufax, LA, P	1972 Gene Tenace, Oak., C	1981 Pedro Guerrero, LA, OF;

Year	Year	Year
Ron Cey, LA, 3B; & Steve Yeager, LA, C	1987 Frank Viola, Min., P	1994 Series not held.
1982 Darrell Porter, St.L., C	1988 Orel Hershiser, LA, P	1995 Tom Glavine, Atl., P
1983 Rick Dempsey, Bal., C	1989 Dave Stewart, Oak., P	1996 John Wetteland, NY, P
1984 Alan Trammell, Det., SS	1990 Jose Rijo, Cin., P	1997 Livan Hernandez, Fla., P
1985 Bret Saberhagen, KC, P	1991 Jack Morris, Min., P	1998 Scott Brosius, NY, 3B
1986 Ray Knight, NY, 3B	1992 Pat Borders, Tor., C	1999 Mariano Rivera, NY, P
	1993 Paul Molitor, Tor., DH/1B/3B	2000 Derek Jeter, NY, SS

All-Time World Series Leaders
CAREER
World Series leaders through 2000. Years listed indicate number of World Series appearances.

Hitting

Games
	Yrs	Gm
Yogi Berra, NY Yankees	14	75
Mickey Mantle, NY Yankees	12	65
Elston Howard, NY Yankees-Boston	10	54
Hank Bauer, NY Yankees	9	53
Gil McDougald, NY Yankees	8	53

At Bats
	Yrs	AB
Yogi Berra, NY Yankees	14	259
Mickey Mantle, NY Yankees	12	230
Joe DiMaggio, NY Yankees	10	199
Frankie Frisch, NY Giants-St.L. Cards	8	197
Gil McDougald, NY Yankees	8	190

Batting Avg. (minimum 50 AB)
	AB	H	Avg
Pepper Martin, St.L. Cards	55	23	.418
Paul Molitor, Mil. Brewers-Tor. Blue Jays	55	23	.418
Lou Brock, St. Louis	87	34	.391
Marquis Grissom, Atl-Cle.	77	30	.390
Thurman Munson, NY Yankees	67	25	.373
George Brett, Kansas City	51	19	.373
Hank Aaron, Milw. Braves	55	20	.364

Hits
	AB	H	Avg
Yogi Berra, NY Yankees	259	71	.274
Mickey Mantle, NY Yankees	230	59	.257
Frankie Frisch, NYG-St.L. Cards.	197	58	.294
Joe DiMaggio, NY Yankees	199	54	.271
Hank Bauer, NY Yankees	188	46	.245
Pee Wee Reese, Brooklyn	169	46	.272

Runs
	Gm	R
Mickey Mantle, NY Yankees	65	42
Yogi Berra, NY Yankees	75	41
Babe Ruth, Boston Red Sox-NY Yankees	41	37
Lou Gehrig, NY Yankees	34	30
Joe DiMaggio, NY Yankees	51	27

Home Runs
	AB	HR
Mickey Mantle, NY Yankees	230	18
Babe Ruth, Boston Red Sox-NY Yankees	129	15
Yogi Berra, NY Yankees	259	12
Duke Snider, Brooklyn-LA	133	11
Lou Gehrig, NY Yankees	119	10
Reggie Jackson, Oakland-NY Yankees	98	10

Runs Batted In
	Gm	RBI
Mickey Mantle, NY Yankees	65	40
Yogi Berra, NY Yankees	75	39
Lou Gehrig, NY Yankees	34	35
Babe Ruth, Boston Red Sox-NY Yankees	41	33
Joe DiMaggio, NY Yankees	51	30

World Series Appearances
In the 96 years that the World Series has been contested, American League teams have won 57 championships while National League teams have won 39.

The following teams are ranked by number of appearances through the 2000 World Series; (*) indicates AL teams.

	App	W	L	Pct.	Last Series	Last Title
NY Yankees*	37	26	11	.703	2000	2000
Bklyn/LA Dodgers	18	6	12	.333	1988	1988
NY/SF Giants	16	5	11	.313	1989	1954
St.L. Cardinals	15	9	6	.600	1987	1982
Phi/KC/Oak.A's*	14	9	5	.643	1990	1989
Chicago Cubs	10	2	8	.200	1945	1908
Boston Red Sox*	9	5	4	.556	1986	1918
Cincinnati Reds	9	5	4	.556	1990	1990
Detroit Tigers*	9	4	5	.444	1984	1984
Bos/Mil/Atl.Braves	9	3	6	.333	1999	1995
Pittsburgh Pirates	7	5	2	.714	1979	1979
St.L/Bal.Orioles*	7	3	4	.429	1983	1983
Wash/Min.Twins*	6	3	3	.500	1991	1991
Cle.Indians*	5	2	3	.400	1997	1948
Phi.Phillies	5	1	4	.200	1993	1980
Chi.White Sox*	4	2	2	.500	1959	1917
NY Mets	4	2	2	.500	2000	1986
Tor. Blue Jays*	2	2	0	1.000	1993	1993
KC Royals*	2	1	1	.500	1985	1985
SD Padres	2	0	2	.000	1998	—
Fla. Marlins	1	1	0	1.000	1997	1997
Sea/Mil.Brewers*	1	0	1	.000	1982	—

Stolen Bases
	Gm	SB
Lou Brock, St. Louis	21	14
Eddie Collins, Phi. A's-Chisox	34	14
Frank Chance, Chi. Cubs	20	10
Davey Lopes, Los Angeles	23	10
Phil Rizzuto, NY Yankees	52	10

Total Bases
	Gm	TB
Mickey Mantle, NY Yankees	65	123
Yogi Berra, NY Yankees	75	117
Babe Ruth, Boston Red Sox-NY Yankees	41	96
Lou Gehrig, NY Yankees	34	87
Joe DiMaggio, NY Yankees	51	84

Slugging Pct. (minimum 50 AB)
	AB	Pct
Reggie Jackson, Oakland-NY Yankees	98	.755
Babe Ruth, Boston Red Sox-NY Yankees	129	.744
Lou Gehrig, NY Yankees	119	.731
Al Simmons, Phi. A's-Cincinnati	73	.658
Lou Brock, St. Louis	87	.655

Pitching

Games

	Yrs	Gm
Whitey Ford, NY Yankees	11	22
Rollie Fingers, Oakland	3	16
Allie Reynolds, NY Yankees	6	15
Bob Turley, NY Yankees	5	15
Mike Stanton, Atlanta-NY Yankees	5	15
Clay Carroll, Cincinnati	3	14
Mariano Rivera, NY Yankees	4	14

Wins

	Gm	W-L
Whitey Ford, NY Yankees	22	10-8
Bob Gibson, St. Louis	9	7-2
Allie Reynolds, NY Yankees	15	7-2
Red Ruffing, NY Yankees	10	7-2
Lefty Gomez, NY Yankees	7	6-0
Chief Bender, Philadelphia A's	10	6-4
Waite Hoyt, NY Yankees-Phi. A's	12	6-4

ERA (minimum 25 IP)

	Gm	IP	ERA
Jack Billingham, Cincinnati	7	25.1	0.36
Harry Brecheen, St. Louis	7	32.2	0.83
Babe Ruth, Boston Red Sox	3	31.0	0.87
Sherry Smith, Brooklyn	3	30.1	0.89
Sandy Koufax, Los Angeles	8	57.0	0.95

Saves

	Gm	IP	Sv
Mariano Rivera, NY Yankees	14	20.2	7
Rollie Fingers, Oakland	16	33.1	6
Allie Reynolds, NY Yankees	15	77.1	4
Johnny Murphy, NY Yankees	8	16.1	4
John Wetteland, NY Yankees	5	4.1	4
Eight pitchers tied with 3 each.			

Shutouts

	GS	CG	ShO
Christy Mathewson, NY Giants	11	10	4
Three Finger Brown, Chi. Cubs	7	5	3
Whitey Ford, NY Yankees	22	7	3
Seven pitchers tied with 2 each.			

Innings Pitched

	Gm	IP
Whitey Ford, NY Yankees	22	146.0
Christy Mathewson, NY Giants	11	101.2
Red Ruffing, NY Yankees	10	85.2
Chief Bender, Philadelphia A's	10	85.0
Waite Hoyt, NY Yankees-Phi. A's	12	83.2

Complete Games

	GS	CG	W-L
Christy Mathewson, NY Giants	11	10	5-5
Chief Bender, Philadelphia A's	10	9	6-4
Bob Gibson, St. Louis	9	8	7-2
Whitey Ford, NY Yankees	22	7	10-8
Red Ruffing, NY Yankees	10	7	7-2

Strikeouts

	Gm	IP	SO
Whitey Ford, NY Yankees	22	146.0	94
Bob Gibson, St. Louis	9	81.0	92
Allie Reynolds, NY Yankees	15	77.1	62
Sandy Koufax, Los Angeles	8	57.0	61
Red Ruffing, NY Yankees	10	85.2	61

Losses

	Gm	W-L
Whitey Ford, NY Yankees	22	10-8
Christy Mathewson, NY Giants	11	5-5
Joe Bush, Phi. A's-Bosox-NY Yankees	9	2-5
Rube Marquard, NY Giants-Brooklyn	11	2-5
Eddie Plank, Philadelphia A's	7	2-5
Schoolboy Rowe, Detroit	8	2-5

League Championship Series

Division play came to the major leagues in 1969 when both the American and National Leagues expanded to 12 teams. With an East and West Division in each league, League Championship Series (LCS) became necessary to determine the NL and AL pennant winners. In 1994, teams were realigned into three divisions, the East, Central, and West with division winners and one wildcard team playing a best of five series to determine the LCS competitors. In the charts below, the East Division champions are noted by the letter E, the Central division champions by C and the West Division champions by W. A wildcard winner is noted by WC. Also, each playoff winner's wins and losses are noted in parentheses after the series score. The LCS changed from best-of-5 to best-of-7 in 1985. Each league's LCS was cancelled in 1994 due to the players' strike.

National League

Multiple champions: Atlanta, Cincinnati and LA Dodgers (5); NY Mets (4); Philadelphia and St. Louis (3); Pittsburgh and San Diego (2).

Year	Winner	Manager	Series		Loser	Manager
1969	E- New York	Gil Hodges	3-0		W- Atlanta	Lum Harris
1970	W- Cincinnati	Sparky Anderson	3-0		E- Pittsburgh	Danny Murtaugh
1971	E- Pittsburgh	Danny Murtaugh	3-1 (LWWW)		W- San Francisco	Charlie Fox
1972	W- Cincinnati	Sparky Anderson	3-2 (LWLWW)		E- Pittsburgh	Bill Virdon
1973	E- New York	Yogi Berra	3-2 (LWWLW)		W- Cincinnati	Sparky Anderson
1974	W- Los Angeles	Walter Alston	3-1 (WWLW)		E- Pittsburgh	Danny Murtaugh
1975	W- Cincinnati	Sparky Anderson	3-0		E- Pittsburgh	Danny Murtaugh
1976	W- Cincinnati	Sparky Anderson	3-0		E- Philadelphia	Danny Ozark
1977	W- Los Angeles	Tommy Lasorda	3-1 (LWWW)		E- Philadelphia	Danny Ozark
1978	W- Los Angeles	Tommy Lasorda	3-1 (WWLW)		E- Philadelphia	Danny Ozark
1979	E- Pittsburgh	Chuck Tanner	3-0		W- Cincinnati	John McNamara
1980	E- Philadelphia	Dallas Green	3-2 (WLLWW)		W- Houston	Bill Virdon
1981	W- Los Angeles	Tommy Lasorda	3-2 (WLLWW)		E- Montreal	Jim Fanning
1982	E- St. Louis	Whitey Herzog	3-0		W- Atlanta	Joe Torre
1983	E- Philadelphia	Paul Owens	3-1 (WLWW)		W- Los Angeles	Tommy Lasorda
1984	W- San Diego	Dick Williams	3-2 (LLWWW)		E- Chicago	Jim Frey
1985	E- St. Louis	Whitey Herzog	4-2 (LWWWW)		W- Los Angeles	Tommy Lasorda
1986	E- New York	Davey Johnson	4-2 (LWWLWW)		W- Houston	Hal Lanier
1987	E- St. Louis	Whitey Herzog	4-3 (WLWWLLWW)		W- San Francisco	Roger Craig
1988	W- Los Angeles	Tommy Lasorda	4-3 (LWLWLWW)		E- New York	Davey Johnson
1989	W- San Francisco	Roger Craig	4-1 (WLWWW)		E- Chicago	Don Zimmer
1990	W- Cincinnati	Lou Piniella	4-2 (LWWWLW)		E- Pittsburgh	Jim Leyland
1991	W- Atlanta	Bobby Cox	4-3 (LWWWLLW)		E- Pittsburgh	Jim Leyland

Year	Winner	Manager	Series	Loser	Manager
1992	W- Atlanta	Bobby Cox	4-3 (WWLWLLW)	E- Pittsburgh	Jim Leyland
1993	E- Philadelphia	Jim Fregosi	4-2 (WLLWWW)	W- Atlanta	Bobby Cox
1994	Not held				
1995	E- Atlanta	Bobby Cox	4-0	C- Cincinnati	Davey Johnson
1996	E- Atlanta	Bobby Cox	4-3 (WLLLWWW)	C- St. Louis	Tony La Russa
1997	WC-Florida	Jim Leyland	4-2 (WLWLWW)	E-Atlanta	Bobby Cox
1998	W-San Diego	Bruce Bochy	4-2 (WWWLLW)	E-Atlanta	Bobby Cox
1999	E-Atlanta	Bobby Cox	4-2 (WWWWLLW)	WC-New York	Bobby Valentine
2000	WC-New York	Bobby Valentine	4-1 (WWLWW)	C- St. Louis	Tony La Russa

NLCS Most Valuable Players

Winners who did not play for NLCS champions are in **bold** type.

Multiple winner: Steve Garvey (2).

Year		
1977 Dusty Baker, LA, OF	1986 **Mike Scott,** Hou., P	1994 LCS not held.
1978 Steve Garvey, LA, 1B	1987 **Jeff Leonard,** SF, OF	1995 Mike Devereaux, Atl., OF
1979 Willie Stargell, Pit., 1B	1988 Orel Hershiser, LA, P	1996 Javy Lopez, Atl., C
1980 Manny Trillo, Phi., 2B	1989 Will Clark, SF, 1B	1997 Livan Hernandez, Fla., P
1981 Burt Hooton, LA, P	1990 Rob Dibble, Cin., P	1998 Sterling Hitchcock, SD, P
1982 Darrell Porter, St.L., C	& Randy Myers, Cin., P	1999 Eddie Perez, Atl., C
1983 Gary Matthews, Phi., OF	1991 Steve Avery, Atl., P	2000 Mike Hampton, NY, P
1984 Steve Garvey, SD, 1B	1992 John Smoltz, Atl., P	
1985 Ozzie Smith, St.L., SS	1993 Curt Schilling, Phi., P	

American League

Multiple champions: NY Yankees (8); Oakland (6); Baltimore (5); Boston, Cleveland, Kansas City, Minnesota and Toronto (2).

Year	Winner	Manager	Series	Loser	Manager
1969	E- Baltimore	Earl Weaver	3-0	W- Minnesota	Billy Martin
1970	E- Baltimore	Earl Weaver	3-0	W- Minnesota	Bill Rigney
1971	E- Baltimore	Earl Weaver	3-0	W- Oakland	Dick Williams
1972	W- Oakland	Dick Williams	3-2 (WWLLW)	E- Detroit	Billy Martin
1973	W- Oakland	Dick Williams	3-2 (LWWLW)	E- Baltimore	Earl Weaver
1974	W- Oakland	Alvin Dark	3-1 (LWWW)	E- Baltimore	Earl Weaver
1975	E- Boston	Darrell Johnson	3-0	W- Oakland	Alvin Dark
1976	E- New York	Billy Martin	3-2 (WLWLW)	W- Kansas City	Whitey Herzog
1977	E- New York	Billy Martin	3-2 (LWLWW)	W- Kansas City	Whitey Herzog
1978	E- New York	Bob Lemon	3-1 (WLWW)	W- Kansas City	Whitey Herzog
1979	E- Baltimore	Earl Weaver	3-1 (WWLW)	W- California	Jim Fregosi
1980	W- Kansas City	Jim Frey	3-0	E- New York	Dick Howser
1981	E- New York	Bob Lemon	3-0	W- Oakland	Billy Martin
1982	E- Milwaukee	Harvey Kuenn	3-2 (LLWWW)	W- California	Gene Mauch
1983	E- Baltimore	Joe Altobelli	3-1 (LWWW)	W- Chicago	Tony La Russa
1984	E- Detroit	Sparky Anderson	3-0	W- Kansas City	Dick Howser
1985	W- Kansas City	Dick Howser	4-3 (LLWLWWW)	E- Toronto	Bobby Cox
1986	E- Boston	John McNamara	4-3 (LWLLWWW)	W- California	Gene Mauch
1987	W- Minnesota	Tom Kelly	4-1 (WWLWW)	E- Detroit	Sparky Anderson
1988	W- Oakland	Tony La Russa	4-0	E- Boston	Joe Morgan
1989	W- Oakland	Tony La Russa	4-1 (WWLWW)	E- Toronto	Cito Gaston
1990	W- Oakland	Tony La Russa	4-0	E- Boston	Joe Morgan
1991	W- Minnesota	Tom Kelly	4-1 (WLWWW)	E- Toronto	Cito Gaston
1992	E- Toronto	Cito Gaston	4-2 (LWWWLW)	W- Oakland	Tony La Russa
1993	E- Toronto	Cito Gaston	4-2 (WWLLWW)	W- Chicago	Gene Lamont
1994	Not held				
1995	C- Cleveland	Mike Hargrove	4-2 (LWLWWW)	W- Seattle	Lou Piniella
1996	E- New York	Joe Torre	4-1 (WLWWW)	WC- Baltimore	Davey Johnson
1997	C- Cleveland	Mike Hargrove	4-2 (LWWWLW)	E- Baltimore	Davey Johnson
1998	E- New York	Joe Torre	4-2 (WLLWWW)	C- Cleveland	Mike Hargrove
1999	E- New York	Joe Torre	4-1 (WLWWW)	WC- Boston	Jimy Williams
2000	E- New York	Joe Torre	4-2 (LWWWLW)	WC- Seattle	Lou Piniella

ALCS Most Valuable Players

Winner who did not play for ALCS champions is in **bold** type.

Multiple winner: Dave Stewart (2).

Year		
1980 Frank White, KC, 2B	1987 Gary Gaetti, Min., 3B	1994 LCS not held.
1981 Graig Nettles, NY, 3B	1988 Dennis Eckersley, Oak., P	1995 Orel Hershiser, Cle., P
1982 **Fred Lynn,** Cal., CF	1989 Rickey Henderson, Oak., LF	1996 Bernie Williams, NY, OF
1983 Mike Boddicker, Bal., P	1990 Dave Stewart, Oak., P	1997 Marquis Grissom, Cle., OF
1984 Kirk Gibson, Det., OF	1991 Kirby Puckett, Min., OF	1998 David Wells, NY, P
1985 George Brett, KC, 3B	1992 Roberto Alomar, Tor., 2B	1999 Orlando Hernandez, NY, P
1986 Marty Barrett, Bos., 2B	1993 Dave Stewart, Tor., P	2000 Dave Justice, NY, OF

Other Playoffs

Ten times since 1946, playoffs have been necessary to decide league or division championships or wild card berths when two teams were tied at the end of the regular season. Additionally, in the strike year of 1981 there were playoffs between the first and second half-season champions in both leagues.

National League

Year	NL	W	L	Manager	Year	NL East	W	L	Manager
1946	Brooklyn	96	58	Leo Durocher	1981	(1st Half) Philadelphia	34	21	Dallas Green
	St. Louis	96	58	Eddie Dyer		(2nd Half) Montreal	30	23	Jim Fanning
	Playoff: (Best-of-3) St. Louis, 2-0					Playoff: (Best-of-5) Montreal, 3-2 (WWLLW)			

Year	NL	W	L	Manager		NL West	W	L	Manager
1951	Brooklyn	96	58	Charlie Dressen	1981	(1st Half) Los Angeles	36	21	Tommy Lasorda
	New York	96	58	Leo Durocher		(2nd Half) Houston	33	20	Bill Virdon
	Playoff: (Best-of-3) New York, 2-1 (WLW)					Playoff: (Best-of-5) Los Angeles, 3-2 (LLWWW)			

Year	NL	W	L	Manager		NL Wild Card	W	L	Manager
1959	Milwaukee	86	68	Fred Haney	1998	Chicago	89	73	Jim Riggleman
	Los Angeles	86	68	Walter Alston		San Francisco	89	73	Dusty Baker
	Playoff: (Best-of-3) Los Angeles, 2-0					Playoff: (1 game) Chicago, 5-3 (at Chicago)			

Year	NL	W	L	Manager		NL Wild Card	W	L	Manager
1962	Los Angeles	101	61	Walter Alston	1999	Cincinnati	96	66	Jack McKeon
	San Francisco	101	61	Alvin Dark		New York	96	66	Bobby Valentine
	Playoff: (Best-of-3) San Francisco, 2-1 (WLW)					Playoff: (1 game) New York, 5-0 (at Cincinnati)			

Year	NL West	W	L	Manager
1980	Houston	92	70	Bill Virdon
	Los Angeles	92	70	Tommy Lasorda
	Playoff: (1 game) Houston, 7-1 (at LA)			

American League

Year	AL	W	L	Manager	Year	AL West	W	L	Manager
1948	Boston	96	58	Joe McCarthy	1981	(1st Half) Oakland	37	23	Billy Martin
	Cleveland	96	58	Lou Boudreau		(2nd Half) Kan. City	30	23	Jim Frey
	Playoff: (1 game) Cleveland, 8-3 (at Boston)					Playoff: (Best-of-5), Oakland, 3-0			

Year	AL East	W	L	Manager		AL West	W	L	Manager
1978	Boston	99	63	Don Zimmer	1995	Seattle	78	66	Lou Piniella
	New York	99	63	Bob Lemon		California	78	66	M. Lachemann
	Playoff: (1 game) New York, 5-4 (at Boston)					Playoff: (1 game) Seattle, 9-1 (at Seattle)			

Year	AL East	W	L	Manager
1981	(1st Half) N.Y.	34	22	Bob Lemon
	(2nd Half) Milw.	31	22	Buck Rodgers
	Playoff: (Best-of-5) New York, 3-2 (WWLLW)			

Regular Season League & Division Winners

Regular season National and American League pennant winners from 1900-68, as well as West and East divisional champions from 1969-93. In 1994, both leagues went to three divisions, West, Central and East, and each league also sent a wild card (WC) team to the playoffs. Note that (*) indicates 1994 divisional champion is unofficial (due to the players' strike). Note that **GA** column indicates games ahead of the second place club.

National League

Year		W	L	Pct	GA	Year		W	L	Pct	GA
1900	Brooklyn	82	54	.603	4½	1925	Pittsburgh	95	58	.621	8½
1901	Pittsburgh	90	49	.647	7½	1926	St. Louis	89	65	.578	2
1902	Pittsburgh	103	36	.741	27½	1927	Pittsburgh	94	60	.610	1½
1903	Pittsburgh	91	49	.650	6½	1928	St. Louis	95	59	.617	2
1904	New York	106	47	.693	13	1929	Chicago	98	54	.645	10½
1905	New York	105	48	.686	9	1930	St. Louis	92	62	.597	2
1906	Chicago	116	36	.763	20	1931	St. Louis	101	53	.656	13
1907	Chicago	107	45	.704	17	1932	Chicago	90	64	.584	4
1908	Chicago	99	55	.643	1	1933	New York	91	61	.599	5
1909	Pittsburgh	110	42	.724	6½	1934	St. Louis	95	58	.621	2
1910	Chicago	104	50	.675	13	1935	Chicago	100	54	.649	4
1911	New York	99	54	.647	7½	1936	New York	92	62	.597	5
1912	New York	103	48	.682	10	1937	New York	95	57	.625	3
1913	New York	101	51	.664	12½	1938	Chicago	89	63	.586	2
1914	Boston	94	59	.614	10½	1939	Cincinnati	97	57	.630	4½
1915	Philadelphia	90	62	.592	7	1940	Cincinnati	100	53	.654	12
1916	Brooklyn	94	60	.610	2½	1941	Brooklyn	100	54	.649	2½
1917	New York	98	56	.636	10	1942	St. Louis	106	48	.688	2
1918	Chicago	84	45	.651	10½	1943	St. Louis	105	49	.682	18
1919	Cincinnati	96	44	.686	9	1944	St. Louis	105	49	.682	14½
1920	Brooklyn	93	61	.604	7	1945	Chicago	98	56	.636	3
1921	New York	94	59	.614	4	1946	St. Louis†	98	58	.628	2
1922	New York	93	61	.604	7	1947	Brooklyn	94	60	.610	5
1923	New York	95	58	.621	4½	1948	Boston	91	62	.595	6½
1924	New York	93	60	.608	1½	1949	Brooklyn	97	57	.630	1

Year		W	L	Pct	GA
1950	Philadelphia	91	63	.591	2
1951	New York†	98	59	.624	1
1952	Brooklyn	96	57	.627	4½
1953	Brooklyn	105	49	.682	13
1954	New York	97	57	.630	5
1955	Brooklyn	98	55	.641	13½
1956	Brooklyn	93	61	.604	1
1957	Milwaukee	95	59	.617	8
1958	Milwaukee	92	62	.597	8
1959	Los Angeles†	88	68	.564	2
1960	Pittsburgh	95	59	.617	7
1961	Cincinnati	93	61	.604	4
1962	San Francisco†	103	62	.624	1
1963	Los Angeles	99	63	.611	6
1964	St. Louis	93	69	.574	1
1965	Los Angeles	97	65	.599	2
1966	Los Angeles	95	67	.586	1½
1967	St. Louis	101	60	.627	10½
1968	St. Louis	97	65	.599	9
1969	West—Atlanta	93	69	.574	3
	East—N.Y. Mets	100	62	.617	8
1970	West—Cincinnati	102	60	.630	14½
	East—Pittsburgh	89	73	.549	5
1971	West—San Francisco	90	72	.556	1
	East—Pittsburgh	97	65	.599	7
1972	West—Cincinnati	95	59	.617	10½
	East—Pittsburgh	96	59	.619	11
1973	West—Cincinnati	99	63	.611	3½
	East—N.Y. Mets	82	79	.509	1½
1974	West—Los Angeles	102	60	.630	4
	East—Pittsburgh	88	74	.543	1½
1975	West—Cincinnati	108	54	.667	20
	East—Pittsburgh	92	69	.571	6½
1976	West—Cincinnati	102	60	.630	10
	East—Philadelphia	101	61	.623	9
1977	West—Los Angeles	98	64	.605	10
	East—Philadelphia	101	61	.623	5
1978	West—Los Angeles	95	67	.586	2½
	East—Philadelphia	90	72	.556	1½
1979	West—Cincinnati	90	71	.559	1½
	East—Pittsburgh	98	64	.605	2
1980	West—Houston †	93	70	.571	1
	East—Philadelphia	91	71	.562	1
1981	West—Los Angeles$	63	47	.573	—
	East—Montreal$	60	48	.556	—
1982	West—Atlanta	89	73	.549	1
	East—St. Louis	92	70	.568	3
1983	West—Los Angeles	91	71	.562	3
1984	East—Philadelphia	90	72	.556	6
	West—San Diego	92	70	.568	12
	East—Chicago	96	65	.596	6½
1985	West—Los Angeles	95	67	.586	5½
	East—St. Louis	101	61	.623	3
1986	West—Houston	96	66	.593	10
	East—N.Y. Mets	108	54	.667	21½
1987	West—San Francisco	90	72	.556	6
	East—St. Louis	95	67	.586	3
1988	West—Los Angeles	94	67	.584	7
	East—N.Y. Mets	100	60	.625	15
1989	West—San Francisco	92	70	.568	3
	East—Chicago	93	69	.574	6
1990	West—Cincinnati	91	71	.562	5
	East—Pittsburgh	95	67	.586	4
1991	West—Atlanta	94	68	.580	1
	East—Pittsburgh	98	64	.605	14
1992	West—Atlanta	98	64	.605	8
	East—Pittsburgh	96	66	.593	9
1993	West—Atlanta	104	58	.642	1
	East—Philadelphia	97	65	.599	3
1994	West—Los Angeles*	58	56	.509	3½
	Central—Cincinnati*	66	48	.579	½
	East—Montreal*	74	40	.649	6
1995	West—Los Angeles	78	66	.542	1
	Central—Cincinnati	85	59	.590	9
	East—Atlanta	90	54	.625	21
	WC—Colorado	77	67	.535	—
1996	West—San Diego	91	71	.562	1
	Central—St. Louis	88	74	.543	6
	East—Atlanta	96	66	.593	8
	WC—Los Angeles	90	72	.556	—
1997	West—San Francisco	90	72	.556	2
	Central—Houston	84	78	.519	5
	East—Atlanta	101	61	.623	9
	WC—Florida	92	70	.568	—
1998	West—San Diego	98	64	.605	9½
	Central—Houston	102	60	.630	12½
	East—Atlanta	106	56	.654	18
	WC—Chicago†	90	73	.552	—
1999	West—Arizona	100	62	.617	14
	Central—Houston	97	65	.599	1½
	East—Atlanta	103	59	.636	6½
	WC—N.Y. Mets†	97	66	.595	—
2000	West—San Francisco	97	65	.599	11
	Central—St. Louis	95	67	.586	10
	East—Atlanta	95	67	.586	1
	WC—N.Y. Mets	94	68	.580	—

†**Regular season playoffs:** See "Other Playoffs" on page 96 for details.
$**Divsional playoffs:** See "Other Playoffs" on page 96 for details.

American League

Year		W	L	Pct	GA
1901	Chicago	83	53	.610	4
1902	Philadelphia	83	53	.610	5
1903	Boston	91	47	.659	14½
1904	Boston	95	59	.617	1½
1905	Philadelphia	92	56	.622	2
1906	Chicago	93	58	.616	3
1907	Detroit	92	58	.613	1½
1908	Detroit	90	63	.588	½
1909	Detroit	98	54	.645	3½
1910	Philadelphia	102	48	.680	14½
1911	Philadelphia	101	50	.669	13½
1912	Boston	105	47	.691	14
1913	Philadelphia	96	57	.627	6½
1914	Philadelphia	99	53	.651	8½
1915	Boston	101	50	.669	2½
1916	Boston	91	63	.591	2
1917	Chicago	100	54	.649	9
1918	Boston	75	51	.595	2½
1919	Chicago	88	52	.629	3½
1920	Cleveland	98	56	.636	2
1921	New York	98	55	.641	4½
1922	New York	94	60	.610	1
1923	New York	98	54	.645	16
1924	Washington	92	62	.597	2
1925	Washington	96	55	.636	8½
1926	New York	91	63	.591	3
1927	New York	110	44	.714	19
1928	New York	101	53	.656	2½
1929	Philadelphia	104	46	.693	18
1930	Philadelphia	102	52	.662	8
1931	Philadelphia	107	45	.704	13½
1932	New York	107	47	.695	13
1933	Washington	99	53	.651	7
1934	Detroit	101	53	.656	7
1935	Detroit	93	58	.616	3
1936	New York	102	51	.667	19½
1937	New York	102	52	.662	13
1938	New York	99	53	.651	9½
1939	New York	106	45	.702	17
1940	Detroit	90	64	.584	1

Year		W	L	Pct	GA	Year		W	L	Pct	GA
1941	New York	101	53	.656	17	1981	West—Oakland$	64	45	.587	—
1942	New York	103	51	.669	9		East—New York$	59	48	.551	—
1943	New York	98	56	.636	13½	1982	West—California	93	69	.574	3
1944	St. Louis	89	65	.578	1		East—Milwaukee	95	67	.586	1
1945	Detroit	88	65	.575	1½	1983	West—Chicago	99	63	.611	20
1946	Boston	104	50	.675	12		East—Baltimore	98	64	.605	6
1947	New York	97	57	.630	12	1984	West—Kansas City	84	78	.519	3
1948	Cleveland†	97	58	.626	1		East—Detroit	104	58	.642	15
1949	New York	97	57	.630	1	1985	West—Kansas City	91	71	.562	1
1950	New York	98	56	.636	3		East—Toronto	99	62	.615	2
1951	New York	98	56	.636	5	1986	West—California	92	70	.568	5
1952	New York	95	59	.617	2		East—Boston	95	66	.590	5½
1953	New York	99	52	.656	8½	1987	West—Minnesota	85	77	.525	2
1954	Cleveland	111	43	.721	8		East—Detroit	98	64	.605	2
1955	New York	96	58	.623	3	1988	West—Oakland	104	58	.642	13
1956	New York	97	57	.630	9		East—Boston	89	73	.549	1
1957	New York	98	56	.636	8	1989	West—Oakland	99	63	.611	7
1958	New York	92	62	.597	10		East—Toronto	89	73	.549	2
1959	Chicago	94	60	.610	5	1990	West—Oakland	103	59	.636	9
1960	New York	97	57	.630	8		East—Boston	88	74	.543	2
1961	New York	109	53	.673	8	1991	West—Minnesota	95	67	.586	8
1962	New York	96	66	.593	5		East—Toronto	91	71	.562	7
1963	New York	104	57	.646	10½	1992	West—Oakland	96	66	.593	6
1964	New York	99	63	.611	1		East—Toronto	96	66	.593	4
1965	Minnesota	102	60	.630	7	1993	West—Chicago	94	68	.580	8
1966	Baltimore	97	63	.606	9		East—Toronto	95	67	.586	7
1967	Boston	92	70	.568	1	1994	West—Texas*	52	62	.456	1
1968	Detroit	103	59	.636	12		Central—Chicago*	67	46	.593	1
1969	West—Minnesota	97	65	.599	9		East—New York*	70	43	.619	6½
	East—Baltimore	109	53	.673	19	1995	West—Seattle†	79	66	.545	1
1970	West—Minnesota	98	64	.605	9		Central—Cleveland	100	44	.694	30
	East—Baltimore	108	54	.667	15		East—Boston	86	58	.597	7
1971	West—Oakland	101	60	.627	16		WC—New York	79	65	.549	—
	East—Baltimore	101	57	.639	12	1996	West—Texas	90	72	.556	4½
1972	West—Oakland	93	62	.600	5½		Central—Cleveland	99	62	.615	14½
	East—Detroit	86	70	.551	½		East—New York	92	70	.568	4
1973	West—Oakland	94	68	.580	6		WC—Baltimore	88	74	.543	—
	East—Baltimore	97	65	.599	8	1997	West—Seattle	90	72	.556	6
1974	West—Oakland	90	72	.556	5		Central—Cleveland	86	75	.534	6
	East—Baltimore	91	71	.562	2		East—Baltimore	98	64	.605	2
1975	West—Oakland	98	64	.605	7		WC—New York	96	66	.593	—
	East—Boston	95	65	.594	4½	1998	West—Texas	88	74	.543	3
1976	West—Kansas City	90	72	.556	2½		Central—Cleveland	89	73	.549	9
	East—New York	97	62	.610	10½		East—New York	114	48	.704	22
1977	West—Kansas City	102	60	.630	8		WC—Boston	92	70	.568	—
	East—New York	100	62	.617	2½	1999	West—Texas	95	67	.586	8
1978	West—Kansas City	92	70	.568	5		Central—Cleveland	97	65	.599	21½
	East—New York†	100	63	.613	1		East—New York	98	64	.605	4
1979	West—California	88	74	.543	3		WC—Boston	94	68	.580	—
	East—Baltimore	102	57	.642	8	2000	West—Oakland	91	70	.565	½
1980	West—Kansas City	97	65	.599	14		Central—Chicago	95	67	.586	5
	East—New York	103	59	.636	3		East—New York	87	74	.540	2½
							WC—Seattle	91	71	.562	—

†**Regular season playoffs:** See "Other Playoffs" on page 96 for details.
$**Divsional playoffs:** See "Other Playoffs" on page 96 for details.

The All-Star Game

Baseball's first All-Star Game was held on July 6, 1933, before 47,595 at Comiskey Park in Chicago. From that year on, the All-Star Game has matched the best players in the American League against the best in the National. From 1959-62, two All-Star Games were played. The only year an All-Star Game wasn't played was 1945, when World War II travel restrictions made it necessary to cancel the meeting. The NL leads the series, 40-30-1. In the chart below, the American League is listed in **bold** type.

The All-Star Game MVP Award is named after Arch Ward, the *Chicago Tribune* sports editor who founded the game in 1933. First given at the two All-Star games in 1962, the name of the award was changed to the Commissioner's Trophy in 1970 and back to the Ward Memorial Award in 1985.

Multiple winners: Gary Carter, Steve Garvey and Willie Mays (2).

Year		Host	AL Manager	NL Manager	MVP
1933	**American,** 4-2	Chicago (AL)	Connie Mack	John McGraw	No award
1934	**American,** 9-7	New York (NL)	Joe Cronin	Bill Terry	No award
1935	**American,** 4-1	Cleveland	Mickey Cochrane	Frankie Frisch	No award
1936	National, 4-3	Boston (NL)	Joe McCarthy	Charlie Grimm	No award
1937	**American,** 8-3	Washington	Joe McCarthy	Bill Terry	No award
1938	National, 4-1	Cincinnati	Joe McCarthy	Bill Terry	No award

Year		Host	AL Manager	NL Manager	MVP
1939	**American,** 3-1	New York (AL)	Joe McCarthy	Gabby Hartnett	No award
1940	National, 4-0	St. Louis (NL)	Joe Cronin	Bill McKechnie	No award
1941	**American,** 7-5	Detroit	Del Baker	Bill McKechnie	No award
1942	**American,** 3-1	New York (NL)	Joe McCarthy	Leo Durocher	No award
1943	**American,** 5-3	Philadelphia (AL)	Joe McCarthy	Billy Southworth	No award
1944	National, 7-1	Pittsburgh	Joe McCarthy	Billy Southworth	No award
1945	Not held				
1946	**American,** 12-0	Boston (AL)	Steve O'Neill	Charlie Grimm	No award
1947	**American,** 2-1	Chicago (NL)	Joe Cronin	Eddie Dyer	No award
1948	**American,** 5-2	St. Louis (AL)	Bucky Harris	Leo Durocher	No award
1949	**American,** 11-7	Brooklyn	Lou Boudreau	Billy Southworth	No award
1950	National, 4-3 (14)	Chicago (AL)	Casey Stengel	Burt Shotton	No award
1951	National, 8-3	Detroit	Casey Stengel	Eddie Sawyer	No award
1952	National, 3-2 (5, rain)	Philadelphia (NL)	Casey Stengel	Leo Durocher	No award
1953	National, 5-1	Cincinnati	Casey Stengel	Charlie Dressen	No award
1954	**American,** 11-9	Cleveland	Casey Stengel	Walter Alston	No award
1955	National, 6-5 (12)	Milwaukee	Al Lopez	Leo Durocher	No award
1956	National, 7-3	Washington	Casey Stengel	Walter Alston	No award
1957	**American,** 6-5	St. Louis	Casey Stengel	Walter Alston	No award
1958	**American,** 4-3	Baltimore	Casey Stengel	Fred Haney	No award
1959-a	National, 5-4	Pittsburgh	Casey Stengel	Fred Haney	No award
1959-b	**American,** 5-3	Los Angeles	Casey Stengel	Fred Haney	No award
1960-a	National, 5-3	Kansas City	Al Lopez	Walter Alston	No award
1960-b	National, 6-0	New York	Al Lopez	Walter Alston	No award
1961-a	National, 5-4 (10)	San Francisco	Paul Richards	Danny Murtaugh	No award
1961-b	TIE, 1-1 (9, rain)	Boston	Paul Richards	Danny Murtaugh	No award
1962-a	National, 3-1	Washington	Ralph Houk	Fred Hutchinson	Maury Wills, LA (NL), SS
1962-b	**American,** 9-4	Chicago (NL)	Ralph Houk	Fred Hutchinson	Leon Wagner, LA (AL), OF
1963	National, 5-3	Cleveland	Ralph Houk	Alvin Dark	Willie Mays, SF, OF
1964	National, 7-4	New York (NL)	Al Lopez	Walter Alston	Johnny Callison, Phi., OF
1965	National, 6-5	Minnesota	Al Lopez	Gene Mauch	Juan Marichal, SF, P
1966	National, 2-1 (10)	St. Louis	Sam Mele	Walter Alston	Brooks Robinson, Bal., 3B
1967	National, 2-1 (15)	California	Hank Bauer	Walter Alston	Tony Perez, Cin., 3B
1968	National, 1-0	Houston	Dick Williams	Red Schoendienst	Willie Mays, SF, OF
1969	National, 9-3	Washington	Mayo Smith	Red Schoendienst	Willie McCovey, SF, 1B
1970	National, 5-4 (12)	Cincinnati	Earl Weaver	Gil Hodges	Carl Yastrzemski, Bos., OF-1B
1971	**American,** 6-4	Detroit	Earl Weaver	Sparky Anderson	Frank Robinson, Bal., OF
1972	National, 4-3 (10)	Atlanta	Earl Weaver	Danny Murtaugh	Joe Morgan, Con., 2B
1973	National, 7-1	Kansas	Dick Williams	Sparky Anderson	Bobby Bonds, SF, OF
1974	National, 7-2	Pittsburgh	Dick Williams	Yogi Berra	Steve Garvey, LA, 1B
1975	National, 6-3	Milwaukee	Alvin Dark	Walter Alston	Bill Madlock, Chi. (NL), 3B & Jon Matlack, NY (NL), P
1976	National, 7-1	Philadelphia	Darrell Johnson	Sparky Anderson	George Foster, Cin., OF
1977	National, 7-5	New York (AL)	Billy Martin	Sparky Anderson	Don Sutton, LA, P
1978	National, 7-3	San Diego	Billy Martin	Tommy Lasorda	Steve Garvey, LA, 1B
1979	National, 7-6	Seattle	Bob Lemon	Tommy Lasorda	Dave Parker, Pit, OF
1980	National, 4-2	Los Angeles	Earl Weaver	Chuck Tanner	Ken Griffey, Cin., OF
1981	National, 5-4	Cleveland	Jim Frey	Dallas Green	Gary Carter, Mon., C
1982	National, 4-1	Montreal	Billy Martin	Tommy Lasorda	Dave Concepcion, Cin., SS
1983	**American,** 13-3	Chicago (AL)	Harvey Kuenn	Whitey Herzog	Fred Lynn, Cal., OF
1984	National, 3-1	San Francisco	Joe Altobelli	Paul Owens	Gary Carter, Mon., C
1985	National, 6-1	Minnesota	Sparky Anderson	Dick Williams	LaMarr Hoyt, SD, P
1986	**American,** 3-2	Houston	Dick Howser	Whitey Herzog	Roger Clemens, Bos., P
1987	National, 2-0 (13)	Oakland	John McNamara	Davey Johnson	Tim Raines, Mon., OF
1988	**American,** 2-1	Cincinnati	Tom Kelly	Whitey Herzog	Terry Steinbach, Oak., C
1989	**American,** 5-3	California	Tony La Russa	Tommy Lasorda	Bo Jackson, KC, OF
1990	**American,** 2-0	Chicago (NL)	Tony La Russa	Roger Craig	Julio Franco, Tex., 2B
1991	**American,** 4-2	Toronto	Tony La Russa	Lou Piniella	Cal Ripken Jr., Bal., SS
1992	**American,** 13-6	San Diego	Tom Kelly	Bobby Cox	Ken Griffey Jr., Sea., OF
1993	**American,** 9-3	Baltimore	Cito Gaston	Bobby Cox	Kirby Puckett, Min., OF
1994	National, 8-7 (10)	Pittsburgh	Cito Gaston	Jim Fregosi	Fred McGriff, Atl., 1B
1995	National, 3-2	Texas	Buck Showalter	Felipe Alou	Jeff Conine, Fla., PH
1996	National, 6-0	Philadelphia	Mike Hargrove	Bobby Cox	Mike Piazza, LA, C
1997	**American,** 3-1	Cleveland	Joe Torre	Bobby Cox	Sandy Alomar Jr., Cle., C
1998	**American,** 13-8	Colorado	Mike Hargrove	Jim Leyland	Roberto Alomar, Bal., 2B
1999	**American,** 4-1	Boston	Joe Torre	Bruce Bochy	Pedro Martinez, Bos., P
2000	**American,** 6-3	Atlanta	Joe Torre	Bobby Cox	Derek Jeter, NY (AL), SS

Major League Franchise Origins

Here is what the current 30 teams in Major League Baseball have to show for the years they have put in as members of the National League (NL) and American League (AL). Pennants and World Series championships are since 1901.

National League

	1st Year	Pennants & World Series	Franchise Stops
Arizona Diamondbacks	1998	None	• Phoenix (1998—)

Atlanta Braves	1876	9 NL (1914,48,57-58,91-92,95,96,99)
		3 WS (1914,57,95)
			• Boston (1876-1952)
			  Milwaukee (1953-65)
			  Atlanta (1966—)

Chicago Cubs	1876	10 NL (1906-08,10,18,29,32,35,38,45) 2 WS (1907-08)	• Chicago (1876—)
Cincinnati Reds	1876	9 NL (1919,39-40,61,70,72,75-76,90) 5 WS (1919,40,75-76,90)	• Cincinnati (1876-80) Cincinnati (1890—)
Colorado Rockies	1993	None	• Denver (1993—)
Florida Marlins	1993	1 NL (1997) 1 WS (1997)	• Miami (1993—)
Houston Astros	1962	None	• Houston (1962—)
Los Angeles Dodgers	1890	18 NL (1916,20,41,47,49,52-53,55-56, 59,63, 65-66,74,77-78, 81,88) 6 WS (1955,59,63,65,81,88)	• Brooklyn (1890-1957) Los Angeles (1958—)
Milwaukee Brewers	1969	1 AL (1982)	• Seattle (1969) Milwaukee (1970—)
Montreal Expos	1969	None	• Montreal (1969—)
New York Mets	1962	4 NL (1969,73,86,00) 2 WS (1969,86)	• New York (1962—)
Philadelphia Phillies	1883	5 NL (1915,50,80,83,93) 1 WS (1980)	• Philadelphia (1883—)
Pittsburgh Pirates	1887	7 NL (1903,09,25,27,60,71,79) 5 WS (1909,25,60,71,79)	• Pittsburgh (1887—)
St. Louis Cardinals	1892	15 NL (1926,28,30-31,34,42-44,46,64, 67-68,82,85,87) 9 WS (1926,31,34,42,44,46,64,67,82)	• St. Louis (1892—)
San Diego Padres	1969	2 NL (1984,98)	• San Diego (1969—)
San Francisco Giants	1883	16 NL (1905,11-13,17,21-24,33,36-37,51, 54,62,89) 5 WS (1905,21-22,33,54)	• New York (1883-1957) San Francisco (1958—)

American League

	1st Year	Pennants & World Series	Franchise Stops
Anaheim Angels	1961	None	• Los Angeles (1961-65) Anaheim, CA (1966—)

Baltimore Orioles	1901	7 AL (1944,66,69-71,79,83)
		3 WS (1966,70,83)
			• Milwaukee (1901)
			  St. Louis (1902-53)
			  Baltimore (1954—)

Boston Red Sox	1901	9 AL (1903,12,15-16,18,46,67,75,86) 5 WS (1903,12,15-16,18)	• Boston (1901—)
Chicago White Sox	1901	4 AL (1906,17,19,59) 2 WS (1906,17)	• Chicago (1901—)
Cleveland Indians	1901	5 AL (1920,48,54,95,97) 2 WS (1920,48)	• Cleveland (1901—)
Detroit Tigers	1901	9 AL (1907-09,34-35,40,45,68,84) 4 WS (1935,45,68,84)	• Detroit (1901—)
Kansas City Royals	1969	2 AL (1980,85) 1 WS (1985)	• Kansas City (1969—)

Minnesota Twins	1901	6 AL (1924-25,33,65,87,91)
		3 WS (1924,87,91)
			• Washington, DC (1901-60)
			  Bloomington, MN (1961-81)
			  Minneapolis (1982—)

New York Yankees	1901	37 AL (1921-23,26-28,32,36-39,41-43,47, 49-53,55-58,60-64,76-78,81,96,98-00) 26 WS (1923,27-28,32,36-39,41,43,47, 49-53,56,58,61-62,77-78,96,98-00)	• Baltimore (1901-02) New York (1903—)

Oakland Athletics	1901	14 AL (1905,10-11,13-14,29-31,72-74,
		88-90) 9 WS (1910-11,13,29-30,72-74,89)
			• Philadelphia (1901-54)
			  Kansas City (1955-67)
			  Oakland (1968—)

Seattle Mariners	1977	None	• Seattle (1977—)
Tampa Bay Devil Rays	1998	None	• Tampa Bay (1998—)
Texas Rangers	1961	None	• Washington, DC (1961-71) Arlington, TX (1972—)
Toronto Blue Jays	1977	2 AL (1992-93) 2 WS (1992-93)	• Toronto (1977—)

The Growth of Major League Baseball

The National League (founded in 1876) and the American League (founded in 1901) were both eight-team circuits at the turn of the century and remained that way until expansion finally came to Major League Baseball in the 1960s. The AL added two teams in 1961 and the NL did the same a year later. Both leagues went to 12 teams and split into two divisions in 1969. The AL then grew by two more teams in 1977, but the NL didn't follow suit until adding its 13th and 14th clubs in 1993. The NL added two teams in 1998 when the expansion Arizona Diamondbacks entered the league and the Milwaukee Brewers moved over from the AL.

Expansion Timetable (Since 1901)

1961—Los Angeles Angels (now Anaheim) and Washington Senators (now Texas Rangers) join AL; **1962**—Houston Colt .45s (now Astros) and New York Mets join NL; **1969**—Kansas City Royals and Seattle Pilots (now Milwaukee Brewers) join AL, while Montreal Expos and San Diego Padres join NL; **1977**—Seattle Mariners and Toronto Blue Jays join AL; **1993**—Colorado Rockies and Florida Marlins join NL; **1998**—Arizona Diamondbacks join NL and Tampa Bay Devil Rays join AL.

City and Nickname Changes
National League

1953—Boston Braves move to Milwaukee; **1958**—Brooklyn Dodgers move to Los Angeles and New York Giants move to San Francisco; **1965**—Houston Colt .45s renamed Astros; **1966**—Milwaukee Braves move to Atlanta.

Other nicknames: Boston (Beaneaters and Doves through 1908, and Bees from 1936-40); **Brooklyn** (Superbas through 1926, then Robins from 1927-31; then Dodgers from 1932-57); **Cincinnati** (Red Legs from 1944-45, then Redlegs from 1954-60, then Reds since 1961); **Philadelphia** (Blue Jays from 1943-44).

American League

1902—Milwaukee Brewers move to St. Louis and become Browns; **1903**—Baltimore Orioles move to New York and become Highlanders; **1913**—NY Highlanders renamed Yankees; **1954**—St. Louis Browns move to Baltimore and become Orioles; **1955**—Philadelphia Athletics move to Kansas City; **1961**—Washington Senators move to Bloomington, Minn., and become Minnesota Twins; **1965**—LA Angels renamed California Angels; **1966**—California Angels move to Anaheim; **1968**—KC Athletics move to Oakland and become A's; **1970**—Seattle Pilots move to Milwaukee and become Brewers; **1972**—Washington Senators move to Arlington, Texas, and become Rangers; **1982**—Minnesota Twins move to Minneapolis; **1987**—Oakland A's renamed Athletics; **1997**—California Angels renamed Anaheim Angels.

Other nicknames: Boston (Pilgrims, Puritans, Plymouth Rocks and Somersets through 1906); **Cleveland** (Broncos, Blues, Naps and Molly McGuires through 1914); **Washington** (Senators through 1904, then Nationals from 1905-44, then Senators again from 1945-60).

National League Pennant Winners from 1876-99

Founded in 1876, the National League played 24 seasons before the turn of the century and its eventual rivalry with the younger American League.

Multiple winners: Boston (8); Chicago (6); Baltimore (3); Brooklyn, New York and Providence (2).

Year		Year		Year		Year	
1876	Chicago	1882	Chicago	1888	New York	1894	Baltimore
1877	Boston	1883	Boston	1889	New York	1895	Baltimore
1878	Boston	1884	Providence	1890	Brooklyn	1896	Baltimore
1879	Providence	1885	Chicago	1891	Boston	1897	Boston
1880	Chicago	1886	Chicago	1892	Boston	1898	Boston
1881	Chicago	1887	Detroit	1893	Boston	1899	Brooklyn

Champions of Leagues That No Longer Exist

A Special Baseball Records Committee appointed by the commissioner found in 1968 that four extinct leagues qualified for major league status—the American Association (1882-91), the Union Association (1884), the Players' League (1890) and the Federal League (1914-15). The first years of the American League (1900) and Federal League (1913) were not recognized.

American Association

Year	Champion	Manager	Year	Champion	Manager	Year	Champion	Manager
1882	Cincinnati	Pop Snyder	1886	St. Louis	Charlie Comiskey	1890	Louisville	Jack Chapman
1883	Philadelphia	Lew Simmons	1887	St. Louis	Charlie Comiskey	1891	Boston	Arthur Irwin
1884	New York	Jim Mutrie	1888	St. Louis	Charlie Comiskey			
1885	St. Louis	Charlie Comiskey	1889	Brooklyn	Bill McGunnigle			

Union Association

Year	Champion	Manager
1884	St. Louis	Henry Lucas

Players' League

Year	Champion	Manager
1890	Boston	King Kelly

Federal League

Year	Champion	Manager
1914	Indianapolis	Bill Phillips
1915	Chicago	Joe Tinker

Annual Batting Leaders (since 1900)
Batting Average
National League

Multiple winners: Tony Gwynn and Honus Wagner (8); Rogers Hornsby and Stan Musial (7); Roberto Clemente and Bill Madlock (4); Pete Rose and Paul Waner (3); Hank Aaron, Richie Ashburn, Jake Daubert, Tommy Davis, Ernie Lombardi, Willie McGee, Lefty O'Doul, Dave Parker, Edd Roush and Larry Walker (2).

Year		Avg	Year		Avg	Year		Avg
1900	Honus Wagner, Pit	.381	1934	Paul Waner, Pit	.362	1968	Pete Rose, Cin	.335
1901	Jesse Burkett, St.L	.382	1935	Arky Vaughan, Pit	.385	1969	Pete Rose, Cin	.348
1902	Ginger Beaumont, Pit	.357	1936	Paul Waner, Pit	.373	1970	Rico Carty, Atl	.366
1903	Honus Wagner, Pit	.355	1937	Joe Medwick, St.L	.374	1971	Joe Torre, St.L	.363
1904	Honus Wagner, Pit	.349	1938	Ernie Lombardi, Cin	.342	1972	Billy Williams, Chi	.333
1905	Cy Seymour, Cin	.377	1939	Johnny Mize, St.L	.349	1973	Pete Rose, Cin	.338
1906	Honus Wagner, Pit	.339	1940	Debs Garms, Pit	.355	1974	Ralph Garr, Atl	.353
1907	Honus Wagner, Pit	.350	1941	Pete Reiser, Bklyn	.343	1975	Bill Madlock, Chi	.354
1908	Honus Wagner, Pit	.354	1942	Ernie Lombardi, Bos	.330	1976	Bill Madlock, Chi	.339
1909	Honus Wagner, Pit	.339	1943	Stan Musial, St.L	.357	1977	Dave Parker, Pit	.338
1910	Sherry Magee, Phi	.331	1944	Dixie Walker, Bklyn	.357	1978	Dave Parker, Pit	.334
1911	Honus Wagner, Pit	.334	1945	Phil Cavarretta, Chi	.355	1979	Keith Hernandez, St.L	.344
1912	Heinie Zimmerman, Chi	.372	1946	Stan Musial, St.L	.365	1980	Bill Buckner, Chi	.324
1913	Jake Daubert, Bklyn	.350	1947	Harry Walker, St.L-Phi	.363	1981	Bill Madlock, Pit	.341
1914	Jake Daubert, Bklyn	.329	1948	Stan Musial, St.L	.376	1982	Al Oliver, Mon	.331
1915	Larry Doyle, NY	.320	1949	Jackie Robinson, Bklyn	.342	1983	Bill Madlock, Pit	.323
1916	Hal Chase, Cin	.339	1950	Stan Musial, St.L	.346	1984	Tony Gwynn, SD	.351
1917	Edd Roush, Cin	.341	1951	Stan Musial, St.L	.355	1985	Willie McGee, St.L	.353
1918	Zack Wheat, Bklyn	.335	1952	Stan Musial, St.L	.336	1986	Tim Raines, Mon	.334
1919	Edd Roush, Cin	.321	1953	Carl Furillo, Bklyn	.344	1987	Tony Gwynn, SD	.370
1920	Rogers Hornsby, St.L	.370	1954	Willie Mays, NY	.345	1988	Tony Gwynn, SD	.313
1921	Rogers Hornsby, St.L	.397	1955	Richie Ashburn, Phi	.338	1989	Tony Gwynn, SD	.336
1922	Rogers Hornsby, St.L	.401	1956	Hank Aaron, Mil	.328	1990	Willie McGee, St.L	.335
1923	Rogers Hornsby, St.L	.384	1957	Stan Musial, St.L	.351	1991	Terry Pendleton, Atl	.319
1924	Rogers Hornsby, St.L	.424	1958	Richie Ashburn, Phi	.350	1992	Gary Sheffield, SD	.330
1925	Rogers Hornsby, St.L	.403	1959	Hank Aaron, Mil	.355	1993	Andres Galarraga, Col	.370
1926	Bubbles Hargrave, Cin	.353	1960	Dick Groat, Pit	.325	1994	Tony Gwynn, SD	.394
1927	Paul Waner, Pit	.380	1961	Roberto Clemente, Pit	.351	1995	Tony Gwynn, SD	.368
1928	Rogers Hornsby, Bos	.387	1962	Tommy Davis, LA	.346	1996	Tony Gwynn, SD	.353
1929	Lefty O'Doul, Phi	.398	1963	Tommy Davis, LA	.326	1997	Tony Gwynn, SD	.372
1930	Bill Terry, NY	.401	1964	Roberto Clemente, Pit	.339	1998	Larry Walker, Col.	.363
1931	Chick Hafey, St.L	.349	1965	Roberto Clemente, Pit	.329	1999	Larry Walker, Col.	.379
1932	Lefty O'Doul, Bklyn	.368	1966	Matty Alou, Pit	.342	2000	Todd Helton, Col	.372
1933	Chuck Klein, Phi	.368	1967	Roberto Clemente, Pit	.357			

American League

Multiple winners: Ty Cobb (12); Rod Carew (7); Ted Williams (6); Wade Boggs (5); Harry Heilmann (4); George Brett, Nap Lajoie, Tony Oliva and Carl Yastrzemski (3); Luke Appling, Joe DiMaggio, Ferris Fain, Jimmie Foxx, Nomar Garciaparra, Edgar Martinez, Pete Runnels, Al Simmons, George Sisler and Mickey Vernon (2).

Year		Avg	Year		Avg	Year		Avg
1901	Nap Lajoie, Phi	.422	1924	Babe Ruth, NY	.378	1947	Ted Williams, Bos	.343
1902	Ed Delahanty, Wash	.376	1925	Harry Heilmann, Det	.393	1948	Ted Williams, Bos	.369
1903	Nap Lajoie, Cle	.355	1926	Heinie Manush, Det	.378	1949	George Kell, Det	.343
1904	Nap Lajoie, Cle	.381	1927	Harry Heilmann, Det	.398	1950	Billy Goodman, Bos	.354
1905	Elmer Flick, Cle	.306	1928	Goose Goslin, Wash	.379	1951	Ferris Fain, Phi	.344
1906	George Stone, St.L	.358	1929	Lew Fonseca, Cle	.369	1952	Ferris Fain, Phi	.327
1907	Ty Cobb, Det	.350	1930	Al Simmons, Phi	.381	1953	Mickey Vernon, Wash	.337
1908	Ty Cobb, Det	.324	1931	Al Simmons, Phi	.390	1954	Bobby Avila, Clev	.341
1909	Ty Cobb, Det	.377	1932	Dale Alexander, Det-Bos	.367	1955	Al Kaline, Det	.340
1910	Ty Cobb, Det	.385	1933	Jimmie Foxx, Phi	.356	1956	Mickey Mantle, NY	.353
1911	Ty Cobb, Det	.420	1934	Lou Gehrig, NY	.363	1957	Ted Williams, Bos	.388
1912	Ty Cobb, Det	.410	1935	Buddy Myer, Wash	.349	1958	Ted Williams, Bos	.328
1913	Ty Cobb, Det	.390	1936	Luke Appling, Chi	.388	1959	Harvey Kuenn, Det	.353
1914	Ty Cobb, Det	.368	1937	Charlie Gehringer, Det	.371	1960	Pete Runnels, Bos	.320
1915	Ty Cobb, Det	.369	1938	Jimmie Foxx, Bos	.349	1961	Norm Cash, Det	.361*
1916	Tris Speaker, Cle	.386	1939	Joe DiMaggio, NY	.381	1962	Pete Runnels, Bos	.326
1917	Ty Cobb, Det	.383	1940	Joe DiMaggio, NY	.352	1963	Carl Yastrzemski, Bos	.321
1918	Ty Cobb, Det	.382	1941	Ted Williams, Bos	.406	1964	Tony Oliva, Min	.323
1919	Ty Cobb, Det	.384	1942	Ted Williams, Bos	.356	1965	Tony Oliva, Min	.321
1920	George Sisler, St.L	.407	1943	Luke Appling, Chi	.328	1966	Frank Robinson, Bal	.316
1921	Harry Heilmann, Det	.394	1944	Lou Boudreau, Clev	.327	1967	Carl Yastrzemski, Bos	.326
1922	George Sisler, St.L	.420	1945	Snuffy Stirnweiss, NY	.309	1968	Carl Yastrzemski, Bos	.301
1923	Harry Heilmann, Det	.403	1946	Mickey Vernon, Wash	.353	1969	Rod Carew, Min	.332

Year	Avg	Year	Avg	Year	Avg
1970 Alex Johnson, Cal	.329	1982 Willie Wilson, KC	.332	1994 Paul O'Neill, NY	.359
1971 Tony Oliva, Min	.337	1983 Wade Boggs, Bos	.361	1995 Edgar Martinez, Sea	.356
1972 Rod Carew, Min	.318	1984 Don Mattingly, NY	.343	1996 Alex Rodriguez, Sea	.358
1973 Rod Carew, Min	.350	1985 Wade Boggs, Bos	.368	1997 Frank Thomas, Chi	.347
1974 Rod Carew, Min	.364	1986 Wade Boggs, Bos	.357	1998 Bernie Williams, NY	.339
1975 Rod Carew, Min	.359	1987 Wade Boggs, Bos	.363	1999 Nomar Garciaparra, Bos	.357
1976 George Brett, KC	.333	1988 Wade Boggs, Bos	.366		
1977 Rod Carew, Min	.388	1989 Kirby Puckett, Min	.339	2000 Nomar Garciaparra, Bos	.372
1978 Rod Carew, Min	.333			*Norm Cash later admitted to using a	
1979 Fred Lynn, Bos	.333	1990 George Brett, KC	.329	corked bat the entire season. He	
		1991 Julio Franco, Tex	.341	played 16 other seasons and never hit	
1980 George Brett, KC	.390	1992 Edgar Martinez, Sea	.343	better than .286.	
1981 Carney Lansford, Bos	.336	1993 John Olerud, Tor	.363		

Home Runs
National League

Multiple winners: Mike Schmidt (8); Ralph Kiner (7); Gavvy Cravath and Mel Ott (6); Hank Aaron, Chuck Klein, Willie Mays, Johnny Mize, Cy Williams and Hack Wilson (4); Willie McCovey (3); Ernie Banks, Johnny Bench, George Foster, Rogers Hornsby, Tim Jordan, Dave Kingman, Eddie Mathews, Mark McGwire, Dale Murphy, Bill Nicholson, Dave Robertson, Wildfire Schulte and Willie Stargell (2).

Year	HR	Year	HR	Year	HR
1900 Herman Long, Bos	12	1934 Rip Collins, St.L	35	1968 Willie McCovey, SF	36
1901 Sam Crawford, Cin	16	& Mel Ott, NY	35	1969 Willie McCovey, SF	45
1902 Tommy Leach, Pit	6	1935 Wally Berger, Bos	34		
1903 Jimmy Sheckard, Bklyn	9	1936 Mel Ott, NY	33	1970 Johnny Bench, Cin	45
1904 Harry Lumley, Bklyn	9	1937 Joe Medwick, St.L	31	1971 Willie Stargell, Pit	48
1905 Fred Odwell, Cin	9	& Mel Ott, NY	31	1972 Johnny Bench, Cin	40
1906 Tim Jordan, Bklyn	12	1938 Mel Ott, NY	36	1973 Willie Stargell, Pit	44
1907 Dave Brain, Bos	10	1939 Johnny Mize, St.L	28	1974 Mike Schmidt, Phi	36
1908 Tim Jordan, Bklyn	12			1975 Mike Schmidt, Phi	38
1909 Red Murray, NY	7	1940 Johnny Mize, St.L	43	1976 Mike Schmidt, Phi	38
		1941 Dolph Camilli, Bklyn	34	1977 George Foster, Cin	52
1910 Fred Beck, Bos	10	1942 Mel Ott, NY	30	1978 George Foster, Cin	40
& Wildfire Schulte, Chi	10	1943 Bill Nicholson, Chi	29	1979 Dave Kingman, Chi	48
1911 Wildfire Schulte, Chi	21	1944 Bill Nicholson, Chi	33		
1912 Heinie Zimmerman, Chi	14	1945 Tommy Holmes, Bos	28	1980 Mike Schmidt, Phi	48
1913 Gavvy Cravath, Phi	19	1946 Ralph Kiner, Pit	23	1981 Mike Schmidt, Phi	31
1914 Gavvy Cravath, Phi	19	1947 Ralph Kiner, Pit	51	1982 Dave Kingman, NY	37
1915 Gavvy Cravath, Phi	24	& Johnny Mize, NY	51	1983 Mike Schmidt, Phi	40
1916 Cy Williams, Chi	12	1948 Ralph Kiner, Pit	40	1984 Dale Murphy, Atl	36
& Dave Robertson, NY	12	& Johnny Mize, NY	40	& Mike Schmidt, Phi	36
1917 Gavvy Cravath, Phi	12	1949 Ralph Kiner, Pit	54	1985 Dale Murphy, Atl	37
& Dave Robertson, NY	12			1986 Mike Schmidt, Phi	37
1918 Gavvy Cravath, Phi	8	1950 Ralph Kiner, Pit	47	1987 Andre Dawson, Chi	49
1919 Gavvy Cravath, Phi	12	1951 Ralph Kiner, Pit	42	1988 Darryl Strawberry, NY	39
		1952 Ralph Kiner, Pit	37	1989 Kevin Mitchell, SF	47
1920 Cy Williams, Phi	15	& Hank Sauer, Chi	37		
1921 George Kelly, NY	23	1953 Eddie Mathews, Mil	47	1990 Ryne Sandberg, Chi	40
1922 Rogers Hornsby, St.L	42	1954 Ted Kluszewski, Cin	49	1991 Howard Johnson, NY	38
1923 Cy Williams, Phi	41	1955 Willie Mays, NY	51	1992 Fred McGriff, SD	35
1924 Jack Fournier, Bklyn	27	1956 Duke Snider, Bklyn	43	1993 Barry Bonds, SF	46
1925 Rogers Hornsby, St.L	39	1957 Hank Aaron, Mil	44	1994 Matt Williams, SF	43
1926 Hack Wilson, Chi	21	1958 Ernie Banks, Chi	47	1995 Dante Bichette, Col	40
1927 Cy Williams, Phi	30	1959 Eddie Mathews, Mil	46	1996 Andres Galarraga, Col	47
& Hack Wilson, Chi	30			1997 Larry Walker, Col	49
1928 Jim Bottomley, St.L	31	1960 Ernie Banks, Chi	41	1998 Mark McGwire, St.L	70
& Hack Wilson, Chi	31	1961 Orlando Cepeda, SF	46	1999 Mark McGwire, St.L	65
1929 Chuck Klein, Phi	43	1962 Willie Mays, SF	49		
		1963 Hank Aaron, Mil	44	2000 Sammy Sosa, Chi	50
1930 Hack Wilson, Chi	56	& Willie McCovey, SF	44	**Note:** In 1997 Mark McGwire hit 58	
1931 Chuck Klein, Phi	31	1964 Willie Mays, SF	47	home runs but hit 34 of them in the AL	
1932 Chuck Klein, Phi	38	1965 Willie Mays, SF	52	with Oakland before getting traded to	
& Mel Ott, NY	38	1966 Hank Aaron, Atl	44	St. Louis.	
1933 Chuck Klein, Phi	28	1967 Hank Aaron, Atl	39		

American League

Multiple winners: Babe Ruth (12); Harmon Killebrew (6); Home Run Baker, Harry Davis, Jimmie Foxx, Hank Greenberg, Ken Griffey Jr., Reggie Jackson, Mickey Mantle and Ted Williams (4); Lou Gehrig and Jim Rice (3); Dick Allen, Tony Armas, Jose Canseco, Joe DiMaggio, Larry Doby, Cecil Fielder, Juan Gonzalez, Mark McGwire, Wally Pipp, Al Rosen and Gorman Thomas (2).

Year	HR	Year	HR	Year	HR
1901 Nap Lajoie, Phi	14	1905 Harry Davis, Phi	8	1909 Ty Cobb, Det	9
1902 Socks Seybold, Phi	16	1906 Harry Davis, Phi	12		
1903 Buck Freeman, Bos	13	1907 Harry Davis, Phi	8	1910 Jake Stahl, Bos	10
1904 Harry Davis, Phi	10	1908 Sam Crawford, Det	7	1911 Home Run Baker, Phi	11

Year	HR	Year	HR	Year	HR
1912	Home Run Baker, Phi 10	1944	Nick Etten, NY 22	1977	Jim Rice, Bos 39
	& Tris Speaker, Bos.......10	1945	Vern Stephens, St.L........24	1978	Jim Rice, Bos 46
1913	Home Run Baker, Phi 12	1946	Hank Greenberg, Det......44	1979	Gorman Thomas, Mil.......45
1914	Home Run Baker, Phi 9	1947	Ted Williams, Bos 32	1980	Reggie Jackson, NY 41
1915	Braggo Roth, Chi-Cle 7	1948	Joe DiMaggio, NY 39		& Ben Oglivie, Mil.........41
1916	Wally Pipp, NY............12	1949	Ted Williams, Bos 43	1981	Tony Armas, Oak 22
1917	Wally Pipp, NY............9	1950	Al Rosen, Cle.............37		Dwight Evans, Bos 22
1918	Babe Ruth, Bos 11	1951	Gus Zernial, Chi-Phi.......33		Bobby Grich, Cal 22
	& Tilly Walker, Phi 11	1952	Larry Doby, Cle...........32		& Eddie Murray, Bal.......22
1919	Babe Ruth, Bos 29	1953	Al Rosen, Cle.............43	1982	Reggie Jackson, Cal.......39
1920	Babe Ruth, NY 54	1954	Larry Doby, Cle...........32		& Gorman Thomas, Mil....39
1921	Babe Ruth, NY 59	1955	Mickey Mantle, NY 37	1983	Jim Rice, Bos 39
1922	Ken Williams, St.L..........39	1956	Mickey Mantle, NY 52	1984	Tony Armas, Bos 43
1923	Babe Ruth, NY 41	1957	Roy Sievers, Wash 42	1985	Darrell Evans, Det.........40
1924	Babe Ruth, NY 46	1958	Mickey Mantle, NY 42	1986	Jesse Barfield, Tor 40
1925	Bob Meusel, NY 33	1959	Rocky Colavito, Cle 42	1987	Mark McGwire, Oak 49
1926	Babe Ruth, NY 47		& Harmon Killebrew, Wash .42	1988	Jose Canseco, Oak 42
1927	Babe Ruth, NY 60	1960	Mickey Mantle, NY 40	1989	Fred McGriff, Tor 36
1928	Babe Ruth, NY 54	1961	Roger Maris, NY...........61	1990	Cecil Fielder, Det 51
1929	Babe Ruth, NY 46	1962	Harmon Killebrew, Min 48	1991	Jose Canseco, Oak 44
1930	Babe Ruth, NY 49	1963	Harmon Killebrew, Min 45		& Cecil Fielder, Det 44
1931	Lou Gehrig, NY............46	1964	Harmon Killebrew, Min 49	1992	Juan Gonzalez, Tex 43
	& Babe Ruth, NY 46	1965	Tony Conigliaro, Bos 32	1993	Juan Gonzalez, Tex 46
1932	Jimmie Foxx, Phi 58	1966	Frank Robinson, Bal 49	1994	Ken Griffey Jr., Sea 40
1933	Jimmie Foxx, Phi 48	1967	Harmon Killebrew, Min 44	1995	Albert Belle, Cle 50
1934	Lou Gehrig, NY............49		& Carl Yastrzemski, Bos....44	1996	Mark McGwire, Oak 52
1935	Jimmie Foxx, Phi 36	1968	Frank Howard, Wash.......44	1997	Ken Griffey Jr., Sea 56
	& Hank Greenberg, Det....36	1969	Harmon Killebrew, Min 49	1998	Ken Griffey Jr., Sea 56
1936	Lou Gehrig, NY............49	1970	Frank Howard, Wash......44	1999	Ken Griffey Jr., Sea 48
1937	Joe DiMaggio, NY 46	1971	Bill Melton, Chi 33	2000	Troy Glaus, Ana 47
1938	Hank Greenberg, Det......58	1972	Dick Allen, Chi 37		
1939	Jimmie Foxx, Bos...........35	1973	Reggie Jackson, Oak 32		
1940	Hank Greenberg, Det......41	1974	Dick Allen, Chi 32		
1941	Ted Williams, Bos..........37	1975	Reggie Jackson, Oak 36		
1942	Ted Williams, Bos..........36		& George Scott, Mil........36		
1943	Rudy York, Det.............34	1976	Graig Nettles, NY 32		

Note: In 1997 Mark McGwire hit 58 home runs but hit 24 of them in the NL with St. Louis after getting traded from Oakland.

Runs Batted In
National League

Multiple winners: Hank Aaron, Rogers Hornsby, Sherry Magee, Mike Schmidt and Honus Wagner (4); Johnny Bench, George Foster, Joe Medwick, Johnny Mize and Heinie Zimmerman (3); Ernie Banks, Jim Bottomley, Orlando Cepeda, Gavvy Cravath, Andres Galarraga, George Kelly, Chuck Klein, Willie McCovey, Dale Murphy, Stan Musial, Bill Nicholson and Hack Wilson (2).

Year	RBI	Year	RBI	Year	RBI
1900	Elmer Flick, Phi 110	1924	George Kelly, NY.........136	1950	Del Ennis, Phi 126
1901	Honus Wagner, Pit........126	1925	Rogers Hornsby, St.L......143	1951	Monte Irvin, NY 121
1902	Honus Wagner, Pit 91	1926	Jim Bottomley, St.L 120	1952	Hank Sauer, Chi...........121
1903	Sam Mertes, NY 104	1927	Paul Waner, Pit...........131	1953	Roy Campanella, Bklyn 142
1904	Bill Dahlen, NY 80	1928	Jim Bottomley, St.L 136	1954	Ted Kluszewski, Cin 141
1905	Cy Seymour, Cin 121	1929	Hack Wilson, Chi..........159	1955	Duke Snider, Bklyn 136
1906	Jim Nealon, Pit 83	1930	Hack Wilson, Chi..........191	1956	Stan Musial, St.L...........109
	& Harry Steinfeldt, Chi......83	1931	Chuck Klein, Phi 121	1957	Hank Aaron, Mil 132
1907	Sherry Magee, Phi 85	1932	Don Hurst, Phi............143	1958	Ernie Banks, Chi..........129
1908	Honus Wagner, Pit........109	1933	Chuck Klein, Phi 120	1959	Ernie Banks, Chi..........143
1909	Honus Wagner, Pit........100	1934	Mel Ott, NY 135	1960	Hank Aaron, Mil 126
1910	Sherry Magee, Phi........123	1935	Wally Berger, Bos 130	1961	Orlando Cepeda, SF 142
1911	Wildfire Schulte, Chi.......121	1936	Joe Medwick, St.L.........138	1962	Tommy Davis, LA 153
1912	Heinie Zimmerman, Chi ...103	1937	Joe Medwick, St.L.........154	1963	Hank Aaron, Mil 130
1913	Gavvy Cravath, Phi 128	1938	Joe Medwick, St.L.........122	1964	Ken Boyer, St.L 119
1914	Sherry Magee, Phi........103	1939	Frank McCormick, Cin 128	1965	Deron Johnson, Cin 130
1915	Gavvy Cravath, Phi 115	1940	Johnny Mize, St.L..........137	1966	Hank Aaron, Atl 127
1916	Heinie Zimmerman, Chi-NY .83	1941	Dolph Camilli, Bklyn 120	1967	Orlando Cepeda, St.L......111
1917	Heinie Zimmerman, NY....102	1942	Johnny Mize, NY 110	1968	Willie McCovey, SF........105
1918	Sherry Magee, Cin.........76	1943	Bill Nicholson, Chi.........128	1969	Willie McCovey, SF 126
1919	Hy Myers, Bklyn 73	1944	Bill Nicholson, Chi.........122	1970	Johnny Bench, Cin 148
1920	Rogers Hornsby, St.L........94	1945	Dixie Walker, Bklyn 124	1971	Joe Torre, St.L 137
	& George Kelly, NY........94	1946	Enos Slaughter, St.L.......130	1972	Johnny Bench, Cin 125
1921	Rogers Hornsby, St.L.......126	1947	Johnny Mize, NY 138	1973	Willie Stargell, Pit.........119
1922	Rogers Hornsby, St.L.......152	1948	Stan Musial, St.L...........131	1974	Johnny Bench, Cin 129
1923	Irish Meusel, NY...........125	1949	Ralph Kiner, Pit 127	1975	Greg Luzinski, Phi 120

Year		RBI
1976	George Foster, Cin	121
1977	George Foster, Cin	149
1978	George Foster, Cin	120
1979	Dave Winfield, SD	118
1980	Mike Schmidt, Phi	121
1981	Mike Schmidt, Phi	91
1982	Dale Murphy, Atl	109
	& Al Oliver, Mon	109
1983	Dale Murphy, Atl	121

Year		RBI
1984	Gary Carter, Mon	106
	& Mike Schmidt, Phi.	106
1985	Dave Parker, Cin	125
1986	Mike Schmidt, Phi.	119
1987	Andre Dawson, Chi	137
1988	Will Clark, SF	109
1989	Kevin Mitchell, SF.	125
1990	Matt Williams, SF.	122
1991	Howard Johnson, NY	117

Year		RBI
1992	Darren Daulton, Phi	109
1993	Barry Bonds, SF	123
1994	Jeff Bagwell, Hou	116
1995	Dante Bichette, Col	128
1996	Andres Galarraga, Col	150
1997	Andres Galarraga, Col	140
1998	Sammy Sosa, Chi.	158
1999	Mark McGwire, St.L.	147
2000	Todd Helton, Col	147

American League

Multiple winners: Babe Ruth (6); Lou Gehrig (5); Ty Cobb, Hank Greenberg and Ted Williams (4); Albert Belle, Sam Crawford, Cecil Fielder, Jimmie Foxx, Jackie Jensen, Harmon Killebrew, Vern Stephens and Bobby Veach (3); Home Run Baker, Cecil Cooper, Harry Davis, Joe DiMaggio, Buck Freeman, Nap Lajoie, Roger Maris, Jim Rice, Al Rosen, and Bobby Veach (2).

Year		RBI
1901	Nap Lajoie, Phi.	125
1902	Buck Freeman, Bos.	121
1903	Buck Freeman, Bos.	104
1904	Nap Lajoie, Cle	102
1905	Harry Davis, Phi	83
1906	Harry Davis, Phi	96
1907	Ty Cobb, Det.	116
1908	Ty Cobb, Det.	108
1909	Ty Cobb, Det.	107
1910	Sam Crawford, Det	120
1911	Ty Cobb, Det.	144
1912	Home Run Baker, Phi	133
1913	Home Run Baker, Phi	126
1914	Sam Crawford, Det	104
1915	Sam Crawford, Det	112
	& Bobby Veach, Det	112
1916	Del Pratt, St.L.	103
1917	Bobby Veach, Det	103
1918	Bobby Veach, Det.	78
1919	Babe Ruth, Bos	114
1920	Babe Ruth, NY	137
1921	Babe Ruth, NY	171
1922	Ken Williams, St.L	155
1923	Babe Ruth, NY	131
1924	Goose Goslin, Wash	129
1925	Bob Meusel, NY	138
1926	Babe Ruth, NY	145
1927	Lou Gehrig, NY	175
1928	Lou Gehrig, NY	142
	& Babe Ruth, NY	142
1929	Al Simmons, Phi	157
1930	Lou Gehrig, NY	174
1931	Lou Gehrig, NY	184
1932	Jimmie Foxx, Phi	169
1933	Jimmie Foxx, Phi	163
1934	Lou Gehrig, NY	165
1935	Hank Greenberg, Det	170

Year		RBI
1936	Hal Trosky, Cle	162
1937	Hank Greenberg, Det	183
1938	Jimmie Foxx, Bos	175
1939	Ted Williams, Bos.	145
1940	Hank Greenberg, Det	150
1941	Joe DiMaggio, NY	125
1942	Ted Williams, Bos.	137
1943	Rudy York, Det	118
1944	Vern Stephens, St.L.	109
1945	Nick Etten, NY	111
1946	Hank Greenberg, Det	127
1947	Ted Williams, Bos.	114
1948	Joe DiMaggio, NY	155
1949	Ted Williams, Bos.	159
	& Vern Stephens, Bos.	159
1950	Walt Dropo, Bos.	144
	& Vern Stephens, Bos.	144
1951	Gus Zernial, Chi-Phi.	129
1952	Al Rosen, Cle	105
1953	Al Rosen, Cle	145
1954	Larry Doby, Cle.	126
1955	Ray Boone, Det.	116
	& Jackie Jensen, Bos	116
1956	Mickey Mantle, NY	130
1957	Roy Sievers, Wash	114
1958	Jackie Jensen, Bos	122
1959	Jackie Jensen, Bos	112
1960	Roger Maris, NY	112
1961	Roger Maris, NY	142
1962	Harmon Killebrew, Min	126
1963	Dick Stuart, Bos	118
1964	Brooks Robinson, Bal.	118
1965	Rocky Colavito, Det	108
1966	Frank Robinson, Bal.	122
1967	Carl Yastrzemski, Bos	121
1968	Ken Harrelson, Bos	109
1969	Harmon Killebrew, Min	140

Year		RBI
1970	Frank Howard, Wash	126
1971	Harmon Killebrew, Min	119
1972	Dick Allen, Chi	113
1973	Reggie Jackson, Oak	117
1974	Jeff Burroughs, Tex	118
1975	George Scott, Mil.	109
1976	Lee May, Bal	109
1977	Larry Hisle, Min	119
1978	Jim Rice, Bos	139
1979	Don Baylor, Cal	139
1980	Cecil Cooper, Mil.	122
1981	Eddie Murray, Bal.	78
1982	Hal McRae, KC.	133
1983	Cecil Cooper, Mil.	126
	& Jim Rice, Bos	126
1984	Tony Armas, Bos.	123
1985	Don Mattingly, NY	145
1986	Joe Carter, Cle	121
1987	George Bell, Tor	134
1988	Jose Canseco, Oak	124
1989	Ruben Sierra, Tex	119
1990	Cecil Fielder, Det	132
1991	Cecil Fielder, Det	133
1992	Cecil Fielder, Det	124
1993	Albert Belle, Cle	129
1994	Kirby Puckett, Min	112
1995	Albert Belle, Cle	126
	& Mo Vaughn, Bos.	126
1996	Albert Belle, Cle	148
1997	Ken Griffey Jr., Sea	147
1998	Juan Gonzalez, Tex	157
1999	Manny Ramirez, Cle	165
2000	Edgar Martinez, Sea	145

Batting Triple Crown Winners

Players who led either league in Batting Average, Home Runs and Runs Batted In over a single season.

National League

	Year	Avg	HR	RBI
Paul Hines, Providence	1878	.358	4	50
Hugh Duffy, Boston	1894	.438	18	145
Heinie Zimmerman, Chicago	1912	.372	14	103
Rogers Hornsby, St. Louis	1922	.401	42	152
Rogers Hornsby, St. Louis	1925	.403	39	143
Chuck Klein, Philadelphia	1933	.368	28	120
Joe Medwick, St. Louis	1937	.374	31*	154

*Tied for league lead in HRs with Mel Ott, NY.

American League

	Year	Avg	HR	RBI
Nap Lajoie, Philadelphia	1901	.422	14	125
Ty Cobb, Detroit	1909	.377	9	115
Jimmie Foxx, Philadelphia	1933	.356	48	163
Lou Gehrig, New York	1934	.363	49	165
Ted Williams, Boston	1942	.356	36	137
Ted Williams, Boston	1947	.343	32	114
Mickey Mantle, New York	1956	.353	52	130
Frank Robinson, Baltimore	1966	.316	49	122
Carl Yastrzemski, Boston	1967	.326	44*	121

*Tied for league lead in HRs with Harmon Killebrew, Min.

Stolen Bases
National League

Multiple winners: Max Carey (10); Lou Brock (8); Vince Coleman and Maury Wills (6); Honus Wagner (5); Bob Bescher, Kiki Cuyler, Willie Mays and Tim Raines (4); Bill Bruton, Frankie Frisch, Pepper Martin and Tony Womack (3); George Burns, Frank Chance, Augie Galan, Marquis Grissom, Stan Hack, Sam Jethroe, Davey Lopes, Omar Moreno, Pete Reiser and Jackie Robinson (2).

Year		SB
1900	Patsy Donovan, St.L	.45
	& George Van Haltren, NY	.45
1901	Honus Wagner, Pit	.49
1902	Honus Wagner, Pit	.42
1903	Frank Chance, Chi	.67
	& Jimmy Sheckard, Bklyn	.67
1904	Honus Wagner, Pit	.53
1905	Art Devlin, NY	.59
	& Billy Maloney, Chi	.59
1906	Frank Chance, Chi	.57
1907	Honus Wagner, Pit	.61
1908	Honus Wagner, Pit	.53
1909	Bob Bescher, Cin	.54
1910	Bob Bescher, Cin	.70
1911	Bob Bescher, Cin	.81
1912	Bob Bescher, Cin	.67
1913	Max Carey, Pit	.61
1914	George Burns, NY	.62
1915	Max Carey, Pit	.36
1916	Max Carey, Pit	.63
1917	Max Carey, Pit	.46
1918	Max Carey, Pit	.58
1919	George Burns, NY	.40
1920	Max Carey, Pit	.52
1921	Frankie Frisch, NY	.49
1922	Max Carey, Pit	.51
1923	Max Carey, Pit	.51
1924	Max Carey, Pit	.49
1925	Max Carey, Pit	.46
1926	Kiki Cuyler, Pit	.35
1927	Frankie Frisch, St.L	.48
1928	Kiki Cuyler, Chi	.37
1929	Kiki Cuyler, Chi	.43
1930	Kiki Cuyler, Chi	.37
1931	Frankie Frisch, St.L	.28
1932	Chuck Klein, Phi	.20

Year		SB
1933	Pepper Martin, St.L	.26
1934	Pepper Martin, St.L	.23
1935	Augie Galan, Chi	.22
1936	Pepper Martin, St.L	.23
1937	Augie Galan, Chi	.23
1938	Stan Hack, Chi	.16
1939	Stan Hack, Chi	.17
	& Lee Handley, Pit	.17
1940	Lonny Frey, Cin	.22
1941	Danny Murtaugh, Phi	.18
1942	Pete Reiser, Bklyn	.20
1943	Arky Vaughan, Bklyn	.20
1944	Johnny Barrett, Pit	.28
1945	Red Schoendienst, St.L	.26
1946	Pete Reiser, Bklyn	.34
1947	Jackie Robinson, Bklyn	.29
1948	Richie Ashburn, Phi	.32
1949	Jackie Robinson, Bklyn	.37
1950	Sam Jethroe, Bos	.35
1951	Sam Jethroe, Bos	.35
1952	Pee Wee Reese, Bklyn	.30
1953	Bill Bruton, Mil	.26
1954	Bill Bruton, Mil	.34
1955	Bill Bruton, Mil	.25
1956	Willie Mays, NY	.40
1957	Willie Mays, NY	.38
1958	Willie Mays, SF	.31
1959	Willie Mays, SF	.27
1960	Maury Wills, LA	.50
1961	Maury Wills, LA	.35
1962	Maury Wills, LA	.104
1963	Maury Wills, LA	.40
1964	Maury Wills, LA	.53
1965	Maury Wills, LA	.94
1966	Lou Brock, St.L	.74
1967	Lou Brock, St.L	.52

Year		SB
1968	Lou Brock, St.L	.62
1969	Lou Brock, St.L	.53
1970	Bobby Tolan, Cin	.57
1971	Lou Brock, St.L	.64
1972	Lou Brock, St.L	.63
1973	Lou Brock, St.L	.70
1974	Lou Brock, St.L	.118
1975	Davey Lopes, LA	.77
1976	Davey Lopes, LA	.63
1977	Frank Taveras, Pit	.70
1978	Omar Moreno, Pit	.71
1979	Omar Moreno, Pit	.77
1980	Ron LeFlore, Mon	.97
1981	Tim Raines, Mon	.71
1982	Tim Raines, Mon	.78
1983	Tim Raines, Mon	.90
1984	Tim Raines, Mon	.75
1985	Vince Coleman, St.L	.110
1986	Vince Coleman, St.L	.107
1987	Vince Coleman, St.L	.109
1988	Vince Coleman, St.L	.81
1989	Vince Coleman, St.L	.65
1990	Vince Coleman, St.L	.77
1991	Marquis Grissom, Mon	.76
1992	Marquis Grissom, Mon	.78
1993	Chuck Carr, Fla	.58
1994	Craig Biggio, Hou	.39
1995	Quilvio Veras, Fla	.56
1996	Eric Young, Col	.53
1997	Tony Womack, Pit	.60
1998	Tony Womack, Pit	.58
1999	Tony Womack, Ari	.72
2000	Luis Castillo, Fla	.62

30 Homers & 30 Stolen Bases in One Season
National League

	Year	Gm	HR	SB
Willie Mays, NY Giants	1956	152	36	40
Willie Mays, NY Giants	1957	152	35	38
Hank Aaron, Milwaukee	1963	161	44	31
Bobby Bonds, San Francisco	1969	158	32	45
Bobby Bonds, San Francisco	1973	160	39	43
Dale Murphy, Atlanta	1983	162	36	30
Eric Davis, Cincinnati	1987	129	37	50
Howard Johnson, NY Mets	1987	157	36	32
Darryl Strawberry, NY Mets	1987	154	39	36
Howard Johnson, NY Mets	1989	153	36	41
Ron Gant, Atlanta	1990	152	32	33
Barry Bonds, Pittsburgh	1990	151	33	52
Ron Gant, Atlanta	1991	154	32	34
Howard Johnson, NY Mets	1991	156	38	30
Barry Bonds, Pittsburgh	1992	140	34	39
Sammy Sosa, Chicago	1993	159	33	36
Barry Bonds, San Francisco	1995	144	33	31
Sammy Sosa, Chicago	1995	144	36	34
Barry Bonds, San Francisco	1996	158	42	40
Ellis Burks, Colorado	1996	156	40	32
Dante Bichette, Colorado	1996	159	31	31

	Year	Gm	HR	SB
Larry Walker, Colorado	1997	153	49	33
Barry Bonds, San Francisco	1997	159	40	37
Raul Mondesi, Los Angeles	1997	159	30	32
Jeff Bagwell, Houston	1997	162	43	31
Jeff Bagwell, Houston	1999	162	42	30
Raul Mondesi, Los Angeles	1999	159	33	36
Preston Wilson, Florida	2000	161	31	36

American League

	Year	Gm	HR	SB
Kenny Williams, St. Louis	1922	153	39	37
Tommy Harper, Milwaukee	1970	154	31	38
Bobby Bonds, New York	1975	145	32	30
Bobby Bonds, California	1977	158	37	41
Bobby Bonds, Chicago-Texas	1978	156	31	43
Joe Carter, Cleveland	1987	149	32	31
Jose Canseco, Oakland	1988	158	42	40
Alex Rodriguez, Seattle	1998	161	42	46
Shawn Green, Toronto	1998	158	35	35

American League

Multiple winners: Rickey Henderson (12); Luis Aparicio (9); Bert Campaneris, George Case and Ty Cobb (6); Kenny Lofton (5); Ben Chapman, Eddie Collins and George Sisler (4); Bob Dillinger, Minnie Minoso and Bill Werber (3); Elmer Flick, Tommy Harper, Brian Hunter, Clyde Milan, Johnny Mostil, Bill North and Snuffy Stirnweiss (2).

Year	SB	Year	SB	Year	SB
1901 Frank Isbell, Chi	52	1934 Bill Werber, Bos	40	1967 Bert Campaneris, KC	55
1902 Topsy Hartsel, Phi	47	1935 Bill Werber, Bos	29	1968 Bert Campaneris, Oak	62
1903 Harry Bay, Cle	45	1936 Lyn Lary, St.L	37	1969 Tommy Harper, Sea	73
1904 Elmer Flick, Cle	42	1937 Ben Chapman, Wash-Bos	35	1970 Bert Campaneris, Oak	42
1905 Danny Hoffman, Phi	46	& Bill Werber, Phi	35	1971 Amos Otis, KC	52
1906 John Anderson, Wash	39	1938 Frank Crosetti, NY	27	1972 Bert Campaneris, Oak	52
& Elmer Flick, Cle	39	1939 George Case, Wash	51	1973 Tommy Harper, Bos	54
1907 Ty Cobb, Det	49	1940 George Case, Wash	35	1974 Bill North, Oak	54
1908 Patsy Dougherty, Chi	47	1941 George Case, Wash	33	1975 Mickey Rivers, CA	70
1909 Ty Cobb, Det	76	1942 George Case, Wash	44	1976 Bill North, Oak	75
1910 Eddie Collins, Phi	81	1943 George Case, Wash	61	1977 Freddie Patek, KC	53
1911 Ty Cobb, Det	83	1944 Snuffy Stirnweiss, NY	55	1978 Ron LeFlore, Det	68
1912 Clyde Milan, Wash	88	1945 Snuffy Stirnweiss, NY	33	1979 Willie Wilson, KC	83
1913 Clyde Milan, Wash	75	1946 George Case, Cle	28	1980 Rickey Henderson, Oak	100
1914 Fritz Maisel, NY	74	1947 Bob Dillinger, St.L	34	1981 Rickey Henderson, Oak	56
1915 Ty Cobb, Det	96	1948 Bob Dillinger, St.L	28	1982 Rickey Henderson, Oak	130
1916 Ty Cobb, Det	68	1949 Bob Dillinger, St.L	20	1983 Rickey Henderson, Oak	108
1917 Ty Cobb, Det	55	1950 Dom DiMaggio, Bos	15	1984 Rickey Henderson, Oak	66
1918 George Sisler, St.L	45	1951 Minnie Minoso, Cle-Chi	31	1985 Rickey Henderson, NY	80
1919 Eddie Collins, Chi	33	1952 Minnie Minoso, Chi	22	1986 Rickey Henderson, NY	87
1920 Sam Rice, Wash	63	1953 Minnie Minoso, Chi	25	1987 Harold Reynolds, Sea	60
1921 George Sisler, St.L	35	1954 Jackie Jensen, Bos	22	1988 Rickey Henderson, NY	93
1922 George Sisler, St.L	51	1955 Jim Rivera, Chi	25	1989 R. Henderson, NY-Oak	77
1923 Eddie Collins, Chi	47	1956 Luis Aparicio, Chi	21	1990 Rickey Henderson, Oak	65
1924 Eddie Collins, Chi	42	1957 Luis Aparicio, Chi	28	1991 Rickey Henderson, Oak	58
1925 Johnny Mostil, Chi	43	1958 Luis Aparicio, Chi	29	1992 Kenny Lofton, Cle	66
1926 Johnny Mostil, Chi	35	1959 Luis Aparicio, Chi	56	1993 Kenny Lofton, Cle	70
1927 George Sisler, St.L	27	1960 Luis Aparicio, Chi	51	1994 Kenny Lofton, Cle	60
1928 Buddy Myer, Bos	30	1961 Luis Aparicio, Chi	53	1995 Kenny Lofton, Cle	54
1929 Charlie Gehringer, Det	28	1962 Luis Aparicio, Chi	31	1996 Kenny Lofton, Cle	75
1930 Marty McManus, Det	23	1963 Luis Aparicio, Bal	40	1997 Brian Hunter, Det	74
1931 Ben Chapman, NY	61	1964 Luis Aparicio, Bal	57	1998 Rickey Henderson, Oak	66
1932 Ben Chapman, NY	38	1965 Bert Campaneris, KC	51	1999 Brian Hunter, Det-Sea	44
1933 Ben Chapman, NY	27	1966 Bert Campaneris, KC	52	2000 Johnny Damon, KC	46

Consecutive Game Streaks

Regular season games through 2000.

Games Played

Gm		Dates of Streak
2632	Cal Ripken Jr., Bal	5/30/82 to 9/19/98
2130	Lou Gehrig, NY	6/1/25 to 4/30/39
1307	Everett Scott, Bos-NY	6/20/16 to 5/5/25
1207	Steve Garvey, LA-SD	9/3/75 to 7/29/83
1117	Billy Williams, Cubs	9/22/63 to 9/2/70
1103	Joe Sewell, Cle	9/13/22 to 4/30/30
895	Stan Musial, St.L	4/15/52 to 8/23/57
829	Eddie Yost, Wash	4/30/49 to 5/11/55
822	Gus Suhr, Pit	9/11/31 to 6/4/37
798	Nellie Fox, Chisox	8/8/55 to 9/3/60
745	Pete Rose, Cin-Phi	9/2/78 to 8/23/83
740	Dale Murphy, Atl	9/26/81 to 7/8/86
730	Richie Ashburn, Phi	6/7/50 to 4/13/55
717	Ernie Banks, Cubs	8/28/56 to 6/22/61
678	Pete Rose, Cin	9/28/73 to 5/7/78

Hitting

	Gm	Year
Joe DiMaggio, New York (AL)	56	1941
Willie Keeler, Baltimore (NL)	44	1897
Pete Rose, Cincinnati (NL)	44	1978
Bill Dahlen, Chicago (NL)	42	1894
George Sisler, St. Louis (AL)	41	1922
Ty Cobb, Detroit (AL)	40	1911
Paul Molitor, Milwaukee (AL)	39	1987
Tommy Holmes, Boston (NL)	37	1945
Billy Hamilton, Philadelphia (NL)	36	1894
Fred Clarke, Louisville (NL)	35	1895
Ty Cobb, Detroit (AL)	35	1917
Ty Cobb, Detroit (AL)	34	1912
George Sisler, St. Louis (AL)	34	1925
George McQuinn, St. Louis (AL)	34	1938
Dom DiMaggio, Boston (AL)	34	1949
Benito Santiago, San Diego (NL)	34	1987
George Davis, New York (NL)	33	1893
Hal Chase, New York (AL)	33	1907
Rogers Hornsby, St. Louis (NL)	33	1922
Heinie Manush, Washington (AL)	33	1933
Ed Delahanty, Philadelphia (NL)	31	1899
Nap Lajoie, Cleveland (AL)	31	1906
Sam Rice, Washington, (AL)	31	1924
Willie Davis, Los Angeles (NL)	31	1969
Rico Carty, Atlanta (NL)	31	1970
Ken Landreaux, Minnesota (AL)	31	1980
Vladimir Guerrero, Montreal (NL)	31	1999

Others

Gm		Gm	
673	Earl Averill	565	Aaron Ward
652	Frank McCormick	540	Candy LaChance
648	Sandy Alomar Sr.	535	Buck Freeman
618	Eddie Brown	533	Fred Luderus
585	Roy McMillan	511	Clyde Milan
577	George Pinckney	511	Charlie Gehringer
574	Steve Brodie	508	Vada Pinson

Annual Pitching Leaders (since 1900)
Winning Percentage
At least 15 wins, except in strike years of 1981 and 1994 (when the minimum was 10).
National League
Multiple winners: Ed Reulbach and Tom Seaver (3); Larry Benton, Harry Brecheen, Jack Chesbro, Paul Derringer, Freddie Fitzsimmons, Don Gullett, Claude Hendrix, Carl Hubbell, Sandy Koufax, Bill Lee, Greg Maddux, Christy Mathewson, Don Newcombe, Preacher Roe and John Smoltz (2).

Year		W-L	Pct	Year		W-L	Pct
1900	Jesse Tannehill, Pittsburgh	20-6	.769	1951	Preacher Roe, Brooklyn	22-3	.880
1901	Jack Chesbro, Pittsburgh	21-10	.677	1952	Hoyt Wilhelm, New York	15-3	.833
1902	Jack Chesbro, Pittsburgh	28-6	.824	1953	Carl Erskine, Brooklyn	20-6	.769
1903	Sam Leever, Pittsburgh	25-7	.781	1954	Johnny Antonelli, New York	21-7	.750
1904	Joe McGinnity, New York	35-8	.814	1955	Don Newcombe, Brooklyn	20-5	.800
1905	Christy Mathewson, New York	31-8	.795	1956	Don Newcombe, Brooklyn	27-7	.794
1906	Ed Reulbach, Chicago	19-4	.826	1957	Bob Buhl, Milwaukee	18-7	.720
1907	Ed Reulbach, Chicago	17-4	.810	1958	Warren Spahn, Milwaukee	22-11	.667
1908	Ed Reulbach, Chicago	24-7	.774		& Lew Burdette, Milwaukee	20-10	.667
1909	Howie Camnitz, Pittsburgh	25-6	.806	1959	Roy Face, Pittsburgh	18-1	.947
	& Christy Mathewson, New York	25-6	.806				
				1960	Ernie Broglio, St. Louis	21-9	.700
1910	King Cole, Chicago	20-4	.833	1961	Johnny Podres, Los Angeles	18-5	.783
1911	Rube Marquard, New York	24-7	.774	1962	Bob Purkey, Cincinnati	23-5	.821
1912	Claude Hendrix, Pittsburgh	24-9	.727	1963	Ron Perranoski, Los Angeles	16-3	.842
1913	Bert Humphries, Chicago	16-4	.800	1964	Sandy Koufax, Los Angeles	19-5	.792
1914	Bill James, Boston	26-7	.788	1965	Sandy Koufax, Los Angeles	26-8	.765
1915	Grover Alexander, Phila.	31-10	.756	1966	Juan Marichal, San Francisco	25-6	.806
1916	Tom Hughes, Boston	16-3	.842	1967	Dick Hughes, St. Louis	16-6	.727
1917	Ferdie Schupp, New York	21-7	.750	1968	Steve Blass, Pittsburgh	18-6	.750
1918	Claude Hendrix, Chicago	19-7	.731	1969	Tom Seaver, New York	25-7	.781
1919	Dutch Ruether, Cincinnati	19-6	.760				
				1970	Bob Gibson, St. Louis	23-7	.767
1920	Burleigh Grimes, Brooklyn	23-11	.676	1971	Don Gullett, Cincinnati	16-6	.727
1921	Bill Doak, St. Louis	15-6	.714	1972	Gary Nolan, Cincinnati	15-5	.750
1922	Pete Donohue, Cincinnati	18-9	.667	1973	Tommy John, Los Angeles	16-7	.696
1923	Dolf Luque, Cincinnati	27-8	.771	1974	Andy Messersmith, Los Angeles	20-6	.769
1924	Emil Yde, Pittsburgh	16-3	.842	1975	Don Gullett, Cincinnati	15-4	.789
1925	Bill Sherdel, St. Louis	15-6	.714	1976	Steve Carlton, Philadelphia	20-7	.741
1926	Ray Kremer, Pittsburgh	20-6	.769	1977	John Candelaria, Pittsburgh	20-5	.800
1927	Larry Benton, Boston-NY	17-7	.708	1978	Gaylord Perry, San Diego	21-6	.778
1928	Larry Benton, New York	25-9	.735	1979	Tom Seaver, Cincinnati	16-6	.727
1929	Charlie Root, Chicago	19-6	.760				
				1980	Jim Bibby, Pittsburgh	19-6	.760
1930	Freddie Fitzsimmons, NY	19-7	.731	1981	Tom Seaver, Cincinnati	14-2	.875
1931	Paul Derringer, St. Louis	18-8	.692	1982	Phil Niekro, Atlanta	17-4	.810
1932	Lon Warneke, Chicago	22-6	.786	1983	John Denny, Philadelphia	19-6	.760
1933	Ben Cantwell, Boston	20-10	.667	1984	Rick Sutcliffe, Chicago	16-1	.941
1934	Dizzy Dean, St. Louis	30-7	.811	1985	Orel Hershiser, Los Angeles	19-3	.864
1935	Bill Lee, Chicago	20-6	.769	1986	Bob Ojeda, New York	18-5	.783
1936	Carl Hubbell, New York	26-6	.813	1987	Dwight Gooden, New York	15-7	.682
1937	Carl Hubbell, New York	22-8	.733	1988	David Cone, New York	20-3	.870
1938	Bill Lee, Chicago	22-9	.710	1989	Mike Bielecki, Chicago	18-7	.720
1939	Paul Derringer, Cincinnati	25-7	.781				
				1990	Doug Drabek, Pittsburgh	22-6	.786
1940	Freddie Fitzsimmons, Bklyn	16-2	.889	1991	John Smiley, Pittsburgh	20-8	.714
1941	Elmer Riddle, Cincinnati	19-4	.826		& Jose Rijo, Cincinnati	15-6	.714
1942	Larry French, Brooklyn	15-4	.789	1992	Bob Tewksbury, St. Louis	16-5	.762
1943	Mort Cooper, St. Louis	21-8	.724	1993	Mark Portugal, Houston	18-4	.818
1944	Ted Wilks, St. Louis	17-4	.810	1994	Marvin Freeman, Colorado	10-2	.833
1945	Harry Brecheen, St. Louis	14-4	.778	1995	Greg Maddux, Atlanta	19-2	.905
1946	Murray Dickson, St. Louis	15-6	.714	1996	John Smoltz, Atlanta	24-8	.750
1947	Larry Jansen, New York	21-5	.808	1997	Greg Maddux, Atlanta	19-4	.826
1948	Harry Brecheen, St. Louis	20-7	.741	1998	John Smoltz, Atlanta	17-3	.850
1949	Preacher Roe, Brooklyn	15-6	.714	1999	Mike Hampton, Houston	22-4	.846
1950	Sal Maglie, New York	18-4	.818	2000	Randy Johnson, Arizona	19-7	.731

Note: In 1984, Sutcliffe was also 4-5 with Cleveland for a combined AL-NL record of 20-6 (.769).

American League
Multiple winners: Lefty Grove (5); Chief Bender and Whitey Ford (3); Johnny Allen, Eddie Cicotte, Roger Clemens, Mike Cuellar, Lefty Gomez, Catfish Hunter, Randy Johnson, Walter Johnson, Jim Palmer, Pete Vuckovich and Smokey Joe Wood (2).

Year		W-L	Pct	Year		W-L	Pct
1901	Clark Griffith, Chicago	24-7	.774	1904	Jack Chesbro, New York	41-12	.774
1902	Bill Bernhard, Phila-Cleve	18-5	.783	1905	Andy Coakley, Philadelphia	20-7	.741
1903	Cy Young, Boston	28-9	.757	1906	Eddie Plank, Philadelphia	19-6	.760

Year		W-L	Pct	Year		W-L	Pct
1907	Wild Bill Donovan, Detroit	25-4	.862	1956	Whitey Ford, New York	19-6	.760
1908	Ed Walsh, Chicago	40-15	.727	1957	Dick Donovan, Chicago	16-6	.727
1909	George Mullin, Detroit	29-8	.784		& Tom Sturdivant, New York	16-6	.727
1910	Chief Bender, Philadelphia	23-5	.821	1958	Bob Turley, New York	21-7	.750
1911	Chief Bender, Philadelphia	17-5	.773	1959	Bob Shaw, Chicago	18-6	.750
1912	Smokey Joe Wood, Boston	34-5	.872	1960	Jim Perry, Cleveland	18-10	.643
1913	Walter Johnson, Washington	36-7	.837	1961	Whitey Ford, New York	25-4	.862
1914	Chief Bender, Philadelphia	17-3	.850	1962	Ray Herbert, Chicago	20-9	.690
1915	Smokey Joe Wood, Boston	15-5	.750	1963	Whitey Ford, New York	24-7	.774
1916	Eddie Cicotte, Chicago	15-7	.682	1964	Wally Bunker, Baltimore	19-5	.792
1917	Reb Russell, Chicago	15-5	.750	1965	Mudcat Grant, Minnesota	21-7	.750
1918	Sad Sam Jones, Boston	16-5	.762	1966	Sonny Siebert, Cleveland	16-8	.667
1919	Eddie Cicotte, Chicago	29-7	.806	1967	Joe Horlen, Chicago	19-7	.731
1920	Jim Bagby, Cleveland	31-12	.721	1968	Denny McLain, Detroit	31-6	.838
1921	Carl Mays, New York	27-9	.750	1969	Jim Palmer, Baltimore	16-4	.800
1922	Joe Bush, New York	26-7	.788	1970	Mike Cuellar, Baltimore	24-8	.750
1923	Herb Pennock, New York	19-6	.760	1971	Dave McNally, Baltimore	21-5	.808
1924	Walter Johnson, Washington	23-7	.767	1972	Catfish Hunter, Oakland	21-7	.750
1925	Stan Coveleski, Washington	20-5	.800	1973	Catfish Hunter, Oakland	21-5	.808
1926	George Uhle, Cleveland	27-11	.711	1974	Mike Cuellar, Baltimore	22-10	.688
1927	Waite Hoyt, New York	22-7	.759	1975	Mike Torrez, Baltimore	20-9	.690
1928	General Crowder, St. Louis	21-5	.808	1976	Bill Campbell, Minnesota	17-5	.773
1929	Lefty Grove, Philadelphia	20-6	.769	1977	Paul Splittorff, Kansas City	16-6	.727
1930	Lefty Grove, Philadelphia	28-5	.848	1978	Ron Guidry, New York	25-3	.893
1931	Lefty Grove, Philadelphia	31-4	.886	1979	Mike Caldwell, Milwaukee	16-6	.727
1932	Johnny Allen, New York	17-4	.810	1980	Steve Stone, Baltimore	25-7	.781
1933	Lefty Grove, Philadelphia	24-8	.750	1981	Pete Vuckovich, Milwaukee	14-4	.778
1934	Lefty Gomez, New York	26-5	.839	1982	Pete Vuckovich, Milwaukee	18-6	.750
1935	Eldon Auker, Detroit	18-7	.720		& Jim Palmer, Baltimore	15-5	.750
1936	Monte Pearson, New York	19-7	.731	1983	Rich Dotson, Chicago	22-7	.759
1937	Johnny Allen, Cleveland	15-1	.938	1984	Doyle Alexander, Toronto	17-6	.739
1938	Red Ruffing, New York	21-7	.750	1985	Ron Guidry, New York	22-6	.786
1939	Lefty Grove, Boston	15-4	.789	1986	Roger Clemens, Boston	24-4	.857
1940	Schoolboy Rowe, Detroit	16-3	.842	1987	Roger Clemens, Boston	20-9	.690
1941	Lefty Gomez, New York	15-5	.750	1988	Frank Viola, Minnesota	24-7	.774
1942	Ernie Bonham, New York	21-5	.808	1989	Bret Saberhagen, Kansas City	23-6	.793
1943	Spud Chandler, New York	20-4	.833	1990	Bob Welch, Oakland	27-6	.818
1944	Tex Hughson, Boston	18-5	.783	1991	Scott Erickson, Minnesota	20-8	.714
1945	Hal Newhouser, Detroit	25-9	.735	1992	Mike Mussina, Baltimore	18-5	.783
1946	Boo Ferriss, Boston	25-6	.806	1993	Jimmy Key, New York	18-6	.750
1947	Allie Reynolds, New York	19-8	.704	1994	Jason Bere, Chicago	12-2	.857
1948	Jack Kramer, Boston	18-5	.783	1995	Randy Johnson, Seattle	18-2	.900
1949	Ellis Kinder, Boston	23-6	.793	1996	Charles Nagy, Cleveland	17-5	.773
1950	Vic Raschi, New York	21-8	.724	1997	Randy Johnson, Seattle	20-4	.833
1951	Bob Feller, Cleveland	22-8	.733	1998	David Wells, New York	18-4	.818
1952	Bobby Shantz, Philadelphia	24-7	.774	1999	Pedro Martinez, Boston	23-4	.852
1953	Ed Lopat, New York	16-4	.800	2000	Tim Hudson, Oakland	20-6	.769
1954	Sandy Consuegra, Chicago	16-3	.842				
1955	Tommy Byrne, New York	16-5	.762				

Earned Run Average

Earned Run Averages were based on at least 10 complete games pitched (1900-49), at least 154 innings pitched (1950-60), and at least 162 innings pitched since 1961 in the AL and 1962 in the NL. In the strike years of 1981, '94 and '95, qualifiers had to pitch at least as many innings as the total number of games their team played that season.

National League

Multiple winners: Grover Alexander, Sandy Koufax and Christy Mathewson (5); Greg Maddux (4); Carl Hubbell, Tom Seaver, Warren Spahn and Dazzy Vance (3); Kevin Brown, Bill Doak, Ray Kremer, Dolf Luque, Howie Pollet, Nolan Ryan, Bill Walker and Bucky Walters (2).

Year		ERA	Year		ERA	Year		ERA
1900	Rube Waddell, Pit	2.37	1909	Christy Mathewson, NY	1.14	1918	Hippo Vaughn, Chi	1.74
1901	Jesse Tannehill, Pit	2.18	1910	George McQuillan, Phi	1.60	1919	Grover Alexander, Chi	1.72
1902	Jack Taylor, Chi	1.33	1911	Christy Mathewson, NY	1.99	1920	Grover Alexander, Chi	1.91
1903	Sam Leever, Pit	2.06	1912	Jeff Tesreau, NY	1.96	1921	Bill Doak, St.L	2.59
1904	Joe McGinnity, NY	1.61	1913	Christy Mathewson, NY	2.06	1922	Rosy Ryan, NY	3.01
1905	Christy Mathewson, NY	1.27	1914	Bill Doak, St.L	1.72	1923	Dolf Luque, Cin	1.93
1906	Three Finger Brown, Chi	1.04	1915	Grover Alexander, Phi	1.22	1924	Dazzy Vance, Bklyn	2.16
1907	Jack Pfiester, Chi	1.15	1916	Grover Alexander, Phi	1.55	1925	Dolf Luque, Cin	2.63
1908	Christy Mathewson, NY	1.43	1917	Grover Alexander, Phi	1.86	1926	Ray Kremer, Pit	2.61

Year		ERA	Year		ERA	Year		ERA
1927	Ray Kremer, Pit	2.47	1952	Hoyt Wilhelm, NY	2.43	1977	John Candelaria, Pit	2.34
1928	Dazzy Vance, Bklyn	2.09	1953	Warren Spahn, Mil.	2.10	1978	Craig Swan, NY	2.43
1929	Bill Walker, NY	3.09	1954	Johnny Antonelli, NY	2.30	1979	J.R. Richard, Hou	2.71
1930	Dazzy Vance, Bklyn	2.61	1955	Bob Friend, Pit.	2.83	1980	Don Sutton, LA.	2.21
1931	Bill Walker, NY	2.26	1956	Lew Burdette, Mil	2.70	1981	Nolan Ryan, Hou	1.69
1932	Lon Warneke, Chi.	2.37	1957	Johnny Podres, Bklyn	2.66	1982	Steve Rogers, Mon	2.40
1933	Carl Hubbell, NY	1.66	1958	Stu Miller, SF	2.47	1983	Atlee Hammaker, SF	2.25
1934	Carl Hubbell, NY	2.30	1959	Sam Jones, SF	2.83	1984	Alejandro Peña, LA.	2.48
1935	Cy Blanton, Pit.	2.58	1960	Mike McCormick, SF	2.70	1985	Dwight Gooden, NY	1.53
1936	Carl Hubbell, NY	2.31	1961	Warren Spahn, Mil.	3.02	1986	Mike Scott, Hou	2.22
1937	Jim Turner, Bos	2.38	1962	Sandy Koufax, LA	2.54	1987	Nolan Ryan, Hou	2.76
1938	Bill Lee, Chi	2.66	1963	Sandy Koufax, LA.	1.88	1988	Joe Magrane, St.L	2.18
1939	Bucky Walters, Cin	2.29	1964	Sandy Koufax, LA.	1.74	1989	Scott Garrelts, SF	2.28
1940	Bucky Walters, Cin	2.48	1965	Sandy Koufax, LA.	2.04	1990	Danny Darwin, Hou	2.21
1941	Elmer Riddle, Cin	2.24	1966	Sandy Koufax, LA.	1.73	1991	Dennis Martinez, Mon	2.39
1942	Mort Cooper, St.L	1.78	1967	Phil Niekro, Atl	1.87	1992	Bill Swift, SF.	2.08
1943	Howie Pollet, St.L	1.75	1968	Bob Gibson, St.L.	1.12	1993	Greg Maddux, Atl	2.36
1944	Ed Heusser, Cin.	2.38	1969	Juan Marichal, SF	2.10	1994	Greg Maddux, Atl	1.56
1945	Hank Borowy, Chi.	2.13	1970	Tom Seaver, NY	2.81	1995	Greg Maddux, Atl	1.63
1946	Howie Pollet, St.L	2.10	1971	Tom Seaver, NY	1.76	1996	Kevin Brown, Fla	1.89
1947	Warren Spahn, Bos	2.33	1972	Steve Carlton, Phi	1.97	1997	Pedro Martinez, Mon	1.90
1948	Harry Brecheen, St.L.	2.24	1973	Tom Seaver, NY	2.08	1998	Greg Maddux, Atl	2.22
1949	Dave Koslo, NY	2.50	1974	Buzz Capra, Atl	2.28	1999	Randy Johnson, Ari.	2.48
1950	Jim Hearn, St.L-NY	2.49	1975	Randy Jones, SD	2.24	2000	Kevin Brown, LA	2.58
1951	Chet Nichols, Bos	2.88	1976	John Denny, St.L	2.52			

Note: In 1945, Borowy had a 3.13 ERA in 18 games with New York (AL) for a combined ERA of 2.65.

American League

Multiple winners: Lefty Grove (9); Roger Clemens (6); Walter Johnson (5); Spud Chandler, Stan Coveleski, Red Faber, Whitey Ford, Lefty Gomez, Ron Guidry, Addie Joss, Pedro Martinez, Hal Newhouser, Jim Palmer, Gary Peters, Luis Tiant and Ed Walsh (2).

Year		ERA	Year		ERA	Year		ERA
1901	Cy Young, Bos	1.62	1935	Lefty Grove, Bos	2.70	1969	Dick Bosman, Wash	2.19
1902	Ed Siever, Det	1.91	1936	Lefty Grove, Bos	2.81	1970	Diego Segui, Oak.	2.56
1903	Earl Moore, Cle.	1.77	1937	Lefty Gomez, NY	2.33	1971	Vida Blue, Oak	1.82
1904	Addie Joss, Cle	1.59	1938	Lefty Grove, Bos	3.08	1972	Luis Tiant, Bos	1.91
1905	Rube Waddell, Phi	1.48	1939	Lefty Grove, Bos	2.54	1973	Jim Palmer, Bal	2.40
1906	Doc White, Chi	1.52	1940	Ernie Bonham, NY	1.90	1974	Catfish Hunter, Oak	2.49
1907	Ed Walsh, Chi	1.60	1941	Thornton Lee, Chi	2.37	1975	Jim Palmer, Bal	2.09
1908	Addie Joss, Cle	1.16	1942	Ted Lyons, Chi	2.10	1976	Mark Fidrych, Det	2.34
1909	Harry Krause, Phi	1.39	1943	Spud Chandler, NY	1.64	1977	Frank Tanana, Cal	2.54
1910	Ed Walsh, Chi	1.27	1944	Dizzy Trout, Det.	2.12	1978	Ron Guidry, NY	1.74
1911	Vean Gregg, Cle	1.81	1945	Hal Newhouser, Det	1.81	1979	Ron Guidry, NY	2.78
1912	Walter Johnson, Wash	1.39	1946	Hal Newhouser, Det	1.94	1980	Rudy May, NY.	2.47
1913	Walter Johnson, Wash	1.09	1947	Spud Chandler, NY	2.46	1981	Steve McCatty, Oak	2.32
1914	Dutch Leonard, Bos	1.01	1948	Gene Bearden, Cle.	2.43	1982	Rick Sutcliffe, Cle	2.96
1915	Smokey Joe Wood, Bos	1.49	1949	Mel Parnell, Bos	2.77	1983	Rick Honeycutt, Tex.	2.42
1916	Babe Ruth, Bos	1.75	1950	Early Wynn, Cle	3.20	1984	Mike Boddicker, Bal	2.79
1917	Eddie Cicotte, Chi	1.53	1951	Saul Rogovin, Det-Chi	2.78	1985	Dave Stieb, Tor	2.48
1918	Walter Johnson, Wash	1.27	1952	Allie Reynolds, NY	2.06	1986	Roger Clemens, Bos	2.48
1919	Walter Johnson, Wash	1.49	1953	Ed Lopat, NY	2.42	1987	Jimmy Key, Tor.	2.76
1920	Bob Shawkey, NY	2.45	1954	Mike Garcia, Cle	2.64	1988	Allan Anderson, Min	2.45
1921	Red Faber, Chi.	2.48	1955	Billy Pierce, Chi.	1.97	1989	Bret Saberhagen, KC	2.16
1922	Red Faber, Chi.	2.80	1956	Whitey Ford, NY	2.47	1990	Roger Clemens, Bos	1.93
1923	Stan Coveleski, Cle.	2.76	1957	Bobby Shantz, NY	2.45	1991	Roger Clemens, Bos	2.62
1924	Walter Johnson, Wash	2.72	1958	Whitey Ford, NY	2.01	1992	Roger Clemens, Bos	2.41
1925	Stan Coveleski, Wash.	2.84	1959	Hoyt Wilhelm, Bal.	2.19	1993	Kevin Appier, KC	2.56
1926	Lefty Grove, Phi	2.51	1960	Frank Baumann, Chi.	2.67	1994	Steve Ontiveros, Oak.	2.65
1927	Wilcy Moore, NY	2.28	1961	Dick Donovan, Wash	2.40	1995	Randy Johnson, Sea	2.48
1928	Garland Braxton, Wash.	2.51	1962	Hank Aguirre, Det.	2.21	1996	Juan Guzman, Tor.	2.93
1929	Lefty Grove, Phi	2.81	1963	Gary Peters, Chi	2.33	1997	Roger Clemens, Tor.	2.05
1930	Lefty Grove, Phi	2.54	1964	Dean Chance, LA	1.65	1998	Roger Clemens, Tor.	2.65
1931	Lefty Grove, Phi	2.06	1965	Sam McDowell, Cle	2.18	1999	Pedro Martinez, Bos.	2.07
1932	Lefty Grove, Phi	2.84	1966	Gary Peters, Chi	1.98	2000	Pedro Martinez, Bos.	1.74
1933	Monte Pearson, Cle	2.33	1967	Joe Horlen, Chi	2.06			
1934	Lefty Gomez, NY	2.33	1968	Luis Tiant, Cle	1.60			

Strikeouts
National League

Multiple winners: Dazzy Vance (7); Grover Alexander (6); Steve Carlton, Christy Mathewson and Tom Seaver (5); Dizzy Dean, Sandy Koufax and Warren Spahn (4); Don Drysdale, Sam Jones and Johnny Vander Meer (3); David Cone, Dwight Gooden, Bill Hallahan, Randy Johnson, J.R. Richard, Robin Roberts, Nolan Ryan, Curt Schilling, John Smoltz and Hippo Vaughn (2).

Year	SO	Year	SO	Year	SO
1900 Rube Waddell, Pit	130	1935 Dizzy Dean, St.L	190	1968 Bob Gibson, St.L	268
1901 Noodles Hahn, Cin	239	1936 Van Lingle Mungo, Bklyn	238	1969 Ferguson Jenkins, Chi	273
1902 Vic Willis, Bos.	225	1937 Carl Hubbell, NY	159		
1903 Christy Mathewson, NY	267	1938 Clay Bryant, Chi.	135	1970 Tom Seaver, NY	283
1904 Christy Mathewson, NY	212	1939 Claude Passeau, Phi-Chi	137	1971 Tom Seaver, NY	289
1905 Christy Mathewson, NY	206	& Bucky Walters, Cin.	137	1972 Steve Carlton, Phi.	310
1906 Fred Beebe, Chi-St.L.	171			1973 Tom Seaver, NY	251
1907 Christy Mathewson, NY	178	1940 Kirby Higbe, Phi.	137	1974 Steve Carlton, Phi.	240
1908 Christy Mathewson, NY	259	1941 John Vander Meer, Cin	202	1975 Tom Seaver, NY	243
1909 Orval Overall, Chi.	205	1942 John Vander Meer, Cin	186	1976 Tom Seaver, NY	235
		1943 John Vander Meer, Cin	174	1977 Phil Niekro, Atl	262
1910 Earl Moore, Phi.	185	1944 Bill Voiselle, NY	161	1978 J.R. Richard, Hou	303
1911 Rube Marquard, NY	237	1945 Preacher Roe, Pit	148	1979 J.R. Richard, Hou	313
1912 Grover Alexander, Phi.	195	1946 Johnny Schmitz, Chi.	135		
1913 Tom Seaton, Phi	168	1947 Ewell Blackwell, Cin	193	1980 Steve Carlton, Phi.	286
1914 Grover Alexander, Phi.	214	1948 Harry Brecheen, St.L	149	1981 F. Valenzuela, LA	180
1915 Grover Alexander, Phi.	241	1949 Warren Spahn, Bos	151	1982 Steve Carlton, Phi.	286
1916 Grover Alexander, Phi.	167			1983 Steve Carlton, Phi.	275
1917 Grover Alexander, Phi.	201	1950 Warren Spahn, Bos	191	1984 Dwight Gooden, NY	276
1918 Hippo Vaughn, Chi	148	1951 Don Newcombe, Bklyn	164	1985 Dwight Gooden, NY	268
1919 Hippo Vaughn, Chi	141	& Warren Spahn, Bos	164	1986 Mike Scott, Hou	306
		1952 Warren Spahn, Bos	183	1987 Nolan Ryan, Hou	270
1920 Grover Alexander, Chi	173	1953 Robin Roberts, Phi	198	1988 Nolan Ryan, Hou	228
1921 Burleigh Grimes, Bklyn	136	1954 Robin Roberts, Phi	185	1989 Jose DeLeon, St.L	201
1922 Dazzy Vance, Bklyn	134	1955 Sam Jones, Chi.	198		
1923 Dazzy Vance, Bklyn	197	1956 Sam Jones, Chi.	176	1990 David Cone, NY.	233
1924 Dazzy Vance, Bklyn	262	1957 Jack Sanford, Phi	188	1991 David Cone, NY.	241
1925 Dazzy Vance, Bklyn	221	1958 Sam Jones, St.L.	225	1992 John Smoltz, Atl.	215
1926 Dazzy Vance, Bklyn	140	1959 Don Drysdale, LA	242	1993 Jose Rijo, Cin	227
1927 Dazzy Vance, Bklyn	184			1994 Andy Benes, SD	189
1928 Dazzy Vance, Bklyn	200	1960 Don Drysdale, LA	246	1995 Hideo Nomo, LA	236
1929 Pat Malone, Chi	166	1961 Sandy Koufax, LA	269	1996 John Smoltz, Atl	276
		1962 Don Drysdale, LA	232	1997 Curt Schilling, Phi.	319
1930 Bill Hallahan, St.L	177	1963 Sandy Koufax, LA	306	1998 Curt Schilling, Phi.	300
1931 Bill Hallahan, St.L.	159	1964 Bob Veale, Pit	250	1999 Randy Johnson, Ari	364
1932 Dizzy Dean, St.L.	191	1965 Sandy Koufax, LA	382		
1933 Dizzy Dean, St.L.	199	1966 Sandy Koufax, LA	317	2000 Randy Johnson, Ari	347
1934 Dizzy Dean, St.L	195	1967 Jim Bunning, Phi	253		

Pitching Triple Crown Winners

Pitchers who led either league in Earned Run Average, Wins and Strikeouts over a single season.

National League

	Year	ERA	W-L	SO
Tommy Bond, Bos.	1877	2.11	40-17	170
Hoss Radbourne, Prov.	1884	1.38	60-12	441
Tim Keefe, NY	1888	1.74	35-12	333
John Clarkson, Bos	1889	2.73	49-19	284
Amos Rusie, NY	1894	2.78	36-13	195
Christy Mathewson, NY	1905	1.27	31-8	206
Christy Mathewson, NY	1908	1.43	37-11	259
Grover Alexander, Phi	1915	1.22	31-10	241
Grover Alexander, Phi	1916	1.55	33-12	167
Grover Alexander, Phi	1917	1.86	30-13	201
Hippo Vaughn, Chi	1918	1.74	22-10	148
Grover Alexander, Chi	1920	1.91	27-14	173
Dazzy Vance, Bklyn.	1924	2.16	28-6	262
Bucky Walters, Cin	1939	2.29	27-11	137
Sandy Koufax, LA	1963	1.88	25-5	306
Sandy Koufax, LA	1965	2.04	26-8	382
Sandy Koufax, LA	1966	1.73	27-9	317
Steve Carlton, Phi	1972	1.97	27-10	310
Dwight Gooden, NY	1985	1.53	24-4	268

Ties: In 1894, Rusie tied for league lead in wins with Jouett Meekin, NY (36-10); in 1939, Walters tied for league lead in strikeouts with Claude Passeau, Phi-Chi; in 1963, Koufax tied for the league lead in wins with Juan Marichal, SF.

American League

	Year	ERA	W-L	SO
Cy Young, Bos	1901	1.62	33-10	158
Rube Waddell, Phi.	1905	1.48	26-11	287
Walter Johnson, Wash	1913	1.09	36-7	243
Walter Johnson, Wash	1918	1.27	23-13	162
Walter Johnson, Wash	1924	2.72	23-7	158
Lefty Grove, Phi	1930	2.54	28-5	209
Lefty Grove, Phi	1931	2.06	31-4	175
Lefty Gomez, NY	1934	2.33	26-5	158
Lefty Gomez, NY	1937	2.33	21-11	194
Hal Newhouser, Det	1945	1.81	25-9	212
Roger Clemens, Tor	1997	2.05	21-7	292
Roger Clemens, Tor	1998	2.65	20-6	271
Pedro Martinez, Bos	1999	2.07	23-4	313

Ties: In 1998, Clemens tied for league lead in wins with David Cone, NY (20-7) and Rick Helling, Tex (20-7).

American League

Multiple winners: Walter Johnson (12); Nolan Ryan (9); Bob Feller and Lefty Grove (7); Rube Waddell (6); Roger Clemens and Sam McDowell (5); Randy Johnson (4); Lefty Gomez, Mark Langston and Camilo Pascual (3); Len Barker, Tommy Bridges, Jim Bunning, Pedro Martinez, Hal Newhouser, Allie Reynolds, Herb Score, Ed Walsh and Early Wynn (2).

Year	SO	Year	SO	Year	SO
1901 Cy Young, Bos	158	1935 Tommy Bridges, Det	163	1968 Sam McDowell, Cle	283
1902 Rube Waddell, Phi	210	1936 Tommy Bridges, Det	175	1969 Sam McDowell, Cle	279
1903 Rube Waddell, Phi	302	1937 Lefty Gomez, NY	194	1970 Sam McDowell, Cle	304
1904 Rube Waddell, Phi	349	1938 Bob Feller, Cle	240	1971 Mickey Lolich, Det	308
1905 Rube Waddell, Phi	287	1939 Bob Feller, Cle	246	1972 Nolan Ryan, Cal	329
1906 Rube Waddell, Phi	196	1940 Bob Feller, Cle	261	1973 Nolan Ryan, Cal	383
1907 Rube Waddell, Phi	232	1941 Bob Feller, Cle	260	1974 Nolan Ryan, Cal	367
1908 Ed Walsh, Chi	269	1942 Tex Hughson, Bos	113	1975 Frank Tanana, Cal	269
1909 Frank Smith, Chi	177	& Bobo Newsom, Wash	113	1976 Nolan Ryan, Cal	327
1910 Walter Johnson, Wash	313	1943 Allie Reynolds, Cle	151	1977 Nolan Ryan, Cal	341
1911 Ed Walsh, Chi	255	1944 Hal Newhouser, Det	187	1978 Nolan Ryan, Cal	260
1912 Walter Johnson, Wash	303	1945 Hal Newhouser, Det	212	1979 Nolan Ryan, Cal	223
1913 Walter Johnson, Wash	243	1946 Bob Feller, Cle	348	1980 Len Barker, Cle	187
1914 Walter Johnson, Wash	225	1947 Bob Feller, Cle	196	1981 Len Barker, Cle	127
1915 Walter Johnson, Wash	203	1948 Bob Feller, Cle	164	1982 Floyd Bannister, Sea	209
1916 Walter Johnson, Wash	228	1949 Virgil Trucks, Det	153	1983 Jack Morris, Det	232
1917 Walter Johnson, Wash	188	1950 Bob Lemon, Cle	170	1984 Mark Langston, Sea	204
1918 Walter Johnson, Wash	162	1951 Vic Raschi, NY	164	1985 Bert Blyleven, Cle-Min	206
1919 Walter Johnson, Wash	147	1952 Allie Reynolds, NY	160	1986 Mark Langston, Sea	245
1920 Stan Coveleski, Cle	133	1953 Billy Pierce, Chi	186	1987 Mark Langston, Sea	262
1921 Walter Johnson, Wash	143	1954 Bob Turley, Bal	185	1988 Roger Clemens, Bos	291
1922 Urban Shocker, St.L	149	1955 Herb Score, Cle	245	1989 Nolan Ryan, Tex	301
1923 Walter Johnson, Wash	130	1956 Herb Score, Cle	263	1990 Nolan Ryan, Tex	232
1924 Walter Johnson, Wash	158	1957 Early Wynn, Cle	184	1991 Roger Clemens, Bos	241
1925 Lefty Grove, Phi	116	1958 Early Wynn, Chi	179	1992 Randy Johnson, Sea	241
1926 Lefty Grove, Phi	194	1959 Jim Bunning, Det	201	1993 Randy Johnson, Sea	308
1927 Lefty Grove, Phi	174	1960 Jim Bunning, Det	201	1994 Randy Johnson, Sea	204
1928 Lefty Grove, Phi	183	1961 Camilo Pascual, Min	221	1995 Randy Johnson, Sea	294
1929 Lefty Grove, Phi	170	1962 Camilo Pascual, Min	206	1996 Roger Clemens, Bos	257
1930 Lefty Grove, Phi	209	1963 Camilo Pascual, Min	202	1997 Roger Clemens, Tor	292
1931 Lefty Grove, Phi	175	1964 Al Downing, NY	217	1998 Roger Clemens, Tor	271
1932 Red Ruffing, NY	190	1965 Sam McDowell, Cle	325	1999 Pedro Martinez, Bos	313
1933 Lefty Gomez, NY	163	1966 Sam McDowell, Cle	225	2000 Pedro Martinez, Bos	284
1934 Lefty Gomez, NY	158	1967 Jim Lonborg, Bos	246		

Perfect Games

Eighteen pitchers have thrown perfect games (27 up, 27 down) in major league history. However, the games pitched by Harvey Haddix and Ernie Shore are not considered to be official.

National League

	Game	Date	Score
Lee Richmond	Wor. vs Cle.	6/12/1880	1-0
Monte Ward	Prov. vs Bos.	6/17/1880	5-0
Harvey Haddix	Pit. at Mil.	5/26/1959	0-1*
Jim Bunning	Phi. at NY	6/21/1964	6-0
Sandy Koufax	LA vs Chi.	9/9/1965	1-0
Tom Browning	Cin. vs LA	9/16/1988	1-0
Dennis Martinez	Mon. at LA	7/28/1991	2-0

*Haddix pitched 12 perfect innings before losing in the 13th. Braves' lead-off batter Felix Mantilla reached on a throwing error by Pirates 3B Don Hoak, Eddie Mathews sacrificed Mantilla to 2nd, Hank Aaron was walked intentionally, and Joe Adcock hit a 3-run HR. Adcock, however, passed Aaron on the bases and was only credited with a 1-run double.

American League

	Game	Date	Score
Cy Young	Bos. vs Phi.	5/5/1904	3-0
Addie Joss	Cle. vs Chi.	10/2/1908	1-0
Ernie Shore	Bos. vs Wash.	6/23/1917	4-0*
Charlie Robertson	Chi. at Det.	4/30/1922	2-0
Catfish Hunter	Oak. vs Min.	5/8/1968	4-0
Len Barker	Cle. vs Tor.	5/15/1981	3-0
Mike Witt	Cal. at Tex.	9/30/1984	1-0
Kenny Rogers	Tex. vs Cal.	7/28/1994	4-0
David Wells	NY vs Min.	5/17/1998	4-0
David Cone	NY vs Mon.	7/18/1999	6-0

*Babe Ruth started for Boston, walking Senators' lead-off batter Ray Morgan, then was thrown out of game by umpire Brick Owens for arguing the call. Shore came on in relief. Morgan was caught stealing and Shore retired the next 26 batters in a row. While technically not a perfect game—since he didn't start—Shore gets credit anyway.

World Series

Pitcher	Game	Date	Score
Don Larsen	NY vs Bklyn	10/8/1956	2-0

No-Hit Games

Nine innings or more, including perfect games, since 1876. Losing pitchers in **bold** type. **Multiple no-hitters:** Nolan Ryan (7); Sandy Koufax (4); Larry Cocoran, Bob Feller and Cy Young (3); Jim Bunning, Steve Busby, Carl Erskine, Bob Forsch, Pud Galvin, Ken Holtzman, Addie Joss, Hub Leonard, Jim Maloney, Christy Mathewson, Allie Reynolds, Warren Spahn, Bill Stoneham, Virgil Trucks, Johnny Vander Meer and Don Wilson (2).

National League

Year	Date	Pitcher	Result	Year	Date	Pitcher	Result
1876	7/15	George Bradley	St.L vs Har, 2-0		9/25	Sal Maglie	Bklyn vs Phi, 5-0
1880	6/12	Lee Richmond	Wor vs Cle,1-0 (perfect game)	1960	5/15	Don Cardwell	Chi vs St.L, 4-0
	6/17	Monte Ward	Prov vs Buf, 5-0 (perfect game)		8/18	Lew Burdette	Mil vs Phi, 1-0
	8/19	Larry Corcoran	Chi vs Bos, 6-0		9/16	Warren Spahn	Mil vs Phi, 4-0
	8/20	Pud Galvin	Buf at Wor, 1-0	1961	4/28	Warren Spahn	Mil vs SF, 1-0
1882	9/20	Larry Corcoran	Chi vs Wor, 1-0	1962	6/30	Sandy Koufax	LA vs NY, 5-0
1883	7/25	Old Hoss Radbourne	Prov at Cle, 8-0	1963	5/11	Sandy Koufax	LA vs SF, 1-0
	9/13	Hugh Daily	Cle at Phi, 1-0		5/17	Don Nottebart	Hou vs Phi, 4-1
1884	6/27	Larry Cocoran	Chi vs Prov, 6-0		6/15	Juan Marichal	SF vs Hou, 1-0
	8/4	Pud Galvin	Buf at Det, 18-0	1964	4/23	**Ken Johnson**	Hou vs Cin, 0-1
1885	7/27	John Clarkson	Chi vs Prov, 6-0		6/4	Sandy Koufax	LA at Phi, 3-0
	8/29	Charlie Ferguson	Phi vs Prov, 1-0		6/21	Jim Bunning	Phi at NY, 6-0 (perfect game)
1891	6/22	Tom Lovett	Bklyn vs NY, 4-0	1965	8/19	Jim Maloney	Cin at Chi, 1-0 (10)
	7/31	Amos Rusie	NY vs Bklyn, 11-0		9/9	Sandy Koufax	LA vs Chi, 1-0 (perfect game)
1892	8/6	John Stivetts	Bos vs Bklyn, 11-0	1967	6/18	Don Wilson	Hou vs Atl, 2-0
	8/22	Ben Sanders	Lou vs Bal, 6-2	1968	7/29	George Culver	Cin at Phi, 6-1
	10/22	Bumpus Jones	Cin vs Pit, 7-1 (1st major league game)		9/17	Gaylord Perry	SF vs St.L, 1-0
					9/18	Ray Washburn	St.L at SF, 2-0 (next day, same park)
1893	8/16	Bill Hawke	Bal vs Wash, 5-0	1969	4/17	Bill Stoneman	Mon at Phi, 7-0
1897	9/18	Cy Young	Cle vs Cin, 6-0		4/30	Jim Maloney	Cin vs Hou, 10-0
1898	4/22	Ted Breitenstein	Cin vs Pit, 11-0		5/1	Don Wilson	Hou at Cin, 4-0
	4/22	Jim Hughes	Bal vs Bos, 8-0		8/19	Ken Holtzman	Chi vs Atl, 3-0
	7/8	Frank Donahue	Phi vs Bos, 5-0		9/20	Bob Moose	Pit at NY, 4-0
	8/21	Walter Thornton	Chi vs Bklyn, 2-0	1970	6/12	Dock Ellis	Pit at SD, 2-0
1899	5/25	Deacon Phillippe	Lou vs NY, 7-0		7/20	Bill Singer	LA vs Phi, 5-0
1900	7/12	Noodles Hahn	Cin vs Phi, 4-0	1971	6/3	Ken Holtzman	Chi at Cin, 1-0
1901	7/15	Christy Mathewson	NY vs St.L, 5-0		6/23	Rick Wise	Phi at Cin, 4-0
1903	9/18	Chick Fraser	Phi at Chi, 10-0		8/14	Bob Gibson	St.L at Pit, 11-0
1905	6/13	Christy Mathewson	NY at Chi, 1-0	1972	4/16	Burt Hooton	Chi vs Phi, 4-0
1906	5/1	John Lush	Phi at Bklyn, 1-0		9/2	Milt Pappas	Chi vs SD, 8-0
	7/20	Mal Eason	Bklyn at St.L, 2-0		10/2	Bill Stoneman	Mon vs NY, 7-0
1907	5/8	Frank Pfeffer	Bos vs Cin, 6-0	1973	8/5	Phil Niekro	Atl vs SD, 9-0
	9/20	Nick Maddox	Pit vs Bkn, 2-1	1975	8/24	Ed Halicki	SF vs NY, 6-0
1908	7/4	Hooks Wiltse	NY vs Phi, 1-0 (10)	1976	7/9	Larry Dierker	Hou vs Mon, 6-0
	9/5	Nap Rucker	Bklyn vs Bos, 6-0		8/9	John Candelaria	Pit vs LA, 2-0
1912	9/6	Jeff Tesreau	NY at Phi, 3-0		9/29	John Montefusco	SF vs Atl, 9-0
1914	9/9	George Davis	Bos vs Phi, 7-0	1978	4/16	Bob Forsch	St.L vs Phi, 5-0
1915	4/15	Rube Marquard	NY vs Bklyn, 2-0		6/16	Tom Seaver	Cin vs St.L, 4-0
	8/31	Jimmy Lavender	Chi at N.Y, 2-0	1979	4/7	Ken Forsch	Hou vs Atl, 6-0
1916	6/16	Tom Hughes	Bos vs. Pit, 2-0	1980	6/27	Jerry Reuss	LA at SF, 4-0
1917	5/2	Fred Toney	Cin at Chi, 1-0 (10)	1981	5/10	Charlie Lea	Mon vs SF, 4-0
1919	5/11	Hod Eller	Cin at St.L, 6-0		9/26	Nolan Ryan	Hou vs LA, 5-0
1922	5/7	Jesse Barnes	NY vs Phi, 6-0	1983	9/26	Bob Forsch	St.L vs Mon, 3-0
1924	7/17	Jesse Haines	St.L vs Bos, 5-0	1986	9/25	Mike Scott	Hou vs SF, 2-0
1925	9/17	Dazzy Vance	Bklyn vs Phi, 10-1	1988	9/16	Tom Browning	Cin vs LA, 1-0 (perfect game)
1929	5/8	Carl Hubbell	NY vs Pit, 2-0				
1934	9/21	Paul Dean	St.L vs Bklyn, 3-0	1990	6/29	Fernando Valenzuela	LA vs St.L, 6-0
1938	6/11	Johnny Vander Meer	Cin vs Bos, 3-0		8/15	Terry Mulholland	Phi vs SF, 6-0
	6/15	Johnny Vander Meer	Cin at Bklyn, 6-0 (consecutive starts)	1991	5/23	Tommy Greene	Phi at Mon, 2-0
					7/28	Dennis Martinez	Mon at LA, 2-0 (perfect game)
1940	4/30	Tex Carleton	Bklyn at Cin, 3-0		9/11	Kent Mercker (6), Mark Wohlers (2) & Alejandro Peña (1)	Atl vs SD, 1-0 (combined no-hitter)
1941	8/30	Lon Warneke	St.L at Cin, 2-0				
1944	4/27	Jim Tobin	Bos vs Bklyn, 2-0	1992	8/17	Kevin Gross	LA vs SF, 2-0
	5/15	Clyde Shoun	Cin vs Bos, 1-0	1993	9/8	Darryl Kile	Hou vs NY, 7-1
1946	4/23	Ed Head	Bklyn at NY, 2-0	1994	4/8	Kent Mercker	Atl at LA, 6-0
1947	6/18	Ewell Blackwell	Cin vs Bos, 6-0	1995	7/14	Ramon Martinez	LA vs Fla, 7-0
1948	9/9	Rex Barney	Bklyn at NY, 2-0	1996	5/11	Al Leiter	Fla vs Col, 11-0
1950	8/11	Vern Bickford	Bos vs Bklyn, 7-0		9/17	Hideo Nomo	LA at Col, 9-0
1951	5/6	Cliff Chambers	Pit at Bos, 3-0				
1952	6/19	Carl Erskine	Bklyn vs Chi, 5-0				
1954	6/12	Jim Wilson	Mil vs Phi, 2-0				
1955	5/12	Sam Jones	Chi vs Pit, 4-0				
1956	5/12	Carl Erskine	Bklyn vs NY, 3-0				

Year	Date	Pitcher	Result
1997	6/10	Kevin Brown	Fla at SF, 9-0
	7/12	Francisco Cordova (9)	Pit vs. Hou, 3-0 (10 inn.)
		Ricardo Rincon (1)	(combined no-hitter)

Year	Date	Pitcher	Result
1999	6/25	Jose Jimenez	St.L vs Ari, 1-0

American League

Year	Date	Pitcher	Result
1902	9/20	Jimmy Callahan	Chi vs Det, 3-0
1904	5/5	Cy Young	Bos vs Phi, 3-0
			(perfect game)
	8/17	Jesse Tannehill	Bos vs Chi, 6-0
1905	7/22	Weldon Henley	Phi at St. L, 6-0
	9/6	Frank Smith	Chi at Det, 15-0
	9/27	Bill Dinneen	Bos vs Chi, 2-0
1908	6/30	Cy Young	Bos at NY, 8-0
	9/18	Dusty Rhoades	Cle vs Bos, 2-0
	9/20	Frank Smith	Chi vs Phi, 1-0
	10/2	Addie Joss	Cle vs Chi, 1-0
			(perfect game)
1910	4/20	Addie Joss	Cle at Chi, 1-0
	5/12	Chief Bender	Phi vs Cle, 4-0
1911	7/19	Smokey Joe Wood	Bos vs St. L, 5-0
	8/27	Ed Walsh	Chi vs Bos, 5-0
1912	7/4	George Mullin	Det vs St. L, 7-0
	8/30	Earl Hamilton	St. L at Det, 5-1
1914	5/31	Joe Benz	Chi vs Cle, 6-1
1916	6/16	Rube Foster	Bos vs NY, 2-0
	8/26	Joe Bush	Phi vs Cle, 5-0
	8/30	Hub Leonard	Bos vs St. L, 4-0
1917	4/14	Ed Cicotte	Chi at St. L, 11-0
	4/24	George Mogridge	NY at Bos, 2-1
	5/5	Ernie Koob	St. L vs Chi, 1-0
	5/6	Bob Groom	St. L vs Chi, 3-0
	6/23	Babe Ruth (0)	Bos vs Wash, 4-0
		& Ernie Shore (9)	(combined no-hitter)
1918	6/3	Hub Leonard	Bos at Det, 5-0
1919	9/10	Ray Caldwell	Cle at NY, 3-0
1920	7/1	Walter Johnson	Wash at Bos, 1-0
1922	4/30	Charlie Robertson	Chi at Det, 2-0
			(perfect game)
1923	9/4	Sam Jones	NY at Phi, 2-0
	9/7	Howard Ehmke	Bos at Phi, 4-0
1926	8/21	Ted Lyons	Chi at Bos, 6-0
1931	4/29	Wes Ferrell	Cle vs St. L, 9-0
	8/8	Bob Burke	Wash vs Bos, 5-0
1935	8/31	Vern Kennedy	Chi vs Cle, 5-0
1937	6/1	Bill Dietrich	Chi vs St. L, 8-0
1938	8/27	Monte Pearson	NY vs Cle, 13-0
1940	4/16	Bob Feller	Cle at Chi, 1-0
			(Opening Day)
1945	9/9	Dick Fowler	Phi vs St. L, 1-0
1946	4/30	Bob Feller	Cle vs NY, 1-0
1947	7/10	Don Black	Cle vs Phi, 3-0
	9/3	Bill McCahan	Phi vs Wash, 3-0
1948	6/30	Bob Lemon	Cle at Det, 2-0
1951	7/1	Bob Feller	Cle vs Det, 2-1
	7/12	Allie Reynolds	NY vs Cle, 1-0
	9/28	Allie Reynolds	NY vs Bos, 8-0
1952	5/15	Virgil Trucks	Det vs Wash, 1-0
	8/25	Virgil Trucks	Det at NY, 1-0
1953	5/6	Bobo Holloman	St. L vs Phi, 6-0
			(first major league start)
1956	7/14	Mel Parnell	Bos vs Chi, 4-0
	10/8	Don Larsen	NY vs Bklyn, 2-0
			(perfect W. Series game)
1957	8/20	Bob Keegan	Chi vs Wash, 6-0
1958	7/20	Jim Bunning	Det at Bos, 3-0
	9/2	Hoyt Wilhelm	Bal vs NY, 1-0
1962	5/5	Bo Belinsky	LA vs Bal, 2-0
	6/26	Earl Wilson	Bos vs LA, 2-0
	8/1	Bill Monbouquette	Bos at Chi, 1-0
	8/26	Jack Kralick	Min vs KC, 1-0
1965	9/16	Dave Morehead	Bos vs Cle, 2-0
1966	6/10	Sonny Siebert	Cle vs Wash, 2-0
1967	4/30	**Steve Barber** (8⅔)	Bal vs Det, 1-2
		& **Stu Miller** (⅓)	(combined no-hitter)
	8/25	Dean Chance	Min at Cle, 2-1
	9/10	Joel Horlen	Chi vs Det, 6-0
1968	4/27	Tom Phoebus	Bal vs Bos, 6-0
	5/8	Catfish Hunter	Oak vs Min, 4-0
			(perfect game)
1969	8/13	Jim Palmer	Bal vs Oak, 8-0
1970	7/3	Clyde Wright	Cal vs Oak, 4-0
	9/21	Vida Blue	Oak vs Min, 6-0
1973	4/27	Steve Busby	KC at Det, 3-0
	5/15	Nolan Ryan	Cal at KC, 3-0
	7/15	Nolan Ryan	Cal at Det, 6-0
	7/30	Jim Bibby	Tex at Oak, 6-0
1974	6/19	Steve Busby	KC at Mil, 2-0
	7/19	Dick Bosman	Cle at Oak, 4-0
	9/28	Nolan Ryan	Cal at Min, 4-0
1975	6/1	Nolan Ryan	Cal vs Bal, 1-0
	9/28	Vida Blue (5),	Oak vs Cal, 5-0
		Glenn Abbott (1),	(combined no-hitter)
		Paul Lindblad (1),	
		& Rollie Fingers (2)	
1976	7/28	John Odom (5) &	Chi at Oak, 2-1
		Francisco Barrios (4)	(combined no-hitter)
1977	5/14	Jim Colborn	KC vs Tex, 6-0
	5/30	Dennis Eckersley	Cle vs Cal, 1-0
	9/22	Bert Blyleven	Tex at Cal, 6-0
1981	5/15	Len Barker	Cle vs Tor, 3-0
			(perfect game)
1983	7/4	Dave Righetti	NY vs Bos, 4-0
	9/29	Mike Warren	Oak vs Chi, 3-0
1984	4/7	Jack Morris	Det at Chi, 4-0
	9/30	Mike Witt	Cal at Tex, 1-0
			(perfect game)
1986	9/19	Joe Cowley	Chi at Cal, 7-1
1987	4/15	Juan Nieves	Mil at Bal, 7-0
1990	4/11	Mark Langston (7)	Cal vs Sea, 1-0
		& Mike Witt (2)	(combined no-hitter)
	6/2	Randy Johnson	Sea vs Det, 2-0
	6/11	Nolan Ryan	Tex at Oak, 5-0
	6/29	Dave Stewart	Oak at Tor, 5-0
	9/2	Dave Stieb	Tor at Cle, 3-0
1991	5/1	Nolan Ryan	Tex vs Tor, 3-0
	7/13	Bob Milacki (6),	Bal at Oak, 2-0
		Mike Flanagan (1),	(combined no-hitter)
		Mark Williamson (1)	
		& Gregg Olson (1)	
	8/11	Wilson Alvarez	Chi at Bal, 7-0
	8/26	Bret Saberhagen	KC vs Chi, 7-0
1993	4/22	Chris Bosio	Sea vs Bos, 7-0
	9/4	Jim Abbott	NY vs Cle, 4-0
1994	4/27	Scott Erickson	Min vs Mil, 6-0
	7/28	Kenny Rogers	Tex vs Cal, 4-0
			(perfect game)
1996	5/14	Dwight Gooden	NY vs Sea, 2-0
1998	5/17	David Wells	NY vs Min, 4-0
			(perfect game)
1999	7/18	David Cone	NY vs Mon, 6-0
			(perfect game)
	9/11	Eric Milton	Min vs Ana, 7-0

All-Time Major League Leaders

Based on statistics compiled by *The Baseball Encyclopedia* (9th ed.); through 2000 regular season.

CAREER

Players active in 2000 in **bold** type.

Batting

Note that (*) indicates left-handed hitter and (†) indicates switch-hitter.

Batting Average

		Yrs	AB	H	Avg
1	Ty Cobb*	24	11,429	4191	.367
2	Rogers Hornsby	23	8,137	2930	.358
3	Joe Jackson*	13	4,981	1774	.356
4	Ed Delahanty	16	7,509	2597	.346
5	Tris Speaker*	22	10,197	3514	.345
6	Ted Williams*	19	7,706	2654	.344
7	Billy Hamilton*	14	6,284	2163	.344
8	Willie Keeler*	19	8,585	2947	.343
9	Dan Brouthers*	19	6,711	2296	.342
10	Babe Ruth*	22	8,399	2873	.342
11	Harry Heilmann	17	7,787	2660	.342
12	Pete Browning	13	4,820	1646	.341
13	Bill Terry*	14	6,428	2193	.341
14	George Sisler*	15	8,267	2812	.340
15	Lou Gehrig*	17	8,001	2721	.340
16	Jesse Burkett*	16	8,413	2853	.339
17	Tony Gwynn*	19	9,186	3108	.338
18	Nap Lajoie	21	9,592	3244	.338
19	Riggs Stephenson	14	4,508	1515	.336
20	Al Simmons	20	8,761	2927	.334
21	Paul Waner*	20	9,459	3152	.333
22	Eddie Collins*	25	9,951	3313	.333
23	Stan Musial*	22	10,972	3630	.331
24	Sam Thompson*	14	6,005	1986	.331
25	Heinie Manush*	17	7,654	2524	.330

Hits

		Yrs	AB	H	Avg
1	Pete Rose†	24	14,053	**4256**	.303
2	Ty Cobb*	24	11,429	**4191**	.367
3	Hank Aaron	23	12,364	**3771**	.305
4	Stan Musial*	22	10,972	**3630**	.331
5	Tris Speaker*	22	10,197	**3514**	.345
6	Carl Yastrzemski*	23	11,988	**3419**	.285
7	Honus Wagner	21	10,443	**3418**	.327
8	Paul Molitor	21	10,835	**3319**	.306
9	Eddie Collins*	25	9,951	**3313**	.333
10	Willie Mays	22	10,881	**3283**	.302
11	Eddie Murray†	21	11,336	**3255**	.287
12	Nap Lajoie	21	9,592	**3244**	.338
13	George Brett*	21	10,349	**3154**	.305
14	Paul Waner*	20	9,459	**3152**	.333
15	Robin Yount	20	11,008	**3142**	.285
16	Dave Winfield	22	11,003	**3110**	.283
17	Tony Gwynn*	19	9,186	**3108**	.338
18	Cal Ripken Jr.	20	11,074	**3070**	.277
19	Rod Carew*	19	9,315	**3053**	.328
20	Lou Brock*	19	10,332	**3023**	.293
21	Wade Boggs*	18	9,180	**3010**	.328
22	Al Kaline	22	10,116	**3007**	.297
23	Cap Anson	22	9,108	**3000**	.329
	Roberto Clemente	18	9,454	**3000**	.317
25	Sam Rice*	20	9,269	**2987**	.322

Players Active in 2000
(Minimum 3000 AB)

		Yrs	AB	H	Avg
1	Tony Gwynn*	19	9,186	3108	.338
2	Mike Piazza	9	4,135	1356	.328
3	Derek Jeter	6	3,130	1008	.322
4	Frank Thomas	11	5,474	1755	.321
5	Edgar Martinez	14	5,432	1738	.320
6	Manny Ramirez	8	3,470	1086	.313
7	Larry Walker*	12	4,906	1528	.311
8	Jeff Cirillo	7	3,409	1059	.311
9	Alex Rodriguez	7	3,126	966	.309
10	Mark Grace*	13	7,156	2201	.308
11	Rusty Greer*	7	3,385	1040	.307
12	Kenny Lofton*	10	4,922	1507	.306
13	Jeff Bagwell	10	5,349	1630	.305

Players Active in 2000

		Yrs	AB	H	Avg
1	Tony Gwynn*	19	9,186	**3108**	.338
2	Cal Ripken Jr.	20	11,074	**3070**	.277
3	Rickey Henderson	22	10,331	**2914**	.282
4	Harold Baines*	21	9,824	**2855**	.291
5	Rafael Palmeiro*	15	7,846	**2321**	.296
6	Gary Gaetti	20	8,951	**2280**	.255
7	Mark Grace*	13	7,156	**2201**	.308
8	Robero Alomar†	13	7,221	**2196**	.304
9	Will Clark*	15	7,173	**2176**	.303
10	Barry Bonds*	15	7,456	**2157**	.289
11	Fred McGriff*	15	7,352	**2013**	.286
12	Andres Galarraga	15	7,123	**2070**	.291
13	Wally Joyner*	15	6,979	**2024**	.290

Games Played

1	Pete Rose	3562
2	Carl Yastrzemski	3308
3	Hank Aaron	3298
4	Ty Cobb	3034
5	Stan Musial	3026
	Eddie Murray	3026
7	Willie Mays	2992
8	Dave Winfield	2973
9	Rusty Staub	2951
10	Brooks Robinson	2896
11	Cal Ripken Jr.	2873
12	Robin Yount	2856
	Rickey Henderson	2856
14	Al Kaline	2834
15	Eddie Collins	2826
16	Reggie Jackson	2820
17	Frank Robinson	2808
18	Harold Baines	2798
19	Tris Speaker	2789
	Honus Wagner	2789

At Bats

1	Pete Rose	14,053
2	Hank Aaron	12,364
3	Carl Yastrzemski	11,988
4	Ty Cobb	11,429
5	Eddie Murray	11,336
6	Cal Ripken Jr.	11,074
7	Robin Yount	11,008
8	Dave Winfield	11,003
9	Stan Musial	10,972
10	Willie Mays	10,881
11	Paul Molitor	10,835
12	Brooks Robinson	10,654
13	Honus Wagner	10,441
14	George Brett	10,349
15	Lou Brock	10,332
16	Rickey Henderson	10,331
17	Luis Aparicio	10,230
18	Tris Speaker	10,197
19	Al Kaline	10,116
20	Rabbit Maranville	10,078

Total Bases

1	Hank Aaron	6856
2	Stan Musial	6134
3	Willie Mays	6066
4	Ty Cobb	5863
5	Babe Ruth	5793
6	Pete Rose	5752
7	Carl Yastrzemski	5539
8	Eddie Murray	5397
9	Frank Robinson	5373
10	Dave Winfield	5221
11	Tris Speaker	5103
12	Lou Gehrig	5059
13	George Brett	5044
14	Mel Ott	5041
15	Cal Ripken Jr.	4996
16	Jimmie Foxx	4956
17	Ted Williams	4884
18	Honus Wagner	4868
19	Paul Molitor	4854
20	Al Kaline	4852

Home Runs

		Yrs	AB	HR	AB/HR
1	Hank Aaron	.23	12,364	**755**	16.4
2	Babe Ruth*	.22	8,399	**714**	11.8
3	Willie Mays	.22	10,881	**660**	16.5
4	Frank Robinson	.21	10,006	**586**	17.1
5	Harmon Killebrew	.22	8,147	**573**	14.2
6	Reggie Jackson*	.21	9,864	**563**	17.5
7	**Mark McGwire**	.15	5,888	**554**	10.6
8	Mike Schmidt	.18	8,352	**548**	15.2
9	Mickey Mantle†	.18	8,102	**536**	15.1
10	Jimmie Foxx	.20	8,134	**534**	15.2
11	Ted Williams*	.19	7,706	**521**	14.8
	Willie McCovey*	.22	8,197	**521**	15.7
13	Eddie Mathews*	.17	8,537	**512**	16.7
	Ernie Banks	.19	9,421	**512**	18.4
15	Mel Ott*	.22	9,456	**511**	18.5
16	Eddie Murray†	.21	11,336	**504**	22.5
17	**Barry Bonds**	.15	7,456	**494**	15.1
18	Lou Gehrig*	.17	8,001	**493**	16.2
19	Willie Stargell*	.21	7,927	**475**	16.7
	Stan Musial*	.22	10,972	**475**	23.1
21	Dave Winfield	.22	11,003	**465**	23.7
22	Carl Yastrzemski*	.23	11,988	**452**	26.5
23	**Jose Canseco**	.16	6,801	**446**	15.2
24	Dave Kingman	.16	6,677	**442**	15.1
25	**Ken Griffey Jr.***	.12	6,352	**438**	14.5
	Andre Dawson	.21	9,927	**438**	22.7

Runs Batted In

		Yrs	Gm	RBI	P/G
1	Hank Aaron	.23	3298	**2297**	.70
2	Babe Ruth*	.22	2503	**2211**	.88
3	Lou Gehrig*	.17	2164	**1990**	.92
4	Ty Cobb*	.24	3034	**1961**	.65
5	Stan Musial*	.22	3026	**1951**	.64
6	Jimmie Foxx	.20	2317	**1921**	.83
7	Eddie Murray†	.21	2980	**1917**	.64
8	Willie Mays	.22	2992	**1903**	.64
9	Mel Ott*	.22	2732	**1861**	.68
10	Carl Yastrzemski*	.23	3308	**1844**	.56
11	Ted Williams*	.19	2292	**1839**	.80
12	Dave Winfield	.22	2973	**1833**	.62
13	Al Simmons	.20	2215	**1827**	.82
14	Frank Robinson	.21	2808	**1812**	.65
15	Honus Wagner	.21	2786	**1732**	.62
16	Cap Anson	.22	2276	**1715**	.75
17	Reggie Jackson*	.21	2820	**1702**	.60
18	Tony Perez	.23	2777	**1652**	.59
19	Ernie Banks	.19	2528	**1636**	.65
20	**Cal Ripken Jr.**	.20	2873	**1627**	.57
21	**Harold Baines***	.21	2798	**1622**	.58
22	Goose Goslin*	.18	2287	**1609**	.70
23	Nap Lajoie	.21	2475	**1599**	.65
24	Mike Schmidt	.18	2404	**1595**	.66
	George Brett*	.21	2707	**1595**	.59

Players Active in 2000

		Yrs	AB	HR	AB/HR
1	Mark McGwire	.15	5,888	**554**	10.6
2	Barry Bonds*	.15	7,456	**494**	15.1
3	Jose Canseco	.16	6,801	**446**	15.2
4	Ken Griffey Jr.*	.12	6,352	**438**	14.5
5	Fred McGriff*	.15	7,352	**417**	17.6
	Cal Ripken Jr.	.20	11,074	**417**	26.6
7	Rafael Palmeiro*	.15	7,846	**400**	19.6
8	Sammy Sosa	.12	5,893	**386**	15.3
9	Harold Baines*	.21	9,824	**384**	25.6
10	Albert Belle	.12	5,853	**381**	15.4
11	Juan Gonzalez	.12	5,292	**362**	14.6
12	Andres Galarraga	.15	7,123	**360**	19.8
	Gary Gaetti	.20	8,951	**360**	24.9
14	Matt Williams	.14	6,243	**346**	18.0
15	Frank Thomas	.11	5,474	**344**	15.9

Players Active in 2000

		Yrs	Gm	RBI	P/G
1	Cal Ripken Jr.	.20	2873	**1627**	.57
2	Harold Baines*	.21	2798	**1622**	.58
3	Barry Bonds*	.15	2143	**1405**	.66
4	Jose Canseco	.16	1811	**1358**	.75
5	Mark McGwire	.15	1777	**1350**	.76
6	Rafael Palmeiro*	.15	2098	**1347**	.64
7	Gary Gaetti	.20	2507	**1341**	.53
8	Fred McGriff*	.15	2055	**1298**	.63
9	Andres Galarraga	.15	1915	**1272**	.66
10	Ken Griffey Jr.*	.12	1680	**1270**	.76
11	Albert Belle	.12	1539	**1239**	.81
12	Will Clark*	.15	1976	**1205**	.61
13	Paul O'Neill*	.16	1916	**1199**	.63
14	Frank Thomas	.11	1530	**1183**	.77
15	Bobby Bonilla†	.15	2020	**1152**	.57

Runs

1	Ty Cobb	.2245
2	**Rickey Henderson**	.2178
3	Babe Ruth	.2174
	Hank Aaron	.2174
5	Pete Rose	.2165
6	Willie Mays	.2062
7	Stan Musial	.1949
8	Lou Gehrig	.1888
9	Tris Speaker	.1881
10	Mel Ott	.1859
11	Frank Robinson	.1829
12	Eddie Collins	.1820
13	Carl Yastrzemski	.1816
14	Ted Williams	.1798
15	Paul Molitor	.1782
16	Charlie Gehringer	.1774
17	Jimmie Foxx	.1751
18	Honus Wagner	.1735
19	Willie Keeler	.1727
20	Cap Anson	.1719

Extra Base Hits

1	Hank Aaron	.1477
2	Stan Musial	.1377
3	Babe Ruth	.1356
4	Willie Mays	.1323
5	Lou Gehrig	.1190
6	Frank Robinson	.1186
7	Carl Yastrzemski	.1157
8	Ty Cobb	.1139
9	Tris Speaker	.1132
10	George Brett	.1119
11	Ted Williams	.1117
	Jimmie Foxx	.1117
13	Eddie Murray	.1099
14	Dave Winfield	.1093
15	Reggie Jackson	.1075
16	Mel Ott	.1071
17	**Cal Ripken Jr.**	.1048
18	Pete Rose	.1041
19	Andre Dawson	.1039
20	Mike Schmidt	.1015

Slugging Percentage

1	Babe Ruth	.690
2	Ted Williams	.634
3	Lou Gehrig	.632
4	Jimmie Foxx	.609
5	Hank Greenberg	.605
6	**Mark McGwire**	.593
7	**Manny Ramirez**	.592
8	**Mike Piazza**	.580
9	Joe DiMaggio	.579
10	**Frank Thomas**	.579
11	Rogers Hornsby	.577
12	**Ken Griffey Jr.**	.568
13	**Barry Bonds**	.567
14	**Juan Gonzalez**	.566
15	**Albert Belle**	.564
16	**Larry Walker**	.563
17	Johnny Mize	.562
18	**Alex Rodriguez**	.561
19	Stan Musial	.559
20	Willie Mays	.557

Stolen Bases

1	**Rickey Henderson**	1370
2	Lou Brock	938
3	Billy Hamilton	937
4	Ty Cobb	892
5	Tim Raines	807
6	Vince Coleman	752
7	Eddie Collins	743
8	Max Carey	738
9	Honus Wagner	720
10	Joe Morgan	689
11	Arlie Latham	679
12	Willie Wilson	668
13	Bert Campaneris	649
14	Tom Brown	627
15	Otis Nixon	620
16	George Davis	615
17	Dummy Hoy	597
18	Maury Wills	586
19	Hugh Duffy	583
	George Van Haltren	583

Walks

1	Babe Ruth	2062
2	**Rickey Henderson**	2060
3	Ted Williams	2019
4	Joe Morgan	1865
5	Carl Yastrzemski	1845
6	Mickey Mantle	1734
7	Mel Ott	1708
8	Eddie Yost	1614
9	Darrell Evans	1605
10	Stan Musial	1599
11	Pete Rose	1566
12	Harmon Killebrew	1559
13	**Barry Bonds**	1547
14	Lou Gehrig	1508
15	Mike Schmidt	1507
16	Eddie Collins	1503
17	Willie Mays	1463
18	Jimmie Foxx	1452
19	Eddie Mathews	1444
20	Frank Robinson	1420

Strikeouts

1	Reggie Jackson	2597
2	Willie Stargell	1936
3	Mike Schmidt	1883
4	Tony Perez	1867
	Jose Canseco	1867
6	Dave Kingman	1816
7	Bobby Bonds	1757
8	Dale Murphy	1748
9	**Andres Galarraga**	1741
10	Lou Brock	1730
11	Mickey Mantle	1710
12	Harmon Killebrew	1699
13	Chili Davis	1698
14	Dwight Evans	1697
15	Dave Winfield	1686
16	**Gary Gaetti**	1602
17	**Fred McGriff**	1592
18	Lee May	1570
19	Dick Allen	1556
20	Willie McCovey	1550

Pitching

Note that (*) indicates left-handed pitcher. Active pitching leaders are listed for wins and strikeouts.

Wins

		Yrs	GS	W	L	Pct
1	Cy Young	22	815	**511**	316	.618
2	Walter Johnson	21	666	**417**	279	.599
3	Christy Mathewson	17	551	**373**	188	.665
	Grover Alexander	20	598	**373**	208	.642
5	Warren Spahn*	21	665	**363**	245	.597
6	Kid Nichols	15	561	**361**	208	.634
	Pud Galvin	14	682	**361**	308	.540
8	Tim Keefe	14	594	**342**	225	.603
9	Steve Carlton*	24	709	**329**	244	.574
10	Eddie Plank*	17	527	**327**	193	.629
11	John Clarkson	12	518	**326**	177	.648
12	Don Sutton	23	756	**324**	256	.559
	Nolan Ryan	27	773	**324**	292	.526
14	Phil Niekro	24	716	**318**	274	.537
15	Gaylord Perry	22	690	**314**	265	.542
16	Old Hoss Radbourn	12	503	**311**	194	.616
	Tom Seaver	20	647	**311**	205	.603
18	Mickey Welch	13	549	**308**	209	.596
19	Lefty Grove*	17	456	**300**	141	.680
	Early Wynn	23	612	**300**	244	.551
21	Tommy John*	26	700	**288**	231	.555
22	Bert Blyleven	22	685	**287**	250	.534
23	Robin Roberts	19	609	**286**	245	.539
24	Tony Mullane	13	505	**285**	220	.564
25	Ferguson Jenkins	19	594	**284**	226	.557
26	Jim Kaat*	25	625	**283**	237	.544
27	Red Ruffing	22	536	**273**	225	.548
28	Burleigh Grimes	19	495	**270**	212	.560
29	Jim Palmer	19	521	**268**	152	.638
30	Bob Feller	18	484	**266**	162	.621

Strikeouts

		Yrs	IP	SO	P/9
1	Nolan Ryan	27	5387.0	**5714**	9.55
2	Steve Carlton*	24	5217.1	**4136**	7.13
3	Bert Blyleven	22	4970.1	**3701**	6.70
4	Tom Seaver	20	4782.2	**3640**	6.85
5	Don Sutton	23	5282.1	**3574**	6.09
6	Gaylord Perry	22	5350.1	**3534**	5.94
7	Walter Johnson	21	5923.2	**3508**	5.33
8	**Roger Clemens**	17	3666.2	**3504**	8.60
9	Phil Niekro	24	5404.1	**3342**	5.57
10	Ferguson Jenkins	19	4500.2	**3192**	6.38
11	Bob Gibson	17	3884.1	**3117**	7.22
12	**Randy Johnson***	13	2498.2	**3040**	10.95
13	Jim Bunning	17	3760.1	**2855**	6.83
14	Mickey Lolich*	16	3638.1	**2832**	7.01
15	Cy Young	22	7354.2	**2796**	3.42
16	Frank Tanana*	21	4186.2	**2773**	5.96
17	Warren Spahn*	21	5243.2	**2583**	4.43
18	Bob Feller	18	3827.0	**2581**	6.07
19	Jerry Koosman*	19	3839.1	**2556**	5.99
20	**David Cone**	15	2745.0	**2540**	8.33
21	Tim Keefe	14	5061.1	**2527**	4.50
22	Christy Mathewson	17	4781.0	**2502**	4.71
23	Don Drysdale	14	3432.0	**2486**	6.52
24	Jack Morris	18	3824.2	**2478**	5.83
25	Mark Langston*	16	2962.2	**2464**	7.49
26	Jim Kaat*	25	4530.1	**2461**	4.89
27	Sam McDowell*	15	2492.1	**2453**	8.86
28	Luis Tiant	19	3486.1	**2416**	6.24
29	Dennis Eckersley	24	3285.2	**2401**	6.58
30	Sandy Koufax*	12	2324.1	**2396**	9.28

Pitchers Active in 2000

		Yrs	GS	W	L	Pct
1	Roger Clemens	17	511	**260**	142	.647
2	Greg Maddux	15	467	**240**	135	.640
3	Tom Glavine*	14	434	**208**	125	.625
4	Orel Hershiser	18	466	**204**	150	.576
5	Dwight Gooden	16	410	**194**	112	.634
6	David Cone	15	390	**184**	116	.613
7	Chuck Finley*	15	413	**181**	151	.545
8	Randy Johnson*	13	357	**179**	95	.653
9	Kevin Brown	14	380	**170**	114	.599
10	Bret Saberhagen	16	368	**166**	115	.591

Pitchers Active in 2000

		Yrs	IP	SO	P/9
1	Roger Clemens	17	3666.2	**3504**	8.60
2	Randy Johnson*	13	2498.2	**3040**	10.95
3	David Cone	15	2745.0	**2540**	8.33
4	Greg Maddux	15	3318.0	**2350**	6.37
5	Chuck Finley*	15	2893.0	**2340**	7.28
6	Dwight Gooden	16	2800.2	**2293**	7.37
7	John Smoltz	13	2414.1	**2098**	7.82
8	Orel Hershiser	18	3130.1	**2014**	5.79
9	Kevin Brown	14	2660.2	**1917**	6.48
10	Andy Benes	12	2301.0	**1858**	7.27

Winning Pct.

		Yrs	W-L	Pct
1	Bob Caruthers	9	218-97	.692
2	**Pedro Martinez**	9	125-56	.691
3	Dave Foutz	11	147-66	.690
4	Whitey Ford*	16	236-106	.690
5	Don Gullett*	9	109-50	.686
6	Lefty Grove*	17	300-141	.680
7	Vic Raschi	10	132-66	.667
8	Christy Mathewson	17	373-188	.665
9	Larry Corcoran	8	177-90	.663
10	Sam Leever	13	194-101	.658
11	Sal Maglie	10	119-62	.657
12	Sandy Koufax*	12	165-87	.655
13	Johnny Allen	13	142-75	.654
14	**Randy Johnson**	13	179-95	.653
15	Ron Guidry*	14	170-91	.651

Losses

		Yrs	GS	W	L	Pct
1	Cy Young	22	815	511	**316**	.618
2	Pud Galvin	14	682	361	**308**	.540
3	Nolan Ryan	27	773	324	**292**	.526
4	Walter Johnson	21	666	417	**279**	.599
5	Phil Niekro	24	716	318	**274**	.537
6	Gaylord Perry	22	690	314	**265**	.542
7	Jack Powell	16	517	245	**256**	.489
	Don Sutton	23	756	324	**256**	.559
9	Eppa Rixey*	21	552	266	**251**	.515
10	Bert Blyleven	22	685	287	**250**	.534
11	Robin Roberts	19	609	286	**245**	.539
	Warren Spahn*	21	665	363	**245**	.597
13	Early Wynn	23	612	300	**244**	.551
	Steve Carlton*	24	709	329	**244**	.574
15	Jim Kaat*	25	625	283	**237**	.544

Appearances

1	**Jesse Orosco**	1096
2	Dennis Eckersley	1071
3	Hoyt Wilhelm	1070
4	Kent Tekulve	1050
5	Lee Smith	1022
6	Rich Gossage	1002
7	Lindy McDaniel	987
8	Rollie Fingers	944
9	**John Franco**	940
10	Gene Garber	931
11	Cy Young	906
12	Sparky Lyle	899
13	Jim Kaat	898
14	Paul Assenmacher	884
	Dan Pleasc	884

Innings Pitched

1	Cy Young	7356.0
2	Pud Galvin	5941.1
3	Walter Johnson	5923.2
4	Phil Niekro	5403.1
5	Nolan Ryan	5387.0
6	Gaylord Perry	5350.1
7	Don Sutton	5280.1
8	Warren Spahn	5243.2
9	Steve Carlton	5217.1
10	Grover Alexander	5189.2
11	Kid Nichols	5084.0
12	Tim Keefe	5061.1
13	Bert Blyleven	4970.1
14	Mickey Welch	4802.0
15	Tom Seaver	4782.2

Earned Run Avg.

1	Ed Walsh	1.82
2	Addie Joss	1.88
3	Three Finger Brown	2.06
4	Monte Ward	2.10
5	Christy Mathewson	2.13
6	Rube Waddell	2.16
7	Walter Johnson	2.17
8	Orval Overall	2.24
9	Tommy Bond	2.25
10	Will White	2.28
11	Ed Reulbach	2.28
12	Jim Scott	2.32
13	Eddie Plank	2.34
14	Larry Corcoran	2.36
15	Eddie Cicotte	2.37

Shutouts

1	Walter Johnson	110
2	Grover Alexander	90
3	Christy Mathewson	80
4	Cy Young	76
5	Eddie Plank	69
6	Warren Spahn	63
7	Nolan Ryan	61
	Tom Seaver	61
9	Bert Blyleven	60
10	Don Sutton	58
11	Three Finger Brown	57
	Pud Galvin	57
	Ed Walsh	57
14	Bob Gibson	56
15	Steve Carlton	55

Walks Allowed

1	Nolan Ryan	2795
2	Steve Carlton	1833
3	Phil Niekro	1809
4	Early Wynn	1775
5	Bob Feller	1764
6	Bobo Newsom	1732
7	Amos Rusie	1704
8	Charlie Hough	1665
9	Gus Weyhing	1566
10	Red Ruffing	1541
11	Bump Hadley	1442
12	Warren Spahn	1434
13	Earl Whitehill	1431
14	Tony Mullane	1409
15	Sad Sam Jones	1396

HRs Allowed

1	Robin Roberts	505
2	Ferguson Jenkins	484
3	Phil Niekro	482
4	Don Sutton	472
5	Frank Tanana	448
6	Warren Spahn	434
7	Bert Blyleven	430
8	Steve Carlton	414
9	Gaylord Perry	399
10	Jim Kaat	395
11	Jack Morris	389
12	Charlie Hough	383
13	Tom Seaver	380
14	Catfish Hunter	374
15	Jim Bunning	372
	Dennis Martinez	372

Saves

1	Lee Smith	478
2	**John Franco**	420
3	Dennis Eckersley	390
4	Jeff Reardon	367
5	**Randy Myers**	347
6	Rollie Fingers	341
7	**John Wetteland**	330
8	**Rick Aguilera**	318
9	Tom Henke	311
10	Rich Gossage	310
11	Jeff Montgomery	304
12	**Doug Jones**	303
13	Bruce Sutter	300
14	**Trevor Hoffman**	271
15	**Roberto Hernandez**	266
16	**Rod Beck**	260
17	Todd Worrell	256
18	Dave Righetti	252
19	Dan Quisenberry	244
20	Sparky Lyle	238
21	Hoyt Wilhelm	227
22	**Robb Nen**	226
23	Gene Garber	218
24	**Gregg Olson**	217
25	Dave Smith	216
26	Bobby Thigpen	201
27	Roy Face	193
	Mike Henneman	193
29	Mitch Williams	192
30	Jeff Russell	186

SINGLE SEASON
Through 2000 regular season.
Batting

Home Runs

		Year	Gm	AB	HR
1	Mark McGwire, St.L	1998	155	509	70
2	Sammy Sosa, Chi-NL	1998	159	643	66
3	Mark McGwire, St.L	1999	153	521	65
4	Sammy Sosa, Chi-NL	1999	162	625	63
5	Roger Maris, NY-AL	1961	162	590	61
6	Babe Ruth, NY-AL	1927	151	540	60
7	Babe Ruth, NY-AL	1921	152	540	59
8	Mark McGwire, Oak-St.L	1997	156	540	58
	Hank Greenberg, Det	1938	155	556	58
	Jimmie Foxx, Phi-AL	1932	154	585	58
11	Hack Wilson, Chi-NL	1930	155	585	56
	Ken Griffey Jr., Sea	1997	157	608	56
	Ken Griffey Jr., Sea	1998	161	633	56
14	Babe Ruth, NY-AL	1920	142	458	54
	Mickey Mantle, NY-AL	1961	153	514	54
	Babe Ruth, NY-AL	1928	154	536	54
	Ralph Kiner, Pit	1949	152	549	54
18	Mickey Mantle, NY-AL	1956	150	533	52
	Willie Mays, SF	1965	157	558	52
	George Foster, Cin	1977	158	615	52
	Mark McGwire, Oak	1996	130	423	52

Hits

		Year	AB	H	Avg
1	George Sisler, StL-AL	1920	631	257	.407
2	Bill Terry, NY-NL	1930	633	254	.401
	Lefty O'Doul, Phi-NL	1929	638	254	.398
4	Al Simmons, Phi-AL	1925	658	253	.384
5	Rogers Hornsby, StL-NL	1922	623	250	.401
	Chuck Klein, Phi-NL	1930	648	250	.386
7	Ty Cobb, Det	1911	591	248	.420
8	George Sisler, StL-AL	1922	586	246	.420
9	Babe Herman, Bklyn	1930	614	241	.393
	Heinie Manush, StL-AL	1928	638	241	.378
11	Wade Boggs, Bos	1985	653	240	.368
	Darin Erstad, Ana	2000	676	240	.355
13	Rod Carew, Min	1977	616	239	.388
14	Don Mattingly, NY-AL	1986	677	238	.352
15	Harry Heilmann, Det	1921	602	237	.394
	Paul Waner, Pit	1927	623	237	.380
	Joe Medwick, StL-NL	1937	633	237	.374
18	Jack Tobin, StL-AL	1921	671	236	.352
19	Rogers Hornsby, StL-NL	1921	592	235	.397
20	Lloyd Waner, Pit	1929	662	234	.353
	Kirby Puckett, Min	1988	657	234	.356

Batting Average

From 1900-49

		Year	AB	H	Avg
1	Rogers Hornsby, StL-NL	1924	536	227	.424
2	Nap Lajoie, Phi-AL	1901	543	229	.422
3	George Sisler, StL-AL	1922	586	246	.420
4	Ty Cobb, Det	1911	591	248	.420
5	Ty Cobb, Det	1912	533	227	.410
6	Joe Jackson, Cle	1911	571	233	.408
7	George Sisler, StL-AL	1920	631	257	.407
8	Ted Williams, Bos-AL	1941	456	185	.406
9	Rogers Hornsby, StL-NL	1925	504	203	.403
10	Harry Heilmann, Det	1923	524	211	.403

Since 1950

		Year	AB	H	Avg
1	Tony Gwynn, SD	1994	419	175	.394
2	George Brett, KC	1980	449	175	.390
3	Ted Williams, Bos	1957	420	163	.388
4	Rod Carew, Min	1977	616	239	.388
5	Larry Walker, Col	1999	438	166	.379
6	**Todd Helton**, Col	2000	580	216	.372
7	**Nomar Garciaparra**, Bos	2000	529	197	.372
8	Tony Gwynn, SD	1997	592	220	.372
9	Andres Galarraga, Col	1993	470	174	.370
10	Tony Gwynn, SD	1987	589	218	.370

Total Bases

From 1900-49

		Year	TB
1	Babe Ruth, New York-AL	1921	457
2	Rogers Hornsby, St. Louis-NL	1922	450
3	Lou Gehrig, New York-AL	1927	447
4	Chuck Klein, Philadelphia-NL	1930	445
5	Jimmie Foxx, Philadelphia-AL	1932	438
6	Stan Musial, St. Louis-NL	1948	429
7	Hack Wilson, Chicago-NL	1930	423
8	Chuck Klein, Philadelphia-NL	1932	420
9	Lou Gehrig, New York-AL	1930	419
10	Joe DiMaggio, New York-AL	1937	418

Since 1950

		Year	TB
1	Sammy Sosa, Chi-NL	1998	416
2	Larry Walker, Colorado	1997	409
3	Jim Rice, Boston	1978	406
4	**Todd Helton**, Col	2000	405
5	Hank Aaron, Milwaukee	1959	400
6	Albert Belle, Chi-AL	1998	399
7	Sammy Sosa, Chi-NL	1999	397
8	Ken Griffey Jr., Seattle	1997	393
9	Ellis Burks, Colorado	1996	392
10	George Foster, Cincinnati	1977	388
	Don Mattingly, New York-AL	1986	388

Runs Batted In

From 1900-49

		Year	Avg	HR	RBI
1	Hack Wilson, Chi-NL	1930	.356	56	191
2	Lou Gehrig, NY-AL	1931	.341	46	184
3	Hank Greenberg, Det	1937	.337	40	183
4	Lou Gehrig, NY-AL	1927	.373	47	175
	Jimmie Foxx, Bos-AL	1938	.349	50	175
6	Lou Gehrig, NY-AL	1930	.379	41	174
7	Babe Ruth, NY-AL	1921	.378	59	171
8	Chuck Klein, Phi-NL	1930	.386	40	170
	Hank Greenberg, Det	1935	.328	36	170
10	Jimmie Foxx, Phi-AL	1932	.364	58	169

Since 1950

		Year	Avg	HR	RBI
1	Manny Ramirez, Cle	1999	.333	44	165
2	Sammy Sosa, Chi-NL	1998	.308	66	158
3	Juan Gonzalez, Tex	1998	.318	45	157
4	Tommy Davis, LA-NL	1962	.346	27	153
5	Albert Belle, Chi-AL	1998	.328	49	152
6	Andres Galarraga, Col	19.5	.304	47	150
7	George Foster, Cin	1977	.320	52	149
8	Rafael Palmeiro, Tex	1999	.324	47	148
	Johnny Bench, Cin	1970	.293	45	148
	Albert Belle, Cle	1996	.311	48	148

Runs

		Year	Runs
1	Babe Ruth, New York-AL	1921	177
2	Lou Gehrig, New York-AL	1936	167
3	Babe Ruth, New York-AL	1928	163
	Lou Gehrig, New York-AL	1931	163
5	Babe Ruth, New York-AL	1920	158
	Babe Ruth, New York-AL	1927	158
	Chuck Klein, Philadelphia-NL	1930	158
8	Rogers Hornsby, Chicago-NL	1929	156
9	Kiki Cuyler, Chicago-NL	1930	155
10	Lefty O'Doul, Philadelphia-NL	1929	152
	Woody English, Chicago-NL	1930	152
	Al Simmons, Philadelphia-AL	1930	152
	Chuck Klein, Philadelphia-NL	1932	152
	Jeff Bagwell, Houston	2000	152
15	Babe Ruth, New York-AL	1923	151
	Jimmie Foxx, Philadelphia-AL	1932	151
	Joe DiMaggio, New York-AL	1937	151
18	Babe Ruth, New York-AL	1930	150
	Ted Williams, Boston-AL	1940	150
20	Lou Gehrig, New York-AL	1927	149
	Babe Ruth, New York-AL	1931	149

Walks

		Year	BB
1	Babe Ruth, New York-AL	1923	170
2	Ted Williams, Boston-AL	1947	162
	Ted Williams, Boston-AL	1949	162
	Mark McGwire, St. Louis	1998	162
5	Ted Williams, Boston-AL	1946	156
6	Barry Bonds, San Francisco	1996	151
	Eddie Yost, Washington	1956	151
8	Jeff Bagwell, Houston	1999	149
	Eddie Joost, Philadelphia-AL	1949	149
10	Babe Ruth, New York-AL	1920	148
	Eddie Stanky, Brooklyn	1945	148
	Jimmy Wynn, Houston	1969	148

Extra Base Hits

		Year	EBH
1	Babe Ruth, New York-AL	1921	119
2	Lou Gehrig, New York-AL	1927	117
3	Chuck Klein, Philadelphia-NL	1930	107
4	Chuck Klein, Philadelphia-NL	1932	103
	Hank Greenberg, Detroit	1937	103
	Stan Musial, St. Louis-NL	1948	103
	Albert Belle, Cleveland	1995	103
	Todd Helton, Colorado	2000	103
9	Rogers Hornsby, St. Louis-NL	1922	102
10	Lou Gehrig, New York-AL	1930	100
	Jimmie Foxx, Philadelphia-AL	1933	100

Slugging Percentage
From 1900-49

		Year	Pct
1	Babe Ruth, New York-AL	1920	.847
2	Babe Ruth, New York-AL	1921	.846
3	Babe Ruth, New York-AL	1927	.772
4	Lou Gehrig, New York-AL	1927	.765
5	Babe Ruth, New York-AL	1923	.764
6	Rogers Hornsby, St. Louis-NL	1925	.756
7	Jimmie Foxx, Philadelphia-AL	1932	.749
8	Babe Ruth, New York-AL	1924	.739
9	Babe Ruth, New York-AL	1926	.737
10	Ted Williams, Boston-AL	1941	.735

Since 1950

		Year	Pct
1	Mark McGwire, St. Louis	1998	.752
2	Jeff Bagwell, Houston	1994	.750
3	Ted Williams, Boston	1957	.731
4	Mark McGwire, Oakland	1996	.730
5	Frank Thomas, Chicago-AL	1994	.729
6	Larry Walker, Colorado	1997	.720

Stolen Bases

		Year	SB
1	Rickey Henderson, Oakland	1982	130
2	Lou Brock, St. Louis	1974	118
3	Vince Coleman, St. Louis	1985	110
4	Vince Coleman, St. Louis	1987	109
5	Rickey Henderson, Oakland	1983	108
6	Vince Coleman, St. Louis	1986	107
7	Maury Wills, Los Angeles-NL	1962	104
8	Rickey Henderson, Oakland	1980	100
9	Ron LeFlore, Montreal	1980	97
10	Ty Cobb, Detroit	1915	96
	Omar Moreno, Pittsburgh	1980	96
12	Maury Wills, Los Angeles	1965	94
13	Rickey Henderson, New York-AL	1988	93
14	Tim Raines, Montreal	1983	90
15	Clyde Milan, Washington	1912	88
16	Rickey Henderson, New York-AL	1986	87
17	Ty Cobb, Detroit	1911	83
	Willie Wilson, Kansas City	1979	83
19	Bob Bescher, Cincinnati	1911	81
	Eddie Collins, Philadelphia-AL	1910	81
	Vince Coleman, St. Louis	1988	81

Strikeouts

		Year	SO
1	Bobby Bonds, San Francisco	1970	189
2	Bobby Bonds, San Francisco	1969	187
	Preston Wilson, Florida	2000	187
4	Rob Deer, Milwaukee	1987	186
5	Pete Incaviglia, Texas	1986	185
6	Cecil Fielder, Detroit	1990	182
7	**Mo Vaughn**, Anaheim	2000	181
8	Mike Schmidt, Philadelphia	1975	180
9	Rob Deer, Milwaukee	1986	179
10	Dave Nicholson, Chicago-AL	1963	175
	Gorman Thomas, Milwaukee	1979	175
	Jose Canseco, Oakland	1986	175
	Rob Deer, Detroit	1991	175
	Jay Buhner, Seattle	1997	175

Pinch Hits
Career pinch hits in parentheses.

		Year	PH	
1	John Vander Wal, Colorado	1995	28	(98)
2	Jose Morales, Montreal	1976	25	(123)
3	Dave Philley, Baltimore	1961	24	(93)
	Vic Davalillo, St. Louis	1970	24	(95)
	Rusty Staub, New York-NL	1983	24	(100)

Four tied with 22 each.

Note: The all-time career pinch hit leader is Manny Mota (150).

Four Home Runs in One Game
National League

	Date	H/A	Inn
Bobby Lowe, Boston	5/30/1894	H	9
Ed Delahanty, Philadelphia	7/13/1896	A	9
Chuck Klein, Philadelphia	7/10/1936	A	10
Gil Hodges, Brooklyn	8/31/1950	H	9
Joe Adcock, Milwaukee	7/31/1954	H	9
Willie Mays, San Francisco	4/30/1961	A	9
Mike Schmidt, Philadelphia	4/17/1976	A	10
Bob Horner, Atlanta	7/6/1986	H	9
Mark Whiten, St. Louis	9/7/1993	A	9

American League

	Date	H/A	Inn
Lou Gehrig, New York	6/3/1932	A	9
Pat Seerey, Chicago	7/18/1948	A	11
Rocky Colavito, Cleveland	6/10/1959	A	9

Pitching
Wins

From 1900-49

		Year	W	L	Pct
1	Jack Chesbro, NY-AL	1904	41	12	.774
2	Ed Walsh, Chi-AL	1908	40	15	.727
3	Christy Mathewson, NY-NL	1908	37	11	.771
4	Walter Johnson, Wash	1913	36	7	.837
5	Joe McGinnity, NY-NL	1904	35	8	.814
6	Smokey Joe Wood, Bos-AL	1912	34	5	.872
7	Cy Young, Bos-AL	1901	33	10	.767
	Grover Alexander, Phi-NL	1916	33	12	.733
	Christy Mathewson, NY-NL	1904	33	12	.733
10	Cy Young, Bos-AL	1902	32	11	.744

Since 1950

		Year	W	L	Pct
1	Denny McLain, Det.	1968	31	6	.838
2	Robin Roberts, Phi-NL	1952	28	7	.800
3	Bob Welch, Oak	1990	27	6	.818
	Don Newcombe, Bklyn	1956	27	7	.794
	Sandy Koufax, LA	1966	27	9	.750
	Steve Carlton, Phi.	1972	27	10	.730
7	Sandy Koufax, LA	1965	26	8	.765
	Juan Marichal, SF	1968	26	9	.743

Note: 11 pitchers tied with 25 wins, including Marichal twice.

Earned Run Average

From 1900-49

		Year	ShO	ERA
1	Dutch Leonard, Bos-AL	1914	7	1.01
2	Three Finger Brown, Chi-NL	1906	10	1.04
3	Walter Johnson, Wash	1913	11	1.09
4	Christy Mathewson, NY-NL	1909	8	1.14
5	Jack Pfiester, Chi-NL	1907	3	1.15
6	Addie Joss, Cle.	1908	9	1.16
7	Carl Lundgren, Chi-NL	1907	7	1.17
8	Grover Alexander, Phi-NL	1915	12	1.22
9	Cy Young, Bos-AL	1908	3	1.26
10	Three pitchers tied at 1.27			

Since 1950

		Year	ShO	ERA
1	Bob Gibson, St.L	1968	13	1.12
2	Dwight Gooden, NY-NL	1985	8	1.53
3	Greg Maddux, Atl.	1994	3	1.56
4	Luis Tiant, Cle	1968	9	1.60
5	Greg Maddux, Atl.	1995	3	1.63
6	Dean Chance, LA-AL	1964	11	1.65
7	Nolan Ryan, Cal	1981	3	1.69
8	Sandy Koufax, LA	1966	5	1.73
9	Sandy Koufax, LA	1964	7	1.74
10	**Pedro Martinez**, Bos.	2000	4	1.74

Note: Koufax's ERA in 1964 was 1.735. Martinez' ERA in 2000 was 1.742. The Yankees' Ron Guidry narrowly missed the top 10 list with an ERA of 1.743 in 1978.

Winning Pct.

		Year	W-L	Pct
1	Roy Face, Pit	1959	18-1	.947
2	Rick Sutcliffe, Chi-NL*	1984	16-1	.941
3	Johnny Allen, Cle	1937	15-1	.938
4	Greg Maddux, Atl	1995	19-2	.904
5	Randy Johnson, Sea.	1995	18-2	.900
6	Ron Guidry, NY-AL	1978	25-3	.893
7	Freddie Fitzsimmons, Bklyn.	1940	16-2	.889
8	Lefty Grove, Phi-AL	1931	31-4	.886
9	Bob Stanley, Bos.	1978	15-2	.882
10	Preacher Roe, Bklyn.	1951	22-3	.880
11	Tom Seaver, Cin	1981	14-2	.875
12	Smokey Joe Wood, Bos-AL	1912	34-5	.872

*Sutcliffe began 1984 with Cleveland and was 4-5 before being traded to the Cubs; his overall winning pct. was .769 (20-6).

Appearances

		Year	App	Sv
1	Mike Marshall, LA	1974	106	21
2	Kent Tekulve, Pit	1979	94	31
3	Mike Marshall, LA	1973	92	31
4	Kent Tekulve, Pit	1978	91	31
5	Wayne Granger, Cin.	1969	90	27
	Mike Marshall, Min	1979	90	32
	Kent Tekulve, Phi.	1987	90	3

Innings Pitched (since 1920)

		Year	IP	W-L
1	Wilbur Wood, Chi-AL	1972	377	24-17
2	Mickey Lolich, Det	1971	376	25-14
3	Bob Feller, Cle	1946	371	26-15
4	Grover Alexander, Chi-NL	1920	363	27-14
5	Wilbur Wood, Chi-AL	1973	359	24-20

Walks Allowed

		Year	BB	SO
1	Bob Feller, Cle	1938	208	240
2	Nolan Ryan, Cal	1977	204	341
3	Nolan Ryan, Cal	1974	202	367
4	Bob Feller, Cle	1941	194	260
5	Bobo Newsom, St.L-AL	1938	192	226

Strikeouts

		Year	SO	P/G
1	Nolan Ryan, Cal	1973	383	10.57
2	Sandy Koufax, LA	1965	382	10.24
3	Nolan Ryan, Cal	1974	367	9.92
4	Randy Johnson, Ari	1999	364	10.40
5	Rube Waddell, Phi-AL	1904	349	8.12
6	Bob Feller, Cle	1946	348	8.45
7	**Randy Johnson**, Ari	2000	347	9.91
8	Nolan Ryan, Cal	1977	341	10.26
9	Nolan Ryan, Cal	1972	329	10.43
	Randy Johnson, Sea-Hou	1998	329	9.68

Saves

		Year	App	Sv
1	Bobby Thigpen, Chi-AL	1990	77	57
2	Randy Myers, Chi-NL	1993	73	53
	Trevor Hoffman, SD	1998	66	53
4	Dennis Eckersley, Oak.	1992	69	51
	Rod Beck, Chi-NL	1998	81	51
6	Dennis Eckersley, Oak.	1990	63	48
	Rod Beck, SF.	1993	76	48
	Jeff Shaw, Cin-LA	1998	73	48
9	Lee Smith, St.L.	1991	67	47

Shutouts

		Year	ShO	ERA
1	Grover Alexander, Phi-NL	1916	16	1.55
2	Jack Coombs, Phi-AL	1910	13	1.30
	Bob Gibson, St.L	1968	13	1.12
4	Christy Mathewson, NY-NL	1908	12	1.43
	Grover Alexander, Phi-NL	1915	12	1.22

Home Runs Allowed

		Year	HRs
1	Bert Blyleven, Minnesota	1986	50
2	**Jose Lima**, Houston	2000	48
3	Robin Roberts, Philadelphia	1956	46
	Bert Blyleven, Minnesota	1987	46
5	Pedro Ramos, Washington	1957	43

Home Run in First Major League At bat
* on first pitch

A.L.

Luke Stuart, St. Louis, August 8, 1921.

Earl Averill, Cleveland, April 16, 1929.

Ace Parker, Philadelphia, April 30, 1937.

Gene Hasson, Philadelphia, September 9, 1937, first game.

Bill Lefebvre, Boston, June 10, 1938.*

Hack Miller, Detroit, April 23, 1944, second game.

Eddie Pellagrini, Boston, April 22, 1946.

George Vico, Detroit, April 20, 1948.*

Bob Nieman, St. Louis, September 14, 1951.

Bob Tillman, Boston, May 19, 1962.

John Kennedy, Washington, September 5, 1962, first game.

Buster Narum, Baltimore, May 3, 1963.

Gates Brown, Detroit, June 19, 1963.

Bert Campaneris, Kansas City, July 23, 1964.*

Bill Roman, Detroit, September 30, 1964, second game.

Brant Alyea, Washington, September 12, 1965.*

John Miller, New York, September 11, 1966.

Rick Renick, Minnesota, July 11, 1968.

Joe Keough, Oakland, August 7, 1968, second game.

Gene Lamont, Detroit, September 2, 1970, second game.

Don Rose, California, May 24, 1972.*

Reggie Sanders, Detroit, September 1, 1974.

Dave McKay, Minnesota, August 22, 1975.

Al Woods, Toronto, April 7, 1977.

Dave Machemer, California, June 21, 1978.

Gary Gaetti, Minnesota, September 20, 1981.

Andre David, Minnesota, June 29, 1984, first game.

Terry Steinbach, Oakland, September 12, 1986.

Jay Bell, Cleveland, September 29, 1986.*

Junior Felix, Toronto, May 4, 1989.*

Jon Nunnally, Kansas City, April 29, 1995.

Carlos Lee, Chicago, May 7, 1999.

Esteban Yan, Tampa Bay, June 4, 2000*

Total number of players: 33

N.L.

Joe Harrington, Boston, September 10, 1895.

Bill Duggleby, Philadelphia, April 21, 1898.

Johnny Bates, Boston, April 12, 1906.

Walter Mueller, Pittsburgh, May 7, 1922.

Clise Dudley, Brooklyn, April 27, 1929.*

Gordon Slade, Brooklyn, May 24, 1930.

Eddie Morgan, St. Louis, April 14, 1936.*

Ernie Koy, Brooklyn, April 19, 1938.

Emmett Mueller, Philadelphia, April 19, 1938.

Clyde Vollmer, Cincinnati, May 31, 1942, second game.*

Paul Gillespie, Chicago, September 11, 1942.

Buddy Kerr, New York, September 8, 1943.

Whitey Lockman, New York, July 5, 1945.

Dan Bankhead, Brooklyn, August 26, 1947.

Les Layton, New York, May 21, 1948.

Ed Sanicki, Philadelphia, September 14, 1949.

Ted Tappe, Cincinnati, September 14, 1950, first game.

Hoyt Wilhelm, New York, April 23, 1952.

Wally Moon, St. Louis, April 13, 1954.

Chuck Tanner, Milwaukee, April 12, 1955.*

Bill White, New York, May 7, 1956.

Frank Ernaga, Chicago, May 24, 1957.

Don Leppert, Pittsburgh, June 18, 1961, first game.

Cuno Barragan, Chicago, September 1, 1961.

Benny Ayala, New York, August 27, 1974.

John Montefusco, San Francisco, September 3, 1974.

Jose Sosa, Houston, July 30, 1975.

Johnnie LeMaster, San Francisco, September 2, 1975.

Tim Wallach, Montreal, September 6, 1980.

Carmelo Martinez, Chicago, August 22, 1983.

Mike Fitzgerald, New York, September 13, 1983.

Will Clark, San Francisco, April 8, 1986.

Ricky Jordan, Philadelphia, July 17, 1988.

Jose Offerman, Los Angeles, August 19, 1990.

Dave Eiland, San Diego, April 10, 1992.

Jim Bullinger, Chicago, June 8, 1992, first game.

Jay Gainer, Colorado, May 14, 1993.*

Mitch Lyden, Florida, June 16, 1993.

Garey Ingram, Los Angeles, May 19, 1994.

Jermaine Dye, Atlanta, May 17, 1996.

Dustin Hermanson, Montreal, April 16, 1997.

Brad Fullmer, Montreal, Sept. 2, 1997.

Marlon Anderson, Philadelphia, Sept. 8, 1998.

Guillermo Mota, Montreal, June 9, 1999.

Alex Cabrera, Arizona, June 26, 2000.

Keith McDonald, St. Louis, July 4, 2000.

Chris Richard, St. Louis, July 17, 2000.*

Total number of players: 47

Unassisted Triple Plays

One of the rarest feats in baseball, the unassisted triple play has been accomplished only 12 times in major league history. Ironically, in what can only be described as a statistic anomaly, the trick was turned twice in two days in May of 1927.

Player, Position, Team	Date	Opponent
Paul Hines, OF, Providence	May 8, 1878	Boston-NL
Neal Ball, SS, Cleveland	July 19, 1909	Boston-AL
Bill Wambganss, 2B, Cleveland*	Oct. 10, 1920	Brooklyn
George Burns, 1B, Boston-AL	Sept. 14, 1923	Cleveland
Ernie Padgett, SS, Boston-NL	Oct. 6, 1923	Philadelphia
Glenn Wright, SS, Pittsburgh	May 7, 1925	St.Louis-NL
Jimmy Cooney, SS, Chicago-NL	May 30, 1927	Pittsburgh
Johnny Neun, 1B, Detroit	May 31, 1927	Cleveland
Ron Hansen, SS, Washington	July 30, 1968	Cleveland
Mickey Morandini, 2B, Philadelphia	Sept. 20, 1992	Pittsburgh
John Valentin, SS, Boston	July 8, 1994	Seattle
Randy Velarde, 2B, Oakland	May 29, 2000	NY Yankees

*World Series game

All-Time Winningest Managers

Top 20 Major League career victories through the 2000 season. Career, regular season and postseason (playoffs and World Series) records are noted along with AL and NL pennants and World Series titles won. Managers active during 2000 season in **bold** type.

			Career			Regular Season			Postseason			
		Yrs	W	L	Pct	W	L	Pct	W	L	Pct	Titles
1	Connie Mack	53	**3755**	3967	.486	3731	3948	.486	24	19	.558	9 AL, 5 WS
2	John McGraw	33	**2866**	2012	.588	2840	1984	.589	26	28	.482	10 NL, 3 WS
3	Sparky Anderson	26	**2228**	1855	.547	2194	1834	.545	34	21	.618	4 NL, 1 AL, 3 WS
4	Bucky Harris	29	**2168**	2228	.493	2157	2218	.493	11	10	.524	3 AL, 2 WS
5	Joe McCarthy	24	**2155**	1346	.616	2125	1333	.615	30	13	.698	1 NL, 8 AL, 7 WS
6	Walter Alston	23	**2063**	1634	.558	2040	1613	.558	23	21	.523	7 NL, 4 WS
7	Leo Durocher	24	**2015**	1717	.540	2008	1709	.540	7	8	.467	3 NL, 1 WS
8	Casey Stengel	25	**1942**	1868	.510	1905	1842	.508	37	26	.587	10 AL, 7 WS
9	Gene Mauch	26	**1907**	2044	.483	1902	2037	.483	5	7	.417	—None—
10	Bill McKechnie	25	**1904**	1737	.523	1896	1723	.524	8	14	.364	4 NL, 2 WS
11	**Tony La Russa**	22	**1764**	1602	.524	1734	1578	.524	30	24	.565	3 AL, 1 WS
12	**Bobby Cox**	19	**1666**	1317	.558	1616	1271	.560	50	46	.521	5 NL, 1 WS
13	Tommy Lasorda	21	**1630**	1469	.526	1599	1439	.526	31	30	.508	4 NL, 2 WS
14	Ralph Houk	20	**1627**	1539	.514	1619	1531	.514	8	8	.500	3 AL, 2 WS
15	Fred Clarke	19	**1609**	1189	.575	1602	1181	.576	7	8	.467	4 NL, 1 WS
16	Dick Williams	21	**1592**	1474	.519	1571	1451	.520	21	23	.477	3 AL, 1 NL, 2 WS
17	Earl Weaver	17	**1506**	1080	.582	1480	1060	.583	26	20	.565	4 AL, 1 WS
18	Clark Griffith	20	**1491**	1367	.522	1491	1367	.522	0	0	.000	1 AL (1901)
19	Miller Huggins	17	**1431**	1149	.555	1413	1134	.555	18	15	.545	6 AL, 3 WS
20	**Joe Torre**	19	**1427**	1343	.515	1381	1325	.510	46	18	.719	4 AL, 4 WS

Notes: John McGraw's postseason record also includes two World Series tie games (1912,'22); Miller Huggins postseason record also includes one World Series tie game (1922).

Where They Managed

Alston—Brooklyn/Los Angeles NL (1954-76); **Anderson**—Cincinnati NL (1970-78), Detroit AL (1979-95); **Clarke**—Louisville NL (1897-99), Pittsburgh NL (1900-15); **Cox**—Atlanta (1978-81, 1990-), Toronto (1982-85); **Durocher**—Brooklyn NL (1939-46,48), New York NL (1948-55), Chicago NL (1966-72), Houston NL (1972-73); **Griffith**—Chicago AL (1901-02), New York AL (1903-08), Cincinnati NL (1909-11), Washington AL (1912-20); **Harris**—Washington AL (1924-28,35-42,50-54), Detroit AL (1929-33,55-56), Boston AL (1934), Philadelphia NL (1943), New York AL (1947-48); **Houk**—New York AL (1961-63,66-73), Detroit AL (1974-78), Boston AL (1981-84); **Huggins**—St. Louis NL (1913-17), New York AL (1918-29); **La Russa**—Chicago AL (1979-86), Oakland (1986-95); St. Louis (1996-) **Lasorda**—Los Angeles NL (1976-96); **Mack**—Pittsburgh NL (1894-96), Philadelphia AL (1901-50).

Mauch—Philadelphia NL (1960-68), Montreal NL (1969-75), Minnesota AL (1976-80), California AL (1981-82,85-87); **McCarthy**—Chicago NL (1926-30), New York AL (1931-46), Boston AL (1948-50); **McGraw**—Baltimore AL (1899), Baltimore AL (1901-02), New York NL (1902-32); **McKechnie**—Newark FL (1915), Pittsburgh NL (1922-26), St. Louis NL (1928-29), Boston NL (1930-37), Cincinnati NL (1938-46); **Stengel**—Brooklyn NL (1934-36), Boston NL (1938-43), New York AL (1949-60), New York NL (1962-65); **Torre**—New York NL (1977-81), Atlanta (1982-84), St. Louis (1990-95), New York AL (1996-); **Weaver**—Baltimore AL (1968-82,85-86); **Williams**—Boston AL (1967-69), Oakland AL (1971-73), California AL (1974-76), Montreal NL (1977-81), San Diego NL (1982-85), Seattle AL (1986-88).

Regular Season Winning Pct.

Minimum of 750 victories.

		Yrs	W	L	Pct	Pen
1	Joe McCarthy	24	2125	1333	**.615**	9
2	Charlie Comiskey	12	838	541	**.608**	4
3	Frank Selee	16	1284	862	**.598**	5
4	Billy Southworth	13	1044	704	**.597**	4
5	Frank Chance	11	946	648	**.593**	4
6	John McGraw	33	2840	1984	**.589**	10
7	Al Lopez	17	1410	1004	**.584**	2
8	Earl Weaver	17	1480	1060	**.583**	4
9	Cap Anson	20	1296	947	**.578**	5
10	Fred Clarke	19	1602	1181	**.576**	4
11	**Davey Johnson**	14	1148	888	**.564**	1
14	**Bobby Cox**	19	1616	1271	**.560**	5
12	Steve O'Neill	14	1040	821	**.559**	1
13	Walter Alston	23	2040	1613	**.558**	7
15	Bill Terry	10	823	661	**.555**	3
16	Miller Huggins	17	1413	1134	**.555**	6
17	Billy Martin	16	1253	1013	**.553**	2
18	Harry Wright	18	1000	825	**.548**	3
19	Charlie Grimm	19	1287	1067	**.547**	3
20	Sparky Anderson	26	2194	1834	**.545**	5

World Series Victories

		App	W	L	T	Pct	WS
1	Casey Stengel	10	**37**	26	0	.587	7
2	Joe McCarthy	9	**30**	13	0	.698	7
3	John McGraw	9	**26**	28	2	.482	3
4	Connie Mack	8	**24**	19	0	.558	5
5	Walter Alston	7	**20**	20	0	.500	4
6	Miller Huggins	6	**18**	15	1	.544	3
7	**Joe Torre**	4	**16**	3	0	.842	4
	Sparky Anderson	5	**16**	12	0	.571	3
9	Tommy Lasorda	4	**12**	11	0	.522	2
	Dick Williams	4	**12**	14	0	.462	2
11	Frank Chance	4	**11**	9	1	.548	2
	Bucky Harris	3	**11**	10	0	.524	2
	Billy Southworth	4	**11**	11	0	.500	2
	Earl Weaver	4	**11**	13	0	.458	1
	Bobby Cox	5	**11**	18	0	.379	1
16	Whitey Herzog	3	**10**	11	0	.476	1
17	Bill Carrigan	2	**8**	2	0	.800	2
	Danny Murtaugh	2	**8**	6	0	.571	2
	Cito Gaston	2	**8**	6	0	.571	2
	Tom Kelly	2	**8**	6	0	.571	2
	Ralph Houk	3	**8**	8	0	.500	2
	Bill McKechnie	4	**8**	14	0	.364	2

Active Managers' Records
Regular season games only; through 2000 (updated as of Oct. 29).

National League

		Yrs	W	L	Pct
1	Tony La Russa, St.L	22	**1734**	1578	.524
2	Bobby Cox, Atl	19	**1616**	1271	.560
3	Bobby Valentine, NY	13	**960**	906	.514
4	Felipe Alou, Mon.	9	**670**	685	.494
5	Dusty Baker, SF	8	**655**	577	.532
6	Don Baylor, Chi.	7	**505**	566	.472
7	Bruce Bochy, SD	6	**485**	469	.508
8	Larry Dierker, Hou.	4	**355**	293	.548
9	Buddy Bell, Col	4	**266**	357	.427
10	John Boles, Fla	3	**183**	215	.460
11	Davey Lopes, Mil	1	**73**	89	.451
12	Lloyd McClendon, Pit.	0	**0**	0	.000
	Arizona				
	Cincinnati				
	Los Angeles				
	Philadelphia				

American League

		Yrs	W	L	Pct
1	Joe Torre, NY	19	**1381**	1325	.510
2	Lou Piniella, Sea	14	**1110**	1020	.521
3	Tom Kelly, Min.	15	**1055**	1167	.475
4	Mike Hargrove, Bal	10	**795**	679	.539
5	Art Howe, Oak.	10	**787**	832	.486
6	Johnny Oates, Tex.	9	**786**	729	.519
7	Phil Garner, Det.	9	**642**	700	.478
8	Jimy Williams, Bos	8	**630**	540	.538
9	Jerry Manuel, Chi	3	**250**	235	.515
10	Tony Muser, KC	4	**244**	319	.433
11	Larry Rothschild, TB	3	**201**	284	.414
12	Charlie Manuel, Cle	1	**90**	72	.556
13	Mike Scioscia, Ana	1	**82**	80	.506
	Toronto				

Annual Awards

MOST VALUABLE PLAYER

There have been three different Most Valuable Player awards in baseball since 1911—the Chalmers Award (1911-14), presented by the Detroit-based automobile company; the League Award (1922-29), presented by the National and American Leagues; and the Baseball Writers' Award (since 1931), presented by the Baseball Writers' Association of America. Statistics for winning players are provided below. Stats for winning pitchers before advent of Cy Young Award are in MVP Pitchers' Statistics table.

Multiple winners: NL—Barry Bonds, Roy Campanella, Stan Musial and Mike Schmidt (3); Ernie Banks, Johnny Bench, Rogers Hornsby, Carl Hubbell, Willie Mays, Joe Morgan and Dale Murphy (2). **AL**—Yogi Berra, Joe DiMaggio, Jimmie Foxx and Mickey Mantle (3); Mickey Cochrane, Lou Gehrig, Juan Gonzalez, Hank Greenberg, Walter Johnson, Roger Maris, Hal Newhouser, Cal Ripken Jr., Frank Thomas, Ted Williams and Robin Yount (2). **NL & AL**—Frank Robinson (2, one in each).

Chalmers Award

National League

Year		Pos	HR	RBI	Avg
1911	Wildfire Schulte, Chi	OF	21	121	.300
1912	Larry Doyle, NY	2B	10	90	.330
1913	Jake Daubert, Bklyn	1B	2	52	.350
1914	Johnny Evers, Bos	2B	1	40	.279

American League

Year		Pos	HR	RBI	Avg
1911	Ty Cobb, Det	OF	8	144	.420
1912	Tris Speaker, Bos	OF	10	98	.383
1913	Walter Johnson, Wash	P	—	—	—
1914	Eddie Collins, Phi	2B	2	85	.344

League Award

National League

Year		Pos	HR	RBI	Avg
1922	No selection				
1923	No selection				
1924	Dazzy Vance, Bklyn	P	—	—	—
1925	Rogers Hornsby, St.L	2B-Mgr	39	143	.403
1926	Bob O'Farrell, St.L	C	7	68	.293
1927	Paul Waner, Pit	OF	9	131	.380
1928	Jim Bottomley, St.L	1B	31	136	.325
1929	Rogers Hornsby, Chi	2B	39	149	.380

American League

Year		Pos	HR	RBI	Avg
1922	George Sisler, St.L	1B	8	105	.420
1923	Babe Ruth, NY	OF	41	131	.393
1924	Walter Johnson, Wash	P	—	—	—
1925	Roger Peckinpaugh, Wash.	SS	4	64	.294
1926	George Burns, Cle	1B	4	114	.358
1927	Lou Gehrig, NY	1B	47	175	.373
1928	Mickey Cochrane, Phi	C	10	57	.293
1929	No selection				

Most Valuable Player

National League

Year		Pos	HR	RBI	Avg	Year		Pos	HR	RBI	Avg
1931	Frankie Frisch, St.L	2B	4	82	.311	1945	Phil Cavarretta, Chi	1B	6	97	.355
1932	Chuck Klein, Phi	OF	38	137	.348	1946	Stan Musial, St.L	1B-OF	16	103	.365
1933	Carl Hubbell, NY	P	—	—	—	1947	Bob Elliott, Bos	3B	22	113	.317
1934	Dizzy Dean, St.L	P	—	—	—	1948	Stan Musial, St.L	OF	39	131	.376
1935	Gabby Hartnett, Chi	C	13	91	.344	1949	Jackie Robinson, Bklyn	2B	16	124	.342
1936	Carl Hubbell, NY	P	—	—	—	1950	Jim Konstanty, Phi	P	—	—	—
1937	Joe Medwick, St.L	OF	31	154	.374	1951	Roy Campanella, Bklyn	C	33	108	.325
1938	Ernie Lombardi, Cin	C	19	95	.342	1952	Hank Sauer, Chi	OF	37	121	.270
1939	Bucky Walters, Cin	P	—	—	—	1953	Roy Campanella, Bklyn	C	41	142	.312
1940	Frank McCormick, Cin	1B	19	127	.309	1954	Willie Mays, NY	OF	41	110	.345
1941	Dolf Camilli, Bklyn	1B	34	120	.285	1955	Roy Campanella, Bklyn	C	32	107	.318
1942	Mort Cooper, St.L	P	—	—	—	1956	Don Newcombe, Bklyn	P	—	—	—
1943	Stan Musial, St.L	OF	13	81	.357	1957	Hank Aaron, Mil	OF	44	132	.322
1944	Marty Marion, St.L	SS	6	63	.267	1958	Ernie Banks, Chi	SS	47	129	.313

Year		Pos	HR	RBI	Avg
1959	Ernie Banks, Chi	SS	45	143	.304
1960	Dick Groat, Pit	SS	2	50	.325
1961	Frank Robinson, Cin	OF	37	124	.323
1962	Maury Wills, LA	SS	6	48	.299
1963	Sandy Koufax, LA	P	–	–	–
1964	Ken Boyer, St.L	3B	24	119	.295
1965	Willie Mays, SF	OF	52	112	.317
1966	Roberto Clemente, Pit	OF	29	119	.317
1967	Orlando Cepeda, St.L	1B	25	111	.325
1968	Bob Gibson, St.L	P	–	–	–
1969	Willie McCovey, SF	1B	45	126	.320
1970	Johnny Bench, Cin	C	45	148	.293
1971	Joe Torre, St.L	3B	24	137	.363
1972	Johnny Bench, Cin	C	40	125	.270
1973	Pete Rose, Cin	OF	5	64	.338
1974	Steve Garvey, LA	1B	21	111	.312
1975	Joe Morgan, Cin	2B	17	94	.327
1976	Joe Morgan, Cin	2B	27	111	.320
1977	George Foster, Cin	OF	52	149	.320
1978	Dave Parker, Pit	OF	30	117	.334
1979	Keith Hernandez, St.L	1B	11	105	.344
	Willie Stargell, Pit	1B	32	82	.281
1980	Mike Schmidt, Phi	3B	48	121	.286
1981	Mike Schmidt, Phi	3B	31	91	.316
1982	Dale Murphy, Atl	OF	36	109	.281
1983	Dale Murphy, Atl	OF	36	121	.302
1984	Ryne Sandberg, Chi	2B	19	84	.314
1985	Willie McGee, St.L	OF	10	82	.353
1986	Mike Schmidt, Phi	3B	37	119	.290
1987	Andre Dawson, Chi	OF	49	137	.287
1988	Kirk Gibson, LA	OF	25	76	.290
1989	Kevin Mitchell, SF	OF	47	125	.291
1990	Barry Bonds, Pit	OF	33	114	.301
1991	Terry Pendleton, Atl	3B	22	86	.319
1992	Barry Bonds, Pit	OF	34	103	.311
1993	Barry Bonds, SF	OF	46	123	.336
1994	Jeff Bagwell, Hou	1B	39	116	.368
1995	Barry Larkin, Cin	SS	15	66	.319
1996	Ken Caminiti, SD	3B	40	130	.326
1997	Larry Walker, Col	OF	49	130	.366
1998	Sammy Sosa, Chi	OF	66	158	.308
1999	Chipper Jones, Atl	3B	45	110	.319

American League

Year		Pos	HR	RBI	Avg
1931	Lefty Grove, Phi	P	–	–	–
1932	Jimmie Foxx, Phi	1B	58	169	.364
1933	Jimmie Foxx, Phi	1B	48	163	.356
1934	Mickey Cochrane, Det	C-Mgr	2	76	.320
1935	Hank Greenberg, Det	1B	36	170	.328
1936	Lou Gehrig, NY	1B	49	152	.354
1937	Charlie Gehringer, Det	2B	14	96	.371
1938	Jimmie Foxx, Bos	1B	50	175	.349
1939	Joe DiMaggio, NY	OF	30	126	.381
1940	Hank Greenberg, Det	OF	41	150	.340
1941	Joe DiMaggio, NY	OF	30	125	.357

Year		Pos	HR	RBI	Avg
1942	Joe Gordon, NY	2B	18	103	.322
1943	Spud Chandler, NY	P	–	–	–
1944	Hal Newhouser, Det	P	–	–	–
1945	Hal Newhouser, Det	P	–	–	–
1946	Ted Williams, Bos	OF	38	123	.342
1947	Joe DiMaggio, NY	OF	20	97	.315
1948	Lou Boudreau, Cle	SS-Mgr	18	106	.355
1949	Ted Williams, Bos	OF	43	159	.343
1950	Phil Rizzuto, NY	SS	7	66	.324
1951	Yogi Berra, NY	C	27	88	.294
1952	Bobby Shantz, Phi	P	–	–	–
1953	Al Rosen, Cle	3B	43	145	.336
1954	Yogi Berra, NY	C	22	125	.307
1955	Yogi Berra, NY	C	27	108	.272
1956	Mickey Mantle, NY	OF	52	130	.353
1957	Mickey Mantle, NY	OF	34	94	.365
1958	Jackie Jensen, Bos	OF	35	122	.286
1959	Nellie Fox, Chi	2B	2	70	.306
1960	Roger Maris, NY	OF	39	112	.283
1961	Roger Maris, NY	OF	61	142	.269
1962	Mickey Mantle, NY	OF	30	89	.321
1963	Elston Howard, NY	C	28	85	.287
1964	Brooks Robinson, Bal	3B	28	118	.317
1965	Zoilo Versalles, Min	SS	19	77	.273
1966	Frank Robinson, Bal	OF	49	122	.316
1967	Carl Yastrzemski, Bos	OF	44	121	.326
1968	Denny McLain, Det	P	–	–	–
1969	Harmon Killebrew, Min	3B-1B	49	140	.276
1970	Boog Powell, Bal	1B	35	114	.297
1971	Vida Blue, Oak	P	–	–	–
1972	Dick Allen, Chi	1B	37	113	.308
1973	Reggie Jackson, Oak	OF	32	117	.293
1974	Jeff Burroughs, Tex	OF	25	118	.301
1975	Fred Lynn, Bos	OF	21	105	.331
1976	Thurman Munson, NY	C	17	105	.302
1977	Rod Carew, Min	1B	14	100	.388
1978	Jim Rice, Bos	OF-DH	46	139	.315
1979	Don Baylor, Cal	OF-DH	36	139	.296
1980	George Brett, KC	3B	24	118	.390
1981	Rollie Fingers, Mil	P	–	–	–
1982	Robin Yount, Mil	SS	29	114	.331
1983	Cal Ripken Jr., Bal	SS	27	102	.318
1984	Willie Hernandez, Det	P	–	–	–
1985	Don Mattingly, NY	1B	35	145	.324
1986	Roger Clemens, Bos	P	–	–	–
1987	George Bell, Tor	OF	47	134	.308
1988	Jose Canseco, Oak	OF	42	124	.307
1989	Robin Yount, Mil	OF	21	103	.318
1990	Rickey Henderson, Oak	OF	28	61	.325
1991	Cal Ripken Jr., Bal	SS	34	114	.323
1992	Dennis Eckersley, Oak	P	–	–	–
1993	Frank Thomas, Chi	1B	41	128	.317
1994	Frank Thomas, Chi	1B	38	101	.353
1995	Mo Vaughn, Bos	1B	39	126	.300
1996	Juan Gonzalez, Tex	OF-DH	47	144	.314
1997	Ken Griffey Jr., Sea	OF	56	147	.304
1998	Juan Gonzalez, Tex	OF	45	157	.318
1999	Ivan Rodriguez, Tex	C	35	113	.332

MVP Pitchers' Statistics

Pitchers have been named Most Valuable Player on 23 occasions, 10 times in the NL and 13 in the AL. Four have been relief pitchers—Jim Konstanty, Rollie Fingers, Willie Hernandez and Dennis Eckersley.

National League

Year		Gm	W-L	SV	ERA
1924	Dazzy Vance, Bklyn	35	28-6	0	2.16
1933	Carl Hubbell, NY	45	23-12	5	1.66
1934	Dizzy Dean, St.L	50	30-7	7	2.66
1936	Carl Hubbell, NY	42	26-6	3	2.31
1939	Bucky Walters, Cin	39	27-11	0	2.29
1942	Mort Cooper, St.L	37	22-7	0	1.78
1950	Jim Konstanty, Phi	74	16-7	22	2.66

American League

Year		Gm	W-L	SV	ERA
1913	Walter Johnson, Wash	47	36-7	2	1.09
1924	Walter Johnson, Wash	38	23-7	0	2.72
1931	Lefty Grove, Phi	41	31-4	5	2.06
1943	Spud Chandler, NY	30	20-4	0	1.64
1944	Hal Newhouser, Det	47	29-9	2	2.22
1945	Hal Newhouser, Det	40	25-9	2	1.81
1952	Bobby Shantz, Phi	33	24-7	0	2.48

CY YOUNG AWARD

Voted on by the Baseball Writers Association of America. One award was presented from 1956-66, two since 1967. Pitchers who won the MVP and Cy Young awards in the same season are in **bold** type.

Multiple winners: NL—Steve Carlton and Greg Maddux (4); Sandy Koufax and Tom Seaver (3); Bob Gibson and Tom Glavine (2). **AL**—Roger Clemens (5); Jim Palmer (3); Denny McLain (2). **NL & AL**— Randy Johnson, Pedro Martinez and Gaylord Perry (2, one in each).

NL and AL Combined

Year	National League	Gm	W-L	SV	ERA	Year	National League	Gm	W-L	SV	ERA
1956	**Don Newcombe**, Bklyn	.38	27-7	0	3.06	1966	Sandy Koufax, LA	.41	27-9	0	1.73
1957	Warren Spahn, Mil.	.39	21-11	3	2.69						
1960	Vernon Law, Pit	.35	20-9	0	3.08	**Year**	**American League**	**Gm**	**W-L**	**SV**	**ERA**
1962	Don Drysdale, LA	.43	25-9	1	2.83	1958	Bob Turley, NY	.33	21-7	1	2.97
1963	**Sandy Koufax**, LA	.40	25-5	0	1.88	1959	Early Wynn, Chi	.37	22-10	0	3.17
1965	Sandy Koufax, LA	.43	26-8	2	2.04	1961	Whitey Ford, NY	.39	25-4	0	3.21
						1964	Dean Chance, LA	.46	20-9	4	1.65

Separate League Awards

National League

Year		Gm	W-L	SV	ERA
1967	Mike McCormick, SF	.40	22-10	0	2.85
1968	**Bob Gibson**, St.L.	.34	22-9	0	1.12
1969	Tom Seaver, NY	.36	25-7	0	2.21
1970	Bob Gibson, St.L.	.34	23-7	0	3.12
1971	Ferguson Jenkins, Chi	.39	24-13	0	2.77
1972	Steve Carlton, Phi	.41	27-10	0	1.97
1973	Tom Seaver, NY	.36	19-10	0	2.08
1974	Mike Marshall, LA	.106	15-12	21	2.42
1975	Tom Seaver, NY	.36	22-9	0	2.38
1976	Randy Jones, SD	.40	22-14	0	2.74
1977	Steve Carlton, Phi	.36	23-10	0	2.64
1978	Gaylord Perry, SD	.37	21-6	0	2.72
1979	Bruce Sutter, Chi	.62	6-6	37	2.23
1980	Steve Carlton, Phi	.38	24-9	0	2.34
1981	Fernando Valenzuela, LA	.25	13-7	0	2.48
1982	Steve Carlton, Phi	.38	23-11	0	3.10
1983	John Denny, Phi	.36	19-6	0	2.37
1984	Rick Sutcliffe, Chi	.20*	16-1	0	2.69
1985	Dwight Gooden, NY	.35	24-4	0	1.53
1986	Mike Scott, Hou	.37	18-10	0	2.22
1987	Steve Bedrosian, Phi	.65	5-3	40	2.83
1988	Orel Hershiser, LA	.35	23-8	1	2.26
1989	Mark Davis, SD	.70	4-3	44	1.85
1990	Doug Drabek, Pit	.33	22-6	0	2.76
1991	Tom Glavine, Atl	.34	20-11	0	2.55
1992	Greg Maddux, Chi	.35	20-11	0	2.18
1993	Greg Maddux, Atl	.36	20-10	0	2.36
1994	Greg Maddux, Atl	.25	16-6	0	1.56
1995	Greg Maddux, Atl	.28	19-2	0	1.63
1996	John Smoltz, Atl	.35	24-8	0	2.94
1997	Pedro Martinez, Mon	.31	17-8	0	1.90
1998	Tom Glavine, Atl	.33	20-6	0	2.47
1999	Randy Johnson, Ari	.35	17-9	0	2.48

*NL games only, Sutcliffe pitched 15 games with Cleveland before being traded to the Cubs.

American League

Year		Gm	W-L	SV	ERA
1967	Jim Lonborg, Bos	.39	22-9	0	3.16
1968	**Denny McLain**, Det	.41	31-6	0	1.96
1969	Denny McLain, Det	.42	24-9	0	2.80
	Mike Cuellar, Bal	.39	23-11	0	2.38
1970	Jim Perry, Min	.40	24-12	0	3.03
1971	**Vida Blue**, Oak	.39	24-8	0	1.82
1972	Gaylord Perry, Cle	.41	24-16	1	1.92
1973	Jim Palmer, Bal	.38	22-9	1	2.40
1974	Catfish Hunter, Oak	.41	25-12	0	2.49
1975	Jim Palmer, Bal	.39	23-11	1	2.09
1976	Jim Palmer, Bal	.40	22-13	0	2.51
1977	Sparky Lyle, NY	.72	13-5	26	2.17
1978	Ron Guidry, NY	.35	25-3	0	1.74
1979	Mike Flanagan, Bal	.39	23-9	0	3.08
1980	Steve Stone, Bal	.37	25-7	0	3.23
1981	**Rollie Fingers**, Mil	.47	6-3	28	1.04
1982	Pete Vuckovich, Mil	.30	18-6	0	3.34
1983	LaMarr Hoyt, Chi	.36	24-10	0	3.66
1984	**Willie Hernandez**, Det	.80	9-3	32	1.92
1985	Bret Saberhagen, KC	.32	20-6	0	2.87
1986	**Roger Clemens**, Bos	.33	24-4	0	2.48
1987	Roger Clemens, Bos	.36	20-9	0	2.97
1988	Frank Viola, Min	.35	24-7	0	2.64
1989	Bret Saberhagen, KC	.36	23-6	0	2.16
1990	Bob Welch, Oak	.35	27-6	0	2.95
1991	Roger Clemens, Bos	.35	18-10	0	2.62
1992	**Dennis Eckersley**, Oak	.69	7-1	51	1.91
1993	Jack McDowell, Chi	.34	22-10	0	3.37
1994	David Cone, KC	.23	16-5	0	2.94
1995	Randy Johnson, Sea	.30	18-2	0	2.48
1996	Pat Hentgen, Tor	.35	20-10	0	3.22
1997	Roger Clemens, Tor	.34	21-7	0	2.05
1998	Roger Clemens, Tor	.33	20-6	0	2.65
1999	Pedro Martinez, Bos	.31	23-4	0	2.07

ROOKIE OF THE YEAR

Voted on by the Baseball Writers Assn. of America. One award was presented from 1947-48. Two awards (one for each league) have been presented since 1949. Winner who was also named MVP is in **bold** type.

NL and AL Combined

Year		Pos	Year		Pos
1947	Jackie Robinson, Brooklyn	.1B	1948	Alvin Dark, Boston-NL	.SS

National League

Year		Pos	Year		Pos	Year		Pos
1949	Don Newcombe, Bklyn	.P	1956	Frank Robinson, Cin	.OF	1963	Pete Rose, Cin	.2B
1950	Sam Jethroe, Bos	.OF	1957	Jack Sanford, Phi	.P	1964	Richie Allen, Phi	.3B
1951	Willie Mays, NY.	.OF	1958	Orlando Cepeda, SF	.1B	1965	Jim Lefebvre, LA.	.2B
1952	Joe Black, Bklyn	.P	1959	Willie McCovey, SF	.1B	1966	Tommy Helms, Cin	.3B
1953	Jim Gilliam, Bklyn	.2B	1960	Frank Howard, LA	.OF	1967	Tom Seaver, NY	.P
1954	Wally Moon, St.L	.OF	1961	Billy Williams, Chi	.OF	1968	Johnny Bench, Cin	.C
1955	Bill Virdon, St.L.	.OF	1962	Ken Hubbs, Chi	.2B	1969	Ted Sizemore, LA	.2B

Year		Pos	Year		Pos	Year		Pos
1970	Carl Morton, Mon	.P	1980	Steve Howe, LA	.P	1990	David Justice, Atl	.OF
1971	Earl Williams, Atl	.C	1981	Fernando Valenzuela, LA	.P	1991	Jeff Bagwell, Hou	.1B
1972	Jon Matlack, NY	.P	1982	Steve Sax, LA	.2B	1992	Eric Karros, LA	.1B
1973	Gary Matthews, SF	.OF	1983	Darryl Strawberry, NY	.OF	1993	Mike Piazza, LA	.C
1974	Bake McBride, St.L	.OF	1984	Dwight Gooden, NY	.P	1994	Raul Mondesi, LA	.OF
1975	John Montefusco, SF	.P	1985	Vince Coleman, St.L	.OF	1995	Hideo Nomo, LA	.P
1976	Butch Metzger, SD	.P	1986	Todd Worrell, St.L	.P	1996	Todd Hollandsworth, LA	.OF
	& Pat Zachry, Cin	.P	1987	Benito Santiago, SD	.C	1997	Scott Rolen, Phi	.3B
1977	Andre Dawson, Mon	.OF	1988	Chris Sabo, Cin	.3B	1998	Kerry Wood, Chi	.P
1978	Bob Horner, Atl	.3B	1989	Jerome Walton, Chi	.OF	1999	Scott Williamson, Cin	.P
1979	Rick Sutcliffe, LA	.P						

American League

Year		Pos	Year		Pos	Year		Pos
1949	Roy Sievers, St.L	.OF	1967	Rod Carew, Min	.2B	1984	Alvin Davis, Sea	.1B
			1968	Stan Bahnsen, NY	.P	1985	Ozzie Guillen, Chi	.SS
1950	Walt Dropo, Bos	.1B	1969	Lou Piniella, KC	.OF	1986	Jose Canseco, Oak	.OF
1951	Gil McDougald, NY	.3B				1987	Mark McGwire, Oak	.1B
1952	Harry Byrd, Phi	.P	1970	Thurman Munson, NY	.C	1988	Walt Weiss, Oak	.SS
1953	Harvey Kuenn, Det	.SS	1971	Chris Chambliss, Cle	.1B	1989	Gregg Olson, Bal	.P
1954	Bob Grim, NY	.P	1972	Carlton Fisk, Bos	.C			
1955	Herb Score, Cle	.P	1973	Al Bumbry, Bal	.OF	1990	Sandy Alomar Jr., Cle	.C
1956	Luis Aparicio, Chi	.SS	1974	Mike Hargrove, Tex	.1B	1991	Chuck Knoblauch, Min	.2B
1957	Tony Kubek, NY	.INF-OF	1975	**Fred Lynn**, Bos	.OF	1992	Pat Listach, Mil	.SS
1958	Albie Pearson, Wash	.OF	1976	Mark Fidrych, Det	.P	1993	Tim Salmon, Cal	.OF
1959	Bob Allison, Wash	.OF	1977	Eddie Murray, Bal	.DH-1B	1994	Bob Hamelin, KC	.DH
			1978	Lou Whitaker, Det	.2B	1995	Marty Cordova, Min	.OF
1960	Ron Hansen, Bal	.SS	1979	John Castino, Min	.3B	1996	Derek Jeter, NY	.SS
1961	Don Schwall, Bos	.P		& Alfredo Griffin, Tor	.SS	1997	Nomar Garciaparra, Bos	.SS
1962	Tom Tresh, NY	.SS-OF				1998	Ben Grieve, Oak	.OF
1963	Gary Peters, Chi	.P	1980	Joe Charboneau, Cle	.OF-DH	1999	Carlos Beltran, KC	.OF
1964	Tony Oliva, Min	.OF	1981	Dave Righetti, NY	.P			
1965	Curt Blefary, Bal	.OF	1982	Cal Ripken Jr., Bal	.SS-3B			
1966	Tommie Agee, Chi	.OF	1983	Ron Kittle, Chi	.OF			

MANAGER OF THE YEAR

Voted on by the Baseball Writers Association of America. Two awards (one for each league) presented since 1983. Note that (*) indicates manager's team won division championship and (†) indicates unofficial division won in 1994.

Multiple winners: Tony La Russa (3); Sparky Anderson, Dusty Baker, Bobby Cox, Tommy Lasorda, Jim Leyland and Joe Torre (2).

National League

Year		Improvement		
1983	Tommy Lasorda, LA	88-74	to	91-71*
1984	Jim Frey, Chi	71-91	to	96-75*
1985	Whitey Herzog, St. L	84-78	to	101-61*
1986	Hal Lanier, Hou	83-79	to	96-66*
1987	Buck Rodgers, Mon	78-83	to	91-71
1988	Tommy Lasorda, LA	73-89	to	94-67*
1989	Don Zimmer, Chi	77-85	to	93-69*
1990	Jim Leyland, Pit	74-88	to	95-67*
1991	Bobby Cox, Atl	65-97	to	94-68*
1992	Jim Leyland, Pit	98-64*	to	96-66*
1993	Dusty Baker, SF	72-90	to	103-59
1994	Felipe Alou, Mon	94-68	to	74-40†
1995	Don Baylor, Col	53-64	to	77-67
1996	Bruce Bochy, SD	70-74	to	91-71
1997	Dusty Baker, SF	68-94	to	90-72
1998	Larry Dierker, Hou	84-78	to	102-60*
1999	Jack McKeon, Cin	77-85	to	96-67

American League

Year		Improvement		
1983	Tony La Russa, Chi	87-75	to	99-63*
1984	Sparky Anderson, Det	92-70	to	104-58*
1985	Bobby Cox, Tor	89-73	to	99-62*
1986	John McNamara, Bos	81-81	to	95-66*
1987	Sparky Anderson, Det	87-75	to	98-64*
1988	Tony La Russa, Oak	81-81	to	104-58*
1989	Frank Robinson, Bal	54-107	to	87-75
1990	Jeff Torborg, Chi	69-92	to	94-68
1991	Tom Kelly, Min	74-88	to	95-67*
1992	Tony La Russa, Oak	84-78	to	96-66*
1993	Gene Lamont, Chi	86-76	to	94-68*
1994	Buck Showalter, NY	88-74	to	70-43†
1995	Lou Piniella, Sea	49-63	to	79-66*
1996	Joe Torre, NY	79-65	to	92-70
	& Johnny Oates, Tex	74-70	to	90-72
1997	Davey Johnson, Bal	88-74	to	98-64
1998	Joe Torre, NY	96-66	to	114-48*
1999	Jimy Williams, Bos	92-70	to	94-68

HANK AARON AWARD

The inaugural award was presented in 1999 to the best "complete" hitter in both the American and National leagues. In 1999, hitters received one point for every hit, home run and RBI. Beginning in 2000, winners are selected by a panel of broadcasters.

National League

Year		H	HR	RBI	Avg
1999	Sammy Sosa, Chi	180	63	141	.288
2000	Todd Helton, Col	216	42	147	.372

American League

Year		H	HR	RBI	Avg
1999	Manny Ramirez, Cle	174	44	165	.333
2000	Carlos Delgado, Tor	196	41	137	.344

COLLEGE BASEBALL

College World Series

The NCAA Division I College World Series has been held in Kalamazoo, Mich. (1947-48), Wichita, Kan. (1949) and Omaha, Neb. (since 1950).

Multiple winners: USC (12); Arizona St. and LSU (5); Texas (4); Arizona, CS-Fullerton, Miami-FL and Minnesota (3); California, Michigan, Oklahoma and Stanford (2).

Year	Winner	Coach	Score	Runner-up	Year	Winner	Coach	Score	Runner-up
1947	California	Clint Evans	8-7	Yale	1974	USC	Rod Dedeaux	7-3	Miami-FL
1948	USC	Sam Barry	9-2	Yale	1975	Texas	Cliff Gustafson	5-1	S. Carolina
1949	Texas	Bibb Falk	10-3	W. Forest	1976	Arizona	Jerry Kindall	7-1	E. Michigan
1950	Texas	Bibb Falk	3-0	Wash. St.	1977	Arizona St.	Jim Brock	2-1	S. Carolina
1951	Oklahoma	Jack Baer	3-2	Tennessee	1978	USC	Rod Dedeaux	10-3	Ariz. St.
1952	Holy Cross	Jack Barry	8-4	Missouri	1979	CS-Fullerton	Augie Garrido	2-1	Arkansas
1953	Michigan	Ray Fisher	7-5	Texas	1980	Arizona	Jerry Kindall	5-3	Hawaii
1954	Missouri	Hi Simmons	4-1	Rollins	1981	Arizona St.	Jim Brock	7-4	Okla. St.
1955	Wake Forest	Taylor Sanford	7-6	W. Mich.	1982	Miami-FL	Ron Fraser	9-3	Wichita St.
1956	Minnesota	Dick Siebert	12-1	Arizona	1983	Texas	Cliff Gustafson	4-3	Alabama
1957	California	Geo. Wolfman	1-0	Penn St.	1984	CS-Fullerton	Augie Garrido	3-1	Texas
1958	USC	Rod Dedeaux	8-7	Missouri	1985	Miami-FL	Ron Fraser	10-6	Texas
1959	Oklahoma St.	Toby Greene	5-3	Arizona	1986	Arizona	Jerry Kindall	10-2	Fla. St.
1960	Minnesota	Dick Siebert	2-1	USC	1987	Stanford	M. Marquess	9-5	Okla. St.
1961	USC	Rod Dedeaux	1-0	Okla. St.	1988	Stanford	M. Marquess	9-4	Ariz. St.
1962	Michigan	Don Lund	5-4	S. Clara	1989	Wichita St.	G.Stephenson	5-3	Texas
1963	USC	Rod Dedeaux	5-2	Arizona	1990	Georgia	Steve Webber	2-1	Okla. St.
1964	Minnesota	Dick Siebert	5-1	Missouri	1991	LSU	Skip Bertman	6-3	Wichita St.
1965	Arizona St.	Bobby Winkles	2-1	Ohio St.	1992	Pepperdine	Andy Lopez	3-2	CS-Fullerton
1966	Ohio St.	Marty Karow	8-2	Okla. St.	1993	LSU	Skip Bertman	8-0	Wichita St.
1967	Arizona St.	Bobby Winkles	11-2	Houston	1994	Oklahoma	Larry Cochell	13-5	Ga. Tech
1968	USC	Rod Dedeaux	4-3	So. Ill.	1995	CS-Fullerton	Augie Garrido	11-5	USC
1969	Arizona St.	Bobby Winkles	10-1	Tulsa	1996	LSU	Skip Bertman	9-8	Miami-FL
1970	USC	Rod Dedeaux	2-1	Fla. St.	1997	LSU	Skip Bertman	13-6	Alabama
1971	USC	Rod Dedeaux	7-2	So. Ill.	1998	USC	Mike Gillespie	21-14	Arizona St.
1972	USC	Rod Dedeaux	1-0	Ariz. St.	1999	Miami-FL	Jim Morris	6-5	Fla. St.
1973	USC	Rod Dedeaux	4-3	Ariz. St.	2000	LSU	Skip Bertman	6-5	Stanford

Most Outstanding Player

The Most Outstanding Player has been selected every year of the College World Series since 1949. Winners who did not play for the CWS champion are listed in **bold** type. No player has won the award more than once.

Year		Year		Year	
1949	**Charles Teague,** W. Forest, 2B	1967	Ron Davini, Ariz. St., C	1985	Greg Ellena, Miami-FL, LF
1950	**Ray VanCleef,** Rutgers, CF	1968	Bill Seinsoth, USC, 1B	1986	Mike Senne, Arizona, DH
1951	**Sidney Hatfield,** Tenn., P-1B	1969	John Dolinsek, Ariz. St., LF	1987	Paul Carey, Stanford, RF
1952	James O'Neill, Holy Cross, P	1970	**Gene Ammann,** Fla. St., P	1988	Lee Plemel, Stanford, P
1953	**J.L. Smith,** Texas, P	1971	**Jerry Tabb,** Tulsa, 1B	1989	Greg Brummett, Wich. St., P
1954	**Tom Yewcic,** Mich. St., C	1972	Russ McQueen, USC, P	1990	Mike Rebhan, Georgia, P
1955	**Tom Borland,** Okla. St., P	1973	**Dave Winfield,** Minn., P-OF	1991	Gary Hymel, LSU, C
1956	Jerry Thomas, Minn., P	1974	George Milke, USC, P	1992	**Phil Nevin,** CS-Fullerton, 3B
1957	**Cal Emery,** Penn St., P-1B	1975	Mickey Reichenbach, Texas, 1B	1993	Todd Walker, LSU, 2B
1958	Bill Thom, USC, P	1976	Steve Powers, Arizona, P-DH	1994	Chip Glass, Oklahoma, OF
1959	Jim Dobson, Okla. St., 3B	1977	Bob Horner, Ariz. St., 3B	1995	Mark Kotsay, CS-Fullerton, OF
1960	John Erickson, Minn., 2B	1978	Rod Boxberger, USC, P	1996	**Pat Burrell,** Miami-FL, 3B
1961	**Littleton Fowler,** Okla. St., P	1979	Tony Hudson, CS-Fullerton, P	1997	Brandon Larson, LSU, SS
1962	**Bob Garibaldi,** Santa Clara, P	1980	Terry Francona, Arizona, LF	1998	Wes Rachels, USC, 2B
1963	Bud Hollowell, USC, C	1981	Stan Holmes, Ariz. St., LF	1999	**Marshall McDougall,** Fla. St., 2B
1964	**Joe Ferris,** Maine, P	1982	Dan Smith, Miami-FL, P	2000	Trey Hodges, LSU, P
1965	Sal Bando, Ariz. St., 3B	1983	Calvin Schiraldi, Texas, P		
1966	Steve Arlin, Ohio St., P	1984	John Fishel, CS-Fullerton, LF		

Annual Awards
Golden Spikes Award

First presented in 1978 by USA Baseball, honoring the nation's best amateur player. Alex Fernandez, the 1990 winner, has been the only junior college player chosen.

Year		Year		Year	
1978	Bob Horner, Ariz. St, 2B	1984	Oddibe McDowell, Ariz. St., OF	1990	Alex Fernandez, Miami-Dade, P
1979	Tim Wallach, CS-Fullerton, 1B	1985	Will Clark, Miss. St., 1B	1991	Mike Kelly, Ariz. St., OF
1980	Terry Francona, Arizona, OF	1986	Mike Loynd, Fla. St., P	1992	Phil Nevin, CS-Fullerton, 3B
1981	Mike Fuentes, Fla. St., OF	1987	Jim Abbott, Michigan, P	1993	Darren Dreifort, Wichita St., P
1982	Augie Schmidt, N. Orleans, SS	1988	Robin Ventura, Okla. St., 3B	1994	Jason Varitek, Ga. Tech, C
1983	Dave Magadan, Alabama, 1B	1989	Ben McDonald, LSU, P	1995	Mark Kotsay, CS-Fullerton, OF

Year
1996 Travis Lee, San Diego St., 1B
1997 J.D. Drew, Florida St., OF

Year
1998 Pat Burrell, Miami-FL, 3B
1999 Jason Jennings, Baylor, DH/P

Baseball America Player of the Year

Presented to the College Player of the Year since 1981 by *Baseball America*.

Year
1981 Mike Sodders, Ariz. St., 3B
1982 Jeff Ledbetter, Fla. St., OF/P
1983 Dave Magadan, Alabama, 1B
1984 Oddibe McDowell, Ariz. St., OF
1985 Pete Incaviglia, Okla. St., OF
1986 Casey Close, Michigan, OF
1987 Robin Ventura, Okla. St., 3B

Year
1988 John Olerud, Wash. St., 1B/P
1989 Ben McDonald, LSU, P
1990 Mike Kelly, Ariz. St., OF
1991 David McCarty, Stanford, 1B
1992 Phil Nevin, CS-Fullerton, 3B
1993 Brooks Kieschnick, Texas, DH/P
1994 Jason Varitek, Ga. Tech, C

Year
1995 Todd Helton, Tenn., 1B/P
1996 Kris Benson, Clemson, P
1997 J.D. Drew, Florida St., OF
1998 Jeff Austin, Stanford, RHP
1999 Jason Jennings, Baylor, DH/P
2000 Mark Teixeira, Ga. Tech, 3B

Dick Howser Trophy

Presented to the College Player of the Year since 1987, by the American Baseball Coaches Association (ABCA) from 1987-98 and the National Collegiate Baseball Writers Association (NCBWA) beginning in 1999. Beginning in 2000, voting was conducted by the NCBWA in conjunction with *Baseball America*. Named after the late two-time All-America shortstop and college coach at Florida State. Howser was also a major league manager with Kansas City and the New York Yankees.

Multiple winner: Brooks Kieschnick (2).

Year
1987 Mike Fiore, Miami-FL, OF
1988 Robin Ventura, Okla. St., 3B
1989 Scott Bryant, Texas, DH
1990 Paul Ellis, UCLA, C
1991 Bobby Jones, Fresno St., P

Year
1992 Brooks Kieschnick, Texas, DH/P
1993 Brooks Kieschnick, Texas, DH/P
1994 Jason Varitek, Ga. Tech, C
1995 Todd Helton, Tenn., 1B/P
1996 Kris Benson, Clemson, P

Year
1997 J.D. Drew, Florida St., OF
1998 Eddie Furniss, LSU, 1B
1999 Jason Jennings, Baylor, DH/P
2000 Mark Teixeira, Ga. Tech, 3B

Baseball America Coach of the Year

Presented to the College Coach of the Year since 1981 by *Baseball America*.

Multiple winners: Skip Bertman, Dave Snow and Gene Stephenson (2).

Year
1981 Ron Fraser, Miami-FL
1982 Gene Stephenson, Wichita St.
1983 Barry Shollenberger, Alabama
1984 Augie Garrido, CS-Fullerton
1985 Ron Polk, Mississippi St.
1986 Skip Bertman, LSU
   & Dave Snow, Loyola-CA

Year
1987 Mark Marquess, Stanford
1988 Jim Brock, Arizona St.
1989 Dave Snow, Long Beach St.
1990 Steve Webber, Georgia
1991 Jim Hendry, Creighton
1992 Andy Lopez, Pepperdine
1993 Gene Stephenson, Wichita St.

Year
1994 Jim Morris, Miami-FL
1995 Rod Delmonico, Tennessee
1996 Skip Bertman, LSU
1997 Jim Wells, Alabama
1998 Pat Murphy, Arizona St.
1999 Wayne Graham, Rice
2000 Ray Tanner, S. Carolina

All-Time Winningest Coaches

Coaches active in 2000 are in **bold** type. Records given are for four-year colleges only. For winning percentage, a minimum 10 years in Division I is required.

Top 25 Winning Percentage

		Yrs	W	L	T	Pct
1	John Barry	40	619	147	6	.806
2	W.J. Disch	29	465	115	0	.802
3	Cliff Gustafson	29	1427	373	2	.792
4	Harry Carlson	17	143	41	0	.777
5	**Gene Stephenson**	23	1270	383	3	.768
6	Gary Ward	19	953	313	1	.753
7	George Jacobs	11	76	25	0	.752
8	Bobby Winkles	13	524	173	0	.752
9	**Mike Martin**	21	1132	383	3	.747
10	Frank Sancet	23	831	283	8	.744
11	Ron Fraser	30	1271	438	9	.742
12	Bob Wren	23	464	160	4	.742
13	Bob Falk	25	435	152	0	.741
14	**Skip Bertman**	17	826	308	2	.728
15	Bud Middaugh	22	821	319	1	.720
16	J.F. "Pop" McKale	30	302	118	7	.715
17	Jim Brock	28	1100	440	0	.714
18	Toby Green	21	318	132	0	.707
19	**Jim Morris**	19	844	351	2	.706
20	Joe Arnold	18	750	313	2	.705
21	**Jim Wells**	11	480	203	0	.703
22	Joe Bedenk	32	380	159	3	.701
23	Rod Dedeaux	45	1332	571	11	.699
24	Enos Semore	22	851	370	1	.697
25	**Ray Tanner**	13	563	248	3	.693

Top 25 Victories

		Yrs	W	L	T	Pct
1	Cliff Gustafson	29	**1427**	373	2	.792
2	Rod Dedeaux	45	**1332**	571	11	.699
3	**Augie Garrido**	32	**1284**	622	8	.673
4	**Chuck Hartman**	41	**1276**	651	7	.662
5	Ron Fraser	30	**1271**	438	9	.742
6	**Gene Stephenson**	23	**1270**	383	3	.768
7	Jack Stallings	39	**1258**	796	5	.612
8	**Larry Hays**	30	**1235**	666	2	.650
9	**Bob Bennett**	32	**1230**	706	8	.635
10	Al Ogletree	41	**1217**	713	1	.631
11	**Larry Cochell**	34	**1186**	679	2	.636
12	Chuck Brayton	33	**1162**	523	8	.689
13	Bill Wilhelm	36	**1161**	536	10	.683
14	**Jim Dietz**	29	**1154**	701	18	.621
15	**Mike Martin**	21	**1132**	383	3	.746
16	Jim Brock	23	**1100**	440	0	.714
17	**Norm DeBriyn**	31	**1099**	595	6	.648
18	**Richard Jones**	34	**1097**	623	5	.637
19	**Les Murakami**	30	**1079**	570	4	.654
20	**Ron Polk**	27	**1075**	512	0	.677
21	**Bob Hannah**	37	**1053**	464	6	.693
	Gary Adams	31	**1053**	770	12	.577
23	**Mark Marquess**	24	995	498	5	.666
24	Gary Ward	19	953	313	1	.753
25	John Winkin	42	**934**	670	11	.582

Other NCAA Champions
Division II

Multiple winners: Florida Southern (8); Cal Poly Pomona and Tampa (3); CS-Chico, CS-Northridge, Jacksonville St., Troy St., UC-Irvine and UC-Riverside (2).

Year		Year		Year		Year	
1968	Chapman, CA	1977	UC-Riverside	1986	Troy St., AL	1995	Florida Southern
1969	Illinois St.	1978	Florida Southern	1987	Troy St., AL	1996	Kennesaw St., GA
1970	CS-Northridge	1979	Valdosta St., GA	1988	Florida Southern	1997	CS-Chico
1971	Florida Southern	1980	Cal Poly Pomona	1989	Cal Poly SLO	1998	Tampa
1972	Florida Southern	1981	Florida Southern	1990	Jacksonville St., AL	1999	CS-Chico
1973	UC-Irvine	1982	UC-Riverside	1991	Jacksonville St., AL	2000	Southeastern Okla.
1974	UC-Irvine	1983	Cal Poly Pomona	1992	Tampa		
1975	Florida Southern	1984	CS-Northridge	1993	Tampa		
1976	Cal Poly Pomona	1985	Florida Southern	1994	Central Missouri St.		

Division III

Multiple winners: Eastern Conn. St., Marietta, and Montclair St. (3); CS-Stanislaus, Glassboro St., Ithaca, NC-Wesleyan, Southern Maine and Wm. Paterson, NJ (2).

Year		Year		Year		Year	
1976	CS-Stanislaus	1983	Marietta, OH	1990	Eastern Conn. St.	1997	Southern Maine
1977	CS-Stanislaus	1984	Ramapo, NJ	1991	Southern Maine	1998	Eastern Conn. St.
1978	Glassboro St., NJ	1985	Wisconsin-Oshkosh	1992	Wm. Paterson, NJ	1999	NC-Wesleyan
1979	Glassboro St., NJ	1986	Marietta, OH	1993	Montclair St., NJ	2000	Montclair St., NJ
1980	Ithaca, NY	1987	Monclair St., NJ	1994	Wisconsin-Oshkosh		
1981	Marietta, OH	1988	Ithaca, NY	1995	La Verne, CA		
1982	Eastern Conn. St.	1989	NC-Wesleyan	1996	Wm. Paterson, NJ		

Major League Number One Draft Picks

The Major League First-Year Player Draft has been held every year since 1965. Clubs select in reverse order of their won-loss records from the previous regular season with National League and American League teams alternating. AL teams select first in odd-numbered years while NL teams go first in even-numbered years. The pool of draftees consists of graduated high school players, junior or senior college players, Junior college players and anyone over the age of 21. Listed are the top selections from each draft.

Year		Pos	Team	Year		Pos	Team
1965	Rick Monday	OF	Kansas City Athletics	1983	Tim Belcher	P	Minnesota Twins
1966	Steve Chilcott	C	New York Mets	1984	Shawn Abner	OF	New York Mets
1967	Rom Blomberg	1B	New York Yankees	1985	B.J. Surhoff	C	Milwaukee Brewers
1968	Tim Foli	IF	New York Mets	1986	Jeff King	IF	Pittsburgh Pirates
1969	Jeff Burroughs	OF	Washington Senators	1987	Ken Griffey Jr.	OF	Seattle Mariners
1970	Mike Ivie	C	San Diego Padres	1988	Andy Benes	P	San Diego Padres
1971	Danny Goodwin	C	Chicago White Sox	1989	Ben McDonald	P	Baltimore Orioles
1972	Dave Roberts	IF	San Diego Padres	1990	Chipper Jones	SS	Atlanta Braves
1973	David Clyde	P	Texas Rangers	1991	Brien Taylor	P	New York Yankees
1974	Bill Almon	IF	San Diego Padres	1992	Phil Nevin	3B	Houston Astros
1975	Danny Goodwin	C	California Angels	1993	Alex Rodriguez	SS	Seattle Mariners
1976	Floyd Bannister	P	Houston Astros	1994	Paul Wilson	P	New York Mets
1977	Harold Baines	OF	Chicago White Sox	1995	Darin Erstad	OF/P	California Angels
1978	Bob Horner	3B	Atlanta Braves	1996	Kris Benson	P	Pittsburgh Pirates
1979	Al Chambers	OF	Seattle Mariners	1997	Matt Anderson	P	Detroit Tigers
1980	Darryl Strawberry	OF	New York Mets	1998	Pat Burrell	3B	Philadelphia Phillies
1981	Mike Moore	P	Seattle Mariners	1999	Josh Hamilton	OF	T.B. Devil Rays
1982	Shawon Dunston	SS	Chicago Cubs	2000	Adrian Gonzalez	1B	Florida Marlins

Straight to the Majors

Since Major League baseball began its free agent draft in 1965, 17 selections have advanced directly to the major leagues without first playing in the minors

Draft		Pos	Team	Draft		Pos	Team
1967	Mike Adamson, South Carolina	P	Baltimore	1978	Tim Conroy, Gateway HS (Pa.)	P	Oakland
1969	Steve Dunning, Stanford	P	Cleveland		Bob Horner, Arizona St.	IF	Atlanta
1971	Pete Broberg, Dartmouth	P	Washington		Brian Milner, Southwest HS (Tex.)	C	Toronto
	Rob Ellis, Michigan St.	IF	Milwaukee		Mike Morgan, Valley HS (Nev.)	P	Oakland
	Burt Hooton, Texas	P	Chicago	1985	Pete Incaviglia, Oklahoma St.	OF	Montreal
1972	Dave Roberts, Oregon	IF	San Diego	1988	Jim Abbott, Michigan	P	California
1973	Dick Ruthven, Fresno St.	P	Philadelphia	1989	John Olerud, Washington St.	IF	Toronto
1973	David Clyde, Westchester HS (Tex.)	P	Texas				
	Dave Winfield, Minnesota	OF	San Diego				
	Eddie Bane, Arizona St.	P	Minnesota				

College Football

*Sugar Bowl MVP **Peter Warrick** pulls in a ball late in the second half of the national title game at the Superdome.*

AP/Wide World Photos

Warrick Sweeter in Sugar Bowl

FSU receiver leads 'Noles to title over Michael Vick and Va. Tech in New Orleans.

by

Chris Fowler

The script seemed too well crafted to be real: an athletic duel for the ages between two of the most outrageously talented football players in recent history. One, a senior, bent on redemption in his final college performance. The other, a freshman, precociously defying conventional wisdom with deeds beyond his years.

On Jan. 4 in New Orleans, a city long famous for its strange magic, Peter Warrick and Michael Vick were sorcerers, conjuring the impossible, operating on a different plane from the mesmerized mortals. Each man shouldered his team's hopes for a national championship.

But somehow, to many of us watching, the scoreboard seemed hardly the point. This was about experi-

Chris Fowler is the host of ESPN's *College GameDay.*

encing the raw skills and the showmanship of the truly gifted. One of the two was on the field for almost every snap of the Nokia Sugar Bowl in the Superdome that night. And that meant the real possibility for a time capsule highlight existed each play. Lingering in the lavatory was a bad idea.

There was Vick, eluding and evading, creating jaw-dropping shows of athleticism as he darted through a Florida State defense that all week had vowed to shake up and bottle up the youngster with speed he'd never faced. Instead, it was the 'Noles who looked almost slow.

Freshman quarterbacks win national championships about once every couple decades. Could a rookie in his teens really take away the title that everyone figured FSU had won going in? For three quarters, it looked like it.

Of course, this rookie was a freak of nature, with natural born calm and confidence that had only grown during

Virginia Tech freshman quarterback **Michael Vick** certainly gave the Florida State defense all they could handle in the Sugar Bowl, rushing for nearly 100 yards and throwing for 225 more, but Tech's defense simply could not keep down game MVP Peter Warrick.

an 11-0 drive to the title game. Virginia Tech's quarterback had already produced the season's most significant play: a fourth and long scramble to set up the game-winning field goal that rescued the Hokies at West Virginia. It was the kind of moment that made many believe that destiny had been recruited to join Virginia Tech's cause. It still seemed that way with a quarter to play in the Superdome.

Then came Warrick's turn. He'd already dazzled the dome with a long touchdown sprint and then taken a punt to paydirt. But he hadn't yet delivered the dagger.

That came after a time out. FSU fans stacked to the dome's ceiling had started a chant as the players waited for ABC's commercials to play out. "Pe-ter War-rick" they repeated again and again. The sound poured down to

the field, and in the huddle, quarterback Chris Weinke decided to comply. He'd give Warrick a chance to seal the title.

What followed was a catch for the ages: number nine outleaping a Hokie defender who was draped on him—tipping the ball into the air—and then somehow grabbing it, after it had landed on top of his sprawled out body. It was the kind of play you hope you can see once or twice in your life: a moment that you realize during the very seconds you're watching it unfold...that it's something you'll never forget.

Warrick's "called shot" was the final page of his FSU legacy and he knew it as he came to the sidelines with his right fist pounding on his chest, above his heart. He was showing his appreciation right back to the

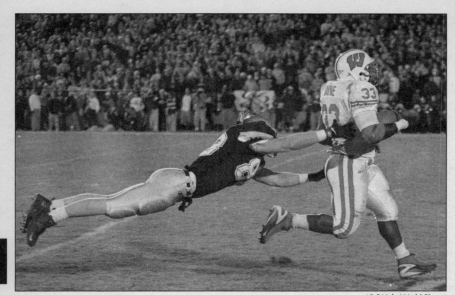

AP/Wide World Photos

Wisconsin tailback **Ron Dayne** ran away with the Heisman Trophy and made everyone in college football forget about Ricky Williams when he eclipsed his one-year-old career rushing record.

Noles' delirious fans, who had been so patient with him during his troubled senior year. If Warrick's poor judgement in accepting the notorious "Dillard's Discount" had ruined his Heisman hopes and brought shame on the program, then all was forgotten and forgiven now.

Warrick won his ring. Vick won boundless respect, which he'll carry into future campaigns for a Tech title. The morning after the loss, Hokie Coach Frank Beamer set aside the sting to savor what he'd seen from his young star.

"Have you ever seen a quarterback make those kinds of plays? So many of them?" he asked.

Coach, I don't believe I have. And how could watching Vick and Warrick showcase such brilliance not get every young kid with dreams excited about the idea of playing college football? It was great for the game and it was great to watch. Four days into the new century, it was a pretty high standard to set for this sport's next century. ■

Lee Corso's Ten Biggest Moments of the Year in College Football

10. **TCU's LaDainian Tomlinson** sets a single-game Div. I-A rushing record with an amazing 406 yards against UTEP.

9. **Oklahoma**, one of the great running teams in college football history in the 1970s and 1980s, transforms into a wide-open passing team under first-year head coach Bob Stoops.

8. **Lou Holtz makes his debut** as head coach at South Carolina with an 0-11 record, the school's only winless season in the 20th Century.

7. **Father beats son** when Bobby Bowden's Florida State Seminoles beat Tommy Bowden's Clemson Tigers, 17-14, in the first father-son head coaching matchup in NCAA history.

6. **Hopping Mad-ison.** Wisconsin becomes the first Big Ten team to win consecutive Rose Bowls and tailback Ron Dayne wins the Heisman Trophy with a Div. I-A career rushing record of 6,397 yards, breaking the mark set by Ricky Williams in 1998.

5. Virginia Tech and their freshman quarterback **Michael Vick** capture the public's fancy with an 11-0 regular-season record and Sugar Bowl berth. Vick cements his spot as favorite for the 2000 Heisman Trophy, which has never been awarded to a sophomore.

4. **Big turnarounds** at Hawaii, Illinois, Minnesota, Oklahoma, Oregon State, Stanford, Vanderbilt and Wake Forest. Hawaii's 8½-game turnaround is the best in NCAA history and Oregon State breaks a record streak of 28 seasons without even a .500 record.

3. **Traditional powers struggle** as Notre Dame, USC, Ohio State and UCLA all fail to post winning seasons.

2. **Florida State wins the national championship** and becomes the first team in the 64-year history of the AP poll to go wire-to-wire as the top-ranked team from pre-season to postseason. FSU also extends its record streaks to 13 consecutive seasons with at least 10 wins and 13 straight finishes in the AP top four.

1. **Tragedy strikes Texas A&M** when the collapse of logs being readied for annual giant bonfire kills 12 students one week before the big game with arch-rival Texas. ■

AP/Wide World Photos

Engineers struggle to clear the massive pile of logs in the aftermath of the tragedy that killed 12 students at Texas A&M on Nov. 18, 1999.

135

inside the numbers

RAINBOW REBOUND

With their win over Oregon St. in the Oahu Bowl, Hawaii earned the record for the most victories ever by a team that was winless the previous season.

Season		From	To
1999	Hawaii	0-12	9-4
1980	Florida	0-10-1	8-4
1965	UTEP	0-8-2	8-3

Note: All of the above teams won bowl games.

HIGH FIVE

Florida State extended their amazing streak of top-five (in the AP Poll) finishes in 1999. The last time the Seminoles finished out of the top five was 1986.

	Top 5s	Seasons
Florida St.	13	1987-99
Miami-FL	7	1986-92
Oklahoma	7	1952-58
Oklahoma	6	1971-76

RUNNING GUNNERS

Yellow Jacket quarterback Joe Hamilton had one of the finest offensive seasons ever by a college QB. Here's a look at the quarterbacks with the most rushing yards who also threw for over 3,000 yards in a season.

Player, School, Year	Yards
Joe Hamilton, Ga. Tech, 1999	734
Shaun King, Tulane, 1998	532
Stoney Case, New Mexico, 1994	532
Daunte Culpepper, UCF, 1998	463
Steve Young, BYU, 1983	444

NO LOSSES, NO RESPECT

Here is a look at the undefeated, untied, uncrowned teams of the last 25 years.

Season		Record
1999	Marshall	13-0
1998	Tulane	12-0
1994	Penn St.	12-0
1993	Auburn	11-0
1976	Rutgers	11-0
1975	Arizona St.	12-0
1975	Arkansas St.	11-0

DOUBLE THREAT

Virginia Tech accomplished the rare double in 1999...leading the nation in scoring offense and defense. The only team on the following list (of teams to lead the nation in scoring offense and defense) to win the national title is Florida State, while Oklahoma played for it and lost in the Orange Bowl to Miami, as Virginia Tech did last season.

	Points For	Points Against
Virginia Tech, 1999	41.4	10.5
Florida St., 1993	43.2	9.4
Oklahoma, 1987	43.5	7.5
Oklahoma, 1986	42.4	7.6
Michigan, 1976	38.7	7.4
UCLA, 1954	40.8	4.4
Army, 1944	56.0	3.9
Duke, 1943	37.2	3.8
Tulsa, 1942	42.7	3.2

LONG-TIME LOSERS

Oregon State snapped a streak of 28 straight losing seasons, passing the baton of sustained futility to Vanderbilt. Here's a look at the longest active losing-season streaks in I-A.

Schools	Years
Vanderbilt	17
Kent	12
UTEP	11
Iowa State	10

COLLEGE FOOTBALL
1999-2000 Season in Review

Final AP Top 25 Poll

Voted on by panel of 70 sportswriters & broadcasters and released on Jan. 5, 2000, following the Sugar Bowl: winning team receives the Bear Bryant Trophy, given since 1983; first place votes in parentheses, records, total points (based on 25 for 1st, 24 for 2nd, etc.) bowl game result, head coach and career record, preseason rank (released Aug. 14, 1999) and final regular season rank (released Dec. 5, 1999).

		Final Record	Points	Bowl Game	Head Coach	Aug. 14 Rank	Dec. 5 Rank
1	Florida St. (70)	12-0	1750	won Sugar	Bobby Bowden (34 yrs: 304-85-4)	1	1
2	Virginia Tech	11-1	1647	lost Sugar	Frank Beamer (19 yrs: 130-83-4)	13	2
3	Nebraska	12-1	1634	won Fiesta	Frank Solich (2 yrs: 21-5-0)	6	3
4	Wisconsin	10-2	1519	won Rose	Barry Alvarez (10 yrs: 70-44-4)	10	4
5	Michigan	10-2	1406	won Orange	Lloyd Carr (5 yrs: 49-13-0)	8	8
6	Kansas St.	11-1	1402	won Holiday	Bill Snyder (11 yrs: 88-40-1)	20t	7
7	Michigan St.	10-2	1357	won Citrus	Nick Saban (6 yrs: 43-26-1) & Bobby Williams (1 yr: 1-0-0)	29	9
8	Alabama	10-3	1236	lost Orange	Mike DuBose (3 yrs: 21-15-0)	20t	5
9	Tennessee	9-3	1168	lost Fiesta	Phillip Fulmer (8 yrs: 76-14-0)	2	6
10	Marshall	13-0	1136	won Motor City	Bob Pruett (4 yrs: 50-4-0)	27	11
11	Penn St.	10-3	1038	won Alamo	Joe Paterno (34 yrs: 317-83-3)	3	13
12	Florida	9-4	941	lost Citrus	Steve Spurrier (13 yrs: 122-35-2)	5	10
13	Mississippi St.	10-2	923	won Peach	Jackie Sherrill (22 yrs: 164-89-4)	28	15
14	Southern Miss.	9-3	788	won Liberty	Jeff Bower (10 yrs: 59-43-1)	40	16
15	Miami-FL	9-4	678	won Gator	Butch Davis (5 yrs: 40-19-0)	12	23
16	Georgia	8-4	640	won Outback	Jim Donnan (10 yrs: 96-36-0)	14	21
17	Arkansas	8-4	575	won Cotton	Houston Nutt (7 yrs: 52-30-0)	22	24
18	Minnesota	8-4	452	lost Sun	Glen Mason (14 yrs: 75-83-1)	NR	12
19	Oregon	9-3	358	won Sun	Mike Bellotti (10 yrs: 60-45-2)	39	NR
20	Georgia Tech	8-4	345	lost Gator	George O'Leary (5 yrs: 36-25-0)	11	17
21	Texas	9-5	340	lost Cotton	Mack Brown (16 yrs: 105-82-1)	17	14
22	Mississippi	8-4	281	won Independence	David Cutcliffe (2 yrs: 9-4-0)	31	NR
23	Texas A&M	8-4	272	lost Alamo	R.C. Slocum (11 yrs: 102-32-2)	7	18
24	Illinois	8-4	201	won Micron PC	Ron Turner (4 yrs: 18-27-0)	NR	NR
25	Purdue	7-5	198	lost Outback	Joe Tiller (9 yrs: 64-42-1)	23	19

Other teams receiving votes: 26. Stanford (8-4, 168 points, lost Rose); **27. East Carolina** (9-3, 97 pts, lost Mobile); **28. Colorado** (7-5, 75 pts, won Insight.com); **29. TCU** (8-4, 45 pts, won Mobile); **30. Syracuse** (7-5, 21 pts, lost Music City); **31. Utah** (9-3, 20 pts, won Las Vegas); **32. Hawaii** (9-4, 19 pts, won Oahu); **33. Washington** (7-5, 7 pts, lost Holiday); **34. Wake Forest** (7-5, 5 pts, won Aloha); **35. Boise St.** (10-3, 3 pts, won Humanitarian) and **Oklahoma** (7-5, 3 pts, lost Independence); **37. Colorado St.** (8-4, 2 pts, lost Liberty).

AP Preseason and Final Regular Season Polls

First place votes in parentheses.

Top 25
(Aug. 14, 1999)

		Pts
1	Florida St. (48)	1720
2	Tennessee (15)	1643
3	Penn St. (4)	1582
4	Arizona (1)	1537
5	Florida (1)	1361
6	Nebraska	1327
7	Texas A&M	1314
8	Michigan	1292
9	Ohio St.	1160
10	Wisconsin	1091
11	Georgia Tech	979
12	Miami-FL	928
13	Virginia Tech (1)	896
14	Georgia	829
15	Colorado	636
16	UCLA	587
17	Texas	487
18	Notre Dame	463
19	USC	455
20	Alabama	445
	Kansas St.	445
22	Arkansas	441
23	Purdue	370
24	Virginia	222
25	Arizona St.	108

Top 25
(Dec. 5, 1999)

		Pts
1	Florida St. (64)	1744
2	Virginia Tech (6)	1685
3	Nebraska	1606
4	Wisconsin	1482
5	Alabama	1450
6	Tennessee	1412
7	Kansas St.	1336
8	Michigan	1226
9	Michigan St.	1193
10	Florida	1095
11	Marshall	1047
12	Minnesota	935
13	Penn St.	772
14	Texas	746
15	Mississippi St.	727
16	Southern Miss.	722
17	Georgia Tech	672
18	Texas A&M	632
19	Purdue	504
20	East Carolina	431
21	Georgia	298
22	Stanford	270
23	Miami-FL	224
24	Arkansas	121
25	Boston College	112

1999-2000 Bowl Games

Listed by bowls matching highest-ranked teams as of final regular season AP poll (released Dec. 5, 1999). Attendance figures indicate tickets sold.

Bowl	Winner	Regular Season		Loser	Regular Season	Score	Date	Attendance
Sugar ....#1	Florida St.	11-0	#2	Virginia Tech	11-0	46-29	Jan. 4	79,280
Fiesta ....#3	Nebraska	11-1	#6	Tennessee	9-2	31-21	Jan. 2	71,526
Rose ....#4	Wisconsin	9-2	#22	Stanford	8-3	17-9	Jan. 1	93,731
Orange...............#8	Michigan	9-2	#5	Alabama	10-2	35-34	Jan. 1	70,461
Holiday..............#7	Kansas St.	10-1		Washington	7-4	24-20	Dec. 29	57,118
Citrus ....#9	Michigan St.	9-2	#10	Florida	9-3	37-34	Jan. 1	62,011
Motor City ....#11	Marshall	12-0		BYU	8-3	21-3	Dec. 27	52,449
Sun.....................	Oregon	8-3	#12	Minnesota	8-3	24-20	Dec. 31	48,757
Alamo...............#13	Penn St.	9-3	#18	Texas A&M	8-3	24-0	Dec. 28	65,380
Cotton ....#24	Arkansas	7-4	#14	Texas	9-4	27-6	Jan. 1	72,723
Peach ....#15	Mississippi St.	9-2		Clemson	6-5	17-7	Dec. 30	73,315
Liberty..............#16	Southern Miss.	8-3		Colorado St.	8-3	23-17	Dec. 31	54,866
Gator ....#23	Miami-FL	8-4	#17	Georgia Tech	8-3	28-13	Jan. 1	43,416
Outback ....#21	Georgia	7-4	#19	Purdue	7-4	28-25	Jan. 1	54,059
Mobile.................	TCU	7-4	#20	East Carolina	9-2	28-14	Dec. 22	34,200
Insight.com	Colorado	6-5	#25	Boston College	8-3	62-28	Dec. 31	35,762
Oahu..................	Hawaii	8-4		Oregon St.	7-4	23-17	Dec. 25	40,974*
Aloha.................	Wake Forest	6-5		Arizona St.	6-5	23-3	Dec. 25	40,974*
Micron PC.............	Illinois	7-4		Virginia	7-4	63-21	Dec. 30	31,089
Independence..........	Mississippi	7-4		Oklahoma	7-4	27-25	Dec. 31	49,873
Humanitarian	Boise St.	9-3		Louisville	6-5	34-31	Dec. 30	29,283
Music City............	Syracuse	6-5		Kentucky	6-5	20-13	Dec. 29	59,221
Las Vegas	Utah	8-3		Fresno St.	8-4	17-16	Dec. 18	28,227

*The Oahu and Aloha Bowls were held as a single-admission doubleheader.

FAVORITES:

Sugar (Florida St. by 5½); **Fiesta** (Nebraska by 4); **Rose** (Wisconsin by 13½); **Orange** (Alabama by 1½); **Holiday** (Kansas St. by 11); **Citrus** (Florida by 2); **Motor City** (Marshall by 3); **Sun** (Minnesota by 3); **Alamo** (Penn St. by 6½); **Cotton** (Texas by 5½); **Peach** (Clemson by 3); **Liberty** (Southern Miss. by 4½); **Gator** (Miami-FL by 5); **Outback** (Purdue by 5½); **Mobile** (East Carolina by 4½); **Insight.com** (Colorado by 8); **Oahu** (Oregon St. by 9); **Aloha** (Arizona St. by 2½); **Micron PC** (Virginia by 2½); **Independence** (Oklahoma by 4); **Humanitarian** (Louisville by 2½); **Music City** (Kentucky by 3); **Las Vegas** (Utah by 6).

PER TEAM PAYOUTS:

Nokia Sugar and **Tostitos Fiesta** ($13 million); **FedEx Orange** ($12.5 million); **Rose** ($12 million); **Ourhouse.com Citrus** ($3.8 million); **Southwestern Bell Cotton** ($2.5 million); **Outback** ($1.9 million); **Culligan Holiday** ($1.8 million); **Chick-fil-A Peach** ($1.6 million); **Toyota Gator** ($1.4 million); **EA Sports Las Vegas, Sylvania Alamo** and **AXA Liberty** ($1.2 million); **Sanford Independence** and **Norwest Sun** ($1 million); **Jeep/Eagle Aloha** and **Jeep/Eagle Oahu** ($800,000); **Insight.com, Mobile, Micron PC, Ford Motor City, Homepoint.com Music City** and **Crucial.com Humanitarian** ($750,000).

Final BCS Rankings

The Bowl Championship Series rankings were used for the first time during the 1998 season to determine BCS bowl match-ups and revised slightly for the 1999 season. The final rankings were released Dec. 15, 1999. Note that S-rank refers to schedule rank and L refers to games lost.

		Polls		Computer Rankings											
		AP	ESPN	Bill.	D.I.	K.M.	NYT	D.R.	Sag.	S.H.	S.T.	Sched.	S-rank	L	Total
1	Florida St.......1	1	1	1	1	1	1	1	1	1	6	0.24	0	2.24
2	Va. Tech.......2	2	2	2	2	2	2	2	2	3	53	2.12	0	6.12
3	Nebraska 3	3	3	3	3	4	3	3	3	2	14	0.56	1	7.42
4	Alabama 5	6	5	7	6	3	4	6	4	4	1	0.04	2	12.11
5	Tennessee 6	5	7	6	5	5	6	5	5	8	16	0.64	2	13.71
6	Kansas St......7	7	4	5	4	6	5	4	6	5	63	2.52	1	15.23
7	Wisconsin......4	4	8	4	7	8	9	7	11	12	75	3.00	2	16.71
8	Michigan 8	8	10	9	8	7	10	9	7	6	2	0.08	2	18.08
9	Michigan St....9	9	6	8	9	10	8	8	8	7	10	0.40	2	19.11
10	Florida......10	10	9	12	12	16	7	11	9	9	5	0.20	3	23.06
11	Penn St. 13	17	11	10	10	20	11	10	10	11	8	0.32	3	28.75
12	Marshall......11	11	33	31	11	11	12	13	22	15	93	3.72	0	31.15
13	Minnesota 12	12	14	19	17	21.5	15	15	15	21	51	2.04	3	33.61
14	Texas A&M....18	13	13	16	15	15	16	17	19	14	28	1.12	3	34.76
15	Texas......14	18	17	13	16	21.5	13	14	14	13	13	0.52	4	34.81

Explanation Key
Schedule Rank—Rank of schedule strength compared to other Division I-A teams divided by 25. This component is calculated by determining the cumulative won/loss records of the team's opponents (66.6 percent) and the cumulative won/loss record of the team's opponents' opponents (33.3 percent).
Losses—One point for each loss during the season.

National Championship Game

Florida State and Virginia Tech were ranked first and second, respectively, in the final Bowl Championship Series rankings (released Dec. 15, 1999) and according to the BCS plan met in the so-called National Championship game at the Sugar Bowl on Jan. 4. Opponents' records and AP rank listed below are day of game.

Florida State Seminoles (11-0)

Date	AP Rank	Opponent	Result
Aug. 28	#1	Louisiana Tech (0-0)	.41-7
Sept. 11	#1	#10 Georgia Tech (1-0)	.41-35
Sept. 18	#1	#20 N.C. State (3-0)	.42-11
Sept. 25	#1	at North Carolina (1-1)	.42-10
Oct. 2	#1	at Duke (0-3)	.51-23
Oct. 9	#1	#19 Miami-FL (2-2)	.31-21
Oct. 16	#1	Wake Forest (3-3)	.33-10
Oct. 23	#1	at Clemson (3-3)	.17-14
Oct. 30	#1	at Virginia (4-3)	.35-10
Nov. 13	#1	Maryland (5-4)	.49-10
Nov. 20	#1	at #3 Florida (9-1)	.30-23

Final Statistics

Passing (5 Att)	Att	Cmp	Pct.	Yds	TD	Rate
Chris Weinke	377	232	61.5	3103	25	145.1
Marcus Outzen	26	12	46.2	169	1	105.8
Jared Jones	13	5	38.5	25	0	23.8

Interceptions: Weinke 14, Jones 2, Outzen 1.

Top Receivers	No	Yds	Avg	Long	TD
Peter Warrick	71	934	13.2	59	8
Ron Dugans	43	644	15.0	84-td	6
Marvin Minnis	19	257	13.5	27-td	3
Robert Morgan	16	245	15.3	38	0
Travis Minor	16	102	6.4	16	0
Atrews Bell	14	202	14.4	30-td	4
Laveranues Coles	12	179	14.9	35-td	1
Dan Kendra	7	31	4.4	17	2

Top Rushers	Car	Yds	Avg	Long	TD
Travis Minor	180	815	4.5	47	7
Jeff Chaney	43	157	3.7	23	2
Nick Maddox	29	111	3.8	9	0
Peter Warrick	16	96	10.7	21	3
Dan Kendra	36	82	2.3	10	2
Davy Ford	19	75	2.9	8	0
Marcus Outzen	20	41	2.1	10	1
Anquan Boldin	4	33	8.3	19	1
Talman Gardner	2	23	11.5	22	0

Most Touchdowns	TD	Run	Rec	Ret	Pts
Peter Warrick	12	3	8	1	72
Travis Minor	7	7	0	0	42
Atrews Bell	4	0	4	0	24
Dan Kendra	4	2	2	0	24
Ron Dugans	3	0	3	0	18
Jeff Chaney	3	2	1	0	18
Marvin Minnis	3	0	3	0	18
Anquan Boldin	3	1	2	0	18

Kicking	FG/Att	Lg	PAT/Att	Pts
S. Janikowski	23/30	54	47/47	116

Punting	No	Yds	Long	Blk	Avg
Keith Cottrell	44	1885	59	0	42.8

Most Interceptions
Chris Hope ... 4
Derrick Gibson ... 4
Clevan Thomas ... 3

Most Sacks
Jamal Reynolds ... 7
Brian Allen ... 5
Corey Simon ... 4
Tony Benford ... 4

Virginia Tech Hokies (11-0)

Date	AP Rank	Opponent	Result
Sept. 4	#11	James Madison* (0-0)	.47-0
Sept. 11	#11	Ala-Birmingham (0-1)	.31-10
Sept. 23	#8	Clemson (1-1)	.31-11
Oct. 2	#8	at #24 Virginia (3-1)	.31-7
Oct. 9	#5	at Rutgers (0-4)	.58-20
Oct. 16	#4	#16 Syracuse (5-1)	.62-0
Oct. 30	#3	at Pittsburgh (4-3)	.30-17
Nov. 6	#3	at West Virginia (3-5)	.22-20
Nov. 13	#2	#19 Miami-FL (5-3)	.43-10
Nov. 20	#2	at Temple (2-7)	.62-7
Nov. 26	#2	#22 Boston College (8-2)	.38-14

*James Madison is in Division 1-AA.

Final Statistics

Passing (5 Att)	Att	Cmp	Pct.	Yds	TD	Rate
Michael Vick	152	90	59.2	1840	12	180.4
Dave Meyer	42	25	59.5	292	1	111.5

Interceptions: Vick 5, Meyer 3.

Top Receivers	No	Yds	Avg	Long	TD
Andre Davis	35	962	27.5	74-td	9
Ricky Hall	25	398	15.9	60	3
Emmett Johnson	10	147	14.7	41-td	1
Terrell Parham	9	98	10.9	22	0
Browning Wynn	7	157	22.4	35	0
Derek Carter	7	132	18.9	30	0

Top Rushers	Car	Yds	Avg	Long	TD
Shyrone Stith	226	1119	5.0	58	13
Andre Kendrick	103	645	6.3	59	7
Michael Vick	108	585	5.4	75-td	8
Jarrett Ferguson	34	173	5.1	33	1
Lee Suggs	44	136	3.1	12	2
Cullen Hawkins	15	75	5.0	18	0
Andre Davis	3	72	24.0	28-td	3
Keith Burnell	7	14	2.0	6	0
Wayne Briggs	1	2	2.0	2	0
Wayne Ward	1	2	2.0	2	0
Dave Meyer	11	-20	-1.8	3	1

Most Touchdowns	TD	Run	Rec	Ret	Pts
Shyrone Stith	13	13	0	0	78
Andre Davis	12	3	9	0	72
Michael Vick	8	8	0	0	48
Andre Kendrick	7	7	0	0	42
Ricky Hall	4	0	3	1	24
Lee Suggs	2	2	0	0	12
Ike Charlton	2	0	0	2	12

Kicking	FG/Att	Lg	PAT/Att	Pts
Shayne Graham	17/22	52	56/57	107

Punting	No	Yds	Long	Blk	Avg
Jimmy Kibble	46	1765	64	0	38.4

Most Interceptions
Anthony Midget ... 4

Most Sacks
Corey Moore ... 17
Cory Bird ... 6

Sugar Bowl

Tuesday, Jan. 4, 2000 at Superdome in New Orleans, Louisiana

#2 **Virginia Tech** (Big East)	7	7	15	0	**—29**
#1 **Florida St.** (ACC)	14	14	0	18	**—46**

1st; 3:22; **Florida St.**—Peter Warrick 64-yd pass from Chris Weinke (Sebastian Janikowski kick). Drive: 4 plays, 80 yards, 0:32.

1st; 2:14; **Florida St.**—Jeff Chaney 6-yd blocked punt return (Janikowski kick).

1st; 00:30; **Virginia Tech**—Andre Davis 49-yd pass from Michael Vick (Shayne Graham kick). Drive: 3 plays, 80 yards, 1:44.

2nd; 13:45; **Florida St.**—Ron Dugans 34-yd pass from Weinke (Janikowski kick). Drive: 5 plays, 80 yards, 1:45.

2nd; 11:40; **Florida St.**—Warrick 59-yd punt return (Janikowski kick).

2nd; 00:37; **Virginia Tech**— Vick 3-yd run (Graham kick). Drive: 7 plays, 80 yards, 3:16.

3rd; 07:54; **Virginia Tech**—Graham 23-yd field goal. Drive: 5 plays, 74 yards, 1:44.

3rd; 05:57; **Virginia Tech**—Andre Kendrick 29-yd run (pass failed). Drive: 3 plays, 36 yards, 0:55.

3rd; 02:13; **Virginia Tech**—Kendrick 6-yd run (pass failed). Drive: 7 plays, 59 yards, 3:14.

4th; 12:59; **Florida St.**—Dugans 14-yd pass from Weinke (Warrick pass from Weinke). Drive: 11 plays, 85 yards, 4:14.

4th; 10:26; **Florida St.**— Janikowski 32-yd field goal. Drive: 5 plays, 19 yards, 1:32.

4th; 07:42; **Florida St.**—Warrick 43-yd pass from Weinke (Janikowski kick). Drive: 1 play, 43 yards, 0:14.

Favorite: Florida St. by 5½   **Attendance:** 79,280
Field: Turf   **Time:** 3:55
Weather: Indoors

MVP: Peter Warrick, FSU, 6 receptions, 163 yards, 3 TDs

Team Statistics

	VT	FSU
Touchdowns	4	6
Rushing	3	0
Passing	1	4
Kick/Punt returns	0	1
Interception returns	0	0
Safeties	0	0
Time of possession	36:25	23:35
First downs	24	15
Rushing	11	4
Passing	10	10
Penalties	3	1
3rd down efficiency	3 of 14	5 of 14
4th down efficiency	0 of 4	1 of 1
Total offense (net yards)	503	359
Plays	81	57
Average gain	6.2	6.3
Carries/yards (includ. sacks)	52/278	23/30
Passing yards	225	329
Completions/attempts	15/29	20/34
Times sacked/yards lost	7/37	4/31
Return yardage	222	155
Punt returns/yards	4/88	4/80
Kickoff returns/yards	4/134	4/75
Interceptions/yards	1/0	0/0
Fumbles/lost	3/3	2/0
Penalties/yards	6/65	7/59
Punts/average	6/29.3	7/44.3

INDIVIDUAL STATISTICS
Florida State Seminoles

Passing (5 Att)	Att	Cmp	Pct.	Yds	TD	Int
Chris Weinke	34	20	58.8	329	4	1

Rushing	Car	Yds	Avg	Long	TD
Jeff Chaney	4	43	10.8	27	0
Travis Minor	9	35	3.9	16	0
Chris Weinke	7	-41	-5.9	9	0
team	3	-7	-2.3	0	0
TOTAL	23	30	1.3	27	0

Receiving	No	Yds	Avg	Long	TD
Peter Warrick	6	163	27.2	64	2
Ron Dugans	5	99	19.8	63	2
Marvin Minnis	2	25	12.5	19	0
Travis Minor	2	23	11.5	28	0
Robert Morgan	2	10	5.0	7	0
Jeff Chaney	2	5	2.5	10	0
Anquan Boldin	1	4	4.0	4	0
TOTAL	20	329	16.4	64	4

Field Goals	20-29	30-39	40-49	50-59	Total
Sebastian Janikowski	0-0	1-1	0-0	0-0	1-1

Punting	No	Yds	Long	Blk	Avg
Keith Cottrell	7	310	56	0	44.3

Punt Returns	Ret		Yds	Lg	TD
Peter Warrick	2		57	59	1
Reggie Durden	1		13	13	0
Tommy Polley	1		4	4	0
Jeff Chaney	0		6	6	0
TOTAL	4		80	59	1

Kickoff Returns	No	Yds	Long	Avg	TD
Talman Gardner	2	36	22	18.0	0
Nick Maddox	1	22	22	22.0	0
Germaine Stringer	1	17	17	17.0	0
TOTAL	4	75	22	18.8	0

Virginia Tech Hokies

Passing (5 Att)	Att	Cmp	Pct.	Yds	TD	Int
Michael Vick	29	15	51.7	225	1	0

Rushing	Car	Yds	Avg	Long	TD
Michael Vick	23	97	4.2	43	1
Andre Kendrick	12	69	5.8	29	2
Shyrone Stith	11	68	6.2	26	0
Andre Davis	1	16	16.0	16	0
Emmett Johnson	1	12	12.0	12	0
Nick Sorensen	1	7	7.0	7	0
Jarrett Ferguson	1	5	5.0	5	0
Cullen Hawkins	1	4	4.0	4	0
Shayne Graham	1	0	0.0	0	0
TOTAL	52	278	5.3	43	3

Receiving	No	Yds	Avg	Long	TD
Andre Davis	7	108	15.4	49	1
Cullen Hawkins	2	49	24.5	26	0
Andre Kendrick	2	27	13.5	15	0
Emmett Johnson	1	23	23.0	23	0
Browning Wynn	1	7	7.0	7	0
Jarrett Ferguson	1	6	6.0	6	0
Derek Carter	1	5	5.0	5	0
TOTAL	15	225	15.0	49	1

Field Goals	20-29	30-39	40-49	50-59	Total
Shayne Graham	1-1	0-0	0-0	0-0	1-1

Punting	No	Yds	Long	Blk	Avg
Jimmy Kibble	5	176	43	1	35.2
Team	1	0	0	0	0
TOTAL	6	176	43	1	29.3

Punt Returns	Ret		Yds	Lg	TD
Ike Charlton	4		88	46	0

Kickoff Returns	No	Yds	Long	Avg	TD
Andre Kendrick	2	75	63	37.5	0
Shyrone Stith	2	59	34	29.5	0
TOTAL	4	134	63	33.5	0

Other Final Division I-A Polls

USA Today/ESPN Coaches' Poll

Voted on by panel of 59 Division I-A head coaches; winning team receives the Sears Trophy (originally the McDonald's Trophy, 1991-93); first place votes in parentheses with total points (based on 25 for 1st, 24 for 2nd, etc.).

	Pts		Pts
1 Florida St. (59)	1475	14 Florida	713
2 Nebraska	1390	15 Miami-FL	605
3 Virginia Tech	1366	16 Georgia	505
4 Wisconsin	1283	17 Minnesota	395
5 Michigan	1189	18 Oregon	375
6 Kansas St.	1188	19 Arkansas	357
7 Michigan St.	1117	20 Texas A&M	344
8 Alabama	1042	21 Georgia Tech	337
9 Tennessee	985	22 Mississippi	231
10 Marshall	956	23 Texas	173
11 Penn St.	840	24 Stanford	155
12 Mississippi St.	810	25 Illinois	139
13 So. Mississippi	763		

Other teams receiving votes: East Carolina (119 pts); Purdue (118); TCU (54); Colorado (49); Hawaii (27); Utah (21); BYU (17); Colorado St. (9); Wake Forest (8); Ohio St. and Syracuse (6); Washington (4); Boise St. and Oklahoma (2).

NY Times Computer Ratings

Based on an analysis of each team's scores with emphasis on three factors: who won, by what margin, and against what quality of opposition. Computer balances lop-sided scores, notes home field advantage, and gives late-season games more weight than those played earlier in the schedule.

The top team is assigned a rating of 1.000; ratings of all other teams reflect their strength relative to strength of No. 1 team. Rankings include all regular season games.

	Rating		Rating
1 Florida St.	1.000	14 Illinois	.748
2 Nebraska	.910	15 Utah	.744
3 Michigan	.858	16 La. Tech	.737
4 Virginia Tech	.840	17 Mississippi St.	.717
5 Michigan St.	.835	18 So. Mississippi	.699
6 Alabama	.831	19 Arkansas	.693
7 Kansas St.	.829	Boise St.	.693
8 Wisconsin	.826	21 Colorado St.	.681
8 Miami-FL	.825	22 Colorado	.677
10 Marshall	.775	23 Florida	.661
11 Tennessee	.773	24 Minnesota	.656
12 Penn St.	.771	25 Georgia Tech	.653
13 Oregon	.759		

FWAA Poll

Voted on by a five-man panel comprised of Tony Barnhart of the *Atlanta Journal-Constitution*, Mark Blaudschun of the *Boston Globe*, Chris Dufresne of the *Los Angeles Times*, Tom Shatel of the *Omaha World-Herald*, and Dick Weiss of the *New York Daily News*. Each selector voted for one team.

Winning team receives the Grantland Rice Award, given since 1954.

Florida St. (5)

Winningest Teams of the 1990s

Division I-A schools with the best overall winning percentage from 1990-99, through the Jan. 4, 2000 bowl games.

National champions: 1990—Colorado (AP, FWAA, NFF) and Georgia Tech (UPI); 1991—Miami-FL (AP) and Washington (FWAA, NFF, *USA Today*/CNN); 1992—Alabama; 1993—Florida St.; 1994—Nebraska; 1995—Nebraska; 1996—Florida; 1997—Michigan (AP, FWAA, NFF) and Nebraska (*USA Today*/ESPN); 1998—Tennessee; 1999—Florida St.

		Overall Record	Bowls W-L-T	Overall Win Pct.
1	Florida St.	109-13-1	8-2-0	.890
2	Nebraska	108-16-1	5-5-0	.868
3	Marshall†	114-25-0	2-1-0	.820
4	Florida	102-22-1	5-4-0	.820
5	Tennessee	99-22-2	6-4-0	.813
6	Penn St.	97-26-0	7-3-0	.789
7	Michigan	93-26-3	7-3-0	.775
8	Miami-FL	92-27-0	5-3-0	.773
9	Texas A&M	94-28-2	2-6-0	.766
10	Ohio St.	91-29-3	3-6-0	.752
11	Colorado	87-29-4	7-2-0	.742
12	Kansas St.	87-30-1	4-3-0	.742
13	Notre Dame	84-35-2	3-5-0	.702
14	Washington	82-35-1	3-5-0	.699
15	Syracuse	82-35-3	6-2-0	.696
16	BYU	86-39-2	2-5-1	.685
17	Alabama	83-40-0	5-3-0	.675
18	Nevada†	80-39-0	1-2-0	.672
19	North Carolina	78-39-1	5-2-0	.665
20	Virginia Tech	77-39-1	3-4-0	.662
21	Virginia	78-40-1	2-5-0	.660
22	Idaho†	77-41-0	1-0-0	.653
23	Toledo	72-38-3	1-0-0	.650
24	Air Force	78-44-0	3-3-0	.639
25	Auburn	72-40-3	3-1-0	.639
26	Texas	74-44-2	2-4-0	.625
	Georgia	72-43-1	5-1-0	.625
28	Colorado St.	74-46-0	2-4-0	.617
29	Miami-OH	65-40-4	0-0-0	.615
30	Arizona	71-46-1	3-3-0	.606

†Joined I-A as follows: Marshall (1997), Idaho (1996) and Nevada (1992).

NFF's MacArthur Bowl

In the past the MacArthur Bowl was awarded following a vote by a panel of members of the National Football Foundation and College Hall of Fame but since the advent of the Bowl Championship Series it has been awarded to the BCS champion; winning team receives the NFF's MacArthur Bowl, given since 1959; The McArthur Bowl was the gift of an anonymous donor in the name of General Douglas MacArthur who served for several years as chairman of the Foundation's National Advisory Board. Almost 400 ounces of silver went into the bowl which represents a huge stadium with rows of seats carved in relief.

Florida St.

NCAA Division I-A Final Standings

Standings based on conference games only; overall records include postseason games.

Atlantic Coast Conference

	Conference				Overall		
	W	L	PF	PA	W	L	PF	PA
*Florida St.	8	0	310	123	12	0	458	203
*Georgia Tech	5	3	307	261	8	4	461	361
*Virginia	5	3	222	210	7	5	345	365
*Clemson	5	3	262	171	6	6	322	253
*Wake Forest	3	5	145	178	7	5	266	209
N.C. State	3	5	167	250	6	6	244	302
Duke	3	5	182	290	3	8	217	363
Maryland	2	6	202	250	5	6	292	260
North Carolina	2	6	129	194	3	8	186	272

Bowls (2-3): Florida St. (won Sugar); Georgia Tech (lost Gator); Virginia (lost Micron PC); Clemson (lost Peach); Wake Forest (won Aloha).

Big East Conference

	Conference				Overall		
	W	L	PF	PA	W	L	PF	PA
*Virginia Tech	7	0	315	88	11	1	484	162
*Miami-FL	6	1	257	107	9	4	432	220
*Boston College	4	3	161	156	8	4	297	308
*Syracuse	3	4	138	189	7	5	300	256
West Virginia	3	4	198	168	4	7	292	289
Pittsburgh	2	5	167	198	5	6	281	278
Temple	2	5	138	261	2	9	153	366
Rutgers	1	6	110	317	1	10	155	427

Bowls (2-2): Virginia Tech (lost Sugar); Miami-FL (won Gator); Boston College (lost Insight.com); Syracuse (won Music City).

Big Ten Conference

	Conference				Overall		
	W	L	PF	PA	W	L	PF	PA
*Wisconsin	7	1	281	108	10	2	409	154
*Michigan	6	2	245	175	10	2	361	204
*Michigan St.	6	2	240	171	10	2	378	245
*Penn St.	5	3	235	163	10	3	417	234
*Minnesota	5	3	225	158	8	4	368	196
*Illinois	4	4	205	205	8	4	388	275
*Purdue	4	4	226	225	7	5	384	305
Ohio St.	3	5	157	208	6	6	285	287
Indiana	3	5	205	291	4	7	291	386
Northwestern	1	7	106	254	3	8	141	301
Iowa	0	8	121	288	1	10	162	347

Bowls (5-2): Wisconsin (won Rose); Michigan (won Orange); Michigan St. (won Citrus); Penn St. (won Alamo); Minnesota (lost Sun); Illinois (won Micron PC); Purdue (lost Outback).

<table>
<tr><td colspan="2" align="center">

Conference Bowling Results

Postseason records for 1999 season.
</td></tr>
</table>

	W-L
Big Ten	5-2
SEC	4-4
Big 12	3-3
WAC	2-1
Big East	2-2
ACC	2-3
Big West	1-0
Mid-American	1-0
Conference USA	1-2
Mountain West	1-2
Pac-10	1-4

Big 12 Conference

	Conference				Overall		
North	W	L	PF	PA	W	L	PF	PA
*Nebraska	8	1	304	130	12	1	442	171
*Kansas St.	7	1	313	137	11	1	457	164
*Colorado	5	3	242	176	7	5	405	311
Kansas	3	5	170	242	5	7	294	354
Iowa St.	1	7	173	255	4	7	247	272
Missouri	1	7	118	292	4	7	224	371

	Conference				Overall		
South	W	L	PF	PA	W	L	PF	PA
*Texas	6	3	299	194	9	5	450	295
*Texas A&M	5	3	196	172	8	4	318	232
*Oklahoma	5	3	284	147	7	5	430	229
Texas Tech	5	3	188	213	6	5	253	282
Oklahoma St.	3	5	186	229	5	6	267	274
Baylor	0	8	61	347	1	10	137	414

Big 12 championship game: Nebraska beat Texas, 22-6 (Dec. 4).

Bowls (3-3): Nebraska (won Fiesta); Kansas St. (won Holiday); Colorado (won Insight.com); Texas (lost Cotton); Texas A&M (lost Alamo); Oklahoma (lost Independence).

Big West Conference

	Conference				Overall		
	W	L	PF	PA	W	L	PF	PA
*Boise St.	5	1	248	111	10	3	430	277
Idaho	4	2	159	157	7	4	304	283
New Mexico St.	3	2	120	97	6	5	311	274
Utah St.	3	3	127	134	4	7	234	301
Arkansas St.	2	3	106	151	4	7	246	332
Nevada	2	4	177	219	3	8	283	418
North Texas	1	5	81	149	2	9	118	291

Bowl (1-0): Boise St. (won Humanitarian).

Conference USA

	Conference				Overall		
	W	L	PF	PA	W	L	PF	PA
*Southern Miss.	6	0	189	88	9	3	333	189
*East Carolina	4	2	191	133	9	3	333	225
*Louisville	4	2	196	180	7	5	443	365
Memphis	4	2	158	96	5	6	232	182
UAB	2	4	140	129	5	6	248	279
Houston	3	3	131	152	7	4	254	211
Army	1	5	125	197	3	8	225	317
Tulane	1	5	127	236	3	8	279	399
Cincinnati	0	6	121	167	3	8	275	289

Bowls (1-2): Southern Miss. (won Liberty); East Carolina (lost Mobile); Louisville (lost Humanitarian).

Mid-American Conference

	Conference				Overall		
Eastern	W	L	PF	PA	W	L	PF	PA
*Marshall	9	0	332	121	13	0	463	137
Miami-OH	6	2	238	166	7	4	335	264
Akron	5	3	231	200	7	4	315	314
Ohio	5	3	227	178	5	6	271	287
Bowling Green	3	5	213	237	5	6	296	312
Kent	2	6	159	257	2	9	213	376
Buffalo	0	8	96	333	0	11	130	426

	Conference				Overall		
Western	W	L	PF	PA	W	L	PF	PA
Western Michigan	6	3	267	211	7	5	373	342
Toledo	5	3	240	157	6	5	293	229
Northern Illinois	5	5	237	204	5	6	289	289
Eastern Michigan	4	4	216	211	4	7	239	338
Central Michigan	3	5	173	222	4	7	229	344
Ball St.	0	8	117	249	0	11	157	361

Bowl (1-0): Marshall (won Motor City).

Mountain West Conference

	Conference				Overall			
	W	L	PF	PA	W	L	PF	PA
*BYU	5	2	185	98	8	4	335	251
*Colorado State	5	2	190	148	8	4	345	269
*Utah	5	2	236	143	9	3	380	210
Wyoming	4	3	178	179	7	4	302	270
San Diego St.	3	4	159	139	5	6	272	226
New Mexico	3	4	148	216	4	7	240	298
Air Force	2	5	149	170	6	5	264	218
UNLV	1	6	95	247	3	8	160	324

Bowls (1-2): BYU (lost Motor City), Colorado St. (lost Liberty), Utah (won Las Vegas).

Pacific 10 Conference

	Conference				Overall			
	W	L	PF	PA	W	L	PF	PA
*Stanford	7	1	313	197	8	4	418	364
*Oregon	6	2	247	199	9	3	410	284
*Washington	6	2	231	188	7	5	331	302
*Arizona St.	5	3	227	192	6	6	285	311
*Oregon St.	4	4	208	177	7	5	347	277
Arizona	3	5	229	252	6	6	339	364
USC	3	5	193	206	6	6	348	278
California	3	5	131	164	4	7	180	254
UCLA	2	6	137	241	4	7	230	311
Washington St.	1	7	158	258	3	9	248	327

Bowls (1-4): Stanford (lost Rose); Oregon (won Sun); Washington (lost Holiday); Arizona St. (lost Aloha); Oregon St. (lost Oahu).

Southeastern Conference

	Conference				Overall			
Eastern	W	L	PF	PA	W	L	PF	PA
*Florida	7	1	233	152	9	4	403	272
*Tennessee	6	2	251	116	9	3	369	194
*Georgia	5	3	198	204	7	5	336	310
*Kentucky	4	4	198	218	6	6	328	343
Vanderbilt	2	6	129	211	5	6	252	256
South Carolina	0	8	63	216	0	11	87	278

	Conference				Overall			
Western	W	L	PF	PA	W	L	PF	PA
*Alabama	8	1	244	177	10	3	378	265
*Mississippi St.	6	2	156	121	10	2	255	156
*Arkansas	4	4	198	196	8	4	353	214
*Mississippi	4	4	235	176	8	4	323	228
Auburn	2	6	153	188	5	6	233	236
LSU	1	7	135	218	3	8	223	259

SEC championship game: Alabama beat Florida, 34-7 (Dec. 4).

Bowls (4-4): Florida (lost Citrus); Tennessee (lost Fiesta); Alabama (lost Orange); Georgia (won Outback); Kentucky (lost Music City); Mississippi St. (won Peach); Arkansas (won Cotton); Mississippi (won Independence).

Western Athletic Conference

	Conference				Overall			
Pacific	W	L	PF	PA	W	L	PF	PA
*Fresno St.	5	2	226	141	8	5	413	282
*Hawaii	5	2	214	161	9	4	371	349
*TCU	5	2	245	123	8	4	362	213
Rice	4	3	198	161	5	6	237	261
SMU	3	3	107	113	4	6	193	235
UTEP	3	4	183	235	5	7	306	389
San Jose St.	1	5	120	268	3	7	258	402
Tulsa	1	6	129	220	2	9	230	386

Bowls (2-1): Fresno St. (lost Las Vegas); Hawaii (won Oahu); TCU (won Mobile).

I-A Independents

	W	L	PF	PA
Louisiana Tech	8	3	389	306
UL-Monroe	5	6	186	322
Navy	5	7	326	306
Notre Dame	5	7	348	331
Central Florida	4	7	277	318
Middle Tennessee	3	8	272	379
UL-Lafayette	2	9	203	415

NCAA Division I-A Individual Leaders

REGULAR SEASON

Total Offense

		Rushing				Passing		Total Offense				
	Cl	Car	Gain	Loss	Net	Att	Yds	Plays	Yds	YdsPP	TDR*	YdsPG
Tim Rattay, La. Tech	Sr.	46	67	179	-112	516	3922	562	3810	6.78	35	381.00
Joe Hamilton, Ga. Tech	Sr.	154	861	127	734	305	3060	459	3798	8.27	35	345.27
Drew Brees, Purdue	Jr.	70	315	134	181	494	3531	564	3712	6.58	25	337.45
David Neill, Nevada	So.	100	505	296	209	423	3402	523	3611	6.90	25	328.27
Chad Pennington, Marshall	Sr.	55	204	99	105	405	3799	460	3904	8.49	39	325.33
Chris Redman, Louisville	Sr.	43	68	178	-110	489	3647	532	3537	6.65	30	321.55
Kevin Feterik, BYU	Sr.	88	256	333	-77	452	3554	540	3477	6.44	26	316.09
Dan Robinson, Hawaii	Sr.	60	105	196	-91	556	3853	616	3762	6.11	32	313.50
Josh Heupel, Oklahoma	Jr.	47	98	196	-98	500	3460	547	3362	6.15	35	305.64
Patrick Ramsey, Tulane	So.	64	99	160	-61	513	3410	577	3349	5.80	24	304.45

*Touchdowns responsible for includes TD passes and TDs scored.

All-Purpose Yards

	Cl	Gm	Rush	Rec	PR	KOR	Total Yds	YdsPG
Trevor Insley, Nevada	Sr.	11	5	2060	111	0	2176	197.82
Dennis Northcutt, Arizona	Sr.	12	200	1422	436	191	2249	187.42
Thomas Jones, Virginia	Sr.	11	1798	239	17	0	2054	186.73
LaDainian Tomlinson, TCU	Jr.	11	1850	55	0	69	1974	179.45
Travis Prentice, Miami-OH	Sr.	11	1659	270	0	0	1929	175.36
Troy Walters, Stanford	Sr.	11	6	1456	131	284	1877	170.64
Deuce McAllister, Mississippi	Jr.	10	809	201	30	652	1692	169.20
Ron Dayne, Wisconsin	Sr.	11	1834	9	0	0	1843	167.55
Lamont Jordan, Maryland	Jr.	11	1632	208	0	0	1840	167.27
Demario Brown, Utah St.	Sr.	11	1536	282	0	0	1818	165.27

TCU
LaDainian Tomlinson
Rushing

Virginia Tech
Michael Vick
Passing Efficiency

Florida St.
Sebastian Janikowski
Field Goals

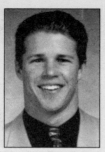

Univ. of Nevada
Trevor Insley
Receptions

Passing Efficiency

(Minimum 15 attempts per game)

	Cl	Gm	Att	Cmp	Cmp Pct	Int	Int Pct	Yds	Yds/ Att	TD	TD Pct	Rating Points
Michael Vick, Va. Tech	Fr.	10	152	90	59.21	5	3.29	1840	12.11	12	7.89	180.4
Joe Hamilton, Ga. Tech	Sr.	11	305	203	66.56	11	3.61	3060	10.03	29	9.51	175.0
Chad Pennington, Marshall	Sr.	12	405	275	67.90	11	2.72	3799	9.38	37	9.14	171.4
Billy Volek, Fresno St.	Sr.	12	355	235	66.20	3	0.85	2559	7.21	30	8.45	152.9
Tim Rattay, La. Tech	Sr.	10	516	342	66.28	12	2.33	3922	7.60	35	6.78	147.9
Jay Stuckey, UTEP	Sr.	12	225	145	64.44	13	5.78	1918	8.52	15	6.67	146.5
Chris Weinke, Florida St.	Jr.	11	377	232	61.54	14	3.71	3103	8.23	25	6.63	145.1
Dan Ellis, Virginia	Jr.	10	258	156	60.47	10	3.88	2050	7.95	20	7.75	145.0
Jeff Kelly, Southern Miss.	So.	11	260	153	58.85	11	4.23	2062	7.93	21	8.08	143.7
Tim Lester, Western Mich.	Sr.	12	470	282	60.00	13	2.77	3639	7.74	34	7.23	143.4
Todd Husak, Stanford	Sr.	10	308	176	57.14	11	3.57	2688	8.73	18	5.84	142.6
Chris Redman, Louisville	Sr.	11	489	317	64.83	13	2.66	3647	7.46	29	5.93	141.7

Rushing

	Cl	Car	Yds	TD	YdsPG
LaDainian Tomlinson, TCU	Jr.	268	1850	18	168.18
Ron Dayne, Wisconsin	Sr.	303	1834	19	166.73
Thomas Jones, Virginia	Sr.	334	1798	16	163.45
Travis Prentice, Miami-OH	Sr.	354	1659	17	150.82
Lamont Jordan, Maryland	Jr.	266	1632	16	148.36
Demario Brown, Utah St.	Sr.	279	1536	14	139.64
Trung Canidate, Arizona	Sr.	253	1602	11	133.50
Frank Moreau, Louisville	Sr.	233	1289	17	128.90
Darren Davis, Iowa St.	Sr.	287	1388	14	126.18
Shaun Alexander, Alabama	Sr.	302	1383	19	125.73
Robert Cooper, Cincinnati	Jr.	248	1245	7	124.50
Thomas Hamner, Minnesota	Sr.	288	1362	10	123.82

Games: All played 11, except Canidate (12), Cooper and Moreau (10).

Receptions

	Cl	No	Yds	TD	P/Gm
Trevor Insley, Nevada	Sr.	134	2060	13	12.18
Chris Daniels, Purdue	Sr.	109	1133	5	9.91
JaJuan Dawson, Tulane	Sr.	96	1051	8	9.60
Arnold Jackson, Louisville	Sr.	101	1209	9	9.18
James Whalen, Kentucky	Sr.	90	1019	10	8.18
Charles Lee, C. Florida	Sr.	87	1133	5	7.91
Peter Warrick, Florida St.	Sr.	71	934	8	7.89
Drew Haddad, Buffalo	Sr.	85	1158	6	7.73
Kwame Cavil, Texas	Jr.	100	1188	6	7.69
James Jordan, La. Tech	So.	81	824	11	7.36
Dennis Northcutt, Arizona	Sr.	88	1422	8	7.33
Adrian Burnette, Tulane	Jr.	79	1095	7	7.18
John Simon, La. Tech	So.	79	757	2	7.18

Games: All played 11, except Dawson (10), Warrick (9), Cavil (13) and Northcutt (12).

Field Goals

	Cl	FG/Att	Pct	Lg
Sebastian Janikowski, Fla. St.	Jr.	23/30	.767	54
Jeff Chandler, Florida	Jr.	21/24	.875	50
Travis Forney, Penn St.	Sr.	21/26	.808	47
Neil Rackers, Illinois	Sr.	20/25	.800	50
Kris Stockton, Texas	Jr.	20/29	.690	50

Six tied with 18 each.

Games: All played 11, except Chandler and Forney (12) and Stockton (13).

Longest FG of season: 62 yards by Terance Kitchens, Texas A&M vs. So. Miss. (Sept. 25).

Interceptions

	Cl	No	Yds	TD	Lg
Deltha O'Neal, California	Sr.	9	280	4	100-td
Deon Grant, Tennessee	Jr.	9	167	1	42
Rodregis Brooks, UAB	Jr.	9	152	1	91
Jamar Fletcher, Wisconsin	So.	7	135	2	93-td
Mike James, Houston	Sr.	7	57	1	29-td
Quincy Lejay, Hawaii	Sr.	7	151	3	54-td

Twelve tied with 6 each.

Games: All played 11 except Lejay (12)

Scoring

Non-Kickers

	Cl	TD	Pts	P/Gm
Shaun Alexander, Alabama	Sr.	24	144	13.09
Travis Prentice, Miami-OH	Sr.	21	126	11.45
Ron Dayne, Wisconsin	Sr.	19	114	10.36
Frank Moreau, Louisville	Sr.	17	102	10.20
LaDainian Tomlinson, TCU	Jr.	18	108	9.82
Ken Simonton, Oregon St.	So.	17	106*	9.64
Travis Zachery, Clemson	So.	16	96	9.60
Lamont Jordan, Maryland	Jr.	17	102	9.27
Thomas Jones, Virginia	Sr.	17	102	9.27
Anthony Thomas, Michigan	Jr.	16	96	8.73
Darren Davis, Iowa St.	Sr.	16	96	8.73

*Includes two 2-point conversions.
Games: All played 11, except Moreau and Zachery (10).

Kickers

	FG/Att	PAT/Att	Pts	P/Gm
Sebastian Janikowski, FSU	23/30	47/47	116	10.55
Shayne Graham, Va. Tech	17/22	56/57	107	9.73
Jamie Rheem, Kansas St.	18/21	41/43	95	9.50
Neil Rackers, Illinois	20/25	35/35	101*	9.18
Travis Forney, Penn St.	21/26	44/44	107	8.92
Jeff Chandler, Florida	21/24	38/41	101	8.42
Paul Edinger, Michigan St.	18/22	38/39	92	8.36
Nick Calaycay, Boise St.	14/17	41/42	83	8.30
Mike Biselli, Stanford	14/17	49/52	91	8.27
Travis Dorsch, Purdue	18/28	37/37	91	8.27

*Includes one touchdown.
Games: All played 11, except Rheem and Calaycay (10) and Forney and Chandler (12).

Punting
(Minimum of 3.6 per game)

	Cl	No	Yds	Avg
Andrew Bayes, E. Carolina	Sr.	47	2259	48.06
Brian Schmitz, N. Carolina	Sr.	74	3538	47.81
Shane Lechler, Texas A&M	Sr.	60	2787	46.45
Ray Cheetany, UNLV	Jr.	65	2950	45.38
Dan Hadenfeldt, Nebraska	Sr.	65	2924	44.98
Drew Hagan, Indiana	Sr.	44	1971	44.80
Nick Harris, California	Jr.	85	3795	44.65

Punt Returns
(Minimum of 1.2 per game)

	Cl	No	Yds	TD	Avg
Dennis Northcutt, Arizona	Sr.	23	436	2	18.96
Bobby Newcombe, Nebraska	Jr.	16	294	1	18.38
Vinny Sutherland, Purdue	Jr.	17	295	2	17.35
Rodregis Brooks, UAB	Jr.	19	325	0	17.11
Stevonne Smith, Utah	Jr.	29	495	3	17.07
Dallas Davis, Colorado St.	Jr.	32	541	2	16.91
Hank Poteat, Pittsburgh	Sr.	19	307	1	16.16
Keith Stokes, E. Carolina	Jr.	26	404	1	15.54
Emmett White, Utah St.	So.	24	361	0	15.04
Terance Richardson, Oklahoma St.	Sr.	40	591	1	14.77

Kickoff Returns
(Minimum of 1.2 per game)

	Cl	No	Yds	TD	Avg
James Williams, Marshall	Sr.	15	493	1	32.87
Brandon Daniels, Oklahoma	Sr.	16	508	1	31.75
John Stone, Wake Forest	So.	13	389	1	29.92
Deltha O'Neal, California	Sr.	19	555	1	29.21
Ben Kelly, Colorado	Jr.	19	547	2	28.79
Sonny Cook, Oregon	Jr.	14	402	0	28.71
Deonce Whitaker, San Jose St.	Jr.	14	396	1	28.29
Scottie Montgomery, Duke	Sr.	21	587	1	27.95
Chris Lacy, Idaho	So.	15	419	1	27.93
Ryan Wells, Stanford	So.	15	412	0	27.47

NCAA Division I-A Team Leaders
REGULAR SEASON

Scoring Offense

	Gm	Record	Pts	Avg
Virginia Tech	11	11-0	455	41.4
Georgia Tech	11	8-3	448	40.7
Kansas St.	11	10-1	433	39.4
Louisville	11	6-5	412	37.5
Florida St.	11	11-0	412	37.5
Stanford	11	8-3	409	37.2
Marshall	12	12-0	442	36.8
Oklahoma	11	7-4	405	36.8
Wisconsin	11	9-2	392	35.6
Louisiana Tech	11	8-3	389	35.4

Scoring Defense

	Gm	Record	Pts	Avg
Virginia Tech	11	11-0	116	10.5
Marshall	12	12-0	134	11.2
Nebraska	12	11-1	150	12.5
Kansas St.	11	10-1	144	13.1
Wisconsin	11	9-2	145	13.2
Mississippi St.	11	9-2	149	13.5
Tennessee	11	9-2	163	14.8
Southern Miss.	11	8-3	172	15.6
Minnesota	11	8-3	172	15.6
Florida St.	11	11-0	174	15.8

Total Offense

	Gm	Plays	Yds	Avg	TD	YdsPG
Georgia Tech	11	822	5603	6.8	58	509.36
Nevada	11	843	5192	6.2	39	472.00
Arizona	12	870	5663	6.5	42	471.92
La. Tech	11	822	5181	6.3	50	471.00
Stanford	11	793	5138	6.5	47	467.09
Louisville	11	851	5136	6.0	48	466.91
Marshall	12	541	5584	6.6	57	465.33
Purdue	11	859	5016	5.8	38	456.00
Virginia Tech	11	758	4970	6.6	49	451.82
Oregon St.	11	857	4774	5.6	41	434.00

Note: Touchdowns scored by rushing and passing only.

Total Defense

	Gm	Plays	Yds	Avg	TD	YdsPG
Mississippi St.	11	734	2448	3.3	14	222.5
Kansas St.	11	693	2585	3.7	18	235.0
Virginia Tech	11	732	2720	3.7	15	247.3
Nebraska	12	815	3022	3.7	17	251.8
TCU	11	729	3129	4.3	24	284.5
Texas	13	876	3727	4.3	28	286.7
Marshall	12	882	3516	4.0	11	293.0
Southern Miss.	11	754	3235	4.3	14	294.1
Alabama	12	749	3568	4.8	26	297.3
Oklahoma St.	11	683	3273	4.8	30	297.5

Note: Opponents' TDs scored by rushing and passing only.

Single Game Highs
INDIVIDUAL

Rushing Yards

Yds
406   LaDainian Tomlinson, TCU vs. UTEP (Nov. 20, 1999)

Total Offense

Yds
541   Tim Rattay, La. Tech vs. C. Fla. (Oct. 23, 1999)

Points Scored

Att
36   LaDainian Tomlinson, TCU vs. UTEP (Nov. 20, 1999)

Rushing TDs

Att
6   LaDainian Tomlinson, TCU vs. UTEP (Nov. 20, 1999)

Passing TDs

Att
6   Tim Rattay, La. Tech vs. C. Fla. (Oct. 23, 1999)

Receptions

No
21   Chris Daniels, Purdue vs. Mich. St. (Oct. 16, 1999)

Receiving Yards

Yds
301   Chris Daniels, Purdue vs. Mich. St. (Oct. 16, 1999)

Passing Yards

Yds
561   Tim Rattay, La. Tech vs. C. Fla. (Oct. 23, 1999)

Passes Completed

No
46   Tim Rattay, La. Tech vs. C. Fla. (Oct. 23, 1999)

Annual Awards

Player of the Year

Ron Dayne, Wisconsin . . . . . .AP, Camp, Heisman, Maxwell

Position Players of the Year

O'Brien Award (Quarterback) . . . . Joe Hamilton, Ga. Tech
Walker Award (Running Back) . . . . .Ron Dayne, Wisconsin
Biletnikoff Award (Receiver) . . . . .Troy Walters, Stanford
Groza Award (Kicker) . . . . .Sebastian Janikowski, Fla. St.
Outland Trophy (Interior Lineman). . . . .Chris Samuels, Ala., OT
Lombardi Award (Lineman) . . . . . . .Corey Moore, Va. Tech, DE
Butkus Award (Linebacker) . . . . .LaVar Arrington, Penn St.
Thorpe Award (Defensive Back) . . . . .Tyrone Carter, Minnesota
Nagurski Award (Defensive Player).Corey Moore, Va. Tech, DE
Payton Award (IAA Player of the Year) . . . . . . .Adrian Peterson,
Georgia Southern, RB
Hill Trophy (Div. II Player of the Year) . . . . .Corte McGuffet,
N. Colorado, QB
Melberger Award (Div. III Player of the Year) . . . . . .Scott Pingel,
Westminster (Mo.), WR

Coach of the Year

Frank Beamer, Va. Tech. . . .AFCA, AP, Camp, Dodd, FWAA

Heisman Trophy Vote

Presented since 1935 by the Downtown Athletic Club of New York City and named after former college coach and DAC athletic director John W. Heisman. Voting done by national media and former Heisman winners. Each ballot allows for three names (points based on 3 for 1st, 2 for 2nd and 1 for 3rd).

Top 10 Vote-Getters

	Pos	1st	2nd	3rd	Pts
Ron Dayne, Wisconsin	RB	586	121	42	2042
Joe Hamilton, Ga. Tech	QB	96	285	136	994
Michael Vick, Va. Tech	QB	25	72	100	319
Drew Brees, Purdue	QB	3	89	121	308
Chad Pennington, Marshall	QB	21	45	94	247
Peter Warrick, Florida St. . . .	WR	14	50	61	203
Shaun Alexander, Alabama . .	RB	11	43	52	171
Thomas Jones, Virginia	RB	10	32	46	140
LaVar Arrington, Penn St. . . .	LB	3	14	17	54
Tim Rattay, La. Tech	QB	1	5	16	29

Consensus All-America Team

NCAA Division I-A players cited most frequently by the following selectors: AFCA, AP, and Walter Camp Foundation. Holdovers from 1998 All-America team are in **bold** type; (*) indicates unanimous selection.

Offense

	Player	Class	Ht	Wt
WR	Troy Walters, Stanford	Sr.	5-8	170
WR	**Peter Warrick***, FSU	Sr.	6-0	190
TE	James Whalen, Kentucky	Sr.	6-4	231
OL	Cosey Coleman*, Tennessee	Jr.	6-5	315
OL	Chris McIntosh*, Wisconsin	Sr.	6-7	307
OL	Jason Whitaker, Florida St.	Sr.	6-5	300
OL	Chris Samuels, Alabama	Sr.	6-6	291
C	Rob Riti, Missouri.	Sr.	6-3	289
QB	Joe Hamilton*, Ga. Tech	Sr.	5-10	189
RB	Ron Dayne*, Wisconsin.	Sr.	5-10	254
RB	Thomas Jones, Virginia	Sr.	5-10	205
K	**Sebastian Janikowski***, Fla. St.. .	Jr.	6-2	255

Defense

	Player	Class	Ht	Wt
DL	Corey Moore*, Va. Tech	Sr.	6-0	225
DL	Corey Simon*, Florida St.	Sr.	6-4	275
DL	Courtney Brown*, Penn St.	Sr.	6-5	270
LB	Brandon Short, Penn St.	Jr.	6-3	233
LB	LaVar Arrington*, Penn St.	Jr.	6-3	242
LB	Mark Simoneau*, Kansas St.	Sr.	6-0	240
LB	Raynoch Thompson, Tennessee	Sr.	6-3	217
DB	Tyrone Carter*, Minnesota	Sr.	5-9	184
DB	Brian Urlacher*, New Mexico	Sr.	6-4	240
DB	Deon Grant, Tennessee	Jr.	6-3	205
DB	Deltha O'Neal, California	Sr.	5-11	195
P	Andrew Bayes, E. Carolina	Sr.	6-3	200

Underclassmen who declared for the 2000 draft

Twenty-nine players forfeited the remainder of their college eligibility and declared for the NFL draft in 2000. NFL teams drafted 21 underclassmen. Players listed in alphabetical order; first round selections in **bold** type.

	Pos	Drafted by	Overall pick		Pos	Drafted by	Overall pick
LaVar Arrington, Penn St.	LB	Washington	2	Keith Jackson, Cheyney (PA)	DT	—	
Rodregis Brooks, UAB	CB	Indianapolis	238	**Sebastian Janikowski**, FSU	PK	Oakland	17
Plaxico Burress, Michigan St.	WR	Pittsburgh	8	Ronney Jenkins, N. Arizona	RB	—	
Kwame Cavil, Texas	WR	—		Ben Kelly, Colorado	CB	Miami	84
Ike Charlton, Va. Tech	CB	Seattle	52	**Jamal Lewis**, Tennessee	TB	Baltimore	5
Cosey Coleman, Tennessee	G	Tampa Bay	51	Tariq McDonald, Arizona St.	WR	—	
Patrick Dennis, LA-Monroe	DB	Kansas City	162	Lewis Sanders, Maryland	CB	Cleveland	95
Na'il Diggs, Ohio St.	LB	Green Bay	98	Jacoby Shepherd, Oklahoma St.	DB	St. Louis	62
Jeffrey Dunlap, Auburn	DT	—		Marvel Smith, Arizona St.	OL	Pittsburgh	38
Shaun Ellis, Tennessee	DE	New York Jets	12	Shyrone Stith, Va. Tech	RB	Jacksonville	243
Bubba Franks, Miami-FL	TE	Green Bay	14	**Travis Taylor**, Florida	WR	Baltimore	10
Deon Grant, Tennessee	DB	Carolina	57	Hubert Thompson, Michigan St.	DE	—	
Jonathan Gray, Texas Tech	OL	—		Raynoch Thompson, Tennessee	LB	Arizona	41
Bud Herring, Louisville	LB	—		Dez White, Ga. Tech	WR	Chicago	69
Darrell Jackson, Florida	WR	Seattle	80				

NCAA Division I-AA Final Standings

Standings based on conference games only; overall records include postseason games.

Atlantic 10 Conference

	Conference				Overall			
	W	L	PF	PA	W	L	PF	PA
*Massachusetts	7	1	314	126	9	4	415	244
*James Madison	7	1	237	149	8	4	273	260
Villanova	6	2	266	253	7	4	334	324
Delaware	5	3	232	202	7	4	322	270
Wm. & Mary	5	3	242	162	6	5	292	266
New Hampshire	3	5	213	193	5	6	325	294
Richmond	3	5	200	235	5	6	278	295
Connecticut	3	5	201	282	4	7	255	383
Maine	3	5	151	211	4	7	226	273
Northeastern	1	7	159	289	2	9	256	362
Rhode Island	1	7	109	222	1	10	168	294

Playoffs (1-2): Massachusetts (1-1), James Madison (0-1).

Big Sky Conference

	Conference				Overall			
	W	L	PF	PA	W	L	PF	PA
*Montana	7	1	407	194	9	3	537	284
Portland St.	6	2	303	244	8	3	399	334
*Northern Arizona	6	2	282	206	8	4	409	370
Eastern Wash.	6	2	254	233	7	4	326	336
CS-Northridge	4	4	230	250	5	6	298	398
CS-Sacramento	3	5	294	250	6	5	414	310
Weber St.	2	6	195	310	3	8	251	393
Idaho St.	1	7	202	335	3	8	345	429
Montana St.	1	7	147	292	3	8	269	350

Playoffs (0-2): Montana (0-1), Northern Arizona (0-1).
Note: Following the season, N. Arizona had to forfeit 6 games (4 wins, 2 losses) for using an ineligible player.

Best Conference Playoff Records

Postseason records for 1999 season.

	W-L
Gateway Athletic	5-2
Southern	4-2
Mid-Eastern Athletic	3-2
Atlantic 10	1-2
Southland	1-1
Patriot	0-2

Gateway Athletic Conference

	Conference				Overall			
	W	L	PF	PA	W	L	PF	PA
*Illinois St.	6	0	237	193	11	3	487	356
*Youngstown St.	5	1	176	154	12	3	421	362
Northern Iowa	3	3	182	174	8	3	400	254
Western Ill.	2	4	221	186	7	4	383	241
SW Missouri St.	2	4	180	175	5	6	373	265
Indiana St.	2	4	185	207	3	8	284	373
Southern Ill.	1	5	223	315	5	6	424	432

Playoffs (5-2): Youngstown St. (3-1), Illinois St. (2-1).

Ivy League

	Conference				Overall			
	W	L	PF	PA	W	L	PF	PA
Brown	6	1	225	168	9	1	324	239
Yale	6	1	216	138	9	1	315	159
Cornell	5	2	165	152	7	3	254	235
Pennsylvania	4	3	188	140	5	5	245	216
Harvard	3	4	171	120	5	5	254	190
Dartmouth	2	5	111	215	2	8	138	300
Columbia	1	6	124	218	3	7	175	301
Princeton	1	6	135	184	3	7	184	225

Playoffs: League does not play postseason games.

Metro-Atlantic Conference

	Conference				Overall			
	W	L	PF	PA	W	L	PF	PA
Duquesne	6	1	335	155	8	3	393	224
Georgetown	6	1	252	101	9	2	364	166
Marist	5	2	226	195	6	5	259	266
Iona	4	3	176	182	5	5	239	271
La Salle	3	4	127	224	4	6	181	252
Siena	3	4	127	159	3	7	141	215
St. Peters	1	6	99	239	1	10	125	328
Canisius	0	7	84	277	1	10	133	431
†Fairfield	0	0	0	0	9	2	408	147

Playoffs: No teams invited.
†Fairfield was ineligible for the MAAC title in 1999 and its games did not count in the league standings.

Mid-Eastern Athletic Conference

	Conference				Overall			
	W	L	PF	PA	W	L	PF	PA
*N. Carolina A&T	8	0	250	97	11	2	324	202
*Florida A&M	7	1	405	137	10	4	583	320
†Hampton	5	3	207	211	8	4	290	255
Bethune-Cookman	4	4	206	241	7	4	277	277
Howard	4	4	237	291	5	6	323	395
Delaware St.	4	4	191	207	4	7	261	354
South Carolina St.	2	5	181	258	4	6	241	315
Norfolk St.	1	7	126	236	2	9	160	286
Morgan St.	0	7	129	254	2	8	191	334

*Playoffs (3-2): North Carolina A&T (1-1), Florida A&M (2-1).
†Heritage Bowl: Hampton defeated Southern-BR (24-3).

Northeast Conference

	Conference				Overall			
	W	L	PF	PA	W	L	PF	PA
Robert Morris	7	0	261	100	8	2	328	156
Albany	6	1	256	118	7	2	333	156
Wagner	5	2	214	104	5	5	257	186
Stony Brook	4	3	158	162	5	5	215	232
Central Conn.	3	4	167	170	4	6	227	256
Monmouth (N.J.)	2	5	116	154	2	8	159	274
St. Francis (Pa.)	1	6	82	251	2	9	117	359
Sacred Heart	0	7	73	268	2	9	132	349

Playoffs: No teams invited.

Ohio Valley Conference

	Conference				Overall			
	W	L	PF	PA	W	L	PF	PA
*Tennessee St.	7	0	249	169	11	1	426	274
Murray St.	5	2	267	168	7	4	415	302
Eastern Ky.	4	3	216	163	7	4	311	258
Western Ky.	4	3	155	131	6	5	270	245
Tennessee Tech	3	4	153	103	5	5	201	177
SE Missouri St.	2	5	172	204	3	8	245	359
Eastern Ill.	2	5	179	212	2	10	267	365
Tenn.-Martin	0	7	75	316	1	10	128	499

*Playoffs (0-1): Tennessee St. (0-1).

Patriot League

	Conference				Overall			
	W	L	PF	PA	W	L	PF	PA
*Colgate	5	1	232	123	10	2	430	253
*Lehigh	5	1	141	121	10	2	478	220
Towson	4	2	154	132	7	4	302	255
Bucknell	3	3	166	149	7	4	320	233
Lafayette	2	4	94	163	4	7	207	271
Holy Cross	2	4	122	179	3	8	219	323
Fordham	0	6	90	232	0	11	170	410

*Playoffs (0-2): Colgate (0-1), Lehigh (0-1).

Pioneer League

	Conference				Overall			
	W	L	PF	PA	W	L	PF	PA
Dayton	4	0	137	31	6	4	325	210
Valparaiso	3	1	89	78	9	2	290	199
Drake	2	2	125	73	7	4	330	173
San Diego	1	3	69	110	5	5	215	201
Butler	0	4	47	175	5	5	217	305

Playoffs: No teams invited.

Southern Conference

	Conference				Overall			
	W	L	PF	PA	W	L	PF	PA
*Ga. Southern	7	1	382	109	13	2	747	262
*Appalachian St.	7	1	263	121	9	3	369	219
*Furman	7	1	307	157	9	3	432	220
Wofford	5	3	253	201	6	5	364	303
E. Tenn St.	4	4	180	215	6	5	272	251
Tenn.-Chatt.	3	5	220	275	5	6	328	360
W. Carolina	2	6	259	279	3	8	260	365
The Citadel	1	7	111	251	2	9	147	349
VMI	0	8	42	309	1	10	77	400

*Playoffs (4-2): Georgia Southern (4-0), Appalachian St. (0-1), Furman (0-1).

Southland Conference

	Conference				Overall			
	W	L	PF	PA	W	L	PF	PA
*Troy St.	6	1	178	101	11	2	362	224
Stephen F. Austin	6	1	220	126	8	3	389	260
McNeese St.	5	2	148	127	6	5	220	244
Sam Houston St.	4	3	222	143	6	5	331	298
Northwestern St.	3	4	165	139	4	7	243	243
SW Texas St.	2	5	108	129	3	8	217	210
Jacksonville St.	1	6	151	248	2	9	271	383
Nicholls St.	1	6	86	265	1	10	133	362

*Playoffs (1-1): Troy St. (1-1)

Southwestern Athletic Conference

	Conference				Overall			
Eastern	W	L	PF	PA	W	L	PF	PA
Jackson St.	4	0	193	41	9	3	448	220
Alabama A&M	3	2	111	106	6	5	287	230
Alcorn St.	1	3	96	150	3	7	267	302
Miss. Valley St.	1	3	76	150	3	8	170	373
Alabama St.	1	3	89	124	2	9	240	363

	Conference				Overall			
Western	W	L	PF	PA	W	L	PF	PA
†Southern-BR	4	0	119	54	11	2	331	237
Texas Southern	3	1	89	50	6	5	236	220
Grambling	2	2	122	96	7	4	315	265
Ark.-Pine Bluff	2	3	88	84	6	5	226	226
Prairie View	0	4	25	153	2	8	109	324

†Heritage Bowl: Hampton defeated Southern-BR (24-3).

NCAA I-AA Independents

	W	L	PF	PA
*Hofstra	11	2	419	224
Elon College	9	2	344	193
Davidson	8	3	257	217
Southern Utah	8	3	399	277
Samford	7	4	335	238
South Florida	7	4	246	248
St. John's	7	4	247	142
Morehead St.	5	5	359	310
Charleston Southern	4	6	219	256
Liberty	4	7	225	276
Jacksonville	3	6	201	251
Austin Peay	3	8	240	423
Cal Poly-SLO	3	8	246	345
St. Mary's (Ca.)	2	9	169	345

*Playoffs (1-1): Hofstra (1-1)

Villanova
Murle Sango
Receptions

Univ. of Montana
Drew Miller
Passing Efficiency

William & Mary
Brett Sterba
Field Goals

CS-Sacramento
Charles Roberts
Rushing

NCAA Division I-AA Regular Season Leaders
INDIVIDUAL
Passing Efficiency
(Minimum 15 attempts per game)

	Cl	Gm	Att	Cmp	Cmp Pct	Int	Int Pct	Yds	Yds/ Att	TD	TD Pct	Rating Points
Drew Miller, Montana	Jr.	10	368	240	65.22	8	2.17	3461	9.40	32	8.70	168.6
Mark Washington, Jackson St.	Sr.	12	287	147	51.22	10	3.48	2788	9.71	29	10.10	159.2
Jimmy Blanchard, Portland St.	Jr.	11	355	212	59.72	3	.85	3098	8.73	29	8.17	158.3
Phil Stambaugh, Lehigh	Sr.	11	347	236	68.01	13	3.75	2995	8.63	26	7.49	157.7
JaJuan Seider, Florida A&M	Sr.	11	253	150	59.29	2	.79	2086	8.25	23	9.09	157.0
Chris Chaloupka, Sam Houston St.	Sr.	10	271	168	61.99	13	4.80	2503	9.24	21	7.75	155.6
Ryan Helming, Northern Iowa	Jr.	11	403	253	62.78	14	3.47	3469	8.61	31	7.69	153.5
Justin Fuente, Murray St.	Sr.	11	400	240	60.00	9	2.25	3497	8.74	27	6.75	151.2
Jay Rodgers, SW Mo. St.	Sr.	11	326	206	63.19	13	3.99	2741	8.41	24	7.36	150.1
Ricky Ray, CS-Sacramento	Jr.	10	291	182	62.54	8	2.75	2422	8.32	20	6.87	149.6

Total Offense

	Cl	Rush	Pass	Yds	YdsPG
Joe Lee, Towson	Sr.	-137	4168	4031	366.45
Drew Miller, Montana	Jr.	-146	3461	3315	331.50
James Perry, Brown	Sr.	-72	467	3255	318.30
Chris Sanders, Chattanooga	Jr.	-48	3539	3491	317.36
Ryan Helming, N. Iowa	Jr.	0	3469	3469	315.36
David Dinkins, Morehead St.	Jr.	1138	2011	3149	314.90
Marcus Brady, CS-Northridge	So.	93	3326	3419	310.82
Justin Fuente, Murray St.	Sr.	-90	3497	3407	309.73
Sherard Poteete, S. Illinois	Jr.	527	2777	3304	300.36
Joe Walland, Yale	Sr.	363	2207	2570	285.56

Rushing

	Cl	Car	Yds	TD	YdsPG
Charles Roberts, CS-Sacramento	Jr.	303	2082	22	189.27
Adrian Peterson, Ga. So.	So.	248	1807	28	164.27
Randall Joseph, Colgate	Jr.	193	1446	15	160.67
Corey Holmes, Miss. Valley	Jr.	331	1692	11	153.82
Curtis Keaton, James Madison	Sr.	290	1659	19	150.82
Marcel Shipp, UMass	Jr.	327	1572	20	142.91
Ralph Saldiveri, Iona	Jr.	255	1400	16	140.00
Rick Sarille, Wagner	Jr.	274	1373	15	137.30
Destry Wright, Jackson St.	Sr.	296	1643	12	136.92
Derek O'Neal, S. Carolina St.	Sr.	297	1352	15	135.20
Charles Dunn, Portland St.	Jr.	279	1478	16	134.36

Games: All played 11, except Joseph (9), Saldiveri, Sarille and O'Neal (10).

Receptions

	Cl	No	Yds	TD	P/Gm
Murle Sango, Villanova	So.	98	1064	10	8.91
Stephen Campbell, Brown	Jr.	89	1107	11	8.90
Elijah Thurmon, Howard	Sr.	84	1366	9	7.64
Jamal White, Towson	So.	82	1322	8	7.45
Phil Wendler, Princeton	Sr.	74	822	4	7.40
Joe Splendorio, Cornell	Jr.	65	944	10	7.22
Jason Corle, Towson	Sr.	72	864	8	7.20
Cornell Craig, Southern Ill.	Sr.	77	1419	15	7.00
Gerry McDermott, Fordham	Sr.	77	911	7	7.00
Cos Dematteo, Chattanooga	So.	76	977	11	6.91

Games: All played 11, except Corle and Wendler (10) and Splendorio (9).

Interceptions

	Cl	No	Yds	TD	LG
Edreece Brown, Southern	Sr.	12	22	0	11
Ryan Crawford, Davidson	Jr.	8	63	0	23
Jim Gallagher, Georgetown	Sr.	7	84	1	66-td
Dan Mulhern, Delaware	Fr.	7	60	0	22
Lance Small, Rhode Island	So.	7	60	0	39
Eric Kenesie, Valparaiso	Sr.	7	35	0	22

Games: All played 11, except Brown (14).

Scoring
Non-Kickers

	Cl	TD	XPt	Pts	P/Gm
Adrian Peterson, Ga. Southern	So.	29	0	174	15.82
Ronald Jean, Lehigh	Sr.	26	0	156	14.18
Charles Roberts, CS-Sac.	Jr.	22	6	138	12.55
Matt Cannon, Southern Utah	Jr.	23	0	138	12.55
David Dinkins, Morehead St.	Jr.	20	2	122	12.20
Marcel Shipp, UMass	Jr.	21	0	126	11.45

Games: All played 11, except Dinkins (10).

Kickers

	Cl	FG/Att	PAT/Att	Pts
Kris Heppner, Montana	Sr.	12/20	56/63	92
Dan Frantz, Portland St.	Jr.	14/19	47/49	89
Chris Chambers, Ga. Southern	Sr.	6/14	69/72	87
Brett Sterba, Wm. & Mary	Jr.	18/23	32/32	86
Jeremy Edwards, Fla. A&M	Sr.	10/17	56/61	86

Games: All played 11, except Heppner (12).

Field Goals

		Cl	FG/Att	Pct	LG
Brett Sterba, Wm. & Mary		Jr.	18/23	.783	44
David Collett, Tenn. Tech.		So.	16/24	.667	48
Jason Feinberg, Penn.		Jr.	15/21	.714	48

Five tied with 14 each.

Games: Sterba (11), Collett and Feinberg (10).

Longest FG of season: 57 yds by Chris Chambers, Ga. Southern vs. Oregon St. (Sept. 18).

Punt/Kickoff Leaders

Punting		Cl	No	Yds	Avg
Matthew Peot, Montana St.		Jr.	48	2195	45.73

Punt Returns	Cl	No	Yds	TD	Avg
KaRon Coleman, S.F. Austin	Sr.	17	348	1	20.47

Kickoff Returns	Cl	No	Yds	TD	Avg
Cordell Roane, Richmond	Fr.	13	470	1	36.15

TEAM
Scoring Offense

	Gm	Record	Pts	Avg
Ga. Southern	11	9-2	550	50.0
Montana	11	9-2	510	46.4
Florida A&M	11	8-3	498	45.3
Lehigh	11	10-1	463	42.1
Southern Ill.	11	5-6	424	38.5
Colgate	11	10-1	417	37.9
Tennessee St.	11	11-0	416	37.8
Murray St.	11	7-4	415	37.7
CS-Sacramento	11	6-5	414	37.6
Jackson St.	12	9-3	448	37.3
Furman	11	9-2	409	37.2
Fairfield	11	9-2	408	37.1
Albany	9	7-2	333	37.0
Northen Iowa	11	8-3	400	36.4
Portland St.	11	8-3	399	36.3
Southern Utah	11	8-3	399	36.3

Scoring Defense

	Gm	Record	Pts	Avg
St. John's	11	7-4	142	12.9
Fairfield	11	9-2	147	13.4
N. Carolina A&T	11	10-1	151	13.7
Georgetown	11	9-2	166	15.1
Ga. Southern	11	9-2	171	15.5
Robert Morris	10	8-2	156	15.6
Hofstra	11	10-1	172	15.6
Drake	11	7-4	173	15.7
Appalachian St.	11	9-2	175	15.9
Yale	10	9-1	160	16.0
Massachusetts	11	8-3	183	16.6
Furman	11	9-2	190	17.3
Albany	9	7-2	156	17.3
Lehigh	11	10-1	193	17.5
Elon	11	9-2	193	17.5

Total Offense

	Record	Plays	Yds	Avg
Ga. Southern	9-2	795	6069	551.73
Montana	9-2	810	5691	517.36
Jackson St.	9-3	1023	6588	488.83
Morehead St.	5-5	756	4822	482.20
Towson	7-4	927	5258	478.00
Southern Utah	8-3	801	5251	477.36
Northern Iowa	8-3	823	5235	475.91
Wofford	6-5	834	5212	473.82
Murray St.	7-4	789	5175	470.45
CS-Sacramento	6-5	793	5174	470.36
Florida A&M	8-3	806	5096	463.27
Lehigh	10-1	806	5084	462.18
Portland St.	8-3	796	5063	460.27
Brown	9-1	789	4593	459.30
Colgate	10-1	835	5043	458.45

Total Defense

	Record	Plays	Yds	Avg
St. John's	7-4	677	2197	199.7
Fairfield	9-2	681	2610	237.3
North Carolina A&T	10-1	763	2853	259.4
Wagner	5-5	608	2619	261.9
Drake	7-4	733	2893	263.0
SW Texas St.	3-8	697	3012	273.8
Elon	9-2	670	3037	276.1
Tennessee Tech	5-5	635	2783	278.3
Robert Morris	8-2	633	2795	279.5
Siena	3-7	685	2797	279.7
Georgetown	9-2	789	3100	281.8
Troy St.	10-1	715	3146	286.0
Valparaiso	9-2	722	3152	286.5
Colgate	10-1	745	3175	288.6
Northwestern St.	4-7	718	3181	289.2

NCAA Playoffs

Division I-AA
First Round (Nov. 27)

N. Carolina A&T 24 . . . . .at Tennessee St. 10
at Georgia Southern 72 . . . . .N. Arizona 29
at Hofstra 27. . . . . .Lehigh 15
Florida A&M 44 . . . . .at Appalachian St. 29
at Troy St. 27. . . . . .James Madison 7
at Illinois St. 56 . . . . .Colgate 13
Massachusetts 30 . . . . .OT . . . . .at Furman 23
Youngstown St. 30. .at Montana 27

Quarterfinals (Dec. 4)

at Georgia Southern 38. . . . . .Massachusetts 21
Illinois St. 37 . . . . .at Hofstra 20
Florida A&M 17. . . . . .at Troy St. 10
at Youngstown St. 41. . . . . .N. Carolina A&T 3

Semifinals (Dec. 11)

at Georgia Southern 28. . . . . .Illinois St. 17
at Youngstown St. 27 . . . . .Florida A&M 24

Championship Game
Dec. 18 at Chattanooga, Tenn. (Att: 20,052)

Georgia Southern 59 . . . . .Youngstown St. 24
(13-2)   (12-3)

Division II
First Round (Nov. 20)

at NW Missouri St. 20 . . . .OT . . . . .North Dakota 13
at N. Colorado 34 . . . . .Pittsburg St. 31
at Millersville (Pa.) 21. . . . . .Shepherd 14
Indiana (Pa.) 27 . . . . .OT . .at Slippery Rock (Pa.) 20
at N'eastern St. (Okla.) 27 . .OT. . . . . . .W. Washington 24
at UC-Davis 42. .C. Oklahoma 21
at Catawba (N.C.) 48 . . . . .Fort Valley St. 17
at Carson-Newman (Tenn.) 40 . . . . .Arkansas Tech 28

Quarterfinals (Nov. 27)

NW Missouri St. 41 . . . . .at N. Colorado 35
Indiana (Pa.) 26. . . . . .at Millersville (Pa.) 21
Northeastern St. (Okla.) 19. . . . . .at UC-Davis 14
at Carson-Newman (Tenn.) 28 . . . . .Catawba (N.C.) 25

Semifinals (Dec. 4)

at Carson-Newman (Tenn.) 42 . . .Northeastern St. (Okla.) 7
at NW Missouri St. 20. . . . . .Indiana (Pa.) 12

Championship Game
Dec. 11 at Florence, Ala. (Att: 8,451)

NW Missouri St. 58 . . . . . 4 OT . . . . .Carson-Newman 52
(14-1)   (13-1)

Division I-AA, II and III Awards

Players of the Year

Payton Award (Div. I-AA) .Adrian Peterson, Ga. Southern, RB
Hill Trophy (Div. II) . .Corte McGuffet, N. Colorado, QB

Gagliardi Trophy (Div. III).Scott Pingel, Westminster (Mo.), WR

Coaches of the Year

AFCA (NCAA Div. I-AA) . . . . .Paul Johnson, Ga. Southern
AFCA (College Div. II) . . .Mel Tjeerdsma, NW Missouri St.
AFCA (College Div. III) . . .Frost Westering, Pacific Lutheran

Division III
First Round (Nov. 20)

Wash. & Jeff. (Pa.) 14 . . . . .at Lycoming (Pa.) 7
at Hardin-Simmons (Tex.) 28. . . . . . . .Washington (Mo.) 21
at W. Maryland 20. . . . . .Catholic (D.C.) 17
at St. John's (Minn.) 23 . . . . .WI-Stevens Point 10
Central (Iowa) 38. . . . . .at WI-La Crosse 17
Pacific Lutheran (Wash.) 28 . . . . . . .at Willamette (Ore.) 24
Ursinus (Pa.) 43 . . . . .at Bridgewater St. (Mass.) 38
Rowan (N.J.) 29. . . . . .at Rensselaer (N.Y.) 10
at Montclair St. (N.J.) 37. . . . . .Buffalo St. (N.Y.) 34
at Wittenberg (Ohio) 42 . . . . .Alma (Mich.) 19
Ohio Northern (Ind.) 56. . . . . at Hanover 14
at Augustana (Ill.) 39 . . . . .St. Norbert (Wisc.) 32

Second Round (Nov. 27)

at Hardin-Simmons 51. . . . . .Wash. & Jeff. 3
at Trinity (Tex.) 20. . . . . .W. Maryland 16
at St. John's 10 . . . . .Central 9
Pacific Lutheran 49. . . . . .at Wartburg (Iowa) 14
at Rowan 55. . . . . .Ursinus 0
Montclair St. 33 . . . . .at W. Connecticut St. 28
Ohio Northern 58 . . . . .at Wittenberg 24
at Mt. Union (Ohio) 42 . . . . .Augustana 33

Quarterfinals (Dec. 4)

at Trinity 40 . . . . .Hardin-Simmons 33
Pacific Lutheran 19 . . . . .at St. John's 9
Rowan 42. . . . . .at Montclair St. 13
at Mt. Union 56 . . . . .Ohio Northern 31

Semifinals (Dec. 11)

Rowan 24. . . . . .at Mt. Union 17
Pacific Lutheran 49 .at Trinity 28

Amos Alonzo Stagg Bowl
Dec. 18 at Salem, Va. (Att: 4,101)

Pacific Lutheran 42 . . . . .Rowan 13
(13-1)   (12-2)

NAIA Playoffs
Division I

NAIA returned to a single division playoff for its football championship in 1997.

First Round (Nov. 20)

at Taylor (Ind.) 38. . . . . .Mo. Valley College 12
at Hastings (Neb.) 45 . . . . .Bethany (Kan.) 23
at Georgetown (Ky.) 38 . . . . .St. Francis (Ind.) 0
at Mary (N.D.) 34 . . . . .Huron (S.D.) 3
at NW Oklahoma St. 44. . . . . .Southwestern (Kan.) 10
Lambuth (Tenn.) 41 . . . . .at McKendree (Ill.) 38
Rocky Mtn. (Mont.) 38 . . . . .at Dickinson St. (N.D.) 32
at Azusa Pacific (Calif.) 31 . . . . .Doane (Neb.) 12

Quarterfinals (Nov. 27)

at Georgetown 55. . . . . .Taylor 3
at Mary 7 . . . . .Rocky Mtn. College 3
at NW Oklahoma St. 56. . . . . .Lambuth 13
at Azusa Pacific 38. . . . . Hastings 35

Semifinals (Dec. 4)

at NW Oklahoma 21 . . . . .Mary 6
Georgetown 66 . . . . .at Azusa Pacific 35

Championship
Dec. 18 at Savannah, Tenn. (Att: 6,000 est.)

NW Oklahoma St. 34 . . . . .Georgetown 26
(13-0)   (13-1)

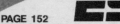
National Champions

Over the last 130 years, there have been 25 major selectors of national champions by way of polls (11), mathematical rating systems (10) and historical research (4). The best-known and most widely circulated of these surveys, the Associated Press poll of sportswriters and broadcasters, first appeared during the 1936 season. Champions prior to 1936 have been determined by retro polls, ratings, and historical research.

The Early Years (1869-1935)

National champions based on the Dickinson mathematical system (DS) and three historical retro polls taken by the College Football Researchers Association (CFRA), the National Championship Foundation (NCF) and the Helms Athletic Foundation (HF). The CFRA and NCF polls start in 1869, college football's inaugural year, while the Helms poll begins in 1883, the first season the game adopted a point system for scoring. Frank Dickinson, an economics professor at Illinois, introduced his system in 1926 and retro-picked winners in 1924 and '25. Bowl game results were counted in the Helms selections, but not in the other three.

Multiple champions: Yale (18); Princeton (17); Harvard (9); Michigan (7); Notre Dame and Penn (4); Alabama, California, Cornell, Illinois, Pittsburgh and USC (3); Georgia Tech, Minnesota and Penn St. (2).

Year		Record	Year		Record	Year		Record
1869	**Princeton**	1-1-0	1880	**Yale** (CFRA)	4-0-1	1891	**Yale**	13-0-0
1870	**Princeton**	1-0-0		& **Princeton** (NCF)	4-0-1	1892	**Yale**	13-0-0
1871	No games played		1881	**Yale**	5-0-1	1893	**Princeton**	11-0-0
1872	**Princeton**	1-0-0	1882	**Yale**	8-0-0	1894	**Yale**	16-0-0
1873	**Princeton**	1-0-0	1883	**Yale**	8-0-0	1895	**Penn**	14-0-0
1874	**Yale**	3-0-0	1884	**Yale**	8-0-1	1896	**Princeton** (CFRA)	10-0-1
1875	**Princeton** (CFRA)	2-0-0	1885	**Princeton**	9-0-0		& **Lafayette** (NCF)	11-0-1
	& **Harvard** (NCF)	4-0-0	1886	**Yale**	9-0-1	1897	**Penn**	15-0-0
1876	**Yale**	3-0-0	1887	**Yale**	9-0-0	1898	**Harvard**	11-0-0
1877	**Yale**	3-0-1	1888	**Yale**	13-0-0	1899	**Princeton** (CFRA)	12-1-0
1878	**Princeton**	6-0-0	1889	**Princeton**	10-0-0		& **Harvard** (NCF, HF)	10-0-1
1879	**Princeton**	4-0-1	1890	**Harvard**	11-0-0			

Year		Record	Bowl Game	Head Coach	Outstanding Player
1900	**Yale**	12-0-0	No bowl	Malcolm McBride	Perry Hale, HB
1901	**Harvard** (CFRA)	12-0-0	No bowl	Bill Reid	Bob Kernan, HB
	& **Michigan** (NCF, HF)	11-0-0	Won Rose	Hurry Up Yost	Neil Snow, E
1902	**Michigan**	11-0-0	No bowl	Hurry Up Yost	Boss Weeks, QB
1903	**Princeton**	11-0-0	No bowl	Art Hillebrand	John DeWitt, G
1904	**Penn** (CFRA, HF)	12-0-0	No bowl	Carl Williams	Andy Smith, FB
	& **Michigan** (NCF)	10-0-0	No bowl	Hurry Up Yost	Willie Heston, HB
1905	**Chicago**	10-0-0	No bowl	Amos Alonzo Stagg	Walter Eckersall, QB
1906	**Princeton**	9-0-1	No bowl	Bill Roper	Cap Wister, E
1907	**Yale**	9-0-1	No bowl	Bill Knox	Tad Jones, HB
1908	**Penn** (CFRA, HF)	11-0-1	No bowl	Sol Metzger	Hunter Scarlett, E
	& **LSU** (NCF)	10-0-0	No bowl	Edgar Wingard	Doc Fenton, QB
1909	**Yale**	12-1-0	No bowl	Howard Jones	Ted Coy, FB
1910	**Harvard** (CFRA, HF)	8-0-1	No bowl	Percy Haughton	Percy Wendell, HB
	& **Pittsburgh** (NCF)	9-0-0	No bowl	Joe Thompson	Ralph Galvin, C
1911	**Princeton** (CFRA, HF)	8-0-2	No bowl	Bill Roper	Sam White, E
	& **Penn St.** (NCF)	8-0-1	No bowl	Bill Hollenback	Dexter Very, E
1912	**Harvard** (CFRA, HF)	9-0-0	No bowl	Percy Haughton	Charley Brickley, HB
	& **Penn St.** (NCF)	8-0-0	No bowl	Bill Hollenback	Dexter Very, E
1913	**Harvard**	9-0-0	No bowl	Percy Haughton	Eddie Mahan, FB
1914	**Army**	9-0-0	No bowl	Charley Daly	John McEwan, C
1915	**Cornell**	9-0-0	No bowl	Al Sharpe	Charley Barrett, QB
1916	**Pittsburgh**	8-0-0	No bowl	Pop Warner	Bob Peck, C
1917	**Georgia Tech**	9-0-0	No bowl	John Heisman	Ev Strupper, HB
1918	**Pittsburgh** (CFRA, HF)	4-1-0	No bowl	Pop Warner	Tom Davies, HB
	& **Michigan** (NCF)	5-0-0	No bowl	Hurry Up Yost	Frank Steketee, FB
1919	**Harvard** (CFRA-tie, HF)	9-0-1	Won Rose	Bob Fisher	Eddie Casey, HB
	Illinois (CFRA-tie)	6-1-0	No bowl	Bob Zuppke	Chuck Carney, E
	& **Notre Dame** (NCF)	9-0-0	No bowl	Knute Rockne	George Gipp, HB
1920	**California**	9-0-0	Won Rose	Andy Smith	Dan McMillan, T

Year		Record	Bowl Game	Head Coach	Outstanding Player
1921	**California** (CFRA)	9-0-1	Tied Rose	Andy Smith	Brick Muller, E
	& **Cornell** (NCF, HF)	8-0-0	No bowl	Gil Dobie	Eddie Kaw, HB
1922	**Princeton** (CFRA)	8-0-0	No bowl	Bill Roper	Herb Treat, T
	California (NCF)	9-0-0	No bowl	Andy Smith	Brick Muller, E
	& **Cornell** (HF)	8-0-0	No bowl	Gil Dobie	Eddie Kaw, HB
1923	**Illinois** (CFRA, HF)	8-0-0	No bowl	Bob Zuppke	Red Grange, HB
	& **Michigan** (NCF)	8-0-0	No bowl	Hurry Up Yost	Jack Blott, C
1924	**Notre Dame**	10-0-0	Won Rose	Knute Rockne	"The Four Horsemen"*
1925	**Alabama** (CFRA, HF)	10-0-0	Won Rose	Wallace Wade	Johnny Mack Brown, HB
	& **Dartmouth** (DS)	8-0-0	No bowl	Jesse Hawley	Swede Oberlander, HB
1926	**Alabama** (CFRA, HF)	9-0-1	Tied Rose	Wallace Wade	Hoyt Winslett, E
	& **Stanford** (DS)	10-0-1	Tied Rose	Pop Warner	Ted Shipkey, E
1927	**Yale** (CFRA)	7-1-0	No bowl	Tad Jones	Bill Webster, G
	& **Illinois** (NCF, HF, DS)	7-0-1	No bowl	Bob Zuppke	Bob Reitsch, C
1928	**Georgia Tech** (CFRA, NCF, HF)	10-0-0	Won Rose	Bill Alexander	Pete Pund, C
	& **USC** (DS)	9-0-1	No bowl	Howard Jones	Jesse Hibbs, T
1929	**Notre Dame**	9-0-0	No bowl	Knute Rockne	Frank Carideo, QB
1930	**Alabama** (CFRA)	10-0-0	Won Rose	Wallace Wade	Fred Sington, T
	& **Notre Dame** (NCF, HF, DS)	10-0-0	No bowl	Knute Rockne	Marchy Schwartz, HB
1931	**USC**	10-1-0	Won Rose	Howard Jones	John Baker, G
1932	**USC** (CFRA, NCF, HF)	10-0-0	Won Rose	Howard Jones	Ernie Smith, T
	& **Michigan** (DS)	8-0-0	No bowl	Harry Kipke	Harry Newman, QB
1933	**Michigan**	8-0-0	No bowl	Harry Kipke	Chuck Bernard, C
1934	**Minnesota**	8-0-0	No bowl	Bernie Bierman	Pug Lund, HB
1935	**Minnesota** (CFRA, NCF, HF)	8-0-0	No bowl	Bernie Bierman	Dick Smith, T
	& **SMU** (DS)	12-1-0	Lost Rose	Matty Bell	Bobby Wilson, HB

*Notre Dame's Four Horsemen were Harry Stuhldreher (QB), Jim Crowley (HB), Don Miller (HB-P) and Elmer Layden (FB).

The Media Poll Years (since 1936)

National champions according to seven media and coaches' polls: Associated Press (since 1936), United Press (1950-57), International News Service (1952-57), United Press International (1958-92), Football Writers Association of America (since 1954), National Football Foundation and Hall of Fame (since 1959 and *USA Today*/CNN (since 1991). In 1991, the American Football Coaches Association switched outlets for its poll from UPI to *USA Today*/CNN and then to *USA Today*/ESPN in 1997.

After 29 years of releasing its final Top 20 poll in early December, AP named its 1965 national champion following that season's bowl games. AP returned to a pre-bowls final vote in 1966 and '67, but has polled its writers and broadcasters after the bowl games since the 1968 season. The FWAA has selected its champion after the bowl games since the 1955 season, the NFF-Hall of Fame since 1971, UPI after 1974, *USA Today*/CNN 1991-96, and *USA Today*/ESPN since 1997.

The Associated Press changed the name of its national championship award from the AP trophy to the Bear Bryant Trophy after the legendary Alabama coach's death in 1983. The Football Writers' trophy is called the Grantland Rice Award (after the celebrated sportswriter) and the NFF-Hall of Fame trophy is called the MacArthur Bowl (in honor of Gen. Douglas MacArthur).

Multiple champions: Notre Dame (9); Alabama (7); Ohio St. and Oklahoma (6); USC and Nebraska (5); Miami-FL and Minnesota (4); Michigan St. and Texas (3); Army, Florida St., Georgia Tech, Michigan, Penn St., Pittsburgh and Tennessee (2).

Year		Record	Bowl Game	Head Coach	Outstanding Player
1936	**Minnesota**	7-1-0	No bowl	Bernie Bierman	Ed Widseth, T
1937	**Pittsburgh**	9-0-1	No bowl	Jock Sutherland	Marshall Goldberg, HB
1938	**TCU**	11-0-0	Won Sugar	Dutch Meyer	Davey O'Brien, QB
1939	**Texas A&M**	11-0-0	Won Sugar	Homer Norton	John Kimbrough, FB
1940	**Minnesota**	8-0-0	No Bowl	Bernie Bierman	George Franck, HB
1941	**Minnesota**	8-0-0	No bowl	Bernie Bierman	Bruce Smith, HB
1942	**Ohio St.**	9-1-0	No bowl	Paul Brown	Gene Fekete, FB
1943	**Notre Dame**	9-1-0	No bowl	Frank Leahy	Angelo Bertelli, QB
1944	**Army**	9-0-0	No bowl	Red Blaik	Glenn Davis, HB
1945	**Army**	9-0-0	No bowl	Red Blaik	Doc Blanchard, FB
1946	**Notre Dame**	8-0-1	No bowl	Frank Leahy	Johnny Lujack, QB
1947	**Notre Dame**	9-0-0	No bowl	Frank Leahy	Johnny Lujack, QB
1948	**Michigan**	9-0-0	No bowl	Bennie Oosterbaan	Dick Rifenburg, E
1949	**Notre Dame**	10-0-0	No bowl	Frank Leahy	Leon Hart, E
1950	**Oklahoma**	10-1-0	Lost Sugar	Bud Wilkinson	Leon Heath, FB
1951	**Tennessee**	10-1-0	Lost Sugar	Bob Neyland	Hank Lauricella, TB
1952	**Michigan St.** (AP, UP)	9-0-0	No bowl	Biggie Munn	Don McAuliffe, HB
	& **Georgia Tech** (INS)	12-0-0	Won Sugar	Bobby Dodd	Hal Miller, T
1953	**Maryland**	10-1-0	Lost Orange	Jim Tatum	Bernie Faloney, QB
1954	**Ohio St.** (AP, INS)	10-0-0	Won Rose	Woody Hayes	Howard Cassady, HB
	& **UCLA** (UP, FW)	9-0-0	No bowl	Red Sanders	Jack Ellena, T
1955	**Oklahoma**	11-0-0	Won Orange	Bud Wilkinson	Jerry Tubbs, C
1956	**Oklahoma**	10-0-0	No bowl	Bud Wilkinson	Tommy McDonald, HB
1957	**Auburn** (AP)	10-0-0	No bowl	Shug Jordan	Jimmy Phillips, E
	& **Ohio St.** (UP, FW, INS)	9-1-0	Won Rose	Woody Hayes	Bob White, FB
1958	**LSU** (AP, UPI)	11-0-0	Won Sugar	Paul Dietzel	Billy Cannon, HB
	& **Iowa** (FW)	8-1-1	Won Rose	Forest Evashevski	Randy Duncan, QB
1959	**Syracuse**	11-0-0	Won Cotton	Ben Schwartzwalder	Ernie Davis, HB

National Champions (Cont.)

Year		Record	Bowl Game	Head Coach	Outstanding Player
1960	**Minnesota** (AP, UPI, NFF) 8-2-0		Lost Rose	Murray Warmath	Tom Brown, G
	& **Mississippi** (FW)................10-0-1		Won Sugar	Johnny Vaught	Jake Gibbs, QB
1961	**Alabama** (AP, UPI, NFF)..........11-0-0		Won Sugar	Bear Bryant	Billy Neighbors, T
	& **Ohio St.** (FW) 8-0-1		No bowl	Woody Hayes	Bob Ferguson, HB
1962	**USC**...........................11-0-0		Won Rose	John McKay	Hal Bedsole, E
1963	**Texas**.........................11-0-0		Won Cotton	Darrell Royal	Scott Appleton, T
1964	**Alabama** (AP, UPI)..............10-1-0		Lost Orange	Bear Bryant	Joe Namath, QB
	Arkansas (FW)..................11-0-0		Won Cotton	Frank Broyles	Ronnie Caveness, LB
	& **Notre Dame** (NFF) 9-1-0		No bowl	Ara Parseghian	John Huarte, QB
1965	**Alabama** (AP, FW-tie)...........9-1-1		Won Orange	Bear Bryant	Paul Crane, C
	& **Michigan St.** (UPI, NFF, FW-tie)..10-1-0		Lost Rose	Duffy Daugherty	George Webster, LB
1966	**Notre Dame** (AP, UPI, FW, NFF-tie)..9-0-1		No bowl	Ara Parseghian	Jim Lynch, LB
	& **Michigan St.** (NFF-tie)..........9-0-1		No bowl	Duffy Daugherty	Bubba Smith, DE
1967	**USC**...........................10-1-0		Won Rose	John McKay	O.J. Simpson, HB
1968	**Ohio St.**.......................10-0-0		Won Rose	Woody Hayes	Rex Kern, QB
1969	**Texas**.........................11-0-0		Won Cotton	Darrell Royal	James Street, QB
1970	**Nebraska** (AP, FW)..............11-0-1		Won Orange	Bob Devaney	Jerry Tagge, QB
	Texas (UPI, NFF-tie), ...10-1-0		Lost Cotton	Darrell Royal	Steve Worster, RB
	& **Ohio St.** (NFF-tie)............9-1-0		Lost Rose	Woody Hayes	Jim Stillwagon, MG
1971	**Nebraska**......................13-0-0		Won Orange	Bob Devaney	Johnny Rodgers, WR
1972	**USC**...........................12-0-0		Won Rose	John McKay	Charles Young, TE
1973	**Notre Dame** (AP, FW, NFF) 11-0-0		Won Sugar	Ara Parseghian	Mike Townsend, DB
	& **Alabama** (UPI)................11-1-0		Lost Sugar	Bear Bryant	Buddy Brown, OT
1974	**Oklahoma** (AP).................11-0-0		No bowl	Barry Switzer	Joe Washington, RB
	& **USC** (UPI, FW, NFF)...........10-1-1		Won Rose	John McKay	Anthony Davis, RB
1975	**Oklahoma**.....................11-1-0		Won Orange	Barry Switzer	Lee Roy Selmon, DE
1976	**Pittsburgh** 12-0-0		Won Sugar	Johnny Majors	Tony Dorsett, RB
1977	**Notre Dame** 11-1-0		Won Cotton	Dan Devine	Ross Browner, DE
1978	**Alabama** (AP, FW, NFF) 11-1-0		Won Sugar	Bear Bryant	Marty Lyons, DT
	& **USC** (UPI) 12-1-0		Won Rose	John Robinson	Charles White, RB
1979	**Alabama** 12-0-0		Won Sugar	Bear Bryant	Jim Bunch, OT
1980	**Georgia** 12-0-0		Won Sugar	Vince Dooley	Herschel Walker, RB
1981	**Clemson** 12-0-0		Won Orange	Danny Ford	Jeff Davis, LB
1982	**Penn St.** 11-1-0		Won Sugar	Joe Paterno	Todd Blackledge, QB
1983	**Miami-FL** 11-1-0		Won Orange	H. Schnellenberger	Bernie Kosar, QB
1984	**BYU**..........................13-0-0		Won Holiday	LaVell Edwards	Robbie Bosco, QB
1985	**Oklahoma** 11-1-0		Won Orange	Barry Switzer	Brian Bosworth, LB
1986	**Penn St.** 12-0-0		Won Fiesta	Joe Paterno	D.J. Dozier, RB
1987	**Miami-FL** 12-0-0		Won Orange	Jimmy Johnson	Steve Walsh, QB
1988	**Notre Dame** 12-0-0		Won Fiesta	Lou Holtz	Tony Rice, QB
1989	**Miami-FL** 11-1-0		Won Sugar	Dennis Erickson	Craig Erickson, QB
1990	**Colorado** (AP, FW, NFF)..........11-1-1		Won Orange	Bill McCartney	Eric Bieniemy, RB
	& **Georgia Tech** (UPI)...........11-0-1		Won Citrus	Bobby Ross	Shawn Jones, QB
1991	**Miami-FL** (AP) 12-0-0		Won Orange	Dennis Erickson	Gino Torretta, QB
	& **Washington** (USA, FW, NFF)....12-0-0		Won Rose	Don James	Steve Emtman, DT
1992	**Alabama** 13-0-0		Won Sugar	Gene Stallings	Eric Curry, DE
1993	**Florida St.** 12-1-0		Won Orange	Bobby Bowden	Charlie Ward, QB
1994	**Nebraska**......................13-0-0		Won Orange	Tom Osborne	Zach Wiegert, OT
1995	**Nebraska** 12-0-0		Won Fiesta	Tom Osborne	Tommie Frazier, QB
1996	**Florida** 12-1*		Won Sugar	Steve Spurrier	Danny Wuerffel, QB
1997	**Michigan** (AP, FW, NFF) 12-0		Won Rose	Lloyd Carr	Charles Woodson, DB
	& **Nebraska** (ESPN/USA).........13-0		Won Orange	Tom Osborne	Ahman Green, RB
1998	**Tennessee** 13-0		Won Fiesta	Phillip Fulmer	Peerless Price, WR
1999	**Florida St.** 12-0		Won Sugar	Bobby Bowden	Peter Warrick, WR

*The NCAA instituted overtime for regular season games in 1996.

Number 1 vs. Number 2

Since the Associated Press writers poll started keeping track of such things in 1936, the No. 1 and No. 2 ranked teams in the country have met 33 times; 20 during the regular season and 13 in bowl games. Since the first showdown in 1943, the No. 1 team has beaten the No. 2 team 21 times, lost 10 and there have been two ties. Each showdown is listed below with the date, the match-up, each team's record going into the game, the final score, the stadium and site.

Date	Match-up		Stadium	Date	Match-up		Stadium
Oct. 9 1943	#1 Notre Dame (2-0)	35	Michigan	1944	#2 Navy (6-2)	7	(Baltimore)
	#2 Michigan (3-0)	12	(Ann Arbor)	Nov. 10 1945	#1 Army (6-0)	48	Yankee
Nov. 20 1943	#1 Notre Dame (8-0)	14	Notre Dame		#2 Notre Dame (5-0-1)	0	(New York)
	#2 Iowa Pre-Flight (8-0)	13	(South Bend)	Dec. 1 1945	#1 Army (8-0)	32	Municipal
Dec. 2	#1 Army (8-0)	23	Municipal		#2 Navy (7-0-1)	13	(Philadelphia)

Date	Match-up		Stadium
Nov. 9 1946	#1 Army (7-0)	0	Yankee (New York)
	#2 Notre Dame (5-0)	0	
Jan. 1 1963	#1 USC (10-0)	42	ROSE BOWL (Pasadena)
	#2 Wisconsin (8-1)	37	
Oct. 12 1963	#2 Texas (3-0)	28	Cotton Bowl (Dallas)
	#1 Oklahoma (2-0)	7	
Jan. 1 1964	#1 Texas (10-0)	28	COTTON BOWL (Dallas)
	#2 Navy (9-1)	6	
Nov. 19 1966	#1 Notre Dame (8-0)	10	Spartan (East Lansing)
	#2 Michigan St. (9-0)	10	
Sept. 28 1968	#1 Purdue (1-0)	37	Notre Dame (South Bend)
	#2 Notre Dame (1-0)	22	
Jan. 1 1969	#1 Ohio St. (9-0)	27	ROSE BOWL (Pasadena)
	#2 USC (9-0-1)	16	
Dec. 6 1969	#1 Texas (9-0)	15	Razorback (Fayetteville)
	#2 Arkansas (9-0)	14	
Nov. 25 1971	#1 Nebraska (10-0)	35	Owen Field (Norman)
	#2 Oklahoma (9-0)	31	
Jan. 1 1972	#1 Nebraska (12-0)	38	ORANGE BOWL (Miami)
	#2 Alabama (11-0)	6	
Jan. 1 1979	#2 Alabama (10-1)	14	SUGAR BOWL (New Orleans)
	#1 Penn St. (11-0)	7	
Sept. 26 1981	#1 USC (2-0)	28	Coliseum (Los Angeles)
	#2 Oklahoma (1-0)	24	
Jan. 1 1983	#2 Penn St. (10-1)	27	SUGAR BOWL (New Orleans)
	#1 Georgia (11-0)	23	
Oct. 19 1985	#1 Iowa (5-0)	12	Kinnick (Iowa City)
	#2 Michigan (5-0)	10	

Date	Match-up		Stadium
Sept. 27 1986	#2 Miami-FL (3-0)	28	Orange Bowl (Miami)
	#1 Oklahoma (2-0)	16	
Jan. 2 1987	#1 Penn St. (11-0)	14	FIESTA BOWL (Tempe)
	#2 Miami-FL (11-0)	10	
Nov. 21 1987	#2 Oklahoma (10-0)	17	Memorial (Lincoln)
	#1 Nebraska (10-0)	7	
Jan. 1 1988	#2 Miami-FL (11-0)	20	ORANGE BOWL (Miami)
	#1 Oklahoma (11-0)	14	
Nov. 26 1988	#1 Notre Dame (10-0)	27	Coliseum (Los Angeles)
	#2 USC (10-0)	10	
Sept. 16 1989	#1 Notre Dame (1-0)	24	Michigan (Ann Arbor)
	#2 Michigan (0-0)	19	
Nov. 16 1991	#2 Miami-FL (8-0)	17	Doak Campbell (Tallahassee)
	#1 Florida St. (10-0)	16	
Jan. 1 1993	#2 Alabama (12-0)	34	SUGAR BOWL (New Orleans)
	#1 Miama-FL (11-0)	13	
Nov. 13 1993	#2 Notre Dame (9-0)	31	Notre Dame (South Bend)
	#1 Florida St. (9-0)	24	
Jan. 1 1994	#1 Florida St. (11-1)	18	ORANGE BOWL (Miami)
	#2 Nebraska (11-0)	16	
Jan. 2 1996	#1 Nebraska (11-0)	62	FIESTA BOWL (Tempe)
	#2 Florida (12-0)	24	
Nov. 30 1996	#2 Florida St. (10-0)	24	Doak Campbell (Tallahassee)
	#1 Florida (10-1)	21	
Jan. 4 1999	#1 Tennessee (12-0)	23	FIESTA BOWL (Tempe)
	#2 Florida St. (11-1)	16	
Jan. 4 2000	#1 Florida St. (11-0)	46	SUGAR BOWL (New Orleans)
	#2 Virginia Tech (11-0)	29	

Top 50 Rivalries

Top Division I-A and I-AA series records, including games through the 1999 season. All rivalries listed below are renewed annually with the following exceptions. **LSU-Tulane** stopped playing in 1996 but have made plans to renew rivalry no later than 2001. **Nebraska-Oklahoma** now play only when matched up as part of the rotating Big 12 schedule.

RECENTLY DISCONTINUED SERIES: **Baylor vs TCU** in 1995 after 102 games (Baylor ahead 48-47-7); **Florida vs Miami-FL** in 1991 after 49 games (Florida ahead, 25-24); **Miami-FL vs Notre Dame** in 1990 after 23 games (ND ahead, 15-7-1).

	Gm	Series Leader		Gm	Series Leader
Air Force-Army	34	Air Force (21-12-1)	**Michigan-Notre Dame**	29	Michigan (17-11-1)
Air Force-Navy	32	Air Force (22-10-0)	**Michigan-Ohio St.**	96	Michigan (55-35-6)
Alabama-Auburn	64	Alabama (37-26-1)	**Minnesota-Wisconsin**	109	Minnesota (57-44-8)
Alabama-Tennessee	82	Alabama (42-33-7)	**Mississippi-Miss. St.**	96	Ole Miss (54-36-6)
Arizona-Arizona St.	73	Arizona (42-30-1)	**Missouri-Kansas**	108	Missouri (50-49-9)
Army-Navy	100	Army (48-45-7)	**Nebraska-Oklahoma**	78	Oklahoma (39-36-3)
Auburn-Georgia	103	Auburn (49-46-8)	**N. Mexico-N. Mexico St.**	89	New Mexico (57-27-5)
California-Stanford	102	Stanford (52-39-11)	**N. Carolina-N.C. State**	89	N. Carolina (59-24-6)
The Citadel-VMI	59	The Citadel (29-28-2)	**Notre Dame-Purdue**	71	Notre Dame (46-23-2)
Clemson-S. Carolina	97	Clemson (58-35-4)	**Notre Dame-USC**	71	Notre Dame (40-26-5)
Colorado-Nebraska	58	Nebraska (42-14-2)	**Oklahoma-Okla. St.**	94	Oklahoma (73-14-7)
Colo. St.-Wyoming	89	Colorado St. (46-38-5)	**Oregon-Oregon St.**	103	Oregon (52-41-10)
Duke-N. Carolina	85	N. Carolina (46-35-4)	**Penn-Cornell**	106	Penn (60-41-5)
Florida-Florida St.	44	Florida (26-16-2)	**Penn St.-Pittsburgh**	95	Penn St. (50-41-4)
Florida-Georgia	78	Georgia (46-30-2)	**Pittsburgh-West Va**	92	Pitt (56-33-3)
Florida St.-Miami,FL	43	Miami (23-20-0)	**Princeton-Yale**	122	Yale (66-46-10)
Georgia-Georgia Tech	94	Georgia (52-37-5)	**Purdue-Indiana**	102	Purdue (62-34-6)
Grambling-Southern	48	Southern (25-23-0)	**Richmond-Wm. & Mary**	109	Wm. & Mary (56-48-5)
Harvard-Yale	116	Yale (63-45-8)	**Tennessee-Vanderbilt**	93	Tennessee (62-26-5)
Kansas-Kansas St.	97	Kansas (61-31-5)	**Texas-Oklahoma**	94	Texas (55-34-5)
Kentucky-Tennessee	95	Tennessee (63-23-9)	**Texas-Texas A&M**	106	Texas (67-34-5)
Lafayette-Lehigh	135	Lafayette (71-59-5)	**UCLA-USC**	69	USC (35-27-7)
LSU-Tulane	93	LSU (64-22-7)*	**Utah-BYU**	75	Utah (45-26-4)
Miami,OH-Cincinnati	104	Miami (55-42-7)	**Utah-Utah St.**	97	Utah (64-29-4)
Michigan-Michigan St.	92	Michigan (60-27-5)	**Washington-Wash. St.**	92	Washington (60-26-6)

*Disputed series record: Tulane claims LSU leads 61-23-7

Associated Press Final Polls

The Associated Press introduced its weekly college football poll of sportswriters (later, sportswriters and broadcasters) in 1936. The final AP poll was released at the end of the regular season until 1965, when bowl results were included for one year. After a two-year return to regular season games only, the final poll has come out after the bowls since 1968. Starting in 1989, the AP Poll has ranked 25 teams.

1936

Final poll released Nov. 30. Top 20 regular season results after that: **Dec. 5**–#8 Notre Dame tied USC, 13-13; #17 Tennessee tied Ole Miss, 0-0; #18 Arkansas over Texas, 6-0. **Dec. 12**–#16 TCU over #6 Santa Clara, 9-0.

		As of Nov. 30	Head Coach	After Bowls
1	Minnesota	7-1-0	Bernie Bierman	same
2	LSU	9-0-1	Bernie Moore	9-1-1
3	Pittsburgh	7-1-1	Jock Sutherland	8-1-1
4	Alabama	8-0-1	Frank Thomas	same
5	Washington	7-1-1	Jimmy Phelan	7-2-1
6	Santa Clara	7-0-0	Buck Shaw	8-1-0
7	Northwestern	7-1-0	Pappy Waldorf	same
8	Notre Dame	6-2-0	Elmer Layden	6-2-1
9	Nebraska	7-2-0	Dana X. Bible	same
10	Penn	7-1-0	Harvey Harman	same
11	Duke	9-1-0	Wallace Wade	same
12	Yale	7-1-0	Ducky Pond	same
13	Dartmouth	7-1-1	Red Blaik	same
14	Duquesne	7-2-0	John Smith	8-2-0
15	Fordham	5-1-2	Jim Crowley	same
16	TCU	7-2-2	Dutch Meyer	9-2-2
17	Tennessee	6-2-1	Bob Neyland	6-2-2
18	Arkansas	6-3-0	Fred Thomsen	7-3-0
	Navy	6-3-0	Tom Hamilton	same
20	Marquette	7-1-0	Frank Murray	7-2-0

Key Bowl Games
Sugar–#6 Santa Clara over #2 LSU, 21-14; **Rose**– #3 Pitt over #5 Washington, 21-0; **Orange**–#14 Duquesne over Mississippi St., 13-12; **Cotton**–#16 TCU over #20 Marquette, 16-6.

1937

Final poll released Nov. 29. Top 20 regular season results after that: **Dec. 4**–#18 Rice over SMU, 15-7.

		As of Nov. 29	Head Coach	After Bowls
1	Pittsburgh	9-0-1	Jock Sutherland	same
2	California	9-0-1	Stub Allison	10-0-1
3	Fordham	7-0-1	Jim Crowley	same
4	Alabama	9-0-0	Frank Thomas	9-1-0
5	Minnesota	6-2-0	Bernie Bierman	same
6	Villanova	8-0-1	Clipper Smith	same
7	Dartmouth	7-0-2	Red Blaik	same
8	LSU	9-1-0	Bernie Moore	9-2-0
9	Notre Dame	6-2-1	Elmer Layden	same
	Santa Clara	8-0-0	Buck Shaw	9-0-0
11	Nebraska	6-1-2	Biff Jones	same
12	Yale	6-1-1	Ducky Pond	same
13	Ohio St.	6-2-0	Francis Schmidt	same
14	Holy Cross	8-0-2	Eddie Anderson	same
	Arkansas	6-2-2	Fred Thomsen	same
16	TCU	4-2-2	Dutch Meyer	same
17	Colorado	8-0-0	Bunnie Oakes	8-1-0
18	Rice	4-3-2	Jimmy Kitts	6-3-2
19	North Carolina	7-1-1	Ray Wolf	same
20	Duke	7-2-1	Wallace Wade	same

Key Bowl Games
Rose–#2 Cal over #4 Alabama, 13-0; **Sugar**–#9 Santa Clara over #8 LSU, 6-0; **Cotton**–#18 Rice over #17 Colorado, 28-14; **Orange**–Auburn over Michigan St., 6-0.

1938

Final poll released Dec. 5. Top 20 regular season results after that: **Dec. 26**–#14 Cal over Georgia Tech, 13-7.

		As of Dec. 5	Head Coach	After Bowls
1	TCU	10-0-0	Dutch Meyer	11-0-0
2	Tennessee	10-0-0	Bob Neyland	11-0-0
3	Duke	9-0-0	Wallace Wade	9-1-0
4	Oklahoma	10-0-0	Tom Stidham	10-1-0
5	Notre Dame	8-1-0	Elmer Layden	same
6	Carnegie Tech	7-1-0	Bill Kern	7-2-0
7	USC	8-2-0	Howard Jones	9-2-0
8	Pittsburgh	8-2-0	Jock Sutherland	same
9	Holy Cross	8-1-0	Eddie Anderson	same
10	Minnesota	6-2-0	Bernie Bierman	same
11	Texas Tech	10-0-0	Pete Cawthon	10-1-0
12	Cornell	5-1-1	Carl Snavely	same
13	Alabama	7-1-1	Frank Thomas	same
14	California	9-1-0	Stub Allison	10-1-0
15	Fordham	6-1-2	Jim Crowley	same
16	Michigan	6-1-1	Fritz Crisler	same
17	Northwestern	4-2-2	Pappy Waldorf	same
18	Villanova	8-0-1	Clipper Smith	same
19	Tulane	7-2-1	Red Dawson	same
20	Dartmouth	7-2-0	Red Blaik	same

Key Bowl Games
Sugar–#1 TCU over #6 Carnegie Tech, 15-7; **Orange**–#2 Tennessee over #4 Oklahoma, 17-0; **Rose**–#7 USC over #3 Duke, 7-3; **Cotton**–St. Mary's over #11 Texas Tech 20-13.

1939

Final poll released Dec. 11. Top 20 regular season results after that: None.

		As of Dec. 11	Head Coach	After Bowls
1	Texas A&M	10-0-0	Homer Norton	11-0-0
2	Tennessee	10-0-0	Bob Neyland	10-1-0
3	USC	7-0-2	Howard Jones	8-0-2
4	Cornell	8-0-0	Carl Snavely	same
5	Tulane	8-0-1	Red Dawson	8-1-1
6	Missouri	8-1-0	Don Faurot	8-2-0
7	UCLA	6-0-4	Babe Horrell	same
8	Duke	8-1-0	Wallace Wade	same
9	Iowa	6-1-1	Eddie Anderson	same
10	Duquesne	8-0-1	Buff Donelli	same
11	Boston College	9-1-0	Frank Leahy	9-2-0
12	Clemson	8-1-0	Jess Neely	9-1-0
13	Notre Dame	7-2-0	Elmer Layden	same
14	Santa Clara	5-1-3	Buck Shaw	same
15	Ohio St.	6-2-0	Francis Schmidt	same
16	Georgia Tech	7-2-0	Bill Alexander	8-2-0
17	Fordham	6-2-0	Jim Crowley	same
18	Nebraska	7-1-1	Biff Jones	same
19	Oklahoma	6-2-1	Tom Stidham	same
20	Michigan	6-2-0	Fritz Crisler	same

Key Bowl Games
Sugar–#1 Texas A&M over #5 Tulane, 14-13; **Rose**–#3 USC over #2 Tennessee, 14-0; **Orange**–#16 Georgia Tech over #6 Missouri, 21-7; **Cotton**–#12 Clemson over #11 Boston College, 6-3.

1940

Final poll released Dec. 2. Top 20 regular season results after that: **Dec. 7**–#16 SMU over Rice, 7-6.

		As of Dec. 2	Head Coach	After Bowls
1	Minnesota	8-0-0	Bernie Bierman	same
2	Stanford	9-0-0	Clark Shaughnessy	10-0-0
3	Michigan	7-1-0	Fritz Crisler	same
4	Tennessee	10-0-0	Bob Neyland	10-1-0
5	Boston College	10-0-0	Frank Leahy	11-0-0
6	Texas A&M	8-1-0	Homer Norton	9-1-0
7	Nebraska	8-1-0	Biff Jones	8-2-0
8	Northwestern	6-2-0	Pappy Waldorf	same
9	Mississippi St.	9-0-1	Allyn McKeen	10-0-1
10	Washington	7-2-0	Jimmy Phelan	same
11	Santa Clara	6-1-1	Buck Shaw	same
12	Fordham	7-1-0	Jim Crowley	7-2-0
13	Georgetown	8-1-0	Jack Hagerty	8-2-0
14	Penn	6-1-1	George Munger	same
15	Cornell	6-2-0	Carl Snavely	same
16	SMU	7-1-1	Matty Bell	8-1-1
17	Hardin-Simmons	9-0-0	Warren Woodson	same
18	Duke	7-2-0	Wallace Wade	same
19	Lafayette	9-0-0	Hooks Mylin	same
20	–			

Note: Only 19 teams ranked.

Key Bowl Games

Rose–#2 Stanford over #7 Nebraska, 21-13; **Sugar**– #5 Boston College over #4 Tennessee, 19-13; **Cotton**–#6 Texas A&M over #12 Fordham, 13-12; **Orange**–#9 Mississippi St. over #13 Georgetown, 14-7.

1941

Final poll released Dec. 1. Top 20 regular season results after that: **Dec. 6**–#4 Texas over Oregon, 71-7; #9 Texas A&M over #19 Washington St., 7-0; #16 Mississippi St. over San Francisco, 26-13.

		As of Dec. 1	Head Coach	After Bowls
1	Minnesota	8-0-0	Bernie Bierman	same
2	Duke	9-0-0	Wallace Wade	9-1-0
3	Notre Dame	8-0-1	Frank Leahy	same
4	Texas	7-1-1	Dana X. Bible	8-1-1
5	Michigan	6-1-1	Fritz Crisler	same
6	Fordham	7-1-0	Jim Crowley	8-1-0
7	Missouri	8-1-0	Don Faurot	8-2-0
8	Duquesne	8-0-0	Buff Donelli	same
9	Texas A&M	8-1-0	Homer Norton	9-2-0
10	Navy	7-1-1	Swede Larson	same
11	Northwestern	5-3-0	Pappy Waldorf	same
12	Oregon St.	7-2-0	Lon Stiner	8-2-0
13	Ohio St.	6-1-1	Paul Brown	same
14	Georgia	8-1-1	Wally Butts	9-1-1
15	Penn	7-1-1	George Munger	same
16	Mississippi St.	7-1-1	Allyn McKeen	8-1-1
17	Mississippi	6-2-1	Harry Mehre	same
18	Tennessee	8-2-0	John Barnhill	same
19	Washington St.	6-3-0	Babe Hollingbery	6-4-0
20	Alabama	8-2-0	Frank Thomas	9-2-0

Note: 1942 Rose Bowl moved to Durham, N.C., for one year after outbreak of World War II.

Key Bowl Games

Rose–#12 Oregon St. over #2 Duke, 20-16; **Sugar**– #6 Fordham over #7 Missouri, 2-0; **Cotton**–#20 Alabama over #9 Texas A&M, 29-21; **Orange**–#14 Georgia over TCU, 40-26.

1942

Final poll released Nov. 30. Top 20 regular season results after that: **Dec. 5**–#6 Notre Dame tied Great Lakes Naval Station, 13-13; #13 UCLA over Idaho, 40-13; #14 William & Mary over Oklahoma, 14-7; #17 Washington St. lost to Texas A&M, 21-0; #18 Mississippi St. over San Francisco, 19-7. **Dec. 12**–#13 UCLA over USC, 14-7.

		As of Nov. 30	Head Coach	After Bowls
1	Ohio St.	9-1-0	Paul Brown	same
2	Georgia	10-1-0	Wally Butts	11-1-0
3	Wisconsin	8-1-1	Harry Stuhldreher	same
4	Tulsa	10-0-0	Henry Frnka	10-1-0
5	Georgia Tech	9-1-0	Bill Alexander	9-2-0
6	Notre Dame	7-2-1	Frank Leahy	7-2-2
7	Tennessee	8-1-1	John Barnhill	9-1-1
8	Boston College	8-1-0	Denny Myers	8-2-0
9	Michigan	7-3-0	Fritz Crisler	same
10	Alabama	7-3-0	Frank Thomas	8-3-0
11	Texas	8-2-0	Dana X. Bible	9-2-0
12	Stanford	6-4-0	Marchie Schwartz	same
13	UCLA	5-3-0	Babe Horrell	7-4-0
14	William & Mary	8-1-1	Carl Voyles	9-1-1
15	Santa Clara	7-2-0	Buck Shaw	same
16	Auburn	6-4-1	Jack Meagher	same
17	Washington St.	6-1-2	Babe Hollingbery	6-2-2
18	Mississippi St.	7-2-0	Allyn McKeen	8-2-0
19	Minnesota	5-4-0	George Hauser	same
	Holy Cross	5-4-1	Ank Scanlon	same
	Penn St.	6-1-1	Bob Higgins	same

Key Bowl Games

Rose–#2 Georgia over #13 UCLA, 9-0; **Sugar**–#7 Tennessee over #4 Tulsa, 14-7; **Cotton**–#11 Texas over #5 Georgia Tech, 14-7; **Orange**–#10 Alabama over #8 Boston College, 37-21.

1943

Final poll released Nov. 29. Top 20 regular season results after that: **Dec.11**–#10 March Field over #19 Pacific, 19-0.

		As of Nov. 29	Head Coach	After Bowls
1	Notre Dame	9-1-0	Frank Leahy	same
2	Iowa Pre-Flight	9-1-0	Don Faurot	same
3	Michigan	8-1-0	Fritz Crisler	same
4	Navy	8-1-0	Billick Whelchel	same
5	Purdue	9-0-0	Elmer Burnham	same
6	Great Lakes Naval Station	10-2-0	Tony Hinkle	same
7	Duke	8-1-0	Eddie Cameron	same
8	DelMonte Pre-Flight	7-1-0	Bill Kern	same
9	Northwestern	6-2-0	Pappy Waldorf	same
10	March Field	8-1-0	Paul Schissler	9-1-0
11	Army	7-2-1	Red Blaik	same
12	Washington	4-0-0	Ralph Welch	4-1-0
13	Georgia Tech	7-3-0	Bill Alexander	8-3-0
14	Texas	7-1-0	Dana X. Bible	7-1-1
15	Tulsa	6-0-1	Henry Frnka	6-1-1
16	Dartmouth	6-1-0	Earl Brown	same
17	Bainbridge Navy Training School	7-0-0	Joe Maniaci	same
18	Colorado College	7-0-0	Hal White	same
19	Pacific	7-1-0	Amos A. Stagg	7-2-0
20	Penn	6-2-1	George Munger	same

Key Bowl Games

Rose–USC over #12 Washington, 29-0; **Sugar**–#13 Georgia Tech over #15 Tulsa, 20-18; **Cotton**–#14 Texas tied Randolph Field, 7-7; **Orange**–LSU over Texas A&M, 19-14.

Associated Press Final Polls (Cont.)

1944

Final poll released Dec. 4. Top 20 regular season results after that: **Dec. 10**–#3 Randolph Field over #10 March Field, 20-7; #18 Fort Pierce over Kessler Field, 34-7; Morris Field over #20 Second Air Force, 14-7.

	As of Dec. 4	Head Coach	After Bowls
1 Army	9-0-0	Red Blaik	same
2 Ohio St.	9-0-0	Carroll Widdoes	same
3 Randolph Field	10-0-0	Frank Tritico	12-0-0
4 Navy	6-3-0	Oscar Hagberg	same
5 Bainbridge Navy Training School	10-0-0	Joe Maniaci	same
6 Iowa Pre-Flight	10-1-0	Jack Meagher	same
7 USC	7-0-2	Jeff Cravath	8-0-2
8 Michigan	8-2-0	Fritz Crisler	same
9 Notre Dame	8-2-0	Ed McKeever	same
10 March Field	7-0-2	Paul Schissler	7-1-2
11 Duke	5-4-0	Eddie Cameron	6-4-0
12 Tennessee	7-0-1	John Barnhill	7-1-1
13 Georgia Tech	8-2-0	Bill Alexander	8-3-0
14 Norman Pre-Flight	6-0-0	John Gregg	same
15 Illinois	5-4-1	Ray Eliot	same
16 El Toro Marines	8-1-0	Dick Hanley	same
17 Great Lakes Naval Station	9-2-1	Paul Brown	same
18 Fort Pierce	8-0-0	Hamp Pool	9-0-0
19 St. Mary's Pre-Flight	4-4-0	Jules Sikes	same
20 Second Air Force	10-2-1	Bill Reese	10-4-1

Key Bowl Games

Treasury–#3 Randolph Field over #20 Second Air Force, 13-6; **Rose**–#7 USC over #12 Tennessee, 25-0; **Sugar**–#11 Duke over Alabama, 29-26; **Orange**–Tulsa over #13 Georgia Tech, 26-12; **Cotton**–Oklahoma A&M over TCU, 34-0.

1945

Final poll released Dec. 3. Top 20 regular season results after that: None.

	As of Dec. 3	Head Coach	After Bowls
1 Army	9-0-0	Red Blaik	same
2 Alabama	9-0-0	Frank Thomas	10-0-0
3 Navy	7-1-1	Oscar Hagberg	same
4 Indiana	9-0-1	Bo McMillan	same
5 Oklahoma A&M	8-0-0	Jim Lookabaugh	9-0-0
6 Michigan	7-3-0	Fritz Crisler	same
7 St. Mary's-CA	7-1-0	Jimmy Phelan	7-2-0
8 Penn	6-2-0	George Munger	same
9 Notre Dame	7-2-1	Hugh Devore	same
10 Texas	9-1-0	Dana X. Bible	10-1-0
11 USC	7-3-0	Jeff Cravath	7-4-0
12 Ohio St.	7-2-0	Carroll Widdoes	same
13 Duke	6-2-0	Eddie Cameron	same
14 Tennessee	8-1-0	John Barnhill	same
15 LSU	7-2-0	Bernie Moore	same
16 Holy Cross	8-1-0	John DeGrosa	8-2-0
17 Tulsa	8-2-0	Henry Frnka	8-3-0
18 Georgia	8-2-0	Wally Butts	9-2-0
19 Wake Forest	4-3-1	Peahead Walker	5-3-1
20 Columbia	8-1-0	Lou Little	same

Key Bowl Games

Rose–#2 Alabama over #11 USC, 34-14; **Sugar**–#5 Oklahoma A&M over #7 St. Mary's, 33-13; **Cotton**–#10 Texas over Missouri, 40-27; **Orange**–Miami-FL over #16 Holy Cross, 13-6.

1946

Final poll released Dec. 2. Top 20 regular season results after that: None.

	As of Dec. 2	Head Coach	After Bowls
1 Notre Dame	8-0-1	Frank Leahy	same
2 Army	9-0-1	Red Blaik	same
3 Georgia	10-0-0	Wally Butts	11-0-0
4 UCLA	10-0-0	Bert LaBrucherie	10-1-0
5 Illinois	7-2-0	Ray Eliot	8-2-0
6 Michigan	6-2-1	Fritz Crisler	same
7 Tennessee	9-1-0	Bob Neyland	9-2-0
8 LSU	9-1-0	Bernie Moore	9-1-1
9 North Carolina	8-1-1	Carl Snavely	8-2-1
10 Rice	8-2-0	Jess Neely	9-2-0
11 Georgia Tech	8-2-0	Bobby Dodd	9-2-0
12 Yale	7-1-1	Howard Odell	same
13 Penn	6-2-0	George Munger	same
14 Oklahoma	7-3-0	Jim Tatum	8-3-0
15 Texas	8-2-0	Dana X. Bible	same
16 Arkansas	6-3-1	John Barnhill	6-3-2
17 Tulsa	9-1-0	J.O. Brothers	same
18 N.C. State	8-2-0	Beattie Feathers	8-3-0
19 Delaware	9-0-0	Bill Murray	10-0-0
20 Indiana	6-3-0	Bo McMillan	same

Key Bowl Games

Sugar–#3 Georgia over #9 N. Carolina, 20-10; **Rose**–#5 Illinois over #4 UCLA, 45-14; **Orange**–#10 Rice over #7 Tennessee, 8-0; **Cotton**–#8 LSU tied #16 Arkansas, 0-0.

1947

Final poll released Dec. 8. Top 20 regular season results after that: None.

	As of Dec. 8	Head Coach	After Bowls
1 Notre Dame	9-0-0	Frank Leahy	same
2 Michigan	9-0-0	Fritz Crisler	10-0-0
3 SMU	9-0-1	Matty Bell	9-0-2
4 Penn St.	9-0-0	Bob Higgins	9-0-1
5 Texas	9-1-0	Blair Cherry	10-1-0
6 Alabama	8-2-0	Red Drew	8-3-0
7 Penn	7-0-1	George Munger	same
8 USC	7-1-1	Jeff Cravath	7-2-1
9 North Carolina	8-2-0	Carl Snavely	same
10 Georgia Tech	9-1-0	Bobby Dodd	10-1-0
11 Army	5-2-2	Red Blaik	same
12 Kansas	8-0-2	George Sauer	8-1-2
13 Mississippi	8-2-0	Johnny Vaught	9-2-0
14 William & Mary	9-1-0	Rube McCray	9-2-0
15 California	9-1-0	Pappy Waldorf	same
16 Oklahoma	7-2-1	Bud Wilkinson	same
17 N.C. State	5-3-1	Beattie Feathers	same
18 Rice	6-3-1	Jess Neely	same
19 Duke	4-3-2	Wallace Wade	same
20 Columbia	7-2-0	Lou Little	same

Key Bowl Games

Rose–#2 Michigan over #8 USC, 49-0; **Cotton**–#3 SMU tied #4 Penn St., 13-13; **Sugar**–#5 Texas over #6 Alabama, 27-7; **Orange**–#10 Georgia Tech over #12 Kansas, 20-14.

Note: An unprecedented "Who's No. 1?" poll was conducted by AP after the Rose Bowl game, pitting Notre Dame against Michigan. The Wolverines won the vote, 226-119, but AP ruled that the Irish would be the No. 1 team of record. For more information see the box on page 169.

1948

Final poll released Nov. 29. Top 20 regular season results after that: **Dec. 3**–#12 Vanderbilt over Miami-FL, 33-6. **Dec. 4**–#2 Notre Dame tied USC, 14-14; #11 Clemson over The Citadel, 20-0.

	As of Nov. 29	Head Coach	After Bowls
1	Michigan 9-0-0	Bennie Oosterbaan	same
2	Notre Dame 9-0-0	Frank Leahy	9-0-1
3	North Carolina . . .9-0-1	Carl Snavely	9-1-1
4	California 10-0-0	Pappy Waldorf	10-1-0
5	Oklahoma 9-1-0	Bud Wilkinson	10-1-0
6	Army 8-0-1	Red Blaik	same
7	Northwestern 7-2-0	Bob Voigts	8-2-0
8	Georgia 9-1-0	Wally Butts	9-2-0
9	Oregon 9-1-0	Jim Aiken	9-2-0
10	SMU 8-1-1	Matty Bell	9-1-1
11	Clemson 9-0-0	Frank Howard	11-0-0
12	Vanderbilt 7-2-1	Red Sanders	8-2-1
13	Tulane 9-1-0	Henry Frnka	same
14	Michigan St. 6-2-2	Biggie Munn	same
15	Mississippi 8-1-0	Johnny Vaught	same
16	Minnesota 7-2-0	Bernie Bierman	same
17	William & Mary . .6-2-2	Rube McCray	7-2-2
18	Penn St. 7-1-1	Bob Higgins	same
19	Cornell 8-1-0	Lefty James	same
20	Wake Forest 6-3-0	Peahead Walker	6-4-0

Note: Big Nine "no-repeat" rule kept Michigan from Rose Bowl.

Key Bowl Games

Sugar–#5 Oklahoma over #3 North Carolina, 14-6; **Rose**–#7 Northwestern over #4 Cal, 20-14; **Orange**–Texas over #8 Georgia, 41-28; **Cotton**–#10 SMU over #9 Oregon, 21-13.

1949

Final poll released Nov. 28. Top 20 regular season results after that: **Dec. 2**–#14 Maryland over Miami-FL, 13-0. **Dec. 3**–#1 Notre Dame over SMU, 27-20; #10 Pacific over Hawaii, 75-0.

	As of Nov. 28	Head Coach	After Bowls
1	Notre Dame 9-0-0	Frank Leahy	10-0-0
2	Oklahoma 10-0-0	Bud Wilkinson	11-0-0
3	California 10-0-0	Pappy Waldorf	10-1-0
4	Army 9-0-0	Red Blaik	same
5	Rice 9-1-0	Jess Neely	10-1-0
6	Ohio St. 6-1-2	Wes Fesler	7-1-2
7	Michigan 6-2-1	Bennie Oosterbaan	same
8	Minnesota 7-2-0	Bernie Bierman	same
9	LSU 8-2-0	Gaynell Tinsley	8-3-0
10	Pacific 10-0-0	Larry Siemering	11-0-0
11	Kentucky 9-2-0	Bear Bryant	9-3-0
12	Cornell 8-1-0	Lefty James	same
13	Villanova 8-1-0	Jim Leonard	same
14	Maryland 7-1-0	Jim Tatum	9-1-0
15	Santa Clara 7-2-1	Len Casanova	8-2-1
16	North Carolina . . .7-3-0	Carl Snavely	7-4-0
17	Tennessee 7-2-1	Bob Neyland	same
18	Princeton 6-3-0	Charlie Caldwell	same
19	Michigan St. 6-3-0	Biggie Munn	same
20	Missouri 7-3-0	Don Faurot	7-4-0
	Baylor 8-2-0	Bob Woodruff	same

Key Bowl Games

Sugar–#2 Oklahoma over #9 LSU, 35-0; **Rose**–#6 Ohio St. over #3 Cal, 17-14; **Cotton**–#5 Rice over #16 North Carolina, 27-13; **Orange**–#15 Santa Clara over #11 Kentucky, 21-13.

1950

Final poll released Nov. 27. Top 20 regular season results after that: **Nov. 30**–#3 Texas over Texas A&M, 17-0. **Dec. 1**–#15 Miami-FL over Missouri, 27–9. **Dec. 2**–#1 Oklahoma over Okla. A&M, 41-14; Navy over #2 Army, 14-2; #4 Tennessee over Vanderbilt, 43-0; #16 Alabama over Auburn, 34-0; #19 Tulsa over Houston, 28-21; #20 Tulane tied LSU, 14-14. **Dec. 9**–#3 Texas over LSU, 21-6.

	As of Nov. 27	Head Coach	After Bowls
1	Oklahoma 9-0-0	Bud Wilkinson	10-1-0
2	Army 8-0-0	Red Blaik	8-1-0
3	Texas 7-1-0	Blair Cherry	9-2-0
4	Tennessee 9-1-0	Bob Neyland	11-1-0
5	California 9-0-1	Pappy Waldorf	9-1-1
6	Princeton 9-0-0	Charlie Caldwell	same
7	Kentucky 10-1-0	Bear Bryant	11-1-0
8	Michigan St. 8-1-0	Biggie Munn	same
9	Michigan 5-3-1	Bennie Oosterbaan	6-3-1
10	Clemson 8-0-1	Frank Howard	9-0-1
11	Washington 8-2-0	Howard Odell	same
12	Wyoming 9-0-0	Bowden Wyatt	10-0-0
13	Illinois 7-2-0	Ray Eliot	same
14	Ohio St. 6-3-0	Wes Fesler	same
15	Miami-FL 8-0-1	Andy Gustafson	9-1-1
16	Alabama 8-2-0	Red Drew	9-2-0
17	Nebraska 6-2-1	Bill Glassford	same
18	Wash. & Lee 8-2-0	George Barclay	8-3-0
19	Tulsa 8-1-1	J.O. Brothers	9-1-1
20	Tulane 6-2-0	Henry Frnka	6-2-1

Key Bowl Games

Sugar–#7 Kentucky over #1 Oklahoma, 13-7; **Cotton**–#4 Tennessee over #3 Texas, 20-14; **Rose**–#9 Michigan over #5 Cal, 14-6; **Orange**–#10 Clemson over #15 Miami-FL, 15-14.

1951

Final poll released Dec. 3. Top 20 regular season results after that: None.

	As of Dec. 3	Head Coach	After Bowls
1	Tennessee 10-0-0	Bob Neyland	10-1-0
2	Michigan St. 9-0-0	Biggie Munn	same
3	Maryland 9-0-0	Jim Tatum	10-0-0
4	Illinois 8-0-1	Ray Eliot	9-0-1
5	Georgia Tech 10-0-1	Bobby Dodd	11-0-1
6	Princeton 9-0-0	Charlie Caldwell	same
7	Stanford 9-1-0	Chuck Taylor	9-2-0
8	Wisconsin 7-1-1	Ivy Williamson	same
9	Baylor 8-1-1	George Sauer	8-2-1
10	Oklahoma 8-2-0	Bud Wilkinson	same
11	TCU 6-4-0	Dutch Meyer	6-5-0
12	California 8-2-0	Pappy Waldorf	same
13	Virginia 8-1-0	Art Guepe	same
14	San Francisco 9-0-0	Joe Kuharich	same
15	Kentucky 7-4-0	Bear Bryant	8-4-0
16	Boston Univ. 6-4-0	Buff Donelli	same
17	UCLA 5-3-1	Red Sanders	same
18	Washington St. 7-3-0	Forest Evashevski	same
19	Holy Cross 8-2-0	Eddie Anderson	same
20	Clemson 7-2-0	Frank Howard	7-3-0

Key Bowl Games

Sugar–#3 Maryland over #1 Tennessee, 28-13; **Rose**– #4 Illinois over #7 Stanford, 40-7; **Orange**–#5 Georgia Tech over #9 Baylor, 17-14; **Cotton**–#15 Kentucky over #11 TCU, 20-7.

Associated Press Final Polls (Cont.)

1952

Final poll released Dec. 1. Top 20 regular season results after that: **Dec. 6**–#15 Florida over #20 Kentucky, 27-20.

		As of Dec. 1	Head Coach	After Bowls
1	Michigan St.	9-0-0	Biggie Munn	same
2	Georgia Tech	11-0-0	Bobby Dodd	12-0-0
3	Notre Dame	7-2-1	Frank Leahy	same
4	Oklahoma	8-1-1	Bud Wilkinson	same
5	USC	9-1-0	Jess Hill	10-1-0
6	UCLA	8-1-0	Red Sanders	same
7	Mississippi	8-0-2	Johnny Vaught	8-1-2
8	Tennessee	8-1-1	Bob Neyland	8-2-1
9	Alabama	9-2-0	Red Drew	10-2-0
10	Texas	8-2-0	Ed Price	9-2-0
11	Wisconsin	6-2-1	Ivy Williamson	6-3-1
12	Tulsa	8-1-1	J.O. Brothers	8-2-1
13	Maryland	7-2-0	Jim Tatum	same
14	Syracuse	7-2-0	Ben Schwartzwalder	7-3-0
15	Florida	6-3-0	Bob Woodruff	8-3-0
16	Duke	8-2-0	Bill Murray	same
17	Ohio St.	6-3-0	Woody Hayes	same
18	Purdue	4-3-2	Stu Holcomb	same
19	Princeton	8-1-0	Charlie Caldwell	same
20	Kentucky	5-3-2	Bear Bryant	5-4-2

Note: Michigan St. would officially join Big Ten in 1953.

Key Bowl Games

Sugar–#2 Georgia Tech over #7 Ole Miss, 24-7; **Rose**–#5 USC over #11 Wisconsin, 7-0; **Cotton**–#10 Texas over #8 Tennessee, 16-0; **Orange**–#9 Alabama over #14 Syracuse, 61-6.

1953

Final poll released Nov. 30. Top 20 regular season results after that: **Dec. 5**–#2 Notre Dame over SMU, 40-14.

		As of Nov. 30	Head Coach	After Bowls
1	Maryland	10-0-0	Jim Tatum	10-1-0
2	Notre Dame	8-0-1	Frank Leahy	9-0-1
3	Michigan St.	8-1-0	Biggie Munn	9-1-0
4	Oklahoma	8-1-1	Bud Wilkinson	9-1-1
5	UCLA	8-1-0	Red Sanders	8-2-0
6	Rice	8-2-0	Jess Neely	9-2-0
7	Illinois	7-1-1	Ray Eliot	same
8	Georgia Tech	8-2-1	Bobby Dodd	9-2-1
9	Iowa	5-3-1	Forest Evashevski	same
10	West Virginia	8-1-0	Art Lewis	8-2-0
11	Texas	7-3-0	Ed Price	same
12	Texas Tech	10-1-0	DeWitt Weaver	11-1-0
13	Alabama	6-2-3	Red Drew	6-3-3
14	Army	7-1-1	Red Blaik	same
15	Wisconsin	6-2-1	Ivy Williamson	same
16	Kentucky	7-2-1	Bear Bryant	same
17	Auburn	7-2-1	Shug Jordan	7-3-1
18	Duke	7-2-1	Bill Murray	same
19	Stanford	6-3-1	Chuck Taylor	same
20	Michigan	6-3-0	Bennie Oosterbaan	same

Key Bowl Games

Orange–#4 Oklahoma over #1 Maryland, 7-0; **Rose**–#3 Michigan St. over #5 UCLA, 28-20; **Cotton**–#6 Rice over #13 Alabama, 28-6; **Sugar**–#8 Georgia Tech over #10 West Virginia, 42-19.

1954

Final poll released Nov. 29. Top 20 regular season results after that: **Dec. 4**–#4 Notre Dame over SMU, 26-14.

		As of Nov. 29	Head Coach	After Bowls
1	Ohio St.	9-0-0	Woody Hayes	10-0-0
2	UCLA	9-0-0	Red Sanders	same
3	Oklahoma	10-0-0	Bud Wilkinson	same
4	Notre Dame	8-1-0	Terry Brennan	9-1-0
5	Navy	7-2-0	Eddie Erdelatz	8-2-0
6	Mississippi	9-1-0	Johnny Vaught	9-2-0
7	Army	7-2-0	Red Blaik	same
8	Maryland	7-2-1	Jim Tatum	same
9	Wisconsin	7-2-0	Ivy Williamson	same
10	Arkansas	8-2-0	Bowden Wyatt	8-3-0
11	Miami-FL.	8-1-0	Andy Gustafson	same
12	West Virginia	8-1-0	Art Lewis	same
13	Auburn	7-3-0	Shug Jordan	8-3-0
14	Duke	7-2-1	Bill Murray	8-2-1
15	Michigan	6-3-0	Bennie Oosterbaan	same
16	Virginia Tech	8-0-1	Frank Moseley	same
17	USC	8-3-0	Jess Hill	8-4-0
18	Baylor	7-3-0	George Sauer	7-4-0
19	Rice	7-3-0	Jess Neely	same
20	Penn St.	7-2-0	Rip Engle	same

Note: PCC and Big Seven "no-repeat" rules kept UCLA and Oklahoma from Rose and Orange bowls, respectively.

Key Bowl Games

Rose–#1 Ohio St. over #17 USC, 20-7; **Sugar**–#5 Navy over #6 Ole Miss, 21-0; **Cotton**–Georgia Tech over #10 Arkansas, 14-6; **Orange**–#14 Duke over Nebraska, 34-7.

1955

Final poll released Nov. 28. Top 20 regular season results after that: None.

		As of Nov. 28	Head Coach	After Bowls
1	Oklahoma	10-0-0	Bud Wilkinson	11-0-0
2	Michigan St.	8-1-0	Duffy Daugherty	9-1-0
3	Maryland	10-0-0	Jim Tatum	10-1-0
4	UCLA	9-1-0	Red Sanders	9-2-0
5	Ohio St.	7-2-0	Woody Hayes	same
6	TCU	9-1-0	Abe Martin	9-2-0
7	Georgia Tech	8-1-1	Bobby Dodd	9-1-1
8	Auburn	8-1-1	Shug Jordan	8-2-1
9	Notre Dame	8-2-0	Terry Brennan	same
10	Mississippi	9-1-0	Johnny Vaught	10-1-0
11	Pittsburgh	7-3-0	John Michelosen	7-4-0
12	Michigan	7-2-0	Bennie Oosterbaan	same
13	USC	6-4-0	Jess Hill	same
14	Miami-FL.	6-3-0	Andy Gustafson	same
15	Miami-OH	9-0-0	Ara Parseghian	same
16	Stanford	6-3-1	Chuck Taylor	same
17	Texas A&M	7-2-1	Bear Bryant	same
18	Navy	6-2-1	Eddie Erdelatz	same
19	West Virginia	8-2-0	Art Lewis	same
20	Army	6-3-0	Red Blaik	same

Note: Big Ten "no-repeat" rule kept Ohio St. from Rose Bowl.

Key Bowl Games

Orange–#1 Oklahoma over #3 Maryland, 20-6; **Rose**–#2 Michigan St. over #4 UCLA, 17-14; **Cotton**–#10 Ole Miss over #6 TCU, 14-13; **Sugar**–#7 Georgia Tech over #11 Pitt, 7-0; **Gator**–Vanderbilt over #8 Auburn, 25-13.

1956

Final poll released Dec. 3. Top 20 regular season results after that: **Dec. 8**—#13 Pitt over #6 Miami-FL, 14-7.

		As of Dec. 3	Head Coach	After Bowls
1	Oklahoma	10-0-0	Bud Wilkinson	same
2	Tennessee	10-0-0	Bowden Wyatt	10-1-0
3	Iowa	8-1-0	Forest Evashevski	9-1-0
4	Georgia Tech	9-1-0	Bobby Dodd	10-1-0
5	Texas A&M	9-0-1	Bear Bryant	same
6	Miami-FL	8-0-1	Andy Gustafson	8-1-1
7	Michigan	7-2-0	Bennie Oosterbaan	same
8	Syracuse	7-1-0	Ben Schwartzwalder	7-2-0
9	Michigan St.	7-2-0	Duffy Daugherty	same
10	Oregon St.	7-2-1	Tommy Prothro	7-3-1
11	Baylor	8-2-0	Sam Boyd	9-2-0
12	Minnesota	6-1-2	Murray Warmath	same
13	Pittsburgh	6-2-1	John Michelosen	7-3-1
14	TCU	7-3-0	Abe Martin	8-3-0
15	Ohio St.	6-3-0	Woody Hayes	same
16	Navy	6-1-2	Eddie Erdelatz	same
17	G. Washington	7-1-1	Gene Sherman	8-1-1
18	USC	8-2-0	Jess Hill	same
19	Clemson	7-1-2	Frank Howard	7-2-2
20	Colorado	7-2-1	Dallas Ward	8-2-1

Note: Big Seven "no-repeat" rule kept Oklahoma from Orange Bowl and Texas A&M was on probation.

Key Bowl Games

Sugar—#11 Baylor over #2 Tennessee, 13-7; **Rose**— #3 Iowa over #10 Oregon St., 35-19; **Gator**—#4 Georgia Tech over #13 Pitt, 21-14; **Cotton**—#14 TCU over #8 Syracuse, 28-27; **Orange**—#20 Colorado over #19 Clemson, 27-21.

1957

Final poll released Dec. 2. Top 20 regular season results after that: **Dec. 7**—#10 Notre Dame over SMU, 54-21.

		As of Dec. 2	Head Coach	After Bowls
1	Auburn	10-0-0	Shug Jordan	same
2	Ohio St.	8-1-0	Woody Hayes	9-1-0
3	Michigan St.	8-1-0	Duffy Daugherty	same
4	Oklahoma	9-1-0	Bud Wilkinson	10-1-0
5	Navy	8-1-1	Eddie Erdelatz	9-1-1
6	Iowa	7-1-1	Forest Evashevski	same
7	Mississippi	8-1-1	Johnny Vaught	9-1-1
8	Rice	7-3-0	Jess Neely	7-4-0
9	Texas A&M	8-2-0	Bear Bryant	8-3-0
10	Notre Dame	6-3-0	Terry Brennan	7-3-0
11	Texas	6-3-1	Darrell Royal	6-4-1
12	Arizona St.	10-0-0	Dan Devine	same
13	Tennessee	7-3-0	Bowden Wyatt	8-3-0
14	Mississippi St.	6-2-1	Wade Walker	same
15	N.C. State	7-1-2	Earle Edwards	same
16	Duke	6-2-2	Bill Murray	6-3-2
17	Florida	6-2-1	Bob Woodruff	same
18	Army	7-2-0	Red Blaik	same
19	Wisconsin	6-3-0	Milt Bruhn	same
20	VMI	9-0-1	John McKenna	same

Note: Auburn on probation, ineligible for bowl game.

Key Bowl Games

Rose—#2 Ohio St. over Oregon, 10-7; **Orange**—#4 Oklahoma over #16 Duke, 48-21; **Cotton**—#5 Navy over #8 Rice, 20-7; **Sugar**—#7 Ole Miss over #11 Texas, 39-7; **Gator**—#13 Tennessee over #9 Texas A&M, 3-0.

1958

Final poll released Dec. 1. Top 20 regular season results after that: None.

		As of Dec. 1	Head Coach	After Bowls
1	LSU	10-0-0	Paul Dietzel	11-0-0
2	Iowa	7-1-1	Forest Evashevski	8-1-1
3	Army	8-0-1	Red Blaik	same
4	Auburn	9-0-1	Shug Jordan	same
5	Oklahoma	9-1-0	Bud Wilkinson	10-1-0
6	Air Force	9-0-1	Ben Martin	9-0-2
7	Wisconsin	7-1-1	Milt Bruhn	same
8	Ohio St.	6-1-2	Woody Hayes	same
9	Syracuse	8-1-0	Ben Schwartzwalder	8-2-0
10	TCU	8-2-0	Abe Martin	8-2-1
11	Mississippi	8-2-0	Johnny Vaught	9-2-0
12	Clemson	8-2-0	Frank Howard	8-3-0
13	Purdue	6-1-2	Jack Mollenkopf	same
14	Florida	6-3-1	Bob Woodruff	6-4-1
15	South Carolina	7-3-0	Warren Giese	same
16	California	7-3-0	Pete Elliott	7-4-0
17	Notre Dame	6-4-0	Terry Brennan	same
18	SMU	6-4-0	Bill Meek	same
19	Oklahoma St.	7-3-0	Cliff Speegle	8-3-0
20	Rutgers	8-1-0	John Stiegman	same

Key Bowl Games

Sugar—#1 LSU over #12 Clemson, 7-0; **Rose**—#2 Iowa over #16 Cal, 38-12; **Orange**—#5 Oklahoma over #9 Syracuse, 21-6; **Cotton**—#6 Air Force tied #10 TCU, 0-0.

1959

Final poll released Dec. 7. Top 20 regular season results after that: None.

		As of Dec. 7	Head Coach	After Bowls
1	Syracuse	10-0-0	Ben Schwartzwalder	11-0-0
2	Mississippi	9-1-0	Johnny Vaught	10-1-0
3	LSU	9-1-0	Paul Dietzel	9-2-0
4	Texas	9-1-0	Darrell Royal	9-2-0
5	Georgia	9-1-0	Wally Butts	10-1-0
6	Wisconsin	7-2-0	Milt Bruhn	7-3-0
7	TCU	8-2-0	Abe Martin	8-3-0
8	Washington	9-1-0	Jim Owens	10-1-0
9	Arkansas	8-2-0	Frank Broyles	9-2-0
10	Alabama	7-1-2	Bear Bryant	7-2-2
11	Clemson	8-2-0	Frank Howard	9-2-0
12	Penn St.	8-2-0	Rip Engle	9-2-0
13	Illinois	5-3-1	Ray Eliot	same
14	USC	8-2-0	Don Clark	same
15	Oklahoma	7-3-0	Bud Wilkinson	same
16	Wyoming	9-1-0	Bob Devaney	same
17	Notre Dame	5-5-0	Joe Kuharich	same
18	Missouri	6-4-0	Dan Devine	6-5-0
19	Florida	5-4-1	Bob Woodruff	same
20	Pittsburgh	6-4-0	John Michelosen	same

Note: Big Seven "no-repeat" rule kept Oklahoma from Orange Bowl.

Key Bowl Games

Cotton—#1 Syracuse over #4 Texas, 23-14; **Sugar**— #2 Ole Miss over #3 LSU, 21-0; **Orange**—#5 Georgia over #18 Missouri, 14-0; **Rose**—#8 Washington over #6 Wisconsin, 44-8; **Bluebonnet**—#11 Clemson over #7 TCU, 23-7; **Gator**—#9 Arkansas over Georgia Tech, 14-7; **Liberty**—#12 Penn St. over #10 Alabama, 7-0.

Associated Press Final Polls (Cont.)

1960

Final poll released Nov. 28. Top 20 regular season results after that: **Dec. 3**–UCLA over #10 Duke, 27-6.

	As of Nov. 28	Head Coach	After Bowls
1	Minnesota 8-1-0	Murray Warmath	8-2-0
2	Mississippi 9-0-1	Johnny Vaught	10-0-1
3	Iowa 8-1-0	Forest Evashevski	same
4	Navy. 9-1-0	Wayne Hardin	9-2-0
5	Missouri 9-1-0	Dan Devine	10-1-0
6	Washington 9-1-0	Jim Owens	10-1-0
7	Arkansas 8-2-0	Frank Broyles	8-3-0
8	Ohio St. 7-2-0	Woody Hayes	same
9	Alabama 8-1-1	Bear Bryant	8-1-2
10	Duke 7-2-0	Bill Murray	8-3-0
11	Kansas 7-2-1	Jack Mitchell	same
12	Baylor. 8-2-0	John Bridgers	8-3-0
13	Auburn. 8-2-0	Shug Jordan	same
14	Yale. 9-0-0	Jordan Olivar	same
15	Michigan St. 6-2-1	Duffy Daugherty	same
16	Penn St. 6-3-0	Rip Engle	7-3-0
17	New Mexico St. . .10-0-0	Warren Woodson	11-0-0
18	Florida 8-2-0	Ray Graves	9-2-0
19	Syracuse. 7-2-0	Ben Schwartzwalder	same
	Purdue 4-4-1	Jack Mollenkopf	same

Key Bowl Games
Rose–#6 Washington over #1 Minnesota, 17-7; **Sugar**–#2 Ole Miss over Rice, 14-6; **Orange**–#5 Missouri over #4 Navy, 21-14; **Cotton**–#10 Duke over #7 Arkansas, 7-6; **Bluebonnet**–#9 Alabama tied Texas, 3-3.

1961

Final poll released Dec. 4. Top 20 regular season results after that: None.

	As of Dec. 4	Head Coach	After Bowls
1	Alabama 10-0-0	Bear Bryant	11-0-0
2	Ohio St. 8-0-1	Woody Hayes	same
3	Texas. 9-1-0	Darrell Royal	10-1-0
4	LSU 9-1-0	Paul Dietzel	10-1-0
5	Mississippi 9-1-0	Johnny Vaught	9-2-0
6	Minnesota 7-2-0	Murray Warmath	8-2-0
7	Colorado 9-1-0	Sonny Grandelius	9-2-0
8	Michigan St. 7-2-0	Duffy Daugherty	same
9	Arkansas 8-2-0	Frank Broyles	8-3-0
10	Utah St. 9-0-1	John Ralston	9-1-1
11	Missouri 7-2-1	Dan Devine	same
12	Purdue 6-3-0	Jack Mollenkopf	same
13	Georgia Tech. 7-3-0	Bobby Dodd	7-4-0
14	Syracuse. 7-3-0	Ben Schwartzwalder	8-3-0
15	Rutgers 9-0-0	John Bateman	same
16	UCLA 7-3-0	Bill Barnes	7-4-0
17	Rice. 7-3-0	Jess Neely	7-4-0
	Penn St. 7-3-0	Rip Engle	8-3-0
	Arizona 8-1-1	Jim LaRue	same
20	Duke 7-3-0	Bill Murray	same

Note: Ohio St. faculty council turned down Rose Bowl invitation citing concern with OSU's overemphasis on sports.

Key Bowl Games
Sugar–#1 Alabama over #9 Arkansas, 10-3; **Cotton**–#3 Texas over #5 Ole Miss, 12-7; **Orange**–#4 LSU over #7 Colorado, 25-7; **Rose**–#6 Minnesota over #16 UCLA, 21-3; **Gotham**–Baylor over #10 Utah St., 24-9.

1962

Final poll released Dec. 3. Top 10 regular season results after that: None.

	As of Dec. 3	Head Coach	After Bowls
1	USC 10-0-0	John McKay	11-0-0
2	Wisconsin 8-1-0	Milt Bruhn	8-2-0
3	Mississippi 9-0-0	Johnny Vaught	10-0-0
4	Texas. 9-0-1	Darrell Royal	9-1-1
5	Alabama 9-1-0	Bear Bryant	10-1-0
6	Arkansas 9-1-0	Frank Broyles	9-2-0
7	LSU 8-1-1	Charlie McClendon	9-1-1
8	Oklahoma 8-2-0	Bud Wilkinson	8-3-0
9	Penn St. 9-1-0	Rip Engle	9-2-0
10	Minnesota 6-2-1	Murray Warmath	same

Key Bowl Games
Rose–#1 USC over #2 Wisconsin, 42-37; **Sugar**–#3 Ole Miss over #6 Arkansas, 17-13; **Cotton**–#7 LSU over #4 Texas, 13-0; **Orange**–#5 Alabama over #8 Oklahoma, 17-0; **Gator**–Florida over #9 Penn St.,17-7.

1963

Final poll released Dec. 9. Top 10 regular season results after that: **Dec.14**–#8 Alabama over Miami-FL, 17-12.

	As of Dec. 9	Head Coach	After Bowls
1	Texas 10-0-0	Darrell Royal	11-0-0
2	Navy. 9-1-0	Wayne Hardin	9-2-0
3	Illinois 7-1-1	Pete Elliott	8-1-1
4	Pittsburgh 9-1-0	John Michelosen	same
5	Auburn 9-1-0	Shug Jordan	9-2-0
6	Nebraska 9-1-0	Bob Devaney	10-1-0
7	Mississippi 7-0-2	Johnny Vaught	7-1-2
8	Alabama 7-2-0	Bear Bryant	9-2-0
9	Michigan St. 6-2-1	Duffy Daugherty	same
10	Oklahoma 8-2-0	Bud Wilkinson	same

Key Bowl Games
Cotton–#1 Texas over #2 Navy, 28-6; **Rose**–#3 Illinois over Washington, 17-7; **Orange**–#6 Nebraska over #5 Auburn, 13-7; **Sugar**–#8 Alabama over #7 Ole Miss, 12-7.

1964

Final poll released Nov. 30. Top 10 regular season results after that: **Dec. 5**–Florida over #7 LSU, 20-6.

	As of Nov. 30	Head Coach	After Bowls
1	Alabama 10-0-0	Bear Bryant	10-1-0
2	Arkansas 10-0-0	Frank Broyles	11-0-0
3	Notre Dame. 9-1-0	Ara Parseghian	same
4	Michigan 8-1-0	Bump Elliott	9-1-0
5	Texas. 9-1-0	Darrell Royal	10-1-0
6	Nebraska 9-1-0	Bob Devaney	9-2-0
7	LSU 7-1-1	Charlie McClendon	8-2-1
8	Oregon St. 8-2-0	Tommy Prothro	8-3-0
9	Ohio St. 7-2-0	Woody Hayes	same
10	USC 7-3-0	John McKay	same

Key Bowl Games
Orange–#5 Texas over #1 Alabama, 21-17; **Cotton**–#2 Arkansas over #6 Nebraska, 10-7; **Rose**– #4 Michigan over #8 Oregon St., 34-7; **Sugar**–#7 LSU over Syracuse, 13-10.

1965

Final poll taken after bowl games for the first time.

		After Bowls	Head Coach	Regular Season
1	Alabama	9-1-1	Bear Bryant	8-1-1
2	Michigan St.	10-1-0	Duffy Daugherty	10-0-0
3	Arkansas	10-1-0	Frank Broyles	10-0-0
4	UCLA	8-2-1	Tommy Prothro	7-1-1
5	Nebraska	10-1-0	Bob Devaney	10-0-0
6	Missouri	8-2-1	Dan Devine	7-2-1
7	Tennessee	8-1-2	Doug Dickey	6-1-2
8	LSU	8-3-0	Charlie McClendon	7-3-0
9	Notre Dame	7-2-1	Ara Parseghian	same
10	USC	7-2-1	John McKay	same

Key Bowl Games

Rankings below reflect final regular season poll, released Nov. 29. No bowls for then #8 USC or #9 Notre Dame. **Rose**–#5 UCLA over #1 Michigan St., 14-12; **Cotton**–LSU over #2 Arkansas, 14-7; **Orange**–#4 Alabama over #3 Nebraska, 39-28; **Sugar**–#6 Missouri over Florida, 20-18; **Bluebonnet**–#7 Tennessee over Tulsa, 27-6; **Gator**–Georgia Tech over #10 Texas Tech, 31-21.

1966

Final poll released Dec. 5, returning to pre-bowl status. Top 10 regular season results after that: None.

		As of Dec. 5	Head Coach	After Bowls
1	Notre Dame	9-0-1	Ara Parseghian	same
2	Michigan St.	9-0-1	Duffy Daugherty	same
3	Alabama	10-0-0	Bear Bryant	11-0-0
4	Georgia	9-1-0	Vince Dooley	10-1-0
5	UCLA	9-1-0	Tommy Prothro	same
6	Nebraska	9-1-0	Bob Devaney	9-2-0
7	Purdue	8-2-0	Jack Mollenkopf	9-2-0
8	Georgia Tech	9-1-0	Bobby Dodd	9-2-0
9	Miami-FL	7-2-1	Charlie Tate	8-2-1
10	SMU	8-2-0	Hayden Fry	8-3-0

Key Bowl Games

Sugar–#3 Alabama over #6 Nebraska, 34-7; **Cotton**–#4 Georgia over #10 SMU, 24-9; **Rose**–#7 Purdue over USC, 14-13; **Orange**–Florida over #8 Georgia Tech, 27-12; **Liberty**–#9 Miami-FL over Virginia Tech, 14-7.

1967

Final poll released Nov. 27. Top 10 regular season results after that: **Dec. 2**–#2 Tennessee over Vanderbilt, 41-14; #3 Oklahoma over Oklahoma St., 38-14; #8 Alabama over Auburn, 7-3.

		As of Nov. 27	Head Coach	After Bowls
1	USC	9-1-0	John McKay	10-1-0
2	Tennessee	8-1-0	Doug Dickey	9-2-0
3	Oklahoma	8-1-0	Chuck Fairbanks	10-1-0
4	Indiana	9-1-0	John Pont	9-2-0
5	Notre Dame	8-2-0	Ara Parseghian	same
6	Wyoming	10-0-0	Lloyd Eaton	10-1-0
7	Oregon St.	7-2-1	Dee Andros	same
8	Alabama	7-1-1	Bear Bryant	8-2-1
9	Purdue	8-2-0	Jack Mollenkopf	same
10	Penn St.	8-2-0	Joe Paterno	8-2-1

Key Bowl Games

Rose–#1 USC over #4 Indiana, 14-3; **Orange**–#3 Oklahoma over #2 Tennessee, 26-24; **Sugar**–LSU over #6 Wyoming, 20-13; **Cotton**–Texas A&M over #8 Alabama, 20-16; **Gator**–#10 Penn St. tied Florida St. 17-17.

1968

Final poll taken after bowl games for first time since close of 1965 season.

		After Bowls	Head Coach	Regular Season
1	Ohio St.	10-0-0	Woody Hayes	9-0-0
2	Penn St.	11-0-0	Joe Paterno	10-0-0
3	Texas	9-1-1	Darrell Royal	8-1-1
4	USC	9-1-1	John McKay	9-0-1
5	Notre Dame	7-2-1	Ara Parseghian	same
6	Arkansas	10-1-0	Frank Broyles	9-1-0
7	Kansas	9-2-0	Pepper Rodgers	9-1-0
8	Georgia	8-1-2	Vince Dooley	8-0-2
9	Missouri	8-3-0	Dan Devine	7-3-0
10	Purdue	8-2-0	Jack Mollenkopf	same
11	Oklahoma	7-4-0	Chuck Fairbanks	7-3-0
12	Michigan	8-2-0	Bump Elliott	same
13	Tennessee	8-2-1	Doug Dickey	8-1-1
14	SMU	8-3-0	Hayden Fry	7-3-0
15	Oregon St.	7-3-0	Dee Andros	same
16	Auburn	7-4-0	Shug Jordan	6-4-0
17	Alabama	8-3-0	Bear Bryant	8-2-0
18	Houston	6-2-2	Bill Yeoman	same
19	LSU	8-3-0	Charlie McClendon	7-3-0
20	Ohio Univ.	10-1-0	Bill Hess	10-0-0

Key Bowl Games

Rankings below reflect final regular season poll, released Dec. 2. No bowls for then #7 Notre Dame and #11 Purdue. **Rose**–#1 Ohio St. over #2 USC, 27-16; **Orange**–#3 Penn St. over #6 Kansas, 15-14; **Sugar**–#9 Arkansas over #4 Georgia, 16-2; **Cotton**–#5 Texas over #8 Tennessee, 36-13; **Bluebonnet**–#20 SMU over #10 Oklahoma, 28-27; **Gator**–#16 Missouri over #12 Alabama, 35-10.

1969

Final poll taken after bowl games.

		After Bowls	Head Coach	Regular Season
1	Texas	11-0-0	Darrell Royal	10-0-0
2	Penn St.	11-0-0	Joe Paterno	10-0-0
3	USC	10-0-1	John McKay	9-0-1
4	Ohio St.	8-1-0	Woody Hayes	same
5	Notre Dame	8-2-1	Ara Parseghian	8-1-1
6	Missouri	9-2-0	Dan Devine	9-1-0
7	Arkansas	9-2-0	Frank Broyles	9-1-0
8	Mississippi	8-3-0	Johnny Vaught	7-3-0
9	Michigan	8-3-0	Bo Schembechler	8-2-0
10	LSU	9-1-0	Charlie McClendon	same
11	Nebraska	9-2-0	Bob Devaney	8-2-0
12	Houston	9-2-0	Bill Yeoman	8-2-0
13	UCLA	8-1-1	Tommy Prothro	same
14	Florida	9-1-1	Ray Graves	8-1-1
15	Tennessee	9-2-0	Doug Dickey	9-1-0
16	Colorado	8-3-0	Eddie Crowder	7-3-0
17	West Virginia	10-1-0	Jim Carlen	9-1-0
18	Purdue	8-2-0	Jack Mollenkopf	same
19	Stanford	7-2-1	John Ralston	same
20	Auburn	8-3-0	Shug Jordan	8-2-0

Key Bowl Games

Rankings below reflect final regular season poll, released Dec. 8. No bowls for then #4 Ohio St., #8 LSU and #10 UCLA. **Cotton**–#1 Texas over #9 Notre Dame, 21-17; **Orange**–#2 Penn St. over #6 Missouri, 10-3; **Sugar**–#13 Ole Miss over #3 Arkansas, 27-22; **Rose**–#5 USC over #7 Michigan, 10-3.

Associated Press Final Polls (Cont.)

1970

		After Bowls	Head Coach	Regular Season
1	Nebraska	11-0-1	Bob Devaney	10-0-1
2	Notre Dame	10-1-0	Ara Parseghian	9-0-1
3	Texas	10-1-0	Darrell Royal	10-0-0
4	Tennessee	11-1-0	Bill Battle	10-1-0
5	Ohio St.	9-1-0	Woody Hayes	9-0-0
6	Arizona St.	11-0-0	Frank Kush	10-0-0
7	LSU	9-3-0	Charlie McClendon	9-2-0
8	Stanford	9-3-0	John Ralston	8-3-0
9	Michigan	9-1-0	Bo Schembechler	same
10	Auburn	9-2-0	Shug Jordan	8-2-0
11	Arkansas	9-2-0	Frank Broyles	same
12	Toledo	12-0-0	Frank Lauterbur	11-0-0
13	Georgia Tech.	9-3-0	Bud Carson	8-3-0
14	Dartmouth	9-0-0	Bob Blackman	same
15	USC	6-4-1	John McKay	same
16	Air Force	9-3-0	Ben Martin	9-2-0
17	Tulane	8-4-0	Jim Pittman	7-4-0
18	Penn St.	7-3-0	Joe Paterno	same
19	Houston	8-3-0	Bill Yeoman	same
20	Oklahoma	7-4-1	Chuck Fairbanks	7-4-0
	Mississippi	7-4-0	Johnny Vaught	7-3-0

Key Bowl Games

Rankings below reflect final regular season poll, released Dec. 7. No bowls for then #4 Arkansas and #7 Michigan.
Cotton–#6 Notre Dame over #1 Texas, 24-11; **Rose**– #12 Stanford over #2 Ohio St., 27-17; **Orange**–#3 Nebraska over #8 LSU, 17-12; **Sugar**– #5 Tennessee over #11 Air Force, 34-13; **Peach**–#9 Ariz. St. over N. Carolina, 48-26.

1971

		After Bowls	Head Coach	Regular Season
1	Nebraska	13-0-0	Bob Devaney	12-0-0
2	Oklahoma	11-1-0	Chuck Fairbanks	10-1-0
3	Colorado	10-2-0	Eddie Crowder	9-2-0
4	Alabama	11-1-0	Bear Bryant	11-0-0
5	Penn St.	11-1-0	Joe Paterno	10-1-0
6	Michigan	11-1-0	Bo Schembechler	11-0-0
7	Georgia	11-1-0	Vince Dooley	10-1-0
8	Arizona St.	11-1-0	Frank Kush	10-1-0
9	Tennessee	10-2-0	Bill Battle	9-2-0
10	Stanford	9-3-0	John Ralston	8-3-0
11	LSU	9-3-0	Charlie McClendon	8-3-0
12	Auburn	9-2-0	Shug Jordan	9-1-0
13	Notre Dame	8-2-0	Ara Parseghian	same
14	Toledo	12-0-0	John Murphy	11-0-0
15	Mississippi	10-2-0	Billy Kinard	9-2-0
16	Arkansas	8-3-1	Frank Broyles	8-2-1
17	Houston	9-3-0	Bill Yeoman	9-2-0
18	Texas	8-3-0	Darrell Royal	8-2-0
19	Washington	8-3-0	Jim Owens	same
20	USC	6-4-1	John McKay	same

Key Bowl Games

Rankings below reflect final regular season poll, released Dec. 6.
Orange–#1 Nebraska over #2 Alabama, 38-6; **Sugar**–#3 Oklahoma over #5 Auburn, 40-22; **Rose**–#16 Stanford over #4 Michigan, 13-12; **Gator**–#6 Georgia over N. Carolina, 7-3; **Bluebonnet**–#7 Colorado over #15 Houston, 29-17; **Fiesta**–#8 Ariz. St. over Florida St., 45-38; **Cotton**–#10 Penn St. over #12 Texas, 30-6.

1972

		After Bowls	Head Coach	Regular Season
1	USC	12-0-0	John McKay	11-0-0
2	Oklahoma	11-1-0	Chuck Fairbanks	10-1-0
3	Texas	10-1-0	Darrell Royal	9-1-0
4	Nebraska	9-2-1	Bob Devaney	8-2-1
5	Auburn	10-1-0	Shug Jordan	9-1-0
6	Michigan	10-1-0	Bo Schembechler	same
7	Alabama	10-2-0	Bear Bryant	10-1-0
8	Tennessee	10-2-0	Bill Battle	9-2-0
9	Ohio St.	9-2-0	Woody Hayes	9-1-0
10	Penn St.	10-2-0	Joe Paterno	10-1-0
11	LSU	9-2-1	Charlie McClendon	9-1-1
12	North Carolina	11-1-0	Bill Dooley	10-1-0
13	Arizona St.	10-2-0	Frank Kush	9-2-0
14	Notre Dame	8-3-0	Ara Parseghian	8-2-0
15	UCLA	8-3-0	Pepper Rodgers	same
16	Colorado	8-4-0	Eddie Crowder	8-3-0
17	N.C. State	8-3-1	Lou Holtz	7-3-1
18	Louisville	9-1-0	Lee Corso	same
19	Washington St.	7-4-0	Jim Sweeney	same
20	Georgia Tech.	7-4-1	Bill Fulcher	6-4-1

Key Bowl Games

Rankings below reflect final regular season poll, released Dec. 4. No bowl for then #8 Michigan.
Rose–#1 USC over #3 Ohio St., 42-17; **Sugar**–#2 Oklahoma over #5 Penn St., 14-0; **Cotton**–#7 Texas over #4 Alabama, 17-13; **Orange**–#9 Nebraska over #12 Notre Dame, 40-6; **Gator**–#6 Auburn over #13 Colorado, 24-3; **Bluebonnet**–#11 Tennessee over #10 LSU, 24-17.

1973

		After Bowls	Head Coach	Regular Season
1	Notre Dame	11-0-0	Ara Parseghian	10-0-0
2	Ohio St.	10-0-1	Woody Hayes	9-0-1
3	Oklahoma	10-0-1	Barry Switzer	same
4	Alabama	11-1-0	Bear Bryant	11-0-0
5	Penn St.	12-0-0	Joe Paterno	11-0-0
6	Michigan	10-0-1	Bo Schembechler	same
7	Nebraska	9-2-1	Tom Osborne	8-2-1
8	USC	9-2-1	John McKay	9-1-1
9	Arizona St.	11-1-0	Frank Kush	10-1-0
	Houston	11-1-0	Bill Yeoman	10-1-0
11	Texas Tech	11-1-0	Jim Carlen	10-1-0
12	UCLA	9-2-0	Pepper Rodgers	same
13	LSU	9-3-0	Charlie McClendon	9-2-0
14	Texas	8-3-0	Darrell Royal	8-2-0
15	Miami-OH	11-0-0	Bill Mallory	10-0-0
16	N.C. State	9-3-0	Lou Holtz	8-3-0
17	Missouri	8-4-0	Al Onofrio	7-4-0
18	Kansas	7-4-1	Don Fambrough	7-3-1
19	Tennessee	8-4-0	Bill Battle	8-3-0
20	Maryland	8-4-0	Jerry Claiborne	8-3-0
	Tulane	9-3-0	Bennie Ellender	9-2-0

Key Bowl Games

Rankings below reflect final regular season poll, released Dec. 3. No bowls for then #2 Oklahoma (probation), #5 Michigan and #9 UCLA.
Sugar–#3 Notre Dame over #1 Alabama, 24-23; **Rose**–#4 Ohio St. over #7 USC, 42-21; **Orange**–#6 Penn St. over #13 LSU, 16-9; **Cotton**–#12 Nebraska over #8 Texas, 19-3; **Fiesta**–#10 Ariz. St. over Pitt, 28-7; **Bluebonnet**–#14 Houston over #17 Tulane, 47-7.

1974

	After Bowls	Head Coach	Regular Season
1	Oklahoma 11-0-0	Barry Switzer	same
2	USC 10-1-1	John McKay	9-1-1
3	Michigan 10-1-0	Bo Schembechler	same
4	Ohio St. 10-2-0	Woody Hayes	10-1-0
5	Alabama 11-1-0	Bear Bryant	11-0-0
6	Notre Dame 10-2-0	Ara Parseghian	9-2-0
7	Penn St. 10-2-0	Joe Paterno	9-2-0
8	Auburn..........10-2-0	Shug Jordan	9-2-0
9	Nebraska........9-3-0	Tom Osborne	8-3-0
10	Miami-OH 10-0-1	Dick Crum	9-0-1
11	N.C. State 9-2-1	Lou Holtz	9-2-0
12	Michigan St. 7-3-1	Denny Stolz	same
13	Maryland........8-4-0	Jerry Claiborne	8-3-0
14	Baylor...........8-4-0	Grant Teaff	8-3-0
15	Florida 8-4-0	Doug Dickey	8-3-0
16	Texas A&M 8-3-0	Emory Ballard	same
17	Mississippi St. 9-3-0	Bob Tyler	8-3-0
	Texas..........8-4-0	Darrell Royal	8-3-0
19	Houston 8-3-1	Bill Yeoman	8-3-0
20	Tennessee 7-3-2	Bill Battle	6-3-2

Key Bowl Games

Rankings below reflect final regular season poll, released Dec. 2. No bowls for #1 Oklahoma (probation) and then #4 Michigan.

Orange–#9 Notre Dame over #2 Alabama, 13-11; **Rose**–#5 USC over #3 Ohio St., 18-17; **Gator**–#6 Auburn over #11 Texas, 27-3; **Cotton**–#7 Penn St. over #12 Baylor, 41-20; **Sugar**–#8 Nebraska over #18 Florida, 13-10; **Liberty**–Tennessee over #10 Maryland, 7-3.

1975

	After Bowls	Head Coach	Regular Season
1	Oklahoma 11-1-0	Barry Switzer	10-1-0
2	Arizona St. 12-0-0	Frank Kush	11-0-0
3	Alabama 11-1-0	Bear Bryant	10-1-0
4	Ohio St...........11-1-0	Woody Hayes	11-0-0
5	UCLA 9-2-1	Dick Vermeil	8-2-1
6	Texas 10-2-0	Darrell Royal	9-2-0
7	Arkansas 10-2-0	Frank Broyles	9-2-0
8	Michigan 8-2-2	Bo Schembechler	8-1-2
9	Nebraska........10-2-0	Tom Osborne	10-1-0
10	Penn St. 9-3-0	Joe Paterno	9-2-0
11	Texas A&M 10-2-0	Emory Bellard	10-1-0
12	Miami-OH 11-1-0	Dick Crum	10-1-0
13	Maryland........9-2-1	Jerry Claiborne	8-2-1
14	California........8-3-0	Mike White	same
15	Pittsburgh 8-4-0	Johnny Majors	7-4-0
16	Colorado 9-3-0	Bill Mallory	9-2-0
17	USC 8-4-0	John McKay	7-4-0
18	Arizona 9-2-0	Jim Young	same
19	Georgia 9-3-0	Vince Dooley	9-2-0
20	West Virginia 9-3-0	Bobby Bowden	8-3-0

Key Bowl Games

Rankings below reflect final regular season poll, released Dec. 1. Texas A&M was unbeaten and ranked 2nd in that poll, but lost to #18 Arkansas, 31-6, in its final regular season game on Dec.6.

Rose–#11 UCLA over #1 Ohio St., 23-10; **Liberty**–#17 USC over #2 Texas A&M, 20-0; **Orange**–#3 Oklahoma over #5 Michigan, 14-6; **Sugar**–#4 Alabama over #8 Penn St., 13-6; **Fiesta**–#7 Ariz. St. over #6 Nebraska, 17-14; **Bluebonnet**–#9 Texas over #10 Colorado, 38-21; **Cotton**–#18 Arkansas over #12 Georgia, 31-10.

1976

	After Bowls	Head Coach	Regular Season
1	Pittsburgh 12-0-0	Johnny Majors	11-0-0
2	USC 11-1-0	John Robinson	10-1-0
3	Michigan 10-2-0	Bo Schembechler	10-1-0
4	Houston 10-2-0	Bill Yeoman	9-2-0
5	Oklahoma 9-2-1	Barry Switzer	8-2-1
6	Ohio St. 9-2-1	Woody Hayes	8-2-1
7	Texas A&M 10-2-0	Emory Bellard	9-2-0
8	Maryland........11-1-0	Jerry Claiborne	11-0-0
9	Nebraska........9-3-1	Tom Osborne	8-3-1
10	Georgia 10-2-0	Vince Dooley	10-1-0
11	Alabama 9-3-0	Bear Bryant	8-3-0
12	Notre Dame 9-3-0	Dan Devine	8-3-0
13	Texas Tech 10-2-0	Steve Sloan	10-1-0
14	Oklahoma St. 9-3-0	Jim Stanley	8-3-0
15	UCLA 9-2-1	Terry Donahue	9-1-1
16	Colorado 8-4-0	Bill Mallory	8-3-0
17	Rutgers 11-0-0	Frank Burns	same
18	Kentucky 8-4-0	Fran Curci	7-4-0
19	Iowa St. 8-3-0	Earle Bruce	same
20	Mississippi St. 9-2-0	Bob Tyler	same

Key Bowl Games

Rankings below reflect final regular season poll, released Nov. 29. No bowl for then #20 Miss. St. (probation).

Sugar–#1 Pitt over #5 Georgia, 27-3; **Rose**–#3 USC over #2 Michigan, 14-6; **Cotton**–#6 Houston over #4 Maryland, 30-21; **Liberty**–#16 Alabama over #7 UCLA, 36-6; **Fiesta**–#8 Oklahoma over Wyoming, 41-7; **Bluebonnet**–#13 Nebraska over #9 Texas Tech, 27-24; **Sun**–#10 Texas A&M over Florida, 37-14; **Orange**–#11 Ohio St. over #12 Colorado, 27-10.

1977

	After Bowls	Head Coach	Regular Season
1	Notre Dame 11-1-0	Dan Devine	10-1-0
2	Alabama 11-1-0	Bear Bryant	10-1-0
3	Arkansas 11-1-0	Lou Holtz	10-1-0
4	Texas 11-1-0	Fred Akers	11-0-0
5	Penn St. 11-1-0	Joe Paterno	10-1-0
6	Kentucky 10-1-0	Fran Curci	same
7	Oklahoma 10-2-0	Barry Switzer	10-1-0
8	Pittsburgh 9-2-1	Jackie Sherrill	8-2-1
9	Michigan 10-2-0	Bo Schembechler	10-1-0
10	Washington 8-4-0	Don James	7-4-0
11	Ohio St. 9-3-0	Woody Hayes	9-2-0
12	Nebraska........9-3-0	Tom Osborne	8-3-0
13	USC 8-4-0	John Robinson	7-4-0
14	Florida St. 10-2-0	Bobby Bowden	9-2-0
15	Stanford 9-3-0	Bill Walsh	8-3-0
16	San Diego St. 10-1-0	Claude Gilbert	same
17	North Carolina ...8-3-1	Bill Dooley	8-2-1
18	Arizona St........9-3-0	Frank Kush	9-2-0
19	Clemson.........8-3-1	Charley Pell	8-2-1
20	BYU.............9-2-0	LaVell Edwards	same

Key Bowl Games

Rankings below reflect final regular season poll, released Nov. 28. No bowl for then #7 Kentucky (probation).

Cotton–#5 Notre Dame over #1 Texas, 38-10; **Orange**–#6 Arkansas over #2 Oklahoma, 31-6; **Sugar**–#3 Alabama over #9 Ohio St., 35-6; **Rose**–#13 Washington over #4 Michigan, 27-20; **Fiesta**–#8 Penn St. over #15 Ariz. St., 42-30; **Gator**–#10 Pitt over #11 Clemson, 34-3.

Associated Press Final Polls (Cont.)

1978

		After Bowls	Head Coach	Regular Season
1	Alabama	11-1-0	Bear Bryant	10-1-0
2	USC	12-1-0	John Robinson	11-1-0
3	Oklahoma	11-1-0	Barry Switzer	10-1-0
4	Penn St.	11-1-0	Joe Paterno	11-0-0
5	Michigan	10-2-0	Bo Schembechler	10-1-0
6	Clemson	11-1-0	Charley Pell	10-1-0
7	Notre Dame	9-3-0	Dan Devine	8-3-0
8	Nebraska	9-3-0	Tom Osborne	9-2-0
9	Texas	9-3-0	Fred Akers	8-3-0
10	Houston	9-3-0	Bill Yeoman	9-2-0
11	Arkansas	9-2-1	Lou Holtz	9-2-0
12	Michigan St.	8-3-0	Darryl Rogers	same
13	Purdue	9-2-1	Jim Young	8-2-1
14	UCLA	8-3-1	Terry Donahue	8-3-0
15	Missouri	8-4-0	Warren Powers	7-4-0
16	Georgia	9-2-1	Vince Dooley	9-1-1
17	Stanford	8-4-0	Bill Walsh	7-4-0
18	N.C. State	9-3-0	Bo Rein	8-3-0
19	Texas A&M	8-4-0	Emory Bellard (4-2) & Tom Wilson (4-2)	7-4-0
20	Maryland	9-3-0	Jerry Claiborne	9-2-0

Key Bowl Games

Rankings below reflect final regular season poll, released Dec. 4. No bowl for then #12 Michigan St. (probation). **Sugar**–#2 Alabama over #1 Penn St., 14-7; **Rose**–#3 USC over #5 Michigan, 17-10; **Orange**–#4 Oklahoma over #6 Nebraska, 31-24; **Gator**–#7 Clemson over #20 Ohio St., 17-15; **Fiesta**–#8 Arkansas tied #15 UCLA, 10-10; **Cotton**–#10 Notre Dame over #9 Houston, 35-34.

1979

		After Bowls	Head Coach	Regular Season
1	Alabama	12-0-0	Bear Bryant	11-0-0
2	USC	11-0-1	John Robinson	10-0-1
3	Oklahoma	11-1-0	Barry Switzer	10-1-0
4	Ohio St.	11-1-0	Earle Bruce	11-0-0
5	Houston	11-1-0	Bill Yeoman	10-1-0
6	Florida St.	11-1-0	Bobby Bowden	11-0-0
7	Pittsburgh	11-1-0	Jackie Sherrill	10-1-0
8	Arkansas	10-2-0	Lou Holtz	10-1-0
9	Nebraska	10-2-0	Tom Osborne	10-1-0
10	Purdue	10-2-0	Jim Young	9-2-0
11	Washington	9-3-0	Don James	8-3-0
12	Texas	9-3-0	Fred Akers	9-2-0
13	BYU	11-1-0	LaVell Edwards	11-0-0
14	Baylor	8-4-0	Grant Teaff	7-4-0
15	North Carolina	8-3-1	Dick Crum	7-3-1
16	Auburn	8-3-0	Doug Barfield	same
17	Temple	10-2-0	Wayne Hardin	9-2-0
18	Michigan	8-4-0	Bo Schembechler	8-3-0
19	Indiana	8-4-0	Lee Corso	7-4-0
20	Penn St.	8-4-0	Joe Paterno	7-4-0

Key Bowl Games

Rankings below reflect final regular season poll, released Dec. 3. No bowl for then #17 Auburn (probation). **Sugar**–#2 Alabama over #6 Arkansas, 24-9; **Rose**–#3 USC over #1 Ohio St., 17-16; **Orange**–#5 Oklahoma over #4 Florida St., 24-7; **Sun**–#13 Washington over #11 Texas, 14-7; **Cotton**–#8 Houston over #7 Nebraska, 17-14; **Fiesta**–#10 Pitt over Arizona, 16-10.

1980

		After Bowls	Head Coach	Regular Season
1	Georgia	12-0-0	Vince Dooley	11-0-0
2	Pittsburgh	11-1-0	Jackie Sherrill	10-1-0
3	Oklahoma	10-2-0	Barry Switzer	9-2-0
4	Michigan	10-2-0	Bo Schembechler	9-2-0
5	Florida St.	10-2-0	Bobby Bowden	10-1-0
6	Alabama	10-2-0	Bear Bryant	9-2-0
7	Nebraska	10-2-0	Tom Osborne	9-2-0
8	Penn St.	10-2-0	Joe Paterno	9-2-0
9	Notre Dame	9-2-1	Dan Devine	9-1-1
10	North Carolina	11-1-0	Dick Crum	10-1-0
11	USC	8-2-1	John Robinson	same
12	BYU	12-1-0	LaVell Edwards	11-1-0
13	UCLA	9-2-0	Terry Donahue	same
14	Baylor	10-2-0	Grant Teaff	10-1-0
15	Ohio St.	9-3-0	Earle Bruce	9-2-0
16	Washington	9-3-0	Don James	9-2-0
17	Purdue	9-3-0	Jim Young	8-3-0
18	Miami-FL.	9-3-0	H. Schnellenberger	8-3-0
19	Mississippi St.	9-3-0	Emory Bellard	9-2-0
20	SMU	8-4-0	Ron Meyer	8-3-0

Key Bowl Games

Rankings below reflect final regular season poll, released Dec. 8. **Sugar**–#1 Georgia over #7 Notre Dame, 17-10; **Orange**–#4 Oklahoma over #2 Florida St., 18-17; **Gator**–#3 Pitt over #18 S. Carolina, 37-9; **Rose**–#5 Michigan over #16 Washington, 23-6; **Cotton**–#9 Alabama over #6 Baylor, 30-2; **Sun**–#8 Nebraska over #17 Miss. St., 31-17; **Fiesta**–#10 Penn St. over #11 Ohio St., 31-19; **Bluebonnet**–#13 N. Carolina over Texas, 16-7.

1981

		After Bowls	Head Coach	Regular Season
1	Clemson	12-0-0	Danny Ford	11-0-0
2	Texas	10-1-1	Fred Akers	9-1-1
3	Penn St.	10-2-0	Joe Paterno	9-2-0
4	Pittsburgh	11-1-0	Jackie Sherrill	10-1-0
5	SMU	10-1-0	Ron Meyer	same
6	Georgia	10-2-0	Vince Dooley	10-1-0
7	Alabama	9-2-1	Bear Bryant	9-1-1
8	Miami-FL.	9-2-0	H. Schnellenberger	same
9	North Carolina	10-2-0	Dick Crum	9-2-0
10	Washington	10-2-0	Don James	9-2-0
11	Nebraska	9-3-0	Tom Osborne	9-2-0
12	Michigan	9-3-0	Bo Schembechler	8-3-0
13	BYU	11-2-0	LaVell Edwards	10-2-0
14	USC	9-3-0	John Robinson	9-2-0
15	Ohio St.	9-3-0	Earle Bruce	8-3-0
16	Arizona St.	9-2-0	Darryl Rogers	same
17	West Virginia	9-3-0	Don Nehlen	8-3-0
18	Iowa	8-4-0	Hayden Fry	8-3-0
19	Missouri	8-4-0	Warren Powers	7-4-0
20	Oklahoma	7-4-1	Barry Switzer	6-4-1

Key Bowl Games

Rankings below reflect final regular season poll, released Nov. 30. No bowl for then #5 SMU (probation), #9 Miami-FL (probation), and #17 Ariz. St. (probation). **Orange**–#1 Clemson over #4 Nebraska, 22-15; **Sugar**–#10 Pitt over #2 Georgia, 24-20; **Cotton**–#6 Texas over #3 Alabama, 14-12; **Fiesta**–#7 Penn St. over #8 USC, 26-10; **Gator**–#11 N. Carolina over Arkansas, 31-27; **Rose**–#12 Washington over #13 Iowa, 28-0.

1982

		After Bowls	Head Coach	Regular Season
1	Penn St.	11-1-0	Joe Paterno	10-1-0
2	SMU	11-0-1	Bobby Collins	10-0-1
3	Nebraska	12-1-0	Tom Osborne	11-1-0
4	Georgia	11-1-0	Vince Dooley	11-0-0
5	UCLA	10-1-1	Terry Donahue	9-1-1
6	Arizona St.	10-2-0	Darryl Rogers	9-2-0
7	Washington	10-2-0	Don James	9-2-0
8	Clemson	9-1-1	Danny Ford	same
9	Arkansas	9-2-1	Lou Holtz	8-2-1
10	Pittsburgh	9-3-0	Foge Fazio	9-2-0
11	LSU	8-3-1	Jerry Stovall	8-2-1
12	Ohio St.	9-3-0	Earle Bruce	8-3-0
13	Florida St.	9-3-0	Bobby Bowden	8-3-0
14	Auburn	9-3-0	Pat Dye	8-3-0
15	USC	8-3-0	John Robinson	same
16	Oklahoma	8-4-0	Barry Switzer	8-3-0
17	Texas	9-3-0	Fred Akers	9-2-0
18	North Carolina	8-4-0	Dick Crum	7-4-0
19	West Virginia	9-3-0	Don Nehlen	9-2-0
20	Maryland	8-4-0	Bobby Ross	8-3-0

Key Bowl Games

Rankings below reflect final regular season poll, released Dec. 6. No bowl for then #7 Clemson (probation) and #15 USC (probation).
Sugar–#2 Penn St. over #1 Georgia, 27-23; **Orange**–#3 Nebraska over #13 LSU, 21-20; **Cotton**–#4 SMU over #6 Pitt, 7-3; **Rose**–#5 UCLA over #19 Michigan, 24-14; **Aloha**–#9 Washington over #16 Maryland, 21-20; **Fiesta**–#11 Ariz. St. over #12 Oklahoma, 32-21; **Bluebonnet**–#14 Arkansas over Florida, 28-24.

1983

		After Bowls	Head Coach	Regular Season
1	Miami-FL	11-1-0	H. Schnellenberger	10-1-0
2	Nebraska	12-1-0	Tom Osborne	12-0-0
3	Auburn	11-1-0	Pat Dye	10-1-0
4	Georgia	10-1-1	Vince Dooley	9-1-1
5	Texas	11-1-0	Fred Akers	11-0-0
6	Florida	9-2-1	Charley Pell	8-2-1
7	BYU	11-1-0	LaVell Edwards	10-1-0
8	Michigan	9-3-0	Bo Schembechler	9-2-0
9	Ohio St.	9-3-0	Earle Bruce	8-3-0
10	Illinois	10-2-0	Mike White	10-1-0
11	Clemson	9-1-1	Danny Ford	same
12	SMU	10-2-0	Bobby Collins	10-1-0
13	Air Force	10-2-0	Ken Hatfield	9-2-0
14	Iowa	9-3-0	Hayden Fry	9-2-0
15	Alabama	8-4-0	Ray Perkins	7-4-0
16	West Virginia	9-3-0	Don Nehlen	8-3-0
17	UCLA	7-4-1	Terry Donahue	6-4-1
18	Pittsburgh	8-3-1	Foge Fazio	8-2-1
19	Boston College	9-3-0	Jack Bicknell	9-2-0
20	East Carolina	8-3-0	Ed Emory	same

Key Bowl Games

Rankings below reflect final regular season poll, released Dec. 5. No bowl for then #12 Clemson (probation).
Orange–#5 Miami-FL over #1 Nebraska, 31-30; **Cotton**–#7 Georgia over #2 Texas, 10-9; **Sugar**– #3 Auburn over #8 Michigan, 9-7; **Rose**–UCLA over #4 Illinois, 45-9; **Holiday**–#9 BYU over Missouri, 21-17; **Gator**–#11 Florida over #10 Iowa, 14-6; **Fiesta**–#14 Ohio St. over #15 Pitt, 28-23.

1984

		After Bowls	Head Coach	Regular Season
1	BYU	13-0-0	LaVell Edwards	12-0-0
2	Washington	11-1-0	Don James	10-1-0
3	Florida	9-1-1	Charley Pell (0-1-1) & Galen Hall (9-0)	same
4	Nebraska	10-2-0	Tom Osborne	9-2-0
5	Boston College	10-2-0	Jack Bicknell	9-2-0
6	Oklahoma	9-2-1	Barry Switzer	9-1-1
7	Oklahoma St.	10-2-0	Pat Jones	9-2-0
8	SMU	10-2-0	Bobby Collins	9-2-0
9	UCLA	9-3-0	Terry Donahue	8-3-0
10	USC	9-3-0	Ted Tollner	8-3-0
11	South Carolina	10-2-0	Joe Morrison	10-1-0
12	Maryland	9-3-0	Bobby Ross	8-3-0
13	Ohio St.	9-3-0	Earle Bruce	9-2-0
14	Auburn	9-4-0	Pat Dye	8-4-0
15	LSU	8-3-1	Bill Arnsparger	8-2-1
16	Iowa	8-4-1	Hayden Fry	7-4-1
17	Florida St.	7-3-2	Bobby Bowden	7-3-1
18	Miami-FL	8-5-0	Jimmy Johnson	8-4-0
19	Kentucky	9-3-0	Jerry Claiborne	8-3-0
20	Virginia	8-2-2	George Welsh	7-2-2

Key Bowl Games

Rankings below reflect final regular season poll, released Dec. 3. No bowl for then #3 Florida (probation).
Holiday–#1 BYU over Michigan, 24-17;
Orange–#4 Washington over #2 Oklahoma, 28-17; **Sugar**–#5 Nebraska over #11 LSU, 28-10; **Rose**–#18 USC over #6 Ohio St., 20-17; **Gator**–#9 Okla. St. over #7 S. Carolina, 21-14; **Cotton**–#8 BC over Houston, 45-28; **Aloha**–#10 SMU over #17 Notre Dame, 27-20.

1985

		After Bowls	Head Coach	Regular Season
1	Oklahoma	11-1-0	Barry Switzer	10-1-0
2	Michigan	10-1-1	Bo Schembechler	9-1-1
3	Penn St.	11-1-0	Joe Paterno	11-0-0
4	Tennessee	9-1-2	Johnny Majors	8-1-2
5	Florida	9-1-1	Galen Hall	same
6	Texas A&M	10-2-0	Jackie Sherrill	9-2-0
7	UCLA	9-2-1	Terry Donahue	8-2-1
8	Air Force	12-1-0	Fisher DeBerry	11-1-0
9	Miami-FL	10-2-0	Jimmy Johnson	10-1-0
10	Iowa	10-2-0	Hayden Fry	10-1-0
11	Nebraska	9-3-0	Tom Osborne	9-2-0
12	Arkansas	10-2-0	Ken Hatfield	9-2-0
13	Alabama	9-2-1	Ray Perkins	8-2-1
14	Ohio St.	9-3-0	Earle Bruce	8-3-0
15	Florida St.	9-3-0	Bobby Bowden	8-3-0
16	BYU	11-3-0	LaVell Edwards	11-2-0
17	Baylor	9-3-0	Grant Teaff	8-3-0
18	Maryland	9-3-0	Bobby Ross	8-3-0
19	Georgia Tech	9-2-1	Bill Curry	8-2-1
20	LSU	9-2-1	Bill Arnsparger	9-1-1

Key Bowl Games

Rankings below reflect final regular season poll, released Dec. 9. No bowl for then #6 Florida (probation).
Orange–#3 Oklahoma over #1 Penn St., 25-10; **Sugar**–#8 Tennessee over #2 Miami-FL, 35-7; **Rose**–#13 UCLA over #4 Iowa, 45-28; **Fiesta**–#5 Michigan over #7 Nebraska, 27-23; **Bluebonnet**–#10 Air Force over Texas, 24-16; **Cotton**–#11 Texas A&M over #16 Auburn, 36-16.

Associated Press Final Polls (Cont.)

1986

		After Bowls	Head Coach	Regular Season
1	Penn St.	12-0-0	Joe Paterno	11-0-0
2	Miami-FL	11-1-0	Jimmy Johnson	11-0-0
3	Oklahoma	11-1-0	Barry Switzer	10-1-0
4	Arizona St.	10-1-1	John Cooper	9-1-1
5	Nebraska	10-2-0	Tom Osborne	9-2-0
6	Auburn	10-2-0	Pat Dye	9-2-0
7	Ohio St.	10-3-0	Earle Bruce	9-3-0
8	Michigan	11-2-0	Bo Schembechler	11-1-0
9	Alabama	10-3-0	Ray Perkins	9-3-0
10	LSU	9-3-0	Bill Arnsparger	9-2-0
11	Arizona	9-3-0	Larry Smith	8-3-0
12	Baylor	9-3-0	Grant Teaff	8-3-0
13	Texas A&M	9-3-0	Jackie Sherrill	9-2-0
14	UCLA	8-3-1	Terry Donahue	7-3-1
15	Arkansas	9-3-0	Ken Hatfield	9-2-0
16	Iowa	9-3-0	Hayden Fry	8-3-0
17	Clemson	8-2-2	Danny Ford	7-2-2
18	Washington	8-3-1	Don James	8-2-1
19	Boston College	9-3-0	Jack Bicknell	8-3-0
20	Virginia Tech	9-2-1	Bill Dooley	8-2-1

Key Bowl Games

Rankings below reflect final regular season poll, released Dec. 1.

Fiesta—#2 Penn St. over #1 Miami-FL, 14-10; **Orange**—#3 Oklahoma over #9 Arkansas, 42-8; **Rose**— #7 Ariz. St. over #4 Michigan, 22-15; **Sugar**—#6 Nebraska over #5 LSU, 30-15; **Cotton**—#11 Ohio St. over #8 Texas A&M, 28-12; **Citrus**—#10 Auburn over USC, 16-7; **Sun**—#13 Alabama over #12 Washington, 28-6.

1987

		After Bowls	Head Coach	Regular Season
1	Miami-FL	12-0-0	Jimmy Johnson	11-0-0
2	Florida St.	11-1-0	Bobby Bowden	10-1-0
3	Oklahoma	11-1-0	Barry Switzer	11-0-0
4	Syracuse	11-0-1	Dick MacPherson	11-0-0
5	LSU	10-1-1	Mike Archer	9-1-1
6	Nebraska	10-2-0	Tom Osborne	10-1-0
7	Auburn	9-1-2	Pat Dye	9-1-1
8	Michigan St.	9-2-1	George Perles	8-2-1
9	UCLA	10-2-0	Terry Donahue	9-2-0
10	Texas A&M	10-2-0	Jackie Sherrill	9-2-0
11	Oklahoma St.	10-2-0	Pat Jones	9-2-0
12	Clemson	10-2-0	Danny Ford	9-2-0
13	Georgia	9-3-0	Vince Dooley	8-3-0
14	Tennessee	10-2-1	Johnny Majors	9-2-1
15	South Carolina	8-4-0	Joe Morrison	8-3-0
16	Iowa	10-3-0	Hayden Fry	9-3-0
17	Notre Dame	8-4-0	Lou Holtz	8-3-0
18	USC	8-4-0	Larry Smith	8-3-0
19	Michigan	8-4-0	Bo Schembechler	7-4-0
20	Arizona St.	7-4-1	John Cooper	6-4-1

Key Bowl Games

Rankings below reflect final regular season poll, released Dec. 7.

Orange—#2 Miami-FL over #1 Oklahoma, 20-14; **Fiesta**—#3 Florida St. over #5 Nebraska, 31-28; **Sugar**—#4 Syracuse tied #6 Auburn 16-16; **Gator**—#7 LSU over #9 S. Carolina, 30-13; **Rose**—#8 Mich. over #16 USC, 20-17; **Aloha**—#10 UCLA over Florida, 20-16; **Cotton**—#13 Texas A&M over #12 Notre Dame, 35-10.

1988

		After Bowls	Head Coach	Regular Season
1	Notre Dame	12-0-0	Lou Holtz	11-0-0
2	Miami-FL	11-1-0	Jimmy Johnson	10-1-0
3	Florida St.	11-1-0	Bobby Bowden	10-1-0
4	Michigan	9-2-1	Bo Schembechler	8-2-1
5	West Virginia	11-1-0	Don Nehlen	11-0-0
6	UCLA	10-2-0	Terry Donahue	9-2-0
7	USC	10-2-0	Larry Smith	10-1-0
8	Auburn	10-2-0	Pat Dye	10-1-0
9	Clemson	10-2-0	Danny Ford	9-2-0
10	Nebraska	11-2-0	Tom Osborne	11-1-0
11	Oklahoma St.	10-2-0	Pat Jones	9-2-0
12	Arkansas	10-2-0	Ken Hatfield	10-1-0
13	Syracuse	10-2-0	Dick MacPherson	9-2-0
14	Oklahoma	9-3-0	Barry Switzer	9-2-0
15	Georgia	9-3-0	Vince Dooley	8-3-0
16	Washington St.	9-3-0	Dennis Erickson	8-3-0
17	Alabama	9-3-0	Bill Curry	8-3-0
18	Houston	9-3-0	Jack Pardee	9-2-0
19	LSU	8-4-0	Mike Archer	8-3-0
20	Indiana	8-3-1	Bill Mallory	7-3-1

Key Bowl Games

Rankings below reflect final regular season poll, released Dec. 5.

Fiesta—#1 Notre Dame over #3 West Va., 34-21; **Orange**—#2 Miami-FL over #6 Nebraska, 23-3; **Sugar**—#4 Florida St. over #7 Auburn, 13-7; **Rose**—#11 Michigan over #5 USC, 22-14; **Cotton**—#9 UCLA over #8 Arkansas, 17-3; **Citrus**—#13 Clemson over #10 Oklahoma, 13-6.

1989

		After Bowls	Head Coach	Regular Season
1	Miami-FL	11-1-0	Dennis Erickson	10-1-0
2	Notre Dame	12-1-0	Lou Holtz	11-1-0
3	Florida St.	10-2-0	Bobby Bowden	9-2-0
4	Colorado	11-1-0	Bill McCartney	11-0-0
5	Tennessee	11-1-0	Johnny Majors	10-1-0
6	Auburn	10-2-0	Pat Dye	9-2-0
7	Michigan	10-2-0	Bo Schembechler	10-1-0
8	USC	9-2-1	Larry Smith	8-2-1
9	Alabama	10-2-0	Bill Curry	10-1-0
10	Illinois	10-2-0	John Mackovic	9-2-0
11	Nebraska	10-2-0	Tom Osborne	10-1-0
12	Clemson	10-2-0	Danny Ford	9-2-0
13	Arkansas	10-2-0	Ken Hatfield	10-1-0
14	Houston	9-2-0	Jack Pardee	same
15	Penn St.	8-3-1	Joe Paterno	7-3-1
16	Michigan St.	8-4-0	George Perles	7-4-0
17	Pittsburgh	8-3-1	Mike Gottfried (7-3-1) & Paul Hackett (1-0)	7-3-1
18	Virginia	10-3-0	George Welsh	10-2-0
19	Texas Tech	9-3-0	Spike Dykes	8-3-0
20	Texas A&M	8-4-0	R.C. Slocum	8-3-0
21	West Virginia	8-3-1	Don Nehlen	8-2-1
22	BYU	10-3-0	LaVell Edwards	10-2-0
23	Washington	8-4-0	Don James	7-4-0
24	Ohio St.	8-4-0	John Cooper	8-3-0
25	Arizona	8-4-0	Dick Tomey	7-4-0

Key Bowl Games

Rankings below reflect final regular season poll, released Dec. 11. No bowl for then #13 Houston (probation).

Orange—#4 Notre Dame over #1 Colorado, 21-6; **Sugar**—#2 Miami-FL over #7 Alabama, 33-25; **Rose**— #12 USC over #3 Michigan, 17-10; **Fiesta**—#5 Florida St. over #6 Nebraska, 41-17; **Cotton**—#8 Tennessee over #10 Arkansas, 31-27; **Hall of Fame**—#9 Auburn over #21 Ohio St., 31-14; **Citrus**—#11 Illinois over #15 Virginia, 31-21.

1990

	After Bowls	Head Coach	Regular Season
1 Colorado	11-1-1	Bill McCartney	10-1-1
2 Georgia Tech	11-0-1	Bobby Ross	10-0-1
3 Miami-FL	10-2-0	Dennis Erickson	9-2-0
4 Florida St.	10-2-0	Bobby Bowden	9-2-0
5 Washington	10-2-0	Don James	9-2-0
6 Notre Dame	9-3-0	Lou Holtz	9-2-0
7 Michigan	9-3-0	Gary Moeller	8-3-0
8 Tennessee	9-2-2	Johnny Majors	8-2-2
9 Clemson	10-2-0	Ken Hatfield	9-2-0
10 Houston	10-1-0	John Jenkins	same
11 Penn St.	9-3-0	Joe Paterno	9-2-0
12 Texas	10-2-0	David McWilliams	10-1-0
13 Florida	9-2-0	Steve Spurrier	same
14 Louisville	10-1-1	H. Schnellenberger	9-1-1
15 Texas A&M	9-3-1	R.C. Slocum	8-3-1
16 Michigan St.	8-3-1	George Perles	7-3-1
17 Oklahoma	8-3-0	Gary Gibbs	same
18 Iowa	8-4-0	Hayden Fry	8-3-0
19 Auburn	8-3-1	Pat Dye	7-3-1
20 USC	8-4-1	Larry Smith	8-3-1
21 Mississippi	9-3-0	Billy Brewer	9-2-0
22 BYU	10-3-0	LaVell Edwards	10-2-0
23 Virginia	8-4-0	George Welsh	8-3-0
24 Nebraska	9-3-0	Tom Osborne	9-2-0
25 Illinois	8-4-0	John Mackovic	8-3-0

Key Bowl Games

Rankings below reflect final regular season poll, released Dec. 3. No bowl for then #9 Houston (probation), #11 Florida (probation) and #20 Oklahoma (probation).

Orange–#1 Colorado over #5 Notre Dame, 10-9; **Citrus**–#2 Ga. Tech over #19 Nebraska, 45-21; **Cotton**–#4 Miami-FL over #3 Texas, 46-3; **Blockbuster**–#6 Florida St. over #7 Penn St., 24-17; **Rose**–#8 Washington over #17 Iowa, 46-34; **Sugar**–#10 Tennessee over Virginia, 23-22; **Gator**–#12 Michigan over #15 Ole Miss, 35-3.

1991

	After Bowls	Head Coach	Regular Season
1 Miami-FL	12-0-0	Dennis Erickson	11-0-0
2 Washington	12-0-0	Don James	11-0-0
3 Penn St.	11-2-0	Joe Paterno	10-2-0
4 Florida St.	11-2-0	Bobby Bowden	10-2-0
5 Alabama	11-1-0	Gene Stallings	10-1-0
6 Michigan	10-2-0	Gary Moeller	10-1-0
7 Florida	10-2-0	Steve Spurrier	10-1-0
8 California	10-2-0	Bruce Snyder	9-2-0
9 East Carolina	11-1-0	Bill Lewis	10-1-0
10 Iowa	10-1-1	Hayden Fry	10-1-0
11 Syracuse	10-2-0	Paul Pasqualoni	9-2-0
12 Texas A&M	10-2-0	R.C. Slocum	10-1-0
13 Notre Dame	10-3-0	Lou Holtz	9-3-0
14 Tennessee	9-3-0	Johnny Majors	9-2-0
15 Nebraska	9-2-1	Tom Osborne	9-1-1
16 Oklahoma	9-3-0	Gary Gibbs	8-3-0
17 Georgia	9-3-0	Ray Goff	8-3-0
18 Clemson	9-2-1	Ken Hatfield	9-1-1
19 UCLA	9-3-0	Terry Donahue	8-3-0
20 Colorado	8-3-1	Bill McCartney	8-2-1
21 Tulsa	10-2-0	David Rader	9-2-0
22 Stanford	8-4-0	Dennis Green	8-3-0
23 BYU	8-3-2	LaVell Edwards	8-3-1
24 N.C. State	9-3-0	Dick Sheridan	9-2-0
25 Air Force	10-3-0	Fisher DeBerry	9-3-0

Key Bowl Games

Rankings below reflect final regular season poll, taken Dec. 2.

Orange–#1 Miami-FL over #11 Nebraska, 22-0; **Rose**–#2 Washington over #4 Michigan, 34-14; **Sugar**–#18 Notre Dame over #3 Florida, 39-28; **Cotton**–#5 Florida St. over #9 Texas A&M, 10-2; **Fiesta**–#6 Penn St. over #10 Tennessee, 42-17; **Holiday**–#7 Iowa tied BYU, 13-13; **Blockbuster**–#8 Alabama over #15 Colorado, 30-25; **Citrus**–#14 California over #13 Clemson, 37-13; **Peach**–#12 East Carolina over #21 N.C. State, 37-34.

1992

	After Bowls	Head Coach	Regular Season
1 Alabama	13-0-0	Gene Stallings	12-0-0
2 Florida St.	11-1-0	Bobby Bowden	10-1-0
3 Miami-FL	11-1-0	Dennis Erickson	11-0-0
4 Notre Dame	10-1-1	Lou Holtz	9-1-1
5 Michigan	9-0-3	Gary Moeller	8-0-3
6 Syracuse	10-2-0	Paul Pasqualoni	9-2-0
7 Texas A&M	12-1-0	R.C. Slocum	12-0-0
8 Georgia	10-2-0	Ray Goff	9-2-0
9 Stanford	10-3-0	Bill Walsh	9-3-0
10 Florida	9-4-0	Steve Spurrier	8-4-0
11 Washington	9-3-0	Don James	9-2-0
12 Tennessee	9-3-0	Johnny Majors (5-3) & Phillip Fulmer (4-0)	8-3-0
13 Colorado	9-2-1	Bill McCartney	9-1-1
14 Nebraska	9-3-0	Tom Osborne	9-2-0
15 Washington St.	9-3-0	Mike Price	8-3-0
16 Mississippi	9-3-0	Billy Brewer	8-3-0
17 N.C. State	9-3-1	Dick Sheridan	9-2-1
18 Ohio St.	8-3-1	John Cooper	8-2-1
19 North Carolina	9-3-0	Mack Brown	8-3-0
20 Hawaii	11-2-0	Bob Wagner	10-2-0
21 Boston College	8-3-1	Tom Coughlin	8-2-1
22 Kansas	8-4-0	Glen Mason	7-4-0
23 Mississippi St.	7-5-0	Jackie Sherrill	7-4-0
24 Fresno St.	9-4-0	Jim Sweeney	9-3-0
25 Wake Forest	8-4-0	Bill Dooley	7-4-0

Key Bowl Games

Rankings below reflect final regular season poll, taken Dec. 5.

Sugar–#2 Alabama over #1 Miami-FL, 34-13; **Orange**–#3 Florida St. over #11 Nebraska, 27-14; **Cotton**–#5 Notre Dame over #4 Texas A&M, 28-3; **Fiesta**–#6 Syracuse over #10 Colorado, 26-22; **Rose**–#7 Michigan over #9 Washington, 38-31; **Citrus**–#8 Georgia over #15 Ohio St., 21-14.

The Special Election That Didn't Count

There was one No. 1 vs No. 2 confrontation not noted in the Number 1 vs. Number 2 table on pages 154-5. It came in a special election or re-vote of AP selectors following the 1948 Rose Bowl. Here's what happened: Unbeaten Notre Dame was declared 1947 national champion by AP on Dec. 8, two days after closing out an undefeated season with a 38-7 rout of then third-ranked USC in Los Angeles. Twenty-four days later, however, unbeaten Michigan, AP's final No. 2 team, clobbered No. 8-ranked USC, 49-0, in the Rose Bowl. An immediate cry went up for an unprecedented two-team, "Who's No. 1" ballot and AP gave in. Michigan won the election, 226-119, with 12 voters calling it even. However, AP ruled that the Dec. 8 final poll won by Notre Dame would be the vote of record.

Associated Press Final Polls (Cont.)

1993

		After Bowls	Head Coach	Regular Season
1	Florida St	12-1-0	Bobby Bowden	11-1-0
2	Notre Dame	11-1-0	Lou Holtz	10-1-0
3	Nebraska	11-1-0	Tom Osborne	11-0-0
4	Auburn	11-0-0	Terry Bowden	11-0-0
5	Florida	11-2-0	Steve Spurrier	10-2-0
6	Wisconsin	10-1-1	Barry Alvarez	9-1-1
7	West Virginia	11-1-0	Don Nehlen	11-0-0
8	Penn St.	10-2-0	Joe Paterno	9-2-0
9	Texas A&M	10-2-0	R.C. Slocum	10-1-0
10	Arizona	10-2-0	Dick Tomey	9-2-0
11	Ohio St	10-1-1	John Cooper	9-1-1
12	Tennessee	9-2-1	Phillip Fulmer	9-1-1
13	Boston College	9-3-0	Tom Coughlin	8-3-0
14	Alabama	9-3-1	Gene Stallings	8-3-1
15	Miami-FL	9-3-0	Dennis Erickson	9-2-0
16	Colorado	8-3-1	Bill McCartney	7-3-1
17	Oklahoma	9-3-0	Gary Gibbs	8-3-0
18	UCLA	8-4-0	Terry Donahue	8-3-0
19	North Carolina	10-3-0	Mack Brown	10-2-0
20	Kansas St	9-2-1	Bill Snyder	8-2-1
21	Michigan	8-4-0	Gary Moeller	7-4-0
22	Va. Tech	9-3-0	Frank Beamer	9-2-0
23	Clemson	9-3-0	Ken Hatfield (8-3)	8-3-0
			& Tommy West (1-0)	
24	Louisville	9-3-0	H. Schnellenberger	8-3-0
25	California	9-4-0	Keith Gilbertson	8-4-0

Key Bowl Games

Rankings below reflect final regular season poll, taken Dec. 5. No bowl for then #5 Auburn (probation).
Orange–#1 Florida St. over #2 Nebraska, 18-16; **Sugar**–#8 Florida over #3 West Virginia, 41-7; **Cotton**–#4 Notre Dame over #7 Texas A&M, 24-21; **Citrus**–#13 Penn St. over #6 Tennessee, 31-13; **Rose**–#9 Wisconsin over #14 UCLA, 21-16; **Fiesta**–#16 Arizona over #10 Miami-FL, 29-0; **Holiday**–#11 Ohio St. over BYU, 28-21; **Gator**–#18 Alabama over #12 North Carolina, 24-10; **Carquest**–#15 Boston College over Virginia, 31-13.

1994

		After Bowls	Head Coach	Regular Season
1	Nebraska	13-0-0	Tom Osborne	12-0-0
2	Penn St.	12-0-0	Joe Paterno	11-0-0
3	Colorado	11-1-0	Bill McCartney	10-1-0
4	Florida St.	10-1-1	Bobby Bowden	9-1-1
5	Alabama	12-1-0	Gene Stallings	11-1-0
6	Miami-FL	10-2-0	Dennis Erickson	10-1-0
7	Florida	10-2-1	Steve Spurrier	10-1-1
8	Texas A&M	10-0-1	R.C. Slocum	same
9	Auburn	9-1-1	Terry Bowden	same
10	Utah	10-2-0	Ron McBride	9-2-0
11	Oregon	9-4-0	Rich Brooks	9-3-0
12	Michigan	8-4-0	Gary Moeller	7-4-0
13	USC	8-3-1	John Robinson	7-3-1
14	Ohio St.	9-4-0	John Cooper	9-3-0
15	Virginia	9-3-0	George Welsh	8-3-0
16	Colorado St.	10-2-0	Sonny Lubick	10-1-0
17	N.C. State	9-3-0	Mike O'Cain	8-3-0
18	BYU	10-3-0	LaVell Edwards	9-3-0
19	Kansas St	9-3-0	Bill Snyder	9-2-0
20	Arizona	8-4-0	Dick Tomey	8-3-0
21	Washington St.	8-4-0	Mike Price	7-4-0
22	Tennessee	8-4-0	Phillip Fulmer	7-4-0
23	Boston College	7-4-1	Dan Henning	6-4-1
24	Mississippi St.	8-4-0	Jackie Sherrill	8-3-0
25	Texas	8-4-0	John Mackovic	7-4-0

Key Bowl Games

Rankings below reflect final regular season poll, taken Dec. 4. No bowls for then #8 Texas A&M (probation) and #9 Auburn (probation).
Orange– #1 Nebraska over #3 Miami-FL, 24-17; **Rose**– #2 Penn St. over #12 Oregon, 38-20; **Fiesta**–#4 Colorado over Notre Dame, 41-24; **Sugar**– #7 Florida St. over #5 Florida, 23-17; **Citrus**– #6 Alabama over #13 Ohio St., 24-17; **Freedom**– #14 Utah over #15 Arizona, 16-13.

1995

		After Bowls	Head Coach	Regular Season
1	Nebraska	12-0-0	Tom Osborne	11-0-0
2	Florida	12-1-0	Steve Spurrier	12-0-0
3	Tennessee	11-1-0	Phillip Fulmer	10-1-0
4	Florida St	10-2-0	Bobby Bowden	9-2-0
5	Colorado	10-2-0	Rick Neuheisel	9-2-0
6	Ohio St.	11-2-0	John Cooper	11-1-0
7	Kansas St.	10-2-0	Bill Snyder	9-2-0
8	Northwestern	10-2-0	Gary Barnett	10-1-0
9	Kansas	10-2-0	Glen Mason	9-2-0
10	Va. Tech	10-2-0	Frank Beamer	9-2-0
11	Notre Dame	9-3-0	Lou Holtz	9-2-0
12	USC	9-2-1	John Robinson	8-2-1
13	Penn St.	9-3-0	Joe Paterno	8-3-0
14	Texas	10-2-1	John Mackovic	10-1-1
15	Texas A&M	9-3-0	R.C. Slocum	8-3-0
16	Virginia	9-4-0	George Welsh	8-4-0
17	Michigan	9-4-0	Lloyd Carr	9-3-0
18	Oregon	9-3-0	Mike Bellotti	9-2-0
19	Syracuse	9-3-0	Paul Pasqualoni	8-3-0
20	Miami-FL	8-3-0	Butch Davis	same
21	Alabama	8-3-0	Gene Stallings	same
22	Auburn	8-4-0	Terry Bowden	8-3-0
23	Texas Tech	9-3-0	Spike Dykes	8-3-0
24	Toledo	11-0-1	Gary Pinkel	10-0-1
25	Iowa	8-4-0	Hayden Fry	7-4-0

Key Bowl Games

Rankings below reflect final regular season poll, taken Dec. 3. No bowl for then #21 Alabama (probation) and #22 Miami-FL (probation).
Fiesta– #1 Nebraska over #2 Florida, 62-24; **Rose**– #17 USC over #3 Northwestern, 41-32; **Citrus**– #4 (tie) Tennessee over #4 (tie) Ohio St., 20-14; **Orange**– #8 Florida St. over #6 Notre Dame, 31-26; **Cotton**– #7 Colorado over #12 Oregon, 38-6; **Sugar**– #13 Va. Tech over #9 Texas, 28-10; **Holiday**– #10 Kansas St. over Colo. St., 54-21; **Aloha**– #11 Kansas over UCLA, 51-30; **Alamo**– #19 Texas A&M over #14 Michigan, 22-20; **Outback**– #15 Penn St. over #16 Auburn, 43-14; **Peach**– #18 Virginia over Georgia, 34-27; **Gator**– Syracuse over #23 Clemson, 41-0.

1996

	After Bowls	Head Coach	Regular Season
1	Florida........12-1	Steve Spurrier	11-1
2	Ohio St...........11-1	John Cooper	10-1
3	Florida St........11-1	Bobby Bowden	11-0
4	Arizona St........11-1	Bruce Snyder	11-0
5	BYU 14-1	LaVell Edwards	13-1
6	Nebraska........11-2	Tom Osborne	10-2
7	Penn St..........11-2	Joe Paterno	10-2
8	Colorado.........10-2	Rick Neuheisel	9-2
9	Tennessee........10-2	Phillip Fulmer	9-2
10	North Carolina.....10-2	Mack Brown	9-2
11	Alabama..........10-3	Gene Stallings	9-3
12	LSU..............10-2	Gerry DiNardo	9-2
13	Virginia Tech......10-2	Frank Beamer	10-1
14	Miami-FL 9-3	Butch Davis	8-3
15	Northwestern......9-3	Gary Barnett	9-2
16	Washington......9-3	Jim Lambright	9-2
17	Kansas St..........9-3	Bill Snyder	9-2
18	Iowa...............9-3	Hayden Fry	8-3
19	Notre Dame.......8-3	Lou Holtz	same
20	Michigan..........8-4	Lloyd Carr	8-3
21	Syracuse 9-3	Paul Pasqualoni	8-3
22	Wyoming 10-2	Joe Tiller	same
23	Texas 8-5	John Mackovic	8-4
24	Auburn............8-4	Terry Bowden	7-4
25	Army 10-2	Bob Sutton	10-1

Key Bowl Games
Rankings below reflect final regular season poll, taken Dec. 8. No bowl for then #18 Notre Dame and #22 Wyoming.
Sugar– #3 Florida over #1 Florida St., 52-20; **Rose–** #4 Ohio St. over #2 Arizona St., 20-17; **Fiesta–** #7 Penn St. over #20 Texas, 38-15; **Cotton–** #5 BYU over #14 Kansas St., 19-15; **Citrus–** #9 Tennessee over #11 Northwestern, 48-28; **Orange–** #6 Nebraska over #10 Virginia Tech, 41-21; **Gator–** #12 North Carolina over #25 West Virginia, 20-13; **Outback–** #16 Alabama over #15 Michigan, 17-14. **Carquest–** #19 Miami over Virginia, 31-21.

1997

	After Bowls	Head Coach	Regular Season
1	Michigan.........12-0	Lloyd Carr	11-0
2	Nebraska 13-0	Tom Osborne	12-0
3	Florida St 11-1	Bobby Bowden	10-1
4	Florida............10-2	Steve Spurrier	9-2
5	UCLA.............10-2	Bob Toledo	9-2
6	North Carolina.....11-1	Mack Brown (10-1) & Carl Torbush (1-0)	10-1
7	Tennessee........11-2	Phillip Fulmer	11-1
8	Kansas St.........11-1	Bill Snyder	10-1
9	Washington St.....10-2	Mike Price	10-1
10	Georgia 10-2	Jim Donnan	9-2
11	Auburn 10-3	Terry Bowden	9-3
12	Ohio St...........10-3	John Cooper	10-2
13	LSU 9-3	Gerry DiNardo	8-3
14	Arizona St. 8-3	Bruce Snyder	7-3
15	Purdue 9-3	Joe Tiller	8-3
16	Penn St. 9-3	Joe Paterno	9-2
17	Colorado St........11-2	Sonny Lubick	10-2
18	Washington........8-4	Jim Lambright	7-4
19	So. Mississippi 9-3	Jeff Bower	8-3
20	Texas A&M 9-4	R.C. Slocum	9-3
21	Syracuse 9-4	Paul Pasqualoni	9-3
22	Mississippi........8-4	Tommy Tuberville	7-4
23	Missouri...........7-5	Larry Smith	6-5
24	Oklahoma St.......8-4	Bobby Simmons	8-3
25	Georgia Tech 7-5	George O'Leary	6-5

Key Bowl Games
Rankings below reflect final regular season poll, taken Dec. 7.
Rose– #1 Michigan over #7 Washington St., 21-16; **Orange–** #2 Nebraska over #3 Tennessee, 42-17; **Sugar–** #4 Florida St. over #10 Ohio St., 31-14; **Gator–** #5 North Carolina over Virginia Tech, 42-3; **Cotton–** #6 UCLA over #19 Texas A&M, 29-23; **Citrus–** #8 Florida over #12 Penn St., 21-6; **Fiesta–** #9 Kansas St. over #14 Syracuse, 35-18; **Outback–** #11 Georgia over Wisconsin, 33-6; **Peach–** #13 Auburn over Clemson, 21-17; **Independence–** #15 LSU over Notre Dame, 27-9; **Alamo–** #16 Purdue over #24 Oklahoma St., 33-20; **Holiday–** #17 Colorado St. over #20 Missouri, 35-24.

1998

	After Bowls	Head Coach	Regular Season
1	Tennessee 13-0	Phillip Fulmer	12-0
2	Ohio St............11-1	John Cooper	10-1
3	Florida St 11-2	Bobby Bowden	11-1
4	Arizona...........12-1	Dick Tomey	11-1
5	Florida 10-2	Steve Spurrier	9-2
6	Wisconsin.........11-1	Barry Alvarez	10-1
7	Tulane 12-0	Tommy Bowden	11-0
8	UCLA.............10-2	Bob Toledo	10-1
9	Georgia Tech 10-2	George O'Leary	9-2
10	Kansas St..........11-2	Bill Snyder	11-1
11	Texas A&M 11-3	R.C. Slocum	11-2
12	Michigan..........10-3	Lloyd Carr	9-3
13	Air Force 12-1	Fisher DeBerry	11-1
14	Georgia...........9-3	Jim Donnan	8-3
15	Texas 9-3	Mack Brown	8-3
16	Arkansas..........9-3	Houston Nutt	9-2
17	Penn St............9-3	Joe Paterno	8-3
18	Virginia 9-3	George Welsh	9-2
19	Nebraska..........9-4	Frank Solich	9-3
20	Miami-FL 9-3	Butch Davis	8-3
21	Missouri...........8-4	Larry Smith	7-4
22	Notre Dame 9-3	Bob Davie	9-2
23	Va. Tech...........9-3	Frank Beamer	8-3
24	Purdue 9-4	Joe Tiller	8-4
25	Syracuse 8-4	Paul Pasqualoni	8-3

Key Bowl Games
Rankings below reflect final regular season poll, taken Dec. 6.
Fiesta– #1 Tennessee over #2 Florida St., 23-16; **Sugar–** #3 Ohio St. over #8 Texas A&M, 24-14; **Orange–** #7 Florida over #18 Syracuse, 31-10; **Rose–** #9 Wisconsin over #6 UCLA, 38-31; **Holiday–** #5 Arizona over #14 Nebraska, 23-20; **Citrus–** #15 Michigan over #11 Arkansas, 45-31; **Gator–** #12 Georgia Tech over #17 Notre Dame, 35-28; **Cotton–** #20 Texas over #25 Mississippi St., 38-11; **Peach–** #19 Georgia over #13 Virginia, 35-33; **Alamo–** Purdue over #4 Kansas St., 37-34; **Outback–** #22 Penn St. over Kentucky, 26-14.

Associated Press Final Polls (Cont.)

1999

		After Bowls	Head Coach	Regular Season
1	Florida St.	12-0	Bobby Bowden	11-0
2	Va. Tech.	11-1	Frank Beamer	11-0
3	Nebraska	12-1	Frank Solich	11-1
4	Wisconsin	10-2	Barry Alvarez	9-2
5	Michigan	10-2	Lloyd Carr	9-2
6	Kansas St.	11-1	Bill Snyder	10-1
7	Michigan St.	10-2	Nick Saban (9-2) & Bobby Williams (1-0)	9-2
8	Alabama	10-3	Mike DuBose	10-2
9	Tennessee	9-3	Phillip Fulmer	8-3
10	Marshall	13-0	Bob Pruett	12-0
11	Penn St.	10-3	Joe Paterno	9-3
12	Florida	9-4	Steve Spurrier	9-3
13	Mississippi St.	10-2	Jackie Sherrill	9-2
14	Southern Miss.	9-3	Jeff Bower	8-3
15	Miami-FL	9-4	Butch Davis	8-4
16	Georgia	8-4	Jim Donnan	7-4
17	Arkansas	8-4	Houston Nutt	7-4
18	Minnesota	8-4	Glen Mason	8-3
19	Oregon	9-3	Mike Bellotti	8-3
20	Georgia Tech	8-4	George O'Leary	8-3
21	Texas	9-5	Mack Brown	9-4
22	Mississippi	8-4	David Cutcliffe	7-4
23	Texas A&M	8-4	R.C. Slocum	8-3
24	Illinois	8-4	Ron Turner	7-4
25	Purdue	7-5	Joe Tiller	7-4

All-Time AP Top 20

The composite AP Top 20 from the 1936 season through the 1999 season, based on the final rankings of each year. The final AP poll has been taken after the bowl games in 1965 and since 1968. Team point totals are based on 20 points for all 1st place finishes, 19 for each 2nd, etc. Also listed are the number of times each team has been named national champion by AP and times ranked in the final Top 10 and Top 20.

Final AP

		Pts	No.1	Top 10	Top 20
1	Notre Dame	626	8	34	44
2	Michigan	591	2	34	47
3	Alabama	564	6	31	42
4	Oklahoma	558	6	29	41
5	Nebraska	520	4	28	39
6	Ohio St.	518	3	24	41
7	Tennessee	433	2	21	36
8	USC	414	3	20	36
9	Texas	406	2	19	32
10	Penn St.	403	2	21	35
11	UCLA	322	0	16	29
12	Florida St.	292	2	15	19
13	Auburn	281	1	14	26
14	LSU	277	1	14	25
15	Miami-FL	271	4	13	23
16	Arkansas	267	0	13	25
17	Georgia	261	1	14	23
18	Michigan St.	252	1	13	20
19	Florida	228	1	11	20
20	Texas A&M	216	1	11	22

Key Bowl Games

Rankings below reflect final regular season poll, taken Dec. 5. **Sugar–** #1 Florida St. over #2 Va. Tech, 46-29; **Fiesta–** #3 Nebraska over #6 Tennessee, 31-21; **Rose–** #4 Wisconsin over #22 Stanford, 17-9; **Orange–** #8 Michigan over #5 Alabama, 35-34; **Holiday–** #7 Kansas St. over Washington, 24-20; **Citrus–** #9 Michigan St. over #10 Florida, 37-34; **Motor City–** #11 Marshall over BYU, 21-3; **Sun–** Oregon over #12 Minnesota, 24-20; **Alamo–** #13 Penn St. over #18 Texas A&M, 24-0; **Cotton–** #24 Arkansas over #14 Texas, 27-6; **Peach–** #15 Mississippi St. over Clemson, 17-7; **Liberty–** #16 Southern Miss. over Colorado St., 23-17; **Gator–** #23 Miami-FL over #17 Georgia Tech, 28-13; **Outback–** #21 Georgia over #19 Purdue, 28-25.

Bowl Games

From Jan. 1, 1902 through Jan. 4, 2000. Corporate title sponsors and automatic berths updated through Jan. 4, 2000. Please note that the Bowl selection process is now dominated by the recently inaugurated Bowl Championship Series (which includes the Fiesta, Orange, Rose and Sugar bowls) and the following non-BCS bowls' so called "automatic berths" are contingent upon several factors, including the leftovers from the BCS, Notre Dame's record and the record of their designated choices.

Rose Bowl

City: Pasadena, Calif. **Stadium:** Rose Bowl. **Capacity:** 102,083. **Playing surface:** Grass. **First game:** Jan. 1, 1902. **Playing sites:** Tournament Park (1902, 1916-22), Rose Bowl (1923-41 and since 1943) and Duke Stadium in Durham, N.C. (1942, due to wartime restrictions following Japan's attack at Pearl Harbor on Dec. 7, 1941). **Corporate sponsor:** AT&T (since 1998).

    Automatic berths: Pacific Coast Conference champion vs. opponent selected by PCC (1924-45 seasons); Big Ten champion vs. Pac-10 champion (1946-97); Bowl Championship Series: Big Ten champion vs. Pac-10 champion, if available (1998-2000 seasons) and #1 vs. #2 on Jan. 3, 2002.

    Multiple wins: USC (20); Michigan (8); Ohio St. and Washington (6); Stanford and UCLA (5); Alabama (4); Illinois, Michigan St. and Wisconsin (3); California and Iowa (2).

Year		Year		Year	
1902*	Michigan 49, Stanford 0	1929	Georgia Tech 8, California 7	1943	Georgia 9, UCLA 0
1916	Washington St. 14, Brown 0	1930	USC 47, Pittsburgh 14	1944	USC 29, Washington 0
1917	Oregon 14, Penn 0	1931	Alabama 24, Washington St. 0	1945	USC 25, Tennessee 0
1918	Mare Island 19, Camp Lewis 7	1932	USC 21, Tulane 12	1946	Alabama 34, USC 14
1919	Great Lakes 17, Mare Island 0	1933	USC 35, Pittsburgh 0	1947	Illinois 45, UCLA 14
1920	Harvard 7, Oregon 6	1934	Columbia 7, Stanford 0	1948	Michigan 49, USC 0
1921	California 28, Ohio St. 0	1935	Alabama 29, Stanford 13	1949	Northwestern 20, California 14
1922	0-0, California vs Wash. & Jeff.	1936	Stanford 7, SMU 0	1950	Ohio St. 17, California 14
1923	USC 14, Penn St. 0	1937	Pittsburgh 21, Washington 0	1951	Michigan 14, California 6
1924	14-14, Navy vs Washington	1938	California 13, Alabama 0	1952	Illinois 40, Stanford 7
1925	Notre Dame 27, Stanford 10	1939	USC 7, Duke 3	1953	USC 7, Wisconsin 0
1926	Alabama 20, Washington 19	1940	USC 14, Tennessee 0	1954	Michigan St. 28, UCLA 20
1927	7-7, Alabama vs Stanford	1941	Stanford 21, Nebraska 13	1955	Ohio St. 20, USC 7
1928	Stanford 7, Pittsburgh 6	1942	Oregon St. 20, Duke 16	1956	Michigan St. 17, UCLA 14

Year		Year		Year	
1957	Iowa 35, Oregon St. 19	1973	USC 42, Ohio St. 17	1989	Michigan 22, USC 14
1958	Ohio St. 10, Oregon 7	1974	Ohio St. 42, USC 21	1990	USC 17, Michigan 10
1959	Iowa 38, California 12	1975	USC 18, Ohio St. 17	1991	Washington 46, Iowa 34
		1976	UCLA 23, Ohio St. 10	1992	Washington 34, Michigan 14
1960	Washington 44, Wisconsin 8	1977	USC 14, Michigan 6	1993	Michigan 38, Washington 31
1961	Washington 17, Minnesota 7	1978	Washington 27, Michigan 20	1994	Wisconsin 21, UCLA 16
1962	Minnesota 21, UCLA 3	1979	USC 17, Michigan 10	1995	Penn St. 38, Oregon 20
1963	USC 42, Wisconsin 37			1996	USC 41, Northwestern 32
1964	Illinois 17, Washington 7	1980	USC 17, Ohio St. 16	1997	Ohio St. 20, Arizona St. 17
1965	Michigan 34, Oregon St. 7	1981	Michigan 23, Washington 6	1998	Michigan 21, Washington St. 16
1966	UCLA 14, Michigan St. 12	1982	Washington 28, Iowa 0	1999	Wisconsin 38, UCLA 31
1967	Purdue 14, USC 13	1983	UCLA 24, Michigan 14		
1968	USC 14, Indiana 3	1984	UCLA 45, Illinois 9	2000	Wisconsin 17, Stanford 9
1969	Ohio St. 27, USC 16	1985	USC 20, Ohio St. 17	*January game since 1902.
		1986	UCLA 45, Iowa 28		
1970	USC 10, Michigan 3	1987	Arizona St. 22, Michigan 15		
1971	Stanford 27, Ohio St. 17	1988	Michigan St. 20, USC 17		
1972	Stanford 13, Michigan 12				

Fiesta Bowl

City: Tempe, Ariz. **Stadium:** Sun Devil. **Capacity:** 73,656. **Playing surface:** Grass. **First game:** Dec. 27, 1971. **Playing site:** Sun Devil Stadium (since 1971). **Corporate title sponsors:** Sunkist Citrus Growers (1986-91), IBM OS/2 (1993-95) and Frito-Lay Tostitos chips (since 1996).

Automatic berths: Western Athletic Conference champion vs. at-large opponent (1971-79 seasons); Two of first five picks from 8-team Bowl Coalition pool (1992-94); Bowl Alliance (#1 vs. #2 on Jan. 2, 1996; #3 vs. #5 on Jan. 1, 1997; and #4 vs. #6 on Dec. 31, 1997); Big 12 champion vs. next best team in pool (New Bowl Alliance 1995-1997 seasons); Bowl Championship Series: #1 vs. #2 on Jan. 4, 1999 and Big 12 champion, if available, vs. at-large (1999-2001 seasons).

Multiple wins: Penn St. (6); Arizona St. (5); Florida St. and Nebraska (2).

Year		Year		Year	
1971†	Arizona St. 45, Florida 38	1983	Arizona St. 32, Oklahoma 21	1994	Arizona 29, Miami-FL 0
1972	Arizona St. 49, Missouri 35	1984	Ohio St. 28, Pittsburgh 23	1995	Colorado 41, Notre Dame 24
1973	Arizona St. 28, Pittsburgh 7	1985	UCLA 39, Miami-FL 37	1996	Nebraska 62, Florida 24
1974	Oklahoma St. 16, BYU 6	1986	Michigan 27, Nebraska 23	1997	Penn St. 38, Texas 15
1975	Arizona St. 17, Nebraska 14	1987	Penn St. 14, Miami-FL 10	1997†	Kansas St. 35, Syracuse 18
1976	Oklahoma 41, Wyoming 7	1988	Florida St. 31, Nebraska 28	1999	Tennessee 23, Florida St. 16
1977	Penn St. 42, Arizona St. 30	1989	Notre Dame 34, West Va. 21		
1978	10-10, Arkansas vs UCLA			2000	Nebraska 31, Tennessee 21
1979	Pittsburgh 16, Arizona 10	1990	Florida St. 41, Nebraska 17	†December game from 1971-80 and
		1991	Louisville 34, Alabama 7	in '97.
1980	Penn St. 31, Ohio St. 19	1992	Penn St. 42, Tennessee 17	* January game since 1982.
1982*	Penn St. 26, USC 10	1993	Syracuse 26, Colorado 22		

Sugar Bowl

City: New Orleans, La. **Stadium:** Louisiana Superdome. **Capacity:** 77,446. **Playing surface:** AstroTurf. **First game:** Jan. 1, 1935. **Playing sites:** Tulane Stadium (1935-74) and Superdome (since 1975). **Corporate title sponsors:** USF&G Financial Services (1987-95) and Nokia cellular telephones of Finland (starting in 1995).

Automatic berths: SEC champion vs. at-large opponent (1976-91 seasons); SEC champion vs. one of first five picks from 8-team Bowl Coalition pool (1992-94 seasons); #4 vs. #6 on Dec. 31, 1995; #1 vs. #2 on Jan. 2, 1997; and #3 vs. #5 on Jan. 1, 1998; Bowl Championship Series: SEC champion, if available, vs. at-large (1998-99, 2000 seasons) and #1 vs. #2 on Jan. 4, 2000.

Multiple wins: Alabama (8); Mississippi (5); Florida St., Georgia Tech, Oklahoma and Tennessee (4); LSU and Nebraska (3); Florida, Georgia, Notre Dame, Pittsburgh, Santa Clara and TCU (2).

Year		Year		Year	
1935*	Tulane 20, Temple 14	1954	Georgia Tech 42, West Va. 19	1972†	Oklahoma 14, Penn St. 0
1936	TCU 3, LSU 2	1955	Navy 21, Mississippi 0	1973	Notre Dame 24, Alabama 23
1937	Santa Clara 21, LSU 14	1956	Georgia Tech 7, Pittsburgh 0	1974	Nebraska 13, Florida 10
1938	Santa Clara 6, LSU 0	1957	Baylor 13, Tennessee 7	1975	Alabama 13, Penn St. 6
1939	TCU 15, Carnegie Tech 7	1958	Mississippi 39, Texas 7	1977*	Pittsburgh 27, Georgia 3
		1959	LSU 7, Clemson 0	1978	Alabama 35, Ohio St. 6
1940	Texas A&M 14, Tulane 13			1979	Alabama 14, Penn St. 7
1941	Boston College 19, Tennessee 13	1960	Mississippi 21, LSU 0		
1942	Fordham 2, Missouri 0	1961	Mississippi 14, Rice 6	1980	Alabama 24, Arkansas 9
1943	Tennessee 14, Tulsa 7	1962	Alabama 10, Arkansas 3	1981	Georgia 17, Notre Dame 10
1944	Georgia Tech 20, Tulsa 18	1963	Mississippi 17, Arkansas 13	1982	Pittsburgh 24, Georgia 20
1945	Duke 29, Alabama 26	1964	Alabama 12, Mississippi 7	1983	Penn St. 27, Georgia 23
1946	Okla. A&M 33, St.Mary's 13	1965	LSU 13, Syracuse 10	1984	Auburn 9, Michigan 7
1947	Georgia 20, N. Carolina 10	1966	Missouri 20, Florida 18	1985	Nebraska 28, LSU 10
1948	Texas 27, Alabama 7	1967	Alabama 34, Nebraska 7	1986	Tennessee 35, Miami-FL 7
1949	Oklahoma 14, N. Carolina 6	1968	LSU 20, Wyoming 13	1987	Nebraska 30, LSU 15
		1969	Arkansas 16, Georgia 2	1988	16-16, Syracuse vs Auburn
1950	Oklahoma 35, LSU 0			1989	Florida St. 13, Auburn 7
1951	Kentucky 13, Oklahoma 7	1970	Mississippi 27, Arkansas 22		
1952	Maryland 28, Tennessee 13	1971	Tennessee 34, Air Force 13	1990	Miami-FL 33, Alabama 25
1953	Georgia Tech 24, Mississippi 7	1972	Oklahoma 40, Auburn 22	1991	Tennessee 23, Virginia 22

Bowl Games (Cont.)

Year		Year		Year	
1992	Notre Dame 39, Florida 28	1995†	Va. Tech 28, Texas 10	2000	Florida St. 46, Va. Tech 29
1993	Alabama 34, Miami-FL 13	1997	Florida 52, Florida St. 20	*January game from 1935-72 and
1994	Florida 41, West Va. 7	1998	Florida St. 31, Ohio St. 14	since 1977 (except in 1995).
1995	Florida St. 23, Florida 17	1999	Ohio St. 24, Texas A&M 14	†Game played on Dec. 31 from 1972-75 and in 1995.

Orange Bowl

City: Miami, Fla. **Stadium:** Pro Player. **Capacity:** 74,916. **Playing surface:** Grass. **First game:** Jan. 1, 1935. **Playing sites:** Orange Bowl (1935-95); Pro Player Stadium (since 1996). **Corporate title sponsor:** Federal Express (since 1989).

Automatic berths: Big 8 champion vs. Atlantic Coast Conference champion (1953-57 seasons); Big 8 champion vs. at-large opponent (1958-63 seasons and 1975-91 seasons); Big 8 champion vs. one of first five picks from 8-team Bowl Coalition pool (1992-94 seasons); #3 vs. #5 on Jan. 1, 1996; #4 vs. #6 on Dec. 31, 1996; and #1 vs. #2 on Jan. 2, 1998 (New Bowl Alliance 1995-97 seasons); Bowl Championship Series: Big East or ACC champion, if available, vs. at-large (1998-99, 2001 seasons) and #1 vs. #2 Jan. 3, 2001.

Multiple wins: Oklahoma (11); Nebraska (8); Miami-FL (5); Alabama (4); Florida State, Georgia Tech and Penn St. (3); Clemson, Colorado, Florida, Georgia, LSU, Notre Dame and Texas (2).

Year		Year		Year	
1935*	Bucknell 26, Miami-FL 0	1959	Oklahoma 21, Syracuse 6	1983	Nebraska 21, LSU 20
1936	Catholic U. 20, Mississippi 19	1960	Georgia 14, Missouri 0	1984	Miami-FL 31, Nebraska 30
1937	Duquesne 13, Mississippi St. 12	1961	Missouri 21, Navy 14	1985	Washington 28, Oklahoma 17
1938	Auburn 6, Michigan St. 0	1962	LSU 25, Colorado 7	1986	Oklahoma 25, Penn St. 10
1939	Tennessee 17, Oklahoma 0	1963	Alabama 17, Oklahoma 0	1987	Oklahoma 42, Arkansas 8
		1964	Nebraska 13, Auburn 7	1988	Miami-FL 20, Oklahoma 14
1940	Georgia Tech 21, Missouri 7	1965†	Texas 21, Alabama 17	1989	Miami-FL 23, Nebraska 3
1941	Mississippi 14, Georgetown 7	1966	Alabama 39, Nebraska 28		
1942	Georgia 40, TCU 26	1967	Florida 27, Georgia Tech 12	1990	Notre Dame, 21, Colorado 6
1943	Alabama 37, Boston College 21	1968	Oklahoma 26, Tennessee 24	1991	Colorado 10, Notre Dame 9
1944	LSU 19, Texas A&M 14	1969	Penn St. 15, Kansas 14	1992	Miami-FL 22, Nebraska 0
1945	Tulsa 26, Georgia Tech 12			1993	Florida St. 27, Nebraska 14
1946	Miami-FL 13, Holy Cross 6	1970	Penn St. 10, Missouri 3	1994	Florida St. 18, Nebraska 16
1947	Rice 8, Tennessee 0	1971	Nebraska 17, LSU 12	1995	Nebraska 24, Miami-FL 17
1948	Georgia Tech 20, Kansas 14	1972	Nebraska 38, Alabama 6	1996	Florida St. 31, Notre Dame 26
1949	Texas 41, Georgia 28	1973	Nebraska 40, Notre Dame 6	1996**	Nebraska 41, Virginia Tech 21
		1974	Penn St. 16, LSU 9	1998*	Nebraska 42, Tennessee 17
1950	Santa Clara 21, Kentucky 13	1975	Notre Dame 13, Alabama 11	1999	Florida 31, Syracuse 10
1951	Clemson 15, Miami-FL 14	1976	Oklahoma 14, Michigan 6		
1952	Georgia Tech 17, Baylor 14	1977	Ohio St. 27, Colorado 10	2000	Michigan 35, Alabama 34
1953	Alabama 61, Syracuse 6	1978	Arkansas 31, Oklahoma 6	*January game 1935-1996 and since
1954	Oklahoma 7, Maryland 0	1979	Oklahoma 31, Nebraska 24	'98.
1955	Duke 34, Nebraska 7	1980	Oklahoma 24, Florida St. 7	**December game in 1996
1956	Oklahoma 20, Maryland 6	1981	Oklahoma 18, Florida St. 17	†Night game since 1965.
1957	Colorado 27, Clemson 21	1982	Clemson 22, Nebraska 15		
1958	Oklahoma 48, Duke 21				

Cotton Bowl

City: Dallas, Tex. **Stadium:** Cotton Bowl. **Capacity:** 68,252. **Playing surface:** Grass. **First game:** Jan 1, 1937. **Playing sites:** Fair Park Stadium (1937) and Cotton Bowl (since 1938). **Corporate title sponsor:** Mobil Corporation (1988-95), SBC Communications Inc., previously Southwestern Bell, (since 1997).

Automatic berths: SWC champion vs. at-large opponent (1941-91 seasons); SWC champion vs. one of first five picks from 8-team Bowl Coalition pool (1992-1994 seasons); second pick from Big 12 vs. first choice of WAC champion or second pick from Pac-10 (1995-97 seasons); Big 12 vs. SEC (since 1998).

Multiple wins: Texas (10); Notre Dame (5); Texas A&M (4); Arkansas and Rice (3); Alabama, Georgia, Houston, LSU, Penn St., SMU, Tennessee, TCU and UCLA (2).

Year		Year		Year	
1937*	TCU 16, Marquette 6	1954	Rice 28, Alabama 6	1971	Notre Dame 24, Texas 11
1938	Rice 28, Colorado 14	1955	Georgia Tech 14, Arkansas 6	1972	Penn St. 30, Texas 6
1939	St. Mary's 20, Texas Tech 13	1956	Mississippi 14, TCU 13	1973	Texas 17, Alabama 13
1940	Clemson 6, Boston College 3	1957	TCU 28, Syracuse 27	1974	Nebraska 19, Texas 3
1941	Texas A&M 13, Fordham 12	1958	Navy 20, Rice 7	1975	Penn St. 41, Baylor 20
1942	Alabama 29, Texas A&M 21	1959	0-0, TCU vs Air Force	1976	Arkansas 31, Georgia 10
1943	Texas 14, Georgia Tech 7	1960	Syracuse 23, Texas 14	1977	Houston 30, Maryland 21
1944	7-7, Texas vs Randolph Field	1961	Duke 7, Arkansas 6	1978	Notre Dame 38, Texas 10
1945	Oklahoma A&M 34, TCU 0	1962	Texas 12, Mississippi 7	1979	Notre Dame 35, Houston 34
1946	Texas 40, Missouri 27	1963	LSU 13, Texas 0	1980	Houston 17, Nebraska 14
1947	0-0, Arkansas vs LSU	1964	Texas 28, Navy 6	1981	Alabama 30, Baylor 2
1948	13-13, SMU vs Penn St.	1965	Arkansas 10, Nebraska 7	1982	Texas 14, Alabama 12
1949	SMU 21, Oregon 13	1966	LSU 14, Arkansas 7	1983	SMU 7, Pittsburgh 3
1950	Rice 27, N. Carolina 13	1966†	Georgia 24, SMU 9	1984	Georgia 10, Texas 9
1951	Tennessee 20, Texas 14	1968*	Texas A&M 20, Alabama 16	1985	Boston College 45, Houston 28
1952	Kentucky 20, TCU 7	1969	Texas 36, Tennessee 13	1986	Texas A&M 36, Auburn 16
1953	Texas 16, Tennessee 0	1970	Texas 21, Notre Dame 17	1987	Ohio St. 28, Texas A&M 12

Year		Year		Year	
1988	Texas A&M 35, Notre Dame 10	1994	Notre Dame 24, Texas A&M 21	2000	Arkansas 27, Texas 6
1989	UCLA 17, Arkansas 3	1995	USC 55, Texas Tech 14	*January game from 1937-66 and
1990	Tennessee 31, Arkansas 27	1996	Colorado 38, Oregon 6	since 1968.
1991	Miami-FL 46, Texas 3	1997	BYU 19, Kansas St. 15	†Game played on Dec. 31, 1966.
1992	Florida St. 10, Texas A&M 2	1998	UCLA 29, Texas A&M 23	
1993	Notre Dame 28, Texas A&M 3	1999	Texas 38, Mississippi St. 11	

Florida Citrus Bowl

City: Orlando, Fla. **Stadium:** Florida Cirtus Bowl. **Capacity:** 70,188. **Playing surface:** Grass. **First game:** Jan. 1, 1947. **Name change:** Tangerine Bowl (1947-82) and Florida Citrus Bowl (since 1983). **Playing sites:** Tangerine Bowl (1947-72, 1974-82), Florida Field in Gainesville (1973), Orlando Stadium (1983-85) and Florida Citrus Bowl (since 1986). The Tangerine Bowl, Orlando Stadium and Florida Citrus Bowl are all the same stadium. **Corporate title sponsors:** Florida Department of Citrus (since 1983), CompUSA (1992-99) and Ourhouse.com (since 2000).

Automatic berths: Championship game of Atlantic Coast Regional Conference (1964-67 seasons); Mid-American Conference champion vs. Southern Conference champion (1968-71 seasons); ACC champion vs. at-large opponent (1988-91 seasons); second pick from SEC, if available, vs. second pick from Big 10, if available (since 1992 season).

Multiple wins: East Texas St., Miami-OH, Tennessee and Toledo (3); Auburn, Catawba, Clemson, East Carolina and Florida (2).

Year		Year		Year	
1947*	Catawba 31, Maryville 6	1965	E. Carolina 31, Maine 0	1984	17-17, Florida St. vs Georgia
1948	Catawba 7, Marshall 0	1966	Morgan St. 14, West Chester 6	1985	Ohio St. 10, BYU 7
1949	21-21, Murray St. vs Sul Ross St.	1967	Tenn-Martin 25, West Chester 8	1987*	Auburn 16, USC 7
1950	St. Vincent 7, Emory & Henry 6	1968	Richmond 49, Ohio U. 42	1988	Clemson 35, Penn St. 10
1951	M. Harvey 35, Emory & Henry 14	1969	Toledo 56, Davidson 33	1989	Clemson 13, Oklahoma 6
1952	Stetson 35, Arkansas St. 20	1970	Toledo 40, Wm. & Mary 12	1990	Illinois 31, Virginia 21
1953	E. Texas St. 33, Tenn. Tech 0	1971	Toledo 28, Richmond 3	1991	Georgia Tech 45, Nebraska 21
1954	7-7, E. Texas St. vs Arkansas St.	1972	Tampa 21, Kent St. 18	1992	California 37, Clemson 13
1955	Neb.-Omaha 7, Eastern Ky. 6	1973	Miami-OH 16, Florida 7	1993	Georgia 21, Ohio St. 14
1956	6-6, Juniata vs Missouri Valley	1974	Miami-OH 21, Georgia 10	1994	Penn St. 31, Tennessee 13
1957	W. Texas St. 20, So. Miss. 13	1975	Miami-OH 20, S. Carolina 7	1995	Alabama 24, Ohio St. 17
1958	E. Texas St. 10, So. Miss. 3	1976	Oklahoma 49, BYU 21	1996	Tennessee 20, Ohio St. 14
1958†	E. Texas St. 26, Mo. Valley 7	1977	Florida St. 40, Texas Tech 17	1997	Tennessee 48, Northwestern 28
1960*	Mid. Tenn. 21, Presbyterian 12	1978	N.C. State 30, Pittsburgh 17	1998	Florida 21, Penn St. 6
1960†	Citadel 27, Tenn. Tech 0	1979	LSU 34, Wake Forest 10	1999	Michigan 45, Arkansas 31
1961	Lamar 21, Middle Tenn. 14	1980	Florida 35, Maryland 20	2000	Michigan St. 37, Florida 34
1962	Houston 49, Miami-OH 21	1981	Missouri 19, Southern Miss. 17	*January game from 1947-58, in
1963	Western Ky. 27, Coast Guard 0	1982	Auburn 33, Boston College 26	1960 and since 1987.
1964	E. Carolina 14, Massachusetts 13	1983	Tennessee 30, Maryland 23	†December game in 1958 and 1960-85.

Gator Bowl

City: Jacksonville, Fla. **Stadium:** ALLTEL Stadium. **Capacity:** 73,000. **Playing surface:** Grass. **First game:** Jan. 1, 1946. **Playing sites:** Gator Bowl (1946-93), Florida Field in Gainesville (1994) and New Gator Bowl (since 1995). Name was changed to ALLTEL Stadium in 1997. **Corporate title sponsors:** Mazda Motors of America, Inc. (1986-91), Outback Steakhouse, Inc. (1992-94) and Toyota Motor Co. (since 1995).

Automatic berths: Third pick from SEC vs. sixth pick from 8-team Bowl Coalition pool (1992-94 seasons); second pick from ACC, if available, vs. second pick from Big East or Notre Dame, if available (since 1995 season).

Multiple wins: Florida (6); North Carolina (5); Auburn and Clemson (4); Florida St., Georgia Tech and Tennessee (3); Georgia, Maryland, Miami-FL, Oklahoma, Pittsburgh, and Texas Tech (2).

Year		Year		Year	
1946*	Wake Forest 26, S. Carolina 14	1966	Tennessee 18, Syracuse 12	1987	LSU 30, S. Carolina 13
1947	Oklahoma 34, N.C. State 13	1967	17-17, Florida St. vs Penn St.	1989*	Georgia 34, Michigan St. 27
1948	20-20, Maryland vs Georgia	1968	Missouri 35, Alabama 10	1989†	Clemson 27, West Va. 7
1949	Clemson 24, Missouri 23	1969	Florida 14, Tennessee 13	1991*	Michigan 35, Mississippi 3
1950	Maryland 20, Missouri 7	1971*	Auburn 35, Mississippi 28	1991†	Oklahoma 48, Virginia 14
1951	Wyoming 20, Wash. & Lee 7	1971†	Georgia 7, N. Carolina 3	1992	Florida 27, N.C. State 10
1952	Miami-FL 14, Clemson 0	1972	Auburn 24, Colorado 3	1993	Alabama 24, N. Carolina 10
1953	Florida 14, Tulsa 13	1973	Texas Tech 28, Tennessee 19	1994	Tennessee 45, Va. Tech 23
1954	Texas Tech 35, Auburn 13	1974	Auburn 27, Texas 3	1996*	Syracuse 41, Clemson 0
1954†	Auburn 33, Baylor 13	1975	Maryland 13, Florida 0	1997	N. Carolina 20, West Va. 13
1955	Vanderbilt 25, Auburn 13	1976	Notre Dame 20, Penn St. 9	1998	N. Carolina 42, Va. Tech 3
1956	Georgia Tech 21, Pittsburgh 14	1977	Pittsburgh 34, Clemson 3	1999	Ga. Tech 35, Notre Dame 28
1957	Tennessee 3, Texas A&M 0	1978	Clemson 17, Ohio St. 15	2000	Miami-FL 28, Ga. Tech 13
1958	Mississippi 7, Florida 3	1979	N. Carolina 17, Michigan 15	*January game from 1946-54, 1960,
1960*	Arkansas 14, Georgia Tech 7	1980	Pittsburgh 37, S. Carolina 9	1965, 1971, 1989, 1991 and since
1960†	Florida 13, Baylor 12	1981	N. Carolina 31, Arkansas 27	1996.
1961	Penn St. 30, Georgia Tech 15	1982	Florida St. 31, West Va. 12	†December game from 1954-58,
1962	Florida 17, Penn St. 7	1983	Florida 14, Iowa 6	1960-63, 1965-69, 1971-87, 1989
1963	N. Carolina 35, Air Force 0	1984	Oklahoma St. 21, S. Carolina 14	and 1991-94.
1965*	Florida St. 36, Oklahoma 19	1985	Florida St. 34, Oklahoma St. 23	
1965†	Georgia Tech 31, Texas Tech 21	1986	Clemson 27, Stanford 21	

Bowl Games (Cont.)
Holiday Bowl

City: San Diego, Calif. **Stadium:** Qualcomm. **Capacity:** 71,000. **Playing surface:** Grass. **First game:** Dec. 22, 1978. **Playing site:** San Diego/Jack Murphy Stadium (since 1978). Name changed to Qualcomm Stadium in 1997. **Corporate title sponsors:** Sea World (1986-90), Thrifty Car Rental (1991-94), Chrysler-Plymouth Division of Chrysler Corp. (1995-97) and U.S. Filter/Culligan Water Tech. (since 1998).

Automatic berths: WAC champion vs. at-large opponent (1978-84, 1986-90 seasons); WAC champ vs. second pick from Big 10 (1991 season); WAC champ vs. third pick from Big 10 (1992-94 seasons); choice of WAC champion, if available, or second pick from Pac-10, if available vs. third pick from Big 12, if available (1995-99); second pick from Pac-10 vs. third pick from Big 12 (2000 season).

Multiple wins: BYU (4); Iowa, Kansas St. and Ohio St. (2).

Year		Year		Year	
1978†	Navy 23, BYU 16	1986	Iowa 39, San Diego St. 38	1994	Michigan 24, Colo. St. 14
1979	Indiana 38, BYU 37	1987	Iowa 20, Wyoming 19	1995	Kansas St. 54, Colorado St. 21
		1988	Oklahoma St. 62, Wyoming 14	1996	Colorado 33, Washington 21
1980	BYU 46, SMU 45	1989	Penn St. 50, BYU 39	1997	Colorado St. 35, Missouri 24
1981	BYU 38, Washington St. 36			1998	Arizona 20, Nebraska 20
1982	Ohio St. 47, BYU 17	1990	Texas A&M 65, BYU 14	1999	Kansas St. 24, Washington 20
1983	BYU 21, Missouri 17	1991	13-13, Iowa vs BYU	†December game since 1978.	
1984	BYU 24, Michigan 17	1992	Hawaii 27, Illinois 17		
1985	Arkansas 18, Arizona St. 17	1993	Ohio St. 28, BYU 21		

Outback Bowl

City: Tampa, Fla. **Stadium:** Raymond James. **Capacity:** 66,005. **Playing surface:** Grass. **First game:** Dec. 23, 1986. **Name change:** Hall of Fame Bowl (1986-95) and Outback Bowl (since 1995). **Playing sites:** Tampa Stadium (since 1986). Name changed to Houlihan's Stadium in 1996, Raymond James Stadium (since 1999). **Corporate title sponsor:** Outback Steakhouse, Inc. (since 1995).

Automatic berths: Fourth pick from ACC vs. fourth pick from Big 10 (1993-94 seasons); third pick from Big 10, if available, vs. third pick from SEC, if available (1995-99); fourth pick from Big 10 vs. third pick from SEC (2000 season).

Multiple wins: Georgia, Michigan, Penn St. and Syracuse (2).

Year		Year		Year	
1986†	Boston College 27, Georgia 24	1993	Tennessee 38, Boston Col. 23	1999	Penn St. 26, Kentucky 14
1988*	Michigan 28, Alabama 24	1994	Michigan 42, N.C. State 7		
1989	Syracuse 23, LSU 10	1995	Wisconsin 34, Duke 20	2000	Georgia 28, Purdue 25
		1996	Penn St. 43, Auburn 14	†December game in 1986.	
1990	Auburn 31, Ohio St. 14	1997	Alabama 17, Michigan 14	*January game since 1988.	
1991	Clemson 30, Illinois 0	1998	Georgia 33, Wisconsin 6		
1992	Syracuse 24, Ohio St. 17				

Peach Bowl

City: Atlanta, Ga. **Stadium:** Georgia Dome. **Capacity:** 71,228. **Playing surface:** AstroTurf. **First game:** Dec. 30, 1968. **Playing sites:** Grant Field (1968-70), Atlanta-Fulton County Stadium (1971-92) and Georgia Dome (since 1993). **Corporate title sponsor:** Chick-fil-A (since 1998).

Automatic berths: Third pick from ACC vs. at-large opponent (1992 season); third pick from ACC vs. fourth pick from SEC (1993-94 seasons); third pick from ACC, if available, vs. fourth pick from SEC, if available (since 1995 season).

Multiple wins: N.C. State (4); West Virginia (3); Auburn, Georgia, LSU and Virginia (2).

Year		Year		Year	
1968†	LSU 31, Florida St. 27	1981*	Miami-FL 20, Va. Tech 10	1993	N. Carolina 21, Miss. St. 17
1969	West Va. 14, S. Carolina 3	1981†	West Va. 26, Florida 6	1993†	Clemson 14, Kentucky 13
		1982	Iowa 28, Tennessee 22	1995*	N.C. State 24, Miss. St. 24
1970	Arizona St. 48, N. Carolina 26	1983	Florida St. 28, N. Carolina 3	1995†	Virginia 34, Georgia 27
1971	Mississippi 41, Georgia Tech 18	1984	Virginia 27, Purdue 24	1996	LSU 10, Clemson 7
1972	N.C. State 49, West Va. 13	1985	Army 31, Illinois 29	1998*	Auburn 21, Clemson 17
1973	Georgia 17, Maryland 16	1986	Va. Tech 25, N.C. State 24	1998†	Georgia 35, Virginia 33
1974	6-6, Vanderbilt vs Texas Tech	1988*	Tennessee 27, Indiana 22	1999*	Mississippi St. 17, Clemson 7
1975	West Va. 13, N.C. State 10	1988†	N.C. State 28, Iowa 23	†December game from 1968-79,
1976	Kentucky 21, N. Carolina 0	1989	Syracuse 19, Georgia 18	1981-86, 1988-90, 1993, 1995,
1977	N.C. State 24, Iowa St. 14	1990	Auburn 27, Indiana 23	1996, 1998 and 1999.
1978	Purdue 41, Georgia Tech 21	1992*	E. Carolina 37, N.C. State 34	*January game in 1981, 1988, 1992-
1979	Baylor 24, Clemson 18			93, 1995 and 1998.

Alamo Bowl

City: San Antonio, Tex. **Stadium:** Alamodome. **Capacity:** 65,000. **Playing surface:** AstroTurf. **First game:** Dec. 31, 1993. **Playing site:** Alamodome (since 1993). **Corporate title sponsor:** Builders Square (1993-98) and Sylvania (since 1999).

Automatic berths: third pick from SWC vs. fourth pick from Pac-10 (1993-94 seasons); fourth pick from Big 10, if available vs. fourth pick from Big 12, if available (1995-99 seasons); fourth pick from Big 12 vs. third pick from Big 10 (2000 season).

Multiple wins: Purdue (2).

Year		Year		Year	
1993†	California 37, Iowa 3	1996	Iowa 27, Texas Tech 0	1999	Penn St. 24, Texas A&M 0
1994	Washington St. 10, Baylor 3	1997	Purdue 33, Oklahoma St. 20	†December game since 1993.	
1995	Texas A&M 22, Michigan 20	1998	Purdue 37, Kansas St. 34		

Sun Bowl

City: El Paso, Tex. **Stadium:** Sun Bowl. **Capacity:** 52,000. **Playing surface:** AstroTurf. **First game:** Jan. 1, 1936.
Name changes: Sun Bowl (1936-85), John Hancock Sun Bowl (1986-88), John Hancock Bowl (1989-93) and Sun Bowl
(since 1994). **Playing sites:** Kidd Field (1936-62) and Sun Bowl (since 1963). **Corporate title sponsors:** John Hancock
Financial Services (1986-93), Norwest Bank (1996-98), Wells Fargo (since 1999).

Automatic berths: Eighth pick from 8-team Bowl Coalition pool vs. at-large opponent (1992); Seventh and eighth picks
from 8-team Bowl Coalition pool (1993-94 seasons); third pick from Pac-10, if available, vs. fifth pick from Big 10, if available
(since 1995 season).

Multiple wins: Texas Western/UTEP (5); Alabama and Wyoming (3); Nebraska, New Mexico St., North Carolina, Oklahoma, Oregon, Pittsburgh, SW Texas, Stanford, Texas, West Texas St. and West Virginia (2).

Year		Year		Year	
1936*	14-14, Hardin-Simmons vs New Mexico St.	1958*	Louisville 34, Drake 20	1981	Oklahoma 40, Houston 14
1937	Hardin-Simmons 34, Texas Mines 6	1958†	Wyoming 14, Hardin-Simmons 6	1982	N. Carolina 26, Texas 10
1938	West Va. 7, Texas Tech 6	1959	New Mexico St. 28, N. Texas 8	1983	Alabama 28, SMU 7
1939	Utah 26, New Mexico 0	1960	New Mexico St. 20, Utah St. 13	1984	Maryland 28, Tennessee 27
1940	0-0, Catholic U. vs Arizona St.	1961	Villanova 17, Wichita 9	1985	13-13, Georgia vs Arizona
1941	W. Reserve 26, Arizona St. 13	1962	West Texas 15, Ohio U. 14	1986	Alabama 28, Washington 6
1942	Tulsa 6, Texas Tech 0	1963	Oregon 21, SMU 14	1987	Oklahoma St. 35, West Va. 33
1943	Second Air Force 13, Hardin-Simmons 7	1964	Georgia 7, Texas Tech 0	1988	Alabama 29, Army 28
1944	SW Texas 7, New Mexico 0	1965	Texas Western 13, TCU 12	1989	Pittsburgh 31, Texas A&M 28
1945	SW Texas 35, U. of Mexico 0	1966	Wyoming 28, Florida St. 20	1990	Michigan St. 17, USC 16
1946	New Mexico 34, Denver 24	1967	UTEP 14, Mississippi 7	1991	UCLA 6, Illinois 3
1947	Cincinnati 18, Va. Tech 6	1968	Auburn 34, Arizona 10	1992	Baylor 20, Arizona 15
1948	Miami-OH 13, Texas Tech 12	1969	Nebraska 45, Georgia 6	1993	Oklahoma 41, Texas Tech 10
1949	West Va. 21, Texas Mines 12	1970	Georgia Tech 17, Texas Tech 9	1994	Texas 35, N. Carolina 31
1950	Tex. Western 33, Georgetown 20	1971	LSU 33, Iowa St. 15	1995	Iowa 38, Washington 18
1951	West Texas 14, Cincinnati 13	1972	N. Carolina 32, Texas Tech 28	1996	Stanford 38, Michigan St. 0
1952	Texas Tech 25, Pacific 14	1973	Missouri 34, Auburn 17	1997	Arizona St. 17, Iowa 7
1953	Pacific 26, Southern Miss. 7	1974	Miss. St. 26, N. Carolina 24	1998	TCU 28, USC 19
1954	Tex. Western 37, So. Miss. 14	1975	Pittsburgh 33, Kansas 19	1999	Oregon 24, Minnesota 20
1955	Tex. Western 47, Florida St. 20	1977*	Texas A&M 37, Florida 14	*January game from 1936-58 and in 1977.
1956	Wyoming 21, Texas Tech 14	1977†	Stanford 24, LSU 14	†December game from 1958-75 and since 1977.
1957	Geo. Wash. 13, Tex. Western 0	1978	Texas 42, Maryland 0	
		1979	Washington 14, Texas 7	
		1980	Nebraska 31, Miss. St. 17	

Insight.com Bowl

City: Tucson, Ariz. **Stadium:** Arizona. **Capacity:** 57,803. **Playing surface:** Grass. **First game:** Dec. 31, 1989.
Name change: Copper Bowl (1989-1996), Insight.com Bowl (since 1997). **Playing site:** Arizona Stadium (since 1989).
Corporate title sponsors: Domino's Pizza (1990-91), Weiser Lock (1992-1996) and Insight Enterprises (since 1997).

Automatic berths: Third pick from WAC vs. at-large opponent (1992 season); third pick from WAC vs. fourth pick from
Big Eight (1993-94 seasons); second pick from WAC vs. sixth pick from Big 12 (1995-97); third pick from Big East or Notre
Dame, if available vs. fifth pick from Big 12, if available (since 1998 season).

Multiple wins: Arizona (2).

Year		Year		Year	
1989†	Arizona 17, N.C. State 10	1993	Kansas St. 52, Wyoming 17	1997	Arizona 20, New Mexico 14
1990	California 17, Wyoming 15	1994	BYU 31, Oklahoma 6	1998	Missouri 34, W. Virginia 31
1991	Indiana 24, Baylor 0	1995	Texas Tech 55, Air Force 41	1999	Colorado 62, Boston College 28
1992	Washington St. 31, Utah 28	1996	Wisconsin 38, Utah 10	†December game since 1989.

Liberty Bowl

City: Memphis, Tenn. **Stadium:** Liberty Bowl Memorial. **Capacity:** 62,380. **Playing surface:** Grass. **First game:** Dec.
19, 1959. **Playing sites:** Municipal Stadium in Philadelphia (1959-63), Convention Hall in Atlantic City, N.J. (1964), Memphis Memorial Stadium (1965-75) and Liberty Bowl Memorial Stadium (since 1976). Memphis Memorial Stadium renamed
Liberty Bowl Memorial in 1976. **Corporate title sponsors:** St. Jude's Hospital (since 1993), AXA/Equitable (since 1997).

Automatic berths: Commander-in-Chief's Trophy winner (Army, Navy or Air Force) vs. at-large opponent (1989-92 seasons); none (1993 season); first pick from independent group of Cincinnati, East Carolina, Memphis, Southern Miss. and
Tulane vs. at-large opponent (for 1994 and '95 seasons); Conference USA champion vs. fourth pick from the Big East (1996-97
seasons); Conference USA champion, if available, vs. fifth, sixth or seventh pick or at-large from SEC (1998-99 seasons); Mountain West champion vs. Conference USA champion, if available (2000 season).

Multiple wins: Mississippi (4); Penn St. and Tennessee (3); Air Force, Alabama, N.C. State, Southern Miss., Syracuse and
Tulane (2).

Year		Year		Year	
1959†	Penn St. 7, Alabama 0	1969	Colorado 47, Alabama 33	1979	Penn St. 9, Tulane 6
1960	Penn St. 41, Oregon 12	1970	Tulane 17, Colorado 3	1980	Purdue 28, Missouri 25
1961	Syracuse 15, Miami-FL 14	1971	Tennessee 14, Arkansas 13	1981	Ohio St. 31, Navy 28
1962	Oregon St. 6, Villanova 0	1972	Georgia Tech 31, Iowa St. 30	1982	Alabama 21, Illinois 15
1963	Mississippi St. 16, N.C. State 12	1973	N.C. State 31, Kansas 18	1983	Notre Dame 19, Boston Col. 18
1964	Utah 32, West Virginia 6	1974	Tennessee 7, Maryland 3	1984	Auburn 21, Arkansas 15
1965	Mississippi 13, Auburn 7	1975	USC 20, Texas A&M 0	1985	Baylor 21, LSU 7
1966	Miami-FL 14, Virginia Tech 7	1976	Alabama 36, UCLA 6	1986	Tennessee 21, Minnesota 14
1967	N.C. State 14, Georgia 7	1977	Nebraska 21, N. Carolina 17	1987	Georgia 20, Arkansas 17
1968	Mississippi 34, Virginia Tech 17	1978	Missouri 20, LSU 15	1988	Indiana 34, S. Carolina 10

Bowl Games (Cont.)

Year		Year		Year	
1989	Mississippi 42, Air Force 29	1993	Louisville 18, Michigan St. 7	1997	Southern Miss. 41, Pittsburgh 7
1990	Air Force 23, Ohio St. 11	1994	Illinois 30, E. Carolina 0	1998	Tulane 41, BYU 27
1991	Air Force 38, Mississippi St. 15	1995	E. Carolina 19, Stanford 13	1999	Southern Miss. 23, Colorado St. 17
1992	Mississippi 13, Air Force 0	1996	Syracuse 30, Houston 17	†December game since 1959.	

Micron PC Bowl

City: Miami, Fla. **Stadium:** Pro Player. **Capacity:** 74,915. **Playing surface:** Grass. **First game:** Dec. 28, 1990. **Name change:** Blockbuster Bowl (1990-93), Carquest Bowl (1994-97) and Micron PC Bowl (since 1998). The game was called the Sunshine Football Classic for a short time in the offseason after Carquest Auto Parts dropped its sponsorship and before Micron signed on. **Playing site:** Joe Robbie Stadium (since 1990). Name changed to Pro Player Stadium in 1996. **Corporate title sponsors:** Blockbuster Video (1990-93), Carquest Auto Parts (1993-97) and Micron Electronics (since 1998).
   Automatic berths: Penn St. vs. seventh pick from 8-team Bowl Coalition pool (1992 season); third pick from Big East vs. fifth pick from SEC (1993-94 seasons); third pick from Big East vs. fifth pick from SEC (1995 season); third pick from Big East vs. fourth pick from ACC (1996-97 season); sixth pick from Big Ten, if available, vs. fourth pick from ACC, if available (since 1998 season).
   Multiple wins: Miami-FL (2).

Year		Year		Year	
1990†	Florida St. 24, Penn St. 17	1995	S. Carolina 24, West Va. 21	1998	Miami-FL 46, N.C. State 23
1991	Alabama 30, Colorado 25	1995†	N. Carolina 20, Arkansas 10	1999	Illinois 63, Virginia 21
1993*	Stanford 24, Penn St. 3	1996	Miami-FL 31, Virginia 21	†December game from 1990-91 and	
1994	Boston College 31, Virginia 13	1997	Ga. Tech 35, W. Virginia 30	since 1995.	
				*January game 1993-95.	

Aloha Bowl

City: Honolulu, Hawaii. **Stadium:** Aloha. **Capacity:** 50,000. **Playing surface:** AstroTurf. **First game:** Dec. 25, 1982. **Playing site:** Aloha Stadium (since 1982). **Corporate title sponsor:** Jeep Eagle Division of Chrysler (since 1987).
   Automatic berths: Second pick from WAC vs. third pick from Big Eight (1992-93 seasons); fifth pick from Big 12 vs. fourth pick from Pac-10 (1995-97 seasons); fourth pick from Pac-10, if available vs. at-large (1998-99 seasons); fourth or fifth pick from Pac-10 vs. fourth or fifth pick from Big East or fourth pick from ACC (2000 season).
   Multiple wins: Colorado, Kansas and Washington (2).

Year		Year		Year	
1982†	Washington 21, Maryland 20	1988	Washington St. 24, Houston 22	1994	Boston Col. 12, Kansas St. 7
1983	Penn St. 13, Washington 10	1989	Michigan St. 33, Hawaii 13	1995	Kansas 51, UCLA 30
1984	SMU 27, Notre Dame 20	1990	Syracuse 28, Arizona 0	1996	Navy 42, California 38
1985	Alabama 24, USC 3	1991	Georgia Tech 18, Stanford 17	1997	Washington 51, Michigan St. 23
1986	Arizona 30, N. Carolina 21	1992	Kansas 23, BYU 20	1998	Colorado 51, Oregon 43
1987	UCLA 20, Florida 16	1993	Colorado 41, Fresno St. 30	1999	Wake Forest 23, Arizona St. 3
				†December game since 1982.	

Oahu Bowl

City: Honolulu, Hawaii. **Stadium:** Aloha. **Capacity:** 50,000. **Playing surface:** AstroTurf. **First game:** Dec. 25, 1998. **Playing site:** Aloha Stadium (since 1998). **Corporate title sponsor:** Jeep Eagle Division of Chrysler (since 1998).
   Automatic berths: second or third pick from WAC, if available, vs. fifth pick from Pac-10, if available (1998-99 seasons); fourth or fifth pick from Pac-10 vs. fourth or fifth pick from Big East or fourth pick from ACC (2000 season).

Year		Year			
1998†	Air Force 45, Washington 25	1999	Hawaii 23, Oregon St. 17	†December game since 1998.	

Humanitarian Bowl

City: Boise, Idaho. **Stadium:** Bronco. **Capacity:** 30,000. **Playing surface:** AstroTurf. **First game:** Dec. 29, 1997. **Playing sites:** Bronco Stadium (since 1997). **Corporate title sponsor:** World Sports Humanitarian Hall of Fame (since 1997) and Crucial.com (since 1999).
   Automatic berths: Big West champion, if available, vs. at-large (since 1997 season).

Year		Year			
1997†	Cincinnati 35, Utah St. 19	1999	Boise St. 34, Louisville 31	†December game since 1997.	
1998	Idaho 42, Southern Miss. 35				

Las Vegas Bowl

City: Las Vegas, Nev. **Stadium:** Sam Boyd. **Capacity:** 40,000. **Playing surface:** AstroTurf. **First game:** Dec. 18, 1992. **Playing site:** Sam Boyd Stadium (since 1992). **Corporate title sponsor:** EA Sports (since 1999).

Automatic berths: Mid-American champion vs. Big West champion (1992-96 season); none (1997 season); second or third pick from WAC, if available vs. at-large (since 1998 season).

Note: The MAC and Big West champs met in a bowl game from 1981 to 1996, originally in Fresno at the California Bowl (1981-88, 1992) and California Raisin Bowl (1989-91). The results from 1981-91 are included below.

Multiple wins: Fresno St. (4); Bowling Green, San Jose St. and Toledo (2).

Year		Year		Year	
1981†	Toledo 27, San Jose St. 25	1989	Fresno St. 27, Ball St. 6	1996	Nevada 18, Ball St. 15
1982	Fresno St. 29, Bowling Green 28	1990	San Jose St. 48, C. Michigan 24	1997	Oregon 41, Air Force 13
1983	Northern Ill. 20, CS-Fullerton 13	1991	Bowling Green 28, Fresno St. 21	1998	N. Carolina 20, San Diego St. 13
1984*	UNLV 30, Toledo 13	1992	Bowling Green 35, Nevada 34	1999	Utah 17, Fresno St. 16
1985	Fresno St. 51, Bowling Green 7	1993	Utah St. 42, Ball St. 33	†December game since 1981.
1986	San Jose St. 37, Miami-OH 7	1994	UNLV 52, C. Michigan 24	* Toledo later ruled winner of 1984
1987	E. Michigan 30, San Jose St. 27	1995	Toledo 40, Nevada 37 (OT)	game by forfeit because UNLV used
1988	Fresno St. 35, W. Michigan 30			ineligible players.

Independence Bowl

City: Shreveport, La. **Stadium:** Independence. **Capacity:** 50,832. **Playing surface:** Grass. **First game:** Dec. 13, 1976. **Playing site:** Independence Stadium (since 1976). **Corporate title sponsors:** Poulan/Weed Eater (1990-97) and Sanford (since 1998).

Automatic berths: Southland Conference champion vs. at-large opponent (1976-81 seasons); none (1982-95 seasons); fifth pick from SEC, if available, vs. at-large (1995-97 season); fifth, sixth or seventh pick from SEC, if available, vs. at-large (1998-99 season); sixth pick from Big 12 vs. SEC (2000 season).

Multiple wins: Mississippi (3); Air Force, LSU and Southern Miss (2).

Year		Year		Year	
1976†	McNeese St. 20, Tulsa 16	1984	Air Force 23, Va. Tech 7	1992	Wake Forest 39, Oregon 35
1977	La. Tech 24, Louisville 14	1985	Minnesota 20, Clemson 13	1993	Va. Tech 45, Indiana 20
1978	E. Carolina 35, La. Tech 13	1986	Mississippi 20, Texas Tech 17	1994	Virginia 20, TCU 10
1979	Syracuse 31, McNeese St. 7	1987	Washington 24, Tulane 12	1995	LSU 45, Michigan St. 26
		1988	Southern Miss 38, UTEP 18	1996	Auburn 32, Army 29
1980	Southern Miss 16, McNeese St. 14	1989	Oregon 27, Tulsa 24	1997	LSU 27, Notre Dame 9
1981	Texas A&M 33, Oklahoma St. 16			1998	Mississippi 35, Texas Tech 18
1982	Wisconsin 14, Kansas St. 3	1990	34-34, La. Tech vs Maryland	1999	Mississippi 27, Oklahoma 25
1983	Air Force 9, Mississippi 3	1991	Georgia 24, Arkansas 15	†December game since 1976.

Bowl Championship Series

Division I-A football remains the only NCAA sport on any level that does not have a sanctioned national champion. To that end, the Bowl Coalition was formed in 1992 and was updated and renamed the Bowl Alliance in 1995 in an attempt to keep the bowl system intact while forcing an annual championship game between the regular season's two top-ranked teams.

The Bowl Championship Series is the organizers' latest attempt to finally guarantee that the teams ranked #1 and #2 will play each other in a "national title game" come January. The key difference from the 1992-97 Bowl Coalition/Bowl Alliance is that the Bowl Championship Series includes the Big 10 and Pac-10 champions. These teams, which were originally locked into playing in the Rose Bowl, are allowed under the new system to move to another bowl game in order to create a match-up featuring the #1 and #2 teams.

The bowls (the Fiesta, Orange, and Sugar) which made up the old Bowl Alliance kept their spots in this new four-bowl alliance. The Fiesta Bowl held the first national championship (#1 vs. #2) game under the Bowl Championship Series contract on Jan. 4, 1999, it was followed by the Sugar (Jan. 4, 2000) and the series will continue with the Orange (Jan. 3, 2001) and the Fiesta (Jan. 3, 2002). Originally, ABC paid the BCS members $525 million over seven years in rights fees for the four "title" games, with a three year option clause. The option was exercised in January 2000 and ABC and the BCS agreed on an eighth year as well.

The 1992 Coalition, which lasted three seasons, consolidated the resources of four major bowl games (the Cotton, Fiesta, Orange and Sugar), the champions of five major conferences (the ACC, Big East, Big Eight, Southeastern and Southwest) and the national independent Notre Dame. It worked two out of three years with #1 vs. #2 showdowns in the 1993 Sugar Bowl (#2 Alabama over #1 Miami-FL) and 1994 Orange Bowl (#1 Florida St. over #2 Nebraska). The 1995 Orange Bowl had to settle for #1 Nebraska beating #3 Miami-FL because #2 Penn St., the Big Ten champion, was obligated to play in the Rose Bowl.

The Bowl Alliance, which ended a three-year run after the 1997 season, was an updated version of the Coalition.

Non-BCS matchups: ALAMO (fourth pick from Big 12 vs. third pick from Big 10); ALOHA (fourth or fifth pick from Pac-10 vs. fourth from Big East or fourth from Big 10); CITRUS (second pick from Big 10 vs. second pick from SEC); COTTON (second pick from Big 12 vs. SEC pick); GALLERYFUNITURE.COM (seventh pick from Big 12 vs. third pick from CUSA); GATOR (second pick from ACC vs. second pick from Big East/ND); HOLIDAY (second pick from Pac-10 vs. third pick from Big 12); HUMANITARIAN (Big West champ vs. third pick from WAC); INDEPENDENCE (sixth pick from Big 12 vs. SEC); INSIGHT.COM (third pick from Big East/ND vs. fifth pick from the Big 12); LAS VEGAS (second pick from Mtn West vs. at-large); LIBERTY (first pick from Mtn West vs. first from CUSA); MICRON PC (sixth pick from Big 10 vs. ACC); MOBILE (first pick from WAC if team is from east or second from WAC vs. second from CUSA); MOTOR CITY (MAC champ vs. fourth from CUSA); MUSIC CITY (SEC vs. fourth pick from Big East/ND); OAHU (fourth or fifth pick from Pac-10 vs. fourth from Big East or fourth from ACC); OUTBACK (fourth pick from Big 10 vs. third pick from SEC); PEACH (third pick from ACC vs. SEC); SILICON VALLEY CLASSIC (first pick from WAC if team is from the west or second from WAC vs. at-large); SUN (third pick from Pac-10 vs. fifth pick from Big 10). Note that if the champion of CUSA qualifies for the BCS, Liberty gets choice two, Mobile gets choice 3, etc.

Bowl Games (Cont.)
Motor City Bowl

City: Pontiac, Mich. **Stadium:** Pontiac Silverdome. **Capacity:** 80,368. **Playing surface:** Turf. **First game:** Dec. 26, 1997. **Playing site:** Pontiac Silverdome (since 1997). **Corporate title sponsor:** Ford Division of Ford Motor Company (since 1997).

Automatic berths: Mid-American champions vs at-large (1997-99 season); Mid-American champions vs. fourth pick from Conference USA (2000 season).

Multiple wins: Marshall (2).

Year		Year		
1997†	Mississippi 34, Marshall 31	1999	Marshall 21, BYU 3	†December game since 1997.
1998	Marshall 48, Louisville 29			

Music City Bowl

City: Nashville, Tenn. **Stadium:** Adelphia Coliseum **Capacity:** 67,000. **Playing surface:** Grass. **First game:** Dec. 29, 1998. **Playing sites:** Vanderbilt Stadium (1998) and Adelphia Coliseum (1999–). **Corporate title sponsors:** American General (1998) and HomePoint.com (since 1999).

Automatic berths: sixth choice from the SEC, if available, vs. at-large (1998-99 season); fourth pick from Big East, if available vs. SEC (2000 season).

Year
1998† Va. Tech 38, Alabama 7   †December game since 1998.
1999 Syracuse 20, Kentucky 13

Mobile Bowl

City: Mobile, Ala. **Stadium:** Ladd-Peebles **Capacity:** 40,646. **Playing surface:** Grass. **First game:** Dec. 22, 1999. **Playing sites:** Ladd-Peebles Stadium (since 1999).

Automatic berths: WAC champions (if team is from the east) or second pick from WAC vs. second pick from Conference USA, if available (2000 season).

Year
1999† TCU 28, E. Carolina 14   †December game since 1999.

All-Time Winningest Division I-A Teams

Schools classified as Division I-A for at least 10 years; through 1999 season (including bowl games).

Top 25 Winning Percentage

		Yrs	Gm	W	L	T	Pct	Bowls App	Bowls Record	1999 Season Bowl	1999 Season Record
1	Notre Dame	111	1047	767	238	42	.753	23	13-10-0	None	5-7
2	Michigan	120	1091	796	259	36	.746	31	16-15-0	Won Orange	10-2
3	Alabama*	105	1045	734	268	43	.723	50	28-19-3	Lost Orange	10-3
4	Ohio St.	110	1052	717	282	53	.707	31	14-17-0	None	6-6
5	Nebraska	110	1080	743	297	40	.706	38	19-19-0	Won Fiesta	12-1
6	Texas	107	1067	735	299	33	.704	39	18-19-2	Lost Cotton	9-5
7	Oklahoma	105	1020	689	278	53	.701	33	20-12-1	Lost Independence	7-5
8	Penn St.	113	1080	734	305	41	.699	36	23-11-2	Won Alamo	10-3
9	Tennessee*	103	1039	699	288	52	.698	40	22-18-0	Lost Fiesta	9-3
10	USC*	107	1008	673	281	54	.694	39	25-14-0	None	6-6
11	Florida St.*	53	581	381	183	17	.670	28	17-9-2	Won Sugar	12-0
12	Miami-OH*	111	962	591	327	44	.637	7	5-2-0	None	7-4
13	Washington*	110	992	606	336	50	.636	26	13-12-1	Lost Holiday	7-5
14	Georgia	106	1045	633	358	54	.632	35	18-14-3	Won Outback	8-4
15	Central Michigan	99	838	510	292	36	.630	2	0-2-0	None	4-7
16	Arizona St.	87	792	484	284	24	.626	18	10-7-1	Lost Aloha	6-6
17	LSU*	106	1013	610	356	47	.625	31	14-16-1	None	3-8
18	Army	110	1032	617	364	51	.623	4	2-2-0	None	3-8
19	Auburn*	107	1009	601	361	47	.619	26	14-10-2	None	5-6
20	Colorado*	110	1012	608	368	36	.619	23	11-12-0	Won Insight.com	7-5
21	Miami-FL	73	761	461	281	19	.618	24	13-11-0	Won Gator	9-4
22	Florida	93	938	554	344	40	.612	27	13-14-0	Lost Citrus	9-4
23	UCLA	81	823	481	308	37	.607	22	11-10-1	None	4-7
24	Texas A&M	105	1031	602	381	48	.607	25	12-13-0	Lost Alamo	8-4
25	Syracuse	110	1087	632	406	49	.604	20	11-8-1	Won Music City	7-4

*Includes games forfeited following rulings by the NCAA Executive Council and/or the Committee on Infractions.

Top 50 Victories

		Wins			Wins			Wins
1	Michigan	.796	18	Auburn	.601	35	Missouri	.537
2	Notre Dame	.767	19	West Virginia	.596	36	Maryland	.530
3	Nebraska	.743	20	North Carolina	.594	37	Boston College	.529
4	Texas	.735	21	Georgia Tech	.592	38	Wisconsin	.526
5	Alabama	.734	22	Miami-OH	.591	39	Vanderbilt	.522
	Penn St	.734	23	Pittsburgh	.589	40	Illinois	.521
7	Ohio St.	.717	24	Arkansas	.588	41	Utah	.520
8	Tennessee	.699	25	Minnesota	.581	42	Kentucky	.517
9	Oklahoma	.689	26	Navy	.578	43	Stanford	.513
10	USC	.673	27	Virginia Tech	.568	44	Kansas	.511
11	Georgia	.633	28	Clemson	.562	45	Central Michigan	.510
12	Syracuse	.632	29	Michigan St	.556	46	Purdue	.508
13	Army	.617	30	California	.555	47	Arizona	.503
14	LSU	.610	31	Florida	.554	48	Iowa	.498
15	Colorado	.608	32	Mississippi	.552	49	Tulsa	.493
16	Washington	.606	33	Virginia	.549	50	Baylor	.491
17	Texas A&M	.602	34	Rutgers	.547		Louisiana Tech	.491

Top 30 Bowl Appearances

		App	Record			App	Record			App	Record
1	Alabama	50	28-19-3		Michigan	31	16-15-0	21	Texas Tech	23	5-17-1
2	Tennessee	40	22-18-0	12	Arkansas	30	10-17-3		Notre Dame	23	13-10-0
3	USC	39	25-14-0	13	Georgia Tech	28	19-9-0		Clemson	23	12-11-0
	Texas	39	18-19-2		Florida St	28	17-9-2		North Carolina	23	11-12-0
5	Nebraska	38	19-19-0		Mississippi	28	17-11-0		Colorado	23	11-12-0
6	Penn St	36	23-11-2	16	Florida	27	13-14-0	26	UCLA	22	11-10-1
7	Georgia	35	18-14-3	17	Auburn	26	14-10-2		BYU	22	7-14-1
8	Oklahoma	33	20-12-1		Washington	26	13-12-1	28	Missouri	21	9-12-0
9	LSU	31	14-16-1	19	Texas A&M	25	12-13-0	29	West Virginia	20	8-12-0
	Ohio St.	31	14-17-0	20	Miami-FL	24	13-11-0	30	Syracuse	20	11-8-1

Note: Alabama, Georgia, Georgia Tech, Notre Dame, Ohio State and Penn State are the only schools that have won all four of the traditional major bowl games—the Rose, Orange, Sugar and Cotton. Ohio State, Penn State and Notre Dame are the only schools to have won those four and the recently prestigious Fiesta bowl.

Major Conference Champions
Atlantic Coast Conference

Founded in 1953 when charter members all left Southern Conference to form ACC. **Charter members** (7): Clemson, Duke, Maryland, North Carolina, N.C. State, South Carolina and Wake Forest. **Admitted later** (3): Virginia in 1953 (began play in '54), Georgia Tech in 1979 (began play in '83); Florida St. in 1990 (began play in '92). **Withdrew later** (1): South Carolina in 1971 (became an independent after '70 season).

2000 playing membership (9): Clemson, Duke, Florida St., Georgia Tech, Maryland, North Carolina, N.C. State, Virginia and Wake Forest.

Multiple titles: Clemson (13); Florida St. and Maryland (8); Duke and N.C. State (7); North Carolina (5); Georgia Tech & Virginia (2).

Year		Year		Year		Year	
1953	Duke (4-0) & Maryland (3-0)	1964	N.C. State (5-2)	1977	North Carolina (5-0-1)	1989	Virginia (6-1) & Duke (6-1)
1954	Duke (4-0)	1965	Clemson (5-2) & N.C. State (5-2)	1978	Clemson (6-0)	1990	Georgia Tech (6-0-1)
1955	Maryland (4-0) & Duke (4-0)	1966	Clemson (6-1)	1979	N.C. State (5-1)	1991	Clemson (6-0-1)
1956	Clemson (4-0-1)	1967	Clemson (6-0)	1980	North Carolina (6-0)	1992	Florida St. (8-0)
1957	N.C. State (5-0-1)	1968	N.C. State (6-1)	1981	Clemson (6-0)	1993	Florida St. (8-0)
1958	Clemson (5-1)	1969	South Carolina (6-0)	1982	Clemson (6-0)	1994	Florida St. (8-0)
1959	Clemson (6-1)	1970	Wake Forest (5-1)	1983	Clemson (7-0) † & Maryland (5-0)	1995	Virginia (7-1) & Florida St. (7-1)
1960	Duke (5-1)	1971	North Carolina (6-0)	1984	Maryland (5-0)	1996	Florida St. (8-0)
1961	Duke (5-1)	1972	North Carolina (6-0)	1985	Maryland (6-0)	1997	Florida St. (8-0)
1962	Duke (6-0)	1973	N.C. State (6-0)	1986	Clemson (5-1-1)	1998	Florida St. (7-1) & Georgia Tech (7-1)
1963	North Carolina (6-1) & N.C. State (6-1)	1974	Maryland (6-0)	1987	Clemson (6-1)	1999	Florida St. (8-0)
		1975	Maryland (5-0)	1988	Clemson (6-1)		† On probation, ineligible for championship.
		1976	Maryland (5-0)				

Major Conference Champions (Cont.)
Big East Conference

Founded in 1991 when charter members gave up independent football status to form Big East. **Charter members** (8): Boston College, Miami-FL, Pittsburgh, Rutgers, Syracuse, Temple, Virginia Tech and West Virginia. **Note:** Temple and Virginia Tech are Big East members in football only.

2000 playing membership (8): Boston College, Miami-FL, Pittsburgh, Rutgers, Syracuse, Temple, Virginia Tech and West Virginia.

Conference champion: Member schools needed two years to adjust their regular season schedules in order to begin round-robin conference play in 1993. In the meantime, the 1991 and '92 Big East titles went to the highest-ranked member in the final regular season *USA Today*/CNN coaches' poll.

Multiple titles: Miami-FL (5); Syracuse (4); Virginia Tech (3).

Year		Year		Year		Year	
1991	Miami-FL (2-0, #1)	1994	Miami-FL (7-0)	1996	Virginia Tech (6-1),	1997	Syracuse (6-1)
	& Syracuse (5-0, #16)	1995	Virginia Tech (6-1)		Miami-FL (6-1)	1998	Syracuse (6-1)
1992	Miami-FL (4-0, #1)		& Miami-FL (6-1)		& Syracuse (6-1)	1999	Virginia Tech (7-0)
1993	West Virginia (7-0)						

Big Ten Conference

Originally founded in 1895 as the Intercollegiate Conference of Faculty Representatives, better known as the Western Conference. **Charter members** (7): Chicago, Illinois, Michigan, Minnesota, Northwestern, Purdue and Wisconsin. **Admitted later** (5): Indiana and Iowa in 1899; Ohio St. in 1912; Michigan St. in 1950 (began play in '53); Penn St. in 1990 (began play in '93). **Withdrew later** (2): Michigan in 1907 (rejoined in '17); Chicago in 1940 (dropped football after '39 season). **Note:** Iowa belonged to both the Western and Missouri Valley conferences from 1907-10.

Unofficially called the **Big Ten** from 1912 until Chicago's withdrawal in 1939, then the **Big Nine** from 1940 until Michigan St. began conference play in 1953. Formally named the **Big Ten** in 1984 and has kept the name even after adding Penn St. as its 11th member in 1990.

2000 playing membership (11): Illinois, Indiana, Iowa, Michigan, Michigan St., Minnesota, Northwestern, Ohio St., Penn St., Purdue, and Wisconsin.

Multiple titles: Michigan (39); Ohio St. (28); Minnesota (18); Illinois (14); Wisconsin (11); Iowa (9); Purdue and Northwestern (7); Chicago and Michigan St. (6); Indiana (2).

Year		Year		Year		Year	
1896	Wisconsin (2-0-1)	1922	Iowa (5-0)	1948	Michigan (6-0)	1975	Ohio St. (8-0)
1897	Wisconsin (3-0)		& Michigan (4-0)	1949	Ohio St. (4-1-1)	1976	Michigan (7-1)
1898	Michigan (3-0)	1923	Illinois (5-0)		& Michigan (4-1-1)		& Ohio St. (7-1)
1899	Chicago (4-0)		& Michigan (4-0)	1950	Michigan (4-1-1)	1977	Michigan (7-1)
1900	Iowa (3-0-1)	1924	Chicago (3-0-3)	1951	Illinois (5-0-1)		& Ohio St. (7-1)
	& Minnesota (3-0-1)	1925	Michigan (5-1)	1952	Wisconsin (4-1-1)	1978	Michigan (7-1)
1901	Michigan (4-0)	1926	Michigan (5-0)		& Purdue (4-1-1)		& Michigan St. (7-1)
	& Wisconsin (2-0)		& Northwestern (5-0)	1953	Michigan St. (5-1)	1979	Ohio St. (8-0)
1902	Michigan (5-0)	1927	Illinois (5-0)		& Illinois (5-1)	1980	Michigan (8-0)
1903	Michigan (3-0-1),		& Minnesota (3-0-1)	1954	Ohio St. (7-0)	1981	Iowa (6-2)
	Minnesota (3-0-1)	1928	Illinois (4-1)	1955	Ohio St. (6-0)		& Ohio St. (6-2)
	& Northwestern (1-0-2)	1929	Purdue (5-0)	1956	Iowa (5-1)	1982	Michigan (8-1)
1904	Minnesota (3-0)	1930	Michigan (5-0)	1957	Ohio St. (7-0)	1983	Illinois (9-0)
	& Michigan (2-0)		& Northwestern (5-0)	1958	Iowa (5-1)	1984	Ohio St. (7-2)
1905	Chicago (7-0)	1931	Purdue (5-1),	1959	Wisconsin (5-2)	1985	Iowa (7-1)
1906	Wisconsin (3-0),		Michigan (5-1)	1960	Minnesota (5-1)	1986	Michigan (7-1)
	Minnesota (2-0)		& Northwestern (5-1)		& Iowa (5-1)		& Ohio St. (7-1)
	& Michigan (1-0)	1932	Michigan (6-0)	1961	Ohio St. (6-0)	1987	Michigan St. (7-0-1)
1907	Chicago (4-0)		& Purdue (5-0-1)	1962	Wisconsin (6-1)	1988	Michigan (7-0-1)
1908	Chicago (5-0)	1933	Michigan (5-0-1)	1963	Illinois (5-1-1)	1989	Michigan (8-0)
1909	Minnesota (3-0)		& Minnesota (2-0-4)	1964	Michigan (6-1)	1990	Iowa (6-2),
1910	Illinois (4-0)	1934	Minnesota (5-0)	1965	Michigan St. (7-0)		Michigan (6-2),
	& Minnesota (2-0)	1935	Minnesota (5-0)	1966	Michigan St. (7-0)		Michigan St. (6-2)
1911	Minnesota (3-0-1)		& Ohio St. (5-0)	1967	Indiana (6-1),		& Illinois (6-2)
1912	Wisconsin (6-0)	1936	Northwestern (6-0)		Purdue (6-1)	1991	Michigan (8-0)
1913	Chicago (7-0)	1937	Minnesota (5-0)		& Minnesota (6-1)	1992	Michigan (6-0-2)
1914	Illinois (6-0)	1938	Minnesota (4-1)	1968	Ohio St. (7-0)	1993	Wisconsin (6-1-1)
1915	Minnesota (3-0-1)	1939	Ohio St. (5-1)	1969	Ohio St. (6-1)		& Ohio St. (6-1-1)
	& Illinois (3-0-2)	1940	Minnesota (6-0)		& Michigan (6-1)	1994	Penn St. (8-0)
1916	Ohio St. (4-0)	1941	Minnesota (5-0)	1970	Ohio St. (7-0)	1995	Northwestern (8-0)
1917	Ohio St. (4-0)	1942	Ohio St. (5-1)	1971	Michigan (8-0)	1996	Ohio St. (7-1)
1918	Illinois (4-0),	1943	Purdue (6-0)	1972	Ohio St. (7-1)		& Northwestern (7-1)
	Michigan (2-0)		& Michigan (6-0)		& Michigan (7-1)	1997	Michigan (8-0)
	& Purdue (1-0)	1944	Ohio St. (6-0)	1973	Ohio St. (7-0-1)	1998	Ohio St. (7-1),
1919	Illinois (6-1)	1945	Indiana (5-0-1)		& Michigan (7-0-1)		Wisconsin (7-1)
1920	Ohio St. (5-0)	1946	Illinois (6-1)	1974	Ohio St. (7-1)		& Michigan (7-1)
1921	Iowa (5-0)	1947	Michigan (6-0)		& Michigan (7-1)	1999	Wisconsin (7-1)

Big 12 Conference

Originally founded in 1907 as the Missouri Valley Intercollegiate Athletic Assn. **Charter members** (5): Iowa, Kansas, Missouri, Nebraska and Washington University of St. Louis. **Admitted later** (11): Drake and Iowa St. (then Ames College) in 1908; Kansas St. (then Kansas College of Applied Science and Agriculture) in 1913; Grinnell (Iowa) College in 1919; Oklahoma in 1920; Oklahoma A&M (now Oklahoma St.) in 1925; Colorado in 1947 (began play in '48); Baylor, Texas, Texas A&M and Texas Tech in 1994 (all four began play in 1996).

Withdrew later (1): Iowa in 1911 (left for Big Ten after 1910 season); **Excluded later** (4): Drake, Grinnell, Oklahoma A&M and Washington-MO (left out when MVIAA cut membership to six teams in 1928).

Streamlined MVIAA unofficially called **Big Six** from 1928-47 with surviving members Iowa St., Kansas, Kansas St., Missouri, Nebraska and Oklahoma. Became the **Big Seven** after 1947 season when Colorado came over from the Skyline Conference, and then the **Big Eight** with the return of Oklahoma A&M in 1957. A&M, which resumed conference play in '60, became Oklahoma St. on July 10, 1957. The MVIAA was officially renamed the Big Eight in 1964 and became the **Big 12** after the 1995-96 academic year with the arrival of Baylor, Texas, Texas A&M and Texas Tech from the defunct Southwest Conference.

2000 playing membership (12): Baylor, Colorado, Iowa St., Kansas, Kansas St., Missouri, Nebraska, Oklahoma, Oklahoma St., Texas, Texas A&M and Texas Tech.

Multiple titles: Nebraska (43); Oklahoma (33); Missouri (12); Colorado and Kansas (5); Iowa St. and Oklahoma St. (2).

Year		Year		Year		Year	
1907	Iowa (1-0)	1929	Nebraska (3-0-2)	1954	Oklahoma (6-0)		& Oklahoma St. (5-2)
	& Nebraska (1-0)	1930	Kansas (4-1)	1955	Oklahoma (6-0)	1977	Oklahoma (7-0)
1908	Kansas (4-0)	1931	Nebraska (5-0)	1956	Oklahoma (6-0)	1978	Nebraska (6-1)
1909	Missouri (4-0-1)	1932	Nebraska (5-0)	1957	Oklahoma (6-0)		& Oklahoma (6-1)
1910	Nebraska (2-0)	1933	Nebraska (5-0)	1958	Oklahoma (6-0)	1979	Oklahoma (7-0)
1911	Iowa St. (2-0-1)	1934	Kansas St. (5-0)	1959	Oklahoma (5-1)	1980	Oklahoma (7-0)
	& Nebraska (2-0-1)	1935	Nebraska (4-0-1)	1960	Missouri (7-0)	1981	Nebraska (7-0)
1912	Iowa St. (2-0)	1936	Nebraska (5-0)	1961	Colorado (7-0)	1982	Nebraska (7-0)
	& Nebraska (2-0)	1937	Nebraska (3-0-2)	1962	Oklahoma (7-0)	1983	Nebraska (7-0)
1913	Missouri (4-0)	1938	Oklahoma (5-0)	1963	Nebraska (7-0)	1984	Oklahoma (6-1)
	& Nebraska (3-0)	1939	Missouri (5-0)	1964	Nebraska (6-1)		& Nebraska (6-1)
1914	Nebraska (3-0)	1940	Nebraska (5-0)	1965	Nebraska (7-0)	1985	Oklahoma (7-0)
1915	Nebraska (4-0)	1941	Missouri (5-0)	1966	Nebraska (6-1)	1986	Oklahoma (7-0)
1916	Nebraska (3-1)	1942	Missouri (4-0-1)	1967	Oklahoma (7-0)	1987	Oklahoma (7-0)
1917	Nebraska (2-0)	1943	Oklahoma (5-0)	1968	Kansas (6-1)	1988	Nebraska (7-0)
1918	Vacant (WW I)	1944	Oklahoma (4-0-1)		& Oklahoma (6-1)	1989	Colorado (7-0)
1919	Missouri (4-0-1)	1945	Missouri (5-0)	1969	Missouri (6-1)	1990	Colorado (7-0)
1920	Oklahoma (4-0-1)	1946	Oklahoma (4-1)		& Nebraska (6-1)	1991	Nebraska (6-0-1)
1921	Nebraska (3-0)		& Kansas (4-1)	1970	Nebraska (7-0)		& Colorado (6-0-1)
1922	Nebraska (5-0)	1947	Kansas (4-0-1)	1971	Nebraska (7-0)	1992	Nebraska (6-1)
1923	Nebraska (3-0-2)		& Oklahoma (4-0-1)	1972	Nebraska (5-1-1)*	1993	Nebraska (7-0)
	& Kansas (3-0-3)	1948	Oklahoma (5-0)	1973	Oklahoma (7-0)	1994	Nebraska (7-0)
1924	Missouri (5-1)	1949	Oklahoma (5-0)	1974	Oklahoma (7-0)	1995	Nebraska (7-0)
1925	Missouri (5-1)	1950	Oklahoma (6-0)	1975	Nebraska (6-1)	*Oklahoma (6-1) forfeited
1926	Okla. A&M (3-0-1)	1951	Oklahoma (6-0)		& Oklahoma (6-1)	title in 1972 after a player
1927	Missouri (5-1)	1952	Oklahoma (5-0-1)	1976	Colorado (5-2),	was ruled ineligible.
1928	Nebraska (4-0)	1953	Oklahoma (6-0)		Oklahoma (5-2)	

Big 12 Championship Game

After expanding to 12 teams and splitting into two divisions in 1996, the Big 12 (formerly the Big Eight) now stages a conference championship game between the two division winners on the first Saturday in December. The game has been played at the Trans World Dome in St. Louis (1996, 1998) and the Alamodome in San Antonio (1997, 1999). The divisions: NORTH— Colorado, Iowa St., Kansas, Kansas St., Missouri and Nebraska; SOUTH— Baylor, Oklahoma, Oklahoma St., Texas, Texas A&M and Texas Tech.

Year	Year	Year
1996 Texas 37, Nebraska 27	1998 Texas A&M 36, Kansas St. 33	1999 Nebraska 22, Texas 6
1997 Nebraska 54, Texas A&M 15		

Major Conference Champions (Cont.)
Big West Conference

Originally founded in 1969 as Pacific Coast Athletic Assn. **Charter members** (7): CS-Los Angeles, Fresno St., Long Beach St., Pacific, San Diego St., San Jose St. and UC-Santa Barbara. **Admitted later** (12): CS-Fullerton in 1974; Utah St. in 1977 (began play in '78); UNLV in 1982; New Mexico St. in 1983 (began play in '84); Nevada in 1991 (began play in '92); Arkansas St., Louisiana Tech, Northern Illinois and SW Louisiana in 1992 (all four began play in football only in '93); Boise St., Idaho and North Texas in 1994 (all three began play in '96); Arkansas St. rejoined in 1999 (in football only). **Withdrew later** (13): CS-Los Angeles and UC-Santa Barbara in 1972 (both dropped football after '71 season); San Diego St. in 1975 (became an independent after '75 season); Fresno St. in 1991 (left for WAC after '91 season); Long Beach St. in 1991 (dropped football after '91 season); CS-Fullerton in 1992 (dropped football after '92 season); San Jose St. and UNLV in 1994 (left for WAC after '95 season); Pacific in 1995 (dropped football after '95 season); Arkansas St., Louisiana Tech, Northern Illinois and SW Louisiana in 1995 (all four returned to independent football status after '95 season). **Conference renamed** Big West in 1988.

2000 playing membership (7): Arkansas St., Boise St., Idaho, Nevada, New Mexico St., North Texas and Utah St.

Multiple titles: San Jose St. (8); Fresno St. (6); Nevada, San Diego St. and Utah St. (5); Long Beach St. (3); CS-Fullerton and SW Louisiana (2).

Year		Year		Year		Year	
1969	San Diego St. (6-0)	1980	Long Beach St. (5-0)	1992	Nevada (5-1)	1999	Boise St. (5-1)
1970	Long Beach St. (5-1)	1981	San Jose St. (5-0)	1993	Utah St. (5-1)		*San Jose St. (4-0-1) for-
	& San Diego St. (5-1)	1982	Fresno St. (6-0)		& SW Louisiana (5-1)		feited share of title in 1979
1971	Long Beach St. (5-1)	1983	CS-Fullerton (5-1)	1994	UNLV (5-1),		for use of an ineligible
1972	San Diego St. (4-0)	1984	CS-Fullerton (6-1)†		Nevada (5-1),		player.
1973	San Diego St. (3-0-1)	1985	Fresno St. (7-0)		& SW Louisiana (5-1)		†UNLV (7-0) forfeited title in
1974	San Diego St. (4-0)	1986	San Jose St. (7-0)	1995	Nevada (6-0)		1984 for use of ineligible
1975	San Jose St. (5-0)	1987	San Jose St. (7-0)	1996	Nevada (4-1)		players.
1976	San Jose St. (4-0)	1988	Fresno St. (7-0)		& Utah St. (4-1)		
1977	Fresno St. (4-0)	1989	Fresno St. (7-0)				
1978	San Jose St. (4-1)	1990	San Jose St. (7-0)	1997	Utah St. (4-1)		
	& Utah St. (4-1)	1991	Fresno St. (6-1)		& Nevada (4-1)		
1979	Utah St. (4-0-1)*		& San Jose St. (6-1)	1998	Idaho (4-1)		

Conference USA

Founded in 1994 by six independent football schools which began play as a conference in 1996. **Charter members** (6): Cincinnati, Houston, Louisville, Memphis, Southern Mississippi and Tulane. **Admitted later** (2): East Carolina in 1997, Army in 1998 and Univ. of Alabama-Birmingham in 1999; **2000 playing members** (9): Alabama-Birmingham, Army, Cincinnati, East Carolina, Houston, Louisville, Memphis, Southern Mississippi and Tulane.

Multiple titles: Southern Mississippi (3).

Year		Year		Year	
1996	Southern Mississippi (4-1)	1997	Southern Mississippi (6-0)	1999	Southern Mississippi (6-0)
	& Houston (4-1)	1998	Tulane (6-0)		

Ivy League

First called the "Ivy League" in 1937 by sportswriter Caswell Adams of the *New York Herald Tribune*. Unofficial conference of 10 eastern teams was occasionally referred to as the "Old 10" and included: Army, Brown, Columbia, Cornell, Dartmouth, Harvard, Navy, Pennsylvania, Princeton and Yale. Army and Navy were dropped from the group after 1940. **League formalized** in 1954 for play beginning in 1956. **Charter members** (8): Brown, Columbia, Cornell, Dartmouth, Harvard, Pennsylvania, Princeton, and Yale. League downgraded from Division I to Division I-AA after 1977 season. **2000 playing membership:** the same.

Multiple titles: Dartmouth (17); Yale (12); Penn (10); Harvard (9); Princeton (8); Cornell (3).

Year		Year		Year		Year	
1956	Yale (7-0)	1968	Harvard (6-0-1)	1978	Dartmouth (6-1)	1989	Princeton (6-1)
1957	Princeton (6-1)		& Yale (6-0-1)	1979	Yale (6-1)		& Yale (6-1)
1958	Dartmouth (6-1)	1969	Dartmouth (6-1),	1980	Yale (6-1)	1990	Cornell (6-1)
1959	Penn (6-1)		Yale (6-1)	1981	Yale (6-1)		& Dartmouth (6-1)
1960	Yale (7-0)		& Princeton (6-1)		& Dartmouth (6-1)	1991	Dartmouth (6-0-1)
1961	Columbia (6-1)	1970	Dartmouth (7-0)	1982	Harvard (5-2),	1992	Dartmouth (6-1)
	& Harvard (6-1)	1971	Cornell (6-1)		Penn (5-2)		& Princeton (6-1)
1962	Dartmouth (7-0)		& Dartmouth (6-1)		& Dartmouth (5-2)	1993	Penn (7-0)
1963	Dartmouth (5-2)	1972	Dartmouth (5-1-1)	1983	Harvard (5-1-1)	1994	Penn (7-0)
	& Princeton (5-2)	1973	Dartmouth (6-1)		& Penn (5-1-1)	1995	Princeton (5-1-1)
1964	Princeton (7-0)	1974	Harvard (6-1)	1984	Penn (6-1)	1996	Dartmouth (7-0)
1965	Dartmouth (7-0)		& Yale (6-1)	1985	Penn (6-1)	1997	Harvard (7-0)
1966	Dartmouth (6-1),	1975	Harvard (6-1)	1986	Penn (7-0)	1998	Penn (6-1)
	Harvard (6-1)	1976	Brown (6-1)	1987	Harvard (6-1)	1999	Brown (6-1)
	& Princeton (6-1)		& Yale (6-1)	1988	Penn (6-1)		& Yale (6-1)
1967	Yale (7-0)	1977	Yale (6-1)		& Cornell (6-1)		

Mid-American Conference

Founded in 1946. **Charter members** (6): Butler, Cincinnati, Miami-OH, Ohio University, Western Michigan and Western Reserve (Miami and WMU began play in '48). **Admitted later** (12): Kent St. (now Kent) and Toledo in 1951 (Toledo began play in '52); Bowling Green in 1952; Marshall in 1954; Central Michigan and Eastern Michigan in 1972 (CMU began play in '75 and EMU in '76); Ball St. and Northern Illinois in 1973 (both began play in '75); Akron in 1991 (began play in '92); Marshall and Northern Illinois in 1995 (both resumed play in '97); Buffalo in 1995 (resumed play in '99). **Withdrew later** (5): Butler in 1950 (left for the Indiana Collegiate Conference); Cincinnati in 1953 (went independent); Western Reserve (now Case Western) in 1955 (left for President's Athletic Conference); Marshall in 1969 (went independent); and Northern Illinois in 1986 (went independent).

2000 playing membership (12): Akron, Ball St., Bowling Green, Central Michigan, Eastern Michigan, Kent, Marshall, Miami-OH, Northern Illinois, Ohio University, Toledo and Western Michigan.

Multiple titles: Miami-OH (13); Bowling Green (10); Toledo (8); Ball St. and Ohio University (5); Central Michigan and Cincinnati (4); Marshall (3); Western Michigan (2).

Year		Year		Year		Year	
1947	Cincinnati (3-1)	1960	Ohio Univ. (6-0)	1972	Kent St. (4-1)	1987	Eastern Mich. (7-1)
1948	Miami-OH (4-0)	1961	Bowling Green (5-1)	1973	Miami-OH (5-0)	1988	Western Mich. (7-1)
1949	Cincinnati (4-0)	1962	Bowling Green (5-0-1)	1974	Miami-OH (5-0)	1989	Ball St. (6-1-1)
1950	Miami-OH (4-0)	1963	Ohio Univ. (5-1)	1975	Miami-OH (6-0)	1990	Central Mich. (7-1)
1951	Cincinnati (3-0)	1964	Bowling Green (5-1)	1976	Ball St. (4-1)		& Toledo (7-1)
1952	Cincinnati (3-0)	1965	Bowling Green (5-1)	1977	Miami-OH (5-0)	1991	Bowling Green (8-0)
1953	Ohio Univ. (5-0-1)		& Miami-OH (5-1)	1978	Ball St. (8-0)	1992	Bowling Green (8-0)
	& Miami-OH (3-0-1)	1966	Miami-OH (5-1)	1979	Central Mich. (8-0-1)	1993	Ball St. (7-0-1)
1954	Miami-OH (4-0)		& Western Mich. (5-1)	1980	Central Mich. (7-2)	1994	Central Mich. (8-1)
1955	Miami-OH (5-0)	1967	Toledo (5-1)	1981	Toledo (8-1)	1995	Toledo (7-0-1)
1956	Bowling Green (5-0-1)		& Ohio Univ. (5-1)	1982	Bowling Green (7-2)	1996	Ball St. (7-1)
	& Miami-OH (4-0-1)	1968	Ohio Univ. (6-0)	1983	Northern Ill. (8-1)	1997	Marshall (8-1)
1957	Miami-OH (5-0)	1969	Toledo (5-0)	1984	Toledo (7-1-1)	1998	Marshall (8-1)
1958	Miami-OH (5-0)	1970	Toledo (5-0)	1985	Bowling Green (9-0)	1999	Marshall (9-0)
1959	Bowling Green (6-0)	1971	Toledo (5-0)	1986	Miami-OH (6-2)		

Mountain West Conference

Founded in 1999. **Charter members** (8): Air Force, Brigham Young, Colorado St., New Mexico, Nevada-Las Vegas, San Diego St., Utah and Wyoming.

2000 playing membership (8): Air Force, Brigham Young, Colorado St., New Mexico, Nevada-Las Vegas, San Diego St., Utah and Wyoming.

Year	
1999	BYU (5-2),
	Colorado St. (5-2)
	& Utah (5-2)

Pacific-10 Conference

Originally founded in 1915 as Pacific Coast Conference. **Charter members** (4): California, Oregon, Oregon St. and Washington. **Admitted later** (6): Washington St. in 1917; Stanford in 1918; Idaho and USC (Southern Cal) in 1922; Montana in 1924; and UCLA in 1928. **Withdrew later** (1): Montana in 1950 (left for the Mountain States Conf.).

The **PCC** dissolved in 1959 and the **AAWU** (Athletic Assn. of Western Universities) was founded. **Charter members** (5): California, Stanford, UCLA, USC and Washington. **Admitted later** (5): Washington St. in 1962; Oregon and Oregon St. in 1964; Arizona and Arizona St. in 1978. **Conference renamed** Pacific-8 in 1968 and Pacific-10 in 1978.

2000 playing membership (10): Arizona, Arizona St., California, Oregon, Oregon St., Stanford, UCLA, USC, Washington and Washington St.

Multiple titles: USC (31); UCLA (17); Washington (14); California (13); Stanford (12); Oregon (5); Oregon St. (4); Washington St. (3); Arizona St. (2).

Year		Year		Year		Year	
1916	Washington (3-0-1)	1931	USC (7-0)	1943	USC (4-0)	1958	California (6-1)
1917	Washington St. (3-0)	1932	USC (6-0)	1944	USC (3-0-2)	1959	Washington (3-1),
1918	California (3-0)	1933	Oregon (4-1)	1945	USC (5-1)		USC (3-1)
1919	Oregon (2-1)		& Stanford (4-1)	1946	UCLA (7-0)		& UCLA (3-1)
	& Washington (2-1)	1934	Stanford (5-0)	1947	USC (6-0)	1960	Washington (4-0)
1920	California (3-0)	1935	California (4-1),	1948	California (6-0)	1961	UCLA (3-1)
1921	California (5-0)		Stanford (4-1)		& Oregon (6-0)	1962	USC (4-0)
1922	California (3-0)		& UCLA (4-1)	1949	California (7-0)	1963	Washington (4-1)
1923	California (5-0)	1936	Washington (6-0-1)	1950	California (5-0-1)	1964	Oregon St. (3-1)
1924	Stanford (3-0-1)	1937	California (6-0-1)	1951	Stanford (6-1)		& USC (3-1)
1925	Washington (5-0)	1938	USC (6-1)	1952	USC (6-0)	1965	UCLA (4-0)
1926	Stanford (4-0)		& California (6-1)	1953	UCLA (6-1)	1966	USC (4-1)
1927	USC (4-0-1)	1939	USC (5-0-2)	1954	UCLA (6-0)	1967	USC (6-1)
	& Stanford (4-0-1)		& UCLA (5-0-3)	1955	UCLA (6-0)	1968	USC (6-0)
1928	USC (4-0-1)	1940	Stanford (7-0)	1956	Oregon St. (6-1-1)	1969	USC (6-0)
1929	USC (6-1)	1941	Oregon St. (7-2)	1957	Oregon (6-2)	1970	Stanford (6-1)
1930	Washington St. (6-0)	1942	UCLA (6-1)		& Oregon St. (6-2)	1971	Stanford (6-1)

Major Conference Champions (Cont.)

Year		Year		Year		Year	
1972	USC (7-0)	1980	Washington (6-1)	1988	USC (8-0)	1994	Oregon (7-1)
1973	USC (7-0)	1981	Washington (6-2)	1989	USC (6-0-1)	1995	USC (6-1-1)
1974	USC (6-0-1)	1982	UCLA (5-1-1)	1990	Washington (7-1)		& Washington (6-1-1)
1975	UCLA (6-1)	1983	UCLA (6-1-1)	1991	Washington (8-0)	1996	Arizona St. (8-0)
	& California (6-1)	1984	USC (7-1)	1992	Washington (6-2)	1997	Washington St. (7-1)
1976	USC (7-0)	1985	UCLA (6-2)		& Stanford (6-2)		& UCLA (7-1)
1977	Washington (6-1)	1986	Arizona St. (5-1-1)	1993	UCLA (6-2),	1998	UCLA (8-0)
1978	USC (6-1)	1987	USC (7-1)		Arizona (6-2)	1999	Stanford (7-1)
1979	USC (6-0-1)		& UCLA (7-1)		& USC (6-2)		

Southeastern Conference

Founded in 1933 when charter members all left Southern Conference to form SEC. **Charter members** (13): Alabama, Auburn, Florida, Georgia, Georgia Tech, Kentucky, LSU (Louisiana St.), Mississippi, Mississippi St., Sewanee, Tennessee, Tulane and Vanderbilt. **Admitted later** (2): Arkansas and South Carolina in 1990 (both began play in '92). **Withdrew later** (3): Sewanee in 1940; Georgia Tech in 1964; and Tulane in 1966.

2000 playing membership (12): Alabama, Arkansas, Auburn, Florida, Georgia, Kentucky, LSU, Mississippi, Mississippi St., South Carolina, Tennessee and Vanderbilt. **Note:** Conference title decided by championship game between Western and Eastern division winners since 1992.

Multiple titles: Alabama (21); Tennessee (13); Georgia (10); Florida (8); LSU (7); Mississippi (6); Auburn and Georgia Tech (5); Kentucky and Tulane (3).

Year		Year		Year		Year	
1933	Alabama (5-0-1)	1941	Mississippi St. (4-0-1)	1951	Georgia Tech (7-0)	1961	Alabama (7-0)
1934	Tulane (8-0)	1942	Georgia (6-1)		& Tennessee (5-0)		& LSU (6-0)
	& Alabama (7-0)	1943	Georgia Tech (3-0)	1952	Georgia Tech (6-0)	1962	Mississippi (6-0)
1935	LSU (5-0)	1944	Georgia Tech (4-0)	1953	Alabama (4-0-3)	1963	Mississippi (5-0-1)
1936	LSU (6-0)	1945	Alabama (6-0)	1954	Mississippi (5-1)	1964	Alabama (8-0)
1937	Alabama (6-0)	1946	Georgia (5-0)	1955	Mississippi (5-1)	1965	Alabama (6-1-1)
1938	Tennessee (7-0)		& Tennessee (5-0)	1956	Tennessee (6-0)	1966	Alabama (6-0)
1939	Tennessee (6-0),	1947	Mississippi (6-1)	1957	Auburn (7-0)		& Georgia (6-0)
	Georgia Tech (6-0)	1948	Georgia (6-0)	1958	LSU (6-0)	1967	Tennessee (6-0)
	& Tulane (5-0)	1949	Tulane (5-1)	1959	Georgia (7-0)	1968	Georgia (5-0-1)
1940	Tennessee (5-0)	1950	Kentucky (5-1)	1960	Mississippi (5-0-1)	1969	Tennessee (5-1)

Southwest Conference (1914-95)

Founded in 1914 as Southwest Intercollegiate Athletic Conference. **Charter members** (8): Arkansas, Baylor, Oklahoma, Oklahoma A&M (now Oklahoma St.), Rice, Southwestern, Texas and Texas A&M. **Admitted later** (5): SMU (Southern Methodist) in 1918; Phillips University in 1920; TCU (Texas Christian) in 1923; Texas Tech in 1956 (began play in '60); Houston in 1971 (began play in '76). **Withdrew later** (9): Southwestern in 1917 (went independent); Oklahoma in 1920 (left for Missouri Valley after '19 season); Phillips in 1921; Oklahoma A&M (now Oklahoma St.) in 1925 (left for Big Six); Arkansas in 1990 (left for SEC after '91 season); Baylor, Texas, Texas A&M and Texas Tech in 1994 (all four left for Big 12 after '95 season); Rice, SMU and TCU in 1994 (all three left for WAC after '95 season); Houston in 1994 (left for Conference USA after '95 season).

2000 playing membership: Conference folded on June 30, 1996.

Multiple titles: Texas (25); Texas A&M (17); Arkansas (13); SMU (9); TCU (9); Rice (7); Baylor (5); Houston (4); Texas Tech (2).

Year		Year		Year		Year	
1914	No champion	1940	Texas A&M (5-1)	1961	Texas (6-1)	1981	SMU (7-1)
1915	Oklahoma (3-0)	1941	Texas A&M (5-1)		& Arkansas (6-1)	1982	SMU (7-0-1)
1916	No champion	1942	Texas (5-1)	1962	Texas (6-0-1)	1983	Texas (8-0)
1917	Texas A&M (2-0)	1943	Texas (5-0)	1963	Texas (7-0)	1984	SMU (6-2)
1918	No champion	1944	TCU (3-1-1)	1964	Arkansas (7-0)		& Houston (6-2)
1919	Texas A&M (4-0)	1945	Texas (5-1)	1965	Arkansas (7-0)	1985	Texas A&M (7-1)
1920	Texas (5-0)	1946	Rice (5-1)	1966	SMU (6-1)	1986	Texas A&M (7-1)
1921	Texas A&M (3-0-2)		& Arkansas (5-1)	1967	Texas A&M (6-1)	1987	Texas A&M (6-1)
1922	Baylor (5-0)	1947	SMU (5-0-1)	1968	Arkansas (6-1)	1988	Arkansas (7-0)
1923	SMU (5-0)	1948	SMU (5-0-1)		& Texas (6-1)	1989	Arkansas (7-1)
1924	Baylor (4-0-1)	1949	Rice (6-0)	1969	Texas (7-0)	1990	Texas (8-0)
1925	Texas A&M (4-1)	1950	Texas (6-0)	1970	Texas (7-0)	1991	Texas A&M (8-0)
1926	SMU (5-0)	1951	TCU (5-1)	1971	Texas (6-1)	1992	Texas A&M (7-0)
1927	Texas A&M (4-0-1)	1952	Texas (6-0)	1972	Texas (7-0)	1993	Texas A&M (7-0)
1928	Texas (5-1)	1953	Rice (5-1)	1973	Texas (7-0)	1994	Baylor, Rice, TCU,
1929	TCU (4-0-1)		& Texas (5-1)	1974	Baylor (6-1)		Texas and Texas Tech†
1930	Texas (4-1)	1954	Arkansas (5-1)	1975	Arkansas (6-1),		(4-3)
1931	SMU (5-0-1)	1955	TCU (5-1)		Texas (6-1)	1995	Texas (7-0)
1932	TCU (6-0)	1956	Texas A&M (6-0)		& Texas A&M (6-1)	
1933	Arkansas (4-1)*	1957	Rice (5-1)	1976	Houston (7-1)	*Arkansas (4-1) forced to
1934	Rice (5-1)	1958	TCU (5-1)		& Texas Tech (7-1)	vacate 1933 title for use of
1935	SMU (6-0)	1959	Texas (5-1),	1977	Texas (8-0)	ineligible player.
1936	Arkansas (5-1)		TCU (5-1)	1978	Houston (7-1)	†Texas A&M had the best
1937	Rice (4-1-1)		& Arkansas (5-1)	1979	Houston (7-1)	record (6-0-1) in 1994 but
1938	TCU (6-0)	1960	Arkansas (6-1)		& Arkansas (7-1)	was on probation and there-
1939	Texas A&M (6-0)			1980	Baylor (8-0)	fore ineligible for the South-
							west championship.

Year		Year		Year		Year	
1970	LSU (5-0)	1978	Alabama (6-0)	1986	LSU (5-1)	1991	Florida (7-0)
1971	Alabama (7-0)	1979	Alabama (6-0)	1987	Auburn (5-0-1)	*Title vacated.	
1972	Alabama (7-1)	1980	Georgia (6-0)	1988	Auburn (6-1)	†On probation, ineligible	
1973	Alabama (8-0)	1981	Georgia (6-0)		& LSU (6-1)	for championship.	
1974	Alabama (6-0)		& Alabama (6-0)	1989	Alabama (6-1),		
1975	Alabama (6-0)	1982	Georgia (6-0)		Tennessee (6-1)		
1976	Georgia (5-1)	1983	Auburn (6-0)		& Auburn (6-1)		
	& Kentucky (5-1)	1984	Florida (5-0-1)*	1990	Florida (6-1)†		
1977	Alabama (7-0)	1985	Florida (5-1)†		& Tennessee (5-1-1)		
	& Kentucky (6-0)		& Tennessee (5-1)				

SEC Championship Game

Since expanding to 12 teams and splitting into two divisions in 1992, the SEC has staged a conference championship game between the two division winners on the first Saturday in December. The game has been played at Legion Field in Birmingham, Ala., (1992-93) and the Georgia Dome in Atlanta (since 1994). The divisions: EAST— Florida, Georgia, Kentucky, South Carolina, Tennessee and Vanderbilt; WEST— Alabama, Arkansas, Auburn, LSU, Mississippi and Mississippi St.

Year	Year	Year
1992 Alabama 28, Florida 21	1995 Florida 34, Arkansas 3	1998 Tennessee 24, Miss. St. 14
1993 Florida 28, Alabama 23	1996 Florida 45, Alabama 30	1999 Alabama 34, Florida 7
1994 Florida 24, Alabama 23	1997 Tennessee 30, Auburn 29	

Western Athletic Conference

Founded in 1962 when charter members left the Skyline and Border conferences to form the WAC. **Charter members** (6): Arizona and Arizona St. from Border; BYU (Brigham Young), New Mexico, Utah and Wyoming from Skyline. **Admitted later** (12): Colorado St. and UTEP (Texas-El Paso) in 1967 (both began play in '68); San Diego St. in 1978; Hawaii in 1979; Air Force in 1980; Fresno St. in 1991 (began play in '92); Rice, San Jose St., SMU (Southern Methodist), TCU (Texas Christian), Tulsa and UNLV (Nevada-Las Vegas) in 1994 (all began play in '96); Nevada set to join in 2000. **Withdrew later** (10): Arizona and Arizona St. in 1978 (left for Pac-10 after '77 season); Air Force, BYU, Colorado St., New Mexico, San Diego St., UNLV, Utah and Wyoming (left to form Mountain West conference in '99).

2000 playing membership (8): Fresno St., Hawaii, Rice, San Jose St., SMU, TCU, Tulsa and UTEP.

Multiple titles: BYU (19); Arizona St. and Wyoming (7); Air Force, Fresno St., New Mexico and Colorado St. (3); Arizona, Hawaii and Utah (2).

Year		Year		Year		Year	
1962	New Mexico (2-1-1)	1965	BYU (4-1)	1970	Arizona St. (7-0)	1974	BYU (6-0-1)
1963	New Mexico (3-1)	1966	Wyoming (5-0)	1971	Arizona St. (7-0)	1975	Arizona St. (7-0)
1964	Utah (3-1),	1967	Wyoming (5-0)	1972	Arizona St. (5-1)	1976	BYU (6-1)
	New Mexico (3-1)	1968	Wyoming (6-1)	1973	Arizona St. (6-1)		& Wyoming (6-1)
	& Arizona (3-1)	1969	Arizona St. (6-1)		& Arizona (6-1)		

Longest Division I Streaks

Winning Streaks
(Including bowl games)

No		Seasons	Spoiler	Score
47	Oklahoma	1953-57	Notre Dame	7-0
39	Washington	1908-14	Oregon St.	0-0
37	Yale	1890-93	Princeton	6-0
37	Yale	1887-89	Princeton	10-0
35	Toledo	1969-71	Tampa	21-0
34	Penn	1894-96	Lafayette	6-4
31	Oklahoma	1948-50	Kentucky	13-7*
31	Pittsburgh	1914-18	Cleve. Naval	10-9
31	Penn	1896-98	Harvard	10-0
30	Texas	1968-70	Notre Dame	24-11*
29	Miami-FL	1990-93	Alabama	34-13
29	Michigan	1901-03	Minnesota	6-6
28	Alabama†	1991-93	Tennessee	17-17
28	Alabama	1978-80	Mississippi St.	6-3
28	Oklahoma	1973-75	Kansas	23-3
28	Michigan St.	1950-53	Purdue	6-0
27	Nebraska	1901-04	Colorado	6-0
26	Nebraska	1994-96	Arizona St.	19-0
26	Cornell	1921-24	Williams	14-7
26	Michigan	1903-05	Chicago	2-0
25	BYU	1983-85	UCLA	27-24
25	San Diego St.	1965-67	Utah St.	31-25
25	Michigan	1946-49	Army	21-7
25	Army	1944-46	Notre Dame	0-0
25	USC	1931-33	Oregon St.	0-0

*Kentucky beat Oklahoma in 1951 Sugar Bowl and Notre Dame beat Texas in 1971 Cotton Bowl.
†Alabama was forced to forfeit eight victories and one tie in 1993 by the NCAA Committee on Infractions.

Unbeaten Streaks
(Including bowl games)

No	W-T	Seasons	Spoiler	Score
63	59-4	Washington	1907-17	California	27-0
56	55-1	Michigan	1901-05	Chicago	2-0
50	46-4	California	1920-25	Olympic Club	15-0
48	47-1	Oklahoma	1953-57	N. Dame	7-0
48	47-1	Yale	1885-89	Princeton	10-0
47	42-5	Yale	1879-85	Princeton	6-5
44	42-2	Yale	1894-96	Princeton	24-6
42	39-3	Yale	1904-08	Harvard	4-0
39	37-2	N. Dame	1946-50	Purdue	28-14
37	36-1	Oklahoma	1972-75	Kansas	23-3
37	37-0	Yale	1890-93	Princeton	6-0
35	35-0	Toledo	1967-71	Tampa	21-0
35	34-1	Minnesota	1903-05	Wisconsin	16-12

Losing Streaks

No		Seasons	Victim	Score
80	Prairie View	1989-98	Langston	14-12
44	Columbia	1983-88	Princeton	16-14
34	Northwestern	1979-82	No. Illinois	31-6
28	Virginia	1958-60	Wm. & Mary	21-6
28	Kansas St.	1944-48	Arkansas St.	37-6
27	Eastern Mich.	1980-82	Kent St.	9-7
27	New Mexico St.	1988-90	CS-Fullerton	43-9

Note: Virginia ended its losing streak in the opening game of the 1961 season.

Major Conference Champions (Cont.)

Year		Year		Year		Year	
1977	Arizona St. (6-1)	1984	BYU (8-0)	1991	BYU (7-0-1)	1995	Colorado St. (6-2),
	& BYU (6-1)	1985	Air Force (7-1)	1992	Hawaii (6-2),		Air Force (6-2),
1978	BYU (5-1)		& BYU (7-1)		BYU (6-2)		BYU (6-2)
1979	BYU (7-0)	1986	San Diego St. (7-1)		& Fresno St. (6-2)		& Utah (6-2)
1980	BYU (6-1)	1987	Wyoming (8-0)	1993	BYU (6-2),	1999	Fresno St. (5-2),
1981	BYU (7-1)	1988	Wyoming (8-0)		Fresno St. (6-2)		Hawaii (7-2)
1982	BYU (7-1)	1989	BYU (7-1)		& Wyoming (6-2)		& TCU (7-2)
1983	BYU (7-0)	1990	BYU (7-1)	1994	Colorado St. (7-1)		

WAC Championship Game

In addition to expanding to 16 teams and splitting into two divisions in 1996, the WAC staged a conference championship game between the two division winners on the first Saturday in December at Sam Boyd Stadium in Las Vegas until eight teams split off and formed the Mountain West Conference in 1999. The divisions: Pacific Division—BYU, Fresno St., Hawaii, New Mexico, San Diego St., San Jose St., UTEP, Utah; Mountain Division—Air Force, Colorado St., Rice, SMU, TCU, Tulsa, UNLV, Wyoming.

Year		Year		Year	
1996	BYU 28, Wyoming 25 (OT)	1997	Colorado St. 41, New Mexico 13	1998	Air Force 20, BYU 13

Annual NCAA Division I-A Leaders

Note that Oklahoma A&M is now Oklahoma St. and Texas Mines is now UTEP.

Rushing

Individual championship decided on Rushing Yards (1937-69), and on Yards Per Game (since 1970).

Multiple winners: Troy Davis, Marshall Faulk, Art Luppino, Ed Marinaro, Rudy Mobley, Jim Pilot, O.J. Simpson and Ricky Williams (2).

Year		Car	Yards	Year		Car	Yards	P/Gm
1937	Byron (Whizzer) White, Colorado	181	1121	1969	Steve Owens, Oklahoma	358	1523	
1938	Len Eshmont, Fordham	132	831					
1939	John Polanski, Wake Forest	137	882	Year		Car	Yards	P/Gm
1940	Al Ghesquiere, Detroit	146	957	1970	Ed Marinaro, Cornell	285	1425	158.3
1941	Frank Sinkwich, Georgia	209	1103	1971	Ed Marinaro, Cornell	356	1881	209.0
1942	Rudy Mobley, Hardin-Simmons	187	1281	1972	Pete VanValkenburg, BYU	232	1386	138.6
1943	Creighton Miller, Notre Dame	151	911	1973	Mark Kellar, Northern Ill	291	1719	156.3
1944	Red Williams, Minnesota	136	911	1974	Louie Giammona, Utah St.	329	1534	153.4
1945	Bob Fenimore, Oklahoma A&M	142	1048	1975	Ricky Bell, USC	357	1875	170.5
1946	Rudy Mobley, Hardin-Simmons	227	1262	1976	Tony Dorsett, Pittsburgh	338	1948	177.1
1947	Wilton Davis, Hardin-Simmons	193	1173	1977	Earl Campbell, Texas	267	1744	158.5
1948	Fred Wendt, Texas Mines	184	1570	1978	Billy Sims, Oklahoma	231	1762	160.2
1949	John Dottley, Ole Miss	208	1312	1979	Charles White, USC	293	1803	180.3
1950	Wilford White, Arizona St	199	1502	1980	George Rogers, S. Carolina	297	1781	161.9
1951	Ollie Matson, San Francisco	245	1566	1981	Marcus Allen, USC	403	2342	212.9
1952	Howie Waugh, Tulsa	164	1372	1982	Ernest Anderson, Okla. St.	353	1877	170.6
1953	J.C. Caroline, Illinois	194	1256	1983	Mike Rozier, Nebraska	275	2148	179.0
1954	Art Luppino, Arizona	179	1359	1984	Keith Byars, Ohio St.	313	1655	150.5
1955	Art Luppino, Arizona	209	1313	1985	Lorenzo White, Mich. St.	386	1908	173.5
1956	Jim Crawford, Wyoming	200	1104	1986	Paul Palmer, Temple	346	1866	169.6
1957	Leon Burton, Arizona St	117	1126	1987	Ickey Woods, UNLV	259	1658	150.7
1958	Dick Bass, Pacific	205	1361	1988	Barry Sanders, Okla. St.	344	2628	238.9
1959	Pervis Atkins, New Mexico St.	130	971	1989	Anthony Thompson, Ind	358	1793	163.0
1960	Bob Gaiters, New Mexico St	197	1338	1990	Gerald Hudson, Okla. St.	279	1642	149.3
1961	Jim Pilot, New Mexico St.	191	1278	1991	Marshall Faulk, S. Diego St.	201	1429	158.8
1962	Jim Pilot, New Mexico St.	208	1247	1992	Marshall Faulk, S. Diego St.	265	1630	163.0
1963	Dave Casinelli, Memphis St	219	1016	1993	LeShon Johnson, No. Ill.	327	1976	179.6
1964	Brian Piccolo, Wake Forest	252	1044	1994	Rashaan Salaam, Colorado	298	2055	186.8
1965	Mike Garrett, USC	267	1440	1995	Troy Davis, Iowa St.	345	2010	182.7
1966	Ray McDonald, Idaho	259	1329	1996	Troy Davis, Iowa St.	402	2185	198.6
1967	O.J. Simpson, USC	266	1415	1997	Ricky Williams, Texas	279	1893	172.1
1968	O.J. Simpson, USC	355	1709	1998	Ricky Williams, Texas	361	2124	193.1
				1999	LaDainian Tomlinson, TCU	268	1850	168.2

All-Purpose Yardage

Multiple winners: Marcus Allen, Pervis Atkins, Ryan Benjamin, Troy Davis, Troy Edwards, Louie Giammona, Tom Harmon, Art Luppino, Napolean McCallum, O.J. Simpson, Charles White and Gary Wood (2).

Year		Yards	P/Gm	Year		Yards	P/Gm
1937	Byron (Whizzer) White, Colorado	1970	246.3	1942	Complete records not available		
1938	Parker Hall, Ole Miss	1420	129.1	1943	Stan Koslowski, Holy Cross	1411	176.4
1939	Tom Harmon, Michigan	1208	151.0	1944	Red Williams, Minnesota	1467	163.0
1940	Tom Harmon, Michigan	1312	164.0	1945	Bob Fenimore, Oklahoma A&M	1577	197.1
1941	Bill Dudley, Virginia	1674	186.0	1946	Rudy Mobley, Hardin-Simmons	1765	176.5

Year		Yards	P/Gm	Year		Yards	P/Gm
1947	Wilton Davis, Hardin-Simmons	1798	179.8	1974	Louie Giammona, Utah St	1984	198.4
1948	Lou Kusserow, Columbia	1737	193.0	1975	Louie Giammona, Utah St	2045	185.9
1949	Johnny Papit, Virginia	1611	179.0	1976	Tony Dorsett, Pittsburgh	2021	183.7
1950	Wilford White, Arizona St.	2065	206.5	1977	Earl Campbell, Texas	1855	168.6
1951	Ollie Matson, San Francisco	2037	226.3	1978	Charles White, USC	2096	174.7
1952	Billy Vessels, Oklahoma	1512	151.2	1979	Charles White, USC	1941	194.1
1953	J.C. Caroline, Illinois	1470	163.3	1980	Marcus Allen, USC	1794	179.4
1954	Art Luppino, Arizona	2193	219.3	1981	Marcus Allen, USC	2559	232.6
1955	Jim Swink, TCU	1702	170.2	1982	Carl Monroe, Utah	2036	185.1
	& Art Luppino, Arizona	1702	170.2	1983	Napoleon McCallum, Navy	2385	216.8
1956	Jack Hill, Utah St.	1691	169.1	1984	Keith Byars, Ohio St.	2284	207.6
1957	Overton Curtis, Utah St	1608	160.8	1985	Napoleon McCallum, Navy	2330	211.8
1958	Dick Bass, Pacific	1878	187.8	1986	Paul Palmer, Temple	2633	239.4
1959	Pervis Atkins, New Mexico St.	1800	180.0	1987	Eric Wilkerson, Kent St.	2074	188.6
1960	Pervis Atkins, New Mexico St.	1613	161.3	1988	Barry Sanders, Oklahoma St.	3250	295.5
1961	Jim Pilot, New Mexico St	1606	160.6	1989	Mike Pringle, CS-Fullerton	2690	244.6
1962	Gary Wood, Cornell	1395	155.0	1990	Glyn Milburn, Stanford	2222	202.0
1963	Gary Wood, Cornell	1508	167.6	1991	Ryan Benjamin, Pacific.	2995	249.6
1964	Donny Anderson, Texas Tech	1710	171.0	1992	Ryan Benjamin, Pacific.	2597	236.1
1965	Floyd Little, Syracuse	1990	199.0	1993	LeShon Johnson, Northern Ill.	2082	189.3
1966	Frank Quayle, Virginia	1616	161.6	1994	Rashaan Salaam, Colorado	2349	213.5
1967	O.J. Simpson, USC	1700	188.9	1995	Troy Davis, Iowa St.	2466	224.2
1968	O.J. Simpson, USC	1966	196.6	1996	Troy Davis, Iowa St.	2364	214.9
1969	Lynn Moore, Army	1795	179.5	1997	Troy Edwards, La. Tech	2144	194.9
1970	Don McCauley, North Carolina	2021	183.7	1998	Troy Edwards, La. Tech	2784	232.0
1971	Ed Marinaro, Cornell	1932	214.7	1999	Trevor Insley, Nevada	2176	197.8
1972	Howard Stevens, Louisville	2132	213.2				
1973	Willard Harrell, Pacific	1777	177.7				

Total Offense

Individual championship decided on Total Yards (1937-69) and on Yards Per Game (since 1970).

Multiple winners: Tim Rattay (3); Johnny Bright, Bob Fenimore, Mike Maxwell and Jim McMahon (2).

Year		Plays	Yards	Year		Plays	Yards	P/Gm
1937	Byron (Whizzer) White, Colorado	224	1596	1970	Pat Sullivan, Auburn	333	2856	285.6
1938	Davey O'Brien, TCU	291	1847	1971	Gary Huff, Florida St	386	2653	241.2
1939	Kenny Washington, UCLA	259	1370	1972	Don Strock, Va. Tech	480	3170	288.2
1940	Johnny Knolla, Creighton	298	1420	1973	Jesse Freitas, San Diego St.	410	2901	263.7
1941	Bud Schwenk, Washington-MO	354	1928	1974	Steve Joachim, Temple	331	2227	222.7
1942	Frank Sinkwich, Georgia	341	2187	1975	Gene Swick, Toledo	490	2706	246.0
1943	Bob Hoernschemeyer, Indiana	355	1648	1976	Tommy Kramer, Rice	562	3272	297.5
1944	Bob Fenimore, Oklahoma A&M	241	1758	1977	Doug Williams, Gambling	377	3229	293.5
1945	Bob Fenimore, Oklahoma A&M	203	1641	1978	Mike Ford, SMU	459	2957	268.8
1946	Travis Bidwell, Auburn	339	1715	1979	Marc Wilson, BYU	488	3580	325.5
1947	Fred Enke, Arizona	329	1941	1980	Jim McMahon, BYU	540	4627	385.6
1948	Stan Heath, Nevada-Reno	233	1992	1981	Jim McMahon, BYU	487	3458	345.8
1949	Johnny Bright, Drake	275	1950	1982	Todd Dillon, Long Beach St	585	3587	326.1
1950	Johnny Bright, Drake	320	2400	1983	Steve Young, BYU	531	4346	395.1
1951	Dick Kazmaier, Princeton	272	1827	1984	Robbie Bosco, BYU	543	3932	327.7
1952	Ted Marchibroda, Detroit	305	1813	1985	Jim Everett, Purdue	518	3589	326.3
1953	Paul Larson, California	262	1572	1986	Mike Perez, San Jose St.	425	2969	329.9
1954	George Shaw, Oregon	276	1536	1987	Todd Santos, San Diego St.	562	3688	307.3
1955	George Welsh, Navy	203	1348	1988	Scott Mitchell, Utah	589	4299	390.8
1956	John Brodie, Stanford	295	1642	1989	Andre Ware, Houston	628	4661	423.7
1957	Bob Newman, Washington St	263	1444	1990	David Klingler, Houston	704	5221	474.6
1958	Dick Bass, Pacific	218	1440	1991	Ty Detmer, BYU	478	4001	333.4
1959	Dick Norman, Stanford	319	2018	1992	Jimmy Klingler, Houston	544	3768	342.6
1960	Billy Kilmer, UCLA	292	1889	1993	Chris Vargas, Nevada	535	4332	393.8
1961	Dave Hoppmann, Iowa St.	320	1638	1994	Mike Maxwell, Nevada	477	3498	318.0
1962	Terry Baker, Oregon St	318	2276	1995	Mike Maxwell, Nevada	443	3623	402.6
1963	George Mira, Miami-FL	394	2318	1996	Josh Wallwork, Wyoming	525	4209	350.8
1964	Jerry Rhome, Tulsa	470	3128	1997	Tim Rattay, La. Tech	541	3968	360.7
1965	Bill Anderson, Tulsa	580	3343	1998	Tim Rattay, La. Tech	602	4840	403.3
1966	Virgil Carter, BYU	388	2545	1999	Tim Rattay, La. Tech	562	3810	381.0
1967	Sal Olivas, New Mexico St.	368	2184					
1968	Greg Cook Cincinnati	507	3210					
1969	Dennis Shaw, San Diego St	388	3197					

Annual NCAA Division I-A Leaders (Cont.)
Passing

Individual championship decided on Completions (1937-69), on Completions Per Game (1970-78) and on Passing Efficiency rating points (since 1979).

Multiple winners: Elvis Grbac, Don Heinrich, Jim McMahon, Davey O'Brien and Don Trull (2).

Year		Cmp	Pct	TD	Yds
1937	Davey O'Brien, TCU	.94	.402	–	969
1938	Davey O'Brien, TCU	.93	.557	–	1457
1939	Kay Eakin, Arkansas	.78	.404	–	962
1940	Billy Sewell, Wash. St.	.86	.494	–	1023
1941	Bud Schwenk, Wash.-MO	.114	.487	–	1457
1942	Ray Evans, Kansas	.101	.505	–	1117
1943	Johnny Cook, Georgia	.73	.465	–	1007
1944	Paul Rickards, Pittsburgh	.84	.472	–	997
1945	Al Dekdebrun, Cornell	.90	.464	–	1227
1946	Travis Tidwell, Auburn	.79	.500	5	943
1947	Charlie Conerly, Ole Miss	.133	.571	18	1367
1948	Stan Heath, Nev-Reno	.126	.568	22	2005
1949	Adrian Burk, Baylor	.110	.576	14	1428
1950	Don Heinrich, Washington	.134	.606	14	1846
1951	Don Klosterman, Loyola-CA	.159	.505	9	1843
1952	Don Heinrich, Washington	.137	.507	13	1647
1953	Bob Garrett, Stanford	.118	.576	17	1637
1954	Paul Larson, California	.125	.641	10	1537
1955	George Welsh, Navy	.94	.627	8	1319
1956	John Brodie, Stanford	.139	.579	12	1633
1957	Ken Ford, H-Simmons	.115	.561	14	1254
1958	Buddy Humphrey, Baylor	.112	.574	7	1316
1959	Dick Norman, Stanford	.152	.578	11	1963
1960	Harold Stephens, H-Simm.	.145	.566	3	1254
1961	Chon Gallegos, S. Jose St.	.117	.594	14	1480
1962	Don Trull, Baylor	.125	.546	11	1627
1963	Don Trull, Baylor	.174	.565	12	2157
1964	Jerry Rhome, Tulsa	.224	.687	32	2870
1965	Bill Anderson, Tulsa	.296	.582	30	3464
1966	John Eckman, Wichita St.	.195	.426	7	2339
1967	Terry Stone, N. Mexico	.160	.476	9	1946
1968	Chuck Hixson, SMU	.265	.566	21	3103
1969	John Reaves, Florida	.222	.561	24	2896

Year		Cmp	P/Gm	TD	Yds
1970	Sonny Sixkiller, Wash	.186	18.6	15	2303
1971	Brian Sipe, S. Diego St.	.196	17.8	17	2532
1972	Don Strock, Va. Tech	.228	20.7	16	3243
1973	Jesse Freitas, S. Diego St.	.227	20.6	21	2993
1974	Steve Bartkowski, Cal	.182	16.5	12	2580
1975	Craig Penrose, S. Diego St.	.198	18.0	15	2660
1976	Tommy Kramer, Rice	.269	24.5	21	3317
1977	Guy Benjamin, Stanford	.208	20.8	19	2521
1978	Steve Dils, Stanford	.247	22.5	22	2943

Year		Cmp	TD	Yds	Rating
1979	Turk Schonert, Stanford	.148	19	1922	163.0
1980	Jim McMahon, BYU	.284	47	4571	176.9
1981	Jim McMahon, BYU	.272	30	3555	155.0
1982	Tom Ramsey, UCLA	.191	21	2824	153.5
1983	Steve Young, BYU	.306	33	3902	168.5
1984	Doug Flutie, BC	.233	27	3454	152.9
1985	Jim Harbaugh, Michigan	.139	18	1913	163.7
1986	Vinny Testaverde, Miami-FL	.175	26	2557	165.8
1987	Don McPherson, Syracuse	.129	22	2341	164.3
1988	Timm Rosenbach, Wash. St.	.199	23	2791	162.0
1989	Ty Detmer, BYU	.265	32	4560	175.6
1990	Shawn Moore, Virginia	.144	21	2262	160.7
1991	Elvis Grbac, Michigan	.152	24	1955	169.0
1992	Elvis Grbac, Michigan	.112	15	1465	154.2
1993	Trent Dilfer, Fresno St.	.217	28	3276	173.1
1994	Kerry Collins, Penn St.	.176	21	2679	172.9
1995	Danny Wuerffel, Florida	.210	35	3266	178.4
1996	Steve Sarkisian, BYU	.278	33	4027	173.6
1997	Cade McNown, UCLA	.173	22	2877	168.6
1998	Shaun King, Tulane	.223	36	3232	183.3
1999	Michael Vick, Va. Tech	.90	12	1840	180.4

Receptions

Championship decided on Passes Caught (1937-69) and on Catches Per Game (since 1970). Touchdown totals unavailable in 1939 and 1941-45.

Multiple winners: Neil Armstrong, Hugh Campbell, Manny Hazard, Reid Moseley, Jason Phillips, Howard Twilley and Alex Van Dyke (2).

Year		No	TD	Yds
1937	Jim Benton, Arkansas	.47	7	754
1938	Sam Boyd, Baylor	.32	5	537
1939	Ken Kavanaugh, LSU	.30	–	467
1940	Eddie Bryant, Virginia	.30	4	222
1941	Hank Stanton, Arizona	.50	–	820
1942	Bill Rogers, Texas A&M	.39	–	432
1943	Neil Armstrong, Okla. A&M	.39	–	317
1944	Reid Moseley, Georgia	.32	–	506
1945	Reid Moseley, Georgia	.31	–	662
1946	Neil Armstrong, Okla. A&M	.32	1	479
1947	Barney Poole, Ole Miss	.52	8	513
1948	Red O'Quinn, Wake Forest	.39	7	605
1949	Art Weiner, N. Carolina	.52	7	762
1950	Gordon Cooper, Denver	.46	6	569
1951	Dewey McConnell, Wyoming	.47	9	725
1952	Ed Brown, Fordham	.57	6	774
1953	John Carson, Georgia	.45	4	663
1954	Jim Hanifan, California	.44	7	569
1955	Hank Burnine, Missouri	.44	2	594
1956	Art Powell, San Jose St.	.40	5	583
1957	Stuart Vaughan, Utah	.53	5	756
1958	Dave Hibbert, Arizona	.61	4	606
1959	Chris Burford, Stanford	.61	6	756
1960	Hugh Campbell, Wash. St.	.66	10	881
1961	Hugh Campbell, Wash. St.	.53	5	723
1962	Vern Burke, Oregon St.	.69	10	1007

Year		No	TD	Yds
1963	Lawrence Elkins, Baylor	.70	8	873
1964	Howard Twilley, Tulsa	.95	13	1178
1965	Howard Twilley, Tulsa	.134	16	1779
1966	Glenn Meltzer, Wichita St	.91	4	1115
1967	Bob Goodridge, Vanderbilt	.79	6	1114
1968	Ron Sellers, Florida St.	.86	12	1496
1969	Jerry Hendren, Idaho	.95	12	1452

Year		No	P/Gm	TD	Yds
1970	Mike Mikolayunas, Davidson	.87	8.7	8	1128
1971	Tom Reynolds, San Diego St	.67	6.7	7	1070
1972	Tom Forzani, Utah St	.85	7.7	8	1169
1973	Jay Miller, BYU	.100	9.1	8	1181
1974	D. McDonald, San Diego St	.86	7.8	7	1157
1975	Bob Farnham, Brown	.56	6.2	2	701
1976	Billy Ryckman, La. Tech	.77	7.0	10	1382
1977	W. Tolleson, W. Carolina	.73	6.6	7	1101
1978	Dave Petzke, Northern Ill	.91	8.3	11	1217
1979	Rick Beasley, Appalach. St	.74	6.7	12	1205
1980	Dave Young, Purdue	.67	6.1	8	917
1981	Pete Harvey, N. Texas St	.57	6.3	3	743
1982	Vincent White, Stanford	.68	6.8	8	677
1983	Keith Edwards, Vanderbilt	.97	8.8	8	909
1984	David Williams, Illinois	.101	9.2	8	1278
1985	Rodney Carter, Purdue	.98	8.9	4	1099
1986	Mark Templeton, L. Beach St	.99	9.0	2	688

Year		No	P/Gm	TD	Yds
1987 Jason Phillips, Houston		99	9.0	3	875
1988 Jason Phillips, Houston		108	9.8	15	1444
1989 Manny Hazard, Houston		142	12.9	22	1689
1990 Manny Hazard, Houston		78	7.8	9	946
1991 Fred Gilbert, Houston		106	9.6	7	957
1992 Sherman Smith, Houston		103	9.4	6	923
1993 Chris Penn, Tulsa		105	9.6	12	1578

Year		No	P/Gm	TD	Yds
1994 Alex Van Dyke, Nevada		98	8.9	10	1246
1995 Alex Van Dyke, Nevada		129	11.7	16	1854
1996 Damond Wilkins, Nevada		114	10.4	4	1121
1997 Eugene Baker, Kent		103	9.4	18	1549
1998 Troy Edwards, La. Tech		140	11.7	27	1996
1999 Trevor Insley, Nevada		134	12.2	13	2060

Scoring

Championship decided on Total Points (1937-69) and on Points Per Game (since 1970).

Multiple winners: Tom Harmon and Billy Sims (2).

Year		TD	XP	FG	Pts
1937 Byron (Whizzer) White, Colo		16	23	1	122
1938 Parker Hall, Ole Miss		11	7	0	73
1939 Tom Harmon, Michigan		14	15	1	102
1940 Tom Harmon, Michigan		16	18	1	117
1941 Bill Dudley, Virginia		18	23	1	134
1942 Bob Steuber, Missouri		18	13	0	121
1943 Steve Van Buren, LSU		14	14	0	98
1944 Glenn Davis, Army		20	0	0	120
1945 Doc Blanchard, Army		19	1	0	115
1946 Gene Roberts, Tenn-Chatt.		18	9	0	117
1947 Lou Gambino, Maryland		16	0	0	96
1948 Fred Wendt, Texas Mines		20	32	0	152
1949 George Thomas, Oklahoma		19	3	0	117
1950 Bobby Reynolds, Nebraska		22	25	0	157
1951 Ollie Matson, San Francisco		21	0	0	126
1952 Jackie Parker, Miss. St.		16	24	0	120
1953 Earl Lindley, Utah St.		13	3	0	81
1954 Art Luppino, Arizona		24	22	0	166
1955 Jim Swink, TCU		20	5	0	125
1956 Clendon Thomas, Oklahoma		18	0	0	108
1957 Leon Burton, Ariz. St.		16	0	0	96
1958 Dick Bass, Pacific		18	8	0	116
1959 Pervis Atkins, N. Mexico St.		17	5	0	107
1960 Bob Gaiters, N. Mexico St.		23	7	0	145
1961 Jim Pilot, N. Mexico St.		21	12	0	138
1962 Jerry Logan, W. Texas St.		13	32	0	110
1963 Cosmo Iacavazzi, Princeton		14	0	0	84
& Dave Casinelli, Memphis St.		14	0	0	84
1964 Brian Piccolo, Wake Forest		17	9	0	111
1965 Howard Twilley, Tulsa		16	31	0	127
1966 Ken Hebert, Houston		11	41	2	113
1967 Leroy Keyes, Purdue		19	0	0	114
1968 Jim O'Brien, Cincinnati		12	31	13	142

Year		TD	XP	FG	Pts
1969 Steve Owens, Oklahoma		23	0	0	138

Year		TD	XP	FG	Pts	P/Gm
1970 Brian Bream, Air Force		20	0	0	120	12.0
& Gary Kosins, Dayton		18	0	0	108	12.0
1971 Ed Marinaro, Cornell		24	4	0	148	16.4
1972 Harold Henson, Ohio St		20	0	0	120	12.0
1973 Jim Jennings, Rutgers		21	2	0	128	11.6
1974 Bill Marek, Wisconsin		19	0	0	114	12.7
1975 Pete Johnson, Ohio St.		25	0	0	150	13.6
1976 Tony Dorsett, Pitt		22	2	0	134	12.2
1977 Earl Campbell, Texas		19	0	0	114	10.4
1978 Billy Sims, Oklahoma		20	0	0	120	10.9
1979 Billy Sims, Oklahoma		22	0	0	132	12.0
1980 Sammy Winder, So. Miss		20	0	0	120	10.9
1981 Marcus Allen, USC		23	0	0	138	12.5
1982 Greg Allen, Fla. St		21	0	0	126	11.5
1983 Mike Rozier, Nebraska		29	0	0	174	14.5
1984 Keith Byars, Ohio St		24	0	0	144	13.1
1985 Bernard White, B. Green.		19	0	0	114	10.4
1986 Steve Bartalo, Colo. St.		19	0	0	114	10.4
1987 Paul Hewitt, S. Diego St.		24	0	0	144	12.0
1988 Barry Sanders, Okla.St.		39	0	0	234	21.3
1989 Anthony Thompson, Ind		25	4	0	154	14.0
1990 Stacey Robinson, No. Ill.		19	6	0	120	10.9
1991 Marshall Faulk, S.D. St.		23	2	0	140	15.6
1992 Garrison Hearst, Georgia		21	0	0	126	11.5
1993 Bam Morris, Texas Tech		22	2	0	134	12.2
1994 Rashaan Salaam, Colo		24	0	0	144	13.1
1995 Eddie George, Ohio St.		24	0	0	144	12.0
1996 Corey Dillon, Washington		23	0	0	138	12.6
1997 Ricky Williams, Texas		25	2	0	152	13.8
1998 Troy Edwards, La. Tech		31	2	0	188	15.7
1999 Shaun Alexander, Alabama		24	0	0	144	13.1

All-Time NCAA Division I-A Leaders

Through the 1999 regular season. The NCAA does not recognize active players among career Per Game leaders.

CAREER

Passing
(Minimum 500 Completions)

Passing Efficiency

		Years	Rating
1	Danny Wuerffel, Florida	1993-96	163.6
2	Ty Detmer, BYU	1988-91	162.7
3	Steve Sarkisian, BYU	1995-96	162.0
4	Billy Blanton, San Diego St.	1993-96	157.1
5	Jim McMahon, BYU	1977-78, 80-81	156.9

Yards Gained

		Years	Yards
1	Ty Detmer, BYU	1988-91	15,031
2	Tim Rattay, La. Tech	1997-99	12,746
3	Chris Redman, Louisville	1996-99	12,541
4	Todd Santos, San Diego St	1984-87	11,425
5	Tim Lester, W. Michigan	1996-99	11,299

Completions

		Years	No
1	Chris Redman, Louisville	1996-99	1031
2	Tim Rattay, La. Tech	1997-99	1015
3	Ty Detmer, BYU	1988-91	958
4	Todd Santos, San Diego St	1984-87	910
5	Brian McClure, Bowling Green	1982-85	900

Receptions

Catches

		Years	No
1	Trevor Insley, Nevada	1996-99	298
2	Geoff Noisy, Nevada	1995-98	295
3	Troy Edwards, La. Tech	1996-98	280
4	Aaron Turner, Pacific	1989-92	266
5	Chad Mackey, La. Tech	1993-96	264

Catches Per Game

		Years	No	P/Gm
1	Manny Hazard, Houston	1989-90	220	10.5
2	Alex Van Dyke, Nevada	1994-95	227	10.3
3	Howard Twilley, Tulsa	1963-65	261	10.0
4	Jason Phillips, Houston	1987-88	207	9.4
5	Troy Edwards, La. Tech	1996-98	280	8.2

Yards Gained

		Years	No	Yards
1	Trevor Insley, Nevada	1996-99	298	5005
2	Marcus Harris, Wyoming	1993-96	259	4518
3	Ryan Yarborough, Wyoming	1990-93	229	4357
4	Troy Edwards, La. Tech	1996-98	280	4352
5	Aaron Turner, Pacific	1989-92	266	4345

All-Time NCAA Division I-A Leaders (Cont.)

Rushing

	Yards Gained	Years	Yards
1	Ron Dayne, Wisconsin	1996-99	6397
2	Ricky Williams, Texas	1995-98	6279
3	Tony Dorsett, Pittsburgh	1973-76	6082
4	Charles White, USC	1976-79	5598
5	Travis Prentice, Miami-OH	1996-99	5596

	Yards Per Game	Years	Yards	P/Gm
1	Ed Marinaro, Cornell	1969-71	4715	174.6
2	O.J. Simpson, USC	1967-68	3124	164.4
3	Herschel Walker, Georgia	1980-82	5259	159.4
4	LeShon Johnson, No. Ill.	1992-93	3314	150.6
5	Ron Dayne, Wisconsin	1996-99	6397	148.8

Total Offense

	Yards Gained	Years	Yards
1	Ty Detmer, BYU	1988-91	14,665
2	Tim Rattay, La. Tech	1997-99	12,689
3	Chris Redman, Louisville	1996-99	12,129
4	Doug Flutie, Boston College	1981-84	11,317
5	Tim Lester, W. Michigan	1996-99	11,081

	Yards Per Game	Years	Yards	P/Gm
1	Tim Rattay, La. Tech	1997-99	12,689	382.4
2	Chris Vargas, Nevada	1992-93	6,417	320.9
3	Ty Detmer, BYU	1988-91	14,665	318.8
4	Daunte Culpepper*, C. Fla.	1996-98	10,344	313.5
5	Mike Perez, San Jose St	1986-87	6,182	309.1

*Culpepper played I-AA with Central Florida in 1995.

All-Purpose Yardage

	Yards Gained	Years	Yards
1	Ricky Williams, Texas	1995-98	7206
2	Napoleon McCallum, Navy	1981-85	7172
3	Darrin Nelson, Stanford	1977-78, 80-81	6885
4	Kevin Faulk, LSU	1995-98	6833
5	Ron Dayne, Wisconsin	1996-99	6701

	Yards Per Game	Years	Yards	P/Gm
1	Ryan Benjamin, Pacific	1990-92	5706	237.8
2	Sheldon Canley, S. Jose St.	1988-90	5146	205.8
3	Howard Stevens, Louisville	1971-72	3873	193.7
4	O.J. Simpson, USC	1967-68	3666	192.9
5	Alex Van Dyke, Nevada	1994-95	4146	188.5

Miscellaneous

	Interceptions	Years	No
1	Al Brosky, Illinois	1950-52	29
2	John Provost, Holy Cross	1972-74	27
	Martin Bayless, Bowling Green	1980-83	27
4	Tom Curtis, Michigan	1967-69	25
	Tony Thurman, Boston College	1981-84	25
	Tracy Saul, Texas Tech.	1989-92	25

	Punt Return Average*	Years	Avg
1	Jack Mitchell, Oklahoma	1946-48	23.6
2	Gene Gibson, Cincinnati	1949-50	20.5
3	Eddie Macon, Pacific.	1949-51	18.9
4	Jackie Robinson, UCLA	1939-40	18.8
5	Two tied at 17.7 each.		

*Minimum 1.2 punt returns per game and 30 career returns.

	Punting Average*	Years	Avg
1	Todd Sauerbrun, West Va.	1991-94	46.3
2	Reggie Roby, Iowa	1979-82	45.6
3	Greg Montgomery, Mich. St.	1985-87	45.4
4	Tom Tupa, Ohio St.	1984-87	45.2
5	Barry Helton, Colorado	1984-87	44.9

*At least 150 punts.

	Kickoff Return Average*	Years	Avg
1	Anthony Davis, USC	1972-74	35.1
2	Eric Booth, So. Miss.	1994-97	32.4
3	Overton Curtis, Utah St.	1957-58	31.0
4	Fred Montgomery, New Mexico St.	1991-92	30.5
5	Allie Taylor, Utah St.	1966-68	29.3

*Minimum 1.2 kickoff returns per game and 30 career returns.

Scoring
Non-kickers

	Points	Years	TD	Xpt	FG	Pts
1	Travis Prentice, Miami-OH	1996-99	78	0	0	468
2	Ricky Williams, Texas	1995-98	75	2	0	452
3	Anthony Thompson, Ind.	1986-89	65	4	0	394
4	Ron Dayne, Wisconsin	1996-99	63	0	0	378
5	Marshall Faulk, S.D. St.	1991-93	62	4	0	376

	Touchdown Catches	Years	No
1	Troy Edwards, La. Tech	1996-98	50
2	Aaron Turner, Pacific	1989-92	43
3	Ryan Yarborough, Wyoming	1990-93	42
4	Clarkston Hines, Duke	1986-89	38
	Marcus Harris, Wyoming	1993-96	38

	Points Per Game	Years	Pts	P/Gm
1	Marshall Faulk, S. Diego St.	1991-93	376	12.1
2	Ed Marinaro, Cornell	1969-71	318	11.8
3	Bill Burnett, Arkansas	1968-70	294	11.3
4	Steve Owens, Oklahoma	1967-69	336	11.2
5	Eddie Talboom, Wyoming	1948-50	303	10.8

	Touchdowns Rushing	Years	No
1	Travis Prentice, Miami-OH	1996-99	73
2	Ricky Williams, Texas	1995-98	72
3	Anthony Thompson, Indiana	1986-89	64
4	Ron Dayne, Wisconsin	1996-99	63
5	Marshall Faulk, S. Diego St.	1991-93	57

	Touchdowns Passing	Years	No
1	Ty Detmer, BYU	1988-91	121
2	Tim Rattay, La. Tech	1997-99	115
3	Danny Wuerffel, Florida	1993-96	114
4	Chad Pennington, Marshall	1997-99	100
5	David Klingler, Houston	1988-91	91

Kickers

	Points	Years	FG	XP	Pts
1	Roman Anderson, Hou	1988-91	70	213	423
2	Carlos Huerta, Mia-FL	1988-91	73	178	397
3	Jason Elam, Hawaii	1988-89, 91-92	79	158	395
4	Derek Schmidt, Fla. St	1984-87	73	174	393
5	Kris Brown, Nebraska	1995-98	57	217	388
6	Jeff Hall, Tennessee	1995-98	61	188	371
	Shayne Graham, Va. Tech	1996-99	68	167	371
8	Luis Zendejas, Ariz. St	1981-84	78	134	368
9	Jeff Jaeger, Wash.	1983-86	80	118	358
10	John Lee, UCLA	1982-85	79	116	353
	Max Zendejas, Arizona	1982-85	77	122	353
	Kevin Butler, Georgia	1981-84	77	122	353

	Field Goals	Years	No
1	Jeff Jaeger, Washington	1983-86	80
2	John Lee, UCLA	1982-85	79
	Jason Elam, Hawaii	1988-89, 91-92	79
4	Philip Doyle, Alabama	1987-90	78
	Luis Zendejas, Arizona St	1981-84	78

SINGLE SEASON
Rushing

Yards Gained	Year	Gm	Car	Yards
Barry Sanders, Okla. St	1988	11	344	2628
Marcus Allen, USC	1981	11	403	2342
Troy Davis, Iowa St.	1996	11	402	2185
Mike Rozier, Nebraska	1983	12	275	2148
Ricky Williams, Texas	1998	11	361	2124

Yards Per Game	Year	Gm	Yards	P/Gm
Barry Sanders, Okla. St	1988	11	2628	238.9
Marcus Allen, USC	1981	11	2342	212.9
Ed Marinaro, Cornell	1971	9	1881	209.0
Troy Davis, Iowa St.	1996	11	2185	198.6
Ricky Williams, Texas	1998	11	2124	193.1

Passing
(Minimum 15 Attempts Per Game)

Passing Efficiency	Year	Rating
Shaun King, Tulane	1998	183.3
Michael Vick, Va. Tech	1999	180.4
Danny Wuerffel, Florida	1995	178.4
Jim McMahon, BYU	1980	176.9
Ty Detmer, BYU	1989	175.6

Yards Gained	Year	Yards
Ty Detmer, BYU	1990	5188
David Klingler, Houston	1990	5140
Tim Rattay, La. Tech	1998	4943
Andre Ware, Houston	1989	4699
Jim McMahon, BYU	1980	4571

Completions	Year	Att	No
Tim Rattay, La. Tech	1998	559	380
David Klingler, Houston	1990	643	374
Andre Ware, Houston	1989	578	365
Tim Couch, Kentucky	1997	547	363
Ty Detmer, BYU	1990	562	361

Total Offense

Yards Gained	Year	Gm	Plays	Yards
David Klingler, Houston	1990	11	704	5221
Ty Detmer, BYU	1990	12	635	5022
Tim Rattay, La. Tech	1998	12	602	4840
Andre Ware, Houston	1989	11	628	4661
Jim McMahon, BYU	1980	12	540	4627

Yards Per Game	Year	Gm	Yards	P/Gm
David Klingler, Houston	1990	11	5221	474.6
Andre Ware, Houston	1989	11	4661	423.7
Ty Detmer, BYU	1990	12	5022	418.5
Tim Rattay, La. Tech	1998	12	4840	403.3
Mike Maxwell, Nevada	1995	9	3623	402.6

Receptions

Catches	Year	Gm	No
Manny Hazard, Houston	1989	11	142
Troy Edwards, La. Tech	1998	12	140
Howard Twilley, Tulsa	1965	10	134
Trevor Insley, Nevada	1999	11	134
Alex Van Dyke, Nevada	1995	11	129

Catches Per Game	Year	No	P/Gm
Howard Twilley, Tulsa	1965	134	13.4
Manny Hazard, Houston	1989	142	12.9
Trevor Insley, Nevada	1999	134	12.2
Alex Van Dyke, Nevada	1995	129	11.7
Troy Edwards, La. Tech	1998	140	11.7
Damond Wilkins, Nevada	1996	114	10.4

Yards Gained	Year	No	Yards
Trevor Insley, Nevada	1999	134	2060
Troy Edwards, La. Tech	1998	140	1996
Alex Van Dyke, Nevada	1995	129	1854
Howard Twilley, Tulsa	1965	134	1779
Troy Edwards, La. Tech	1997	102	1707

All-Purpose Yardage

Yards Gained	Year	Yards
Barry Sanders, Okla. St	1988	3250
Ryan Benjamin, Pacific	1991	2995
Troy Edwards, La. Tech	1998	2784
Mike Pringle, CS-Fullerton	1989	2690
Paul Palmer, Temple	1986	2633

Yards Per Game	Year	Yards	P/Gm
Barry Sanders, Okla. St	1988	3250	295.5
Ryan Benjamin, Pacific	1991	2995	249.6
Byron (Whizzer) White, Colo	1937	1970	246.3
Mike Pringle, CS-Fullerton	1989	2690	244.6
Paul Palmer, Temple	1986	2633	239.4

Scoring

Points	Year	TD	Xpt	FG	Pts
Barry Sanders, Okla. St	1988	39	0	0	234
Troy Edwards, La. Tech	1998	31	2	0	188
Mike Rozier, Nebraska	1983	29	0	0	174
Lydell Mitchell, Penn St	1971	29	0	0	174
Art Luppino, Arizona	1954	24	22	0	166

Points Per Game	Year	Pts	P/Gm
Barry Sanders, Okla. St	1988	234	21.3
Bobby Reynolds, Nebraska	1950	157	17.4
Art Luppino, Arizona	1954	166	16.6
Ed Marinaro, Cornell	1971	148	16.4
Lydell Mitchell, Penn St	1971	174	15.8

Touchdowns Rushing	Year	No
Barry Sanders, Okla. St	1988	37
Mike Rozier, Nebraska	1983	29
Ricky Williams, Texas	1998	27
Ricky Williams, Texas	1997	25
Travis Prentice, Miami-OH	1997	25

Touchdowns Passing	Year	No
David Klingler, Houston	1990	54
Jim McMahon, BYU	1980	47
Andre Ware, Houston	1989	46
Tim Rattay, La. Tech	1998	46
Ty Detmer, BYU	1990	41

Touchdown Catches	Year	No
Troy Edwards, La. Tech	1998	27
Randy Moss, Marshall	1997	25
Manny Hazard, Houston	1989	22
Desmond Howard, Michigan	1991	19
Five tied with 18 each.		

Field Goals	Year	No
John Lee, UCLA	1984	29
Paul Woodside, West Virginia	1982	28
Luis Zendejas, Arizona St	1983	28
Fuad Reveiz, Tennessee	1982	27
Sebastian Janikowski, FSU	1998	27
Three tied with 25 each.		

All-Time NCAA Division I-A Leaders (Cont.)
Miscellaneous

Interceptions	Year	No
Al Worley, Washington	1968	14
George Shaw, Oregon	1951	13
Eight tied with 12 each.		

Punting Average*	Year	Avg
Chad Kessler, LSU	1997	50.3
Reggie Roby, Iowa	1981	49.8
Kirk Wilson, UCLA	1956	49.3
Todd Sauerbrun, West Virginia	1994	48.4
Zack Jordan, Colorado	1950	48.2
*Qualifiers for championship.		

Punt Return Average*	Year	Avg
Bill Blackstock, Tennessee	1951	25.9
George Sims, Baylor	1948	25.0
Gene Derricotte, Michigan	1947	24.8
*At least 1.2 returns per game.		

Kickoff Return Average*	Year	Avg
Paul Allen, BYU	1961	40.1
Tremain Mack, Miami-FL	1996	39.5
Leeland McElroy, Texas A&M	1993	39.3
Forrest Hall, San Francisco	1946	38.2
Tony Ball, Tenn-Chattanooga	1977	36.4
*At least 1.2 kickoff returns per game.		

SINGLE GAME

Rushing

Yards Gained	Opponent	Year	Yds
LaDainian Tomlinson, TCU	UTEP	1999	406
Tony Sands, Kansas	Missouri	1991	396
Marshall Faulk, San Diego St	Pacific	1991	386
Troy Davis, Iowa St.	Missouri	1996	378
Anthony Thompson, Indiana	Wisconsin	1989	377

Passing

Yards Gained	Opponent	Year	Yds
David Klingler, Houston	Arizona St.	1990	716
Matt Vogler, TCU	Houston	1990	690
Scott Mitchell, Utah	Air Force	1988	631
Jeremy Leach, New Mexico	Utah	1989	622
Dave Wilson, Illinois	Ohio St.	1980	621

Completions	Opponent	Year	No
Drew Brees, Purdue	Wisconsin	1998	55
Rusty LaRue, Wake Forest	Duke	1995	55
Rusty LaRue, Wake Forest	N.C. St.	1995	50
David Klingler, Houston	SMU	1990	48
Tim Couch, Kentucky	Arkansas	1998	47

Scoring

Points	Opponent	Year	Pts
Howard Griffith, Illinois	So. Ill.	1990	48
Marshall Faulk, S. Diego St	Pacific	1991	44
Jim Brown, Syracuse	Colgate	1956	43
Showboat Boykin, Ole Miss	Miss. St.	1951	42
Fred Wendt, UTEP*	N. Mex. St.	1948	42
*UTEP was Texas Mines in 1948.			

Touchdowns Rushing	Opponent	Year	No
Howard Griffith, Illinois	So. Ill	1990	8
Showboat Boykin, Ole Miss	Miss. St.	1951	7
Note: Griffith's TD runs (5-51-7-41-5-18-5-3).			

Touchdowns Passing	Opponent	Year	No
David Klingler, Houston	E. Wash.	1990	11
Dennis Shaw, San Diego St	N. Mex. St.	1969	9
Note: Klingler's TD passes (5-48-29-7-3-7-40-8-7-8-51).			

Total Offense

Yards Gained	Opponent	Year	Yds
David Klingler, Houston	Arizona St.	1990	732
Matt Vogler, TCU	Houston	1990	696
David Klingler, Houston	TCU	1990	625
Scott Mitchell, Utah	Air Force	1988	625
Jimmy Klingler, Houston	Rice	1992	612

Receiving

Catches	Opponent	Year	No
Randy Gatewood, UNLV	Idaho	1994	23
Jay Miller, BYU	New Mexico	1973	22
Troy Edwards, La. Tech	Nebraska	1998	21
Chris Daniels, Purdue	Mich. St.	1999	21
Rick Eber, Tulsa	Idaho St.	1967	20

Yards Gained	Opponent	Year	Yds
Troy Edwards, La. Tech	Nebraska	1998	405
Randy Gatewood, UNLV	Idaho	1994	363
Chuck Hughes, UTEP*	N. Texas St.	1965	349
Rick Eber, Tulsa	Idaho St.	1967	322
Harry Wood, Tulsa	Idaho St.	1967	318
*UTEP was Texas Western in 1965.			

Touchdown Catches	Opponent	Year	No
Tim Delaney, S. Diego St	N. Mex. St.	1969	6
Note: Delaney's TD catches (2-22-34-31-30-9).			

Field Goals	Opponent	Year	No
Dale Klein, Nebraska	Missouri	1985	7
Mike Prindle, W. Mich.	Marshall	1984	7
Note: Klein's FGs (32-22-43-44-29-43-43); Prindle's FGs (32-44-42-23-48-41-27).			

Extra Points (Kick)	Opponent	Year	No
Terry Leiweke, Houston	Tulsa	1968	13
Derek Mahoney, Fresno St	New Mexico	1991	13

Longest Plays (since 1941)

Rushing	Opponent	Year	Yds
Gale Sayers, Kansas	Nebraska	1963	99
Max Anderson, Ariz. St.	Wyoming	1967	99
Ralph Thompson, W. Texas St	Wich. St.	1970	99
Kelsey Finch, Tennessee	Florida	1977	99
Eric Vann, Kansas	Oklahoma	1997	99
Eleven tied at 98 each.			

Passing	Opponent	Year	Yds
Fred Owens to Jack Ford, Portland	St. Mary's	1947	99
Bo Burris to Warren McVea, Houston	Wash. St.	1966	99
Colin Clapton to Eddie Jenkins, Holy Cross	Boston U.	1970	99
Terry Peel to Robert Ford, Houston	Syracuse	1970	99

Passing	Opponent	Year	Yds
Terry Peel to Robert Ford, Houston	S. Diego St.	1972	99
Cris Collinsworth to Derrick Gaffney, Florida	Rice	1977	99
Scott Ankrom to James Maness, TCU	Rice	1984	99
Gino Torretta to Horace Copeland, Miami-FL	Ark.	1991	99
John Paci to Thomas Lewis, Indiana	Penn St.	1993	99
Drew Brees to Vinny Sutherland, Purdue	Northwestern	1999	99

Field Goals	Opponent	Year	Yds	Field Goals	Opponent	Year	Yds
Steve Little, Arkansas	Texas	1977	67	Tony Franklin, Tex. A&M	Baylor	1976	65
Russell Erxleben, Texas	Rice	1977	67	Martin Gramatica, Kan. St.	No. Ill.	1998	65
Joe Williams, Wichita St	So. Ill.	1978	67				

Annual Awards
Heisman Trophy

Originally presented in 1935 as the DAC Trophy by the Downtown Athletic Club of New York City to the best college football player east of the Mississippi. In 1936, players across the country were eligible and the award was renamed the Heisman Trophy following the death of former college coach and DAC athletic director John W. Heisman.

Multiple winner: Archie Griffin (2).

Winners in junior year (13): Doc Blanchard (1945), Ty Detmer (1990); Archie Griffin (1974), Desmond Howard (1991), Vic Janowicz (1950), Rashaan Salaam (1994), Barry Sanders (1988), Billy Sims (1978), Roger Staubach (1963), Doak Walker (1948), Herschel Walker (1982), Andre Ware (1989) and Charles Woodson (1997).

Winners on AP national champions (10): Angelo Bertelli (Notre Dame, 1943); Doc Blanchard (Army, 1945); Tony Dorsett (Pittsburgh, 1976); Leon Hart (Notre Dame, 1949); Johnny Lujack (Notre Dame, 1947); Davey O'Brien (TCU, 1938); Bruce Smith (Minnesota, 1941); Charlie Ward (Florida St., 1993); Danny Wuerffel (Florida, 1996); and Charles Woodson (Michigan, 1997).

Year	Points	Year	Points
1935 **Jay Berwanger,** Chicago, HB	84	1948 **Doak Walker,** SMU, HB	778
2nd–Monk Meyer, Army, HB	29	2nd–Charlie Justice, N. Carolina, HB	443
3rd–Bill Shakespeare, Notre Dame, HB	23	3rd–Chuck Bednarik, Penn, C	336
4th–Pepper Constable, Princeton, FB	20	4th–Jackie Jensen, California, HB	143
1936 **Larry Kelley,** Yale, E	219	1949 **Leon Hart,** Notre Dame, E	995
2nd–Sam Francis, Nebraska, FB	47	2nd–Charlie Justice, N. Carolina, HB	272
3rd–Ray Buivid, Marquette, HB	43	3rd–Doak Walker, SMU, HB	229
4th–Sammy Baugh, TCU, HB	39	4th–Arnold Galiffa, Army QB	196
1937 **Clint Frank,** Yale, HB	524	1950 **Vic Janowicz,** Ohio St., HB	633
2nd–Byron (Whizzer) White, Colo., HB	264	2nd–Kyle Rote, SMU, HB	280
3rd–Marshall Goldberg, Pitt, HB	211	3rd–Reds Bagnell, Penn, HB	231
4th–Alex Wojciechowicz, Fordham, C	85	4th–Babe Parilli, Kentucky, QB	214
1938 **Davey O'Brien,** TCU, QB	519	1951 **Dick Kazmaier,** Princeton, TB	1777
2nd–Marshall Goldberg, Pitt, HB	294	2nd–Hank Lauricella, Tennessee, HB	424
3rd–Sid Luckman, Columbia, QB	154	3rd–Babe Parilli, Kentucky, QB	344
4th–Bob MacLeod, Dartmouth, HB	78	4th–Bill McColl, Stanford, E	313
1939 **Nile Kinnick,** Iowa, HB	651	1952 **Billy Vessels,** Oklahoma, HB	525
2nd–Tom Harmon, Michigan, HB	405	2nd–Jack Scarbath, Maryland, QB	367
3rd–Paul Christman, Missouri, QB	391	3rd–Paul Giel, Minnesota, HB	329
4th–George Cafego, Tennessee, QB	296	4th–Donn Moomaw, UCLA, C	257
1940 **Tom Harmon,** Michigan, HB	1303	1953 **Johnny Lattner,** Notre Dame, HB	1850
2nd–John Kimbrough, Texas A&M, FB	841	2nd–Paul Giel, Minnesota, HB	1794
3rd–George Franck, Minnesota, HB	102	3rd–Paul Cameron, UCLA, HB	444
4th–Frankie Albert, Stanford, QB	90	4th–Bernie Faloney, Maryland, QB	258
1941 **Bruce Smith,** Minnesota, HB	554	1954 **Alan Ameche,** Wisconsin, FB	1068
2nd–Angelo Bertelli, Notre Dame, QB	345	2nd–Kurt Burris, Oklahoma, C	838
3rd–Frankie Albert, Stanford, QB	336	3rd–Howard Cassady, Ohio St., HB	810
4th–Frank Sinkwich, Georgia, HB	249	4th–Ralph Guglielmi, Notre Dame, QB	691
1942 **Frank Sinkwich,** Georgia, TB	1059	1955 **Howard Cassady,** Ohio St., HB	2219
2nd–Paul Governali, Columbia, QB	218	2nd–Jim Swink, TCU, HB	742
3rd–Clint Castleberry, Ga. Tech, HB	99	3rd–George Welsh, Navy, QB	383
4th–Mike Holovak, Boston College, FB	95	4th–Earl Morrall, Michigan St., QB	323
1943 **Angelo Bertelli,** Notre Dame, QB	648	1956 **Paul Hornung,** Notre Dame, QB	1066
2nd–Bob Odell, Penn, HB	177	2nd–Johnny Majors, Tennessee, HB	994
3rd–Otto Graham, Northwestern, QB	140	3rd–Tommy McDonald, Oklahoma, HB	973
4th–Creighton Miller, Notre Dame, HB	134	4th–Jerry Tubbs, Oklahoma, C	724
1944 **Les Horvath,** Ohio St., TB-QB	412	1957 **John David Crow,** Texas A&M, HB	1183
2nd–Glenn Davis, Army, HB	287	2nd–Alex Karras, Iowa, T	693
3rd–Doc Blanchard, Army, FB	237	3rd–Walt Kowalczyk, Mich. St., HB	630
4th–Don Whitmire, Navy, T	115	4th–Lou Michaels, Kentucky, T	330
1945 **Doc Blanchard,** Army, FB	860	1958 **Pete Dawkins,** Army, HB	1394
2nd–Glenn Davis, Army, HB	638	2nd–Randy Duncan, Iowa, QB	1021
3rd–Bob Fenimore, Oklahoma A&M, HB	187	3rd–Billy Cannon, LSU, HB	975
4th–Herman Wedemeyer, St. Mary's, HB	152	4th–Bob White, Ohio St., FB	365
1946 **Glenn Davis,** Army, HB	792	1959 **Billy Cannon,** LSU, HB	1929
2nd–Charlie Trippi, Georgia, HB	435	2nd–Richie Lucas, Penn St., QB	613
3rd–Johnny Lujack, Notre Dame, QB	379	3rd–Don Meredith, SMU, QB	286
4th–Doc Blanchard, Army, FB	267	4th–Bill Burrell, Illinois, G	196
1947 **Johnny Lujack,** Notre Dame, QB	742	1960 **Joe Bellino,** Navy, HB	1793
2nd–Bob Chappuis, Michigan, HB	555	2nd–Tom Brown, Minnesota, G	731
3rd–Doak Walker, SMU, HB	196	3rd–Jake Gibbs, Mississippi, QB	453
4th–Charlie Conerly, Mississippi, QB	186	4th–Ed Dyas, Auburn, HB	319

Annual Awards (Cont.)

Year		Points
1961	**Ernie Davis,** Syracuse, HB	824
	2nd–Bob Ferguson, Ohio St., HB	771
	3rd–Jimmy Saxton, Texas, HB	551
	4th–Sandy Stephens, Minnesota, QB	543
1962	**Terry Baker,** Oregon St., QB	707
	2nd–Jerry Stovall, LSU, HB	618
	3rd–Bobby Bell, Minnesota, T.	429
	4th–Lee Roy Jordan, Alabama, C	321
1963	**Roger Staubach,** Navy, QB	1860
	2nd–Billy Lothridge, Ga. Tech, QB	504
	3rd–Sherman Lewis, Mich. St., HB	369
	4th–Don Trull, Baylor, QB	253
1964	**John Huarte,** Notre Dame, QB	1026
	2nd–Jerry Rhome, Tulsa, QB	952
	3rd–Dick Butkus, Illinois, C	505
	4th–Bob Timberlake, Michigan, QB	361
1965	**Mike Garrett,** USC, HB	926
	2nd–Howard Twilley, Tulsa, E	528
	3rd–Jim Grabowski, Illinois, FB	481
	4th–Donny Anderson, Texas Tech, HB	408
1966	**Steve Spurrier,** Florida, QB	1679
	2nd–Bob Griese, Purdue, QB	816
	3rd–Nick Eddy, Notre Dame, HB	456
	4th–Gary Beban, UCLA, QB	318
1967	**Gary Beban,** UCLA, QB	1968
	2nd–O.J. Simpson, USC, HB	1722
	3rd–Leroy Keyes, Purdue, HB	1366
	4th–Larry Csonka, Syracuse, FB	136
1968	**O.J. Simpson,** USC, HB	2853
	2nd–Leroy Keyes, Purdue, HB	1103
	3rd–Terry Hanratty, Notre Dame, QB	387
	4th–Ted Kwalick, Penn St., TE	254
1969	**Steve Owens,** Oklahoma, HB	1488
	2nd–Mike Phipps, Purdue, QB	1344
	3rd–Rex Kern, Ohio St., QB	856
	4th–Archie Manning, Mississippi, QB	582
1970	**Jim Plunkett,** Stanford, QB	2229
	2nd–Joe Theismann, Notre Dame, QB	1410
	3rd–Archie Manning, Mississippi, QB	849
	4th–Steve Worster, Texas, RB	398
1971	**Pat Sullivan,** Auburn, QB	1597
	2nd–Ed Marinaro, Cornell, RB	1445
	3rd–Greg Pruitt, Oklahoma, RB	586
	4th–Johnny Musso, Alabama, RB	365
1972	**Johnny Rodgers,** Nebraska, FL	1310
	2nd–Greg Pruitt, Oklahoma, RB	966
	3rd–Rich Glover, Nebraska, MG	652
	4th–Bert Jones, LSU, QB	351
1973	**John Cappelletti,** Penn St., RB	1057
	2nd–John Hicks, Ohio St., OT	524
	3rd–Roosevelt Leaks, Texas, RB	482
	4th–David Jaynes, Kansas, QB	394
1974	**Archie Griffin,** Ohio St., RB	1920
	2nd–Anthony Davis, USC, RB	819
	3rd–Joe Washington, Oklahoma, RB	661
	4th–Tom Clements, Notre Dame, QB	244
1975	**Archie Griffin,** Ohio St., RB	1800
	2nd–Chuck Muncie, California, RB	730
	3rd–Ricky Bell, USC, RB	708
	4th–Tony Dorsett, Pitt, RB	616
1976	**Tony Dorsett,** Pittsburgh, RB	2357
	2nd–Ricky Bell, USC, RB	1346
	3rd–Rob Lytle, Michigan, RB	413
	4th–Terry Miller, Oklahoma St., RB	197
1977	**Earl Campbell,** Texas, RB	1547
	2nd–Terry Miller, Oklahoma St., RB	812
	3rd–Ken MacAfee, Notre Dame, TE	343
	4th–Doug Williams, Grambling, QB	266

Year		Points
1978	**Billy Sims,** Oklahoma, RB	827
	2nd–Chuck Fusina, Penn St., QB	750
	3rd–Rick Leach, Michigan, QB	435
	4th–Charles White, USC, RB	354
1979	**Charles White,** USC, RB	1695
	2nd–Billy Sims, Oklahoma, RB	773
	3rd–Marc Wilson, BYU, QB	589
	4th–Art Schlichter, Ohio St., QB	251
1980	**George Rogers,** South Carolina, RB	1128
	2nd–Hugh Green, Pittsburgh, DE	861
	3rd–Herschel Walker, Georgia, RB	683
	4th–Mark Herrmann, Purdue, QB	405
1981	**Marcus Allen,** USC, RB	1797
	2nd–Herschel Walker, Georgia, RB	1199
	3rd–Jim McMahon, BYU, QB	706
	4th–Dan Marino, Pitt, QB	256
1982	**Herschel Walker,** Georgia, RB	1926
	2nd–John Elway, Stanford, QB	1231
	3rd–Eric Dickerson, SMU, RB	465
	4th–Anthony Carter, Michigan, WR	142
1983	**Mike Rozier,** Nebraska, RB	1801
	2nd–Steve Young, BYU, QB	1172
	3rd–Doug Flutie, Boston College, QB	253
	4th–Turner Gill, Nebraska, QB	190
1984	**Doug Flutie,** Boston College, QB	2240
	2nd–Keith Byars, Ohio St., RB	1251
	3rd–Robbie Bosco, BYU, QB	443
	4th–Bernie Kosar, Miami-FL, QB	320
1985	**Bo Jackson,** Auburn, RB	1509
	2nd–Chuck Long, Iowa, QB	1464
	3rd–Robbie Bosco, BYU, QB	459
	4th–Lorenzo White, Michigan St., RB	391
1986	**Vinny Testaverde,** Miami-FL, QB	2213
	2nd–Paul Palmer, Temple, RB	672
	3rd–Jim Harbaugh, Michigan, QB	458
	4th–Brian Bosworth, Oklahoma, LB	395
1987	**Tim Brown,** Notre Dame, WR	1442
	2nd–Don McPherson, Syracuse, QB	831
	3rd–Gordie Lockbaum, Holy Cross, WR-DB	657
	4th–Lorenzo White, Michigan St., RB	632
1988	**Barry Sanders,** Oklahoma St., RB	1878
	2nd–Rodney Peete, USC, QB	912
	3rd–Troy Aikman, UCLA, QB	582
	4th–Steve Walsh, Miami-FL, QB	341
1989	**Andre Ware,** Houston, QB	1073
	2nd–Anthony Thompson, Ind., RB	1003
	3rd–Major Harris, West Va., QB	709
	4th–Tony Rice, Notre Dame, QB	523
1990	**Ty Detmer,** BYU, QB	1482
	2nd–Rocket Ismail, Notre Dame, FL	1177
	3rd–Eric Bieniemy, Colorado, RB	798
	4th–Shawn Moore, Virginia, QB	465
1991	**Desmond Howard,** Michigan, WR	2077
	2nd–Casey Weldon, Florida St., QB	503
	3rd–Ty Detmer, BYU, QB	445
	4th–Steve Emtman, Washington, DT	357
1992	**Gino Torretta,** Miami-FL, QB	1400
	2nd–Marshall Faulk, San Diego St., RB	1080
	3rd–Garrison Hearst, Georgia, RB	982
	4th–Marvin Jones, Florida St., LB	392
1993	**Charlie Ward,** Florida St., QB	2310
	2nd–Heath Shuler, Tennessee, QB	688
	3rd–David Palmer, Alabama, RB	292
	4th–Marshall Faulk, S. Diego St., RB	250
1994	**Rashaan Salaam,** Colorado, RB	1743
	2nd–Ki-Jana Carter, Penn St., RB	901
	3rd–Steve McNair, Alcorn St., QB	655
	4th–Kerry Collins, Penn St., QB	639

Year		Points	Year		Points
1995	**Eddie George,** Ohio St., RB	1460	1998	**Ricky Williams,** Texas, RB	2355
	2nd–Tommie Frazier, Nebraska, QB	1196		2nd–Michael Bishop, Kansas St., QB	792
	3rd–Danny Wuerffel, Florida, QB	987		3rd–Cade McNown, UCLA, QB	696
	4th–Darnell Autry, Northwestern, RB	535		4th–Tim Couch, Kentucky, QB	527
1996	**Danny Wuerffel,** Florida, QB	1363	1999	**Ron Dayne,** Wisconsin, RB	2042
	2nd–Troy Davis, Iowa St., RB	1174		2nd–Joe Hamilton, Ga. Tech, QB	994
	3rd–Jake Plummer, Arizona St., QB	685		3rd–Michael Vick, Va. Tech, QB	319
	4th–Orlando Pace, Ohio St., OT	599		4th–Drew Brees, Purdue, QB	308
1997	**Charles Woodson,** Michigan, DB-WR	1815			
	2nd–Peyton Manning, Tennessee, QB	1543			
	3rd–Ryan Leaf, Washington St., QB	861			
	4th–Randy Moss, Marshall, WR	253			

Maxwell Award

First presented in 1937 by the Maxwell Memorial Football Club of Philadelphia, the award is named after Robert (Tiny) Maxwell, a Philadelphia native who was a standout lineman at the University of Chicago at the turn of the century. Like the Heisman, the Maxwell is given to the outstanding college player in the nation. Both awards have gone to the same player in the same season 34 times. Those players are preceded by (#). Glenn Davis of Army and Doak Walker of SMU won both but in different years.

Multiple winner: Johnny Lattner (2).

Year	Year	Year
1937 #Clint Frank, Yale, HB	1958 #Pete Dawkins, Army, HB	1979 #Charles White, USC, RB
1938 #Davey O'Brien, TCU, QB	1959 Rich Lucas, Penn St., QB	1980 Hugh Green, Pitt, DE
1939 #Nile Kinnick, Iowa, HB		1981 #Marcus Allen, USC, RB
1940 #Tom Harmon, Michigan, HB	1960 #Joe Bellino, Navy, HB	1982 #Herschel Walker, Georgia, RB
1941 Bill Dudley, Virginia, HB	1961 Bob Ferguson, Ohio St., HB	1983 #Mike Rozier, Nebraska, RB
1942 Paul Governali, Columbia, QB	1962 #Terry Baker, Oregon St., QB	1984 #Doug Flutie, Boston Col., QB
1943 Bob Odell, Penn, HB	1963 #Roger Staubach, Navy, QB	1985 Chuck Long, Iowa, QB
1944 Glenn Davis, Army, HB	1964 Glenn Ressler, Penn St., G	1986 #V. Testaverde, Miami-FL, QB
1945 #Doc Blanchard, Army, FB	1965 Tommy Nobis, Texas, LB	1987 Don McPherson, Syracuse, QB
1946 Charley Trippi, Georgia, HB	1966 Jim Lynch, Notre Dame, LB	1988 #Barry Sanders, Okla. St., RB
1947 Doak Walker, SMU, HB	1967 #Gary Beban, UCLA, QB	1989 Anthony Thompson, Indiana, RB
1948 Chuck Bednarik, Penn, C	1968 #O.J. Simpson, USC, HB	
1949 #Leon Hart, Notre Dame, E	1969 Mike Reid, Penn St., DT	1990 #Ty Detmer, BYU, QB
		1991 #Desmond Howard, Mich., WR
1950 Reds Bagnell, Penn, HB	1970 #Jim Plunkett, Stanford, QB	1992 #Gino Torretta, Miami-FL, QB
1951 #Dick Kazmaier, Princeton, TB	1971 Ed Marinaro, Cornell, RB	1993 #Charlie Ward, Florida St., QB
1952 Johnny Lattner, Notre Dame, HB	1972 Brad Van Pelt, Michigan St., DB	1994 Kerry Collins, Penn St., QB
1953 #Johnny Lattner, N. Dame, HB	1973 #John Cappelletti, Penn St., RB	1995 #Eddie George, Ohio St., RB
1954 Ron Beagle, Navy, E	1974 Steve Joachim, Temple, QB	1996 #Danny Wuerffel, Florida, QB
1955 #Howard Cassady, Ohio St., HB	1975 #Archie Griffin, Ohio St., RB	1997 Peyton Manning, Tennessee, QB
1956 Tommy McDonald, Okla., HB	1976 #Tony Dorsett, Pitt, RB	1998 #Ricky Williams, Texas, RB
1957 Bob Reifsnyder, Navy, T	1977 Ross Browner, Notre Dame, DE	1999 #Ron Dayne, Wisconsin, RB
	1978 Chuck Fusina, Penn St., QB	

Outland Trophy

First presented in 1946 by the Football Writers Association of America, honoring the nation's outstanding interior lineman. The award is named after its benefactor, Dr. John H. Outland (Kansas, Class of 1898). Players listed in **bold** type helped lead their team to a national championship (according to AP).

Multiple winner: Dave Rimington (2). **Winners in junior year:** Ross Browner (1976), Steve Emtman (1991), Orlando Pace (1996) and Rimington (1981).

Year	Year	Year
1946 **George Connor**, N. Dame, T	1965 Tommy Nobis, Texas, G	1984 Bruce Smith, Virginia Tech, DT
1947 Joe Steffy, Army, G	1966 Loyd Phillips, Arkansas, T	1985 Mike Ruth, Boston College, NG
1948 Bill Fischer, Notre Dame, G	1967 **Ron Yary**, USC, T	1986 Jason Buck, BYU, DT
1949 Ed Bagdon, Michigan St., G	1968 Bill Stanfill, Georgia, T	1987 Chad Hennings, Air Force, DT
	1969 Mike Reid, Penn St., T	1988 Tracy Rocker, Auburn, DT
1950 Bob Gain, Kentucky, T		1989 Mohammed Elewonibi, BYU, G
1951 Jim Weatherall, Oklahoma, T	1970 Jim Stillwagon, Ohio St., MG	
1952 Dick Modzelewski, Maryland, T	1971 **Larry Jacobson**, Neb., DT	1990 Russell Maryland, Miami-FL, NT
1953 J.D. Roberts, Oklahoma, G	1972 Rich Glover, Nebraska, MG	1991 Steve Emtman, Washington, DT
1954 Bill Brooks, Arkansas, G	1973 John Hicks, Ohio St., OT	1992 Will Shields, Nebraska, G
1955 Calvin Jones, Iowa, G	1974 Randy White, Maryland, DT	1993 Rob Waldrop, Arizona, NG
1956 Jim Parker, Ohio St., G	1975 **Lee Roy Selmon**, Okla., DT	1994 **Zach Wiegert**, Nebraska, OT
1957 Alex Karras, Iowa, T	1976 Ross Browner, Notre Dame, DE	1995 Jonathan Ogden, UCLA, OT
1958 Zeke Smith, Auburn, G	1977 Brad Shearer, Texas, DT	1996 Orlando Pace, Ohio St., OT
1959 Mike McGee, Duke, T	1978 Greg Roberts, Oklahoma, G	1997 Aaron Taylor, Nebraska, G
	1979 Jim Richter, N.C. State, C	1998 Kris Farris, UCLA, OT
1960 **Tom Brown**, Minnesota, G		1999 Chris Samuels, Alabama, OT
1961 Merlin Olsen, Utah St., T	1980 Mark May, Pittsburgh, OT	
1962 Bobby Bell, Minnesota, T	1981 Dave Rimington, Nebraska, C	
1963 **Scott Appleton**, Texas, T	1982 Dave Rimington, Nebraska, C	
1964 Steve DeLong, Tennessee, T	1983 Dean Steinkuhler, Nebraska, G	

Annual Awards (Cont.)
Butkus Award

First presented in 1985 by the Downtown Athletic Club of Orlando, Fla., to honor the nation's outstanding linebacker. The award is named after Dick Butkus, two-time consensus All-America at Illinois and six-time All-Pro with the Chicago Bears.

Multiple winner: Brian Bosworth (2).

Year	Year	Year
1985 Brian Bosworth, Oklahoma	1990 Alfred Williams, Colorado	1995 Kevin Hardy, Illinois
1986 Brian Bosworth, Oklahoma	1991 Erick Anderson, Michigan	1996 Matt Russell, Colorado
1987 Paul McGowan, Florida St.	1992 Marvin Jones, Florida St.	1997 Andy Katzenmoyer, Ohio St.
1988 Derrick Thomas, Alabama	1993 Trev Alberts, Nebraska	1998 Chris Claiborne, USC
1989 Percy Snow, Michigan St.	1994 Dana Howard, Illinois	1999 LaVar Arrington, Penn St.

Lombardi Award

First presented in 1970 by the Rotary Club of Houston, honoring the nation's best lineman. The award is named after pro football coach Vince Lombardi, who, as a guard, was a member of the famous "Seven Blocks of Granite" at Fordham in the 1930s. The Lombardi and Outland awards have gone to the same player in the same year ten times. Those players are preceded by (#). Ross Browner of Notre Dame won both, but in different years.

Multiple winner: Orlando Pace (2).

Year	Year	Year
1970 #Jim Stillwagon, Ohio St., MG	1980 Hugh Green, Pitt, DE	1990 Chris Zorich, Notre Dame, NT
1971 Walt Patulski, Notre Dame, DE	1981 Kenneth Sims, Texas, DT	1991 #Steve Emtman, Wash., DT
1972 #Rich Glover, Nebraska, MG	1982 #Dave Rimington, Neb., C	1992 Marvin Jones, Florida St., LB
1973 #John Hicks, Ohio St., OT	1983 #Dean Steinkuhler, Neb., G	1993 Aaron Taylor, Notre Dame, OT
1974 #Randy White, Maryland, DT	1984 Tony Degrate, Texas, DT	1994 Warren Sapp, Miami-FL, DT
1975 #Lee Roy Selmon, Okla., DT	1985 Tony Casillas, Oklahoma, NG	1995 Orlando Pace, Ohio St., OT
1976 Wilson Whitley, Houston, DT	1986 Cornelius Bennett, Alabama, LB	1996 #Orlando Pace, Ohio St., OT
1977 Ross Browner, Notre Dame, DE	1987 Chris Spielman, Ohio St., LB	1997 Grant Wistrom, Nebraska, DE
1978 Bruce Clark, Penn St., DT	1988 #Tracy Rocker, Auburn, DT	1998 Dat Nguyen, Tex. A&M, LB
1979 Brad Budde, USC, G	1989 Percy Snow, Michigan St., LB	1999 Corey Moore, Va. Tech, DE

O'Brien Quarterback Award

First presented in 1977 as the O'Brien Memorial Trophy, the award went to the outstanding player in the Southwest. In 1981, however, the Davey O'Brien Educational and Charitable Trust of Ft. Worth renamed the prize the O'Brien National Quarterback Award and now honors the nation's best quarterback. The award is named after 1938 Heisman Trophy-winning QB Davey O'Brien of Texas Christian.

Multiple winners: Ty Detmer, Mike Singletary and Danny Wuerffel (2).

Memorial Trophy

Year	Year	Year
1977 Earl Campbell, Texas, RB	1979 Mike Singletary, Baylor, LB	1980 Mike Singletary, Baylor, LB
1978 Billy Sims, Oklahoma, RB		

National QB Award

Year	Year	Year
1981 Jim McMahon, BYU	1988 Troy Aikman, UCLA	1995 Danny Wuerffel, Florida
1982 Todd Blackledge, Penn St.	1989 Andre Ware, Houston	1996 Danny Wuerffel, Florida
1983 Steve Young, BYU	1990 Ty Detmer, BYU	1997 Peyton Manning, Tennessee
1984 Doug Flutie, Boston College	1991 Ty Detmer, BYU	1998 Michael Bishop, Kansas St.
1985 Chuck Long, Iowa	1992 Gino Torretta, Miami-FL	1999 Joe Hamilton, Ga. Tech
1986 Vinny Testaverde, Miami, FL	1993 Charlie Ward, Florida St.	
1987 Don McPherson, Syracuse	1994 Kerry Collins, Penn St.	

Thorpe Award

First presented in 1986 by the Jim Thorpe Athletic Club of Oklahoma City to honor the nation's outstanding defensive back. The award is named after Jim Thorpe—Olympic champion and two-time consensus All-America halfback at Carlisle.

Year	Year	Year
1986 Thomas Everett, Baylor	1990 Darryl Lewis, Arizona	1995 Greg Myers, Colorado St.
1987 Bennie Blades, Miami-FL	1991 Terrell Buckley, Florida St.	1996 Lawrence Wright, Florida
& Rickey Dixon, Oklahoma	1992 Deon Figures, Colorado	1997 Charles Woodson, Michigan
1988 Deion Sanders, Florida St.	1993 Antonio Langham, Alabama	1998 Antoine Winfield, Ohio St.
1989 Mike Carrier, USC	1994 Chris Hudson, Colorado	1999 Tyrone Carter, Minnesota

Payton Award

First presented in 1987 by the Sports Network and Division I-AA sports information directors to honor the nation's outstanding Division I-AA player. The award is named after Walter Payton, the NFL's all-time leading rusher who was an All-America running back at Jackson St.

Year	Year	Year
1987 Kenny Gamble, Colgate, RB	1992 Michael Payton, Marshall, QB	1997 Brian Finneran, Villanova, WR
1988 Dave Meggett, Towson St., RB	1993 Doug Nussmeier, Idaho, QB	1998 Jerry Azumah, N. Hampshire, RB
1989 John Friesz, Idaho, QB	1994 Steve McNair, Alcorn St., QB	1999 Adrian Peterson, Ga. Southern, RB
1990 Walter Dean, Grambling, RB	1995 Dave Dickenson, Montana, QB	
1991 Jamie Martin, Weber St., QB	1996 Archie Amerson, N. Arizona, RB	

Hill Trophy

First presented in 1986 by the Harlon Hill Awards Committee in Florence, AL, to honor the nation's outstanding Division II player. The award is named after three-time NFL All-Pro Harlon Hill, who played college ball at North Alabama.

Multiple winner: Johnny Bailey (3).

Year	Year	Year
1986 Jeff Bentrim, N. Dakota St., QB	1991 Ronnie West, Pittsburg St., WR	1996 Jarrett Anderson, Truman St., RB
1987 Johnny Bailey, Texas A&I, RB	1992 Ronald Moore, Pittsburg St., RB	1997 Irv Sigler, Bloomsburg, RB
1988 Johnny Bailey, Texas A&I, RB	1993 Roger Graham, New Haven, RB	1998 Brian Shay, Emporia St., RB
1989 Johnny Bailey, Texas A&I, RB	1994 Chris Hatcher, Valdosta St., QB	1999 Corte McGuffet, N. Colo., QB
1990 Chris Simdorn, N. Dakota St., QB	1995 Ronald McKinnon, N. Alabama, LB	

All-Time Winningest Division I-A Coaches

Minimum of 10 years in Division I-A through 1999 season. Regular season and bowl games included. Coaches active in 1999 in **bold** type.

Top 25 Winning Percentage

		Yrs	W	L	T	Pct
1	Knute Rockne	13	105	12	5	.881
2	Frank Leahy	13	107	13	9	.864
3	George Woodruff	12	142	25	2	.846
4	Barry Switzer	16	157	29	4	.837
5	Tom Osborne	25	255	49	3	.836
6	Percy Haughton	13	96	17	6	.832
7	Bob Neyland	21	173	31	12	.829
8	Hurry Up Yost	29	196	36	12	.828
9	Bud Wilkinson	17	145	29	4	.826
10	Jock Sutherland	20	144	28	14	.812
11	Bob Devaney	16	136	30	7	.806
12	Frank Thomas	19	141	33	9	.795
13	**Joe Paterno**	34	317	83	3	.790
14	Henry Williams	23	141	34	12	.786
15	Gil Dobie	33	180	45	15	.781
16	Bear Bryant	38	323	85	17	.780
17	**Bobby Bowden**	34	304	85	4	.779
18	Fred Folsom	19	106	28	6	.779
19	Bo Schembechler	27	234	65	8	.775
20	**Steve Spurrier**	13	122	35	2	.774
21	Fritz Crisler	18	116	32	9	.768
22	Charley Moran	18	122	33	12	.766
23	Wallace Wade	24	171	49	10	.765
24	Frank Kush	22	176	54	1	.764
25	Dan McGugin	30	197	55	19	.762

Top 25 Victories

		Yrs	W	L	T	Pct
1	Bear Bryant	38	**323**	85	17	.780
2	Pop Warner	44	**319**	106	32	.733
3	**Joe Paterno**	34	**317**	83	3	.790
4	Amos Alonzo Stagg	57	**314**	199	35	.605
5	**Bobby Bowden**	34	**304**	85	4	.779
6	Tom Osborne	25	**255**	49	3	.836
7	**LaVell Edwards**	28	**251**	95	3	.723
8	Woody Hayes	33	**238**	72	10	.759
9	Bo Schembechler	27	**234**	65	8	.775
10	Hayden Fry	37	**232**	178	10	.564
11	**Lou Holtz**	28	**216**	106	7	.667
12	Jess Neely	40	**207**	176	19	.539
13	Warren Woodson	31	**203**	95	14	.673
14	Vince Dooley	25	**201**	77	10	.715
	Eddie Anderson	39	**201**	128	15	.606
16	Jim Sweeney	32	**200**	154	4	.564
17	Dana X. Bible	33	**198**	72	23	.715
18	Dan McGugin	30	**197**	55	19	.762
19	Hurry Up Yost	29	**196**	36	12	.828
20	**Don Nehlen**	29	**195**	123	8	.610
21	Howard Jones	29	**194**	64	21	.733
22	Johnny Vaught	25	**190**	61	12	.745
23	John Heisman	36	**185**	70	17	.711
	Johnny Majors	29	**185**	137	10	.572
25	Darrell Royal	23	**184**	60	5	.749
	John Cooper	23	**184**	80	6	.693

Note: Eddie Robinson of Division I-AA Grambling St. (1941-42, 1945-97) is the all-time NCAA leader in coaching wins with a 408-165-15 record and .708 winning pct. over 55 seasons.

Where They Coached

Anderson–Loras (1922-24), DePaul (1925-31), Holy Cross (1933-38), Iowa (1939-42), Holy Cross (1950-64); **Bible**–Mississippi College (1913-15), LSU (1916), Texas A&M (1917,1919-28), Nebraska (1929-36), Texas (1937-46); **Bowden**–Samford (1959-62), West Virginia (1970-75), Florida St. (1976–); **Bryant**–Maryland (1945), Kentucky (1946-53), Texas A&M (1954-57), Alabama (1958-82); **Cooper**– Tulsa (1977-84), Arizona St. (1985-87), Ohio St. (1988–); **Crisler**–Minnesota (1930-31), Princeton (1932-37), Michigan (1938-47); **Devaney**–Wyoming (1957-61), Nebraska (1962-72); **V. Dooley**–Georgia (1964-88); **Edwards**–BYU (1972–); **Folsom**–Colorado (1895-99, 1901-02), Dartmouth (1903-06), Colorado (1908-15).

Fry–SMU (1962-72), North Texas (1973-78), Iowa (1979-98); **Haughton**–Cornell (1899-1900), Harvard (1908-16), Columbia (1923-24); **Hayes**–Denison (1946-48), Miami-OH (1949-50), Ohio St. (1951-78); **Heisman**–Oberlin (1892), Akron (1893), Oberlin (1894), Auburn (1895-99), Clemson (1900-03), Georgia Tech (1904-19), Penn (1920-22), Washington & Jefferson (1923), Rice (1924-27); **Holtz**–William & Mary (1969-71), N.C. State (1972-75), Arkansas (1977-83), Minnesota (1984-85), Notre Dame (1986-96), South Carolina (1999–); **Jones**–Syracuse (1909), Ohio St. (1910), Yale (1913), Iowa (1916-23), Duke (1924), USC (1925-40); **Kush**–Arizona St. (1958-79); **Leahy**–Boston College (1939-40), Notre Dame (1941-43, 1946-53); **Majors**–Iowa St. (1968-72), Pittsburgh (1973-76, 93-96), Tennessee (1977-92); **McGugin**–Michigan (1904), Vanderbilt (1904-17, 1919-34); **Moran**–Texas A&M (1909-14), Centre (1919-23), Bucknell (1924-26), Catawba (1930-33).

Neely–Rhodes (1924-27), Clemson (1931-39), Rice (1940-66); **Nehlen**–Bowling Green (1968-76), West Virginia (1980–); **Neyland**–Tennessee (1926-34, 1936-40, 1946-52); **Osborne**–Nebraska (1973-97); **Paterno**–Penn St. (1966–); **Rockne**–Notre Dame (1918-30); **Royal**–Mississippi St. (1954-55), Washington (1956), Texas (1957-76); **Schembechler**–Miami-OH (1963-68), Michigan (1969-89); **Spurrier**–Duke (1987-89), Florida (1990–); **Stagg**–Springfield College (1890-91), Chicago (1892-1932), Pacific (1933-46); **Sutherland**–Lafayette (1919-23), Pittsburgh (1924-38); **Sweeney**–Montana St. (1963-67), Washington St. (1968-75), Fresno St. (1976-96); **Switzer**–Oklahoma (1973-88).

Thomas–Chattanooga (1925-28), Alabama (1931-42, 1944-46); **Vaught**–Mississippi (1947-70); **Wade**–Alabama (1923-30), Duke (1931-41, 1946-50); **Warner**–Georgia (1895-96), Cornell (1897-98), Carlisle (1899-1903), Cornell (1904-06), Carlisle (1907-13), Pittsburgh (1915-23), Stanford (1924-32), Temple (1933-38); **Wilkinson**–Oklahoma (1947-63); **Williams**–Army (1891), Minnesota (1900-21); **Woodruff**–Penn (1892-1901), Illinois (1903), Carlisle (1905); **Woodson**–Central Arkansas (1935-39), Hardin-Simmons (1941-42, 1946-51), Arizona (1952-56), New Mexico St. (1958-67), Trinity-TX (1972-73); **Yost**–Ohio Wesleyan (1897), Nebraska (1898), Kansas (1899), Stanford (1900), Michigan (1901-23, 1925-26).

All-Time Winningest Division I-A Coaches (Cont.)

All-Time Bowl Appearances
Coaches active in 1999 in **bold** type.

Active Coaches' Victories
(Minimum 5 years in Division I-A.)

		Overall		
		App	W	L	T
1	**Joe Paterno**	30	20	9	1
2	Bear Bryant	29	15	12	2
3	Tom Osborne	25	12	13	0
4	**Bobby Bowden**	23	17	5	1
5	**LaVell Edwards**	22	7	14	1
6	Lou Holtz	20	10	8	2
	Vince Dooley	20	8	10	2
8	Johnny Vaught	18	10	8	0
9	Hayden Fry	17	7	9	1
	Bo Schembechler	17	5	12	0
11	Johnny Majors	16	9	7	0
	Darrell Royal	16	8	7	1
13	Don James	15	10	5	0
14	**George Welsh**	14	5	9	0
15	Bobby Dodd	13	9	4	0
	Terry Donahue	13	8	4	1
	Barry Switzer	13	8	5	0
	Charlie McClendon	13	7	6	0
	Jackie Sherrill	13	7	6	0
	John Cooper	13	5	8	0

		Yrs	W	L	T	Pct
1	Joe Paterno, Penn St.	34	**317**	83	3	.790
2	Bobby Bowden, Fla. St.	34	**304**	85	4	.779
3	LaVell Edwards, BYU	28	**251**	95	3	.725
4	Lou Holtz, South Carolina	28	**216**	106	7	.667
5	Don Nehlen, West Va.	29	**195**	123	8	.610
6	John Cooper, Ohio St.	23	**184**	80	6	.693
7	George Welsh, Virginia	27	**183**	126	4	.591
8	Jackie Sherrill, Miss. St.	22	**164**	89	4	.646
9	Dick Tomey, Arizona	23	**153**	104	7	.593
10	Ken Hatfield, Rice	21	**144**	96	4	.598
11	Larry Smith, Missouri	23	**140**	118	7	.542
12	Frank Beamer, Va. Tech	19	**130**	83	4	.608
13	Dennis Franchione, TCU	17	**128**	64	2	.665
14	Fisher DeBerry, Air Force	16	**126**	69	1	.645
15	Steve Spurrier, Florida	13	**122**	35	2	.774
16	Dennis Erickson, Oregon St.	14	**120**	45	1	.726
17	Bruce Snyder, Arizona St.	20	**118**	101	6	.538
18	Paul Pasqualoni, Syracuse	14	**109**	48	1	.693
19	John Robinson, UNLV	13	**107**	43	4	.708
20	Mike Price, Wash. St.	19	**105**	110	0	.488

Note: Only four coaches— **Bill Alexander** of Georgia Tech (1920-44); **Bob Neyland** of Tennessee (1926-34, 36-40, 46-52); **Frank Thomas** of Alabama (1931-42, 44-46) and **Joe Paterno** of Penn State (1966–)— have taken teams to the Rose, Orange, Sugar and Cotton Bowls. Paterno has won all four, while Alexander and Thomas won three and Neyland two.

AFCA Coach of the Year
First presented in 1935 by the American Football Coaches Association.
Multiple winners: Joe Paterno (4), Bear Bryant (3), John McKay and Darrell Royal (2).

Years
1935 Pappy Waldorf, Northwestern
1936 Dick Harlow, Harvard
1937 Hooks Mylin, Lafayette
1938 Bill Kern, Carnegie Tech
1939 Eddie Anderson, Iowa
1940 Clark Shaughnessy, Stanford
1941 Frank Leahy, Notre Dame
1942 Bill Alexander, Georgia Tech
1943 Amos Alonzo Stagg, Pacific
1944 Carroll Widdoes, Ohio St.
1945 Bo McMillin, Indiana
1946 Red Blaik, Army
1947 Fritz Crisler, Michigan
1948 Bennie Oosterbaan, Michigan
1949 Bud Wilkinson, Oklahoma
1950 Charlie Caldwell, Princeton
1951 Chuck Taylor, Stanford
1952 Biggie Munn, Michigan St.
1953 Jim Tatum, Maryland
1954 Red Sanders, UCLA
1955 Duffy Daugherty, Michigan St.
1956 Bowden Wyatt, Tennessee
1957 Woody Hayes, Ohio St.

Years
1958 Paul Dietzel, LSU
1959 Ben Schwartzwalder, Syracuse
1960 Murray Warmath, Minnesota
1961 Bear Bryant, Alabama
1962 John McKay, USC
1963 Darrell Royal, Texas
1964 Frank Broyles, Arkansas
 & Ara Parseghian, Notre Dame
1965 Tommy Prothro, UCLA
1966 Tom Cahill, Army
1967 John Pont, Indiana
1968 Joe Paterno, Penn St.
1969 Bo Schembechler, Michigan
1970 Charlie McClendon, LSU
 & Darrell Royal, Texas
1971 Bear Bryant, Alabama
1972 John McKay, USC
1973 Bear Bryant, Alabama
1974 Grant Teaff, Baylor
1975 Frank Kush, Arizona St.
1976 Johnny Majors, Pittsburgh
1977 Don James, Washington
1978 Joe Paterno, Penn St.

Years
1979 Earle Bruce, Ohio St.
1980 Vince Dooley, Georgia
1981 Danny Ford, Clemson
1982 Joe Paterno, Penn St.
1983 Ken Hatfield, Air Force
1984 LaVell Edwards, BYU
1985 Fisher DeBerry, Air Force
1986 Joe Paterno, Penn St.
1987 Dick MacPherson, Syracuse
1988 Don Nehlen, West Virginia
1989 Bill McCartney, Colorado
1990 Bobby Ross, Georgia Tech
1991 Bill Lewis, East Carolina
1992 Gene Stallings, Alabama
1993 Barry Alvarez, Wisconsin
1994 Tom Osborne, Nebraska
1995 Gary Barnett, Northwestern
1996 Bruce Snyder, Arizona St.
1997 Lloyd Carr, Michigan
1998 Phillip Fulmer, Tennessee
1999 Frank Beamer, Va. Tech

FWAA Coach of the Year
First presented in 1957 by the Football Writers Association of America. The FWAA and AFCA awards have both gone to the same coach in the same season 28 times. Those double winners are preceded by (#).
Multiple winners: Woody Hayes and Joe Paterno (3); Lou Holtz, Johnny Majors and John McKay (2).

Year
1957 #Woody Hayes, Ohio St.
1958 #Paul Dietzel, LSU
1959 #Ben Schwartzwalder, Syracuse
1960 #Murray Warmath, Minnesota
1961 Darrell Royal, Texas
1962 #John McKay, USC
1963 #Darrell Royal, Texas
1964 #Ara Parseghian, Notre Dame
1965 Duffy Daugherty, Michigan St.

Year
1966 #Tom Cahill, Army
1967 #John Pont, Indiana
1968 Woody Hayes, Ohio St.
1969 #Bo Schembechler, Michigan
1970 Alex Agase, Northwestern
1971 Bob Devaney, Nebraska
1972 #John McKay, USC
1973 Johnny Majors, Pitt
1974 #Grant Teaff, Baylor

Year
1975 Woody Hayes, Ohio St.
1976 #Johnny Majors, Pitt
1977 Lou Holtz, Arkansas
1978 #Joe Paterno, Penn St.
1979 #Earle Bruce, Ohio St.
1980 #Vince Dooley, Georgia
1981 #Danny Ford, Clemson
1982 #Joe Paterno, Penn St.
1983 Howard Schnellenberger, Miami-FL

Year	Year	Year
1984 #LaVell Edwards, BYU	1990 #Bobby Ross, Georgia Tech	1996 #Bruce Snyder, Arizona St.
1985 #Fisher DeBerry, Air Force	1991 Don James, Washington	1997 Mike Price, Washington St.
1986 #Joe Paterno, Penn St.	1992 #Gene Stallings, Alabama	1998 #Phillip Fulmer, Tennessee
1987 #Dick MacPherson, Syracuse	1993 Terry Bowden, Auburn	1999 #Frank Beamer, Va. Tech
1988 Lou Holtz, Notre Dame	1994 Rich Brooks, Oregon	
1989 #Bill McCartney, Colorado	1995 #Gary Barnett, Northwestern	

All-Time NCAA Division I-AA Leaders
CAREER

Total Offense

Yards Gained

		Years	Yards
1	Steve McNair, Alcorn St.	1991-94	16,823
2	Willie Totten, Miss. Valley	1982-85	13,007
3	Jamie Martin, Weber St.	1989-92	12,287
4	Doug Nussmeier, Idaho	1990-93	12,054
5	Neil Lomax, Portland St.	1978-80	11,647

Yards per Game

		Years	Yards	P/Gm
1	Steve McNair, Alcorn St.	1991-94	16,823	400.5
2	Neil Lomax, Portland St.	1978-80	11,647	352.9
3	Dave Dickenson, Montana	1992-95	11,523	329.2
4	Willie Totten, Miss. Valley	1982-85	13,007	325.2
5	Tom Ehrhardt, Rhode Island	1984-85	6,492	309.1

Passing
(Minimum 500 Completions)

Passing Efficiency

		Years	Rating
1	Shawn Knight, William & Mary	1991-94	170.8
2	Dave Dickenson, Montana	1992-95	166.3
3	Doug Nussmeier, Idaho	1990-93	154.4
4	Mike Simpson, E. Illinois	1996-97	148.9
5	Jay Johnson, Northern Iowa	1989-92	148.9

Yards Gained

		Years	Yards
1	Steve McNair, Alcorn St.	1991-94	14,496
2	Willie Totten, Miss. Valley	1982-85	12,711
3	Jamie Martin, Weber St.	1989-92	12,207
4	Neil Lomax, Portland St.	1978-80	11,550
5	Travis Brown, N. Arizona	1996-99	11,400

Receiving

Catches

		Years	No
1	Jerry Rice, Miss. Valley	1981-84	301
2	Kasey Dunn, Idaho	1988-91	268
3	Sean Morey, Brown	1995-98	251
4	Brian Forster, Rhode Island	1983-85,87	245
5	Mike Furrey, N. Iowa	1997-99	242

Yards Gained

		Years	No	Yards
1	Jerry Rice, Miss. Valley	1981-84	301	4693
2	Kasey Dunn, Idaho	1988-91	268	3847
3	Sean Morey, Brown	1995-98	251	3850
4	Rennie Benn, Lehigh	1982-85	237	3662
5	David Rhodes, Central Fla.	1991-94	213	3618

Rushing

Yards Gained

		Years	Yards
1	Jerry Azumah, N. Hampshire	1995-98	6193
2	Reggie Green, Siena	1994-97	5415
3	Thomas Haskins, VMI	1993-96	5355
4	Frank Hawkins, Nevada	1977-80	5333
5	Rick Sarille, Wagner	1995-99	5290

Yards per Game

		Years	Yards	P/Gm
1	Arnold Mickens, Butler	1994-95	2908	190.7
2	Aaron Stecker, W. Ill.	1997-98	3081	151.1
3	Tim Hall, Robert Morris	1994-95	2908	153.1
4	Jerry Azumah, N. Hampshire	1995-98	6193	151.0
5	Reggie Green, Siena	1994-97	5415	150.4

Miscellaneous

Interceptions

		Years	No
1	Dave Murphy, Holy Cross	1986-89	28
2	Cedric Walker, S.F. Austin	1990-93	25
3	Issiac Holt, Alcorn St.	1981-84	24
	Bill McGovern, Holy Cross	1981-84	24
	Darren Sharper, Wm. & Mary	1993-96	24

Punting Average

		Years	Avg
1	Pumpy Tudors, Tenn.-Chatt.	1989-91	44.4
2	Case de Brujin, Idaho St.	1978-81	43.7
3	Terry Belden, Northern Ariz.	1990-93	43.4
4	Chad Stanley, SF Austin	1996-98	43.3
5	George Cimadevilla, East Tenn. St.	1983-86	43.0

Punt Return Average*

		Years	Avg
1	Willie Ware, Miss. Valley	1982-85	16.4
2	Buck Phillips, Western Ill.	1994-95	16.4
3	Tim Egerton, Delaware St.	1986-89	16.1
4	Mark Orlando, Towson St.	1991-94	15.7
5	John Armstrong, Richmond	1984-85	14.5

Kickoff Return Average*

		Years	Avg
1	Troy Brown, Marshall	1991-92	29.7
2	Charles Swann, Indiana St.	1989-91	29.3
3	Craig Richardson, Eastern Wash.	1983-86	28.5
4	Kenyatta Sparks, Southern-BR	1992-95	28.2
5	Kerry Hayes, Western Caro.	1991-94	28.2
*(Minimum 1.2 returns per game)			

Scoring
NON-KICKERS

Points

		Years	TD	XP	Pts
1	Jerry Azumah, N. Hampshire	1995-98	69	4	418
2	Sherriden May, Idaho	1991-94	61	0	366
3	Charvez Foger, Nevada	1985-88	60	2	362
4	Kenny Gamble, Colgate	1984-87	57	0	342
5	Rick Sarille, Wagner	1995-99	55	4	334

Touchdowns Passing

		Years	No
1	Willie Totten, Miss. Valley	1982-85	139
2	Steve McNair, Alcorn St.	1991-94	119
3	Dave Dickenson, Montana	1992-95	96
4	Chris Boden, Villanova	1996-99	93
5	Ted White, Howard	1995-98	92

Touchdowns Rushing

		Years	No
1	Jerry Azumah, N. Hampshire	1995-98	60
2	Kenny Gamble, Colgate	1984-87	55
3	Rene Ingoglia, UMass	1992-95	54
4	Adrian Peterson, Ga. Southern	1998–	53
5	Charvez Foger, Nevada	1985-88	52

Touchdown Catches

		Years	No
1	Jerry Rice, Miss. Valley	1981-84	50
2	Rennie Benn, Lehigh	1982-85	44
3	Dedric Ward, N. Iowa	1993-96	41
4	Sean Morey, Brown	1995-98	39
5	Roy Banks, Eastern Ill.	1983-86	38
	Mike Jones, Tennessee St.	1979-92	38

All-Time NCAA Division I-AA Leaders (Cont.)
KICKERS

	Points	Years	FG	XP	Pts		Field Goals	Years	No
1	Marty Zendejas, Nevada	1984-87	72	169	385	1	Marty Zendejas, Nevada	1984-87	72
2	Dave Ettinger, Hofstra	1994-97	62	140	326	2	Kirk Roach, Western Carolina	1984-87	71
3	B. Mitchell, Marshall/N. Iowa	1987, 89-91	64	130	322	3	Tony Zendejas, Nevada	1981-83	70
	Scott Shields, Weber St.	1995-98	67	109	322	4	Scott Shields, Weber St.	1995-98	67
5	Thayne Doyle, Idaho	1988-91	49	160	307	5	B. Mitchell, Marshall/N. Iowa	1987,89-91	64

All-Time Winningest Division I-AA Teams
Includes record at a senior college only, minimum of 20 seasons of competition. Bowl and playoff games are included.

Top 25 Winning Percentage

		Yrs	Gm	W	L	T	Pct.	Playoffs W-L-T
1	Yale	127	1151	799	297	55	.718	0-0-0
2	Florida A&M	67	680	474	188	18	.710	5-6-0
3	Tennessee St.	72	672	458	184	30	.704	8-4-1
4	Grambling St.	57	610	420	175	15	.701	9-7-0
5	Princeton	130	1104	737	317	50	.690	0-0-0
6	Harvard	125	1133	729	354	50	.665	1-0-0
7	Jackson St.	54	555	355	187	13	.651	1-11-1
8	Georgia Southern	31	348	219	122	7	.639	31-6-0
9	Southern-BR	78	759	469	265	25	.634	6-1-0
10	Dartmouth	118	1020	624	350	46	.634	0-0-0
11	Fordham	101	1126	686	387	53	.633	2-3-0
12	Eastern Kentucky	76	756	464	271	27	.632	17-17-0
13	Pennsylvania	123	1205	735	429	42	.627	0-1-0
14	Hofstra	59	566	347	208	11	.623	3-10-0
15	Dayton	92	870	525	319	26	.618	16-11-0
16	S. Carolina St.	72	666	398	241	27	.618	6-5-0
17	Appalachian St.	70	734	438	267	29	.616	6-13-0
18	McNeese St.	49	529	318	197	14	.614	11-10-0
19	Youngstown St.	59	601	352	232	17	.600	26-8-0
20	Delaware	108	968	559	366	43	.600	22-13-0
21	Georgetown	88	748	433	284	31	.600	0-2-0
22	Northern Iowa	101	900	513	340	47	.596	8-10-0
23	Western Kentucky	81	767	440	296	31	.594	8-5-0
24	Alcorn St.	76	667	372	256	39	.587	1-4-0
25	Cornell	112	1019	581	404	34	.587	0-0-0

Top 50 Victories

		Wins			Wins			Wins
1	Yale	799	18	Drake	489	35	VMI	428
2	Princeton	737	19	Villanova	483		Howard	428
3	Pennsylvania	735	20	Florida A&M	474	37	Maine	422
4	Harvard	729	21	Furman	473	38	Grambling St.	420
5	Fordham	686	22	William & Mary	469		Western Ill.	420
6	Dartmouth	624		Southern-BR	469	40	SW Texas St.	418
7	Lafayette	588	24	Massachusetts	468		Richmond	418
8	Cornell	581	26	E. Kentucky	464	42	Citadel	414
9	Delaware	559	27	Tennessee St.	458	43	Montana	411
10	Lehigh	553	28	Hampton	447	44	Connecticut	410
11	Holy Cross	537	29	Tenn-Chat	443	45	Idaho St.	402
12	Dayton	525	30	W. Kentucky	440	46	Murray St.	399
13	Bucknell	517	31	Appalachian St.	438	47	S. Carolina St.	398
14	Brown	514	32	Northwestern St.	435	48	Eastern Ill.	396
	Colgate	514		New Hampshire	435	49	E. Washington	392
16	N. Iowa	513	34	Georgetown	433	50	SW Missouri St.	391
17	Butler	500						

Top 10 Playoff Game Appearances
Ranked by NCAA playoff games played from 1978-1999. CH refers to championships won.

		Years	Games	Record	CH			Years	Games	Record	CH
1	Georgia Southern	11	36	30-6	5	8	Northern Iowa	9	18	9-9	0
2	Eastern Ky.	17	31	16-15	2	9	Idaho*	11	17	6-11	0
3	Marshall*	8	29	23-6	2	10	Nevada*	7	16	9-7	0
4	Youngstown St.	9	28	23-5	4						
5	Montana	10	20	11-9	1						
6	Delaware	10	19	9-10	0						
	Furman	9	19	11-8	1						

*Marshall (1997), Idaho (1996) and Nevada (1992) have all moved up to I-A.

Active Division I-AA Coaches

Minimum of 5 years as a Division I-A and/or Division I-AA through 1999 season.

Top 10 Winning Percentage

		Yrs	W	L	T	Pct
1	Mike Kelly, Dayton	19	177	36	1	.829
2	Pete Richardson, Southern	12	107	32	1	.768
3	Al Bagnoli, Pennsylvania	18	138	46	0	.750
	Larry Blakeney, Troy St.	9	82	27	1	.750
5	Greg Gattuso, Duquesne	7	57	21	0	.731
6	Joe Gardi, Hofstra	10	81	29	3	.730
7	Roy Kidd, Eastern Ky.	36	293	112	8	.719
8	Tubby Raymond, Delaware	34	284	111	3	.717
9	Walt Hameline, Wagner	19	141	56	2	.714
10	Billy Joe, Florida A&M	26	205	82	4	.711

Top 10 Victories

		Yrs	W	L	T	Pct
1	Roy Kidd, Eastern Ky.	36	293	112	8	.719
2	Tubby Raymond, Delaware	34	284	111	3	.717
3	Billy Joe, Florida A&M	26	205	82	4	.711
4	Ron Randleman, Sam Houston St.	31	184	141	6	.565
5	Mike Kelly, Dayton	19	177	36	1	.829
6	Bill Hayes, N. Carolina A&T	24	175	90	2	.659
7	Willie Jeffries, S. Carolina St.	27	170	119	6	.586
8	Walt Hameline, Wagner	19	141	56	2	.714
9	Bob Ricca, St. John's	22	140	85	1	.622
10	Al Bagnoli, Pennsylvania	18	138	46	0	.750

Note: Eddie Robinson of Grambling St. (1941-42, 1945-97) retired following the 1997 season as the all-time NCAA leader in coaching wins with a 408-165-15 record and a .707 winning pct. over 55 seasons.

Division I-AA Coach of the Year

First presented in 1983 by the American Football Coaches Association.

Multiple winners: Mark Duffner and Erk Russell (2).

Year		Year		Year	
1983	Rey Dempsey, Southern Ill.	1989	Erk Russell, Ga. Southern	1995	Don Read, Montana
1984	Dave Arnold, Montana St.	1990	Tim Stowers, Ga. Southern	1996	Ray Tellier, Columbia
1985	Dick Sheridan, Furman	1991	Mark Duffner, Holy Cross	1997	Andy Talley, Villanova
1986	Erk Russell, Ga. Southern	1992	Charlie Taafe, Citadel	1998	Mark Whipple, Massachusetts
1987	Mark Duffner, Holy Cross	1993	Dan Allen, Boston Univ.	1999	Paul Johnson, Ga. Southern
1988	Jimmy Satterfield, Furman	1994	Jim Tressel, Youngstown St.		

NCAA Playoffs

Division I-AA

Established in 1978 as a four-team playoff. Tournament field increased to eight teams in 1981, 12 teams in 1982 and 16 teams in 1986. Automatic berths have been awarded to champions of the Big Sky, Gateway, Ohio Valley, Southern, Southland and Atlantic 10 (formerly Yankee) conferences since 1992.

Multiple winners: Georgia Southern (5); Youngstown St. (4); Eastern Kentucky and Marshall (2).

Year	Winner	Score	Loser	Year	Winner	Score	Loser
1978	Florida A&M	35-28	Massachusetts	1989	Georgia Southern	37-34	S.F. Austin St.
1979	Eastern Kentucky	30-7	Lehigh, PA	1990	Georgia Southern	36-13	Nevada-Reno
1980	Boise St., ID	31-29	Eastern Kentucky	1991	Youngstown St., OH	25-17	Marshall
1981	Idaho St.	34-23	Eastern Kentucky	1992	Marshall	31-28	Youngstown St.
1982	Eastern Kentucky	17-14	Delaware	1993	Youngstown St.	17-5	Marshall
1983	Southern Illinois	43-7	Western Carolina	1994	Youngstown St.	28-14	Boise St.
1984	Montana St.	19-6	Louisiana Tech	1995	Montana	22-20	Marshall
1985	Georgia Southern	44-42	Furman, SC	1996	Marshall	49-29	Montana
1986	Georgia Southern	48-21	Arkansas St.	1997	Youngstown St.	10-9	McNeese St.
1987	NE Louisiana	43-42	Marshall, WV	1998	Massachusetts	55-43	Georgia Southern
1988	Furman, SC	17-12	Georgia Southern	1999	Georgia Southern	59-24	Youngstown St.

Division II

Established in 1973 as an eight-team playoff. Tournament field increased to 16 teams in 1988. From 1964-72, eight qualifying NCAA College Division member institutions competed in four regional bowl games, but there was no tournament and no national championship until 1973.

Multiple winners: North Dakota St. (5); North Alabama (3); Northern Colorado, Northwest Missouri St., Southwest Texas St. and Troy St. (2).

Year	Winner	Score	Loser	Year	Winner	Score	Loser
1973	Louisiana Tech	34-0	Western Kentucky	1987	Troy St., AL	31-17	Portland St., OR
1974	Central Michigan	54-14	Delaware	1988	North Dakota St.	35-21	Portland St., OR
1975	Northern Michigan	16-14	Western Kentucky	1989	Mississippi Col.	3-0	Jacksonville St., AL
1976	Montana St.	24-13	Akron, OH				
1977	Lehigh, PA	33-0	Jacksonville St., AL	1990	North Dakota St.	51-11	Indiana, PA
1978	Eastern Illinois	10-9	Delaware	1991	Pittsburg St., KS	23-6	Jacksonville St., AL
1979	Delaware	38-21	Youngstown St., OH	1992	Jacksonville St., AL	17-13	Pittsburg St., KS
				1993	North Alabama	41-34	Indiana, PA
1980	Cal Poly-SLO	21-13	Eastern Illinois	1994	North Alabama	16-10	Tex. A&M (Kings.)
1981	SW Texas St.	42-13	North Dakota St.	1995	North Alabama	27-7	Pittsburg St., KS
1982	SW Texas St.	34-9	UC-Davis	1996	Northern Colorado	23-14	Carson-Newman
1983	North Dakota St.	41-21	Central St., OH	1997	Northern Colorado	51-0	New Haven
1984	Troy St., AL	18-17	North Dakota St.	1998	NW Missouri St.	24-6	Carson-Newman
1985	North Dakota St.	35-7	North Alabama	1999	NW Missouri St.	58-52*	Carson-Newman
1986	North Dakota St.	27-7	South Dakota		*Four overtimes		

Division III

Established in 1973 as a four-team playoff. Tournament field increased to eight teams in 1975 and 16 teams in 1985. From 1969-72, four qualifying NCAA College Division member institutions competed in two regional bowl games, but there was no tournament and no national championship until 1973.

Multiple winners: Augustana and Mt. Union (4); Ithaca (3); Dayton, Widener, WI-La Crosse and Wittenberg (2).

Year	Winner	Score	Loser	Year	Winner	Score	Loser
1973	Wittenberg, OH	41-0	Juniata, PA	1987	Wagner, NY	19-3	Dayton
1974	Central, IA	10-8	Ithaca, NY	1988	Ithaca	39-24	Central, IA
1975	Wittenberg	28-0	Ithaca	1989	Dayton	17-7	Union
1976	St. John's, MN	31-28	Towson St., MD	1990	Allegheny, PA	21-14*	Lycoming, PA
1977	Widener, PA.	39-36	Wabash, IN	1991	Ithaca	34-20	Dayton
1978	Baldwin-Wallace	24-10	Wittenberg	1992	WI-La Crosse	16-12	Wash. & Jeff., PA
1979	Ithaca, NY	14-10	Wittenberg	1993	Mt. Union, OH	34-24	Rowan, NJ
1980	Dayton, OH	63-0	Ithaca	1994	Albion, MI.	38-15	Wash. & Jeff.
1981	Widener, PA.	17-10	Dayton, OH	1995	WI-La Crosse.	36-7	Rowan
1982	West Georgia.	14-0	Augustana, IL	1996	Mt. Union	56-24	Rowan
1983	Augustana	21-17	Union, NY	1997	Mt. Union	61-12	Lycoming
1984	Augustana	21-12	Central, IA	1998	Mt. Union	44-24	Rowan
1985	Augustana.	20-7	Ithaca	1999	Pacific Lutheran	42-13	Rowan
1986	Augustana.	31-3	Salisbury St., MD		*Overtime		

NAIA Playoffs

Division I

Established in 1956 as two-team playoff. Tournament field increased to four teams in 1958, eight teams in 1978 and 16 teams in 1987 before cutting back to eight teams in 1989. NAIA went back to a single division 16-team playoff in 1997. The title game has ended in a tie four times (1956, '64, '84 and '85).

Multiple winners: Texas A&I (7); Carson-Newman (5); Central Arkansas and Central St., OH (3); Abilene Christian, Central St-OK, Elon, Pittsburg St. and St. John's-MN (2).

Year	Winner	Score	Loser	Year	Winner	Score	Loser
1956	Montana St.	0-0	St. Joseph's, IN	1978	Angelo St., TX	34-14	Elon, NC
1957	Pittsburg St., KS	27-26	Hillsdale, MI	1979	Texas A&I	20-14	Central St., OK
1958	NE Oklahoma	19-13	Northern Arizona	1980	Elon, NC.	17-10	NE Oklahoma
1959	Texas A&I	20-7	Lenoir-Rhyne, NC	1981	Elon, NC	3-0	Pittsburg St., KS
1960	Lenoir-Rhyne, NC	15-14	Humboldt St., CA	1982	Central St., OK	14-11	Mesa, CO
1961	Pittsburg St., KS	12-7	Linfield, OR	1983	Car-Newman, TN	36-28	Mesa, CO
1962	Central St., OK	28-13	Lenoir-Rhyne, NC	1984	Car-Newman, TN	19-19	Central Arkansas
1963	St. John's, MN	33-27	Prairie View, TX	1985	Hillsdale, MI.	10-10	Central Arkansas
1964	Concordia, MN	7-7	Sam Houston, TX	1986	Car-Newman, TN	17-0	Cameron, OK
1965	St. John's, MN	33-0	Linfield, OR	1987	Cameron, OK.	30-2	Car-Newman, TN
1966	Waynesburg, PA	42-21	WI-Whitewater	1988	Car-Newman, TN	56-21	Adams St., CO
1967	Fairmont St., WV	28-21	Eastern Wash.	1989	Car-Newman, TN	34-20	Emporia St., KS
1968	Troy St., AL	43-35	Texas A&I	1990	Central St., OH	38-16	Mesa, CO
1969	Texas A&I	32-7	Concordia, MN	1991	Central Arkansas	19-16	Central St., OH
1970	Texas A&I	48-7	Wofford, SC	1992	Central St., OH	19-16	Gardner-Webb, NC
1971	Livingston, AL	14-12	Arkansas Tech	1993	E. Central, OK	49-35	Glenville St., WV
1972	East Texas St.	21-18	Car-Newman, TN	1994	N'eastern St., OK	13-12	Ark-Pine Bluff
1973	Abilene Christian	42-14	Elon, NC	1995	Central St., OH	37-7	N'eastern St., OK
1974	Texas A&I	34-23	Henderson St., AR	1996	SW Oklahoma St.	33-31	Montana Tech
1975	Texas A&I	37-0	Salem, WV	1997	Findlay, OH	14-7	Willamette, ORE
1976	Texas A&I	26-0	Central Arkansas	1998	Azusa Pacific, CA	17-14	Olivet Nazarene, IL
1977	Abilene Christian	24-7	SW Oklahoma	1999	NW Oklahoma St.	34-26	Georgetown, KY

Division II

Established in 1970 as four-team playoff. Tournament field increased to eight teams in 1978 and 16 teams in 1987. NAIA went back to a single division playoff in 1997. The title game has ended in a tie twice (1981 and '87).

Multiple winners: Westminster (6); Findlay, Linfield and Pacific Lutheran (3); Concordia-MN, Northwestern-IA and Texas Lutheran (2).

Year	Winner	Score	Loser	Year	Winner	Score	Loser
1970	Westminster, PA	21-16	Anderson, IN	1984	Linfield, OR	33-22	Northwestern, IA
1971	Calif. Lutheran	20-14	Westminster, PA	1985	WI-La Crosse	24-7	Pacific Lutheran
1972	Missouri Southern	21-14	Northwestern, IA	1986	Linfield, OR	17-0	Baker, KS
1973	Northwestern, IA	10-3	Glenville St., WV	1987	Pacific Lutheran	16-16	WI-Stevens Pt.*
1974	Texas Lutheran	42-0	Missouri Valley	1988	Westminster, PA	21-14	WI-La Crosse
1975	Texas Lutheran	34-8	Calif. Lutheran	1989	Westminster, PA	51-30	WI-La Crosse
1976	Westminster, PA	20-13	Redlands, CA	1990	Peru St., NE.	17-7	Westminster, PA
1977	Westminster, PA	17-9	Calif. Lutheran	1991	Georgetown-KY	28-20	Pacific Lutheran
1978	Concordia, MN	7-0	Findlay, OH	1992	Findlay, OH	26-13	Linfield, OR
1979	Findlay, OH	51-6	Northwestern, IA	1993	Pacific Lutheran	50-20	Westminster, PA
1980	Pacific Lutheran	38-10	Wilmington, OH	1994	Westminster, PA	27-7	Pacific Lutheran
1981	Austin College, TX	24-24	Concordia, MN	1995	Findlay, OH	21-21	Central Wash.
1982	Linfield, OR	33-15	Wm. Jewell, MO	1996	Sioux Falls, S.D.	47-25	W. Washington
1983	Northwestern, IA	25-21	Pacific Lutheran	1997	discontinued		

*Wisconsin-Stevens Point forfeited its entire 1987 schedule due to its use of an ineligible player.

Pro Football

*Former Arena League quarterback **Kurt Warner** led the Rams to their first Super Bowl win in 2000.*

AP/Wide World Photos

Out of Nowhere

Rams quarterback Kurt Warner goes from supermarket stock boy to Super Bowl MVP.

by

Chris Berman

Born in 1920, the National Football League proved to be pretty spry for an 80-year old in 1999. And in a story even Hollywood probably would have rejected, an old friend and a new face were the keys to an unexpected championship.

Of course, Hollywood had already rejected the Rams four years earlier as the well-traveled franchise, whose roots began in Cleveland, set up shop in St. Louis in 1995 and wasted little time picking up where it left off in Southern California. Entering the season, the Rams were an NFL-worst 45-99 in the '90s and had suffered through nine straight losing campaigns. Dick Vermeil, the team's fourth head coach of the decade, had won just nine games in his two years with the club. And despite the offseason additions of Pro Bowl runner Marshall Faulk, rookie wideout Torry Holt and promising passer Trent Green, it figured to be another

Chris Berman is the host of ESPN's *NFL Prime Time.*

long year in the Gateway City, especially after Green went down in mid-August with a season-ending knee injury.

"We will rally around Kurt Warner," said Vermeil, "and we'll play good football."

In what may be the biggest understatement in recent NFL history, the Rams played amazing football behind Warner, a former Arena Football star who would add his name to the record books by becoming just the second player in NFL annals to throw at least 40 touchdown passes in one season (some guy named Marino did it twice). Along the way, Warner captured league MVP honors.

Warner led the Rams to a 13-3 regular season and into Super Bowl XXXIV, where he passed for a game-record 414 yards in St. Louis' remarkable 23-16 victory over the equally incredible Tennessee Titans at the Georgia Dome. Jeff Fisher's team took their own amazing path to Atlanta. After three straight 8-8 seasons in three different home stadiums, the Houston/Tennessee/Oilers/Titans

AP/Wide World Photos

Missed it by *that* much. Tennessee Titans receiver **Kevin Dyson** lunges but is brought down by St. Louis' Mike Jones just a yard shy of the end zone in the final play of Super Bowl XXXIV.

became the first team to win 13 games and settle for a wild card invitation. And after edging the Bills, 22-16, in the AFC Wild Card Game thanks to the "Music City Miracle" (TE Frank Wycheck's controversial lateral and WR Kevin Dyson's kickoff return for a touchdown on the final play of the game), Fisher's club surprised the Colts and Jaguars on the road to advance to their first Super Bowl. Trailing 16-0 in the second half, the resilient Titans eventually forged a tie, then watched Warner and WR Isaac Bruce connect on a 73-yard score with 1:54 to play to put the Rams ahead again. Tennessee drove to the St. Louis 10-yard line, but QB Steve McNair's completion to Dyson came up less than a yard short of the end zone as time expired thanks to Rams' LB Mike Jones' game-saving tackle.

But as exciting as '99 was for its new faces, it will also be remembered for who wasn't around. Before the season, future Hall of Famers John Elway, Barry Sanders and Reggie White had retired, and by mid-October perennial stars such as Steve Young, Vinny Testaverde, Jamal Anderson, Michael Irvin and Terrell Davis were shelved for the year with injuries. Hence both Super Bowl teams from the previous season, Denver (6-10) and Atlanta (5-11), combined to win only 11 games, while playoff mainstays such as the 49ers and Packers were home for the holidays.

Still, it was a year of transition as a Pro Bowl record 41 players earned their first invitation to Honolulu, while teams such as the Seahawks (1988), Rams ('89), Redskins ('92) and Titans ('93) made their first postseason appearance in a long time. St. Louis' amazing turnaround was mirrored by the Indianapolis Colts, who behind

Andy Lyons/Allsport

Titans tight end **Frank Wycheck** (89) prepares to make a lateral pass to **Kevin Dyson** in the final play of their Wild Card game against the Bills. Dyson would race 75 yards down the left sideline to give Tennessee a 22-16 victory in the most controversial play of the year.

their young trio of QB Peyton Manning, WR Marvin Harrison and Offensive Rookie of the Year and NFL rushing champion RB Edgerrin James won 10 more games (13) than they did in 1998 and won their first AFC East title since 1987. And in a league that stressed offense, Tony Dungy's Tampa Bay Buccaneers proved a great defense can still take you far, leading those explosive Rams by the unlikely score of 6-5 late in the final quarter of the NFC Championship Game before falling, 11-6.

Say it once again. The Rams won the Super Bowl. Is it any wonder that all 31 teams enter the next decade with legitimate championship aspirations? ∎

John Clayton's Top Ten Highlights of the 1999 NFL season

10. **The Redskins-Cowboys rivalry** continues to escalate. In the season opener at FedEx Field, the Cowboys rally from a 35-14 deficit to win in overtime, 41-35. The Redskins lose in Dallas, 38-20, but finally pass the Cowboys as the NFC East's best team with a 10-6 record for first-year owner Daniel Snyder.

9. **The Year of The Freak.** Titans defensive end Jevon Kearse, considered by some to be too skinny and too raw to be a defensive end, registers 10½ sacks in the final eight games to lead the Titans to the Super Bowl. The Freak was

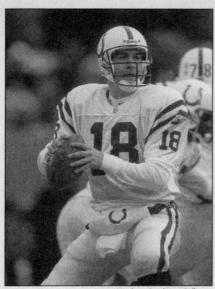

Matthew Stockman/Allsport

Field general **Peyton Manning** connected on 26 touchdown passes and threw for over 4,000 yards in 1999 as Indianapolis went from league laughing-stock to AFC East champion.

6. **An easy schedule has the Jaguars** ticketed to go to the AFC title game with homefield advantage, but they just can't solve the Tennessee Titans. Coughlin and Co. won't soon forget how the Titans destroyed them 33-14 in ALLTEL Stadium and taunted and celebrated on the Jags' home turf while accepting the AFC trophy.

5. **Peyton Manning**, in only his second year in the NFL, shows that hard work in the offseason really works by leading the Colts' miraculous turnaround from 3-13 to 13-3, the greatest single-season improvement in NFL history. Manning completes 115 passes to Marvin Harrison despite constant double-coverage during the second half of the season. It doesn't hurt having rookie Edgerrin James rush for 1,553 yards.

virtually unstoppable when going against left tackles.

8. **Rookie Shaun King** has to take over as the Buccaneers quarterback for a key Monday night game in Tampa in Week 13. The St. Petersburg, Fla. native throws two second-half touchdown passes to beat the rival Vikings, 24-17, and goes on to finish the season with a 4-1 record and an eventual trip the NFC title game.

7. **Carolina's Steve Beuerlein** always wondered what would happen if he had a full season at quarterback. Carrying over from a hot finish in 1998, Beuerlein earns a trip to the Pro Bowl with a 36-touchdown season in which he has 17 touchdown passes in his final five games.

4. **Bills coach Wade Phillips** benches popular QB Doug Flutie for their AFC Wild Card game against the Titans in favor of strong-armed Rob Johnson, who threw only 34 passes all season. Johnson starts slow but rallies the Bills from a 12-0 halftime deficit to a 16-15 lead with 16 seconds left, until...

3. In a play almost the equal of Franco Harris' "Immaculate Reception," Titans TE Frank Wycheck makes the **"Music City Miracle"** happen by turning a Bills squib kick into a kickoff touchdown pass to teammate Kevin Dyson. After the Bills take a 16-15 lead with 16 seconds left, Wycheck rifles the infamous "Home Run Throwback" across

the field to Dyson, who takes the lateral for a 75-yard kickoff return.

2. In the last play of perhaps the most exciting Super Bowl in history, **Rams LB Mike Jones stops** Titans WR Kevin Dyson on the 1-yard line to save a 23-16 victory. Jones executes perfect tackling technique in a perfect finish to the 1999 season.

1. Does it get any better than former Arena League QB **Kurt Warner**? After starter Trent Green goes down for the season on Aug. 28, Warner throws for 41 touchdowns, wins the league and the Super Bowl MVP awards and proves that fairy tales can come true in the NFL. Warner is the league's ultimate Cinderella story. ∎

SPLIT PERSONALITY

Tennessee truly brought out the worst in Jacksonville in 1999-00. Including the playoffs, the Jaguars finished the season with a 15-3 record overall. All three losses were to the Titans (two in the regular season and one in the playoffs).

	vs Tenn.	vs others
W-L	0-3	15-0
PPG	15.7	28.3
Opp. PPG	31.3	10.9
Total Giveaways	13	13
Brunell Interceptions	6	5

TURNABOUT IS FAIR PLAY

The 13-3 Indianapolis Colts won ten more games in 1999 than they had the previous year for the largest single-season improvement in NFL history. The Super Bowl champion Rams were right behind them with a nine-game swing.

Most Improved Team	Years	Win Diff.
Indianapolis Colts	1998-99	**+10**
St. Louis Rams	1998-99	**+9**
Oakland Raiders	1962-63	**+9**
New York Giants	1928-29	**+9**
New York Jets	1996-97	**+8**
Indianapolis Colts	1991-92	**+8**
Cincinnati Bengals	1987-88	**+8**
New England Patriots	1975-76	**+8**
Baltimore Colts	1974-75	**+8**

IN (TWO) GRAND STYLE

Rams running back Marshall Faulk joined former 49er back Roger Craig as the only two players with 1,000 yards rushing and receiving in one year. He also set the NFL mark for yards from scrimmage in a single season (top five listed below).

	Rush	Rec	Yards
Marshall Faulk, St.L, '99	1381	1048	**2429**
Barry Sanders, Det., '97	2053	305	**2358**
Marcus Allen, Raid., '85	1759	555	**2314**
Eric Dickerson, Rams, '84	2105	139	**2244**
O.J. Simpson, Buf., '75	1817	426	**2243**

RUSHING BREAKDOWN

The top four rushers in 1998 gained a total of 6,915 yards between them — and then thanks to three injuries and a retirement combined for a mere 270 in 1999.

	1998	1999
Terrell Davis	2008	211
Jamal Anderson	1846	59
Garrison Hearst	1570	0
Barry Sanders	1491	0
TOTAL	6915	270

∎

PRO FOOTBALL
1999-2000 Season in Review

information please
SPORTS ALMANAC

Final NFL Standings

Division champions (*) and Wild Card playoff qualifiers (†) are noted; division champions with two best records received first round byes. Number of seasons listed after each head coach refers to latest tenure with club through 1999 season.

American Football Conference

Eastern Division

	W	L	T	PF	PA	vs Div	vs AFC
*Indianapolis	13	3	0	423	333	5-3	9-3
†Buffalo	11	5	0	320	229	6-2	8-4
†Miami	9	7	0	326	336	3-5	7-5
NY Jets	8	8	0	308	309	4-4	6-6
New England	8	8	0	299	284	2-6	5-7

1999 Head Coaches: Ind—Jim Mora (2nd season); **Buf**—Wade Phillips (2nd); **Mia**—Jimmy Johnson (4th); **NY**—Bill Parcells (3rd); **NE**—Pete Carroll (3rd).
1998 Standings: 1. NY Jets (12-4); 2. Miami (10-6); 3. Buffalo (10-6); 4. New England (9-7); 5. Indianapolis (3-13).

Central Division

	W	L	T	PF	PA	vs Div	vs AFC
*Jacksonville	14	2	0	396	217	8-2	10-2
†Tennessee	13	3	0	392	324	9-1	10-2
Baltimore	8	8	0	324	277	6-4	6-7
Pittsburgh	6	10	0	317	320	3-7	3-10
Cincinnati	4	12	0	283	460	3-7	3-10
Cleveland	2	14	0	217	437	1-9	1-12

1999 Head Coaches: Jax—Tom Coughlin (5th season); **Ten**—Jeff Fisher (6th); **Bal**—Brian Billick (1st); **Pit**—Bill Cowher (8th); **Cin**—Bruce Coslet (4th); **Cle**—Chris Palmer (1st).
1998 Standings: 1. Jacksonville (11-5); 2. Tennessee (8-8); 3. Pittsburgh (7-9); 4. Baltimore (6-10); 5. Cincinnati (3-13). **Note:** Cleveland rejoined the division in 1999.

Western Division

	W	L	T	PF	PA	vs Div	vs AFC
*Seattle	9	7	0	338	298	4-4	7-5
Kansas City	9	7	0	390	322	4-4	7-5
San Diego	8	8	0	269	316	5-3	7-5
Oakland	8	8	0	390	329	3-5	5-7
Denver	6	10	0	314	318	4-4	4-8

1999 Head Coaches: Sea—Mike Holmgren (1st season); **KC**—Gunther Cunningham (1st); **SD**—Mike Riley (1st); **Oak**—Jon Gruden (2nd); **Den**—Mike Shanahan (5th).
1998 Standings: 1. Denver (14-2); 2. Oakland (8-8); 3. Seattle (8-8); 4. Kansas City (7-9); 5. San Diego (5-11).

National Football Conference

Eastern Division

	W	L	T	PF	PA	vs Div	vs NFC
*Washington	10	6	0	443	377	5-3	8-4
†Dallas	8	8	0	352	276	5-3	7-5
NY Giants	7	9	0	299	358	3-5	5-7
Arizona	6	10	0	245	382	5-3	6-6
Philadelphia	5	11	0	272	357	2-6	4-8

1999 Head Coaches: Wash—Norv Turner (6th season); **Dal**—Chan Gailey (2nd); **NY**—Jim Fassel (3rd); **Ariz**—Vince Tobin (4th); **Phi**—Andy Reid (1st).
1998 Standings: 1. Dallas (10-6); 2. Arizona (9-7); 3. NY Giants (8-8); Washington (6-10); Philadelphia (3-13).

Central Division

	W	L	T	PF	PA	vs Div	vs NFC
*Tampa Bay	11	5	0	270	235	5-3	8-4
†Minnesota	10	6	0	399	335	4-4	8-4
†Detroit	8	8	0	322	323	4-4	7-5
Green Bay	8	8	0	357	341	4-4	6-6
Chicago	6	10	0	272	341	3-5	4-8

1999 Head Coaches: TB—Tony Dungy (4th season); **Min**—Dennis Green (8th); **Det**—Bobby Ross (3rd); **GB**—Ray Rhodes (1st); **Chi**—Dick Jauron (1st).
1998 Standings: 1. Minnesota (15-1); 2. Green Bay (11-5); 3. Tampa Bay (8-8); 4. Detroit (5-11); 5. Chicago (4-12).

Western Division

	W	L	T	PF	PA	vs Div	vs NFC
*St. Louis	13	3	0	526	242	8-0	10-2
Carolina	8	8	0	421	381	4-4	6-6
Atlanta	5	11	0	285	380	4-4	5-7
San Francisco	4	12	0	295	453	2-6	3-9
New Orleans	3	13	0	260	434	2-6	3-9

1999 Head Coaches: St.L—Dick Vermeil (3rd season); **Car**—George Seifert (1st); **Atl**—Dan Reeves (3rd); **SF**—Steve Mariucci (3rd); **NO**—Mike Ditka (3rd).
1998 Standings: 1. Atlanta (14-2); 2. San Francisco (12-4); 3. New Orleans (6-10); 4. Carolina (4-12); 5. St. Louis (4-12).

Playoff Tiebreakers

Division Championship—AFC: Seattle (9-7) qualified over Kansas City (9-7) in the West by winning both regular season head-to-head matchups.
Wild Card berths—AFC: Miami (9-7) qualified over Kansas City (9-7) due to a better winning percentage vs. common opponents. NFC: Carolina, Dallas, Detroit and Green Bay all finished with 8-8 records. Green Bay was eliminated because Detroit came from the same division and had a better conference record. Carolina was eliminated because both Dallas and Detroit had better conference records.

NFL Regular Season Individual Leaders
(* indicates rookies)
Passing Efficiency
(Minimum of 224 attempts)

AFC	Att	Cmp	Cmp Pct	Yds	Yds/ Att	TD	Long	Int	Sack/Lost	Rating Points
Peyton Manning, Ind............533		331	62.1	4135	7.76	26	80-td	15	14/116	90.7
Rich Gannon, Oak..............515		304	59.0	3840	7.46	24	50	14	49/241	86.5
Ray Lucas, NYJ.................272		161	59.2	1678	6.17	14	56-td	6	11/69	85.1
Mark Brunell, Jax...............441		259	58.7	3060	6.94	14	62	9	29/174	82.0
Elvis Grbac, KC................499		294	58.9	3389	6.79	22	86-td	15	26/170	81.7
Tony Banks, Bal................320		169	52.8	2136	6.68	17	76-td	8	33/190	81.2
Steve McNair, Ten...............331		187	56.5	2179	6.58	12	65-td	8	16/74	78.6
Jon Kitna, Sea..................495		270	54.5	3346	6.76	23	51	16	32/198	77.7
Jeff Blake, Cin.................389		215	55.3	2670	6.86	16	76-td	12	30/168	77.6
Mike Tomczak, Pit..............258		139	53.9	1625	6.30	12	49	8	15/104	75.8
Brian Griese, Den...............452		261	57.7	3032	6.71	14	88	14	27/176	75.6
Drew Bledsoe, NE...............539		305	56.6	3985	7.39	19	68-td	21	55/342	75.6
Doug Flutie, Buf................478		264	55.2	3171	6.63	19	54-td	16	26/176	75.1
Tim Couch*, Cle................399		223	55.9	2447	6.13	15	78-td	13	56/359	73.2
Jim Harbaugh, SD...............434		249	57.4	2761	6.36	10	80-td	10	37/208	70.6

NFC	Att	Cmp	Cmp Pct	Yds	Yds/ Att	TD	Long	Int	Sack/Lost	Rating Points
Kurt Warner, St.L...............499		325	65.1	4353	8.72	41	75-td	13	29/201	109.2
Steve Beuerlein, Car............571		343	60.1	4436	7.77	36	88-td	15	50/284	94.6
Jeff George, Min...............329		191	58.1	2816	8.56	23	80-td	12	28/228	94.2
Brad Johnson, Wash.............519		316	60.9	4005	7.72	24	65-td	13	29/177	90.0
Charlie Batch, Det..............270		151	55.9	1957	7.25	13	74-td	7	36/186	84.1
Gus Frerotte, Det...............288		175	60.8	2117	7.35	9	77-td	7	28/202	83.6
Chris Chandler, Atl..............307		174	56.7	2339	7.61	16	60-td	11	32/230	83.5
Troy Aikman, Dal...............442		263	59.5	2964	6.71	17	90-td	12	19/130	81.1
Shane Matthews, Chi............275		167	60.7	1645	5.98	10	56	6	13/79	80.6
Jeff Garcia, SF................375		225	60.0	2544	6.78	11	62	11	14/94	77.9
Trent Dilfer, TB...............244		146	59.8	1619	6.64	11	62-td	11	26/189	75.8
Brett Favre, GB................595		341	57.3	4091	6.88	22	74-td	23	35/223	74.7
Kent Graham, NYG..............271		160	59.0	1697	6.26	9	56	9	26/184	74.6
Kerry Collins, NYG..............332		191	57.5	2316	6.98	8	80-td	11	16/112	73.3
Cade McNown*, Chi.............235		127	54.0	1465	6.23	8	80-td	10	18/94	66.7

Receptions

AFC	No	Yds	Avg	Long	TD
Jimmy Smith, Jax..........116		1636	14.1	62	6
Marvin Harrison, Ind. 115		1663	14.5	57-td	12
Tim Brown, Oak...........90		1344	14.9	47	6
Keyshawn Johnson, NYJ 89		1170	13.1	65	8
Rod Smith, Den. 79		1020	12.9	71	4
Keenan McCardell, Jax 78		891	11.4	49	5
Tony Gonzalez, KC 76		849	11.2	73-td	11
Ed McCaffrey, Den. 71		1018	14.3	78-td	7
Terry Glenn, NE 69		1147	16.6	67	4
Frank Wycheck, Ten. 69		641	9.3	35	2
Qadry Ismail, Bal. 68		1105	16.3	76-td	6
Darnay Scott, Cin..........68		1022	15.0	76-td	7
Tony Martin, Mia...........67		1037	15.5	69-td	5
Kevin Johnson*, Cle........66		986	14.9	64-td	8

NFC	No	Yds	Avg	Long	TD
Mushin Muhammad, Car......96		1253	13.1	60-td	8
Cris Carter, Min............90		1241	13.8	68	13
Bobby Engram, Chi.........88		947	10.8	56	4
Marshall Faulk, St.L........87		1048	12.0	57-td	5
Marcus Robinson, Chi.......84		1400	16.7	80-td	9
Germane Crowell, Det. 81		1338	16.5	77-td	7
Terance Mathis, Atl..........81		1016	12.5	52	6
Raghib Ismail, Dal..........80		1097	13.7	76-td	6
Johnnie Morton, Det. 80		1129	14.1	48	5
Randy Moss, Min...........80		1413	17.7	67-td	11
Frank Sanders, Ari..........79		954	12.1	63	1
Amani Toomer, NYG 79		1183	15.0	80-td	6
Isaac Bruce, St.L 77		1165	15.1	60	12
Antonio Freeman, GB........74		1074	14.5	51	6
Bill Schroeder, GB..........74		1051	14.2	51	5

Rushing

AFC	Att	Yards	Avg	Long	TD
Edgerrin James*, Ind. 369		1553	4.2	72	13
Curtis Martin, NYJ 367		1464	4.0	50	5
Eddie George, Ten. 320		1304	4.1	40	9
Ricky Watters, Sea. 325		1210	3.7	45	5
Corey Dillon, Cin..........263		1200	4.6	50	5
Olandis Gary*, Den........276		1159	4.2	71	7
Jerome Bettis, Pit...........299		1091	3.6	35	7
Tyrone Wheatley, Oak......242		936	3.9	30-td	8
James Stewart, Jax..........249		931	3.7	44-td	13
Terry Allen, NE 254		896	3.5	39	8
Errict Rhett, Bal. 236		852	3.6	52-td	5
Fred Taylor, Jax............159		732	4.6	52	6
Napoleon Kaufman, Oak. .138		714	5.2	75-td	2
Jonathan Linton, Buf. 205		695	3.4	18	5

NFC	Att	Yards	Avg	Long	TD
Stephen Davis, Wash......290		1405	4.8	76-td	17
Emmitt Smith, Dal..........329		1397	4.2	63-td	11
Marshall Faulk, St.L........253		1381	5.5	58	7
Duce Staley, Phi...........325		1273	3.9	29	4
Charlie Garner, SF.........241		1229	5.1	53	4
Dorsey Levens, GB 279		1034	3.7	36	9
Robert Smith, Min..........221		1015	4.6	70-td	2
Mike Alstott, TB...........242		949	3.9	30	7
Curtis Enis, Chi............287		916	3.2	19	3
Ricky Williams*, NO........253		884	3.5	25	2
Tim Biakabutuka, Car.......138		718	5.2	67-td	6
Warrick Dunn, TB 195		616	3.2	33	0
Leroy Hoard, Min..........138		555	4.0	53	10
Adrian Murrell, Ari.........193		553	2.9	22	0
Greg Hill, Det. 144		542	3.8	45	2

St. Louis Rams	Washington Redskins	Indianapolis Colts	Jacksonville Jaguars
Kurt Warner	**Stephen Davis**	**Edgerrin James**	**Jimmy Smith**
Passing Efficiency	Scoring – Nonkickers	Rushing	Receptions

All-Purpose Yardage

AFC	Rush	Rec	Ret	Total	NFC	Rush	Rec	Ret	Total
Edgerrin James*, Ind.	1553	586	0	2139	Marshall Faulk, St.L	1381	1048	0	2429
Terrence Wilkins*, Ind.	2	565	1522	2089	Glyn Milburn, Chi.	102	151	1772	2025
Eddie George, Ten.	1304	458	0	1762	Tim Dwight, Atl.	28	669	1164	1861
Napoleon Kaufman, Oak.	714	181	831	1726	Charlie Garner, SF	1229	535	0	1764
Curtis Martin, NYJ	1464	259	0	1723	Brian Mitchell, Wash.	220	305	1225	1750
Marvin Harrison, Ind.	4	1663	0	1667	Randy Moss, Min.	43	1413	162	1618
Jimmy Smith, Jax.	0	1636	0	1636	Dorsey Levens, GB	1034	573	0	1607
Ricky Watters, Sea.	1210	387	0	1597	Allen Rossum, Phi.	0	0	1597	1597
Kevin Williams, Buf.	13	381	1171	1565	Duce Staley, Phi.	1273	294	0	1567
Brock Marion, Mia.	0	0	1554	1554	Stephen Davis, Wash.	1405	111	0	1516
Tamarick Vanover, KC	0	0	1513	1513	Emmitt Smith, Dal.	1397	119	0	1516
Corey Dillon, Cin.	1200	290	4	1494	Mario Bates, Ari.	202	34	1231	1467
Chris Watson*, Den.	0	0	1472	1472	Marcus Robinson, Chi.	0	1400	0	1400

Ret column indicates all kickoff, punt, fumble and interception returns.

Scoring

Touchdowns

AFC	TD	Rush	Rec	Ret	Pts
Edgerrin James*, Ind.	17	13	4	0	102
Eddie George, Ten.	13	9	4	0	78
James Stewart, Jax.	13	13	0	0	78
Marvin Harrison, Ind.	12	0	12	0	74†
Tony Gonzalez, KC	11	0	11	0	66
Tyrone Wheatley, Oak.	11	8	3	0	66
Derrick Mayes, Sea.	10	0	10	0	60
Terry Allen, NE	9	8	1	0	54
Rickey Dudley, Oak.	9	0	9	0	54
Terry Kirby, Cle.	9	6	3	0	54
Five tied with 8 each for 48 pts.					

NFC	TD	Rush	Rec	Ret	Pts
Stephen Davis, Wash.	17	17	0	0	104†
Cris Carter, Min.	13	0	13	0	78
Emmitt Smith, Dal.	13	11	2	0	78
Isaac Bruce, St.L	12	0	12	0	74†
Marshall Faulk, St.L	12	7	5	0	74†
Patrick Jeffers, Car.	12	0	12	0	72
Randy Moss, Min.	12	0	11	1	72
Wesley Walls, Car.	12	0	12	0	72
Leroy Hoard, Min.	10	10	0	0	60
Dorsey Levens, GB	10	9	1	0	60
Michael Westbrook, Wash.	9	0	9	0	56†
Mike Alstott, TB	9	7	2	0	54
Mario Bates, Ari.	9	9	0	0	54
Tim Dwight, Atl.	9	1	7	1	54
Az-zahir Hakim, St.L	9	0	8	1	54
Marcus Robinson, Chi.	9	0	9	0	54

† Includes one 2-point conversion.

Kickers

AFC	PAT	FG	Long	Pts
Mike Vanderjagt, Ind.	43/43	34/38	53	145
Olindo Mare, Mia.	27/27	39/46	54	144
Todd Peterson, Sea.	32/32	34/40	51	134
Mike Hollis, Jax.	37/37	31/38	50	130
Jason Elam, Den.	29/29	29/36	55	116
Matt Stover, Bal.	32/32	28/33	50	116
John Carney, SD	22/23	31/36	50	115
Steve Christie, Buf.	33/33	25/34	52	108
John Hall, NYJ	27/29	27/33	48	108
Pete Stoyanovich, KC	45/45	21/28	51	108
Adam Vinatieri, NE	29/30	26/33	51	107
Al Del Greco, Ten.	43/43	21/25	50	106
Kris Brown*, Pit.	30/31	25/29	51	105
Michael Husted, Oak.	30/30	20/31	49	90

NFC	PAT	FG	Long	Pts
Jeff Wilkins, St.L	64/64	20/28	51	124
Brett Conway, Wash.	49/50	22/32	51	115
Ryan Longwell, GB	38/38	25/30	50	113
Martin Gramatica*, TB	25/25	27/32	53	106
Jason Hanson, Det.	28/29	26/32	52	106
Gary Anderson, Min.	46/46	19/30	44	103
John Kasay, Car.	33/33	22/25	52	99
Wade Richey, SF	30/31	21/23	52	93
Doug Brien, NO	20/21	24/29	52	92
R. Cunningham, Dal.-Car.	44/45	1./25	47	89
Chris Jacke, Ari.	26/26	19/27	49	83
Morten Andersen, Atl.	34/34	15/21	49	79
Norm Johnson, Phi.	25/25	18/25	49	79
Cary Blanchard, NYG	19/19	18/21	48	73

Interceptions

AFC	No	Yds	Long	TD
James Hasty, KC	7	98	56-td	2
Sam Madison, Mia.	7	164	42	1
Rod Woodson, Bal.	7	195	66-td	2
Aaron Beasley, Jax.	6	200	93-td	2
Marcus Coleman, NYJ	6	165	98-td	1

NFC	No	Yds	Long	TD
Donnie Abraham, TB	7	115	55-td	2
Troy Vincent, Phi.	7	91	35	0
Ashley Ambrose, NO	6	27	16	0
Percy Ellsworth, NYG	6	80	26	0
Todd Lyght, St.L	6	112	57-td	1
Mike McKenzie*, GB	6	4	4	0
Lance Schulters, SF	6	127	64-td	1
Matt Stevens, Wash.	6	61	25	0

Sacks

AFC	No
Jevon Kearse*, Ten.	14.5
Trevor Pryce, Den.	13.0
Tony Brackens, Jax.	12.0
Chad Bratzke, Ind.	12.0
Michael McCrary, Bal.	11.5
Kevin Hardy, Jax.	10.5
Raylee Johnson, SD	10.5

NFC	No
Kevin Carter, St.L	17.0
Simeon Rice, Ari.	16.5
Robert Porcher, Det.	15.0
Warren Sapp, TB	12.5
Kevin Greene, Car.	12.0
Bryant Young, SF	11.0

Punting

AFC	No	Yds	Lg	Avg	In20
Tom Rouen, Den.	84	3908	65	46.5	19
Josh Miller, Pit.	84	3795	75	45.2	27
Tom Tupa, NYJ	81	3659	69	45.2	25
Darren Bennett, SD	89	3910	60	43.9	32
Chris Gardocki, Cle.	106	4645	61	43.8	20

NFC	No	Yds	Lg	Avg	In20
Mitch Berger, Min.	61	2769	75	45.4	18
Toby Gowin, Dal.	81	3500	64	43.2	24
Mark Royals, TB	90	3882	66	43.1	23
John Jett, Det.	86	3637	62	42.3	27
Sean Landeta, Phi.	107	4524	60	42.3	21

Punt Returns
(Minimum of 20 returns)

AFC	No	Yards	Avg	Long	TD
Charlie Rogers*, Sea.	22	318	14.5	94-td	1
Nate Jacquet, Mia.	28	351	12.5	45	0
Tamarick Vanover, KC	51	627	12.3	84-td	2
Reggie Barlow, Jax.	38	414	10.9	74-td	1
Troy Brown, NE	38	405	10.7	52	0

NFC	No	Yds	Avg	Long	TD
Mac Cody*, Ari.	32	373	11.7	31	0
Tiki Barber, NYG	44	506	11.5	85-td	1
Glyn Milburn, Chi.	30	346	11.5	54	0
Deion Sanders, Dal.	30	344	11.5	76	1
Tim Dwight, Atl.	20	220	11.0	70-td	1

Kickoff Returns
(Minimum of 20 returns)

AFC	No	Yards	Avg	Long	TD
Tremain Mack, Cin.	51	1382	27.1	99-td	1
Brock Marion, Mia	62	1524	24.6	93	0
Dwight Stone, Mia.	28	689	24.6	50	0
Kevin Faulk*, NE	39	943	24.2	95	0
Chris Watson*, Den.	48	1138	23.7	71	0

NFC	No	Yards	Avg	Long	TD
Tony Horne, St.L	30	892	29.7	101-td	2
Jason Tucker*, Dal.	22	613	27.9	79	0
Robert Tate, Min.	25	627	25.1	76-td	1
Allen Rossum, Phi.	54	1347	24.9	89-td	1
Michael Bates, Car.	52	1287	24.8	100-td	2

Single Game Highs

Passing

AFC	Cmp/Att	Yds	TD
Peyton Manning, Ind. vs. SD (9/26)	29/54	404	2
Jim Harbaugh, SD vs. Min. (11/28)	25/39	404	1
Drew Bledsoe, NE vs. Cle. (10/3)	29/43	393	1
Dan Marino, Mia. vs. Ind. (10/10)	25/38	393	2
Drew Bledsoe, NE vs. Ind. (12/12)	31/44	379	1

NFC	Cmp/Att	Yds	TD
Brad Johnson, Wash. vs. SF (12/26)	32/47	471	2
Jeff Garcia, SF vs. Cin. (12/5)	33/49	437	3
Jim Miller, Chi. vs. Min. (11/14)	34/48	422	3
Jake Plummer, Ari. vs. GB (1/2)	35/57	396	2
Brett Favre, GB vs. TB (10/10)	22/40	390	2

Rushing

AFC	Car	Yds	TD
Eddie George, Ten. vs. Oak. (12/9)	28	199	2
Corey Dillon, Cin. vs. Cle. (12/12)	28	192	3
Olandis Gary*, Den. vs. Det. (12/25)	29	185	1
Olandis Gary*, Den. vs. Sea. (12/19)	22	183	0
Jermaine Fazande*, SD vs. Den. (1/2)	30	183	1

NFC	Car	Yds	TD
Stephen Davis, Wash. vs. Ari. (12/12)	37	189	1
Stephen Davis, Wash. vs. NYG (11/21)	33	183	1
Marshall Faulk, St.L vs. Atl. (10/17)	18	181	1
Ricky Williams*, NO vs. Cle. (10/31)	40	179	0
Charlie Garner, SF vs. Pit. (11/7)	20	166	0

Receiving Yards

AFC	Ct	Yds	TD
Qadry Ismail, Bal. vs. Pit. (12/12)	6	258	3
Jimmy Smith, Jax. vs. NO (11/21)	9	220	1
Terry Glenn, NE vs. Cle. (10/3)	13	214	1
Marvin Harrison, Ind. vs. SD (9/26)	13	196	1
Keyshawn Johnson, NYJ vs. NE (9/12)	8	194	1

NFC	Ct	Yds	TD
Randy Moss, Min. vs. Chi. (11/14)	12	204	0
Marshall Faulk, St.L vs. Chi. (12/26)	12	204	1
Amani Toomer, NYG vs. NYJ (12/5)	6	181	3
Marcus Robinson, Chi. vs. Det. (12/19)	11	170	3
Terance Mathis, Atl. vs. Pit. (10/25)	12	166	1

NFL Bests

Longest Field Goal
55 yds . . . . Jason Elam, Den. vs. SD (11/7)
Longest Run from Scrimmage
82 yds . . . . Derrick Alexander, KC vs. Pit. (12/18) TD
Longest Pass Play
90 yds . . Troy Aikman to Jason Tucker, Dal. vs. NYG (1/2) TD
90 yds . . . . . Billy Joe Hobert to Eddie Kennison, NO vs. Atl.
(10/10) TD
Longest Interception Return
98 yds . . . . Marcus Coleman, NYJ vs. Mia. (12/27) TD
Longest Punt Return
94 yds . . . . Charlie Rogers, Sea. vs. Pit. (9/26) TD
Longest Kickoff Return
101 yds . . . . Tony Horne, St.L vs. Atl. (10/17) TD

NFL Regular Season Team Leaders

Offense

AFC	Points For	Avg	Yardage Rush	Pass	Total	Avg
Indianapolis	423	26.4	1660	4066	5726	357.9
Oakland	390	24.4	2084	3609	5693	355.8
Jacksonville	396	24.8	2091	3495	5586	349.1
Buffalo	320	20.0	2040	3293	5333	333.3
Kansas City	390	24.4	2082	3239	5321	332.6
Tennessee	392	24.5	1811	3485	5296	331.0
Denver	314	19.6	1864	3419	5283	330.2
Cincinnati	283	17.7	2051	3226	5277	329.8
New England	299	18.7	1426	3636	5062	316.4
Miami	326	20.4	1453	3485	4938	308.6
Pittsburgh	317	19.8	1991	2883	4874	304.6
Seattle	338	21.1	1408	3397	4805	300.3
Baltimore	324	20.3	1754	3024	4778	298.6
NY Jets	308	19.3	1961	2791	4752	297.0
San Diego	269	16.8	1246	3343	4589	286.8
Cleveland	217	13.6	1150	2612	3762	235.1

NFC	Points For	Avg	Yardage Rush	Pass	Total	Avg
St. Louis	526	32.9	2059	4353	6412	400.8
Washington	443	27.7	2039	3926	5965	372.8
Minnesota	399	24.9	1804	3989	5793	362.1
Carolina	421	26.3	1525	4161	5686	355.4
Chicago	272	17.0	1387	4136	5523	345.2
Green Bay	357	22.3	1519	3900	5419	338.7
San Francisco	295	18.4	2085	3295	5380	336.3
Dallas	352	22.0	2051	3127	5178	323.6
NY Giants	299	18.7	1410	3717	5127	320.4
New Orleans	260	16.3	1690	3293	4983	311.4
Detroit	322	20.1	1245	3686	4931	308.2
Atlanta	285	17.8	1196	3346	4542	283.9
Tampa Bay	270	16.9	1776	2478	4254	265.9
Arizona	245	15.3	1207	2803	4010	250.6
Philadelphia	272	17.0	1746	2084	3830	239.4

Defense

AFC	Points Opp	Avg	Yardage Rush	Pass	Total	Avg
Buffalo	229	14.3	1370	2675	4045	252.8
Baltimore	277	17.3	1231	2991	4222	263.9
Jacksonville	217	13.6	1444	2890	4334	270.9
Miami	336	21.0	1476	2928	4404	275.3
Denver	318	19.9	1737	3016	4753	297.1
New England	284	17.8	1795	3013	4808	300.5
Oakland	329	20.6	1559	3321	4880	305.0
Pittsburgh	320	20.0	1958	2926	4884	305.3
San Diego	316	19.8	1321	3584	4905	306.6
Kansas City	322	20.1	1557	3482	5039	314.9
Indianapolis	333	20.8	1715	3506	5221	326.3
Tennessee	324	20.3	1550	3695	5245	327.8
NY Jets	309	19.3	1703	3676	5379	336.2
Seattle	298	18.6	1934	3492	5426	339.1
Cincinnati	460	28.8	1699	3798	5497	343.6
Cleveland	437	27.3	2736	3310	6046	377.9

NFC	Points Opp	Avg	Yardage Rush	Pass	Total	Avg
Tampa Bay	235	14.7	1407	2873	4280	267.5
St. Louis	242	15.1	1189	3509	4698	293.6
Dallas	276	17.3	1444	3396	4840	302.5
NY Giants	358	22.4	1560	3421	4981	311.3
Atlanta	380	23.8	2062	3161	5223	326.4
Detroit	323	20.2	1531	3760	5291	330.7
Green Bay	341	21.3	1804	3505	5309	331.8
New Orleans	434	27.1	1774	3544	5318	332.4
Arizona	382	23.9	2265	3157	5422	338.9
Philadelphia	357	22.3	2001	3461	5462	341.4
Carolina	381	23.8	1898	3605	5503	343.9
Minnesota	335	20.9	1617	3980	5597	349.8
San Francisco	453	28.3	1619	4068	5687	355.4
Chicago	341	21.3	1882	3822	5704	356.5
Washington	377	23.6	1973	3732	5705	356.6

Offensive Downs

AFC	Tot	First Downs Rush	Pass	Pen	3rd Downs Made	Att	Pct	4th Downs Made	Att	Pct
Jacksonville	331	116	194	21	92	230	40.0	5	10	50.0
Indianapolis	327	89	200	38	73	186	39.2	2	6	33.3
Oakland	326	110	196	20	85	216	39.4	7	8	87.5
Buffalo	313	117	173	23	93	228	40.8	11	21	52.4
Denver	308	107	168	33	84	229	36.7	6	14	42.9
Pittsburgh	295	111	159	25	90	234	38.5	7	24	29.2
Tennessee	294	109	167	18	83	217	38.2	7	12	58.3
Cincinnati	293	111	161	21	93	235	39.6	7	23	30.4
Miami	287	81	188	18	80	236	33.9	8	14	57.1
Kansas City	282	108	164	10	96	243	39.5	6	11	54.5
New England	280	72	184	24	79	223	35.4	4	13	30.8
Seattle	276	65	179	32	68	210	32.4	2	8	25.0
NY Jets	268	111	139	18	78	226	34.5	11	25	44.0
San Diego	262	69	171	22	89	242	36.8	6	14	42.9
Baltimore	259	87	148	24	65	229	28.4	3	11	27.3
Cleveland	220	64	134	22	59	203	29.1	9	13	69.2

NFC	Tot	First Downs Rush	Pass	Pen	3rd Downs Made	Att	Pct	4th Downs Made	Att	Pct
Washington	338	121	183	34	77	203	37.9	9	18	50.0
St. Louis	335	102	207	26	91	194	46.9	5	8	62.5
Minnesota	324	96	192	36	89	204	43.6	6	11	54.5
Green Bay	314	87	196	31	77	209	36.8	2	9	22.2
NY Giants	308	87	197	24	84	232	36.2	12	19	63.2
Carolina	307	78	208	21	77	201	38.3	10	20	50.0
Chicago	302	82	203	17	91	247	36.8	11	27	40.7
San Francisco	300	102	172	26	70	206	34.0	8	23	34.8
Dallas	295	129	139	27	77	219	35.2	6	17	35.3
New Orleans	288	97	159	32	74	220	33.6	8	22	36.4
Atlanta	273	68	179	26	68	196	34.7	5	14	35.7
Detroit	269	67	179	23	81	222	36.5	6	17	35.3
Arizona	254	77	150	27	72	221	32.6	4	17	23.5
Tampa Bay	245	97	132	16	81	230	35.2	7	15	46.7
Philadelphia	218	76	123	19	74	238	31.1	6	9	66.7

AFC Team by Team Results
Home games are listed in **bold** type.

Baltimore Ravens (8-8)

10	ST.L	27
20	**PIT**	**23**
17	**CLE**	**10**
19	ATL (OT)	13
11	TEN	14
	OPEN	
8	**KC**	**35**
10	**BUF**	**13**
41	CLE	9
3	JAX	6
34	CIN	31
23	**JAX**	**30**
41	**TEN**	**14**
31	PIT	24
31	**NO**	**8**
22	**CIN**	**0**
3	NE	20

Buffalo Bills (11-5)

14	IND	31
17	**NYJ**	**3**
26	**PHI**	**0**
23	MIA	18
24	**PIT**	**21**
14	**OAK**	**20**
16	SEA	26
13	BAL	10
34	WASH	17
23	**MIA**	**3**
7	NYJ	17
17	**NE**	**7**
	OPEN	
17	**NYG**	**19**
31	ARI	21
13	NE (OT)	10
31	**IND**	**6**

Cincinnati Bengals (4-12)

35	TEN	36
7	**SD**	**34**
3	CAR	27
10	ST.L	38
18	CLE	17
3	**PIT**	**17**
10	IND	31
10	**JAX**	**41**
20	SEA	37
14	**TEN**	**24**
31	**BAL**	**34**
27	PIT	20
44	**SF**	**30**
44	**CLE**	**28**
	OPEN	
0	BAL	22
7	JAX	24

Cleveland Browns (2-14)

0	**PIT**	**43**
9	TEN	26
10	BAL	17
7	**NE**	**19**
17	**CIN**	**18**
7	JAX	24
3	ST.L	34
21	NO	16
9	**BAL**	**41**
16	PIT	15
17	**CAR**	**31**
21	**TEN**	**33**
10	SD	23
28	CIN	44
14	**JAX**	**24**
28	**IND**	**29**
	OPEN	

Denver Broncos (6-10)

21	**MIA**	**38**
10	KC	26
10	TB	13
13	**NYJ**	**21**
16	**OAK**	**13**
31	**GB**	**10**
23	NE	24
20	**MIN**	**23**
33	SD	17
17	SEA	20
27	**OAK (OT)**	**21**
	OPEN	
10	**KC**	**16**
24	JAX	27
36	**SEA (OT)**	**30**
17	DET	7
6	SD	12

Indianapolis Colts (13-3)

31	**BUF**	**14**
28	NE	31
27	SD	19
	OPEN	
31	**MIA**	**34**
16	NYJ	13
31	**CIN**	**10**
34	**DAL**	**24**
25	**KC**	**17**
27	NYG	19
44	PHI	17
13	**NYJ**	**6**
37	MIA	34
20	**NE**	**15**
24	**WASH**	**21**
29	CLE	28
6	BUF	31

Jacksonville Jaguars (14-2)

41	**SF**	**3**
22	CAR	20
19	**TEN**	**20**
17	PIT	3
16	NYJ	6
24	**CLE**	**7**
	OPEN	
41	CIN	10
30	ATL	7
6	**BAL**	**3**
41	**NO**	**23**
30	BAL	23
20	**PIT**	**6**
27	**DEN**	**24**
24	CLE	14
14	TEN	41
24	**CIN**	**7**

Kansas City Chiefs (9-7)

17	CHI	20
26	**DEN**	**10**
31	**DET**	**21**
14	SD	21
16	**NE**	**14**
	OPEN	
35	BAL	8
34	**SD**	**0**
17	IND	25
10	TB	17
19	**SEA**	**31**
37	OAK	34
16	**DEN**	**10**
31	**MIN**	**28**
35	PIT	19
14	SEA	23
38	**OAK (OT)**	**41**

Miami Dolphins (9-7)

38	DEN	21
19	**ARI**	**16**
	OPEN	
18	**BUF**	**23**
34	IND	31
31	NE	30
16	**PHI**	**13**
16	OAK	9
17	**TEN**	**0**
3	BUF	23
27	**NE**	**17**
0	DAL	20
34	**IND**	**37**
20	NYJ	28
12	**SD**	**9**
31	**NYJ**	**38**
10	WASH	21

New England Patriots (8-8)

30	NYJ	28
31	**IND**	**28**
16	**NYG**	**14**
19	CLE	7
14	KC	16
30	**MIA**	**31**
24	**DEN**	**23**
27	ARI	3
	OPEN	
17	**NYJ**	**24**
17	MIA	27
7	BUF	17
13	**DAL**	**6**
15	IND	20
9	PHI	24
10	**BUF (OT)**	**13**
20	**BAL**	**3**

New York Jets (8-8)

28	**NE**	**30**
3	BUF	17
20	**WASH**	**27**
21	DEN	13
6	**JAX**	**16**
13	**IND**	**16**
23	OAK	24
	OPEN	
12	**ARI**	**7**
24	NE	17
17	**BUF**	**7**
6	IND	13
28	NYG	41
28	**MIA**	**20**
22	DAL	21
38	MIA	31
19	**SEA**	**9**

Oakland Raiders (8-8)

24	GB	28
22	MIN	17
24	**CHI**	**17**
21	SEA	22
13	DEN	16
20	BUF	14
24	**NYJ**	**23**
9	**MIA**	**16**
	OPEN	
28	**SD**	**9**
21	DEN (OT)	27
34	**KC**	**37**
30	**SEA**	**21**
14	TEN	21
45	**TB**	**0**
20	SD	23
41	KC (OT)	38

Pittsburgh Steelers (6-10)

43	CLE	0
23	BAL	20
10	**SEA**	29
3	**JAX**	17
21	BUF	24
17	CIN	3
13	**ATL**	9
	OPEN	
27	SF	6
15	**CLE**	16
10	TEN	16
20	**CIN**	27
6	JAX	20
24	**BAL**	31
19	KC	35
30	**CAR**	20
36	TEN	47

San Diego Chargers (8-8)

	OPEN	
34	CIN	7
19	**IND**	27
21	**KC**	14
20	DET	10
13	**SEA**	10
3	**GB**	31
0	KC	34
17	**DEN**	33
9	OAK	28
20	**CHI (OT)**	23
27	MIN	35
23	**CLE**	10
19	SEA	16
9	MIA	12
23	**OAK**	20
12	DEN	6

Seattle Seahawks (9-7)

20	**DET**	28
14	CHI	13
29	PIT	10
22	**OAK**	21
	OPEN	
10	SD	13
26	**BUF**	16
27	GB	7
37	**CIN**	20
20	**DEN**	17
31	KC	19
3	**TB**	16
21	OAK	30
16	**SD**	19
30	DEN (OT)	36
23	**KC**	14
9	NYJ	19

Tennessee Titans (13-3)

36	**CIN**	35
26	**CLE**	9
20	JAX	19
22	SF	24
14	**BAL**	11
24	NO	21
	OPEN	
24	**ST.L**	21
0	MIA	17
24	CIN	14
16	**PIT**	10
33	CLE	21
14	BAL	41
21	**OAK**	14
30	**ATL**	17
41	**JAX**	14
47	PIT	36

NFC Team by Team Results

Home games are listed in **bold** type.

Arizona Cardinals (6-10)

25	PHI	24
16	MIA	19
10	**SF**	24
7	DAL	35
14	**NYG**	3
10	WASH	24
	OPEN	
3	**NE**	27
7	NYJ	12
23	**DET**	19
13	**DAL**	9
34	NYG	24
21	**PHI**	17
3	WASH	28
21	**BUF**	31
14	ATL	37
24	GB	49

Atlanta Falcons (5-11)

14	**MIN**	17
7	DAL	24
7	ST.L	35
13	**BAL (OT)**	19
20	NO	17
13	**ST.L**	41
9	PIT	13
27	**CAR**	20
7	**JAX**	30
	OPEN	
10	TB	19
28	CAR	34
35	**NO**	12
7	SF	26
17	TEN	30
37	**ARI**	14
34	**SF**	29

Carolina Panthers (8-8)

10	NO	19
20	**JAX**	22
27	**CIN**	3
36	WASH	38
	OPEN	
31	SF	29
9	**DET**	24
20	ATL	27
33	**PHI**	7
10	ST.L	35
31	CLE	17
34	**ATL**	28
21	**ST.L**	34
33	GB	31
41	**SF**	24
20	PIT	30
45	**NO**	13

Chicago Bears (6-10)

20	**KC**	17
13	**SEA**	14
17	OAK	24
14	**NO**	10
24	MIN	22
16	**PHI**	20
3	TB	6
22	WASH	48
14	GB	13
24	**MIN (OT)**	27
23	SD (OT)	20
17	DET	21
19	GB	35
	OPEN	
28	**DET**	10
12	ST.L	34
6	TB	20

Dallas Cowboys (8-8)

41	WASH (OT)	35
24	**ATL**	7
	OPEN	
35	**ARI**	7
10	PHI	13
10	NYG	13
38	**WASH**	20
24	IND	34
17	MIN	27
27	**GB**	13
9	ARI	13
20	**MIA**	0
6	NE	13
20	**PHI**	10
21	**NYJ**	22
24	NO	31
26	**NYG**	18

Detroit Lions (8-8)

28	SEA	20
23	**GB**	15
21	KC	31
	OPEN	
10	**SD**	20
25	**MIN**	23
24	CAR	9
20	**TB**	3
31	**ST.L**	27
19	ARI	23
17	GB	26
21	**CHI**	17
33	**WASH**	17
16	TB	23
10	CHI	28
7	**DEN**	17
17	MIN	24

Green Bay Packers (8-8)

28	**OAK**	24
15	DET	23
23	**MIN**	20
	OPEN	
26	**TB**	23
10	DEN	31
31	SD	3
7	**SEA**	27
13	**CHI**	14
13	DAL	27
26	**DET**	17
20	SF	3
35	CHI	19
31	**CAR**	33
20	MIN	24
10	TB	29
49	**ARI**	24

Minnesota Vikings (10-6)

17	ATL	14
17	**OAK**	22
20	GB	23
21	**TB**	14
22	**CHI**	24
23	DET	25
40	**SF**	16
23	DEN	20
27	**DAL**	14
27	CHI (OT)	24
	OPEN	
35	**SD**	27
17	TB	24
28	KC	31
24	**GB**	20
34	NYG	17
24	**DET**	17

New Orleans Saints (3-13)

19	CAR	10
21	SF	28
	OPEN	
10	CHI	14
17	ATL	20
21	TEN	24
3	NYG	31
16	CLE	21
16	TB	31
24	SF	6
23	JAX	41
12	ST.L	43
12	ATL	35
14	ST.L	30
8	BAL	31
31	DAL	24
13	CAR	45

New York Giants (7-9)

17	TB	13
21	WASH	50
14	NE	16
16	PHI	15
3	ARI	14
13	DAL	10
31	NO	3
23	PHI (OT)	17
	OPEN	
19	IND	27
13	WASH	23
24	ARI	34
41	NYJ	28
19	BUF	17
10	ST.L	31
17	MIN	34
18	DAL	26

Philadelphia Eagles (5-11)

24	ARI	25
5	TB	19
0	BUF	26
15	NYG	16
13	DAL	10
20	CHI	16
13	MIA	16
17	NYG (OT)	23
7	CAR	33
35	WASH	28
17	IND	44
17	WASH (OT)	20
17	ARI	21
10	DAL	20
24	NE	9
	OPEN	
38	ST.L	31

St. Louis Rams (13-3)

27	BAL	10
	OPEN	
35	ATL	7
38	CIN	10
42	SF	20
41	ATL	13
34	CLE	3
21	TEN	24
27	DET	31
35	CAR	10
23	SF	7
43	NO	12
34	CAR	21
30	NO	14
31	NYG	10
34	CHI	12
31	PHI	38

San Francisco 49ers (4-12)

3	JAX	41
28	NO	21
24	ARI	10
24	TEN	22
20	ST.L	42
29	CAR	31
16	MIN	40
	OPEN	
6	PIT	27
6	NO	24
7	ST.L	23
3	GB	20
30	CIN	44
26	ATL	7
24	CAR	41
20	WASH (OT)	26
29	ATL	34

Tampa Bay Buccaneers (11-5)

13	NYG	17
19	PHI	5
13	DEN	10
14	MIN	21
23	GB	26
	OPEN	
6	CHI	3
3	DET	20
31	NO	16
17	KC	10
19	ATL	10
16	SEA	3
24	MIN	17
23	DET	16
0	OAK	45
29	GB	10
20	CHI	6

Washington Redskins (10-6)

35	DAL (OT)	41
50	NYG	21
27	NYJ	20
38	CAR	36
	OPEN	
24	ARI	10
20	DAL	38
48	CHI	22
17	BUF	34
28	PHI	35
23	NYG	13
20	PHI (OT)	17
17	DET	33
28	ARI	3
21	IND	24
26	SF (OT)	20
21	MIA	10

Takeaways/Giveaways

AFC	Takeaways Int	Fum	Total	Giveaways Int	Fum	Total	Net Diff
Kansas City	25	20	45	15	9	24	+21
Tennessee	16	24	40	13	9	22	+18
NY Jets	24	11	35	16	6	22	+13
Jacksonville	19	11	30	11	7	18	+12
Oakland	20	13	33	14	15	29	+4
Pittsburgh	14	14	28	18	7	25	+3
Seattle	30	6	36	16	17	33	+3
Baltimore	21	10	31	20	11	31	0
Denver	15	11	26	18	10	28	-2
New England	16	15	31	21	12	33	-2
Cincinnati	12	15	27	18	14	32	-5
Indianapolis	10	13	23	17	11	28	-5
Buffalo	12	9	21	16	11	27	-6
Miami	18	10	28	21	13	34	-6
San Diego	15	12	27	24	11	35	-8
Cleveland	8	12	20	15	16	31	-11
TOTALS	275	206	481	273	179	452	+29

NFC	Takeaways Int	Fum	Total	Giveaways Int	Fum	Total	Net Diff
Washington	24	13	37	14	11	25	+12
Dallas	24	9	33	13	10	23	+10
Detroit	16	16	32	14	8	22	+10
Philadelphia	28	18	46	18	21	39	+7
Green Bay	26	15	41	23	13	36	+5
St. Louis	29	7	36	15	16	31	+5
Chicago	14	19	33	22	15	37	-4
Tampa Bay	21	10	31	16	19	35	-4
Carolina	15	14	29	15	19	34	-5
New Orleans	19	15	34	30	9	39	-5
NY Giants	17	7	24	20	12	32	-8
Minnesota	12	18	30	21	19	40	-10
San Francisco	13	7	20	19	13	32	-12
Arizona	17	10	27	30	10	40	-13
Atlanta	12	6	18	19	16	35	-17
TOTALS	287	184	471	289	211	500	-29

AFC Team by Team Statistics

Players with more than one team during the regular season are listed with club they ended season with; (*) indicates rookies.

Baltimore Ravens

Passing (5 Att)	Att	Cmp	Pct	Yds	TD	Rate
Tony Banks	320	169	52.8	2136	17	81.2
Stoney Case	170	77	45.3	988	3	50.3
Scott Mitchell	56	24	42.9	236	1	31.5

Interceptions: Banks 8, Case 8, Mitchell 4.

Top Receivers	No	Yds	Avg	Long	TD
Qadry Ismail	68	1105	16.3	76-td	6
Justin Armour	37	538	14.5	54-td	4
Chuck Evans	32	235	7.3	27	1
Pat Johnson	29	526	18.1	76-td	3
Jermaine Lewis	25	281	11.2	46	2
Errict Rhett	24	169	7.0	20-td	2

Top Rushers	Car	Yds	Avg	Long	TD
Errict Rhett	236	852	3.6	52-td	5
Priest Holmes	89	506	5.7	72	1
Stoney Case	36	141	3.9	28	3
Chuck Evans	38	134	3.5	12	0

Most Touchdowns	TD	Run	Rec	Ret	Pts
Errict Rhett	7	5	2	0	42
Qadry Ismail	6	0	6	0	36
Justin Armour	4	0	4	0	24
Stoney Case	3	3	0	0	18
Pat Johnson	3	0	3	0	18

2-Pt. Conversions: (1-1) Evans.

Kicking	PAT/Att	FG/Att	Lg	Pts
Matt Stover	32/32	28/33	50	116

Punts (10 or more)	No	Yds	Long	Avg	In20
Kyle Richardson	103	4355	63	42.3	39

Most Interceptions		Most Sacks	
Rod Woodson	7	Michael McCrary	11.5

Buffalo Bills

Passing (5 Att)	Att	Cmp	Pct	Yds	TD	Rate
Doug Flutie	478	264	55.2	3171	19	75.1
Rob Johnson	34	25	73.5	298	2	119.5

Interceptions: Flutie 16.

Top Receivers	No	Yds	Avg	Long	TD
Eric Moulds	65	994	15.3	54-td	7
Andre Reed	52	536	10.3	30	1
Jay Riemersma	37	496	13.4	38	4
Peerless Price*	31	393	12.7	45	3
Kevin Williams	31	381	12.3	35	0
Jonathan Linton	29	228	7.9	28	1
Sam Gash	20	163	8.2	31-td	2

Top Rushers	Car	Yds	Avg	Long	TD
Jonathan Linton	205	695	3.4	18	5
Antowain Smith	165	614	3.7	52-td	6
Doug Flutie	88	476	5.4	24-td	1
Thurman Thomas	36	152	4.2	31	0

Most Touchdowns	TD	Run	Rec	Ret	Pts
Eric Moulds	7	0	7	0	42
Jonathan Linton	6	5	1	0	38
Antowain Smith	6	6	0	0	36
Jay Riemersma	4	0	4	0	24
Peerless Price*	3	0	3	0	18

2-Pt. Conversions: (1-2) Linton.

Kicking	PAT/Att	FG/Att	Lg	Pts
Steve Christie	33/33	25/34	52	108

Punts (10 or more)	No	Yds	Long	Avg	In20
Chris Mohr	73	2840	60	38.9	20

Most Interceptions		Most Sacks	
Kurt Schulz	3	Bruce Smith	7

Cincinnati Bengals

Passing (5 Att)	Att	Cmp	Pct	Yds	TD	Rate
Jeff Blake	389	215	55.3	2670	16	77.6
Akili Smith*	153	80	52.3	805	2	55.6
Scott Covington*	5	4	80.0	23	0	85.8

Interceptions: Blake 12, Smith 6.

Top Receivers	No	Yds	Avg	Long	TD
Darnay Scott	68	1022	15.0	76-td	7
Carl Pickens	57	737	12.9	75-td	6
Willie Jackson	31	369	11.9	29	2
Corey Dillon	31	290	9.4	23	1
Tony McGee	26	344	13.2	35	2
Clif Groce	25	154	6.2	14	0

Top Rushers	Car	Yds	Avg	Long	TD
Corey Dillon	263	1200	4.6	50	5
Jeff Blake	63	332	5.3	16	2
Michael Basnight*	62	308	5.0	46	0
Akili Smith*	19	114	6.0	24	1

Most Touchdowns	TD	Run	Rec	Ret	Pts
Darnay Scott	7	0	7	0	42
Corey Dillon	6	5	1	0	36
Carl Pickens	6	0	6	0	36
Willie Jackson	2	0	2	0	14

2-Pt. Conversions: (2-6) Jackson, Brian Milne.

Kicking	PAT/Att	FG/Att	Lg	Pts
Doug Pelfrey	27/27	18/27	50	81

Punts (10 or more)	No	Yds	Long	Avg	In20
Will Brice	60	2475	72	41.3	12
Brad Costello	22	744	44	33.8	1

Most Interceptions		Most Sacks	
Rodney Heath*	3	Michael Bankston	6

Cleveland Browns

Passing (5 Att)	Att	Cmp	Pct	Yds	TD	Rate
Tim Couch*	399	223	55.9	2447	15	73.2
Ty Detmer	91	47	51.6	548	4	75.7

Interceptions: Couch 13, Detmer 2.

Top Receivers	No	Yds	Avg	Long	TD
Kevin Johnson*	66	986	14.9	64-td	8
Terry Kirby	58	528	9.1	78-td	3
Darrin Chiaverini*	44	487	11.1	28-td	4
Marc Edwards	27	212	7.9	27-td	2
Irv Smith	24	222	9.3	22	1

Top Rushers	Car	Yds	Avg	Long	TD
Terry Kirby	130	452	3.5	28	6
Karim Abdul-Jabbar	143	445	3.1	21	1
MIA	28	95	3.4	12	1
CLE	115	350	3.0	21	0
Tim Couch*	40	267	6.7	40	1

Acquired: Abdul-Jabbar from Miami for a 2000 sixth-round draft pick and a conditional 2001 fifth-round pick (Oct. 19).

Most Touchdowns	TD	Run	Rec	Ret	Pts
Terry Kirby	9	6	3	0	54
Kevin Johnson*	8	0	8	0	48
Darrin Chiaverini*	4	0	4	0	24

2-Pt. Conversions: (1-4) Couch.

Kicking	PAT/Att	FG/Att	Lg	Pts
Phil Dawson*	23/24	8/12	49	53

Punts (10 or more)	No	Yds	Long	Avg	In20
Chris Gardocki	106	4645	61	43.8	20

Most Interceptions		Most Sacks	
Marquez Pope	2	John Thierry	7

Denver Broncos

Passing (5 Att)	Att	Cmp	Pct	Yds	TD	Rate
Brian Griese	.452	261	57.7	3032	14	75.6
Chris Miller	.81	46	56.8	527	2	79.6
Bubby Brister	.20	12	60.0	87	0	30.6

Interceptions: Griese 14, Brister 3, Miller 1.

Top Receivers	No	Yds	Avg	Long	TD
Rod Smith	.79	1020	12.9	71	4
Ed McCaffrey	.71	1018	14.3	78-td	7
Byron Chamberlain	.32	488	15.3	88	2
Howard Griffith	.26	192	7.4	20	1
Dwayne Carswell	.24	201	8.4	20	2
Shannon Sharpe	.23	224	9.7	24	0
Olandis Gary*	.21	159	7.6	21	0

Top Rushers	Car	Yds	Avg	Long	TD
Olandis Gary*	.276	1159	4.2	71	7
Terrell Davis	.67	211	3.1	26	2
Derek Loville	.40	203	5.1	36-td	1
Brian Griese	.46	138	3.0	23	2
Howard Griffith	.17	66	3.9	13	1

Most Touchdowns	TD	Run	Rec	Ret	Pts
Olandis Gary*	.7	7	0	0	44
Ed McCaffrey	.7	0	7	0	42
Rod Smith	.4	0	4	0	24

Five tied with 2 each for 12 pts.

2-Pt. Conversions: (1-1) Gary.

Kicking	PAT/Att	FG/Att	Lg	Pts
Jason Elam	.29/29	29/36	55	116

Punts (10 or more)	No	Yds	Long	Avg	In20
Tom Rouen	.84	3098	65	46.5	19

Most Interceptions		Most Sacks	
Tory James	.5	Trevor Pryce	.13

Indianapolis Colts

Passing (5 Att)	Att	Cmp	Pct	Yds	TD	Rate
Peyton Manning	...533	331	62.1	4135	26	90.7
Steve Walsh	.13	7	53.8	47	0	22.4

Interceptions: Manning 15, Walsh 2.

Top Receivers	No	Yds	Avg	Long	TD
Marvin Harrison	.115	1663	14.5	57-td	12
Edgerrin James*	.62	586	9.5	54	4
Terrence Wilkins*	.42	565	13.5	80-td	4
Ken Dilger	.40	479	12.0	30	2
Marcus Pollard	.34	374	11.0	33	4
E.G. Green	.21	287	13.7	50	0
Jerome Pathon	.14	163	11.6	38	0

Top Rushers	Car	Yds	Avg	Long	TD
Edgerrin James*	.369	1553	4.2	72	13
Peyton Manning	.35	73	2.1	13	2
Keith Elias	.13	28	2.2	8	0

Most Touchdowns	TD	Run	Rec	Ret	Pts
Edgerrin James*	.17	13	4	0	102
Marvin Harrison	.12	0	12	0	74
Terrence Wilkins*	.7	0	4	3	42
Marcus Pollard	.4	0	4	0	24
Peyton Manning	.2	2	0	0	12
Ken Dilger	.2	0	2	0	12

2-Pt. Conversions: (1-3) Harrison.

Kicking	PAT/Att	FG/Att	Lg	Pts
Mike Vanderjagt	.43/43	34/38	53	145

Punts (10 or more)	No	Yds	Long	Avg	In20
Hunter Smith*	.58	2467	61	42.5	16

Most Interceptions		Most Sacks	
Tyrone Poole	.3	Chad Bratzke	.12

Jacksonville Jaguars

Passing (5 Att)	Att	Cmp	Pct	Yds	TD	Rate
Mark Brunell	.441	259	58.7	3060	14	82.0
Jay Fiedler	.94	61	64.9	656	2	83.5

Interceptions: Brunell 9, Fiedler 2.

Top Receivers	No	Yds	Avg	Long	TD
Jimmy Smith	.116	1636	14.1	62	6
Keenan McCardell	.78	891	11.4	49	5
Kyle Brady	.32	346	10.8	30	1
James Stewart	.21	108	5.1	19	0
Damon Jones	.19	221	11.6	31	4
Reggie Barlow	.16	202	12.6	31	0

Top Rushers	Car	Yds	Avg	Long	TD
James Stewart	.249	931	3.7	44-td	13
Fred Taylor	.159	732	4.6	52	6
Mark Brunell	.47	208	4.4	15	1
Tavian Banks	.23	82	3.6	21	0
Chris Howard	.13	55	4.2	22	0

Most Touchdowns	TD	Run	Rec	Ret	Pts
James Stewart	.13	13	0	0	78
Jimmy Smith	.6	0	6	0	38
Fred Taylor	.6	6	0	0	36
Keenan McCardell	.5	0	5	0	32
Damon Jones	.4	0	4	0	24

2-Pt. Conversions: (4-5) Brady, Brunell, McCardell, Smith.

Kicking	PAT/Att	FG/Att	Lg	Pts
Mike Hollis	.37/37	31/38	50	130

Punts (10 or more)	No	Yds	Long	Avg	In20
Bryan Barker	.78	3260	83	41.8	32

Most Interceptions		Most Sacks	
Aaron Beasley	.6	Tony Brackens	.12

Kansas City Chiefs

Passing (5 Att)	Att	Cmp	Pct	Yds	TD	Rate
Elvis Grbac	.499	294	58.9	3389	22	81.7

Interceptions: Grbac 15.

Top Receivers	No	Yds	Avg	Long	TD
Tony Gonzalez	.76	849	11.2	73-td	11
Derrick Alexander	.54	832	15.4	86-td	2
Joe Horn	.35	586	16.7	76-td	6
Kevin Lockett	.34	426	12.5	39-td	2
Tony Richardson	.24	141	5.9	29	0
Andre Rison	.21	218	10.4	20	0

Top Rushers	Car	Yds	Avg	Long	TD
Donnell Bennett	.161	627	3.9	44	8
Bam Morris	.120	414	3.5	24	3
Tony Richardson	.84	387	4.6	26	1
Rashaan Shehee	.65	238	3.7	18	1
Kimble Anders	.32	181	5.7	46	0
Mike Cloud*	.35	128	3.7	14	0

Most Touchdowns	TD	Run	Rec	Ret	Pts
Tony Gonzalez	.11	0	11	0	66
Donnell Bennett	.8	8	0	0	48
Joe Horn	.6	0	6	0	36
Derrick Alexander	.3	1	2	0	18
Bam Morris	.3	3	0	0	18

2-Pt. Conversions: (0-2).

Kicking	PAT/Att	FG/Att	Lg	Pts
Pete Stoyanovich	.45/45	21/28	51	108

Punts (10 or more)	No	Yds	Long	Avg	In20
Daniel Pope*	.101	4218	64	41.8	20

Most Interceptions		Most Sacks	
James Hasty	.7	Derrick Thomas	.7
		Marvcus Patton	.7

Miami Dolphins

Passing (5 Att)

	Att	Cmp	Pct	Yds	TD	Rate
Dan Marino	.369	204	55.3	2448	12	67.4
Damon Huard	.216	125	57.9	1288	8	79.8

Interceptions: Marino 17, Huard 4.

Top Receivers

	No	Yds	Avg	Long	TD
Tony Martin	.67	1037	15.5	69-td	5
Oronde Gadsden	.48	803	16.7	62	6
O.J. McDuffie	.43	516	12.0	34	2
Stanley Pritchett	.43	312	7.3	30	4
Rob Konrad*	.34	251	7.4	25	1
Troy Drayton	.32	299	9.3	26	1
Yatil Green	.18	234	13.0	27	0

Top Rushers

	Car	Yds	Avg	Long	TD
J.J. Johnson*	.164	558	3.4	34	4
Cecil Collins*	.131	414	3.2	25-td	2
Stanley Pritchett	.47	158	3.4	25	1
Damon Huard	.28	124	4.4	25	0
Autry Denson*	.28	98	3.5	20	0

Most Touchdowns

	TD	Run	Rec	Ret	Pts
Oronde Gadsden	.6	0	6	0	36
Tony Martin	.5	0	5	0	30
Stanley Pritchett	.5	1	4	0	30
J.J. Johnson*	.4	4	0	0	24

2-Pt. Conversions: (0-3).

Kicking

	PAT/Att	FG/Att	Lg	Pts
Olindo Mare	.27/27	39/46	54	144

Punts (10 or more)

	No	Yds	Long	Avg	In20
Tom Hutton	.73	2978	63	40.8	22

Most Interceptions
Sam Madison 7

Most Sacks
Rich Owens 8.5

New England Patriots

Passing (5 Att)

	Att	Cmp	Pct	Yds	TD	Rate
Drew Bledsoe	.539	305	56.6	3985	19	75.6

Interceptions: Bledsoe 21.

Top Receivers

	No	Yds	Avg	Long	TD
Terry Glenn	.69	1147	16.6	67	4
Shawn Jefferson	.40	698	17.5	68-td	6
Troy Brown	.36	471	13.1	37	1
Ben Coates	.32	370	11.6	27	2
Lamont Warren	.29	262	9.0	21	1
Tony Carter	.20	108	5.4	20	0

Top Rushers

	Car	Yds	Avg	Long	TD
Terry Allen	.254	896	3.5	39	8
Kevin Faulk*	.67	227	3.4	43	1
Lamont Warren	.35	120	3.4	18	0
Drew Bledsoe	.42	101	2.4	25	0

Most Touchdowns

	TD	Run	Rec	Ret	Pts
Terry Allen	.9	8	1	0	54
Shawn Jefferson	.6	0	6	0	36
Terry Glenn	.4	0	4	0	24
Ben Coates	.2	0	2	0	12
Kevin Faulk*	.2	1	1	0	12
Tony Simmons	.2	0	2	0	12

2-Pt. Conversions: (0-2).

Kicking

	PAT/Att	FG/Att	Lg	Pts
Adam Vinatieri	.29/30	26/33	51	107

Punts (10 or more)

	No	Yds	Long	Avg	In20
Lee Johnson	.90	3735	58	41.5	23

Most Interceptions
Lawyer Milloy 4

Most Sacks
Willie McGinest 9

New York Jets

Passing (5 Att)

	Att	Cmp	Pct	Yds	TD	Rate
Ray Lucas	.272	161	59.2	1678	14	85.1
Rick Mirer	.176	95	54.0	1062	5	60.4
Vinny Testaverde	.15	10	66.7	96	1	78.8
Tom Tupa	.11	6	54.5	165	2	139.2

Interceptions: Mirer 9, Lucas 6, Testaverde 1.

Top Receivers

	No	Yds	Avg	Long	TD
Keyshawn Johnson	.89	1170	13.1	65	8
Wayne Chrebet	.48	631	13.1	50-td	3
Curtis Martin	.45	259	5.8	34	0
Richie Anderson	.29	302	10.4	29	3
Dedric Ward	.22	325	14.8	56-td	3

Top Rushers

	No	Yds	Avg	Long	TD
Curtis Martin	.367	1464	4.0	50	5
Ray Lucas	.41	144	3.5	21	1
Bernie Parmalee	.27	133	4.9	18	0
Rick Mirer	.21	89	4.2	12	1

Most Touchdowns

	TD	Run	Rec	Ret	Pts
Keyshawn Johnson	.8	0	8	0	48
Curtis Martin	.5	5	0	0	30
Richie Anderson	.3	0	3	0	18
Wayne Chrebet	.3	0	3	0	18

2-Pt. Conversions: (0-4).

Kicking

	PAT/Att	FG/Att	Lg	Pts
John Hall	.27/29	27/33	48	108

Punts (10 or more)

	No	Yds	Long	Avg	In20
Tom Tupa	.81	3659	69	45.2	25

Most Interceptions
Marcus Coleman 6

Most Sacks
Mo Lewis 5.5

Oakland Raiders

Passing (5 Att)

	Att	Cmp	Pct	Yds	TD	Rate
Rich Gannon	.515	304	59.0	3840	24	86.5
Bobby Hoying	.5	2	40.0	10	0	47.9

Interceptions: Gannon 14.

Top Receivers

	No	Yds	Avg	Long	TD
Tim Brown	.90	1344	14.9	47	6
Jon Ritchie	.45	408	9.1	20-td	1
Rickey Dudley	.39	555	14.2	35	9
James Jett	.39	552	14.2	43	2
Tyrone Wheatley	.21	196	9.3	28	3

Top Rushers

	Car	Yds	Avg	Long	TD
Tyrone Wheatley	.242	936	3.9	30-td	8
Napoleon Kaufman	.138	714	5.2	75-td	2
Rich Gannon	.46	298	6.5	39	2
Zack Crockett	.45	91	2.0	7	4

Most Touchdowns

	TD	Run	Rec	Ret	Pts
Tyrone Wheatley	.11	8	3	0	66
Rickey Dudley	.9	0	9	0	54
Tim Brown	.6	0	6	0	36

2-Pt. Conversions: (1-2) Jett.

Kicking

	PAT/Att	FG/Att	Lg	Pts
Michael Husted	.30/30	20/31	49	90
Joe Nedney	.13/13	5/7	52	28

Signed: Nedney (Dec. 14).

Punts (10 or more)

	No	Yds	Long	Avg	In20
Leo Araguz	.76	3045	56	40.1	25

Most Interceptions
Eric Allen 3
Darrien Gordon 3
Eric Turner 3

Most Sacks
Lance Johnstone 10

Pittsburgh Steelers

Passing (5 Att)	Att	Cmp	Pct	Yds	TD	Rate
Kordell Stewart	.275	160	58.2	1464	6	64.9
Mike Tomczak	.258	139	53.9	1625	12	75.8

Interceptions: Stewart 10, Tomczak 8.

Top Receivers	No	Yds	Avg	Long	TD
Troy Edwards*	.61	714	11.7	41	5
Hines Ward	.61	638	10.5	42	7
Courtney Hawkins	.30	285	9.5	23	0
Bobby Shaw	.28	387	13.8	49	3
Richard Huntley	.27	253	9.4	25	3
Jerome Bettis	.21	110	5.2	17	0

Top Rushers	Car	Yds	Avg	Long	TD
Jerome Bettis	.299	1091	3.6	35	7
Richard Huntley	.93	567	6.1	52	5
Kordell Stewart	.56	258	4.6	21	2
Amos Zereoue	.18	48	2.7	8	0

Most Touchdowns	TD	Run	Rec	Ret	Pts
Richard Huntley	.8	5	3	0	48
Hines Ward	.7	0	7	0	44
Jerome Bettis	.7	7	0	0	42
Troy Edwards*	.5	0	5	0	30
Bobby Shaw	.3	0	3	0	18
Kordell Stewart	.3	2	1	0	18

2-Pt. Conversions: (1-4) Ward.

Kicking	PAT/Att	FG/Att	Lg	Pts
Kris Brown*	.30/31	25/29	51	105

Punts (10 or more)	No	Yds	Long	Avg	In20
Josh Miller	.84	3795	75	45.2	27

Most Interceptions
Scott Shields* 4
Dewayne Washington ...4

Most Sacks
Jason Gildon 11

Seattle Seahawks

Passing (5 Att)	Att	Cmp	Pct	Yds	TD	Rate
Jon Kitna	.495	270	54.5	3346	23	77.7
Glenn Foley	.30	18	60.0	283	2	113.6

Interceptions: Kitna 16.

Top Receivers	No	Yds	Avg	Long	TD
Derrick Mayes	.62	829	13.4	43-td	10
Sean Dawkins	.58	992	17.1	45-td	7
Ricky Watters	.40	387	9.7	25	2
Christian Fauria	.35	376	10.7	25	0
Reggie Brown	.34	228	6.7	26	1
Mike Pritchard	.26	375	14.4	51	2
Joey Galloway	.22	335	15.2	48	1

Top Rushers	Car	Yds	Avg	Long	TD
Ricky Watters	.325	1210	3.7	45	5
Ahman Green	.26	120	4.6	21	0
Jon Kitna	.35	56	1.6	10	0
Reggie Brown	.14	38	2.7	9	0

Most Touchdowns	TD	Run	Rec	Ret	Pts
Derrick Mayes	.10	0	10	0	60
Sean Dawkins	.7	0	7	0	42
Ricky Watters	.7	5	2	0	42
Mike Pritchard	.2	0	2	0	12

2-Pt. Conversions: (0-2).

Kicking	PAT/Att	FG/Att	Lg	Pts
Todd Peterson	.32/32	34/40	51	134

Punts (10 or more)	No	Yds	Lg	Avg	In20
Jeff Feagles	.84	3425	59	40.8	34

Most Interceptions
Shawn Springs 5
Willie Williams 5

Most Sacks
Phillip Daniels 9

San Diego Chargers

Passing (5 Att)	Att	Cmp	Pct	Yds	TD	Rate
Jim Harbaugh	.434	249	57.4	2761	10	70.6
Erik Kramer	.141	78	55.3	788	2	46.6
Moses Moreno	.7	5	71.4	78	0	108.0

Interceptions: Harbaugh 14, Kramer 10.

Top Receivers	No	Yds	Avg	Long	TD
Jeff Graham	.57	968	17.0	54	2
Freddie Jones	.56	670	12.0	36	2
Terrell Fletcher	.45	360	8.0	25	0
Mikhael Ricks	.40	429	10.7	50	0
Fred McCrary	.37	201	5.4	38	1
Tremayne Stephens	.18	133	7.4	22	1

Top Rushers	No	Yds	Avg	Long	TD
Jermaine Fazande*	.91	365	4.0	54	2
Kenny Bynum	.92	287	3.1	25	1
Natrone Means	.112	277	2.5	15	4
Terrell Fletcher	.48	126	2.6	16	0
Jim Harbaugh	.34	126	3.7	16	0

Most Touchdowns	TD	Run	Rec	Ret	Pts
Natrone Means	.5	4	1	0	30
Tremayne Stephens	.4	3	1	0	24
Kenny Bynum	.3	1	2	0	18

Four tied with 2 each for 12 pts.

2-Pt. Conversions: (1-2) Ricks.

Kicking	PAT/Att	FG/Att	Lg	Pts
John Carney	.22/23	31/36	50	115

Punts (10 or more)	No	Yds	Long	Avg	In20
Darren Bennett	.89	3910	60	43.9	32

Most Interceptions
Darryll Lewis 4
Jimmy Spencer 4

Most Sacks
Raylee Johnson 10.5

Tennessee Oilers

Passing (5 Att)	Att	Cmp	Pct	Yds	TD	Rate
Steve McNair	.331	187	56.5	2179	12	78.6
Neil O'Donnell	.195	116	59.5	1382	10	87.6

Interceptions: McNair 8, O'Donnell 5.

Top Receivers	No	Yds	Avg	Long	TD
Frank Wycheck	.69	641	9.3	35	2
Kevin Dyson	.54	658	12.2	47-td	4
Eddie George	.47	458	9.7	54-td	4
Yancey Thigpen	.38	648	17.1	35	4
Jackie Harris	.26	297	11.4	62-td	1
Chris Sanders	.20	336	16.8	48-td	1
Isaac Byrd	.14	261	18.6	65-td	2

Top Rushers	Car	Yds	Avg	Long	TD
Eddie George	.320	1304	4.1	40	9
Steve McNair	.72	337	4.7	38	8
Rodney Thomas	.43	164	3.8	22	1

Most Touchdowns	TD	Run	Rec	Ret	Pts
Eddie George	.13	9	4	0	78
Steve McNair	.8	8	0	0	48
Kevin Dyson	.4	0	4	0	24
Yancey Thigpen	.4	0	4	0	24
Lorenzo Neal	.3	1	2	0	18
Michael Roan	.3	0	3	0	18

2-Pt. Conversions: (1-3) Harris.

Kicking	PAT/Att	FG/Att	Lg	Pts
Al Del Greco	.43/43	21/25	50	106

Punts (10 or more)	No	Yds	Long	Avg	In20
Craig Hentrich	.90	3824	78	42.5	35

Most Interceptions
Samari Rolle 4

Most Sacks
Jevon Kearse* 14.5

NFC Team by Team Statistics

Players with more than one team during the regular season are listed with club they ended season with; (*) indicates rookies.

Arizona Cardinals

Passing (5 Att)	Att	Cmp	Pct	Yds	TD	Rate
Jake Plummer	381	201	52.8	2111	9	50.8
Dave Brown	169	84	49.7	944	2	55.9
Chris Greisen*	6	1	16.7	4	0	39.6

Interceptions: Plummer 24, Brown 6.

Top Receivers	No	Yds	Avg	Long	TD
Frank Sanders	79	954	12.1	63	1
Adrian Murrell	49	335	6.8	23	0
David Boston*	40	473	11.8	43	2
Rob Moore	37	621	16.8	71	5
Terry Hardy	30	222	7.4	23	0
Michael Pittman	16	196	12.3	46	0

Top Rushers	Car	Yds	Avg	Long	TD
Adrian Murrell	193	553	2.9	22	0
Michael Pittman	64	289	4.5	58-td	2
Mario Bates	72	202	2.8	16	9
Jake Plummer	39	121	3.1	17	2
Dave Brown	13	49	3.8	10	0

Most Touchdowns	TD	Run	Rec	Ret	Pts
Mario Bates	9	9	0	0	54
Rob Moore	5	0	5	0	30
David Boston*	2	0	2	0	12
Michael Pittman	2	2	0	0	12
Jake Plummer	2	2	0	0	12

2-Pt. Conversions: (0-1).

Kicking	PAT/Att	FG/Att	Lg	Pts
Chris Jacke	26/26	19/27	49	83

Punts (10 or more)	No	Yds	Long	Avg	In20
Scott Player	94	3948	60	42.0	18

Most Interceptions
Five tied with 2 each.

Most Sacks
Simeon Rice 16.5

Atlanta Falcons

Passing (5 Att)	Att	Cmp	Pct	Yds	TD	Rate
Chris Chandler	307	174	56.7	2339	16	83.5
Tony Graziani	118	62	52.5	759	2	64.2
Danny Kanell	84	42	50.0	593	4	69.2

Interceptions: Chandler 11, Graziani 4, Kanell 2.

Top Receivers	No	Yds	Avg	Long	TD
Terance Mathis	81	1016	12.5	52	6
Bob Christian	40	354	8.9	36	2
Tim Dwight	32	669	20.9	60-td	7
Chris Calloway	22	314	14.3	33	1
Ken Oxendine	17	172	10.1	32	1
O.J. Santiago	15	174	11.6	46	0
Jammi German	12	219	18.3	62	3

Top Rushers	Car	Yds	Avg	Long	TD
Ken Oxendine	141	452	3.2	20	1
Byron Hanspard	136	383	2.8	15	1
Bob Christian	38	174	4.6	33-td	5
Jamal Anderson	19	59	3.1	20	0

Most Touchdowns	TD	Run	Rec	Ret	Pts
Tim Dwight	9	1	7	1	54
Bob Christian	7	5	2	0	42
Terance Mathis	6	0	6	0	36
Jammi German	3	0	3	0	18

2-Pt. Conversions: (0-0).

Kicking	PAT/Att	FG/Att	Lg	Pts
Morten Anderson	34/34	15/21	49	79

Punts (10 or more)	No	Yds	Long	Avg	In20
Dan Stryzinski	80	3163	55	39.5	27

Most Interceptions
Ray Buchanan 4

Most Sacks
Chuck Smith 10

Carolina Panthers

Passing (5 Att)	Att	Cmp	Pct	Yds	TD	Rate
Steve Beuerlein	571	343	60.1	4436	36	94.6

Interceptions: Beuerlein 15.

Top Receivers	No	Yds	Avg	Long	TD
Mushin Muhammad	96	1253	13.1	60-td	8
Patrick Jeffers	63	1082	17.2	88-td	12
Wesley Walls	63	822	13.0	37-td	12
Tim Biakabutuka	23	189	8.2	32	0
Fred Lane	23	163	7.1	23	0

Top Rushers	Car	Yds	Avg	Long	TD
Tim Biakabutuka	138	718	5.2	67-td	6
Fred Lane	115	475	4.1	41-td	1
Steve Beuerlein	27	124	4.6	16	2
William Floyd	35	78	2.2	16	3

Most Touchdowns	TD	Run	Rec	Ret	Pts
Patrick Jeffers	12	0	12	0	72
Wesley Walls	12	0	12	0	72
Mushin Muhammad	8	0	8	0	48
Tim Biakabutuka	6	6	0	0	36

2-Pt. Conversions: (0-3).

Kicking	PAT/Att	FG/Att	Lg	Pts
John Kasay	33/33	22/25	52	99
Richie Cunningham	44/45	15/25	47	89
DAL	31/31	12/22	47	67
CAR	13/14	3/3	43	22

Signed: Cunningham (Dec. 14).

Punts (10 or more)	No	Yds	Long	Avg	In20
Ken Walter	65	2562	56	39.4	18

Most Interceptions
Eric Davis 5

Most Sacks
Kevin Greene 12

Chicago Bears

Passing (5 Att)	Att	Cmp	Pct	Yds	TD	Rate
Shane Matthews	275	167	60.7	1645	10	80.6
Cade McNown*	235	127	54.0	1465	8	66.7
Jim Miller	174	110	63.2	1242	7	83.5

Interceptions: McNown 10, Matthews 6, Miller 6.

Top Receivers	No	Yds	Avg	Long	TD
Bobby Engram	88	947	10.8	56	4
Marcus Robinson	84	1400	16.7	80-td	9
Curtis Enis	45	340	7.6	28	2
Curtis Conway	44	426	9.7	30-td	4

Top Rushers	Car	Yds	Avg	Long	TD
Curtis Enis	287	916	3.2	19	3
Cade McNown*	32	160	5.0	18	0
James Allen	32	119	3.7	13	0
Glyn Milburn	16	102	6.4	49-td	1

Most Touchdowns	TD	Run	Rec	Ret	Pts
Marcus Robinson	9	0	9	0	54
Curtis Enis	5	3	2	0	30
Curtis Conway	4	0	4	0	24
Bobby Engram	4	0	4	0	24

2-Pt. Conversions: (1-3) McNown.

Kicking	PAT/Att	FG/Att	Lg	Pts
Chris Boniol	17/18	11/18	46	50
Brian Gowins*	3/3	4/6	43	15
Jeff Jaeger	7/7	2/8	52	13
Jaret Holmes*	0/0	2/2	39	6

Punts (10 or more)	No	Yds	Lg	Avg	In20
Todd Sauerbrun	85	3478	65	40.9	20

Most Interceptions
Chris Hudson 3

Most Sacks
Clyde Simmons 7

Dallas Cowboys

Passing (5 Att)	Att	Cmp	Pct	Yds	TD	Rate
Troy Aikman	442	263	59.5	2964	17	81.1
Jason Garrett	64	32	50.0	314	3	73.3

Interceptions: Aikman 12, Garrett 1.

Top Receivers	No	Yds	Avg	Long	TD
Raghib Ismail	80	1097	13.7	76-td	6
David LaFleur	35	322	9.2	25	7
Chris Warren	34	224	6.6	24	0
Ernie Mills	30	325	10.8	36	0
Emmitt Smith	27	119	4.4	14-td	2
Jason Tucker*	23	439	19.1	90-td	2

Top Rushers	Car	Yds	Avg	Long	TD
Emmitt Smith	329	1397	4.2	63-td	11
Chris Warren	99	403	4.1	25	2
Raghib Ismail	13	110	8.5	27-td	1
Robert Chancey	14	57	4.1	11	0

Most Touchdowns	TD	Run	Rec	Ret	Pts
Emmitt Smith	13	11	2	0	78
Raghib Ismail	7	1	6	0	42
David LaFleur	7	0	7	0	42
Michael Irvin	3	0	3	0	18

Four tied at 2 each for 12 pts.

2-Pt. Conversions: (0-0).

Kicking	PAT/Att	FG/Att	Lg	Pts
Eddie Murray	10/10	7/9	40	31

Released: Richie Cunningham on Dec. 7 (see Carolina).

Punts (10 or more)	No	Yds	Long	Avg	In20
Toby Gowin	81	3500	64	43.2	24

Most Interceptions	Most Sacks
Dexter Coakley ... 4	Greg Ellis ... 7.5

Detroit Lions

Passing (5 Att)	Att	Cmp	Pct	Yds	TD	Rate
Gus Frerotte	288	175	60.8	2117	9	83.6
Charlie Batch	270	151	55.9	1957	13	84.1

Interceptions: Frerotte 7, Batch 7.

Top Receivers	No	Yds	Avg	Long	TD
Germane Crowell	81	1338	16.5	77-td	7
Johnnie Morton	80	1129	14.1	48	5
David Sloan	47	591	12.6	74-td	4
Sedrick Irvin*	25	233	9.3	31	0
Ron Rivers	22	173	7.9	31-td	1
Cory Schlesinger	21	151	7.2	25	1
Herman Moore	16	197	12.3	26	2

Top Rushers	Car	Yds	Avg	Long	TD
Greg Hill	144	542	3.8	45	2
Ron Rivers	82	295	3.6	37	0
Sedrick Irvin*	36	133	3.7	51	4
Cory Schlesinger	43	124	2.9	16	0

Most Touchdowns	TD	Run	Rec	Ret	Pts
Germane Crowell	7	0	7	0	44
Johnnie Morton	5	0	5	0	30
Sedrick Irvin*	4	4	0	0	24
David Sloan	4	0	4	0	24

Four tied with 2 each for 12 pts.

2-Pt. Conversions: (2-6) Crowell, Brian Stablein.

Kicking	PAT/Att	FG/Att	Lg	Pts
Jason Hanson	28/29	26/32	52	106

Punts (10 or more)	No	Yds	Long	Avg	In20
John Jett	86	3637	62	42.3	27

Most Interceptions	Most Sacks
Ron Rice ... 5	Robert Porcher ... 15

Green Bay Packers

Passing (5 Att)	Att	Cmp	Pct	Yds	TD	Rate
Brett Favre	595	341	57.3	4091	22	74.7
Matt Hasselbeck	10	3	30.0	41	1	77.5

Interceptions: Favre 23.

Top Receivers	No	Yds	Avg	Long	TD
Antonio Freeman	74	1074	14.5	51	6
Bill Schroeder	74	1051	14.2	51	5
Dorsey Levens	71	573	8.1	53	1
Corey Bradford	37	637	17.2	74-td	5
William Henderson	30	203	6.8	22	1
Tyrone Davis	20	204	10.2	33	2
Jeff Thomason	14	140	10.0	22	2

Top Rushers	Car	Yds	Avg	Long	TD
Dorsey Levens	279	1034	3.7	36	9
De'Mond Parker*	36	184	5.1	26	2
Brett Favre	28	142	5.1	20	0
Basil Mitchell*	29	117	4.0	15	0

Most Touchdowns	TD	Run	Rec	Ret	Pts
Dorsey Levens	10	9	1	0	60
Antonio Freeman	6	0	6	0	36
Corey Bradford	5	0	5	0	32
Bill Schroeder	5	0	5	0	30
William Henderson	3	2	1	0	18

2-Pt. Conversions: (1-2) Bradford.

Kicking	PAT/Att	FG/Att	Lg	Pts
Ryan Longwell	38/38	25/30	50	113

Punts (10 or more)	No	Yds	Long	Avg	In20
Louie Aguiar	75	2954	64	39.4	20

Most Interceptions	Most Sacks
Mike McKenzie* ... 6	Keith McKenzie ... 8

Minnesota Vikings

Passing (5 Att)	Att	Cmp	Pct	Yds	TD	Rate
Jeff George	329	191	58.1	2816	23	94.2
Randall Cunningham	200	124	62.0	1475	8	79.1

Interceptions: George 12, Cunningham 9.

Top Receivers	No	Yds	Avg	Long	TD
Cris Carter	90	1241	13.8	68	13
Randy Moss	80	1413	17.7	67-td	11
Jake Reed	44	643	14.6	50	2
Andrew Glover	28	327	11.7	31	1
Robert Smith	24	166	6.9	34	0
Leroy Hoard	17	166	9.8	29	0

Top Rushers	Car	Yds	Avg	Long	TD
Robert Smith	221	1015	4.6	70-td	2
Leroy Hoard	138	555	4.0	53	10
Moe Williams	24	69	2.9	10	1
Randall Cunningham	10	58	5.8	14	0
Randy Moss	4	43	10.8	15	0

Most Touchdowns	TD	Run	Rec	Ret	Pts
Cris Carter	13	0	13	0	78
Randy Moss	12	0	11	1	72
Leroy Hoard	10	10	0	0	60
Matt Hatchette	2	0	2	0	12
Jake Reed	2	0	2	0	12
Robert Smith	2	2	0	0	12
Moe Williams	2	1	0	1	12

2-Pt. Conversions: (0-3).

Kicking	PAT/Att	FG/Att	Lg	Pts
Gary Anderson	46/46	19/30	44	103

Punts (10 or more)	No	Yds	Long	Avg	In20
Mitch Berger	61	2769	75	45.4	18

Most Interceptions	Most Sacks
Robert Griffith ... 3	John Randle ... 9

New Orleans Saints

Passing (5 Att)

	Att	Cmp	Pct	Yds	TD	Rate
Billy Joe Tolliver	.268	139	51.9	1916	7	58.9
Billy Joe Hobert	.159	85	53.5	970	6	68.9
Jake Delhomme	.76	42	55.3	521	3	62.4
Danny Wuerffel	.48	22	45.8	191	0	30.8

Interceptions: Tolliver 16, Hobert 6, Delhomme 5, Wuerffel 3.

Top Receivers

	No	Yds	Avg	Long	TD
Eddie Kennison	.61	835	13.7	90-td	4
Keith Poole	.42	796	19.0	67-td	6
Andre Hastings	.40	564	14.1	42	1
Ricky Williams*	.28	172	6.1	29	0
Cameron Cleeland	.26	325	12.5	31	1

Top Rushers

	Car	Yds	Avg	Long	TD
Ricky Williams*	.253	884	3.5	25	2
Lamar Smith	.60	250	3.4	24	0
Wilmont Perry	.48	180	3.8	22	0
Billy Joe Tolliver	.26	142	5.5	33	3

Most Touchdowns

	TD	Run	Rec	Ret	Pts
Keith Poole	.6	0	6	0	36
Eddie Kennison	.4	0	4	0	26
Billy Joe Tolliver	.3	3	0	0	18
Jake Delhomme	.2	2	0	0	12
Ricky Williams*	.2	2	0	0	12

2-Pt. Conversions: (3-6) Brett Bech, Cleeland, Kennison.

Kicking

	PAT/Att	FG/Att	Lg	Pts
Doug Brien	20/21	24/29	52	92

Punts (10 or more)

	No	Yds	Long	Avg	In20
Tommy Barnhardt	.82	3262	52	39.8	14

Most Interceptions
Ashley Ambrose 6

Most Sacks
La'Roi Glover 8.5

New York Giants

Passing (5 Att)

	Att	Cmp	Pct	Yds	TD	Rate
Kerry Collins	.332	191	57.5	2316	8	73.3
Kent Graham	.271	160	59.0	1697	9	74.6

Interceptions: Collins 11, Graham 9.

Top Receivers

	No	Yds	Avg	Long	TD
Amani Toomer	.79	1183	15.0	80-td	6
Ike Hilliard	.72	996	13.8	46	3
Tiki Barber	.66	609	9.2	56	2
Pete Mitchell	.58	520	9.0	25	3
Joe Jurevicius	.18	318	17.7	71	1
LeShon Johnson	.12	86	7.2	28	1

Top Rushers

	Car	Yds	Avg	Long	TD
Joe Montgomery*	.115	348	3.0	14	3
Tiki Barber	.62	258	4.2	30	0
Gary Brown	.55	177	3.2	28	0
LeShon Johnson	.61	143	2.3	17	2
Charles Way	.49	141	2.9	17	2

Most Touchdowns

	TD	Run	Rec	Ret	Pts
Amani Toomer	.6	0	6	0	36
Joe Montgomery*	.3	3	0	0	20
Tiki Barber	.3	0	2	1	18
Ike Hilliard	.3	0	3	0	18
LeShon Johnson	.3	2	1	0	18
Pete Mitchell	.3	0	3	0	18

2-Pt. Conversions: (2-3) Collins, Montgomery.

Kicking

	PAT/Att	FG/Att	Lg	Pts
Cary Blanchard	19/19	18/21	48	73
Brad Daluiso	9/9	7/9	36	30

Punts (10 or more)

	No	Yds	Long	Avg	In20
Brad Maynard	.89	3651	63	41.0	31

Most Interceptions
Percy Ellsworth 6

Most Sacks
Jessie Armstead 9

Philadelphia Eagles

Passing (5 Att)

	Att	Cmp	Pct	Yds	TD	Rate
Doug Pederson	.227	119	52.4	1276	7	62.9
Donovan McNabb*	.216	106	49.1	948	8	60.1
Koy Detmer	.29	10	34.5	181	3	62.6

Interceptions: Pederson 9, McNabb 7, Detmer 2.

Top Receivers

	No	Yds	Avg	Long	TD
Torrance Small	.49	655	13.4	84-td	4
Duce Staley	.41	294	7.2	19	2
Charles Johnson	.34	414	12.2	36	1
Luther Broughton	.26	295	11.3	33	4
Na Brown*	.18	188	10.4	27	1

Top Rushers

	Car	Yds	Avg	Long	TD
Duce Staley	.325	1273	3.9	29	4
Donovan McNabb*	.47	313	6.7	27	0
Eric Bieniemy	.12	75	6.3	28	1
Doug Pederson	.20	33	1.7	19	0

Most Touchdowns

	TD	Run	Rec	Ret	Pts
Duce Staley	.6	4	2	0	36
Luther Broughton	.4	0	4	0	24
Torrance Small	.4	0	4	0	24
Chad Lewis	.3	0	3	0	18
Dietrich Jells	.2	0	2	0	12

2-Pt. Conversions: (2-2) McNabb, Jed Weaver.

Kicking

	PAT/Att	FG/Att	Lg	Pts
Norm Johnson	25/25	18/25	49	79
David Akers	2/2	3/6	53	11

Punts (10 or more)

	No	Yds	Long	Avg	In20
Sean Landeta	.107	4524	60	42.3	21

Most Interceptions
Troy Vincent 7

Most Sacks
Mike Mamula 8.5

St. Louis Rams

Passing (5 Att)

	Att	Cmp	Pct	Yds	TD	Rate
Kurt Warner	.499	325	65.1	4353	41	109.2
Joe Germaine*	.16	9	56.3	136	1	65.6
Paul Justin	.14	9	64.3	91	0	82.7

Interceptions: Warner 13, Germaine 2.

Top Receivers

	No	Yds	Avg	Long	TD
Marshall Faulk	.87	1048	12.0	57-td	5
Isaac Bruce	.77	1165	15.1	60	12
Torry Holt*	.52	788	15.2	63-td	6
Az-zahir Hakim	.36	677	18.8	75-td	8
Ricky Proehl	.33	349	10.6	30	0
Roland Williams	.25	226	9.0	24	6

Top Rushers

	Car	Yds	Avg	Long	TD
Marshall Faulk	.253	1381	5.5	58	7
Robert Holcombe	.78	294	3.8	34	4
Justin Watson	.47	179	3.8	21	0
Kurt Warner	.23	92	4.0	22	1

Most Touchdowns

	TD	Run	Rec	Ret	PTS
Isaac Bruce	.12	0	12	0	74
Marshall Faulk	.12	7	5	0	74
Az-zahir Hakim	.9	0	8	1	54
Torry Holt*	.6	0	6	0	36
Roland Williams	.6	0	6	0	36

2-Pt. Conversions: (2-2) Bruce, Faulk.

Kicking

	PAT/Att	FG/Att	Lg	Pts
Jeff Wilkins	64/64	20/28	51	124

Punts (10 or more)

	No	Yds	Long	Avg	In20
Rick Tuten	.32	1359	70	42.5	9
Mike Horan	.26	1048	57	40.3	7

Most Interceptions
Todd Lyght 6

Most Sacks
Kevin Carter 17

San Francisco 49ers

Passing (5 Att)	Att	Cmp	Pct	Yds	TD	Rate
Jeff Garcia	.375	225	60.0	2544	11	77.9
Steve Stenstrom	.100	54	54.0	536	0	52.8
Steve Young	.84	45	53.6	446	3	60.9

Interceptions: Garcia 11, Stenstrom 4, Young 4.

Top Receivers	No	Yds	Avg	Long	TD
Jerry Rice	.67	830	12.4	62	5
Terrell Owens	.60	754	12.6	36	4
Charlie Garner	.56	535	9.6	53	2
J.J. Stokes	.34	429	12.6	47	3
Greg Clark	.34	347	10.2	24	0
Fred Beasley	.32	282	8.8	24	0

Top Rushers	Car	Yds	Avg	Long	TD
Charlie Garner	.241	1229	5.1	53	4
Fred Beasley	.58	276	4.8	44-td	4
Jeff Garcia	.45	231	5.1	25	2
Lawrence Phillips	.30	144	4.8	68-td	2
Terry Jackson*	.15	75	5.0	11	0

Most Touchdowns	TD	Run	Rec	Ret	Pts
Charlie Garner	.6	4	2	0	36
Jerry Rice	.5	0	5	0	30
Fred Beasley	.4	4	0	0	24
Terrell Owens	.4	0	4	0	24
J.J. Stokes	.3	0	3	0	20

2-Pt. Conversions: (1-2) Stokes.

Kicking	PAT/Att	FG/Att	Lg	Pts
Wade Richey	.30/31	21/23	52	93

Punts (10 or more)	No	Yds	Long	Avg	In20
Chad Stanley*	.69	2737	70	39.7	20

Most Interceptions		Most Sacks	
Lance Schulters	.6	Bryant Young	11

Tampa Bay Buccaneers

Passing (5 Att)	Att	Cmp	Pct	Yds	TD	Rate
Trent Dilfer	.244	146	59.8	1619	11	75.8
Shaun King*	.146	89	61.0	875	7	82.4
Eric Zeier	.55	32	58.2	270	0	63.4

Interceptions: Dilfer 11, King 4, Zeier 1.

Top Receivers	No	Yds	Avg	Long	TD
Warrick Dunn	.64	589	9.2	68	2
Jacquez Green	.56	791	14.1	62-td	3
Reidel Anthony	.30	296	9.9	30	1
Mike Alstott	.27	239	8.9	24	2
Dave Moore	.23	276	12.0	35-td	5
Bert Emanuel	.22	238	10.8	39	1
Karl Williams	.21	176	8.4	14	0

Top Rushers	Car	Yds	Avg	Long	TD
Mike Alstott	.242	949	3.9	30	7
Warrick Dunn	.195	616	3.2	33	0
Trent Dilfer	.35	144	4.1	28	0

Most Touchdowns	TD	Run	Rec	Ret	Pts
Mike Alstott	.9	7	2	0	54
Dave Moore	.5	0	5	0	30
Jacquez Green	.3	0	3	0	18
Donnie Abraham	.2	0	0	2	12
Warrick Dunn	.2	0	2	0	12

2-Pt. Conversions: (0-2).

Kicking	PAT/Att	FG/Att	Lg	Pts
Martin Gramatica	.25/25	27/32	53	106

Punts (10 or more)	No	Yds	Long	Avg	In20
Mark Royals	.90	3882	66	43.1	23

Most Interceptions		Most Sacks	
Donnie Abraham	.7	Warren Sapp	12.5

Washington Redskins

Passing (5 Att)	Att	Cmp	Pct	Yds	TD	Rate
Brad Johnson	.519	316	60.9	4005	24	90.0
Rodney Peete	.17	8	47.1	107	2	82.2

Interceptions: Johnson 13, Peete 1.

Top Receivers	No	Yds	Avg	Long	TD
Larry Centers	.69	544	7.9	33-td	3
Michael Westbrook	.65	1191	18.3	65-td	9
Albert Connell	.62	1132	18.3	62-td	7
Brian Mitchell	.31	305	9.8	36	0
Stephen Alexander	.29	324	11.2	27-td	3
Irving Fryar	.26	254	9.8	30-td	2
Stephen Davis	.23	111	4.8	21	0

Top Rushers	Car	Yds	Avg	Long	TD
Stephen Davis	.290	1405	4.8	76-td	17
Skip Hicks	.78	257	3.3	24	3
Brian Mitchell	.40	220	5.5	16	1
Larry Centers	.13	51	3.9	12	0

Most Touchdowns	TD	Run	Rec	Ret	Pts
Stephen Davis	.17	17	0	0	104
Michael Westbrook	.9	0	9	0	56
Albert Connell	.7	0	7	0	42
Three tied at 3 each for 18 pts.					

2-Pt. Conversions: (2-3) Davis, Westbrook.

Kicking	PAT/Att	FG/Att	Lg	Pts
Brett Conway	.49/50	22/32	51	115

Punts (10 or more)	No	Yds	Long	Avg	In20
Matt Turk	.62	2564	57	41.4	16

Most Interceptions		Most Sacks	
Matt Stevens	.6	Dan Wilkinson	8

Overall Club Rankings

Combined AFC and NFC rankings by yards gained on offense and yards given up on defense. Teams are ranked by offense with AFC teams in *italics*.

	Offense			Defense		
	Rush	Pass	Rank	Rush	Pass	Rank
St. Louis	.5	1	**1**	1	20	6
Washington	.9	6	**2**	27	26	30
Minnesota	.14	5	**3**	14	30	27
Indianapolis	.19	4	**4**	18	19	15
Oakland	.3	11	**5**	12	12	10
Carolina	.20	2	**6**	24	23	26
Jacksonville	.1	12	**7**	6	3	4
Chicago	.26	3	**8**	23	29	29
Green Bay	.21	7	**9**	22	18	19
San Francisco	.2	19	**10**	15	31	28
Buffalo	.8	20	**11**	4	1	1
Kansas City	.4	22	**12**	11	16	14
Tennessee	.13	13	**13**	10	25	17
Denver	.12	15	**14**	19	8	7
Cincinnati	.6	23	**15**	16	28	25
Dallas	.7	24	**16**	7	13	9
NY Giants	.24	8	**17**	13	14	13
New England	.23	10	**18**	21	7	8
New Orleans	.18	21	**19**	20	21	20
Miami	.22	14	**20**	8	5	5
Detroit	.28	9	**21**	9	27	18
Pittsburgh	.10	26	**22**	26	4	11
Seattle	.25	16	**23**	25	17	23
Baltimore	.16	25	**24**	2	6	2
NY Jets	.11	28	**25**	17	24	21
San Diego	.27	18	**26**	3	22	12
Atlanta	.30	17	**27**	29	10	16
Tampa Bay	.15	30	**28**	5	2	3
Arizona	.29	27	**29**	30	9	22
Philadelphia	.17	31	**30**	28	15	24
Cleveland	.31	29	**31**	31	11	31

NFL PLAYOFFS

| 1ST ROUND | SEMIFINALS | FINAL | | FINAL | SEMIFINALS | 1ST ROUND |

AFC

†Buffalo 16
†Tennessee 22
Tennessee 19
Indianapolis 16
Tennessee 33

†Miami 20
Seattle 17
Miami 7
Jacksonville 14
Jacksonville 62

†Wild Card Team

St. Louis 23
Tennessee 16

Jan. 30, 2000
Georgia Dome, Atlanta

NFC

Tampa Bay 6
Tampa Bay 14
Washington 13

St. Louis 11
St. Louis 49
Minnesota 37

†Detroit 13
Washington 27

†Dallas 10
†Minnesota 27

†Wild Card Team

Playoff Game Summaries

Team records listed in parentheses indicate records before game.

WILD CARD ROUND

AFC

Titans, 22-16

Buffalo (11-5)	0	0	7	9—	**16**
Tennessee (13-3)	0	12	0	10—	**22**

Date—Jan. 8. **Att**—66,672. **Time**—3:19.

2nd Quarter: TEN—Safety, Rob Johnson tackled by Jevon Kearse in end zone, 3:41; TEN—Steve McNair 1-yd run (Al Del Greco kick), 7:05; TEN—Del Greco 40-yd FG, 15:00.

3rd Quarter: BUF—Antowain Smith 4-yd run (Steve Christie kick), 2:32.

4th Quarter: BUF—Smith 1-yd run (two-pt attempt failed), 3:52; TEN—Del Greco 36-yd FG, 13:12; BUF—Christie 41-yd FG, 14:44; TEN—Kevin Dyson 75-yd kickoff return, lateral from Frank Wycheck (Del Greco kick), 14:57.

Dolphins, 20-17

Miami (9-7)	3	0	10	7—	**20**
Seattle (9-7)	7	3	7	0—	**17**

Date—Jan. 9. **Att**—66,170. **Time**—2:55.

1st Quarter: SEA—Sean Dawkins 9-yd pass from Jon Kitna (Todd Peterson kick), 8:42; MIA—Olindo Mare 32-yd FG, 12:55.

2nd Quarter: SEA—Peterson 50-yd FG, 14:15.

3rd Quarter: MIA—Oronde Gadsden 1-yd pass from Dan Marino (Mare kick), 6:05; SEA—Charlie Rogers 85-yd kickoff return (Peterson kick), 6:23; MIA—Mare 50-yd FG, 12:38.

4th Quarter: MIA—J.J. Johnson 2-yd run (Mare kick), 10:12.

NFC

Redskins, 27-13

Detroit (8-8)	0	0	0	13—	**13**
Washington (10-6)	14	13	0	0—	**27**

Date—Jan. 8. **Att**—79,411. **Time**—3:14.

1st Quarter: WASH—Stephen Davis 1-yd run (Brett Conway kick), 5:51; WASH—Davis 4-yd run (Conway kick), 12:32.

2nd Quarter: WASH—Conway 33-yd FG, 1:10; WASH—Conway 23-yd FG, 5:10; WASH—Albert Connell 30-yd pass from Brad Johnson (Conway kick), 13:41.

4th Quarter: DET—Ron Rice 94-yd return of blocked FG (2-pt attempt failed), 5:37; DET—Ron Rivers 5-yd pass from Gus Frerotte (Jason Hanson kick), 15:00.

Vikings, 27-10

Dallas (8-8)	10	0	0	0—	**10**
Minnesota (10-6)	3	14	3	7—	**27**

Date—Jan. 9. **Att**—64,056. **Time**—3:03.

1st Quarter: DAL—Eddie Murray 18-yd FG, 3:51; MIN—Gary Anderson 47-yd FG, 7:01; DAL—Emmitt Smith 5-yd run (Murray kick), 10:00.

2nd Quarter: MIN—Robert Smith 26-yd pass from Jeff George (Anderson kick), 5:39; MIN—Randy Moss 58-yd pass from George (Anderson kick), 14:32.

3rd Quarter: MIN—Anderson 38-yd FG, 11:50.

4th Quarter: MIN—Cris Carter 5-yd pass from George (Anderson kick), 2:20.

DIVISIONAL SEMIFINALS

● AFC

● Jaguars, 62-7

Miami (10-7) ....0 7 0 0— **7**
Jacksonville (14-2) ....24 17 14 7— **62**
Date—Jan. 15. **Att**—75,173. **Time**—3:23.

1st Quarter: JAX—Jimmy Smith 8-yd pass from Mark Brunell (Mike Hollis kick), 4:28; JAX—Hollis 45-yd FG, 8:41; JAX—Fred Taylor 90-yd run (Hollis kick), 11:14; JAX—Tony Brackens 16-yd fumble return (Hollis kick), 11:39.

2nd Quarter: JAX—Taylor 39-yd pass from Brunell (Hollis kick), 0:12; JAX—James Stewart 25-yd run (Hollis kick), 2:55; JAX—Hollis 28-yd FG, 13:13; MIA—Oronde Gadsden 20-yd pass from Dan Marino (Olindo Mare kick), 14:57.

3rd Quarter: JAX—Smith 70-yd pass from Jay Fiedler (Hollis kick), 2:57; JAX—Alvis Whitted 38-yd pass from Fiedler (Hollis kick), 8:41.

4th Quarter: JAX—Chris Howard 5-yd run (Hollis kick), 4:23.

● Titans, 19-16

Tennessee (14-3) ....0 6 7 6— **19**
Indianapolis (13-3) ....3 6 0 7— **16**
Date—Jan. 16. **Att**—57,097. **Time**—3:20.

1st Quarter: IND—Mike Vanderjagt 40-yd FG, 7:47.

2nd Quarter: TEN—Al Del Greco 49-yd FG, 0:04; IND—Vanderjagt 40-yd FG, 9:22; TEN—Del Greco 37-yd FG, 11:45; IND—Vanderjagt 34-yd FG, 14:59.

3rd Quarter: TEN—Eddie George 68-yd run (Del Greco kick), 1:41.

4th Quarter: TEN—Del Greco 25-yd FG, 2:03; TEN—Del Greco 43-yd FG, 10:41; IND—Peyton Manning 15-yd run (Vanderjagt kick), 13:09.

● NFC

● Buccaneers, 14-13

Washington (11-6) ....0 3 10 0— **13**
Tampa Bay (11-5) ....0 0 7 7— **14**
Date—Jan. 15. **Att**—65,835. **Time**—3:01.

2nd Quarter: WASH—Brett Conway 28-yd FG, 9:23.

3rd Quarter: WASH—Brian Mitchell 100-yd kickoff return (Conway kick), 0:19; WASH—Conway 48-yd FG, 6:50; TB—Mike Alstott 2-yd run (Martin Gramatica kick), 12:57.

4th Quarter: TB—John Davis 1-yd pass from Shaun King (Gramatica kick), 7:31.

● Rams, 49-37

Minnesota (11-6) ....3 14 0 20— **37**
St. Louis (13-3) ....14 0 21 14— **49**
Date—Jan. 16. **Att**—66,194. **Time**—3:34.

1st Quarter: MIN—Gary Anderson 31-yd FG, 5:37; ST.L—Isaac Bruce 77-yd pass from Kurt Warner (Jeff Wilkins kick), 5:58; ST.L—Marshall Faulk 41-yd pass from Warner (Wilkins kick), 10:41.

2nd Quarter: MIN—Cris Carter 22-yd pass from Jeff George (Anderson kick), 5:07; MIN—Leroy Hoard 4-yd run (Anderson kick), 12:20.

3rd Quarter: ST.L—Tony Horne 95-yd kickoff return (Wilkins kick), 0:18; ST.L—Faulk 1-yd run (Wilkins kick), 6:32; ST.L—Jeff Robinson 13-yd pass from Warner (Wilkins kick), 14:38.

4th Quarter: ST.L—Ryan Tucker 1-yd pass from Warner (Wilkins kick), 1:24; ST.L—Roland Williams 2-yd pass from Warner (Wilkins kick), 6:47; MIN—Jake Reed 4-yd pass from George (Hoard, run), 10:04; MIN—Randy Moss 44-yd pass from George (2-pt attempt failed), 11:12; MIN—Moss 2-yd pass from George (2-pt attempt failed), 14:29.

CONFERENCE CHAMPIONSHIPS

● AFC

● Titans, 33-14

Tennessee (15-3) ....7 3 16 7— **33**
Jacksonville (15-2) ....7 7 0 0— **14**
Date—Jan. 23. **Att**—75,206. **Time**—2:59.

1st Quarter: JAX—Kyle Brady 7-yd pass from Mark Brunell (Mike Hollis kick), 3:40; TEN—Yancey Thigpen 9-yd pass from Steve McNair (Al Del Greco kick), 9:30.

2nd Quarter: JAX—James Stewart 33-yd run (Hollis kick), 10:24; TEN—Del Greco 34-yd FG, 14:40.

3rd Quarter: TEN—McNair 1-yd run (Del Greco kick), 5:36; TEN—Safety, Brunell tackled by Josh Evans in end zone, 9:47; TEN—Derrick Mason 80-yd kickoff return (Del Greco kick), 10:04.

4th Quarter: TEN—McNair 1-yd run (Del Greco kick), 8:01.

● NFC

● Rams, 11-6

Tampa Bay (12-5) ....3 0 3 0— **6**
St. Louis (14-3) ....3 2 0 6— **11**
Date—Jan. 23. **Att**—66,396. **Time**—3:07.

1st Quarter: TB—Martin Gramatica 25-yd FG, 2:38; ST.L—Jeff Wilkins 24-yd FG, 10:43

2nd Quarter: ST.L—Safety, Snap went over QB Shaun King's head and out of the end zone, 0:05.

3rd Quarter: TB—Gramatica 23-yd FG, 4:32.

4th Quarter: ST.L—Ricky Proehl 30-yd pass from Kurt Warner (2-pt attempt failed), 10:16.

Super Bowl XXXIV

Sunday, Jan. 30, 2000 at the Georgia Dome, Atlanta, Ga.

St. Louis (15-3) 3   6   7   7— **23**
Tennessee (16-3) 0   0   6 10— **16**

1st: ST.L—Jeff Wilkins 27-yd FG, 12:00. Drive: 54 yards in 6 plays. Key play: Torry Holt 32-yd pass from Kurt Warner to TEN 42.

2nd: ST.L—Wilkins 29-yd FG, 10:44. Drive: 73 yards in 11 plays. Key play: Holt 15-yd pass from Warner to TEN 16. **ST.L**—Wilkins 28-yd FG, 14:45. Drive: 67 yards in 13 plays. Key play: Az-zahir Hakim 17-yd pass from Warner to TEN 21.

3rd: ST.L—Holt 9-yd pass from Warner (Wilkins kick), 7:40. Drive: 68 yards in 8 plays. Key play: Isaac Bruce 31-yd pass from Warner to TEN 27. **TEN**—Eddie George 1-yd run (2-pt attempt failed), 14:46. Drive: 66 yards in 12 plays. Key play: Steve McNair 23-yd run to ST.L 2.

4th: TEN—George 2-yd run (Al Del Greco kick), 7:39. Drive: 79 yards in 13 plays. Key play: McNair 2-yd run on 4th-and-1 to TEN 45. **TEN**—Del Greco 43-yd FG, 12:48. Drive: 28 yards in 8 plays. Key play: Jackie Harris 6-yd pass from McNair to ST.L 28 and then Isaac Byrd's recovery of Harris' fumble on the same play. **ST.L**—Bruce 73-yd pass from Warner (Wilkins kick), 13:06. Drive: 73 yards in 1 play.

Favorite: Rams by 7   **Attendance:** 72,625
Field: Artificial Turf   **Time:** 3:28
Start time: 6:18 EST   **TV Rating:** 43.2/62 share (ABC)
MVP—Kurt Warner, St. Louis QB (24-45 for 414 yds, 2 TD, 0 INT)

Officials: Bob McElwee (referee); Ron Botchan (umpire); Byron Boston (LJ); Tom Fincken (SJ); Earnie Frantz (HL); Bill Leavy (BJ); Al Jury (FJ).

Team Statistics

	Rams	Titans
Touchdowns	2	2
Rushing	0	2
Passing	2	0
Returns	0	0
Field Goals made/attempted	3/4	1/3
Time of possession	23:34	36:26
First downs	23	27
Rushing	1	12
Passing	18	13
Penalty	4	2
3rd down efficiency	5/12	6/13
4th down efficiency	0/1	1/1
Total offense (net yards)	436	367
Plays	59	73
Average gain	7.4	5.0
Carries/yards	13/29	36/159
Yards per carry	2.2	4.4
Passing yards	414	214
Completions/attempts	24/45	22/36
Yards per pass	9.2	5.9
Times intercepted	0	0
Times sacked/yards lost	1/7	1/6
Return yardage	63	121
Punt returns/yards	2/8	1/-1
Kickoff returns/yards	4/55	5/122
Interceptions/yards	0/0	0/0
Fumbles/lost	2/0	1/0
Penalties/yards	8/60	7/45
Punts/average	2/38.5	3/43.0

Individual Statistics

St. Louis Rams

Passing	Att	Cmp	Pct.	Yds	TD	Int
Kurt Warner	45	24	53.3	414	2	0

Receiving	No	Yds	Avg	Long	TD
Torry Holt	7	109	15.6	32	1
Isaac Bruce	6	162	27.0	73-td	1
Marshall Faulk	5	90	18.0	52	0
Az-zahir Hakim	1	17	17.0	17	0
Ernie Conwell	1	16	16.0	16	0
Ricky Proehl	1	11	11.0	11	0
Roland Williams	1	9	9.0	9	0
Robert Holcombe	1	1	1.0	1	0
Fred Miller	1	-1	-1.0	-1	0
TOTAL	24	414	17.3	73-td	0

Rushing	Car	Yds	Avg	Long	TD
Marshall Faulk	10	17	1.7	4	0
Robert Holcombe	1	11	11.0	11	0
Kurt Warner	1	1	1.0	1	0
Mike Horan	1	0	0.0	0	0
TOTAL	13	29	2.2	11	0

Field Goals	20-29	30-39	40-49	50-59	Total
Jeff Wilkins	3-3	0-1	0-0	0-0	3-4

Punting	No	Yds	Avg	Long	In 20	TB
Mike Horan	2	77	38.5	47	0	0

Punt Returns	Ret	Yds	Long	Avg	FC	TD
Az-zahir Hakim	2	8	10	4.0	0	0

Kickoff Returns	Ret	Yds	Long	Avg	FC	TD
Tony Horne	4	55	25	13.8	0	0

Interceptions	No	Yds	Long	Avg	TD
none

Sacks
Kevin Carter 1

Most Tackles
Billy Jenkins 12

Tennessee Titans

Passing	Att	Cmp	Pct.	Yds	TD	Int
Steve McNair	36	22	61.1	214	0	0

Receiving	No	Yds	Avg	Long	TD
Jackie Harris	7	64	9.1	21	0
Frank Wycheck	5	35	7.0	13	0
Kevin Dyson	4	41	10.3	16	0
Eddie George	2	35	17.5	32	0
Isaac Byrd	2	21	10.5	21	0
Derrick Mason	2	18	9.0	9	0
TOTAL	22	214	9.7	32	0

Rushing	Car	Yds	Avg	Long	TD
Eddie George	28	95	3.4	13	2
Steve McNair	8	64	8.0	23	0
TOTAL	36	159	4.4	23	2

Field Goals	20-29	30-39	40-49	50-59	Total
Al Del Greco	0-0	0-0	1-3	0-0	1-3

Punting	No	Yds	Avg	Long	In 20	TB
Craig Hentrich	3	129	43.0	49	1	0

Punt Returns	Ret	Yds	Long	Avg	FC	TD
Derrick Mason	1	-1	-1	-1.0	0	0

Kickoff Returns	No	Yds	Long	Avg	FC	TD
Derrick Mason	5	122	35	24.4	0	0

Interceptions	No	Yds	Long	Avg	TD
none

Sacks
Jason Fisk 1

Most Tackles
Blaine Bishop 5
Anthony Dorsett 5

Super Bowl Finalists' Playoff Statistics

St. Louis Rams (3-0)

Passing	Att	Cmp	Pct.	Yds	TD	Rating
Kurt Warner........121	77	63.6	1063	8	100.0

Interceptions: Warner 4.

Top Receivers	No	Yds	Avg	Long	TD
Torry Holt.................20	242	12.1	32	1
Isaac Bruce 13	317	24.4	77-td	2
Marshall Faulk..............13	175	13.5	52	1
Ricky Proehl................8	121	15.1	30-td	1
Az-zahir Hakim 8	93	11.6	20	0
Roland Williams 4	51	12.8	22	1
Robert Holcombe............4	18	4.5	12	0

Top Rushers	Car	Yds	Avg	Long	TD
Marshall Faulk..............38	82	2.2	11	1
Robert Holcombe...........3	15	5.0	11	0
Az-zahir Hakim 2	10	5.0	6	0
Kurt Warner 6	2	0.3	4	0

Touchdowns	TD	Run	Rec	Ret	Pts
Isaac Bruce..................2	0	2	0	12
Marshall Faulk 2	1	1	0	12
Jeff Robinson 1	0	1	0	6
Ricky Proehl.................1	0	1	0	6
Tony Horne..................1	0	0	1	6
Roland Williams 1	0	1	0	6
Ryan Tucker.................1	0	1	0	6
Torry Holt 1	0	1	0	6

Kicking	PAT/Att	FG/Att	Lg	Pts
Jeff Wilkins 9/9	4/7	29	21

Punts	No	Yds	Avg	Long	In20
Mike Horan 9	368	40.9	48	1

Interceptions		Sacks	
Todd Lyght..............1		Kevin Carter............3
Dexter McCleon.........1		Charlie Clemons 2
Dre' Bly................1		Five tied with 1 each.

Tennessee (3-1)

Passing	Att	Cmp	Pct.	Yds	TD	Rate
Steve McNair 107	62	57.9	514	1	65.7

Interceptions: McNair 2.

Top Receivers	No	Yds	Avg	Long	TD
Jackie Harris 14	117	8.4	21	0
Frank Wycheck.............14	92	6.6	14	0
Eddie George 10	72	7.2	32	0
Kevin Dyson.................8	82	10.3	16	0
Yancey Thigpen 6	43	7.2	9-td	0
Isaac Byrd...................4	40	10.0	21	0
Chris Sanders................3	49	16.3	26	0
Derrick Mason...............2	18	9.0	9	0
Lorenzo Neal................1	1	1.0	1	0

Top Rushers	Car	Yds	Avg	Long	TD
Eddie George 108	449	4.2	68-td	3
Steve McNair 30	209	7.0	51	3
Rodney Thomas 4	14	3.5	13	0

Touchdowns	TD	Run	Rec	Ret	Pts
Steve McNair 3	3	0	0	18
Eddie George 3	3	0	0	18
Yancey Thigpen 1	0	1	0	6
Derrick Mason...............1	0	0	1	6
Kevin Dyson.................1	0	0	1	6

Kicking	PAT/Att	FG/Att	Lg	Pts
Al Del Greco.....................8/8	8/11	49	32

Punts	No	Yds	Avg	Long	In20
Craig Hentrich.............20	877	43.9	57	7

Interceptions		Sacks	
Donald Mitchell 1		Jason Fisk 2.5
Marcus Robertson 1		Jevon Kearse 2
		Kenny Holmes 2
		Josh Evans............1.5
		Two tied with 1 each.

Rams' 1999 Schedule

Date	Regular Season (13-3)	Result	W-L
Sept. 12	Baltimore (0-0)	W, 27-10	1-0
Sept. 19	OPEN DATE	—	—
Sept. 26	Atlanta (0-2)	W, 35-7	2-0
Oct. 3	at Cincinnati (0-3)	W, 38-10	3-0
Oct. 10	San Francisco (3-1)	W, 42-20	4-0
Oct. 17	at Atlanta (1-4)	W, 41-13	5-0
Oct. 24	Cleveland (0-6)	W, 34-3	6-0
Oct. 31	at Tennessee (5-1)	L, 21-24	6-1
Nov. 7	at Detroit (5-2)	L, 27-31	6-2
Nov. 14	Carolina (3-5)	W, 35-10	7-2
Nov. 21	at San Francisco (3-6)	W, 23-7	8-2
Nov. 28	New Orleans (2-8)	W, 43-12	9-2
Dec. 5	at Carolina (5-6)	W, 34-21	10-2
Dec. 12	at New Orleans (2-10)	W, 30-14	11-2
Dec. 19	NY Giants (7-6)	W, 31-10	12-2
Dec. 26	Chicago (6-8)	W, 34-12	13-2
Jan. 2	at Philadelphia (4-11)	L, 31-38	13-3

Date	Playoffs (3-0)	Result	W-L
Jan. 9	Bye	—	—
Jan. 16	Minnesota (11-6)	W, 49-37	14-3
Jan. 23	Tampa Bay (12-5)	W, 11-6	15-3
Jan. 30	Tennessee (16-3)	W, 23-16	16-3

Titans' 1999 Schedule

Date	Regular Season (13-3)	Results	W-L
Sept. 12	Cincinnati (0-0)	W, 36-35	1-0
Sept. 19	Cleveland (0-1)	W, 26-9	2-0
Sept. 26	at Jacksonville (2-0)	W, 20-19	3-0
Oct. 3	at San Francisco (2-1)	L, 22-24	3-1
Oct. 10	Baltimore (2-2)	W, 14-11	4-1
Oct. 17	at New Orleans (1-3)	W, 24-21	5-1
Oct. 24	OPEN DATE	—	—
Oct. 31	St. Louis (5-1)	W, 24-21	6-1
Nov. 7	at Miami (6-1)	L, 0-17	6-2
Nov. 14	at Cincinnati (1-8)	W, 24-14	7-2
Nov. 21	Pittsburgh (5-4)	W, 16-10	8-2
Nov. 28	at Cleveland (2-9)	W, 33-21	9-2
Dec. 5	at Baltimore (4-7)	L, 14-41	9-3
Dec. 9*	Oakland (6-6)	W, 21-14	10-3
Dec. 19	Atlanta (3-10)	W, 30-17	11-3
Dec. 26	Jacksonville (13-1)	W, 41-14	12-3
Jan. 2	at Pittsburgh (6-9)	W, 47-36	13-3

Date	Playoffs (3-1)	Result	W-L
Jan. 8†	Buffalo (11-5)	W, 22-16	14-3
Jan. 16	at Indianapolis (13-3)	W, 19-16	15-3
Jan. 23	at Jacksonville (15-2)	W, 33-14	16-3
Jan. 30	St. Louis (15-3)	L, 16-23	16-4

*Thursday; †Saturday.

NFL Pro Bowl

50th NFL Pro Bowl Game and 30th AFC-NFC contest (NFC leads series, 16-14). **Date:** Feb. 6, 2000 at Aloha Stadium in Honolulu. **Coaches:** Tom Coughlin, Jax. (AFC) and Tony Dungy, TB (NFC). **Most Valuable Player:** WR Randy Moss, Min. with 9 catches for 212 yards and 1 TD.

AFC	7	14	0	10—	**31**
NFC	10	17	10	14—	**51**

1st: NFC—Aeneas Williams 62-yd interception return (Jason Hanson kick), 2:46; NFC—Hanson 21-yd FG, 10:36; AFC—Jimmy Smith 5-yd pass from Mark Brunell (Olindo Mare kick), 14:30.

2nd: NFC—Mike Alstott 1-yd run (Hanson kick), 2:03; AFC—Tony Gonzalez 10-yd pass from Rich Gannon (Mare kick), 4:55; NFC—Alstott 3-yd run (Hanson kick), 10:15; AFC—Smith 21-yd pass from Peyton Manning (Mare kick), 14:40; NFC—Hanson 51-yd FG, 15:00.

3rd: NFC—Alstott 1-yd run (Hanson kick), 7:52; NFC—Hanson 23-yd FG, 12:57.

4th: AFC—Mare 33-yd FG, 0:11; NFC—Derrick Brooks 20-yd interception return (Hanson kick), 3:48; AFC—Smith 52-yd pass from Manning (Mare kick), 8:30; NFC—Randy Moss 25-yd pass from Steve Beuerlein (Hanson kick), 13:55.

Attendance— 50,112. **TV Rating**— 8.6/15 share (ABC). **Time**— 3:16.

STARTING LINEUPS

As voted on by NFL players and coaches.

American Conference

Pos	Offense	Pos	Defense
WR	Marvin Harrison, Ind.	E	Tony Brackens, Jax.
WR	Jimmy Smith, Jax.	E	Jevon Kearse, Ten.
TE	Tony Gonzalez, KC	T	Trevor Pryce, Den.
T	Tony Boselli*, Jax.	T	Darrell Russell, Oak.
T	Jonathan Ogden, Bal.	LB	Peter Boulware, Bal.
G	Ruben Brown, Buf.	LB	Kevin Hardy, Jax.
G	Bruce Matthews, Ten.	LB	Ray Lewis*, Bal.
C	Tom Nalen*, Den.	CB	Sam Madison, Mia.
QB	Peyton Manning, Ind.	CB	Charles Woodson, Oak.
RB	Edgerrin James, Ind.	SS	Lawyer Milloy, NE
FB	Sam Gash, Buf.	FS	Carnell Lake, Jax.
K	Olindo Mare, Mia.	P	Tom Tupa, NYJ
KR	Tremain Mack, Cin.	ST	Detron Smith, Den.

* injured and unable to play.

National Conference

Pos	Offense	Pos	Defense
WR	Isaac Bruce, St.L	E	Kevin Carter, St.L
WR	Cris Carter, Min	E	Michael Strahan, NYG
TE	Wesley Walls, Car.	T	Luther Elliss, Det.
T	Orlando Pace, St.L	T	Warren Sapp, TB
T	William Roaf, NO	LB	Jessie Armstead, NYG
G	Larry Allen*, Dal.	LB	Derrick Brooks, TB
G	Randall McDaniel, Min.	LB	Hardy Nickerson, TB
C	Jeff Christy, Min.	CB	Todd Lyght, St.L
QB	Kurt Warner, St.L	CB	Deion Sanders*, Dal.
RB	Marshall Faulk, St.L	SS	John Lynch, TB
FB	Mike Alstott, TB	FS	Lance Schulters, SF
K	Jason Hanson, Det.	P	Mitch Berger, Min.
KR	Glyn Milburn, Chi.	ST	Michael Bates, Car.

* injured and unable to play.

Reserves

Offense: WR—Tim Brown, Oak. and Keyshawn Johnson, NYJ; **TE**—Frank Wycheck, Ten.; **T**—Leon Searcy, Jax.; **G**—Will Shields, KC; **C**—Kevin Mawae, NYJ.; **QB**—Mark Brunell, Jax. and Rich Gannon, Oak.; **RB**—Corey Dillon, Cin. and Eddie George, Ten.

Defense: E—Michael McCrary, Bal.; **T**—Cortez Kennedy, Sea.; **LB**—Chad Brown, Sea. and Zach Thomas, Mia.; **CB**—James Hasty, KC; **FS**—Rod Woodson, Bal.

Replacements: OFFENSE—WR Terry Glenn, NE for Brown; Walter Jones, Sea. for Boselli; C Tim Grunhard, KC for Nalen. DEFENSE—LB Junior Seau, SD for Lewis. NEED PLAYER—LB Mo Lewis, NYJ.

Reserves

Offense: WR—Randy Moss, Min. and Mushin Muhammad, Car.; **TE**—David Sloan, Det.; **T**— Erik Williams, Dal.; **G**—Tré Johnson, Wash.; **C**— Tony Mayberry, TB; **QB**—Steve Beuerlein, Car. and Brad Johnson, Wash.; **RB**—Stephen Davis, Wash. and Emmitt Smith, Dal.

Defense: E—Robert Porcher, Det.; **T**—D'Marco Farr, St.L; **LB**—Dexter Coakley, Dal. and Stephen Boyd, Det.; **CB**—Aeneas Williams, Ari.; **S**—Brian Dawkins, Phi.

Replacements: OFFENSE—G Adam Timmerman, St.L for Allen. DEFENSE—CB Troy Vincent, Phi. for Sanders. NEED PLAYER—E Simeon Rice, Ari.

Annual Awards

The NFL does not sanction any of the major postseason awards for players and coaches, but many are given out. Among the presenters for the 1999 regular season were AP, The Maxwell Football Club of Philadelphia (Bert Bell Award), *The Sporting News* and the Pro Football Writers of America/*Pro Football Weekly*.

Most Valuable Player

Kurt Warner, St. Louis, QB ....AP, Bell, *TSN*, PFWA

Offensive Players of the Year

Marshall Faulk, St. Louis, RB ....AP
Kurt Warner, St. Louis, QB.............................PFWA

Defensive Player of the Year

Warren Sapp, Tampa Bay, DT ....AP, PFWA

Rookies of the Year

NFL	Edgerrin James, Indianapolis, RB	............*TSN*
Offense	Edgerrin James, Indianapolis, RB	......AP, PFWA
Defense	Jevon Kearse, Tennessee, DE	.........AP, PFWA

Coach of the Year

Dick Vermeil, St. Louis ....AP, Bell, *TSN*, PFWA

1999 All-NFL Team

The 1999 All-NFL team combining the All-Pro selections of the Associated Press, *The Sporting News (TSN)* and the Pro Football Writers of America/*Pro Football Weekly* (PFWA). Holdovers from the 1998 All-NFL Team in **bold** type.

Offense

Pos		Selectors
WR—	Marvin Harrison, Indianapolis	AP, PFWA, *TSN*
WR—	Cris Carter, Minnesota	AP, PFWA
WR—	Isaac Bruce, St. Louis	*TSN*
TE—	Tony Gonzalez, Kansas City	AP, PFWA, *TSN*
T—	**Tony Boselli**, Jacksonville	AP, PFWA, *TSN*
T—	Orlando Pace, St. Louis	AP, PFWA, *TSN*
G—	**Larry Allen**, Dallas	AP, PFWA, *TSN*
G—	**Bruce Matthews**, Tennessee	AP, PFWA
G—	Will Shields, Kansas City	*TSN*
C—	Kevin Mawae, NY Jets	AP, *TSN*
C—	Tom Nalen, Denver	*TSN*
C—	Jeff Christy, Minnesota	PFWA
QB—	Kurt Warner, St. Louis	AP, PFWA, *TSN*
RB—	Marshall Faulk, St. Louis	AP, PFWA, *TSN*
RB—	Edgerrin James, Indianapolis	AP, PFWA, *TSN*
FB—	**Mike Alstott**, Tampa Bay	AP

Defense

Pos		Selectors
DE—	Jevon Kearse, Tennessee	AP, PFWA, *TSN*
DE—	Kevin Carter, St. Louis	AP, PFWA, *TSN*
DT—	Warren Sapp, Tampa Bay	AP, PFWA, *TSN*
DT—	**Darrell Russell**, Oakland	PFWA, *TSN*
DT—	Trevor Pryce, Denver	AP
LB—	Derrick Brooks, Tampa Bay	AP, PFWA, *TSN*
LB—	Kevin Hardy, Jacksonville	AP, PFWA, *TSN*
LB—	Ray Lewis, Baltimore	AP, PFWA, *TSN*
LB—	Zach Thomas, Miami	AP
CB—	Sam Madison, Miami	AP, PFWA, *TSN*
CB—	Charles Woodson, Oakland	AP, PFWA
CB—	**Deion Sanders**, Dallas	*TSN*
S—	John Lynch, Tampa Bay	AP, PFWA, *TSN*
S—	Lawyer Milloy, New England	AP, *TSN*
S—	Carnell Lake, Jacksonville	PFWA

Specialists

Pos		Selectors
PK—	Olindo Mare, Miami	AP, PFWA, *TSN*
P—	Mitch Berger, Minnesota	PFWA, *TSN*
P—	Tom Tupa, NY Jets	AP
KR—	Glyn Milburn, Chicago	AP, *TSN*

Pos		Selectors
KR—	Tony Horne, St. Louis	PFWA, *TSN*
PR—	Charlie Rogers, Seattle	PFWA
ST—	Michael Bates, Carolina	PFWA

2000 College Draft

First and second round selections at the 65th annual NFL College Draft held April 15-16, 2000, in New York City. Thirteen underclassmen were among the first 62 players chosen and are listed in capital LETTERS.

First Round

No	Team		Pos
1	Cleveland	Courtney Brown, Penn St.	DE
2	Washington	LAVAR ARRINGTON, Penn St.	LB
3	Washington	Chris Samuels, Alabama	OT
4	Cincinnati	Peter Warrick, Florida St.	WR
5	Baltimore	JAMAL LEWIS, Tennessee	RB
6	Philadelphia	Corey Simon, Florida St.	DT
7	Arizona	Thomas Jones, Virginia	RB
8	Pittsburgh	PLAXICO BURRESS, Michigan St.	WR
9	Chicago	Brian Urlacher, New Mexico	LB
10	Baltimore	TRAVIS TAYLOR, Florida	WR
11	NY Giants	Ron Dayne, Wisconsin	RB
12	NY Jets	SHAUN ELLIS, Tennessee	DE
13	NY Jets	John Abraham, South Carolina	LB
14	Green Bay	BUBBA FRANKS, Miami-FL	TE
15	Denver	Deltha O'Neal, California	CB
16	San Francisco	Julian Peterson, Michigan St.	LB
17	Oakland	SEBASTIAN JANIKOWSKI, Florida St.	K
18	NY Jets	Chad Pennington, Marshall	QB
19	Seattle	Shaun Alexander, Alabama	RB
20	Detroit	Stockar McDougle, Oklahoma	OT
21	Kansas City	Sylvester Morris, Jackson St.	WR
22	Seattle	Chris McIntosh, Wisconsin	OT
23	Carolina	Rashard Anderson, Jackson St.	CB
24	San Francisco	Ahmed Plummer, Ohio St.	CB
25	Minnesota	Chris Hovan, Boston College	DT
26	Buffalo	Erik Flowers, Arizona St.	DE
27	NY Jets	Anthony Becht, West Virginia	TE
28	Indianapolis	Rob Morris, BYU	LB
29	Jacksonville	R. Jay Soward, USC	WR
30	Tennessee	Keith Bulluck, Syracuse	LB
31	St. Louis	Trung Canidate, Arizona	RB

Second Round

No	Team		Pos
32	Cleveland	Dennis Northcutt, Arizona	WR
33	New Orleans	Darren Howard, Kansas St.	DE
34	Cincinnati	Mark Roman, LSU	S
35	San Francisco	John Engelberger, Virginia Tech	DE
36	Philadelphia	Todd Pinkston, Southern Miss.	WR
37	Atlanta	Travis Claridge, USC	G
38	Pittsburgh	MARVEL SMITH, Arizona St.	OT
39	Chicago	Mike Brown, Nebraska	S
40	Denver	Ian Gold, Michigan	LB
41	Arizona	RAYNOCH THOMPSON, Tennessee	LB
42	NY Giants	Cornelius Griffin, Alabama	DT
43	San Diego	Rogers Beckett, Marshall	S
44	Green Bay	Chad Clifton, Tennessee	G
45	Denver	Kenoy Kennedy, Arkansas	S
46	New England	Adrian Klemm, Hawaii	OT
47	Oakland	Jerry Porter, West Virginia	WR
48	San Francisco	Jason Webster, Texas A&M	CB
49	Dallas	Dwayne Goodrich, Tennessee	CB
50	Detroit	Barrett Green, West Virginia	LB
51	Tampa Bay	COSEY COLEMAN, Tennessee	G
52	Seattle	IKE CHARLTON, Virginia Tech	CB
53	Miami	Todd Wade, Mississippi	OT
54	Kansas City	William Bartee, Oklahoma	CB
55	Minnesota	Fred Robbins, Wake Forest	DT
56	Minnesota	Mike Boireau, Miami-FL	DE
57	Carolina	DEON GRANT, Tennessee	S
58	Buffalo	Travares Tillman, Georgia Tech	S
59	Indianapolis	Marcus Washington, Auburn	LB
60	Jacksonville	Brad Meester, Northern Iowa	C
61	Philadelphia	Bobby Williams, Arkansas	OT
62	St. Louis	JACOBY SHEPHERD, Oklahoma St.	CB

Canadian Football League
Final 1999 Standings
Division champions (*) and playoff qualifiers (†) are noted.

East Division

	W	L	T	Pts	PF	PA
*Montreal	12	6	0	24	495	385
†Hamilton	11	7	0	22	603	368
†Toronto	9	9	0	18	386	373
Winnipeg	6	12	0	12	360	601

West Division

	W	L	T	Pts	PF	PA
*Brit. Columbia	13	5	0	26	429	373
†Calgary	12	6	0	24	493	393
†Edmonton	6	12	0	12	483	502
Saskatchewan	3	15	0	6	370	592

Playoffs
Division Semifinals (Nov. 14)
East: at Hamilton 27 ....Toronto 6
West: at Calgary 30 ....Edmonton 17

Division Finals (Nov. 21)
East: Hamilton 27 ....at Montreal 26
West: Calgary 26 ....at B.C. 24

87th Grey Cup Championship
November 28, 1999 at B.C. Place in Vancouver, British Columbia

(Att: 45,118)

Hamilton	10	11	4	7	—	32
Calgary	0	0	14	7	—	21

MVP: Danny McManus, Hamilton, QB (22-34 for 347 yds, 2 TDs)

Regular Season Individual Leaders
Passing Efficiency

	Att	Cmp	Cmp Pct	Yds	Yds/ Att	TD	TD Pct	Int	Int Pct	Rating
Anthony Calvillo, Mon	249	166	66.7	2592	10.4	13	5.2	6	2.4	108.3
Tracy Ham, Mon	214	128	59.8	1931	9.0	11	5.1	3	1.4	100.6
Dave Dickenson, Calg	343	219	63.8	3048	8.9	16	4.7	11	3.2	94.6
Danny McManus, Ham	611	364	59.6	5318	8.7	28	4.6	16	2.6	92.4
Damon Allen, B.C.	521	315	60.5	4219	8.1	22	4.2	13	2.5	89.8

Scoring

Touchdowns

	TD	Rus	Rec	Ret	Pts
Ronald Williams, Ham	15	14	1	0	90
Mike Pringle, Mon	14	13	1	0	84
Curtis Mayfield, Sask	12	0	9	3	72
Terry Vaughn, Edm	11	0	11	0	66
Deland McCullough, Win	11	11	0	0	66
Kelvin Anderson, Calg	11	8	3	0	66
Robert Drummond, B.C.	11	8	3	0	66

Kicking

	PAT	FG	S*	Pts
Paul Osbaldiston, Ham	63/63	43/53	11	203
Mark McLoughlin, Calg	44/44	48/59	4	192
Terry Baker, Mon	51/51	40/52	17	188
Dan Giancola, Tor	28/28	48/61	9	181
Lui Passaglia, B.C.	39/40	30/47	14	143
*Singles (or Rouges)				

Rushing

	Car	Yards	Avg	TD
Mike Pringle, Mon	322	1656	5.1	13
Robert Drummond, B.C.	257	1309	5.1	8
Kelvin Anderson, Calg	262	1306	5.0	8
Ronald Williams, Ham	207	1025	5.0	14
Troy Mills, Edm	172	1022	5.9	6

Receptions

	No	Yards	Avg	TD
Allen Pitts, Calg	97	1449	14.9	10
Darren Flutie, Ham	84	1155	13.8	7
Terry Vaughn, Edm	75	1057	14.1	11
Milt Stegall, Win	73	1193	16.3	6
Vince Danielsen, Calg	71	923	13.0	7

All-CFL Team

Offense
- WR Travis Moore, Calg.
- WR Ben Cahoon, Mon.
- T Rocco Romano, Calg.
- T Uzooma Okeke, Mon.
- G Pierre Vercheval, Mon.
- G Leo Groenewegen, Edm.
- G Jamie Taras, B.C.
- QB Danny McManus, Ham.
- RB Kelvin Anderson, Calg.
- RB Mike Pringle, Mon.
- SB Allen Pitts, Calg.
- SB Darren Flutie, Ham.

Defense
- E Joe Montford, Ham.
- E Daved Benefield, B.C.
- T Johnny Scott, B.C.
- T Demetrious Maxie, Tor.
- LB Calvin Tiggle, Ham.
- LB Maurice Kelly, B.C.
- LB Mike O'Shea, Tor.
- DB Adrion Smith, Tor.
- DB Barron Miles, Mon.
- DB William Hampton, Calg.
- DB Gerald Vaughn, Ham.
- S Rob Hitchcock, Ham.

Specialists
K—Mark McLoughlin, Calg.
P/K—Noel Prefontaine, Tor.
Special Teams—Jimmy Cunningham, B.C.

Most Outstanding Awards

Player ....Danny McManus, Hamilton, QB
Canadian ....Mike O'Shea, Toronto, LB
Offensive Lineman ....Uzooma Okeke, Montreal, T
Defensive Player ....Calvin Tiggle, Hamilton, LB
Rookie ....Paul Lacoste, B.C., LB
Tom Pate Award (Sportsmanship) ..Jamie Taras, B.C., G
Coach ....Charlie Taaffe, Montreal

NFL Europe

Final 2000 Standings

	W	L	T	Pct.	PF	PA
*Rhein	7	3	0	.700	279	209
*Scotland	6	4	0	.600	273	165
Barcelona	5	5	0	.500	194	212
Amsterdam	4	6	0	.400	206	243
Frankfurt	4	6	0	.400	206	269
Berlin	4	6	0	.400	189	249

*World Bowl participants

Note: The teams with the top two records after the regular season advance directly to the World Bowl.

World Bowl 2000

June 25, 2000 at Waldstadion in Frankfurt, Germany
(Att: 35,860)

Scotland (6-4)	7	3	0	0	—	10
Rhein (7-3)	3	3	0	7	—	13

MVP: Aaron Stecker, Scotland, RB (13 rushes for 92 yards, including a record 36-yd TD run.)

Regular Season Individual Leaders

Passing Efficiency
(Min. 140 pass attempts)

	Att	Cmp	Cmp Pct	Yds	Yds/ Att	TD	TD Pct	Long	Int	Int Pct	Rating
Kevin Daft, Sco	185	111	60.0	1231	6.65	19	10.3	65-td	3	1.6	107.3
Danny Wuerffel, Rhe	260	161	61.9	2042	7.85	25	9.6	59	7	2.7	107.2
Pat Barnes, Fra	250	138	55.2	1954	7.82	18	7.2	69-td	10	4.0	88.0
Cory Sauter, Bar	163	102	62.6	961	5.83	6	3.7	38-td	2	1.2	84.8
Ron Powlus, Ams	287	156	54.4	1784	6.22	13	4.5	57	5	1.7	81.2

Scoring

Touchdowns	TD	Rus	Rec	Ret	Pts
Kevin Drake, Rhe	12	0	12	0	72
Aaron Stecker, Sco	11	7	4	0	66
Mario Bailey, Fra	10	0	10	0	60
Jason Shelley, Ams	8	0	8	0	48
Jeff Ogden, Rhe	7	0	7	0	42

Kicking	PAT	FG/FGA	Lg	Pts
Rob Hart, Sco	34/34	7/11	42	55
Jesus Angoy, Bar	23/23	9/16	48	50
Ralf Kleinmann, Fra	22/24	6/13	35	40
Manfred Burgsmuller, Rhe	32/32	2/3	27	38
Silvio Diliberto, Ams	16/17	7/7	32	37

Rushing

	Car	Yards	Avg	Long	TD
Aaron Stecker, Sco	176	774	4.4	59-td	7
Pepe Pearson, Rhe	102	486	4.8	46	3
Brian Shay, Ber	125	460	3.7	29	3
Terry Battle, Bar	80	444	5.6	69-td	4
Jesse Haynes, Bar	77	341	4.4	27	3

Punting

	No	Yards	Avg	Long	In20
Brian Moorman, Ber	41	1902	46.4	64	11
Rodney Williams, Rhe	42	1865	44.4	72	11
Chris Hanson, Bar	50	2141	42.8	69	16
F. Biancamano, Ams	58	2346	40.4	59	12
Nick Gallery, Fra	43	1693	39.4	62	12
Jon Ballantyne, Sco	55	2146	39.0	60	17

Receptions

	No	Yards	Avg	Long	TD
Jermaine Copeland, Bar	74	821	11.1	42	6
Mario Bailey, Fra	53	873	16.5	69-td	10
L.C. Stevens, Ams	48	619	12.9	64-td	6
Todd Floyd, Fra	45	757	16.8	71-td	5
Jeff Ogden, Rhe	44	635	14.4	59	7

Sacks

	No
Jonathan Brown, Ber	10
Derrick Ham, Rhe	9
Marques Douglas, Rhe	9
Mike Sutton, Ber	9
Chartric Darby, Bar	8.5

All-NFL Europe League Team

The All-NFL Europe League Team as selected by members of the NFL Europe media and by fan vote.

Pos	Offense	Pos	Defense
QB	Danny Wuerffel, Rhe	DE	Derrick Ham, Rhe
RB	Aaron Stecker, Sco	DE	Marques Douglas, Rhe
WR	Mario Bailey, Fra	DE	Mike Sutton, Ber
WR	Jeff Ogden, Rhe	DT	Antonio Dingle, Sco
WR	Kevin Drake, Rhe	LB	Jaime Baisley, Rhe
TE	Damian Vaughan, Bar	LB	Richard Hogans, Ber
G	Craig Heimburger, Rhe	LB	John Hesse, Sco
G	Lennie Friedman, Bar	CB	DeShone Mallard, Rhe
C	Mike Newell, Sco	CB	D. Hawthorne, Sco
T	Scott Curry, Sco	S	Blaine McElmurry, Sco
T	Dan Collins, Rhe	S	Brad Trout, Bar

Pos	Special Teams
K	Jaret Holmes, Ber
P	Chris Hanson, Bar
Spec.	Bashir Levingston, Ams

Interceptions

	No	Yds	Long	TD
Blaine McElmurry, Sco	4	89	52	0
Duane Hawthorne, Sco	4	51	27	0
Bashir Levingston, Ams	3	60	45-td	1
Samyr Hamoudi, Bar	3	56	24	1
Steve Fisher, Rhe	3	37	32-td	1
Deshone Mallard, Rhe	3	20	13	0
Quincy Coleman, Fra	3	5	5	0

Annual Awards

Offensive MVP . . . . Aaron Stecker, Scotland, RB
Defensive MVP . . . . Jonathan Brown, Berlin, DE
& Duane Hawthorne, Scotland, CB
Coach of the Year . . . . Galen Hall, Rhein

Arena Football
Final 2000 Standings

Division champions (*) and playoff qualifiers (†) are noted; top six seeds from each conference advance to the playoffs.

American Conference
Central Division

	W	L	T	Pct.	PF	PA
*Iowa	9	5	0	.643	797	677
†Milwaukee	7	7	0	.500	750	714
†Grand Rapids	6	8	0	.429	628	721
Houston	3	11	0	.214	709	810

Western Division

	W	L	T	Pct.	PF	PA
*San Jose	12	2	0	.857	871	648
†Arizona	12	2	0	.857	727	592
†Oklahoma	7	7	0	.500	654	605
Los Angeles	3	11	0	.214	659	831

National Conference
Eastern Division

	W	L	T	Pct.	PF	PA
*Albany	9	5	0	.643	815	706
†New England	8	6	0	.571	694	696
†Buffalo	5	9	0	.357	615	767
New Jersey	4	10	0	.286	698	773

Southern Division

	W	L	T	Pct.	PF	PA
*Orlando	11	3	0	.786	663	568
†Nashville	9	5	0	.643	671	593
†Tampa Bay	8	6	0	.571	657	598
Carolina	3	11	0	.214	641	783
Florida	3	11	0	.214	611	800

Annual Awards

Tinactin Ironman of the Year . . . . Hunkie Cooper, Ari.
Offensive Player of the Year . . . . Mike Horacek, Iowa
Defensive Player of the Year . . . . Kenny McEntyre, Orlando
Rookie of the Year . . . . Chris Jackson, LA
Coach of the Year . . . . Darren Arbet, SJ

ArenaBowl XIV

August 20, 2000 at the TD Waterhouse Centre in Orlando

(Att: 15,989)

Nashville	7	16	7	8	—	**38**
Orlando	15	14	3	9	—	**41**

MVP: Connell Maynor, Orlando, quarterback (17-28 for 202 yards and 4 TDs.)

Regular Season Individual Leaders
Passing Efficiency

	Att	Cmp	Cmp Pct	Yds	Yds/ Att	TD	TD Pct	Int	Int Pct	Rating
Mark Grieb, SJ	337	216	64.1	3095	9.18	62	18.4	3	0.9	129.6
Aaron Garcia, Iowa	469	297	63.3	4026	8.58	92	19.6	8	1.7	123.1
Mike Pawlawski, Alb	479	324	67.6	3772	7.87	70	14.6	8	1.7	120.8
Kevin McDougal, Mil	442	285	64.5	3889	8.80	73	16.5	17	3.8	116.0
Robert Hall, Hou	496	325	65.5	4053	8.17	64	12.9	11	2.2	113.8

Scoring

Touchdowns	TD	Rus	Rec	Ret	PAT	Pts
Mike Horacek, Iowa	46	0	46	0	0	276
Steve Papin, SJ	38	11	23	4	0	228
Greg Hopkins, Alb	32	0	30	2	2	196
Sean Riley, Mil	28	0	27	1	0	168
Chris Jackson, LA	26	0	26	0	0	156

Kicking	PAT	2PAT	FG/FGA	Pts
Clay Rush, Iowa	99/105	0/0	16/28	147
Mike Black, Buf	70/76	0/0	23/42	139
Steve Videtich, Mil	90/98	0/0	16/32	138
Nelson Garner, Alb	96/102	0/0	13/25	135
Brian Gowins, GR	59/68	0/0	25/44	134

Rushing

	Car	Yards	Avg	TD
Rick Hamilton, Orl	72	210	2.9	9
Connell Maynor, Orl	60	200	3.3	6
Leroy Thompson, Alb	59	190	3.2	14
Terrence Melton, Hou	47	179	3.8	11
Rupert Grant, Nash	38	161	4.2	9

arenafootball2

arenafootball2 was launched in 2000 with 15 teams located primarily in the southeast. Teams play a 16-game schedule. The top four teams advance to the playoffs with the final two surviving teams competing in the ArenaCup.

ArenaCup

August 10, 2000 at The Mark of the Quad Cities in Moline, Ill.

(Att: 9,200)

Tennessee Valley	14	17	28	0	—	**59**
Quad City	21	20	14	13	—	**68**

MVP: Shon King, Quad City, offensive specialist (5 KR for 237 yards and 3 TDs; 6 catches for 111 yards and 2 TDs.)

Receptions

	No	Yards	Avg	TD
Carlos Johnson, Okl	121	1400	11.6	23
Mike Horacek, Iowa	119	1880	15.8	46
Ben Bronson, Hou	112	1494	13.3	21
Greg Hopkins, Alb	111	1295	11.7	30
Bobby Olive, Buf	106	1184	11.2	15

The Super Bowl

The first AFL-NFL World Championship Game, as it was originally called, was played seven months after the two leagues agreed to merge in June of 1966. It became the Super Bowl (complete with roman numerals) by the third game in 1969. The Super Bowl winner has been presented the Vince Lombardi Trophy since 1971. Lombardi, whose Green Bay teams won the first two title games, died in 1970. NFL champions (1966-69) and NFC champions (since 1970) are listed in CAPITAL letters.

Multiple winners: Dallas and San Francisco (5); Pittsburgh (4); Green Bay, Oakland-LA Raiders and Washington (3); Denver, Miami and NY Giants (2).

Bowl	Date	Winner	Head Coach	Score	Loser	Head Coach	Site
I	1/15/67	GREEN BAY	Vince Lombardi	35-10	Kansas City	Hank Stram	Los Angeles
II	1/14/68	GREEN BAY	Vince Lombardi	33-14	Oakland	John Rauch	Miami
III	1/12/69	NY Jets	Weeb Ewbank	16- 7	BALTIMORE	Don Shula	Miami
IV	1/11/70	Kansas City	Hank Stram	23- 7	MINNESOTA	Bud Grant	New Orleans
V	1/17/71	Baltimore	Don McCafferty	16-13	DALLAS	Tom Landry	Miami
VI	1/16/72	DALLAS	Tom Landry	24- 3	Miami	Don Shula	New Orleans
VII	1/14/73	Miami	Don Shula	14- 7	WASHINGTON	George Allen	Los Angeles
VIII	1/13/74	Miami	Don Shula	24- 7	MINNESOTA	Bud Grant	Houston
IX	1/12/75	Pittsburgh	Chuck Noll	16- 6	MINNESOTA	Bud Grant	New Orleans
X	1/18/76	Pittsburgh	Chuck Noll	21-17	DALLAS	Tom Landry	Miami
XI	1/ 9/77	Oakland	John Madden	32-14	MINNESOTA	Bud Grant	Pasadena
XII	1/15/78	DALLAS	Tom Landry	27-10	Denver	Red Miller	New Orleans
XIII	1/21/79	Pittsburgh	Chuck Noll	35-31	DALLAS	Tom Landry	Miami
XIV	1/20/80	Pittsburgh	Chuck Noll	31-19	LA RAMS	Ray Malavasi	Pasadena
XV	1/25/81	Oakland	Tom Flores	27-10	PHILADELPHIA	Dick Vermeil	New Orleans
XVI	1/24/82	SAN FRANCISCO	Bill Walsh	26-21	Cincinnati	Forrest Gregg	Pontiac, MI
XVII	1/30/83	WASHINGTON	Joe Gibbs	27-17	Miami	Don Shula	Pasadena
XVIII	1/22/84	LA Raiders	Tom Flores	38- 9	WASHINGTON	Joe Gibbs	Tampa
XIX	1/20/85	SAN FRANCISCO	Bill Walsh	38-16	Miami	Don Shula	Stanford
XX	1/26/86	CHICAGO	Mike Ditka	46-10	New England	Raymond Berry	New Orleans
XXI	1/25/87	NY GIANTS	Bill Parcells	39-20	Denver	Dan Reeves	Pasadena
XXII	1/31/88	WASHINGTON	Joe Gibbs	42-10	Denver	Dan Reeves	San Diego
XXIII	1/22/89	SAN FRANCISCO	Bill Walsh	20-16	Cincinnati	Sam Wyche	Miami
XXIV	1/28/90	SAN FRANCISCO	George Seifert	55-10	Denver	Dan Reeves	New Orleans
XXV	1/27/91	NY GIANTS	Bill Parcells	20-19	Buffalo	Marv Levy	Tampa
XXVI	1/26/92	WASHINGTON	Joe Gibbs	37-24	Buffalo	Marv Levy	Minneapolis
XXVII	1/31/93	DALLAS	Jimmy Johnson	52-17	Buffalo	Marv Levy	Pasadena
XXVIII	1/30/94	DALLAS	Jimmy Johnson	30-13	Buffalo	Marv Levy	Atlanta
XXIX	1/29/95	SAN FRANCISCO	George Seifert	49-26	San Diego	Bobby Ross	Miami
XXX	1/28/96	DALLAS	Barry Switzer	27-17	Pittsburgh	Bill Cowher	Tempe, AZ
XXXI	1/26/97	GREEN BAY	Mike Holmgren	35-21	New England	Bill Parcells	New Orleans
XXXII	1/25/98	Denver	Mike Shanahan	31-24	GREEN BAY	Mike Holmgren	San Diego
XXXIII	1/31/99	Denver	Mike Shanahan	34-19	ATLANTA	Dan Reeves	Miami
XXXIV	1/30/00	ST. LOUIS	Dick Vermeil	23-16	Tennessee	Jeff Fisher	Atlanta

Pete Rozelle Award (MVP)

The Most Valuable Player in the Super Bowl. Currently selected by an 11-member panel made up of national pro football writers and broadcasters chosen by the NFL. Presented by *Sport* magazine from 1967-89 and by the NFL since 1990. Named after former NFL commissioner Pete Rozelle in 1990. Winner who did not play for Super Bowl champion is in **bold** type.

Multiple winners: Joe Montana (3); Terry Bradshaw and Bart Starr (2).

Bowl		Bowl		Bowl	
I	Bart Starr, Green Bay, QB	XII	Harvey Martin, Dallas, DE	XXIII	Jerry Rice, San Francisco, WR
II	Bart Starr, Green Bay, QB		& Randy White, Dallas, DT	XXIV	Joe Montana, San Francisco, QB
III	Joe Namath, NY Jets, QB	XIII	Terry Bradshaw, Pittsburgh, QB	XXV	Ottis Anderson, NY Giants, RB
IV	Len Dawson, Kansas City, QB	XIV	Terry Bradshaw, Pittsburgh, QB	XXVI	Mark Rypien, Washington, QB
V	**Chuck Howley**, Dallas, LB	XV	Jim Plunkett, Oakland, QB	XXVII	Troy Aikman, Dallas, QB
VI	Roger Staubach, Dallas, QB	XVI	Joe Montana, San Francisco, QB	XXVIII	Emmitt Smith, Dallas, RB
VII	Jake Scott, Miami, S	XVII	John Riggins, Washington, RB	XXIX	Steve Young, San Francisco, QB
VIII	Larry Csonka, Miami, RB	XVIII	Marcus Allen, LA Raiders, RB	XXX	Larry Brown, Dallas, CB
IX	Franco Harris, Pittsburgh, RB	XIX	Joe Montana, San Francisco, QB	XXXI	Desmond Howard, Green Bay, KR
X	Lynn Swann, Pittsburgh, WR	XX	Richard Dent, Chicago, DE	XXXII	Terrell Davis, Denver, RB
XI	Fred Biletnikoff, Oakland, WR	XXI	Phil Simms, NY Giants, QB	XXXIII	John Elway, Denver, QB
		XXII	Doug Williams, Washington, QB	XXXIV	Kurt Warner, St. Louis, QB

All-Time Super Bowl Leaders
Through 2000; participants in Super Bowl XXXIV in **bold** type.

CAREER
Passing Efficiency

		Gm	Att	Cmp	Cmp%	Yards	Avg Gain	TD	TD%	Int	Int%	Rating
1	Phil Simms, NYG	1	25	22	88.0	268	10.72	3	12.0	0	0.0	160.1
2	Steve Young, SF	2	39	26	66.7	345	8.85	6	15.4	0	0.0	145.8
3	Doug Williams, Wash.	1	29	18	62.1	340	11.72	4	13.8	1	3.4	134.3
4	Joe Montana, SF	4	122	83	68.0	1142	9.36	11	9.0	0	0.0	127.8
5	Jim Plunkett, Raiders	2	46	29	63.0	433	9.41	4	8.7	0	0.0	122.8
6	Terry Bradshaw, Pit	4	84	49	58.3	932	11.10	9	10.7	4	4.8	112.8
7	Troy Aikman, Dal.	3	80	56	70.0	689	8.61	5	6.3	1	1.3	111.9
8	Bart Starr, GB.	2	47	29	61.7	452	9.62	3	6.4	1	2.1	106.0
9	**Kurt Warner**, St.L	1	45	24	53.3	414	9.20	2	4.4	0	0.0	99.7
10	Brett Favre, GB	2	69	39	56.5	502	7.28	5	7.2	1	1.4	97.6

Ratings based on performance standards established for completion percentage, average gain, touchdown percentage and interception percentage. Quarterbacks are allocated points according to how their statistics measure up to those standards. Minimum 25 passing attempts.

Passing Yards

		Gm	Att	Cmp	Pct	Yds
1	Joe Montana, SF	4	122	83	68.0	1142
2	John Elway, Den	5	152	76	50.0	1128
3	Terry Bradshaw, Pit	4	84	49	58.3	932
4	Jim Kelly, Buf	4	145	81	55.9	829
5	Roger Staubach, Dal	4	98	61	62.2	734
6	Troy Aikman, Dal	3	80	56	70.0	689
7	Brett Favre, GB	2	69	39	56.5	502
8	Fran Tarkenton, Min	3	89	46	51.7	489
9	Bart Starr, GB	2	47	29	61.7	452
10	Jim Plunkett, Raiders	2	46	29	63.0	433
11	**Kurt Warner**, St.L	1	45	24	53.3	414
12	Joe Theismann, Wash	2	58	31	53.4	386
13	Len Dawson, KC	2	44	28	63.6	353
14	Steve Young, SF	2	26	39	66.7	345
15	Doug Williams, Wash.	1	29	18	62.1	340

Receptions

		Gm	No	Yds	Avg	TD
1	Jerry Rice, SF	3	28	512	18.3	7
2	Andre Reed, Buf	4	27	323	12.0	0
3	Roger Craig, SF	3	20	212	10.6	3
	Thurman Thomas, Buf	4	20	144	7.2	0
5	Jay Novacek, Dal	3	17	148	8.7	2
6	Lynn Swann, Pit	4	16	364	22.8	3
7	Michael Irvin, Dal	3	16	256	16.0	2
8	Chuck Foreman, Min.	3	15	139	9.3	0
9	Cliff Branch, Raiders	3	14	181	12.9	3
10	Don Beebe, Buf	3	12	171	14.3	2
	Preston Pearson, Bal-Pit-Dal	5	12	105	8.8	0
	Kenneth Davis, Buf	4	12	72	6.0	0
	Antonio Freeman, GB	2	12	231	19.3	3
14	John Stallworth, Pit	4	11	268	24.4	3
	Dan Ross, Cin	1	11	104	9.5	2

Super Bowl Appearances
Through Super Bowl XXXIV, nine NFL teams have yet to play for the Vince Lombardi Trophy. In alphabetical order, they are: Arizona, Baltimore Ravens, Carolina, Cleveland, Detroit, Jacksonville, New Orleans, Seattle and Tampa Bay. Of the 22 teams that have participated, Dallas has the most appearances (8) and, along with San Francisco, has the most titles (5).

App		W	L	Pct	PF	PA
8	Dallas	5	3	.625	221	132
6	Denver	2	4	.333	115	206
5	San Francisco	5	0	1.000	188	89
5	Pittsburgh	4	1	.800	120	100
5	Washington	3	2	.600	122	103
5	Miami	2	3	.400	74	103
4	Green Bay	3	1	.750	127	76
4	Oak/LA Raiders	3	1	.750	111	66
4	Buffalo	0	4	.000	73	139
4	Minnesota	0	4	.000	34	95
2	NY Giants	2	0	1.000	59	39
2	Baltimore Colts	1	1	.500	23	29
2	Kansas City	1	1	.500	33	42
2	LA/St.L Rams	1	1	.500	42	47
2	Cincinnati	0	2	.000	37	46
2	New England	0	2	.000	31	81
1	Chicago	1	0	1.000	46	10
1	NY Jets	1	0	1.000	16	7
1	Atlanta	0	1	.000	19	34
1	Philadelphia	0	1	.000	10	27
1	San Diego	0	1	.000	26	49
1	Tennessee	0	1	.000	16	23

Rushing

		Gm	Car	Yds	Avg	TD
1	Franco Harris, Pit.	4	101	354	3.5	4
2	Larry Csonka, Mia.	3	57	297	5.2	2
3	Emmitt Smith, Dal.	3	70	289	4.1	5
4	Terrell Davis, Den.	2	55	259	4.7	3
5	John Riggins, Wash.	2	64	230	3.6	2
6	Timmy Smith, Wash.	1	22	204	9.3	2
	Thurman Thomas, Buf	4	52	204	3.9	4
8	Roger Craig, SF	3	52	201	3.9	2
9	Marcus Allen, Raiders	1	20	191	9.5	2
10	Tony Dorsett, Dal	2	31	162	5.2	1
11	Mark van Eeghen, Raiders	2	37	153	4.1	0
12	Dorsey Levens, GB	2	33	151	4.6	0
13	Kenneth Davis, Buf	4	30	145	4.8	0
14	Rocky Bleier, Pit	4	44	144	3.3	0
15	Walt Garrison, Dal	2	26	139	5.3	0

All-Purpose Yards

		Gm	Rush	Rec	Ret	Total
1	Jerry Rice, SF	3	15	512	0	527
2	Franco Harris, Pit.	4	354	114	0	468
3	Roger Craig, SF	3	201	212	0	413
4	Lynn Swann, Pit	4	-7	364	34	391
5	Thurman Thomas, Buf	4	204	144	0	348
6	Emmitt Smith, Dal.	3	289	56	0	345
7	Antonio Freeman, GB	2	0	231	104	335
8	Andre Reed, Buf	3	0	323	0	323
9	Terrell Davis, Den.	2	259	58	0	317
10	Larry Csonka, Mia.	3	297	17	0	314

Scoring

Points

		Gm	TD	FG	PAT	Pts
1	Jerry Rice, SF	3	7	0	0	42
2	Emmitt Smith, Dal	3	5	0	0	30
3	Roger Craig, SF	3	4	0	0	24
	Franco Harris, Pit	4	4	0	0	24
	Thurman Thomas, Buf	4	4	0	0	24
	John Elway, Den	5	4	0	0	24
7	Ray Wersching, SF	2	0	5	7	22
8	Don Chandler, GB	2	0	4	8	20
9	Cliff Branch, Raiders	3	3	0	0	18
	John Stallworth, Pit	4	3	0	0	18
	Lynn Swann, Pit	4	3	0	0	18
	Ricky Watters, SF	1	3	0	0	18
	Terrell Davis, Den	2	3	0	0	18
	Antonio Freeman, GB	2	3	0	0	18
15	Chris Bahr, Raiders	2	0	3	8	17
	Jason Elam, Den	2	0	3	8	17

Punting
(Minimum 10 Punts)

		Gm	No	Yds	Avg.
1	Jerrel Wilson, KC	2	11	511	46.5
2	Ray Guy, Raiders	3	14	587	41.9
3	Larry Seiple, Mia	3	15	620	41.3
4	Mike Eischeid, Raiders-Min	3	17	698	41.1
5	**Craig Hentrich**, GB-Ten	3	14	570	40.7

Punt Returns
(Minimum 4 returns)

		Gm	No	Yds	Avg.	TD
1	John Taylor, SF	3	6	94	15.7	0
2	Desmond Howard, GB	1	6	90	15.0	0
3	Neal Colzie, Raiders	1	4	43	10.8	0
4	Dana McLemore, SF	1	5	51	10.2	0
5	Mike Fuller, Cin	1	4	35	8.8	0

Kickoff Returns
(Minimum 4 returns)

		Gm	No	Yds	Avg.	TD
1	Tim Dwight, Atl	1	5	210	42.0	1
2	Desmond Howard, GB	1	4	154	38.5	1
3	Fulton Walker, Mia	2	8	283	35.4	1
4	Andre Coleman, SD	1	8	242	30.3	1
5	Larry Anderson, Pit	2	8	207	25.9	0

Touchdowns

		Gm	Rush	Rec	Ret	TD
1	Jerry Rice, SF	3	0	7	0	7
2	Emmitt Smith, Dal	3	5	0	0	5
3	Roger Craig, SF	3	2	2	0	4
	Franco Harris, Pit	4	4	0	0	4
	John Elway, Den	5	4	0	0	4
	Thurman Thomas, Buf	4	4	0	0	4
7	Cliff Branch, Raiders	3	0	3	0	3
	John Stallworth, Pit	4	0	3	0	3
	Lynn Swann, Pit	4	0	3	0	3
	Ricky Watters, SF	1	1	2	0	3
	Terrell Davis, Den	2	3	0	0	3
	Antonio Freeman, GB	2	0	3	0	3
13	Twenty-four tied with 2 TDs each:					

Marcus Allen, Raiders; Ottis Anderson, NYG; Pete Banaszak, Raiders; Don Beebe, Buf.; Gary Clark, Wash.; Larry Csonka, Mia.; **Eddie George**, Ten.; Howard Griffith, Den.; Michael Irvin, Dal.; Butch Johnson, Dal.; Jim Kiick, Mia.; Max McGee, GB; Jim McMahon, Chi.; Bill Miller, Raiders; Joe Montana, SF; Elijah Pitts, GB; Tom Rathman, SF; John Riggins, Wash.; Gerald Riggs, Wash.; Dan Ross, Cin.; Ricky Sanders, Wash.; Timmy Smith, Wash.; John Taylor, SF and Duane Thomas, Dal.

Interceptions

		Gm	No	Yds	TD
1	Larry Brown, Dal	2	3	77	0
	Chuck Howley, Dal	2	3	63	0
	Rod Martin, Raiders	2	3	44	0
4	Randy Beverly, NYJ	1	2	0	0
	Mel Blount, Pit	1	2	23	0
	Brad Edwards, Wash	1	2	56	0
	Thomas Everett, Dal	2	2	22	0
	Darrien Gordon, Den	3	2	108	0
	Jake Scott, Mia	3	2	63	0
	Mike Wagner, Pit	3	2	45	0
	James Washington, Dal	2	2	25	0
	Barry Wilburn, Wash	1	2	11	0
	Eric Wright, SF	4	2	25	0

Sacks

		Gm	No
1	Charles Haley, SF-Dal	5	4½
2	Reggie White, GB	2	3
	Leonard Marshall, NYG	2	3
	Danny Stubbs, SF	2	3
	Jeff Wright, Buf	4	3

Before the Super Bowl

The first NFL champion was the Akron Pros in 1920, when the league was called the American Professional Football Association (APFA) and the title went to the team with the best regular season record. The APFA changed its name to the National Football League in 1922.

The first playoff game with the championship at stake came in 1932, when the Chicago Bears (6-1-6) and Portsmouth (Ohio) Spartans (6-1-4) ended the regular season tied for first place. The Bears won the subsequent playoff, 9-0. Due to a snowstorm and cold weather, the game was moved from Wrigley Field to an improvised 80-yard dirt field at Chicago Stadium, making it the first indoor title game as well.

The NFL Championship Game decided the league title until the NFL merged with the AFL and the first Super Bowl was played following the 1966 season.

NFL Champions, 1920-32
Winning player-coaches noted by position.

Multiple winners: Canton-Cleveland Bulldogs and Green Bay (3); Chicago Staleys/Bears (2).

Year	Champion	Head Coach	Year	Champion	Head Coach
1920	Akron Pros	Fritz Pollard, HB & Elgie Tobin, QB	1927	New York Giants	Earl Potteiger, QB
			1928	Providence Steam Roller	Jimmy Conzelman, HB
1921	Chicago Staleys	George Halas, E	1929	Green Bay Packers	Curly Lambeau, QB
1922	Canton Bulldogs	Guy Chamberlin, E	1930	Green Bay Packers	Curly Lambeau
1923	Canton Bulldogs	Guy Chamberlin, E	1931	Green Bay Packers	Curly Lambeau
1924	Cleveland Bulldogs	Guy Chamberlin, E	1932	Chicago Bears	Ralph Jones
1925	Chicago Cardinals	Norm Barry		(Bears beat Portsmouth-OH in playoff, 9-0)	
1926	Frankford Yellow Jackets	Guy Chamberlin, E			

SINGLE GAME

Passing

Yards Gained	Year	Att/Cmp	Yds
1 **Kurt Warner**, St.L vs Ten	.2000	45/24	414
2 Joe Montana, SF vs Cin	.1989	36/23	357
3 Doug Williams, Wash vs Den	.1988	29/18	340
4 John Elway, Den vs Atl	.1999	29/18	336
5 Joe Montana, SF vs Mia	.1985	35/24	331
6 Steve Young, SF vs SD	.1995	36/24	325
7 Terry Bradshaw, Pit vs Dal	.1979	30/17	318
Dan Marino, Mia vs SF	.1985	50/29	318
9 Terry Bradshaw, Pit vs Rams	.1980	21/14	309
10 John Elway, Den vs NYG	.1987	37/22	304

Touchdown Passes	Year	TD	Int
1 Steve Young, SF vs SD	.1995	6	0
2 Joe Montana, SF vs Den	.1990	5	0
3 Terry Bradshaw, Pit vs Dal	.1979	4	1
Doug Williams, Wash vs Den	.1988	4	1
Troy Aikman, Dal vs Buf	.1993	4	0
6 Roger Staubach, Dal vs Pit	.1979	3	1
Jim Plunkett, Raiders vs Phi	.1981	3	0
Joe Montana, SF vs Mia	.1985	3	0
Phil Simms, NYG vs Den	.1987	3	0
Brett Favre, GB vs Den	.1998	3	1

Receiving

Catches	Year	No	Yds	TD
1 Dan Ross, Cin vs SF	.1982	11	104	2
Jerry Rice, SF vs Cin	.1989	11	215	1
3 Tony Nathan, Mia vs SF	.1985	10	83	0
Jerry Rice, SF vs SD	.1995	10	149	3
Andre Hastings, Pit vs Dal	.1996	10	98	0
6 Ricky Sanders, Wash vs Den	.1988	9	193	2
Antonio Freeman, GB vs Den	.1998	9	126	2
8 Five tied with 8 each, including twice by Andre Reed.				

Yards Gained	Year	No	Yds	TD
1 Jerry Rice, SF vs Cin	.1989	11	215	1
2 Ricky Sanders, Wash vs Den	.1988	9	193	2
3 **Isaac Bruce**, St.L vs Ten	.2000	6	162	1
4 Lynn Swann, Pit vs Dal	.1976	4	161	1
5 Andre Reed, Buf vs Dal	.1993	8	152	0
Rod Smith, Den vs Atl	.1999	5	152	1
7 Jerry Rice, SF vs SD	.1995	10	149	3
8 Jerry Rice, SF vs Den	.1990	7	148	3
9 Max McGee, GB vs KC	.1967	7	138	2
10 George Sauer, NYJ vs Bal	.1969	8	133	0

Rushing

Yards Gained	Year	Car	Yds	TD
1 Timmy Smith, Wash vs Den	.1988	22	204	2
2 Marcus Allen, Raiders vs Wash	.1984	20	191	2
3 John Riggins, Wash vs Mia	.1983	38	166	1
4 Franco Harris, Pit vs Min	.1975	34	158	1
5 Terrell Davis, Den vs GB	.1998	30	157	3
6 Larry Csonka, Mia vs Min	.1974	33	145	2
7 Clarence Davis, Raiders vs Min	.1977	16	137	0
8 Thurman Thomas, Buf vs NYG	.1991	15	135	1
9 Emmitt Smith, Dal vs Buf	.1994	30	132	2
10 Matt Snell, NYJ vs Bal	.1969	30	121	1
11 Tom Matte, Bal vs NYJ	.1969	11	116	0
12 Larry Csonka, Mia vs Wash	.1973	15	112	1
13 Emmitt Smith, Dal vs Buf	.1993	22	108	1
14 Ottis Anderson, NYG vs Buf	.1991	21	102	1
Terrell Davis, Den vs Atl	.1999	25	102	0

Scoring

Points	Year	TD	FG	PAT	Pts
1 Roger Craig, SF vs Mia	.1985	3	0	0	18
Jerry Rice, SF vs Den	.1990	3	0	0	18
Jerry Rice, SF vs SD	.1995	3	0	0	18
Ricky Watters, SF vs SD	.1995	3	0	0	18
Terrell Davis, Den vs GB	.1998	3	0	0	18
6 Don Chandler, GB vs Raiders	.1968	0	4	3	15

Touchdowns	Year	TD	Rush	Rec
1 Roger Craig, SF vs Mia	.1985	3	1	2
Jerry Rice, SF vs Den	.1990	3	0	3
Jerry Rice, SF vs SD	.1995	3	0	3
Ricky Watters, SF vs SD	.1995	3	1	2
Terrell Davis, Den vs GB	.1998	3	3	0

Punt Returns
(Minimum 3 returns)

	Year	No	Yds	Avg
1 John Taylor, SF vs Cin	.1989	3	56	18.7
2 Desmond Howard, GB vs NE	.1997	6	90	15.0
3 John Taylor, SF vs Den	.1990	3	38	12.7
4 Kelvin Martin, Dal vs Buf	.1993	3	35	11.7

All-Purpose Yards

Yards Gained	Year	Run	Rec	Tot
1 Desmond Howard, GB vs NE	.1997	0	0	244
2 Andre Coleman, SD vs SF	.1995	0	0	242
3 Ricky Sanders, Wash vs Den	.1988	193	-4	235
4 Antonio Freeman, GB vs Den	.1998	0	126	230
5 Jerry Rice, SF vs Cin	.1989	215	5	220
6 Tim Dwight, Atl vs Den	.1999	5	0	215
7 Timmy Smith, Wash vs Den	.1988	204	9	213
8 Marcus Allen, Raiders vs Wash	.1984	191	18	209
9 Stephen Starring, NE vs Chi	.1986	0	39	192
10 Fulton Walker, Mia vs Wash	.1983	0	0	190
Thurman Thomas, Buf vs NYG	.1991	135	55	190

Return Yardage: Howard 244, Coleman 242, Sanders 46, Freeman 104, Dwight 210, Starring 153, Walker 190.

Interceptions

	Year	No	Yds	TD
1 Rod Martin, Raiders vs Phi	.1981	3	44	0
2 Seven tied with 2 each.				

Punting
(Minimum 4 punts)

	Year	No	Yds	Avg
1 Bryan Wagner, SD vs SF	.1995	4	195	48.8
2 Jerrel Wilson, KC vs Min	.1970	4	194	48.5
3 Jim Miller, SF vs Cin	.1982	4	185	46.3

Kickoff Returns
(Minimum 3 returns)

	Year	No	Yds	Avg
1 Fulton Walker, Mia vs Wash	.1983	4	190	47.5
2 Tim Dwight, Atl vs Den	.1999	5	210	42.0
3 Desmond Howard, GB vs NE	.1997	4	154	38.5
4 Larry Anderson, Pit vs Rams	.1980	5	162	32.4
5 Rick Upchurch, Den vs Dal	.1978	3	94	31.3

Super Bowl Playoffs

The Super Bowl forced the NFL to set up pro football's first guaranteed multiple-game playoff format. Over the years, the NFL-AFL merger, the creation of two conferences comprised of three divisions each and the proliferation of wild card entries has seen the postseason field grow from four teams (1966), to six (1967-68), to eight (1969-77), to 10 (1978-81, 1983-89), to the present 12 (since 1990).

In 1968, there was a special playoff between Oakland and Kansas City which were both 12-2 and tied for first in the AFL's Western Division. In 1982, when a 57-day players' strike shortened the regular season to just nine games, playoff berths were extended to 16 teams (eight from each conference) and a 15-game tournament was played.

Note that in the following year-by-year summary, records of finalists include all games leading up to the Super Bowl; (*) indicates non-division winners or wild card teams.

1966 Season

AFL Playoffs

Championship . . . . .Kansas City 31, at Buffalo 7

NFL Playoffs

Championship . . . . .Green Bay 34, at Dallas 27

Super Bowl I

Jan. 15, 1967
Memorial Coliseum, Los Angeles
Favorite: Packers by 14   Attendance: 61,946

Kansas City (12-2-1) 0	10	0	0	**—10**
Green Bay (13-2) 7	7	14	7	**—35**

MVP: Green Bay QB Bart Starr (16 for 23, 250 yds, 2 TD, 1 Int)

1967 Season

AFL Playoffs

Championship . . . . .at Oakland 40, Houston 7

NFL Playoffs

Eastern Conference . . . . .at Dallas 52, Cleveland 14
Western Conference . . . . .at Green Bay 28, LA Rams 7
Championship . . . . .at Green Bay 21, Dallas 17

Super Bowl II

Jan. 14, 1968
Orange Bowl, Miami
Favorite: Packers by 13½   Attendance: 75,546

Green Bay (11-4-1) 3	13	10	7	**—33**
Oakland (14-1) 0	7	0	7	**—14**

MVP: Green Bay QB Bart Starr (13 for 24, 202 yds, 1 TD)

1968 Season

AFL Playoffs

Western Div. Playoff . . . . .at Oakland 41, Kansas City 6
AFL Championship . . . . .at NY Jets 27, Oakland 23

NFL Playoffs

Eastern Conference . . . . .at Cleveland 31, Dallas 20
Western Conference . . . . . .at Baltimore 24, Minnesota 14
NFL Championship . . . . .Baltimore 34, at Cleveland 0

Super Bowl III

Jan. 12, 1969
Orange Bowl, Miami
Favorite: Colts by 18   Attendance: 75,389

NY Jets (12-3) 0	7	6	3	**—16**
Baltimore (15-1) 0	0	0	7	**—7**

MVP: NY Jets QB Joe Namath (17 for 28, 206 yds)

1969 Season

AFL Playoffs

Inter-Division . . . .*Kansas City 13, at NY Jets 6
                                          at Oakland 56, *Houston 7
AFL Championship . . . . .Kansas City 17, at Oakland 7

NFL Playoffs

Eastern Conference . . . . .Cleveland 38, at Dallas 14
Western Conference . . . . .at Minnesota 23, LA Rams 20
NFL Championship . . . . .at Minnesota 27, Cleveland 7

Super Bowl IV

Jan. 11, 1970
Tulane Stadium, New Orleans
Favorite: Vikings by 12   Attendance: 80,562

Minnesota (14-2) 0	0	7	0	**—7**
Kansas City (13-3) 3	13	7	0	**—23**

MVP: KC QB Len Dawson (12 for 17, 142 yds, 1 TD, 1 Int)

1970 Season

AFC Playoffs

First Round . . . . .at Baltimore 17, Cincinnati 0
                                          at Oakland 21,*Miami 14
Championship . . . . .at Baltimore 27, Oakland 17

NFC Playoffs

First Round. . . . . .at Dallas 5, *Detroit 0
                                          San Francisco 17, at Minnesota 14
Championship . . . . .Dallas 17, at San Francisco 10

Super Bowl V

Jan. 17, 1971
Orange Bowl, Miami
Favorite: Cowboys by 2½   Attendance: 79,204

Baltimore (13-2-1) 0	6	0	10	**—16**
Dallas (12-4) 3	10	0	0	**—13**

MVP: Dallas LB Chuck Howley (2 interceptions for 22 yds)

1971 Season

AFC Playoffs

First Round. . . . . .Miami 27, at Kansas City 24 (OT)
                                          *Baltimore 20, at Cleveland 3
Championship . . . . .at Miami 21, Baltimore 0

NFC Playoffs

First Round . . . . .Dallas 20, at Minnesota 12
                                          at San Francisco 24,*Washington 20
Championship . . . . .at Dallas 14, San Francisco 3

Super Bowl VI

Jan. 16, 1972
Tulane Stadium, New Orleans
Favorite: Cowboys by 6   Attendance: 81,023

Dallas (13-3) 3	7	7	7	**—24**
Miami (12-3-1) 0	3	0	0	**—3**

MVP: Dallas QB Roger Staubach (12 for 19, 119 yds, 2 TD)

1972 Season

AFC Playoffs

First Round . . . . .at Pittsburgh 13, Oakland 7
at Miami 20, *Cleveland 14
Championship. . . . . .Miami 21, at Pittsburgh 17

NFC Playoffs

First Round . . . .*Dallas 30, at San Francisco 28
at Washington 16, Green Bay 3
Championship . . . . .at Washington 26, Dallas 3

Super Bowl VII
Jan. 14, 1973
Memorial Coliseum, Los Angeles
Favorite: Redskins by 1½   Attendance: 90,182

Miami (16-0) 7   7   0   0 **—14**
Washington (13-3) 0   0   0   7   **—7**
MVP: Miami safety Jake Scott (2 Interceptions for 63 yds)

1973 Season

AFC Playoffs

First Round. . . . . .at Oakland 33, *Pittsburgh 14
at Miami 34, Cincinnati 16
Championship. . . . . .at Miami 27, Oakland 10

NFC Playoffs

First Round . . . . .at Minnesota 27, *Washington 20
at Dallas 27, LA Rams 16
Championship . . . . .Minnesota 27, at Dallas 10

Super Bowl VIII
Jan. 13, 1974
Rice Stadium, Houston
Favorite: Dolphins by 6½   Attendance: 71,882

Minnesota (14-2). 0   0   0   7   **—7**
Miami (12-4) 14   3   7   0 **—24**
MVP: Miami FB Larry Csonka (33 carries, 145 yds, 2 TD)

1974 Season

AFC Playoffs

First Round. . . . . .at Oakland 28, Miami 26
at Pittsburgh 32, *Buffalo 14
Championship. . . . . .Pittsburgh 24, at Oakland 13

NFC Playoffs

First Round . . . . .at Minnesota 30, St.Louis 14
at LA Rams 19, *Washington 10
Championship . . . . .at Minnesota 14, LA Rams 10

Super Bowl IX
Jan. 12, 1975
Tulane Stadium, New Orleans
Favorite: Steelers by 3   Attendance: 80,997

Pittsburgh (12-3-1) 0   2   7   7 **—16**
Minnesota (12-4) 0   0   0   6   **—6**
MVP: Pittsburgh RB Franco Harris (34 carries, 158 yds, 1 TD)

1975 Season

AFC Playoffs

First Round . . . . .at Pittsburgh 28, Baltimore 10
at Oakland 31, *Cincinnati 28
Championship. . . . . .at Pittsburgh 16, Oakland 10

NFC Playoffs

First Round . . . . .at LA Rams 35, St. Louis 23
*Dallas 17, at Minnesota 14
Championship . . . . .Dallas 37, at LA Rams 7

Super Bowl X
Jan. 18, 1976
Orange Bowl, Miami
Favorite: Steelers by 6½   Attendance: 80,187

Dallas (12-4) 7   3   0   7 **—17**
Pittsburgh (14-2) 7   0   0   14 **—21**
MVP: Pittsburgh WR Lynn Swann (4 catches, 161 yds, 1 TD)

1976 Season

AFC Playoffs

First Round . . . . .at Oakland 24, *New England 21
Pittsburgh 40, at Baltimore 14
Championship . . . . .at Oakland 24, Pittsburgh 7

NFC Playoffs

First Round . . . . .at Minnesota 35, *Washington 20
LA Rams 14, at Dallas 12
Championship . . . . .at Minnesota 24, LA Rams 13

Super Bowl XI
Jan. 9, 1977
Rose Bowl, Pasadena
Favorite: Raiders by 4½   Attendance: 103,438

Oakland (15-1). 0   16   3   13 **—32**
Minnesota (13-2-1) 0   0   7   7   **—14**
MVP: Oakland WR Fred Biletnikoff (4 catches, 79 yds)

1977 Season

AFC Playoffs

First Round . . . . .at Denver 34, Pittsburgh 21
*Oakland 37, at Baltimore 31 (OT)
Championship . . . . .at Denver 20, Oakland 17

NFC Playoffs

First Round . . . . .at Dallas 37, *Chicago 7
Minnesota 14, at LA Rams 7
Championship. . . . . .at Dallas 23, Minnesota 6

Super Bowl XII
Jan. 15, 1978
Louisiana Superdome, New Orleans
Favorite: Cowboys by 6   Attendance: 75,583

Dallas (14-2) 10   3   7   7 **—27**
Denver (14-2) 0   0   10   0 **—10**
MVPs: Dallas DE Harvey Martin and DT Randy White (Cowboys' defense forced 8 turnovers)

A Year Later . . .
Super Bowl champions who did not qualify for the playoffs the following season.

Season		Record	Finish	Season		Record	Finish
1968	Green Bay	6-7-1	3rd in NFL Central	1987	NY Giants	6-9-0*	5th in NFC East
1970	Kansas City	7-5-2	2nd in AFC West	1988	Washington	7-9-0	3rd in NFC East
1980	Pittsburgh	9-7-0	3rd in AFC Central	1991	NY Giants	8-8-0	4th in NFC East
1981	Oakland	7-9-0	4th in AFC West	1999	Denver	6-10-0	5th in AFC West
1982	San Francisco	3-6-0*	11th in overall NFC				

* Seasons when player strikes interrupted schedule.

Super Bowl Playoffs (Cont.)

1978 Season

AFC Playoffs

First Round . . . .*Houston 17, at *Miami 9
Second Round . . . . .Houston 31, at New England 14
at Pittsburgh 33, Denver 10
Championship . . . . .at Pittsburgh 34, Houston 5

NFC Playoffs

First Round . . . . .at *Atlanta 14, *Philadelphia 13
Second Round . . . . .at Dallas 27, Atlanta 20
at LA Rams 34, Minnesota 10
Championship . . . . .Dallas 28, at LA Rams 0

Super Bowl XIII
Jan. 21, 1979
Orange Bowl, Miami
Favorite: Steelers by 4   Attendance: 79,484

Pittsburgh (16-2) 7	14	0	14	**—35**
Dallas (14-4) 7	7	3	14	**—31**

MVP: Pittsburgh QB Terry Bradshaw (17 for 30, 318 yds, 4 TD, 1 Int)

1979 Season

AFC Playoffs

First Round . . . . .at *Houston 13, *Denver 7
Second Round . . . . .Houston 17, at San Diego 14
at Pittsburgh 34, Miami 14
Championship . . . . .at Pittsburgh 27, Houston 13

NFC Playoffs

First Round . . . . .at *Philadelphia 27, *Chicago 17
Second Round . . . . .at Tampa Bay 24, Philadelphia 17
LA Rams 21, at Dallas 19
Championship . . . . .LA Rams 9, at Tampa Bay 0

Super Bowl XIV
Jan. 20, 1980
Rose Bowl, Pasadena
Favorite: Steelers by 10½   Attendance: 103,985

LA Rams (11-7) 7	6	6	0	**—19**
Pittsburgh (14-4) 3	7	7	14	**—31**

MVP: Pittsburgh QB Terry Bradshaw (14 for 21, 309 yds, 2 TD, 3 Int)

1980 Season

AFC Playoffs

First Round . . . . .at *Oakland 27, *Houston 7
Second Round . . . . .at San Diego 20, Buffalo 14
Oakland 14, at Cleveland 12
Championship . . . . .Oakland 34, at San Diego 27

NFC Playoffs

First Round . . . . .at *Dallas 34, *LA Rams 13
Second Round . . . . .at Philadelphia 31, Minnesota 16
Dallas 30, at Atlanta 27
Championship . . . . .at Philadelphia 20, Dallas 7

Super Bowl XV
Jan. 25, 1981
Louisiana Superdome, New Orleans
Favorite: Eagles by 3   Attendance: 76,135

Oakland (14-5) 14	0	10	3	**—27**
Philadelphia (14-4) 0	3	0	7	**—10**

MVP: Oakland QB Jim Plunkett (13 for 21, 261 yds, 3 TD)

1981 Season

AFC Playoffs

First Round . . . .*Buffalo 31, at *NY Jets 27
Second Round . . . . .San Diego 41, at Miami 38 (OT)
at Cincinnati 28, Buffalo 21
Championship . . . . .at Cincinnati 27, San Diego 7

NFC Playoffs

First Round . . . .*NY Giants 27, at *Philadelphia 21
Second Round . . . . .at Dallas 38, Tampa Bay 0
at San Francisco 38, NY Giants 24
Championship . . . . .at San Francisco 28, Dallas 27

Super Bowl XVI
Jan. 24, 1982
Pontiac Silverdome, Pontiac, Mich.
Favorite: Pick'em   Attendance: 81,270

San Francisco (15-3) 7	13	0	6	**—26**
Cincinnati (14-4) 0	0	7	14	**—21**

MVP: San Francisco QB Joe Montana (14 for 22, 157 yds, 1 TD; 6 carries, 18 yds, 1 TD)

1982 Season

A 57-day players' strike shortened the regular season from 16 games to nine. The playoff format was changed to a 16-team tournament open to the top eight teams in each conference.

AFC Playoffs

First Round . . . . .at LA Raiders 27, Cleveland 10
at Miami 28, New England 3
NY Jets 44, at Cincinnati 17
San Diego 31, at Pittsburgh 28
Second Round . . . . .NY Jets 17, at LA Raiders 14
at Miami 34, San Diego 13
Championship . . . . .at Miami 14, NY Jets 0

NFC Playoffs

First Round . . . . .at Washington 31, Detroit 7
at Dallas 30, Tampa Bay 17
at Green Bay 41, St. Louis 16
at Minnesota 30, Atlanta 24
Second Round . . . . .at Washington 21, Minnesota 7
at Dallas 37, Green Bay 26
Championship . . . . .at Washington 31, Dallas 17

Super Bowl XVII
Jan. 30, 1983
Rose Bowl, Pasadena
Favorite: Dolphins by 3   Attendance: 103,667

Miami (10-2) 7	10	0	0	**—17**
Washington (11-1) 0	10	3	14	**—27**

MVP: Washington RB John Riggins (38 carries, 166 yds, 1 TD; 1 catch, 15 yds)

1983 Season

AFC Playoffs

First Round . . . . .at *Seattle 31, *Denver 7
Second Round . . . . .Seattle 27, at Miami 20
at LA Raiders 38, Pittsburgh 10
Championship . . . . .at LA Raiders 30, Seattle 14

NFC Playoffs

First Round . . . .*LA Rams 24, at *Dallas 17
Second Round . . . . .at San Francisco 24, Detroit 23
at Washington 51, LA Rams 7
Championship . . . . . . .at Washington 24, San Francisco 21

Super Bowl XVIII
Jan. 22, 1984
Tampa Stadium, Tampa
Favorite: Redskins by 3   Attendance: 72,920

Washington (16-2) 0   3   6   0   **—9**
LA Raiders (14-4).............7   14   14   3   **—38**
MVP: LA Raiders RB Marcus Allen (20 carries, 191 yds, 2 TD; 2 catches, 18 yds)

1984 Season

AFC Playoffs
First Round.................at *Seattle 13, *LA Raiders 7
Second Round ....at Miami 31, Seattle 10
Pittsburgh 24, at Denver 17
Championship...............at Miami 45, Pittsburgh 28

NFC Playoffs
First Round ....*NY Giants 16, at *LA Rams 13
Second Round.........at San Francisco 21, NY Giants 10
Chicago 23, at Washington 19
Championship ....at San Francisco 23, Chicago 0

Super Bowl XIX
Jan. 20, 1985
Stanford Stadium, Stanford, Calif.
Favorite: 49ers by 3   Attendance: 84,059

Miami (16-2) 10   6   0   0   **—16**
San Francisco (17-1)..........7   21   10   0   **—38**
MVP: San Francisco QB Joe Montana (24 for 35, 331 yds, 2 TD; 5 carries, 59 yards, 1 TD)

1985 Season

AFC Playoffs
First Round ....*New England 26, at *NY Jets 14
Second Round...............at Miami 24, Cleveland 21
New England 27, at LA Raiders 20
Championship ....New England 31, at Miami 14

NFC Playoffs
First Round ....at *NY Giants 17, *San Francisco 3
Second Round ....at LA Rams 20, Dallas 0
at Chicago 21, NY Giants 0
Championship ....at Chicago 24, LA Rams 0

Super Bowl XX
Jan. 26, 1986
Louisiana Superdome, New Orleans
Favorite: Bears by 10   Attendance: 73,818

Chicago Bears (17-1)........13   10   21   2   **—46**
New England (14-5)..........3   0   0   7   **—10**
MVP: Chicago DE Richard Dent (Bears defense: 7 sacks, 6 turnovers, 1 safety and gave up just 123 total yards)

Most Popular Playing Sites
Stadiums hosting more than one Super Bowl.

No		Years
5	Orange Bowl (Miami)	1968-69, 71, 76, 79
5	Rose Bowl (Pasadena)	1977, 80, 83, 87, 93
5	Superdome (N. Orleans)	1978, 81, 86, 90, 97
3	Tulane Stadium (N. Orleans)	1970, 72, 75
3	Joe Robbie/Pro Player Stadium (Miami)	1989, 95, 99
2	LA Memorial Coliseum	1967, 73
2	Tampa Stadium	1984, 91
2	Jack Murphy/Qualcomm Stadium (San Diego)	1988, 98
2	Georgia Dome (Atlanta)	1994, 2000

1986 Season

AFC Playoffs
First Round..............at *NY Jets 35, *Kansas City 15
Second Round ....at Cleveland 23, NY Jets 20 (OT)
at Denver 22, New England 17
Championship ....Denver 23, at Cleveland 20 (OT)

NFC Playoffs
First Round..............at *Washington 19, *LA Rams 7
Second Round...........Washington 27, at Chicago 13
at NY Giants 49, San Francisco 3
Championship ....at NY Giants 17, Washington 0

Super Bowl XXI
Jan. 25, 1987
Rose Bowl, Pasadena
Favorite: Giants by 9½   Attendance: 101,063

Denver (13-5) 10   0   0   10   **—20**
NY Giants (16-2)..............7   2   17   13   **—39**
MVP: NY Giants QB Phil Simms (22 for 25, 268 yds, 3 TD; 3 carries, 25 yds)

1987 Season
A 24-day players' strike shortened the regular season to 15 games with replacement teams playing for three weeks.

AFC Playoffs
First Round ....at *Houston 23, *Seattle 20 (OT)
Second Round ....at Cleveland 38, Indianapolis 21
at Denver 34, Houston 10
Championship...............at Denver 38, Cleveland 33

NFC Playoffs
First Round.........*Minnesota 44, at *New Orleans 10
Second Round........Minnesota 36, at San Francisco 24
Washington 21, at Chicago 17
Championship ....at Washington 17, Minnesota 10

Super Bowl XXII
Jan. 31, 1988
San Diego/Jack Murphy Stadium
Favorite: Broncos by 3½   Attendance: 73,302

Washington (13-4) 0   35   0   7   **—42**
Denver (12-4-1)...............10   0   0   0   **—10**
MVP: Washington QB Doug Williams (18 for 29, 340 yds, 4 TD, 1 Int)

1988 Season

AFC Playoffs
First Round..............*Houston 24, at *Cleveland 23
Second Round.................at Buffalo 17, Houston 10
at Cincinnati 21, Seattle 13
Championship..............at Cincinnati 21, Buffalo 10

NFC Playoffs
First Round..............at *Minnesota 28, *LA Rams 17
Second Round.........at San Francisco 34, Minnesota 9
at Chicago 20, Philadelphia 12
Championship ....San Francisco 28, at Chicago 3

Super Bowl XXIII
Jan. 22, 1989
Joe Robbie Stadium, Miami
Favorite: 49ers by 7   Attendance: 75,129

Cincinnati (14-4)..............0   3   10   3   **—16**
San Francisco (12-6)...........3   0   3   14   **—20**
MVP: San Francisco WR Jerry Rice (11 catches, 215 yds, 1 TD; 1 carry, 5 yds)

Super Bowl Playoffs (Cont.)

1989 Season

AFC Playoffs

First Round . . . .*Pittsburgh 26, at *Houston 23
Second Round . . . . .at Cleveland 34, Buffalo 30
                                        at Denver 24, Pittsburgh 23
Championship . . . . .at Denver 37, Cleveland 21

NFC Playoffs

First Round . . . .*LA Rams 21, at *Philadelphia 7
Second Round . . . . .LA Rams 19, NY Giants 13 (OT)
                                    at San Francisco 41, Minnesota 13
Championship . . . . .at San Francisco 30, LA Rams 3

Super Bowl XXIV
Jan. 28, 1990
Louisiana Superdome, New Orleans
Favorite: 49ers by 12½   Attendance: 72,919

San Francisco (17-2) 13   14 14 14 **—55**
Denver (13-6) 3   0   7   0 **—10**
MVP: San Francisco QB Joe Montana (22 for 29, 297 yds, 5 TD)

1990 Season

AFC Playoffs

First Round . . . . .at *Miami 17, *Kansas City 16
                                        at Cincinnati 41, *Houston 14
Second Round . . . . .at Buffalo 44, Miami 34
                                        at LA Raiders 20, Cincinnati 10
Championship . . . . .at Buffalo 51, LA Raiders 3

NFC Playoffs

First Round . . . .*Washington 20, at *Philadelphia 6
                                    at Chicago 16, *New Orleans 6
Second Round . . . . . . .at San Francisco 28, Washington 10
                            at NY Giants 31, Chicago 3
Championship . . . . .NY Giants 15, at San Francisco 13

Super Bowl XXV
Jan. 27, 1991
Tampa Stadium, Tampa
Favorite: Bills by 7   Attendance: 73,813

Buffalo (15-4) 3   9   0   7 **—19**
NY Giants (16-3) 3   7   7   3 **—20**
MVP: NY Giants RB Ottis Anderson (21 carries, 102 yds, 1 TD; 1 catch, 7 yds)

1991 Season

AFC Playoffs

First Round . . . . .at *Kansas City 10, *LA Raiders 6
                                    at Houston 17, *NY Jets 10
Second Round . . . . .at Denver 26, Houston 24
                                        at Buffalo 37, Kansas City 14
Championship . . . . .at Buffalo 10, Denver 7

NFC Playoffs

First Round . . . .*Atlanta 27, at New Orleans 20
                                    *Dallas 17, at *Chicago 13
Second Round . . . . .at Washington 24, Atlanta 7
                                        at Detroit 38, Dallas 6
Championship . . . . .at Washington 41, Detroit 10

Super Bowl XXVI
Jan. 26, 1992
Hubert Humphrey Metrodome, Minneapolis
Favorite: Redskins by 7   Attendance: 63,130

Washington (16-2) 0   17 14   6 **—37**
Buffalo (15-3) 0   0 10 14 **—24**
MVP: Washington QB Mark Rypien (18 for 33, 292 yds, 2 TD, 1 Int)

1992 Season

AFC Playoffs

First Round . . . . .at *Buffalo 41, *Houston 38 (OT)
                                    at San Diego 17, *Kansas City 0
Second Round . . . . .Buffalo 24, at Pittsburgh 3
                                        at Miami 31, San Diego 0
Championship . . . . .Buffalo 29, at Miami 10

NFC Playoffs

First Round . . . .*Washington 24, at Minnesota 7
                                    *Philadelphia 36, at *New Orleans 20
Second Round . . . . . . .at San Francisco 20, Washington 13
                            at Dallas 34, Philadelphia 10
Championship . . . . .Dallas 30, at San Francisco 20

Super Bowl XXVII
Jan. 31, 1993
Rose Bowl, Pasadena
Favorite: Cowboys by 7   Attendance: 98,374

Buffalo (14-5) 7   3   7   0 **—17**
Dallas (15-3) 14   14   3 21 **—52**
MVP: Dallas QB Troy Aikman (22 for 30, 273 yds, 4 TD)

1993 Season

AFC Playoffs

First Round . . . . .at Kansas City 27, *Pittsburgh 24 (OT)
                            at *LA Raiders 42, *Denver 24
Second Round . . . . .at Buffalo 29, LA Raiders 23
                                    Kansas City 28, at Houston 20
Championship . . . . .at Buffalo 30, Kansas City 13

NFC Playoffs

First Round . . . .*Green Bay 28, at Detroit 24
                                    at *NY Giants 17, *Minnesota 10
Second Round . . . . .at San Francisco 44, NY Giants 3
                                at Dallas 27, Green Bay 17
Championship . . . . .at Dallas 38, San Francisco 21

Super Bowl XXVIII
Jan. 30, 1994
Georgia Dome, Atlanta
Favorite: Cowboys by 10½   Attendance: 72,817

Dallas (15-4) 6   0 14 10 **—30**
Buffalo (14-5) 3   10   0   0 **—13**
MVP: Dallas RB Emmitt Smith (30 carries, 132 yds, 2 TDs; 4 catches, 26 yds)

1994 Season

AFC Playoffs

First Round . . . . .at Miami 27, *Kansas City 17
                                    at *Cleveland 20, *New England 13
Second Round . . . . .at Pittsburgh 29, Cleveland 9
                                    at San Diego 22, Miami 21
Championship . . . . .San Diego 17, at Pittsburgh 13

NFC Playoffs

First Round . . . . .at *Green Bay 16, *Detroit 12
                                    *Chicago 25, at Minnesota 18
Second Round . . . . .at San Francisco 44, Chicago 15
                                at Dallas 35, Green Bay 9
Championship . . . . .at San Francisco 38, Dallas 28

Super Bowl XXIX
Jan. 29, 1995
Joe Robbie Stadium, Miami
Favorite: 49ers by 18   Attendance: 74,107

San Diego (13-5) 7   3   8   8 **—26**
San Francisco (15-3) 14   14 14   7 **—49**
MVP: San Francisco QB Steve Young (24 for 36, 325 yds, 6 TD)

1995 Season

AFC Playoffs

First Round .at Buffalo 37, *Miami 22
*Indianapolis 35, at *San Diego 20
Second Round . . . . .at Pittsburgh 40, Buffalo 21
*Indianapolis 10, at Kansas City 7
Championship . . . . .at Pittsburgh 20, *Indianapolis 16

NFC Playoffs

First Round . . . . at *Philadelphia 58, *Detroit 37
at Green Bay 37, *Atlanta 20
Second Round . . . . Green Bay 27, at San Francisco 17
at Dallas 30, *Philadelphia 11
Championship . . . . at Dallas 38, Green Bay 27

Super Bowl XXX

Jan. 28, 1996
Sun Devil Stadium, Tempe, Ariz.
Favorite: Cowboys by 13½   Attendance: 76,347

Dallas (14-4)	10	3	7	7	**—27**
Pittsburgh (13-5)	0	7	0	10	**—17**

MVP: Dallas CB Larry Brown (2 interceptions for 77 yds)

1996 Season

AFC Playoffs

First Round . . . .*Jacksonville 30, at *Buffalo 27
at Pittsburgh 42, *Indianapolis 14
Second Round . . . .*Jacksonville 30, at Denver 27
at New England 28, Pittsburgh 3
Championship . . . . .at New England 20, *Jacksonville 6

NFC Playoffs

First Round . . . . at Dallas 40, *Minnesota 15
at *San Francisco 14, *Philadelphia 0
Second Round . . . . . . at Green Bay 35, *San Francisco 14
at Carolina 26, Dallas 17
Championship . . . . at Green Bay 30, Carolina 13

Super Bowl XXXI

Jan. 26, 1997
Louisiana Superdome, New Orleans
Favorite: Packers by 14   Attendance: 72,301

New England (13-5)	14	0	7	0	**—21**
Green Bay (15-3)	10	17	8	0	**—35**

MVP: Green Bay KR Desmond Howard (4 kickoff returns for 154 yds and 1 TD, also 6 punt returns for 90 yds)

1997 Season

AFC Playoffs

First Round . . . . .at *Denver 42, *Jacksonville 17
at New England 17, *Miami 3
Second Round . . . . .at Pittsburgh 7, New England 6
*Denver 14, at Kansas City 10
Championship . . . . *Denver 24, at Pittsburgh 21

NFC Playoffs

First Round . . . .*Minnesota 23, at NY Giants 22
at *Tampa Bay 20, *Detroit 10
Second Round . . . . . . .at San Francisco 38, *Minnesota 22
at Green Bay 21, *Tampa Bay 7
Championship . . . . .Green Bay 23, at San Francisco 10

Super Bowl XXXII

Jan. 25, 1998
Qualcomm Stadium, San Diego
Favorite: Packers by 11½   Attendance: 68,912

Green Bay (15-3)	7	7	3	7	**—24**
Denver (15-4)	7	10	7	7	**—31**

MVP: Denver RB Terrell Davis (30 carries, 157 yds, 3 TDs; 2 catches, 8 yds)

1998 Season

AFC Playoffs

First Round . . . . .at *Miami 24, *Buffalo 17
at Jacksonville 25, *New England 10
Second Round . . . . .at NY Jets 34, Jacksonville 24
at Denver 38, *Miami 3
Championship . . . . at Denver 23, NY Jets 10

NFC Playoffs

First Round . . . . .at *San Francisco 30, *Green Bay 27
*Arizona 20, at Dallas 7
Second Round . . . . .at Atlanta 20, *San Francisco 18
at Minnesota 41, *Arizona 21
Championship . . . . .Atlanta 30, at Minnesota 27 (OT)

Super Bowl XXXIII

Jan. 31, 1999
Pro Player Stadium, Miami
Favorite: Broncos by 7½   Attendance: 74,803

Denver (16-2)	7	10	0	17	**—34**
Atlanta (16-2)	3	3	0	13	**—19**

MVP: Denver QB John Elway (18 for 29, 336 yds, 1 TD, 1 Int and 1 rushing TD)

1999 Season

AFC Playoffs

First Round . . . . .at *Tennessee 22, *Buffalo 16
Miami 20, at Seattle 17
Second Round . . . . .at Jacksonville 62, *Miami 7
*Tennessee 19, at Indianapolis 16
Championship . . . . *Tennessee 33, at Jacksonville 14

NFC Playoffs

First Round . . . . .at Washington 27, *Detroit 13
at *Minnesota 27, *Dallas 10
Second Round . . . . .at Tampa Bay 14, Washington 13
at St. Louis 49, *Minnesota 37
Championship . . . . .at St. Louis 11, Tampa Bay 6

Super Bowl XXXIV

Jan. 30, 2000
Georgia Dome, Atlanta
Favorite: Rams by 7   Attendance: 72,625

St. Louis (15-3)	3	6	7	7	**—23**
Tennessee (16-3)	0	0	6	10	**—16**

MVP: St. Louis QB Kurt Warner (24 for 45, 414 yds, 2 TD)

NFL-NFC Championship Game

NFL Championship games from 1933-69 and NFC Championship games since the completion of the NFL-AFL merger following the 1969 season.

Multiple winners: Green Bay (10); Dallas (8); Chicago Bears and Washington (7); NY Giants and San Francisco (5); Cleveland Browns, Detroit, Minnesota, and Philadelphia (4); Baltimore and Cle-LA-St.L Rams (3).

Season	Winner	Head Coach	Score	Loser	Head Coach	Site
1933	Chicago Bears	George Halas	23-21	New York	Steve Owen	Chicago
1934	New York	Steve Owen	30-13	Chicago Bears	George Halas	New York
1935	Detroit	Potsy Clark	26-7	New York	Steve Owen	Detroit
1936	Green Bay	Curly Lambeau	21-6	Boston Redskins	Ray Flaherty	New York
1937	Washington Redskins	Ray Flaherty	28-21	Chicago Bears	George Halas	Chicago
1938	New York	Steve Owen	23-17	Green Bay	Curly Lambeau	New York
1939	Green Bay	Curly Lambeau	27-0	New York	Steve Owen	Milwaukee
1940	Chicago Bears	George Halas	73-0	Washington	Ray Flaherty	Washington
1941	Chicago Bears	George Halas	37-9	New York	Steve Owen	Chicago
1942	Washington	Ray Flaherty	14-6	Chicago Bears	Hunk Anderson & Luke Johnsos	Washington
1943	Chicago Bears	Hunk Anderson & Luke Johnsos	41-21	Washington	Arthur Bergman	Chicago
1944	Green Bay	Curly Lambeau	14-7	New York	Steve Owen	New York
1945	Cleveland Rams	Adam Walsh	15-14	Washington	Dudley DeGroot	Cleveland
1946	Chicago Bears	George Halas	24-14	New York	Steve Owen	New York
1947	Chicago Cardinals	Jimmy Conzelman	28-21	Philadelphia	Greasy Neale	Chicago
1948	Philadelphia	Greasy Neale	7-0	Chicago Cardinals	Jimmy Conzelman	Philadelphia
1949	Philadelphia	Greasy Neale	14-0	Los Angeles Rams	Clark Shaughnessy	Los Angeles
1950	Cleveland Browns	Paul Brown	30-28	Los Angeles	Joe Stydahar	Cleveland
1951	Los Angeles	Joe Stydahar	24-17	Cleveland	Paul Brown	Los Angeles
1952	Detroit	Buddy Parker	17-7	Cleveland	Paul Brown	Cleveland
1953	Detroit	Buddy Parker	17-16	Cleveland	Paul Brown	Detroit
1954	Cleveland	Paul Brown	56-10	Detroit	Buddy Parker	Cleveland
1955	Cleveland	Paul Brown	38-14	Los Angeles	Sid Gillman	Los Angeles
1956	New York	Jim Lee Howell	47-7	Chicago Bears	Paddy Driscoll	New York
1957	Detroit	George Wilson	59-14	Cleveland	Paul Brown	Detroit
1958	Baltimore	Weeb Ewbank	23-17*	New York	Jim Lee Howell	New York
1959	Baltimore	Weeb Ewbank	31-16	New York	Jim Lee Howell	Baltimore
1960	Philadelphia	Buck Shaw	17-13	Green Bay	Vince Lombardi	Philadelphia
1961	Green Bay	Vince Lombardi	37-0	New York	Allie Sherman	Green Bay
1962	Green Bay	Vince Lombardi	16-7	New York	Allie Sherman	New York
1963	Chicago	George Halas	14-10	New York	Allie Sherman	Chicago
1964	Cleveland	Blanton Collier	27-0	Baltimore	Don Shula	Cleveland
1965	Green Bay	Vince Lombardi	23-12	Cleveland	Blanton Collier	Green Bay
1966	Green Bay	Vince Lombardi	34-27	Dallas	Tom Landry	Dallas
1967	Green Bay	Vince Lombardi	21-17	Dallas	Tom Landry	Green Bay
1968	Baltimore	Don Shula	34-0	Cleveland	Blanton Collier	Cleveland
1969	Minnesota	Bud Grant	27-7	Cleveland	Blanton Collier	Minnesota
1970	Dallas	Tom Landry	17-10	San Francisco	Dick Nolan	San Francisco
1971	Dallas	Tom Landry	14-3	San Francisco	Dick Nolan	Dallas
1972	Washington	George Allen	26-3	Dallas	Tom Landry	Washington
1973	Minnesota	Bud Grant	27-10	Dallas	Tom Landry	Dallas
1974	Minnesota	Bud Grant	14-10	Los Angeles	Chuck Knox	Minnesota
1975	Dallas	Tom Landry	37-7	Los Angeles	Chuck Knox	Los Angeles
1976	Minnesota	Bud Grant	24-13	Los Angeles	Chuck Knox	Minnesota
1977	Dallas	Tom Landry	23-6	Minnesota	Bud Grant	Dallas
1978	Dallas	Tom Landry	28-0	Los Angeles	Ray Malavasi	Los Angeles
1979	Los Angeles	Ray Malavasi	9-0	Tampa Bay	John McKay	Tampa Bay
1980	Philadelphia	Dick Vermeil	20-7	Dallas	Tom Landry	Philadelphia
1981	San Francisco	Bill Walsh	28-27	Dallas	Tom Landry	San Francisco
1982	Washington	Joe Gibbs	31-17	Dallas	Tom Landry	Washington
1983	Washington	Joe Gibbs	24-21	San Francisco	Bill Walsh	Washington
1984	San Francisco	Bill Walsh	23-0	Chicago	Mike Ditka	San Francisco
1985	Chicago	Mike Ditka	24-0	Los Angeles	John Robinson	Chicago
1986	New York	Bill Parcells	17-0	Washington	Joe Gibbs	New York
1987	Washington	Joe Gibbs	17-10	Minnesota	Jerry Burns	Washington
1988	San Francisco	Bill Walsh	28-3	Chicago	Mike Ditka	Chicago
1989	San Francisco	George Seifert	30-3	Los Angeles	John Robinson	San Francisco
1990	New York	Bill Parcells	15-13	San Francisco	George Seifert	San Francisco
1991	Washington	Joe Gibbs	41-10	Detroit	Wayne Fontes	Washington
1992	Dallas	Jimmy Johnson	30-20	San Francisco	George Seifert	San Francisco
1993	Dallas	Jimmy Johnson	38-21	San Francisco	George Seifert	Dallas
1994	San Francisco	George Seifert	38-28	Dallas	Barry Switzer	San Francisco
1995	Dallas	Barry Switzer	38-27	Green Bay	Mike Holmgren	Dallas
1996	Green Bay	Mike Holmgren	30-13	Carolina	Dom Capers	Green Bay
1997	Green Bay	Mike Holmgren	23-10	San Francisco	Steve Mariucci	San Francisco
1998	Atlanta	Dan Reeves	30-27*	Minnesota	Dennis Green	Minnesota
1999	St. Louis	Dick Vermeil	11-6	Tampa Bay	Tony Dungy	St. Louis

*Sudden death overtime

NFL-NFC Championship Game Appearances

App		W	L	Pct	PF	PA	App		W	L	Pct	PF	PA
16	Dallas Cowboys	8	8	.500	361	319	7	Minnesota	4	3	.571	135	110
16	NY Giants	5	11	.313	240	322	6	Detroit	4	2	.667	139	141
13	Green Bay Packers	10	3	.769	303	177	5	Philadelphia	4	1	.800	79	48
13	Chicago Bears	7	6	.538	286	245	4	Baltimore Colts	3	1	.750	88	60
13	Cle-LA-St.L Rams	4	9	.308	134	276	2	Chicago Cardinals	1	1	.500	28	28
12	Boston-Wash.Redskins	7	5	.583	222	255	2	Tampa Bay	0	2	.000	6	20
12	San Francisco	5	7	.417	245	224	1	Atlanta	1	0	1.000	30	27
11	Cleveland Browns	4	7	.364	224	253	1	Carolina	0	1	.000	13	30

AFL-AFC Championship Game

AFL Championship games from 1960-69 and AFC Championship games since the completion of the NFL-AFL merger following the 1969 season.

Multiple winners: Buffalo and Denver (6); Miami and Pittsburgh (5); Oakland-LA Raiders (4); Dallas Texans-KC Chiefs and Houston Oilers-Tennessee Titans (3); Cincinnati, Jacksonville, New England and San Diego (2).

Season	Winner	Head Coach	Score	Loser	Head Coach	Site
1960	Houston	Lou Rymkus	24-16	LA Chargers	Sid Gillman	Houston
1961	Houston	Wally Lemm	10- 3	SD Chargers	Sid Gillman	San Diego
1962	Dallas	Hank Stram	20-17*	Houston	Pop Ivy	Houston
1963	San Diego	Sid Gillman	51-10	Boston Patriots	Mike Holovak	San Diego
1964	Buffalo	Lou Saban	20- 7	San Diego	Sid Gillman	Buffalo
1965	Buffalo	Lou Saban	23- 0	San Diego	Sid Gillman	San Diego
1966	Kansas City	Hank Stram	31- 7	Buffalo	Joel Collier	Buffalo
1967	Oakland	John Rauch	40- 7	Houston	Wally Lemm	Oakland
1968	NY Jets	Weeb Ewbank	27-23	Oakland	John Rauch	New York
1969	Kansas City	Hank Stram	17- 7	Oakland	John Madden	Oakland
1970	Baltimore	Don McCafferty	27-17	Oakland	John Madden	Baltimore
1971	Miami	Don Shula	21- 0	Baltimore	Don McCafferty	Miami
1972	Miami	Don Shula	21-17	Pittsburgh	Chuck Noll	Pittsburgh
1973	Miami	Don Shula	27-10	Oakland	John Madden	Miami
1974	Pittsburgh	Chuck Noll	24-13	Oakland	John Madden	Oakland
1975	Pittsburgh	Chuck Noll	16-10	Oakland	John Madden	Pittsburgh
1976	Oakland	John Madden	24- 7	Pittsburgh	Chuck Noll	Oakland
1977	Denver	Red Miller	20-17	Oakland	John Madden	Denver
1978	Pittsburgh	Chuck Noll	34- 5	Houston	Bum Phillips	Pittsburgh
1979	Pittsburgh	Chuck Noll	27-13	Houston	Bum Phillips	Pittsburgh
1980	Oakland	Tom Flores	34-27	San Diego	Don Coryell	San Diego
1981	Cincinnati	Forrest Gregg	27- 7	San Diego	Don Coryell	Cincinnati
1982	Miami	Don Shula	14- 0	NY Jets	Walt Michaels	Miami
1983	LA Raiders	Tom Flores	30-14	Seattle	Chuck Knox	Los Angeles
1984	Miami	Don Shula	45-28	Pittsburgh	Chuck Noll	Miami
1985	New England	Raymond Berry	31-14	Miami	Don Shula	Miami
1986	Denver	Dan Reeves	23-20*	Cleveland	Marty Schottenheimer	Cleveland
1987	Denver	Dan Reeves	38-33	Cleveland	Marty Schottenheimer	Denver
1988	Cincinnati	Sam Wyche	21-10	Buffalo	Marv Levy	Cincinnati
1989	Denver	Dan Reeves	37-21	Cleveland	Bud Carson	Denver
1990	Buffalo	Marv Levy	51-3	LA Raiders	Art Shell	Buffalo
1991	Buffalo	Marv Levy	10- 7	Denver	Dan Reeves	Buffalo
1992	Buffalo	Marv Levy	29-10	Miami	Don Shula	Miami
1993	Buffalo	Marv Levy	30-13	Kansas City	Marty Schottenheimer	Buffalo
1994	San Diego	Bobby Ross	17-13	Pittsburgh	Bill Cowher	Pittsburgh
1995	Pittsburgh	Bill Cowher	20-16	Indianapolis	Ted Marchibroda	Pittsburgh
1996	New England	Bill Parcells	20-6	Jacksonville	Tom Coughlin	New England
1997	Denver	Mike Shanahan	24-21	Pittsburgh	Bill Cowher	Pittsburgh
1998	Denver	Mike Shanahan	23-10	NY Jets	Bill Parcells	Denver
1999	Tennessee	Jeff Fisher	33-14	Jacksonville	Tom Coughlin	Jacksonville

*Sudden death overtime

AFL-AFC Championship Game Appearances

App		W	L	Pct	PF	PA	App		W	L	Pct	PF	PA
12	Oakland-LA Raiders	4	8	.333	228	264	3	Boston-NE Patriots	2	1	.750	61	71
10	Pittsburgh	5	5	.500	207	188	3	Baltimore-Indy Colts	1	2	.333	43	58
8	Buffalo	6	2	.750	180	92	3	NY Jets	1	2	.333	37	60
8	LA-San Diego Chargers	2	6	.250	128	161	3	Cleveland	0	3	.000	74	111
7	Denver	6	1	.857	172	132	2	Cincinnati	2	0	1.000	48	17
7	Miami	5	2	.714	152	115	2	Jacksonville	0	2	.000	20	53
7	Houston Oilers/Ten. Titans	3	4	.429	109	154	1	Seattle	0	1	.000	14	30
4	Dallas Texans/KC Chiefs	3	1	.750	81	61							

NFL Divisional Champions

The NFL adopted divisional play for the first time in 1967, splitting both conferences into two four-team divisions—the Capitol and Century divisions in the East and the Central and Coastal divisions in the West. Merger with the AFL in 1970 increased NFL membership to 26 teams and made it necessary for realignment. Two 13-team conferences—the AFC and NFC—were formed by moving established NFL clubs in Baltimore, Cleveland and Pittsburgh to the AFC and rearranging both conferences into Eastern, Central and Western divisions. Expansion has since increased the league to 31 teams with 16 teams in the AFC and 15 in the NFC. The AFC Central currently has six teams and all others have five.

Division champions are listed below; teams that went on to win the Super Bowl are in **bold** type. Note that in the 1980 season, Oakland won the Super Bowl as a wild card team, as did Denver in 1997; and in 1982, the players' strike shortened the regular season to nine games and eliminated divisional play for one season.

Multiple champions (since 1970): **AFC**—Pittsburgh (14); Miami (11); Denver and Oakland-LA Raiders (9); Buffalo (7); Baltimore-Indianapolis Colts and Cleveland (6); Cincinnati and San Diego (5); Kansas City and New England (4); Houston, Jacksonville and Seattle (2). **NFC**—San Francisco (16); Dallas (15); Minnesota (13); LA-St. Louis Rams (9); Chicago and Washington (6); Green Bay and NY Giants (4); Detroit and Tampa Bay (3); Atlanta, Philadelphia and St. Louis Cardinals (2).

	American Football League			**National Football League**			
Season	**East**	**West**	**Season**	**East**		**West**	
1966	Buffalo	Kansas City	1966	Dallas		**Green Bay**	
Season	**East**	**West**	**Season**	**Capitol**	**Century**	**Central**	**Coastal**
1967	Houston	Oakland	1967	Dallas	Cleveland	**Green Bay**	LA Rams
1968	**NY Jets**	Oakland	1968	Dallas	Cleveland	Minnesota	Baltimore
1969	NY Jets	Oakland	1969	Dallas	Cleveland	Minnesota	LA Rams

Note: Kansas City, an AFL second-place team, won the Super Bowl in the 1969 season.

	American Football Conference				**National Football Conference**		
Season	**East**	**Central**	**West**	**Season**	**East**	**Central**	**West**
1970	**Baltimore**	Cincinnati	Oakland	1970	Dallas	Minnesota	San Francisco
1971	Miami	Cleveland	Kansas City	1971	**Dallas**	Minnesota	San Francisco
1972	**Miami**	Pittsburgh	Oakland	1972	Washington	Green Bay	San Francisco
1973	**Miami**	Cincinnati	Oakland	1973	Dallas	Minnesota	LA Rams
1974	Miami	**Pittsburgh**	Oakland	1974	St. Louis	Minnesota	LA Rams
1975	Baltimore	**Pittsburgh**	Oakland	1975	St. Louis	Minnesota	LA Rams
1976	Baltimore	Pittsburgh	**Oakland**	1976	Dallas	Minnesota	LA Rams
1977	Baltimore	Pittsburgh	Denver	1977	**Dallas**	Minnesota	LA Rams
1978	New England	**Pittsburgh**	Denver	1978	Dallas	Minnesota	LA Rams
1979	Miami	**Pittsburgh**	San Diego	1979	Dallas	Tampa Bay	LA Rams
1980	Buffalo	Cleveland	San Diego	1980	Philadelphia	Minnesota	Atlanta
1981	Miami	Cincinnati	San Diego	1981	Dallas	Tampa Bay	**San Francisco**
1982	—	—	—	1982	—	—	—
1983	Miami	Pittsburgh	**LA Raiders**	1983	Washington	Detroit	San Francisco
1984	Miami	Pittsburgh	Denver	1984	Washington	Chicago	**San Francisco**
1985	Miami	Cleveland	LA Raiders	1985	Dallas	**Chicago**	LA Rams
1986	New England	Cleveland	Denver	1986	**NY Giants**	Chicago	San Francisco
1987	Indianapolis	Cleveland	Denver	1987	**Washington**	Chicago	San Francisco
1988	Buffalo	Cincinnati	Seattle	1988	Philadelphia	Chicago	**San Francisco**
1989	Buffalo	Cleveland	Denver	1989	NY Giants	Minnesota	**San Francisco**
1990	Buffalo	Cincinnati	LA Raiders	1990	**NY Giants**	Chicago	San Francisco
1991	Buffalo	Houston	Denver	1991	**Washington**	Detroit	New Orleans
1992	Miami	Pittsburgh	San Diego	1992	**Dallas**	Minnesota	San Francisco
1993	Buffalo	Houston	Kansas City	1993	**Dallas**	Detroit	San Francisco
1994	Miami	Pittsburgh	San Diego	1994	Dallas	Minnesota	**San Francisco**
1995	Buffalo	Pittsburgh	Kansas City	1995	**Dallas**	Green Bay	San Francisco
1996	New England	Pittsburgh	Denver	1996	Dallas	**Green Bay**	Carolina
1997	New England	Pittsburgh	Kansas City	1997	NY Giants	Green Bay	San Francisco
1998	NY Jets	Jacksonville	**Denver**	1998	Dallas	Minnesota	Atlanta
1999	Indianapolis	Jacksonville	Seattle	1999	Washington	Tampa Bay	**St. Louis**

Overall Postseason Games

The postseason records of all NFL teams, ranked by number of playoff games participated in from 1933 through the 1999 season.

Gm		W	L	Pct	PF	PA	Gm		W	L	Pct	PF	PA
53	Dallas Cowboys	32	21	.604	1274	979	21	Balt-Indianapolis Colts	10	11	.476	376	408
39	San Francisco 49ers	24	15	.615	984	759	20	Philadelphia Eagles	9	11	.450	356	369
38	Minnesota Vikings	16	22	.421	745	856	19	Dallas Texans/KC Chiefs	8	11	.421	301	384
37	Boston-Wash. Redskins	22	15	.595	778	652	18	LA-San Diego Chargers	7	11	.389	332	428
36	Oakland-LA Raiders	21	15	.583	855	659	17	Boston-NE Patriots	7	10	.412	310	357
36	Pittsburgh Steelers	21	15	.583	801	707	17	Detroit Lions	7	10	.412	365	404
36	Miami Dolphins	19	17	.528	754	784	13	New York Jets	6	7	.462	260	247
36	Cle-LA-St.L Rams	16	20	.444	584	756	12	Cincinnati Bengals	5	7	.417	246	257
33	New York Giants	14	19	.424	551	616	10	Atlanta Falcons	4	6	.400	208	260
32	Green Bay Packers	22	10	.688	772	558	8	Jacksonville Jaguars	4	4	.500	208	200
30	Cleveland Browns	11	19	.367	596	702	8	Seattle Seahawks	3	5	.375	145	159
29	Buffalo Bills	15	14	.483	681	658	8	Tampa Bay Buccaneers	3	5	.375	88	149
28	Chicago Bears	14	14	.500	579	552	7	Chi-St.L.-Ari. Cardinals	2	5	.286	122	182
27	Denver Broncos	16	11	.593	613	636	4	New Orleans Saints	0	4	.000	56	123
26	Houston Oilers/Ten. Titans	12	14	.462	461	602	2	Carolina Panthers	1	1	.500	39	47

All-Time Postseason Leaders

Through Super Bowl XXXIV in 2000; participants in 1999 season playoffs in **bold** type.

CAREER

Passing Efficiency

Ratings based on performance standards established for completion percentage, average gain, touchdown percentage and interception percentage. Minimum 150 passing attempts.

		Gm	Cmp%	Yds	TD	Int	Rtg
1	Bart Starr	10	61.0	1753	15	3	104.8
2	Joe Montana	23	62.7	5772	45	21	95.6
3	Kenny Anderson	6	66.3	1321	9	6	93.5
4	Joe Theismann	10	60.7	1782	11	7	91.4
5	Brett Favre	14	60.1	3390	25	12	91.1
6	**Troy Aikman**	16	63.8	3849	23	17	88.3
7	Steve Young	22	62.0	3325	20	13	85.8
8	Warren Moon	10	64.3	2870	17	14	84.9
9	Ken Stabler	13	57.8	2641	19	13	84.2
10	Bernie Kosar	10	56.3	1953	16	10	83.5

Passing

	Attempts	Gm	Att
1	Joe Montana, S.F.-KC	23	734
2	**Dan Marino**, Miami	18	687
3	John Elway, Denver	22	651

	Completions	Gm	Cmp
1	Joe Montana, SF-KC	23	460
2	**Dan Marino**, Miami	18	385
3	John Elway, Denver	22	355

	Yards Gained	Gm	Yds
1	Joe Montana, SF-KC	23	5772
2	John Elway, Denver	22	4964
3	**Dan Marino**, Miami	18	4510
4	Jim Kelly, Buffalo	17	3863
5	**Troy Aikman**, Dallas	16	3849

Games

	Played	Gm
1	D.D. Lewis, Dallas	27
2	Larry Cole, Dallas	26
3	Charlie Waters, Dallas	25

	Coached	Gm
1	Tom Landry, Dallas	36
	Don Shula, Baltimore-Miami	36
3	Chuck Noll, Pittsburgh	24

Scoring

	Points Scored	Season	Pts
1	Ricky Watters, SF vs. NYG	1993	30
2	Pat Harder, Det. vs. LA	1952	19
	Paul Hornung, GB vs. NYG	1961	19

	Field Goals	Season	FG
1	Chuck Nelson, Min. vs. SF	1987	5
	Matt Bahr, NYG vs. SF	1990	5
	Steve Christie, Buf. vs. Mia.	1992	5
	Brad Daluiso, NYG vs Min	1997	5

Rushing

	Yards Gained	Season	Yds
1	Eric Dickerson, LA Rams vs. Dal.	1985	248
2	Keith Lincoln, SD vs. Bos.	1963	206
3	Timmy Smith, Wash. vs. Den.	1987	204

	Most Attempts	Season	Att
1	Ricky Bell, T.B. vs. Phi	1979	38
	John Riggins, Wash. vs. Mia.	1982	38
3	Lawrence McCutcheon, LA vs. St. L.	1975	37
	John Riggins, Wash. vs. Minn.	1982	37

Rushing

	Yards Gained	Gm	Car	Yds	Avg
1	**Emmitt Smith**	17	349	1586	4.54
2	Franco Harris	19	400	1556	3.89
3	**Thurman Thomas**	21	339	1442	4.25
4	Tony Dorsett	17	302	1383	4.58
5	Marcus Allen	16	267	1347	5.04

	Attempts	Gm	Att
1	Franco Harris, Pittsburgh	19	400
2	**Emmitt Smith**, Dallas	17	349
	Thurman Thomas, Buffalo	21	339

Receiving

	Catches	Gm	No	Yds	Avg
1	Jerry Rice, San Francisco	23	124	1811	14.6
2	Michael Irvin, Dallas	16	87	1315	15.1
3	**Andre Reed**, Buffalo	21	85	1229	14.5

	Yards Gained	Gm	Yds
1	Jerry Rice, San Francisco	23	1811
2	Michael Irvin, Dallas	16	1315
3	Cliff Branch, Oakland-LA	22	1289
4	**Andre Reed**, Buffalo	21	1229
5	Fred Biletnikoff, Oakland	19	1167

	Average Gain (min. 20 rec.)	Gm	Avg
1	Alvin Harper, Dallas	10	27.3
2	Willie Gault, Chicago-LA	12	23.7
3	Harold Jackson, LA-NE-Minn-Sea	14	22.8

Scoring

	Points	Gm	TD	FG	PAT	Pts
1	**Gary Anderson**	19	0	28	49	133
2	**Thurman Thomas**	21	21	0	0	126
	Emmitt Smith	17	21	0	0	126
4	George Blanda	19	0	22	49	115

	Touchdowns	Gm	Run	Rec	Ret	No
1	**Thurman Thomas**	21	16	5	0	21
	Emmitt Smith	17	19	2	0	21
3	Jerry Rice	23	0	19	0	19

	Field Goals	Gm	Att	FG	Pct
1	**Gary Anderson**	19	35	28	.800
2	George Blanda	19	39	22	.564
	Steve Christie	12	25	22	.880
4	Matt Bahr	14	25	21	.840

SINGLE GAME

Passing

	Attempts	Season	Att
1	Steve Young, SF vs. GB	1995	65
2	Bernie Kosar, Cle. vs. NYJ	1986	64
	Dan Marino, Mia. vs. Buf.	1995	64

	Completions	Season	Cmp
1	Warren Moon, Hou. vs. Buf.	1992	36
2	Dan Fouts, SD vs. Mia.	1981	33
	Bernie Kosar, Cle. vs. NYJ	1986	33
	Dan Marino, Mia. vs. Buf.	1995	33

	Yards Gained	Season	Yds
1	Bernie Kosar, Cle. vs. NYJ	1986	489
2	Dan Fouts, SD vs. Mia.	1981	433
3	Dan Marino, Mia. vs. Buf.	1995	422

Receiving

	Catches	Season	Rec
1	Kellen Winslow, SD vs. Mia	1981	13
	Thurman Thomas, Buf. vs. Cle.	1989	13
	Shannon Sharpe, Den. vs. LA Raiders	1993	13

	Yards Gained	Season	Yds
1	Eric Moulds, Buf. vs Mia.	1998	240
2	Anthony Carter, Min. vs. SF	1987	227
3	Jerry Rice, SF vs. Cin.	1988	215

Champions of Leagues That No Longer Exist

No professional league in American sports has had to contend with more pretenders to the throne than the NFL. Seven times in as many decades a rival league has risen up to challenge the NFL and six of them went under in less than five seasons. Only the fourth American Football League (1960-69) succeeded, forcing the older league to sue for peace and a full partnership in 1966.

Of the six leagues that didn't make it, only the All-America Football Conference (1946-49) lives on—the Cleveland Browns and San Francisco 49ers joined the NFL after the AAFC folded in 1949. The champions of leagues past are listed below.

American Football League I

Year		Head Coach
1926	Philadelphia Quakers (8-2)	Bob Folwell

Note: Philadelphia was challenged to a postseason game by the 7th place New York Giants (8-4-1) of the NFL. The Giants won, 31-0, in a snowstorm.

American Football League II

Year		Head Coach
1936	Boston Shamrocks (8-3)	George Kenneally
1937	Los Angeles Bulldogs (9-0)	Gus Henderson

Note: Boston was scheduled to play 2nd place Cleveland (5-2-2) in the '36 championship game, but the Shamrock players refused to participate because they were owed pay for past games.

American Football League III

Year		Head Coach
1940	Columbus Bullies (8-1-1)	Phil Bucklew
1941	Columbus Bullies (5-1-2)	Phil Bucklew

All-America Football Conference

Year	Winner	Head Coach	Score	Loser	Head Coach	Site
1946	Cleveland Browns	Paul Brown	14-9	NY Yankees	Ray Flaherty	Cleveland
1947	Cleveland Browns	Paul Brown	14-3	NY Yankees	Ray Flaherty	New York
1948	Cleveland Browns	Paul Brown	49-7	Buffalo Bills	Red Dawson	Cleveland
1949	Cleveland Browns	Paul Brown	21-7	S.F. 49ers	Buck Shaw	Cleveland

World Football League

Year	Winner	Head Coach	Score	Loser	Head Coach	Site
1974	Birmingham Americans	Jack Gotta	22-21	Florida Blazers	Jack Pardee	Birmingham
1975	WFL folded Oct. 22.					

United States Football League

Year	Winner	Head Coach	Score	Loser	Head Coach	Site
1983	Michigan Panthers	Jim Stanley	24-22	Philadelphia Stars	Jim Mora	Denver
1984	Philadelphia Stars	Jim Mora	23-3	Arizona Wranglers	George Allen	Tampa
1985	Baltimore Stars	Jim Mora	28-24	Oakland Invaders	Charlie Sumner	E. Rutherford

---

Defunct Leagues

AFL I (1926): Boston Bulldogs, Brooklyn Horseman, Chicago Bulls, Cleveland Panthers, Los Angeles Wildcats, New York Yankees, Newark Bears, Philadelphia Quakers, Rock Island Independents.

AFL II (1936-37): Boston Shamrocks (1936-37); Brooklyn Tigers (1936); Cincinnati Bengals (1937); Cleveland Rams (1936); Los Angeles Bulldogs (1937); New York Yankees (1936-37); Pittsburgh Americans (1936-37); Rochester Tigers (1936-37).

AFL III (1940-41): Boston Bears (1940); Buffalo Indians (1940-41); Cincinnati Bengals (1940-41); Columbus Bullies (1940-41); Milwaukee Chiefs (1940-41); New York Yankees (1940) renamed Americans (1941).

AAFC (1946-49): Brooklyn Dodgers (1946-48) merged to become Brooklyn-New York Yankees (1949); Buffalo Bisons (1946) renamed Bills (1947-49); Chicago Rockets (1946-48) renamed Hornets (1949); Cleveland Browns (1946-49); Los Angeles Dons (1946-49); Miami Seahawks (1946) became Baltimore Colts (1947-49); New York Yankees (1946-48) merged to become Brooklyn-New York Yankees (1949); San Francisco 49ers (1946-49).

WFL (1974-75): Birmingham Americans (1974) renamed Vulcans (1975); Chicago Fire (1974) renamed Winds (1975); Detroit Wheels (1974); Florida Blazers (1974) became San Antonio Wings (1975); The Hawaiians (1974-75); Houston Texans (1974) became Shreveport (La.) Steamer (1974-75); Jacksonville Sharks (1974) renamed Express (1975); Memphis Southmen (1974) also known as Grizzlies (1975); New York Stars (1974) became Charlotte Hornets (1974-75); Philadelphia Bell (1974-75); Portland Storm (1974) renamed Thunder (1975); Southern California Sun (1974-75).

USFL (1983-85): Arizona Wranglers (1983-84) merged with Oklahoma to become Arizona Outlaws (1985); Birmingham Stallions (1983-85); Boston Breakers (1983) became New Orleans Breakers (1984) and then Portland Breakers (1985); Chicago Blitz (1983-84); Denver Gold (1983-85); Houston Gamblers (1984-85); Jacksonville Bulls (1984-85); Los Angeles Express (1983-85); Memphis Showboats (1984-85).

Michigan Panthers (1983-84) merged with Oakland (1985); New Jersey Generals (1983-85); Oakland Invaders (1983-85); Oklahoma Outlaws (1984) merged with Arizona to become Arizona Outlaws (1985); Philadelphia Stars (1983-84) became Baltimore Stars (1985); Pittsburgh Maulers (1984); San Antonio Gunslingers (1983-85); Tampa Bay Bandits (1983-85); Washington Federals (1983-84) became Orlando Renegades (1985).

NFL Pro Bowl

A postseason All-Star game between the new league champion and a team of professional all-stars was added to the NFL schedule in 1939. In the first game at Wrigley Field in Los Angeles, the NY Giants beat a team made up of players from NFL teams and two independent clubs in Los Angeles (the LA Bulldogs and Hollywood Stars). An all-NFL All-Star team provided the opposition over the next four seasons, but the game was cancelled in 1943.

The Pro Bowl was revived in 1951 as a contest between conference all-star teams: American vs National (1951-53), Eastern vs Western (1954-70), and AFC vs NFC (since 1971). The NFC leads the current series with the AFC, 16-14.

The MVP trophy was named the Dan McGuire Award in 1984 after the late SF 49ers publicist and *Honolulu Advertiser* sports columnist.

Year	Winner	Score	Loser	Year	Winner	MVP
1939	NY Giants	13-10	All-Stars			Line—Merlin Olsen, LA
1940	Green Bay	16-7	All-Stars	1970	West, 16-13	Back—Gale Sayers, Chi.
1940	Chicago Bears	28-14	All-Stars			Line—George Andrie, Dal.
1942	Chicago Bears	35-24	All-Stars	1971	NFC, 27-6	Back—Mel Renfro, Dal.
1942	All-Stars	17-14	Washington			Line—Fred Carr, GB
1943-50		No game		1972	AFC, 26-13	Off—Jan Stenerud, KC
						Def—Willie Lanier, KC

Year	Winner	MVP	Year	Winner	MVP
1951	American, 28-27	Otto Graham, Cle., QB	1973	AFC, 33-28	O.J. Simpson, Buf., RB
1952	National, 30-13	Dan Towler, LA, HB	1974	AFC, 15-13	Garo Yepremian, Mia., PK
1953	National, 27-7	Don Doll, Det., DB	1975	NFC, 17-10	James Harris, LA Rams, QB
1954	East, 20-9	Chuck Bednarik, Phi., LB	1976	NFC, 23-20	Billy Johnson, Hou., KR
1955	West, 26-19	Billy Wilson, SF, E	1977	AFC, 24-14	Mel Blount, Pit., CB
1956	East, 31-30	Ollie Matson, Cards, HB	1978	NFC, 14-13	Walter Payton, Chi., RB
1957	West, 19-10	Back—Bert Rechichar, Bal.	1979	NFC, 13-7	Ahmad Rashad, Min., WR
		Line—Ernie Stautner, Pit.	1980	NFC, 37-27	Chuck Muncie, NO, RB
1958	West, 26-7	Back—Hugh McElhenny, SF	1981	NFC, 21-7	Eddie Murray, Det., PK
		Line—Gene Brito, Wash.	1982	AFC, 16-13	Kellen Winslow, SD, WR
1959	East, 28-21	Back—Frank Gifford, NY			& Lee Roy Selmon, TB, DE
		Line—Doug Atkins, Chi.	1983	NFC, 20-19	Dan Fouts, SD, QB
1960	West, 38-21	Back—Johnny Unitas, Bal.			& John Jefferson, GB, WR
		Line—Big Daddy Lipscomb, Pit.	1984	NFC, 45-3	Joe Theismann, Wash., QB
1961	West, 35-31	Back—Johnny Unitas, Bal.	1985	AFC, 22-14	Mark Gastineau, NYJ, DE
		Line—Sam Huff, NY	1986	NFC, 28-24	Phil Simms, NYG, QB
1962	West, 31-30	Back—Jim Brown, Cle.	1987	AFC, 10-6	Reggie White, Phi., DE
		Line—Henry Jordan, GB	1988	AFC, 15-6	Bruce Smith, Buf., DE
1963	East, 30-20	Back—Jim Brown, Cle.	1989	NFC, 34-3	Randall Cunningham, Phi., QB
		Line—Big Daddy Lipscomb, Pit.	1990	NFC, 27-21	Jerry Gray, LA Rams, CB
1964	West, 31-17	Back—Johnny Unitas, Bal.	1991	AFC, 23-21	Jim Kelly, Buf., QB
		Line—Gino Marchetti, Bal.	1992	NFC, 21-15	Michael Irvin, Dal., WR
1965	West, 34-14	Back—Fran Tarkenton, Min.	1993	AFC, 23-20 (OT)	Steve Tasker, Buf., Sp. Teams
		Line—Terry Barr, Det.	1994	NFC, 17-3	Andre Rison, Atl., WR
1966	East, 36-7	Back—Jim Brown, Cle.	1995	AFC, 41-13	Marshall Faulk, Ind., RB
		Line—Dale Meinhart, St. L.	1996	NFC, 20-13	Jerry Rice, SF, WR
1967	East, 20-10	Back—Gale Sayers, Chi.	1997	AFC, 26-23 (OT)	Mark Brunell, Jax, QB
		Line—Floyd Peters, Phi.	1998	AFC, 29-24	Warren Moon, Sea., QB
1968	West, 38-20	Back—Gale Sayers, Chi.	1999	AFC, 23-10	Ty Law, NE, CB
		Line—Dave Robinson, GB			& Keyshawn Johnson, NYJ, WR
1969	West, 10-7	Back—Roman Gabriel, LA	2000	NFC, 51-31	Randy Moss, Min., WR

Playing sites: Wrigley Field in Los Angeles (1939); Gilmore Stadium in Los Angeles (1940—both games); Polo Grounds in New York (Jan., 1942); Shibe Park in Philadelphia (Dec., 1942); Memorial Coliseum in Los Angeles (1951-72 and 1979); Texas Stadium in Irving, TX (1973); Arrowhead Stadium in Kansas City (1974); Orange Bowl in Miami (1975); Superdome in New Orleans (1976); Kingdome in Seattle (1977); Tampa Stadium in Tampa (1978) and Aloha Stadium in Honolulu (since 1980).

AFL All-Star Game

The AFL did not play an All-Star game after its first season in 1960 but did stage All-Star games from 1962-70. All-Star teams from the Eastern and Western divisions played each other every year except 1966 with the West winning the series, 6-2. In 1966, the league champion Buffalo Bills met an elite squad made up of the best players from the league's other eight clubs and lost, 30-19.

Year	Winner	MVP	Year	Winner	MVP
1962	West, 47-27	Cotton Davidson, Oak., QB	1967	East, 30-23	Off—Babe Parilli, Bos.
1963	West, 21-14	Off—Curtis McClinton, Dal.			Def—Verlon Biggs, NY
		Def—Earl Faison, SD	1968	East, 25-24	Off—Joe Namath, NY
1964	West, 27-24	Off—Keith Lincoln, SD			& Don Maynard, NY
		Def—Archie Matsos, Oak.			Def—Speedy Duncan, SD
1965	West, 38-14	Off—Keith Lincoln, SD	1969	West, 38-25	Off—Len Dawson, KC
		Def—Willie Brown, Den.			Def—George Webster, Hou.
1966	All-Stars 30	Off—Joe Namath, NY	1970	West, 26-3	John Hadl, SD, QB
	Buffalo 19	Def—Frank Buncom, SD			

Playing sites: Balboa Stadium in San Diego (1962-64); Jeppesen Stadium in Houston (1965); Rice Stadium in Houston (1966); Oakland Coliseum (1967); Gator Bowl in Jacksonville (1968-69) and Astrodome in Houston (1970).

NFL Franchise Origins

Here is what the current 31 teams in the National Football League have to show for the years they have put in as members of the American Professional Football Association (APFA), the NFL, the All-America Football Conference (AAFC) and the American Football League (AFL). Years given for league titles indicate seasons championships were won.

American Football Conference

	First Season	League Titles	Franchise Stops
Baltimore Ravens	1996 (NFL)	None	• Baltimore (1996—)
Buffalo Bills	1960 (AFL)	2 AFL (1964-65)	• Buffalo (1960-72) Orchard Park, NY (1973—)
Cincinnati Bengals	1968 (AFL)	None	• Cincinnati (1968—)
Cleveland Browns	1946 (AAFC)	4 AAFC (1946-49) 4 NFL (1950,54-55,64)	• Cleveland (1946-95, 99—)
Denver Broncos	1960 (AFL)	2 Super Bowls (1997-98)	• Denver (1960—)
Indianapolis Colts	1953 (NFL)	3 NFL (1958-59,68) 1 Super Bowl (1970)	• Baltimore (1953-83) Indianapolis (1984—)
Jacksonville Jaguars	1995 (NFL)	None	• Jacksonville, FL (1995—)
Kansas City Chiefs	1960 (AFL)	3 AFL (1962,66,69) 1 Super Bowl (1969)	• Dallas (1960-62) Kansas City (1963—)
Miami Dolphins	1966 (AFL)	2 Super Bowls (1972-73)	• Miami (1966—)
New England Patriots	1960 (AFL)	None	• Boston (1960-70) Foxboro, MA (1971—)
New York Jets	1960 (AFL)	1 AFL (1968) 1 Super Bowl (1968)	• New York (1960-83) E. Rutherford, NJ (1984—)
Oakland Raiders	1960 (AFL)	1 AFL (1967) 3 Super Bowls (1976,80,83)	• Oakland (1960-81, 1995—) Los Angeles (1982-94)
Pittsburgh Steelers	1933 (NFL)	4 Super Bowls (1974-75,78-79)	• Pittsburgh (1933—)
San Diego Chargers	1960 (AFL)	1 AFL (1963)	• Los Angeles (1960) San Diego (1961—)
Seattle Seahawks	1976 (NFL)	None	• Seattle (1976—)
Tennessee Titans	1960 (AFL)	2 AFL (1960-61)	• Houston (1960-96) Memphis (1997) Nashville (1998—)

National Football Conference

	First Season	League Titles	Franchise Stops
Arizona Cardinals	1920 (APFA)	2 NFL (1925,47)	• Chicago (1920-59) St. Louis (1960-87) Tempe, AZ (1988—)
Atlanta Falcons	1966 (NFL)	None	• Atlanta (1966—)
Carolina Panthers	1995 (NFL)	None	• Clemson, SC (1995) Charlotte, NC (1996—)
Chicago Bears	1920 (APFA)	8 NFL (1921, 32-33,40-41,43,46,63) 1 Super Bowl (1985)	• Decatur, IL (1920) Chicago (1921—)
Dallas Cowboys	1960 (NFL)	5 Super Bowls (1971,77,92-93,95)	• Dallas (1960-70) Irving, TX (1971—)
Detroit Lions	1930 (NFL)	4 NFL (1935,52-53,57)	• Portsmouth, OH (1930-33) Detroit (1934-74) Pontiac, MI (1975—)
Green Bay Packers	1921 (APFA)	11 NFL (1929-31,36,39,44,61-62,65-67) 3 Super Bowls (1966-67,96)	• Green Bay (1921—)
Minnesota Vikings	1961 (NFL)	1 NFL (1969)	• Bloomington, MN (1961-81) Minneapolis, MN (1982—)
New Orleans Saints	1967 (NFL)	None	• New Orleans (1967—)
New York Giants	1925 (NFL)	4 NFL (1927,34,38,56) 2 Super Bowls (1986,90)	• New York (1925-73,75) New Haven, CT (1973-74) E. Rutherford, NJ (1976—)
Philadelphia Eagles	1933 (NFL)	3 NFL (1948-49,60)	• Philadelphia (1933—)
St. Louis Rams	1937 (NFL)	2 NFL (1945,51) 1 Super Bowl (1999)	• Cleveland (1936-45) Los Angeles (1946-79) Anaheim (1980-94) St. Louis (1995—)
San Francisco 49ers	1946 (AAFC)	5 Super Bowls (1981,84,88-89,94)	• San Francisco (1946—)
Tampa Bay Buccaneers	1976 (NFL)	None	• Tampa, FL (1976—)
Washington Redskins	1932 (NFL)	2 NFL (1937,42) 3 Super Bowls (1982,87,91)	• Boston (1932-36) Washington, DC (1937-96) Raljon, MD (1997—)

The Growth of the NFL

Of the 14 franchises that comprised the American Professional Football Association in 1920, only two remain—the Arizona Cardinals (then the Chicago Cardinals) and the Chicago Bears (originally the Decatur-IL Staleys). Green Bay joined the APFC in 1921 and the league changed its name to the NFL in 1922. Since then, 54 NFL clubs have come and gone, five rival leagues have expired and two other leagues have been swallowed up.

The NFL merged with the **All-America Football Conference** (1946-49) following the 1949 season and adopted three of its seven clubs—the Baltimore Colts, Cleveland Browns and San Francisco 49ers. The four remaining AAFC teams—the Brooklyn/NY Yankees, Buffalo Bills, Chicago Hornets and Los Angeles Dons—did not survive. After the 1950 season, the financially troubled Colts were sold back to the NFL. The league folded the team and added its players to the 1951 college draft pool. A new Baltimore franchise, also named the Colts, joined the NFL in 1953.

The formation of the **American Football League** (1960-69) was announced in 1959 with ownership lined up in eight cities—Boston, Buffalo, Dallas, Denver, Houston, Los Angeles, Minneapolis and New York. Set to begin play in the autumn of 1960, the AFL was stunned early that year when Minneapolis withdrew to accept an offer to join the NFL as an expansion team in 1961. The new league responded by choosing Oakland to replace Minneapolis and inherit the departed team's draft picks. Since no AFL team actually played in Minneapolis, it is not considered the original home of the Oakland Raiders.

In 1966, the NFL and AFL agreed to a merger that resulted in the first Super Bowl (originally called the AFL-NFL World Championship Game) following the '66 league playoffs. In 1970, the now 10-member AFL officially joined the NFL, forming a 26-team league made up of two conferences of three divisions each.

Expansion/Merger Timetable

For teams currently in NFL.

1921–Green Bay Packers; **1925**–New York Giants; **1930**–Portsmouth-OH Spartans (now Detroit Lions); **1932**–Boston Braves (now Washington Redskins); **1933**–Philadelphia Eagles and Pittsburgh Pirates (now Steelers); **1937**–Cleveland Rams (now St. Louis); **1950**–added AAFC's Cleveland Browns and San Francisco 49ers; **1953**–Baltimore Colts (now Indianapolis).

1960–Dallas Cowboys; **1961**–Minnesota Vikings; **1966**–Atlanta Falcons; **1967**–New Orleans Saints; **1970**–added AFL's Boston Patriots (now New England), Buffalo Bills, Cincinnati Bengals (1968 expansion team), Denver Broncos, Houston Oilers, Kansas City Chiefs, Miami Dolphins (1966 expansion team), New York Jets, Oakland Raiders and San Diego Chargers (the AFL-NFL merger divided the league into two 13-team conferences with old-line NFL clubs Baltimore, Cleveland and Pittsburgh moving to the AFC); **1976**–Seattle Seahawks and Tampa Bay Buccaneers (Seattle was originally in the NFC West and Tampa Bay in the AFC West, but were switched to their current divisions in 1977); **1995**–Carolina Panthers and Jacksonville Jaguars; **1996**–Cleveland Browns move to Baltimore and become Ravens. City of Cleveland retains rights to team name, colors and all memorabilia; **1999**–Cleveland Browns return to the NFL.

Looking forward: 2002–Houston Texans.

City and Nickname Changes

1921—Decatur Staleys move to Chicago; **1922**—Chicago Staleys renamed Bears; **1933**—Boston Braves renamed Redskins; **1937**—Boston Redskins move to Washington; **1934**—Portsmouth (Ohio) Spartans move to Detroit and become Lions; **1941**—Pittsburgh Pirates renamed Steelers; **1943**—Philadelphia and Pittsburgh merge for one season and become Phil-Pitt, or the "Steagles"; **1944**—Chicago Cardinals and Pittsburgh merge for one season and become Card-Pitt; **1946**—Cleveland Rams move to Los Angeles.

1960—Chicago Cardinals move to St. Louis; **1961**—Los Angeles Chargers (AFL) move to San Diego; **1963**—New York Titans (AFL) renamed Jets and Dallas Texans (AFL) move to Kansas City and become Chiefs; **1971**—Boston Patriots become New England Patriots; **1982**—Oakland Raiders move to Los Angeles; **1984**—Baltimore Colts move to Indianapolis; **1988**—St. Louis Cardinals move to Phoenix; **1994**—Phoenix Cardinals become Arizona Cardinals;. **1995**—L.A. Rams move to St. Louis and L.A. Raiders move back to Oakland; **1996**—Cleveland Browns move to Baltimore and become Ravens. City of Cleveland retains rights to team name, colors and all memorabilia; **1997**—Houston Oilers move to Memphis and become Tennessee Oilers; **1998**— Tennessee Oilers move to Nashville; **1999**— Tennessee Oilers renamed Titans.

Defunct NFL Teams

Teams that once played in the APFA and NFL, but no longer exist.

Akron-OH–Pros (1920-25) and Indians (1926); **Baltimore**–Colts (1950); **Boston**–Bulldogs (1926) and Yanks (1944-48); **Brooklyn**–Lions (1926), Dodgers (1930-43) and Tigers (1944); **Buffalo**–All-Americans (1920-23), Bisons (1924-25), Rangers (1926), Bisons (1927,1929); **Canton-OH**–Bulldogs (1920-23,1925-26); **Chicago**–Tigers (1920); **Cincinnati**–Celts (1921) and Reds (1933-34); **Cleveland**–Tigers (1920), Indians (1921), Indians (1923), Bulldogs (1924-25,1927) and Indians (1931); **Columbus-OH**–Panhandles (1920-22) and Tigers (1923-26); **Dallas**–Texans (1952); **Dayton-OH**–Triangles (1920-29).

Detroit–Heralds (1920-21), Panthers (1925-26) and Wolverines (1928); **Duluth-MN**–Kelleys (1923-25) and Eskimos (1926-27); **Evansville-IN**–Crimson Giants (1921-22); **Frankford-PA**–Yellow Jackets (1924-31); **Hammond-IN**–Pros (1920-26); **Hartford**–Blues (1926); **Kansas City**–Blues (1924) and Cowboys (1925-26); **Kenosha-WI**–Maroons (1924); **Los Angeles**–Buccaneers (1926); **Louisville**–Brecks (1921-23) and Colonels (1926); **Marion-OH**–Oorang Indians (1922-23); **Milwaukee**–Badgers (1922-26); **Minneapolis**–Marines (1922-24) and Red Jackets (1929-30); **Muncie-IN**–Flyers (1920-21).

New York–Giants (1921), Yankees (1927-28), Bulldogs (1949) and Yankees (1950-51); **Newark-NJ**–Tornadoes (1930); **Orange-NJ**–Tornadoes (1929); **Pottsville-PA**–Maroons (1925-31); **Racine-WI**–Legion (1922-24) and Tornadoes (1926); **Rochester-NY**–Jeffersons (1920-25); **Rock Island-IL**–Independents (1920-26); **Staten Island-NY**–Stapletons (1929-32); **St. Louis**–All-Stars (1923) and Gunners (1934); **Toledo-OH**–Maroons (1922-23); **Tonawanda-NY**–Kardex (1921), also called Lumbermen; **Washington**–Senators (1921).

Annual NFL Leaders

Individual leaders in NFL (1932-69), NFC (since 1970), AFL (1960-69) and AFC (since 1970).

Passing

Since 1932, the NFL has used several formulas to determine passing leadership, from Total Yards alone (1932-37), to the current rating system—adopted in 1973—that takes Completions, Completion Percentage, Yards Gained, TD Passes, Interceptions, Interception Percentage and other factors into account. The quarterbacks listed below all led the league according to the system in use at the time.

Multiple winners: Sammy Baugh and Steve Young (6); Joe Montana and Roger Staubach (5); Arnie Herber, Sonny Jurgensen, Bart Starr and Norm Van Brocklin (3); Ed Danowski, Otto Graham, Cecil Isbell, Milt Plum and Bob Waterfield (2).

NFL-NFC

Year		Att	Cmp	Yds	TD	Year		Att	Cmp	Yds	TD
1932	Arnie Herber, GB	101	37	639	9	1966	Bart Starr, GB	251	156	2257	14
1933	Harry Newman, NY	136	53	973	11	1967	Sonny Jurgensen, Wash	508	288	3747	31
1934	Arnie Herber, GB	115	42	799	8	1968	Earl Morrall, Bal	317	182	2909	26
1935	Ed Danowski, NY	113	57	794	10	1969	Sonny Jurgensen, Wash	442	274	3102	22
1936	Arnie Herber, GB	173	77	1239	11	1970	John Brodie, SF	378	223	2941	24
1937	Sammy Baugh, Wash	171	81	1127	8	1971	Roger Staubach, Dal	211	126	1882	15
1938	Ed Danowski, NY	129	70	848	7	1972	Norm Snead, NY	325	196	2307	17
1939	Parker Hall, Cle. Rams	208	106	1227	9	1973	Roger Staubach, Dal	286	179	2428	23
1940	Sammy Baugh, Wash	177	111	1367	12	1974	Sonny Jurgensen, Wash	167	107	1185	11
1941	Cecil Isbell, GB	206	117	1479	15	1975	Fran Tarkenton, Min	425	273	2994	25
1942	Cecil Isbell, GB	268	146	2021	24	1976	James Harris, LA	158	91	1460	8
1943	Sammy Baugh, Wash	239	133	1754	23	1977	Roger Staubach, Dal	361	210	2620	18
1944	Frank Filchock, Wash	147	84	1139	13	1978	Roger Staubach, Dal	413	231	3190	25
1945	Sammy Baugh, Wash	182	128	1669	11	1979	Roger Staubach, Dal	461	267	3586	27
	& Sid Luckman, Chi. Bears	217	117	1725	14	1980	Ron Jaworski, Phi	451	257	3529	27
1946	Bob Waterfield, LA	251	127	1747	18	1981	Joe Montana, SF	488	311	3565	19
1947	Sammy Baugh, Wash	354	210	2938	25	1982	Joe Theismann, Wash	252	161	2033	13
1948	Tommy Thompson, Phi	246	141	1965	25	1983	Steve Bartkowski, Atl	432	274	3167	22
1949	Sammy Baugh, Wash	255	145	1903	18	1984	Joe Montana, SF	432	279	3630	28
1950	Norm Van Brocklin, LA	233	127	2061	18	1985	Joe Montana, SF	494	303	3653	27
1951	Bob Waterfield, LA	176	88	1566	13	1986	Tommy Kramer, Min	372	208	3000	24
1952	Norm Van Brocklin, LA	205	113	1736	14	1987	Joe Montana, SF	398	266	3054	31
1953	Otto Graham, Cle	258	167	2722	11	1988	Wade Wilson, Min	332	204	2746	15
1954	Norm Van Brocklin, LA	260	139	2637	13	1989	Don Majkowski, GB	599	353	4318	27
1955	Otto Graham, Cle	185	98	1721	15	1990	Joe Montana, SF	520	321	3944	26
1956	Ed Brown, Chi. Bears	168	96	1667	11	1991	Steve Young, SF	279	180	2517	17
1957	Tommy O'Connell, Cle.	110	63	1229	9	1992	Steve Young, SF	402	268	3465	25
1958	Eddie LeBaron, Wash	145	79	1365	11	1993	Steve Young, SF	462	314	4023	29
1959	Charlie Conerly, NY	194	113	1706	14	1994	Steve Young, SF	461	324	3969	35
1960	Milt Plum, Cle	250	151	2297	21	1995	Brett Favre, GB	570	359	4413	38
1961	Milt Plum, Cle	302	177	2416	16	1996	Steve Young, SF	316	214	2410	14
1962	Bart Starr, GB	285	178	2438	12	1997	Steve Young, SF	356	241	3029	19
1963	Y.A. Tittle, NY	367	221	3145	36	1998	Randall Cunningham, Min	425	259	3704	34
1964	Bart Starr, GB	272	163	2144	15	1999	Kurt Warner, St.L	499	325	4353	41
1965	Rudy Bukich, Chi	312	176	2641	20						

Note: In 1945, Sammy Baugh and Sid Luckman tied with 8 points on an inverse rating system.

AFL-AFC

Multiple winners: Dan Marino (5); Ken Anderson and Len Dawson (4); Bob Griese, Daryle Lamonica, Warren Moon and Ken Stabler (2).

Year		Att	Cmp	Yds	TD	Year		Att	Cmp	Yds	TD
1960	Jack Kemp, LA	406	211	3018	20	1980	Brian Sipe, Cle	554	337	4132	30
1961	George Blanda, Hou	362	187	3330	36	1981	Ken Anderson, Cin	479	300	3753	29
1962	Len Dawson, Dal	310	189	2759	29	1982	Ken Anderson, Cin	309	218	2495	12
1963	Tobin Rote, SD	286	170	2510	20	1983	Dan Marino, Mia	296	173	2210	20
1964	Len Dawson, KC	354	199	2879	30	1984	Dan Marino, Mia	564	362	5084	48
1965	John Hadl, SD	348	174	2798	20	1985	Ken O'Brien, NY	488	297	3888	25
1966	Len Dawson, KC	284	159	2527	26	1986	Dan Marino, Mia	623	378	4746	44
1967	Daryle Lamonica, Oak	425	220	3228	30	1987	Bernie Kosar, Cle	389	241	3033	22
1968	Len Dawson, KC	224	131	2109	17	1988	Boomer Esiason, Cin	388	223	3572	28
1969	Greg Cook, Cin	197	106	1854	15	1989	Dan Marino, Mia	550	308	3997	24
1970	Daryle Lamonica, Oak	356	179	2516	22	1990	Warren Moon, Hou	584	362	4689	33
1971	Bob Griese, Mia	263	145	2089	19	1991	Jim Kelly, Buf	474	304	3844	33
1972	Earl Morrall, Mia	150	83	1360	11	1992	Warren Moon, Hou	346	224	2521	18
1973	Ken Stabler, Oak	260	163	1997	14	1993	John Elway, Den	551	348	4030	25
1974	Ken Anderson, Cin	328	213	2667	18	1994	Dan Marino, Mia	615	385	4453	30
1975	Ken Anderson, Cin	377	228	3169	21	1995	Jim Harbaugh, Ind	314	200	2575	17
1976	Ken Stabler, Oak	291	194	2737	27	1996	John Elway, Den	466	287	3328	26
1977	Bob Griese, Mia	307	180	2252	22	1997	Mark Brunell, Jax	435	264	3281	18
1978	Terry Bradshaw, Pit	368	207	2915	28	1998	Vinny Testaverde, NYJ	421	259	3256	29
1979	Dan Fouts, SD	530	332	4082	24	1999	Peyton Manning, Ind	533	331	4135	26

Receptions
NFL-NFC

Multiple winners: Don Hutson (8); Raymond Berry, Tom Fears, Pete Pihos, Jerry Rice, Sterling Sharpe and Billy Wilson (3); Dwight Clark, Herman Moore, Ahmad Rashad and Charley Taylor (2).

Year	Player	No	Yds	Avg	TD
1932	Ray Flaherty, NY	21	350	16.7	3
1933	Shipwreck Kelly, Bklyn	22	246	11.2	3
1934	Joe Carter, Phi	16	238	14.9	4
	& Red Badgro, NY	16	206	12.9	1
1935	Tod Goodwin, NY	26	432	16.6	4
1936	Don Hutson, GB	34	536	15.8	8
1937	Don Hutson, GB	41	552	13.5	7
1938	Gaynell Tinsley, Chi. Cards	41	516	12.6	1
1939	Don Hutson, GB	34	846	24.9	6
1940	Don Looney, Phi.	58	707	12.2	4
1941	Don Hutson, GB	58	739	12.7	10
1942	Don Hutson, GB	74	1211	16.4	17
1943	Don Hutson, GB	47	776	16.5	11
1944	Don Hutson, GB	58	866	14.9	9
1945	Don Hutson, GB	47	834	17.7	9
1946	Jim Benton, LA	63	981	15.6	6
1947	Jim Keane, Chi. Bears	64	910	14.2	10
1948	Tom Fears, LA	51	698	13.7	4
1949	Tom Fears, LA	77	1013	13.2	9
1950	Tom Fears, LA	84	1116	13.3	7
1951	Elroy Hirsch, LA	66	1495	22.7	17
1952	Mac Speedie, Cle	62	911	14.7	5
1953	Pete Pihos, Phi	63	1049	16.7	10
1954	Pete Pihos, Phi	60	872	14.5	10
	& Billy Wilson, SF	60	830	13.8	5
1955	Pete Pihos, Phi	62	864	13.9	7
1956	Billy Wilson, SF	60	889	14.8	5
1957	Billy Wilson, SF	52	757	14.6	6
1958	Raymond Berry, Bal	56	794	14.2	9
	& Pete Retzlaff, Phi	56	766	13.7	2
1959	Raymond Berry, Bal	66	959	14.5	14
1960	Raymond Berry, Bal	74	1298	17.5	10
1961	Red Phillips, LA	78	1092	14.0	5
1962	Bobby Mitchell, Wash	72	1384	19.2	11
1963	Bobby Joe Conrad, St. L	73	967	13.2	10
1964	Johnny Morris, Chi. Bears	93	1200	12.9	10
1965	Dave Parks, SF	80	1344	16.8	12
1966	Charley Taylor, Wash	72	1119	15.5	12
1967	Charley Taylor, Wash	70	990	14.1	9
1968	Clifton McNeil, SF	71	994	14.0	7
1969	Dan Abramowicz, NO	73	1015	13.9	7
1970	Dick Gordon, Chi.	71	1026	14.5	13
1971	Bob Tucker, NY	59	791	13.4	4
1972	Harold Jackson, Phi	62	1048	16.9	4
1973	Harold Carmichael, Phi.	67	1116	16.7	9
1974	Charles Young, Phi.	63	696	11.0	3
1975	Chuck Foreman, Min	73	691	9.5	9
1976	Drew Pearson, Dal	58	806	13.9	6
1977	Ahmad Rashad, Min	51	681	13.4	2
1978	Rickey Young, Min	88	704	8.0	5
1979	Ahmad Rashad, Min	80	1156	14.5	9
1980	Earl Cooper, SF	83	567	6.8	4
1981	Dwight Clark, SF	85	1105	13.0	4
1982	Dwight Clark, SF	60	913	12.2	5
1983	Roy Green, St. L	78	1227	15.7	14
	Charlie Brown, Wash	78	1225	15.7	8
	& Earnest Gray, NY	78	1139	14.6	5
1984	Art Monk, Wash	106	1372	12.9	7
1985	Roger Craig, SF	92	1016	11.0	6
1986	Jerry Rice, SF	86	1570	18.3	15
1987	J.T. Smith, St. L	91	1117	12.3	8
1988	Henry Ellard, LA	86	1414	16.4	10
1989	Sterling Sharpe, GB	90	1423	15.8	12
1990	Jerry Rice, SF	100	1502	15.0	13
1991	Michael Irvin, Dal	93	1523	16.4	8
1992	Sterling Sharpe, GB	108	1461	13.5	13
1993	Sterling Sharpe, GB	112	1274	11.4	11
1994	Cris Carter, Min	122	1256	10.3	7
1995	Herman Moore, Det	123	1686	13.7	14
1996	Jerry Rice, SF	108	1254	11.6	8
1997	Herman Moore, Det	104	1293	12.4	8
1998	Frank Sanders, Ari	89	1145	12.9	3
1999	Mushin Muhammad, Car	96	1253	13.1	8

AFL-AFC

Multiple winners: Lionel Taylor (5); Lance Alworth, Haywood Jeffires, Lydell Mitchell and Kellen Winslow (3); Fred Biletnikoff, Todd Christensen, Carl Pickens and Al Toon (2).

Year	Player	No	Yds	Avg	TD
1960	Lionel Taylor, Den	92	1235	13.4	12
1961	Lionel Taylor, Den	100	1176	11.8	4
1962	Lionel Taylor, Den	77	908	11.8	4
1963	Lionel Taylor, Den	78	1101	14.1	10
1964	Charley Hennigan, Hou	101	1546	15.3	8
1965	Lionel Taylor, Den	85	1131	13.3	6
1966	Lance Alworth, SD	73	1383	18.9	13
1967	George Sauer, NY	75	1189	15.9	6
1968	Lance Alworth, SD	68	1312	19.3	10
1969	Lance Alworth, SD	64	1003	15.7	4
1970	Marlin Briscoe, Buf	57	1036	18.2	8
1971	Fred Biletnikoff, Oak.	61	929	15.2	9
1972	Fred Biletnikoff, Oak.	58	802	13.8	7
1973	Fred Willis, Hou	57	371	6.5	1
1974	Lydell Mitchell, Bal	72	544	7.6	2
1975	Reggie Rucker, Cle	60	770	12.8	3
	& Lydell Mitchell, Bal	60	544	9.1	4
1976	MacArthur Lane, KC	66	686	10.4	1
1977	Lydell Mitchell, Bal	71	620	8.7	4
1978	Steve Largent, Sea	71	1168	16.5	8
1979	Joe Washington, Bal	82	750	9.1	3
1980	Kellen Winslow, SD	89	1290	14.5	9
1981	Kellen Winslow, SD	88	1075	12.2	10
1982	Kellen Winslow, SD	54	721	13.4	6
1983	Todd Christensen, LA	92	1247	13.6	12
1984	Ozzie Newsome, Cle	89	1001	11.2	5
1985	Lionel James, SD	86	1027	11.9	6
1986	Todd Christensen, LA	95	1153	12.1	8
1987	Al Toon, NY	68	976	14.4	5
1988	Al Toon, NY	93	1067	11.5	5
1989	Andre Reed, Buf	88	1312	14.9	9
1990	Haywood Jeffires, Hou	74	1048	14.2	8
	& Drew Hill, Hou	74	1019	13.8	5
1991	Haywood Jeffires, Hou	100	1181	11.8	7
1992	Haywood Jeffires, Hou	90	913	10.1	9
1993	Reggie Langhorne, Ind	85	1038	12.2	3
1994	Ben Coates, NE	96	1174	12.2	7
1995	Carl Pickens, Cin	99	1234	12.5	17
1996	Carl Pickens, Cin	100	1180	11.8	12
1997	Tim Brown, Oak.	104	1408	13.5	5
1998	O.J. McDuffie, Mia	90	1050	11.7	7
1999	Jimmy Smith, Jax	116	1636	14.1	6

Annual NFL Leaders (Cont.)
Rushing
NFL-NFC

Multiple winners: Jim Brown (8); Walter Payton and Barry Sanders (5); Emmitt Smith and Steve Van Buren (4); Eric Dickerson (3); Cliff Battles, John Brockington, Larry Brown, Bill Dudley, Leroy Kelly, Bill Paschal, Joe Perry, Gale Sayers and Whizzer White (2).

Year		Car	Yds	Avg	TD	Year		Car	Yds	Avg	TD
1932	Cliff Battles, Bos	148	576	3.9	3	1966	Gale Sayers, Chi	229	1231	5.4	8
1933	Jim Musick, Bos	173	809	4.7	5	1967	Leroy Kelly, Cle	235	1205	5.1	11
1934	Beattie Feathers, Chi. Bears	119	1004	8.4	8	1968	Leroy Kelly, Cle	248	1239	5.0	16
1935	Doug Russell, Chi. Cards	140	499	3.6	0	1969	Gale Sayers, Chi	236	1032	4.4	8
1936	Tuffy Leemans, NY	206	830	4.0	2	1970	Larry Brown, Wash	237	1125	4.7	5
1937	Cliff Battles, Wash	216	874	4.0	5	1971	John Brockington, GB	216	1105	5.1	4
1938	Whizzer White, Pit	152	567	3.7	4	1972	Larry Brown, Wash	285	1216	4.3	8
1939	Bill Osmanski, Chi. Bears	121	699	5.8	7	1973	John Brockington, GB	265	1144	4.3	3
1940	Whizzer White, Det	146	514	3.5	5	1974	Lawrence McCutcheon, LA	236	1109	4.7	3
1941	Pug Manders, Bklyn	111	486	4.4	5	1975	Jim Otis, St. L	269	1076	4.0	5
1942	Bill Dudley, Pit	162	696	4.3	5	1976	Walter Payton, Chi	311	1390	4.5	13
1943	Bill Paschal, NY	147	572	3.9	10	1977	Walter Payton, Chi	339	1852	5.5	14
1944	Bill Paschal, NY	196	737	3.8	9	1978	Walter Payton, Chi	333	1395	4.2	11
1945	Steve Van Buren, Phi	143	832	5.8	15	1979	Walter Payton, Chi	369	1610	4.4	14
1946	Bill Dudley, Pit	146	604	4.1	3	1980	Walter Payton, Chi	317	1460	4.6	6
1947	Steve Van Buren, Phi	217	1008	4.6	13	1981	George Rogers, NO	378	1674	4.4	13
1948	Steve Van Buren, Phi	201	945	4.7	10	1982	Tony Dorsett, Dal	177	745	4.2	5
1949	Steve Van Buren, Phi	263	1146	4.4	11	1983	Eric Dickerson, LA	390	1808	4.6	18
1950	Marion Motley, Cle	140	810	5.8	3	1984	Eric Dickerson, LA	379	2105	5.6	14
1951	Eddie Price, NY Giants	271	971	3.6	7	1985	Gerald Riggs, Atl	397	1719	4.3	10
1952	Dan Towler, LA	156	894	5.7	10	1986	Eric Dickerson, LA	404	1821	4.5	11
1953	Joe Perry, SF	192	1018	5.3	10	1987	Charles White, LA	324	1374	4.2	11
1954	Joe Perry, SF	173	1049	6.1	8	1988	Herschel Walker, Dal	361	1514	4.2	5
1955	Alan Ameche, Bal	213	961	4.5	9	1989	Barry Sanders, Det	280	1470	5.3	14
1956	Rick Casares, Chi. Bears	234	1126	4.8	12	1990	Barry Sanders, Det	255	1304	5.1	13
1957	Jim Brown, Cle	202	942	4.7	9	1991	Emmitt Smith, Dal	365	1563	4.3	12
1958	Jim Brown, Cle	257	1527	5.9	17	1992	Emmitt Smith, Dal	373	1713	4.6	18
1959	Jim Brown, Cle	290	1329	4.6	14	1993	Emmitt Smith, Dal	283	1486	5.3	9
1960	Jim Brown, Cle	215	1257	5.8	9	1994	Barry Sanders, Det	331	1883	5.7	7
1961	Jim Brown, Cle	305	1408	4.6	8	1995	Emmitt Smith, Dal	377	1773	4.7	25
1962	Jim Taylor, GB	272	1474	5.4	19	1996	Barry Sanders, Det	307	1553	5.1	11
1963	Jim Brown, Cle	291	1863	6.4	12	1997	Barry Sanders, Det	335	2053	6.1	11
1964	Jim Brown, Cle	280	1446	5.2	7	1998	Jamal Anderson, Atl	410	1846	4.5	14
1965	Jim Brown, Cle	289	1544	5.3	17	1999	Stephen Davis, Wash	290	1405	4.8	17

Note: Jim Brown led the NFL in rushing eight of his nine years in the league. The one season he didn't win (1962) he finished fourth (996 yds) behind Jim Taylor, John Henry Johnson of Pittsburgh (1,141 yds) and Dick Bass of the LA Rams (1,033 yds).

AFL-AFC

Multiple winners: Earl Campbell and O.J. Simpson (4); Terrell Davis and Thurman Thomas (3); Eric Dickerson, Cookie Gilchrist, Floyd Little, Jim Nance and Curt Warner (2).

Year		Car	Yds	Avg	TD	Year		Car	Yds	Avg	TD
1960	Abner Haynes, Dal	157	875	5.6	9	1980	Earl Campbell, Hou	373	1934	5.2	13
1961	Billy Cannon, Hou	200	948	4.7	6	1981	Earl Campbell, Hou	361	1376	3.8	10
1962	Cookie Gilchrist, Buf	214	1096	5.1	13	1982	Freeman McNeil, NY	151	786	5.2	6
1963	Clem Daniels, Oak	215	1099	5.1	3	1983	Curt Warner, Sea	335	1449	4.3	13
1964	Cookie Gilchrist, Buf	230	981	4.3	6	1984	Earnest Jackson, SD	296	1179	4.0	8
1965	Paul Lowe, SD	222	1121	5.0	7	1985	Marcus Allen, LA	380	1759	4.6	11
1966	Jim Nance, Bos	299	1458	4.9	11	1986	Curt Warner, Sea	319	1481	4.6	13
1967	Jim Nance, Bos	269	1216	4.5	7	1987	Eric Dickerson, Ind	223	1011	4.5	5
1968	Paul Robinson, Cin	238	1023	4.3	8	1988	Eric Dickerson, Ind	388	1659	4.3	14
1969	Dickie Post, SD	182	873	4.8	6	1989	Christian Okoye, KC	370	1480	4.0	12
1970	Floyd Little, Den	209	901	4.3	3	1990	Thurman Thomas, Buf	271	1297	4.8	11
1971	Floyd Little, Den	284	1133	4.0	6	1991	Thurman Thomas, Buf	288	1407	4.9	7
1972	O.J. Simpson, Buf	292	1251	4.3	6	1992	Barry Foster, Pit	390	1690	4.3	11
1973	O.J. Simpson, Buf	332	2003	6.0	12	1993	Thurman Thomas, Buf	355	1315	3.7	6
1974	Otis Armstrong, Den	263	1407	5.3	9	1994	Chris Warren, Sea	333	1545	4.6	9
1975	O.J. Simpson, Buf	329	1817	5.5	16	1995	Curtis Martin, NE	368	1487	4.0	14
1976	O.J. Simpson, Buf	290	1503	5.2	8	1996	Terrell Davis, Den	345	1538	4.5	13
1977	Mark van Eeghen, Oak	324	1273	3.9	7	1997	Terrell Davis, Den	369	1750	4.7	15
1978	Earl Campbell, Hou	302	1450	4.8	13	1998	Terrell Davis, Den	392	2008	5.1	21
1979	Earl Campbell, Hou	368	1697	4.6	19	1999	Edgerrin James, Ind	369	1553	4.2	13

Note: Eric Dickerson was traded to Indianapolis from the NFC's LA Rams during the 1987 season. In three games with the Rams, he carried the ball 60 times for 277 yds, a 4.6 avg and 1 TD. His official AFC statistics above came in nine games with the Colts.

Scoring
NFL-NFC

Multiple winners: Don Hutson (5); Dutch Clark, Pat Harder, Paul Hornung, Chip Lohmiller and Mark Moseley (3); Kevin Butler, Mike Cofer, Fred Cox, Jack Manders, Chester Marcol, Eddie Murray, Emmitt Smith, Gordy Soltau and Doak Walker (2).

Year		TD	FG	PAT	Pts	Year		TD	FG	PAT	Pts
1932	Dutch Clark, Portsmouth	6	3	10	55	1967	Jim Bakken, St.L	0	27	36	117
1933	Glenn Presnell, Portsmouth	6	6	10	64	1968	Leroy Kelly, Cle	20	0	0	120
	& Ken Strong, NY	6	5	13	64	1969	Fred Cox, Min	0	26	43	121
1934	Jack Manders, Chi. Bears	3	10	31	79	1970	Fred Cox, Min	0	30	35	125
1935	Dutch Clark, Det	6	1	16	55	1971	Curt Knight, Wash	0	29	27	114
1936	Dutch Clark, Det	7	4	19	73	1972	Chester Marcol, GB	0	33	29	128
1937	Jack Manders, Chi. Bears	5	8	15	69	1973	David Ray, LA	0	30	40	130
1938	Clarke Hinkle, GB	7	3	7	58	1974	Chester Marcol, GB	0	25	19	94
1939	Andy Farkas, Wash	11	0	2	68	1975	Chuck Foreman, Min	22	0	0	132
1940	Don Hutson, GB	7	0	15	57	1976	Mark Moseley, Wash	0	22	31	97
1941	Don Hutson, GB	12	1	20	95	1977	Walter Payton, Chi	16	0	0	96
1942	Don Hutson, GB	17	1	33	138	1978	Frank Corral, LA	0	29	31	118
1943	Don Hutson, GB	12	3	26	117	1979	Mark Moseley, Wash	0	25	39	114
1944	Don Hutson, GB	9	0	31	85	1980	Eddie Murray, Det	0	27	35	116
1945	Steve Van Buren, Phi	18	0	2	110	1981	Rafael Septien, Dal	0	27	40	121
1946	Ted Fritsch, GB	10	9	13	100		& Eddie Murray, Det	0	25	46	121
1947	Pat Harder, Chi. Cards	7	7	39	102	1982	Wendell Tyler, LA	13	0	0	78
1948	Pat Harder, Chi. Cards	6	7	53	110	1983	Mark Moseley, Wash	0	33	62	161
1949	Gene Roberts, NY Giants	17	0	0	102	1984	Ray Wersching, SF	0	25	56	131
	& Pat Harder, Chi. Cards	8	3	45	102	1985	Kevin Butler, Chi	0	31	51	144
1950	Doak Walker, Det	11	8	38	128	1986	Kevin Butler, Chi	0	28	36	120
1951	Elroy Hirsch, LA	17	0	0	102	1987	Jerry Rice, SF	23	0	0	138
1952	Gordy Soltau, SF	7	6	34	94	1988	Mike Cofer, SF	0	27	40	121
1953	Gordy Soltau, SF	6	10	48	114	1989	Mike Cofer, SF	0	29	49	136
1954	Bobby Walston, Phi	11	4	36	114	1990	Chip Lohmiller, Wash	0	30	41	131
1955	Doak Walker, Det	7	9	27	96	1991	Chip Lohmiller, Wash	0	31	56	149
1956	Bobby Layne, Det	5	12	33	99	1992	Chip Lohmiller, Wash	0	30	30	120
1957	Sam Baker, Wash	1	14	29	77		& Morten Andersen, NO	0	29	33	120
	& Lou Groza, Cle	0	15	32	77	1993	Jason Hanson, Det	0	34	28	130
1958	Jim Brown, Cle	18	0	0	108	1994	Emmitt Smith, Dal	22	0	0	132
1959	Paul Hornung, GB	7	7	31	94		& Fuad Reveiz, Min	0	34	30	132
1960	Paul Hornung, GB	15	15	41	176	1995	Emmitt Smith, Dal	25	0	0	150
1961	Paul Hornung, GB	10	15	41	146	1996	John Kasay, Car	0	37	34	145
1962	Jim Taylor, GB	19	0	0	114	1997	Richie Cunningham, Dal	0	34	24	126
1963	Don Chandler, NY	0	18	52	106	1998	Gary Anderson, Min	0	35	59	164
1964	Lenny Moore, Bal	20	0	0	120	1999	Jeff Wilkins, St.L	0	20	64	124
1965	Gale Sayers, Chi	22	0	0	132						
1966	Bruce Gossett, LA	0	28	29	113						

AFL-AFC

Multiple winners: Gino Cappelletti (5); Gary Anderson (3); Jim Breech, Roy Gerela, Gene Mingo, Nick Lowery, John Smith, Pete Stoyanovich and Jim Turner (2).

Year		TD	FG	PAT	Pts	Year		TD	FG	PAT	Pts
1960	Gene Mingo, Den	6	18	33	123	1981	Nick Lowery, KC	0	26	37	115
1961	Gino Cappelletti, Bos	8	17	48	147		& Jim Breech, Cin	0	22	49	115
1962	Gene Mingo, Den	4	27	32	137	1982	Marcus Allen, LA	14	0	0	84
1963	Gino Cappelletti, Bos	2	22	35	113	1983	Gary Anderson, Pit	0	27	38	119
1964	Gino Cappelletti, Bos	7	25	36	155	1984	Gary Anderson, Pit	0	24	45	117
1965	Gino Cappelletti, Bos	9	17	27	132	1985	Gary Anderson, Pit	0	33	40	139
1966	Gino Cappelletti, Bos	6	16	35	119	1986	Tony Franklin, NE	0	32	44	140
1967	George Blanda, Oak	0	20	56	116	1987	Jim Breech, Cin	0	24	25	97
1968	Jim Turner, NY	0	34	43	145	1988	Scott Norwood, Buf	0	32	33	129
1969	Jim Turner, NY	0	32	33	129	1989	David Treadwell, Den	0	27	39	120
1970	Jan Stenerud, KC	0	30	26	116	1990	Nick Lowery, KC	0	34	37	139
1971	Garo Yepremian, Mia	0	28	33	117	1991	Pete Stoyanovich, Mia	0	31	28	121
1972	Bobby Howfield, NY	0	27	40	121	1992	Pete Stoyanovich, Mia	0	30	34	124
1973	Roy Gerela, Pit	0	29	36	123	1993	Jeff Jaeger, LA	0	35	27	132
1974	Roy Gerela, Pit	0	20	33	93	1994	John Carney, SD	0	34	33	135
1975	O.J. Simpson, Buf	23	0	0	138	1995	Norm Johnson, Pit	0	34	39	141
1976	Toni Linhart, Bal	0	20	49	109	1996	Cary Blanchard, Ind	0	36	27	135
1977	Errol Mann, Oak	0	20	39	99	1997	Mike Hollis, Jax	0	31	41	134
1978	Pat Leahy, NY	0	22	41	107	1998	Steve Christie, Buf	0	33	41	140
1979	John Smith, NE	0	23	46	115	1999	Mike Vanderjagt, Ind	0	34	43	145
1980	John Smith, NE	0	26	51	129						

All-Time NFL Leaders

Through 1999 regular season.

CAREER

Players active in 1999 in **bold** type.

Passing Efficiency

Ratings based on performance standards established for completion percentage, average gain, touchdown percentage and interception percentage. Quarterbacks are allocated points according to how their statistics measure up to those standards. Minimum 1500 passing attempts.

		Yrs	Att	Cmp	Cmp%	Yards	Avg Gain	TD	TD%	Int	Int%	Rating
1	**Steve Young**	15	4149	2667	64.36	33,124	7.98	232	5.6	107	2.6	96.8
2	Joe Montana	15	5391	3409	63.2	40,551	7.52	273	5.1	139	2.6	92.3
3	**Brett Favre**	9	4352	2659	61.1	30,894	7.10	235	5.4	141	3.2	87.1
4	**Dan Marino**	17	8358	4967	59.4	61,361	7.34	420	5.0	252	3.0	86.4
5	**Mark Brunell**	6	2160	1297	60.1	15,572	7.21	86	4.0	52	2.4	85.4
6	Jim Kelly	11	4779	2874	60.1	35,467	7.42	237	5.0	175	3.7	84.4
7	Roger Staubach	11	2958	1685	57.0	22,700	7.67	153	5.2	109	3.7	83.4
8	Neil Lomax	8	3153	1817	57.6	22,771	7.22	136	4.3	90	2.9	82.7
9	**Troy Aikman**	11	4453	2742	61.6	31,310	7.03	158	3.5	127	2.9	82.638
10	Sonny Jurgensen	19	4262	2433	57.1	32,224	7.56	255	6.0	189	4.4	82.625
11	Len Dawson	19	3741	2136	57.1	28,711	7.67	239	6.4	183	4.9	82.555
12	**Neil O'Donnell**	10	3057	1766	57.8	20,408	6.68	114	3.7	62	2.0	82.0
13	Ken Anderson	16	4475	2654	59.3	32,838	7.34	197	4.4	160	3.6	81.9
14	Bernie Kosar	12	3365	1994	59.3	23,301	6.92	124	3.7	87	2.6	81.8
15	Danny White	13	2950	1761	59.7	21,959	7.44	155	5.3	132	4.5	81.7
16	Dave Krieg	19	5311	3105	58.5	38,147	7.18	261	4.9	199	3.7	81.5
17	**Randall Cunningham**	14	4075	2301	56.5	28,557	7.01	198	4.9	128	3.1	81.4
18	**Chris Chandler**	12	2894	1668	57.6	20,865	7.21	135	4.7	101	3.5	81.2
19	**Steve Beuerlein**	11	2615	1469	56.2	19,002	7.27	120	4.6	84	3.2	81.086
20	Boomer Esiason	14	5205	2969	57.0	37,920	7.29	247	4.7	184	3.5	81.062
21	**Warren Moon**	17	6789	3973	58.5	49,117	7.23	290	4.3	232	3.4	80.996
22	**Jeff George**	10	3731	2162	58.0	26,045	6.98	147	3.9	104	2.8	80.978
23	Jeff Hostetler	12	2338	1357	58.0	16,430	7.03	94	4.0	71	3.0	80.480
24	Bart Starr	16	3149	1808	57.4	24,718	7.85	152	4.8	138	4.4	80.465
25	Ken O'Brien	10	3602	2110	58.6	25,094	6.97	128	3.6	98	2.7	80.4

Note: The NFL does not recognize records from the All-American Football Conference (1946-49). If it did, **Otto Graham** would rank 4th (after Favre) with the following stats: 10 Yrs; 2,626 Att; 1,464 Comp; 55.8 Comp Pct; 23,584 Yards; 8.98 Avg Gain; 174 TD; 6.6 TD Pct; 135 Int; 5.1 Int Pct; and 86.6 Rating Pts.

Touchdown Passes

		No			No			No
1	**Dan Marino**	420	16	**Steve Young**	232	31	Ken Stabler	194
2	Fran Tarkenton	342	17	John Brodie	214	32	Bob Griese	192
3	John Elway	300	18	Terry Bradshaw	212	33	Sammy Baugh	187
4	Johnny Unitas	290		Y.A. Tittle	212	34	Craig Morton	183
	Warren Moon	290	20	Jim Hart	209	35	Steve Grogan	182
6	Joe Montana	273	21	**Vinny Testaverde**	205	36	Ron Jaworski	179
7	Dave Krieg	261	22	Jim Everett	203	37	Babe Parilli	178
8	Sonny Jurgensen	255	23	Roman Gabriel	201	38	Charlie Conerly	173
9	Dan Fouts	254	24	Phil Simms	199		Joe Namath	173
10	Boomer Esiason	247	25	**Randall Cunningham**	198		Norm Van Brocklin	173
11	John Hadl	244	26	Ken Anderson	197	41	Charley Johnson	170
12	Len Dawson	239	27	Joe Ferguson	196	42	Daryle Lamonica	164
13	Jim Kelly	237		Bobby Layne	196		Jim Plunkett	164
14	George Blanda	236		Steve Grogan	196	44	Earl Morrall	161
15	**Brett Favre**	235		Norm Snead	196	45	Joe Theismann	160

Note: The NFL does not recognize records from the All-American Football Conference (1946-49). If it did, **Y.A. Tittle** would move up from 18th to 12th (after Hadl) with 242 TDs and **Otto Graham** would rank 38th (after Parilli) with 174 TDs.

Passes Intercepted

		No			No			No
1	George Blanda	277	10	**Warren Moon**	232	19	Steve Grogan	208
2	John Hadl	268	11	John Elway	226	20	Steve DeBerg	204
3	Fran Tarkenton	266	12	John Brodie	224	21	Sammy Baugh	203
4	Norm Snead	257	13	Ken Stabler	222	22	Dave Krieg	199
5	Johnny Unitas	253	14	Y.A. Tittle	221	23	Jim Plunkett	198
6	**Dan Marino**	252	15	Joe Namath	220	24	Tobin Rote	191
7	Jim Hart	247		Babe Parilli	220		**Vinny Testaverde**	191
8	Bobby Layne	245	17	Terry Bradshaw	210			
9	Dan Fouts	242	18	Joe Ferguson	209			

Passing Yards

		Yrs	Att	Comp	Pct	Yards
1	**Dan Marino** 17		8358	4967	59.4	61,361
2	John Elway 16		7250	4123	56.9	51,475
3	**Warren Moon** 16		6789	3973	58.5	49,117
4	Fran Tarkenton 18		6467	3686	57.0	47,003
5	Dan Fouts 15		5604	3297	58.8	43,040
6	Joe Montana........15		5391	3409	63.2	40,551
7	Johnny Unitas 18		5186	2830	54.6	40,239
8	Dave Krieg..........19		5311	3105	58.5	38,147
9	Boomer Esiason......14		5205	2969	57.0	37,920
10	Jim Kelly 11		4779	2874	60.1	35,467
11	Jim Everett 12		4923	2841	57.7	34,837
12	Jim Hart 19		5076	2593	51.1	34,665
13	Steve DeBerg 17		5024	2874	57.2	34,241
14	John Hadl 16		4687	2363	50.4	33,503
15	Phil Simms.........14		4647	2576	55.4	33,462
16	**Steve Young**......15		4149	2667	64.3	33,124
17	Ken Anderson....... 16		4475	2654	59.3	32,838
18	**Vinny Testaverde** .13		4613	2569	55.7	32,575
19	Sonny Jurgensen ... 18		4262	2433	57.1	32,224
20	John Brodie......... 17		4491	2469	55.0	31,548
21	**Troy Aikman** 11		4453	2742	61.6	31,310
22	**Brett Favre** 9		4352	2659	61.1	30,894
23	Norm Snead....... 15		4353	2276	52.3	30,797
24	Joe Ferguson...... 18		4519	2369	52.4	29,817
25	Roman Gabriel...... 16		4498	2366	52.6	29,444

Note: The NFL does not recognize records from the All-American Football Conference (1946-49). If it did, **Y.A. Tittle** would rank 17th (after Young) with the following stats: 17 Yrs; 4,395 Att; 2,427 Comp; 55.2 Pct; and 33,070 Yards.

Receptions

		Yrs	No	Yards	Avg	TD
1	**Jerry Rice** 15		1200	18,299	15.2	169
2	**Andre Reed** 15		941	13,095	13.9	86
3	Art Monk........... 16		940	12,721	13.5	68
4	**Cris Carter** 13		924	11,688	12.6	114
5	Steve Largent 14		819	13,089	16.0	100
6	Henry Ellard........16		814	13,777	16.9	65
7	**Irving Fryar** 16		810	12,237	15.1	79
8	**Tim Brown** 12		770	10,944	14.2	75
9	James Lofton 16		764	14,004	18.3	75
10	Charlie Joiner...... 18		750	12,146	16.2	65
	Michael Irvin 12		750	11,904	15.9	65
12	**Andre Rison** 11		702	9,599	13.7	78
13	Gary Clark 11		699	10,856	15.5	65
14	Ozzie Newsome 13		662	7,980	12.1	47
15	Charley Taylor ... 13		649	9,110	14.0	79
16	Drew Hill 15		634	9,831	15.5	60
17	Don Maynard ... 15		633	11,834	18.7	88
18	Raymond Berry..... 13		631	9,275	14.7	68
19	**Rob Moore** 10		628	9,368	14.9	49
20	**Herman Moore** 9		626	8,664	13.8	59
21	Keith Byars.........13		610	5,661	9.3	31
22	**Larry Centers** 10		604	5,083	8.4	22
23	Sterling Sharpe........7		595	8,134	13.7	65
	Anthony Miller 10		595	9,148	15.4	63
25	Harold Carmichael .. 14		590	8,985	15.2	79

Rushing

		Yrs	Car	Yards	Avg	TD
1	Walter Payton....... 13		3838	16,726	4.4	110
2	Barry Sanders 10		3062	15,269	5.0	99
3	**Emmitt Smith** 10		3242	13,963	4.3	136
4	Eric Dickerson 11		2996	13,259	4.4	90
5	Tony Dorsett 12		2936	12,739	4.3	77
6	Jim Brown 9		2359	12,312	5.2	106
7	Marcus Allen 16		3022	12,243	4.1	123
8	Franco Harris 13		2949	12,120	4.1	91
9	**Thurman Thomas** .12		2849	11,938	4.2	65
10	John Riggins 14		2916	11,352	3.9	104
11	O.J. Simpson 11		2404	11,236	4.7	61
12	Ottis Anderson 14		2562	10,273	4.0	81
13	Earl Campbell........ 8		2187	9,407	4.3	74
14	**Ricky Watters** 8		2272	9,083	4.0	70
15	Jim Taylor 10		1941	8,597	4.4	83
16	**Jerome Bettis** 7		2106	8,463	4.0	41
17	Joe Perry 14		1737	8,378	4.8	53
18	Ernest Byner..........14		2095	8,261	3.9	56
19	Herschel Walker 12		1954	8,225	4.2	61
20	Roger Craig 11		1991	8,189	4.1	56
21	Gerald Riggs 10		1989	8,188	4.1	69
22	Larry Csonka 11		1891	8,081	4.3	64
23	Freeman McNeil ... 12		1798	8,074	4.5	38
24	James Brooks 12		1685	7,962	4.7	49
25	**Terry Allen** 8		1938	7,777	4.0	68

Note: The NFL does not recognize records from the All-American Football Conference (1946-49). If it did, **Joe Perry** would move up from 17th to 13th (after Anderson) with the following stats: 16 Yrs; 1,929 Att; 9,723 Yards; 5.0 Avg; and 71 TD.

All-Purpose Yards

		Rush	Rec	Ret	Total
1	Walter Payton	16,726	4,538	539	21,803
2	**Jerry Rice** 627		18,299	6	18,932
3	Barry Sanders.......15,269		2,921	118	18,308
4	Herschel Walker....8,225		4,859	5,084	18,168
5	Marcus Allen........12,243		5,411	-6	17,648
6	**Brian Mitchell** 1,751		2,087	13,062	16,900
7	**Eric Metcalf** 2,385		5,553	8,789	16,727
8	**Emmitt Smith**......13,963		2,728	0	16,691
9	Tony Dorsett 12,739		3,554	33	16,326
10	**Thurman Thomas** .11,938		4,341	0	16,279
11	Henry Ellard............50		13,777	1,891	15,718
12	Jim Brown..........12,312		2,499	648	15,459
13	Eric Dickerson 13,259		2,137	15	15,411
14	**Tim Brown** 120		10,944	4,344	15,408
15	**Irving Fryar** 230		12,237	2,567	15,084
16	James Brooks 7,962		3,621	3,327	14,910
17	Franco Harris 12,120		2,287	215	14,622
18	O.J. Simpson 11,236		2,142	990	14,368
19	James Lofton............ 246		14,004	27	14,277
20	Bobby Mitchell 2,735		7,954	3,389	14,078
21	Dave Meggett.......1,684		3,038	9,274	13,996
22	**Andre Reed** 500		13,095	12	13,607
23	Earnest Byner........8,261		4,605	631	13,497
24	John Riggins 11,352		2,090	-7	13,435
25	Steve Largent 83		13,089	224	13,396

Years played: Allen (16), Brooks (13), J. Brown (9), T. Brown (12), Byner (14), Dickerson (11), Dorsett (12), Ellard (16), Fryar (16), Harris (13), Largent (14), Lofton (16), Meggett (14), Metcalf (11), Bri. Mitchell (10), Bo. Mitchell (11), Payton (13), Reed (15), Rice (15), Riggins (14), Sanders (10), Simpson (11), Smith (10), Thomas (12) and Walker (12).

All-Time NFL Leaders (Cont.)
Scoring

Points

		Yrs	TD	FG	PAT	Total
1	George Blanda	26	9	335	943	2002
2	Gary Anderson	18	0	439	631	1948
3	Morten Andersen	18	0	416	592	1840
4	Norm Johnson	18	0	366	638	1736
5	Nick Lowery	18	0	383	562	1711
6	Jan Stenerud	19	0	373	580	1699
7	Eddie Murray	18	0	344	531	1563
8	Pat Leahy	18	0	304	558	1470
9	Al Del Greco	16	0	320	506	1466
10	Jim Turner	16	1	304	521	1439
11	Matt Bahr	17	0	300	522	1422
12	Mark Moseley	16	0	300	482	1382
13	Jim Bakken	17	0	282	534	1380
14	Fred Cox	15	0	282	519	1365
15	Lou Groza	17	1	234	641	1349
16	Jim Breech	14	0	243	517	1246
17	Chris Bahr	14	0	241	490	1213
18	Kevin Butler	13	0	265	413	1208
19	Pete Stoyanovich	11	0	267	394	1195
20	Gino Cappelletti	11	42	176	350	1130†
21	Ray Wersching	15	0	222	456	1122
22	Jerry Rice	15	180	0	0	1088†
23	Don Cockroft	13	0	216	432	1080
24	Garo Yepremian	14	0	210	444	1074
25	Steve Christie	10	0	246	327	1065

† Cappelletti's total and Rice's total both include four 2-point conversions.

Note: The NFL does not recognize records from the All-American Football Conference (1946-49). If it did, **Lou Groza** would move up from 15th to 7th (after Stenerud) with the following stats: 21 Yrs; 1 TD; 264 FG, 810 PAT; 1,608 Pts.

Touchdowns

		Yrs	Rush	Rec	Ret	Total
1	Jerry Rice	15	10	169	1	180
2	Emmitt Smith	10	136	11	0	147
3	Marcus Allen	16	123	21	1	145
4	Jim Brown	9	106	20	0	126
5	Walter Payton	13	110	15	0	125
6	John Riggins	14	104	12	0	116
7	Cris Carter	13	0	114	1	115
8	Lenny Moore	12	63	48	2	113
9	Barry Sanders	10	99	10	0	109
10	Don Hutson	11	3	99	3	105
11	Steve Largent	14	1	100	0	101
12	Franco Harris	13	91	9	0	100
13	Eric Dickerson	11	90	6	0	96
14	Jim Taylor	10	83	10	0	93
15	Tony Dorsett	12	77	13	1	91
	Bobby Mitchell	11	18	65	8	91
17	Leroy Kelly	10	74	13	3	90
	Charley Taylor	13	11	79	0	90
19	Don Maynard	15	0	88	0	88
20	Lance Alworth	11	2	85	0	87
	Andre Reed	15	1	86	0	87
	Thurman Thomas	12	65	22	0	87
23	Ottis Anderson	14	81	5	0	86
	Paul Warfield	13	1	85	0	86
25	Mark Clayton	11	0	84	1	85
	Tommy McDonald	12	0	84	1	85

Interceptions

		Yrs	No	Yards	TD
1	Paul Krause	16	81	1185	3
2	Emlen Tunnell	14	79	1282	4
3	Dick (Night Train) Lane	14	68	1207	5
4	Ken Riley	15	65	596	5
5	Ronnie Lott	14	63	730	5

Sacks

		Yrs	No
1	Reggie White	14	192½
2	Bruce Smith	15	171
3	Kevin Greene	15	160
4	Chris Doleman	15	151
5	Richard Dent	15	137½

Note: The NFL did not begin officially compiling sacks until 1982. Deacon Jones, who played with the Rams, Chargers and Redskins from 1961-74, is often credited with 173½ sacks.

Safeties

		Yrs	No
1	Ted Hendricks	15	4
	Doug English	10	4
3	Sixteen players tied with 3 each.		

Kickoff Returns
Minimum 75 returns.

		Yrs	No	Yards	Avg	TD
1	Gale Sayers	7	91	2781	30.6	6
2	Lynn Chandnois	7	92	2720	29.6	3
3	Abe Woodson	9	193	5538	28.7	5
4	Buddy Young	6	90	2514	27.9	2
5	Travis Williams	5	102	2801	27.5	6

Punting
Minimum 300 punts.

		Yrs	No	Yards	Avg
1	Sammy Baugh	16	338	15,245	45.1
2	Tommy Davis	11	511	22,833	44.7
3	Darren Bennett	5	432	19,244	44.5
4	Yale Lary	11	503	22,279	44.3
5	Tom Rouen	7	470	20,784	44.2

Punt Returns
Minimum 75 returns.

		Yrs	No	Yards	Avg	TD
1	George McAfee	8	112	1431	12.8	2
2	Jack Christiansen	8	85	1084	12.8	8
3	Claude Gibson	5	110	1381	12.6	3
4	Darrien Gordon	6	219	2726	12.4	6
5	Karl Williams	4	89	1107	12.4	2

Long-Playing Records

Seasons

		No
1	George Blanda, QB-K	26
2	Earl Morrall, QB	21
3	Jim Marshall, DE	20
	Jackie Slater, OL	20

Games

		No
1	George Blanda, QB-K	340
2	Jim Marshall, DE	282
3	Clay Matthews, LB	278

Consecutive Games

		No
1	Jim Marshall, DE	282
2	Mick Tingelhoff, C	240
3	Jim Bakken, K	234

SINGLE SEASON
Passing

Yards Gained	Year	Att	Cmp	Pct	Yds	Efficiency	Year	Att/Cmp	TD	Rtg
Dan Marino, Mia	1984	564	362	64.2	5084	Steve Young, SF	1994	461/324	35	112.8
Dan Fouts, SD	1981	609	360	59.1	4802	Joe Montana, SF	1989	386/271	26	112.4
Dan Marino, Mia	1986	623	378	60.7	4746	Milt Plum, Cle	1960	250/151	21	110.4
Dan Fouts, SD	1980	589	348	59.1	4715	Sammy Baugh, Wash	1945	182/128	11	109.9
Warren Moon, Hou	1991	655	404	61.7	4690	Kurt Warner, St.L	1999	499/325	41	109.2
Warren Moon, Hou	1990	584	362	62.0	4689	Dan Marino, Mia	1984	564/362	48	108.9
Neil Lomax, St.L	1984	560	345	61.6	4614	Sid Luckman, Bears	1943	202/110	28	107.5
Drew Bledsoe, NE	1994	691	400	57.9	4555	Steve Young, SF	1992	402/268	25	107.0
Lynn Dickey, GB	1983	484	286	59.7	4458	Randall Cunningham, Min	1998	425/259	34	106.0
Steve Beuerlein, Car	1999	571	343	60.1	4436	Bart Starr, GB	1966	251/156	14	105.0

Receptions

Catches	Year	No	Yds
Herman Moore, Det	1995	123	1686
Jerry Rice, SF	1995	122	1848
Cris Carter, Min	1995	122	1371
Cris Carter, Min	1994	122	1256
Isaac Bruce, St. L	1995	119	1781
Jimmy Smith, Jax	1999	116	1636
Marvin Harrison, Ind	1999	115	1663
Jerry Rice, SF	1994	112	1499
Sterling Sharpe, GB	1993	112	1274
Michael Irvin, Dal	1995	111	1603
Terance Mathis, Atl	1994	111	1342
Brett Perriman, Det	1995	108	1488
Sterling Sharpe, GB	1992	108	1461

Rushing

Yards Gained	Year	Car	Yds	Avg
Eric Dickerson, LA Rams	1984	379	2105	5.6
Barry Sanders, Det	1997	335	2053	6.1
Terrell Davis, Den	1998	392	2008	5.1
O.J. Simpson, Buf	1973	332	2003	6.0
Earl Campbell, Hou	1980	373	1934	5.2
Barry Sanders, Det	1994	331	1883	5.7
Jim Brown, Cle	1963	291	1863	6.4
Walter Payton, Chi	1977	339	1852	5.5
Jamal Anderson, Atl	1998	410	1846	4.5
Eric Dickerson, LA Rams	1986	404	1821	4.5
O.J. Simpson, Buf	1975	329	1817	5.5
Eric Dickerson, LA Rams	1983	390	1808	4.6

Scoring
Points

	Year	TD	PAT	FG	Pts
Paul Hornung, GB	1960	15	41	15	176
Gary Anderson, Min	1998	0	59	35	164
Mark Moseley, Wash	1983	0	62	33	161
Gino Cappelletti, Bos	1964	7	38	25	155
Emmitt Smith, Dal	1995	25	0	0	150
Chip Lohmiller, Wash	1991	0	56	31	149
Gino Cappelletti, Bos	1961	8	48	17	147
Paul Hornung, GB	1961	10	41	15	146
Jim Turner, Jets	1968	0	43	34	145
John Kasay, Car	1996	0	34	37	145
Mike Vanderjagt, Ind	1999	0	43	34	145
John Riggins, Wash	1983	24	0	0	144
Kevin Butler, Chi	1985	0	51	31	144
Olindo Mare, Mia	1999	0	27	39	144
Norm Johnson, Pit	1995	0	39	34	141
Tony Franklin, NE	1986	0	44	32	140

Touchdowns

	Year	Rush	Rec	Ret	Total
Emmitt Smith, Dal	1995	25	0	0	25
John Riggins, Wash	1983	24	0	0	24
Terrell Davis, Den	1998	21	2	0	23
O.J. Simpson, Buf	1975	16	7	0	23
Jerry Rice, SF	1987	1	22	0	23
Gale Sayers, Chi	1966	14	6	2	22
Chuck Foreman, Min	1975	13	9	0	22
Emmitt Smith, Dal	1994	21	1	0	22
Jim Brown, Cle	1965	17	4	0	21
Joe Morris, NY Giants	1985	21	0	0	21
Terry Allen, Wash	1996	21	0	0	21
Lenny Moore, Bal	1964	16	3	1	20
Leroy Kelly, Cle	1968	16	4	0	20
Eric Dickerson, LA Rams	1983	18	2	0	20

Note: The NFL regular season schedule grew from 12 games (1947-60) to 14 (1961-77) to 16 (1978-present). The AFL regular season schedule was always 14 games (1960-69).

Touchdowns Passing

	Year	No
Dan Marino, Miami	1984	48
Dan Marino, Miami	1986	44
Kurt Warner, St. Louis	1999	41
Brett Favre, Green Bay	1996	39
Brett Favre, Green Bay	1995	38
George Blanda, Houston	1961	36
Y.A. Tittle, NY Giants	1963	36
Steve Young, San Francisco	1998	36
Steve Beuerlein, Carolina	1999	36
Brett Favre, Green Bay	1997	35
Steve Young, San Francisco	1994	35
Randall Cunningham, Minnesota	1998	34
Y.A. Tittle, NY Giants	1962	33
Dan Fouts, San Diego	1981	33
Warren Moon, Houston	1990	33
Jim Kelly, Buffalo	1991	33
Brett Favre, Green Bay	1994	33
Warren Moon, Minnesota	1995	33
Vinny Testaverde, Baltimore	1996	33

Touchdowns Receiving

	Year	No
Jerry Rice, San Francisco	1987	22
Mark Clayton, Miami	1984	18
Sterling Sharpe, Green Bay	1994	18
Don Hutson, Green Bay	1942	17
Elroy (Crazylegs) Hirsch, LA Rams	1951	17
Bill Groman, Houston	1961	17
Jerry Rice, San Francisco	1989	17
Cris Carter, Minnesota	1995	17
Carl Pickens, Cincinnati	1995	17
Randy Moss, Minnesota	1998	17
Art Powell, Oakland	1963	16
Cloyce Box, Detroit	1952	15
Sonny Randle, St. Louis	1960	15
Jerry Rice, San Francisco	1986	15
Jerry Rice, San Francisco	1993	15
Andre Rison, Atlanta	1993	15
Jerry Rice, San Francisco	1995	15

All-Time NFL Leaders (Cont.)

Touchdowns Rushing

	Year	No
Emmitt Smith, Dallas	1995	25
John Riggins, Washington	1983	24
Joe Morris, NY Giants	1985	21
Emmitt Smith, Dallas	1994	21
Terry Allen, Washington	1996	21
Terrell Davis, Denver	1998	21
Jim Taylor, Green Bay	1962	19
Earl Campbell, Houston	1979	19
Chuck Muncie, San Diego	1981	19
Eric Dickerson, LA Rams	1983	18
George Rogers, Washington	1986	18
Emmitt Smith, Dallas	1992	18
Jim Brown, Cleveland	1958	17
Jim Brown, Cleveland	1965	17
Stephen Davis, Washington	1999	17
Six tied with 16 each.		

Field Goals

	Year	Att	No
Olindo Mare, Miami	1999	46	39
John Kasay, Carolina	1996	45	37
Cary Blanchard, Indianapolis	1996	40	36
Al Del Greco, Tennessee	1998	39	36
Ali Haji-Sheikh, NY Giants	1983	42	35
Jeff Jaeger, LA Raiders	1993	44	35
Gary Anderson, Minnesota	1998	35	35
Jim Turner, NY Jets	1968	46	34
Nick Lowery, Kansas City	1990	37	34
Jason Hanson, Detroit	1993	43	34
John Carney, San Diego	1994	38	34
Fuad Reveiz, Minnesota	1994	39	34
Norm Johnson, Pittsburgh	1995	41	34
Richie Cunningham, Dallas	1997	37	34
Mike Vanderjagt, Indianapolis	1999	38	34
Todd Peterson, Seattle	1999	40	34

Interceptions

	Year	No
Dick (Night Train) Lane, Detroit	1952	14
Dan Sandifer, Washington	1948	13
Spec Sanders, NY Yanks	1950	13
Lester Hayes, Oakland	1980	13

Punting

Qualifiers	Year	Avg
Sammy Baugh, Washington	1940	51.4
Yale Lary, Detroit	1963	48.9
Sammy Baugh, Washington	1941	48.7

Kickoff Returns

	Year	Avg
Travis Williams, Green Bay	1967	41.1
Gale Sayers, Chicago Bears	1967	37.7
Ollie Matson, Chicago Cards	1958	35.5

Punt Returns

	Year	Avg
Herb Rich, Baltimore	1950	23.0
Jack Christiansen, Detroit	1952	21.5
Dick Christy, NY Titans	1961	21.3
Bob Hayes, Dallas	1968	20.8

Sacks

	Year	No		Year	No
Mark Gastineau, NY Jets	1984	22	Chris Doleman, Minnesota	1989	21
Reggie White, Philadelphia	1987	21	Lawrence Taylor, NY Giants	1986	20½

Note: The NFL did not begin officially compiling sacks until 1982. Cincinnati's Coy Bacon is widely, although not officially, credited with 26 sacks during the 1976 season.

SINGLE GAME

Passing

Yards Gained	Date	Yds
Norm Van Brocklin, LA vs NY Yanks	9/28/51	554
Warren Moon, Hou vs KC	12/16/90	527
Boomer Esiason, Ariz vs Wash	11/10/96	522
Dan Marino, Mia vs NYJ	10/23/88	521
Phil Simms, NYG vs Cin	10/13/85	513

Completions	Date	No
Drew Bledsoe, NE vs Min	11/13/94	45
Richard Todd, NYJ vs SF	9/21/80	42
Vinny Testaverde, NYJ vs Sea	12/6/98	42
Warren Moon, Hou vs Dal	11/10/91	41
Ken Anderson, Cin vs SD	12/20/82	40
Phil Simms, NYG vs Cin	10/13/85	40

Receiving

Catches	Date	No
Tom Fears, LA vs GB	12/3/50	18
Clark Gaines, NYJ vs SF	9/21/80	17
Sonny Randle, St.L vs NYG	11/4/62	16
Keenan McCardell, Jax vs St.L	10/20/96	16
Jerry Rice, SF vs LA Rams	11/20/94	16

Yards Gained	Date	Yds
Flipper Anderson, LA Rams vs NO	11/26/89	336
Stephone Paige, KC vs SD	12/22/85	309
Jim Benton, Cle vs Det	11/22/45	303
Cloyce Box, Det vs Bal	12/3/50	302
Jerry Rice, SF vs Det	9/25/95	289
John Taylor, SF vs LA Rams	12/11/89	286

Rushing

Yards Gained	Date	Yds
Walter Payton, Chi vs Min	11/20/77	275
O.J. Simpson, Buf vs Det	11/25/76	273
O.J. Simpson, Buf vs NE	9/16/73	250
Willie Ellison, LA Rams vs NO	12/5/71	247
Corey Dillon, Cin vs Ten	12/4/97	246
Cookie Gilchrist, Buf vs NYJ	12/8/63	243

All-Purpose Yards

	Date	Yds
Glyn Milburn, Den vs Sea	12/10/95	404
Billy Cannon, Hou vs NY Titans	12/10/61	373
Tyrone Hughes, NO vs LA Rams	10/23/94	347
Lionel James, SD vs Raiders	11/10/85	345
Timmy Brown, Phi vs St.L	12/16/62	341
Gale Sayers, Chi vs Min	12/18/66	339
Gale Sayers, Chi vs SF	12/12/65	336
Flipper Anderson, LA Rams vs NO	11/26/89	336

Scoring

Points

	Date	Pts
Ernie Nevers, Chi. Cards vs Chi. Bears	11/28/29	40
Dub Jones, Cle vs Chi. Bears	11/25/51	36
Gale Sayers, Chi vs SF	12/12/65	36
Paul Hornung, GB vs Bal	10/8/61	33
Bob Shaw, Chi. Cards vs Bal	10/2/50	30
Jim Brown, Cle vs Bal	11/1/59	30
Abner Haynes, Dal. Texans vs Oak	11/26/61	30
Billy Cannon, Hou vs NY Titans	12/10/61	30
Cookie Gilchrist, Buf vs NY Jets	12/8/63	30
Kellen Winslow, SD vs Oak	11/22/81	30
Jerry Rice, SF vs Atl	10/14/90	30
James Stewart, Jax vs Phi.	10/12/97	30

Note: Nevers celebrated Thanksgiving, 1929, by scoring all of the Chicago Cardinals' points on six rushing TDs and four PATs. The Cards beat Red Grange and the Chicago Bears, 40-6.

Touchdowns Passing

	Date	No
Sid Luckman, Chi. Bears vs NYG	11/14/43	7
Adrian Burk, Phi vs Wash	10/17/54	7
George Blanda, Hou vs NY Titans	11/19/61	7
Y.A. Tittle, NYG vs Wash	10/28/62	7
Joe Kapp, Min vs Bal	9/28/69	7

Touchdowns Receiving

	Date	No
Bob Shaw, Chi. Cards vs Bal	10/2/50	5
Kellen Winslow, SD vs Oak	11/22/81	5
Jerry Rice, SF vs Atl	10/14/90	5

Touchdowns Rushing

	Date	No
Ernie Nevers, Chi. Cards vs Chi. Bears	11/28/29	6
Jim Brown, Cle vs Bal	11/1/59	5
Cookie Gilchrist, Buf vs NY Jets	12/8/63	5
James Stewart, Jax vs Phi	10/12/97	5

Field Goals

	Date	No
Jim Bakken, St.L vs Pit	9/24/67	7
Chris Boniol, Dal vs GB	11/18/96	7
Rich Karlis, Min vs LA Rams	11/5/89	7

14 players tied with 6 FGs.
Note: Bakken was 7-for-9, Boniol and Karlis 7-for-7.

Extra Point Kicks

	Date	No
Pat Harder, Cards vs NYG	10/17/48	9
Bob Waterfield, LA Rams vs Bal	10/22/50	9
Charlie Gogolak, Wash vs NYG	11/27/66	9

Interceptions

	No
By 17 players	4

Sacks

	Date	No
Derrick Thomas, KC vs Sea	11/11/90	7
Fred Dean, SF vs NO	11/13/83	6
Derrick Thomas, KC vs Oak	9/6/98	6
William Gay, Det vs TB	9/4/83	5½

Longest Plays

Passing (all for TDs)

	Date	Yds
Frank Filchock to Andy Farkas, Wash vs Pit	10/15/39	99
George Izo to Bobby Mitchell, Wash vs Cle.	9/15/63	99
Karl Sweetan to Pat Studstill, Det vs Bal.	10/16/66	99
Sonny Jurgensen to Gerry Allen, Wash vs Chi	9/15/68	99
Jim Plunkett to Cliff Branch, LA Raiders vs Wash	10/2/83	99
Ron Jaworski to Mike Quick, Phi vs Atl	11/10/85	99
Stan Humphries to Tony Martin, SD vs Sea	9/18/94	99
Brett Favre to Robert Brooks, GB vs Chi.	9/11/95	99

Runs from Scrimmage (all for TDs)

	Date	Yds
Tony Dorsett, Dal vs Min	1/3/83	99
Andy Uram, GB vs Chi. Cards	10/8/39	97
Bob Gage, Pit vs Bears	12/4/49	97
Jim Spavital, Balt. Colts vs GB	11/5/50	96
Bob Hoernschemeyer, Det vs NY Yanks	11/23/50	96
Garrison Hearst, SF vs NYJ	9/6/98	96

Punts

	Date	Yds
Steve O'Neal, NYJ vs Den.	9/21/69	98
Joe Lintzenich, Chi. Bears vs NYG	11/15/31	94
Shawn McCarthy, NE vs Buf	11/3/91	93

Field Goals

	Date	Yds
Tom Dempsey, NO vs Det	11/8/70	63
Jason Elam, Den vs Jax	10/25/98	63
Steve Cox, Cle vs Cin	10/21/84	60
Morten Andersen, NO vs Chi	10/27/91	60
Tony Franklin, Phi vs Dal	11/12/79	59
Pete Stoyanovich, Mia vs NYJ	11/12/89	59
Steve Christie, Buf vs Mia	9/26/93	59
Morten Andersen, Atl vs SF	12/24/95	59

Punt Returns (all for TDs)

	Date	Yds
Robert Bailey, Rams vs NO	10/23/94	103
Gil LeFebvre, Cin vs Bklyn	12/3/33	98
Charlie West, Min vs Wash	11/3/68	98
Dennis Morgan, Dal vs St.L	10/13/74	98
Terance Mathis, NYJ vs Dal	11/4/90	98
Greg Pruitt, LA Raiders vs Wash.	10/2/83	97

Kickoff Returns (all for TDs)

	Date	Yds
Al Carmichael, GB vs Chi. Bears	10/7/56	106
Noland Smith, KC vs Den	12/17/67	106
Roy Green, St.L vs Dal	10/21/79	106

Interception Returns (all for TDs)

	Date	Yds
James Willis (14 yds) lateral to Troy Vincent (90 yds), Phi vs Dal	11/3/96	104
Vencie Glenn, SD vs Den.	11/29/87	103
Louis Oliver, Mia vs Buf	10/4/92	103

Six players tied with 102-yd returns.

Chicago College All-Star Game

On Aug. 31, 1934, a year after sponsoring Major League Baseball's first All-Star Game, *Chicago Tribune* sports editor Arch Ward presented the first Chicago College All-Star Game at Soldier Field. A crowd of 79,432 turned out to see an all-star team of graduated college seniors battle the 1933 NFL champion Chicago Bears to a scoreless tie. The preseason game was played at Soldier Field and pitted the College All-Stars against the defending NFL champions (1933-1966) or Super Bowl champions (1967-75) every year except 1935 until it was cancelled in 1977. The NFL champs won the series, 31-9-1.

Year		Year		Year	
1934	Chi. Bears 0, All-Stars 0	1949	Philadelphia 38, All-Stars 0	1964	Chi. Bears 28, All-Stars 17
1935	Chi. Bears 5, All-Stars 0	1950	All-Stars 17, Philadelphia 7	1965	Cleveland 24, All-Stars 16
1936	Detroit 7, All-Stars 0	1951	Cleveland 33, All-Stars 0	1966	Green Bay 38, All-Stars 0
1937	All-Stars 6, Green Bay 0	1952	LA Rams 10, All-Stars 7	1967	Green Bay 27, All-Stars 0
1938	All-Stars 28, Washington 16	1953	Detroit 24, All-Stars 10	1968	Green Bay 34, All-Stars 17
1939	NY Giants 9, All-Stars 0	1954	Detroit 31, All-Stars 6	1969	NY Jets 26, All-Stars 24
1940	Green Bay 45, All-Stars 28	1955	All-Stars 30, Cleveland 27	1970	Kansas City 24, All-Stars 3
1941	Chi. Bears 37, All-Stars 13	1956	Cleveland 26, All-Stars 0	1971	Baltimore 24, All-Stars 17
1942	Chi. Bears 21, All-Stars 0	1957	NY Giants 22, All-Stars 12	1972	Dallas 20, All-Stars 7
1943	All-Stars 27, Washington 7	1958	All-Stars 35, Detroit 19	1973	Miami 14, All-Stars 3
1944	Chi. Bears 24, All-Stars 21	1959	Baltimore 29, All-Stars 0	1974	No Game (NFLPA Strike)
1945	Green Bay 19, All-Stars 7	1960	Baltimore 32, All-Stars 7	1975	Pittsburgh 21, All-Stars 14
1946	All-Stars 16, LA Rams 0	1961	Philadelphia 28, All-Stars 14	1976	Pittsburgh 24, All-Stars 0*
1947	All-Stars 16, Chi. Bears 0	1962	Green Bay 42, All-Stars 20		*Downpour flooded field, game called
1948	Chi. Cards 28, All-Stars 0	1963	All-Stars 20, Green Bay 17		with 1:22 left in 3rd quarter.

Number One Draft Choices

In an effort to blunt the dominance of the Chicago Bears and New York Giants in the 1930s and distribute talent more evenly throughout the league, the NFL established the college draft in 1936. The first player chosen in the first draft was Jay Berwanger, who was also college football's first Heisman Trophy winner. In all, 16 Heisman winners have also been the NFL's No. 1 draft choice. They are noted in **bold** type. The American Football League (formed in 1960) held its own draft for six years before agreeing to merge with the NFL and select players in a common draft starting in 1967.

Year	Team		Year	Team	
1936	Philadelphia	**Jay Berwanger**, HB, Chicago	1966	NFL–Atlanta	Tommy Nobis, LB, Texas
1937	Philadelphia	Sam Francis, FB, Nebraska		AFL–Miami	Jim Grabowski, FB, Illinois
1938	Cleveland Rams	Corbett Davis, FB, Indiana	1967	Baltimore	Bubba Smith, DT, Michigan St.
1939	Chicago Cards	Ki Aldrich, C, TCU	1968	Minnesota	Ron Yary, T, USC
1940	Chicago Cards	George Cafego, HB, Tennessee	1969	Buffalo	**O.J. Simpson**, RB, USC
1941	Chicago Bears	**Tom Harmon**, HB, Michigan	1970	Pittsburgh	Terry Bradshaw, QB, La.Tech
1942	Pittsburgh	Bill Dudley, HB, Virginia	1971	New England	**Jim Plunkett**, QB, Stanford
1943	Detroit	**Frank Sinkwich**, HB, Georgia	1972	Buffalo	Walt Patulski, DE, Notre Dame
1944	Boston Yanks	**Angelo Bertelli**, QB, N. Dame	1973	Houston	John Matuszak, DE, Tampa
1945	Chicago Cards	Charley Trippi, HB, Georgia	1974	Dallas	Ed (Too Tall) Jones, DE, Tenn. St.
1946	Boston Yanks	Frank Dancewicz, QB, N. Dame	1975	Atlanta	Steve Bartkowski, QB, Calif.
1947	Chicago Bears	Bob Fenimore, HB, Okla. A&M	1976	Tampa Bay	Lee Roy Selmon, DE, Oklahoma
1948	Washington	Harry Gilmer, QB, Alabama	1977	Tampa Bay	Ricky Bell, RB, USC
1949	Philadelphia	Chuck Bednarik, C, Penn	1978	Houston	**Earl Campbell**, RB, Texas
1950	Detroit	**Leon Hart**, E, Notre Dame	1979	Buffalo	Tom Cousineau, LB, Ohio St.
1951	NY Giants	Kyle Rote, HB, SMU	1980	Detroit	**Billy Sims**, RB, Oklahoma
1952	LA Rams	Bill Wade, QB, Vanderbilt	1981	New Orleans	**George Rogers**, RB, S. Carolina
1953	San Francisco	Harry Babcock, E, Georgia	1982	New England	Kenneth Sims, DT, Texas
1954	Cleveland	Bobby Garrett, QB, Stanford	1983	Baltimore	John Elway, QB, Stanford
1955	Baltimore	George Shaw, QB, Oregon	1984	New England	Irving Fryar, WR, Nebraska
1956	Pittsburgh	Gary Glick, DB, Colo. A&M	1985	Buffalo	Bruce Smith, DE, Va. Tech
1957	Green Bay	**Paul Hornung**, QB, N. Dame	1986	Tampa Bay	**Bo Jackson**, RB, Auburn
1958	Chicago Cards	King Hill, QB, Rice	1987	Tampa Bay	**V. Testaverde**, QB, Miami-FL
1959	Green Bay	Randy Duncan, QB, Iowa	1988	Atlanta	Aundray Bruce, LB, Auburn
1960	NFL–LA Rams	**Billy Cannon**, HB, LSU	1989	Dallas	Troy Aikman, QB, UCLA
	AFL–No choice		1990	Indianapolis	Jeff George, QB, Illinois
1961	NFL–Minnesota	Tommy Mason, HB, Tulane	1991	Dallas	Russell Maryland, DT, Miami-FL
	AFL–Buffalo	Ken Rice, G, Auburn	1992	Indianapolis	Steve Emtman, DT, Washington
1962	NFL–Washington	**Ernie Davis**, HB, Syracuse	1993	New England	Drew Bledsoe, QB, Washington St.
	AFL–Oakland	Roman Gabriel, QB, N.C. State	1994	Cincinnati	Dan Wilkinson, DT, Ohio St.
1963	NFL–LA Rams	**Terry Baker**, QB, Oregon St.	1995	Cincinnati	Ki-Jana Carter, RB, Penn St.
	AFL–Kan.City	Buck Buchanan, DT, Grambling	1996	NY Jets	Keyshawn Johnson, WR, USC
1964	NFL–San Fran	Dave Parks, E, Texas Tech	1997	St. Louis	Orlando Pace, OT, Ohio St.
	AFL–Boston	Jack Concannon, QB, Boston Col.	1998	Indianapolis	Peyton Manning, QB, Tennessee
1965	NFL–NY Giants	Tucker Frederickson, FB, Auburn	1999	Cleveland	Tim Couch, QB, Kentucky
	AFL–Houston	Lawrence Elkins, E, Baylor	2000	Cleveland	Courtney Brown, DE, Penn St.

AP/Wide World Photos	Atlanta Falcons	New Orleans Saints	AP/Wide World Photos
Don Shula	**Dan Reeves**	**Mike Ditka**	**Vince Lombardi**

All-Time Winningest NFL Coaches

NFL career victories through the 1999 season. Career, regular season and playoff records are noted along with NFL, AFL and Super Bowl titles won. Coaches active during 1999 season in **bold** type.

		Career				Regular Season				Playoffs			
		Yrs	**W**	**L**	**T**	**Pct**	**W**	**L**	**T**	**Pct**	**W**	**L**	**Pct.**	**League Titles**
1	Don Shula............	33	**347**	173	6	.665	328	156	6	.676	19	17	.528	2 Super Bowls and 1 NFL
2	George Halas........	40	**324**	151	31	.671	318	148	31	.671	6	3	.667	5 NFL
3	Tom Landry..........	29	**270**	178	6	.601	250	162	6	.605	20	16	.556	2 Super Bowls
4	Curly Lambeau........	33	**229**	134	22	.623	226	132	22	.624	3	2	.600	6 NFL
5	Chuck Noll	23	**209**	156	1	.572	193	148	1	.566	16	8	.667	4 Super Bowls
6	Chuck Knox	22	**193**	158	1	.550	186	147	1	.558	7	11	.389	—None—
7	**Dan Reeves**........	19	**177**	136	1	.565	167	128	1	.566	10	8	.556	—None—
8	Paul Brown	21	**170**	108	6	.609	166	100	6	.621	4	8	.333	3 NFL
9	Bud Grant............	18	**168**	108	5	.607	158	96	5	.620	10	12	.455	1 NFL
10	Marv Levy	17	**154**	120	0	.562	143	112	0	.561	11	8	.579	—None—
11	Steve Owen	23	**153**	108	17	.581	151	100	17	.595	2	8	.200	2 NFL
12	Marty Schottenheimer..	15	**150**	96	1	.609	145	85	1	.630	5	11	.313	—None—
13	**Bill Parcells**	15	**149**	106	1	.584	138	100	1	.579	11	6	.647	2 Super Bowls
14	Joe Gibbs	12	**140**	65	0	.683	124	60	0	.674	16	5	.762	3 Super Bowls
15	Hank Stram...........	17	**136**	100	10	.573	131	97	10	.571	5	3	.625	1 Super Bowl and 3 AFL
16	Weeb Ewbank	20	**134**	130	7	.507	130	129	7	.502	4	1	.800	1 Super Bowl, 2 NFL, and 1 AFL
17	**Mike Ditka**	14	**127**	101	0	.557	121	95	0	.560	6	6	.500	1 Super Bowl
18	Sid Gillman	18	**123**	104	7	.541	122	99	7	.550	1	5	.167	1 AFL
19	George Allen	12	**118**	54	5	.681	116	47	5	.705	2	7	.222	—None—
20	Don Coryell	14	**114**	89	1	.561	111	83	1	.572	3	6	.333	—None—
21	John Madden	10	**112**	39	7	.731	103	32	7	.750	9	7	.563	1 Super Bowl
22	**George Seifert**.......	9	**116**	43	0	.730	106	38	0	.736	10	5	.667	2 Super Bowls
23	**Jim Mora**............	13	**109**	95	0	.534	109	90	0	.548	0	5	.000	—None—
24	Buddy Parker	15	**107**	76	9	.581	104	75	9	.577	3	1	.750	2 NFL
25	Vince Lombardi	10	**105**	35	6	.740	96	34	6	.728	9	1	.900	2 Super Bowls and 5 NFL
	Tom Flores...........	12	**105**	90	0	.538	97	87	0	.527	8	3	.727	2 Super Bowls

Notes: The NFL does not recognize records from the All-American Football Conference (1946-49). If it did, **Paul Brown** (52-4-3 in four AAFC seasons) would move up from 8th to 5th on the all-time list with the following career stats— 25 Yrs; 222 Wins; 112 Losses; 9 Ties; .660 Pct; 9-8 playoff record; and 4 AAFC titles.
The NFL also considers the Playoff Bowl or "Runner-up Bowl" (officially: the Bert Bell Benefit Bowl) as a post-season exhibition game. The Playoff Bowl was contested every year from 1960-69 in Miami between Eastern and Western Conference second place teams. While the games did not count, six of the coaches above went to the Playoff Bowl at least once and came away with the following records— Allen (2-0), Brown (0-1), Grant (0-1), Landry (1-2), Lombardi (1-1) and Shula (2-0).

Where They Coached

Allen—LA Rams (1966-70), Washington (1971-77); **Brown**—Cleveland (1950-62), Cincinnati (1968-75); **Coryell**—St. Louis (1973-77), San Diego (1978-86); **Ditka**— Chicago (1982-92), New Orleans (1997-99); **Ewbank**— Baltimore (1954-62), NY Jets (1963-73); **Flores**—Oakland-LA Raiders (1979-87), Seattle (1992-94); **Gibbs**—Washington (1981-92); **Gillman**—LA Rams (1955-59), LA-San Diego Chargers (1960-69), Houston (1973-74).

Grant—Minnesota (1967-83,1985); **Halas**—Chicago Bears (1920-29,33-42,46-55,58-67); **Knox**— LA Rams (1973-77, 1992-94); Buffalo (1978-82), Seattle (1983-91); **Lambeau**— Green Bay (1921-49), Chicago Cards (1950-51), Washington (1952-53); **Landry**—Dallas (1960-88); **Levy**— Kansas City (1978-82), Buffalo (1986-97); **Lombardi**— Green Bay (1959-67), Washington (1969); **Madden**—Oakland (1969-78); **Mora**—New Orleans (1986-1995), Indianapolis (1998—).

Noll—Pittsburgh (1969-91); **Owen**—NY Giants (1931-53); **Parcells**— NY Giants (1983-90), New England (1993-97), NY Jets (1997-99); **Parker**—Chicago Cards (1949), Detroit (1951-56), Pittsburgh (1957-64); **Reeves**— Denver (1981-92), NY Giants (1993-96), Atlanta (1997—); **Schottenheimer**— Cleveland (1984-88), Kansas City (1989-98); **Seifert**—San Francisco (1989-96), Carolina (1999—); **Shula**—Baltimore (1963-69), Miami (1970-95); **Stram**—Dallas-Kansas City (1960-74), New Orleans (1976-77).

Top Winning Percentages

Minimum of 85 NFL victories, including playoffs.

		Yrs	W	L	T	Pct
1	Vince Lombardi	10	105	35	6	**.740**
2	John Madden	10	112	39	7	**.731**
3	**George Seifert**	9	116	43	0	**.730**
4	Joe Gibbs	12	140	65	0	**.683**
5	George Allen	12	118	54	5	**.681**
6	George Halas	40	324	151	31	**.671**
7	Don Shula	33	347	173	6	**.665**
8	**Mike Holmgren**	8	93	50	0	**.650**
9	Curly Lambeau	33	229	134	22	**.623**
10	Bill Walsh	10	102	63	1	**.617**
11	Marty Schottenheimer	15	150	96	1	**.609**
12	Paul Brown	21	170	108	6	**.609**
13	Bud Grant	18	168	108	5	**.607**
14	Tom Landry	29	270	178	6	**.601**
15	**Bill Parcells**	15	149	106	1	**.584**
16	Steve Owen	23	153	108	17	**.581**
17	Buddy Parker	15	107	76	9	**.581**
18	Hank Stram	17	136	100	10	**.573**
19	Chuck Noll	23	209	156	1	**.572**
20	**Jimmy Johnson**	9	89	68	0	**.567**
21	**Dan Reeves**	19	177	136	1	**.565**
22	Marv Levy	17	154	120	0	**.562**
23	Don Coryell	14	114	89	1	**.561**
24	Jimmy Conzelman	15	89	68	17	**.560**
25	**Mike Ditka**	14	127	101	0	**.557**

Note: If AAFC records are included, **Paul Brown** moves from 12th to 8th with a percentage of .660 (25 yrs, 222-112-9) and Buck Shaw would be 11th at .619 (8 yrs, 91-55-5).

Active Coaches' Victories

Through 1999 season, including playoffs.

		Yrs	W	L	T	Pct
1	Dan Reeves, Atlanta	19	**177**	136	1	.565
2	George Seifert, Carolina	9	**116**	43	0	.730
3	Jim Mora, Indianapolis	13	**109**	95	0	.534
4	Mike Holmgren, Seattle	8	**93**	50	0	.650
5	Dennis Green, Minnesota	8	**84**	54	0	.609
6	Bill Cowher, Pittsburgh	8	**82**	57	0	.590
7	Bobby Ross, Detroit	8	**72**	64	0	.529
8	Mike Shanahan, Denver	7	**68**	40	0	.630
9	Tom Coughlin, Jacksonville	5	**53**	35	0	.602
10	Jeff Fisher, Tennessee	6	**48**	42	0	.533
11	Bruce Coslet, Cincinnati	8	**47**	75	0	.385
12	Norv Turner, Washington	6	**43**	54	1	.444
13	Dave Wannstedt, Miami	6	**41**	57	0	.418
14	Wade Phillips, Buffalo	5	**38**	33	0	.535
15	Tony Dungy, Tampa Bay	4	**37**	31	0	.544
	Bill Belichick, New England	5	**37**	45	0	.451
17	Steve Mariucci, San Fran	3	**31**	21	0	.596
18	Vince Tobin, Arizona	4	**27**	39	0	.409
19	Jim Fassel, NY Giants	3	**25**	23	1	.520
20	Jon Gruden, Oakland	2	**16**	16	0	.500
21	Gunther Cunningham, KC	1	**9**	7	0	.563
22	Brian Billick, Baltimore	1	**8**	8	0	.500
	Mike Riley, San Diego	1	**8**	8	0	.500
24	Dick Jauron, Chicago	1	**6**	10	0	.375
25	Andy Reid, Philadelphia	1	**5**	11	0	.313
26	Chris Palmer, Cleveland	1	**2**	14	0	.125
27	Dave Campo, Dallas	0	**0**	0	0	.000
	Jim Haslett, New Orleans	0	**0**	0	0	.000
	Al Groh, NY Jets	0	**0**	0	0	.000
	Mike Martz, St. Louis	0	**0**	0	0	.000
	Mike Sherman, Green Bay	0	**0**	0	0	.000

Annual Awards
Most Valuable Player

Currently, the NFL does not sanction an official MVP award. It awarded the Joe F. Carr Trophy (Carr was NFL president from 1921-39) to the league MVP from 1938 to 1946. Since then, four principal MVP awards have been given out throughout the years and are noted below: UPI (1953-69), AP (since 1957), the Maxwell Club of Philadelphia's Bert Bell Trophy (since 1959) and the Pro Football Writers Assn. (since 1976). UPI switched to AFC and NFC Player of the Year awards in 1970 and then discontinued its awards in 1997.

Multiple winners (more than one season): Jim Brown (4); Randall Cunningham, Brett Favre, Johnny Unitas and Y.A. Tittle (3); Earl Campbell, Otto Graham, Don Hutson, Joe Montana, Walter Payton, Barry Sanders, Ken Stabler, Joe Theismann and Steve Young (2).

Year	Awards
1938 Mel Hein, NY Giants, C	Carr
1939 Parker Hall, Cleveland Rams, HB	Carr
1940 Ace Parker, Brooklyn, HB	Carr
1941 Don Hutson, Green Bay, E	Carr
1942 Don Hutson, Green Bay, E	Carr
1943 Sid Luckman, Chicago Bears, QB	Carr
1944 Frank Sinkwich, Detroit, HB	Carr
1945 Bob Waterfield, Cleveland Rams, QB	Carr
1946 Bill Dudley, Pittsburgh, HB	Carr
1947-52 No award	
1953 Otto Graham, Cleveland Browns, QB	UPI
1954 Joe Perry, San Francisco, FB	UPI
1955 Otto Graham, Cleveland, QB	UPI
1956 Frank Gifford, NY Giants, HB	UPI
1957 Y.A. Tittle, San Francisco, QB	UPI
& Jim Brown, Cleveland, FB	AP
1958 Jim Brown, Cleveland, FB	UPI
& Gino Marchetti, Baltimore, DE	AP
1959 Johnny Unitas, Baltimore, QB	UPI, Bell
& Charley Conerly, NY Giants, QB	AP
1960 Norm Van Brocklin, Phi., QB	UPI, AP (tie), Bell
& Joe Schmidt, Detroit, LB	AP (tie)
1961 Paul Hornung, Green Bay, HB	UPI, AP, Bell
1962 Y.A. Tittle, NY Giants, QB	UPI
Jim Taylor, Green Bay, FB	AP
& Andy Robustelli, NY Giants, DE	Bell

Year	Awards
1963 Jim Brown, Cleveland, FB	UPI, Bell
& Y.A. Tittle, NY Giants, QB	AP
1964 Johnny Unitas, Baltimore, QB	UPI, AP, Bell
1965 Jim Brown, Cleveland, FB	UPI, AP
& Pete Retzlaff, Philadelphia, TE	Bell
1966 Bart Starr, Green Bay, QB	UPI, AP
& Don Meredith, Dallas, QB	Bell
1967 Johnny Unitas, Baltimore, QB	UPI, AP, Bell
1968 Earl Morrall, Baltimore, QB	UPI, AP
& Leroy Kelly, Cleveland, RB	Bell
1969 Roman Gabriel, LA Rams, QB	UPI, AP, Bell
1970 John Brodie, San Francisco, QB	AP
& George Blanda, Oakland, QB-PK	Bell
1971 Alan Page, Minnesota, DT	AP
& Roger Staubach, Dallas, QB	Bell
1972 Larry Brown, Washington, RB	AP, Bell
1973 O.J. Simpson, Buffalo, RB	AP, Bell
1974 Ken Stabler, Oakland, QB	AP
& Merlin Olsen, LA Rams, DT	Bell
1975 Fran Tarkenton, Minnesota, QB	AP, Bell
1976 Bert Jones, Baltimore, QB	AP, PFWA
& Ken Stabler, Oakland, QB	Bell
1977 Walter Payton, Chicago, RB	AP, PFWA
& Bob Griese, Miami, QB	Bell
1978 Terry Bradshaw, Pittsburgh, QB	AP, Bell
& Earl Campbell, Houston, RB	PFWA

Year	Awards	Year	Awards
1979 Earl Campbell, Houston, RB	AP, Bell, PFWA	1990 Randall Cunningham, Phila., QB	Bell, PFWA
1980 Brian Sipe, Cleveland, QB	AP, PFWA	& Joe Montana, San Francisco, QB	AP
& Ron Jaworski, Philadelphia, QB	Bell	1991 Thurman Thomas, Buffalo, RB	AP, PFWA
1981 Ken Anderson, Cincinnati, QB	AP, Bell, PFWA	& Barry Sanders, Detroit, RB	Bell
1982 Mark Moseley, Washington, PK	AP	1992 Steve Young, San Francisco, QB	AP, Bell, PFWA
Joe Theismann, Washington, QB	Bell	1993 Emmitt Smith, Dallas, RB	AP, Bell, PFWA
& Dan Fouts, San Diego, QB	PFWA	1994 Steve Young, San Francisco, QB	AP, Bell, PFWA
1983 Joe Theismann, Washington, QB	AP, PFWA	1995 Brett Favre, Green Bay, QB	AP, Bell, PFWA
& John Riggins, Washington, RB	Bell	1996 Brett Favre, Green Bay, QB	AP, Bell, PFWA
1984 Dan Marino, Miami, QB	AP, Bell, PFWA	1997 Barry Sanders, Detroit, RB	AP*, Bell, PFWA
1985 Marcus Allen, LA Raiders, RB	AP, PFWA	& Brett Favre, Green Bay, QB	AP*
& Walter Payton, Chicago, RB	Bell	1998 Terrell Davis, Denver, RB	AP, PFWA
1986 Lawrence Taylor, NY Giants, LB	AP, Bell, PFWA	& Randall Cunningham, Minnesota, QB	Bell
1987 Jerry Rice, San Francisco, WR	Bell, PFWA	1999 Kurt Warner, St. Louis, QB	AP, Bell, PFWA
& John Elway, Denver, QB	AP	*In 1997 for the first time in history, two players tied for the	
1988 Boomer Esiason, Cincinnati, QB	AP, PFWA	AP MVP award.	
& Randall Cunningham, Phila, QB	Bell		
1989 Joe Montana, San Francisco, QB	AP, Bell, PFWA		

AP Offensive Player of the Year

Selected by The Associated Press in balloting by a nationwide media panel. Given out since 1972. Rookie winners are in **bold** type.

Multiple winners: Earl Campbell (3); Terrell Davis, Jerry Rice and Barry Sanders (2).

Year	Pos	Year	Pos	Year	Pos
1972 Larry Brown, Was	RB	1982 Dan Fouts, SD	QB	1992 Steve Young, SF	QB
1973 O.J. Simpson, Buf	RB	1983 Joe Theismann, Was	QB	1993 Jerry Rice, SF	WR
1974 Ken Stabler, Oak	QB	1984 Dan Marino, Mia	QB	1994 Barry Sanders, Det	RB
1975 Fran Tarkenton, Min	S	1985 Marcus Allen, Raiders	RB	1995 Brett Favre, GB	QB
1976 Bert Jones, Bal	QB	1986 Eric Dickerson, Rams	RB	1996 Terrell Davis, Den	RB
1977 Walter Payton, Chi	RB	1987 Jerry Rice, SF	WR	1997 Barry Sanders, Det	RB
1978 **Earl Campbell**, Hou	RB	1988 Roger Craig, SF	RB	1998 Terrell Davis, Den	RB
1979 Earl Campbell, Hou	RB	1989 Joe Montana, SF	QB	1999 Marshall Faulk, St.L	RB
1980 Earl Campbell, Hou	RB	1990 Warren Moon, Hou	QB		
1981 Ken Anderson, Cin	QB	1991 Thurman Thomas, Buf	RB		

AP Defensive Player of the Year

Selected by The Associated Press in balloting by a nationwide media panel. Given out since 1971. Rookie winners are in **bold** type.

Multiple winners: Lawrence Taylor (3); Joe Greene, Mike Singletary, Bruce Smith and Reggie White (2).

Year	Pos	Year	Pos	Year	Pos
1971 Alan Page, Min	DT	1981 **Lawrence Taylor**, NYG	LB	1991 Pat Swilling, NO	LB
1972 Joe Greene, Pit	DT	1982 Lawrence Taylor, NYG	LB	1992 Cortez Kennedy, Sea	DT
1973 Dick Anderson, Mia	S	1983 Doug Betters, Mia	DE	1993 Rod Woodson, Pit	CB
1974 Joe Greene, Pit	DT	1984 Kenny Easley, Sea	S	1994 Deion Sanders, SF	CB
1975 Mel Blount, Pit	CB	1985 Mike Singletary, Chi	LB	1995 Bryce Paup, Buf	LB
1976 Jack Lambert, Pit	LB	1986 Lawrence Taylor, NYG	LB	1996 Bruce Smith, Buf	DE
1977 Harvey Martin, Dal	DE	1987 Reggie White, Phi	DE	1997 Dana Stubblefield, SF	DT
1978 Randy Gradishar, Den	S	1988 Mike Singletary, Chi	LB	1998 Reggie White, GB	DE
1979 Lee Roy Selmon, TB	DE	1989 Keith Millard, Min	DT	1999 Warren Sapp, TB	DT
1980 Lester Hayes, Oak	CB	1990 Bruce Smith, Buf	DE		

UPI NFC Player of the Year

Given out by UPI from 1970-96. Offensive and defensive players honored since 1983. Rookie winners are in **bold** type.

Multiple winners: Eric Dickerson, Reggie White and Mike Singletary (3); Brett Favre, Charles Haley, Walter Payton, Lawrence Taylor and Steve Young (2).

Year	Pos	Year	Pos	Year	Pos
1970 John Brodie, SF	QB	Def–Lawrence Taylor, NYG	LB	Def–Charles Haley, SF	LB
1971 Alan Page, Min	DT	1984 Off–Eric Dickerson, Rams	RB	1991 Off–Mark Rypien, Was	QB
1972 Larry Brown, Was	RB	Def–Mike Singletary, Chi	LB	Def–Reggie White, Phi	DE
1973 John Hadl, Rams	QB	1985 Off–Walter Payton, Chi	RB	1992 Off–Steve Young, SF	QB
1974 Jim Hart, St.L	QB	Def–Mike Singletary, Chi	LB	Def–Chris Doleman, Min	DE
1975 Fran Tarkenton, Min	QB	1986 Off–Eric Dickerson, Rams	RB	1993 Off–Emmitt Smith, Dal	RB
1976 Chuck Foreman, Min	RB	Def–Lawrence Taylor, NYG	LB	Def–Eric Allen, Phi	CB
1977 Walter Payton, Chi	RB	1987 Off–Jerry Rice, SF	WR	1994 Off–Steve Young, SF	QB
1978 Archie Manning, NO	QB	Def–Reggie White, Phi	DE	Def–Charles Haley, Dal	DE
1979 Ottis Anderson, St.L	RB	1988 Off–Roger Craig, SF	RB	1995 Off–Brett Favre, GB	QB
1980 Ron Jaworski, Phi	QB	Def–Mike Singletary, Chi	LB	Def–Reggie White, GB	DE
1981 Tony Dorsett, Dal	RB	1989 Off–Joe Montana, SF	QB	1996 Off–Brett Favre, GB	QB
1982 Mark Moseley, Was	PK	Def–Keith Millard, Min	DT	Def–Kevin Greene, Car	LB
1983 Off–Eric Dickerson, Rams	RB	1990 Off–Randall Cunningham, Phi	QB	1997 Award discontinued.	

Annual Awards (Cont.)
UPI AFL-AFC Player of the Year

Presented by UPI to the top player in the AFL (1960-69) and AFC (1970-96). Offensive and defensive players have been honored since 1983. Rookie winners are in **bold** type.

Multiple winners: Bruce Smith (4); O.J. Simpson (3); Cornelius Bennett, George Blanda, John Elway, Dan Fouts, Daryle Lamonica, Dan Marino and Curt Warner (2).

Year		Pos	Year		Pos	Year		Pos
1960	**Abner Haynes**, Dal	.HB	1978	**Earl Campbell**, Hou	.RB	1989	Off–Christian Okoye, KC	.RB
1961	George Blanda, Hou	.QB	1979	Dan Fouts, SD	.QB		Def–Michael Dean Perry, Cle	.NT
1962	Cookie Gilchrist, Buf	.FB	1980	Brian Sipe, Cle	.QB	1990	Off–Warren Moon, Hou	.QB
1963	Lance Alworth, SD	.FL	1981	Ken Anderson, Cin	.QB		Def–Bruce Smith, Buf	.DE
1964	Gino Cappelletti, Bos	.FL-PK	1982	Dan Fouts, SD	.QB	1991	Off–Thurman Thomas, Buf	.RB
1965	Paul Lowe, SD	.HB	1983	Off–**Curt Warner**, Sea	.RB		Def–Cornelius Bennett, Buf	.LB
1966	Jim Nance, Bos	.FB		Def–Rod Martin, Raiders	.LB	1992	Off–Barry Foster, Pit	.RB
1967	Daryle Lamonica, Raiders	.QB	1984	Off–Dan Marino, Mia	.QB		Def–Junior Seau, SD	.LB
1968	Joe Namath, NYJ	.QB		Def–Mark Gastineau, NYJ	.DE	1993	Off–John Elway, Den	.QB
1969	Daryle Lamonica, Raiders	.QB	1985	Off–Marcus Allen, Raiders	.RB		Def–Rod Woodson, Pit	.CB
1970	George Blanda, Raiders	.QB-PK		Def–Andre Tippett, NE	.LB	1994	Off–Dan Marino, Mia	.QB
1971	Otis Taylor, KC	.WR	1986	Off–Curt Warner, Sea	.RB		Def–Greg Lloyd, Pit	.LB
1972	O.J. Simpson, Buf	.RB		Def–Rulon Jones, Den	.DE	1995	Off–Jim Harbaugh, Ind	.QB
1973	O.J. Simpson, Buf	.RB	1987	Off–John Elway, Den	.QB		Def–Bryce Paup, Buf	.LB
1974	Ken Stabler, Raiders	.QB		Def–Bruce Smith, Buf	.DE	1996	Off–Terrell Davis, Den	.RB
1975	O.J. Simpson, Buf	.RB	1988	Off–Boomer Esiason, Cin	.QB		Def–Bruce Smith, Buf	.DE
1976	Bert Jones, Bal	.QB		Def–Bruce Smith, Buf	.DE	1997	Award discontinued.	
1977	Craig Morton, Den	.QB		& Cornelius Bennett, Buf	.LB			

UPI NFL-NFC Rookie of the Year

Presented by UPI to the top rookie in the NFL (1955-69) and NFC (1970-96). Players who were the overall first pick in the NFL draft are in **bold** type.

Year		Pos	Year		Pos	Year		Pos
1955	Alan Ameche, Bal	.FB	1970	Bruce Taylor, SF	.DB	1985	Jerry Rice, SF	.WR
1956	Lenny Moore, Bal	.HB	1971	John Brockington, GB	.RB	1986	Reuben Mayes, NO	.RB
1957	Jim Brown, Cle	.FB	1972	Chester Marcol, GB	.PK	1987	Robert Awalt, St.L	.TE
1958	Jimmy Orr, Pit	.FL	1973	Charle Young, Phi	.TE	1988	Keith Jackson, Phi	.TE
1959	Boyd Dowler, GB	.FL	1974	John Hicks, NY	.G	1989	Barry Sanders, Det	.RB
1960	Gail Cogdill, Det	.FL	1975	Mike Thomas, Wash	.RB	1990	Mark Carrier, Chi	.S
1961	Mike Ditka, Chi	.TE	1976	Sammy White, Min	.WR	1991	Lawrence Dawsey, TB	.WR
1962	Ronnie Bull, Chi	.FB	1977	Tony Dorsett, Dal	.RB	1992	Robert Jones, Dal	.LB
1963	Paul Flatley, Min	.FL	1978	Bubba Baker, Det	.DE	1993	Jerome Bettis, LA	.RB
1964	Charley Taylor, Wash	.HB	1979	Ottis Anderson, St.L	.RB	1994	Bryant Young, SF	.DT
1965	Gale Sayers, Chi	.HB	1980	**Billy Sims**, Det	.RB	1995	Rashaan Salaam, Chi	.RB
1966	Johnny Roland, St.L	.HB	1981	**George Rogers**, NO	.RB	1996	Simeon Rice, Ari	.DE
1967	Mel Farr, Det	.RB	1982	Jim McMahon, Chi	.QB	1997	Award discontinued.	
1968	Earl McCullough, Det	.FL	1983	Eric Dickerson, LA	.RB			
1969	Calvin Hill, Dal	.RB	1984	Paul McFadden, Phi	.PK			

UPI AFL-AFC Rookie of the Year

Presented by UPI to the top rookie in the AFL (1960-69) and AFC (1970-96). Players who were the overall first pick in the AFL or NFL draft are in **bold** type.

Year		Pos	Year		Pos	Year		Pos
1960	Abner Haynes, Dal	.HB	1973	Bobbie Clark, Cin	.RB	1986	Leslie O'Neal, SD	.DE
1961	Earl Faison, SD	.DE	1974	Don Woods, SD	.RB	1987	Shane Conlan, Buf	.LB
1962	Curtis McClinton, Dal	.FB	1975	Robert Brazile, Hou	.LB	1988	John Stephens, NE	.RB
1963	Billy Joe, Den	.FB	1976	Mike Haynes, NE	.DB	1989	Derrick Thomas, KC	.LB
1964	Matt Snell, NY	.FB	1977	A.J. Duhe, Mia	.DE	1990	Richmond Webb, Mia	.OT
1965	Joe Namath, NY	.QB	1978	**Earl Campbell**, Hou	.RB	1991	Mike Croel, Den	.LB
1966	Bobby Burnett, Buf	.HB	1979	Jerry Butler, Buf	.WR	1992	Dale Carter, KC	.CB
1967	George Webster, Hou	.LB	1980	Joe Cribbs, Buf	.RB	1993	Rick Mirer, Sea	.QB
1968	Paul Robinson, Cin	.RB	1981	Joe Delaney, KC	.RB	1994	Marshall Faulk, Ind	.RB
1969	Greg Cook, Cin	.QB	1982	Marcus Allen, LA	.RB	1995	Curtis Martin, NE	.RB
1970	Dennis Shaw, Buf	.QB	1983	Curt Warner, Sea	.RB	1996	Terry Glenn, NE	.WR
1971	**Jim Plunkett**, NE	.QB	1984	Louis Lipps, Pit	.WR	1997	Award discontinued.	
1972	Franco Harris, Pit	.RB	1985	Kevin Mack, Cle	.RB			

AP Offensive Rookie of the Year

Selected by The Associated Press in balloting by a nationwide media panel. Given out since 1967.

Year		Pos	Year		Pos	Year		Pos
1967	Mel Farr, Det	RB	1978	Earl Campbell, Hou.	RB	1989	Barry Sanders, Det	RB
1968	Earl McCullouch, Det	OE	1979	Ottis Anderson, St.L.	RB	1990	Emmitt Smith, Dal.	RB
1969	Calvin Hill, Dal	RB	1980	Billy Sims, Det	RB	1991	Leonard Russell, NE	RB
1970	Dennis Shaw, Buf	QB	1981	George Rogers, NO	RB	1992	Carl Pickens, Cin	WR
1971	John Brockington, GB	RB	1982	Marcus Allen, Raiders	RB	1993	Jerome Bettis, Rams	RB
1972	Franco Harris, Pit	RB	1983	Eric Dickerson, Rams.	RB	1994	Marshall Faulk, Ind	RB
1973	Chuck Foreman, Min.	RB	1984	Louis Lipps, Pit	WR	1995	Curtis Martin, NE	RB
1974	Don Woods, SD	RB	1985	Eddie Brown, Cin	WR	1996	Eddie George, Hou.	RB
1975	Mike Thomas, Was	RB	1986	Reuben Mayes, NO	RB	1997	Warrick Dunn, TB	RB
1976	Sammy White, Min	WR	1987	Troy Stradford, Mia.	RB	1998	Randy Moss, Min	WR
1977	Tony Dorsett, Dal	RB	1988	John Stephens, NE	RB	1999	Edgerrin James, Ind.	RB

AP Defensive Rookie of the Year

Selected by The Associated Press in balloting by a nationwide media panel. Given out since 1967.

Year		Pos	Year		Pos	Year		Pos
1967	Lem Barney, Det	CB	1979	Jim Haslett, Buf	LB	1990	Mark Carrier, Chi	S
1968	Claude Humphrey, Atl	DE	1980	Buddy Curry, Atl.	LB	1991	Mike Croel, Den.	LB
1969	Joe Greene, Pit	DT		& Al Richardson, Atl	LB	1992	Dale Carter, KC	CB
1970	Bruce Taylor, SF.	CB	1981	Lawrence Taylor, NYG	LB	1993	Dana Stubblefield, SF	DT
1971	Isiah Robertson, Rams	LB	1982	Chip Banks, Cle	LB	1994	Tim Bowens, Mia.	DT
1972	Willie Buchanon, GB	CB	1983	Vernon Maxwell, Bal	LB	1995	Hugh Douglas, NYJ	DE
1973	Wally Chambers, Chi	DT	1984	Bill Maas, KC.	DT	1996	Simeon Rice, Ari	DE
1974	Jack Lambert, Pit.	LB	1985	Duane Bickett, Ind	LB	1997	Peter Boulware, Bal	LB
1975	Robert Brazile, Hou	LB	1986	Leslie O'Neal, SD	DE	1998	Charles Woodson, Raiders	CB
1976	Mike Haynes, NE	CB	1987	Shane Conlan, Buf.	LB	1999	Jevon Kearse, Ten	DE
1977	A.J. Duhe, Mia	DE	1988	Erik McMillan, NYJ	S			
1978	Al Baker, Det	DE	1989	Derrick Thomas, KC.	LB			

Coach of the Year

Presented by UPI to the top coach in the AFL-NFL (1955-69) and AFC-NFC (1970-96). In 1997, the UPI awards were discontinued. Awards beginning in 1997 are the consensus selections from presenters such as AP, The Maxwell Football Club of Philadelphia, *The Sporting News* and the Pro Football Writers Association. Records indicate the team's change in record from the previous season.

Multiple winners: Dan Reeves (4); Paul Brown, Chuck Knox and Don Shula (3); George Allen, Leeman Bennett, Mike Ditka, George Halas, Tom Landry, Marv Levy, Bill Parcells, Jack Pardee, Sam Rutigliano, Lou Saban, Allie Sherman, Marty Schottenheimer, Dick Vermeil and Bill Walsh (2).

Year		Improvement	Year		Improvement
1955	NFL—Joe Kuharich, Washington	3-9 to 8-4	1973	NFC—Chuck Knox, Los Angeles	6-7-1 to 12-2
1956	NFL—Buddy Parker, Detroit.	3-9 to 9-3		AFC—John Ralston, Denver	5-9 to 7-5-2
1957	NFL—Paul Brown, Cleveland.	5-7 to 9-2-1	1974	AFC—Don Coryell, St. Louis	4-9-1 to 10-4
1958	NFL—Weeb Ewbank, Baltimore	7-5 to 9-3		AFC—Sid Gillman, Houston	1-13 to 7-7
1959	NFL—Vince Lombardi, Green Bay	1-10-1 to 7-5	1975	NFC—Tom Landry, Dallas	8-6 to 10-4
1960	NFL—Buck Shaw, Philadelphia	7-5 to 10-2		AFC—Ted Marchibroda, Baltimore	2-12 to 10-4
	AFL—Lou Rymkus, Houston	10-4	1976	NFC—Jack Pardee, Chicago	4-10 to 7-7
1961	NFL—Allie Sherman, New York	6-4-2 to 10-3-1		AFC—Chuck Fairbanks, New England.	3-11 to 11-3
	AFL—Wally Lemm, Houston	10-4 to 10-3-1	1977	NFC—Leeman Bennett, Atlanta	4-10 to 7-7
1962	NFL—Allie Sherman, New York	10-3-1 to 12-2		AFC—Red Miller, Denver	9-5 to 12-2
	AFL—Jack Faulkner, Denver	3-11 to 7-7	1978	NFC—Dick Vermeil, Philadelphia	5-9 to 9-7
1963	NFL—George Halas, Chicago	9-5 to 11-1-2		AFC—Walt Michaels, New York	3-11 to 8-8
	AFL—Al Davis, Oakland	1-13 to 10-4	1979	NFC—Jack Pardee, Washington	8-8 to 10-6
1964	NFL—Don Shula, Baltimore	8-6 to 12-2		AFC—Sam Rutigliano, Cleveland	8-8 to 9-7
	AFL—Lou Saban, Buffalo	7-6-1 to 12-2	1980	NFC—Leeman Bennett, Atlanta	6-10 to 12-4
1965	NFL—George Halas, Chicago	5-9 to 9-5		AFC—Sam Rutigliano, Cleveland	9-7 to 11-5
	AFL—Lou Saban, Buffalo	12-2 to 10-3-1	1981	NFC—Bill Walsh, San Francisco	6-10 to 13-3
1966	NFL—Tom Landry, Dallas	7-7 to 10-3-1		AFC—Forrest Gregg, Cincinnati	6-10 to 12-4
	AFL—Mike Holovak, Boston	4-8-2 to 8-4-2	1982	NFC—Joe Gibbs, Washington	8-8 to 8-1
1967	NFL—George Allen, Los Angeles	8-6 to 11-1-2		AFC—Tom Flores, Los Angeles	7-9 to 8-1
	AFL—John Rauch, Oakland	8-5-1 to 13-1	1983	NFC—John Robinson, Los Angeles	2-7 to 9-7
1968	NFL—Don Shula, Baltimore	11-1-2 to 13-1		AFC—Chuck Knox, Seattle	4-5 to 9-7
	AFL—Hank Stram, Kansas City	9-5 to 12-2	1984	NFC—Bill Walsh, San Francisco	10-6 to 15-1
1969	NFL—Bud Grant, Minnesota	8-6 to 12-2		AFC—Chuck Knox, Seattle	9-7 to 12-4
	AFL—Paul Brown, Cincinnati	3-11 to 4-9-1	1985	NFC—Mike Ditka, Chicago	10-6 to 15-1
1970	NFC—Alex Webster, New York	6-8 to 9-5		AFC—Raymond Berry, New England	9-7 to 11-5
	AFC—Paul Brown, Cincinnati	4-9-1 to 8-6	1986	NFC—Bill Parcells, New York	10-6 to 14-2
1971	NFC—George Allen, Washington	6-8 to 9-4-1		AFC—Marty Schottenheimer, Cleveland.	8-8 to 12-4
	AFC—Don Shula, Miami	10-4 to 10-3-1	1987	NFC—Jim Mora, New Orleans	7-9 to 12-3
1972	NFC—Dan Devine, Green Bay	4-8-2 to 10-4		AFC—Ron Meyer, Indianapolis	3-13 to 9-6
	AFC—Chuck Noll, Pittsburgh	6-8 to 11-3	1988	NFC—Mike Ditka, Chicago	11-4 to 12-4
				AFC—Marv Levy, Buffalo	7-8 to 12-4

Annual Awards (Cont.)

Year		Improvement
1989	NFC–Lindy Infante, Green Bay	4-12 to 10-6
	AFC–Dan Reeves, Denver	8-8 to 11-5
1990	NFC–Jimmy Johnson, Dallas	1-15 to 7-9
	AFC–Art Shell, Los Angeles	8-8 to 12-4
1991	NFC–Wayne Fontes, Detroit	6-10 to 12-4
	AFC–Dan Reeves, Denver	5-11 to 12-4
1992	NFC–Dennis Green, Minnesota	8-8 to 11-5
	AFC–Bobby Ross, San Diego	4-12 to 11-5
1993	NFC–Dan Reeves, New York	6-10 to 11-5
	AFC–Marv Levy, Buffalo	11-5 to 12-4

Year		Improvement
1994	NFC–Dave Wannstedt, Chicago	7-9 to 9-7
	AFC–Bill Parcells, New England	5-11 to 10-6
1995	NFC–Ray Rhodes, Philadelphia	7-9 to 10-6
	AFC–Marty Schottenheimer, Kansas City	9-7 to 13-3
1996	NFC–Dom Capers, Carolina	7-9 to 12-4
	AFC–Tom Coughlin, Jacksonville	4-12 to 9-7
1997	NFL–Jim Fassel, NY Giants	6-10 to 10-5-1
1998	NFL–Dan Reeves, Atlanta	7-9 to 14-2
1999	NFL–Dick Vermeil, St. Louis	4-12 to 13-3

CANADIAN FOOTBALL

The Grey Cup

Earl Grey, the Governor-General of Canada (1904-11), donated a trophy in 1909 for the Rugby Football Championship of Canada. The trophy, which later became known as the Grey Cup, was originally open to competition for teams registered with the Canada Rugby Union. Since 1954, the Cup has gone to the champion of the Canadian Football League (CFL).

Overall multiple winners: Toronto Argonauts (14); Edmonton Eskimos (11); Winnipeg Blue Bombers (9); Hamilton Tiger-Cats (8); Ottawa Rough Riders (7); Hamilton Tigers (5); Calgary Stampeders, Montreal Alouettes and University of Toronto (4); B.C. Lions and Queen's University (3); Ottawa Senators, Sarnia Imperials, Saskatchewan Roughriders and Toronto Balmy Beach (2).

CFL multiple winners (since 1954): Edmonton (11); Hamilton and Winnipeg (7); Ottawa (5); Toronto (4); B.C. Lions, Calgary and Montreal (3); Saskatchewan (2).

Year	Cup Final
1909	Univ. of Toronto 26, Toronto Parkdale 6
1910	Univ. of Toronto 16, Hamilton Tigers 7
1911	Univ. of Toronto 14, Toronto Argonauts 7
1912	Hamilton Alerts 11, Toronto Argonauts 4
1913	Hamilton Tigers 44, Toronto Parkdale 2
1914	Toronto Argonauts 14, Univ. of Toronto 2
1915	Hamilton Tigers 13, Toronto Rowing 7
1916-19	Not held (WWI)
1920	Univ. of Toronto 16, Toronto Argonauts 3
1921	Toronto Argonauts 23, Edmonton Eskimos 0
1922	Queens Univ. 13, Edmonton Elks 1
1923	Queens Univ. 54, Regina Roughriders 0
1924	Queens Univ. 11, Toronto Balmy Beach 3
1925	Ottawa Senators 24, Winnipeg Tigers 1
1926	Ottawa Senators 10, Univ. of Toronto 7
1927	Toronto Balmy Beach 9, Hamilton Tigers 6
1928	Hamilton Tigers 30, Regina Roughriders 0
1929	Hamilton Tigers 14, Regina Roughriders 3
1930	Toronto Balmy Beach 11, Regina Roughriders 6
1931	Montreal AAA 22, Regina Roughriders 0
1932	Hamilton Tigers 25, Regina Roughriders 6
1933	Toronto Argonauts 4, Sarnia Imperials 3

Year	Cup Final
1934	Sarnia Imperials 20, Regina Roughriders 12
1935	Winnipeg 'Pegs 18, Hamilton Tigers 12
1936	Sarnia Imperials 26, Ottawa Rough Riders 20
1937	Toronto Argonauts 4, Winnipeg Blue Bombers 3
1938	Toronto Argonauts 30, Winnipeg Blue Bombers 7
1939	Winnipeg Blue Bombers 8, Ottawa Rough Riders 7
1940	Gm 1: Ottawa Rough Riders 8, Toronto B-Beach 2
	Gm 2: Ottawa Rough Riders 12, Toronto B-Beach 5
1941	Winnipeg Blue Bombers 18, Ottawa Rough Riders 16
1942	Toronto RACF 8, Winnipeg RACF 5
1943	Hamilton Wildcats 23, Winnipeg RACF 14
1944	Montreal HMCS 7, Hamilton Wildcats 6
1945	Toronto Argonauts 35, Winnipeg Blue Bombers 0
1946	Toronto Argonauts 28, Winnipeg Blue Bombers 6
1947	Toronto Argonauts 10, Winnipeg Blue Bombers 9
1948	Calgary Stampeders 12, Ottawa Rough Riders 7
1949	Montreal Alouettes 28, Calgary Stampeders 15
1950	Toronto Argonauts 13, Winnipeg Blue Bombers 0
1951	Ottawa Rough Riders 21, Saskatch. Roughriders 14
1952	Toronto Argonauts 21, Edmonton Eskimos 11
1953	Hamilton Tiger-Cats 12, Winnipeg Blue Bombers 6

Year	Winner	Head Coach	Score	Loser	Head Coach	Site
1954	Edmonton	Frank (Pop) Ivy	26-25	Montreal	Doug Walker	Toronto
1955	Edmonton	Frank (Pop) Ivy	34-19	Montreal	Doug Walker	Vancouver
1956	Edmonton	Frank (Pop) Ivy	50-27	Montreal	Doug Walker	Toronto
1957	Hamilton	Jim Trimble	32-7	Winnipeg	Bud Grant	Toronto
1958	Winnipeg	Bud Grant	35-28	Hamilton	Jim Trimble	Vancouver
1959	Winnipeg	Bud Grant	21-7	Hamilton	Jim Trimble	Toronto
1960	Ottawa	Frank Clair	16-6	Edmonton	Eagle Keys	Vancouver
1961	Winnipeg	Bud Grant	21-14(OT)	Hamilton	Jim Trimble	Toronto
1962	Winnipeg	Bud Grant	28-27*	Hamilton	Jim Trimble	Toronto
1963	Hamilton	Ralph Sazio	21-10	B.C. Lions	Dave Skrien	Vancouver
1964	B.C. Lions	Dave Skrien	34-24	Hamilton	Ralph Sazio	Toronto
1965	Hamilton	Ralph Sazio	22-16	Winnipeg	Bud Grant	Toronto
1966	Saskatchewan	Eagle Keys	29-14	Ottawa	Frank Clair	Vancouver
1967	Hamilton	Ralph Sazio	24-1	Saskatchewan	Eagle Keys	Ottawa
1968	Ottawa	Frank Clair	24-21	Calgary	Jerry Williams	Toronto
1969	Ottawa	Frank Clair	29-11	Saskatchewan	Eagle Keys	Montreal
1970	Montreal	Sam Etcheverry	23-10	Calgary	Jim Duncan	Toronto
1971	Calgary	Jim Duncan	14-11	Toronto	Leo Cahill	Vancouver
1972	Hamilton	Jerry Williams	13-10	Saskatchewan	Dave Skrien	Hamilton
1973	Ottawa	Jack Gotta	22-18	Edmonton	Ray Jauch	Toronto
1974	Montreal	Marv Levy	20-7	Edmonton	Ray Jauch	Vancouver

Year	Winner	Head Coach	Score	Loser	Head Coach	Site
1975	Edmonton	Ray Jauch	9-8	Montreal	Marv Levy	Calgary
1976	Ottawa	George Brancato	23-20	Saskatchewan	John Payne	Toronto
1977	Montreal	Marv Levy	41-6	Edmonton	Hugh Campbell	Montreal
1978	Edmonton	Hugh Campbell	20-13	Montreal	Joe Scannella	Toronto
1979	Edmonton	Hugh Campbell	17-9	Montreal	Joe Scannella	Montreal
1980	Edmonton	Hugh Campbell	48-10	Hamilton	John Payne	Toronto
1981	Edmonton	Hugh Campbell	26-23	Ottawa	George Brancato	Montreal
1982	Edmonton	Hugh Campbell	32-16	Toronto	Bob O'Billovich	Toronto
1983	Toronto	Bob O'Billovich	18-17	B.C. Lions	Don Matthews	Vancouver
1984	Winnipeg	Cal Murphy	47-17	Hamilton	Al Bruno	Edmonton
1985	B.C. Lions	Don Matthews	37-24	Hamilton	Al Bruno	Montreal
1986	Hamilton	Al Bruno	39-15	Edmonton	Jack Parker	Vancouver
1987	Edmonton	Joe Faragalli	38-36	Toronto	Bob O'Billovich	Vancouver
1988	Winnipeg	Mike Riley	22-21	B.C. Lions	Larry Donovan	Ottawa
1989	Saskatchewan	John Gregory	43-40	Hamilton	Al Bruno	Toronto
1990	Winnipeg	Mike Riley	50-11	Edmonton	Joe Faragalli	Vancouver
1991	Toronto	Adam Rita	36-21	Calgary	Wally Buono	Winnipeg
1992	Calgary	Wally Buono	24-10	Winnipeg	Urban Bowman	Toronto
1993	Edmonton	Ron Lancaster	33-23	Winnipeg	Cal Murphy	Calgary
1994	B.C. Lions	Dave Ritchie	26-23	Baltimore	Don Matthews	Vancouver
1995	Baltimore	Don Matthews	37-20	Calgary	Wally Buono	Regina
1996	Toronto	Don Matthews	43-37	Edmonton	Ron Lancaster	Hamilton
1997	Toronto	Don Matthews	47-23	Saskatchewan	Jim Daley	Edmonton
1998	Calgary	Wally Buono	26-24	Hamilton	Ron Lancaster	Winnipeg
1999	Hamilton	Ron Lancaster	32-21	Calgary	Wally Buono	Vancouver

*Halted by fog in 4th quarter, final 9:29 played the following day.

CFL Most Outstanding Player

Regular season Player of the Year as selected by The Football Reporters of Canada since 1953.

Multiple winners: Doug Flutie (6); Russ Jackson and Jackie Parker (3); Dieter Brock, Ron Lancaster and Mike Pringle (2).

Year	Year	Year
1953 Billy Vessels, Edmonton, RB	1969 Russ Jackson, Ottawa, QB	1985 Merv Fernandez, B.C. Lions, WR
1954 Sam Etcheverry, Montreal, QB	1970 Ron Lancaster, Saskatch., QB	1986 James Murphy, Winnipeg, WR
1955 Pat Abbruzzi, Montreal, RB	1971 Don Jonas, Winnipeg, QB	1987 Tom Clements, Winnipeg, QB
1956 Hal Patterson, Montreal, E-DB	1972 Garney Henley, Hamilton, WR	1988 David Williams, B.C. Lions, WR
1957 Jackie Parker, Edmonton, QB	1973 Geo. McGowan, Edmonton, WR	1989 Tracy Ham, Edmonton, QB
1958 Jackie Parker, Edmonton, QB	1974 Tom Wilkinson, Edmonton, QB	1990 Mike Clemons, Toronto, RB
1959 Johnny Bright, Edmonton, RB	1975 Willie Burden, Calgary, RB	1991 Doug Flutie, B.C. Lions, QB
1960 Jackie Parker, Edmonton, QB	1976 Ron Lancaster, Saskatch., QB	1992 Doug Flutie, Calgary, QB
1961 Bernie Faloney, Hamilton, QB	1977 Jimmy Edwards, Hamilton, RB	1993 Doug Flutie, Calgary, QB
1962 George Dixon, Montreal, RB	1978 Tony Gabriel, Ottawa, TE	1994 Doug Flutie, Calgary, QB
1963 Russ Jackson, Ottawa, QB	1979 David Green, Montreal, RB	1995 Mike Pringle, Baltimore, RB
1964 Lovell Coleman, Calgary, RB	1980 Dieter Brock, Winnipeg, QB	1996 Doug Flutie, Toronto, QB
1965 George Reed, Saskatchewan, RB	1981 Dieter Brock, Winnipeg, QB	1997 Doug Flutie, Toronto, QB
1966 Russ Jackson, Ottawa, QB	1982 Condredge Holloway, Tor., QB	1998 Mike Pringle, Montreal, RB
1967 Peter Liske, Calgary, QB	1983 Warren Moon, Edmonton, QB	1999 Danny McManus, Hamilton, QB
1968 Bill Symons, Toronto, RB	1984 Willard Reaves, Winnipeg, RB	

All-Time CFL Leaders

Through the 1999 season. Players active in 1999 are in **bold** type.

Passing Yards

		Yrs	Att	Cmp	Yards	Cmp Pct	Avg Gain	TD	Int	Rating
1	Ron Lancaster	19	6233	3384	50,535	54.3	14.9	333	396	72.4
2	**Damon Allen**	15	5955	3264	45,949	54.8	14.1	253	203	79.9
3	Matt Dunigan	14	5476	3057	43,857	55.8	14.3	306	211	84.5
4	Doug Flutie	8	4854	2975	41,355	61.3	13.9	270	155	93.9
5	**Tracy Ham**	12	4945	2670	40,534	53.9	15.2	284	164	86.4
6	Tom Clements	12	4657	2807	39,041	60.3	13.9	252	214	86.1
7	Kent Austin	10	4700	2709	36,030	57.6	13.3	198	191	79.2
8	Dieter Brock	11	4535	2602	34,830	57.4	13.4	210	158	82.8
9	Tom Burgess	10	4034	2118	30,308	52.5	14.3	190	191	73.1
10	**Danny McManus**	10	3599	1953	29,316	54.3	15.0	146	147	77.7

Rushing Yards

		Yrs	Car	Yards	Avg	TD
1	George Reed	13	3243	16,116	5.0	134
2	Johnny Bright	13	1969	10,909	5.5	69
3	**Mike Pringle**	8	1803	10,579	5.9	69
4	**Damon Allen**	15	1322	9,179	6.9	74
5	Normie Kwong	13	1745	9,022	5.2	78

Receiving Yards

		Yrs	Ct	Yards	Avg	TD
1	**Allen Pitts**	10	889	13,846	15.6	111
2	Ray Elgaard	14	830	13,198	16.0	78
3	**Don Narcisse**	13	919	12,366	13.5	75
4	Brian Kelly	9	575	11,169	19.4	97
5	**Darren Flutie**	9	749	11,104	14.8	52

NFL EUROPE

The World League of American Football was formed in 1991 with hopes of expanding the popularity of the NFL to overseas markets. Funded by the NFL, the inaugural league in 1991 consisted of three European teams (London, Barcelona and Frankfurt), and seven North American teams (New York/New Jersey, Orlando, Montreal, Raleigh-Durham, Birmingham, Sacramento and San Antonio). The second season used the same format with Columbus, Ohio, replacing Raleigh-Durham.

In the fall of 1992, the NFL and WLAF Board of Directors voted to restructure the league to include more European teams. Play was subsequently suspended. In 1993, NFL clubs approved a six-team European-only league to resume play in 1995 with teams in Amsterdam, Barcelona, Frankfurt, London, Rhein and Scotland. In January 1998, the name of the league was changed to NFL Europe. Berlin was added for the 1999 season and London was disbanded.

The World Bowl

The first World Bowl was held in 1991 in front of 61,108 fans at London's Wembley Stadium. In 1991 and 1992, when the league consisted of three divisions, the top team from each division and one wild-card team advanced to the playoffs, with the winners of each game advancing to the World Bowl. There was no game played in 1993 or 1994. Since 1995, the top two regular season teams advance directly to the World Bowl.

Year	Winner	Head Coach	Score	Loser	Head Coach	Site
1991	London	Larry Kennan	21-0	Barcelona	Jack Bicknell	London
1992	Sacramento	Kay Stephenson	21-17	Orlando	Galen Hall	Montreal
1995	Frankfurt	Ernie Stautner	26-22	Amsterdam	Al Luginbill	Amsterdam
1996	Scotland	Jim Criner	32-27	Frankfurt	Ernie Stautner	Edinburgh, Scot.
1997	Barcelona	Jack Bicknell	38-24	Rhein	Galen Hall	Barcelona
1998	Rhein	Galen Hall	34-10	Frankfurt	Dick Curl	Frankfurt
1999	Frankfurt	Dick Curl	38-24	Barcelona	Jack Bicknell	Dusseldorf
2000	Rhein	Galen Hall	13-10	Scotland	Jim Criner	Frankfurt

World Bowl MVP

Year		Year		Year	
1991	Dan Crossman, London, S	1996	Yo Murphy, Scotland, WR	1999	Andy McCullough, Frankfurt, WR
1992	Davis Archer, Sacramento, QB	1997	Jon Kitna, Barcelona, QB	2000	Aaron Stecker, Scotland, RB
1995	Paul Justin, Frankfurt, QB	1998	Jim Arellanes, Rhein, QB		

Most Valuable Player

Regular season Offensive and Defensive Most Valuable Players as selected by league head coaches since 1991.

Year
1991 Off–Stan Gelbaugh, Lon., QB
Def–Anthony Parker, NY/NJ, CB
& Danny Lockett, Lon., LB
1992 Off–David Archer, Sac., QB
Def–Adrian Jones, Bar., CB
1995 Off–Paul Justin, Fra., QB
Def–Malcolm Showell, Ams., DE

Year
1996 Off–Sean LaChapelle, Sco., WR
Def–Ty Parten, Sco., DL
1997 Off–T.J. Rubley, Rhe., QB
Def–Jason Simmons, Sco., DE
1998 Off–Marcus Robinson, Rhe., WR
Def–Josh Taves, Bar., DE

Year
1999 Off–Lawrence Phillips, Bar., RB
Def–Mike Maslowski, Bar., LB
2000 Off–Aaron Stecker, Sco., RB
Def–Jonathan Brown, Ber., DE
& Duane Hawthorne, Sco., CB

ARENA FOOTBALL

The Arena Football League debuted in June of 1987 with four teams in Chicago, Denver, Pittsburgh and Washington D.C. Currently there are 17 teams in the league, divided into two conferences and four divisions.

ArenaBowl

Bowl	Year	Winner	Head Coach	Score	Loser	Head Coach	Site
I	1987	Denver	Tim Marcum	45-16	Pittsburgh	Joe Haering	Pittsburgh
II	1988	Detroit	Tim Marcum	24-13	Chicago	Perry Moss	Chicago
III	1989	Detroit	Tim Marcum	39-26	Pittsburgh	Joe Haering	Detroit
IV	1990	Detroit	Perry Moss	51-27	Dallas	Ernie Stautner	Detroit
V	1991	Tampa Bay	Fran Curci	48-42	Detroit	Tim Marcum	Detroit
VI	1992	Detroit	Tim Marcum	56-38	Orlando	Perry Moss	Orlando
VII	1993	Tampa Bay	Lary Kuharich	51-31	Detroit	Tim Marcum	Detroit
VIII	1994	Arizona	Danny White	36-31	Orlando	Perry Moss	Orlando
IX	1995	Tampa Bay	Tim Marcum	48-35	Orlando	Perry Moss	St. Petersburg
X	1996	Tampa Bay	Tim Marcum	42-38	Iowa	John Gregory	Des Moines
XI	1997	Arizona	Danny White	55-33	Iowa	John Gregory	Phoenix
XII	1998	Orlando	Jay Gruden	62-31	Tampa Bay	Tim Marcum	Tampa
XIII	1999	Albany	Mike Dailey	59-48	Orlando	Jay Gruden	Albany
XIV	2000	Orlando	Jay Gruden	41-38	Nashville	Pat Sperduto	Orlando

ArenaBowl MVP

Year		Year		Year	
1987	Gary Mullen, Denver, WR	1992	George LaFrance, Detroit, OS	1997	Donnie Davis, Arizona, QB
1988	Steve Griffin, Detroit, WR/DB	1993	Jay Gruden, Tampa Bay, QB	1998	Rick Hamilton, Orlando, FB/LB
1989	George LaFrance, Detroit, WR/DB	1994	Sherdrick Bonner, Arizona, QB	1999	Eddie Brown, Albany, OS
1990	Art Schlichter, Detroit, QB	1995	George LaFrance, Tampa Bay, OS	2000	Connell Maynor, Orlando, QB
1991	Jay Gruden, Tampa Bay, QB	1996	Stevie Thomas, Tampa Bay, WR/LB		

College Basketball

Cincinnati's Final Four dreams were broken along with the right leg of **Kenyon Martin**.

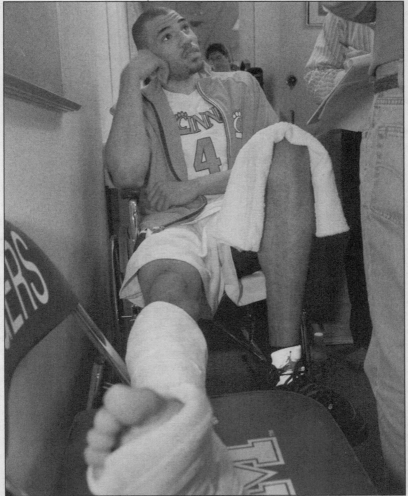

AP/Wide World Photos

Will to Win

A determined Mateen Cleaves leads the Michigan State Spartans to their first national championship since 1979.

by

Chris Fowler

Championship dreams are so fragile. They can shatter in a second, the time it takes for a leg bone to snap.

That is especially true in college basketball, where the value of a single star is higher than in other sports and the title drive entails six straight survival tests. Typically, a few fateful trips down the floor determine whose dreams are fulfilled each March.

As the 2000 edition of March Madness began, fate arrived swiftly and cruelly. The NCAA tournament was ripped open before it even tipped off. When Kenyon Martin crumbled to the floor of The Pyramid in Memphis just three minutes into his team's Conference USA quarterfinal game with Saint Louis, his leg was broken and Cincinnati was finished.

Coach Bob Huggins and the Bearcats put up a brave front, but they

Chris Fowler is the host of ESPN's *College GameDay*.

weren't fooling anyone, not even themselves. It is the only time in memory that a consensus national player of the year (and the eventual NBA top overall draft pick) had fallen on the eve of the dance.

Instead, the season's enduring snapshot is of the fiery, defiant face of Mateen Cleaves, his fist raised toward the roof of Indianapolis' RCA Dome. Has any college basketball player more outwardly embodied the will to win better than Michigan State's little general?

Some may have equaled it, like the guardian of the Spartans' point guard legacy, who watched at courtside flashing that famous smile as Cleaves delivered a title 21 years after he had.

Theirs had become a special bond. So it was natural that Cleaves' wide eyes sought out Magic Johnson following each critical basket of the championship battle with Florida.

In fact, the whole dome was wide-eyed, because these were perimeter jumpers from Cleaves, a guy who had

Michigan State head coach **Tom Izzo**, left, and **Mateen Cleaves**, the tournament's Most Outstanding Player, share the moment and emotions following the Spartans' 89-76 win over the Florida Gators in the 2000 NCAA title game at the RCA Dome in Indianapolis.

been told so many times he couldn't shoot it's a wonder he hadn't just accepted it and moved on.

Even after rolling his right ankle early in the second half, he returned from the locker room, dispelling any thoughts that a leg injury would affect the national championship picture for the second time in two weeks. He was limping a bit, but was willing as ever to do what it took to win, making long passes and sacrificing his body setting picks. When the young Gator horde had finally been worn down, there were Cleaves and his coach wet-eyed and hugging like reunited brothers.

If anyone could match Cleaves' fire, it was his coach, Tom Izzo. We may never see a better matched player-coach tandem: two former football players, the city kid from Flint and the guy from the rural Upper Peninsula-outpost of Iron Mountain, Mich.

In the hours after the Spartans had cut down the nets, Izzo's thoughts briefly drifted to this sobering notion: not only would he never coach Cleaves again, but he'd never coach another player like him again. A touch of bittersweet on a night filled with joy, the kind only a coach can appreciate.

If not for fate, it might have been Huggins and Martin, another tough-love tandem, sharing those same moments and same emotions.

We'll never know.

10. **LSU snaps a six-year streak** of finishing with a losing record. Shot-blocking forward Stromile Swift leads the Tigers to the Sweet 16 and a 28-6 overall finish.

9. Led by Marcus Fizer, Iowa State goes from a team expected to finish in the second half of the Big 12 standings to league champions with a 32-5 finish. **The Cyclones make the Elite Eight**, losing to the eventual champion Michigan State in the Midwest Regional Final.

AP/Wide World Photos

Fiery head coach **Billy Donovan** and his young Florida Gators made a surprising run to the Final Four before falling to Michigan State in the national championship game.

8. **Eddie House scores 61 points** in Arizona State's double-overtime thrilling win over California. That's the highest single-game scoring effort in Division I all season. House also had a 46-point performance.

7. **North Carolina's roller coaster.** Considered the ACC favorite in the preseason, the Tar Heels go from major disappointment to the Final Four, also as an eight seed.

6. **Wisconsin's Cinderella Story** ...Going from 13-12 at one point to making the Final Four, Dick Bennett's team does it with defense. The Badgers were an eight seed yet they won the West Regional.

5. **Mateen Cleaves**, returns for his senior season and comes back from an injury to perform well for the eventual national champions. He pulls a "Willis Reed" by coming back in the national championship game after suffering an ankle injury.

4. **Kenyon Martin returns to college** for his senior season and dominates for a Cincinnati team which holds down the #1 ranking through most of the regular season. Martin is also involved in the year's most dramatic and disappointing moment, suffering a devastating injury vs. Saint Louis in the Conference USA tournament, which ends his season.

3. **Duke loses four starters yet wins the ACC** and finishes #1 in the

AP/Wide World Photos

After 29 seasons and three national championships, legendary Indiana University head coach **Bob Knight** was fired on Sept. 10 for violating the "zero tolerance" policy that university adminstrators had instituted in May following an investigation into his behavior as coach.

regular season polls for the second straight year, the first team to do that since DePaul in 1980-81. Coach Mike Krzyzewski does one of his best coaching jobs ever.

2. **Billy Donovan's young Florida Gator team**, beats both Duke and North Carolina in the NCAA tournament en route to the national championship game. The Gators also had one of the most exciting finishes in the NCAA tourney in a first-round win over Butler.

1. **Michigan State**, the first team with seven losses to earn a one seed in the tournament, gives coach Tom Izzo a national championship, the school's first since Magic Johnson's team in 1979. ∎

UPSETTING FIRST ROUND

The sixth-seeded Indiana Hoosiers were upset in the first round of the tourney once again in 2000. In fact, Indiana has the most first-round losses as the higher seeded team in the NCAA tournament (since the tournament expanded to 64 teams in 1985 and did away with first-round byes).

Losses	School (seedings)
6	Indiana (3,4,6,6,8,8)
4	Arizona (2,3,4,5)
4	Missouri (3,4,6,8)
4	UCLA (4,4,5,5)

ENLARGIN' MARGIN

Here's a look at Indiana's worst NCAA tournament losses under Bob Knight. Notice that five of the seven have come in the last five years, with the two worst coming in the last two years. Indiana last advanced to the Sweet 16 in 1994. Please note that the numbers in parentheses after the opponents refer to the opponent's seeding.

Year (Round)	Opponent	Margin of Loss (Score)
1999 (2nd)	St. John's (3)	25 (86-61)
2000 (1st)	Pepperdine (11)	20 (77-57)
1997 (1st)	Colorado (9)	18 (80-62)
1991 (3rd)	Kansas (3)	18 (83-65)
1998 (2nd)	Connecticut (2)	13 (64-51)
1996 (1st)	Boston College (11)	13 (64-51)
1989 (3rd)	Seton Hall (3)	13 (78-65)

Note: Indiana was the higher seeded team in every game except for 1998 and 1999.

NOT EVEN CLOSE

Michigan State is the first national champion since Indiana in 1981 to win each game of the NCAA tournament by at least 10 points. The Spartans also pulled off the feat in 1979, the year of their first national championship. See the following list of teams to win all their NCAA tournament games by at least 10 points.

Year	School	Avg. Margin
2000	Michigan St.	15.3
1981	Indiana	22.6
1979	Michigan St.	20.8
1973	UCLA	16.0
1970	UCLA	18.0
1967	UCLA	23.8
1960	Ohio St.	19.5
1956	San Francisco	14.0

OFFENSIVE OFFENSE

Wisconsin, which was bounced from the 1999 tourney after scoring only 32 points in the first round, made it to the Final Four in 2000. But then the Badgers could manage just 41 points in their loss to eventual national champion Michigan State. Here is a look at the fewest points scored by one team in a national semifinal game in the last 50 years.

Points	Year	School
40	1984	Kentucky
41	2000	Wisconsin
44	1951	Oklahoma St.
45	1985	Memphis

Note: Wisconsin's 41 points is the lowest since the shot clock was introduced in the 1985-86 season.

USUAL SUSPECTS

North Carolina's men's basketball team hasn't missed the Big Dance since 1974. Here's a look at the longest active streaks for consecutive tournament appearances for both men's and women's teams.

MEN

School (last miss)	Consecutive Seasons
North Carolina (1974)	26
Arizona (1984)	16
Indiana (1988)	12
UCLA (1988)	12
Kansas (1989)	11
Temple (1989)	11

WOMEN

School (last miss)	Consecutive Seasons
Louisiana Tech (1981)	19
Tennessee (1981)	19
Virginia (1983)	17
Stanford (1987)	13
Stephen F. Austin (1987)	13

■

Final Regular Season AP Men's Top 25 Poll

Taken **before** start of NCAA tournament.

The sportswriters & broadcasters poll: first place votes in parentheses; records through Monday, March 13, 2000; total points (based on 25 for 1st, 24 for 2nd, etc.); record in NCAA tourney and team lost to; head coach (career years and record including 2000 postseason), and preseason ranking. Teams in **bold** type went on to reach NCAA Final Four.

		Mar. 13 Record	Points	NCAA Recap	Head Coach	Preseason Rank
1	Duke (58)	27-4	1729	2-1 (Florida)	Mike Krzyzewski (25 yrs: 571-219)	10
2	**Michigan St.** (6)	26-7	1628	6-0	Tom Izzo (5 yrs: 120-48)	3
3	Stanford (3)	26-3	1522	1-1 (N. Carolina)	Mike Montgomery (22 yrs: 442-220)	13
4	Arizona (2)	26-6	1510	1-1 (Wisconsin)	Lute Olson (27 yrs: 613-220)	9
5	Temple	26-5	1482	1-1 (Seton Hall)	John Chaney (28 yrs: 632-225)	7
6	Iowa St.	29-4	1441	3-1 (Michigan St.)	Larry Eustachy (10 yrs: 206-105)	NR
7	Cincinnati (1)	28-3	1414	1-1 (Tulsa)	Bob Huggins (19 yrs: 444-158)	2
8	Ohio St.	22-6	1192	1-1 (Miami-FL)	Jim O'Brien (18 yrs: 293-255)	5
9	St. John's	24-7	1050	1-1 (Gonzaga)	Mike Jarvis (15 yrs: 306-158)	18
10	LSU	26-5	1035	2-1 (Wisconsin)	John Brady (9 yrs: 138-116)	NR
11	Tennessee	24-6	986	2-1 (N. Carolina)	Jerry Green (17 yrs: 290-202)	19
12	Oklahoma	26-6	919	1-1 (Purdue)	Kelvin Sampson (17 yrs: 306-210)	NR
13	**Florida**	24-7	853	5-1 (Michigan St.)	Billy Donovan (6 yrs: 113-69)	8
14	Oklahoma St.	24-6	748	3-1 (Florida)	Eddie Sutton (30 yrs: 659-259)	22
15	Texas	23-8	729	1-1 (LSU)	Rick Barnes (13 yrs: 245-156)	21
16	Syracuse	24-5	701	2-1 (Michigan St.)	Jim Boeheim (24 yrs: 566-199)	17
17	Maryland	24-9	670	1-1 (UCLA)	Gary Williams (22 yrs: 424-256)	26
18	Tulsa	29-4	550	3-1 (N. Carolina)	Bill Self (7 yrs: 129-81)	39
19	Kentucky	22-9	496	1-1 (Syracuse)	Tubby Smith (9 yrs: 210-85)	14
20	Connecticut	24-9	452	1-1 (Tennessee)	Jim Calhoun (28 yrs: 577-267)	1
21	Illinois	21-9	444	1-1 (Florida)	Lon Kruger (18 yrs: 318-233)	16
22	Indiana	20-8	394	0-1 (Pepperdine)	Bob Knight (35 yrs: 763-290)	30
23	Miami-FL	21-10	181	2-1 (Tulsa)	Leonard Hamilton (yrs: 200-210)	25
24	Auburn	23-9	166	1-1 (Iowa St.)	Cliff Ellis (25 yrs: 468-281)	4
25	Purdue	21-9	100	3-1 (Wisconsin)	Gene Keady (22 yrs: 477-210)	23

Others receiving votes: 26. **Oregon** (22-7) 96 pts; 27. **Kansas** (23-9) 55; 28. **UCLA** (19-11) 50; 29. **Arkansas** (19-14) 39; 30. **Fresno St.** (24-9) 33; 31. **Utah St.** (28-5) 30; 32. **Seton Hall** (20-9) 15; 33. **Ball St.** (22-8), **Louisville** (19-11), **Utah** (22-8) and **Vanderbilt** (19-10) 6; 37. **Pennsylvania** (21-7) and **Wisconsin** (18-13) 3; 39. **Butler** (23-7) and **Gonzaga** (24-8) 2; 41. **Lafayette** (28-6) and **Saint Louis** (19-13) 1.

NCAA Men's Division I Tournament Seeds

	WEST		MIDWEST		SOUTH		EAST
1	Arizona (26-6)	1	Michigan St. (26-7)	1	Stanford (26-3)	1	Duke (27-4)
2	St. John's (24-7)	2	Iowa St. (29-4)	2	Cincinnati (28-3)	2	Temple (26-5)
3	Oklahoma (26-6)	3	Maryland (24-9)	3	Ohio St. (22-6)	3	Oklahoma St. (24-6)
4	LSU (26-5)	4	Syracuse (24-5)	4	Tennessee (24-6)	4	Illinois (21-9)
5	Texas (23-8)	5	Kentucky (22-9)	5	Connecticut (24-9)	5	Florida (24-7)
6	Purdue (21-9)	6	UCLA (19-11)	6	Miami-FL (21-10)	6	Indiana (20-8)
7	Louisville (19-11)	7	Auburn (23-9)	7	Tulsa (29-4)	7	Oregon (22-7)
8	Wisconsin (18-13)	8	Utah (22-8)	8	North Carolina (18-13)	8	Kansas (23-9)
9	Fresno St. (24-9)	9	St. Louis (19-13)	9	Missouri (18-12)	9	DePaul (21-11)
10	Gonzaga (24-8)	10	Creighton (23-9)	10	UNLV (23-7)	10	Seton Hall (20-9)
11	Dayton (22-8)	11	Ball St. (22-8)	11	Arkansas (19-14)	11	Pepperdine (24-8)
12	Indiana St. (22-9)	12	St. Bonaventure (21-9)	12	Utah St. (28-5)	12	Butler (23-7)
13	SE Missouri St. (24-6)	13	Samford (21-10)	13	LA-Lafayette (25-8)	13	Pennsylvania (21-7)
14	Winthrop (21-8)	14	Iona (20-10)	14	Appalachian St. (23-8)	14	Hofstra (24-6)
15	N. Arizona (20-10)	15	C. Connecticut (25-5)	15	NC-Wilmington (18-12)	15	Lafayette (24-6)
16	Jackson St. (17-15)	16	Valparaiso (19-12)	16	S.C. State (20-13)	16	Lamar (15-15)

2000 NCAA BASKETBALL MEN'S DIVISION I

EAST

First Round (March 16-17)
- 1 Duke 82 / 16 Lamar 55
- 8 Kansas (OT) 81 / 9 DePaul 77
- 5 Florida (OT) 69 / 12 Butler 68
- 4 Illinois 68 / 13 Penn 58
- 6 Indiana 57 / 11 Pepperdine 77
- 3 Okla. St. 86 / 14 Hofstra 66
- 7 Oregon 71 / 10 Seton Hall (OT) 72
- 2 Temple 73 / 15 Lafayette 47

Second Round (March 18-19)
- Duke 69 / Kansas 64 → Duke 78
- Florida 93 / Illinois 76 → Florida 87
- Pepperdine 67 / Okla. St. 75 → Okla. St. 68
- Seton Hall (OT) 67 / Temple 65 → Seton Hall 66

Regionals (March 23-26)
- Duke / Florida 77 → Florida 71
- Okla. St. 65 / Seton Hall → Okla. St. 65
- **Florida 71**

SOUTH

First Round (March 16-17)
- 1 Stanford 84 / 16 S. Carolina St. 65
- 8 N. Carolina 84 / 9 Missouri 70
- 5 Connecticut 75 / 12 Utah St. 67
- 4 Tennessee 63 / 13 Louisiana 58
- 6 Miami (Fla.) 75 / 11 Arkansas 71
- 3 Ohio St. 87 / 14 Appalachian St. 61
- 7 Tulsa 89 / 10 UNLV 62
- 2 Cincinnati 64 / 15 NC-Wilmington 47

Second Round (March 18-19)
- Stanford 53 / N. Carolina 60 → N. Carolina 74
- Connecticut 51 / Tennessee 65 → Tennessee 69
- Miami (Fla.) 75 / Ohio St. 62 → Miami (Fla.) 71
- Tulsa 69 / Cincinnati 61 → Tulsa 80

Regionals (March 23-26)
- N. Carolina 74 / Tennessee 69 → N. Carolina 59
- Miami (Fla.) 71 / Tulsa 80 → Tulsa 55
- **N. Carolina 59**

WEST

First Round (March 16-17)
- 1 Arizona 71 / 16 Jackson St. 47
- 8 Wisconsin 66 / 9 Fresno St. 56
- 5 Texas 77 / 12 Indiana St. 61
- 4 LSU 64 / 13 SE Missouri St. 61
- 6 Purdue 62 / 11 Dayton 61
- 3 Oklahoma 74 / 14 Winthrop 50
- 7 Louisville 66 / 10 Gonzaga 77
- 2 St. John's 61 / 15 No. Arizona 56

Second Round (March 18-19)
- Arizona 59 / Wisconsin 66 → Wisconsin 61
- Texas 67 / LSU 72 → LSU 48
- Purdue 66 / Oklahoma 62 → Purdue 75
- Gonzaga 82 / St. John's 76 → Gonzaga 66

Regionals (March 23-26)
- Wisconsin 61 / LSU 48 → Wisconsin 64
- Purdue 75 / Gonzaga 66 → Purdue 60
- **Wisconsin 41**

MIDWEST

First Round (March 16-17)
- 1 Michigan St. 73 / 16 Valparaiso 38
- 8 Utah 48 / 9 St. Louis 45
- 5 Kentucky (2OT) 85 / 12 St. Bonaventure 80
- 4 Syracuse 79 / 13 Samford 65
- 6 UCLA 65 / 11 Ball St. 57
- 3 Maryland 74 / 14 Iona 59
- 7 Auburn 72 / 10 Creighton 69
- 2 Iowa St. 88 / 15 Central Conn. 78

Second Round (March 18-19)
- Michigan St. 73 / Utah 61 → Michigan St. 75
- Kentucky 50 / Syracuse 52 → Syracuse 58
- UCLA 105 / Maryland 70 → UCLA 56
- Auburn 60 / Iowa St. 80 → Iowa St. 64

Regionals (March 23-26)
- Michigan St. 75 / Syracuse 58 → Michigan St.
- UCLA 56 / Iowa St. 64 → Iowa St. 64
- **Michigan St. 53**

NATIONAL CHAMPIONSHIP
Florida 76 / Mich. St. 89

FINAL FOUR
RCA Dome in Indianapolis, IN
***
Semifinals: April 1
Finals: April 3

NCAA Men's Championship Game

62nd NCAA Division I Championship Game. **Date:** Monday, April 3, at the RCA Dome in Indianapolis. **Coaches:** Tom Izzo of Michigan State and Billy Donovan of Florida. **Favorite:** Michigan State by 4.
Attendance: 43,116; **Officials:** Jim Burr, Gerald Boudreaux, David Hall; **TV Rating:** 14.1/23 share (CBS).

Florida 76

	Min	FG M-A	FT M-A	Pts	Reb O-T	A	PF
Brent Wright	29	5-8	3-5	13	4-10	4	4
Mike Miller	31	2-5	5-6	10	1-3	2	0
Udonis Haslem	28	10-12	7-7	27	2-2	0	4
Teddy Dupay	15	0-4	0-0	0	0-0	1	2
Justin Hamilton	14	0-1	0-0	0	0-0	0	1
Brett Nelson	26	4-10	0-0	11	1-4	3	1
Matt Bonner	7	0-3	0-0	0	1-3	0	1
Kenyan Weaks	22	1-3	0-0	3	1-1	1	2
Donnell Harvey	16	3-11	3-4	9	4-6	0	2
Major Parker	12	1-3	0-0	3	0-0	2	2
TOTALS	200	26-60	18-22	76	14-29	13	19

Three-point FG: 6-18 (Wright 0-1. Miller 1-2. Dupay 0-2, Hamilton 0-1, Nelson 3-6, Bonner 0-2, Weaks 1-1. Parker 1-3); **Team Rebounds:** 1; **Blocked Shots:** 2 (Haslem, Harvey); **Turnovers:** 13 (Haslem 3, Nelson 3, Harvey 2, Miller 2, Parker, Weaks, Wright); **Steals:** 5 (Nelson 2, Weaks 2, Wright); **Percentages:** 2-Pt FG (.476), 3-Pt FG (.333), Total FG (.433), Free Throws (.818).

Michigan State 89

	Min	FG M-A	FT M-A	Pts	Reb O-T	A	PF
Andre Hutson	23	2-4	2-2	6	0-1	3	4
Morris Peterson	32	7-14	4-6	21	1-2	5	3
A.J. Granger	34	7-11	2-2	19	2-9	1	2
Mateen Cleaves	33	7-11	1-1	18	0-2	4	1
Charlie Bell	33	3-6	2-3	9	3-8	5	2
Jason Richardson	15	4-7	1-2	9	1-2	0	1
Al Anagonye	11	0-0	0-0	0	2-3	0	0
Mike Chappell	6	2-4	0-0	5	1-1	0	4
Adam Ballinger	6	1-1	0-0	2	0-0	0	2
David Thomas	4	0-0	0-0	0	1-1	1	1
Brandon Smith	1	0-0	0-0	0	0-0	0	0
Steve Cherry	1	0-0	0-0	0	0-0	0	0
Mat Ishbia	1	0-1	0-0	0	0-0	0	0
TOTALS	200	33-59	12-16	89	11-29	19	20

Three-point FG: 11-22 (Peterson 3-8, Granger 3-5, Cleaves 3-4, Bell 1-2, Chappell 1-3); **Team Rebounds:** 3; **Blocked Shots:** 1 (Anagonye); **Turnovers:** 14 (Peterson 3, Anagonye 2, Bell 2, Cleaves 2, Granger 2, Chappell, Hutson, Thomas); **Steals:** 5 (Bell 2, Chappell, Peterson, Richardson). **Percentages:** 2-Pt FG (.595), 3-Pt FG (.500), Total FG (.559), Free Throws (.750).

Florida (SEC)	32 44 —	**76**
Michigan State (Big Ten)	43 46 —	**89**

Final ESPN/*USA Today* Coaches' Poll

Taken **after** NCAA Tournament.

Voted on by a panel of 31 Division I head coaches following the NCAA tournament; first place votes in parentheses with total points (based on 25 for 1st, 24 for 2nd, etc.). Schools on major probation are ineligible to be ranked.

			Before NCAAs	
		W-L	Pts	W-L Rank
1	Michigan State (31)	32-7	775	26-7 1
2	Florida	29-8	735	24-7 11
3	Iowa State	32-5	657	29-4 7
4	Duke	29-5	656	27-4 1
5	Stanford	27-4	594	26-3 3
6	Oklahoma State	27-7	529	24-6 15
7	Cincinnati	29-4	520	28-3 6
8	Arizona	27-7	497	26-6 4
9	Tulsa	32-5	446	29-4 19
10	Temple	27-6	431	26-5 5
11	North Carolina	22-14	400	18-13 NR
12	Syracuse	26-6	387	24-5 14
13	LSU	28-6	378	26-5 9
14	Tennessee	26-7	362	24-6 10
15	Purdue	24-10	347	21-9 24
16	Wisconsin	22-14	339	18-13 NR
17	Ohio State	23-7	301	22-6 8
18	St. John's	25-8	235	24-7 12
19	Oklahoma	27-7	227	26-6 13
20	Miami-FL	23-11	201	21-10 25
21	Texas	24-9	178	23-8 18
22	Kentucky	23-10	160	22-9 20
23	UCLA	21-12	117	19-11 NR
24	Gonzaga	26-9	110	24-8 NR
25	Maryland	25-10	101	24-9 16

Others receiving votes: 26. **Connecticut** (25-10, 94 pts); 27. **Seton Hall** (22-10, 81); 28. **Auburn** (25-10, 63); 29. **Indiana** (20-9, 36); 30. **Kansas** (24-10, 32); 31. **Illinois** (22-10, 29); 32. **Pepperdine** (25-9, 12); 33. **Dayton** (22-9, 8); 34. **Wake Forest** (22-14, 7); 35. **Fresno State** (24-10, 6); 36. **Oregon** (22-8, 5); 37. **Butler** (23-8) and **Utah** (23-9, 4); 39. **DePaul** (21-12) and **Vanderbilt** (19-11, 3); 41. **Arkansas** (19-15, 2); 42. **Ball State** (22-9), **Louisiana-Lafayette** (25-9) and **Utah State** (28-6, 1).

THE FINAL FOUR

RCA Dome in Indianapolis.
(Apr. 1-3).

Semifinal—Game One

Midwest Regional champ Michigan State vs. West Regional champ Wisconsin; Saturday, Apr. 1 (5:31 p.m. tipoff). **Coaches:** Tom Izzo, Michigan State and Dick Bennett, Wisconsin. **Favorite:** Michigan State by 8.

Wisconsin (Big Ten)	17 24—	**41**
Michigan State (Big Ten)	19 34—	**53**

High scorers— Morris Peterson, Michigan State (20) and Roy Boone, Wisconsin (18); **Att—** 43,116; **TV rating—**8.8/21 share (CBS).

Semifinal—Game Two

East Regional champion Florida vs. South Regional champ North Carolina; Saturday, Apr. 1 (8:12 p.m. tipoff). **Coaches:** Billy Donovan, Florida and Bill Guthridge, North Carolina. **Favorite:** Florida by 4½.

North Carolina (ACC)	34 25—	**59**
Florida (SEC)	37 34—	**71**

High scorers— Brendan Haywood, North Carolina (20) and Brett Nelson, Florida (13); **Att—** 43,116; **TV rating—**10.2/19 share (CBS).

Most Outstanding Player

Mateen Cleaves, senior guard, Michigan State. SEMIFINAL—36 minutes, 11 points, 4 rebounds, 1 assist, 2 steals; FINAL—33 minutes, 18 points, 2 rebounds, 4 assists.

All-Tournament Team

Cleaves, guard Charlie Bell and forwards Morris Peterson and A.J. Granger of Michigan State and center Udonis Haslem of Florida.

NCAA Finalists' Tournament and Season Statistics

At least 10 games played during the overall season.

Florida (29-8)

| | NCAA Tournament | | | | | | Overall Season | | | | | |
| | | | | —Per Game— | | | | | | —Per Game— | | |
	Gm	FG%	TPts	Pts	Reb	Ast	Gm	FG%	TPts	Pts	Reb	Ast
Mike Miller	6	.359	79	13.2	7.7	1.7	37	.476	521	14.1	6.6	2.5
Udonis Haslem	6	.660	85	14.2	4.3	1.0	37	.579	437	11.8	5.1	0.9
Donnell Harvey	6	.395	45	7.5	5.8	0.8	37	.507	374	10.1	7.0	1.0
Kenyan Weaks	6	.471	40	6.7	2.8	1.3	37	.524	371	10.0	2.7	2.1
Teddy Dupay	6	.316	43	7.2	1.2	0.8	37	.393	318	8.6	1.6	2.6
Brent Wright	6	.333	41	6.8	5.7	2.8	35	.503	289	8.3	4.5	2.0
Brett Nelson	6	.451	68	11.3	3.2	3.5	37	.420	299	8.1	1.5	3.0
Matt Bonner	6	.591	27	4.5	1.8	0.3	36	.440	174	4.8	3.2	0.4
Justin Hamilton	6	.563	24	4.0	1.7	0.8	37	.490	173	4.7	1.7	1.2
Major Parker	6	.385	21	3.5	0.8	0.5	37	.395	128	3.5	1.8	1.0
FLORIDA	6	.445	473	78.8	38.0	13.7	37	.480	3102	83.8	39.2	16.5
OPPONENTS	6	.418	435	72.5	37.7	15.5	37	.420	2548	68.9	34.0	13.3

Three-pointers: NCAA TOURNAMENT— Nelson (14-27), Dupay (7-23), Parker (5-9), Miller (5-25), Weaks (4-13), Hamilton (2-6), Wright (2-9), Bonner (1-8), Team (40-120 for .333 pct.); OVERALL— Dupay (62-159), Weaks (56-135), Nelson (49-113), Miller (47-139), Bonner (16-56), Hamilton (14-50), Wright (11-37), Parker (11-41), Team (266-732 for .363 pct.).

Michigan State (32-7)

| | NCAA Tournament | | | | | | Overall Season | | | | | |
| | | | | —Per Game— | | | | | | —Per Game— | | |
	Gm	FG%	TPts	Pts	Reb	Ast	Gm	FG%	TPts	Pts	Reb	Ast
Morris Peterson	6	.486	105	17.5	4.3	1.2	39	.465	657	16.8	6.0	1.3
Mateen Cleaves	6	.418	85	14.2	2.0	4.5	26	.421	315	12.1	1.8	6.9
Charlie Bell	6	.317	43	7.2	6.0	2.8	39	.453	449	11.5	4.9	3.2
Andre Hutson	6	.615	67	11.2	6.5	1.7	39	.586	397	10.2	6.2	1.5
A.J. Granger	6	.581	71	11.8	4.3	1.7	39	.500	370	9.5	5.3	1.2
Mike Chappell	6	.438	22	3.7	1.5	0.2	39	.383	230	5.9	2.2	0.6
Jason Richardson	6	.471	20	3.3	3.5	0.0	37	.503	189	5.1	4.1	0.6
Aloysius Anagonye	6	1.000	6	1.0	1.2	0.2	34	.556	99	2.9	3.0	0.3
David Thomas	6	.000	1	0.2	0.8	0.3	34	.408	83	2.4	2.4	1.5
Adam Ballinger	5	.571	10	2.0	1.2	0.2	37	.644	73	2.0	1.7	0.3
Steve Cherry	2	—	0	0.0	0.0	0.5	12	.273	8	0.7	0.2	0.3
MICHIGAN ST.	6	.476	430	71.7	33.3	12.7	39	.474	2889	74.1	39.0	15.4
OPPONENTS	6	.403	338	56.3	27.8	11.0	39	.394	2299	58.9	27.3	11.1

Three-pointers: NCAA TOURNAMENT— Peterson (15-35), Cleaves (12-27), Granger (9-19), Bell (4-18), Chappell (2-9), Richardson (1-2), Team (43-110 for .391 pct.); OVERALL— Peterson (85-200), Granger (49-109), Bell (38-111), Chappell (37-117), Cleaves (32-85), Richardson (8-27), Cherry (2-6), Smith (1-3), Hutson (0-1), Ishbia (0-1), Team (253-669 for .378 pct.).

Florida's Schedule

Reg. Season
(23-6)

W	Florida State	96-91
W	Utah State	60-58
L	at Purdue	68-79
W	at Georgetown	72-62
W	New Hampshire	131-72
W	Florida A&M	96-44
W	Bethune Cookman	93-77
W	High Point	109-60
W	at Rutgers	85-65
W	NC-Wilmington	80-53
W	VMI	113-68
L	at Vanderbilt	77-87
W	at Mississippi	75-71
W	LSU	82-57
L	Tennessee	79-81
W	at Alabama	77-73
L	at DePaul	69-71
W	Vanderbilt	89-63
W	at South Carolina	86-82
W	Georgia	85-66
W	Kentucky	90-73

L	at Tennessee	73-76
W	at Arkansas	80-71
W	Mississippi State	88-58
W	at Georgia	90-68
W	Auburn	88-59
W	South Carolina	87-67
L	at Kentucky	70-85

SEC Tourney
(1-1)

W	Mississippi	89-67
L	at Auburn	70-78

NCAA Tourney
(5-1)

W	Butler	69-68
W	Illinois	93-76
W	Duke	87-78
W	Ohio State	77-65
W	North Carolina	71-59
L	Michigan State	76-89

Michigan State's Schedule

Reg. Season
(23-7)

W	Toledo	78-33
W	at Providence	82-58
W	at South Carolina	59-56
L	at Texas	74-81
W	at North Carolina	86-76
W	Howard	75-45
W	E. Michigan	74-57
W	Kansas	66-54
L	at Arizona	68-79
W	Oakland	86-51
L	at Kentucky	58-60
W	Mississippi Valley St.	96-63
L	at Wright State	49-53
W	Penn State	76-63
W	at Iowa	75-53
W	Indiana	77-71
L	at Ohio State	67-78
W	Northwestern	69-45
W	at Northwestern	59-29
W	Illinois	91-66
W	at Michigan	82-62

W	Connecticut	85-66
L	at Purdue	67-70
W	at Wisconsin	61-44
W	at Penn State	79-63
L	at Indiana	79-81
W	Minnesota	79-43
W	Michigan	114-63

Big Ten Tourney
(3-0)

W	Iowa	75-65
W	Wisconsin	55-46
W	Illinois	76-61

NCAA Tourney
(6-0)

W	Valparaiso	65-38
W	Utah	73-61
W	Syracuse	75-58
W	Iowa State	75-64
W	Wisconsin	53-41
W	Florida	89-76

Final NCAA Men's Division I Standings

Conference records include regular season games only. Overall records include all postseason tournament games.

America East Conference

Team	Conference W	L	Pct	Overall W	L	Pct
*Hofstra	16	2	.859	24	7	.774
Maine	15	3	.833	24	7	.774
†Delaware	14	4	.778	24	8	.750
Vermont	11	7	.611	16	12	.571
Drexel	9	9	.500	13	17	.433
Towson	7	11	.389	11	17	.393
Hartford	6	12	.333	10	19	.345
Boston University	5	13	.278	7	22	.241
Northeastern	5	13	.278	7	21	.250
New Hampshire	2	16	.111	3	25	.107

Conf. Tourney Final: Hofstra 76, Delaware 69.
***NCAA Tourney (0-1):** Hofstra (0-1).
†NIT (0-1): Delaware (0-1).

Atlantic Coast Conference

Team	Conference W	L	Pct	Overall W	L	Pct
*Duke	15	1	.937	29	5	.852
*Maryland	11	5	.688	25	10	.714
†Virginia	9	7	.563	19	12	.613
*North Carolina	9	7	.563	22	14	.611
†Wake Forest	7	9	.438	22	14	.611
†N.C. State	6	10	.375	20	14	.588
Florida St	6	10	.375	12	17	.414
Georgia Tech	5	11	.313	13	17	.433
Clemson	4	12	.250	10	20	.333

Conf. Tourney Final: Duke 81, Maryland 68.
***NCAA Tourney (7-3):** North Carolina (4-1), Duke (2-1), Maryland (1-1).
†NIT (8-3): Wake Forest (5-0, NIT Champion), N.C. State (3-2), Virginia (0-1).

Atlantic 10 Conference

East	Conference W	L	Pct	Overall W	L	Pct
*Temple	14	2	.875	27	6	.818
*St. Bonaventure	11	5	.688	21	10	.677
†Massachusetts	9	7	.563	17	16	.515
St. Joseph's-PA	7	9	.438	13	16	.448
Fordham	7	9	.438	14	15	.483
Rhode Island	2	14	.125	5	25	.167

West	W	L	Pct	W	L	Pct
*Dayton	11	5	.688	22	9	.710
Geo. Washington	9	7	.563	15	15	.500
†Xavier-OH	9	7	.563	21	12	.636
Virginia Tech	8	8	.500	16	15	.516
La Salle	5	11	.313	11	17	.393
Duquesne	4	12	.250	9	20	.310

Note: There are 12 teams in the Atlantic 10.
Conf. Tourney Final: Temple 65, St. Bonaventure 44.
***NCAA Tourney (1-3):** Temple (1-1), Dayton (0-1), St. Bonaventure (0-1).
†NIT (1-2): Xavier-OH (1-1), Massachusetts (0-1).

Big East Conference

Team	Conference W	L	Pct	Overall W	L	Pct
*Syracuse	13	3	.813	26	6	.813
*Miami-FL	13	3	.813	23	11	.676
*St. John's	12	4	.774	25	8	.758
*Connecticut	10	6	.625	25	10	.714
*Seton Hall	10	6	.625	22	10	.688
†Villanova	8	8	.500	20	13	.606
†Notre Dame	8	8	.500	22	15	.595
West Virginia	6	10	.375	14	14	.500
†Georgetown	6	10	.375	19	15	.559
Rutgers	6	10	.375	15	16	.484
Pittsburgh	5	11	.313	13	15	.464
Providence	4	12	.250	11	19	.367
Boston College	3	13	.188	11	19	.367

Conf. Tourney Final: St. John's 80, Connecticut 70.
***NCAA Tourney (8-5):** Miami-FL (2-1), Syracuse (2-1), Seton Hall (2-1), Connecticut (1-1), St. John's (1-1).
†NIT (6-3): Notre Dame (4-1, NIT Runner up), Georgetown (1-1), Villanova (1-1).

Big Sky Conference

Team	Conference W	L	Pct	Overall W	L	Pct
Montana	12	4	.750	17	11	.607
Eastern Washington	12	4	.750	15	12	.556
*Northern Arizona	11	5	.688	20	11	.645
Weber St	10	6	.625	18	10	.643
Cal St.-Northridge	10	6	.625	20	10	.667
Portland St	7	9	.438	15	14	.517
Montana St	4	12	.250	12	17	.414
Cal St.-Sacramento	3	13	.188	9	18	.333
Idaho St	3	13	.188	8	19	.296

Conf. Tourney Final: Northern Arizona 85, Cal State Northridge 81 (OT).
***NCAA Tourney (0-1):** Northern Arizona (0-1).

Big South Conference

Team	Conference W	L	Pct	Overall W	L	Pct
Radford	12	2	.857	18	10	.643
*Winthrop	11	3	.786	21	8	.724
Elon	7	7	.500	13	15	.464
NC-Asheville	7	7	.500	11	19	.367
Coastal Carolina	7	7	.500	10	18	.357
High Point	5	9	.357	11	17	.393
Liberty	4	10	.286	14	14	.500
Charleston Southern	3	11	.214	8	21	.276

Conf. Tourney Final: Winthrop 75, NC-Asheville 62.
***NCAA Tourney (0-1):** Winthrop (0-1).

Best in Show

Conferences with at least two wins in the 2000 NCAA's; number of tournament teams in parentheses.

	W-L		W-L
Big Ten (6)	15-5	ACC (3)	7-3
SEC (6)	11-6	Pac-10 (4)	4-4
Big 12 (6)	9-6	West Coast (2)	3-2
Big East (5)	8-5	WAC (2)	3-2

Final NCAA Men's Division I Standings (Cont.)

Big Ten Conference

	Conference			Overall		
Team	W	L	Pct	W	L	Pct
*Ohio St.	13	3	.813	23	7	.767
*Michigan St	13	3	.813	32	7	.821
*Purdue	12	4	.750	24	10	.706
*Illinois	11	5	.688	21	9	.700
*Indiana	10	6	.625	20	9	.689
*Wisconsin	8	8	.500	22	14	.611
Iowa	6	10	.375	14	16	.467
Michigan	6	10	.375	15	14	.517
†Penn St	5	11	.333	18	17	.514
Minnesota	4	12	.267	12	16	.400
Northwestern	0	16	.000	5	25	.167

Note: There are 11 teams in the Big 10.
Conf. Tourney Final: Michigan St. 76, Illinois 61.
***NCAA Tourney (15-5):** Michigan St. (6-0), Wisconsin (4-1), Purdue (3-1), Ohio St. (1-1), Illinois (1-1), Indiana (0-1).
†NIT (3-1): Penn State (3-1).

Big 12 Conference

	Conference			Overall		
Team	W	L	Pct	W	L	Pct
*Iowa St.	14	2	.875	32	5	.865
*Texas	13	3	.813	24	9	.727
*Oklahoma	12	4	.750	27	7	.794
*Oklahoma St.	12	4	.750	27	7	.794
*Kansas	11	5	.688	24	10	.706
*Missouri	10	6	.625	18	13	.581
†Colorado	7	9	.438	14	14	.563
Nebraska	4	12	.250	11	19	.367
Baylor	4	12	.250	14	15	.483
Texas A&M	4	12	.250	8	20	.286
Texas Tech	3	13	.188	12	16	.429
Kansas St	2	14	.125	9	19	.321

Conf. Tourney Final: Iowa St. 70, Oklahoma 58.
***NCAA Tourney (9-6):** Iowa St. (3-1), Oklahoma St. (3-1), Texas (1-1), Kansas (1-1), Oklahoma (1-1), Missouri (0-1).
†NIT (0-1): Colorado (0-1).

Big West Conference

	Conference			Overall		
Team	W	L	Pct	W	L	Pct
*Utah St.	16	0	1.000	28	6	.824
†New Mexico St.	11	5	.688	22	10	.687
Nevada	6	10	.375	9	20	.310
Idaho	6	10	.375	12	17	.414
Boise St.	6	10	.375	12	15	.444
North Texas	5	11	.312	7	20	.259

	Conference			Overall		
Team	W	L	Pct	W	L	Pct
†Long Beach St	15	1	.938	24	6	.800
UC-Santa Barbara	10	6	.625	14	14	.500
UC-Irvine	7	9	.438	14	14	.500
Pacific	6	10	.375	11	18	.379
Cal Poly-SLO	5	11	.312	10	18	.357
Cal St.-Fullerton	3	13	.188	8	19	.296

Conf. Tourney Final: Utah State 71, New Mexico State 66.
***NCAA Tourney (0-1):** Utah State (0-1).
†NIT (0-2): Long Beach St. (0-1), New Mexico St. (0-1).

Colonial Athletic Association

	Conference			Overall		
Team	W	L	Pct	W	L	Pct
James Madison	12	4	.750	20	9	.690
George Mason	12	4	.750	19	11	.633
Richmond	11	5	.688	18	12	.600
*NC-Wilmington	8	8	.500	18	13	.581
Va. Commonwealth	7	9	.438	14	14	.500
William & Mary	6	10	.375	11	17	.393
Old Dominion	5	11	.312	11	18	.379
American	5	11	.312	11	18	.379
East Carolina	5	11	.312	10	18	.357

Conf. Tourney Final: NC-Wilmington 57, Richmond 47.
***NCAA Tourney (0-1):** NC-Wilmington (0-1).

Conference USA

	Conference			Overall		
American Division	W	L	Pct	W	L	Pct
*Cincinnati	16	0	1.000	29	4	.879
*Louisville	10	6	.625	19	12	.613
*DePaul	9	7	.563	21	12	.636
†Marquette	8	8	.500	15	14	.517
†Saint Louis	7	9	.438	19	14	.576
†NC-Charlotte	7	9	.438	17	15	.531

	Conference			Overall		
National Division	W	L	Pct	W	L	Pct
†Tulane	8	8	.500	20	11	.645
†So. Florida	8	8	.500	17	14	.548
So. Mississippi	7	9	.438	17	12	.586
Ala-Birmingham	7	9	.438	14	14	.500
Memphis	7	9	.438	15	16	.484
Houston	2	14	.125	9	22	.290

Conf. Tourney Final: Saint Louis 56, DePaul 49.
***NCAA Tourney (1-4):** Cincinnati (1-1), Saint Louis (0-1), Louisville (0-1), DePaul (0-1).
†NIT (0-4): Marquette (0-1), Tulane (0-1), South Florida (0-1), NC-Charlotte (0-1).

Ivy League

	Conference			Overall		
Team	W	L	Pct	W	L	Pct
*Pennsylvania	14	0	1.000	21	8	.724
†Princeton	11	3	.786	19	11	.633
Columbia	7	7	.500	13	14	.482
Harvard	7	7	.500	12	15	.444
Dartmouth	5	9	.357	9	18	.333
Yale	5	9	.357	7	20	.259
Brown	4	10	.286	8	19	.296
Cornell	3	11	.214	10	17	.370

Conf. Tourney Final: Ivy League has no tournament.
***NCAA Tourney (0-1):** Pennsylvania (0-1).
†NIT Tourney (0-1): Princeton (0-1).

Metro Atlantic Athletic Conference

	Conference			Overall		
Team	W	L	Pct	W	L	Pct
†Siena	15	3	.833	24	9	.727
*Iona	13	5	.722	20	11	.645
Fairfield	11	7	.611	14	15	.483
Niagara	10	8	.556	17	12	.586
Marist	10	8	.556	14	14	.500
Manhattan	9	9	.500	12	15	.444
Rider	8	10	.444	16	14	.533
Canisius	8	10	.444	10	20	.333
Loyola-MD	4	14	.222	7	21	.250
St. Peter's	2	16	.111	5	23	.179

Conf. Tourney Final: Iona 84, Siena 80.
***NCAA Tourney (0-1):** Iona (0-1).
†NIT Tourney (1-1): Siena (1-1).

Mid-American Conference

East	Conference			Overall		
	W	L	Pct	W	L	Pct
†Bowling Green 14	14	4	.778	22	8	.733
†Kent 13	13	5	.722	23	8	.742
Marshall............11	11	7	.611	21	9	.700
Akron 11	11	7	.611	17	11	.607
Ohio................11	11	7	.611	20	13	.606
Miami-OH 8	8	10	.444	15	15	.500
Buffalo 3	3	15	.167	5	23	.179

West	Conference			Overall		
	W	L	Pct	W	L	Pct
*Ball St.............11	11	7	.611	22	9	.710
Toledo..............11	11	7	.611	18	13	.581
Eastern Mich 9	9	9	.500	15	13	.536
N. Illinois 7	7	11	.389	13	15	.464
Western Mich 6	6	12	.333	10	18	.357
Central Mich 2	2	16	.111	6	23	.207

Conf. Tourney Final: Ball State 61, Miami-OH 58.
***NCAA Tourney (0-1):** Ball State (0-1).
†NIT (2-2): Kent (2-1), Bowling Green (0-1).

Mid-Continent Conference

Team	Conference			Overall		
	W	L	Pct	W	L	Pct
Oakland.............11	11	5	.688	13	17	.433
*Valparaiso 10	10	6	.625	19	13	.594
Missouri-KC 10	10	6	.625	16	13	.552
Southern Utah 10	10	6	.625	16	13	.552
Youngstown St. 9	9	7	.563	12	16	.429
Oral Roberts 8	8	8	.500	13	17	.433
Chicago St. 7	7	9	.438	10	18	.357
Indiana-Purdue.........4	4	12	.250	7	21	.250
Western Illinois 3	3	13	.188	8	22	.267

Conf. Tourney Final: Valparaiso 71, Southern Utah 62.
***NCAA Tourney (0-1):** Valparaiso (0-1).
Note: Oakland and Indiana-Purdue were provisional members of the Mid-Continent Conference in 1999-2000 and were not eligible for the conference championship.

Mid-Eastern Athletic Conference

Team	Conference			Overall		
	W	L	Pct	W	L	Pct
*South Carolina St. 14	14	5	.737	20	14	.588
Hampton 13	13	5	.722	17	12	.586
Coppin St. 13	13	5	.722	15	15	.500
Bethune-Cookman.......12	12	6	.667	14	15	.483
Norfolk St.............11	11	7	.611	12	16	.429
N. Carolina A&T 11	11	8	.579	14	15	.483
MD-Eastern Shore 8	8	10	.444	12	17	.414
Florida A&M 7	7	11	.389	9	22	.290
Delaware St. 5	5	13	.278	6	22	.214
Morgan St.............5	5	13	.278	5	24	.172
Howard 1	1	17	.056	1	27	.036

Conf. Tourney Final: S.C. State 70, Coppin State 53.
***NCAA Tourney (0-1):** S.C. State (0-1).

Midwestern Collegiate Conference

Team	Conference			Overall		
	W	L	Pct	W	L	Pct
*Butler 12	12	2	.857	23	8	.742
Cleveland St..........9	9	5	.643	16	14	.533
Detroit...............8	8	6	.571	20	12	.625
WI-Milwaukee 6	6	8	.429	15	14	.517
WI-Green Bay 6	6	8	.429	14	16	.467
Wright St 6	6	8	.429	11	17	.393
Illinois-Chicago 5	5	9	.357	11	20	.355
Loyola-IL 4	4	10	.286	14	14	.500

Conf. Tourney Final: Butler 62, Detroit 43.
***NCAA Tourney (0-1):** Butler (0-1).

Missouri Valley Conference

Team	Conference			Overall		
	W	L	Pct	W	L	Pct
*Indiana St............14	14	4	.778	22	10	.688
†SW Missouri St. 13	13	5	.722	23	11	.676
†Southern Illinois 12	12	6	.667	20	13	.606
*Creighton 11	11	7	.611	23	10	.697
Bradley...............10	10	8	.556	14	16	.467
Evansville 9	9	9	.500	18	12	.600
Northern Iowa 7	7	11	.389	14	15	.483
Wichita St..............5	5	13	.278	12	17	.414
Illinois St..............5	5	13	.278	10	20	.333
Drake................4	4	14	.222	11	18	.379

Conf. Tourney Final: Creighton 57, SW Missouri St. 45.
***NCAA Tourney (0-2):** Creighton (0-1), Indiana St. (0-1).
†NIT (2-2): SW Missouri St. (1-1), Southern Illinois (1-1).

Mountain West Conference

Team	Conference			Overall		
	W	L	Pct	W	L	Pct
*UNLV 10	10	4	.714	23	8	.742
*Utah 10	10	4	.714	23	9	.719
†New Mexico 9	9	5	.643	18	14	.563
Colorado St...........8	8	6	.571	19	12	.613
Wyoming 8	8	6	.571	19	12	.613
†Brigham Young 7	7	7	.500	22	11	.667
Air Force.............4	4	10	.286	8	20	.286
San Diego St...........0	0	14	.000	5	23	.179

Conf. Tourney Final: UNLV 79, Brigham Young 56.
***NCAA Tourney (1-2):** UNLV (0-1), Utah (1-1).
†NIT (3-2): Brigham Young (2-1), New Mexico (1-1), .

Northeast Conference

Team	Conference			Overall		
	W	L	Pct	W	L	Pct
*Central Connecticut St. ..15	15	3	.833	25	6	.806
Fairleigh Dickinson 13	13	5	.722	17	11	.607
Robert Morris 13	13	5	.722	18	12	.600
Quinnipiac.............12	12	6	.667	18	10	.643
St. Francis-NY 12	12	6	.667	18	12	.600
Monmouth 9	9	9	.500	12	18	.429
MD-Baltimore County 7	7	11	.389	11	18	.379
Mt. St. Mary's 7	7	11	.389	9	20	.310
St. Francis-PA 7	7	11	.389	10	18	.357
Wagner 6	6	12	.333	11	16	.407
LIU Brooklyn 5	5	13	.278	8	19	.296
Sacred Heart 2	2	16	.111	3	25	.107

Conf. Tourney Final: Central Connecticut St. 63, Robert Morris 46.
***NCAA Tourney (0-1):** Central Connecticut St. (0-1).
Note: Quinnipiac and Sacred Heart were provisional members of the Northeast Conference in 1999-2000 and ineligible for the conference championship.

Ohio Valley Conference

Team	Conference			Overall		
	W	L	Pct	W	L	Pct
*SE Missouri St 14	14	4	.778	24	7	.774
Murray St..............14	14	4	.778	23	9	.719
Austin Peay 11	11	7	.611	18	10	.643
Eastern Illinois 11	11	7	.611	17	12	.586
Tennessee Tech 11	11	7	.611	16	12	.571
Middle Tenn. St.........10	10	8	.556	15	13	.536
Tennessee-Martin 7	7	11	.389	10	19	.345
Tennessee St............6	6	12	.333	7	22	.241
Morehead St 4	4	14	.222	9	18	.333
Eastern Kentucky 2	2	16	.111	6	21	.222

Conf. Tourney Final: SE Missouri St. 67, Murray St. 56.
***NCAA Tourney (0-1):** SE Missouri St. (0-1).

Final NCAA Men's Division I Standings (Cont.)

Pacific-10 Conference

Team	Conference			Overall		
	W	L	Pct	W	L	Pct
*Stanford	15	3	.833	27	4	.871
*Arizona	15	3	.833	27	7	.794
*Oregon	13	5	.722	22	8	.733
*UCLA	10	8	.555	21	12	.636
†Arizona St	10	8	.555	19	13	.594
USC	9	9	.500	16	14	.533
†California	7	11	.389	18	15	.545
Oregon St	5	13	.278	13	16	.448
Washington	5	13	.278	10	20	.333
Washington St	1	17	.056	6	22	.214

Conf. Tourney Final: Pac-10 has no tournament.
***NCAA Tourney (4-4):** UCLA (2-1), Stanford (1-1), Arizona (1-1), Oregon (0-1).
†NIT (3-2): California (2-1), Arizona St. (1-1).

Patriot League

Team	Conference			Overall		
	W	L	Pct	W	L	Pct
*Lafayette	11	1	.917	24	7	.774
Navy	11	1	.917	23	6	.793
Bucknell	8	4	.667	17	11	.607
Colgate	4	8	.333	13	16	.448
Holy Cross	3	9	.250	10	18	.357
Lehigh	3	9	.250	8	21	.276
Army	2	10	.167	5	23	.179

Conf. Tourney Final: Lafayette 87, Navy 61.
***NCAA Tourney (0-1):** Lafayette (0-1).

Southeastern Conference

Eastern Div.	Conference			Overall		
	W	L	Pct	W	L	Pct
*Tennessee	12	4	.750	26	7	.788
*Kentucky	12	4	.750	23	10	.697
*Florida	12	4	.750	29	8	.784
†Vanderbilt	8	8	.500	19	11	.633
South Carolina	5	11	.313	15	17	.469
Georgia	3	13	.188	10	20	.333

Western Div.	Conference			Overall		
	W	L	Pct	W	L	Pct
*LSU	12	4	.750	28	6	.824
*Auburn	9	7	.563	24	10	.706
*Arkansas	7	9	.438	19	15	.559
Alabama	6	10	.375	13	16	.448
Mississippi St	5	11	.313	14	16	.467
†Mississippi	5	11	.313	19	14	.576

Conf. Tourney Final: Arkansas 75, Auburn 61.
***NCAA Tourney (11-6):** Florida (5-1), LSU (2-1), Tennessee (2-1), Kentucky (1-1), Auburn (1-1), Arkansas (0-1).
†NIT (2-2): Mississippi (2-1), Vanderbilt (0-1).

Southern Conference

North Div.	Conference			Overall		
	W	L	Pct	W	L	Pct
*Appalachian St	13	3	.813	23	9	.719
Davidson	10	6	.625	15	13	.536
NC-Greensboro	9	7	.563	15	13	.536
East Tennessee St	8	8	.500	14	15	.483
W. Carolina	7	9	.438	14	14	.500
Virginia Military	1	15	.063	6	23	.207

South Div.	Conference			Overall		
	W	L	Pct	W	L	Pct
College of Charleston	13	3	.813	24	6	.800
Georgia Southern	10	6	.625	16	12	.571
Wofford	8	8	.500	14	16	.467
Tenn-Chattanooga	6	10	.375	10	19	.345
The Citadel	5	10	.333	9	20	.310
Furman	5	10	.333	14	18	.438

Conf. Tourney Final: Appalachian St. 68, College of Charleston 56.
***NCAA Tourney (0-1):** Appalachian St. (0-1).

Southland Conference

Team	Conference			Overall		
	W	L	Pct	W	L	Pct
Sam Houston St	15	3	.833	22	7	.759
Louisiana-Monroe	13	5	.722	19	9	.679
Texas-San Antonio	12	6	.667	15	13	.536
Northwestern St	11	7	.611	17	13	.567
Texas-Arlington	11	7	.611	15	12	.556
*Lamar	8	10	.444	15	16	.484
SW Texas St	8	10	.444	12	17	.414
Nicholls St	8	10	.444	11	17	.393
SE Louisiana	5	13	.278	10	17	.370
McNeese St	5	13	.278	6	21	.222
Stephen F. Austin	3	15	.167	6	21	.222

Conf. Tourney Final: Lamar 62, Northwestern St. 55.
***NCAA Tourney (0-1):** Lamar (0-1).

Southwestern Athletic Conference

Team	Conference			Overall		
	W	L	Pct	W	L	Pct
Alcorn St	15	3	.833	19	10	.655
Alabama A&M	14	4	.778	18	10	.643
Southern	14	4	.778	18	11	.621
Texas Southern	10	8	.556	15	14	.517
*Jackson St	10	8	.556	17	16	.515
Alabama St	10	8	.556	13	15	.464
Miss. Valley St	7	11	.389	7	21	.250
Prairie View A&M	5	13	.278	7	27	.250
Ark-Pine Bluff	5	13	.278	6	21	.222
Grambling	0	18	.000	1	30	.032

Conf. Tourney Final: Jackson St. 76, Southern 61.
***NCAA Tourney (0-1):** Jackson St. (0-1).

Sun Belt Conference

Team	Conference			Overall		
	W	L	Pct	W	L	Pct
*Louisiana-Lafayette	13	3	.813	25	9	.735
South Alabama	13	3	.813	20	10	.667
Louisiana Tech	12	4	.750	21	8	.724
Florida International	9	7	.563	16	14	.533
Western Kentucky	8	8	.500	11	18	.379
Arkansas St	7	9	.438	10	18	.357
New Orleans	6	10	.375	11	18	.379
Denver	3	13	.188	6	22	.214
Ark-Little Rock	1	15	.063	4	24	.143

Conf. Tourney Final: Louisiana-Lafayette 51, South Alabama 50.
***NCAA Tourney (0-1):** Louisiana-Lafayette (0-1).

Trans America Athletic Conference

Team	Conference			Overall		
	W	L	Pct	W	L	Pct
Troy St.	13	5	.722	17	11	.607
Georgia St.	13	5	.722	17	12	.586
*Samford	12	6	.667	21	11	.656
Jacksonville St.	12	6	.667	17	11	.607
Central Florida	10	8	.556	14	18	.438
Campbell	10	8	.556	12	16	.429
Stetson	8	10	.444	13	15	.464
Mercer	7	11	.389	12	21	.364
Jacksonville	5	13	.278	8	19	.296
Florida Atlantic	0	18	.000	2	28	.070

Conf. Tourney Final: Samford 78, Central Florida 69.
***NCAA Tourney (0-1):** Samford (0-1).

West Coast Conference

Team	Conference			Overall		
	W	L	Pct	W	L	Pct
*Pepperdine	12	2	.857	25	9	.735
*Gonzaga	11	3	.786	26	9	.743
San Diego	10	4	.714	20	9	.690
Santa Clara	9	5	.643	19	12	.613
San Francisco	7	6	.538	19	8	.704
Portland	4	10	.286	10	18	.357
Loyola Marymount	3	11	.214	8	20	.286
St. Mary's-CA	0	14	.000	2	26	.071

Conf. Tourney Final: Gonzaga 69, Pepperdine 65 (OT).
***NCAA Tourney (3-2):** Gonzaga (2-1), Pepperdine (1-1).

Western Athletic Conference

Pacific	Conference			Overall		
	W	L	Pct	W	L	Pct
*Tulsa	12	2	.857	32	5	.865
*Fresno St.	11	3	.786	24	10	.706
†SMU	9	5	.643	21	9	.700
TCU	8	6	.571	18	14	.563
San Jose St.	6	8	.429	15	15	.500
Hawaii	5	9	.357	17	12	.583
UTEP	4	10	.286	13	15	.464
Rice	1	13	.071	5	22	.185

Conf. Tourney Final: Fresno St. 75, Tulsa 72.
***NCAA Tourney (3-2):** Tulsa (3-1), Fresno St. (0-1).
†NIT (0-1): SMU (0-1).

Division I Independents

Team	W	L	Pct
Texas A&M-Corpus Christi	13	13	.500
Texas-Pan American	12	16	.429
Albany	10	18	.357
Centenary	10	18	.357
Belmont	7	21	.250
Stony Brook	6	23	.222

Annual Awards

Player of the Year

Kenyon Martin, Cincinnati . . . . . .AP, NABC, *TSN*, USBWA, Naismith, Wooden

Wooden Award Voting

Presented since 1977 by the Los Angeles Athletic Club and named after the former Purdue All-America and UCLA coach John Wooden. Voting done by 1,047-member panel of national media; candidates must have a cumulative college grade point average of 2.0 (out of 4.0) and be making progress toward graduation.

		Cl	Pos	Pts
1	Kenyon Martin, Cincinnati	Sr.	C	4365
2	Marcus Fizer, Iowa St.	Jr.	F	2993
3	Mateen Cleaves, Michigan St.	Sr.	G	2296
4	Shane Battier, Duke	Jr.	F	1990
5	A.J. Guyton, Indiana	Sr.	G	1831
6	Troy Murphy, Notre Dame	So.	F	1446
7	Chris Carrawell, Duke	Sr.	F	1407
8	Morris Peterson, Michigan St.	Sr.	F	1274
9	Chris Mihm, Texas	Jr.	C	1160
10	Mark Madsen, Stanford	Sr.	F	1150

Div. II and III Annual Awards

Awarded by the National Association of Basketball Coaches.

Players of the Year
Div. II . . . . Ajamu Gaines, Charleston (W.Va.), G
Div. III . . . . Aaron Winkle, Calvin (Mich.), F
Coaches of the Year
Div. II . . . . Mike Dunlap, Metro St. (Colo.)
Div. III . . . . Kevin Vande Streek, Calvin (Mich.)
NAIA . . . . Roger Kaiser, Life (Ga.)
JuCo . . . . Joe O'Brien, SE Iowa

Coaches of the Year

Larry Eustachy, Iowa St. .AP, USBWA
Gene Keady, Purdue . . . . NABC
Mike Montgomery, Stanford . . . . .Naismith

Consensus All-America Team

The NCAA Division I players cited most frequently by the following All-America selectors: AP, U.S. Basketball Writers, National Assn. of Basketball Coaches and Wooden Award Committee. (*) indicates unanimous first team selection.

First Team

	Class	Hgt	Pos
Kenyon Martin*, Cincinnati	Sr.	6-8	C
Marcus Fizer*, Iowa St.	Jr.	6-8	F
A.J. Guyton*, Indiana	Sr.	6-1	G
Chris Mihm, Texas	Jr.	7-0	C
Troy Murphy, Notre Dame	So.	6-9	F

Second Team

	Class	Hgt	Pos
Chris Carrawell, Duke	Sr.	6-6	F
Morris Peterson, Michigan St.	Sr.	6-6	F
Shane Battier, Duke	Jr.	6-8	F
Scoonie Penn, Ohio St.	Sr.	5-10	G
Courtney Alexander, Fresno St.	Sr.	6-6	G

Third Team

	Class	Hgt	Pos
Mateen Cleaves, Michigan St.	Sr.	6-2	G
Stromile Swift, LSU	So.	6-9	F
Mark Madsen, Stanford	Sr.	6-9	F
Pepe Sanchez, Temple	Sr.	6-4	G
Eduardo Najera, Oklahoma	Sr.	6-8	F

NCAA Men's Division I Leaders

Includes games through NCAA and NIT tourneys.

INDIVIDUAL

Scoring

	Cl	Gm	FG%	3FG/Att	FT%	Reb	Ast	Stl	Blk	Pts	Avg	Hi
Courtney Alexander, Fresno St.	Sr.	27	.444	58/175	.781	128	92	36	4	669	24.8	43
SirValiant Brown, Geo. Wash.	Fr.	30	.333	73/277	.840	100	64	45	3	738	24.6	42
Ronnie McCollum, Centenary	Jr.	28	.392	92/258	.804	103	27	29	0	667	23.8	38
Eddie House, Arizona St.	Sr.	32	.424	73/198	.835	169	109	69	2	736	23.0	61
Harold Arceneaux, Weber St.	Sr.	28	.512	38/103	.796	205	50	40	26	664	23.0	40
Rashard Phillips, Detroit	Sr.	32	.441	102/252	.870	96	169	51	3	735	23.0	34
Demond Stewart, Niagara	Jr.	29	.421	55/166	.721	195	55	60	23	665	22.9	37
Marcus Fizer, Iowa St.	Jr.	37	.582	15/42	.732	285	41	29	37	844	22.8	38
Craig Claxton, Hofstra	Sr.	31	.470	51/134	.764	168	186	102	5	706	22.8	40
Troy Murphy, Notre Dame	So.	37	.492	30/92	.808	380	58	52	38	839	22.7	35
Dan Langhi, Vanderbilt.	Sr.	30	.477	58/144	.871	181	24	13	9	664	22.1	33
Tierre Brown, McNeese St.	Jr.	27	.463	30/94	.729	135	121	45	1	593	22.0	38
Maurice Bell, LA-Monroe	Sr.	28	.482	0/1	.793	193	41	26	10	612	21.9	39
Chris Davis, North Texas	Fr.	27	.379	77/229	.693	137	82	10	4	587	21.7	35
Durelle Brown, Manhattan	Jr.	27	.500	28/88	.767	165	44	24	13	576	21.3	36
Will Solomon, Clemson	So.	30	.418	93/248	.684	123	95	38	14	627	20.9	43
Damion Woolfolk, Norfolk St.	Sr.	28	.411	39/120	.786	118	52	37	13	585	20.9	34
Mike Pegues, Delaware	Sr.	32	.512	17/54	.766	245	83	33	37	667	20.8	34
Brandon Wolfram, UTEP	Jr.	28	.553	12/30	.831	191	48	27	19	580	20.7	33
Marquise Gainous, TCU	Sr.	32	.495	12/35	.843	265	46	29	41	662	20.7	38

Rebounding

	Cl	Gm	No	Avg
Darren Phillip, Fairfield	Sr.	29	405	14.0
Josh Sankes, Holy Cross	Jr.	28	334	11.9
Larry Abney, Fresno St.	Sr.	34	402	11.8
Shaun Stonerook, Ohio	Sr.	33	387	11.7
Jarrett Stephens, Penn St.	Sr.	35	368	10.5
Darren Fenn, Canisius	Jr.	30	315	10.5
Chris Mihm, Texas	Jr.	33	346	10.5
Darryl Neal, Norfolk St.	Jr.	27	282	10.4
Troy Murphy, Notre Dame	So.	37	380	10.3
Matt Williams, Montana	Sr.	28	287	10.3
Quentin Richardson, DePaul	So.	33	325	9.8
Ricardo Greer, Pittsburgh	Jr.	28	275	9.5
Kenyon Martin, Cincinnati	Sr.	31	300	9.7
Chris Marcus, Western Ky.	So.	29	275	9.5
Mike Smith, LA-Monroe	Sr.	28	264	9.4

Assists

	Cl	Gm	No	Avg
Mark Dickel, UNLV	Sr.	31	280	9.0
Doug Gottlieb, Oklahoma St.	Sr.	34	293	8.6
Chico Fletcher, Arkansas St.	Sr.	28	232	8.3
Brandon Granville, USC	So.	30	248	8.3
Ed Cota, N. Carolina	Sr.	35	284	8.1
Pepe Sanchez, Temple	Jr.	25	201	8.0
Casey Rogers, W. Carolina	So.	28	213	7.6
Cornelius Jackson, Marshall	Jr.	30	218	7.3
Elliott Prasse-Freeman, Harvard	Fr.	27	196	7.3
Eddie Gill, Weber St.	Sr.	28	195	7.0
Flinder Boyd, Dartmouth	So.	26	181	7.0
Andy Bedard, Maine	Jr.	28	193	6.9
Markus Carr, CS-Northridge	So.	30	206	6.9
Vernon Jennings, Miami-FL	Sr.	32	218	6.8
Tyson Patterson, Appalachian St.	Sr.	32	218	6.8

Field Goal Percentage

Minimum 5 Field Goals made per game.

	Cl	Gm	FG	FGA	Pct
Brendan Haywood, N. Carolina	Jr.	36	191	274	69.7
John Whorton, Kent	Sr.	31	159	250	63.6
Joel Przybilla, Minnesota	So.	21	122	199	61.3
Stomile Swift, LSU	So.	34	208	342	60.8
Patrick Chambers, AR-Pine Bluff	Sr.	27	174	287	60.6
Melvin Ely, Fresno St.	Jr.	31	180	297	60.6
Roderick Johnson, SE Missouri	Jr.	31	163	270	60.4
Etan Thomas, Syracuse	Sr.	29	148	246	60.2
Dan McClintock, N. Arizona	Sr.	31	190	318	59.7
Oliver Morton, Chattanooga	Jr.	28	153	258	59.3

Free Throw Percentage

Minimum 2.5 Free Throws made per game.

	Cl	Gm	FT	FTA	Pct
Clay McKnight, Pacific	Sr.	24	74	78	94.9
Troy Bell, Boston Coll.	Fr.	27	161	180	89.4
Lee Nosse, Mid. Tenn St.	Jr.	28	83	93	89.2
Khalid El-Amin, UConn	Jr.	35	107	120	89.2
Brad Buddenborg, Oakland	So.	28	107	120	89.2
Joe Crispin, Penn St.	Jr.	35	181	203	89.2
Josh Heard, Tenn. Tech	Sr.	28	89	100	89.0
Ross Land, N. Arizona	Sr.	31	116	131	88.5
Rimas Kaukenas, Seton Hall	Sr.	32	97	110	88.2
B.J. Proffitt, Belmont	So.	28	72	82	87.8
Nathan Jameson, NC-Greensboro	Jr.	28	72	82	87.8

Fresno St.
Courtney Alexander
Scoring

UNLV
Mark Dickel
Assists

Ohio St.
Ken Johnson
Blocked Shots

Liberty
Carl Williams
Steals

3-Pt Field Goal Percentage

Minimum 1.5 Three-Point FG made per game.

	Cl	Gm	FG	FGA	Pct
Jonathan Whitworth, Mid. Tenn St. . . .Jr.		28	50	99	50.5
Jason Thornton, C. Florida . . . . . .So.		32	94	190	49.5
Aki Palmer, Colorado St. . . . . . . .Fr.		30	70	143	49.0
Pete Conway, Montana St. . . . . . .Fr.		29	44	90	48.9
Stephen Brown, Idaho St. . . . . . . .Sr.		27	65	133	48.9
Albert Mouring, UConn. . . . . .Jr.		35	86	180	47.8
Keith McLeod, Bowling Green . . .So.		30	51	107	47.7
Jason Kapono, UCLA . . . . .Fr.		33	82	173	47.4
John Sivesind, Colorado St. . . . . .Jr.		30	74	158	46.8
Brett Blizzard, NC-Wilmington . . .Fr.		31	94	201	46.8

3-Pt Field Goals Per Game

	Cl	Gm	No	Avg
Brian Merriweather, TX-Pan Am . . . .Jr.		28	114	4.1
Josh Heard, Tennessee Tech . . . . . . .Sr.		28	112	4.0
Tevis Stukes, Baylor . . . . .Sr.		29	100	3.4
Adam Fellers, Campbell . . . . .So.		28	96	3.4
Gordon Scott, Idaho . . . . .Jr.		28	96	3.4
Matthew Haggarty, Albany . . . . . . .Jr.		28	94	3.4
Ryan Hercek, Fla. Atlantic . . . . .Sr.		29	97	3.3
Angel Santana, St. Francis. . . . . . . .Sr.		30	100	3.3
Alan Barksdale, AR-Little Rock . . . . .Sr.		24	80	3.3
Jason Harris, Fordham. . . . . .Jr.		28	93	3.3

Blocked Shots

	Cl	Gm	No	Avg
Ken Johnson, Ohio St. . . . . .Sr.		30	161	5.4
Wojciech Myrda, LA-Monroe . . . . . .So.		28	144	5.1
Loren Woods, Arizona . . . . .Jr.		26	102	3.9
Joel Przybilla, Minnesota . . . . .So.		21	81	3.9
Sitapha Savane, Navy . . . . .Sr.		29	111	3.8
Etan Thomas, Syracuse. . . . . .Sr.		29	107	3.7
Samuel Dalembert, Seton Hall . . . . . .Fr.		30	107	3.6
Kenyon Martin, Cincinnati . . . . .Sr.		31	107	3.5
Brian Carroll, Loyola-MD. . . . . .Jr.		27	89	3.3
Nakiea Miller, Iona . . . . .Jr.		30	98	3.3
Jody Lumpkin, Col. of Charleston. . .So.		30	93	3.1
Ndongo Ndiaye, Delaware. . . . . . . .Sr.		32	99	3.1

Steals

	Cl	Gm	No	Avg
Carl Williams, Liberty . . . . .Sr.		28	107	3.8
Rick Mickens, C. Conn. St. . . . . .Sr.		26	93	3.6
Pepe Sanchez, Temple. . . . . .Sr.		25	85	3.4
Fred House, Southern Utah . . . . .Jr.		29	98	3.4
Eric Coley, Tulsa . . . . .Sr.		37	123	3.3
Tim Winn, St. Bonaventure. . . . . .Sr.		31	103	3.3
Craig Claxton, Hofstra . . . . .Sr.		31	102	3.3
Jarion Childs, American . . . . .Sr.		29	95	3.3
Jeff Trepagnier, USC . . . . .Jr.		29	94	3.2
Eddie Gill, Weber St. . . . . .Sr.		29	95	3.2

Single Game Highs

Points

No		Opponent	Date
61	Eddie House, Ariz. St. . . . . . . .Cal. (2 OT)		Jan. 8
51	David Webber, C. Mich . . . . .Ball St.		Feb. 24

Rebounds

No		Opponent	Date
35	Larry Abney, Fresno St. . . . . .SMU		Feb. 17

Assists

No		Opponent	Date
20	Mateen Cleaves, Mich. St. . . . . .Michigan		Mar. 4

Blocks

No		Opponent	Date
14	Loren Woods, Arizona . . . . .Oregon		Feb. 3

Steals

No		Opponent	Date
10	Jeff Trepagnier, USC . . . . .Utah St.		Nov. 24
10	Mike Kelley, Wisconsin . . . . .Texas		Dec. 7
10	Collis Temple, LSU . . . . .Florida		Jan. 12

NCAA Men's Division I Leaders (Cont.)
TEAM

Scoring Offense

	Gm	W-L	Pts	Avg
Duke	.34	29-5	2992	88.0
TCU	.32	18-14	2813	87.9
Siena	.33	24-9	2862	86.7
Florida	.37	29-8	3102	83.8
Wyoming	.31	19-12	2567	82.8
Fresno St.	.34	24-10	2799	82.3
UNLV	.31	23-8	2548	82.2
Virginia	.31	19-12	2526	81.5
Marshall	.30	21-9	2442	81.4
Tennessee Tech	.28	16-12	2279	81.4
Long Beach St.	.30	24-6	2435	81.2
George Washington	.30	15-15	2417	80.6
Eastern Ill.	.29	17-12	2336	80.6
Tulsa	.37	32-5	2974	80.4
Tennessee	.33	26-7	2629	79.7

Scoring Defense

	Gm	W-L	Pts	Avg
Princeton	.30	19-11	1637	54.6
Temple	.33	27-6	1808	54.8
Butler	.31	23-8	1728	55.7
Wisconsin	.36	22-14	2007	55.8
NC-Wilmington	.31	18-13	1781	57.5
WI-Green Bay	.30	14-16	1735	57.8
Col. of Charleston	.30	24-6	1759	58.6
Michigan St.	.39	32-7	2299	58.9
Stanford	.31	27-4	1850	59.7
San Jose St.	.30	15-15	1792	59.7
Pennsylvania	.29	21-9	1742	60.1
Monmouth	.28	12-16	1702	60.8
Utah St.	.34	28-6	2080	61.2
Columbia	.27	13-14	1654	61.3
Bucknell	.28	17-11	1719	61.4

Scoring Margin

	Off	Def	Mar.
Stanford	.78.9	59.7	19.3
Tulsa	.80.4	62.9	17.5
Duke	.88.0	71.3	16.7
Cincinnati	.77.6	61.5	16.1
Michigan St.	.74.1	58.9	15.1
Florida	.83.8	68.9	15.0
Oklahoma St.	.77.1	62.3	14.8
Temple	.68.5	54.8	13.7
Iowa St.	.78.3	65.1	13.2
LSU	.75.8	62.7	13.1
Oklahoma	.74.9	62.3	12.6
Long Beach St.	.81.2	68.7	12.5
Navy	.76.0	63.7	12.2
Butler	.68.0	55.7	12.2
Tennessee	.79.7	67.8	11.8

Won-Lost Percentage

	W	L	Pct.
Cincinnati	.29	4	.879
Stanford	.27	4	.871
Iowa St.	.32	5	.865
Tulsa	.32	5	.865
Duke	.29	5	.853
LSU	.28	6	.824
Utah St.	.28	6	.824
Michigan St.	.32	7	.821
Temple	.27	6	.818
Syracuse	.26	6	.813
C. Conn. St.	.25	6	.806
Long Beach St.	.24	6	.800
Col. of Charleston	.24	6	.800
Arizona	.27	7	.794
Oklahoma St.	.27	7	.794
Oklahoma	.27	7	.794

Field Goal Percentage

	FG	FGA	PCT.
Samford	.825	1649	50.0
Long Beach St.	.884	1784	49.6
Austin Peay	.797	1618	49.3
Bowling Green	.777	1578	49.2
North Carolina	1014	2066	49.1
UMKC	.765	1566	48.9
Maine	.851	1744	48.8
LSU	.915	1880	48.7
Appalachian St.	.915	1882	48.6
Iowa St.	1038	2140	48.5
Hawaii	.818	1696	48.2
Utah	.782	1624	48.2
Duke	1045	2172	48.1
Florida	1104	2299	48.0
Cincinnati	.898	1871	48.0

Field Goal Percentage Defense

	FG	FGA	PCT.
Stanford	.667	1893	35.2
Temple	.633	1747	36.2
Princeton	.577	1558	37.0
Ohio St.	.654	1730	37.8
SE Missouri St.	.670	1765	38.0
Bucknell	.571	1500	38.1
LSU	.781	2046	38.2
Col. of Charleston	.640	1676	38.2
Cincinnati	.743	1941	38.3
C. Conn. St.	.703	1835	38.3
Texas	.741	1920	38.6
Butler	.614	1590	38.6
NC-Wilmington	.607	1571	38.6
Oklahoma St.	.779	2007	38.8
Indiana	.696	1792	38.8

Rebound Margin

	Off	Def	Mar
Michigan St.	39.0	27.3	11.7
Stanford	42.2	32.5	9.7
Texas Southern	39.3	30.7	8.6
Kansas	44.3	36.0	8.2
LSU	40.4	32.4	8.0
DePaul	39.5	31.5	8.0
TX-San Antonio	44.3	36.3	8.0
Navy	42.6	34.7	7.9
Stetson	40.3	32.5	7.8
East Carolina	39.3	32.6	6.6
Iowa St.	38.4	32.1	6.4
San Diego	39.1	33.1	6.0
San Francisco	38.8	32.8	6.0
C. Conn. St.	40.7	34.9	5.8
Holy Cross	37.6	31.9	5.7

Free Throw Percentage

	FT	FTA	Pct
Montana St.	481	609	79.0
Tennessee Tech	532	693	76.8
TCU	621	812	76.5
Akron	585	767	76.3
Morehead St.	390	515	75.7
Delaware	522	693	75.3
NC-Asheville	528	701	75.3
Maine	413	549	75.2
Weber St.	540	718	75.2
N. Arizona	467	622	75.1
Siena	657	876	75.0
Troy St.	407	544	74.8
Miami-FL	516	690	74.8
Fordham	421	563	74.8
Oregon	481	646	74.5

3-point FG Percentage

	3PT	3PTA	Pct
Colorado St.	255	579	44.0
Creighton	289	694	41.6
Coastal Carolina	224	551	40.7
Troy St.	253	625	40.5
E. Illinois	206	512	40.2
Morehead St.	224	560	40.0
Stanford	245	613	40.0
Ball St.	215	538	40.0
Montana	197	493	40.0
C. Florida	233	586	39.8
NC-Asheville	174	439	39.6
Siena	283	721	39.3
N. Arizona	263	673	39.1
Marshall	246	631	39.0
Lafayette	249	639	39.0

3-point FG Made Per Game

	Gm	No	Avg
Tennessee Tech	28	279	10.0
Samford	32	313	9.8
Belmont	28	273	9.8
Missouri	31	291	9.4
TX-Arlington	27	247	9.1
Troy St.	28	253	9.0
Oakland	30	271	9.0
WI-Milwaukee	29	256	8.8
Creighton	33	289	8.8
Arkansas	34	292	8.6
Siena	33	283	8.6
Colorado St.	30	255	8.5
St. Francis	30	255	8.5
N. Arizona	31	263	8.5
Albany	28	236	8.4

Underclassmen in NBA Draft

Twenty-three division I players (11 juniors, 9 sophomores and 3 freshmen), 2 high school seniors, 2 junior college players, 1 division II junior and 1 NAIA junior forfeited the remainder of their college eligibility and declared for the 2000 NBA Draft which took place at the Target Center in Minneapolis, Minn. on June 28.

Players are listed in alphabetical order; first round selections in **bold** type, high school players in *italics*.

	Cl	Drafted by	Overall Pick
Erick Barkley, St. John's	So.	Portland	28
E. Brown, Indian Hills (Iowa) CC	So.	Miami	52
Schea Cotton, Alabama	So.	Not drafted	—
Jamal Crawford, Michigan	Fr.	Cleveland	8
Joshua Cross, S. Illinois	Jr.	Not drafted	—
Kaniel Dickens, Idaho	Jr.	Utah	50
Keyon Dooling, Missouri	So.	Orlando	10
Khalid El-Amin, UConn	Jr.	Chicago	34
Steve Eldridge, Henderson St.	Jr.	Not drafted	—
Marcus Fizer, Iowa St.	Jr.	Chicago	4
Donnell Harvey, Florida	Fr.	New York	22
Cory Hightower, Indian Hills CC	So.	San Antonio	54
R. Hines, Tex. A&M-Corp. Christi	Jr.	Not drafted	—
Jimmie Hunter, Life (Ga.)	Jr.	Not drafted	—
DerMarr Johnson, Cincinnati	Fr.	Atlanta	6
Mark Karcher, Temple	Jr.	Philadelphia	48
Andre Mahorn, Utah St.	Jr.	Not drafted	—
Paul McPherson, DePaul	Jr.	Not drafted	—
Chris Mihm, Texas	Jr.	Chicago	7
Darius Miles, East St. Louis, Ill.	HS	LA Clippers	3
Mike Miller, Florida	So.	Orlando	5
Jerome Moiso, UCLA	So.	Boston	11
Joel Przybilla, Minnesota	So.	Houston	9
Michael Redd, Ohio St.	Jr.	Milwaukee	43
Quentin Richardson, DePaul	So.	LA Clippers	18
JaRon Rush, UCLA	So.	Not drafted	—
DeShawn Stevenson, Fresno	HS	Utah	23
Stromile Swift, LSU	So.	Vancouver	2
Derrick Worrell, Pittsburgh	Jr.	Not drafted	—

Note: Jason Kapono (UCLA), D.A. Layne (Georgia), Brian Merriweather (Texas-PanAm), Jeryl Sasser (SMU), Kenny Satterfield (Cincinnati), Karim Shabazz (Providence) and Joe White (Texas A&M) declared for the draft and then withdrew their names before the June 21 deadline.

High School Players to enter NBA

Player	Pro career
Tony Kappen	1946-47
Connie Simmons	1946-56
Joe Graboski	1948-62
Reggie Harding	1963-68
Moses Malone	1974-95
Bill Willoughby	1975-84
Darryl Dawkins	1975-89
Kevin Garnett	1995—
Kobe Bryant	1996—
Jermaine O'Neal	1996—
Tracy McGrady	1997—
Al Harrington	1998—
Rashard Lewis	1998—
Korleone Young	1998-99
Darius Miles	2000—
DeShawn Stevenson	2000—

Note: Kappen started out in the American Basketball League and Malone started out in the American Basketball Association. Because they enrolled in a college, Lloyd Daniels (Mount St. Antonio), Thomas Hamilton (Pittsburgh) and Shawn Kemp (Kentucky/Trinity Valley CC) were not included on this list.

Other 2000 Men's Tournaments

NIT Tournament

The 63rd annual National Invitation Tournament had a 32-team field. First three rounds played on home courts of higher seeded teams. Semifinal, Third Place and Championship games played March 28-30 at Madison Square Garden in New York City.

1st Round

at Siena 66	Massachusetts 65
at Penn St. 55	Princeton 41
at Kent 73	Rutgers 62
at Villanova 72	Delaware 63
at Notre Dame 75	Michigan 65
at Xavier 67	Marquette 63
at BYU 81	Bowling Green 54
S. Illinois 94	at Colorado 92
at N.C. State 64	Tulane 60
at Arizona St. 83	N. Mexico St. 77
at SW Mo. St. 77	SMU 64
at Mississippi 62	NC-Charlotte 45
Wake Forest 83	at Vanderbilt 68
at New Mexico 64	S. Florida 58
Georgetown 115	3 OT	at Virginia 111
at California 70	Long Beach St. 66

2nd Round

at Penn St. 105	Siena 103
Kent 81	at Villanova 67
at Notre Dame 76	Xavier 64
at BYU 82	S. Illinois 57
at N.C. State 60	Arizona St. 57
at Mississippi 70	SW Missouri St. 48
at Wake Forest 72	New Mexico 65
at California 60	Georgetown 49

Quarterfinals

at Penn St. 81	Kent 74
at Notre Dame 64	BYU 52
at N.C. State 77	Mississippi 54
at Wake Forest 76	California 59

Semifinals

Wake Forest 62	OT	N.C. State 59
Notre Dame 73	Penn St. 52

Third Place

Penn St. 74	N.C. State 72

Championship

Wake Forest 71	Notre Dame 61

Most Valuable Players

NIT
Robert O'Kelley, Wake Forest guard

NCAA Division II
DeMarcos Anzures, Metropolitan St. guard

NCAA Division III
Sherm Carstensen, WI-Eau Claire guard

NAIA Division I
Jimmie Hunter, Life (Ga.) guard

NAIA Division II
Jason Cruse, Embry-Riddle forward/center

NCAA Division II

The eight regional winners of the 48-team field: NORTHEAST— St. Anslem, N.H. (23-8); EAST— Indiana, Pa. (24-7); SOUTH ATLANTIC— Georgia College & State University (25-5); SOUTH— Florida Southern (32-1); SOUTH CENTRAL— Mo. Southern St. (29-2); GREAT LAKES— Kentucky Wesleyan (29-2); NORTH CENTRAL— Metropolitan State, Colo. (30-4); WEST— Seattle Pacific (26-4).

The Elite Eight was played March 22-25, at the Commonwealth Convention Center in Louisville, Ky. There was no Third Place game.

Quarterfinals

Mo. Southern St. 76	Florida Southern 65
Metropolitan St. 81	St. Anslem 61
Seattle Pacific 77	GC & SU 65
Ky. Wesleyan 84	Indiana-PA 68

Semifinals

Metropolitan St. 75	Mo. Southern St. 74
Ky. Wesleyan 87	Seattle Pacific 81

Championship

Metropolitan St. 97	Ky. Wesleyan 79

NCAA Division III

Sixty-four teams played into the 32-team Division III field. The four sectional winners: MIDDLE ATLANTIC— Franklin & Marshall (Pa.) (25-5); EAST/NORTHEAST— Salem (Mass.) St. (26-4); NORTH— Calvin (Mich.) (28-2); MIDWEST— WI-Eau Claire (26-6).

The Final Four was played March 17-18, at Salem Civic Center in Salem, Va.

Semifinals

WI-Eau Claire 72	Salem St. 42
Calvin 79	Franklin & Marshall 77

Third Place

Salem St. 79	Franklin & Marshall 75

Championship

Calvin 79	WI-Eau Claire 74

NAIA Division I

The quarterfinalists, in alphabetical order, after two rounds of the 32-team NAIA tournament: Biola, Calif. (27-7); Faulkner, Ala. (26-10); Georgetown, Ky. (32-7); Life, Ga. (31-2); Lipscomb, Tenn. (34-3); The Master's, Calif. (28-5); Olivet Nazarene, Ill. (29-8); Spring Hill, Ala. (29-7).

All tournament games played, March 14-20, at the Donald W. Reynolds Center in Tulsa, Okla. There was no Third Place game.

Quarterfinals: Georgetown def. Faulkner, 80-61; Life def. The Master's, 79-68; Olivet Nazarene def. Spring Hill, 62-44; Biola def. Lipscomb, 82-71.

Semifinals: Life def. Olivet Nazarene, 85-69; Georgetown def. Biola, 118-108 (4 OT).

Championship: Life def. Georgetown, 61-59.

NAIA Division II

The semifinalists, in alphabetical order, after three rounds of the 32-team NAIA tournament: Embry-Riddle, Fla. (29-7); Huntington, Ind. (34-4); Ozarks, Mo. (24-8); Siena Heights, Mich. (31-7).

All tournament games played, March 8-14, at Point Lookout, Missouri. There was no Third Place game.

Semifinals: Ozarks def. Huntington, 83-81; Embry-Riddle def. Siena Heights, 92-80.

Championship: Embry-Riddle def. Ozarks, 75-63.

Nearly Perfect

by Jay Bilas

The Connecticut Huskies entered the 2000 season with the No. 1 ranking and high expectations, yet the season began with one lingering question: Could UConn unseat Tennessee as the gold standard of women's college basketball? The Huskies were widely considered to have the best talent, while the Lady Vols could boast the nation's top player in Tamika Catchings. Even though the Lady Vols had dominated the college basketball landscape for so long, many thought the 2000 season would bring the Tennessee program down a peg. But Pat Summitt methodically molded her young players into a championship-caliber team yet again, even without Chamique Holdsclaw.

In November, Tennessee pulled off the unthinkable when it upset the United States national team, becoming the only college team to come within shouting distance of our country's best and brightest. Behind the versatility of Catchings, the defense and intensity of Semeka Randall, and the tenacious play of freshman Kara Lawson, Tennessee served notice that a coronation of UConn was a bit premature. Next, Tennessee opened the season with a loss to

Shea Ralph

Louisiana Tech. Summitt immediately got her team's attention, and guided the Lady Vols down a collision course with Connecticut in the first of two regular season meetings between the two giants of the women's game.

Meanwhile, UConn coach Geno Auriemma was looking to promote team chemistry and to challenge his team in innovative ways. Auriemma assembled a team that led the nation in field goal percentage and three point percentage and would prove to be the best defensive team in the country. After a summer trip to Europe where the players could bond, UConn worked tirelessly on its halfcourt execution, so that they would not be so reliant upon their full court pressure to generate scoring. The return of point guard Sue Bird from a knee injury gave the Huskies a leader at the point of attack that could make superior reads. Bird's injury had deflated UConn's chances of success in 1999, but in 2000 her stabilizing influence took pressure off of Shea Ralph and Svetlana Abrosimova to concentrate on their strengths. Auriemma put all of the pressure of the season squarely on Bird's shoulders and she took the reins of the team and never wavered.

Tennessee and UConn were not alone in their quests for the title. Georgia coach Andy Landers assembled one of his best teams, finishing 32-4 behind the twin scoring machines Kelly and Coco Miller. C. Vivian Stringer watched her original recruiting class at Rutgers, led by Shawnetta Stewart and Tasha Pointer, become seniors and blossom into Final Four contenders with a smash-mouth style of play.

UConn and Tennessee met twice before the NCAA tournament, each winning on the other's court. In the first meeting at Tennessee in January, Bird was magnificent, scoring 25 points and dictating the action in the Huskies' 74-67 win. However, in the rematch at UConn, Tennessee would not be intimidated. In a physical contest that UConn seemed to have in hand, Tennessee's Randall came up with the big plays to avenge the Lady Vols' earlier loss with a 72-71 win in Storrs. That loss would prove to be the only blemish on UConn's otherwise perfect season.

As expected, UConn and Tennessee met in the title game, but the Lady Vols came into the rubber match without Kristen "Ace" Clement, who badly sprained her ankle at the morning shoot-around. Without Clement, UConn dominated the game, and put the Lady Vols on their heels with stifling defense and precision passing and cutting. Ralph set the tone early, and finished with 15 points, seven assists and six steals to take Most Outstanding Player honors, while Kelly Schumacher demonstrated the brilliance she had flashed at times by blocking an NCAA Final-record nine shots. Asjha Jones, Tamika Williams, Kennitra Johnson and Swin Cash assisted Bird, Ralph and Abrosimova in ruthlessly forcing 26 Tennessee turnovers and holding down Catchings and Randall on the way to the 71-52 win and wire-to-wire run as the nation's top ranked team. ∎

Jay Bilas is ESPN's women's college basketball analyst.

Photo source: AP/Wide World Photos

Final Regular Season AP Women's Top 25 Poll

Taken **before** start of NCAA tournament.

The sportswriters & broadcasters poll: first place votes in parentheses; records through Sunday, March 12, 2000; total points (based on 25 for 1st, 24 for 2nd, etc.); record in NCAA tourney and team lost to; head coach (career years and career record including 2000 postseason), and preseason ranking. Teams in **bold** type went on to reach the NCAA Final Four.

		Mar. 12 Record	Points	NCAA Recap	Head Coach	Preseason Rank
1	**Connecticut** (41)	30-1	1097	6-0	Geno Auriemma (15 yrs: 393-95)	1
2	**Tennessee** (3)	28-3	1055	5-1 (UConn)	Pat Summitt (26 yrs: 728-150)	2
3	Louisiana Tech	28-2	1001	3-1 (Penn St.)	Leon Barmore (18 yrs: 520-77)	6
4	Georgia	29-3	970	3-1 (Rutgers)	Andy Landers (25 yrs: 600-173)	3
5	Notre Dame	25-4	860	2-1 (Texas Tech)	Muffet McGraw (18 yrs: 376-156)	8
6	**Penn St.**	26-4	843	4-1 (UConn)	Rene Portland (24 yrs: 553-185)	10
7	Iowa St.	25-5	785	2-1 (Penn St.)	Bill Fennelly (12 yrs: 277-97)	7
8	**Rutgers**	22-7	770	4-1 (Tennessee)	C. Vivian Stringer (28 yrs: 621-191)	4
9	UC-Santa Barbara	30-3	736	0-1 (Rice)	Mark French (21 yrs: 364-229)	14
10	Duke	26-5	712	2-1 (LSU)	Gail Goestenkors (8 yrs: 176-74)	21
11	Texas Tech	25-4	662	3-1 (Tennessee)	Marsha Sharp (18 yrs: 434-134)	22
12	Mississippi St.	23-7	605	1-1 (UAB)	Sharon Fanning (24 yrs: 402-290)	NR
13	Purdue	22-7	567	1-1 (Oklahoma)	Kristy Curry (1 yr: 23-8)	23
14	Old Dominion	27-4	543	2-1 (La. Tech)	Wendy Larry (16 yrs: 359-130)	15
15	LSU	22-6	503	3-1 (UConn)	Sue Gunter (30 yrs: 613-273)	13
16	Auburn	21-7	377	1-1 (Penn St.)	Joe Ciampi (23 yrs: 529-168)	11
17	Boston College	25-8	312	1-1 (Virginia)	Cathy Inglese (14 yrs: 232-164)	19
18	Oklahoma	23-7	270	2-1 (UConn)	Sherri Coale (4 yrs: 53-63)	NR
19	Virginia	23-8	265	2-1 (Tennessee)	Debbie Ryan (23 yrs: 526-183)	NR
20	Oregon	23-7	226	0-1 (UAB)	Jody Runge (7 yrs: 143-61)	16
21	Arizona	24-6	216	1-1 (Tennessee)	Joan Bonvicini (21 yrs: 484-176)	25
22	Tulane	26-4	214	1-1 (Texas Tech)	Lisa Stockton (9 yrs: 202-70)	NR
23	N.C. State	20-8	210	0-1 (SMU)	Kay Yow (29 yrs: 589-242)	20
24	Xavier	26-4	96	0-1 (S.F. Austin)	Melanie Balcomb (7 yrs: 120-82)	NR
25	Michigan	22-7	89	0-1 (Stanford)	Sue Guevara (4 yrs: 74-41)	NR

Others receiving votes: 26. **Texas** (21-12) 79.5 pts; 27. **North Carolina** (18-12) 40; 28. **George Washington** (25-5) 33; 29. **Stanford** (20-8) 32; 30. **Marquette** (22-6) 26.5; 31. **Drake** (23-6) 20; 32. **Illinois** (22-10) 19; 33. **Kent** (25-5) and **Vanderbilt** (20-12) 13; 35. **Utah** (23-7) 12; 36. **UCLA** (18-10) 11; 37. **Stephen F. Austin** (27-3) 6; 38. **Kansas** (20-9), **St. Joseph's-PA** (24-5) 4; 40. **Nebraska** (18-12), **Rice** (21-9) and **Wisconsin** (21-8) 1.

NCAA Women's Division I Tournament Seeds

	WEST		MIDWEST		MIDEAST		EAST
1	Georgia (29-3)	1	Louisiana Tech (28-2)	1	Tennessee (28-3)	1	Connecticut (30-1)
2	Rutgers (22-7)	2	Penn St. (26-4)	2	Notre Dame (25-4)	2	Duke (26-5)
3	Mississippi St. (23-7)	3	Iowa St. (25-5)	3	Texas Tech (25-4)	3	LSU (22-6)
4	UC-Santa Barbara (30-3)	4	Old Dominion (27-4)	4	Virginia (23-8)	4	Purdue (22-7)
5	North Carolina (18-12)	5	N.C. State (20-8)	5	Boston College (25-8)	5	Oklahoma (23-7)
6	Oregon (23-7)	6	Illinois (22-10)	6	Tulane (26-4)	6	Xavier (26-4)
7	Texas (21-12)	7	Auburn (21-7)	7	George Washington (25-5)	7	Marquette (22-6)
8	Michigan (22-7)	8	Kansas (20-9)	8	Arizona (24-6)	8	Drake (23-6)
9	Stanford (20-8)	9	Vanderbilt (20-12)	9	Kent (25-5)	9	Clemson (18-11)
10	St. Joseph's (24-5)	10	SW Missouri St. (23-8)	10	UCLA (18-10)	10	Western Ky. (21-9)
11	UAB (19-12)	11	Utah (23-7)	11	Vermont (25-5)	11	Stephen F. Austin (27-3)
12	Maine (20-10)	12	SMU (21-8)	12	Nebraska (18-12)	12	BYU (22-8)
13	Rice (21-9)	13	Wisc-Green Bay (21-8)	13	Pepperdine (21-9)	13	Dartmouth (20-7)
14	St. Peters (23-7)	14	St. Francis-PA (23-7)	14	Tennessee Tech (24-8)	14	Liberty (23-7)
15	Holy Cross (23-6)	15	Youngstown St. (22-8)	15	San Diego (17-13)	15	Campbell (22-7)
16	Montana (22-7)	16	Alcorn St. (22-8)	16	Furman (20-10)	16	Hampton (16-14)

2000 NCAA BASKETBALL WOMEN'S DIVISION I

2000 NCAA Women's Final Four — PHILADELPHIA

MIDEAST

FIRST ROUND — March 17-18
- 1 Tennessee 90 / 16 Furman 38
- 8 Arizona 73 / 9 Kent 61
- 5 Boston College 93 / 12 Nebraska 76
- 4 Virginia 74 / 13 Pepperdine 62
- 6 Tulane 65 / 11 Vermont 60
- 3 Texas Tech 83 / 14 Tennessee Tech 54
- 7 G. Washington 79 / 10 UCLA 72
- 2 Notre Dame 81 / 15 San Diego 61

SECOND ROUND — March 19-20
- Tennessee 75
- Arizona 60
- Boston College 70
- Virginia 74
- Tulane 59
- Texas Tech 76
- G. Washington 60
- Notre Dame 95

REGIONALS — March 25-27
- Tennessee 77 / Virginia 56
- Texas Tech 69 / Notre Dame 65
- Tennessee 57 / Texas Tech 44
- **Tennessee 64**

WEST

FIRST ROUND — March 17-18
- 1 Georgia 74 / 16 Montana 46
- 8 Stanford (OT) 81 / 9 Michigan 74
- 5 N. Carolina 62 / 12 Maine 57
- 4 Rice 67 / 13 UC-SB 64
- 6 UAB (OT) 80 / 11 Oregon 79
- 3 Mississippi St. 94 / 14 St. Peter's 60
- 7 Texas 48 / 10 St. Joseph's 69
- 2 Rutgers 91 / 15 Holy Cross 70

SECOND ROUND — March 19-20
- Georgia 83
- Stanford 64
- N. Carolina 83
- Rice 50
- UAB 78
- Mississippi St. 72
- St. Joseph's 39
- Rutgers 59

REGIONALS — March 25-27
- Georgia 83 / UNC 57
- UAB 45 / Rutgers 60
- Georgia 51 / Rutgers 59
- **Rutgers 54**

EAST

FIRST ROUND — March 17-18
- 1 Connecticut 116 / 16 Hampton 45
- 8 Drake 50 / 9 Clemson 64
- 5 Oklahoma 86 / 12 BYU 81
- 4 Purdue 70 / 13 Dartmouth 66
- 6 Xavier 72 / 11 S. F. Austin 73
- 3 Louisiana St. 77 / 14 Liberty 54
- 7 W. Kentucky 65 / 10 Marquette 63
- 2 Duke 71 / 15 Campbell 42

SECOND ROUND — March 19-20
- Connecticut 83
- Clemson 45
- Oklahoma 76
- Purdue 74
- S. F. Austin 45
- Louisiana St. 57
- W. Kentucky 70
- Duke 90

REGIONALS — March 25-27
- UConn 102 / Oklahoma 80
- LSU 79 / Duke 66
- UConn 86 / LSU 71
- **UConn 89**

MIDWEST

FIRST ROUND — March 17-18
- 1 Louisiana Tech 95 / 16 Alcorn St. 53
- 8 Vanderbilt (2OT) 71 / 9 Kansas 69
- 5 SMU 64 / 12 N.C. State 63
- 4 Old Dominion 94 / 13 WI-Green Bay 85
- 6 Illinois 73 / 11 Utah 58
- 3 Iowa St. 92 / 14 St. Francis (Pa.) 63
- 7 Auburn 78 / 10 SW Missouri St. 74
- 2 Penn St. 83 / 15 Youngstown St. 63

SECOND ROUND — March 19-20
- Louisiana Tech 66
- Vanderbilt 65
- SMU 76
- Old Dominion 96
- Illinois 68
- Iowa St. 79
- Auburn 69
- Penn St. 75

REGIONALS — March 25-27
- La. Tech 86 / ODU 74
- Iowa St. 65 / Penn St. 86
- La. Tech 65 / Penn St. 66
- **Penn St. 67**

NATIONAL CHAMPIONSHIP

- UConn 71
- Tennessee 52

FINAL FOUR

First Union Center in Philadelphia, PA
***
Semifinals: March 31
Finals: April 2

NCAA Championship Game
Tennessee 52

	Min	FG M-A	FT M-A	Pts	Reb O-T	A	PF
Semeka Randall	.35	1-11	4-6	6	4-8	2	1
Tamika Catchings	.36	4-6	5-10	16	2-4	1	4
Michelle Snow	.26	2-9	1-2	5	4-4	0	4
Kyra Elzy	.19	3-5	2-2	8	2-5	0	2
Kara Lawson	.35	3-13	0-0	6	0-6	3	2
April McDivitt	.21	1-2	2-2	5	0-0	0	2
Gwen Jackson	.12	2-4	0-0	4	2-7	0	0
Shalon Pillow	.11	0-1	2-2	2	1-2	0	1
Niya Butts	.5	0-0	0-0	0	0-0	0	1
TOTALS	.200	16-51	16-24	52	15-36	6	17

Three-point FG: 4-7 (Catchings 3-3, Lawson 0-2, McDivitt 1-2); **Team Rebounds:** 3; **Blocked Shots:** 3 (Snow 2, Jackson); **Turnovers:** 25 (Catchings 7, Elzy 6, Randall 6, Jackson 2, Lawson, McDivitt, Pillow, Snow); **Steals:** 7 (Catchings 2, Lawson 2, Jackson, Randall, Snow); **Percentages:** 2-Pt FG (.273); 3-Pt FG (.571); Total FG (.314); Free Throws (.667).

Connecticut 71

	Min	FG M-A	FT M-A	Pts	Reb O-T	A	PF
S. Abrosimova	.28	5-9	3-4	14	1-5	2	2
Swin Cash	.18	4-8	1-2	9	1-3	0	4
Kelly Schumacher	.20	3-4	0-0	6	2-6	0	2
Sue Bird	.35	2-8	0-0	4	1-3	4	1
Shea Ralph	.28	7-8	1-2	15	1-3	7	3
Tamika Williams	.14	3-4	0-0	6	2-2	2	4
Asjha Jones	.22	5-14	2-3	12	4-8	2	1
Kennitra Johnson	.23	1-3	1-2	3	0-1	3	2
Stacy Hansmeyer	.5	0-1	0-2	0	0-0	1	1
Paige Sauer	.3	1-1	0-0	2	0-1	0	0
Marci Czel	.2	0-0	0-0	0	0-0	0	0
Christine Rigby	.2	0-1	0-0	0	0-0	0	0
TOTALS	.200	31-61	8-15	71	12-32	21	20

Three-point FG: 1-9 (Abrosimova 1-3, Bird 0-3, Johnson 0-2, Hansmeyer 0-1); **Team Rebounds:** 2; **Blocked Shots:** 11 (Schumacher 9, Ralph, Jones); **Turnovers:** 14 (Abrosimova 5, Williams 3, Cash, Czel, Hansmeyer, Johnson, Ralph, Schumacher); **Steals:** 12 (Ralph 6, Cash 2, Abrosimova, Johnson, Schumacher, Williams); **Percentages:** 2-Pt FG (.577); 3-Pt FG (.111); Total FG (.508); Free Throws (.533).

Tennessee (SEC)	19	33—	**52**
Connecticut (Big East)	32	39—	**71**

Technical Fouls: None. **Officials:** Sally Bell, Dennis Demayo, Art Bomengen. **Attendance:** 20,060. **TV Rating:** 3.5/5 share (ESPN).

Final ESPN/USA Today Coaches' Poll

Taken **after** NCAA tournament.

Voted on by panel of 40 women's coaches and media following the NCAA tournament: first place votes in parentheses.

		Pts			Pts
1	UConn (40)	1,000	14	Virginia	433
2	Tennessee	954	15	Mississippi St.	380
3	Penn State	909	16	Purdue	362
4	Rutgers	890	17	Boston College	268
5	Georgia	830	18	North Carolina	243
6	Louisiana Tech	752	19	Auburn	239
7	Texas Tech	725	20	Arizona	214
8	LSU	702	21	UC-SB	209
9	Notre Dame	647	22	Ala-Birmingham	170
10	Iowa State	638	23	N.C. State	153
11	Duke	614	24	Tulane	142
12	Old Dominion	508	25	Vanderbilt	111
13	Oklahoma	434			

WOMEN'S FINAL FOUR

at First Union Center, Philadelphia, Penn. (March 31-April 2).

Semifinals

Tennessee 64	Rutgers 54
Connecticut 89	Penn St. 67

Championship

Connecticut 71 .... Tennessee 52

Final Records: Connecticut (36-1), Tennessee (33-4), Penn St. (30-5), Rutgers (26-8).

Most Outstanding Player: Shea Ralph, junior guard-forward. SEMIFINAL— 28 minutes, 9 points, 4 rebounds, 3 assists, 2 steals; FINAL— 28 minutes, 15 points, 3 rebounds, 6 steals, 7 assists.

All-Tournament Team: Ralph, guard Sue Bird, forward Svetlana Abrosimova and forward Asjha Jones of Connecticut and forward Tamika Catchings of Tennessee.

Annual Awards

Player of the Year

Tamika Catchings, Tennessee .... AP, Naismith, USBWA, WBCA

Edwina Brown, Texas .... Wade

Coach of the Year

Geno Auriemma, Connecticut .... AP, Naismith, WBCA

Consensus All-America Team

The NCAA Division I players cited most frequently by the Associated Press, US Basketball Writers Assn., the Women's Basketball Coaches Assn. and the Women's Basketball News Service. Holdover from the 1998-99 All-America first team are in **bold** type; (*) indicates unanimous first team selection.

First Team

	Class	Hgt	Pos
Tamika Catchings, Tennessee*	Jr.	6-1	F
Kelly Miller, Georgia*	Jr.	5-10	G
Svetlana Abrosimova, Connecticut	Jr.	6-2	F
Edwina Brown, Texas	Sr.	5-10	G/F
Semeka Randall, Tennessee	Jr.	5-10	G

Second Team

	Class	Hgt	Pos
Katie Douglas, Purdue	Jr.	6-1	G
Shea Ralph, Connecticut	Jr.	6-0	G/F
Jackie Stiles, SW Missouri St.	Jr.	5-8	G
Phylesha Waley, Oklahoma	Sr.	5-10	F
LaToya Thomas, Mississippi St.	Fr.	6-2	C

Other Women's Tournaments

WNIT (Mar. 29 at Madison, Wisc.): Final— Wisconsin def. Florida, 75-74.

NCAA Division II (Mar. 25 at Pine Bluff, Ark.): Final— Northern Kentucky def. North Dakota St., 71-62.

NCAA Division III (Mar. 18 at Danbury, Conn.): Final— Washington (Mo.) def. Southern Maine, 79-33.

NAIA Division I (Mar. 21 at Jackson, Tenn.): Final— Oklahoma City def. Simon Fraser (B.C.), 64-55.

NAIA Division II (Mar. 14 at Sioux City, Iowa): Final— University of Mary (N.D.) def. Northwestern College (Iowa), 59-49.

NCAA Women's Division I Leaders

Includes games through NCAA and NIT tourneys.

INDIVIDUAL

Scoring

	Cl	Gm	Pts	Avg
Jackie Stiles, SW Missouri St.	Jr.	32	890	27.8
Diana Caramanico, Pennsylvania	Jr.	28	694	24.8
Jess Zinobile, St. Francis-PA	Sr.	31	724	23.4
Madinah Slaise, Cincinnati	Sr.	30	654	21.8
Grace Daley, Tulane	Sr.	32	692	21.6
Linda Frohlich, UNLV	So.	28	604	21.6
Jamie Cassidy, Maine	Sr.	31	668	21.5
Edwina Brown, Texas	Sr.	34	722	21.2
Jennifer Crow, Oklahoma St.	Sr.	30	633	21.1
Rhonda Smith, Long Beach St.	Sr.	32	675	21.1
Julie Szabo, Stony Brook	Fr.	28	589	21.0
LaToya Thomas, Mississippi	Fr.	32	672	21.0
Phylesha Whaley, Oklahoma	Sr.	33	686	20.8
Alli Nieman, Idaho	Sr.	28	576	20.6
Shauna Geronzin, Canisius	So.	29	595	20.5
Kim MacMillan, LIU	Fr.	29	594	20.5
Katie Douglas, Purdue	Jr.	30	613	20.4
Lisa Baswell, Jacksonville St.	Sr.	28	569	20.3
Brooke Armistead, Austin Peay	Fr.	30	608	20.3
Kiesha Brooks, Coppin St.	Jr.	27	540	20.0

Assists

	Cl	Gm	No	Avg
Helen Darling, Penn. St.	Sr.	35	274	7.8
Angela Zampella, St. Joseph's-PA	Sr.	31	241	7.8
Sharin Milner, Troy St.	Fr.	27	206	7.6
Michele Koclanes, Richmond	So.	27	206	7.6
Rochelle Luckett, VCU	So.	30	214	7.1
Clarissa Tomlinson, Samford	Sr.	29	201	6.9
Shala Crook, Ball St.	So.	29	197	6.8
Tricia Brenitsky, Canisius	So.	29	197	6.8
Amy Vachon, Maine	Sr.	31	209	6.7
Lindsay Logan, Fresno St.	Fr.	29	192	6.6
Kara Wile, St. Louis	Sr.	28	183	6.5
Sonia Ortega, Buffalo	Sr.	29	188	6.5
Gina Graziani, Miami-FL	Sr.	29	182	6.3
Nikki Teasley, North Carolina	Jr.	26	162	6.2
Juli Grant, Cleveland St.	Sr.	30	184	6.1
Jennifer Monti, Harvard	So.	25	152	6.1
Niele Ivey, Notre Dame	Sr.	32	194	6.1
Tombi Bell, Florida	Jr.	34	204	6.0
Edwina Brown, Texas	Sr.	34	203	6.0
Brooke Gallert, Western Mich.	So.	26	155	6.0

Rebounding

	Cl	Gm	No	Avg
Malveata Johnson, N.C. A&T	Jr.	27	363	13.4
Elise James, Robert Morris	Sr.	28	367	13.1
Diana Caramanico, Pennsylvania	Jr.	28	334	11.9
Jess Zinobile, St. Francis-PA	Sr.	31	366	11.8
Mercy Aghedo, St. Peter's	Sr.	30	352	11.7
Deanna Jackson, UAB	So.	33	385	11.7
Nekesha Jewell, Grambling	Sr.	30	350	11.7
Gail Strumpf, Fairfield	Jr.	33	378	11.5
Linda Frohlich, UNLV	So.	28	319	11.4
Andrea Gardner, Howard	So.	28	316	11.3
Audra Cook, Cleveland St.	Sr.	30	333	11.1
Erin Whiteside, CS-Fullerton	Sr.	24	263	11.0
Mandi Carver, Idaho St.	So.	29	316	10.9
Jackie Smith, Furman	Sr.	31	335	10.8
Shniece Perry, Towson St.	Sr.	27	288	10.7

Blocked Shots

	Cl	Gm	No	Avg
Rhonda Smith, Long Beach St.	Sr.	32	111	3.5
Sissel Pierce, Oregon St.	Sr.	29	85	2.9
Malveata Johnson, N.C. A&T	Jr.	27	75	2.8
Michaela Pavlickova, Denver	Sr.	27	72	2.7
Ruth Riley, Notre Dame	Jr.	32	85	2.7

Steals

	Cl	Gm	No	Avg
Shakira Smith, Morgan St.	Jr.	29	126	4.3
Jennifer O'Brien, Davidson	Sr.	27	117	4.3
Jessica Burch, Stony Brook	Jr.	27	111	4.1
Courtney Banghart, Dartmouth	Sr.	28	108	3.9
Natarsua Player, Sam Houston St.	Sr.	27	104	3.9
Cher Dyson, Stetson	Jr.	27	104	3.9

TEAM

Scoring Offense

	Gm	W-L	Pts	Avg
Grambling	30	25-5	2666	88.9
Louisiana Tech	34	31-3	2960	87.1
Connecticut	37	36-1	3184	86.1
Old Dominion	34	29-5	2757	81.1
UC-Santa Barbara	34	30-4	2756	81.1
Tulane	32	27-5	2576	80.5
Iowa St.	33	27-6	2638	79.9
Richmond	28	12-16	2231	79.7
Kent	31	25-6	2469	79.6

Scoring Defense

	Gm	W-L	Pts	Avg
Utah	31	23-8	1618	52.2
St. Joseph's-PA	31	25-6	1647	53.1
Montana	30	22-8	1624	54.1
Rutgers	34	26-8	1850	55.5
Connecticut	37	36-1	2053	55.5
Texas-Arlington	28	13-15	1561	55.8
Vanderbilt	34	21-13	1912	56.2
Texas Tech	33	28-5	1857	56.3
Duke	34	28-6	1919	56.4
Northeastern	30	17-13	1700	56.7

Scoring Margin

	Off	Def	Mar
Connecticut	86.1	55.5	30.6
Louisiana Tech	87.1	59.2	27.8
Stephen F. Austin	76.0	57.0	19.0
Duke	74.5	56.4	18.1
Grambling	88.9	70.8	18.1
Old Dominion	81.1	63.1	18.0
Georgia	78.3	61.0	17.4
Tennessee	79.3	62.6	16.7
UC-Santa Barbara	81.1	64.6	16.5

High-Point Games

Individual

No		Opponent	Date
56	Jackie Stiles, SW Mo. St.	Evansville	3/10
46	Jess Zinobile, St. Francis-PA	Long Island	3/4
43	Jackie Stiles, SW Mo. St.	UMKC	12/18
43	Jackie Stiles, SW Mo. St.	Bradley	2/25
42	Lisa Oldenburg, Marquette	Pacific	11/26
42	Shauna Geronzin, Canisius	Niagara	2/20

National Champions

The Helms Foundation of Los Angeles, under the direction of founder Bill Schroeder, selected national college basketball champions from 1942-82 and researched retroactive picks from 1901-41. The first NIT tournament and then the NCAA tournament have settled the national championship since 1938, but there are four years (1939, '40, '44 and '54) where the Helms selections differ. Please note that the column titled Outstanding Player is not a list of the official NCAA tournament Most Outstanding Players but rather a subjective list of each team's best player over the course of the season. For a list of official tournament Most Outstanding Players turn to page 301.

Multiple champions (1901-37): Chicago, Columbia and Wisconsin (3); Kansas, Minnesota, Notre Dame, Penn, Pittsburgh, Syracuse and Yale (2). **Multiple champions (since 1938):** UCLA (11); Kentucky (7); Indiana (5); North Carolina (3); Cincinnati, Duke, Kansas, Louisville, Michigan St., N.C. State, Oklahoma A&M (now Oklahoma St.) and San Francisco (2).

Year		Record	Head Coach	Outstanding Player
1901	Yale	10-4	No coach	G.M. Clark, F
1902	Minnesota	11-0	Louis Cooke	W.C. Deering, F
1903	Yale	15-1	W.H. Murphy	R.B. Hyatt, F
1904	Columbia	17-1	No coach	Harry Fisher, F
1905	Columbia	19-1	No coach	Harry Fisher, F
1906	Dartmouth	16-2	No coach	George Grebenstein, F
1907	Chicago	22-2	Joseph Raycroft	John Schommer, C
1908	Chicago	21-2	Joseph Raycroft	John Schommer, C
1909	Chicago	12-0	Joseph Raycroft	John Schommer, C
1910	Columbia	11-1	Harry Fisher	Ted Kiendl, F
1911	St. John's-NY	14-0	Claude Allen	John Keenan, F/C
1912	Wisconsin	15-0	Doc Meanwell	Otto Stangel, F
1913	Navy	9-0	Louis Wenzell	Laurence Wild, F
1914	Wisconsin	15-0	Doc Meanwell	Gene Van Gent, C
1915	Illinois	16-0	Ralph Jones	Ray Woods, G
1916	Wisconsin	20-1	Doc Meanwell	George Levis, F
1917	Washington St	25-1	Doc Bohler	Roy Bohler, G
1918	Syracuse	16-1	Edmund Dollard	Joe Schwarzer, G
1919	Minnesota	13-0	Louis Cooke	Arnold Oss, F
1920	Penn	22-1	Lon Jourdet	George Sweeney, F
1921	Penn	21-2	Edward McNichol	Danny McNichol, G
1922	Kansas	16-2	Phog Allen	Paul Endacott, G
1923	Kansas	17-1	Phog Allen	Paul Endacott, G
1924	North Carolina	25-0	Bo Shepard	Jack Cobb, F
1925	Princeton	21-2	Al Wittmer	Art Loeb, G
1926	Syracuse	19-1	Lew Andreas	Vic Hanson, F
1927	Notre Dame	19-1	George Keogan	John Nyikos, C
1928	Pittsburgh	21-0	Doc Carlson	Chuck Hyatt, F
1929	Montana St.	36-2	Schubert Dyche	John (Cat) Thompson, F
1930	Pittsburgh	23-2	Doc Carlson	Chuck Hyatt, F
1931	Northwestern	16-1	Dutch Lonborg	Joe Reiff, C
1932	Purdue	17-1	Piggy Lambert	John Wooden, G
1933	Kentucky	20-3	Adolph Rupp	Forest Sale, F
1934	Wyoming	26-3	Willard Witte	Les Witte, G
1935	NYU	19-1	Howard Cann	Sid Gross, F
1936	Notre Dame	22-2-1	George Keogan	John Moir, F
1937	Stanford	25-2	John Bunn	Hank Luisetti, F

Year		Record	Winner	Head Coach	Outstanding Player
1938	Temple	23-2	NIT	James Usilton	Meyer Bloom, G
1939	Oregon	29-5	NCAA	Howard Hobson	Slim Wintermute, C
	& LIU-Brooklyn (Helms)	24-0	NIT	Clair Bee	Irv Torgoff, F
1940	Indiana	20-3	NCAA	Branch McCracken	Marv Huffman, G
	& USC (Helms)	20-3	*	Sam Barry	Ralph Vaughn, F
1941	Wisconsin	20-3	NCAA	Bud Foster	Gene Englund, F
1942	Stanford	27-4	NCAA	Everett Dean	Jim Pollard, F
1943	Wyoming	31-2	NCAA	Everett Shelton	Kenny Sailors, G
1944	Utah	21-4	NCAA	Vadal Peterson	Arnie Ferrin, F
	& Army (Helms)	15-0	**	Ed Kelleher	Dale Hall, F

Year		Record	Winner	Head Coach	Outstanding Player
1945	Oklahoma A&M	27-4	NCAA	Hank Iba	Bob Kurland, C
1946	Oklahoma A&M	31-2	NCAA	Hank Iba	Bob Kurland, C
1947	Holy Cross	27-3	NCAA	Doggie Julian	George Kaftan, F
1948	Kentucky	36-3	NCAA	Adolph Rupp	Ralph Beard, G
1949	Kentucky	32-2	NCAA	Adolph Rupp	Alex Groza, C
1950	CCNY	24-5	NCAA & NIT	Nat Holman	Irwin Dambrot, G
1951	Kentucky	32-2	NCAA	Adolph Rupp	Bill Spivey, C
1952	Kansas	28-3	NCAA	Phog Allen	Clyde Lovellette, C
1953	Indiana	23-3	NCAA	Branch McCracken	Don Schlundt, C
1954	La Salle	26-4	NCAA	Ken Loeffler	Tom Gola, F
	& Kentucky (Helms)	25-0	***	Adolph Rupp	Cliff Hagan, G
1955	San Francisco	28-1	NCAA	Phil Woolpert	Bill Russell, C
1956	San Francisco	29-0	NCAA	Phil Woolpert	Bill Russell, C
1957	North Carolina	32-0	NCAA	Frank McGuire	Lennie Rosenbluth, F
1958	Kentucky	23-6	NCAA	Adolph Rupp	Vern Hatton, G
1959	California	25-4	NCAA	Pete Newell	Darrall Imhoff, C
1960	Ohio St	25-3	NCAA	Fred Taylor	Jerry Lucas, C
1961	Cincinnati	27-3	NCAA	Ed Jucker	Bob Wiesenhahn, F
1962	Cincinnati	29-2	NCAA	Ed Jucker	Paul Hogue, C
1963	Loyola-IL	29-2	NCAA	George Ireland	Jerry Harkness, F
1964	UCLA	30-0	NCAA	John Wooden	Walt Hazzard, G
1965	UCLA	28-2	NCAA	John Wooden	Gail Goodrich, G
1966	Texas Western	28-1	NCAA	Don Haskins	Bobby Joe Hill, G
1967	UCLA	30-0	NCAA	John Wooden	Lew Alcindor, C
1968	UCLA	29-1	NCAA	John Wooden	Lew Alcindor, C
1969	UCLA	29-1	NCAA	John Wooden	Lew Alcindor, C
1970	UCLA	28-2	NCAA	John Wooden	Sidney Wicks, F
1971	UCLA	29-1	NCAA	John Wooden	Sidney Wicks, F
1972	UCLA	30-0	NCAA	John Wooden	Bill Walton, C
1973	UCLA	30-0	NCAA	John Wooden	Bill Walton, C
1974	N.C. State	30-1	NCAA	Norm Sloan	David Thompson, F
1975	UCLA	28-3	NCAA	John Wooden	Dave Meyers, F
1976	Indiana	32-0	NCAA	Bob Knight	Scott May, F
1977	Marquette	25-7	NCAA	Al McGuire	Butch Lee, G
1978	Kentucky	30-2	NCAA	Joe B. Hall	Jack Givens, F
1979	Michigan St	26-6	NCAA	Jud Heathcote	Magic Johnson, G
1980	Louisville	33-3	NCAA	Denny Crum	Darrell Griffith, G
1981	Indiana	26-9	NCAA	Bob Knight	Isiah Thomas, G
1982	North Carolina	32-2	NCAA	Dean Smith	James Worthy, F
1983	N.C. State	26-10	NCAA	Jim Valvano	Sidney Lowe, G
1984	Georgetown	34-3	NCAA	John Thompson	Patrick Ewing, C
1985	Villanova	25-10	NCAA	Rollie Massimino	Ed Pinckney, C
1986	Louisville	32-7	NCAA	Denny Crum	Pervis Ellison, C
1987	Indiana	30-4	NCAA	Bob Knight	Steve Alford, G
1988	Kansas	27-11	NCAA	Larry Brown	Danny Manning, C
1989	Michigan	30-7	NCAA	Steve Fisher	Glen Rice, F
1990	UNLV	35-5	NCAA	Jerry Tarkanian	Larry Johnson, F
1991	Duke	32-7	NCAA	Mike Krzyzewski	Christian Laettner, F/C
1992	Duke	34-2	NCAA	Mike Krzyzewski	Christian Laettner, C
1993	North Carolina	34-4	NCAA	Dean Smith	Eric Montross, C
1994	Arkansas	31-3	NCAA	Nolan Richardson	Corliss Williamson, F
1995	UCLA	31-2	NCAA	Jim Harrick	Ed O'Bannon, F
1996	Kentucky	34-2	NCAA	Rick Pitino	Tony Delk, G
1997	Arizona	25-9	NCAA	Lute Olson	Miles Simon, G
1998	Kentucky	35-4	NCAA	Tubby Smith	Jeff Sheppard, G
1999	Connecticut	34-2	NCAA	Jim Calhoun	Richard Hamilton, G
2000	Michigan St	32-7	NCAA	Tom Izzo	Mateen Cleaves, G

*USC was beaten by Kansas in the West Regional of the NCAA tournament.
**Army did not lift its policy against postseason play until accepting a bid to the 1961 NIT.
***Unbeaten Kentucky turned down a bid to the 1954 NCAA tournament after the NCAA declared seniors Cliff Hagan, Frank Ramsey and Lou Tsioropoulos ineligible for postseason play.

The Red Cross Benefit Games, 1943-45

For three seasons during World War II, the NCAA and NIT champions met in a benefit game at Madison Square Garden in New York to raise money for the Red Cross. The NCAA champs won all three games.

Year	Winner	Score	Loser
1943	Wyoming (NCAA)	52-47	St. John's (NIT)
1944	Utah (NCAA)	43-36	St. John's (NIT)
1945	Oklahoma A&M (NCAA)	52-44	DePaul (NIT)

NCAA Final Four

The NCAA basketball tournament began in 1939 under the sponsorship of the National Association of Basketball Coaches, but was taken over by the NCAA in 1940. From 1939-51, the winners of the Eastern and Western Regionals played for the national championship, while regional runners-up shared third place. The concept of a Final Four originated in 1952 when four teams qualified for the first national semifinals. Consolation games to determine overall third place were held between regional finalists from 1946-51 and then national semifinalists in 1952-81. Consolation games were discontinued in 1982.

Multiple champions: UCLA (11); Kentucky (7); Indiana (5); Cincinnati, Duke, Kansas, Louisville, Michigan St., N.C. State, Oklahoma A&M (now Oklahoma St.) and San Francisco (2).

Year	Champion	Runner-up	Score	Final Four	——Third Place——	
1939	Oregon	Ohio St.	46-33	@ Evanston, IL	Oklahoma	Villanova
1940	Indiana	Kansas	60-42	@ Kansas City	Duquesne	USC
1941	Wisconsin	Washington St.	39-34	@ Kansas City	Arkansas	Pittsburgh
1942	Stanford	Dartmouth	53-38	@ Kansas City	Colorado	Kentucky
1943	Wyoming	Georgetown	46-34	@ New York	DePaul	Texas
1944	Utah	Dartmouth	42-40 (OT)	@ New York	Iowa St.	Ohio St.
1945	Oklahoma A&M	NYU	49-45	@ New York	Arkansas	Ohio St.

Year	Champion	Runner-up	Score	Final Two	Third Place	Fourth Place
1946	Oklahoma A&M	North Carolina	43-40	@ New York	Ohio St.	California
1947	Holy Cross	Oklahoma	58-47	@ New York	Texas	CCNY
1948	Kentucky	Baylor	58-42	@ New York	Holy Cross	Kansas St.
1949	Kentucky	Oklahoma A&M	46-36	@ Seattle	Illinois	Oregon St.
1950	CCNY	Bradley	71-68	@ New York	N.C. State	Baylor
1951	Kentucky	Kansas St.	68-58	@ Minneapolis	Illinois	Oklahoma A&M

Year	Champion	Runner-up	Score	Third Place	Fourth Place	Final Four
1952	Kansas	St. John's	80-63	Illinois	Santa Clara	@ Seattle
1953	Indiana	Kansas	69-68	Washington	LSU	@ Kansas City
1954	La Salle	Bradley	92-76	Penn St.	USC	@ Kansas City
1955	San Francisco	La Salle	77-63	Colorado	Iowa	@ Kansas City
1956	San Francisco	Iowa	83-71	Temple	SMU	@ Evanston, IL
1957	North Carolina	Kansas	54-53 (3OT)	San Francisco	Michigan St.	@ Kansas City
1958	Kentucky	Seattle	84-72	Temple	Kansas St.	@ Louisville
1959	California	West Virginia	71-70	Cincinnati	Louisville	@ Louisville
1960	Ohio St.	California	75-55	Cincinnati	NYU	@ San Francisco
1961	Cincinnati	Ohio St.	70-65 (OT)	St. Joseph's-PA	Utah	@ Kansas City
1962	Cincinnati	Ohio St.	71-59	Wake Forest	UCLA	@ Louisville
1963	Loyola-IL	Cincinnati	60-58 (OT)	Duke	Oregon St.	@ Louisville
1964	UCLA	Duke	98-83	Michigan	Kansas St.	@ Kansas City
1965	UCLA	Michigan	91-80	Princeton	Wichita St.	@ Portland, OR
1966	Texas Western	Kentucky	72-65	Duke	Utah	@ College Park, MD
1967	UCLA	Dayton	79-64	Houston	North Carolina	@ Louisville
1968	UCLA	North Carolina	78-55	Ohio St.	Houston	@ Los Angeles
1969	UCLA	Purdue	92-72	Drake	North Carolina	@ Louisville
1970	UCLA	Jacksonville	80-69	New Mexico St.	St. Bonaventure	@ College Park, MD
1971	UCLA	Villanova	68-62	Western Ky.	Kansas	@ Houston
1972	UCLA	Florida St.	81-76	North Carolina	Louisville	@ Los Angeles
1973	UCLA	Memphis St.	87-66	Indiana	Providence	@ St. Louis
1974	N.C. State	Marquette	76-64	UCLA	Kansas	@ Greensboro, NC
1975	UCLA	Kentucky	92-85	Louisville	Syracuse	@ San Diego
1976	Indiana	Michigan	86-68	UCLA	Rutgers	@ Philadelphia
1977	Marquette	North Carolina	67-59	UNLV	NC-Charlotte	@ Atlanta
1978	Kentucky	Duke	94-88	Arkansas	Notre Dame	@ St. Louis
1979	Michigan St.	Indiana St.	75-64	DePaul	Penn	@ Salt Lake City
1980	Louisville	UCLA	59-54	Purdue	Iowa	@ Indianapolis
1981	Indiana	North Carolina	63-50	Virginia	LSU	@ Philadelphia

Year	Champion	Runner-up	Score	——Third Place——		Final Four
1982	North Carolina	Georgetown	63-62	Houston	Louisville	@ New Orleans
1983	N.C. State	Houston	54-52	Georgia	Louisville	@ Albuquerque
1984	Georgetown	Houston	84-75	Kentucky	Virginia	@ Seattle
1985	Villanova	Georgetown	66-64	Memphis St.	St. John's	@ Lexington
1986	Louisville	Duke	72-69	Kansas	LSU	@ Dallas
1987	Indiana	Syracuse	74-73	Providence	UNLV	@ New Orleans
1988	Kansas	Oklahoma	83-79	Arizona	Duke	@ Kansas City
1989	Michigan	Seton Hall	80-79 (OT)	Duke	Illinois	@ Seattle
1990	UNLV	Duke	103-73	Arkansas	Georgia Tech	@ Denver
1991	Duke	Kansas	72-65	North Carolina	UNLV	@ Indianapolis
1992	Duke	Michigan	71-51	Cincinnati	Indiana	@ Minneapolis
1993	North Carolina	Michigan	77-71	Kansas	Kentucky	@ New Orleans
1994	Arkansas	Duke	76-72	Arizona	Florida	@ Charlotte
1995	UCLA	Arkansas	89-78	North Carolina	Oklahoma St.	@ Seattle
1996	Kentucky	Syracuse	76-67	UMass	Mississippi St.	@ E. Rutherford, NJ
1997	Arizona	Kentucky	84-79 (OT)	Minnesota	North Carolina	@ Indianapolis
1998	Kentucky	Utah	78-69	Stanford	North Carolina	@ San Antonio
1999	Connecticut	Duke	77-74	Michigan St.	Ohio St.	@ St. Petersburg, FL
2000	Michigan St.	Florida	89-76	Wisconsin	North Carolina	@ Indianapolis

Note: Six teams have had their standing in the Final Four vacated for using ineligible players: 1961–St. Joseph's-PA (3rd place); 1971–Villanova (Runner-up) and Western Kentucky (3rd place); 1980–UCLA (Runner-up); 1985–Memphis St. (3rd place); 1996–UMass (3rd place).

Most Outstanding Player

A Most Outstanding Player has been selected every year of the NCAA tournament. Winners who did not play for the tournament champion are listed in **bold** type. The 1939 and 1951 winners are unofficial and not recognized by the NCAA. Statistics listed are for Final Four games only.

Multiple winners: Lew Alcindor (3); Alex Groza, Bob Kurland, Jerry Lucas and Bill Walton (2).

Year		Gm	FGM	Pct	3PTM	3PTA	FTM	Pct	Reb	Ast	Blk	Stl	PPG
1939	**Jimmy Hull**, Ohio St.	2	15	—	—	—	10	.833	—	—	—	—	20.0
1940	Marv Huffman, Indiana	2	7	—	—	—	4	—	—	—	—	—	9.0
1941	John Kotz, Wisconsin	2	8	—	—	—	6	—	—	—	—	—	11.0
1942	Howie Dallmar, Stanford	2	8	—	—	—	4	.667	—	—	—	—	10.0
1943	Kenny Sailors, Wyoming	2	10	—	—	—	8	.727	—	—	—	—	14.0
1944	Arnie Ferrin, Utah	2	11	—	—	—	6	—	—	—	—	—	14.0
1945	Bob Kurland, Okla. A&M	2	16	—	—	—	5	—	—	—	—	—	18.5
1946	Bob Kurland, Okla. A&M	2	21	—	—	—	10	.667	—	—	—	—	26.0
1947	George Kaftan, Holy Cross	2	18	—	—	—	12	.706	—	—	—	—	24.0
1948	Alex Groza, Kentucky	2	16	—	—	—	5	—	—	—	—	—	18.5
1949	Alex Groza, Kentucky	2	19	—	—	—	14	—	—	—	—	—	26.0
1950	Irwin Dambrot, CCNY	2	12	.429	—	—	4	.500	—	—	—	—	14.0
1951	Bill Spivey, Kentucky	2	20	.400	—	—	10	.625	37	—	—	—	25.0
1952	Clyde Lovellette, Kansas	2	24	—	—	—	18	—	—	—	—	—	33.0
1953	**B.H. Born**, Kansas	2	17	—	—	—	17	—	—	—	—	—	25.5
1954	Tom Gola, La Salle	2	12	—	—	—	14	—	—	—	—	—	19.0
1955	Bill Russell, San Francisco	2	19	—	—	—	9	—	—	—	—	—	23.5
1956	**Hal Lear**, Temple	2	32	—	—	—	16	—	—	—	—	—	40.0
1957	**Wilt Chamberlain**, Kansas	2	18	.514	—	—	19	.704	25	—	—	—	32.5
1958	**Elgin Baylor**, Seattle	2	18	.340	—	—	12	.750	41	—	—	—	24.0
1959	**Jerry West**, West Virginia	2	22	.667	—	—	22	.688	25	—	—	—	33.0
1960	Jerry Lucas, Ohio St.	2	16	.667	—	—	3	1.000	23	—	—	—	17.5
1961	**Jerry Lucas**, Ohio St.	2	20	.714	—	—	16	.941	25	—	—	—	28.0
1962	Paul Hogue, Cincinnati	2	23	.639	—	—	12	.632	38	—	—	—	29.0
1963	**Art Heyman**, Duke	2	18	.409	—	—	15	.682	19	—	—	—	25.5
1964	Walt Hazzard, UCLA	2	11	.550	—	—	8	.667	10	—	—	—	15.0
1965	**Bill Bradley**, Princeton	2	34	.630	—	—	19	.950	24	—	—	—	43.5
1966	**Jerry Chambers**, Utah	2	25	.532	—	—	20	.833	35	—	—	—	35.0
1967	Lew Alcindor, UCLA	2	14	.609	—	—	11	.458	38	—	—	—	19.5
1968	Lew Alcindor, UCLA	2	22	.629	—	—	9	.900	34	—	—	—	26.5
1969	Lew Alcindor, UCLA	2	23	.676	—	—	16	.640	41	—	—	—	31.0
1970	Sidney Wicks, UCLA	2	15	.714	—	—	9	.600	34	—	—	—	19.5
1971	**Howard Porter**, Villanova	2	20	.488	—	—	7	.778	24	—	—	—	23.5
1972	Bill Walton, UCLA	2	20	.690	—	—	17	.739	41	—	—	—	28.5
1973	Bill Walton, UCLA	2	28	.824	—	—	2	.400	30	—	—	—	29.0
1974	David Thompson, N.C. State	2	19	.514	—	—	11	.786	17	—	—	—	24.5
1975	Richard Washington, UCLA	2	23	.548	—	—	8	.727	20	—	—	—	27.0
1976	Kent Benson, Indiana	2	17	.500	—	—	7	.636	18	—	—	—	20.5
1977	Butch Lee, Marquette	2	11	.344	—	—	8	1.000	6	2	1	1	15.0
1978	Jack Givens, Kentucky	2	28	.651	—	—	8	.667	17	4	1	3	32.0
1979	Magic Johnson, Michigan St.	2	17	.680	—	—	19	.864	17	3	0	2	26.5
1980	Darrell Griffith, Louisville	2	23	.622	—	—	11	.688	7	15	0	2	28.5
1981	Isiah Thomas, Indiana	2	14	.560	—	—	9	.818	4	9	3	4	18.5
1982	James Worthy, N. Carolina	2	20	.741	—	—	2	.286	8	9	0	4	21.0
1983	**Akeem Olajuwon**, Houston	2	16	.552	—	—	9	.643	40	3	2	5	20.5
1984	Patrick Ewing, Georgetown	2	8	.571	—	—	2	1.000	18	1	15	1	9.0
1985	Ed Pinckney, Villanova	2	8	.571	—	—	12	.750	15	6	3	0	14.0
1986	Pervis Ellison, Louisville	2	15	.600	—	—	6	.750	24	2	3	1	18.0
1987	Keith Smart, Indiana	2	14	.636	0	1	7	.778	7	7	0	2	17.5
1988	Danny Manning, Kansas	2	25	.556	0	1	6	.667	17	4	8	9	28.0
1989	Glen Rice, Michigan	2	24	.490	7	16	4	1.000	16	1	0	3	29.5
1990	Anderson Hunt, UNLV	2	19	.613	9	16	2	.500	4	9	1	1	24.5
1991	Christian Laettner, Duke	2	12	.545	1	1	21	.913	17	2	1	2	23.0
1992	Bobby Hurley, Duke	2	10	.417	7	12	8	.800	3	11	0	3	17.5
1993	Donald Williams, N. Carolina	2	15	.652	10	14	10	1.000	4	1	0	2	25.0
1994	Corliss Williamson, Arkansas	2	21	.500	0	0	10	.714	21	8	3	4	26.0
1995	Ed O'Bannon, UCLA	2	16	.457	3	8	10	.769	25	3	1	7	22.5
1996	Tony Delk, Kentucky	2	15	.417	8	16	6	.546	9	2	3	2	22.0
1997	Miles Simon, Arizona	2	17	.459	3	10	17	.773	8	6	0	1	27.0
1998	Jeff Sheppard, Kentucky	2	16	.552	4	10	7	.778	10	7	0	4	21.5
1999	Richard Hamilton, Connecticut	2	20	.513	3	7	8	.727	12	4	1	2	25.5
2000	Mateen Cleaves, Michigan St.	2	8	.444	3	4	10	.833	6	5	0	2	14.5

Final Four All-Decade Teams

To celebrate the 50th anniversary of the NCAA tournament in 1989, five All-Decade teams were selected by a blue ribbon panel of coaches and administrators. An All-Time Final Four team was also chosen. Selections were actually made prior to the 1988 tournament.

Selection panel: Vic Bubas, Denny Crum, Wayne Duke, Dave Gavitt, Joe B. Hall, Jud Heathcote, Hank Iba, Pete Newell, Dean Smith, John Thompson and John Wooden.

All-Time Team

	Years
Lew Alcindor, UCLA	1967-69
Larry Bird, Indiana St.	1979
Wilt Chamberlain, Kansas	1957
Magic Johnson, Mich. St.	1979
Michael Jordan, N. Carolina	1982

All-1950s

	Years
Elgin Baylor, Seattle	1958
Wilt Chamberlain, Kansas	1957
Tom Gola, La Salle	1954
K.C. Jones, San Francisco	1955
Clyde Lovellette, Kansas	1952
Oscar Robertson, Cinn.	1959-60
Guy Rodgers, Temple	1958
Lennie Rosenbluth, N. Carolina	1957
Bill Russell, San Francisco	1955-56
Jerry West, West Virginia	1959

All-1970s

	Years
Kent Benson, Indiana	1976
Larry Bird, Indiana St.	1979
Jack Givens, Kentucky	1978
Magic Johnson, Mich. St.	1979
Marques Johnson, UCLA	1975-76
Scott May, Indiana	1976
David Thompson, N.C. State	1974
Bill Walton, UCLA	1972-74
Sidney Wicks, UCLA	1969-71
Keith Wilkes, UCLA	1972-74

All-1940s

	Years
Ralph Beard, Kentucky	1948-49
Howie Dallmar, Stanford	1942
Dwight Eddleman, Illinois	1949
Arnie Ferrin, Utah	1944
Alex Groza, Kentucky	1948-49
George Kaftan, Holy Cross	1947
Bob Kurland, Okla. A&M	1945-46
Jim Pollard, Stanford	1942
Kenny Sailors, Wyoming	1943
Gerry Tucker, Oklahoma	1947

All-1960s

	Years
Lew Alcindor, UCLA	1967-69
Bill Bradley, Princeton	1965
Gail Goodrich, UCLA	1964-65
John Havlicek, Ohio St.	1961-62
Elvin Hayes, Houston	1967
Walt Hazzard, UCLA	1964
Jerry Lucas, Ohio St	1960-61
Jeff Mullins, Duke	1964
Cazzie Russell, Michigan	1965
Charlie Scott, N. Carolina	1968-69

All-1980s

	Years
Steve Alford, Indiana	1987
Johnny Dawkins, Duke	1986
Patrick Ewing, Georgetown	1982-84
Darrell Griffith, Louisville	1980
Michael Jordan, N. Carolina	1982
Rodney McCray, Louisville	1980
Akeem Olajuwon, Houston	1983-84
Ed Pinckney, Villanova	1985
Isiah Thomas, Indiana	1981
James Worthy, N. Carolina	1982

Note: Lew Alcindor later changed his name to Kareem Abdul-Jabbar; Keith Wilkes later changed his first name to Jamaal; and Akeem Olajuwon later changed the spelling of his first name to Hakeem.

Seeds at the Final Four

Year	Seeds (Total)	Teams
1979	1,2,2,9 (14)	Indiana St., **Michigan St.**, DePaul, Pennsylvania
1980	2,5,6,8 (21)	**Louisville**, Iowa, Purdue, UCLA
1981	1,1,2,3 (7)	Virginia, LSU, N. Carolina, **Indiana**
1982	1,1,3,6 (11)	**N. Carolina**, Georgetown, Louisville, Houston
1983	1,1,4,6 (12)	Houston, Louisville, Georgia, **N.C. State**
1984	1,1,2,7 (11)	Kentucky, **Georgetown**, Houston, Virginia
1985	1,1,2,8 (12)	St. John's, Georgetown, Memphis, **Villanova**
1986	1,1,2,11 (15)	Duke, Kansas, **Louisville**, LSU
1987	1,1,2,6 (10)	UNLV, **Indiana**, Syracuse, Providence
1988	1,1,2,6 (10)	Arizona, Oklahoma, Duke, **Kansas**
1989	1,2,3,3 (9)	Illinois, Duke, Seton Hall, **Michigan**
1990	1,3,4,4 (12)	**UNLV**, Duke, Ga. Tech, Arkansas
1991	1,1,2,3 (7)	UNLV, N. Carolina, **Duke**, Kansas
1992	1,2,4,6 (13)	**Duke**, Indiana, Cincinnati, Michigan
1993	1,1,1,2 (5)	**N. Carolina**, Kentucky, Michigan, Kansas
1994	1,2,2,3 (8)	**Arkansas**, Arizona, Duke, Florida
1995	1,2,2,4 (9)	**UCLA**, Arkansas, N. Carolina, Okla. St.
1996	1,1,4,5 (11)	**Kentucky**, UMass, Syracuse, Miss. St.
1997	1,1,1,4 (7)	Kentucky, N. Carolina, Minnesota, **Arizona**
1998	1,2,3,3 (9)	N. Carolina, **Kentucky**, Stanford, Utah
1999	1,1,1,4 (7)	**Connecticut**, Duke, Michigan St., Ohio St.
2000	1,5,8,8 (22)	**Michigan St.**, Florida, Wisconsin, N. Carolina

All-Time Seeds Records

All-time records of NCAA tournament seeds since tourney began seeding teams in 1979. Records are through the 2000 NCAA Tournament. Note that 1st refers to championships. 2nd refers to runners-up and FF refers to Final Four appearances not including 1st and 2nd place finishes.

Seed	W	L	Pct.	1st	2nd	FF
1	264	78	.772	11	9	23
2	192	83	.698	5	5	11
3	130	86	.602	2	4	4
4	124	87	.588	1	1	8
5	101	89	.532	0	1	2
6	123	86	.589	2	1	3
7	71	88	.447	0	0	1
8	70	87	.446	1	1	2
9	51	89	.364	0	0	1
10	59	88	.401	0	0	0
11	36	84	.300	0	0	1
12	31	84	.270	0	0	0
13	15	64	.190	0	0	0
14	15	64	.190	0	0	0
15	3	64	.045	0	0	0
16	0	64	.000	0	0	0

Collegiate Commissioners Association Tournament

The Collegiate Commissioners Association staged an eight-team tournament for teams that didn't make the NCAA tournament in 1974 and '75.

Most Valuable Players: 1974—Kent Benson, Indiana; 1975—Bob Elliot, Arizona.

Year	Winner	Score	Loser	Site
1974	Indiana	85-60	USC	St. Louis
1975	Drake	83-76	Arizona	Louisville

NCAA Tournament Appearances

App	W-L	F4	Championships	App	W-L	F4	Championships
42 Kentucky	87-37	13	7 (1948-49,51,58,78,96,98)	20 Illinois	24-21	4	None
36 UCLA	77-28	15	11 (1964-65,67-73,75,95)	19 Arizona	27-18	3	1 (1997)
34 N. Carolina	80-34	15	3 (1957,82,93)	19 Cincinnati	35-18	6	2 (1961-62)
29 Indiana	52-24	7	5 (1940,53,76,81,87)	19 Iowa	26-21	3	None
29 Kansas	59-29	10	2 (1952,88)	19 Oklahoma	23-19	3	None
29 Louisville	48-31	7	2 (1980,86)	19 Purdue	26-19	2	None
26 St. John's	27-28	2	None	18 Houston	26-23	5	None
26 Syracuse	39-27	3	None	18 BYU	11-21	0	None
25 Arkansas	39-25	6	1 (1994)	18 West Virginia	13-18	1	None
25 Villanova	37-25	3	1 (1985)	18 Texas	17-21	2	None
24 Duke	67-22	12	2 (1991-92)	18 Missouri	13-18	0	None
24 Notre Dame	25-28	1	None	18 Pennsylvania	13-20	1	None
24 Temple	28-24	2	None	17 N.C. State	27-16	3	2 (1974,83)
22 Connecticut	27-22	1	1 (1999)	17 Maryland	22-17	0	None
22 Kansas St.	27-26	4	None	17 Oklahoma St.	30-16	5	2 (1945-46)
22 Utah	32-25	4	1 (1944)	16 San Francisco	21-14	3	2 (1955-56)
21 Georgetown	36-20	4	1 (1984)	16 LSU	19-19	3	None
21 Marquette	28-22	2	1 (1977)	16 Memphis	18-16	2	None
21 DePaul	20-24	2	None	16 Oregon St.	12-19	2	None
21 Princeton	13-25	1	None	16 Western Ky.	15-17	1	None
20 Michigan	41-19	6	1 (1989)	16 Miami-OH	6-18	0	None
20 Ohio St.	36-19	9	1 (1960)	16 New Mexico St.	10-18	1	None

Note: Although all NCAA tournament appearances are included above, the NCAA has officially voided the records of Villanova (4-1) and Western Ky. (4-1) in 1971, UCLA (5-1) in 1980, Oregon St. (2-3) from 1980-82, Memphis (9-5) from 1982-86, DePaul (6-4) from 1986-89, N.C. State (0-2) from 1987-88 and Kentucky (2-1) in 1988.

All-Time NCAA Division I Tournament Leaders

Through 2000; minimum of six games; **Last** column indicates final year played.

CAREER

Scoring

Points

		Yrs	Last	Gm	Pts
1	Christian Laettner, Duke	4	1992	23	407
2	Elvin Hayes, Houston	3	1968	13	358
3	Danny Manning, Kansas	4	1988	16	328
4	Oscar Robertson, Cincinnati	3	1960	10	324
5	Glen Rice, Michigan	4	1989	13	308
6	Lew Alcindor, UCLA	3	1969	12	304
7	Bill Bradley, Princeton	3	1965	9	303
	Corliss Williamson, Arkansas	3	1995	15	303
9	Austin Carr, Notre Dame	3	1971	7	289
10	Juwan Howard, Michigan	3	1994	16	280

Average

		Yrs	Last	Pts	Avg
1	Austin Carr, Notre Dame	3	1971	289	41.3
2	Bill Bradley, Princeton	3	1965	303	33.7
3	Oscar Robertson, Cincinnati	3	1960	324	32.4
4	Jerry West, West Virginia	3	1960	275	30.6
5	Bob Pettit, LSU	2	1954	183	30.5
6	Dan Issel, Kentucky	3	1970	176	29.3
	Jim McDaniels, Western Ky	2	1971	176	29.3
8	Dwight Lamar, SW Louisiana	2	1973	175	29.2
9	Bo Kimble, Loyola-CA	3	1990	204	29.1
10	David Robinson, Navy	3	1987	200	28.6

Rebounds

Total

		Yrs	Last	Gm	No
1	Elvin Hayes, Houston	3	1968	13	222
2	Lew Alcindor, UCLA	3	1969	12	201
3	Jerry Lucas, Ohio St.	3	1962	12	197
4	Bill Walton, UCLA	3	1974	12	176
5	Christian Laettner, Duke	4	1992	23	169
6	Tim Duncan, Wake Forest	4	1997	11	165
7	Paul Hogue, Cincinnati	3	1962	12	160
8	Sam Lacey, New Mexico St.	3	1970	11	157
9	Derrick Coleman, Syracuse	4	1990	14	155
10	Akeem Olajuwon, Houston	3	1984	15	153

Average

		Yrs	Last	Reb	Avg
1	Johnny Green, Michigan St.	2	1959	118	19.7
2	Artis Gilmore, Jacksonville	2	1971	115	19.2
3	Paul Silas, Creighton	3	1964	111	18.5
4	Len Chappell, Wake Forest	2	1962	137	17.1
5	Elvin Hayes, Houston	3	1968	222	17.1
6	Lew Alcindor, UCLA	3	1969	201	16.8
7	Jerry Lucas, Ohio St.	3	1962	197	16.4
8	Tim Duncan, Wake Forest	4	1997	165	15.0
9	Bill Walton, UCLA	3	1974	176	14.7
10	Sam Lacey, New Mexico St.	3	1970	157	14.3

3-Pt Field Goals

Total

		Yrs	Last	Gm	No
1	Bobby Hurley, Duke	4	1993	20	42
2	Tony Delk, Kentucky	4	1996	17	40
3	Jeff Fryer, Loyola-CA	3	1990	7	38
	Donald Williams, North Carolina	4	1995	15	38
5	Scotty Thurman, Arkansas	3	1995	15	36

Assists

Total

		Yrs	Last	Gm	No
1	Bobby Hurley, Duke	4	1993	20	145
2	Sherman Douglas, Syracuse	4	1989	14	106
3	Greg Anthony, UNLV	3	1991	15	100
4	Mark Wade, UNLV	2	1987	8	93
	Rumeal Robinson, Michigan	3	1990	11	93
	Jacque Vaughn, Kansas	4	1997	13	93
	Anthony Epps, Kentucky	4	1997	18	93

SINGLE TOURNAMENT

Scoring

Points

		Year	Gm	Pts
1	Glen Rice, Michigan	1989	6	184
2	Bill Bradley, Princeton	1965	5	177
3	Elvin Hayes, Houston	1968	5	167
4	Danny Manning, Kansas	1988	6	163
5	Hal Lear, Temple	1956	5	160
	Jerry West, West Virginia	1959	5	160

Average

		Year	Gm	Pts	Avg
1	Austin Carr, Notre Dame	1970	3	158	52.7
2	Austin Carr, Notre Dame	1971	3	125	41.7
3	Jerry Chambers, Utah	1966	4	143	35.8
	Bo Kimble, Loyola-CA	1990	4	143	35.8
5	Bill Bradley, Princeton	1965	5	177	35.4
6	Clyde Lovellette, Kansas	1952	4	141	35.3

Rebounds

	Total	Year	Gm	No	Avg
1	Elvin Hayes, Houston	1968	5	97	19.4
2	Artis Gilmore, Jacksonville	1970	5	93	18.6
3	Elgin Baylor, Seattle	1958	5	91	18.2
4	Sam Lacey, New Mexico St.	1970	5	90	18.0
5	Clarence Glover, Western Ky.	1971	5	89	17.8

Assists

	Total	Year	Gm	No	Avg
1	Mark Wade, UNLV	1987	5	61	12.2
2	Rumeal Robinson, Michigan	1989	6	56	9.3
3	Sherman Douglas, Syracuse	1987	6	49	8.2
4	Bobby Hurley, Duke	1992	6	47	7.8
5	Lazarus Sims, Syracuse	1996	6	46	7.7

SINGLE GAME

Scoring

	Points	Year	Pts
1	Austin Carr, Notre Dame vs Ohio Univ	1970	61
2	Bill Bradley, Princeton vs Wichita St.	1965	58
3	Oscar Robertson, Cincinnati vs Arkansas	1958	56
4	Austin Carr, Notre Dame vs Kentucky	1970	52
	Austin Carr, Notre Dame vs TCU	1971	52
6	David Robinson, Navy vs Michigan	1987	50
7	Elvin Hayes, Houston vs Loyola-IL	1968	49
8	Hal Lear, Temple vs SMU	1956	48
9	Austin Carr, Notre Dame vs Houston	1971	47
10	Dave Corzine, DePaul vs Louisville	1978	46
11	Bob Houbregs, Washington vs Seattle	1953	45
	Austin Carr, Notre Dame vs Iowa	1970	45
	Bo Kimble, Loyola-CA vs New Mexico St.	1990	45
14	Seven players tied with 44 each.		

Rebounds

	Total	Year	No
1	Fred Cohen, Temple vs UConn	1956	34
2	Nate Thurmond, Bowl. Green vs Miss. St.	1963	31
3	Jerry Lucas, Ohio St. vs Kentucky	1961	30
4	Toby Kimball, UConn vs St. Joseph's-PA	1965	29
5	Elvin Hayes, Houston vs Pacific	1966	28

Assists

	Total	Year	No
1	Mark Wade, UNLV vs Indiana	1987	18
2	Sam Crawford, N. Mexico St. vs Nebraska	1993	16
3	Kenny Patterson, DePaul vs Syracuse	1985	15
	Keith Smart, Indiana vs Auburn	1987	15
5	Six players tied with 14 each.		

SINGLE FINAL FOUR GAME

Letters in the **Year** column indicate the following: C for Consolation Game, F for Final and S for Semifinal.

Scoring

	Points	Year	Pts
1	Bill Bradley, Princeton vs Wichita St	1965-C	58
2	Hal Lear, Temple vs SMU	1956-C	48
3	Bill Walton, UCLA vs Memphis St	1973-F	44
4	Bob Houbregs, Washington vs LSU	1953-C	42
	Jack Egan, St. Joseph's-PA vs Utah	1961-C	42*
	Gail Goodrich, UCLA vs Michigan	1965-C	42
7	Jack Givens, Kentucky vs Duke	1978-F	41
8	Oscar Robertson, Cincinnati vs L'ville	1959-C	39
	Al Wood, N. Carolina vs Virginia	1981-S	39
10	Jerry West, West Va. vs Louisville	1959-S	38
	Jerry Chambers, Utah vs Texas Western	1966-S	38
	Freddie Banks, UNLV vs Indiana	1987-S	38

*Four overtimes.

Rebounds

	Total	Year	No
1	Bill Russell, San Francisco vs Iowa	1956-F	27
2	Elvin Hayes, Houston vs UCLA	1967-S	24
3	Bill Russell, San Francisco vs SMU	1956-S	23
4	Four players tied with 22 each.		

Assists

	Total	Year	No
1	Mark Wade, UNLV vs Indiana	1987-S	18
2	Rumeal Robinson, Michigan vs Illinois	1989-S	12
	Edgar Padilla, UMass vs. Ky.	1996-S	12
4	Michael Jackson, G'town vs St. John's	1985-S	11
	Milt Wagner, Louisville vs LSU	1986-S	11
	Rumeal Robinson, Mich. vs Seton Hall	1989-F	11*

*Overtime.

Teams in Both NCAA and NIT

Fourteen teams played in both the NCAA and NIT tournaments from 1940-52. Colorado (1940), Utah (1944), Kentucky (1949) and BYU (1951) won one of the titles, while CCNY won two in 1950, beating Bradley in both championship games.

Year		NIT	NCAA
1940	Colorado	**Won Final**	Lost 1st Rd
	Duquesne	Lost Final	Lost 2nd Rd
1944	Utah	Lost 1st Rd	**Won Final**
1949	Kentucky	Lost 2nd Rd	**Won Final**
1950	CCNY	**Won Final**	**Won Final**
	Bradley	Lost Final	Lost Final
1951	BYU	**Won Final**	Lost 2nd Rd
	St. John's	Lost 3rd Rd	Lost 2nd Rd
	N.C. State	Lost 2nd Rd	Lost 2nd Rd
	Arizona	Lost 2nd Rd	Lost 1st Rd
1952	St. John's	Lost 2nd Rd	Lost Final
	Dayton	Lost 1st Rd	Lost Final
	Duquesne	Lost 2nd Rd	Lost 2nd Rd
	Saint Louis	Lost 2nd Rd	Lost 2nd Rd

Most Popular Final Four Sites

The NCAA has staged its Men's Division I championship–the Final Two (1939-51) and Final Four (since 1952)–at 31 different arenas and indoor stadiums in 27 different cities. The following facilities have all hosted the event more than once. Note that the HHH Metrodome in Minneapolis, which hosted the Final Four in 1992, was set to host the event again in 2001.

No	Arena	Years
9	Municipal Auditorium (KC)	1940-42, 53-55, 57, 61, 64
7	Madison Sq. Garden (NYC)	1943-48, 50
6	Freedom Hall (Louisville)	1958-59, 62-63, 67, 69
3	Kingdome (Seattle)	1984, 89, 95
	RCA Dome (Indianapolis)	1991, 97, 2000
	Superdome (New Orleans)	1982, 87, 93
2	Cole Field House (College Park, Md.)	1966, 70
	Edmundson Pavilion (Seattle)	1949, 52
	LA Sports Arena	1968, 72
	St. Louis Arena	1973, 78
	Spectrum (Philadelphia)	1976, 81

NIT Championship

The National Invitation Tournament began under the sponsorship of the Metropolitan New York Basketball Writers Association in 1938. The NIT is now administered by the Metropolitan Intercollegiate Basketball Association. All championship games have been played at Madison Square Garden.

Multiple winners: St. John's (5); Bradley (4); BYU, Dayton, Kentucky, LIU-Brooklyn, Michigan, Minnesota, Providence, Temple, Virginia and Virginia Tech (2).

Year	Winner	Score	Loser	Year	Winner	Score	Loser
1938	Temple	60-36	Colorado	1970	Marquette	65-53	St. John's
1939	LIU-Brooklyn	44-32	Loyola-IL	1971	North Carolina	84-66	Georgia Tech
1940	Colorado	51-40	Duquesne	1972	Maryland	100-69	Niagara
1941	LIU-Brooklyn	56-42	Ohio Univ.	1973	Virginia Tech	92-91 (OT)	Notre Dame
1942	West Virginia	47-45	Western Ky.	1974	Purdue	97-81	Utah
1943	St. John's	48-27	Toledo	1975	Princeton	80-69	Providence
1944	St. John's	47-39	DePaul	1976	Kentucky	71-67	NC-Charlotte
1945	DePaul	71-54	Bowling Green	1977	St. Bonaventure	94-91	Houston
1946	Kentucky	46-45	Rhode Island	1978	Texas	101-93	N.C. State
1947	Utah	49-45	Kentucky	1979	Indiana	53-52	Purdue
1948	Saint Louis	65-52	NYU	1980	Virginia	58-55	Minnesota
1949	San Francisco	48-47	Loyola-IL	1981	Tulsa	86-84 (OT)	Syracuse
1950	CCNY	69-61	Bradley	1982	Bradley	67-58	Purdue
1951	BYU	62-43	Dayton	1983	Fresno St.	69-60	DePaul
1952	La Salle	75-64	Dayton	1984	Michigan	83-63	Notre Dame
1953	Seton Hall	58-46	St. John's	1985	UCLA	65-62	Indiana
1954	Holy Cross	71-62	Duquesne	1986	Ohio St.	73-63	Wyoming
1955	Duquesne	70-58	Dayton	1987	Southern Miss.	84-80	La Salle
1956	Louisville	93-80	Dayton	1988	Connecticut	72-67	Ohio St.
1957	Bradley	84-83	Memphis St.	1989	St. John's	73-65	Saint Louis
1958	Xavier-OH	78-74 (OT)	Dayton	1990	Vanderbilt	74-72	Saint Louis
1959	St. John's	76-71 (OT)	Bradley	1991	Stanford	78-72	Oklahoma
1960	Bradley	88-72	Providence	1992	Virginia	81-76 (OT)	Notre Dame
1961	Providence	62-59	Saint Louis	1993	Minnesota	62-61	Georgetown
1962	Dayton	73-67	St. John's	1994	Villanova	80-73	Vanderbilt
1963	Providence	81-66	Canisius	1995	Virginia Tech	65-64 (OT)	Marquette
1964	Bradley	86-54	New Mexico	1996	Nebraska	60-56	St. Joseph's
1965	St. John's	55-51	Villanova	1997	Michigan	82-72	Florida St.
1966	BYU	97-84	NYU	1998	Minnesota	79-72	Penn St.
1967	Southern Illinois	71-56	Marquette	1999	California	61-60	Clemson
1968	Dayton	61-48	Kansas	2000	Wake Forest	71-61	Notre Dame
1969	Temple	89-76	Boston Coll.				

Most Valuable Player

A Most Valuable Player has been selected every year of the NIT tournament. Winners who did not play for the tournament champion are listed in **bold** type.

Multiple winners: None. However, Tom Gola of La Salle is the only player to be named MVP in the NIT (1952) and Most Outstanding Player of the NCAA tournament (1954).

Year
1938 Don Shields, Temple
1939 **Bill Lloyd**, St. John's
1940 Bob Doll, Colorado
1941 **Frank Baumholtz**, Ohio U.
1942 Rudy Baric, West Virginia
1943 Harry Boykoff, St. John's
1944 Bill Kotsores, St. John's
1945 George Mikan, DePaul
1946 **Ernie Calverley**, Rhode Island
1947 Vern Gardner, Utah
1948 Ed Macauley, Saint Louis
1949 Don Lofgan, San Francisco
1950 Ed Warner, CCNY
1951 Roland Minson, BYU
1952 Tom Gola, La Salle
    & Norm Grekin, La Salle
1953 Walter Dukes, Seton Hall
1954 Togo Palazzi, Holy Cross
1955 **Maurice Stokes**, St. Francis-PA
1956 Charlie Tyra, Louisville
1957 **Win Wilfong**, Memphis St.
1958 Hank Stein, Xavier-OH
1959 Tony Jackson, St. John's
1960 **Lenny Wilkens**, Providence
1961 Vinny Ernst, Providence
1962 Bill Chmielewski, Dayton

Year
1963 Ray Flynn, Providence
1964 Lavern Tart, Bradley
1965 Ken McIntyre, St. John's
1966 **Bill Melchionni**, Villanova
1967 Walt Frazier, So. Illinois
1968 Don May, Dayton
1969 **Terry Driscoll,** Boston College
1970 Dean Meminger, Marquette
1971 Bill Chamberlain, N. Carolina
1972 Tom McMillen, Maryland
1973 **John Shumate,** Notre Dame
1974 **Mike Sojourner,** Utah
1975 **Ron Lee,** Oregon
1976 **Cedric Maxwell**, NC-Charlotte
1977 Greg Sanders, St. Bonaventure
1978 Ron Baxter, Texas
    & Jim Krivacs, Texas
1979 Clarence Carter, Indiana
    & Ray Tolbert, Indiana
1980 Ralph Sampson, Virginia
1981 Greg Stewart, Tulsa
1982 Mitchell Anderson, Bradley
1983 Ron Anderson, Fresno St.
1984 Tim McCormick, Michigan
1985 Reggie Miller, UCLA
1986 Brad Sellers, Ohio St.

Year
1987 Randolph Keys, So. Miss.
1988 Phil Gamble, Connecticut
1989 Jayson Williams, St. John's
1990 Scott Draud, Vanderbilt
1991 Adam Keefe, Stanford
1992 Bryant Stith, Virginia
1993 Voshon Lenard, Minnesota
1994 **Doremus Bennerman,** Siena
1995 Shawn Smith, Va. Tech
1996 Erick Strickland, Nebraska
1997 Robert Traylor, Michigan
1998 Kevin Clark, Minnesota
1999 Sean Lampley, California
2000 Robert O'Kelley, Wake Forest

All-Time NIT Team

As selected by a media panel
(Mar. 15, 1997).

Walt Frazier, S. Illinois
George Mikan, DePaul
Tom Gola, La Salle
Maurice Stokes, St. Francis-PA
Ralph Beard, Kentucky

All-Time Winningest Division I Teams

Top 25 Winning Percentage

Division I schools with best winning percentages through 1999-2000 season (including tournament games). Years in Division I only; minimum 20 years. NCAA tournament columns indicate years in tournament, record and number of championships.

		First Year	Yrs	Games	Won	Lost	Tied	Pct	NCAA Tourney Yrs	W-L	Titles
1	Kentucky	1903	97	2320	1771	548	1	.764	41	87-37	7
2	North Carolina	1911	90	2378	1755	623	0	.738	34	80-34	3
3	UNLV	1959	42	1197	869	328	0	.726	14	30-13	1
4	Kansas	1899	102	2445	1711	734	0	.700	29	59-29	2
5	UCLA	1920	81	2099	1465	634	0	.698	36	81-29	11
6	St. John's	1908	93	2330	1607	723	0	.690	26	27-28	0
7	Syracuse	1901	99	2233	1523	710	0	.682	26	39-27	0
8	Duke	1906	95	2374	1614	760	0	.680	24	67-22	2
9	Western Kentucky	1915	81	2092	1389	703	0	.664	16	15-17	0
10	Arkansas	1924	77	2031	1334	697	0	.657	25	39-25	1
11	Utah	1909	92	2171	1425	746	0	.656	22	32-25	1
12	Indiana	1901	100	2260	1473	787	0	.652	29	52-24	5
13	Temple	1895	104	2376	1547	829	0	.651	23	27-23	0
14	Louisville	1912	86	2114	1375	739	0	.650	28	48-31	2
15	Purdue	1897	102	2209	1428	781	0	.646	19	26-19	0
16	DePaul	1924	77	1897	1226	671	0	.646	21	20-24	0
17	Weber St.	1963	38	1075	694	381	0	.646	12	6-13	0
18	Notre Dame	1898	95	2270	1463	806	1	.644	24	25-28	0
19	Illinois	1906	94	2154	1380	774	0	.641	20	24-21	0
20	Arizona	1906	95	2125	1358	761	0	.639	19	27-18	1
21	Penn	1897	100	2344	1496	846	2	.639	18	13-20	0
22	Villanova	1921	80	2054	1308	746	0	.637	25	37-25	1
23	Murray St.	1926	75	1925	1219	706	0	.633	10	1-10	0
24	New Orleans	1970	31	883	555	328	0	.629	4	1-4	0
25	N.C. State	1913	88	2171	1365	806	0	.629	17	27-16	1

Top 35 All-Time Victories

Division I schools with most victories through 1999-2000 (including postseason tournaments). Minimum 20 years in Division I.

		Wins			Wins			Wins			Wins
1	Kentucky	1771	10	Indiana	1473	19	Louisville	1375	28	Washington St.	1326
2	North Carolina	1755	11	UCLA	1465	20	West Virginia	1373	29	Ohio St	1314
3	Kansas	1711	12	Notre Dame	1463	21	Bradley	1369	30	Montana St.	1309
4	Duke	1614	13	Purdue	1428	22	Cincinnati	1367	31	Villanova	1308
5	St. John's	1607	14	Princeton	1426	23	N.C. State	1365	32	Iowa	1298
6	Temple	1547	15	Utah	1425	24	Arizona	1358	33	Alabama	1296
7	Syracuse	1523	16	Washington	1412	25	Fordham	1346	34	USC	1289
8	Penn	1496	17	Western Ky.	1389	26	Texas	1339	35	St. Joseph's-PA	1284
9	Oregon St.	1480	18	Illinois	1380	27	Arkansas	1334			

Top 28 Single-Season Victories

Division I schools with most victories in a season through 1999-2000 (including postseason tournaments). NCAA champions in **bold** type.

		Year	Record			Year	Record			Year	Record
1	UNLV	1987	37-2		Kentucky	1947	34-3		Duke	1998	32-4
	Duke	1999	37-2		**Georgetown**	1984	34-3		Louisville	1983	32-4
	Duke	1986	37-3		Arkansas	1991	34-4		Kentucky	1986	32-4
4	**Kentucky**	1948	36-3		**N. Carolina**	1993	34-4		N. Carolina	1987	32-4
5	Massachusetts*	1996	35-2		N. Carolina	1998	34-4		Temple	1987	32-4
	Georgetown	1985	35-3	24	Indiana St	1979	33-1		Bradley	1950	32-5
	Arizona	1988	35-3		**Louisville**	1980	33-3		Connecticut	1998	32-5
	Kansas	1986	35-4		Michigan St.	1999	33-5		Tulsa	2000	32-5
	Kansas	1998	35-4		UNLV	1986	33-5		Iowa St.	2000	32-5
	Kentucky	1998	35-4	28	**N. Carolina**	1957	32-0		Marshall	1947	32-5
	Oklahoma	1988	35-4		**Indiana**	1976	32-0		Houston	1984	32-5
	UNLV	1990	35-5		**Kentucky**	1949	32-2		Bradley	1951	32-6
	Kentucky	1997	35-5		**Kentucky**	1951	32-2		**Louisville**	1986	32-7
14	UNLV	1991	34-1		**N. Carolina**	1982	32-2		**Duke**	1991	32-7
	Connecticut	1999	34-2		Temple	1988	32-2		Arkansas	1995	32-7
	Duke	1992	34-2		Arkansas	1978	32-3		**Michigan St.**	2000	32-7
	Kentucky	1996	34-2		Bradley	1986	32-3				
	Kansas	1997	34-2		Connecticut*	1996	32-3				

*NCAA later stripped UMass of its four 1996 tournament victories after learning that center Marcus Camby accepted gifts from an agent. UConn was stripped of its two 1996 tournament victories because two players illegally accepted plane tickets.

Associated Press Final Polls

Taken before NCAA, NIT and Collegiate Commissioner's Association (1974-75) tournaments.

The Associated Press introduced its weekly college basketball poll of sportswriters (later, sportswriters and broadcasters) during the 1948-49 season.

Since the NCAA Division I tournament has determined the national champion since 1939, the final AP poll ranks the nation's best teams through the regular season and conference tournaments.

Except for four seasons (see AP Post-Tournament Final Polls), the final AP poll has been released prior to the NCAA and NIT tournaments and has gone from a Top 10 (1949 and 1963-67) to a Top 20 (1950-62 and 1968-89) to a Top 25 (since 1990).

Tournament champions are in **bold** type.

1949

		Before Tourns	Head Coach	Final Record
1	**Kentucky**	29-1	Adolph Rupp	32-2
2	Oklahoma A&M	21-4	Hank Iba	23-5
3	Saint Louis	22-3	Eddie Hickey	22-4
4	Illinois	19-3	Harry Combes	21-4
5	Western Ky.	25-3	Ed Diddle	25-4
6	Minnesota	18-3	Ozzie Cowles	same
7	Bradley	25-6	Forddy Anderson	27-8
8	**San Francisco**	21-5	Pete Newell	25-5
9	Tulane	24-4	Cliff Wells	same
10	Bowling Green	21-6	Harold Anderson	24-7

NCAA Final Four (at Edmundson Pavilion, Seattle): **Third Place**—Illinois 57, Oregon St. 53. **Championship**—Kentucky 46, Oklahoma A&M 36.

NIT Final Four (at Madison Square Garden): **Semifinals**—San Francisco 49, Bowling Green 39; Loyola-IL 55, Bradley 50. **Third Place**—Bowling Green 82, Bradley 77. **Championship**—San Francisco 48, Loyola-IL 47.

1950

		Before Tourns	Head Coach	Final Record
1	Bradley	28-3	Forddy Anderson	32-5
2	Ohio St.	21-3	Tippy Dye	22-4
3	Kentucky	25-4	Adolph Rupp	25-5
4	Holy Cross	27-2	Buster Sheary	27-4
5	N.C. State	25-5	Everett Case	27-6
6	Duquesne	22-5	Dudey Moore	23-6
7	UCLA	24-5	John Wooden	24-7
8	Western Ky.	24-5	Ed Diddle	25-6
9	St. John's	23-4	Frank McGuire	24-5
10	La Salle	20-3	Ken Loeffler	21-4
11	Villanova	25-4	Al Severance	same
12	San Francisco	19-6	Pete Newell	19-7
13	LIU-Brooklyn	20-4	Clair Bee	20-5
14	Kansas St.	17-7	Jack Gardner	same
15	Arizona	26-4	Fred Enke	26-5
16	Wisconsin	17-5	Bud Foster	same
17	San Jose St.	21-7	Walter McPherson	same
18	Washington St.	19-13	Jack Friel	same
19	Kansas	14-11	Phog Allen	same
20	Indiana	17-5	Branch McCracken	same

Note: Unranked **CCNY**, coached by Nat Holman, won both the NCAAs and NIT. The Beavers entered the postseason at 17-5 and had a final record of 24-5.

NCAA Final Four (at Madison Square Garden): **Third Place**—N. Carolina St. 53, Baylor 41. **Championship**—CCNY 71, Bradley 68.

NIT Final Four (at Madison Square Garden): **Semifinals**—Bradley 83, St. John's 72; CCNY 62, Duquesne 52. **Third Place**—St. John's 69, Duquesne 67 (OT). **Championship**—CCNY 69, Bradley 61.

1951

		Before Tourns	Head Coach	Final Record
1	**Kentucky**	28-2	Adolph Rupp	32-2
2	Oklahoma A&M	27-4	Hank Iba	29-6
3	Columbia	22-0	Lou Rossini	22-1
4	Kansas St.	22-3	Jack Gardner	25-4
5	Illinois	19-4	Harry Combes	22-5
6	Bradley	32-6	Forddy Anderson	same
7	Indiana	19-3	Branch McCracken	same
8	N.C. State	29-4	Everett Case	30-7
9	St. John's	22-3	Frank McGuire	26-5
10	Saint Louis	21-7	Eddie Hickey	22-8
11	**BYU**	22-8	Stan Watts	26-10
12	Arizona	24-4	Fred Enke	24-6
13	Dayton	24-4	Tom Blackburn	27-5
14	Toledo	23-8	Jerry Bush	same
15	Washington	22-5	Tippy Dye	24-6
16	Murray St.	21-6	Harlan Hodges	same
17	Cincinnati	18-3	John Wiethe	18-4
18	Siena	19-8	Dan Cunha	same
19	USC	21-6	Forrest Twogood	same
20	Villanova	25-6	Al Severance	25-7

NCAA Final Four (at Williams Arena, Minneapolis): **Third Place**—Illinois 61, Oklahoma St. 46. **Championship**—Kentucky 68, Kansas St. 58.

NIT Final Four (at Madison Sq. Garden): **Semifinals**—Dayton 69, St. John's 62 (OT); BYU 69, Seton Hall 59. **Third Place**—St. John's 70, Seton Hall 68 (2 OT). **Championship**—BYU 62, Dayton 43.

1952

		Before Tourns	Head Coach	Final Record
1	Kentucky	28-2	Adolph Rupp	29-3
2	Illinois	19-3	Harry Combes	22-4
3	Kansas St.	19-5	Jack Gardner	same
4	Duquesne	21-1	Dudey Moore	23-4
5	Saint Louis	22-6	Eddie Hickey	23-8
6	Washington	25-6	Tippy Dye	same
7	Iowa	19-3	Bucky O'Connor	same
8	**Kansas**	24-3	Phog Allen	28-3
9	West Virginia	23-4	Red Brown	same
10	St. John's	22-3	Frank McGuire	25-5
11	Dayton	24-3	Tom Blackburn	28-5
12	Duke	24-6	Harold Bradley	24-4
13	Holy Cross	23-3	Buster Sheary	24-4
14	Seton Hall	25-2	Honey Russell	25-3
15	St. Bonaventure	19-5	Ed Melvin	21-6
16	Wyoming	27-6	Everett Shelton	28-7
17	Louisville	20-5	Peck Hickman	20-6
18	Seattle	29-7	Al Brightman	29-8
19	UCLA	19-10	John Wooden	19-12
20	SW Texas St.	30-1	Milton Jowers	same

Note: Unranked La Salle, coached by Ken Loeffler, won the NIT. The Explorers entered the postseason at 21-7 and had a final record of 25-7.

NCAA Final Four (at Edmundson Pavillion, Seattle): **Semifinals**—St. John's 61, Illinois 59; Kansas 74, Santa Clara 59. **Third Place**—Illinois 67, Santa Clara 64. **Championship**—Kansas 80, St. John's 63.

NIT Final Four (at Madison Sq. Garden): **Semifinals**—La Salle 59, Duquesne 46; Dayton 69, St. Bonaventure 62. **Third Place**—St. Bonaventure 48, Duquesne 34. **Championship**—La Salle 75, Dayton 64.

COLLEGE BASKETBALL

Associated Press Final Polls (Cont.)

1953

		Before Tourns	Head Coach	Final Record
1	Indiana	18-3	Branch McCracken	23-3
2	La Salle	25-2	Ken Loeffler	25-3
3	Seton Hall	28-2	Honey Russell	31-2
4	Washington	27-2	Tippy Dye	30-3
5	LSU	22-1	Harry Rabenhorst	24-3
6	Kansas	16-5	Phog Allen	19-6
7	Oklahoma A&M	22-6	Hank Iba	23-7
	Kansas St.	17-4	Jack Gardner	same
9	Western Ky.	25-5	Ed Diddle	25-6
10	Illinois	18-4	Harry Combes	same
11	Oklahoma City	18-4	Doyle Parrick	18-6
12	N.C. State	26-6	Everett Case	same
13	Notre Dame	17-4	John Jordan	19-5
14	Louisville	21-5	Peck Hickman	22-6
	Seattle	27-3	Al Brightman	29-4
16	Miami-OH	17-5	Bill Rohr	17-6
17	Eastern Ky.	16-8	Paul McBrayer	16-9
18	Duquesne	18-7	Dudey Moore	21-8
	Navy	16-4	Ben Carnevale	16-5
20	Holy Cross	18-5	Buster Sheary	20-6

NCAA Final Four (at Municipal Auditorium, Kansas City): **Semifinals**–Indiana 80, LSU 67; Kansas 79, Washington 53. **Third Place**–Washington 88, LSU 69. **Championship**–Indiana 69, Kansas 68.
NIT Final Four (at Madison Sq. Garden): **Semifinals**–Seton Hall 74, Manhattan 56; St. John's 64, Duquesne 55. **Third Place**–Duquesne 81, Manhattan 67. **Championship**–Seton Hall 58, St. John's 46.

1955

		Before Tourns	Head Coach	Final Record
1	San Francisco	23-1	Phil Woolpert	28-1
2	Kentucky	22-2	Adolph Rupp	23-3
3	La Salle	22-4	Ken Loeffler	26-5
4	N.C. State	28-4	Everett Case	same
5	Iowa	17-5	Bucky O'Connor	19-7
6	Duquesne	19-4	Dudey Moore	22-4
7	Utah	23-3	Jack Gardner	24-4
8	Marquette	22-2	Jack Nagle	24-3
9	Dayton	23-3	Tom Blackburn	25-4
10	Oregon St.	21-7	Slats Gill	22-8
11	Minnesota	15-7	Ozzie Cowles	same
12	Alabama	19-5	Johnny Dee	same
13	UCLA	21-5	John Wooden	same
14	G. Washington	24-6	Bill Reinhart	same
15	Colorado	16-5	Bebe Lee	19-6
16	Tulsa	20-6	Clarence Iba	21-7
17	Vanderbilt	16-6	Bob Polk	same
18	Illinois	17-5	Harry Combes	same
19	West Virginia	19-10	Fred Schaus	19-11
20	Saint Louis	19-7	Eddie Hickey	20-8

NCAA Final Four (at Municipal Auditorium, Kansas City): **Semifinals**–La Salle 76, Iowa 73; San Francisco 62, Colorado 50. **Third Place**–Colorado 75, Iowa 74. **Championship**–San Francisco 77, La Salle 63.
NIT Final Four (at Madison Square Garden): **Semifinals**–Dayton 79, St. Francis-PA 73 (OT); Duquesne 65, Cincinnati 51. **Third Place**–Cincinnati 96, St. Francis-PA 91 (OT). **Championship**–Duquesne 70, Dayton 58.

1954

		Before Tourns	Head Coach	Final Record
1	Kentucky	25-0	Adolph Rupp	same*
2	Indiana	19-3	Branch McCracken	20-4
3	Duquesne	24-2	Dudey Moore	26-3
4	Western Ky.	28-1	Ed Diddle	29-3
5	Oklahoma A&M	23-4	Hank Iba	24-5
6	Notre Dame	20-2	John Jordan	22-3
7	Kansas	16-5	Phog Allen	same
8	Holy Cross	23-2	Buster Sheary	26-2
9	LSU	21-3	Harry Rabenhorst	21-5
10	La Salle	21-4	Ken Loeffler	26-4
11	Iowa	17-5	Bucky O'Connor	same
12	Duke	22-6	Harold Bradley	same
13	Colorado A&M	22-5	Bill Strannigan	22-7
14	Illinois	17-5	Harry Combes	same
15	Wichita	27-3	Ralph Miller	27-4
16	Seattle	26-1	Al Brightman	26-2
17	N.C. State	26-6	Everett Case	28-7
18	Dayton	24-6	Tom Blackburn	25-7
	Minnesota	17-5	Ozzie Cowles	same
20	Oregon St.	19-10	Slats Gill	same
	UCLA	18-7	John Wooden	same
	USC	17-12	Forrest Twogood	19-14

*Kentucky turned down invitation to NCAA tournament after NCAA declared seniors Cliff Hagan, Frank Ramsey and Lou Tsioropoulos ineligible for postseason play.
NCAA Final Four (at Municipal Auditorium, Kansas City): **Semifinals**–La Salle 69, Penn St. 54; Bradley 74, USC 72. **Third Place**–Penn St. 70, USC 61. **Championship**–La Salle 92, Bradley 76.
NIT Final Four (at Madison Square Garden): **Semifinals**–Duquesne 66, Niagara 51; Holy Cross 75, Western Ky. 69. **Third Place**–Niagara 71, Western Ky. 65. **Championship**–Holy Cross 71, Duquesne 62.

1956

		Before Tourns	Head Coach	Final Record
1	San Francisco	25-0	Phil Woolpert	29-0
2	N.C. State	24-3	Everett Case	24-4
3	Dayton	23-3	Tom Blackburn	25-4
4	Iowa	17-5	Bucky O'Connor	20-6
5	Alabama	21-3	Johnny Dee	same
6	Louisville	23-3	Peck Hickman	26-3
7	SMU	22-2	Doc Hayes	25-4
8	UCLA	21-5	John Wooden	22-6
9	Kentucky	19-5	Adolph Rupp	20-6
10	Illinois	18-4	Harry Combes	same
11	Oklahoma City	18-6	Abe Lemons	20-7
12	Vanderbilt	19-4	Bob Polk	same
13	North Carolina	18-5	Frank McGuire	same
14	Holy Cross	22-4	Roy Leenig	22-5
15	Temple	23-3	Harry Litwack	27-4
16	Wake Forest	19-9	Murray Greason	same
17	Duke	19-7	Harold Bradley	same
18	Utah	21-5	Jack Gardner	22-6
19	Oklahoma A&M	18-8	Hank Iba	18-9
20	West Virginia	21-8	Fred Schaus	21-9

NCAA Final Four (at McGaw Hall, Evanston, IL): **Semifinals**–Iowa 83, Temple 76; San Francisco 86, SMU 68. **Third Place**–Temple 90, SMU 81. **Championship**–San Francisco 83, Iowa 71.
NIT Final Four (at Madison Square Garden): **Semifinals**–Dayton 89, St. Francis-NY 58; Louisville 89, St. Joseph's-PA 79. **Third Place**–St. Joseph's-PA 93, St. Francis-NY 82. **Championship**–Louisville 93, Dayton 80.

1957

		Before Tourns	Head Coach	Final Record
1	N. Carolina	27-0	Frank McGuire	32-0
2	Kansas	21-2	Dick Harp	24-3
3	Kentucky	22-4	Adolph Rupp	23-5
4	SMU	21-3	Doc Hayes	22-4
5	Seattle	24-2	John Castellani	24-3
6	Louisville	21-5	Peck Hickman	same
7	West Va.	25-4	Fred Schaus	25-5
8	Vanderbilt	17-5	Bob Polk	same
9	Oklahoma City	17-8	Abe Lemons	19-9
10	Saint Louis	19-7	Eddie Hickey	19-9
11	Michigan St.	14-8	Forddy Anderson	16-10
12	Memphis St.	21-5	Bob Vanatta	24-6
13	California	20-4	Pete Newell	21-5
14	UCLA	22-4	John Wooden	same
15	Mississippi St.	17-8	Babe McCarthy	same
16	Idaho St.	24-2	John Grayson	25-4
17	Notre Dame	18-7	John Jordan	20-8
18	Wake Forest	19-9	Murray Greason	same
19	Canisius	20-5	Joe Curran	22-6
20	Oklahoma A&M	17-9	Hank Iba	same

Note: Unranked **Bradley**, coached by Chuck Orsborn, won the NIT. The Braves entered the tourney at 19-7 and had a final record of 22-7.

NCAA Final Four (at Municipal Auditorium, Kansas City): **Semifinals**—North Carolina 74, Michigan 70 (3 OT); Kansas 80, San Francisco 56. **Third Place**—San Francisco 67, Michigan 56. **Championship**—North Carolina 54, Kansas 53 (3 OT).

NIT Final Four (at Madison Square Garden): **Semifinals**—Memphis St. 80, St. Bonaventure 78; Bradley 78, Temple 66. **Third Place**—Temple 67, St. Bonaventure 50. **Championship**—Bradley 84, Memphis St. 83.

1958

		Before Tourns	Head Coach	Final Record
1	West Virginia	26-1	Fred Schaus	26-2
2	Cincinnati	24-2	George Smith	25-3
3	Kansas St.	20-3	Tex Winter	22-5
4	San Francisco	24-1	Phil Woolpert	25-2
5	Temple	24-2	Harry Litwack	27-3
6	Maryland	20-6	Bud Millikan	22-7
7	Kansas	18-5	Dick Harp	same
8	Notre Dame	22-4	John Jordan	24-5
9	Kentucky	19-6	Adolph Rupp	23-6
10	Duke	18-7	Harold Bradley	same
11	Dayton	23-3	Tom Blackburn	25-4
12	Indiana	12-10	Branch McCracken	13-11
13	North Carolina	19-7	Frank McGuire	same
14	Bradley	20-6	Chuck Orsborn	20-7
15	Mississippi St.	20-5	Babe McCarthy	same
16	Auburn	16-6	Joel Eaves	same
17	Michigan St.	16-6	Forddy Anderson	same
18	Seattle	20-6	John Castellani	24-7
19	Oklahoma St.	19-7	Hank Iba	21-8
20	N.C. State	18-6	Everett Case	same

Note: Unranked **Xavier-OH**, coached by Jim McCafferty, won the NIT. The Musketeers entered the tourney at 15-11 and had a final record of 19-11.

NCAA Final Four (at Freedom Hall, Louisville): **Semifinals**—Kentucky 61, Temple 60; Seattle 73, Kansas St. 51. **Third Place**—Temple 67, Kansas St. 57. **Championship**—Kentucky 84, Seattle 72.

NIT Final Four (at Madison Square Garden): **Semifinals**—Dayton 80, St. John's 56; Xavier-OH 72, St. Bonaventure 53. **Third Place**—St. Bonaventure 84, St. John's 69. **Championship**—Xavier-OH 78, Dayton 74 (OT).

1959

		Before Tourns	Head Coach	Final Record
1	Kansas St.	24-1	Tex Winter	25-2
2	Kentucky	23-2	Adolph Rupp	24-3
3	Mississippi St.	24-1	Babe McCarthy	same*
4	Bradley	23-3	Chuck Orsborn	25-4
5	Cincinnati	23-3	George Smith	26-4
6	N.C. State	22-4	Everett Case	same
7	Michigan St.	18-3	Forddy Anderson	19-4
8	Auburn	20-2	Joel Eaves	same
9	North Carolina	20-4	Frank McGuire	20-5
10	West Virginia	25-4	Fred Schaus	29-5
11	California	21-4	Pete Newell	25-4
12	Saint Louis	20-5	John Benington	20-6
13	Seattle	23-6	Vince Cazzetta	same
14	St. Joseph's-PA	22-3	Jack Ramsay	22-5
15	St. Mary's-CA	18-5	Jim Weaver	19-6
16	TCU	19-5	Buster Brannon	20-6
17	Oklahoma City	20-6	Abe Lemons	20-7
18	Utah	21-5	Jack Gardner	21-7
19	St. Bonaventure	20-2	Eddie Donovan	20-3
20	Marquette	22-4	Eddie Hickey	23-6

*Mississippi St. turned down invitation to NCAA tournament because it was an integrated event.

Note: Unranked **St. John's**, coached by Joe Lapchick, won the NIT. The Redmen entered the tourney at 16-6 and had a final record of 20-6.

NCAA Final Four (at Freedom Hall, Louisville): **Semifinals**—West Virginia 94, Louisville 79; California 64, Cincinnati 58. **Third Place**—Cincinnati 98, Louisville 85. **Championship**—California 71, West Virginia 70.

NIT Final Four (at Madison Square Garden): **Semifinals**—Bradley 59, NYU 57; St. John's 76, Providence 55. **Third Place**—NYU 71, Providence 57. **Championship**—St. John's 76, Bradley 71 (OT).

1960

		Before Tourns	Head Coach	Final Record
1	Cincinnati	25-1	George Smith	28-2
2	California	24-1	Pete Newell	28-2
3	Ohio St.	21-3	Fred Taylor	25-3
4	Bradley	24-2	Chuck Orsborn	27-2
5	West Virginia	24-4	Fred Schaus	26-5
6	Utah	24-2	Jack Gardner	26-3
7	Indiana	20-4	Branch McCracken	same
8	Utah St.	22-4	Cecil Baker	24-5
9	St. Bonaventure	19-3	Eddie Donovan	21-5
10	Miami-FL	23-3	Bruce Hale	23-4
11	Auburn	19-3	Joel Eaves	same
12	NYU	19-4	Lou Rossini	22-5
13	Georgia Tech	21-5	Whack Hyder	22-6
14	Providence	21-4	Joe Mullaney	24-5
15	Saint Louis	19-7	John Benington	19-8
16	Holy Cross	20-5	Roy Leenig	20-6
17	Villanova	19-5	Al Severance	20-6
18	Duke	15-10	Vic Bubas	17-11
19	Wake Forest	21-7	Bones McKinney	same
20	St. John's	17-7	Joe Lapchick	17-8

NCAA Final Four (at the Cow Palace, San Fran.): **Semifinals**—Ohio St. 76, NYU 54; California 77, Cincinnati 69. **Third Place**—Cincinnati 95, NYU 71. **Championship**—Ohio St. 75, California 55.

NIT Final Four (at Madison Square Garden): **Semifinals**—Bradley 82, St. Bonaventure 77; Providence 68, Utah St. 62. **Third Place**—Utah St. 99, St. Bonaventure 93. **Championship**—Bradley 88, Providence 72.

Associated Press Final Polls (Cont.)

1961

		Before Tourns	Head Coach	Final Record
1	Ohio St.	24-0	Fred Taylor	27-1
2	**Cincinnati**	23-3	Ed Jucker	27-3
3	St. Bonaventure	22-3	Eddie Donovan	24-4
4	Kansas St.	22-3	Tex Winter	23-4
5	North Carolina	19-4	Frank McGuire	same
6	Bradley	21-5	Chuck Orsborn	same
7	USC	20-6	Forrest Twogood	21-8
8	Iowa	18-6	S. Scheuerman	same
9	West Virginia	23-4	George King	same
10	Duke	22-6	Vic Bubas	same
11	Utah	21-6	Jack Gardner	23-8
12	Texas Tech	14-9	Polk Robison	15-10
13	Niagara	16-4	Taps Gallagher	16-5
14	Memphis St.	20-2	Bob Vanatta	20-3
15	Wake Forest	17-10	Bones McKinney	19-11
16	St. John's	20-4	Joe Lapchick	20-5
17	St. Joseph's-PA	22-4	Jack Ramsay	25-5
18	Drake	19-7	Maury John	same
19	Holy Cross	19-4	Roy Leenig	22-5
20	Kentucky	18-8	Adolph Rupp	19-9

Note: Unranked **Providence**, coached by Joe Mullaney, won the NIT. The Friars entered the tourney at 20-5 and had a final record of 24-5.
NCAA Final Four (at Municipal Auditorium, Kansas City): **Semifinals**–Ohio St. 95, St. Joseph's-PA 69; Cincinnati 82, Utah 67. **Third Place**–St. Joseph's-PA 127, Utah 120 (4 OT). **Championship**–Cincinnati 70, Ohio St. 65 (OT).
NIT Final Four (at Madison Square Garden) **Semifinals**– St. Louis 67, Dayton 60; Providence 90, Holy Cross 83 (OT). **Third Place**–Holy Cross 85, Dayton 67. **Championship**– Providence 62, St. Louis 59.

1962

		Before Tourns	Head Coach	Final Record
1	Ohio St.	23-1	Fred Taylor	26-2
2	**Cincinnati**	25-2	Ed Jucker	29-2
3	Kentucky	22-2	Adolph Rupp	23-3
4	Mississippi St.	19-6	Babe McCarthy	same
5	Bradley	21-6	Chuck Orsborn	21-7
6	Kansas St.	22-3	Tex Winter	same
7	Utah	23-3	Jack Gardner	same
8	Bowling Green	21-3	Harold Anderson	same
9	Colorado	18-6	Sox Walseth	19-7
10	Duke	20-5	Vic Bubas	same
11	Loyola-IL	21-3	George Ireland	23-4
12	St. John's	19-4	Joe Lapchick	21-5
13	Wake Forest	18-8	Bones McKinney	22-9
14	Oregon St.	22-4	Slats Gill	24-5
15	West Virginia	24-5	George King	24-6
16	Arizona St.	23-3	Ned Wulk	23-4
17	Duquesne	20-5	Red Manning	22-7
18	Utah St.	21-5	Ladell Andersen	22-7
19	UCLA	16-9	John Wooden	18-11
20	Villanova	19-6	Jack Kraft	21-7

Note: Unranked **Dayton**, coached by Tom Blackburn, won the NIT. The Flyers entered the tourney at 20-6 and had a final record of 24-6.
NCAA Final Four (at Freedom Hall, Louisville): **Semifinals**–Ohio St. 84, Wake Forest 68; Cincinnati 72, UCLA 70. **Third Place**–Wake Forest 82, UCLA 80. **Championship**–Cincinnati 71, Ohio St. 59.
NIT Final Four (at Madison Square Garden): **Semifinals**–Dayton 98, Loyola-IL 82; St. John's 76, Duquesne 65. **Third Place**–Loyola-IL 95, Duquesne 84. **Championship**–Dayton 73, St. John's 67.

1963

AP ranked only 10 teams from the 1962-63 season through 1967-68.

		Before Tourns	Head Coach	Final Record
1	Cincinnati	23-1	Ed Jucker	26-2
2	Duke	24-2	Vic Bubas	27-3
3	**Loyola-IL**	24-2	George Ireland	29-2
4	Arizona St.	24-2	Ned Wulk	26-3
5	Wichita	19-7	Ralph Miller	19-8
6	Mississippi St.	21-5	Babe McCarthy	22-6
7	Ohio St.	20-4	Fred Taylor	same
8	Illinois	19-5	Harry Combes	20-6
9	NYU	17-3	Lou Rossini	18-5
10	Colorado	18-6	Sox Walseth	19-7

Note: Unranked **Providence**, coached by Joe Mullaney, won the NIT. The Friars entered the tourney at 21-4 and had a final record of 24-4.
NCAA Final Four (at Freedom Hall, Louisville): **Semifinals**–Loyola-IL 94, Duke 75; Cincinnati 80, Oregon St. 46. **Third Place**–Duke 85, Oregon St. 63. **Championship**–Loyola-IL 60, Cincinnati 58 (OT).
NIT Final Four (at Madison Square Garden): **Semifinals**–Providence 70, Marquette 64; Canisius 61, Villanova 46. **Third Place**–Marquette 66, Villanova 58. **Championship**–Providence 81, Canisius 66.

1964

AP ranked only 10 teams from the 1962-63 season through 1967-68.

		Before Tourns	Head Coach	Final Record
1	**UCLA**	26-0	John Wooden	30-0
2	Michigan	20-4	Dave Strack	23-5
3	Duke	23-4	Vic Bubas	26-5
4	Kentucky	21-4	Adolph Rupp	21-6
5	Wichita St.	22-5	Ralph Miller	23-6
6	Oregon St.	25-3	Slats Gill	25-4
7	Villanova	22-3	Jack Kraft	24-4
8	Loyola-IL	20-5	George Ireland	22-6
9	DePaul	21-3	Ray Meyer	21-4
10	Davidson	22-4	Lefty Driesell	same

Note: Unranked **Bradley**, coached by Chuck Orsborn, won the NIT. The Braves entered the tourney at 20-6 and finished with a record of 23-6.
NCAA Final Four (at Municipal Auditorium, Kansas City): **Semifinals**–Duke 91, Michigan 80; UCLA 90, Kansas St. 84. **Third Place**–Michigan 100, Kansas St. 90. **Championship**–UCLA 98, Duke 83.
NIT Final Four (at Madison Square Garden): **Semifinals**–New Mexico 72, NYU 65; Bradley 67, Army 52. **Third Place**–Army 60, NYU 59. **Championship**–Bradley 86, New Mexico 54.

Undefeated National Champions

Seven NCAA seasons have ended with an undefeated national champion. UCLA has accomplished the feat four times.

Year		W-L
1956	San Francisco	29-0
1957	North Carolina	32-0
1964	UCLA	30-0
1967	UCLA	30-0
1972	UCLA	30-0
1973	UCLA	30-0
1976	Indiana	32-0

1965

AP ranked only 10 teams from the 1962-63 season through 1967-68.

		Before Tourns	Head Coach	Final Record
1	Michigan	21-3	Dave Strack	24-4
2	**UCLA**	24-2	John Wooden	28-2
3	St. Joseph's-PA	25-1	Jack Ramsay	26-3
4	Providence	22-1	Joe Mullaney	24-2
5	Vanderbilt	23-3	Roy Skinner	24-4
6	Davidson	24-2	Lefty Driesell	same
7	Minnesota	19-5	John Kundla	same
8	Villanova	21-4	Jack Kraft	23-5
9	BYU	21-5	Stan Watts	21-7
10	Duke	20-5	Vic Bubas	same

Note: Unranked **St. John's**, coached by Joe Lapchick, won the NIT. The Redmen entered the tourney at 17-8 and finished with a record of 21-8.
NCAA Final Four (at Memorial Coliseum, Portland, OR): **Semifinals**–Michigan 93, Princeton 76; UCLA 108, Wichita St. 89. **Third Place**–Princeton 118, Wichita St. 82. **Championship**–UCLA 91, Michigan 80.
NIT Final Four (at Madison Square Garden): **Semifinals**–Villanova 91, NYU 69; St. John's 67, Army 60. **Third Place**–Army 75, NYU 74. **Championship**– St. John's 55, Villanova 51.

1966

AP ranked only 10 teams from the 1962-63 season through 1967-68.

		Before Tourns	Head Coach	Final Record
1	Kentucky	24-1	Adolph Rupp	27-2
2	Duke	23-3	Vic Bubas	26-4
3	**Texas Western**	23-1	Don Haskins	28-1
4	Kansas	22-3	Ted Owens	23-4
5	St. Joseph's-PA	22-4	Jack Ramsay	24-5
6	Loyola-IL	22-2	George Ireland	22-3
7	Cincinnati	21-5	Tay Baker	21-7
8	Vanderbilt	22-4	Roy Skinner	same
9	Michigan	17-7	Dave Strack	18-8
10	Western Ky.	23-2	Johnny Oldham	25-3

Note: Unranked **BYU**, coached by Stan Watts, won the NIT. The Cougars entered the tourney at 17-5 and had a final record of 20-5.
NCAA Final Four (at Cole Fieldhouse, College Park, MD): **Semifinals**–Kentucky 83, Duke 79; Texas Western 85, Utah 78. **Third Place**–Duke 79, Utah 77. **Championship**–Texas Western 72, Kentucky 65.
NIT Final Four (at Madison Square Garden): **Semifinals**–BYU 66, Army 60; NYU 69, Villanova 63. **Third Place**–Villanova 76, Army 65. **Championship**–BYU 97, NYU 84.

1967

AP ranked only 10 teams from the 1962-63 season through 1967-68.

		Before Tourns	Head Coach	Final Record
1	**UCLA**	26-0	John Wooden	30-0
2	Louisville	23-3	Peck Hickman	23-5
3	Kansas	22-3	Ted Owens	23-4
4	North Carolina	24-4	Dean Smith	26-6
5	Princeton	23-2	B. van Breda Kolff	25-3
6	Western Ky.	23-2	Johnny Oldham	23-3
7	Houston	23-3	Guy Lewis	27-4
8	Tennessee	21-5	Ray Mears	21-7
9	Boston College	19-2	Bob Cousy	21-3
10	Texas Western	20-5	Don Haskins	22-6

Note: Unranked **Southern Illinois**, coached by Jack Hartman, won the NIT. The Salukis entered the tourney at 20-2 and had a final record of 24-2.
NCAA Final Four (at Freedom Hall, Louisville): **Semifinals**–Dayton 76, N. Carolina 62; UCLA 73, Houston 58. **Third Place**–Houston 84, N. Carolina 62. **Championship**–UCLA 79, Dayton 64.
NIT Final Four (at Madison Square Garden): **Semifinals**–Marquette 83, Marshall 78; Southern Ill. 79, Rutgers 70. **Third Place**–Rutgers 93, Marshall 76. **Championship**–Southern Ill. 71, Marquette 56.

1968

AP ranked only 10 teams from the 1962-63 season through 1967-68.

		Before Tourns	Head Coach	Final Record
1	Houston	28-0	Guy Lewis	31-2
2	**UCLA**	25-1	John Wooden	29-1
3	St. Bonaventure	22-0	Larry Weise	23-2
4	North Carolina	25-3	Dean Smith	28-4
5	Kentucky	21-4	Adolph Rupp	22-5
6	New Mexico	23-3	Bob King	23-5
7	Columbia	21-4	Jack Rohan	23-5
8	Davidson	22-4	Lefty Driesell	24-5
9	Louisville	20-6	John Dromo	21-7
10	Duke	21-5	Vic Bubas	22-6

Note: Unranked **Dayton**, coached by Don Donoher, won the NIT. The Flyers entered the tourney at 17-9 and had a final record of 21-9.
NCAA Final Four (at the Sports Arena, Los Angeles): **Semifinals**–N. Carolina 80, Ohio St. 66; UCLA 101, Houston 69. **Third Place**–Ohio St. 89, Houston 85. **Championship**–UCLA 78, N. Carolina 55.
NIT Final Four (at Madison Square Garden): **Semifinals**–Dayton 76, Notre Dame 74 (OT); Kansas 58, St. Peter's 46. **Third Place**–Notre Dame 81, St.Peter's 78. **Championship**–Dayton 61, Kansas 48.

All-Time AP Top 20

The composite AP Top 20 from the 1948-49 season through 1999-2000, based on the final regular season rankings of each year. The final AP poll has been taken before the NCAA and NIT tournaments each season since 1949 except in 1953 and '54 and again in 1974 and '75 when the final poll came out after the postseason. Team point totals are based on 20 points for all 1st place finishes, 19 for each 2nd, etc. Also listed are the number of times ranked No.1 by AP going into the tournaments, and times ranked in the pre-tournament Top 10 and Top 20.

		Pts	No.1	Top 10	Top 20			Pts	No.1	Top 10	Top 20
1	Kentucky	602	7	34	40	11	Arizona	184	1	8	16
2	North Carolina	495	5	27	35	12	N.C. State	176	1	9	16
3	UCLA	443	7	22	34	13	UNLV	173	2	8	13
4	Duke	375	4	21	30	14	Ohio St	169	2	10	12
5	Kansas	312	1	17	24	15	Marquette	166	0	11	15
6	Indiana	292	4	16	23		Arkansas	166	0	9	15
7	Cincinnati	233	2	12	17	17	Illinois	164	0	8	18
	Louisville	233	0	11	22	18	Syracuse	156	0	9	16
9	Michigan	200	2	10	15	19	Utah	152	0	7	16
10	Notre Dame	195	0	13	17	20	Kansas St	147	1	8	12

Associated Press Final Polls (Cont.)

1969

		Before Tourns	Head Coach	Final Record
1	UCLA	25-1	John Wooden	29-1
2	La Salle	23-1	Tom Gola	same*
3	Santa Clara	26-1	Dick Garibaldi	27-2
4	North Carolina	25-3	Dean Smith	27-5
5	Davidson	24-2	Lefty Driesell	26-3
6	Purdue	20-4	George King	23-5
7	Kentucky	22-4	Adolph Rupp	23-5
8	St. John's	22-4	Lou Carnesecca	23-6
9	Duquesne	19-4	Red Manning	21-5
10	Villanova	21-4	Jack Kraft	21-5
11	Drake	23-4	Maury John	26-5
12	New Mexico St.	23-3	Lou Henson	24-5
13	South Carolina	20-6	Frank McGuire	21-7
14	Marquette	22-4	Al McGuire	24-5
15	Louisville	20-5	John Dromo	21-6
16	Boston College	21-3	Bob Cousy	24-4
17	Notre Dame	20-6	Johnny Dee	20-7
18	Colorado	20-6	Sox Walseth	21-7
19	Kansas	20-6	Ted Owens	20-7
20	Illinois	19-5	Harvey Schmidt	same

*On probation

Note: Unranked **Temple**, coached by Harry Litwack, won the NIT. The Owls entered the tourney at 18-8 and finished with a record of 22-8.

NCAA Final Four (at Freedom Hall, Louisville): **Semifinals**—Purdue 92, N. Carolina 65; UCLA 85, Drake 82. **Third Place**—Drake 104, N. Carolina 84. **Championship**—UCLA 92, Purdue 72.

NIT Final Four (at Madison Square Garden): **Semifinals**—Temple 63, Tennessee 58; Boston College 73, Army 61. **Third Place**—Tennessee 64, Army 52. **Championship**—Temple 89, Boston College 76.

1971

		Before Tourns	Head Coach	Final Record
1	UCLA	25-1	John Wooden	29-1
2	Marquette	26-0	Al McGuire	28-1
3	Penn	26-0	Dick Harter	28-1
4	Kansas	25-1	Ted Owens	27-3
5	USC	24-2	Bob Boyd	24-2
6	South Carolina	23-4	Frank McGuire	23-6
7	Western Ky.	20-5	John Oldham	24-6
8	Kentucky	22-4	Adolph Rupp	22-6
9	Fordham	25-1	Digger Phelps	26-3
10	Ohio St.	19-5	Fred Taylor	20-6
11	Jacksonville	22-3	Tom Wasdin	22-4
12	Notre Dame	19-7	Johnny Dee	20-9
13	N. Carolina	22-6	Dean Smith	26-6
14	Houston	20-6	Guy Lewis	22-7
15	Duquesne	21-3	Red Manning	21-4
16	Long Beach St.	21-4	Jerry Tarkanian	23-5
17	Tennessee	20-6	Ray Mears	21-7
18	Villanova	19-5	Jack Kraft	23-6
19	Drake	20-7	Maury John	21-8
20	BYU	18-9	Stan Watts	18-11

NCAA Final Four (at the Astrodome, Houston): **Semifinals**—Villanova 92, Western Ky. 89 (2 OT); UCLA 68, Kansas 60. **Third Place**—Western Ky. 77, Kansas 75. **Championship**—UCLA 68, Villanova 62.

NIT Final Four (at Madison Square Garden): **Semifinals**—N. Carolina 73, Duke 69; Ga.Tech 76, St. Bonaventure 71 (2 OT). **Third Place**—St. Bonaventure 92, Duke 88 (OT). **Championship**—N. Carolina 84, Ga.Tech 66.

1970

		Before Tourns	Head Coach	Final Record
1	Kentucky	25-1	Adolph Rupp	26-2
2	UCLA	24-2	John Wooden	28-2
3	St. Bonaventure	22-1	Larry Weise	25-3
4	Jacksonville	23-1	Joe Williams	27-2
5	New Mexico St.	23-2	Lou Henson	27-3
6	South Carolina	25-3	Frank McGuire	25-3
7	Iowa	19-4	Ralph Miller	20-5
8	Marquette	22-3	Al McGuire	26-3
9	Notre Dame	20-6	Johnny Dee	21-8
10	N.C. State	22-6	Norm Sloan	23-7
11	Florida St.	23-3	Hugh Durham	23-3
12	Houston	24-3	Guy Lewis	25-5
13	Penn	25-1	Dick Harter	25-2
14	Drake	21-6	Maury John	22-7
15	Davidson	22-4	Terry Holland	22-5
16	Utah St.	20-6	Ladell Andersen	22-7
17	Niagara	21-5	Frank Layden	22-7
18	Western Ky.	22-2	John Oldham	22-3
19	Long Beach St.	23-3	Jerry Tarkanian	24-5
20	USC	18-8	Bob Boyd	18-8

NCAA Final Four (at Cole Fieldhouse, College Park, MD): **Semifinals**—Jacksonville 91, St. Bonaventure 83; UCLA 93, New Mexico St. 77. **Third Place**—N. Mexico St. 79, St. Bonaventure 73. **Championship**—UCLA 80, Jacksonville 69.

NIT Final Four (at Madison Square Garden): **Semifinals**—St. John's 60, Army 59; Marquette 101, LSU 79. **Third Place**—Army 75, LSU 68. **Championship**—Marquette 65, St. John's 53.

1972

		Before Tourns	Head Coach	Final Record
1	UCLA	26-0	John Wooden	30-0
2	North Carolina	23-4	Dean Smith	26-5
3	Penn	23-2	Chuck Daly	25-3
4	Louisville	23-4	Denny Crum	26-5
5	Long Beach St.	23-3	Jerry Tarkanian	25-4
6	South Carolina	22-4	Frank McGuire	24-5
7	Marquette	24-2	Al McGuire	25-4
8	SW Louisiana	23-3	Beryl Shipley	25-4
9	BYU	21-4	Stan Watts	21-5
10	Florida St.	23-5	Hugh Durham	27-6
11	Minnesota	17-6	Bill Musselman	18-7
12	Marshall	23-3	Carl Tacy	23-4
13	Memphis St.	21-6	Gene Bartow	21-7
14	Maryland	23-5	Lefty Driesell	27-5
15	Villanova	19-6	Jack Kraft	20-8
16	Oral Roberts	25-1	Ken Trickey	26-2
17	Indiana	17-7	Bob Knight	17-8
18	Kentucky	20-6	Adolph Rupp	21-7
19	Ohio St.	18-6	Fred Taylor	same
20	Virginia	21-6	Bill Gibson	21-7

NCAA Final Four (at the Sports Arena, Los Angeles): **Semifinals**—Florida St. 79, N. Carolina 75; UCLA 96, Louisville 77. **Third Place**—N. Carolina 105, Louisville 91. **Championship**—UCLA 81, Florida St. 76.

NIT Final Four (at Madison Square Garden): **Semifinals**—Maryland 91, Jacksonville 77; Niagara 69, St. John's 67. **Third Place**—Jacksonville 83, St. John's 80. **Championship**—Maryland 100, Niagara 69.

1973

	Before Tourns	Head Coach	Final Record
1	UCLA 26-0	John Wooden	30-0
2	N.C. State...... 27-0	Norm Sloan	same*
3	Long Beach St... 24-2	Jerry Tarkanian	26-3
4	Providence 24-2	Dave Gavitt	27-4
5	Marquette 23-3	Al McGuire	25-4
6	Indiana 19-5	Bob Knight	22-6
7	SW Louisiana ... 23-2	Beryl Shipley	24-5
8	Maryland 22-6	Lefty Driesell	23-7
9	Kansas St....... 22-4	Jack Hartman	23-5
10	Minnesota...... 20-4	Bill Musselman	21-5
11	North Carolina.. 22-7	Dean Smith	25-8
12	Memphis St..... 21-5	Gene Bartow	24-6
13	Houston........ 23-3	Guy Lewis	23-4
14	Syracuse 22-4	Roy Danforth	24-5
15	Missouri........ 21-5	Norm Stewart	21-6
16	Arizona St...... 18-7	Ned Wulk	19-9
17	Kentucky 19-7	Joe B. Hall	20-8
18	Penn........... 20-5	Chuck Daly	21-7
19	Austin Peay..... 21-5	Lake Kelly	22-7
20	San Francisco... 22-4	Bob Gaillard	23-5

*N.C. State was ineligible for NCAA tournament for using improper methods to recruit David Thompson.
Note: Unranked **Virginia Tech**, coached by Don DeVoe, won the NIT. The Hokies entered the tourney at 18-5 and finished with a record of 22-5.
NCAA Final Four (at The Arena, St. Louis): **Semifinals**–Memphis St. 98, Providence 85; UCLA 70, Indiana 59. **Third Place**–Indiana 97, Providence 79. **Championship**–UCLA 87, Memphis St. 66.
NIT Final Four (at Madison Square Garden): **Semifinals**–Va. Tech 74, Alabama 73; Notre Dame 78, N. Carolina 71. **Third Place**–N. Carolina 88, Alabama 69. **Championship**–Va. Tech 92, Notre Dame 91 (OT).

1974

	Before Tourns	Head Coach	Final Record
1	N.C. State 26-1	Norm Sloan	30-1
2	UCLA 23-3	John Wooden	26-4
3	Notre Dame 24-2	Digger Phelps	26-3
4	Maryland 23-5	Lefty Driesell	same
5	Providence 26-3	Dave Gavitt	28-4
6	Vanderbilt 23-3	Roy Skinner	23-5
7	Marquette 22-4	Al McGuire	26-5
8	North Carolina.. 22-5	Dean Smith	22-6
9	Long Beach St... 24-2	Lute Olson	same
10	Indiana 20-5	Bob Knight	23-5
11	Alabama....... 22-4	C.M. Newton	same
12	Michigan....... 21-4	Johnny Orr	22-5
13	Pittsburgh 23-3	Buzz Ridl	25-4
14	Kansas......... 21-5	Ted Owens	23-7
15	USC........... 22-4	Bob Boyd	24-5
16	Louisville 21-6	Denny Crum	21-7
17	New Mexico.... 21-6	Norm Ellenberger	22-7
18	South Carolina.. 22-4	Frank McGuire	22-5
19	Creighton 22-6	Eddie Sutton	23-7
20	Dayton........ 19-7	Don Donoher	20-9

NCAA Final Four (at Greensboro, NC, Coliseum): **Semifinals**–N.C. State 80, UCLA 77 (2 OT); Marquette 64, Kansas 51. **Third Place**–UCLA 78, Kansas 61. **Championship**–N.C. State 76, Marquette 64.
NIT Final Four (at Madison Square Garden): **Semifinals**–Purdue 78, Jacksonville 63; Utah 117, Boston Col. 93. **Third Place**–Boston Col. 87, Jacksonville 77. **Championship**–Purdue 87, Utah 81.
CCA Final Four (at The Arena, St. Louis): **Semifinals**–Indiana 73, Toledo 72; USC 74, Bradley 73. **Championship**–Indiana 85, USC 60.

1975

	Before Tourns	Head Coach	Final Record
1	Indiana 29-0	Bob Knight	31-1
2	UCLA 23-3	John Wooden	28-3
3	Louisville 24-2	Denny Crum	28-3
4	Maryland 22-4	Lefty Driesell	24-5
5	Kentucky 22-4	Joe B. Hall	26-5
6	North Carolina.. 21-7	Dean Smith	23-8
7	Arizona St...... 23-3	Ned Wulk	25-4
8	N.C.State 22-6	Norm Sloan	22-6
9	Notre Dame ... 18-8	Digger Phelps	19-10
10	Marquette 23-3	Al McGuire	23-4
11	Alabama....... 22-4	C.M. Newton	22-5
12	Cincinnati 21-5	Gale Catlett	23-6
13	Oregon St...... 18-10	Ralph Miller	19-12
14	Drake 16-10	Bob Ortegel	19-10
15	Penn........... 23-4	Chuck Daly	23-5
16	UNLV.......... 22-4	Jerry Tarkanian	24-5
17	Kansas St....... 18-8	Jack Hartman	20-9
18	USC........... 18-7	Bob Boyd	18-8
19	Centenary...... 25-4	Larry Little	same
20	Syracuse 20-7	Roy Danforth	23-9

NCAA Final Four (at San Diego Sports Arena): **Semifinals**–Kentucky 95, Syracuse 79; UCLA 75, Louisville 74 (OT). **Third Place**–Louisville 96, Syracuse 88 (OT). **Championship**–UCLA 92, Kentucky 85.
NIT Championship (at Madison Sq. Garden): Princeton 80, Providence 69. No Top 20 teams played in NIT.
CCA Championship (at Freedom Hall, Louisville): Drake 83, Arizona 76. No.14 Drake and No.18 USC were only Top 20 teams in CCA.

1976

	Before Tourns	Head Coach	Final Record
1	Indiana 27-0	Bob Knight	32-0
2	Marquette 25-1	Al McGuire	27-2
3	UNLV.......... 28-1	Jerry Tarkanian	29-2
4	Rutgers........ 28-0	Tom Young	31-2
5	UCLA 24-3	Gene Bartow	28-4
6	Alabama....... 22-4	C.M. Newton	23-5
7	Notre Dame ... 22-5	Digger Phelps	23-6
8	North Carolina.. 25-3	Dean Smith	25-4
9	Michigan....... 21-6	Johnny Orr	25-7
10	Western Mich... 24-2	Eldon Miller	25-3
11	Maryland 22-6	Lefty Driesell	same
12	Cincinnati 25-5	Gale Catlett	25-6
13	Tennessee 21-5	Ray Mears	21-6
14	Missouri....... 24-4	Norm Stewart	26-5
15	Arizona........ 22-8	Fred Snowden	24-9
16	Texas Tech..... 24-5	Gerald Myers	25-6
17	DePaul......... 19-8	Ray Meyer	20-9
18	Virginia........ 18-11	Terry Holland	18-12
19	Centenary...... 22-5	Larry Little	same
20	Pepperdine 21-5	Gary Colson	22-6

NCAA Final Four (at the Spectrum, Phila.); **Semifinals**–Michigan 86, Rutgers 70; Indiana 65, UCLA 51. **Third Place**–UCLA 106, Rutgers 92. **Championship**–Indiana 86, Michigan 68.
NIT Championship (at Madison Square Garden): Kentucky 71, NC-Charlotte 67. No Top 20 teams played in NIT.

Associated Press Final Polls (Cont.)

1977

		Before Tourns	Head Coach	Final Record
1	Michigan	24-3	Johnny Orr	26-4
2	UCLA	24-3	Gene Bartow	25-4
3	Kentucky	24-3	Joe B. Hall	26-4
4	UNLV	25-2	Jerry Tarkanian	29-3
5	North Carolina	24-4	Dean Smith	28-5
6	Syracuse	25-3	Jim Boeheim	26-4
7	**Marquette**	20-7	Al McGuire	25-7
8	San Francisco	29-1	Bob Gaillard	29-2
9	Wake Forest	20-7	Carl Tacy	22-8
10	Notre Dame	21-6	Digger Phelps	22-7
11	Alabama	23-4	C.M. Newton	25-6
12	Detroit	24-3	Dick Vitale	25-4
13	Minnesota	24-3	Jim Dutcher	same*
14	Utah	22-6	Jerry Pimm	23-7
15	Tennessee	22-5	Ray Mears	22-6
16	Kansas St.	23-6	Jack Hartman	24-7
17	NC-Charlotte	25-3	Lee Rose	28-5
18	Arkansas	26-1	Eddie Sutton	26-2
19	Louisville	21-6	Denny Crum	21-7
20	VMI	25-3	Charlie Schmaus	26-4

*On probation

NCAA Final Four (at the Omni, Atlanta): **Semifinals**–Marquette 51, NC-Charlotte, 49; N. Carolina 84, UNLV 83. **Third Place**–UNLV 106, NC-Charlotte 94. **Championship**–Marquette 67, N. Carolina 59.
NIT Championship (at Madison Square Garden): St. Bonaventure 94, Houston 91. No.11 Alabama was only Top 20 team in NIT.

1979

		Before Tourns	Head Coach	Final Record
1	Indiana St.	29-0	Bill Hodges	33-1
2	UCLA	23-4	Gary Cunningham	25-5
3	**Michigan St.**	21-6	Jud Heathcote	26-6
4	Notre Dame	22-5	Digger Phelps	24-6
5	Arkansas	23-4	Eddie Sutton	25-5
6	DePaul	22-5	Ray Meyer	26-6
7	LSU	22-5	Dale Brown	23-6
8	Syracuse	25-3	Jim Boeheim	26-4
9	North Carolina	23-5	Dean Smith	23-6
10	Marquette	21-6	Hank Raymonds	22-7
11	Duke	22-7	Bill Foster	22-8
12	San Francisco	21-6	Dan Belluomini	22-7
13	Louisville	23-7	Denny Crum	24-8
14	Penn	21-5	Bob Weinhauer	25-7
15	Purdue	23-7	Lee Rose	27-8
16	Oklahoma	20-9	Dave Bliss	21-10
17	St. John's	18-10	Lou Carnesecca	21-11
18	Rutgers	21-8	Tom Young	22-9
19	Toledo	21-6	Bob Nichols	22-7
20	Iowa	20-7	Lute Olson	20-8

NCAA Final Four (at Special Events Center, Salt Lake City): **Semifinals**–Michigan St. 101, Penn 67; Indiana St. 76, DePaul 74; **Third Place**–DePaul 96, Penn 93; **Championship**–Michigan St. 75, Indiana St. 64.
NIT Championship (at Madison Square Garden): Indiana 53, Purdue 52. No. 15 Purdue was the only Top 20 team in NIT.

1978

		Before Tourns	Head Coach	Final Record
1	**Kentucky**	25-2	Joe B. Hall	30-2
2	UCLA	24-2	Gary Cunningham	25-3
3	DePaul	25-2	Ray Meyer	27-3
4	Michigan St.	23-4	Jud Heathcote	25-5
5	Arkansas	28-3	Eddie Sutton	32-3
6	Notre Dame	20-6	Digger Phelps	23-8
7	Duke	23-6	Bill Foster	27-7
8	Marquette	24-3	Hank Raymonds	24-4
9	Louisville	22-6	Denny Crum	23-7
10	Kansas	24-4	Ted Owens	24-5
11	San Francisco	22-5	Bob Gaillard	23-6
12	New Mexico	24-3	Norm Ellenberger	24-4
13	Indiana	20-7	Bob Knight	21-8
14	Utah	22-5	Jerry Pimm	23-6
15	Florida St.	23-5	Hugh Durham	23-6
16	North Carolina	23-7	Dean Smith	23-8
17	**Texas**	22-5	Abe Lemons	26-5
18	Detroit	24-3	Dave Gaines	25-4
19	Miami-OH.	18-8	Darrell Hedric	19-9
20	Penn	19-7	Bob Weinhauer	20-8

NCAA Final Four (at the Checkerdome, St. Louis): **Semifinals**–Kentucky 64, Arkansas 59; Duke 90, Notre Dame 86. **Third Place**–Arkansas 71, Notre Dame 69. **Championship**–Kentucky 94, Duke 88.
NIT Championship (at Madison Square Garden): Texas 101, N.C. State 93. No. 17 Texas and No. 18 Detroit were only Top 20 teams in NIT.

1980

		Before Tourns	Head Coach	Final Record
1	DePaul	26-1	Ray Meyer	26-2
2	**Louisville**	28-3	Denny Crum	33-3
3	LSU	24-5	Dale Brown	26-6
4	Kentucky	28-5	Joe B. Hall	29-6
5	Oregon St.	26-3	Ralph Miller	26-4
6	Syracuse	25-3	Jim Boeheim	26-4
7	Indiana	20-7	Bob Knight	21-8
8	Maryland	23-6	Lefty Driesell	24-7
9	Notre Dame	20-7	Digger Phelps	20-8
10	Ohio St.	24-5	Eldon Miller	21-8
11	Georgetown	24-5	John Thompson	26-6
12	BYU	24-4	Frank Arnold	24-5
13	St. John's	24-4	Lou Carnesecca	24-5
14	Duke	22-8	Bill Foster	24-9
15	North Carolina	21-7	Dean Smith	21-8
16	Missouri	23-5	Norm Stewart	25-6
17	Weber St.	26-2	Neil McCarthy	26-3
18	Arizona St.	21-6	Ned Wulk	22-7
19	Iona	28-4	Jim Valvano	29-5
20	Purdue	19-9	Lee Rose	23-10

NCAA Final Four (at Market Square Arena, Indianapolis): **Semifinals**–Louisville 80, Iowa 72; UCLA 67, Purdue 62; **Championship**–Louisville 59, UCLA 54.
NIT Championship (at Madison Square Garden): Virginia 58, Minnesota 55. No Top 20 teams played in NIT.

1981

		Head Coach	Before Tourns	Final Record
1	DePaul	Ray Meyer	27-1	27-2
2	Oregon St.	Ralph Miller	26-1	26-2
3	Arizona St.	Ned Wulk	24-3	24-4
4	LSU	Dale Brown	28-3	31-5
5	Virginia	Terry Holland	25-3	29-4
6	North Carolina	Dean Smith	25-7	29-8
7	Notre Dame	Digger Phelps	22-5	23-6
8	Kentucky	Joe B. Hall	22-5	22-6
9	**Indiana**	Bob Knight	21-9	26-9
10	UCLA	Larry Brown	20-6	20-7
11	Wake Forest	Carl Tacy	22-6	22-7
12	Louisville	Denny Crum	21-8	21-9
13	Iowa	Lute Olson	21-6	21-7
14	Utah	Jerry Pimm	24-4	25-5
15	Tennessee	Don DeVoe	20-7	21-8
16	BYU	Frank Arnold	22-6	25-7
17	Wyoming	Jim Brandenburg	23-5	24-6
18	Maryland	Lefty Driesell	20-9	21-10
19	Illinois	Lou Henson	20-7	21-8
20	Arkansas	Eddie Sutton	22-7	24-8

NCAA Final Four (at the Spectrum, Phila.):
Semifinals–N. Carolina 78, Virginia 65; Indiana 67, LSU
49. **Third Place**–Virginia 78, LSU 74. **Championship**–
Indiana 63, N. Carolina 50.
NIT Championship (at Madison Square Garden): Tulsa
86, Syracuse 84. No Top 20 teams played in NIT.

1982

		Head Coach	Before Tourns	Final Record
1	N. Carolina	Dean Smith	27-2	32-2
2	DePaul	Ray Meyer	26-1	26-2
3	Virginia	Terry Holland	29-3	30-4
4	Oregon St.	Ralph Miller	23-4	25-5
5	Missouri	Norm Stewart	26-3	27-4
6	Georgetown	John Thompson	26-6	30-7
7	Minnesota	Jim Dutcher	22-5	23-6
8	Idaho	Don Monson	26-2	27-3
9	Memphis St.	Dana Kirk	23-4	24-5
10	Tulsa	Nolan Richardson	24-5	24-6
11	Fresno St.	Boyd Grant	26-2	27-3
12	Arkansas	Eddie Sutton	23-5	23-6
13	Alabama	Wimp Sanderson	23-6	24-7
14	West Virginia	Gale Catlett	26-3	27-4
15	Kentucky	Joe B. Hall	22-7	22-8
16	Iowa	Lute Olson	20-7	21-8
17	Ala-Birmingham	Gene Bartow	23-5	25-6
18	Wake Forest	Carl Tacy	20-8	21-9
19	UCLA	Larry Farmer	21-6	21-6
20	Louisville	Denny Crum	20-9	23-10

NCAA Final Four (at the Superdome, New Orleans):
Semifinals–N. Carolina 68, Houston 63; Georgetown 50,
Louisville 46. **Championship**–N. Carolina 63, George-
town 62.
NIT Championship (at Madison Square Garden): Bradley
67, Purdue 58. No Top 20 teams played in NIT.

1983

		Head Coach	Before Tourns	Final Record
1	Houston	Guy Lewis	27-2	31-3
2	Louisville	Denny Crum	29-3	32-4
3	St. John's	Lou Carnesecca	27-4	28-5
4	Virginia	Terry Holland	27-4	29-5
5	Indiana	Bob Knight	23-5	24-6
6	UNLV	Jerry Tarkanian	28-2	28-3
7	UCLA	Larry Farmer	23-5	23-6
8	North Carolina	Dean Smith	26-7	28-8
9	Arkansas	Eddie Sutton	25-3	26-4
10	Missouri	Norm Stewart	26-7	26-8
11	Boston College	Gary Williams	24-6	25-7
12	Kentucky	Joe B. Hall	22-7	23-8
13	Villanova	Rollie Massimino	22-7	24-8
14	Wichita St.	Gene Smithson	25-3	same*
15	Tenn-Chatt.	Murray Arnold	26-3	26-4
16	**N.C. State**	Jim Valvano	20-10	26-10
17	Memphis St.	Dana Kirk	22-7	23-8
18	Georgia	Hugh Durham	21-9	24-10
19	Oklahoma St.	Paul Hansen	24-6	24-7
20	Georgetown	John Thompson	21-9	22-10

*On probation
NCAA Final Four (at The Pit, Albuquerque, NM):
Semifinals–N.C. State 67, Georgia 60; Houston 94, Louis-
ville 81. **Championship**–N.C. State 54, Houston 52.
NIT Championship (at Madison Square Garden): Fresno
St. 69, DePaul 60. No Top 20 teams played in NIT.

1984

		Head Coach	Before Tourns	Final Record
1	North Carolina	Dean Smith	27-2	28-3
2	**Georgetown**	John Thompson	29-3	34-3
3	Kentucky	Joe B. Hall	26-4	29-5
4	DePaul	Ray Meyer	26-2	27-3
5	Houston	Guy Lewis	28-4	32-5
6	Illinois	Lou Henson	24-4	26-5
7	Oklahoma	Billy Tubbs	29-4	29-5
8	Arkansas	Eddie Sutton	25-6	25-7
9	UTEP	Don Haskins	27-3	27-4
10	Purdue	Gene Keady	22-6	22-7
11	Maryland	Lefty Driesell	23-7	24-8
12	Tulsa	Nolan Richardson	27-3	27-4
13	UNLV	Jerry Tarkanian	27-5	29-6
14	Duke	Mike Krzyzewski	24-9	24-10
15	Washington	Marv Harshman	22-6	24-7
16	Memphis St.	Dana Kirk	24-6	26-7
17	Oregon St.	Ralph Miller	22-6	22-7
18	Syracuse	Jim Boeheim	22-8	23-9
19	Wake Forest	Carl Tacy	21-8	23-9
20	Temple	John Chaney	25-4	26-5

NCAA Final Four (at the Kingdome, Seattle): **Semifinals**–
Houston 49, Virginia 47 (OT); Georgetown 53, Kentucky
40. **Championship**–Georgetown 84, Houston 75.
NIT Championship (at Madison Square Garden): Michigan 83, Notre Dame 63. No Top 20 teams played in NIT.

Highest-Rated College Games on TV

The dozen highest-rated college basketball games seen on U.S. television have been NCAA tournament championship games, led by the 1979 Michigan State-Indiana State final that featured Magic Johnson and Larry Bird.
Listed below are the finalists (winning team first), date of game, TV network, and TV rating and audience share
(according to Nielson Media Research).

		Date	Net	Rtg/Sh			Date	Net	Rtg/Sh
1	Michigan St.-Indiana St.	3/26/79	NBC	24.1/38	7	N. Carolina-Georgetown	3/29/82	CBS	21.6/31
2	Villanova-Georgetown	4/1/85	CBS	23.3/33	8	UCLA-Kentucky	3/31/75	NBC	21.3/33
3	Duke-Michigan	4/6/92	CBS	22.7/35	9	Michigan-Seton Hall	4/3/89	CBS	21.3/33
4	N.C. State-Houston	4/4/83	CBS	22.3/32	10	Louisville-Duke	3/31/86	CBS	20.7/31
5	N. Carolina-Michigan	4/5/93	CBS	22.2/34	11	Indiana-N. Carolina	3/30/81	NBC	20.7/29
6	Arkansas-Duke	4/4/94	CBS	21.6/33	12	UCLA-Memphis St.	3/26/73	NBC	20.5/32

Associated Press Final Polls (Cont.)

1985

		Before Tourns	Head Coach	Final Record
1	Georgetown	30-2	John Thompson	35-3
2	Michigan	25-3	Bill Frieder	26-4
3	St. John's	27-3	Lou Carnesecca	31-4
4	Oklahoma	28-5	Billy Tubbs	31-6
5	Memphis St.	27-3	Dana Kirk	31-4
6	Georgia Tech	24-7	Bobby Cremins	27-8
7	North Carolina	24-8	Dean Smith	27-9
8	Louisiana Tech	27-2	Andy Russo	29-3
9	UNLV	27-3	Jerry Tarkanian	28-4
10	Duke	22-7	Mike Krzyzewski	23-8
11	VCU	25-5	J.D. Barnett	26-6
12	Illinois	24-8	Lou Henson	26-9
13	Kansas	25-7	Larry Brown	26-8
14	Loyola-IL	25-5	Gene Sullivan	27-6
15	Syracuse	21-8	Jim Boeheim	22-9
16	N.C. State	20-9	Jim Valvano	23-10
17	Texas Tech	23-7	Gerald Myers	23-8
18	Tulsa	23-7	Nolan Richardson	23-8
19	Georgia	21-8	Hugh Durham	22-9
20	LSU	19-9	Dale Brown	19-10

Note: Unranked **Villanova**, coached by Rollie Massimino, won the NCAAs. The Wildcats entered the tourney at 19-10 and had a final record of 25-10.

NCAA Final Four (at Rupp Arena, Lexington, KY): **Semifinals**— Georgetown 77, St. John's 59; Villanova 52, Memphis St. 45. **Championship**–Villanova 66, Georgetown 64.

NIT Championship (at Madison Square Garden): UCLA 65, Indiana 62. No Top 20 teams played in NIT.

1986

		Before Tourns	Head Coach	Final Record
1	Duke	32-2	Mike Krzyzewski	37-3
2	Kansas	31-3	Larry Brown	35-4
3	Kentucky	29-3	Eddie Sutton	32-4
4	St. John's	30-4	Lou Carnesecca	31-5
5	Michigan	27-4	Bill Frieder	28-5
6	Georgia Tech	25-6	Bobby Cremins	27-7
7	**Louisville**	26-7	Denny Crum	32-7
8	North Carolina	26-5	Dean Smith	28-6
9	Syracuse	25-5	Jim Boeheim	26-6
10	Notre Dame	23-5	Digger Phelps	23-6
11	UNLV	31-4	Jerry Tarkanian	33-5
12	Memphis St.	27-5	Dana Kirk	28-6
13	Georgetown	23-7	John Thompson	24-8
14	Bradley	31-2	Dick Versace	32-3
15	Oklahoma	25-8	Billy Tubbs	26-9
16	Indiana	21-7	Bob Knight	21-8
17	Navy	27-4	Paul Evans	30-5
18	Michigan St.	21-7	Jud Heathcote	23-8
19	Illinois	21-9	Lou Henson	22-10
20	UTEP	27-5	Don Haskins	27-6

NCAA Final Four (at Reunion Arena, Dallas): **Semifinals**–Duke 71, Kansas 67; Louisville 88, LSU 77. **Championship**–Louisville 72, Duke 69.

NIT Championship (at Madison Square Garden): Ohio St. 73, Wyoming 63. No Top 20 teams played in NIT.

1987

		Before Tourns	Head Coach	Final Record
1	UNLV	33-1	Jerry Tarkanian	37-2
2	North Carolina	29-3	Dean Smith	32-4
3	**Indiana**	24-4	Bob Knight	30-4
4	Georgetown	26-4	John Thompson	29-5
5	DePaul	26-2	Joey Meyer	28-3
6	Iowa	27-4	Tom Davis	30-5
7	Purdue	24-4	Gene Keady	25-5
8	Temple	31-3	John Chaney	32-4
9	Alabama	26-4	Wimp Sanderson	28-5
10	Syracuse	26-6	Jim Boeheim	31-7
11	Illinois	23-7	Lou Henson	23-8
12	Pittsburgh	24-7	Paul Evans	25-8
13	Clemson	25-5	Cliff Ellis	25-6
14	Missouri	24-9	Norm Stewart	24-10
15	UCLA	24-6	Walt Hazzard	25-7
16	New Orleans	25-3	Benny Dees	26-4
17	Duke	22-8	Mike Krzyzewski	24-9
18	Notre Dame	22-7	Digger Phelps	24-8
19	TCU	23-6	Jim Killingsworth	24-7
20	Kansas	23-10	Larry Brown	25-11

NCAA Final Four (at the Superdome, New Orleans): **Semifinals**–Syracuse 77, Providence 63; Indiana 97, UNLV 93. **Championship**–Indiana 74, Syracuse 73.

NIT Championship (at Madison Square Garden): Southern Miss. 84, La Salle 80. No Top 20 teams played in NIT.

1988

		Before Tourns	Head Coach	Final Record
1	Temple	29-1	John Chaney	32-2
2	Arizona	31-2	Lute Olson	35-3
3	Purdue	27-3	Gene Keady	29-4
4	Oklahoma	30-3	Billy Tubbs	35-4
5	Duke	24-6	Mike Krzyzewski	28-7
6	Kentucky	25-5	Eddie Sutton	27-6
7	North Carolina	24-6	Dean Smith	27-7
8	Pittsburgh	23-6	Paul Evans	24-7
9	Syracuse	25-8	Jim Boeheim	26-9
10	Michigan	24-7	Bill Frieder	26-8
11	Bradley	26-4	Stan Albeck	26-5
12	UNLV	27-5	Jerry Tarkanian	28-6
13	Wyoming	26-5	Benny Dees	26-6
14	N.C. State	24-7	Jim Valvano	24-8
15	Loyola-CA	27-3	Paul Westhead	28-4
16	Illinois	22-9	Lou Henson	23-10
17	Iowa	22-9	Tom Davis	24-10
18	Xavier-OH	26-3	Pete Gillen	26-4
19	BYU	25-5	Ladell Andersen	26-6
20	Kansas St.	22-8	Lon Kruger	25-9

Note: Unranked **Kansas**, coached by Larry Brown, won the NCAAs. The Jayhawks entered the tourney at 21-11 and had a final record of 27-11.

NCAA Final Four (at Kemper Arena, Kansas City): **Semifinals**–Kansas 66, Duke 59; Oklahoma 86, Arizona 78. **Championship**–Kansas 83, Oklahoma 79.

NIT Championship (at Madison Square Garden): Connecticut 72, Ohio St. 67. No Top 20 teams played in NIT.

1989

	Before Tourns	Head Coach	Final Record
1	Arizona.........27-3	Lute Olson	29-4
2	Georgetown.....26-4	John Thompson	29-5
3	Illinois..........27-4	Lou Henson	31-5
4	Oklahoma.......28-5	Billy Tubbs	30-6
5	North Carolina..27-7	Dean Smith	29-8
6	Missouri.........27-7	Norm Stewart & Rich Daly*	29-8
7	Syracuse........27-7	Jim Boeheim	30-8
8	Indiana.........25-7	Bob Knight	27-8
9	Duke...........24-7	Mike Krzyzewski	28-8
10	**Michigan**......24-7	Bill Frieder (24-7) & Steve Fisher (6-0)	30-7
11	Seton Hall......26-6	P.J. Carlesimo	31-7
12	Louisville.......22-8	Denny Crum	24-9
13	Stanford........26-6	Mike Montgomery	26-7
14	Iowa...........22-9	Tom Davis	23-10
15	UNLV..........26-7	Jerry Tarkanian	29-8
16	Florida St.......22-7	Pat Kennedy	22-8
17	West Virginia...25-4	Gale Catlett	26-5
18	Ball State.......28-2	Rick Majerus	29-3
19	N.C. State......20-8	Jim Valvano	22-9
20	Alabama.......23-7	Wimp Sanderson	23-8

NCAA Final Four (at The Kingdome, Seattle): **Semifinals**—Seton Hall 95, Duke 78; Michigan 83, Illinois 81. **Championship**—Michigan 80, Seton Hall 79 (OT). **NIT Championship** (at Madison Square Garden): St. John's 73, St. Louis 65. No Top 20 teams played in NIT.

*Norm Stewart's assistant Rich Daly temporarily took over for his ailing boss (Daly coached the final 14 games of the season) but returned to his role as an assistant when Stewart recovered before the start of the following season.

1990

	Before Tourns	Head Coach	Final Record
1	Oklahoma.......26-4	Billy Tubbs	27-5
2	**UNLV**..........29-5	Jerry Tarkanian	35-5
3	Connecticut......28-5	Jim Calhoun	31-6
4	Michigan St.....26-5	Jud Heathcote	28-6
5	Kansas.........29-4	Roy Williams	30-5
6	Syracuse........24-6	Jim Boeheim	26-7
7	Arkansas........26-4	Nolan Richardson	30-5
8	Georgetown......23-6	John Thompson	24-7
9	Georgia Tech....24-6	Bobby Cremins	28-7
10	Purdue.........21-7	Gene Keady	22-8
11	Missouri.........26-5	Norm Stewart	26-6
12	La Salle.........29-1	Speedy Morris	30-2
13	Michigan........22-7	Steve Fisher	23-8
14	Arizona.........24-6	Lute Olson	25-7
15	Duke...........24-8	Mike Krzyzewski	29-9
16	Louisville.......26-7	Denny Crum	27-8
17	Clemson........24-8	Cliff Ellis	26-9
18	Illinois..........21-7	Lou Henson	21-8
19	LSU.............22-8	Dale Brown	23-9
20	Minnesota......20-8	Clem Haskins	23-9
21	Loyola-CA......23-5	Paul Westhead	26-6
22	Oregon St.......22-6	Jim Anderson	22-7
23	Alabama........24-8	Wimp Sanderson	26-9
24	New Mexico St...26-4	Neil McCarthy	26-5
25	Xavier-OH......26-4	Pete Gillen	28-5

NCAA Final Four (at McNichols Sports Arena, Denver): **Semifinals**—Duke 97, Arkansas 83; UNLV 90, Georgia Tech 81. **Championship**—UNLV 103, Duke 73. **NIT Championship** (at Madison Square Garden): Vanderbilt 74, St.Louis 72. No Top 25 teams played in NIT.

1991

	Before Tourns	Head Coach	Final Record
1	UNLV...........30-0	Jerry Tarkanian	34-1
2	Arkansas........31-3	Nolan Richardson	34-4
3	Indiana.........27-4	Bob Knight	29-5
4	North Carolina..25-5	Dean Smith	29-6
5	Ohio St........25-3	Randy Ayers	27-4
6	**Duke**..........26-7	Mike Krzyzewski	32-7
7	Syracuse........26-5	Jim Boeheim	26-6
8	Arizona.........26-6	Lute Olson	28-7
9	Kentucky........22-6	Rick Pitino	same*
10	Utah............28-3	Rick Majerus	30-4
11	Nebraska.......26-7	Danny Nee	26-8
12	Kansas.........22-7	Roy Williams	27-8
13	Seton Hall......22-8	P.J. Carlesimo	25-9
14	Oklahoma St....22-7	Eddie Sutton	24-8
15	New Mexico St..23-5	Neil McCarthy	23-6
16	UCLA..........23-8	Jim Harrick	23-9
17	E.Tennessee St..28-4	Alan LaForce	28-5
18	Princeton........24-2	Pete Carril	24-3
19	Alabama........21-9	Wimp Sanderson	23-10
20	St. John's.......20-8	Lou Carnesecca	23-9
21	Mississippi St....20-8	Richard Williams	20-9
22	LSU.............20-9	Dale Brown	20-10
23	Texas..........22-8	Tom Penders	23-9
24	DePaul..........20-8	Joey Meyer	20-9
25	Southern Miss...21-7	M.K. Turk	21-8

*On probation

NCAA Final Four (at the Hoosier Dome, Indianapolis): **Semifinals**—Kansas 79, North Carolina 73; Duke 79, UNLV 77. **Championship**—Duke 72, Kansas 65. **NIT Championship** (at Madison Square Garden): Stanford 78, Oklahoma 72. No Top 25 teams played in NIT.

1992

	Before Tourns	Head Coach	Final Record
1	**Duke**..........28-2	Mike Krzyzewski	34-2
2	Kansas.........26-4	Roy Williams	27-5
3	Ohio St.........23-5	Randy Ayers	26-6
4	UCLA..........25-4	Jim Harrick	28-5
5	Indiana.........23-6	Bob Knight	27-7
6	Kentucky........26-6	Rick Pitino	29-7
7	UNLV..........26-2	Jerry Tarkanian	same*
8	USC............23-5	George Raveling	24-6
9	Arkansas........25-7	Nolan Richardson	26-8
10	Arizona.........24-6	Lute Olson	24-7
11	Oklahoma St....26-7	Eddie Sutton	28-8
12	Cincinnati......25-4	Bob Huggins	29-5
13	Alabama........25-8	Wimp Sanderson	26-9
14	Michigan St.....21-7	Jud Heathcote	22-8
15	Michigan.......20-8	Steve Fisher	25-9
16	Missouri.........20-8	Norm Stewart	21-9
17	Massachusetts...28-4	John Calipari	30-5
18	North Carolina..21-9	Dean Smith	23-10
19	Seton Hall......21-8	P.J. Carlesimo	23-9
20	Florida St.......20-9	Pat Kennedy	22-10
21	Syracuse........21-9	Jim Boeheim	22-10
22	Georgetown....21-9	John Thompson	22-10
23	Oklahoma.......21-8	Billy Tubbs	21-9
24	DePaul..........20-8	Joey Meyer	20-9
25	LSU.............20-9	Dale Brown	21-10

*On probation

NCAA Final Four (at the Metrodome, Minneapolis): **Semifinals**—Michigan 76, Cincinnati 72; Duke 81, Indiana 78. **Championship**—Duke 71, Michigan 51. **NIT Championship** (at Madison Square Garden): Virginia 81, Notre Dame 76 (OT). No Top 25 teams played in NIT.

Associated Press Final Polls (Cont.)

1993

		Before Tourns	Head Coach	Final Record
1	Indiana	28-3	Bob Knight	31-4
2	Kentucky	26-3	Rick Pitino	30-4
3	Michigan	26-4	Steve Fisher	31-5
4	N. Carolina	28-4	Dean Smith	34-4
5	Arizona	24-3	Lute Olson	24-4
6	Seton Hall	27-6	P.J. Carlesimo	28-7
7	Cincinnati	24-4	Bob Huggins	27-5
8	Vanderbilt	26-5	Eddie Fogler	28-6
9	Kansas	25-6	Roy Williams	29-7
10	Duke	23-7	Mike Krzyzewski	24-8
11	Florida St.	22-9	Pat Kennedy	25-10
12	Arkansas	20-8	Nolan Richardson	22-9
13	Iowa	22-8	Tom Davis	23-9
14	Massachusetts	23-6	John Calipari	24-7
15	Louisville	20-8	Denny Crum	22-9
16	Wake Forest	19-8	Dave Odom	21-9
17	New Orleans	26-3	Tim Floyd	26-4
18	Georgia Tech	19-10	Bobby Cremins	19-11
19	Utah	23-6	Rick Majerus	24-7
20	Western Ky.	24-5	Ralph Willard	26-6
21	New Mexico	24-6	Dave Bliss	24-7
22	Purdue	18-9	Gene Keady	18-10
23	Oklahoma St.	19-8	Eddie Sutton	20-9
24	New Mexico St.	25-7	Neil McCarthy	26-8
25	UNLV	21-7	Rollie Massimino	20-10

NCAA Final Four (at the Superdome, New Orleans): **Semifinals**–North Carolina 78, Kansas 68; Michigan 81, Kentucky 78 (OT). **Championship**–North Carolina 77, Michigan 71.
NIT Championship (at Madison Square Garden): Minnesota 62, Georgetown 61. No. 25 UNLV was the only Top 25 team that played in the NIT.

1995

		Before Tourns	Head Coach	Final Record
1	UCLA	25-2	Jim Harrick	31-2
2	Kentucky	25-4	Rick Pitino	28-5
3	Wake Forest	24-5	Dave Odom	26-6
4	North Carolina	24-5	Dean Smith	28-6
5	Kansas	23-5	Roy Williams	25-6
6	Arkansas	27-6	Nolan Richardson	32-7
7	Massachusetts	26-4	John Calipari	26-5
8	Connecticut	25-4	Jim Calhoun	28-5
9	Villanova	25-7	Steve Lappas	25-8
10	Maryland	24-7	Gary Williams	26-8
11	Michigan St.	22-5	Jud Heathcote	22-6
12	Purdue	24-6	Gene Keady	25-7
13	Virginia	22-8	Jeff Jones	25-9
14	Oklahoma St.	23-9	Eddie Sutton	27-10
15	Arizona	23-7	Lute Olson	23-8
16	Arizona St.	22-8	Bill Frieder	24-9
17	Oklahoma	23-8	Kelvin Sampson	23-9
18	Mississippi St.	20-7	Richard Williams	22-8
19	Utah	27-5	Rick Majerus	28-6
20	Alabama	22-9	David Hobbs	23-10
21	Western Ky.	26-3	Matt Kilcullen	27-4
22	Georgetown	19-9	John Thompson	21-10
23	Missouri	19-8	Norm Stewart	20-9
24	Iowa St.	22-10	Tim Floyd	23-11
25	Syracuse	19-9	Jim Boeheim	20-10

NCAA Final Four (at the Kingdome, Seattle): **Semifinals**– UCLA 74, Oklahoma St. 61; Arkansas 75, North Carolina 68. **Championship**– UCLA 89, Arkansas 78.
NIT Championship (at Madison Square Garden): Virginia Tech 65, Marquette 64 (OT). No top 25 teams played in NIT.

1994

		Before Tourns	Head Coach	Final Record
1	North Carolina	27-6	Dean Smith	28-7
2	Arkansas	25-3	Nolan Richardson	31-3
3	Purdue	26-4	Gene Keady	29-5
4	Connecticut	27-4	Jim Calhoun	29-5
5	Missouri	25-3	Norm Stewart	28-4
6	Duke	23-5	Mike Krzyzewski	28-6
7	Kentucky	26-6	Rick Pitino	27-7
8	Massachusetts	27-6	John Calipari	28-7
9	Arizona	25-5	Lute Olson	29-6
10	Louisville	26-5	Denny Crum	28-6
11	Michigan	21-7	Steve Fisher	24-8
12	Temple	22-7	John Chaney	23-8
13	Kansas	25-7	Roy Williams	27-8
14	Florida	25-7	Lon Kruger	29-8
15	Syracuse	21-6	Jim Boeheim	23-7
16	California	22-7	Todd Bozeman	22-8
17	UCLA	21-6	Jim Harrick	21-7
18	Indiana	19-8	Bob Knight	21-9
19	Oklahoma St.	23-9	Eddie Sutton	24-10
20	Texas	25-7	Tom Penders	26-8
21	Marquette	22-8	Kevin O'Neill	24-9
22	Nebraska	20-9	Danny Nee	20-10
23	Minnesota	20-11	Clem Haskins	21-12
24	Saint Louis	23-5	Charlie Spoonhour	23-6
25	Cincinnati	22-9	Bob Huggins	22-11

NCAA Final Four (at the Charlotte Coliseum): **Semifinals**– Arkansas 91, Arizona 82; Duke 70, Florida 65. **Championship**– Arkansas 76, Duke 72.
NIT Championship (at Madison Square Garden): Villanova 80, Vanderbilt 73. No top 25 teams played in NIT.

1996

		Before Tourns	Head Coach	Final Record
1	Massachusetts	31-1	John Calipari	35-2
2	Kentucky	28-2	Rick Pitino	34-2
3	Connecticut	30-2	Jim Calhoun	32-3
4	Georgetown	26-7	John Thompson	29-8
5	Kansas	26-4	Roy Williams	29-5
6	Purdue	25-5	Gene Keady	26-6
7	Cincinnati	25-4	Bob Huggins	28-5
8	Texas Tech	28-1	James Dickey	30-2
9	Wake Forest	23-5	Dave Odom	26-6
10	Villanova	25-6	Steve Lappas	26-7
11	Arizona	24-6	Lute Olson	26-7
12	Utah	25-6	Rick Majerus	27-7
13	Georgia Tech	22-11	Bobby Cremins	24-12
14	UCLA	23-7	Jim Harrick	23-8
15	Syracuse	24-8	Jim Boeheim	29-9
16	Memphis	22-7	Larry Finch	22-8
17	Iowa St.	23-8	Tim Floyd	24-9
18	Penn St.	21-6	Jerry Dunn	21-7
19	Mississippi St.	22-7	Richard Williams	26-8
20	Marquette	22-7	Mike Deane	23-8
21	Iowa	22-8	Tom Davis	23-9
22	Virginia Tech	22-5	Bill Foster	23-6
23	New Mexico	27-4	Dave Bliss	28-5
24	Louisville	20-11	Denny Crum	22-12
25	North Carolina	20-10	Dean Smith	21-11

NCAA Final Four (at the Meadowlands, E. Rutherford, N.J.): **Semifinals**– Kentucky 81, Massachusetts 74; Syracuse 77, Mississippi St. 69. **Championship**– Kentucky 76, Syracuse 67.
NIT Championship (at Madison Square Garden): Nebraska 60, St. Joseph's 56. No top 25 teams played in NIT.

1997

	Before Tourns	Head Coach	Final Record
1	Kansas..........32-1	Roy Williams	34-2
2	Utah..........26-3	Rick Majerus	29-4
3	Minnesota......27-3	Clem Haskins	31-4
4	North Carolina..24-6	Dean Smith	28-7
5	Kentucky.......30-4	Rick Pitino	35-5
6	South Carolina..24-7	Eddie Fogler	24-8
7	UCLA...........21-7	Steve Lavin	24-8
8	Duke 23-8	Mike Krzyzewski	24-9
9	Wake Forest 23-6	Dave Odom	24-7
10	Cincinnati 25-7	Bob Huggins	26-8
11	New Mexico....24-7	Dave Bliss	25-8
12	St. Joseph's 24-6	Phil Martelli	26-7
13	Xavier 22-5	Skip Prosser	23-6
14	Clemson.........21-9	Rick Barnes	23-10
15	**Arizona**.......19-9	Lute Olsen	25-9
16	Charleston......28-2	John Kresse	29-3
17	Georgia 24-8	Tubby Smith	24-9
18	Iowa St..........20-8	Tim Floyd	22-9
19	Illinois 21-9	Lon Kruger	22-10
20	Villanova.......23-9	Steve Lappas	24-10
21	Stanford 20-7	Mike Montgomery	22-8
22	Maryland 21-10	Gary Williams	21-11
23	Boston College...21-8	Jim O'Brien	22-9
24	Colorado........21-9	Ricardo Patton	22-10
25	Louisville 23-8	Denny Crum	26-9

NCAA Final Four (at the RCA Dome, Indianapolis): **Semifinals**– Kentucky 78, Minnesota 69; Arizona 66, North Carolina 58. **Championship**– Arizona 84, Kentucky 79 (OT).

NIT Championship (at Madison Square Garden): Michigan 82, Florida St. 72. No top 25 teams played in NIT.

1998

	Before Tourns	Head Coach	Final Record
1	North Carolina...30-3	Bill Guthridge	34-4
2	Kansas..........34-3	Roy Williams	35-4
3	Duke 29-3	Mike Krzyzewski	32-4
4	Arizona.........27-4	Lute Olsen	30-5
5	**Kentucky**......29-4	Tubby Smith	35-4
6	Connecticut 29-4	Jim Calhoun	32-5
7	Utah.............25-3	Rick Majerus	30-4
8	Princeton.......26-1	Bill Carmody	27-2
9	Cincinnati 26-5	Bob Huggins	27-6
10	Stanford 26-4	Mike Montgomery	30-5
11	Purdue..........26-7	Gene Keady	28-8
12	Michigan........24-8	Brian Ellerbe	25-9
13	Mississippi 22-6	Rob Evans	22-7
14	South Carolina..23-7	Eddie Fogler	23-8
15	TCU 27-5	Billy Tubbs	27-6
16	Michigan St......20-7	Tom Izzo	22-8
17	Arkansas........23-8	Nolan Richardson	24-9
18	New Mexico....23-7	Dave Bliss	24-8
19	UCLA...........22-8	Steve Lavin	24-9
20	Maryland 19-10	Gary Williams	21-11
21	Syracuse 24-8	Jim Boeheim	26-9
22	Illinois 22-9	Lon Kruger	23-10
23	Xavier 22-7	Skip Prosser	22-8
24	Temple 21-8	John Chaney	21-9
25	Murray St........29-3	Mark Gottfried	29-4

NCAA Final Four (at the Alamodome, San Antonio): **Semifinals**– Kentucky 86, Stanford 85 (OT); Utah 65, North Carolina 59. **Championship**– Kentucky 78, Utah 69.

NIT Championship (at Madison Square Garden): Minnesota 79, Penn St. 72. No top 25 teams played in NIT.

AP Post-Tournament Final Polls

The final AP Top 20 poll has been released after the NCAA tournament and NIT four times– in 1953 and '54 and again in 1974 and '75. Those four polls are listed below; teams that were not included in the last regular season polls are in CAPITAL italic letters.

1953

		Final Record
1	Indiana	23-3
2	Seton Hall	31-2
3	Kansas	19-6
4	Washington	30-3
5	LSU	24-3
6	La Salle	25-3
7	*ST. JOHN'S*	17-6
8	Okla. A&M	23-7
9	Duquesne	21-8
10	Notre Dame	19-5
11	Illinois	18-4
12	Kansas St.	17-4
13	Holy Cross	20-6
14	Seattle	29-4
15	*WAKE FOREST*	22-7
16	*SANTA CLARA*	20-7
17	Western Ky.	25-6
18	N.C. State	26-6
19	*DEPAUL*	19-9
20	*SW MISSOURI*	24-4

1954

		Final Record
1	Kentucky	25-0
2	La Salle	26-4
3	Holy Cross	26-2
4	Indiana	20-4
5	Duquesne	26-3
6	Notre Dame	22-3
7	*BRADLEY*	19-13
8	Western Ky.	29-3
9	*PENN ST.*	18-6
10	Okla. A&M	24-5
11	USC	19-14
12	*GEO. WASH.*	23-3
13	Iowa	17-5
14	LSU	21-5
15	Duke	22-6
16	*NIAGARA*	24-6
17	Seattle	26-2
18	Kansas	16-5
19	Illinois	17-5
20	*MARYLAND*	23-7

1974

		Final Record
1	N.C. State	30-1
2	UCLA	26-4
3	Marquette	26-5
4	Maryland	23-5
5	Notre Dame	26-3
6	Michigan	22-5
7	Kansas	23-7
8	Providence	28-4
9	Indiana	23-5
10	Long Beach St.	24-2
11	*PURDUE*	22-8
12	North Carolina	22-6
13	Vanderbilt	23-5
14	Alabama	22-4
15	*UTAH*	22-8
16	Pittsburgh	25-4
17	USC	24-5
18	*ORAL ROBERTS*	23-6
19	South Carolina	22-5
20	Dayton	20-9

1975

		Final Record
1	UCLA	28-3
2	Kentucky	26-5
3	Indiana	31-1
4	Louisville	28-3
5	Maryland	24-5
6	Syracuse	23-9
7	N.C. State	22-6
8	Arizona St.	25-4
9	North Carolina	23-8
10	Alabama	22-5
11	Marquette	23-4
12	*PRINCETON*	22-8
13	Cincinnati	23-6
14	Notre Dame	19-10
15	Kansas St.	20-9
16	Drake	19-10
17	UNLV	24-5
18	Oregon St.	19-12
19	*MICHIGAN*	19-8
20	Penn	23-5

Pre-Tournament Records

1953– St. John's (Al DeStefano, 14-5); Wake Forest (Murray Greason, 21-6); Santa Clara (Bob Feerick, 18-6); DePaul (Ray Meyer, 18-7); SW Missouri St. (Bob Vanatta, 19-4 before NAIA tourney). **1954**– Bradley (Forddy Anderson, 15-12); Penn St. (Elmer Gross, 14-5); George Washington (Bill Reinhart, 23-2); Niagara (Taps Gallagher, 22-5); Maryland (Bud Millikan, 23-7). **1974**– Purdue (Fred Schaus, 18-8); Utah (Bill Foster, 19-7); Oral Roberts (Ken Trickey, 21-5). **1975**– Princeton (Pete Carril, 18-8); Michigan (Johnny Orr, 19-7).

Associated Press Final Polls (Cont.)

1999

		Before Tourns	Head Coach	Final Record
1	Duke	32-1	Mike Krzyzewski	37-2
2	Michigan St.	29-4	Tom Izzo	33-5
3	**Connecticut**	28-2	Jim Calhoun	34-2
4	Auburn	27-3	Cliff Ellis	29-4
5	Maryland	26-5	Gary Williams	28-6
6	Utah	27-4	Rick Majerus	28-5
7	Stanford	25-6	Mike Montgomery	26-7
8	Kentucky	25-8	Tubby Smith	28-9
9	St. John's	25-8	Mike Jarvis	28-9
10	Miami-FL	22-6	Leonard Hamilton	23-7
11	Cincinnati	26-5	Bob Huggins	27-6
12	Arizona	22-6	Lute Olsen	22-7
13	North Carolina	24-9	Bill Guthridge	24-10
14	Ohio St.	23-8	Jim O'Brien	27-9
15	UCLA	22-8	Steve Lavin	22-9
16	College of Charleston	28-2	John Kresse	28-3
17	Arkansas	22-10	Nolan Richardson	23-11
18	Wisconsin	22-9	Dick Bennett	22-10
19	Indiana	22-10	Bobby Knight	23-11
20	Tennessee	20-8	Jerry Green	21-9
21	Iowa	18-9	Tom Davis	20-10
22	Kansas	22-9	Roy Williams	23-10
23	Florida	20-8	Billy Donovan	22-9
24	NC-Charlotte	22-10	Bob Lutz	23-11
25	New Mexico	24-8	Dave Bliss	25-9

NCAA Final Four (at the Tropicana Field, St. Petersburg): **Semifinals**— Duke 68, Michigan St. 62; Connecticut 64, Ohio St. 58. **Championship**— Connecticut 77, Duke 74.
NIT Championship (at Madison Square Garden): California 61, Clemson 60. No top 25 teams played in NIT.

2000

		Before Tourns	Head Coach	Final Record
1	Duke	27-4	Mike Krzyzewski	29-5
2	**Michigan St.**	26-7	Tom Izzo	32-7
3	Stanford	26-3	Mike Montgomery	27-4
4	Arizona	26-6	Lute Olsen	27-7
5	Temple	26-5	John Chaney	27-6
6	Iowa St.	29-4	Larry Eustachy	32-5
7	Cincinnati	28-3	Bob Huggins	29-4
8	Ohio St.	22-6	Jim O'Brien	23-7
9	St. John's	24-7	Mike Jarvis	25-8
10	LSU	26-5	John Brady	28-6
11	Tennessee	24-6	Jerry Green	26-7
12	Oklahoma	26-6	Kelvin Sampson	27-7
13	Florida	24-7	Billy Donovan	29-8
14	Oklahoma St.	24-6	Eddie Sutton	27-7
15	Texas	23-8	Rick Barnes	24-9
16	Syracuse	26-6	Jim Boeheim	26-6
17	Maryland	24-9	Gary Williams	25-10
18	Tulsa	29-4	Bill Self	32-5
19	Kentucky	22-9	Tubby Smith	23-10
20	Connecticut	24-9	Jim Calhoun	25-10
21	Illinois	21-9	Lon Kruger	22-10
22	Indiana	20-8	Bobby Knight	20-9
23	Miami-FL	21-10	Leonard Hamilton	23-11
24	Auburn	23-9	Cliff Ellis	24-10
25	Purdue	21-9	Gene Keady	24-10

NCAA Final Four (at the RCA Dome, Indianapolis): **Semifinals**— Michigan St. 53, Wisconsin 41; Florida 71, North Carolina 59. **Championship**— Michigan St. 89, Florida 76.
NIT Championship (at Madison Square Garden): Wake Forest 71, Notre Dame 61. No top 25 teams played in NIT.

Division I Winning Streaks

Full Season
(Including tournaments)

No		Seasons	Broken by	Score
88	UCLA	1971-74	Notre Dame	71-70
60	San Francisco	1955-57	Illinois	62-33
47	UCLA	1966-68	Houston	71-69
45	UNLV	1990-91	Duke	79-77
44	Texas	1913-14	Rice	24-18
43	Seton Hall	1939-41	LIU-Bklyn	49-26
43	LIU-Brooklyn	1935-37	Stanford	45-31
41	UCLA	1968-69	USC	46-44
39	Marquette	1970-71	Ohio St.	60-59
37	Cincinnati	1962-63	Wichita St.	65-64
37	North Carolina	1957-58	West Virginia	75-64
36	N.C. State	1974-75	Wake Forest	83-78
35	Arkansas	1927-29	Texas	26-25

Regular Season
(Not including tournaments)

No		Seasons	Broken by	Score
76	UCLA	1971-74	Notre Dame	71-70
57	Indiana	1975-77	Toledo	59-57
56	Marquette	1970-72	Detroit	70-49
54	Kentucky	1952-55	Georgia Tech	59-58
51	San Francisco	1955-57	Illinois	62-33
48	Penn	1970-72	Temple	57-52
47	Ohio St	1960-62	Wisconsin	86-67
44	Texas	1913-17	Rice	24-18
43	UCLA	1966-68	Houston	71-69
43	LIU-Brooklyn	1935-37	Stanford	45-31
42	Seton Hall	1939-41	LIU-Bklyn	49-26

Home Court

No		Seasons	Broken By	Score
129	Kentucky	1943-55	Georgia Tech	59-58
99	St. Bonaventure	1948-61	Detroit	77-70
98	UCLA	1970-76	Oregon	65-45
86	Cincinnati	1957-64	Kansas	51-47
81	Arizona	1945-51	Kansas St.	76-57
81	Marquette	1967-73	Notre Dame	71-69
80	Lamar	1978-84	Louisiana Tech	68-65
75	Long Beach St.	1968-74	San Francisco	94-84
72	UNLV	1974-78	New Mexico	102-98
71	Arizona	1987-92	UCLA	89-87

All-Time Highest Scoring Teams
SINGLE SEASON
Scoring Offense

Team	Season	Gm	Pts	Avg
Loyola-CA	1990	32	3918	122.4
Loyola-CA	1989	31	3486	112.5
UNLV	1976	31	3426	110.5
Loyola-CA	1988	32	3528	110.3
UNLV	1977	32	3426	107.1
Oral Roberts	1972	28	2943	105.1
Southern-BR	1991	28	2924	104.4
Loyola-CA	1991	31	3211	103.6
Oklahoma	1988	39	4012	102.9
Oklahoma	1989	36	3680	102.2

Annual NCAA Division I Leaders
Scoring

The NCAA did not begin keeping individual scoring records until the 1947-48 season. All averages include postseason games where applicable.

Multiple winners: Pete Maravich and Oscar Robertson (3); Darrell Floyd, Charles Jones, Harry Kelly, Frank Selvy and Freeman Williams (2).

Year		Gm	Pts	Avg	Year		Gm	Pts	Avg
1948	Murray Wier, Iowa	19	399	21.0	1975	Bob McCurdy, Richmond	26	855	32.9
1949	Tony Lavelli, Yale	30	671	22.4	1976	Marshall Rodgers, Texas-Pan Am	25	919	36.8
1950	Paul Arizin, Villanova	29	735	25.3	1977	Freeman Williams, Portland St.	26	1010	38.8
1951	Bill Mlkvy, Temple	25	731	29.2	1978	Freeman Williams, Portland St.	27	969	35.9
1952	Clyde Lovellette, Kansas	28	795	28.4	1979	Lawrence Butler, Idaho St.	27	812	30.1
1953	Frank Selvy, Furman	25	738	29.5	1980	Tony Murphy, Southern-BR	29	932	32.1
1954	Frank Selvy, Furman	29	1209	41.7	1981	Zam Fredrick, S. Carolina	27	781	28.9
1955	Darrell Floyd, Furman	25	897	35.9	1982	Harry Kelly, Texas Southern	29	862	29.7
1956	Darrell Floyd, Furman	28	946	33.8	1983	Harry Kelly, Texas Southern	29	835	28.8
1957	Grady Wallace, S. Carolina	29	906	31.2	1984	Joe Jakubick, Akron	27	814	30.1
1958	Oscar Robertson, Cincinnati	28	984	35.1	1985	Xavier McDaniel, Wichita St	31	844	27.2
1959	Oscar Robertson, Cincinnati	30	978	32.6	1986	Terrance Bailey, Wagner	29	854	29.4
1960	Oscar Robertson, Cincinnati	30	1011	33.7	1987	Kevin Houston, Army	29	953	32.9
1961	Frank Burgess, Gonzaga	26	842	32.4	1988	Hersey Hawkins, Bradley	31	1125	36.3
1962	Billy McGill, Utah	26	1009	38.8	1989	Hank Gathers, Loyola-CA	31	1015	32.7
1963	Nick Werkman, Seton Hall	22	650	29.5	1990	Bo Kimble, Loyola-CA	32	1131	35.3
1964	Howie Komives, Bowling Green	23	844	36.7	1991	Kevin Bradshaw, US Int'l	28	1054	37.6
1965	Rick Barry, Miami-FL	26	973	37.4	1992	Brett Roberts, Morehead St	29	815	28.1
1966	Dave Schellhase, Purdue	24	781	32.5	1993	Greg Guy, Texas-Pan Am	19	556	29.3
1967	Jimmy Walker, Providence	28	851	30.4	1994	Glenn Robinson, Purdue	34	1030	30.3
1968	Pete Maravich, LSU	26	1138	43.8	1995	Kurt Thomas, TCU	27	781	28.9
1969	Pete Maravich, LSU	26	1148	44.2	1996	Kevin Granger, Texas Southern	24	648	27.0
1970	Pete Maravich, LSU	31	1381	44.5	1997	Charles Jones, LIU-Brooklyn	30	903	30.1
1971	Johnny Neumann, Ole Miss	23	923	40.1	1998	Charles Jones, LIU-Brooklyn	30	869	29.0
1972	Dwight Lamar, SW La.	29	1054	36.3	1999	Alvin Young, Niagara	29	728	25.1
1973	Bird Averitt, Pepperdine	25	848	33.9	2000	Courtney Alexander, Fresno St.	27	669	24.8
1974	Larry Fogle, Canisius	25	835	33.4					

Note: Seventeen underclassmen have won the title. **Sophomores** (4)–Robertson (1958), Maravich (1968), Neumann (1971) and Fogle (1974); **Juniors** (13)–Selvy (1953), Floyd (1955), Robertson (1959), Werkman (1963), Maravich (1969), Lamar (1972), Williams (1977), Kelly (1982), Bailey (1986), Gathers (1989), Guy (1993), Robinson (1994) and Jones (1997).

Rebounds

The NCAA did not begin keeping individual rebounding records until the 1950-51 season. From 1956-62, the championship was decided on highest percentage of recoveries out of all rebounds made by both teams in all games. All averages include postseason games where applicable.

Multiple winners: Artis Gilmore, Jerry Lucas, Xavier McDaniel, Kermit Washington and Leroy Wright (2).

Year		Gm	No	Avg	Year		Gm	No	Avg
1951	Ernie Beck, Penn	27	556	20.6	1976	Sam Pellom, Buffalo	26	420	16.2
1952	Bill Hannon, Army	17	355	20.9	1977	Glenn Mosley, Seton Hall	29	473	16.3
1953	Ed Conlin, Fordham	26	612	23.5	1978	Ken Williams, N. Texas	28	411	14.7
1954	Art Quimby, Connecticut	26	588	22.6	1979	Monti Davis, Tennessee St.	26	421	16.2
1955	Charlie Slack, Marshall	21	538	25.6	1980	Larry Smith, Alcorn State	26	392	15.1
1956	Joe Holup, G. Washington	26	604	25.6	1981	Darryl Watson, Miss. Valley St.	27	379	14.0
1957	Elgin Baylor, Seattle	25	508	23.5	1982	LaSalle Thompson, Texas	27	365	13.5
1958	Alex Ellis, Niagara	25	536	26.2	1983	Xavier McDaniel, Wichita St.	28	403	14.4
1959	Leroy Wright, Pacific	26	652	23.8	1984	Akeem Olajuwon, Houston	37	500	13.5
1960	Leroy Wright, Pacific	17	380	23.4	1985	Xavier McDaniel, Wichita St.	31	460	14.8
1961	Jerry Lucas, Ohio St.	27	470	19.8	1986	David Robinson, Navy	35	455	13.0
1962	Jerry Lucas, Ohio St.	28	499	21.1	1987	Jerome Lane, Pittsburgh	33	444	13.5
1963	Paul Silas, Creighton	27	557	20.6	1988	Kenny Miller, Loyola-IL	29	395	13.6
1964	Bob Pelkington, Xavier-OH	26	567	21.8	1989	Hank Gathers, Loyola-CA	31	426	13.7
1965	Toby Kimball, Connecticut	23	483	21.0	1990	Anthony Bonner, St. Louis	33	456	13.8
1966	Jim Ware, Oklahoma City	29	607	20.9	1991	Shaquille O'Neal, LSU	28	411	14.7
1967	Dick Cunningham, Murray St.	22	479	21.8	1992	Popeye Jones, Murray St.	30	431	14.4
1968	Neal Walk, Florida	25	494	19.8	1993	Warren Kidd, Mid. Tenn. St.	26	386	14.8
1969	Spencer Haywood, Detroit	22	472	21.5	1994	Jerome Lambert, Baylor	24	355	14.8
1970	Artis Gilmore, Jacksonville	28	621	22.2	1995	Kurt Thomas, TCU	27	393	14.6
1971	Artis Gilmore, Jacksonville	26	603	23.2	1996	Marcus Mann, Miss. Valley St.	29	394	13.6
1972	Kermit Washington, American	23	455	19.8	1997	Tim Duncan, Wake Forest	31	457	14.7
1973	Kermit Washington, American	22	439	20.0	1998	Ryan Perryman, Dayton	33	412	12.5
1974	Marvin Barnes, Providence	32	597	18.7	1999	Ian McGinnis, Dartmouth	26	317	12.2
1975	John Irving, Hofstra	21	323	15.4	2000	Darren Phillip, Fairfield	29	405	14.0

Note: Only three players have ever led the NCAA in scoring and rebounding in the same season: Xavier McDaniel of Wichita St. (1985), Hank Gathers of Loyola-Marymount (1989) and Kurt Thomas of TCU (1995).

Assists

The NCAA did not begin keeping individual assist records until the 1983-84 season. All averages include postseason games where applicable.

Multiple winner: Avery Johnson (2).

Year		Gm	No	Avg
1984	Craig Lathen, IL-Chicago	29	274	9.45
1985	Rob Weingard, Hofstra	24	228	9.50
1986	Mark Jackson, St. John's	36	328	9.11
1987	Avery Johnson, Southern-BR	31	333	10.74
1988	Avery Johnson, Southern-BR	30	399	13.30
1989	Glenn Williams, Holy Cross	28	278	9.93
1990	Todd Lehmann, Drexel	28	260	9.29
1991	Chris Corchiani, N.C. State	31	299	9.65
1992	Van Usher, Tennessee Tech	29	254	8.76
1993	Sam Crawford, N. Mexico St	34	310	9.12
1994	Jason Kidd, California	30	272	9.06
1995	Nelson Haggerty, Baylor	28	284	10.14
1996	Raimonds Miglinieks, UC-Irvine	27	230	8.52
1997	Kenny Mitchell, Dartmouth	26	203	7.81
1998	Ahlon Lewis, Arizona St.	32	294	9.19
1999	Doug Gottlieb, Oklahoma St.	34	299	8.79
2000	Mark Dickel, UNLV	31	280	9.03

Blocked Shots

The NCAA did not begin keeping individual blocked shots records until the 1985-86 season. All averages include post-season games where applicable.

Multiple winner: Keith Closs and David Robinson (2).

Year		Gm	No	Avg
1986	David Robinson, Navy	35	207	5.91
1987	David Robinson, Navy	32	144	4.50
1988	Rodney Blake, St. Joe's-PA	29	116	4.00
1989	Alonzo Mourning, G'town	34	169	4.97
1990	Kenny Green, Rhode Island	26	124	4.77
1991	Shawn Bradley, BYU	34	177	5.21
1992	Shaquille O'Neal, LSU	30	157	5.23
1993	Theo Ratliff, Wyoming	28	124	4.43
1994	Grady Livingston, Howard	26	115	4.42
1995	Keith Closs, Cen. Conn. St.	26	139	5.35
1996	Keith Closs, Cen. Conn. St.	28	178	6.36
1997	Adonal Foyle, Colgate	28	180	6.43
1998	Jerome James, Florida A&M	27	125	4.63
1999	Tarvis Williams, Hampton	27	135	5.00
2000	Ken Johnson, Ohio St.	30	161	5.37

All-Time NCAA Division I Individual Leaders

Through 1999-00; includes regular season and tournament games; **Last** column indicates final year played.

CAREER

Scoring

Points		Yrs	Last	Gm	Pts
1	Pete Maravich, LSU	3	1970	83	3667
2	Freeman Williams, Port. St.	4	1978	106	3249
3	Lionel Simmons, La Salle	4	1990	131	3217
4	Alphonso Ford, Miss. Val. St.	4	1993	109	3165
5	Harry Kelly, Texas Southern	4	1983	110	3066
6	Hersey Hawkins, Bradley	4	1988	125	3008
7	Oscar Robertson, Cincinnati	3	1960	88	2973
8	Danny Manning, Kansas	4	1988	147	2951
9	Alfredrick Hughes, Loyola-IL	4	1985	120	2914
10	Elvin Hayes, Houston	3	1968	93	2884
11	Larry Bird, Indiana St.	3	1979	94	2850
12	Otis Birdsong, Houston	4	1977	116	2832
13	Kevin Bradshaw, Beth-Cook/US Int'l	4	1991	111	2804
14	Allan Houston, Tennessee	4	1993	128	2801
15	Hank Gathers, USC/Loyola-CA	4	1990	117	2723
16	Reggie Lewis, Northeastern	4	1987	122	2708
17	Daren Queenan, Lehigh	4	1988	118	2703
18	Byron Larkin, Xavier-OH	4	1988	121	2696
19	David Robinson, Navy	4	1987	127	2669
20	Wayman Tisdale, Oklahoma	3	1985	104	2661

Average		Yrs	Last	Pts	Avg
1	Pete Maravich, LSU	3	1970	3667	44.2
2	Austin Carr, Notre Dame	3	1971	2560	34.6
3	Oscar Robertson, Cinn	3	1960	2973	33.8
4	Calvin Murphy, Niagara	3	1970	2548	33.1
5	Dwight Lamar, SW La	2	1973	1862	32.7
6	Frank Selvy, Furman	3	1954	2538	32.5
7	Rick Mount, Purdue	3	1970	2323	32.3
8	Darrell Floyd, Furman	3	1956	2281	32.1
9	Nick Werkman, Seton Hall	3	1964	2273	32.0
10	Willie Humes, Idaho St.	2	1971	1510	31.5
11	William Averitt, Pepperdine	2	1973	1541	31.4
12	Elgin Baylor, Idaho/Seattle	3	1958	2500	31.3
13	Elvin Hayes, Houston	3	1968	2884	31.0
14	Freeman Williams, Port. St.	4	1978	3249	30.7
15	Larry Bird, Indiana St.	3	1979	2850	30.3
16	Bill Bradley, Princeton	3	1965	2503	30.2
17	Rich Fuqua, Oral Roberts	2	1973	1617	29.9
18	Wilt Chamberlain, Kansas	2	1958	1433	29.9
19	Rick Barry, Miami-FL	3	1965	2298	29.8
20	Doug Collins, Illinois St.	3	1973	2240	29.1

Field Goal Pct.		Yrs	Last	FG	FGA	Pct
1	Steve Johnson, Ore. St.	4	1981	828	1222	.678
2	Murray Brown, Fla. St.	4	1980	566	847	.668
3	Lee Campbell, M.Tenn St./ SW Mo.St.	3	1990	411	618	.665
4	Warren Kidd, M.Tenn.St.	3	1993	496	747	.664
5	Todd MacCulloch, Wash.	4	1999	702	1058	.664
6	Joe Senser, West Chester	4	1979	476	719	.662
7	Kevin McGee, UC-Irvine	2	1982	552	841	.656
8	O. Phillips, Pepperdine	2	1983	404	618	.654
9	Bill Walton, UCLA	3	1974	747	1147	.651
10	William Herndon, UMass.	4	1992	472	728	.648

Note: minimum 400 FGs made and an average of four per game.

Free Throw Pct.		Yrs	Last	FT	FTA	Pct
1	Greg Starrick, Ky/So.Ill	4	1972	341	375	.909
2	Jack Moore, Nebraska	4	1982	446	495	.901
3	Steve Henson, Kansas St.	4	1990	361	401	.900
4	Steve Alford, Indiana	4	1987	535	596	.898
5	Bob Lloyd, Rutgers	3	1967	543	605	.898
6	Jim Barton, Dartmouth	4	1989	394	440	.895
7	Tommy Boyer, Arkansas	3	1963	315	353	.892
8	Rob Robbins, N. Mexico	4	1991	309	348	.888
9	Marcus Wilson, Evansville	4	1999	455	513	.887
10	Sean Miller, Pitt	4	1992	317	358	.885

Note: minimum 300 FTs made and an average of two per game.

3-Pt Field Goals		Yrs	Last	Gm	3FG
1	Curtis Staples, Virginia	4	1998	122	413
2	Keith Veney, Lamar/Marshall	4	1997	111	409
3	Doug Day, Radford	4	1993	117	401
4	Ronnie Schmitz, Missouri-KC	4	1993	112	378
5	Mark Alberts, Akron	4	1993	107	375

3-Pt Field Goal Pct.		Yrs	Last	3FG	Att	Pct
1	Tony Bennett, Wisc-GB	4	1992	290	584	.497
2	Keith Jennings, E.Tenn.St.	4	1991	223	452	.493
3	Kirk Manns, Michigan St.	4	1990	212	446	.475
4	Tim Locum, Wisconsin	4	1991	227	481	.472
5	David Olson, Eastern Ill.	4	1992	262	562	.466

Note: minimum 200 3FGs made.

Rebounds

Total (before 1973)

		Yrs	Last	Gm	No
1	Tom Gola, La Salle	4	1955	118	2201
2	Joe Holup, G. Washington	4	1956	104	2030
3	Charlie Slack, Marshall	4	1956	88	1916
4	Ed Conlin, Fordham	4	1955	102	1884
5	Dickie Hemric, Wake Forest	4	1955	104	1802
6	Paul Silas, Creighton	3	1964	81	1751
7	Art Quimby, Connecticut	4	1955	80	1716
8	Jerry Harper, Alabama	4	1956	93	1688
9	Jeff Cohen, Wm. & Mary	4	1961	103	1679
10	Steve Hamilton, Morehead St.	4	1958	102	1675

Total (since 1973)

		Yrs	Last	Gm	No
1	Tim Duncan, Wake Forest	4	1997	128	1570
2	Derrick Coleman, Syracuse	4	1990	143	1537
3	Malik Rose, Drexel	4	1996	120	1514
4	Ralph Sampson, Virginia	4	1983	132	1511
5	Pete Padgett, Nevada-Reno	4	1976	104	1464
6	Lionel Simmons, La Salle	4	1990	131	1429
7	Anthony Bonner, St. Louis	4	1990	133	1424
8	Tyrone Hill, Xavier-OH	4	1990	126	1380
9	Popeye Jones, Murray St.	4	1992	123	1374
10	Michael Brooks, La Salle	4	1980	114	1372

Average (before 1973)

		Yrs	Last	No	Avg
1	Artis Gilmore, Jacksonville	2	1971	1224	22.7
2	Charlie Slack, Marshall	4	1956	1916	21.8
3	Paul Silas, Creighton	3	1964	1751	21.6
4	Leroy Wright, Pacific	3	1960	1442	21.5
5	Art Quimby, Connecticut	4	1955	1716	21.5

Note: minimum 800 rebounds.

Average (since 1973)

		Yrs	Last	No	Avg
1	Glenn Mosley, Seton Hall	4	1977	1263	15.2
2	Bill Campion, Manhattan	3	1975	1070	14.2
3	Pete Padgett, Nevada-Reno	4	1976	1464	14.1
4	Bob Warner, Maine	4	1976	1304	13.6
5	Shaquille O'Neal, LSU	3	1992	1217	13.5

Note: minimum 650 rebounds.

Assists

Total

		Yrs	Last	Gm	No
1	Bobby Hurley, Duke	4	1993	140	1076
2	Chris Corchiani, N.C. State	4	1991	124	1038
3	Ed Cota, N. Carolina	4	2000	138	1030
4	Keith Jennings, E. Tenn. St.	4	1991	127	983
5	Sherman Douglas, Syracuse	4	1989	138	960
6	Tony Miller, Marquette	4	1995	123	956
7	Greg Anthony, Portland/UNLV	4	1991	138	950
8	Doug Gottlieb, ND/Okla St.	4	2000	124	947
9	Gary Payton, Oregon St.	4	1990	120	938
10	Orlando Smart, San Fran	4	1994	116	902
11	Andre LaFleur, Northeastern	4	1987	128	894

Average

		Yrs	Last	No	Avg
1	A. Johnson, Cameron/Southern	3	1988	838	8.91
2	Sam Crawford, N. Mexico St.	2	1993	592	8.84
3	Mark Wade, Okla/UNLV	3	1987	693	8.77
4	Chris Corchiani, N.C. State	4	1991	1038	8.37
5	Taurence Chisholm, Delaware	4	1988	877	7.97
6	Van Usher, Tennessee Tech	3	1992	676	7.95
7	Anthony Manuel, Bradley	3	1989	855	7.92
8	Chico Fletcher, Ark. St.	4	2000	893	7.83
9	Gary Payton, Oregon St.	4	1990	938	7.82
10	Orlando Smart, San Fran	4	1994	902	7.78

Note: minimum 550 assists.

Blocked Shots

Average

		Yrs	Last	No	Avg
1	Keith Closs, Cen. Conn. St.	2	1996	317	5.87
2	Adonal Foyle, Colgate	3	1997	492	5.66
3	David Robinson, Navy	2	1987	351	5.24
4	Shaquille O'Neal, LSU	3	1992	412	4.58
5	Jerome James, Fla. A&M	3	1998	363	4.48

Note: minimum 225 blocked shots.

Steals

Average

		Yrs	Last	No	Avg
1	Mookie Blaylock, Oklahoma	2	1989	281	3.80
2	Ronn McMahon, Eastern Wash.	3	1990	225	3.52
3	Eric Murdock, Providence	4	1991	376	3.21
4	Van Usher, Tennessee Tech	3	1992	270	3.18
5	Pepe Sanchez, Temple	4	2000	365	3.15

Note: minimum 225 steals.

2000 Points/1000 Rebounds

For a combined total of 4000 or more.

		Gm	Pts	Reb	Total
1	Tom Gola, La Salle	118	2462	2201	4663
2	Lionel Simmons, La Salle	131	3217	1429	4646
3	Elvin Hayes, Houston	93	2884	1602	4486
4	Dickie Hemric, W. Forest	104	2587	1802	4389
5	Oscar Robertson, Cinn.	88	2973	1338	4311
6	Joe Holup, G. Wash	104	2226	2030	4256
7	Harry Kelly, TX-Southern	110	3066	1085	4151
8	Danny Manning, Kansas	147	2951	1187	4138
9	Larry Bird, Indiana St.	94	2850	1247	4097
10	Elgin Baylor, Col. Idaho/ Seattle	80	2500	1559	4059
11	Michael Brooks, La Salle	114	2628	1372	4000

Years Played– Baylor (1956-58); **Bird** (1977-79); **Brooks** (1977-80); **Gola** (1952-55); **Hayes** (1966-68); **Hemric** (1952-55); **Holup** (1953-56); **Kelly** (1980-83); **Manning** (1985-88); **Robertson** (1958-60); **Simmons** (1987-90).

SINGLE SEASON
Scoring

Points

		Year	Gm	Pts
1	Pete Maravich, LSU	1970	31	1381
2	Elvin Hayes, Houston	1968	33	1214
3	Frank Selvy, Furman	1954	29	1209
4	Pete Maravich, LSU	1969	26	1148
5	Pete Maravich, LSU	1968	26	1138
6	Bo Kimble, Loyola-CA	1990	32	1131
7	Hersey Hawkins, Bradley	1988	31	1125
8	Austin Carr, Notre Dame	1970	29	1106
9	Austin Carr, Notre Dame	1971	29	1101
10	Otis Birdsong, Houston	1977	36	1090

Average

		Year	Gm	Pts	Avg
1	Pete Maravich, LSU	1970	31	1381	44.5
2	Pete Maravich, LSU	1969	26	1148	44.2
3	Pete Maravich, LSU	1968	26	1138	43.8
4	Frank Selvy, Furman	1954	29	1209	41.7
5	Johnny Neumann, Ole Miss	1971	23	923	40.1
6	Freeman Williams, Port. St.	1977	26	1010	38.8
7	Billy McGill, Utah	1962	26	1009	38.8
8	Calvin Murphy, Niagara	1968	24	916	38.2
9	Austin Carr, Notre Dame	1970	29	1106	38.1
10	Austin Carr, Notre Dame	1971	29	1101	38.0

All-Time NCAA Division I Individual Leaders (Cont.)

Field Goal Pct.	Year	FG	FGA	Pct
1 Steve Johnson, Oregon St.	1981	235	315	.746
2 Dwayne Davis, Florida	1989	179	248	.722
3 Keith Walker, Utica	1985	154	216	.713
4 Steve Johnson, Oregon St.	1980	211	297	.710
5 Oliver Miller, Arkansas	1991	254	361	.704

Free Throw Pct.	Year	FT	FTA	Pct
1 Craig Collins, Penn St.	1985	94	98	.959
2 Rod Foster, UCLA	1982	95	100	.950
3 Clay McKnight, Pacific	2000	74	78	.949
4 Carlos Gibson, Marshall	1978	84	89	.944
5 Danny Basile, Marist	1994	84	89	.944

3-Pt Field Goal Pct.	Year	3FG	Att	Pct
1 Glenn Tropf, Holy Cross	1988	52	82	.634
2 Sean Wightman, W. Mich	1992	48	76	.632
3 Keith Jennings, E. Tenn. St.	1991	84	142	.592
4 Dave Calloway, Monmouth	1989	48	82	.585
5 Steve Kerr, Arizona	1988	114	199	.573

Assists

Average	Year	Gm	No	Avg
1 Avery Johnson, Southern-BR	1988	30	399	13.3
2 Anthony Manuel, Bradley	1988	31	373	12.0
3 Avery Johnson, Southern-BR	1987	31	333	10.7
4 Mark Wade, UNLV	1987	38	406	10.7
5 Glenn Williams, Holy Cross	1989	28	278	9.9

Rebounds

Average (before 1973)	Year	Gm	No	Avg
1 Charlie Slack, Marshall	1955	21	538	25.6
2 Leroy Wright, Pacific	1959	26	652	25.1
3 Art Quimby, Connecticut	1955	25	611	24.4
4 Charlie Slack, Marshall	1956	22	520	23.6
5 Ed Conlin, Fordham	1953	26	612	23.5

Average (since 1973)	Year	Gm	No	Avg
1 Kermit Washington, American	1973	25	511	20.4
2 Marvin Barnes, Providence	1973	30	571	19.0
3 Marvin Barnes, Providence	1974	32	597	18.7
4 Pete Padgett, Nevada	1973	26	462	17.8
5 Jim Bradley, Northern Ill	1973	24	426	17.8

Blocked Shots

Average	Year	Gm	No	Avg
1 Adonal Foyle, Colgate	1997	28	180	6.42
2 Keith Closs, Cen. Conn. St.	1996	28	178	6.36
3 David Robinson, Navy	1986	35	207	5.91
4 Ken Johnson, Ohio St.	2000	30	161	5.37
5 Keith Closs, Cen. Conn. St.	1995	26	139	5.35

Steals

Average	Year	Gm	No	Avg
1 Darron Brittman, Chicago St.	1986	28	139	4.96
2 Aldwin Ware, Florida A&M	1988	29	142	4.90
3 Ronn McMahon, East Wash.	1990	29	130	4.48
4 Pointer Williams, McNeese St.	1996	27	118	4.37
5 Jim Paguaga, St. Francis-NY	1986	28	120	4.29

SINGLE GAME

Scoring

Points vs Div. I Team	Year	Pts
1 Kevin Bradshaw, US Int'l vs Loyola-CA	1991	72
2 Pete Maravich, LSU vs Alabama	1970	69
3 Calvin Murphy, Niagara vs Syracuse	1969	68
4 Jay Handlan, Wash. & Lee vs Furman	1951	66
Pete Maravich, LSU vs Tulane	1969	66
Anthony Roberts, Oral Rbts vs N.C. A&T	1977	66
7 Anthony Roberts, Oral Rbts vs Ore	1977	65
Scott Haffner, Evansville vs Dayton	1989	65
9 Pete Maravich, LSU vs Kentucky	1970	64
10 Johnny Neumann, Ole Miss vs LSU	1971	63
Hersey Hawkins, Bradley vs Detroit	1988	63

Points vs Non-Div. I Team	Year	Pts
1 Frank Selvy, Furman vs Newberry	1954	100
2 Paul Arizin, Villanova vs Phi. NAMC	1949	85
3 Freeman Williams, Port. St. vs Rocky Mt	1978	81
4 Bill Mlkvy, Temple vs Wilkes	1951	73
5 Freeman Williams, Port. St. vs So. Ore	1977	71

Note: Bevo Francis of Division II Rio Grande (Ohio) scored an overall collegiate record 113 points against Hillsdale in 1954. He also scored 84 against Alliance and 82 against Bluffton that same season.

Assists

	Year	No
1 Tony Fairley, Baptist vs Armstrong St.	1987	22
Avery Johnson, Southern-BR vs TX-South	1988	22
Sherman Douglas, Syracuse vs Providence	1989	22
4 Mark Wade, UNLV vs Navy	1986	21
Kelvin Scarborough, N. Mexico vs Hawaii	1987	21
Anthony Manuel, Bradley vs UC-Irvine	1987	21
Avery Johnson, Southern-BR vs Ala. St.	1988	21

3-Pt Field Goals

	Year	No
1 Keith Veney, Marshall vs Morehead St.	1996	15
2 Dave Jamerson, Ohio U. vs Charleston	1989	14
Askia Jones, Kansas St. vs Fresno St.	1994	14
4 Gary Bosserd, Niagara vs Siena	1987	12
Darrin Fitzgerald, Butler vs Detroit	1987	12
Al Dillard, Arkansas vs Delaware St.	1993	12
Mitch Taylor, South-BR vs La. Christian	1995	12
David McMahan, Winthrop vs C. Carolina	1996	12

Rebounds

Total (before 1973)	Year	No
1 Bill Chambers, Wm. & Mary vs Virginia	1953	51
2 Charlie Slack, Marshall vs M. Harvey	1954	43
3 Tom Heinsohn, Holy Cross vs BC	1955	42
4 Art Quimby, UConn vs BU	1955	40
5 Three players tied with 39 each.		

Total (since 1973)	Year	No
1 Larry Abney, Fresno St. vs SMU	2000	35
2 David Vaughn, Oral Roberts vs Brandeis	1973	34
3 Robert Parish, Centenary vs So. Miss	1973	33
4 Durand Macklin, LSU vs Tulane	1976	32
Jervaughn Scales, South-BR vs Grambling	1994	32

Blocked Shots

	Year	No
1 David Robinson, Navy vs NC-Wilmington	1986	14
Shawn Bradley, BYU vs Eastern Ky	1990	14
Roy Rogers, Alabama vs Georgia	1996	14
Loren Woods, Arizona vs Oregon	2000	14
5 Kevin Roberson, Vermont vs UNH	1992	13
Jim McIlvaine, Marquette vs No. Ill	1993	13
Keith Closs, C. Conn. St. vs St. Fran-PA	1994	13

Steals

	Year	No
1 Mookie Blaylock, Oklahoma vs Centenary	1987	13
Mookie Blaylock, Oklahoma vs Loyola-CA	1988	13
3 Kenny Robertson, Cleve. St. vs Wagner	1988	12
Terry Evans, Oklahoma vs Florida A&M	1993	12
Richard Duncan, Mid. Tenn St. vs E. Ky.	1999	12

Annual Awards

UPI picked the first national Division I Player of the Year in 1955. Since then, the U.S. Basketball Writers Assn. (1959), the Commonwealth Athletic Club of Kentucky's Adolph Rupp Trophy (1961), the Atlanta Tip-Off Club (1969), the National Assn. of Basketball Coaches (1975), and the LA Athletic Club's John Wooden Award (1977) have joined in. UPI discontinued its award in 1997.

Since 1977, the first year all the following awards were given out, the same player has won all of them in the same season 13 times: Marques Johnson in 1977, Larry Bird in 1979, Ralph Sampson in both 1982 and '83, Michael Jordan in 1984, David Robinson in 1987, Lionel Simmons in 1990, Calbert Cheaney in 1993, Glenn Robinson in 1994, Tim Duncan in 1997, Antawn Jamison in 1998, Elton Brand in 1999 and Kenyon Martin in 2000.

United Press International

Voted on by a panel of UPI college basketball writers and first presented in 1955.
Multiple winners: Oscar Robertson, Ralph Sampson and Bill Walton (3); Lew Alcindor and Jerry Lucas (2).

Year	Year	Year
1955 Tom Gola, La Salle	1970 Pete Maravich, LSU	1985 Chris Mullin, St. John's
1956 Bill Russell, San Francisco	1971 Austin Carr, Notre Dame	1986 Walter Berry, St. John's
1957 Chet Forte, Columbia	1972 Bill Walton, UCLA	1987 David Robinson, Navy
1958 Oscar Robertson, Cincinnati	1973 Bill Walton, UCLA	1988 Hersey Hawkins, Bradley
1959 Oscar Robertson, Cincinnati	1974 Bill Walton, UCLA	1989 Danny Ferry, Duke
1960 Oscar Robertson, Cincinnati	1975 David Thompson, N.C. State	1990 Lionel Simmons, La Salle
1961 Jerry Lucas, Ohio St.	1976 Scott May, Indiana	1991 Shaquille O'Neal, LSU
1962 Jerry Lucas, Ohio St.	1977 Marques Johnson, UCLA	1992 Jim Jackson, Ohio St.
1963 Art Heyman, Duke	1978 Butch Lee, Marquette	1993 Calbert Cheaney, Indiana
1964 Gary Bradds, Ohio St.	1979 Larry Bird, Indiana St.	1994 Glenn Robinson, Purdue
1965 Bill Bradley, Princeton	1980 Mark Aguirre, DePaul	1995 Joe Smith, Maryland
1966 Cazzie Russell, Michigan	1981 Ralph Sampson, Virginia	1996 Ray Allen, UConn
1967 Lew Alcindor, UCLA	1982 Ralph Sampson, Virginia	1997 award discontinued
1968 Elvin Hayes, Houston	1983 Ralph Sampson, Virginia	
1969 Lew Alcindor, UCLA	1984 Michael Jordan, N. Carolina	

U.S. Basketball Writers Association

Voted on by the USBWA and first presented in 1959.
Multiple winners: Ralph Sampson and Bill Walton (3); Lew Alcindor, Jerry Lucas and Oscar Robertson (2).

Year	Year	Year
1959 Oscar Robertson, Cincinnati	1973 Bill Walton, UCLA	1987 David Robinson, Navy
1960 Oscar Robertson, Cincinnati	1974 Bill Walton, UCLA	1988 Hersey Hawkins, Bradley
1961 Jerry Lucas, Ohio St.	1975 David Thompson, N.C. State	1989 Danny Ferry, Duke
1962 Jerry Lucas, Ohio St.	1976 Adrian Dantley, Notre Dame	1990 Lionel Simmons, La Salle
1963 Art Heyman, Duke	1977 Marques Johnson, UCLA	1991 Larry Johnson, UNLV
1964 Walt Hazzard, UCLA	1978 Phil Ford, North Carolina	1992 Christian Laettner, Duke
1965 Bill Bradley, Princeton	1979 Larry Bird, Indiana St.	1993 Calbert Cheaney, Indiana
1966 Cazzie Russell, Michigan	1980 Mark Aguirre, DePaul	1994 Glenn Robinson, Purdue
1967 Lew Alcindor, UCLA	1981 Ralph Sampson, Virginia	1995 Ed O'Bannon, UCLA
1968 Elvin Hayes, Houston	1982 Ralph Sampson, Virginia	1996 Marcus Camby, UMass
1969 Lew Alcindor, UCLA	1983 Ralph Sampson, Virginia	1997 Tim Duncan, Wake Forest
1970 Pete Maravich, LSU	1984 Michael Jordan, N. Carolina	1998 Antawn Jamison, N. Carolina
1971 Sidney Wicks, UCLA	1985 Chris Mullin, St. John's	1999 Elton Brand, Duke
1972 Bill Walton, UCLA	1986 Walter Berry, St. John's	2000 Kenyon Martin, Cincinnati

Rupp Trophy

Voted on by AP sportswriters and broadcasters and first presented in 1961 by the Commonwealth Athletic Club of Kentucky in the name of former University of Kentucky coach Adolph Rupp.
Multiple winners: Ralph Sampson (3); Lew Alcindor, Jerry Lucas, David Thompson and Bill Walton (2).

Year	Year	Year
1961 Jerry Lucas, Ohio St.	1975 David Thompson, N.C. State	1989 Sean Elliott, Arizona
1962 Jerry Lucas, Ohio St.	1976 Scott May, Indiana	1990 Lionel Simmons, La Salle
1963 Art Heyman, Duke	1977 Marques Johnson, UCLA	1991 Shaquille O'Neal, LSU
1964 Gary Bradds, Ohio St.	1978 Butch Lee, Marquette	1992 Christian Laettner, Duke
1965 Bill Bradley, Princeton	1979 Larry Bird, Indiana St.	1993 Calbert Cheaney, Indiana
1966 Cazzie Russell, Michigan	1980 Mark Aguirre, DePaul	1994 Glenn Robinson, Purdue
1967 Lew Alcindor, UCLA	1981 Ralph Sampson, Virginia	1995 Joe Smith, Maryland
1968 Elvin Hayes, Houston	1982 Ralph Sampson, Virginia	1996 Marcus Camby, UMass
1969 Lew Alcindor, UCLA	1983 Ralph Sampson, Virginia	1997 Tim Duncan, Wake Forest
1970 Pete Maravich, LSU	1984 Michael Jordan, N. Carolina	1998 Antawn Jamison, N. Carolina
1971 Austin Carr, Notre Dame	1985 Patrick Ewing, Georgetown	1999 Elton Brand, Duke
1972 Bill Walton, UCLA	1986 Walter Berry, St. John's	2000 Kenyon Martin, Cincinnati
1973 Bill Walton, UCLA	1987 David Robinson, Navy	
1974 David Thompson, N.C. State	1988 Hersey Hawkins, Bradley	

Naismith Award

Voted on by a panel of coaches, sportswriters and broadcasters and first presented in 1969 by the Atlanta Tip-Off Club in 1969 in the name of the inventor of basketball, Dr. James Naismith.

Multiple winners: Ralph Sampson and Bill Walton (3).

Year	Year	Year
1969 Lew Alcindor, UCLA	1980 Mark Aguirre, DePaul	1991 Larry Johnson, UNLV
1970 Pete Maravich, LSU	1981 Ralph Sampson, Virginia	1992 Christian Laettner, Duke
1971 Austin Carr, Notre Dame	1982 Ralph Sampson, Virginia	1993 Calbert Cheaney, Indiana
1972 Bill Walton, UCLA	1983 Ralph Sampson, Virginia	1994 Glenn Robinson, Purdue
1973 Bill Walton, UCLA	1984 Michael Jordan, N. Carolina	1995 Joe Smith, Maryland
1974 Bill Walton, UCLA	1985 Patrick Ewing, Georgetown	1996 Marcus Camby, UMass
1975 David Thompson, N.C. State	1986 Johnny Dawkins, Duke	1997 Tim Duncan, Wake Forest
1976 Scott May, Indiana	1987 David Robinson, Navy	1998 Antawn Jamison, N. Carolina
1977 Marques Johnson, UCLA	1988 Danny Manning, Kansas	1999 Elton Brand, Duke
1978 Butch Lee, Marquette	1989 Danny Ferry, Duke	2000 Kenyon Martin, Cincinnati
1979 Larry Bird, Indiana St.	1990 Lionel Simmons, La Salle	

National Association of Basketball Coaches

Voted on by the National Assn. of Basketball Coaches and presented by the Eastman Kodak Co. from 1975-94.

Multiple winner: Ralph Sampson (2).

Year	Year	Year
1975 David Thompson, N.C. State	1984 Michael Jordan, N. Carolina	1993 Calbert Cheaney, Indiana
1976 Scott May, Indiana	1985 Patrick Ewing, Georgetown	1994 Glenn Robinson, Purdue
1977 Marques Johnson, UCLA	1986 Walter Berry, St. John's	1995 Shawn Respert, Mich. St.
1978 Phil Ford, North Carolina	1987 David Robinson, Navy	1996 Marcus Camby, UMass
1979 Larry Bird, Indiana St.	1988 Danny Manning, Kansas	1997 Tim Duncan, Wake Forest
1980 Michael Brooks, La Salle	1989 Sean Elliott, Arizona	1998 Antawn Jamison, N. Carolina
1981 Danny Ainge, BYU	1990 Lionel Simmons, La Salle	1999 Elton Brand, Duke
1982 Ralph Sampson, Virginia	1991 Larry Johnson, UNLV	2000 Kenyon Martin, Cincinnati
1983 Ralph Sampson, Virginia	1992 Christian Laettner, Duke	

Wooden Award

Voted on by a panel of coaches, sportswriters and broadcasters and first presented in 1977 by the Los Angeles Athletic Club in the name of former Purdue All-America and UCLA coach John Wooden. Unlike the other five Player of the Year awards, candidates for the Wooden must have a minimum grade point average of 2.00 (out of 4.00).

Multiple winner: Ralph Sampson (2).

Year	Year	Year
1977 Marques Johnson, UCLA	1985 Chris Mullin, St. John's	1993 Calbert Cheaney, Indiana
1978 Phil Ford, North Carolina	1986 Walter Berry St. John's	1994 Glenn Robinson, Purdue
1979 Larry Bird, Indiana St.	1987 David Robinson, Navy	1995 Ed O'Bannon, UCLA
1980 Darrell Griffith, Louisville	1988 Danny Manning, Kansas	1996 Marcus Camby, UMass
1981 Danny Ainge, BYU	1989 Sean Elliott, Arizona	1997 Tim Duncan, Wake Forest
1982 Ralph Sampson, Virginia	1990 Lionel Simmons, La Salle	1998 Antawn Jamison, N. Carolina
1983 Ralph Sampson, Virginia	1991 Larry Johnson, UNLV	1999 Elton Brand, Duke
1984 Michael Jordan, N. Carolina	1992 Christian Laettner, Duke	2000 Kenyon Martin, Cincinnati

Players of the Year and Top Draft Picks

Consensus College Players of the Year and first overall selections in NBA draft since the abolition of the NBA's territorial draft in 1966. Top draft picks who became Rookie of the Year are in **bold** type; (*) indicates top draft pick chosen as junior and (**) indicates top draft pick chosen as sophomore.

Year	Player of the Year	Top Draft Pick	Year	Player of the Year	Top Draft Pick
1966	Cazzie Russell, Mich.	Cazzie Russell, NY	1985	Patrick Ewing, G'town	
1967	Lew Alcindor, UCLA	Jimmy Walker, Det.		& Chris Mullin, St. John's	**Patrick Ewing**, NY
1968	Elvin Hayes, Houston	Elvin Hayes, SD	1986	Walter Berry, St. John's	Brad Daugherty, Cle.
1969	Lew Alcindor, UCLA	**Lew Alcindor**, Mil.	1987	David Robinson, Navy	**David Robinson**, SA
1970	Pete Maravich, LSU	Bob Lanier, Det.	1988	Hersey Hawkins, Bradley	
1971	Sidney Wicks, UCLA	Austin Carr, Cle.		& Danny Manning, Kan.	Danny Manning, LAC
1972	Bill Walton, UCLA	LaRue Martin, Por.	1989	Sean Elliott, Arizona	
1973	Bill Walton, UCLA	Doug Collins, Phi.		& Danny Ferry, Duke	Pervis Ellison, Sac.
1974	Bill Walton, UCLA	Bill Walton, Por.	1990	Lionel Simmons, La Salle	**Derrick Coleman**, NJ
1975	David Thompson, N.C. St.	David Thompson, Atl.	1991	Larry Johnson, UNLV	
1976	Scott May, Indiana	John Lucas, Hou.		& Shaquille O'Neal, LSU	**Larry Johnson**, Cha.
1977	Marques Johnson, UCLA	Kent Benson, Ind.	1992	Christian Laettner, Duke	**Shaquille O'Neal**, Orl.*
1978	Butch Lee, Marquette		1993	Calbert Cheaney, Ind.	**Chris Webber**, Orl.**
	& Phil Ford, N. Caro.	Mychal Thompson, Por.	1994	Glenn Robinson, Purdue	Glenn Robinson, Mil.*
1979	Larry Bird, Indiana St.	Magic Johnson, LAL**	1995	Ed O'Bannon, UCLA	
1980	Mark Aguirre, DePaul	Joe Barry Carroll, G. St.		& Joe Smith, Maryland	Joe Smith, G. St.**
1981	Ralph Sampson, Va.		1996	Marcus Camby, UMass	**Allen Iverson**, Phi.**
	& Danny Ainge, BYU	Mark Aguirre, Dal.	1997	Tim Duncan, Wake Forest	**Tim Duncan**, SA
1982	Ralph Sampson, Va.	James Worthy, LAL*	1998	Antawn Jamison, N. Caro.	M. Olowokandi, LAC
1983	Ralph Sampson, Va.	**Ralph Sampson**, Hou.	1999	Elton Brand, Duke	**Elton Brand**, Chi.**
1984	Michael Jordan, N. Caro.	Akeem Olajuwon, Hou.	2000	Kenyon Martin, Cincinnati	Kenyon Martin, NJ

All-Time Winningest Division I Coaches

Minimum of 10 seasons as Division I head coach; regular season and tournament games included; coaches active during 1999-2000 in **bold** type.

Top 30 Winning Percentage

		Yrs	W	L	Pct
1	Clair Bee	21	412	87	.826
2	Adolph Rupp	41	876	190	.822
3	John Wooden	29	664	162	.804
4	Jerry Tarkanian	29	731	179	.803
5	**Roy Williams**	12	328	82	.800
6	Dean Smith	36	879	254	.776
7	Harry Fisher	13	147	44	.770
8	Frank Keaney	27	387	117	.768
9	George Keogan	24	385	117	.767
10	Jack Ramsay	11	231	71	.765
11	Vic Bubas	10	213	67	.761
12	Chick Davies	21	314	106	.748
13	Ray Mears	21	399	135	.747
14	**Rick Majerus**	16	358	125	.741
15	**Jim Boeheim**	24	566	199	.740
16	Rick Pitino	15	352	124	.739
17	Al McGuire	20	405	143	.739
18	Everett Case	18	376	133	.739
19	Phog Allen	48	746	264	.739
20	**Bob Huggins**	19	444	158	.738
21	**John Chaney**	28	632	225	.737
22	**Lute Olson**	27	613	220	.736
23	Walter Meanwell	22	280	101	.735
24	Bill Musselman	12	232	85	.732
25	Lew Andreas	25	355	134	.726
26	**Bob Knight**	35	763	290	.725
27	Lou Carnesecca	24	526	200	.725
28	**Nolan Richardson**	20	475	181	.724
29	Fred Schaus	12	251	96	.723
30	**Mike Krzyzewski**	25	571	219	.723

Top 30 Victories

		Yrs	W	L	Pct
1	Dean Smith	36	**879**	254	.776
2	Adolph Rupp	41	**876**	190	.822
3	**Jim Phelan**	46	**809**	463	.636
4	Hank Iba	41	**767**	338	.694
5	**Bob Knight**	35	**763**	290	.725
6	Ed Diddle	42	**759**	302	.715
7	Phog Allen	48	**746**	264	.739
8	**Lefty Driesell**	38	**733**	372	.663
9	Norm Stewart	38	**731**	375	.661
	Jerry Tarkanian	29	**731**	179	.803
11	Ray Meyer	42	**724**	354	.672
	Lou Henson	37	**724**	362	.667
13	Don Haskins	38	**719**	353	.671
14	John Wooden	29	**664**	162	.804
15	Denny Crum	30	**663**	276	.706
16	**Eddie Sutton**	30	**659**	259	.718
17	Ralph Miller	38	**657**	382	.632
18	Marv Harshman	40	**654**	449	.593
19	Gene Bartow	34	**647**	353	.647
20	**John Chaney**	28	**632**	225	.737
21	Cam Henderson	35	**630**	243	.722
22	Norm Sloan	37	**624**	393	.614
23	**Lute Olson**	27	**613**	220	.736
24	Slats Gill	36	**599**	392	.604
25	Abe Lemons	34	**597**	344	.634
26	John Thompson	27	**596**	239	.714
27	Guy Lewis	30	**592**	279	.680
28	**Jim Calhoun**	28	**577**	267	.684
29	**Mike Kryzewski**	25	**571**	219	.723
30	Eldon Miller	36	**568**	419	.575

Note: Clarence (Bighouse) Gaines of Division II Winston-Salem St. (1947-93) retired after the 1992-93 season to finish his 47-year career ranked No. 3 on the all-time NCAA list of all coaches regardless of division. His record is 828-446 with a .650 winning percentage.

Where They Coached

Allen–Baker (1906-08), Kansas (1908-09), Haskell (1909), Central Mo. St. (1913-19), Kansas (1920-56); **Andreas**–Syracuse (1925-43; 45-50); **Bartow**–Central Mo. St. (1962-64), Valparaiso (1965-70), Memphis St. (1971-74), Illinois (1975), UCLA (1976-77), UAB (1979-96); **Bee**–Rider (1929-31), LIU-Brooklyn (1932-45, 46-51); **Boeheim**–Syracuse (1977–); **Bubas**–Duke (1960-69); **Calhoun**–Northeastern (1973-86), Connecticut (1987–); **Carnesecca**–St. John's (1966-70, 74-92); **Case**–N.C. State (1947-64); **Chaney**–Cheyney St. (1973-82), Temple (1983–); **Crum**–Louisville (1972–); **Davies**–Duquesne (1925-43, 47-48), **Diddle**–Western Ky. (1923-64); **Driesell**–Davidson (1961-69), Maryland (1970-86), J. Madison (1989-97), Georgia St. (1997–); **Fisher**–Columbia (1907-16), Army (1922-23, 25).

Gill–Oregon St. (1929-64); **Harshman**–Pacific Lutheran (1946-58), Wash. St. (1959-71), Washington (1972-85); **Haskins**–UTEP (1962-99); **Henderson**–Muskingum (1920-22), Davis & Elkins (1923-35), Marshall (1936-55); **Henson**–Hardin-Simmons (1963-66), N. Mexico St. (1967-75), Illinois (1976-96), N. Mexico St. (1997–); **Huggins**–Walsh (1981-83), Akron (1985-89), Cincinnati (1990–); **Iba**–NW Missouri St. (1930-33), Colorado (1934), Oklahoma St. (1935-70); **Keaney**–Rhode Island (1921-48); **Keogan**–St. Louis (1916), Allegheny (1919), Valparaiso (1920-21), Notre Dame (1924-43); **Knight**–Army (1966-71), Indiana (1972-00); **Kryzewski**–Army (1976-80), Duke (1981–).

Lemons–Okla. City (1956-73), Pan American (1974-76), Texas (1977-82), Okla. City (1984-90); **Lewis**– Houston (1957-86); **Majerus**–Marquette (1984-86), Ball St. (1988-89), Utah (1991–); **A. McGuire**–Belmont Abbey (1958-64), Marquette (1965-77); **Meanwell**–Wisconsin (1912-17, 21-34), Missouri (1918-20); **Mears**–Wittenberg (1957-62), Tennessee (1963-77); **Meyer**–DePaul (1943-84); **E. Miller**–Western Mich. (1970-75), Ohio St. (1976-85), Northern Iowa (1986-98); **R. Miller**–Wichita St. (1952-64), Iowa (1965-70), Oregon St. (1971-89); **Musselman**–Ashland (1966-71), Minnesota (1972-75), S. Alabama (1996-97); **Olson**–Long Beach St. (1974), Iowa (1975-83), Arizona (1984–); **Phelan**–Mount St. Mary's (1955–); **Pitino**–Boston Univ. (1979-83), Providence (1986-87), Kentucky (1990-97).

Ramsay–St. Joseph's-PA (1956-66); **Richardson**–Tulsa (1981-85), Arkansas (1986–); **Rupp**–Kentucky (1931-72); **Schaus**–West Va. (1955-60), Purdue (1973-78); **Sloan**–Presbyterian (1952-55), Citadel (1957-60), Florida (1961-66), N.C. State (1967-80), Florida (1981-89); **Smith**–North Carolina (1962-97); **Stewart**–No. Iowa (1962-67), Missouri (1968-99); **Sutton**–Creighton (1970-74), Arkansas (1975-85), Kentucky (1986-89), Oklahoma St. (1991–); **Tarkanian**–Long Beach St. (1969-73), UNLV (1974-92), Fresno St. (1995–); **Thompson**–Georgetown (1973-99); **Williams**– Kansas (1989–); **Wooden**–Indiana St. (1947-48), UCLA (1949-75).

Most NCAA Tournaments

Through 2000; listed are number of appearances, overall tournament record, times reaching Final Four, and number of NCAA championships.

App		W-L	F4	Championships
27	Dean Smith	65-27	11	2 (1982, 93)
24	**Bob Knight**	42-21	5	3 (1976, 81, 87)
23	Denny Crum	42-23	6	2 (1980, 86)
21	**Lute Olson**	32-21	4	1 (1997)
21	**Eddie Sutton**	32-21	2	None
20	Adolph Rupp	30-18	6	4 (1948-49, 51, 58)
20	John Thompson	34-19	3	1 (1984)
20	**Jim Boeheim**	31-20	2	None
19	**Lou Henson**	19-20	2	None
18	Lou Carnesecca	17-20	1	None
17	**Jerry Tarkanian**	37-17	4	1 (1990)
17	**Gene Keady**	18-17	0	None
16	John Wooden	47-10	12	10 (1964-65, 67-73, 75)
16	Norm Stewart	12-16	0	None
16	**Mike Krzyzewski**	50-14	8	2 (1991-92)
16	**John Chaney**	20-16	0	None
15	Digger Phelps	17-17	1	None
14	Don Haskins	14-13	1	1 (1966)
14	Guy Lewis	26-18	5	None
14	**Jim Calhoun**	26-13	1	1 (1999)
13	Dale Brown	15-14	2	None
13	Ray Meyer	14-16	2	None

Active Coaches' Victories

Minimum five seasons in Division I.

		Yrs	W	L	Pct
1	Jim Phelan, Mt. St. Mary's	46	**809**	463	.636
2	Lefty Driesell, Georgia St.	38	**733**	372	.663
3	Jerry Tarkanian, Fresno St.	29	**731**	179	.803
4	Lou Henson, N. Mexico St.	37	**724**	362	.667
5	Denny Crum, Louisville	30	**663**	276	.706
6	Eddie Sutton, Okla. St.	30	**659**	259	.718
7	John Chaney, Temple	28	**632**	225	.737
8	Lute Olson, Arizona	27	**613**	220	.736
9	Jim Calhoun, UConn.	28	**577**	267	.684
10	Mike Krzyzewski, Duke	25	**571**	219	.723
11	Jim Boeheim, Syracuse	24	**566**	199	.740
12	Billy Tubbs, TCU	26	**556**	272	.671
13	Hugh Durham, Jacksonville	32	**553**	362	.604
14	Gale Catlett, West Va.	28	**540**	292	.649
15	John Kresse, C. of Charleston	21	**514**	127	.802
16	Tom Penders, Geo. Wash.	29	**513**	342	.600
	Davey Whitney, Alcorn St.	29	**513**	312	.622
18	Larry Hunter, Ohio	24	**489**	213	.697
19	Dave Bliss, Baylor	25	**479**	286	.626
20	Gene Keady, Purdue	22	**477**	210	.694
21	Rollie Massimino, Cleveland St.	26	**476**	340	.583
22	Nolan Richardson, Arkansas	20	**475**	181	.724
23	Don DeVoe, Navy	26	**470**	314	.599
24	Cliff Ellis, Auburn	25	**468**	281	.625
25	Homer Drew, Valparaiso	24	**455**	291	.610

Annual Awards

UPI picked the first national Division I Coach of the Year in 1955. Since then, the U.S. Basketball Writers Assn. (1959), AP (1967), the National Assn. of Basketball Coaches (1969), and the Atlanta Tip-Off Club (1987) have joined in. Since 1987, the first year all five awards were given out, no coach has won all of them in the same season.

United Press International

Voted on by a panel of UPI college basketball writers and first presented in 1955.

Multiple winners: John Wooden (6); Bob Knight, Ray Meyer, Adolph Rupp, Norm Stewart, Fred Taylor and Phil Woolpert (2).

Year	Year	Year
1955 Phil Woolpert, San Francisco	1970 John Wooden, UCLA	1985 Lou Carnesecca, St. John's
1956 Phil Woolpert, San Francisco	1971 Al McGuire, Marquette	1986 Mike Krzyzewski, Duke
1957 Frank McGuire, North Carolina	1972 John Wooden, UCLA	1987 John Thompson, Georgetown
1958 Tex Winter, Kansas St.	1973 John Wooden, UCLA	1988 John Chaney, Temple
1959 Adolph Rupp, Kentucky	1974 Digger Phelps, Notre Dame	1989 Bob Knight, Indiana
1960 Pete Newell, California	1975 Bob Knight, Indiana	1990 Jim Calhoun, Connecticut
1961 Fred Taylor, Ohio St.	1976 Tom Young, Rutgers	1991 Rick Majerus, Utah
1962 Fred Taylor, Ohio St.	1977 Bob Gaillard, San Francisco	1992 Perry Clark, Tulane
1963 Ed Jucker, Cincinnati	1978 Eddie Sutton, Arkansas	1993 Eddie Fogler, Vanderbilt
1964 John Wooden, UCLA	1979 Bill Hodges, Indiana St.	1994 Norm Stewart, Missouri
1965 Dave Strack, Michigan	1980 Ray Meyer, DePaul	1995 Leonard Hamilton, Miami-FL
1966 Adolph Rupp, Kentucky	1981 Ralph Miller, Oregon St.	1996 Gene Keady, Purdue
1967 John Wooden, UCLA	1982 Norm Stewart, Missouri	1997 award discontinued
1968 Guy Lewis, Houston	1983 Jerry Tarkanian, UNLV	
1969 John Wooden, UCLA	1984 Ray Meyer, DePaul	

U.S. Basketball Writers Association

Voted on by the USBWA and first presented in 1959.

Multiple winners: John Wooden (5); Bob Knight (3); Lou Carnesecca, John Chaney, Ray Meyer and Fred Taylor (2).

Year	Year	Year
1959 Eddie Hickey, Marquette	1973 John Wooden, UCLA	1987 John Chaney, Temple
1960 Pete Newell, California	1974 Norm Sloan, N.C. State	1988 John Chaney, Temple
1961 Fred Taylor, Ohio St.	1975 Bob Knight, Indiana	1989 Bob Knight, Indiana
1962 Fred Taylor, Ohio St.	1976 Bob Knight, Indiana	1990 Roy Williams, Kansas
1963 Ed Jucker, Cincinnati	1977 Eddie Sutton, Arkansas	1991 Randy Ayers, Ohio St.
1964 John Wooden, UCLA	1978 Ray Meyer, DePaul	1992 Perry Clark, Tulane
1965 Butch van Breda Kolff, Princeton	1979 Dean Smith, North Carolina	1993 Eddie Fogler, Vanderbilt
1966 Adolph Rupp, Kentucky	1980 Ray Meyer, DePaul	1994 Charlie Spoonhour, St. Louis
1967 John Wooden, UCLA	1981 Ralph Miller, Oregon St.	1995 Kelvin Sampson, Oklahoma
1968 Guy Lewis, Houston	1982 John Thompson, Georgetown	1996 Gene Keady, Purdue
1969 Maury John, Drake	1983 Lou Carnesecca, St. John's	1997 Clem Haskins, Minnesota
1970 John Wooden, UCLA	1984 Gene Keady, Purdue	1998 Tom Izzo, Michigan St.
1971 Al McGuire, Marquette	1985 Lou Carnesecca, St. John's	1999 Cliff Ellis, Auburn
1972 John Wooden, UCLA	1986 Dick Versace, Bradley	2000 Larry Eustachy, Iowa St.

Associated Press

Voted on by AP sportswriters and broadcasters and first presented in 1967.

Multiple winners: John Wooden (5); Bob Knight (3); Guy Lewis, Ray Meyer, Ralph Miller and Eddie Sutton (2).

Year	Year	Year
1967 John Wooden, UCLA	1979 Bill Hodges, Indiana St.	1991 Randy Ayers, Ohio St.
1968 Guy Lewis, Houston	1980 Ray Meyer, DePaul	1992 Roy Williams, Kansas
1969 John Wooden, UCLA	1981 Ralph Miller, Oregon St.	1993 Eddie Fogler, Vanderbilt
1970 John Wooden, UCLA	1982 Ralph Miller, Oregon St.	1994 Norm Stewart, Missouri
1971 Al McGuire, Marquette	1983 Guy Lewis, Houston	1995 Kelvin Sampson, Oklahoma
1972 John Wooden, UCLA	1984 Ray Meyer, DePaul	1996 Gene Keady, Purdue
1973 John Wooden, UCLA	1985 Bill Frieder, Michigan	1997 Clem Haskins, Minnesota
1974 Norm Sloan, N.C. State	1986 Eddie Sutton, Kentucky	1998 Tom Izzo, Michigan St.
1975 Bob Knight, Indiana	1987 Tom Davis, Iowa	1999 Cliff Ellis, Auburn
1976 Bob Knight, Indiana	1988 John Chaney, Temple	2000 Larry Eustachy, Iowa St.
1977 Bob Gaillard, San Francisco	1989 Bob Knight, Indiana	
1978 Eddie Sutton, Arkansas	1990 Jim Calhoun, Connecticut	

National Association of Basketball Coaches

Voted on by NABC membership and first presented in 1969.

Multiple winners: John Wooden (3); Gene Keady and Mike Krzyzewski (2).

Year	Year	Year
1969 John Wooden, UCLA	1980 Lute Olson, Iowa	1991 Mike Krzyzewski, Duke
1970 John Wooden, UCLA	1981 Ralph Miller, Oregon St.	1992 George Raveling, USC
1971 Jack Kraft, Villanova	& Jack Hartman, Kansas St.	1993 Eddie Fogler, Vanderbilt
1972 John Wooden, UCLA	1982 Don Monson, Idaho	1994 Nolan Richardson, Arkansas
1973 Gene Bartow, Memphis St.	1983 Lou Carnesecca, St. John's	& Gene Keady, Purdue
1974 Al McGuire, Marquette	1984 Marv Harshman, Washington	1995 Jim Harrick, UCLA
1975 Bob Knight, Indiana	1985 John Thompson, Georgetown	1996 John Calipari, UMass
1976 Johnny Orr, Michigan	1986 Eddie Sutton, Kentucky	1997 Clem Haskins, Minnesota
1977 Dean Smith, North Carolina	1987 Rick Pitino, Providence	1998 Bill Guthridge, N. Carolina
1978 Bill Foster, Duke	1988 John Chaney, Temple	1999 Mike Krzyzewski, Duke
& Abe Lemons, Texas	1989 P.J. Carlesimo, Seton Hall	& Jim O'Brien, Ohio St.
1979 Ray Meyer, DePaul	1990 Jud Heathcote, Michigan St.	2000 Gene Keady, Purdue

Naismith Award

Voted on by a panel of coaches, sportswriters and broadcasters and first presented by the Atlanta Tip-Off Club in 1987 in the name of the inventor of basketball, Dr. James Naismith.

Multiple winner: Mike Krzyzewski (3).

Year	Year	Year
1987 Bob Knight, Indiana	1992 Mike Krzyzewski, Duke	1997 Roy Williams, Kansas
1988 Larry Brown, Kansas	1993 Dean Smith, North Carolina	1998 Bill Guthridge, N. Carolina
1989 Mike Krzyzewski, Duke	1994 Nolan Richardson, Arkansas	1999 Mike Krzyzewski, Duke
1990 Bobby Cremins, Georgia Tech	1995 Jim Harrick, UCLA	2000 Mike Montgomery, Stanford
1991 Randy Ayers, Ohio St.	1996 John Calipari, UMass	

Other Men's Champions

The NCAA has sanctioned national championship tournaments for Division II since 1957 and Division III since 1975. The NAIA sanctioned a single tournament from 1937-91, then split into two divisions in 1992.

NCAA Div. II Finals

Multiple winners: Kentucky Wesleyan (7); Evansville (5); CS-Bakersfield (3); North Alabama and Virginia Union (2).

Year	Winner	Score	Loser	Year	Winner	Score	Loser
1957	Wheaton, IL	89-65	Ky. Wesleyan	1965	Evansville	85-82*	Southern Illinois
1958	South Dakota	75-53	St. Michael's, VT	1966	Ky. Wesleyan	54-51	Southern Illinois
1959	Evansville, IN	83-67	SW Missouri St.	1967	Winston-Salem, NC	77-74	SW Missouri St.
1960	Evansville	90-69	Chapman, CA	1968	Ky. Wesleyan	63-52	Indiana St.
1961	Wittenberg, OH	42-38	SE Missouri St.	1969	Ky. Wesleyan	75-71	SW Missouri St.
1962	Mt. St. Mary's, MD	58-57*	CS-Sacramento	1970	Phila. Textile	76-65	Tennessee St.
1963	South Dakota St.	42-40	Wittenberg, OH	1971	Evansville	97-82	Old Dominion, VA
1964	Evansville	72-59	Akron, OH	1972	Roanoke, VA	84-72	Akron, OH

Player of the Year and NBA MVP

College Players of the Year who have gone on to win the NBA's Most Valuable Player award:

Bill Russell COLLEGE–San Francisco (1956); PROS–Boston Celtics (1958, 1961, 1962, 1963 and 1965).

Oscar Robertson COLLEGE–Cincinnati (1958, 1959 and 1960); PROS–Cincinnati Royals (1964).

Kareem Abdul-Jabbar COLLEGE–UCLA (1967 and 1969); PROS–Milwaukee Bucks (1971, 1972 and 1974) and LA Lakers (1976, 1977 and 1980).

Bill Walton COLLEGE–UCLA (1972, 1973 and 1974); PROS–Portland Trail Blazers (1978).

Larry Bird COLLEGE–Indiana St. (1979); PROS–Boston Celtics (1984, 1985, and 1986).

Michael Jordan COLLEGE–North Carolina (1984); PROS–Chicago Bulls (1988, 1991, 1992, 1996 and 1998).

David Robinson COLLEGE–Navy (1987); PROS–San Antonio Spurs (1995).

Shaquille O'Neal COLLEGE–LSU (1991); PROS–LA Lakers (2000).

Year	Winner	Score	Loser	Year	Winner	Score	Loser
1973	Ky. Wesleyan	78-76*	Tennessee St.	1988	Lowell, MA	75-72	AK-Anchorage
1974	Morgan St., MD	67-52	SW Missouri St.	1989	N.C. Central	73-46	SE Missouri St.
1975	Old Dominion	76-74	New Orleans	1990	Ky. Wesleyan	93-79	CS-Bakersfield
1976	Puget Sound, WA	83-74	Tennessee-Chatt.	1991	North Alabama	79-72	Bridgeport, CT
1977	Tennessee-Chatt.	71-62	Randolph-Macon	1992	Virginia Union	100-75	Bridgeport
1978	Cheyney, PA	47-40	WI-Green Bay	1993	CS-Bakersfield	85-72	Troy St., AL
1979	North Alabama	64-50	WI-Green Bay	1994	CS-Bakersfield	92-86	Southern Ind.
1980	Virginia Union	80-74	New York Tech	1995	Southern Indiana	71-63	UC-Riverside
1981	Florida Southern	73-68	Mt. St. Mary's, MD	1996	Fort Hays St.	70-63	N. Kentucky
1982	Dist. of Columbia	73-63	Florida Southern	1997	CS-Bakersfield	57-56	N. Kentucky
1983	Wright St., OH	92-73	Dist. of Columbia	1998	UC-Davis	83-77	Ky. Wesleyan
1984	Central Mo. St.	81-77	St. Augustine's, NC	1999	Ky. Wesleyan	75-60	Metropolitan St.
1985	Jacksonville St.	74-73	South Dakota St.	2000	Metropolitan St.	97-79	Ky. Wesleyan
1986	Sacred Heart, CT	93-87	SE Missouri St.				
1987	Ky. Wesleyan	92-74	Gannon, PA				

*Overtime

NCAA Div. III Finals

Multiple winners: North Park (5); WI-Platteville (4); Calvin, Potsdam St., Scranton and WI-Whitewater (2).

Year	Winner	Score	Loser	Year	Winner	Score	Loser
1975	LeMoyne-Owen, TN	57-54	Glassboro St., NJ	1989	WI-Whitewater	94-86	Trenton St., NJ
1976	Scranton, PA	60-57	Wittenberg, OH	1990	Rochester, NY	43-42	DePauw, IN
1977	Wittenberg, OH	79-66	Oneonta St., NY	1991	WI-Platteville	81-74	Franklin Marshall
1978	North Park, IL	69-57	Widener, PA	1992	Calvin, MI	62-49	Rochester, NY
1979	North Park, IL	66-62	Potsdam St., NY	1993	Ohio Northern	71-68	Augustana, IL
1980	North Park, IL	83-76	Upsala, NJ	1994	Lebanon Valley, PA	66-59*	NYU
1981	Potsdam St., NY	67-65*	Augustana, IL	1995	WI-Platteville	69-55	Manchester, IN
1982	Wabash, IN	83-62	Potsdam St., NY	1996	Rowan, NJ	100-93	Hope, MI
1983	Scranton, PA	64-63	Wittenberg, OH	1997	Illinois Wesleyan	89-86	Neb-Wesleyan
1984	WI-Whitewater	103-86	Clark, MA	1998	WI-Platteville	69-56	Hope, MI
1985	North Park, IL	72-71	Potsdam St., NY	1999	WI-Platteville	76-75**	Hampden-Sydney
1986	Potsdam St., NY	76-73	LeMoyne-Owen, TN	2000	Calvin, MI	79-74	WI-Eau Claire
1987	North Park, IL	106-100	Clark, MA				
1988	Ohio Wesleyan	92-70	Scranton, PA				

*Overtime
**Double overtime

NAIA Finals, 1937-91

Multiple winners: Grand Canyon, Hamline, Kentucky St. and Tennessee St. (3); Central Missouri, Central St., Fort Hays St. and SW Missouri St. (2).

Year	Winner	Score	Loser	Year	Winner	Score	Loser
1937	Central Missouri	35-24	Morningside, IA	1972	Kentucky St.	71-62	WI-Eau Claire
1938	Central Missouri	45-30	Roanoke, VA	1973	Guilford, NC	99-96	MD-Eastern Shore
1939	Southwestern, KS	32-31	San Diego St.	1974	West Georgia	97-79	Alcorn St., MS
1940	Tarkio, MO	52-31	San Diego St.	1975	Grand Canyon, AZ	65-54	M'western St., TX
1941	San Diego St.	36-32	Murray St., KY	1976	Coppin St., MD	96-91	Henderson St., AR
1942	Hamline, MN	33-31	SE Oklahoma	1977	Texas Southern	71-44	Campbell, NC
1943	SE Missouri St.	34-32	NW Missouri St.	1978	Grand Canyon	79-75	Kearney St., NE
1944	Not held			1979	Drury, MO	60-54	Henderson St., AR
1945	Loyola-LA	49-36	Pepperdine, CA	1980	Cameron, OK	84-77	Alabama St.
1946	Southern Illinois	49-40	Indiana St.	1981	Beth. Nazarene, OK	86-85*	AL-Huntsville
1947	Marshall, WV	73-59	Mankato St., MN	1982	SC-Spartanburg	51-38	Biola, CA
1948	Louisville, KY	82-70	Indiana St.	1983	Charleston, SC	57-53	WV-Wesleyan
1949	Hamline, MN	57-46	Regis, CO	1984	Fort Hays St., KS	48-46*	WI-Stevens Pt.
1950	Indiana St.	61-47	East Central, OK	1985	Fort Hays St.	82-80*	Wayland Bapt., TX
1951	Hamline, MN	69-61	Millikin, IL	1986	David Lipscomb, TN	67-54	AR-Monticello
1952	SW Missouri St.	73-64	Murray St., KY	1987	Washburn, KS	79-77	West Virginia St.
1953	SW Missouri St.	79-71	Hamline, MN	1988	Grand Canyon	88-86*	Auburn-Montg, AL
1954	St.Benedict's, KS	62-56	Western Illinois	1989	St.Mary's, TX	61-58	East Central, OK
1955	East Texas St.	71-54	SE Oklahoma	1990	Birm-Southern, AL	88-80	WI-Eau Claire
1956	McNeese St., LA	60-55	Texas Southern	1991	Oklahoma City	77-74	Central Arkansas
1957	Tennessee St.	92-73	SE Oklahoma				
1958	Tennessee St.	85-73	Western Illinois				
1959	Tennessee St.	97-87	Pacific-Luth., WA				
1960	SW Texas St.	66-44	Westminster, PA				
1961	Grambling, LA	95-75	Georgetown, KY				
1962	Prairie View, TX	62-53	Westminster, PA				
1963	Pan American, TX	73-62	Western Carolina				
1964	Rockhurst, MO	66-56	Pan American, TX				
1965	Central St., OH	85-51	Oklahoma Baptist				
1966	Oklahoma Baptist	88-59	Georgia Southern				
1967	St.Benedict's, KS	71-65	Oklahoma Baptist				
1968	Central St., OH	51-48	Fairmont St., WV				
1969	Eastern N. Mex	99-76	MD-Eastern Shore				
1970	Kentucky St.	79-71	Central Wash.				
1971	Kentucky St.	102-82	Eastern Michigan				

*Overtime

NAIA Div. I Finals

NAIA split tournament into two divisions in 1992.
Multiple winner: Life, GA and Oklahoma City (3).

Year	Winner	Score	Loser
1992	Oklahoma City	82-73*	Central Arkansas
1993	Hawaii Pacific	88-83	Okla. Baptist
1994	Oklahoma City	99-81	Life, GA
1995	Birm-Southern	92-76	Pfeiffer, NC
1996	Oklahoma City	86-80	Georgetown, KY
1997	Life, GA	73-64	Okla. Baptist
1998	Georgetown, KY	83-69	So. Nazarene
1999	Life, GA	63-60	Mobile, AL
2000	Life, GA	61-59	Georgetown, KY

*Overtime

NAIA Div. II Finals

NAIA split tournament into two divisions in 1992.

Multiple winner: Bethel, IN (3).

Year	Winner	Score	Loser	Year	Winner	Score	Loser
1992	Grace, IN	85-79*	Northwestern-IA	1997	Bethel	95-94	Siena Heights, MI
1993	Williamette, OR	63-56	Northern St., SD	1998	Bethel	89-87	Oregon Tech
1994	Eureka, IL	98-95*	Northern St.	1999	Cornerstone, MI	113-109	Bethel
1995	Bethel, IN	103-95*	NW Nazarene, ID	2000	Embry-Riddle, FL	75-63	Ozarks, MO
1996	Albertson, ID	81-72*	Whitworth, WA		*Overtime		

WOMEN

NCAA Final Four

Replaced the Association of Intercollegiate Athletics for Women (AIAW) tournament in 1982 as the official playoff for the national championship.

Multiple winners: Tennessee (6); Connecticut, Louisiana Tech, Stanford and USC (2).

Year	Champion	Head Coach	Score	Runner-up	——Third Place——	
1982	Louisiana Tech	Sonya Hogg	76-62	Cheyney	Maryland	Tennessee
1983	USC	Linda Sharp	69-67	Louisiana Tech	Georgia	Old Dominion
1984	USC	Linda Sharp	72-61	Tennessee	Cheyney	Louisiana Tech
1985	Old Dominion	Marianne Stanley	70-65	Georgia	NE Louisiana	Western Ky.
1986	Texas	Jody Conradt	97-81	USC	Tennessee	Western Ky.
1987	Tennessee	Pat Summitt	67-44	Louisiana Tech	Long Beach St.	Texas
1988	Louisiana Tech	Leon Barmore	56-54	Auburn	Long Beach St.	Tennessee
1989	Tennessee	Pat Summitt	76-60	Auburn	Louisiana Tech	Maryland
1990	Stanford	Tara VanDerveer	88-81	Auburn	Louisiana Tech	Virginia
1991	Tennessee	Pat Summitt	70-67 (OT)	Virginia	Connecticut	Stanford
1992	Stanford	Tara VanDerveer	78-62	Western Kentucky	SW Missouri St.	Virginia
1993	Texas Tech	Marsha Sharp	84-82	Ohio St.	Iowa	Vanderbilt
1994	North Carolina	Sylvia Hatchell	60-59	Louisiana Tech	Alabama	Purdue
1995	Connecticut	Geno Auriemma	70-64	Tennessee	Georgia	Stanford
1996	Tennessee	Pat Summitt	83-65	Georgia	Connecticut	Stanford
1997	Tennessee	Pat Summitt	68-59	Old Dominion	Stanford	Notre Dame
1998	Tennessee	Pat Summitt	93-75	Louisiana Tech	Arkansas	N.C. State
1999	Purdue	Carolyn Peck	62-45	Duke	Louisiana Tech	Georgia
2000	Connecticut	Geno Auriemma	71-52	Tennessee	Penn St.	Rutgers

Final Four sites: 1982 (Norfolk, Va.), **1983** (Norfolk, Va.), **1984** (Los Angeles), **1985** (Lexington), **1986** (Austin), **1987** (Austin), **1988** (Tacoma), **1989** (Tacoma), **1990** (Knoxville), **1991** (New Orleans), **1992** (Los Angeles), **1993** (Atlanta), **1994** (Richmond), **1995** (Minneapolis), **1996** (Charlotte), **1997** (Cincinnati), **1998** (Kansas City), **1999** (San Jose), **2000** (Philadelphia).

Most Outstanding Player

A Most Outstanding Player has been selected every year of the NCAA tournament. Winner who did not play for the tournament champion is listed in **bold**, type.

Multiple winner: Chamique Holdsclaw and Cheryl Miller (2).

Year
1982 Janice Lawrence, La. Tech
1983 Cheryl Miller, USC
1984 Cheryl Miller, USC
1985 Tracy Claxton, Old Dominion
1986 Clarissa Davis, Texas
1987 Tonya Edwards, Tennessee
1988 Erica Westbrooks, La. Tech

Year
1989 Bridgette Gordon, Tennessee
1990 Jennifer Azzi, Stanford
1991 **Dawn Staley**, Virginia
1992 Molly Goodenbour, Stanford
1993 Sheryl Swoopes, Texas Tech
1994 Charlotte Smith, N. Carolina
1995 Rebecca Lobo, Connecticut

Year
1996 Michelle Marciniak, Tennessee
1997 Chamique Holdsclaw, Tenn.
1998 Chamique Holdsclaw, Tenn.
1999 Ukari Figgs, Purdue
2000 Shea Ralph, Connecticut

All-Time NCAA Division I Tournament Leaders

Through 1999-00; minimum of six games; **Last** column indicates final year played.

CAREER

Scoring

	Total Points	Yrs	Last	Pts	Avg
1	Chamique Holdsclaw, Tenn	4	1999	**479**	21.8
2	Bridgette Gordon, Tenn	4	1989	**388**	21.6
3	Cheryl Miller, USC	4	1986	**333**	20.8
4	Janice Lawrence, La. Tech	3	1984	**312**	22.3
5	Penny Toler, Long Beach St.	4	1989	**291**	22.4
6	Dawn Staley, Virginia	4	1992	**274**	18.3
7	Cindy Brown, Long Beach St	4	1987	**263**	21.9
	Venus Lacy, La. Tech	3	1990	**263**	18.8
9	Clarissa Davis, Texas	3	1989	**261**	21.8
10	Janet Harris, Georgia	4	1985	**254**	19.5

Rebounds

	Total Rebounds	Yrs	Last	No	Avg
1	Chamique Holdsclaw, Tenn	4	1999	**188**	8.5
2	Cheryl Miller, USC	4	1986	**170**	10.6
3	Sheila Frost, Tennessee	4	1989	**162**	9.0
4	Val Whiting, Stanford	4	1993	**161**	10.1
5	Venus Lacy, La. Tech	3	1990	**148**	10.6
6	Bridgette Gordon, Tenn	4	1989	**142**	7.9
7	Kirsten Cummings, Long Beach St.	4	1985	**136**	10.5
8	Nora Lewis, La. Tech	3	1989	**130**	9.3
9	Pam McGee, USC	3	1984	**127**	9.8
10	Daedra Charles, Tenn	3	1991	**125**	9.6
	Paula McGee, USC	3	1984	**125**	9.6

SINGLE GAME

Scoring

		Year	Pts
1	Lorri Bauman, Drake vs Maryland	1982	50
2	Sheryl Swoopes, Texas Tech vs Ohio St	1993	47
3	Barbara Kennedy, Clemson vs Penn St	1982	43
4	LaTaunya Pollard, L. Beach St. vs Howard	1982	40
	Cindy Brown, L. Beach St. vs Ohio St.	1987	40
6	Kerry Bascom, UConn vs Toledo	1991	39
	Portia Hill, S.F. Austin St. vs Arkansas	1990	39
	Delmonica DeHorney, Ark. vs Stanford	1990	39
	Sheri Sam, Vanderbilt vs. Harvard	1996	39
	Chamique Holdsclaw, Tenn. vs. Boston Col.	1999	39

Rebounds

		Year	No
1	Cheryl Taylor, Tenn. Tech vs Georgia	1985	23
	Charlotte Smith, N. Car. vs La. Tech	1994	23
3	Daedra Charles, Tenn. vs SW Missouri	1991	22
4	Cherie Nelson, USC vs Western Ky	1987	21
5	Alison Lang, Oregon vs Missouri	1982	20
	Shelda Arceneaux, S.D. St. vs L. Beach St.	1984	20
	Tracy Claxton, ODU vs Georgia	1985	20
	Brigette Combs, West. Ky. vs West Va	1989	20
	Tandreia Green, West. Ky. vs West Va	1989	20
10	Seven tied with 19 each.		

Associated Press Final Top 10 Polls

The Associated Press weekly women's college basketball poll was begun by Mel Greenberg of *The Philadelphia Inquirer* during the 1976-77 season. Although the poll was started as a Top 20 in 1977 and was expanded to a Top 25 in 1990, only the Top 10 from each poll are listed below due to space constraints. The Association of Intercollegiate Athletics for Women (AIAW) Tournament determined the Division I national champion for 1972-81. The NCAA began its women's Division I tournament in 1982. The final AP Polls were taken before the NCAA tournament. Eventual national champions are in **bold** type.

1977
1 **Delta St.**
2 Immaculata
3 St. Joseph's-PA
4 CS-Fullerton
5 Tennessee
6 Tennessee Tech
7 Wayland Baptist
8 Montclair St.
9 S.F. Austin St.
10 N.C. State

1978
1 Tennessee
2 Wayland Baptist
3 N.C. State
4 Montclair St.
5 **UCLA**
6 Maryland
7 Queens-NY
8 Valdosta St.
9 Delta St.
10 LSU

1979
1 Old Dominion
2 Louisiana Tech
3 Tennessee
4 Texas
5 S.F. Austin St.
6 UCLA
7 Rutgers
8 Maryland
9 Cheyney
10 Wayland Baptist

1980
1 **Old Dominion**
2 Tennessee
3 Louisiana Tech
4 South Carolina
5 S.F. Austin St.
6 Maryland
7 Texas
8 Rutgers
9 Long Beach St.
10 N.C. State

1981
1 **Louisiana Tech**
2 Tennessee
3 Old Dominion
4 USC
5 Cheyney
6 Long Beach St.
7 UCLA
8 Maryland
9 Rutgers
10 Kansas

1982
1 **Louisiana Tech**
2 Cheyney
3 Maryland
4 Tennessee
5 Texas
6 USC
7 Old Dominion
8 Rutgers
9 Long Beach St.
10 Penn St.

1983
1 **USC**
2 Louisiana Tech
3 Texas
4 Old Dominion
5 Cheyney
6 Long Beach St.
7 Maryland
8 Penn St.
9 Georgia
10 Tennessee

1984
1 Texas
2 Louisiana Tech
3 Georgia
4 Old Dominion
5 **USC**
6 Long Beach St.
7 Kansas St.
8 LSU
9 Cheyney
10 Mississippi

1985
1 Texas
2 NE Louisiana
3 Long Beach St.
4 Louisiana Tech
5 **Old Dominion**
6 Mississippi
7 Ohio St.
8 Georgia
9 Penn St.
10 Auburn

1986
1 **Texas**
2 Georgia
3 USC
4 Louisiana Tech
5 Western Ky.
6 Virginia
7 Auburn
8 Long Beach St.
9 LSU
10 Rutgers

1987
1 Texas
2 Auburn
3 Louisiana Tech
4 Long Beach St.
5 Rutgers
6 Georgia
7 **Tennessee**
8 Mississippi
9 Iowa
10 Ohio St.

1988
1 Tennessee
2 Iowa
3 Auburn
4 Texas
5 **Louisiana Tech**
6 Ohio St.
7 Long Beach St.
8 Rutgers
9 Maryland
10 Virginia

1989
1 **Tennessee**
2 Auburn
3 Louisiana Tech
4 Stanford
5 Maryland
6 Texas
7 Long Beach St.
8 Iowa
9 Colorado
10 Georgia

1990
1 Louisiana Tech
2 **Stanford**
3 Washington
4 Tennessee
5 UNLV
6 S.F. Austin St.
7 Georgia
8 Texas
9 Auburn
10 Iowa

1991
1 Penn St.
2 Virginia
3 Georgia
4 **Tennessee**
5 Purdue
6 Auburn
7 N.C. State
8 LSU
9 Arkansas
10 Western Ky.

1992
1 Virginia
2 Tennessee
3 **Stanford**
4 S.F. Austin St.
5 Mississippi
6 Miami-FL
7 Iowa
8 Maryland
9 Penn St.
10 SW Missouri St.

1993

1 Vanderbilt
2 Tennessee
3 Ohio St.
4 Iowa
5 **Texas Tech**
6 Stanford
7 Auburn
8 Penn St.
9 Virginia
10 Colorado

1994

1 Tennessee
2 Penn St.
3 Connecticut
4 **North Carolina**
5 Colorado
6 Louisiana Tech
7 USC
8 Purdue
9 Texas Tech
10 Virginia

1995

1 **Connecticut**
2 Colorado
3 Tennessee
4 Stanford
5 Texas Tech
6 Vanderbilt
7 Penn St.
8 Louisiana Tech
9 Western Ky.
10 Virginia

1996

1 Louisiana Tech
2 Connecticut
3 Stanford
4 **Tennessee**
5 Georgia
6 Old Dominion
7 Iowa
8 Penn St.
9 Texas Tech
10 Alabama

1997

1 Connecticut
2 Old Dominion
3 Stanford
4 North Carolina
5 Louisiana Tech
6 Georgia
7 Florida
8 Alabama
9 LSU
10 **Tennessee**

1998

1 **Tennessee**
2 Old Dominion
3 Connecticut
4 Louisiana Tech
5 Stanford
6 Texas Tech
7 North Carolina
8 Duke
9 Arizona
10 N.C. State

1999

1 **Purdue**
2 Tennessee
3 Louisiana Tech
4 Colorado St.
5 Old Dominion
6 Connecticut
7 Rutgers
8 Notre Dame
9 Texas Tech
10 Duke

2000

1 **Connecticut**
2 Tennessee
3 Louisiana Tech
4 Georgia
5 Notre Dame
6 Penn St.
7 Iowa St.
8 Rutgers
9 UC-Santa Barbara
10 Duke

All-Time AP Top 10

The composite AP Top 10 from the 1976-77 season through 1999-2000, based on the final regular season rankings of each year. Team points are based on 10 points for all 1st place finishes, 9 for each 2nd, etc. Also listed are the number of times ranked No. 1 by AP going into the tournaments, and times ranked in the pre-tournament Top 10.

			Pts	No. 1	Top 10
1	Tennessee	169		5	22
2	Louisiana Tech	156		4	20
3	Old Dominion	81		2	11
4	Texas	80		4	17
5	Georgia	65		0	12
6	Connecticut	60		3	7
7	Stanford	58		0	8
8	Penn St.	46		1	10
9	Long Beach St.	45		0	10
10	Auburn	42		0	8

All-Time Winningest Division I Teams

Division I schools with best winning percentages and most victories through 1999-00 (including postseason tournaments). Although official NCAA women's basketball records didn't begin until the 1981-82 season, results from previous seasons are included below.

Top 10 Winning Percentage

		Yrs	W	L	Pct
1	Louisiana Tech	26	737	123	.857
2	Tennessee	55	821	207	.799
3	Montana	22	515	139	.787
4	Texas	26	667	191	.777
5	S. F. Austin St.	28	664	214	.756
6	Old Dominion	31	679	222	.754
7	Mount St. Mary's*	26	519	182	.740
8	Virginia	27	573	215	.727
9	Norfolk St.	25	514	199	.721
10	Auburn	29	586	227	.721

*Includes records prior to Division I.

Top 10 Victories

		Yrs	W	L	Pct
1	Tennessee	55	821	207	.799
2	Louisiana Tech	26	737	123	.857
3	Old Dominion	31	679	222	.754
4	James Madison	78	668	377	.639
5	Texas	26	667	191	.777
6	S.F. Austin St.	28	664	214	.756
7	Long Beach St.	38	660	273	.707
8	Tennessee Tech	30	651	269	.708
9	Richmond	80	614	420	.594
10	Penn St.	36	596	233	.719
	Western Ky.	38	596	283	.678

Annual NCAA Division I Leaders

All averages include postseason games

Scoring

Multiple winner: Cindy Blodgett and Andrea Congreaves (2).

Year		Gm	Pts	Avg
1982	Barbara Kennedy, Clemson	31	908	29.3
1983	LaTaunya Pollard, L. Beach St	31	907	29.3
1984	Deborah Temple, Delta St	28	873	31.2
1985	Anucha Browne, Northwestern	28	855	30.5
1986	Wanda Ford, Drake	30	919	30.6
1987	Tresa Spaulding, BYU	28	810	28.9
1988	LeChandra LeDay, Grambling	28	850	30.4
1989	Patricia Hoskins, Miss. Valley	27	908	33.6
1990	Kim Perrot, SW Louisiana	28	839	30.0
1991	Jan Jensen, Drake	30	888	29.6

Year		Gm	Pts	Avg
1992	Andrea Congreaves, Mercer	28	925	33.0
1993	Andrea Congreaves, Mercer	26	805	31.0
1994	Kristy Ryan, CS-Sacramento	26	727	28.0
1995	Koko Lahanas, CS-Fullerton	29	778	26.8
1996	Cindy Blodgett, Maine	32	889	27.8
1997	Cindy Blodgett, Maine	30	810	27.0
1998	Allison Feaster, Harvard	28	797	28.5
1999	Tamika Whitmore, Memphis	32	843	26.3
2000	Jackie Stiles, SW Missouri St.	32	890	27.8

Rebounds

Multiple winner: Patricia Hoskins (2).

Year		Gm	No	Avg	Year		Gm	No	Avg
1982	Anne Donovan, Old Dominion	.28	412	14.7	1992	Christy Greis, Evansville	.28	383	13.7
1983	Deborah Mitchell, Miss. Col	.28	447	16.0	1993	Ann Barry, Nevada	.25	355	14.2
1984	Joy Kellog, Oklahoma City	.23	373	16.2	1994	DeShawne Blocker, E. Tenn. St.	.26	450	17.3
1985	Rosina Pearson, Beth-Cookman	.26	480	18.5	1995	Tera Sheriff, Jackson St	.29	401	13.8
1986	Wanda Ford, Drake	.30	506	16.9	1996	Dana Wynne, Seton Hall	.29	372	12.8
1987	Patricia Hoskins, Miss. Valley St.	.28	476	17.0	1997	Etolia Mitchell, Georgia St.	.25	330	13.2
1988	Katie Beck, East Tenn. St.	.25	441	17.6	1998	Alisha Hill, Howard	.30	397	13.2
1989	Patricia Hoskins, Miss. Valley St.	.27	440	16.3	1999	Monica Logan, UMBC	.27	364	13.5
1990	Pam Hudson, Northwestern St	.29	438	15.1	2000	Malveata Johnson, N.C. A&T	.27	363	13.4
1991	Tarcha Hollis, Grambling	.29	443	15.3					

Note: Wanda Ford (1986) and Patricia Hoskins (1989) each led the country in scoring and rebounds in the same year.

All-Time NCAA Division I Individual Leaders

Through 1999-00; includes regular season and tournament games; Official NCAA women's basketball records began with 1981-82 season. Players who competed earlier than that are not included below; **Last** column indicates final year played.

CAREER

Scoring

Average		Yrs	Last	Pts	Avg
1	Patricia Hoskins, Miss. Valley St.	.4	1989	3122	28.4
2	Sandra Hodge, New Orleans	.4	1984	2860	26.7
3	Lorri Bauman, Drake	.4	1984	3115	26.0
4	Andrea Congreaves, Mercer	.4	1993	2796	25.9
5	Cindy Blodgett, Maine	.4	1998	3005	25.5
6	Valorie Whiteside, Aplach St.	.4	1988	2944	25.4
7	Joyce Walker, LSU	.4	1984	2906	24.8
8	Tarcha Hollis, Grambling	.4	1991	2058	24.2
9	Korie Hlede, Duquesne	.4	1998	2631	24.1
10	Karen Pelphrey, Marshall	.4	1986	2746	24.1

Rebounds

		Yrs	Last	Reb	Avg
1	Wanda Ford, Drake	.4	1986	1887	16.1
2	Patricia Hoskins, Miss. Valley St.	.4	1989	1662	15.1
3	Tarcha Hollis, Grambling	.4	1991	1185	13.9
4	Katie Beck, East Tenn. St.	.4	1988	1404	13.4
5	Marilyn Stephens, Temple	.4	1984	1519	13.0
6	Natalie Williams, UCLA	.4	1994	1137	12.8
7	Cheryl Taylor, Tenn. Tech	.4	1987	1532	12.8
8	DeShawne Blocker, E. Tenn. St.	.4	1995	1361	12.7
9	Olivia Bradley, West Virginia	.4	1985	1484	12.7
10	Judy Mosley, Hawaii	.4	1990	1441	12.6

SINGLE SEASON
Scoring

Average		Year	Gm	Pts	Avg
1	Patricia Hoskins, Miss.Valley St.	.1989	27	908	33.6
2	Andrea Congreaves, Mercer	.1992	28	925	33.0
3	Deborah Temple, Delta St.	.1984	28	873	31.2
4	Andrea Congreaves, Mercer	.1993	26	805	31.0
5	Wanda Ford, Drake	.1986	30	919	30.6
6	Anucha Browne, Northwestern	.1985	28	855	30.5
7	LeChandra LeDay, Grambling	.1988	28	850	30.4
8	Kim Perrot, SW Louisiana	.1990	28	841	30.0
9	Tina Hutchinson, San Diego St.	.1984	30	898	29.9
10	Jan Jensen, Drake	.1991	30	888	29.6

SINGLE GAME
Scoring

		Year	Pts
1	Cindy Brown, Long Beach St. vs San Jose St.	.1987	60
2	Lorri Bauman, Drake vs SW Missouri St.	.1984	58
	Kim Perrot, SW La. vs SE La	.1990	58
4	Jackie Stiles, SW Mo. St. vs Evansville	.2000	56
5	Patricia Hoskins, Miss.Valley St. vs South-BR	.1989	55
	Patricia Hoskins, Miss.Valley St. vs Ala. St.	.1989	55
7	Wanda Ford, Drake vs SW Missouri St.	.1986	54
	Anjinea Hopson, Grambling vs Jackson St.	.1994	54
	Mary Lowry, Baylor vs Texas	.1994	54
10	Chris Starr, Nevada vs CS-Sacramento	.1983	53
	Felisha Edwards, NE La. vs Southern Miss.	.1991	53
	Sheryl Swoopes, Texas Tech vs Texas	.1993	53

Winningest Active Division I Coaches

Minimum of five seasons as Division I head coach; regular season and tournament games included.

Top 10 Winning Percentage

		Yrs	W	L	Pct
1	Leon Barmore, La. Tech	18	520	77	**.871**
2	Pat Summitt, Tennessee	26	728	150	**.829**
3	Geno Auriemma, Connecticut	15	393	95	**.805**
4	Robin Selvig, Montana	22	515	139	**.790**
5	Tara VanDerveer, Stanford	21	497	142	**.778**
6	Andy Landers, Georgia	21	518	152	**.773**
7	Vivian Stringer, Rutgers	28	621	191	**.765**
8	Marsha Sharp, Texas Tech	18	433	134	**.764**
8	Jody Conradt, Texas	31	746	235	**.760**
10	Joe Ciampi, Auburn	23	529	168	**.759**

Top 10 Victories

		Yrs	W	L	Pct
1	Jody Conradt, Texas	31	**746**	235	.760
2	Pat Summitt, Tennessee	26	**728**	150	.829
4	Vivian Stringer, Rutgers	28	**621**	191	.765
3	Sue Gunter, LSU	30	**613**	273	.692
5	Kay Yow, N.C. State	29	**589**	242	.709
6	Sylvia Hatchell, N. Carolina	25	**561**	226	.713
7	Theresa Grentz, Illinois	26	**560**	211	.726
8	Rene Portland, Penn St.	25	**553**	185	.749
9	Mike Granelli, St. Peter's	28	**536**	203	.725
10	Joe Ciampi, Auburn	23	**529**	168	.759

Annual Awards

The Broderick Award was first given out to the Women's Division I or Large School Player of the Year in 1977. Since then, the National Assn. for Girls and Women in Sports (1978), the Women's Basketball Coaches Assn. (1983), the Atlanta Tip-Off Club (1983) and the Associated Press (1995) have joined in.

Since 1983, the first year as many as four awards were given out, the same player has won all of them in the same season twice: Cheryl Miller of USC in 1985 and Rebecca Lobo of Connecticut in 1995.

Associated Press

Voted on by AP sportswriters and broadcasters and first presented in 1995.
Multiple winners: Chamique Holdsclaw (2).

Year	Year	Year
1995 Rebecca Lobo, Connecticut	1997 Kara Wolters, Connecticut	1999 Chamique Holdsclaw, Tennessee
1996 Jennifer Rizzotti, Connecticut	1998 Chamique Holdsclaw, Tennessee	2000 Tamika Catchings, Tennessee

Broderick Award

Voted on by a national panel of women's collegiate athletic directors and first presented by the late Thomas Broderick, an athletic outfitter, in 1977. Honda has presented the award since 1987. Basketball Player of the Year is one of 10 nominated for Collegiate Woman Athlete of the Year; (*) indicates player also won Athlete of the Year.
Multiple winners: Chamique Holdsclaw, Nancy Lieberman, Cheryl Miller and Dawn Staley (2).

Year	Year	Year
1977 Lucy Harris, Delta St.*	1985 Cheryl Miller, USC	1993 Sheryl Swoopes, Texas Tech
1978 Ann Meyers, UCLA*	1986 Kamie Ethridge, Texas*	1994 Lisa Leslie, USC
1979 Nancy Lieberman, Old Dominion*	1987 Katrina McClain, Georgia	1995 Rebecca Lobo, Connecticut
1980 Nancy Lieberman, Old Dominion*	1988 Teresa Weatherspoon, La. Tech*	1996 Jennifer Rizzotti, Connecticut
1981 Lynette Woodard, Kansas	1989 Bridgette Gordon, Tennessee	1997 Chamique Holdsclaw, Tennessee
1982 Pam Kelly, La. Tech	1990 Jennifer Azzi, Stanford	1998 Chamique Holdsclaw, Tennessee*
1983 Anne Donovan, Old Dominion	1991 Dawn Staley, Virginia	1999 Stephanie White-McCarty, Purdue
1984 Cheryl Miller, USC*	1992 Dawn Staley, Virginia	

Wade Trophy

Voted on by the National Assn. for Girls and Women in Sports (NAGWS) and awarded for academics and community service as well as player performance. First presented in 1978 in the name of former Delta St. coach Margaret Wade.
Multiple winner: Nancy Lieberman (2).

Year	Year	Year
1978 Carol Blazejowski, Montclair St.	1986 Kamie Ethridge, Texas	1994 Carol Ann Shudlick, Minnesota
1979 Nancy Lieberman, Old Dominion	1987 Shelly Pennefather, Villanova	1995 Rebecca Lobo, Connecticut
1980 Nancy Lieberman, Old Dominion	1988 Teresa Weatherspoon, La. Tech	1996 Jennifer Rizzotti, Connecticut
1981 Lynette Woodard, Kansas	1989 Clarissa Davis, Texas	1997 DeLisha Milton, Florida
1982 Pam Kelly, La. Tech	1990 Jennifer Azzi, Stanford	1998 Ticha Penicheiro, Old Dominion
1983 LaTaunya Pollard, L. Beach St.	1991 Daedra Charles, Tennessee	1999 Stephanie White-McCarty, Purdue
1984 Janice Lawrence, La. Tech	1992 Susan Robinson, Penn St.	2000 Edwina Brown, Texas
1985 Cheryl Miller, USC	1993 Karen Jennings, Nebraska	

Naismith Trophy

Voted on by a panel of coaches, sportswriters and broadcasters and first presented in 1983 by the Atlanta Tip-Off Club in the name of the inventor of basketball, Dr. James Naismith.
Multiple winners: Cheryl Miller (3); Clarissa Davis, Chamique Holdsclaw and Dawn Staley (2).

Year	Year	Year
1983 Anne Donovan, Old Dominion	1989 Clarissa Davis, Texas	1995 Rebecca Lobo, Connecticut
1984 Cheryl Miller, USC	1990 Jennifer Azzi, Stanford	1996 Saudia Roundtree, Georgia
1985 Cheryl Miller, USC	1991 Dawn Staley, Virgina	1997 Kate Starbird, Stanford
1986 Cheryl Miller, USC	1992 Dawn Staley, Virginia	1998 Chamique Holdsclaw, Tennessee
1987 Clarissa Davis, Texas	1993 Sheryl Swoopes, Texas Tech	1999 Chamique Holdsclaw, Tennessee
1988 Sue Wicks, Rutgers	1994 Lisa Leslie, USC	2000 Tamika Catchings, Tennessee

Women's Basketball Coaches Association

Voted on by the WBCA and first presented by Champion athletic outfitters in 1983.
Multiple winners: Chamique Holdsclaw, Cheryl Miller and Dawn Staley (2).

Year	Year	Year
1983 Anne Donovan, Old Dominion	1989 Clarissa Davis, Texas	1995 Rebecca Lobo, Connecticut
1984 Janice Lawrence, La. Tech	1990 Venus Lacy, La. Tech	1996 Saudia Roundtree, Georgia
1985 Cheryl Miller, USC	1991 Dawn Staley, Virginia	1997 Kate Starbird, Stanford
1986 Cheryl Miller, USC	1992 Dawn Staley, Virginia	1998 Chamique Holdsclaw, Tennessee
1987 Katrina McClain, Georgia	1993 Sheryl Swoopes, Texas Tech	1999 Chamique Holdsclaw, Tennessee
1988 Michelle Edwards, Iowa	1994 Lisa Leslie, USC	2000 Tamika Catchings, Tennessee

Coach of the Year Award

Voted on by the Women's Basketball Coaches Assn. and first presented by Converse athletic outfitters in 1983.
Multiple winners: Pat Summitt (3), Geno Auriemma, Jody Conradt and Vivian Stringer (2).

Year		Year		Year	
1983	Pat Summitt, Tennessee	1989	Tara VanDerveer, Stanford	1995	Pat Summitt, Tennessee
1984	Jody Conradt, Texas	1990	Kay Yow, N.C. State	1996	Leon Barmore, La. Tech
1985	Jim Foster, St. Joseph's-PA	1991	Rene Portland, Penn St.	1997	Geno Auriemma, Connecticut
1986	Jody Conradt, Texas	1992	Ferne Labati, Miami-FL	1998	Pat Summitt, Tennessee
1987	Theresa Grentz, Rutgers	1993	Vivian Stringer, Iowa	1999	Carolyn Peck, Purdue
1988	Vivian Stringer, Iowa	1994	Marsha Sharp, Texas Tech	2000	Geno Auriemma, Connecticut

Other Women's Champions

The NCAA has sanctioned national championship tournaments for Division II and Division III since 1982. The NAIA sanctioned a single tournament from 1981-91, then split in to two divisions in 1992.

NCAA Div. II Finals

Multiple winners: North Dakota St. (5); Cal Poly Pomona, Delta St. and North Dakota (3).

Year	Winner	Score	Loser
1982	Cal Poly Pomona	93-74	Tuskegee, AL
1983	Virginia Union	73-60	Cal Poly Pomona
1984	Central Mo.St.	80-73	Virginia Union
1985	Cal Poly Pomona	80-69	Central Mo.St.
1986	Cal Poly Pomona	70-63	North Dakota St.
1987	New Haven, CT	77-75	Cal Poly Pomona
1988	Hampton, VA	65-48	West Texas St.
1989	Delta St., MS	88-58	Cal Poly Pomona
1990	Delta St., MS	77-43	Bentley, MA
1991	North Dakota St.	81-74	SE Missouri St.
1992	Delta St., MS	65-63	North Dakota St.
1993	North Dakota St.	95-63	Delta St.
1994	North Dakota St.	89-56	CS-San Bernardino
1995	North Dakota St.	98-85	Portland St.
1996	North Dakota St.	104-78	Shippensburg, PA
1997	North Dakota	94-78	S. Indiana
1998	North Dakota	92-76	Emporia St.
1999	North Dakota	80-63	Arkansas Tech
2000	Northern Kentucky	71-62	North Dakota St.

NCAA Div. III Finals

Multiple winners: Washington (3); Capital and Elizabethtown.

Year	Winner	Score	Loser
1982	Elizabethtown, PA	67-66*	NC-Greensboro
1983	North Central, IL	83-71	Elizabethtown, PA
1984	Rust College, MS	51-49	Elizabethtown, PA
1985	Scranton, PA	68-59	New Rochelle, NY
1986	Salem St., MA	89-85	Bishop, TX
1987	WI-Stevens Pt.	81-74	Concordia, MN
1988	Concordia, MN	65-57	St. John Fisher, NY
1989	Elizabethtown, PA	66-65	CS-Stanislaus
1990	Hope, MI	65-63	St. John Fisher
1991	St. Thomas, MN	73-55	Muskingum, OH
1992	Alma, MI	79-75	Moravian, PA
1993	Central Iowa	71-63	Capital, OH
1994	Capital, OH	82-63	Washington, MO
1995	Capital, OH	59-55	WI-Oshkosh
1996	WI-Oshkosh	66-50	Mt. Union, OH
1997	NYU	72-70	WI-Eau Claire
1998	Washington, MO	77-69	So. Maine
1999	Washington, MO	74-65	College of St. Benedict, MN
2000	Washington, MO	79-33	So. Maine

*Overtime

NAIA Finals

Multiple winners: One tournament-SW Oklahoma (4); Div. I tourney-Southern Nazarene (4), Oklahoma City (3); Arkansas Tech (2); Div. II tourney-Northern St. and Western Oregon (2).

Year	Winner	Score	Loser
1981	Kentucky St.	73-67	Texas Southern
1982	SW Oklahoma	80-45	Mo. Southern
1983	SW Oklahoma	80-68	AL-Huntsville
1984	NC-Asheville	72-70*	Portland, OR
1985	SW Oklahoma	55-54	Saginaw Val., MI
1986	Francis Marion, SC	75-65	Wayland Baptist, TX
1987	SW Oklahoma	60-58	North Georgia
1988	Oklahoma City	113-95	Claflin, SC
1989	So. Nazarene, OK	98-96	Claflin, SC
1990	SW Oklahoma	82-75	AR-Monticello
1991	Ft. Hays St., KS	57-53	SW Oklahoma
1992	I- Arkansas Tech	84-68	Wayland Baptist, TX
	II- Northern St., SD	73-56	Tarleton St., TX
1993	I- Arkansas Tech	76-75	Union, TN
	II- No. Montana	71-68	Northern St., SD
1994	I- So. Nazarene	97-74	David Lipscomb, TN
	II- Northern St., SD	48-45	Western Oregon
1995	I- So. Nazarene	78-77	SE Oklahoma
	II- Western Oregon	75-67	NW Nazarene, ID
1996	I- So. Nazarene	80-79	SE Oklahoma
	II- Western Oregon	80-77	Huron, SD
1997	I- So. Nazarene	78-73	Union, TN
	II- NW Nazarene	64-46	Black Hills St., SD
1998	I- Union, TN	73-70	So. Nazarene
	II- Walsh, OH	73-66	Mary Hardin-Baylor
1999	I- Oklahoma City	72-55	Simon Fraser, B.C.
	II- Shawnee St., OH	80-65	St. Francis, IN
2000	I- Oklahoma City	64-55	Simon Fraser, B.C.
	II- Mary, N.D.	59-49	Northwestern, IA

*Overtime

AIAW Finals

The Association of Intercollegiate Athletics for Women Large College tournament determined the women's national champion for 10 years until supplanted by the NCAA.

In 1982, most Division I teams entered the first NCAA tournament rather than the last one staged by the AIAW.

Year	Winner	Score	Loser
1972	Immaculata, PA	52-48	West Chester, PA
1973	Immaculata, PA	59-52	Queens College, NY
1974	Immaculata, PA	68-53	Mississippi College
1975	Delta St., MS	90-81	Immaculata, PA
1976	Delta St., MS	69-64	Immaculata, PA
1977	Delta St., MS	68-55	LSU
1978	UCLA	90-74	Maryland
1979	Old Dominion	75-65	Louisiana Tech
1980	Old Dominion	68-53	Tennessee
1981	Louisiana Tech	79-59	Tennessee
1982	Rutgers	83-77	Texas

Pro Basketball

Vince Carter *captured the Slam Dunk contest and attention of the rest of the NBA in 2000.*

Youth Movement

The Lakers rise to the top of the NBA, a league going in a new, younger direction.

by

Ric Bucher

Seeing a chance for a makeover entering the 1999-2000 season, the NBA didn't merely go for some new eye shadow and a little lip gloss. It went for the full facial after a labor-strife-shortened 1998-99 season and the retirement of Michael Jordan exposed some unsightly blemishes and wrinkles.

What was the most noticeable change? It embraced the impetuous youths once considered the league's bane and shifted the rules in their favor. Rather than punish the ever-younger stars for their inexperience, commissioner David Stern opted to showcase what makes them special–out-of-this-world athleticism and creativity–by opening up the game.

"We had an interesting transitional year where the fans are getting to know our new players," said Stern at his annual mid-Finals state of the league address. Translation: Goodbye, Karl Malone and Hakeem

Ric Bucher is ESPN's NBA analyst.

Olajuwon. Hello, Vince Carter and Steve Francis. Stern added, "We're committed to making sure that the fans get to understand really how extraordinary our players are." Translation: the most entertaining aspect of our young players is how high they jump and how fast they run, so we better let them!

No one, of course, took more advantage of the league's swing in allegiance than Shaquille O'Neal and Kobe Bryant, who led an otherwise creaky crew of Los Angeles Lakers past the Indiana Pacers, 4 games to 2, in the best-of-seven NBA Finals. You want proof of how their athleticism overcame their technical inefficiency? The Finals had always been won by the better free-throw shooting team until last season–when the Pacers posted the *best* all-time Finals free-throw shooting percentage and the Lakers put up the all-time *worst*.

Credit O'Neal for up-ending that stat. Quietly putting aside his rap microphone and actors' guild card, he got his body right and his free throws,

A happy **Shaquille O'Neal**, the regular season and Finals MVP center for the World Champion Los Angeles Lakers, gets a closer look at the Lakers' first Larry O'Brien Trophy in 12 years.

uh, better. Result: averaging 40 minutes a night, he anchored new coach Phil Jackson's defense as well as his vaunted triangle offense, winning one-vote-short-of-unanimous regular-season MVP honors and the Finals MVP trophy unanimously while leading the Lakers to their first title since 1988.

While the rule changes limiting physical contact allowed Shaq to use his devastating combination of size and quickness, the true benefactors were perimeter players who could dribble-drive knowing any contact would result in a foul. Six of the league's top 10 scorers were guards in the 1999-2000 season, twice as many as in either of the two previous seasons. Detroit Pistons shooting guard Jerry Stackhouse led the way, making a league-leading 618 free throws to climb to eighth in scoring after not making the top 15 the previous two years. Rules that re-started the 24-second shot clock at 14 seconds after certain infractions also resulted in more shots and thereby more points. Seven teams averaged 100 or more last season, six more than in the 1998-99 season.

Youth will continue to be served. High schooler Darius Miles was the number three draft pick and, after Tim Duncan and Grant Hill, three of the hottest potential free agent properties were direct-from-preps Rashard Lewis, Tracy McGrady and Jermaine O'Neal. The NBA has a new motto–play fast, draft young and leave a good-looking score for the nightly news. ■

AP/Wide World Photos

Michael Jordan (and his famous tongue) has returned to the NBA, but this time as president of the Washington Wizards.

Ric Bucher's Top 10 Stories of the NBA Season

10. **Bobby Phills and Malik Sealy die in car crashes** – The seeming invincibility and charmed life of NBA players is rocked when Phills, 30, dies while drag-racing teammate David Wesley on their way home from practice on January 12. Sealy, also 30, is killed by a drunk driver on May 20.

9. **First Canadian team reaches playoffs** – Led by Vince Carter, who also inspired and then dominated the return of the All-Star Game dunk contest, the first team north of the border makes a postseason appearance.

8. **Doc Rivers makes Magic** – Leading a young, athletic group of no-names, the former all-star guard earns coach of the year honors in his debut with the Orlando Magic

for taking a team under construction to the brink of a playoff berth.

7. **Michael Jordan returns, again** – Pro hoops, left for dead in D.C., is electrified by his Airness returning, albeit in a suit to an upstairs' office as president of the Washington Wizards. MJ quickly finds dominating from behind a desk less easy.

6. **Sean Elliott's new kidney** – The Spurs small forward makes history on March 14 by becoming the first professional athlete to return to competition after receiving a kidney transplant.

5. **Pacers reach Finals** – The window in Indiana was supposed to have closed after four fruitless conference finals and Antonio Davis' trade to Toronto, but the

AP/Wide World Photos

Veteran player, and veteran trash-talker, **Reggie Miller** made his first trip to the Finals in 2000.

emergence of Jalen Rose and Austin Croshere and resurgence of Reggie Miller and Dale Davis did the trick.

4. **Larry Legend steps down** – Pacers coach and former Boston Celtics legend Larry Bird retires after a three-year stint which included coach of the year honors as a rookie and the Pacers' first trip to the Finals. Another legend, former Detroit Pistons great Isiah Thomas, is picked to replace him.

3. **Sir Charles abdicates his throne** – A ruptured knee tendon in Philly (his first NBA home) finally forces one of the most entertaining players, on and off the court, to make good on his vow to retire. He still

Wilt Chamberlain, perhaps the most dominating player in basketball history, died Oct. 12, 1999. In the picture above, Wilt celebrates his 100-point game in Hershey, Pa. on Mar. 2, 1962.

Charles Barkley returned from injury, for one game, and then retired from the league after 16 NBA seasons.

goes out defiantly, waddling onto the floor in Houston for one last appearance in the season finale.

2. **The Logo Goes** – Longtime Lakers VP of Basketball Operations Jerry West, in part because of health problems, finally makes good on his vow to retire as well, ending an illustrious run of 18 front-office years and 14 All-Star seasons, all with the Lakers.

1. **Wilt Chamberlain, R.I.P.** – The only 100-point scorer in NBA history and the holder of several other unapproachable records dies unexpectedly, a shock to the basketball community not only because of his legacy but also his seemingly inextinguishable vitality. ∎

insidethenumbers

FIRST TIME'S THE CHARM

The Lakers have had a lot of luck with new head coaches. Phil Jackson became the fifth head coach in franchise history to win an NBA title in his first year with the team. Only 10 coaches have done it in the history of the league. In the list below the coaches are listed in chronological order.

	Team	Year
Ed Gottlieb	Philadelphia	1947
Buddy Jeannette	Baltimore	1948
John Kundla	Minn. Lakers	1949
George Senesky	Philadelphia	1956
Bill Sharman	LA Lakers	1972
Jack Ramsay	Portland	1977
Paul Westhead	LA Lakers	1980
Pat Riley	LA Lakers	1982
K.C. Jones	Boston	1984
Phil Jackson	LA Lakers	2000

Note: Jackson won his first NBA title with the Chicago Bulls (1991) in his second season.

LOW FIVE

In just five seasons, the Vancouver Grizzlies have managed to post the worst win percentage of ANY team during ANY five-season span in NBA history. No other team approaches the Grizzlies in this category, although the Timberwolves did have a woeful seven-year stretch from 1989 through 1996 that saw them make this list three times.

Team	W-L	Pct.
Grizzlies, 1995-00	78-300	.206
Timberwolves, 1991-96	101-309	.246
Timberwolves, 1990-95	104-306	.254
Timberwolves, 1989-94	105-305	.256
Mavericks, 1990-95	110-300	.268

FINALS PERFORMANCE

Phil Jackson remains the only head coach with at least three NBA Finals appearances to never lose a Finals series. Take a look at the list of coaches with the highest Finals series winning percentage (minimum of three Finals appearances) below.

Coach	W-L	Win pct.
Phil Jackson	7-0	1.000
John Kundla	5-1	.833
Red Auerbach	9-2	.818
Chuck Daly	2-1	.667
Red Holzman	2-1	.667

IN AND OUT

The New Jersey Nets have not made it past the first round of the playoffs in 16 years. The last and only time they did advance past the first round, the Nets lost in the next round to Milwaukee in six games. Here is a look at the longest streaks without surviving the first stage of the postseason.

Team	Years
LA Clippers	24
Sacramento Kings	19
Washington Wizards	18
New Jersey Nets	16
Dallas Mavericks	12
Milwaukee Bucks	11

STREAKY COACHES

Phil Jackson is closing in on the immortal Red Auerbach in the category of most consecutive postseason series won by a head coach in NBA history. Jackson has now won 16 consecutive playoff series, dating back to his three-year run of NBA titles with the Chicago Bulls from 1996-98.

	Series
Red Auerbach, 1959-66	17
Phil Jackson, 1996–	16
Phil Jackson, 1991-94	13
Pat Riley, 1987-89	11
Chuck Daly, 1989-91	10
John Kundla, 1952-55	10

■

PRO BASKETBALL
1999-2000 Season in Review

ESPN
information please
SPORTS ALMANAC

PAGE 343

Final NBA Standings

Division champions (*) and playoff qualifiers (†) are noted. Number of seasons listed after each head coach refers to current tenure with club.

Western Conference
Midwest Division

	W	L	Pct	GB	Per Game For	Opp
*Utah	55	27	.671	—	96.5	92.0
†San Antonio	53	29	.646	2	96.1	90.2
†Minnesota	50	32	.610	5	98.5	96.0
Dallas	40	42	.488	15	101.4	101.9
Denver	35	47	.427	20	98.9	101.0
Houston	34	48	.415	21	99.4	100.3
Vancouver	22	60	.268	33	93.9	99.5

Head Coaches: Utah— Jerry Sloan (12th season); **SA—** Gregg Popovich (4th); **Min—** Phil Saunders (5th); **Dal—** Don Nelson (3rd); **Den—** Dan Issel (1st); **Hou—** Rudy Tomjanovich (9th); **Van—** Brian Hill (3rd, 4-18) was fired and replaced on an interim basis by assistant Lionel Hollins (18-42) on Dec. 16, 1999.
1998-99 Standings: 1. San Antonio (37-13); 2. Utah (37-13); 3. Houston (31-19); 4. Minnesota (25-25); 5. Dallas (19-31); 6. Denver (14-36); 7. Vancouver (8-42).

Pacific Division

	W	L	Pct	GB	Per Game For	Opp
*LA Lakers	67	15	.817	—	100.8	92.2
†Portland	59	23	.720	8	97.4	91.0
†Phoenix	53	29	.646	14	98.9	93.6
†Seattle	45	37	.549	22	99.0	98.1
†Sacramento	44	38	.537	23	104.9	102.0
Golden St.	19	63	.232	48	95.5	103.8
LA Clippers	15	67	.183	52	92.0	103.5

Head Coaches: LAL— Phil Jackson (1st season); **Port—** Mike Dunleavy (3rd); **Pho—** Danny Ainge (4th, 13-7) resigned and was replaced by assistant Scott Skiles (40-22); **Sea—** Paul Westphal (2nd); **Sac—** Rick Adelman (3rd); **GS—** P.J. Carlesimo (3rd, 6-21) was fired on Dec. 27, 1999 and replaced by GM Garry St. Jean (13-42); **LAC—** Chris Ford (2nd, 11-34) was fired and replaced on an interim basis by assistant Jim Todd (4-33).
1998-99 Standings: 1. Portland (35-15); 2. LA Lakers (31-19); 3. Sacramento (27-23); 4. Phoenix (27-23); 5. Seattle (25-25); 6. Golden St. (21-29); 7. LA Clippers (9-41).

Eastern Conference
Atlantic Division

	W	L	Pct	GB	Per Game For	Opp
*Miami	52	30	.634	—	94.3	91.2
†New York	50	32	.610	2	92.1	90.6
†Philadelphia	49	33	.598	3	94.7	93.4
Orlando	41	41	.500	11	100.0	99.3
Boston	35	47	.427	17	99.3	100.0
New Jersey	31	51	.378	21	98.0	99.0
Washington	29	53	.354	23	96.5	99.8

Head Coaches: Mia— Pat Riley (5th season); **NY—** Jeff Van Gundy (5th); **Phi—** Larry Brown (3rd); **Orl—** Doc Rivers (1st); **Bos—** Rick Pitino (3rd); **NJ—** Don Casey (2nd); **Wash—** Gar Heard (1st, 16-33) was fired and replaced with Darrell Walker (15-23) on an interim basis on Jan. 31, 2000.
1998-99 Standings: 1. Miami (33-17); 2. Orlando (33-17); 3. Philadelphia (28-22); 4. New York (27-23); 5. Boston (19-31); 6. Washington (18-32); 7. New Jersey (16-34).

Central Division

	W	L	Pct	GB	Per Game For	Opp
*Indiana	56	26	.683	—	101.2	96.6
†Charlotte	49	33	.598	7	98.4	95.7
†Toronto	45	37	.549	11	97.1	97.3
†Detroit	42	40	.512	14	103.4	102.0
†Milwaukee	42	40	.512	14	101.2	101.0
Cleveland	32	50	.390	24	96.9	100.4
Atlanta	28	54	.341	28	94.3	99.7
Chicago	17	65	.207	39	84.7	94.1

Head Coaches: Ind— Larry Bird (3rd season); **Char—** Paul Silas (2nd); **Tor—** Butch Carter (3rd); **Det—** Alvin Gentry (3rd, 28-30) was fired and replaced by assistant George Irvine (14-10) on an interim basis on Mar. 6, 2000; **Mil—** George Karl (2nd); **Cle—** Randy Wittman (1st); **Atl—** Lenny Wilkens (7th); **Chi—** Tim Floyd (2nd).
1998-99 Standings: 1. Indiana (33-17); 2. Atlanta (31-19); 3. Detroit (29-21); 4. Milwaukee (28-22); 5. Charlotte (26-24); 6. Toronto (23-27); 7. Cleveland (22-28); 8. Chicago (13-37).

Overall Conference Standings

Sixteen teams—eight from each conference—qualify for the NBA Playoffs; (*) indicates division champions.

Western Conference

		W	L	Home	Away	Div	Conf
1	LA Lakers*	67	15	36-5	31-10	20-4	40-12
2	Portland	59	23	30-11	29-12	21-3	38-14
3	Utah*	55	27	31-10	24-17	14-10	33-19
4	San Antonio	53	29	31-10	22-19	16-8	33-19
5	Phoenix	53	29	32-9	21-20	15-9	30-22
6	Minnesota	50	32	26-15	24-17	18-6	32-20
7	Seattle	45	37	24-17	21-20	12-12	31-21
8	Sacramento	44	38	30-11	14-27	9-15	25-27
	Dallas	40	42	22-19	18-23	12-12	28-24
	Denver	35	47	25-16	10-31	10-14	22-30
	Houston	34	48	22-19	12-29	8-16	23-29
	Vancouver	22	60	12-29	10-31	6-18	12-40
	Golden St.	19	63	12-29	7-34	2-22	9-43
	LA Clippers	15	67	10-31	5-36	5-19	8-44

Eastern Conference

		W	L	Home	Away	Div	Conf
1	Indiana*	56	26	36-5	20-21	20-8	36-18
2	Miami*	52	30	33-8	19-22	18-6	34-20
3	New York	50	32	33-8	17-24	14-10	32-22
4	Charlotte	49	33	30-11	19-22	20-8	36-18
5	Philadelphia	49	33	29-12	20-21	13-11	36-18
6	Toronto	45	37	26-15	19-22	16-12	29-25
7	Detroit	42	40	27-14	15-26	16-12	30-24
8	Milwaukee	42	40	23-18	19-22	16-12	28-26
	Orlando	41	41	26-15	15-26	12-13	27-27
	Boston	35	47	26-15	9-32	12-12	24-30
	Cleveland	32	50	22-19	10-31	8-20	8-20
	New Jersey	31	51	22-19	9-32	9-16	21-33
	Washington	29	53	17-24	12-29	7-17	19-35
	Atlanta	28	54	21-10	7-34	11-17	20-34
	Chicago	17	65	12-29	5-36	13-41	5-23

2000 NBA All-Star Game
West, 137-126

49th NBA All-Star Game. **Date:** Feb. 13, at The Arena in Oakland, Calif.; **Coaches:** Jeff Van Gundy, New York (East) and Phil Jackson, LA Lakers (West); **Co-MVPs:** Tim Duncan (33 minutes, 24 points, 14 rebounds) and Shaquille O'Neal (25 minutes, 22 points, 3 blocks); Starters chosen by fan vote, (Toronto's Vince Carter, a first-time All-Star, was the leading vote-getter, receiving 1,911,973); bench chosen by conference coaches' vote.

Eastern Conference

Pos	Starters	Min	FG M-A	Pts	Reb	A
F	Vince Carter, Tor	28	6-11	12	4	2
F	Grant Hill, Det	19	3-7	7	3	5
C	Alonzo Mourning, Mia	27	7-11	15	7	1
G	Eddie Jones, Cha	21	4-7	10	4	3
G	Allen Iverson, Phi	28	10-18	26	2	9
Bench						
G	Allan Houston, NY	18	3-10	11	0	2
F	Glenn Robinson, Mil	17	5-10	10	6	0
G	Ray Allen, Mil	17	4-13	14	1	2
C	Dikembe Mutombo, Atl	16	2-4	4	8	0
F	Dale Davis, Ind	14	2-3	4	8	1
G	Jerry Stackhouse, Det	14	4-7	8	1	2
G	Reggie Miller, Ind	21	1-7	5	2	3
	TOTALS	240	51-108	126	46	30

Three-Point FG: 7-23 (Iverson 2-2, Jones 2-3, Houston 1-3, Allen 1-6, Miller 1-6, Hill 0-1, Carter 0-2); **Free Throws:** 17-20 (Allen 5-6, Houston 4-4, Iverson 4-5, Miller 2-2, Hill 1-1, Mourning 1-2); **Percentages:** FG (.472), Three-Pt. FG (.304), Free Throws (.850); **Turnovers:** 20 (Iverson 5, Allen 3, Hill 3, Carter 2, Mutombo 2, Houston, Jones, Miller, Mourning, Stackhouse); **Steals:** 14 (Allen 3, Mourning 3, Carter 2, Iverson 2, Hill, Houston, Jones, Miller); **Blocked Shots:** 5 (Mourning 4, Allen); **Fouls:** 11 (Mourning, Allen 2, Stackhouse 2, Houston, Jones, Miller); **Team Rebounds:** 8.

	1	2	3	4	F
East	26	33	38	29	—**126**
West	33	31	35	38	—**137**

Western Conference

Pos	Starters	Min	FG M-A	Pts	Reb	A
F	Kevin Garnett, Minn.	35	10-19	24	10	5
F	Tim Duncan, SA	33	12-14	24	14	4
C	Shaquille O'Neal, LAL	25	11-20	22	9	3
G	Kobe Bryant, LAL	28	7-16	15	1	3
G	Jason Kidd, Pho	34	4-9	11	5	14
Bench						
G	Gary Payton, Sea	20	1-8	5	4	8
G	John Stockton, Utah	11	5-5	10	0	2
F	Karl Malone, Utah	3	0-1	0	0	0
C	David Robinson, SA	7	0-1	0	2	0
F	Rasheed Wallace, Por	21	3-6	9	4	0
F	Michael Finley, Dal	10	5-6	11	1	0
F	Chris Webber, Sac	13	3-10	6	8	3
	TOTALS	240	61-115	137	58	42

Three-Point FG: 5-17 (Kidd 3-6, Finley 1-2, Bryant 1-4, Garnett 0-1, Payton 0-4); **Free Throws:** 10-13 (Garnett 4-4, Payton 3-3, Wallace 3-4, O'Neal 0-2); **Percentages:** FG (.530), Three-Pt. FG (.294), Free Throws (.769); **Turnovers:** 19 (Kidd 6, O'Neal 4, Duncan 2, Payton 2, Webber 2, Bryant, Finley, Robinson); **Steals:** 13 (Kidd 4, Bryant 2, Payton 2, Duncan, Garnett, Stockton, Wallace, Webber); **Blocked Shots:** 6 (O'Neal 3, Duncan, Garnett, Wallace); **Fouls:** 15 (Bryant 3, Duncan 3, O'Neal 2, Stockton 2, Webber 2, Garnett, Payton, Robinson); **Team Rebounds:** 5.

Halftime— West, 64-59; **Third Quarter—** West, 99-97; **Technical Fouls—** none; **Officials—** Joe Crawford, Terry Durham, Joe Forte; **Attendance—** 18,325; **Time—** 2:12; **TV Rating—** 6.9/12 (NBC).

NBA 3-point Shootout

Eight players are invited to compete in the annual three-point shooting contest held during All-Star weekend, since 1986. Each shooter has 60 seconds to shoot the 25 balls in five racks outside the three-point line. Each ball is worth one point, except the last ball in each rack, which is worth two. Highest scores advance. First prize: $25,000.

First Round	Pts
Dirk Nowitzki, Dal	18
Jeff Hornacek, Utah	17
Ray Allen, Mil	16
Failed to advance	
Mike Bibby, Van	15
Terry Porter, SA	15
Hubert Davis, Dal	14
Allen Iverson, Phi	10
Bob Sura, Cle	9

Finals	
Jeff Hornacek	13
Dirk Nowitzki	11
Ray Allen	10

Slam Dunk Contest

Six players are invited to compete in the slam dunk contest based on "the creativity and artistry they have displayed in dunking" over the course of the season. In the first round, everyone attempts three dunks, one of which must involve a teammate. The dunks are judged by five judges on a scale from six to ten. The top three advance to the final round and attempt two dunks. The combined score of the two dunks determines the winner. First prize: $25,000.

First Round	Pts
Vince Carter, Tor	100
Tracy McGrady, Tor	99
Steve Francis, Hou	95
Ricky Davis, Cha	88
Jerry Stackhouse, Det	83
Larry Hughes, Phi	67

Finals	Pts
Vince Carter	98
Steve Francis	91
Tracy McGrady	77

NBA/WNBA All-Star 2Ball

In 2Ball one NBA and one WNBA player, who compete on teams from the same city, are paired up in a competition in which they alternate taking shots from seven designated spots on the half court, accumulating points for every made basket. Each team has one minute to perform, and the point amounts differ according to each spot's distance away from the basket. First prize: $25,000. **Teams: Detroit—** Grant Hill and Jennifer Azzi; **Houston—** Steve Francis and Cynthia Cooper; **Los Angeles—** Derek Fisher and Lisa Leslie; **New York—** Allan Houston and Becky Hammon; **Phoenix—** Jason Kidd and Jennifer Gillom; **Sacramento—** Jason Williams and Yolanda Griffith; **Utah—** Jeff Hornacek and Natalie Williams; **Washington—** Richard Hamilton and Chamique Holdsclaw. **Finals:** Utah def. Phoenix, 68-61.

| Phoenix Suns
Jason Kidd
Assists & Triple Doubles | Utah Jazz
Jeff Hornacek
Free Throw Pct. | Atlanta Hawks
Dikembe Mutombo
Rebounds | Miami Heat
Alonzo Mourning
Blocked Shots |

NBA Regular Season Individual Leaders
Scoring

	Gm	Min	FG	FG%	3pt/Att	FT	FT%	Reb	Ast	Stl	Blk	Pts	Avg	Hi
Shaquille O'Neal, LAL	79	3163	956	.574	0/1	432	.524	1078	299	36	239	2344	**29.7**	61
Allen Iverson, Phi.	70	2853	729	.421	89/261	442	.713	267	328	144	5	1989	**28.4**	50
Grant Hill, Det	74	2776	696	.489	34/98	478	.795	489	385	102	44	1904	**25.8**	42
Vince Carter, Tor	82	3126	788	.465	95/236	436	.791	476	322	110	92	2107	**25.7**	51
Karl Malone, Utah	82	2947	752	.509	2/8	589	.797	779	304	79	71	2095	**25.5**	40
Chris Webber, Sac	75	2880	748	.483	27/95	311	.751	788	345	120	128	1834	**24.5**	39
Gary Payton, Sea	82	3425	747	.448	177/520	311	.735	529	732	153	18	1982	**24.2**	43
Jerry Stackhouse, Det	82	3149	619	.428	83/288	618	.815	315	365	104	40	1939	**23.6**	40
Tim Duncan, SA.	74	2865	628	.490	1/11	459	.761	918	234	66	165	1718	**23.2**	46
Kevin Garnett, Min	81	3243	759	.497	30/81	309	.765	956	401	120	126	1857	**22.9**	40
Michael Finley, Dal	82	3464	748	.457	99/247	260	.820	518	438	109	32	1855	**22.6**	38
Kobe Bryant, LAL.	66	2524	554	.468	46/144	331	.821	416	323	106	62	1485	**22.5**	40
Stephon Marbury, NJ	74	2881	569	.432	66/233	436	.813	240	622	112	15	1640	**22.2**	42
Ray Allen, Mil	82	3070	642	.455	172/407	353	.887	360	308	110	19	1809	**22.1**	36
Alonzo Mourning, Mia	79	2748	652	.551	0/4	414	.711	753	123	40	294	1718	**21.7**	43
Glenn Robinson, Mil.	81	2909	690	.472	86/237	227	.802	485	193	78	41	1693	**20.9**	38
Antoine Walker, Bos.	82	3003	648	.430	73/285	311	.699	652	305	116	32	1680	**20.5**	39
Shareef Abdur-Rahim, Van.	82	3223	594	.465	29/96	446	.809	825	271	89	87	1663	**20.3**	36
Eddie Jones, Cha	72	2807	630	.427	128/341	362	.864	343	305	192	49	1446	**20.1**	34
Elton Brand, Chi	81	2999	478	.482	0/2	367	.685	810	155	66	132	1627	**20.1**	44
Allan Houston, NY	82	3169	614	.483	106/242	280	.838	271	224	65	14	1614	**19.7**	37
Antawn Jamison, GS	43	1556	486	.471	2/7	127	.611	359	90	30	15	841	**19.6**	37
Paul Pierce, Bos.	73	2583	559	.442	96/280	359	.798	396	221	152	62	1427	**19.5**	38
Isaiah Rider, Atl.	60	2084	614	.419	56/180	204	.785	258	219	41	6	1158	**19.3**	38
Keith Van Horn, NJ	80	2782	545	.445	84/228	333	.847	676	158	64	60	1535	**19.2**	32

Rebounds

	Gm	Off	Def	Tot	Avg
Dikembe Mutombo, Atl	82	304	853	1157	14.1
Shaquille O'Neal, LAL	79	336	742	1078	13.6
Tim Duncan, SA.	74	262	656	918	12.4
Kevin Garnett, Min	81	223	733	956	11.8
Chris Webber, Sac	75	189	598	787	10.5
Shareef Abdur-Rahim, Van.	82	218	607	825	10.1
Elton Brand, Chi	81	348	462	810	10.0
Dale Davis, Ind	74	256	473	729	9.9
David Robinson, SA	80	193	577	770	9.6
Jerome Williams, Det	82	277	512	789	9.6
Karl Malone, Utah	82	169	610	779	9.5
Alonzo Mourning, Mia	79	215	538	753	9.5
Jamie Feick, NJ	81	264	491	755	9.3
Antonio Davis, Tor.	79	235	461	696	8.8
Shawn Kemp, Cle	82	231	494	725	8.8

Assists

	Gm	Ast	Avg
Jason Kidd, Pho.	67	678	10.1
Sam Cassell, Mil	81	729	9.0
Nick Van Exel, Den.	79	714	9.0
Terrell Brandon, Min.	71	629	8.9
Gary Payton, Sea	82	732	8.9
John Stockton, Utah	82	703	8.6
Stephon Marbury, Min	74	622	8.4
Mike Bibby, Van	82	665	8.1
Mark Jackson, Ind.	81	650	8.0
Eric Snow, Phi	82	624	7.6
Rod Strickland, Was.	69	519	7.5
Jason Williams, Sac	81	589	7.3
Brevin Knight, Cle.	65	458	7.0
Mookie Blaylock, GS	73	489	6.7
Steve Francis, Hou	77	507	6.6

Field Goal Pct.

	Gm	FG	Att	Pct
Shaquille O'Neal, LAL	.79	956	1665	.574
Dikembe Mutombo, Atl	.82	322	573	.562
Alonzo Mourning, Mia	.79	652	1184	.551
Ruben Patterson, Sea	.81	354	661	.536
Rasheed Wallace, Por	.81	542	1045	.519
David Robinson, SA	.80	528	1031	.512
Wally Szczerbiak, Min.	.73	342	669	.511
Karl Malone, Utah	.82	752	1476	.509
Antonio McDyess, Den.	.81	614	1211	.507
Othella Harrington, Van.	.82	420	830	.506
Arvydas Sabonis, Por.	.66	302	598	.505
Vlade Divac, Sac	.82	384	765	.503

Free Throw Pct.

	Gm	FT	Att	Pct
Jeff Hornacek, Utah	.77	171	180	.950
Reggie Miller, Ind	.81	373	406	.919
Darrell Armstrong, Orl	.82	225	247	.911
Terrell Brandon, Min	.71	187	208	.889
Ray Allen, Mil	.82	353	398	.887
Predrag Stojakovic, Sac.	.74	135	153	.882
Derek Anderson, LAC	.64	271	309	.877
Jim Jackson, Atl	.79	186	212	.877
Sam Cassell, Mil	.81	390	445	.876
Mitch Richmond, Was	.74	298	340	.876
Glen Rice, LAL	.80	346	396	.874
Latrell Sprewell, NY	.82	344	397	.866

3-Point Field Goal Pct.

	Gm	3FG	Att	Pct
Hubert Davis, Dal	.79	82	167	.491
Jeff Hornacek, Utah	.77	66	138	.478
Matt Bullard, Hou	.56	79	177	.446
Rodney Rogers, Pho	.82	115	262	.439
Allan Houston, NY	.82	106	243	.436
Terry Porter, SA	.68	90	207	.435
Lindsey Hunter, Det	.82	168	389	.432
Jon Barry, Sac	.62	66	154	.429
Wesley Person, Cle	.79	106	250	.424

High-Point Games

	Opp	Date	FG-FT—Pts
Shaquille O'Neal, LAL...	at LAC	3/6/00	24-13—61
Vince Carter, Tor	vs Pho	2/27/00	17-13—51
Allen Iverson, Phi	vs Sac	2/6/00	20-9—50
Cliff Robinson, Pho	vs Den	1/16/00	17-13—50
Shaquille O'Neal, LAL...	at GS	4/5/00	19-11—49
Vince Carter, Tor	vs Mil.	1/14/00	20-4—47
Tim Duncan, SA	vs Utah	1/10/00	16-14—46
Allen Iverson, Phi	at Orl	11/10/99	18-5—46

Personal Fouls

Shawn Kemp, Cle	.371
Christian Laettner, Det.	.326
Antonio McDyess, Den.	.316
Alonzo Mourning, Mia.	.308
Michael Olowokandi, LAC	.304

Triple Doubles

Jason Kidd, Pho	.5
Chris Webber, Sac.	.5
Michael Finely, Dal	.4
Anthony Mason, Cha	.3
Lamar Odom, LAC	.3

Blocked Shots

	Gm	Blk	Avg
Alonzo Mourning, Mia	.79	294	3.72
Dikembe Mutombo, Atl	.82	269	3.28
Shaquille O'Neal, LAL	.79	239	3.03
Theo Ratliff, Phi	.57	171	3.00
Shawn Bradley, Phi.	.77	190	2.47
David Robinson, SA	.80	183	2.29
Tim Duncan, SA.	.74	165	2.23
Raef LaFrentz, Den	.81	180	2.22
Greg Ostertag, Uta.	.81	172	2.12
Marcus Camby, NY	.59	116	1.97

Steals

	Gm	Stl	Avg
Eddie Jones, Cha	.72	192	2.67
Paul Pierce, Bos.	.73	152	2.08
Darrell Armstrong, Orl	.82	169	2.06
Allen Iverson, Phi.	.70	144	2.06
Mookie Blaylock, GS	.73	146	2.00
Terrell Brandon, Min	.71	134	1.89
Gary Payton, Sea	.82	153	1.87
Kendall Gill, NJ	.76	139	1.83
John Stockton, Utah	.82	143	1.74

Rookie Leaders

Scoring	Gm	FG	FT	Pts	Avg
Elton Brand, Chi	.81	630	367	1627	20.1
Steve Francis, Hou	.77	497	287	1388	18.0
Lamar Odom, LAC	.76	449	302	1259	16.6
Ron Artest, Chi	.72	309	188	866	12.0
Wally Szczerbiak, Min.	.73	342	133	845	11.6

Field Goal Pct.	Gm	FG	Att	Pct
Eddie Robinson, Cha	.67	212	386	.549
Wally Szczerbiak, Min.	.73	342	669	.511
Elton Brand, Chi	.81	630	1306	.482
Corey Maggette, LAC	.77	224	469	.478
Shawn Marion, Pho	.51	222	471	.471

Rebounds	Gm	Off	Def	Tot	Avg
Elton Brand, Chi	.81	348	462	810	10.0
Lamar Odom, LAC	.76	159	436	595	7.8
Shawn Marion, Pho	.51	105	227	332	6.5
Kenny Thomas, Hou	.72	147	290	437	6.1
Steve Francis, Hou	.77	152	257	409	5.3

Assists			Gm	No	Avg
Steve Francis, Hou			.77	507	6.6
Andre Miller, Cle.			.82	476	5.8
Anthony Carter, Mia.			.79	378	4.8
Jason Terry, Atl			.81	346	4.3
Lamar Odom, LAC			.76	317	4.2

Disqualifications

Lamar Odom, LAC.	.13
Shawn Kemp, Cle	.13
Antonio McDyess, Den	.12
Jason Caffey, GS	.11

Minutes Played

Michael Finley, Dal	.3464
Gary Payton, Sea	.3425
Latrell Sprewell, NY	.3276
Kevin Garnett, Min	.3243
Shareef Abdur-Rahim, Van	.3223

Turnovers

Jerry Stackhouse, Det	.311
Steve Francis, Hou	.306
Jason Williams, Sac	.296
Shawn Kemp, Cle	.291
Stephon Marbury, NJ	.270

Technical Fouls

Rasheed Wallace, Por.	.38
Gary Payton, Sea	.18
Vlade Divac, Sac.	.18
Antoine Walker, Bos	.17
Karl Malone, Utah	.17

Team by Team Statistics

Players who competed for more than one team during the regular season are listed with their final club; (*) indicates rookies.

Atlanta Hawks

	Gm	FG%	Tpts	PPG	RPG	APG
Isaiah Rider	.60	.419	1158	19.3	4.3	3.7
Jim Jackson	.79	.411	1317	16.7	5.0	2.9
Alan Henderson	.82	.461	1083	13.2	7.0	0.9
Dikembe Mutombo	.82	.562	942	11.5	14.1	1.3
LaPhonso Ellis	.58	.450	487	8.4	5.0	1.0
Jason Terry*	.81	.415	657	8.1	2.0	4.3
Bimbo Coles	.80	.455	645	8.1	2.2	3.6
Roshown McLeod	.44	.395	318	7.2	3.1	1.2
Dion Glover*	.30	.386	195	6.5	1.3	0.9
Lorenzen Wright	.75	.499	448	6.0	4.1	0.3
Chris Crawford	.55	.397	252	4.6	1.8	0.6
Cal Bowdler*	.46	.426	122	2.7	1.8	0.3
Drew Barry	.16	.455	41	2.6	0.8	2.1

Triple Doubles: Mutombo (1). **3-pt FG leader:** Jackson (117).
Steals leader: Terry (90). **Blocks leader:** Mutombo (269).
Signed: G Barry (Mar. 27).

Boston Celtics

	Gm	FG%	Tpts	PPG	RPG	APG
Antoine Walker	.82	.430	1680	20.5	8.0	3.7
Paul Pierce	.73	.442	1427	19.5	5.4	3.0
Kenny Anderson	.82	.440	1149	14.0	2.7	5.1
Vitaly Potapenko	.79	.499	723	9.2	6.3	1.0
Danny Fortson	.55	.528	419	7.6	6.7	0.5
Eric Williams	.68	.427	489	7.2	2.3	1.4
Dana Barros	.72	.451	517	7.2	1.4	1.9
Adrian Griffin*	.72	.424	485	6.7	5.2	2.5
Tony Battie	.82	.477	541	6.6	5.0	0.8
Calbert Cheaney	.67	.440	267	4.0	2.1	1.2
Walter McCarty	.61	.339	229	3.8	1.8	1.1
Doug Overton	.48	.396	152	3.2	0.7	1.1
Pervis Ellison	.30	.442	53	1.8	2.2	0.4
Wayne Turner	.30	.167	4	1.3	1.0	1.7

Triple Doubles: Walker (1). **3-pt FG leader:** Pierce (96).
Steals leader: Pierce (152). **Blocks leader:** Battie (70).
Signed G Overton (Nov. 8).

Charlotte Hornets

	Gm	FG%	Tpts	PPG	RPG	APG
Eddie Jones	.72	.427	1446	20.1	4.8	4.2
Derrick Coleman	.74	.456	1239	16.7	8.5	2.4
David Wesley	.82	.426	1116	13.6	2.7	5.7
Bobby Phills	.28	.454	381	13.6	2.5	2.8
Elden Campbell	.78	.480	987	12.7	7.6	1.7
Anthony Mason	.82	.480	948	11.6	8.5	4.5
Brad Miller	.55	.461	423	7.7	5.3	0.8
Eddie Robinson*	.67	.549	471	7.0	2.8	0.5
Baron Davis*	.82	.420	486	5.9	2.0	3.8
Chucky Brown	.63	.451	334	5.3	2.7	1.1
Ricky Davis	.48	.503	227	4.7	1.7	1.3
Dale Ellis	.42	.415	178	4.2	1.3	0.3
Todd Fuller	.41	.418	134	3.3	2.7	0.1
Eldridge Recasner	.7	.429	7	1.0	0.6	0.7
Michael Hawkins	.12	.231	8	0.7	0.6	1.1
Derek Hood	.2	.000	0	0.0	0.5	0.0
Jason Miskiri	.1	.000	0	0.0	0.0	1.0

Triple Doubles: Mason (3). **3-pt FG leader:** Jones (128).
Steals leader: Jones (192). **Blocks leader:** Campbell (150).
Signed: G Hawkins (Nov. 9).

Individual Single Game Highs
Most Field Goals Made
24 . . . . Shaquille O'Neal, LAL at LAC (3/6)
Most Field Goals Attempted
37 . . . . Chris Webber, Sac. vs. Port. (2/20)

Chicago Bulls

	Gm	FG%	Tpts	PPG	RPG	APG
Elton Brand*	.81	.482	1627	20.1	10.0	1.9
John Starks	.37	.375	515	13.9	2.8	4.9
Ron Artest*	.72	.407	866	12.0	4.3	2.7
Chris Carr	.57	.395	531	9.3	3.0	1.5
Rusty LaRue	.4	.349	37	9.3	2.5	2.8
Fred Hoiberg	.31	.387	279	9.0	3.6	2.7
Hersey Hawkins	.61	.424	480	7.9	2.9	2.2
Corey Benjamin	.48	.414	370	7.7	1.8	1.1
Dedric Willoughby	.25	.341	190	7.6	2.0	2.6
B.J. Armstrong	.28	.446	201	7.2	1.7	2.8
Randy Brown	.59	.361	379	6.4	2.4	3.4
Matt Maloney	.51	.358	327	6.4	1.3	2.7
Chris Anstey	.73	.442	439	6.0	3.8	0.9
Dickey Simpkins	.69	.405	287	4.2	5.4	1.5
Khalid Reeves	.3	.250	11	3.7	1.3	4.3
Will Perdue	.67	.351	168	2.5	3.9	0.9
Michael Ruffin*	.71	.420	159	2.2	3.5	0.6

Triple Doubles: none. **3-pt FG leader:** Maloney (62).
Steals leader: Artest (119). **Blocks leader:** Brand (132).
Signed: G Reeves (Dec. 29), G Carr and G Willoughby (Jan. 10).

Cleveland Cavaliers

	Gm	FG%	Tpts	PPG	RPG	APG
Shawn Kemp	.82	.418	1463	17.8	8.9	1.7
Lamond Murray	.74	.451	1175	15.9	5.7	1.8
Bob Sura	.73	.437	1009	13.8	4.0	3.9
Andre Miller*	.82	.449	917	11.2	3.4	5.8
Brevin Knight	.65	.413	602	9.3	3.0	7.0
Wesley Person	.79	.427	724	9.2	3.4	1.9
Danny Ferry	.63	.497	463	7.4	3.8	1.1
Andrew Declercq	.82	.508	544	6.6	5.4	0.7
Mark Bryant	.75	.503	424	5.7	4.7	0.8
Kornel David	.32	.427	179	5.6	2.5	0.5
Cedric Henderson	.61	.396	328	5.4	2.3	0.9
Earl Boykins	.26	.483	138	5.3	1.0	1.9
Trajan Langdon*	.10	.375	49	4.9	1.5	1.1
Ryan Stack	.25	.333	52	2.1	1.8	0.2
Donny Marshall	.6	.273	11	1.8	0.2	0.0
Lari Ketner*	.22	.406	34	1.6	1.6	0.1
A.J. Bramlett	.8	.190	8	1.0	2.8	0.0
Benoit Benjamin	.3	.333	2	0.7	0.3	0.0

Triple Doubles: Miller (1). **3-pt FG leader:** Sura (122).
Steals leader: Knight (107). **Blocks leader:** Kemp (96).
Signed: F David (Jan. 6), G Boykins (Feb. 8), C/F Ketner (Feb. 22), F Marshall (Feb. 25).
Claimed: C Benjamin off waivers (Nov. 1).

Dallas Mavericks

	Gm	FG%	Tpts	PPG	RPG	APG
Michael Finley	.82	.457	1855	22.6	6.3	5.3
Dirk Nowitzki	.82	.461	1435	17.5	6.5	2.5
Cedric Ceballos	.69	.446	1147	16.6	6.7	1.3
Gary Trent	.11	.493	151	13.7	4.7	2.0
Erick Strickland	.68	.433	867	12.8	4.8	3.1
Robert Pack	.29	.417	259	8.9	1.5	5.8
Steve Nash	.56	.477	481	8.6	2.2	4.9
Shawn Bradley	.77	.479	647	8.4	6.5	0.8
Hubert Davis	.79	.468	583	7.4	1.7	1.8
Greg Buckner*	.48	.476	275	5.7	3.6	1.2
Sean Rooks	.71	.431	309	4.4	3.5	1.0
Damon Jones	.55	.385	233	4.2	1.0	1.8
Rick Hughes	.21	.486	82	3.9	2.3	0.4
Dennis Rodman	.12	.387	34	2.8	14.3	1.2
Bruno Sundov	.14	.387	26	1.9	0.9	0.1
Roderick Rhodes	.1	.000	0	0.0	1.0	0.0

Triple Doubles: Finley (4). **3-pt FG leader:** Nowitzki (116).
Steals leader: Finley (109). **Blocks leader:** Bradley (190).
Signed: F Hughes (Nov. 4), G Jones (Dec. 2), G Buckner (Jan. 26), G/F Rhodes (Apr. 10).

Denver Nuggets

	Gm	FG%	Tpts	PPG	RPG	APG
Antonio McDyess	.81	.507	1551	19.2	8.5	2.0
Nick Van Exel	.79	.390	1275	16.1	3.9	9.0
Raef LaFrentz	.81	.446	1006	12.4	7.9	1.2
Chris Gatling	.85	.455	1014	11.9	5.9	0.8
Tariq Abdul-Wahad	.61	.424	697	11.4	4.8	1.6
George McCloud	.78	.417	787	10.1	3.7	3.2
Keon Clark	.81	.542	694	8.6	6.2	0.9
James Posey*	.81	.429	662	8.2	3.9	1.8
Bryant Smith	.45	.455	253	5.6	1.9	1.4
Chris Herren*	.45	.363	141	3.1	1.2	2.5
Cory Alexander	.29	.286	82	2.8	1.5	2.0
Popeye Jones	.40	.423	104	2.6	2.6	0.5
Ryan Bowen*	.52	.393	131	2.5	2.2	0.4
Roy Rogers	.40	.398	89	2.2	2.0	0.2

Triple Doubles: none. **3-pt FG leader:** Van Exel (133).
Steals leader: Posey (98). **Blocks leader:** Lafrentz (180).

Detroit Pistons

	Gm	FG%	Tpts	PPG	RPG	APG
Grant Hill	.74	.489	1904	25.7	6.6	5.2
Jerry Stackhouse	.82	.428	1939	23.7	3.8	4.5
Lindsey Hunter	.82	.425	1043	12.7	3.1	4.0
Christian Laettner	.82	.473	1002	12.2	6.7	2.3
Jerome Williams	.82	.562	691	8.4	9.6	0.8
Mikki Moore	.29	.621	228	7.9	3.9	0.6
Terry Mills	.82	.439	548	6.7	4.8	1.0
Michael Curry	.82	.480	506	6.2	1.3	1.1
John Crotty	.69	.422	325	4.7	1.1	1.9
Jud Buechler	.58	.353	130	2.2	1.6	0.6
Loy Vaught	.43	.360	75	1.7	2.1	0.3
Marcus Brown	.6	.286	10	1.7	1.2	0.5
Jermaine Jackson*	.7	.091	7	1.0	1.6	0.6
Eric Montross	.51	.309	40	0.8	1.4	0.1

Triple Doubles: none. **3-pt FG leader:** Hunter (168).
Steals leader: Hunter (129). **Blocks leader:** Laettner (47).
Signed: G Crotty (Nov. 13).

Golden St. Warriors

	Gm	FG%	Tpts	PPG	RPG	APG
Antawn Jamison	.43	.471	841	19.6	8.4	2.1
Chris Mills	.20	.421	322	16.1	6.2	2.4
Larry Hughes	.82	.400	1226	15.0	4.3	2.5
Donyell Marshall	.64	.394	910	14.2	9.9	2.6
Jason Caffey	.71	.479	852	12.0	6.8	1.7
Mookie Blaylock	.73	.391	822	11.3	3.7	6.7
V. Cummings	.75	.405	706	9.4	2.5	3.3
Terry Cummings	.22	.429	184	8.4	4.9	1.0
Erick Dampier	.21	.405	167	8.0	6.4	0.9
Tony Farmer	.74	.407	465	6.3	4.0	1.0
Mark Davis	.23	.409	143	6.2	3.7	1.7
Billy Owens	.61	.417	367	6.0	4.8	1.5
Adonal Foyle	.76	.507	420	5.5	5.6	0.6
Sam Mack	.23	.303	114	5.0	1.7	1.0
Sam Jacobson	.52	.509	255	4.9	1.4	0.6
Tim Legler	.23	.359	77	3.4	1.0	1.0
Jamel Thomas	.8	.476	24	3.0	1.8	1.5
Drew Barry	.8	.500	22	2.8	1.0	2.1
Bill Curley	.28	.426	76	2.7	1.8	0.5
Tim Young*	.25	.333	54	2.2	1.4	0.2

Triple Doubles: none. **3-pt FG leader:** Blaylock (101).
Steals leader: Hughes (205). **Blocks leader:** Foyle (136).
Signed: G/F Thomas (Dec. 29), G Jacobson (Jan. 11), F Curley (Mar. 21), G/F Davis (Mar. 22).

Houston Rockets

	Gm	FG%	Tpts	PPG	RPG	APG
Steve Francis*	.77	.445	1388	18.0	5.3	6.6
Cuttino Mobley	.81	.430	1277	15.8	3.6	2.6
Charles Barkley	.20	.477	289	14.5	10.5	3.2
Shandon Anderson	.82	.473	1009	12.3	4.7	2.9
Walt Williams	.76	.458	827	10.9	4.0	2.1
Hakeem Olajuwon	.44	.458	455	10.3	6.2	1.4
Kelvin Cato	.65	.537	567	8.7	6.0	0.4
Kenny Thomas*	.72	.399	594	8.3	6.1	1.6
Carlos Rogers	.53	.525	422	8.0	5.2	0.8
Moochie Norris	.30	.437	207	6.9	2.3	3.1
Matt Bullard	.56	.409	382	6.8	2.5	1.1
Bryce Drew	.72	.383	420	5.8	1.4	2.3
Tony Massenburg	.10	.444	46	4.6	2.7	0.3
Thomas Hamilton	.22	.443	82	3.7	4.1	0.7
Anthony Miller	.35	.536	130	3.7	4.7	0.5
Devin Gray	.21	.405	49	2.3	1.2	0.2

Triple Doubles: Francis (1). **3-pt FG leader:** Francis (107).
Steals leader: Francis (118). **Blocks leader:** Cato (124).
Signed: F/C Miller (Jan. 16), F Gray (Jan.17), G Norris (Feb. 8).

Indiana Pacers

	Gm	FG%	Tpts	PPG	RPG	APG
Jalen Rose	.80	.471	1457	18.2	4.8	4.0
Reggie Miller	.81	.448	1470	18.2	3.0	2.3
Rik Smits	.79	.484	1018	12.9	5.1	1.1
Austin Croshere	.81	.441	835	10.3	6.4	1.1
Dale Davis	.74	.502	743	10.0	9.9	0.9
Travis Best	.82	.483	733	8.9	1.7	3.3
Mark Jackson	.81	.432	660	8.2	3.7	8.0
Sam Perkins	.81	.417	537	6.6	3.6	0.8
Al Harrington	.50	.458	328	6.6	3.2	0.8
Chris Mullin	.47	.428	242	5.2	1.6	0.8
Derrick McKey	.32	.398	139	4.3	4.2	1.1
Jonathan Bender*	.24	.329	64	2.7	0.9	0.1
Jeff Foster*	.19	.565	43	2.3	1.7	0.3
Zan Tabak	.18	.471	37	2.1	1.8	0.2

Triple Doubles: Jackson (1). **3-pt FG leader:** Miller (165).
Steals leader: Miller (85). **Blocks leader:** Smits (100).

Los Angeles Clippers

	Gm	FG%	Tpts	PPG	RPG	APG
Maurice Taylor	.62	.464	1060	17.1	6.5	1.6
Derek Anderson	.64	.438	1080	16.9	4.0	3.4
Lamar Odom*	.76	.438	1259	16.6	7.8	4.2
Tyrone Nesby	.73	.398	973	13.3	3.8	1.7
Michael Olowokandi	.80	.437	783	9.8	8.2	0.5
Troy Hudson	.62	.377	545	8.8	2.4	3.9
Eric Piatkowski	.75	.415	654	8.7	3.0	1.1
Jeff McInnis	.25	.430	180	7.2	2.9	3.6
Eric Murdock	.40	.385	225	5.6	1.9	2.7
Brian Skinner	.33	.507	179	5.4	6.1	0.3
Keith Closs	.57	.487	238	4.2	3.1	0.4
Charles Jones	.56	.328	188	3.4	1.1	1.7
Etdrick Bohannon	.13	.538	29	2.2	2.4	0.4
Pete Chilcutt	.56	.417	120	2.1	2.3	0.5
Anthony Avent	.49	.302	81	1.7	1.5	0.2
Marty Conlon	.3	.500	2	0.7	0.7	0.0
Mario Bennett	.1	.000	0	0.0	2.0	0.0

Triple Doubles: Odom (3), Anderson (1). **3-pt FG leader:** Nesby (94).
Steals leader: Odom (91). **Blocks leader:** Olowokandi (140).
Signed: F Chilcutt and G McInnis (Feb. 26), F Bohannon (Apr. 6).

Los Angeles Lakers

	Gm	FG%	Tpts	PPG	RPG	APG
Shaquille O'Neal 79		.574	2344	29.7	13.7	3.8
Kobe Bryant.........66		.468	1485	22.5	6.3	4.9
Glen Rice 80		.430	1272	15.9	4.1	2.2
Ron Harper 80		.399	557	7.0	4.2	3.4
Rick Fox 82		.414	534	6.5	2.4	1.7
Derek Fisher 78		.346	491	6.3	1.8	2.8
Tyronn Lue 8		.487	48	6.0	1.5	2.1
Robert Horry 76		.438	436	5.7	4.8	1.6
A.C. Green 82		.447	413	5.0	5.9	1.0
Brian Shaw 74		.382	305	4.1	2.9	2.7
Devean George* 49		.389	155	3.2	1.5	0.2
John Celestand* 16		.333	37	2.3	0.7	1.3
Travis Knight 63		.390	109	1.7	2.1	0.4
John Salley.........45		.362	71	1.6	1.4	0.6

Triple Doubles: none. **3-pt FG leader:** Rice (84).
Steals leader: Bryant (106). **Blocks leader:** O'Neal (239).

Miami Heat

	Gm	FG%	Tpts	PPG	RPG	APG
Alonzo Mourning 79		.551	1718	21.8	9.5	1.6
Jamal Mashburn 76		.445	1328	17.5	5.0	3.9
Tim Hardaway 52		.386	696	13.4	2.9	7.4
Voshon Lenard 53		.407	629	11.9	2.9	2.6
P.J. Brown 80		.480	764	9.6	7.5	1.8
Dan Majerle 69		.403	506	7.3	4.8	3.0
C. Weatherspoon 78		.513	656	7.2	5.8	1.2
Anthony Carter* 80		.395	498	6.2	2.5	4.7
Otis Thorpe 51		.514	279	5.5	3.3	0.7
Mark Strickland.....58		.545	284	4.9	2.4	0.4
Rodney Buford*.....34		.411	147	4.3	1.4	0.6
Bruce Bowen 69		.371	196	2.8	1.4	0.5
Rex Walters 33		.418	93	2.8	1.1	2.0
Tim James* 4		.357	11	2.8	1.0	0.5
Duane Causwell 25		.541	66	2.6	1.9	0.1
Harold Jamison* 12		.350	18	1.5	1.8	0.3

Triple Doubles: none. **3-pt FG leader:** Mashburn (112).
Steals leader: Mashburn (79). **Blocks leader:** Mourning (294).
Claimed: G/F Bowen off waivers (Feb. 23).

Milwaukee Bucks

	Gm	FG%	Tpts	PPG	RPG	APG
Ray Allen 82		.455	1809	22.1	4.4	3.8
Glenn Robinson 81		.472	1693	20.9	6.0	2.4
Sam Cassell 81		.466	1506	18.6	3.7	9.0
Tim Thomas 80		.461	945	11.8	4.2	1.4
Scott Williams 68		.499	518	7.6	6.6	0.4
Vinny Del Negro 67		.471	349	5.2	1.6	2.4
Darvin Ham 35		.555	177	5.1	4.9	1.2
Ervin Johnson.......80		.518	385	4.8	8.1	0.6
Danny Manning 72		.440	333	4.6	2.9	1.0
J.R. Reid 34		.417	150	4.4	3.4	0.5
Robert Traylor* 44		.475	157	3.6	2.6	0.5
Rafer Alston* 27		.284	60	2.2	0.9	2.6
Mirsad Turkcan* 17		.368	33	1.9	1.9	0.3

Triple Doubles: none. **3-pt FG leader:** Allen (172).
Steals leader: Allen (110). **Blocks leader:** Johnson (127).
Signed: F Turkcan (Feb. 16).

Minnesota Timberwolves

	Gm	FG%	Tpts	PPG	RPG	APG
Kevin Garnett.......81		.497	1857	22.9	11.8	5.0
Terrell Brandon 71		.466	1212	17.1	3.4	8.9
Wally Szczerbiak* ...73		.511	845	11.6	9.7	2.8
Malik Sealy 82		.476	929	11.3	4.3	2.4
Joe Smith 78		.464	774	9.9	6.2	1.1
Anthony Peeler 82		.436	804	9.8	2.8	2.4
Sam Mitchell 66		.447	427	6.5	2.1	1.7
Radoslav Nesterovic .82		.476	471	5.7	4.6	1.1
Bobby Jackson.......73		.405	369	5.1	2.1	2.4
William Avery*......59		.309	154	2.6	0.7	1.5
Tom Hammonds......56		.433	117	2.1	1.8	0.2
Dean Garrett 56		.444	114	2.0	2.5	0.3
Andrae Patterson....5		.750	6	1.2	0.4	0.2

Triple Doubles: Brandon (1), Garnett (1), Jackson (1). **3-pt FG leader:** Peeler (85).
Steals leader: Brandon (134). **Blocks leader:** Garnett (126).

New Jersey Nets

	Gm	FG%	Tpts	PPG	RPG	APG
Stephon Marbury 74		.432	1640	22.2	3.2	8.4
Keith Van Horn 80		.445	1535	19.2	8.4	2.0
Kendall Gill 76		.414	993	13.1	3.7	2.8
Kerry Kittles 62		.437	807	13.0	3.6	2.3
Johnny Newman 82		.446	820	10.0	1.9	0.8
Lucious Harris 77		.428	513	6.7	2.4	1.3
Scott Burrell 74		.394	451	6.1	3.5	1.0
Sherman Douglas 20		.500	120	6.0	1.5	1.7
Jamie Feick.........81		.428	459	5.7	9.3	0.8
Elliot Perry 60		.435	317	5.3	1.0	2.3
Gheorghe Muresan ...30		.456	105	3.5	2.3	0.3
Evan Eschmeyer* 31		.521	91	2.9	3.5	0.7
Jim McIlvaine.......66		.416	157	2.4	3.5	0.6
Michael Cage 20		.500	27	1.4	4.1	0.5
Mark Hendrickson....15		.625	13	0.9	0.9	0.4

Triple Doubles: none. **3-pt FG leader:** Van Horn (84).
Steals leader: Gill (139). **Blocks leader:** McIlvaine (117).
Signed: F Hendrickson (Apr. 17).

New York Knicks

	Gm	FG%	Tpts	PPG	RPG	APG
Allan Houston 82		.483	1614	19.7	3.3	2.7
Latrell Sprewell 82		.435	1524	18.6	4.3	4.0
Patrick Ewing 62		.466	929	15.0	9.7	0.9
Larry Johnson........70		.433	750	10.7	5.4	2.5
Marcus Camby 59		.481	601	10.2	7.8	0.8
Kurt Thomas 80		.505	641	8.0	6.3	1.0
Charlie Ward 72		.423	528	7.3	3.2	4.2
John Wallace 60		.467	392	6.5	2.3	0.4
Chris Childs 71		.410	376	5.3	2.1	4.0
Andrew Lang 19		.438	59	3.1	3.2	0.2
Rick Brunson 37		.414	71	1.9	0.7	1.3
DeMarco Johnson 5		.333	6	1.2	1.4	0.0
Chris Dudley 47		.343	55	1.2	2.9	0.1
David Wingate 11		.111	2	0.3	0.3	0.4

Triple Doubles: none. **3-pt FG leader:** Houston (106).
Steals leader: Sprewell (109). **Blocks leader:** Camby (116).

More Individual Single Game Highs

Most Assists

20 ....Nick Van Exel, Den. vs. Atl (11/8)

Most Rebounds

29 ....Dikembe Mutombo, Atl. vs. Minn. (12/14)

Most 3-point Field Goals Made

9 ....Dan Majerle, Mia. at Minn. (1/11)

Most 3-point Field Goals Attempted

17.................Gary Payton, Sea. at Minn. (12/23)

Most Free Throws Made

19 ....Reggie Miller, Ind. at NJ (11/2)
Shaquille O'Neal, LAL vs. Chi. (11/19)

Most Free Throws Attempted

31 ....Shaquille O'Neal, LAL vs. Chi. (11/19)

Orlando Magic

	Gm	FG%	Tpts	PPG	RPG	APG
Ron Mercer	.68	.426	1148	16.9	3.7	2.3
Darrell Armstrong	.82	.433	1330	16.2	3.3	6.1
John Amaechi	.80	.437	836	10.5	3.3	1.2
Chucky Atkins*	.82	.424	782	9.5	1.5	3.7
Monty Williams	.75	.489	651	8.7	3.3	1.4
Chauncey Billups	.13	.337	112	8.6	2.6	3.0
Corey Maggette*	.77	.478	646	8.4	3.9	0.8
Pat Garrity	.82	.441	675	8.2	2.6	0.7
Michael Doleac	.81	.452	565	7.0	4.1	0.8
Bo Outlaw	.82	.601	491	6.0	6.6	3.0
Ben Wallace	.81	.503	389	4.8	8.0	0.8
Matt Harpring	.4	.235	16	4.0	3.0	2.0
Anthony Parker	.19	.431	65	3.4	1.5	0.6
Anthony Johnson	.53	.372	146	2.8	0.9	1.3
Derek Strong	.20	.438	54	2.7	2.2	0.2
Johnny Taylor	.6	.357	11	1.8	1.0	0.2
Kiwane Garris	.3	.200	4	1.3	0.3	0.7

Triple Doubles: Outlaw (1). **3-pt FG leader:** Armstrong (137).
Steals leader: Armstrong (169). **Blocks leader:** Outlaw (146).
Signed: G Garris (Dec. 21).

Philadelphia 76ers

	Gm	FG%	Tpts	PPG	RPG	APG
Allen Iverson	.70	.421	1989	28.4	3.8	4.7
Toni Kukoc	.56	.408	830	14.8	4.9	4.7
Tyrone Hill	.68	.485	815	12.0	9.2	0.8
Theo Ratliff	.57	.503	676	11.9	7.6	0.6
Matt Geiger	.65	.441	629	9.7	6.0	0.6
George Lynch	.75	.461	722	9.6	7.8	1.8
Aaron McKie	.82	.411	653	8.0	3.0	2.9
Eric Snow	.82	.430	651	7.9	3.2	7.6
Todd MacCulloch*	.56	.553	206	3.7	2.6	0.2
Stanley Roberts	.5	.313	10	2.0	3.0	0.6
Nazr Mohammed	.28	.389	54	1.9	1.8	0.1
Kevin Ollie	.40	.449	72	1.8	0.8	1.2
Jumaine Jones*	.32	.379	57	1.8	1.2	0.2
Antonio Lang	.10	.167	6	0.6	0.5	0.2
Ira Bowman*	.11	1.000	5	0.5	0.2	0.1

Triple Doubles: Kukoc (1). **3-pt FG leader:** Iverson (89).
Steals leader: Iverson (144). **Blocks leader:** Ratliff (171).
Signed: G Bowman (Mar. 15), F Lang (Apr. 3).

Phoenix Suns

	Gm	FG%	Tpts	PPG	RPG	APG
Clifford Robinson	.80	.464	1478	18.5	4.5	2.8
Anfernee Hardaway	.60	.474	1015	16.9	5.8	5.3
Jason Kidd	.67	.410	961	14.3	7.2	10.1
Rodney Rogers	.82	.486	1130	13.8	5.5	2.1
Tom Gugliotta	.54	.481	738	13.7	7.9	2.3
Shawn Marion*	.51	.471	520	10.2	6.5	1.4
Todd Day	.58	.394	395	6.8	2.2	1.1
Kevin Johnson	.6	.571	40	6.7	2.7	4.0
Rex Chapman	.53	.386	346	6.5	1.5	1.2
Oliver Miller	.51	.588	323	6.3	5.1	1.3
Luc Longley	.72	.466	452	6.3	4.5	1.1
Randy Livingston	.79	.416	381	4.8	1.7	2.2
Toby Bailey	.46	.414	164	3.6	1.6	0.7
Corie Blount	.38	.494	107	2.8	3.0	0.3
Don MacLean	.16	.367	42	2.6	1.4	0.5
Ben Davis	.5	.333	4	0.8	1.8	0.4
Mark West	.22	.417	15	0.7	1.4	0.1

Triple Doubles: Kidd (5), Hardaway (1). **3-pt FG leader:** Robinson (120).
Steals leader: Kidd (134). **Blocks leader:** Miller (80).
Signed: G Johnson and F MacLean (Mar. 23).

Portland Trailblazers

	Gm	FG%	Tpts	PPG	RPG	APG
Rasheed Wallace	.81	.519	1325	16.4	7.0	1.8
Steve Smith	.82	.467	1225	14.9	3.8	2.6
Damon Stoudamire	.78	.432	974	12.5	3.1	5.2
Scottie Pippen	.82	.451	1022	12.5	6.3	5.0
Arvydas Sabonis	.66	.505	778	11.8	7.8	1.8
Bonzi Wells	.66	.492	580	8.8	2.8	1.5
Detlef Schrempf	.77	.432	574	7.5	4.3	2.6
Brian Grant	.63	.491	459	7.3	5.5	1.0
Greg Anthony	.82	.406	514	6.3	1.6	2.5
Gary Grant	.3	.429	12	4.0	1.0	0.3
Jermaine O'Neal	.70	.486	273	3.9	3.3	0.3
Stacey Augmon	.59	.474	203	3.4	2.0	0.9
Antonio Harvey	.19	.567	41	2.2	1.7	0.3
Joe Kleine	.7	.364	11	1.6	0.9	0.3

Triple Doubles: none. **3-pt FG leader:** Smith (96).
Steals leader: Pippen (117). **Blocks leader:** Wallace (107).

Sacramento Kings

	Gm	FG%	Tpts	PPG	RPG	APG
Chris Webber	.75	.483	1834	24.5	10.5	4.6
Jason Williams	.81	.373	999	12.3	2.8	7.3
Vlade Divac	.82	.503	1005	12.3	8.0	3.0
Predrag Stojakovic	.74	.448	877	11.9	3.7	1.4
Nick Anderson	.72	.391	781	10.9	4.7	1.7
Corliss Williamson	.76	.500	785	10.3	3.8	1.1
Jon Barry	.62	.465	495	8.0	2.6	2.4
L. Funderburke	.75	.523	483	6.4	3.1	0.4
Tony Delk	.46	.430	296	6.4	1.9	1.2
Darrick Martin	.71	.380	402	5.7	0.6	1.7
Scott Pollard	.76	.527	412	5.4	5.3	0.6
Ryan Robertson*	.1	.333	5	5.0	0.0	0.0
Tyrone Corbin	.54	.356	219	4.1	3.1	1.1
Bill Wennington	.7	.300	14	2.0	2.7	0.1

Triple Doubles: Webber (5), Divac (1). **3-pt FG leader:** Anderson (132).
Steals leader: Webber (120). **Blocks leader:** Webber (128).

More Individual Single Game Highs

Most Blocked Shots

11 . . . . Dikembe Mutombo, Atl. vs. NJ (2/15)

Most Steals

9 . . . . Eddie Jones, Cha. vs. Ind. (11/4)
Allen Iverson, Phi. vs. Orl. (3/19)
Paul Pierce, Bos. vs. Mia. (12/3)

Most Turnovers

10 . . . . Toni Kukoc, Chi. vs. Atl. (1/14)

Most Minutes

55 . . . . Shaquille O'Neal, LAL at Utah (1/24)*
Shareef Abdur-Rahim, Van. vs. Minn. (4/14)*
*double overtime

Most Offensive Rebounds

13 . . . . Dikembe Mutombo, Atl. vs. NY (1/28)

Most Defensive Rebounds

18 . . . . Derrick Coleman, Cha. vs SA (2/24)
Dikembe Mutombo, Atl. vs. Min. (12/14)
Keon Clark, Den. at Ind. (3/7)
Tim Duncan, SA at Sac. (1/13)
Shareef Abdur-Rahim, Van. at Cha. (11/24)

San Antonio Spurs

	Gm	FG%	Tpts	PPG	RPG	APG
Tim Duncan	74	.491	1718	23.2	12.4	3.2
David Robinson	80	.511	1425	17.8	9.6	1.8
Avery Johnson	82	.473	919	11.2	1.9	6.0
Terry Porter	68	.446	641	9.4	2.8	3.3
Mario Elie	79	.427	590	7.5	3.2	2.4
Malik Rose	74	.457	496	6.7	4.5	0.6
Jaren Jackson	81	.381	513	6.3	2.2	1.5
Antonio Daniels	68	.474	420	6.2	1.3	2.6
Sean Elliott	19	.358	114	6.0	2.5	1.5
Samaki Walker	71	.449	360	5.1	3.8	0.5
Derrick Dial*	8	.370	40	5.0	3.3	0.6
Jerome Kersey	72	.412	321	4.5	3.1	1.0
Steve Kerr	32	.432	89	2.8	0.6	0.4
Felton Spencer	26	.455	50	1.9	1.5	0.1

Triple Doubles: Duncan (1). **3-pt FG leader:** Jackson (108).
Steals leader: Robinson (97). **Blocks leader:** Robinson (182).

Seattle Supersonics

	Gm	FG%	Tpts	PPG	RPG	APG
Gary Payton	82	.448	1982	24.2	6.5	8.9
Vin Baker	79	.455	1311	16.6	7.7	1.9
Brent Barry	80	.463	945	11.8	4.7	3.6
Ruben Patterson	81	.536	942	11.6	5.4	1.6
Vernon Maxwell	47	.345	513	10.9	1.7	1.6
Rashard Lewis	82	.486	674	8.2	4.1	0.9
Horace Grant	76	.444	612	8.1	7.8	2.5
Shammond Williams	43	.373	225	5.2	1.2	1.8
Jelani McCoy	58	.576	249	4.3	3.1	0.4
Emanual Davis	54	.364	217	4.0	1.9	1.3
Lazaro Borrell*	17	.444	62	3.7	2.4	0.6
Greg Foster	60	.406	203	3.4	1.8	0.7
Chuck Person	37	.301	102	2.8	1.4	0.6
Vladimir Stepania	30	.367	75	2.5	1.6	0.1
Fred Vinson	8	.294	13	1.6	0.1	0.0

Triple Doubles: Payton (2). **3-pt FG leader:** Payton (177).
Steals leader: Payton (153). **Blocks leader:** Baker (66).

Toronto Raptors

	Gm	FG%	Tpts	PPG	RPG	APG
Vince Carter	82	.465	2107	25.7	5.8	3.9
Tracy McGrady	79	.451	1213	15.4	6.3	3.3
Doug Christie	73	.407	903	12.4	3.9	4.4
Antonio Davis	79	.440	910	11.5	8.8	1.3
Kevin Willis	79	.415	604	7.7	6.1	0.6
Dell Curry	67	.427	507	7.6	1.5	1.3
Dee Brown	38	.360	264	7.0	1.4	2.3
Charles Oakley	80	.418	548	6.9	6.8	3.2
Alvin Williams	55	.397	292	5.3	1.6	2.3
Muggsy Bogues	80	.439	410	5.1	1.7	3.7
Haywoode Workman	36	.344	86	2.4	0.7	1.7
Aleksander Radojevic*	3	.286	7	2.3	2.7	0.3
John Thomas	55	.458	114	2.1	1.4	0.2
Sean Marks	5	.333	8	1.6	0.4	0.0
Michael Stewart	42	.377	58	1.4	2.2	0.1

Triple Doubles: Carter (1). **3-pt FG leader:** Carter and Curry (95).
Steals leader: Carter (110). **Blocks leader:** McGrady (151).
Claimed: G Workman off waivers (Feb. 9).

Utah Jazz

	Gm	FG%	Tpts	PPG	RPG	APG
Karl Malone	82	.509	2095	25.6	9.5	3.7
Bryon Russell	82	.446	1159	14.1	5.2	1.9
Jeff Hornacek	77	.492	953	12.4	2.4	2.6
John Stockton	82	.501	990	12.1	2.6	8.6
Howard Eisley	82	.418	708	8.6	2.1	4.2
Armen Gilliam	50	.436	333	6.7	4.2	0.8
Olden Polynice	82	.510	435	5.3	5.5	0.5
Greg Ostertag	81	.464	367	4.5	6.0	0.2
Quincy Lewis*	74	.372	283	3.8	1.5	0.5
Jacque Vaughn	78	.416	289	3.7	0.8	1.6
Scott Padgett*	47	.314	120	2.6	1.9	0.5
Adam Keefe	62	.408	135	2.2	2.2	0.6

Triple Doubles: none. **3-pt FG leader:** Russell (106).
Steals leader: Stockton (143). **Blocks leader:** Ostertag (172).

Vancouver Grizzlies

	Gm	FG%	Tpts	PPG	RPG	APG
Shareef Abdur-Rahim	82	.465	1663	20.3	10.1	3.3
Michael Dickerson	82	.436	1496	18.2	3.4	2.5
Michael Bibby	82	.445	1188	14.5	3.7	8.1
Othella Harrington	82	.507	1078	13.2	6.9	1.2
Bryant Reeves	69	.448	611	8.9	5.7	1.2
Dennis Scott	66	.375	369	5.6	1.6	1.1
Grant Long	42	.443	203	4.8	5.6	1.0
Felipe Lopez	65	.425	292	4.5	1.9	0.7
Doug West	38	.410	152	4.0	1.9	1.1
Brent Price	41	.345	141	3.4	0.9	1.7
Obinna Ekezie*	39	.466	125	3.2	2.4	0.2
Antoine Carr	21	.438	67	3.2	1.5	0.3
Joe Stephens	13	.373	41	3.2	2.8	0.9
Cherokee Parks	56	.497	168	3.0	3.3	0.6
Milt Palacio*	53	.439	108	2.0	1.0	0.9

Triple Doubles: Bibby (1). **3-pt FG leader:** Dickerson (119).
Steals leader: Bibby (132). **Blocks leader:** Abdur-Rahim (87).

Washington Wizards

	Gm	FG%	Tpts	PPG	RPG	APG
Mitch Richmond	74	.426	1285	17.4	2.9	2.5
Juwan Howard	82	.459	1220	14.9	5.7	3.0
Rod Strickland	69	.429	869	12.6	3.8	7.5
Tracy Murray	80	.433	813	10.2	3.4	0.9
Richard Hamilton*	71	.420	639	9.0	1.8	1.5
Chris Whitney	82	.417	642	7.8	1.6	3.8
Aaron Williams	81	.522	616	7.6	5.1	0.7
Jahidi White	80	.507	569	7.1	6.9	0.2
Isaac Austin	59	.429	397	6.7	4.8	1.3
Michael Smith	46	.563	289	6.3	7.2	1.2
Randell Jackson	2	.625	12	6.0	4.0	0.5
Gerard King	62	.502	327	5.3	4.0	0.8
Calvin Booth*	11	.348	42	3.8	2.9	0.6
Don Reid	37	.529	132	3.6	2.5	0.3
Lorenzo Williams	8	.778	14	1.8	3.1	0.1
Laron Profit*	33	.356	49	1.5	0.8	0.8
Reggie Jordan	36	.321	41	1.1	1.1	0.9

Triple Doubles: none. **3-pt FG leader:** Murray (113).
Steals leader: Richmond (110). **Blocks leader:** Williams (92).
Signed: F/C Reid (Mar. 14).

NBA Regular Season Team Leaders
Offense

—Per Game—

WEST	Pts	Reb	Ast	FGM-FGA	FG%	3PM-3PA	3Pt%	FTM-FTA	FT%	OFF-DEF	TRB	TO	BLKS
Sacramento	105.0	45.0	23.8	3276-7288	.450	534-1656	.322	1521-2017	.754	1057-2635	3692	1324	381
Dallas	101.4	41.1	22.1	3195-7047	.453	519-1326	.391	1407-1751	.804	931-2444	3375	1124	416
LA Lakers	100.8	47.0	23.4	3137-6836	.459	344-1047	.329	1649-2368	.696	1117-2738	3855	1143	532
Houston	99.5	43.8	21.6	3001-6663	.450	581-1624	.358	1573-2145	.733	1008-2586	3594	1425	438
Seattle	99.1	43.0	22.9	3108-6946	.447	546-1611	.339	1363-1960	.695	1042-2483	3525	1153	345
Denver	99.0	44.7	23.3	3057-6911	.442	470-1397	.336	1531-2116	.724	1073-2590	3663	1280	618
Phoenix	98.9	43.7	25.6	3093-6771	.457	458-1245	.368	1467-1934	.759	1022-2558	3580	1367	433
Minnesota	98.5	42.5	26.9	3226-6910	.467	248-716	.346	1379-1769	.780	1016-2471	3487	1139	444
Portland	97.5	43.0	23.5	3021-6430	.470	407-1128	.361	1542-2029	.760	966-2560	3526	1243	402
Utah	96.5	41.0	24.9	2962-6380	.464	329-854	.385	1661-2150	.773	936-2427	3363	1220	445
San Antonio	96.2	43.8	22.2	2952-6394	.462	330-883	.374	1652-2214	.746	927-2666	3593	1234	549
Golden State	95.5	45.6	22.6	2996-7141	.420	345-1067	.323	1497-2147	.697	1300-2436	3736	1301	363
Vancouver	93.9	40.1	20.7	2892-6440	.449	324-898	.361	1594-2060	.774	1007-2321	3328	1379	345
LA Clippers	92.0	40.6	18.0	2877-6757	.426	429-1267	.339	1363-1826	.746	955-2377	3332	1326	494

—Per Game—

EAST	Pts	Reb	Ast	FGM-FGA	FG%	3PM-3PA	3Pt%	FTM-FTA	FT%	ORB-DRB	TRB	TO	BLKS
Detroit	103.5	41.1	20.8	3044-6636	.459	439-1223	.359	1956-2506	.781	917-2458	3375	1289	292
Indiana	101.3	42.1	22.6	3047-6640	.459	583-1487	.392	1629-2008	.811	842-2612	3454	1159	422
Milwaukee	101.2	41.3	22.6	3174-6827	.465	394-1069	.369	1558-1982	.786	1017-2373	3390	1230	383
Orlando	100.1	44.9	20.8	3169-7014	.452	294-870	.338	1574-2142	.735	1145-2540	3685	1443	467
Boston	99.3	43.0	21.2	3054-6879	.444	417-1259	.331	1621-2175	.745	1108-2420	3528	1259	287
Charlotte	98.4	42.9	24.7	2935-6533	.449	339-1001	.339	1863-2458	.758	884-2635	3519	1206	480
New Jersey	98.0	40.9	26.0	2979-6882	.433	477-1374	.347	1601-2041	.784	1040-2315	3355	1119	393
Toronto	97.2	43.3	23.7	2980-6882	.433	425-1171	.363	1583-2068	.765	1098-2449	3547	1137	544
Cleveland	97.0	42.8	23.7	2977-6734	.442	343-920	.373	1653-2205	.750	1011-2499	3510	1427	363
Washington	96.6	42.7	21.6	3010-6681	.451	335-890	.376	1566-2107	.743	1064-2438	3502	1320	380
Philadelphia	94.8	44.1	22.2	2993-6776	.442	208-643	.323	1577-2226	.708	1147-2468	3615	1284	386
Miami	94.4	43.2	23.5	2974-6462	.460	446-1202	.371	1345-1827	.736	921-2619	3540	1231	524
Atlanta	94.3	45.3	18.9	3000-6807	.441	258-814	.317	1477-1987	.743	1146-2570	3716	1266	466
New York	92.1	40.5	19.4	2897-6372	.455	351-936	.375	1410-1805	.781	802-2521	3323	1200	360
Chicago	84.8	40.9	20.0	2565-6180	.415	340-1031	.330	1482-2089	.709	1032-2324	3356	1557	383

Defense

—Per Game—

WEST	Pts	Reb	Ast	FGM-FGA	FG%	3PM-3PA	3Pt%	FTM-FTA	FT%	OFF-DEF	TRB	TO	BLKS
San Antonio	90.2	41.4	20.3	2884-6781	.425	355-1036	.343	1276-1726	.739	986-2411	3397	1180	429
Portland	91.1	39.0	20.8	2825-6557	.431	394-1195	.330	1422-1985	.716	978-2220	3198	1186	350
Utah	92.1	38.1	19.8	2781-6240	.446	388-1097	.354	1598-2141	.746	887-2236	3123	1270	416
LA Lakers	92.3	43.1	19.5	2838-6824	.416	372-1142	.326	1518-2045	.742	1007-2531	3538	1196	359
Phoenix	93.7	43.1	20.7	2825-6665	.424	403-1146	.352	1630-2205	.739	1071-2465	3536	1421	425
Minnesota	96.0	40.9	21.2	2924-6577	.445	380-1067	.356	1644-2185	.752	916-2441	3357	1232	344
Seattle	98.1	45.1	23.6	3132-6941	.451	440-1292	.341	1343-1795	.748	1084-2611	3695	1258	433
Vancouver	99.6	40.3	23.5	3136-6612	.474	361-1083	.333	1530-1990	.769	972-2335	3307	1235	516
Houston	100.3	42.4	22.7	3226-7074	.456	350-990	.354	1425-1829	.779	1027-2451	3478	1126	433
Denver	101.1	44.3	24.4	3129-6953	.450	399-1126	.354	1632-2174	.751	1027-2606	3633	1178	462
Dallas	102.0	48.4	23.2	3225-7053	.457	429-1243	.345	1484-2005	.740	1251-2719	3970	1318	421
Sacramento	102.1	47.6	23.8	3269-7240	.452	396-1123	.353	1434-1910	.751	1143-2761	3904	1438	403
LA Clippers	103.6	45.6	24.1	3281-6879	.477	417-1077	.387	1512-2041	.741	1038-2699	3737	1172	382
Golden State	103.8	46.1	24.8	3165-6775	.467	427-1162	.367	1755-2328	.754	1091-2691	3782	1337	493

—Per Game—

EAST	Pts	Reb	Ast	FGM-FGA	FG%	3PM-3PA	3Pt%	FTM-FTA	FT%	OFF-DEF	TRB	TO	BLKS
New York	90.7	41.0	19.6	2711-6399	.424	404-1195	.338	1609-2153	.747	927-2439	3366	1160	353
Miami	91.3	40.4	19.3	2782-6596	.422	408-1130	.361	1512-2022	.748	974-2341	3315	1150	372
Philadelphia	93.4	43.5	22.3	2867-6595	.435	417-1172	.356	1510-2001	.755	1065-2501	3566	1445	529
Chicago	94.2	41.7	23.2	2916-6396	.456	358-1049	.341	1533-2070	.741	1000-2416	3416	1244	461
Charlotte	95.8	42.9	23.2	3048-6811	.448	410-1086	.378	1347-1807	.745	965-2551	3516	1297	421
Indiana	96.7	43.7	21.2	3113-6982	.446	329-1006	.327	1374-1821	.755	1040-2545	3585	1126	325
Toronto	97.3	42.8	21.8	3002-6615	.454	346-1021	.339	1631-2136	.764	961-2552	3513	1250	442
New Jersey	99.0	46.2	22.6	3125-6741	.464	368-1013	.363	1503-2012	.747	1129-2657	3786	1366	469
Orlando	99.4	43.5	24.3	3076-6919	.445	431-1127	.338	1567-2104	.745	1094-2473	3567	1488	475
Atlanta	99.7	43.0	23.0	3211-7060	.455	373-1015	.367	1381-1796	.769	1052-2474	3526	1001	400
Washington	99.9	41.2	21.9	3005-6547	.459	390-1052	.371	1790-2405	.744	962-2419	3381	1227	503
Boston	100.1	41.3	21.9	2960-6304	.470	359-995	.361	1929-2563	.753	857-2534	3391	1394	478
Cleveland	100.5	43.9	23.7	2983-6733	.443	420-1227	.342	1851-2385	.776	1015-2583	3598	1387	501
Milwaukee	101.0	41.5	24.2	3033-6644	.457	531-1357	.391	1685-2241	.752	1037-2367	3404	1303	344
Detroit	102.0	42.4	23.1	3119-6706	.465	458-1235	.371	1669-2237	.746	975-2504	3479	1400	396

NBA PLAYOFFS

1ST ROUND	SEMIFINALS	FINAL		FINAL	SEMIFINALS	1ST ROUND

EASTERN CONFERENCE

Indiana 3
Milwaukee 2
— Indiana 4
Indiana 4

Charlotte 1
Philadelphia 3
— Philadelphia 2

New York 3
Toronto 0
— New York 4
New York 2

Miami 3
Detroit 0
— Miami 3

Indiana 2
LA Lakers 4

WESTERN CONFERENCE

LA Lakers 4
— LA Lakers 4
Phoenix 1
LA Lakers 3
Sacramento 2

San Antonio 1
Phoenix 3

Portland 3
— Portland 4
Utah 1
Portland 3
Minnesota 1

Utah 3
Seattle 2

Series Summaries

WESTERN CONFERENCE

FIRST ROUND (Best of 5)

	W-L	Avg.	Leading Scorer
Sacramento	2-3	96.4	Webber (24.4)
LA Lakers	3-2	104.4	O'Neal (29.4)

Date	Winner	Home Court
Apr. 23	Lakers, 117-107	at Los Angeles
Apr. 27	Lakers, 113-89	at Los Angeles
Apr. 30	Kings, 99-91	at Sacramento
May 2	Kings, 101-88	at Sacramento
May 5	Lakers, 113-86	at Los Angeles

	W-L	Avg.	Leading Scorer
Seattle	2-3	93.2	Payton (25.8)
Utah	3-2	94.4	Malone (30.6)

Date	Winner	Home Court
Apr. 22	Jazz, 104-93	at Utah
Apr. 24	Jazz, 101-87	at Utah
Apr. 29	Supersonics, 89-78	at Seattle
May 3	Supersonics, 104-93	at Seattle
May 5	Jazz, 96-93	at Utah

	W-L	Avg.	Leading Scorer
Minnesota	1-3	85.3	Brandon (19.5)
Portland	3-1	87.3	Pippen (18.8)

Date	Winner	Home Court
Apr. 23	Trailblazers, 91-88	at Portland
Apr. 26	Trailblazers, 86-82	at Portland
Apr. 30	Timberwolves, 94-87	at Minnesota
May 2	Trailblazers, 85-77	at Minnesota

	W-L	Avg.	Leading Scorer
Phoenix	3-1	83.0	Hardaway (19.0)
San Antonio	1-3	81.8	Robinson (23.5)

Date	Winner	Home Court
Apr. 22	Suns, 72-70	at San Antonio
Apr. 25	Spurs, 85-70	at San Antonio
Apr. 29	Suns, 101-94	at Phoenix
May 2	Suns, 89-78	at Phoenix

SEMIFINALS (Best of 7)

	W-L	Avg.	Leading Scorer
Phoenix	1-4	97.4	Hardaway (20.3)
LA Lakers	4-1	99.8	O'Neal (29.8)

Date	Winner	Home Court
May 7	Lakers, 105-77	at Los Angeles
May 10	Lakers, 97-96	at Los Angeles
May 12	Lakers, 105-99	at Phoenix
May 14	Suns, 117-98	at Phoenix
May 16	Lakers, 87-65	at Los Angeles

	W-L	Avg.	Leading Scorer
Portland	4-1	93.2	Smith (16.2)
Utah	1-4	82.2	Malone (27.2)

Date	Winner	Home Court
May 7	Trailblazers, 94-75	at Portland
May 9	Trailblazers, 103-85	at Portland
May 11	Trailblazers, 103-84	at Utah
May 14	Jazz, 88-85	at Utah
May 16	Trailblazers, 81-79	at Portland

CHAMPIONSHIP (Best of 7)

	W-L	Avg.	Leading Scorer
Portland	3-4	95.0	Wallace & Smith (17.9)
LA Lakers	4-3	93.1	O'Neal (28.2)

Date	Winner	Home Court
May 20	Lakers, 109-94	at Los Angeles
May 22	Trailblazers, 106-77	at Los Angeles
May 26	Lakers, 93-91	at Portland
May 28	Lakers, 103-91	at Portland
May 30	Trailblazers, 96-88	at Los Angeles
June 2	Trailblazers, 103-91	at Portland
June 4	Lakers, 89-84	at Los Angeles

EASTERN CONFERENCE

FIRST ROUND (Best of 5)

	W-L	Avg.	Leading Scorer
Milwaukee	2-3	96.0	Allen (22.0)
Indiana	3-2	94.2	Miller (24.2)

Date	Winner	Home Court
Apr. 23	Pacers, 88-85	at Indiana
Apr. 27	Bucks, 104-91	at Indiana
Apr. 29	Pacers, 109-96	at Milwaukee
May 1	Bucks, 100-87	at Milwaukee
May 4	Pacers, 96-95	at Indiana

	W-L	Avg.	Leading Scorer
Toronto	0-3	83.7	Carter (19.3)
New York	3-0	87.7	Sprewell (19.0)

Date	Winner	Home Court
Apr. 23	Knicks, 92-88	at New York
Apr. 26	Knicks, 84-83	at New York
Apr. 30	Knicks, 87-80	at Toronto

	W-L	Avg.	Leading Scorer
Detroit	0-3	79.7	Stackhouse (24.7)
Miami	3-0	90.0	Mashburn (23.1)

Date	Winner	Home Court
Apr. 22	Heat, 95-85	at Miami
Apr. 25	Heat, 84-82	at Miami
Apr. 29	Heat, 91-72	at Detroit

	W-L	Avg.	Leading Scorer
Philadelphia	3-1	94.0	Iverson (25.8)
Charlotte	1-3	91.3	Coleman (20.3)

Date	Winner	Home Court
Apr. 22	76ers, 92-82	at Charlotte
Apr. 24	Hornets, 108-98 OT	at Charlotte
Apr. 28	76ers, 81-76	at Philadelphia
May 1	76ers, 105-99	at Philadelphia

SEMIFINALS (Best of 7)

	W-L	Avg.	Leading Scorer
Philadelphia	2-4	94.3	Iverson (26.5)
Indiana	4-2	98.3	Miller (25.8)

Date	Winner	Home Court
May 6	Pacers, 108-91	at Indiana
May 8	Pacers, 103-97	at Indiana
May 10	Pacers, 97-89	at Philadelphia
May 13	76ers, 92-90	at Philadelphia
May 15	76ers, 107-86	at Indiana
May 19	Pacers, 106-90	at Philadelphia

	W-L	Avg.	Leading Scorer
New York	3-4	81.1	Sprewell (18.1)
Miami	4-3	80.3	Mourning (21.6)

Date	Winner	Home Court
May 7	Heat, 87-83	at Miami
May 9	Knicks, 82-76	at Miami
May 12	Heat, 77-76 OT	at New York
May 14	Knicks, 91-83	at New York
May 17	Heat, 87-81	at Miami
May 19	Knicks, 72-70	at New York
May 21	Knicks, 83-82	at Miami

CHAMPIONSHIP (Best of 7)

	W-L	Avg.	Leading Scorer
New York	2-4	86.7	Sprewell (18.7)
Indiana	4-2	92.5	Miller (23.8)

Date	Winner	Home Court
May 23	Pacers, 102-88	at Indiana
May 25	Pacers, 88-84	at Indiana
May 27	Knicks, 98-95	at New York
May 29	Knicks, 91-89	at New York
May 31	Pacers, 88-79	at Indiana
June 2	Pacers, 93-80	at New York

NBA FINALS (Best of 7)

	W-L	Avg.	Leading Scorer
LA Lakers	4-2	104.8	O'Neal (38.0)
Indiana	2-4	106.7	Miller (24.3)

Date	Winner	Home Court
June 7	Lakers, 104-87	at Los Angeles
June 9	Lakers, 111-104	at Los Angeles
June 11	Pacers, 100-91	at Indiana
June 14	Lakers, 120-118 OT	at Indiana
June 16	Pacers, 120-87	at Indiana
June 19	Lakers, 116-111	at Los Angeles

Most Valuable Player
Shaquille O'Neal, Lakers, C
38.0 points, 15.4 rebounds, 2.7 blocks

Final Playoff Standings

(Ranked by victories)

	Gm	W	L	Pct	Per Game For	Opp
LA Lakers	23	15	8	.652	99.8	97.4
Indiana	23	13	10	.565	98.1	95.4
Portland	16	10	6	.625	92.5	87.8
New York	16	9	7	.563	84.4	85.5
Miami	10	6	4	.600	83.2	80.7
Philadelphia	10	5	5	.500	94.2	95.5
Utah	10	4	6	.400	88.3	93.2
Phoenix	9	4	5	.444	87.3	91.0
Seattle	5	2	3	.400	93.2	94.4
Sacramento	5	2	3	.400	96.4	104.4
Milwaukee	5	2	3	.400	96.0	94.2
San Antonio	4	1	3	.250	81.8	83.0
Minnesota	4	1	3	.250	85.3	87.3
Charlotte	4	1	3	.250	91.3	94.0
Toronto	3	0	3	.000	83.7	87.7
Detroit	3	0	3	.000	79.7	90.0

Off-Season Coaching Changes in 2000

Team	Old Coach	Why left?	New Coach	Old Job
Atlanta	Lenny Wilkens	resigned	Lon Kruger	Coach, Univ. of Illinois
Golden St.	Garry St. Jean	interim	Dave Cowens	Asst., Warriors
Indiana	Larry Bird	retired	Isiah Thomas	Owner, CBA
LA Clippers	Jim Todd	interim	Alvin Gentry	Asst., Spurs
New Jersey	Don Casey	fired	Byron Scott	Asst., Kings
Toronto	Butch Carter	fired	Lenny Wilkens	Coach, Hawks
Vancouver	Lionel Hollins	interim	Sidney Lowe	Asst., Timberwolves
Washington	Darrell Walker	interim	Leonard Hamilton	Coach, Univ. of Miami

NBA Finals Box Scores

Game 1

Attendance: 18,997; **Time:** 2:17; **Officials:** Danny Crawford, Jack Nies, Terry Durham

	1	2	3	4	F
Indiana	18	25	28	16	— 87
LA Lakers	33	22	22	27	—104

		FG	FT		Reb		
Indiana	Min	M-A	M-A	Pts	O-T	A	PF
Jalen Rose	36	5-12	0-0	12	0-2	2	4
Dale Davis	28	4-5	1-2	9	3-8	0	3
Rik Smits	20	5-12	2-2	12	0-5	0	6
Reggie Miller	41	1-16	5-5	7	0-2	4	1
Mark Jackson	28	6-8	4-5	18	1-5	7	3
Austin Croshere	26	6-7	4-7	16	1-6	0	3
Sam Perkins	21	1-5	2-2	5	0-2	0	3
Travis Best	19	2-7	0-0	4	1-2	2	0
Derrick McKey	12	0-1		0	0-4	0	0
Chris Mullin	4	0-0	0-0	0	0-4	1	0
Zan Tabak	3	0-0	0-0	0	0-0	0	0
Jonathan Bender	2	2-3	0-0	4	0-0	0	0
TOTALS	240	32-76	18-23	87	6-36	16	23

Three-point FG: 5-14 (Rose 2-3, Jackson 2-3, Perkins 1-3, Miller 0-3, Croshere 0-1, McKey 0-1); **Team Rebounds:** 7; **Blocked Shots:** 5 (Smits 2, Davis, Croshere, Best); **Turnovers:** 14 (Smits 4, Rose 3, Croshere 3, Perkins, Best, McKey, Mullin); **Steals:** 6 (Best 2, Davis, Smits, Miller, Perkins); **Percentages:** Total FG (.421), 3-Pt FG (.357), Free Throws (.783).

		FG	FT		Reb		
LA Lakers	Min	M-A	M-A	Pts	O-T	A	PF
Glen Rice	27	1-8	1-2	3	1-3	1	2
A.C. Green	22	2-6	0-0	4	1-5	1	1
Shaquille O'Neal	44	21-31	1-6	43	6-19	4	2
Kobe Bryant	38	6-13	2-2	14	0-3	5	4
Ron Harper	21	4-6	3-5	12	1-1	5	2
Rick Fox	24	3-4	4-4	11	0-4	2	1
Robert Horry	23	3-5	0-0	6	1-4	2	4
Derek Fisher	19	2-4	0-0	5	1-2	2	2
Brian Shaw	18	2-9		4	1-5	3	0
John Salley	3	0-0	0-0	0	0-0	0	0
Travis Knight	1	1-2	0-0	2	0-2	0	1
TOTALS	240	45-88	11-19	104	14-48	25	19

Three-point FG: 3-12 (Harper 1-2, Fox, 1-1, Fisher 1-1, Rice 0-2, Bryant 0-2, Shaw 0-4); **Team Rebounds:** 9; **Blocked Shots:** 6 (O'Neal 3, Rice, Horry); **Turnovers:** 11 (Rice 2, O'Neal 2, Bryant 2, Harper, Fox, Horry, Fisher, Shaw); **Steals:** 9 (Horry 3, Rice 2, Fisher 2, Bryant, Fox); **Percentages:** Total FG (.511), 3-Pt FG (.250), Free Throws (.579).

Game 2

Attendance: 18,997; **Time:** 2:55; **Officials:** Joe Crawford, Bennett Salvatore, Eddie F. Rush

	1	2	3	4	F
Indiana	28	21	20	35	—104
LA Lakers	28	24	21	38	—111

		FG	FT		Reb		
Indiana	Min	M-A	M-A	Pts	O-T	A	PF
Jalen Rose	48	10-23	10-14	30	1-9	1	3
Dale Davis	34	4-9	1-1	9	4-10	1	6
Rik Smits	16	2-6	0-0	4	1-2	5	5
Reggie Miller	36	7-16	6-6	21	0-2	4	4
Mark Jackson	29	2-9	1-2	7	0-9	8	4
Austin Croshere	25	6-15	12-12	24	4-6	1	4
Sam Perkins	24	2-5	0-0	6	0-3	1	6
Travis Best	19	2-5	2-2	6	0-1	0	1
Derrick McKey	6	0-1	1-2	0	2-3	1	2
Zan Tabak	3	0-1	0-0	0	1-1	0	3
TOTALS	240	33-88	33-39	104	13-46	19	38

Three-point FG: 5-20 (Jackson 2-7, Perkins 2-4, Miller 1-5, Croshere 0-2, Rose 0-1, Best 0-1); **Team Rebounds:** 13; **Blocked Shots:** 5 (Davis 2, Croshere 2, Rose); **Turnovers:** 4 (Rose 2, Jackson, McKey); **Steals:** 5 (Jackson 2, Rose, Croshere, Perkins); **Percentages:** Total FG (.375), 3-Pt FG (.250), Free Throws (.846); **Technical:** Croshere.

		FG	FT		Reb		
LA Lakers	Min	M-A	M-A	Pts	O-T	A	PF
Glen Rice	35	7-15	2-2	21	0-4	3	4
A.C. Green	15	2-4	0-0	4	3-4	1	1
Shaquille O'Neal	46	11-18	18-39	40	5-24	4	5
Ron Harper	37	8-12	4-5	21	0-3	6	4
Kobe Bryant	9	1-3	0-0	2	0-1	4	1
Robert Horry	33	2-6	3-4	7	1-6	1	5
Brian Shaw	32	1-9	2-2	4	1-3	7	1
Derek Fisher	16	2-4	1-2	6	0-0	3	1
Rick Fox	15	2-3	2-3	6	1-2	0	4
Travis Knight	1	0-0	0-0	0	0-0	0	0
John Salley	1	0-1	0-0	0	0-0	0	0
TOTALS	240	36-75	32-57	111	11-47	29	26

Three-point FG: 7-15 (Rice 5-6, Harper 1-2, Fisher 1-1, Shaw 0-3, Horry 0-2, Bryant 0-1); **Team Rebounds:** 19; **Blocked Shots:** 8 (Horry 4, O'Neal 3, Bryant); **Turnovers:** 9 (Harper 3, O'Neal 2, Rice, Green, Horry, Fox); **Steals:** 3 (Shaw, Fox, Salley); **Percentages:** Total FG (.480), 3-Pt FG (.467), Free Throws (.561); **Technical:** Fisher.

Game 3

Attendance: 18,345; **Time:** 2:32; **Officials:** Ron Garretson, Bernie Fryer, Hugh Evans

	1	2	3	4	F
LA Lakers	15	27	24	25	— 91
Indiana	23	30	26	21	—100

		FG	FT		Reb		
LA Lakers	Min	M-A	M-A	Pts	O-T	A	PF
Glen Rice	27	3-9	0-0	7	0-1	1	4
A.C. Green	14	1-2	2-2	4	0-1	1	3
Shaquille O'Neal	47	15-24	3-13	33	4-13	1	3
Ron Harper	38	6-14	0-0	14	1-5	2	2
Brian Shaw	31	3-10	0-0	6	0-5	1	4
Robert Horry	33	5-8	0-0	10	3-7	6	4
Derek Fisher	27	3-5	2-2	10	0-1	10	4
Rick Fox	21	2-4	1-2	7	0-0	1	5
Travis Knight	2	0-0	0-0	0	0-0	0	0
TOTALS	240	38-76	8-19	91	8-33	23	27

Three-point FG: 7-17 (Harper 2-3, Fisher 2-3, Fox 2-3, Rice 1-3, Shaw 0-3, Horry 0-2); **Team Rebounds:** 10; **Blocked Shots:** 4 (O'Neal 2, Rice, Harper); **Turnovers:** 16 (Harper 5, O'Neal 3, Horry 3, Shaw 2, Fox); **Steals:** 5 (O'Neal 2, Rice, Shaw); **Percentages:** Total FG (.500), 3-Pt FG (.412), Free Throws (.421); **Technical:** Harper.

		FG	FT		Reb		
Indiana	Min	M-A	M-A	Pts	O-T	A	PF
Jalen Rose	45	9-18	3-3	21	0-6	2	2
Dale Davis	28	1-5	0-0	2	4-12	1	6
Rik Smits	19	3-11	0-0	6	3-6	0	4
Reggie Miller	46	11-22	9-9	33	0-2	2	0
Mark Jackson	27	2-5	1-2	6	0-2	6	1
Austin Croshere	27	4-6	3-4	12	0-3	0	1
Sam Perkins	22	1-4	0-0	3	0-4	1	2
Travis Best	21	5-7	2-2	14	1-1	2	2
Derrick McKey	5	0-0	3-4	3	1-3	0	1
TOTALS	240	36-78	21-24	100	9-39	14	19

Three-point FG: 7-18 (Miller 2-7, Best 2-2, Perkins 1-3, Jackson 1-1, Croshere 1-1, Rose 0-4); **Team Rebounds:** 12; **Blocked Shots:** 3 (Smits 2, Croshere); **Turnovers:** 12 (Miller 3, Jackson 3, Rose 2, Smits, Perkins, Best, McKey); **Steals:** 8 (Jackson 2, Best 2, Rose, Smits, Miller, Perkins); **Percentages:** Total FG (.462), 3-Pt FG (.389), Free Throws (.875); **Technical:** Jackson.

Game 4

Attendance: 18,345; **Time:** 2:55; **Officials:** Dick Bavetta, Steve Javie, Ronnie Nunn.

	1	2	3	4	OT	F
LA Lakers	23	28	29	24	16	—120
Indiana	33	21	23	27	14	—118

		FG	FT		Reb		
LA Lakers	Min	M-A	M-A	Pts	O-T	A	PF
Glen Rice	39	3-8	3-3	11	0-1	1	3
A.C. Green	16	2-2	1-2	5	1-3	0	3
Shaquille O'Neal	47	13-25	10-17	36	7-21	1	6
Kobe Bryant	47	14-27	0-0	28	2-4	5	4
Ron Harper	26	2-6	0-0	4	0-3	2	2
Robert Horry	37	6-10	5-7	17	2-6	2	4
Derek Fisher	20	3-6	0-0	7	0-0	4	2
Rick Fox	15	3-5	1-1	8	1-3	2	5
Brian Shaw	13	2-4	0-0	4	1-1	3	0
John Salley	5	0-0	0-0	0	0-0	0	2
TOTALS	265	48-93	20-30	120	14-42	20	31

Three-point FG: 4-12 (Rice 2-3, Fisher 1-2, Fox 1-2, Harper 0-2, Horry 0-2, Shaw 0-1); **Team Rebounds:** 10; **Blocked Shots:** 4 (O'Neal 2, Bryant 2); **Turnovers:** 12 (Rice 3, O'Neal 3, Bryant 3, Horry, Fisher, Fox); **Steals:** 6 (O'Neal 2, Horry 2, Bryant, Fisher); **Percentages:** Total FG (.516), 3-Pt FG (.333), Free Throws (.667); **Technical:** Harper.

		FG	FT		Reb		
Indiana	Min	M-A	M-A	Pts	O-T	A	PF
Jalen Rose	44	5-16	4-4	14	0-3	5	3
Dale Davis	29	2-4	0-2	4	2-8	0	6
Rik Smits	22	11-14	2-2	24	1-3	0	4
Reggie Miller	50	9-19	11-12	35	0-5	3	1
Mark Jackson	32	2-8	2-2	7	0-2	7	2
Derrick McKey	23	2-2	0-0	4	3-5	0	2
Sam Perkins	22	3-6	1-2	10	0-4	2	5
Travis Best	21	5-9	0-0	10	2-2	4	2
Austin Croshere	19	3-6	4-4	10	1-7	1	3
TOTALS	265	42-84	24-28	118	9-39	22	28

Three-point FG: 10-19 (Miller 6-9, Perkins 3-5, Jackson 1-3, Best 0-1, Croshere 0-1); **Team Rebounds:** 10; **Blocked Shots:** 3 (Smits 2, Miller); **Turnovers:** 12 (Rose 3, O'Neal 2, Miller, Jackson, McKey, Perkins, Croshere); **Steals:** 5 (Rose, Davis, Smits, Miller, McKey); **Percentages:** Total FG (.500), 3-Pt FG (.526), Free Throws (.857).

Game 5

Attendance: 18,345; **Time:** 2:29; **Officials:** Bennett Salvatore, Jack Nies, Danny Crawford.

	1	2	3	4	F
LA Lakers	28	17	22	20	— 87
Indiana	39	25	22	34	—120

		FG	FT		Reb		
LA Lakers	Min	M-A	M-A	Pts	O-T	A	PF
Glen Rice	30	3-8	4-7	11	0-0	2	2
A.C. Green	16	3-4	1-1	7	1-2	0	2
Shaquille O'Neal	42	17-27	1-6	35	7-11	3	2
Kobe Bryant	37	4-20	0-0	8	1-5	3	5
Ron Harper	25	3-8	0-0	8	2-5	5	2
Robert Horry	29	3-8	0-0	7	0-4	2	5
Derek Fisher	22	0-6	2-2	2	1-2	1	3
Rick Fox	15	0-1	1-1	1	0-0	0	2
Brian Shaw	12	0-4	0-0	0	0-1	2	4
Travis Knight	5	1-1	1-2	3	0-0	0	2
John Salley	4	2-2	0-0	4	1-3	0	1
Devean George	3	0-1	1-2	1	0-1	0	0
TOTALS	240	36-90	11-21	87	13-34	18	33

Three-point FG: 4-19 (Harper 2-4, Rice 1-3, Horry 1-6, Bryant 0-1, Fisher 0-3, Fox 0-1, Shaw 0-1, George 0-1); **Team Rebounds:** 12; **Blocked Shots:** 4 (O'Neal 2, Bryant 2); **Turnovers:** 12 (O'Neal 3, Harper 2, Shaw 2, Rice, Horry, Fisher, Knight, George); **Steals:** 2 (O'Neal 2); **Percentages:** Total FG (.400), 3-Pt FG (.211), Free Throws (.524); **Technicals:** 2 (Fisher, Fox).

		FG	FT		Reb		
Indiana	Min	M-A	M-A	Pts	O-T	A	PF
Jalen Rose	44	12-18	4-4	32	0-6	5	4
Dale Davis	23	4-7	0-0	8	1-8	1	3
Rik Smits	14	5-7	2-2	12	1-2	0	5
Reggie Miller	39	7-12	7-7	25	0-4	6	1
Mark Jackson	30	4-9	2-2	10	2-6	7	0
Sam Perkins	29	2-7	0-0	6	1-7	1	3
Austin Croshere	25	1-3	11-12	13	0-9	3	3
Derrick McKey	12	0-0	0-0	0	0-3	0	1
Travis Best	10	2-2	1-2	5	0-0	3	1
Chris Mullin	5	1-2	2-3	4	0-0	0	0
Zan Tabak	5	1-1	0-0	2	1-3	0	3
Jonathan Bender	4	0-0	3-4	3	0-1	0	0
TOTALS	240	39-68	32-36	120	6-46	26	24

Three-point FG: 10-20 (Rose 4-5, Miller 4-6, Perkins 2-6, Jackson 0-2, Mullin 0-1); **Team Rebounds:** 5; **Blocked Shots:** 4 (Rose, Miller, Croshere, Mullin); **Turnovers:** 14 (Rose 5, Jackson 5, Miller 2, Croshere, McKey, Mullin); **Steals:** 7 (Rose 2, Miller 1, Croshere, McKey, Mullin, Bender); **Percentages:** Total FG (.574), 3-Pt FG (.500), Free Throws (.889); **Technicals:** 2 (Miller, Jackson).

Game 6

Attendance: 18,997; **Time:** 2:46; **Officials:** Hugh Evans, Ron Garretson, Joe Crawford.

	1	2	3	4	F
Indiana	26	30	28	27	—111
LA Lakers	24	29	26	37	—116

		FG	FT		Reb		
Indiana	Min	M-A	M-A	Pts	O-T	A	PF
Jalen Rose	42	9-20	9-11	29	1-1	3	3
Dale Davis	35	8-10	4-6	20	5-14	3	4
Rik Smits	25	1-8	0-0	2	2-6	1	5
Mark Jackson	40	3-7	2-2	10	0-8	11	3
Reggie Miller	40	8-19	7-7	25	0-1	3	1
Austin Croshere	23	4-7	5-6	16	1-5	0	5
Derrick McKey	14	1-2	0-0	3	0-1	0	4
Sam Perkins	13	2-2	0-0	6	0-4	1	1
Travis Best	8	0-2	0-0	0	0-1	2	1
TOTALS	240	36-77	27-32	111	9-41	24	27

Three-point FG: 12-25 (Croshere 3-5, Miller 2-10, Perkins 2-2, Rose 2-3, Jackson 2-4, McKey 1-1); **Team Rebounds:** 8; **Blocked Shots:** 6 (Davis 3, Smits, Croshere, McKey); **Turnovers:** 9 (Rose 2, Miller 2, Smits, Jackson, Croshere, McKey, Perkins); **Steals:** 2 (Jackson, Miller); **Percentages:** Total FG (.468), 3-Pt FG (.480), Free Throws (.844).

		FG	FT		Reb		
LA Lakers	Min	M-A	M-A	Pts	O-T	A	PF
Glen Rice	35	5-7	3-6	16	0-6	2	3
A.C. Green	20	2-3	2-2	6	3-5	0	1
Shaquille O'Neal	47	19-32	3-12	41	5-12	1	2
Kobe Bryant	45	8-27	8-9	26	3-10	4	4
Ron Harper	37	3-10	0-0	6	0-3	9	2
Robert Horry	27	3-6	0-0	8	1-4	4	6
Rick Fox	14	1-1	4-4	7	1-1	1	3
Derek Fisher	8	2-3	0-0	6	0-1	3	1
Brian Shaw	7	0-1	0-0	0	0-2	1	2
TOTALS	240	43-90	20-33	116	13-44	25	24

Three-point FG: 10-17 (Rice 3-3, Bryant 2-6, Horry 2-3, Fisher 2-2, Fox 1-1, Harper 0-2); **Team Rebounds:** 13; **Blocked Shots:** 7 (O'Neal 4, Bryant 2, Horry); **Turnovers:** 7 (Horry 2, Green, Bryant, Harper); **Steals:** 5 (Harper 2, Rice, Green, Bryant); **Percentages:** Total FG (.478), 3-Pt FG (.588), Free Throws (.606).

NBA Playoff Leaders

Scoring

	Gm	FG	FT	Pts	Avg
Shaquille O'Neal, LA Lakers	23	286	135	707	30.7
Karl Malone, Utah	10	103	64	272	27.2
Allen Iverson, Philadelphia	10	91	68	262	26.2
Gary Payton, Seattle	5	50	20	129	25.8
Jerry Stackhouse, Detroit	3	24	23	74	24.7
Chris Webber, Sacramento	5	47	27	122	24.4
Reggie Miller, Indiana	22	174	121	527	24.0
David Robinson, San Antonio	4	31	32	94	23.5
Ray Allen, Milwaukee	5	40	20	110	22.0
Kobe Bryant, LA Lakers	22	174	95	465	21.1
Alonzo Mourning, Miami	10	76	64	216	21.6
Jalen Rose, Indiana	23	171	107	479	20.8
Derrick Coleman, Charlotte	4	27	22	81	20.3
Anfernee Hardaway, Phoenix	9	67	44	183	20.3
Terrell Brandon, Minnesota	4	32	10	78	19.5
Vince Carter, Toronto	3	15	27	58	19.3
Kevin Garnett, Minnesota	4	30	13	75	18.8
Latrell Sprewell, New York	16	110	69	299	18.7
Rasheed Wallace, Portland	16	110	58	286	17.9

High Point Games

	Date	FG-FT—Pts
Shaquille O'Neal, LAL vs. Port	Apr. 23	21-4—46
Shaquille O'Neal, LAL vs. Ind	June 7	21-1—43
Shaquille O'Neal, LAL vs. Ind	June 19	19-3—41
Shaquille O'Neal, LAL vs. Port	May 20	14-13—41
Reggie Miller, Ind. vs. Mil	May 4	15-8—41

Rebounds

	Gm	Off	Def	Tot	Avg
Shaquille O'Neal, LAL	23	119	236	355	15.4
David Robinson, SA	4	17	38	55	13.8
Derrick Coleman, Cha	4	10	40	50	12.5
Dale Davis, Ind	23	83	180	263	11.4
Samaki Walker, SA	4	13	32	45	11.3

Assists

	Gm	No	Avg
John Stockton, Utah	10	103	10.3
Sam Cassell, Mil	5	45	9.0
Kevin Garnett, Min	4	35	8.8
Jason Kidd, Pho	23	178	7.7
Gary Payton, Sea	5	37	7.4

NBA Finalists' Composite Box Scores

Indiana Pacers (13-10)

		Overall Playoffs						Finals vs. Los Angeles				
				—Per Game—						—Per Game—		
	Gm	FG%	TPts	Pts	Reb	Ast	Gm	FG%	TPts	Pts	Reb	Ast
Reggie Miller	22	.452	527	24.0	2.4	2.7	6	.413	146	24.3	2.7	3.7
Jalen Rose	23	.437	479	20.8	4.4	3.4	6	.432	138	23.0	4.5	3.0
Rik Smits	22	.498	241	11.0	3.5	1.0	6	.466	60	10.0	4.0	0.5
Austin Croshere	23	.545	216	9.4	4.7	0.8	6	.545	91	15.2	6.0	0.8
Travis Best	23	.430	204	8.9	2.5	2.9	6	.467	35	5.8	1.2	2.2
Dale Davis	23	.523	190	8.3	11.4	0.7	6	.575	52	8.7	10.0	1.0
Mark Jackson	23	.392	187	8.1	3.7	7.7	6	.413	58	9.7	5.3	7.7
Sam Perkins	23	.324	110	4.8	3.2	0.4	6	.478	36	6.0	4.0	1.0
Chris Mullin	9	.476	31	3.4	1.6	0.6	3	.500	4	1.3	0.0	0.3
Derrick McKey	23	.469	47	2.0	3.4	0.6	6	.500	11	1.8	3.2	0.2
Jonathan Bender	9	.667	12	1.3	0.3	0.0	2	.667	7	3.5	0.5	0.0
Zan Tabak	10	.500	12	1.2	1.6	0.0	3	.500	2	0.7	0.3	0.0
PACERS	23	.443	2256	98.1	40.5	20.3	6	.463	640	106.7	41.2	20.2
OPPONENTS	23	.454	2195	95.4	41.3	19.7	6	.480	629	104.8	41.3	23.3

Three-pointers: PLAYOFFS—Miller (58-for-147), Rose (30-70), Perkins (23-66), Jackson (21-67), Croshere (15-37), Best (13-30), Mullin (2-8), Bender (1-1), McKey (1-6), Smits (0-1), Team (164-433 for .379 pct.); FINALS—Miller (15-for-40), Perkins (11-23), Rose (8-16), Jackson (8-20), Croshere (4-10), Best (2-4), McKey (1-2), Mullin (0-1), Team (49-116 for .422 pct.).

Los Angeles Lakers (15-8)

		Overall Playoffs						Finals vs. Indiana				
				—Per Game—						—Per Game—		
	Gm	FG%	TPts	Pts	Reb	Ast	Gm	FG%	TPts	Pts	Reb	Ast
Shaquille O'Neal	23	.566	707	30.7	15.4	3.1	6	.611	228	38.0	16.7	2.3
Kobe Bryant	22	.442	465	21.1	4.5	4.4	5	.367	78	15.6	4.6	4.2
Glen Rice	23	.408	285	12.4	4.0	2.1	6	.632	69	11.5	2.5	1.7
Ron Harper	23	.431	198	8.6	3.7	3.2	6	.464	65	10.8	3.3	4.8
Robert Horry	23	.407	175	7.6	5.3	2.5	6	.512	55	9.2	5.2	2.8
Brian Shaw	22	.421	119	5.4	2.3	3.0	6	.216	18	3.0	2.8	2.8
Derek Fisher	21	.430	99	4.7	1.0	2.0	6	.429	36	6.0	1.0	3.8
Rick Fox	23	.452	100	4.3	1.7	1.2	6	.611	40	6.7	1.7	1.0
A.C. Green	23	.411	90	3.9	4.2	0.6	6	.571	30	5.0	3.3	0.5
Devean George	9	.368	22	2.4	1.1	0.2	1	.000	1	1.0	1.0	0.0
Travis Knight	14	.533	18	1.3	0.4	0.0	4	.667	5	1.3	0.5	0.0
John Salley	18	.385	17	0.9	1.2	0.2	4	.667	4	1.0	0.8	0.0
LAKERS	23	.465	2295	99.8	43.3	21.8	6	.480	629	104.8	41.3	23.3
OPPONENTS	23	.436	2241	97.4	40.7	19.0	6	.463	640	106.7	41.2	20.2

Three-pointers: PLAYOFFS— Rice (28-for-67), Bryant (22-64), Fox (18-39), Horry (17-59), Shaw (16-48), Fisher (12-29), Harper (9-39), George (2-10), Team (124-355 for .369 pct.); FINALS—Rice (12-for-19), Fisher (7-12), Harper (6-15), Fox (5-8), Horry (3-15), Bryant (2-10), Shaw (0-12), George (0-1), Team (35-92 for .380 pct.).

Annual Awards

Most Valuable Player

The Maurice Podoloff Trophy; voting by 121-member panel of local and national pro basketball writers and broadcasters. Each ballot has five entries; points awarded on 10-7-5-3-1 basis.

	1st	2nd	3rd	4th	5th	Pts
Shaquille O'Neal, LAL	120	1	0	0	0	1207
Kevin Garnett, Minnesota	0	30	25	20	13	408
Alonzo Mourning, Miami	0	28	24	14	6	367
Karl Malone, Utah	0	22	15	23	14	312
Tim Duncan, San Antonio	0	11	20	18	17	248
Gary Payton, Seattle	0	11	9	14	16	180
Allen Iverson, Philadelphia	1	4	9	12	13	132
Grant Hill, Detroit	0	7	6	7	13	113
Chris Webber, Sacramento	0	4	8	6	10	96
Vince Carter, Toronto	0	3	3	3	6	51
Jason Kidd, Phoenix	0	0	1	3	6	25
Kobe Bryant, LA Lakers	0	0	0	1	0	3
Jalen Rose, Indiana	0	0	0	0	1	1
Reggie Miller, Indiana	0	0	0	0	1	1
Michael Finley, Dallas	0	0	0	0	1	1
Darrell Armstrong, Orlando	0	0	0	0	1	1

All-NBA Teams

Voting by a 121-member panel of local and national pro basketball writers and broadcasters. Each ballot has entries for three teams; points awarded on 5-3-1 basis. First Team repeaters from 1998-99 are in **bold** type.

Pos	First Team	1st	Pts
F	Kevin Garnett, Minnesota	77	495
F	**Tim Duncan**, San Antonio	61	460
C	Shaquille O'Neal, LA Lakers	121	605
G	Gary Payton, Seattle	95	541
G	**Jason Kidd**, Phoenix	48	445

Pos	Second Team	1st	Pts
F	Karl Malone, Utah	51	409
F	Grant Hill, Detroit	32	342
C	Alonzo Mourning, Miami	0	354
G	Allen Iverson, Philadelphia	52	420
G	Kobe Bryant, LA Lakers	45	411

Pos	Third Team	1st	Pts
F	Chris Webber, Sacramento	8	254
F	Vince Carter, Toronto	13	194
C	David Robinson, San Antonio	0	91
G	Eddie Jones, Charlotte	2	125
G	Stephon Marbury, New Jersey	0	53

All-Defensive Teams

Voting by NBA head coaches. Each ballot has entries for two teams; two points given for 1st team, one for 2nd. Coaches cannot vote for own players. First Team repeaters from 1998-99 are in **bold** type.

Pos	First Team	1st	Pts
F	**Tim Duncan**, San Antonio	12	29
F	Kevin Garnett, Minnesota	14	31
C	**Alonzo Mourning**, Miami	16	42
G	**Gary Payton**, Seattle	24	52
G	Kobe Bryant, LA Lakers	12	33

Pos	Second Team	1st	Pts
F	Scottie Pippen, Portland	7	19
F	Clifford Robinson, Phoenix	4	18
C	Shaquille O'Neal, LA Lakers	11	29
G	Eddie Jones, Charlotte	8	27
G	Jason Kidd, Phoenix	7	26

Coach of the Year

The Red Auerbach Trophy; voting by 121-member panel of local and national pro basketball writers and broadcasters. Each ballot has one entry.

	Votes	Improvement
Doc Rivers, Orlando	60	33-17 to 41-41
Phil Jackson, LA Lakers	53	31-19 to 67-15
Paul Silas, Charlotte	3	26-24 to 49-33
Jerry Sloan, Utah	2	37-13 to 55-27
Pat Riley, Miami	1	33-17 to 52-30
Scott Skiles, Phoenix	1	27-23 to 53-29
Butch Carter, Toronto	1	23-27 to 45-37

Rookie of the Year

The Eddie Gottlieb Trophy; voting by 121-member panel of local and national pro basketball writers and broadcasters. Each ballot has one entry.

	Pos	Votes
Elton Brand, Chicago	F	58
Steve Francis, Houston	G	58
Lamar Odom, LA Clippers	F	3
Andre Miller, Cleveland	G	2

All-Rookie Team

Voting by NBA's 29 head coaches, who cannot vote for players on their team. Each ballot has entries for two five-man teams, regardless of position; two points given for 1st team, one for 2nd. First team votes in parentheses.

First Team	College	Pts
Elton Brand, Chicago (28)	Duke	56
Steve Francis, Houston (28)	Maryland	56
Lamar Odom, LA Clippers (27)	Rhode Island	55
Wally Szczerbiak, Minnesota (23)	Miami-OH	51
Andre Miller, Cleveland (21)	Utah	49

Second Team	College	Pts
Shawn Marion, Phoenix (8)	UNLV	34
Ron Artest, Chicago (2)	St. John's	28
James Posey, Denver (1)	Xavier-OH	23
Jason Terry, Atlanta (1)	Arizona	15
Chucky Atkins, Orlando (2)	S. Florida	13

IBM Award

Created prior to the 1983-84 season to honor the player who contributes most to his team's overall success and utilizes a computer evaluation of key offensive and defensive statistics to determine an overall leader. The formula is as follows: (Player pts.-FGA+REB+AST+STL+BLK-PF-TO+(team wins x 10) x 250)/(team pts.-FGA+REB+AST+STL+BLK-PF-TO).

	Pos	Pts
Shaquille O'Neal, LA Lakers	C	117.46
Dikembe Mutombo, Atlanta	C	107.04
Karl Malone, Utah	F	101.59
Kevin Garnett, Minnesota	F	100.56
Gary Payton, Seattle	G	96.43
Alonzo Mourning, Miami	C	92.97
Tim Duncan, San Antonio	F	92.56
Shareef Abdur-Rahim, Vancouver	F	86.95
David Robinson, San Antonio	C	83.33

Other Awards

Defensive Player of the Year— Alonzo Mourning, Miami; **Most Improved Player**—Jalen Rose, Indiana; **Sixth Man Award**— Rodney Rogers, Phoenix; **Kennedy PBWAA Citizenship Award**— Vlade Divac, Sacramento; **NBA Sportsmanship Award**— Eric Snow, Philadelphia; *The Sporting News* Executive of the Year— John Gabriel, Orlando.

2000 College Draft

First and second round picks at the 54th annual NBA College Draft held June 28, 2000 at the Target Center in Minneapolis. The order of the first 13 positions were determined by a Draft Lottery held May 21, in Secaucus, N.J. Positions 14 through 29 reflect regular season records in reverse order. Underclassmen selected are noted in CAPITAL letters.

First Round

Team		Pos
1 New Jersey	Kenyon Martin, Cincinnati	C/F
2 Vancouver	STROMILE SWIFT, LSU	F
3 LA Clippers	DARIUS MILES, E. St. Louis HS	F
4 Chicago	MARCUS FIZER, Iowa St.	F
5 a-Orlando	MIKE MILLER, Florida	F
6 Atlanta	DERMARR JOHNSON, Cincinnati	G
7 bc-Chicago	CHRIS MIHM, Texas	C
8 d-Cleveland	JAMAL CRAWFORD, Michigan	G
9 Houston	JOEL PRZYBILLA, Minnesota	C
10 ef-Orlando	KEYON DOOLING, Missouri	G
11 Boston	JEROME MOISO, UCLA	F
12 Dallas	Etan Thomas, Syracuse	F
13 Orlando	Courtney Alexander, Fresno St.	G
14 Detroit	Mateen Cleaves, Michigan St.	G
15 Milwaukee	Jason Collier, Georgia Tech	F
16 Sacramento	Hidayet Turkoglu, Turkey	F
17 Seattle	Desmond Mason, Oklahoma St.	F
18 g-LA Clippers	QUENTON RICHARDSON, Depaul	G
19 Charlotte	Jamaal Magloire, Kentucky	C
20 Philadelphia	Craig Claxton, Hofstra	G
21 h-Toronto	Morris Peterson, Michigan St.	F
22 New York	Donnell Harvey, Florida	F
23 i-Utah	DeSHAWN STEVENSON, Wash. Union HS	F
24 j-Chicago	Dalibor Bagaric, Benston Zagreb (CRO)	C
25 Phoenix	Iakovos Tsakalidis, AEK (GRE)	C
26 k-Denver	Mamadou N'diaye, Auburn	C
27 Indiana	Primoz Brezec, Olympija Ljubljana (SLO)	F
28 Portland	Erick Barkley, St. John's	G
29 LA Lakers	Mark Madsen, Stanford	F

Second Round

Team		Pos
30 LA Clippers	Marko Jaric, Fortitudo Bologna (ITA)	G
31 l-Dallas	Dan Langhi, Vanderbilt	F
32 m-Chicago	A.J. Guyton, Indiana	G
33 n-Chicago	Jake Voskuhl, Connecticut	C
34 o-Chicago	KHALID EL-AMIN, Connecticut	G
35 Washington	Mike Smith, LA-Monroe	F
36 New Jersey	Soumaila Samake, Mali	C
37 p-Miami	Eddie House, Arizona St.	G
38 Houston	Eduardo Najera, Oklahoma	F
39 q-New York	Lavor Postell, St. John's	G
40 r-Atlanta	Hanno Möttölä, Utah	F
41 s-San Antonio	Chris Carrawell, Duke	F
42 t-Seattle	OLUMIDE OYEDEJI, DJK Wurzburg	F
43 Milwaukee	MICHAEL REDD, Ohio St.	G
44 Detroit	Brian Cardinal, Purdue	F
45 Sacramento	Jabari Smith, LSU	C
46 Toronto	DeeAndre Hulett, College of the Sequoias	G
47 Seattle	Josip Sesar, Cibona Zagreb (CRO)	G
48 Philadelphia	MARK KARCHER, Temple	G
49 u-Milwaukee	Jason Hart, Syracuse	G
50 v-Utah	Kaniel Dickens, Idaho	F
51 Minnesota	Igor Rakocevic, Yugoslavia	G
52 Miami	ERNEST BROWN, Indian Hills CC	C
53 w-Denver	Dan McClintock, N. Arizona	C
54 San Antonio	COREY HIGHTOWER, Indian Hills CC	G
55 x-Golden State	Chris Porter, Auburn	F
56 Indiana	Jaquay Walls, Colorado	G
57 y-Atlanta	Scoonie Penn, Ohio St.	G
58 z-Dallas	Pete Mickeal, Cincinnati	F

Acquired Picks

FIRST ROUND: **a**-from Golden St.; **b**-from Washington; **c**-Chicago traded Mihm to Cleveland for rights to Jamal Crawford and cash; **d**-Houston traded Przybilla to Milwaukee for rights to Jason Collier and a future first-round draft pick; **e**-from Denver; **f**-Orlando traded Dooling, Corey Maggette, Derek Strong and cash to the LA Clippers for a future first-round draft pick; **g**-from Toronto via Atlanta, Philadelphia and New York; **h**-from Minnesota; **i**-from Miami; **j**-from San Antonio; **k**-from Utah; **l**-from Chicago; **m**-from Golden St.; **n**-from Vancouver via Houston; **o**-from Atlanta; **p**-from Denver via Cleveland; **q**-from Boston; **r**-from Denver; **s**-from Dallas; **t**-from Orlando; **u**-from Charlotte; **v**-from New York; **w**-from Phoenix; **x**-from Utah; **y**-from Portland via Detroit; **z**-from LA Lakers.

2000 EuroLeague Championships

The European Championships of Men's Clubs. The semifinals and finals of the EuroLeague were played April 18 and 20 at Thessaloniki, Greece. FIBA, the international basketball federation, announced plans at the championships for a new format and name for the EuroLeague. The newly-dubbed SuproLeague, featuring 24 European clubs, debuted in September of 2000 and will climax in spring 2001 with the "FIBA SuproLeague Final Four".

Round of 16

Games played Feb. 29-Mar. 2, 2000. Series were best-of-three.

FC Barcelona (Spain) 2	Ülker SC (Turkey)	1
KK Cibona VIP (Croatia) 2	CSKA (Russia)	1
Winnington Group (Italy) 2	Benetton (Italy)	0
Efes Pilsen (Turkey) 2	ALBA (Germany)	0
Panathinaikos BSA (Greece) 2	Olympiacos BC (Greece)	1
Union Olimpija (Slovenia) 2	Olympiakos BC (Greece)	1
ASVEL (France) 2	Real Madrid Teka (Spain)	0
Maccabi Elite (Israel) 2	PAOK BC (Greece)	1

Quarterfinals

Games played Mar. 21-30, 2000.

FC Barcelona 2	Union Olimpija	1
Panathinaikos BSA 2	KK Cibona VIP	1
Efes Pilsen 2	ASVEL	1
Maccabi Elite 2	Winnington Group	1

Semifinals

Maccabi Elite 65	FC Barcelona	51
Panathinaikos BSA 81	Efes Pilsen	71

Third Place Game

Efes Pilsen 75	FC Barcelona	69

Championship

	1	2	F
Panathinaikos BSA	36	37 —	73
Maccabi Elite	36	31 —	67

Continental Basketball Association
Final Standings

The CBA abandoned their point standings system based on games and quarters won for the 2000 season. All teams made the postseason with the eight and nine seeds facing off in a play-in game for the last spot in the first round of the postseason tournament.

American Conference

	W	L	Pct	GB	Home	Road
Rockford	30	26	.536	—	19-9	11-17
Connecticut	29	27	.518	1	21-7	8-20
Grand Rapids	29	27	.518	1	19-9	10-18
Fort Wayne	26	30	.464	4	16-12	10-18

National Conference

	W	L	Pct	GB	Home	Road
Quad City	35	21	.625	—	21-7	14-14
Yakima	33	23	.589	2	20-8	13-15
Sioux Falls	30	26	.536	5	20-8	10-18
La Crosse	21	35	.375	14	15-13	6-22
Idaho	19	37	.339	16	14-14	5-23

Playoffs
Play-in Game

Mar. 27   at La Crosse 107 . . . . Idaho 94

First Round

Mar. 28	at Rockford 104 . . . . Fort Wayne 94
Mar. 29	La Crosse 111 . . . . at Quad City 101
Mar. 29	at Sioux Falls 109 . . . . Connecticut 90
Mar. 29	at Yakima 98 . . . . Grand Rapids 96

Semifinals

Mar. 31	La Crosse 99 . . . . at Sioux Falls 90
Mar. 31	at Yakima 124 . . . . Rockford 102

Final

April 2 at Yakima Valley SunDome in Yakima, Wash.
Attendance: 3,945. **Time:** 2:15.

	1	2	3	4	F
La Crosse Bobcats	31	22	23	17	— **93**
Yakima Sun Kings	28	24	27	30	—**109**

Playoff MVP: Silas Mills, Yakima, F (26.3 ppg, 6.0 rpg)

CBA Annual Awards

Most Valuable Player	Jeff McInnis, Quad City
Newcomer of the Year	Charles Smith, Rockford
Rookie of the Year	Jamel Thomas, Quad City
Def. Player of the Year	Maceo Baston, Quad City
Coach of the Year	Dan Panaggio, Quad City

CBA Regular Season Individual Leaders

Scoring

	Gm	Pts	Avg
Brandon Williams, La Crosse	46	913	19.8
Jamel Thomas, Quad City	29	553	19.1
Kebu Stewart, Sioux Falls	30	569	19.0
Damian Owens, Connecticut	44	832	18.9
Jerald Honeycutt, Idaho	36	671	18.6
Silas Mills, Yakima	56	1015	18.1
Victor Page, Sioux Falls	51	854	16.7
Charles Smith, Rockford	56	936	16.7

Field Goal Pct.

	FGM	FGA	Pct
Rosell Ellis, Yakima	236	387	.610
Maceo Baston, Quad City	261	441	.592
Jason Lawson, Grand Rapids	216	368	.587
Shawnelle Scott, Connecticut	178	319	.558
Wille Sims, Grand Rapids	244	445	.548
Mark Hendrickson, La Crosse	221	404	.547
Etdrick Bohannon, Ft. Wayne	193	353	.547
Michael McDonald, Grand Rapids	196	360	.544

Rebounding

	Gm	Reb	Avg
Nick Davis, Sioux Falls	56	654	11.7
Shawnelle Scott, Connecticut	50	568	11.4
Etdrick Bohannon, Ft. Wayne	39	417	10.7
Torraye Braggs, Rockford	55	533	9.7
Kebu Stewart, Sioux Falls	30	282	9.4
Derek Hood, Quad City	51	462	9.1
Maceo Baston, Quad City	46	381	8.3
Jerald Honeycutt, Idaho	36	284	7.9

Assists

	Gm	Ast	Avg
Rusty LaRue, Idaho	38	318	8.4
Tyson Wheeler, Quad City	47	279	5.9
David Vanterpool, Yakima	55	318	5.8
Sean Colson, Grand Rapids	55	311	5.7
Jerry McCullough, Sioux Falls	54	302	5.6
Darren McLinton, Idaho	38	191	5.0
Dan Cross, Connecticut	54	261	4.8
Gerald Brown, La Crosse	29	129	4.4

Women's National Basketball Association
Final WNBA Standings

Conference champions (*) and playoff qualifiers (†) are noted. GB refers to Games Behind leader. Number of seasons listed after each head coach refers to current tenure with club.

Eastern Conference

	W	L	Pct	GB	Home	Road
*New York	20	12	.625	—	12-4	8-8
†Cleveland	17	15	.531	3	13-3	4-12
†Orlando	16	16	.500	4	11-5	5-11
†Washington	14	18	.438	6	7-9	7-9
Detroit	14	18	.438	6	8-8	6-10
Miami	13	19	.406	7	9-7	4-12
Indiana	9	23	.281	11	5-11	4-12
Charlotte	8	24	.250	12	5-11	3-13

Head Coaches: NY–Richie Adubato (2nd season); **Cle**–Dan Hughes (1st); **Orl**–Carolyn Peck (2nd); **Wash**–Darrell Walker (1st); **Det**–Nancy Lieberman-Cline (3rd); **Mia**–Ron Rothstein (1st); **Ind**–Anne Donovan (1st); **Cha**– T.R. Dunn (1st).

1999 Standings: 1. New York (18-14); 2. Charlotte (15-17); 3. Detroit (15-17); 4. Orlando (15-17); 5. Washington (12-20); 6. Cleveland (7-25). Miami and Indiana were expansion teams in 2000.

Western Conference

	W	L	Pct	GB	Home	Road
*Los Angeles	28	4	.875	—	15-1	13-3
†Houston	27	5	.844	1	14-2	13-3
†Sacramento	21	11	.656	7	13-3	8-8
†Phoenix	20	12	.625	8	11-5	9-7
Utah	18	14	.563	10	12-4	6-10
Minnesota	15	17	.469	13	8-8	7-9
Portland	10	22	.313	18	6-10	4-12
Seattle	6	26	.188	22	4-12	2-14

Head Coaches: LA–Michael Cooper (1st season); **Hou**–Van Chancellor (4th); **Sac**–Sonny Allen (2nd); **Pho**–Cheryl Miller (3rd); **Utah**–Fred Williams (2nd); **Min**–Brian Agler (2nd); **Port**–Linda Hargrove (1st); **Sea**–Lin Dunn (1st).

1999 Standings: 1. Houston (26-6); 2. Los Angeles (20-12); 3. Sacramento (19-13); 4. Phoenix (15-17); 5. Minnesota (15-15); 6. Utah (15-17). Portland and Seattle are expansion teams in 2000.

WNBA Regular Season Individual Leaders

Scoring

	Gm	Pts	Avg
Sheryl Swoopes, Houston	31	643	20.7
Katie Smith, Minnesota	32	646	20.2
Brandy Reed, Phoenix	32	608	19.0
Natalie Williams, Utah	29	543	18.7
Lisa Leslie, Los Angeles	32	570	17.8
Cynthia Cooper, Houston	31	550	17.7
Andrea Stinson, Charlotte	32	565	17.7
Chamique Holdsclaw, Washington	32	561	17.5
Adrienne Goodson, Utah	29	498	17.2
Betty Lennox, Minnesota	32	541	16.9

Rebounding

	Gm	Reb	Avg
Natalie Williams, Utah	29	336	11.6
Yolanda Griffith, Sacramento	32	331	10.3
Lisa Leslie, Los Angeles	32	306	9.6
Tari Phillips, New York	31	247	8.0
Tina Thompson, Houston	32	245	7.7
Taj McWilliams, Orlando	32	244	7.6
Chamique Holdsclaw, Washington	32	240	7.5
Marlies Askamp, Miami	32	231	7.2
Rhonda Mapp, Charlotte	30	205	6.8
Wendy Palmer, Detroit	32	219	6.8

Field Goal Pct.

	Gm	FGM	FGA	Pct
Muriel Page, Washington	32	131	222	.590
Kara Wolters, Indiana	31	148	264	.561
Yolanda Griffith, Sacramento	32	193	361	.535
Taj McWilliams, Orlando	32	173	330	.524
Alicia Thompson, Indiana	31	131	255	.514

Assists

	Gm	Ast	Avg
Ticha Penicheiro, Sacramento	30	236	7.9
Teresa Weatherspoon, New York	32	205	6.4
Dawn Staley, Charlotte	32	190	5.9
Shannon Johnson, Orlando	32	169	5.3
Andrea Nagy, Washington	23	118	5.1

Free Throw Pct.

	Gm	FTM	FTA	Pct
Jennifer Azzi, Utah	15	40	43	.930
Elena Tornikidou, Detroit	32	85	93	.914
Brandy Reed, Phoenix	32	128	142	.901
Becky Hammon, New York	32	61	69	.884
Vickie Johnson, New York	31	67	76	.882

Blocks

	Gm	Blk	Avg
Margo Dydek, Utah	32	96	3.00
Lisa Leslie, Los Angeles	32	74	2.31
Tangela Smith, Sacramento	32	64	2.00
Cintia Dos Santos, Orlando	32	63	1.97
Yolanda Griffith, Sacramento	32	61	1.91

3-Point Field Goal Pct.

	Gm	FGM	FGA	Pct
Korie Hlede, Utah	31	25	58	.431
Tina Thompson, Houston	32	55	132	.417
Eva Nemcova, Cleveland	14	29	71	.408
Monica Maxwell, Indiana	32	62	156	.397
Betty Lennox, Minnesota	32	55	139	.396

Steals

	Gm	Stl	Avg
Sheryl Swoopes, Houston	31	87	2.81
Yolanda Griffith, Sacramento	32	83	2.59
Rita Williams, Indiana	32	76	2.38
Ticha Penicheiro, Sacramento	30	70	2.33
Brandy Reed, Phoenix	32	66	2.06

WNBA Annual Awards

Most Valuable Player	Sheryl Swoopes, Hou	**Def. Player of the Year**	Sheryl Swoopes, Hou
Rookie of the Year	Betty Lennox, Min	**Coach of the Year**	Michael Cooper, LA
Most Improved	Tari Phillips, NY	**Sportsmanship Award**	Suzie McConnell Serio, Cle

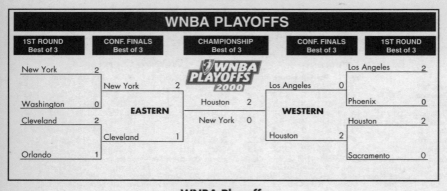

WNBA Playoffs
First Round (Best of 3)

East

Aug. 12 New York 72 .Washington 63
Aug. 14 New York 78 .Washington 57
New York Liberty win series, 2-0

Aug. 11 Orlando 62 . . . . .Cleveland 55
Aug. 13 Cleveland 63 . . . . .Orlando 54
Aug. 15 Cleveland 72 . . . . .Orlando 43
Cleveland Rockers win series, 2-1

West

Aug. 11 Los Angeles 86 .Phoenix 71
Aug. 13 Los Angeles 101 . . . . .Phoenix 76
Los Angeles Sparks win series, 2-0

Aug. 12 Houston 72 . . . . .Sacramento 64
Aug. 14 Houston 75 . . . . .Sacramento 70
Houston Comets win series, 2-0

Conference Finals (Best of 3)

East

Aug. 17 Cleveland 56 .New York 43
Aug. 20 New York 51 .Cleveland 45
Aug. 21 New York 81 . . . . .Cleveland 67
New York Liberty win series, 2-1

West

Aug. 17 Houston 77 . . . . .Los Angeles 56
Aug. 20 Houston 74 . . . . .Los Angeles 69
Houston Comets win series, 2-0

Championship Series (Best of 3)
Houston wins series, 2 games to 0

	W-L	Avg	Leading Scorer
Houston	2-0	69.0	Cooper (22.5 ppg)
New York	0-2	62.5	Phillips (22.0 ppg)

Date	Winner	Home Court
Aug. 24 . . . . Comets, 59-52		at New York
Aug. 26 . . . . .Comets, 79-73 OT		at Houston

Finals MVP: Cynthia Cooper, Houston, G (22.5 ppg, 3.5 rpg, 6.0 apg, 1.5 spg)

WNBA 2000 Attendance
Attendance figures below are for the regular season and teams are listed in alphabetical order.

Team	Home Games	Total Attendance	Average Attendance
Charlotte Sting 16		90,963	5,685
Cleveland Rockers 16		137,532	8,596
Detroit Shock 16		107,449	6,716
Houston Comets 16		196,077	12,255
Indiana Fever 16		180,270	11,267
Los Angeles Sparks 16		105,005	6,563
Miami Sol 16		127,721	7,983
Minnesota Lynx 16		116,638	7,290
New York Liberty 16		231,962	14,498
Orlando Miracle 16		117,810	7,363
Phoenix Mercury 16		162,078	10,130
Portland Fire 16		133,076	8,317
Sacramento Monarchs 16		126,841	7,928
Seattle Storm 16		142,594	8,912
Utah Starzz 16		102,672	6,417
Washington Mystics 16		244,134	15,258
WNBA TOTALS 256		2,322,822	9,074

The NBA Finals

Although the National Basketball Association traces its first championship back to the 1946-47 season, the league was then called the Basketball Association of America (BAA). It did not become the NBA until after the 1948-49 season when the BAA and the National Basketball League (NBL) agreed to merge.

In the chart below, the Eastern finalists (representing the NBA Eastern Division from 1947-70, and the NBA Eastern Conference since 1971) are listed in CAPITAL letters. Also, each NBA champion's wins and losses are noted in parentheses after the series score.

Multiple winners: Boston (16); Minneapolis-LA Lakers (12); Chicago Bulls (6); Phi-SF-Golden St. Warriors and Syracuse Nationals-Phi. 76ers (3); Detroit, Houston and New York (2).

Year	Winner	Head Coach	Series	Loser	Head Coach
1947	PHILADELPHIA WARRIORS	Eddie Gottlieb	4-1 (WWWLW)	Chicago Stags	Harold Olsen
1948	Baltimore Bullets	Buddy Jeannette	4-2 (LWWWLW)	PHILA. WARRIORS	Eddie Gottlieb
1949	Minneapolis Lakers	John Kundla	4-2 (WWWLLW)	WASH. CAPITOLS	Red Auerbach
1950	Minneapolis Lakers	John Kundla	4-2 (WLWLW)	SYRACUSE	Al Cervi
1951	Rochester	Les Harrison	4-3 (WWWLLLLW)	NEW YORK	Joe Lapchick
1952	Minneapolis Lakers	John Kundla	4-3 (WLWLWLW)	NEW YORK	Joe Lapchick
1953	Minneapolis Lakers	John Kundla	4-1 (LWWW)	NEW YORK	Joe Lapchick
1954	Minneapolis Lakers	John Kundla	4-3 (WLWLWLW)	SYRACUSE	Al Cervi
1955	SYRACUSE	Al Cervi	4-3 (WWLLLWW)	Ft. Wayne Pistons	Charley Eckman
1956	PHILADELPHIA WARRIORS	George Senesky	4-1 (LWWLW)	Ft. Wayne Pistons	Charley Eckman
1957	BOSTON	Red Auerbach	4-3 (LWLWWLW)	St. Louis Hawks	Alex Hannum
1958	St. Louis Hawks	Alex Hannum	4-2 (WLWLWW)	BOSTON	Red Auerbach
1959	BOSTON	Red Auerbach	4-0	Mpls. Lakers	John Kundla
1960	BOSTON	Red Auerbach	4-3 (WLWLWLW)	St. Louis Hawks	Ed Macauley
1961	BOSTON	Red Auerbach	4-1 (WWLWW)	St. Louis Hawks	Paul Seymour
1962	BOSTON	Red Auerbach	4-3 (WLLWLWW)	LA Lakers	Fred Schaus
1963	BOSTON	Red Auerbach	4-2 (WWLWLW)	LA Lakers	Fred Schaus
1964	BOSTON	Red Auerbach	4-1 (WWLWW)	SF Warriors	Alex Hannum
1965	BOSTON	Red Auerbach	4-1 (WWLWW)	LA Lakers	Fred Schaus
1966	BOSTON	Red Auerbach	4-3 (LWWWLLW)	LA Lakers	Fred Schaus
1967	PHILADELPHIA 76ERS	Alex Hannum	4-2 (WWLWLW)	SF Warriors	Bill Sharman
1968	BOSTON	Bill Russell	4-2 (WLWLWW)	LA Lakers	B.van Breda Kolff
1969	BOSTON	Bill Russell	4-3 (LLWWLWW)	LA Lakers	B.van Breda Kolff
1970	NEW YORK	Red Holzman	4-3 (WLWLWLW)	LA Lakers	Joe Mullaney
1971	Milwaukee	Larry Costello	4-0	BALT. BULLETS	Gene Shue
1972	LA Lakers	Bill Sharman	4-1 (LWWWW)	NEW YORK	Red Holzman
1973	NEW YORK	Red Holzman	4-1 (LWWWW)	LA Lakers	Bill Sharman
1974	BOSTON	Tommy Heinsohn	4-3 (WLWLWLW)	Milwaukee	Larry Costello
1975	Golden St. Warriors	Al Attles	4-0	WASH. BULLETS	K.C. Jones
1976	BOSTON	Tommy Heinsohn	4-2 (WWLLWW)	Phoenix	John MacLeod
1977	Portland	Jack Ramsay	4-2 (LLWWWW)	PHILA. 76ERS	Gene Shue
1978	WASHINGTON BULLETS	Dick Motta	4-3 (LWLWLWW)	Seattle	Lenny Wilkens
1979	Seattle	Lenny Wilkens	4-1 (LWWWW)	WASH. BULLETS	Dick Motta
1980	LA Lakers	Paul Westhead	4-2 (WLWLWW)	PHILA. 76ERS	Billy Cunningham
1981	BOSTON	Bill Fitch	4-2 (WLWLWW)	Houston	Del Harris
1982	LA Lakers	Pat Riley	4-2 (WLWLWLW)	PHILA. 76ERS	Billy Cunningham
1983	PHILADELPHIA 76ERS	Billy Cunningham	4-0	LA Lakers	Pat Riley
1984	BOSTON	K.C. Jones	4-3 (LWWLWWLW)	LA Lakers	Pat Riley
1985	LA Lakers	Pat Riley	4-2 (LWWLWW)	BOSTON	K.C. Jones
1986	BOSTON	K.C. Jones	4-2 (WWLWLW)	Houston	Bill Fitch
1987	LA Lakers	Pat Riley	4-2 (WWLWLW)	BOSTON	K.C. Jones
1988	LA Lakers	Pat Riley	4-3 (LWWWLLWW)	DETROIT PISTONS	Chuck Daly
1989	DETROIT PISTONS	Chuck Daly	4-0	LA Lakers	Pat Riley
1990	DETROIT	Chuck Daly	4-1 (WLWWW)	Portland	Rick Adelman
1991	CHICAGO	Phil Jackson	4-1 (LWWWW)	LA Lakers	Mike Dunleavy
1992	CHICAGO	Phil Jackson	4-2 (WLWLWW)	Portland	Rick Adelman
1993	CHICAGO	Phil Jackson	4-2 (WWLWLW)	Phoenix	Paul Westphal

Year	Winner	Head Coach	Series	Loser	Head Coach
1994	Houston	Rudy Tomjanovich	4-3 (WLWLLWW)	NEW YORK	Pat Riley
1995	Houston	Rudy Tomjanovich	4-0	ORLANDO	Brian Hill
1996	CHICAGO	Phil Jackson	4-2 (WWWLLW)	Seattle	George Karl
1997	CHICAGO	Phil Jackson	4-2 (WWLLWW)	Utah	Jerry Sloan
1998	CHICAGO	Phil Jackson	4-2 (LWWWLW)	Utah	Jerry Sloan
1999	San Antonio	Gregg Popovich	4-1 (WWLWW)	NEW YORK	Jeff Van Gundy
2000	LA Lakers	Phil Jackson	4-2 (WWLWLW)	INDIANA	Larry Bird

Note: Four finalists were led by player-coaches: **1948**—Buddy Jeannette (guard) of Baltimore; **1950**—Al Cervi (guard) of Syracuse; **1968**—Bill Russell (center) of Boston; **1969**—Bill Russell (center) of Boston.

Most Valuable Player

Selected by an 11-member media panel. Winner who did not play for the NBA champion is in **bold** type.

Multiple winners: Michael Jordan (6); Magic Johnson (3); Kareem Abdul-Jabbar, Larry Bird, Hakeem Olajuwon and Willis Reed (2).

Year		Year		Year	
1969	**Jerry West**, LA Lakers, G	1980	Magic Johnson, LA Lakers, G/C	1991	Michael Jordan, Chicago, G
1970	Willis Reed, New York, C	1981	Cedric Maxwell, Boston, F	1992	Michael Jordan, Chicago, G
1971	Lew Alcindor, Milwaukee, C	1982	Magic Johnson, LA Lakers, G	1993	Michael Jordan, Chicago, G
1972	Wilt Chamberlain, LA Lakers, C	1983	Moses Malone, Philadelphia, C	1994	Hakeem Olajuwon, Houston, C
1973	Willis Reed, New York, C	1984	Larry Bird, Boston, F	1995	Hakeem Olajuwon, Houston, C
1974	John Havlicek, Boston, F	1985	K. Abdul-Jabbar, LA Lakers, C	1996	Michael Jordan, Chicago, G
1975	Rick Barry, Golden State, F	1986	Larry Bird, Boston, F	1997	Michael Jordan, Chicago, G
1976	Jo Jo White, Boston, G	1987	Magic Johnson, LA Lakers, G	1998	Michael Jordan, Chicago, G
1977	Bill Walton, Portland, C	1988	James Worthy, LA Lakers, F	1999	Tim Duncan, San Antonio, F/C
1978	Wes Unseld, Washington, C	1989	Joe Dumars, Detroit, G	2000	Shaquille O'Neal, LAL, C
1979	Dennis Johnson, Seattle, G	1990	Isiah Thomas, Detroit, G		

Note: Lew Alcindor changed his name to Kareem Abdul-Jabbar after the 1970-71 season.

All-Time NBA Playoff Leaders

Through the 2000 playoffs.

CAREER

Years listed indicate number of playoff appearances. Players active in 2000 in **bold** type. DNP indicates player that was active in 2000 but did not participate in playoffs.

Points

		Yrs	Gm	Pts	Avg
1	Michael Jordan	13	179	5987	33.4
2	Kareem Abdul-Jabbar	18	237	5762	24.3
3	Jerry West	13	153	4457	29.1
4	**Karl Malone**	15	158	4203	26.6
5	Larry Bird	12	164	3897	23.8
6	John Havlicek	13	172	3776	22.0
7	**Hakeem Olajuwon** (DNP)	14	140	3727	26.6
8	Magic Johnson	13	190	3701	19.5
9	Elgin Baylor	12	134	3623	27.0
10	Wilt Chamberlain	13	160	3607	22.5
11	**Scottie Pippen**	13	198	3529	17.8
12	Kevin McHale	13	169	3182	18.8
13	Dennis Johnson	13	180	3116	17.3
14	Julius Erving	11	141	3088	21.9
15	James Worthy	9	143	3022	21.1
16	Clyde Drexler	15	145	2963	20.4
17	Sam Jones	12	154	2909	18.9
18	**Charles Barkley** (DNP)	13	123	2833	23.0
19	Robert Parish	16	184	2820	15.3
20	**Patrick Ewing**	13	135	2787	20.6

Scoring Average

Minimum of 25 games or 700 points.

		Yrs	Gm	Pts	Avg
1	Michael Jordan	13	179	5987	33.4
2	Jerry West	13	153	4457	29.1
3	**Shaquille O'Neal**	7	89	2469	27.7
4	Elgin Baylor	12	134	3623	27.0
5	George Gervin	9	59	1592	27.0
6	**Hakeem Olajuwon** (DNP)	14	140	3727	26.6
7	**Karl Malone**	15	158	4203	26.6
8	Dominique Wilkins	9	55	1421	25.8
9	Bob Pettit	9	88	2240	25.5
10	Rick Barry	7	74	1833	24.8
11	Bernard King	5	28	687	24.5
12	Alex English	10	68	1661	24.4
13	Kareem Abdul-Jabbar	18	237	5762	24.3
14	Paul Arizin	8	49	1186	24.2
15	Larry Bird	12	164	3897	23.8
16	George Mikan	9	91	2141	23.5
17	**Reggie Miller**	10	100	2320	23.2
18	**Charles Barkley** (DNP)	13	123	2833	23.0
19	Bob Love	6	47	1076	22.9
20	**Tim Duncan** (DNP)	2	26	581	22.3

Field Goals

		Yrs	FG	Att	Pct
1	Kareem Abdul-Jabbar	18	2356	4422	.533
2	Michael Jordan	13	2188	4497	.487
3	Jerry West	13	1622	3460	.469
4	**Karl Malone**	15	1532	3272	.468
5	**Hakeem Olajuwon** (DNP)	12	1469	2771	.530
6	Larry Bird	12	1458	3090	.472
7	John Havlicek	13	1451	3329	.436
8	Wilt Chamberlain	13	1425	2728	.522
9	Elgin Baylor	12	1388	3161	.439
10	**Scottie Pippen**	13	1292	2910	.444

Free Throws

		Yrs	FT	Att	Pct
1	Michael Jordan	13	1463	1766	.828
2	Jerry West	13	1213	1507	.805
3	**Karl Malone**	15	1134	1534	.739
4	Kareem Abdul-Jabbar	18	1050	1419	.740
5	Magic Johnson	13	1040	1241	.838
6	Larry Bird	12	901	1012	.891
7	John Havlicek	13	874	1046	.836
8	Elgin Baylor	12	847	1101	.769
9	Kevin McHale	13	766	972	.788
10	Wilt Chamberlain	13	757	1627	.465
	Scottie Pippen	13	757	1048	.722

Assists

		Yrs	Gm	No	Avg
1	Magic Johnson	13	190	2346	12.3
2	**John Stockton**	16	168	1716	10.2
3	Larry Bird	12	164	1062	6.5
4	Michael Jordan	13	179	1022	5.7
5	**Scottie Pippen**	13	198	1011	5.1

Rebounds

		Yrs	Gm	No	Avg
1	Bill Russell	13	165	4104	24.9
2	Wilt Chamberlain	13	160	3913	24.5
3	Kareem Abdul-Jabbar	18	237	2481	10.5
4	Wes Unseld	12	119	1777	14.9
5	**Karl Malone**	15	158	1769	11.2

Appearances

	No		No
Kareem Abdul-Jabbar	18	**Karl Malone**	15
Robert Parish	16	Dolph Schayes	15
John Stockton	16	Paul Silas	14
Jerome Kersey	15	H. Olajuwon (DNP)	14

Games Played

	No		No
K. Abdul-Jabbar	237	John Havlicek	170
Scottie Pippen	198	Kevin McHale	169
Danny Ainge	193	Michael Cooper	168
Magic Johnson	190	**John Stockton**	168
Robert Parish	184	Bill Russell	165
Byron Scott	183	Larry Bird	164
Dennis Johnson	180	Paul Silas	163
Michael Jordan	179	Wilt Chamberlain	160

SINGLE GAME

Points

	Date	FG-FT–Pts
Michael Jordan, Chi at Bos*	4/20/86	22-19–63
Elgin Baylor, LA at Bos	4/14/62	22-17–61
Wilt Chamberlain, SF vs Syr	3/22/62	22-12–56
Michael Jordan, Chi at Mia.	4/29/92	20-16–56
Charles Barkley, Pho vs G.St.	5/4/94	23- 7–56
Rick Barry, SF vs Phi	4/18/67	22-11–55
Michael Jordan, Chi vs Cle	5/1/88	24- 7–55
Michael Jordan, Chi vs Pho	4/16/93	21-13–55
Michael Jordan, Chi vs. Wash	4/27/97	22-10–55

*Double overtime.

Field Goals

	Date	FG	Att
Wilt Chamberlain, Phi vs Syr	3/14/60	24	42
John Havlicek, Bos vs Atl	4/1/73	24	36
Michael Jordan, Chi vs Cle	5/1/88	24	45

Eight tied with 22 each.

Miscellaneous

3-Pt Field Goals	Date	No
Rex Chapman, Pho at Sea	4/25/97	9
Dan Majerle, Pho vs Sea	6/1/93	8

Eight tied with 7 each.

Assists	Date	No
Magic Johnson, LA vs Pho	5/15/84	24
John Stockton, Utah at LA Lakers	5/17/88	24
Magic Johnson, LA Lakers at Port	5/3/85	23
John Stockton, Utah vs Port	4/25/96	23
Doc Rivers, Atl vs Bos	5/16/88	22

Four tied with 21 each.

Rebounds	Date	No
Wilt Chamberlain, Phi vs Bos	4/5/67	41
Bill Russell, Bos vs Phi	3/23/58	40
Bill Russell, Bos vs St.L	3/29/60	40
Bill Russell, Bos vs LA*	4/18/62	40

Three tied with 39 each.

*Overtime.

Appearances in NBA Finals

Standings of all NBA teams that have reached the NBA Finals since 1947.

App		Titles	Last Won
25	Minneapolis-LA Lakers	12	2000
19	Boston Celtics	16	1986
8	Syracuse Nats-Phila. 76ers	3	1983
8	New York Knicks	2	1973
6	Chicago Bulls	6	1998
6	Phila-SF-Golden St. Warriors	3	1975
5	Ft. Wayne-Detroit Pistons	2	1990
4	Houston Rockets	2	1995
4	St. Louis Hawks	1	1958
4	Baltimore-Washington Bullets	1	1978
3	Portland Trail Blazers	1	1977
3	Seattle SuperSonics	1	1979
2	Milwaukee Bucks	1	1971
2	Phoenix Suns	0	—
2	Utah Jazz	0	—
1	Baltimore Bullets	1	1948
1	Rochester Royals	1	1951
1	San Antonio Spurs	1	1999
1	Chicago Stags	0	—
1	Orlando Magic	0	—
1	Washington Capitols	0	—
1	Indiana Pacers	0	—

Change of address: The St. Louis Hawks now play in Atlanta and the Rochester Royals are now the Sacramento Kings.

Teams now defunct: Baltimore Bullets (1947-55), Chicago Stags (1946-50) and Washington Capitols (1946-51).

NBA FINALS

Points

Series		Year	Pts
4-Gm	Hakeem Olajuwon, Hou vs Orl	1995	131
5-Gm	Jerry West, LA vs Bos	1965	169
6-Gm	Michael Jordan, Chi vs Pho	1993	246
7-Gm	Elgin Baylor, LA vs Bos	1962	284

Field Goals

Series		Year	No
4-Gm	Hakeem Olajuwon, Hou vs Orl	1995	56
5-Gm	Michael Jordan, Chi vs LAL	1991	63
6-Gm	Michael Jordan, Chi vs Pho	1993	101
7-Gm	Elgin Baylor, LA vs Bos	1962	101

Assists

Series		Year	No
4-Gm	Bob Cousy, Bos vs Mpls	1959	51
5-Gm	Magic Johnson, LAL vs Chi	1991	62
6-Gm	Magic Johnson, LAL vs Bos	1985	84
7-Gm	Magic Johnson, LA vs Bos	1984	95

Rebounds

Series		Year	No
4-Gm	Bill Russell, Bos vs Mpls	1959	118
5-Gm	Bill Russell, Bos vs St.L	1961	144
6-Gm	Wilt Chamberlain, Phi vs SF	1967	171
7-Gm	Bill Russell, Bos vs LA	1962	189

The National Basketball League

Formed in 1937 by three corporations– General Electric and the Firestone and Goodyear rubber companies of Akron, Ohio– which were interested in moving up from their midwestern industrial league origins and backing a fully professional league. The NBL started with 13 previously independent teams in 1937-38 and although GE, Firestone and Goodyear were gone by late 1942, ran 12 years before merging with the three-year-old Basketball Association of America in 1949 to form the NBA.

Multiple champions: Akron Firestone Non-Skids, Fort Wayne Zollner Pistons, Oshkosh All-Stars (2).

Year	Winner	Series	Loser	Year	Winner	Series	Loser
1938	Goodyear Wingfoots	2-1	Oshkosh All-Stars	1944	Ft. Wayne Pistons	3-0	Sheboygan Redskins
1939	Firestone Non-Skids	3-2	Oshkosh All-Stars	1945	Ft. Wayne Pistons	3-2	Sheboygan Redskins
1940	Firestone Non-Skids	3-2	Oshkosh All-Stars	1946	Rochester Royals	3-0	Sheboygan Redskins
1941	Oshkosh All-Stars	3-0	Sheboygan Redskins	1947	Chicago Gears	3-2	Rochester Royals
1942	Oshkosh All-Stars	2-1	Ft. Wayne Pistons	1948	Minneapolis Lakers	3-1	Rochester Royals
1943	Sheboygan Redskins	2-1	Ft. Wayne Pistons	1949	Anderson Packers	3-0	Oshkosh All-Stars

NBA All-Star Game

The NBA staged its first All-Star Game before 10,094 at Boston Garden on March 2, 1951. From that year on, the game has matched the best players in the East against the best in the West. Winning coaches are listed first. East leads series, 31-18.

Multiple MVP winners: Bob Pettit (4); Michael Jordan and Oscar Robertson (3); Bob Cousy, Julius Erving, Magic Johnson, Karl Malone and Isiah Thomas (2).

Year		Host	Coaches	Most Valuable Player
1951	East 111, West 94	Boston	Joe Lapchick, John Kundla	Ed Macauley, Boston
1952	East 108, West 91	Boston	Al Cervi, John Kundla	Paul Arizin, Philadelphia
1953	West 79, East 75	Ft. Wayne	John Kundla, Joe Lapchick	George Mikan, Minneapolis
1954	East 98, West 93 (OT)	New York	Joe Lapchick, John Kundla	Bob Cousy, Boston
1955	East 100, West 91	New York	Al Cervi, Charley Eckman	Bill Sharman, Boston
1956	West 108, East 94	Rochester	Charley Eckman, George Senesky	Bob Pettit, St. Louis
1957	East 109, West 97	Boston	Red Auerbach, Bobby Wanzer	Bob Cousy, Boston
1958	East 130, West 118	St. Louis	Red Auerbach, Alex Hannum	Bob Pettit, St. Louis
1959	West 124, East 108	Detroit	Ed Macauley, Red Auerbach	Bob Pettit, St. Louis & Elgin Baylor, Minneapolis
1960	East 125, West 115	Philadelphia	Red Auerbach, Ed Macauley	Wilt Chamberlain, Philadelphia
1961	West 153, East 131	Syracuse	Paul Seymour, Red Auerbach	Oscar Robertson, Cincinnati
1962	West 150, East 130	St. Louis	Fred Schaus, Red Auerbach	Bob Pettit, St. Louis
1963	East 115, West 108	Los Angeles	Red Auerbach, Fred Schaus	Bill Russell, Boston
1964	East 111, West 107	Boston	Red Auerbach, Fred Schaus	Oscar Robertson, Cincinnati
1965	East 124, West 123	St. Louis	Red Auerbach, Alex Hannum	Jerry Lucas, Cincinnati
1966	East 137, West 94	Cincinnati	Red Auerbach, Fred Schaus	Adrian Smith, Cincinnati
1967	West 135, East 120	San Francisco	Fred Schaus, Red Auerbach	Rick Barry, San Francisco
1968	East 144, West 124	New York	Alex Hannum, Bill Sharman	Hal Greer, Philadelphia
1969	East 123, West 112	Baltimore	Gene Shue, Richie Guerin	Oscar Robertson, Cincinnati
1970	East 142, West 135	Philadelphia	Red Holzman, Richie Guerin	Willis Reed, New York
1971	West 108, East 107	San Diego	Larry Costello, Red Holzman	Lenny Wilkens, Seattle
1972	West 112, East 110	Los Angeles	Bill Sharman, Tom Heinsohn	Jerry West, Los Angeles
1973	East 104, West 84	Chicago	Tom Heinsohn, Bill Sharman	Dave Cowens, Boston
1974	West 134, East 123	Seattle	Larry Costello, Tom Heinsohn	Bob Lanier, Detroit
1975	East 108, West 102	Phoenix	K.C. Jones, Al Attles	Walt Frazier, New York
1976	East 123, West 109	Philadelphia	Tom Heinsohn, Al Attles	Dave Bing, Washington
1977	West 125, East 124	Milwaukee	Larry Brown, Gene Shue	Julius Erving, Philadelphia
1978	East 133, West 125	Atlanta	Billy Cunningham, Jack Ramsay	Randy Smith, Buffalo
1979	West 134, East 129	Detroit	Lenny Wilkens, Dick Motta	David Thompson, Denver
1980	East 144, West 136 (OT)	Washington	Billy Cunningham, Lenny Wilkens	George Gervin, San Antonio
1981	East 123, West 120	Cleveland	Billy Cunningham, John MacLeod	Nate Archibald, Boston
1982	East 120, West 118	New Jersey	Bill Fitch, Pat Riley	Larry Bird, Boston
1983	East 132, West 123	Los Angeles	Billy Cunningham, Pat Riley	Julius Erving, Philadelphia
1984	East 154, West 145 (OT)	Denver	K.C. Jones, Frank Layden	Isiah Thomas, Detroit
1985	West 140, East 129	Indiana	Pat Riley, K.C. Jones	Ralph Sampson, Houston
1986	East 139, West 132	Dallas	K.C. Jones, Pat Riley	Isiah Thomas, Detroit
1987	West 154, East 149 (OT)	Seattle	Pat Riley, K.C. Jones	Tom Chambers, Seattle
1988	East 138, West 133	Chicago	Mike Fratello, Pat Riley	Michael Jordan, Chicago
1989	West 143, East 134	Houston	Pat Riley, Lenny Wilkens	Karl Malone, Utah
1990	East 130, West 113	Miami	Chuck Daly, Pat Riley	Magic Johnson, LA Lakers
1991	East 116, West 114	Charlotte	Chris Ford, Rick Adelman	Charles Barkley, Philadelphia
1992	West 153, East 113	Orlando	Don Nelson, Phil Jackson	Magic Johnson, LA Lakers
1993	West 135, East 132 (OT)	Salt Lake City	Paul Westphal, Pat Riley	Karl Malone, Utah & John Stockton, Utah
1994	East 127, West 118	Minneapolis	Lenny Wilkens, George Karl	Scottie Pippen, Chicago
1995	West 139, East 112	Phoenix	Paul Westphal, Brian Hill	Mitch Richmond, Sacramento
1996	East 129, West 118	San Antonio	Phil Jackson, George Karl	Michael Jordan, Chicago
1997	East 132, West 120	Cleveland	Doug Collins, Rudy Tomjanovich	Glen Rice, Charlotte
1998	East 135, West 114	New York	Larry Bird, George Karl	Michael Jordan, Chicago
1999	Not held–due to lockout			
2000	West 137, East 126	Oakland	Jeff Van Gundy, Phil Jackson	Tim Duncan, San Antonio & Shaquille O'Neal, LA Lakers

NBA Franchise Origins

Here is what the current 29 teams in the National Basketball Association have to show for the years they have put in as members of the National Basketball League (NBL), Basketball Association of America (BAA), the NBA, and the American Basketball Association (ABA). League titles are noted by year won.

Western Conference

	First Season		League Titles	Franchise Stops
Dallas Mavericks	1980-81	(NBA)	None	•Dallas (1980–)
Denver Nuggets	1967-68	(ABA)	None	•Denver (1967–)
Golden St. Warriors	1946-47	(BAA)	1 BAA (1947) 2 NBA (1956,75)	•Philadelphia (1946-62) San Francisco (1962-71) Oakland (1971–)
Houston Rockets	1967-68	(NBA)	2 NBA (1994-95)	•San Diego (1967-71) Houston (1971–)
Los Angeles Clippers	1970-71	(NBA)	None	•Buffalo (1970-78) San Diego (1978-84) Los Angeles (1984–)
Los Angeles Lakers	1947-48	(NBL)	1 NBL (1948) 1 BAA (1949) 11 NBA (1950,52-54,72, 80,82,85,87-88,00)	•Minneapolis (1947-60) Los Angeles (1960-67) Inglewood, CA (1967-99) Los Angeles (1999–)
Minnesota Timberwolves	1989-90	(NBA)	None	•Minneapolis (1989–)
Phoenix Suns	1968-69	(NBA)	None	•Phoenix (1968–)
Portland Trail Blazers	1970-71	(NBA)	1 NBA (1977)	•Portland (1970–)
Sacramento Kings	1945-46	(NBL)	1 NBL (1946) 1 NBA (1951)	•Rochester, NY (1945-58) Cincinnati (1958-72) KC-Omaha (1972-75) Kansas City (1975-85) Sacramento (1985–)
San Antonio Spurs	1967-68	(ABA)	1 NBA (1999)	•Dallas (1967-73) San Antonio (1973–)
Seattle SuperSonics	1967-68	(NBA)	1 NBA (1979)	•Seattle (1967–)
Utah Jazz	1974-75	(NBA)	None	•New Orleans (1974-79) Salt Lake City (1979–)
Vancouver Grizzlies	1995-96	(NBA)	None	•Vancouver (1995–)

Eastern Conference

	First Season		League Titles	Franchise Stops
Atlanta Hawks	1946-47	(NBL)	1 NBA (1958)	•Tri-Cities (1946-51) Milwaukee (1951-55) St. Louis (1955-68) Atlanta (1968–)
Boston Celtics	1946-47	(BAA)	16 NBA (1957,59-66,68-69 74,76,81,84,86)	•Boston (1946–)
Charlotte Hornets	1988-89	(NBA)	None	•Charlotte (1988–)
Chicago Bulls	1966-67	(NBA)	6 NBA (1991-93,96-98)	•Chicago (1966–)
Cleveland Cavaliers	1970-71	(NBA)	None	•Cleveland (1970-74) Richfield, OH (1974-94) Cleveland (1994–)
Detroit Pistons	1941-42	(NBL)	2 NBL (1944-45) 2 NBA (1989-90)	•Ft. Wayne, IN (1941-57) Detroit (1957-78) Pontiac, MI (1978-88) Auburn Hills, MI (1988–)
Indiana Pacers	1967-68	(ABA)	3 ABA (1970,72-73)	•Indianapolis (1967–)
Miami Heat	1988-89	(NBA)	None	•Miami (1988–)
Milwaukee Bucks	1968-69	(NBA)	1 NBA (1971)	•Milwaukee (1968–)
New Jersey Nets	1967-68	(ABA)	2 ABA (1974,76)	•Teaneck, NJ (1967-68) Commack, NY (1968-69) W. Hempstead, NY (1969-71) Uniondale, NY (1971-77) Piscataway, NJ (1977-81) E. Rutherford, NJ (1981–)
New York Knicks	1946-47	(BAA)	2 NBA (1970,73)	•New York (1946–)
Orlando Magic	1989-90	(NBA)	None	•Orlando, FL (1989–)
Philadelphia 76ers	1949-50	(NBA)	3 NBA (1955,67,83)	•Syracuse, NY (1949-63) Philadelphia (1963–)
Toronto Raptors	1995-96	(NBA)	None	•Toronto (1995–)
Washington Wizards	1961-62	(NBA)	1 NBA (1978)	•Chicago (1961-63) Baltimore (1963-73) Landover, MD (1973–)

Note: The Tri-Cities Blackhawks represented Moline and Rock Island, Ill., and Davenport, Iowa.

The Growth of the NBA

Of the 11 franchises that comprised the Basketball Association of America (BAA) at the start of the 1946-47 season, only three remain—the Boston Celtics, New York Knickerbockers and Golden State Warriors (originally Philadelphia Warriors).

Just before the start of the 1948-49 season, four teams from the more established **National Basketball League** (NBL)— the Ft. Wayne Pistons (now Detroit), Indianapolis Jets, Minneapolis Lakers (now Los Angeles) and Rochester Royals (now Sacramento Kings)—joined the BAA.

A year later, the six remaining NBL franchises—Anderson (Ind.), Denver, Sheboygan (Wisc.), the Syracuse Nationals (now Philadelphia 76ers), Tri-Cities Blackhawks (now Atlanta Hawks) and Waterloo (Iowa)—joined along with the new Indianapolis Olympians and the BAA became the 17-team **National Basketball Association**.

The NBA was down to 10 teams by the 1950-51 season and slipped to eight by 1954-55 with Boston, New York, Philadelphia and Syracuse in the Eastern Division, and Ft. Wayne, Milwaukee (formerly Tri-Cities), Minneapolis and Rochester in the West.

By 1960, five of those surviving eight teams had moved to other cities but by the end of the decade the NBA was a 14-team league. It also had a rival, the **American Basketball Association**, which began play in 1967 with a red, white and blue ball, a three-point line and 11 teams. After a nine-year run, the ABA merged four clubs—the Denver Nuggets, Indiana Pacers, New York Nets and San Antonio Spurs—with the NBA following the 1975-76 season. The NBA adopted the three-point play in 1979-80.

Expansion/Merger Timetable

For teams currently in NBA.

1948—Added NBL's Ft. Wayne Pistons (now Detroit), Minneapolis Lakers (now Los Angeles) and Rochester Royals (now Sacramento Kings); **1949**—Syracuse Nationals (now Philadelphia 76ers) and Tri-Cities Blackhawks (now Atlanta Hawks).

1961—Chicago Packers (now Washington Wizards); **1966**—Chicago Bulls; **1967**—San Diego Rockets (now Houston) and Seattle SuperSonics; **1968**—Milwaukee Bucks and Phoenix Suns.

1970—Buffalo Braves (now Los Angeles Clippers), Cleveland Cavaliers and Portland Trail Blazers; **1974**—New Orleans Jazz (now Utah); **1976**—added ABA's Denver Nuggets, Indiana Pacers, New York Nets (now New Jersey) and San Antonio Spurs.

1980—Dallas Mavericks; **1988**—Charlotte Hornets and Miami Heat; **1989**—Minnesota Timberwolves and Orlando Magic.

1995—Toronto Raptors and Vancouver Grizzlies.

City and Nickname Changes

1951—Tri-Cities Blackhawks, who divided home games between Moline and Rock Island, Ill., and Davenport, Iowa, move to Milwaukee and become the Hawks; **1955**—Milwaukee Hawks move to St. Louis; **1957**—Ft. Wayne Pistons move to Detroit, while Rochester Royals move to Cincinnati.

1960—Minneapolis Lakers move to Los Angeles; **1962**—Chicago Packers renamed Zephyrs, while Philadelphia Warriors move to San Francisco; **1963**—Chicago Zephyrs move to Baltimore and become Bullets, while Syracuse Nationals move to Philadelphia and become 76ers; **1968**—St. Louis Hawks move to Atlanta.

1971—San Diego Rockets move to Houston, while San Francisco Warriors move to Oakland and become Golden State Warriors; **1972**—Cincinnati Royals move to Midwest, divide home games between Kansas City, Mo., and Omaha, Neb., and become Kings; **1973**—Baltimore Bullets move to Landover, Md., outside Washington and become Capital Bullets; **1974**—Capital Bullets renamed Washington Bullets; **1975**—KC-Omaha Kings settle in Kansas City; **1977**—New York Nets move from Uniondale, N.Y., to Piscataway, N.J. (later East Rutherford) and become New Jersey Nets; **1978**—Buffalo Braves move to San Diego and become Clippers; **1979**—New Orleans Jazz move to Salt Lake City and become Utah Jazz.

1984—San Diego Clippers move to Los Angeles; **1985**—Kansas City Kings move to Sacramento; **1997**—Washington Bullets become Washington Wizards.

Defunct NBA Teams

Teams that once played in the BAA and NBA, but no longer exist.

Anderson (Ind.)—Packers (1949-50); **Baltimore**—Bullets (1947-55); **Chicago**—Stags (1946-50); **Cleveland**—Rebels (1946-47); **Denver**—Nuggets (1949-50); **Detroit**—Falcons (1946-47); **Indianapolis**—Jets (1948-49) and Olympians (1949-53); **Pittsburgh**—Ironmen (1946-47); **Providence**—Steamrollers (1946-49); **St. Louis**—Bombers (1946-50); **Sheboygan (Wisc.)**—Redskins (1949-50); **Toronto**—Huskies (1946-47); **Washington**—Capitols (1946-51); **Waterloo (Iowa)**—Hawks (1949-50).

ABA Teams (1967-76)

Anaheim—Amigos (1967-68, moved to LA); **Baltimore**—Claws (1975, never played); **Carolina**—Cougars (1969-74, moved to St. Louis); **Dallas**—Chaparrals (1967-73, called Texas Chaparrals in 1970-71, moved to San Antonio); **Denver**—Rockets (1967-76, renamed Nuggets in 1974-76); **Miami**—Floridians (1968-72, called simply Floridians from 1970-72).

Houston—Mavericks (1967-69, moved to North Carolina); **Indiana**—Pacers (1967-76); **Kentucky**—Colonels (1967-76); **Los Angeles**—Stars (1968-70, moved to Utah); **Memphis**—Pros (1970-75, renamed Tams in 1972 and Sounds in 1974, moved to Baltimore); **Minnesota**—Muskies (1967-68, moved to Miami) and Pipers (1968-69, moved back to Pittsburgh); **New Jersey**—Americans (1967-68, moved to New York).

New Orleans—Buccaneers (1967-70, moved to Memphis); **New York**—Nets (1968-76); **Oakland**—Oaks (1967-69, moved to Washington); **Pittsburgh**—Pipers (1967-68, moved to Minnesota), Pipers (1969-72, renamed Condors in 1970); **St. Louis**—Spirits of St. Louis (1974-76); **San Antonio**—Spurs (1973-76); **San Diego**—Conquistadors (1972-75, renamed Sails in 1975); **Utah**—Stars (1970-75); **Virginia**—Squires (1970-76); **Washington**—Caps (1969-70, moved to Virginia).

Annual NBA Leaders
Scoring

Decided by total points from 1947-69, and per game average since 1970. A lockout in 1999 shortened the regular season to 50 games.

Multiple winners: Michael Jordan (10); Wilt Chamberlain (7); George Gervin (4); Neil Johnston, Bob McAdoo and George Mikan (3); Kareem Abdul-Jabbar, Paul Arizin, Adrian Dantley, Shaquille O'Neal and Bob Pettit (2).

Year		Gm	Pts	Avg	Year		Gm	Pts	Avg
1947	Joe Fulks, Phi	60	1389	23.2	1974	Bob McAdoo, Buf	74	2261	30.6
1948	Max Zaslofsky, Chi	48	1007	21.0	1975	Bob McAdoo, Buf	82	2831	34.5
1949	George Mikan, Mpls	60	1698	28.3	1976	Bob McAdoo, Buf	78	2427	31.1
					1977	Pete Maravich, NO	73	2273	31.1
1950	George Mikan, Mpls	68	1865	27.4	1978	George Gervin, SA	82	2232	27.2
1951	George Mikan, Mpls	68	1932	28.4	1979	George Gervin, SA	80	2365	29.6
1952	Paul Arizin, Phi	66	1674	25.4					
1953	Neil Johnston, Phi	70	1564	22.3	1980	George Gervin, SA	78	2585	33.1
1954	Neil Johnston, Phi	72	1759	24.4	1981	Adrian Dantley, Utah	80	2452	30.7
1955	Neil Johnston, Phi	72	1631	22.7	1982	George Gervin, SA	79	2551	32.3
1956	Bob Pettit, St.L	72	1849	25.7	1983	Alex English, Den	82	2326	28.4
1957	Paul Arizin, Phi	71	1817	25.6	1984	Adrian Dantley, Utah	79	2418	30.6
1958	George Yardley, Det	72	2001	27.8	1985	Bernard King, NY	55	1809	32.9
1959	Bob Pettit, St.L	72	2105	29.2	1986	Dominique Wilkins, Atl	78	2366	30.3
					1987	Michael Jordan, Chi	82	3041	37.1
1960	Wilt Chamberlain, Phi	72	2707	37.6	1988	Michael Jordan, Chi	82	2868	35.0
1961	Wilt Chamberlain, Phi	79	3033	38.4	1989	Michael Jordan, Chi	81	2633	32.5
1962	Wilt Chamberlain, Phi	80	4029	50.4					
1963	Wilt Chamberlain, SF	80	3586	44.8	1990	Michael Jordan, Chi	82	2753	33.6
1964	Wilt Chamberlain, SF	80	2948	36.9	1991	Michael Jordan, Chi	82	2580	31.5
1965	Wilt Chamberlain, SF-Phi	73	2534	34.7	1992	Michael Jordan, Chi	80	2404	30.1
1966	Wilt Chamberlain, Phi	79	2649	33.5	1993	Michael Jordan, Chi	78	2541	32.6
1967	Rick Barry, SF	78	2775	35.6	1994	David Robinson, SA	80	2383	29.8
1968	Dave Bing, Det	79	2142	27.1	1995	Shaquille O'Neal, Orl	79	2315	29.3
1969	Elvin Hayes, SD	82	2327	28.4	1996	Shaquille O'Neal, Orl	82	2491	30.4
					1997	Michael Jordan, Chi	82	2431	29.7
1970	Jerry West, LA	74	2309	31.2	1998	Michael Jordan, Chi	82	2357	28.7
1971	Lew Alcindor, Mil	82	2596	31.7	1999	Allen Iverson, Phi	48	1284	26.8
1972	Kareem Abdul-Jabbar, Mil	81	2822	34.8					
1973	Nate Archibald, KC-Omaha	80	2719	34.0	2000	Shaquille O'Neal, LAL	79	2344	29.7

Note: Lew Alcindor changed his name to Kareem Abdul-Jabbar after the 1970-71 season.

Rebounds

Decided by total rebounds from 1951-69 and per game average since 1970.

Multiple winners: Wilt Chamberlain (11); Dennis Rodman (7); Moses Malone (6); Bill Russell (4); Elvin Hayes and Hakeem Olajuwon (2).

Year		Gm	No	Avg	Year		Gm	No	Avg
1951	Dolph Schayes, Syr	66	1080	16.4	1976	Kareem Abdul-Jabbar, LA	82	1383	16.9
1952	Larry Foust, Ft. Wayne	66	880	13.3	1977	Bill Walton, Port	65	934	14.4
	& Mel Hutchins, Mil	66	880	13.3	1978	Len Robinson, NO	82	1288	15.7
1953	George Mikan, Mpls	70	1007	14.4	1979	Moses Malone, Hou	82	1444	17.6
1954	Harry Gallatin, NY	72	1098	15.3					
1955	Neil Johnston, Phi	72	1085	15.1	1980	Swen Nater, SD	81	1216	15.0
1956	Bob Pettit, St.L	72	1164	16.2	1981	Moses Malone, Hou	80	1180	14.8
1957	Maurice Stokes, Roch	72	1256	17.4	1982	Moses Malone, Hou	81	1188	14.7
1958	Bill Russell, Bos	69	1564	22.7	1983	Moses Malone, Phi	78	1194	15.3
1959	Bill Russell, Bos	70	1612	23.0	1984	Moses Malone, Phi	71	950	13.4
					1985	Moses Malone, Phi	79	1031	13.1
1960	Wilt Chamberlain, Phi	72	1941	27.0	1986	Bill Laimbeer, Det	82	1075	13.1
1961	Wilt Chamberlain, Phi	79	2149	27.2	1987	Charles Barkley, Phi	68	994	14.6
1962	Wilt Chamberlain, Phi	80	2052	25.7	1988	Michael Cage, LA Clippers	72	938	13.0
1963	Wilt Chamberlain, SF	80	1946	24.3	1989	Hakeem Olajuwon, Hou	82	1105	13.5
1964	Bill Russell, Bos	78	1930	24.7					
1965	Bill Russell, Bos	78	1878	24.1	1990	Hakeem Olajuwon, Hou	82	1149	14.0
1966	Wilt Chamberlain, Phi	79	1943	24.6	1991	David Robinson, SA	82	1063	13.0
1967	Wilt Chamberlain, Phi	81	1957	24.2	1992	Dennis Rodman, Det	82	1530	18.7
1968	Wilt Chamberlain, Phi	82	1952	23.8	1993	Dennis Rodman, Det	62	1232	18.3
1969	Wilt Chamberlain, LA	81	1712	21.1	1994	Dennis Rodman, SA	79	1132	17.3
					1995	Dennis Rodman, SA	49	823	16.8
1970	Elvin Hayes, SD	82	1386	16.9	1996	Dennis Rodman, Chi	64	952	14.9
1971	Wilt Chamberlain, LA	82	1493	18.2	1997	Dennis Rodman, Chi	55	883	16.1
1972	Wilt Chamberlain, LA	82	1572	19.2	1998	Dennis Rodman, Chi	80	1201	15.0
1973	Wilt Chamberlain, LA	82	1526	18.6	1999	Chris Webber, Sac	42	545	13.0
1974	Elvin Hayes, Cap*	81	1463	18.1	2000	Dikembe Mutombo, Atl	82	1157	14.1
1975	Wes Unseld, Wash	73	1077	14.8					

*The Baltimore Bullets moved to Landover, Md. in 1973-74 and became first the Capital Bullets, then the Washington Bullets in 1974-75.

Assists

Decided by total assists from 1952-69 and per game average since 1970.

Multiple winners: John Stockton (9); Bob Cousy (8); Oscar Robertson (6); Magic Johnson and Kevin Porter (4); Jason Kidd, Andy Phillip and Guy Rodgers (2).

Year		No	Year		No	Year		No
1947	Ernie Calverly, Prov	.202	1965	Oscar Robertson, Cin	.861	1983	Magic Johnson, LA	.10.5
1948	Howie Dallmar, Phi	.120	1966	Oscar Robertson, Cin	.847	1984	Magic Johnson, LA	.13.1
1949	Bob Davies, Roch	.321	1967	Guy Rodgers, Chi	.908	1985	Isiah Thomas, Det	.13.9
1950	Dick McGuire, NY	.386	1968	Wilt Chamberlain, Phi	.702	1986	Magic Johnson, Lakers	.12.6
1951	Andy Phillip, Phi	.414	1969	Oscar Robertson, Cin	.772	1987	Magic Johnson, Lakers	.12.2
1952	Andy Phillip, Phi	.539				1988	John Stockton, Utah	.13.8
1953	Bob Cousy, Bos	.547	1970	Lenny Wilkens, Sea	.9.1	1989	John Stockton, Utah	.13.6
1954	Bob Cousy, Bos	.518	1971	Norm Van Lier, Chi	.10.1			
1955	Bob Cousy, Bos	.557	1972	Jerry West, LA	.9.7	1990	John Stockton, Utah	.14.5
1956	Bob Cousy, Bos	.642	1973	Nate Archibald, KC-O	.11.4	1991	John Stockton, Utah	.14.2
1957	Bob Cousy, Bos	.478	1974	Ernie DiGregorio, Buf	.8.2	1992	John Stockton, Utah	.13.7
1958	Bob Cousy, Bos	.463	1975	Kevin Porter, Wash	.8.0	1993	John Stockton, Utah	.12.0
1959	Bob Cousy, Bos	.557	1976	Slick Watts, Sea	.8.1	1994	John Stockton, Utah	.12.6
1960	Bob Cousy, Bos	.715	1977	Don Buse, Ind	.8.5	1995	John Stockton, Utah	.12.3
1961	Oscar Robertson, Cin	.690	1978	Kevin Porter, Det-NJ	.10.2	1996	John Stockton, Utah	.11.2
1962	Oscar Robertson, Cin	.899	1979	Kevin Porter, Det	.13.4	1997	Mark Jackson, Den-Ind	.11.4
1963	Guy Rodgers, SF	.825	1980	M.R. Richardson, NY	.10.1	1998	Rod Strickland, Wash	.10.5
1964	Oscar Robertson, Cin	.868	1981	Kevin Porter, Wash	.9.1	1999	Jason Kidd, Pho	.10.8
			1982	Johnny Moore, SA	.9.6	2000	Jason Kidd, Pho	.10.1

Field Goal Percentage

Multiple winners: Wilt Chamberlain (9); Artis Gilmore and Shaquille O'Neal (4); Neil Johnston (3); Bob Feerick, Johnny Green, Alex Groza, Cedric Maxwell, Kevin McHale, Gheorghe Muresan, Kenny Sears and Buck Williams (2).

Year		Pct	Year		Pct	Year		Pct
1947	Bob Feerick, Wash	.401	1965	W. Chamberlain, SF-Phi	.510	1983	Artis Gilmore, SA	.626
1948	Bob Feerick, Wash	.340	1966	Wilt Chamberlain, Phi	.540	1984	Artis Gilmore, SA	.631
1949	Arnie Risen, Roch	.423	1967	Wilt Chamberlain, Phi	.683	1985	James Donaldson, LAC	.637
1950	Alex Groza, Indpls	.478	1968	Wilt Chamberlain, Phi	.595	1986	Steve Johnson, SA	.632
1951	Alex Groza, Indpls	.470	1969	Wilt Chamberlain, LA	.583	1987	Kevin McHale, Bos	.604
1952	Paul Arizin, Phi	.448	1970	Johnny Green, Cin	.559	1988	Kevin McHale, Bos	.604
1953	Neil Johnston, Phi	.452	1971	Johnny Green, Cin	.587	1989	Dennis Rodman, Det.	.595
1954	Ed Macauley, Bos	.486	1972	Wilt Chamberlain, LA	.649			
1955	Larry Foust, Ft.W	.487	1973	Wilt Chamberlain, LA	.727	1990	Mark West, Pho.	.625
1956	Neil Johnston, Phi	.457	1974	Bob McAdoo, Buf	.547	1991	Buck Williams, Port	.602
1957	Neil Johnston, Phi.	.447	1975	Don Nelson, Bos	.539	1992	Buck Williams, Port	.604
1958	Jack Twyman, Cin	.452	1976	Wes Unseld, Wash	.561	1993	Cedric Ceballos, Pho	.576
1959	Kenny Sears, NY	.490	1977	K. Abdul-Jabbar, LA	.579	1994	Shaquille O'Neal, Orl	.599
1960	Kenny Sears, NY	.477	1978	Bobby Jones, Den	.578	1995	Chris Gatling, G.St	.633
1961	Wilt Chamberlain, Phi	.509	1979	Cedric Maxwell, Bos	.584	1996	Gheorghe Muresan, Wash.	.584
1962	Walt Bellamy, Chi	.519	1980	Cedric Maxwell, Bos	.609	1997	Gheorghe Muresan, Wash.	.604
1963	Wilt Chamberlain, SF	.528	1981	Artis Gilmore, Chi.	.670	1998	Shaquille O'Neal, LAL.	.584
1964	Jerry Lucas, Cin	.527	1982	Artis Gilmore, Chi.	.652	1999	Shaquille O'Neal, LAL.	.576
						2000	Shaquille O'Neal, LAL.	.574

Free Throw Percentage

Multiple winners: Bill Sharman (7); Rick Barry (6); Larry Bird (4); Mark Price and Dolph Schayes (3); Mahmoud Abdul-Rauf, Larry Costello, Ernie DiGregorio, Bob Feerick, Kyle Macy, Reggie Miller, Calvin Murphy, Oscar Robertson and Larry Siegfried (2).

Year		Pct	Year		Pct	Year		Pct
1947	Fred Scolari, Wash	.811	1965	Larry Costello, Phi	.877	1983	Calvin Murphy, Hou	.920
1948	Bob Feerick, Wash	.788	1966	Larry Siegfried, Bos	.881	1984	Larry Bird, Bos	.888
1949	Bob Feerick, Wash	.859	1967	Adrian Smith, Cin	.903	1985	Kyle Macy, Pho	.907
1950	Max Zaslofsky, Chi	.843	1968	Oscar Robertson, Cin	.873	1986	Larry Bird, Bos	.896
1951	Joe Fulks, Phi	.855	1969	Larry Siegfried, NY	.864	1987	Larry Bird, Bos	.910
1952	Bob Wanzer, Roch	.904	1970	Flynn Robinson, Mil	.898	1988	Jack Sikma, Mil	.922
1953	Bill Sharman, Bos	.850	1971	Chet Walker, Chi	.859	1989	Magic Johnson, LAL	.911
1954	Bill Sharman, Bos	.844	1972	Jack Marin, Bal	.894			
1955	Bill Sharman, Bos	.897	1973	Rick Barry, G.St.	.902	1990	Larry Bird, Bos	.930
1956	Bill Sharman, Bos	.867	1974	Ernie DiGregorio, Buf	.902	1991	Reggie Miller, Ind	.918
1957	Bill Sharman, Bos	.905	1975	Rick Barry, G.St.	.904	1992	Mark Price, Cle	.947
1958	Dolph Schayes, Syr	.904	1976	Rick Barry, G.St.	.923	1993	Mark Price, Cle	.948
1959	Bill Sharman, Bos	.932	1977	Ernie DiGregorio, Buf	.945	1994	M. Abdul-Rauf, Den	.956
1960	Dolph Schayes, Syr	.892	1978	Rick Barry, G.St.	.924	1995	Spud Webb, Sac	.934
1961	Bill Sharman, Bos	.921	1979	Rick Barry, Hou	.947	1996	M. Abdul-Rauf, Den	.930
1962	Dolph Schayes, Syr	.896	1980	Rick Barry, Hou	.935	1997	Mark Price, G.St.	.906
1963	Larry Costello, Syr	.881	1981	Calvin Murphy, Hou	.958	1998	Chris Mullin, Ind.	.939
1964	Oscar Robertson, Cin	.853	1982	Kyle Macy, Pho	.899	1999	Reggie Miller, Ind	.915
						2000	Jeff Hornacek, Utah	.950

Blocked Shots

Decided by per game average since 1973-74 season.

Multiple winners: Kareem Abdul-Jabbar and Mark Eaton (4); George Johnson, Dikembe Mutombo and Hakeem Olajuwon (3); Manute Bol and Alonzo Mourning (2).

Year		Gm	No	Avg
1974	Elmore Smith, LA	.81	393	4.85
1975	Kareem Abdul-Jabbar, Mil	.65	212	3.26
1976	Kareem Abdul-Jabbar, LA	.82	338	4.12
1977	Bill Walton, Port	.65	211	3.25
1978	George Johnson, NJ	.81	274	3.38
1979	Kareem Abdul-Jabbar, LA	.80	316	3.95
1980	Kareem Abdul-Jabbar, LA	.82	280	3.41
1981	George Johnson, SA	.82	278	3.39
1982	George Johnson, SA	.75	234	3.12
1983	Tree Rollins, Atl	.80	343	4.29
1984	Mark Eaton, Utah	.82	351	4.28
1985	Mark Eaton, Utah	.82	456	5.56
1986	Manute Bol, Wash	.80	397	4.96
1987	Mark Eaton, Utah	.79	321	4.06
1988	Mark Eaton, Utah	.82	304	3.71
1989	Manute Bol, G.St.	.80	345	4.31
1990	Akeem Olajuwon, Hou	.82	376	4.59
1991	Hakeem Olajuwon, Hou	.56	221	3.95
1992	David Robinson, SA	.68	305	4.49
1993	Hakeem Olajuwon, Hou	.82	342	4.17
1994	Dikembe Mutombo, Den	.82	336	4.10
1995	Dikembe Mutombo, Den	.82	321	3.91
1996	Dikembe Mutombo, Den	.74	332	4.49
1997	Shawn Bradley, Dal-NJ	.73	248	3.40
1998	Marcus Camby, Tor	.63	230	3.65
1999	Alonzo Mourning, Mia	.46	180	3.91
2000	Alonzo Mourning, Mia	.79	294	3.72

Note: Akeem Olajuwon changed the spelling of his first name to Hakeem during the 1990-91 season.

Steals

Decided by per game average since 1973-74 season.

Multiple winners: Michael Jordan, Micheal Ray Richardson and Alvin Robertson (3); Mookie Blaylock, Magic Johnson and John Stockton (2).

Year		Gm	No	Avg
1974	Larry Steele, Port	.81	217	2.68
1975	Rick Barry, G.St.	.80	228	2.85
1976	Slick Watts, Sea	.82	261	3.18
1977	Don Buse, Ind	.81	281	3.47
1978	Ron Lee, Pho	.82	225	2.74
1979	M.L. Carr, Det	.80	197	2.46
1980	Micheal Ray Richardson, NY	.82	265	3.23
1981	Magic Johnson, LA	.37	127	3.43
1982	Magic Johnson, LA	.78	208	2.67
1983	Micheal Ray Richardson, G. ST-NJ	.64	182	2.84
1984	Rickey Green, Utah	.81	215	2.65
1985	Micheal Ray Richardson, NJ	.82	243	2.96
1986	Alvin Robertson, SA	.82	301	3.67
1987	Alvin Robertson, SA	.81	260	3.21
1988	Michael Jordan, Chi	.82	259	3.16
1989	John Stockton, Utah	.82	263	3.21
1990	Michael Jordan, Chi	.82	227	2.77
1991	Alvin Robertson, SA	.81	246	3.04
1992	John Stockton, Utah	.82	244	2.98
1993	Michael Jordan, Chi	.78	221	2.83
1994	Nate McMillan, Sea	.73	216	2.96
1995	Scottie Pippen, Chi	.79	232	2.94
1996	Gary Payton, Sea	.81	231	2.85
1997	Mookie Blaylock, Atl	.78	212	2.72
1998	Mookie Blaylock, Atl	.70	183	2.61
1999	Kendall Gill, NJ	.50	134	2.68
2000	Eddie Jones, Cha	.72	192	2.67

All-Time NBA Regular Season Leaders

Through the 1999-2000 regular season.

CAREER

Players active in 1999-2000 in **bold** type.

Points

		Yrs	Gm	Pts	Avg
1	Kareem Abdul-Jabbar	20	1560	38,387	24.6
2	Wilt Chamberlain	14	1045	31,419	30.1
3	**Karl Malone**	15	1192	31,041	26.0
4	Michael Jordan	13	930	29,277	31.5
5	Moses Malone	19	1329	27,409	20.6
6	Elvin Hayes	16	1303	27,313	21.0
7	Oscar Robertson	14	1040	26,710	25.7
8	Dominique Wilkins	15	1074	26,668	24.8
9	John Havlicek	16	1270	26,395	20.8
10	**Hakeem Olajuwon**	16	1119	25,822	23.1
11	Alex English	15	1193	25,613	21.5
12	Jerry West	14	932	25,192	27.0
13	**Charles Barkley**	16	1073	23,757	22.1
14	**Patrick Ewing**	15	1039	23,665	22.8
15	Robert Parish	21	1611	23,334	14.5
16	Adrian Dantley	15	955	23,177	24.3
17	Elgin Baylor	14	846	23,149	27.4
18	Clyde Drexler	15	1086	22,195	20.4
19	Larry Bird	13	897	21,791	24.3
20	Hal Greer	15	1122	21,586	19.2
21	Walt Bellamy	14	1043	20,941	20.1
22	Bob Pettit	11	792	20,880	26.4
23	George Gervin	10	791	20,708	26.2
24	Tom Chambers	16	1107	20,049	18.1
25	**Reggie Miller**	13	1013	19,792	19.5
26	Bernard King	14	874	19,655	22.5
27	**Mitch Richmond**	12	875	19,639	22.4
28	Walter Davis	15	1033	19,521	18.9
29	**Terry Cummings**	18	1183	19,460	16.4
30	Bob Lanier	14	959	19,248	20.1

Scoring Average

Minimum of 400 games and 10,000 points.

		Yrs	Gm	Pts	Avg
1	Michael Jordan	13	930	29,277	31.5
2	Wilt Chamberlain	14	1045	31,419	30.1
3	**Shaquille O'Neal**	8	534	14,687	27.5
4	Elgin Baylor	14	846	23,149	27.4
5	Jerry West	14	932	25,192	27.0
6	Bob Pettit	11	792	20,880	26.4
7	George Gervin	10	791	20,708	26.2
8	**Karl Malone**	15	1192	31,041	26.0
9	Oscar Robertson	14	1040	26,710	25.7
10	Dominique Wilkins	15	1074	26,668	24.8
11	Kareem Abdul-Jabbar	20	1560	38,387	24.6
12	**David Robinson**	11	765	18,142	23.7
13	Larry Bird	13	897	21,791	24.3
14	Adrian Dantley	15	955	23,177	24.3
15	Pete Maravich	10	658	15,948	24.2
16	Rick Barry	10	794	18,395	23.2
17	**Hakeem Olajuwon**	16	1119	25,822	23.1
18	Paul Arizin	10	713	16,266	22.8
19	**Patrick Ewing**	15	1039	23,665	22.8
20	George Mikan	9	520	11,764	22.6
21	Bernard King	14	874	19,655	22.5
22	**Mitch Richmond**	12	875	19,639	22.4
23	**Charles Barkley**	16	1073	23,757	22.1
24	David Thompson	8	509	11,264	22.1
25	Bob McAdoo	14	852	18,787	22.1
26	Julius Erving	11	836	18,364	22.0
27	Alex English	15	1193	25,613	21.5
28	Elvin Hayes	16	1303	27,313	21.0
29	Billy Cunningham	9	654	13,626	20.8
30	John Havlicek	16	1270	26,395	20.8

NBA-ABA Top 20

Points

All-Time combined regular season scoring leaders, including ABA service (1968-76). NBA players with ABA experience are listed in CAPITAL letters. Players active during 1999-2000 are in **bold** type.

		Yrs	Pts	Avg
1	Kareem Abdul-Jabbar	20	38,387	24.6
2	Wilt Chamberlain	14	31,419	30.1
3	**Karl Malone**	15	31,041	26.0
4	JULIUS ERVING	16	30,026	24.2
5	MOSES MALONE	21	29,580	20.3
5	Michael Jordan	13	29,277	31.5
7	DAN ISSEL	15	27,482	22.6
8	Elvin Hayes	16	27,313	21.0
9	Oscar Robertson	14	26,710	25.7
10	Dominique Wilkins	15	26,668	24.8
11	GEORGE GERVIN	14	26,595	25.1
12	John Havlicek	16	26,395	20.8
13	**Hakeem Olajuwon**	16	25,822	23.1
14	Alex English	15	25,613	21.5
15	RICK BARRY	14	25,279	24.8
16	Jerry West	14	25,192	27.0
17	ARTIS GILMORE	17	24,941	18.8
18	**Charles Barkley**	16	23,757	22.1
19	**Patrick Ewing**	15	23,655	22.8
20	Robert Parish	21	23,334	14.5

ABA Totals: BARRY (4 yrs, 226 gm, 6884 pts, 30.5 avg); ERVING (5 yrs, 407 gm, 11,662 pts, 28.7 avg); GERVIN (4 yrs, 269 gm, 5887 pts, 21.9 avg); GILMORE (5 yrs, 420 gm, 9362 pts, 22.3 avg); ISSEL (6 yrs, 500 gm, 12,823 pts, 25.6 avg); MALONE (2 yrs, 126 gm, 2171 pts, 17.2 avg).

Field Goals

		Yrs	FG	Att	Pct
1	Kareem Abdul-Jabbar	20	15,837	28,307	.559
2	Wilt Chamberlain	14	12,681	23,497	.540
3	**Karl Malone**	15	11,432	21,777	.525
4	Elvin Hayes	16	10,976	24,272	.452
5	Michael Jordan	13	10,958	21,686	.505
6	Alex English	15	10,659	21,036	.507
7	John Havlicek	16	10,513	23,930	.439
8	**Hakeem Olajuwon**	16	10,272	20,005	.511
9	Dominique Wilkins	15	9,963	21,589	.461
10	Robert Parish	21	9,614	17,914	.537

Note: If field goals made in the ABA are included, consider these NBA-ABA totals: Julius Erving (11,818), Dan Issel (10,431), George Gervin (10,368), Moses Malone (10,277) and Rick Barry (9,695).

Free Throws

		Yrs	FT	Att	Pct
1	Moses Malone	19	8531	11,090	.769
2	**Karl Malone**	15	8100	11,027	.735
3	Oscar Robertson	14	7694	9,185	.838
4	Jerry West	14	7160	8,801	.814
5	Dolph Schayes	16	6979	8,273	.844
6	Adrian Dantley	15	6832	8,351	.818
7	Michael Jordan	13	6798	8,115	.838
8	Kareem Abdul-Jabbar	20	6712	9,304	.721
9	**Charles Barkley**	16	6349	8,643	.734
10	Bob Pettit	11	6182	8,119	.761

Note: If free throws made in the ABA are included, consider these totals: Moses Malone (9,018), Dan Issel (6,591), and Julius Erving (6,256).

Assists

		Yrs	Gm	No	Avg
1	**John Stockton**	16	1258	13,790	11.0
2	Magic Johnson	13	906	10,141	11.2
3	Oscar Robertson	14	1040	9,887	9.5
4	Isiah Thomas	13	979	9,061	9.3
5	**Mark Jackson**	13	1007	8,574	8.5
6	Maurice Cheeks	15	1101	7,392	6.7
7	Lenny Wilkens	15	1077	7,211	6.7
8	Bob Cousy	14	924	6,955	7.5
9	Guy Rodgers	12	892	6,917	7.8
10	**Kevin Johnson**	12	735	6,711	9.1

Rebounds

		Yrs	Gm	No	Avg
1	Wilt Chamberlain	14	1045	23,924	22.9
2	Bill Russell	13	963	21,620	22.5
3	Kareem Abdul-Jabbar	20	1560	17,440	11.2
4	Elvin Hayes	16	1303	16,279	12.5
5	Moses Malone	19	1329	16,212	12.2
6	Robert Parish	21	1611	14,715	9.1
7	Nate Thurmond	14	964	14,464	15.0
8	Walt Bellamy	14	1043	14,241	13.7
9	Wes Unseld	13	984	13,769	14.0
10	Buck Williams	17	1307	13,017	10.0

Note: If rebounds accumulated in the ABA are included, consider the following totals: Moses Malone (17,834) and Artis Gilmore (16,330).

Steals

		Yrs	Gm	No
1	**John Stockton**	16	1258	2844
2	Maurice Cheeks	15	1101	2310
3	Michael Jordan	13	930	2306
4	Clyde Drexler	15	1086	2207
5	Alvin Robertson	10	779	2112

Note: Steals have only been an official stat since the 1973-74 season.

Blocked Shots

		Yrs	Gm	No
1	**Hakeem Olajuwon**	16	1119	3652
2	Kareem Abdul-Jabbar	20	1560	3189
3	Mark Eaton	11	875	3064
4	**Patrick Ewing**	15	1039	2758
5	Tree Rollins	18	1156	2542

Note: Blocked shots have only been an official stat since the 1973-74 season. Also, note that if ABA records are included, consider the following block totals: Artis Gilmore (3,178).

Games Played

		Yrs	Career	Gm
1	Robert Parish	21	1976-97	1611
2	Kareem Abdul-Jabbar	20	1970-89	1560
3	Moses Malone	19	1976-95	1329
4	Buck Williams	17	1982-98	1307
5	Elvin Hayes	16	1969-84	1303

Note: If ABA records are included, consider the following game totals: Moses Malone (1,455) and Artis Gilmore (1,329).

Personal Fouls

		Yrs	Gm	Fouls	DQ
1	Kareem Abdul-Jabbar	20	1560	4657	48
2	Robert Parish	21	1611	4443	86
3	Buck Williams	17	1307	4267	58
4	Elvin Hayes	16	1303	4193	53
5	**Hakeem Olajuwon**	16	1119	4095	80

Note: If ABA records are included, consider the following personal foul totals: Artis Gilmore (4,529) and Caldwell Jones (4,436).

SINGLE SEASON

Scoring Average

		Season	Avg
1	Wilt Chamberlain, Phi	1961-62	50.4
2	Wilt Chamberlain, SF	1962-63	44.8
3	Wilt Chamberlain, Phi	1960-61	38.4
4	Elgin Baylor, LA	1961-62	38.3
5	Wilt Chamberlain, Phi	1959-60	37.6
6	Michael Jordan, Chi	1986-87	37.1
7	Wilt Chamberlain, SF	1963-64	36.9
8	Rick Barry, SF	1966-67	35.6
9	Michael Jordan, Chi	1987-88	35.0
10	Elgin Baylor, LA	1960-61	34.8
	Kareem Abdul-Jabbar, Mil	1971-72	34.8

Assists

		Season	Avg
1	John Stockton, Utah	1989-90	14.5
2	John Stockton, Utah	1990-91	14.2
3	Isiah Thomas, Det	1984-85	13.9
4	John Stockton, Utah	1987-88	13.8
5	John Stockton, Utah	1991-92	13.7
6	John Stockton, Utah	1988-89	13.6
7	Kevin Porter, Det	1978-79	13.4
8	Magic Johnson, LA Lakers	1983-84	13.1
9	Magic Johnson, LA Lakers	1988-89	12.8
10	Magic Johnson, LA Lakers	1984-85	12.6
	John Stockton, Utah	1993-94	12.6

Field Goal Pct.

		Season	Pct
1	Wilt Chamberlain, LA	1972-73	.727
2	Wilt Chamberlain, SF	1966-67	.683
3	Artis Gilmore, Chi	1980-81	.670
4	Artis Gilmore, Chi	1981-82	.652
5	Wilt Chamberlain, LA	1971-72	.649

Rebounds

		Season	Avg
1	Wilt Chamberlain, Phi	1960-61	27.2
2	Wilt Chamberlain, Phi	1959-60	27.0
3	Wilt Chamberlain, Phi	1961-62	25.7
4	Bill Russell, Bos	1963-64	24.7
5	Wilt Chamberlain, Phi	1965-66	24.6

Free Throw Pct.

		Season	Pct
1	Calvin Murphy, Hou	1980-81	.958
2	Mahmoud Abdul-Rauf, Den	1993-94	.956
3	Mark Price, Cle	1992-93	.948
4	Mark Price, Cle	1991-92	.947
	Rick Barry, Hou	1978-79	.947

Blocked Shots

		Season	Avg
1	Mark Eaton, Utah	1984-85	5.56
2	Manute Bol, Wash	1985-86	4.96
3	Elmore Smith, LA	1973-74	4.85
4	Mark Eaton, Utah	1985-86	4.61
5	Hakeem Olajuwon, Hou	1989-90	4.59

3-Pt Field Goal Pct.

		Season	Pct
1	Steve Kerr, Chi	1994-95	.524
2	Jon Sundvold, Mia	1988-89	.522
3	Tim Legler, Wash	1995-96	.522
4	Steve Kerr, Chi	1995-96	.515
5	Detlef Schrempf, Sea	1994-95	.514

Steals

		Season	Avg
1	Alvin Robertson, SA	1985-86	3.67
2	Don Buse, Ind	1976-77	3.47
3	Magic Johnson, LA Lakers	1980-81	3.43
4	Micheal Ray Richardson, NY	1979-80	3.23
5	Alvin Robertson, SA	1986-87	3.21

SINGLE GAME

Points

	Date	FG-FT	Pts
Wilt Chamberlain, Phi vs NY	3/2/62	36-28–	100
Wilt Chamberlain, Phi vs LA***	12/8/61	31-16–	78
Wilt Chamberlain, Phi vs Chi	1/13/62	29-15–	73
Wilt Chamberlain, SF at NY	11/16/62	29-15–	73
David Thompson, Den at Det	4/9/78	28-17–	73
Wilt Chamberlain, SF at LA	11/3/62	29-14–	72
Elgin Baylor, LA at NY	11/15/60	28-15–	71
David Robinson, SA at LAC	4/24/94	26-18–	71
Wilt Chamberlain, SF at Syr	3/10/63	27-16–	70
Michael Jordan, Chi at Cle*	3/28/90	23-21–	69
Wilt Chamberlain, Phi at Chi	12/16/67	30- 8–	68
Pete Maravich, NO at NYK	2/25/77	26-16–	68
Wilt Chamberlain, Phi vs NY	3/9/61	27-13–	67
Wilt Chamberlain, Phi at St. L	2/17/62	26-15–	67
Wilt Chamberlain, Phi vs NY	2/25/62	25-17–	67
Wilt Chamberlain, SF vs LA	1/11/63	28-11–	67
Wilt Chamberlain, LA vs Pho	2/9/69	29- 8–	66
Wilt Chamberlain, Phi at Cin	2/13/62	24-17–	65
Wilt Chamberlain, Phi at St. L	2/27/62	25-15–	65
Wilt Chamberlain, Phi vs LA	2/7/66	28- 9–	65
Elgin Baylor, Mpls vs Bos	11/8/59	25-14–	64
Rick Barry, G.St. vs Port	3/26/74	30- 4–	64
Michael Jordan, Chi vs Orl	1/16/93	27- 9–	64

*Overtime
***Triple overtime.

Note: Wilt Chamberlain's 100-point game vs New York was played at Hershey, Penn.

Field Goals

	Date	FG	Att
Wilt Chamberlain, Phi vs NY	3/2/62	36	63
Wilt Chamberlain, Phi vs LA***	12/8/61	31	62
Wilt Chamberlain, Phi at Chi	12/16/67	30	40
Rick Barry, G.St. vs Port	2/26/74	30	45

Wilt Chamberlain made 29 four times.

***Triple overtime.

Free Throws

	Date	FT	Att
Wilt Chamberlain, Phi vs NY	3/2/62	28	32
Adrian Dantley, Utah vs Hou	1/4/84	28	29
Adrian Dantley, Utah vs Den	11/25/83	27	31
Adrian Dantley, Utah vs Dal	10/31/80	26	29
Michael Jordan, Chi vs NJ	2/26/87	26	27

3-Pt Field Goals

	Date	No
Dennis Scott, Orl vs Atl	4/18/96	11
Brian Shaw, Mia at Mil	4/8/93	10
Joe Dumars, Det vs Min	11/8/94	10
George McCloud, Dal vs Pho	12/16/95	10*

Many tied with 9 each

* Overtime

Assists

	Date	No
Scott Skiles, Orl vs Den	12/30/90	30
Kevin Porter, NJ vs Hou	2/24/78	29
Bob Cousy, Bos vs Mpls	2/27/59	28
Guy Rodgers, SF vs St.L	3/14/63	28
John Stockton, Utah vs SA	1/15/91	28

Rebounds

	Date	No
Wilt Chamberlain, Phi vs Bos	11/24/60	55
Bill Russell, Bos vs Syr	2/5/60	51
Bill Russell, Bos vs Phi	11/16/57	49
Bill Russell, Bos vs Det	3/11/65	49
Wilt Chamberlain, Phi vs Syr	2/6/60	45
Wilt Chamberlain, Phi vs LA	1/21/61	45

Blocked Shots

	Date	No
Elmore Smith, LA vs Port	10/28/73	17
Manute Bol, Wash vs Atl	1/25/86	15
Manute Bol, Wash vs Ind	2/26/87	15
Shaquille O'Neal, Orl at NJ	11/20/93	15

Steals

	Date	No
Larry Kenon, San Antonio at KC	12/26/76	11
Kendall Gill, NJ vs Mia	4/3/99	11
14 different players tied with 10 each, including Alvin Robertson, who had 10 steals in a game four times.		

All-Time Winningest NBA Coaches

Top 25 NBA career victories through the 1999-2000 season. Career, regular season and playoff records are noted along with NBA titles won. Coaches active during 1999-2000 season in **bold** type.

		Career			Regular Season			Playoffs			
		Yrs	W	L	Pct	W	L	Pct	W	L	Pct	NBA Titles
1	**Lenny Wilkens**	27	**1251**	1066	.540	1179	981	.546	72	85	.459	1 (1979)
2	**Pat Riley**	18	**1154**	531	.685	999	434	.697	155	97	.616	4 (1982,85,87-88)
3	Red Auerbach	20	**1037**	548	.654	938	479	.662	99	69	.589	9 (1957, 59-66)
4	Bill Fitch	25	**999**	1157	.463	944	1106	.460	55	54	.505	1 (1981)
5	Dick Motta	25	**991**	1087	.477	935	1017	.479	56	70	.444	1 (1978)
6	**Don Nelson**	21	**977**	813	.546	926	752	.552	51	61	.455	None
7	Jack Ramsay	21	**908**	841	.519	864	783	.525	44	58	.431	1 (1977)
8	Cotton Fitzsimmons	21	**867**	824	.513	832	775	.518	35	49	.417	None
9	Gene Shue	22	**814**	908	.473	784	861	.477	30	47	.390	None
10	**Jerry Sloan**	15	**805**	489	.622	731	419	.636	74	70	.514	None
11	**Larry Brown**	17	**781**	638	.550	732	586	.555	49	52	.485	None
12	Red Holzman	18	**754**	652	.536	696	604	.535	58	48	.547	2 (1970, 73)
	John MacLeod	18	**754**	711	.515	707	657	.518	47	54	.465	None
14	**Phil Jackson**	10	**738**	257	.742	612	208	.746	126	49	.720	7 (1991-93,96-98,00)
15	Chuck Daly	14	**713**	488	.594	638	437	.593	75	51	.595	2 (1989-90)
16	Doug Moe	15	**661**	579	.533	628	529	.543	33	50	.398	None
17	**George Karl**	14	**620**	443	.583	573	388	.596	47	55	.460	None
18	K.C. Jones	10	**603**	309	.661	522	252	.674	81	57	.587	2 (1984,86)
19	Del Harris	14	**594**	507	.540	556	457	.549	38	50	.432	None
20	Mike Fratello	14	**592**	499	.543	572	465	.552	20	34	.370	None
21	Al Attles	14	**588**	548	.518	557	518	.518	31	30	.508	1 (1975)
22	Billy Cunningham	8	**520**	235	.689	454	196	.698	66	39	.629	1 (1983)
23	Alex Hannum	12	**518**	446	.536	471	412	.533	47	34	.580	2 (1958, 67)
24	John Kundla	11	**485**	338	.589	423	302	.583	62	36	.633	5 (1949-50, 52-54)
25	Kevin Loughery	17	**480**	683	.413	474	662	.417	6	21	.222	None

Note: The NBA does not recognize records from the National Basketball League (1937-49), the American Basketball League (1961-62) or the American Basketball Assn. (1968-76), so the following NBL, ABL and ABA overall coaching records are not included above: NBL–**John Kundla** (51-19 and a title in 1 year). ABA– **Larry Brown** (249-129 in 4 yrs), **Alex Hannum** (194-164 and one title in 4 yrs), **K.C. Jones** (30-58 in 1 yr); **Kevin Loughery** (189-95 and one title in 3 yrs).

Where They Coached

Attles–Golden St. (1970-80,80-83); **Auerbach**–Washington (1946-49), Tri-Cities (1949-50), Boston (1950-66); **Brown**–Denver (1976-79), New Jersey (1981-83), San Antonio (1988-92), LA Clippers (1992-93), Indiana (1993-97), Philadelphia (1997–); **Cunningham**–Philadelphia (1977-85); **Daly**–Cleveland (1981-82), Detroit (1983-92), New Jersey (1992-94), Orlando (1997-99); **Fitch**–Cleveland (1970-79), Boston (1979-83), Houston (1983-88), New Jersey (1989-92), LA Clippers (1994-98); **Fitzsimmons**–Phoenix (1970-72), Atlanta (1972-76), Buffalo (1977-78), Kansas City (1978-84), San Antonio (1984-86), Phoenix (1988-92, 95-96); **Fratello**–Atlanta (1980-90), Cleveland (1993-99).

Hannum–St. Louis (1957-58), Syracuse (1960-63), San Francisco (1963-66), Phila. 76ers (1966-68), Houston (1970-71); **Harris**–Houston (1979-83), Milwaukee (1987-92), LA Lakers (1994-99); **Holzman**–Milwaukee-St. Louis Hawks (1954-57), NY Knicks (1968-77,78-82); **Jackson**–Chicago (1989-98), LA Lakers (1999–); **Jones**–Washington (1973-76), Boston (1983-88), Seattle (1990-92); **Karl**–Cleveland (1984-86), Golden St. (1986-88), Seattle (1991-98), Milwaukee (1999–); **Kundla**–Minneapolis (1948-57,58-59); **Loughery**–Philadelphia (1972-73), NY-NJ Nets (1973-81), Atlanta (1981-83), Chicago (1983-85), Washington (1985-88), Miami (1991-95); **MacLeod**–Phoenix (1973-87), Dallas (1987-89), NY Knicks (1990-91); **Moe**–San Antonio (1976-80), Denver (1981-90), Philadelphia (1992-93).

Motta–Chicago (1968-76), Washington (1976-80), Dallas (1980-87), Sacramento (1990-91), Denver (1997); **Nelson**–Milwaukee (1976-87), Golden St. (1988-95), New York (1995-96), Dallas (1997–); **Ramsay**–Philadelphia (1968-72), Buffalo (1972-76), Portland (1976-86), Indiana (1986-89); **Riley**–LA Lakers (1981-90), New York (1991-95), Miami (1995–); **Shue**–Baltimore (1967-73), Philadelphia (1973-77), San Diego Clippers (1978-80), Washington (1980-86), LA Clippers (1987-89); **Sloan**–Chicago (1979-82), Utah (1988–); **Wilkens**–Seattle (1969-72), Portland (1974-76), Seattle (1977-85), Cleveland (1986-93), Atlanta (1993-00).

Top Winning Percentages

Minimum of 350 victories, including playoffs; coaches active during 1999-2000 season in **bold** type.

		Yrs	W	L	Pct
1	**Phil Jackson**	10	738	257	**.742**
2	Billy Cunningham	8	520	235	**.689**
3	**Pat Riley**	18	1154	531	**.685**
4	K.C. Jones	10	603	309	**.661**
5	Red Auerbach	20	1037	548	**.654**
6	**Jerry Sloan**	15	805	489	**.622**
7	Tommy Heinsohn	9	474	296	**.616**
8	Chuck Daly	14	713	488	**.594**
9	Larry Costello	10	467	323	**.591**
10	**Rudy Tomjanovich**	9	438	306	**.589**
11	John Kundla	11	485	338	**.589**
12	**George Karl**	13	620	443	**.583**
13	Bill Sharman	7	368	267	**.580**
14	Al Cervi	9	359	267	**.573**
15	**Rick Adelman**	10	468	352	**.571**
16	Joe Lapchick	9	356	277	**.562**
17	**Larry Brown**	17	781	638	**.550**
18	**Don Nelson**	22	977	813	**.546**
19	Mike Fratello	14	592	499	**.543**
20	Bill Russell	8	375	317	**.542**
21	**Lenny Wilkens**	27	1251	1066	**.540**
22	Del Harris	14	594	507	**.540**
23	Alex Hannum	12	518	446	**.537**
24	Red Holzman	18	754	651	**.536**
25	Doug Moe	15	661	579	**.533**

Active Coaches' Victories

Through 1999-2000 season, including playoffs.

		Yrs	W	L	Pct
1	Lenny Wilkens, Toronto	27	1251	1066	.540
2	Pat Riley, Miami	18	1154	531	.685
3	Don Nelson, Dallas	22	977	813	.546
4	Jerry Sloan, Utah	15	805	489	.622
5	Larry Brown, Philadelphia	17	781	638	.550
6	Phil Jackson, LA Lakers	10	738	257	.742
7	George Karl, Milwaukee	13	620	443	.583
8	Rick Adelman, Sacramento	10	468	352	.571
9	Rudy Tomjanovich, Houston	9	438	306	.589
10	Mike Dunleavy, Portland	9	379	403	.485
11	Paul Westphal, Seattle	6	288	172	.626
12	Jeff Van Gundy, New York	5	225	158	.587
13	Rick Pitino, Boston	5	186	205	.476
14	Phil Saunders, Minnesota	5	184	189	.493
15	Gregg Popovich, San Antonio	4	183	125	.594
16	Paul Silas, Charlotte	5	150	217	.409
17	Dan Issel, Denver	4	137	155	.469
18	Dave Cowens, Golden St.	5	136	111	.551
19	Alvin Gentry, LA Clippers	4	90	96	.484
20	George Irvine, Detroit	4	68	140	.327
21	Scott Skiles, Phoenix	1	44	27	.620
22	Doc Rivers, Orlando	1	41	41	.500
23	Sidney Lowe, Vancouver	2	33	102	.244
24	Randy Wittman, Cleveland	1	32	50	.390
25	Tim Floyd, Chicago	2	30	102	.227
26	Leonard Hamilton, Washington	0	0	0	—
27	Lon Kruger, Atlanta	0	0	0	—
28	Byron Scott, New Jersey	0	0	0	—
29	Isiah Thomas, Indiana	0	0	0	—

Annual Awards

Most Valuable Player

The Maurice Podoloff Trophy for regular season MVP. Named after the first commissioner (then president) of the NBA. Winners first selected by the NBA players (1956-80) then a national panel of pro basketball writers and broadcasters (since 1981). Winners' scoring averages are provided; (*) indicates led league.

Multiple winners: Kareem Abdul-Jabbar (6); Michael Jordan and Bill Russell (5); Wilt Chamberlain (4); Larry Bird, Magic Johnson and Moses Malone (3); Karl Malone and Bob Pettit (2).

Year		Avg
1956	Bob Pettit, St. Louis, F	25.7*
1957	Bob Cousy, Boston, G	20.6
1958	Bill Russell, Boston, C	16.6
1959	Bob Pettit, St. Louis, F	29.2*
1960	Wilt Chamberlain, Philadelphia, C	37.6*
1961	Bill Russell, Boston, C	16.9
1962	Bill Russell, Boston, C	18.9
1963	Bill Russell, Boston, C	16.8
1964	Oscar Robertson, Cincinnati, G	31.4
1965	Bill Russell, Boston, C	14.1
1966	Wilt Chamberlain, Philadelphia, C	33.5*
1967	Wilt Chamberlain, Philadelphia, C	24.1
1968	Wilt Chamberlain, Philadelphia, C	24.3
1969	Wes Unseld, Baltimore, C	13.8
1970	Willis Reed, New York, C	21.7
1971	Lew Alcindor, Milwaukee, C	31.7*
1972	Kareem Abdul-Jabbar, Milwaukee, C	34.8*
1973	Dave Cowens, Boston, C	20.5
1974	Kareem Abdul-Jabbar, Milwaukee, C	27.0
1975	Bob McAdoo, Buffalo, F	34.5*
1976	Kareem Abdul-Jabbar, LA, C	27.7
1977	Kareem Abdul-Jabbar, LA, C	26.2
1978	Bill Walton, Portland, C	18.9

Year		Avg
1979	Moses Malone, Houston, C	24.8
1980	Kareem Abdul-Jabbar, LA, C	24.8
1981	Julius Erving, Philadelphia, F	24.6
1982	Moses Malone, Houston, C	31.1
1983	Moses Malone, Philadelphia, C	24.5
1984	Larry Bird, Boston, F	24.2
1985	Larry Bird, Boston, F	28.7
1986	Larry Bird, Boston, F	25.8
1987	Magic Johnson, LA Lakers, G	23.9
1988	Michael Jordan, Chicago, G	35.0*
1989	Magic Johnson, LA Lakers, G	22.5
1990	Magic Johnson, LA Lakers, G	22.3
1991	Michael Jordan, Chicago, G	31.5*
1992	Michael Jordan, Chicago, G	30.1*
1993	Charles Barkley, Phoenix, F	25.6
1994	Hakeem Olajuwon, Houston, C	27.3
1995	David Robinson, San Antonio, C	27.6
1996	Michael Jordan, Chicago, G	30.4*
1997	Karl Malone, Utah, F	27.4
1998	Michael Jordan, Chicago, G	28.7*
1999	Karl Malone, Utah, F	23.8
2000	Shaquille O'Neal, LA Lakers, C	29.7*

Note: Lew Alcindor changed his name to Kareem Abdul-Jabbar after the 1970-71 season.

Rookie of the Year

The Eddie Gottlieb Trophy for outstanding rookie of the regular season. Named after the pro basketball pioneer and owner-coach of the first NBA champion Philadelphia Warriors. Winners selected by a national panel of pro basketball writers and broadcasters. Winners' scoring averages provided; (*) indicates led league; winners who were also named MVP are in **bold** type.

Year		Avg	Year		Avg
1953	Don Meineke, Ft. Wayne, F	10.8	1978	Walter Davis, Phoenix, G	24.2
1954	Ray Felix, Baltimore, C	17.6	1979	Phil Ford, Kansas City, G	15.9
1955	Bob Pettit, Milwaukee Hawks, F	20.4	1980	Larry Bird, Boston, F	21.3
1956	Maurice Stokes, Rochester, F/C	16.8	1981	Darrell Griffith, Utah, G	20.6
1957	Tommy Heinsohn, Boston, F	16.2	1982	Buck Williams, New Jersey, F	15.5
1958	Woody Sauldsberry, Philadelphia, F/C	12.8	1983	Terry Cummings, San Diego, F	23.7
1959	Elgin Baylor, Minneapolis, F	24.9	1984	Ralph Sampson, Houston, C	21.0
1960	**Wilt Chamberlain**, Philadelphia, C	37.6*	1985	Michael Jordan, Chicago, G	28.2
1961	Oscar Robertson, Cincinnati, G	30.5	1986	Patrick Ewing, New York, C	20.0
1962	Walt Bellamy, Chicago Packers, C	31.6	1987	Chuck Person, Indiana, F	18.8
1963	Terry Dischinger, Chicago Zephyrs, F	25.5	1988	Mark Jackson, New York, G	13.6
1964	Jerry Lucas, Cincinnati, F/C	17.7	1989	Mitch Richmond, Golden St., G	22.0
1965	Willis Reed, New York, C	19.5	1990	David Robinson, San Antonio, C	24.3
1966	Rick Barry, San Francisco, F	25.7	1991	Derrick Coleman, New Jersey, F	18.4
1967	Dave Bing, Detroit, G	20.0	1992	Larry Johnson, Charlotte, F	19.2
1968	Earl Monroe, Baltimore, G	24.3	1993	Shaquille O'Neal, Orlando,C	23.4
1969	**Wes Unseld**, Baltimore, C	13.8	1994	Chris Webber, Golden St., F	17.5
1970	Lew Alcindor, Milwaukee Bucks, C	28.8	1995	Grant Hill, Detroit, F	19.9
1971	Dave Cowens, Boston, C	17.0		& Jason Kidd, Dallas, G	11.7
	& Geoff Petrie, Portland, G	24.8	1996	Damon Stoudamire, Toronto, G	19.0
1972	Sidney Wicks, Portland, F	24.5	1997	Allen Iverson, Philadelphia, G	23.5
1973	Bob McAdoo, Buffalo, C/F	18.0	1998	Tim Duncan, San Antonio, F/C	21.6
1974	Ernie DiGregorio, Buffalo, G	15.2	1999	Vince Carter, Toronto, F	18.3
1975	Keith Wilkes, Golden St., F	14.2	2000	Elton Brand, Chicago, F	20.1
1976	Alvan Adams, Phoenix, C	19.0		& Steve Francis, Houston, G	18.0
1977	Adrian Dantley, Buffalo, F	20.3			

Note: The Chicago Packers changed their name to the Zephyrs after 1961-62 season. Also, Lew Alcindor changed his name to Kareem Abdul-Jabbar after the 1970-71 season.

Sixth Man Award

Awarded to the Best Player Off the Bench for the regular season. Winners selected by a national panel of pro basketball writers and broadcasters.

Multiple winners: Kevin McHale, Ricky Pierce and Detlef Schrempf (2).

Year	Year	Year
1983 Bobby Jones, Phi., F	1989 Eddie Johnson, Pho., F	1995 Anthony Mason, NY, F
1984 Kevin McHale, Bos., F	1990 Ricky Pierce, Mil., G/F	1996 Toni Kukoc, Chi., F
1985 Kevin McHale, Bos., F	1991 Detlef Schrempf, Ind., F	1997 John Starks, NY, G
1986 Bill Walton, Bos., F/C	1992 Detlef Schrempf, Ind., F	1998 Danny Manning, Pho., F
1987 Ricky Pierce, Mil., G/F	1993 Cliff Robinson, Port., F	1999 Darrell Armstrong, Orl., G
1988 Roy Tarpley, Dal., F	1994 Dell Curry, Char., G	2000 Rodney Rogers, Pho., F

Number One Draft Choices

Overall first choices in the NBA draft since the abolition of the territorial draft in 1966. Players who became Rookie of the Year are in **bold** type. The draft lottery began in 1985.

Year	Overall 1st Pick	Year	Overall 1st Pick
1966 New York	Cazzie Russell, Michigan	1984 Houston	Akeem Olajuwon, Houston
1967 Detroit	Jimmy Walker, Providence	1985 New York	**Patrick Ewing**, Georgetown
1968 San Diego	Elvin Hayes, Houston	1986 Cleveland	Brad Daugherty, N. Carolina
1969 Milwaukee	**Lew Alcindor**, UCLA	1987 San Antonio	**David Robinson**, Navy
1970 Detroit	Bob Lanier, St. Bonaventure	1988 LA Clippers	Danny Manning, Kansas
1971 Cleveland	Austin Carr, Notre Dame	1989 Sacramento	Pervis Ellison, Louisville
1972 Portland	LaRue Martin, Loyola-Chicago	1990 New Jersey	**Derrick Coleman**, Syracuse
1973 Philadelphia	Doug Collins, Illinois St.	1991 Charlotte	**Larry Johnson**, UNLV
1974 Portland	Bill Walton, UCLA	1992 Orlando	**Shaquille O'Neal**, LSU
1975 Atlanta	David Thompson, N.C. State	1993 Orlando	**Chris Webber**, Michigan
1976 Houston	John Lucas, Maryland	1994 Milwaukee	Glenn Robinson, Purdue
1977 Milwaukee	Kent Benson, Indiana	1995 Golden St.	Joe Smith, Maryland
1978 Portland	Mychal Thompson, Minnesota	1996 Philadelphia	**Allen Iverson**, Georgetown
1979 LA Lakers	Magic Johnson, Michigan St.	1997 San Antonio	**Tim Duncan**, Wake Forest
1980 Golden St	Joe Barry Carroll, Purdue	1998 LA Clippers	Michael Olowokandi, Pacific
1981 Dallas	Mark Aguirre, DePaul	1999 Chicago	**Elton Brand**, Duke
1982 LA Lakers	James Worthy, N. Carolina		
1983 Houston	**Ralph Sampson**, Virginia	2000 New Jersey	Kenyon Martin, Cincinnati

Note: Lew Alcindor changed his name to Kareem Abdul-Jabbar after the 1970-71 season; Akeem Olajuwon changed his first name to Hakeem in 1991; in 1975 David Thompson signed with Denver of the ABA and did not play for Atlanta; David Robinson joined NBA for 1989-90 season after fulfilling military obligation.

Defensive Player of the Year

Awarded to the Best Defensive Player for the regular season. Winners selected by a national panel of pro basketball writers and broadcasters.

Multiple winners: Dikembe Mutombo (3); Mark Eaton, Sidney Moncrief, Alonzo Mourning, Hakeem Olajuwon and Dennis Rodman (2).

Year		Year		Year	
1983	Sidney Moncrief, Mil., G	1989	Mark Eaton, Utah, C	1995	Dikembe Mutombo, Den., C
1984	Sidney Moncrief, Mil., G	1990	Dennis Rodman, Det., F	1996	Gary Payton, Sea., G
1985	Mark Eaton, Utah, C	1991	Dennis Rodman, Det., F	1997	Dikembe Mutombo, Atl., C
1986	Alvin Robertson, SA, G	1992	David Robinson, SA, C	1998	Dikembe Mutombo, Atl., C
1987	Michael Cooper, LAL, F	1993	Hakeem Olajuwon, Hou., C	1999	Alonzo Mourning, Mia., C
1988	Michael Jordan, Chi., G	1994	Hakeem Olajuwon, Hou., C	2000	Alonzo Mourning, Mia., C

Most Improved Player

Awarded to the Most Improved Player for the regular season. Winners selected by a national panel of pro basketball writers and broadcasters.

Year		Year		Year	
1986	Alvin Robertson, SA, G	1991	Scott Skiles, Orl., G	1996	Gheorghe Muresan, Wash., C
1987	Dale Ellis, Sea., G	1992	Pervis Ellison, Wash., C	1997	Isaac Austin, Miami, C
1988	Kevin Duckworth, Port., C	1993	Mahmoud Abdul-Rauf, Den., G	1998	Alan Henderson, Atl., F
1989	Kevin Johnson, Pho., G	1994	Don MacLean, Wash., F	1999	Darrell Armstrong, Orl., G
1990	Rony Seikaly, Mia., C	1995	Dana Barros, Phi., G	2000	Jalen Rose, Ind., G

Coach of the Year

The Red Auerbach Trophy for outstanding coach of the year. Renamed in 1967 for the former Boston coach who led the Celtics to nine NBA titles. Winners selected by a national panel of pro basketball writers and broadcasters. Previous season and winning season records are provided; (*) indicates division title.

Multiple winners: Don Nelson and Pat Riley (3); Bill Fitch, Cotton Fitzsimmons and Gene Shue (2).

Year			Improvement		Year			Improvement	
1963	Harry Gallatin, St. L	29-51	to	48-32	1982	Gene Shue, Wash	39-43	to	43-39
1964	Alex Hannum, SF	31-49	to	48-32*	1983	Don Nelson, Mil.	55-27*	to	51-31*
1965	Red Auerbach, Bos	59-21*	to	61-18*	1984	Frank Layden, Utah	30-52	to	45-37*
1966	Dolph Schayes, Phi	40-40	to	55-25*	1985	Don Nelson, Mil.	50-32*	to	59-23*
1967	Johnny Kerr, Chi	Expan.	to	33-48	1986	Mike Fratello, Atl	34-48	to	50-32
1968	Richie Guerin, St. L	39-42	to	56-26*	1987	Mike Schuler, Port	40-42	to	49-33
1969	Gene Shue, Balt	36-46	to	57-25*	1988	Doug Moe, Den	37-45	to	54-28*
1970	Red Holzman, NY	54-28	to	60-22*	1989	Cotton Fitzsimmons, Pho	28-54	to	55-27
1971	Dick Motta, Chi	39-43	to	51-31	1990	Pat Riley, LA Lakers	57-25*	to	63-19*
1972	Bill Sharman, LA	48-34*	to	69-13*	1991	Don Chaney, Hou.	41-41	to	52-30
1973	Tommy Heinsohn, Bos	56-26*	to	68-14*	1992	Don Nelson, GS	44-38	to	55-27
1974	Ray Scott, Det	40-42	to	52-30	1993	Pat Riley, NY	51-31	to	60-22
1975	Phil Johnson, KC-Omaha	33-49	to	44-38	1994	Lenny Wilkens, Atl	43-39	to	57-25*
1976	Bill Fitch, Cle	40-42	to	49-33*	1995	Del Harris, LA Lakers	33-49	to	48-34
1977	Tom Nissalke, Hou	40-42	to	49-33*	1996	Phil Jackson, Chi.	47-35	to	72-10*
1978	Hubie Brown, Atl	31-51	to	41-41	1997	Pat Riley, Mia	42-40	to	61-21
1979	Cotton Fitzsimmons, KC	31-51	to	48-34*	1998	Larry Bird, Ind	39-43	to	58-24
1980	Bill Fitch, Bos	29-53	to	61-21*	1999	Mike Dunleavy, Port.	46-36	to	35-15*
1981	Jack McKinney, Ind	37-45	to	44-38	2000	Doc Rivers, Orlando	33-17	to	41-41

World Championships

The World Basketball Championships for men and women have been played regularly at four-year intervals (give or take a year) since 1970. The men's tournament began in 1950 and the women's in 1953. The Federation Internationale de Basketball Amateur (FIBA), which governs the World and Olympic tournaments, was founded in 1932. FIBA first allowed professional players from the NBA to participate in 1994. A team of collegians represented the USA in 1998.

Men

Multiple wins: Yugoslavia (4); Soviet Union and USA (3); Brazil (2).

Year	
1950	**Argentina**, United States, Chile
1954	**United States**, Brazil, Philippines
1959	**Brazil**, United States, Chile
1963	**Brazil**, Yugoslavia, Soviet Union
1967	**Soviet Union**, Yugoslavia, Brazil
1970	**Yugoslavia**, Brazil, Soviet Union
1974	**Soviet Union**, Yugoslavia, United States
1978	**Yugoslavia**, Soviet Union, Brazil
1982	**Soviet Union**, United States, Yugoslavia
1986	**United States**, Soviet Union, Yugoslavia
1990	**Yugoslavia**, Soviet Union, United States
1994	**United States**, Russia, Croatia
1998	**Yugoslavia**, Russia, United States
2002	at Indianapolis (August)

Women

Multiple wins: Soviet Union and USA (6).

Year	
1953	**United States**, Chile, France
1957	**United States**, Soviet Union, Czechoslovakia
1959	**Soviet Union**, Bulgaria, Czechoslovakia
1964	**Soviet Union**, Czechoslovakia, Bulgaria
1967	**Soviet Union**, South Korea, Czechoslovakia
1971	**Soviet Union**, Czechoslovakia, Brazil
1975	**Soviet Union**, Japan, Czechoslovakia
1979	**United States**, South Korea, Canada
1983	**Soviet Union**, United States, China
1986	**United States**, Soviet Union, Canada
1990	**United States**, Yugoslavia, Cuba
1994	**Brazil**, China, United States
1998	**United States**, Russia, Australia
2002	at China (May)

NBA Photos

NBA's 50 Greatest Players

In October 1996, as part of its 50th anniversary celebration, the NBA named the 50 greatest players in league history. The voting was done by a league-approved panel of media, former players and coaches, current and former general managers and team executives. The players are listed alphabetically along with the dates of their professional careers and positions. Active players are in **bold** type.

Player	Pos	Player	Pos	Player	Pos
Kareem Abdul-Jabbar, 1969-89	C	George Gervin, 1972-86	G	Bob Pettit, 1954-65	F/C
Nate Archibald, 1970-84	G	Hal Greer, 1958-73	G	**Scottie Pippen**, 1987—	F
Paul Arizin, 1950-61	F/G	John Havlicek, 1962-78	F/G	Willis Reed, 1964-74	C
Charles Barkley, 1984-00	F	Elvin Hayes, 1968-84	F/C	Oscar Robertson, 1960-74	G
Rick Barry, 1965-80	F	Magic Johnson, 1979-91, 96	G	**David Robinson**, 1989—	C
Elgin Baylor, 1958-72	F	Sam Jones, 1957-69	G	Bill Russell, 1956-69	C
Dave Bing, 1966-78	G	Michael Jordan, 1984-93, 95-98	G	Dolph Schayes, 1948-64	F/C
Larry Bird, 1979-92	F	Jerry Lucas, 1963-74	F/C	Bill Sharman, 1950-61	G
Wilt Chamberlain, 1959-73	C	**Karl Malone**, 1985—	F	**John Stockton**, 1984—	G
Bob Cousy, 1950-63, 69-70	G	Moses Malone, 1974-95	C	Isiah Thomas, 1981-94	G
Dave Cowens, 1970-80, 1982-83	C	Pete Maravich, 1970-80	G	Nate Thurmond, 1963-77	C/F
Billy Cunningham, 1965-76	G	Kevin McHale, 1980-93	F	Wes Unseld, 1968-81	C/F
Dave DeBusschere, 1962-74	F	George Mikan, 1946-54, 55-56	C	Bill Walton, 1974-88	C
Clyde Drexler, 1983-98	G	Earl Monroe, 1967-80	G	Jerry West, 1960-74	G
Julius Erving, 1971-87	F	**Hakeem Olajuwon**, 1984—	C	Lenny Wilkens, 1960-75	G
Patrick Ewing, 1985—	C	**Shaquille O'Neal**, 1992—	C	James Worthy, 1982-94	F
Walt Frazier, 1967-80	G	Robert Parish, 1976-97	C		

Note: Rick Barry, Billy Cunningham, Julius Erving, George Gervin and Moses Malone all played part of their pro careers in the ABA.

NBA's 10 Greatest Coaches

In December 1996, as part of its 50th anniversary celebration, the NBA named the 10 greatest coaches in league history. The voting was done by a league-approved panel of media. The coaches are listed alphabetically along with the dates of their professional coaching careers and overall records, including playoff games, and number of NBA titles won. Active coaches are in **bold** type.

Coach	W	L	Pct.	Titles	Coach	W	L	Pct.	Titles
Red Auerbach, 1946-66	1037	548	.654	9	**Don Nelson**, 1976-96, 97—	.977	813	.546	0
Chuck Daly, 1981-94, 97-99	.713	488	.594	2	Jack Ramsay, 1968-89	.908	841	.519	1
Bill Fitch, 1970-98	.999	1157	.463	1	**Pat Riley**, 1981—	1154	531	.685	4
Red Holzman, 1953-82	.754	652	.536	2	**Lenny Wilkens**, 1969—	1251	1066	.540	1
Phil Jackson, 1989-98, 99—	.738	257	.742	7	TOTALS	.9016	6691	.574	32
John Kundla, 1947-59	.485	338	.589	5					

American Basketball Association
ABA Finals

The American Basketball Assn. began play in 1967-68 as a 10-team rival of the 21-year-old NBA. The ABA, which introduced the three-point basket, a multi-colored ball and the All-Star Game Slam Dunk Contest, lasted nine seasons before folding following the 1975-76 season. Four ABA teams–Denver, Indiana, New York and San Antonio–survived to enter the NBA in 1976-77. The NBA also adopted the three-point basket (in 1979-80) and the All-Star Game Slam Dunk Contest. The older league, however, refused to take in the ABA ball.

Multiple winners: Indiana (3); New York (2).

Year	Winner	Head Coach	Series	Loser	Head Coach
1968	Pittsburgh Pipers	Vince Cazzetta	4-3 (WLLWLWW)	New Orleans Bucs	Babe McCarthy
1969	Oakland Oaks	Alex Hannum	4-1 (WLWWW)	Indiana Pacers	Bob Leonard
1970	Indiana Pacers	Bob Leonard	4-2 (WWLWW)	Los Angeles Stars	Bill Sharman
1971	Utah Stars	Bill Sharman	4-3 (WWLLWLW)	Kentucky Colonels	Frank Ramsey
1972	Indiana Pacers	Bob Leonard	4-2 (WLWLWW)	New York Nets	Lou Carnesecca
1973	Indiana Pacers	Bob Leonard	4-3 (WLLWWLW)	Kentucky Colonels	Joe Mullaney
1974	New York Nets	Kevin Loughery	4-1 (WWWLW)	Utah Stars	Joe Mullaney
1975	Kentucky Colonels	Hubie Brown	4-1 (WWWLW)	Indiana Pacers	Bob Leonard
1976	New York Nets	Kevin Loughery	4-2 (WLWWLW)	Denver Nuggets	Larry Brown

Most Valuable Player

Winners' scoring averages provided; (*) indicates led league.

Multiple winners: Julius Erving (3); Mel Daniels (2).

Year		Avg
1968	Connie Hawkins, Pittsburgh, C	26.8*
1969	Mel Daniels, Indiana, C	24.0
1970	Spencer Haywood, Denver, C	30.0*
1971	Mel Daniels, Indiana, C	21.0
1972	Artis Gilmore, Kentucky, C	23.8
1973	Billy Cunningham, Carolina, F	24.1
1974	Julius Erving, New York, F	27.4*
1975	George McGinnis, Indiana, F	29.8*
	& Julius Erving, New York, F	27.9
1976	Julius Erving, New York, F	29.3*

Rookie of the Year

Winners' scoring averages provided; (*) indicates led league. Rookies who were also named Most Valuable Player are in **bold** type.

Year		Avg
1968	Mel Daniels, Minnesota, C	22.2
1969	Warren Armstrong, Oakland, G	21.5
1970	**Spencer Haywood**, Denver, C	30.0*
1971	Dan Issel, Kentucky, C	29.8*
	& Charlie Scott, Virginia, G	27.1
1972	**Artis Gilmore**, Kentucky, C	23.8
1973	Brian Taylor, New York, G	15.3
1974	Swen Nater, Virginia-SA, C	14.1
1975	Marvin Barnes, St. Louis, C	24.0
1976	David Thompson, Denver, F	26.0

Note: Warren Armstrong changed his name to Warren Jabali after the 1970-71 season.

Coach of the Year

Previous season and winning season records are provided; (*) indicates division title.

Multiple winner: Larry Brown (3).

Year		Improvement
1968	Vince Cazzetta, Pittsburgh	54-24*
1969	Alex Hannum, Oakland	22-56 to 60-18*
1970	Joe Belmont, Denver	44-34 to 51-33*
	& Bill Sharman, LA Stars	33-45 to 43-41
1971	Al Bianchi, Virginia	44-40 to 55-29*
1972	Tom Nissalke, Dallas	30-54 to 42-42
1973	Larry Brown, Carolina	35-49 to 57-27*
1974	Babe McCarthy, Kentucky	56-28 to 53-31
	& Joe Mullaney, Utah	55-29* to 51-33*
1975	Larry Brown, Denver	37-47 to 65-19*
1976	Larry Brown, Denver	65-19* to 60-24*

Scoring Leaders

Scoring championship decided by per game point average every season.

Multiple winner: Julius Erving (3).

Year		Gm	Avg	Pts
1968	Connie Hawkins, Pittsburgh	70	1875	26.8
1969	Rick Barry, Oakland	35	1190	34.0
1970	Spencer Haywood, Denver	84	2519	30.0
1971	Dan Issel, Kentucky	83	2480	29.8
1972	Charlie Scott, Virginia	73	2524	34.6
1973	Julius Erving, Virginia	71	2268	31.9
1974	Julius Erving, New York	84	2299	27.4
1975	George McGinnis, Indiana	79	2353	29.8
1976	Julius Erving, New York	84	2462	29.3

ABA All-Star Game

The ABA All-Star Game was an Eastern Division vs. Western Division contest from 1968-75. League membership had dropped to seven teams by 1976, the ABA's last season, so the team in first place at the break (Denver) played an All-Star team made up from the other six clubs.

Series: East won 5, West 3 and Denver 1.

Year	Result	Host	Coaches	Most Valuable Player
1968	East 126, West 120	Indiana	Jim Pollard, Babe McCarthy	Larry Brown, New Orleans
1969	West 133, East 127	Louisville	Alex Hannum, Gene Rhodes	John Beasley, Dallas
1970	West 128, East 98	Indiana	Babe McCarthy, Bob Leonard	Spencer Haywood, Denver
1971	East 126, West 122	Carolina	Al Bianchi, Bill Sharman	Mel Daniels, Indiana
1972	East 142, West 115	Louisville	Joe Mullaney, Ladell Andersen	Dan Issel, Kentucky
1973	West 123, East 111	Utah	Ladell Andersen, Larry Brown	Warren Jabali, Denver
1974	East 128, West 112	Virginia	Babe McCarthy, Joe Mullaney	Artis Gilmore, Kentucky
1975	East 151, West 124	San Antonio	Kevin Loughery, Larry Brown	Freddie Lewis, St. Louis
1976	Denver 144, ABA 138	Denver	Larry Brown, Kevin Loughery	David Thompson, Denver

Continental Basketball Association

Formed on April 23, 1946, the CBA is the oldest professional basketball league in the world. Originally named the Eastern Pennsylvania Basketball League, the league changed names several times before becoming known as the Eastern Basketball Association. In 1978, the EBA was redubbed the CBA.

Multiple champions: Allentown and Wilkes-Barre (8); Scranton, Tampa Bay and Williamsport (3); Albany, La Crosse, Pottsville, Rochester, Wilmington and Yakima (2).

Year		Year		Year		Year	
1947	Wilkes-Barre Barons	1963	Allentown Jets	1977	Scranton Apollos	1992	La Crosse Catbirds
1948	Reading Keys	1964	Camden Bullets	1978	Wilkes-Barre Barons	1993	Omaha Racers
1949	Pottsville Packers	1965	Allentown Jets	1979	Rochester Zeniths	1994	Quad City Thunder
1950	Williamsport Billies	1966	Wilmington Blue	1980	Anchorage Northern	1995	Yakima Sun Kings
1951	Sunbury Mercuries		Bombers		Knights	1996	Sioux Falls Skyforce
1952	Pottsville Packers	1967	Wilmington Blue	1981	Rochester Zeniths	1997	Oklahoma City
1953	Williamsport Billies		Bombers	1982	Lancaster Lightning		Calvary
1954	Williamsport Billies	1968	Allentown Jets	1983	Detroit Spirits	1998	Quad City Thunder
1955	Wilkes-Barre Barons	1969	Wilkes-Barre Barons	1984	Albany Patroons	1999	Connecticut Pride
1956	Wilkes-Barre Barons	1970	Allentown Jets	1985	Tampa Bay Thrillers	2000	Yakima Sun Kings
1957	Scranton Miners	1971	Scranton Apollos	1986	Tampa Bay Thrillers		
1958	Wilkes-Barre Barons	1972	Allentown Jets	1987	Rapid City Thrillers*		*The Tampa Bay Thrillers
1959	Wilkes-Barre Barons	1973	Wilkes-Barre Barons	1988	Albany Patroons		moved to Rapid City, S.D.
1960	Easton Madisons	1974	Hartford Capitols	1989	Tulsa Fast Breakers		at the end of the 1987 regu-
1961	Baltimore Bullets	1975	Allentown Jets	1990	La Crosse Catbirds		lar season.
1962	Allentown Jets	1976	Allentown Jets	1991	Wichita Falls Texans		

WOMEN

American Basketball League

League Champions

The American Basketball League began play in 1996 as an eight-team league. Before the 1997-98 season the league added an expansion franchise in Long Beach, Calif. while the Richmond Rage was relocated to Philadelphia. In the spring of 1998, the league announced plans to dissolve an original franchise, the Atlanta Glory, and expand to Chicago and Nashville before the 1998-99 season, increasing the league's size to 10 teams. The ABL finals was a best of five series. Each ABL champion's wins and losses are noted in parentheses after the series score. The ABL folded before the 1999 season.

Multiple winner: Columbus (2).

Year	Champions	Head Coach	Series	Runners-up	Head Coach
1997	Columbus Quest	Brian Agler	3-2 (WLLWW)	Richmond Rage	Lisa Boyer
1998	Columbus Quest	Brian Agler	3-2 (LLWWW)	Long Beach StingRays	Maura McHugh
1999	league folded				

Most Valuable Player

Winner's scoring averages provided; (*) indicates led league.

Year		Avg
1997	Nikki McCray, Columbus	19.9
1998	Natalie Williams, Portland	21.9*

Coach of the Year

Previous season and winning season's record are provided; (*) indicates division title.

Year		Improvement
1997	Brian Agler, Columbus	31-9*
1998	Lin Dunn, Portland	14-26 to 27-17

Women's National Basketball Association

League Champions

The WNBA, owned and operated by the NBA, began play in 1997 as an eight-team summer league. The league added two teams prior to its second season (1998) and again expanded by two teams before its third season in 1999. Four more teams were added before the 2000 season, bringing the total number of teams to 16. The WNBA champion was determined by a single-game playoff between the winners of the semifinals in the league's 1997 inaugural season, before going to a best-of-three championship series in 1998.

Multiple winner: Houston (4).

Year	Champions	Head Coach	Score	Runners-up	Head Coach
1997	Houston Comets	Van Chancellor	65-51	New York Liberty	Nancy Darsch
1998	Houston Comets	Van Chancellor	2-1 (LWW)	Phoenix Mercury	Cheryl Miller
1999	Houston Comets	Van Chancellor	2-1 (WLW)	New York Liberty	Richie Adubato
2000	Houston Comets	Van Chancellor	2-0	New York Liberty	Richie Adubato

Most Valuable Player

Winner's scoring averages provided; (*) indicates led league.

Multiple winner: Cynthia Cooper (2).

Year		Avg
1997	Cynthia Cooper, Houston	22.2*
1998	Cynthia Cooper, Houston	22.7*
1999	Yolanda Griffith, Sacramento	18.8
2000	Sheryl Swoopes, Houston	20.7*

Coach of the Year

Previous season and winning season's record are provided; (*) indicates division title.

Multiple winner: Van Chancellor (3).

Year		Improvement
1997	Van Chancellor, Houston	18-10*
1998	Van Chancellor, Houston	18-10 to 27-3*
1999	Van Chancellor, Houston	27-3 to 26-6*
2000	Michael Cooper, Los Angeles	20-12 to 28-4*

Hockey

*New Jersey head coach **Larry Robinson** raises the Stanley Cup while wearing the jersey of injured star center Petr Sykora.*

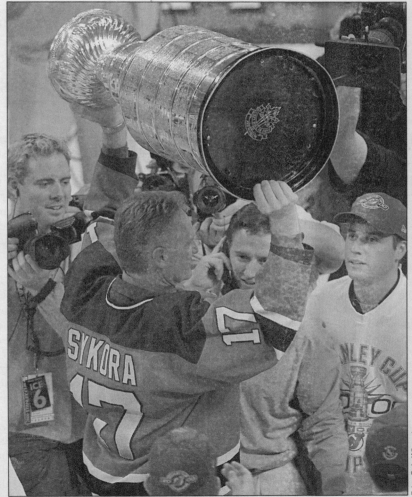

Brian Bahr/Allsport

Give the Devils their Due

Jason Arnott's double OT goal lifts New Jersey to its second cup in six years.

by

Steve Levy

You heard all the talk before the playoffs even started. The West was the best — by far the NHL's dominant conference. There was absolutely no way one of the big four teams (Dallas, Detroit, Colorado, and St. Louis) would fail to win the Stanley Cup. It was just a matter of which one. The Western Conference Finals would be the real Stanley Cup Finals. Oh sure, the East had some solid teams, but none really stood out from the pack. Each team could be eliminated in the first round or win the conference — but not the cup. Right? *Wrong!*

The New Jersey Devils proved that all that talk was just that — talk. New Jersey didn't just win the Stanley Cup, they dominated Dallas, making the defending

Steve Levy is a *SportsCenter* anchor and host of ESPN's *National Hockey Night.*

champs look slow and old. It was amazing the series even lasted six games. And as opposed to the "boring" defensive style the Devils used to win their first cup in 1995, this year's team was actually fun to watch. European forwards Patrik Elias and Petr Sykora were electrifying and huge winger Jason Arnott was an immovable force in front of the net. As usual, goaltender Martin Brodeur was great, but thanks to the impenetrable defense in front of him, he really didn't have to be. You're just not supposed to have a career year at the age of 36, but that's exactly what captain Scott Stevens did. He was a dominant force in the playoffs and the obvious choice for the Conn Smythe Trophy as playoff MVP.

Sometimes it's the moves made *off* the ice that are more important than the ones on it. The Devils proved that they continue to have one of the smartest management teams in the

New Jersey's **Jason Arnott** watches his shot sail past Dallas goaltender Ed Belfour 8:20 into the second overtime of Game 6 of the Stanley Cup Finals. The goal gave the Devils a 2-1 win in the game and their second Stanley Cup in the last six years.

league, led by general manager Lou Lamoriello. Player agents might not always like him, but you can't argue with his results. Lamoriello drafted rookie of the year Scott Gomez, made mid-season acquisitions of veterans Claude Lemieux and Alexander Mogilny, and even had the guts to fire coach Robbie Ftorek in favor of Larry Robinson with just eight games remaining in the regular season.

Overall, 1999-2000 wouldn't be considered a classic NHL season. There were just too many negatives subtracting from the positives. The image of Toronto's Bryan Berard taking an inadvertent stick to the eye from Ottawa's Marian Hossa is something I'll never forget, as much as I'd like to. Montreal's Trent McCleary suffered a horrendous injury as well after a slap shot to the throat left him

gasping for air with a fractured larynx and a collapsed lung. Emergency surgery was required to save his life. And then there were all the concussions and, of course, the most famous and unnecessary one caused by Marty McSorley's "mistake."

Off the ice, there was way too much attention paid to Ottawa's holdout Alexei Yashin. I'd like to give him the benefit of the doubt that he's just been getting bad advice, but ultimately it was Yashin who decided to sit out and take a season out of his prime playing years.

There were disappointments on the ice as well. After that regular season, how is it possible that the Blues were eliminated in the first round of the playoffs? Defenseman Chris Pronger is the best player in the NHL and has been for the last three years but his

AP/Wide World Photos

Opposing teams tried whatever they could in 1999-2000 to slow down Panthers winger **Pavel Bure**. Not many succeeded as the "Russian Rocket" tallied 58 goals to lead the league.

team's 114 regular season points and Presidents Trophy were meaningless once the playoffs began.

Speaking of disappointments, I'm sure the entire league enjoyed a good laugh in the direction of the New York Rangers — all that money, all those losses, and no playoff berth for the third consecutive year. They're truly hockey's version of baseball's Baltimore Orioles.

Eric Lindros' concussion troubles continued throughout the season, and when he publicly ripped team management after a concussion was misdiagnosed, his team captaincy was stripped. Of course it didn't stop him from coming back and performing better than any other Flyer on the ice in Game 6 of the Eastern Conference Finals against the Devils, before being devastated by Stevens in Game 7 with what we can only hope is his final

concussion. The Lindros saga was just one of the crazy stories surrounding the Flyers this year. Craig Ramsey took over the head coaching duties late in the season after Roger Neilson was stricken with cancer. And then when Neilson was ready to return behind the bench, his request was denied.

Do you think distractions were a factor for this team? You better believe it. Through it all, rookie goaltender Brian Boucher led the team deep into the playoffs, making one of the greatest saves in history in the process. Newly acquired Keith Primeau ended the third-longest game in NHL history against the Penguins. But it all came crashing down when they blew a 3-1 series lead against the Devils to lose 4-3.

So while the entire NHL season featured peaks and valleys, the Devils

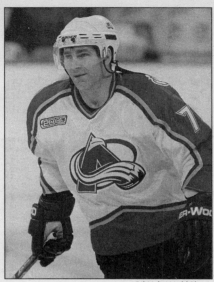

AP/Wide World Photos

Still looks weird, huh? After two decades and no Stanley Cups with the Bruins, defenseman **Ray Bourque** was traded late in the season to the cup-contending Colorado Avalanche.

and Stars saw to it that it finished on an up note. With Game 5 ending in triple overtime and Arnott's goal ending Game 6 in double overtime, the last two games of the Stanley Cup Finals were simply breathtaking. ∎

Steve Levy's Top Ten Memories from the 1999-00 Hockey Season.

10. **Ray Bourque in a Colorado Avalanche sweater.** After almost 21 seasons with the Bruins, the future hall of famer finally asks for a trade to a Stanley Cup contender. He comes close but again misses out on the ultimate prize.

9. **Buffalo's run of bad breaks continues.** I thought these things are supposed to even out? This time, the Sabres are done in by John LeClair's phantom goal in Game 2 of their first round series with the Flyers. The goal, which goes through a hole in the side of the net, gives the Flyers an insurmountable 2-0 lead in the series.

8. **The ugly feud** between the Lindros family and the Flyers boils over. The bulk of the bickering is done by Flyers' general manager Bobby Clarke and Eric's father/agent Carl but Eric's the one who pays.

7. **The Blues are ousted** in the first round of the playoffs. After losing just 20 games in the regular season, St. Louis goes down three games to one to Steve Shields and the San Jose Sharks before losing in seven.

6. **Marty McSorley's slash.** Even he couldn't believe he did it. After being whipped by Vancouver's Donald Brashear earlier in the game, McSorley returns to the ice with 2.7 seconds left in the game and levies a two-handed slash to Brashear's head, leaving him unconscious and twitching on the ice with a concussion.

5. **Toronto's Bryan Berard** takes a stick blade directly to the eye after a follow through on a fanned shot by Ottawa's Marion Hossa. He hopes someday to return to the ice but unfortunately the vision in his right eye may never be the same.

4. **Philadelphia's Keith Primeau finally** beats Pittsburgh goalie Ron Tugnutt with a wrist shot at 12:01 of the fifth overtime of Game 4 of the Eastern Conference semifinals in the third-longest NHL game ever played. The game ends at 2:35 a.m.

3. **Brian Boucher's miraculous save.** The rookie netminder does his best Dominik Hasek impression, flopping on his back and reaching with an outstretched arm to stop Devils sniper Patrik Elias on a breakaway to lead the Flyers to a 4-2 win in Game 3 of the Eastern Conference finals.

2. **Conn Smythe Award winner Scott Stevens** delivers a thunderous hit to recently-returned Eric Lindros in Game 7 of the Eastern Conference finals, giving the former Flyers captain his sixth concussion in the past two years.

1. **Devils head coach Larry Robinson** dons Petr Sykora's sweater as New Jersey celebrates its Stanley Cup victory on Dallas' ice. Sykora had been taken to the hospital earlier in the game after being drilled by Stars defenseman Derian Hatcher. ■

BEGINNER'S LUCK

In NHL history no goaltender has won more games in their first season with a new club than Roman Turek did with the Blues in 1999-00.

Player	Season	Wins
Roman Turek, St. Louis	'99-00	42
Pete Peeters, Boston	'82-83	40
Tony Esposito, Chicago	'69-70	38
Bill Durnan, Montreal	'43-44	38

WHO NEEDS 82?

Only four times in NHL history has a player missed over ten games in a regular season and still won the Art Ross Trophy (scoring title). Jaromir Jagr did it this season, winning by two points over Florida's Pavel Bure, and some guy named Mario did it the other three times.

Player	GP	Points	Games Missed
Mario Lemieux ('92-93)	60	160	24
Jaromir Jagr ('99-00)	63	96	19
Mario Lemieux ('91-92)	64	131	16
Mario Lemieux ('95-96)	70	161	12

DESERT DROUGHT

With their five-game loss to Colorado in the first round of the 2000 playoffs, the Phoenix Coyotes have now lost ten consecutive playoff series, tying the Montreal Canadiens for the all-time record.

	Years	Series
Phoenix Coyotes*	'87-00	10
Montreal Canadiens	'32-43	10
New York Rangers	'50-70	9
Carolina Hurricanes*	'86-99	8
Buffalo Sabres	'83-92	8
* current streak		

BROTHERLY LOVE

This season Pavel and Valeri Bure broke the NHL record for goals scored by a pair of brothers in a single season. Listed are the top five seasons for brotherly duos.

Season		Brothers	Goals
'99-00	Bure	Pavel (58)/Valeri (35)	93
'68-69	Hull	Bobby (58)/Dennis (30)	88
'70-71	Hull	Bobby (44)/Dennis (40)	84
'92-93	Turgeon	Pierre (58)/Sylvain (25)	83
'82-83	Stastny	Peter (47)/Marian (36)	83

Note: For the record, in both the 1983-84 and '84-85 seasons, the six Sutter brothers combined for 138 goals. ■

HOCKEY
1999-2000 Season in Review

ESPN information please SPORTS ALMANAC

Final NHL Standings

Division champions (*) and playoff qualifiers (†) are noted. T denotes any game that was tied after regulation play and a five-minute overtime period. RT signifies any game that was tied after regulation play but lost in overtime. They are each worth one point in the standings. Number of seasons listed after each head coach refers to current tenure with club through 1999-00 season.

Western Conference

Central Division

	W	L	RT	T	Pts	GF	GA
*St. Louis	51	20	1	11	114	248	165
†Detroit	48	24	2	10	108	278	210
Chicago	33	39	2	10	78	242	245
Nashville	28	47	7	7	70	199	240

Head Coaches: St.L— Joel Quenneville (4th season); **Det—** Scotty Bowman (7th); **Chi—** Bob Pulford (3rd, 28-25-0-6) replaced Lorne Molleken (5-14-2-4) on Dec. 2; **Nash—** Barry Trotz (2nd).

Northwest Division

	W	L	RT	T	Pts	GF	GA
*Colorado	42	29	1	11	96	233	201
†Edmonton	32	34	8	16	88	226	212
Vancouver	30	37	8	15	83	227	237
Calgary	31	41	5	10	77	211	256

Head Coaches: Col— Bob Hartley (2nd season); **Edm—** Kevin Lowe (1st); **Van—** Marc Crawford (2nd); **Calg—** Brian Sutter (3rd).

Pacific Division

	W	L	RT	T	Pts	GF	GA
*Dallas	43	29	6	10	102	211	184
†Los Angeles	39	31	4	12	94	245	228
†Phoenix	39	35	4	8	90	232	228
†San Jose	35	37	7	10	87	225	214
Anaheim	34	36	3	12	83	217	227

Head Coaches: Dal— Ken Hitchcock (5th season); **LA—** Andy Murray (1st); **Pho—** Bob Francis (1st); **SJ—** Darryl Sutter (3rd); **Ana—** Craig Hartsburg (2nd).

Eastern Conference

Northeast Division

	W	L	RT	T	Pts	GF	GA
*Toronto	45	30	3	7	100	246	222
†Ottawa	41	30	2	11	95	244	210
†Buffalo	35	36	4	11	85	213	204
Montreal	35	38	4	9	83	196	194
Boston	24	39	6	19	73	210	248

Head Coaches: Tor— Pat Quinn (2nd season); **Ott—** Jacques Martin (5th); **Buf—** Lindy Ruff (3rd); **Mon—** Alain Vigneault (3rd); **Bos—** Pat Burns (3rd).

Atlantic Division

	W	L	RT	T	Pts	GF	GA
*Philadelphia	45	25	3	12	105	237	179
†New Jersey	45	29	5	8	103	251	203
†Pittsburgh	37	37	6	8	88	241	236
NY Rangers	29	41	3	12	73	218	246
NY Islanders	24	49	1	9	58	194	275

Head Coaches: Phi— Roger Neilson (3rd season); **NJ—** Robbie Ftorek (2nd, 41-25-5-8) was replaced by Larry Robinson (4-4-0-0) on March 23; **Pit—** Kevin Constantine (3rd, 8-14-4-3) was replaced by Herb Brooks (29-23-2-5) on Dec. 9; **NYR—** John Muckler (3rd, 29-38-3-11) was replaced on an interim basis by John Tortorella (0-3-0-1) on March 28; **NYI—** Butch Goring (1st).

Southeast Division

	W	L	RT	T	Pts	GF	GA
*Washington	44	26	2	12	102	227	194
†Florida	43	33	6	6	98	244	209
Carolina	37	35	0	10	84	217	216
Tampa Bay	19	54	7	9	54	204	310
Atlanta	14	61	4	7	39	170	313

Head Coaches: Wash— Ron Wilson (3rd season); **Fla—** Terry Murray (2nd); **Car—** Paul Maurice (5th); **TB—** Steve Ludzik (1st); **Atl—** Curt Fraser (1st).

Home & Away, Division, Conference Records

Sixteen teams— eight from each conference— qualify for the Stanley Cup Playoffs; (*) indicates division champions.

Western Conference

	Pts	Home	Away	Div	Conf
1 St. Louis*	114	24-10-7	27-10-4	8-6-3	34-15-9
2 Dallas*	102	21-15-5	22-14-5	12-11-1	29-24-7
3 Colorado*	96	25-12-4	17-17-7	13-3-2	31-19-8
4 Detroit	108	28-10-3	20-14-7	10-6-2	32-19-7
5 Los Angeles	94	21-15-5	18-16-7	8-13-3	27-24-8
6 Phoenix	90	22-17-2	17-18-6	13-10-1	28-26-4
7 Edmonton	88	18-14-9	14-20-7	6-9-2	20-30-7
8 San Jose	87	21-17-3	14-20-7	11-11-2	23-28-8
Anaheim	83	19-15-7	15-21-5	11-10-3	26-23-8
Vancouver	83	16-20-5	14-17-10	4-11-3	16-28-11
Chicago	78	16-20-5	17-19-5	6-8-3	22-27-7
Calgary	77	20-15-6	11-26-4	8-9-1	20-28-7
Nashville	70	15-23-3	13-24-4	6-10-2	17-34-5

Eastern Conference

	Pts	Home	Away	Div	Conf
1 Philadelphia*	105	25-9-7	20-16-5	12-6-2	36-18-8
2 Washington*	102	26-7-8	18-19-4	14-4-2	37-19-6
3 Toronto*	100	24-12-5	21-18-2	10-8-2	32-21-6
4 New Jersey	103	28-10-3	17-19-5	13-5-2	36-19-6
5 Florida	98	26-11-4	17-22-2	10-7-3	31-26-3
6 Ottawa	95	24-12-5	17-18-6	11-5-4	33-19-10
7 Pittsburgh	88	23-11-7	14-26-1	9-10-1	32-26-4
8 Buffalo	85	21-15-5	14-21-6	9-9-2	25-29-8
Carolina	84	20-16-5	17-19-5	12-5-3	29-26-5
Montreal	83	18-18-5	17-20-4	7-10-3	26-26-8
NY Rangers	73	15-21-5	14-20-7	5-12-3	21-29-10
Boston	73	12-18-11	12-21-8	5-10-5	20-27-13
NY Islanders	58	10-26-5	14-23-4	6-12-2	19-36-5
Tampa Bay	54	13-24-4	6-30-5	2-15-3	14-40-5
Atlanta	39	9-29-3	5-32-4	5-12-3	11-41-7

2000 NHL All-Star Game

The World 9, North America 4

50th NHL All-Star Game. **Date:** Feb. 6 at the Air Canada Centre in Toronto; **Coaches:** Scotty Bowman, Detroit (World) and Pat Quinn, Toronto (North America); **MVP:** Pavel Bure, Florida right wing (World) — three goals, one assist.

For the third consecutive year, the NHL decided to abandon its usual all-star game format of Eastern Conference vs. Western Conference in favor of a game pitting the North American all-stars vs. the rest of the world's all-stars.

Starters were chosen by fan vote while reserves were selected by the NHL's Hockey Operations Department, after consultation with NHL general managers. Head coaches whose teams had the best winning percentage in the Eastern Conference (North America) and Western Conference (World) on Jan. 4 were named all-star head coaches.

Goaltender Roman Turek, left wing Patrik Elias and defenseman Dimitri Yushkevich were added to the **World** team as injury replacements for Dominik Hasek, Peter Forsberg and Kimmo Timonen, respectively.

Left wing Ray Whitney was added to the **North American** team as an injury replacement for Pierre Turgeon.

The World

Starters		G	A	Pts	PM
W	Jaromir Jagr, Pittsburgh	1	1	2	0
D	Niklas Lidstrom, Detroit	0	1	1	0
D	Sandis Ozolinsh, Colorado	0	0	0	2
W	Teemu Selanne, Anaheim	0	0	0	0
C	Mats Sundin, Toronto	0	0	0	0

Reserves		G	A	Pts	PM
W	Pavel Bure, Florida	3	1	4	0
C	Viktor Kozlov, Florida	0	3	3	0
C	Radek Bonk, Ottawa	1	1	2	0
W	Valeri Bure, Calgary	0	2	2	0
W	Pavol Demitra, St. Louis	2	0	2	0
W	Patrik Elias, New Jersey	0	2	2	0
W	Martin Rucinsky, Montreal	0	2	2	0
D	Dimitri Yushkevich, Toronto	1	1	2	0
W	Mariusz Czerkawski, NYI	0	1	1	0
W	Milan Hejduk, Colorado	0	1	1	0
W	Miroslav Satan, Buffalo	1	0	1	0
D	Petr Buzek, Atlanta	0	0	0	0
W	Sami Kapanen, Carolina	0	0	0	0
D	Teppo Numminen, Phoenix	0	0	0	0
D	Petr Svoboda, Tampa Bay	0	0	0	0
D	Sergei Zubov, Dallas	0	0	0	0
	TOTALS	9	16	25	2

Goaltenders	Mins	Shots	Saves	GA
Roman Turek, St.L	20:00	13	11	2
Tommy Salo, Edm (W)	20:00	11	9	2
Olaf Kolzig, Wash.	20:00	8	8	0
TOTALS	60:00	32	28	4

North America

Starters		G	A	Pts	PM
D	Rob Blake, Los Angeles	0	0	0	0
W	Paul Kariya, Anaheim	0	0	0	0
D	Chris Pronger, St. Louis	0	0	0	0
W	Brendan Shanahan, Detroit	0	0	0	0
C	Steve Yzerman, Detroit	0	0	0	0

Reserves		G	A	Pts	PM
W	Ray Whitney, Florida	1	1	2	0
C	Mike Modano, Dallas	0	2	2	0
W	Tony Amonte, Chicago	1	0	1	0
D	Ray Bourque, Boston	0	1	1	0
D	Eric Desjardins, Philadelphia	0	1	1	0
C	Mark Messier, Vancouver	0	1	1	0
W	Mark Recchi, Philadelphia	0	1	1	0
C	Jeremy Roenick, Phoenix	1	0	1	0
C	Joe Sakic, Colorado	1	0	1	0
C	Chris Chelios, Detroit	0	0	0	0
C	Scott Gomez, New Jersey	0	0	0	0
C	Phil Housley, Calgary	0	0	0	0
W	John LeClair, Philadelphia	0	0	0	0
C	Eric Lindros, Philadelphia	0	0	0	0
C	Al MacInnis, St. Louis	0	0	0	0
W	Owen Nolan, San Jose	0	0	0	0
D	Scott Stevens, New Jersey	0	0	0	0
	TOTALS	4	7	11	0

Goaltenders	Mins	Shots	Saves	GA
Curtis Joseph, Tor.	20:00	20	17	3
Martin Brodeur, NJ (L)	20:00	13	11	2
Mike Richter, NYR	20:00	15	11	4
TOTALS	60:00	48	39	9

Score by Periods

	1	2	3	Final
World	3	2	4	— 9
North America	2	2	0	— 4

Power plays: World — 0/0; North America — 0/1. **Officials:** Kerry Fraser and Don Koharski (referees), Gerry Gauthier and Ray Scapinello (linesmen). **Attendance:** 19,300. **TV Rating:** 2.7/6 share (ABC).

2000 NHL Skills Competition

The World, 13-11

Puck Control Relay
Team: World
Individual: Paul Kariya (North America)

Fastest Skater
Team: World (14.016 sec.)
Individual: Sami Kapanen, World (13.649 sec.)

Hardest Shot
Team: North America (99.9 mph)
Individual: Al MacInnis, North America (100.1 mph)

Rapid Fire Relay
Team: North America (47 saves—Richter, Brodeur and Joseph)

Shooting Accuracy (targets/shots)
Team: World (13/28)
Individual: Viktor Kozlov, World and Ray Bourque, North America (4/5)

Breakaway Relay
Team: World wins, 8-6

Goaltender Competition
Individual: Mike Richter, North America (14 saves)

Pittsburgh Penguins	Florida Panthers	Detroit Red Wings	New Jersey Devils
Jaromir Jagr	**Pavel Bure**	**Nicklas Lidstrom**	**Martin Brodeur**
Scoring	Goals, Shots	Defensemen Points	Wins

NHL Regular Season Individual Leaders

(*) indicates rookie eligible for Calder Trophy.

Scoring

	Pos	Gm	G	A	Pts	+/-	PM	PP	SH	GW	GT	Shots	Pct
Jaromir Jagr, Pittsburgh	R	63	42	54	**96**	25	50	10	0	5	1	290	14.5
Pavel Bure, Florida	R	74	58	36	**94**	21	16	11	2	14	0	361	16.1
Mark Recchi, Philadelphia	R	82	28	63	**91**	19	52	7	1	5	1	223	12.6
Paul Kariya, Anaheim	L	74	42	44	**86**	22	24	11	3	3	0	324	13.0
Tony Amonte, Chicago	R	82	43	42	**85**	8	48	11	5	2	1	259	16.6
Teemu Selanne, Anaheim	R	79	33	52	**85**	6	12	8	0	6	2	236	14.0
Owen Nolan, San Jose	R	78	44	40	**84**	-1	110	18	4	6	2	261	16.9
Joe Sakic, Colorado	C	60	28	54	**82**	30	28	5	1	5	0	242	11.6
Mike Modano, Dallas	C	77	38	43	**81**	-1	48	11	1	8	3	188	20.2
Steve Yzerman, Detroit	C	78	35	44	**79**	29	34	15	2	6	1	234	15.0
Brendan Shanahan, Detroit	L	78	41	37	**78**	25	105	13	1	9	1	284	14.4
Jeremy Roenick, Phoenix	C	78	34	44	**78**	12	102	6	3	12	1	192	17.7
John LeClair, Philadelphia	L	82	40	37	**77**	8	36	13	0	7	2	249	16.1
Valeri Bure, Calgary	R	82	35	40	**75**	-7	50	13	0	6	1	310	11.3
Pavol Demitra, St. Louis	R	71	28	47	**75**	34	8	8	0	4	0	241	11.6
Luc Robitaille, Los Angeles	L	71	36	37	**73**	11	68	13	0	7	0	220	16.4
Mats Sundin, Toronto	C	73	32	41	**73**	16	46	10	2	7	0	184	17.4
Doug Gilmour, Chi-Buf	C	74	25	48	**73**	-9	63	10	0	3	1	113	22.1
Nicklas Lidstrom, Detroit	D	81	20	53	**73**	21	18	9	4	3	0	218	9.2
Milan Hejduk, Colorado	R	82	36	36	**72**	14	16	13	0	9	2	228	15.8
Ron Francis, Carolina	C	78	23	48	**72**	12	18	7	0	4	0	150	15.3
Doug Weight, Edmonton	C	77	21	51	**72**	6	54	3	1	4	0	167	12.6

Goals

Bure, Fla	58
Nolan, SJ	44
Amonte, Chi	43
Jagr, Pit	42
Kariya, Ana	42
Shanahan, Det	41
LeClair, Phi	40
Modano, Dal	38
Robitaille, LA	36
Hejduk, Col	36

Plus/Minus

Pronger, St.L	52
Chelios, Det	48
Demitra, St.L	34
Sakic, Col	30
Turgeon, St.L	30
Stevens, NJ	30
Yzerman, Det	28
Bergevin, St.L	27
Finley, St.L	26
Gonchar, Wash	26
Klemm, Col	26

Assists

Recchi, Phi	63
Oates, Wash	56
Sakic, Col	54
Jagr, Pit	54
Lidstrom, Det	53
Selanne, Ana	52
Kozlov, Fla	52
Weight, Edm	51
Gomez*, NJ	51
Damphousse, SJ	50
Francis, Car	49
Fleury, NYR	49

Penalty Minutes

Lambert, Atl	219
Simpson, Fla	202
Domi, Tor	198
Barnaby, Pit	197
Cairns, NYI	196
Brown, Edm	192
Laperriere, LA	185
Oliwa, NJ	184
Laus, Fla	172
Svoboda, TB	170

Defensemen Points

Lidstrom, Det	73
Pronger, St.L	62
R. Blake, LA	57
Housley, Calg	55
Desjardins, Phi	55
Gonchar, Wash	54
Ozolinsh, Col	52
Bourque, Bos-Col	52
Tverdovsky, Ana	51
Svehla, Fla	49

Power Play Goals

Nolan, SJ	18
Czerkawski, NYI	16
Yzerman, Det	15
LeClair, Phi	13
Bure, Calg	13
Robitaille, LA	13
Lang, Pit	13
Hejduk, Col	13
Bourque, Bos-Col	13
Shanahan, Det	13

Rookie Points

Gomez, NJ	70
Tanguay, Col	51
York, NYR	50
Gagne, Phi	48
Hlavac, NYR	42
Letowski, Pho	39
Stuart, SJ	36
Connolly, NYI	34
Hecht, St.L	34
Afinogenov, Buf	34
Morrow, Dal	33

Short-Handed Goals

Madden*, NJ	6
Amonte, Chi	5
Lidstrom, Det	4
Keane, Dal	4
Fedorov, Det	4
Halpern*, Wash	4
Handzus, St.L	4
Letowski*, Pho	4
Nolan, SJ	4
Sturm, SJ	4

Shots

Bure, Fla.	360
Blake, LA	327
Kariya, Ana.	324
Bure, Calg.	308
Jagr, Pit	290
Shanahan, Det	283
Czerkawski, NYI	276
Naslund, Van	271
Satan, Buf	265
Fedorov, Det	263

Shooting Pct.
(Min. 70 shots)

Tanguay*, Col	23.0
Eastwood, St.L.	22.9
Selivanov, Edm	22.1
Gilmour, Chi-Buf	22.1
Brunette, Atl	21.5
Bartecko, St.L.	21.3
Modano, Dal	20.2
Korolev, Tor	19.8
Nylander, TB-Chi	19.7
Elias, NJ	19.1

Hits

Witt, Wash	322
Chara, NYI	309
Klee, Wash	307
Sweeney, Bos	301
McLaren, Bos	282
Yushkevich, Tor	266
McGillis, Phi	264
Kasparaitis, Pit	261
Norstrom, LA.	261
Smith, Edm	260

Minutes/Game
(Min. 50 Games)

Pronger, St.L.	30.2
Zubov, Dal	28.8
Lidstrom, Det	28.7
Blake, LA	28.5
Hatcher, Dal.	27.5
Bourque, Bos-Col.	27.2
Desjardins, Phi.	27.0
Leetch, NYR	26.9
MacInnis, St.L.	26.1
Foote, Col.	25.9
Weinrich, Mon.	25.3

Goaltending
(Minimum 26 games)

	Gm	Min	GAA	GA	Shots	Sv%	EN	ShO	Record	G	A	Pts	PM
Brian Boucher*, Philadelphia	35	2038	**1.91**	65	790	.918	3	4	20-10-3	0	1	1	4
Roman Turek, St. Louis	67	3960	**1.95**	129	1470	.912	3	7	42-15-9	0	1	1	4
Ed Belfour, Dallas	62	3620	**2.10**	127	1571	.919	6	4	32-21-7	0	3	3	10
Jose Theodore, Montreal	30	1655	**2.10**	58	717	.919	2	5	12-13-2	0	0	0	0
John Vanbiesbrouck, Philadelphia	50	2950	**2.20**	108	1143	.906	3	3	25-15-9	0	1	1	6
Dominik Hasek, Buffalo	35	2066	**2.21**	76	937	.919	2	3	15-11-6	0	1	1	12
Martin Brodeur, New Jersey	72	4312	**2.24**	161	1797	.910	3	6	43-20-8	1	4	5	16
Olaf Kolzig, Washington	73	4371	**2.24**	163	1957	.917	1	5	41-20-11	0	2	2	4
Patrick Roy, Colorado	63	3704	**2.28**	141	1640	.914	5	2	32-21-8	0	3	3	10
Patrick Lalime, Ottawa	38	2038	**2.33**	79	834	.905	1	3	19-14-3	0	0	0	4
Tommy Salo, Edmonton	70	4164	**2.33**	162	1875	.914	0	2	27-28-13	0	1	1	8
Mikhail Shtalenkov, Florida	30	1786	**2.35**	70	739	.905	3	2	15-10-4	0	3	3	4
Jeff Hackett, Montreal	56	3301	**2.40**	132	1543	.914	2	3	23-25-7	0	0	0	4
Chris Osgood, Detroit	53	3148	**2.40**	126	1349	.907	2	6	30-14-8	0	1	1	18
Martin Biron*, Buffalo	41	2229	**2.42**	90	988	.909	2	5	19-18-2	0	0	0	6

Wins

Brodeur, NJ	43
Turek, St.L.	42
Kolzig, Wash.	41
Joseph, Tor	36
Irbe, Car.	34
Belfour, Dal	32
Roy, Col	32
Osgood, Det	30
Hebert, Ana.	28
Two tied with 27 each.	

Shutouts

Turek, St.L.	7
Brodeur, NJ	6
Osgood, Det	6
Biron*, Buf	5
Brathwaite, Calg	5
Irbe, Car.	5
Kolzig, Wash	5
Theodore, Mon	5
Six tied with 4 each.	

Save Pct.

Belfour, Dal.	.919
Hasek, Buf.	.919
Theodore, Buf.	.919
Boucher*, Phi	.918
Kolzig, Wash	.917
Vernon, Fla	.917
Joseph, Tor	.915
Kidd, Fla	.915
Aubin*, Pit	.914
Burke, Pho.	.914

Losses

Hebert, Ana.	31
Richter, NYR.	31
Cloutier, TB	30
Shields, SJ	30
Irbe, Car.	28
Salo, Edm.	28
Dunham, Nash	27
Potvin, NYI-Van	27
Weekes, Van-NYI	27
Thibault, Chi	26

Team Goaltending

WESTERN	GAA	Mins	GA	Shots	Sv%	EN	SO	EASTERN	GAA	Mins	GA	Shots	Sv%	EN	SO
St. Louis	**1.98**	4988	165	1814	.909	3	9	Philadelphia	**2.14**	5008	179	1939	.908	6	6
Dallas	**2.21**	4992	184	2183	.916	9	5	Washington	**2.33**	4999	194	2270	.915	3	7
Colorado	**2.42**	4990	201	2283	.912	7	5	Montreal	**2.34**	4983	194	2264	.914	4	8
Edmonton	**2.53**	5030	212	2318	.909	0	2	New Jersey	**2.45**	4975	203	2101	.903	8	5
Detroit	**2.53**	4985	210	2169	.903	3	6	Buffalo	**2.45**	4996	204	2208	.908	6	8
San Jose	**2.57**	5004	214	2357	.909	5	5	Ottawa	**2.53**	4986	210	2064	.898	3	7
Anaheim	**2.73**	4992	227	2259	.900	9	5	Florida	**2.53**	4966	209	2431	.914	4	2
Los Angeles	**2.74**	4997	228	2290	.900	10	2	Carolina	**2.61**	4974	216	2141	.899	9	6
Phoenix	**2.74**	4987	228	2334	.902	8	6	Toronto	**2.67**	4983	222	2386	.907	5	6
Vancouver	**2.83**	5033	237	2292	.897	8	1	Pittsburgh	**2.84**	4984	236	2356	.900	7	4
Nashville	**2.89**	4986	240	2499	.904	7	1	NY Rangers	**2.95**	4996	246	2446	.899	7	0
Chicago	**2.95**	4984	245	2397	.898	14	4	Boston	**2.96**	5028	248	2274	.891	7	6
Calgary	**3.07**	5007	256	2381	.892	6	5	NY Islanders	**3.31**	4981	275	2742	.900	9	3
								Tampa Bay	**3.73**	4982	310	2494	.876	8	0
								Atlanta	**3.78**	4966	313	2543	.877	10	2

Power Play/Penalty Killing

Power play and penalty killing conversions. Power play: No— number of opportunities; GF— goals for; Pct— percentage. Penalty killing: No— number of times shorthanded; GA— goals against; Pct— percentage of penalties killed; SH— shorthanded goals for.

WESTERN	—Power Play—			—Penalty Killing—				EASTERN	—Power Play—			—Penalty Killing—			
	No	GF	Pct	No	GA	Pct	SH		No	GF	Pct	No	GA	Pct	SH
Detroit.........338	338	69	**20.4**	311	44	85.9	15	Philadelphia ...340	340	69	**20.3**	316	42	86.7	7
Colorado 302	302	59	**19.5**	335	52	84.5	3	New Jersey ...274	274	55	**20.1**	313	39	87.5	9
Calgary 330	330	59	**17.9**	365	74	79.7	4	Toronto 321	321	57	**17.8**	330	58	82.4	11
St. Louis 342	342	61	**17.8**	345	42	87.8	13	Florida 338	338	58	**17.2**	323	47	85.4	2
Los Angeles ...356	356	60	**16.9**	373	66	82.3	4	Carolina......342	342	58	**17.0**	253	40	84.2	3
Anaheim 332	332	55	**16.6**	296	62	79.1	4	NY Rangers...325	325	55	**16.9**	292	49	83.2	5
San Jose.......377	377	62	**16.4**	372	61	83.6	16	Ottawa........310	310	52	**16.8**	273	34	87.5	6
Chicago......325	325	52	**16.0**	355	58	83.7	10	Montreal 323	323	54	**16.7**	302	40	86.8	7
Vancouver 323	323	51	**15.8**	322	63	80.4	9	Pittsburgh 346	346	54	**15.6**	321	56	82.6	7
Edmonton 336	336	53	**15.8**	369	54	85.4	9	Washington ...287	287	43	**15.0**	341	47	86.2	9
Dallas.........343	343	54	**15.7**	307	33	89.3	9	Boston 355	355	51	**14.4**	268	55	79.5	0
Nashville 304	304	41	**13.5**	309	46	85.1	9	NY Islanders ...320	320	45	**14.1**	420	84	80.0	8
Phoenix 310	310	37	**11.9**	306	43	85.9	14	Tampa Bay....365	365	51	**14.0**	399	77	80.7	9
								Atlanta........348	348	44	**12.6**	386	76	80.3	6
								Buffalo.........351	351	37	**10.5**	361	54	85.0	8

Hat Tricks

Players scored three or more goals in one game a total of 53 times during the 1999-00 regular season. Pavel Bure of Florida accomplished the feat four times to lead all players. (*) indicates rookie.

Four Goals	Date	Career Total
Dave Andreychuk, Bos vs TB ....Oct. 28	Oct. 28	11
Alexander Selivanov, Edm at Chi ....Nov. 14	Nov. 14	2
Michael Nylander, Chi at Bos ....Dec. 4	Dec. 4	2
Pavel Bure, Fla vs TB................Jan. 1	Jan. 1	14
Marc Savard, Calg at St.L...........Apr. 5	Apr. 5	1

Three Goals	Date	Career Total
Jeff Friesen, SJ vs Chi...............Oct. 4	Oct. 4	2
Owen Nolan, SJ vs Chi ....Oct. 4	Oct. 4	10
Alexei Morozov, Pit at NJ ....Oct. 7	Oct. 7	1
Luc Robitaille, LA at TB.............Oct. 7	Oct. 7	14
Brian Savage, Mon at Calg ....Oct. 8	Oct. 8	4
Peter Bondra, Wash vs Phi ....Oct. 12	Oct. 12	14
Brian Savage, Mon at Phi...........Oct. 14	Oct. 14	5
Glen Murray, LA at Edm ....Oct. 16	Oct. 16	2
Rob Valicevic, Nash at Chi ....Nov. 10	Nov. 10	1
Dean Sylvester, Atl vs Van ....Nov. 22	Nov. 22	1
Jeremy Roenick, Pho vs NJ..........Nov. 25	Nov. 25	7
Jaromir Jagr, Pit vs Ott ....Nov. 26	Nov. 26	5
Jeremy Roenick, Pho vs Col ....Nov. 26	Nov. 26	8
Teemu Selanne, Ana at Dal ....Nov. 26	Nov. 26	16
Pierre Turgeon, St.L vs Nash........Dec. 2	Dec. 2	14
Sandis Ozolinsh, Col vs Van ....Dec. 6	Dec. 6	1
Pavel Bure, Fla vs Pho ....Dec. 8	Dec. 8	12
Eric Lindros, Phi vs Tor ....Dec. 9	Dec. 9	11
Pavel Bure, Fla at Buf ....Dec. 17	Dec. 17	13
Nikolai Antropov*, Tor at Fla........Dec. 20	Dec. 20	1
Mike Eastwood, St.L at Pho ....Dec. 21	Dec. 21	1

Three Goals	Date	Career Total
Scott Gomez*, NJ at NYR ....Dec. 26	Dec. 26	1
Jaromir Jagr, Pit vs NYI ....Dec. 30	Dec. 30	6
Sergei Gonchar, Wash vs Mon.......Jan. 4	Jan. 4	1
Adam Deadmarsh, Col vs Calg.......Jan. 5	Jan. 5	1
Viktor Kozlov, Fla at Ana ....Jan. 5	Jan. 5	1
Miroslav Satan, Buf at Ott ....Jan. 8	Jan. 8	3
Petr Nedved, NYR at Tor ....Jan. 8	Jan. 8	3
Petr Nedved, NYR at Atl ....Jan. 24	Jan. 24	4
Radek Dvorak, NYR vs Nash.........Jan. 31	Jan. 31	1
Trevor Linden, Mon vs Edm ....Feb. 8	Feb. 8	5
Jan Hlavac*, NYR vs Bos ....Feb. 11	Feb. 11	1
Pavol Demitra, St.L vs Ana ....Feb. 12	Feb. 12	1
Shjon Podein, Col at NYR...........Feb. 18	Feb. 18	1
Georges Laraque, Edm vs LA ....Feb. 21	Feb. 21	1
Michael Peca, Buf vs NYR...........Feb. 25	Feb. 25	1
Petr Nedved, NYR at Buf............Feb. 25	Feb. 25	5
Stephane Richer, St.L vs Col ....Feb. 25	Feb. 25	10
Joe Sakic, Col at Calg...............Mar. 7	Mar. 7	8
Bates Battaglia, Car vs Chi..........Mar. 8	Mar. 8	1
Tony Amonte, Chi at TB ....Mar. 12	Mar. 12	7
Ryan Smyth, Edm at Atl..............Mar. 13	Mar. 13	2
Boyd Devereaux, Edm vs Ott ....Mar. 17	Mar. 17	1
Pavel Bure, Fla at NYI...............Mar. 18	Mar. 18	15
Joe Sakic, Col at Pho ....Mar. 23	Mar. 23	9
Martin Lapointe, Det vs NYR ....Mar. 26	Mar. 26	1
Alexander Selivanov, Edm at Calg......Apr. 8	Apr. 8	3
Mariusz Czerkawski, NYI vs Fla........Apr. 9	Apr. 9	3

NHL Expansion through 2000-2001

In the 2000-2001 season, the Columbus Blue Jackets and Minnesota Wild will each join the Western Conference, with Columbus going to the Central Division and Minnesota to the Northwest.

WESTERN			EASTERN		
Central	Northwest	Pacific	Northeast	Atlantic	Southeast
Chicago	Calgary	Anaheim	Boston	New Jersey	Atlanta
Columbus	Colorado	Dallas	Buffalo	NY Islanders	Carolina
Detroit	Edmonton	Los Angeles	Montreal	NY Rangers	Florida
Nashville	Minnesota	Phoenix	Ottawa	Philadelphia	Tampa Bay
St. Louis	Vancouver	San Jose	Toronto	Pittsburgh	Washington

Team by Team Statistics

High scorers and goaltenders with at least ten games played. Players who competed for more than one team during the regular season are listed with their final club; (*) indicates rookies eligible for Calder Trophy.

Mighty Ducks of Anaheim

Top Scorers	Gm	G	A	Pts	+/-	PM	PP
Paul Kariya	74	42	44	86	22	24	11
Teemu Selanne	79	33	52	85	6	12	8
Steve Rucchin	71	19	38	57	9	16	10
Oleg Tverdovsky	82	15	36	51	5	30	5
Kip Miller	74	10	32	42	0	14	2
PIT	44	4	15	19	-1	10	0
ANA	30	6	17	23	1	4	2
Matt Cullen	80	13	26	39	5	24	1
Fredrik Olausson	70	15	19	34	-13	28	8
Jorgen Jonsson	81	12	19	31	-8	16	1
NYI	68	11	17	28	-6	16	1
ANA	13	1	2	3	-2	0	0
Ted Donato	81	11	19	30	-3	26	2
Marty McInnis	62	16	12	28	-4	26	2
Ladislav Kohn*	77	5	16	21	-17	27	1
Mike LeClerc	69	8	11	19	-15	70	0
Jeff Nielsen	79	8	10	18	4	14	1
Antti Aalto	63	7	11	18	-13	26	1
Pavel Trnka	57	2	15	17	12	34	0

Acquired: C Miller from Pit. for future considerations (Jan. 29); LW Jonsson from NYI for C Johan Davidsson and a conditional pick (Mar. 11).

Goalies (10 Gm)	Gm	Min	GAA	Record	SV%
Guy Hebert	68	3976	2.51	28-31-9	.908
Dominic Roussel	20	988	3.16	6-5-3	.883
ANAHEIM	82	4992	2.73	34-36-12	.900

Shutouts: Hebert (4), Roussel (1). **Assists:** Hebert (2). **PM:** Roussel (6), Hebert (2).

Atlanta Thrashers

Top Scorers	Gm	G	A	Pts	+/-	PM	PP
Andrew Brunette	81	23	27	50	-32	30	9
Ray Ferraro	81	19	25	44	-33	88	10
Donald Audette	63	19	24	43	2	57	1
LA	49	12	20	32	6	45	1
ATL	14	7	4	11	-4	12	0
Yannick Tremblay	75	10	21	31	-42	22	4
Hnat Domenichelli	59	11	18	29	-21	16	1
CALG	32	5	9	14	0	12	1
ATL	27	6	9	15	-21	4	0
Stephen Guolla	66	10	19	29	-11	15	4
TB	46	6	10	16	2	11	2
ATL	20	4	9	13	-13	4	2
Dean Sylvester	52	16	10	26	-14	24	1
Patrick Stefan*	72	5	20	25	-20	30	1
Mike Stapleton	62	10	12	22	-29	30	4
Petr Buzek*	63	5	14	19	-22	41	3
Johan Garpenlov	73	2	14	16	-30	31	0
Frantisek Kaberle*	51	1	15	16	-10	10	0
LA	37	0	9	9	3	4	0
ATL	14	1	6	7	-13	6	0
Andreas Karlsson*	51	5	9	14	-17	14	1

Acquired: LW Domenichelli and LW Dmitri Vlasenkov from Calg. for D Darryl Shannon and LW Jason Botterill (Feb. 11); RW Audette and D Kaberle from LA for RW Nelson Emerson and LW Kelly Buchberger (Mar. 13). **Claimed:** C Guolla off waivers from TB (Mar. 1).

Goalies (10 Gm)	Gm	Min	GAA	Record	SV%
Scott Fankhouser*	16	920	3.20	2-11-2	.891
Norm Maracle*	32	1618	3.49	4-19-2	.890
Damian Rhodes	28	1561	3.88	5-19-3	.874
Scott Langkow*	15	765	4.31	3-11-0	.861
ATLANTA	82	4966	3.78	14-61-7	.877

Shutouts: Maracle and Rhodes (1). **Assists:** none. **PM:** Fankhouser (4), Rhodes (2).

Boston Bruins

Top Scorers	Gm	G	A	Pts	+/-	PM	PP
Joe Thornton	81	23	37	60	-5	82	5
Anson Carter	59	22	25	47	8	14	4
Sergei Samsonov	77	19	26	45	-6	4	6
Brian Rolston	77	16	15	31	-12	18	5
NJ	11	3	1	4	-2	0	1
COL	50	8	10	18	-6	12	1
BOS	16	5	4	9	-4	6	3
Jason Allison	37	10	18	28	5	20	3
Darren Van Impe	79	5	23	28	-19	73	4
P.J. Axelsson	81	10	16	26	1	24	0
Steve Heinze	75	12	13	25	-8	36	2
Mike Knuble	73	12	8	20	-7	26	2
NYR	59	9	5	14	-5	18	1
BOS	14	3	3	6	-2	8	1
Andre Savage*	43	7	13	20	-8	10	2
Kyle McLaren	71	8	11	19	-4	67	2
Mikko Eloranta	50	6	12	18	-10	36	1
Don Sweeney	81	1	13	14	-14	48	0

Acquired: LW Rolston, D Martin Grenier, C Sami Pahlsson and either a '00 or '01 1st-round pick from Col. for D Ray Bourque and LW Dave Andreychuk (Mar. 6); RW Knuble from NYR for RW Rob DiMaio (Mar. 10).

Goalies (10 Gm)	Gm	Min	GAA	Record	SV%
John Grahame*	24	1344	2.46	7-10-5	.910
Byron Dafoe	41	2307	2.96	13-16-10	.889
Rob Tallas	27	1363	3.17	4-13-4	.885
BOSTON	82	5028	2.96	24-39-19	.891

Shutouts: Dafoe (3), Grahame (2). Tallas and Grahame also combined for a shutout. **Assists:** Grahame (8), Tallas (6). **PM:** Grahame (10).

Buffalo Sabres

Top Scorers	Gm	G	A	Pts	+/-	PM	PP
Doug Gilmour	74	25	48	73	-9	63	10
CHI	63	22	34	56	-12	51	8
BUF	11	3	14	17	3	12	2
Miroslav Satan	81	33	34	67	16	32	5
Curtis Brown	74	22	29	51	19	42	5
Chris Gratton	72	15	34	49	-23	136	4
TB	58	14	27	41	-24	121	4
BUF	14	1	7	8	1	15	0
Stu Barnes	82	20	25	45	-3	16	8
Michael Peca	73	20	21	41	6	67	2
Vaclav Varada	76	10	27	37	12	62	0
Maxim Afinogenov*	65	16	18	34	-4	41	2
Jason Woolley	74	8	25	33	14	52	2
Vladimir Tsyplakov	63	12	20	32	23	14	1
LA	29	6	7	13	6	4	1
BUF	34	6	13	19	17	10	0
Geoff Sanderson	67	13	13	26	4	22	4
Dixon Ward	71	11	9	20	1	41	1
J.P. Dumont*	47	10	8	18	-6	18	0
CHI	47	10	8	18	-6	18	0
BUF	0	0	0	0	0	0	0
Jay McKee	78	5	12	17	5	50	1
Erik Rasmussen	67	8	6	14	1	43	0

Acquired: LW Tsyplakov from LA for a '00 8th-round pick (Jan. 24); C Gratton from TB for C Brian Holzinger, C Wayne Primeau and D Cory Sarich (Mar. 9); C Gilmour and RW Dumont from Chi. for LW Michal Grosek (Mar. 10).

Goalies (10 Gm)	Gm	Min	GAA	Record	Sv%
Dominik Hasek	35	2066	2.21	15-11-6	.919
Martin Biron*	41	2229	2.42	19-18-2	.909
Dwayne Roloson	14	677	2.84	1-7-3	.884
BUFFALO	82	4996	2.45	35-36-11	.908

Shutouts: Biron (5), Hasek (3). **Assists:** Hasek (1). **PM:** Hasek (12), Biron (6).

Calgary Flames

Top Scorers	Gm	G	A	Pts	+/-	PM	PP
Valeri Bure	82	35	40	75	-7	50	13
Jarome Iginla	77	29	34	63	0	26	12
Phil Housley	78	11	44	55	-12	24	5
Marc Savard	78	22	31	53	-2	56	4
Derek Morris	78	9	29	38	2	80	3
Sergei Krivokrasov ...	75	10	27	37	-5	44	3
NASH	63	9	17	26	-7	40	3
CALG	12	1	10	11	2	4	0
Andrei Nazarov	76	10	22	32	3	78	1
Jeff Shantz	74	13	18	31	-13	30	6
Darryl Shannon	76	6	21	27	-27	87	1
ATL	49	5	13	18	-14	65	1
CALG	27	1	8	9	-13	22	0
Jason Wiemer	64	11	11	22	-10	120	2
Clarke Wilm	78	10	12	22	-6	67	1
Cory Stillman	37	12	9	21	-9	12	6
Bill Lindsay	80	8	12	20	-7	86	0
Martin St. Louis*	56	3	15	18	-5	22	0
Andreas Johansson	40	5	10	15	-2	22	1
TB	12	2	3	5	1	8	0
CALG	28	3	7	10	-3	14	1
Brad Werenka	73	4	9	13	13	90	0
PIT	61	3	8	11	15	69	0
CALG	12	1	1	2	-2	21	0
Robyn Regehr*	57	5	7	12	-2	46	2

Acquired: LW Johansson from TB for LW Nils Ekman and a '00 4th-round pick (Nov. 20); D Shannon and LW Jason Botterill from Atl. for LW Hnat Domenichelli and LW Dmitri Vlasenkov (Feb. 11); RW Krivokrasov from Nash. for D Cale Hulse and '01 3rd-round pick (Mar. 14); D Werenka from Pit. for G Tyler Moss and LW Rene Corbet (Mar. 14).

Goalies (10 Gm)	Gm	Min	GAA	Record	SV%
Fred Brathwaite	61	3448	2.75	25-25-7	.905
Grant Fuhr	23	1205	3.83	5-13-2	.856
CALGARY	82	5007	3.07	31-41-10	.892

Shutouts: Brathwaite (5). **Assists:** Brathwaite (4), Fuhr (2). **PM:** Brathwaite (4), Fuhr (2).

Carolina Hurricanes

Top Scorers	Gm	G	A	Pts	+/-	PM	PP
Ron Francis	78	23	50	73	10	18	7
Jeff O'Neill..........	80	25	38	63	-9	72	4
Gary Roberts	69	23	30	53	-10	62	12
Sami Kapanen	76	24	24	48	10	12	7
Sean Hill...........	62	13	31	44	3	59	8
Robert Kron	81	13	27	40	-4	8	2
Paul Coffey	69	11	29	40	-6	40	6
Andrei Kovalenko	76	15	24	39	-13	38	2
Bates Battaglia........	77	16	18	34	20	39	3
Martin Gelinas	81	14	16	30	-10	40	3
Rod Brind'Amour	45	9	13	22	-13	26	4
PHI...............	12	5	3	8	-1	4	4
CAR..............	33	4	10	14	-12	22	0
Paul Ranheim	79	9	13	22	-14	6	0
Glen Wesley	78	7	15	22	-4	38	1
Marek Malik	57	4	10	14	13	63	0
Tommy Westlund*	81	4	8	12	-10	19	0
Sandy McCarthy	71	6	5	11	-3	120	1
PHI..............	58	6	5	11	-5	111	1
CAR..............	13	0	0	0	-2	9	0
Steve Halko	58	0	8	8	0	25	0
Jeff Daniels..........	69	3	4	7	-8	10	0
David Karpa	27	1	4	5	9	52	0

Acquired: C Brind'Amour, G Jean-Marc Pelletier and a '00 2nd-round pick from Phi. for C Keith Primeau and a '00 5th-round pick (Jan. 23); RW McCarthy from Phi. for C Kent Manderville (Mar. 14).

Goalies (10 Gm)	Gm	Min	GAA	Record	Sv%
Arturs Irbe	75	4345	2.42	34-28-9	.906
CAROLINA	82	4974	2.61	37-35-10	.899

Shutouts: Irbe (5). **Assists:** Irbe (1). **PM:** Irbe (14).

Chicago Blackhawks

Top Scorers	Gm	G	A	Pts	+/-	PM	PP
Tony Amonte	82	43	41	84	10	48	11
Steve Sullivan..........	80	22	43	65	19	56	2
TOR	7	0	1	1	-1	4	0
CHI	73	22	42	64	20	52	2
Alex Zhamnov	71	23	37	60	7	61	5
Michael Nylander	77	24	30	54	6	30	5
TB	11	1	2	3	-3	4	1
CHI	66	23	28	51	9	26	4
Michal Grosek........	75	13	27	40	11	47	3
BUF	61	11	23	34	12	35	2
CHI	14	2	4	6	-1	12	1
Boris Mironov	58	9	28	37	-3	72	4
Eric Daze	59	23	13	36	-16	28	6
Dean McAmmond......	76	14	18	32	11	72	1
Anders Eriksson	73	3	25	28	4	20	0
Bryan McCabe	79	6	19	25	-8	139	2
Josef Marha	81	10	12	22	-10	18	2
Bob Probert	69	4	11	15	10	114	0
Blair Atcheynum	47	5	7	12	-8	6	0
Kevin Dean	64	3	8	11	3	36	0
ATL	23	1	0	1	-5	14	0
DAL	14	0	0	0	-1	10	0
CHI	27	2	8	10	9	12	0
Doug Zmolek	43	2	7	9	6	60	0
Brad Brown	57	0	9	9	-1	134	0

Acquired: RW Nylander from TB for D Bryan Muir and LW Reid Simpson (Nov. 12); D Dean, C Derek Plante and a '01 2nd-round pick from Dal. for D Sylvain Cote and D Dave Manson (Feb. 8); LW Grosek from Buf. for C Doug Gilmour and RW J.P. Dumont (Mar. 10). **Claimed:** C Sullivan off waivers from Tor. (Oct. 23).

Goalies (10 Gm)	Gm	Min	GAA	Record	SV%
Steve Passmore	24	1388	2.72	7-12-3	.904
Jocelyn Thibault........	60	3438	2.76	25-26-7	.906
CHICAGO	82	4984	2.95	33-39-10	.898

Shutouts: Thibault (3), Passmore (1). **Assists:** none. **PM:** Passmore (9), Thibault (2).

Colorado Avalanche

Top Scorers	Gm	G	A	Pts	+/-	PM	PP
Joe Sakic	60	28	53	81	30	28	5
Milan Hejduk..........	82	36	36	72	14	16	13
Chris Drury	82	20	47	67	8	42	7
Ray Bourque	79	18	34	52	-2	26	13
BOS	65	10	28	38	-11	20	6
COL	14	8	6	14	9	6	7
Sandis Ozolinsh	82	16	36	52	17	46	6
Alex Tanguay*	76	17	34	51	6	22	5
Peter Forsberg	49	14	37	51	9	52	3
Adam Deadmarsh	71	18	27	45	-10	106	5
Dave Andreychuk	77	20	16	36	-20	30	8
BOS	63	19	14	33	-11	28	7
COL	14	1	2	3	-9	2	1
Stephane Yelle	79	14	22	9	28	0	
Shjon Podein	75	11	8	19	12	29	0
Dave Reid..........	65	11	7	18	12	28	0
Adam Foote	59	5	13	18	5	98	1
Martin Skoula*	80	3	13	16	5	20	2
Jon Klemm	73	5	7	12	26	34	0
Chris Dingman	68	8	3	11	-2	132	2
Eric Messier	61	3	6	9	0	24	1
Greg de Vries	69	2	7	9	-7	73	0
Aaron Miller	53	5	7	8	3	36	0

Acquired: D Bourque and LW Andreychuk from Bos. for LW Brian Rolston, D Martin Grenier, C Sami Pahlsson and either a '00 or '01 1st-round pick (Mar. 6). **Signed:** free agent LW Reid (Oct. 6).

Goalies (10 Gm)	Gm	Min	GAA	Record	SV%
Patrick Roy	63	3704	2.28	32-21-8	.914
Marc Denis*	23	1203	2.54	9-8-3	.917
COLORADO	82	4990	2.42	42-29-11	.912

Shutouts: Denis (3), Roy (2). **Assists:** Roy (3), Denis (2). **PM:** Roy (10), Denis (6).

Dallas Stars

Top Scorers

Top Scorers	Gm	G	A	Pts	+/-	PM	PP
Mike Modano	77	38	43	81	0	48	11
Brett Hull	79	24	35	59	-21	43	11
Sergei Zubov	77	9	33	42	-2	18	3
Jamie Langenbrunner	65	18	21	39	16	68	4
Sylvain Cote	76	8	27	35	3	28	5
TOR	3	0	1	1	1	0	0
CHI	45	6	18	24	-4	14	5
DAL	28	2	8	10	6	14	0
Joe Nieuwendyk	48	15	19	34	-1	26	7
Mike Keane	81	13	21	34	9	41	0
Darryl Sydor	74	8	26	34	6	32	5
Brenden Morrow*	64	14	19	33	8	81	3
Richard Matvichuk	70	4	21	25	7	42	0
Derian Hatcher	57	2	22	24	6	68	0
Kirk Muller	47	7	15	22	-3	24	3
Blake Sloan*	67	4	13	17	11	50	0
Guy Carbonneau	69	10	6	16	10	36	0
Scott Thornton	65	8	6	14	-12	108	1
MON	35	2	3	5	-7	70	0
DAL	30	6	3	9	-5	38	1
Aaron Gavey	41	7	6	13	0	44	1
Roman Lyashenko*	58	6	6	12	-2	10	0
Dave Manson	63	1	9	10	12	62	0
CHI	37	0	7	7	2	40	0
DAL	26	1	2	3	10	22	0

Acquired: C Thornton from Mon. for LW Juha Lind (Jan. 22); D Cote and D Manson from Chi. for D Kevin Dean, C Derek Plante and a '01 2nd-round pick (Feb. 8). **Signed:** free agent C Muller (Dec. 15).

Goalies (10 Gm)

Goalies (10 Gm)	Gm	Min	GAA	Record	SV%
Ed Belfour	62	3620	2.10	32-21-7	.919
Manny Fernandez*	24	1353	2.13	11-8-3	.920
DALLAS	82	4992	2.21	43-29-10	.916

Shutouts: Belfour (4), Fernandez (1). **Assists:** Belfour (3), Fernandez (2). **PM:** Belfour (10), Fernandez (2).

Detroit Red Wings

Top Scorers

Top Scorers	Gm	G	A	Pts	+/-	PM	PP
Steve Yzerman	78	35	44	79	28	34	15
Brendan Shanahan	78	41	37	78	24	105	13
Nicklas Lidstrom	81	20	53	73	19	18	9
Sergei Fedorov	68	27	35	62	8	22	4
Pat Verbeek	68	22	26	48	22	95	7
Igor Larionov	79	9	38	47	13	28	3
Martin Lapointe	82	16	25	41	17	121	1
Steve Duchesne	79	10	31	41	12	42	1
Larry Murphy	81	10	30	40	4	45	7
Vyacheslav Kozlov	72	18	18	36	11	28	4
Tomas Holmstrom	72	13	22	35	4	43	4
Chris Chelios	81	3	31	34	48	103	0
Doug Brown	51	10	8	18	8	12	0
Mathieu Dandenault	81	6	12	18	-12	20	0
Stacy Roest	49	7	9	16	-1	12	1
Kirk Maltby	41	6	8	14	1	24	0
Darren McCarty	24	6	6	12	1	48	0
Kris Draper	51	5	7	12	3	28	0
Todd Gill	54	3	6	9	-8	45	0
PHO	41	1	6	7	-10	30	0
DET	13	2	0	2	2	15	0
Yuri Butsayev*	57	5	3	8	-6	12	0
Jiri Fischer*	52	0	8	8	1	45	0
Brent Gilchrist	24	4	2	6	1	24	0
Darryl Laplante*	30	0	6	6	3	10	0

Acquired: D Gill from Pho. for LW Philippe Audet (Mar. 14). **Signed:** free agent RW Verbeek (Nov. 10).

Goalies (10 Gm)

Goalies (10 Gm)	Gm	Min	GAA	Record	Sv%
Chris Osgood	53	3148	2.40	30-14-8	.907
Ken Wregget	29	1579	2.66	14-10-2	.900
DETROIT	82	4985	2.53	48-24-10	.903

Shutouts: Osgood (6). **Assists:** Osgood (1), Wregget (1). **PM:** Osgood (18).

Edmonton Oilers

Top Scorers

Top Scorers	Gm	G	A	Pts	+/-	PM	PP
Doug Weight	77	21	51	72	6	54	3
Ryan Smyth	82	28	26	54	-2	58	11
Alexander Selivanov	67	27	20	47	2	46	10
Bill Guerin	70	24	22	46	4	123	11
German Titov	70	17	29	46	-1	38	4
PIT	63	17	25	42	-3	34	4
EDM	7	0	4	4	2	4	0
Roman Hamrlik	80	8	37	45	1	68	5
Todd Marchant	82	17	23	40	7	70	0
Tom Poti	76	9	26	35	8	65	2
Janne Niinimaa	81	8	25	33	14	89	2
Mike Grier	65	9	22	31	9	68	0
Ethan Moreau	73	17	10	27	8	62	1
Boyd Devereaux	76	8	19	27	7	20	0
Jim Dowd	69	5	18	23	10	45	2
Georges Laraque	76	8	16	24	5	123	0
Rem Murray	44	9	5	14	-2	8	2
Jason Smith	80	3	11	14	16	60	0
Sean Brown	72	4	8	12	1	192	0
Igor Ulanov	57	1	8	9	-14	86	0
MON	43	1	5	6	-11	76	0
EDM	14	0	3	3	-3	10	0

Acquired: D Ulanov and D Alain Nasreddine from Mon. for D Christian Laflamme and D Matthieu Descoteaux (Mar. 9); LW Titov from Pit. for C Josef Beranek (Mar. 14).

Goalies (10 Gm)

Goalies (10 Gm)	Gm	Min	GAA	Record	Sv%
Tommy Salo	70	4164	2.33	27-28-13	.914
Bill Ranford	16	785	3.59	4-6-3	.885
EDMONTON	82	5030	2.53	32-34-16	.909

Shutouts: Salo (2). **Assists:** Salo (1). **PM:** Salo (8), Ranford (2).

Florida Panthers

Top Scorers

Top Scorers	Gm	G	A	Pts	+/-	PM	PP
Pavel Bure	74	58	36	94	25	16	11
Ray Whitney	81	29	42	71	16	35	5
Viktor Kozlov	80	17	53	70	24	16	6
Mike Sillinger	80	23	29	52	-30	102	8
TB	67	19	25	44	-29	86	6
FLA	13	4	4	8	-1	16	2
Robert Svehla	82	9	40	49	23	64	3
Scott Mellanby	77	18	28	46	14	126	6
Mark Parrish	81	26	18	44	1	39	6
Jaroslav Spacek	82	10	26	36	7	53	4
Rob Niedermayer	81	10	23	33	-5	46	1
Bret Hedican	76	6	19	25	4	68	2
Oleg Kvasha	78	5	20	25	3	34	2
Len Barrie	60	9	14	23	9	62	0
LA	46	5	8	13	5	56	0
FLA	14	4	6	10	4	6	0
Ray Sheppard	47	10	10	20	-4	4	5
Mike Wilson	60	4	16	20	10	35	0
Cam Stewart	65	9	7	16	-2	50	0
Paul Laus	77	3	8	11	-1	172	0

Acquired: G Shtalenkov and a '00 4th-round pick from Pho. for G Sean Burke and a '00 5th-round pick (Nov. 19); G Vernon and a '00 3rd-round pick from SJ for RW Radek Dvorak (Dec. 30); C Sillinger from TB for C Ryan Johnson and LW Dwayne Hay (Mar. 14). **Claimed:** C Barrie off waivers from LA (Mar. 10). **Signed:** free agent RW Sheppard (Nov. 15).

Goalies (10 Gm)

Goalies (10 Gm)	Gm	Min	GAA	Record	Sv%
Mikhail Shtalenkov	30	1786	2.35	15-10-4	.905
PHO	15	904	2.39	7-6-2	.903
FLA	15	882	2.31	8-4-2	.908
Mike Vernon	49	2791	2.47	24-18-3	.917
SJ	15	772	2.49	6-5-1	.911
FLA	34	2019	2.47	18-13-2	.919
Trevor Kidd	28	1574	2.63	14-11-2	.915
FLORIDA	82	4966	2.53	43-33-6	.914

Shutouts: Shtalenkov (2 with PHO), Vernon and Kidd (1). **Assists:** Shtalenkov and Vernon (3). **PM:** Shtalenkov (4), Vernon (2)

Los Angeles Kings

Top Scorers

	Gm	G	A	Pts	+/-	PM	PP
Luc Robitaille	.71	36	38	74	11	68	13
Zigmund Palffy	.64	27	39	66	18	32	4
Glen Murray	.78	29	33	62	13	60	10
Jozef Stumpel	.57	17	41	58	23	10	3
Rob Blake	.77	18	39	57	10	112	12
Bryan Smolinski	.79	20	36	56	2	48	2
Nelson Emerson	.63	15	20	35	-23	47	4
ATL	.58	14	19	33	-24	47	4
LA	.5	1	1	2	1	0	0
Garry Galley	.70	9	21	30	9	52	2
Craig Johnson	.76	9	14	23	-10	28	1
Jason Blake	.64	5	18	23	4	26	0
Ian Laperriere	.79	9	13	22	-14	185	0
Kelly Buchberger	.81	7	13	20	-36	152	0
ATL	.68	5	12	17	-34	139	0
LA	.13	2	1	3	-2	13	0
Marko Tuomainen	.63	9	8	17	-12	80	2
Jere Karalahti*	.48	6	10	16	3	18	4
Aki Berg	.70	3	13	16	-1	45	0
Sean O'Donnell	.80	2	12	14	4	114	0
Mattias Norstrom	.82	1	13	14	22	66	0
Brad Chartrand*	.50	6	6	12	4	17	0
Bob Corkum	.45	5	6	11	0	14	0

Acquired: RW Emerson and LW Buchberger from Atl. for RW Donald Audette and D Frantisek Kaberle (Mar. 13).

Goalies (10 Gm)

	Gm	Min	GAA	Record	Sv%
Jamie Storr	.42	2206	2.53	18-15-5	.908
Stephane Fiset	.47	2592	2.75	20-15-7	.901
LOS ANGELES	.82	4997	2.74	39-31-12	.900

Shutouts: Storr and Fiset (1). **Assists:** Fiset (2), Storr (1). **PM:** Storr and Fiset (4).

Montreal Canadiens

Top Scorers

	Gm	G	A	Pts	+/-	PM	PP
Martin Rucinsky	.80	25	24	49	1	70	7
Dainius Zubrus	.73	14	28	42	-1	54	3
Sergei Zholtok	.68	26	12	38	2	28	9
Patrice Brisebois	.54	10	25	35	-1	18	5
Trevor Linden	.50	13	17	30	-3	34	4
Brian Savage	.38	17	12	29	-4	19	6
Benoit Brunet	.50	14	15	29	3	13	6
Eric Weinrich	.77	4	25	29	4	39	2
Shayne Corson	.70	8	20	28	-2	115	2
Oleg Petrov	.44	2	24	26	10	8	1
Turner Stevenson	.64	8	13	21	-1	61	0
Saku Koivu	.24	3	18	21	7	14	1
Karl Dykhuis	.72	7	13	20	-5	46	3
PHI	.5	0	1	1	-2	6	0
MON	.67	7	12	19	-3	40	3
Craig Darby	.76	7	10	17	-14	14	0
Craig Rivet	.61	3	14	17	11	76	0
Francis Bouillon*	.74	3	13	16	-7	38	2
Patrick Poulin	.82	10	5	15	-15	17	0
Sheldon Souray	.71	3	8	11	1	114	0
NJ	.52	0	8	8	-6	70	0
MON	.19	3	0	3	7	44	0
Juha Lind	.47	4	6	10	-3	10	0
DAL	.34	3	4	7	-1	6	0
MON	.13	1	2	3	-2	4	0
Jesse Belanger	.16	3	6	9	2	2	0

Acquired: D Dykhuis from Phi. for future considerations (Oct. 20); LW Lind from Dal. for C Scott Thornton (Jan. 22); D Souray, D Joshua De Wolf and a '01 2nd-round pick from NJ for D Vladimir Malakhov (Mar. 1).

Goalies (10 Gm)

	Gm	Min	GAA	Record	Sv%
Jose Theodore	.30	1655	2.10	12-13-2	.919
Jeff Hackett	.56	3301	2.40	23-25-7	.914
MONTREAL	.82	4983	2.34	35-38-9	.914

Shutouts: Theodore (5), Hackett (3). **Assists:** none. **PM:** Hackett (4).

Nashville Predators

Top Scorers

	Gm	G	A	Pts	+/-	PM	PP
Cliff Ronning	.82	26	36	62	-13	34	7
Patric Kjellberg	.82	23	23	46	-11	14	9
Greg Johnson	.82	11	33	44	-15	40	2
Kimmo Timonen	.51	8	25	33	-5	26	2
Vitali Yachmenev	.68	16	16	32	5	12	1
Drake Berehowsky	.79	12	20	32	-4	87	5
David Legwand*	.71	13	15	28	-6	30	4
Scott Walker	.69	7	21	28	-16	90	0
Ville Peltonen	.79	6	22	28	-1	22	2
Rob Valicevic	.80	14	11	25	-11	21	2
Randy Robitaille*	.69	11	14	25	-13	10	2
Sebastien Bordeleau	.60	10	13	23	-12	30	0
Tom Fitzgerald	.82	13	9	22	-18	66	0
Bill Houlder	.71	3	14	17	-9	26	2
TB	.14	1	2	3	-3	2	1
NASH	.57	2	12	14	-6	24	1
Craig Millar	.57	3	11	14	-6	28	0
Karlis Skrastins*	.59	5	6	11	-7	20	1
Niklas Andersson	.24	3	8	11	-3	8	1
NYI	.17	3	7	10	-3	8	1
NASH	.7	0	1	1	0	0	0
Mark Mowers	.41	4	5	9	0	10	0
Richard Lintner*	.33	1	5	6	-6	22	0

Claimed: D Houlder off waivers from TB (Nov. 10); LW Andersson off waivers from NYI (Jan. 20).

Goalies (10 Gm)

	Gm	Min	GAA	Record	Sv%
Tomas Vokoun	.33	1879	2.78	9-20-1	.904
Mike Dunham	.52	3077	2.85	19-27-6	.908
NASHVILLE	.82	4986	2.89	28-47-7	.904

Shutouts: Vokoun (1). **Assists:** Vokoun (1). **PM:** Vokoun (8), Dunham (6).

New Jersey Devils

Top Scorers

	Gm	G	A	Pts	+/-	PM	PP
Patrik Elias	.72	35	37	72	16	58	9
Scott Gomez*	.82	19	51	70	14	78	7
Petr Sykora	.79	25	43	68	24	26	5
Jason Arnott	.76	22	34	56	22	51	7
Claude Lemieux	.83	20	27	47	-3	90	7
COL	.13	3	6	9	0	4	0
NJ	.70	17	21	38	-3	86	7
Bobby Holik	.79	23	23	46	7	106	7
Alexander Mogilny	.59	24	20	44	3	20	5
VAN	.47	21	17	38	7	16	3
NJ	.12	3	3	6	-4	4	2
Randy McKay	.67	16	23	39	8	80	3
Scott Niedermayer	.71	7	31	38	19	48	1
Brian Rafalski*	.75	5	27	32	21	28	1
Scott Stevens	.78	8	21	29	30	103	0
Sergei Nemchinov	.53	10	16	26	1	18	0
John Madden*	.74	16	9	25	7	6	0
Sergei Brylin	.64	9	11	20	0	20	1
Krzysztof Oliwa	.69	6	10	16	-2	184	1
Jay Pandolfo	.71	7	8	15	0	4	0
Deron Quint	.54	4	7	11	-2	24	0
PHO	.50	3	7	10	0	22	0
NJ	.4	1	0	1	-2	2	0
Ken Daneyko	.78	0	6	6	13	98	0

Acquired: RW Lemieux, a '00 2nd-round pick and a cond. swap of '00 1st-round picks from Col. for LW Brian Rolston (Nov. 3); D Quint and a cond. pick in the '01 draft from Pho. for D Lyle Odelein (Mar. 7); RW Mogilny from Van. for C Brendan Morrison and C Denis Pederson (Mar. 14).

Goalies (10 Gm)

	Gm	Min	GAA	Record	Sv%
Martin Brodeur	.72	4312	2.24	43-20-8	.910
Chris Terreri	.12	649	3.42	2-9-0	.876
NEW JERSEY	.82	4975	2.45	45-29-8	.903

Shutouts: Brodeur (6). **Assists:** Brodeur (4). **PM:** Brodeur (16), Terreri (2).

New York Islanders

Top Scorers	Gm	G	A	Pts	+/-	PM	PP
Mariusz Czerkawski	79	35	35	70	-16	34	16
Brad Isbister	64	22	20	42	-18	100	9
Tim Connolly*	81	14	20	34	-25	44	2
Claude Lapointe	76	15	16	31	-22	60	2
Dave Scatchard	65	12	18	30	-3	117	0
VAN	21	0	4	4	-3	24	0
NYI	44	12	14	26	0	93	0
Josh Green	49	12	14	26	-7	41	2
Kenny Jonsson	65	1	24	25	-15	32	1
Olli Jokinen	82	11	10	21	0	80	1
Bill Muckalt	45	8	11	19	11	21	1
VAN	33	4	8	12	6	17	1
NYI	12	4	3	7	5	4	0
Jamie Heward	54	6	11	17	-9	26	2
Jamie Rivers	75	1	16	17	-4	84	1
Mats Lindgren	43	9	7	16	0	24	1
Mike Watt	45	5	6	11	-8	17	0
Dmitri Nabokov*	26	4	7	11	-8	16	0
Zdeno Chara	65	2	9	11	-27	57	0
Eric Cairns	67	2	7	9	-5	196	0
Ray Giroux*	14	0	9	9	0	10	0

Acquired: C Scatchard, RW Muckalt and G Weekes from Van. for G Felix Potvin and '00 2nd and 3rd-round picks (Dec. 19).

Goalies (10 Gm)	Gm	Min	GAA	Record	Sv%
Kevin Weekes	56	3012	3.23	16-27-8	.901
VAN	20	987	2.86	6-7-4	.898
NYI	36	2026	3.41	10-20-4	.902
Roberto Luongo*	24	1292	3.25	7-14-1	.904
NY ISLANDERS	82	4981	3.31	24-49-9	.900

Shutouts: Weekes (2), Luongo (1). **Assists:** Weekes (1). **PM:** none.

New York Rangers

Top Scorers	Gm	G	A	Pts	+/-	PM	PP
Petr Nedved	76	24	44	68	2	40	6
Theo Fleury	80	15	49	64	-4	68	1
Mike York*	82	26	24	50	-17	18	8
Radek Dvorak	81	18	32	50	5	16	2
FLA	35	7	10	17	5	6	0
NYR	46	11	22	33	0	10	2
Jan Hlavac*	67	19	23	42	3	16	6
John MacLean	77	18	24	42	-2	52	6
Adam Graves	77	23	17	40	-15	14	11
Valeri Kamensky	58	13	19	32	-13	24	3
Mathieu Schneider	80	10	20	30	-6	78	3
Alex Daigle	58	8	18	26	-5	23	1
Brian Leetch	50	7	19	26	-16	20	3
Rob DiMaio	62	6	19	25	-9	50	0
BOS	50	5	16	21	-1	42	0
NYR	12	1	3	4	-8	8	0
Kevin Hatcher	74	4	19	23	-10	38	2
Kim Johnsson*	76	6	15	21	-13	46	1
Tim Taylor	76	9	11	20	-4	72	0
Stephane Quintal	75	2	14	16	-10	77	0
Eric Lacroix	70	4	8	12	-12	24	0
Sylvain Lefebvre	82	2	10	12	-13	43	0
Kevin Stevens	38	3	5	8	-7	43	1
Rich Pilon	54	0	6	6	-2	70	0
NYI	9	0	2	2	-2	34	0
NYR	45	0	4	4	0	36	0

Acquired: RW Daigle from TB for future considerations (Oct. 3); RW Dvorak from SJ (see Fla.) for RW Todd Harvey and a '01 4th-round pick (Dec. 30); RW DiMaio from Bos. for RW Mike Knuble (Mar. 10). **Claimed:** D Pilon off waivers from NYI (Dec. 1).

Goalies (10 Gm)	Gm	Min	GAA	Record	Sv%
Mike Richter	61	3622	2.87	22-31-8	.905
Kirk McLean	22	1206	2.89	7-8-4	.896
NY RANGERS	82	4996	2.95	29-41-12	.899

Shutouts: none. **Assists:** McLean (1). **PM:** Richter (4), McLean (2).

Ottawa Senators

Top Scorers	Gm	G	A	Pts	+/-	PM	PP
Radek Bonk	80	23	37	60	-2	53	10
Daniel Alfredsson	57	21	38	59	11	28	4
Marian Hossa	78	29	27	56	5	32	5
Vaclav Prospal	79	22	33	55	-2	40	5
Shawn McEachern	69	29	22	51	2	24	10
Joe Juneau	65	13	24	37	3	22	2
Wade Redden	81	10	26	36	-1	49	3
Andreas Dackell	82	10	25	35	5	18	0
Jason York	79	8	22	30	-3	60	1
Magnus Arvedson	47	15	13	28	4	36	1
Shaun Van Allen	75	9	19	28	20	37	0
Patrick Traverse	66	6	17	23	17	21	1
Rob Zamuner	57	9	12	21	-6	32	0
Chris Phillips	65	5	14	19	12	39	0
Igor Kravchuk	64	6	12	18	-5	20	5
Sami Salo	37	6	8	14	6	2	3
Kevin Dineen	67	4	8	12	2	57	0
Mike Fisher*	32	4	5	9	-6	15	0
Andre Roy*	73	4	3	7	3	145	0
Petr Schastlivy*	13	2	5	7	4	2	1
Colin Forbes	53	2	5	7	-5	30	0
TB	8	0	0	0	0	18	0
OTT	45	2	5	7	-1	12	0

Acquired: LW Forbes from TB for C Bruce Gardiner (Nov. 11); G Barrasso from Pit. for G Ron Tugnutt and D Janne Laukkanen (Mar. 14). **Signed:** free agent C Juneau (Oct. 25); free agent D Ledyard (Nov. 17).

Goalies (10 Gm)	Gm	Min	GAA	Record	Sv%
Patrick Lalime	38	2038	2.33	19-14-3	.905
Tom Barrasso	25	1288	3.17	8-11-2	.880
PIT	18	870	3.17	5-7-2	.881
OTT	7	418	3.16	3-4-0	.879
OTTAWA	82	4986	2.53	41-30-11	.898

Shutouts: Lalime (3), Barrasso (1 with Pit.). **Assists:** none. **PM:** Barrasso (6), Lalime (4).

Philadelphia Flyers

Top Scorers	Gm	G	A	Pts	+/-	PM	PP
Mark Recchi	82	28	63	91	20	50	7
John LeClair	82	40	37	77	8	36	13
Eric Lindros	55	27	32	59	11	83	10
Eric Desjardins	81	14	41	55	20	32	8
Daymond Langkow	82	18	32	50	1	56	5
Simon Gagne*	80	20	28	48	11	22	8
Rick Tocchet	80	15	20	35	-1	90	4
PHO	64	12	17	29	-5	67	2
PHI	16	3	3	6	4	23	2
Valeri Zelepukin	77	11	21	32	-3	55	2
Keith Jones	57	9	16	25	8	82	1
Gino Odjick	59	8	11	19	-5	100	0
NYI	46	5	10	15	-7	90	0
PHI	13	3	1	4	2	10	0
Dan McGillis	68	4	14	18	16	55	3
Keith Primeau	23	7	10	17	10	31	1
Jody Hull	67	10	3	13	8	4	0
Chris Therien	80	4	9	13	11	66	1
Craig Berube	77	4	8	12	3	162	0
Kent Manderville	69	1	7	8	-6	16	0
CAR	56	1	4	5	-8	12	0
PHI	13	0	3	3	2	4	0

Acquired: RW Hull from Atl. for future considerations (Oct. 15); C Primeau and a '00 5th-round pick from Car. for C Rod Brind'Amour, G Jean-Marc Pelletier and a '00 2nd-round pick (Jan. 30); LW Odjick from NYI for LW Mikael Andersson and a 5th-round '00 pick (Feb. 15); RW Tocchet from Pho. for RW Mikael Renberg (Mar. 8); C Manderville from Car. for RW Sandy McCarthy (Mar. 14).

Goalies (10 Gm)	Gm	Min	GAA	Record	Sv%
Brian Boucher*	35	2038	1.91	20-10-3	.918
John Vanbiesbrouck	50	2950	2.20	25-15-9	.906
PHILADELPHIA	82	5008	2.14	45-25-12	.908

Shutouts: Boucher (4), Vanbiesbrouck (3). **Assists:** Boucher and Vanbiesbrouck (1). **PM:** Vanbiesbrouck (6), Boucher (4).

Phoenix Coyotes

Top Scorers

Top Scorers	Gm	G	A	Pts	+/-	PM	PP
Jeremy Roenick	.75	34	44	78	11	102	6
Shane Doan	.81	26	25	51	6	66	1
Travis Green	.78	25	21	46	-4	45	6
Greg Adams	.69	19	27	46	-1	14	5
Dallas Drake	.79	15	30	45	11	62	0
Keith Tkachuk	.50	22	21	43	7	82	5
Teppo Numminen	.79	8	34	42	21	16	2
Jyrki Lumme	.74	8	32	40	9	44	4
Trevor Letowski*	.82	19	20	39	2	20	3
Mikael Renberg	.72	10	25	35	-1	32	3
PHI.	.62	8	21	29	-1	30	3
PHO	.10	2	4	6	0	2	0
Juha Ylonen	.76	6	23	29	-6	12	0
Mika Alatalo	.82	10	17	27	-3	36	1
Keith Carney	.82	4	20	24	11	87	0
Lyle Odelein	.73	2	22	24	-9	123	1
NJ	.57	1	15	16	-10	104	0
PHO	.16	1	7	8	1	19	1
Mike Sullivan	.79	5	10	15	-4	10	0
Benoit Hogue	.27	3	10	13	-1	10	0

Acquired: G Burke and a '00 5th-round pick from Fla. for G Mikhail Shtalenkov and a '00 4th-round pick (Nov. 19); D Odelein from NJ for D Deron Quint and a cond. pick in the '01 draft (Mar. 7); RW Renberg from Phi. for RW Rick Tocchet (Mar. 8).

Goalies (10 Gm)

Goalies (10 Gm)	Gm	Min	GAA	Record	Sv%
Sean Burke	.42	2493	2.55	19-19-3	.914
FLA.	.7	418	2.58	2-5-0	.913
PHO	.35	2074	2.55	17-14-3	.914
Bob Essensa	.30	1573	2.78	13-10-3	.898
PHOENIX	.82	4987	2.74	39-35-8	.902

Shutouts: Burke (3), Essensa (1). **Assists:** none. **PM:** Burke (12).

Pittsburgh Penguins

Top Scorers

Top Scorers	Gm	G	A	Pts	+/-	PM	PP
Jaromir Jagr	.63	42	54	96	25	50	10
Alexei Kovalev	.82	26	40	66	-3	94	9
Robert Lang	.78	23	42	65	-9	14	13
Martin Straka	.71	20	39	59	24	26	3
Jan Hrdina	.70	13	33	46	13	43	3
Aleksey Morozov	.68	12	19	31	12	14	0
Jiri Slegr	.74	11	20	31	20	82	0
Pat Falloon	.63	9	22	31	4	14	1
EDM	.33	5	13	18	6	4	1
PIT	.30	4	9	13	-2	10	0
Josef Beranek	.71	13	12	25	-12	57	4
EDM	.58	9	8	17	-6	39	3
PIT	.13	4	4	8	-6	18	1
Matthew Barnaby	.64	12	12	24	3	197	0
Rob Brown	.50	10	13	23	-13	10	4
Tyler Wright	.50	12	10	22	4	45	0
Michal Rozsival*	.75	4	17	21	11	48	1
Janne Laukkanen	.71	2	18	20	17	67	1
OTT	.60	1	11	12	14	55	0
PIT	.11	1	7	8	3	12	1

Acquired: C Beranek from Edm. for LW German Titov (Mar. 14); G Tugnutt and D Laukkanen from Ott. for G Tom Barrasso (Mar. 14). **Claimed:** RW Falloon off waivers from Edm. (Feb. 4).

Goalies (10 Gm)

Goalies (10 Gm)	Gm	Min	GAA	Record	Sv%
Ron Tugnutt	.51	2809	2.52	22-14-8	.903
OTT	.44	2435	2.54	18-12-8	.899
PIT	.7	374	2.41	4-2-0	.924
J-S Aubin*	.51	2789	2.58	23-21-3	.914
Peter Skudra	.20	922	3.12	5-7-3	.872
PITTSBURGH	.82	4984	2.84	37-37-8	.900

Shutouts: Tugnutt (4 with Ottawa), Aubin (2), Skudra (1). **Assists:** Aubin (1). **PM:** Aubin (2).

St. Louis Blues

Top Scorers

Top Scorers	Gm	G	A	Pts	+/-	PM	PP
Pavol Demitra	.71	28	47	75	34	8	8
Pierre Turgeon	.52	26	40	66	30	8	8
Chris Pronger	.79	14	48	62	52	92	8
Michal Handzus	.81	25	28	53	19	44	3
Scott Young	.75	24	15	39	12	18	6
Lubos Bartecko	.67	16	23	39	25	51	3
Al MacInnis	.61	11	28	39	20	34	6
Stephane Richer	.56	15	22	37	9	18	5
TB	.20	7	5	12	2	4	1
STL.	.36	8	17	25	7	14	4
Mike Eastwood	.79	19	15	34	5	32	1
Jochen Hecht*	.63	13	21	34	20	28	5
Craig Conroy	.79	12	15	27	5	36	1
Todd Reirden	.56	4	21	25	18	32	0
Marty Reasoner*	.32	10	14	24	9	20	3
Scott Pellerin	.80	8	15	23	8	48	0
Jamal Mayers	.79	7	10	17	0	90	0
Tyson Nash*	.66	4	9	13	6	150	0
Dave Ellett	.52	2	8	10	-4	12	0
Jeff Finley	.74	2	8	10	26	38	0
Derek King	.22	2	7	9	-2	8	1
TOR	.3	0	0	0	-2	2	0
STL	.19	2	7	9	0	6	1
Marc Bergevin	.81	1	8	9	27	75	0
Ricard Persson*	.41	0	8	8	-2	38	0
Ladislav Nagy*	.11	2	4	6	2	2	1

Acquired: LW King from Tor. for D Tyler Harlton and an exchange of '00 8th-round picks (Oct. 20); RW Richer from TB for D Chris McAlpine and G Rich Parent (Jan. 13).

Goalies (10 Gm)

Goalies (10 Gm)	Gm	Min	GAA	Record	Sv%
Roman Turek	.67	3960	1.95	42-15-9	.912
Jamie McLennan	.19	1009	1.96	9-5-2	.903
ST. LOUIS	.82	4988	1.98	51-20-11	.909

Shutouts: Turek (7), McLennan (2). **Assists:** Turek (1). **PM:** Turek (4), McLennan (2).

San Jose Sharks

Top Scorers

Top Scorers	Gm	G	A	Pts	+/-	PM	PP
Owen Nolan	.78	44	40	84	-1	110	18
Vincent Damphousse	.82	21	49	70	4	58	3
Jeff Friesen	.82	26	35	61	-2	47	11
Mike Ricci	.82	20	24	44	14	60	10
Patrick Marleau	.81	17	23	40	-9	36	3
Niklas Sundstrom	.79	12	25	37	9	22	2
Brad Stuart*	.82	10	26	36	3	32	5
Alex Korolyuk	.57	14	21	35	4	35	3
Gary Suter	.76	6	28	34	7	52	2
Marco Sturm	.74	12	15	27	4	22	2
Stephane Matteau	.69	12	12	24	-3	61	0
Jeff Norton	.62	0	20	20	-2	49	0
Todd Harvey	.71	11	7	18	-11	140	2
NYR	.31	3	3	6	-9	62	0
SJ	.40	8	4	12	-2	78	2
Magnus Ragnarsson	.63	3	13	16	13	38	0
Mike Rathje	.66	2	14	16	-2	31	0
Tony Granato	.48	6	7	13	2	39	1
Ron Sutter	.78	5	6	11	-3	34	0
Ronnie Stern	.67	4	5	9	-9	151	0
Dave Lowry	.32	1	4	5	1	18	0
Bryan Marchment	.49	0	4	4	3	72	0

Acquired: RW Harvey and a '01 4th-round pick from NYR for RW Radek Dvorak (Dec. 30).

Goalies (10 Gm)

Goalies (10 Gm)	Gm	Min	GAA	Record	Sv%
Evgeni Nabokov*	.11	414	2.17	2-2-1	.910
Steve Shields	.67	3797	2.56	27-30-8	.911
SAN JOSE	.82	5004	2.57	35-37-10	.909

Shutouts: Shields (4), Nabokov (1). **Assists:** Shields (1). **PM:** Shields (29).

Tampa Bay Lightning

Top Scorers	Gm	G	A	Pts	+/-	PM	PP
Vincent Lecavalier	.80	25	42	67	-25	43	6
Fredrik Modin	.80	22	26	48	-26	18	3
Mike Johnson	.80	21	26	47	6	27	6
TOR	.52	11	14	25	8	23	2
TB	.28	10	12	22	-2	4	4
Stan Drulia	.68	11	22	33	-18	24	1
Brian Holzinger	.73	10	20	30	-3	51	1
BUF	.59	7	17	24	4	30	0
TB	.14	3	3	6	-7	21	1
Todd Warriner	.73	14	14	28	-8	36	3
TOR	.18	3	1	4	6	2	0
TB	.55	11	13	24	-14	34	3
Pavel Kubina	.69	8	18	26	-19	93	6
Petr Svoboda	.70	2	23	25	-11	170	2
Paul Mara*	.54	7	11	18	-27	73	4
Ryan Johnson*	.80	4	14	18	-7	16	0
FLA	.66	4	12	16	1	14	0
TB	.14	0	2	2	-8	2	0
Robert Petrovicky	.43	7	10	17	2	14	1
Wayne Primeau	.58	7	10	17	-12	63	2
BUF	.41	5	7	12	-8	38	2
TB	.17	2	3	5	-4	25	0

Acquired: C Warriner from Tor. for a '00 3rd-round pick (Nov. 29); G Parent and D Chris McAlpine from St.L for RW Stephane Richer (Jan. 13); RW M. Johnson and D Marek Posmyk from Tor. for LW Darcy Tucker, a '00 4th-round pick and a cond. exchange of mid-round picks in '01 (Feb. 9); C Holzinger, C Primeau and D Cory Sarich from Buf. for C Chris Gratton (Mar. 9); C R. Johnson and LW Dwayne Hay from Fla. for C Mike Sillinger (Mar. 14).

Goalies (10 Gm)	Gm	Min	GAA	Record	Sv%
Dan Cloutier	.52	2492	3.49	9-30-3	.885
Zac Bierk*	.12	509	3.65	4-4-1	.899
Kevin Hodson	.24	769	3.67	2-7-4	.856
Rich Parent	.14	698	3.70	2-7-1	.878
TAMPA BAY	.82	4982	3.73	19-54-9	.876

Shutouts: none. **Assists:** Bierk (1). **PM:** Cloutier (29), Hodson and Parent (2).

Toronto Maple Leafs

Top Scorers	Gm	G	A	Pts	+/-	PM	PP
Mats Sundin	.73	32	41	73	16	46	10
Steve Thomas	.81	26	37	63	1	68	9
Jonas Hoglund	.82	29	27	56	-2	10	9
Darcy Tucker	.77	21	30	51	-12	163	1
TB	.50	14	20	34	-15	108	1
TOR	.27	7	10	17	3	55	0
Igor Korolev	.80	20	26	46	12	22	5
Yanic Perreault	.58	18	27	45	3	22	5
Tomas Kaberle	.82	7	33	40	3	24	2
Sergei Berezin	.61	26	13	39	8	2	5
Dmitri Khristich	.53	12	18	30	8	24	3
Nikolai Antropov*	.66	12	18	30	14	41	0
Bryan Berard	.64	3	27	30	11	42	1
Dimitri Yushkevich	.77	3	24	27	2	55	2
Garry Valk	.73	10	14	24	-2	44	0
Alexander Karpovtsev	.69	3	14	17	9	54	3
Cory Cross	.71	4	11	15	13	64	0
Tie Domi	.70	5	9	14	-5	198	0
Kevyn Adams*	.52	5	8	13	-7	39	0
Alyn McCauley	.45	5	5	10	-6	10	1
Danny Markov	.59	0	10	10	13	28	0

Acquired: LW Khristich from Bos. for a '00 2nd-round pick (Oct. 21); LW Tucker, a '00 4th-round pick and a cond. exchange of mid-round picks in '01 from TB for RW Mike Johnson and D Marek Posmyk (Feb. 9).

Goalies (10 Gm)	Gm	Min	GAA	Record	Sv%
Curtis Joseph	.63	3801	2.49	36-20-7	.915
Glenn Healy	.20	1164	3.04	9-10-0	.888
TORONTO	.82	4983	2.67	45-30-7	.907

Shutouts: Joseph (4), Healy (2). **Assists:** Joseph and Healy (1). **PM:** Joseph (14), Healy (2).

Vancouver Canucks

Top Scorers	Gm	G	A	Pts	+/-	PM	PP
Markus Naslund	.82	27	38	65	-5	64	6
Andrew Cassels	.79	17	45	62	8	16	6
Mark Messier	.66	17	37	54	-15	30	6
Todd Bertuzzi	.80	25	25	50	-2	126	4
Brendan Morrison	.56	7	28	35	12	18	2
NJ	.44	5	21	26	8	8	2
VAN	.12	2	7	9	4	10	0
Peter Schaefer*	.71	16	15	31	0	20	2
Ed Jovanovski	.75	5	21	26	-3	54	1
Adrian Aucoin	.57	10	14	24	7	30	4
Greg Hawgood	.79	5	17	22	5	26	2
Trent Klatt	.47	10	10	20	-8	26	8
Mattias Ohlund	.42	4	16	20	6	24	2
Steve Kariya*	.45	8	11	19	9	22	0
Harry York	.54	4	13	17	-4	20	1
Brad May	.59	9	7	16	-2	90	0
Harold Druken*	.33	7	9	16	14	10	2
Donald Brashear	.60	11	2	13	-9	136	1
Matt Cooke	.51	5	7	12	3	39	0
Murray Baron	.81	2	10	12	8	67	0
Denis Pederson	.47	6	5	11	-6	18	0
NJ	.35	3	3	6	-7	16	0
VAN	.12	3	2	5	1	2	0

Acquired: G Potvin and '00 2nd and 3rd-round pick from NYI for C Dave Scatchard, RW Bill Muckalt and G Kevin Weekes (Dec. 19); C Morrison and C Pederson from NJ for RW Alexander Mogilny (Mar. 14).

Goalies (10 Gm)	Gm	Min	GAA	Record	Sv%
Garth Snow	.32	1712	2.66	10-15-3	.902
Felix Potvin	.56	3239	2.83	17-27-10	.901
NYI	.22	1273	3.21	5-14-3	.892
VAN	.34	1966	2.59	12-13-7	.906
VANCOUVER	.82	5033	2.83	30-37-15	.897

Shutouts: Potvin (1 with NYI). **Assists:** Snow and Potvin (2). **PM:** Snow (8), Potvin (4).

Washington Capitals

Top Scorers	Gm	G	A	Pts	+/-	PM	PP
Adam Oates	.82	15	56	71	13	14	5
Sergei Gonchar	.73	18	36	54	27	52	5
Chris Simon	.75	29	20	49	11	146	7
Steve Konowalchuk	.82	16	27	43	19	80	3
Peter Bondra	.62	21	17	38	5	30	5
Ulf Dahlen	.75	15	23	38	11	8	5
Richard Zednik	.49	19	16	35	6	54	1
Calle Johansson	.82	7	25	32	13	24	1
Jan Bulis	.56	9	22	31	7	30	0
Jeff Halpern*	.79	18	11	29	21	39	4
Joe Murphy	.55	12	15	27	1	94	4
BOS	.26	7	7	14	-7	41	3
WASH	.29	5	8	13	8	53	1
Andrei Nikolishin	.76	11	14	25	6	28	0
Terry Yake	.61	10	14	24	4	34	3
STL	.26	4	9	13	2	22	2
WASH	.35	6	5	11	2	12	1
Joe Sacco	.79	7	16	23	7	50	0
Dmitri Mironov	.73	3	19	22	6	28	1
Ken Klee	.80	7	13	20	8	79	0
Glen Metropolit*	.30	6	13	19	5	4	1
James Black	.49	8	9	17	-1	6	1
Jim McKenzie	.61	4	5	9	-5	64	0
ANA	.31	3	3	6	-5	48	0
WASH	.30	1	2	3	0	16	0
Brendan Witt	.77	1	7	8	0	114	0

Claimed: RW Yake off waivers from St.L (Jan. 18); LW McKenzie off waivers from Ana. (Jan. 20); RW Murphy off waivers from Bos. (Feb. 10).

Goalies (10 Gm)	Gm	Min	GAA	Record	Sv%
Olaf Kolzig	.73	4371	2.24	41-20-11	.917
Craig Billington	.13	611	2.75	3-6-1	.910
WASHINGTON	.82	4999	2.33	44-26-12	.915

Shutouts: Kolzig (5), Billington (2). **Assists:** Kolzig (2). **PM:** Kolzig (6).

STANLEY CUP PLAYOFFS

QUARTERFINAL	SEMIFINAL	FINAL		FINAL	SEMIFINAL	QUARTERFINAL

Philadelphia 4
Buffalo 1
— Philadelphia 4
Washington 1 — Philadelphia 3
Pittsburgh 2
Pittsburgh 4

EASTERN CONFERENCE — New Jersey 4

Toronto 4
Ottawa 2 — Toronto 2
New Jersey 4 — New Jersey 4
Florida 0 — New Jersey 4

Dallas 2

Dallas 4

San Jose 1
Dallas 4

Colorado 4
Colorado 3
Detroit 1

WESTERN CONFERENCE

St. Louis 3
San Jose 4
Dallas 4
Edmonton 1
Colorado 4
Phoenix 1
Detroit 4
Los Angeles 0

Stanley Cup Playoffs
Series Summaries

WESTERN CONFERENCE

FIRST ROUND (Best of 7)

	W-L	GF	Leading Scorers
San Jose	4-3	20	Nolan (6-2-8)
St. Louis	3-4	22	Hecht (4-6-10)

Date	Winner	Home Ice
April 12	Blues, 5-3	at St. Louis
April 15	Sharks, 4-2	at St. Louis
April 17	Sharks, 2-1	at San Jose
April 19	Sharks, 3-2	at San Jose
April 21	Blues, 5-3	at St. Louis
April 23	Blues, 6-2	at San Jose
April 25	Sharks, 3-1	at St. Louis

	W-L	GF	Leading Scorers
Colorado	4-1	17	Ozolinsh (3-4-7)
Phoenix	1-4	10	Roenick (2-2-4)

Date	Winner	Home Ice
April 13	Avalanche, 6-3	at Colorado
April 15	Avalanche, 3-1	at Colorado
April 17	Avalanche, 4-2	at Phoenix
April 19	Coyotes, 3-2	at Phoenix
April 21	Avalanche, 2-1	at Colorado

	W-L	GF	Leading Scorers
Dallas	4-1	14	Hull (3-3-6)
Edmonton	1-4	11	Weight (3-2-5) & Guerin (3-2-5)

Date	Winner	Home Ice
April 12	Stars, 2-1	at Dallas
April 13	Stars, 3-0	at Dallas
April 16	Oilers, 5-2	at Edmonton
April 18	Stars, 4-3	at Edmonton
April 21	Stars, 3-2	at Dallas

Shutout: Belfour, Dallas.

	W-L	GF	Leading Scorers
Detroit	4-0	15	Fedorov (3-2-5)
Los Angeles	0-4	6	Robitaille (2-2-4) & Stumpel (0-4-4)

Date	Winner	Home Ice
April 13	Red Wings, 2-0	at Detroit
April 15	Red Wings, 8-5	at Detroit
April 17	Red Wings, 2-1	at Los Angeles
April 19	Red Wings, 3-0	at Los Angeles

Shutouts: Osgood, Detroit (2).

SEMIFINALS (Best of 7)

	W-L	GF	Leading Scorers
Dallas	4-1	15	Hull (1-5-6)
San Jose	1-4	7	Damphousse (1-2-3)

Date	Winner	Home Ice
April 28	Stars, 4-0	at Dallas
April 30	Stars, 1-0	at Dallas
May 2	Sharks, 2-1	at San Jose
May 5	Stars, 5-4	at San Jose
May 7	Stars, 4-1	at Dallas

Shutouts: Belfour, Dallas (2).

	W-L	GF	Leading Scorers
Colorado	4-1	13	Forsberg (4-2-6) & Drury (2-4-6)
Detroit	1-4	8	Fedorov (1-2-3) & Murphy (1-2-3)

Date	Winner	Home Ice
April 27	Avalanche, 2-0	at Colorado
April 29	Avalanche, 3-1	at Colorado
May 1	Red Wings, 3-1	at Detroit
May 3	Avalanche, 3-2 (OT)	at Detroit
May 5	Avalanche, 4-2	at Colorado

Shutout: Roy, Colorado.

CHAMPIONSHIP (Best of 7)

	W-L	GF	Leading Scorers
Dallas	4-3	14	Modano (3-6-9)
Colorado	3-4	13	Forsberg (2-3-5)

Date	Winner	Home Ice
May 13	Avalanche, 2-0	at Dallas
May 15	Stars, 3-2	at Dallas
May 19	Avalanche, 2-0	at Colorado

Date	Winner	Home Ice
May 21	Stars, 4-1	at Colorado
May 23	Stars, 3-2 (OT)	at Dallas
May 25	Avalanche, 2-1	at Colorado
May 27	Stars, 3-2	at Dallas

Shutouts: Roy, Colorado (2).

EASTERN CONFERENCE

FIRST ROUND (Best of 7)

	W-L	GF	Leading Scorers
Philadelphia	4-1	14	Gagne (2-3-5)
			& Desjardins (1-4-5)
Buffalo	1-4	8	Satan (3-2-5)

Date	Winner	Home Ice
April 13	Flyers, 3-2	at Philadelphia
April 14	Flyers, 2-1	at Philadelphia
April 16	Flyers, 2-0	at Buffalo
April 18	Sabres, 3-2 (OT)	at Buffalo
April 20	Flyers, 5-2	at Philadelphia

Shutout: Boucher, Philadelphia.

	W-L	GF	Leading Scorers
Pittsburgh	4-1	17	Jagr (3-7-10)
Washington	1-4	8	Three tied with 3 each.

Date	Winner	Home Ice
April 13	Penguins, 7-0	at Washington
April 15	Penguins, 2-1 (OT)	at Washington
April 17	Penguins, 4-3	at Pittsburgh
April 19	Capitals, 3-2	at Pittsburgh
April 21	Penguins, 2-1	at Washington

Shutout: Tugnutt, Pittsburgh.

	W-L	GF	Leading Scorers
Toronto	4-2	17	Thomas (6-2-8)
Ottawa	2-4	10	Alfredsson (1-3-4)
			& Prospal (0-4-4)

Date	Winner	Home Ice
April 12	Maple Leafs, 2-0	at Toronto
April 15	Maple Leafs, 5-1	at Toronto
April 17	Senators, 4-3	at Ottawa
April 19	Senators, 2-1	at Ottawa
April 22	Maple Leafs, 2-1 (OT)	at Toronto
April 24	Maple Leafs, 4-2	at Ottawa

Shutout: Joseph, Toronto.

	W-L	GF	Leading Scorers
New Jersey	4-0	12	Stevens (2-2-4)
			& Elias (1-3-4)
Florida	0-4	6	Bure (1-3-4)

Date	Winner	Home Ice
April 13	Devils, 4-3	at New Jersey
April 16	Devils, 2-1	at New Jersey
April 18	Devils, 2-1	at Florida
April 20	Devils, 4-1	at Florida

SEMIFINALS (Best of 7)

	W-L	GF	Leading Scorers
Philadelphia	4-2	15	Recchi (2-6-8)
Pittsburgh	2-4	14	Straka (2-6-8)

Date	Winner	Home Ice
April 27	Penguins, 2-0	at Philadelphia
April 29	Penguins, 4-1	at Philadelphia
May 2	Flyers, 4-3 (OT)	at Pittsburgh
May 4	Flyers, 2-1 (5OT)	at Pittsburgh
May 7	Flyers, 6-3	at Philadelphia
May 9	Flyers, 2-1	at Pittsburgh

Shutout: Tugnutt, Pittsburgh.

	W-L	GF	Leading Scorers
New Jersey	4-2	16	Elias (2-4-6)
Toronto	2-4	9	Three tied with 3 each.

Date	Winner	Home Ice
April 27	Maple Leafs, 2-1	at Toronto
April 29	Devils, 1-0	at Toronto
May 1	Devils, 5-1	at New Jersey
May 3	Maple Leafs, 3-2	at New Jersey
May 6	Devils, 4-3	at Toronto
May 8	Devils, 3-0	at New Jersey

Shutouts: Brodeur, New Jersey (2).

CHAMPIONSHIP (Best of 7)

	W-L	GF	Leading Scorers
New Jersey	4-3	18	Arnott (2-4-6)
Philadelphia	3-4	15	Tocchet (4-2-6)
			& Recchi (3-3-6)

	Winner	Home Ice
May 14	Devils, 4-1	at Philadelphia
May 16	Flyers, 4-3	at Philadelphia
May 18	Flyers, 4-2	at New Jersey
May 20	Flyers, 3-1	at New Jersey
May 22	Devils, 4-1	at Philadelphia
May 24	Devils, 2-1	at New Jersey
May 26	Devils, 2-1	at Philadelphia

STANLEY CUP FINAL (Best of 7)

	W-L	GF	Leading Scorers
New Jersey	4-2	15	Arnott (4-3-7)
Dallas	2-4	9	Hull (2-2-4)
			& Modano (1-3-4)

	Winner	Home Ice
May 30	Devils, 7-3	at New Jersey
June 1	Stars, 2-1	at New Jersey
June 3	Devils, 2-1	at Dallas
June 5	Devils, 3-1	at Dallas
June 8	Stars, 1-0 (3OT)	at New Jersey
June 10	Devils, 2-1 (2OT)	at Dallas

Shutout: Belfour, Dallas.

Conn Smythe Trophy (Playoff MVP)
Scott Stevens, New Jersey, D
23 games, 3 goals, 8 assists, 11 points, plus-9

Stanley Cup Final Box Scores

Game 1
Tuesday, May 30, at New Jersey

Dallas 1   0   2 — 3
New Jersey 1   3   3 — 7

1st Period: NJ— Arnott 5 (Sykora, Elias) 7:22; DAL— Sydor 1 (Lehtinen, Keane) 13:13.
2nd Period: NJ— Daneyko 1 (Brylin, Madden) 2:52; NJ— Sykora 7 (Elias, Arnott) 10:28; NJ— Stevens 3 (Pandolfo, Rafalski) 16:04.
3rd Period: NJ— Brylin 2 (McKay) 2:21; NJ— Sykora 8 (Arnott, Elias) 3:02; NJ— Arnott 6 (Holik, Sykora) 5:12 (pp); DAL— Sim 1 (Carbonneau) 7:43; DAL— Muller 2 (Carbonneau) 7:55.
Shots on Goal: Dallas— 5-7-6–18; New Jersey— 7-9-10–26. **Power plays:** Dallas 0-0; New Jersey 1-4. **Goalies:** Dallas, Belfour (18 shots, 12 saves) and Fernandez (3:02 of 3rd period, 8 shots, 7 saves); New Jersey, Brodeur (18 shots, 15 saves). **Attendance:** 19,040.

Game 2
Thursday, June 1, at New Jersey

Dallas 1   0   1 — 2
New Jersey 1   0   0 — 1

1st Period: DAL— Hull 10 (Modano, Matvichuk) 4:25; NJ— Mogilny 4 (Gomez, Stevens) 12:42.
3rd Period: DAL— Hull 11 (Lehtinen, Modano) 15:44.
Shots on Goal: Dallas— 3-7-7–17; New Jersey— 9-8-11–28. **Power plays:** Dallas 0-1; New Jersey 0-2. **Goalies:** Dallas, Belfour (28 shots, 27 saves); New Jersey, Brodeur (17 shots, 15 saves). **Attendance:** 19,040.

Game 3
Saturday, June 3, at Dallas

New Jersey 1   1   0 — 2
Dallas 1   0   0 — 1

1st Period: DAL— Cote 2 (unassisted) 13:08 (pp); NJ— Arnott 7 (Rafalski, White) 18:06.
2nd Period: NJ— Sykora 9 (Arnott, Rafalski) 12:27 (pp).
Shots on Goal: New Jersey— 10-16-5–31; Dallas— 7-9-7–23. **Power plays:** Dallas 1-2; Dallas 1-4. **Goalies:** New Jersey, Brodeur (23 shots, 22 saves); Dallas, Belfour (31 shots, 29 saves). **Attendance:** 17,001.

Game 4
Monday, June 5, at Dallas

New Jersey 0   0   3 — 3
Dallas 0   1   0 — 1

2nd Period: DAL— Nieuwendyk 7 (Sydor, Hull) 18:02 (pp).
3rd Period: NJ— Brylin 3 (Mogilny, Malakhov) 2:27; NJ— Madden 3 (Nemchinov, Daneyko) 4:51 (sh); NJ— Rafalski 2 (Elias) 6:08.
Shots on Goal: New Jersey— 8-8-15–31; Dallas— 6-7-4–17. **Power plays:** New Jersey 0-4; Dallas 1-5. **Goalies:** New Jersey, Brodeur (17 shots, 16 saves); Dallas, Belfour (31 shots, 28 saves). **Attendance:** 17,001.

Game 5
Thursday, June 8, at New Jersey

Dallas 0   0   0   0   0   1 — 1
New Jersey 0   0   0   0   0   0 — 0

3rd Overtime: DAL— Modano 10 (Hull, Lehtinen) 6:21.
Shots on Goal: Dallas— 11-6-5-5-12-2–41; New Jersey— 7-11-9-10-8-3–48. **Power plays:** Dallas 0-2; New Jersey 0-3. **Goalies:** Dallas, Belfour (48 shots, 48 saves); New Jersey, Brodeur (41 shots, 40 saves). **Attendance:** 19,040.

Game 6
Saturday, June 10, at Dallas

New Jersey 0   1   0   0   1 — 2
Dallas 0   1   0   0   0 — 1

2nd Period: NJ— Niedermayer 5 (Lemieux, Pandolfo) 5:18 (sh); DAL— Keane 2 (Thornton, Modano) 6:27.
2nd Overtime: NJ— Arnott 8 (Elias, Stevens) 8:20.
Shots on Goal: New Jersey— 11-13-7-11-3–45; Dallas— 7-9-13-1-1–31. **Power plays:** New Jersey 0-1; Dallas 0-4. **Goalies:** New Jersey, Brodeur (31 shots, 30 saves); Dallas, Belfour (45 shots, 43 saves). **Attendance:** 17,001.

Stanley Cup Leaders

Scoring

	Gm	G	A	Pts	+/-	PM	PP
Brett Hull, Dal	23	11	13	24	3	4	3
Mike Modano, Dal	23	10	13	23	3	10	4
Jason Arnott, NJ	23	8	12	20	7	18	3
Patrik Elias, NJ	23	7	13	20	9	9	2
Mark Recchi, Phi	18	6	12	18	3	6	2
Petr Sykora, NJ	23	9	8	17	8	10	1
Jaromir Jagr, Pit	11	8	8	16	5	6	2
Peter Forsberg, Col	16	7	8	15	9	12	2
Adam Deadmarsh, Col	17	4	11	15	7	21	1

Plus/Minus

Hrdina, Pit	9
Forsberg, Col	9
Elias, NJ	9
Stevens, NJ	9
White*, NJ	9
Sundin, Tor	8
Thomas, Tor	8
Sykora, NJ	8

Penalty Minutes

Tocchet, Phi	49
Richardson, Phi	41
Manson, Dal	33
Pronger, St.L	32
Barnaby, Pit	29
Hatcher, Dal	29
Foote, Col	28
Lemieux, NJ	28
Thornton, Dal	28

Goals

Hull, Dal	11
Modano, Dal	10
Sykora, NJ	9
Nolan, SJ	8
Jagr, Pit	8
Arnott, NJ	8
Forsberg, Col	7
Elias, NJ	7
Nieuwendyk, Dal	7

Assists

Elias, NJ	13
Hull, Dal	13
Modano, Dal	13
Recchi, Phi	12
Arnott, NJ	12
Deadmarsh, Col	11
Primeau, Phi	11
Drury, Col	10
Desjardins, Phi	10

Goaltending
(Minimum 420 minutes)

	Gm	Min	W-L	ShO	GAA
Martin Brodeur, NJ	23	1450	16-7	2	1.61
Ron Tugnutt, Pit	11	747	6-5	2	1.77
Patrick Roy, Col	17	1039	11-6	3	1.79
Ed Belfour, Dal	23	1443	14-9	4	1.87
Chris Osgood, Det	9	546	5-4	2	1.97
Brian Boucher*, Phi	18	1184	11-7	1	2.03
Curtis Joseph, Tor	12	730	6-6	1	2.06

Power Play Goals

Modano, Dal	4
LeClair, Phi	4
Seven tied with 3 each.	

Game Winning Goals

Jagr, Pit	4
Forsberg, Col	4
Hull, Dal	4

Wins

Brodeur, NJ	16-7
Belfour, Dal	14-9
Boucher*, Phi	11-7
Roy, Col	11-6
Joseph, Tor	6-6
Tugnutt, Phi	6-5

Save Pct.

Tugnutt, Pit	.945
Joseph, Tor	.932
Belfour, Dal	.931
Roy, Col	.928
Brodeur, NJ	.927
Osgood, Det	.924

Finalists' Composite Box Scores
New Jersey Devils (16-7)

Top Scorers	Pos	Overall Playoffs								Finals vs Dallas							
		Gm	G	A	Pts	+/-	PM	PP	S	Gm	G	A	Pts	+/-	PM	PP	S
Jason Arnott	R	23	8	12	20	7	18	3	56	6	4	3	7	+3	2	1	22
Patrik Elias	L	23	7	13	20	9	9	2	60	6	0	5	5	+2	0	0	22
Petr Sykora	C	23	9	8	17	8	10	1	45	6	3	2	5	+2	4	1	14
Scott Stevens	D	23	3	8	11	9	6	0	29	6	1	2	3	+3	2	0	8
Scott Gomez*	C	23	4	6	10	1	4	1	53	6	0	1	1	0	0	0	12
Claude Lemieux	R	23	4	6	10	7	28	1	78	6	0	1	1	+2	4	0	19
Bobby Holik	C	23	3	7	10	-1	14	0	73	6	0	1	1	0	4	0	18
Sergei Brylin	C	17	3	5	8	2	0	0	24	6	2	1	3	+1	0	0	13
Brian Rafalski*	D	23	2	6	8	5	8	0	31	6	1	3	4	+3	4	0	6
Scott Niedermayer	D	22	5	2	7	5	10	0	40	6	1	0	1	+3	2	0	10
Alexander Mogilny	R	23	4	3	7	1	4	2	55	6	1	1	2	+2	0	0	14
John Madden	L	20	3	4	7	4	0	0	38	6	1	1	2	+1	0	0	15
Colin White*	D	23	1	5	6	9	18	0	23	6	0	1	1	+2	4	0	9
Randy McKay	R	23	0	6	6	-1	9	0	31	6	0	1	1	0	2	0	8
Sergei Nemchinov	C	21	3	2	5	1	2	1	20	6	0	1	1	0	2	0	6
Vladimir Malakhov	D	23	1	4	5	3	18	1	29	6	0	1	1	+1	4	0	6
Jay Pandolfo	L	23	0	5	5	3	0	0	28	6	0	2	2	+2	0	0	6
Ken Daneyko	D	23	1	2	3	-2	14	0	9	6	1	1	2	0	4	0	2
Steve Brule*	C	1	0	0	0	0	0	0	0	0	0	0	0	0	0	0	0
Brad Bombardir	D	1	0	0	0	0	0	0	0	0	0	0	0	0	0	0	0
Steve Kelly	C	10	0	0	0	-1	4	0	5	0	0	0	0	0	0	0	0

Overtime goals— OVERALL (Arnott); FINALS (Arnott). **Shorthanded goals—** OVERALL (Niedermayer 2, Elias, Madden); FINALS (Niedermayer, Madden). **Power Play conversions—**OVERALL (12 for 70, 17.1%); FINALS (2 for 16, 12.5%).

Goaltending	Gm	Min	GAA	GA	SA	Sv%	W-L	Gm	Min	GAA	GA	SA	Sv%	W-L
Martin Brodeur	23	1450	1.61	39	537	.927	16-7	6	435	1.24	9	147	.939	4-2
TOTAL	23	1455	1.57	39	537	.927	16-7	6	435	1.24	9	147	.939	4-2

Empty Net Goals— OVERALL (none), FINALS (none). **Shutouts—** OVERALL (Brodeur 2), FINALS (none). **Assists—** OVERALL (none), FINALS (none). **Penalty Minutes—** OVERALL (Brodeur 10), FINALS (Brodeur 2).

Dallas Stars (14-9)

Top Scorers	Pos	Overall Playoffs								Finals vs New Jersey							
		Gm	G	A	Pts	+/-	PM	PP	S	Gm	G	A	Pts	+/-	PM	PP	S
Brett Hull	R	23	11	13	24	3	4	3	79	6	2	2	4	-2	2	0	18
Mike Modano	C	23	10	13	23	3	10	4	67	6	1	3	4	0	0	0	17
Joe Nieuwendyk	C	23	7	3	10	-2	18	3	45	6	0	1	1	-4	0	1	13
Sergei Zubov	D	18	2	7	9	1	6	1	34	6	0	0	0	-5	0	0	12
Scott Thornton	C	23	2	7	9	1	28	0	33	6	0	1	1	-1	4	0	8
Jamie Langenbrunner	R	15	1	7	8	-1	18	1	27	1	0	0	0	-2	0	0	4
Richard Matvichuk	D	23	2	5	7	7	14	0	19	6	0	1	1	+1	4	0	5
Darryl Sydor	D	23	1	6	7	1	6	0	39	6	1	1	2	-3	0	0	8
Brenden Morrow*	L	21	2	4	6	2	22	1	30	6	0	0	0	-4	4	0	5
Guy Carbonneau	C	23	2	4	6	2	12	0	12	6	0	2	2	-1	0	0	4
Mike Keane	R	23	2	4	6	1	14	0	27	6	1	1	2	-2	2	0	7
Jere Lehtinen	L	13	1	5	6	1	2	0	23	6	0	3	3	+1	2	0	9
Kirk Muller	C	23	2	3	5	-2	18	0	19	6	1	0	1	-1	0	0	6
Derian Hatcher	D	23	1	3	4	-4	29	0	34	6	0	0	0	-2	6	0	7
Roman Lyashenko*	C	16	2	1	3	-1	0	0	15	4	0	0	0	-1	0	0	1
Sylvain Cote	D	23	2	1	3	0	8	2	24	6	1	0	1	-3	2	1	11
Aaron Gavey	C	13	1	2	3	1	10	0	6	1	0	0	0	0	0	0	0
Jon Sim*	C	7	1	0	1	0	6	0	9	6	1	0	1	0	0	0	7
Grant Marshall	R	14	0	1	1	0	4	0	15	3	0	0	0	0	0	0	5
Jamie Pushor	D	5	0	0	0	-1	5	0	2	0	0	0	0	0	0	0	0
Blake Sloan*	R	16	0	0	0	2	10	0	10	3	0	0	0	0	2	0	1
Dave Manson	D	23	0	0	0	2	33	0	19	6	0	0	0	-6	6	0	3

Overtime goals— OVERALL (Modano, Nieuwendyk); FINALS (Modano). **Shorthanded goals—** OVERALL (Zubov, Carbonneau); FINALS (none). **Power Play conversions—** OVERALL (15 for 93, 16.1%); FINALS (2 for 16, 12.5%).

Goaltending	Gm	Min	GAA	GA	SA	Sv%	W-L	Gm	Min	GAA	GA	SA	Sv%	W-L
Ed Belfour	23	1443	1.87	45	651	.931	14-9	6	416	2.02	14	201	.930	2-4
Manny Fernandez*	1	17	3.53	1	8	.875	0-0	1	17	3.53	1	8	.875	0-0
TOTAL	23	1507	1.83	46	659	.930	14-9	6	435	2.07	15	209	.928	2-4

Empty Net Goals— OVERALL (none); FINALS (none). **Shutouts—** OVERALL (Belfour 4); FINALS (Belfour). **Assists—** OVERALL (none); FINALS (none). **Penalty Minutes—** OVERALL (Belfour 8); FINALS (none).

Annual Awards

Voting for the Hart, Calder, Norris, Lady Byng, Selke, and Masterton Trophies is conducted after the regular season by the Professional Hockey Writers Association. The Vezina Trophy is selected by the NHL general managers, while the Jack Adams Award is selected by NHL broadcasters. Points are awarded on 10–7–5–3–1 basis except for the Vezina Trophy and the Adams Award which are awarded 5–3–1.

Hart Trophy
For Most Valuable Player

	Pos	1st	2nd	3rd	4th	5th	Pts
Chris Pronger, St.L	D	25	9	11	8	4–	396
Jaromir Jagr, Pit	R	18	22	9	4	4–	395
Pavel Bure, Fla	R	11	18	16	9	3–	346
Olaf Kolzig, Wash	G	2	3	12	10	8–	139
Owen Nolan, SJ	R	1	0	3	7	16–	62
Roman Turek, St.L	G	0	2	1	3	2–	30

Calder Trophy
For Rookie of the Year

	Pos	1st	2nd	3rd	4th	5th	Pts
Scott Gomez, NJ	C	49	9	0	0	0–	553
Brad Stuart, SJ	D	6	19	3	12	6–	250
Michael York, NYR	C	1	11	15	13	8–	209
Simon Gagne, Phi	C	0	12	11	6	4–	161
Alex Tanguay, Col	C	0	4	6	10	10–	98

Norris Trophy
For Best Defenseman

	1st	2nd	3rd	4th	5th	Pts
Chris Pronger, St.L	53	5	0	0	0–	565
Nicklas Lidstrom, Det	5	46	5	1	0–	400
Rob Blake, LA	0	3	25	15	5–	196
Eric Desjardins, Phi	0	2	8	19	8–	119
Sergei Gonchar, Wash	0	0	7	10	13–	78

Vezina Trophy
For Outstanding Goaltender

	1st	2nd	3rd	Pts
Olaf Kolzig, Wash	14	13	1–	110
Roman Turek, St.L	9	9	7–	79
Curtis Joseph, Tor	2	3	4–	23
Ed Belfour, Dal	2	0	4–	14
Martin Brodeur, NJ	0	1	5–	8

Lady Byng Trophy
For Sportsmanship and Gentlemanly Play

	Pos	1st	2nd	3rd	4th	5th	Pts
Pavol Demitra, St.L	R	18	8	7	9	4–	302
Nicklas Lidstrom, Det	D	17	8	6	2	1–	263
Teemu Selanne, Ana	R	5	7	11	3	6–	169
Pavel Bure, Fla	R	4	13	2	6	5–	164
Mike Modano, Dal	C	3	5	1	2	0–	76

Selke Trophy
For Best Defensive Forward

	Pos	1st	2nd	3rd	4th	5th	Pts
Steve Yzerman, Det	C	32	11	5	2	3–	431
Michal Handzus, St.L	C	6	10	10	2	2–	188
Mike Ricci, SJ	C	3	6	5	9	1–	125
Adam Oates, Wash	C	4	5	3	6	4–	112
Michael Peca, Buf	C	1	5	2	3	2–	66

Adams Award
For Coach of the Year

	1st	2nd	3rd	Pts
Joel Quenneville, St.L	61	16	2–	355
Alain Vigneault, Mon	9	18	18–	117
Ron Wilson, Wash	5	26	13–	116
Ken Hitchcock, Dal	3	8	14–	53
Andy Murray, LA	1	6	10–	33

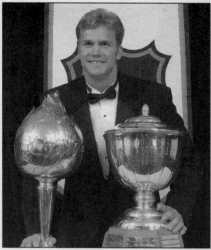

AP/Wide World Photos

St. Louis Blues captain **Chris Pronger** became the first defenseman since Bobby Orr to win both the Hart and Norris Trophies in the same season.

Other Awards

Lester B. Pearson Award (NHL Players Assn. MVP)— Jaromir Jagr, Pittsburgh; **Jennings Trophy** (goaltenders with a minimum of 25 games played for team with fewest goals against)— Roman Turek, St. Louis; **Maurice "Rocket" Richard Trophy** (regular season goal-scoring leader)— Pavel Bure, Florida; **Art Ross Trophy** (regular season points leader)— Jaromir Jagr, Pittsburgh; **Masterton Trophy** (perseverance, sportsmanship, and dedication to hockey)— Ken Daneyko, New Jersey; **King Clancy Trophy** (leadership and humanitarian contributions to community)— Curtis Joseph, Toronto; **Lester Patrick Trophy** (outstanding service to hockey in the U.S.)— Pittsburgh Penguins owner Mario Lemieux, Pittsburgh Penguins general manager Craig Patrick, and USA Hockey executive Lou Vairo.

All-NHL Team

Voting by Pro Hockey Writers' Association (PHWA). Holdovers from 1998-99 All-NHL first team in **bold** type.

	First Team		Second Team
G	Olaf Kolzig, Wash	G	Roman Turek, St.L
D	Chris Pronger, St.L	D	Rob Blake, LA
D	**Nicklas Lidstrom, Det**	D	Eric Desjardins, Phi
C	Steve Yzerman, Det	C	Mike Modano, Dal
R	**Jaromir Jagr**, Pit	R	Pavel Bure, Fla
L	Brendan Shanahan, Det	L	**Paul Kariya, Ana**

All-Rookie Team

Voting by PHWA. Vote totals not released.

Pos		Pos	
G	Brian Boucher, Phi	F	Simon Gagne, Phi
D	Brian Rafalski, NJ	F	Scott Gomez, NJ
D	Brad Stuart, SJ	F	Michael York, NYR

2000 NHL Draft

The top 50 selections at the 38th annual NHL Entry Draft held June 24, 2000, in Calgary. The order of the first 14 positions (12 non-playoff teams plus expansion Columbus and Minnesota) were determined by a draft lottery held June 1 in New Jersey. Positions 15 through 30 reflect regular season records in reverse order. The top 30 picks are first round selections and the remaining 20 are from the second round.

Top 50 Picks

Team	Player, Last Team	Pos	Team	Player, Last Team	Pos
1 NY Islanders	Rick DiPietro, Boston Univ.	G	26 Washington	Brian Sutherby, Moose Jaw	C
2 Atlanta	Dany Heatley, U of Wisconsin	L	27 **h**-Boston	Martin Samuelsson, MoDo (Swe)	D
3 Minnesota	Marian Gaborik, Trencin (Slo)	L	28 Philadelphia	Justin Williams, Plymouth	R
4 Columbus	Rostislav Klesla, Brampton	D	29 Detroit	Niklas Kronvall, Djurgarden (Swe)	D
5 **a**-NY Islanders	Raffi Torres, Brampton	L	30 St. Louis	Jeff Taffe, U of Minnesota	C
6 Nashville	Scott Hartnell, Prince Albert	R	31 Atlanta	Ilja Nikulin, Tver (Rus)	D
7 Boston	Lars Jonsson, Leksand (Swe)	D	32 **i**-Carolina	Tomas Kurka, Plymouth	L
8 **b**-Tampa Bay	Nikita Alexeev, Erie	R	33 Minnesota	Nick Schultz, Prince Albert	D
9 Calgary	Brent Krahn, Calgary	G	34 Tampa Bay	Ruslan Zainullan, Kazan (Rus)	R
10 Chicago	Mikhail Yakubov, Togliatti (Rus)	C	35 **j**-Edmonton	Brad Winchester, U of Wisconsin	L
11 **c**-Chicago	Pavel Vorobiev, Yaroslavl (Rus)	R	36 Nashville	Daniel Widing, Leksand (Swe)	R
12 Anaheim	Alexei Smirnov, Dynamo (Rus)	L	37 Boston	Andy Hilbert, U of Michigan	L
13 Montreal	Ron Hainsey, UMass-Lowell	D	38 **k**-Detroit	Tomas Kopecky, Trencin (Slo)	L
14 **d**-Colorado	Vaclav Nedorost, Budejovice (Cze)	C	39 **l**-New Jersey*	Teemu Laine, Jokerit (Fin)	R
15 Buffalo	Artem Kriukov, Yaroslavl (Rus)	C	40 Calgary	Kurtis Foster, Peterborough	D
16 **e**-Montreal	Marcel Hossa, Portland	C	41 **m**-San Jose	Tero Maatta, Jokerit (Fin)	D
17 Edmonton	Alexei Mikhnov, Yaroslavl (Rus)	L	42 **n**-Atlanta	Libor Ustrnul, Plymouth	D
18 Pittsburgh	Brooks Orpik, Boston Coll.	D	43 **o**-Washington	Matt Pettinger, Calgary	L
19 Phoenix	Krystofer Kolanos, Boston Coll.	C	44 **p**-Anaheim	Ilja Bryzgalov, Togliatti (Rus)	G
20 Los Angeles	Alexander Frolov, Yaroslavl (Rus)	L	45 Ottawa*	Mathieu Chouinard, Shawinigan	G
21 Ottawa	Anton Volchenkov, CSKA (Rus)	D	46 **q**-Calgary*	Jarret Stoll, Kootenay	C
22 **f**-New Jersey	David Hale, Sioux City	D	47 Colorado	Jared Aulin, Kamloops	C
23 **g**-Vancouver	Nathan Smith, Swift Current	C	48 Buffalo	Gerard Dicaire, Seattle	D
24 Toronto	Brad Boyes, Erie	C	49 **s**-Chicago	Jonas Nordqvist, Leksand (Swe)	C
25 Dallas	Steve Ott, Windsor	C	50 Colorado*	Sergei Soin, Krylja Sovetov (Rus)	C

Acquired picks: a— from Tampa Bay; **b—** from NY Rangers; **c—** from Vancouver; **d—** from Carolina; **e—** from San Jose; **f—** from Colorado; **g—** from Florida; **h—** from Colorado; **i—** from Colorado via Columbus; **j—** from NY Islanders; **k—** from NY Rangers; **l—** from NY Islanders via Vancouver; **m—** from Chicago; **n—** from Vancouver; **o—** from Calgary via Anaheim; **p—** from Montreal; **q—** from Colorado; **r—** from Carolina; **s—** from San Jose.
*compensatory pick

U.S. Division I College Hockey

Final regular season standings; overall records, including all postseason tournament games, in parentheses.

Central Collegiate Hockey Assn.

	W	L	T	Pts	GF	GA
*Michigan (27-10-4)	19	6	3	41	112	65
*Michigan St. (27-11-4)	18	8	2	38	84	46
Lake Superior St. (18-16-2)	17	9	2	36	76	66
N. Michigan (22-13-4)	16	8	4	36	93	64
Notre Dame (16-18-8)	11	10	7	29	65	76
Ferris St. (21-16-2)	13	13	2	28	85	79
Nebraska-Omaha (16-19-7)	10	12	6	26	83	95
Bowling Green (17-19-1)	12	15	1	25	90	88
Miami-OH (13-20-3)	10	15	3	23	75	89
W. Michigan (12-21-3)	10	15	3	23	83	109
Ohio St. (13-19-4)	9	16	3	21	56	90
Alaska-Fairbanks (6-25-3)	4	22	2	10	65	100

Conf. Tourney Final: Michigan St. 6, Nebraska-Omaha 0.

***NCAA Tourney (1-2):** Michigan (1-1), Michigan St. (0-1).

College Hockey America

	W	L	T	Pts	GF	GA
Niagara (30-8-4)	15	0	2	38	86	18
Alab.-Huntsville (17-10-4)	12	5	1	29	73	46
Bemidji State (13-20-1)	8	8	1	21	63	69
Air Force (19-18-2)	6	10	0	18	44	50
Findlay (9-22-0)	4	14	0	10	38	101
Army (13-17-2)	1	9	0	4	21	41

Conf. Tourney Final: Niagara 3, Alabama-Huntsville 2.
***NCAA Tourney (1-1):** Niagara (1-1).
Note: Army played fewer conference games than the other five members. Therefore all conference games with Army were worth four points instead of two.

Eastern Collegiate Athletic Conf.

	W	L	T	Pct	GF	GA
*St. Lawrence (27-8-2)	16	3	1	.825	76	47
*Colgate (24-9-2)	14	4	2	.750	85	61
Rensselaer (22-13-2)	11	9	1	.548	61	49
Cornell (16-14-2)	10	9	1	.525	70	54
Clarkson (17-15-3)	9	8	3	.525	69	71
Princeton (10-16-4)	9	9	4	.476	66	66
Harvard (11-17-2)	9	10	2	.476	65	63
Dartmouth (9-17-4)	8	10	3	.452	54	63
Yale (9-16-5)	6	11	4	.381	45	63
Union (8-24-1)	6	14	1	.310	48	75
Brown (6-19-3)	4	15	2	.238	52	78
Vermont (5-9-3)	3	2	2	.571	25	26

Conf. Tourney Final: St. Lawrence 2, Rensselaer 0.
***NCAA Tourney (1-2):** St. Lawrence (1-1), Colgate (0-1).
Note: Due to a hazing scandal, Vermont cancelled the remainder of its season. The ECAC voted to rank teams by winning percentage and place Vermont 12th.

Hockey East Association

	W	L	T	Pts	GF	GA
*Boston University (25-10-7)	15	3	6	36	85	69
*New Hampshire (23-9-6)	13	5	6	32	75	68
*Boston College (29-12-1)	15	8	1	31	91	50
*Maine (27-8-5)	13	7	4	30	88	67
Providence (18-18-2)	10	13	1	21	65	79
Northeastern (12-19-5)	8	11	5	21	67	76
Merrimack (11-19-6)	7	12	6	18	58	81
UMass-Amherst (11-20-5)	5	15	4	14	50	71
UMass-Lowell (9-22-3)	5	16	3	13	60	78

Conf. Tourney Final: Maine 2, Boston College 1.
***NCAA Tourney (5-4):** Boston College (3-1), Boston University (1-1), Maine (1-1), New Hampshire (0-1).

Metro Atlantic Athletic Conf.

	W	L	T	Pts	GF	GA
Quinnipiac (27-6-3) 23	1	3		49	152	60
Mercyhurst (22-10-4) 19	6	2		40	113	64
Canisius (21-10-4) 16	8	3		35	93	79
Connecticut (19-16-1).......15	11	1		31	104	77
Sacred Heart (16-15-3) 14	10	3		31	86	74
Iona (17-17-3)...............13	12	2		28	93	93
Holy Cross (8-24-3)..........8	16	3		19	83	110
Bentley (7-23-2)..............7	18	2		16	90	130
American Int'l (7-20-3) 5	19	3		13	72	124
Fairfield (3-28-3) 3	22	2		8	69	144

Conf. Tourney Final: Connecticut 6, Iona 1.
NCAA Tourney: No teams invited.

Western Collegiate Hockey Assn.

	W	L	T	Pts	GF	GA
*Wisconsin (31-9-1)..........23	5	0		46	112	70
*North Dakota (31-8-5)......17	6	5		39	113	61
*St. Cloud St. (23-14-3).......16	9	3		35	105	66
MSU-Mankato (21-14-4) 15	10	3		33	90	82
Colorado College (18-18-3)..14	11	3		31	88	69
Minnesota (20-19-2) 13	13	2		28	95	84
Alaska-Anchorage (15-18-3)..11	14	3		25	65	87
Minnesota-Duluth (15-22-0)...10	18	0		20	59	114
Denver (16-23-2)..............9	18	1		19	92	97
Michigan Tech (4-34-0) 2	26	0		4	47	136

Conf. Tourney Final: North Dakota 5, Wisconsin 3.
*NCAA Tourney (3-2): North Dakota (3-0), St. Cloud St. (0-1), Wisconsin (0-1).

USA Today/American Hockey Magazine Coaches Poll

Taken April 12, 2000 after the NCAA Tournament. First place votes are in parentheses.

	League	W	L	T	Pts
1 North Dakota (15) ....WCHA		31	8	5	225
2 Boston College ....HE	29	12	1	210	
3 Maine.......................HE	27	8	5	189	
4 St. Lawrence..............ECAC	27	8	2	186	
5 Wisconsin ....WCHA		31	9	1	165
6 Boston University............HE	25	10	7	150	
7 Michigan ....CCHA	27	10	4	135	
8 Niagara ....CHA		30	8	4	119
9 Colgate...................ECAC	24	9	2	106	
10 Michigan State ....CCHA	27	11	4	84	

Scoring Leaders

Including postseason games; minimum 20 games.

	Cl	Gm	G	A	Pts	Avg
Steve Reinprecht, Wisc........Sr	37	26	40	66	**1.78**
Andy McDonald, Colg.........Sr	34	25	33	58	**1.71**
Shawn Mansoff, Quinn........Jr	35	29	27	56	**1.60**
Brian Herbert, Quinn..........Fr	34	22	32	54	**1.59**
Shawn Horcoff, Mich. St. ......Sr	42	14	51	65	**1.55**

Goaltending Leaders

Including postseason games; minimum 15 games.

	Cl	Record	Sv%	GAA
Greg Gardner, Niag. ....Sr	29-8-4	.936	1.53
Ryan Miller, Mich. St...........Fr	16-5-3	.932	1.53
Joel Laing, Rens...............Sr	17-7-2	.947	1.82

Hobey Baker Award

For College Hockey Player of the Year. Voting is done by a 20-member panel of national media, college coaches, pro scouts, and one USA Hockey member.

	Cl	Pos
Winner: Mike Mottau, Boston College ....Sr.		D

NCAA Division I Tournament
Regional Seeds

Frozen Four teams in **bold**.

West
1 Wisconsin (31-8-1)
2 **North Dakota** (28-8-5)
3 New Hampshire (23-8-6)
4 **Boston College** (26-11-1)
5 Michigan St. (27-10-4)
6 Niagara (29-7-4)

East
1 Maine (26-7-5)
2 **St. Lawrence** (26-7-2)
3 Boston University (24-9-7)
4 Colgate (24-8-2)
5 Michigan (26-9-4)
6 St. Cloud St. (23-13-3)

West Regional

Held at Mariucci Arena in Minneapolis, Minn., March 24-25. Single elimination, two second round winners advance to Frozen Four.

First Round

Niagara 4......................................New Hampshire 1
Boston College 6 ....OT ....Michigan St. 5
(Byes: North Dakota and Wisconsin)

Second Round

North Dakota 4...........................Niagara 1
Boston College 4 ....Wisconsin 1

East Regional

Held at Pepsi Arena in Albany, N.Y., March 25-26. Single elimination, two second round winners advance to Frozen Four.

First Round

Michigan 4 ....OT...............Colgate 3
Boston University 5......................St. Cloud St. 3
(Byes: Maine and St. Lawrence)

Second Round

Maine 5 ....Michigan 2
St. Lawrence 3 ....4OT ....Boston University 2

THE FROZEN FOUR

Held at Providence (R.I.) Civic Center, April 6 and April 8. Single elimination; no consolation game.

Semifinals

North Dakota 2........................Maine 0
Boston College 4 ....St. Lawrence 2

Championship Game

North Dakota, 4-2

North Dakota (WCHA) 1	0	3	**— 4**
Boston College (HE) 1	1	0	**— 2**

1st Period: ND— Mike Commodore 5 (Bryan Lundbohm, Tim Skarperud), 3:48; BC— Jeff Farkas 32 (Blake Bellefeuille, Brian Gionta), 16:47 (pp).
2nd Period: BC— Marty Hughes 5 (Gionta), 6:59.
3rd Period: ND— Lee Goren 33 (Ryan Bayda), 2:43; ND— Jason Ulmer 18 (Goren), 14:22; ND— Goren 34 (unassisted), 19:14 (en).
Goalies: ND— Karl Goehring (23 shots, 21saves); BC— Scott Clemmensen (35 shots, 32 saves). **Attendance:** 11,484.
Final records: North Dakota (31-8-5); Boston College (29-12-1); Maine (27-8-5); St. Lawrence (27-8-2).
Most Outstanding Player: Lee Goren, North Dakota senior forward; 2 goals, 1 assist in final game.
All-Tournament Team: Goren, forward Bryan Lundbohm, defenseman Mike Commodore and goalie Karl Goehring of North Dakota; forward Jeff Farkas and defenseman Mike Mottau of Boston College.

Division I All-America

First team JOFA Division I All-Americans as chosen by the American Hockey Coaches Association. Holdovers from 1998-99 All-America first team are in **bold** type.

West Team

Pos		Yr	Hgt	Wgt
G	Karl Goehring, North Dakota ......Jr.	5-7	150
D	Jeff Dessner, Wisconsin............Jr.	6-2	195
D	Jeff Jillson, Michigan ....So.	6-3	220
F	Steve Reinprecht, Wisconsin ......Sr.	6-0	190
F	Jeff Panzer, North Dakota.........Jr.	5-10	160
F	Shawn Horcoff, Michigan St........Sr.	6-1	202

East Team

Pos		Yr	Hgt	Wgt
G	Joel Laing, Rensselaer ....Sr.	5-10	185
D	Justin Harney, St. Lawrence ....Sr.	6-0	195
D	**Mike Mottau**, Boston College ....Sr.	6-0	198
F	**Brian Gionta**, Boston College ....Jr.	5-7	165
F	Andy McDonald, Colgate...........Sr.	5-10	165
F	Jeff Farkas, Boston College.........Sr.	6-1	190

Division III

Final Four

March 17-18 in Superior, Wisc.

Semifinals

Norwich (Vt.) 5...........OT ....Wisc.-Superior 4
St. Thomas (Minn.) 7 ....Plattsburgh St. (N.Y.) 1

Third Place: Plattsburgh St. 2..........Wisc.-Superior 0
Championship Game: Norwich 2 ....St. Thomas 1
Final records: Norwich (29-2-1); St. Thomas (27-4-2); Plattsburgh St. (26-4-3); Wisconsin-Superior (24-10-1).

Women's College Hockey

Women's hockey is not an officially sanctioned NCAA sport, but championships are sponsored by the American Women's College Hockey Alliance (AWCHA).

Division I Championship

March 25 in Boston, Mass.

Third Place: Dartmouth 5 ....Minn.-Duluth 4
Championship Game: Minnesota 4.............Brown 2
Final records: Minnesota (32-6-1); Brown (25-4-3); Dartmouth (21-12-0); Minnesota-Duluth (25-5-3).

Division III Championship

March 24-25 in Boston, Mass.

Game 1: Middlebury 5 ....Augsburg 1
Game 2: Middlebury 8 ....Augsburg 1
Final records: Middlebury (24-2-0); Augsburg (21-7-1).

MINOR LEAGUE HOCKEY

American Hockey League

Division champions (*) and playoff qualifiers (†) are noted. GF and GA refer to goals for and against. Losses in overtime are designated in parentheses and worth one point in the standings.

Eastern Conference
Atlantic Division

Team (Affiliate)	W	L	T	Pts	GF	GA
*Quebec (Mon.)...........37	38(4)	5	83	227	238
†Saint John (Calg.)......32	37(5)	11	80	267	283
†Lowell (LA & NYI) 33	40(4)	7	77	228	240
St. John's (Tor.) 23	49(4)	8	58	202	277

New England Division

Team (Affiliate)	W	L	T	Pts	GF	GA
*Hartford (NYR) 49	24(2)	7	107	249	198
†Portland (Wash.).........46	24(1)	10	103	256	202
†Worcester (St.L.)........34	35(4)	11	83	249	250
†Springfield (Pho.) 33	36(1)	11	78	272	252
†Providence (Bos.) 33	41(3)	6	75	231	269

Western Conference
Empire Division

Team (Affiliate)	W	L	T	Pts	GF	GA
*Rochester (Buf.)..........46	25(3)	9	104	247	201
†Syracuse (Van.)..........35	36(1)	9	80	290	294
†Hamilton (Edm.) 27	40(6)	13	73	225	262
†Albany (NJ)..............30	43(3)	7	70	225	250
Wilkes-Barre (Pit) 23	48(5)	9	60	236	306

Mid-Atlantic Division

Team (Affiliate)	W	L	T	Pts	GF	GA
*Kentucky (SJ)............42	29(4)	9	97	250	211
†Hershey (Col.)...........43	32(3)	5	94	297	267
†Philadelphia (Phi.)........44	33(2)	3	93	281	239
†Louisville (Fla.)...........42	31(1)	7	92	278	254
Cincinnati (Ana. & Det.) ...30	41(4)	9	73	227	244

Scoring Leaders

	Gm	G	A	Pts	PM
Christian Matte, Her..............73	43	61	104	83
Mike Maneluk, Phi 73	47	40	87	156
Mark Greig, Phi 68	34	48	82	112
Derek Armstrong, Har 77	28	54	82	101
Serge Aubin, Her 58	42	38	80	50

Goaltending Leaders

	GP	GAA	Sv%	Record
Mika Noronen, Roch 54	2.18	.920	33-13-4
Milan Hnilicka, Har 36	2.19	.927	22-11-0
Martin Brochu, Por 54	2.19	.925	32-15-6

Calder Cup Finals

	W-L	GF	Leading Scorers
Hartford..........4-2	14	Smyth (3-3-6)
			& Armstrong (2-4-6)
Rochester.........2-4	10	Dumont (4-0-4)

Date	Winner	Home Ice
May 24 ....Hartford, 1-0	at Hartford
May 26..................Rochester, 4-1	at Hartford
May 28 ....Hartford, 3-1	at Rochester
May 31 ....Rochester, 4-2	at Rochester
June 2 ....Hartford, 3-0	at Hartford
June 4 ....Hartford, 4-1	at Rochester

International Hockey League

Division champions (*) and playoff qualifiers (†) are noted. GF and GA refer to goals for and against. SOL refers to shootout losses and are worth one point in the standings.

Eastern Conference

Team (Affiliate)	W	L	SOL	Pts	GF	GA
*Grand Rapids (Ott.)	51	22	9	111	254	200
†Orlando (Atl.)	47	23	12	106	250	202
†Cincinnati (Car.)	44	30	8	96	244	246
†Cleveland (Chi.)	40	30	12	92	225	238
†Milwaukee (Nash.)	37	36	9	83	222	246
Michigan (Dal.)	33	37	12	78	178	223
Detroit (TB)	22	52	8	52	163	277

Western Conference

Team (Affiliate)	W	L	SOL	Pts	GF	GA
*Chicago (Indep.)	53	21	8	114	270	228
†Utah (Indep.)	45	25	12	102	265	220
†Houston (Indep.)	44	29	9	97	219	197
†Long Beach (Indep.)	44	31	7	95	234	216
†Manitoba (Indep.)	37	31	14	88	227	237
Kansas City (Indep.)	36	37	9	81	249	270

Scoring Leaders

	Gm	G	A	Pts	PM
Steve Maltais, Chi.	82	44	46	90	78
Steve Larouche, Chi	82	31	57	88	52
David Ling, KC	82	35	48	83	210
Gilbert Dionne, Cin	81	34	49	83	88
Jarrod Skalde, Utah	77	25	54	79	98

Goaltending Leaders

	GP	GAA	Sv%	Record
Nikolai Khabibulin, LB	33	1.83	.930	21-11-1
Frederic Chabot, Hou	62	2.13	.920	36-19-7
Jani Hurme, GR	52	2.18	.921	29-15-4

Turner Cup Finals

	W-L	GF	Leading Scorers
Chicago	4-2	23	C. Ferraro (3-5-8)
Grand Rapids	2-4	18	Schastlivy (3-4-7)

Date	Winner	Home Ice
May 26	Chicago, 4-3 (OT)	at Chicago
May 28	Chicago, 4-0	at Chicago
May 30	Grand Rapids, 5-3	at Grand Rapids
June 1	Chicago, 5-3	at Grand Rapids
June 3	Grand Rapids, 6-4	at Chicago
June 5	Chicago, 3-1	at Grand Rapids

East Coast Hockey League

Division champions (*) and playoff qualifiers (†) are noted. GF and GA refer to goals for and against. SOL refers to shootout losses and are worth one point in the standings.

Northern Conference
Northeast Division

Team (Affiliate)	W	L	SOL	Pts	GF	GA
*Roanoke (Indep.)	44	20	6	94	221	181
†Richmond (SJ)	44	21	5	93	258	205
†Hampton Roads (Chi./Wash./Nash.)	44	22	4	92	241	198
†Trenton (Phi./LA/NYI)	37	29	4	78	233	199
Charlotte (NYR)	25	38	7	57	186	254
Greensboro (Indep.)	20	43	7	47	229	337

Northwest Division

Team (Affiliate)	W	L	SOL	Pts	GF	GA
*Peoria (St.L)	45	20	5	95	273	216
†Huntington (Indep.)	35	25	10	80	230	238
†Johnstown (Calg.)	33	28	9	75	235	233
†Dayton (Dal.)	32	28	10	74	229	226
Wheeling (Pit.)	25	40	5	55	202	246
Toledo (TB)	22	41	7	51	214	306

Southern Conference
Southeast Division

Team (Affiliate)	W	L	SOL	Pts	GF	GA
*Florida (Car.)	53	15	2	108	277	181
†Pee Dee (Indep.)	47	18	5	99	233	175
†Greenville (Bos.)	46	18	6	98	277	197
†South Carolina (Buf.)	35	25	10	80	253	242
†Augusta (NJ)	34	31	5	73	243	248
Tallahassee (Edm./Mon.)	31	33	6	68	256	261
Jacksonville (Indep.)	27	34	9	63	246	291

Southwest Division

Team (Affiliate)	W	L	SOL	Pts	GF	GA
*Louisiana (Det./Tor.)	43	18	9	95	281	241
†Mobile (Ott.)	40	28	2	82	275	230
†New Orleans (SJ)	36	27	7	79	230	219
†Mississippi (LA/Pho.)	35	27	8	78	241	221
†Pensacola (Col.)	35	29	6	76	215	216
†Baton Rouge (Indep.)	33	32	5	71	253	277
Jackson (Indep.)	32	32	6	70	201	227
Birmingham (Indep.)	29	37	4	62	255	297
Arkansas (Indep.)	18	49	3	39	191	316

Scoring Leaders

	Gm	G	A	Pts	PM
John Spoltore, Lou	66	27	92	119	89
Andrew Williamson, Tol	63	63	39	102	114
Sean Venedam, Grv	68	33	60	93	70
Lars Pettersen, Aug	70	31	62	93	70
Chris Gignac, Tol	59	33	56	89	36

Goaltending Leaders

	GP	GAA	Sv%	Record
Sandy Allan, PD	33	2.26	.924	21-8-3
Marc Magliarditi, Fla	33	2.31	.923	22-9-0
Paxton Schafer, PD	41	2.42	.920	26-10-2

Kelly Cup Finals

	W-L	GF	Leading Scorers
Peoria	4-2	24	Boutin (5-5-10)
Louisiana	2-4	23	Spoltore (5-7-12)

Date	Winner	Home Ice
May 19	Louisiana, 5-3	at Peoria
May 20	Louisiana, 4-2	at Peoria
May 24	Peoria, 5-4 (2OT)	at Louisiana
May 25	Peoria, 4-2	at Louisiana
May 28	Peoria, 6-5 (2OT)	at Louisiana
May 31	Peoria, 4-3 (OT)	at Peoria

World Hockey Championships

MEN

The World Hockey Championships, held in St. Petersburg, Russia from April 29-May 14, 2000. Top three teams (*) in each group after preliminary round-robin advance to the second round. Fourth-place teams play in a consolation round. Top four teams from each group of the second round advance to the quarterfinals.

Final Round Robin Standings

GROUP A	W-L-T	Pts	GF	GA
*Sweden	3-0-0	6	17	3
*Latvia	2-1-0	4	9	7
*Belarus	1-2-0	2	10	16
Ukraine	0-3-0	0	6	16

GROUP B	W-L-T	Pts	GF	GA
*Slovakia	2-0-1	5	10	4
*Finland	1-0-2	4	11	5
*Italy	1-2-0	2	5	12
Austria	0-2-1	1	3	8

GROUP C	W-L-T	Pts	GF	GA
*Czech Republic	3-0-0	6	12	4
*Norway	2-1-0	4	13	7
*Canada	1-2-0	2	10	6
Japan	0-3-0	0	3	21

GROUP D	W-L-T	Pts	GF	GA
*United States	2-0-1	5	9	5
*Switzerland	1-1-1	3	8	9
*Russia	1-2-0	2	10	7
France	1-2-0	2	7	13

Second Round

GROUP E	W-L-T	Pts	GF	GA
*United States	3-0-2	8	13	7
*Switzerland	2-1-2	6	14	12
*Sweden	2-2-1	5	16	11
*Latvia	2-2-1	5	11	10
Belarus	2-3-0	4	9	17
Russia	1-4-0	2	8	12

GROUP F	W-L-T	Pts	GF	GA
*Czech Republic	4-1-0	8	25	11
*Finland	3-1-1	7	22	15
*Canada	3-2-0	6	19	10
*Slovakia	2-2-1	5	22	15
Norway	1-3-1	3	10	24
Italy	0-4-1	1	5	28

Quarterfinals

Slovakia 4 .... United States 1
Finland 2 .... Sweden 1
Canada 5 .... Switzerland 3
Czech Republic 3 .... Latvia 1

Semifinals

Slovakia 3 .... Finland 1
Czech Republic 2 .... Canada 1

Bronze Medal: Finland 2 .... Canada 1
Gold Medal: Czech Republic 5 .... Slovakia 3

Scoring Leaders

	Gm	G	A	Pts	PM
Miroslav Satan, Slovakia	9	10	2	12	14
Jiri Dopita, Czech Republic	9	4	7	11	16
David Vyborny, Czech Republic	9	4	6	10	6
Todd Bertuzzi, Canada	9	5	4	9	47
Tomas Vlasak, Czech Republic	9	4	5	9	0
Trond Magnussen, Norway	6	3	6	9	10
Ryan Smyth, Canada	9	3	6	9	0

Goaltending Leaders

(At least 200 minutes)	Gm	Min	GAA
Jose Theodore, Canada	8	478	1.63
Tommy Salo, Sweden	6	358	1.67
Roman Cechmanek, Czech Rep.	8	480	2.00
Damian Rhodes, USA	5	300	2.40
Arturs Irbe, Latvia	7	420	2.43

WOMEN

The sixth sanctioned Women's World Hockey Championship, held in Ontario, Canada April 4-9, 2000. This tournament served as the main qualifier for the 2002 Olympics in Salt Lake City. The top six finishers (Canada, United States, Finland, Sweden, China, and Russia) qualified. The remaining two teams will be determined at a tournament held in February, 2001.

Pool A Final Standings

Top two teams (*) in each group after preliminary round-robin advance to the medal round.

GROUP A	W-L-T	Pts	GF	GA
*Canada	3-0-0	6	21	1
*Sweden	1-1-1	3	11	5
China	1-1-1	3	5	9
Japan	0-3-0	0	0	22

GROUP B	W-L-T	Pts	GF	GA
*United States	3-0-0	6	35	4
*Finland	2-1-0	4	14	6
Russia	1-2-0	2	8	24
Germany	0-3-0	0	4	27

Medal Round

Canada 3 .... Finland 2
United States 7 .... Sweden 1

Bronze Medal: Finland 7 .... Sweden 1
Gold Medal: Canada 3 .... United States 2

Scoring Leaders

	Gm	G	A	Pts	PM
Krissy Wendell, USA	5	2	11	13	6
Stephanie O'Sullivan, USA	5	5	7	12	2
Karyn Bye, USA	5	8	2	10	2
Alana Blahoski, USA	5	7	2	9	0
Five tied with 8 points each.					

The Stanley Cup

The Stanley Cup was originally donated to the Canadian Amateur Hockey Association by Sir Frederick Arthur Stanley, Lord Stanley of Preston and 16th Earl of Derby, who had become interested in the sport while Governor General of Canada from 1888 to 1893. Stanley wanted the trophy to be a challenge cup, contested for each year by the best amateur hockey teams in Canada.

In 1893, the Cup was presented without a challenge to the AHA champion Montreal Amateur Athletic Association team. Every year since, however, there has been a playoff. In 1914, Cup trustees limited the field challenging for the trophy to the champion of the eastern professional National Hockey Association (NHA, organized in 1910) and the western professional Pacific Coast Hockey Association (PCHA, organized in 1912).

The NHA disbanded in 1917 and the National Hockey League (NHL) was formed. From 1918 to 1926, the NHL and PCHA champions played for the Cup with the Western Canada Hockey League (WCHL) champion joining in a three-way challenge in 1923 and '24. The PCHA disbanded in 1924, while the WCHL became the Western Hockey League (WHL) for the 1925-26 season and folded the following year. The NHL playoffs have decided the winner of the Stanley Cup ever since.

Champions, 1893-1917

Multiple winners: Montreal Victorias and Montreal Wanderers (4); Montreal Amateur Athletic Association and Ottawa Silver Seven (3); Montreal Shamrocks, Ottawa Senators, Quebec Bulldogs and Winnipeg Victorias (2).

Year		Year		Year	
1893	Montreal AAA	1901	Winnipeg Victorias	1909	Ottawa Senators
1894	Montreal AAA	1902	Montreal AAA	1910	Montreal Wanderers
1895	Montreal Victorias	1903	Ottawa Silver Seven	1911	Ottawa Senators
1896	(Feb.) Winnipeg Victorias	1904	Ottawa Silver Seven	1912	Quebec Bulldogs
	(Dec.) Montreal Victorias	1905	Ottawa Silver Seven	1913	Quebec Bulldogs
1897	Montreal Victorias	1906	Montreal Wanderers	1914	Toronto Blueshirts (NHA)
1898	Montreal Victorias	1907	(Jan.) Kenora Thistles	1915	Vancouver Millionaires (PCHA)
1899	Montreal Shamrocks		(Mar.) Montreal Wanderers	1916	Montreal Canadiens (NHA)
1900	Montreal Shamrocks	1908	Montreal Wanderers	1917	Seattle Metropolitans (PCHA)

Champions Since 1918

Multiple winners: Montreal Canadiens (23); Toronto Arenas-St. Pats-Maple Leafs (13); Detroit Red Wings (9); Boston Bruins and Edmonton Oilers (5); NY Islanders, NY Rangers and Ottawa Senators (4); Chicago Blackhawks (3); Montreal Maroons, New Jersey Devils, Philadelphia Flyers and Pittsburgh Penguins (2).

Year	Winner	Head Coach	Series	Loser	Head Coach
1918	Toronto Arenas	Dick Carroll	3-2 (WLWLW)	Vancouver (PCHA)	Frank Patrick
1919	No Decision*				
1920	Ottawa	Pete Green	3-2 (WWLLW)	Seattle (PCHA)	Pete Muldoon
1921	Ottawa	Pete Green	3-2 (LWWLW)	Vancouver (PCHA)	Frank Patrick
1922	Toronto St. Pats	Eddie Powers	3-2 (LWLWW)	Vancouver (PCHA)	Frank Patrick
1923	Ottawa	Pete Green	3-1 (WLWW)	Vancouver (PCHA)	Frank Patrick
			2-0	Edmonton (WCHL)	K.C. McKenzie
1924	Montreal	Leo Dandurand	2-0	Vancouver (PCHA)	Frank Patrick
			2-0	Calgary (WCHL)	Eddie Oatman
1925	Victoria (WCHL)	Lester Patrick	3-1 (WWLW)	Montreal	Leo Dandurand
1926	Montreal Maroons	Eddie Gerard	3-1 (WWLW)	Victoria (WHL)	Lester Patrick
1927	Ottawa	Dave Gill	2-0 (TWTW)	Boston	Art Ross
1928	NY Rangers	Lester Patrick	3-2 (LWLWW)	Montreal Maroons	Eddie Gerard
1929	Boston	Cy Denneny	2-0	NY Rangers	Lester Patrick
1930	Montreal	Cecil Hart	2-0	Boston	Art Ross
1931	Montreal	Cecil Hart	3-2 (WLLWW)	Chicago	Art Duncan
1932	Toronto	Dick Irvin	3-0	NY Rangers	Lester Patrick
1933	NY Rangers	Lester Patrick	3-1 (WWLW)	Toronto	Dick Irvin
1934	Chicago	Tommy Gorman	3-1 (WWLW)	Detroit	Jack Adams
1935	Montreal Maroons	Tommy Gorman	3-0	Toronto	Dick Irvin
1936	Detroit	Jack Adams	3-1 (WWLW)	Toronto	Dick Irvin
1937	Detroit	Jack Adams	3-2 (LWLWW)	NY Rangers	Lester Patrick
1938	Chicago	Bill Stewart	3-1 (WWLW)	Toronto	Dick Irvin
1939	Boston	Art Ross	4-1 (WLWWW)	Toronto	Dick Irvin
1940	NY Rangers	Frank Boucher	4-2 (WWLLWW)	Toronto	Dick Irvin

Year	Winner	Head Coach	Series	Loser	Head Coach
1941	Boston	Cooney Weiland	4-0	Detroit	Jack Adams
1942	Toronto	Hap Day	4-3 (LLLWWWW)	Detroit	Jack Adams
1943	Detroit	Ebbie Goodfellow	4-0	Boston	Art Ross
1944	Montreal	Dick Irvin	4-0	Chicago	Paul Thompson
1945	Toronto	Hap Day	4-3 (WWWLLLW)	Detroit	Jack Adams
1946	Montreal	Dick Irvin	4-1 (WWWLW)	Boston	Dit Clapper
1947	Toronto	Hap Day	4-2 (LWWWLW)	Montreal	Dick Irvin
1948	Toronto	Hap Day	4-0	Detroit	Tommy Ivan
1949	Toronto	Hap Day	4-0	Detroit	Tommy Ivan
1950	Detroit	Tommy Ivan	4-3 (WLWLLWW)	NY Rangers	Lynn Patrick
1951	Toronto	Joe Primeau	4-1 (WLWWW)	Montreal	Dick Irvin
1952	Detroit	Tommy Ivan	4-0	Montreal	Dick Irvin
1953	Montreal	Dick Irvin	4-1 (WLWWW)	Boston	Lynn Patrick
1954	Detroit	Tommy Ivan	4-3 (WLWWLLW)	Montreal	Dick Irvin
1955	Detroit	Jimmy Skinner	4-3 (WWLLWLW)	Montreal	Dick Irvin
1956	Montreal	Toe Blake	4-1 (WWWLW)	Detroit	Jimmy Skinner
1957	Montreal	Toe Blake	4-1 (WWWLW)	Boston	Milt Schmidt
1958	Montreal	Toe Blake	4-2 (WLWLWW)	Boston	Milt Schmidt
1959	Montreal	Toe Blake	4-1 (WWWLW)	Toronto	Punch Imlach
1960	Montreal	Toe Blake	4-0	Toronto	Punch Imlach
1961	Chicago	Rudy Pilous	4-2 (WLWLWW)	Detroit	Sid Abel
1962	Toronto	Punch Imlach	4-2 (WWLLWW)	Chicago	Rudy Pilous
1963	Toronto	Punch Imlach	4-1 (WWLWW)	Detroit	Sid Abel
1964	Toronto	Punch Imlach	4-3 (WLLWLWW)	Detroit	Sid Abel
1965	Montreal	Toe Blake	4-3 (WWLLWLW)	Chicago	Billy Reay
1966	Montreal	Toe Blake	4-2 (LLWWWW)	Detroit	Sid Abel
1967	Toronto	Punch Imlach	4-2 (LWWLWW)	Montreal	Toe Blake
1968	Montreal	Toe Blake	4-0	St. Louis	Scotty Bowman
1969	Montreal	Claude Ruel	4-0	St. Louis	Scotty Bowman
1970	Boston	Harry Sinden	4-0	St. Louis	Scotty Bowman
1971	Montreal	Al MacNeil	4-3 (LLWWLWW)	Chicago	Billy Reay
1972	Boston	Tom Johnson	4-2 (WWLWLW)	NY Rangers	Emile Francis
1973	Montreal	Scotty Bowman	4-2 (WWLWLW)	Chicago	Billy Reay
1974	Philadelphia	Fred Shero	4-2 (LWWWLW)	Boston	Bep Guidolin
1975	Philadelphia	Fred Shero	4-2 (WWLLWW)	Buffalo	Floyd Smith
1976	Montreal	Scotty Bowman	4-0	Philadelphia	Fred Shero
1977	Montreal	Scotty Bowman	4-0	Boston	Don Cherry
1978	Montreal	Scotty Bowman	4-2 (WWLLWW)	Boston	Don Cherry
1979	Montreal	Scotty Bowman	4-1 (LWWWW)	NY Rangers	Fred Shero
1980	NY Islanders	Al Arbour	4-2 (WLWWLW)	Philadelphia	Pat Quinn
1981	NY Islanders	Al Arbour	4-1 (WWWLW)	Minnesota	Glen Sonmor
1982	NY Islanders	Al Arbour	4-0	Vancouver	Roger Neilson
1983	NY Islanders	Al Arbour	4-0	Edmonton	Glen Sather
1984	Edmonton	Glen Sather	4-1 (WLWWW)	NY Islanders	Al Arbour
1985	Edmonton	Glen Sather	4-1 (LWWWW)	Philadelphia	Mike Keenan
1986	Montreal	Jean Perron	4-1 (LWWWW)	Calgary	Bob Johnson
1987	Edmonton	Glen Sather	4-3 (WWLWLLW)	Philadelphia	Mike Keenan
1988	Edmonton	Glen Sather	4-0	Boston	Terry O'Reilly
1989	Calgary	Terry Crisp	4-2 (WLLWWW)	Montreal	Pat Burns
1990	Edmonton	John Muckler	4-1 (WWWLW)	Boston	Mike Milbury
1991	Pittsburgh	Bob Johnson	4-2 (LWLWWW)	Minnesota	Bob Gainey
1992	Pittsburgh	Scotty Bowman	4-0	Chicago	Mike Keenan
1993	Montreal	Jacques Demers	4-1 (LWWWW)	Los Angeles	Barry Melrose
1994	NY Rangers	Mike Keenan	4-3 (LWWWLLW)	Vancouver	Pat Quinn
1995	New Jersey	Jacques Lemaire	4-0	Detroit	Scotty Bowman
1996	Colorado	Marc Crawford	4-0	Florida	Doug MacLean
1997	Detroit	Scotty Bowman	4-0	Philadelphia	Terry Murray
1998	Detroit	Scotty Bowman	4-0	Washington	Ron Wilson
1999	Dallas	Ken Hitchcock	4-2 (LWWLWW)	Buffalo	Lindy Ruff
2000	New Jersey	Larry Robinson	4-2 (WLWLWW)	Dallas	Ken Hitchcock

* The 1919 finals were cancelled after five games due to an influenza epidemic with Montreal and Seattle (PCHA) tied at 2-2-1.

M.J. O'Brien Trophy

Donated by Canadian mining magnate M.J. O'Brien, whose son Ambrose founded the National Hockey Association in 1910. Originally presented to the NHA champion until the league's demise in 1917, the trophy then passed to the NHL champion through 1927. It was awarded to the NHL's Canadian Division winner from 1927-38 and the Stanley Cup runner-up from 1939-50 before being retired in 1950.

NHA winners included the Montreal Wanderers (1910), original Ottawa Senators (1911 and '15), Quebec Bulldogs (1912 and '13), Toronto Blueshirts (1914) and Montreal Canadiens (1916 and '17).

Conn Smythe Trophy

The Most Valuable Player of the Stanley Cup Playoffs, as selected by the Pro Hockey Writers Association. Presented since 1965 by Maple Leaf Gardens Limited in the name of the former Toronto coach, GM and owner, Conn Smythe. Winners who did not play for the Cup champion are in **bold** type.

Multiple winners: Wayne Gretzky, Mario Lemieux, Bobby Orr, Bernie Parent and Patrick Roy (2).

Year	Year	Year
1965 Jean Beliveau, Mon., C	1977 Guy Lafleur, Mon., RW	1989 Al MacInnis, Calg., D
1966 **Roger Crozier**, Det., G	1978 Larry Robinson, Mon., D	1990 Bill Ranford, Edm., G
1967 Dave Keon, Tor., C	1979 Bob Gainey, Mon., LW	1991 Mario Lemieux, Pit., C
1968 **Glenn Hall**, St.L., G	1980 Bryan Trottier, NYI, C	1992 Mario Lemieux, Pit., C
1969 Serge Savard, Mon., D	1981 Butch Goring, NYI, C	1993 Patrick Roy, Mon., G
1970 Bobby Orr, Bos., D	1982 Mike Bossy, NYI, RW	1994 Brian Leetch, NYR, D
1971 Ken Dryden, Mon., G	1983 Billy Smith, NYI, G	1995 Claude Lemieux, NJ, RW
1972 Bobby Orr, Bos., D	1984 Mark Messier, Edm., LW	1996 Joe Sakic, Col., C
1973 Yvan Cournoyer, Mon., RW	1985 Wayne Gretzky, Edm., C	1997 Mike Vernon, Det., G
1974 Bernie Parent, Phi., G	1986 Patrick Roy, Mon., G	1998 Steve Yzerman, Det., C
1975 Bernie Parent, Phi., G	1987 **Ron Hextall**, Phi., G	1999 Joe Nieuwendyk, Dal., C
1976 **Reggie Leach**, Phi., RW	1988 Wayne Gretzky, Edm., C	2000 Scott Stevens, NJ, D

Note: Ken Dryden (1971) and Patrick Roy (1986) are the only players to win as rookies.

All-Time Stanley Cup Playoff Leaders
CAREER

Stanley Cup Playoff leaders through 2000. Years listed indicate number of playoff appearances. Players active in 2000 are in **bold** type; (DNP) indicates player that was active in 2000 but did not participate in playoffs.

Scoring

Points

		Yrs	Gm	G	A	Pts
1	Wayne Gretzky	16	208	122	260	382
2	**Mark Messier** (DNP)	17	236	109	186	295
3	Jari Kurri	14	200	106	127	233
4	Glenn Anderson	15	225	93	121	214
5	**Paul Coffey** (DNP)	16	194	59	137	196
6	Bryan Trottier	17	221	71	113	184
7	Jean Beliveau	17	162	79	97	176
8	Denis Savard	16	169	66	109	175
9	**Doug Gilmour**	15	157	54	118	172
10	**Ray Bourque**	20	193	37	133	170
11	Denis Potvin	14	185	56	108	164
12	Mike Bossy	10	129	85	75	160
	Gordie Howe	20	157	68	92	160
	Bobby Smith	13	184	64	96	160
15	**Brett Hull**	15	153	88	71	159
16	**Claude Lemieux**	15	221	80	77	157
17	Mario Lemieux	7	89	70	85	155
18	**Steve Yzerman**	15	153	61	91	152
19	**Larry Murphy**	19	209	37	114	151
20	Stan Mikita	18	155	59	91	150
21	Brian Propp	13	160	64	84	148
22	Larry Robinson	20	227	28	116	144
23	**Al MacInnis**	16	149	37	105	142
24	**Adam Oates**	12	131	38	103	141
25	Jacques Lemaire	11	145	61	78	139

Goals

		Yrs	Gm	G
1	Wayne Gretzky	16	208	122
2	**Mark Messier** (DNP)	17	236	109
3	Jari Kurri	15	200	106
4	Glenn Anderson	15	225	93
5	**Brett Hull**	15	153	88
6	Mike Bossy	10	129	85
7	Maurice Richard	15	133	82
8	**Claude Lemieux**	15	221	80
9	Jean Beliveau	17	162	79
10	Dino Ciccarelli	14	141	73
11	Esa Tikkanen	13	186	72
12	Bryan Trottier	17	221	71
13	Mario Lemieux	7	89	70
14	Gordie Howe	20	157	68
15	Denis Savard	16	169	66

Assists

		Yrs	Gm	A
1	Wayne Gretzky	16	208	260
2	**Mark Messier** (DNP)	17	236	186
3	**Paul Coffey** (DNP)	16	194	137
4	**Ray Bourque**	20	193	133
5	Jari Kurri	15	200	127
6	Glenn Anderson	15	225	121
7	**Doug Gilmour**	15	157	118
8	Larry Robinson	20	227	116
9	**Larry Murphy**	19	209	114
10	Bryan Trottier	17	221	113
11	Denis Savard	16	169	109
12	Denis Potvin	14	185	108
13	**Al MacInnis**	16	149	105
14	**Adam Oates**	12	131	103
15	Jean Beliveau	17	162	97

Goaltending
Wins

		Gm	W-L	Pct	GAA
1	**Patrick Roy**	196	121-73	.624	2.36
2	Grant Fuhr	150	92-50	.648	2.92
3	Billy Smith	132	88-36	.710	2.73
4	Ken Dryden	112	80-32	.714	2.40
5	**Mike Vernon**	138	77-56	.579	2.68
6	**Ed Belfour**	131	75-51	.595	2.13
7	Jacques Plante	112	71-37	.657	2.17
8	Andy Moog	132	68-57	.544	3.04
9	**Tom Barrasso**	119	61-54	.530	3.01
10	Turk Broda	102	58-42	.580	1.98
11	Terry Sawchuk	106	54-48	.529	2.54
12	**Martin Brodeur**	84	50-34	.595	1.86
13	Glenn Hall	115	49-65	.430	2.79
14	Gerry Cheevers	88	47-35	.573	2.69
	Ron Hextall	93	47-43	.522	3.04

Shutouts

		Gm	GAA	No
1	Clint Benedict	48	1.80	15
	Jacques Plante	112	2.17	15
	Patrick Roy	196	2.36	15
4	Turk Broda	102	1.98	13
5	Terry Sawchuk	106	2.54	12

Goals Against Average
Minimum of 50 games played

		Gm	Min	GA	GAA
1	**Martin Brodeur**..........84	5325	165	1.86
2	George Hainsworth 52	3486	112	1.93
3	Turk Broda.............101	6389	211	1.98
4	**Dominik Hasek**..........61	3684	128	2.08
5	**Ed Belfour**.............131	7968	283	2.13
6	**Chris Osgood** 62	3624	129	2.14
7	Jacques Plante..........112	6652	240	2.16
8	**Patrick Roy** 196	12094	475	2.36
9	Ken Dryden.............112	6846	274	2.40
10	Bernie Parent............71	4302	174	2.43

Note: Clint Benedict had an average of 1.80 but played in only 48 games.

Games Played

		Yrs	Gm
1	**Patrick Roy**, Mon-Col..............14	196
2	Grant Fuhr, Edm-Buf-St.L..........14	150
3	**Mike Vernon**, Calg-Det-SJ-Fla 14	138
4	Billy Smith, NY Islanders 13	132
	Andy Moog, Edm-Bos-Dal-Mon...........16	132

Appearances in Cup Finals

Standings of all teams that have reached the Stanley Cup championship round, since 1918.

App		Cups	Last Won
32	Montreal Canadiens	23*	1993
21	Toronto Maple Leafs	13†	1967
21	Detroit Red Wings	9	1998
17	Boston Bruins	5	1972
10	New York Rangers	4	1994
10	Chicago Blackhawks	3	1961
7	Philadelphia Flyers	2	1975
6	Edmonton Oilers	5	1990
5	New York Islanders	4	1983
5	Vancouver Millionaires (PCHA) ...	0	—
4	(original) Ottawa Senators	4	1927
4	Minnesota/Dallas (North) Stars ...	1	1999
3	Montreal Maroons	2	1935
3	St. Louis Blues	0	—
2	New Jersey Devils	2	2000
2	Pittsburgh Penguins	2	1992
2	Calgary Flames	1	1989
2	Victoria Cougars (WCHL-WHL) ...	1	1925
2	Buffalo Sabres	0	—
2	Seattle Metropolitans (PCHA)	0	—
2	Vancouver Canucks	0	—
1	Colorado Avalanche	1	1996
1	Calgary Tigers (WCHL)	0	—
1	Edmonton Eskimos (WCHL)	0	—
1	Florida Panthers	0	—
1	Los Angeles Kings	0	—
1	Washington Capitals..............	0	—

*Les Canadiens also won the Cup in 1916 for a total of 24. Also, their final with Seattle in 1919 was cancelled due to an influenza epidemic that claimed the life of the Habs' Joe Hall.

†Toronto has won the Cup under three nicknames—Arenas (1918), St. Pats (1922) and Maple Leafs (1932,42,45,47-49,51,62-64,67).

Teams now defunct (7): Calgary Tigers, Edmonton Eskimos, Montreal Maroons, (original) Ottawa Senators, Seattle, Vancouver Millionaires and Victoria. Edmonton (1923) and Calgary (1924) represented the WCHL and later the WHL, while Vancouver (1918,1921-24) and Seattle (1919-20) played out of the PCHA.

Miscellaneous
Championships

		Yrs	Cups
1	Henri Richard, Montreal................18	11
2	Yvan Cournoyer, Montreal..............15	10
	Jean Beliveau, Montreal................17	10
4	Claude Provost, Montreal 14	9
5	Jacques Lemaire, Montreal 11	8
	Maurice Richard, Montreal 15	8
	Red Kelly, Detroit-Toronto 19	8

Years in Playoffs

		Yrs	Gm
1	Gordie Howe, Detroit-Hartford 20	157
	Larry Robinson, Montreal-Los Angeles 20	227
	Ray Bourque, Boston-Colorado 20	193
4	**Larry Murphy**, LA-Wash-Min-Pit-Tor-Det ..19	209
	Red Kelly, Detroit-Toronto 19	164

Games Played

		Yrs	Gm
1	**Mark Messier**, Edm-NYR-Van (DNP) 17	236
2	**Guy Carbonneau**, Mon-St.L-Dal........17	231
3	Larry Robinson, Montreal-Los Angeles 20	227
4	Glenn Anderson, Edm-Tor-NYR-St.L......15	225
5	Bryan Trottier, NY Isles-Pittsburgh 17	221
	Claude Lemieux, Mon-NJ-Col-NJ........15	221

Penalty Minutes

		Yrs	Gm	Min
1	Dale Hunter, Que-Wash-Col 18	186	729
2	Chris Nilan, Mon-NYR-Bos-Mon 12	111	541
3	**Claude Lemieux**, Mon-NJ-Col-NJ...15	221	517
4	Willi Plett, Atl-Calg-Min-Bos 10	83	466
5	**Rick Tocchet**, Phi-Pit-Bos-Pho-Phi.....12	139	465

SINGLE SEASON
Scoring
Points

		Year	Gm	G	A	Pts
1	Wayne Gretzky, Edm 1985	18	17	30	47
2	Mario Lemieux, Pit.........1991	23	16	28	44
3	Wayne Gretzky, Edm 1988	19	12	31	43
4	Wayne Gretzky, LA 1993	24	15	25	40
5	Wayne Gretzky, Edm 1983	16	12	26	38
6	Paul Coffey, Edm 1985	18	12	25	37
7	Mike Bossy, NYI..........1981	18	17	18	35
	Wayne Gretzky, Edm 1984	19	13	22	35
	Doug Gilmour, Tor 1993	21	10	25	35
10	Mario Lemieux, Pit.........1992	15	16	18	34
	Mark Messier, Edm 1988	19	11	23	34
	Mark Recchi, Pit 1991	24	10	24	34
	Wayne Gretzky, Edm 1987	21	5	29	34
	Brian Leetch, NYR 1994	23	11	23	34
	Joe Sakic, Col............1996	22	18	16	34

Goals

		Year	Gm	No
1	Reggie Leach, Philadelphia 1976	16	19
	Jari Kurri, Edmonton 1985	18	19
3	Joe Sakic, Colorado 1996	22	18
4	Newsy Lalonde, Montreal 1919	10	17
	Mike Bossy, NY Islanders 1981	18	17
	Wayne Gretzky, Edmonton...........1985	18	17
	Steve Payne, Minnesota 1981	19	17
	Mike Bossy, NY Islanders 1982	19	17
	Mike Bossy, NY Islanders 1983	19	17
	Kevin Stevens, Pittsburgh............1991	24	17

Assists

		Year	Gm	No
1	Wayne Gretzky, Edmonton	1988	19	31
2	Wayne Gretzky, Edmonton	1985	18	30
3	Wayne Gretzky, Edmonton	1987	21	29
4	Mario Lemieux, Pittsburgh	1991	23	28
5	Wayne Gretzky, Edmonton	1983	16	26
6	Paul Coffey, Edmonton	1985	18	25
	Doug Gilmour, Toronto	1993	21	25
	Wayne Gretzky, Los Angeles	1993	24	25
9	Al MacInnis, Calgary	1989	22	24
	Mark Recchi, Pittsburgh	1991	24	24

Goaltending
Wins

		Year	Gm	Min	W-L
1	Grant Fuhr, Edm	1988	19	1136	16-2
	Mike Vernon, Det	1997	20	1229	16-4
	Patrick Roy, Mon	1993	20	1293	16-4
	Martin Brodeur, NJ	1995	20	1222	16-4
	Mike Vernon, Calg	1989	22	1381	16-5
	Tom Barrasso, Pit	1992	21	1233	16-5
	Chris Osgood, Det	1998	22	1361	16-6
	Bill Ranford, Edm	1990	22	1401	16-6
	Patrick Roy, Col	1996	22	1454	16-6
	Mike Richter, NYR	1994	23	1417	16-7
	Ed Belfour, Dal	1999	23	1544	16-7
	Martin Brodeur, NJ	2000	23	1450	16-7

Shutouts

		Year	Gm	No
1	Clint Benedict, Mon. Maroons	1926	8	4
	Terry Sawchuk, Detroit	1952	8	4
	Clint Benedict, Mon. Maroons	1928	9	4
	Dave Kerr, NY Rangers	1937	9	4
	Frank McCool, Toronto	1945	13	4
	Ken Dryden, Montreal	1977	14	4
	Bernie Parent, Philadelphia	1975	17	4
	Olaf Kolzig, Washington	1998	21	4
	Mike Richter, NY Rangers	1994	23	4
	Ed Belfour, Dallas	2000	23	4
	Kirk McLean, Vancouver	1994	24	4

Goals Against Average

	Min. 8 games played	Year	Gm	Min	GA	GAA
1	Terry Sawchuk, Det	1952	8	480	5	0.63
2	Clint Benedict, Mon-M.	1928	9	555	8	0.89
3	Turk Broda, Tor	1951	9	509	9	1.06
4	Dave Kerr, NYR	1937	9	553	10	1.11
5	Jacques Plante, Mon	1960	8	489	11	1.35
6	Rogie Vachon, Mon	1968	8	507	12	1.42
7	Jacques Plante, St.L	1969	10	589	14	1.43
8	Frankie Brimsek, Bos	1939	12	863	18	1.50
9	Chuck Gardiner, Chi	1934	8	602	12	1.50
10	Ken Dryden, Mon	1977	14	849	22	1.55

Note: Average determined by games played through 1942-43 season and by minutes played since then.

SINGLE SERIES
Scoring
Points

	Year	Rd	G-A—Pts
Rick Middleton, Bos vs Buf	1983	DF	5-14—19
Wayne Gretzky, Edm vs Chi	1985	CF	4-14—18
Mario Lemieux, Pit vs Wash	1992	DSF	7-10—17
Barry Pedersen, Bos vs Buf	1983	DF	7-9—16
Doug Gilmour, Tor vs SJ	1994	CSF	3-13—16
Jari Kurri, Edm vs Chi	1985	CF	12-3—15
Tim Kerr, Phi vs Pit	1989	DF	10-5—15
Mario Lemieux, Pit vs Bos	1991	CF	6-9—15
Wayne Gretzky, Edm vs LA	1987	DSF	2-13—15

Goals

	Year	Rd	No
Jari Kurri, Edm vs Chi	1985	CF	12
Newsy Lalonde, Mon vs Ott	1919	SF*	11
Tim Kerr, Phi vs Pit	1989	DF	10
Five tied with 9 each.			

*NHL final prior to Stanley Cup series with Seattle.

Assists

	Year	Rd	No
Rick Middleton, Bos vs Buf	1983	DF	14
Wayne Gretzky, Edm vs Chi	1985	CF	14
Wayne Gretzky, Edm vs LA	1987	DSF	13
Doug Gilmour, Tor vs SJ	1994	CSF	13
Four tied with 11 each.			

SINGLE GAME
Scoring
Points

	Date	G	A	Pts
Patrik Sundstrom, NJ vs Wash	4/22/88	3	5	8
Mario Lemieux, Pit vs Phi	4/25/89	5	3	8
Wayne Gretzky, Edm at Calg	4/17/83	4	3	7
Wayne Gretzky, Edm at Win	4/25/85	3	4	7
Wayne Gretzky, Edm vs LA	4/9/87	1	6	7

Goals

	Date	No
Newsy Lalonde, Mon vs Ott	3/1/19	5
Maurice Richard, Mon vs Tor	3/23/44	5
Darryl Sittler, Tor vs Phi.	4/22/76	5
Reggie Leach, Phi vs Bos	5/6/76	5
Mario Lemieux, Pit vs Phi	4/25/89	5

Assists

	Date	No
Mikko Leinonen, NYR vs Phi	4/8/82	6
Wayne Gretzky, Edm vs LA	4/9/87	6
Ten tied with 5 each.		

Ten Longest Playoff Overtime Games

The 10 longest overtime games in Stanley Cup history. Note the following Series initials: SF (semifinals), CQF (conference quarterfinal), CSF (conference semifinal), DSF (division semifinal), QF (quarterfinal) and Final (Cup final). Series winners are in **bold** type; (*) indicates deciding game of series.

		OTs	Elapsed Time	Goal Scorer	Date	Series	Location
1	**Detroit** 1, Montreal Maroons 0	6	176:30	Mud Bruneteau	3/24/36	SF, Gm 1	Montreal
2	**Toronto** 1, Boston 0	6	164:46	Ken Doraty	4/3/33	SF, Gm 5	Toronto
3	**Philadelphia** 2, Pittsburgh 1	5	152:01	Keith Primeau	5/4/00	CSF, Gm 4	Pittsburgh
4	**Pittsburgh** 3 Washington 2	4	139:15	Petr Nedved	4/24/96	CQF, Gm 4	Washington
5	Toronto 3, **Detroit** 2	4	130:18	Jack McLean	3/23/43	SF, Gm 6	Detroit
6	**Montreal** 2, NY Rangers 1	4	128:52	Gus Rivers	3/28/30	SF, Gm 1	Montreal
7	**NY Islanders** 3, Washington 2	4	128:47	Pat LaFontaine	4/18/87	DSF, Gm 7*	Washington
8	Buffalo 1, **New Jersey** 0	4	125:43	Dave Hannan	4/27/94	QF, Gm 6	Buffalo
9	**Montreal** 3, Detroit 2	4	121:09	Maurice Richard	3/27/51	SF, Gm 1	Detroit
10	**NY Americans** 3, NY Rangers 2	4	120:40	Lorne Carr	3/27/38	QF, Gm 3*	New York

NHL All-Star Game

Three benefit NHL All-Star Games were staged in the 1930s for forward Ace Bailey and the families of Howie Morenz and Babe Siebert. Bailey, of Toronto, suffered a fractured skull on a career-ending check by Boston's Eddie Shore. Morenz, the Montreal Canadiens' legend, died of a heart attack at 35 after a severely broken leg ended his career. Siebert, who played with both Montreal teams, drowned at age 35.

The All-Star Game was revived at the start of the 1947-48 season as an annual exhibition match between the defending Stanley Cup champion and All-Stars from the league's other five teams. The format has changed several times since then. The game was moved to midseason in 1966-67 and became an East vs. West contest in 1968-69. The Eastern (East, 1968-1974; Wales, 1975-93) Conference leads the series 18-7-1. In 1998, the East-West format was abandoned for one pitting North American all-stars against all-stars from the rest of the world. North America leads that series 2-1.

Benefit Games

Date	Occasion		Host	Coaches
2/14/34	Ace Bailey Benefit	Toronto 7, All-Stars 3	Toronto	Dick Irvin, Lester Patrick
11/3/37	Howie Morenz Memorial	All-Stars 6, Montreals* 5	Montreal	Jack Adams, Ceil Hart
10/29/39	Babe Seibert Memorial	All-Stars 5, Canadiens 3	Montreal	Art Ross, Pit Lepine

*Combined squad of Montreal Canadiens and Montreal Maroons.

All-Star Games

Multiple MVP winners: Wayne Gretzky and Mario Lemieux (3); Bobby Hull and Frank Mahovlich (2).

Year		Host	Coaches	Most Valuable Player
1947	All-Stars 4, Toronto 3	Toronto	Dick Irvin, Hap Day	No award
1948	All-Stars 3, Toronto 1	Chicago	Tommy Ivan, Hap Day	No award
1949	All-Stars 3, Toronto 1	Toronto	Tommy Ivan, Hap Day	No award
1950	Detroit 7, All-Stars 1	Detroit	Tommy Ivan, Lynn Patrick	No award
1951	1st Team 2, 2nd Team 2	Toronto	Joe Primeau, Hap Day	No award
1952	1st Team 1, 2nd Team 1	Detroit	Tommy Ivan, Dick Irvin	No award
1953	All-Stars 3, Montreal 1	Montreal	Lynn Patrick, Dick Irvin	No award
1954	All-Stars 2, Detroit 2	Detroit	King Clancy, Jim Skinner	No award
1955	Detroit 3, All-Stars 1	Detroit	Jim Skinner, Dick Irvin	No award
1956	All-Stars 1, Montreal 1	Montreal	Jim Skinner, Toe Blake	No award
1957	All-Stars 5, Montreal 3	Montreal	Milt Schmidt, Toe Blake	No award
1958	Montreal 6, All-Stars 3	Montreal	Toe Blake, Milt Schmidt	No award
1959	Montreal 6, All-Stars 1	Montreal	Toe Blake, Punch Imlach	No award
1960	All-Stars 2, Montreal 1	Montreal	Punch Imlach, Toe Blake	No award
1961	All-Stars 3, Chicago 1	Chicago	Sid Abel, Rudy Pilous	No award
1962	Toronto 4, All-Stars 1	Toronto	Punch Imlach, Rudy Pilous	Eddie Shack, Tor., RW
1963	All-Stars 3, Toronto 3	Toronto	Sid Abel, Punch Imlach	Frank Mahovlich, Tor., LW
1964	All-Stars 3, Toronto 2	Toronto	Sid Abel, Punch Imlach	Jean Beliveau, Mon., C
1965	All-Stars 5, Montreal 2	Montreal	Billy Reay, Toe Blake	Gordie Howe, Det., RW
1966	No game (see below)			
1967	Montreal 3, All-Stars 0	Montreal	Toe Blake, Sid Abel	Henri Richard, Mon., C
1968	Toronto 4, All-Stars 3	Toronto	Punch Imlach, Toe Blake	Bruce Gamble, Tor., G
1969	West 3, East 3	Montreal	Scotty Bowman, Toe Blake	Frank Mahovlich, Det., LW
1970	East 4, West 1	St. Louis	Claude Ruel, Scotty Bowman	Bobby Hull, Chi., LW
1971	West 2, East 1	Boston	Scotty Bowman, Harry Sinden	Bobby Hull, Chi., LW
1972	East 3, West 2	Minnesota	Al MacNeil, Billy Reay	Bobby Orr, Bos., D
1973	East 5, West 4	NY Rangers	Tom Johnson, Billy Reay	Greg Polis, Pit., LW
1974	West 6, East 4	Chicago	Billy Reay, Scotty Bowman	Garry Unger, St.L., C
1975	Wales 7, Campbell 1	Montreal	Bep Guidolin, Fred Shero	Syl Apps Jr., Pit., C
1976	Wales 7, Campbell 5	Philadelphia	Floyd Smith, Fred Shero	Peter Mahovlich, Mon., C
1977	Wales 4, Campbell 3	Vancouver	Scotty Bowman, Fred Shero	Rick Martin, Buf., LW
1978	Wales 3, Campbell 2 (OT)	Buffalo	Scotty Bowman, Fred Shero	Billy Smith, NYI, G
1979	No game (see below)			
1980	Wales 6, Campbell 3	Detroit	Scotty Bowman, Al Arbour	Reggie Leach, Phi., RW
1981	Campbell 4, Wales 1	Los Angeles	Pat Quinn, Scotty Bowman	Mike Liut, St.L., G
1982	Wales 4, Campbell 2	Washington	Al Arbour, Glen Sonmor	Mike Bossy, NYI, RW
1983	Campbell 9, Wales 3	NY Islanders	Roger Neilson, Al Arbour	Wayne Gretzky, Edm., C
1984	Wales 7, Campbell 6	New Jersey	Al Arbour, Glen Sather	Don Maloney, NYR, LW
1985	Wales 6, Campbell 4	Calgary	Al Arbour, Glen Sather	Mario Lemieux, Pit., C
1986	Wales 4, Campbell 3 (OT)	Hartford	Mike Keenan, Glen Sather	Grant Fuhr, Edm., G
1987	No game (see below)			
1988	Wales 6, Campbell 5 (OT)	St. Louis	Mike Keenan, Glen Sather	Mario Lemieux, Pit., C
1989	Campbell 9, Wales 5	Edmonton	Glen Sather, Terry O'Reilly	Wayne Gretzky, LA, C
1990	Wales 12, Campbell 7	Pittsburgh	Pat Burns, Terry Crisp	Mario Lemieux, Pit., C
1991	Campbell 11, Wales 5	Chicago	John Muckler, Mike Milbury	Vincent Damphousse, Tor., LW
1992	Campbell 10, Wales 6	Philadelphia	Bob Gainey, Scotty Bowman	Brett Hull, St.L., RW
1993	Wales 16, Campbell 6	Montreal	Scotty Bowman, Mike Keenan	Mike Gartner, NYR, RW
1994	East 9, West 8	NY Rangers	Jacques Demers, Barry Melrose	Mike Richter, NYR, G
1995	No game (see below)			
1996	East 5, West 4	Boston	Doug MacLean, Scotty Bowman	Ray Bourque, Bos., D
1997	East 11, West 7	San Jose	Doug MacLean, Ken Hitchcock	Mark Recchi, Mon., RW
1998	North America 8, World 7	Vancouver	Jacques Lemaire, Ken Hitchcock	Teemu Selanne, World, RW
1999	North America 8, World 6	Tampa	Ken Hitchcock, Lindy Ruff	Wayne Gretzky, N. Amer., C
2000	World 9, North America 4	Toronto	Scotty Bowman, Pat Quinn	Pavel Bure, World, RW

No All-Star Game: in 1966 (moved from start of season to mid-season); in 1979 (replaced by Challenge Cup series with USSR); in 1987 (replaced by Rendez-Vous '87 series with USSR); and in 1995 (cancelled when NHL lockout shortened season to 48 games).

NHL Franchise Origins

Here is what the current 30 teams in the National Hockey League have to show for the years they have put in as members of the NHL, the early National Hockey Association (NHA) and the more recent World Hockey Association (WHA). League titles and Stanley Cup championships are noted by year won. The Stanley Cup has automatically gone to the NHL champion since the 1926-27 season. Following the 1992-93 season, the NHL renamed the Clarence Campbell Conference the Western Conference, while the Prince of Wales Conference became the Eastern Conference.

Western Conference

	First Season	League Titles	Franchise Stops
Anaheim, Mighty Ducks of	1993-94 (NHL)	None	•Anaheim, CA (1993—)
Calgary Flames	1972-73 (NHL)	1 Cup (1989)	•Atlanta (1972-80)
			Calgary (1980—)
Chicago Blackhawks	1926-27 (NHL)	3 Cups (1934,38,61)	•Chicago (1926—)
Colorado Avalanche	1972-73 (WHA)	1 WHA (1977)	•Quebec City (1972-95)
		1 Cup (1996)	Denver (1995—)
Columbus Blue Jackets	2000-01 (NHL)	None	•Columbus, OH (2000—)
Dallas Stars	1967-68 (NHL)	1 Cup (1999)	•Bloomington, MN (1967-93)
			Dallas (1993—)
Detroit Red Wings	1926-27 (NHL)	9 Cups (1936-37,43,50,52,54-	•Detroit (1926—)
		55,97,98)	
Edmonton Oilers	1973-74 (WHA)	5 Cups (1984-85,87-88,90)	•Edmonton (1972—)
Los Angeles Kings	1967-68 (NHL)	None	•Inglewood, CA (1967-99)
			Los Angeles (1999—)
Minnesota Wild	2000-01 (NHL)	None	•St. Paul, MN (2000—)
Nashville Predators	1998-99 (NHL)	None	•Nashville, TN (1998—)
Phoenix Coyotes	1972-73 (WHA)	3 WHA (1976, 78-79)	•Winnipeg (1972-96)
			Phoenix (1996—)
St. Louis Blues	1967-68 (NHL)	None	•St. Louis (1967—)
San Jose Sharks	1991-92 (NHL)	None	•San Francisco (1991-93)
			San Jose (1993—)
Vancouver Canucks	1970-71 (NHL)	None	•Vancouver (1970—)

Eastern Conference

	First Season	League Titles	Franchise Stops
Atlanta Thrashers	1999-00 (NHL)	None	•Atlanta (1999—)
Boston Bruins	1924-25 (NHL)	5 Cups (1929,39,41,70,72)	•Boston (1924—)
Buffalo Sabres	1970-71 (NHL)	None	•Buffalo (1970—)
Carolina Hurricanes	1972-73 (WHA)	1 WHA (1973)	•Boston (1972-74)
			W. Springfield, MA (1974-75)
			Hartford, CT (1975-78)
			Springfield, MA (1978-80)
			Hartford (1980-97)
			Greensboro (1997-99)
			Raleigh (1999—)
Florida Panthers	1993-94 (NHL)	None	•Miami (1993-98)
			Sunrise, FL (1998—)
Montreal Canadiens	1909-10 (NHA)	2 NHA (1916-17)	•Montreal (1909—)
		2 NHL (1924-25)	
		24 Cups (1916,24,30-	
		31,44,46,53,56-60,65-66,68-	
		69,71,73,76-79,86,93)	
New Jersey Devils	1974-75 (NHL)	2 Cups (1995, 2000)	•Kansas City (1974-76)
			Denver (1976-82)
			E. Rutherford, NJ (1982—)
New York Islanders	1972-73 (NHL)	4 Cups (1980-83)	•Uniondale, NY (1972—)
New York Rangers	1926-27 (NHL)	4 Cups (1928,33,40,94)	•New York (1926—)
Ottawa Senators	1992-93 (NHL)	None	•Ottawa (1992-1996)
			Kanata, Ont. (1996—)
Philadelphia Flyers	1967-68 (NHL)	2 Cups (1974-75)	•Philadelphia (1967—)
Pittsburgh Penguins	1967-68 (NHL)	2 Cups (1991-92)	•Pittsburgh (1967—)
Tampa Bay Lightning	1992-93 (NHL)	None	•Tampa, FL (1992-93)
			St. Petersburg, FL (1993-96)
			Tampa, FL (1996—)
Toronto Maple Leafs	1916-17 (NHA)	2 NHL (1918,22)	•Toronto (1916—)
		13 Cups (1918,22,32,42,45,47-	
		49,51,62-64,67)	
Washington Capitals	1974-75 (NHL)	None	•Landover, MD (1974-97)
			Washington, D.C. (1997—)

Note: The Hartford Civic Center roof collapsed after a snowstorm in January 1978, forcing the Whalers to move their home games to Springfield, Mass., for two years.

The Growth of the NHL

Of the four franchises that comprised the National Hockey League (NHL) at the start of the 1917-18 season, only two remain—the Montreal Canadiens and the Toronto Maple Leafs (originally the Toronto Arenas). From 1919-26, eight new teams joined the league, but only four—the Boston Bruins, Chicago Blackhawks (originally Black Hawks), Detroit Red Wings (originally Cougars) and New York Rangers—survived.

It was 41 years before the NHL expanded again, doubling in size for the 1967-68 season with new teams in Los Angeles, Minnesota, Oakland, Philadelphia, Pittsburgh and St. Louis. The league had 16 clubs by the start of the 1972-73 season, but it also had a rival in the **World Hockey Association,** which debuted that year with 12 teams.

The NHL added two more teams in 1974 and merged the struggling Cleveland Barons (originally the Oakland Seals) and Minnesota North Stars in 1978, before absorbing four WHA clubs—the Edmonton Oilers, Hartford Whalers, Quebec Nordiques and Winnipeg Jets—in time for the 1979-80 season. Seven expansion teams joined the league in the 1990s, with two more being added in 2000 to make it an even 30.

Expansion/Merger Timetable
For teams currently in NHL.

1919—Quebec Bulldogs finally take the ice after sitting out NHL's first two seasons; **1924**—Boston Bruins and Montreal Maroons; **1925**–New York Americans and Pittsburgh Pirates; **1926**—Chicago Black Hawks (now Blackhawks), Detroit Cougars (now Red Wings) and New York Rangers; **1932**—Ottawa Senators return after sitting out 1931-32 season.

1967—California Seals (later Cleveland Barons), Los Angeles Kings, Minnesota North Stars, Philadelphia Flyers, Pittsburgh Penguins and St. Louis Blues.

1970—Buffalo Sabres and Vancouver Canucks; **1972**—Atlanta Flames (now Calgary) and New York Islanders; **1974**—Kansas City Scouts (now New Jersey Devils) and Washington Capitals; **1978**—Cleveland Barons merge with Minnesota North Stars (now Dallas Stars) and team remains in Minnesota; **1979**—added WHA's Edmonton Oilers, Hartford Whalers, Quebec Nordiques (now Colorado Avalanche) and Winnipeg Jets (now Phoenix Coyotes).

1991—San Jose Sharks; **1992**—Ottawa Senators and Tampa Bay Lightning; **1993**—Mighty Ducks of Anaheim and Florida Panthers; **1998**—Nashville Predators; **1999**—Atlanta Thrashers.

2000—Columbus Blue Jackets and Minnesota Wild.

City and Nickname Changes

1919—Toronto Arenas renamed St. Pats; **1920**—Quebec moves to Hamilton and becomes Tigers (will fold in 1925); **1926**—Toronto St. Pats renamed Maple Leafs; **1929**—Detroit Cougars renamed Falcons.

1930—Pittsburgh Pirates move to Philadelphia and become Quakers (will fold in 1931); **1932**—Detroit Falcons renamed Red Wings; **1934**—Ottawa Senators move to St. Louis and become Eagles (will fold in 1935); **1941**—New York Americans renamed Brooklyn Americans (will fold in 1942).

1967—California Seals renamed Oakland Seals three months into first season; **1970**—Oakland Seals renamed California Golden Seals; **1975**—California Golden Seals renamed Seals; **1976**—California Seals move to Cleveland and become Barons, while Kansas City Scouts move to Denver and become Colorado Rockies; **1978**—Cleveland Barons merge with Minnesota North Stars and become Minnesota North Stars.

1980—Atlanta Flames move to Calgary; **1982**—Colorado Rockies move to East Rutherford, N.J., and become New Jersey Devils; **1986**—Chicago Black Hawks renamed Blackhawks; **1993**—Minnesota North Stars move to Dallas and become Stars. **1995**—Quebec Nordiques move to Denver and become Colorado Avalanche; **1996**—Winnipeg Jets move to Phoenix and become Coyotes; **1997**—Hartford Whalers move to Greensboro and become Carolina Hurricanes; **1999**—Carolina Hurricanes move to Raleigh.

Defunct NHL Teams
Teams that once played in the NHL, but no longer exist.

Brooklyn—Americans (1941-42, formerly NY Americans from 1925-41); **Cleveland**—Barons (1976-78, originally California-Oakland Seals from 1967-76); **Hamilton (Ont.)**—Tigers (1920-25, originally Quebec Bulldogs from 1919-20); **Montreal**—Maroons (1924-38) and Wanderers (1917-18); **New York**—Americans (1925-41, later Brooklyn Americans for 1941-42); **Oakland**—Seals (1967-76, also known as California Seals and Golden Seals and later Cleveland Barons from 1976-78); **Ottawa**—Senators (1917-31) and 1932-34, later St. Louis Eagles for 1934-35); **Philadelphia**—Quakers (1930-31, originally Pittsburgh Pirates from 1925-30); **Pittsburgh**—Pirates (1925-30, later Philadelphia Quakers for 1930-31); **Quebec**—Bulldogs (1919-20, later Hamilton Tigers from 1920-25); **St. Louis**—Eagles (1934-35), originally Ottawa Senators (1917-31 and 1932-34).

WHA Teams (1972-79)

Baltimore—Blades (1975); **Birmingham**—Bulls (1976-78); **Calgary**—Cowboys (1975-77); **Chicago**—Cougars (1972-75); **Cincinnati**—Stingers (1975-79); **Cleveland**—Crusaders (1972-76, moved to Minnesota); **Denver**—Spurs (1975-76, moved to Ottawa); **Edmonton**—Oilers (1972-79, originally called Alberta Oilers in 1972-73); **Houston**—Aeros (1972-78); **Indianapolis**—Racers (1974-78).

Los Angeles—Sharks (1972-74, moved to Michigan); **Michigan**—Stags (1974-75, moved to Baltimore); **Minnesota**—Fighting Saints (1972-76) and New Fighting Saints (1976-77); **New England**—Whalers (1972-79, played in Boston from 1972-74, West Springfield, MA from 1974-75, Hartford from 1975-78 and Springfield, MA in 1979); **New Jersey**—Knights (1973-74, moved to San Diego); **New York**—Raiders (1972-73, renamed Golden Blades in 1973, moved to New Jersey).

Ottawa—Nationals (1972-73, moved to Toronto) and Civics (1976); **Philadelphia**—Blazers (1972-73, moved to Vancouver); **Phoenix**—Roadrunners (1974-77); **Quebec**—Nordiques (1972-79); **San Diego**—Mariners (1974-77); **Toronto**—Toros (1973-76, moved to Birmingham, AL); **Vancouver**—Blazers (1973-75, moved to Calgary); **Winnipeg**—Jets (1972-79).

Annual NHL Leaders
Art Ross Trophy (Scoring)

Given to the player who leads the league in points scored and named after the former Boston Bruins general manager-coach. First presented in 1948, names of prior leading scorers have been added retroactively. A tie for the scoring championship is broken three ways: 1. total goals; 2. fewest games played; 3. first goal scored.

Multiple Winners: Wayne Gretzky (10); Gordie Howe and Mario Lemieux (6); Phil Esposito (5); Jaromir Jagr and Stan Mikita (4); Bobby Hull and Guy Lafleur (3); Max Bentley, Charlie Conacher, Bill Cook, Babe Dye, Bernie Geoffrion, Elmer Lach, Newsy Lalonde, Joe Malone, Dickie Moore, Howie Morenz, Bobby Orr and Sweeney Schriner (2).

Year		Gm	G	A	Pts	Year		Gm	G	A	Pts
1918	Joe Malone, Mon	20	44	0	44	1960	Bobby Hull, Chi	70	39	42	81
1919	Newsy Lalonde, Mon	17	23	9	32	1961	Bernie Geoffrion, Mon	64	50	45	95
1920	Joe Malone, Que	24	39	6	45	1962	Bobby Hull, Chi	70	50	34	84
1921	Newsy Lalonde, Mon	24	33	8	41	1963	Gordie Howe, Det	70	38	48	86
1922	Punch Broadbent, Ott	24	32	14	46	1964	Stan Mikita, Chi	70	39	50	89
1923	Babe Dye, Tor	22	26	11	37	1965	Stan Mikita, Chi	70	28	59	87
1924	Cy Denneny, Ott	21	22	1	23	1966	Bobby Hull, Chi	65	54	43	97
1925	Babe Dye, Tor	29	38	6	44	1967	Stan Mikita, Chi	70	35	62	97
1926	Nels Stewart, Maroons	36	34	8	42	1968	Stan Mikita, Chi	72	40	47	87
1927	Bill Cook, NYR	44	33	4	37	1969	Phil Esposito, Bos	74	49	77	126
1928	Howie Morenz, Mon	43	33	18	51	1970	Bobby Orr, Bos	76	33	87	120
1929	Ace Bailey, Tor	44	22	10	32	1971	Phil Esposito, Bos	78	76	76	152
1930	Cooney Weiland, Bos	44	43	30	73	1972	Phil Esposito, Bos	76	66	67	133
1931	Howie Morenz, Mon	39	28	23	51	1973	Phil Esposito, Bos	78	55	75	130
1932	Busher Jackson, Tor	48	28	25	53	1974	Phil Esposito, Bos	78	68	77	145
1933	Bill Cook, NYR	48	28	22	50	1975	Bobby Orr, Bos	80	46	89	135
1934	Charlie Conacher, Tor	42	32	20	52	1976	Guy Lafleur, Mon	80	56	69	125
1935	Charlie Conacher, Tor	47	36	21	57	1977	Guy Lafleur, Mon	80	56	80	136
1936	Sweeney Schriner, NYA	48	19	26	45	1978	Guy Lafleur, Mon	79	60	72	132
1937	Sweeney Schriner, NYA	48	21	25	46	1979	Bryan Trottier, NYI	76	47	87	134
1938	Gordie Drillon, Tor	48	26	26	52	1980	Marcel Dionne, LA	80	53	84	137
1939	Toe Blake, Mon	48	24	23	47	1981	Wayne Gretzky, Edm	80	55	109	164
1940	Milt Schmidt, Bos	48	22	30	52	1982	Wayne Gretzky, Edm	80	92	120	212
1941	Bill Cowley, Bos	46	17	45	62	1983	Wayne Gretzky, Edm	80	71	125	196
1942	Bryan Hextall, NYR	48	24	32	56	1984	Wayne Gretzky, Edm	74	87	118	205
1943	Doug Bentley, Chi	50	33	40	73	1985	Wayne Gretzky, Edm	80	73	135	208
1944	Herbie Cain, Bos	48	36	46	82	1986	Wayne Gretzky, Edm	80	52	163	215
1945	Elmer Lach, Mon	50	26	54	80	1987	Wayne Gretzky, Edm	79	62	121	183
1946	Max Bentley, Chi	47	31	30	61	1988	Mario Lemieux, Pit	77	70	98	168
1947	Max Bentley, Chi	60	29	43	72	1989	Mario Lemieux, Pit	76	85	114	199
1948	Elmer Lach, Mon	60	30	31	61	1990	Wayne Gretzky, LA	73	40	102	142
1949	Roy Conacher, Chi	60	26	42	68	1991	Wayne Gretzky, LA	78	41	122	163
1950	Ted Lindsay, Det	69	23	55	78	1992	Mario Lemieux, Pit	64	44	87	131
1951	Gordie Howe, Det	70	43	43	86	1993	Mario Lemieux, Pit	60	69	91	160
1952	Gordie Howe, Det	70	47	39	86	1994	Wayne Gretzky, LA	81	38	92	130
1953	Gordie Howe, Det	70	49	46	95	1995	Jaromir Jagr, Pit	48	32	38	70
1954	Gordie Howe, Det	70	33	48	81	1996	Mario Lemieux, Pit	70	69	92	161
1955	Bernie Geoffrion, Mon	70	38	37	75	1997	Mario Lemieux, Pit	76	50	72	122
1956	Jean Beliveau, Mon	70	47	41	88	1998	Jaromir Jagr, Pit	77	35	67	102
1957	Gordie Howe, Det	70	44	45	89	1999	Jaromir Jagr, Pit	81	44	83	127
1958	Dickie Moore, Mon	70	36	48	84	2000	Jaromir Jagr, Pit	63	42	54	96
1959	Dickie Moore, Mon	70	41	55	96						

Note: The three times players have tied for total points in one season the player with more goals has won the trophy. In 1961-62, Hull outscored Andy Bathgate of NY Rangers, 50 goals to 28. In 1979-80, Dionne outscored Wayne Gretzky of Edmonton, 53-51. In 1995, Jagr outscored Eric Lindros of Philadelphia, 32-29.

NHL 500-Goal Scorers

Of the 28 500-goal scorers listed below, seven (Ciccarelli, Bobby Hull, Brett Hull, Kurri, Lemieux, Messier and Yzerman) went on to score over 600, three (Dionne, Esposito and Gartner) scored over 700, and two (Gretzky and Howe) have scored over 800. Players active in 2000 are in **bold** type.

	Date	Game #		Date	Game #
Maurice Richard, Mon vs Chi	10/19/57	863	Bryan Trottier, NYI vs Calg	2/13/90	1104
Gordie Howe, Det at NYR	3/14/62	1045	Mike Gartner, NYR vs Wash	10/14/91	936
Bobby Hull, Chi vs NYR	2/21/70	861	Michel Goulet, Chi vs Calg	2/16/91	951
Jean Beliveau, Mon vs Min	2/11/71	1101	Jari Kurri, LA vs Bos	10/17/92	833
Frank Mahovlich, Mon vs Van	3/21/73	1105	Dino Ciccarelli, Det at LA	1/8/94	946
Phil Esposito, Bos vs Det	12/22/74	803	Mario Lemieux, Pit at NYI	10/26/95	605
John Bucyk, Bos vs St.L	10/30/75	1370	**Mark Messier,** NYR vs Calg	11/6/95	1141
Stan Mikita, Chi vs Van	2/27/77	1221	**Steve Yzerman,** Det vs Col	1/17/96	906
Marcel Dionne, LA at Wash	12/14/82	887	Dale Hawerchuk, St.L at Tor	1/31/96	1103
Guy Lafleur, Mon at NJ	12/20/83	918	**Brett Hull,** St.L vs LA	12/22/96	693
Mike Bossy, NYI vs Bos	1/2/86	647	Joe Mullen, Pit at Col	3/14/97	1052
Gilbert Perreault, Buf vs NJ	3/9/86	1159	**Dave Andreychuk,** NJ vs Wash	3/15/97	1070
Wayne Gretzky, Edm vs Van	11/22/86	575	**Luc Robitaille,** LA vs Buf	1/7/99	928
Lanny McDonald, Calg vs NYI	3/21/89	1107	**Pat Verbeek,** Det vs Calg	3/22/00	1285

Goals

Multiple Winners: Bobby Hull (7); Phil Esposito (6); Charlie Conacher, Wayne Gretzky, Gordie Howe and Maurice Richard (5); Bill Cooke, Babe Dye, Brett Hull, Mario Lemieux and Teemu Selanne (3); Jean Beliveau, Doug Bentley, Peter Bondra, Mike Bossy, Pavel Bure, Bernie Geoffrion, Bryan Hextall, Joe Malone and Nels Stewart (2).

Year		No	Year		No	Year		No
1918	Joe Malone, Mon	44	1945	Maurice Richard, Mon	50	1974	Phil Esposito, Bos	68
1919	Odie Cleghorn, Mon	23	1946	Gaye Stewart, Tor	37	1975	Phil Esposito, Bos	61
	& Newsy Lalonde, Mon	23	1947	Maurice Richard, Mon	45	1976	Reggie Leach, Phi	61
1920	Joe Malone, Mon	39	1948	Ted Lindsay, Det	33	1977	Steve Shutt, Mon	60
1921	Babe Dye, Ham-Tor	35	1949	Sid Abel, Det	28	1978	Guy Lafleur, Mon	60
1922	Punch Broadbent, Ott	32	1950	Maurice Richard, Mon	43	1979	Mike Bossy, NYI	69
1923	Babe Dye, Tor	26	1951	Gordie Howe, Det	43	1980	Danny Gare, Buf	56
1924	Cy Denneny, Ott	22	1952	Gordie Howe, Det	47		Charlie Simmer, LA	56
1925	Babe Dye, Tor	38	1953	Gordie Howe, Det	49		& Blaine Stoughton, Hart	56
1926	Nels Stewart, Maroons	34	1954	Maurice Richard, Mon	37	1981	Mike Bossy, NYI	68
1927	Bill Cook, NYR	33	1955	Bernie Geoffrion, Mon	38	1982	Wayne Gretzky, Edm	92
1928	Howie Morenz, Mon	33		& Maurice Richard, Mon	38	1983	Wayne Gretzky, Edm	71
1929	Ace Bailey, Tor	22	1956	Jean Beliveau, Mon	47	1984	Wayne Gretzky, Edm	87
1930	Cooney Weiland, Bos	43	1957	Gordie Howe, Det	44	1985	Wayne Gretzky, Edm	73
1931	Charlie Conacher, Tor	31	1958	Dickie Moore, Mon	36	1986	Jari Kurri, Edm	68
1932	Charlie Conacher, Tor	34	1959	Jean Beliveau, Mon	45	1987	Wayne Gretzky, Edm	62
	& Bill Cook, NYR	34	1960	Bronco Horvath, Bos	39	1988	Mario Lemieux, Pit	70
1933	Bill Cook, NYR	28		& Bobby Hull, Chi	39	1989	Mario Lemieux, Pit	85
1934	Charlie Conacher, Tor	32	1961	Bernie Geoffrion, Mon	50	1990	Brett Hull, St.L	72
1935	Charlie Conacher, Tor	36	1962	Bobby Hull, Chi	50	1991	Brett Hull, St.L	86
1936	Charlie Conacher, Tor	23	1963	Gordie Howe, Det	38	1992	Brett Hull, St.L	70
	& Bill Thoms, Tor	23	1964	Bobby Hull, Chi	43	1993	Alexander Mogilny, Buf	76
1937	Larry Aurie, Det	23	1965	Norm Ullman, Tor	42		& Teemu Selanne, Win	76
	& Nels Stewart, Bos-NYA	23	1966	Bobby Hull, Chi	54	1994	Pavel Bure, Van	60
1938	Gordie Drillon, Tor	26	1967	Bobby Hull, Chi	52	1995	Peter Bondra, Wash	34
1939	Roy Conacher, Bos	26	1968	Bobby Hull, Chi	44	1996	Mario Lemieux, Pit	69
1940	Bryan Hextall, NYR	24	1969	Bobby Hull, Chi	58	1997	Keith Tkachuk, Pho	52
1941	Bryan Hextall, NYR	26	1970	Phil Esposito, Bos	43	1998	Teemu Selanne, Ana	52
1942	Lynn Patrick, NYR	32	1971	Phil Esposito, Bos	76		& Peter Bondra, Wash	52
1943	Doug Bentley, Chi	33	1972	Phil Esposito, Bos	66	1999	Teemu Selanne, Ana	47
1944	Doug Bentley, Chi	38	1973	Phil Esposito, Bos	55	2000	Pavel Bure, Fla	58

Assists

Multiple Winners: Wayne Gretzky (16); Bobby Orr (5); Frank Boucher, Bill Cowley, Phil Esposito, Gordie Howe, Elmer Lach, Mario Lemieux, Stan Mikita and Joe Primeau (3); Syl Apps, Andy Bathgate, Jean Beliveau, Doug Bentley, Art Chapman, Bobby Clarke, Ron Francis, Jaromir Jagr, Ted Lindsay, Bert Olmstead, Henri Richard and Bryan Trottier (2).

Year		No	Year		No	Year		No
1918	No official records kept.		1947	Billy Taylor, Det	46	1975	Bobby Clarke, Phi	89
1919	Newsy Lalonde, Mon	9	1948	Doug Bentley, Chi	37		& Bobby Orr, Bos	89
1920	Corbett Denneny, Tor	12	1949	Doug Bentley, Chi	43	1976	Bobby Clarke, Phi	89
1921	Louis Berlinquette, Mon	9	1950	Ted Lindsay, Det	55	1977	Guy Lafleur, Mon	80
	Harry Cameron, Tor	9	1951	Gordie Howe, Det	43	1978	Bryan Trottier, NYI	77
	& Joe Matte, Ham	9		& Teeder Kennedy, Tor	43	1979	Bryan Trottier, NYI	87
1922	Punch Broadbent, Ott	14	1952	Elmer Lach, Mon	50	1980	Wayne Gretzky, Edm	86
	& Leo Reise, Ham	14	1953	Gordie Howe, Det	46	1981	Wayne Gretzky, Edm	109
1923	Ed Bouchard, Ham	12	1954	Gordie Howe, Det	48	1982	Wayne Gretzky, Edm	120
1924	King Clancy, Ott	8	1955	Bert Olmstead, Mon	48	1983	Wayne Gretzky, Edm	125
1925	Cy Denneny, Ott	15	1956	Bert Olmstead, Mon	56	1984	Wayne Gretzky, Edm	118
1926	Frank Nighbor, Ott	13	1957	Ted Lindsay, Det	55	1985	Wayne Gretzky, Edm	135
1927	Dick Irvin, Chi	18	1958	Henri Richard, Mon	52	1986	Wayne Gretzky, Edm	163
1928	Howie Morenz, Mon	18	1959	Dickie Moore, Mon	55	1987	Wayne Gretzky, Edm	121
1929	Frank Boucher, NYR	16	1960	Don McKenney, Bos	49	1988	Wayne Gretzky, Edm	109
1930	Frank Boucher, NYR	36	1961	Jean Beliveau, Mon	58	1989	Wayne Gretzky, LA	114
1931	Joe Primeau, Tor	32	1962	Andy Bathgate, NYR	56		& Mario Lemieux, Pit	114
1932	Joe Primeau, Tor	37	1963	Henri Richard, Mon	50	1990	Wayne Gretzky, LA	102
1933	Frank Boucher, NYR	28	1964	Andy Bathgate, NYR-Tor	58	1991	Wayne Gretzky, LA	122
1934	Joe Primeau, Tor	32	1965	Stan Mikita, Chi	59	1992	Wayne Gretzky, LA	90
1935	Art Chapman, NYA	34	1966	Jean Beliveau, Mon	48	1993	Adam Oates, Bos	97
1936	Art Chapman, NYA	28		Stan Mikita, Chi	48	1994	Wayne Gretzky, LA	92
1937	Syl Apps, Tor	29		& Bobby Rousseau, Mon	48	1995	Ron Francis, Pit	48
1938	Syl Apps, Tor	29	1967	Stan Mikita, Chi	62	1996	Ron Francis, Pit	92
1939	Bill Cowley, Bos	34	1968	Phil Esposito, Bos	49		& Mario Lemieux, Pit	92
1940	Milt Schmidt, Bos	30	1969	Phil Esposito, Bos	77	1997	Mario Lemieux, Pit	72
1941	Bill Cowley, Bos	45	1970	Bobby Orr, Bos	87		& Wayne Gretzky, NYR	72
1942	Phil Watson, NYR	37	1971	Bobby Orr, Bos	102	1998	Jaromir Jagr, Pit	67
1943	Bill Cowley, Bos	45	1972	Bobby Orr, Bos	80		& Wayne Gretzky, NYR	67
1944	Clint Smith, Chi	49	1973	Phil Esposito, Bos	75	1999	Jaromir Jagr, Pit	83
1945	Elmer Lach, Mon	54	1974	Bobby Orr, Bos	90	2000	Mark Recchi, Phi	63
1946	Elmer Lach, Mon	34						

Goals Against Average

Average determined by games played through 1942-43 season and by minutes played since then. Minimum of 15 games from 1917-18 season through 1925-26; minimum of 25 games since 1926-27 season. Not to be confused with the Vezina Trophy. Goaltenders who posted the season's lowest goals against average, but did not win the Vezina are in **bold** type.

Multiple Winners: Jacques Plante (9); Clint Benedict and Bill Durnan (6); Johnny Bower, Ken Dryden and Tiny Thompson (4); Patrick Roy and Georges Vezina (3); Ed Belfour, Frankie Brimsek, Turk Broda, George Hainsworth, Dominik Hasek, Harry Lumley, Bernie Parent, Pete Peeters and Terry Sawchuk (2).

Year		GAA	Year		GAA	Year		GAA
1918	Georges Vezina, Mon	3.82	1946	Bill Durnan, Mon	2.60	1974	Bernie Parent, Phi	1.89
1919	Clint Benedict, Ott	2.94	1947	Bill Durnan, Mon	2.30	1975	Bernie Parent, Phi	2.03
1920	Clint Benedict, Ott	2.67	1948	Turk Broda, Tor	2.38	1976	Ken Dryden, Mon	2.03
1921	Clint Benedict, Ott	3.13	1949	Bill Durnan, Mon	2.10	1977	Bunny Larocque, Mon	2.09
1922	Clint Benedict, Ott	3.50	1950	Bill Durnan, Mon	2.20	1978	Ken Dryden, Mon	2.05
1923	Clint Benedict, Ott	2.25	1951	Al Rollins, Tor	1.77	1979	Ken Dryden, Mon	2.30
1924	Georges Vezina, Mon	2.00	1952	Terry Sawchuk, Det	1.90	1980	Bob Sauve, Buf	2.36
1925	Georges Vezina, Mon	1.87	1953	Terry Sawchuk, Det	1.90	1981	Richard Sevigny, Mon	2.40
1926	Alex Connell, Ott	1.17	1954	Harry Lumley, Tor	1.86	1982	**Denis Herron,** Mon	2.64
1927	**Clint Benedict,** Mon-M	1.51	1955	**Harry Lumley,** Tor	1.94	1983	Pete Peeters, Bos	2.36
1928	Geo. Hainsworth, Mon	1.09	1956	Jacques Plante, Mon	1.86	1984	**Pat Riggin,** Wash	2.66
1929	Geo. Hainsworth, Mon	0.98	1957	Jacques Plante, Mon	2.02	1985	**Tom Barrasso,** Buf	2.66
1930	Tiny Thompson, Bos	2.23	1958	Jacques Plante, Mon	2.11	1986	**Bob Froese,** Phi	2.55
1931	Roy Worters, NYA	1.68	1959	Jacques Plante, Mon	2.16	1987	**Brian Hayward,** Mon	2.81
1932	Chuck Gardiner, Chi	1.92	1960	Jacques Plante, Mon	2.54	1988	**Pete Peeters,** Wash	2.78
1933	Tiny Thompson, Bos	1.83	1961	Johnny Bower, Tor	2.50	1989	Patrick Roy, Mon	2.47
1934	**Wilf Cude,** Det-Mon	1.57	1962	Jacques Plante, Mon	2.37	1990	**Mike Liut,** Hart-Wash	2.53
1935	Lorne Chabot, Chi	1.83	1963	**Jacques Plante,** Mon	2.49	1991	Ed Belfour, Chi	2.47
1936	Tiny Thompson, Bos	1.71	1964	**Johnny Bower,** Tor	2.11	1992	Patrick Roy, Mon	2.36
1937	Norm Smith, Det	2.13	1965	Johnny Bower, Tor	2.38	1993	**Felix Potvin,** Tor	2.50
1938	Tiny Thompson, Bos	1.85	1966	**Johnny Bower,** Tor	2.25	1994	Dominik Hasek, Buf	1.95
1939	Frankie Brimsek, Bos	1.58	1967	Glenn Hall, Chi	2.38	1995	Dominik Hasek, Buf	2.11
1940	Dave Kerr, NYR	1.60	1968	Gump Worsley, Mon	1.98	1996	**Ron Hextall,** Phi	2.17
1941	Turk Broda, Tor	2.06	1969	Jacques Plante, St.L	1.96	1997	**Martin Brodeur,** NJ	1.88
1942	Frankie Brimsek, Bos	2.45	1970	**Ernie Wakely,** St.L	2.11	1998	**Ed Belfour,** Dal	1.88
1943	John Mowers, Det	2.47	1971	**Jacques Plante,** Tor	1.88	1999	**Ron Tugnutt,** Ott	1.79
1944	Bill Durnan, Mon	2.18	1972	Tony Esposito, Chi	1.77	2000	**Brian Boucher,** Phi	1.91
1945	Bill Durnan, Mon	2.42	1973	Ken Dryden, Mon	2.26			

Penalty Minutes

Multiple Winners: Red Horner (8); Gus Mortson and Dave Schultz (4); Bert Corbeau, Lou Fontinato and Tiger Williams (3); Billy Boucher, Carl Brewer, Red Dutton, Pat Egan, Bill Ezinicki, Joe Hall, Tim Hunter, Keith Magnuson, Chris Nilan, Jimmy Orlando and Rob Ray (2).

Year		Min	Year		Min	Year		Min
1918	Joe Hall, Mon	60	1946	Jack Stewart, Det	73	1974	Dave Schultz, Phi	348
1919	Joe Hall, Mon	85	1947	Gus Mortson, Tor	133	1975	Dave Schultz, Phi	472
1920	Cully Wilson, Tor	79	1948	Bill Barilko, Tor	147	1976	Steve Durbano, Pit-KC	370
1921	Bert Corbeau, Mon	86	1949	Bill Ezinicki, Tor	145	1977	Tiger Williams, Tor	338
1922	Sprague Cleghorn, Mon	63	1950	Bill Ezinicki, Tor	144	1978	Dave Schultz, LA-Pit	405
1923	Billy Boucher, Mon	52	1951	Gus Mortson, Tor	142	1979	Tiger Williams, Tor	298
1924	Bert Corbeau, Tor	55	1952	Gus Kyle, Bos	127	1980	Jimmy Mann, Win	287
1925	Billy Boucher, Mon	92	1953	Maurice Richard, Mon	112	1981	Tiger Williams, Van	343
1926	Bert Corbeau, Tor	121	1954	Gus Mortson, Chi	132	1982	Paul Baxter, Pit	409
1927	Nels Stewart, Mon-M	133	1955	Fern Flaman, Bos	150	1983	Randy Holt, Wash	275
1928	Eddie Shore, Bos	165	1956	Lou Fontinato, NYR	202	1984	Chris Nilan, Mon	338
1929	Red Dutton, Mon-M	139	1957	Gus Mortson, Chi	147	1985	Chris Nilan, Mon	358
1930	Joe Lamb, Ott	119	1958	Lou Fontinato, NYR	152	1986	Joey Kocur, Det	377
1931	Harvey Rockburn, Det	118	1959	Ted Lindsay, Chi	184	1987	Tim Hunter, Calg	361
1932	Red Dutton, NYA	107	1960	Carl Brewer, Tor	150	1988	Bob Probert, Det	398
1933	Red Horner, Tor	144	1961	Pierre Pilote, Chi	165	1989	Tim Hunter, Calg	375
1934	Red Horner, Tor	146	1962	Lou Fontinato, Mon	167	1990	Basil McRae, Min	351
1935	Red Horner, Tor	125	1963	Howie Young, Det	273	1991	Rob Ray, Buf	350
1936	Red Horner, Tor	167	1964	Vic Hadfield, NYR	151	1992	Mike Peluso, Chi	408
1937	Red Horner, Tor	124	1965	Carl Brewer, Tor	177	1993	Marty McSorley, LA	399
1938	Red Horner, Tor	82	1966	Reg Fleming, Bos-NYR	166	1994	Tie Domi, Win	347
1939	Red Horner, Tor	85	1967	John Ferguson, Mon	177	1995	Enrico Ciccone, TB	225
1940	Red Horner, Tor	87	1968	Barclay Plager, St.L	153	1996	Matthew Barnaby, Buf	335
1941	Jimmy Orlando, Det	99	1969	Forbes Kennedy, Phi-Tor	219	1997	Gino Odjick, Van	371
1942	Pat Egan, NYA	124	1970	Keith Magnuson, Chi	213	1998	Donald Brashear, Van	372
1943	Jimmy Orlando, Det	99	1971	Keith Magnuson, Chi	291	1999	Rob Ray, Buf	261
1944	Mike McMahon, Mon	98	1972	Bryan Watson, Pit	212	2000	Denny Lambert, Atl	219
1945	Pat Egan, Bos	86	1973	Dave Schultz, Phi	259			

All-Time NHL Regular Season Leaders

Through 2000 regular season.

CAREER

Players active during 2000 season in **bold** type.

Points

		Yrs	Gm	G	A	Pts
1	Wayne Gretzky	20	1487	894	1963	2857
2	Gordie Howe	26	1767	801	1049	1850
3	Marcel Dionne	18	1348	731	1040	1771
4	**Mark Messier**	21	1479	627	1087	1714
5	Phil Esposito	18	1282	717	873	1590
6	**Steve Yzerman**	17	1256	627	935	1562
7	**Ron Francis**	19	1407	472	1087	1559
8	**Paul Coffey**	20	1391	396	1131	1527
9	**Ray Bourque**	21	1532	403	1117	1520
10	Mario Lemieux	12	745	613	881	1494
11	Stan Mikita	22	1394	541	926	1467
12	Bryan Trottier	18	1279	524	901	1425
13	Dale Hawerchuk	16	1188	518	891	1409
14	Jari Kurri	17	1251	601	797	1398
15	John Bucyk	23	1540	556	813	1369
16	Guy Lafleur	17	1126	560	793	1353
17	Denis Savard	17	1196	473	865	1338
18	Mike Gartner	19	1432	708	627	1335
19	Gilbert Perreault	17	1191	512	814	1326
20	**Doug Gilmour**	17	1271	422	883	1305
21	Alex Delvecchio	24	1549	456	825	1281
22	Jean Ratelle	21	1281	491	776	1267
23	Peter Stastny	15	977	450	789	1239
24	Norm Ullman	20	1410	490	739	1229
25	Jean Beliveau	20	1125	507	712	1219
26	Bobby Clarke	15	1144	358	852	1210
27	Bernie Nicholls	18	1127	475	734	1209
28	Dino Ciccarelli	19	1232	608	592	1200
29	**Adam Oates**	15	1049	303	894	1197
30	**Larry Murphy**	20	1558	285	910	1195

Goals

		Yrs	Gm	No
1	Wayne Gretzky	20	1487	894
2	Gordie Howe	26	1767	801
3	Marcel Dionne	18	1348	731
4	Phil Esposito	18	1282	717
5	Mike Gartner	19	1432	708
6	**Mark Messier**	21	1479	627
	Steve Yzerman	17	1256	627
8	Mario Lemieux	12	745	613
9	Bobby Hull	16	1063	610
	Brett Hull	15	940	610
11	Dino Ciccarelli	19	1232	608
12	Jari Kurri	17	1251	601
13	Mike Bossy	10	752	573
14	Guy Lafleur	17	1126	560
15	John Bucyk	23	1540	556
16	**Luc Robitaille**	14	1042	553
17	**Dave Andreychuk**	18	1287	552
18	Michel Goulet	15	1089	548
19	Maurice Richard	18	978	544
20	Stan Mikita	22	1394	541
21	Frank Mahovlich	18	1181	533
22	Bryan Trottier	18	1279	524
23	Dale Hawerchuk	16	1188	518
24	Gilbert Perreault	17	1191	512
25	Jean Beliveau	20	1125	507
26	Joe Mullen	17	1062	502
27	Lanny McDonald	16	1111	500
	Pat Verbeek	18	1293	500
29	Glenn Anderson	16	1128	498
30	Jean Ratelle	21	1281	491

Assists

		Yrs	Gm	No
1	Wayne Gretzky	20	1487	1963
2	**Paul Coffey**	20	1391	1131
3	**Ray Bourque**	21	1532	1117
4	**Mark Messier**	21	1479	1087
	Ron Francis	19	1407	1087
6	Gordie Howe	26	1767	1049
7	Marcel Dionne	18	1348	1040
8	**Steve Yzerman**	17	1256	935
9	Stan Mikita	22	1394	926
10	**Larry Murphy**	20	1558	910
11	Bryan Trottier	18	1279	901
12	**Adam Oates**	15	1049	894
13	Dale Hawerchuk	16	1188	891
14	**Doug Gilmour**	17	1271	883
15	Mario Lemieux	12	745	881
16	Phil Esposito	18	1281	873
17	Denis Savard	17	1196	865
18	Bobby Clarke	15	1144	852
19	Alex Delvecchio	24	1549	825
20	**Phil Housley**	18	1288	817

Penalty Minutes

		Yrs	Gm	Min
1	Tiger Williams	14	962	3966
2	Dale Hunter	19	1407	3565
3	**Marty McSorley**	17	961	3381
4	Tim Hunter	16	815	3146
5	Chris Nilan	13	688	3043
6	**Bob Probert**	14	795	3021
7	**Rick Tocchet**	16	1070	2863
8	**Craig Berube**	14	873	2813
9	**Pat Verbeek**	18	1293	2760
10	**Rob Ray**	11	714	2687
11	**Dave Manson**	14	982	2666
12	**Tie Domi**	11	628	2656
13	**Scott Stevens**	18	1353	2607
14	Willi Plett	12	834	2519
15	Joey Kocur	15	820	2519

NHL-WHA Top 15

All-time regular season scoring leaders, including games played in World Hockey Association (1972-79). NHL players with WHA experience are listed in CAPITAL letters. Players active during 2000 are in **bold** type.

Points

		Yrs	G	A	Pts
1	WAYNE GRETZKY	21	940	2027	2967
2	GORDIE HOWE	32	975	1383	2358
3	BOBBY HULL	23	913	895	1808
4	Marcel Dionne	18	731	1040	1771
5	**MARK MESSIER**	22	628	1097	1725
6	Phil Esposito	18	717	873	1590
7	**Steve Yzerman**	17	627	935	1562
8	**Ron Francis**	19	472	1087	1559
9	**Paul Coffey**	20	396	1131	1527
10	**Ray Bourque**	21	403	1117	1520
11	Mario Lemieux	12	613	881	1494
12	Stan Mikita	22	541	926	1467
13	Bryan Trottier	18	524	901	1425
14	Dale Hawerchuk	16	512	891	1409
15	Jari Kurri	17	601	797	1398

WHA Totals: GRETZKY (1 yr, 80 gm, 46-64—110); HOWE (6 yrs, 419 gm, 174-334—508); HULL (7 yrs, 411 gm, 303-335—638); MESSIER (1 yr, 52 gm, 1-10—11).

Years Played

		Yrs	Career	Gm
1	Gordie Howe	26	1946-71, 79-80	1767
2	Alex Delvecchio	24	1950-74	1549
	Tim Horton	24	1949-50, 51-74	1446
4	John Bucyk	23	1955-78	1540
5	Stan Mikita	22	1958-80	1394
	Doug Mohns	22	1953-75	1390
	Dean Prentice	22	1952-74	1378
8	**Ray Bourque**	21	1979—	1532
	Mark Messier	21	1979—	1479
	Harry Howell	21	1952-73	1411
	Ron Stewart	21	1952-73	1353
	Jean Ratelle	21	1960-81	1281
	Allan Stanley	21	1948-69	1244
	Eric Nesterenko	21	1951-72	1219
	Marcel Pronovost	21	1950-70	1206
	George Armstrong	21	1949-50, 51-71	1187
	Terry Sawchuk	21	1949-70	971
	Gump Worsley	21	1952-53, 54-74	862

Note: Combined NHL-WHA years played: Howe (32); Howell (24); Bobby Hull (23); Norm Ullman, Messier, Nesterenko, Frank Mahovlich and Dave Keon (22); Wayne Gretzky (21).

Games Played

		Yrs	Career	Gm
1	Gordie Howe	26	1946-71, 79-80	1767
2	**Larry Murphy**	20	1980—	1558
3	Alex Delvecchio	24	1950-74	1549
4	John Bucyk	23	1955-78	1540
5	**Ray Bourque**	21	1979—	1532
6	Wayne Gretzky	20	1979-99	1487
7	**Mark Messier**	21	1979—	1479
8	Tim Horton	24	1949-50, 51-74	1446
9	Mike Gartner	19	1979-98	1432
10	Harry Howell	21	1952-73	1411
11	Norm Ullman	20	1955-75	1410
12	Dale Hunter	19	1980-99	1407
	Ron Francis	19	1981—	1407
14	Stan Mikita	22	1958-80	1394
15	**Paul Coffey**	20	1980—	1391

Note: Combined NHL-WHA games played: Howe (2,186), Dave Keon (1,597), Howell (1,581), Gretzky (1,567), Ullman (1,554), Messier (1,531), Gartner (1,510), Bobby Hull (1,474) and Frank Mahovlich (1,418).

Goaltending

Wins

		Yrs	Gm	W	L	T	Pct
1	Terry Sawchuk	21	971	**447**	330	172	.562
2	**Patrick Roy**	16	841	**444**	264	103	.611
3	Jacques Plante	18	837	**434**	247	146	.614
4	Tony Esposito	16	886	**423**	306	152	.566
5	Glenn Hall	18	906	**407**	326	163	.545
6	**Grant Fuhr**	19	868	**403**	295	114	.567
7	Andy Moog	18	713	**372**	209	88	.622
8	**Mike Vernon**	17	722	**371**	241	86	.593
9	**J. Vanbiesbrouck**	18	829	**358**	318	114	.525
10	Rogie Vachon	16	795	**355**	291	127	.541
11	**Tom Barrasso**	17	733	**353**	259	81	.568
12	Gump Worsley	21	861	**335**	352	150	.490
13	Harry Lumley	16	804	**330**	329	143	.501
14	**Ed Belfour**	12	612	**308**	195	82	.597
15	Billy Smith	18	680	**305**	233	105	.556
16	Turk Broda	12	629	**302**	224	101	.562
17	Ron Hextall	13	608	**296**	214	69	.571
18	Mike Liut	13	663	**294**	271	74	.518
19	Ed Giacomin	13	610	**289**	208	97	.568
20	Dan Bouchard	14	655	**286**	232	113	.543

Losses

		Yrs	Gm	W	L	T	Pct
1	Gump Worsley	21	861	335	**352**	150	.490
2	Gilles Meloche	18	788	270	**351**	131	.446
3	Terry Sawchuk	21	971	447	**330**	172	.562
4	Harry Lumley	16	804	330	**329**	143	.501
5	Glenn Hall	18	906	407	**326**	163	.545

Goals Against Average

Minimum of 300 games played.

Before 1950

		Gm	Min	GA	GAA
1	George Hainsworth	465	29,415	937	1.91
2	Alex Connell	417	26,050	830	1.91
3	Chuck Gardiner	316	19,687	664	2.02
4	Lorne Chabot	411	25,307	860	2.04
5	Tiny Thompson	553	34,175	1183	2.08

Since 1950

		Gm	Min	GA	GAA
1	**Martin Brodeur**	447	25,939	950	2.20
2	Ken Dryden	397	23,352	870	2.24
3	**Dominik Hasek**	449	25,968	977	2.26
4	**Chris Osgood**	337	19,639	773	2.36
5	Jacques Plante	837	49,533	1965	2.38

Shutouts

		Yrs	Games	No
1	Terry Sawchuk	21	971	103
2	George Hainsworth	11	465	94
3	Glenn Hall	18	906	84
4	Jacques Plante	18	837	82
5	Alex Connell	12	417	81
	Tiny Thompson	12	553	81
7	Tony Esposito	16	886	76
8	Lorne Chabot	11	411	73
9	Harry Lumley	16	804	71
10	Roy Worters	12	484	66
11	Turk Broda	14	629	62
12	John Roach	14	491	58
13	Clint Benedict	13	362	57
14	Bernie Parent	13	608	54
	Ed Giacomin	13	610	54

NHL-WHA Top 15

All-Time regular season wins leaders, including games played in World Hockey Association (1972-79). NHL goaltenders with WHA experience are listed in CAPITAL letters. Players active during 2000 are in **bold** type.

Wins

		Yrs	W	L	T	Pct
1	JACQUES PLANTE	19	449	261	147	.610
2	Terry Sawchuk	21	447	330	172	.562
3	**Patrick Roy**	16	444	264	103	.611
4	Tony Esposito	16	423	306	152	.566
5	Glenn Hall	18	407	326	163	.545
6	**Grant Fuhr**	19	403	295	114	.567
7	Andy Moog	18	372	209	88	.622
8	**Mike Vernon**	17	371	241	86	.593
9	**J. Vanbiesbrouck**	18	358	318	114	.525
10	Rogie Vachon	16	355	291	127	.541
11	**Tom Barrasso**	17	353	259	81	.568
12	Gump Worsley	21	335	352	150	.490
13	Harry Lumley	16	330	329	143	.501
14	GERRY CHEEVERS	17	329	180	83	.626
15	MIKE LIUT	15	329	310	78	.511

WHA Totals: PLANTE (1 yr, 31 gm, 15-14-1); CHEEVERS (4 yrs, 191 gm, 99-78-9); LIUT (2 yrs, 81 gm, 31-39-4).

All-Time NHL Regular Season Leaders (Cont.)
SINGLE SEASON

Scoring
Points

		Season	G	A	Pts
1	Wayne Gretzky, Edm	1985-86	52	163	215
2	Wayne Gretzky, Edm	1981-82	92	120	212
3	Wayne Gretzky, Edm	1984-85	73	135	208
4	Wayne Gretzky, Edm	1983-84	87	118	205
5	Mario Lemieux, Pit	1988-89	85	114	199
6	Wayne Gretzky, Edm	1982-83	71	125	196
7	Wayne Gretzky, Edm	1986-87	62	121	183
8	Mario Lemieux, Pit	1987-88	70	98	168
9	Wayne Gretzky, LA	1988-89	54	114	168
10	Wayne Gretzky, Edm	1980-81	55	109	164
11	Wayne Gretzky, LA	1990-91	41	122	163
12	Mario Lemieux, Pit	1995-96	69	92	161
13	Mario Lemieux, Pit	1992-93	69	91	160
14	Steve Yzerman, Det	1988-89	65	90	155
15	Phil Esposito, Bos	1970-71	76	76	152
16	Bernie Nicholls, LA.	1988-89	70	80	150
17	Jaromir Jagr, Pit	1995-96	62	87	149
	Wayne Gretzky, Edm	1987-88	40	109	149
19	Pat LaFontaine, Buf.	1992-93	53	95	148
20	Mike Bossy, NYI	1981-82	64	83	147

WHA 150 points or more: 154—Marc Tardif, Que. (1977-78).

Goals

		Season	Gm	No
1	Wayne Gretzky, Edm	1981-82	80	92
2	Wayne Gretzky, Edm	1983-84	74	87
3	Brett Hull, St.L	1990-91	78	86
4	Mario Lemieux, Pit	1988-89	76	85
5	Alexander Mogilny, Buf.	1992-93	77	76
	Phil Esposito, Bos	1970-71	78	76
	Teemu Selanne, Win	1992-93	84	76
8	Wayne Gretzky, Edm	1984-85	80	73
9	Brett Hull, St.L	1989-90	80	72
10	Jari Kurri, Edm	1984-85	73	71
	Wayne Gretzky, Edm	1982-83	80	71
12	Brett Hull, St.L	1991-92	73	70
	Mario Lemieux, Pit	1987-88	77	70
	Bernie Nicholls, LA.	1988-89	79	70
15	Mario Lemieux, Pit	1992-93	60	69
	Mario Lemieux, Pit	1995-96	70	69
	Mike Bossy, NYI	1978-79	80	69
18	Phil Esposito, Bos	1973-74	78	68
	Jari Kurri, Edm	1985-86	78	68
	Mike Bossy, NYI	1980-81	79	68

WHA 70 goals or more: 77—Bobby Hull, Win. (1974-75); 75—Real Cloutier, Que. (1978-79); 71—Marc Tardif, Que. (1975-76); 70—Anders Hedberg, Win. (1976-77).

Assists

		Season	Gm	No
1	Wayne Gretzky, Edm	1985-86	80	163
2	Wayne Gretzky, Edm	1984-85	80	135
3	Wayne Gretzky, Edm	1982-83	80	125
4	Wayne Gretzky, LA	1990-91	78	122
5	Wayne Gretzky, Edm	1986-87	79	121
6	Wayne Gretzky, Edm	1981-82	80	120
7	Wayne Gretzky, Edm	1983-84	74	118
8	Mario Lemieux, Pit	1988-89	76	114
	Wayne Gretzky, LA	1988-89	78	114
10	Wayne Gretzky, Edm	1987-88	64	109
	Wayne Gretzky, Edm	1980-81	80	109
12	Wayne Gretzky, LA	1989-90	73	102
	Bobby Orr, Bos.	1970-71	78	102
14	Mario Lemieux, Pit	1987-88	77	98
15	Adam Oates, Bos	1992-93	84	97

WHA 95 assists or more: 106—Andre Lacroix, S.Diego (1974-75).

Goaltending
Wins

		Season	Record
1	Bernie Parent, Phi	1973-74	47-13-12
2	Bernie Parent, Phi	1974-75	44-14- 9
	Terry Sawchuk, Det	1950-51	44-13-13
	Terry Sawchuk, Det	1951-52	44-14-12
5	**Martin Brodeur**, NJ.	1999-00	43-20- 8
	Martin Brodeur, NJ.	1997-98	43-17- 8
	Tom Barrasso, Pit	1992-93	43-14- 5
	Ed Belfour, Chi	1990-91	43-19- 7
9	**Roman Turek**, St.L	1999-00	42-15- 9
	Jacques Plante, Mon	1955-56	42-12-10
	Jacques Plante, Mon	1961-62	42-14-14
	Ken Dryden, Mon.	1975-76	42-10- 8
	Mike Richter, NYR	1993-94	42-12- 6

Most WHA wins in one season: 44—Richard Brodeur, Que. (1975-76).

Losses

		Season	Record
1	Gary Smith, Cal	1970-71	19-48- 4
2	Al Rollins, Chi	1953-54	12-47- 7
3	Peter Sidorkiewicz, Ott	1992-93	8-46- 3
4	Harry Lumley, Chi	1951-52	17-44- 9
5	Harry Lumley, Chi	1950-51	12-41-10
	Craig Billington, Ott.	1993-94	11-41- 4

Most WHA losses in one season: 36—Don McLeod, Van. (1974-75) and Andy Brown, Ind. (1974-75).

Shutouts

		Season	Gm	No
1	George Hainsworth, Mon	1928-29	44	22
2	Alex Connell, Ottawa	1925-26	36	15
	Alex Connell, Ottawa	1927-28	44	15
	Hal Winkler, Bos	1927-28	44	15
	Tony Esposito, Chi	1969-70	63	15

Most WHA shutouts in one season: 5—Gerry Cheevers, Cle. (1972-73) and Joe Daly, Win. (1975-76).

Goals Against Average
Before 1950

		Season	Gm	GAA
1	George Hainsworth, Mon	1928-29	44	0.98
2	George Hainsworth, Mon	1927-28	44	1.09
3	Alex Connell, Ottawa	1925-26	36	1.17
4	Tiny Thompson, Bos	1928-29	44	1.18
5	Roy Worters, NY Americans	1928-29	38	1.21

Since 1950

		Season	Gm	GAA
1	Tony Esposito, Chi	1971-72	48	1.77
2	Al Rollins, Tor	1950-51	40	1.77
3	Ron Tugnutt, Ott	1998-99	43	1.79
4	Harry Lumley, Tor	1953-54	69	1.86
5	Jacques Plante, Mon	1955-56	64	1.86

Penalty Minutes

		Season	PM
1	Dave Schultz, Phi	1974-75	472
2	Paul Baxter, Pit	1981-82	409
3	Mike Peluso, Chi	1991-92	408
4	Dave Schultz, LA-Pit	1977-78	405
5	Marty McSorley, LA	1992-93	399
6	Bob Probert, Det	1987-88	398
7	Basil McRae, Min	1987-88	382
8	Joey Kocur, Det	1985-86	377
9	Tim Hunter, Calg	1988-89	375
10	Donald Brashear, Van	1997-98	372

WHA 355 minutes or more: 365—Curt Brackenbury, Min-Que. (1975-76).

SINGLE GAME
Scoring

Points

	Date	G-A—Pts
Darryl Sittler, Tor vs Bos	2/7/76	6-4—10
Maurice Richard, Mon vs Det	12/28/44	5-3— 8
Bert Olmstead, Mon vs Chi	1/9/54	4-4— 8
Tom Bladon, Phi vs Cle	12/11/77	4-4— 8
Bryan Trottier, NYI vs NYR	12/23/78	5-3— 8
Peter Stastny, Que at Wash	2/22/81	4-4— 8
Anton Stastny, Que at Wash	2/22/81	3-5— 8
Wayne Gretzky, Edm vs NJ	11/19/83	3-5— 8
Wayne Gretzky, Edm vs Min	1/4/84	4-4— 8
Paul Coffey, Edm vs Det	3/14/86	2-6— 8
Mario Lemieux, Pit vs St.L	10/15/88	2-6— 8
Bernie Nicholls, LA vs Tor	12/1/88	2-6— 8
Mario Lemieux, Pit vs NJ	12/31/88	5-3— 8

Goals

	Date	No
Joe Malone, Que vs Tor	1/31/20	7
Newsy Lalonde, Mon vs Tor	1/10/20	6
Joe Malone, Que vs Ott	3/10/20	6
Corb Denneny, Tor vs Ham	1/26/21	6
Cy Denneny, Ott vs Ham	3/7/21	6
Syd Howe, Det vs NYR	2/3/44	6
Red Berenson, St.L at Phi	11/7/68	6
Darryl Sittler, Tor vs Bos	2/7/76	6

Assists

	Date	No
Billy Taylor, Det at Chi	3/16/47	7
Wayne Gretzky, Edm vs Wash	2/15/80	7
Wayne Gretzky, Edm at Chi	12/11/85	7
Wayne Gretzky, Edm vs Que	2/14/86	7
24 players tied with 6 each.		

Penalty Minutes

	Date	Min
Randy Holt, LA at Phi	3/11/79	67
Frank Bathe, Phi vs LA	3/11/79	55
Russ Anderson, Pit vs Edm	1/19/80	51

Penalties

	Date	No
Chris Nilan, Bos vs Har	3/31/91	10*

Eight tied with 9 each.
* Nilan accumulated six minors, two majors, one 10-minute misconduct and one game misconduct.

The NHL Top 50

To celebrate its 50th anniversary, *The Hockey News* presented its list of the "Top 50 NHL Players of All-Time" on January 9, 1998. The list was determined by a panel of 50 hockey experts representing past and present NHL players, coaches, executives and journalists. Voting was conducted before the 1997 Stanley Cup playoffs. Players active during the 1999-00 season are in **bold** type.

No.	Player	Pos	No.	Player	Pos
1	Wayne Gretzky, 1979-99	C	26	Frank Mahovlich, 1956-74	LW
2	Bobby Orr, 1966-79	D	27	Milt Schmidt, 1936-42, 45-55	C
3	Gordie Howe, 1946-71, 79-80	RW	28	**Paul Coffey**, 1980—	D
4	Mario Lemieux, 1984-97	C	29	Henri Richard, 1955-75	C
5	Maurice Richard, 1942-60	RW	30	Bryan Trottier, 1975-92, 93-94	C
6	Doug Harvey, 1947-69	D			
7	Jean Beliveau, 1950-71	C	31	Dickie Moore, 1951-65, 67-68	LW
8	Bobby Hull, 1957-72, 79-80	LW	32	Newsy Lalonde, 1917-21, 25-27	C
9	Terry Sawchuk, 1949-70	G	33	Syl Apps, 1936-48	C
10	Eddie Shore, 1926-40	D	34	Bill Durnan, 1943-50	G
			35	**Patrick Roy**, 1984—	G
11	Guy Lafleur, 1971-85, 88-91	RW	36	Charlie Conacher, 1929-41	RW
12	**Mark Messier**, 1979—	C	37	**Jaromir Jagr**, 1990—	RW
13	Jacques Plante, 1952-65, 67-73	G	38	Marcel Dionne, 1971-89	C
14	**Ray Bourque**, 1979—	D	39	Joe Malone, 1917-24	C
15	Howie Morenz, 1923-37	C	40	**Chris Chelios**, 1983—	D
16	Glenn Hall, 1952-71	G			
17	Stan Mikita, 1958-80	C	41	Dit Clapper, 1927-47	D
18	Phil Esposito, 1963-81	C	42	Bernie Geoffrion, 1950-64, 66-68	RW
19	Denis Potvin, 1973-88	D	43	Tim Horton, 1949-50, 51-74	D
20	Mike Bossy, 1977-87	RW	44	Bill Cook, 1926-37	RW
			45	Johnny Bucyk, 1955-78	LW
21	Ted Lindsay, 1944-60, 64-65	LW	46	George Hainsworth, 1926-37	G
22	Red Kelly, 1947-67	D	47	Gilbert Perreault, 1970-87	C
23	Bobby Clarke, 1969-84	C	48	Max Bentley, 1940-43, 45-54	C
24	Larry Robinson, 1972-92	D	49	Brad Park, 1968-85	D
25	Ken Dryden, 1970-79	G	50	Jari Kurri, 1980-98	RW

All-Time Winningest NHL Coaches

Top 20 NHL career victories through the 2000 season. Career, regular season and playoff records are noted along with NHL titles won. Coaches active during 2000 season in **bold** type.

		Career				Regular Season				Playoffs				
		Yrs	W	L	T	Pct	W	L	T	Pct	W	L	T	Pct Stanley Cups
1	**Scotty Bowman**	28	**1353**	658	295	.651	1148	539	295	.654	205	119	0	.633 8 (1973, 76-79, 92, 97-98)
2	Al Arbour	22	**904**	663	248	.566	781	577	248	.564	123	86	0	.589 4 (1980-83)
3	Dick Irvin	26	**790**	609	228	.556	690	521	226	.559	100	88	2	.532 4 (1932,44,46,53)
4	Billy Reay	16	**599**	445	175	.563	542	385	175	.571	57	60	0	.487 None
5	Mike Keenan	14	**597**	441	117	.568	506	372	117	.567	91	69	0	.569 1 (1994)
6	Toe Blake	13	**582**	292	159	.640	500	255	159	.634	82	37	0	.689 8 (1956-60,65-66,68)
7	Glen Sather	11	**553**	305	110	.628	464	268	110	.616	89	37	0	.706 4 (1984-85,87-88)
8	Bryan Murray	13	**518**	412	123	.550	484	368	123	.559	34	44	0	.436 None
9	**Pat Quinn**	14	**515**	409	116	.551	447	345	116	.556	68	64	0	.515 None
10	**Roger Neilson**	15	**483**	420	158	.530	443	372	158	.536	40	48	0	.455 None
11	Jack Adams	21	**449**	449	163	.512	423	397	162	.513	52	52	1	.500 3 (1936-37, 43)
12	**Pat Burns**	11	**470**	369	128	.552	409	310	128	.558	61	59	0	.508 None
13	Jacques Demers	14	**464**	510	130	.479	409	467	130	.471	55	43	0	.561 1 (1993)
14	Fred Shero	10	**451**	272	119	.606	390	225	119	.612	61	47	0	.565 2 (1974-75)
15	Punch Imlach	15	**439**	384	148	.528	395	336	148	.534	44	48	0	.478 4 (1962-64,67)
16	Emile Francis	13	**433**	326	112	.561	393	273	112	.577	40	53	0	.430 None
17	Sid Abel	16	**414**	470	155	.473	382	426	155	.477	32	44	0	.421 None
18	**Terry Murray**	10	**400**	308	82	.558	354	265	82	.563	46	43	0	.517 None
19	Bob Berry	11	**395**	377	121	.510	384	355	121	.517	11	22	0	.333 None
20	Art Ross	18	**393**	310	95	.552	361	277	90	.558	32	33	5	.493 1 (1939)

Where They Coached

Abel—Chicago (1952-54), Detroit (1957-68,69-70), St. Louis (1971-72), Kansas City (1975-76); **Adams**—Toronto (1922-23), Detroit (1927-47); **Arbour**—St. Louis (1970-73), NY Islanders (1973-86,88-94); **Berry**—Los Angeles (1978-81), Montreal (1981-84), Pittsburgh (1984-87), St. Louis (1992-94); **Blake**—Montreal (1955-68); **Bowman**—St. Louis (1967-71), Montreal (1971-79), Buffalo (1979-87), Pittsburgh (1991-93), Detroit (1993—); **Burns**—Montreal (1988-92), Toronto (1992-96), Boston (1997—).

Demers—Quebec (1979-80), St. Louis (1983-86), Detroit (1986-90), Montreal (1992-95), Tampa Bay (1997-99); **Francis**—NY Rangers (1965-75), St. Louis (1976-77,81-83); **Imlach**—Toronto (1958-69), Buffalo (1970-72), Toronto (1979-81); **Irvin**—Chicago (1930-31,55-56), Toronto (1931-40), Montreal (1940-55); **Keenan**—Philadelphia (1984-88), Chicago (1988-92), NY Rangers (1993-94), St. Louis (1994-96), Vancouver (1997-99); **B. Murray**—Washington (1982-90), Detroit (1990-93), Florida (1997-98); **T. Murray**—Washington (1990-94), Philadelphia (1994-97), Florida (1998—).

Neilson—Toronto (1977-79), Buffalo (1979-81), Vancouver (1982-83), Los Angeles (1984), NY Rangers (1989-93), Florida (1993-95), Philadelphia (1998-00); **Quinn**—Philadelphia (1978-82), Los Angeles (1984-87), Vancouver (1990-94, 96), Toronto (1998—); **Reay**—Toronto (1957-59), Chicago (1963-77); **Ross**—Montreal Wanderers (1917-18), Hamilton (1922-23), Boston (1924-28,29-34,36-39,41-45); **Sather**—Edmonton (1979-89, 93-94); **Shero**—Philadelphia (1971-78), NY Rangers (1978-81).

Top Winning Percentages

Minimum of 275 victories, including playoffs.

		Yrs	W	L	T	Pct.
1	**Scotty Bowman**	28	1353	658	295	**.651**
2	Toe Blake	13	582	292	159	**.640**
3	Glen Sather	11	553	305	110	**.628**
4	Fred Shero	10	451	272	119	**.606**
5	Don Cherry	6	281	177	77	**.597**
6	Tommy Ivan	9	324	205	111	**.593**
7	Jacques Lemaire	7	296	193	69	**.592**
8	Mike Keenan	14	597	441	117	**.568**
9	Al Arbour	22	904	663	248	**.566**
10	Billy Reay	16	599	445	175	**.563**
11	Emile Francis	13	433	326	112	**.561**
12	**Terry Murray**	10	400	308	82	**.558**
13	Hap Day	10	308	237	81	**.557**
14	Dick Irvin	26	790	609	228	**.556**
15	Lester Patrick	13	312	242	115	**.552**
16	**Pat Burns**	11	470	369	128	**.552**
17	Art Ross	18	393	310	95	**.552**
18	**Pat Quinn**	14	515	409	116	**.551**
19	Bryan Murray	13	518	412	123	**.550**
20	Bob Johnson	6	275	223	58	**.547**
21	**Roger Neilson**	15	483	420	158	**.530**
22	Punch Imlach	15	439	384	148	**.528**
23	**Brian Sutter**	10	387	355	103	**.519**
24	Terry Crisp	9	310	286	78	**.518**
25	Jack Adams	21	475	449	163	**.512**

Active Coaches' Victories

Through 2000 season, including playoffs.

		Yrs	W	L	T	Pct.
1	Scotty Bowman, Det.	28	**1353**	658	295	.651
2	Pat Quinn, Tor.	14	**515**	409	116	.551
3	Pat Burns, Bos.	11	**470**	369	128	.552
4	Terry Murray, Fla.	10	**400**	308	82	.558
5	Jacques Lemaire, Min.	7	**296**	193	69	.592
6	Ron Wilson, Wash.	7	**252**	266	61	.488
7	Ken Hitchcock, Dal.	5	**249**	146	46	.617
8	Jacques Martin, Ott.	7	**243**	244	83	.499
9	Marc Crawford, Van.	6	**234**	169	62	.570
10	Darryl Sutter, SJ	6	**230**	218	64	.512
11	Craig Hartsburg, Ana.	5	**181**	184	65	.497
12	Joel Quenneville, St.L.	4	**168**	115	39	.582
13	Paul Maurice, Car.	5	**167**	182	55	.481
14	Ron Low, NYR	5	**149**	180	40	.458
15	Larry Robinson, NJ	5	**142**	176	45	.453
16	Lindy Ruff, Buf.	3	**133**	109	45	.542
17	Dave King, Clb.	3	**117**	88	31	.561
18	Bob Hartley, Col.	2	**108**	71	21	.593
	Alain Vigneault, Mon.	3	**108**	115	33	.486
20	Butch Goring, NYI	3	**66**	90	22	.433
21	Barry Trotz, Nash.	2	**56**	94	14	.384
22	Don Hay, Calg.	1	**41**	41	7	.500
23	Bobby Francis, Pho.	1	**40**	39	8	.506
24	Andy Murray, LA	1	**39**	35	12	.523
25	Craig Ramsey, Phi.	1	**27**	15	1	.640
26	Steve Ludzik, TB	1	**19**	54	9	.287
27	Curt Fraser, Atl.	1	**14**	61	7	.213
28	Ivan Hlinka, Pit.	0	**0**	0	0	.000
	Alpo Suhonen, Chi.	0	**0**	0	0	.000
	Craig MacTavish, Edm.	0	**0**	0	0	.000

Annual Awards
Hart Memorial Trophy

Awarded to the player "adjudged to be the most valuable to his team" and named after Cecil Hart, the former manager-coach of the Montreal Canadiens. Winners selected by Pro Hockey Writers Assn. (PHWA). Winners' scoring statistics or goaltender W-L records and goals against average are provided; (*) indicates led or tied for league lead.

Multiple Winners: Wayne Gretzky (9); Gordie Howe (6); Eddie Shore (4); Bobby Clarke, Mario Lemieux, Howie Morenz and Bobby Orr (3); Jean Beliveau, Bill Cowley, Phil Esposito, Dominik Hasek, Bobby Hull, Guy Lafleur, Mark Messier, Stan Mikita and Nels Stewart (2).

Year		G	A	Pts	Year		G	A	Pts
1924	Frank Nighbor, Ottawa, C	10	3	13	1963	Gordie Howe, Det., RW	38	48	86*
1925	Billy Burch, Hamilton, C	20	4	24	1964	Jean Beliveau, Mon., C	28	50	78
1926	Nels Stewart, Maroons, C	34	8	42*	1965	Bobby Hull, Chi., LW	39	32	71
1927	Herb Gardiner, Mon., D	6	6	12	1966	Bobby Hull, Chi., LW	54	43	97*
1928	Howie Morenz, Mon., C	33	18	51	1967	Stan Mikita, Chi., C	35	62	97*
1929	Roy Worters, NYA, G	16-13-9,	1.21		1968	Stan Mikita, Chi., C	40	47	87*
1930	Nels Stewart, Maroons, C	39	16	55	1969	Phil Esposito, Bos., C	49	77	126*
1931	Howie Morenz, Mon., C	28	23	51*	1970	Bobby Orr, Bos., D	33	87	120*
1932	Howie Morenz, Mon., C	24	25	49	1971	Bobby Orr, Bos., D	37	102	139
1933	Eddie Shore, Bos., D	8	27	35	1972	Bobby Orr, Bos., D	37	80	117
1934	Aurel Joliat, Mon., LW	22	15	37	1973	Bobby Clarke, Phi., C	37	67	104
1935	Eddie Shore, Bos., D	7	26	33	1974	Phil Esposito, Bos., C	68	77	145*
1936	Eddie Shore, Bos., D	3	16	19	1975	Bobby Clarke, Phi., C	27	89	116
1937	Babe Siebert, Mon., D	8	20	28	1976	Bobby Clarke, Phi., C	30	89	119
1938	Eddie Shore, Bos., D	3	14	17	1977	Guy Lafleur, Mon., RW	56	80	136*
1939	Toe Blake, Mon., LW	24	23	47*	1978	Guy Lafleur, Mon., RW	60	72	132*
1940	Ebbie Goodfellow, Det., D	11	17	28	1979	Bryan Trottier, NYI., C	47	87	134*
1941	Bill Cowley, Bos., C	17	45	62*	1980	Wayne Gretzky, Edm., C	51	86	137*
1942	Tommy Anderson, NYA, D	12	29	41	1981	Wayne Gretzky, Edm., C	55	109	164*
1943	Bill Cowley, Bos., C	27	45	72	1982	Wayne Gretzky, Edm., C	92	120	212*
1944	Babe Pratt, Tor., D	17	40	57	1983	Wayne Gretzky, Edm., C	71	125	196*
1945	Elmer Lach, Mon., C	26	54	80*	1984	Wayne Gretzky, Edm., C	87	118	205*
1946	Max Bentley, Chi., C	31	30	61*	1985	Wayne Gretzky, Edm., C	73	135	208*
1947	Maurice Richard, Mon., RW	45	26	71	1986	Wayne Gretzky, Edm., C	52	163	215*
1948	Buddy O'Connor, NYR, C	24	36	60	1987	Wayne Gretzky, Edm., C	62	121	183*
1949	Sid Abel, Det., C	28	26	54	1988	Mario Lemieux, Pit., C	70	98	168*
1950	Chuck Rayner, NYR, G	28-30-11;	2.62		1989	Wayne Gretzky, LA, C	54	114	168
1951	Milt Schmidt, Bos., C	22	39	61	1990	Mark Messier, Edm., C	45	84	129
1952	Gordie Howe, Det., RW	47	39	86*	1991	Brett Hull, St. L., RW	86	45	131
1953	Gordie Howe, Det., RW	49	46	95*	1992	Mark Messier, NYR, C	35	72	107
1954	Al Rollins, Chi., G	12-47-7;	3.23		1993	Mario Lemieux, Pit., C	69	91	160*
1955	Ted Kennedy, Tor., C	10	42	52	1994	Sergei Fedorov, Det., C	56	64	120
1956	Jean Beliveau, Mon., C	47	41	88	1995	Eric Lindros, Phi., C	29	41	70*
1957	Gordie Howe, Det., RW	44	45	89*	1996	Mario Lemieux, Pit., C	69	92	161*
1958	Gordie Howe, Det., RW	33	44	77	1997	Dominik Hasek, Buf., G	37-20-10;	2.27	
1959	Andy Bathgate, NYR, RW	40	48	88	1998	Dominik Hasek, Buf., G	33-23-13,	2.09	
1960	Gordie Howe, Det., RW	28	45	73	1999	Jaromir Jagr, Pit., RW	44	83	127*
1961	Bernie Geoffrion, Mon., RW	50	45	95*	2000	Chris Pronger, St.L, D	14	48	62
1962	Jacques Plante, Mon., G	42-14-14;	2.37*						

Calder Memorial Trophy

Awarded to the most outstanding rookie of the year and named after Frank Calder, the late NHL president (1917-43). Since the 1990-91 season, all eligible candidates must not have attained their 26th birthday by Sept. 15 of their rookie year. Winners selected by PHWA. Winners' scoring statistics or goaltender W-L record & goals against average are provided.

Year		G	A	Pts	Year		G	A	Pts
1933	Carl Voss, NYR-Det., C	8	15	23	1951	Terry Sawchuk, Det., G	44-13-13;	1.99	
1934	Russ Blinco, Maroons, C	14	9	23	1952	Bernie Geoffrion, Mon., RW	30	24	54
1935	Sweeney Schriner, NYA, LW	18	22	40	1953	Gump Worsley, NYR, G	13-29-8;	3.06	
1936	Mike Karakas, Chi., G	21-19-8;	1.92		1954	Camille Henry, NYR, LW	24	15	39
1937	Syl Apps, Tor., C	16	29	45	1955	Ed Litzenberger, Mon-Chi., RW	23	28	51
1938	Cully Dahlstrom, Chi., C	10	9	19	1956	Glenn Hall, Det., G	30-24-16;	2.11	
1939	Frankie Brimsek, Bos., G	33-9-1;	1.58		1957	Larry Regan, Bos., RW	14	19	33
1940	Kilby MacDonald, NYR, LW	15	13	28	1958	Frank Mahovlich, Tor., LW	20	16	36
1941	John Quilty, Mon., C	18	16	34	1959	Ralph Backstrom, Mon., C	18	22	40
1942	Knobby Warwick, NYR, RW	16	17	33	1960	Billy Hay, Chi., C	18	37	55
1943	Gaye Stewart, Tor., LW	24	23	47	1961	Dave Keon, Tor., C	20	25	45
1944	Gus Bodnar, Tor., C	22	40	62	1962	Bobby Rousseau, Mon., RW	21	24	45
1945	Frank McCool, Tor., G	24-22-4;	3.22		1963	Kent Douglas, Tor., D	7	15	22
1946	Edgar Laprade, NYR, C	15	19	34	1964	Jacques Laperriere, Mon., D	2	28	30
1947	Howie Meeker, Tor., RW	27	18	45	1965	Roger Crozier, Det., G	40-23-7;	2.42	
1948	Jim McFadden, Det., C	24	24	48	1966	Brit Selby, Tor., LW	14	13	27
1949	Penny Lund, NYR, RW	14	16	30	1967	Bobby Orr, Bos., D	13	28	41
1950	Jack Gelineau, Bos., G	22-30-15;	3.28		1968	Derek Sanderson, Bos., C	24	25	49

Annual Awards (Cont.)

Year		G	A	Pts	Year		G	A	Pts
1969	Danny Grant, Min., LW	34	31	65	1985	Mario Lemieux, Pit., C	43	57	100
1970	Tony Esposito, Chi., G	38-17-8;		2.17	1986	Gary Suter, Calg., D	18	50	68
1971	Gilbert Perreault, Buf., C	38	34	72	1987	Luc Robitaille, LA, LW	45	39	84
1972	Ken Dryden, Mon., G	39-8-15;		2.24	1988	Joe Nieuwendyk, Calg., C	51	41	92
1973	Steve Vickers, NYR, LW	30	23	53	1989	Brian Leetch, NYR, D	23	48	71
1974	Denis Potvin, NYI, D	17	37	54	1990	Sergei Makarov, Calg., RW	24	62	86
1975	Eric Vail, Atl., LW	39	21	60	1991	Ed Belfour, Chi., G	43-19-7;		2.47
1976	Bryan Trottier, NYI, C	32	63	95	1992	Pavel Bure, Van., RW	34	26	60
1977	Willi Plett, Atl., RW	33	23	56	1993	Teemu Selanne, Win., RW	76	56	132
1978	Mike Bossy, NYI, RW	53	38	91	1994	Martin Brodeur, NJ, G	27-11-8;		2.40
1979	Bobby Smith, Min., C	30	44	74	1995	Peter Forsberg, Que., C	15	35	50
1980	Ray Bourque, Bos., D	17	48	65	1996	Daniel Alfredsson, Ott., RW	26	35	61
1981	Peter Stastny, Que., C	39	70	109	1997	Bryan Berard, NYI, D	8	40	48
1982	Dale Hawerchuk, Win., C	45	58	103	1998	Sergei Samsonov, Bos., LW	22	25	47
1983	Steve Larmer, Chi., RW	43	47	90	1999	Chris Drury, Col., C	20	24	44
1984	Tom Barrasso, Buf., G	26-12-3;		2.84	2000	Scott Gomez, NJ, C	19	51	70

Vezina Trophy

From 1927-80, given to the principal goaltender(s) on the team allowing the fewest goals during the regular season. Trophy named after 1920's goalie Georges Vezina of the Montreal Canadiens, who died of tuberculosis in 1926. Since the 1980-81 season, the trophy has been awarded to the most outstanding goaltender of the year as selected by the league's general managers.

Multiple Winners: Jacques Plante (7, one of them shared); Bill Durnan (6); Ken Dryden (5, three shared); Dominik Hasek (5); Bunny Larocque (4, all shared); Terry Sawchuk (4, one shared); Tiny Thompson (4, one shared); Tony Esposito (3, one shared); George Hainsworth (3); Glenn Hall (3, two shared); Patrick Roy (3); Ed Belfour (2); Johnny Bower (2, one shared); Frankie Brimsek (2); Turk Broda (2); Chuck Gardiner (2); Charlie Hodge (2, one shared); Bernie Parent (2, one shared); Gump Worsley (2, both shared).

Year		Record	GAA	Year		Record	GAA
1927	George Hainsworth, Mon	28-14-2	1.52	1968	Gump Worsley, Mon	19-9-8	1.98
1928	George Hainsworth, Mon	26-11-7	1.09		& Rogie Vachon, Mon	23-13-2	2.48
1929	George Hainsworth, Mon	22-7-15	0.98	1969	Jacques Plante, St.L	18-12-6	1.96
1930	Tiny Thompson, Bos	38-5-1	2.23		& Glenn Hall, St.L	19-12-8	2.17
1931	Roy Worters, NYA	18-16-10	1.68	1970	Tony Esposito, Chi	38-17-8	2.17
1932	Chuck Gardiner, Chi	18-19-11	1.92	1971	Ed Giacomin, NYR	27-10-7	2.16
1933	Tiny Thompson, Bos	25-15-8	1.83		& Gilles Villemure, NYR	22-8-4	2.30
1934	Chuck Gardiner, Chi	20-17-11	1.73	1972	Tony Esposito, Chi	31-10-6	1.77
1935	Lorne Chabot, Chi	26-17-5	1.83		& Gary Smith, Chi	14-5-6	2.42
1936	Tiny Thompson, Bos	22-20-6	1.71	1973	Ken Dryden, Mon	33-7-13	2.26
1937	Norm Smith, Det	25-14-9	2.13	1974	(Tie) Bernie Parent, Phi	47-13-12	1.89
1938	Tiny Thompson, Bos	30-11-7	1.85		Tony Esposito, Chi	34-14-21	2.04
1939	Frankie Brimsek, Bos	33-9-1	1.58	1975	Bernie Parent, Phi	44-14-10	2.03
1940	Dave Kerr, NYR	27-11-10	1.60	1976	Ken Dryden, Mon	42-10-8	2.03
1941	Turk Broda, Tor	28-14-6	2.06	1977	Ken Dryden, Mon	41-6-8	2.14
1942	Frankie Brimsek, Bos	24-17-6	2.45		& Bunny Larocque, Mon	19-2-4	2.09
1943	John Mowers, Det	25-14-11	2.47	1978	Ken Dryden, Mon	37-7-7	2.05
1944	Bill Durnan, Mon	38-5-7	2.18		& Bunny Larocque, Mon	22-3-4	2.67
1945	Bill Durnan, Mon	38-8-4	2.42	1979	Ken Dryden, Mon	30-10-7	2.30
1946	Bill Durnan, Mon	24-11-5	2.60		& Bunny Larocque, Mon	22-7-4	2.84
1947	Bill Durnan, Mon	34-16-10	2.30	1980	Bob Sauve, Buf	20-8-4	2.36
1948	Turk Broda, Tor	32-15-13	2.38		& Don Edwards, Buf.	27-9-12	2.57
1949	Bill Durnan, Mon	28-23-9	2.10	1981	Richard Sevigny, Mon	20-4-3	2.40
1950	Bill Durnan, Mon	26-21-17	2.20		Denis Herron, Mon	6-9-6	3.50
1951	Al Rollins, Tor	27-5-8	1.77		& Bunny Larocque, Mon	16-9-3	3.03
1952	Terry Sawchuk, Det	44-14-12	1.90	1982	Billy Smith, NYI	32-9-4	2.97
1953	Terry Sawchuk, Det	32-15-16	1.90	1983	Pete Peeters, Bos.	40-11-9	2.36
1954	Harry Lumley, Tor	32-24-13	1.86	1984	Tom Barrasso, Buf.	26-12-3	2.84
1955	Terry Sawchuk, Det	40-17-11	1.96	1985	Pelle Lindbergh, Phi	40-17-7	3.02
1956	Jacques Plante, Mon	42-12-10	1.86	1986	John Vanbiesbrouck, NYR	31-21-5	3.32
1957	Jacques Plante, Mon	31-18-12	2.02	1987	Ron Hextall, Phi	37-21-6	3.00
1958	Jacques Plante, Mon	34-14-8	2.11	1988	Grant Fuhr, Edm	40-24-9	3.43
1959	Jacques Plante, Mon	38-16-13	2.16	1989	Patrick Roy, Mon	33-5-6	2.47
1960	Jacques Plante, Mon	40-17-12	2.54	1990	Patrick Roy, Mon	31-16-5	2.53
1961	Johnny Bower, Tor	33-15-10	2.50	1991	Ed Belfour, Chi	43-19-7	2.47
1962	Jacques Plante, Mon	42-14-14	2.37	1992	Patrick Roy, Mon	36-22-8	2.36
1963	Glenn Hall, Chi	30-20-16	2.55	1993	Ed Belfour, Chi	41-18-11	2.59
1964	Charlie Hodge, Mon	33-18-11	2.26	1994	Dominik Hasek, Buf	30-20-6	1.95
1965	Johnny Bower, Tor	13-13-8	2.38	1995	Dominik Hasek, Buf	19-14-7	2.11
	& Terry Sawchuk, Tor	17-13-6	2.56	1996	Jim Carey, Wash	35-24-9	2.26
1966	Gump Worsley, Mon	29-14-6	2.36	1997	Dominik Hasek, Buf	37-20-10	2.27
	& Charlie Hodge, Mon	12-7-2	2.58	1998	Dominik Hasek, Buf	33-23-13	2.09
1967	Glenn Hall, Chi	19-5-5	2.38	1999	Dominik Hasek, Buf	30-18-14	1.87
	& Denis Dejordy, Chi	22-12-7	2.46	2000	Olaf Kolzig, Wash	41-20-11	2.24

Lady Byng Memorial Trophy

Awarded to the player "adjudged to have exhibited the best type of sportsmanship and gentlemanly conduct combined with a high standard of playing ability" and named after Lady Evelyn Byng, the wife of former Canadian Governor General (1921-26) Baron Byng of Vimy. Winners selected by PHWA.

Multiple winners: Frank Boucher (7); Wayne Gretzky (5); Red Kelly (4); Bobby Bauer, Mike Bossy and Alex Delvecchio (3); Johnny Bucyk, Marcel Dionne, Ron Francis, Paul Kariya, Dave Keon, Stan Mikita, Joey Mullen, Frank Nighbor, Jean Ratelle, Clint Smith and Sid Smith (2).

Year	Year	Year
1925 Frank Nighbor, Ott., C	1951 Red Kelly, Det., D	1977 Marcel Dionne, LA, C
1926 Frank Nighbor, Ott., C	1952 Sid Smith, Tor., LW	1978 Butch Goring, LA, C
1927 Billy Burch, NYA, C	1953 Red Kelly, Det., D	1979 Bob MacMillan, Atl., RW
1928 Frank Boucher, NYR, C	1954 Red Kelly, Det., D	1980 Wayne Gretzky, Edm., C
1929 Frank Boucher, NYR, C	1955 Sid Smith, Tor., LW	1981 Rick Kehoe, Pit., RW
1930 Frank Boucher, NYR, C	1956 Earl Reibel, Det., C	1982 Rick Middleton, Bos., RW
1931 Frank Boucher, NYR, C	1957 Andy Hebenton, NYR, RW	1983 Mike Bossy, NYI, RW
1932 Joe Primeau, Tor., C	1958 Camille Henry, NYR, LW	1984 Mike Bossy, NYI, RW
1933 Frank Boucher, NYR, C	1959 Alex Delvecchio, Det., LW	1985 Jari Kurri, Edm., RW
1934 Frank Boucher, NYR, C	1960 Don McKenney, Bos., C	1986 Mike Bossy, NYI, RW
1935 Frank Boucher, NYR, C	1961 Red Kelly, Tor., D	1987 Joey Mullen, Calg., RW
1936 Doc Romnes, Chi., F	1962 Dave Keon, Tor., C	1988 Mats Naslund, Mon., LW
1937 Marty Barry, Det., C	1963 Dave Keon, Tor., C	1989 Joey Mullen, Calg., RW
1938 Gordie Drillon, Tor., RW	1964 Ken Wharram, Chi., RW	1990 Brett Hull, St.L., RW
1939 Clint Smith, NYR, C	1965 Bobby Hull, Chi., LW	1991 Wayne Gretzky, LA, C
1940 Bobby Bauer, Bos., RW	1966 Alex Delvecchio, Det., LW	1992 Wayne Gretzky, LA, C
1941 Bobby Bauer, Bos., RW	1967 Stan Mikita, Chi., C	1993 Pierre Turgeon, NYI, C
1942 Syl Apps, Tor., C	1968 Stan Mikita, Chi., C	1994 Wayne Gretzky, LA, C
1943 Max Bentley, Chi., C	1969 Alex Delvecchio, Det., LW	1995 Ron Francis, Pit., C
1944 Clint Smith, Chi., C	1970 Phil Goyette, St.L., C	1996 Paul Kariya, Ana., LW
1945 Bill Mosienko, Chi., RW	1971 Johnny Bucyk, Bos., LW	1997 Paul Kariya, Ana., LW
1946 Toe Blake, Mon., LW	1972 Jean Ratelle, NYR, C	1998 Ron Francis, Pit., C
1947 Bobby Bauer, Bos., RW	1973 Gilbert Perreault, Buf., C	1999 Wayne Gretzky, NYR, C
1948 Buddy O'Connor, NYR, C	1974 Johnny Bucyk, Bos., LW	2000 Pavol Demitra, St.L, RW
1949 Bill Quackenbush, Det., D	1975 Marcel Dionne, Det., C	
1950 Edgar Laprade, NYR, C	1976 Jean Ratelle, NY-Bos., C	

Note: Bill Quackenbush and Red Kelly are the only defensemen to win the Lady Byng.

James Norris Memorial Trophy

Awarded to the most outstanding defenseman of the year and named after James Norris, the late Detroit Red Wings owner-president. Winners selected by PHWA.

Multiple winners: Bobby Orr (8); Doug Harvey (7); Ray Bourque (5); Chris Chelios, Paul Coffey, Pierre Pilote and Denis Potvin (3); Rod Langway, Brian Leetch and Larry Robinson (2).

Year	Year	Year
1954 Red Kelly, Detroit	1970 Bobby Orr, Boston	1986 Paul Coffey, Edmonton
1955 Doug Harvey, Montreal	1971 Bobby Orr, Boston	1987 Ray Bourque, Boston
1956 Doug Harvey, Montreal	1972 Bobby Orr, Boston	1988 Ray Bourque, Boston
1957 Doug Harvey, Montreal	1973 Bobby Orr, Boston	1989 Chris Chelios, Montreal
1958 Doug Harvey, Montreal	1974 Bobby Orr, Boston	1990 Ray Bourque, Boston
1959 Tom Johnson, Montreal	1975 Bobby Orr, Boston	1991 Ray Bourque, Boston
1960 Doug Harvey, Montreal	1976 Denis Potvin, NY Islanders	1992 Brian Leetch, NY Rangers
1961 Doug Harvey, Montreal	1977 Larry Robinson, Montreal	1993 Chris Chelios, Chicago
1962 Doug Harvey, NY Rangers	1978 Denis Potvin, NY Islanders	1994 Ray Bourque, Boston
1963 Pierre Pilote, Chicago	1979 Denis Potvin, NY Islanders	1995 Paul Coffey, Detroit
1964 Pierre Pilote, Chicago	1980 Larry Robinson, Montreal	1996 Chris Chelios, Chicago
1965 Pierre Pilote, Chicago	1981 Randy Carlyle, Pittsburgh	1997 Brian Leetch, NY Rangers
1966 Jacques Laperriere, Montreal	1982 Doug Wilson, Chicago	1998 Rob Blake, Los Angeles
1967 Harry Howell, NY Rangers	1983 Rod Langway, Washington	1999 Al MacInnis, St. Louis
1968 Bobby Orr, Boston	1984 Rod Langway, Washington	2000 Chris Pronger, St. Louis
1969 Bobby Orr, Boston	1985 Paul Coffey, Edmonton	

Frank Selke Trophy

Awarded to the outstanding defensive forward of the year and named after the late Montreal Canadiens general manager. Winners selected by the PHWA.

Multiple winners: Bob Gainey (4); Guy Carbonneau (3); Sergei Fedorov and Jere Lehtinen (2).

Year	Year	Year
1978 Bob Gainey, Mon., LW	1986 Troy Murray, Chi., C	1994 Sergei Fedorov, Det., C
1979 Bob Gainey, Mon., LW	1987 Dave Poulin, Phi., C	1995 Ron Francis, Pit., C
1980 Bob Gainey, Mon., LW	1988 Guy Carbonneau, Mon., C	1996 Sergei Fedorov, Det., C
1981 Bob Gainey, Mon., LW	1989 Guy Carbonneau, Mon., C	1997 Michael Peca, Buf., C
1982 Steve Kasper, Bos., C	1990 Rick Meagher, St.L., C	1998 Jere Lehtinen, Dal., RW
1983 Bobby Clarke, Phi., C	1991 Dirk Graham, Chi., RW	1999 Jere Lehtinen, Dal., RW
1984 Doug Jarvis, Wash., C	1992 Guy Carbonneau, Mon., C	2000 Steve Yzerman, Det. C
1985 Craig Ramsay, Buf., LW	1993 Doug Gilmour, Tor., C	

Annual Awards (Cont.)
Jack Adams Award

Awarded to the coach "adjudged to have contributed the most to his team's success" and named after the late Detroit Red Wings coach and general manager. Winners selected by NHL Broadcasters' Assn.; (*) indicates division champion.

Multiple winners: Pat Burns (3); Scotty Bowman, Jacques Demers and Pat Quinn (2).

Year		Improvement		Year		Improvement	
1974	Fred Shero, Phi	37-30-11	to 50-16-12*	1988	Jacques Demers, Det	34-36-10	to 41-28-11*
1975	Bob Pulford, LA	41-14-23	to 37-35-8	1989	Pat Burns, Mon	45-22-13	to 53-18- 9*
1976	Don Cherry, Bos	40-26-14	to 48-15-17*	1990	Bob Murdoch, Win	26-42-12	to 37-32-11
1977	Scotty Bowman, Mon	58-11-11*	to 60- 8-12*	1991	Brian Sutter, St.L	37-34-9	to 47-22-11
1978	Bobby Kromm, Det	6-55-9	to 32-34-14	1992	Pat Quinn, Van	28-43-9	to 42-26-12*
1979	Al Arbour, NYI	48-17-15*	to 51-15-14*	1993	Pat Burns, Tor	30-43-7	to 44-29-11
1980	Pat Quinn, Phi	40-25-15	to 48-12-20*	1994	Jacques Lemaire, NJ	40-37-7	to 47-25-12
1981	Red Berenson, St.L	34-34-12	to 45-18-17*	1995	Marc Crawford, Que	34-42-8	to 30-13-5*
1982	Tom Watt, Win	9-57-14	to 33-33-14	1996	Scotty Bowman, Det	33-11-4*	to 62-13-7*
1983	Orval Tessier, Chi	30-38-12	to 47-23-10	1997	Ted Nolan, Buf	33-42-7	to 40-30-12*
1984	Bryan Murray, Wash	39-25-16	to 48-27-5	1998	Pat Burns, Bos	26-47-9	to 39-30-13
1985	Mike Keenan, Phi	44-26-10	to 53-20-7*	1999	Jacques Martin, Ott	34-33-15	to 44-23-15*
1986	Glen Sather, Edm	49-20-11*	to 56-17-7*	2000	Joel Quenneville, St.L	37-32-13	to 51-20-11*
1987	Jacques Demers, Det	17-57-6	to 34-36-10				

Lester B. Pearson Award

Awarded to the season's most outstanding player and named after the former diplomat, Nobel Peace Prize winner and Canadian prime minister. Winners selected by the NHL Players Assn.

Multiple winners: Wayne Gretzky (5); Mario Lemieux (4); Guy Lafleur (3); Marcel Dionne, Phil Esposito, Dominik Hasek, Jaromir Jagr and Mark Messier (2).

Year		Year		Year	
1971	Phil Esposito, Bos., C	1981	Mike Liut, St.L., G	1991	Brett Hull, St.L., RW
1972	Jean Ratelle, NYR, C	1982	Wayne Gretzky, Edm., C	1992	Mark Messier, NYR, C
1973	Bobby Clarke, Phi., C	1983	Wayne Gretzky, Edm., C	1993	Mario Lemieux, Pit., C
1974	Phil Esposito, Bos., C	1984	Wayne Gretzky, Edm., C	1994	Sergei Fedorov, Det., C
1975	Bobby Orr, Bos., D	1985	Wayne Gretzky, Edm., C	1995	Eric Lindros, Phi., C
1976	Guy Lafleur, Mon., RW	1986	Mario Lemieux, Pit., C	1996	Mario Lemieux, Pit., C
1977	Guy Lafleur, Mon., RW	1987	Wayne Gretzky, Edm., C	1997	Dominik Hasek, Buf., G
1978	Guy Lafleur, Mon., RW	1988	Mario Lemieux, Pit., C	1998	Dominik Hasek, Buf., G
1979	Marcel Dionne, LA, C	1989	Steve Yzerman, Det., C	1999	Jaromir Jagr, Pit., RW
1980	Marcel Dionne, LA, C	1990	Mark Messier, Edm., C	2000	Jaromir Jagr, Pit., RW

Bill Masterton Trophy

Awarded to the player who "best exemplifies the qualities of perseverance, sportsmanship and dedication to hockey" and named after the 29-year-old rookie center of the Minnesota North Stars who died of a head injury sustained in a 1968 NHL game. Presented by the PHWA.

Year		Year		Year	
1968	Claude Provost, Mon., RW	1979	Serge Savard, Mon., D	1990	Gord Kluzak, Bos., D
1969	Ted Hampson, Oak., C	1980	Al MacAdam, Min., RW	1991	Dave Taylor, LA, RW
1970	Pit Martin, Chi., C	1981	Blake Dunlop, St.L., C	1992	Mark Fitzpatrick, NYI, G
1971	Jean Ratelle, NYR, C	1982	Chico Resch, Colo., G	1993	Mario Lemieux, Pit., C
1972	Bobby Clarke, Phi., C	1983	Lanny McDonald, Calg., RW	1994	Cam Neely, Bos., RW
1973	Lowell MacDonald, Pit., RW	1984	Brad Park, Det., D	1995	Pat LaFontaine, Buf., C
1974	Henri Richard, Mon., C	1985	Anders Hedberg, NYR, RW	1996	Gary Roberts, Calg., LW
1975	Don Luce, Buf., C	1986	Charlie Simmer, Bos., LW	1997	Tony Granato, SJ, LW
1976	Rod Gilbert, NYR, RW	1987	Doug Jarvis, Hart., C	1998	Jamie McLennan, St.L, G
1977	Ed Westfall, NYI, RW	1988	Bob Bourne, LA, C	1999	John Cullen, TB, C
1978	Butch Goring, LA, C	1989	Tim Kerr, Phi., C	2000	Ken Daneyko, NJ, D

Number One Draft Choices

Overall first choices in the NHL draft since the league staged its first universal amateur draft in 1969. Players are listed with team that selected them; those who became Rookie of the Year are in **bold** type.

Year		Year		Year	
1969	Rejean Houle, Mon., LW	1980	Doug Wickenheiser, Mon., C	1991	Eric Lindros, Que., C
1970	**Gilbert Perreault,** Buf., C	1981	**Dale Hawerchuk,** Win., C	1992	Roman Hamrlik, TB, D
1971	Guy Lafleur, Mon., RW	1982	Gord Kluzak, Bos., D	1993	Alexandre Daigle, Ott., C
1972	Billy Harris, NYI, RW	1983	Brian Lawton, Min., C	1994	Ed Jovanovski, Fla., D
1973	**Denis Potvin,** NYI, D	1984	**Mario Lemieux,** Pit., C	1995	**Bryan Berard,** Ott., D
1974	Greg Joly, Wash., D	1985	Wendel Clark, Tor., LW/D	1996	Chris Phillips, Ott., D
1975	Mel Bridgman, Phi., C	1986	Joe Murphy, Det., C	1997	Joe Thornton, Bos., C
1976	Rick Green, Wash., D	1987	Pierre Turgeon, Buf., C	1998	Vincent Lecavalier, TB, C
1977	Dale McCourt, Det., C	1988	Mike Modano, Min., C	1999	Patrik Stefan, Atl., C
1978	**Bobby Smith,** Min., C	1989	Mats Sundin, Que., RW	2000	Rick DiPietro, NYI, G
1979	Rob Ramage, Colo., D	1990	Owen Nolan, Que., RW		

World Hockey Association
WHA Finals

The World Hockey Association began play in 1972-73 as a 12-team rival of the 56-year-old NHL. The WHA played for the AVCO World Trophy in its seven playoff finals (Avco Financial Services underwrote the playoffs).

Multiple winners: Winnipeg (3); Houston (2).

Year	Winner	Head Coach	Series	Loser	Head Coach
1973	New England Whalers	Jack Kelley	4-1 (WWLWW)	Winnipeg Jets	Bobby Hull
1974	Houston Aeros	Bill Dineen	4-0	Chicago Cougars	Pat Stapleton
1975	Houston Aeros	Bill Dineen	4-0	Quebec Nordiques	Jean-Guy Gendron
1976	Winnipeg Jets	Bobby Kromm	4-0	Houston Aeros	Bill Dineen
1977	Quebec Nordiques	Marc Boileau	4-3 (LWLWWLW)	Winnipeg Jets	Bobby Kromm
1978	Winnipeg Jets	Larry Hillman	4-0	NE Whalers	Harry Neale
1979	Winnipeg Jets	Larry Hillman	4-2 (WWLWLW)	Edmonton Oilers	Glen Sather

Playoff MVPs—1973—No award; **1974**—No award; **1975**—Ron Grahame, Houston, G; **1976**—Ulf Nilsson, Winnipeg, C; **1977**—Serg Bernier, Quebec, C; **1978**—Bobby Guindon, Winnipeg, C; **1979**—Rich Preston, Winnipeg, RW.

Most Valuable Player
(Gordie Howe Trophy, 1976-79)

Year		G	A	Pts
1973	Bobby Hull, Win., LW	.51	52	103
1974	Gordie Howe, Hou., RW	.31	69	100
1975	Bobby Hull, Win., LW	.77	65	142
1976	Marc Tardif, Que., LW	.71	77	148
1977	Robbie Ftorek, Pho., C	.46	71	117
1978	Marc Tardif, Que., LW	.65	89	154
1979	Dave Dryden, Edm., G	.41-17-2; 2.89		

Scoring Leaders

Year		Gm	G	A	Pts
1973	Andre Lacroix, Phi.	.78	50	74	124
1974	Mike Walton, Min.	.78	57	60	117
1975	Andre Lacroix, S. Diego.	.78	41	106	147
1976	Marc Tardif, Que	.81	71	77	148
1977	Real Cloutier, Que	.76	66	75	141
1978	Marc Tardif, Que	.78	65	89	154
1979	Real Cloutier, Que	.77	75	54	129

Note: In 1979, 18 year-old Rookie of the Year Wayne Gretzky finished third in scoring (46-64—110).

Rookie of the Year

Year		G	A	Pts
1973	Terry Caffery, N. Eng., C	.39	61	100
1974	Mark Howe, Hou., LW	.38	41	79
1975	Anders Hedberg, Win., RW	.53	47	100
1976	Mark Napier, Tor., RW	.43	50	93
1977	George Lyle, N. Eng., LW	.39	33	72
1978	Kent Nilsson, Win., C	.42	65	107
1979	Wayne Gretzky, Ind.-Edm., C	.46	64	110

Best Goaltender

Year		Record	GAA
1973	Gerry Cheevers, Cleveland	.32-20-0	2.84
1974	Don McLeod, Houston	.33-13-3	2.56
1975	Ron Grahame, Houston	.33-10-0	3.03
1976	Michel Dion, Indianapolis	.14-15-1	2.74
1977	Ron Grahame, Houston	.27-10-2	2.74
1978	Al Smith, New England	.30-20-3	3.22
1979	Dave Dryden, Edmonton	.41-17-2	2.89

Best Defenseman

Year	
1973	J.C. Tremblay, Quebec
1974	Pat Stapleton, Chicago
1975	J.C. Tremblay, Quebec
1976	Paul Shmyr, Cleveland
1977	Ron Plumb, Cincinnati
1978	Lars-Erik Sjoberg, Winnipeg
1979	Rick Ley, New England

Coach of the Year

Year		Improvement	
1973	Jack Kelley, N. Eng		46-30-2*
1974	Billy Harris, Tor	.35-39-4	to 41-33-4
1975	Sandy Hucul, Pho	.Expan.	to 39-31-8
1976	Bobby Kromm, Win	.38-35-5	to 52-27-2*
1977	Bill Dineen, Hou	.53-27-0*	to 50-24-6*
1978	Bill Dineen, Hou	.50-24-6*	to 42-34-4
1979	John Brophy, Birm	.36-41-3	to 32-42-6

*Won Division.

WHA All-Star Game

The WHA All-Star Game was an Eastern Division vs Western Division contest from 1973-75. In 1976, the league's five Canadian-based teams played the nine teams in the US. Over the final three seasons–East played West in 1977; AVCO Cup champion Quebec played a WHA All-Star team in 1978; and in 1979, a full WHA All-Star team played a three-game series with Moscow Dynamo of the Soviet Union.

Year	Result	Host	Coaches	Most Valuable Player
1973	East 6, West 2	Quebec	Jack Kelley, Bobby Hull	Wayne Carleton, Ottawa
1974	East 8, West 4	St. Paul, MN	Jack Kelley, Bobby Hull	Mike Walton, Minnesota
1975	West 6, East 4	Edmonton	Bill Dineen, Ron Ryan	Rejean Houle, Quebec
1976	Canada 6, USA 1	Cleveland	Jean-Guy Gendron, Bill Dineen	Can—Real Cloutier, Que. USA—Paul Shmyr, Cleve.
1977	East 4, West 2	Hartford	Jacques Demers, Bobby Kromm	East—L. Levasseur, Min. West—W. Lindstrom, Win.
1978	Quebec 5, WHA 4	Quebec	Marc Boileau, Bill Dineen	Quebec—Marc Tardif WHA—Mark Howe, NE
1979	WHA def. Moscow Dynamo 3 games to none (4-2, 4-2, 4-3)	Edmonton	Larry Hillman, P. Iburtovich	No awards

World Championship
Men

The World Hockey Championship tournament has been played regularly since 1930. The International Ice Hockey Federation (IIHF), which governs both the World and Winter Olympic tournaments, considers the Olympic champions from 1920-68 to also be the World champions. However the IIHF has not recognized an Olympic champion as World champion since 1968. The IIHF has sanctioned separate World Championships in Olympic years three times—in 1972, 1976 and again in 1992. The world championship is officially vacant for the three Olympic years from 1980-88.

Multiple winners: Soviet Union/Russia (23); Canada (21); Sweden (7); Czechoslovakia (6) Czech Republic (3), USA (2).

Year		Year		Year		Year	
1920	Canada	1950	Canada	1967	Soviet Union	1984	Not held
1924	Canada	1951	Canada	1968	Soviet Union	1985	Czechoslovakia
1928	Canada	1952	Canada	1969	Soviet Union	1986	Soviet Union
1930	Canada	1953	Sweden	1970	Soviet Union	1987	Sweden
1931	Canada	1954	Soviet Union	1971	Soviet Union	1988	Not held
1932	Canada	1955	Canada	1972	Czechoslovakia	1989	Soviet Union
1933	United States	1956	Soviet Union	1973	Soviet Union	1990	Soviet Union
1934	Canada	1957	Sweden	1974	Soviet Union	1991	Sweden
1935	Canada	1958	Canada	1975	Soviet Union	1992	Sweden
1936	Great Britain	1959	Canada	1976	Czechoslovakia	1993	Russia
1937	Canada	1960	United States	1977	Czechoslovakia	1994	Canada
1938	Canada	1961	Canada	1978	Soviet Union	1995	Finland
1939	Canada	1962	Sweden	1979	Soviet Union	1996	Czech Republic
1940-46	Not held	1963	Soviet Union	1980	Not held	1997	Canada
1947	Czechoslovakia	1964	Soviet Union	1981	Soviet Union	1998	Sweden
1948	Canada	1965	Soviet Union	1982	Soviet Union	1999	Czech Republic
1949	Czechoslovakia	1966	Soviet Union	1983	Soviet Union	2000	Czech Republic

Women

The women's World Hockey Championship tournament is governed by the International Ice Hockey Federation (IIHF).

Multiple winners: Canada (6).

Year		Year		Year		Year	
1990	Canada	1994	Canada	1999	Canada	2000	Canada
1992	Canada	1997	Canada				

Canada vs. USSR Summits

The first competition between the Soviet National Team and the NHL took place Sept. 2-28, 1972. A team of NHL All-Stars emerged as the winner of the heralded 8-game series, but just barely—winning with a record of 4-3-1 after trailing 1-3-1.

Two years later a WHA All-Star team played the Soviet Nationals and could win only one game and tie three others in eight contests. Two other Canada vs USSR series took place during NHL All-Star breaks: the three-game Challenge Cup at New York in 1979, and the two-game Rendez-Vous '87 in Quebec City in 1987.

The NHL All-Stars played the USSR in a three-game Challenge Cup series in 1979.

1972 Team Canada vs. USSR
NHL All-Stars vs Soviet National Team.

Date	City	Result	Goaltenders
9/2	Montreal	USSR, 7-3	Tretiak/Dryden
9/4	Toronto	Canada, 4-1	Esposito/Tretiak
9/6	Winnipeg	Tie, 4-4	Tretiak/Esposito
9/8	Vancouver	USSR, 5-3	Tretiak/Dryden
9/22	Moscow	USSR, 5-4	Tretiak/Esposito
9/24	Moscow	Canada, 3-2	Dryden/Tretiak
9/26	Moscow	Canada, 4-3	Esposito/Tretiak
9/28	Moscow	Canada, 6-5	Dryden/Tretiak

Standings

	W	L	T	Pts	GF	GA
Team Canada (NHL)	4	3	1	9	32	32
Soviet Union	3	4	1	7	32	32

Leading Scorers

1. Phil Esposito, Canada, (7-6—13); **2.** Aleksandr Yakushev, USSR (7-4—11); **3.** Paul Henderson, Canada (7-2—9); **4.** Boris Shadrin, USSR (3-5—8); **5.** Valeri Kharlamov, USSR (3-4—7) and Vladimir Petrov, USSR (3-4—7); **7.** Bobby Clarke, Canada (2-4—6) and Yuri Liapkin, USSR (1-5—6).

1974 Team Canada vs. USSR
WHA All-Stars vs Soviet National Team.

Date	City	Result	Goaltenders
9/17	Quebec City	Tie, 3-3	Tretiak/Cheevers
9/19	Toronto	Canada, 4-1	Cheevers/Tretiak
9/21	Winnipeg	USSR, 8-5	Tretiak/McLeod
9/23	Vancouver	Tie, 5-5	Tretiak/Cheevers
10/1	Moscow	USSR, 3-2	Tretiak/Cheevers
10/3	Moscow	USSR, 5-2	Tretiak/Cheevers
10/5	Moscow	Tie, 4-4	Cheevers/Tretiak
10/6	Moscow	USSR, 3-2	Sidelinkov/Cheevers

Standings

	W	L	T	Pts	GF	GA
Soviet Union	4	1	3	11	32	27
Team Canada (WHA)	1	4	3	5	27	32

Leading Scorers

1. Bobby Hull, Canada (7-2—9); **2.** Aleksandr Yakushev, USSR (6-2—8), Ralph Backstrom, Canada (4-4—8) and Valeri Kharlamov, USSR (2-6—8); **5.** Gordie Howe, Canada (3-4—7), Andre Lacroix, Canada (1-6—7) and Vladimir Petrov, USSR (1-6—7).

1979 Challenge Cup Series
NHL All-Stars vs Soviet National Team

Date	City	Result	Goaltenders
2/8	New York	NHL, 4-2	K. Dryden/Tretiak
2/10	New York	USSR, 5-4	Tretiak/K. Dryden
2/11	New York	USSR, 6-0	Myshkin/Cheevers

Rendez-Vous '87
NHL All-Stars vs Soviet National Team

Date	City	Result	Goaltenders
2/11	Quebec	NHL, 4-3	Fuhr/Belosheykhin
2/13	Quebec	USSR, 5-3	Belosheykhin/Fuhr

The Canada Cup

After organizing the historic 8-game Team Canada-Soviet Union series of 1972, NHL Players Association executive director Alan Eagleson and the NHL created the Canada Cup in 1976. For the first time, the best players from the world's six major hockey powers—Canada, Czechoslovakia, Finland, Russia, Sweden and the USA—competed together in one tournament.

1976
Round Robin Standings

	W	L	T	Pts	GF	GA
Canada	4	1	0	8	22	6
Czechoslovakia	3	1	1	7	19	9
Soviet Union	2	2	1	5	23	14
Sweden	2	2	1	5	16	18
United States	1	3	1	3	14	21
Finland	1	4	0	2	16	42

Finals (Best of 3)

Date	City	Score
9/13	Toronto	Canada 6, Czechoslovakia 0
9/15	Montreal	Canada 5, Czechoslovakia 4 (OT)

Note: Darryl Sittler scored the winning goal for Canada at 11:33 in overtime to clinch the Cup, 2 games to none.

Leading Scorers

1. Victor Hluktov, USSR (5-4—9), Bobby Orr, Canada (2-7—9) and Denis Potvin, Canada (1-8—9); **4.** Bobby Hull, Canada (5-3—8) and Milan Novy, Czechoslovakia (5-3—8).

Team MVPs

Canada—Rogie Vachon
Czech.—Milan Novy
USSR—Alexandr Maltsev
Sweden—Borje Salming
USA—Robbie Ftorek
Finland—Matti Hagman
Tournament MVP—Bobby Orr, Canada

1981
Round Robin Standings

	W	L	T	Pts	GF	GA
Canada	4	0	1	9	32	13
Soviet Union	3	1	1	7	20	13
Czechoslovakia	2	1	2	6	21	13
United States	2	2	1	5	17	19
Sweden	1	4	0	2	13	20
Finland	0	4	1	1	6	31

Semifinals

Date	City	Score
9/11	Ottawa	USSR 4, Czechoslovakia 1
9/11	Montreal	Canada 4, United States 1

Finals

Date	City	Score
9/13	Montreal	USSR 8, Canada 1

Leading Scorers

1. Wayne Gretzky, Canada (5-7—12); **2.** Mike Bossy, Canada (8-3—11), Bryan Trottier, Canada (3-8—11), Guy Lafleur, Canada (2-9—11), Alexei Kasatonov, USSR (1-10—11).

All-Star Team

Goal—Vladislav Tretiak, USSR; **Defense**—Arnold Kadlec, Czech. and Alexei Kasatonov, USSR; **Forwards**—Mike Bossy, Canada, Gil Perreault, Canada, and Sergei Shepelev, USSR. **Tournament MVP**—Tretiak.

1984
Round Robin Standings

	W	L	T	Pts	GF	GA
Soviet Union	5	0	0	10	22	7
United States	3	1	1	7	21	13
Sweden	3	2	0	6	15	16
Canada	2	2	1	5	23	18
West Germany	0	4	1	1	13	29
Czechoslovakia	0	4	1	1	10	21

Semifinals

Date	City	Score
9/12	Edmonton	Sweden 9, United States 2
9/15	Montreal	Canada 3, USSR 2 (OT)

Note: Mike Bossy scored the winning goal for Canada at 12:29 in overtime.

Finals (Best of 3)

Date	City	Score
9/16	Calgary	Canada 5, Sweden 2
9/18	Edmonton	Canada 6, Sweden 5

Leading Scorers

1. Wayne Gretzky, Canada (5-7—12); **2.** Michel Goulet, Canada (5-6—11), Kent Nilsson, Sweden (3-8—11), Paul Coffey, Canada (3-8—11); **5.** Hakan Loob, Sweden (6-4—10).

All-Star Team

Goal—Vladimir Myshkin, USSR; **Defense**—Paul Coffey, Canada and Rod Langway, USA; **Forwards**—Wayne Gretzky, Canada, John Tonelli, Canada, and Sergei Makarov, USSR. **Tournament MVP**—Tonelli.

1987
Round Robin Standings

	W	L	T	Pts	GF	GA
Canada	3	0	2	8	19	13
Soviet Union	3	1	1	7	22	13
Sweden	3	2	0	6	17	14
Czechoslovakia	2	2	1	5	12	15
United States	2	3	0	4	13	14
Finland	0	5	0	0	9	23

Semifinals

Date	City	Score
9/8	Hamilton	USSR 4, Sweden 2
9/9	Montreal	Canada 5, Czechoslovakia 3

Finals (Best of 3)

Date	City	Score
9/11	Montreal	USSR 6, Canada 5 (OT)
9/13	Hamilton	Canada 6, USSR 5 (2 OT)
9/15	Hamilton	Canada 6, USSR 5

Note: In Game 1, Alexander Semak of USSR scored at 5:33 in overtime. In Game 2, Mario Lemieux of Canada scored at 10:01 in the second overtime period. Lemieux also won Game 3 on a goal with 1:26 left in regulation time.

Leading Scorers

1. Wayne Gretzky, Canada (3-18—21); **2.** Mario Lemieux, Canada (11-7—18); **3.** Sergei Makarov, USSR (7-8—15); **4.** Vladimir Krutov, USSR (7-7—14); **5.** Viacheslav Bykov, USSR (2-7—9); **6.** Ray Bourque, Canada (2-6—8).

All-Star Team

Goal—Grant Fuhr, Canada; **Defense**—Ray Bourque, Canada and Viacheslav Fetisov, USSR; **Forwards**—Wayne Gretzky, Canada, Mario Lemieux, Canada, and Vladimir Krutov, USSR. **Tournament MVP**—Gretzky.

1991

Round Robin Standings

	W	L	T	Pts	GF	GA
Canada	3	0	2	8	21	11
United States	4	1	0	8	19	15
Finland	2	2	1	5	10	13
Sweden	2	3	0	4	13	17
Soviet Union	1	3	1	3	14	14
Czechoslovakia	1	4	0	2	11	18

Semifinals

Date	City	Score
9/11	Hamilton	United States 7, Finland 3
9/12	Toronto	Canada 4, Sweden 0

Finals (Best of 3)

Date	City	Score
9/14	Montreal	Canada 4, United States 1
9/16	Hamilton	Canada 4, United States 2

Leading Scorers

1. Wayne Gretzky, Canada (4-8—12); **2.** Steve Larmer, Canada (6-5—11); **3.** Brett Hull, USA (2-7—9); **4.** Mike Modano, USA (2-7—9); **5.** Mark Messier, Canada (2-6—8).

All-Star Team

Goal—Bill Ranford, Canada; **Defense**—Al MacInnis, Canada and Chris Chelios, USA; **Forwards**—Wayne Gretzky, Canada, Jeremy Roenick, USA and Mats Sundin, Sweden. **Tournament MVP**—Bill Ranford.

The World Cup

Formed jointly by the NHL and the NHL Players Association in cooperation with the International Ice Hockey Federation. The inaugural World Cup held games in nine different cities throughout North America and Europe, the most ever by a single international hockey tournament.

1996

Round Robin Standings

European Pool	W	L	T	Pts	GF	GA
Sweden	3	0	0	6	14	3
Finland	2	1	0	4	17	11
Germany	1	2	0	2	11	15
Czech Republic	0	3	0	0	4	17

North American Pool	W	L	T	Pts	GF	GA
United States	3	0	0	6	19	8
Canada	2	1	0	4	11	10
Russia	1	2	0	2	12	14
Slovakia	0	3	0	0	10	18

Semifinals

Date	City	Score
9/7	Philadelphia	Canada 3, Sweden 2 (OT)
9/8	Ottawa	United States 5, Russia 2

Finals (Best of 3)

Date	City	Score
9/10	Philadelphia	Canada 4, United States 3 (OT)
9/12	Montreal	United States 5, Canada 2
9/14	Montreal	United States 5, Canada 2

Leading Scorers

1. Brett Hull, USA (7-4—11); **2.** John LeClair, USA (6-4—10); **3.** Mats Sundin, Sweden (4-3—7); Wayne Gretzky, Canada (3-4—7); Doug Weight, USA (3-4—7); Paul Coffey, Canada (0-7—7); Brian Leetch, USA (0-7—7).

All-Tournament Team

Goal—Mike Richter, USA; **Defense**—Calle Johansson, Sweden and Chris Chelios, USA; **Forwards**—Brett Hull, USA; John LeClair, USA and Mats Sundin, Sweden. **Tournament MVP**—Mike Richter, USA.

U.S. DIVISION I COLLEGE HOCKEY

NCAA Final Four

The NCAA Division I hockey tournament began in 1948 and was played at the Broadmoor Ice Palace in Colorado Springs from 1948-57. Since 1958, the tournament has moved around the country, stopping for consecutive years only at Boston Garden from 1972-74. Consolation games to determine third place were played from 1949-89 and discontinued in 1990.

Multiple Winners: Michigan (9); North Dakota (7); Denver and Wisconsin (5); Boston University (4); Lake Superior St., Michigan Tech and Minnesota (3); Colorado College, Cornell, Maine, Michigan St. and RPI (2).

Year	Champion	Head Coach	Score	Runner-up		Third Place		
1948	Michigan	Vic Heyliger	8-4	Dartmouth		Colorado College and Boston College		

Year	Champion	Head Coach	Score	Runner-up	Third Place	Score	Fourth Place
1949	Boston College	Snooks Kelley	4-3	Dartmouth	Michigan	10-4	Colorado Col.
1950	Colorado College	Cheddy Thompson	13-4	Boston Univ.	Michigan	10-6	Boston College
1951	Michigan	Vic Heyliger	7-1	Brown	Boston Univ.	7-4	Colorado College
1952	Michigan	Vic Heyliger	4-1	Colorado Col.	Yale	4-1	St. Lawrence
1953	Michigan	Vic Heyliger	7-3	Minnesota	RPI	6-3	Boston Univ.
1954	RPI	Ned Harkness	5-4*	Minnesota	Michigan	7-2	Boston College
1955	Michigan	Vic Heyliger	5-3	Colorado Col.	Harvard	6-3	St. Lawrence
1956	Michigan	Vic Heyliger	7-5	Michigan Tech	St. Lawrence	6-2	Boston College
1957	Colorado College	Tom Bedecki	13-6	Michigan	Clarkson	2-1†	Harvard
1958	Denver	Murray Armstrong	6-2	North Dakota	Clarkson	5-1	Harvard
1959	North Dakota	Bob May	4-3*	Michigan St.	Boston College	7-6†	St. Lawrence
1960	Denver	Murray Armstrong	5-3	Michigan Tech	Boston Univ.	7-6	St. Lawrence
1961	Denver	Murray Armstrong	12-2	St. Lawrence	Minnesota	4-3	RPI
1962	Michigan Tech	John MacInnes	7-1	Clarkson	Michigan	5-1	St. Lawrence
1963	North Dakota	Barry Thorndycraft	6-5	Denver	Clarkson	5-3	Boston College
1964	Michigan	Allen Renfrew	6-3	Denver	RPI	2-1	Providence
1965	Michigan Tech	John MacInnes	8-2	Boston College	North Dakota	9-5	Brown
1966	Michigan St.	Amo Bessone	6-1	Clarkson	Denver	4-3	Boston Univ.
1967	Cornell	Ned Harkness	4-1	Boston Univ.	Michigan St.	6-1	North Dakota
1968	Denver	Murray Armstrong	4-0	North Dakota	Cornell	6-1	Boston College
1969	Denver	Murray Armstrong	4-3	Cornell	Harvard	6-5†	Michigan Tech
1970	Cornell	Ned Harkness	6-4	Clarkson	Wisconsin	6-5	Michigan Tech
1971	Boston Univ.	Jack Kelley	4-2	Minnesota	Denver	1-0	Harvard
1972	Boston Univ.	Jack Kelley	4-0	Cornell	Wisconsin	5-2	Denver

Year	Champion	Head Coach	Score	Runner-up	Third Place	Score	Fourth Place
1973	Wisconsin	Bob Johnson	4-2	Denver	Boston College	3-1	Cornell
1974	Minnesota	Herb Brooks	4-2	Michigan Tech	Boston Univ.	7-5	Harvard
1975	Michigan Tech	John MacInnes	6-1	Minnesota	Boston Univ.	10-5	Harvard
1976	Minnesota	Herb Brooks	6-4	Michigan Tech	Brown	8-7	Boston Univ.
1977	Wisconsin	Bob Johnson	6-5*	Michigan	Boston Univ.	6-5	N. Hampshire
1978	Boston Univ.	Jack Parker	5-3	Boston College	Bowl. Green	4-3	Wisconsin
1979	Minnesota	Herb Brooks	4-3	North Dakota	Dartmouth	7-3	N. Hampshire
1980	North Dakota	Gino Gasparini	5-2	N. Michigan	Dartmouth	8-4	Cornell
1981	Wisconsin	Bob Johnson	6-3	Minnesota	Mich. Tech	5-2	N. Michigan
1982	North Dakota	Gino Gasparini	5-2	Wisconsin	Northeastern	10-4	N. Hampshire
1983	Wisconsin	Jeff Sauer	6-2	Harvard	Providence	4-3	Minnesota
1984	Bowling Green	Jerry York	5-4*	Minn-Duluth	North Dakota	6-5†	Michigan St.
1985	RPI	Mike Addesa	2-1	Providence	Minn-Duluth	7-6†	Boston College
1986	Michigan St.	Ron Mason	6-5	Harvard	Minnesota	6-4	Denver
1987	North Dakota	Gino Gasparini	5-3	Michigan St.	Minnesota	6-3	Harvard
1988	Lake Superior St.	Frank Anzalone	4-3*	St. Lawrence	Maine	5-2	Minnesota
1989	Harvard	Billy Cleary	4-3*	Minnesota	Michigan St.	7-4	Maine

Year	Champion	Head Coach	Score	Runner-up	Third Place
1990	Wisconsin	Jeff Sauer	7-3	Colgate	Boston College and Boston Univ.
1991	Northern Michigan	Rick Comley	8-7*	Boston Univ.	Maine and Clarkson
1992	Lake Superior St.	Jeff Jackson	5-3	Wisconsin	Michigan and Michigan St.
1993	Maine	Shawn Walsh	5-4	Lake Superior St.	Boston Univ. and Michigan
1994	Lake Superior St.	Jeff Jackson	9-1	Boston Univ.	Harvard and Minnesota
1995	Boston Univ.	Jack Parker	6-2	Maine	Michigan and Minnesota
1996	Michigan	Red Berenson	3-2*	Colorado Col.	Vermont and Boston Univ.
1997	North Dakota	Dean Blais	6-4	Boston Univ.	Colorado College and Michigan
1998	Michigan	Red Berenson	3-2*	Boston College	New Hampshire and Ohio St.
1999	Maine	Shawn Walsh	3-2*	New Hampshire	Boston College and Michigan St.
2000	North Dakota	Dean Blais	4-2	Boston College	St. Lawrence and Maine

*Championship game overtime goals:1954—1:54; **1959**—4:22; **1977**—0: 23; **1984**—7:11 in 4th OT; **1988**—4:46; **1989**—4:16; **1991**—1:57 in 3rd OT; **1996**—3:35; **1998**—17:51; **1999**—10:50.
†Consolation game overtimes ended in 1st OT except in 1957, '59, and '69, which all ended in 2nd OT.
Note: Runners-up Denver (1973) and Wisconsin (1992) had participation voided by the NCAA for using ineligible players.

Most Outstanding Player

The Most Outstanding Players of each NCAA Div. I tournament since 1948. Winners of the award who did not play for the tournament champion are in **bold** type. In 1960, three players, none on the winning team, shared the award.
   Multiple Winners: Lou Angotti and Marc Behrend (2).

Year		Year		Year	
1948	**Joe Riley,** Dartmouth, F	1965	Gary Milroy, Mich. Tech, F	1984	Gary Kruzich, Bowl. Green, G
1949	**Dick Desmond,** Dart., G	1966	Gaye Cooley, Mich. St., G	1985	**Chris Terreri**, Prov., G
1950	**Ralph Bevins,** Boston U., G	1967	Walt Stanowski, Cornell, D	1986	Mike Donnelly, Mich. St., F
1951	**Ed Whiston,** Brown, G	1968	Gerry Powers, Denver, G	1987	Tony Hrkac, N. Dakota, F
1952	**Ken Kinsley,** Colo. Col., G	1969	Keith Magnuson, Denver, D	1988	Bruce Hoffort, Lk. Superior, G
1953	John Matchetts, Mich., F	1970	Dan Lodboa, Cornell, D	1989	Ted Donato, Harvard, F
1954	Abbie Moore, RPI, F	1971	Dan Brady, Boston U., G	1990	Chris Tancill, Wisconsin, F
1955	**Phil Hilton,** Colo. Col., D	1972	Tim Regan, Boston, U., G	1991	Scott Beattie, No. Mich., F
1956	Lorne Howes, Mich., G	1973	Dean Talafous, Wisc., F	1992	Paul Constantin, Lk. Superior, F
1957	Bob McCusker, Colo. Col., F	1974	Brad Shelstad, Minn., G	1993	Jim Montgomery, Maine, F
1958	Murray Massier, Denver, F	1975	Jim Warden, Mich. Tech, G	1994	Sean Tallaire, Lk. Superior, F
1959	Reg Morelli, N. Dakota, F	1976	Tom Vanelli, Minn., F	1995	Chris O'Sullivan, Boston U., F
1960	**Lou Angotti,** Mich. Tech, F;	1977	Julian Baretta, Wisc., G	1996	Brendan Morrison, Michigan, F
	Bob Marquis, Boston U., F;	1978	Jack O'Callahan, Boston U., D	1997	Matt Henderson, N. Dakota, F
	& **Barry Urbanski,** BU, G	1979	Steve Janaszak, Minn., F	1998	Marty Turco, Michigan, G
1961	Bill Masterton, Denver, F	1980	Doug Smail, N. Dakota, F	1999	Alfie Michaud, Maine, G
1962	Lou Angotti, Mich. Tech, F	1981	Marc Behrend, Wisc., G	2000	Lee Goren, N. Dakota, F
1963	Al McLean, N. Dakota, F	1982	Phil Sykes, N. Dakota, F		
1964	Bob Gray, Michigan, G	1983	Marc Behrend, Wisc., G		

Hobey Baker Award

College hockey's Player of the Year award; voted on by a national panel of sportswriters, broadcasters, college coaches and pro scouts. First presented in 1981 by the Decathlon Athletic Club of Bloomington, Minn., in the name of the Princeton collegiate hockey and football star who was killed in a plane crash.

Year		Year		Year	
1981	Neal Broten, Minnesota, F	1988	Robb Stauber, Minnesota, G	1995	Brian Holzinger, Bowl. Green, F
1982	George McPhee, Bowl. Green, F	1989	Lane MacDonald, Harvard, F	1996	Brian Bonin, Minnesota, F
1983	Mark Fusco, Harvard, D	1990	Kip Miller, Michigan St., F	1997	Brendan Morrison, Michigan, F
1984	Tom Kurvers, Minn-Duluth, D	1991	Dave Emma, Boston College, F	1998	Chris Drury, Boston U., F
1985	Bill Watson, Minn-Duluth, F	1992	Scott Pellerin, Maine, F	1999	Jason Krog, UNH, F
1986	Scott Fusco, Harvard, F	1993	Paul Kariya, Maine, F	2000	Mike Mottau, Boston College, D
1987	Tony Hrkac, North Dakota, F	1994	Chris Marinucci, Minn-Duluth, F		

Coach of the Year

The Penrose Memorial Trophy, voted on by the American Hockey Coaches Association and first presented in 1951 in the name of Colorado gold and copper magnate Spencer T. Penrose. Penrose built the Broadmoor hotel and athletic complex in Colorado Springs that originally hosted the NCAA hockey championship from 1948-57.

Multiple winners: Len Ceglarski and Charlie Holt (3); Rick Comley, Eddie Jeremiah, Snooks Kelly, John MacInnes, Joe Marsh, Jack Parker, Jack Riley and Cooney Weiland (2).

Year
1951 Eddie Jeremiah, Dartmouth
1952 Cheddy Thompson, Colo. Col.
1953 John Mariucci, Minnesota
1954 Vic Heyliger, Michigan
1955 Cooney Weiland, Harvard
1956 Bill Harrison, Clarkson
1957 Jack Riley, Army
1958 Harry Cleverly, BU
1959 Snooks Kelly, BC

1960 Jack Riley, Army
1961 Murray Armstrong, Denver
1962 Jack Kelley, Colby
1963 Tony Frasca, Colorado Col.
1964 Tom Eccleston, Providence
1965 Jim Fulllerton, Brown
1966 Amo Bessone, Michigan St.
    & Len Ceglarski, Clarkson
1967 Eddie Jeremiah, Dartmouth
1968 Ned Harkness, Cornell

Year
1969 Charlie Holt, New Hampshire

1970 John MacInnes, Michigan Tech
1971 Cooney Weiland, Harvard
1972 Snooks Kelly, BC
1973 Len Ceglarski, BC
1974 Charlie Holt, New Hampshire
1975 Jack Parker, BU
1976 John MacInnes, Michigan Tech
1977 Jerry York, Clarkson
1978 Jack Parker, BU
1979 Charlie Holt, New Hampshire

1980 Rick Comley, No. Michigan
1981 Bill O'Flarety, Clarkson
1982 Fern Flaman, Northeastern
1983 Bill Cleary, Harvard
1984 Mike Sertich, Minn-Duluth
1985 Len Ceglarski, BC
1986 Ralph Backstrom, Denver
1987 Gino Gasparini, N. Dakota

Year
1988 Frank Anzalone, Lk. Superior
1989 Joe Marsh, St. Lawrence

1990 Terry Slater, Colgate
1991 Rick Comley, No. Michigan
1992 Ron Mason, Michigan St.
1993 George Gwozdecky, Miami-OH
1994 Don Lucia, Colorado Col.
1995 Shawn Walsh, Maine
1996 Bruce Crowder, UMass-Lowell
1997 Dean Blais, N. Dakota
1998 Tim Taylor, Yale
1999 Dick Umile, UNH

2000 Joe Marsh, St. Lawrence
Note: 1960 winner Jack Riley won the award for coaching the USA to its first hockey gold medal in the Winter Olympics at Squaw Valley.

All-Time Tournament Appearances

	App	Record		App	Record
Boston Univ.	25	33-29-0	Providence	7	9-12-0
Michigan	23	36-16-0	N. Michigan	7	8-8-0
Minnesota	22	28-24-0	Dartmouth	5	4-5-0
Boston College	21	20-30-0	Minn.-Duluth	4	5-6-0
Michigan St.	20	23-23-1	Brown	4	2-5-0
Wisconsin	18	29-16-1	Northeastern	3	3-3-1
North Dakota	17	28-13-0	UMass-Lowell	3	2-3-1
Clarkson	17	12-20-0	Ala-Anchorage	3	2-5-0
Harvard	16	14-24-1	Vermont	3	1-4-0
Denver	14	19-12-0	W. Michigan	3	0-4-0
Colorado Coll.	14	12-15-0	Colgate	2	3-2-0
St. Lawrence	14	6-23-0	Ohio St.	2	2-2-0
Cornell	11	10-12-0	Yale	2	1-2-0
New Hampshire	11	7-15-0	St. Cloud St.	2	0-3-0
Lake Superior St.	10	20-11-1	Miami-OH.	2	0-2-0
Michigan Tech	10	13-9-0	Merrimack	1	2-2-0
Maine	9	19-11-0	Niagara	1	1-1-0
Bowling Green	9	8-12-1	Princeton	1	0-1-0
RPI	8	8-8-1			

Note: The NCAA voided tournament participation of Denver in 1973 and Wisconsin in 1992 for using ineligible players.

NCAA All-Time Team

To celebrate the 50th anniversary of the NCAA tournament in 1997, the NCAA announced its 50th Anniversary Team and introduced it during the 1997 championship game in Milwaukee. The team was chosen by current Division I coaches, coaches of teams that have participated in the NCAA tournament, and members of the Division I Hockey Committee. Players named to the team had to have played in at least one NCAA tournament game. Tournament years are listed below.

Forwards

Tony Amonte, Boston Univ., 1981, '83
Lou Angotti, Michigan Tech, 1960, '62
Red Berenson, Michigan, 1962
Bill Cleary, Harvard, 1955
Tony Hrkac, North Dakota, 1987
Paul Kariya, Maine, 1993
Bill Masterton, Denver, 1960, '61
John Matchetts, Michigan, 1951, '53
John Mayasich, Minnesota, 1953, '54
Jim Montgomery, Maine, 1990, '91, '92, '93
Tom Rendall, Michigan, 1955, '56, '57
Phil Sykes, North Dakota, 1979, '80, '82

Defensemen

Chris Chelios, Wisconsin, 1982, '83
Bruce Driver, Wisconsin, 1981, '82, '83
George Konik, Denver, 1960, '61
Dan Lodboa, Cornell, 1970
Keith Magnuson, Denver, 1968, '69
Jack O'Callahan, Boston Univ., 1976, '77, '78

Goaltenders

Marc Behrend, Wisconsin, 1981, '83
Ken Dryden, Cornell, 1967, '68, '69
Chris Terreri, Providence, 1983, '85

College Sports

Double winner **Brad Hauser** helped Stanford snap Arkansas' men's outdoor track championship streak at eight.

Pictures and Frames

Far too many team van crashes marred the world of college athletics this year.

by

Steve Cyphers

The picture of big-time college sports is found on the screen of prime time TV. Top of the line treatment and chartered jets. Pampered athletes who aspire to the "next level" while wading through the scandals that come with the scrutiny.

But that glitzy picture is framed by the reality found in Divisions II and III with twice as many NCAA member schools (655) as Division I (318). Down here, athletes get little or no scholarship money and even less exposure. The "love of the game" drives them to compete and more often than not, they get there by way of buses . . . or vans.

Kenyon College in Gambier, Ohio, is one of those Division III schools. Entering the 1999-2000 season, the Kenyon

Steve Cyphers is a reporter for ESPN's *SportsCenter* and *College GameDay*.

Ladies amassed 16 consecutive swimming and diving national championships, the longest streak in women's college sports at any level.

But on the night of January 13, 2000, the streak became meaningless. Returning home from a meet in North Carolina, less than an hour away from campus, the last van in the caravan carrying the Kenyon swimming team hit a patch of ice. Careening out of control the van flipped and rolled several times before coming to a stop. And Molly Hatcher — the middle child of seven, the outgoing senior captain from Evanston, Illinois — was killed. Her younger sister Emily, a freshman, was among the other ten passengers who survived.

With the national championships less than two months away, competition and practice gave way to grief and pain. Meets were postponed. Training resumed when swimmers were ready to return to the water. For

Philip Williams/NCAA Photos

In an emotional ceremony, the **Kenyon Ladies** stood upon the podium and celebrated their 17th consecutive Division III women's swimming and diving championship. The Ladies dedicated their win to teammate Molly Hatcher, who was killed earlier in the season in a team van accident.

some it took days. For others, weeks.

Sadly, in just a two month period, the Kenyon tragedy was one of five college sports-related van accidents. Four athletes died when a Prairie View A&M van carrying members of the track team rolled near Karnack, Texas. Students from Wisconsin-Oshkosh (swimming), Urbana (basketball) and DePaul (track) were also injured in crashes. The rash of serious accidents might have been the most important yet under-reported story of the year. But across the country schools re-evaluated and, in many cases, revised travel procedure and policy. None wants to suffer the way others had.

Seventeen Kenyon Ladies qualified for the Division III national championships at Emory University in early March. Eighteen . . . when you count the inspirational presence of the captain, Molly Hatcher.

"We had to keep going to keep her alive in us," said Erica Carroll, who was in Molly's van that January night. Carroll won the 100-yard butterfly and 100-yard backstroke. She also swam on the school's two winning relay teams. Against enormous odds the Ladies built a commanding lead during the first day of competition. The meet ended with Kenyon claiming its 17th consecutive title. The winning margin over three-time runner-up Denison was even greater than the previous year. When it was over, when it was time to accept another championship trophy, the team posed for one more picture. A picture of victory and joy. A picture, framed in loss and sorrow. ■

With a launch of 200 feet, nine inches in the discus, UCLA's **Seilala Sua** became the first woman to win four titles in a single field event in the NCAA Championships. She also won the shot put for the second consecutive year. Her six titles make her the all-time winningest female athlete at the outdoor championships.

Steve Cyphers' Top Highlights of the 2000 College Sports Season

10. **Former NBA stars** Sidney Moncrief and Clyde Drexler find the going rougher than when they were in college and make less than graceful exits from their coaching positions at Arkansas-Little Rock and Houston, respectively. Their teams finish a combined 13-46 for the year.

9. **The venerable Bill Guthridge** exits North Carolina after leading the Heels to a surprising Final Four run, but didn't it seem like it took a long time to settle on Matt Doherty as his replacement? (p.s. Yes, Roy Williams really does like Lawrence and his players).

8. **Don't mess with Alaska-Fairbanks.** The Nanooks win their second straight National Championship in men's and women's rifle. Kelly Mansfield successfully defends her title in air rifle but not in smallbore. Nebraska freshman Nicole Allaire upsets her, setting a meet record in the process.

7. **Nebraska overhauls its backfield** after the first two weeks of the season. Running back DeAngelo Evans quits the team, quarterback Bobby Newcombe is shifted to wingback and Eric Crouch is given the starting quarterback job. By the end of the year the Huskers were playing as well as (maybe better than) any team in the nation.

AP/Wide World Photos

Georgia senior co-captain **Kristy Kowal** ended her collegiate career in style, winning three individual events to pace the Bulldogs to their second consecutive Division I swimming and diving title. She was named co-NCAA Swimmer of the Year, along with teammate Courtney Shealey.

6. **But could it match Mt. Union?** On a glorious October afternoon, the Purple Raiders beat Otterbein, 44-20, for their 48th consecutive win, breaking the NCAA record held by the Oklahoma teams of the 1950s. They would win six more to bring the streak to 54, but it ended when Rowan beat them, 24-17, in the semifinal round of the Division III playoffs.

5. After 32 years, one of the really good guys and really good coaches resigns. **Jerry Sandusky**, the Penn State defensive coordinator who helped the Nittany Lions earn the "Linebacker U" moniker, decides to devote more time to his "The Second Mile" foundation which serves disadvantaged youth.

4. **California's Anthony Ervin** sweeps the 50- and 100-meter freestyle races at the NCAA Division I Swimming and Diving Championships and sets a new world record in the 50. But he really makes a splash in August when he becomes the first swimmer of African-American descent to make the U.S. Olympic team.

3. **Stanford's Gabe Jennings** wins the 1500-meter event at the Division I Outdoor Track and Field Championships in June to spark the Cardinal to their first title since 1934...and then wins the same event six weeks later at the U.S. Olympic Trials to open the eyes of the country to this quirky free-spirit who was raised and schooled in a commune.

2. **Northwest Missouri State** successfully defends its Division II football crown, but not before some last-second heroics to force overtime with Carson-Newman. The teams then play four overtime periods before the Bearcats pull out a 58-52 victory in one of the most exciting games I've ever seen.

1. **The freeze frame of the year:** Michigan State's Mateen Cleaves crawls on the floor after injuring his ankle in the NCAA men's basketball title game against Florida. Cleaves returns to the game at 12:58 of the second half and his will ripples through the Spartans who claim their first national championship since 1979.

■

inside the numbers

BIG TEN BALANCE

If Florida had beaten Michigan St. in the Men's Basketball Division I Championship Game, it would have become just the fourth Division I school to have won a national football championship (as named by the Associated Press) and a national basketball championship. The three schools that have accomplished the feat are all from the Big Ten and are listed below.

School	Basketball	Football
Michigan	1989	1948, '97
Ohio St.	1960	1942, '54, '68
Michigan St.	1979, 2000	1952

SPLENDID SPARTANS

Magic who? Michigan State's 2000 senior class, led by Mateen Cleaves, Morris Peterson and A.J. Granger, is the most accomplished Spartan senior class of all-time.

Overall Record	104-32
Conference Record	50-17
Overall Winning Pct.	.765
Big Ten titles	3
Final Fours	2
National titles	1

A MEAN STREAK

Division III Mt. Union won 54 consecutive football games from 1996-99, breaking the all-time NCAA record held by Oklahoma (47 from 1953-57). Below is just a sampling of the dominating statistics put up by the Purple Raiders during the streak.

Record:	54-0
Points (for-against):	2,576-750
Points Per Game:	47.7-13.9
Shutouts:	11
Offensive Yards Per Game:	511.9
Yards Allowed Per Game:	283.7
Turnover Margin:	+63
Trailed in 4th Quarter:	3 times

STATE OF CHAMPIONS

Eight teams from the state of California won championships during the 1999-00 school year, the most of any state in the U.S. The UCLA Bruins led the charge with four while Stanford added two.

State	Titles
California	8
Pennsylvania	7
Texas	6
Colorado	4
North Carolina	4

Six states tied with 3 each.

Note: There were 82 NCAA-sponsored team championships in 1999-2000 (33 Division I/National; 23 Division II; 26 Division III). ■

NCAA Division I Basketball Schools
2000-2001 Season
Conferences and coaches as of Sept. 10, 2000.

Joining Big East in 2000-2001: VIRGINIA TECH from Atlantic 10.

Joining Sun Belt in 2000-2001: MIDDLE TENN. ST. from Ohio Valley and NORTH TEXAS and NEW MEXICO ST. from Big West.

Joining WAC in 2000-2001: NEVADA from Big West.

Joining Atlantic 10 in 2001-2002: RICHMOND from Colonial.

Joining Big West in 2001-2002: CAL STATE NORTHRIDGE from Big Sky.

Joining Conference USA in 2001-2002: EAST CAROLINA from Colonial.

Joining Patriot in 2001-2002: AMERICAN from Colonial.

Joining Sun Belt in 2001-2002: UC-IRVINE from Big West.

	Nickname	Conference	Head Coach	Location	Colors
Air Force	Falcons	Mountain West	Joe Scott	Colo. Springs, CO	Blue/Silver
Akron	Zips	Mid-American	Dan Hipsher	Akron, OH	Blue/Gold
Alabama	Crimson Tide	SEC-West	Mark Gottfried	Tuscaloosa, AL	Crimson/White
Alabama A&M	Bulldogs	SWAC	Vann Pettaway	Huntsville, AL	Maroon/White
Ala.-Birmingham	Blazers	USA	Murray Bartow	Birmingham, AL	Green/Gold
Alabama St.	Hornets	SWAC	Rob Spivery	Montgomery, AL	Black/Gold
Albany	Great Danes	Independent	Scott Beeten	Albany, NY	Purple/Gold
Alcorn St.	Braves	SWAC	Davey Whitney	Lorman, MS	Purple/Gold
American	Eagles	Colonial	Jeff Jones	Washington, DC	Red/Blue
Appalachian St.	Mountaineers	Southern	Houston Fancher	Boone, NC	Black/Gold
Arizona	Wildcats	Pac-10	Lute Olson	Tucson, AZ	Cardinal/Navy
Arizona St.	Sun Devils	Pac-10	Rob Evans	Tempe, AZ	Maroon/Gold
Arkansas	Razorbacks	SEC-West	Nolan Richardson	Fayetteville, AR	Cardinal/White
Ark.-Little Rock	Trojans	Sun Belt	Porter Moser	Little Rock, AR	Maroon/White
Ark.-Pine Bluff	Golden Lions	SWAC	Harold Blevins	Pine Bluff, AR	Black/Gold
Arkansas St.	Indians	Sun Belt	Dickey Nutt	State Univ., AR	Scarlet/Black
Army	Black Knights	Patriot	Pat Harris	West Point, NY	Black/Gold/Gray
Auburn	Tigers	SEC-West	Cliff Ellis	Auburn, AL	Orange/Blue
Austin Peay St.	Governors	Ohio Valley	Dave Loos	Clarksville, TN	Red/White
Ball St.	Cardinals	Mid-American	Tim Buckley	Muncie, IN	Cardinal/White
Baylor	Bears	Big 12	Dave Bliss	Waco, TX	Green/Gold
Belmont	Bruins	Independent	Rick Byrd	Nashville, TN	Navy Blue/Red
Bethune-Cookman	Wildcats	Mid-Eastern	Horace Broadnax	Daytona Beach, FL	Maroon/Gold
Boise St.	Broncos	Big West	Rod Jensen	Boise, ID	Orange/Blue
Boston College	Eagles	Big East	Al Skinner	Chestnut Hill, MA	Maroon/Gold
Boston University	Terriers	America East	Dennis Wolff	Boston, MA	Scarlet/White
Bowling Green	Falcons	Mid-American	Dan Dakich	Bowling Green, OH	Orange/Brown
Bradley	Braves	Mo. Valley	Jim Molinari	Peoria, IL	Red/White
Brigham Young	Cougars	Mountain West	Steve Cleveland	Provo, UT	Royal Blue/White
Brown	Bears	Ivy	Glen Miller	Providence, RI	Brown/Cardinal/White
Bucknell	Bison	Patriot	Pat Flannery	Lewisburg, PA	Orange/Blue
Buffalo	Bulls	Mid-American	R. Witherspoon	Buffalo, NY	Royal Blue/White
Butler	Bulldogs	Midwestern	Thad Matta	Indianapolis, IN	Blue/White
California	Golden Bears	Pac-10	Ben Braun	Berkeley, CA	Blue/Gold
Cal Poly SLO	Mustangs	Big West	Jeff Schneider	San Luis Obispo, CA	Green/Gold
CS-Fullerton	Titans	Big West	Donny Daniels	Fullerton, CA	Blue/Orange/White
CS-Northridge	Matadors	Big Sky	Bobby Braswell	Northridge, CA	Red/White/Black
CS-Sacramento	Hornets	Big Sky	Jerome Jenkins	Sacramento, CA	Green/Gold
Campbell	Fighting Camels	Trans Am	Billy Lee	Buies Creek, NC	Orange/Black
Canisius	Golden Griffins	Metro Atlantic	Mike MacDonald	Buffalo, NY	Blue/Gold
Centenary	Gentlemen	Independent	Kevin Johnson	Shreveport, LA	Maroon/White
Central Conn. St.	Blue Devils	Northeast	Howie Dickenman	New Britain, CT	Blue/White
Central Florida	Golden Knights	Trans Am	Kirk Speraw	Orlando, FL	Black/Gold
Central Michigan	Chippewas	Mid-American	Jay Smith	Mt. Pleasant, MI	Maroon/Gold
Charleston So.	Buccaneers	Big South	Jim Platt	Charleston, SC	Blue/Gold

NCAA Division I Basketball Schools (Cont.)

	Nickname	Conference	Head Coach	Location	Colors
Chicago St.	Cougars	Mid-Continent	Bo Ellis	Chicago, IL	Green/White
Cincinnati	Bearcats	USA	Bob Huggins	Cincinnati, OH	Red/Black
The Citadel	Bulldogs	Southern	Pat Dennis	Charleston, SC	Blue/White
Clemson	Tigers	ACC	Larry Shyatt	Clemson, SC	Purple/Orange
Cleveland St.	Vikings	Midwestern	Rollie Massimino	Cleveland, OH	Forest Green/White
Coastal Carolina	Chanticleers	Big South	Pete Strickland	Conway, SC	Green/Bronze/Black
Colgate	Red Raiders	Patriot	Emmett Davis	Hamilton, NY	Maroon/Gray/White
College of Charleston	Cougars	Southern	John Kresse	Charleston, SC	Maroon/White
Colorado	Buffaloes	Big 12	Ricardo Patton	Boulder, CO	Silver/Gold/Black
Colorado St.	Rams	Mountain West	Dale Layer	Ft. Collins, CO	Green/Gold
Columbia	Lions	Ivy	Armond Hill	New York, NY	Lt. Blue/White
Connecticut	Huskies	Big East	Jim Calhoun	Storrs, CT	Blue/White
Coppin St.	Eagles	Mid-Eastern	Ron Mitchell	Baltimore, MD	Royal Blue/Gold
Cornell	Big Red	Ivy	Steve Donahue	Ithaca, NY	Carnelian/White
Creighton	Bluejays	Mo. Valley	Dana Altman	Omaha, NE	Blue/White
Dartmouth	Big Green	Ivy	Dave Faucher	Hanover, NH	Green/White
Davidson	Wildcats	Southern	Bob McKillop	Davidson, NC	Red/Black
Dayton	Flyers	Atlantic 10	Oliver Purnell	Dayton, OH	Red/Blue
Delaware	Fightin' Blue Hens	America East	David Henderson	Newark, DE	Blue/Gold
Delaware St.	Hornets	Mid-Eastern	Greg Jackson	Dover, DE	Red/Columbia Blue
Denver	Pioneers	Sun Belt	Marty Fletcher	Denver, CO	Crimson/Gold
DePaul	Blue Demons	USA	Pat Kennedy	Chicago, IL	Scarlet/Blue
Detroit Mercy	Titans	Midwestern	Perry Watson	Detroit, MI	Red/White/Blue
Drake	Bulldogs	Mo. Valley	Kurt Kanaskie	Des Moines, IA	Blue/White
Drexel	Dragons	America East	Steve Seymour	Philadelphia, PA	Navy Blue/Gold
Duke	Blue Devils	ACC	Mike Krzyzewski	Durham, NC	Royal Blue/White
Duquesne	Dukes	Atlantic 10	Darelle Porter	Pittsburgh, PA	Red/Blue
East Carolina	Pirates	Colonial	Bill Herrion	Greenville, NC	Purple/Gold
East Tenn. St.	Buccaneers	Southern	Ed DeChellis	Johnson City, TN	Blue/Gold
Eastern Illinois	Panthers	Ohio Valley	Rick Samuels	Charleston, IL	Blue/Gray
Eastern Kentucky	Colonels	Ohio Valley	Travis Ford	Richmond, KY	Maroon/White
Eastern Michigan	Eagles	Mid-American	Jim Boone	Ypsilanti, MI	Green/White
Eastern Washington	Eagles	Big Sky	Ray Giacoletti	Cheney, WA	Red/White
Elon	Phoenix	Big South	Mark Simons	Elon, NC	Maroon/Gold
Evansville	Aces	Mo. Valley	Jim Crews	Evansville, IN	Purple/White
Fairfield	Stags	Metro Atlantic	Tim O'Toole	Fairfield, CT	Cardinal Red
Fairleigh Dickinson	Knights	Northeast	Tom Green	Teaneck, NJ	Blue/Black
Florida	Gators	SEC-East	Billy Donovan	Gainesville, FL	Orange/Blue
Florida A&M	Rattlers	Mid-Eastern	Mickey Clayton	Tallahassee, FL	Orange/Green
Florida Atlantic	Owls	Trans Am	Sidney Green	Boca Raton, FL	Blue/Red
Florida Int'l	Golden Panthers	Sun Belt	Donnie Marsh	Miami, FL	Blue/Gold
Florida St.	Seminoles	ACC	Steve Robinson	Tallahassee, FL	Garnet/Gold
Fordham	Rams	Atlantic 10	Bob Hill	Bronx, NY	Maroon/White
Fresno St.	Bulldogs	WAC	Jerry Tarkanian	Fresno, CA	Cardinal/Blue
Furman	Paladins	Southern	Larry Davis	Greenville, SC	Purple/White
George Mason	Patriots	Colonial	Jim Larranaga	Fairfax, VA	Green/Gold
George Washington	Colonials	Atlantic 10	Tom Penders	Washington, DC	Buff/Blue
Georgetown	Hoyas	Big East	Craig Esherick	Washington, DC	Blue/Gray
Georgia	Bulldogs, 'Dawgs	SEC-East	Jim Harrick	Athens, GA	Red/Black
Georgia Southern	Eagles	Southern	Jeff Price	Statesboro, GA	Blue/White
Georgia St.	Panthers	Trans Am	Lefty Driesell	Atlanta, GA	Roy. Blue/White
Georgia Tech	Yellow Jackets	ACC	Paul Hewitt	Atlanta, GA	Old Gold/White
Gonzaga	Bulldogs, Zags	West Coast	Mark Few	Spokane, WA	Blue/White/Red
Grambling St.	Tigers	SWAC	Larry Wright	Grambling, LA	Black/Gold
Hampton	Pirates	Mid-Eastern	Steve Merfeld	Hampton, VA	Royal Blue/White
Hartford	Hawks	America East	Larry Harrison	W. Hartford, CT	Scarlet/White
Harvard	Crimson	Ivy	Frank Sullivan	Cambridge, MA	Crimson/Black/White
Hawaii	Rainbows	WAC	Riley Wallace	Honolulu, HI	Green/White
High Point	Panthers	Big South	Jerry Steele	High Point, NC	Purple/White
Hofstra	Flying Dutchmen	America East	Jay Wright	Hempstead, NY	Blue/White/Gold
Holy Cross	Crusaders	Patriot	Ralph Willard	Worcester, MA	Royal Purple
Houston	Cougars	USA	Ray McCallum	Houston, TX	Scarlet/White
Howard	Bison	Mid-Eastern	Frankie Allen	Washington, DC	Blue/White/Red
Idaho	Vandals	Big West	David Farrar	Moscow, ID	Silver/Gold
Idaho St.	Bengals	Big Sky	Doug Oliver	Pocatello, ID	Orange/Black
Illinois	Fighting Illini	Big Ten	Bill Self	Champaign, IL	Orange/Blue
Illinois-Chicago	Flames	Midwestern	Jim Collins	Chicago, IL	Navy Blue/Red
Illinois St.	Redbirds	Mo. Valley	Tom Richardson	Normal, IL	Red/White
Indiana	Hoosiers	Big Ten	Mike Davis	Bloomington, IN	Cream/Crimson

	Nickname	Conference	Head Coach	Location	Colors
IU/PU-Indianapolis	Jaguars	Mid-Continent	Ron Hunter	Indianapolis, IN	Red/Gold
Indiana St.	Sycamores	Mo. Valley	Royce Waltman	Terre Haute, IN	Blue/White
Iona	Gaels	Metro Atlantic	Jeff Ruland	New Rochelle, NY	Maroon/Gold
Iowa	Hawkeyes	Big Ten	Steve Alford	Iowa City, IA	Old Gold/Black
Iowa St.	Cyclones	Big 12	Larry Eustachy	Ames, IA	Cardinal/Gold
Jackson St.	Tigers	SWAC	Andy Stoglin	Jackson, MS	Blue/White
Jacksonville	Dolphins	Trans Am	Hugh Durham	Jacksonville, FL	Green/White
Jacksonville St.	Gamecocks	Trans Am	Mike LaPlante	Jacksonville, AL	Red/White
James Madison	Dukes	Colonial	Sherman Dillard	Harrisonburg, VA	Purple/Gold
Kansas	Jayhawks	Big 12	Roy Williams	Lawrence, KS	Crimson/Blue
Kansas St.	Wildcats	Big 12	Jim Wooldridge	Manhattan, KS	Purple/White
Kent St.	Golden Flashes	Mid-American	Gary Waters	Kent, OH	Navy Blue/Gold
Kentucky	Wildcats	SEC-East	Tubby Smith	Lexington, KY	Blue/White
La Salle	Explorers	Atlantic 10	Speedy Morris	Philadelphia, PA	Blue/Gold
Lafayette	Leopards	Patriot	Fran O'Hanlon	Easton, PA	Maroon/White
Lamar	Cardinals	Southland	Mike Deane	Beaumont, TX	Red/White
Lehigh	Mountain Hawks, Engineers	Patriot	Sal Mentesana	Bethlehem, PA	Brown/White
Liberty	Flames	Big South	Mel Hankinson	Lynchburg, VA	Red/White/Blue
Long Beach St.	49ers	Big West	Wayne Morgan	Long Beach, CA	Black/Gold
LIU-Brooklyn	Blackbirds	Northeast	Ray Martin	Brooklyn, NY	Blue/White
LSU	Fighting Tigers	SEC-West	John Brady	Baton Rouge, LA	Purple/Gold
LA-Lafayette	Ragin' Cajuns	Sun Belt	Jessie Evans	Lafayette, LA	Vermilion/White
LA-Monroe	Indians	Southland	Mike Vining	Monroe, LA	Maroon/Gold
Louisiana Tech	Bulldogs	Sun Belt	Keith Richard	Ruston, LA	Red/Blue
Louisville	Cardinals	USA	Denny Crum	Louisville, KY	Red/Black/White
Loyola Marymount	Lions	West Coast	Steve Aggers	Los Angeles, CA	Crimson/Blue
Loyola-IL	Ramblers	Midwestern	Larry Farmer	Chicago, IL	Maroon/Gold
Loyola-MD	Greyhounds	Metro Atlantic	Scott Hicks	Baltimore, MD	Green/Gray
Maine	Black Bears	America East	John Giannini	Orono, ME	Blue/White
Manhattan	Jaspers	Metro Atlantic	Bobby Gonzalez	Riverdale, NY	Kelly Green/White
Marist	Red Foxes	Metro Atlantic	Dave Magarity	Poughkeepsie, NY	Red/White
Marquette	Golden Eagles	USA	Tom Crean	Milwaukee, WI	Blue/Gold
Marshall	Thundering Herd	Mid-American	Greg White	Huntington, WV	Green/White
Maryland	Terrapins, Terps	ACC	Gary Williams	College Park, MD	Red/Wt./Black/Gold
MD-Balt. County	Retrievers	Northeast	Tom Sullivan	Baltimore, MD	Black/Gold/Red
MD-Eastern Shore	Hawks	Mid-Eastern	Thomas Trotter	Princess Anne, MD	Maroon/Gray
Massachusetts	Minutemen	Atlantic 10	James Bruiser Flint	Amherst, MA	Maroon/White
McNeese St.	Cowboys	Southland	Ron Everhart	Lake Charles, LA	Blue/Gold
Memphis	Tigers	USA	John Calipari	Memphis, TN	Blue/Gray
Mercer	Bears	Trans Am	Mark Slonaker	Macon, GA	Orange/Black
Miami-FL	Hurricanes	Big East	Perry Clark	Coral Gables, FL	Orange/Green/White
Miami-OH	RedHawks	Mid-American	Charlie Coles	Oxford, OH	Red/White
Michigan	Wolverines	Big Ten	Brian Ellerbe	Ann Arbor, MI	Maize/Blue
Michigan St.	Spartans	Big Ten	Tom Izzo	East Lansing, MI	Green/White
Middle Tenn. St.	Blue Raiders	Sun Belt	Randy Wiel	Murfreesboro, TN	Blue/White
Minnesota	Golden Gophers	Big Ten	Dan Monson	Minneapolis, MN	Maroon/Gold
Mississippi	Ole Miss, Rebels	SEC-West	Rod Barnes	Oxford, MS	Red/Blue
Mississippi St.	Bulldogs	SEC-West	Rick Stansbury	Starkville, MS	Maroon/White
Miss. Valley St.	Delta Devils	SWAC	Lafayette Stribling	Itta Bena, MS	Green/White
Missouri	Tigers	Big 12	Quin Snyder	Columbia, MO	Old Gold/Black
Missouri-KC	Kangaroos	Mid-Continent	Dean Demopoulos	Kansas City, MO	Blue/Gold
Monmouth	Hawks	Northeast	Dave Calloway	W. Long Branch, NJ	Royal Blue/White
Montana	Grizzlies	Big Sky	Don Holst	Missoula, MT	Copper/Silver/Gold
Montana St.	Bobcats	Big Sky	Mick Durham	Bozeman, MT	Blue/Gold
Morehead St.	Eagles	Ohio Valley	Kyle Macy	Morehead, KY	Blue/Gold
Morgan St.	Bears	Mid-Eastern	Chris Fuller	Baltimore, MD	Blue/Orange
Mt. St. Mary's	Mountaineers	Northeast	Jim Phelan	Emmitsburg, MD	Blue/White
Murray St.	Racers	Ohio Valley	Tevester Anderson	Murray, KY	Blue/Gold
Navy	Midshipmen	Patriot	Don DeVoe	Annapolis, MD	Navy Blue/Gold
Nebraska	Cornhuskers	Big 12	Barry Collier	Lincoln, NE	Scarlet/Cream
Nevada	Wolf Pack	WAC	Trent Johnson	Reno, NV	Silver/Blue
New Hampshire	Wildcats	America East	Phil Rowe	Durham, NH	Blue/White
New Mexico	Lobos	Mountain West	Fran Fraschilla	Albuquerque, NM	Cherry/Silver
New Mexico St.	Aggies	Sun Belt	Lou Henson	Las Cruces, NM	Crimson/White
New Orleans	Privateers	Sun Belt	Joey Stiebing	New Orleans, LA	Royal Blue/Silver
Niagara	Purple Eagles	Metro Atlantic	Joe Mihalich	Lewiston, NY	Purple/White/Gold
Nicholls St.	Colonels	Southland	Rickey Broussard	Thibodaux, LA	Red/Gray
Norfolk State	Spartans	Mid-Eastern	Mel Coleman	Norfolk, VA	Green/Gold
North Carolina	Tar Heels	ACC	Matt Doherty	Chapel Hill, NC	Carolina Blue/White
North Carolina A&T	Aggies	Mid-Eastern	Curtis Hunter	Greensboro, NC	Blue/Gold
North Carolina St.	Wolfpack	ACC	Herb Sendek	Raleigh, NC	Red/White

COLLEGE SPORTS

NCAA Division I Basketball Schools (Cont.)

	Nickname	Conference	Head Coach	Location	Colors
NC-Asheville	Bulldogs	Big South	Eddie Biedenbach	Asheville, NC	Royal Blue/White
NC-Charlotte	49ers	USA	Bobby Lutz	Charlotte, NC	Green/White
NC-Greensboro	Spartans	Southern	Fran McCaffrey	Greensboro, NC	Gold/White/Navy
NC-Wilmington	Seahawks	Colonial	Jerry Wainwright	Wilmington, NC	Green/Gold/Navy
North Texas	Mean Green	Sun Belt	Vic Trilli	Denton, TX	Green/White
Northeastern	Huskies	America East	Rudy Keeling	Boston, MA	Red/Black
Northern Arizona	Lumberjacks	Big Sky	Mike Adras	Flagstaff, AZ	Blue/Gold
Northern Illinois	Huskies	Mid-American	Brian Hammel	De Kalb, IL	Cardinal/Black
Northern Iowa	Panthers	Mo. Valley	Sam Weaver	Cedar Falls, IA	Purple/Old Gold
Northwestern	Wildcats	Big Ten	Bill Carmody	Evanston, IL	Purple/White
Northwestern St.	Demons	Southland	Mike McConathy	Natchitoches, LA	Purple/Orange/Wt.
Notre Dame	Fighting Irish	Big East	Mike Brey	Notre Dame, IN	Gold/Blue
Oakland-MI	Pioneers	Mid-Continent	Greg Kampe	Rochester, MI	Black/Gold
Ohio	Bobcats	Mid-American	Larry Hunter	Athens, OH	Hunter Green/White
Ohio St.	Buckeyes	Big Ten	Jim O'Brien	Columbus, OH	Scarlet/Gray
Oklahoma	Sooners	Big 12	Kelvin Sampson	Norman, OK	Crimson/Cream
Oklahoma St.	Cowboys	Big 12	Eddie Sutton	Stillwater, OK	Orange/Black
Old Dominion	Monarchs	Colonial	Jeff Capel	Norfolk, VA	Slate Blue/Silver
Oral Roberts	Golden Eagles	Mid-Continent	Scott Sutton	Tulsa, OK	Navy Blue/White
Oregon	Ducks	Pac-10	Ernie Kent	Eugene, OR	Green/Yellow
Oregon St.	Beavers	Pac-10	Ritchie McKay	Corvallis, OR	Orange/Black
Pacific	Tigers	Big West	Bob Thomason	Stockton, CA	Orange/Black
Pennsylvania	Quakers	Ivy	Fran Dunphy	Philadelphia, PA	Red/Blue
Penn St.	Nittany Lions	Big Ten	Jerry Dunn	University Park, PA	Blue/White
Pepperdine	Waves	West Coast	Jan Van Breda Kolff	Malibu, CA	Blue/Orange
Pittsburgh	Panthers	Big East	Ben Howland	Pittsburgh, PA	Gold/Blue
Portland	Pilots	West Coast	Rob Chavez	Portland, OR	Purple/White
Portland St.	Vikings	Big Sky	Joel Sobotka	Portland, OR	Green/White
Prairie View A&M	Panthers	SWAC	Elwood Plummer	Prairie View, TX	Purple/Gold
Princeton	Tigers	Ivy	J. Thompson III	Princeton, NJ	Orange/Black
Providence	Friars	Big East	Tim Welsh	Providence, RI	Black/White
Purdue	Boilermakers	Big Ten	Gene Keady	W. Lafayette, IN	Old Gold/Black
Quinnipiac	Braves	Northeast	Joe DeSantis	Hamden, CT	Blue/Gold
Radford	Highlanders	Big South	Ron Bradley	Radford, VA	Blue/Red/Green/Wt.
Rhode Island	Rams	Atlantic 10	Jerry DeGregorio	Kingston, RI	Lt. Blue/White/Navy
Rice	Owls	WAC	Willis Wilson	Houston, TX	Blue/Gray
Richmond	Spiders	Colonial	John Beilein	Richmond, VA	Red/Blue
Rider	Broncs	Metro Atlantic	Don Harnum	Lawrenceville, NJ	Cranberry/White
Robert Morris	Colonials	Northeast	Danny Nee	Moon Township, PA	Blue/White
Rutgers	Scarlet Knights	Big East	Kevin Bannon	New Brunswick, NJ	Scarlet
Sacred Heart	Pioneers	Northeast	Dave Bike	Fairfield, CT	Scarlet/White
St. Bonaventure	Bonnies	Atlantic 10	Jim Baron	St. Bonaventure, NY	Brown/White
St. Francis-NY	Terriers	Northeast	Ron Ganulin	Brooklyn, NY	Red/Blue
St. Francis-PA	Red Flash	Northeast	Bobby Jones	Loretto, PA	Red/White
St. John's	Red Storm	Big East	Mike Jarvis	Jamaica, NY	Red/White
St. Joseph's-PA	Hawks	Atlantic 10	Phil Martelli	Philadelphia, PA	Crimson/Gray
Saint Louis	Billikens	USA	Lorenzo Romar	St. Louis, MO	Blue/White
St. Mary's-CA	Gaels	West Coast	Dave Bollwinkel	Moraga, CA	Red/Blue
St. Peter's	Peacocks	Metro Atlantic	Bob Leckie	Jersey City, NJ	Blue/White
Sam Houston St.	Bearkats	Southland	Bob Marlin	Huntsville, TX	Orange/White
Samford	Bulldogs	Trans Am	Jimmy Tillette	Birmingham, AL	Red/Blue
San Diego	Toreros	West Coast	Brad Holland	San Diego, CA	Lt. Blue/Navy
San Diego St.	Aztecs	Mountain West	Steve Fisher	San Diego, CA	Scarlet/Black
San Francisco	Dons	West Coast	Phil Mathews	San Francisco, CA	Green/Gold
San Jose St.	Spartans	WAC	Steve Barnes	San Jose, CA	Gold/White/Blue
Santa Clara	Broncos	West Coast	Dick Davey	Santa Clara, CA	Bronco Red/White
Seton Hall	Pirates	Big East	Tommy Amaker	South Orange, NJ	Blue/White
Siena	Saints	Metro Atlantic	Louis Orr	Loudonville, NY	Green/Gold
South Alabama	Jaguars	Sun Belt	Bob Weltlich	Mobile, AL	Red/White/Blue
South Carolina	Gamecocks	SEC-East	Eddie Fogler	Columbia, SC	Garnet/Black
South Carolina St.	Bulldogs	Mid-Eastern	Cy Alexander	Orangeburg, SC	Garnet/Blue
South Florida	Bulls	USA	Seth Greenberg	Tampa, FL	Green/Gold
SE Missouri St.	Indians	Ohio Valley	Gary Garner	Cape Girardeau, MO	Red/Black
SE Louisiana	Lions	Southland	Billy Kennedy	Hammond, LA	Green/Gold
Southern Illinois	Salukis	Mo. Valley	Bruce Weber	Carbondale, IL	Maroon/White
SMU	Mustangs	WAC	Mike Dement	Dallas, TX	Red/Blue
Southern Miss	Golden Eagles	USA	James Green	Hattiesburg, MS	Black/Gold
Southern Utah	Thunderbirds	Mid-Continent	Bill Evans	Cedar City, UT	Scarlet/White
Southern-BR	Jaguars	SWAC	Tommy Green	Baton Rouge, LA	Blue/Gold

	Nickname	Conference	Head Coach	Location	Colors
SW Missouri St.	Bears	Mo. Valley	Barry Hinson	Springfield, MO	Maroon/White
SW Texas St.	Bobcats	Southland	Dennis Nutt	San Marcos, TX	Maroon/Gold
Stanford	Cardinal	Pac-10	Mike Montgomery	Stanford, CA	Cardinal/White
S.F. Austin St.	Lumberjacks	Southland	Danny Kaspar	Nacogdoches, TX	Purple/White
Stetson	Hatters	Trans Am	Murray Arnold	DeLand, FL	Green/White
Stony Brook	Seawolves	Independent	Nick Macarchuk	Stony Brook, NY	Scarlet/Gray
Syracuse	Orangemen	Big East	Jim Boeheim	Syracuse, NY	Orange
Temple	Owls	Atlantic 10	John Chaney	Philadelphia, PA	Cherry/White
Tennessee	Volunteers	SEC-East	Jerry Green	Knoxville, TN	Orange/White
Tenn-Chattanooga	Mocs	Southern	Henry Dickerson	Chattanooga, TN	Navy Blue/Old Gold
Tenn-Martin	Skyhawks	Ohio Valley	Bret Campbell	Martin, TN	Orange/Wt./Royal Blue
Tennessee St.	Tigers	Ohio Valley	N. Richardson III	Nashville, TN	Blue/White
Tennessee Tech	Golden Eagles	Ohio Valley	Jeff Lebo	Cookeville, TN	Purple/Gold
Texas	Longhorns	Big 12	Rick Barnes	Austin, TX	Burnt Orange/White
Texas A&M	Aggies	Big 12	Melvin Watkins	College Station, TX	Maroon/White
TX A&M Corpus-Christi	Islanders	Independent	Ronnie Arrow	Corpus Christi, TX	Blue/Green/Silver
TCU	Horned Frogs	WAC	Billy Tubbs	Ft. Worth, TX	Purple/White
Texas Southern	Tigers	SWAC	Robert Moreland	Houston, TX	Maroon/Gray
Texas Tech	Red Raiders	Big 12	James Dickey	Lubbock, TX	Scarlet/Black
TX-Arlington	Mavericks	Southland	Eddie McCarter	Arlington, TX	Royal Blue/White
TX-Pan American	Broncs	Independent	TBA	Edinburg, TX	Green/White
TX-San Antonio	Roadrunners	Southland	Tim Carter	San Antonio, TX	Orange/Navy/White
Toledo	Rockets	Mid-American	Stan Joplin	Toledo, OH	Blue/Gold
Towson	Tigers	America East	Mike Jaskulski	Towson, MD	Gold/White/Black
Troy St.	Trojans	Trans Am	Don Maestri	Troy, AL	Cardinal/Silver/Black
Tulane	Green Wave	USA	Shawn Finney	New Orleans, LA	Olive Green/Sky Blue
Tulsa	Golden Hurricane	WAC	Buzz Peterson	Tulsa, OK	Blue/Red/Gold
UC-Irvine	Anteaters	Big West	Pat Douglass	Irvine, CA	Blue/Gold
UCLA	Bruins	Pac-10	Steve Lavin	Los Angeles, CA	Blue/Gold
UC-Santa Barbara	Gauchos	Big West	Bob Williams	Santa Barbara, CA	Blue/Gold
UNLV	Runnin' Rebels	Mountain West	Billy Bayno	Las Vegas, NV	Scarlet/Gray
USC	Trojans	Pac-10	Henry Bibby	Los Angeles, CA	Cardinal/Gold
Utah	Utes	Mountain West	Rick Majerus	Salt Lake City, UT	Crimson/White
Utah St.	Aggies	Big West	Stew Morrill	Logan, UT	Navy Blue/White
UTEP	Miners	WAC	Jason Rabedeaux	El Paso, TX	Orange/Blue/Wt.
Valparaiso	Crusaders	Mid-Continent	Homer Drew	Valparaiso, IN	Brown/Gold
Vanderbilt	Commodores	SEC-East	Kevin Stallings	Nashville, TN	Black/Gold
Vermont	Catamounts	America East	Tom Brennan	Burlington, VT	Green/Gold
Villanova	Wildcats	Big East	Steve Lappas	Villanova, PA	Blue/White
Virginia	Cavaliers	ACC	Pete Gillen	Charlottesville, VA	Orange/Blue
VCU	Rams	Colonial	Mack McCarthy	Richmond, VA	Black/Gold
VMI	Keydets	Southern	Bart Bellairs	Lexington, VA	Red/White/Yellow
Virginia Tech	Hokies, Gobblers	Big East	Ricky Stokes	Blacksburg, VA	Orange/Maroon
Wagner	Seahawks	Northeast	Dereck Whittenburg	Staten Island, NY	Green/White
Wake Forest	Demon Deacons	ACC	Dave Odom	Winston-Salem, NC	Old Gold/Black
Washington	Huskies	Pac-10	Bob Bender	Seattle, WA	Purple/Gold
Washington St.	Cougars	Pac-10	Paul Graham	Pullman, WA	Crimson/Gray
Weber St.	Wildcats	Big Sky	Joe Cravens	Ogden, UT	Purple/White
West Virginia	Mountaineers	Big East	Gale Catlett	Morgantown, WV	Old Gold/Blue
Western Carolina	Catamounts	Southern	Steve Shurina	Cullowhee, NC	Purple/Gold
Western Illinois	Leathernecks	Mid-Continent	Jim Kerwin	Macomb, IL	Purple/Gold
Western Kentucky	Hilltoppers	Sun Belt	Dennis Felton	Bowling Green, KY	Red/White
Western Michigan	Broncos	Mid-American	Robert McCullum	Kalamazoo, MI	Brown/Gold
Wichita St.	Shockers	Mo. Valley	Mark Turgeon	Wichita, KS	Yellow/Black
William & Mary	Tribe	Colonial	Rick Boyages	Williamsburg, VA	Green/Gold/Silver
Winthrop	Eagles	Big South	Gregg Marshall	Rock Hill, SC	Garnet/Gold
Wisconsin	Badgers	Big Ten	Dick Bennett	Madison, WI	Cardinal/White
WI-Green Bay	Phoenix	Midwestern	Mike Heideman	Green Bay, WI	Green/White/Red
WI-Milwaukee	Panthers	Midwestern	Bo Ryan	Milwaukee, WI	Black/Gold
Wofford	Terriers	Southern	Richard Johnson	Spartanburg, SC	Old Gold/Black
Wright St.	Raiders	Midwestern	Ed Schilling	Dayton, OH	Green/Gold
Wyoming	Cowboys	Mountain West	Steve McClain	Laramie, WY	Brown/Yellow
Xavier	Musketeers	Atlantic 10	Skip Prosser	Cincinnati, OH	Blue/White
Yale	Bulldogs, Elis	Ivy	James Jones	New Haven, CT	Yale Blue/White
Youngstown St.	Penguins	Mid-Continent	John Robic	Youngstown, OH	Red/White

NCAA Division I-A Football Schools
2000 Season
Conferences and coaches as of Sept. 10, 2000.

Joining WAC in 2000: NEVADA from Big West.
Moving up from Division I-AA in 2000: CONNECTICUT to I-A Independent from I-AA Atlantic 10.
New Conference in 2001: Sun Belt (7 teams)— ARKANSAS ST., IDAHO, NEW MEXICO ST., NORTH TEXAS from Big West, plus Independents LA-LAFAYETTE, LA-MONROE, and MIDDLE TENN. ST.
Joining WAC in 2001: BOISE ST. from Big West.
To I-A Independent in 2001: UTAH ST. from Big West.
Joining Conference USA in 2002: TCU from WAC.

	Nickname	Conference	Head Coach	Location	Colors
Air Force	Falcons	Mountain West	Fisher DeBerry	Colo. Springs, CO	Blue/Silver
Akron	Zips	Mid-American	Lee Owens	Akron, OH	Blue/Gold
Alabama	Crimson Tide	SEC-West	Mike DuBose	Tuscaloosa, AL	Crimson/White
Ala.-Birmingham	Blazers	USA	Watson Brown	Birmingham, AL	Green/Gold
Arizona	Wildcats	Pac-10	Dick Tomey	Tucson, AZ	Cardinal/Navy
Arizona St.	Sun Devils	Pac-10	Bruce Snyder	Tempe, AZ	Maroon/Gold
Arkansas	Razorbacks	SEC-West	Houston Nutt	Fayetteville, AR	Cardinal/White
Arkansas St.	Indians	Big West	Joe Hollis	State Univ., AR	Scarlet/Black
Army	Cadets, Black Knights	USA	Todd Berry	West Point, NY	Black/Gold/Gray
Auburn	Tigers	SEC-West	Tommy Tuberville	Auburn, AL	Orange/Blue
Ball St.	Cardinals	Mid-American	Bill Lynch	Muncie, IN	Cardinal/White
Baylor	Bears	Big 12	Kevin Steele	Waco, TX	Green/Gold
Boise St.	Broncos	Big West	Dirk Koetter	Boise, ID	Orange/Blue
Boston College	Eagles	Big East	Tom O'Brien	Chestnut Hill, MA	Maroon/Gold
Bowling Green	Falcons	Mid-American	Gary Blackney	Bowling Green, OH	Orange/Brown
Buffalo	Bulls	Mid-American	Craig Cirbus	Buffalo, NY	Royal Blue/White
Brigham Young	Cougars	Mountain West	LaVell Edwards	Provo, UT	Royal Blue/White
California	Golden Bears	Pac-10	Tom Holmoe	Berkeley, CA	Blue/Gold
Central Florida	Golden Knights	Independent	Mike Kruczek	Orlando, FL	Black/Gold
Central Michigan	Chippewas	Mid-American	Mike DeBord	Mt. Pleasant, MI	Maroon/Gold
Cincinnati	Bearcats	USA	Rick Minter	Cincinnati, OH	Red/Black
Clemson	Tigers	ACC	Tommy Bowden	Clemson, SC	Purple/Orange
Colorado	Buffaloes	Big 12	Gary Barnett	Boulder, CO	Silver/Gold/Black
Colorado St.	Rams	Mountain West	Sonny Lubick	Ft. Collins, CO	Green/Gold
Connecticut	Huskies	Independent	Randy Edsall	Storrs, CT	Blue/White
Duke	Blue Devils	ACC	Carl Franks	Durham, NC	Royal Blue/White
East Carolina	Pirates	USA	Steve Logan	Greenville, NC	Purple/Gold
Eastern Michigan	Eagles	Mid-American	Jeff Woodruff	Ypsilanti, MI	Green/White
Florida	Gators	SEC-East	Steve Spurrier	Gainesville, FL	Orange/Blue
Florida St.	Seminoles	ACC	Bobby Bowden	Tallahassee, FL	Garnet/Gold
Fresno St.	Bulldogs	WAC	Pat Hill	Fresno, CA	Cardinal/Blue
Georgia	Bulldogs	SEC-East	Jim Donnan	Athens, GA	Red/Black
Georgia Tech	Yellow Jackets	ACC	George O'Leary	Atlanta, GA	Old Gold/White
Hawaii	Warriors	WAC	June Jones	Honolulu, HI	Green/White
Houston	Cougars	USA	Dana Dimel	Houston, TX	Scarlet/White
Idaho	Vandals	Big West	Tom Cable	Moscow, ID	Silver/Gold
Illinois	Fighting Illini	Big Ten	Ron Turner	Champaign, IL	Orange/Blue
Indiana	Hoosiers	Big Ten	Cam Cameron	Bloomington, IN	Cream/Crimson
Iowa	Hawkeyes	Big Ten	Kirk Ferentz	Iowa City, IA	Old Gold/Black
Iowa St.	Cyclones	Big 12	Dan McCarney	Ames, IA	Cardinal/Gold
Kansas	Jayhawks	Big 12	Terry Allen	Lawrence, KS	Crimson/Blue
Kansas St.	Wildcats	Big 12	Bill Snyder	Manhattan, KS	Purple/White
Kent St.	Golden Flashes	Mid-American	Dean Pees	Kent, OH	Navy Blue/Gold
Kentucky	Wildcats	SEC-East	Hal Mumme	Lexington, KY	Blue/White
LSU	Fighting Tigers	SEC-West	Nick Saban	Baton Rouge, LA	Purple/Gold
LA-Lafayette	Ragin' Cajuns	Independent	Jerry Baldwin	Lafayette, LA	Vermilion/White
LA-Monroe	Indians	Independent	Bobby Keasler	Monroe, LA	Maroon/Gold
Louisiana Tech	Bulldogs	Independent	Jack Bicknell III	Ruston, LA	Red/Blue
Louisville	Cardinals	USA	John L. Smith	Louisville, KY	Red/Black/White
Marshall	Thundering Herd	Mid-American	Bob Pruett	Huntington, WV	Green/White
Maryland	Terrapins, Terps	ACC	Ron Vanderlinden	College Park, MD	Red/White/Black/Gold
Memphis	Tigers	USA	Rip Scherer	Memphis, TN	Blue/Gray
Miami-FL	Hurricanes	Big East	Butch Davis	Coral Gables, FL	Orange/Green/White
Miami-OH	RedHawks	Mid-American	Terry Hoeppner	Oxford, OH	Red/White
Michigan	Wolverines	Big Ten	Lloyd Carr	Ann Arbor, MI	Maize/Blue
Michigan St.	Spartans	Big Ten	Bobby Williams	E. Lansing, MI	Green/White
Middle Tenn. St.	Blue Raiders	Independent	Andy McCollum	Murfreesboro, TN	Blue/White
Minnesota	Golden Gophers	Big Ten	Glen Mason	Minneapolis, MN	Maroon/Gold
Mississippi	Ole Miss, Rebels	SEC-West	David Cutcliffe	Oxford, MS	Cardinal/Navy Blue

	Nickname	Conference	Head Coach	Location	Colors
Mississippi St.	Bulldogs	SEC-West	Jackie Sherrill	Starkville, MS	Maroon/White
Missouri	Tigers	Big 12	Larry Smith	Columbia, MO	Old Gold/Black
Navy	Midshipmen	Independent	Charlie Weatherbie	Annapolis, MD	Navy Blue/Gold
Nebraska	Cornhuskers	Big 12	Frank Solich	Lincoln, NE	Scarlet/Cream
Nevada	Wolf Pack	WAC	Chris Tormey	Reno, NV	Silver/Blue
New Mexico	Lobos	Mountain West	Rocky Long	Albuquerque, NM	Cherry/Silver
New Mexico St.	Aggies	Big West	Tony Samuel	Las Cruces, NM	Crimson/White
North Carolina	Tar Heels	ACC	Carl Torbush	Chapel Hill, NC	Carolina Blue/White
North Carolina St.	Wolfpack	ACC	Chuck Amato	Raleigh, NC	Red/White
North Texas	Mean Green	Big West	Darrell Dickey	Denton, TX	Green/White
Northern Illinois	Huskies	Mid-American	Joe Novak	De Kalb, IL	Cardinal/Black
Northwestern	Wildcats	Big Ten	Randy Walker	Evanston, IL	Purple/White
Notre Dame	Fighting Irish	Independent	Bob Davie	Notre Dame, IN	Gold/Blue
Ohio University	Bobcats	Mid-American	Jim Grobe	Athens, OH	Ohio Green/White
Ohio St.	Buckeyes	Big Ten	John Cooper	Columbus, OH	Scarlet/Gray
Oklahoma	Sooners	Big 12	Bob Stoops	Norman, OK	Crimson/Cream
Oklahoma St.	Cowboys	Big 12	Bob Simmons	Stillwater, OK	Orange/Black
Oregon	Ducks	Pac-10	Mike Bellotti	Eugene, OR	Green/Yellow
Oregon St.	Beavers	Pac-10	Dennis Erickson	Corvallis, OR	Orange/Black
Penn St.	Nittany Lions	Big Ten	Joe Paterno	University Park, PA	Blue/White
Pittsburgh	Panthers	Big East	Walt Harris	Pittsburgh, PA	Blue/Gold
Purdue	Boilermakers	Big Ten	Joe Tiller	W. Lafayette, IN	Old Gold/Black
Rice	Owls	WAC	Ken Hatfield	Houston, TX	Blue/Gray
Rutgers	Scarlet Knights	Big East	Terry Shea	New Brunswick, NJ	Scarlet
San Diego St.	Aztecs	Mountain West	Ted Tollner	San Diego, CA	Scarlet/Black
San Jose St.	Spartans	WAC	Dave Baldwin	San Jose, CA	Gold/White/Blue
South Carolina	Gamecocks	SEC-East	Lou Holtz	Columbia, SC	Garnet/Black
SMU	Mustangs	WAC	Mike Cavan	Dallas, TX	Red/Blue
Southern Miss.	Golden Eagles	USA	Jeff Bower	Hattiesburg, MS	Black/Gold
Stanford	Cardinal	Pac-10	Tyrone Willingham	Stanford, CA	Cardinal/White
Syracuse	Orangemen	Big East	Paul Pasqualoni	Syracuse, NY	Orange
Temple	Owls	Big East	Bobby Wallace	Philadelphia, PA	Cherry/White
Tennessee	Volunteers	SEC-East	Phillip Fulmer	Knoxville, TN	Orange/White
Texas	Longhorns	Big 12	Mack Brown	Austin, TX	Burnt Orange/White
Texas A&M	Aggies	Big 12	R.C. Slocum	College Station, TX	Maroon/White
TCU	Horned Frogs	WAC	Dennis Franchione	Ft. Worth, TX	Purple/White
Texas Tech	Red Raiders	Big 12	Mike Leach	Lubbock, TX	Scarlet/Black
Toledo	Rockets	Mid-American	Gary Pinkel	Toledo, OH	Blue/Gold
Tulane	Green Wave	USA	Chris Scelfo	New Orleans, LA	Olive Green/Sky Blue
Tulsa	Golden Hurricane	WAC	Keith Burns	Tulsa, OK	Blue/Gold
UCLA	Bruins	Pac-10	Bob Toledo	Los Angeles, CA	Blue/Gold
UNLV	Rebels	Mountain West	John Robinson	Las Vegas, NV	Scarlet/Gray
USC	Trojans	Pac-10	Paul Hackett	Los Angeles, CA	Cardinal/Gold
Utah	Utes	Mountain West	Ron McBride	Salt Lake City, UT	Crimson/White
Utah St.	Aggies	Big West	Mick Dennehy	Logan, UT	Navy Blue/White
UTEP	Miners	WAC	Gary Nord	El Paso, TX	Orange/Blue/Wt.
Vanderbilt	Commodores	SEC-East	Woody Widenhofer	Nashville, TN	Black/Gold
Virginia	Cavaliers	ACC	George Welsh	Charlottesville, VA	Orange/Blue
Virginia Tech	Hokies, Gobblers	Big East	Frank Beamer	Blacksburg, VA	Orange/Maroon
Wake Forest	Demon Deacons	ACC	Jim Caldwell	Winston-Salem, NC	Old Gold/Black
Washington	Huskies	Pac-10	Rick Neuheisel	Seattle, WA	Purple/Gold
Washington St.	Cougars	Pac-10	Mike Price	Pullman, WA	Crimson/Gray
West Virginia	Mountaineers	Big East	Don Nehlen	Morgantown, WV	Old Gold/Blue
Western Michigan	Broncos	Mid-American	Gary Darnell	Kalamazoo, MI	Brown/Gold
Wisconsin	Badgers	Big Ten	Barry Alvarez	Madison, WI	Cardinal/White
Wyoming	Cowboys	Mountain West	Vic Koennig	Laramie, WY	Brown/Yellow

Soaring Attendance

In 1999-00, more fans attended Division I men's basketball and football games than ever before. Overall Division I basketball totals topped the 24 million mark for the first time in history, while Division I-A and I-AA combined for 35 million. Listed are the top five schools in Division I basketball and football with the highest home attendance figures. Source: NCAA.

Basketball	Avg. Att.	I-A Football	Avg. Att.	I-AA Football	Avg. Att.
Kentucky	22,448	Michigan	111,108	Jackson St.	28,933
Syracuse	20,807	Tennessee	106,839	Yale	27,518
North Carolina	20,163	Penn St.	96,500	Southern	25,734
Louisville	19,180	Ohio St.	93,456	South Florida	25,053
Ohio St.	18,702	Georgia	86,117	North Carolina A&T	21,954

NCAA Division I-AA Football Schools
2000 Season
Conferences and coaches as of Sept. 10, 2000.

Joining Northeast in 2000: ST. JOHN'S from Independent.
Joining Gateway in 2001: WESTERN KENTUCKY from Ohio Valley.
Joining Patriot in 2001: GEORGETOWN from Metro Atlantic.
To I-AA Independent in 2001: CAL STATE NORTHRIDGE from Big Sky.

	Nickname	Conference	Head Coach	Location	Colors
Alabama A&M	Bulldogs	SWAC	Ron Cooper	Huntsville, AL	Maroon/White
Alabama St.	Hornets	SWAC	L.C. Cole	Montgomery, AL	Black/Gold
Albany	Great Danes	Northeast	Bob Ford	Albany, NY	Purple/Gold
Alcorn St.	Braves	SWAC	Johnny Thomas	Lorman, MS	Purple/Gold
Appalachian St.	Mountaineers	Southern	Jerry Moore	Boone, NC	Black/Gold
Ark.-Pine Bluff	Golden Lions	SWAC	Lee Hardman	Pine Bluff, AR	Black/Gold
Austin Peay St.	Governors	Independent	Bill Schmitz	Clarksville, TN	Red/White
Bethune-Cookman	Wildcats	Mid-Eastern	Alvin Wyatt	Daytona Beach, FL	Maroon/Gold
Brown	Bears	Ivy	Phil Estes	Providence, RI	Brown/Red/White
Bucknell	Bison	Patriot	Tom Gadd	Lewisburg, PA	Orange/Blue
Butler	Bulldogs	Pioneer	Ken LaRose	Indianapolis, IN	Blue/White
Cal Poly SLO	Mustangs	Independent	Larry Welsh	San Luis Obispo, CA	Green/Gold
CS-Northridge	Matadors	Big Sky	Jeff Kearin	Northridge, CA	Red/White/Black
CS-Sacramento	Hornets	Big Sky	John Volek	Sacramento, CA	Green/Gold
Canisius	Golden Griffins	Metro Atlantic	Edward Argast	Buffalo, NY	Blue/Gold
Central Conn. St.	Blue Devils	Northeast	Sal Cintorino	New Britain, CT	Blue/White
Charleston So.	Buccaneers	Independent	David Dowd	Charleston, SC	Blue/Gold
The Citadel	Bulldogs	Southern	Don Powers	Charleston, SC	Blue/White
Colgate	Red Raiders	Patriot	Dick Biddle	Hamilton, NY	Maroon/White/Gray
Columbia	Lions	Ivy	Ray Tellier	New York, NY	Lt. Blue/White
Cornell	Big Red	Ivy	Pete Mangurian	Ithaca, NY	Carnelian/White
Dartmouth	Big Green	Ivy	John Lyons	Hanover, NH	Green/White
Davidson	Wildcats	Independent	Joe Susan	Davidson, NC	Red/Black
Dayton	Flyers	Pioneer	Mike Kelly	Dayton, OH	Red/Blue
Delaware	Blue Hens	Atlantic 10	Tubby Raymond	Newark, DE	Blue/Gold
Delaware St.	Hornets	Mid-Eastern	Ben Blacknall	Dover, DE	Red/Blue
Drake	Bulldogs	Pioneer	Rob Ash	Des Moines, IA	Blue/White
Duquesne	Dukes	Metro Atlantic	Greg Gattuso	Pittsburgh, PA	Red/Blue
East Tenn. St.	Buccaneers	Southern	Paul Hamilton	Johnson City, TN	Blue/Gold
Eastern Illinois	Panthers	Ohio Valley	Bob Spoo	Charleston, IL	Blue/Gray
Eastern Kentucky	Colonels	Ohio Valley	Roy Kidd	Richmond, KY	Maroon/White
Eastern Washington	Eagles	Big Sky	Paul Wulff	Cheney, WA	Red/White
Elon	Phoenix	Independent	Al Seagraves	Elon, NC	Maroon/Gold
Fairfield	Stags	Metro Atlantic	Kevin Kiesel	Fairfield, CT	Cardinal Red
Florida A&M	Rattlers	Mid-Eastern	Billy Joe	Tallahassee, FL	Orange/Green
Fordham	Rams	Patriot	Dave Clawson	Bronx, NY	Maroon/White
Furman	Paladins	Southern	Bobby Johnson	Greenville, SC	Purple/White
Georgetown	Hoyas	Metro Atlantic	Bob Benson	Washington, DC	Blue/Gray
Georgia Southern	Eagles	Southern	Paul Johnson	Statesboro, GA	Blue/White
Grambling St.	Tigers	SWAC	Doug Williams	Grambling, LA	Black/Gold
Hampton	Pirates	Mid-Eastern	Joe Taylor	Hampton, VA	Royal Blue/White
Harvard	Crimson	Ivy	Tim Murphy	Cambridge, MA	Crimson/Black/White
Hofstra	Flying Dutchmen	Independent	Joe Gardi	Hempstead, NY	Gray/White/Gold
Holy Cross	Crusaders	Patriot	Dan Allen	Worcester, MA	Royal Purple
Howard	Bison	Mid-Eastern	Steve Wilson	Washington, DC	Blue/Wt./Red
Idaho St.	Bengals	Big Sky	Larry Lewis	Pocatello, ID	Orange/Black
Illinois St.	Redbirds	Gateway	Denver Johnson	Normal, IL	Red/White
Indiana St.	Sycamores	Gateway	Tim McGuire	Terre Haute, IN	Royal Blue/White
Iona	Gaels	Metro Atlantic	Fred Mariani	New Rochelle, NY	Maroon/Gold
Jackson St.	Tigers	SWAC	Robert Hughes	Jackson, MS	Blue/White
Jacksonville	Dolphins	Independent	Steve Gilbert	Jacksonville, FL	Green/White
Jacksonville St.	Gamecocks	Southland	Jack Crowe	Jacksonville, AL	Red/White
James Madison	Dukes	Atlantic 10	Mickey Matthews	Harrisonburg, VA	Purple/Gold
Lafayette	Leopards	Patriot	Frank Tavani	Easton, PA	Maroon/White
La Salle	Explorers	Metro Atlantic	Bill Manlove	Philadelphia, PA	Blue/Gold
Lehigh	Engineers	Patriot	Kevin Higgins	Bethlehem, PA	Brown/White
Liberty	Flames	Independent	Ken Karcher	Lynchburg, VA	Red/White/Blue
Maine	Black Bears	Atlantic 10	Jack Cosgrove	Orono, ME	Blue/White
Marist	Red Foxes	Metro Atlantic	Jim Parady	Poughkeepsie, NY	Red/White
Massachusetts	Minutemen	Atlantic 10	Mark Whipple	Amherst, MA	Maroon/White
McNeese St.	Cowboys	Southland	Tommy Tate	Lake Charles, LA	Blue/Gold

	Nickname	Conference	Head Coach	Location	Colors
Miss. Valley St.	Delta Devils	SWAC	LaTraia Jones	Itta Bena, MS	Green/White
Monmouth	Hawks	Northeast	Kevin Callahan	W. Long Branch, NJ	Royal Blue/White
Montana	Grizzlies	Big Sky	Joe Glenn	Missoula, MT	Maroon/Gray
Montana St.	Bobcats	Big Sky	Mike Kramer	Bozeman, MT	Blue/Gold
Morehead St.	Eagles	Independent	Matt Ballard	Morehead, KY	Blue/Gold
Morgan St.	Bears	Mid-Eastern	Stanley Mitchell	Baltimore, MD	Blue/Orange
Murray St.	Racers	Ohio Valley	Joe Pannunzio	Murray, KY	Blue/Gold
New Hampshire	Wildcats	Atlantic 10	Sean McDonnell	Durham, NH	Blue/White
Nicholls St.	Colonels	Southland	Daryl Daye	Thibodaux, LA	Red/Gray
Norfolk State	Spartans	Mid-Eastern	Maurice Forte	Norfolk, VA	Green/Gold
North Carolina A&T	Aggies	Mid-Eastern	Bill Hayes	Greensboro, NC	Blue/Gold
Northeastern	Huskies	Atlantic 10	Don Brown	Boston, MA	Red/Black
Northern Arizona	Lumberjacks	Big Sky	Jerome Souers	Flagstaff, AZ	Blue/Gold
Northern Iowa	Panthers	Gateway	Mike Dunbar	Cedar Falls, IA	Purple/Old Gold
Northwestern St.	Demons	Southland	Steve Roberts	Natchitoches, LA	Purple/White
Pennsylvania	Quakers	Ivy	Al Bagnoli	Philadelphia, PA	Red/Blue
Portland St.	Vikings	Big Sky	Tim Walsh	Portland, OR	Green/Gray
Prairie View A&M	Panthers	SWAC	Gregory Johnson	Prairie View, TX	Purple/Gold
Princeton	Tigers	Ivy	Roger Hughes	Princeton, NJ	Orange/Black
Rhode Island	Rams	Atlantic 10	Tim Stowers	Kingston, RI	Light Blue/Navy/Wt.
Richmond	Spiders	Atlantic 10	Jim Reid	Richmond, VA	Red/Blue
Robert Morris	Colonials	Northeast	Joe Walton	Moon Township, PA	Blue/White
Sacred Heart	Pioneers	Northeast	Jim Fleming	Fairfield, CT	Scarlet/White
St. Francis-PA	Red Flash	Northeast	David Jaumotte	Loretto, PA	Red/White
St. John's-NY	Red Storm	Northeast	Bob Ricca	Jamaica, NY	Red/White
St. Mary's-CA	Gaels	Independent	Tim Landis	Moraga, CA	Red/Blue
St. Peter's	Peacocks	Metro Atlantic	Rob Stern	Jersey City, NJ	Blue/White
Sam Houston St.	Bearkats	Southland	Ron Randleman	Huntsville, TX	Orange/White
Samford	Bulldogs	Independent	Pete Hurt	Birmingham, AL	Crimson/Blue
San Diego	Toreros	Pioneer	Kevin McGarry	San Diego, CA	Lt. Blue/Navy
Siena	Saints	Metro Atlantic	Jay Bateman	Loudonville, NY	Green/Gold
South Carolina St.	Bulldogs	Mid-Eastern	Willie Jeffries	Orangeburg, SC	Garnet/Blue
South Florida	Bulls	Independent	Jim Leavitt	Tampa, FL	Green/Gold
SE Missouri St.	Indians	Ohio Valley	Tim Billings	Cape Girardeau, MO	Red/Black
Southern-BR	Jaguars	SWAC	Pete Richardson	Baton Rouge, LA	Blue/Gold
Southern Illinois	Salukis	Gateway	Jan Quarless	Cardondale, IL	Maroon/White
Southern Utah	Thunderbirds	Independent	C. Ray Gregory	Cedar City, UT	Scarlet/White
SW Missouri St.	Bears	Gateway	Randy Ball	Springfield, MO	Maroon/White
SW Texas St.	Bobcats	Southland	Bob DeBesse	San Marcos, TX	Maroon/Gold
S.F. Austin St.	Lumberjacks	Southland	Mike Santiago	Nacogdoches, TX	Purple/White
Stony Brook	Seawolves	Northeast	Ron Cooper	Stony Brook, NY	Scarlet/Gray
Tenn-Chattanooga	Mocs	Southern	Donnie Kirkpatrick	Chattanooga, TN	Navy Blue/Old Gold
Tennessee-Martin	Skyhawks	Ohio Valley	Sam McCorkle	Martin, TN	Orange/White/Blue
Tennessee St.	Tigers	Ohio Valley	James Reese	Nashville, TN	Blue/White
Tennessee Tech	Golden Eagles	Ohio Valley	Mike Hennigan	Cookeville, TN	Purple/Gold
Texas Southern	Tigers	SWAC	Bill Thomas	Houston, TX	Maroon/Gray
Towson	Tigers	Patriot	Gordy Combs	Towson, MD	Gold/White
Troy St.	Trojans	Southland	Larry Blakeney	Troy, AL	Cardinal/Gray/Black
Valparaiso	Crusaders	Pioneer	Tom Horne	Valparaiso, IN	Brown/Gold
Villanova	Wildcats	Atlantic 10	Andy Talley	Villanova, PA	Blue/White
VMI	Keydets	Southern	Cal McCombs	Lexington, VA	Red/White/Yellow
Wagner	Seahawks	Northeast	Walt Hameline	Staten Island, NY	Green/White
Weber St.	Wildcats	Big Sky	Jerry Graybeal	Ogden, UT	Royal Purple/White
Western Carolina	Catamounts	Southern	Bill Bleil	Cullowhee, NC	Purple/Gold
Western Illinois	Leathernecks	Gateway	Don Patterson	Macomb, IL	Purple/Gold
Western Kentucky	Hilltoppers	Ohio Valley	Jack Harbaugh	Bowling Green, KY	Red/White
William & Mary	Tribe	Atlantic 10	Jimmye Laycock	Williamsburg, VA	Green/Gold/Silver
Wofford	Terriers	Southern	Mike Ayers	Spartanburg, SC	Old Gold/Black
Yale	Bulldogs, Elis	Ivy	Jack Siedlecki	New Haven, CT	Yale Blue/White
Youngstown St.	Penguins	Gateway	Jim Tressel	Youngstown, OH	Red/White

Native American Nicknames at 9

At the start of the 2000-01 academic year the number of Native American nickname variations remained at 9 in Division I basketball and football: INDIANS (3)– Arkansas St., Louisiana-Monroe, and Southeast Missouri St.; BRAVES (2)– Alcorn St. and Bradley; CHIPPEWAS– Central Michigan; FIGHTING ILLINI– Illinois; SEMINOLES– Florida St.; TRIBE– William & Mary.

Memphis
John Calipari
NBA 76ers to Memphis

Georgia Tech
Paul Hewitt
Siena to Georgia Tech

Michigan St.
Bobby Williams
Michigan St.

N.C. State
Chuck Amato
Florida St. to N.C. State

Coaching Changes

New head coaches were named at 51 Division 1 basketball schools while 14 Division 1-A and 23 Division 1-AA football schools changed head coaches after the 1999-00 season. Coaching changes listed below are as of September 10, 2000.

Division I Basketball

	Old Coach	Record	Why Left?	New Coach	Old Job
Air Force	Reggie Minton	8-20	fired	Joe Scott	Asst., Princeton
Albany	Scott Hicks	10-18	to Loyola-MD*	Scott Beeten	Assoc. head, California
American	Art Perry	11-18	fired	Jeff Jones	Assoc. head, URI
Appalachian St.	Buzz Peterson	23-9	to Tulsa*	Houston Fancher	Assoc. head, App. St.
Ark.-Little Rock	Sidney Moncrief	4-24	to NBA Dallas**	Porter Moser	Asst., Ark.-Little Rock
Ball St.	Ray McCallum	22-9	to Houston*	Tim Buckley	Asst., Marquette
Buffalo	Tim Cohane	5-23#	resigned	Reggie Witherspoon	Coach, Erie CC
Butler	Barry Collier	23-8	to Nebraska*	Thad Matta	Asst., Butler
CS-Fullerton	Bob Hawking	8-19	resigned	Donny Daniels	Asst., Utah
CS-Sacramento	Tom Abatemarco	9-18	resigned	Jerome Jenkins	Asst., CS-Sacramento
Charleston Southern	Tom Conrad	8-21	fired	Jim Platt	Asst., Florida St.
Colorado St.	Ritchie McKay	19-12	to Oregon St.*	Dale Layer	Asst., Colorado St.
Cornell	Scott Thompson	10-17	resigned	Steve Donahue	Asst., Pennsylvania
Delaware	Mike Brey	24-8	to Notre Dame*	David Henderson	Asst., Duke
Delaware St.	Tony Sheals	6-22	resigned	Greg Jackson	Coach, NC Central
Eastern Kentucky	Scott Perry	6-21	resigned	Travis Ford	Coach, Campbellsville
Eastern Michigan	Milton Barnes	15-13	fired	Jim Boone	Coach, Robert Morris
Eastern Washington	Steve Aggers	15-12	to Loyola-Marymount*	Ray Giacoletti	Coach, N. Dakota St.
Florida International	Shakey Rodriguez	16-14	resigned	Donnie Marsh	Assoc. head, Va. Tech
Georgia Tech	Bobby Cremins	13-17	retired	Paul Hewitt	Coach, Siena
Hartford	Paul Brazeau	10-19	resigned	Larry Harrison	Asst., DePaul
Houston	Clyde Drexler	9-22	resigned	Ray McCallum	Coach, Ball St.
Howard	Kirk Saulny	1-27†	fired	Frankie Allen	Coach, Tennessee St.
Illinois	Lon Kruger	21-9	to NBA Atlanta*	Bill Self	Coach, Tulsa
Indiana	Bobby Knight	20-9	fired	Mike Davis	Asst., Indiana
Jacksonville St.	Mark Turgeon	17-11	to Wichita St.*	Mike LaPlante	Asst., Auburn
Kansas St.	Tom Asbury	9-19	resigned	Jim Wooldridge	Asst., NBA Bulls
Loyola Marymount	Charles Bradley	8-20	resigned	Steve Aggers	Coach, Eastern Wash.
Loyola-MD	Dino Gaudio	7-21	resigned	Scott Hicks	Coach, Albany
MD-Eastern Shore	Lonnie Williams	12-17	fired	Thomas Trotter	Asst., New Mexico St.
Memphis	Johnny Jones	15-16	interim@	John Calipari	Asst., NBA 76ers
Miami-FL	Leonard Hamilton	23-11	to NBA Wash.*	Perry Clark	Coach, Tulane
Missouri-KC	Bob Sundvold	16-13	fired	Dean Demopoulos	Asst., Temple
Nebraska	Danny Nee	11-19	fired	Barry Collier	Coach, Butler
North Carolina	Bill Guthridge	22-14	resigned	Matt Doherty	Coach, Notre Dame
Northwestern	Kevin O'Neill	5-25	to NBA N.Y.**	Bill Carmody	Coach, Princeton
Notre Dame	Matt Doherty	22-15	to N. Carolina*	Mike Brey	Coach, Delaware
Oregon St.	Eddie Payne	13-16	fired	Ritchie McKay	Coach, Colorado St.
Princeton	Bill Carmody	19-11	to Northwestern*	John Thompson III	Asst., Princeton
Robert Morris	Jim Boone	18-12	to Eastern Mich.*	Danny Nee	Coach, Nebraska
St. Peter's	Rodger Blind	5-23	fired	Bob Leckie	Coach, Bishop Loughlin HS (NY)
Siena	Paul Hewitt	24-9	to Georgia Tech*	Louis Orr	Asst., Syracuse
SW Texas St.	Mike Miller	12-17	to Kansas St.**	Dennis Nutt	Asst., Arkansas St.

	Old Coach	Record	Why Left?	New Coach	Old Job
S.F. Austin St.	Derek Allister	6-21	resigned	Danny Kaspar	Coach, Incarnate Word
Tennessee St.	Frankie Allen	7-22	to Howard*	Nolan Richardson III	Asst., Arkansas
Tulane	Perry Clark	20-11	to Miami-FL*	Shawn Finney	Asst., Kentucky
Tulsa	Bill Self	32-5	to Illinois*	Buzz Peterson	Coach, App. St.
W. Carolina	Phil Hopkins	14-14	fired	Steve Shurina	Asst., Vanderbilt
W. Michigan	Bob Donewald	10-18	reassigned	Robert McCullum	Asst., Illinois
Wichita St.	Randy Smithson	12-17	resigned	Mark Turgeon	Coach, Jacksonville St.
William & Mary	Charlie Woollum	11-17	retired	Rick Boyages	Assoc. head, Ohio St.

* as head coach
** as assistant coach
# Cohane (2-3) resigned on Dec. 3, 1999 and was replaced by Witherspoon for the rest of the season.
† Saulny (0-9) was fired on Jan. 7, 2000 and was replaced by football assistant coach William Coward for the remainder of the season.
@ Jones replaced Tic Price, who resigned on Nov. 14, 1999, just before the start of the season.

Division I-A Football

	Old Coach	Record	Why Left?	New Coach	Old Job
Army	Bob Sutton	3-8	fired	Todd Berry	Coach, Illinois St.
Central Michigan	Dick Flynn	4-7	resigned	Mike DeBord	Off. coord., Michigan
Eastern Michigan	Rick Rasnick	4-7#	fired	Jeff Woodruff	Asst., Arizona
Houston	Kim Helton	7-4	fired	Dana Dimel	Coach, Wyoming
Idaho	Chris Tormey	7-4	to Nevada*	Tom Cable	Off. coord., Colorado
LSU	Gerry DiNardo	3-8@	fired	Nick Saban	Coach, Michigan St.
Michigan St.	Nick Saban	10-2&	to LSU*	Bobby Williams	Asst., Michigan St.
Nevada	Jeff Tisdel	3-8	resigned	Chris Tormey	Coach, Idaho
N.C. State	Mike O'Cain	6-6	fired	Chuck Amato	Asst., Florida St.
Texas Tech	Spike Dykes	6-5	retired	Mike Leach	Off. coord., Oklahoma
Tulsa	Dave Rader	2-9%	fired	Keith Burns	Def. coord., Arkansas
Utah St.	Dave Arslanian	4-7	fired	Mick Dennehy	Coach, Montana
UTEP	Charlie Bailey	5-7	retired	Gary Nord	Off. coord., UTEP
Wyoming	Dana Dimel	7-4	to Houston*	Vic Koenning	Def. coord., Wyoming

* as head coach
# Rasnick (4-6) was fired on Nov. 16, 1999 and replaced by defensive coordinator Tony Lombardi for the final game of the season.
@ DiNardo (2-8) was fired on Nov. 15, 1999 and replaced by assistant coach Hal Hunter for the final game of the season.
& Saban (9-2) left the team on Nov. 30, 1999 and was replaced by Williams for the final game of the season, the Citrus Bowl.
% Rader (1-6) was fired on Oct. 25, 1999 and was replaced by defensive coordinator Pat Henderson for the final four games of the season.

Division I-AA Football

	Old Coach	Record	Why Left?	New Coach	Old Job
Alabama St.	Ron Dickerson	2-9	fired	L.C. Cole	Coach, Tennessee St.
Canisius	Chuck Williams	1-10	resigned	Edward Argast	Asst., Colgate
Davidson	Tim Landis	8-3	to St. Mary's*	Joe Susan	Off. coord., Princeton
Delaware St.	John McKenzie	4-7	fired	Ben Blacknall	Def. coord., Morehouse
Eastern Washington	Mike Kramer	7-4	to Montana St.*	Paul Wulff	Off. coord., E. Wash.
Illinois St.	Todd Berry	11-3	to Army*	Denver Johnson	Coach, Murray St.
Jacksonville St.	Mike Williams	2-9@	resigned	Jack Crowe	Off. coord., Baylor
Lafayette	Bill Russo	4-7	resigned	Frank Tavani	Assoc. head, Lafayette
Liberty	Sam Rutigliano	4-7	retired	Ken Karcher	Off. coord, NFL Europe Rhein
McNeese St.	Kirby Bruchhaus	6-5	resigned	Tommy Tate	Def. coord., McNeese
Montana	Mick Dennehy	9-3	to Utah St.*	Joe Glenn	Coach, Northern Colo.
Montana St.	Cliff Hysell	3-8	resigned	Mike Kramer	Coach, E. Washington
Murray St.	Denver Johnson	7-4	to Illinois St.*	Joe Pannunzio	Asst., Auburn
Northeastern	Barry Gallup	2-9	resigned	Don Brown	Def. coord., UMass
Northwestern St.	Sam Goodwin	4-7	retired	Steve Roberts	Coach, S. Arkansas
Princeton	Steve Tosches	3-7	resigned	Roger Hughes	Off. coord., Dartmouth
Rhode Island	Floyd Keith	1-10	resigned	Tim Stowers	Asst., Temple
Sacred Heart	Tom Radulski	2-9†	fired	Jim Fleming	Def. coord., Villanova
St. Mary's-CA	Mike Rasmussen	2-9	fired	Tim Landis	Coach, Davidson
Siena	Chris Phelps	3-7	resigned	Jay Bateman	Def. coord., Siena
SE Missouri St.	John Mumford	3-8	resigned	Tim Billings	Def. coord., Marshall
Tennessee-Martin	Jim Marshall	1-10	resigned	Sam McCorkle	Off. coord., Miss. Delta
Tennessee St.	L.C. Cole	11-1	to Alabama St.*	James Reese	Off. coord., Tenn. St.

* as head coach
@ Williams (1-3) resigned on Oct. 4, 1999 and was replaced by offensive coordinator Jeff Richards for the remainder of the season.
† Radulski (1-5) was fired on Oct. 12, 1999 and was replaced by assistant Walt Czekaj for the remainder of the season.

1999-00 Directors' Cup

Officially, the Sears Directors' Cup and sponsored by the National Association of Collegiate Directors of Athletics. Introduced in 1993-94 to honor the nation's best overall NCAA Division I athletic department (combining men's and women's sports), winners in NCAA Division II and III and NAIA were named for the first time following the 1995-96 season.

Standings are computed by NACDA with points awarded for each Div. I school's finish in 20 sports (top 10 scoring sports for both men and women). Div. II schools are awarded points in 14 sports (top 7 scoring sports for both men and women). Div III schools are awarded points in 18 sports (top 9 scoring sports for both men and women). NAIA schools are awarded points in 12 sports (top 6 scoring sports for both men and women). National champions in each sport earn 100 points, while 2nd through 64th-place finishers earn decreasing points depending on the size of the tournament field. Division I-A football points are based on the final ESPN/*USA Today* Coaches' Top 25 poll. Listed below are team conferences (for Div. I only), combined Final Four finishes (1st through 4th place) for men's and women's programs, overall points in **bold** type, and the previous year's ranking (for Div. I only).

Multiple Winners: Stanford (6); Simon Fraser, BC and Williams, MA (4); UC-Davis (3)

Division I

		Conf	1-2-3-4	Pts	98-99 Rank			Conf	1-2-3-4	Pts	98-99 Rank
1	Stanford	Pac-10	2-6-2-3	**1359.5**	1	14	Ohio St.	Big Ten	0-1-0-0	**682**	15
2	UCLA	Pac-10	4-1-2-0	**1153.5**	5	15	California	Pac-10	0-0-1-2	**669.5**	23
3	Michigan	Big Ten	0-2-0-0	**965**	6	16	USC	Pac-10	0-1-0-1	**666.5**	9
4	Penn St.	Big Ten	3-0-3-0	**909**	3	17	Wisconsin	Big Ten	0-1-1-2	**661.5**	25
5	N. Carolina	ACC	1-0-1-0	**908.5**	17	18	BYU	Mountain West	1-0-0-1	**657.5**	12
6	Nebraska	Big 12	0-1-1-1	**906**	12	19	Minnesota	Big Ten	0-0-1-0	**627**	21
7	Florida	SEC	0-1-2-1	**842**	4	20	Tennessee	SEC	0-1-1-0	**621**	17
8	Arizona	Pac-10	1-1-3-0	**837.5**	9	21	Notre Dame	Big East	0-2-0-0	**594.5**	25
9	Texas	Big 12	1-0-1-0	**801**	11	22	Michigan St.	Big Ten	1-0-0-0	**587**	34
10	LSU	SEC	2-0-0-1	**764**	16	23	Auburn	SEC	0-1-1-0	**572**	20
11	Arizona St.	Pac-10	0-0-0-0	**733**	12	24	Duke	ACC	0-0-0-0	**566**	7
12	Georgia	SEC	2-0-1-0	**728.5**	2	25	Oklahoma	Big 12	1-0-0-2	**563.5**	51
13	Virginia	ACC	0-0-2-0	**698.5**	8						

Division II

		1-2-3-4	Pts			1-2-3-4	Pts
1	UC-Davis	0-0-2-1	**670.5**	14	Northern Colorado	0-0-0-0	**316.5**
2	North Dakota St.	2-2-0-1	**583.5**	15	St. Cloud St., MN	0-0-0-0	**306.5**
3	North Dakota	1-0-1-1	**553.5**	16	Bloomsburg, PA	1-0-1-0	**298.5**
4	Florida Southern	2-0-0-0	**473**	17	Fort Hays St., KS	0-1-0-0	**298**
5	Western St., CO	1-1-0-1	**462.5**	18	South Dakota	0-0-1-0	**297**
6	CS-Bakersfield	1-1-0-0	**435.5**	19	Nebraska-Kearney	0-0-0-0	**292.5**
7	Indiana, PA	0-0-1-0	**394**	20	Lewis, IL	0-0-0-1	**289.5**
8	Adams St., CO	1-1-1-1	**392.5**	21	Gardner-Webb, NC	0-0-0-0	**289**
9	Truman St., MO	0-1-0-0	**364.5**	22	Southern Connecticut St.	1-0-0-0	**287**
10	Grand Valley St., MI	0-0-0-0	**359.5**	23	Northern Kentucky	1-0-2-0	**280**
11	Central Missouri St.	0-0-0-0	**346**	24	Edinboro, PA	0-0-1-0	**275.5**
12	Abilene Christian, TX	3-1-0-1	**333**	25	Central Washington	0-0-0-0	**271.5**
13	Ashland, OH	0-0-0-0	**319.5**				

Division III

		1-2-3-4	Pts			1-2-3-4	Pts
1	Williams, MA	0-1-3-2	**849**	14	Emory, GA	0-0-1-0	**491**
2	UC-San Diego	1-1-2-1	**788.5**	15	Wisconsin-Whitewater	0-0-0-1	**488.5**
3	College of New Jersey	2-0-1-0	**702.5**	16	Wheaton, IL	0-1-0-0	**486.5**
4	St. Thomas, MN	0-2-1-0	**586**	17	Cortland St., NY	0-0-1-0	**419**
5	Middlebury, VT	1-1-1-0	**573.5**	18	Salisbury St., MD	0-1-1-0	**405**
6	Calvin, MI	2-0-0-1	**551**	19	St. Olaf, MN	0-0-0-1	**385.5**
7	Wisconsin-Stevens Pt.	0-0-0-1	**548**	20	Pacific Lutheran, WA	1-0-0-0	**368.5**
8	Wisconsin-Eau Claire	0-1-0-1	**545**	21	Ithaca, NY	0-0-0-0	**361**
9	Rowan, NJ	0-1-0-0	**537**	22	Johns Hopkins, MD	0-0-1-0	**347**
10	Trinity, TX	2-1-1-0	**525**	23	Washington, MO	1-0-0-0	**340**
11	Wisconsin-La Crosse	0-0-2-1	**508**	24	Hamilton, NY	0-0-0-0	**339**
12	Amherst, MA	0-1-0-1	**501**	25	Central, IA	1-0-1-0	**329**
13	Springfield, MA	0-0-1-0	**497**				

NAIA

		1-2-3-4	Pts			1-2-3-4	Pts
1	Simon Fraser, BC	2-1-2-2	**778.5**	14	McKendree, IL	1-2-0-0	**381.5**
2	Lindenwood, MO	0-0-0-0	**626.5**	15	Westmont, CA	1-0-1-0	**367**
3	Azusa Pacific, CA	0-1-3-1	**607**	16	Pt. Loma Nazarene, CA	0-1-0-0	**357.5**
4	Mary, ND	1-0-2-0	**589**	17	CS-San Marcos	0-0-1-0	**356.5**
5	Oklahoma City	3-0-2-0	**567.5**	18	Biola, CA	0-0-1-0	**349.5**
6	Findlay, OH	0-0-1-0	**516**	19	Briar Cliff, IA	0-0-0-0	**338.5**
7	California Baptist	0-2-0-0	**496.5**	20	Embry-Riddle, FL	1-0-0-0	**335**
8	Life, GA	5-1-0-0	**490**	21	Auburn-Montgomery, AL	1-1-0-0	**320**
9	Malone, OH	2-0-1-0	**422**	22	Taylor, IN	0-1-1-0	**305.5**
10	Hastings, NE	0-0-1-0	**410**	23	Oklahoma Baptist	0-0-0-1	**296.5**
11	Mobile, AL	0-1-0-1	**409**	24	Huntington, IN	0-0-1-0	**291**
12	Lewis-Clark St., ID	1-0-0-0	**408.5**	25	Lindsey Wilson, KY	1-0-0-0	**290**
13	Cumberland, KY	0-0-0-0	**396.5**				

NCAA Division I Schools on Probation

As of September 1, 2000, there were 22 Division I member institutions serving NCAA probations.

School	Sport	Yrs	Penalty To End	School	Sport	Yrs	Penalty To End
Texas-Pan American	M Basketball	8	7/25/00	Texas Tech	M & W Basketball	4	4/24/02
Cincinnati	M Basketball	2	8/7/00		Football	4	4/24/02
Weber St.	M Basketball	4	8/7/00		Baseball	4	4/24/02
Wisconsin	No Specific Sport	2	11/13/00		Golf	4	4/24/02
SE Missouri St.	M Basketball	3	1/31/01		M Track	4	4/24/02
Purdue	M & W Basketball	2	4/8/01		W Soccer	4	4/24/02
UCLA	Softball	4	4/30/01		W Volleyball	4	4/24/02
	& M Basketball	4	4/30/01		& M Tennis	4	4/24/02
Louisville	M Basketball	5	8/9/01	Texas-El Paso	M & W Basketball	5	5/1/02
	& W Volleyball	5	8/9/01		Football	5	5/1/02
Texas Southern	M/W Track and XC	5	8/11/01		& W Rifle	5	5/1/02
	Football	5	8/11/01	Gonzaga	M Basketball	4	6/5/02
	Baseball	5	8/11/01	CS-Fullerton	M Basketball	4	11/14/02
	M Tennis	5	8/11/01	Tennessee St.	Football	3	1/5/03
	& M Golf	5	8/11/01		M Tennis	3	1/5/03
Arkansas-LR	M & W Basketball	2	9/24/01		& M Golf	3	1/5/03
LSU	M Basketball	3	9/26/01	Bucknell	M Wrestling	4	2/6/03
Michigan St.	Wrestling	6	12/2/01	Dayton	M Basketball	3	4/18/03
	& W Track	6	12/2/01	CS-Northridge	Football	3	5/31/03
Notre Dame	Football	2	12/17/01	Jackson St.	M Track and XC	5	5/16/05

Remaining postseason and TV sanctions
2000-2001 postseason ban: CS-Northridge football; Jackson St. mens track and XC.
2000-2001 television ban: None.

NCAA Graduation Rates

The following table compares graduation rates of NCAA Division I student athletes with the entire student body in those schools. Years given denote the year in which students entered college. Rates are based on students who enrolled as freshmen, received an athletics scholarship and graduated in six years or less. All figures are percentages.
Source: NCAA Graduation-Rate Report, 1999.

	1987	1988	1989	1990	1991	1992
All Student Athletes	57	58	58	58	57	58
Entire Student Body	56	57	57	56	56	56
Male Student Athletes	53	53	53	53	51	52
Male Student Body	54	55	55	54	53	54
Female Student Athletes	67	69	67	68	67	68
Female Student Body	58	58	59	58	58	59
Div. I-A Football Players	55	56	56	52	50	51
Male Basketball Players	46	42	44	45	41	41
Female Basketball Players	62	65	65	67	66	62

1999-00 NCAA Team Champions

Seventeen schools won two or more national championships during the 1999-00 academic year, led by Division I UCLA with four.

Multiple winners: Four— UCLA (National Div. men's volleyball, National Div. men's water polo, National Div. women's gymnastics, Div. I women's indoor track). **Three**— ABILENE CHRISTIAN (Div. II men's indoor track and women's indoor track, Div. II men's outdoor track); LINCOLN, PA (Div. III men's indoor track, Div. III men's and women's outdoor track); PENN ST. (Nat'l Div. men's gymnastics, Div. I women's volleyball, Nat'l Div. fencing).

Two— ARKANSAS (Div. I men's cross country and Div. I men's indoor track); BRIGHAM YOUNG-HAWAII (Div. II women's volleyball and Div. II women's tennis); CALVIN, MI (Div. III men's basketball and Div. III women's cross country); COLLEGE OF NEW JERSEY (Division III field hockey and Div. III women's lacrosse); FLORIDA SOUTHERN (Div. II men's golf and women's golf); GEORGIA (Div. I women's swimming & diving and Div. I women's tennis); KENYON (Div. III men's swimming & diving and women's swimming & diving); LSU (Div. I baseball and Div. I women's outdoor track); MARYLAND (Div. I field hockey and Div. I women's lacrosse); NORTH CENTRAL, IL (Div. III men's cross country and men's outdoor track); NORTH DAKOTA ST. (Div. II wrestling and Div. II softball); STANFORD (Div. I men's tennis and Div. I men's outdoor track); TRINITY, TX (Div. III men's tennis and women's tennis).

Overall titles in parentheses; (*) indicates defending champions.

FALL

Cross Country

Men

Div.	Winner		Runner-Up	Score
I	Arkansas*	(10)	Wisconsin	58-185
II	Western St., CO	(2)	Adams St., CO*	27-95
III	North Central, IL*	(12)	Keene St., NH	84-100

Women

Div.	Winner		Runner-Up	Score
I	Brigham Young	(2)	Arkansas	72-125
II	Adams St., CO*	(8)	Western St., CO	23-47
III	Calvin, MI*	(2)	Middlebury, VT	85-119

Field Hockey

Div.	Winner		Runner-Up	Score
I	Maryland	(3)	Michigan	2-1
II	Bloomsburg, PA*	(6)	Bentley, MA	2-0
III	College of NJ	(9)	Amherst, MA	4-1

Football

Div.	Winner	Runner-Up		Score
I-A	Florida St.	(2) Virginia Tech		AP poll
I-AA	Georgia Southern	(5) Youngstown St.		59-24
II	NW Missouri St.*	(2) Carson-Newman	58-52 (4OT)	
III	Pacific Lutheran	(1) Rowan, NJ		42-13

Note: There is no official Div. I-A playoff.

Soccer

Men

Div.	Winner		Runner-Up	Score
I	Indiana*	(5)	Santa Clara	1-0
II	Southern Conn. St.*	(6)	Fort Lewis, CO	2-1 (OT)
III	St. Lawrence, NY	(1)	Wheaton, IL	2-0

Women

Div.	Winner		Runner-Up	Score
I	North Carolina	(15)	Notre Dame	2-0
II	Franklin Pierce, NH	(5)	Cal Poly Pomona	3-1
III	UC San Diego	(5)	Macalester, MN*	1-0

Volleyball

Women

Div.	Winner		Runner-Up	Score
I	Penn St.	(1)	Stanford	3 games
II	BYU-Hawaii	(1)	Tampa	3 games
III	Central, IA*	(2)	Trinity, TX	3 games

Water Polo

Men

Div.	Winner		Runner-Up	Score
National	UCLA	(6)	Stanford	6-5

WINTER

Basketball

Men

Div.	Winner		Runner-Up	Score
I	Michigan St.	(2)	Florida	89-76
II	Metropolitan St., CO	(1)	Kentucky Wesleyan*	97-79
III	Calvin, MI	(2)	Wisc.-Eau Claire	79-74

Women

Div.	Winner		Runner-Up	Score
I	Connecticut	(2)	Tennessee	71-52
II	Northern Kentucky	(1)	North Dakota St.	71-62 (OT)
III	Washington, MO*	(3)	Southern Maine	79-33

Fencing

Div.	Winner		Runner-Up	Score
Combined	Penn St.*	(8)	Notre Dame & St. John's	175-171

Gymnastics

	Winner		Runner-Up	Margin
Men	Penn St.	(10)	Michigan*	by .125
Women	UCLA	(2)	Utah	by .425

Ice Hockey

Div.	Winner		Runner-Up	Score
I	North Dakota	(7)	Boston College	4-2
III	Norwich, VT	(1)	St. Thomas, MN	2-1

Real Gender Equity

Schools whose men's and women's teams won NCAA championships in the same sport, or its equivalent during the 1999-00 season.

School	Div.	Sports	School	Div.	Sports
Abilene Christian	II	Men's Indoor Track Women's Indoor Track	Lincoln, PA	III	Men's Outdoor Track Women's Outdoor Track
Florida Southern	II	Men's Golf Women's Golf	Trinity, TX	III	Men's Tennis Women's Tennis
Kenyon, OH	III	Men's Swimming Women's Swimming			

Rifle

Div.	Winner		Runner-Up	Score
Combined	..AK-Fairbanks*	(3)	Xavier	6285-6156

Skiing

Div.	Winner		Runner-Up	Score
Combined	.......Denver	(15)	Colorado*	729-621

Swimming & Diving
Men

Div.	Winner		Runner-Up	Score
I	.............Texas	(7)	Auburn*	538-385
II	.....CS-Bakersfield	(10)	Drury, MO*	687-630
III	.....Kenyon, OH*	(21)	Denison, OH	670½-317

Women

Div.	Winner		Runner-Up	Score
I	..............Georgia*	(2)	Arizona	490½-472
II	.......Drury, MO*	(4)	Truman, MO	663-556
III	......Kenyon, OH*	(17)	Denison, OH	619½-417½

Indoor Track
Men

Div.	Winner		Runner-Up	Score
I	...........Arkansas*	(16)	Stanford	69½-52
II	....Abilene Christian*	(8)	St. Augustine's	80-77
III	.........Lincoln, PA*	(6)	North Central, IL	59-40

Women

Div.	Winner		Runner-Up	Score
I	...............UCLA	(1)	South Carolina	51-41
II	....Abilene Christian*	(12)	North Dakota St.	48-47
III	......Wheaton, MA*	(2)	Lincoln, PA	47-41

Wrestling

Div.	Winner		Runner-Up	Score
I	.............Iowa*	(20)	Iowa St.	116-109½
II	...North Dakota St.	(3)	Central Oklahoma	91½-75
III	....Augsburg, MN	(6)	Wartburg, IA*	136-88

SPRING
Baseball

Div.	Winner		Runner-Up	Score
I	..................LSU	(5)	Stanford	6-5
II	......SE Oklahoma St.	(1)	Fort Hays St., KS	7-2
III	.....Montclair St., NJ	(3)	St. Thomas, MN	6-2

Golf
Men

Div.	Winner		Runner-Up	Score
I	........Oklahoma St.	(9)	Georgia Tech	1116-1116†
II	.....Florida Southern*	(11)	Grand Canyon & CS-Bakers.	1140-1169
III	.....Greensboro, NC	(1)	Methodist, NC*	881-882@

†Oklahoma St. won on the first sudden death playoff hole.
@rain shortened

Women

Div.	Winner		Runner-Up	Score
I	...............Arizona	(2)	Stanford	1175-1196
II	..........Fla. Southern	(1)	Rollins, FL	1259-1266
III	........Methodist, NC*	(3)	Concordia, MN	1285-1336

Lacrosse
Men

Div.	Winner		Runner-Up	Score
I	.............Syracuse	(6)	Princeton	13-7
II	........Limestone, SC	(1)	C.W. Post	10-9
III	......Middlebury, VT	(1)	Salisbury St., MD*	16-12

Women

Div.	Winner		Runner-Up	Score
National	.....Maryland*	(8)	Princeton	16-8
III	.......College of NJ	(10)	Williams, MA	14-8

Rowing
Women

Div.	Winner		Runner-Up	Score
National	........Brown*	(2)	Washington	59-55

Note: The 1997 National Collegiate Women's Rowing Championships were the first to be sponsored by the NCAA. National championships had been held without NCAA sponsorship since 1979.

Softball

Div.	Winner		Runner-Up	Score
I	...........Oklahoma	(1)	UCLA	3-1
II	.....N. Dakota St.	(1)	Kennesaw St., GA	3-1
III	......St. Mary's, MN	(1)	Chapman, CA	5-0

Tennis

Note that both Div. II tournaments were team-only.

Men

Div.	Winner		Runner-Up	Score
I	...........Stanford	(17)	Virginia Comm.	4-0
II	........Lander, SC*	(8)	Hawaii Pacific	5-2
III	.........Trinity, TX	(1)	Gustavus Adolphus, MN	4-3

Women

Div.	Winner		Runner-Up	Score
I	............Georgia	(2)	Stanford*	5-4
II	..........BYU-Hawaii*	(2)	Lynn, FL	5-0
III	...........Trinity, TX	(1)	UC-San Diego	5-4

Outdoor Track
Men

Div.	Winner		Runner-Up	Score
I	.............Stanford	(4)	Arkansas*	72-59
II	....Abilene Christian*	(11)	St. Augustine's	115-71
III	.........Lincoln, PA* & North Central, IL	(6) (4)	Central, IA	52 (tie)-38

Women

Div.	Winner		Runner-Up	Score
I	..................LSU	(12)	USC	59-56
II	....St. Augustine's	(2)	Abilene Christian*	77-66
III	..........Lincoln, PA*	(3)	Christopher Newport	65-50

Volleyball
Men

Div.	Winner		Runner-Up	Score
National	.........UCLA	(18)	Ohio St.	3 games

Wisconsin
Erica Palmer
Cross Country

Stanford
Felix Reichling
Fencing

Iowa St.
Cael Sanderson
Wrestling

Ohio St.
Jamie Natalie
Gymnastics

1999-00 Division I Individual Champions
Repeat champions in **bold** type.

FALL
Cross Country

Men (10,000 meters)	**Time**
1 David Kimani, S. Alabama	30:06.6
2 Michael Power, Arkansas	30:09.6
3 Steve Fein, Oregon	30:14.3

Women (5,000 meters)	**Time**
1 Erica Palmer, Wisconsin	16:39.5
2 Amy Yoder, Arkansas	16:44.1
3 Larissa Kleinman, Arkansas	16:48.8

WINTER
Fencing
Men

Event		Score
Foil	**Felix Reichling**, Stanford	15-10
Epee	Daniel Landgren, Penn St.	15-12
Sabre	Gabor Szelle, Notre Dame	15-12

Women

Event		Score
Foil	Eva Petschnigg, Princeton	15-13
Epee	Jessica Burke, Penn St.	15-13
Sabre	Caroline Purcell, MIT	15-6

Gymnastics
Men

Event		Points
All-Around	Jamie Natalie, Ohio St.	58.375
Floor Exercise	Jamie Natalie, Ohio St.	9.9000
Pommel Horse	**Brandon Stefaniak**, Penn St.	9.9125
	& Don Jackson, Iowa	9.9125
Rings	**Cortney Bramwell**, BYU	9.9500
Vault	**Guard Young**, BYU	9.8250
Parallel Bars	**Justin Toman**, Michigan	9.9000
	& Kris Zimmerman, Michigan	9.9000
Horizontal Bar	Michael Ashe, California	9.9000

Women

Event		Points
All-Around	Heather Brink, Nebraska	39.600
Vault	Heather Brink, Nebraska	9.9500
Uneven Bars	Mohini Bhardwaj, UCLA	9.9500
Balance Beam	Lena Degteva, UCLA	9.9130
Floor Exercise	Suzanne Sears, Georgia	9.9500

Rifle
Combined
Smallbore

		Points
1	Nicole Allaire, Nebraska	1183
2	Matthew Emmons, AK-Fairbanks	1183
3	Melissa Mulloy, AK-Fairbanks	1174

Note: Allaire won the event over Emmons with more inner tens (80-78).

Air Rifle

		Points
1	**Kelly Mansfield**, AK-Fairbanks	398
2	Emily Caruso, Norwich	396
3	Matthew Emmons, AK-Fairbanks	393

Skiing
Men

Event		Time
Slalom	Andy Leroy, Colorado	1:39.12
Giant Slalom	Matthew Knittle, Vermont	2:21.32
10-k Freestyle	Pietro Broggini, Denver	29:06.8
20-k Classic	Pietro Broggini, Denver	45:46.0

Women

Event		Time
Slalom	Cecile Hagen Larsen, Denver	1:41.96
Giant Slalom	**Aimee-Noel Hartley**, Colorado	2:24.46
5-k Freestyle	Katerina Hanusova, Colorado	17:19.3
15-k Classic	Kristina Strandberg, New Mexico	45:55.6

Wrestling

Wgt	Champion	Runner-Up
125	Jeremy Hunter, Penn St.	Steve Garland, Virginia
133	Eric Juergens, Iowa	Cody Sanderson, Iowa St.
141	Carl Perry, Illinois	Michael Lightner, Okla.
149	Tony Davis, N. Iowa	Adam Tirapelle, Illinois
157	Brett Matter, Penn	Larry Quisel, Boise St.
165	Don Pritzlaff, Wisconsin	Joe Heskett, Iowa St.
174	Byron Tucker, Oklahoma	Josh Koscheck, Edinboro
184	**Cael Sanderson**, Iowa St.	Vertus Jones, W. Virginia
197	Brad Vering, Nebraska	Zach Thompson, Iowa St.
Hvy	Brock Lesnar, Minnesota	Wes Hand, Iowa

Columbia	South Carolina	UCLA	Arizona
Cristina Teuscher	**Terrence Trammell**	**Seilala Sua**	**Jenna Daniels**
Swimming	Track & Field	Track & Field	Golf

Swimming & Diving

(*) indicates world record. (†) indicates tied world record.

Men

Event (meters)		Time
50 free	**Anthony Ervin**, California	21.21*
100 free	Anthony Ervin, California	47.36
200 free	**Ryk Neethling**, Arizona	1:43.90
400 free	**Ryk Neethling**, Arizona	3:40.47
1500 free	Erik Vendt, USC	14:31.02
100 back	Matt Ulrickson, Texas	52.05
200 back	Matt Cole, Florida	1:53.68
100 breast	Ed Moses, Virginia	57.66*
200 breast	Ed Moses, Virginia	2:06.40*
100 butterfly	Adam Pine, Nebraska	51.23
200 butterfly	Adam Messner, Stanford	1:55.79
200 IM	Atilla Czene, Arizona St.	1:54.65†
400 IM	**Tim Siciliano**, Michigan	4:06.02
200 free relay	**Auburn**	1:25.14
400 free relay	Texas	3:31.23
800 free relay	**Texas**	7:05.05
200 medley relay	Texas	1:35.66
400 medley relay	Texas	3:31.23

Diving		Points
1-meter	Troy Dumais, Texas	605.20
3-meter	**Troy Dumais**, Texas	662.65
Platform	Tyce Routson, Miami-FL	596.10

Women

Event (meters)		Time
50 free	Courtney Shealy, Georgia	24.80
100 free	Courtney Shealy, Georgia	53.99
200 free	Maritza Correja, Georgia	1:57.33
400 free	Cristina Teuscher, Columbia	4:04.09
1500 free	Cara Lane, Virginia	16:03.59
100 back	Courtney Shealy, Georgia	58.66
200 back	Beth Botsford, Arizona	2:06.70
100 breast	**Kristy Kowal**, Georgia	1:05.74
200 breast	**Kristy Kowal**, Georgia	2:22.05
100 butterfly	Limin Liu, Nevada	57.97
200 butterfly	**Limin Liu**, Nevada	2:06.04
200 IM	Kristy Kowal, Georgia	2:10.69
400 IM	Cristina Teuscher, Columbia	4:33.81
200 free relay	California	1:40.18
400 free relay	Georgia	3:37.67
800 free relay	Arizona	7:55.51
200 medley relay	California	1:49.23*
400 medley relay	Georgia	3:57.46*

Diving		Points
1-meter	Jamie Watkins, LSU	439.70
3-meter	Ashley Culpepper, LSU	538.25
Platform	Jenny Keim, Miami-FL	538.80

Indoor Track

(*) indicates meet record

Men

Event		Time
60 meters	Terrence Trammell, S. Carolina	6.54
200 meters	Shawn Crawford, Clemson	20.26*
400 meters	Brandon Couts, Baylor	45.79
800 meters	Jess Strutzel, UCLA	1:46.57
Mile	Gabriel Jennings, Stanford	3:59.46
3000 meters	David Kimani, S. Alabama	7:52.64
5000 meters	David Kimani, S. Alabama	13:52.58
60-m hurdles	**Terrence Trammell**, S. Carolina	7.55
4x400-m relay	Texas Christian	3:06.69
Distance medley relay	Stanford	9:28.83*

Event		Hgt/Dist
High Jump	**Mark Boswell**, Texas	7-7¾
Pole Vault	Russ Buller, LSU	18-8¼
Long Jump	Melvin Lister, Arkansas	26-8½
Triple Jump	**Melvin Lister**, Arkansas	54-7½
Shot Put	Janus Robberts, SMU	65-1¼
35-lb Throw	**Libor Charfreitag**, SMU	78-3¾*

Women

Event		Time
60 meters	Tonya Carter, Florida St.	7.21*
200 meters	Mikele Barber, S. Carolina	23.06
400 meters	Aliann Pompey, Manhattan	52.21
800 meters	Chantee Earl, Pittsburgh	2:02.19
Mile	Carman Douma, Villanova	4:39.91
3000 meters	**Carrie Tollefson**, Villanova	9:13.68
5000 meters	Amy Yoder, Arkansas	15:46.89
60-m hurdles	Vonette Dixon, Auburn	7.94*
4x400-m relay	**Texas**	3:32.56
Distance medley relay	Stanford	11:01.56*

Event		Hgt/Dist
High Jump	Dora Gyorffy, Harvard	6-4¼
Pole Vault	Tracy O'Hara, UCLA	14-6*
Long Jump	Keyon Soley, UCLA	21-4¾
Triple Jump	Keisha Spencer, LSU	46-1½
Shot Put	Seilala Sua, UCLA	56-8
20-lb Throw	Florence Ezeh, SMU	69-11½

SPRING

Golf

Men

		Total
1	Charles Howell, Oklahoma St.	67-66-63-69—265
2	Chris Morris, Houston	71-69-67-66—273
3	Three-way tie at 275.	

Women

		Total
1	Jenna Daniels, Arizona	73-69-68-77—287
2	Julia Kraschinski, Arizona	73-67-70-80—290
3	Marta Prieto, Wake Forest	77-70-71-74—292

Tennis

Men

Singles— Alex Kim (Stanford) def. Carlos Drada (Kentucky), 6-1, 6-1.

Doubles— Cary Franklin & Graydon Oliver (Illinois) def. Ryan Moore & Nick Rainey (USC), 6-4, 6-2.

Women

Singles— Laura Granville (Stanford) def. Marissa Irvin (Stanford), 6-0, 6-4.

Doubles— Amy Jensen & Claire Curran (California) def. Lori Grey & Marissa Catlin (Georgia), 4-6, 6-1, 7-5.

Outdoor Track

(*) indicates meet record

Men

Event		Time
100 meters	Bernard Williams, Florida	10.03
200 meters	Shawn Crawford, Clemson	20.09
400 meters	Avard Moncur, Auburn	44.72
800 meters	Patrick Nduwimana, Arizona	1:45.08
1500 meters	Gabe Jennings, Stanford	3:37.76
5000 meters	Brad Hauser, Stanford	13:48.80
10,000 meters	Brad Hauser, Stanford	30:38.57
110-m hurdles	**Terrence Trammell**, S. Carolina	13.43
400-m hurdles	Felix Sanchez, USC	48.41
3000-m steeple	Tim Broe, Alabama	8:39.03
4x100-m relay	Florida	38.35
4x400-m relay	Baylor	3:01.46

Event		Hgt/Dist
High Jump	**Mark Boswell**, Texas	7-7
Pole Vault	Russ Buller, LSU	18-4½
Long Jump	Savante Stringfell, Mississippi	26-9¾
Triple Jump	Melvin Lister, Arkansas	55-7¾
Shot Put	Joachim Olsen, Idaho	66-5¾
Discus	**Gábor Máté**, Auburn	215-8
Javelin	Esko Mikkola, Arizona	238-3
Hammer	Libor Charfreitag, SMU	253-4
Decathlon	Bevan Hart, California	8002 pts

Women

Event		Time
100 meters	**Angela Williams**, USC	11.12
200 meters	Peta-Gaye Dowdie, LSU	22.51
400 meters	Mikele Barber, S. Carolina	51.14
800 meters	Tytti Reho, BYU	2:01.43
1500 meters	Susan Taylor, BYU	4:13.03
3000 meters	Cara Wheeler, Colorado	9:02.15
5000 meters	Cara Wheeler, Colorado	15:54.30
10,000 meters	Tara Rohatinski, BYU	33:49.24
100-m hurdles	Joyce Bates, LSU	12.85
400-m hurdles	Natasha Danvers, USC	55.26
4x100-m relay	USC	43.14
4x400-m relay	South Carolina	3:28.64

Event		Hgt/Dist
High Jump	Erin Aldrich, Texas	6-2¾
Pole Vault	Tracy O'Hara, UCLA	14-5¼*
Long Jump	Jenny Adams, Houston	21-5½
Triple Jump	Keisha Spencer, LSU	45-10
Shot Put	**Seilala Sua**, UCLA	56-11½
Discus	**Seilala Sua**, UCLA	200-9
Javelin	Angeliki Tsiolakoudi, UTEP	197-8*
Hammer	**Florence Ezeh**, SMU	211-10*
Heptathlon	Christie Smith, Akron	5797 pts

Championships
Most Outstanding Players
Men

Baseball	Trey Hodges, LSU
Basketball	Mateen Cleaves, Michigan St.
Cross Country	David Kimani, S. Alabama*
Golf	Charles Howell, Oklahoma St.*
Gymnastics	Jamie Natalie, Ohio St.*
Ice Hockey	Lee Goren, North Dakota
Lacrosse	Liam Banks, Syracuse
Soccer: Offense	Yuri Lavrinenko, Indiana
Soccer: Defense	Nick Garcia, Indiana
Swimming & Diving	Ed Moses, Virginia
Tennis	Alex Kim, Stanford*
Track: Indoor	Melvin Lister, Arkansas* Terrence Trammell, S. Carolina* & David Kimani, S. Alabama*
Track: Outdoor	Brad Hauser, Stanford*
Volleyball	Brandon Taliaferro, UCLA
Water Polo	Sean Kern, UCLA
Wrestling	Cael Sanderson, Iowa St.

Women

Basketball	Shea Ralph, Connecticut
Cross Country	Erica Palmer, Wisconsin*
Golf	Jenna Daniels, Arizona*
Gymnastics	Heather Brink, Nebraska
Lacrosse	Jen Adams, Maryland
Soccer: Offense	Susan Bush, N. Carolina
Soccer: Defense	Lorrie Fair, N. Carolina
Softball	Jennifer Stewart, Oklahoma
Swimming & Diving	Kristy Kowal, Georgia & Courtney Shealy, Georgia
Tennis	Laura Granville, Stanford*
Track: Indoor	Mikele Barber, S. Carolina* Seilala Sua, UCLA* & Carrie Tollefson, Villanova*
Track: Outdoor	Cara Wheeler, Colorado* & Seilala Sua, UCLA*
Volleyball	Lauren Cacciamani, Penn St.

(*) indicates won individual or all-around NCAA championship; There were no official Outstanding Players in field hockey, rowing, or the men's and women's combined sports of fencing, riflery and skiing. Outstanding players in indoor and outdoor track are the individuals earning the most points in the NCAA Championships.

1999-00 NAIA Team Champions

Total NAIA titles in parentheses.

FALL

Cross Country: MEN'S–Life, GA (2); WOMEN'S– Malone, OH (1). **Football:** MEN'S– Northwestern Oklahoma St. (1). **Soccer:** MEN'S– Lindsey Wilson, KY (4); WOMEN'S– Westmont, CA (2). **Volleyball:** WOMEN'S– Columbia, MO (2).

WINTER

Basketball: MEN'S– Division I: Life, GA (3) and Division II: Embry-Riddle, FL (1); WOMEN'S– Division I: Oklahoma City (3) and Division II: Mary, ND (1). **Swimming & Diving:** MEN'S– Simon Fraser, BC (3); WOMEN'S– Simon Fraser, BC (7). **Indoor Track:** MEN'S– Life, GA (2); WOMEN'S– McKendree, IL (2). **Volleyball:** MEN'S– Columbia, MO (1); **Wrestling:** MEN'S– Montana St.-Northern (5).

SPRING

Baseball: MEN'S– Lewis-Clark, ID (11); **Golf:** MEN'S– Malone, OH (1); WOMEN'S– Mary Hardin-Baylor (1); **Softball:** WOMEN'S– Oklahoma City (5); **Tennis:** MEN'S– Oklahoma City (3); WOMEN'S– Auburn-Montgomery, AL (3); **Outdoor Track:** MEN'S– Life, GA (4); WOMEN'S– Life, GA (1).

Annual NCAA Division I Team Champions

Men's and women's NCAA Division I team champions from Cross Country to Wrestling. Rowing is included, although the NCAA does not sanction championships on the men's side. Also see team champions for baseball, basketball, football, golf, ice hockey, soccer and tennis in the appropriate chapters throughout the almanac. See pages 456-458 for list of 1999-00 individual champions.

CROSS COUNTRY

Men

Arkansas placed three finishers in the top 10 to run away with their second consecutive men's cross country title and 10th overall. They amassed a total of 58 points, ahead of runner-up Wisconsin (185) and North Carolina St. (201) in the largest margin of victory in the championships' 61-year history. Second-place finisher Michael Power (30:09.6) was the first Razorback to complete the 10,000-meter course. South Alabama freshman David Kimani won his first individual crown with a time of 30:06.6. (Bloomington, IN; Nov. 22, 1999.)

Multiple winners: Arkansas (10); Michigan St. (8); UTEP (7); Oregon and Villanova (4); Drake, Indiana, Penn St. and Wisconsin (3); Iowa St., San Jose St., Stanford and Western Michigan (2).

Year		Year		Year		Year		Year	
1938	Indiana	1950	Penn St.	1963	San Jose St.	1976	UTEP	1989	Iowa St.
1939	Michigan St.	1951	Syracuse	1964	Western Mich.	1977	Oregon	1990	Arkansas
1940	Indiana	1952	Michigan St.	1965	Western Mich.	1978	UTEP	1991	Arkansas
1941	Rhode Island	1953	Kansas	1966	Villanova	1979	UTEP	1992	Arkansas
1942	Indiana	1954	Oklahoma St.	1967	Villanova	1980	UTEP	1993	Arkansas
	& Penn St.	1955	Michigan St.	1968	Villanova	1981	UTEP	1994	Iowa St.
1943	Not held	1956	Michigan St.	1969	UTEP	1982	Wisconsin	1995	Arkansas
1944	Drake	1957	Notre Dame	1970	Villanova	1983	Vacated	1996	Stanford
1945	Drake	1958	Michigan St.	1971	Oregon	1984	Arkansas	1997	Stanford
1946	Drake	1959	Michigan St.	1972	Tennessee	1985	Wisconsin	1998	Arkansas
1947	Penn St.	1960	Houston	1973	Oregon	1986	Arkansas	1999	Arkansas
1948	Michigan St.	1961	Oregon St.	1974	Oregon	1987	Arkansas		
1949	Michigan St.	1962	San Jose St.	1975	UTEP	1988	Wisconsin		

Women

Despite having no runners finish in the top 10, Brigham Young reclaimed its spot atop the women's cross country world, after finishing second last year. It was truly a team effort as the well-balanced Cougars scored 72 points and had all their scorers finish within 18 seconds of each other. Wisconsin's Erica Palmer celebrated her 20th birthday by winning the individual title, finishing the 5,000-meter course in 16:39.5. (Bloomington, IN; Nov. 22, 1999.)

Multiple winners: Villanova (7); Brigham Young, Oregon, Virginia and Wisconsin (2).

Year		Year		Year		Year		Year	
1981	Virginia	1985	Wisconsin	1989	Villanova	1993	Villanova	1997	Brigham Young
1982	Virginia	1986	Texas	1990	Villanova	1994	Villanova	1998	Villanova
1983	Oregon	1987	Oregon	1991	Villanova	1995	Providence	1999	Brigham Young
1984	Wisconsin	1988	Kentucky	1992	Villanova	1996	Stanford		

FENCING

Men & Women

Penn St. narrowly recorded its sixth consecutive NCAA fencing championship and eighth overall. The Nittany Lions scored 175 total points, edging out perennial runner-up Notre Dame and St. John's, which tied for second with 171. Penn St. ruled the epee matches as Jessica Burke defeated Emese Takcs of St. John's in the championship round of the women's epee while Daniel Landgren defeated Alex Roytblat of St. John's for the individual men's epee title. (Stanford, CA; Mar. 23-26, 2000.)

Multiple winners: Penn St. (8); Columbia/Barnard (5). **Note:** Prior to 1990, men and women held separate championships. Men's multiple winners included: NYU (12); Columbia (11); Wayne St. (7); Navy, Notre Dame and Penn (3); Illinois (2). Women's multiple winners included: Wayne St. (3); Yale (2).

Year		Year		Year		Year	
1990	Penn St.	1993	Columbia/Barnard	1996	Penn St.	1999	Penn St.
1991	Penn St.	1994	Notre Dame	1997	Penn St.	2000	Penn St.
1992	Columbia/Barnard	1995	Penn St.	1998	Penn St.		

FIELD HOCKEY

Women

Maryland jumped out to a 2-0 first-half lead and hung on to beat Michigan, 2-1, in the NCAA Field Hockey championship game. It was the Terrapins' third field hockey title and first since 1993. Keli Smith broke the scoreless tie at 10:06 of the first half when she scooped up a loose ball in front of the net and rammed it past goalie Kati Oakes. As time expired in the first half, Carissa Messimer tipped in a Dina Rizzo shot for the game winner. (Boston, MA; Nov. 21, 1999.)

Multiple winners: Old Dominion (8); North Carolina (4); Maryland (3); Connecticut (2).

Year		Year		Year		Year		Year	
1981	Connecticut	1985	Connecticut	1989	North Carolina	1993	Maryland	1997	North Carolina
1982	Old Dominion	1986	Iowa	1990	Old Dominion	1994	J. Madison	1998	Old Dominion
1983	Old Dominion	1987	Maryland	1991	Old Dominion	1995	North Carolina	1999	Maryland
1984	Old Dominion	1988	Old Dominion	1992	Old Dominion	1996	North Carolina		

Annual NCAA Division I Team Champions (Cont.)

GYMNASTICS

Men

Penn St. came out of nowhere to win their 10th overall men's gymnastics title and their first since 1976. Buoyed by an individual title by Brandon Stefaniak in the pommel horse, Penn St. amassed a total of 231.975 points to edge Michigan (231.850) and third-place Iowa (231.525). Ohio State's Jamie Natalie won the individual all-around title and added another individual victory in the floor exercise. (Iowa City, IA; Mar. 31-Apr. 1, 2000.)

Multiple winners: Penn St. (10); Illinois (9); Nebraska (8); California and So. Illinois (4); Iowa St., Michigan, Oklahoma and Stanford (3); Florida St., Ohio St. and UCLA (2).

Year		Year		Year		Year		Year	
1938	Chicago	1956	Illinois	1969	Iowa	1980	Nebraska	1994	Nebraska
1939	Illinois	1957	Penn St.		& Michigan (T)	1981	Nebraska	1995	Stanford
1940	Illinois	1958	Michigan St.	1970	Michigan &	1982	Nebraska	1996	Ohio St.
1941	Illinois		& Illinois		Michigan (T)	1983	Nebraska	1997	California
1942	Illinois	1959	Penn St.	1971	Iowa St.	1984	UCLA	1998	California
1943-47	Not held	1960	Penn St.	1972	So. Illinois	1985	Ohio St.	1999	Michigan
1948	Penn St.	1961	Penn St.	1973	Iowa St.	1986	Arizona St.	2000	Penn St.
1949	Temple	1962	USC	1974	Iowa St.	1987	UCLA	(T) indicates won
1950	Illinois	1963	Michigan	1975	California	1988	Nebraska	trampoline competi-
1951	Florida St.	1964	So. Illinois	1976	Penn St.	1989	Illinois	tion (1969-70).
1952	Florida St.	1965	Penn St.	1977	Indiana St.	1990	Nebraska	
1953	Penn St.	1966	So. Illinois		& Oklahoma	1991	Oklahoma	
1954	Penn St.	1967	So. Illinois	1978	Oklahoma	1992	Stanford	
1955	Illinois	1968	California	1979	Nebraska	1993	Stanford	

Women

On the strength of their performances in the beam, floor, and vault, the UCLA Bruins won their second NCAA gymnastics title in the last four years. They wound up with 197.3 points to beat Utah (196.875) and last year's champion Georgia (196.8), which finished in second and third, respectively. Seniors Lena Degteva and Heidi Moneymaker provided invaluable leadership and experience while the Bruins' tremendous freshman class put them over the top. Nebraska's Heather Brink was the top individual performer, taking home the individual all-around title. (Boise, ID; Apr. 13-15, 2000.)

Multiple winners: Utah (9); Georgia (5); Alabama (3), UCLA (2).

Year		Year		Year		Year		Year	
1982	Utah	1986	Utah	1990	Utah	1994	Utah	1998	Georgia
1983	Utah	1987	Georgia	1991	Alabama	1995	Utah	1999	Georgia
1984	Utah	1988	Alabama	1992	Utah	1996	Alabama	2000	UCLA
1985	Utah	1989	Georgia	1993	Georgia	1997	UCLA		

LACROSSE

Men

Sophomore Liam Banks netted six goals and added one assist to lead Syracuse to a 13-7 victory over Princeton in the NCAA Division I Men's Lacrosse Championship Game. It was Syracuse's sixth men's lacrosse title, first since 1995, and first for coach John Desko. The Orangemen went up 4-0 in the first period and then 6-0 in the second before Princeton could put one past netminder Rob Mulligan. (College Park, MD; May 27-29, 2000.)

Multiple winners: Johns Hopkins (7); Syracuse (6); Princeton (5); North Carolina (4); Cornell (3); Maryland and Virginia (2).

Year		Year		Year		Year		Year	
1971	Cornell	1977	Cornell	1983	Syracuse	1989	Syracuse	1995	Syracuse
1972	Virginia	1978	Johns Hopkins	1984	Johns Hopkins	1990	Syracuse*	1996	Princeton
1973	Maryland	1979	Johns Hopkins	1985	Johns Hopkins	1991	North Carolina	1997	Princeton
1974	Johns Hopkins	1980	Johns Hopkins	1986	North Carolina	1992	Princeton	1998	Princeton
1975	Maryland	1981	North Carolina	1987	Johns Hopkins	1993	Syracuse	1999	Virginia
1976	Cornell	1982	North Carolina	1988	Syracuse	1994	Princeton	2000	Syracuse

*Title was later vacated due to action by the NCAA Committee on Infractions.

Women

Down 4-3 at halftime, Maryland went on a torrid second-half scoring spree to roll past Princeton, 16-8, at the NCAA Division I Women's Lacrosse Championship Game. The Terps blitzed Princeton and goaltender Laura Field, scoring a championship-record 13 goals in the second half. Tournament Most Outstanding Player Jen Adams set a championship single-game mark with 10 points (five goals, five assists) to lead the attack. (Trenton, NJ; May 19-21, 2000.)

Multiple winners: Maryland (8); Penn St., Temple and Virginia (2).

Year		Year		Year		Year		Year	
1982	Massachusetts	1986	Maryland	1990	Harvard	1994	Princeton	1998	Maryland
1983	Delaware	1987	Penn St.	1991	Virginia	1995	Maryland	1999	Maryland
1984	Temple	1988	Temple	1992	Maryland	1996	Maryland	2000	Maryland
1985	New Hampshire	1989	Penn St.	1993	Virginia	1997	Maryland		

RIFLE

Men & Women

Alaska-Fairbanks successfully defended its title, and in record fashion, at the 2000 NCAA Rifle Championships. The Nanooks broke the meet record with an aggregate score of 6,285, well ahead of runner-up Xavier (6,156) and third place Nebraska (6,121). It was the third title overall for Alaska-Fairbanks. Matt Emmons was the Nanooks' top scorer in both the smallbore and air rifle team competitions. (*Lexington, VA; Mar. 9-11, 2000.*)

Multiple winners: West Virginia (13); Alaska-Fairbanks and Tennessee Tech (3); Murray St. (2).

Year		Year		Year		Year		Year	
1980	Tenn. Tech	1985	Murray St.	1990	West Virginia	1995	West Virginia	2000	AK-Fairbanks
1981	Tenn. Tech	1986	West Virginia	1991	West Virginia	1996	West Virginia		
1982	Tenn. Tech	1987	Murray St.	1992	West Virginia	1997	West Virginia		
1983	West Virginia	1988	West Virginia	1993	West Virginia	1998	West Virginia		
1984	West Virginia	1989	West Virginia	1994	AK-Fairbanks	1999	AK-Fairbanks		

ROWING

NCAA Championships
Women

On the strength of victories in both the I and II Varsity Eights races, the Brown Bears won their second consecutive title at the NCAA Rowing Championships. Washington, the 1997 and 98 champ, won the Fours event, catapulting them to a 29-28 lead over Brown going into the I Varsity Eights final. But Brown jumped out to a lead in the first 500 meters and never relinquished it, completing the 2,000 meter course in 6:37.20. Washington finished the race second in 6:41.10 and also finished runner-up to Brown in overall points, 59-55. Virginia came in third with 48. (*Camden, NJ; May 26-28, 2000*).

Multiple winners: Brown and Washington (2).

Year	Overall winner	Varsity Eights	Year	Overall winner	Varsity Eights
1997	Washington	Washington	1999	Brown	Brown
1998	Washington	Washington	2000	Brown	Brown

Intercollegiate Rowing Association Regatta
VARSITY EIGHTS
Men

California successfully defended its title at the 98th IRA Championships Regatta for their 12th overall win. In a span of only 100 meters, the Golden Bears surged from three seats down to eight seats up by the 1,000-meter mark and cruised home for the victory in 5:39.58. Brown finished in second at 5:44.5, followed by Princeton at 5:44.87. (*Cooper River, Camden NJ; June 1-3, 2000.*)

The IRA was formed in 1895 by several Northeastern colleges after Harvard and Yale quit the Rowing Association (established in 1871) to stage an annual race of their own. Since then the IRA Regatta has been contested over courses of varing lengths in Poughkeepsie, N.Y., Marietta, Ohio, Syracuse, N.Y. and Camden, N.J.

Distances: 4 miles (1895-97,1899-1916,1925-41); 3 miles (1898,1921-24,1947-49,1952-63,1965-67); 2 miles (1920,1950-51); 2000 meters (1964, since 1968).

Multiple winners: Cornell (24); Navy (13); California (12); Washington (11); Penn (9); Brown and Wisconsin (7); Syracuse (6); Columbia (4); Princeton (3); Northeastern (2).

Year		Year		Year		Year		Year	
1895	Columbia	1916	Syracuse	1939	California	1964	California	1985	Princeton
1896	Cornell	1917-19	Not held	1940	Washington	1965	Navy	1986	Brown
1897	Cornell	1920	Syracuse	1941	Washington	1966	Wisconsin	1987	Brown
1898	Penn	1921	Navy	1942-46	Not held	1967	Penn	1988	Northeastern
1899	Penn	1922	Navy	1947	Navy	1968	Penn	1989	Penn
1900	Penn	1923	Washington	1948	Washington	1969	Penn	1990	Wisconsin
1901	Cornell	1924	Washington	1949	California	1970	Washington	1991	Northeastern
1902	Cornell	1925	Navy	1950	Washington	1971	Cornell	1992	Dartmouth,
1903	Cornell	1926	Washington	1951	Wisconsin	1972	Penn		Navy & Penn†
1904	Syracuse	1927	Columbia	1952	Navy	1973	Wisconsin	1993	Brown
1905	Cornell	1928	California	1953	Navy	1974	Wisconsin	1994	Brown
1906	Cornell	1929	Columbia	1954	Navy*	1975	Wisconsin	1995	Brown
1907	Cornell	1930	Cornell	1955	Cornell	1976	California	1996	Princeton
1908	Syracuse	1931	Navy	1956	Cornell	1977	Cornell	1997	Washington
1909	Cornell	1932	California	1957	Cornell	1978	Syracuse	1998	Princeton
1910	Cornell	1933	Not held	1958	Cornell	1979	Brown	1999	California
1911	Cornell	1934	California	1959	Wisconsin	1980	Navy	2000	California
1912	Cornell	1935	California	1960	California	1981	Cornell		
1913	Syracuse	1936	Washington	1961	California	1982	Cornell		
1914	Columbia	1937	Washington	1962	Cornell	1983	Brown		
1915	Cornell	1938	Navy	1963	Cornell	1984	Navy		

*In 1954, Navy was disqualified because of an ineligible coxswain; no trophies were given.
†First dead heat in history of IRA Regatta.

Annual NCAA Division I Team Champions (Cont.)

The Harvard-Yale Regatta

After losing last year's event to Yale, the Harvard varsity heavyweights had a point to prove. And they wasted no time in proving it, jumping out to a lead after a half-mile and coasting to an easy win in the 135th running of the Harvard/Yale Regatta on June 10, 2000. Harvard completed the four-mile course on the Thames River in New London, Conn. in 19:44.4, well ahead of the Bulldogs, who recorded a time of 19:54.2. Yale actually held the lead very early on but was overmatched by the Crimson the rest of the way. The Harvard/Yale Regatta is the nation's oldest intercollegiate sporting event. Harvard holds an 82-53 series edge.

National Rowing Championship
VARSITY EIGHTS
Men

National championship raced annually from 1982-96 in Bantam, Ohio over a 2,000-meter course on Lake Harsha. Winner received the Herschede Cup. Regatta discontinued in 1997.

Multiple winners: Harvard (6); Brown (3); Wisconsin (2).

Year	Champion	Time	Runner-up	Time	Year	Champion	Time	Runner-up	Time
1982	Yale	5:50.8	Cornell	5:54.15	1990	Wisconsin	5:52.5	Harvard	5:56.84
1983	Harvard	5:59.6	Washington	6:00.0	1991	Penn	5:58.21	Northeastern	5:58.48
1984	Washington	5:51.1	Yale	5:55.6	1992	Harvard	5:33.97	Dartmouth	5:34.28
1985	Harvard	5:44.4	Princeton	5:44.87	1993	Brown	5:54.15	Penn	5:56.98
1986	Wisconsin	5:57.8	Brown	5:59.9	1994	Brown	5:24.52	Harvard	5:25.83
1987	Harvard	5:35.17	Brown	5:35.63	1995	Brown	5:23.40	Princeton	5:25.83
1988	Harvard	5:35.98	Northeastern	5:37.07	1996	Princeton	5:57.47	Penn	6:03.28
1989	Harvard	5:36.6	Washington	5:38.93	1997	discontinued			

Women

National championship held over various distances at 10 different venues from 1979-96. Distances– 1000 meters (1979-81); 1500 meters (1982-83); 1000 meters (1984); 1750 meters (1985); 2000 meters (1986-88, since 1991); 1852 meters (1989-90). Winner received the Ferguson Bowl. Regatta discontinued in 1997.

Multiple winners: Washington (7); Princeton (4); Boston University (2).

Year	Champion	Time	Runner-up	Time	Year	Champion	Time	Runner-up	Time
1979	Yale	3:06	California	3:08.6	1988	Washington	6:41.0	Yale	6:42.37
1980	California	3:05.4	Oregon St.	3:05.8	1989	Cornell	5:34.9	Wisconsin	5:37.5
1981	Washington	3:20.6	Yale	3:22.9	1991	Boston Univ.	7:03.2	Cornell	7:06.21
1982	Washington	4:56.4	Wisconsin	4:59.83	1992	Boston Univ.	6:28.79	Cornell	6:32.79
1983	Washington	4:57.5	Dartmouth	5:03.02	1993	Princeton	6:40.75	Washington	6:43.86
1984	Washington	3:29.48	Radcliffe	3:31.08	1994	Princeton	6:11.38	Yale	6:14.46
1985	Washington	5:28.4	Wisconsin	5:32.0	1995	Princeton	6:11.98	Washington	6:12.69
1986	Wisconsin	6:53.28	Radcliffe	6:53.34	1996	Brown	6:45.7	Princeton	6:49.3
1987	Washington	6:33.8	Yale	6:37.4	1997	discontinued			

SKIING

Men & Women

Back in the 1950s and 60s, when it came to college skiing, there was Denver and everyone else. The Pioneers won 14 championships between 1954-71. And none since. That all changed in 2000 as they dethroned two-time defending champ Colorado to reclaim their position atop the college skiing world. Denver scored a net total of 720 points, ahead of Colorado in second (621) and third-place Vermont (592). Denver was propelled to victory by three individual titles: Pietro Broggini in the men's 10-k freestyle cross country and men's 20-k classical cross-country, and Cecile Hagen Larsen in the women's slalom. Not only did Broggini win both men's Nordic events, but Denver swept the top three spots in each. (*Soldier Hollow, UT; March 8-11, 2000.*)

Multiple winners: Colorado and Denver (15); Utah (9); Vermont (5); Dartmouth and Wyoming (2).

Year		Year		Year		Year		Year	
1954	Denver	1964	Denver	1974	Colorado	1983	Utah	1993	Utah
1955	Denver	1965	Denver	1975	Colorado	1984	Utah	1994	Vermont
1956	Denver	1966	Denver	1976	Colorado	1985	Wyoming	1995	Colorado
1957	Denver	1967	Denver		& Dartmouth	1986	Utah	1996	Utah
1958	Dartmouth	1968	Wyoming	1977	Colorado	1987	Utah	1997	Utah
1959	Colorado	1969	Denver	1978	Colorado	1988	Utah	1998	Colorado
1960	Colorado	1970	Denver	1979	Colorado	1989	Vermont	1999	Colorado
1961	Denver	1971	Denver	1980	Vermont	1990	Vermont	2000	Denver
1962	Denver	1972	Colorado	1981	Utah	1991	Colorado		
1963	Denver	1973	Colorado	1982	Colorado	1992	Vermont		

SOFTBALL

Women

First baseman Lisa Carey blasted a two-run homer to lead underdog Oklahoma to a 3-1 victory over UCLA in the Division I softball championship game for the Sooners' first softball championship in history. It was the 20th homer of the year for Carey, who also added two singles in the win. Jennifer Stewart was stellar on the mound for Oklahoma, limiting a powerful UCLA squad to eight hits and just one run. Overall she allowed just two runs in 23 innings during the World Series to win most outstanding player honors. Oklahoma ended the season at 66-8 while UCLA finished at 46-12-1. (*Oklahoma City, OK; May 25-29, 2000.*)

Multiple winners: UCLA (8); Arizona (5); Texas A&M (2).

Year		Year		Year		Year		Year	
1982	UCLA	1986	CS-Fullerton	1990	UCLA	1994	Arizona	1998	Fresno St.
1983	Texas A&M	1987	Texas A&M	1991	Colorado	1995	UCLA*	1999	UCLA
1984	UCLA	1988	UCLA	1992	UCLA	1996	Arizona	2000	Oklahoma
1985	UCLA	1989	UCLA	1993	Arizona	1997	Arizona		

*Title was later vacated due to action by the NCAA Committee on Infractions.

SWIMMING & DIVING

Men

Texas opened up a huge lead in the first two days of competition and cruised to their seventh men's swimming and diving championship and their first since 1996. The Longhorns registered a total of 538 points, well ahead of runner-up and defending champ Auburn (385) and Arizona (360½). The bulk of Texas' points came in the relays where they absolutely dominated, winning the 200- and 400-meter medleys and the 800-meter freestyle relay. Matt Ulrickson won the individual 100-meter backstroke and diver Troy Dumais captured the one-meter and three-meter diving titles and was runner-up in the platform diving competition.

Arizona's Ryk Neethling defended his title in the 200- and 400-meter freestyle events but placed third in the 1500-meter freestyle. He finished his collegiate career with nine NCAA titles. Ed Moses of Virginia set world records in the 100- and 200-meter breaststroke events and was voted Swimmer of the Meet for his efforts. (*Minneapolis, MN; Mar. 23-25, 2000.*)

Multiple winners: Michigan and Ohio St. (11); USC (9); Stanford (8); Texas (7); Indiana (6); Yale (4); Auburn, California and Florida (2).

Year		Year		Year		Year		Year	
1937	Michigan	1950	Ohio St.	1963	USC	1976	USC	1989	Texas
1938	Michigan	1951	Yale	1964	USC	1977	USC	1990	Texas
1939	Michigan	1952	Ohio St.	1965	USC	1978	Tennessee	1991	Texas
1940	Michigan	1953	Yale	1966	USC	1979	California	1992	Stanford
1941	Michigan	1954	Ohio St.	1967	Stanford	1980	California	1993	Stanford
1942	Yale	1955	Ohio St.	1968	Indiana	1981	Texas	1994	Stanford
1943	Ohio St.	1956	Ohio St.	1969	Indiana	1982	UCLA	1995	Michigan
1944	Yale	1957	Michigan	1970	Indiana	1983	Florida	1996	Texas
1945	Ohio St.	1958	Michigan	1971	Indiana	1984	Florida	1997	Auburn
1946	Ohio St.	1959	Ohio St.	1972	Indiana	1985	Stanford	1998	Stanford
1947	Ohio St.	1960	USC	1973	Indiana	1986	Stanford	1999	Auburn
1948	Michigan	1961	Michigan	1974	USC	1987	Stanford	2000	Texas
1949	Ohio St.	1962	Ohio St.	1975	USC	1988	Texas		

Women

Senior co-captains Kristy Kowal and Courtney Shealy each won three individual events to lead Georgia to their second consecutive win at the NCAA Division I Women's Swimming and Diving Championships. The pair also swam legs on Georgia's winning 400-meter medley relay team. The Lady Bulldogs also gained victories in the 400-meter freestyle relay and from Maritza Correia in the 200-meter freestyle. As impressive as Georgia was, it just couldn't pull away from a gritty Arizona team. The meet was still in question until the final race, the 400-meter freestyle relay. Georgia needed to finish at least fifth to win the title. They won the race and the meet with a total of 490½ points, followed by Arizona with 472 and Stanford with 397.

Other double winners were Columbia-Barnard's Cristina Teuscher in the 400-meter freestyle and 400-meter individual medley and Nevada's Limin Liu in the 100- and 200-meter butterflies. For the first time in history, the championship meet was conducted in short-course meters, resulting in many meet records. (*Indianapolis, IN; Mar. 16-18, 2000.*)

Multiple winners: Stanford (8); Texas (7); Georgia (2).

Year		Year		Year		Year		Year	
1982	Florida	1986	Texas	1990	Texas	1994	Stanford	1998	Stanford
1983	Stanford	1987	Texas	1991	Texas	1995	Stanford	1999	Georgia
1984	Texas	1988	Texas	1992	Stanford	1996	Stanford	2000	Georgia
1985	Texas	1989	Stanford	1993	Stanford	1997	USC		

Annual NCAA Division I Team Champions (Cont.)

INDOOR TRACK

Men

It was almost a foregone conclusion that Arkansas would win the indoor track and field title at their sold-out home track, but it came down to the final race before they could wrap it up. The Razorbacks held a slim four-point lead over Stanford heading into the 3,000-meters but Sharif Karie and James Karanu finished third and fifth, respectively, to clinch the victory. It was the Razorbacks' fourth consecutive indoor title and 16th win over the last 17 years. Arkansas scored 69½ points to outdistance Stanford (52) and Southern Methodist (38).

The Razorbacks' Melvin Lister won the long jump and successfully defended his title in the triple jump with a leap of 54-7½. South Carolina's Terrence Trammell was also a double winner, taking the 60-meter dash and 60-meter hurdles, and South Alabama's David Kimani won two events as well, the 3000- and 5000-meter runs. (Fayetteville, AR; March 10-11, 2000.)

Multiple winners: Arkansas (16); UTEP (7); Kansas and Villanova (3); USC (2).

Year		Year		Year		Year		Year	
1965	Missouri	1973	Manhattan	1981	UTEP	1989	Arkansas	1997	Arkansas
1966	Kansas	1974	UTEP	1982	UTEP	1990	Arkansas	1998	Arkansas
1967	USC	1975	UTEP	1983	SMU	1991	Arkansas	1999	Arkansas
1968	Villanova	1976	UTEP	1984	Arkansas	1992	Arkansas	2000	Arkansas
1969	Kansas	1977	Washington St.	1985	Arkansas	1993	Arkansas		
1970	Kansas	1978	UTEP	1986	Arkansas	1994	Arkansas		
1971	Villanova	1979	Villanova	1987	Arkansas	1995	Arkansas		
1972	USC	1980	UTEP	1988	Arkansas	1996	George Mason		

Women

After placing second the past two years, UCLA finally got over the hump and won its first Division I Women's Indoor Track and Field Championship. On the strength of three individual titles, the Bruins amassed 51 points to best South Carolina (41) and host Arkansas (37). Tracy O'Hara set an NCAA meet record (14-6) in winning the pole vault for UCLA, Keyon Soley took the top prize in the long jump (21-4¾), and Seilala Sua won the shot put championship.

Mikele Barber was the top scorer for runner-up South Carolina, winning the 200-meter dash and placing second in the 400. Villanova's outstanding distance runner Carrie Tollefson was the only woman to successfully defend a title from last year as she won the 3,000-meter run in 9:13.68. (Fayetteville, AR; March 10-11, 2000.)

Multiple winners: LSU (8); Texas (5); Nebraska (2).

Year		Year		Year		Year		Year	
1983	Nebraska	1987	LSU	1991	LSU	1995	LSU	1999	Texas
1984	Nebraska	1988	Texas	1992	Florida	1996	LSU	2000	UCLA
1985	Florida St.	1989	LSU	1993	LSU	1997	LSU		
1986	Texas	1990	Texas	1994	LSU	1998	Texas		

OUTDOOR TRACK

Men

Stanford's Brad Hauser won the 5,000- and 10,000-meter runs to help break Arkansas' eight-year stranglehold on the NCAA outdoor track and field championships and give the Cardinal their first title since 1934. Stanford totaled 72 points to cruise past Arkansas (59) and Auburn (51). Aisde from Hauser's heroics, Stanford was also helped immensely by a 1-2 finish by Gabe Jennings and Michael Stember in the 1,500-meter event.

Arkansas' Melvin Lister won the triple jump and placed fourth in the long jump as his Razorbacks came up just short in their bid for a ninth consecutive title. Three athletes successfully defended titles they won in 1999 — Auburn's Gábor Máté in the discus, South Carolina's Terrence Trammell in the 110-meter hurdles, and Texas' Mark Boswell in the high jump. (Durham, NC; May 31-June 3, 2000.)

Multiple winners: USC (26); Arkansas (9); UCLA (8); UTEP (6); Illinois and Oregon (5); Stanford (4); Kansas and LSU (3); SMU and Tennessee (2).

Year		Year		Year		Year		Year	
1921	Illinois	1938	USC	1955	USC	1971	UCLA	1988	UCLA
1922	California	1939	USC	1956	UCLA	1972	UCLA	1989	LSU
1923	Michigan	1940	USC	1957	Villanova	1973	UCLA	1990	LSU
1924	Not held	1941	USC	1958	USC	1974	Tennessee	1991	Tennessee
1925	Stanford*	1942	USC	1959	Kansas	1975	UTEP	1992	Arkansas
1926	USC*	1943	USC	1960	Kansas	1976	USC	1993	Arkansas
1927	Illinois*	1944	Illinois	1961	USC	1977	Arizona St.	1994	Arkansas
1928	Stanford	1945	Navy	1962	Oregon	1978	UCLA & UTEP	1995	Arkansas
1929	Ohio St.	1946	Illinois	1963	USC	1979	UTEP	1996	Arkansas
1930	USC	1947	Illinois	1964	Oregon	1980	UTEP	1997	Arkansas
1931	USC	1948	Minnesota	1965	Oregon & USC	1981	UTEP	1998	Arkansas
1932	Indiana	1949	USC	1966	UCLA	1982	UTEP	1999	Arkansas
1933	LSU	1950	USC	1967	USC	1983	SMU		
1934	Stanford	1951	USC	1968	USC	1984	Oregon	2000	Stanford
1935	USC	1952	USC	1969	San Jose St.	1985	Arkansas		
1936	USC	1953	USC	1970	BYU, Kansas	1986	SMU		
1937	USC	1954	USC		& Oregon	1987	UCLA		

(*) indicates unofficial championship.

AP/Wide World Photos

Stanford teammates **Gabe Jennings** (313) and **Michael Stember** (318) took first and second place, respectively, in the 1,500-meter run to vault the Cardinal to their first men's outdoor track and field championship since 1934.

Women

After a two-year hiatus, LSU returned to prominence at the Division I Women's Track and Field Championships winning its 12th overall title. Their four-day total of 58 points was just barely enough to edge runner-up USC (54) and third-place UCLA (47). In fact, USC actually held a 54-48 lead over LSU until Keisha Spencer came through with a victory in the triple jump to give the Tigers the championship.

LSU was also led by Peta-Gaye Dowdie and Joyce Bates, who recorded victories in the 200-meter dash and the 100-meter hurdles, respectively. USC's Natasha Danvers won the 400-meter hurdles and Angela Williams repeated as champion in the 100-meter dash to help the Trojans to their best finish at the championships in school history. (*Durham, NC; May 31-June 3, 2000.*)

Multiple winners: LSU (12); Texas (3); UCLA (2).

Year		Year		Year		Year		Year	
1982	UCLA	1986	Texas	1990	LSU	1994	LSU	1998	Texas
1983	UCLA	1987	LSU	1991	LSU	1995	LSU	1999	Texas
1984	Florida St.	1988	LSU	1992	LSU	1996	LSU	2000	LSU
1985	Oregon	1989	LSU	1993	LSU	1997	LSU		

VOLLEYBALL

Men

It wasn't quite as easy as the scoreboard might have indicated, but when all was said and done, UCLA had scored a straight-set victory over Ohio State at the NCAA Division I Men's Volleyball Championship for its 18th overall title. The Bruins put away the Buckeyes, 15-8, 15-10, 17-15 but the match took two hours and 15 minutes to complete. Outside hitter Evan Thatcher recorded 25 kills in the championship match, most set up by setter extraordinaire Brandon Taliaferro. Seth Burnham added 14 kills for the champions while Chris Fash led the Buckeyes with 21. (*Ft. Wayne, IN; May 6, 2000.*)

Multiple winners: UCLA (18); Pepperdine and USC (4).

Year		Year		Year		Year		Year	
1970	UCLA	1977	USC	1984	UCLA	1991	Long Beach St.	1998	UCLA
1971	UCLA	1978	Pepperdine	1985	Pepperdine	1992	Pepperdine	1999	Brigham Young
1972	UCLA	1979	UCLA	1986	Pepperdine	1993	UCLA	2000	UCLA
1973	San Diego St.	1980	USC	1987	UCLA	1994	Penn St.		
1974	UCLA	1981	UCLA	1988	USC	1995	UCLA		
1975	UCLA	1982	UCLA	1989	UCLA	1996	UCLA		
1976	UCLA	1983	UCLA	1990	USC	1997	Stanford		

Annual NCAA Division I Team Champions (Cont.)
Women

Penn St. had reached the championship final the past two years and three times in the last six years, only to come out on the losing end each time. This year the Nittany Lions' hard work finally paid off as they recorded a straight-set victory over Stanford to win their first NCAA women's volleyball title. The Nittany Lions left no doubt, pounding No. 2 Stanford 15-2, 15-10, 15-7.

National Co-Player of the Year Lauren Cacciamani led the way with 20 kills to take home yet another award — the tournament MVP. Penn State opened up an early 8-0 lead in the first game and kept the pressure on, leaving Kerri Walsh and the rest of her Cardinal teammates mesmerized. Stanford's combined three-game total of 19 points is the second-lowest ever. (*Honolulu, HI; Dec. 18, 1999.*)

Multiple winners: Stanford (4); Hawaii, Long Beach St. and UCLA (3); Pacific (2).

Year		Year		Year		Year		Year	
1981	USC	1985	Pacific	1989	Long Beach St.	1993	Long Beach St.	1997	Stanford
1982	Hawaii	1986	Pacific	1990	UCLA	1994	Stanford	1998	Long Beach St.
1983	Hawaii	1987	Hawaii	1991	UCLA	1995	Nebraska	1999	Penn St.
1984	UCLA	1988	Texas	1992	Stanford	1996	Stanford		

WATER POLO
Men

Behind four goals from tournament MVP Sean Kern, the UCLA Bruins defeated the Stanford Cardinal, 6-5, for their sixth NCAA water polo championship. Stanford jumped out to an early 4-1 lead, but then Kern, a two-time All-American, went to work in the second half. Adam Wright and Matt Armato also scored for UCLA and Kern's final goal put UCLA up 6-4. The Cardinal crawled back to within a goal but UCLA goaltender Brandon Brooks stopped Jeff Nesmith's two-point attempt with just 10 seconds left to preserve the victory. UCLA finished out the year at 22-3, while Stanford ended at 22-6. (*San Diego, CA; Dec. 5, 1999.*)

Multiple winners: California (11); Stanford (8); UCLA (6); UC-Irvine (3).

Year		Year		Year		Year		Year	
1969	UCLA	1976	Stanford	1983	California	1990	California	1997	Pepperdine
1970	UC-Irvine	1977	California	1984	California	1991	California	1998	USC
1971	UCLA	1978	Stanford	1985	Stanford	1992	California	1999	UCLA
1972	UCLA	1979	UC-S. Barbara	1986	Stanford	1993	Stanford		
1973	California	1980	Stanford	1987	California	1994	Stanford		
1974	California	1981	Stanford	1988	California	1995	UCLA		
1975	California	1982	UC-Irvine	1989	UC-Irvine	1996	UCLA		

WRESTLING
Men

Wrestling juggernaut Iowa made it six titles in a row, nine of the last ten, and 20 of the last 26 by winning the 2000 NCAA Division I Wrestling Championship. Heading into the final day of action, it appeared as though Iowa's reign would be over as cross-state rival Iowa State had opened up a formidable 9½ point lead. But alas there was no stopping the Hawkeyes. Iowa's Eric Juergens defeated Iowa State's Cody Sanderson in a pivotal match and the championship was all theirs.

Iowa accumulated a total of 116 points, followed by Iowa State with 109½, and Minnesota with 80. Iowa State's sophomore star Cael Sanderson easily won the 184-pound class, defeating West Virginia's Vertus Jones to run his record to an amazing 79-0. For the second consecutive year, he won the award for Most Outstanding Wrestler. (*St. Louis, MO; Mar. 16-18, 2000.*)

Multiple winners: Oklahoma St. (30); Iowa (20); Iowa St. (8); Oklahoma (7).

Year		Year		Year		Year		Year	
1928	Okla. A&M*	1942	Okla. A&M	1959	Okla. St.	1974	Oklahoma	1989	Okla. St.
1929	Okla. A&M	1943-45	Not held	1960	Oklahoma	1975	Iowa	1990	Okla. St.
1930	Okla. A&M	1946	Okla. A&M	1961	Okla. St.	1976	Iowa	1991	Iowa
1931	Okla. A&M*	1947	Cornell Col.	1962	Okla. St.	1977	Iowa St.	1992	Iowa
1932	Indiana*	1948	Okla. A&M	1963	Oklahoma	1978	Iowa	1993	Iowa
1933	Okla. A&M*	1949	Okla. A&M	1964	Okla. St.	1979	Iowa	1994	Okla. St.
	& Iowa St.*	1950	Northern Iowa	1965	Iowa St.	1980	Iowa	1995	Iowa
1934	Okla. A&M	1951	Oklahoma	1966	Okla. St.	1981	Iowa	1996	Iowa
1935	Okla. A&M	1952	Oklahoma	1967	Michigan St.	1982	Iowa	1997	Iowa
1936	Oklahoma	1953	Penn St.	1968	Okla. St.	1983	Iowa	1998	Iowa
1937	Okla. A&M	1954	Okla. A&M	1969	Iowa St.	1984	Iowa	1999	Iowa
1938	Okla. A&M	1955	Okla. A&M	1970	Iowa St.	1985	Iowa	2000	Iowa
1939	Okla. A&M	1956	Okla. A&M	1971	Okla. St.	1986	Iowa		
1940	Okla. A&M	1957	Oklahoma	1972	Iowa St.	1987	Iowa St.		
1941	Okla. A&M	1958	Okla. St.	1973	Iowa St.	1988	Arizona St.		

(*) indicates unofficial champions. **Note:** Oklahoma A&M became Oklahoma St. in 1958.

Halls of Fame & Awards

Martina Navratilova, winner of a record 167 singles titles, was inducted into the Tennis Hall of Fame in 2000.

BASEBALL

National Baseball Hall of Fame & Museum

Established in 1935 by Major League Baseball to celebrate the game's 100th anniversary. **Address:** P.O. Box 590, Cooperstown, NY 13326. **Telephone:** (607) 547-7200.

Eligibility: Nominated players must have played at least part of 10 seasons in the major leagues and be retired for at least five but no more than 20 years. Voting done by Baseball Writers' Association of America. Certain nominated players not elected by the writers can become eligible via the Veterans' Committee 23 years after retirement. The Hall of Fame board of directors voted unanimously on Feb. 4, 1991, to exclude players on baseball's ineligible list from consideration. Pete Rose is the only living ex-player on that list.

Class of 2000 (5): BBWAA vote—catcher **Carlton Fisk**, Boston (1969, 1971-80), Chicago-AL (1981-93); first baseman **Tony Perez**, Cincinnati (1964-76), Montreal (1977-79), Boston (1980-82), Philadelphia (1983), Cincinnati (1984-86); VETERAN'S COMMITTEE vote—second baseman **Bid McPhee**, Cincinnati (1882-99); Negro Leagues center field **Turkey Stearns**, several clubs (1921-42); manager **Sparky Anderson**, Cincinnati (1970-78), Detroit (1979-95).

2000 Top 10 vote-getters (499 BBWAA ballots cast, 375 needed to elect): 1. **Carlton Fisk** (397), 2. **Tony Perez** (385), 3. **Jim Rice** (257), 4. **Gary Carter** (248), 5. **Bruce Sutter** (192), 6. **Rich Gossage** (166), 7. **Steve Garvey** (160), 8. **Tommy John** (135), 9. **Jim Kaat** (125), 10. **Dale Murphy** (116).

Elected first year on ballot (34): Hank Aaron, Ernie Banks, Johnny Bench, George Brett, Lou Brock, Rod Carew, Steve Carlton, Ty Cobb, Bob Feller, Bob Gibson, Reggie Jackson, Walter Johnson, Al Kaline, Sandy Koufax, Mickey Mantle, Christy Mathewson, Willie Mays, Willie McCovey, Joe Morgan, Stan Musial, Jim Palmer, Brooks Robinson, Frank Robinson, Jackie Robinson, Babe Ruth, Nolan Ryan, Mike Schmidt, Tom Seaver, Warren Spahn, Willie Stargell, Honus Wagner, Ted Williams, Carl Yastrzemski and Robin Yount.

Members are listed with years of induction; (+) indicates deceased members.

Catchers

Bench, Johnny 1989	+ Cochrane, Mickey. 1947	Fisk, Carlton 2000
Berra, Yogi 1972	+ Dickey, Bill 1954	+ Hartnett, Gabby 1955
+ Bresnahan, Roger 1945	+ Ewing, Buck 1939	+ Lombardi, Ernie 1986
+ Campanella, Roy. 1969	+ Ferrell, Rick 1984	+ Schalk, Ray 1955

1st Basemen

+ Anson, Cap 1939	+ Connor, Roger 1976	McCovey, Willie 1986
+ Beckley, Jake 1971	+ Foxx, Jimmie 1951	+ Mize, Johnny 1981
+ Bottomley, Jim. 1974	+ Gehrig, Lou 1939	Perez, Tony 2000
+ Brouthers, Dan 1945	+ Greenberg, Hank 1956	+ Sisler, George 1939
Cepeda, Orlando 1999	+ Kelly, George. 1973	+ Terry, Bill 1954
+ Chance, Frank 1946	Killebrew, Harmon 1984	

2nd Basemen

Carew, Rod 1991	+ Frisch, Frankie 1947	+ Lazzeri, Tony 1991
+ Collins, Eddie 1939	+ Gehringer, Charlie 1949	+ McPhee, Bid 2000
Doerr, Bobby 1986	+ Herman, Billy 1975	Morgan, Joe. 1990
+ Evers, Johnny 1946	+ Hornsby, Rogers 1942	+ Robinson, Jackie 1962
+ Fox, Nellie 1997	+ Lajoie, Nap 1937	Schoendienst, Red. 1989

Shortstops

Aparicio, Luis. 1984	+ Jackson, Travis. 1982	+ Vaughan, Arky. 1985
+ Appling, Luke 1964	+ Jennings, Hugh 1945	+ Wagner, Honus 1936
+ Bancroft, Dave 1971	+ Maranville, Rabbit. 1954	+ Wallace, Bobby 1953
Banks, Ernie 1977	+ Reese, Pee Wee. 1984	+ Ward, Monte 1964
Boudreau, Lou 1970	Rizzuto, Phil 1994	Yount, Robin 1999
+ Cronin, Joe 1956	+ Sewell, Joe 1977	
Davis, George 1998	+ Tinker, Joe. 1946	

3rd Basemen

+ Baker, Frank 1955	Kell, George. 1983	Robinson, Brooks. 1983
Brett, George 1999	+ Lindstrom, Fred 1976	Schmidt, Mike 1995
+ Collins, Jimmy 1945	Mathews, Eddie. 1978	+ Traynor, Pie 1948

Left Fielders

Brock, Lou. 1985	Kiner, Ralph 1975	+ Wheat, Zack 1959
+ Burkett, Jesse 1946	+ Manush, Heinie 1964	Williams, Billy 1987
+ Clarke, Fred 1945	+ Medwick, Joe. 1968	Williams, Ted 1966
+ Delahanty, Ed. 1945	Musial, Stan 1969	Yastrzemski, Carl 1989
+ Goslin, Goose 1968	+ O'Rourke, Jim. 1945	
+ Hafey, Chick 1971	+ Simmons, Al 1953	
+ Kelley, Joe. 1971	Stargell, Willie. 1988	

Center Fielders

+ Ashburn, Richie 1995	Doby, Larry................1998	Snider, Duke...............1980
+ Averill, Earl................1975	+ Duffy, Hugh 1945	+ Speaker, Tris..............1937
+ Carey, Max 1961	+ Hamilton, Billy 1961	+ Waner, Lloyd 1967
+ Cobb, Ty....................1936	+ Mantle, Mickey 1974	+ Wilson, Hack..............1979
+ Combs, Earle 1970	Mays, Willie 1979	
+ DiMaggio, Joe.............1955	+ Roush, Edd 1962	

Right Fielders

Aaron, Hank 1982	Jackson, Reggie...........1993	+ Rice, Sam 1963
+ Clemente, Roberto.........1973	Kaline, Al 1980	Robinson, Frank............1982
+ Crawford, Sam 1957	+ Keeler, Willie 1939	+ Ruth, Babe 1936
+ Cuyler, Kiki 1968	+ Kelly, King 1945	Slaughter, Enos 1985
+ Flick, Elmer................1963	+ Klein, Chuck...............1980	+ Thompson, Sam 1974
+ Heilmann, Harry 1952	+ McCarthy, Tommy 1946	+ Waner, Paul 1952
+ Hooper, Harry 1971	+ Ott, Mel 1951	+ Youngs, Ross 1972

Pitchers

+ Alexander, Grover 1938	+ Chesbro, Jack 1946	+ Faber, Red 1964
+ Bender, Chief..............1953	+ Clarkson, John 1963	Feller, Bob 1962
+ Brown, Mordecai 1949	+ Coveleski, Stan 1969	Fingers, Rollie...............1992
Bunning, Jim................1996	+ Dean, Dizzy 1953	Ford, Whitey 1974
Carlton, Steve 1994	+ Drysdale, Don 1984	+ Galvin, Pud 1965

Major League Baseball's All-Time Team—Then and Now

The Baseball Writers' Association of America originally selected an all-time team as part of major league baseball's 100th anniversary, announcing the outcome of its vote on July 21, 1969. Vote totals were not released. Recently, another vote was released when a panel of 36 BWAA members picked an all-time team for the Classic Sports Network just before the 1997 All-Star Game. This time vote totals were given, the single outfield category was divided into three (left, center and right) and two recently popularized positions—the designated hitter and relief pitcher—were added. In the most recent vote two points were awarded for first-place votes and one point for second place. Point totals follow the names with the number of first-place votes in parentheses. All-time team members are listed in **bold** type

1969 Vote

C	**Mickey Cochrane**, Bill Dickey, Roy Campanella
1B	**Lou Gehrig**, George Sisler, Stan Musial
2B	**Rogers Hornsby**, Charlie Gehringer, Eddie Collins
SS	**Honus Wagner**, Joe Cronin, Ernie Banks
3B	**Pie Traynor**, Brooks Robinson, Jackie Robinson

OF	**Babe Ruth, Ty Cobb, Joe DiMaggio**, Ted Williams, Tris Speaker, Willie Mays
RHP	**Walter Johnson**, Christy Mathewson, Cy Young
LHP	**Lefty Grove**, Sandy Koufax, Carl Hubbell
Mgr.	**John McGraw**, Casey Stengel, Joe McCarthy

1969 Vote All-Time Outstanding Player: **Ruth**, Cobb, Wagner, DiMaggio

1997 Vote

C **Johnny Bench** (24) 52; Yogi Berra (4) 22; Roy Campanella (4) 17; Mickey Cochrane (1) 5; Bill Dickey (1) 4; Gabby Hartnett (1) 3; Carlton Fisk 2.

1B **Lou Gehrig** (31) 66½; Jimmie Foxx (3) 19; George Sisler (2) 8; Willie McCovey 6; Hank Greenberg 2½; Stan Musial, Eddie Murray, Mark McGwire and Frank Thomas 1.

2B **Rogers Hornsby** (17) 44; Joe Morgan (6) 23; Jackie Robinson (6) 15; Charley Gehringer (4) and Napolean Lajoie (3) 11; Eddie Collins (1) 3; Rod Carew 2; Ryne Sandberg 1.

SS **Honus Wagner** (23) 55; Cal Ripken Jr. (6) 24; Ozzie Smith (5) 16; Ernie Banks (1) 8; Lou Boudreau and Luke Appling 1.

3B **Mike Schmidt** (21) 50; Brooks Robinson (13) 37; Eddie Mathews 5; George Brett (1) 8; Pie Traynor (1) 5; Pete Rose (1) 2; Frank Baker, Al Rosen and Wade Boggs 1.

LF **Ted Williams** (32) 68; Stan Musial (4) 36; Pete Rose, Ralph Kiner, Rickey Henderson and Barry Bonds 1.

CF **Willie Mays** (25) 57; Ty Cobb (7) 22; Joe DiMaggio (3) 17; Mickey Mantle (1) 10; Tris Speaker 2.

RF **Babe Ruth** (31) 67; Hank Aaron (5) 36; Frank Robinson 2; Al Kaline, Roberto Clemente and Tony Gwynn 1.

DH **Paul Molitor** (22) 48; Harold Baines (3) 12; Don Baylor (1) 10; Edgar Martinez (2) 9; Ty Cobb (2) 6; Hal McRae (1) 5; Mickey Mantle (1) and Dave Parker (1) 3; Joe DiMaggio (1) 2; Lee May, Frank Robinson and Tony Oliva 1.

RHP **Walter Johnson** (9) 30; Cy Young (12) 25; Christy Mathewson (5) 18; Bob Feller (4) 10; Bob Gibson (2) 9; Nolan Ryan (2) 7; Tom Seaver (1) 3; Greg Maddux (1), Grover Cleveland Alexander and Juan Marichal 2.

LHP **Sandy Koufax** (11) 32; Warren Spahn (11) 28; Lefty Grove (8) 25; Steve Carlton (4) 12; Carl Hubbell 6; Whitey Ford (1) 3; Eddie Plank (1) 2.

RP **Dennis Eckersley** (16) 40; Rollie Fingers (9) 29; Lee Smith (4) 13; Hoyt Wilhelm (3) 10; Rich Gossage (3) 9; Bruce Sutter (1) 6, Dan Quisenberry 1.

Mgr. **Casey Stengel** (6) 22; Joe McCarthy (6) 18; Connie Mack (7) 17; John McGraw (6) 14; Sparky Anderson (3) 11; Leo Durocher (2) 6; Dick Williams (1) 4; Billy Martin (1) 3; Al Lopez (1), Ned Hanlon (1), Whitey Herzog (1), Earl Weaver and Bobby Cox 2; Tony La Russa 1.

Baseball (Cont.)

Gibson, Bob..............1981
+ Gomez, Lefty 1972
+ Grimes, Burleigh 1964
+ Grove, Lefty 1947
+ Haines, Jess 1970
+ Hoyt, Waite 1969
+ Hubbell, Carl 1947
+ Hunter, Catfish 1987
  Jenkins, Ferguson..........1991
+ Johnson, Walter 1936
+ Joss, Addie................1978
+ Keefe, Tim................1964
  Koufax, Sandy 1972
+ Lemon, Bob 1976

+ Lyons, Ted 1955
  Marichal, Juan............1983
+ Marquard, Rube 1971
+ Mathewson, Christy 1936
+ McGinnity, Joe 1946
  Niekro, Phil 1997
+ Newhouser, Hal............1992
+ Nichols, Kid..............1949
  Palmer, Jim 1990
+ Pennock, Herb 1948
  Perry, Gaylord 1991
+ Plank, Eddie 1946
+ Radbourne, Old Hoss......1939
+ Rixey, Eppa 1963

Roberts, Robin 1976
+ Ruffing, Red 1967
+ Rusie, Amos 1977
  Ryan, Nolan 1999
  Seaver, Tom 1992
  Spahn, Warren 1973
  Sutton, Don 1998
+ Vance, Dazzy 1955
+ Waddell, Rube............1946
+ Walsh, Ed................1946
+ Welch, Mickey............1973
  Wilhelm, Hoyt 1985
+ Willis, Vic................1995
+ Wynn, Early 1972
+ Young, Cy................1937

Managers

+ Alston, Walter 1983
  Anderson, Sparky 2000
+ Durocher, Leo 1994
+ Hanlon, Ned 1996
+ Harris, Bucky 1975
+ Huggins, Miller 1964

  Lasorda, Tommy............1997
  Lopez, Al 1977
+ Mack, Connie 1937
+ McCarthy, Joe 1957
+ McGraw, John 1937
+ McKechnie, Bill 1962

+ Robinson, Wilbert 1945
+ Selee, Frank 1999
+ Stengel, Casey............1966
  Weaver, Earl 1996

Umpires

+ Barlick, Al..............1989
+ Chylak, Nestor............1999
+ Conlan, Jocko 1974

+ Connolly, Tom 1953
+ Evans, Billy................1973
+ Hubbard, Cal..............1976

+ Klem, Bill................1953
+ McGowan, Bill............1992

From Negro Leagues

+ Bell, Cool Papa (OF)......1974
+ Charleston, Oscar (1B-OF)...1976
+ Dandridge, Ray (3B)......1987
+ Day, Leon (P-OF-2B) 1995
+ Dihigo, Martin (P-OF)......1977
+ Foster, Rube (P-Mgr) 1981

+ Foster, Willie (P)..........1996
+ Gibson, Josh (C) 1972
  Irvin, Monte (OF)..........1973
+ Johnson, Judy (3B)........1975
+ Leonard, Buck (1B) 1972
+ Lloyd, Pop (SS)............1977

+ Paige, Satchel (P) 1971
+ Rogan, Wilber (P) 1998
+ Stearns, Turkey (OF) 2000
+ Wells, Willie (SS)..........1997
+ Williams, Joe (P) 1999

Pioneers and Executives

+ Barrow, Ed 1953
+ Bulkeley, Morgan..........1937
+ Cartwright, Alexander 1938
+ Chadwick, Henry 1938
+ Chandler, Happy............1982
+ Comiskey, Charles..........1939
+ Cummings, Candy..........1939
+ Frick, Ford 1970

+ Giles, Warren 1979
+ Griffith, Clark..............1946
+ Harridge, Will 1972
+ Hulbert, William 1995
+ Johnson, Ban 1937
+ Landis, Kenesaw 1944
+ MacPhail, Larry............1978
  MacPhail, Lee 1998

+ Rickey, Branch 1967
+ Spalding, Al................1939
+ Veeck, Bill................1991
+ Weiss, George............1971
+ Wright, George............1937
+ Wright, Harry 1953
+ Yawkey, Tom..............1980

Ford Frick Award

First presented in 1978 by the Hall of Fame for meritorious contributions by baseball broadcasters. Named in honor of the late newspaper reporter, broadcaster, National League president and commissioner, the Frick Award does not constitute induction into the Hall of Fame.

Year		Year		Year	
1978	Mel Allen & Red Barber	1986	Bob Prince	1994	Bob Murphy
1979	Bob Elson	1987	Jack Buck	1995	Bob Wolff
1980	Russ Hodges	1988	Lindsey Nelson	1996	Herb Carneal
1981	Ernie Harwell	1989	Harry Caray	1997	Jimmy Dudley
1982	Vin Scully	1990	Byrum Saam	1998	Jaime Jarrin
1983	Jack Brickhouse	1991	Joe Garagiola	1999	Arch McDonald
1984	Curt Gowdy	1992	Milo Hamilton	2000	Marty Brennaman
1985	Buck Canel	1993	Chuck Thompson		

J.G. Taylor Spink Award

First presented in 1962 by the Baseball Writers' Association of America for meritorious contributions by members of the BBWAA. Named in honor of the late publisher of *The Sporting News*, the Spink Award does not constitute induction into the Hall of Fame. Winners are honored in the year following their selection.

Year		Year		Year	
1962	J.G. Taylor Spink	1967	Damon Runyon	1972	Dan Daniel, Fred Lieb
1963	Ring Lardner	1968	H.G. Salsinger		& J. Roy Stockton
1964	Hugh Fullerton	1969	Sid Mercer	1973	Warren Brown, John Drebinger
1965	Charley Dryden	1970	Heywood C. Broun		& John F. Kieran
1966	Grantland Rice	1971	Frank Graham		

Year		Year		Year	
1974	John Carmichael & James Isaminger	1982	Si Burick	1992	Leonard Koppett & Buzz Saidt
1975	Tom Meany & Shirley Povich	1983	Ken Smith	1993	John Wendell Smith
1976	Harold Kaese & Red Smith	1984	Joe McGuff	1994	No award
1977	Gordon Cobbledick & Edgar Munzel	1985	Earl Lawson	1995	Joseph Durso
		1986	Jack Lang	1996	Charley Feeney
1978	Tim Murnane & Dick Young	1987	Jim Murray	1997	Sam Lacy
1979	Bob Broeg & Tommy Holmes	1988	Bob Hunter & Ray Kelly	1998	Bob Stevens
1980	Joe Reichler & Milt Richman	1989	Jerome Holtzman	1999	Hal Lebovitz
1981	Bob Addie & Allen Lewis	1990	Phil Collier		
		1991	Ritter Collett		

BASKETBALL

Naismith Memorial Basketball Hall of Fame

Established in 1949 by the National Association of Basketball Coaches in memory of the sport's inventor, Dr. James Naismith. Original Hall opened in 1968 and current Hall in 1985. **Address:** 1150 West Columbus Avenue, Springfield, MA 01105. **Telephone:** (413) 781-6500.

Eligibility: Nominated players and referees must be retired for five years, coaches must have coached 25 years or be retired for five, and contributors must have already completed their noteworthy service to the game. Voting done by 24-member honors committee made up of media representatives, Hall of Fame members and trustees. Any nominee not elected after five years becomes eligible for consideration by the Veterans' Committee after a five-year wait.

Class of 2000 (6): PLAYERS—guard **Isiah Thomas**, NBA (Detroit 1981-94); center/forward **Bob McAdoo**, NBA (Buffalo 1973-76, Buffalo/New York 1976-77, New York 1977-78, New York/Boston 1978-79, Detroit 1979-80, Detroit/New Jersey 1980-81, Los Angeles Lakers 1981-85, Philadelphia 1985-86) COACHES— **Pat Summitt**, women's college (Tennessee, 1974–); **Morgan Wooten**, boy's high school (Dematha High School 1956–). CONTRIBUTORS— **Danny Biasone**, owner, Syracuse Nationals (1946-63); **Charles Martin Newton**, 40 year career as player, coach, and administrator.

2000 finalists (nominated but not elected): PLAYERS—Bobby Jones, Sidney Moncrief, and James Worthy. COACHES— Lute Olson and Jim Phelan. CONTRIBUTERS—Junius Kellogg and Grady Lewis. INTERNATIONAL—Drazen Dalipagic and Mirko Novosel. WOMEN'S—Cathy Rush.

Note: John Wooden and **Lenny Wilkens**, who was rehonored by the Hall in 1998, are the only members to be inducted as both a player and a coach.

Members are listed with years of induction; (+) indicates deceased members.

Men

Abdul-Jabbar, Kareem	1995	Goodrich, Gail	1996	Mikkelsen, Vern	1995
Archibald, Nate	1991	Greer, Hal	1981	Monroe, Earl	1990
Arizin, Paul	1977	+ Gruenig, Robert	1963	Murphy, Calvin	1993
+ Barlow, Thomas (Babe)	1980	Hagan, Cliff	1977	+ Murphy, Charles (Stretch)	1960
Barry, Rick	1987	+ Hanson, Victor	1960	+ Page, Harlan (Pat)	1962
Baylor, Elgin	1976	Havlicek, John	1983	Pettit, Bob	1970
+ Beckman, John	1972	Hawkins, Connie	1992	Phillip, Andy	1961
Bellamy, Walt	1993	Hayes, Elvin	1990	+ Pollard, Jim	1977
Belov, Sergei	1992	Haynes, Marques	1998	Ramsey, Frank	1981
Bing, Dave	1990	Heinsohn, Tom	1986	Reed, Willis	1981
Bird, Larry	1998	+ Holman, Nat	1964	Risen, Arnie	1998
+ Borgmann, Benny	1961	Houbregs, Bob	1987	Robertson, Oscar	1979
Bradley, Bill	1982	Howell, Bailey	1997	+ Roosma, John	1961
+ Brennan, Joe	1974	+ Hyatt, Chuck	1959	Russell, Bill	1974
Cervi, Al	1984	Issel, Dan	1993	+ Russell, John (Honey)	1964
+ Chamberlain, Wilt	1978	+ Jeannette, Buddy	1994	Schayes, Dolph	1972
+ Cooper, Charles (Tarzan)	1976	+ Johnson, Bill (Skinny)	1976	+ Schmidt, Ernest J	1973
+ Cosic, Kresimir	1996	+ Johnston, Neil	1990	+ Schommer, John	1959
Cousy, Bob	1970	Jones, K. C.	1989	+ Sedran, Barney	1962
Cowens, Dave	1991	Jones, Sam	1983	Sharman, Bill	1975
Cunningham, Billy	1986	+ Krause, Edward (Moose)	1975	+ Steinmetz, Christian	1961
+ Davies, Bob	1969	Kurland, Bob	1961	Thomas, Isiah	2000
+ DeBernardi, Forrest	1961	Lanier, Bob	1992	Thompson, David	1996
DeBusschere, Dave	1982	+ Lapchick, Joe	1966	+ Thompson, John (Cat)	1962
+ Dehnert, Dutch	1968	Lovellette, Clyde	1988	Thurmond, Nate	1984
+ Endacott, Paul	1971	Lucas, Jerry	1979	Twyman, Jack	1982
English, Alex	1997	Luisetti, Hank	1959	Unseld, Wes	1988
Erving, Julius (Dr. J)	1993	Macauley, Ed	1960	+ Vandivier, Robert (Fuzzy)	1974
Foster, Bud	1964	+ Maravich, Pete	1987	+ Wachter, Ed	1961
Frazier, Walt	1987	Martin, Slater	1981	Walton, Bill	1993
+ Friedman, Marty	1971	McAdoo, Bob	2000	Wanzer, Bobby	1987
+ Fulks, Joe	1977	+ McCracken, Branch	1960	West, Jerry	1979
Gale, Laddie	1976	+ McCracken, Jack	1962	Wilkens, Lenny	1989
Gallatin, Harry	1991	+ McDermott, Bobby	1988	Wooden, John	1960
+ Gates, William (Pop)	1989	McGuire, Dick	1993	Yardley, George	1996
Gervin, George	1996	McHale, Kevin	1999		
Gola, Tom	1975	Mikan, George	1959		

Basketball (Cont.)

Women

Blazejowski, Carol 1994	Harris, Lucy 1992	Semenova, Juliana 1993
Crawford, Joan 1997	Lieberman-Cline, Nancy.....1996	White, Nera...............1992
Curry, Denise..............1997	Meyers, Ann...............1993	
Donovan, Anne 1995	Miller, Cheryl 1995	

Teams

Buffalo Germans 1961	New York Renaissance 1963	Original Celtics 1959
First Team 1959		

Referees

+ Enright, Jim................1978	+ Leith, Lloyd 1982	+ Shirley, J. Dallas 1979
+ Hepbron, George 1960	+ Mihalik, Red...............1986	+ Strom, Earl 1995
+ Hoyt, George..............1961	Nucatola, John..............1977	Tobey, Dave 1961
+ Kennedy, Pat 1959	+ Quigley, Ernest (Quig) 1961	+ Walsh, David..............1961

Coaches

+ Allen, Forrest (Phog) 1959	Gomelsky, Aleksandr 1995	Meyer, Ray................1978
+ Anderson, Harold (Andy)....1984	Hannum, Alex 1998	Miller, Ralph...............1988
Auerbach, Red.............1968	Harshman, Marv 1984	Moore, Billie...............1999
+ Barry, Sam 1978	Haskins, Don 1997	Nikolic, Aleksandar 1998
+ Blood, Ernest (Prof) 1960	+ Hickey, Eddie..............1978	Ramsay, Jack 1992
+ Cann, Howard.............1967	+ Hobson, Howard (Hobby) ...1965	Rubini, Cesare 1994
+ Carlson, Henry (Doc) 1959	+ Holzman, Red.............1986	+ Rupp, Adolph..............1968
Carnesecca, Lou 1992	+ Iba, Hank 1968	+ Sachs, Leonard 1961
Carnevale, Ben 1969	+ Julian, Alvin (Doggie) 1967	+ Shelton, Everett 1979
Carril, Pete 1997	+ Keaney, Frank 1960	Smith, Dean 1982
+ Case, Everett 1981	+ Keogan, George 1961	Summitt, Pat 2000
Conradt, Judy.............1998	Knight, Bob 1991	Taylor, Fred................1985
Crum, Denny 1994	Kundla, John 1995	Thompson, John............1999
Daly, Chuck 1994	+ Lambert, Ward (Piggy) 1960	+ Wade, Margaret 1984
+ Dean, Everett 1966	Litwack, Harry 1975	Watts, Stan................1985
Diaz-Miguel, Antonio 1997	+ Loeffler, Ken 1964	Wilkens, Lenny.............1998
+ Diddle, Ed 1971	+ Lonborg, Dutch 1972	Wooden, John 1972
+ Drake, Bruce 1972	+ McCutchan, Arad 1980	+ Woolpert, Phil 1992
Gaines, Clarence (Bighouse).1981	McGuire, Al 1992	Wooten, Morgan............2000
+ Gardner, Jack 1983	+ McGuire, Frank 1976	
+ Gill, Amory (Slats)..........1967	+ Meanwell, Walter (Doc) 1959	

Contributors

+ Abbott, Senda Berenson.....1984	+ Hinkle, Tony 1965	+ Porter, Henry (H.V.)........1960
+ Bee, Clair..................1967	+ Irish, Ned 1964	+ Reid, William A............1963
+ Biasone, Danny 2000	+ Jones, R. William...........1964	+ Ripley, Elmer..............1972
+ Brown, Walter A 1965	+ Kennedy, Walter 1980	+ St. John, Lynn W 1962
+ Bunn, John 1964	+ Liston, Emil (Liz) 1974	+ Saperstein, Abe 1970
+ Douglas, Bob 1971	McLendon, John............1978	+ Schabinger, Arthur 1961
+ Duer, Al 1981	+ Mokray, Bill 1965	+ Stagg, Amos Alonzo........1959
Embry, Wayne.............1999	+ Morgan, Ralph.............1959	Stankovic, Boris 1991
Fagen, Clifford B 1983	+ Morgenweck, Frank (Pop) ...1962	+ Steitz, Ed.................1983
+ Fisher, Harry 1973	+ Naismith, James............1959	+ Taylor, Chuck 1968
+ Fleisher, Larry 1991	Newell, Pete...............1978	+ Teague, Bertha 1984
+ Gottlieb, Eddie.............1971	Newton, Charles M........2000	+ Tower, Oswald.............1959
+ Gulick, Luther..............1959	+ O'Brien, John J. (Jack).......1961	+ Trester, Arthur (A.L.) 1961
+ Harrison, Les 1979	+ O'Brien, Larry 1991	+ Wells, Cliff 1971
+ Hepp, Ferenc 1980	+ Olsen, Harold G 1959	+ Wilke, Lou 1982
+ Hickox, Ed 1959	+ Podoloff, Maurice 1973	+ Zollner, Fred..............1999

Curt Gowdy Award

First presented in 1990 by the Hall of Fame Board of Trustees for meritorious contributions by the media. Named in honor of the former NBC sportscaster, the Gowdy Award does not constitute induction into the Hall of Fame.

Year	**Year**	**Year**
1990 Curt Gowdy & Dick Herbert	1995 Dick Enberg & Bob Hammel	2000 Dave Kindred & Hubie Brown
1991 Dave Dorr & Marty Glickman	1996 Billy Packer & Bob Hentzen	
1992 Sam Goldaper & Chick Hearn	1997 Marv Albert & Bob Ryan	
1993 Leonard Lewin & Johnny Most	1998 Dick Vitale, Larry Donald &	
1994 Leonard Koppett	Dick Weiss	
& Cawood Ledford	1999 Smith Barrier & Bob Costas	

BOWLING

National Bowling Hall of Fame & Museum

The National Bowling Hall is one museum with separate wings for honorees of the American Bowling Congress (ABC), Professional Bowlers' Association (PBA) and Women's International Bowling Congress (WIBC). The museum does not include the new Ladies Pro Bowlers Tour Hall of Fame, which is located in Las Vegas. **Address:** 111 Stadium Plaza, St. Louis, MO 63102. **Telephone:** (314) 231-6340.

Professional Bowlers Association

Established in 1975. **Eligibility:** Nominees must be PBA members and at least 35 years old. Voting done by 50-member panel that includes writers who have covered bowling for at least 12 years.

Class of 2000 (2): PERFORMANCE—**Parker Bohn III**; MERITORIOUS SERVICE—**Jim Fitzgerald**.

Members are listed with years of induction; (+) indicates deceased members.

Performance

+ Allen, Bill 1983	+ Fazio, Buzz 1976	Roth, Mark 1987
Anthony, Earl 1986	Ferraro, Dave 1997	Salvino, Carmen 1975
Aulby, Mike 1996	Godman, Jim 1987	Semiz, Teata...............1998
Berardi, Joe 1990	Hardwick, Billy 1977	Smith, Harry...............1975
Bluth, Ray 1975	Holman, Marshall 1990	Soutar, Dave 1979
Bohn, Parker III...........2000	Hudson, Tommy 1989	Stefanich, Jim 1980
Buckley, Roy...............1992	Husted, Dave 1996	Voss, Brian 1994
Burton, Nelson Jr...........1979	Johnson, Don 1977	Webb, Wayne...............1993
Carter, Don 1975	Laub, Larry 1985	Weber, Dick 1975
Colwell, Paul 1991	Monacelli, Amleto...........1997	Weber, Pete 1998
Cook, Steve 1993	Ozio, David...............1995	+ Welu, Billy 1975
Davis, Dave 1978	Pappas, George 1986	Williams, Mark 1999
Dickinson, Gary...............1988	Petraglia, John 1982	Williams, Walter Ray Jr......1995
Durbin, Mike 1984	Ritger, Dick...............1978	Zahn, Wayne...............1981

Veterans

Allison, Glenn 1984	+ Joseph, Joe...............1985	Schlegel, Ernie...............1997
Asher, Barry...............1988	Limongello, Mike 1994	+ St. John, Jim 1989
Baker, Tom 1999	Marzich, Andy...............1990	Strampe, Bob...............1987
Foremsky, Skee 1992	McCune, Don...............1991	
Guenther, Johnny...........1986	McGrath, Mike 1988	

Meritorious Service

+ Antenora, Joe...............1993	Fitzgerald, Jim 2000	Nakano, Keijiro...........1999
Archibald, John 1989	+ Frantz, Lou 1978	Pezzano, Chuck...........1975
Clemens, Chuck...............1994	Golden, Harry 1983	Reichert, Jack...............1992
+ Elias, Eddie 1976	Hoffman, Ted Jr 1985	+ Richards, Joe 1976
Esposito, Frank...............1975	Jowdy, John 1988	Schenkel, Chris 1976
Evans, Dick...............1986	Kelley, Joe...............1989	Stitzlein, Lorraine...........1980
Firestone, Raymond...........1987	Lichstein, Larry 1996	Thompson, Al...............1991
Fisher, E.A. (Bud)...........1984	+ Nagy, Steve 1977	Zeller, Roger...............1995

American Bowling Congress

Established in 1941 and open to professional and amateur bowlers. **Eligibility:** Nominated bowlers must have competed in at least 20 years of ABC tournaments. Voting done by 170-member panel made up of ABC officials, Hall of Fame members and media representatives.

Class of 2000 (2): PERFORMANCE—**Bill Spigner**; MERITORIOUS SERVICE— **John Jowdy**.

Members are listed with years of induction; (+) indicates deceased members.

Performance

Allison, Glenn 1979	Burton, Nelson Jr...........1981	Ellis, Don...............1981
Anthony, Earl...............1986	+ Burton, Nelson Sr 1964	+ Falcaro, Joe 1968
Asher, Barry...............1998	+ Campi, Lou...............1968	+ Faragalli, Lindy 1968
+ Asplund, Harold 1978	+ Carlson, Adolph 1941	+ Fazio, Buzz 1963
Baer, Gordy 1987	Carter, Don 1970	Fehr, Steve 1993
Beach, Bill 1991	+ Caruana, Frank 1977	+ Gersonde, Russ 1968
+ Benkovic, Frank...............1958	+ Cassio, Marty 1972	+ Gibson, Therm...........1965
Berlin, Mike 1994	+ Castellano, Graz...........1976	Godman, Jim 1987
+ Billick, George...............1982	+ Clause, Frank 1980	Goike, Robert...............1996
+ Blouin, Jimmy 1953	Cohn, Alfred 1985	+ Golembiewski, Billy...........1979
Bluth, Ray 1973	Colwell, Paul 1999	Griffo, Greg...............1995
+ Bodis, Joe...............1941	+ Crimmins, Johnny 1962	Guenther, Johnny...........1988
+ Bomar, Buddy 1966	Davis, Dave 1990	Hardwick, Billy 1985
+ Brandt, Allie 1960	+ Daw, Charlie 1941	Hart, Bob 1994
+ Brosius, Eddie 1976	+ Day, Ned 1952	Hennessey, Tom 1976
+ Bujack, Fred...............1967	Dickinson, Gary...............1992	Hoover, Dick 1974
Bunetta, Bill 1968	+ Easter, Sarge 1963	Horn, Bud 1992

Bowling (Cont.)

Howard, George..........1986	+ McMahon, Junie 1967	+ Steers, Harry 1941

Howard, George..........1986
Jackson, Eddie............1988
Johnson, Don 1982
Johnson, Earl 1987
+ Joseph, Joe 1969
+ Jouglard, Lee 1979
+ Kartheiser, Frank 1967
+ Kawolics, Ed 1968
+ Kissoff, Joe 1976
+ Klares, John 1982
+ Knox, Billy 1954
+ Koster, John 1941
+ Krems, Eddie 1973
Kristof, Joe 1968
+ Krumske, Paul............1968
+ Lange, Herb 1941
+ Lauman, Hank 1976
Lillard, Bill................1972
Lindemann, Tony 1979
+ Lindsey, Mort 1941
+ Lippe, Harry 1989
Lubanski, Ed..............1971
Lucci, Vince Sr 1978
+ Marino, Hank..............1941
+ Martino, John..............1969
Marzich, Andy............1993
McGrath, Mike 1993

+ McMahon, Junie 1967
+ Meisel, Darold............1998
+ Mercurio, Skang 1967
+ Meyers, Norm 1984
+ Nagy, Steve 1963
Norris, Joe 1954
O'Donnell, Chuck 1968
Pappas, George 1989
+ Patterson, Pat 1974
Ritger, Dick 1984
+ Rogoznica, Andy............1993
Salvino, Carmen 1979
Schissler, Les..............1991
Schlegel, Ernie............1997
Schroeder, Jim 1990
+ Schwoegler, Connie 1968
Scudder, Don 1999
Semiz, Teata 1991
+ Sielaff, Lou 1968
+ Sinke, Joe 1977
+ Sixty, Billy 1961
Smith, Harry 1978
+ Smith, Jimmy 1941
Soutar, Dave 1985
Spigner, Bill 2000
+ Sparando, Tony 1968
+ Spinella, Barney 1968

+ Steers, Harry 1941
Stefanich, Jim 1983
+ Stein, Otto Jr 1971
Stoudt, Bud..............1991
Strampe, Bob 1977
+ Thoma, Sykes 1971
Toft, Rod 1991
Tountas, Pete 1989
+ Totsky, Mike 1996
Tucker, Bill................1988
Tuttle, Tommy 1995
+ Varipapa, Andy............1957
+ Ward, Walter..............1959
Weber, Dick 1970
+ Welu, Billy 1975
+ Wilman, Joe..............1951
+ Wolf, Phil 1961
Wonders, Rich 1990
+ Young, George 1959
Zahn, Wayne............1980
Zikes, Les 1983
+ Zunker, Gil 1941

Pioneers

+ Allen, Lafayette Jr. 1994
+ Briell, Frank 1996
+ Carow, Rev. Charles 1995
+ Celestine, Sydney 1993
+ Curtis, Thomas............1993
+ de Freitas, Eric............1994
Hall, William Sr. 1994

Hirashima, Hirohito.........1995
+ Karpf, Samuel 1993
+ Moore, Henry 1996
+ Pasdeloup, Frank 1993
+ Rhodman, Bill..............1997
+ Satow, Masao 1994
+ Schutte, Louis 1993

Shimada, Fuzzy............1997
+ Stein, Louis 1997
+ Thompson, William V.......1993
+ Timm, Dr. Henry............1993
Wilcox, John 1999

Meritorious Service

+ Allen, Harold 1966
Archibald, John 1996
+ Baker, Frank..............1975
+ Baumgarten, Elmer 1963
+ Bellisimo, Lou 1986
+ Bensinger, Bob.............1969
+ Chase, LeRoy..............1972
+ Coker, John 1980
+ Collier, Chuck 1963
+ Cruchon, Steve 1983
+ Ditzen, Walt..............1973
+ Dobs, Darold 1999
+ Doehrman, Bill............1968
+ Elias, Eddie 1985
Esposito, Frank............1997
Evans, Dick................1992

Franklin, Bill 1992
+ Hagerty, Jack 1963
+ Hattstrom, H.A. (Doc) 1980
+ Hermann, Cornelius 1968
+ Howley, Pete 1941
Jowdy, John 2000
+ Kennedy, Bob..............1981
+ Langtry, Abe..............1963
+ Levine, Sam 1971
+ Luby, David................1969
Luby, Mort Jr................1988
+ Luby, Mort Sr..............1974
Matzelle, Al 1995
+ McCullough, Howard.......1971
+ Patterson, Morehead........1985
+ Petersen, Louie 1963

Pezzano, Chuck............1982
Picchietti, Remo 1993
Pluckhahn, Bruce............1989
Powell, John 2000
+ Raymer, Milt..............1972
+ Reed, Elmer 1978
Reichert, Jack 1998
Rudo, Milt................1984
Schenkel, Chris 1988
+ Sweeney, Dennis 1974
Tessman, Roger 1994
+ Thum, Joe 1980
Weinstein, Sam 1970
+ Whitney, Eli 1975
Wolf, Fred 1976

Women's International Bowling Congress

Established in 1953. **Eligibility:** Performance nominees must have won at least one WIBC Championship Tournament title, a WIBC Queens tournament title or an international competition title and have bowled at least 15 national WIBC Championship Tournaments (unless injury or illness cut career short).

Class of 2000 (6): PERFORMANCE—**Dana Miller-Mackey, Susie Reichley** and **Lisa Wagner**; MERITORIOUS SERVICE—**Elaine Hagin, Hazel McCleary** and **Jeanette Robinson**.

Members are listed with years of induction; (+) indicates deceased members.

Performance

Abel, Joy..................1984
Adamek, Donna 1996
Ann, Patty..................1995
Bolt, Mae 1978
Bouvia, Gloria 1987
Boxberger, Loa............1984
Buckner, Pam 1990

+ Burling, Catherine 1958
+ Burns, Nina 1977
Cantaline, Anita 1979
Carter, LaVerne 1977
Carter, Paula 1994
Coburn, Cindy C...........1998
Coburn, Doris 1976

Costello, Pat..............1986
Costello, Patty 1989
Dryer, Pat 1978
Duval, Helen 1970
Fellmeth, Catherine 1970
Fothergill, Dotty 1980
+ Fritz, Deane 1966

Garms, Shirley	1971	Ladewig, Marion	1964	+ Robinson, Leona	1969
Gianulias, Nikki	1997	Martin, Sylvia Wene	1966	Romeo, Robin	1995
Giovinco-Sandelin, Lucy	1999	Martorella, Millie	1975	+ Rump, Anita	1962
Gloor, Olga	1976	+ Matthews, Merle	1974	+ Ruschmeyer, Addie	1961
Gonzalez, Ashie	1998	+ McCutcheon, Floretta	1956	+ Ryan, Esther	1963
Graham, Linda	1992	Merrick, Marge	1980	+ Sablatnik, Ethel	1979
Graham, Mary Lou	1989	+ Mikiel, Val	1979	+ Schulte, Myrtle	1965
+ Greenwald, Goldie	1953	Miller-Mackey, Dana	2000	+ Shablis, Helen	1977
Grinfelds, Vesma	1991	Miller, Carol	1997	Sill, Aleta	1996
+ Harman, Janet	1985	+ Miller, Dorothy	1954	+ Simon, Violet (Billy)	1960
+ Hartrick, Stella	1972	Mivelaz, Betty	1991	+ Small, Tess	1971
+ Hatch, Grayce	1953	Mohacsi, Mary	1994	+ Smith, Grace	1968
Havlish, Jean	1987	Morris, Betty	1983	Soutar, Judy	1976
+ Hoffman, Martha	1979	Naccarato, Jeanne	1999	+ Stockdale, Louise	1953
Holm, Joan	1974	Nichols, Lorrie	1989	Toepfer, Elvira	1976
+ Humphreys, Birdie	1979	Norman, Edie Jo	1993	+ Twyford, Sally	1964
Ignizio, Mildred	1975	Norton, Virginia	1988	Wagner, Lisa	2000
Jacobson, D.D	1981	Notaro, Phyllis	1979	+ Warmbier, Marie	1953
+ Jaeger, Emma	1953	Ortner, Bev	1972	Wilkinson, Dorothy	1990
Kelly, Annese	1985	+ Powers, Connie	1973	+ Winandy, Cecelia	1975
+ Knechtges, Doris	1983	Reichley, Susie	2000	Zimmerman, Donna	1982
Kuczynski, Betty	1981	Rickard, Robbie	1994		

Meritorious Service

Baetz, Helen	1977	Herold, Mitzi	1998	+ Phaler, Emma	1965
+ Baker, Helen	1989	+ Higley, Margaret	1969	+ Porter, Cora	1986
+ Banker, Gladys	1994	+ Hochstadter, Bee	1967	+ Quin, Zoe	1979
+ Bayley, Clover	1992	+ Kay, Nora	1964	+ Rishling, Gertrude	1972
+ Berger, Winifred	1976	Keller, Pearl	1999	Robinson, Jeanette	2000
+ Bohlen, Philena	1955	+ Kelly, Ellen	1979	Simone, Anne	1991
Borschuk, Lo	1988	Kelone, Theresa	1978	Sloan, Catherine	1985
+ Botkin, Freda	1986	+ Knepprath, Jeannette	1963	+ Speck, Berdie	1966
+ Chapman, Emily	1957	+ Lasher, Iolia	1967	Spitalnick, Mildred	1994
+ Crowe, Alberta	1982	Marrs, Mabel	1979	+ Spring, Alma	1979
+ Dornblaser, Gertrude	1979	+ McBride, Bertha	1968	+ Switzer, Pearl	1973
Duffy, Agnes	1987	McCleary, Hazel	2000	Todd, Trudy	1993
Finke, Gertrude	1990	+ Menne, Catherine	1979	+ Veatch, Georgia	1974
+ Fisk, Rae	1983	Mitchell, Flora	1996	+ White, Mildred	1975
+ Haas, Dorothy	1977	+ Mraz, Jo	1959	+ Wood, Ann	1970
Hagin, Elaine	2000	O'Connor, Billie	1992		

Professional Women Bowlers Hall of Fame

Established in 1995 by the Ladies Pro Bowlers Tour. The LPBT has since been renamed the Professional Women Bowlers Association. **Address:** Sam's Town Hotel, Gambling Hall and Bowling Center, 5111 Boulder Highway, Las Vegas, NV 89122. **Telephone:** (815) 332-5756.

Eligibility: Nominees in performance category must have at least five titles from organizations including All-Star, World Invitational, LPBT, WPBA, PWBA, TPA and LPBA. Voting done by 10-member committee of bowling writers appointed by PWBA president John Falzone.

Members are listed with year of induction; (+) indicates deceased member.

Performance

Adamek, Donna	1995	Gianulias, Nikki	1996	Morris, Betty	1995
Colburn-Carroll, Cindy	1997	Grinfelds, Vesma	1997	Nichols, Lorrie	1996
Costello, Pat	1997	Johnson, Tish	1998	Romeo, Robin	1996
Costello, Patty	1995	Ladewig, Marion	1995	Sill, Aleta	1998
Fothergill, Dotty	1995	Martorella, Millie	1995	Wagner, Lisa	1996

Pioneers

Able, Joy	1998	Coburn, Doris	1996	Ortner, Bev	1998
Boxberger, Loa	1997	Duval, Helen	1995	Soutar, Judy	1997
Carter, LaVerne	1995	Garms, Shirley	1995	Zimmerman, Donna	1996

Builders

Buhler, Janet	1996	Robinson, Jeanette	1996	+ Veatch, Georgia	1995
Keller, Pearl	1997	Sommer Jr., John	1997		

BOXING

International Boxing Hall of Fame

Established in 1989 and opened in 1990. **Address:** 1 Hall of Fame Drive, Canastota, NY 13032. **Telephone:** (315) 697-7095.

Eligibility: All nominees must be retired for five years. Voting done by 142-member panel made up of Boxing Writers' Association members and world-wide boxing historians.

Class of 2000 (12): MODERN ERA—**Ken Buchanan** (lightweight), **Jimmy Carter** (lightweight), **Jeff Chandler** (bantamweight), **Carl Olson** (middleweight). OLD TIMERS—**Jimmy Barry** (bantamweight), **Battling Levinsky** (light heavyweight), **Billy Petrolle** (lightweight), **Ad Wolgast** (lightweight). PIONEER—**Arthur Chambers** (lightweight). NON-PARTICIPANTS— **Jeff Dickson** (promoter), **Tito Lectoure** (promoter), **Dan Morgan** (manager).

Members are listed with year of induction; (+) indicates deceased member.

Modern Era

Ali, Muhammad...........1990	Gavilan, Kid............1990	Olivares, Ruben...........1991
+ Angott, Sammy 1998	Giardello, Joey 1993	Olson, Carl...............2000
Arguello, Alexis...........1992	Gomez, Wilfredo 1995	Ortiz, Carlos 1991
+ Armstrong, Henry 1990	+ Graham, Billy 1992	+ Ortiz, Manuel 1996
Basilio, Carmen...........1990	+ Graziano, Rocky 1991	Patterson, Floyd 1991
Benitez, Wilfredo 1996	Griffith, Emile 1990	Pedroza, Eusebio 1999
Benvenuti, Nino 1992	Hagler, Marvelous Marvin...1993	Pep, Willie 1990
+ Berg, Jackie (Kid).........1994	Harada, Masahiko (Fighting) .1995	+ Perez, Pascual 1995
Bivins, Jimmy 1999	Jack, Beau 1991	Pryor, Aaron..............1996
+ Brown, Joe 1996	+ Jenkins, Lew 1999	+ Robinson, Sugar Ray.......1990
Buchanan, Ken 2000	Jofre, Eder 1992	+ Rodriguez, Luis 1997
+ Burley, Charley 1992	Johnson, Harold...........1993	Saddler, Sandy 1990
Canto, Miguel 1998	LaMotta, Jake 1990	+ Saldivar, Vicente 1999
+ Carter, Jimmy 2000	Leonard, Sugar Ray 1997	+ Sanchez, Salvador 1991
+ Cerdan, Marcel 1991	+ Liston, Sonny 1991	Schmeling, Max............1992
Cervantes, Antonio 1998	+ Louis, Joe 1990	Spinks, Michael 1994
Chandler, Jeff.............2000	+ Marciano, Rocky 1990	+ Tiger, Dick 1991
+ Charles, Ezzard 1990	Maxim, Joey 1994	Torres, Jose...............1997
+ Conn, Billy 1990	+ Montgomery, Bob 1995	+ Walcott, Jersey Joe 1990
+ Elorde, Gabriel (Flash) 1993	+ Monzon, Carlos 1990	+ Williams, Ike 1990
Foster, Bob 1990	+ Moore, Archie 1990	+ Wright, Chalky 1997
Frazier, Joe..............1990	Muhammad, Matthew Saad .1998	+ Zale, Tony...............1991
Fullmer, Gene 1991	Napoles, Jose 1990	Zarate, Carlos 1994
Galaxy, Khaosai 1999	Norton, Ken 1992	+ Zivic, Fritzie 1993

Old-Timers

Ambers, Lou 1992	+ Genaro, Frankie 1998	+ McFarland, Packey 1992
+ Attell, Abe................1990	+ Gibbons, Mike 1992	+ McGovern, Terry 1990
+ Baer, Max...............1995	+ Gibbons, Tommy 1993	McLarnin, Jimmy 1991
+ Barry, Jimmy..............2000	+ Greb, Harry 1990	+ McVey, Sam 1999
+ Britton, Jack 1990	+ Griffo, Young 1991	+ Miller, Freddie 1997
+ Brown, Panama Al 1992	+ Herman, Pete 1997	+ Nelson, Battling 1992
+ Burns, Tommy 1996	+ Jackson, Peter...........1990	+ O'Brien, Philadelphia Jack...1994
+ Canzoneri, Tony 1990	+ Jeanette, Joe 1997	+ Petrolle, Billy............2000
+ Carpentier, Georges 1991	+ Jeffries, James J 1990	+ Rosenbloom, Maxie 1993
+ Chocolate, Kid 1991	+ Johnson, Jack 1990	+ Ross, Barney 1990
+ Choynski, Joe.............1998	+ Ketchel, Stanley 1990	+ Ryan, Tommy 1991
+ Corbett, James J...........1990	+ Kilbane, Johnny 1995	+ Sharkey, Jack 1994
+ Coulon, Johnny 1999	+ LaBarba, Fidel 1996	+ Steele, Freddie 1999
+ Darcy, Les...............1993	+ Langford, Sam 1990	+ Stribling, Young 1996
+ Delaney, Jack 1996	+ Lavigne, George (Kid) 1998	+ Tendler, Lew 1999
+ Dempsey, Jack 1990	+ Leonard, Benny 1990	+ Tunney, Gene 1990
+ Dempsey, Jack (Nonpareil) ..1992	+ Levinsky, Battling 2000	+ Villa, Pancho 1994
+ Dillon, Jack 1995	+ Lewis, John Henry 1994	+ Walcott, Joe (Barbados) 1991
+ Dixon, George 1990	+ Lewis, Ted (Kid) 1992	+ Walker, Mickey 1990
+ Driscoll, Jim 1990	+ Loughran, Tommy 1991	+ Welsh, Freddie...........1997
+ Dundee, Johnny 1991	+ Lynch, Benny 1998	+ Wilde, Jimmy 1990
+ Fitzsimmons, Bob...........1990	+ Mandell, Sammy 1998	+ Williams, Kid 1996
+ Flowers, Theodore (Tiger)....1993	+ McAuliffe, Jack 1995	+ Wills, Harry 1992
+ Gans, Joe 1990	+ McCoy, Charles (Kid) 1991	+ Wolgast, Ad..............2000

Pioneers

+ Belcher, Jem 1992	+ Cribb, Tom 1991	+ Johnson, Tom 1995
+ Brain, Ben................1994	+ Donovan, Prof. Mike........1998	+ King, Tom 1992
+ Broughton, Jack 1990	+ Duffy, Paddy 1994	+ Langham, Nat 1992
+ Burke, James (Deaf)........1992	+ Figg, James 1992	+ Mace, Jem 1990
+ Chambers, Arthur 2000	+ Jackson, Gentleman John 1992	+ Mendoza, Daniel 1990

+ Molineaux, Tom 1997
+ Morrissey, John 1996
+ Pearce, Henry 1993
+ Richmond, Bill 1999

+ Sam, Dutch 1997
+ Sayers, Tom 1990
  Spring, Tom 1992
+ Sullivan, John L 1990

+ Thompson, William 1991
+ Ward, Jem 1995

Non-Participants

+ Andrews, Thomas S 1992
+ Arcel, Ray 1991
  Arum, Bob 1999
+ Ballarati, Giuseppe 1999
+ Blackburn, Jack 1992
+ Brady, William A. 1998
  Brenner, Teddy 1993
+ Chambers, John Graham 1990
  Clancy, Gil 1993
+ Coffroth, James W. 1991
+ D'Amato, Cus. 1995
  Dickson, Jeff 2000
+ Donovan, Arthur 1993
  Duff, Mickey 1999
  Dundee, Angelo. 1992
+ Dundee, Chris 1994
+ Dunphy, Don 1993

  Duva, Lou 1998
+ Egan, Pierce 1991
+ Fleischer, Nat. 1990
+ Fox, Richard K. 1997
  Futch, Eddie 1994
+ Goldman, Charley 1992
+ Goldstein, Ruby 1994
  Goodman, Murray 1999
+ Humphreys, Joe 1997
+ Jacobs, Jimmy 1993
+ Jacobs, Mike 1990
+ Johnston, Jimmy 1999
+ Kearns, Jack (Doc). 1990
  King, Don 1997
  Lectoure, Tito 2000
+ Liebling, A.J. 1992
+ Lonsdale, Lord 1990

+ Markson, Harry 1992
  Mercante, Arthur 1995
+ Morgan, Dan 2000
+ Muldoon, William 1996
  Odd, Gilbert 1995
+ O'Rourke, Tom 1999
+ Parker, Dan 1996
+ Parnassus, George 1991
+ Queensberry, Marquis of 1990
+ Rickard, Tex 1990
  Rudd, Irving 1999
+ Siler, George 1995
+ Solomons, Jack 1995
  Steward, Emanuel 1996
+ Taub, Sam. 1994
+ Taylor, Herman 1998
+ Walker, James J. (Jimmy) 1992

Old *Ring* Hall Members Not in Int'l. Boxing Hall

Nat Fleischer, the late founder and editor-in-chief of *The Ring*, established his magazine's Boxing Hall of Fame in 1954, but it was abandoned after the 1987 inductions. One hundred and sixteen members of the old *Ring* Hall have been elected to the International Hall since 1989. The 38 boxers and one sportswriter who have yet to be elected to the International Hall are listed below with their year of induction into the *Ring* Hall.

Modern Group

+ Apostoli, Fred. 1978
+ Braddock, James J 1964

+ Escobar, Sixto 1975
+ Garcia, Ceferino 1977

+ Lesnevich, Gus. 1973
+ Shirai, Yoshio 1977

Old-Timers

+ Berlenbach, Paul 1971
+ Britt, Jimmy 1976
+ Chaney, George (K.O.) 1974
+ Corbett, Young II 1965
+ Fields, Jackie 1977
+ Houck, Leo 1969

+ Jeffra, Harry 1982
+ Kid, The Dixie 1975
+ Klaus, Frank 1974
+ Maher, Peter. 1978
+ Mitchell, Charley 1957
+ Papke, Billy. 1972

+ Ritchie, Willie 1962
+ Root, Jack 1961
+ Sharkey, Tom 1959
+ Smith, Jeff 1969
+ Taylor, Bud 1986
+ Willard, Jess. 1977

Pioneers

+ Aaron, Barney (Young) 1967
+ Chandler, Tom 1972
+ Clark, Nobby 1971
+ Collyer, Sam 1964
+ Donnelly, Dan 1960
+ Goss, Joe 1969

+ Gully, John 1959
+ Heenan, John C 1954
+ Hyer, Jacob 1968
+ Hyer, Tom 1954
+ Jackling, Thomas 1985
+ Kilrain, Jack 1965

+ Price, Ned. 1962
+ Ryan, Paddy 1973

Non-Participant

+ Daniel, Dan (sportswriter). . . .1977

FOOTBALL

College Football Hall of Fame

Established in 1955 by the National Football Foundation. **Address:** 111 South St. Joseph St., South Bend, IN 46601. **Telephone:** (219) 235-9999.

Eligibility: Nominated players must be out of college 10 years and a first team All-America pick by a major selector during their careers; coaches must be retired three years. Voting done by 12-member panel of athletic directors, conference and bowl officials and media representatives. The first year representatives from NCAA Div. I-AA, II, and III, and the NAIA were eligible for induction was 1996.

Class of 2000 (24): LARGE COLLEGE—RB **Marcus Allen**, USC (1978-81); C/LB **Kurt Burris**, Oklahoma (1951-54); OT **Dan Dierdorf**, Michigan (1968-70); E **Bob Dove**, Notre Dame (1940-42); QB **John Elway**, Stanford (1979-82); DB **Michael Haynes**, Arizona St. (1972-75); DB **Terry Hoage**, Georgia (1980-83); OT/DT **Stan Jones**, Maryland (1951-53); HB **Johnny Musso**, Alabama (1969-71); WB **Johnny Rodgers**, Nebraska (1970-72); FB/LB **Joe Schmidt**, Pittsburgh (1950-52); OG **Harley Sewell**, Texas (1950-52); DE **Billy Ray Smith**, Arkansas (1979-82); TB **Eddie Talboom**, Wyoming (1948-50). COACHES—**Tom Donahue**, UCLA (1976-95); **Forest Evashevski**, Hamilton (1941), Washington St. (1950-51), Iowa (1950-60); SMALL COLLEGE—RB/DB **Johnny Bailey**, Texas A&M (1986-89); RB/DB **Bill Cooper**, Muskingum, OH (1957-60); DB **Brad Crawford**, Franklin, IN (1974-77); OG/LB **Willie Lanier Sr.**, Morgan State, MD (1963-66); RB/LB **Paul Younger**, Grambling St. (1945-48); COACHES—**Darrell Mudra**, Adams St. (1959-62), N. Dakota (1963-65), Arizona (1967-68), W. Illinois (1969-73), Florida St. (1974-75), E. Illinois (1978-82), Northern Iowa (1983-87); **Ron Schipper**, Central College (1961-96); **Frank Waters**, Hillside College (1954-73), Saginaw Valley St. (1975-79), Michigan St. (1980-82).

Note: Bobby Dodd and **Amos Alonzo Stagg** are the only members to be honored as both players and coaches.

Football (Cont.)

Players are listed with final year they played in college and coaches are listed with year of induction; (+) indicates deceased members.

Players

+ Abell, Earl-Colgate 1915
Agase, Alex-Purdue/Ill 1946
+ Agganis, Harry-Boston U 1952
Albert, Frank-Stanford......1941
+ Aldrich, Ki-TCU............1938
+ Aldrich, Malcolm-Yale.......1921
+ Alexander, Joe-Syracuse.....1920
Allen, Marcus-USC...........1981
Alworth, Lance-Arkansas 1961
+ Ameche, Alan-Wisconsin 1954
Ames, Knowlton-Princeton ...1889
Amling, Warren-Ohio St......1946
Anderson, Dick-Colorado.....1967
Anderson, Donny-Tex.Tech ...1966
+ Anderson, Hunk-N.Dame.....1921
Atkins, Doug-Tennessee......1952
Babich, Bob-Miami-OH 1968
+ Bacon, Everett-Wesleyan 1912
+ Bagnell, Reds-Penn 1950
+ Baker, Hobey-Princeton......1913
+ Baker, John-USC 1931
+ Baker, Moon-N'western 1926
Baker, Terry-Oregon St 1962
+ Ballin, Harold-Princeton 1914
+ Banker, Bill-Tulane 1929
Banonis, Vince-Detroit.......1941
+ Barnes, Stan-California......1921
+ Barrett, Charles-Cornell......1915
+ Baston, Bert-Minnesota......1916
+ Battles, Cliff-WV Wesleyan ..1931
Baugh, Sammy-TCU 1936
Baughan, Maxie-Ga.Tech.....1959
+ Bausch, James-Kansas.......1930
Beagle, Ron-Navy...........1955
Beban, Gary-UCLA 1967
Bechtol, Hub-Texas 1946
Beck, Ray-Ga. Tech 1951
+ Beckett, John-Oregon 1916
Bednarik, Chuck-Penn 1948
Behm, Forrest-Nebraska......1940
Bell, Bobby-Minnesota 1962
Bellino, Joe-Navy...........1960
Below, Marty-Wisconsin.....1923
+ Benbrook, Al-Michigan 1910
+ Berry, Charlie-Lafayette......1924
+ Bertelli, Angelo-N.Dame......1943
Berwanger, Jay-Chicago 1935
+ Bettencourt, L.-St.Mary's 1927
Biletnikoff, Fred-Fla.St.......1964
Blanchard, Doc-Army 1946
+ Blozis, Al-Georgetown 1942
Bock, Ed-Iowa St 1938
Bomar, Lynn-Vanderbilt 1924
+ Bomeisler, Bo-Yale 1913
+ Booth, Albie-Yale 1931
+ Borries, Fred-Navy 1934
+ Bosley, Bruce-West Va.......1955
Bosseler, Don-Miami,FL......1956
Bottari, Vic-California 1938
+ Boynton, Ben-Williams 1920
Brewer, Charles-Harvard.....1895
+ Bright, Johnny-Drake 1951
Brodie, John-Stanford 1956
+ Brooke, George-Penn 1895
Brosky, Al-Illinois 1952
Brown, Bob-Nebraska 1963
Brown, Geo-Navy/S.Diego St.1947
+ Brown, Gordon-Yale 1900
Brown, Jim-Syracuse 1956
+ Brown, John, Jr.-Navy.......1913
+ Brown, Johnny Mack-Ala....1925

+ Brown, Tay-USC............1932
Browner, Ross-Notre Dame ..1977
Buddie, Brad-USC 1979
+ Bunker, Paul-Army 1902
Burford, Chris-Stanford......1959
+ Burris, Kurt-Oklahoma.......1954
Burton, Ron-N'western 1959
Butkus, Dick-Illinois 1964
+ Butler, Robert-Wisconsin 1912
+ Cafego, George-Tenn 1939
+ Cagle, Red-SWLa/Army......1929
+ Cain, John-Alabama 1932
Cameron, Ed-Wash.& Lee ...1924
+ Campbell, David-Harvard 1901
+ Campbell, Earl-Texas........1977
+ Cannon, Jack-N.Dame 1929
Cappelletti, John-Penn St 1973
+ Carideo, Frank-N.Dame......1930
+ Carney, Charles-Illinois 1921
Caroline, J.C.-Illinois 1954
Carpenter, Bill-Army 1959
+ Carpenter, Hunter-Va.Tech ...1905
Carroll, Chas.-Washington....1928
Casanova, Tommy-LSU 1971
+ Casey, Edward-Harvard......1919
Cassady, Howard-Ohio St ...1955
+ Chamberlin, Guy-Neb.......1915
Chapman, Sam-California 1938
Chappuis, Bob-Michigan.....1947
+ Christman, Paul-Missouri 1940
+ Clark, Dutch-Colo. Col. 1929
Cleary, Paul-USC...........1947
+ Clevenger, Zora-Indiana......1903
Cloud, Jack-Wm. & Mary ...1948
+ Cochran, Gary-Princeton 1897
+ Cody, Josh-Vanderbilt 1919
Coleman, Don-Mich.St 1951
+ Conerly, Charlie-Miss 1947
Connor, George-HC/ND 1947
+ Corbin, William-Yale.........1888
Corbus, William-Stanford.....1933
+ Cowan, Hector-Princeton 1889
+ Coy, Edward (Tad)-Yale 1909
+ Crawford, Fred-Duke........1933
Crow, John David-Tex.A&M...1957
+ Crowley, Jim-Notre Dame....1924
Csonka, Larry-Syracuse 1967
Cutter, Slade-Navy 1934
+ Czarobski, Ziggie-N.Dame ..1947
Dale, Carroll-Va.Tech 1959
+ Dalrymple, Gerald-Tulane ...1931
+ Dalton, John-Navy..........1911
+ Daly, Chas.-Harvard/Army ...1902
Daniell, Averell-Pitt.........1936
+ Daniell, James-Ohio St 1941
Davies, Tom-Pittsburgh 1921
Davis, Ernie-Syracuse 1961
Davis, Glenn-Army 1946
Davis, Robert-Ga.Tech 1947
Dawkins, Pete-Army 1958
DeLong, Steve-Tennessee 1964
+ DeRogatis, Al-Duke.........1948
+ DesJardien, Paul-Chicago....1914
Devine, Aubrey-Iowa 1921
+ DeWitt, John-Princeton 1903
Dial, Buddy-Rice 1958
Dicus, Chuck-Arkansas 1970
Dierdorf, Dan-Michigan 1970
Ditka, Mike-Pittsburgh 1960
Dobbs, Glenn-Tulsa 1942
+ Dodd, Bobby-Tennessee 1930

Donan, Holland-Princeton....1950
+ Donchess, Joseph-Pitt.......1929
Dorsett, Tony-Pitt...........1976
+ Dougherty, Nathan-Tenn....1909
Dove, Bob-Notre Dame 1942
Drahos, Nick-Cornell........1940
+ Driscoll, Paddy-N'western ...1917
Drury, Morley-USC 1927
Dudley, Bill-Virginia.........1941
Duncan, Randy-Iowa........1958
Easley, Kenny-UCLA 1980
+ Eckersall, Walter-Chicago ...1906
+ Edwards, Turk-Wash.St......1931
+ Edwards, Wm.-Princeton 1899
+ Eichenlaub, Ray-N.Dame ...1914
Eisenhauer, Steve-Navy......1953
Elkins, Larry-Baylor 1964
Elliott, Bump-Mich/Purdue ..1947
Elliott, Pete-Michigan........1948
Elmendorf, Dave-Tex. A&M ..1970
Elway, John-Stanford........1982
+ Evans, Ray-Kansas..........1947
+ Exendine, Albert-Carlisle 1907
Falaschi, Nello-S.Clara.......1936
Fears, Tom-S.Clara/UCLA 1947
+ Feathers, Beattie-Tenn 1933
Fenimore, Bob-Okla.St 1946
+ Fenton, Doc-LSU 1909
Ferguson, Bob-Ohio St.......1961
Ferraro, John-USC 1944
Fesler, Wes-Ohio St.........1930
+ Fincher, Bill-Ga.Tech 1920
Fischer, Bill-Notre Dame 1948
+ Fish, Hamilton-Harvard......1909
+ Fisher, Robert-Harvard 1911
+ Flowers, Allen-Ga.Tech 1920
Flowers, Charlie-Ole Miss....1959
+ Fortmann Danny-Colgate ...1935
Fralic, Bill-Pittsburgh 1984
Francis, Sam-Nebraska 1936
Franco, Ed-Fordham 1937
+ Frank, Clint-Yale............1937
Franz, Rodney-California 1949
Frederickson, Tucker-Auburn .1964
+ Friedman, Benny-Michigan ..1926
Gabriel, Roman-N.C. State ..1961
Gain, Bob-Kentucky 1950
+ Galiffa, Arnold-Army 1949
+ Gallarneau, Hugh-Stanford ..1940
+ Garbisch, Edgar-W.& J./Army.1924
Garrett, Mike-USC..........1965
+ Gelbert, Charles-Penn.......1896
+ Geyer, Forest-Oklahoma.....1915
Gibbs, Jake-Miss 1960
Giel, Paul-Minnesota 1953
Gifford, Frank-USC..........1951
Gilbert, Chris-Texas 1968
+ Gilbert, Walter-Auburn 1936
Gilmer, Harry-Alabama 1947
+ Gipp, George-N.Dame 1920
+ Gladchuk, Chet-Boston Col ..1940
Glass, Bill-Baylor 1956
Glover, Rich-Nebraska 1972
Goldberg, Marshall-Pitt......1938
Goodreault, Gene-BC 1940
+ Gordon, Walter-Calif........1918
+ Governali, Paul-Columbia ...1942
Grabowski, Jim-Illinois 1965
Gradishar, Randy-Ohio St....1973
Graham, Otto-N'western 1943
+ Grange, Red-Illinois.........1925

Football (Cont.)

Olds, Robin-Army 1942
+ Oliphant, Elmer-Army/Pur ...1917
Olsen, Merlin-Utah St 1961
Onkotz, Dennis-Penn St......1969
+ Oosterbaan, Bennie-Mich ...1927
O'Rourke, Charles-BC.......1940
+ Orsi, John-Colgate..........1931
+ Osgood, Win-Cornell/Penn..1892
Osmanski, Bill-Holy Cross ...1938
+ Owen, George-Harvard.....1922
Owens, Jim-Oklahoma 1949
Owens, Steve-Oklahoma 1969
Page, Alan-Notre Dame 1966
Palumbo, Joe-Virginia.......1951
Pardee, Jack-Texas A&M 1956
Parilli, Babe-Kentucky 1951
Parker, Ace-Duke 1936
Parker, Jackie-Miss.St 1953
Parker, Jim-Ohio St 1956
+ Pazzetti, Vince-Lehigh 1912
+ Peabody, Chub-Harvard....1941
+ Peck, Robert-Pittsburgh 1916
Pellegrini, Bob-Maryland 1955
+ Pennock, Stan-Harvard......1914
Pfann, George-Cornell 1923
Phillips, H.D.-Sewanee 1904
Phillips, Loyd-Arkansas 1966
Pihos, Pete-Indiana 1946
Pingel, John-Michigan St ...1938
+ Pinckert, Erny-USC..........1931
+ Plunkett, Jim-Stanford.......1970
+ Poe, Arthur-Princeton 1899
+ Pollard, Fritz-Brown.........1916
Poole, B.-Miss/NC/Army....1947
Powell, Marvin-USC 1976
Pregulman, Merv-Michigan ..1943
+ Price, Eddie-Tulane 1949
Pruitt, Greg-Oklahoma 1972
+ Pund, Peter-Georgia Tech ...1928
Ramsey, G.-Wm&Mary 1942
Redman, Rick-Wash 1964
+ Reeds, Claude-Oklahoma ...1913
Reid, Mike-Penn St..........1969
Reid, Steve-Northwestern 1936
+ Reid, William-Harvard 1899
Reifsnyder, Bob-Navy 1958
Renfro, Mel-Oregon 1963
+ Rentner, Pug-N'western.....1932
+ Reynolds, Bob-Stanford.....1935
+ Reynolds, Bobby-Nebraska ..1952
Rhome, Jerry-SMU/Tulsa 1964
Richter, Les-California 1951
Richter, Pat-Wisconsin 1962
+ Riley, Jack-Northwestern.....1931
Rimington, Dave-Nebraska ..1982
+ Rinehart, Chas.-Lafayette 1897
Ritcher, Jim-NC St...........1979
Roberts, J. D.-Oklahoma 1953
+ Robeson, Paul-Rutgers......1918
Robinson, Dave-Penn St......1962
Robinson, Jerry-UCLA 1978
+ Rodgers, Ira-West Va........1919
Rodgers, Johnny-Nebraska ..2000
+ Rogers, Ed-Carlisle/Minn...1903
Rogers, George-S. Carolina..1980
Roland, Johnny-Missouri 1965
Romig, Joe-Colorado........1961
+ Rosenberg, Aaron-USC......1933
Rote, Kyle-SMU 1950
+ Routt, Joe-Texas A&M 1937
+ Salmon, Red-Notre Dame...1903
Sarkisian, Alex.............1948
+ Sauer, George-Nebraska 1933

Savitsky, George-Penn 1947
Saxton, Jimmy-Texas 1961
Sayers, Gale-Kansas 1964
Scarbath, Jack-Maryland 1952
+ Scarlett, Hunter-Penn........1908
Schloredt, Bob-Wash 1960
Schmidt, Joe-Pittsburgh 1952
+ Schoonover, Wear-Ark. 1929
+ Schreiner, Dave-Wisconsin...1942
+ Schultz, Germany-Mich 1908
+ Schwab, Dutch-Lafayette....1922
+ Schwartz, Marchy-N.Dame..1931
+ Schwegler, Paul-Wash 1931
Scott, Clyde-Navy/Arkansas..1948
Scott, Richard-Navy 1947
Scott, Tom-Virginia.........1953
+ Seibels, Henry-Sewanee.....1899
Sellers, Ron-Florida St 1968
Selmon, Lee Roy-Okla.......1975
Sewell, Harley-Texas 1952
+ Shakespeare, Bill-N.Dame ...1935
Shell, Donnie-S.Carolina St...1998
+ Shelton, Murray-Cornell 1915
+ Shevlin, Tom-Yale..........1905
+ Shively, Bernie-Illinois 1926
+ Simons, Monk-Tulane 1934
Simpson, O.J.-USC..........1968
Sims, Billy-Oklahoma 1979
Singletary, Mike-Baylor......1980
Sington, Fred-Alabama......1930
+ Sinkwich, Frank-Georgia 1942
+ Sitko, Emil-Notre Dame......1949
+ Skladany, Joe-Pittsburgh 1933
+ Slater, Duke-Iowa...........1921
Smith, Billy Ray-Arkansas ...1982
Smith, Bruce-Minnesota 1941
Smith, Bubba-Michigan St ...1966
+ Smith, Clipper-N.Dame......1927
Smith, Ernie-USC 1932
Smith, Harry-USC 1939
Smith, Jim Ray-Baylor 1954
Smith, Riley-Alabama 1935
+ Smith, Vernon-Georgia 1931
+ Snow, Neil-Michigan 1901
Sparlis, Al-UCLA 1945
+ Spears, Clarence-Dart.......1915
Spears, W.D.-Vanderbilt 1927
+ Sprackling, Wm.-Brown......1911
+ Sprague, Bud-Army/Texas...1928
Spurrier, Steve-Florida.......1966
Stafford, Harrison-Texas 1932
+ Stagg, Amos Alonzo-Yale....1889
Stanfill, Bill-Georgia 1968
+ Starcevich, Max-Wash 1936
Staubach, Roger-Navy 1964
+ Steffen, Walter-Chicago 1908
Steffy, Joe-Tenn/Army 1947
+ Stein, Herbert-Pitt..........1921
Steuber, Bob-Missouri 1943
+ Stevens, Mal-Yale..........1923
Stillwagon, Jim-Ohio St......1970
+ Stinchcomb, Pete-Ohio St....1920
+ Stevenson, Vincent-Penn 1905
Strom, Brock-Air Force 1959
+ Strong, Ken-NYU 1928
+ Strupper, Ev-Ga.Tech.......1917
+ Stuhldreher, Harry-N.Dame ..1924
+ Sturhan, Herb-Yale.........1926
+ Stydahar, Joe-West Va 1935
+ Suffridge, Bob-Tennessee ...1940
+ Suhey, Steve-Penn St 1947
Sullivan, Pat-Auburn 1971
+ Sundstrom, Frank-Cornell 1923

Swann, Lynn-USC 1973
+ Swanson, Clarence-Neb.....1921
+ Swiacki, Bill-Columbia/HC ..1947
Swink, Jim-TCU 1956
+ Talboom, Eddie-Wyoming ..1950
Taliafarro, Geo.-Indiana 1948
Tarkenton, Fran-Georgia.....1960
+ Tavener, John-Indiana 1944
+ Taylor, Chuck-Stanford 1942
Thomas, Aurelius-Ohio St....1957
+ Thompson, Joe-Pittsburgh ...1907
+ Thorne, Samuel-Yale 1895
+ Thorpe, Jim-Carlisle.........1912
+ Ticknor, Ben-Harvard 1930
+ Tigert, John-Vanderbilt.......1904
Tinsley, Gaynell-LSU 1936
Tipton, Eric-Duke 1938
+ Tonnemaker, Clayton-Minn..1949
+ Torrey, Bob-Pennsylvania ...1905
+ Travis, Brick-Missouri........1920
Trippi, Charley-Georgia 1946
+ Tryon, Edward-Colgate......1925
Tubbs, Jerry-Oklahoma 1956
Turner, Bulldog-H.Simmons...1939
Twilley, Howard-Tulsa 1965
+ Utay, Joe-Texas A&M 1907
+ Van Brocklin, Norm-Ore.....1948
+ Van Sickel, Dale-Florida 1929
+ Van Surdam, H.-Wesleyan...1905
+ Very, Dexter-Penn St 1912
Vessels, Billy-Oklahoma 1952
+ Vick, Ernie-Michigan 1921
+ Wagner, Hube-Pittsburgh ...1913
+ Walker, Doak-SMU 1949
Walker, Herschel-Georgia ...1982
+ Wallace, Bill-Rice...........1935
+ Walsh, Adam-N.Dame 1924
+ Warburton, Cotton, USC 1934
Ward, Bob-Maryland 1951
+ Warner, William-Cornell 1904
+ Washington, Kenny-UCLA ...1939
+ Weatherall, Jim-Okla........1951
Webster, George-Mich. St...1966
+ Wedemeyer, H.-St. Mary's...1947
+ Weekes, Harold-Columbia ...1902
Weiner, Art-N. Carolina......1949
+ Weir, Ed-Nebraska 1925
+ Welch, Gus-Carlisle..........1914
+ Weller, John-Princeton 1935
+ Wendell, Percy-Harvard 1912
+ West, Belford-Colgate 1919
Westfall, Bob-Michigan 1941
+ Weyand, Babe-Army.........1915
+ Wharton, Buck-Penn 1896
+ Wheeler, Arthur-Princeton ...1894
White, Byron-Colorado 1938
White, Charles-USC 1979
White, Danny-Ariz. St........1973
White, Ed-Cal.Berkeley......1968
White, Randy-Maryland......1974
Whitmire, Don-Navy/Ala....1944
+ Wickhorst, Frank-Navy 1926
Widseth, Ed-Minnesota......1936
+ Wildung, Dick-Minnesota....1942
Williams, Bob-N. Dame 1950
Williams, Froggie-Rice 1949
Willis, Bill-Ohio St 1944
+ Wilson, Bobby-SMU 1935
+ Wilson, George-Wash 1925
+ Wilson, Harry-Army/Penn St.1926
Wilson, Marc-BYU 1979
Wilson, Mike-Lafayette 1928
Wistert, Albert-Michigan 1942

Coaches

Small College

Players

Coaches

Pro Football Hall of Fame

Established in 1963 by National Football League to commemorate the sport's professional origins. **Address:** 2121 George Halas Drive NW, Canton, OH 44708. **Telephone:** (330) 456-8207.

Eligibility: Nominated players must be retired five years, coaches must be retired, and contributors can still be active. Voting done by 36-member panel made up of media representatives from all 30 NFL cities, one PFWA representative and five selectors-at-large.

Class of 2000 (5): PLAYERS—DE **Howie Long**, LA/Oakland Raiders (1981-93); CB/S **Ronnie Lott**, SF 49ers (1981-90), LA Raiders (1991-92), NY Jets (1993-94); QB **Joe Montana**, SF 49ers (1979-92), KC Chiefs (1993-94); LB **Dave Wilcox**, SF 49ers (1964-74); CONTRIBUTERS—**Dan Rooney**, executive of Pittsburgh Steelers.

Quarterbacks

Baugh, Sammy............1963	Graham, Otto 1965	Parker, Clarence (Ace) 1972
Blanda, George (also PK) ...1981	Griese, Bob 1990	Starr, Bart 1977
Bradshaw, Terry 1989	+ Herber, Arnie 1966	Staubach, Roger 1985
+ Clark, Dutch 1963	Jurgensen, Sonny 1983	Tarkenton, Fran 1986
+ Conzelman, Jimmy 1964	+ Layne, Bobby 1967	Tittle, Y.A. 1971
Dawson, Len...............1987	+ Luckman, Sid 1965	Unitas, Johnny 1979
+ Driscoll, Paddy............1965	Montana, Joe..............2000	+ Van Brocklin, Norm........1971
Fouts, Dan 1993	Namath, Joe.............../....1985	+ Waterfield, Bob............1965

Running Backs

+ Battles, Cliff 1968	+ Hinkle, Clarke 1964	+ Nevers, Ernie 1963
Brown, Jim 1971	Hornung, Paul 1986	+ Payton, Walter 1993
Campbell, Earl............1991	Johnson, John Henry 1987	Perry, Joe 1969
Canadeo, Tony 1974	Kelly, Leroy...............1994	Riggins, John 1992
Csonka, Larry 1987	+ Leemans, Tuffy 1978	Sayers, Gale 1977
Dickerson, Eric...........1999	Matson, Ollie 1972	Simpson, O.J. 1985
Dorsett, Tony.............1994	McAfee, George 1966	+ Strong, Ken 1967
Dudley, Bill 1966	McElhenny, Hugh 1970	Taylor, Jim 1976
Gifford, Frank 1977	+ McNally, Johnny (Blood) 1963	+ Thorpe, Jim 1963
+ Grange, Red 1963	Moore, Lenny 1975	Trippi, Charley 1968
+ Guyon, Joe...............1966	+ Motley, Marion 1968	Van Buren, Steve 1965
Harris, Franco 1990	+ Nagurski, Bronko 1963	+ Walker, Doak 1986

Ends & Wide Receivers

Alworth, Lance............1978	Hirsch, Elroy (Crazylegs) ...1968	+ Millner, Wayne 1968
+ Badgro, Red 1981	+ Hutson, Don 1963	Mitchell, Bobby 1983
Berry, Raymond 1973	Joiner, Charlie 1996	Newsome, Ozzie 1999
Biletnikoff, Fred 1988	Largent, Steve 1995	Pihos, Pete 1970
+ Chamberlin, Guy 1965	Lavelli, Dante 1975	Smith, Jackie 1994
Ditka, Mike 1988	Mackey, John 1992	Taylor, Charley 1984
+ Fears, Tom 1970	Maynard, Don 1987	Warfield, Paul 1983
+ Hewitt, Bill 1971	McDonald, Tommy 1998	Winslow, Kellen 1995

Linemen (pre-World War II)

+ Edwards, Turk (T)...........1969	+ Hubbard, Cal (T) 1963	+ Musso, George (T-G)........1982
+ Fortmann, Dan (G) 1985	+ Kiesling, Walt (G) 1966	+ Stydahar, Joe (T) 1967
+ Healey, Ed (T)..............1964	+ Kinard, Bruiser (T) 1971	+ Trafton, George (C).........1964
+ Hein, Mel (C) 1963	+ Lyman, Link (T) 1964	+ Turner, Bulldog (C).........1966
+ Henry, Pete (T) 1963	+ Michalske, Mike (G) 1964	+ Wojciechowicz, Alex (C) 1968

Offensive Linemen

Bednarik, Chuck (C-LB)......1967	Langer, Jim (C)............1987	Ringo, Jim (C)............1981
Brown, Roosevelt (T) ...1975	Little, Larry (G) 1993	St. Clair, Bob (T) 1990
Dierdorf, Dan (T)...........1996	Mack, Tom (G) 1999	Shaw, Billy (G)...........1999
Gatski, Frank (C)...........1985	McCormack, Mike (T).......1984	Shell, Art (T)...........1989
Gregg, Forrest (T-G) 1977	Mix, Ron (T-G) 1979	Stephenson, Dwight (C) 1998
Groza, Lou (T-PK).........1974	Munoz, Anthony (T) 1998	Upshaw, Gene (G) 1987
Hannah, John (G) 1991	Otto, Jim (C)..............1980	Webster, Mike (C) 1997
Jones, Stan (T-G-DT).......1991	Parker, Jim (G).............1973	

Defensive Linemen

Atkins, Doug..............1982	Jones, Deacon 1980	Page, Alan 1988
+ Buchanan, Buck............1990	+ Jordan, Henry 1995	Robustelli, Andy............1971
Creekmur, Lou 1996	Lilly, Bob 1980	Selmon, Lee Roy 1995
Davis, Willie.............1981	Long, Howie 2000	Stautner, Ernie 1969
Donovan, Art 1968	Marchetti, Gino 1972	+ Weinmeister, Arnie 1984
+ Ford, Len 1976	Nomellini, Leo 1969	White, Randy 1994
Greene, Joe 1987	Olsen, Merlin 1982	Willis, Bill 1977

Linebackers

Bell, Bobby...............1983	Hendricks, Ted 1990	Schmidt, Joe................1973
Butkus, Dick 1979	Huff, Sam 1982	Singletary, Mike............1998
Connor, George (DT-OT) ...1975	Lambert, Jack 1990	Taylor, Lawrence 1999
+ George, Bill 1974	Lanier, Willie 1986	Wilcox, Dave..............2000
Ham, Jack..................1988	+ Nitschke, Ray 1978	

Defensive Backs

Adderley, Herb 1980	Houston, Ken 1986	Renfro, Mel................1996
Barney, Lem 1992	Johnson, Jimmy 1994	+ Tunnell, Emlen 1967
Blount, Mel................1989	Krause, Paul 1998	Wilson, Larry 1978
Brown, Willie...............1984	Lane, Dick (Night Train) 1974	Wood, Willie...............1989
+ Christiansen, Jack 1970	Lary, Yale 1979	
Haynes, Michael...........1997	Lott, Ronnie...............2000	

Placekicker
Stenerud, Jan 1991

Coaches

+ Brown, Paul 1967	Grant, Bud 1994	+ Neale, Earle (Greasy).......1969
+ Ewbank, Weeb 1978	+ Halas, George............1963	Noll, Chuck 1993
+ Flaherty, Ray 1976	+ Lambeau, Curly 1963	+ Owen, Steve 1966
Gibbs, Joe 1996	+ Landry, Tom 1990	Shula, Don 1997
Gillman, Sid...............1983	+ Lombardi, Vince...........1971	Walsh, Bill 1993

Contributors

+ Bell, Bert..................1963	Hunt, Lamar 1972	+ Rooney, Art................1964
+ Bidwill, Charles 1967	+ Mara, Tim................1963	Rooney, Dan..............2000
+ Carr, Joe..................1963	Mara, Wellington 1997	+ Rozelle, Pete...............1985
Davis, Al 1992	+ Marshall, George 1963	Schramm, Tex..............1991
+ Finks, Jim 1995	+ Ray, Hugh (Shorty) 1966	
+ Halas, George............1963	+ Reeves, Dan 1967	

Dick McCann Award

First presented in 1969 by the Pro Football Writers of America for long and distinguished reporting on pro football. Named in honor of the first director of the Hall, the McCann Award does not constitute induction into the Hall of Fame.

Year	Year	Year	Year
1969 George Strickler	1977 Art Daley	1985 Cooper Rollow	1993 Ira Miller
1970 Arthur Daley	1978 Murray Olderman	1986 Bill Wallace	1994 Don Pierson
1971 Joe King	1979 Pat Livingston	1987 Jerry Magee	1995 Ray Didinger
1972 Lewis Atchison	1980 Chuck Heaton	1988 Gordon Forbes	1996 Paul Zimmerman
1973 Dave Brady	1981 Norm Miller	1989 Vito Stellino	1997 Bob Roesler
1974 Bob Oates	1982 Cameron Snyder	1990 Will McDonough	1998 Dave Anderson
1975 John Steadman	1983 Hugh Brown	1991 Dick Connor	1999 Art Spander
1976 Jack Hand	1984 Larry Felser	1992 Frank Luska	2000 Tom McEwen

Pete Rozelle Award

First presented in 1989 by the Hall of Fame for exceptional longtime contributions to radio and TV in pro football. Named in honor of the former NFL commissioner, who was also a publicist and GM for the LA Rams, the Rozelle Award does not constitute induction into the Hall of Fame.

Year	Year	Year	Year
1989 Bill McPhail	1992 Chris Schenkel	1995 Frank Gifford	1998 Val Pinchbeck Jr.
1990 Lindsey Nelson	1993 Curt Gowdy	1996 Jack Buck	1999 Dick Enberg
1991 Ed Sabol	1994 Pat Summerall	1997 Charlie Jones	2000 Ray Scott

NFL's All-Time Team

Selected by the Pro Football Hall of Fame voters and released Aug. 1, 2000 as part of the NFL Century celebration.

Offense

Wide Receivers:	Don Hutson and Jerry Rice
Tight End:	John Mackey
Tackles:	Roosevelt Brown and Anthony Munoz
Guards:	John Hannah and Jim Parker
Center:	Mike Webster
Quarterback:	Johnny Unitas
Running Backs:	Jim Brown and Walter Payton

Defense

Ends:	Deacon Jones and Reggie White
Tackles:	Joe Greene and Bob Lilly
Linebackers:	Dick Butkus, Jack Ham and Lawrence Taylor
Cornerbacks:	Mel Blount and Dick (Night Train) Lane
Safties:	Ronnie Lott and Larry Wilson

Specialists

Placekicker: Jan Stenerud	**Punt Returner:** Deion Sanders
Punter: Ray Guy	**Special Teams:** Steve Tasker
Kick Returner: Gale Sayers	

Canadian Football Hall of Fame

Established in 1963. Current Hall opened in 1972. **Address:** 58 Jackson Street West, Hamilton, Ontario, L8P 1L4. **Telephone:** (905) 528-7566.

Eligibility: Nominated players must be retired three years, but coaches and builders can still be active. Voting done by 15-member panel of Canadian pro and amateur football officials.

Class of 2000 (5): PLAYERS—LB **Danny Bass**, Toronto (1980), Calgary (1981-83), Edmonton (1984-91); DE **Grover Covington**, Hamilton (1981-91); WR **James Murphy**, Winnipeg (1982-90); RB/DB **Dave Raimey**, Winnipeg (1965-69), Toronto (1969-74); BUILDER—**Hugh Cambell**.

Members are listed with year of induction; (+) indicates deceased members.

Players

Ah You, Junior	1997	Grant, Tom	1995	Parker, Jackie	1971
Atchison, Ron	1978	Gray, Herbert	1983	Patterson, Hal	1971
+ Bailey, Byron	1975	+ Griffing, Dean	1965	Poplawski, Joe	1998
Baker, Bill	1994	Halloway, Condredge	1999	Perry, Gordon	1970
Barrow, John	1976	+ Hanson, Fritz	1963	+ Perry, Norm	1963
Bass, Danny	2000	Harris, Dickie	1999	Ploen, Ken	1975
+ Batstone, Harry	1963	Harris, Wayne	1976	+ Quilty, S.P. (Silver)	1966
+ Beach, Ormond	1963	Harrison, Herm	1993	Raimey, Dave	2000
Benecick, Al	1996	Helton, John	1986	+ Rebholz, Russ	1963
Box, Ab	1965	Henley, Garney	1979	Reed, George	1979
+ Breen, Joe	1963	Hinton, Tom	1991	+ Reeve, Ted	1963
+ Bright, Johnny	1970	+ Huffman, Dick	1987	Rigney, Frank	1985
Brown, Tom	1984	+ Isbister, Bob Sr	1965	Robinson, Larry	1998
Brock, Dieter	1995	Jackson, Russ	1973	+ Rodden, Mike	1964
Campbell, Jerry (Soupy)	1996	+ Jacobs, Jack	1963	+ Rowe, Paul	1964
Casey, Tom	1964	+ James, Eddie (Dynamite)	1963	Ruby, Martin	1974
Charlton, Ken	1992	James, Gerry	1981	+ Russel, Jeff	1963
Clarke, Bill	1996	+ Kabat, Greg	1966	Scott, Tom	1998
Clements, Tom	1994	Kapp, Joe	1984	+ Scott, Vince	1982
Coffey, Tommy Joe	1977	Keeling, Jerry	1989	Shatto, Dick	1975
+ Conacher, Lionel	1963	Kelly, Brian	1991	+ Simpson, Ben	1963
Copeland, Royal	1988	Kelly, Ellison	1992	Simpson, Bob	1976
Corrigall, Jim	1990	Kepley, Dan	1996	+ Sprague, David	1963
Covington, Grover	2000	Krol, Joe	1963	Stevenson, Art	1969
+ Cox, Ernest	1963	Kwong, Normie	1969	Stewart, Ron	1977
+ Craig, Ross	1964	Lancaster, Ron	1982	+ Stirling, Hugh (Bummer)	1966
+ Cronin, Carl	1967	+ Lawson, Smirle	1963	Sutherin, Don	1992
Cutler, Dave	1998	+ Leadlay, Frank (Pep)	1963	Symons, Bill	1997
+ Cutler, Wes	1968	+ Lear, Les	1974	Thelen, Dave	1989
Dalla Riva, Peter	1993	Lewis, Leo	1973	+ Timmis, Brian	1963
DiPietro, Rocky	1997	Lunsford, Earl	1983	Tinsley, Bud	1982
+ Dixon, George	1974	Luster, Marv	1990	+ Tommy, Andy	1989
+ Eliowitz, Abe	1969	Luzzi, Don	1986	+ Trawick, Herb	1975
+ Emerson, Eddie	1963	+ McCance, Ches	1976	+ Tubman, Joe	1968
Etcheverry, Sam	1969	+ McGill, Frank	1965	Tucker, Whit	1993
Evanshen, Terry	1984	McQuarters, Ed	1988	Urness, Ted	1989
+ Faloney, Bernie	1974	Miles, Rollie	1980	Vaughan, Kaye	1978
+ Fear, A.H. (Cap)	1967	+ Molson, Percy	1963	Wagner, Virgil	1980
Fennell, Dave	1990	Morris, Frank	1983	+ Welch, Hawley (Huck)	1964
+ Ferraro, John	1966	+ Morris, Ted	1964	Wilkinson, Tom	1987
Fieldgate, Norm	1979	Mosca, Angelo	1987	Wilson, Al	1997
Fleming, Willie	1982	Murphy, James	2000	Wylie, Harvey	1980
Gabriel, Tony	1985	+ Nelson, Roger	1986	Young, Jim	1991
Gaines, Gene	1994	Neumann, Peter	1979	+ Zock, Bill	1985
+ Gall, Hugh	1963	O'Quinn, John (Red)	1981		
Golab, Tony	1964	Pajaczkowski, Tony	1988		

Builders

+ Back, Leonard	1971	+ DeGruchy, John	1963	Kimball, Norman	1991
+ Bailey, Harold	1965	Dojack, Paul	1978	+ Kramer, R.A. (Bob)	1987
+ Ballard, Harold	1987	+ Duggan, Eck	1981	+ Lieberman, M.I. (Moe)	1973
Barker, Donald	1999	+ DuMoulin, Seppi	1963	+ McBrien, Harry	1978
+ Berger, Sam	1993	+ Foulds, Willliam	1963	+ McCaffrey, Jimmy	1967
+ Brook, Tom	1975	Fulton, Greg	1995	+ McCann, Dave	1966
+ Brown, D. Wes	1963	Gaudaur, J.G. (Jake)	1984	McNaughton, Don	1994
Cambell, Hugh	2000	Gibson, Frank	1996	+ McPherson, Don	1983
+ Chipman, Arthur	1969	Grant, Bud	1983	+ Metras, Johnny	1980
Clair, Frank	1981	+ Grey, Lord Earl	1963	+ Montgomery, Ken	1970
+ Cooper, Ralph	1992	+ Griffith, Dr. Harry	1963	+ Newton, Jack	1964
Coulter, Bruce	1997	+ Halter, Sydney	1966	+ Preston, Ken	1990
+ Crighton, Hec	1986	+ Hannibal, Frank	1963	+ Ritchie, Alvin	1963
+ Currie, Andrew	1974	+ Hayman, Lew	1975	+ Ryan, Joe B.	1968
Custis, Bernard	1998	+ Hughes, W.P. (Billy)	1974	Sazio, Ralph	1988
+ Davies, Dr. Andrew	1969	Keys, Eagle	1990	+ Shaughnessy, Frank (Shag)	1963

+ Shouldice, W.T. (Hap)......1977	+ Stukus, Annis 1974	+ Warwick, Bert 1964
+ Simpson, Jimmie 1986	+ Taylor, N.J. (Piffles) 1963	+ Wilson, Seymour...........1984
+ Slocomb, Karl 1989	+ Tindall, Frank 1985	
+ Spring, Harry..............1976	+ Warner, Clair...............1965	

GOLF

World Golf Hall of Fame

A new World Golf Hall of Fame opened its doors in 1998 at the World Golf Village outside of Jacksonville, Fla. The 71 members of the former Hall of Fame (established in 1974 but inactive since 1993) in Pinehurst, N.C. and LPGA Hall of Fame were "grandfathered" into the new Hall. **Address:** 21 World Golf Place, St. Augustine, FL 32092. **Telephone:** (904) 940-4000.

Eligibility: Professionals have three avenues into the WGHF. A PGA Tour player qualifies for the ballot if he has at least 10 victories in approved tournaments, or at least two victories among The Players Championship, Masters, U.S. Open, British Open and PGA Championship, is at least 40 years old and has been a member of the Tour for 10 years. A senior PGA Tour player qualifies if he has been a Senior Tour member for five years and has 20 wins between the PGA Tour and Senior Tour or five wins among the PGA majors, the Players Championship and the senior majors (U.S. Senior Open, Tradition, PGA Seniors' Championship and Senior Players Championship).

Any player qualifying for the LPGA Hall automatically qualifies for the WGHF. Until 1999, nominees must have had played 10 years on the LPGA tour and won 30 official events, including two major championships; 35 official events and one major; or 40 official events and no majors. The eligibility requirements were loosened somewhat in 1999. The new guidelines are based on a system which awards two points for winning a major and one point for winning other tournaments, the Vare trophy (for lowest scoring average) and the player of the year award. Players must win at least one major, Vare trophy, or player of the year award and accumulate a total of 27 points to be inducted. For players not eligible for either the PGA Tour or the LPGA Hall of Fame, a body of over 300 international golf writers and historians will vote each year.

Members are listed with year of induction; (+) indicates deceased members.

Class of 2000 (8): MEN—**Deane Beman, Sir Michael Bonallack, Jack Burke Jr., Neil Coles,** and **John Jacobs;** WOMEN—**Beth Daniel, Julie Inkster** and **Judy Rankin.**

Note: Annika Sorenstam (2003) and Karie Webb (2005) already have enough points for entrance into the Hall but will be inducted after their 10th LPGA season.

Men

+ Anderson, Willie 1975	Faldo, Nick 1998	Nelson, Byron 1974
+ Armour, Tommy 1976	Floyd, Ray 1989	Nicklaus, Jack 1974
+ Ball, John, Jr. 1977	+ Guldahl, Ralph.............1981	+ Ouimet, Francis 1974
Ballesteros, Seve 1999	+ Hagen, Walter.............1974	Palmer, Arnold 1974
+ Barnes, Jim 1989	+ Hilton, Harold 1978	Player, Gary 1974
Beman, Deane..............2000	+ Hogan, Ben 1974	Runyan, Paul 1990
Bonallack, Sir Michael 2000	Irwin, Hale 1992	+ Sarazen, Gene 1974
+ Boros, Julius 1982	Jacobs, John 2000	+ Smith, Horton..............1990
+ Braid, James...............1976	+ Jones, Bobby 1974	Snead, Sam 1974
Burke, Jack Jr...............2000	+ Little, Lawson 1980	+ Taylor, John H 1975
Casper, Billy 1978	Littler, Gene 1990	Thomson, Peter..............1988
Coles, Neil 2000	+ Locke, Bobby 1977	+ Travers, Jerry 1976
Cooper, Lighthorse Harry....1992	+ Mangrum, Lloyd............1999	+ Travis, Walter..............1979
+ Cotton, Thomas 1980	+ Middlecoff, Cary 1986	Trevino, Lee 1981
+ Demaret, Jimmy 1983	Miller, Johnny...............1998	+ Vardon, Harry 1974
De Vicenzo, Roberto 1989	+ Morris, Tom Jr. 1975	Watson, Tom 1988
+ Evans, Chick 1975	+ Morris, Tom Sr 1976	

Women

Alcott, Amy.................1999	Inkster, Julie 2000	Sheehan, Patty 1993
Berg, Patty 1974	Jameson, Betty 1951	Suggs, Louise 1979
Bradley, Pat 1991	King, Betsy 1995	+ Vare, Glenna Collett 1975
Carner, JoAnne 1985	Lopez, Nancy 1989	+ Wethered, Joyce 1975
Daniel, Beth 2000	Mann, Carol.................1977	Whitworth, Kathy 1982
Haynie, Sandra 1977	Rankin, Judy 2000	Wright, Mickey 1976
+ Howe, Dorothy C.H 1978	Rawls, Betsy 1987	+ Zaharias, Babe Didrikson ...1974

Contributors

Campbell, William 1990	+ Harlow, Robert..............1988	+ Ross, Donald 1977
+ Corcoran, Fred 1975	Hope, Bob 1983	+ Shore, Dinah 1994
+ Crosby, Bing...............1978	+ Jones, Robert Trent 1987	+ Tufts, Richard 1992
+ Dey, Joe 1975	+ Roberts, Clifford 1978	
+ Graffis, Herb 1977	Rodriguez, Chi Chi 1992	

Old PGA Hall Members Not in PGA/World Hall

The original PGA Hall of Fame was established in 1940 by the PGA of America, but abandoned after the 1982 inductions in favor of the PGA/World Hall of Fame. Twenty-nine members of the old PGA Hall have been elected to the PGA/World Hall since then. Players yet to make the cut are listed below with year of induction into old PGA Hall.

+ Brady, Mike 1960	Ford, Doug.................1975	+ McLeod, Fred.............1960
+ Burke, Billy 1966	+ Ghezzi, Vic 1965	+ Picard, Henry.............1961
+ Cruickshank, Bobby 1967	+ Harbert, Chick 1968	+ Revolta, Johnny 1963
+ Diegel, Leo 1955	Harper, Chandler 1969	+ Shute, Denny 1957
+ Dudley, Ed 1964	+ Harrison, Dutch 1962	+ Smith, Alex...............1940
+ Dutra, Olin 1962	+ Hutchison, Jock Sr 1959	+ Smith, Macdonald..........1954
+ Farroll, Johnny 1961	+ McDermott, John 1940	+ Wood, Craig 1956

HOCKEY

Hockey Hall of Fame

Established in 1945 by the National Hockey League and opened in 1961. **Address:** BCE Place, 30 Yonge Street, Toronto, Ontario, M5E 1X8. **Telephone:** (416) 360-7735.

Eligibility: Nominated players and referees must be retired three years. However that waiting period has now been waived ten times. Players that have had the waiting period waived are indicated with an asterisk. Voting done by 15-member panel made up of pro and amateur hockey personalities and media representatives. A 15-member Veterans Committee selects older players.

Class of 2000 (3): PLAYERS— forward **Joe Mullen**, St. Louis (1979-86), Calgary (1986-90), Pittsburgh (1990-95), Boston (1995-96), Pittsburgh (1996-97); forward **Denis Savard**, Chicago (1990-93), Montreal (1993-95), Tampa Bay (1993-95), Chicago (1995-97); BUILDER— **Walter Bush**, president of USA Hockey.

Members are listed with year of induction; (+) indicates deceased members.

Forwards

+ Abel, Sid 1969	Gainey, Bob 1992	+ O'Connor, Buddy 1988
+ Adams, Jack 1959	+ Gardner, Jimmy 1962	+ Oliver, Harry 1967
+ Apps, Syl 1961	Geoffrion, Bernie 1972	Olmstead, Bert 1985
Armstrong, George 1975	+ Gerard, Eddie 1945	+ Patrick, Lynn 1980
+ Bailey, Ace 1975	Gilbert, Rod 1982	Perreault, Gilbert 1990
+ Bain, Dan 1945	+ Gilmour, Billy 1962	+ Phillips, Tom 1945
+ Baker, Hobey 1945	Goulet, Michel 1998	+ Primeau, Joe 1963
Barber, Bill 1990	Gretzky, Wayne* 1999	Pulford, Bob 1991
+ Barry, Marty 1965	+ Griffis, Si 1950	+ Rankin, Frank 1961
Bathgate, Andy 1978	+ Hay, George 1958	Ratelle, Jean 1985
+ Bauer, Bobby 1996	+ Hextall, Bryan 1969	Richard, Henri 1979
Beliveau, Jean* 1972	+ Hooper, Tom 1962	+ Richard, Maurice (Rocket)* . .1961
+ Bentley, Doug 1964	Howe, Gordie* 1972	+ Richardson, George 1950
+ Bentley, Max 1966	+ Howe, Syd 1965	Roberts, Gordie 1971
+ Blake, Toe 1966	Hull, Bobby 1983	+ Russel, Blair 1965
Bossy, Mike 1991	+ Hyland, Harry 1962	+ Russell, Ernie 1965
+ Boucher, Frank 1958	+ Irvin, Dick 1958	+ Ruttan, Jack 1962
+ Bowie, Dubbie 1945	+ Jackson, Busher 1971	Savard, Denis 2000
+ Broadbent, Punch 1962	+ Joliat, Aurel 1947	+ Scanlan, Fred 1965
Bucyk, John (Chief) 1981	+ Keats, Duke 1958	Schmidt, Milt 1961
+ Burch, Billy 1974	Kennedy, Ted (Teeder) 1966	+ Schriner, Sweeney 1962
Clarke, Bobby 1987	Keon, Dave 1986	+ Seibert, Oliver 1961
+ Colville, Neil 1967	Lach, Elmer 1966	Shutt, Steve 1993
+ Conacher, Charlie 1961	Lafleur, Guy 1988	+ Siebert, Babe 1964
Conacher, Roy 1998	+ Lalonde, Newsy 1950	Sittler, Darryl 1989
+ Cook, Bill 1952	Laprade, Edgar 1993	+ Smith, Alf 1962
+ Cook, Bun 1995	Lemaire, Jacques 1984	Smith, Clint 1991
Cournoyer, Yvan 1982	Lemieux, Mario* 1997	+ Smith, Hooley 1972
+ Cowley, Bill 1968	+ Lewis, Herbie 1989	+ Smith, Tommy 1973
+ Crawford, Rusty 1962	Lindsay, Ted* 1966	+ Stanley, Barney 1962
+ Darragh, Jack 1962	+ MacKay, Mickey 1952	Stastny, Peter 1998
+ Davidson, Scotty 1950	Mahovlich, Frank 1981	+ Stewart, Nels 1962
+ Day, Hap 1961	+ Malone, Joe 1950	+ Stuart, Bruce 1961
Delvecchio, Alex 1977	+ Marshall, Jack 1965	+ Taylor, Fred (Cyclone) 1947
+ Denneny, Cy 1959	+ Maxwell, Fred 1962	+ Trihey, Harry 1950
Dionne, Marcel 1992	McDonald, Lanny 1992	Trottier, Bryan 1997
+ Drillon, Gordie 1975	+ McGee, Frank 1945	Ullman, Norm 1982
+ Drinkwater, Graham 1950	+ McGimsie, Billy 1962	+ Walker, Jack 1960
Dumart, Woody 1992	Mikita, Stan 1983	+ Walsh, Marty 1962
+ Dunderdale, Tommy 1974	Moore, Dickie 1974	Watson, Harry 1994
+ Dye, Babe 1970	+ Morenz, Howie 1945	+ Watson, Harry (Moose) 1962
Esposito, Phil 1984	+ Mosienko, Bill 1965	+ Weiland, Cooney 1971
+ Farrell, Arthur 1965	Mullen, Joe 2000	+ Westwick, Harry (Rat) 1962
+ Foyston, Frank 1958	+ Nighbor, Frank 1947	+ Whitcroft, Fred 1962
+ Frederickson, Frank 1958	+ Noble, Reg 1962	

Goaltenders

+ Benedict, Clint 1965	Giacomin, Eddie 1987	Parent, Bernie 1984
Bower, Johnny 1976	+ Hainsworth, George 1961	+ Plante, Jacques 1978
+ Brimsek, Frankie 1966	Hall, Glenn 1975	Rayner, Chuck 1973
+ Broda, Turk 1967	+ Hern, Riley 1962	+ Sawchuk, Terry* 1971
Cheevers, Gerry 1985	+ Holmes, Hap 1972	Smith, Billy 1993
+ Connell, Alex 1958	+ Hutton, J.B. (Bouse) 1962	+ Thompson, Tiny 1959
Dryden, Ken 1983	+ Lehman, Hughie 1958	Tretiak, Vladislav 1989
+ Durnan, Bill 1964	+ LeSueur, Percy 1961	+ Vezina, Georges 1945
Esposito, Tony 1988	+ Lumley, Harry 1980	Worsley, Gump 1980
+ Gardiner, Chuck 1945	+ Moran, Paddy 1958	+ Worters, Roy 1969

Defensemen

Boivin, Leo 1986
+ Boon, Dickie...............1952
Bouchard, Butch 1966
+ Boucher, George..........1960
+ Cameron, Harry 1962
+ Clancy, King...............1958
+ Clapper, Dit* 1947
+ Cleghorn, Sprague 1958
+ Conacher, Lionel 1994
Coulter, Art................1974
+ Dutton, Red...............1958
Flaman, Fernie............1990
Gadsby, Bill 1970
+ Gardiner, Herb 1958
+ Goheen, F.X. (Moose) 1952
+ Goodfellow, Ebbie 1963
+ Grant, Mike 1950
+ Green, Wilf (Shorty) 1962

+ Hall, Joe 1961
+ Harvey, Doug.............1973
Horner, Red 1965
+ Horton, Tim...............1977
Howell, Harry 1979
+ Johnson, Ching 1958
+ Johnson, Ernie 1952
Johnson, Tom 1970
Kelly, Red* 1969
Laperriere, Jacques 1987
Lapointe, Guy 1993
+ Laviolette, Jack 1962
+ Mantha, Sylvio............1960
+ McNamara, George........1958
Orr, Bobby* 1979
Park, Brad.................1988
+ Patrick, Lester 1947
Pilote, Pierre 1975

+ Pitre, Didier 1962
Potvin, Denis..............1991
+ Pratt, Babe 1966
Pronovost, Marcel 1978
+ Pulford, Harvey 1945
Quackenbush, Bill 1976
Reardon, Kenny...........1966
Robinson, Larry 1995
+ Ross, Art 1945
Salming, Borje 1996
Savard, Serge 1986
Seibert, Earl 1963
+ Shore, Eddie 1947
+ Simpson, Joe 1962
Stanley, Allan 1981
+ Stewart, Jack 1964
+ Stuart, Hod...............1945
+ Wilson, Gordon (Phat) 1962

Referees & Linesmen

Armstrong, Neil...........1991
Ashley, John 1981
Chadwick, Bill 1964
D'Amico, John 1993
+ Elliott, Chaucer 1961

+ Hayes, George 1988
+ Hewitson, Bobby 1963
+ Ion, Mickey...............1961
Pavelich, Matt 1987
+ Rodden, Mike 1962

+ Smeaton, J. Cooper 1961
Storey, Red 1967
Udvari, Frank 1973
van Hellemond, Andy......1999

Builders

+ Adams, Charles...........1960
+ Adams, Weston W. Sr 1972
+ Ahearn, Frank 1962
+ Ahearne, J.F. (Bunny) 1977
+ Allan, Sir Montagu 1945
Allen, Keith...............1992
Arbour, Al................1996
+ Ballard, Harold 1977
+ Bauer, Fr. David...........1989
+ Bickell, J.P...............1978
Bowman, Scotty...........1991
+ Brown, George 1961
+ Brown, Walter 1962
+ Buckland, Frank 1975
Bush, Walter..............2000
Butterfield, Jack 1980
+ Calder, Frank.............1945
+ Campbell, Angus..........1964
+ Campbell, Clarence 1966
+ Cattarinich, Joseph 1977
+ Dandurand, Leo...........1963
Dilio, Frank...............1964
+ Dudley, George 1958
+ Dunn, James..............1968
Francis, Emile.............1982
+ Gibson, Jack 1976
+ Gorman, Tommy 1963
+ Griffiths, Frank A. 1993
+ Hanley, Bill 1986

+ Hay, Charles 1984
+ Hendy, Jim 1968
+ Hewitt, Foster 1965
+ Hewitt, W.A. 1945
+ Hume, Fred...............1962
+ Imlach, Punch 1984
+ Ivan, Tommy 1964
+ Jennings, Bill..............1975
+ Johnson, Bob 1992
+ Juckes, Gordon 1979
+ Kilpatrick, John 1960
+ Knox, Seymour III 1993
+ Leader, Al 1969
LeBel, Bob................1970
+ Lockhart, Tom 1965
+ Loicq, Paul 1961
+ Mariucci, John 1985
Mathers, Frank............1992
+ McLaughlin, Frederic 1963
+ Milford, Jake 1984
Molson, Hartland 1973
Morrison, Ian (Scotty) 1999
+ Murray, Athol (Pere) 1998
+ Nelson, Francis 1945
+ Norris, Bruce 1969
+ Norris, James D 1962
+ Norris, James Sr 1958
+ Northey, William..........1945
+ O'Brien, J.A. 1962

O'Neill, Brian 1994
Page, Fred 1993
+ Patrick, Frank 1958
+ Pickard, Allan 1958
+ Pilous, Rudy 1985
Poile, Bud................1990
Pollock, Sam..............1978
+ Raymond, Donat 1958
+ Robertson, John Ross.......1945
+ Robinson, Claude 1945
+ Ross, Philip 1976
Sather, Glen 1997
Sebetzki, Gunther 1995
+ Selke, Frank 1960
Sinden, Harry 1983
+ Smith, Frank 1962
+ Smythe, Conn.............1958
Snider, Ed................1988
+ Stanley, Lord of Preston 1945
+ Sutherland, James 1945
+ Tarasov, Anatoli 1974
Torrey, Bill...............1995
+ Turner, Lloyd 1958
+ Tutt, William Thayer 1978
Voss, Carl 1974
+ Waghorne, Fred 1961
+ Wirtz, Arthur 1971
Wirtz, Bill 1976
Ziegler, John..............1987

Note: Alan Eagleson was inducted into the Hockey Hall of Fame in 1989 but resigned in 1998 after being found guilty of fraud.

Elmer Ferguson Award

First presented in 1984 by the Professional Hockey Writers' Association for meritorious contributions by members of the PHWA. Named in honor of the late Montreal newspaper reporter, the Ferguson Award does not constitute induction into the Hall of Fame and is not necessarily an annual presentation.

1984 Jacques Beauchamp, Jim Burchard, Red Burnett, Dink Carroll, Jim Coleman, Ted Damata, Marcel Desjardins, Jack Dulmage, Milt Dunnell, Elmer Ferguson, Tom Fitzgerald, Trent Frayne, Al Laney, Joe Nichols, Basil O'Meara, Jim Vipond & Lewis Walter
1985 Charlie Barton, Red Fisher, George Gross, Zotique L'Esperance, Charles Mayer & Andy O'Brien
1986 Dick Johnston, Leo Monahan & Tim Moriarty
1987 Bill Brennan, Rex MacLeod, Ben Olan & Fran Rosa
1988 Jim Proudfoot & Scott Young
1989 Claude Larochelle & Frank Orr

1990 Bertrand Raymond
1991 Hugh Delano
1992 No award
1993 Al Strachan
1994 No award
1995 Jake Gatecliff
1996 No award
1997 Ken McKenzie
1998 Yvon Pedneault
1999 Russ Conway
2000 Jim Matheson

Hockey (Cont.)
Foster Hewitt Award

First presented in 1984 by the NHL Broadcasters' Association for meritorious contributions by members of the NHLBA. Named in honor of Canada's legendary "Voice of Hockey," the Hewitt Award does not constitute induction into the Hall of Fame and is not necessarily an annual presentation.

1985 Budd Lynch &	1987 Bob Wilson	1991 Bruce Martyn	1995 Brian McFarlane	1999 Richard Garneau
Doug Smith	1988 Dick Irvin	1992 Jim Robson	1996 Bob Cole	2000 Bob Miller
1986 Wes McKnight &	1989 Dan Kelly	1993 Al Shaver	1997 Gene Hart	
Lloyd Pettit	1990 Jiggs McDonald	1994 Ted Darling	1998 Howie Meeker	

U.S. Hockey Hall of Fame

Established in 1968 by the Eveleth (Minn.) Civic Association Project H Committee and opened in 1973. **Address:** 801 Hat Trick Ave., P.O. Box 657, Eveleth, MN 55734. **Telephone:** (218) 744-5167.

Eligibility: Nominated players and referees must be American-born and retired five years; coaches must be American-born and must have coached predominantly American teams. Voting done by 12-member panel made up of Hall of Fame members and U.S. hockey officials.

Class of 2000 (3): PLAYERS—**Neal Broten**. ADMINISTRATORS—**Doug Palazzari** and **Larry Pleau**.

Members are listed with year of induction; (+) indicates deceased members.

Players

+ Abel, Clarence (Taffy) 1973	Ftorek, Robbie 1991	Moe, Bill 1974
+ Baker, Hobey 1973	+ Garrison, John 1974	Morrow, Ken 1995
Bartholome, Earl 1977	Garrity, Jack 1986	+ Moseley, Fred. 1975
+ Bessone, Peter 1978	+ Goheen, Frank (Moose) 1973	Mullen, Joe 1998
Blake, Bob 1985	Grant, Wally 1994	+ Murray, Hugh (Muzz) Sr. 1987
Boucha, Henry. 1995	+ Harding, Austie 1975	+ Nelson, Hub. 1978
+ Brimsek, Frankie 1973	Iglehart, Stewart 1975	+ Nyrop, William D. 1997
Broten, Neal. 2000	Ikola, Willard 1990	Olson, Eddie 1977
Cavanaugh, Joe 1994	Johnson, Virgil 1974	+ Owen, George 1973
+ Chaisson, Ray 1974	+ Karakas, Mike 1973	+ Palmer, Winthrop 1973
Chase, John 1973	Kirrane, Jack 1987	Paradise, Bob 1989
Christian, Bill 1984	+ Lane, Myles 1973	Purpur, Clifford (Fido) 1974
Christian, Roger. 1989	Langevin, Dave 1993	Riley, Bill 1977
Cleary, Bill 1976	Langway, Rod 1999	+ Romnes, Elwin (Doc) 1973
Cleary, Bob 1981	Larson, Reed. 1996	Rondeau, Dick 1985
+ Conroy, Tony 1975	+ Linder, Joe. 1975	Sheehey, Timothy. 1997
Curran, Mike 1998	+ LoPresti, Sam 1973	Watson, Gordie 1999
Dahlstrom, Carl (Cully) 1973	+ Mariucci, John 1973	+ Williams, Tom 1981
+ DesJardins, Vic. 1974	Matchefts, John 1991	+ Winters, Frank (Coddy) 1973
+ Desmond, Richard. 1988	Mather, Bruce. 1998	+ Yackel, Ken. 1986
+ Dill, Bob 1979	Mayasich, John 1976	
Everett, Doug 1974	McCartan, Jack 1983	

Coaches

+ Almquist, Oscar. 1983	Heyliger, Vic. 1974	Pleban, Connie 1990
Bessone, Amo 1992	+ Holt Jr., Charles E. 1997	Riley, Jack 1979
Brooks, Herb 1990	Ikola, Willard 1990	+ Ross, Larry 1988
Ceglarski, Len 1992	+ Jeremiah, Eddie 1973	+ Thompson, Cliff 1973
+ Fullerton, James 1992	+ Johnson, Bob 1991	+ Stewart, Bill 1982
Gambucci, Sergio 1996	Kelley, Jack 1993	Watson, Sid 1999
+ Gordon, Malcolm 1973	+ Kelly, John (Snooks) 1974	+ Winsor, Ralph 1973
Harkness, Ned. 1994	Nanne, Lou. 1998	

Referee

Chadwick, Bill 1974

Contributor

+ Schulz, Charles M. 1993

+ Brown, George 1973	
+ Brown, Walter 1973	
Bush, Walter. 1980	
+ Clark, Don 1978	
Claypool, Jim 1995	
+ Gibson, J.L. (Doc) 1973	

Administrators

+ Jennings, Bill. 1981	Pleau, Larry 2000	
+ Kahler, Nick 1980	Ridder, Bob 1976	
+ Lockhart, Tom 1973	Trumble, Hal. 1970	
Marvin, Cal 1982	+ Tutt, Thayer. 1973	
Palazzari, Doug. 2000	Wirtz, Bill 1967	
Patrick, Craig. 1996	+ Wright, Lyle 1973	

Members of Both Hockey and U.S. Hockey Halls of Fame

Players	Coach		Builders
Hobey Baker	Bob Johnson	George Brown	Bill Jennings
Frankie Brimsek		Walter Brown	Tom Lockhart
Frank (Moose) Goheen	**Referee**	Walter Bush	Thayer Tutt
John Mariucci	Bill Chadwick	Doc Gibson	Bill Wirtz
Joe Mullen			

HORSE RACING

National Horse Racing Hall of Fame

Established in 1950 by the Saratoga Springs Racing Association and opened in 1955. **Address:** National Museum of Racing and Hall of Fame, 191 Union Ave., Saratoga Springs, NY 12866. **Telephone:** (518) 584-0400.

Eligibility: Nominated horses must be retired five years; jockeys must be active at least 15 years; trainers must be active at least 25 years. Voting done by 100-member panel of horse racing media.

Class of 2000 (5): JOCKEY—**Julie Krone**. TRAINER—**Neil Drysdale**. HORSES—**A.P. Indy**, **Winning Colors** and **Needles**.

Members are listed with year of induction; (+) indicates deceased members.

Jockeys

+ Adams, Frank (Dooley)*.....1970	+ Garner, Andrew (Mack).....1969	+ Parke, Ivan 1978
+ Adams, John 1965	+ Garrison, Snapper 1955	+ Patrick, Gil 1970
+ Aitcheson, Joe Jr.*.........1978	+ Gomez, Avelino...........1982	Pincay, Laffit Jr. 1975
+ Arcaro, Eddie 1958	+ Griffin, Henry............1956	+ Purdy, Sam 1970
Atkinson, Ted 1957	+ Guerin, Eric 1972	+ Reiff, John................1956
Baeza, Braulio.............1976	Hartack, Bill 1959	+ Robertson, Alfred...........1971
Bailey, Jerry 1995	Hawley, Sandy 1992	Rotz, John L................1983
+ Barbee, George...........1996	+ Johnson, Albert 1971	+ Sande, Earl...............1955
+ Bassett, Carroll* 1972	+ Knapp, Willie............1969	+ Schilling, Carroll 1970
Baze, Russell 1999	Krone, Julie...............2000	Shoemaker, Bill 1958
+ Blum, Walter 1987	+ Kummer, Clarence 1972	+ Simms, Willie 1977
+ Bostwick, George H.* 1968	+ Kurtsinger, Charley 1967	+ Sloan, Todhunter 1955
+ Boulmetis, Sam 1973	+ Loftus, Johnny............1959	+ Smithwick, A. Patrick* 1973
+ Brooks, Steve 1963	+ Longden, Johnny 1958	Stevens, Gary 1997
Brumfield, Don............1996	Maher, Danny 1955	+ Stout, James 1968
+ Burns, Tommy 1983	+ McAtee, Linus............1956	+ Taral, Fred 1955
+ Butwell, Jimmy 1984	McCarron, Chris 1989	+ Tuckman, Bayard Jr.* 1973
+ Byers, J.D. (Dolly) 1967	+ McCreary, Conn 1975	Turcotte, Ron..............1979
Cauthen, Steve............1994	+ McKinney, Rigan 1968	+ Turner, Nash..............1955
+ Coltiletti, Frank...........1970	+ McLaughlin, James 1955	Ussery, Robert 1980
Cordero, Angel Jr...........1988	+ Miller, Walter............1955	Vasquez, Jacinto 1998
+ Crawford, Robert (Specs)*...1973	+ Murphy, Isaac 1955	Velasquez, Jorge 1990
Day, Pat 1991	+ Neves, Ralph 1960	+ Woolfe, George 1955
Delahoussaye, Eddie 1993	+ Notter, Joe 1963	+ Workman, Raymond 1956
+ Ensor, Lavelle (Buddy)......1962	+ O'Connor, Winnie 1956	Ycaza, Manuel 1977
+ Fator, Laverne 1955	+ Odom, George 1955	
Fishback, Jerry*...........1992	+ O'Neill, Frank 1956	*Steeplechase jockey

Trainers

+ Barrera, Laz 1979	+ Hyland, John 1956	Nerud, John 1972
+ Bedwell, H. Guy 1971	+ Jacobs, Hirsch 1958	+ Parke, Burley 1986
+ Brown, Edward D..........1984	Jerkens, H. Allen 1975	+ Penna, Angel Sr...........1988
Burch, Elliot 1980	Johnson, Philip 1997	+ Pincus, Jacob 1988
+ Burch, Preston M. 1963	+ Johnson, William R. 1986	+ Rogers, John..............1955
+ Burch, W.P...............1955	+ Jolley, LeRoy 1987	+ Rowe, James Sr............1955
+ Burlew, Fred..............1973	+ Jones, Ben A..............1958	Schulhofer, Scotty 1992
+ Childs, Frank E............1968	Jones, H.A. (Jimmy).........1959	Sheppard, Jonathan 1990
+ Clark, Henry 1982	+ Joyner, Andrew 1955	+ Smith, Robert A............1976
+ Cocks, W. Burling 1985	Kelly, Tom 1993	+ Smithwick, Mike 1976
Conway, James P...........1996	+ Laurin, Lucien 1977	+ Stephens, Woody 1976
Croll, Jimmy 1994	+ Lewis, J. Howard 1969	Tenny, Mesh 1991
Drysdale, Neil 2000	Lukas, D. Wayne 1999	+ Thompson, H.J. 1969
+ Duke, William 1956	+ Luro, Horatio 1980	+ Trotsek, Harry 1984
+ Feustel, Louis 1964	+ Madden, John 1983	Van Berg, Jack 1985
+ Fitzsimmons, J. (Sunny Jim) ..1958	+ Maloney, Jim 1989	+ Van Berg, Marion 1970
Frankel, Bobby.............1995	Martin, Frank (Pancho) 1981	+ Veitch, Sylvester 1977
+ Gaver, John M. 1966	McAnally, Ron 1990	+ Walden, Robert 1970
+ Healey, Thomas...........1955	+ McDaniel, Henry 1956	Walsh, Michael 1997
+ Hildreth, Samuel 1955	+ Miller, MacKenzie 1987	+ Ward, Sherrill 1978
+ Hirsch, Max 1959	+ Molter, William, Jr. 1960	Whiteley, Frank Jr...........1978
+ Hirsch, W.J. (Buddy) 1982	Mott, Bill 1998	+ Whittingham, Charlie 1974
+ Hitchcock, Thomas Sr. 1973	+ Mulholland, Winbert........1967	+ Williamson, Ansel 1998
+ Hughes, Hollie 1973	+ Neloy, Eddie 1983	Winfrey, W.C. (Bill).........1971

Horses

Year foaled in parentheses.

A.P. Indy (1989) 2000	All-Along (1979) 1990	+ American Eclipse (1814) 1970
+ Ack Ack (1966)............1986	+ Alsab (1939) 1976	+ Armed (1941) 1963
Affectionately (1960) 1989	+ Alydar (1975) 1989	+ Artful (1902) 1956
Affirmed (1975)............1980	Alysheba (1984)............1993	+ Arts and Letters (1966)......1994

Horse Racing (Cont.)

+ Assault (1943) 1964
+ Battleship (1927) 1969
+ Bayakoa (1984) 1998
+ Bed O'Roses (1947) 1976
+ Beldame (1901) 1956
+ Ben Brush (1893) 1955
+ Bewitch (1945) 1977
+ Bimelech (1937) 1990
+ Black Gold (1919) 1989
+ Black Helen (1932) 1991
+ Blue Larkspur (1926) 1957
+ Bold 'n Determined (1977) . .1997
+ Bold Ruler (1954) 1973
+ Bon Nouvel (1960) 1976
+ Boston (1833) 1955
+ Broomstick (1901) 1956
+ Buckpasser (1963) 1970
+ Busher (1942) 1964
+ Bushranger (1930) 1967
+ Cafe Prince (1970) 1985
+ Carry Back (1958) 1975
+ Cavalcade (1931) 1993
+ Challendon (1936) 1977
+ Chris Evert (1971) 1988
+ Cicada (1959) 1967
+ Citation (1945) 1959
+ Coaltown (1945) 1983
+ Colin (1905) 1956
+ Commando (1898) 1956
+ Count Fleet (1940) 1961
+ Crusader (1923) 1995
+ Dahlia (1971) 1981
+ Damascus (1964) 1974
+ Dark Mirage (1965) 1974
+ Davona Dale (1976) 1985
+ Desert Vixen (1970) 1979
+ Devil Diver (1939) 1980
+ Discovery (1931) 1969
+ Domino (1891) 1955
+ Dr. Fager (1964) 1971
  Easy Goer (1986) 1997
+ Eight 30 (1936) 1994
+ Elkridge (1938) 1966
+ Emperor of Norfolk (1885) . .1988
+ Equipoise (1928) 1957
+ Exceller (1973) 1999
+ Exterminator (1915) 1957
+ Fairmount (1921) 1985

+ Fair Play (1905) 1956
+ Firenze (1885) 1981
  Flatterer (1979) 1994
+ Foolish Pleasure (1972) 1995
+ Forego (1971) 1979
+ Fort Marcy (1964) 1998
+ Gallant Bloom (1966) 1977
+ Gallant Fox (1927) 1957
+ Gallant Man (1954) 1987
+ Gallorette (1942) 1962
+ Gamely (1964) 1980
  Genuine Risk (1977) 1986
+ Good and Plenty (1900) 1956
+ Go For Wand (1987) 1996
+ Granville (1933) 1997
+ Grey Lag (1918) 1957
+ Gun Bow (1960) 1999
+ Hamburg (1895) 1986
+ Hanover (1884) 1955
+ Henry of Navarre (1891) . . .1985
+ Hill Prince (1947) 1991
+ Hindoo (1878) 1955
+ Imp (1894) 1965
+ Jay Trump (1957) 1971
  John Henry (1975) 1990
+ Johnstown (1936) 1992
+ Jolly Roger (1922) 1965
+ Kingston (1884) 1955
+ Kelso (1957) 1967
+ Kentucky (1861) 1983
  Lady's Secret (1982) 1992
+ La Prevoyante (1970) 1995
+ L'Escargot (1963) 1977
+ Lexington (1850) 1955
+ Longfellow (1867) 1971
+ Luke Blackburn (1877) 1956
+ Majestic Prince (1966) 1988
+ Man o' War (1917) 1957
  Miesque (1984) 1999
+ Miss Woodford (1880) 1967
+ Myrtlewood (1933) 1979
+ Nashua (1952) 1965
+ Native Dancer (1950) 1963
+ Native Diver (1959) 1978
+ Needles (1953) 2000
+ Northern Dancer (1961) 1976
+ Neji (1950) 1966
+ Oedipus (1941) 1978

+ Old Rosebud (1911) 1968
+ Omaha (1932) 1965
+ Pan Zareta (1910) 1972
+ Parole (1873) 1984
  Personal Ensign (1984) 1993
+ Peter Pan (1904) 1956
  Princess Rooney (1980) 1991
+ Real Delight (1949) 1987
+ Regret (1912) 1957
+ Reigh Count (1925) 1978
  Riva Ridge (1969) 1998
+ Roamer (1911) 1981
+ Roseben (1901) 1956
+ Round Table (1954) 1972
+ Ruffian (1972) 1976
+ Ruthless (1864) 1975
+ Salvator (1886) 1955
+ Sarazen (1921) 1957
+ Seabiscuit (1933) 1958
+ Searching (1952) 1978
  Seattle Slew (1974) 1981
+ Secretariat (1970) 1974
+ Shuvee (1966) 1975
+ Silver Spoon (1956) 1978
+ Sir Archy (1805) 1955
+ Sir Barton (1916) 1957
  Slew o'Gold (1980) 1992
+ Sun Beau (1925) 1996
  Sunday Silence (1986) 1996
+ Stymie (1941) 1975
+ Susan's Girl (1969) 1976
+ Swaps (1952) 1966
+ Sword Dancer (1956) 1977
+ Sysonby (1902) 1956
+ Ta Wee (1966) 1994
+ Tim Tam (1955) 1985
+ Tom Fool (1949) 1960
+ Top Flight (1929) 1966
+ Tosmah (1961) 1984
+ Twenty Grand (1928) 1957
+ Twilight Tear (1941) 1963
+ War Admiral (1934) 1958
+ Whirlaway (1938) 1959
+ Whisk Broom II (1907) 1979
  Winning Colors (1985) 2000
  Zaccio (1976) 1990
+ Zev (1920) 1983

Harness Racing Living Hall of Fame

Established by the U.S. Harness Writers Association (USHWA) in 1958. **Address:** Trotting Horse Museum, 240 Main Street, P.O. Box 590, Goshen, NY 10924; **Telephone:** (914) 294-6330.

Eligibility: Open to all harness racing drivers, trainers and executives. Voting done by USHWA membership. There are 73 members of the Living Hall of Fame, but only the 37 drivers and trainer-drivers are listed below.

Class of 1999 (2): HORSES— **Abercrombie** and **Peace Corps.**

Members are listed with years of induction; (+) indicates deceased members.

Trainer-Drivers

Abbatiello, Carmine 1986
Abbatiello, Tony. 1995
Ackerman, Doug 1995
+ Avery, Earle 1975
+ Baldwin, Ralph. 1972
Beissinger, Howard. 1975
Bostwick, Dunbar 1989
+ Cameron, Del. 1975
Campbell, John 1991
+ Chapman, John 1980
Cruise, Jimmy 1987
Dancer, Stanley 1970
+ Ervin, Frank 1969

Farrington, Bob 1980
Filion, Herve 1976
+ Garnsey, Glen 1983
Galbraith, Clint 1990
Gilmour, Buddy 1990
Harner, Levi 1986
+ Haughton, Billy 1969
Hodgins, Clint 1973
Insko, Del 1981
Kopas, Jack 1996
Lachance, Mike 1996
Miller, Del. 1969
+ O'Brien, Joe 1971

O'Donnell, Bill 1991
Patterson, John Sr 1994
+ Pownall, Harry. 1971
Remmem, Ray 1998
Riegle, Gene 1992
+ Russell, Sanders 1971
+ Shively, Bion. 1968
Sholty, George. 1985
Simpson, John Sr 1972
+ Smart, Curly 1970
Sylvester, Charles 1998
Waples, Keith 1987
Waples, Ron. 1994

Exemplars of Racing

+ Hanes, John W ....1982 + Mellon, Paul 1989   Widener, George D 1971
+ Jeffords, Walter M.........1973

National Sportscasters and Sportswriters Hall of Fame

Established in 1959 by the National Sportscasters and Sportswriters Association. A permanent museum for the NSSA Hall of Fame opened on May 1, 2000. **Address:** 322 East Innes St., Salisbury, NC 28144. **Telephone:** (704) 633-4275.

Eligibility: Nominees must be active for at least 25 years. Voting done by NSSA membership and other media representatives.

Class of 2000 (2): **Jim Simpson** and **Jerry Izenberg**.

Members are listed with year of induction; (+) indicates deceased members.

Sportscasters

+ Allen, Mel................1972	Gowdy, Curt 1981	Miller, Jon................1999
+ Barber, Walter (Red)........1973	Harwell, Ernie 1989	+ Nelson, Lindsey 1979
+ Brickhouse, Jack 1983	Hearn, Chick 1997	+ Prince, Bob..............1986
Buck, Jack................1990	+ Hodges, Russ 1975	Schenkel, Chris 1981
+ Caray, Harry 1989	+ Hoyt, Waite 1987	+ Scott, Ray 1982
+ Cosell, Howard 1993	+ Husing, Ted 1963	Scully, Vin 1991
+ Dean, Dizzy..............1976	Jackson, Keith 1995	Simpson, Jim 2000
+ Dunphy, Don 1986	+ McCarthy, Clem..........1970	+ Stern, Bill 1974
+ Elson, Bob 1995	McKay, Jim..............1987	Summerall, Pat..........1994
Enberg, Dick 1996	+ McNamee, Graham 1964	
Glickman, Marty 1992	Michaels, Al..............1998	

Sportswriters

Anderson, Dave..........1990	+ Graham, Frank Sr........1995	+ Povich, Shirley 1984
Bisher, Furman 1989	+ Grimsley, Will 1987	+ Rice, Grantland 1962
Broeg, Bob 1997	Heinz, W.C..............1987	+ Runyon, Damon 1964
Burick, Si................1985	Izenberg, Jerry 2000	Russell, Fred 1988
+ Cannon, Jimmy 1986	Jenkins, Dan..............1996	Sherrod, Blackie 1991
+ Carmichael, John P........1994	+ Kieran, John 1971	+ Smith, Walter (Red) 1977
+ Connor, Dick 1992	+ Lardner, Ring 1967	+ Spink, J.G. Taylor 1969
+ Considine, Bob 1980	+ Murphy, Jack 1988	Stedman, John 1999
+ Daley, Arthur 1976	+ Murray, Jim............1978	+ Ward, Arch 1973
Deford, Frank............1998	Olderman, Murray 1993	+ Woodward, Stanley 1974
Durslag, Mel.............1995	+ Parker, Dan 1975	
+ Gould, Alan 1990	Pope, Edwin.............1994	

American Sportscasters Hall of Fame

Established in 1984 by the American Sportscasters Association. **Mailing Address:** 5 Beekman Street, Suite 814, New York, NY 10038. **Permanent Address:** MCI Center, 601 F St. NW, Washington, D.C. 20001. **Telephone:** (212) 227-8080.

Eligibility: nominations made by selection committee of previous winners, voting by ASA membership.

Class of 1999 (1): **Ray Scott**.

Members are listed with year of induction; (+) indicates deceased members.

+ Allen, Mel................1985	Gowdy, Curt 1985	+ Nelson, Lindsey 1986
+ Barber, Walter (Red)........1984	Harwell, Ernie 1991	Schenkel, Chris 1997
+ Brickhouse, Jack 1985	Hearn, Chick 1995	+ Scott, Ray 1999
Buck, Jack................1990	+ Husing, Ted 1984	Scully, Vin 1992
+ Caray, Harry 1989	Jackson, Keith 1994	+ Stern, Bill 1984
+ Cosell, Howard 1993	+ McCarthy, Clem..........1987	Whitaker, Jack 1998
+ Dunphy, Don 1984	McKay, Jim..............1987	
Glickman, Marty 1993	+ McNamee, Graham 1984	

Motorsports Hall of Fame of America

Established in 1989. **Mailing Address:** P.O. Box 194, Novi, MI 48376. **Telephone:** (248) 349-7223.

Eligibility: Nominees must be retired at least three years or engaged in their area of motorsports for at least 20 years. Areas include: open wheel, stock car, dragster, sports car, motorcycle, off road, power boat, air racing, land speed records, historic and at-large.

Class of 2000 (10): DRIVERS—**Tom D'Eath** (powerboats), **Peter Gregg** (sportscar), **Bob Hannah** (motorcycle), **Sam Hanks** (open wheel), **Ray Harroun** (historic) and **Danny Ongais** (drag racing). PILOTS—**Cook Cleland**. CONTRIBUTORS—**Glen Wood**, **Leonard Wood**, and **Smokey Yunick**.

Members are listed with year of induction; (+) indicates deceased members.

Drivers

Allison, Bobby 1992	Bettenhausen, Tony 1997	+ Campbell, Sir Malcolm......1994
Andretti, Mario 1990	Brabham, Jack 1998	Cantrell, Bill 1992
Arfons, Art 1991	Breedlove, Craig..........1993	+ Chenoweth, Dean 1991
+ Baker, Cannonball 1989	Bryan, Jimmy 1999	Chrisman, Art............1997

Motorsports (Cont.)

+ Clark, Jim 1990	+ Holbert, Al 1993	Ongais, Danny 2000
+ Cook, Betty 1996	+ Horn, Ted 1993	Parks, Wally 1993
Cunningham, Briggs 1997	Jarrett, Ned 1997	Pearson, David 1993
+ Davis, Tom 1997	Jenkins, Bill (Grumpy) 1996	+ Petrali, Joe 1992
D'Eath, Tom 2000	Johnson, Junior 1991	+ Petty, Lee 1996
DeCoster, Roger 1994	Jones, Parnelli 1992	Petty, Richard 1989
+ DePalma, Ralph 1992	Kalitta, Connie 1992	Prudhomme, Don 1991
+ DePaolo, Peter 1995	Kurtis, Frank 1999	+ Revson, Peter 1996
+ Donahue, Mark 1990	Leonard, Joe 1991	+ Roberts, Fireball 1995
Follmer, George 1999	Lockhart, Frank 1999	Roberts, Kenny 1990
Foyt, A.J. 1989	+ McLaren, Bruce 1995	Rutherford, Johnny 1996
Garlits, Don 1989	Mann, Dick 1993	Seebold, Bill 1999
Glidden, Bob 1994	Markle, Bart 1999	+ Shaw, Wilbur 1991
+ Gregg, Peter 2000	+ Mays, Rex. 1995	Slock, Tim 1999
Gurney, Dan 1991	Mears, Rick 1998	Smith, Malcolm 1996
Hanauer, Chip 1995	+ Meyer, Louis 1993	+ Thompson, Mickey 1990
Hannah, Bob 2000	Muldowney, Shirley 1990	Unser, Al 1991
+ Hanks, Sam 2000	+ Muncy, Bill 1989	Unser, Bobby 1994
+ Harroun, Ray 2000	+ Musson, Ron. 1993	+ Vukovich, Bill Sr 1992
Hart, C.J. 1999	Nordskog, Bob 1997	Ward, Rodger 1995
Hill, Phil 1989	+ Oldfield, Barney 1989	+ Wood, Gar. 1990
		Yarborough, Cale 1994

Pilots

Cleland, Cook 2000	+ Doolittle, Jimmy 1989	Greenmayer, Darryl 1997
+ Cochran, Jacqueline 1993	+ Earhart, Amelia 1992	Shelton, Lyle 1999
+ Curtiss, Glenn 1990	+ Falck, Bill 1994	+ Turner, Roscoe 1991

Contributors

+ Agajanian, J.C. 1992	+ Ford, Henry 1996	+ Rickenbacker, Eddie 1994
Bignotti, George 1993	+ France, Bill Sr. 1990	+ Rose, Mauri 1996
+ Black, Keith 1995	Hall, Jim 1994	Shelby, Carroll 1992
Chapman, Colin 1997	+ Hulman, Tony 1991	Watson, A.J. 1996
+ Chevrolet, Louis 1995	Little, Bernie 1994	Wood, Glen 2000
Duesenberg, Fred 1997	Miller, Harry 1999	Wood, Leonard 2000
Economaki, Chris 1994	Penske, Roger 1995	Yunick, Smokey 2000

International Motorsports Hall of Fame

Established in 1990 by the International Motorsports Hall of Fame Commission. **Mailing Address:** P.O. Box 1018, Talladega, AL 35160. **Telephone:** (256) 362-5002.

Eligibility: Nominees must be retired from their specialty in motorsports for five years. Voting done by 150-member panel made up of the world-wide auto racing media.

Class of 2000 (6): DRIVERS—**Mario Andretti, A.J. Foyt, Nelson Piquet, Don Prodhomme** and **Ayrton Senna**. CONTRIBUTOR—**Craig Breedlove.**

Members are listed with year of induction; (+) indicates deceased members.

Drivers

Allison, Bobby 1993	Hill, Phil 1991	Prodhomme, Don. 2000
Andretti, Mario 2000	+ Holbert, Al 1993	Prost, Alain 1999
+ Ascari, Alberto. 1992	+ Isaac, Bobby 1996	+ Roberts, Fireball. 1990
+ Ascari, Alberto. 1992	Jarrett, Ned 1991	Roberts, Kenny. 1992
Baker, Buck. 1990	Johncock, Gordon 1999	Rose, Mauri 1994
+ Bettenhausen, Tony 1991	Johnson, Junior 1990	Rutherford, Johnny 1996
Brabham, Jack 1990	Jones, Parnelli 1990	Scott, Wendell 1999
+ Campbell, Sir Malcolm. 1990	Lauda, Niki. 1993	+ Senna, Ayrton 2000
+ Caracciola, Rudolph. 1998	Lorenzen, Fred 1991	+ Shaw, Wilbur 1991
+ Clark, Jim 1990	+ Lund, Tiny 1994	Smith, Louise 1999
+ DePalma, Ralph 1991	+ Mays, Rex. 1993	Stewart, Jackie. 1990
+ Donahue, Mark 1990	+ McLaren, Bruce 1991	Surtees, John 1996
+ Evans, Richie 1996	+ Meyer, Louis 1992	Thomas, Herb. 1994
+ Fangio, Juan Manuel 1990	Moss, Stirling 1990	+ Turner, Curtis 1992
+ Flock, Tim 1991	+ Nuvolari, Tazio 1998	Unser, Al Sr. 1998
Foyt, A.J. 2000	+ Oldfield, Barney 1990	Unser, Bobby 1990
+ Gregg, Peter 1992	Parsons, Benny 1994	+ Vukovich, Bill 1991
Gurney, Dan. 1990	Pearson, David 1993	Ward Rodger 1992
+ Haley, Donald 1996	+ Petty, Lee 1990	+ Weatherly, Joe 1994
+ Hill, Graham 1990	Piquet, Nelson 2000	Yarborough, Cale 1993

Contributors

Bignotti, George 1993	Granatelli, Andy 1992	Penske, Roger 1998
Breedlove, Craig 2000	+ Hulman, Tony 1990	+ Porsche, Ferdinand 1996
+ Chapman, Colin 1994	Hyde, Harry. 1999	+ Rickenbacker, Eddie 1992
+ Chevrolet, Louis 1992	Marcum, John 1994	Shelby, Carroll 1991
+ Ferrari, Enzo 1994	+ Matthews, Banjo 1998	+ Thompson, Mickey 1990
+ Ford, Henry 1993	Moody, Ralph 1994	Yunick, Smokey 1990
+ France, Bill Sr. 1990	Parks, Wally. 1992	

OLYMPICS

U.S. Olympic Hall of Fame

Established in 1983 by the United States Olympic Committee. **Mailing Address:** U.S. Olympic Committee, 1750 East Boulder Street, Colorado Springs, CO 80909. Plans for a permanent museum site have been suspended due to lack of funding. **Telephone:** (719) 578-4529.

Eligibility: Nominated athletes must be five years removed from active competition. Voting done by National Sportscasters and Sportswriters Association, Hall of Fame members and the USOC board members of directors.

Voting for membership in the Hall was suspended in 1993.

Members are listed with year of induction; (+) indicates deceased members.

Teams

1956 Basketball Dick Boushka, Carl Cain, Chuck Darling, Bill Evans, Gib Ford, Burdy Haldorson, Bill Hougland, Bob Jeangerard, K.C. Jones, Bill Russell, Ron Tomsic, +Jim Walsh and coach +Gerald Tucker.

1960 Basketball Jay Arnette, Walt Bellamy, Bob Boozer, Terry Dischinger, Burdy Haldorson, Darrall Imhoff, Allen Kelley, +Lester Lane, Jerry Lucas, Oscar Robertson, Adrian Smith, Jerry West and coach Pete Newell.

1964 Basketball Jim Barnes, Bill Bradley, Larry Brown, Joe Caldwell, Mel Counts, Richard Davies, Walt Hazzard, Luke Jackson, John McCaffrey, Jeff Mullins, Jerry Shipp, George Wilson and coach +Hank Iba.

1960 Ice Hockey Billy Christian, Roger Christian, Billy Cleary, Bob Cleary, Gene Grazia, Paul Johnson, Jack Kirrane, John Mayasich, Jack McCartan, Bob McKay, Dick Meredith, Weldon Olson, Ed Owen, Rod Paavola, Larry Palmer, Dick Rodenheiser, +Tom Williams and coach Jack Riley.

1980 Ice Hockey Bill Baker, Neal Broten, Dave Christian, Steve Christoff, Jim Craig, Mike Eruzione, Jim Harrington, Steve Janaszak, Mark Johnson, Ken Morrow, Rob McClanahan, Jack O'Callahan, Mark Pavelich, Mike Ramsey, Buzz Schneider, Dave Silk, Eric Strobel, Bob Suter, Phil Verchota, Mark Wells and coach Herb Brooks.

Alpine Skiing

Mahre, Phil 1992

Bobsled

+ Eagan, Eddie (see Boxing) . . . 1983

Boxing

Clay, Cassius* 1983
+ Eagan, Eddie (see Bobsled) . . 1983
Foreman, George 1990
Frazier, Joe 1989
Leonard, Sugar Ray 1985
Patterson, Floyd 1987
*Clay changed name to Muhammad Ali in 1964.

Cycling

Carpenter-Phinney, Connie . . . 1992

Diving

King, Miki 1992
Lee, Sammy 1990
Louganis, Greg 1985
McCormick, Pat 1985

Figure Skating

Albright, Tenley 1988
Button, Dick 1983
Fleming, Peggy 1983
Hamill, Dorothy 1991
Hamilton, Scott 1990

Gymnastics

Conner, Bart 1991
Retton, Mary Lou 1985
Vidmar, Peter 1991

Rowing

+ Kelly, Jack Sr. 1990

Speed Skating

Heiden, Eric 1983

Swimming

Babashoff, Shirley 1987
Caulkins, Tracy 1990
+ Daniels, Charles 1988
de Varona, Donna 1987
+ Kahanamoku, Duke 1984
+ Madison, Helene 1992
Meyer, Debbie 1986
Naber, John 1984
Schollander, Don 1983
Spitz, Mark 1983
+ Weissmuller, Johnny 1983

Track & Field

Beamon, Bob 1983
Boston, Ralph 1985
+ Calhoun, Lee 1991
Campbell, Milt 1992
Davenport, Willie 1991
Davis, Glenn 1986
+ Didrikson, Babe 1983
Dillard, Harrison 1983
Evans, Lee 1989
+ Ewry, Ray 1983
Fosbury, Dick 1992
Jenner, Bruce 1986
Johnson, Rafer 1983
+ Kraenzlein, Alvin 1985
Lewis, Carl 1985
Mathias, Bob 1983

(Track & Field cont.)

Mills, Billy 1984
Morrow, Bobby 1989
Moses, Edwin 1985
O'Brien, Parry 1984
Oerter, Al 1983
+ Owens, Jesse 1983
+ Paddock, Charley 1991
Richards, Bob 1983
+ Rudolph, Wilma 1983
+ Sheppard, Mel 1989
Shorter, Frank 1984
+ Thorpe, Jim 1983
Toomey, Bill 1984
Tyus, Wyomia 1985
Whitfield, Mal 1988
+ Wykoff, Frank 1984

Weight Lifting

+ Davis, John 1989
Kono, Tommy 1990

Wrestling

Gable, Dan 1985

Contributors

Arledge, Roone 1989
+ Brundage, Avery 1983
+ Bushnell, Asa 1990
Hull, Col. Don 1992
+ Iba, Hank 1985
+ Kane, Robert 1986
+ Kelly, Jack Jr. 1992
McKay, Jim 1988
Miller, Don 1984
+ Simon, William 1991
Walker, LeRoy 1987

The Olympic Order

Established in 1974 by the International Olympic Committee (IOC) to honor athletes, officials and media members who have made remarkable contributions to the Olympic movement. The IOC's Council of the Olympic Order is presided over by the IOC president and active IOC members are not eligible for consideration. Through 1998, only three American officials have received the Order's highest commendation—the gold medal:

Avery Brundage, president of USOC (1928-53) and IOC (1952-72), was given the award posthumously in 1975.

Peter Ueberroth, president of Los Angeles Olympic Organizing Committee, was given the award in 1984.

Billy Payne, president of the Atlanta Committee for the Olympic Games, was given the award in 1996.

SOCCER

International Soccer Hall of Champions

Established in 1998 by FIFA, soccer's international governing body. Located at Disneyland Paris.

Eligibility: Nominated players and coaches must be retired at least five years. Nominations made by a committee composed of FIFA members, the Hall of Champions management and three ad hoc members then submit a list to a panel of 32 soccer journalists from around the world who also have the chance to add nominees of their own as well as voting for a specific number of candidates in each category.

Class of 2000: The IFHOC was set to induct its next group in January, 2001.

Players

Beckenbauer, Franz (W. Ger)..1998	Fontaine, Just (FRA) 1999	Pele (BRA)..................1998
Charlton, Sir Bobby (ENG)....1998	+ Garrincha (BRA) 1999	Plantini, Michel (FRA) 1998
Cruyff, Johan (NED) 1998	+ Matthews, Sir Stanley (ENG).1998	Puskas, Ferenc (HUN/SPA) ..1998
Distefano, Alfredo (ARG/SPA).1998	+ Moore, Bobby (ENG) 1999	+ Yashin, Lev (RUS)...........1998
Eusebio (POR) 1998	Müller, Gerd (W. Ger) 1999	Zoff, Dino (ITA).............1999

Managers

+ Busby, Sir Matt (SCO).......1998	Michels, Rinus (NED) 1998	+ Shankly, Bill (SCO) 1999

Referees

Taylor, Jack (ENG)..........1999	Vautrot, Michel (FRA) 1998

Pioneers

Havelange, Joao (BRA)......1999	+ Rimet, Jules (FRA)...........1998

Club Teams

Ajax Amsterdam (NED) 1999	Real Madrid (SPA)..........1998

National Teams

Brazil.....................1998	Germany...................1999

Media

Ferran, Jacques (FRA) 1999	Goddett, Jacques (FRA) 1998

For the Good of the Game

+ Dassler, Horst (GER) 1998	+ Sastre, Fernard (FRA) 1999

National Soccer Hall of Fame

Established in 1950 by the Philadelphia Oldtimers Association. First exhibit unveiled in Oneonta, NY in 1982. Moved into new Hall of Fame building in the summer of 1999. **Address:** 18 Stadium Circle, Oneonta, NY 13820. **Telephone:** (607) 432-3351.

Eligibility: Nominated players must have represented the U.S. in international competition and be retired five years; other categories include Meritorious Service and Special Commendation.

Nominations made by state organizations and a veterans' committee. Voting done by nine-member committee made up of Hall of Famers, U.S. Soccer officials and members of the national media.

Class of 2000 (2): Giorgio Chinaglia and **Carin Jennings Gabarra.**

Members are listed with home state and year of induction; (+) indicates deceased members.

Members

Abronzino, Umberto (CA) ...1971	+ Boxer, Matt (CA) 1961	+ Colombo, Charlie (MO).....1976
Aimi, Milton (TX) 1991	Bradley, Gordon (Eng) 1996	+ Commander, Colin (OH) 1967
+ Alonso, Julie (NY) 1972	+ Briggs, Lawrence E. (MA)....1978	+ Cordery, Ted (CA)..........1975
+ Andersen, William (NY).....1956	+ Brittan, Harold (PA).........1951	+ Craddock, Robert (PA) 1959
+ Ardizzone, John (CA) 1971	+ Brock, John (MA) 1950	+ Craggs, Edmund (WA)......1969
+ Armstrong, James (NY)......1952	+ Brown, Andrew M. (OH) 1950	Craggs, George (WA) 1981
+ Auld, Andrew (RI) 1986	+ Brown, David (NJ)..........1951	+ Cummings, Wilfred R. (IL) ...1953
Bahr, Walter (PA)...........1976	Brown, George (NJ) 1995	+ Delach, Joseph (PA).........1973
Barr, George (NY)..........1983	Brown, James (NY) 1986	DeLuca, Enzo (NY) 1979
+ Barriskill, Joe (NY).........1953	+ Cahill, Thomas W (NY) 1950	+ Dick, Walter (CA) 1989
+ Beardsworth, Fred (MA) 1965	+ Carenza, Joe (MO).........1982	Diorio, Nick (PA) 1974
Beckenbauer, Franz (Ger) ...1998	+ Caraffi, Ralph (OH).........1959	+ Donaghy, Edward J. (NY) ...1951
Berling, Clay (CA)..........1995	Chacurian, Chico (CT) 1992	+ Donelli, Buff (PA) 1954
Bernabei, Ray (PA)..........1978	+ Chesney, Stan (NY)........1966	+ Donnelly, George (NY)......1989
Best, John O. (CA)..........1982	Chinaglia, Giorgio (Italy)....2000	+ Douglas, Jimmy (NJ) 1954
+ Bookie, Michael (PA)........1986	Chyzowych, Walter (PA) ...1997	+ Dresmich, John W. (PA) 1968
+ Booth, Joseph (CT)..........1952	+ Coll, John (NY) 1986	+ Duff, Duncan (CA)..........1972
Borghi, Frank (MO)..........1976	+ Collins, George M. (MA)....1951	+ Dugan, Thomas (NJ) 1951
Boulos, Frenchy (NY) 1980	Collins, Peter (NY)..........1998	+ Dunn, James (MO) 1974

Edwards, Gene (WI)........1985	+ Koszma, Oscar (CA).......1964	Peters, Wally (NJ) 1967
Ely, Alexander (PA) 1997	Kracher, Frank (IL) 1983	Phillipson, Don (CO) 1987
+ Epperleim, Rudy (NJ) 1951	Kraft, Granny (MD) 1984	+ Piscopo, Giorgio (NY) 1978
+ Fairfield, Harry (PA) 1951	+ Kraus, Harry (NY) 1963	+ Pomeroy, Edgar (CA) 1955
Feibusch, Ernst (CA) 1984	Kropfelder, Nicholas.........1996	+ Ramsden, Arnold (TX) 1957
+ Ferguson, John (PA).........1950	+ Kunter, Rudy (NY) 1963	+ Ratican, Harry (MO).........1950
+ Fernley, John A. (MA) 1951	+ Lamm, Kurt (NY) 1979	Reese, Doc (MD)............1957
+ Ferro, Charles (NY).........1958	Lang, Millard (MD) 1950	+ Renzulli, Pete (NY)..........1951
+ Fishwick, George E. (IL) 1974	Larson, Bert (CT) 1988	Ringsdorf, Gene (MD).......1979
+ Flamhaft, Jack (NY).........1964	Leonard, Abbot (Eng) 1996	Roe, James (MO).............1997
+ Fleming, Harry G. (PA).......1967	+ Lewis, H. Edgar (PA) 1950	Roth, Werner (NY)...........1989
+ Florie, Thomas (NJ) 1986	Lombardo, Joe (NY) 1984	+ Rottenberg, Jack (NJ) 1971
+ Foulds, Pal (MA) 1953	Long, Denny (MO)...........1993	Roy, Willy (IL) 1989
+ Foulds, Sam (MA)...........1969	+ MacEwan, John J. (MI) 1953	+ Ryan, Hun (PA)..............1958
+ Fowler, Dan (NY)...........1970	+ Maca, Joe (NY) 1976	+ Sager, Tom (PA) 1968
+ Fowler, Peg (NY) 1979	Magnozzi, Enzo (NY).......1978	Saunders, Harry (NY) 1981
Fricker, Werner (PA) 1992	+ Maher, Jack (IL) 1970	Schaller, Willy (IL) 1995
+ Fryer, William J. (NJ) 1951	+ Manning, Dr. Randolf (NY) ..1950	Schellscheidt, Mannie (NJ)...1990
Gabarra, Carin (CA) 2000	+ Marre, John (MO)...........1953	Schillinger, Emil (PA) 1960
+ Gaetjens, Joe (NY) 1976	McBride, Pat (MO)...........1994	+ Schroeder, Elmer (PA) 1951
+ Gallagher, James (NY) 1986	+ McClay, Allan (MA) 1971	+ Scwarcz, Erno (NY)..........1951
+ Garcia, Pete (MO)...........1964	+ McGhee, Bart (NY)..........1986	+ Shields, Fred (PA) 1968
+ Gentle, James (PA)...........1986	+ McGrath, Frank (MA) 1978	+ Single, Erwin (NY)...........1981
Getzinger, Rudy (IL)..........1991	+ McGuire, Jimmy (NY) 1951	+ Slone, Philip (NY) 1986
+ Giesler, Walter (MO) 1962	+ McGuire, John (NY) 1951	+ Smith, Alfred (PA) 1951
Glover, Teddy (NY) 1965	+ McIlveney, Eddie (PA) 1976	Smith, Patrick (OH) 1998
+ Gonsalves, Billy (MA) 1950	McLaughlin, Bennie (PA).....1977	+ Souza, Ed (MA).............1976
Gormley, Bob (PA)...........1989	+ McSkimming, Dent (MO) 1951	Souza, Clarkie (MA).........1976
+ Gould, David L. (PA) 1953	Merovich, Pete (PA)..........1971	+ Spalding, Dick (PA)..........1951
+ Govier, Sheldon (IL)..........1950	+ Mieth, Werner (NJ) 1974	+ Stark, Archie (NJ)............1950
Greer, Don (CA) 1985	+ Millar, Robert (NY) 1950	+ Steelink, Nicolaas (CA) 1971
Gryzik, Joe (IL)................1973	Miller, Al (OH) 1995	+ Steur, August (NY)...........1969
+ Guelker, Bob (MO)...........1980	+ Miller, Milton (NY)...........1971	+ Stewart, Douglas (PA) 1950
Guennel, Joe (CO) 1980	+ Mills, Jimmy (PA) 1954	+ Stone, Robert T. (CO) 1971
Harker, Al (PA)...............1979	Monson, Lloyd (NY) 1994	+ Swords, Thomas (MA) 1976
+ Healy, George (MI) 1951	Moore, James F. (MO) 1971	+ Tintle, Joseph (NJ) 1952
Heilpern, Herb (NY) 1988	Moore, Johnny (CA) 1997	+ Tracey, Ralph (MO)..........1986
Heinrichs, April (CO) 1998	+ Moorehouse, George (NY) ...1986	+ Triner, Joseph (IL)............1951
+ Hemmings, William (IL).......1961	+ Morrison, Robert (PA) 1951	+ Vaughan, Frank (MO)........1986
+ Hudson, Maurice (CA) 1966	+ Morrissette, Bill (MA) 1967	+ Walder, Jimmy (PA)..........1971
Hunt, Lamar (TX) 1982	Nanoski, Jukey (PA)..........1993	+ Wallace, Frank (MO) 1976
Hynes, John (NY).............1977	+ Netto, Fred (IL) 1958	+ Washauer, Adolph (CA).......1977
+ Iglehart, Alfredda (MD) 1951	Newman, Ron (CA).........1992	+ Webb, Tom (WA)............1987
+ Japp, John (PA) 1953	+ Niotis, D.J. (IL) 1963	+ Weir, Alex (NY) 1975
+ Jeffrey, William (PA) 1951	+ O'Brien, Shamus (NY) 1990	+ Weston, Victor (WA)........1956
Jewell, Frank (FA)............1996	Olaff, Gene (NJ) 1971	+ Wilson, Peter (NJ)............1950
+ Johnson, Jack (IL) 1952	+ Oliver, Arnie (MA)...........1968	+ Wood, Alex (MI) 1986
Kabanica, Mike (WI) 1987	Oliver, Len (PA) 1996	+ Woods, John W. (IL) 1952
Kehoe, Bob (MO) 1990	+ Palmer, William (PA) 1952	Woosnam, Phil (GA).........1997
Kelly, Frank (NJ)..............1994	Pariani, Gino (MO)...........1976	Yeagley, Jerry (IN)...........1989
+ Kempton, George (WA).......1950	+ Patenaude, Bert (MA) 1971	+ Young, John (CA)............1958
Keough, Harry (MO)..........1976	+ Pearson, Eddie (GA) 1990	+ Zampini, Dan (PA)...........1963
+ Klein, Paul (NJ) 1953	+ Peel, Peter (IL)...............1951	Zerhusen, Al (CA) 1978
Kleinaitis, Al (IN)............1995	Pelé (Brazil) 1993	

SWIMMING

International Swimming Hall of Fame

Established in 1965 by the U.S. College Coaches' Swim Forum. **Address:** One Hall of Fame Drive, Ft. Lauderdale, FL 33316. **Telephone:** (954) 462-6536.

Categories for induction are: swimming, diving, water polo, synchronized swimming, coaching, pioneers and contributors. Contributors are not included in the following list. Only U.S. men, women and coaches listed below.

Class of 2000 (5): U.S. WOMEN–**Lynne Cox**, **Barbara Dunbar** and **Mary Wayte**; U.S. COACHES–**Gail Emery** and **Richard Quick**.

Members are listed with year of induction; (+) indicates deceased members.

U.S. Men

+ Anderson, Miller 1967	+ Browning, Skippy 1975	Clark, Steve 1966
Barrowman, Mike 1997	Bruner, Mike................1988	Cleveland, Dick 1991
Biondi, Matt................1997	Burton, Mike...............1977	Clotworthy, Robert..........1980
+ Boggs, Phil 1985	+ Cann, Tedford 1967	+ Crabbe, Buster.............1965
Brack, Walter...............1997	Carey, Rick 1993	+ Daniels, Charlie............1965
Breen, George 1975	Clark, Earl 1972	Degener, Dick 1971

U.S. Women

U.S. Coaches

+ Armbruster, Dave..........1966
+ Bachrach, Bill..............1966
Billingsley, Hobie.........1983
+ Brandsten, Ernst...........1966
+ Brauninger, Stan 1972
Bussard, Ray 1999
+ Cady, Fred 1969
+ Center, George (Dad)......1991
Chavoor, Sherman 1977
+ Cody, Jack 1970
Counsilman, Dr. James 1976
+ Curtis, Katherine 1979
Daland, Peter...............1977
+ Daughters, Ray 1971
Emery, Gail 2000

Gambril, Don..............1983
Gambril, Don..............1983
Haines, George...........1977
Handley, L. de B...........1967
Hannula, Dick 1987
Kimball, Dick 1985
+ Kiphuth, Bob 1965
Mann, Matt II.............1965
+ McCormick, Glen 1995
Moriarty, Phil 1980
Mowerson, Robert.........1986
Muir, Bob 1989
+ Neuschaufer, Al...........1967
Nitzkowski, Monte 1991
O'Brien, Ron 1988

+ Papenguth, Richard........1986
+ Peppe, Mike..............1966
+ Pinkston, Clarence 1966
Quick, Richard............2000
+ Robinson, Tom 1965
Sakamoto, Soichi 1966
+ Sava, Charlie.............1970
+ Schlueter, Walt...........1978
Schubert, Mark 1997
Smith, Dick 1979
Stager, Gus 1982
Thornton, Nort 1995
Tinkham, Stan 1989

TENNIS

International Tennis Hall of Fame

Originally the National Tennis Hall of Fame. Established in 1953 by James Van Alen and sanctioned by the U.S. Tennis Association in 1954. Renamed the International Tennis Hall of Fame in 1976. **Address:** 194 Bellevue Ave., Newport, RI 02840. **Telephone:** (401) 849-3990.

Eligibility: Nominated players must be five years removed from being a "significant factor" in competitive tennis. Voting done by members of the international tennis media.

Class of 2000 (3): PLAYERS— **Malcolm Anderson**, **Robert Kelleher** and **Martina Navratilova**.

Members are listed with year of induction; (+) indicates deceased members.

Men

+ Adee, George 1964
+ Alexander, Fred...........1961
+ Allison, Wilmer...........1963
+ Alonso, Manuel...........1977
Anderson, Malcolm........2000
+ Ashe, Arthur 1985
+ Behr, Karl 1969
Borg, Bjorn...............1987
+ Borotra, Jean 1976
Bromwich, John 1984
+ Brookes, Norman 1977
+ Brugnon, Jacques 1976
+ Budge, Don 1964
+ Campbell, Oliver..........1955
+ Chace, Malcolm 1961
+ Clark, Clarence 1983
+ Clark, Joseph 1955
+ Clothier, William 1956
+ Cochet, Henri 1976
Connors, Jimmy 1998
Cooper, Ashley 1991
+ Crawford, Jack 1979
David, Herman 1998
+ Doeg, John...............1962
+ Doherty, Lawrence.........1980
+ Doherty, Reginald 1980
Drobny, Jaroslav 1983
+ Dwight, James 1955
Emerson, Roy 1982
+ Etchebaster, Pierre 1978
Falkenburg, Bob 1974
Fraser, Neale.............1984
+ Garland, Chuck 1969
+ Gonzales, Pancho 1968
+ Grant, Bryan (Bitsy).......1972
Griffin, Clarence 1970

+ Hackett, Harold 1961
Hewitt, Bob...............1992
+ Hoad, Lew 1980
+ Hovey, Fred 1974
+ Hunt, Joe.................1966
+ Hunter, Frank 1961
+ Johnston, Bill.............1958
+ Jones, Perry 1970
Kelleher, Robert 2000
Kodes, Jan 1990
+ Kramer, Jack.............1968
+ Lacoste, Rene 1976
+ Larned, William 1956
Larsen, Art 1969
Laver, Rod 1981
+ Lott, George 1964
Mako, Gene...............1973
McEnroe, John............1999
McGregor, Ken 1999
+ McKinley, Chuck 1986
+ McLoughlin, Maurice 1957
McMillan, Frew 1992
+ McNeill, Don 1965
Mulloy, Gardnar 1972
+ Murray, Lindley 1958
+ Myrick, Julian 1963
Nastase, Ilie..............1991
Newcombe, John...........1986
+ Nielsen, Arthur 1971
Olmedo, Alex 1987
+ Osuna, Rafael 1979
Parker, Frank 1966
+ Patterson, Gerald 1989
Patty, Budge 1977
+ Perry, Fred 1975
+ Pettitt, Tom...............1982

Pietrangeli, Nicola 1986
+ Quist, Adrian 1984
Ralston, Dennis 1987
+ Renshaw, Ernest..........1983
+ Renshaw, William 1983
+ Richards, Vincent 1961
+ Riggs, Bobby 1967
Roche, Tony 1986
Rosewall, Ken 1980
Santana, Manuel 1984
+ Savitt, Dick 1976
Schroeder, Ted............1966
+ Sears, Richard 1955
Sedgman, Frank 1979
+ Segura, Pancho 1984
Seixas, Vic 1971
+ Shields, Frank 1964
+ Slocum, Henry 1955
Smith, Stan 1987
Stolle, Fred 1985
+ Talbert, Bill 1967
+ Tilden, Bill 1959
Trabert, Tony 1970
Van Ryn, John............1963
Vilas, Guillermo 1991
+ Vines, Ellsworth 1962
+ von Cramm, Gottfried......1977
+ Ward, Holcombe..........1956
+ Washburn, Watson 1965
+ Whitman, Malcolm 1955
+ Wilding, Anthony 1978
+ Williams, Richard 2nd 1957
Wood, Sidney 1964
+ Wrenn, Robert 1955
+ Wright, Beals.............1956

+ Atkinson, Juliette 1974
Austin, Bunny.............1997
Austin, Tracy 1992
+ Barger-Wallach, Maud 1958
Betz Addie, Pauline........1965
+ Bjurstedt Mallory, Molla 1958

Women

Bowrey, Lesley Turner 1997
Brough Clapp, Louise 1967
+ Browne, Mary 1957
Bueno, Maria 1978
+ Cahill, Mabel 1976
Casals, Rosie 1996

+ Connolly Brinker, Maureen ..1968
+ Dod, Charlotte (Lottie).......1983
+ Douglass Chambers, Dorothy .1981
Evert, Chris 1995
Fry Irvin, Shirley 1970
Gibson, Althea 1971

Tennis (Cont.)

Goolagong Cawley, Evonne ..1988	Mandlikova, Hana 1994	+ Round Little, Dorothy 1986
+ Hansell, Ellen 1965	+ Marble, Alice 1964	+ Ryan, Elizabeth 1972
Hard, Darlene 1973	+ McKane Godfree, Kitty 1978	+ Sears, Eleanora 1968
Hart, Doris 1969	+ Moore, Elisabeth 1971	Smith Court, Margaret 1979
Haydon Jones, Ann..........1985	Mortimer Barrett, Angela 1993	+ Sutton Bundy, May 1956
Heldman, Gladys 1979	Navratilova, Martina 2000	+ Townsend Toulmin, Bertha...1974
+ Hotchkiss Wightman, Hazel ..1957	+ Nuthall Shoemaker, Betty 1977	Wade, Virginia 1989
+ Jacobs, Helen Hull..........1962	Osborne duPont, Margaret....1967	+ Wagner, Marie 1969
King, Billie Jean 1987	+ Palfrey Danzig, Sarah 1963	+ Wills Moody Roark, Helen 1959
+ Lenglen, Suzanne 1978	+ Roosevelt, Ellen 1975	

Contributors

+ Baker, Lawrence Sr 1975	+ Gustaf, V (King of Sweden)..1980	Maskell, Dan 1996
Chatrier, Philippe............1992	+ Hester, W.E. (Slew)........1981	+ Outerbridge, Mary 1981
Collins, Bud 1994	+ Hopman, Harry 1978	+ Pell, Theodore 1966
Cullman, Joseph F. 3rd.......1990	Hunt, Lamar 1993	+ Tingay, Lance 1982
+ Danzig, Allison 1968	+ Laney, Al.................1979	+ Tinling, Ted...............1986
+ Davis, Dwight..............1956	Martin, Alastair 1973	+ Van Alen, James 1965
+ Gray, David 1985	Martin, William M.........1982	+ Wingfield, Walter Clopton...1997

TRACK & FIELD

National Track & Field Hall of Fame

Established in 1974 by the The Athletics Congress (now USA Track & Field). Originally located in Charleston, WV, the Hall moved to Indianapolis in 1983 and reopened at the Hoosier Dome (now RCA Dome) in 1986. **Address:** One RCA Dome, Indianapolis, IN 46225. **Telephone:** (317) 261-0500.

Eligibility: Nominated athletes must be retired three years and coaches must have coached at least 20 years if retired or 35 years if still coaching. Voting done by 800-member panel made up of Hall of Fame and USA Track & Field officials, Hall of Fame members, current U.S. champions and members of the Track & Field Writers of America.

Class of 1999 (4): MEN—**Willie Banks, Larry Ellis, Charles Moore** and **Bill Rodgers**.

Members are listed with year of induction; (+) indicates deceased members.

Men

+ Albritton, Dave.............1980	+ Houser, Bud 1979	+ Prefontaine, Steve 1976
Ashenfelter, Horace........1975	+ Hubbard, DeHart 1979	+ Ray, Joie 1976
Banks, Willie 2000	Jenkins, Charlie 1992	+ Rice, Greg 1977
+ Bausch, James 1979	Jenner, Bruce 1980	Richards, Bob...............1975
Beamon, Bob 1977	+ Johnson, Cornelius 1994	Rodgers, Bill 2000
Beatty, Jim................1990	Johnson, Rafer 1974	+ Rose, Ralph 1976
Bell, Greg 1988	Jones, Hayes 1976	Ryun, Jim..................1980
+ Boeckmann, Dee 1976	Kelley, John 1980	+ Scholz, Jackson 1977
Boston, Ralph 1974	Kiviat, Abel................1985	Schul, Bob 1991
Bragg, Don 1996	+ Kraenzlein, Alvin 1974	Seagren, Bob 1986
+ Calhoun, Lee 1974	Laird, Ron 1986	+ Sheppard, Mel..............1976
Campbell, Milt..............1989	+ Lash, Don 1995	+ Sheridan, Martin 1988
Carr, Henry 1997	+ Laskau, Henry 1997	Shorter, Frank..............1989
+ Clark, Ellery 1991	Liquori, Marty..............1995	Silvester, Jay...............1998
Connolly, Harold 1984	Long, Dr. Dallas 1996	Sime, Dave 1981
Courtney, Tom 1978	Mathias, Bob 1974	+ Simpson, Robert............1974
+ Cunningham, Glenn 1974	Matson, Randy..............1984	Smith, Tommie 1978
+ Curtis, William 1979	McCluskey, Joe 1996	+ Stanfield, Andy 1977
Davenport, Willie 1982	+ Meadows, Earle 1996	Steers, Les.................1974
Davis, Glenn 1974	+ Meredith, Ted 1982	Stones, Dwight..............1998
Davis, Harold 1974	Metcalfe, Ralph 1975	+ Tewksbury, Dr. Walter......1996
Dillard, Harrison 1974	+ Milburn, Rod 1993	Thomas, John 1985
Dumas, Charley............1990	Mills, Billy 1976	+ Thomson, Earl 1977
+ Ellis, Larry................2000	Moore, Charles 2000	+ Thorpe, Jim 1975
Evans, Lee................1983	Moore, Tom 1988	+ Tolan, Eddie 1982
+ Ewell, Barney..............1986	Morrow, Bobby 1975	Toomey, Bill 1975
+ Ewry, Ray 1974	+ Mortensen, Jess 1992	+ Towns, Forrest (Spec) 1976
+ Flanagan, John 1975	Moses, Edwin...............1994	Warmerdam, Cornelius 1974
Fosbury, Dick 1981	+ Myers, Lawrence 1974	Whitfield, Mal 1974
Foster, Greg 1998	Nehemiah, Renaldo 1997	Wilkins, Mac 1993
+ Gordien, Fortune 1979	O'Brien, Parry 1974	+ Williams, Archie 1992
Greene, Charlie 1992	Oerter, Al 1974	Wohlhuter, Rick 1990
+ Hahn, Archie 1983	+ Osborn, Harold 1974	Woodruff, John 1978
+ Hardin, Glenn 1978	+ Owens, Jesse 1974	Wottle, Dave 1982
Hayes, Bob 1976	+ Paddock, Charley 1976	+ Wykoff, Frank 1977
Held, Bud 1987	Patton, Mel 1985	Young, George 1981
Hines, Jim.................1979	+ Peacock, Eulace 1987	

Women

Ashford, Evelyn	1997	Heritage, Doris Brown	1990	+ Schmidt, Kate	1994
Brisco, Valerie	1995	+ Jackson, Nell	1989	+ Shiley Newhouse, Jean	1993
Coachman, Alice	1975	Larrieu Smith, Francie	1998	+ Stephens, Helen	1975
+ Copeland, Lillian	1994	Manning, Madeline	1984	Tyus, Wyomia	1980
+ Didrikson, Babe	1974	McDaniel, Mildred	1983	+ Walsh, Stella	1975
Faggs, Mae	1976	McGuire, Edith	1979	Watson, Martha	1987
Ferrell, Barbara	1988	Ritter, Louise	1995	White, Willye	1981
+ Griffith Joyner, Florence	1995	+ Robinson, Betty	1977		
+ Hall Adams, Evelyne	1988	+ Rudolph, Wilma	1974		

Coaches

+ Abbott, Cleve	1996	+ Hamilton, Brutus	1974	+ Murphy, Michael	1974
+ Baskin, Weems	1982	+ Haydon, Ted	1975	Rosen, Mel	1995
+ Beard, Percy	1981	+ Hayes, Billy	1976	+ Snyder, Larry	1978
Bell, Sam	1992	+ Haylett, Ward	1979	Temple, Ed	1989
+ Botts, Tom	1983	+ Higgins, Ralph	1982	+ Templeton, Dink	1976
+ Bowerman, Bill	1981	+ Hillman, Harry	1976	Walker, LeRoy	1983
Bush, Jim	1987	+ Hurt, Edward	1975	+ Wilt, Fred	1981
+ Cromwell, Dean	1974	+ Hutsell, Wilbur	1977	+ Winter, Bud	1985
+ Doherty, Ken	1976	+ Jones, Thomas	1977	Wolfe, Vern	1996
+ Easton, Bill	1975	Jordan, Payton	1982	Wright, Stan	1993
+ Elliott, Jumbo	1981	+ Littlefield, Clyde	1981	+ Yancy, Joseph	1984
+ Giegengack, Bob	1978	+ Moakley, Jack	1988		

Contributors

+ Abramson, Jesse	1981	+ Ferris, Dan	1974	Nelson, Cordner	1988
Andersen, Roxanne	1991	+ Griffith, John	1979	+ Sullivan, James	1977
+ Bakjian, Andy	1986	+ Lebow, Fred	1994		
+ Brundage, Avery	1974	+ Nelson, Bert	1991		

VOLLEYBALL

Volleyball Hall of Fame

Established in 1985. **Address:** P.O. Box 1895, 444 Dwight St., Holyoke, MA 01041 **Telephone:** (413) 536-0926.

Eligibility: Nominees must have contributed at least seven years of outstanding service to volleyball within his/her respective category. Nominees in the player or official category must be retired for five years. A nominee may appear on the ballot a maximum of seven times at which point he/she can be nominated in the Veterans category an unlimited number of times. Voting is done by a panel of no more than 30 individuals from the greater volleyball community.

Class of 2000 (5): MEN—**Yuri Tchesnokov**; WOMEN—**Inna Ryskal** and **Takako Shirai**; COACH—**Hirofumi Daimatsu**; VETERAN—**Harold Wendt**.

Members are listed with year of induction; (+) indicates deceased members.

Men

Bright, Mike	1993	O'Hara, Michael	1989	Tchesnokov, Yuri	2000
Buck, Craig	1998	Rundle, Larry	1994	Velasco, Pedro "Pete"	1997
Dvorak, Dusty	1998	Selznick, Eugene	1988	Von Hagen, Ron	1992
Engen, Rolf	1991	Stanley, Jon	1992		
+ Haine, Thomas	1991	Timmons, Steve	1998		

Women

Bright, Patti	1996	+ Hyman, Flo	1988	Ward, Jane	1988
Dowdell, Patty	1994	Peppler, Mary Jo	1990	Weishoff, Paula	1998
Gregory, Kathy	1989	Ryskal, Inna	2000		
Green, Debbie	1995	Shirai, Takako	2000		

Coaches

Banachowski, Andy	1997	DeGroot, Col. Edward	1990	Selinger, Arie	1995
Beal, Douglas	1989	Dunphy, Marv	1994	Shondell, Donald	1996
Coleman, Dr. James	1992	Matsudaira, Yasutaka	1998	+ Wilson, Harry	1988
+ Daimatsu, Hirofumi	2000	Scates, Al	1993		

Veteran

+ Wendt, Harold	2000	+ Wortham, James	1999

Leaders

Baird, Bill	1998	+ Gibson, Leonard	1988	Monaco, Jr., Albert	1997
+ Fisher, Dr. George J.	1991	+ Koch, John	1994	+ Morgan, Dr. William G.	1985
+ Friermood, Dr. Harold T.	1986	+ Lindsey, Robert L.	1995	Peck, Wilber H.	1999

Officials

Davies, Glen	1989	Ignacio, Catalino	1991	Miller, C.L. (Bobb)	1995
+ Fish, Alton	1990	Kennedy, Merton H.	1992		

WOMEN

International Women's Sports Hall of Fame

Established in 1980 by the Women's Sports Foundation. **Address:** Women's Sports Foundation, Eisenhower Park, East Meadow, NY 11554. **Telephone:** (516) 542-4700.

Eligibility: Nominees' achievements and commitment to the development of women's sports must be internationally recognized. Athletes are elected in two categories—Pioneer (before 1960) and Contemporary (since 1960). Members are divided below by sport for the sake of easy reference; (*) indicates member inducted in Pioneer category. Coaching nominees must have coached at least 10 years.

Class of 1999 (4): CONTEMPORARY—**Sandra Haynie** (golf), **Joan Benoit Samuelson** (marathon). PIONEER—**Betty Jameson** (golf). COACH—**Tina Sloan Green** (Lacrosse).

Members are listed with year of induction; (+) indicates deceased members.

Alpine Skiing

Cranz, Christl*	1991
Golden Brosnihan, Diana	1997
Lawrence, Andrea Mead*	1983
Moser-Pröll, Annemarie	1982

Auto Racing

Guthrie, Janet	1980

Aviation

+ Coleman, Bessie*	1992
+ Earhart, Amelia*	1980
+ Marvingt, Marie*	1987

Badminton

Hashman, Judy Devlin*	1995

Baseball

Stone, Toni*	1993

Basketball

Meyers, Ann	1985
Miller, Cheryl	1991

Bowling

Ladewig, Marion*	1984

Cycling

Carpenter Phinney, Connie	1990

Diving

King, Micki	1983
McCormick, Pat*	1984
Riggin, Aileen*	1988

Equestrian

Hartel, Lis	1994

Fencing

Schacherer-Elek, Ilona*	1989

Figure Skating

Albright, Tenley*	1983
+ Blanchard, Theresa Weld*	1989
Fleming, Peggy	1981
Heiss Jenkins, Carol*	1992
+ Henie, Sonja*	1982
Protopopov, Ludmila	1992
Rodnina, Irena	1988
Scott-King, Barbara Ann*	1997

Golf

Berg, Patty*	1980
Carner, JoAnne	1987
Haynie, Sandra	1999
Hicks, Betty*	1995
Jameson, Betty*	1999
Mann, Carol	1982
Rawls, Betsy*	1986
Suggs, Louise*	1987
+ Vare, Glenna Collett*	1981
Whitworth, Kathy	1984
Wright, Mickey	1981

Golf/Track & Field

+ Zaharias, Babe Didrikson*	1980

Gymnastics

Caslavska, Vera	1991
Comaneci, Nadia	1990
Korbut, Olga	1982
Latynina, Larysa*	1985
Retton, Mary Lou	1993
Tourischeva, Lyudmila	1987

Shooting

Murdock, Margaret	1988

Softball

Joyce, Joan	1989

Speed Skating

+ Klein Outland, Kit*	1993
Young, Sheila	1981

Swimming

Caulkins, Tracy	1986
+ Chadwick, Florence*	1996
Curtis Cuneo, Ann*	1985
de Varona, Donna	1983
Ederle, Gertrude*	1980
Fraser, Dawn	1985
Holm, Eleanor*	1980
Meagher, Mary T.	1993
Meyer-Reyes, Debbie	1987

Tennis

+ Connolly, Maureen*	1987
+ Dod, Charlotte (Lottie)*	1986
Evert, Chris	1981

Golf (cont.)

Gibson, Althea*	1980
Goolagong Cawley, Evonne	1989
+ Hotchkiss Wightman, Hazel*	1986
King, Billie Jean	1980
+ Lenglen, Suzanne*	1984
Navratilova, Martina	1984
Osbourne du Pont, Margaret*	1998
+ Sears, Eleanora*	1984
Smith Court, Margaret	1986

Track & Field

Ashford, Evelyn	1997
Blankers-Koen, Fanny*	1982
Cheng, Chi	1994
Coachman Davis, Alice*	1991
+ Faggs Star, Aeriwentha Mae*	1996
+ Griffith Joyner, Florence	1998
Manning Mims, Madeline	1987
+ Rudolph, Wilma	1980
Samuelson, Joan Benoit	1999
+ Stephens, Helen*	1983
Strickland de la Hunty, Shirley*	1998
Szewinska, Irena	1992
Tyus, Wyomia	1981
Waitz, Grete	1995
White, Willye	1988

Volleyball

+ Hyman, Flo	1986

Water Skiing

McGuire, Willa Worthington*	1990

Orienteering

Kringstad, Annichen	1995

Coaches

Applebee, Constance	1991
Backus, Sharron	1993
Conradt, Judy	1995
Emery, Gail	1997
Green, Tina Sloan	1999
Grossfeld, Muriel	1991
Holum, Diana	1996
Jacket, Barbara	1995
+ Jackson, Nell	1990
Kanakogi, Rusty	1994
Summitt, Pat Head	1990
Van Derveer, Tara	1998
+ Wade, Margaret	1992

RETIRED NUMBERS

Major League Baseball

The New York Yankees have retired the most uniform numbers (14) in the major leagues; followed the Brooklyn/Los Angeles Dodgers (10), the St. Louis Cardinals (9), the Chicago White Sox and the Pittsburgh Pirates (8) and the New York/San Francisco Giants (7). **Jackie Robinson** had his #42 retired by Major League Baseball in 1997. Players who were already wearing the number were allowed to continue to do so. Los Angeles had already retired Robinson's number so he's only listed with the Dodgers below. **Nolan Ryan** has had his number retired by three teams—#34 by Texas and Houston and #30 by California. Five players and a manager have had their numbers retired by two teams: **Hank Aaron**—#44 by the Boston/Milwaukee/Atlanta Braves and the Milwaukee Brewers; **Rod Carew**—#29 by Minnesota and California; **Rollie Fingers**—#34 by Milwaukee and Oakland; **Carlton Fisk**—#27 by Boston and #72 by the Chicago White Sox; **Frank Robinson**—#20 by Cincinnati and Baltimore; **Casey Stengel**—#37 by the New York Yankees and New York Mets.

Numbers retired in 2000 (3) DETROIT—#23 worn by outfielder **Willie Horton** (1963-77 with Tigers); BOSTON—#27 worn by catcher **Carlton Fisk** (1969, 1971-80 with Red Sox); TAMPA BAY—#12 worn by third baseman **Wade Boggs** (1998-99 with Devil Rays).

American League

Two AL teams—the Seattle Mariners and the Toronto Blue Jays—have not retired any numbers. The Blue Jays have a "level of excellence" which includes Dave Steib (#11), George Bell (#37), and Cito Gaston (#43). All numbers have been used in recent years, however.

Anaheim Angels

11 Jim Fregosi
26 Gene Autry
29 Rod Carew
30 Nolan Ryan
50 Jimmie Reese

Baltimore Orioles

4 Earl Weaver
5 Brooks Robinson
20 Frank Robinson
22 Jim Palmer
33 Eddie Murray

Boston Red Sox

1 Bobby Doerr
4 Joe Cronin
8 Carl Yastrzemski
9 Ted Williams
27 Carlton Fisk

Chicago White Sox

2 Nellie Fox
3 Harold Baines
4 Luke Appling
9 Minnie Minoso
11 Luis Aparicio
16 Ted Lyons
19 Billy Pierce
72 Carlton Fisk

Cleveland Indians

3 Earl Averill
5 Lou Boudreau
14 Larry Doby
18 Mel Harder
19 Bob Feller
21 Bob Lemon

Detroit Tigers

2 Charlie Gehringer
5 Hank Greenberg
6 Al Kaline
16 Hal Newhouser
23 Willie Horton

Kansas City Royals

5 George Brett
10 Dick Howser
20 Frank White

Minnesota Twins

3 Harmon Killebrew
6 Tony Oliva
14 Kent Hrbek
29 Rod Carew
34 Kirby Puckett

New York Yankees

1 Billy Martin
3 Babe Ruth
4 Lou Gehrig
5 Joe DiMaggio
7 Mickey Mantle
8 Yogi Berra & Bill Dickey
9 Roger Maris
10 Phil Rizzuto
15 Thurman Munson
16 Whitey Ford
23 Don Mattingly
32 Elston Howard
37 Casey Stengel
44 Reggie Jackson

Oakland Athletics

27 Catfish Hunter
34 Rollie Fingers

Tampa Bay Devil Rays

12 Wade Boggs

Texas Rangers

34 Nolan Ryan

National League

Two NL teams—the Arizona Diamondbacks and Colorado Rockies—have not retired any numbers. San Francisco has honored former NY Giants Christy Mathewson and John McGraw even though they played before numbers were worn.

Atlanta Braves

3 Dale Murphy
21 Warren Spahn
35 Phil Niekro
41 Eddie Mathews
44 Hank Aaron

Chicago Cubs

14 Ernie Banks
26 Billy Williams

Cincinnati Reds

1 Fred Hutchinson
5 Johnny Bench
8 Joe Morgan
18 Ted Kluszewski
20 Frank Robinson

Florida Marlins

5 Carl Barger

Houston Astros

25 Jose Cruz
32 Jim Umbricht
33 Mike Scott
34 Nolan Ryan
40 Don Wilson

Los Angeles Dodgers

1 Pee Wee Reese
2 Tommy Lasorda
4 Duke Snider
19 Jim Gilliam
20 Don Sutton
24 Walter Alston
32 Sandy Koufax
39 Roy Campanella
42 Jackie Robinson
53 Don Drysdale

Milwaukee Brewers

4 Paul Molitor
19 Robin Yount
34 Rollie Fingers
44 Hank Aaron

Montreal Expos

8 Gary Carter
10 Rusty Staub
   & Andre Dawson

New York Mets

14 Gil Hodges
37 Casey Stengel
41 Tom Seaver

Philadelphia Phillies

1 Richie Ashburn
20 Mike Schmidt
32 Steve Carlton
36 Robin Roberts

Pittsburgh Pirates

1 Billy Meyer
4 Ralph Kiner
8 Willie Stargell
9 Bill Mazeroski
20 Pie Traynor
21 Roberto Clemente
33 Honus Wagner
40 Danny Murtaugh

St. Louis Cardinals

1 Ozzie Smith
2 Red Schoendienst
6 Stan Musial
9 Enos Slaughter
14 Ken Boyer
17 Dizzy Dean
20 Lou Brock
45 Bob Gibson
85 August (Gussie) Busch

San Diego Padres

6 Steve Garvey
35 Randy Jones

San Francisco Giants

3 Bill Terry
4 Mel Ott
11 Carl Hubbell
24 Willie Mays
27 Juan Marichal
30 Orlando Cepeda
44 Willie McCovey

Retired Numbers (Cont.)
National Basketball Association

Boston has retired the most numbers (20) in the NBA, followed by Portland (8); Detroit Pistons, Los Angeles Lakers, Milwaukee, New York Knicks and the KC/Sacramento Kings have (7); Cleveland, New Jersey, the Rochester/Cincinnati Royals and the Syracuse Nats/Philadelphia 76ers have (6). **Wilt Chamberlain** is the only player to have his number retired by three teams: #13 by the LA Lakers, Golden State and Philadelphia; Five players have had their numbers retired by two teams: **Kareem Abdul-Jabbar**—#33 by LA Lakers and Milwaukee; **Julius Erving**—#6 by Philadelphia and #32 by New Jersey; **Bob Lanier**—#16 by Detroit and Milwaukee; **Oscar Robertson**—#1 by Milwaukee and #14 by Sacramento; **Nate Thurmond**—#42 by Cleveland and Golden State.

Numbers retired in 1999-2000 (6): DETROIT—#4 worn by guard **Joe Dumars** (1985-99 with Pistons); CHARLOTTE—#13 worn by guard **Bobby Phills** (1997-00 with Hornets); CLEVELAND—#25 worn by guard **Mark Price** (1986-95 with Cavaliers); DALLAS—#22 worn by guard **Rolando Blackman** (1981-92 with Mavericks); GOLDEN STATE—#13 worn by center **Wilt Chamberlain** (1959-65 with Warriors); HOUSTON—#22 worn by guard **Clyde Drexler** (1995-98 with Rockets).

Eastern Conference

Three Eastern teams—the Miami Heat, Orlando Magic, and Toronto Raptors—have not retired any numbers.

Boston Celtics
1 Walter A. Brown
2 Red Auerbach
3 Dennis Johnson
6 Bill Russell
10 Jo Jo White
14 Bob Cousy
15 Tom Heinsohn
16 Tom (Satch) Sanders
17 John Havlicek
18 Dave Cowens
19 Don Nelson
21 Bill Sharman
22 Ed Macauley
23 Frank Ramsey
24 Sam Jones
25 K.C. Jones
32 Kevin McHale
33 Larry Bird
35 Reggie Lewis
00 Robert Parish
Loscy Jim Loscutoff
Radio mic Johnny Most

Atlanta Hawks
9 Bob Pettit
23 Lou Hudson

Charlotte Hornets
13 Bobby Phills

Chicago Bulls
4 Jerry Sloan
10 Bob Love
23 Michael Jordan

Cleveland Cavaliers
7 Bingo Smith
22 Larry Nance
25 Mark Price
34 Austin Carr
42 Nate Thurmond
43 Brad Daugherty

Detroit Pistons
2 Chuck Daly
4 Joe Dumars
11 Isiah Thomas
15 Vinnie Johnson
16 Bob Lanier
21 Dave Bing
40 Bill Laimbeer

Indiana Pacers
30 George McGinnis
34 Mel Daniels
35 Roger Brown

Milwaukee Bucks
1 Oscar Robertson
2 Junior Bridgeman
4 Sidney Moncrief
14 Jon McGlocklin
16 Bob Lanier
32 Brian Winters
33 Kareem Abdul-Jabbar

New York Knicks
10 Walt Frazier
12 Dick Barnett
15 Dick McGuire
    & Earl Monroe
19 Willis Reed
22 Dave DeBusschere
24 Bill Bradley
613 Red Holzman

New Jersey Nets
3 Drazen Petrovic
4 Wendell Ladner
23 John Williamson
25 Bill Melchionni
32 Julius Erving
52 Buck Williams

Philadelphia 76ers
6 Julius Erving
10 Maurice Cheeks
13 Wilt Chamberlain
15 Hal Greer
24 Bobby Jones
32 Billy Cunningham
P.A. mic Dave Zinkoff

Washington Wizards
11 Elvin Hayes
25 Gus Johnson
41 Wes Unseld

Western Conference

Three Western teams—the Los Angeles Clippers, Minnesota Timberwolves and Vancouver Grizzlies—have not retired any numbers.

Dallas Mavericks
15 Brad Davis
22 Rolando Blackman

Denver Nuggets
2 Alex English
33 David Thompson
40 Byron Beck
44 Dan Issel

Golden St. Warriors
13 Wilt Chamberlain
14 Tom Meschery
16 Al Attles
24 Rick Barry
42 Nate Thurmond

Houston Rockets
22 Clyde Drexler
23 Calvin Murphy
24 Moses Malone
45 Rudy Tomjanovich

Los Angeles Lakers
13 Wilt Chamberlain
22 Elgin Baylor
25 Gail Goodrich
32 Magic Johnson
33 Kareem Abdul-Jabbar
42 James Worthy
44 Jerry West

Phoenix Suns
5 Dick Van Arsdale
6 Walter Davis
33 Alvan Adams
42 Connie Hawkins
44 Paul Westphal

Portland Trail Blazers
1 Larry Weinberg
13 Dave Twardzik
15 Larry Steele
20 Maurice Lucas
32 Bill Walton
36 Lloyd Neal
45 Geoff Petrie
77 Jack Ramsay

Sacramento Kings
1 Nate Archibald
6 Fans ("Sixth Man")
11 Bob Davies
12 Maurice Stokes
14 Oscar Robertson
27 Jack Twyman
44 Sam Lacey

San Antonio Spurs
13 James Silas
44 George Gervin
00 Johnny Moore

Seattle SuperSonics
10 Nate McMillan
19 Lenny Wilkens
32 Fred Brown
43 Jack Sikma
Radio Mic Bob Blackburn

Utah Jazz
1 Frank Layden
7 Pete Maravich
35 Darrell Griffith
53 Mark Eaton

National Football League

The Chicago Bears have retired the most uniform numbers (13) in the NFL; followed by the New York Giants (10); the Dallas Texans/Kansas City Chiefs and San Francisco (8); the Baltimore-Indianapolis Colts and the Boston-New England Patriots (7); Detroit and Philadelphia (6); Cleveland (5). No player has ever had his number retired by more than one NFL team. The NFL has recently discouraged (though not eliminated) the practice of retiring numbers. As a result, the Green Bay Packers retired the jersey (but not the #92) of defensive end Reggie White in 1999. Nonetheless, Packers GM Ron Wolf announced that there are no plans to reissue the number.

Numbers retired in 2000 (3): MIAMI—#13 worn by quarterback **Dan Marino** (1983-99 with Dolphins); MINNESOTA—#22 worn by defensive back **Paul Krause** (1968-79 with Vikings), #70 worn by defensive lineman **Jim Marshall** (1961-79 with Vikings).

AFC

Five AFC teams—the Baltimore Ravens, Buffalo Bills, Oakland Raiders, Pittsburgh Steelers and Jacksonville Jaguars—have not retired any numbers.

Cincinnati Bengals
54 Bob Johnson

Cleveland Browns
14 Otto Graham
32 Jim Brown
45 Ernie Davis
46 Don Fleming
76 Lou Groza

Denver Broncos
7 John Elway
18 Frank Tripucka
44 Floyd Little

Indianapolis Colts
19 Johnny Unitas
22 Buddy Young
24 Lenny Moore
70 Art Donovan
77 Jim Parker
82 Raymond Berry
89 Gino Marchetti

Kansas City Chiefs
3 Jan Stenerud
16 Len Dawson
28 Abner Haynes
33 Stone Johnson
36 Mack Lee Hill
63 Willie Lanier
78 Bobby Bell
86 Buck Buchanan

Miami Dolphins
12 Bob Griese
13 Dan Marino

New England Patriots
14 Steve Grogan
20 Gino Cappelletti
40 Mike Haynes
57 Steve Nelson
73 John Hannah
79 Jim Hunt
89 Bob Dee

New York Jets
12 Joe Namath
13 Don Maynard

San Diego Chargers
14 Dan Fouts

Seattle Seahawks
12 Fans ("12th Man")
80 Steve Largent

Tennessee Titans
34 Earl Campbell
43 Jim Norton
63 Mike Munchak
65 Elvin Bethea

NFC

Atlanta, Dallas and the Carolina Panthers are the only NFC teams that haven't officially retired any numbers. The Falcons haven't issued uniforms #10 (Steve Bartkowski), #31 (William Andrews), #57 (Jeff Van Note and Clay Matthews), #60 (Tommy Nobis) and #78 (Mike Kenn) since those players retired. The Cowboys have a "Ring of Honor" at Texas Stadium that includes nine players and one coach—Tony Dorsett, Chuck Howley, Lee Roy Jordan, Tom Landry, Bob Lilly, Don Meredith, Don Perkins, Mel Renfro, Roger Staubach and Randy White.

Arizona Cardinals
8 Larry Wilson
77 Stan Mauldin
88 J.V. Cain
99 Marshall Goldberg

Chicago Bears
3 Bronko Nagurski
5 George McAfee
7 George Halas
28 Willie Galimore
34 Walter Payton
40 Gale Sayers
41 Brian Piccolo
42 Sid Luckman
51 Dick Butkus
56 Bill Hewitt
61 Bill George
66 Bulldog Turner
77 Red Grange

Detroit Lions
7 Dutch Clark
22 Bobby Layne
37 Doak Walker
56 Joe Schmidt
85 Chuck Hughes
88 Charlie Sanders

Green Bay Packers
3 Tony Canadeo
14 Don Hutson
15 Bart Starr
66 Ray Nitschke

Minnesota Vikings
10 Fran Tarkenton
22 Paul Krause
70 Jim Marshall
88 Alan Page

New Orleans Saints
31 Jim Taylor
81 Doug Atkins

New York Giants
1 Ray Flaherty
4 Tuffy Leemans
7 Mel Hein
11 Phil Simms
14 Y.A. Tittle
32 Al Blozis
40 Joe Morrison
42 Charlie Conerly
50 Ken Strong
56 Lawrence Taylor

Philadelphia Eagles
15 Steve Van Buren
40 Tom Brookshier
44 Pete Retzlaff
60 Chuck Bednarik
70 Al Wistert
99 Jerome Brown

St. Louis Rams
7 Bob Waterfield
29 Eric Dickerson
74 Merlin Olsen
78 Jackie Slater

San Francisco 49ers
12 John Brodie
16 Joe Montana
34 Joe Perry
37 Jimmy Johnson
39 Hugh McElhenny
70 Charlie Krueger
73 Leo Nomellini
87 Dwight Clark

Tampa Bay Bucs
63 Lee Roy Selmon

Wash. Redskins
33 Sammy Baugh

National Hockey League

The Boston Bruins and Montreal Canadiens have retired the most uniform numbers (7) in the NHL; followed by Detroit (6); Chicago and N.Y. Islanders (5); Buffalo, St. Louis and Philadelphia (4). Following his retirement in 1999, the NHL announced that the league would retire **Wayne Gretzky**'s #99. Two players have had their numbers retired by two teams: **Gordie Howe**—#9 by Detroit and Hartford; and **Bobby Hull**—#9 by Chicago and Winnipeg.

Numbers retired in 2000 (1): WASHINGTON—# 32 **Dale Hunter** (1987-99 with Capitals).

Eastern Conference

Five Eastern teams—the Atlanta Thrashers, Carolina Hurricanes, New Jersey Devils, Tampa Bay Lightning and Florida Panthers—have not retired any numbers. The Hartford Whalers had retired three numbers: #2 Rick Ley, #9 Gordie Howe and #19 John McKenzie.

Boston Bruins

2 Eddie Shore
3 Lionel Hitchman
4 Bobby Orr
5 Dit Clapper
7 Phil Esposito
9 John Bucyk
15 Milt Schmidt

Buffalo Sabres

2 Tim Horton
7 Rick Martin
11 Gilbert Perreault
14 Rene Robert

Montreal Canadiens

1 Jacques Plante
2 Doug Harvey
4 Jean Beliveau
7 Howie Morenz
9 Maurice Richard
10 Guy Lafleur
16 Henri Richard

New York Islanders

5 Denis Potvin
9 Clark Gilles
22 Mike Bossy
23 Bob Nystrom
31 Billy Smith

New York Rangers

1 Eddie Giacomin
7 Rod Gilbert

Ottawa Senators

8 Frank Finnigan

Philadelphia Flyers

1 Bernie Parent
4 Barry Ashbee
7 Bill Barber
16 Bobby Clarke

Pittsburgh Penguins

21 Michel Briere
66 Mario Lemieux

Toronto Maple Leafs

5 Bill Barilko
6 Ace Bailey

Washington Capitals

5 Rod Langway
7 Yvon Labre
32 Dale Hunter

Western Conference

Six Western teams—the Colorado Avalanche, Columbus Blue Jackets, Mighty Ducks of Anaheim, Minnesota Wild, Nashville Predators and San Jose Sharks —have not retired any numbers. Note, the Quebec Nordiques retired the numbers of J.C. Tremblay (3), Marc Tardiff (8) and Michel Goulet (16) but these numbers have been worn since the team moved to Colorado.

Calgary Flames

9 Lanny McDonald

Chicago Blackhawks

1 Glenn Hall
9 Bobby Hull
18 Denis Savard
21 Stan Mikita
35 Tony Esposito

Dallas Stars

7 Neal Broten
8 Bill Goldsworthy
19 Bill Masterton

Detroit Red Wings

1 Terry Sawchuk
6 Larry Aurie
7 Ted Lindsay
9 Gordie Howe
10 Alex Delvecchio
12 Sid Abel

Edmonton Oilers

3 Al Hamilton

Los Angeles Kings

16 Marcel Dionne
18 Dave Taylor
30 Rogie Vachon

Phoenix Coyotes

9 Bobby Hull
25 Thomas Steen

St. Louis Blues

3 Bob Gassoff
8 Barclay Plager
11 Brian Sutter
24 Bernie Federko

Vancouver Canucks

12 Stan Smyl

AWARDS

Associated Press Athletes of the Year

Selected annually by AP newspaper sports editors since 1931.

Male

Tiger Woods won his second of what could be many AP Athlete of the Year Awards in 1999. His season climaxed with a victory in the 1999 PGA Championship for his second career major win. Woods, the 1999 PGA Tour and PGA of America Player of the Year, as well as the world's top-ranked golfer, set a record with $6,616,585 in earnings with eight wins in 21 Tour events.

The Top 10 vote-getters (first place votes in parentheses): 1. **Tiger Woods**, golf (29), 144 pts; 2. **Lance Armstrong**, cycling (31), 130 pts; 3. **Pedro Martinez**, baseball (6), 45 pts; 4. **John Elway**, football (2), 21 pts; 5. **Ron Dayne**, college football (2), 20 pts; 6. **Andre Agassi**, tennis (2), 19 pts; 7. **Tim Duncan**, basketball (1), 17 pts; 8. **Payne Stewart**, golf (1), 11 pts; 9. **Sammy Sosa**, baseball (2) and **Peyton Manning**, football (1), 10 pts.

Multiple winners: Michael Jordan (3); Don Budge, Sandy Koufax, Carl Lewis, Joe Montana, Byron Nelson and Tiger Woods (2).

Year		Year		Year	
1931	**Pepper Martin**, baseball	1943	**Gunder Haegg**, track	1954	**Willie Mays**, baseball
1932	**Gene Sarazen**, golf	1944	**Byron Nelson**, golf	1955	**Hopalong Cassady**, col.
1933	**Carl Hubbell**, baseball	1945	**Byron Nelson**, golf		football
1934	**Dizzy Dean**, baseball	1946	**Glenn Davis**, college football	1956	**Mickey Mantle**, baseball
1935	**Joe Louis**, boxing	1947	**Johnny Lujack**, college	1957	**Ted Williams**, baseball
1936	**Jesse Owens**, track		football	1958	**Herb Elliott**, track
1937	**Don Budge**, tennis	1948	**Lou Boudreau**, baseball	1959	**Ingemar Johansson**, boxing
1938	**Don Budge**, tennis	1949	**Leon Hart**, college football	1960	**Rafer Johnson**, track
1939	**Nile Kinnick**, college football	1950	**Jim Konstanty**, baseball	1961	**Roger Maris**, baseball
1940	**Tom Harmon**, college football	1951	**Dick Kazmaier**, college	1962	**Maury Wills**, baseball
1941	**Joe DiMaggio**, baseball		football	1963	**Sandy Koufax**, baseball
1942	**Frank Sinkwich**, college	1952	**Bob Mathias**, track	1964	**Don Schollander**, swimming
	football	1953	**Ben Hogan**, golf	1965	**Sandy Koufax**, baseball

Year	Year	Year
1966 **Frank Robinson**, baseball	1978 **Ron Guidry**, baseball	1990 **Joe Montana**, pro football
1967 **Carl Yastrzemski**, baseball	1979 **Willie Stargell**, baseball	1991 **Michael Jordan**, pro basketball
1968 **Denny McLain**, baseball	1980 **U.S. Olympic hockey team**	1992 **Michael Jordan**, pro basketball
1969 **Tom Seaver**, baseball	1981 **John McEnroe**, tennis	1993 **Michael Jordan**, pro basketball
1970 **George Blanda**, pro football	1982 **Wayne Gretzky**, hockey	1994 **George Foreman**, boxing
1971 **Lee Trevino**, golf	1983 **Carl Lewis**, track	1995 **Cal Ripken Jr.**, baseball
1972 **Mark Spitz**, swimming	1984 **Carl Lewis**, track	1996 **Michael Johnson**, track
1973 **O.J. Simpson**, pro football	1985 **Dwight Gooden**, baseball	1997 **Tiger Woods**, golf
1974 **Muhammad Ali**, boxing	1986 **Larry Bird**, pro basketball	1998 **Mark McGwire**, baseball
1975 **Fred Lynn**, baseball	1987 **Ben Johnson**, track	1999 **Tiger Woods**, golf
1976 **Bruce Jenner**, track	1988 **Orel Hershiser**, baseball	
1977 **Steve Cauthen**, horse racing	1989 **Joe Montana**, pro football	

Female

The U.S. Women's Soccer Team captured the nation's attention during the summer of 1999. Their overtime, 5-4 shoot-out win over China in the championship game of the 1999 Women's World Cup at the Rose Bowl culminated with a shirtless Brandi Chastain and her teammates celebrating in front of 90,185 roaring fans, the largest crowd in women's soccer history.

The Top 10 vote-getters (first place votes in parentheses): 1. **U.S. Soccer Team** (55), 179 points; 2. **Cynthia Cooper**, basketball (1), 38 pts; 3. **Mia Hamm**, soccer (9), 37 pts; 4. **Serena Williams**, tennis (2), 34 pts; 5. **Marion Jones**, track and field (2), 31 pts; 6. **Steffi Graf**, tennis (3), 28 pts; 7. **Julie Inkster**, golf (1), 27 pts; 8. **Se Ri Pak**, golf (2), 16 pts; 9. **Martina Hingis**, tennis, and **Chamique Holdsclaw**, basketball, 15 pts.

Multiple winners: Babe Didrikson Zaharias (6); Chris Evert (4); Patty Berg and Maureen Connolly (3); Tracy Austin, Althea Gibson, Billie Jean King, Nancy Lopez, Alice Marble, Martina Navratilova, Wilma Rudolph, Monica Seles, Kathy Whitworth and Mickey Wright (2).

Year	Year	Year
1931 **Helene Madison**, swimming	1954 **Babe Didrikson Zaharias**, golf	1977 **Chris Evert**, tennis
1932 **Babe Didrikson**, track	1955 **Patty Berg**, golf	1978 **Nancy Lopez**, golf
1933 **Helen Jacobs**, tennis	1956 **Pat McCormick**, diving	1979 **Tracy Austin**, tennis
1934 **Virginia Van Wie**, golf	1957 **Althea Gibson**, tennis	1980 **Chris Evert Lloyd**, tennis
1935 **Helen Wills Moody**, tennis	1958 **Althea Gibson**, tennis	1981 **Tracy Austin**, tennis
1936 **Helen Stephens**, track	1959 **Maria Bueno**, tennis	1982 **Mary Decker Tabb**, track
1937 **Katherine Rawls**, swimming	1960 **Wilma Rudolph**, track	1983 **Martina Navratilova**, tennis
1938 **Patty Berg**, golf	1961 **Wilma Rudolph**, track	1984 **Mary Lou Retton**, gymnastics
1939 **Alice Marble**, tennis	1962 **Dawn Fraser**, swimming	1985 **Nancy Lopez**, golf
1940 **Alice Marble**, tennis	1963 **Mickey Wright**, golf	1986 **Martina Navratilova**, tennis
1941 **Betty Hicks Newell**, golf	1964 **Mickey Wright**, golf	1987 **Jackie Joyner-Kersee**, track
1942 **Gloria Callen**, swimming	1965 **Kathy Whitworth**, golf	1988 **Florence Griffith Joyner**, track
1943 **Patty Berg**, golf	1966 **Kathy Whitworth**, golf	1989 **Steffi Graf**, tennis
1944 **Ann Curtis**, swimming	1967 **Billie Jean King**, tennis	1990 **Beth Daniel**, golf
1945 **Babe Didrikson Zaharias**, golf	1968 **Peggy Fleming**, skating	1991 **Monica Seles**, tennis
1946 **Babe Didrikson Zaharias**, golf	1969 **Debbie Meyer**, swimming	1992 **Monica Seles**, tennis
1947 **Babe Didrikson Zaharias**, golf	1970 **Chi Cheng**, track	1993 **Sheryl Swoopes**, basketball
1948 **Fanny Blankers-Koen**, track	1971 **Evonne Goolagong**, tennis	1994 **Bonnie Blair**, speed skating
1949 **Marlene Bauer**, golf	1972 **Olga Korbut**, gymnastics	1995 **Rebecca Lobo**, col. basketball
1950 **Babe Didrikson Zaharias**, golf	1973 **Billie Jean King**, tennis	1996 **Amy Van Dyken**, swimming
1951 **Maureen Connolly**, tennis	1974 **Chris Evert**, tennis	1997 **Martina Hingis**, tennis
1952 **Maureen Connolly**, tennis	1975 **Chris Evert**, tennis	1998 **Se Ri Pak**, golf
1953 **Maureen Connolly**, tennis	1976 **Nadia Comaneci**, gymnastics	1999 **U.S. Soccer Team**

UPI International Athletes of the Year

Selected annually by United Press International's European newspaper sports editors from 1974-95.

Male

Multiple winners: Sebastian Coe, Alberto Juantorena and Carl Lewis (2).

Year	Year	Year
1974 **Muhammad Ali**, boxing	1982 **Daley Thompson**, track	1990 **Stefan Edberg**, tennis
1975 **Joao Oliveira**, track	1983 **Carl Lewis**, track	1991 **Sergei Bubka**, track
1976 **Alberto Juantorena**, track	1984 **Carl Lewis**, track	1992 **Kevin Young**, track
1977 **Alberto Juantorena**, track	1985 **Steve Cram**, track	1993 **Miguel Indurain**, cycling
1978 **Henry Rono**, track	1986 **Diego Maradona**, soccer	1994 **Johan Olav Koss**, speed skating
1979 **Sebastian Coe**, track	1987 **Ben Johnson**, track	
1980 **Eric Heiden**, speed skating	1988 **Matt Biondi**, swimming	1995 **Jonathan Edwards**, track
1981 **Sebastian Coe**, track	1989 **Boris Becker**, tennis	1996 discontinued

Female

Multiple winners: Nadia Comaneci, Steffi Graf, Marita Koch and Monica Seles (2).

Year	Year	Year
1974 **Irena Szewinska**, track	1978 **Tracy Caulkins**, swimming	1982 **Marita Koch**, track
1975 **Nadia Comaneci**, gymnastics	1979 **Marita Koch**, track	1983 **Jarmila Kratochvilova**, track
1976 **Nadia Comaneci**, gymnastics	1980 **Hanni Wenzel**, alpine skiing	1984 **Martina Navratilova**, tennis
1977 **Rosie Ackermann**, track	1981 **Chris Evert Lloyd**, tennis	1985 **Mary Decker Slaney**, track

Awards (Cont.)

Year		Year		Year	
1986	**Heike Drechsler**, track	1990	**Merlene Ottey**, track	1994	**Le Jingyi**, swimming
1987	**Steffi Graf**, tennis	1991	**Monica Seles**, tennis	1995	**Gwen Torrence**, track
1988	**Florence Griffith Joyner**, track	1992	**Monica Seles**, tennis	1996	discontinued
1989	**Steffi Graf**, tennis	1993	**Wang Junxia**, track		

Jesse Owens International Trophy

Presented annually by the International Amateur Athletic Association since 1981 and selected by a worldwide panel of electors. The Jesse Owens International Trophy is named after the late American Olympic champion, who won four gold medals at the 1936 Summer Games in Berlin.

Year		Year		Year	
1981	**Eric Heiden**, speed skating	1988	**Ben Johnson**, track	1995	**Johan Olva Koss**, speed skating
1982	**Sebastian Coe**, track	1990	**Roger Kingdom**, track	1996	**Michael Johnson**, track
1983	**Mary Decker**, track	1991	**Greg LeMond**, cycling	1997	**Michael Johnson**, track
1984	**Edwin Moses**, track	1992	**Mike Powell**, track	1998	**Haile Gebrselassie**, track
1985	**Carl Lewis**, track	1993	**Vitaly Scherbo**, gymnastics	1999	**Marion Jones**, track
1986	**Said Aouita**, track	1994	**Wang Junxia**, track	2000	**Lance Armstrong**, cycling
1987	**Greg Louganis**, diving				

James E. Sullivan Memorial Award

Presented annually by the Amateur Athletic Union since 1930. The Sullivan Award is named after the former AAU president and given to the athlete who, "by his or her performance, example and influence as an amateur, has done the most during the year to advance the cause of sportsmanship." An athlete cannot win the award more than once.

For the first time in its 70-year history two people shared the Sullivan Award in 1999. The winners were college basketball players and twin sisters **Coco Miller** and **Kelly Miller** from the University of Georgia. The Miller sisters were both named All-America and helped lead the Lady Bulldogs to a school record 32 wins and the 1999 Women's Final Four before losing to Duke in the national semifinals. The five finalists are listed alphabetically: **Ron Dayne**, football; **Kelly and Coco Miller**, basketball; **Stephen Neal**, wrestling; **Stacey Nuveman**, softball; **Mark Ruiz**, diving. Vote totals were not released.

Year		Year		Year	
1930	**Bobby Jones**, golf	1954	**Mal Whitfield**, track	1978	**Tracy Caulkins**, swimming
1931	**Barney Berlinger**, track	1955	**Harrison Dillard**, track	1979	**Kurt Thomas**, gymnastics
1932	**Jim Bausch**, track	1956	**Pat McCormick**, diving	1980	**Eric Heiden**, speed skating
1933	**Glenn Cunningham**, track	1957	**Bobby Morrow**, track	1981	**Carl Lewis**, track
1934	**Bill Bonthron**, track	1958	**Glenn Davis**, track	1982	**Mary Decker**, track
1935	**Lawson Little**, golf	1959	**Parry O'Brien**, track	1983	**Edwin Moses**, track
1936	**Glenn Morris**, track	1960	**Rafer Johnson**, track	1984	**Greg Louganis**, diving
1937	**Don Budge**, tennis	1961	**Wilma Rudolph**, track	1985	**Joan B. Samuelson**, track
1938	**Don Lash**, track	1962	**Jim Beatty**, track	1986	**Jackie Joyner-Kersee**, track
1939	**Joe Burk**, rowing	1963	**John Pennel**, track	1987	**Jim Abbott**, baseball
1940	**Greg Rice**, track	1964	**Don Schollander**, swimming	1988	**Florence Griffith Joyner**, track
1941	**Leslie MacMitchell**, track	1965	**Bill Bradley**, basketball	1989	**Janet Evans**, swimming
1942	**Cornelius Warmerdam**, track	1966	**Jim Ryun**, track	1990	**John Smith**, wrestling
1943	**Gilbert Dodds**, track	1967	**Randy Matson**, track	1991	**Mike Powell**, track
1944	**Ann Curtis**, swimming	1968	**Debbie Meyer**, swimming	1992	**Bonnie Blair**, speed skating
1945	**Doc Blanchard**, football	1969	**Bill Toomey**, track	1993	**Charlie Ward**, football
1946	**Arnold Tucker**, football	1970	**John Kinsella**, swimming	1994	**Dan Jansen**, speed skating
1947	**John B. Kelly, Jr.**, rowing	1971	**Mark Spitz**, swimming	1995	**Bruce Baumgartner**, wrestling
1948	**Bob Mathias**, track	1972	**Frank Shorter**, track	1996	**Michael Johnson**, track
1949	**Dick Button**, skating	1973	**Bill Walton**, basketball	1997	**Peyton Manning**, football
1950	**Fred Wilt**, track	1974	**Rich Wohlhuter**, track	1998	**Chamique Holdsclaw**, basketball
1951	**Bob Richards**, track	1975	**Tim Shaw**, swimming		
1952	**Horace Ashenfelter**, track	1976	**Bruce Jenner**, track	1999	**Coco and Kelly Miller**, basketball
1953	**Sammy Lee**, diving	1977	**John Naber**, swimming		

USOC Sportsman & Sportswoman of the Year

To the outstanding overall male and female athletes from within the U.S. Olympic Committee member organizations. Winners are chosen from nominees of the national governing bodies for Olympic and Pan American Games and affiliated organizations. Voting is done by members of the national media, USOC board of directors and Athletes' Advisory Council.

Sportsman

Multiple winners: Eric Heiden and Michael Johnson (3); Matt Biondi and Greg Louganis (2).

Year		Year		Year	
1974	**Jim Bolding**, track	1983	**Rick McKinney**, archery	1992	**Pablo Morales**, swimming
1975	**Clint Jackson**, boxing	1984	**Edwin Moses**, track	1993	**Michael Johnson**, track
1976	**John Naber**, swimming	1985	**Willie Banks**, track	1994	**Dan Jansen**, speed skating
1977	**Eric Heiden**, speed skating	1986	**Matt Biondi**, swimming	1995	**Michael Johnson**, track
1978	**Bruce Davidson**, equestrian	1987	**Greg Louganis**, diving	1996	**Michael Johnson**, track
1979	**Eric Heiden**, speed skating	1988	**Matt Biondi**, swimming	1997	**Pete Sampras**, tennis
1980	**Eric Heiden**, speed skating	1989	**Roger Kingdom**, track	1998	**Jonny Moseley**, skiing
1981	**Scott Hamilton**, fig. skating	1990	**John Smith**, wrestling	1999	**Lance Armstrong**, cycling
1982	**Greg Louganis**, diving	1991	**Carl Lewis**, track		

Sportswoman

Multiple winners: Bonnie Blair, Tracy Caulkins, Jackie Joyner-Kersee, Picabo Street and Sheila Young Ochowicz (2).

Year		Year		Year	
1974	**Shirley Babashoff**, swimming	1982	**Melanie Smith**, equestrian	1991	**Kim Zmeskal**, gymnastics
1975	**Kathy Heddy**, swimming	1983	**Tamara McKinney**, skiing	1992	**Bonnie Blair**, speed skating
1976	**Sheila Young**, speedskating	1984	**Tracy Caulkins**, swimming	1993	**Gail Devers**, track
1977	**Linda Fratianne**, fig. skating	1985	**Mary Decker Slaney**, track	1994	**Bonnie Blair**, speed skating
1978	**Tracy Caulkins**, swimming	1986	**Jackie Joyner-Kersee**, track	1995	**Picabo Street**, skiing
1979	**Sippy Woodhead**, swimming	1987	**Jackie Joyner-Kersee**, track	1996	**Amy Van Dyken**, swimming
1980	**Beth Heiden**, speed skating	1988	**Florence Griffith Joyner**, track	1997	**Tara Lipinski**, figure skating
1981	**Sheila Ochowicz**, speed skating & cycling	1989	**Janet Evans**, swimming	1998	**Picabo Street**, skiing
		1990	**Lynn Jennings**, track	1999	**Jenny Thompson**, swimming

Honda Broderick Cup

To the outstanding collegiate woman athlete of the year in NCAA competition. Winner is chosen from nominees in each of the NCAA's 10 competitive sports. Final voting is done by member athletic directors. Award is named after founder and sportswear manufacturer Thomas Broderick.

Multiple winner: Tracy Caulkins (2).

Year		Year		
1977	**Lucy Harris**, Delta St ....basketball	1989	**Vicki Huber**, Villanova ....track
1978	**Ann Meyers**, UCLA ....basketball	1990	**Suzy Favor**, Wisconsin....................track
1979	**Nancy Lieberman**, Old Dominion .....basketball	1991	**Dawn Staley**, Virginia................basketball
1980	**Julie Shea**, N.C. State ....track & field	1992	**Missy Marlowe**, Utah ....gymnastics
1981	**Jill Sterkel**, Texas ....swimming	1993	**Lisa Fernandez**, UCLA..................softball
1982	**Tracy Caulkins**, Florida ....swimming	1994	**Mia Hamm**, North Carolina ....soccer
1983	**Deitre Collins**, Hawaii ....volleyball	1995	**Rebecca Lobo**, UConn................basketball
1984	**Tracy Caulkins**, Florida ....swimming & **Cheryl Miller**, USC.................basketball	1996	**Jennifer Rizzotti**, UConn ....basketball
		1997	**Cindy Daws**, Notre Dame ....soccer
1985	**Jackie Joyner**, UCLA................track & field	1998	**Chamique Holdsclaw**, Tennessee ......basketball
1986	**Kamie Ethridge**, Texas ....basketball	1999	**Misty May**, Long Beach St..............volleyball
1987	**Mary T. Meagher**, California...........swimming	2000	**Cristina Teuscher**, Columbia ....swimming
1988	**Teresa Weatherspoon**, La. Tech ....basketball		

Flo Hyman Award

Presented annually since 1987 by the Women's Sports Foundation for "exemplifying dignity, spirit and commitment to excellence" and named in honor of the late captain of the 1984 U.S. Women's Volleyball team. Voting by WSF members.

Year		Year		Year	
1987	**Martina Navratilova**, tennis	1992	**Nancy Lopez**, golf	1997	**Billie Jean King**, tennis
1988	**Jackie Joyner-Kersee**, track	1993	**Lynette Woodward**, basketball	1998	**Nadia Comaneci**, gymnastics
1989	**Evelyn Ashford**, track	1994	**Patty Sheehan**, golf	1999	**Bonnie Blair**, speed skating
1990	**Chris Evert**, tennis	1995	**Mary Lou Retton**, gymnastics	2000	**Monica Seles**, tennis
1991	**Diana Golden**, skiing	1996	**Donna de Varona**, swimming		

ESPY Awards

The ESPY Awards, which represent the convergence of the sports and entertainment communities, were created by ESPN in 1993 and are given for Excellence in Sports Performance in more than 30 categories. ESPYs are awarded by a panel of sports executives, journalists and retired athletes whose decisions are based on the performances of the nominees during the year preceding the awards ceremony. Note that not all categories are listed below.

Breakthrough Athlete of the Year

1993	Gary Sheffield, San Diego Padres
1994	Mike Piazza, Los Angeles Dodgers
1995	Jeff Bagwell, Houston Astros
1996	Hideo Nomo, Los Angeles Dodgers
1997	Tiger Woods, golf
1998	Nomar Garciaparra, Boston Red Sox
1999	Randy Moss, Minnesota Vikings
2000	Kurt Warner, St. Louis Rams

Comeback Athlete of the Year

1993	Dave Winfield, Toronto Blue Jays
1994	Mario Lemieux, Pittsburgh Penguins
1995	Dan Marino, Miami Dolphins
1996	Michael Jordan, Chicago Bulls
1997	Evander Holyfield, boxer
1998	Roger Clemens, Toronto Blue Jays
1999	Eric Davis, Baltimore Orioles
2000	Lance Armstrong, cycling

Coach/Manager of the Year

1993	Jimmy Johnson, Dallas Cowboys
1994	Jimmy Johnson, Dallas Cowboys
1995	George Siefert, San Francisco 49ers
1996	Gary Barnett, Northwestern
1997	Joe Torre, New York Yankees
1998	Jim Leyland, Florida Marlins
1999	Joe Torre, New York Yankees
2000	Joe Torre, New York Yankees

Outstanding Female Athlete of the Year

1993	Monica Seles, tennis
1994	Julie Krone, jockey
1995	Bonnie Blair, speed skater
1996	Rebecca Lobo, basketball
1997	Amy Van Dyken, swimming
1998	Mia Hamm, soccer
1999	Chamique Holdsclaw, college basketball
2000	Mia Hamm, soccer

Awards (Cont.)

Outstanding Male Athlete of the Year

1993 Michael Jordan, Chicago Bulls
1994 Barry Bonds, San Francisco Giants
1995 Steve Young, San Francisco 49ers
1996 Cal Ripken, Baltimore Orioles
1997 Michael Johnson, Olympic sprinter
1998 Tiger Woods, golf
1999 Mark McGwire, St. Louis Cardinals
2000 Tiger Woods, golf

Outstanding Performance Under Pressure

1993 Christian Laettner, Duke
1994 Joe Carter, Toronto Blue Jays
1995 Mark Messier, New York Rangers
1996 Martin Broduer, New Jersey Devils
1997 Kerri Strug, Olympic gymnast
1998 Terrell Davis, Denver Broncos
1999 Mark O'Meara, golf
2000 Not Awarded

Outstanding Team

1993 Dallas Cowboys
1994 Toronto Blue Jays
1995 New York Rangers
1996 UConn women's hoops
1997 New York Yankees
1998 Denver Broncos
1999 New York Yankees
2000 U.S. Women's World Cup Soccer Team

Outstanding Baseball Performer of the Year

1993 Dennis Eckersley, Oakland A's
1994 Barry Bonds, San Francisco Giants
1995 Jeff Bagwell, Houston Astros
1996 Greg Maddux, Atlanta Braves
1997 Ken Caminiti, San Diego Padres
1998 Larry Walker, Colorado Rockies
1999 Mark McGwire, St. Louis Cardinals
2000 Pedro Martinez, Boston Red Sox

Outstanding Pro Football Performer of the Year

1993 Emmitt Smith, Dallas Cowboys
1994 Emmitt Smith, Dallas Cowboys
1995 Barry Sanders, Detroit Lions
1996 Brett Favre, Green Bay Packers
1997 Brett Favre, Green Bay Packers
1998 Barry Sanders, Detroit Lions
1999 Terrell Davis, Denver Broncos
2000 Kurt Warner, St. Louis Rams

Outstanding Pro Basketball Performer of the Year

1993 Michael Jordan, Chicago Bulls
1994 Charles Barkley, Phoenix Suns
1995 Hakeem Olajuwon, Houston Rockets
1996 Hakeem Olajuwon, Houston Rockets
1997 Michael Jordan, Chicago Bulls
1998 Michael Jordan, Chicago Bulls
1999 Michael Jordan, Chicago Bulls
2000 Tim Duncan, San Antonio Spurs

Outstanding Women's Pro Basketball Performer of the Year

1998 Cynthia Cooper, Houston Comets
1999 Cynthia Cooper, Houston Comets
2000 Cynthia Cooper, Houston Comets

Outstanding Pro Hockey Performer of the Year

1993 Mario Lemieux, Pittsburgh Penguins
1994 Mario Lemieux, Pittsburgh Penguins
1995 Mark Messier, New York Rangers
1996 Eric Lindros, Philadelphia Flyers
1997 Joe Sakic, Colorado Avalanche
1998 Mario Lemieux, Pittsburgh Penguins
1999 Dominik Hasek, Buffalo Sabres
2000 Dominik Hasek, Buffalo Sabres

Outstanding College Football Performer of the Year

1993 Garrison Hearst, Georgia
1994 Charlie Ward, Florida State
1995 Rashaan Salaam, Colorado
1996 Eddie George, Ohio State
1997 Danny Wuerffel, Florida
1998 Peyton Manning, Tennessee
1999 Ricky Williams, Texas
2000 Michael Vick, Virginia Tech

Outstanding College Basketball Performer of the Year

1993 Christian Laettner, Duke
1994 Bobby Hurley, Duke
1995 Grant Hill, Duke
1996 Ed O'Bannon, UCLA
1997 Tim Duncan, Wake Forest
1998 Keith Van Horn, Utah
1999 Antawn Jamison, North Carolina
2000 Elton Brand, Duke

Outstanding Women's College Hoops Performer of the Year

1993 Dawn Staley, Virginia
1994 Sheryl Swoopes, Texas Tech
1995 Charlotte Smith, North Carolina
1996 Rebecca Lobo, Connecticut
1997 Saudia Roundtree, Georgia
1998 Chamique Holdsclaw, Tennessee
1999 Chamique Holdsclaw, Tennessee
2000 Chamique Holdsclaw, Tennessee

Outstanding Men's Tennis Performer of the Year

1993 Jim Courier
1994 Pete Sampras
1995 Pete Sampras
1996 Pete Sampras
1997 Pete Sampras
1998 Pete Sampras
1999 Pete Sampras
2000 Andre Agassi

Outstanding Women's Tennis Performer of the Year

1993 Monica Seles
1994 Steffi Graf
1995 Aranxta Sanchez-Vicario
1996 Steffi Graf
1997 Steffi Graf
1998 Martina Hingis
1999 Lindsay Davenport
2000 Lindsay Davenport

Outstanding Men's Golf Performer of the Year

1993	Fred Couples
1994	Nick Price
1995	Nick Price
1996	Corey Pavin
1997	Tom Lehman
1998	Tiger Woods
1999	Mark O'Meara
2000	Tiger Woods

Outstanding Women's Golf Performer of the Year

1993	Dottie Monroe
1994	Betsy King
1995	Laura Davies
1996	Annika Sorenstam
1997	Karrie Webb
1998	Annika Sorenstam
1999	Annika Sorenstam
2000	Julie Inkster

Outstanding Jockey of the Year

1994	Mike Smith
1995	Chris McCarron
1996	Jerry Bailey
1997	Jerry Bailey
1998	Gary Stevens
1999	Kent Desormeaux
2000	Chris Antley

Outstanding Bowling Performer of the Year

1995	Norm Duke
1996	Mike Aulby
1997	Bob Learn Jr.
1998	Walter Ray Williams Jr.
1999	Walter Ray Williams Jr.
2000	Parker Bohn III

Outstanding Auto Racing Performer of the Year

1993	Nigel Mansell	1997	Jimmy Vasser
1994	Nigel Mansell	1998	Jeff Gordon
1995	Al Unser Jr.	1999	Jeff Gordon
1996	Jeff Gordon	2000	Dale Jarrett

Outstanding Men's Track Performer of the Year

1993	Kevin Young
1994	Michael Johnson
1995	Dennis Mitchell
1996	Michael Johnson
1997	Michael Johnson
1998	Wilson Kipketer
1999	Maurice Greene
2000	Michael Johnson

Outstanding Women's Track Performer of the Year

1993	Evelyn Ashford
1994	Gail Devers
1995	Gwen Torrence
1996	Kim Batten
1997	Marie-Jose Perec
1998	Marion Jones
1999	Marion Jones
2000	Marion Jones

Outstanding Boxing Performer of the Year

1993	Riddick Bowe
1994	Evander Holyfield
1995	George Foreman
1996	Roy Jones Jr.
1997	Evander Holyfield
1998	Evander Holyfield
1999	Oscar De La Hoya
2000	Roy Jones Jr.

Game of the Year

1996	AFC championship between Colts and Steelers
1997	Ohio State edges Arizona State in the Rose Bowl
1998	Super Bowl XXXII, Broncos over Packers
1999	Not Awarded
2000	Not Awarded

Arthur Ashe Award for Courage

Presented since 1993 on the annual ESPN "ESPYs" telecast. Given to a member of the sports community who has exemplified the same courage, spirit and determination to help others despite personal hardship that characterized Arthur Ashe, the late tennis champion and humanitarian. Voting done by select 26-member committee of media and sports personalities.

Year		Year		Year	
1993	**Jim Valvano**, basketball	1996	**Loretta Clairborne**, special	1998	**Dean Smith**, college basketball
1994	**Steve Palermo**, baseball		olympics	1999	**Billie Jean King**, tennis
1995	**Howard Cosell**, TV & radio	1997	**Muhammad Ali**, boxing	2000	**Dave Sanders**, Columbine H.S. coach

Presidential Medal of Freedom

Since President John F. Kennedy established the Medal of Freedom as America's highest civilian honor in 1963, only nine sports figures have won the award. Note that (*) indicates the presentation was made posthumously.

Year		President	Year		President
1963	**Bob Kiphuth**, swimming	Kennedy	1986	**Earl (Red) Blaik**, football	Reagan
1976	**Jesse Owens**, track & field	Ford	1991	**Ted Williams**, baseball	Bush
1977	**Joe DiMaggio**, baseball	Ford	1992	**Richard Petty**, auto racing	Bush
1983	**Paul (Bear) Bryant***, football	Reagan	1993	**Arthur Ashe***, tennis	Clinton
1984	**Jackie Robinson***, baseball	Reagan			

Awards (Cont.)
The Hickok Belt

Officially known as the S. Rae Hickok Professional Athlete of the Year Award and presented by the Kickik Manufacturing Co. of Arlington, Texas, from 1950-76. The trophy was a large belt of gold, diamonds and other jewels, reportedly worth $30,000 in 1976, the last year it was handed out. Voting was done by 270 newspaper sports editors from around the country.

Multiple winner: Sandy Koufax (2).

Year	Year	Year
1950 **Phil Rizzuto**, baseball	1960 **Arnold Palmer**, golf	1970 **Brooks Robinson**, baseball
1951 **Allie Reynolds**, baseball	1961 **Roger Maris**, baseball	1971 **Lee Trevino**, golf
1952 **Rocky Marciano**, boxing	1962 **Maury Wills**, baseball	1972 **Steve Carlton**, baseball
1953 **Ben Hogan**, golf	1963 **Sandy Koufax**, baseball	1973 **O.J. Simpson**, football
1954 **Willie Mays**, baseball	1964 **Jim Brown**, football	1974 **Muhammad Ali**, boxing
1955 **Otto Graham**, football	1965 **Sandy Koufax**, baseball	1975 **Pete Rose**, baseball
1956 **Mickey Mantle**, baseball	1966 **Frank Robinson**, baseball	1976 **Ken Stabler**, football
1957 **Carmen Basilio**, boxing	1967 **Carl Yastrzemski**, baseball	1977 Discontinued
1958 **Bob Turley**, baseball	1968 **Joe Namath**, football	
1959 **Ingemar Johansson**, boxing	1969 **Tom Seaver**, baseball	

ABC's "Wide World of Sports" Athlete of the Year

Selected annually by the producers of ABC Sports since 1962.

Multiple winner: Greg LeMond (2).

Year	Year	Year
1962 **Jim Beatty**, track	1975 **Jack Nicklaus**, golf	1989 **Greg LeMond**, cycling
1963 **Valery Brumel**, track	1976 **Nadia Comaneci**, gymnastics	1990 **Greg LeMond**, cycling
1964 **Don Schollander**, swimming	1977 **Steve Cauthen**, horse racing	1991 **Carl Lewis**, track
1965 **Jim Clark**, auto racing	1978 **Ron Guidry**, baseball	& **Kim Zmeskal**, gymnastics
1966 **Jim Ryun**, track	1979 **Willie Stargell**, baseball	1992 **Bonnie Blair**, speed skating
1967 **Peggy Fleming**, figure skating	1980 **U.S. Olympic hockey team**	1993 **Evander Holyfield**, boxing
1968 **Bill Toomey**, track	1981 **Sugar Ray Leonard**, boxing	1994 **Al Unser Jr.**, auto racing
1969 **Mario Andretti**, auto racing	1982 **Wayne Gretzky**, hockey	1995 **Miguel Induráin**, cycling
1970 **Willis Reed**, basketball	1983 **Australia II**, yachting	1996 **Michael Johnson**, track
1971 **Lee Trevino**, golf	1984 **Edwin Moses**, track	1997 **Tiger Woods**, golf
1972 **Olga Korbut**, gymnastics	1985 **Pete Rose**, baseball	1998 **Mark McGwire**, baseball
1973 **O.J. Simpson**, football	1986 **Debi Thomas**, figure skating	1999 **Lance Armstrong**, cycling
& **Jackie Stewart**, auto racing	1987 **Dennis Conner**, yachting	
1974 **Muhammad Ali**, boxing	1988 **Greg Louganis**, diving	

The Sporting News Sportsman of the Year

Selected annually by the editors of *The Sporting News* since 1968. 'Man of the Year' changed to 'Sportsman' of the Year in 1993.

Multiple Winner: Mark McGwire (2).

Year	Year	Year
1968 **Denny McLain**, baseball	1980 **George Brett**, baseball	1992 **Mike Krzyzewski**, col. bask.
1969 **Tom Seaver**, baseball	1981 **Wayne Gretzky**, hockey	1993 **Cito Gaston**
1970 **John Wooden**, basketball	1982 **Whitey Herzog**, baseball	& **Pat Gillick**, baseball
1971 **Lee Trevino**, golf	1983 **Bowie Kuhn**, baseball	1994 **Emmitt Smith**, pro football
1972 **Charles O. Finley**, baseball	1984 **Peter Ueberroth**, LA Olympics	1995 **Cal Ripken Jr.**, baseball
1973 **O.J. Simpson**, pro football	1985 **Pete Rose**, baseball	1996 **Joe Torre**, baseball
1974 **Lou Brock**, baseball	1986 **Larry Bird**, pro basketball	1997 **Mark McGwire**, baseball
1975 **Archie Griffin**, football	1987 No award	1998 **Mark McGwire**
1976 **Larry O'Brien**, basketball	1988 **Jackie Joyner-Kersee**, track	& **Sammy Sosa**, baseball
1977 **Steve Cauthen**, horse racing	1989 **Joe Montana**, football	1999 **New York Yankees**, base-
1978 **Ron Guidry**, baseball	1990 **Nolan Ryan**, baseball	ball
1979 **Willie Stargell**, baseball	1991 **Michael Jordan**, basketball	

Time Man of the Year

Since Charles Lindbergh was named *Time* magazine's first Man of the Year for 1927, two individuals with significant sports credentials have won the honor.

Year	
1984	**Peter Ueberroth**, president of the Los Angeles Olympic Organizing Committee.
1991	**Ted Turner**, owner-president of Turner Broadcasting System, founder of CNN cable news network, owner of the Atlanta Braves (NL) and Atlanta Hawks (NBA), and former winning America's Cup skipper.

TROPHY CASE

From the first organized track meet at Olympia in 776 B.C., to the Sydney Summer Olympics over 2,700 years later, championships have been officially recognized with prizes that are symbolically rich and eagerly pursued. Here are 15 of the most coveted trophies in America.

(Illustrations by Lynn Mercer Michaud)

America's Cup

First presented by England's Royal Yacht Squadron to the winner of an invitational race around the Isle of Wight on Aug. 22, 1851. . . originally called the Hundred Guinea Cup. . . renamed after the U.S. boat America, winner of the first race. . . made of sterling silver and designed by London jewelers R. & G. Garrard. . . measures 2 feet, 3 inches high and weighs 16 lbs. . . originally cost 100 guineas ($500), now valued at $250,000 . . . bell-shaped base added in 1958. . . challenged for every three to four years. . . trophy held by yacht club sponsoring winning boat...Cup was badly damaged when a Maori protester repeatedly smashed it with a sledgehammer on March 14, 1997. It was sent back to the original maker and fully restored.

Vince Lombardi Trophy

First presented at the AFL-NFL World Championship Game (now Super Bowl) on Jan. 15, 1967. . . originally called the World Championship Game Trophy . . . renamed in 1971 in honor of former Green Bay Packers GM-coach and two-time Super Bowl winner Vince Lombardi, who died in 1970 as coach of Washington . . . made of sterling silver and designed by Tiffany & Co. of New York . . . measures 21 inches high and weighs 7 lbs (football depicted is regulation size). . . valued at $12,500. . . competed for annually- . . . winning team keeps trophy.

Olympic Gold Medal

First presented by International Olympic Committee in 1908 (until then winners received silver medals). . . second and third place finishers also got medals of silver and bronze for first time in 1908. . . each medal must be at least 2.4 inches in diameter and 0.12 inches thick. . . the gold medal is actually made of silver, but must be gilded with at least 6 grams (0.21 ounces) of pure gold. . . the medals for the 1996 Atlanta Games were designed by Malcolm Grear Designers and produced by Reed & Barton of Taunton, Mass...604 gold, 604 silver and 630 bronze medals were made. . . competed for every two years as Winter and Summer Games alternate. . . winners keep medals.

Stanley Cup

Donated by Lord Stanley of Preston, the Governor General of Canada and first presented in 1893. . . original cup was made of sterling silver by an unknown London silversmith and measured 7 inches high with an 11½-inch diameter. . . in order to accommodate all the rosters of winning teams, the cup now measures 35½ inches high with a base 54 inches around and weighs 32 lbs. . . in order to add new names each year, bands on the trophy are often retired and displayed at the Hall of Fame. . . originally bought for 10 guineas ($48.67), it is now insured for $75,000. . . actual cup retired to Hall of Fame and replaced in 1970. . . presented to NHL playoff champion since 1918. . . trophy loaned to winning team for one year.

World Cup

First presented by the Federation Internationale de Football Association (FIFA). . . originally called the World Cup Trophy. . . renamed the Jules Rimet Cup (after the then FIFA president) in 1946, but retired by Brazil after that country's third title in 1970. . . new World Cup trophy created in 1974. . . designed by Italian sculptor Silvio Gazzaniga and made of solid 18 carat gold with two malachite rings inlaid at the base. . . measures 14.2 inches high and weighs 11 lbs. . . insured for $200,000 (U.S.). . . competed for every four years. . . winning team gets gold-plated replica.

Commissioner's Trophy

First presented by the Commissioner of baseball to the winner of the 1967 World Series. . . also known as the World Championship Trophy. . . made of brass and gold plate with an ebony base and a baseball in the center made of pewter with a silver finish. . . designed by Balfour & Co. of Attleboro, Mass. . . 30 pennants represent 14 AL and 16 NL teams . . . measures 30 inches high and 36 inches around at the base and weighs 30 lbs. . . valued at $15,000. . . competed for annually. . . winning team keeps trophy.

Larry O'Brien Trophy

First presented in 1978 to winner of NBA Finals. . . originally called the Walter A. Brown Trophy after the league pioneer and Boston Celtics owner (an earlier NBA championship bowl was also named after Brown). . . renamed in 1984 in honor of outgoing commissioner O'Brien, who served from 1975-84 . . . made of sterling silver with 24 carat gold overlay and designed by Tiffany & Co. of New York. . . measures 2 feet high and weighs 14½ lbs (basketball depicted is regulation size). . . valued at $13,500. . . competed for annually. . . winning team keeps trophy.

Heisman Trophy

First presented in 1935 to the best college football player east of the Mississippi by the Downtown Athletic Club of New York. . . players across the entire country eligible since 1936. . . originally called the DAC Trophy. . . renamed in 1936 following the death of DAC athletic director and former college coach John W. Heisman. . . made of bronze and designed by New York sculptor Frank Eliscu, it measures 13½ in. high, 6½ in. wide and 14 in. long at the base and weighs 25 lbs. . . valued at $2,000 . . . voting done by national media and former Heisman winners. . . trophy sponsor American Suzuki announced plans for limited fan voting starting in 1999. . . awarded annually. . . winner keeps trophy.

James E. Sullivan Memorial Award

First presented by the Amateur Athletic Union (AAU) in 1930 as a gold medal and given to the nation's outstanding amateur athlete. . . trophy given since 1933. . . named after the amateur sports movement pioneer, who was a founder and past president of AAU and the director of the 1904 Olympic Games in St. Louis. . . made of bronze with a marble base, it measures 17½ in. high and 11 in. wide at the base and weighs 13½ lbs. . . valued at $2,500. . . voting done by AAU and USOC officials, former winners and selected media. . . awarded annually. . . winner keeps trophy.

Ryder Cup

Donated in 1927 by English seed merchant Samuel Ryder, who offered the gold cup for a biennial match between teams of golfing pros from Great Britain and the United States. . . the format changed in 1977 to include the best players on the European PGA Tour . . . made of 14 carat gold on a wood base and designed by Mappin and Webb of London. . . the golfer depicted on the top of the trophy is Ryder's friend and teaching pro Abe Mitchell. . . . the cup measures 16 in. high and weighs 4 lbs. . . insured for $50,000 . . . competed for every two years at alternating European and U.S. sites . . . the cup is held by the PGA headquarters of the winning side.

Davis Cup

Donated by American college student and U.S. doubles champion Dwight F. Davis in 1900 and presented by the International Tennis Federation (ITF) to the winner of the annual 16-team men's competition. . . officially called the International Lawn Tennis Challenge Trophy. . . made of sterling silver and designed by Shreve, Crump and Low of Boston, the cup has a matching tray (added in 1921) and a very heavy two-tiered base containing rosters of past winning teams. . . it stands 34½ in. high and 108 in. around at the base and weighs 400 lbs. . . insured for $150,000. . . competed for annually. . . trophy loaned to winning country for one year.

Borg-Warner Trophy

First presented by the Borg-Warner Automotive Co. of Chicago in 1936 to the winner of the Indianapolis 500. . . replaced the Wheeler-Schebler Trophy which went to the 400-mile leader from 1911-32. . . made of sterling silver with bas-relief sculptured heads of each winning driver and a gold bas-relief head of Tony Hulman, the owner of the Indy Speedway from 1945-77 . . . designed by Robert J. Hill and made by Gorham, Inc. of Rhode Island . . . measures 51½ in. high and weighs over 80 lbs. . . new base added in 1988 and the entire trophy restored in 1991. . . competed for annually. . . insured for $1 million. . . trophy stays at Speedway Hall of Fame. . . winner gets a 14-in. high replica valued at $30,000.

NCAA Championship Trophy

First presented in 1952 by the NCAA to all 1st, 2nd and 3rd place teams in sports with sanctioned tournaments. . . 1st place teams receive gold-plated awards, 2nd place award is silver-plated and 3rd is bronze. . . replaced silver cup given to championship teams from 1939-1951. . . made of walnut, the trophy stands 24¾ in. high, 14⅛ in. wide and 4½ in. deep at the base and weighs 15 lbs . . . designed by Medallic Art Co. of Danbury, Conn. and made by House of Usher of Kansas City since 1990. . . valued at $500. . . competed for annually. . . winning teams keep trophies.

World Championship Belt

First presented in 1921 by the World Boxing Association, one of the three organizations (the World Boxing Council and International Boxing Federation are the others) generally accepted as sanctioning legitimate world championship fights. . . belt weighs 8 lbs. and is made of hand tanned leather. . . the outsized buckle measures 10½ in. high and 8 in. wide, is made of pewter with 24 carat gold plate and contains crystal and semi-precious stones . . . side panels of polished brass are for engraving title bout results . . . currently made by Phil Valentino Originals of Jersey City, N.J.. . . champions keep belts even if they lose their title.

World Championship Ring

Rings decorated with gems and engraving date back to ancient Egypt where the wealthy wore heavy gold and silver rings to indicate social status. . . championship rings in sports serve much the same purpose, indicating the wearer is a champion. . . As an example, the Dallas Cowboys' ring for winning Superbowl XXX on Jan. 28, 1996 was designed by Diamond Cutters International of Houston. . . each ring is made of 14-carat yellow gold, weighs 48–51 penny weights and features five trimmed marquis diamonds interlocking in the shape of the Cowboys' star logo as well as five more marquis diamonds (for the team's five Super Bowl wins) on a bed of 51 smaller diamonds. . . rings were appraised at over $30,000 each.

Who's Who

The classy **Arthur Ashe** won three Grand Slam events and 33 overall singles tournaments during his career.

Sports Personalities

Nine hundred eleven entries dating back to the turn of the century. Entries updated through September 21, 2000.

Hank Aaron (b. Feb. 5, 1934): Baseball OF; led NL in HRs and RBI 4 times each and batting twice with Milwaukee and Atlanta Braves; MVP in 1957; played in 24 All-Star Games, all-time leader in HRs (755) and RBI (2,297), 3rd in hits (3,771); executive with Braves and TBS, Inc.

Jim Abbott (b. Sept. 19, 1967): Baseball LHP; born without a right hand; All-America hurler at Michigan; won Sullivan Award in 1987; threw 4-0 no-hitter for NY Yankees vs. Cleveland (Sept. 4, 1993).

Kareem Abdul-Jabbar (b. Lew Alcindor, Apr. 16, 1947): Basketball C; led UCLA to 3 NCAA titles (1967-69); Final 4 MOP 3 times; Player of Year twice; led Milwaukee (1) and LA Lakers (5) to 6 NBA titles; playoff MVP twice (1971,85), regular season MVP 6 times (1971-72,74,76-77,80); retired in 1989 after 20 seasons as all-time leader in over 20 categories.

Andre Agassi (b. Apr. 29, 1970): Tennis; 44 career tournament wins through 1999 including the career grand slam; Wimbledon (1992), U.S. Open (1994,99), Australian Open (1995,2000), French Open (1999); helped U.S. win 2 Davis Cup finals (1990,92); regained the world No. 1 ranking in 1999 for the first time since 1996.

Troy Aikman (b. Nov. 21, 1966): Football QB; consensus All-America at UCLA (1988); 1st overall pick in 1989 NFL Draft (by Dallas); led Cowboys to 3 Super Bowl titles (1992,93,95 seasons); MVP in Super Bowl XXVII.

Marv Albert (b. June 12, 1941): Radio-TV; NBC announcer and radio broadcaster for the New York Knicks, Rangers and Giants who pled guilty to a misdemeanor assault charge amid embarrassing allegations of his sex life. Rehired to MSG and Turner networks in 1998 and NBC in '99.

Tenley Albright (b. July 18, 1935): Figure skater; 2-time world champion (1953,55); won Olympic silver (1952) and gold (1956) medals; became a surgeon.

Amy Alcott (b. Feb. 22, 1956): Golfer; 29 career wins, including five majors; inducted into World Golf Hall of Fame in 1999.

Grover Cleveland (Pete) Alexander (b. Feb. 26, 1887, d. Nov. 4, 1950): Baseball RHP; won 20 or more games 9 times; 373 career wins and 90 shutouts.

Muhammad Ali (b. Cassius Clay, Jan. 17, 1942): Boxer; 1960 Olympic light heavyweight champion; 3-time world heavyweight champ (1964-67, 1974-78,1978-79); defeated Sonny Liston (1964), George Foreman (1974) and Leon Spinks (1978) for title; fought Joe Frazier in 3 memorable bouts (1971-75), winning twice; adopted Black Muslim faith in 1964 and changed name; stripped of title in 1967 after conviction for refusing induction into U.S. Army; verdict reversed by Supreme Court in 1971; career record of 56-5 with 37 KOs and 19 successful title defenses; lit the flaming cauldron to signal the beginning of the 1996 Summer Olympics in Atlanta.

Forrest (Phog) Allen (b. Nov. 18, 1885, d. Sept. 16, 1974): Basketball; college coach 48 years; directed Kansas to NCAA title (1952); 7th on all-time Div. I list with 746 career wins.

Bobby Allison (b. Dec. 3, 1937): Auto racer; 3-time winner of Daytona 500 (1978,82,88); NASCAR national champ in 1983; father of Davey.

Davey Allison (b. Feb. 25, 1961, d. July 13, 1993): Auto racer; stock car Rookie of Year (1987); winner of 19 NASCAR races, including 1992 Daytona 500; killed at age 32 in helicopter accident at Talladega Superspeedway; son of Bobby.

Roberto Alomar (b. Feb. 5, 1968): Baseball; perennial Gold Glove second baseman and All-Star; MVP of 1992 ALCS; became known well beyond baseball for spitting in the face of umpire John Hirschbeck during final weekend of 1996 season; named MVP of 1998 All-Star Game.

Walter Alston (b. Dec. 1, 1911, d. Oct. 1, 1984): Baseball; managed Brooklyn-LA Dodgers 23 years, won 7 pennants and 4 World Series (1955,59,63,65); retired after 1976 season with 2,063 wins (2,040 regular season and 23 postseason).

Sparky Anderson (b. Feb. 22, 1934): Baseball; only manager to win World Series in each league—Cincinnati in NL (1975-76) and Detroit in AL (1984); 3rd-ranked skipper on all-time career list with 2,228 wins (2,194 regular season and 34 postseason); inducted into the Baseball Hall of Fame in 2000.

Willie Anderson (b. May 1878, d. Oct. 25, 1910): Scottish golfer; became a US citizen and won 4 U.S. Opens, including 3 straight (1901,03-05).

Mario Andretti (b. Feb. 28, 1940): Auto racer; 4-time USAC-CART national champion (1965-66,69,84); only driver to win Daytona 500 (1967), Indy 500 (1969) and Formula One world title (1978); Indy 500 Rookie of Year (1965); retired after 1994 racing season ranked 1st in poles (67) and starts (407) and 2nd in wins (52) on all-time CART list; father of Michael and Jeff, uncle of John.

Michael Andretti (b. Oct. 5, 1962): Auto racer; 1991 CART national champion with single-season record 8 wins; Indy 500 Rookie of Year (1984); left IndyCar circuit for ill-fated Formula One try in 1993; returned to IndyCar (now CART) in '94; son of Mario.

Earl Anthony (b. Apr. 27, 1938): Bowler; 6-time PBA Bowler of Year; 41 career titles; first to earn $100,000 in 1 season (1975); first to earn $1 million in career. Came out of retirement in '96; ranked 11th on list of PBA career money leaders through 1999.

Said Aouita (b. Nov. 2, 1959): Moroccan runner; won gold (5000m) and bronze (800m) in 1984 Olympics; won 5000m at 1987 World Championships; formerly held 2 world records recognized by IAAF—2000m and 5000m.

Luis Aparicio (b. Apr. 29, 1934): Baseball SS; retired as all-time leader in most games, assists and double plays by shortstop; led AL in stolen bases 9 times (1956-64); 506 career steals.

Al Arbour (b. Nov. 1, 1932): Hockey; coached NY Islanders to 4 straight Stanley Cup titles (1980-83); retired after 1993-94 season; 2nd on all-time career list with 904 wins (781 regular season and 123 postseason); elected to Hockey Hall of Fame in 1996.

Eddie Arcaro (b. Feb. 19, 1916, d. Nov. 14, 1997): Jockey; 2-time Triple Crown winner (Whirlaway in 1941, Citation in '48); from 1938-55, he won Kentucky Derby 5 times, Preakness and Belmont 6 times each.

Roone Arledge (b. July 8, 1931): Sports TV innovator of live events, anthology shows, Olympic coverage and "Monday Night Football"; ran ABC Sports from 1968-86; ran ABC News from 1977-98.

Henry Armstrong (b. Dec. 12, 1912, d. Oct. 22, 1988): Boxer; held feather-, light- and welterweight titles simultaneously in 1938; pro record 152-21-8 with 100 KOs.

Lance Armstrong (b. Sept. 18, 1971): Cyclist; returned from treatment for testicular cancer to become improbable winner of 1999 Tour de France, becoming only the second American winner in the race's history; won the Tour de France again in 2000, besting runner-up Jan Ullrich by just over six minutes.

Arthur Ashe (b. July 10, 1943, d. Feb. 6, 1993): Tennis; first black man to win U.S. Championship (1968) and Wimbledon (1975); 1st U.S. player to earn $100,000 in 1 year (1970); won Davis Cup as player (1968-70) and captain (1981-82); wrote black sports history, Hard Road to Glory; announced in 1992 that he was infected with AIDS virus from a blood transfusion during 1983 heart surgery; in 1997, the new home for the U.S. Open was named Arthur Ashe Stadium.

Evelyn Ashford (b. Apr. 15, 1957): Track & Field; winner of 4 Olympic gold medals—100m in 1984, and 4x100m in 1984, '88 and '92; also won silver medal in 100m in '88; member of 5 U.S. Olympic teams (1976-92); Inducted into Track and Field and Women's Sports Halls of Fame in 1998.

Red Auerbach (b. Sept. 20, 1917): Basketball; 3rd winningest coach (regular season and playoffs) in NBA history; won 1,037 times in 20 years; as coach-GM, led Boston to 9 NBA titles, including 8 in a row (1959-66); also coached defunct Washington Capitols (1946-49); NBA Coach of the Year award named after him; retired as Celtics coach in 1966 and as GM in '84; club president from 1970 to 1997.

Tracy Austin (b. Dec. 12, 1962): Tennis; youngest player to win U.S. Open (age 16 in 1979); won 2nd U.S. Open in '81; named AP Female Athlete of Year twice before she was 20; recurring neck and back injuries shortened career after 1983; youngest player ever inducted into Tennis Hall of Fame (age 29 in 1992).

Paul Azinger (b. Jan. 6, 1960): Golf; PGA Player of Year (1987); 11 career wins, including '93 PGA Championship; missed most of '94 season overcoming lymphoma (a form of cancer) in right shoulder blade; won his first tournament since his hiatus at the Sony Open in Honolulu in Jan. 2000.

Donovan Bailey (b. Dec. 16, 1967): Track; Jamaican-born Canadian sprinter who set world record in the 100m (9.84) in gold medal-winning performance at 1996 Olympics which stood until '99; set indoor record in 50m (5.56) in 1996; member of Canadian 4x100 relay that won gold in 1996 Olympics.

Oksana Baiul (b. Feb. 26, 1977): Ukrainian figure skater; 1993 world champion at age 15; edged Nancy Kerrigan by a 5-4 judges' vote for 1994 Olympic gold medal.

Hobey Baker (b. Jan. 15, 1892, d. Dec. 21, 1918): Football and hockey star at Princeton (1911-14); member of college football and pro hockey Halls of Fame; college hockey Player of Year award named after him; killed in plane crash.

Bob Baffert (b. Jan. 13, 1953): Horse racing; 3-time Eclipse Award winner as outstanding trainer; trained 2 Kentuckey Derby winners (1997,98) and 2 Preakness winners (1997,98); leading annual money leader for trainers in 1998 and '99.

Seve Ballesteros (b. Apr. 9, 1957): Spanish golfer; has won British Open 3 times (1979,84,88) and Masters twice (1980,83); 3-time European Golfer of Year (1986,88,91); has led Europe to 5 Ryder Cup titles (1985,87,89,95,97); 72 world-wide victories.

Ernie Banks (b. Jan. 31, 1931): Baseball SS-1B; led NL in home runs and RBI twice each; 2-time MVP (1958-59) with Chicago Cubs; 512 career HRs.

Roger Bannister (b. Mar. 23, 1929): British runner; first to run mile in less than 4 minutes (3:59.4 on May 6, 1954).

Walter (Red) Barber (b. Feb. 17, 1908, d. Oct. 22, 1992): Radio-TV; renowned baseball play-by-play broadcaster for Cincinnati, Brooklyn and N.Y. Yankees from 1934-66; won Peabody Award for radio commentary in 1991.

Charles Barkley (b. Feb. 20, 1963): Basketball F; 5-time All-NBA 1st team with Philadelphia and Phoenix; traded to Suns for 3 players (June 17, 1992); U.S. Olympic Dream Team member in '92; NBA regular season MVP in 1993; traded to Houston Rockets in 1996; retired after the 1999-00 season and became a studio analyst with Turner Sports beginning with the 2000-01 season.

Leon Barmore (b. June 3, 1944): college basketball coach; respected coach of Louisiana Tech Lady Techsters; career win pct. of .871 (520-77, 18 yrs) entering 2000-01 season is best all-time; won national championship with Louisiana Tech in 1988.

Rick Barry (b. Mar. 28, 1944): Basketball F; only player to lead both NBA and ABA in scoring; 5-time All-NBA 1st team; Finals MVP with Golden St. in 1975.

Hank Bauer (b. July 31, 1922): Baseball RF; 3-time all-star with the N.Y. Yankees and a member of nine pennant-winning teams; managed Baltimore to its first pennant and World Series Championship in 1966.

Sammy Baugh (b. Mar. 17, 1914): Football QB-DB-P; led Washington to NFL titles in 1937 (his rookie year) and '42; led league in passing 6 times, punting 4 times and interceptions once.

Elgin Baylor (b. Sept. 16, 1934): Basketball F; MOP of Final 4 in 1958; led Minneapolis-LA Lakers to 8 NBA Finals; 10-time All-NBA 1st team (1959-65,67-69); LA Clippers' vice president of basketball operations.

Bob Beamon (b. Aug. 29, 1946): Track & Field; won 1968 Olympic gold medal in long jump with world record (29-ft, 2½in.) that shattered old mark by nearly 2 feet; record finally broken by 2 inches in 1991 by Mike Powell.

Franz Beckenbauer (b. Sept. 11, 1945): Soccer; captain of West German World Cup champions in 1974 then coached West Germany to World Cup title in 1990; invented sweeper position; played in U.S. for NY Cosmos (1977-80,83); Member of International Soccer Hall of Champions.

Boris Becker (b. Nov. 22, 1967): German tennis player; 3-time Wimbledon champ (1985-86,89); youngest male (17) to win Wimbledon; led country to 1st Davis Cup win in 1988; has also won U.S. (1989) and Australian (1991,96) Opens.

Chuck Bednarik (b. May 1, 1925): Football C-LB; 2-time All-America at Penn and 7-time All-Pro with NFL Eagles as both center (1950) and linebacker (1951-56); missed only 3 games in 14 seasons; led Eagles to 1960 NFL title as a 35-year-old two-way player.

Clair Bee (b. Mar. 2, 1896, d. May 20, 1983): Basketball coach who led LIU to 2 undefeated seasons (1936,39) and 2 NIT titles (1939,41); his teams won 95 percent of their games between 1931-51, including 43 in a row from 1935-37; coached NBA Baltimore Bullets from 1952-54, but was only 34-116; contributions to game include 1-3-1 zone defense, 3-second rule and NBA 24-second clock.

Jean Beliveau (b. Aug. 31, 1931): Hockey C; led Montreal to 10 Stanley Cups in 17 playoffs; playoff MVP (1965); 2-time regular season MVP (1956,64).

Bert Bell (b. Feb. 25, 1895, d. Oct. 11, 1959): Football; team owner and 2nd NFL commissioner (1946-59); proposed college draft in 1935 and instituted TV blackout rule.

James (Cool Papa) Bell (b. May 17, 1903, d. Mar. 8, 1991): Baseball; member of the Negro Leagues; widely considered the fastest player ever to play baseball; tremendous hitter and base runner; also coached for the Kansas City Monarchs, teaching such players as Jackie Robinson; member of the National Baseball Hall of Fame.

Albert Belle (b. August 25, 1966): Baseball OF; tremendous hitter and stupendous troublemaker; in strike-shortened 1995 season, became first player in major league history to hit 50 homers and 50 doubles in a season; five-time All-Star; three-time AL RBI leader; was fined $50,000 for a profanity-laced tirade aimed at NBC's Hannah Storm during 1995 World Series; in 1996, was suspended for a brutal hit on Brewers' Fernando Vina; suspended 10 games in 1994 for using a corked bat.

Deane Beman (b. Apr. 22, 1938): Golf; 1st commissioner of PGA Tour (1974-94); introduced "stadium golf"; as player, won U.S. Amateur twice and British Amateur once; inducted into the World Golf Hall of Fame in 2000.

Johnny Bench (b. Dec. 7, 1947): Baseball C; led NL in HRs twice and RBI 3 times; 2-time regular season MVP (1970,72) with Cincinnati, World Series MVP in 1976; 389 career HRs.

Patty Berg (b. Feb. 13, 1918): Golfer; 57 career pro wins, including 15 majors; 3-time AP Female Athlete of Year (1938,43,55).

Chris Berman (b. May 10, 1955): Radio-TV; 5-time National Sportscaster of Year known for his nicknames and jovial studio anchoring on ESPN; play-by-play man only year Brown University football team won Ivy League (1976); narrated weekly highlights on "Monday Night Football" 1996-99.

Yogi Berra (b. May 12, 1925): Baseball C; played on 10 World Series winners with NY Yankees; holds WS records for games played (75), at bats (259) and hits (71); 3-time AL MVP (1951,54-55); managed both Yankees (1964) and NY Mets (1973) to pennants.

Jay Berwanger (b. Mar. 19, 1914): Football HB; Univ. of Chicago star; won 1st Heisman Trophy in 1935.

Gary Bettman (b. June 2, 1952): Hockey; former NBA executive, who was named first commissioner of NHL on Dec. 11, 1992; took office on Feb. 1, 1993.

Abebe Bikila (b. Aug. 7, 1932, d. Oct. 25, 1973): Ethiopian runner; 1st to win consecutive Olympic marathons (1960,64).

Matt Biondi (b. Oct. 8, 1965): Swimmer; won 7 medals in 1988 Olympics, including 5 gold (2 individual, 3 relay); has won a total of 11 medals (8 gold, 2 silver and a bronze) in 3 Olympics (1984,88,92).

Larry Bird (b. Dec. 7, 1956): Basketball F; college Player of Year (1979) at Indiana St.; 1980 NBA Rookie of Year; 9-time All-NBA 1st team; 3-time regular season MVP (1984-86); led Boston to 3 NBA titles (1981,84,86); 2-time Finals MVP (1984,86); U.S. Olympic Dream Team member in '92; inducted into Hall of Fame in 1998; in 1997, named coach of Indiana Pacers and won Coach of the Year honors in first season; led the Pacers to the NBA finals in 2000 but lost in 6 games to the Lakers; retired from coaching in 2000.

The Black Sox: Eight Chicago White Sox players who were banned from baseball for life in 1921 for allegedly throwing the 1919 World Series— RHP Eddie Cicotte (1884-1969), OF Happy Felsch (1891-1964), 1B Chick Gandil (1887-1970), OF Shoeless Joe Jackson (1889-1951), INF Fred McMullin (1891-1952), SS Swede Risberg (1894-1975), 3B-SS Buck Weaver (1890-1956), and LHP Lefty Williams (1893-1959).

Earl (Red) Blaik (b. Feb. 15, 1897, d. May 6, 1989): Football; coached Army to consecutive national titles in 1944-45; 166 career wins and 3 Heisman winners (Blanchard, Davis, Dawkins).

Bonnie Blair (b. Mar. 18, 1964): Speedskater; only American woman to win 5 Olympic gold medals in Winter Games; won 500-meters in 1988, then 500m and 1,000m in both 1992 and '94; added 1,000m bronze in 1988; Sullivan Award winner (1992); retired on 31st birthday as reigning world sprint champ.

Hector (Toe) Blake (b. Aug. 21, 1912, d. May 17, 1995): Hockey LW; led Montreal to 2 Stanley Cups as a player and 8 more as coach; regular season MVP in 1939.

Felix (Doc) Blanchard (b. Dec. 11, 1924): Football FB; 3-time All-America; led Army to national titles in 1944-45; Glenn Davis' running mate; won Heisman Trophy and Sullivan Award in 1945.

George Blanda (b. Sept. 17, 1927): Football QB-PK; pro football's all-time leading scorer (2,002 points); led Houston to 2 AFL titles (1960-61); played 26 pro seasons; retired at 48.

Fanny Blankers-Koen (b. Apr. 26, 1918): Dutch sprinter; 30-year-old mother of two, who won 4 gold medals (100m, 200m, 800m hurdles and 4x100m relay) at 1948 Olympics.

Drew Bledsoe (b. Feb. 14, 1972): Football QB; 1st overall pick in 1993 NFL draft (by New England); holds NFL season record for most passes attempted (691) and game records for most passes completed (45) and attempted (70).

Wade Boggs (b. June 15, 1958): Baseball 3B; 5 AL batting titles (1983,85-88) with Boston Red Sox; 11-time All-Star; two Gold Gloves; since played with NY Yankees and Tampa Bay; got 3000th career hit with a home run Aug. 7, 1999 against Cleveland; retired after the 1999 season.

Barry Bonds (b. July 24, 1964): Baseball OF; 3-time NL MVP, twice with Pittsburgh (1990,92) and once with San Francisco (1993); NL's HR and RBI leader in 1993; one of only three players with 40 homers and 40 stolen bases in same season (1996); son of Bobby.

Bjorn Borg (b. June 6, 1956): Swedish tennis player; 2-time Player of Year (1979-80); won 6 French Opens and 5 straight Wimbledons (1976-80); led Sweden to 1st Davis Cup win in 1975; retired in 1983 at age 26; attempted unsuccessful comeback in 1991.

Mike Bossy (b. Jan. 22, 1957): Hockey RW; led NY Isles to 4 Stanley Cups; playoff MVP in 1982; 50 goals or more 9 straight years; 573 career goals.

Ralph Boston (b. May 9, 1939): Track & Field; medaled in 3 consecutive Olympic long jumps— gold (1960), silver (1964), bronze (1968).

Ray Bourque (b. Dec. 28, 1960): Hockey D; 12-time All-NHL 1st team; won Norris Trophy 5 times (1987-88,1990-91,94) with Boston; '96 All-Star Game MVP; one of only seven NHL players to have recorded 1,000 assists; entered the 2000-01 season ranked 9th overall in career scoring (1,520 points) and 5th overall in games played (1,532); traded to Colorado Avalanche in 2000.

Bobby Bowden (b. Nov. 8, 1929): Football; coached Florida St. to a national title in 1993 and again in 1999; heading into the 2000 season, amassed 304 wins including a 17-5-1 bowl record in 34 years as coach at Samford, West Va. and FSU; father of Clemson head coach Tommy and former Auburn coach Terry.

Riddick Bowe (b. Aug. 10, 1967): Boxing; won world heavyweight title with unanimous decision over champion Evander Holyfield on Nov. 13, 1992; lost title to Holyfield on majority decision Nov. 6, 1993; in 1996, was fined $250,000 because members of his entourage caused a riot at Madison Square Garden after opponent Andrew Golota was disqualified for repeated low blows.

Scotty Bowman (b. Sept. 18, 1933): Hockey coach; all-time winningest NHL coach in both regular season (1,100) and playoffs (200) over 27 seasons entering 2000-01; coached a record-tying eight Stanley Cup winners with Montreal (1973,76-79), Pittsburgh (1992) and Detroit (1997,98).

Jack Brabham (b. Apr. 2, 1926): Australian auto racer; 3-time Formula One champion (1959-60,66); 14 career wins; member of the Hall of Fame.

Bill Bradley (b. July 28, 1943): Basketball F; 2-time All-America at Princeton; Player of the Year and Final 4 MOP in 1965; captain of gold medal-winning 1964 U.S. Olympic team; Sullivan Award winner (1965); led NY Knicks to 2 NBA titles (1970,73); U.S. Senator (D, N.J.) 1979-95; ran for President in 2000.

Pat Bradley (b. Mar. 24, 1951): Golfer; 2-time LPGA Player of Year (1986,91); has won all four majors on LPGA tour, including 3 du Maurier Classics; inducted into the LPGA Hall of Fame on Jan. 18, 1992; among all-time LPGA money leaders and tournament winners (31); captained the 2000 U.S. Solheim Cup team.

Terry Bradshaw (b. Sept. 2, 1948): Football QB; led Pittsburgh to 4 Super Bowl titles (1975-76,79-80); 2-time Super Bowl MVP (1979-80) and regular season MVP in 1978; Fox TV studio analyst.

George Brett (b. May 15, 1953): Baseball 3B-1B; AL batting champion in 3 different decades (1976,80,90); MVP in 1980; led KC to World Series title in 1985; retired after 1993 season with 3,154 hits and .305 career average; inducted into Hall of Fame in '99.

Valerie Brisco-Hooks (b. July 6, 1960): Track & Field; won three gold medals at the 1984 Olympics (200 meters, 400 meters and 4x100 relay); first athlete to ever win the 200 and 400 in the same Olympics.

Lou Brock (b. June 18, 1939): Baseball OF; former all-time stolen base leader (938); led NL in steals 8 times; led St. Louis to 2 World Series titles (1964,67); had 3,023 career hits.

Herb Brooks (b. Aug. 5, 1937): Hockey; former U.S. Olympic player (1964,68) who coached 1980 team to gold medal; coached Minnesota to 3 NCAA titles (1974,76,78); also coached NY Rangers, Minnesota, New Jersey and Pittsburgh in NHL.

Jim Brown (b. Feb. 17, 1936): Football FB; All-America at Syracuse (1956) and NFL Rookie of Year (1957); led NFL in rushing 8 times; 8-time All-Pro (1957-61,63-65); 3-time MVP (1958,63,65) with Cleveland; ran for 12,312 yards and scored 126 touchdowns in just 9 seasons.

Larry Brown (b. Sept. 14, 1940): Basketball; played in ACC, AAU, 1964 Olympics and ABA; 3-time assist leader (1968-70) and 3-time Coach of Year (1973,75-76) in ABA; coached ABA's Carolina and Denver and NBA's Denver, N. J., San Antonio, LA Clippers, Indiana and Phila.; also coached UCLA to NCAA Final (1980) and Kansas to NCAA title (1988).

Mordecai (Three-Finger) Brown (b. Oct. 18, 1876, d. Feb. 14, 1948): Baseball; nickname derived from loss of three fingers in a childhood accident; injury gave him a particularly nasty curve ball; won the decisive game of the 1907 World Series as a Chicago Cub; in 1908, first pitcher to record 4 consecutive shutouts and finished at 29-9; career record of 239-130 with lifetime ERA of 2.06; member of Hall of Fame.

Paul Brown (b. Sept. 7, 1908, d. Aug. 5, 1991): Football innovator; coached Ohio St. to national title in 1942; in pros, directed Cleveland Browns to 4 straight AAFC titles (1946-49) and 3 NFL titles (1950,54-55); formed Cincinnati Bengals as head coach and part-owner in 1968 (reached playoffs in '70).

Sergi Bruguera (b. Jan. 16, 1971): Spanish tennis player; won consecutive French Opens in 1993 and '94.

Valery Brumel (b. Apr. 14, 1942): Soviet high jumper; dominated event from 1961-64; broke world record 5 times; won silver medal in 1960 Olympics and gold in 1964; highest jump was 7-5 ¾.

Avery Brundage (b. Sept. 28, 1887, d. May 5, 1975): Amateur sports czar for over 40 years as president of AAU (1928-35), U.S. Olympic Committee (1929-53) and Int'l Olympic Committee (1952-72).

Kobe Bryant (b. Aug. 23, 1978): Basketball; guard/forward for the Los Angeles Lakers; graduated from Lower Merion HS in Pennsylvania and made the jump directly to the NBA; youngest player (18 yrs., 2 mos., 11 days) ever to appear in an NBA game; became the youngest all-star in NBA history in 1998 and scored a team-high 18 points; won title with the Lakers in 2000.

Paul (Bear) Bryant (b. Sept. 11, 1913, d. Jan. 26, 1983): Football; coached at 4 colleges over 38 years; directed Alabama to 5 national titles (1961,64-65,78-79); retired as the winningest coach of all time (323-85-17 record); 15 bowl wins, including 8 Sugar Bowls.

Sergey Bubka (b. Dec. 4, 1963): Ukrainian pole vaulter; 1st man to clear 20 feet both indoors and out (1991); holder of indoor (20-2) and outdoor (20-1¾) world records at Sept. 21, 2000; 6-time world champion (1983,87,91,93,95,97); won Olympic gold medal in 1988, but failed to clear any height in 1992 Games.

Buck Buchanan (b. Sept. 10, 1940, d. July 16, 1992): Football; played both ways in college at Grambling; first player chosen in first AFL draft by the Dallas Texans who later became the KC Chiefs; missed one game in a 13-year pro career; played in six AFL All-Star games and two Pro Bowls at def. tackle; defensive star of the Chiefs team that won Super Bowl IV; later coached for the New Orleans Saints and Cleveland Browns; member of Pro Football Hall of Fame.

Don Budge (b. June 13, 1915, d. Jan. 26, 2000): Tennis; in 1938 became 1st player to win the Grand Slam— the French, Wimbledon, U.S. and Australian titles in 1 year; led U.S. to 2 Davis Cups (1937-38); turned pro in late '38.

Maria Bueno (b. Oct. 11, 1939): Brazilian tennis player; won 4 U.S. Championships (1959,63-64,66) and 3 Wimbledons (1959-60,64).

Leroy Burrell (b. Feb. 21, 1967): Track & Field; set former world record of 9.85 in 100 meters, July 6, 1994; previously held record (9.90) in 1991; member of 4 world record-breaking 4x100m relay teams.

George Bush (b. June 12, 1924): 41st President of U.S. (1989-93) and avid sportsman; played 1B on 1947 and '48 Yale baseball teams that placed 2nd in College World Series; captain of 1948 team.

Susan Butcher (b. Dec. 26, 1956): Sled Dog racer; 4-time winner of Iditarod Trail race (1986-88,90).

Dick Butkus (b. Dec. 9, 1942): Football LB; 2-time All-America at Illinois (1963-64); All-Pro 7 of 9 NFL seasons with Chicago Bears; head coach of the XFL's Chicago Enforcers beginning in 2001.

Dick Button (b. July 18, 1929): Figure skater; 5-time world champion (1948-52); 2-time Olympic champ (1948,52); Sullivan Award winner (1949); won Emmy Award as Best Analyst for 1980-81 TV season.

Walter Byers (b. Mar. 13, 1922): College athletics; 1st exec. director of NCAA, serving from 1951-88.

Frank Calder (b. Nov. 17, 1877, d. Feb. 4, 1943): Hockey; 1st NHL president (1917-43); guided league through its formative years; NHL's Rookie of the Year award named after him.

Lee Calhoun (b. Feb. 23, 1933, d. June 22, 1989): Track & Field; won consecutive Olympic gold medals in the 110m hurdles (1956,60).

Walter Camp (b. Apr. 7, 1859, d. Mar. 14, 1925): Football coach and innovator; established scrimmage line, center snap, downs, 11 players per side; elected 1st All-America team (1889).

Roy Campanella (b. Nov. 19, 1921, d. June 26, 1993): Baseball C; 3-time NL MVP (1951,53,55); led Brooklyn to 5 pennants and 1st World Series title (1955); career cut short when 1958 car accident left him paralyzed.

Clarence Campbell (b. July 9, 1905, d. June 24, 1984): Hockey; 3rd NHL president (1946-77), league tripled in size from 6 to 18 teams during his tenure.

Earl Campbell (b. Mar. 29, 1955): Football RB; won Heisman Trophy in 1977; led NFL in rushing 3 times; 3-time All-Pro; 2-time MVP (1978-79) at Houston.

John Campbell (b. Apr. 8, 1955): Harness racing; 5-time winner of Hambletonian (1987,88,90,95,98); 3-time Driver of Year; first driver to go over $100 million in career winnings.

Milt Campbell (b. Dec. 9, 1933): Track & Field; won silver medal in 1952 Olympic decathlon and gold medal in '56.

Jimmy Cannon (b. 1910, d. Dec. 5, 1973): Tough, opinionated New York sportswriter and essayist who viewed sports as an extension of show business; protégé of Damon Runyon; covered World War II for *Stars & Stripes*.

Jose Canseco (b. July 2, 1964): Baseball OF/DH; AL Rookie of the Year in 1986 and Most Valuable Player in 1988 with the Oakland A's; in 1988 he became the first player in history with 40 HRs and 40 steals in a season; led AL in HRs in 1988 and tied for lead in 1991.

Tony Canzoneri (b. Nov. 6, 1908, d. Dec. 9, 1959): Boxer; 2-time world lightweight champion (1930-33,35-36); pro record 141-24-10 with 44 KOs.

Jennifer Capriati (b. Mar. 29, 1976): Tennis; youngest Grand Slam semifinalist ever (age 14 in 1990 French Open); as youngest to win a match at Wimbledon (1990); upset Steffi Graf to win gold medal at 1992 Olympics; left tour from 1994 to '96 due to personal problems including an arrest for marijuana possession.

Harry Caray (b. Mar. 1, 1917, d. Feb. 18, 1998): Radio-TV; baseball play-by-play broadcaster for St. Louis Cardinals, Oakland, Chicago White Sox and Cubs 1945-98; father of sportscaster Skip and grandfather of sportscaster Chip.

Rod Carew (b. Oct. 1, 1945): Baseball 2B-1B; led AL in batting 7 times (1969,72-75,77-78) with Minnesota; MVP in 1977; had 3,053 career hits.

Steve Carlton (b. Dec. 22, 1944): Baseball LHP; won 20 or more games 6 times; 4-time Cy Young winner (1972,77,80,82) with Philadelphia; 329-244 career record.

JoAnne Carner (b. Apr. 4, 1939): Golfer; 5-time U.S. Amateur champion; 2-time U.S. Open champ; 3-time LPGA Player of Year (1974,81-82); 7th in career wins (42).

Cris Carter (b. Nov. 25, 1965): Football; wide receiver for the Minnesota Vikings; does more than just catch touchdowns; twice caught 122 passes in a season (1994, '95), the first time establishing an NFL record for catches in a season that was beaten by Detroit's Herman Moore a year later.

Don Carter (b. July 29, 1926): Bowler; 6-time Bowler of Year (1953-54,57-58,60-61); voted Greatest of All-Time in 1970.

Joe Carter (b. Mar. 7, 1960): Baseball OF; 3-time All-America at Wichita St. (1979-81); won 1993 World Series for Toronto with 3-run HR in bottom of the 9th of Game 6; retired after the 1998 season.

Alexander Cartwright (b. Apr. 17, 1820, d. July 12, 1892): Baseball; engineer and draftsman who spread gospel of baseball from New York City to California gold fields; widely regarded as the father of modern game; his guidelines included setting 3 strikes for an out and 3 outs for each half inning.

Billy Casper (b. June 4, 1931): Golfer; 2-time PGA Player of Year (1966,70); has won U.S. Open (1959,66), Masters (1970), U.S. Senior Open (1983); compiled 51 PGA Tour wins and 9 on Senior Tour.

Tracy Caulkins (b. Jan. 11, 1963): Swimmer; won 3 gold medals (2 individual) at 1984 Olympics; set 5 world records and won 48 U.S. national titles from 1978-84; Sullivan Award winner (1978); 2-time Honda Broderick Cup winner (1982,84).

Steve Cauthen (b. May 1, 1960): Jockey; became youngest jockey (18) to win the Triple Crown with Affirmed in 1978; won a record $6.1 million in 1977, winning the Eclipse Award as the nation's top rider and the award for AP male athlete of the year.

Evonne Goolagong Cawley (b. July 31, 1951): Australian tennis player; won Australian Open 4 times, Wimbledon twice (1971,80), French once (1971).

Florence Chadwick (b. Nov. 9, 1917, d. Mar. 15, 1995): Dominant distance swimmer of 1950s; set English Channel records from France to England (1950) and England to France (1951 and '55).

Wilt Chamberlain (b. Aug. 21, 1936, d. Oct. 12, 1999): Basketball C; consensus All-America in 1957 and '58 at Kansas; Final Four MOP in 1957; led NBA in scoring 7 times and rebounding 11 times; 7-time All-NBA first team; 4-time MVP (1960,66-68); led Philadelphia; scored 100 points vs. NY Knicks in Hershey, Pa., Mar. 2, 1962; led 76ers (1967) and LA Lakers (1972) to NBA titles; Finals MVP in 1972.

A.B. (Happy) Chandler (b. July 14, 1898, d. June 15, 1991): Baseball; former Kentucky governor and U.S. Senator who succeeded Judge Landis as commissioner in 1945; backed Branch Rickey's move in 1947 to make Jackie Robinson 1st black player in major leagues; deemed too pro-player and ousted by owners in 1951.

Julio Cesar Chavez (b. July 12, 1962): Mexican boxer; world jr. welterweight champ (1989-94); also held titles as jr. lightweight (1984-87) and lightweight (1987-89); fought Pernell Whitaker to controversial draw for welterweight title on Sept. 10, 1993; career record of 101-2-2 record with 84 KOs; 90-bout unbeaten streak ended Jan. 29, 1994 when Frankie Randall won title on split decision; Chavez won title back four months later.

Linford Christie (b. Apr. 2, 1960): British sprinter; won 100-meter gold medals at both 1992 Olympics (9.96) and '93 World Championships (9.87).

Jim Clark (b. Mar. 14, 1936, d. Apr. 7, 1968): Scottish auto racer; 2-time Formula One world champion (1963,65); won Indy 500 in 1965; killed in car crash.

Bobby Clarke (b. Aug. 13, 1949): Hockey C; led Philadelphia Flyers to consecutive Stanley Cups in 1974-75; 3-time regular season MVP (1973,75-76); currently Flyers general manager.

Ron Clarke (b. Feb. 21, 1937): Australian runner; from 1963-70 set 17 world records in races from 2 miles to 20,000m; never won Olympic gold medal.

Roger Clemens (b. Aug. 4, 1962): Baseball RHP; twice fanned MLB record 20 batters in 9-inning game (April 29, 1986 and Sept. 18, 1996); 5 Cy Young Awards with Boston (1986-87,91) and Toronto (1997,98); AL MVP in 1986; won pitching Triple Crown in 1997 and 98; traded from Toronto to the New York Yankees and won a World Series ring with them in 1999.

Roberto Clemente (b. Aug. 18, 1934, d. Dec. 31, 1972): Baseball OF; hit over .300 13 times with Pittsburgh; led NL in batting 4 times; World Series MVP in 1971; regular season MVP in 1966; had 3,000 career hits; killed in plane crash.

Alice Coachman (b. Nov. 9, 1923): Track & Field; became the first black woman to win an Olympic gold medal with her win in the high jump in 1948 (London); broke the high school and college high jump records despite not wearing any shoes; member of the National Track & Field Hall of Fame.

Ty Cobb (b. Dec. 18, 1886, d. July 17, 1961): Baseball OF; all-time highest career batting average (.367); hit over .400 3 times; led AL in batting 12 times and stolen bases 6 times with Detroit; MVP in 1911; had 4,191 career hits and 892 steals.

Mickey Cochrane (b. Apr. 6, 1903, d. June 28, 1962): Baseball C; led Philadelphia A's (1929-30) and Detroit (1935) to 3 World Series titles; 2-time AL MVP (1928,34).

Sebastian Coe (b. Sept. 29, 1956): British runner; won gold medal in 1500m and silver medal in 800m at both 1980 and '84 Olympics; long-time world record holder in 800m and 1000m; elected to Parliament as Conservative in 1992.

Paul Coffey (b. June 1, 1961): Hockey D; holds NHL record for assists and points by a defenseman; member of four Stanley Cup championship teams in Edmonton (1984-85,87) and Pittsburgh (1991).

Rocky Colavito (b. August 10, 1933): Baseball OF; six-time all-star who hit 374 HRs over his 14-year career; hugely popular in Cleveland where he played from 1955-59 and then 1965-67; led the league in HRs in 1959 with 42 and RBI in 1965 with 108; hit four consecutive HRs in one game.

Eddie Collins (b. May 2, 1887, d. Mar. 25, 1951): Baseball 2B; led Phila. A's (1910-11) and Chicago White Sox (1917) to 3 World Series titles; AL MVP in 1914; had 3,311 career hits and 743 stolen bases.

Nadia Comaneci (b. Nov. 12, 1961): Romanian gymnast; first to record perfect 10 in Olympics; won 3 individual golds at 1976 Olympics and 2 more in '80.

Lionel Conacher (b. May 24, 1901, d. May 26, 1954): Canada's greatest all-around athlete; NHL hockey (2 Stanley Cups), CFL football (1 Grey Cup), minor league baseball, soccer, lacrosse, track, amateur boxing champion; member of Parliament (1949-54).

Tony Conigliaro (b. Jan. 7, 1945, d. Feb. 24, 1990): Baseball OF; hit 24 HRs as a 19-year-old rookie (1964) with the Red Sox; became youngest in history to lead the AL in HRs (32) the following year; won the pennant with the 1967 "Impossible Dream" Red Sox; hit in the face with a fastball earlier in the season; came back to hit 36 HRs in 1970 but was never the same.

Gene Conley (b. Nov. 10, 1930): Baseball and Basketball; played for World Series and NBA champions with Milwaukee Braves (1957) and Boston Celtics (1959-61); winning pitcher in 1954 All-Star Game; 91-96 record in 11 seasons.

Billy Conn (b. Oct. 8, 1917, d. May 29, 1993): Boxer; Pittsburgh native and world light heavyweight champion from 1939-41; nearly upset heavyweight champ Joe Louis in 1941 title bout, but was knocked out in 13th round; pro record 63-11-1 with 14 KOs.

Dennis Conner (b. Sept. 16, 1942): Sailing; 3-time America's Cup-winning skipper aboard *Freedom* (1980), *Stars & Stripes* (1987) and the *Stars & Stripes* catamaran (1988); only American skipper to lose Cup, first in 1983 when *Australia II* beat *Liberty* and again in '95 when New Zealand's *Black* Magic swept Conner and his *Stars & Stripes* crew aboard the borrowed *Young America.*

Maureen Connolly (b. Sept. 17, 1934, d. June 21, 1969): Tennis; in 1953 1st woman to win Grand Slam (at age 18); riding accident ended her career in '54; won both Wimbledon and U.S. titles 3 times (1951-53); 3-time AP Female Athlete of Year (1951-53).

Jimmy Connors (b. Sept. 2, 1952): Tennis; No. 1 player in world 5 times (1974-78); won 5 U.S. Opens, 2 Wimbledons and 1 Australian; rose from No. 936 at the close of 1990 to U.S. Open semifinals in 1991 at age 39; NCAA singles champ (1971); all-time leader in pro singles titles (109) and matches won at U.S. Open (98) and Wimbledon (84); inducted into Hall of Fame in 1998.

Jack Kent Cooke (b. Oct. 25, 1912, d. April 6, 1997): Football; sole owner of NFL Washington Redskins from 1985-97; teams won 2 Super Bowls (1988,92); also owned NBA Lakers and NHL Kings in LA; built LA Forum for $12 million in 1967.

Cynthia Cooper (b. April 14, 1963): Women's basketball G; won two NCAA basketball titles at USC (1983-84); 2-time WNBA MVP and 4-time league champion with Houston Comets.

Angel Cordero Jr. (b. Nov. 8, 1942): Jockey; retired third on all-time list with 7,057 wins in 38,646 starts; won Kentucky Derby 3 times (1974,76,85), Preakness twice and Belmont once; 2-time Eclipse Award winner (1982-83).

Howard Cosell (b. Mar. 25, 1920, d. Apr. 23, 1995): Radio-TV; former ABC commentator on *Monday Night Football* and *Wide World of Sports*, who energized TV sports journalism with abrasive "tell it like it is" style.

Bob Costas (b. Mar. 22, 1952): Radio-TV; NBC anchor for NBA, NFL and Summer Olympics as well as baseball play-by-play man; 8-time Emmy winner and 9-time National Sportscaster of Year.

James (Doc) Counsilman (b. Dec. 28, 1920): Swimming; coached Indiana men's swim team to 6 NCAA championships (1968-73); coached the 1964 and '76 U.S. men's Olympic teams that won a combined 21 of 24 gold medals; in 1979 became oldest person (59) to swim English Channel; retired in 1990 with dual meet record of 287-36-1.

Fred Couples (b. Oct. 3, 1959): Golfer; 2-time PGA Tour Player of the Year (1991,92); 14 Tour victories, including 1992 Masters.

Jim Courier (b. Aug. 17, 1970): Tennis; No. 1 player in world in 1992; won 2 Australian Opens (1992-93) and 2 French Opens (1991-92); played on 1992 Davis Cup winner; Nick Bollettieri Academy classmate of Andre Agassi; announced retirement in May, 2000.

Margaret Smith Court (b. July 16, 1942): Australian tennis player; won Grand Slam in both singles (1970) and mixed doubles (1963 with Ken Fletcher); record 24 Grand Slam singles titles—11 Australian, 5 U.S., 5 French and 3 Wimbledon.

Bob Cousy (b. Aug. 9, 1928): Basketball G; led NBA in assists 8 times; 10-time All-NBA 1st team; 1957 MVP; led Boston to 6 NBA titles (1957,59-63).

Buster Crabbe (b. Feb. 7, 1910, d. Apr. 23, 1983): Swimmer; 2-time Olympic freestyle medalist with bronze in 1928 (1500m) and gold in '32 (400m); became movie star and King of Serials as Flash Gordon and Buck Rogers.

Ben Crenshaw (b. Jan. 11, 1952): Golfer; co-NCAA champion with Tom Kite in 1972; battled Graves' disease in mid-1980s; 19 career Tour victories; won Masters for second time on April 9, 1995 and dedicated it to 90-year-old mentor Harvey Penick, who had died on April 2; captain of 1999 Ryder Cup team.

Joe Cronin (b. Oct. 12, 1906, d. Sept. 7, 1984): Baseball SS; hit over .300 and drove in over 100 runs 8 times each; player-manager in Washington and Boston (1933-47); AL president (1959-73).

Larry Csonka (b. Dec. 25, 1946): Football RB; powerful runner and blocker who gained 8,081 yards in 11 seasons in the AFL and NFL; won two consecutive Super Bowls with the Miami Dolphins (1973-74) and was named MVP in the latter, rushing for 145 yards and two TDs; member of the College and Pro Football Halls of Fame.

Ann Curtis (b. Mar. 6, 1926): Swimming; won 2 gold medals and 1 silver in 1948 Olympics; set 4 world and 18 U.S. records during career; 1st woman and swimmer to win Sullivan Award (1944).

Betty Cuthbert (b. Apr. 20, 1938): Australian runner; won gold medals in 100 and 200 meters and 4x100m relay at 1956 Olympics; also won 400m gold at 1964 Olympics.

Bjorn Dæhlie (b. June 19, 1967): Norwegian cross-country skier; winner of a record eight gold and 12 overall Winter Olympic medals from 1992-98.

Chuck Daly (b. July 20, 1930): Basketball; coached Detroit to two NBA titles (1989-90) before leaving in 1992 to coach New Jersey; coached NBA "Dream Team" to gold medal in 1992 Olympics; retired in 1994 but returned in 1997 to coach Orlando Magic for two seasons.

John Daly (b. Apr. 28, 1966): Golfer; surprise winner of 1991 PGA Championship as unknown 25-year-old; battled through personal troubles in 1994 to return in '95 and win 2nd major at British Open, beating Italy's Costantino Rocca in 4-hole playoff.

Stanley Dancer (b. July 25, 1927): Harness racing; winner of 4 Hambletonians; trainer-driver of Triple Crown winners in trotting (Nevele Pride in 1968 and Super Bowl in '72) and pacing (Most Happy Fella in 1970).

Beth Daniel (b. Oct. 14, 1956): Golfer; 32 career wins, including 1 major; inducted into World Golf Hall of Fame in 1999.

Alvin Dark (b. Jan. 7, 1922): Baseball OF and MGR; hit .322 to win the NL Rookie of the Year award in 1948 with the Boston Braves; traded to the N.Y. Giants where he led the league in doubles (41) in 1951; won 994 games as a manager and led the Oakland A's to a World Series win in 1974.

Tamas Darnyi (b. June 3, 1967): Hungarian swimmer; 2-time double gold medal winner in 200m and 400m individual medley at 1988 and '92 Olympics; also won both events in 1986 and '91 world championships; set world records in both at '91 worlds; 1st swimmer to break 2 minutes in 200m IM (1:59:36).

Lindsay Davenport (b. June 8, 1976): Tennis player; first American female to be ranked No. 1 in the world (1998) since Chris Evert in 1985; won U.S. Open (1998), Wimbledon (1999) and Australian Open (2000); Olympic gold medalist at Atlanta in 1996.

Al Davis (b. July 4, 1929): Football; GM-coach of Oakland 1963-66; helped force AFL-NFL merger as AFL commissioner in 1966; returned to Oakland as managing general partner and directed club to 3 Super Bowl wins (1977,81,84); defied fellow NFL owners and moved Raiders to LA in 1982; turned down owners' 1995 offer to build him a new stadium in LA and moved back to Oakland instead.

Dwight Davis (b. July 5, 1879, d. Nov. 28, 1945): Tennis; donor of Davis Cup; played for winning U.S. team in 1st two Cup finals (1900,02); won U.S. and Wimbledon doubles titles in 1901; Secretary of War (1925-29) under President Coolidge.

Ernie Davis (b. Dec. 14, 1939, d. May 18, 1963): Football; star running back at Syracuse University; first black to win the Heisman Trophy in 1961; drafted by the Washington Redskins and traded to Cleveland but died the following year of leukemia before playing a pro game.

Glenn Davis (b. Dec. 26, 1924): Football HB; 3-time All-America; led Army to national titles in 1944-45; Doc Blanchard's running mate; won Heisman Trophy in 1946.

John Davis (b. Jan. 12, 1921, d. July 13, 1984): Weightlifting; 6-time world champion; 2-time Olympic super-heavyweight champ (1948,52); undefeated from 1938-53.

Terrell Davis (b. Oct. 28, 1972): Football RB; 1998 NFL MVP, rushing for an league-leading 2,008 yards (3rd all-time); played for two Super Bowl winners in Denver (XXXII and XXXIII), earning MVP honors in the former with Super Bowl-record 3 rushing TDs, missed most of the 1999 season with a torn knee ligament.

Pat Day (b. Oct. 13, 1953): Jockey; 4-time Eclipse award winner; ranked 3rd all-time in career wins through 1999; won Kentucky Derby (1992), 5 Preaknesses (1985,90,94-96) and 3 Belmonts (1989,94,2000); inducted into Hall of Fame in 1991.

Dizzy Dean (b. Jan. 16 1911, d. July 17, 1974): Baseball RHP; led NL in strikeouts and complete games 4 times; last NL pitcher to win 30 games (30-7 in 1934); MVP in 1934 with St. Louis; 150-83 record.

Dave DeBusschere (b. Oct. 16, 1940): Basketball F; youngest coach in NBA history (24 in 1964); player-coach of Detroit Pistons (1964-67); played in 8 All-Star games; won 2 NBA titles as player with NY Knicks; ABA commissioner (1975-76); also pitched 2 seasons for Chicago White Sox (1962-63) with 3-4 record.

Pierre de Coubertin (b. Jan. 1, 1863, d. Sept. 2, 1937): French educator; father of the Modern Olympic Games; IOC president from 1896-1925.

Anita DeFrantz (b. Oct. 4, 1952): Olympics; attorney who is one of 2 American delegates to the International Olympic Committee (the other is); first woman to represent U.S. on IOC; member of USOC Executive Committee; member of bronze medal U.S. women's eight-oared shell at Montreal in 1976.

Oscar De La Hoya (b. Feb. 4, 1973): Boxing; won the IBF lightweight title with a TKO of Rafael Ruelas in 1995; won WBC Super Lightweight title over Julio Cesar Chavez in 1996 and the WBC Welterweight title over Pernell Whitaker in 1997; won Olympic gold medal in 1992 as a lightweight; lost WBC Welterweight belt to Felix Trinidad in a majority decision on Sept. 18, 1999; lost to Sugar Shane Mosely in May, 2000 for his 2nd career defeat.

Cedric Dempsey (b. Apr. 14, 1932): College sports; named to succeed Dick Schultz as NCAA executive director on Nov. 5, 1993; served as athletic director at Pacific (1967-79), San Diego St. (1979), Houston (1979-82) and Arizona (1983-93).

Jack Dempsey (b. June 24, 1895, d. May 31, 1983): Boxer; world heavyweight champion from 1919-26; lost title to Gene Tunney, then lost "Long Count" rematch in 1927 when he floored Tunney in 7th round but failed to retreat to neutral corner; pro record 64-6-9 with 49 KOs.

Bob Devaney (b. April 13, 1915, d. May 9, 1997): Football; head coach at Wyoming from 1957-1961; from 1962 to 1972 built Nebraska into a college football power; won two consecutive national championships in 1970-'71; won eight Big Eight Conference titles; overall record of 136-30-11; later served as Nebraska's athletic director; College Football Hall of Famer.

Donna de Varona (b. Apr. 26, 1947): Swimming; won gold medals in 400 IM and 400 freestyle relay at 1964 Olympics; set 18 world records during career; co-founder of Women's Sports Foundation in 1974.

Gail Devers (b. Nov. 19, 1966): Track & Field; fastest-ever woman sprinter-hurdler; overcame thyroid disorder (Graves' disease) that sidelined her in 1989-90 and nearly resulted in having both feet amputated; won Olympic gold medal in 100 meters in 1992 and '96; world champion in 100 meters (1993) and 100-meter hurdles (1993, 95).

Klaus Dibiasi (b. Oct. 6, 1947): Italian diver; won 3 consecutive Olympic gold medals in platform event (1968,72,76).

Eric Dickerson (b. Sept. 2, 1960): Football RB; led NFL in rushing 4 times (1983-84,86,88); ran for single-season record 2,105 yards in 1984; NFC Rookie of Year in 1983; All-Pro 5 times; traded from LA Rams to Indianapolis (Oct. 31, 1987) in 3-team, 10-player deal (including draft picks) that also involved Buffalo; 3rd on all-time career rushing list with 13,259 yards in 11 seasons; entered Pro Football Hall of Fame in '99, became Monday Night Football sideline reporter in 2000.

Harrison Dillard (b. July 8, 1923): Track & Field; only man to win Olympic gold medals in both sprints (100m in 1948) and hurdles (110m in 1952).

Joe DiMaggio (b. Nov. 25, 1914, d. Mar. 8, 1999): Baseball OF; hit safely in 56 straight games (1941); led AL in batting, HRs and RBI twice each; 3-time MVP (1939,41,47); hit .325 with 361 HRs over 13 seasons; led NY Yankees to 10 World Series titles.

Marcel Dionne (b. Aug. 3, 1951): Hockey C; third on NHL's all-time points list (1,771) and goals list (731); tied Wayne Gretzky for the league lead in points (137) in 1980; scored 50 goals in a season 6 times; won the Lady Byng Award for gentlemanly play in 1975 with Detroit and in 1977 with the L.A. Kings; member of the Hockey Hall of Fame.

Mike Ditka (b. Oct. 18, 1939): Football; All-America at Pitt (1960); NFL Rookie of Year (1961); 5-time Pro Bowl tight end for Chicago Bears; also played for Philadelphia and Dallas in 12-year career; returned to Chicago as head coach in 1982 and won Super Bowl XX, 46-10, against the Patriots in 1986; left Bears in 1992 and worked as a broadcaster at NBC for four years; coached the New Orleans Saints from 1997-99; compiled 127-101-0 record in 14 seasons.

Larry Doby (b. Dec. 13, 1924): Baseball OF; first black player in the AL; joined the Cleveland Indians in July 1947, three months after Jackie Robinson entered the Majors with the NL's Brooklyn Dodgers; an all-star centerfielder from 1949-55; managed the Chicago White Sox in 1978, becoming the second black major league manager; inducted into the Hall of Fame in 1998.

Charlotte (Lottie) Dod (b. Sept. 24, 1871, d. June 27, 1960): British athlete; was 5-time Wimbledon singles champion (1887-88,91-93); youngest player ever to win Wimbledon (15 in 1887); archery silver medalist at 1908 Olympics; member of national field hockey team in 1899; British Amateur golf champ in 1904.

Tony Dorsett (b. Apr. 7, 1954): Football RB; won Heisman Trophy leading Pitt to national title in 1976; 3rd all-time in NCAA Div. I-A rushing with 6,082 yards; led Dallas to Super Bowl title as NFC Rookie of Year (1977); NFC Player of Year (1981); ranks 5th on all-time NFL list with 12,739 yards gained in 12 years.

James (Buster) Douglas (b. Apr. 7, 1960): Boxing; 42-1 shot who knocked out undefeated Mike Tyson in 10th round on Feb. 10, 1990 to win heavyweight title in Tokyo; 8 1/2 months later, lost only title defense to Evander Holyfield by KO in 3rd round.

The Dream Team Head coach Chuck Daly's "Best Ever" 12-man NBA All-Star squad that headlined the 1992 Summer Olympics in Barcelona and easily won the basketball gold medal; co-captained by Larry Bird and Magic Johnson, with veterans Charles Barkley, Clyde Drexler, Patrick Ewing, Michael Jordan, Karl Malone, Chris Mullin, Scottie Pippen, David Robinson, John Stockton and Duke's Christian Laettner.

Heike Drechsler (b. Dec. 16, 1964): German long jumper and sprinter; East German before reunification in 1991; set world long jump record (24-2¼) in 1988; won long jump gold medals at 1992 Olympics and 1983 and '93 World Championships; won silver medal in long jump and bronze medals in both 100- and 200-meter sprints at 1988 Olympics.

Ken Dryden (b. Aug. 8, 1947): Hockey G; led Montreal to 6 Stanley Cup titles; playoff MVP as rookie in 1971; won or shared 5 Vezina trophies; 2.24 career GAA; currently President of Toronto Maple Leafs.

Don Drysdale (b. July 23, 1936, d. July 3, 1993): Baseball RHP; led NL in strikeouts 3 times and games started 4 straight years; pitched record 6 shutouts in a row in 1968; won Cy Young (1962); had 209-166 record and hit 29 HRs in 14 years.

Charley Dumas (b. Feb. 12, 1937): U.S. high jumper; first man to clear 7 feet (7-0½) on June 29, 1956; won gold medal at 1956 Olympics.

Tim Duncan (b. Apr. 25, 1976): Basketball; consensus College Player of the Year as a senior at Wake Forest; #1 overall pick by the San Antonio Spurs (1997); 1998 NBA Rookie of the Year; became only the ninth rookie in NBA history to be named to the All-NBA first team (1998); 1999 NBA Finals MVP as he led Spurs to NBA title.

Margaret Osborne du Pont (b. Mar. 4, 1918): Tennis; won 5 French, 7 Wimbledon and an unprecedented 25 U.S. national titles in singles, doubles and mixed doubles from 1941-62.

Roberto Duran (b. June 16, 1951): Panamanian boxer; one of only 4 fighters to hold 4 different world titles— lightweight (1972-79), welterweight (1980), junior middleweight (1983) and middleweight (1989-90); lost famous "No Mas" welterweight title bout when he quit in 8th round against Sugar Ray Leonard (1980); pro record of 102-14 (69 KOs).

Leo Durocher (b. July 27, 1905, d. Oct. 7, 1991): Baseball; managed in NL 24 years; won 2,015 games, including postseason; 3 pennants with Brooklyn (1941) and NY Giants (1951,54); won World Series in 1954.

Eddie Eagan (b. Apr. 26, 1898, d. June 14, 1967): Only athlete to win gold medals in both Summer and Winter Olympics (Boxing–1920, Bobsled–1932).

Alan Eagleson (b. Apr. 24, 1933): Hockey; Toronto lawyer, agent and 1st executive director of NHL Players Assn. (1967-90); midwived Team Canada vs. Soviet series (1972) and Canada Cup; charged with racketeering and defrauding NHLPA in indictment handed down by U.S. grand jury in 1994; was sentenced to 18 months in jail in Jan. 1998 after pleading guilty but only served 6 months; resigned from Hall of Fame in 1998.

Dale Earnhardt (b. Apr. 29, 1952): Auto racer; 7-time NASCAR national champion (1980,86-87,90-91,93-94); Rookie of Year in 1979; all-time NASCAR money leader with over $34 million won and 6th on career wins list with 73 heading into the 2000 season; finally won Daytona 500 in 1998 on 20th attempt.

James Easton (b. July 26, 1935): Olympics; archer and sporting goods manufacturer (Easton softball bats); one of 2 American delegates to the International Olympic Committee; president of International Archery Federation (FITA); member of LA Olympic Organizing Committee in 1984.

Dick Ebersol (b. July 28, 1947): Radio-TV; protégé of ABC Sports czar Roone Arledge; key NBC exec in launching of *Saturday Night Live* in 1975; became president of NBC Sports in 1989.

Dennis Eckersley (b. Oct. 3, 1954): Baseball P; began his career as a starter in 1975 with the Cleveland Indians; pitched a no-hitter against California in 1977; won 20 games in 1978 with Boston; moved to the bullpen after 12 seasons as a starter and became one of the best closers of all time with Oakland; won the AL Cy Young Award and MVP (1992); retired after '99 season.

Stefan Edberg (b. Jan. 19, 1966): Swedish tennis player; 2-time No.1 player (1990-91); 2-time winner of Australian Open (1985,87), Wimbledon (1988,90) and U.S. Open (1991-92).

Gertrude Ederle (b. Oct. 23, 1906): Swimmer; 1st woman to swim English Channel, breaking men's record by 2 hours in 1926; won 3 medals in 1924 Olympics.

Krisztina Egerszegi (b. Aug. 16, 1974): Hungarian swimmer; 3-time gold medal winner (100m and 200m backstroke and 400m IM) in 1992 Olympics; also won a gold (200m back) and silver (100m back) in 1988 Games; youngest (14) ever to win swimming gold. Won fifth gold medal (200m back) at '96 Games.

Lee Elder (b. July 14, 1934): Golf; in 1975, he became the first black golfer to play in the Masters Tournament; also played in the 1977 Masters; member of the 1979 U.S. Ryder Cup team; played in South Africa's first integrated tournament in 1972.

Todd Eldredge (b. Aug. 28, 1971): Figure Skater; five-time U.S. champion (1990,91,95,97,98); 1996 World Champion; has won U.S. titles at all three levels (novice, junior and senior); most decorated American figure skater without an Olympic medal.

Bill Elliott (b. Oct. 8, 1955): Auto racer; 2-time winner of Daytona 500 (1985,87); NASCAR national champ in 1988; 40 NASCAR wins as of Sept. 1999.

Herb Elliott (b. Feb. 25, 1938): Australian runner; undefeated from 1958-60; ran 17 sub-4:00 miles; 3 world records; won gold medal in 1500 meters at 1960 Olympics; retired at age 22.

John Elway (b. June 28, 1960): Football QB; All-American at Stanford; first overall pick in the famous quarterback draft of 1983; known for his last-minute, game-winning scoring drives; led Broncos to three Super Bowl losses before back-to-back wins in Super Bowl XXXII and XXXIII; 1987 NFL MVP; four-time Pro Bowl selection; first QB to receive a pass in the Super Bowl (1987); one of only two QBs in league history (Marino) to throw for over 3,000 yards in 12 seasons; retired after '98 season.

Roy Emerson (b. Nov. 3, 1936): Australian tennis player; won 12 majors in singles— 6 Australian, 2 French, 2 Wimbledon and 2 U.S. from 1961-67.

Kornelia Ender (b. Oct. 25, 1958): East German swimmer; 1st woman to win 4 gold medals at one Olympics (1976), all in world-record time.

Julius Erving (b. Feb. 22, 1950): Basketball F; in ABA (1971-76)— 3-time MVP, 2-time playoff MVP, led NY Nets to 2 titles (1974,76); in NBA (1976-87)— 5-time All-NBA 1st team, MVP in 1981, led Philadelphia 76ers to title in 1983.

Phil Esposito (b. Feb. 20, 1942): Hockey C; 1st NHL player to score 100 points in a season (126 in 1969); 6-time All-NHL 1st team with Boston (1969-74); 2-time MVP (1969,74); 5-time scoring champ; star of 1972 Canada-Soviet series; former president-GM of Tampa Bay Lightning.

Janet Evans (b. Aug. 28, 1971): Swimmer; won 3 individual gold medals (400m & 800m freestyle, 400m IM) at 1988 Olympics; 1989 Sullivan Award winner; won 1 gold (800m) and 1 silver (400m) at 1992 Olympics.

Lee Evans (b. Feb. 25, 1947): Track & Field; dominant quarter-miler in world from 1966-72; world record in 400m set at 1968 Olympics stood 20 years.

Chris Evert (b. Dec. 21, 1954): Tennis; No.1 player in world 5 times (1975-77,80-81); won at least 1 Grand Slam singles title every year from 1974-86; 18 majors in all— 7 French, 6 U.S., 3 Wimbledon and 2 Australian; retired after 1989 season with 154 singles titles and $8,896,195 in career earnings.

Weeb Ewbank (b. May 6, 1907, d. Nov. 18, 1998): Football; only coach to win NFL and AFL titles; led Baltimore to 2 NFL titles (1958-59) and NY Jets to Super Bowl III win.

Patrick Ewing (b. Aug. 5, 1962): Basketball C; 3-time All-America; led Georgetown to 3 NCAA Finals and 1984 title; Final 4 MOP in '84; NBA Rookie of Year with New York in '86; All-NBA in 1990; on U.S. Olympic gold medal-winning teams in 1984 and '92; named one of the NBA's 50 greatest players of all-time; traded to Seattle Supersonics before the 2000 season.

Ray Ewry (b. Oct. 14, 1873, d. Sept. 29, 1937): Track & Field; won 10 gold medals (although 2 are not recognized by IOC) over 4 consecutive Olympics (1900,04,06,08); all events he won (Standing HJ, LJ and TJ) were discontinued in 1912.

Nick Faldo (b. July 18, 1957): British golfer; 3-time winner of British Open (1987,90,92) and Masters (1989, 90, 96); 3-time European Golfer of Year (1989-90,92); PGA Player of Year in 1990.

Juan Manuel Fangio (b. June 24, 1911, d. July 17, 1995): Argentine auto racer; 5-time Formula One world champion (1951,54-57); 24 career wins, retired in 1958.

Brett Favre (b. Oct. 10, 1969): Football QB; Selected in the second round (33rd overall) by the Atlanta Falcons in the 1991 NFL draft; traded to Green Bay Packers in 1992; league MVP in 1995, '96 and '97; five-time Pro Bowl QB; 100th TD pass came in his 62nd game, third-fastest in league history; 39 TD passes in 1996 season broke his own NFC record of 38 set in 1995 (since broken by Kurt Warner – 41 in 1999); led Packers to Super Bowl victory in 1997.

Sergei Fedorov (b. Dec. 13, 1969): Hockey C; first Russian to win NHL Hart Trophy as 1993-94 regular season MVP; 3-time All-Star with Detroit.

Donald Fehr (b. July 18, 1948): Baseball labor leader; protégé of Marvin Miller; executive director and general counsel of Major League Players Assn. since 1983; led players in 1994 "salary cap" strike that lasted eight months and resulted in first cancellation of World Series since 1904.

Bob Feller (b. Nov. 3, 1918): Baseball RHP; led AL in strikeouts 7 times and wins 6 times with Cleveland; threw 3 no-hitters and 12 one-hitters; 266-162 record.

Tom Ferguson (b. Dec. 20, 1950): Rodeo; 6-time All-Around champion (1974-79); 1st cowboy to win $100,000 in one season (1978); 1st to win $1 million in career (1986).

Herve Filion (b. Feb. 1, 1940): Harness racing; 10-time Driver of Year; all-time leader in races won with 14,783 in 35 years.

Rollie Fingers (b. Aug. 25, 1946): Baseball RHP; relief ace with 341 career saves; won AL MVP and Cy Young awards in 1981 with Milwaukee; World Series MVP in 1974 with Oakland.

Charles O. Finley (b. Feb. 22, 1918, d. Feb, 19, 1997): Baseball owner; moved KC A's to Oakland in 1968; won 3 straight World Series from 1972-74; also owned teams in NHL and ABA.

Bobby Fischer (b. Mar. 9, 1943): Chess; at 15, became youngest international grandmaster in chess history; only American to hold world championship (1972-75); was stripped of title in 1975 after refusing to defend against Anatoly Karpov and became recluse; re-emerged to defeat old foe and former world champion Boris Spassky in 1992.

Carlton Fisk (b. Dec. 26, 1947): Baseball C; holds all-time major league record for games caught (2,229); also all-time HR leader for catchers (376); AL Rookie of Year (1972) and 10-time All-Star; hit epic, 12th-inning Game 6 homer for Boston Red Sox in 1975 World Series; inducted into the Baseball Hall of Fame and had his number retired by the Red Sox in 2000.

Emerson Fittipaldi (b. Dec. 12, 1946): Brazilian auto racer; 2-time Formula One world champion (1972,74); 2-time winner of Indy 500 (1989,93); won overall IndyCar title in 1989.

Bob Fitzsimmons (b. May 26, 1863, d. Oct. 22, 1917): British boxer; held three world titles— middleweight (1881-97), heavyweight (1897-99) and light heavyweight (1903-05); pro record 40-11 with 32 KOs.

James (Sunny Jim) Fitzsimmons (b. July 23, 1874, d. Mar. 11, 1966): Horse racing; trained horses that won over 2,275 races, including 2 Triple Crown winners— Gallant Fox in 1930 and Omaha in '35.

Jim Fixx (b. Apr. 23, 1932, d. July 20, 1984): Running; author who popularized the sport of running; his 1977 bestseller *The Complete Book of Running*, is credited with helping start America's fitness revolution; died of a heart attack while running.

Larry Fleisher (b. Sept. 26, 1930, d. May 4, 1989): Basketball; led NBA players union from 1961-89; increased average yearly salary from $9,400 in 1967 to $600,000 without a strike.

Peggy Fleming (b. July 27, 1948): Figure skating; 3-time world champion (1966-68); won Olympic gold medal in 1968.

Curt Flood (b. Jan. 18, 1938, d. Jan. 20, 1997): Baseball OF; played 15 years (1956-69,71) mainly with St. Louis; hit over .300 6 times with 7 Gold Gloves; refused trade to Phillies in 1969; lost challenge to baseball's reserve clause in Supreme Court in 1972 (see Peter Seitz).

Ray Floyd (b. Sept. 14, 1942): Golfer; has 22 PGA victories in 4 decades; joined Senior PGA Tour in 1992; has won Masters (1976), U.S. Open (1986), PGA twice (1969,82) and PGA Seniors Championship (1995); only player to ever win on PGA and Senior tours in same year (1992); member of 8 Ryder Cup teams and captain in 1989.

Doug Flutie (b. Oct. 23, 1962): Football QB; won Heisman Trophy with Boston College (1984); has played in USFL, NFL and CFL; 6-time CFL MVP with B.C. Lions (1991), Calgary (1992-94) and Toronto (1996-97); led Calgary to Grey Cup title in '92 and Toronto in 1996-97; returned to NFL in 1998 with Buffalo Bills and threw 20 TD passes in '98 and 19 in '99 before being benched for the '99 playoffs.

Gerald Ford (b. July 14, 1913): 38th President of the U.S.; lettered as center on undefeated Michigan football teams in 1932 and '33; MVP on 1934 squad.

Whitey Ford (b. Oct. 21, 1928): Baseball LHP; all-time leader in World Series wins (10); led AL in wins 3 times; won Cy Young and World Series MVP in 1961 with NY Yankees; 236-106 record.

George Foreman (b. Jan. 10, 1949): Boxer; Olympic heavyweight champ (1968); world heavyweight champ (1973-74 and 94-95); lost title to Muhammad Ali (KO-8th) in '74; recaptured it on Nov. 5, 1994 at age 45 with a 10-round KO of WBA/IBF champ Michael Moorer, becoming the oldest man to win heavyweight crown; named AP Male Athlete of Year 20 years after losing title to Ali; stripped of WBA title on Mar. 4, 1995 after declining to fight No. 1 contender; successfully defended title at age 46 against 26-year-old Axel Schultz of Germany in controversial majority decision on Apr. 22; gave up IBF title in June after refusing rematch with Schultz.

Dick Fosbury (b. Mar. 6, 1947): Track & Field; revolutionized high jump with back-first "Fosbury Flop"; won gold medal at 1968 Olympics.

Greg Foster (b. Aug. 4, 1958): Track & Field; 3-time winner of World Championship gold medal in 110-meter hurdles (1983,87,91); best Olympic performance a silver in 1984; world indoor champion in 1991; made world Top 10 rankings 15 years (a record for running events).

The Four Horsemen Senior backfield that led Notre Dame to national collegiate football championship in 1924; put together as sophomores by Irish coach Knute Rockne; immortalized by sportswriter Grantland Rice, whose report of the Oct. 19, 1924, Notre Dame-Army game began: "Outlined against a blue, gray October sky the Four Horsemen rode again . . ."; HB Jim Crowley (b. Sept. 10, 1902, d. Jan. 15, 1986), FB Elmer Layden (b. May 4, 1903, d. June 30, 1973), HB Don Miller (b. May 30, 1902, d. July 28, 1979) and QB Harry Stuhldreher (b. Oct. 14, 1901, d. Jan. 26, 1965).

The celebrated **Four Horsemen** backfield of Notre Dame's 1924 national championship team (from left to right): halfback **Don Miller**, fullback **Elmer Layden**, halfback **Jim Crowley** and quarterback **Harry Stuhldreher.**

The Four Musketeers French quartet that dominated men's tennis in 1920s and '30s, winning 8 straight French singles titles (1925-32), 6 Wimbledons in a row (1924-29) and 6 consecutive Davis Cups (1927-32)— Jean Borotra (b. Aug. 13, 1898, d. July 17, 1994), Jacques Brugnon (b. May 11, 1895, d. Mar. 20, 1978), Henri Cochet (b. Dec. 14, 1901, d. Apr. 1, 1987), Rene Lacoste (b. July 2, 1905, d. Oct. 13, 1996).

Nellie Fox (b. Dec. 25, 1927, d. Dec. 1, 1975): Baseball 2B; batted .306 in 1959 to win the AL MVP award with the pennant-winning Chicago White Sox; led the league in fielding percentage six times, hits four times and triples once; ended his 19-year career with 2,663 hits, 1,279 runs and .288 average.

Jimmie Foxx (b. Oct. 22, 1907, d. July 21, 1967): Baseball 1B; led AL in HRs 4 times and batting twice; won Triple Crown in 1933; 3-time MVP (1932-33,38) with Philadelphia and Boston; hit 30 HRs or more 12 years in a row; 534 career HRs.

A.J. Foyt (b. Jan. 16, 1935): Auto racer; 7-time USAC-CART national champion (1960-61,63-64,67,75,79); 4-time Indy 500 winner (1961,64,67,77); only driver in history to win Indy 500, Daytona 500 (1972) and 24 Hours of LeMans (1967 with Dan Gurney); retired in 1993 as all-time CART wins leader with 67.

Bill France Sr. (b. Sept. 26, 1909, d. June 7, 1992): Stock car pioneer and promoter; founded NASCAR in 1948; guided race circuit through formative years; built both Daytona (Fla.) Int'l Speedway and Talladega (Ala.) Superspeedway.

Dawn Fraser (b. Sept. 4, 1937): Australian swimmer; won gold medals in 100m freestyle at 3 consecutive Olympics (1956,60,64).

Joe Frazier (b. Jan. 12, 1944): Boxer; 1964 Olympic heavyweight champion; world heavyweight champ (1970-73); fought Muhammad Ali 3 times and won once; pro record 32-4-1 with 27 KOs.

Walt Frazier (b. March 29, 1945): Basketball G; won the NBA championship two times (1970 and 73) with the New York Knicks; 35 points and 19 assists in the 1970 championship game vs. the Lakers; averaged 18.9 PPG and 6.1 APG over his career; four-time all-NBA and a member of the Hall of Fame; nicknamed "Clyde" after well-dressed gangster Clyde Barrow.

Ford Frick (b. Dec. 19, 1894, d. Apr. 8, 1978): Baseball; sportswriter and radio announcer who served as NL president (1934-51) and commissioner (1951-65); convinced record-keepers to list Roger Maris' and Babe Ruth's season records separately; major leagues moved to West Coast and expanded from 16 to 20 teams during his tenure.

Frankie Frisch (b. Sept. 9, 1898, d. Mar. 12, 1973): Baseball 2B; played on 8 NL pennant winners in 19 years with NY and St. Louis; hit .300 or better 11 years in a row (1921-31); MVP in 1931; player-manager from 1933-37.

Dan Gable (b. Oct. 25, 1948): Wrestling; career wrestling record of 118-1 at Iowa St., where he was a 2-time NCAA champ (1968,69) and tourney MVP in 1969 (137 lbs); won gold medal (149 lbs) at 1972 Olympics; coached U.S. freestyle team in 1988; coached Iowa to 9 straight NCAA titles (1978-86) and 15 overall in 21 years.

Eddie Gaedel (b. June 8, 1925, d. June 18, 1961): Baseball PH; St. Louis Browns' 3-foot-7 player whose career lasted one at bat (he walked) on Aug 19, 1951; hired as a publicity stunt by eccentric owner Bill Veeck.

Clarence (Big House) Gaines (b. May 21, 1924): Basketball; retired as coach of Div. II Winston-Salem after 1992-93 season with 828-447 record in 47 years; ranks 3rd on all-time NCAA list behind Dean Smith (879) and Adolph Rupp (876).

Alonzo (Jake) Gaither (b. Apr. 11, 1903, d. Feb. 18, 1994): Football; head coach at Florida A&M for 25 years; led Rattlers to 6 national black college titles; retired after 1969 season with record of 203-36-4 and a winning percentage of .844; coined phrase, "I like my boys agile, mobile and hostile."

Lou Gehrig (b. June 19, 1903, d. June 2, 1941): Baseball 1B; played in 2,130 consecutive games from 1925-39 a major league record until Cal Ripken Jr. surpassed it in 1995; led AL in RBI 5 times and HRs 3 times; drove in 100 runs or more 13 years in a row; 2-time MVP (1927,36); hit .340 with 493 HRs over 17 seasons; led NY Yankees to 6 World Series titles; died at age 37 of Amyotrophic Lateral Sclerosis (ALS), a rare and incurable disease of the nervous system now better known as Lou Gehrig's disease.

Charley Gehringer (b. May 11, 1903, d. Jan. 21, 1993): Baseball 2B; hit .300 or better 13 times; AL batting champion and MVP with Detroit in 1937.

Bernie Geoffrion (b. Feb. 14, 1931): Hockey RW; credited with popularizing the slap shot, earning his nickname "Boom Boom"; scored 30 goals in 1952 to win the NHL's Calder Trophy (Rookie of the Year Award); won the MVP award (Hart) in 1955; became the second player in history to score 50 goals in one season; led the league in points in 1955 and 61; won 6 Stanley Cups with Montreal; member of the Hockey Hall of Fame.

George Gervin (b. April 27, 1952): Basketball G/F; joined the ABA in 1972 and came to the NBA with San Antonio in 1976; a five-time NBA all-star; led the league in scoring four times; scored 26,595 points with an average of 25.1 per game; known as the "Iceman" because of his cool style; elected to the Basketball Hall of Fame in 1996.

A. Bartlett Giamatti (b. April 14, 1938, d. Sept. 1, 1989): Scholar and 7th commissioner of baseball; banned Pete Rose for life for betting on Major League games and associating with known gamblers; also served as president of Yale (1978-86) and National League (1986-89).

Joe Gibbs (b. Nov. 25, 1940): Football; coached Washington to 140 victories and 3 Super Bowl titles in 12 seasons before retiring in 1993; owner of NASCAR racing team that won 1993 Daytona 500.

Althea Gibson (b. Aug. 25, 1927): Tennis; won both Wimbledon and U.S. championships in 1957 and '58; 1st black to play in either tourney and 1st to win each title.

Bob Gibson (b. Nov. 9, 1935): Baseball RHP; won 20 or more games 5 times; won 2 NL Cy Youngs (1968,70); MVP in 1968; led St. Louis to 2 World Series titles (1964,67); 251-174 record.

Josh Gibson (b. Dec. 21, 1911, d. Jan. 20, 1947): Baseball C; the "Babe Ruth of the Negro Leagues"; Satchel Paige's battery mate with Pittsburgh Crawfords. The Negro Leagues did not keep accurate records but Gibson hit 84 home runs in one season and his Baseball Hall of Fame plaque says he hit "almost 800" home runs in his seventeen-year career.

Kirk Gibson (b. May 28, 1957): Baseball OF; All-America flanker at Mich. St. in 1978; chose baseball career and was AL playoff MVP with Detroit in 1984 and NL regular season MVP with Los Angeles in 1988; hit famous pinch-hit home run against Oakland's Dennis Eckersley in Game 1 of the 1988 World Series to vault the Dodgers to the title.

Frank Gifford (b. Aug. 16, 1930): Football HB; 4-time All-Pro (1955-57,59); NFL MVP in 1956; led NY Giants to 3 NFL title games; TV sportscaster since 1958, beginning career while still a player.

Sid Gillman (b. Oct. 26, 1911): Football innovator; only coach in both College and Pro Football Halls of Fame; led college teams at Miami-OH and Cincinnati to combined 81-19-2 record from 1944-54; coached LA Rams (1955-59) in NFL, then led LA-San Diego Chargers to 5 Western titles and 1 league championship in first six years of AFL.

George Gipp (b. Feb. 18, 1895, d. Dec. 14, 1920): Football FB; died of throat infection 2 weeks before he made All-America; rushed for 2,341 yards, scored 156 points and averaged 38 yards a punt in 4 years (1917-20).

Marc Girardelli (b. July 18, 1963): Luxembourg Alpine skier; Austrian native who refused to join Austrian Ski Federation because he wanted to be coached by his father; won unprecedented 5th overall World Cup title in 1993; winless at Olympics, although he won 2 silver medals in 1992.

Tom Glavine (b. Mar. 26, 1966): Baseball LHP; Atlanta Braves' pitcher led the majors in wins from 1991-95 with 91; NL Cy Young winner in 1991 and '98; seven-time All-Star and was the NL starter twice; World Series MVP (1995).

Tom Gola (b. Jan. 13, 1933): Basketball F; 4-time All-America and 1955 Player of Year at La Salle; MOP in 1952 NIT and '54 NCAA Final 4, leading Pioneers to both titles; won NBA title as rookie with Philadelphia Warriors in 1956; 4-time NBA All-Star.

Marshall Goldberg (b. Oct. 24, 1917): Football HB; 2-time consensus All-America at Pittsburgh (1937-38); led Pitt to national championship in 1937; played with NFL champion Chicago Cardinals 10 years later.

Lefty Gomez (b. Nov. 26, 1908, d. Feb. 17, 1989): Baseball LHP; 4-time 20-game winner with NY Yankees; holds World Series record for most wins (6) without a defeat; pitched on 5 world championship clubs in 1930s.

Pancho Gonzales (b. May 9, 1928, d. July 3, 1995): Tennis; won consecutive U.S. Championships in 1947-48 before turning pro at 21; dominated pro tour from 1950-61; in 1969 at age 41, played longest Wimbledon match ever (5:12), beating Charlie Pasarell 22-24,1-6,16-14,6-3,11-9.

Bob Goodenow (b. Oct. 29, 1952): Hockey; succeeded Alan Eagleson as executive director of NHL Players Assn. in 1990; led players out on 10-day strike (Apr. 1-10) in 1992 and during 103-day owners' lockout in 1994-95.

Gail Goodrich (b. April 23, 1943): Basketball G; starred at UCLA and won two national championships in 1964 and 1965 under legendary coach John Wooden's tutelage; won the NBA championship with the L.A. Lakers in 1972 and led the team in scoring (25.9 ppg); averaged 18.6 ppg over his 14-year career.

Jeff Gordon (b. Aug. 4, 1971): Auto racer; NASCAR Rookie of Year (1993); 3-time Winston Cup champion (1995,97,98); won inaugural Brickyard 400 in 1994; in 1997, at 25 became youngest winner of the Daytona 500; in 1998 he tied Richard Petty for the modern-era record for wins in a single season with 13.

Dr. Harold Gores (b. Sept. 20, 1909, d. May 28, 1993): Educator and first president of Education Facilities Laboratories in New York; in 1964 hired Monsanto Co. to produce a synthetic turf that kids could play on in city schoolyards; resulting ChemGrass proved too expensive for playground use, but it was just what the Houston Astros were looking for in 1966 to cover the floor of the Astrodome, where grass refused to grow. Thus, AstroTurf was born.

Goose Gossage (b. July 5, 1951): Baseball RHP; Nine-time All Star (1975-78, 80-82, 84-85); intimidating relief pitcher; Fireman of the Year in 1975 with White Sox and 1978 with Yankees; led AL in saves with 26 (1975), 27 (1978); 1,002 career appearances; 310 saves.

Shane Gould (b. Nov. 23, 1956): Australian swimmer; set world records in 5 different freestyle events between July 1971 and Jan. 1972; won 3 gold medals, a silver and bronze in 1972 Olympics then retired at age 16.

Alf Goullet (b. Apr. 5, 1891, d. Mar. 11, 1995): Cycling; Australian who gained fame and fortune early in century as premier performer on U.S. 6-day bike race circuit; won 8 annual races at Madison Square Garden with 6 different partners from 1913-23.

Curt Gowdy (b. July 31, 1919): Radio-TV; former radio voice of NY Yankees and then Boston Red Sox from 1949-66; TV play-by-play man for AFL, NFL and major league baseball; has broadcast World Series, All-Star Games, Rose Bowls, Super Bowls, Olympics and NCAA Final Fours for all 3 networks; hosted "The American Sportsman."

Steffi Graf (b. June 14, 1969): German tennis player; won Grand Slam and Olympic gold medal in 1988 at age 19; won three of four majors in 1993, '95 and '96; won 22 Grand Slam singles titles — 7 at Wimbledon, 6 French, 5 U.S. and 4 Australian Opens; retired in 1999 as 3rd all-time with 107 career singles titles and as all-time tour leader in career earnings with over $21 million in prize money.

Otto Graham (b. Dec. 6, 1921): Football QB and basketball All-America at Northwestern; in pro ball, led Cleveland Browns to 7 league titles in 10 years, winning 4 AAFC championships (1946-49) and 3 NFL (1950,54-55); 5-time All-Pro; 2-time NFL MVP (1953,55).

Red Grange (b. June 13, 1903, d. Jan. 28, 1991): Football HB; 3-time All-America at Illinois who brought 1st huge crowds to pro football when he signed with Chicago Bears in 1925; formed 1st AFL with manager-promoter C.C. Pyle in 1926, but league folded and he returned to Bears.

Bud Grant (b. May 20, 1927): Football and Basketball; only coach to win 100 games in both CFL and NFL and only member of both CFL and U.S. Pro Football Halls of Fame; led Winnipeg to 4 Grey Cup titles (1958-59,61-62) in 6 appearances, but his Minnesota Vikings lost all 4 Super Bowl attempts in 1970s; accumulated 122 CFL wins and 168 NFL wins; also All-Big Ten at Minnesota in both football and basketball in late 1940s; a three-time CFL All-Star offensive end; also member of 1950 NBA champion Minneapolis Lakers.

Rocky Graziano (b. June 7, 1922, d. May 22, 1990): Boxer; world middleweight champion (1946-47); fought Tony Zale for title 3 times in 21 months, losing twice; pro record 67-10-6 with 52 KOs; movie "Somebody Up There Likes Me" based on his life.

Hank Greenberg (b. Jan. 1, 1911, d. Sept. 4, 1986): Baseball 1B; led AL in HRs and RBI 4 times each; 2-time MVP (1935,40) with Detroit; 331 career HRs, including 58 in 1938.

Joe Greene (b. Sept. 24, 1946): Football DT; 5-time All-Pro (1972-74,77,79); led Pittsburgh to 4 Super Bowl titles in 1970s; nicknamed "Mean Joe".

Maurice Greene (b. July 23, 1974): Track & Field; world 100m champion in 1997 and 99 and 200m champion in 1999; current world record holder (9.79) in the 100m as of Sept. 24, 2000; injury forced him out of the 1996 Olympics in Atlanta; won the gold medal in the 100m at the 2000 Olympics in Sydney, though his anticipated meeting with Michael Johnson in the 200m never transpired.

Bud Greenspan (b. Sept. 18, 1926): Filmmaker specializing in the Olympic Games; has won Emmy awards for 22-part "The Olympiad" (1976-77) and historical vignettes for ABC-TV's coverage of 1980 Winter Games; won 1994 Emmy award for edited special on Lillehammer Winter Olympics; won The Peabody Award in 1996 for his outstanding service in chronicling the Olympic Games.

Wayne Gretzky (b. Jan. 26, 1961): Hockey C; 10-time NHL scoring champion; 9-time regular season MVP (1979-87,89) and 9-time All-NHL first team; has scored 200 points or more in a season 4 times; led Edmonton to 4 Stanley Cups (1984-85,87-88); 2-time playoff MVP (1985,88); traded to LA Kings (Aug. 9, 1988); broke Gordie Howe's all-time NHL goal scoring record of 801 on Mar. 23, 1994; all-time NHL leader in points (2857), goals (894) and assists (1963); also all-time Stanley Cup leader in points, goals and assists; spent the end of the 1996 season with the St. Louis Blues and then signed a free agent contract with the New York Rangers; retired in 1999 at age 38 with 61 NHL scoring records in 20 seasons.

Bob Griese (b. Feb. 3, 1945): Football QB; 2-time All-Pro (1971,77); led Miami to undefeated season (17-0) in 1972 and consecutive Super Bowl titles (1973-74); father of Brian.

Ken Griffey Jr. (b. Nov. 21, 1969): Baseball OF; overall 1st pick of 1987 draft by Seattle; 10-time Gold Glove winner; 10-time All-Star; 1997 AL MVP; Mariners all-time leader in home runs and RBIs; MVP of 1992 All-Star game at age 23; hit home runs in 8 consecutive games in 1993; son of Ken Sr. and in 1990 they became the first father-son combination to appear in the same major league lineup; traded to the Cincinnati Reds before the 2000 season.

Archie Griffin (b. Aug. 21, 1954): Football RB; only college player to win two Heisman Trophies (1974-75); rushed for 5,177 yards in career at Ohio St.

Emile Griffith (b. Feb. 3, 1938): Boxer; world welterweight champion (1961,62-63,63-65); world middleweight champ (1966-67,67-68); pro record 85-24-2 with 23 KOs.

Dick Groat (b. Nov. 4, 1930): Basketball G and Baseball SS; 2-time basketball All-America at Duke and college Player of Year in 1951; won NL MVP award as shortstop with Pittsburgh in 1960; won World Series with Pirates (1960) and St. Louis (1964).

Lefty Grove (b. Mar. 6, 1900, d. May 23, 1975): Baseball LHP; won 20 or more games 8 times; led AL in ERA 9 times and strikeouts 7 times; 31-4 record and MVP in 1931 with Philadelphia; 300-141 record.

Lou Groza (b. Jan. 25, 1924): Football T-PK; 6-time All-Pro; played in 13 championship games for Cleveland from 1946-67; kicked winning field goal in 1950 NFL title game; 1,608 career points (1,349 in NFL).

Janet Guthrie (b. Mar. 7, 1938): Auto racer; in 1977, became 1st woman to race in Indianapolis 500; placed 9th at Indy in 1978.

Tony Gwynn (b. May 9, 1960): Baseball OF; 8-time NL batting champion (1984,87-89,94-97) with San Diego, 15-time All-Star; got 3,000th career hit Aug. 6, 1999 at Montreal; played basketball at San Diego St. leaving as school's all-time assist leader; drafted in 10th round of 1981 NBA draft by San Diego Clippers.

Harvey Haddix (b. Sept. 18, 1925, d. Jan. 9, 1994): Baseball LHP; pitched 12 perfect innings for Pittsburgh, but lost to Milwaukee in the 13th, 1-0 (May 26, 1959); won Game 7 of 1960 World Series.

Walter Hagen (b. Dec. 21, 1892, d. Oct. 5, 1969): Pro golf pioneer; won 2 U.S. Opens (1914,19), 4 British Opens (1922,24,28-29), 5 PGA Championships (1921,24-27) and 5 Western Opens; retired with 40 PGA wins; 6-time U.S. Ryder Cup captain.

Marvin Hagler (b. May 23, 1954): Boxer; world middleweight champion 1980-87; enjoyed his nickname "Marvelous Marvin" so much he had his name legally changed; pro record of 62-3-2 with 52 KOs.

Mika Hakkinen (b. Sept. 28, 1968): Finnish auto racer; won two consecutive Formula One world drivers championships in 1998 and '99; recorded eight wins in '98 and five in '99, 18 career F1 wins as of Sept. 21, 2000.

George Halas (b. Feb. 2, 1895, d. Oct. 31, 1983): Football pioneer; MVP in 1919 Rose Bowl; player-coach-owner of Chicago Bears from 1920-83; signed Red Grange in 1925; coached Bears for 40 seasons and won 8 NFL titles (1921,32-33,40-41,43,46,63); 2nd on all-time career list with 324 wins; elected to NFL Hall of Fame in 1963.

Dorothy Hamill (b. July 26, 1956): Figure skater; won Olympic gold medal and world championship in 1976; Ice Capades headliner from 1977-84; bought the financially-strapped Ice Capades in 1993 and sold it several years later.

Scott Hamilton (b. Aug. 28, 1958): Figure skater; 4-time world champion (1981-84); won gold medal at 1984 Olympics.

Mia Hamm (b. Mar. 17, 1972): Soccer F; became all-time leading scorer in international soccer with her 108th goal on May 22, 1999; member of 1996 and 2000 U.S. Olympic teams, the 1991 and 1999 U.S. World Cup championship teams, and the third-place 1995 World Cup team; named U.S. Soccer's Female Athlete of the Year for five consecutive years (1994-98); MVP of both U.S. Women's Cup '97, and U.S. Women's Cup '95; made the U.S. National Team at 15; a three-time collegiate All-American; led the Univ. of North Carolina to four national championships (1989,90,92,93).

Tonya Harding (b. Nov. 12, 1970): Figure skater; 1991 U.S. women's champion; involved in bizarre plot hatched by ex-husband Jeff Gillooly to injure rival Nancy Kerrigan on Jan. 6, 1994 and keep her off Olympic team; won '94 U.S. women's title in Kerrigan's absence; denied any role in assault and sued USOC when her berth on Olympic team was threatened; finished 8th at Lillehammer (Kerrigan recovered and won silver medal); pled guilty on Mar. 16 to conspiracy to hinder investigation; stripped of 1994 title by U.S. Figure Skating Assn.

Tom Harmon (b. Sept. 28, 1919, d. Mar. 17, 1990): Football HB; 2-time All-America at Michigan; won Heisman Trophy in 1940; played with AFL NY Americans in 1941 and NFL LA Rams (1946-47); World War II fighter pilot who won Silver Star and Purple Heart; became radio-TV commentator.

Franco Harris (b. Mar. 7, 1950): Football RB; ran for over 1,000 yards a season 8 times; rushed for 12,120 yards in 13 years; led Pittsburgh to 4 Super Bowl titles.

Leon Hart (b. Nov. 2, 1928): Football E; only player to win 3 national championships in college and 3 more in the NFL; won his titles at Notre Dame (1946-47,49) and with Detroit Lions (1952-53,57); 3-time All-America and last lineman to win Heisman Trophy (1949); All-Pro on both offense and defense in 1951.

Bill Hartack (b. Dec. 9, 1932): Jockey; won Kentucky Derby 5 times (1957,60,62,64,69), Preakness 3 times (1956,64,69), and the Belmont once (1960).

Doug Harvey (b. Dec. 19, 1924, d. Dec. 26, 1989): Hockey D; 10-time All-NHL 1st team; won Norris Trophy 7 times (1955-58,60-62); led Montreal to 6 Stanley Cups.

Dominik Hasek (b. Jan. 29, 1965): Czech hockey G; 2-time NHL MVP (1997,98) with Buffalo; 5-time Vezina Trophy winner (1994,95,97,98,99); led Czech Republic to Olympic gold medal in 1998 at Nagano; plans to retire following 2000-01 season.

Billy Haughton (b. Nov. 2, 1923, d. July 15, 1986): Harness racing; 4-time winner of Hambletonian; trainer-driver of one Pacing Triple Crown winner (1968); 4,910 career wins.

João Havelange (b. May 8, 1916): Soccer; Brazilian-born president of Federation Internationale de Football Assoc. (FIFA) 1974-98; also member of International Olympic Committee.

John Havlicek (b. Apr. 8, 1940): Basketball F; played in 3 NCAA Finals at Ohio St. (1960-62); led Boston to 8 NBA titles (1963-66,68-69,74,76); Finals MVP in 1974; 4-time All-NBA 1st team.

Bob Hayes (b. Dec. 20, 1942): Track & Field and Football; won gold medal in 100m at 1964 Olympics; all-pro SE for Dallas in 1966; convicted of drug trafficking in 1979 and served 18 months of a 5-year sentence.

Elvin Hayes (b. Nov. 17, 1945): Basketball C; Known as "the Big E"; Overall number one pick of the 1968 NBA draft; three-time All-NBA first team (1975,77,79); 1978 Finals MVP; 12-time NBA all-star (1969-80); named to NBA's 50 Greatest Players; 6th leading scorer in NBA history with 27,313 points and fourth leading rebounder with 16,279; member of NBA Hall of Fame.

Woody Hayes (b. Feb. 14, 1913, d. Mar. 12, 1987): Football; coached Ohio St. to 3 national titles (1954,57,68) and 4 Rose Bowl victories; 238 career wins in 28 seasons at Denison, Miami-OH and OSU; his coaching career ended abruptly in 1978 after he attacked an opposing player on the sidelines.

Thomas Hearns (b. Oct. 18, 1958): Boxer; has held world titles as welterweight, junior middleweight, middleweight and light heavyweight; four career losses have come against Sugar Ray Leonard, Marvin Hagler and twice to Iran Barkley; pro record of 59-4-1 and 46 KOs.

Eric Heiden (b. June 14, 1958): Speedskater; 3-time overall world champion (1977-79); won all 5 men's gold medals at 1980 Olympics, setting records in each; Sullivan Award winner (1980).

Mel Hein (b. Aug. 22, 1909, d. Jan. 31, 1992): Football C; NFL All-Pro 8 straight years (1933-40); MVP in 1938 with Giants; didn't miss a game in 15 years.

John W. Heisman (b. Oct. 23, 1869, d. Oct. 3, 1936): Football; coached at 9 colleges from 1892-1927; won 185 games; Director of Athletics at Downtown Athletic Club in NYC (1928-36); DAC named Heisman Trophy after him.

Carol Heiss (b. Jan. 20, 1940): Figure skater; 5-time world champion (1956-60); won Olympic silver medal in 1956 and gold in '60; married 1956 men's gold medalist Hayes Jenkins.

Rickey Henderson (b. Dec. 25, 1958): Baseball OF; AL playoff MVP (1989) and AL regular season MVP (1990); set single-season base stealing record of 130 in 1982; has led AL in steals a record 12 times; broke Lou Brock's all-time record of 938 on May 1, 1991; all-time leader in steals and HRs as leadoff batter.

Sonja Henie (b. Apr. 8, 1912, d. Oct. 12, 1969): Norwegian figure skater; 10-time world champion (1927-36); won 3 consecutive Olympic gold medals (1928,32,36); became movie star.

Foster Hewitt (b. Nov. 21, 1902, d. Apr. 21, 1985): Radio-TV; Canada's premier hockey play-by-play broadcaster from 1923-81; coined phrase, "He shoots, he scores!"

Damon Hill (b. Sept. 17, 1960): British auto racer; 1996 Formula One champion; 22 F1 wins for second place among active drivers as of Sept. 21, 2000.

Graham Hill (b. Feb. 15, 1929, d. Nov. 29, 1975): British auto racer; 2-time Formula One world champion (1962,68); won Indy 500 in 1966; killed in plane crash; father of driver Damon.

Phil Hill (b. Apr. 20, 1927): Auto racer; first U.S. driver to win Formula One championship (1961); 3 career wins (1958-64).

Martina Hingis (b. Sept. 30, 1980): Tennis player; in March 1997 at 16 years, 6 months, became the youngest No. 1 ranked player since the ranking system began in 1975; has won Wimbledon (1997), U.S. Open (1997) and 3 Australian Opens (1997,98,99); first woman to surpass the $3 million mark in earnings for one season (1997).

Max Hirsch (b. July 30, 1880, d. Apr. 3, 1969): Horse racing; trained 1,933 winners from 1908-68; won Triple Crown with Assault in 1946.

Tommy Hitchcock (b. Feb. 11, 1900, d. Apr. 19, 1944): Polo; world class player at 20; achieved 10-goal rating 18 times from 1922-40.

Lew Hoad (b. Nov. 23, 1934, d. July 3, 1994): Australian tennis player; 2-time Wimbledon winner (1956-57); won Australian, French and Wimbledon titles in 1956, but missed capturing Grand Slam at Forest Hills when beaten by Ken Rosewall in 4-set final.

Gil Hodges (b. Apr. 4, 1924, d. Apr. 2, 1972): Baseball 1B-Manager; tied Major League record with four home runs in one game on Aug 31, 1950; won three Gold Gloves (1957-59); drove in 100 runs in seven consecutive seasons (1949-55); hit 370 home runs and 1,274 RBIs lifetime; won 660 games as a manager (Senators and Mets).

Ben Hogan (b. Aug. 13, 1912, d. July 25, 1997): Golfer; 4-time PGA Player of Year; one of only five players to win all four Grand Slam titles (others are Nicklaus, Player, Sarazen and Woods); won 4 U.S. Opens, 2 Masters, 2 PGAs and 1 British Open between 1946-53; one of only two players (Woods is the other) to win three of the four current majors in one year when he won Masters, U.S. Open and British Open in 1953; nearly killed in Feb. 2, 1949 car accident, but came back to win U.S. Open in '50; third on all-time list with 63 career wins.

Chamique Holdsclaw (b. Aug. 9, 1977): Basketball F; 2-time national player of the year, leading Tennessee to 3 straight national championships (1996,97,98); 1998 Sullivan Award winner; 1999 WNBA No. 1 draft choice and Rookie of the Year.

Eleanor Holm (b. Dec. 6, 1913): Swimmer; won gold medal in 100m backstroke at 1932 Olympics; thrown off '36 U.S. team for drinking champagne in public and shooting craps on boat to Germany.

Nat Holman (b. Oct. 18, 1896, d. Feb. 12, 1995): Basketball pioneer; played with Original Celtics (1920-28); coached CCNY to both NCAA and NIT titles in 1950 (a year later, several of his players were caught up in a point-shaving scandal); 423 career wins.

Larry Holmes (b. Nov. 3, 1949): Boxer; heavyweight champion (WBC or IBF) from 1978-85; successfully defended title 20 times before losing to Michael Spinks; returned from first retirement in 1988 and was KO'd in 4th by champ Mike Tyson; launched second comeback in 1991; fought and lost title bids against Evander Holyfield in '92 and Oliver McCall in '95; record of 67-6 and 43 KOs.

Lou Holtz (b. Jan. 6, 1937): Football; coached Notre Dame to national title in 1988; 2-time Coach of Year (1977,88) retired after 1996 season but came back in 1999 to coach South Carolina; coached six schools in all — Wm. & Mary (3 years), N.C. State (4), Arkansas (7), Minnesota (2), ND (11) and SC (2); also coached NFL NY Jets for 13 games (3-10) in 1976.

Evander Holyfield (b. Oct. 19, 1962): Boxer; KO'd Buster Douglas in 3rd round to become world hvywt. champion in 1990; 2 of first 4 title defenses included wins over 42-year-old ex-champ George Foreman and Larry Holmes; lost title to Riddick Bowe by unanimous dec. in 1992; beat Bowe by majority dec. to reclaim title in 1993; lost title again to Michael Moorer by majority dec. in 1994; after retiring in '94 due to an apparent heart defect, he returned to the ring in 1995 with a clean bill of health; defeated Mike Tyson in 1996 to win WBA belt; in 1997 rematch, Tyson was DQ'd for twice biting Holyfield's ear; escaped with controversial draw in 1999 unification bout with Lennox Lewis, then lost the rematch later that year; in another controversial decision, defeated John Ruiz in Aug., 2000 to claim the vacant WBA belt.

Red Holzman (b. Aug. 10, 1920, d. Nov. 13, 1998): Basketball; played for NBL and NBA champions at Rochester (1946,51), coached NY Knicks to 2 NBA titles (1970,73); Coach of Year (1970); ranks 12th on all-time NBA list with 754 wins.

Rogers Hornsby (b. Apr. 27, 1896, d. Jan. 5, 1963): Baseball 2B; hit .400 three times, including .424 in 1924; led NL in batting 7 times; 2-time MVP (1925,29); career average of .358 over 23 years is all-time highest in NL.

Paul Hornung (b. Dec. 23, 1935): Football HB-PK; only Heisman Trophy winner to play for losing team (2-8 Notre Dame in 1956); 3-time NFL scoring leader (1959-61) at Green Bay; 176 points in 1960, an all-time record; MVP in 1961; suspended by NFL for 1963 season for betting on his own team.

Gordie Howe (b. Mar. 31, 1928): Hockey RW; played 32 seasons in NHL and WHA from 1946-80; led NHL in scoring 6 times; All-NHL 1st team 12 times; MVP 6 times in NHL (1952-53,57-58,60,63) with Detroit and once in WHA (1974) with Houston; ranks 2nd on all-time NHL list in goals (801) and points (1,850) to Wayne Gretzky; played with sons Mark and Marty in Houston (1973-77) and New England-Hartford (1977-80).

Cal Hubbard (b. Oct. 31, 1900, d. Oct. 17, 1977): Member of college football, pro football and baseball halls of fame; 9 years in NFL; 4-time All-Pro at end and tackle; AL umpire (1936-51).

William DeHart Hubbard (b. Nov. 25, 1903, d. June 23, 1976): Track & Field; won the long jump at the 1924 Olympics, becoming the first black athlete to win an Olympic gold medal in an individual event; set the long jump world record in 1925 (25-10¾) and tied the 100-yard dash record (9.6) in 1926.

Carl Hubbell (b. June 22, 1903, d. Nov. 21, 1988): Baseball LHP; led NL in wins and ERA 3 times each; 2-time MVP (1933,36) with NY Giants; fanned Ruth, Gehrig, Foxx, Simmons and Cronin in succession in 1934 All-Star Game; 253-154 career record.

Sam Huff (b. Oct. 4, 1934): Football LB; glamorized NFL's middle linebacker position with NY Giants from 1956-63; subject of "The Violent World of Sam Huff" TV special in 1961; helped club win 6 division titles and a world championship (1956).

Miller Huggins (b. Mar. 27, 1878, d. Sept. 25, 1929): Baseball; managed NY Yankees from 1918 until his death late in '29 season; led Yanks to 6 pennants and 3 World Series titles from 1921-28.

H. Wayne Huizenga (b. Dec. 29, 1937): Owner; formerly vice chairman of Viacom Inc. and chairman/CEO of Blockbuster Entertainment; owner of NFL Miami Dolphins, NHL Florida Panthers and Pro Player Stadium and former majority owner of MLB's Florida Marlins; criticized for dismantling 1997 World Champion Marlins in off-season to cut payroll.

Bobby Hull (b. Jan. 3, 1939): Hockey LW; led NHL in scoring 3 times; 2-time MVP (1965-66) with Chicago; All-NHL first team 10 times; jumped to WHA in 1972, 2-time MVP there (1973,75) with Winnipeg; scored 913 goals in both leagues; father of Brett.

Brett Hull (b. Aug. 9, 1964): Hockey RW; NHL MVP in 1991 with St. Louis; holds single season RW scoring record with 86 goals; he and father Bobby have both won Hart (MVP), Lady Byng (sportsmanship) and All-Star Game MVP trophies; won Stanley Cup with Dallas in 1999.

Jim (Catfish) Hunter (b. Apr. 8, 1946, d. Sept. 9, 1999): Baseball RHP; won 20 games or more 5 times (1971-75); played on 5 World Series winners with Oakland and NY Yankees; threw perfect game in 1968; won AL Cy Young Award in 1974; 224-166 career record.

Ibrahim Hussein (b. June 3, 1958): Kenyan distance runner; 3-time winner of Boston Marathon (1988,91-92) and 1st African runner to win in Boston; won New York Marathon in 1987.

Don Hutson (b. Jan. 31, 1913, d. June 24, 1997): Football E-PK; led NFL in receptions 8 times and interceptions once; 9-time All-Pro (1936,38-45) for Green Bay; 99 career TD catches.

Flo Hyman (b. July 31, 1954, d. Jan. 24, 1986): Volleyball; 3-time All-America spiker at Houston and captain of 1984 U.S. Women's Olympic team; died of heart attack caused by Marfan Syndrome during a match in Japan in 1986; namesake of award given out annually by the Women's Sports Foundation.

Hank Iba (b. Aug. 6, 1904, d. Jan. 15, 1993): Basketball; coached Oklahoma A&M to 2 straight NCAA titles (1945-46); 767 career wins in 41 years; coached U.S. Olympic team to 2 gold medals (1964,68), but lost to Soviets in controversial '72 final.

Mike Ilitch (b. July 20, 1929): Baseball and Hockey owner; owns Little Caesar's, the international pizza chain; bought Detroit Red Wings for $8 million in 1982 and Detroit Tigers for $85 million in 1992.

Punch Imlach (b. Mar. 15, 1918, d. Dec. 1, 1987): Hockey; directed Toronto to 4 Stanley Cups (1962-64,67) in 11 seasons as GM-coach.

Miguel Induráin (b. July 16, 1964): Spanish cyclist; won a record 5th straight Tour de France in 1995, joining legends Jacques Anquetil and Bernard Hinault of France and Eddy Merckx of Belgium as the only 5-time winners; won gold in time trial at '96 Olympics; retired in 1997.

Hale Irwin (b. June 3, 1945): Golfer; oldest player ever to win U.S. Open (45 in 1990); NCAA champion in 1967; 20 PGA victories, including 3 U.S. Opens (1974,79,90); 5-time Ryder Cup team member; joined senior PGA tour in 1995 and had already won 28 titles through Sept. 2000.

Bo Jackson (b. Nov. 30, 1962): Baseball OF and Football RB; won Heisman Trophy in 1985 and MVP of baseball All-Star Game in 1989; starter for both baseball's KC Royals and NFL's LA Raiders in 1988 and '89; severely injured left hip Jan. 13, 1991, in NFL playoffs; waived by Royals but signed by Chicago White Sox in 1991; missed entire 1992 season recovering from hip surgery; played for White Sox in 1993 and California in '94 before retiring.

Joe Jackson (b. July 16, 1889, d. Dec. 5, 1951): Baseball OF; hit .300 or better 11 times; nicknamed "Shoeless Joe"; career average of .356 (see Black Sox).

Phil Jackson (b. Sept. 17, 1945): Basketball; NBA champion as reserve forward with New York in 1973 (injured when Knicks won in '70); coached Chicago to six NBA titles in eight plays (1991-93, 96-98); coach of the year in 1996 and 97; all-time leader in winning percentage for NBA coaches with 500 or more wins; returned to coach the LA Lakers in 1999 and won the NBA title with them in 2000, his seventh title overall.

Reggie Jackson (b. May 18, 1946): Baseball OF; led AL in HRs 4 times; MVP in 1973; played on 5 World Series winners with Oakland, NY Yankees; 1977 Series MVP with 5 HRs; 563 career HRs; all-time strikeout leader (2,597); member of the Hall of Fame.

Dr. Robert Jackson (b. Aug. 6, 1932): Surgeon; revolutionized sports medicine by popularizing the use of arthroscopic surgery to treat injuries; learned technique from Japanese physician that allowed athletes to return quickly from potentially career-ending injuries.

Helen Jacobs (b. Aug. 6, 1908): Tennis; 4-time winner of U.S. Championship (1932-35); Wimbledon winner in 1936; lost 4 Wimbledon finals to arch-rival Helen Wills Moody.

Jaromir Jagr (b. Feb. 15, 1972): Czech Hockey RW; fifth overall pick by Pittsburgh (1990); NHL All-Rookie team (1991); NHL MVP (1999); Won Art Ross Trophy (1995,98,99,00); NHL All-Star First Team (1995,96,97,98,99,00); NHL single season record for most points by a right wing (149); NHL single season record for most assists by a right wing (87).

Dan Jansen (b. June 17, 1965): Speedskater; 1993 world record-holder in 500m; fell in 500m and 1,000m in 1988 Olympics at Calgary after learning of death of sister Jane; placed 4th in 500m and didn't attempt 1,000m 4 years later in Albertville; fell in 500m at '94 Games in Lillehammer, but finally won an Olympic medal with world record (1:12.43) effort in 1,000m, then took victory lap with baby daughter Jane in his arms; won 1994 Sullivan Award.

James J. Jeffries (b. Apr. 15, 1875, d. Mar. 3, 1953): Boxer; world heavyweight champion (1899-1905); retired undefeated but came back to fight Jack Johnson in 1910 and lost (KO, 15th).

David Jenkins (b. June 29, 1936): Figure skater; brother of Hayes; 3-time world champion (1957-59); won gold medal at 1960 Olympics.

Hayes Jenkins (b. Mar. 23, 1933): Figure skater; 4-time world champion (1953-56); won gold medal at 1956 Olympics; married 1960 women's gold medalist Carol Heiss.

Bruce Jenner (b. Oct. 28, 1949): Track & Field; won gold medal in 1976 Olympic decathlon.

Jackie Jensen (b. Mar. 9, 1927, d. July 14, 1982): Football RB and Baseball OF; All-America at California in 1948; American League MVP with Boston Red Sox in 1958.

Ben Johnson (b. Dec. 30, 1961): Canadian sprinter; set 100m world record (9.83) at 1987 World Championships; won 100m at 1988 Olympics, but flunked drug test and forfeited gold medal; 1987 world record revoked in '89 for admitted steroid use; returned drug-free in 1991, but performed poorly; banned for life by IAAF in 1993 for testing positive after a meet in Montreal.

Bob Johnson (b. Mar. 4, 1931, d. Nov. 26, 1991): Hockey; coached Pittsburgh Penguins to 1st Stanley Cup title in 1991; led Wisconsin to 3 NCAA titles (1973,77,81) in 15 years; also coached 1976 U.S. Olympic team and NHL Calgary (1982-87).

Earvin (Magic) Johnson (b. Aug. 14, 1959): Basketball G; led Michigan St. to NCAA title in 1979 and was Final 4 MOP; All-NBA 1st team 9 times; 3-time MVP (1987,89-90); led LA Lakers to 5 NBA titles; 3-time Finals MVP (1980, 82, 87); 2nd all-time in NBA assists with 10,141; retired on Nov. 7, 1991 after announcing he was HIV-positive; returned to score 25 points in 1992 NBA All-Star Game; U.S. Olympic Dream Team member in '92; announced NBA comeback then retired again before start of 1992-93 season; named head coach of Lakers on Mar. 23, 1994, but finished season at 5-11 and quit; later became minority owner of team; came back a final time and played 32 games during 1995-96 season before retiring for good.

Jack Johnson (b. Mar. 31, 1878, d. June 10, 1946): Boxer; controversial heavyweight champion (1908-15) and 1st black to hold title; defeated Tommy Burns for crown at age 30; fled to Europe in 1913 after Mann Act conviction; lost title to Jess Willard in Havana, but claimed to have taken a dive; pro record 78-8-12 with 45 KOs.

Jimmy Johnson (b. July 16, 1943): Football; All-SWC defensive lineman on Arkansas' 1964 national championship team; coached Miami-FL to national title in 1987; college record of 81-34-3 in 10 years; hired by old friend and new Dallas owner Jerry Jones to succeed Tom Landry in 1989; went 1-15 in '89, then led Cowboys to consecutive Super Bowl victories in 1992 and '93 seasons; quit in 1994 after feuding with Jones; became TV analyst; replaced Don Shula as Miami Dolphins head coach from 1996-99.

Judy Johnson (b. Oct. 26, 1899, d. June 13, 1989): Baseball IF; one of the great stars of the Negro Leagues; a terrific fielding third baseman who regularly batted over .300; when baseball integrated Johnson's playing days were over but he coached and scouted for the Philadelphia Athletics, Boston Braves and Philadelphia Phillies; member of Hall of Fame.

Junior Johnson (b. 1930): Auto Racing; won the second Daytona 500 in 1960; also won 13 NASCAR races in 1965, including the Rebel 300 at Darlington; retired from racing to become a highly successful car owner; his first driver was Bobby Allison.

Michael Johnson (b. Sep 13, 1967): Track & Field; Shattered world record in 200m (19.32) and set Olympic record in 400m (43.49) to become first man to win the gold in both races in the same Olympic Games at Atlanta in 1996; two-time world champion in 200 (1991,95) and four-time world champ in 400 (1993,95,97,99); set world record in 400m (43.18) at '99 world championships in Seville; won the 400 in Sydney in 2000 to become the only man to win the event in two consecutive Olympics.

Rafer Johnson (b. Aug. 18, 1935): Track & Field; won silver medal in 1956 Olympic decathlon and gold medal in 1960.

Randy Johnson (b. Sept. 10, 1963): Baseball LHP; 6'10" flamethrower; threw no-hitter June 2, 1990 for Seattle; struck out over 300 batters 3 times (1993,98,99); led majors in Ks in 1993,94,98,99; AL Cy Young Award winner (1995) and NL Cy Young Award winner (1999); traded to Houston in 1998 and signed a free agent contract with Arizona in 1999.

Walter Johnson (b. Nov. 6, 1887, d. Dec. 10, 1946): Baseball RHP; won 20 games or more 10 straight years; led AL in ERA 5 times, wins 6 times and strikeouts 12 times; twice MVP (1913, 24) with Washington; all-time leader in shutouts (110) and 2nd in wins (417); nicknamed "Big Train."

Ben A. Jones (b. Dec. 31, 1882, d. June 13, 1961): Horse racing; Calumet Farm trainer (1939-47); saddled 6 Kentucky Derby champions, including 2 Triple Crown winners—Whirlaway in 1941 and Citation in '48.

Bobby Jones (b. Mar. 17, 1902, d. Dec. 18, 1971): Won U.S. and British Opens plus U.S. and British Amateurs in 1930 to become golf's only Grand Slam winner ever; from 1922-30, won 4 U.S. Opens, 5 U.S. Amateurs, 3 British Opens, and played in 6 Walker Cups; founded Masters tournament in 1934.

Deacon Jones (b. Dec. 9, 1938): Football DE; 5-time All-Pro (1965-69) with LA Rams; unofficially 2nd all-time in NFL sacks with 173½ in 14 years.

Jerry Jones (b. Oct. 13, 1942): Football; owner-GM of Dallas Cowboys; maverick who bought declining team (3-13) and Texas Stadium for $140 million in 1989; hired old pal Jimmy Johnson to replace legendary Tom Landry as coach; their partnership led Cowboys to 2 Super Bowl titles (1993-94); when feud developed in 1994, he fired Johnson and hired Barry Switzer, who won Super Bowl in 1996; defied NFL Properties by signing separate sponsorship deals with Pepsi and Nike in 1995, causing NFL to file a $300 million lawsuit against him.

Marion Jones (b. Oct. 12, 1975): Track & Field; American sprinter who aimed to be first to win 5 track golds (100, 200, LJ, 4x100, 4x400) in an Olympics at Sydney in 2000; 2-time world champion in 100m (1997,99); former college basketball star at North Carolina and a member of the Tar Heel team that won the national title in 1994; voted Women's Athlete of the Year by *Track & Field News* in 1997 and 1998; winner of the 1999 Jesse Owens Award.

Roy Jones Jr. (b. Jan. 16, 1969): Boxing; robbed of gold medal at 1988 Summer Olympics due to an error in scoring; still voted Outstanding Boxer of the Games; won IBF middleweight crown by beating Bernard Hopkins in 1993; moved up to super middleweight and won IBF title from James Toney in 1994; moved up to light heavyweight division winning WBC (in 1997), WBA (1998) and IBF titles (1999).

Michael Jordan (b. Feb. 17, 1963): Basketball G; College Player of Year with North Carolina in 1984; NBA Rookie of the Year (1985); led NBA in scoring 7 years in a row (1987-93) and also 1996-98; 10-time All-NBA 1st team; 5-time regular season MVP (1988,91-92,96,98) and 6-time MVP of NBA Finals (1991-93,96-98); 3-time AP Male Athlete of Year; led U.S. Olympic team to gold medals in 1984 and '92; stunned sports world when he retired at age 30 on Oct. 6, 1993; signed as OF with Chi. White Sox and spent summer of '94 in AA with Birmingham; struggled with .204 average; made one of the most anticipated comebacks in sports history when he returned to the Bulls lineup on Mar. 19, 1995 but Bulls were eliminated by Orlando in second round of playoffs later that year; led Bulls to NBA titles for the next three years for 6 titles in all (1991-93,96-98); retired in 1999; currently president of Washington Wizards.

Florence Griffith Joyner (b. Dec. 21, 1959, d. Sept. 21, 1998): Track & Field; set world records in 100 and 200 meters in 1988; won 3 gold medals at '88 Olympics (100m, 200m, 4x100m relay); Sullivan Award winner (1988); retired in 1989; named as co-chairperson of President's Council on Physical Fitness and Sports in 1993; sister-in-law of Jackie Joyner-Kersee; died of suffocation during an epilectic seizure in 1998.

Jackie Joyner-Kersee (b. Mar. 3, 1962): Track & Field; 2-time world champion in both long jump (1987,91) and heptathlon (1987,93); won heptathlon gold medals at 1988 and '92 Olympics and LJ gold at '88 Games; also won Olympic silver (1984) in heptathlon and bronze (1992,96) in LJ; Sullivan Award winner (1986); only woman to receive *The Sporting News* Man of Year award.

Alberto Juantorena (b. Nov. 21, 1950): Cuban runner; won both 400m and 800m gold medals at 1976 Olympics.

Sonny Jurgensen (b. Aug. 23, 1934): Football QB; played 18 seasons with Philadelphia and Washington; led NFL in passing twice (1967,69); All-Pro in 1961; 255 career TD passes.

Duke Kahanamoku (b. Aug. 24, 1890, d. Jan. 22, 1968): Swimmer; won 3 gold medals and 2 silver over 3 Olympics (1912,20,24); also surfing pioneer.

Al Kaline (b. Dec. 19, 1934): Baseball; youngest player (at age 20) to win batting title (led AL with .340 in 1955); had 3,007 hits, 399 HRs in 22 years with Detroit.

Anatoly Karpov (b. May 23, 1951): Chess; Soviet world champion from 1975-85; regained International Chess Federation (FIDE) version of championship in 1993 when countryman Garry Kasparov was stripped of title after forming new Professional Chess Association; held FIDE title until 1999.

Garry Kasparov (b. Apr. 13, 1963): Chess; Azerbaijani who became youngest player (22 years, 210 days) ever to win world championship as Soviet in 1985; defeated countryman Anatoly Karpov for title; split with International Chess Federation (FIDE) to form Professional Chess Association (PCA) in 1993; stripped of FIDE title in '93 but successfully defended PCA title against Briton Nigel Short; beat IBM supercomputer "Deep Blue" 4 games to 2 in 1996 much-publicized match in New York; lost rematch to computer in 1997.

Ewing Kauffman (b. Sept. 21, 1916, d. Aug. 1, 1993): Baseball; pharmaceutical billionaire and long-time owner of Kansas City Royals; Royals Stadium renamed for Kauffman on July 2, 1993, one month before his death.

Mike Keenan (b. Oct. 21, 1949): Hockey; coach who finally led NY Rangers to Stanley Cup title in 1994 after 53 unsuccessful years; quit a month later in pay dispute and signed with St. Louis as coach-GM; since moved on to Vancouver; left coaching in 1999 tied for fifth all-time with 597 wins (including playoffs).

Kipchoge (Kip) Keino (b. Jan. 17, 1940): Kenyan runner; policeman who beat USA's Jim Ryun to win 1,500m gold medal at 1968 Olympics; won again in steeplechase at 1972 Summer Games; his success spawned long line of international distance champions from Kenya.

Johnny Kelley (b. Sept. 6, 1907): Distance runner; ran in his 61st and final Boston Marathon at age 84 in 1992, finishing in 5:58:36; won Boston twice (1935,45) and was 2nd 7 times.

Leroy Kelly (b. May 20, 1942): Football; replaced Jim Brown in the Cleveland Brown's backfield; in 1967, Kelly led the NFL in rushing yards (1,205), rushing average (5.1 per carry) and rushing touchdowns (11); in 1968, he led the league again in yards (1,269) and touchdowns (16); played in six Pro Bowls; retired with 7,274 yards and 74 touchdowns; member of Pro Football Hall of Fame.

Jim Kelly (b. Feb. 14, 1960): Football QB; led Buffalo to four consecutive Super Bowl appearances, but is only QB to lose four times; named to AFC Pro Bowl team 5 times.

Walter Kennedy (b. June 8, 1912, d. June 26, 1977): Basketball; 2nd NBA commissioner (1963-75), league doubled in size to 18 teams during his term of office.

Nancy Kerrigan (b. Oct. 13, 1969): Figure skating; 1993 U.S. women's champion and Olympic medalist in 1992 (bronze) and '94 (silver); victim of Jan. 6, 1994 assault at U.S. nationals in Detroit when Shane Stant clubbed her in right knee with metal baton after a practice session; conspiracy hatched by Jeff Gillooly, ex-husband of rival Tonya Harding; although unable to compete in nationals, she recovered and was granted berth on Olympic team; finished 2nd in Lillehammer to Oksana Baiul of Ukraine by a 5-4 judges' vote.

Billy Kidd (b. Apr. 13, 1943): Skiing; the first great Amercian male Alpine skier; first American male to win an Olympic medal when he won a silver in the slalom and a bronze in the Alpine combined in 1964; competed respectably with the great Jean-Claude Killy; won the world Alpine combined event in 1970, which was the first world championship for an American male.

Harmon Killebrew (b. June 29, 1936): Baseball 3B-1B; led AL in HRs 6 times and RBI 3 times; MVP in 1969 with Minnesota; 573 career homers ranks him fifth all-time.

Jean-Claude Killy (b. Aug. 30, 1943): French alpine skier; 2-time World Cup champion (1967-68); won 3 gold medals at 1968 Olympics in Grenoble; co-president of 1992 Winter Games in Albertville.

Ralph Kiner (b. Oct. 27, 1922): Baseball OF; led NL in home runs 7 straight years (1946-52) with Pittsburgh; 369 career HRs and 1,015 RBI in 10 seasons; long-time NY Mets announcer.

Betsy King (b. Aug. 13, 1955): Golfer; 2-time LPGA Player of Year (1984,89); 3-time winner of Dinah Shore (1987,90,97) and 2-time winner of U.S. Open (1989,90); 31 overall Tour wins; member of LPGA Hall of Fame; Tour's all-time leading money winner with $6.4 million in earnings through 1999.

Billie Jean King (b. Nov. 22, 1943): Tennis; women's rights pioneer; Wimbledon singles champ 6 times; U.S. champ 4 times; first woman athlete to earn $100,000 in one year (1971); beat 55-year-old Bobby Riggs 6-4,6-3,6-3, in "Battle of the Sexes" to win $100,000 at Astrodome in 1973; captained the U.S. Olympic team in 1996 and 2000.

Don King (b. Aug. 20, 1931): Boxing promoter; first major black promoter who controlled heavyweight title from 1978-90 while Larry Holmes and Mike Tyson were champions; first big promotion was Muhammad Ali's fight against George Foreman in 1974; former numbers operator who served 4 years for manslaughter (1967-70); acquitted of tax evasion and fraud in 1985; regained control of heavyweight title in 1994 with wins by Oliver McCall (WBC) and Bruce Seldon (WBA); also promoted Evander Holyfield, Roberto Duran and Julio Cesar Chavez among others; also famous for his gravity-defying hairstyle.

Karch Kiraly (b. Nov. 3, 1960): Volleyball; USA's preeminent volleyball player; led UCLA to three NCAA championships (1979,81,82); played on US national teams that won Olympic gold medals in 1984 and '88, world championships in '82 and '86; won the inaugural gold medal for Olympic beach volleyball with Kent Steffes in 1996.

Tom Kite (b. Dec. 9, 1949): Golfer; entered 2000 as 8th on all-time PGA Tour money list with $10.5 million; finally won 1st major with victory in 1992 U.S. Open at Pebble Beach; co-NCAA champion with Ben Crenshaw (1972); PGA Rookie of Year (1973); PGA Player of Year (1989); captain of losing 1997 US Ryder Cup team; 19 career PGA wins, played on the Senior tour in 2000, winning twice through Sept.

Gene Klein (b. Jan. 29, 1921, d. Mar. 12, 1990): Horseman; won 3 Eclipse awards as top owner (1985-87); his filly Winning Colors won 1988 Kentucky Derby; also owned San Diego Chargers football team (1966-84).

Bob Knight (b. Oct. 25, 1940): Basketball; coached Indiana to 3 NCAA titles (1976,81,87); 3-time Coach of Year (1975-76,89); coached 1984 U.S. Olympic team to gold medal; 5th on all-time NCAA list with 763 wins in 35 years; his volatile temper finally cost him when he was fired from Indiana in Sept. 2000 after a string of unacceptable incidents that included choking one of his players.

Phil Knight (b. Feb. 24, 1938): Founder and chairman of Nike, Inc., the multi-billion dollar shoe and fitness company founded in 1972 and based in Beaverton, Ore.; stable of endorsers includes Michael Jordan, Tiger Woods and Brazilian soccer phenom Ronaldo; named "The Most Powerful Man in Sports" by The Sporting News in 1992.

Bill Koch (b. June 7, 1955): Cross-country skiing; first highly accomplished American male in his sport; first American male to win a cross-country Olympic medal when he took home a silver in the 30-kilometer race in 1976; in 1982, he was the first American male to win the Nordic World Cup.

Olga Korbut (b. May 16, 1955): Soviet gymnast; became the media darling of the 1972 Olympics in Munich by winning 3 gold medals (balance beam, floor exercise and team all-around); came back in the 1976 Olympics in Montreal and was a part of the USSR's gold medal winning all-around team; first to perform back somersault on balance beam; was inducted into the International Women's Sports Hall of Fame in 1982, the first gymnast to be inducted.

Johann Olav Koss (b. Oct. 29, 1968): Norwegian speedskater; won three gold medals at 1994 Olympics in Lillehammer with world records in the 1,500m, 5,000m and 10,000m; also won 1,500m gold and 10,000m silver in 1992 Games; retired shortly after '94 Olympics.

Sandy Koufax (b. Dec. 30, 1935): Baseball LHP; led NL in strikeouts 4 times and ERA 5 straight years; won 3 Cy Young Awards (1963,65,66) with LA Dodgers; MVP in 1963; 2-time World Series MVP (1963, 65); threw perfect game against Chicago Cubs (1-0, Sept. 9, 1965) and had 3 other no-hitters in career.

Alvin Kraenzlein (b. Dec. 12, 1876, d. Jan. 6, 1928): Track & Field; won 4 individual gold medals in 1900 Olympics (60m, long jump and the 110m and 200m hurdles).

Jack Kramer (b. Aug. 1, 1921): Tennis; Wimbledon singles champ 1947; U.S. champ 1946-47; promoter and Open pioneer.

Lenny Krayzelburg (b. Sept. 28, 1975): Swimming; born in Ukraine but became an American citizen in 1995; won gold for U.S. in the 100m backstroke and 200m backstroke at the Sydney Games in 2000; was also part of U.S. team that set a world record in the 4x100m medley relay in Sydney; world record holder in the 50, 100 and 200 meter backstrokes as of Sept. 2000.

Ingrid Kristiansen (b. Mar. 21, 1956): Norwegian runner; 2-time Boston Marathon winner (1986,89); won New York City Marathon in 1989; former world record holder in the marathon.

Julie Krone (b. July 24, 1963): Jockey; only woman to ride winning horse in a Triple Crown race when she captured Belmont Stakes aboard Colonial Affair in 1993; retired in 1999 as all-time winningest female jockey with over 3,000 wins; in 2000 became the first female jockey elected to thoroughbred racing's hall of fame.

Mike Krzyzewski (b. Feb. 13, 1947): Basketball; has coached Duke to 8 Final Four appearances; won consecutive NCAA titles in 1991 and '92; 25-year record of 571-219 at Army (1976-80) and Duke.

Bowie Kuhn (b. Oct. 28, 1926): Baseball Commissioner; Elected commissioner on Feb. 4, 1969 and served until Sept. 30, 1984; kept Willie Mays and Mickey Mantle out of baseball for their employment with casinos; handed down one-year suspensions of several players for drug involvement; nixed Charlie Finley's sale of three players for $3.5 million; baseball enjoyed unprecedented attendance and television contracts during his reign.

Alan Kulwicki (b. Dec. 14, 1954, d. Apr. 1, 1993): Auto racer; 1992 NASCAR national champion; 1st college grad and Northerner to win title; NASCAR Rookie of Year in 1986; famous for driving car backwards on victory lap; killed at age 38 in plane crash near Bristol, Tenn.

Michelle Kwan (b. July 7, 1980): Figure Skater; 1998 Olympic silver medalist at Nagano; 4-time U.S. Champion (1996,98,99,00) and 3-time World Champ (1996,98,00); was U.S. alternate to the Olympics in 1994 as a 13-year-old.

Marion Ladewig (b. Oct. 30, 1914): Bowler; named Woman Bowler of the Year 9 times (1950-54,57-59,63).

Guy Lafleur (b. Sept. 20, 1951): Hockey RW; led NHL in scoring 3 times (1976-78); 2-time MVP (1977-78), played for 5 Stanley Cup winners in Montreal; playoff MVP in 1977; returned to NHL as player in 1988 after election to Hall of Fame; retired again in 1991 with 560 goals and 1,353 points.

Napoleon (Nap) Lajoie (b. Sept. 5, 1874, d. Feb. 7, 1959): Baseball 2B; led AL in batting 3 times (1901,03-04); batted .422 in 1901; hit .339 for career with 3,251 hits.

Jack Lambert (b. July 8, 1952): Football LB; 6-time All-Pro (1975-76,79-82); led Pittsburgh to 4 Super Bowls.

Kenesaw Mountain Landis (b. Nov. 20, 1866, d. Nov. 25, 1944): U.S. District Court judge who became first baseball commissioner (1920-44); banned eight Chicago Black Sox from baseball for life.

Tom Landry (b. Sept. 11, 1924, d. Feb. 12, 2000): Football; All-Pro DB for NY Giants (1954); coached Dallas for 29 years (1960-88); won 2 Super Bowls (1972,78); 3rd on NFL all-time list with 270 wins.

Steve Largent (b. Sept. 28, 1954): Football WR; retired in 1989 after 14 years in Seattle with then NFL records in passes caught (819) and TD passes caught (100); elected to U.S. House of Representatives (R, Okla.) in 1994 and Pro Football Hall of Fame in '95.

Don Larsen (b. Aug. 7, 1929): Baseball RHP; NY Yankees hurler who pitched the only perfect game in World Series history— a 2-0 victory over Brooklyn in Game 5 of the 1956 Series (Oct. 8); Series MVP that year; had career record of 81-91 in 14 seasons with 6 clubs.

Tommy Lasorda (b. Sept. 22, 1927): Baseball; managed LA Dodgers to 2 World Series titles (1981,88) in 4 appearances; retired as manager during 1996 season with 1,599 regular-season wins in 21 years; named interim GM of Dodgers in 1998; member of Baseball Hall of Fame, managed U.S. Olympic team in 2000 at Sydney.

Larissa Latynina (b. Dec. 27, 1934): Soviet gymnast; won total of 18 medals, (9 gold) in 3 Olympics (1956,60,64).

Nikki Lauda (b. Feb. 22, 1949): Austrian auto racer; 3-time world Formula One champion (1975,77,84); 25 career wins from 1971-85.

Rod Laver (b. Aug. 9, 1938): Australian tennis player; only player to win Grand Slam twice (1962,69); Wimbledon champion 4 times; 1st to earn $1 million in prize money, won 11 Grand Slam singles titles.

Andrea Mead Lawrence (b. Apr. 19, 1932): Alpine skier; won 2 gold medals at 1952 Olympics.

Bobby Layne (b. Dec. 19, 1926, d. Dec. 1, 1986): Football QB; college star at Texas; master of 2-minute offense; led Detroit to 4 divisional titles and 3 NFL championships in 1950s.

Frank Leahy (b. Aug. 27, 1908, d. June 21, 1973): Football; coached Notre Dame to four national titles (1943,46-47,49); career record of 107-13-9 for a winning pct. of .864.

Brian Leetch (b. Mar. 3, 1968): Hockey D; NHL Rookie of Year in 1989; won Norris Trophy as top defenseman in 1992; Conn Smythe Trophy winner as playoffs' MVP in 1994 when he helped lead NY Rangers to 1st Stanley Cup title in 54 years.

Jacques Lemaire (b. Sept. 7, 1945): Hockey C; member of 8 Stanley Cup champions in Montreal; scored 366 goals in 12 seasons; coached Canadiens from 1983-85; coached New Jersey from 1993-98 and directed the Devils to a surprising 4-game sweep of Detroit to win 1995 Stanley Cup; returned to the NHL in 2000 as coach of the expansion Minnesota Wild.

Claude Lemieux (b. July 16, 1965): Hockey RW; member of Stanley Cup championship teams in Montreal (1986), New Jersey (1995, 2000) and Colorado (1996); playoff MVP with Devils in '95 and Colorado in 96; no relation to Mario.

Mario Lemieux (b. Oct. 5, 1965): Hockey C; 6-time NHL scoring leader (1988-89,92-93,96,97); Rookie of Year (1985); 4-time All-NHL 1st team (1988-89,93,96); 3-time regular season MVP (1988,93,96); 3-time All-Star Game MVP; led Pittsburgh to consecutive Stanley Cup titles (1991 and '92) and was playoff MVP both years; won 1993 scoring title despite missing 24 games to undergo radiation treatments for Hodgkin's disease; missed 62 games during 1993-94 season and entire 94-95 season due to back injuries and fatigue; returned in 1995-96 to lead NHL in scoring and win the MVP trophy; retired after 1996-97 season and inducted into the Hall of Fame; headed group of investors that bought bankrupt Penguins in 1999.

Greg LeMond (b. June 26, 1961): Cyclist; 3-time Tour de France winner (1986,89-90); only non-European to win the event until Lance Armstrong in 1999; retired in Dec. 1994 after being diagnosed with a rare muscular disease known as mitochondrial myopathy.

Ivan Lendl (b. Mar. 7, 1960): Czech tennis player; No. 1 player in world 4 times (1985-87,89); has won both French and U.S. Opens 3 times and Australian twice; owns 94 career tournament wins.

Suzanne Lenglen (b. May 24, 1899, d. July 4, 1938): French tennis player; dominated women's tennis from 1919-26; won both Wimbledon and French singles titles 6 times.

Sugar Ray Leonard (b. May 17, 1956): Boxer; light welterweight Olympic champ (1976); won world welterweight title 1979 and four more titles; retired after losing to Terry Norris on Feb. 9, 1991, with record of 36-2-1 and 25 KOs; misguided comeback in 1997 resulted in resounding defeat by Hector Camacho.

Walter (Buck) Leonard (b. Sept. 8, 1907, d. Nov. 27, 1997): Baseball 1B; won Negro League championship nine years in a row with the Homestead Grays; hit .391 in 1948 to lead the league; usually batted cleanup behind Josh Gibson; retired at the age of 48; member of the National Baseball Hall of Fame.

Marv Levy (b. Aug. 3, 1928): Football; coached Buffalo to four consecutive Super Bowls, but is one of two coaches who are 0-4 (Bud Grant is the other); won 50 games and two CFL Grey Cups with Montreal (1974,77).

Bill Lewis (b. Nov. 30, 1868, d. Jan. 1, 1949): Football; college star at Amherst College and then Harvard; first black player to be selected as an All-American (1892-93); also the first black admitted to the American Bar Association (1911); was U.S. Assistant Attorney General.

Carl Lewis (b. July 1, 1961): Track & Field; won 9 Olympic gold medals; 4 in 1984 (100m, 200m, 4x100m, LJ), 2 in '88 (100m, LJ), 2 in '92 (4x100m, LJ) and 1 in '96 (LJ); has record 8 World Championship titles and 9 medals in all; Sullivan Award winner (1981); two-time AP Male Athlete of the Year (1983-84).

Lennox Lewis (b. Sept. 2, 1965): British boxer; won 1988 Olympic super heavyweight gold medal for Canada; current WBC and IBF heavyweight champion; originally missed out on the IBF title when his apparent win over champ Evander Holyfield in March, 1999 was controversially ruled a draw; won the rematch with Holyfield in Nov. 1999; pro record of 37-1-1 (29 KOs) as of Sept. 21, 2000.

Nancy Lieberman-Cline (b. July 1, 1958): Basketball; 3-time All-America and 2-time Player of Year (1979-80); led Old Dominion to consecutive AIAW titles in 1979 and '80; played in defunct WPBL and WABA and became 1st woman to play in men's pro league (USBL) in 1986; played in the inaugural season of the WNBA for the Phoenix Mercury and served as coach/GM of Detroit Shock in from 1998-2000.

Eric Lindros (b. Feb. 28, 1973): Hockey C; No. 1 pick in 1991 NHL draft by the Nordiques; sat out 1991-92 season rather than play in Quebec; traded to Philadelphia in 1992 for 6 players, 2 No. 1 picks and $15 million; elected Flyers captain at age 22; won Hart Trophy as league MVP in 1995; suffered series of concussions in 1999-00 that placed his all-star career in jeopardy.

Tara Lipinski (b. June 10, 1982): Figure Skater; won the 1998 women's figure skating gold medal at the Olympics in Nagano, becoming the youngest in history (15 yrs., 7 mos.) to do so; she and Michelle Kwan gave the U.S. its first 1-2 finish in that event since 1956; 1997 U.S. and World champion; turned pro in April 1998.

Sonny Liston (b. May 8, 1932, d. Dec. 30, 1970): Boxer; heavyweight champion (1962-64), who knocked out Floyd Patterson twice in the first round, then lost title to Muhammad Ali (then Cassius Clay) in 1964; pro record of 50-4 with 39 KOs.

Rebecca Lobo (b. Oct. 6, 1973): Basketball F; women's college basketball Player of the Year in 1995; led Connecticut to undefeated season (35-0) and national title; member of 1996 U.S. Olympic team; helped lead NY Liberty to WNBA's first championship game in 1997 but lost to Houston Comets; suffered a torn ACL in June, 1999.

Vince Lombardi (b. June 11, 1913, d. Sept. 3, 1970): Football; coached Green Bay to 5 NFL titles; won first 2 Super Bowls (1967-68); died as NFL's all-time winningest coach with percentage of .740 (105-35-6); Super Bowl trophy named in his honor.

Johnny Longden (b. Feb. 14, 1907): Jockey; first to win 6,000 races; rode Count Fleet to Triple Crown in 1943.

Nancy Lopez (b. Jan. 6, 1957): Golfer; 4-time LPGA Player of the Year (1978-79,85,88); Rookie of Year (1977); 3-time winner of LPGA Championship; reached Hall of Fame by age 30 with 35 victories; 48 career wins.

Donna Lopiano (b. Sept. 11, 1946): Former basketball and softball star who was women's athletic director at Texas for 18 years before leaving to become executive director of Women's Sports Foundation in 1992.

Greg Louganis (b. Jan. 29, 1960): U.S. diver; widely considered the greatest diver in history; won platform and springboard gold medals at both 1984 and '88 Olympics; also won a silver medal at the 1976 Olympics at the age of 16; won five world championships and 47 U.S. National Diving titles; revealed on Feb. 22, 1995 that he has AIDS.

Joe Louis (b. May 13, 1914, d. Apr. 12, 1981): Boxer; world heavyweight champion from June 22, 1937 to Mar. 1, 1949; his reign of 11 years, 8 months longest in division history; successfully defended title 25 times; retired in 1949, but returned to lose title shot against successor Ezzard Charles in 1950 and then to Rocky Marciano in '51; pro record of 63-3 with 49 KOs.

Sid Luckman (b. Nov. 21, 1916, d. July 5, 1998): Football QB; 6-time All-Pro; led Chicago Bears to 4 NFL titles (1940-41,43,46); MVP in 1943.

Hank Luisetti (b. June 16, 1916): Basketball F; 3-time All-America at Stanford (1935-38); revolutionized game with one-handed shot.

Johnny Lujack (b. Jan. 4, 1925): Football QB; led Notre Dame to three national titles (1943,46-47); won Heisman Trophy in 1947.

Darrell Wayne Lukas (b. Sept. 2, 1935): Horse racing; 4-time Eclipse-winning trainer who saddled Horses of Year Lady's Secret in 1988 and Criminal Type in 1990; first trainer to earn over $100 million in purses; led nation in earnings 14 times since 1983; Grindstone's Kentucky Derby win in 1996 gave him six Triple Crown wins in a row; has won Preakness 5 times, Kentucky Derby 4 times and Belmont 4 times; his most recent Triple Crown victory came in the 2000 Belmont with Commendable; leads all Breeders Cup trainers with 15 victories.

Gen. Douglas MacArthur (b. Jan. 26, 1880, d. Apr. 5, 1964): Controversial U.S. general of World War II and Korea; president of U.S. Olympic Committee (1927-28); college football devotee, National Football Foundation MacArthur Bowl named after him.

Connie Mack (b. Dec. 22, 1862, d. Feb. 8, 1956): Baseball owner; managed Philadelphia A's until he was 87 (1901-50); all-time major league wins leader with 3,755, including World Series; won 9 AL pennants and 5 World Series (1910-11,13,29-30); also finished last 17 times.

Andy MacPhail (b. Apr. 5, 1953): Baseball; Chicago Cubs president/CEO and now general manager, who was GM of 2 World Series champions in Minnesota (1987,91); won first title at age 34; son of Lee, grandson of Larry.

Larry MacPhail (b. Feb. 3, 1890, d. Oct. 1, 1975): Baseball executive and innovator; introduced major leagues to night games at Cincinnati (May 24, 1935); won pennant in Brooklyn (1941) and World Series with NY Yankees (1947); father of Lee.

Lee MacPhail (b. Oct. 25, 1917): Baseball; AL president (1974-83); president of owners' Player Relations Committee (1984-85); also GM of Baltimore (1959-65) and NY Yankees (1967-74); son of Larry and father of Andy.

Wendy Macpherson (b. Jan. 28, 1968): Bowling; voted Bowler of the Decade for the 1990s; Major titles include the 1986 BPAA U.S. Open, 1988 and 2000 WIBC Queens and 1999 Sam's Town Invitational; annual PWBA money winner 3 times (1996,97,99).

John Madden (b. Apr. 10, 1936): Football and Radio-TV; won 112 games and a Super Bowl (1976 season) as coach of Oakland Raiders; has won 13 Emmy Awards since 1982 as NFL analyst; signed 4-year, $32 million deal with Fox in 1994— a richer contract than any NFL player at the time.

Greg Maddux (b. Apr. 14, 1966): Baseball RHP; won unprecedented 4 straight NL Cy Young Awards with Cubs (1992) and Atlanta (1993-95); has led NL in ERA four times (1993-95,98); won 10th straight gold glove in 1999.

Larry Mahan (b. Nov. 21, 1943): Rodeo; 6-time All-Around world champion (1966-70,73).

Phil Mahre (b. May 10, 1957): Alpine skier; 3-time World Cup overall champ (1981-83); finished 1-2 with twin brother Steve in 1984 Olympic slalom.

Karl Malone (b. July 24, 1963): Basketball F; 11-time All-NBA 1st team (1989-99) with Utah; member of the 1992 and '96 Olympic Dream Teams; 2-time NBA MVP (1997,99); third-highest all-time scorer with 31,041 points, third-most field goals (11,432) and second-most free throws (8,100) entering the 2000-01 season; named one of the NBA's 50 greatest players.

Moses Malone (b. Mar. 23, 1955): Basketball C; signed with Utah of ABA at age 19; led NBA in rebounding 6 times; 4-time All-NBA 1st team; 3-time NBA MVP (1979,82-83); Finals MVP with Philadelphia in 1983; played in 21st pro season in 1994-95; made more free throws (8,531) than any player in NBA history.

Nigel Mansell (b. Aug. 8, 1953): British auto racer; won 1992 Formula One driving championship with record 9 victories and 14 poles; quit Grand Prix circuit to race Indy cars in 1993; 1st rookie to win IndyCar title; 3rd driver to win IndyCar and F1 titles; returned to F1 after 1994 IndyCar season and won '94 Australian Grand Prix; left F1 again on May 23, 1995 with 31 wins and 32 poles in 15 years.

Mickey Mantle (b. Oct. 20, 1931, d. Aug. 13, 1995): Baseball OF; led AL in home runs 4 times; won Triple Crown in 1956; hit 52 HRs in 1956 and 54 in '61; 3-time MVP (1956-57,62); hit 536 career HRs; played in 12 World Series with NY Yankees and won 7 times; all-time Series leader in HRs (18), RBI (40), runs (42) and strikeouts (54).

Diego Maradona (b. Oct. 30, 1960): Soccer F; captain and MVP of 1986 World Cup champion Argentina; also led national team to 1990 World Cup final; consensus Player of Decade in 1980s; led Napoli to 2 Italian League titles (1987,90) and UEFA Cup (1989); tested positive for cocaine and suspended 15 months by FIFA in 1991; returned to World Cup as Argentine captain in 1994, but was kicked out of tournament after two games when doping test found 5 banned substances in his urine.

Pete Maravich (b. June 27, 1947, d. Jan. 5, 1988): Basketball; NCAA scoring leader 3 times at LSU (1968-70); averaged NCAA-record 44.2 points a game over career; Player of Year in 1970; NBA scoring champ in '77 with New Orleans.

Alice Marble (b. Sept. 28, 1913, d. Dec. 13, 1990): Tennis; 4-time U.S. champion (1936,38-40); won Wimbledon in 1939; swept U.S. singles, doubles and mixed doubles from 1938-40.

Gino Marchetti (b. Jan. 2, 1927): Football DE; 8-time NFL All-Pro (1957-64) with Baltimore Colts.

Rocky Marciano (b. Sept. 1, 1923, d. Aug. 31, 1969): Boxer; heavyweight champion (1952-56); retired undefeated; pro record of 49-0 with 43 KOs; killed in plane crash in Iowa.

Juan Marichal (b. Oct. 20, 1938): Baseball RHP; won 21 or more games 6 times for S.F. Giants from 1963-69; ended 16-year career at 243-142.

Dan Marino (b. Sept. 15, 1961): Football QB; 4-time leading passer in AFC (1983-84,86,89); set NFL single-season records for TD passes (48) and passing yards (5,084) with Miami in 1984; all-time leader in career TD passes, passing yards, attempts and completions; retired after the 1999 season and had his number 13 retired by the Dolphins.

Roger Maris (b. Sept. 10, 1934, d. Dec. 14, 1985): Baseball OF; broke Babe Ruth's season HR record with 61 in 1961 (since broken by McGwire and Sosa); 2-time AL MVP (1960-61) with NY Yankees; 275 HRs in 12 years.

Billy Martin (b. May 16, 1928, d. Dec. 25, 1989): Baseball; 5-time manager of NY Yankees; won 2 pennants and 1 World Series (1977); also managed Minnesota, Detroit, Texas and Oakland; played on 5 Yankee world champions in 1950s.

Casey Martin (b. June 2, 1972): Golfer; suffers from a birth defect in his right leg known as Klippel-Trenauney-Webber Syndrome; won lawsuit against the PGA Tour for the right to use a golf cart during competition under the Americans with Disabilities Act.

Pedro Martinez (b. Oct. 25, 1971): Baseball RHP; one of baseball's premier pitchers; won 1997 NL Cy Young award with Montreal; traded to Boston Red Sox on Nov. 18, 1997 for pitchers Carl Pavano and Tony Armas; won AL Cy Young Award and pitching Triple Crown with Boston in 1999.

Eddie Mathews (b. Oct. 13, 1931): Baseball 3B; led NL in HRs twice (1953,59); hit 30 or more home runs 9 straight years; 512 career HRs.

Christy Mathewson (b. Aug. 12, 1880, d. Oct. 7, 1925): Baseball RHP; won 22 or more games 12 straight years (1903-14); 373 career wins; pitched 3 shutouts in 1905 World Series.

Bob Mathias (b. Nov. 17, 1930): Track & Field; youngest winner of decathlon with gold medal in 1948 Olympics at age 17; first to repeat as decathlon champ in 1952; Sullivan Award winner (1948); 4-term member of U.S. Congress (R, Calif.) from 1967-74.

Ollie Matson (b. May 1, 1930): Football HB; All-America at San Francisco (1951); bronze medal winner in 400m at 1952 Olympics; 4-time All-Pro for NFL Chicago Cardinals (1954-57); traded to LA Rams for 9 players in 1959; accounted for 12,884 all-purpose yards and scored 73 TDs in 14 seasons.

Don Mattingly (b. Apr. 20, 1961): Baseball 1B; American League MVP (1985); won AL batting title in 1984 (.343) and led AL with 207 hits and 44 doubles; led majors with 145 RBI in 1985; led AL with 238 hits (Yankee record), 53 doubles and a .573 slugging percentage in 1986; won 9 Gold Glove Awards (1985-89, 91-94); Back injury shortened career.

Willie Mays (b. May 6, 1931): Baseball OF; nicknamed the "Say Hey Kid"; led NL in HRs and stolen bases 4 times each; 2-time MVP (1954,65) with NY-SF Giants; Hall of Famer who played in 24 All-Star Games; 660 HRs and 3,283 hits in career.

Bill Mazeroski (b. Sept. 5, 1936): Baseball 2B; career .260 hitter who won the 1960 World Series for Pittsburgh with a lead-off HR in the bottom of the 9th inning of Game 7; the pitcher was Ralph Terry of the NY Yankees, the count was 1-0 and the score was tied 9-9; also a sure-fielder, Maz won 8 Gold Gloves in 17 seasons.

Bob McAdoo (b. Sept. 25, 1951): Basketball F/C; 1972 *Sporting News* First Team All-American; NBA Rookie of the Year (1973); NBA MVP (1975); All-NBA First Team (1975); Led NBA in scoring three consecutive years (1974-76); 5-time All-Star (1974-78); two championships with LA Lakers (1982,85).

Joe McCarthy (b. Apr. 21, 1887, d. Jan. 13, 1978): Baseball; first manager to win pennants in both leagues (Chicago Cubs in 1929 and NY Yankees in 1932); greatest success came with Yankees when he won seven pennants and six World Series championships from 1936 to 1943; first manager to win four World Series in a row (1936-39); finished his career with the Boston Red Sox (1948-'50); lifetime record of 2125-1333; member of Baseball Hall of Fame.

Pat McCormick (b. May 12, 1930): U.S. diver; won women's platform and springboard gold medals in both 1952 and '56 Olympics.

Willie McCovey (b. Jan. 10, 1938): Baseball 1B; led NL in HRs 3 times and RBI twice; MVP in 1969 with SF; 521 career HRs; indicted for tax evasion in July 1995, pled guilty; namesake of "McCovey Cove," which is the bay outside the rightfield fence at San Francisco's Pacific Bell Park

John McEnroe (b. Feb. 16, 1959): Tennis; No.1 player in the world 4 times (1981-84); 4-time U.S. Open champ (1979-81,84); 3-time Wimbledon champ (1981,83-84); played on 5 Davis Cup winners (1978,79,81,82,92); won NCAA singles title (1978); finished career with 77 singles championships, 77 more in men's doubles (including 9 Grand Slam titles), and U.S. Davis Cup records for years played (13) and singles matches won (41); current captain of U.S. Davis Cup team.

John McGraw (b. Apr. 7, 1873, d. Feb. 25, 1934): Baseball; managed NY Giants to 9 NL pennants between 1905-24; won 3 World Series (1905,21-22); 2nd on all-time career list with 2,866 wins in 33 seasons (2,840 regular season and 26 World Series).

Frank McGuire (b. Nov. 8, 1916, d. Oct. 11, 1994): Basketball; winner of 731 games as high school, college and pro coach; only coach to win 100 games at 3 colleges— St. John's (103), North Carolina (164) and South Carolina (283); won 550 games in 30 college seasons; 1957 UNC team went 32-0 and beat Kansas 54-53 in triple OT to win NCAA title; coached NBA Philadelphia Warriors to 49-31 record in 1961-62 season, but refused to move with team to San Francisco.

Mark McGwire (b. Oct. 1, 1963): Baseball 1B; *Sporting News* college player of the year (1984); Member of 1984 U.S. Olympic baseball team; won AL Rookie of the Year and hit rookie-record 49 HRs in 1987; broke Roger Maris' season home run record (61) in 1998 with the St. Louis Cardinals finishing with 70; followed that magical season with 65 HRs and 147 RBI in 1999.

Jim McKay (b. Sept. 24, 1921): Radio-TV; host and commentator of ABC's Olympic coverage and "Wide World of Sports" show since 1961; 12-time Emmy winner; also given Peabody Award in 1988 and Life Achievement Emmy in 1990; became part owner of Baltimore Orioles in 1993.

John McKay (b. July 5, 1923): Football; coached USC to 3 national titles (1962,67,72); won Rose Bowl 5 times; reached NFL playoffs 3 times with Tampa Bay.

Tamara McKinney (b. Oct. 16, 1962): Skiing; first American woman to win overall Alpine World Cup championship (1983); won World Cup slalom (1984) and giant slalom titles twice (1981,83).

Denny McLain (b. Mar. 29, 1944): Baseball RHP; last pitcher to win 30 games (1968); 2-time Cy Young winner (1968-69) with Detroit; convicted of racketeering, extortion and drug possession in 1985, served 29 months of 25-year jail term, sentence overturned when court ruled he had not received a fair trial; he has faced subsequent legal troubles.

Rick Mears (b. Dec. 3, 1951): Auto racer; 3-time CART national champ (1979,81-82); 4-time winner of Indy 500 (1979,84,88,91) and only driver to win 6 Indy 500 poles; Indy 500 Rookie of Year (1978); retired after 1992 season with 29 CART wins and 40 poles.

Mark Messier (b. Jan. 18, 1961): Hockey C; 2-time NHL MVP with Edmonton (1990) and NY Rangers (1992); captain of 1994 Rangers team that won 1st Stanley Cup since 1940; ranks 2nd in all-time playoff points, goals and assists; signed free agent contract with Vancouver Canucks in 1997 but returned to the Rangers in 2000.

Anne Meyers (b. Mar. 26, 1955): Basketball G; In 1974, became first high school student to play for U.S. national team; 4-time All-American at UCLA (1976-79); member of 1976 U.S. Olympic team; Broderick Award and Cup winner (1978); Signed $50,000 no cut contract with NBA's Indiana Pacers (1980); married Dodger great Don Drysdale.

Debbie Meyer (b. Aug. 14, 1952): Swimmer; 1st swimmer to win 3 individual gold medals at one Olympics (1968).

George Mikan (b. June 18, 1924): Basketball C; 3-time All-America (1944-46); led DePaul to NIT title (1945); led Minneapolis Lakers to 5 NBA titles in 6 years (1949-54); first commissioner of ABA (1967-69).

Stan Mikita (b. May 20, 1940): Hockey C; led NHL in scoring 4 times; won both MVP and Lady Byng awards in 1967 and '68 with Chicago.

Cheryl Miller (b. Jan. 3, 1964): Basketball; 3-time College Player of Year (1984-86); led USC to NCAA title and U.S. to Olympic gold medal in 1984; coached USC to 44-14 record in 2 seasons before quitting to join Turner Sports as NBA reporter; coach/GM of WNBA's Phoenix Mercury; sister of NBA star Reggie Miller.

Del Miller (b. July 5, 1913): Harness racing; driver, trainer, owner, breeder, seller and track owner; drove to 2,441 wins from 1939-90.

Marvin Miller (b. Apr. 14, 1917): Baseball labor leader; executive director of Players' Assn. from 1966-82; increased average salary from $19,000 to over $240,000; led 13-day strike in 1972 and 50-day walkout in '81.

Shannon Miller (b. Mar. 10, 1977): Gymnast; won 5 medals in 1992 Olympics and 2 golds in '96 Games; All-Around women's world champion in 1993 and '94.

Billy Mills (b. June 30, 1938): Track & Field; upset winner of 10,000m gold medal at 1964 Olympics.

Bora Milutinovic (b. Sept. 7, 1944): Soccer; Serbian who coached United States national team from 1991-95, but was fired on Apr. 14, 1995 when he refused to accept additional duties as director of player development; hired 4 months later to revive Mexican national team; known as a miracle worker, he led Mexico, Costa Rica, the U.S. and Nigeria into the 2nd round of the last four World Cups.

Tommy Moe (b. Feb. 17, 1970): Alpine skier; won Downhill gold and Super-G silver at 1994 Winter Olympics; 1st U.S. man to win 2 Olympic alpine medals in one year.

Paul Molitor (b. Aug. 22, 1956): Baseball DH-1B; All-America SS at Minnesota in 1976; signed as free agent by Toronto in 1992, after 15 years with Milwaukee; led Blue Jays to 2nd straight World Series title as MVP (1993); hit .418 in 2 Series appearances (1982,93); holds World Series record with five hits in one game; got career hit 3,000 with a triple in Sept., 1996.

Joe Montana (b. June 11, 1956): Football QB; led Notre Dame to national title in 1977; led San Francisco to 4 Super Bowl titles in 1980s; only 3-time Super Bowl MVP; 2-time NFL MVP (1989-90); led NFL in passing 5 times; traded to Kansas City in 1993; ranks 2nd in all-time in passing efficiency (92.3), 6th in TD passes (273) and yards passing (40,551); inducted into Pro Football Hall of Fame in 2000.

Helen Wills Moody (b. Oct. 6, 1905, d. Jan. 1, 1998): Tennis; won 8 Wimbledon singles titles, 7 U.S. and 4 French from 1923-38.

Warren Moon (b. Nov. 18, 1956): Football QB; MVP of 1978 Rose Bowl with Washington; MVP of CFL with Edmonton in 1983; led Eskimos to 5 consecutive Grey Cup titles (1978-82) and was playoff MVP twice (1980,82); entered NFL in 1984 and has played for four different teams; picked for 9 Pro Bowls including a QB-record 8 staight (1988-95).

Archie Moore (b. Dec. 13, 1913, d. Dec. 9, 1998): Boxer; world light-heavyweight champion (1952-60); pro record 199-26-8 with a record 145 KOs.

Michael Moorer (b. Nov. 12, 1967): Boxer; became first left-hander to win heavyweight title when he scored majority decision over Evander Holyfield on Apr. 22, 1994; lost title to George Foreman on 10th round KO Nov. 5, 1994; won IBF belt in 1996, defended it twice before losing it to Holyfield on Nov. 8, 1997; pro record of 39-2 with 31 KOs.

Noureddine Morceli (b. Feb. 28, 1970): Algerian runner; 3-time world champion at 1,500 meters (1991,93,95); former holder of world records in several middle distance events.

Howie Morenz (b. June 21, 1902, d. Mar. 8, 1937): Hockey C; 3-time NHL MVP (1928,31,32); led Montreal Canadiens to 3 Stanley Cups; voted Outstanding Player of the Half-Century in 1950.

Joe Morgan (b. Sept. 19, 1943): Baseball 2B; led NL in walks 4 times; regular-season MVP both years he led Cincinnati to World Series titles (1975-76); 4th behind Rickey Henderson, Babe Ruth and Ted Williams in career walks with 1,865.

Bobby Morrow (b. Oct. 15, 1935): Track & Field; won 3 gold medals at 1956 Olympics (100m, 200m and 4x400m relay).

Willie Mosconi (b. June 27, 1913, d. Sept. 12, 1993): Pocket Billiards; 14-time world champion from 1941-57.

Annemarie Moser-Pröll (b. Mar. 27, 1953): Austrian alpine skier; won World Cup overall title 6 times (1971-75,79); all-time women's World Cup leader in career wins with 61; won Downhill in 1980 Olympics.

Edwin Moses (b. Aug. 31, 1955): Track & Field; won 400m hurdles at 1976 and '84 Olympics, bronze medal in '88; also winner of 122 consecutive races from 1977-87.

Stirling Moss (b. Sept. 17, 1929): Auto racer; won 194 of 466 career races and 16 Formula One events, but was never world champion.

Marion Motley (b. June 5, 1920, d. June 27, 1999): Football FB; all-time leading AAFC rusher; rushed for over 4,700 yards and 31 TDs for Cleveland Browns (1946-53).

Rupert Murdoch (b. Mar. 11, 1931): Australian media magnate and Los Angeles Dodgers owner; Bought the Dodgers and Dodger Stadium on Mar. 19, 1998 for a reported $350 million.

Calvin Murphy (b. May 9, 1948): Basketball G; NBA All-Rookie team (1971); holds NBA single season free throw percentage (.958); third all-time career free throw pct. (.892); elected to Basketball Hall of Fame in 1992; though only 5'9" and 165 pounds, he is regarded as one of the best guards ever.

Dale Murphy (b. Mar. 12, 1956): Baseball OF; led NL in RBI 3 times and HRs twice; 2-time MVP (1982-83) with Atlanta; also played with Philadelphia and Colorado; retired in 1993 with 398 HRs.

Jack Murphy (b. Feb. 5, 1923, d. Sept. 24, 1980): Sports editor and columnist of *The San Diego Union* from 1951-80; instrumental in bringing AFL Chargers south from LA in 1961, landing Padres as NL expansion team in '69; and lobbying for 54,000-seat San Diego stadium that would later bear his name.

Eddie Murray (b. Feb. 24, 1956): Baseball 1B-DH; AL Rookie of Year in 1977; became 20th player in history, but only 2nd switch hitter (after Pete Rose) to get 3,000 hits; one of only 3 men (Aaron and Mays) with 500 HRs and 3,000 hits.

Jim Murray (b. Dec. 29, 1919, d. Aug. 16, 1998): Sports columnist for *LA Times* 1961-98; 14-time Sportswriter of the Year; won Pulitzer Prize for commentary in 1990.

Ty Murray (b. Oct. 11, 1969): Rodeo cowboy; 6-time All-Around world champion (1989-94); Rookie of Year in 1988; youngest (age 20) to win All-Around title; set single season earnings mark with $297,896 in 1993; career shortened by injury.

Stan Musial (b. Nov. 21, 1920): Baseball OF-1B; led NL in batting 7 times; 3-time MVP (1943,46,48) with St. Louis; played in 24 All-Star Games; had 3,630 career hits and .331 average.

John Naber (b. Jan. 20, 1956): Swimmer; won 4 gold medals and a silver in 1976 Olympics.

Bronko Nagurski (b. Nov. 3, 1908, d. Jan. 7, 1990): Football FB-T; All-America at Minnesota (1929); All-Pro with Chicago Bears (1932-34); charter member of college and pro Halls of Fame.

James Naismith (b. Nov. 6, 1861, d. Nov. 28, 1939): Canadian physical education instructor who invented basketball in 1891 at the YMCA Training School (now Springfield College) in Springfield, Mass.

Joe Namath (b. May 31, 1943): Football QB; signed for unheard-of $400,000 as rookie with AFL's NY Jets in 1965; 2-time All-AFL (1968-69) and All-NFL (1972); led Jets to Super Bowl upset as MVP in '69 after making brash prediction of victory.

Ilie Nastase (b. July 19, 1946): Romanian tennis player; No.1 in the world twice (1972-73); won U.S. (1972) and French (1973) Opens; has since entered Romanian politics.

Martina Navratilova (b. Oct. 18, 1956): Tennis player; No.1 player in the world 7 times (1978-79,82-86); won her record 9th Wimbledon singles title in 1990; also won 4 U.S. Opens, 3 Australian and 2 French; in all, won 18 Grand Slam singles titles and 37 Grand Slam doubles titles; retired as all-time leader among men and women in singles titles (167) and money won ($20.3 million) over 21 years; inducted into International Tennis Hall of Fame in 2000.

Cosmas Ndeti (b. Nov. 24, 1971): Kenyan distance runner; winner of three consecutive Boston Marathons (1993-95), set what is still the course record of 2:07:15 in 1994.

Earle (Greasy) Neale (b. Nov. 5, 1891, d. Nov. 2, 1973): Baseball and Football; hit .357 for Cincinnati in 1919 World Series; also played with pre-NFL Canton Bulldogs; later coached Philadelphia Eagles to 2 NFL titles (1948-49).

Primo Nebiolo (b. July 14, 1923, d. Nov. 7, 1999): Italian president of International Amateur Athletic Federation (IAAF) since 1981; also an at-large member of International Olympic Committee; regarded as dictatorial, but credited with elevating track & field to world class financial status.

Byron Nelson (b. Feb. 4, 1912): Golfer; 2-time winner of both Masters (1937,42) and PGA (1940,45); also U.S. Open champion in 1939; won 19 tournaments in 1945, including 11 in a row; also set all-time PGA stroke average with 68.33 strokes per round over 120 rounds in '45.

Lindsey Nelson (b. May 25, 1919, d. June 10, 1995): Radio-TV; all-purpose play-by-play broadcaster for CBS, NBC and others; 4-time Sportscaster of the Year (1959-62); voice of Cotton Bowl for 25 years and NY Mets from 1962-78; given Life Achievement Emmy Award in 1991.

Ernie Nevers (b. July 11, 1903, d. May 3, 1976): Football FB; earned 11 letters in four sports at Stanford; played pro football, baseball and basketball; scored 40 points for Chicago Cardinals in one NFL game (1929).

Paula Newby-Fraser (b. June 2, 1962): Zimbabwean triathlete; 8-time winner of Ironman Triathlon in Hawaii; established women's record of 8:55:28 in 1992.

John Newcombe (b. May 23, 1944): Australian tennis player; No.1 player in world 3 times (1967,70-71); won Wimbledon 3 times and U.S. and Australian championships twice each.

Pete Newell (b. Aug. 31, 1915): Basketball; coached at Univ. of San Francisco, Michigan St. and the Univ. of California; first coach to win NIT (San Francisco-1949), NCAA (California-1959) and Olympic gold medal (1960); later served as the general manager of the San Diego Rockets and LA Lakers in the NBA; member of Basketball Hall of Fame.

Bob Neyland (b. Feb. 17, 1892, d. Mar. 28, 1962): Football; 3-time coach at Tennessee; had 173-31-12 record in 21 years; won national title in 1951; Vols' stadium named for him; also Army general who won Distinguished Service Cross as supply officer in World War II.

Jack Nicklaus (b. Jan. 21, 1940): Golfer; all-time leader in major tournament wins with 20— including 6 Masters, 5 PGAs, 4 U.S. Opens and 3 British Opens; oldest player to win Masters (46 in 1986); PGA Player of Year 5 times (1967,72-73,75-76); named Golfer of the Century by PGA in 1988; 6-time Ryder Cup player and 2-time captain (1983,87); won NCAA title (1961) and 2 U.S. Amateurs (1959,61); 70 PGA Tour wins (2nd to Sam Snead's 81); fourth win in Tradition in 1996 gave him 8 majors on Senior PGA Tour; nicknamed "the Golden Bear."

Chuck Noll (b. Jan. 5, 1932): Football; coached Pittsburgh to 4 Super Bowl titles (1975-76,79-80); retired after 1991 season ranked 5th on all-time list with 209 wins (including playoffs) in 23 years.

Greg Norman (b. Feb. 10, 1955): Australian golfer; PGA Tour's all-time leading money winner through 1999 with $12.5 million (since passed by Tiger Woods); 73 tournament wins worldwide including 18 PGA Tour victories; 2-time British Open winner (1986,93); lost Masters by a stroke in both 1986 (to Jack Nicklaus) and '87 (to Larry Mize in sudden death); 1995 PGA Tour Player of the Year.

James D. Norris (b. Nov. 6, 1906, d. Feb. 25, 1966): Boxing promoter and NHL owner; president of International Boxing Club from 1949 until U.S. Supreme Court ordered its break-up (for anti-trust violations) in 1958; only NHL owner to win Stanley Cups in two cities: Detroit (1936-37,43) and Chicago (1961).

Paavo Nurmi (b. June 13, 1897, d. Oct. 2, 1973): Finnish runner; won 9 gold medals (6 individual) in 1920, '24 and '28 Olympics; from 1921-31 broke 23 world outdoor records in events ranging from 1,500 to 20,000 meters.

Dan O'Brien (b. July 18, 1966): Track & Field; Olympic decathlon gold medalist (1996); set former world record in decathlon (8,891 pts) in 1992, after shockingly failing to qualify for event at U.S. Olympic Trials; three-time gold medalist at World Championships (1991,93,95).

Larry O'Brien (b. July 7, 1917, d. Sept. 27, 1990): Basketball; former U.S. Postmaster General and 3rd NBA commissioner (1975-84), league absorbed 4 ABA teams and created salary cap during his term in office.

Parry O'Brien (b. Jan. 28, 1932): Track & Field; in 4 consecutive Olympics, won two gold medals, a silver and placed 4th in the shot put (1952-64).

Al Oerter (b. Sept. 19, 1936): Track & Field; his 4 discus gold medals in consecutive Olympics from 1956-68 is an unmatched Olympic record.

Sadaharu Oh (b. May 20, 1940): Baseball 1B; led Japan League in HRs 15 times; 9-time MVP for Tokyo Giants; hit 868 HRs in 22 years.

Hakeem Olajuwon (b. Jan. 21, 1963): Basketball C; Nigerian native who was consensus All-America in 1984 and Final Four MOP in 1983 for Houston; overall 1st pick by Houston Rockets in 1984 NBA draft; led Rockets to back-to-back NBA titles (1994-95); regular season MVP ('94) and Finals MVP (1994-95); 6-time All-NBA 1st team (1987-89,93-95); member of Dream Team III; all-time NBA leader in blocked shots.

Jose Maria Olazabal (b. Feb. 5, 1966): Spanish golfer; has 25 worldwide victories including 2 Masters (1994,99); played on 6 European Ryder Cup teams.

Barney Oldfield (b. Jan. 29, 1878, d. Oct. 4, 1946): Auto racing pioneer; drove cars built by Henry Ford; first man to drive car a mile per minute (1903).

Walter O'Malley (b. Oct. 9, 1903, d. Aug. 9, 1979): Baseball owner; moved Brooklyn Dodgers to Los Angeles after 1957 season; won 4 World Series (1955,59,63,65).

Shaquille O'Neal (b. Mar. 6, 1972): Basketball C; 2-time All-America at LSU (1991-92); overall 1st pick (as a junior) by Orlando in 1992 NBA draft; Rookie of Year in 1993; led NBA in scoring in 1995 and 2000; MVP of 1999-00 regular season and 2000 NBA Finals; scored at least 30 points in each of the Lakers' six games against the Pacers in 2000 Finals; member of Dream Teams II and III.

Bobby Orr (b. Mar. 20, 1948): Hockey D; 8-time Norris Trophy winner as best defenseman; led NHL in scoring twice and assists 5 times; All-NHL 1st team 8 times; regular season MVP 3 times (1970-72); playoff MVP twice (1970,72) with Boston.

Tom Osborne (b. Feb. 23, 1937): Football; Nebraska head coach from 1973-97; career record of 255-49-3; his win pct. of .836 is fifth all-time; finally won national championship in 1994; followed it with 2nd national title in '95 and shared national title with Michigan in '97.

Mel Ott (b. Mar. 2, 1909, d. Nov. 21, 1958): Baseball OF; joined NY Giants at age 16; led NL in HRs 6 times; had 511 HRs and 1,860 RBI in 22 years.

Kristin Otto (b. Feb. 7, 1966): East German swimmer; 1st woman to win 6 gold medals (4 individual) at one Olympics (1988).

Francis Ouimet (b. May 8, 1893, d. Sept. 3, 1967): Golfer; won 1913 U.S. Open as 20-year-old amateur playing on Brookline, Mass. course where he used to caddie; won U.S. Amateur twice; 8-time Walker Cup player.

Steve Owen (b. Apr. 21, 1898, d. May 17, 1964): Football; All-Pro guard (1927); coached NY Giants for 23 years (1931-53); won 153 career games and 2 NFL titles (1934,38).

Jesse Owens (b. Sept. 12, 1913, d. Mar. 31, 1980): Track & Field; broke 5 world records in one afternoon at Big Ten Championships (May 25, 1935); a year later, he upstaged Hitler by winning 4 golds (100m, 200m, 4x100m relay and long jump) at 1936 Olympics in Berlin.

Alan Page (b. Aug. 7, 1945): Football DE; All-America at Notre Dame in 1966 and member of two national championship teams; 6-time NFL All-Pro and 1971 Player of Year with Minnesota Vikings; later a lawyer who was elected to Minnesota Supreme Court in 1992.

Satchel Paige (b. July 7, 1906, d. June 6, 1982): Baseball RHP; pitched 55 career no-hitters over 20 seasons in Negro Leagues; entered major leagues with Cleveland in 1948 at age 42; had 28-31 record in 5 years; returned to AL at age 59 to start 1 game for Kansas City in 1965 (went 3 innings, gave up a hit and got a strikeout).

Se Ri Pak (b. Sept. 28, 1977): Golfer; won two Majors as a rookie in 1998; won the LPGA Championship and then the U.S. Open on the second hole of sudden death with amateur Jenny Chuasiriporn after an additional 18 holes failed to break the tie; finished second on the 1998 money list; won four tournaments overall in 1998 and another four in 1999.

Arnold Palmer (b. Sept. 10, 1929): Golfer; winner of 4 Masters, 2 British Opens and a U.S. Open; 2-time PGA Player of Year (1960,62); 1st player to earn over $1 million in career (1968); annual PGA Tour money leader award named after him; 60 wins on PGA Tour and 10 more on Senior Tour.

Jim Palmer (b. Oct. 15, 1945): Baseball RHP; 3-time Cy Young Award winner (1973,75-76); won 20 or more games 8 times with Baltimore; 1991 comeback attempt at age 45 scrubbed in spring training.

Bill Parcells (b. Aug. 22, 1941): Football; coached NY Giants to 2 Super Bowl titles (1987,91); retired after 1990 season then returned in '93 as coach of New England; led Patriots to Super Bowl loss against Green Bay in 1997; left Patriots in 1997 to coach the New York Jets; coached three seasons with the Jets (1997-99), turning them from 1-15 doormat to AFC East champ in two years; retired from coaching again in 2000 and became director of football operations with the club.

Jack Pardee (b. Apr. 19, 1936): Football; All-America linebacker at Texas A&M; 2-time All-Pro with LA Rams (1963) and Washington (1971); 2-time NFL Coach of Year (1976,79) and winner of 87 games in 11 seasons; only man hired as head coach in NFL, WFL, USFL and CFL; also coached at University of Houston.

Bernie Parent (b. Apr. 3, 1945): Hockey G; led Philadelphia Flyers to 2 Stanley Cups as playoff MVP (1974,75); 2-time Vezina Trophy winner; posted 55 career shutouts and 2.55 GAA in 13 seasons.

Joe Paterno (b. Dec. 21, 1926): Football; has coached Penn St. to 2 national titles (1982,86) and 20-9-1 bowl record in 34 years; also had three unbeaten teams that didn't finish No. 1; 4-time Coach of Year (1968,78,82,86); entered 2000 season 3rd on all-time list with 317 wins, needing 7 more to become the all-time leader.

Craig Patrick (b. May 20, 1946): Hockey; 3rd generation Patrick to have name inscribed on Stanley Cup; GM of 2-time Cup champion Pittsburgh Penguins (1991-92); also captain of 1969 NCAA champion at Denver; assistant coach-GM of 1980 gold medal-winning U.S. Olympic team; scored 72 goals in 8 NHL seasons and won 69 games in 3 years as coach; grandson of Lester.

Lester Patrick (b. Dec. 30, 1883, d. June 1, 1960): Hockey; pro hockey pioneer as player, coach and general manager for 43 years; led NY Rangers to Stanley Cups as coach (1928,33) and GM (1940); grandfather of Craig.

Floyd Patterson (b. Jan. 4, 1935): Boxer; Olympic middleweight champ in 1952; world heavyweight champion (1956-59,60-62); 1st to regain heavyweight crown; fought Ingemar Johansson 3 times in 22 months from 1959-61 and won last two; pro record 55-8-1 with 40 KOs.

Walter Payton (b. July 25, 1954, d. Nov. 1, 1999): Football RB; NFL's all-time leading rusher with 16,726 yards; scored 125 career TDs; All-Pro 7 times with Chicago; MVP in 1977; led Bears to Super Bowl title in Jan. 1986.

Calvin Peete (b. July 18, 1943): Golf; began playing golf at the age of 23; earned over $2 million in career earnings; selected to the U.S. Ryder Cup teams in 1983 and 1985.

Pelé (b. Oct. 23, 1940): Brazilian soccer F; given name— Edson Arantes do Nascimento; led Brazil to 3 World Cup titles (1958,62,70); came to U.S. in 1975 to play for NY Cosmos in NASL; scored 1,281 goals in 22 years; currently Brazil's minister of sport.

Roger Penske (b. Feb. 20, 1937): Auto racing; national sports car driving champion (1964); established racing team in 1961; co-founder of Championship Auto Racing Teams (CART); Penske Racing has won 10 Indianapolis 500s, 9 CART points titles and the team recorded its 100th overall victory with Gil de Ferran's win at Nazareth in May, 2000.

Willie Pep (b. Sept. 19, 1922): Boxer; 2-time world featherweight champion (1942-48,49-50); pro record 230-11-1 with 65 KOs.

Marie-Jose Perec (b. 1968): Track & Field; French sprinter who became 2nd woman to win the 200m and 400m events in the same Olympics (1996); her time in the 400 (48.25) set an Olympic record; Valerie Brisco-Hooks did it in the boycotted 1984 games; also won the 400M in 1992 Games; left the 2000 Olympics in Sydney after saying she was accosted by a man in her hotel room.

Fred Perry (b. May 18, 1909, d. Feb. 2, 1995): British tennis player; 3-time Wimbledon champ (1934-36); first player to win all four Grand Slam singles titles, though not in same year; last native to win All-England men's title.

Gaylord Perry (b. Sept. 15, 1938): Baseball RHP; was only pitcher to win a Cy Young Award in both leagues until 1999 when Randy Johnson and Pedro Martinez joined him; retired in 1983 with 314-265 record and 3,534 strikeouts over 22 years and with 8 teams; brother Jim won 215 games for family total of 529.

Bob Pettit (b. Dec. 12, 1932): Basketball F; All-NBA 1st team 10 times (1955-64); 2-time MVP (1956,59) with St. Louis Hawks; first player to score 20,000 points.

Richard Petty (b. July 2, 1937): Auto racer; 7-time winner of Daytona 500; 7-time NASCAR national champ (1964,67,71-72,74-75,79); first stock car driver to win $1 million in career; all-time NASCAR leader in races won (200), poles (127) and wins in a single season (27 in 1967); retired after 1992 season; son of Lee (54 career wins) and father of Kyle (7 career wins).

Laffit Pincay Jr. (b. Dec. 29, 1946): Jockey; 5-time Eclipse Award winner (1971,73-74,79,85); winner of 3 Belmonts and 1 Kentucky Derby (aboard Swale in 1984); with his 8834th win in Dec., 1999 he passed Bill Shoemaker to become thoroughbred racing's all-time winningest jockey.

Scottie Pippen (b. Sept. 25, 1965): Basketball F; started on six NBA champions with Chicago (1991-93, 96-98); 3-time all-NBA first team (1994-96). Voted one of NBA's 50 Greatest Players.

Uta Pippig (b. Sept. 7, 1965): German marathoner; won three-straight Boston Marathons (1994,95,96); she set a new course record in '94.

Nelson Piquet (b. Aug. 17, 1952): Brazilian auto racer; 3-time Formula One world champion (1981,83, 87); left circuit in 1991 with 23 career wins.

Rick Pitino (b. Sept. 18, 1952): Basketball; won 1996 NCAA title in his 7th year at Kentucky; previously coached the New York Knicks in the NBA (96-81 overall), Providence College (42-23) and Boston University (46-24); in 1997, became coach and president of Boston Celtics.

Jacques Plante (b. Jan. 17, 1929, d. Feb. 27, 1986): Hockey G; led Montreal to 6 Stanley Cups (1953,56-60); won 7 Vezina Trophies; MVP in 1962; first goalie to regularly wear a mask; posted 82 shutouts with 2.38 GAA.

Gary Player (b. Nov. 1, 1936): South African golfer; 3-time winner of Masters and British Open; only player in 20th century to win British Open in three different decades (1959,68,74); one of only five players to win all four Grand Slam titles (others are Hogan, Nicklaus, Sarazen and Woods), has also won 2 PGAs, a U.S. Open and 2 U.S. Senior Opens; owner of 21 wins on PGA Tour and 19 more on Senior Tour.

Jim Plunkett (b. Dec. 5, 1947): Football QB; Heisman Trophy winner (Stanford) in 1970; AFL Rookie of the Year in 1971; led Oakland-LA Raiders to Super Bowl wins in 1981 and '84; MVP in '81.

Maurice Podoloff (b. Aug. 18, 1890, d. Nov. 24, 1985): Basketball; engineered merger of Basketball Assn. of America and National Basketball League into NBA in 1949; NBA commissioner (1949-63); league MVP trophy named after him.

Fritz Pollard (b. Jan. 27, 1894, d. May 11, 1986): Football; 1st black All-America RB (1916 at Brown); 1st black to play in Rose Bowl; 7-year NFL pro (1920-26); 1st black NFL coach, at Milwaukee and Hammond, Ind.

Sam Pollock (b. Dec. 15, 1925): Hockey GM; managed NHL Montreal Canadiens to 9 Stanley Cups in 14 years (1965-78).

Denis Potvin (b. Oct. 29, 1953): Hockey D; won Norris Trophy 3 times (1976,78-79); 5-time All-NHL 1st-team; led NY Islanders to 4 Stanley Cups.

Mike Powell (b. Nov. 10, 1963): Track & Field; broke Bob Beamon's 23-year-old long jump world record by 2 inches with leap of 29-ft., 4½ in. at the 1991 World Championships; Sullivan Award winner (1991); won long jump silver medals in 1988 and '92 Olympics; repeated as world champ in 1993.

Steve Prefontaine (b. Jan. 25, 1951, d. June 1, 1975): Track & Field; All-America distance runner at Oregon; first athlete to win same event at NCAA championships 4 straight years (5,000 meters from 1970-73); finished 4th in 5,000 at 1972 Munich Olympics; first athlete to endorse Nike running shoes; killed in a one-car accident.

Nick Price (b. Jan. 28, 1957): Zimbabwean golfer; PGA Tour Player of Year in 1993 and '94; became 1st since Nick Faldo in 1990 to win 2 Grand Slam titles in same year when he took British Open and PGA Championship in 1994; also won PGA in '92.

Alain Prost (b. Feb. 24, 1955): French auto racer; 4-time Formula One world champion (1985-86,89,93); sat out 1992 then returned to win title in 1993; retired after '93 season as all-time F1 wins leader with 51.

Kirby Puckett (b. Mar. 14, 1961): Baseball OF; led Minnesota Twins to World Series titles in 1987 and '91; retired in 1996 due to an eye ailment with a batting title (1989), 2,304 hits and a .318 career average in 12 seasons.

C.C. Pyle (b. 1882, d. Feb. 3, 1939): Promoter; known as "Cash and Carry"; hyped Red Grange's pro football debut by arranging 1925 barnstorming tour with Chicago Bears; had Grange bolt NFL for new AFL in 1926 (AFL folded in '27); also staged 2 Transcontinental Races (1928-29), known as "Bunion Derbies."

Bobby Rahal (b. Jan. 10, 1953): Auto racer; 3-time PPG Cup champ (1986,87,92); 24 career Indy-Car wins, including 1986 Indy 500; current CART team owner; acted as interim president-CEO of CART until Dec., 2000 but resigned to assume position with Jaguar Formula One team.

Jack Ramsay (b. Feb. 21, 1925): Basketball; coach who won 239 college games with St. Joseph's-PA in 11 seasons and 906 NBA games (including playoffs) with 4 teams over 21 years; placed 3rd in 1961 Final Four; led Portland to NBA title in 1977.

Bill Rassmussen (b. Oct. 15, 1932): Radio-TV; unemployed radio broadcaster who founded ESPN, the nation's first 24-hour all-sports cable-TV network, in 1978; bought out by Getty Oil in 1981.

Willis Reed (b. June 25, 1942): Basketball C; led NY Knicks to NBA titles in 1970 and '73, Finals MVP both years; regular season MVP 1970. Voted one of NBA's 50 Greatest Players.

Pee Wee Reese (b. July 23, 1919, d. Aug. 14, 1999): Baseball SS; member of Brooklyn/Los Angeles Dodgers from 1940-58; led NL in runs scored (132) in 1949 and stolen bases (30) in 1952; hit over .300 in a season once (.309 in 1954); led the NL in putouts four times; real name was Harold H. Reese.

Mary Lou Retton (b. Jan. 24, 1968): Gymnast; won gold medal in women's All-Around at the 1984 Olympics; also won 2 silvers and 2 bronzes.

Butch Reynolds (b. June 8, 1964): Track & Field; held world record in 400 meters from 1988 to 1999 when it was finally broken by Michael Johnson; banned for 2½ years for allegedly failing drug test in 1990; sued IAAF and won $27.4 million judgment in 1992, but award was voided in '94; won silver medal in 400 meters and gold as member of U.S. 4x400-meter relay team at both 1993 and '95 World Championships.

Grantland Rice (b. Nov. 1, 1880, d. July 13, 1954): First celebrated American sportswriter; chronicled the Golden Age of Sport in 1920s; immortalized Notre Dame's "Four Horsemen."

Jerry Rice (b. Oct. 13, 1962): Football WR; 2-time Div. I-AA All-America at Mississippi Valley St. (1983-84); 10-time all-Pro; regular season MVP in 1987 and Super Bowl MVP in 1989 with San Francisco; NFL all-time leader in touchdowns and receptions.

Henri Richard (b. Feb. 29, 1936): Hockey C; leap year baby who played on more Stanley Cup championship teams (11) than anybody else; at 5-foot-7, known as the "Pocket Rocket"; brother of Maurice.

Maurice Richard (b. Aug. 4, 1921, d. May 27, 2000): Hockey RW; the "Rocket"; 8-time NHL 1st team All-Star; MVP in 1947; 1st to score 50 goals in one season (1944-45); 544 career goals; played on 8 Stanley Cup winners in Montreal.

Bob Richards (b. Feb. 2, 1926): Track & Field; pole vaulter, ordained minister and original *Wheaties* pitchman, who won gold medals at 1952 and '56 Olympics; remains only 2-time Olympic pole vault champ.

Nolan Richardson (b. Dec. 27, 1941): Basketball; coached Arkansas to consecutive NCAA finals, beating Duke in 1994 and losing to UCLA in '95.

Tex Rickard (b. Jan. 2, 1870, d. Jan. 6, 1929): Promoter who handled boxing's first $1 million gate (Dempsey vs. Carpentier in 1921); built Madison Square Garden in 1925; founded NY Rangers as Garden tenant in 1926 and named NHL team after himself (Tex's Rangers); also built Boston Garden in 1928.

Eddie Rickenbacker (b. Oct. 8, 1890, d. July 23, 1973): Mechanic and auto racer; became America's top flying ace (22 kills) in World War I; owned Indianapolis Speedway (1927-45) and ran Eastern Air Lines (1938-59).

Branch Rickey (b. Dec. 20, 1881, d. Dec. 9, 1965): Baseball innovator; revolutionized game with creation of modern farm system while general manager of St. Louis Cardinals (1917-42); integrated major leagues in 1947 as president-GM of Brooklyn Dodgers when he brought up Jackie Robinson (whom he had signed on Oct. 23, 1945); later GM of Pittsburgh Pirates.

Leni Riefenstahl (b. Aug. 22, 1902): German filmmaker of 1930s; directed classic sports documentary "Olympia" on 1936 Berlin Summer Olympics; infamous, however, for also making 1934 Hitler propaganda film "Triumph of the Will."

Roy Riegels (b. Apr. 4, 1908, d. Mar. 26, 1993): Football; California center who picked up fumble in 2nd quarter of 1929 Rose Bowl and raced 70 yards in wrong direction to set up a 2-point safety in 8-7 loss to Georgia Tech.

Bobby Riggs (b. Feb. 25, 1918, d. Oct. 25, 1995): Tennis; won Wimbledon once (1939) and U.S. title twice (1939,41); legendary hustler who made his biggest score in 1973 as 55-year-old male chauvinist challenging the best women players; beat No. 1 Margaret Smith Court 6-2,6-1, but was thrashed by No. 2 Billie Jean King, 6-4,6-3,6-3 in nationally televised "Battle of the Sexes" on Sept. 20, before 30,492 at the Astrodome.

Pat Riley (b. Mar. 20, 1945): Basketball; coached LA Lakers to 4 of their 5 NBA titles in 1980s (1982,85,87-88); coached New York (1991-95; 2-time Coach of Year (1990,93) and all-time NBA leader in playoff wins (155); quit Knicks after 1994-95 season with year left on contract; signed with Miami Heat on Sept. 2 as coach, team president and part-owner after Knicks agreed to drop tampering charges in exchange for $1 million and a conditional first round draft pick.

Cal Ripken Jr. (b. Aug. 24, 1960): Baseball SS; broke Lou Gehrig's major league Iron Man record of 2,130 consecutive games played on Sept. 6, 1995; record streak began on May 30, 1982 and ended Sept. 19, 1998 after 2,632 games; 2-time AL MVP (1983,91) for Baltimore; AL Rookie of Year (1982); AL starter in All-Star Game since 1984; holds record for career home runs by a shortstop.

Phil Rizzuto (b. Sept. 25, 1918): Baseball SS; nicknamed "the Scooter"; AL MVP with the Yankees in 1950; 5-time All-Star; retired in 1956 and became Yankees radio and television announcer; elected to the Hall of Fame in 1994.

Joe Robbie (b. July 7, 1916, d. Jan. 7, 1990): Football; original owner of Miami Dolphins (1966-90); won 2 Super Bowls (1973-74); built $115-million Joe Robbie Stadium (now named Pro Player Stadium) with private funds in 1987.

Oscar Robertson (b. Nov. 24, 1938): Basketball G; 3-time College Player of Year (1958-60) at Cincinnati; led 1960 U.S. Olympic team to gold medal; NBA Rookie of Year (1961); 9-time All-NBA 1st team; MVP in 1964 with Cincinnati Royals; NBA champion in 1971 with Milwaukee Bucks; 3rd in career assists with 9,887.

Paul Robeson (b. Apr. 8, 1898, d. Jan. 23, 1976): Black 4-sport star and 2-time football All-America (1917-18) at Rutgers; 3-year NFL pro; also scholar, lawyer, singer, actor and political activist; long-tainted by Communist sympathies, he was finally inducted into College Football Hall of Fame in 1995.

Brooks Robinson (b. May 18, 1937): Baseball 3B; led AL in fielding 12 times from 1960-72 with Baltimore; AL MVP in 1964; World Series MVP in 1970; 16 Gold Gloves; entered Hall of Fame in 1983.

David Robinson (b. Aug. 6, 1965): Basketball C; College Player of Year at Navy in 1987; overall 1st pick by San Antonio in 1987 NBA draft; served in military from 1987-89; NBA Rookie of Year in 1990 and MVP in '95; 2-time All-NBA 1st team (1991,92); led NBA in scoring in 1994; member of 1988, '92 and '96 U.S. Olympic teams.

Eddie Robinson (b. Feb. 13, 1919): Football; head coach at Div. I-AA Grambling from 1941-97; winningest coach in college history (408-165-15); led Tigers to 8 national black college titles.

Frank Robinson (b. Aug. 31, 1935): Baseball OF; won MVP in NL (1961) and AL (1966); Triple Crown winner and World Series MVP in 1966 with Baltimore; 1st black manager in major leagues with Cleveland in 1975; also managed in SF and Baltimore; hired by MLB in 2000 to be the league's vice president of on-field operations.

Jackie Robinson (b. Jan. 31, 1919, d. Oct. 24, 1972): Baseball 1B-2B-3B; 4-sport athlete at UCLA (baseball, basketball, football and track); hit .387 with K.C. Monarchs of Negro Leagues in 1945; signed by Brooklyn Dodgers on Oct. 23, 1945 and broke major league baseball's color line in 1947; Rookie of Year in 1947 and NL's MVP in '49; hit .311 over 10 seasons. His #42 was retired by MLB in 1997.

Sugar Ray Robinson (b. May 3, 1921, d. Apr. 12, 1989): Boxer; world welterweight champion (1946-51); 5-time middleweight champ; retired at age 45 after 25 years in the ring; pro record 174-19-6 with 109 KOs.

Knute Rockne (b. Mar. 4, 1888, d. Mar. 31, 1931): Football; coached Notre Dame to 3 consensus national titles (1924,29,30), highest winning percentage in college history (.881) with record of 105-12-5 over 13 seasons; killed in plane crash.

Bill Rodgers (b. Dec. 23, 1947): Distance runner; won Boston and New York City marathons 4 times each from 1975-80.

Dennis Rodman (b. May 13, 1961): Basketball F; ferocious rebounder and tenacious defender; also known for dyeing his hair various colors and for getting suspended regularly; in 1997, he was suspended for 11 games for kicking a courtside cameraman; led the NBA in rebounding 7 years in a row, 1992-98; member of 5 NBA champion teams, Detroit (1989,90) and Chicago(1996-98); 2-time All Star (1990,92), 2-time defensive player of the year (1990-91) and 6-time member of the NBA All-Defensive team (1989-93,96).

Irina Rodnina (b. Sept. 12, 1949): Soviet figure skater; won 10 world championships and 3 Olympic gold medals in pairs competition from 1971-80.

Alex Rodriguez (b. July 27, 1975): Baseball SS; one of baseball's best all-around players; led AL in his first full season in the majors (1996) with .358 batting average and 141 runs; in 1998 became just third player ever to hit 40 HRs and steal 40 bases in one season; hit 42 HRs in 1999 despite missing 33 games with an injury.

Ronaldo (b. Sept. 22, 1976): Soccer; Brazilian forward who has been compared to the great Pele; signed with a first division club in Brazil, Cruzeiro Belo Horizonte, before he was 18 and scored 58 goals in 60 games; named to the Brazilian National Team when he was 17; named FIFA Player of the Year in 1996 and '97; European Player of the Year in '97; named 1998 World Cup MVP, has been plagued by injuries since.

Art Rooney (b. Jan. 27, 1901, d. Aug. 25, 1988): Race track legend and pro football pioneer; bought Pittsburgh Steelers franchise in 1933 for $2,500; finally won NFL title with 1st of 4 Super Bowls in 1974 season.

Theodore Roosevelt (b. Oct. 27, 1858, d. Jan. 6, 1919): 26th President of the U.S.; physical fitness buff who boxed as undergraduate at Harvard; credited with presidential assist in forming of Intercollegiate Athletic Assn. (now NCAA) in 1905-06.

Mauri Rose (b. May 26, 1906, d. Jan. 1, 1981): Auto racer; 3-time winner of Indy 500 (1941,47-48).

Murray Rose (b. Jan. 6, 1939): Australian swimmer; won 3 gold medals at 1956 Olympics; added a gold, silver and bronze in 1960.

Pete Rose (b. Apr. 14, 1941): Baseball OF-IF; all-time hits leader with 4,256; led NL in batting 3 times; regular-season MVP in 1973; World Series MVP in 1975; had 44-game hitting streak in '78; managed Cincinnati (1984-89); banned for life in 1989 for conduct detrimental to baseball; convicted of tax evasion in 1990 and sentenced to 5 months in prison; released Jan. 7, 1991.

Ken Rosewall (b. Nov. 2, 1934): Tennis; won French and Australian singles titles at age 18; U.S. champ twice, but never won Wimbledon.

Mark Roth (b. Apr. 10, 1951): Bowler; 4-time PBA Player of Year (1977-79,84); entered 1999 with 36 tournament wins and over $1.5 million in career earnings; victory in Apr. 15, 1995 Foresters Open was first in 7 years; U.S. Open champ in 1984.

Alan Rothenberg (b. Apr. 10, 1939): Soccer; president of U.S. Soccer 1990-98; surprised European skeptics by directing hugely successful 1994 World Cup tournament; successfully got off-delayed outdoor Major League Soccer off ground in 1996.

Patrick Roy (b. Oct. 5, 1965): Hockey G; led Montreal to 2 Stanley Cup titles; playoff MVP as rookie in 1986 and again in '93; has won Vezina Trophy 3 times (1989-90,92); won 3rd Stanley Cup with Colorado ('96); all-time leader in career playoff wins (121) and needed just four wins heading into 2000-01 season to become regular season career win leader.

Pete Rozelle (b. Mar. 1, 1926, d. December 6, 1996): Football; NFL Commissioner from 1960-89; presided over growth of league from 12 to 28 teams, merger with AFL, creation of Super Bowl and advent of huge TV rights fees.

Wilma Rudolph (b. June 23, 1940, d. Nov. 12, 1994): Track & Field; won 3 gold medals (100m, 200m and 4x100m relay) at 1960 Olympics; also won relay silver in '56 Games; 2-time AP Athlete of Year (1960-61) and Sullivan Award winner in 1961.

Damon Runyon (b. Oct. 4, 1884, d. Dec. 10, 1946): Kansas native who gained fame as New York journalist, sports columnist and short-story writer; best known for 1932 story collection, "Guys and Dolls."

Adolph Rupp (b. Sept. 2, 1901, d. Dec. 10, 1977): Basketball; 2nd in all-time college coaching wins with 876; led Kentucky to 4 NCAA championships (1948-49,51,58) and 1 NIT title (1946).

Bill Russell (b. Feb. 12, 1934): Basketball C; won titles in college, Olympics and pros; 5-time NBA MVP; led Boston to 11 titles from 1957-69; also became first black NBA head coach in 1966.

Babe Ruth (b. Feb. 6, 1895, d. Aug. 16, 1948): Baseball LHP-OF; two-time 20-game winner with Boston Red Sox (1916-17); had a 94-46 record with a 2.28 ERA, while he was 3-0 in the World Series with an ERA of 0.87; sold to New York Yankees for $100,000 in 1920; AL MVP in 1923; led AL in slugging average 13 times, HRs 12 times, RBI 6 times and batting once (.378 in 1924); hit 60 HRs in 1927 and at least 54 3 other times; ended career with Boston Braves in 1935 with 714 HRs, 2,211 RBI, 2,062 walks and a batting average of .342; remains all-time leader in slugging percentage (.690); member of the Hall of Fame's inaugural class of 1936.

Johnny Rutherford (b. Mar. 12, 1938): Auto racer; 3-time winner of Indy 500 (1974,76,80); CART national champion in 1980.

Nolan Ryan (b. Jan. 31, 1947): Baseball RHP; recorded 7 no-hitters against Kansas City and Detroit (1973), Minnesota (1974), Baltimore (1975), LA Dodgers (1981), Oakland A's (1990) and Toronto (1991 at age 44); 2-time 20-game winner (1973-74); 2-time NL leader in ERA (1981,87); led AL in strikeouts 9 times and NL twice in 27 years; retired after 1993 season with 324 wins, 292 losses and all-time records for strikeouts (5,714) and walks (2,795); never won Cy Young Award; had his number retired by three teams (California, Houston, Texas); inducted into Hall of Fame in 1999.

Samuel Ryder (b. Mar. 24, 1858, d. Jan. 2, 1936): Golf; English seed merchant who donated the Ryder Cup in 1927 for competition between pro golfers from Great Britain and the U.S.; made his fortune by coming up with idea of selling seeds in small packages.

Toni Sailer (b. Nov. 17, 1935): Austrian skier; 1st to win 3 alpine gold medals in Winter Olympics, winning downhill, slalom and giant slalom.

Alberto Salazar (b. Aug. 7, 1958): Track and Field; set one world and six U.S. records during his career; broke 12-year-old record at New York Marathon in 1981 and broke Boston Marathon record in 1982; won three straight NY Marathons (1980-82); qualified for the 1980 and 1984 U.S. Olympic teams

Juan Antonio Samaranch (b. July 17, 1920): president of International Olympic Committee since 1980; the native of Barcelona was re-elected in 1996 after IOC's move in '95 to bump membership age limit to 80.

Pete Sampras (b. Aug. 12, 1971): Tennis; No.1 player in world from 1993-98; youngest ever U.S. Open men's champion (19 years, 28 days) in 1990; his win at Wimbledon in 2000 gave him 13 grand slam singles titles for his career, more than any other male player; has won 2 Australian Opens (1994,97), 7 Wimbledons (1993,94,95,97,98,99,00) and 4 U.S. Opens (1990,93,95,96).

Joan Benoit Samuelson (b. May 16, 1957): Distance runner; has won Boston Marathon twice (1979,83); won first women's Olympic marathon in 1984 Games at Los Angeles; Sullivan Award recipient in 1985.

Arantxa Sanchez Vicario (b. Dec. 18, 1971): Spanish tennis player; 28 tour victories through Sept. 2000 including 3 French Opens (1989,94,98) and 1 U.S. Open (1994); finalist in three of four Grand Slam finals in '95; teamed with Conchita Martinez to win 5 Federation Cups from 1991-98.

Earl Sande (b. Nov. 13, 1898, d. Aug. 19, 1968): Jockey; rode Gallant Fox to Triple Crown in 1930; won 5 Belmonts and 3 Kentucky Derbies.

Barry Sanders (b. July 16, 1968): Football RB; won 1988 Heisman Trophy as junior at Oklahoma St.; all-time NCAA single season leader in rushing (2,628 yards), scoring (234 points) and TDs (39); 4-time NFL rushing leader with Detroit Lions (1990,94,96,97); NFC Rookie of Year (1988); 2-time NFL Player of Year (1991,97); NFC MVP (1994); rushed for 2,053 yards in 1997, second-best season total ever; No. 2 all-time rusher with 15,269 yards; abruptly retired just prior to 1999 season.

Deion Sanders (b. Aug. 9, 1967): Baseball OF and Football DB-KR-WR; 2-time All-America at Florida St. in football (1987-88); 7-time NFL All-Pro CB with Atlanta, San Francisco and Dallas (1991-94,96-98); signed by Washington Redskins in 2000; led majors in triples (14) with Atlanta in 1992 and hit .533 in World Series the same year; played on 2 Super Bowl winners (SF in XXIX, and Dallas in XXX); first 2-way starter in NFL since Chuck Bednarik in 1962; only athlete to play in both World Series and Super Bowl.

Abe Saperstein (b. July 4, 1901, d. Mar. 15, 1966): Basketball; founded all-black, Harlem Globetrotters barnstorming team in 1927; coached sharpshooting comedians to 1940 world pro title in Chicago and established troupe as game's foremost goodwill ambassadors; also served as 1st commissioner of American Basketball League (1961-62).

Gene Sarazen (b. Feb. 27, 1902, d. May 13, 1999): Golfer; one of only five players to win all four Grand Slam titles (others are Hogan, Nicklaus, Player and Woods); won Masters, British Open, 2 U.S. Opens and 3 PGA titles between 1922-35; invented sand wedge in 1930.

Glen Sather (b. Sept. 2, 1943): Hockey; GM-coach of 4 Stanley Cup winners in Edmonton ͏̸84-85,87-88) and GM-only for another in 1990; ͏̸7th on all-time NHL coaching list with 553 wins ͏̸ playoffs); entered Hockey Hall of Fame in ͏̸ ed as president-GM of New York Rang-

͏̸ b. Dec. 28, 1929, d. May 31, ͏̸ ed 103 shutouts in 21 NHL ͏̸ y winner; played on 4 ͏̸ and Toronto; posted

Gale Sayers (b. May 30, 1943): Football HB; 2-time All-America at Kansas; NFL Rookie of Year (1965) and 5-time All-Pro with Chicago; scored then-record 22 TDs in rookie year.

Chris Schenkel (b. Aug. 21, 1923): Radio-TV; 4-time Sportscaster of Year; easy-going baritone who covered basketball, bowling, football, golf and the Olympics for ABC and CBS; host of ABC's Pro Bowlers Tour for 33 years; received lifetime achievement Emmy Award in 1993.

Vitaly Scherbo (b. Jan. 13, 1972): Russian gymnast; winner of unprecedented 6 gold medals in gymnastics, including men's All-Around, for Unified Team in 1992 Olympics; won 3 bronze in '96 Games.

Mike Schmidt (b. Sept. 27, 1949): Baseball 3B; led NL in HRs 8 times; 3-time MVP (1980,81,86) with Philadelphia; 548 career HRs and 10 Gold Gloves; inducted into Hall of Fame in 1995.

Don Schollander (b. Apr. 30, 1946): Swimming; won 4 gold medals at 1964 Olympics, plus one gold and one silver in 1968; won Sullivan Award in 1964.

Dick Schultz (b. Sept. 5, 1929): Reform-minded executive director of NCAA from 1988-93; announced resignation on May 11, 1993 in wake of special investigator's report citing Univ. of Virginia with improper student-athlete loan program during Schultz's tenure as athletic director (1981-87); named executive director of the USOC on June 23, 1995.

Michael Schumacher (b. Jan. 3, 1969): German auto racer; Formula One's active win leader (and 2nd all-time) with 42 career victories as of Sept. 21, 2000; world champion in 1994 and '95.

Bob Seagren (b. Oct. 17, 1946): Track & Field; won gold medal in pole vault at 1968 Olympics; broke world outdoor record 5 times.

Tom Seaver (b. Nov. 17, 1944): Baseball RHP; won 3 Cy Young Awards (1969,73,75); had 311 wins, 3,640 strikeouts and 2.86 ERA over 20 years.

George Seifert (b. Jan. 22, 1940): Football; coached San Francisco to a record 17 wins in his 1st season as head coach in 1989; 2-time Super Bowl-winning coach with 49ers (1989,94); returned to NFL in 1999 with Carolina; third all-time in coaching winning pct. (.740).

Peter Seitz (b. May 17, 1905, d. Oct. 17, 1983): Baseball arbitrator; ruled on Dec. 23, 1975 that players who perform for one season without a signed contract can become free agents; decision ushered in big money era for players.

Monica Seles (b. Dec. 2, 1973): Tennis; No. 1 in the world in 1991 and '92 after winning Australian, French and U.S. Opens both years; won 4 Australian, 3 French and 2 US Opens; winner of 30 singles titles in just 5 years before she was stabbed in the back by Steffi Graf fan Gunter Parche on Apr. 30, 1993 during match in Hamburg, Germany; spent remainder of 1993, all of '94 and most of '95 recovering; returned to WTA Tour with win at the Canadian Open in 1995; comeback complete with 1996 Australian Open win; winner of 47 WTA tournaments through Sept., 2000.

Bud Selig (b. July 30, 1934): Baseball; Milwaukee car dealer who bought AL Seattle Pilots for $10.8 million in 1970 and moved team to Midwest; as de facto comissioner, he presided over 232-day players' strike that resulted in cancellation of World Series for first time since 1904 and delayed opening of 1995 season until Apr. 25; officially named baseball's ninth commissioner on July 2, 1998.

Frank Selke (b. May 7, 1893, d. July 3, 1985): Hockey; GM of 6 Stanley Cup champions in Montreal (1953,56-60); the annual NHL trophy for best defensive forward bears his name.

Ayrton Senna (b. Mar. 21, 1960, d. May 1, 1994): Brazilian auto racer; 3-time Formula One champion (1988,90-91); died as all-time F1 leader in poles (65) and 2nd in wins (41, currently in 3rd place); killed in crash at Imola, Italy during '94 San Marino Grand Prix.

Wilbur Shaw (b. Oct. 13, 1902, d. Oct. 30, 1954): Auto racer; 3-time winner and 3-time runner-up of Indy 500 from 1933-1940.

Patty Sheehan (b. Oct. 27, 1956): Golfer; LPGA Player of Year in 1983; clinched entry into LPGA Hall of Fame with her 30th career win in 1993; 3 LPGA titles (1983-84,93) and 2 U.S. Opens (1992,94).

Bill Shoemaker (b. Aug. 19, 1931): Jockey; ranks second all-time in career wins with 8,833 (passed by Laffit Pincay Jr. in Dec. 1999); 3-time Eclipse Award winner as jockey (1981) and special award recipient (1976,81); won Belmont 5 times, Kentucky Derby 4 times and Preakness twice; oldest jockey to win Kentucky Derby (age 54, aboard Ferdinand in 1986); retired in 1990 to become trainer; paralyzed in 1991 auto accident but continued to train horses.

Eddie Shore (b. Nov. 25, 1902, d. Mar. 16, 1985): Hockey D; only NHL defenseman to win Hart Trophy as MVP 4 times (1933,35-36,38); led Boston Bruins to Stanley Cup titles in 1929 and '39; had 105 goals and 1,047 penalty minutes in 14 seasons.

Frank Shorter (b. Oct. 31, 1947): Track & Field; won gold medal in marathon at 1972 Olympics, 1st American to win in 64 years.

Don Shula (b. Jan. 4, 1930): Football; retired after 1995 season with an NFL-record 347 career wins (including playoffs) and a winning percentage of .665; took six teams to Super Bowl and won twice with Miami (VII, VIII); 4-time Coach of Year, twice with Baltimore (1964,68) and twice with Miami (1970-71); coached 1972 Dolphins to 17-0 record, the only undefeated team in NFL history.

Charlie Sifford (b. June 2, 1922): Golf; won the Hartford Open in 1967 with a final-round 64, becoming the first black player to win a PGA event; won PGA Seniors Championship in 1975; amassed over $1 million in career earnings; published his autobiography "Just Let Me Play" in 1992.

Al Simmons (b. May 22, 1902, d. May 26, 1956): Baseball OF; led AL in batting twice (1930-31) with Philadelphia A's and knocked in 100 runs or more 11 straight years (1924-34).

O.J. Simpson (b. July 9, 1947): Football RB; won Heisman Trophy in 1968 at USC; ran for 2,003 yards in NFL in 1973; All-Pro 5 times; MVP in 1973; rushed for 11,236 career yards; TV analyst and actor after career ended; arrested June 17, 1994 as suspect in double murder of ex-wife Nicole Brown Simpson and her friend Ronald Goldman; acquitted on Oct. 3, 1995 by a Los Angeles jury in criminal trial but forced to make financial reparations after losing wrongful death civil suit.

George Sisler (b. Mar. 24, 1893, d. Mar. 26, 1973): Baseball 1B; hit over .400 twice (1920,22) and batted over .300 in 13 of his 15 seasons; his 257 hits in 1920 is still a major league record; played most of his career with the St. Louis Browns; inducted into Baseball Hall of Fame in 1939.

Mary Decker Slaney (b. Aug. 4, 1958): U.S. middle distance runner; has held 7 separate American track & field records from the 800 to 10,000 meters; won both 1,500 and 3,000 meters at 1983 World Championships in Helsinki, but no Olympic medals.

Raisa Smetanina (b. Feb. 29, 1952): Russian Nordic skier; all-time Winter Olympics medalist with 10 cross-country medals (4 gold, 5 silver and a bronze) in 5 appearances (1976,80,84,88,92) for USSR and Unified Team.

Billy Smith (b. Dec. 12, 1950): Hockey G; led NY Islanders to 4 consecutive Stanley Cups (1980-83); won Vezina Trophy in 1982; Stanley Cup MVP in 1983.

Dean Smith (b. Feb. 28, 1931): Basketball; No. 1 on all-time NCAA coaches victory list (879); led North Carolina to 25 NCAA tournaments in 34 years, reaching Final Four 10 times and winning championship twice (1982,93); coached U.S. Olympic team to gold medal in 1976.

Emmitt Smith (b. May 15, 1969): Football RB; consensus All-America (1989) at Florida; 4-time NFL rushing leader (1991-93,95); regular season and Super Bowl MVP in 1993; played on three Super Bowl champions (1993,94,96); entered the 2000 season with 136 rushing TDs, more than any player in history; set single-season mark for TDs with 25 in 1995.

John Smith (b. Aug. 9, 1965): Wrestler; 2-time NCAA champion for Oklahoma St. at 134 lbs (1987-88) and Most Outstanding Wrestler of '88 championships; 3-time world champion; gold medal winner at 1988 and '92 Olympics at 137 lbs; won Sullivan Award (1990); coached Oklahoma St. to 1994 NCAA title and brother Pat was Most Outstanding Wrestler.

Lee Smith (b. Dec. 4, 1957): Baseball RHP; 3-time NL saves leader (1983,91-92); retired as all-time saves leader with 478 and an ERA of 3.03; 10 seasons with 30 or more saves and 3 times saved over 40.

Michelle Smith deBruin (b. Apr. 7, 1969): Irish swimmer; won three gold medals at the 1996 Olympics; accused of using performance-enhancing drugs but passed all tests until she was suspended for 4 years by FINA in 1998 for tampering with a urine sample.

Ozzie Smith (b. Dec. 26, 1954): Baseball SS; won 13 straight Gold Gloves (1980-92); played in 12 straight All-Star Games (1981-92); MVP of 1985 NL playoffs; holds all-time assist record for SS with 8,375.

Walter (Red) Smith (b. Sept. 25, 1905, d. Jan. 15, 1982): Sportswriter for newspapers in Philadelphia and New York from 1936-82; won Pulitzer Prize for commentary in 1976.

Conn Smythe (b. Feb. 1, 1895, d. Nov. 18, 1980): Hockey pioneer; built Maple Leaf Gardens in 1931; managed Toronto to 7 Stanley Cups before retiring in 1961.

Sam Snead (b. May 27, 1912): Golfer; won both Masters and PGA 3 times and British Open once; runner-up in U.S. Open 4 times; PGA Player of Year in 1949; oldest player (52 years, 10 months) to win PGA event with Greater Greensboro Open title in 1965; all-time PGA Tour career victory leader with 81.

Peter Snell (b. Dec. 17, 1938): Track & Field; New Zealander who won gold medal in 800m at 1960 Olympics, then won both the 800m and 1,500m at 1964 Games.

Duke Snider (b. Sept. 19, 1926): Baseball OF; hit 40 or more home runs five straight seasons (1953-57); led the league in runs scored 1953-55; played in six World Series with the Dodgers and blasted .286 with 11 home runs; nicknamed "Duke of Flatbush"; in 18 seasons hit 407 home runs, scored 1,259 runs and had 1,333 RBI.

Annika Sorenstam (b. Oct. 9, 1970): Swedish golfer; won the 1995 U.S. Women's Open as her first LPGA victory; won the event again in 1996; College Player of the Year and NCAA champion in 1991; won more LPGA tournaments (18) than any other player in the 1990s; amassed 23 tour wins through Sept., 2000.

Sammy Sosa (b. Nov. 12, 1968): Baseball OF; slugging Chicago Cub who surpassed Roger Maris' season home run record (61), just after Mark McGwire did, in 1998 and finished the year with 66; NL MVP (1998); followed up his amazing 1998 by hitting 63 bombs in 1999 with 141 RBI; 4-time NL all-star (1995,98,99,00) and winner of the 2000 Home Run Derby.

Javier Sotomayor (b. Oct. 13, 1967): Cuban high jumper; first man to clear 8 feet (8-0) on July 29, 1989; won gold medal at 1992 Olympics with jump of only 7-ft, 8-in.; broke world record with leap of 8-0½ in 1993; had a controversial drug suspension reduced, which allowed him to participate in 2000 Olympics; won the silver medal in Sydney with a leap of 7-7¼.

Warren Spahn (b. Apr. 23, 1921): Baseball LHP; led NL in wins 8 times; won 20 or more games 13 times; Cy Young winner in 1957; most career wins (363) by a left-hander.

Tris Speaker (b. Apr. 4, 1888, d. Dec. 8, 1958): Baseball OF; all-time leader in outfield assists (449) and doubles (792); had .344 career BA and 3,515 hits.

J.G. Taylor Spink (b. Nov. 6, 1888, d. Dec. 7, 1962): Publisher of *The Sporting News* from 1914-62; Baseball Writers' Assn. annual meritorious service award named after him.

Leon Spinks (b. July 11, 1953): Boxing; won heavyweight crown in split decision over Muhammad Ali in Feb.1978; Ali regained title seven months later; won gold medal in light heavyweight division at 1976 Olympics; brother Michael won the heavyweight title in 1983; were the only brothers to hold world titles; known more for frequent traffic violations and lavish lifestyle than bouts late in career; filed for bankruptcy in 1986.

Mark Spitz (b. Feb. 10, 1950): Swimmer; set 23 world and 35 U.S. records; won all-time record 7 gold medals (4 individual, 3 relay) in 1972 Olympics; also won 4 medals (2 gold, a silver and a bronze) in 1968 Games for a total of 11; comeback attempt at age 41 foundered in 1991.

Latrell Sprewell (b. Sept. 8, 1970): Basketball G; became an NBA All-Star in just his second pro season out of Alabama; led Golden State in scoring four years in a row; made headlines in 1997 after being suspended by the NBA for attacking Warriors head coach P.J. Carlesimo during a practice; currently a member of the N.Y. Knicks.

Amos Alonzo Stagg (b. Aug. 16, 1862, d. Mar. 17, 1965): Football innovator; coached at U. of Chicago for 41 seasons and College of the Pacific for 14 more; 314-199-35 record; elected to both college football and basketball Halls of Fame.

Willie Stargell (b. Mar. 6, 1940): Baseball OF-1B; led NL in home runs twice (1971,73); 475 career HRs; NL co-MVP and World Series MVP in 1979.

Bart Starr (b. Jan. 9, 1934): Football QB; led Green Bay to 5 NFL titles and 2 Super Bowl wins from 1961-67; regular season MVP in 1966; MVP of Super Bowls I and II.

Roger Staubach (b. Feb. 5, 1942): Football QB; Heisman Trophy winner as Navy junior in 1963; led Dallas to 2 Super Bowl titles (1972,78) and was Super Bowl MVP in 1972; 5-time leading passer in NFC (1971,73,77-79).

George Steinbrenner (b. July 4, 1930): Baseball; principal owner of NY Yankees since 1973; teams have won 7 pennants and 5 World Series (1977-78,96,98,99); has changed managers 21 times and GMs 11 times in 27 years; ordered by baseball commish Fay Vincent in 1990 to surrender control of club for dealings with small-time gambler; reinstated in 1993.

Casey Stengel (b. July 30, 1890, d. Sept. 29, 1975): Baseball; player for 14 years and manager for 25; outfielder and lifetime .284 hitter with 5 clubs (1912-25); guided NY Yankees to 10 AL pennants and 7 World Series titles from 1949-60; 1st NY Mets skipper from 1962-65.

Ingemar Stenmark (b. Mar. 18, 1956): Swedish alpine skier; 3-time World Cup overall champ (1976-78); posted 86 World Cup wins in 16 years; won 2 gold medals at 1980 Olympics.

Helen Stephens (b. Feb. 3, 1918, d. Jan. 17, 1994): Track & Field; set 3 world records in 100-yard dash and 4 more in 100 meters in 1935-36; won gold medals in 100 meters and 4x100-meter relay in 1936 Olympics; retired in 1937.

Woody Stephens (b. Sept. 1, 1913, d. Aug. 22, 1998): Horse racing; trainer who saddled an unprecedented 5 straight winners in Belmont Stakes (1982-86); also had two Kentucky Derby winners (1974,84) and one Preakness winner (1952); trained 1982 Horse of Year Conquistador Cielo; won Eclipse award as nation's top trainer in 1983.

David Stern (b. Sept. 22, 1942): Basketball; marketing expert and NBA commissioner since 1984; took office the year Michael Jordan turned pro; has presided over stunning artistic and financial success of NBA both nationally and internationally; league has grown from 23 teams to 29 during his watch and opened offices worldwide; oversaw launch of WNBA in 1997.

Teófilo Stevenson (b. Mar. 29, 1952): Cuban boxer; won 3 consecutive gold medals as Olympic heavyweight (1972,76,80); did not turn pro.

Jackie Stewart (b. June 11, 1939): Auto racer; won 27 Formula One races and 3 world driving titles from 1965-73.

John Stockton (b. Mar 26, 1962): Basketball G; all-time NBA leader in every major assist category, including most in a season (1,164), highest average in a season (14.5 per game) and most overall (13,790); also holds the NBA record for career steals (2,844); All-NBA team in '94 and '95; member of 1992 and '96 US Olympic basketball Dream Teams; 10-time All-Star.

Dwight Stones (b. Dec. 6, 1953): Track & Field; set three world records in the high jump, the last in 1976 (7-7 1/4); won bronze medal at 1972 and 76 Summer Games; won NCAA indoor and outdoor titles in 1976; was suspended in 1978 for taking money for a television appearance; made 1984 Olympic squad with his 13th American record (7-8), finishing fourth at Games; member of the National Track & Field Hall of Fame.

Curtis Strange (b. Jan. 30, 1955): Golfer; won consecutive U.S. Open titles (1988-89); 3-time leading money winner on PGA Tour (1985,87-88); first PGA player to win $1 million in one year (1988).

Picabo Street (b. Apr. 3, 1971): Skiing; 2-time Olympic medalist, gold (Super G in 1998) and silver (downhill in 1994); her 1995 World Cup downhill series title first-ever by U.S. woman, she repeated the feat in 1996.

Kerri Strug (b. Nov. 19, 1977): Gymnastics; delivered the most dramatic moment of the 1996 Summer Olympics when she completed a vault (9.712) after spraining her ankle; the second vault assured the first all-around gold medal for a US Women's gymnastics team; a poor performance by the Russian team on the beam had clinched the gold medal for the US but Strug was unaware when she made the second vault; the injury prevented her from participating in any individual events.

Louise Suggs (b. Sept. 7, 1923): Golfer; won 11 majors and 50 LPGA events overall from 1949-62.

James E. Sullivan (b. Nov. 18, 1862, d. Sept. 16, 1914): Track & Field; pioneer who founded Amateur Athletic Union (AAU) in 1888; director of St. Louis Olympic Games in 1904; AAU's Sullivan Award for performance and sportsmanship named after him.

John L. Sullivan (b. Oct. 15, 1858, d. Feb. 2, 1918): Boxer; world heavyweight champion (1882-92); last of bare-knuckle champions.

Pat Summitt (b. June 14, 1952): Basketball; women's basketball coach at Tennessee (1974—); 2nd all-time in career victories to Jody Conradt of Texas; coached 1984 US women's basketball team to its first Olympic gold medal; has coached Lady Vols to 6 national championships (1987,89,91,96,97,98).

Don Sutton (b. April 2, 1945): Baseball RHP; won 324 games and tossed 58 shutouts in his 23-year career; recorded NL record five career 1-hitters; played with Dodgers, Astros, Brewers, Athletics, Angels and was a 4-time All-Star; elected to Hall of Fame in 1998.

Lynn Swann (b. Mar. 7, 1952): Football WR; played nine seasons with Pittsburgh (1974-82); appeared in four Super Bowls and had 16 catches for 364 yards and three TDs; named MVP of Super Bowl X for 4-161, 1 TD performance.

Barry Switzer (b. Oct. 5, 1937): Football; coached Oklahoma to 3 national titles (1974-75,85); 4th on all-time winning pct list at .837 (157-29-4); resigned in 1989 after OU was slapped with 3-year NCAA probation and 5 players were brought up on criminal charges; hired as Dallas Cowboys head coach in 1994 and led team to victory in Super Bowl XXX in 1996, resigning before '98 season.

Paul Tagliabue (b. Nov. 24, 1940): Football; NFL attorney who was elected league's 4th commissioner in 1989; ushered in salary cap in 1994; the league expanded by 2 teams in 1995 for 1st time since '76 (will expand to 32 by 2002).

Anatoli Tarasov (b. 1918, d. June 23, 1995): Hockey; coached Soviet Union to 9 straight world championships and 3 Olympic gold medals (1964,68,72).

Jerry Tarkanian (b. Aug. 30, 1930): Basketball; 4th all-time winningest college coach with .803 win pct.; has amassed over 700 wins in 29 years at Long Beach St., UNLV and Fresno St.; led UNLV to 4 Final Fours and 1 national title (1990); fought 16-year battle with NCAA over purity of UNLV program; quit as coach after going 26-2 in 1991-92; fired after 20 games (9-11) as coach of NBA San Antonio Spurs in 1992; unretired in 1995 to coach his alma mater, Fresno St.

Fran Tarkenton (b. Feb. 3, 1940): Football QB; 2-time NFL All-Pro (1973,75); Player of Year (1975); threw for 47,003 yards and 342 TDs (both former NFL records) in 18 seasons with Vikings and Giants.

Chuck Taylor (b. June 24, 1901, d. June 23, 1969): Converse traveling salesman whose name came to grace the classic, high-top canvas basketball sneakers known as "Chucks"; over 500 million pairs have been sold since 1917; he also ran clinics worldwide and edited Converse Basketball Yearbook (1922-68).

Lawrence Taylor (b. Feb. 4, 1959): Football LB; All-America at North Carolina (1980); only defensive player in NFL history to be consensus Player of Year (1986); led NY Giants to Super Bowl titles in 1986 and '90 seasons; played in a record 10 Pro Bowls (1981-90); retired after 1993 season with 132½ sacks and has had several drug-related arrests since; inducted into Hall of Fame in 1999.

Marshall (Major) Taylor (b. Nov. 26, 1878, d. June 21, 1932): Cyclist; Considered one of the first African-American sports heroes; held seven world cycling records at the turn of the century, racing mostly in Europe, Australia and New Zealand after being barred from many events in the U.S. due to racial prejudices; won the world 1-mile championship in 1899.

Gustavo Thoeni (b. Feb. 28, 1951): Italian alpine skier; 4-time World Cup overall champion (1971-73,75); won giant slalom at 1972 Olympics.

Frank Thomas (b. May 27, 1968): Baseball 1B; All-America at Auburn in 1989; won AL MVP with Chicago in 1993 and 94; five-time All Star; first player in major league history to hit .300, hit at least 20 home runs and have over 100 walks, RBIs and runs scored in seven straight seasons; has hit 40 home runs 4 times (1993,95,96,00); nicknamed "the Big Hurt."

Isiah Thomas (b. Apr. 30, 1961): Basketball; led Indiana to NCAA title as sophomore and Final 4 MOP in 1981; consensus All-America guard in '81; led Detroit to 2 NBA titles in 1989 and '90; NBA Finals MVP in 1990; 3-time All-NBA 1st team (1984-86); retired in 1994 at age 33 after tearing right Achilles tendon; returned to NBA in 2000 as coach of the Indiana Pacers; inducted into Basketball Hall of Fame in 2000.

Thurman Thomas (b. May 16, 1966): Football RB; 3-time AFC rushing leader (1990-91,93); 2-time All-Pro (1990-91); NFL Player of Year (1991); led Buffalo to 4 straight Super Bowls (1991-94); signed by Miami before 2000 season.

Daley Thompson (b. July 30, 1958): British Track & Field; won consecutive gold medals in decathlon at 1980 and '84 Olympics.

John Thompson (b. Sept. 2, 1941): Basketball; coached centers Patrick Ewing, Alonzo Mourning and Dikembe Mutombo at Georgetown; reached NCAA tourney final 3 out of 4 years with Ewing, winning title in 1984; also led Hoyas to 6 Big East tourney titles; coached 1988 U.S. Olympic team to bronze medal; retired abruptly during 1999 season with 27-year mark of 596-239.

Bobby Thomson (b. Oct. 25, 1923): Baseball OF; career .270 hitter who won the 1951 NL pennant for the NY Giants with a 1-out, 3-run HR in the bottom of the 9th inning of Game 3 of a best-of-3 playoff with Brooklyn; the pitcher was Ralph Branca, the count was 0-1 and the Dodgers were ahead 4-2; the Giants had trailed Brooklyn by 13½ games on Aug. 11.

Ian Thorpe (b. Oct. 13, 1982): Swimming; Australian who won gold at Sydney Olympics in the 400m freestyle (breaking his own world record) and silver in the 200m freestyle; was also part of Australian relay team that won gold and broke the world record in the 4x100m and 4x200 freestyle relays.

Jim Thorpe (b. May 28, 1888, d. May 28, 1953): 2-time All-America in football; won both pentathlon and decathlon at 1912 Olympics; stripped of medals a month later for playing semi-pro baseball prior to Games; medals restored in 1982; played major league baseball (1913-19) and pro football (1920-26,28); chosen "Athlete of the Half Century" by AP in 1950.

Bill Tilden (b. Feb. 10, 1893, d. June 5, 1953): Tennis; won 7 U.S. and 3 Wimbledon titles in 1920s; led U.S. to 7 straight Davis Cup victories (1920-26).

Tinker to Evers to Chance Chicago Cubs double play combination from 1903-10; immortalized in poem by New York sportswriter Franklin P. Adams— SS Joe Tinker (1880-1948), 2B Johnny Evers (1883-1947) and 1B Frank Chance (1877-1924); all 3 managed the Cubs and made the Hall of Fame.

Y.A. Tittle (b. Oct. 24, 1926): Football QB; played 17 years in AAFC and NFL; All-Pro 4 times; league MVP with San Francisco (1957) and NY Giants (1962); passed for 28,339 career yards.

Alberto Tomba (b. Dec. 19, 1966): Italian alpine skier; all-time Olympic alpine medalist with 5 (3 gold, 2 silver); became 1st alpine skier to win gold medals in 2 consecutive Winter Games when he won the slalom and giant slalom in 1988 then repeated in the GS in '92; also won silvers in slalom in 1992 and '94.

Vladislav Tretiak (b. Apr. 25, 1952): Hockey G; led USSR to Olympic gold medals in 1972 and '76; starred for Soviets against Team Canada in 1972, and again in 2 Canada Cups (1976,81).

Lee Trevino (b. Dec. 1, 1939): Golfer; 2-time winner of 3 majors—U.S. Open (1968,71), British Open (1971-72) and PGA (1974,84); Player of Year once on PGA Tour (1971) and 3 times with Seniors (1990,92,94); 27 PGA Tour and 29 Senior Tour wins.

Felix Trinidad (b. Jan. 10, 1973): Puerto Rican boxer; former WBC/IBF welterweight champion; won WBC belt with a majority decision over the slightly-favored Oscar De La Hoya in their highly-anticipated meeting in Sept., 1999; stepped up to junior middleweight and won the WBA title from David Reid in March, 2000; record of 38-0 with 31 KOs as of Sept., 2000.

Bryan Trottier (b. July 17, 1956): Hockey C; led NY Islanders to 4 straight Stanley Cups (1980-83); Rookie of Year (1976); scoring champion (134 points) and regular season MVP in 1979; playoff MVP (1980); added 5th and 6th Cups with Pittsburgh in 1991 and '92; entered Hockey Hall of Fame in 1997.

Gene Tunney (b. May 25, 1897, d. Nov. 7, 1978): Boxer; world heavyweight champion from 1926-28; beat 31-year-old champ Jack Dempsey unanimous 10 round decision in 1926; beat him in famous "long count" rematch in '27; c' ' champion in 1928 with 65-1-1 record

Ted Turner (b. Nov. 19, 1938): Sportsman and TV mogul; skippered *Courageous* to America's Cup win in 1977; owner of MLB Atlanta Braves, NBA Hawks and NHL Thrashers; owner of CNN, TNT and TBS; founder of Goodwill Games; 1991 *Time* Man of Year.

Mike Tyson (b. June 30, 1966): Boxer; youngest (age 19) to win heavyweight title (WBC in 1986); undisputed champ from 1987 until upset loss to 42-1 shot Buster Douglas on Feb. 10, 1990, in Tokyo; found guilty on Feb. 10, 1992, of raping 18-year-old Miss Black America contestant Desiree Washington in Indianapolis on July 19, 1991; sentenced to 6-year prison term; released May 9, 1995 after serving 3 years; reclaimed WBC and WBA belts with wins over Frank Bruno and Bruce Seldon in 1996; lost WBA title to Evander Holyfield in 1996; brought his career to a halt when he bit Holyfield twice in the ear during their WBA championship fight in 1997; returned to jail in 1999 for assaulting two motorists during a 1998 traffic dispute; see career fight record in Boxing chapter.

Wyomia Tyus (b. Aug. 29, 1945): Track & Field; 1st woman to win consecutive Olympic gold medals in 100m (1964-68).

Peter Ueberroth (b. Sept. 2, 1937): Organizer of 1984 Summer Olympics in LA; 1984 *Time* Man of Year; baseball commissioner from 1984-89; headed Rebuild Los Angeles for one year after 1992 riots.

Johnny Unitas (b. May 7, 1933): Football QB; led Baltimore Colts to 2 NFL titles (1958-59) and a Super Bowl win (1971); All-Pro 5 times; 3-time MVP (1959,64,67); passed for 40,239 career yards and 290 TDs.

Al Unser Jr. (b. Apr. 19, 1962): Auto racer; 2-time CART-IndyCar national champion (1990,94); captured Indy 500 for 2nd time in 3 years in '94, giving Unser family 9 overall titles at the Brickyard; 31 CART wins in 18 years; left CART for Indy Racing League at the start of the 2000 season; won the Vegas Indy 300 in April; son of Al and nephew of Bobby.

Al Unser Sr. (b. May 29, 1939): Auto racer; 3-time USAC-CART national champion (1970,83,85); 4-time winner of Indy 500 (1970-71,78,87); retired in 1994 ranked 3rd on all-time CART list with 39 wins; younger brother of Bobby and father of Al Jr.

Bobby Unser (b. Feb. 20, 1934): Auto racer; 2-time USAC-CART national champion (1968,74); 3-time winner of Indy 500 (1968,75,81); retired after 1981 season; ranks 5th on all-time CART list with 35 career wins.

Gene Upshaw (b. Aug. 15, 1945): Football G; 2-time All-AFL and 3-time All-NFL selection with Oakland; helped lead Raiders to 2 Super Bowl titles in 1976 and '80 seasons; executive director of NFL Players Assn. since 1987; agreed to application of salary cap in 1994.

Jim Valvano (b. Mar. 10, 1946, d. Apr. 28, 1993): Basketball; coach at N.C. State whose team upset Houston to win national title in 1983; in 19 seasons as a coach appeared in 8 NCAA tournaments; twice voted ACC Coach of the Year; career record 346-212; AD at N.C. State (1986-89) when a recruiting and admissions scandal forced him out of the job; worked as a broadcaster for ESPN and ABC; died after a year-long battle with cancer; The V Foundation for cancer resear~ is named for him.

Van Brocklin (b. Mar. 15, 1926, d. May ~~ball QB-P; led NFL in passing 3 times and ~~ LA Rams (1951) and Philadelphia ~~ MVP in 1960.

~~b. Feb. 17, 1973): Swimming; ~~win four gold medals in one ~~individual 50M freestyle, ~~e US team for the 4x100 ~~n gold at Sydney in ~~estyle relay.

~~2, 1914, d. Oct. ~~leaguer to pitch ~~38).

Harold S. Vanderbilt (b. July 6, 1884, d. July 4, 1970): Sportsman; successfully defended America's Cup 3 times (1930, 34,37); also invented contract bridge in 1926.

Glenna Collett Vare (b. June 20, 1903, d. Feb. 10, 1989): Golfer; won record 6 U.S. Women's Amateur titles from 1922-35; "the female Bobby Jones."

Andy Varipapa (b. Mar. 31, 1891, d. Aug. 25, 1984): Bowler; trick-shot artist; won consecutive All-Star match games titles (1947-48) at age 55 and 56.

Mo Vaughn (b. Dec. 15, 1967): Baseball 1B; 1995 AL MVP with Boston; 3-time All-Star; signed a 6-year, $80 million deal with Anaheim in 1999.

Bill Veeck (b. Feb. 9, 1914, d. Jan. 2, 1986): Maverick baseball executive; owned AL teams in Cleveland, St. Louis and Chicago from 1946-80; introduced ballpark giveaways, exploding scoreboards, Wrigley Field's ivy-covered walls and midget Eddie Gaedel; won World Series with Indians (1948) and pennant with White Sox (1959).

Jacques Villeneuve (b. Apr. 9, 1971): Canadian auto racer; Indianapolis 500 runner-up and IndyCar Rookie of Year in 1994; won 500 and IndyCar driving championship in 1995; jumped to Formula One racing in 1996 and won the F1 title in 1997.

Fay Vincent (b. May 29, 1938): Baseball; became 8th commissioner after death of A. Bartlett Giamatti in 1989; presided over World Series earthquake, owners' lockout and banishment of NY Yankees owner George Steinbrenner in his first year on the job; contentious relationship with owners resulted in his resignation on Sept. 7, 1992, four days after 18-9 "no confidence" vote.

Lasse Viren (b. July 22, 1949): Finnish runner; won gold medals at 5,000 and 10,00 meters in 1972 Munich Olympics; repeated 5,000/10,000 double in 1976 Games and added a 5th place in the marathon.

Dick Vitale (b. June 9, 1939): Broadcaster; Radio and television commentator for ESPN and ABC Sports known for his enthusiastic, almost spastic style; had successful college and pro basketball coaching career with the University of Detroit (1973-77) and the Detroit Pistons (1978-79); he's been nominated for a Cable ACE award eight times and won once in 1995.

Lanny Wadkins (b. Dec. 5, 1949): Golfer; member of 8 Ryder Cup teams and captain of 1995 team; 21 PGA Tour wins.

Honus Wagner (b. Feb. 24, 1874, d. Dec. 6, 1955): Baseball SS; hit .300 for 17 consecutive seasons (1897-1913) with Louisville and Pittsburgh; led NL in batting 8 times; ended career with 3,430 career hits, a .329 average and 722 stolen bases.

Lisa Wagner (b. May 19, 1961): Bowler; 4-time LPBT Player of Year (1983,86,88,93); 1980's Bowler of Decade; first woman to earn $100,000 in a season; winner of 32 pro titles as of Sept. 2000.

Grete Waitz (b. Oct. 1, 1953): Norwegian runner; 9-time winner of New York City Marathon from 1978-88; won silver medal at 1984 Olympics.

Jersey Joe Walcott (b. Jan. 31, 1914, d. Feb. 27, 1994): Boxer; oldest heavyweight (37) to ever win the championship; lost four championship bouts before knocking out Ezzard Charles in the seventh round in 1951; lost the title the following year, losing to Rocky Marciano; won 50 bouts, 30 by knockout, lost 17 and fought one draw as a professional; later became sheriff of Camden County, NJ.

Doak Walker (b. Jan. 1, 1927, d. Sept. 27, 1998): Football HB; won Heisman Trophy as SMU junior in 1948; led Detroit to 2 NFL titles (1952-53); All-Pro 4 times in 6 years.

Herschel Walker (b. Mar. 3, 1962): Football RB; led Georgia to national title as freshman in 1980; won Heisman in 1982 then jumped to upstart USFL in '83; signed by Dallas Cowboys after USFL folded; led NFL in rushing in 1988; traded to Minnesota in 1989 for 5 players and 6 draft picks; later played for Philadelphia and NY Giants and again with Dallas.

Rusty Wallace (b. Aug. 14, 1956): Auto racing; NASCAR Winston Cup champion in 1989 and runner-up in 1980, 1988 and 1993; recorded 53 victories and has won over $22 million in earnings in 21 years of racing as of Sept. 21, 2000; has earned $1 million in earnings ten different seasons.

Bill Walsh (b. Nov. 30, 1931): Football; Hall of Fame coach and GM of 3 Super Bowl winners with San Francisco (1982,85,89); retired after 1989 Super Bowl; returned to college coaching in 1992 for his second stint at Stanford; retired again after 1994 season; returned as 49er GM in 1999.

Bill Walton (b. Nov. 5, 1952): Basketball C; 3-time College Player of Year (1972-74); led UCLA to 2 national titles (1972-73); led Portland to NBA title as MVP in 1977; regular season MVP in 1978.

Darrell Waltrip (b. Feb. 5, 1947): Auto racing; 3-time NASCAR Winston Cup champion (1981,82,85); active leader with 84 career Winston Cup wins and 59 poles; announced plans to retire after the 2000 Winston Cup season.

Arch Ward (b. Dec. 27, 1896, d. July 9, 1955): Promoter and sports editor of *Chicago Tribune* from 1930-55; founder of baseball All-Star Game (1933), Chicago College All-Star Football Game (1934) and the All-America Football Conference (1946-49).

Charlie Ward (b. Oct. 12, 1970): Football QB and Basketball G; first Heisman winner to play for national champs (Florida St. in 1993) since Tony Dorsett in 1976, won Sullivan Award (1993); not taken in NFL Draft; 1st round pick of NY Knicks in 1994 NBA draft.

Glenn (Pop) Warner (b. Apr. 5, 1871, d. Sept. 7, 1954): Football innovator; coached at 7 colleges over 49 years; 319 career wins 2nd only to Bear Bryant's 323 in Div. I-A; produced 47 All-Americas, including Jim Thorpe and Ernie Nevers.

Tom Watson (b. Sept. 4, 1949): Golfer; 6-time PGA Player of the Year (1977-80,82,84); has won 5 British Opens, 2 Masters and a U.S. Open; 4-time Ryder Cup member; 34 PGA tour wins; began playing on the Senior Tour in 1999.

Earl Weaver (b. Aug. 14, 1930): Baseball; managed the Baltimore Orioles to 6 Eastern Division titles, four AL pennants and a World Series victory in 1970; was ejected 91 times and suspended four times for outbursts against umpires; record of 1,480-1,060 from 1968-82 and 1985-86.

Dick Weber (b. Dec. 23, 1929): Bowler; 3-time PBA Bowler of the Year (1961,63,65); won 30 PBA titles in 4 decades.

Johnny Weissmuller (b. June 2, 1904, d. Jan. 20 1984): Swimmer; won 3 gold medals at 1924 Olympics and 2 more at 1928 Games; became Hollywood's most famous Tarzan.

Jerry West (b. May 28, 1938): Basketball G; 2-time All-America and NCAA Final 4 MOP (1959) at West Virginia; led 1960 U.S. Olympic team to gold medal; 10-time All-NBA 1st-team; NBA finals MVP (1969); led LA Lakers to NBA title once as player (1972) and then 6 more times (1980,82,85,87,88,00) as an executive in various positions with the club, most recently VP of basketball operations; retired after the 2000 season; his silhouette serves as the NBA's logo.

Pernell Whitaker (b. Jan. 2, 1964): Boxer; won Olympic gold medal as lightweight in 1984; has won 4 world championships at lightweight, jr. welterweight, welterweight and jr. middleweight; outfought but failed to beat Julio Cesar Chavez when Sept. 10, 1993 welterweight title defense ended in controversial draw; pro record of 41-3-1 (17 KOs).

Bill White (b. Jan. 28, 1934): Baseball; NL president and highest ranking black executive in sports from 1989-94; as 1st baseman, won 7 Gold Gloves and hit .286 with 202 HRs in 13 seasons.

Byron (Whizzer) White (b. June 8, 1917): Football; All-America HB at Colorado (1937); signed with Pittsburgh in 1938 for the then largest contract in pro history ($15,800); took Rhodes Scholarship in 1939; returned to NFL in 1940 to lead league in rushing and retired in 1941; named to U.S. Supreme Court by President Kennedy in 1962 and stepped down in 1993.

Reggie White (b. Dec. 19, 1961): Football DE; consensus All-America in 1983 at Tennessee; 7-time All-NFL (1986-92) with Philadelphia; signed as free agent with Green Bay in 1993 for $17 million over 4 years; played key role in Packers 1997 Super Bowl victory; made headlines in 1998 after making controversial public comments about gays and minorities; retired in 1999 but returned with the Carolina Panthers in 2000; all-time NFL leader in sacks (192½) going into the 2000 season.

Kathy Whitworth (b. Sept. 27, 1939): Golf; 7-time LPGA Player of the Year (1966-69,71-73); won 6 majors; 88 tour wins, most on LPGA or PGA tour.

Hazel Hotchkiss Wightman (b. Dec. 20, 1886, d. Dec. 5, 1974): Tennis; won 16 U.S. national titles; 4-time U.S. Women's champion (1909-11,19); donor of Wightman Cup.

Hoyt Wilhelm (b. July 26, 1923): Baseball RHP; Knuckleballer who is 3rd all-time in games pitched (1,070) and 1st in games finished (651) and games won in relief (123); career ERA of 2.52 and 227 saves; 1st reliever inducted into Hall of Fame (1985); threw no-hitter vs. NY Yankees (1958); also hit lone HR of career in first major league at bat (1952).

Lenny Wilkens (b. Oct. 28, 1937): Basketball; NBA's all-time winningest coach (1251-1066 including playoffs); MVP of 1960 NIT as Providence guard; played 15 years in NBA, including 4 as player-coach; MVP of 1971 All-Star Game; coached Seattle to NBA title in 1979; Coach of Year in 1994 with Atlanta; one of only two men (John Wooden) to be honored by the Hall of Fame as player and coach; left Atlanta in 2000 to coach the Toronto Raptors.

Dominique Wilkins (b. Jan. 12, 1960): Basketball F; last player to lead NBA in scoring (1986) before Michael Jordan's reign; All-NBA 1st team in 1986; elder statesman of Dream Team II.

Bud Wilkinson (b. Apr. 23, 1916, d. Feb. 9, 1994): Football; played on 1936 national championship team at Minnesota; coached Oklahoma to 3 national titles (1950,55,56); won 4 Orange and 2 Sugar Bowls; teams had winning streaks of 47 (1953-57) and 31 (1948-50); retired after 1963 season with 145-29-4 record in 17 years; also coached St. Louis of NFL to 9-20 record in 1978-79.

Ricky Williams (b. May 21, 1977): Football RB; became all-time NCAA Div. I-A leader in rushing yards (6,279) and touchdowns (75) at Texas but has since been passed in both categories; 1998 Heisman Trophy winner; Mike Ditka and New Orleans Saints made history by trading their entire draft to take him fifth overall in 1999 NFL draft.

Serena Williams (b. Sept. 26, 1981): Tennis; beat Martina Hingis for 1999 U.S. Open championship becoming the first African-American woman to win a Grand Slam title since Althea Gibson in 1958; won doubles title at the 1999 U.S. and French Opens with sister Venus; the sisters also paired to win the doubles title at Wimbledon in 2000.

Ted Williams (b. Aug. 30, 1918): Baseball OF; led AL in batting 6 times, and HRs and RBI 4 times each; won Triple Crown twice (1942,47); 2-time MVP (1946,49); last player to bat .400 when he hit .406 in 1941; Marine Corps combat pilot who missed three full seasons during World War II (1943-45) and most of two others (1952-53) during Korean War; hit .344 lifetime with 521 HRs in 19 years with Boston Red Sox.

Venus Williams (b. June 17, 1980): Tennis; won doubles title at the 1999 U.S. and French Opens with sister Serena; recorded fastest serve in WTA history with 127 mph blast; won first Grand Slam singles championship at Wimbledon in 2000 and followed it up with her second just two months later at the U.S. Open, defeating Lindsay Davenport in both; paired with sister Serena to win the 2000 Wimbledon doubles title.

Walter Ray Williams Jr. (b. Oct. 6, 1959): Bowling and Horseshoes; 5-time PBA Bowler of Year (1986,93,96,97,98); all-time leading money winner on the PBA Tour through 1999; won 6 World Horseshoe Pitching titles.

Hack Wilson (b. Apr. 26, 1900, d. Nov. 23, 1948): Baseball; as a Chicago Cub, he produced one of baseball's most outstanding seasons in 1930 with 56 homeruns, .356 batting average, 105 walks and, most amazingly, a major league record 191 RBIs that still stands; finished with 1,461 hits, 244 homers, 1,062 RBIs; member of Baseball Hall of Fame.

Dave Winfield (b. Oct. 3, 1951): Baseball OF-DH; selected in 4 major sports league drafts in 1973— NFL, NBA, ABA, and MLB; chose baseball and has played in 12 All-Star Games over 22-year career; at age 41, helped lead Toronto to World Series title in 1992; 3,110 hits and 465 HRs.

Katarina Witt (b. Dec. 3, 1965): East German figure skater; 4-time world champion (1984-85,87-88); won consecutive Olympic gold medals (1984,88).

John Wooden (b. Oct. 14, 1910): Basketball; College Player of Year at Purdue in 1932; coached UCLA to 10 national titles (1964-65,67-73,75); one of only two men (Lenny Wilkens) to be honored by the Hall of Fame as player and coach.

Tiger Woods (b. Dec. 30, 1975): Golfer; youngest (18) and first minority to win U.S. Amateur in 1994, won it again in '95 and '96; turned pro in Sept. of '96 and won the fifth event he entered, the Las Vegas Invitational; in first full year on the tour, he won 6 of 25 events and broke the single season money record; won 1997 Masters by a record 18 under par and 13 stroke margin of victory; won second major at 1999 PGA Championship; in 2000 won the U.S. Open at Pebble Beach by a record 15 strokes, the British Open by 8 strokes and the PGA Championship in a playoff; one of only five players to win all four Grand Slam titles (others are Hogan, Nicklaus, Player and Sarazen); is already the all-time career money leader on the PGA Tour.

Mickey Wright (b. Feb. 14, 1935): Golfer; won 3 of 4 majors (LPGA, U.S. Open, Titleholders) in 1961; 4-time winner of both U.S. Open and LPGA titles; 82 career wins including 13 majors.

Early Wynn (b. Jan. 6, 1920, d. Mar. 4, 1999): Baseball RHP; won 20 games 5 times; Cy Young winner in 1959; 300-244 record in 23 years.

Kristi Yamaguchi (b. July 12, 1971): Figure Skating; finished second in the 1991 American nationals but won the world title that year; dominated the sport in 1992 by winning the national, world and Olympic titles and then turned professional.

Cale Yarborough (b. Mar. 27, 1940): Auto racer; 3-time NASCAR national champion (1976-78); 4-time winner of Daytona 500 (1968,77,83-84); ranks 5th on NASCAR all-time list with 83 wins.

Carl Yastrzemski (b. Aug. 22, 1939): Baseball OF; led AL in batting 3 times; won Triple Crown and MVP in 1967; had 3,419 hits and 452 HRs in 23 years with Boston; member of Hall of Fame.

Cy Young (b. Mar. 29, 1867, d. Nov. 4, 1955): Baseball RHP; all-time leader in wins (511), losses (313), complete games (751) and innings pitched (7,356); had career 2.63 ERA in 22 years (1890-1911); 30-game winner 5 times and 20-game winner 11 other times; threw 3 no-hitters and perfect game (1904); AL and NL pitching awards named after him.

Sheila Young (b. Oct. 14, 1950): Speed skater and cyclist; 1st U.S. athlete to win 3 medals at Winter Olympics (1976); won speed skating overall and sprint cycling world titles in 1976.

Steve Young (b. Oct. 11, 1961): Football QB; All-America at BYU (1983); NFL Player of Year (1992) with SF 49ers; only QB to lead NFL in passer rating 4 straight years (1991-94); rating of 112.8 in 1994 was highest ever; threw record 6 TD passes in MVP performance in Super Bowl XXIX; holds NFL career records for highest passer rating (96.8) and completion percentage (64.4); retired after the 1999 season with 232 TD passes and 33,124 yards.

Robin Yount (b. Sept. 16, 1955): Baseball SS-OF; AL MVP at 2 positions— as SS in 1982 and OF in '89; retired after 1993 season with 3,142 hits, 251 HRs and a major-league-record 123 sacrifice flies after 20 seasons with Milwaukee Brewers; inducted into Hall of Fame in 1999.

Steve Yzerman (b. May 9, 1965): Hockey C; Captained the Detroit Red Wings to back-to-back Stanley Cup sweeps in '96-97 and '97-98; took home the Conn Smythe Trophy as the playoff MVP in 1998; one of only 12 NHL players to score 600 goals; entered the 2000-01 season in sixth place in career scoring (1,562 points).

Mario Zagalo (b. Aug. 9, 1931): Soccer; Brazilian forward who is one of only two men (Franz Beckenbauer is the other) to serve as both captain (1962) and coach (1970,94) of World Cup champion.

Babe Didrikson Zaharias (b. June 26, 1911, d. Sept. 27, 1956): All-around athlete who was chosen AP Female Athlete of Year 6 times from 1932-54; won 2 gold medals (javelin and 80-meter hurdles) and a silver (high jump) at 1932 Olympics; played baseball and acquired the nickname "Babe" for her tape measure home runs; took up golf in 1935 and went on to win 55 pro and amateur events; won 10 majors, including 3 U.S. Opens (1948,50,54); helped found LPGA in 1949; chosen female "Athlete of the Half Century" by AP in 1950; when asked if there was anything she didn't play, she replied, "Yeah, dolls."

Tony Zale (b. May 29, 1913, d. March 20, 1997): Boxer; 2-time world middleweight champion (1941-47,48); fought Rocky Graziano for title 3 times in 21 months in 1947-48, winning twice; pro record 67-18-2 with 44 KOs.

Frank Zamboni (b. Jan. 16, 1901, d. July 27, 1988): Mechanic, ice salesman and skating rink owner in Paramount, Calif.; invented 1st ice-resurfacing machine in 1949; now there are very few skating rinks without one as over 4,000 have been sold in more than 35 countries worldwide

Emil Zatopek (b. Sept. 19, 1922): Czech distance runner; winner of 1948 Olympic gold medal at 10,000 meters; 4 years later, won unprecedented Olympic triple crown (5,000 meters, 10,000 meters and marathon) at 1952 Games in Helsinki.

John Ziegler (b. Feb. 9, 1934): Hockey; NHL president from 1977-92; negotiated settlement with rival WHA in 1979 that led to inviting four WHA teams (Edmonton, Hartford, Quebec and Winnipeg) to join NHL; stepped down June 12, 1992, 2 months after settling 10-day players' strike.

Kim Zmeskal (b. Feb 6, 1976): Gymnastics; Won three U.S. all-around championships in a row (1990-'92); first American gymnast to win the all-around competition in the world championships (1991); only athlete to win two golds in the 1992 world championships (balance beam and floor exercise).

Pirmin Zurbriggen (b. Feb. 4, 1963): Swiss alpine skier; 4-time World Cup overall champ (1984,87-88,90) and 3-time runner-up; 40 World Cup wins in 10 years; won gold and bronze medals at 1988 Olympics.

Ballparks & Arenas

Houston's **Enron Field** *opened for business in 2000.*

World Photos

BALLPARKS & ARENAS
COMING ATTRACTIONS

BASEBALL

Detroit (AL): Comerica Park (Comerica Bank is the title sponsor) celebrated its grand opening on April 11, 2000 as the Tigers beat Seattle 5-2 in front of 39,168 fans who braved the 36-degree game-time temperature. Located near a new stadium for the Detroit Lions in downtown Detroit's Foxtown Theater district about one mile from Tiger Stadium; baseball-only park seats 40,000 and has 80 luxury suites; the centerfield in-play flag pole from Tiger Stadium was re-created; estimated cost: $290 million.

Houston (NL): Enron Field (Enron Oil & Gas Co. is the title sponsor) opened on March 30, 2000 with a 6-5 Astros exhibition win over the New York Yankees before a crowd of 40,624. The natural grass ballpark features a retractable roof which can open and close in 12 minutes and a vintage locomotive atop the left field wall which is connected to Union train station, which will also house the Astros administrative offices, retail stores and a cafe; seats 40,950 and has more than 60 luxury suites; estimated cost: $248 million.

San Francisco (NL): Pacific Bell Park (Pacific Bell is the title sponsor) opened on March 31, 2000 and the home team Giants beat Milwaukee 8-3 in a preseason game in front of 40,930; the park is located right on the waterfront at China Basin; Barry Bonds became the first player to hit a ball into San Francisco Bay on April 1 when he knocked one over the right field wall into what is now known as McCovey Cove; the open-air baseball-only park seats 40,800, including 5,300 club seats and 67 luxury suites; estimated cost: $319 million.

NBA BASKETBALL

Miami (East): Although the official grand opening was held Dec. 31, 1999 with a New Year's Eve Gloria Estefan concert, the first basketball game to be played at Miami's AmericanAirlines Arena was held January 2, 2000 with a 111-103 Heat win over the Orlando Magic in front of a sell-out crowd of 19,600; estimated cost: $215 million.

NFL FOOTBALL

Cincinnati (AFC): Paul Brown Stadium celebrated its grand opening on Aug. 19, 2000 with a Bengals preseason 24-20 win over the Chicago Bears in front of 56,180 fans. The project cost approximately $453 million. The stadium will form the western "bookend" of Cincinnati's "Rebirth of the Riverfront." A new Cincinnati Reds baseball stadium, slated for completion in 2003, will be the eastern "bookend." In between, plans are underway for the National Underground [Freedom] Center, celebrating Cincinnati's role [in the campaign] for runaway slaves in the mid-1800s. The [open-air, gr]ass-field stadium seats 65,600 for foot[ball including cl]ub seats and 114 luxury suites.

[H]OCKEY

[Columbus: Nati]onwide Arena (Nationwide [Insurance]'s grand opening on Sept. [with a] Faith Hill concert. The [arena will house the] expansion Columbus [Blue Jackets an]d cost an estimated [... lu]xury suites and 26

Minnesota (expansion): The XCel Energy Center (XCel Energy Inc. is the title sponsor) was scheduled to open September 29, 2000 with an NHL preseason game between the expansion Minnesota Wild and the Mighty Ducks of Anaheim. The multi-purpose arena will seat 18,600 for the NHL Wild, including 74 luxury suites, and feature a transparent glass exterior. The building, located in downtown St. Paul in front of the old St. Paul Civic Center, cost an estimated $175 million.

BASEBALL

Milwaukee (AL): Groundbreaking for Miller Park (Miller Brewing Co. is the title sponsor) on a site adjacent to the existing County Stadium took place Nov. 9, 1996. The retractable-roof (which will take 10 minutes to open or close) stadium will have natural grass, an asymmetrical outfield and seat approximately 43,000 including 70 luxury suites; Brewers' home opener originally scheduled for April 2000 but that has been delayed to April 1, 2001 in wake of an accident that killed three ironworkers when a 567-foot, 2,100-ton crane collapsed on July 14, 1999 during construction on the new park; estimated cost: $250 million plus an estimated $50-75 million to repair accident damage.

Pittsburgh (NL): Groundbreaking for PNC Park (PNC Bank is the title sponsor) took place April 7, 1999. To be located on a site on the Allegheny River between Three Rivers Stadium and the Roberto Clemente Bridge (formerly Sixth Street Bridge). The baseball-only park will seat 38,127, have 69 luxury suites and cost an estimated $228 million; Stadium will be part of city's larger construction project, including enlarged convention center and new ballpark for NFL's Steelers; earliest Pirates' home opener would be April 9, 2001.

NBA BASKETBALL

Dallas (West): Groundbreaking for the American Airlines Center (American Airlines is also the title sponsor of AmericanAirlines Arena in Miami) took place Sept. 7, 1999. The building will be located due north of Dallas' West End, east of Interstate 35E as part of the new Victory development and will seat 19,200 for the Dallas Mavericks and 18,000 for NHL Stars and include 144 luxury suites; estimated cost: $325 million. Earliest opening would be fall 2001.

NFL FOOTBALL

Denver (AFC): Groundbreaking for the new open-air, grass-field stadium took place August 17, 1999. The as-yet unnamed stadium will seat 76,125 including 106 luxury suites. The stadium will be located adjacent to the existing Mile High Stadium and cost an estimated $364.2 million. Earliest opening would be September 2001.

Pittsburgh (AFC): Groundbreaking for the new open-air, grass-field stadium took place June 18, 1999. The as-yet unnamed stadium will seat 65,000 and contain 120 luxury suites. To be located 300 yards west of Three Rivers Stadium as part of city's larger construction project, including enlarged convention center and PNC Park for MLB's Pirates. Estimated cost for new football stadium: $233 million. Earliest opening would be September 2001.

San Francisco's new **Pacific Bell Park** opened its doors in 2000 as the new home of the Giants. The ballpark is located right on the waterfront and it didn't take long for a flotilla of fans to start trolling for home runs balls on the body of water now called McCovey Cove. Hometown slugger Barry Bonds was the first player to get one wet when he splashed one over the right field fence on April 1 in a preseason game with the Yankees.

NHL HOCKEY

Dallas (West): Groundbreaking for the American Airlines Center (American Airlines is also the title sponsor of AmericanAirlines Arena in Miami) took place Sept. 7, 1999. The building will be located due north of Dallas' West End, east of Interstate 35E as part of the new Victory development and will seat 18,000 for hockey and 19,200 for the NBA Mavericks and include 144 luxury suites; estimated cost: $325 million. Earliest opening would be fall 2001.

2002

BASEBALL

San Diego (NL): The last parcel of land for the as-yet-unnamed baseball-only park was cleared with the Aug. 12, 2000 implosion of the vacant San Diego Refrigeration Building. The open-air, grass-field park will be located on a one-square-block downtown lot and be part of a larger redevelopment project that will include a new hotel, office space and retail space. The park will seat approximately 46,000, including 60 luxury suites, and cost an estimated $267.5 million. Earliest Padres' home opener would be April 2002.

NBA BASKETBALL

San Antonio (West): Groundbreaking for the SBC Center (SBC Communications Inc. is the title sponsor) took place on Aug. 23, 2000. The new arena will seat 18,500 for basketball and be home to the Spurs as well as the popular San Antonio Livestock Exposition and Rodeo; estimated cost: $175 million; to be located adjacent to the Freeman Coliseum in East San Antonio. Opening is scheduled for September 2002.

NFL FOOTBALL

Detroit (NFC): Groundbreaking of Ford Field (Ford Motor Co., is the title sponsor) took place Nov. 16, 1999. Stadium will be located in downtown Detroit and incorporate the adjacent Old Hudson's Warehouse which will house all the stadium's suites and club level seating. Fans will have a view of the city skyline with natural light shining through the glass wall at the main entrance at Adams and Brush. The domed stadium will seat 65,000, including 120 luxury suites for football; estimated cost: $300 million. The Lions are tentatively planning to move in for the 2002 season but their lease with the Pontiac Silverdome doesn't expire until 2004.

New England (AFC): Construction of CMGI Field (Internet company CMGI is the title sponsor) is underway; to be located next to existing Foxboro Stadium. The new open-air, grass-field stadium will have 68,000 seats and include 80 luxury suites and over 7,000 club seats; estimated cost: $325 million. Earliest opening would be April 2002 for the MLS New England Revolution season.

Houston (expansion): Groundbreaking for the new Harris County Stadium (title sponsor pending) took place on March 9, 2000. The new home of the expansion NFL Houston Texans and annual Houston Livestock Show and Rodeo will be the world's first retractable roof football stadium with a grass playing surface. The roof will be able to open or close in 10 minutes. The stadium will seat 69,500, including 166 luxury suites, but will be expandable up to 72,000 seats for events like the Super Bowl; estimated cost: $367 million. Scheduled opening is August 2002.

Seattle (AFC): Construction for the as-yet-unnamed stadium is well underway. Stadium and exhibition center will be located on old site of Kingdome, which was imploded on Mar. 26, 2000; open-air, grass-field stadium will seat 67,000 (expanded capacity: 72,000) and include 82 luxury suites and 7,000 club seats; approximately 70 percent of the seats will be protected from the elements; stadium and exhibition center will cost an estimated $400 million. The Seahawks will compete at University of Washington's Husky Stadium for two years during construction. Earliest Seahawks home opener would be August 2002.

NHL HOCKEY

Phoenix (West): Groundbreaking for the Los Arcos Regional Entertainment Center was scheduled for late 2000/early 2001. The new arena for the Coyotes would be part of a 72-acre complex that includes restaurants and retail components and will be located on the site of the current Los Arcos mall in southern Scottsdale, Ariz. The arena will seat 17,500 including 70 luxury suites for Coyotes' games; estimated cost of entire project: $550 million. Earliest opening would be fall 2002.

2003

BASEBALL

Cincinnati (NL): New as-yet-unnamed ballpark is in planning stages. The stadium site overlaps the current site of Cinergy Field (formerly known as Riverfront Stadium). The left field stands at Cinergy will be removed after the 2000 season to clear space for the new construction to begin. The grass-field, baseball-only park is not expected to have any unusual nooks and crannies in the outfield and will seat an estimated 42,060. Home plate of the new park will be set 568 feet from the Ohio River, probably a little too far for splashdown homers that have been made famous at San Francisco's Pacific Bell Park. Estimated cost of project: $297 million. Earliest opening would be spring 2003.

Boston (AL): New Fenway Park is in the planning stages. The open-air, grass field park would be located adjacent to the existing Fenway Park and emulate many of the Fenway's features including the Green Monster and Pesky's Pole; part of the project includes preserving portions of the old ballpark as a public park; estimated cost of entire project: $627 million; would seat 44,130 and the earliest Red Sox home opener would be April 2003.

Philadelphia (NL): New ballpark is in the planning stages. Several key factors for the baseball only, grass-field park, including location and financing, need to be finalized. Ballpark would seat 45,000 and be part of a retail complex. Estimated cost of entire project: $650-675 million but could be less depending on what site is eventually chosen. Earliest Phillies home opener would be April 2003.

NBA BASKETBALL

Houston (West): New arena for the Rockets is in the planning stages. Voters were set to decide on the partially publicly-funded project on November 7, 2000. The new arena would seat 18,500 for basketball and 17,500 for hockey; estimated cost: $255 million; to be located in downtown Houston near Enron Field, the new home of Major League Baseball's Houston Astros. Earliest opening would be fall 2003.

~~New Je~~ ~~~~st): New arena for the Nets is in the plan-~~~~ would be located in downtown Newark ~~~~ would house the Nets and NHL's New ~~~~ cost: $325 million. Earliest opening

NFL FOOTBALL

Green Bay (NFC): In September 2000, voters approved a plan to use a new 0.5 percent sales tax in Brown County to help fund a $295 million renovation of 43-year-old Lambeau Field. Unlike most stadium renovations, lack of luxury suites was not the issue here. The newly renovated stadium will actually have 32 fewer suites. Approximately 10,000 seats (including about 4,300 additional club seats) will be added bringing the total seating capacity to about 71,100 including 167 luxury suites. Plans also call for the team and the City of Green Bay to seek naming rights before the 2003 season. A minimum bid of $120 million would have to be considered; the team and city would split the proceeds; renovation is scheduled to be completed in September 2003.

Philadelphia (NFC): New stadium for the Eagles is in the planning stages. Several key factors including financing and location need to be finalized. Estimated cost: $300 million. Earliest Eagles home opener could be August 2003.

NHL HOCKEY

New Jersey (East): New arena for the Devils is in the planning stages. Arena would be located in downtown Newark near Penn Station and would house the Devils and NBA's New Jersey Nets; estimated cost: $325 million. Earliest opening would be fall 2003.

SOCCER

England: Construction of new Wembley National Stadium is getting underway. Demolition of the existing Wembley Stadium with its famous twin towers was set to begin in November 2000. The roof on the East, South and West sides partly retracts allowing the sunlight to help grass growth and while the roof will provide protection from the elements to all spectators, the field will be left uncovered. Instead of the twin towers, the new stadium's most distinguishing feature will be a giant 400-foot tall arch. New stadium will seat 90,000 and is scheduled to be completed in March 2003. Estimated cost: £326 million ($456 million USD).

2004

BASEBALL

New York (NL): New ballpark for the Mets is in the planning stages. To be located adjacent to Shea Stadium in Queens. The retractable-roof stadium would seat 45,000, including 78 luxury suites and 5,000 club seats. The stadium will have a grass field on a platform that can be rolled out into the parking lot to receive enough sunshine and moisture. With the field out, the stadium could seat 60,000 for hockey, basketball or other events. Estimated cost: $500 million. Earliest opening would be April 2004.

St. Louis (NL): New ballpark for the Cardinals is in the planning stages. The proposed site is south of the existing Busch Stadium on the south stadium parking lot. The proposed open-air baseball-only ballpark would offer a spectacular view of the Gateway Arch. Since the new site partially overlaps the current stadium site, for the first year the park would offer about 40,000 permanent and temporary seats but, by year two, the stadium would be complete and the seating capacity would grow to 47,900. Estimated cost including a new Cardinals Hall of Fame and Museum is $370 million. Earliest opening would be April 2004.

NFL FOOTBALL

Arizona (NFC): New stadium for the Cardinals is in the planning stages. Several key factors including financing and location need to be determined. The 67,000-seat stadium would be domed with a partially-retractable roof and feature a grass field that could be rolled out into the adjoining parking lot in order to help it grow. Estimated cost: $331 million. Earliest Cardinals home opener could be August 2004.

Home, Sweet Home

The home fields, home courts and home ice of the AL, NL, NBA, NFL, CFL, NHL, WNBA, NCAA Division I-A college football and Division I basketball. Also included are Formula One, IndyCar, Indy Racing League and NASCAR auto racing tracks.

Attendance figures for the 1999 NFL regular season and the 1999-00 NBA and NHL regular seasons are provided. See Baseball chapter for 2000 AL and NL attendance figures.

MAJOR LEAGUE BASEBALL

American League

	Built	Capacity	LF	LCF	CF	RCF	RF	Field
Anaheim Angels . . . .**Edison International Field of Anaheim**	1966	**45,050**	365	387	400	370	365	Grass
Baltimore Orioles. . . . .**Oriole Park at Camden Yards**	1992	**48,876**	333	364	410	373	318	Grass
Boston Red Sox. . . . .**Fenway Park**	1912	**33,871**	310	379	390*	380	302	Grass
Chicago White Sox . . . .**Comiskey Park**	1991	**44,321**	347	375	400	375	347	Grass
Cleveland Indians. . . . .**Jacobs Field**	1994	**43,368**	325	370	405	375	325	Grass
Detroit Tigers . . . .**Comerica Park**	2000	**40,000**	345	398	420	370	330	Grass
Kansas City Royals . . . .**Kauffman Stadium**	1973	**40,529**	330	375	400	375	330	Grass
Minnesota Twins. . . . .**Hubert H. Humphrey Metrodome**	1982	**48,678**	343	385	408	367	327	Turf
New York Yankees. . . . .**Yankee Stadium**	1923	**57,746**	318	399	408	385	314	Grass
Oakland Athletics. . . . . .**Network Associates Coliseum**	1966	**43,662**	330	367	400	367	330	Grass
Seattle Mariners . . . .**SAFECO Field**	1999	**47,116**	331	390	405	386	326	Grass
Tampa Bay Devil Rays . . . .**Tropicana Field**	1990	**47,000**	315	370	404	370	322	Turf
Texas Rangers. . . . .**The Ballpark in Arlington**	1994	**52,000**	332	390	400	407	325	Grass
Toronto Blue Jays . . . .**SkyDome**	1989	**50,516**	328	375	400	375	328	Turf

*The staight-away centerfield fence at Fenway Park is 390 feet from home plate but the deepest part of centerfield, a.k.a. "the Triangle," is 420 feet away. The left-field fence, known as "the Green Monster," is 37 feet tall topped with a 23-foot screen.

National League

	Built	Capacity	LF	LCF	CF	RCF	RF	Field
Arizona Diamondbacks. . . . .**Bank One Ballpark**	1998	**49,075**	330	376	407	374	334	Grass
Atlanta Braves . . . .**Turner Field**	1996	**50,062**	335	380	401	385	330	Grass
Chicago Cubs. . . . .**Wrigley Field**	1914	**39,086**	355	368	400	368	353	Grass
Cincinnati Reds . . . .**Cinergy Field**	1970	**52,953**	330	375	404	375	330	Turf
Colorado Rockies . . . .**Coors Field**	1995	**50,381**	347	390	415	375	350	Grass
Florida Marlins. . . . .**Pro Player Stadium**	1987	**42,531**	330	385	434	385	345	Grass
Houston Astros. . . . .**Enron Field**	2000	**40,950**	315	362	436	373	326	Grass
Los Angeles Dodgers . . . .**Dodger Stadium**	1962	**56,000**	330	385	395	385	330	Grass
Milwaukee Brewers . . . .**Miller Park**	2001	**43,000**	342	374	400	378	345	Grass
Montreal Expos. . . . .**Olympic Stadium**	1976	**46,500**	325	375	404	375	325	Turf
New York Mets . . . .**Shea Stadium**	1964	**55,775**	338	371	410	371	338	Grass
Philadelphia Phillies . . . .**Veterans Stadium**	1971	**62,411**	330	378	408	378	330	Turf
Pittsburgh Pirates . . . .**PNC Park**	2001	**38,127**	326	368	399*	375	324	Grass
St. Louis Cardinals. . . . .**Busch Stadium**	1966	**49,738**	330	372	402	372	330	Grass
San Diego Padres . . . .**Qualcomm Stadium**	1967	**66,307**	327	370	405	370	327	Grass
San Francisco Giants . . . .**Pacific Bell Park**	2000	**40,800**	335	364	404	420	307	Grass

*The deepest part of PNC Park is 410 feet between straight-away center and left-center.

Rank by Capacity

AL		NL	
New York. 57,746		San Diego 66,307	
Texas 52,000		Philadelphia 62,411	
Toronto. 50,516		Los Angeles. 56,000	
Baltimore 48,876		New York. 55,775	
Minnesota 48,678		Cincinnati 52,953	
Seattle 47,116		Colorado 50,381	
Tampa Bay 47,000		Atlanta 50,062	
Anaheim 45,050		St. Louis 49,738	
Chicago. 44,321		Arizona 49,075	
Oakland 43,662		Montreal 46,500	
Cleveland 43,368		Milwaukee 43,000	
Kansas City 40,529		Florida 42,531	
Detroit 40,000		Houston 40,950	
Boston 33,871		San Francisco 40,800	
		Chicago. 39,086	
		Pittsburgh. 38,127	

Rank by Age

AL		NL	
Boston 1912		Chicago. 1914	
New York 1923		Los Angeles. 1962	
Anaheim 1966		New York 1964	
Oakland 1966		St. Louis 1966	
Kansas City. 1973		San Diego 1967	
Minnesota 1982		Cincinnati 1970	
Toronto. 1989		Philadelphia 1971	
Tampa Bay 1990		Montreal 1976	
Chicago. 1991		Florida 1987	
Baltimore 1992		Atlanta 1993	
Cleveland 1994		Colorado 1995	
Texas 1994		Arizona 1998	
Seattle 1999		Houston 2000	
Detroit 2000		San Francisco 2000	
		Milwaukee 2001	
		Pittsburgh. 2001	

Note: New York's Yankee Stadium (AL) was rebuilt in 1976.

Major League Baseball (Cont.)
Home Fields

Listed below are the principal home fields used through the years by current American and National League teams. The NL became a major league in 1876, the AL in 1901.

The capacity figures in the right-hand column indicate the largest seating capacity of the ballpark while the club played there. Capacity figures before 1915 (and the introduction of concrete grandstands) are sketchy at best and have been left blank.

American League

Anaheim Angels

1961	Wrigley Field (Los Angeles)	20,457
1962-65	Dodger Stadium	56,000
1966-	Edison International Field of Anaheim	45,050
	(1966 capacity-43,250)	

Baltimore Orioles

1901	Lloyd Street Grounds (Milwaukee)	-
1902-53	Sportsman's Park II (St. Louis)	30,500
1954-91	Memorial Stadium (Baltimore)	53,371
1992-	Oriole Park at Camden Yards	48,876

Boston Red Sox

1901-11	Huntington Ave. Grounds	-
1912-	Fenway Park	33,871
	(1934 capacity-27,000)	

Chicago White Sox

1901-10	Southside Park	-
1910-90	Comiskey Park I	43,931
1991-	Comiskey Park II	44,321

Cleveland Indians

1901-09	League Park I	-
1910-46	League Park II	21,414
1932-93	Cleveland Stadium	74,483
1994-	Jacobs Field	43,368

Detroit Tigers

1901-11	Bennett Park	-
1912-99	Tiger Stadium	46,945
2000-	Comerica Park	40,000
	(1912 capacity-23,000)	

Kansas City Royals

1969-72	Municipal Stadium	35,020
1973-	Kauffman Stadium	40,529
	(1973 capacity-40,762)	

Minnesota Twins

1901-02	American League Park (Washington, DC)	-
1903-60	Griffith Stadium	27,410
1960-81	Metropolitan Stadium (Bloomington, MN)	45,919
1982-	HHH Metrodome (Minneapolis)	48,678
	(1982 capacity-54,000)	

New York Yankees

1901-02	Oriole Park (Baltimore)	-
1903-12	Hilltop Park (New York)	-
1913-22	Polo Grounds II	38,000
1923-73	Yankee Stadium I	67,224
1974-75	Shea Stadium	55,101
1976-	Yankee Stadium II	57,746
	(1976 capacity-57,145)	

Oakland Athletics

1901-08	Columbia Park (Philadelphia)	-
1909-54	Shibe Park	33,608
1955-67	Municipal Stadium (Kansas City)	35,020
1968-	Network Associates Coliseum	43,662
	(1968 capacity-48,621)	

Seattle Mariners

1977-99	The Kingdome	59,166
1999-	SAFECO Field	47,116

Tampa Bay Devil Rays

1990-	Tropicana Field	47,000

Texas Rangers

1961	Griffith Stadium (Washington, DC)	27,410
1962-71	RFK Stadium	45,016
1972-93	Arlington Stadium (Texas)	43,521
1994-	The Ballpark in Arlington	52,000

Toronto Blue Jays

1977-89	Exhibition Stadium	43,737
1989-	SkyDome	50,516
	(1989 capacity-49,500)	

Ballpark Name Changes: ANAHEIM—**Edison International Field of Anaheim** originally Anaheim Stadium (1966-98); CHICAGO—**Comiskey Park I** originally White Sox Park (1910-12), then Comiskey Park in 1913, then White Sox Park again in 1962, then Comiskey Park again in 1976; CLEVELAND—**League Park** renamed Dunn Field in 1920, then League Park again in 1928; **Cleveland Stadium** originally Municipal Stadium (1932-74); DETROIT—**Tiger Stadium** originally Navin Field (1912-37), then Briggs Stadium (1938-60); KANSAS CITY—**Kauffman Stadium** originally Royals Stadium (1973-93); LOS ANGELES—**Dodger Stadium** referred to as Chavez Revine by AL while Angels played there (1962-65); OAKLAND—**Network Associates Coliseum** originally Oakland Alameda Coliseum (1968-98); PHILADELPHIA—**Shibe Park** renamed Connie Mack Stadium in 1953; ST. LOUIS—**Sportsman's Park** renamed Busch Stadium in 1953; WASHINGTON—**Griffith Stadium** originally National Park (1892-1920), **RFK Stadium** originally D.C. Stadium (1961-68).

National League

Arizona Diamondbacks

1998-	Bank One Ballpark	49,075

Atlanta Braves

1876-94	South End Grounds I (Boston)	-
1894-1914	South End Grounds II	-
1915-52	Braves Field	40,000
1953-65	County Stadium (Milwaukee)	43,394
1966-96	Atlanta-Fulton County Stadium	52,769
	(1966 capacity-50,000)	
1997-	Turner Field	50,062

Chicago Cubs

1876-77	State Street Grounds	-
1878-84	Lakefront Park	-
1885-91	West Side Park	-
1891-93	Brotherhood Park	-
1893-1915	West Side Grounds	-
1916-	Wrigley Field	39,086
	(1916 capacity-16,000)	

Cincinnati Reds

1876-79	Avenue Grounds	.–
1880	Bank Street Grounds	.–
1890-1901	Redland Field I	.–
1902-11	Palace of the Fans	.–
1912-70	Crosley Field	.29,603
1970–	Cinergy Field	.52,953
	(1970 capacity-52,000)	

Colorado Rockies

1993-94	Mile High Stadium (Denver)	.76,100
1995–	Coors Field	.50,381

Florida Marlins

1993–	Pro Player Stadium (Miami)	.42,531

Houston Astros

1962-64	Colt Stadium	.32,601
1965-99	The Astrodome	.54,370
	(1965 capacity-45,011)	
2000–	Enron Field	.40,950

Los Angeles Dodgers

1890	Washington Park I (Brooklyn)	.–
1891-97	Eastern Park	.–
1898-1912	Washington Park II	.–
1913-56	Ebbets Field	.31,497
1957	Ebbets Field	.31,497
	& Roosevelt Stadium (Jersey City)	.24,167
1958-61	Memorial Coliseum (Los Angeles)	.93,600
1962–	Dodger Stadium	.56,000

Milwaukee Brewers

1969	Sick's Stadium (Seattle)	.59,166
1970-00	County Stadium (Milwaukee)	.53,192
	(1970 capacity-46,620)	
2001–	Miller Park	.43,000

Montreal Expos

1969-76	Jarry Park	.28,000
1977–	Olympic Stadium	.46,500
	(1977 capacity-58,500)	

New York Mets

1962-63	Polo Grounds	.55,987
1964–	Shea Stadium	.55,775
	(1964 capacity-55,101)	

Philadelphia Phillies

1883-86	Recreation Park	.–
1887-94	Huntingdon Ave. Grounds	.–
1895-1938	Baker Bowl	.18,800
1938-70	Shibe Park	.33,608
1971–	Veterans Stadium	.62,411
	(1971 capacity-56,371)	

Pittsburgh Pirates

1887-90	Recreation Park	.–
1891-1909	Exposition Park	.–
1909-70	Forbes Field	.35,000
1970-00	Three Rivers Stadium	.47,687
	(1970 capacity-50,235)	
2001–	PNC Park	.38,127

St. Louis Cardinals

1876-77	Sportsman's Park I	.–
1885-86	Vandeventer Lot	.–
1892-1920	Robison Field	.18,000
1920-66	Sportsman's Park II	.30,500
1966–	Busch Stadium	.49,738
	(1966 capacity-50,126)	

San Diego Padres

1969–	Qualcomm Stadium	.66,307
	(1969 capacity-47,634)	

San Francisco Giants

1876	Union Grounds (Brooklyn)	.–
1883-88	Polo Grounds I (New York)	.–
1889-90	Manhattan Field	.–
1891-1957	Polo Grounds II	.55,987
1958-59	Seals Stadium (San Francisco)	.22,900
1960-99	3Com Park	.63,000
	(1960 capacity-42,553)	
2000–	Pacific Bell Park	.40,800

Ballpark Name Changes: ATLANTA—**Atlanta-Fulton County Stadium** originally Atlanta Stadium (1966-74); **Turner Field** originally Centennial Olympic Stadium (1996); CHICAGO—**Wrigley Field** originally Weeghman Park (1914-17), then Cubs Park (1918-25); CINCINNATI—**Redland Field** originally League Park (1890-93), **Crosley Field** originally Redland Field II (1912-33) and **Cinergy Field** originally Riverfront Stadium (1970-96); FLORIDA—**Pro Player Stadium** originally Joe Robbie Stadium (1987-96); HOUSTON—**Astrodome** originally Harris County Domed Stadium before it opened in 1965; PHILADELPHIA—**Shibe Park** renamed Connie Mack Stadium in 1953; ST. LOUIS—**Robison Field** originally Vandeventer Lot, then League Park, then Cardinal Park all before becoming Robison Field in 1901, **Sportsman's Park** renamed Busch Stadium in 1953, and **Busch Stadium** originally Busch Memorial Stadium (1966-82); SAN DIEGO—**Qualcomm Stadium** originally San Diego Stadium (1967-81) and San Diego/Jack Murphy Stadium (1982-96); SAN FRANCISCO—**3Com Park** originally Candlestick Park (1960-95).

NATIONAL BASKETBALL ASSOCIATION

Western Conference

		Location	Built	Capacity
Dallas Mavericks	**Reunion Arena**	Dallas, Texas	1980	**18,187**
Denver Nuggets	**Pepsi Center**	Denver, Colo.	1999	**19,099**
Golden State Warriors	**The Arena in Oakland**	Oakland, Calif.	1997	**19,596**
Houston Rockets	**Compaq Center**	Houston, Texas	1975	**16,285**
Los Angeles Clippers	**Staples Center**	Los Angeles, Calif.	1999	**18,694**
Los Angeles Lakers	**Staples Center**	Los Angeles, Calif.	1999	**19,282**
Minnesota Timberwolves	**Target Center**	Minneapolis, Minn.	1990	**19,006**
Phoenix Suns	**America West Arena**	Phoenix, Ariz.	1992	**19,023**
Portland Trail Blazers	**Rose Garden**	Portland, Ore.	1995	**19,980**
Sacramento Kings	**ARCO Arena**	Sacramento, Calif.	1988	**17,317**
San Antonio Spurs	**The Alamodome**	San Antonio, Texas	1993	**20,557**
Seattle SuperSonics	**KeyArena at Seattle Center**	Seattle, Wash.	1962	**17,072**
Utah Jazz	**Delta Center**	Salt Lake City, Utah	1991	**19,911**
Vancouver Grizzlies	**General Motors Place**	Vancouver, B.C.	1995	**19,193**

Notes: Seattle's KeyArena was originally the Seattle Coliseum before being rebuilt in 1995; San Antonio's Alamodome seating is expandable to 34,215 while Portland's Rose Garden was "downsized" from a capacity of 21,538 to 19,980 prior to the 1998-99 season. The Staples Center has different listed capacities for Clippers games and Lakers games because of different floor seating arrangements.

National Basketball Association (Cont.)
Eastern Conference

		Location	Built	Capacity
Atlanta Hawks	**Philips Arena**	Atlanta, Ga.	1999	**19,445**
Boston Celtics	**FleetCenter**	Boston, Mass.	1995	**18,624**
Charlotte Hornets	**Charlotte Coliseum**	Charlotte, N.C.	1988	**23,799**
Chicago Bulls	**United Center**	Chicago, Ill.	1994	**21,711**
Cleveland Cavaliers	**Gund Arena**	Cleveland, Ohio	1994	**20,562**
Detroit Pistons	**The Palace of Auburn Hills**	Auburn Hills, Mich.	1988	**22,076**
Indiana Pacers	**Conseco Fieldhouse**	Indianapolis, Ind.	1999	**18,345**
Miami Heat	**AmericanAirlines Arena**	Miami, Fla	1999	**19,600**
Milwaukee Bucks	**Bradley Center**	Milwaukee, Wisc.	1988	**18,717**
New Jersey Nets	**Continental Airlines Arena**	E. Rutherford, N.J.	1981	**20,049**
New York Knicks	**Madison Square Garden**	New York, N.Y.	1968	**19,763**
Orlando Magic	**TD Waterhouse Centre**	Orlando, Fla.	1989	**17,248**
Philadelphia 76ers	**First Union Center**	Philadelphia, Pa.	1996	**20,444**
Toronto Raptors	**Air Canada Centre**	Toronto, Ont.	1999	**19,800**
Washington Wizards	**MCI Center**	Washington, D.C.	1997	**20,674**

Rank by Capacity

West		East	
San Antonio	20,557	Charlotte	23,799
Portland	19,980	Detroit	22,076
Utah	19,911	Chicago	21,711
Golden State	19,596	Washington	20,674
LA Lakers	19,282	Cleveland	20,562
Vancouver	19,193	Philadelphia	20,444
Denver	19,099	New Jersey	20,049
Phoenix	19,023	Toronto	19,800
Minnesota	19,006	New York	19,763
LA Clippers	18,694	Miami	19,600
Dallas	18,187	Atlanta	19,445
Sacramento	17,317	Milwaukee	18,717
Seattle	17,072	Boston	18,624
Houston	16,285	Indiana	18,345
		Orlando	17,248

Note: Alamodome seating is expandable to 32,500.

Rank by Age

West		East	
Seattle	1962	New York	1968
Houston	1975	New Jersey	1981
Dallas	1980	Charlotte	1988
Sacramento	1988	Detroit	1988
Minnesota	1990	Milwaukee	1988
Utah	1991	Orlando	1989
Phoenix	1992	Chicago	1994
San Antonio	1993	Cleveland	1994
Portland	1995	Boston	1995
Vancouver	1995	Philadelphia	1996
Golden St.	1997	Washington	1997
Denver	1999	Toronto	1999
LA Clippers	1999	Atlanta	1999
LA Lakers	1999	Indiana	1999
		Miami	1999

Note: The Seattle Coliseum was rebuilt and renamed KeyArena in 1995.

2000 NBA Attendance

Official overall attendance in the NBA for the 1999-2000 season was 20,058,536 for an average per game crowd of 16,870 over 82 games. Teams in each conference are ranked by attendance over 41 home games based on total tickets distributed; sellouts are listed in S/O column. Numbers in parentheses indicate rank in 1999.

Western Conference

	Attendance	S/O	Average
1 San Antonio (1)	889,444	8	21,694
2 Portland (3)	835,078	41	20,368
3 Utah (2)	801,268	15	19,543
4 Phoenix (4)	773,115	29	18,856
5 LA Lakers (5)	771,420	26	18,815
6 Sacramento (8)	687,410	38	17,185
7 Minnesota (6)	655,999	8	16,400
8 Denver (13)	637,698	3	15,554
9 Houston (10)	624,594	12	15,234
10 Seattle (7)	615,730	9	15,018
11 Dallas (11)	666,177	5	14,785
12 Vancouver (9)	569,864	1	13,899
13 LA Clippers (14)	559,714	2	13,652
14 Golden St. (12)	509,172	1	12,419
TOTAL	9,596,683	198	16,719

Eastern Conference

	Attendance	S/O	Average
1 Chicago (1)	907,064	41	22,124
2 New York (3)	810,283	41	19,763
3 Philadelphia (12)	756,929	9	18,762
4 Toronto (11)	756,496	20	18,451
5 Indiana (13)	752,145	41	18,345
6 Charlotte (2)	732,827	3	17,874
7 Miami (15)	707,325	31	17,252
8 Boston (6)	683,608	9	16,673
9 Detroit (5)	678,470	5	16,548
10 New Jersey (7)	643,623	3	15,698
11 Milwaukee (14)	628,605	3	15,332
12 Washington (4)	616,593	4	15,039
13 Cleveland (10)	603,702	6	14,724
14 Atlanta (8)	601,138	3	14,662
15 Orlando (9)	576,409	4	14,059
TOTAL	10,455,217	223	17,000

Note: There were two neutral site games with a total attendance of 66,636 with an average of 33,318.

Home Courts

Listed below are the principal home courts used through the years by current NBA teams. The largest capacity of each arena is noted in the right-hand column. ABA arenas (1972-76) are included for Denver, Indiana, New Jersey and San Antonio.

Western Conference

Dallas Mavericks

1980–	Reunion Arena	18,187

Denver Nuggets

1967-75	Auditorium Arena	6,841
1975-99	McNichols Sports Arena	17,171
	(1975 capacity-16,700)	
1999–	Pepsi Center	19,099

Golden State Warriors

1946-52	Philadelphia Arena	7,777
1952-62	Convention Hall (Philadelphia)	9,200
	& Philadelphia Arena	7,777
1962-64	Cow Palace (San Francisco)	13,862
1964-66	Civic Auditorium	7,500
	& (USF Memorial Gym)	6,000
1966-67	Cow Palace, Civic Auditorium	
	& Oakland Coliseum Arena	15,000
1967-71	Cow Palace	14,500
1971-96	Oakland Coliseum Arena	15,025
	(1971 capacity-12,905)	
1996-97	San Jose Arena	18,500
1997–	The Arena in Oakland	19,596

Houston Rockets

1967-71	San Diego Sports Arena	14,000
1971-72	Hofheinz Pavilion (Houston)	10,218
1972-73	Hofheinz Pavilion	10,218
	& HemisFair Arena (San Antonio)	10,446
1973-75	Hofheinz Pavilion	10,218
1975–	Compaq Center	16,285
	(1975 capacity-15,600)	

Los Angeles Clippers

1970-78	Memorial Auditorium (Buffalo)	17,300
1978-84	San Diego Sports Arena	12,167
1985-94	Los Angeles Sports Arena	16,005
1994-99	Los Angeles Sports Arena	16,021
	& Arrowhead Pond	18,211
1999–	Staples Center	18,694

Los Angeles Lakers

1948-60	Minneapolis Auditorium	10,000
1960-67	Los Angeles Sports Arena	14,781
1967-99	Great Western Forum (Inglewood, CA)	17,505
	(1967 capacity-17,086)	
1999–	Staples Center	19,282

Minnesota Timberwolves

1989-90	Hubert H. Humphrey Metrodome	23,000
1990–	Target Center	19,006

Phoenix Suns

1968-92	Arizona Veterans' Memorial Coliseum	14,487
1992–	America West Arena	19,023

Portland Trail Blazers

1970-95	Memorial Coliseum	12,888
1995–	Rose Garden	19,980
	(1995 capacity-21,538)	

Sacramento Kings

1948-55	Edgarton Park Arena (Rochester, NY)	5,000
1955-58	Rochester War Memorial	10,000
1958-72	Cincinnati Gardens	11,438
1972-74	Municipal Auditorium (Kansas City)	9,929
	& Omaha (NE) Civic Auditorium	9,136
1974-78	Kemper Arena (Kansas City)	16,785
	& Omaha Civic Auditorium	9,136
1978-85	Kemper Arena	16,785
1985-88	ARCO Arena I	10,333
1988–	ARCO Arena II	17,317
	(1988 capacity-16,517)	

San Antonio Spurs

1967-70	Memorial Auditorium (Dallas)	8,088
	& Moody Coliseum (Dallas)	8,500
1970-71	Moody Coliseum	8,500
	Tarrant Convention Center (Ft. Worth)	13,500
	& Municipal Coliseum (Lubbock)	10,400
1971-73	Moody Coliseum	9,500
	& Memorial Auditorium	8,088
1973-93	HemisFair Arena (San Antonio)	16,057
1993–	The Alamodome	20,557

Seattle SuperSonics

1967-78	Seattle Center Coliseum	14,098
1978-85	Kingdome	40,192
1985-94	Seattle Center Coliseum	14,252
1994-95	Tacoma Dome	19,000
1995–	KeyArena at Seattle Center	17,072

Utah Jazz

1974-75	Municipal Auditorium	7,853
	& Louisiana Superdome	47,284
1975-79	Superdome	47,284
1979-83	Salt Palace (Salt Lake City)	12,519
1983-84	Salt Palace	12,519
	& Thomas & Mack Center (Las Vegas)	18,500
1985-91	Salt Palace	12,616
1991–	Delta Center	19,911

Vancouver Grizzlies

1995–	General Motors Place	19,193

Eastern Conference

Atlanta Hawks

1949-51	Wharton Field House (Moline, IL)	6,000
1951-55	Milwaukee Arena	11,000
1955-68	Kiel Auditorium (St. Louis)	10,000
1968-72	Alexander Mem. Coliseum (Atlanta)	7,166
1972-96	The Omni	16,378
1997-99	Georgia Dome	21,570
	& Alexander Mem. Coliseum	9,300
1999–	Philips Arena	19,445

Boston Celtics

1946-95	Boston Garden	14,890
1995–	FleetCenter	18,624

Note: From 1975-95 the Celtics played some regular season games at the Hartford Civic Center (15,418).

Charlotte Hornets

1988–	Charlotte Coliseum	23,799
	(1988 capacity-23,500)	

Chicago Bulls

1966-67	Chicago Amphitheater	11,002
1967-94	Chicago Stadium	18,676
1994–	United Center	21,711

Cleveland Cavaliers

1970-74	Cleveland Arena	11,000
1974-94	The Coliseum (Richfield, OH)	20,273
1994–	Gund Arena	20,562

National Basketball Association (Cont.)

Detroit Pistons

1948-52	North Side H.S. Gym (Ft. Wayne, IN)....3,800
1952-57	Memorial Coliseum (Ft. Wayne)........9,306
1957-61	Olympia Stadium (Detroit)............14,000
1961-78	Cobo Arena 11,147
1978-88	Silverdome (Pontiac, MI) 22,366
1988–	The Palace of Auburn Hills 22,076

Indiana Pacers

1967-74	State Fairgrounds (Indianapolis)........9,479
1974-99	Market Square Arena 16,530
	(1974 capacity-17,287)
1999–	Conseco Fieldhouse 18,345

Miami Heat

1988-99	Miami Arena 15,200
2000–	AmericanAirlines Arena 19,600

Milwaukee Bucks

1968-88	Milwaukee Arena (The Mecca) 11,052
1988–	Bradley Center 18,717

New Jersey Nets

1967-68	Teaneck (NJ) Armory 3,500
1968-69	Long Island Arena (Commack, NY) 6,500
1969-71	Island Garden (W. Hempstead, NY) 5,200
1971-77	Nassau Coliseum (Uniondale, NY) 15,500
1977-81	Rutgers Ath. Center (Piscataway, NJ)....9,050
1981–	Continental Airlines Arena (E. Ruth., NJ) ..20,049

New York Knicks

1946-68	Madison Sq. Garden III (50th St.) 18,496
1968–	Madison Sq. Garden IV (33rd St.) 19,763
	(1968 capacity-19,694)

Orlando Magic

1989–	TD Waterhouse Centre 17,248

Philadelphia 76ers

1949-51	State Fair Coliseum (Syracuse, NY) 7,500
1951-63	Onondaga County (NY) War Memorial ..8,000
1963-67	Convention Hall (Philadelphia).........12,000
	& Philadelphia Arena 7,777
1967-96	CoreStates Spectrum 18,136
1996–	First Union Center....................20,444

Toronto Raptors

1995-99	SkyDome...........................20,125
1999–	Air Canada Centre 19,800

Washington Wizards

1961-62	Chicago Amphitheater................11,000
1962-63	Chicago Coliseum 7,100
1963-73	Baltimore Civic Center...............12,289
1973-97	USAir Arena (Landover, MD) 18,756
1997–	MCI Center 20,674

Note: From 1988-96 the Wizards (then Bullets) played four regular season games at Baltimore Arena (12,756).

Building Name Changes: HOUSTON– **Compaq Center** originally The Summit (1975-97); NEW JERSEY– **Continental Airlines Arena** originally Byrne Meadowlands Arena (1981-96); ORLANDO– **TD Waterhouse Centre** originally Orlando Arena (1989-99); PHILADELPHIA– **First Union Center** originally the CoreStates Center (1996-98) and **CoreStates Spectrum** originally The Spectrum (1967-94); WASHINGTON– **USAir Arena** originally Capital Centre (1973-93).

NATIONAL FOOTBALL LEAGUE

American Football Conference

		Location	Built	Capacity	Field
Baltimore Ravens	**PSInet Stadium**	Baltimore, Md.	1998	**69,084**	Grass
Buffalo Bills	**Ralph Wilson Stadium**	Orchard Park, N.Y.	1973	**73,800**	Turf
Cincinnati Bengals	**Paul Brown Stadium**	Cincinnati, Ohio	2000	**65,600**	Grass
Cleveland Browns	**Cleveland Browns Stadium**	Cleveland, Ohio	1999	**73,200**	Grass
Denver Broncos	**Mile High Stadium**	Denver, Colo.	1948	**76,123**	Grass
Indianapolis Colts	**RCA Dome**	Indianapolis, Ind.	1984	**56,120**	Turf
Jacksonville Jaguars	**ALLTEL Stadium**	Jacksonville, Fla.	1995	**73,000**	Grass
Kansas City Chiefs	**Arrowhead Stadium**	Kansas City, Mo.	1972	**79,409**	Grass
Miami Dolphins	**Pro Player Stadium**	Miami, Fla.	1987	**74,916**	Grass
New England Patriots	**Foxboro Stadium**	Foxboro, Mass.	1971	**60,292**	Grass
New York Jets	**Giants Stadium**	E. Rutherford, N.J.	1976	**79,466**	Grass
Oakland Raiders	**Network Associates Coliseum**	Oakland, Calif.	1966	**63,142**	Grass
Pittsburgh Steelers	**Three Rivers Stadium**	Pittsburgh, Pa.	1970	**59,600**	Turf
San Diego Chargers	**Qualcomm Stadium**	San Diego, Calif.	1967	**71,000**	Grass
Seattle Seahawks	**Husky Stadium**	Seattle, Wash.	1920	**72,500**	Turf
Tennessee Titans	**Adelphia Coliseum**	Nashville, Tenn.	1999	**67,000**	Grass

National Football Conference

		Location	Built	Capacity	Field
Arizona Cardinals	**Sun Devil Stadium**	Tempe, Ariz.	1958	**73,273**	Grass
Atlanta Falcons	**Georgia Dome**	Atlanta, Ga.	1992	**71,228**	Turf
Carolina Panthers	**Ericsson Stadium**	Charlotte, N.C.	1996	**72,350**	Grass
Chicago Bears	**Soldier Field**	Chicago, Ill.	1924	**66,944**	Grass
Dallas Cowboys	**Texas Stadium**	Irving, Texas	1971	**65,675**	Turf
Detroit Lions	**Pontiac Silverdome**	Pontiac, Mich.	1975	**80,311**	Turf
Green Bay Packers	**Lambeau Field**	Green Bay, Wisc.	1957	**60,790**	Grass
Minnesota Vikings	**Hubert H. Humphrey Metrodome**	Minneapolis, Minn.	1982	**64,121**	Turf
New Orleans Saints	**Louisiana Superdome**	New Orleans, La.	1975	**70,200**	Turf
New York Giants	**Giants Stadium**	E. Rutherford, N.J.	1976	**79,466**	Grass
Philadelphia Eagles	**Veterans Stadium**	Philadelphia, Pa.	1971	**65,352**	Turf
St. Louis Rams	**Trans World Dome**	St. Louis, Mo.	1995	**66,000**	Turf
San Francisco 49ers	**3Com Park**	San Francisco, Calif.	1960	**70,140**	Grass
Tampa Bay Buccaneers	**Raymond James Stadium**	Tampa, Fla.	1998	**66,321**	Grass
Washington Redskins	**FedEx Field**	Raljon, MD	1997	**80,166**	Grass

Rank by Capacity

AFC		NFC	
NY Jets	.79,466	Detroit	.80,311
Kansas City	.79,409	Washington	.80,166
Denver	.76,123	NY Giants	.79,466
Miami	.74,916	Arizona	.73,273
Buffalo	.73,800	Carolina	.72,350
Cleveland	.73,200	Atlanta	.71,228
Jacksonville	.73,000	New Orleans	.70,200
Seattle	.71,500	San Francisco	.70,140
San Diego	.71,000	Chicago	.66,944
Baltimore	.69,084	Tampa Bay	.66,321
Tennessee	.67,000	St. Louis	.66,000
Cincinnati	.65,600	Dallas	.65,675
Oakland	.63,142	Philadelphia	.65,352
New England	.60,292	Minnesota	.64,121
Pittsburgh	.59,600	Green Bay	.60,790
Indianapolis	.56,120		

Rank by Age

AFC		NFC	
Seattle	.1920	Chicago	.1924
Denver	.1948	Green Bay	.1957
Oakland	.1966	Arizona	.1958
San Diego	.1967	San Francisco	.1960
Pittsburgh	.1970	Dallas	.1971
New England	.1971	Philadelphia	.1971
Kansas City	.1972	New Orleans	.1975
Buffalo	.1973	Detroit	.1975
NY Jets	.1976	NY Giants	.1976
Indianapolis	.1984	Minnesota	.1982
Miami	.1987	Atlanta	.1992
Jacksonville	.1995	St. Louis	.1995
Baltimore	.1998	Carolina	.1996
Cleveland	.1999	Washington	.1997
Tennessee	.1999	Tampa Bay	.1998
Cincinnati	.2000		

1999 NFL Attendance

Official overall paid attendance in the NFL for the 1999 season was 15,710,970 for an average per game crowd of 63,351 over 248 games. Teams in each conference are ranked by attendance over eight home games. Rank column indicates rank in entire league. Numbers in parentheses indicate conference rank in 1998. Note that Cleveland did not play in 1998.

AFC

		Attendance	Rank	Average
1	Kansas City (3)	.629,544	1	78,693
2	Miami (4)	.592,161	4	74,020
3	Cleveland	.580,934	5	72,617
4	Denver (1)	.577,309	7	72,164
5	Buffalo (6)	.561,269	8	70,159
6	N.Y. Jets (2)	.548,012	9	68,502
7	Baltimore (7)	.547,118	10	68,390
8	Jacksonville (5)	.540,085	12	67,511
9	Tennessee (15)	.528,891	13	66,111
10	San Diego (9)	.476,999	20	59,625
11	Seattle (8)	.464,188	21	58,024
12	New England (10)	.461,624	22	57,703
13	Indianapolis (13)	.453,270	24	56,659
14	Pittsburgh (11)	.416,618	27	52,077
15	Cincinnati (12)	.404,617	28	50,585
16	Oakland (14)	.398,140	29	49,768
	TOTAL	.8,180,842	—	63,912

NFC

		Attendance	Rank	Average
1	NY Giants (1)	.620,362	2	77,545
2	Washington (3)	.619,749	3	74,469
3	Detroit (2)	.579,314	6	72,414
4	San Francisco (4)	.544,231	11	68,029
5	Tampa Bay (6)	.522,691	14	65,336
6	St. Louis (13)	.520,926	15	65,116
7	Philadelphia (5)	.519,835	16	64,979
8	Dallas (8)	.513,295	17	64,162
9	Minnesota (7)	.513,051	18	64,131
10	Carolina (9)	.489,515	19	61,189
11	Atlanta (11)	.460,922	23	57,615
12	Chicago (15)	.452,635	25	56,579
13	Green Bay (10)	.419,032	26	52,379
14	Arizona (14)	.393,240	30	49,155
15	New Orleans (15)	.361,330	31	45,166
	TOTAL	.7,530,128	—	62,751

Home Fields

Listed below are the principal home fields used through the years by current NFL teams. The largest capacity of each stadium is noted in the right-hand column. All-America Football Conference stadiums (1946-49) are included for Cleveland and San Francisco.

AFC

Baltimore Ravens

1996-97	Memorial Stadium	.65,000
1998–	PSInet Stadium	.69,084

Buffalo Bills

1960-72	War Memorial Stadium	.45,748
1973–	Ralph Wilson Stadium (Orchard Park, NY)	.73,800
	(1973 capacity-80,020)	

Cincinnati Bengals

1968-69	Nippert Stadium (Univ. of Cincinnati)	.26,500
1970-99	Cinergy Field	.60,389
	(1970 capacity-56,200)	
2000–	Paul Brown Stadium	.65,600

Cleveland Browns

1946-95	Cleveland Stadium	.78,512
	(1946 capacity-85,703)	
1999–	Cleveland Browns Stadium	.73,200

Denver Broncos

1960–	Mile High Stadium	.76,123
	(1960 capacity-34,000)	

Indianapolis Colts

1953-83	Memorial Stadium (Baltimore)	.60,020
1984–	RCA Dome (Indianapolis)	.56,120
	(1984 capacity-60,127)	

Jacksonville Jaguars

1995–	ALLTEL Stadium	.73,000

Kansas City Chiefs

1960-62	Cotton Bowl (Dallas)	.72,000
1963-71	Municipal Stadium (Kansas City)	.47,000
1972–	Arrowhead Stadium	.79,409
	(1972 capacity-78,097)	

Miami Dolphins

1966-86	Orange Bowl	.75,206
1987–	Pro Player Stadium	.74,916
	(1987 capacity-75,500)	

New England Patriots

1960-62	Nickerson Field (Boston Univ.)	.17,369
1963-68	Fenway Park	.33,379
1969	Alumni Stadium (Boston College)	.26,000
1970	Harvard Stadium	.37,300
1971–	Foxboro Stadium	.60,292
	(1971 capacity-61,114)	

National Football League (Cont.)

New York Jets

1960-63	Polo Grounds	55,987
1964-83	Shea Stadium	60,372
1984–	Giants Stadium (E. Rutherford, NJ)	79,466

Oakland Raiders

1960	Kesar Stadium (San Francisco)	59,636
1961	Candlestick Park	42,500
1962-65	Frank Youell Field (Oakland)	20,000
1966-81	Oakland-Alameda County Coliseum	54,587
1982-94	Memorial Coliseum (Los Angeles)	67,800
1995–	Network Associates Coliseum	63,142

Pittsburgh Steelers

1933-57	Forbes Field	35,000
1958-63	Forbes Field	35,000
	& Pitt Stadium	54,500
1964-69	Pitt Stadium	54,500
1970–	Three Rivers Stadium	59,600
	(1970 capacity-49,000)	

San Diego Chargers

1960	Memorial Coliseum (Los Angeles)	92,604
1961-66	Balboa Stadium (San Diego)	34,000
1967–	Qualcomm Stadium	71,000
	(1967 capacity-54,000)	

Seattle Seahawks

1976-94	Kingdome	66,000
1994	Kingdome	66,400
	& Husky Stadium	72,500
1995-99	Kingdome	66,400
2000–	Husky Stadium	72,500

Tennessee Titans

1960-64	Jeppesen Stadium (Houston)	23,500
1965-67	Rice Stadium (Rice Univ.)	70,000
1968-96	Astrodome	59,969
1997	Liberty Bowl (Memphis)	62,380
1998	Vanderbilt Stadium (Nashville)	41,600
1999–	Adelphia Coliseum (Nashville)	67,000

Ballpark Name Changes: BALTIMORE—**Cleveland Stadium** originally Municipal Stadium (1932-74), **PSInet Stadium** originally Ravens' Stadium (1998-99); BUFFALO—**Ralph Wilson Stadium** originally Rich Stadium (1973-99); CINCINNATI—**Cinergy Field** originally Riverfront Stadium (1970-96); DENVER—**Mile High Stadium** originally Bears Stadium (1948-66); INDIANAPOLIS—**RCA Dome** originally Hoosier Dome (1984-94); JACKSONVILLE—**ALLTEL Stadium** originally Jacksonville Municipal Stadium (1995-97); MIAMI—**Pro Player Stadium** originally Joe Robbie Stadium (1987-96); NEW ENGLAND—**Foxboro Stadium** originally Schaefer Stadium (1971-82), then Sullivan Stadium (1983-89); OAKLAND—**Network Associates Coliseum** originally Oakland Alameda Coliseum (1995-99); SAN DIEGO—**Qualcomm Stadium** originally San Diego Stadium (1967-81) then San Diego/Jack Murphy Stadium (1981-96).

NFC

Arizona Cardinals

1920-21	Normal Field (Chicago)	7,500
1922-25	Comiskey Park	28,000
1926-28	Normal Field	7,500
1929-59	Comiskey Park	52,000
1960-65	Busch Stadium (St. Louis)	34,000
1966-87	Busch Memorial Stadium	54,392
1988–	Sun Devil Stadium (Tempe, AZ)	73,273

Atlanta Falcons

1966-91	Atlanta-Fulton County Stadium	59,643
1992–	Georgia Dome	71,228

Carolina Panthers

1995	Memorial Stadium (Clemson, SC)	81,473
1996–	Ericsson Stadium	72,350

Chicago Bears

1920	Staley Field (Decatur, IL)	–
1921-70	Wrigley Field (Chicago)	37,741
1971–	Soldier Field	66,944
	(1971 capacity-55,049)	

Dallas Cowboys

1960-70	Cotton Bowl	72,132
1971–	Texas Stadium (Irving, TX)	65,675
	(1971 capacity-65,101)	

Detroit Lions

1930-33	Spartan Stadium (Portsmouth, OH)	8,200
1934-37	Univ. of Detroit Stadium	25,000
1938-74	Tiger Stadium	54,468
1975–	Pontiac Silverdome	80,311
	(1975 capacity-80,638)	

Green Bay Packers

1921-22	Hagemeister Brewery Park	–
1923-24	Bellevue Park	–
1925-56	City Stadium I	24,800
1957–	Lambeau Field	60,790
	(1957 capacity-32,150)	

Note: The Packers played games in Milwaukee from 1933-94: at Borchert Field, State Fair Park and Marquette Stadium (1933-52), and County Stadium (1953-94).

Minnesota Vikings

1961-81	Metropolitan Stadium (Bloomington)	48,446
1982–	HHH Metrodome (Minneapolis)	64,121
	(1982 capacity-62,220)	

New Orleans Saints

1967-74	Tulane Stadium	80,997
1975–	Louisiana Superdome	70,200
	(1975 capacity-74,472)	

New York Giants

1925-55	Polo Grounds II	55,200
1956-73	Yankee Stadium I	63,800
1973-74	Yale Bowl (New Haven, CT)	70,896
1975	Shea Stadium	60,372
1976–	Giants Stadium (E. Rutherford, NJ)	79,466
	(1976 capacity-76,800)	

Philadelphia Eagles

1933-35	Baker Bowl	18,800
1936-39	Municipal Stadium	73,702
1940	Shibe Park	33,608
1941	Municipal Stadium	73,702
1942	Shibe Park	33,608
1943	Forbes Field (Pittsburgh)	34,528
1944-57	Shibe Park	33,608
1958-70	Franklin Field (Univ. of Penn.)	60,546
1971–	Veterans Stadium	65,352
	(1971 capacity-65,000)	

St. Louis Rams

1937-42	Municipal Stadium (Cleveland)	85,703
1945	Suspended operations for one year.	
1944-45	Municipal Stadium	85,703
1946-79	Memorial Coliseum (Los Angeles)	92,604
1980-94	Anaheim Stadium	69,008
1995–	Trans World Dome	66,000

San Francisco 49ers

1946-70	Kezar Stadium	59,636
1971–	3Com Park	70,140
	(1971 capacity-61,246)	

Tampa Bay Buccaneers

1976-97	Houlihan's Stadium	74,300
1998–	Raymond James Stadium	66,321

Washington Redskins

1932	Braves Field (Boston)	40,000
1933-36	Fenway Park	27,000
1937-60	Griffith Stadium (Washington, DC)	35,000
1961-97	RFK Stadium	56,454
1997–	FedEx Field (Raljon, MD)	80,166

Ballpark Name Changes: ATLANTA—**Atlanta-Fulton County Stadium** originally Atlanta Stadium (1966-74); CHICAGO— **Wrigley Field** originally Cubs Park (1916-25), also, **Comiskey Park** originally White Sox Park (1910-12); DETROIT—**Tiger Stadium** originally Navin Field (1912-37), then Briggs Stadium (1938-60), also, **Pontiac Silverdome** originally Pontiac Metropolitan Stadium (1975); GREEN BAY—**Lambeau Field** originally City Stadium II (1957-64); PHILADELPHIA—**Shibe Park** renamed Connie Mack Stadium in 1953; ST. LOUIS—**Busch Memorial Stadium** renamed Busch Stadium in 1983; SAN FRANCISCO—**3Com Park** originally Candlestick Park (1960-94); TAMPA BAY—**Raymond James Stadium** originally Tampa Stadium (1976-96), then **Houlihan's Stadium** (1996-98); WASHINGTON—**RFK Stadium** originally D.C. Stadium (1961-68), also, **FedEx Field** originally Jack Kent Cooke Stadium (1997-99).

NATIONAL HOCKEY LEAGUE

Western Conference

		Location	Built	Capacity
Anaheim, Mighty Ducks of	**Arrowhead Pond**	Anaheim, Calif.	1993	**17,174**
Calgary Flames	**Canadian Airlines Saddledome**	Calgary, Alb.	1983	**17,139**
Chicago Blackhawks	**United Center**	Chicago, Ill.	1994	**20,500**
Colorado Avalanche	**Pepsi Center**	Denver, Colo.	1999	**18,129**
Columbus Blue Jackets	**Nationwide Arena**	Columbus, Ohio	2000	**18,500**
Dallas Stars	**Reunion Arena**	Dallas, Texas	1980	**17,001**
Detroit Red Wings	**Joe Louis Arena**	Detroit, Mich.	1979	**19,983**
Edmonton Oilers	**Skyreach Centre**	Edmonton, Alb.	1974	**17,100**
Los Angeles Kings	**Staples Center**	Los Angeles, Calif.	1999	**18,018**
Minnesota Wild	**Xcel Energy Center**	St. Paul, Minn.	2000	**18,600**
Nashville Predators	**Gaylord Entertainment Center**	Nashville, Tenn.	1994	**17,500**
Phoenix Coyotes	**America West Arena**	Phoenix, Ariz.	1992	**16,210**
St. Louis Blues	**Kiel Center**	St. Louis, Mo.	1994	**19,260**
San Jose Sharks	**San Jose Arena**	San Jose, Calif.	1993	**17,483**
Vancouver Canucks	**General Motors Place**	Vancouver, B.C.	1995	**18,422**

Eastern Conference

		Location	Built	Capacity
Atlanta Thrashers	**Philips Arena**	Atlanta, Ga.	1999	**18,750**
Boston Bruins	**FleetCenter**	Boston, Mass.	1995	**17,565**
Buffalo Sabres	**HSBC Arena**	Buffalo, N.Y.	1996	**18,595**
Carolina Hurricanes	**Raleigh Entertainment and Sports Arena**	Raleigh, N.C.	1999	**19,000**
Florida Panthers	**National Car Rental Center**	Sunrise, Fla.	1998	**19,250**
Montreal Canadiens	**Molson Centre**	Montreal, Que.	1996	**21,273**
New Jersey Devils	**Continental Airlines Arena**	E. Rutherford, N.J.	1981	**19,040**
New York Islanders	**Nassau Veterans' Mem. Coliseum**	Uniondale, N.Y.	1972	**16,297**
New York Rangers	**Madison Square Garden**	New York, N.Y.	1968	**18,200**
Ottawa Senators	**Corel Centre**	Kanata, Ont.	1996	**18,500**
Philadelphia Flyers	**First Union Center**	Philadelphia, Pa.	1996	**19,511**
Pittsburgh Penguins	**Civic Arena**	Pittsburgh, Pa.	1961	**17,181**
Tampa Bay Lightning	**Ice Palace**	Tampa Bay, Fla.	1996	**19,758**
Toronto Maple Leafs	**Air Canada Centre**	Toronto, Ont.	1999	**18,800**
Washington Capitals	**MCI Center**	Washington, D.C.	1997	**19,740**

Rank by Capacity

Western		Eastern	
Chicago	20,500	Montreal	21,273
Detroit	19,983	Tampa Bay	19,758
St. Louis	19,260	Washington	19,740
Minnesota	18,600	Philadelphia	19,511
Columbus	18,500	Florida	19,250
Vancouver	18,422	New Jersey	19,040
Colorado	18,129	Carolina	19,000
Los Angeles	18,018	Toronto	18,800
Nashville	17,500	Atlanta	18,750
San Jose	17,483	Buffalo	18,595
Anaheim	17,174	Ottawa	18,500
Calgary	17,139	NY Rangers	18,200
Edmonton	17,100	Boston	17,565
Dallas	17,001	Pittsburgh	17,181
Phoenix	16,210	NY Islanders	16,297

Rank by Age

Western		Eastern	
Edmonton	1974	Pittsburgh	1961
Detroit	1979	NY Rangers	1968
Dallas	1980	NY Islanders	1972
Calgary	1983	New Jersey	1981
Phoenix	1992	Boston	1995
Anaheim	1993	Montreal	1996
San Jose	1993	Ottawa	1996
Chicago	1994	Buffalo	1996
St. Louis	1994	Philadelphia	1996
Nashville	1994	Tampa Bay	1996
Vancouver	1995	Washington	1997
Colorado	1999	Florida	1998
Los Angeles	1999	Toronto	1999
Columbus	2000	Carolina	1999
Minnesota	2000	Atlanta	1999

National Hockey League (Cont.)
1999-2000 NHL Attendance

Official overall paid attendance for the 1999-2000 season according to the NHL accounting office was 18,799,222 (paid tickets) for an average per game crowd of 16,376 over 1,148 games. Teams in each conference are ranked by attendance over 41 home games. There were no neutral site games. Number of sellouts are listed in S/O column. Numbers in parentheses indicate rank in 1998-99.

Western Conference

		Attendance	S/O	Average
1	Detroit (1)	819,303	41	19,983
2	St. Louis (2)	762,222	23	18,591
3	Colorado (8)	738,395	41	18,010
4	San Jose (4)	708,925	35	17,291
5	Dallas (5)	697,041	41	17,001
6	Nashville (7)	680,582	20	16,600
7	Los Angeles (13)	677,264	19	16,519
8	Chicago (3)	667,237	5	16,274
9	Edmonton (6)	647,980	19	15,802
10	Calgary (9)	628,219	5	15,322
11	Phoenix (12)	614,644	0	14,991
12	Vancouver (11)	600,319	3	14,642
13	Anaheim (10)	592,883	8	14,461
	TOTAL	8,835,014	260	16,576

Eastern Conference

		Attendance	S/O	Average
1	Montreal (1)	828,437	13	20,206
2	Philadelphia (2)	804,169	41	19,614
3	Toronto (7)	785,484	39	19,158
4	NY Rangers (4)	746,200	41	18,200
5	Buffalo (10)	736,174	25	17,955
6	Ottawa (6)	717,852	14	17,509
7	Atlanta (N/A)	705,446	12	17,206
8	Boston (9)	669,237	13	16,323
9	Florida (3)	655,260	1	15,982
10	Pittsburgh (11)	633,199	9	15,444
11	New Jersey (8)	623,457	2	15,206
12	Washington (5)	593,670	6	14,480
13	Tampa Bay (12)	557,618	2	13,600
14	Carolina (14)	508,424	0	12,401
15	NY Islanders (13)	399,671	4	9,748
	TOTAL	9,964,208	222	16,202

Home Ice

Listed below are the principal home buildings used through the years by current NHL teams. The largest capacity of each arena is noted in the right hand column. World Hockey Association arenas (1972-76) are included for Edmonton, Hartford (now Carolina), Quebec (now Colorado) and Winnipeg (now Phoenix).

Western Conference

Anaheim, Mighty Ducks of

1993–	Arrowhead Pond	17,174

Calgary Flames

1972-80	The Omni (Atlanta)	15,278
1980-83	Calgary Corral	7,424
1983–	Canadian Airlines Saddledome	17,139
	(1983 capacity-16,674)	

Chicago Blackhawks

1926-29	Chicago Coliseum	5,000
1929-94	Chicago Stadium	17,317
1994–	United Center	20,500

Colorado Avalanche

1972-95	Le Colisee de Quebec	15,399
1995-99	McNichols Arena (Denver)	16,061
1999–	Pepsi Center	18,129

Columbus Blue Jackets

2000–	Nationwide Arena	18,500

Dallas Stars

1967-93	Met Center (Bloomington, MN)	15,174
1993–	Reunion Arena (Dallas)	17,001

Detroit Red Wings

1926-27	Border Cities Arena (Windsor, Ont.)	3,200
1927-79	Olympia Stadium (Detroit)	16,700
1979–	Joe Louis Arena	19,983

Edmonton Oilers

1972-74	Edmonton Gardens	7,200
1974–	Skyreach Centre	17,100
	(1974 capacity-15,513)	

Los Angeles Kings

1967-99	Great Western Forum (Inglewood)	16,005
	(1967 capacity-15,651)	
1999–	Staples Center	18,018

Note: The Kings played 17 games at Long Beach Sports Arena and LA Sports Arena at the start of the 1967-68 season.

Minnesota Wild

2000–	Xcel Energy Center	18,600

Nashville Predators

1998–	Gaylord Entertainment Center	17,500

Phoenix Coyotes

1972-96	Winnipeg Arena	15,393
	(1972 capacity-10,177)	
1996–	America West (Phoenix)	16,210

St. Louis Blues

1967-94	St. Louis Arena	17,188
1994–	Kiel Center	19,260

San Jose Sharks

1991-93	Cow Palace (Daly City, CA)	11,100
1993–	San Jose Arena	17,483

Vancouver Canucks

1970-95	Pacific Coliseum	16,150
1995–	General Motors Place	18,422

Building Name Changes: CALGARY—**Canadian Airlines Saddledome** originally Olympic Saddledome (1983-1995); DALLAS—**Met Center** in Minneapolis originally Metropolitan Sports Center (1967-82); EDMONTON—**Skyreach Centre** formerly named Edmonton Coliseum (1995-99) which was originally Northlands Coliseum (1974-94); LOS ANGELES—**Great Western Forum** originally The Forum (1967-88); NASHVILLE—**Gaylord Entertainment Center** originally Nashville Arena (1994-99); ST. LOUIS—**St. Louis Arena** renamed The Checkerdome in 1977, then St. Louis Arena again in 1982.

Eastern Conference

Atlanta Thrashers

1999–	Philips Arena	18,750

Boston Bruins

1924-28	Boston Arena	6,200
1928-95	Boston Garden	14,448
1995–	FleetCenter	17,565

Buffalo Sabres

1970-96	Memorial Auditorium (The Aud)	16,284
	(1970 capacity-10,429)	
1996–	HSBC Arena	18,595

Carolina Hurricanes

1972-73	Boston Garden	14,442
1973-74	Boston Garden (regular season)	14,442
	West Springfield (MA) Big E (playoffs)	5,513
1974-75	West Springfield Big E	5,513
	& Hartford (CT) Civic Center	10,507
1975-77	Hartford Civic Center	10,507
1977-78	Hartford Civic Center	10,507
	& Springfield (MA) Civic Center	7,725
1978-79	Springfield Civic Center	7,725
1979-80	Springfield Civic Center	7,725
	& Hartford Civic Center II	14,250
1980-97	Hartford Civic Center II	15,635
1997-99	Greensboro Coliseum	21,500
1999–	Raleigh Entertainment and Sports Arena	19,000

Note: The Hartford Civic Center roof caved in January 1978, forcing the Whalers to move their home games to Springfield, MA for two years.

Florida Panthers

1993-98	Miami Arena	14,703
1998–	National Car Rental Center	19,250

Montreal Canadiens

1910-20	Jubilee Arena	3,200
1913-18	Montreal Arena (Westmount)	6,000
1918-26	Mount Royal Arena	6,750
1926-68	Montreal Forum I	15,500
1968-96	Montreal Forum II	17,959
1996–	Molson Centre	21,273

New Jersey Devils

1974-76	Kemper Arena (Kansas City)	16,300
1976-82	McNichols Arena (Denver)	15,900
1982–	Continental Airlines Arena	19,040
	(1982 capacity-19,023)	

New York Islanders

1972–	Nassau Veterans' Mem. Coliseum	16,297
	(1972 capacity-14,500)	

New York Rangers

1925-68	Madison Square Garden III	15,925
1968–	Madison Square Garden IV	18,200
	(1968 capacity-17,250)	

Ottawa Senators

1992-95	Ottawa Civic Center	10,755
1996–	Corel Centre (Kanata)	18,500

Philadelphia Flyers

1967-96	CoreStates Spectrum	17,380
	(1967 capacity-14,558)	
1996–	First Union Center	19,511

Pittsburgh Penguins

1967–	Civic Arena	17,181
	(1967 capacity-12,508)	

Tampa Bay Lightning

1992-93	Expo Hall (Tampa)	10,500
1993-96	ThunderDome (St. Petersburg)	26,000
1996–	Ice Palace	19,758

Toronto Maple Leafs

1917-31	Mutual Street Arena	8,000
1931-99	Maple Leaf Gardens	15,746
	(1931 capacity-13,542)	
1999–	Air Canada Centre	18,800

Washington Capitals

1974-97	USAir Arena (Landover, MD)	18,130
1997–	MCI Center	19,740

Building Name Changes: BUFFALO—**HSBC Arena** originally Marine Midland Arena (1996-99); NEW JERSEY—**Continental Airlines Arena** originally Meadowlands Arena (1982-96); PHILADELPHIA—**First Union Center** originally the CoreStates Center (1996-98) and **CoreStates Spectrum** originally The Spectrum (1967-94); WASHINGTON—**USAir Arena** originally Capital Centre (1974-93).

AUTO RACING

Formula One, NASCAR Winston Cup, CART and Indy Racing League (IRL) racing circuits. Qualifying records accurate as of Sept. 22, 2000. Capacity figures for NASCAR, CART and IRL tracks are approximate and pertain to grandstand seating only. Standing room and hillside terrain seating featured at most road courses are not included.

CART

	Location	Miles	Qual.mph record	Set by	Seats
The Raceway on Belle Isle	Detroit, Mich.	2.346**	114.859	Greg Moore (1998)	18,000
Burke Lakefront Airport	Cleveland, Ohio	2.106**	134.385	Jimmy Vasser (1998)	36,000
California Speedway	Fontana, Calif.	2.029	240.942	Mauricio Gugelmin (1997)	122,000
Chicago Motor Speedway	Cicero, Ill.	1.029	167.567	Juan Montoya (2000)	40,000
Exhibition Place	Toronto, Ont.	1.755**	110.565	Gil de Ferran (1999)	60,000
Gateway International Raceway	Madison, Ill.	1.27	187.963	Raul Boesel (1997)	35,000
Homestead-Miami Speedway	Homestead, Fla.	1.502	217.541	Greg Moore (1998)	72,000
Houston Grand Prix	Houston, Tex.	1.527**	93.651	Juan Montoya (1999)	60,000
Laguna Seca Raceway	Monterey, Calif.	2.238*	118.969	Helio Castro-Neves (2000)	8,000
Long Beach	Long Beach, Calif.	1.824**	111.226	Bryan Herta (1998)	63,000
Michigan Speedway	Brooklyn, Mich.	2.0	234.959	Paul Tracy (2000)	136,000
Mid-Ohio Sports Car Course	Lexington, Ohio	2.258*	124.394	Dario Franchitti (1999) & Gil de Ferran (2000)	6,000
The Milwaukee Mile	West Allis, Wisc.	1.032	185.500	Patrick Carpentier (1998)	36,800
Nazareth Speedway	Nazareth, Pa.	0.946	184.896	Patrick Carpentier (1998)	44,044
Portland International Raceway	Portland, Ore.	1.969*	122.768	Helio Castro-Neves (2000)	50,000
Piquet International Raceway	Rio de Janeiro, Brazil	1.864	174.002	Christian Fittipaldi (1999)	80,000
Road America	Elkhart Lake, Wisc.	4.048*	145.924	Dario Franchitti (2000)	10,000
Surfers Paradise	Queensland, Australia	2.795**	109.724	Dario Franchitti (1999)	55,000
Twin Ring Motegi	Motegi, Japan	1.549	219.000	Gil de Ferran (1999)	50,000
Vancouver	Vancouver, B.C.	1.781**	106.144	Dario Franchitti (2000)	65,000

*Road courses (not ovals). **Temporary street circuits.

Auto Racing (Cont.)
Indy Racing League

Founded by Indianapolis Motor Speedway president Tony George, the Indy Racing League competes with CART and fielded nine races, anchored by the Indianapolis 500, in 2000. Thirteen races were scheduled for 2001. Note that the track records listed are for normally-aspirated IRL cars unless otherwise noted by an asterisk.

	Location	Miles	Qual.mph Record	Set by	Seats
Atlanta Motor Speedway	Hampton, Ga.	1.54	224.145	Billy Boat (1998)	124,000
Chicagoland Speedway	Joliet, Ill.	1.5	—	first race in 2001	75,000
Gateway International Raceway	Madison, Ill.	1.25	—	first race in 2001	35,000
Homestead-Miami Speedway	Homestead, Fla.	1.5	—	first race in 2001	72,000
Indianapolis Motor Speedway	Indianapolis, Ind.	2.5	237.498	Arie Luyendyk (1996)*	265,000
Kansas Speedway	Kansas City, Kans.	1.5	—	first race in 2001	15,000
Kentucky Speedway	Sparta, Kent.	1.5	219.191	Scott Goodyear (2000)	65,989
Las Vegas Motor Speedway	Las Vegas, Nev.	1.5	214.567	Billy Boat (1998)	120,000
Nashville Superspeedway	Nashville, Tenn.	1.33	—	first race in 2001	50,000
Phoenix International Raceway	Phoenix, Ariz.	1.0	177.139	Greg Ray (1999)	78,450
Pikes Peak Int'l. Raceway	Fountain, Colo.	1.0	179.874	Greg Ray (2000)	42,787
Richmond International Raceway	Richmond, Va.	0.75	—	first race in 2001	95,920
Texas Motor Speedway	Fort Worth, Tex.	1.5	225.979	Billy Boat (1998)	154,861
Walt Disney World Speedway	Lake Buena Vista, Fla.	1.1	171.371	Scott Sharp (1999)	43,000

NASCAR Winston Cup

	Location	Miles	Qual.mph Record	Set By	Seats
Atlanta Motor Speedway	Hampton, Ga.	1.54	197.478	Geoff Bodine (1997)	124,000
Bristol Motor Speedway	Bristol, Tenn.	0.533	126.370	Steve Park (2000)	135,000
California Speedway	Fontana, Calif.	2.0	186.061	Mika Skinner (2000)	122,000
Darlington International Raceway	Darlington, N.C.	1.366	173.797	Ward Burton (1996)	62,000
Daytona International Speedway	Daytona Beach, Fla.	2.5	210.364	Bill Elliott (1987)	165,000
Dover Downs International Speedway	Dover, Del.	1.0	159.964	Rusty Wallace (1999)	107,000
Homestead-Miami Speedway	Homestead, Fla.	1.5	155.759	David Green (1999)	72,000
Indianapolis Motor Speedway	Indianapolis, Ind.	2.5	181.068	Ricky Rudd (1999)	265,000
Las Vegas Motor Speedway	Las Vegas, Nev.	1.5	172.563	Ricky Rudd (2000)	120,000
Lowe's Motor Speedway	Concord, N.C.	1.5	186.034	Dale Earnhardt Jr. (2000)	167,000
Martinsville Speedway	Martinsville, Va.	0.526	95.275	Tony Stewart (1999)	77,500
Michigan Speedway	Brooklyn, Mich.	2.0	191.149	Dale Earnhardt Jr. (2000)	126,000
New Hampshire Int'l Speedway	Loudon, N.H.	1.058	132.089	Rusty Wallace (2000)	90,000
North Carolina Speedway	Rockingham, N.C.	1.017	158.035	Rusty Wallace (2000)	60,122
Phoenix International Raceway	Phoenix, Ariz.	1.0	132.714	John Andretti (1999)	78,500
Pocono Raceway	Long Pond, Pa.	2.5	172.391	Tony Stewart (2000)	77,000
Richmond International Raceway	Richmond, Va.	0.75	126.499	Jeff Gordon (1999)	95,920
Sears Point International Raceway	Sonoma, Calif.	1.949	98.711	Jeff Gordon (1998)	42,500
Talladega Superspeedway	Talladega, Ala.	2.66	212.809	Bill Elliott (1987)	108,000
Texas Motor Speedway	Ft. Worth, Tex.	1.5	192.137	Terry Labonte (2000)	204,861
Watkins Glen	Watkins Glen, N.Y.	2.45*	121.234	Rusty Wallace (1999)	40,000

*Road courses (not ovals).

Notes: Richmond sells reserved seats only (no infield) for Winston Cup races.

Formula One

Race track capacity figures unavailable.

Grand Prix		Miles	Qual.mph Record	Set by
Austrian	**A1-Ring** (Zeltwig, Austria)	2.684	137.444	Mika Hakkinen (2000)
Australian	**Albert Park** (Melbourne)	3.274	132.731	Jacques Villeneuve (1997)
Belgian	**Spa-Francorchamps**	4.333	143.418	Mika Hakkinen (1998)
Brazilian	**Interlagos** (Sao Paulo)	2.684	130.067	Mika Hakkinen (2000)
British	**Silverstone** (Towcester)	3.194	148.043	Nigel Mansell (1992)
Canadian	**Circuit Gilles Villeneuve** (Montreal)	2.747	126.442	David Coulthard (1998)
European	**Nürburgring** (Nürburg, Germany)	2.822	131.453	David Coulthard (2000)
French	**Magny Cours** (Nevers)	2.641	128.709	Nigel Mansell (1992)
German	**Hockenheim** (Germany)	4.239	156.722	Nigel Mansell (1991)
Hungarian	**Hungaroring** (Budapest)	2.468	117.602	Riccardo Patrese (1992)
Italian	**Autodromo Nazionale di Monza** (Milan)	3.585	159.951	Ayrton Senna (1991)
Japanese	**Suzuka** (Nagoya)	3.644	138.515	Gerhard Berger (1991)
Malaysian	**Sepang**	3.444	124.358	Michael Schumacher (1999)
Monaco	**Monte Carlo** (Monaco)	2.082	96.286	Heinz-Harald Frentzen (1997)
San Marino	**Autodome Enzo di Ferrari** (Imola, Italy)	3.063	138.265	Ayrton Senna (1994)
Spanish	**Catalunya** (Barcelona)	2.937	138.205	Jacques Villeneuve (1997)
United States	**Indianapolis Motor Speedway**	2.606	126.355	Michael Schumacher (2000)

SOCCER

World's Premier Soccer Stadiums
(Listed by city)

Stadium	Location	Seats	Stadium	Location	Seats
Spiros Louis	Athens, Greece	74,770	Azteca	Mexico City, Mexico	106,000
Eden Park	Auckland, New Zealand	50,000	Guiseppe Meazza	Milan, Italy	85,847
Nou Camp	Barcelona, Spain	109,815	Centenario	Montevideo, Uruguay	73,609
Workers'	Beijing, China	80,000	Luzhniki Stadion	Moscow, Russia	80,840
Olympiastadion	Berlin, Germany	76,243	Olympiastadion	Munich, Germany	63,000
Népstadion	Budapest, Hungary	60,000	Salt Lake	New Dehli, India	120,000
Antonio Liberti	Buenos Aires, Argentina	76,689	San Paolo	Naples, Italy	75,000
National	Cairo, Egypt	90,000	Stade de France	Paris, France	80,000
Millennium	Cardiff, Wales	72,500	Rungnado	Pyongyang, N. Korea	150,000
Westfalenstadion	Dortmund, Germany	68,600	Maracana	Rio de Janeiro, Brazil	165,000
Lansdowne Road	Dublin, Ireland	51,000	King Fahd II	Riyadh, Saudi Arabia	75,000
Celtic Park	Glasgow, Scotland	60,953	Olimpico	Rome, Italy	86,517
Hampden Park	Glasgow, Scotland	52,208	Nacional	Santiago, Chile	75,000
FNB Stadium	Soweto, S. Africa	90,000	Morumbi	Sao Paulo, Brazil	120,000
Central State	Kiev, Ukraine	100,062	Olympic Stadium	Seoul, S. Korea	100,000
Estadio da Luz	Lisbon, Portugal	92,383	Olympic Stadium	Sydney, Australia	120,000
new Wembley	London, England	90,000	Olympic Stadium	Tokyo, Japan	62,000
Santiago Bernabeu	Madrid, Spain	87,000	Delle Alpi	Turin, Italy	69,041
Old Trafford	Manchester, England	55,400	Prater	Vienna, Austria	62,958

Major League Soccer

The 12-team MLS is the only U.S. Division I professional outdoor league sanctioned by FIFA and U.S. Soccer. Note that all capacity figures are approximate given the adjustments of football stadium seating to soccer.

Western Conference

	Stadium	Built	Seats	Field
Chicago Fire	Soldier Field	1924	24,955	Grass
Colorado Rapids	Mile High	1948	17,500	Grass
Dallas Burn	Cotton Bowl	1935	22,528	Grass
Kansas City Wizards	Arrowhead	1972	20,571	Grass
L.A. Galaxy	Rose Bowl	1922	30,000	Grass
San Jose Earthquakes	Spartan	1933	26,000	Grass

Eastern Conference

	Stadium	Built	Seats	Field
Columbus Crew	Columbus Crew	1999	22,500	Grass
D.C. United	RFK	1961	26,169	Grass
Metro Stars (N.Y./N.J.)	Giants	1976	25,576	Grass
Miami Fusion	Lockhart	1959	20,450	Grass
N.E. Revolution	Foxboro	1971	24,871	Grass
Tampa Bay Mutiny	Raymond James	1998	17,482	Grass

MISCELLANEOUS

Minor League Baseball

AAA Ballparks
International League

North		Built	Seats	Field
Buffalo Bisons (Indians)	Dunn Tire Park	1988	20,900	Grass
Ottawa Lynx (Expos)	JetForm Park	1993	10,332	Grass
Pawtucket Red Sox (Red Sox)	McCoy Stadium	1942	10,031	Grass
Rochester Red Wings (Orioles)	Frontier Field	1997	10,840	Grass
Scranton/Wilkes-Barre Red Barons (Phillies)	Lackawanna County Stadium	1989	10,982	Turf
Syracuse Sky Chiefs (Blue Jays)	P&C Stadium	1997	11,604	Turf
West		**Built**	**Seats**	**Field**
Columbus Clippers (Yankees)	Cooper Stadium	1932	15,000	Grass
Indianapolis Indians (Brewers)	Victory Field	1996	15,500	Grass
Louisville RiverBats (Reds)	Louisville Slugger Field	2000	13,000	Grass
Toledo Mud Hens (Tigers)	Ned Skeldon Stadium	1965	10,197	Grass
South		**Built**	**Seats**	**Turf**
Charlotte Knights (White Sox)	Knights Castle	1990	10,002	Grass
Durham Bulls (Devil Rays)	Durham Bulls Athletic Park	1995	10,000	Grass
Norfolk Tides (Mets)	Harbor Park	1993	12,067	Grass
Richmond Braves (Braves)	The Diamond	1985	12,134	Grass

Miscellaneous (Cont.)
Pacific Coast League

East Division		Built	Seats	Field
Oklahoma RedHawks (Rangers)	Southwestern Bell Bricktown Ballpark	1998	13,066	Grass
Memphis Redbirds (Cardinals)	AutoZone Park	2000	14,300	Grass
Nashville Sounds (Pirates)	Herschel Greer Stadium	1978	10,700	Grass
New Orleans Zephyrs (Astros)	Zephyr Field	1997	10,000	Grass
North Division		**Built**	**Seats**	**Field**
Calgary Cannons (Marlins)	Burns Stadium	1966	8,000	Grass
Edmonton Trappers (Twins)	TELUS Field	1995	9,200	Grass
Tacoma Rainiers (Mariners)	Cheney Stadium	1960	9,600	Grass
Salt Lake Buzz (Angels)	Franklin Covey Field	1993	15,500	Grass
Central Division		**Built**	**Seats**	**Field**
Portland (Dodgers)	PGE Park	1926*	TBD	Grass
Colorado Springs Sky Sox (Rockies)	Sky Sox Stadium	1988	9,000	Grass
Iowa Cubs (Cubs)	Sec Taylor Stadium	1992	10,888	Grass
Omaha Golden Spikes (Royals)	Johnny Rosenblatt Stadium	1948	24,000	Turf
South Division		**Built**	**Seats**	**Field**
Las Vegas Stars (Padres)	Cashman Field	1983	9,334	Grass
Fresno Grizzlies (Giants)	Beiden Field	1987	6,575	Grass
Sacramento River Cats (Athletics)	Raley Field	2000	10,500	Grass
Tucson Sidewinders (Diamondbacks)	Tucson Electric Park	1998	11,000	Grass

*PGE Park, formerly known as Civic Stadium, was undergoing extensive renovation prior to the 2001 season.

Japanese Baseball League
Central League

		Location	Built	Seats	Field
Chunichi Dragons	Nagoya Dome	Nagoya	1997	40,500	Turf
Hanshin Tigers	Koshien Stadium	Nisinomiya	1924	55,000	Grass
Hiroshima Carp	Hiroshima Municipal Stadium	Hiroshima	1957	32,000	Grass
Yakult Swallows	Meiji Jingu Stadium	Tokyo	1926	48,785	Turf
Yokohama BayStars	Yokohama Stadium	Yokohama	1978	30,000	Turf
Yomiuri Giants	Tokyo Dome	Tokyo	1988	48,000	Turf

Pacific League

		Location	Built	Seats	Field
Chiba Lotte Marines	Chiba Marine Stadium	Chiba	1991	30,000	Turf
Fukuoka Daiei Hawks	Fukuoka Dome	Fukuoka	1993	48,000	Turf
Kintetsu Buffaloes	Osaka Dome	Osaka	1997	55,000	Turf
Nippon Ham Fighters	Tokyo Dome	Tokyo	1988	48,000	Turf
Orix Blue Wave	Green Stadium Kobe	Kobe	1988	35,000	Grass
Seibu Lions	Seibu Stadium	Tokorozawa	1979	37,000	Turf

Canadian Football League
East Division

		Location	Built	Seats	Field
Hamilton Tiger-Cats	Ivor Wynne Stadium	Hamilton, Ont.	1932	28,830	Turf
Montreal Alouettes	Molson Stadium (McGill)	Montreal, Que.	1976	18,027	Turf
Toronto Argonauts	SkyDome	Toronto, Ont.	1989	31,600	Turf
Winnipeg Blue Bombers	Winnipeg Stadium	Winnipeg, Man.	1953	29,544	Turf

West Division

		Location	Built	Seats	Field
British Columbia Lions	B.C. Place	Vancouver, B.C.	1983	40,800	Turf
Calgary Stampeders	McMahon Stadium	Calgary, Alb.	1960	37,317	Turf
Edmonton Eskimos	Commonwealth Stadium	Edmonton, Alb.	1978	60,081	Grass
Saskatchewan Roughriders	Taylor Field	Regina, Sask.	1948	27,732	Turf

NFL Europe

		Location	Seats
Amsterdam Admirals	Amsterdam Arena	Amsterdam, Netherlands	51,328
Barcelona Dragons	Estadi Olimpic de Monthuic	Barcelona, Spain	54,000
Berlin Thunder	Jahn Sportspark	Berlin, Germany	20,000
Frankfurt Galaxy	WaldStadion	Frankfurt, Germany	54,000
Rhein Fire	Rheinstadion	Dusseldorf, Germany	57,000
Scottish Claymores	Murrayfield Stadium	Edinburgh, Scotland	67,000
	& Hampden Park	Glasgow, Scotland	52,208

Arena Football League
American Conference

Western Division	Arena	Location	Built	Seats
Arizona Rattlers	America West Arena	Phoenix, Ariz.	1992	16,923
Los Angeles Avengers	Staples Center	Los Angeles, Calif.	1999	18,500
Oklahoma Wranglers	Myriad Convention Center	Oklahoma City, Okla.	1973	13,000
San Jose SaberCats	San Jose Arena	San Jose, Calif.	1993	16,929
Central Division				
Detroit Fury	The Palace of Auburn Hills	Auburn Hills, Mich.	1988	22,076
Grand Rapids Rampage	Van Andel Arena	Grand Rapids, Mich.	1996	10,618
Houston ThunderBears	Compaq Center	Houston, Texas	1975	15,050
Iowa Barnstormers	Veterans Memorial Auditorium	Des Moines, Iowa	1955	11,250
Milwaukee Mustangs	Bradley Center	Milwaukee, Wisc.	1988	17,819

National Conference

Southern Division	Arena	Location	Built	Seats
Carolina Cobras	Raleigh Sports & Entertainment Arena	Raleigh, N.C.	1999	16,985
Florida Bobcats	National Car Rental Center	Sunrise, Fla.	1998	17,900
Nashville Kats	Gaylord Entertainment Center	Nashville, Tenn.	1994	16,121
Orlando Predators	TD Waterhouse Centre	Orlando, Fla.	1989	16,613
Tampa Bay Storm	Ice Palace	Tampa Bay, Fla.	1996	20,282
Eastern Division		**Location**	**Built**	**Seats**
Albany Firebirds	Pepsi Arena	Albany, N.Y.	1990	13,652
Buffalo Destroyers	HSBC Arena	Buffalo, N.Y.	1996	18,127
New England Sea Wolves	Hartford Civic Center	Hartford, Conn.	1975	14,716
New Jersey Red Dogs	Continental Airlines Arena	E. Rutherford, N.J.	1981	17,500

Women's Professional Basketball
Women's National Basketball Association

The WNBA teams play in the same arenas as the NBA teams in their respective cities. However, the capacities of some of the venues are "down-sized" for some games. The new, smaller capacity for WNBA games is listed below where applicable.

Eastern	Arena	Location	Built	Seats
Charlotte Sting	Charlotte Coliseum	Charlotte, N.C.	1988	13,133
Cleveland Rockers	Gund Arena	Cleveland, Ohio	1994	11,751
Detroit Shock	The Palace of Auburn Hills	Auburn Hills, Mich.	1988	22,076
Indiana Fever	Conseco Fieldhouse	Indianapolis, Ind.	1999	18,345
Miami Sol	AmericanAirlines Arena	Miami, Fla.	1999	19,600
New York Liberty	Madison Square Garden	New York, N.Y.	1968	19,763
Orlando Miracle	TD Waterhouse Centre	Orlando, Fla.	1989	17,248
Washington Mystics	MCI Center	Washington, D.C.	1997	20,500
Western		**Location**	**Built**	**Seats**
Houston Comets	Compaq Center	Houston, Tex.	1975	16,285
Los Angeles Sparks	Great Western Forum	Inglewood, Calif.	1967	13,000
Minnesota Lynx	Target Center	Minneapolis, Minn.	1990	19,006
Phoenix Mercury	America West Arena	Phoenix, Ariz.	1992	19,023
Portland Fire	Rose Garden	Portland, Ore.	1995	19,980
Sacramento Monarchs	ARCO Arena	Sacramento, Calif.	1988	17,317
Seattle Storm	KeyArena at Seattle Center	Seattle, Wash.	1962	17,072
Utah Starzz	Delta Center	Salt Lake City, Utah	1991	19,911

Horse Racing
Triple Crown race tracks

Race	Racetrack	Seats	Infield
Kentucky Derby	Churchill Downs	48,500	151,000
Preakness	Pimlico Race Course	40,000	60,000
Belmont Stakes	Belmont Park	32,941	55,000

Record crowds: Kentucky Derby– 163,628 (1974); Preakness– 101,000 (1999); Belmont–85,818 (1999).

Tennis
Grand Slam center courts

Event	Main Stadium	Seats
Australian Open	Melbourne Park	15,021
French Open	Stade Roland Garros	16,300
Wimbledon	Centre Court	13,813
U.S. Open	Arthur Ashe Stadium	22,547

COLLEGE BASKETBALL

The 50 Largest Arenas

The 50 largest arenas in Division I for the 2000-2001 NCAA regular season. Note that (*) indicates part-time home court.

		Seats	Home Team			Seats	Home Team
1	Carrier Dome	33,000	Syracuse	26	Pittsburgh Civic Arena	16,725	Pittsburgh*
2	Thompson-Boling Arena	24,535	Tennessee	27	Assembly Hall	16,450	Illinois
3	Rupp Arena	23,000	Kentucky	28	Allen Field House	16,300	Kansas
4	Marriott Center	22,700	BYU	29	Hartford Civic Center	16,294	UConn*
5	Dean Smith Center	21,572	N. Carolina	30	Erwin Center	16,175	Texas
6	First Union Center	21,000	Villanova*	31	LA Sports Arena	15,509	USC
7	MCI Center	20,600	Georgetown*	32	Carver-Hawkeye Arena	15,500	Iowa
8	The Pyramid	20,142	Memphis		Pepsi Arena	15,500	Siena*
9	Continental Airlines Arena	20,029	Seton Hall*	34	Bryce Jordan Center	15,261	Penn St.
10	Ent. and Sports Arena	20,000	N.C. State	35	Miami Arena	15,200	Miami
	Kiel Center	20,000	Saint Louis	36	Breslin Events Center	15,138	Michigan St.
12	The Rose Garden	19,980	Portland St.	37	Coleman Coliseum	15,043	Alabama
13	HSBC Arena	19,500	Canisius* & Niagara*	38	Arena-Auditorium	15,028	Wyoming
14	Bud Walton Arena	19,200	Arkansas	39	Huntsman Center	15,000	Utah
15	Bradley Center	19,150	Marquette		United Spirit Arena	15,000	Texas Tech
16	Freedom Hall	18,865	Louisville	41	McKale Center	14,545	Arizona
17	Thomas & Mack Center	18,500	UNLV	42	Cole Fieldhouse	14,500	Maryland
18	Madison Square Garden	18,470	St. John's*	43	Joel Memorial Coliseum	14,407	Wake Forest
19	University Arena (The Pit)	18,018	New Mexico	44	Williams Arena	14,321	Minnesota
20	Alltel Arena	18,000	Arkansas-Little Rock	45	Devaney Sports Center	14,200	Nebraska
	New Orleans Arena	18,000	Tulane	46	University Activity Center	14,198	Arizona St.
22	All State Arena	17,500	DePaul*	47	Memorial Gym	14,168	Vanderbilt
	Value City Arena	17,500	Ohio St.	48	Maravich Assembly Ctr.	14,164	LSU
24	Assembly Hall	17,357	Indiana	49	Mackey Arena	14,123	Purdue
25	Kohl Center	17,142	Wisconsin	50	Hilton Coliseum	14,092	Iowa St.

Division I Conference Home Courts

NCAA Division I conferences for the 2000-2001 season. Teams with home games in more than one arena are noted.

America East

	Home Floor	Seats
Boston University	Case Gym	1,800
Delaware	Bob Carpenter Center	5,000
Drexel	Phys. Education Center	2,300
Hartford	Chase Family Arena	4,475
Hofstra	Hofstra Arena	5,112
Maine	Alfond Arena	5,712
New Hampshire	Whittemore Center	6,500
Northeastern	Cabot Center	2,500
Towson	Towson Center	5,000
Vermont	Patrick Gym	3,228

Atlantic Coast

	Home Floor	Seats
Clemson	Littlejohn Coliseum	11,020
Duke	Cameron Indoor Stadium	9,314
Florida St.	Leon County Civic Center	12,500
Georgia Tech	Alexander Mem. Stadium	10,000
Maryland	Cole Field House	14,500
North Carolina	Dean Smith Center	21,572
N.C. State	Entertainment and Sports Arena	20,000
Virginia	University Hall	8,457
Wake Forest	Joel Mem. Coliseum	14,407

Atlantic 10

	Home Floor	Seats
Dayton	U. of Dayton Arena	13,511
Duquesne	Palumbo Center	6,200
Fordham	Rose Hill Gym	3,470
G. Washington	Smith Center	5,000
La Salle	Hayman Center	4,000
Massachusetts	Mullins Center	9,493
Rhode Island	Keaney Gymnasium	3,385
	& Providence Civic Center	12,681
St. Bonaventure	Reilly Center	6,000
St. Joseph's-PA	Alumni Mem. Fieldhouse	3,200
Temple	Liacouras Center	10,224
Xavier-OH	Cintas Center	10,200

Big East

	Home Floor	Seats
Boston College	Conte Forum	8,606
Connecticut	Gampel Pavilion	10,027
	& Hartford Civic Center	16,294
Georgetown	MCI Center	20,600
Miami-FL	Miami Arena	15,200
Notre Dame	Joyce Center	11,418
Pittsburgh	Fitzgerald Field House	6,798
	& Pittsburgh Civic Arena	16,725
Providence	Providence Civic Center	12,993
Rutgers	Louis Brown Athletic Center	9,000
St. John's	Alumni Hall	6,008
	& Madison Square Garden	18,470
Seton Hall	Continental Airlines Arena	20,029
Syracuse	Carrier Dome	33,000
Villanova	The Pavilion	6,500
	First Union Center	21,000
Virginia Tech	Cassell Coliseum	10,052
West Virginia	WVU Coliseum	14,000

Big Sky

	Home Floor	Seats
CS-Northridge	The Matadome	1,600
CS-Sacramento	Memorial Auditorium	2,603
Eastern Wash.	Reese Court	6,000
Idaho St.	Holt Arena	8,000
Montana	Adams Center	7,500
Montana St.	Worthington Arena	7,250
Northern Arizona	Walkup Skydome	7,000
Portland St.	Rose Garden	19,980
	& Memorial Coliseum	12,000
Weber St.	Dee Events Center	12,000

Big South

	Home Floor	Seats
Charleston So	CSU Fieldhouse	1,500
Coastal Carolina	Kimbel Gymnasium	1,480
Elon	Koury Center	2,000
High Point	Millis Center	1,800
Liberty	Vines Center	9,000
NC-Asheville	Justice Center	1,570
	& Asheville Civic Center	6,000
Radford	Dedmon Center	5,000
Winthrop	Winthrop Coliseum	6,100

Big Ten

	Home Floor	Seats
Illinois	Assembly Hall	16,450
Indiana	Assembly Hall	17,357
Iowa	Carver-Hawkeye Arena	15,500
Michigan	Crisler Arena	13,562
Michigan St.	Breslin Events Center	15,138
Minnesota	Williams Arena	14,321
Northwestern	Welsh-Ryan Arena	8,117
Ohio St.	Value City Arena	17,500
Penn St.	Bryce Jordan Center	15,261
Purdue	Mackey Arena	14,123
Wisconsin	Kohl Center	17,142

Big 12

North	Home Floor	Seats
Colorado	Coors Events Conference Ctr.	11,198
Iowa St.	Hilton Coliseum	14,092
Kansas	Allen Fieldhouse	16,300
Kansas St.	Bramlage Coliseum	13,500
Missouri	Hearnes Center	13,300
Nebraska	Devaney Sports Center	14,200

South	Home Floor	Seats
Baylor	Ferrell Center	10,284
Oklahoma	Lloyd Noble Center	11,100
Oklahoma St.	Gallagher-Iba Arena	13,611
Texas	Erwin Center	16,175
Texas A&M	Reed Arena	12,700
Texas Tech	United Spirit Arena	15,000

Big West

	Home Floor	Seats
Boise St.	BSU Pavilion	12,380
Cal Poly-SLO	Mott Gym	3,500
CS-Fullerton	Titan Gym	3,500
Idaho	Kibbie Dome	10,000
Long Beach St.	The Pyramid	5,000
Pacific	Spanos Center	6,150
UC-Irvine	Bren Events Center	5,000
UC-Santa Barbara	The Thunderdome	6,000
Utah St.	The Smith Spectrum	10,270

Colonial

	Home Floor	Seats
American	Bender Arena	5,000
East Carolina	Minges Coliseum	7,500
George Mason	Patriot Center	10,000
James Madison	JMU Convocation Center	7,156
NC-Wilmington	Trask Coliseum	6,100
Old Dominion	Norfolk Scope	10,253
Richmond	Robins Center	9,171
VCU	Siegel Center	7,500
Wm. & Mary	William & Mary Hall	8,600

Conference USA

	Home Floor	Seats
UAB	Bartow Arena	8,500
Cincinnati	Shoemaker Center	13,176
DePaul	All State Areana	17,500
Houston	Hofheinz Pavilion	8,479
Louisville	Freedom Hall	18,865
Marquette	Bradley Center	19,150
Memphis	The Pyramid	20,142
UNC Charlotte	Halton Arena	9,105
Saint Louis	Kiel Center	20,000
South Florida	Sun Dome	10,411
Southern Miss	Green Coliseum	8,095
Tulane	New Orleans Arena	18,000

Ivy League

	Home Floor	Seats
Brown	Pizzitola Sports Center	2,800
Columbia	Levien Gymnasium	3,408
Cornell	Newman Arena	4,750
Dartmouth	Leede Arena	2,200
Harvard	Briggs Athletic Center	2,195
Penn	The Palestra	8,700
Princeton	Jadwin Gymnasium	6,854
Yale	Lee Amphitheater	3,100

Metro Atlantic

	Home Floor	Seats
Canisius	HSBC Arena	19,500
	& Koessler Athletic Center	1,800
Fairfield	Alumni Hall	2,479
Iona	Mulcahy Center	3,200
Loyola-MD	Reitz Arena	3,000
Manhattan	Draddy Gymnasium	3,000
Marist	McCann Center	3,944
Niagara	HSBC Arena	19,500
	& Gallagher Center	3,200
Rider	Alumni Gymnasium	1,650
St. Peter's	Yanitelli Center	3,200
Siena	Pepsi Arena	15,500

Mid American

	Home Floor	Seats
Akron	JAR Arena	5,942
Ball St.	John E. Wortham Arena	11,500
Bowling Green	Anderson Arena	5,200
Buffalo	Alumni Arena	8,500
Central Mich.	Rose Arena	5,200
Eastern Mich.	Convocation Center	8,824
Kent	MAC Arena	6,327
Marshall	Henderson Center	9,043
Miami-OH	Millett Hall	9,200
Northern Illinois	Chick Evans Field House	6,044
Ohio Univ.	Convocation Center	13,000
Toledo	Savage Hall	9,000
Western Mich.	University Arena	5,800

Mid-Continent

	Home Floor	Seats
Chicago St.	Dickens Athletic Center	2,500
IU-PUI	IU-PUI Gym	2,000
Missouri-K.C.	Municipal Auditorium	9,287
Oakland	Oakland Arena	3,000
Oral Roberts	Mabee Center	10,575
Southern Utah	Centrum	5,300
Valparaiso	Athletics-Recreation Center	4,500
Western Ill.	Western Hall	5,139
Youngstown St.	Beeghly Center	8,000

College Basketball (Cont.)

Mid-Eastern Athletic

	Home Floor	Seats
Bethune-Cookman	Moore Gym	3,000
Coppin St.	Coppin Center	3,000
Delaware St.	Memorial Hall	3,000
Florida A&M	Gaither Gym	3,350
Hampton	Hampton Convocation Center	7,200
Howard	Burr Gym	3,000
MD-East.Shore	Tawes Gym	1,200
Morgan St.	Hill Fieldhouse	5,000
Norfolk St.	Echols Hall	7,600
N. Carolina A&T	Corbett Sports Center	7,500
S. Carolina St.	SHM Center	3,200

Midwestern

	Home Floor	Seats
Butler	Hinkle Fieldhouse	11,043
Cleveland St.	CSU Convocation Center	13,610
Detroit Mercy	Calihan Hall	8,837
IL-Chicago	UIC Pavilion	8,000
Loyola-IL	Gentile Center	5,200
WI-Green Bay	Brown County Arena	5,600
WI-Milwaukee	Klotsche Center	5,000
Wright St.	Nutter Center	10,632

Missouri Valley

	Home Floor	Seats
Bradley	Carver Arena	10,825
Creighton	Omaha Civic Auditorium	9,493
Drake	Knapp Center	7,002
Evansville	Roberts Stadium	12,300
Illinois St.	Redbird Arena	10,200
Indiana St.	Hulman Center	10,200
Northern Iowa	UNI-Dome	10,000
Southern Ill.	SIU Arena	10,014
SW Missouri St.	Hammons Student Center	8,846
Wichita St.	Levitt Arena	10,423

Mountain West

	Home Floor	Seats
Air Force	Clune Arena	6,003
BYU	Marriott Center	22,700
Colorado St.	Moby Arena	8,754
San Diego St.	Cox Arena at the Aztec Bowl	12,000
UNLV	Thomas & Mack Center	18,500
New Mexico	University Arena (The Pit)	18,018
Utah	Huntsman Center	15,000
Wyoming	Arena-Auditorium	15,028

Northeast

	Home Floor	Seats
Central Conn. St.	Detrick Gym	4,500
Farleigh Dickinson	Rothman Center	5,000
LIU-Brooklyn	Schwartz Athletic Center	1,200
MD-Balt. County	Retriever Activity Center	4,024
Monmouth	Boylan Gym	2,500
Mt. St. Mary's	Knott Arena	3,196
Quinnipiac	Burt Kahn Court	1,500
Robert Morris	Sewall Center	3,056
Sacred Heart	Pitt Center	5,000
St. Francis-NY	Phys. Ed. Center	1,400
St. Francis-PA	DeGol Arena	3,500
Wagner	Spiro Sports Center	2,100

Ohio Valley

	Home Floor	Seats
Austin Peay	Dunn Center	9,000
Eastern Illinois	Lantz Gym	5,300
Eastern Ky.	McBrayer Arena	6,500
Morehead St.	Johnson Arena	6,500
Murray St.	Regional Special Events Ctr.	8,600
SE Missouri St.	Show Me Center	7,000
Tennessee-Martin	Skyhawk Arena	6,700
Tennessee St.	Gentry Complex	10,500
Tennessee Tech	Eblen Center	10,152

Pacific-10

	Home Floor	Seats
Arizona	McKale Center	14,545
Arizona St.	Wells Fargo Arena	14,198
California	Haas Pavillion	12,172
Oregon	McArthur Court	9,087
Oregon St.	Gill Coliseum	10,400
Stanford	Maples Pavilion	7,500
UCLA	Pauley Pavilion	12,819
USC	LA Sports Arena	15,509
Washington	Bank of America Hec Edmundson Pavilion	10,000
Washington. St.	Friel Court	12,058

Patriot League

	Home Floor	Seats
Army	Christl Arena	5,043
Bucknell	Davis Gym	2,380
Colgate	Cotterell Court	3,000
Holy Cross	Hart Recreation Center	3,600
Lafayette	Kirby Field House	3,500
Lehigh	Stabler Arena	5,600
Navy	Alumni Hall	5,710

Southeastern

Eastern	Home Floor	Seats
Florida	O'Connell Center	12,000
Georgia	Stegeman Coliseum	10,523
Kentucky	Rupp Arena	23,000
South Carolina	Frank McGuire Arena	12,401
Tennessee	Thompson-Boling Arena	24,535
Vanderbilt	Memorial Gymnasium	14,168
Western	**Home Floor**	**Seats**
Alabama	Coleman Coliseum	15,043
Arkansas	Bud Walton Arena	19,200
Auburn	Eaves-Memorial Coliseum	10,108
LSU	Maravich Assembly Center	14,164
Mississippi	Tad Smith Coliseum	8,135
Mississippi St.	Humphrey Coliseum	10,500

Southern

	Home Floor	Seats
Appalachian St.	Varsity Gymnasium	8,000
The Citadel	McAlister Field House	6,200
Coll. of Charleston	Kresse Arena	3,500
Davidson	Belk Arena	5,700
E. Tenn. St.	Memorial Center	12,000
Furman	Timmons Arena	5,000
Ga. Southern	Hanner Fieldhouse	5,500
NC-Greensboro	Fleming Gymnasium	2,320
Tenn-Chatt.	UTC Arena	11,218
VMI	Cameron Hall	5,029
W. Carolina	Ramsey Center	7,286
Wofford	Johnson Arena	3,500

Southland

	Home Floor	Seats
Lamar	Montagne Center	10,800
McNeese St.	Burton Coliseum	8,000
Nicholls St.	Stopher Gym	3,800
NE Louisiana	Ewing Coliseum	8,000
Northwestern St.	Prather Coliseum	3,900
Sam Houston St.	Johnson Coliseum	6,172
SE Louisiana	University Center	7,500
SW Texas St.	Strahan Coliseum	7,200
S.F. Austin St.	W.R. Johnson Coliseum	7,200
TX-Arlington	Texas Hall	4,200
TX-San Antonio	Convocation Center	5,100

Southwestern

	Home Floor	Seats
Alabama A&M	T.M. Elmore Gym	8,000
Alabama St.	Joe Reed Acadome	7,000
Alcorn St.	Whitney Complex	7,000
Arkansas-Pine Bluff	Johnson Complex	4,500
Grambling St.	Memorial Gym	4,500
Jackson St.	Williams Center	8,000
Miss.Valley St.	Harrison Athletic Complex	6,000
Prairie View A&M	The Baby Dome	6,600
Southern-BR	Clark Activity Center	7,500
TX Southern	Health & P.E. Building	8,100

Sun Belt

	Home Floor	Seats
Ark-Little Rock	Alltel Arena	18,000
Arkansas St	Convocation Center	10,563
Denver	Magness Arena	7,200
Florida International	Golden Panther Arena	5,000
Louisiana Tech	Thomas Assembly Center	8,000
Middle Tenn. St.	Murphy Center	11,520
New Mexico St.	Pan American Center	13,071
New Orleans	Lakefront Arena	10,000
North Texas	The Super Pit	10,000
South Alabama	Mitchell Center	10,000
SW Louisiana	The Cajundome	12,800
Western Ky.	E.A. Diddle Arena	11,300

Trans America

	Home Floor	Seats
Campbell	Carter Gym	1,050
Central Fla.	UCF Arena	5,100
Fla. Atlantic	FAU Gym	5,000
Georgia St.	GSU Sports Arena	5,500
Jacksonville	Memorial Coliseum	9,150
Jacksonville St.	Mathews Coliseum	5,500
Mercer	Macon Coliseum	2,500
Samford	Seibert Hall	4,000
Stetson	Edmunds Center	5,000
Troy St.	Sartain Hall	3,000

West Coast

	Home Floor	Seats
Gonzaga	Martin Centre	4,000
Loyola Marymount	Gersten Pavilion	4,156
Pepperdine	Firestone Fieldhouse	3,104
Portland	Chiles Center	5,000
St. Mary's-CA	McKeon Pavilion	3,500
San Diego	Jenny Craig Pavilion	5,000
San Francisco	War Memorial Gym	5,300
Santa Clara	Toso Pavilion	5,000

Western Athletic

	Home Floor	Seats
Fresno St.	Selland Arena	10,132
Hawaii	Stan Sherif Center	10,225
Nevada	Lawlor Events Center	11,200
Rice	Autry Court	5,000
San Jose St.	The Events Center	5,000
SMU	Moody Coliseum	8,998
TCU	Daniel-Meyer Coliseum	7,166
Tulsa	Reynolds Center	8,355
UTEP	Haskins Center	12,222

Independents

	Home Floor	Seats
Albany	Rec. and Convocation Center	5,000
Belmont	Striplin Gym	2,500
Centenary	Gold Dome	3,000
Stonybrook	Pritchard Gym	5,226
Texas-Pan Am	Health/PE Fieldhouse	3,500

Future NCAA Final Four Sites

Men

Year	Arena	Seats	Location
2001	Metrodome	50,000	Minneapolis
2002	Georgia Dome	40,000	Atlanta
2003	Louisiana Superdome	53,500	New Orleans
2004	Alamodome	20,557*	San Antonio
2005	Trans World Dome	66,000	St. Louis
2006	RCA Dome	47,100	Indianapolis
2007	Georgia Dome	40,000	Atlanta

*This is the listed capacity for Spurs games at the Alamo-dome. It is likely that the seating will be reconfigured to fit more spectators for the Final Four.

Women

Year	Arena	Seats	Location
2001	Kiel Center	20,000	St. Louis
2002	Alamodome	26,000	San Antonio
2003	Georgia Dome	40,000	Atlanta
2004	New Orleans Sports Arena	17,832	New Orleans

COLLEGE FOOTBALL

The 40 Largest I-A Stadiums

The 40 largest stadiums in NCAA Division I-A college football heading into the 2000 season. Note that (*) indicates stadium not on campus.

		Location	Seats	Home Team	Conference	Built	Field
1	Michigan Stadium	Ann Arbor, Mich.	**107,501**	Michigan	Big Ten	1927	Grass
2	Neyland Stadium	Knoxville, Tenn.	**104,079**	Tennessee	SEC-East	1921	Grass
3	Ohio Stadium	Columbus, Ohio	**103,801**	Ohio St.	Big Ten	1922	Grass
4	Rose Bowl*	Pasadena, Calif.	**98,636**	UCLA	Pac-10	1922	Grass
5	Beaver Stadium	University Park, Pa.	**93,967**	Penn St.	Big Ten	1960	Grass
6	LA Memorial Coliseum*	Los Angeles, Calif.	**92,000**	USC	Pac-10	1923	Grass
7	Tiger Stadium	Baton Rouge, La.	**91,600**	LSU	SEC-West	1924	Grass
8	Sanford Stadium	Athens, Ga.	**86,520**	Georgia	SEC-East	1929	Grass
9	Stanford Stadium	Stanford, Calif.	**85,500**	Stanford	Pac-10	1921	Grass
10	Jordan-Hare Stadium	Auburn, Ala.	**85,214**	Auburn	SEC-West	1939	Grass
11	Bryant-Denny Stadium	Tuscaloosa, Ala.	**83,818**	Alabama	SEC-West	1929	Grass
12	Legion Field*	Birmingham, Ala.	**83,091**	Alabama/UAB	SEC/Indy	1927	Grass
13	Florida Field	Gainesville, Fla.	**83,000**	Florida	SEC-East	1929	Grass
14	Memorial Stadium	Clemson, S.C.	**81,474**	Clemson	ACC	1942	Grass
15	Kyle Field	College Station, Tex.	**80,650**	Texas A&M	Big 12-South	1925	Grass
16	Williams-Brice Stadium	Columbia, S.C.	**80,250**	South Carolina	SEC-East	1934	Grass
17	Royal-Memorial Stadium	Austin, Tex.	**80,082**	Texas	Big 12-South	1924	Grass
18	Notre Dame Stadium	Notre Dame, Ind.	**80,012**	Notre Dame	Independent	1930	Grass
19	Doak Campbell Stadium	Tallahasse, Fla.	**80,000**	Florida St.	ACC	1950	Grass
20	Camp Randall Stadium	Madison, Wisc.	**76,129**	Wisconsin	Big Ten	1917	Turf
21	Memorial Stadium	Berkeley, Calif.	**75,028**	California	Pac-10	1923	Grass
22	Memorial Stadium	Lincoln, Neb.	**74,506**	Nebraska	Big 12-North	1923	Turf
23	Sun Devil Stadium	Tempe, Ariz.	**73,379**	Arizona St.	Pac-10	1959	Grass
24	Oklahoma Memorial Field	Norman, Okla.	**72,765**	Oklahoma	Big 12-South	1924	Grass
25	Husky Stadium	Seattle, Wash.	**72,500**	Washington	Pac-10	1920	Turf
26	Orange Bowl*	Miami, Fla.	**72,314**	Miami-FL	Big East	1935	Grass
27	Spartan Stadium	East Lansing, Mich.	**72,027**	Michigan St.	Big Ten	1957	Turf
28	Qualcomm Stadium*	San Diego, Calif.	**71,000**	San Diego St.	Mountain West	1967	Grass
29	Memorial Stadium	Champaign, Ill.	**70,904**	Illinois	Big Ten	1923	Turf
30	Kinnick Stadium	Iowa City, Iowa	**70,397**	Iowa	Big Ten	1929	Grass
31	Citrus Bowl*	Orlando, Fla.	**70,188**	Central Florida	Independent	1936	Grass
32	Rice Stadium	Houston, Tex.	**70,000**	Rice	WAC	1950	Turf
33	Superdome*	New Orleans, La.	**69,767**	Tulane	USA	1975	Turf
34	HHH Metrodome*	Minneapolis, Minn.	**69,172**	Minnesota	Big Ten	1982	Turf
35	Commonwealth	Lexington, Ky.	**68,000**	Kentucky	SEC	1973	Grass
36	Ross-Ade Stadium	W. Lafayette, Ind.	**67,861**	Purdue	Big Ten	1924	Grass
37	Veterans Stadium*	Philadelphia, Pa.	**66,592**	Temple	Big East	1971	Turf
38	Cougar Stadium	Provo, Utah	**65,000**	BYU	Mountain West	1964	Grass
39	Mountaineer Field	Morgantown, W. Va.	**63,500**	West Virginia	Big East	1980	Turf
40	Liberty Bowl	Memphis, Tenn.	**62,380**	Memphis	USA	1965	Grass

Note: The capacities for several stadiums including the Rose Bowl, Louisiana Superdome and Sun Devil Stadium are often listed differently for other events, such as bowl games, which they host.

2000 Conference Home Fields

NCAA Division I-A conference by conference listing includes member teams heading into the 2000 season. Note that (*) indicates stadium is not on campus.

Atlantic Coast

	Stadium	Built	Seats	Field
Clemson	Memorial	1942	81,474	Grass
Duke	Wallace Wade	1929	33,941	Grass
Florida St.	Doak Campbell	1950	80,000	Grass
Ga. Tech	Bobby Dodd	1913	46,000	Grass
Maryland	Byrd	1950	48,055	Grass
N. Carolina	Kenan Memorial	1927	60,000	Grass
N.C. State	Carter-Finley	1966	51,500	Grass
Virginia	Scott	1931	61,500	Grass
Wake Forest	Groves	1968	31,500	Grass

Big East

	Stadium	Built	Seats	Field
Boston Col.	Alumni	1957	44,500	Turf
Miami-FL	Orange Bowl*	1935	72,314	Grass
Pittsburgh	Three Rivers Stadium	1970	59,600	Turf
Rutgers	Rutgers	1994	41,500	Grass
Syracuse	Carrier Dome	1980	49,550	Turf
Temple	Veterans*	1971	66,592	Turf
Va. Tech	Lane	1965	50,000	Grass
West Va.	Mountaineer Fld.	1980	63,500	Turf

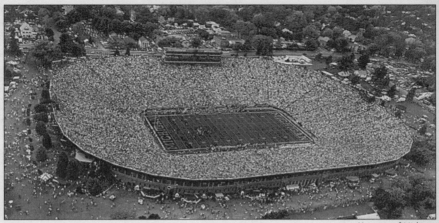

University of Michigan

After getting passed by Tennessee's Neyland Stadium, Michigan Stadium added more than 5,000 seats in 1998. The Wolverines can once again lay claim to playing their home games at the nation's largest college football venue.

Big Ten

	Stadium	Built	Seats	Field
Illinois	Memorial	1923	70,904	Turf
Indiana	Memorial	1960	52,354	Grass
Iowa	Kinnick	1929	70,397	Grass
Michigan	Michigan	1927	107,501	Grass
Michigan St.	Spartan	1957	72,027	Turf
Minnesota	Metrodome*	1982	69,172	Turf
Northwestern	Ryan Field	1926	47,130	Grass
Ohio St.	Ohio	1922	103,801	Grass
Penn St.	Beaver	1960	93,967	Grass
Purdue	Ross-Ade	1924	67,861	Grass
Wisconsin	Camp Randall	1917	76,129	Turf

Big 12

NORTH	Stadium	Built	Seats	Field
Colorado	Folsom Field	1924	51,808	Turf
Iowa St.	Jack Trice Field	1975	43,000	Grass
Kansas	Memorial	1921	50,250	Turf
Kansas St.	Wagner Field	1968	50,000	Turf
Missouri	Faurot Field	1926	62,000	Grass
Nebraska	Memorial	1923	74,506	Turf

SOUTH	Stadium	Built	Seats	Field
Baylor	Floyd Casey	1950	50,000	Grass
Oklahoma	Memorial	1924	72,765	Grass
Oklahoma St.	Lewis Field	1920	48,000	Turf
Texas	Royal-Mem.	1924	80,082	Grass
Texas A&M	Kyle Field	1925	80,650	Grass
Texas Tech	Jones	1947	50,500	Turf

Note: The annual Oklahoma-Texas game has been played at the Cotton Bowl (capacity 68,252) in Dallas since 1937.

Big West

	Stadium	Built	Seats	Field
Arkansas St.	Indian	1974	33,410	Grass
Boise St.	Bronco	1970	30,000	Turf
Idaho	Martin Stadium	1972	37,500	Turf
New Mexico St.	Aggie Memorial	1978	30,343	Grass
North Texas	Fouts Field	1952	30,500	Turf
Utah St.	Romney	1968	30,257	Grass

Conference USA

	Stadium	Built	Seats	Field
UAB	Legion	1927	83,091	Grass
Army	Michie	1924	39,929	Turf
Cincinnati	Nippert	1924	35,000	Turf
E. Carolina	Dowdy-Ficklen	1963	43,000	Grass
Houston	Robertson	1942	31,000	Grass
Louisville	Papa John's Cardinal	1998	42,000	Turf
Memphis	Liberty Bowl*	1965	62,380	Grass
Southern Miss	M.M. Roberts	1976	33,000	Grass
Tulane	Superdome*	1975	69,767	Turf

I-A Independents

	Stadium	Built	Seats	Field
C. Florida	Citrus Bowl	1936	70,188	Grass
Connecticut	Memorial	1953	16,200	Grass
Louisiana Tech	Joe Aillet	1968	30,600	Grass
Middle Tennessee St.	Johnny Red Floyd	1933	30,880	Turf
Navy	Navy-Marine Corps Memorial	1959	30,000	Grass
Louisiana-Monroe	Malone	1978	30,427	Grass
Notre Dame	Notre Dame	1930	80,012	Grass
Louisiana-Lafayette	Cajun Field	1971	31,000	Grass

College Football (Cont.)

Mid-American

	Stadium	Built	Seats	Field
Akron	Rubber Bowl*	1940	35,202	Turf
Ball St.	Ball State	1967	21,581	Grass
Buffalo	UB	1993	31,000	Grass
Bowling Green	Doyt Perry	1966	30,599	Grass
Central Mich.	Kelly/Shorts	1972	30,199	Turf
Eastern Mich.	Rynearson	1969	30,200	Turf
Kent	Dix	1969	30,520	Turf
Marshall	Marshall	1991	40,000	Turf
Miami-OH	Fred Yager	1983	30,012	Grass
Northern Ill.	Huskie	1965	31,000	Turf
Ohio Univ.	Peden	1929	20,000	Grass
Toledo	Glass Bowl	1937	26,248	Turf
Western Mich.	Waldo	1939	30,200	Grass

Mountain West

	Stadium	Built	Seats	Field
Air Force	Falcon	1962	52,480	Grass
BYU	Cougar	1964	65,000	Grass
Colorado St.	Hughes	1968	30,000	Grass
New Mexico	University	1960	31,218	Grass
San Diego St.	Qualcomm*	1967	71,400	Grass
UNLV	Sam Boyd*	1971	40,000	Grass
Utah	Rice-Eccles	1927†	45,634	Grass
Wyoming	War Memorial	1950	33,500	Grass

†Utah's Rice-Eccles Stadium was rebuilt in 1998.

Pacific-10

	Stadium	Built	Seats	Field
Arizona	Arizona	1928	56,002	Grass
Arizona St.	Sun Devil	1959	73,379	Grass
California	Memorial	1923	75,028	Grass
Oregon	Autzen	1967	41,698	Turf
Oregon St.	Reser's	1953	35,362	Turf
Stanford	Stanford	1921	85,500	Grass
UCLA	Rose Bowl*	1922	98,636	Grass
USC	LA Coliseum*	1923	92,000	Grass
Washington	Husky	1920	72,500	Turf
Washington St.	Martin	1972	37,600	Turf

Southeastern

EAST	Stadium	Built	Seats	Field
Florida	Florida Field	1929	83,000	Grass
Georgia	Sanford	1929	86,520	Grass
Kentucky	Commonwealth	1973	68,000	Grass
S. Carolina	Williams-Brice	1934	80,250	Grass
Tennessee	Neyland	1921	104,079	Grass
Vanderbilt	Vanderbilt	1981	41,600	Grass

WEST	Stadium	Built	Seats	Field
Alabama	Bryant-Denny	1929	83,818	Grass
	& Legion	1927	83,091	Grass
Arkansas	Razorback	1938	51,000	Grass
	& War Memorial*	1948	53,727	Grass
Auburn	Jordan-Hare	1939	85,214	Grass
LSU	Tiger	1924	91,600	Grass
Mississippi	Vaught-Hem'way	1915	50,577	Grass
Miss. St.	Scott Field	1915	40,656	Grass

Note: EAST–Vanderbilt Stadium was rebuilt in 1981.

SEC Championship Game

The first two SEC Championship Games were played at Legion Field in Birmingham, Ala., in 1992 and 1993. The game was moved to Atlanta's 71,228-seat Georgia Dome in 1994.

Western Athletic

	Stadium	Built	Seats	Field
Fresno St.	Bulldog	1980	41,031	Grass
Hawaii	Aloha*	1975	50,000	Turf
Nevada	Mackay	1967	31,545	Grass
Rice	Rice	1950	70,000	Turf
San Jose St.	Spartan	1933	30,578	Grass
SMU	Gerald J. Ford Stadium	2000	32,000	Grass
TCU	Amon Carter	1929	44,008	Grass
Tulsa	Skelly	1930	40,385	Turf
UTEP	Sun Bowl*	1963	52,000	Turf

Bowl Games

Listed alphabetically and updated as of Sept. 1, 2000. The Bowl Championship Series calls for the national championship game (No. 1 vs. No. 2) to rotate between the Sugar Bowl (2000), Orange Bowl (2001) and Rose Bowl (2002). See The Bowl Championship Series on page 179.

	Stadium	Built	Seats	Field			Stadium	Built	Seats	Field
Alamo	Alamodome	1993	65,000	Turf		Micron/PC	Pro Player	1987	74,915	Grass
Aloha	Aloha	1975	50,000	Turf		Mobile Alabama	Ladd Peeble	1948	40,646	Grass
Cotton	Cotton	1930	68,252	Grass		Motor City	Pontiac Silverdome	1975	80,368	Turf
Fiesta	Sun Devil	1959	73,656	Grass		Music City	Adelphia	1999	67,000	Grass
Fla. Citrus	Fla. Citrus Bowl	1936	70,188	Grass		Oahu	Aloha	1975	50,000	Turf
Gator	ALLTEL	1995	73,000	Grass		Orange	Pro Player	1987	74,916	Grass
Holiday	Qualcomm	1967	71,000	Grass		Outback	Houlihan's	1967	66,005	Grass
Humanitarian	Bronco	1970	30,000	Turf		Peach	Georgia Dome	1992	71,228	Turf
Independence	Independence	1936	50,832	Grass		Rose	Rose Bowl	1922	102,083	Grass
Insight.com	Arizona	1928	57,803	Grass		Sugar	Superdome	1975	77,446	Turf
Las Vegas	Sam Boyd	1971	40,000	Turf		Sun	Sun Bowl	1963	52,000	Turf
Liberty	Liberty Bowl	1965	62,380	Grass						

Playing Sites

Alamo— San Antonio; **Aloha**— Honolulu; **Cotton**— Dallas; **Fiesta**— Tempe; **Florida Citrus**— Orlando; **Gator**— Jacksonville; **Holiday**— San Diego; **Humanitarian**— Boise; **Independence**— Shreveport; **Insight.com**—Tucson; **Las Vegas**— Las Vegas; **Liberty**— Memphis; **Micron/PC**—Miami; **Mobile Alabama**—Mobile; **Motor City**— Pontiac; **Music City**— Nashville; **Oahu**— Honolulu; **Orange**— Miami; **Outback**— Tampa; **Peach**— Atlanta; **Rose**— Pasadena; **Sugar**— New Orleans; **Sun**— El Paso.

Business

AP/Wide World Photos

Major Windfall

This golf thing is really beginning to pay off for Tiger Woods.

by

Bob Stevens

The morning after he won another million dollars at the NEC Championship at Firestone, in the dark, with the flu, he got up and did a clinic for thousands of Akron, Ohio-area kids. Then he flew nearly all the way across the country to Palm Springs, Calif. to play Sergio Garcia in the made-for-TV *Battle at Bighorn* that he made possible. With the effects of the flu hitting him with full force, he finished the round under the lights — and years from now, no one will remember that he actually lost.

That 24-hour period summarizes the essence of Tiger Woods golfer, and Tiger Woods businessman. He still hasn't starred in a movie (though he did cross the Screen Actors Guild picket line to shoot a Buick commercial in Canada). He doesn't sing (at least not in public) or dance (except when chasing putts toward the hole). He also

Bob Stevens is an anchor for ESPN's *SportsCenter* and *SportsWeekly*.

doesn't abuse alcohol or drugs, get into bar fights, pick up speeding tickets or even wear an earring.

Yet in the words of Mark McCormack, the super-agent who made Arnold Palmer the "King of Endorsements" long after he quit winning on tour and whose firm, IMG, also represents Woods, "Arnold Palmer was the Thomas Edison of golf. Tiger Woods is Bill Gates."

That proclamation was made *before* Woods won the U.S. Open in June by a record-15 strokes at Pebble Beach. The week after his NEC conquest, word got out that Nike, the company that signed Woods to the unheard of $40 million, 5-year deal before he ever hit a ball as a pro, had negotiated a 5-year extension that could make Tiger $100 million, or more with profit sharing.

The 160-pound Tiger is marketing's 500-pound gorilla now. His total from just 11 endorsement deals is over $50 million per year, far surpassing Michael Jordan's top take, reportedly at $35 million. And remember, all of this comes before he wins another

No big deal. Just another press conference announcing yet another multi-million dollar endorsement deal for **Tiger Woods**. The 24-year-old not only dominated the golf world in 2000 but Madison Ave. as well, with endorsements totalling over $50 million for the year.

dime on the tour.

The companies in Tiger's den? A cross-section of world commerce as diverse as American Express, Rolex, Buick and Wheaties on one end, to EA Sports computer games, TLC Laser Eye centers, Asahi Coffee in Japan and, yes, Titleist golf clubs — the same ones he bounced the ball off dozens of times in the commercial for Nike (oops). Chances are he'll end up playing Nike clubs someday, once Nike starts making them as part of their plan to grow their golf business from $200 million annually to $700 million.

Don't think for a minute that Tiger is the only golfer that benefits from all of this. Although the wall-to-wall Tiger TV coverage might actually limit the exposure of other players,

Davis Love III signed a new deal with Titleist worth $50 million over 10 years. And after helping double the TV rights fees the networks paid in 1998, Tiger could be the catalyst to see them double again in 2001, a figure that would make the $5 million dollar tournament commonplace. And that's money Woods would have to win in order to take home.

The most amazing thing about Tiger's outrageous endorsement deal with Nike? Nobody has said he's being overpaid. In the words of his sometimes overbearing father Earl, who's been right more than he's been wrong, "When the next contract comes around, this one will look like chump change." By the way, Tiger turns 25 on December 30, 2000. ■

AP/Wide World Photos

"Here's the thing, Joe. I really think Bernie should be batting behind Paul, and then you've got Tino...and..." Yankees skipper **Joe Torre**, left, can probably stand a little meddling from owner **George Steinbrenner** as long as "The Boss" keeps supplying the cash. The Yankees' payroll topped $100 million in 2000 and the club remained in baseball's elite on the field as well.

Bob Stevens' Top Ten Business Highlights of the Year

10. **Redskins owner Daniel Snyder** charges admission to training camp, allowing Dallas Cowboys scouts to watch, take notes, and subsequently beat the Redskins on Monday Night Football in week three of the regular season. Snyder still loses money on camp.

9. **Ottawa Senators Alexei Yashin** is sued by season-ticket holders for sitting out the final season of his $3.6 million contract, demanding it be tripled. Yashin loses to the team in court and is forced to play the 2000-01 season for the payout that he originally declined.

8. **The St. Louis Cardinals pay** a $500,000 insurance premium to protect themselves for up to $12 million in lost revenue if Mark McGwire misses more than a month of the season. It turns out to be a shrewd move as he misses almost half the season.

7. **Sign of the times?** Mark Martin's Winston Cup car will be sponsored by Viagra for the next 5 years, at a reported $14 million per year.

6. **The WWF announces** a $100 million investment and NBC partnership in the new XFL to debut in February 2001 in eight cities. It will not go head-to-head with the

Doug Pensinger/Allsport

Washington Redskins owner **Daniel Snyder** made the headlines and ruffled some feathers in 2000, first by signing pretty much any free agent he could get his hands on, and then by opening Redskins training camp to the public and charging for admission and parking.

NFL but rather conduct a ten-game schedule in February, March and April.

5. **NBC's $3.5 billion deal** for exclusive rights to the Olympics stumbles out of the blocks in Sydney as the far-off location and the huge time differential causes taped segments and less interest in the U.S., providing some of the lowest television ratings for the Summer Games in the modern era.

4. **Three new Major League ballparks** open and the fans flock to them in record numbers. San Francisco Giants attendance increases 60 percent in the beautiful Pac Bell Park, Detroit Tigers attendance shoots up 29 percent in Comerica, and Houston Astros at-tendance jumps 15 percent in Enron Field.

3. **More Tigermania** (in two parts) – a. Woods admits he endorsed a slightly different Nike golf ball than the one he actually uses on Tour. Not missing a beat, or a chance to make a buck, Nike then announces it will market the "real thing."

b. A bidder at an on-line charity auction reportedly pays $1.7 million to play a round of golf with Woods.

2. **"The Boss," George Steinbrenner,** makes the New York Yankees the first professional sports team with a payroll of over $100 million. Hey, they may spend a lot but at least they win. The Baltimore

Orioles boast quite a payroll as well but become the first losing team with a payroll in excess of $80 million.

1. **Of the 17 dot-com companies** to spend $2 million or more for a 30-second spot in the Super Bowl, only six still had the same advertising agency six months later and one company had already gone out of business. ∎

TIGER'S TAKE

Tiger Woods' reported five-year, $100 million deal with Nike is mere pocket change compared to the deal Salton recently gave George Foreman for the right to use the former champ's name on their grills and other assorted kitchen appliances. Below is the list of top five endorsement deals ever signed by an athlete.

Athlete	Company	Yrs./$M
George Foreman	Salton	5/137.5
Tiger Woods	Nike	5/100.0
Grant Hill	Fila	7/80.0
Allen Iverson	Reebok	10/50.0
Davis Love III	Titleist	10/50.0

Note: Terms of Michael Jordan's last deal with Nike were not disclosed.

WHAT A COUNTRY!

A few world records and gold medals can go a long way when it comes to endorsement deals. American swimming hero Lenny Krayzelburg, who left the Ukraine with his parents in 1989 and became a U.S. citizen in 1995, is already swimming in endorsement deals (companies listed).

Company	Type
Speedo	Clothing – swimwear, etc.
Hebrew National	Food – kosher meats
Powerbar	Food – nutritional bars
IBM	Information technology
Pfizer	Pharmaceuticals
Goodyear	Tires and rubber products
Kellogg's	Food – cereals, etc.

Source: Octagon Marketing

OOH, THAT'S A NICE PURSE

The 2000 U.S. Open tennis tournament is the first annual sporting event to crack the $15 million barrier in prize money. Listed are various major sporting events and their total purses.

Player	Amount (millions)
U.S. Open (tennis)	$15.0
Wimbledon (tennis)	12.6
Daytona 500 (auto racing)	10.0
French Open (tennis)	9.6
Indianapolis 500 (auto racing)	9.0
Australian Open (tennis)	6.5
The Players Championship (golf)	5.0
The Masters (golf)	4.6

Source: USTA and USA Today

RIGHTS ON THE MONEY

Sure, tradition is great, but when you see the kind of dollars being thrown around by companies for the right to stick their name on a stadium or arena, you can understand why owners are going for the cash. And you can understand why names like Fenway Park, RFK Stadium, and Candlestick Park are a thing of the past. Below are the richest naming rights deals in NFL history.

Stadium, Team	Annual Value (millions)
CMGI Field, New England	$7.600
FedEx Field, Washington	7.593
PSINet Stadium, Baltimore	5.275
Raymond James Stadium, Tampa Bay	3.055
Adelphia Coliseum, Tennessee	2.000
Ericsson Stadium, Carolina	2.000
Pro Player Stadium, Miami	2.000

Source: Street & Smith's SportsBusiness Journal ∎

1999-00 Top Rated TV Sports Events

Final 1999-00 network television ratings for nationally-telecast sports events, according to Nielsen Media Research. Covers period from Sept. 1, 1999 through Aug. 31, 2000. Events are listed with ratings points and audience share; each ratings point represents 1,008,000 households and shares indicate percentage of TV sets in use.

Multiple entries: SPORTS—NFL Football (58); Major League Baseball (9); NBA Basketball (4); NCAA Football bowl games (3); NCAA Basketball (1). NETWORKS—FOX (22); ABC (21); CBS (20); NBC (12).

		Date	Net	Rtg/Sh
1	**Super Bowl XXXIV** (Rams vs Titans)	1/30/00	ABC	43.3/63
2	**NFC Championship Game** (Buccaneers at Rams)	1/23/00	FOX	26.9/42
3	**AFC Championship Game** (Titans at Jaguars)	1/23/00	CBS	23.2/48
4	**AFC Playoff Game** (Titans at Colts)	1/16/00	CBS	20.5/38
5	**NFC Playoff Game** (Vikings at Rams)	1/16/00	FOX	20.4/44
6	**AFC Playoff Game** (Dolphins at Seahawks)	1/9/00	CBS	20.3/38
7	**NFC Playoff Game** (Cowboys at Vikings)	1/9/00	FOX	19.1/42
8	**MLB World Series - Game 4** (Braves at Yankees)	10/27/99	NBC	17.8/29
9	**Sugar Bowl** (Florida St. vs Virginia Tech)	1/4/00	ABC	17.5/28
10	**MLB World Series - Game 3** (Braves at Yankees)	10/26/99	NBC	16.3/27
	NFC Playoff Game (Redskins at Buccaneers)	1/15/00	FOX	16.3/34
12	**NFL Monday Night Football** (Cowboys at Vikings)	11/8/99	ABC	16.2/28
13	**NFL Monday Night Football** (Dolphins at Broncos)	9/13/99	ABC	16.1/27
	NFL Thanksgiving Day Late Game (Dolphins at Cowboys)	11/25/99	CBS	16.1/42
	NFL Regular Season Late Game (Various teams)	12/19/99	CBS	16.1/32
16	**NFL Regular Season Late Game** (Various teams)	11/14/99	FOX	15.9/29
17	**MLB NLCS - Game 6** (Mets at Braves)	10/19/99	NBC	15.4/27
	NFL Regular Season Late Game (Various teams)	11/29/99	FOX	15.4/30
19	**NFL Monday Night Football** (Falcons at Cowboys)	9/20/99	ABC	15.2/25
	NFL Regular Season Late Game (Various teams)	10/31/99	FOX	15.2/28
21	**NFL Monday Night Football** (Packers at Vikings)	12/20/99	ABC	15.1/28
22	**MLB World Series - Game 2** (Yankees at Braves)	10/24/99	NBC	15.0/23
23	**NFL Monday Night Football** (Seahawks at Packers)	11/1/99	ABC	14.9/25
	NFC Playoff Game (Lions at Redskins)	1/8/00	ABC	14.9/31
25	**NBA Finals - Game 6** (Pacers at Lakers)	6/19/00	NBC	14.7/26
26	**NFL Regular Season Late Game** (Various teams)	12/12/99	FOX	14.5/34
27	**NFL Monday Night Football** (Jets at Dolphins)	12/27/99	ABC	14.4/25
28	**Monday Night Football** (Vikings at Buccaneers)	12/6/99	ABC	14.3/25
	AFC Playoff Game (Bills at Titans)	1/8/00	ABC	14.3/36
30	**MLB World Series - Game 1** (Yankees at Braves)	10/23/99	NBC	14.2/26
31	**Rose Bowl** (Wisconsin vs Stanford)	1/1/00	ABC	14.1/27
	NCAA Men's Basketball Championship Game (Michigan St. vs Florida)	4/3/00	CBS	14.1/23

AP/Wide World Photos

Over 43 million households watched the fantastic finish between the **Kurt Warner**-led St. Louis Rams and the Tennessee Titans in Super Bowl XXXIV.

		Date	Net	Rtg/Sh
33	**Monday Night Football** (Bills at Dolphins)	10/4/99	ABC	14.0/24
	NFL Regular Season Early Game (Various teams)	10/24/99	FOX	14.0/33
35	**NFL Regular Season Early Game** (Various teams)	1/2/00	CBS	13.9/30
36	**AFC Playoff Game** (Dolphins at Jaguars)	1/15/00	CBS	13.8/34
37	**NFL Regular Season Late Game** (Various teams)	9/26/99	FOX	13.7/29
	NFL Regular Season Late Game (Various teams)	12/5/99	CBS	13.7/27
39	**NFL Regular Season Late Game** (Various Teams)	11/28/99	CBS	13.6/26
	NFL Regular Season Late Game (Various teams)	12/26/99	FOX	13.6/28
41	**NFL Regular Season Late Game** (Various teams)	9/12/99	FOX	13.4/27
	NFL Regular Season Late Game (Various teams)	10/10/99	CBS	13.4/28
	NFL Monday Night Football (Jets at Patriots)	11/15/99	ABC	13.4/22
44	**NFL Monday Night Football** (49ers at Cardinals)	9/27/99	ABC	13.3/22
	NFL Regular Season Late Game (Various teams)	10/3/99	CBS	13.3/27
	NFL Monday Night Football (Broncos at Jaguars)	12/13/99	ABC	13.3/22

		Date	Net	Rtg/Sh
47	**NFL Thanksgiving Day Early Game**			
	(Bears at Lions)	11/25/99	FOX	13.2/34
48	**NFL Monday Night Football**			
	(Packers at 49ers)	11/29/99	ABC	13.1/21
	NFL Regular Season Early Game			
	(Various teams)	1/2/00	FOX	13.1/29
	NBA Finals - Game 4			
	(Lakers at Pacers)	6/14/00	NBC	13.1/24
51	**Monday Night Football**			
	(Raiders at Broncos)	11/22/99	ABC	13.0/22
52	**NFL Regular Season Late Game**			
	(Various teams)	9/19/99	CBS	12.6/27
53	**NFL Regular Season Early Game**			
	(Various teams)	10/10/99	FOX	12.5/28
	NFL Monday Night Football			
	(Falcons at Steelers)	10/25/99	ABC	12.5/21
55	**NBA Playoff Game**			
	(Trailblazers at Lakers)	6/4/00	NBC	12.4/21
56	**NFL Regular Season Early Game**			
	(Various teams)	12/19/99	FOX	12.2/28
57	**NFL Monday Night Football**			
	(Cowboys at Giants)	10/18/99	ABC	12.1/20
58	**MLB NLCS - Game 5**			
	(Braves at Mets)	10/17/99	NBC	12.0/21
	NFL Regular Season Late Game			
	(Various teams)	11/7/99	CBS	12.0/24
60	**NFL Regular Season Early Game**			
	(Various teams)	10/3/99	FOX	11.6/28

		Date	Net	Rtg/Sh
61	**NFL Regular Season Late Game**			
	(Various teams)	10/24/99	CBS	11.4/24
	Orange Bowl			
	(Alabama vs Michigan)	1/1/00	ABC	11.4/21
63	**NFL Regular Season Early Game**			
	(Various teams)	10/17/99	CBS	11.2/26
64	**NFL Regular Season Early Game**			
	(Various teams)	9/12/99	CBS	11.1/27
	NFL Regular Season Early Game			
	(Various teams)	9/19/99	FOX	11.1/27
66	**NFL Regular Season Late Game**			
	(Various teams)	12/12/99	CBS	11.0/22
67	**NFL Regular Season Late Game**			
	(Various teams)	10/17/99	FOX	10.9/21
	NBA Finals - Game 3			
	(Lakers at Pacers)	6/11/00	NBC	10.9/19
69	**MLB NLCS - Game 1**			
	(Mets at Braves)	10/12/99	NBC	10.8/18
	MLB ALCS - Game 1			
	(Red Sox at Yankees)	10/13/99	FOX	10.8/18
	MLB NLCS - Game 3			
	(Braves at Mets)	10/15/99	NBC	10.8/20
	NFL Regular Season Early Game			
	(Various teams)	11/21/99	CBS	10.8/25
	NFL Regular Season Early Game			
	(Various teams)	12/26/99	CBS	10.8/27
74	**NFL Regular Season Early Game**			
	(Various teams)	11/7/99	FOX	10.7/25
	NFL Regular Season Early Game			
	(Various teams)	12/5/99	FOX	10.7/25

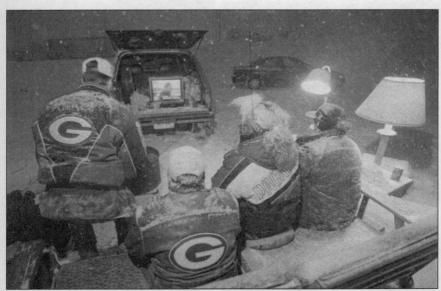

AP/Wide World Photos

These four die-hard Packers fans decided to brave the cold and watch Super Bowl XXXII in the parking lot of Green Bay's Lambeau Field. They came away cold and disappointed as the Packers lost to Denver, but they did help make the game the 28th highest-rated program of all-time.

All-Time Top-Rated TV Programs

NFL Football dominates television's All-Time Top-Rated 50 Programs with 22 Super Bowls and the 1981 NFC Championship Game making the list. Rankings based on surveys taken from January 1961 through August 31, 2000; include only sponsored programs seen on individual networks; and programs under 30 minutes scheduled duration are excluded. Programs are listed with ratings points, audience share and number of households watching, according to Nielsen Media Research.

Multiple entries: The Super Bowl (22); "Roots" (7); "The Beverly Hillbillies" (3); "The Thorn Birds" (3); "The Bob Hope Christmas Show," "The Ed Sullivan Show," "Gone With The Wind" and 1994 Winter Olympics (2).

	Program	Episode/Game	Net	Date	Rating	Share	Households
1	M*A*S*H (series)	Final episode	CBS	2/28/83	**60.2**	77	50,150,000
2	Dallas (series)	"Who Shot J.R.?"	CBS	11/21/80	**53.3**	76	41,470,000
3	Roots (mini-series)	Part 8	ABC	1/30/77	**51.1**	71	36,380,000
4	**Super Bowl XVI**	49ers 26, Bengals 21	CBS	1/24/82	**49.1**	73	40,020,000
5	**Super Bowl XVII**	Redskins 27, Dolphins 17	NBC	1/30/83	**48.6**	69	40,480,000
6	**XVII Winter Olympics**	Women's Figure Skating	CBS	2/23/94	**48.5**	64	45,690,000
7	**Super Bowl XX**	Bears 46, Patriots 10	NBC	1/26/86	**48.3**	70	41,490,000
8	Gone With the Wind (movie)	Part 1	NBC	11/7/76	**47.7**	65	33,960,000
9	Gone With the Wind (movie)	Part 2	NBC	11/8/76	**47.4**	64	33,750,000
10	**Super Bowl XII**	Cowboys 27, Broncos 10	CBS	1/15/78	**47.2**	67	34,410,000
11	**Super Bowl XIII**	Steelers 35, Cowboys 31	NBC	1/21/79	**47.1**	74	35,090,000
12	Bob Hope Special	Christmas Show	NBC	1/15/70	**46.6**	64	27,260,000
13	**Super Bowl XVIII**	Raiders 38, Redskins 9	CBS	1/22/84	**46.4**	71	38,800,000
	Super Bowl XIX	49ers 38, Dolphins 16	ABC	1/20/85	**46.4**	63	39,390,000
15	**Super Bowl XIV**	Steelers 31, Rams 19	CBS	1/20/80	**46.3**	67	35,330,000
16	**Super Bowl XXX**	Cowboys 27, Steelers 17	NBC	1/28/96	**46.0**	68	44,114,400
	ABC Theater (special)	"The Day After"	ABC	11/20/83	**46.0**	62	38,550,000
18	Roots (mini-series)	Part 6	ABC	1/28/77	**45.9**	66	32,680,000
	The Fugitive (series)	Final episode	ABC	8/29/67	**45.9**	72	25,700,000
20	**Super Bowl XXI**	Giants 39, Broncos 20	CBS	1/25/87	**45.8**	66	40,030,000
21	Roots (mini-series)	Part 5	ABC	1/27/77	**45.7**	71	32,540,000
22	**Super Bowl XXVIII**	Cowboys 30, Bills 13	NBC	1/29/94	**45.5**	66	42,860,000
	Cheers (series)	Final episode	NBC	5/20/93	**45.5**	64	42,360,500
24	The Ed Sullivan Show	Beatles' 1st appearance	CBS	2/9/64	**45.3**	60	23,240,000
25	**Super Bowl XXVII**	Cowboys 52, Bills 17	NBC	1/31/93	**45.1**	66	41,988,100
26	Bob Hope Special	Christmas Show	NBC	1/14/71	**45.0**	61	27,050,000
27	Roots (mini-series)	Part 3	ABC	1/25/77	**44.8**	68	31,900,000
28	**Super Bowl XXXII**	Denver 31, Green Bay 24	NBC	1/25/98	**44.5**	67	43,630,000
29	**Super Bowl XI**	Raiders 32, Vikings 14	NBC	1/9/77	**44.4**	73	31,610,000
	Super Bowl XV	Raiders 27, Eagles 10	NBC	1/25/81	**44.4**	63	34,540,000
31	**Super Bowl VI**	Cowboys 24, Dolphins 3	CBS	1/16/72	**44.2**	74	27,450,000
32	**XVII Winter Olympics**	Women's Figure Skating	CBS	2/25/94	**44.1**	64	41,540,000
	Roots (mini-series)	Part 2	ABC	1/24/77	**44.1**	62	31,400,000
34	The Beverly Hillbillies (series)	Regular episode	CBS	1/8/64	**44.0**	65	22,570,000
35	Roots (mini-series)	Part 4	ABC	1/26/77	**43.8**	66	31,190,000
	The Ed Sullivan Show	Beatles' 2nd appearance	CBS	2/16/64	**43.8**	60	22,445,000
37	**Super Bowl XXIII**	49ers 20, Bengals 16	NBC	1/22/89	**43.5**	68	39,320,000
38	The Academy Awards	John Wayne wins Oscar	ABC	4/7/70	**43.4**	78	25,390,000
39	**Super Bowl XXXI**	Packers 35, Patriots 21	FOX	1/26/97	**43.3**	65	42,000,000
	Super Bowl XXXIV	Rams 23, Titans 16	ABC	1/30/00	**43.3**	63	43,618,000
41	The Thorn Birds (mini-series)	Part 3	ABC	3/29/83	**43.2**	62	35,990,000
42	The Thorn Birds (mini-series)	Part 4	ABC	3/30/83	**43.1**	62	35,900,000
43	**NFC Championship Game**	49ers 28, Cowboys 27	CBS	1/10/82	**42.9**	62	34,940,000
44	The Beverly Hillbillies (series)	Regular episode	CBS	1/15/64	**42.8**	62	21,960,000
45	**Super Bowl VII**	Dolphins 14, Redskins 7	NBC	1/14/73	**42.7**	72	27,670,000
46	The Thorn Birds (mini-series)	Part 2	ABC	3/28/83	**42.5**	59	35,400,000
47	**Super Bowl IX**	Steelers 16, Vikings 6	NBC	1/12/75	**42.4**	72	29,040,000
	The Beverly Hillbillies (series)	Regular episode	CBS	2/26/64	**42.4**	60	21,750,000
49	**Super Bowl X**	Steelers 21, Cowboys 17	CBS	1/18/76	**42.3**	78	29,440,000
	ABC Sunday Night Movie	"Airport"	ABC	11/11/73	**42.3**	63	28,000,000
	ABC Sunday Night Movie	"Love Story"	ABC	10/1/72	**42.3**	62	27,410,000
	Cinderella	Musical special	CBS	2/22/65	**42.3**	59	22,250,000
	Roots (mini-series)	Part 7	ABC	1/29/77	**42.3**	65	30,120,000

All-Time Top-Rated Cable TV Sports Events

All-time cable television for sports events, according to ESPN, Turner Sports research and *The Sports Business Daily.* Covers period from Sept. 1, 1980 through Aug. 31, 2000.

NFL Telecasts

		Date	Net	Rtg
1	Chicago at Minnesota	12/6/87	ESPN	17.6
2	Detroit at Miami	12/25/94	ESPN	15.1
3	Chicago at Minnesota	12/3/89	ESPN	14.7
4	Cleveland at San Fran	11/29/87	ESPN	14.2
5	Pittsburgh at Houston	12/30/90	ESPN	13.8

Non-NFL Telecasts

		Date	Net	Rtg
1	MLB: Chicago (NL)-St. Louis	9/7/98	ESPN	9.5
2	NBA: Detroit-Boston	6/1/88	TBS	8.8
3	NBA: Chicago-Detroit	5/31/89	TBS	8.2
4	NBA: Detroit-Boston	5/26/88	TBS	8.1
	MLB: Giants-Chicago (NL)	9/28/98	ESPN	8.1

Teams Bought in 2000

Twelve major league clubs acquired new majority owners from Nov. 1, 1999 through Sept. 10, 2000.

Major League Baseball

Cleveland Indians: Ohio lawyer and long-time Indians fan Larry Dolan purchased the team on Nov. 4, 1999 from Richard Jacobs for approximately $323 million, a record amount for a major league baseball team. The sale was approved in January and subsequently completed on Feb. 15, 2000. Dolan, the brother of Cablevision chairman Charles Dolan, reportedly earned his wealth through his ownership of Cablevision stock.

Though he kept controlling interest, former owner Jacobs offered stock in the Cleveland Indians to the public in June 1998. Dolan acquired all of the outstanding stock in the team at a final price of $22.6612 per share, making the franchise privately owned once again. Dolan will assume the role of President and CEO.

Kansas City Royals: On March 14, 2000 the Royals' board of directors chose former Wal-Mart CEO David Glass as the successful bidder for the team. The $96 million-deal was approved on April 18. Glass had acted as Royals chairman of the board since September 1993 but had no involvement in the bidding process. According to the deal, Glass will ensure that the Royals remain in Kansas City and that all proceeds of the sale will go to the Greater Kansas City Community Foundation for the benefit of the community.

Montreal Expos: On Dec. 1, 1999 New York art dealer Jeffrey Loria was given approval to pay $75 million Canadian (approximately $50 million U.S.) for a 35 percent controlling stake in the Expos. Loria, a Yale graduate and noted art dealer, leads an ownership group that includes the city of Montreal (with a $13 million stake) and Stephen Bronfman, son of original team owner Charles Bronfman.

Toronto Blue Jays: Canada's biggest cable company Rogers Communications purchased controlling interest of the team on Sept. 1, 2000 from Belgian Brewery Interbrew SA for a reported $112 million. The deal gives Rogers an 80 percent stake in the team, while Interbrew still holds onto 20 percent. The Canadian Imperial Bank of Commerce, partial owners since 1977, sold its 10 percent interest. Former Sun Media president Paul Godfrey is expected to become the chairman and CEO of the Blue Jays. The sale is still pending approval from Major League Baseball owners.

NFL Football

New York Jets: On Jan. 11, 2000 Robert Wood Johnson IV purchased the team from the estate of the late Leon Hess for $635 million, outbidding Cablevision founder and chairman Charles Dolan. The price is the highest ever paid for an NFL franchise with no stadium included. The deal was unanimously approved by NFL owners a week later. Johnson is heir to the pharmaceutical company Johnson & Johnson and becomes just the third owner in franchise history. One of the major goals delineated by Johnson when he purchased the team was to have a separate Jets home stadium by the time their lease with the Meadowlands expires in 2008.

NBA Basketball

Dallas Mavericks: On Jan. 14, 2000, internet pioneer Mark Cuban purchased a majority stake in the team from former owner Ross Perot Jr. for $280 million. Perot retains a minority interest in the club. The 41-year-old Cuban co-founded Broadcast.com in 1995 and made his fortune when it was sold to Yahoo Inc. in July, 1999. The Mavericks purchase also includes Cuban becoming partner of the American Airlines Center, now being built in Dallas and scheduled for completion in the fall of 2001.

Denver Nuggets: Wal-Mart heir and St. Louis Rams minority owner Stan Kroenke purchased the Nuggets, along with the NHL's Colorado Avalanche, and the Pepsi Center from Liberty Media Group for $450 million on April 24, 2000. Liberty retains a 6.52 percent interest in the clubs and the arena. The deal ends a tumultuous year that saw two deals collapse at the last minute.

A bid by co-Wal-Mart heirs and St. Louis Blues owners Bill and Nancy Laurie fell apart in March, 1999 when they were sued by Ascent Entertainment Group, and a subsequent deal with Colorado businessman Donald Sturm evaporated when he refused to keep the teams in Denver for at least 25 years. Kroenke, 52, is married to the niece of Wal-Mart founder Sam Walton and is the brother-in-law of the Lauries.

Vancouver Grizzlies: On Jan. 24, 2000 Michael Heisley, the 62-year-old CEO of The Heico Companies, purchased the Grizzlies from John McCaw and Orca Bay Sports & Entertainment for a reported $160 million. The deal was approved by the NBA's Board of Governors in April. Similar to the Nuggets, the Grizzlies also were ready to be sold to Bill and Nancy Laurie until the deal was blocked by the NBA due to the Lauries' unwillingness to keep the team in Vancouver.

NHL Hockey

Colorado Avalanche: See NBA's Denver Nuggets.

New Jersey Devils: On July 12, 2000 the Devils were sold from John McMullen to Puck Holdings LLC, an affiliate of YankeeNets. Puck/YankeeNets now owns over 50 percent of the club, with the rest held by a number of limited partners. The terms of the deal were not disclosed, but were estimated at $175 million. YankeeNets also owns baseball's New York Yankees and the NBA's New Jersey Nets. According to company president Harvey Schiller, talks have begun to build a $325 million arena in Newark which would house the Nets and the Devils, now playing in the Meadowlands.

New York Islanders: On April 26, 2000, Computer Associates executives Charles Wang and Sanjay Kumar purchased the Islanders from Edward Milstein and Steven Gluckstern for an estimated $190 million. The duo become the fourth set of owners the struggling franchise has had in the last six seasons. They admittedly don't know much about hockey but look at the Islanders as a business proposition. "I've been reading my *Hockey for Dummies* book," said Wang, "and Sanjay is reading his textbooks."

Phoenix Coyotes: On May 26, 2000 Steve Ellman, CEO of The Ellman Companies, put a $10 million non-refundable deposit down on behalf of Los Arcos Sports, LLC towards the purchase of the Coyotes. The entire deal has been estimated at $87 million but terms were not fully disclosed. Hockey legend Wayne Gretzky is also on board as a partner. The group, headed by Ellman, is planning to build the brand new Los Arcos Arena in Scottsdale to be ready by the fall of 2002.

Top 10 Salaries In Each Sport

The top 10 highest paid athletes over the 1999-00 season for the NBA, Major League Baseball and NHL and the 1999 season for the NFL. Figures are in millions of dollars.

Source: Street & Smith's SportsBusiness Journal and USA Today.

NFL

		Position	Team	Salary
1	Troy Aikman	Quarterback	Dallas	$6.667
2	Drew Bledsoe	Quarterback	N. England	6.398
3	Brett Favre	Quarterback	Green Bay	6.249
4	Warren Sapp	Def. Lineman	Tampa Bay	6.231
5	Deion Sanders	Cornerback	Dallas	6.200
6	Steve McNair	Quarterback	Tennessee	6.075
7	Steve Young	Quarterback	San Francisco	5.850
8	Joe Johnson	Def. Lineman	New Orleans	5.600
9	Dan Marino	Quarterback	Miami	5.447
10	Levon Kirkland	Linebacker	Pittsburgh	5.346

MLB

		Position	Team	Salary
1	Kevin Brown	Pitcher	Los Angeles	$15.714
2	Randy Johnson	Pitcher	Arizona	13.600
3	Albert Belle	Right Field	Baltimore	13.000
4	Bernie Williams	Center Field	NY Yankees	12.357
5	Larry Walker	Right Field	Colorado	12.143
6	Mike Piazza	Catcher	NY Mets	12.071
7	David Cone	Pitcher	NY Yankees	12.000
8	Pedro Martinez	Pitcher	Boston	11.500
9	Mo Vaughn	First Base	Anaheim	11.167
10	Sammy Sosa	Right Field	Chicago-NL	11.000

NBA

		Position	Team	Salary
1	Shaquille O'Neal	Center	Los Angeles	$17.140
2	Kevin Garnett	Forward	Minnesota	16.810
3	Juwan Howard	Forward	Washington	15.070
4	Patrick Ewing	Center	New York	15.000
	Alonzo Mourning	Center	Miami	15.000
6	Scottie Pippen	Forward	Portland	14.800
7	Hakeem Olajuwon	Center	Houston	14.300
8	Karl Malone	Forward	Utah	14.000
9	Dikembe Mutombo	Center	Atlanta	12.820
10	Jayson Williams	Center	New Jersey	12.380

NHL

		Position	Team	Salary
1	Jaromir Jagr	Right Wing	Pittsburgh	$10.360
2	Paul Kariya	Left Wing	Anaheim	10.000
3	Peter Forsberg	Center	Colorado	9.000
4	Theo Fleury	Right Wing	NY Rangers	8.500
	Eric Lindros	Center	Philadelphia	8.500
6	Pavel Bure	Right Wing	Florida	8.000
7	Patrick Roy	Goalie	Colorado	7.500
8	Dominik Hasek	Goalie	Buffalo	7.000
	Mats Sundin	Center	Toronto	7.000
10	Brian Leetch	Defense	NY Rangers	6.680

Highest and Lowest Ticket Prices

The most expensive and least expensive average ticket prices for NFL, NBA, Major League Baseball and NHL franchises over the 1999-00 season. Note that average ticket prices for each league are as follows: **NFL** $45.63, **MLB** $16.65, **NBA** $48.37, and **NHL** $45.70.

Source: Team Marketing Report

NFL

	Highest	Venue	Avg. Price
1	Washington	Jack Kent Cooke	$74.28
2	Tampa Bay	Raymond James Stad.	64.65
3	Jacksonville	ALLTEL Stadium	57.79
4	Tennessee	Adelphia Coliseum	55.63
5	Carolina	Ericsson Stadium	55.45

	Lowest	Venue	Avg. Price
1	St. Louis	Trans World Dome	$33.99
2	Detroit	Pontiac Silverdome	35.65
3	Seattle	Kingdome	35.68
4	Philadelphia	Veterans Stadium	37.59
5	Cincinnati	Cinergy Field	37.77

MLB

	Highest	Venue	Avg. Price
1	Boston	Fenway Park	$28.33
2	NY Yankees	Yankee Stadium	25.94
3	Detroit	Comerica Park	24.83
4	NY Mets	Shea Stadium	24.29
5	Seattle	Safeco Field	23.43

	Lowest	Venue	Avg. Price
1	Minnesota	HHH Metrodome	$9.33
2	Montreal	Olympic Stadium	10.29
3	Cincinnati	Cinergy Field	10.74
4	Oakland	Network Assoc. Col.	11.35
5	Milwaukee	County Stadium	11.72

NBA

	Highest	Venue	Avg. Price
1	NY Knicks	Madison Sq. Garden	$86.82
2	LA Lakers	Staples Center	81.89
3	Seattle	Key Arena	64.60
4	Houston	Compaq Center	62.63
5	Washington	MCI Center	59.65

	Lowest	Venue	Avg. Price
1	Milwaukee	Bradley Center	$30.83
2	Charlotte	Charlotte Coliseum	32.04
3	Vancouver	General Motors Place	34.71
4	Denver	Pepsi Center	38.34
5	San Antonio	The Alamodome	38.92

NHL

	Highest	Venue	Avg. Price
1	Toronto	Air Canada Centre	$69.92
2	NY Rangers	Madison Sq. Garden	65.82
3	Atlanta	Philips Arena	62.14
4	Colorado	Pepsi Center	59.09
5	Philadelphia	First Union Center	58.19

	Lowest	Venue	Avg. Price
1	Calgary	Canadian Airlines Saddledome	$27.85
2	Edmonton	Skyreach Centre	33.63
3	NY Islanders	Nassau Coliseum	34.68
4	Tampa Bay	Ice Palace	35.74
5	Buffalo	HSBC Arena	37.07

The Rights Stuff

Major sports and their television deals as of Sept. 1, 2000.

League	Network	Yrs (Ends)	Amount	League	Network	Yrs (Ends)	Amount
NFL..............	ESPN	8 (2006)	$4.8 billion	NHL.............	ESPN/ABC	5 (2004)	$600 million
	FOX	8 (2006)	4.4 billion	NCAA Hoops Tourn. ...	CBS	11 (2013)	$6.0 billion†
	ABC	8 (2006)	4.4 billion				
	CBS	8 (2006)	4.0 billion	NCAA Football BCS ...	ABC	8 (2006)	$930 million
NBA	NBC	4 (2002)	$1.75 billion	NASCAR	NBC/Turner	6 (2006)	$1.2 billion
	Turner	4 (2002)	890 million		FOX	8 (2008)	1.6 billion
MLB	FOX	5 (2000)	$575 million	Olympics.............	NBC	13 (2008)	$3.5 billion#
	NBC	5 (2000)	400 million				
	ESPN	6 (2005)	undisclosed*				

* Terms of the deal are undisclosed but estimated to be valued at more than $800 million.
† This deal doesn't begin until the 2003 tournament. CBS's current seven-year, $1.73 billion contract ends in 2002.
# NBC has a deal with the Olympics worth approximately $3.5 billion, which gave them exclusive rights to the 1996 Summer Games in Atlanta, the 2000 Summer Games in Sydney, the 2002 Winter Games in Salt Lake City, the 2004 Summer Games in Athens, the 2006 Winter Games in Turin (ITA), and the 2008 Summer Games (site – TBA). The only Games it didn't have rights to since 1996 were the 1998 Winter Games in Nagano, which were owned by CBS.

Most/Least Valuable Teams

The most valuable and least valuable franchises in North American sports according to *Forbes* magazine. Estimates are based on 1999 revenues and expenses for MLB, NHL and NBA teams and 1998 figures for NFL teams. Note that operating income is defined as earnings minus any interest, taxes, and depreciation.

Dollar amounts given are in millions. Amounts in parentheses denote losses.

NFL

	Most	Operating Income	Value
1	Dallas	$56.7	$663
2	Washington	48.8	607
3	Tampa Bay	41.2	502
4	Carolina	18.8	488
5	New England	13.5	460
6	Miami	32.9	446
7	Denver	5.0	427
8	Jacksonville	29.3	419
9	Baltimore	33.2	408
10	Seattle	6.4	399

	Least	Operating Income	Value
1	Detroit	$16.4	$293
2	Oakland	17.3	299
3	Arizona	10.6	301
4	Indianapolis	15.8	305
5	Atlanta	16.8	306

MLB

	Most	Operating Income	Value
1	NY Yankees	$17.5	$548
2	Atlanta	18.3	388
3	Cleveland	16.5	364
4	Baltimore	(0.7)	348
5	Los Angeles	(21.1)	325
6	NY Mets	(1.2)	314
7	Colorado	7.9	305
8	Texas	(9.5)	294
9	Seattle	5.5	290
10	Boston	2.4	284

	Least	Operating Income	Value
1	Montreal	$1.9	$89
2	Minnesota	2.2	91
3	Kansas City	5.8	122
4	Florida	2.4	125
5	Oakland	3.9	134

NBA

	Most	Operating Income	Value
1	New York	$4.0	$334
2	Chicago	20.4	307
3	LA Lakers	(0.9)	282
4	Portland	(13.5)	257
5	Phoenix	5.8	239
6	Philadelphia	1.8	239
7	Detroit	(1.7)	231
8	Utah	(0.7)	226
9	Washington	(2.8)	215
10	Boston	2.3	209

	Least	Operating Income	Value
1	LA Clippers	$(13.2)	$103
2	Milwaukee	(14.9)	111
3	Denver	(9.8)	124
4	Vancouver	(12.4)	127
5	Charlotte	(2.2)	136

NHL

	Most	Operating Income	Value
1	NY Rangers	$8.7	$236
2	Philadelphia	0.8	211
3	Boston	10.1	197
4	Detroit	(11.6)	194
5	Chicago	6.8	185
6	Montreal	5.8	175
7	Florida	5.1	163
8	Colorado	2.6	160
9	Toronto	2.5	151
10	Dallas	(5.2)	149

	Least	Operating Income	Value
1	Carolina	$(20.6)	$70
2	Edmonton	2.7	72
3	Calgary	0.7	78
4	Ottawa	1.4	79
5	Phoenix	(3.3)	89

The Peabody Award

Presented annually since 1940 for outstanding achievement in radio and television broadcasting. Named after Georgia banker and philanthropist George Foster Peabody, the awards are administered by the Henry W. Grady College of Journalism and Mass Communication at the University of Georgia.

Television

Year
1960 **CBS** for coverage of 1960 Winter and Summer Olympic Games
1966 ABC's **"Wide World of Sports"** (for Outstanding Achievement in Promotion of International Understanding).
1968 **ABC Sports** coverage of both the 1968 Winter and Summer Olympic Games.
1972 **ABC Sports** coverage of the 1972 Summer Olympics in Munich.
1973 **Joe Garagiola** of NBC Sports (for "The Baseball World of Joe Garagiola").
1976 **ABC Sports** coverage of both the 1976 Winter and Summer Olympic Games.
1984 **Roone Arledge**, president of ABC News & Sports (for significant contributions to news and sports programming).
1986 **WFAA-TV**, Dallas for its investigation of the Southern Methodist University football program.
1988 **Jim McKay** of ABC Sports (for pioneering efforts and career accomplishments in the world of TV sports).
1991 **CBS Sports** coverage of the 1991 Masters golf tournament
    & **HBO Sports** and Black Canyon Productions for the baseball special "When It Was A Game."
1995 **Kartemquin Educational Films** and **KTCA-TV** in St. Paul, MN, presented on PBS for "Hoop Dreams"
    & **Turner Original Productions** for the baseball special "Hank Aaron: Chasing the Dream."
1996 **HBO Sports** for its documentary "The Journey of the African-American Athlete"
    & **Bud Greenspan**, a personal award for excellence in chronicling the Olympic Games.
1997 **HBO Pictures** and **The Thomas Carter Company** for the original movie "Don King: Only in America."
1998 **KTVX-TV**, Salt Lake City for its investigation into the policies and practices of the IOC during the Olympic bribery scandal & **HBO Sports** for its ongoing series of sports documentaries.
1999 **WCPO-TV**, Cincinnati for its investigation of fraud and misrepresentation in the construction of new sports stadiums, **HBO Sports** for its documentary "Dare to Compete: The Struggle of Women in Sports," and its documentary "Fists of Freedom: The Story of the '68 Summer Games" & **ESPN** for its "SportsCentury" series.

Radio

Year
1974 **WSB** radio in Atlanta for "Henry Aaron: A Man with a Mission."
1991 **Red Barber** of National Public Radio (for his six decades as a broadcaster and his 10 years as a commentator on NPR's "Morning Edition").

National Emmy Awards
Sports Programming

Presented by the Academy of Television Arts and Sciences since 1948. Eligibility period covered the calendar year from 1948-57 and since 1988.

Multiple major award winners: ABC "Wide World of Sports" (19), NFL Films Football coverage (11); ABC Olympics coverage (9); ABC "Monday Night Football" (8); CBS NFL Football coverage, ESPN "Outside the Lines" series (6); CBS NCAA Basketball coverage, FOX MLB coverage and CBS "NFL Today" (5); ESPN "SportsCenter," NBC Olympics coverage and HBO "Real Sports with Bryant Gumbel" (4); ABC "The American Sportsman," ABC Indianapolis 500 coverage and ESPN "Game-Day" (3); ABC Kentucky Derby coverage, ABC "Sportsbeat," Bud Greenspan Olympic specials, CBS Olympics coverage, CBS Golf coverage, ESPN "Speedworld," Fox "NFL Sunday," MTV Sports series and NBC World Series coverage (2).

1949
Coverage—"Wrestling" (KTLA, Los Angeles)

1950
Program—"Rams Football" (KNBH-TV, Los Angeles)

1954
Program—"Gillette Cavalcade of Sports" (NBC)

1965-66
Programs—"Wide World of Sports" (ABC), "Shell's Wonderful World of Golf" (NBC) and "CBS Golf Classic" (CBS)

1966-67
Program—"Wide World of Sports" (ABC)

1967-68
Program—"Wide World of Sports" (ABC)

1968-69
Program—"1968 Summer Olympics" (ABC)

1969-70
Programs—"NFL Football" (CBS) and "Wide World of Sports" (ABC)

1970-71
Program—"Wide World of Sports" (ABC)

1971-72
Program—"Wide World of Sports" (ABC)

1972-73
News Special—"Coverage of Munich Olympic Tragedy" (ABC)
Sports Programs—"1972 Summer Olympics" (ABC) and "Wide World of Sports" (ABC)

1973-74
Program—"Wide World of Sports" (ABC)

1974-75
Non-Edited Program—"Jimmy Connors vs. Rod Laver Tennis Challenge" (CBS)
Edited Program—"Wide World of Sports" (ABC)

1975-76
Live Special—"1975 World Series: Cincinnati vs. Boston" (NBC)
Live Series—"NFL Monday Night Football" (ABC)
Edited Specials—"1976 Winter Olympics" (ABC) and "Triumph and Tragedy: The Olympic Experience" (ABC)
Edited Series—"Wide World of Sports" (ABC)

1976-77
Live Special—"1976 Summer Olympics" (ABC)
Live Series—"The NFL Today/NFL Football" (CBS)
Edited Special—"1976 Summer Olympics Preview" (ABC)
Edited Series—"The Olympiad" (PBS)

National Emmy Awards (Cont.)

1977-78

Live Special—"Muhammad Ali vs. Leon Spinks Heavyweight Championship Fight" (CBS)
Live Series—"The NFL Today/NFL Football" (CBS)
Edited Special—"The Impossible Dream: Ballooning Across the Atlantic" (CBS)
Edited Series—"The Way It Was" (PBS)

1978-79

Live Special—"Super Bowl XIII: Pittsburgh vs Dallas" (NBC)
Live Series—"NFL Monday Night Football" (ABC)
Edited Special—"Spirit of '78: The Flight of Double Eagle II" (ABC)
Edited Series—"The American Sportsman" (ABC)

1979-80

Live Special—"1980 Winter Olympics" (ABC)
Live Series—"NCAA College Football" (ABC)
Edited Special—"Gossamer Albatross: Flight of Imagination" (CBS)
Edited Series—"NFL Game of the Week" (NFL Films)

1980-81

Live Special—"1981 Kentucky Derby" (ABC)
Live Series—"PGA Golf Tour" (CBS)
Edited Special—"Wide World of Sports 20th Anniversary Show" (ABC)
Edited Series—"The American Sportsman" (ABC)

1981-82

Live Special—"1982 NCAA Basketball Final: North Carolina vs Georgetown" (CBS)
Live Series—"NFL Football" (CBS)
Edited Special—"1982 Indianapolis 500" (ABC)
Edited Series—"Wide World of Sports" (ABC)

1982-83

Live Special—"1982 World Series: St. Louis vs Milwaukee" (NBC)
Live Series—"NFL Football" (CBS)
Edited Special—"Wimbledon '83" (NBC)
Edited Series—"Wide World of Sports" (ABC)
Journalism—"ABC Sportsbeat" (ABC)

1983-84

No awards given—

1984-85

Live Special—"1984 Summer Olympics" (ABC)
Live Series—No award given
Edited Special—"Road to the Super Bowl '85" (NFL Films)
Edited Series—"The American Sportsman" (ABC)
Journalism—"ABC Sportsbeat" (ABC), "CBS Sports Sunday" (CBS), Dick Schaap features (ABC) and 1984 Summer Olympic features (ABC)

1985-86

No awards given—

1986-87

Live Special—"1987 Daytona 500" (CBS)
Live Series—"NFL Football" (CBS)
Edited Special—"Wide World of Sports 25th Anniversary Special" (ABC)
Edited Series—"Wide World of Sports" (ABC)

1987-88

Live Special—"1987 Kentucky Derby" (ABC)
Live Series—"NFL Monday Night Football" (ABC)
Edited Special—"Paris-Roubaix Bike Race" (CBS)
Edited Series—"Wide World of Sports" (ABC)

1988

Live Special—"1988 Summer Olympics" (NBC)
Live Series—"1988 NCAA Basketball" (CBS)
Edited Special—"Road to the Super Bowl '88" (NFL Films)
Edited Series—"Wide World of Sports" (ABC)
Studio Show—"NFL GameDay" (ESPN)
Journalism—1988 Summer Olympic reporting (NBC)

1989

Live Special—"1989 Indianapolis 500" (ABC)
Live Series—"NFL Monday Night Football" (ABC)
Edited Special—"Trans-Antarctical The International Expedition" (ABC)
Edited Series—"This is the NFL" (NFL Films)
Studio Show—"NFL Today" (CBS)
Journalism—1989 World Series Game 3 earthquake coverage (ABC)

1990

Live Special—"1990 Indianapolis 500" (ABC)
Live Series—"1990 NCAA Basketball Tournament" (CBS)
Edited Special—"Road to Super Bowl XXIV" (NFL Films)
Edited Series—"Wide World of Sports" (ABC)
Studio Show—"SportsCenter" (ESPN)
Journalism—"Outside the Lines: The Autograph Game" (ESPN)

1991

Live Special—"1991 NBA Finals: Chicago vs LA Lakers" (NBC)
Live Series—"1991 NCAA Basketball Tournament" (CBS)
Edited Special—"Wide World of Sports 30th Anniversary Special" (ABC)
Edited Series—"This is the NFL" (NFL Films)
Studio Show—"NFL GameDay" (ESPN) and "NFL Live" (NBC)
Journalism—"Outside the Lines: Steroids–Whatever It Takes" (ESPN)

1992

Live Special—"1992 Breeders' Cup" (NBC)
Live Series—"1992 NCAA Basketball Tournament" (CBS)
Edited Special—"1992 Summer Olympics" (NBC)
Edited Series—"MTV Sports" (MTV)
Studio Show—"The NFL Today" (CBS)
Journalism—"Outside the Lines: Portraits in Black and White" (ESPN)

1993

Live Special—"1993 World Series" (CBS)
Live Series—"Monday Night Football" (ABC)
Edited Special—"Road to the Super Bowl" (NFL Films)
Edited Series—"This is the NFL" (NFL Films)
Studio Show—"The NFL Today" (CBS)
Journalism (TIE)—"Outside the Lines: Mitch Ivey Feature" (ESPN) and "SportsCenter: University of Houston Football" (ESPN).
Feature—"Arthur Ashe: His Life, His Legacy" (NBC).

1994

Live Special —"NHL Stanley Cup Finals" (ESPN)
Live Series —"Monday Night Football" (ABC)
Edited Special —"Lillehammer '94: 16 Days of Glory" (Disney/Cappy Productions)
Edited Series —"MTV Sports" (MTV)
Studio Show —"NFL GameDay" (ESPN)
Journalism —"1994 Winter Olympic Games: Mossad feature" (CBS)
Feature (TIE) —"Heroes of Telemark" on Winter Olympic Games (CBS); and "SportsCenter: Vanderbilt running back Brad Gaines" (ESPN).

"Baseball" Wins Prime Time Emmy

Ken Burns's miniseries "Baseball" won the 1994 Emmy Award for Outstanding Informational Series. The nine-part documentary aired from Sept. 18-28, 1994 and ran more than 18 hours, drawing the largest audience in PBS history.

1995

Live Special —"Cal Ripken 2131" (ESPN)
Live Series —"ESPN Speedworld" (ESPN)
Edited Special (quick turn-around) —"Outside the Lines: Playball– Opening Day in America" (ESPN)
Edited Special (long turn-around) —"Lillehammer, an Olympic Diary" (CBS)
Edited Series —"NFL Films Presents" (NFL Films)
Studio Show (TIE) —"NFL GameDay" (ESPN) and "Fox NFL Sunday"(Fox)
Journalism —"Real Sports with Bryant Gumbel: Broken Promises" (HBO)
Feature (TIE) —"SportsCenter: Jerry Quarry" (ESPN) and "Real Sports with Bryant Gumbel: Coach" (HBO).

1996

Live Special —"1996 World Series" (Fox)
Live Series —"ESPN Speedworld" (ESPN)
Edited Special —"Football America" (TNT/NFL Films)
Edited Series —"NFL Films Presents" (NFL Films)
Live Event Turnaround —"The Centennial Olympic Games" (NBC)
Studio Show —"SportsCenter" (ESPN)
Journalism —"Outside the Lines: AIDS in Sports" (ESPN)
Feature —"Real Sports with Bryant Gumbel: 1966 Texas Western NCAA Champs" (HBO).

1997

Live Special —"The NBA Finals" (NBC)
Live Series —"NFL Monday Night Football" (ABC)
Edited Special —"Ironman Triathlon World Championship" (NBC/World Triathlon Corporation)
Edited Series —"NFL Films Presents" (NFL Films)
Live Event Turnaround —"Outside The Lines: Inside The Kentucky Derby" (ESPN)
Studio Show —"Fox NFL Sunday" (FOX)
Journalism —"Real Sports With Bryant Gumbel: Pros and Cons" (HBO)
Feature —"NFL Films Presents: Eddie George" (NFL Films).

1998

Live Special —"McGwire's 62nd Home Run Game" (FOX)
Live Series —"NBC Golf Tour" (NBC)
Edited Special —"A Cinderella Season: The Lady Vols Fight Back" (HBO)
Edited Series —"Real Sports With Bryant Gumbel" (HBO)
Live Event Turnaround —"Wimbledon '98" (NBC)
Studio Show —"Fox NFL Sunday" (FOX)
Journalism (TIE)—"Real Sports With Bryant Gumbel: Winning At All Costs" (HBO) and "Real Sports With Bryant Gumbel: Diamond Bucks" (HBO)
Feature —"NFL Films Presents: Steve Mariucci" (ESPN2 and NFL Films).

1999

Live Special —"2000 MLB All-Star Game" (FOX)
Live Series —"MLB Regular Season" (FOX)
Edited Special —"Ironman Triathlon World Championship" (NBC)
Edited Series —"SportsCentury: 50 Greatest Athletes" (ESPN)

Live Event Turnaround —"The World Track & Field Championships" (NBC)
Studio Show —"MLB Pre-Game Show" (FOX)
Journalism—"Real Sports with Bryant Gumbel: Fake Golf Clubs" (HBO)
Feature —"NFL Films Presents: Lt. Kalsu" (ESPN2)

Sportscasters of the Year
National Emmy Awards

An Emmy Award for Sportscasters was first introduced in 1968 and given for Outstanding Host/Commentator for the 1967-68 TV season. Two awards, one for Outstanding Host or Play-by-Play and the other for Outstanding Analyst, were first presented in 1981 for the 1980-81 season. Three awards, for Outstanding Studio Host, Play-by-Play and Studio Analyst, have been given since the 1993 season, and one more, Sports Event Analyst, was added in 1997.

Multiple winners: John Madden (13); Bob Costas and Jim McKay (9); Dick Enberg (4); Keith Jackson and Al Michaels (3); James Brown and Cris Collinsworth (2). Note that Jim McKay has won a total of 12 Emmy awards: eight for Host/Commentator, one for Host/Play-by-Play, two for Sports Writing, and one for News Commentary.

Season	Host/Commentator	Season	Host/Play-by-Play	Season	Analyst
1967-68	Jim McKay, ABC	1980-81	Dick Enberg, NBC	1980-81	Dick Button, ABC
1968-69	No award	1981-82	Jim McKay, ABC	1981-82	John Madden, CBS
1969-70	No award	1982-83	Dick Enberg, NBC	1982-83	John Madden, CBS
1970-71	Jim McKay, ABC	1983-84	No award	1983-84	No award
	& Don Meredith, ABC	1984-85	George Michael, NBC	1984-85	No award
1971-72	No award	1985-86	No award	1985-86	No award
1972-73	Jim McKay, ABC	1986-87	Al Michaels, ABC	1986-87	John Madden, CBS
1973-74	Jim McKay, ABC	1987-88	Bob Costas, NBC	1987-88	John Madden, CBS
1974-75	Jim McKay, ABC	1988	Bob Costas, NBC	1988	John Madden, CBS
1975-76	Jim McKay, ABC	1989	Al Michaels, ABC	1989	John Madden, CBS
1976-77	Frank Gifford, ABC	1990	Dick Enberg, NBC	1990	John Madden, CBS
1977-78	Jack Whitaker, CBS	1991	Bob Costas, NBC	1991	John Madden, CBS
1978-79	Jim McKay, ABC	1992	Bob Costas, NBC	1992	John Madden, CBS
1979-80	Jim McKay, ABC				

Studio Host

Year		Year		Year	
1993	Bob Costas, NBC	1996	Bob Costas, NBC	1999	James Brown, FOX
1994	Bob Costas, NBC	1997	Dan Patrick, ESPN		
1995	Bob Costas, NBC	1998	James Brown, FOX		

Play-by-Play

Year		Year		Year		Year	
1993	Dick Enberg, NBC	1995	Al Michaels, ABC	1997	Bob Costas, NBC	1999	Joe Buck, FOX
1994	Keith Jackson, ABC	1996	Keith Jackson, ABC	1998	Keith Jackson, ABC		

Studio Analyst

Year		Year		Year	
1993	Billy Packer, CBS	1996	Howie Long, Fox	1999	Terry Bradshaw, FOX
1994	John Madden, Fox	1997	Cris Collinsworth, HBO/NBC		
1995	John Madden, Fox	1998	Cris Collinsworth, HBO/FOX		

Spec. Events Analyst

Year		Year		Year	
1997	Joe Morgan, ESPN	1998	John Madden, FOX	1999	John Madden, FOX

Lifetime Achievement Emmy Award

For outstanding work as an exemplary television sportscaster over many years.

Year		Year		Year		Year	
1989	Jim McKay	1992	Chris Schenkel	1995	Vin Scully	1998	Keith Jackson
1990	Lindsey Nelson	1993	Pat Summerall	1996	Frank Gifford	1999	Jack Buck
1991	Curt Gowdy	1994	Howard Cosell	1997	Jim Simpson		

National Sportscasters and Sportswriters Assn. Award

Sportscaster of the Year presented annually since 1959 by the National Sportcasters and Sportswriters Association, based in Salisbury, N.C. Voting is done by NSSA members and selected national media.

Multiple winners: Bob Costas (7); Chris Berman and Keith Jackson (5); Lindsey Nelson and Chris Schenkel (4); Dick Enberg, Al Michaels and Vin Scully (3); Curt Gowdy and Ray Scott (2).

Year		Year		Year		Year	
1959	Lindsey Nelson	1970	Chris Schenkel	1980	Dick Enberg	1990	Chris Berman
1960	Lindsey Nelson	1971	Ray Scott		& Al Michaels	1991	Bob Costas
1961	Lindsey Nelson	1972	Keith Jackson	1981	Dick Enberg	1992	Bob Costas
1962	Lindsey Nelson	1973	Keith Jackson	1982	Vin Scully	1993	Chris Berman
1963	Chris Schenkel	1974	Keith Jackson	1983	Al Michaels	1994	Chris Berman
1964	Chris Schenkel	1975	Keith Jackson	1984	John Madden	1995	Bob Costas
1965	Vin Scully	1976	Keith Jackson	1985	Bob Costas	1996	Chris Berman
1966	Curt Gowdy	1977	Pat Summerall	1986	Al Michaels	1997	Bob Costas
1967	Chris Schenkel	1978	Vin Scully	1987	Bob Costas	1998	Jim Nantz
1968	Ray Scott	1979	Dick Enberg	1988	Bob Costas	1999	Dan Patrick
1969	Curt Gowdy			1989	Chris Berman		

The Pulitzer Prize

The Pulitzer Prizes for journalism, letters and music have been presented annually since 1917 in the name of Joseph Pulitzer (1847-1911), the publisher of the *New York World*. Prizes are awarded by the president of Columbia University on the recommendation of a board of review. Fifteen Pulitzers have been awarded for newspaper sports reporting, sports commentary and sports photography.

News Coverage

1935 **Bill Taylor,** *NY Herald Tribune,* for his reporting on the 1934 America's Cup yacht races.

Special Citation

1952 **Max Kase**, *NY Journal-American,* for his reporting on the 1951 college basketball point-shaving scandal.

Meritorious Public Service

1954 **Newsday** (Garden City, N.Y.) for its expose of New York State's race track scandals and labor racketeering.

General Reporting

1956 **Arthur Daley,** *NY Times,* for his 1955 columns.

Investigative Reporting

1981 **Clark Hallas** & **Robert Lowe,** *(Tucson) Arizona Daily Star,* for their 1980 investigation of the University of Arizona athletic department.

1986 **Jeffrey Marx** & **Michael York,** Lexington (Ky.) *Herald-Leader,* for their 1985 investigation of the basketball program at the University of Kentucky and other major colleges.

Specialized Reporting

1985 **Randall Savage** & **Jackie Crosby,** Macon (Ga.) *Telegraph and News,* for their 1984 investigation of athletics and academics at the University of Georgia and Georgia Tech.

Beat Reporting

2000 **George Dohrmann,** *St. Paul* (Min.) *Pioneer Press, for his investigation that revealed academic fraud in the men's basketball program at the University of Minnesota.*

Feature Writing

1997 **Lisa Pollak,** *Baltimore Sun,* for her story about baseball umpire John Hirschbeck dealing with the death of one son and the illness of another from the same disease.

Commentary

1976 **Red Smith,** *NY Times,* for his 1975 columns.
1981 **Dave Anderson,** *NY Times,* for his 1980 columns.
1990 **Jim Murray,** *LA Times,* for his 1989 columns.

Photography

1949 **Nat Fein,** *NY Herald Tribune,* for his photo, "Babe Ruth Bows Out."

1952 **John Robinson** & **Don Ultang,** *Des Moines* (Iowa) *Register and Tribune,* for their sequence of six pictures of the 1951 Drake-Oklahoma A&M football game, in which Drake's Johnny Bright had his jaw broken.

1985 **The Photography Staff** of the *Orange County* (Calif.) *Register,* for their coverage of the 1984 Summer Olympics in Los Angeles.

1993 **William Snyder** & **Ken Geiger,** The Dallas Morning News, for their coverage of the 1992 Summer Olympics in Barcelona, Spain.

Sportswriter of the Year
NSSA Award

Presented annually since 1959 by the National Sportscasters and Sportswriters Association, based in Salisbury, N.C. Voting is done by NSSA members and selected national media.

Multiple winners: Jim Murray (14); Frank Deford and Rick Reilly (6); Red Smith (5); Will Grimsley (4); Peter Gammons (3).

Year		Year		Year	
1959	Red Smith, *NY Herald-Tribune*	1973	Jim Murray, *LA Times*	1987	Frank Deford, *Sports Ill.*
1960	Red Smith, *NY Herald-Tribune*	1974	Jim Murray, *LA Times*	1988	Frank Deford, *Sports Ill.*
1961	Red Smith, *NY Herald-Tribune*	1975	Jim Murray, *LA Times*	1989	Peter Gammons, *Sports Ill.*
1962	Red Smith, *NY Herald-Tribune*	1976	Jim Murray, *LA Times*	1990	Peter Gammons, *Boston Globe*
1963	Arthur Daley, *NY Times*	1977	Jim Murray, *LA Times*	1991	Rick Reilly, *Sports Ill.*
1964	Jim Murray, *LA Times*	1978	Will Grimsley, *AP*	1992	Rick Reilly, *Sports Ill.*
1965	Red Smith, *NY Herald-Tribune*	1979	Jim Murray, *LA Times*	1993	Peter Gammons, *Boston Globe*
1966	Jim Murray, *LA Times*	1980	Will Grimsley, *AP*	1994	Rick Reilly, *Sports Ill.*
1967	Jim Murray, *LA Times*	1981	Will Grimsley, *AP*	1995	Rick Reilly, *Sports Ill.*
1968	Jim Murray, *LA Times*	1982	Frank Deford, *Sports Ill.*	1996	Rick Reilly, *Sports Ill.*
1969	Jim Murray, *LA Times*	1983	Will Grimsley, *AP*	1997	Dave Kindred, *The Sporting News*
1970	Jim Murray, *LA Times*	1984	Frank Deford, *Sports Ill.*		
1971	Jim Murray, *LA Times*	1985	Frank Deford, *Sports Ill.*	1998	Mitch Albom, *Detroit Free Press*
1972	Jim Murray, *LA Times*	1986	Frank Deford, *Sports Ill.*	1999	Rick Reilly, *Sports Ill.*

Best Newspaper Sports Sections of 1999

Winners of the Annual Associated Press Sports Editors contest for best daily and Sunday sports sections. Awards are divided into different categories, based on circulation figures. Selections are made by a committee of APSE members.

Circulation Over 250,000

Top 10 Daily		Top 10 Sunday	
Boston Globe	New York Daily News	Atlanta Journal and Constitution	Kansas City Star
Chicago Tribune	New York Times	Boston Globe	Los Angeles Times
Dallas Morning News	St. Petersburg Times	Chicago Sun Times	New York Daily News
Los Angeles Times	USA Today	Chicago Tribune	New York Times
Minneapolis Star Tribune	Washington Post	Dallas Morning News	Toronto Sun

Circulation 100,000-250,000

Top 10 Daily		Top 10 Sunday	
Arkansas Democrat-Gazette	Nashville Tennessean	Charlotte Observer	Pittsburgh
Arlington Heights Daily Herald	Raleigh News and Observer	Contra Costa Times	Post-Gazette Record
Columbia State	Seattle Times	Hartford Courant	San Antonio Express-News
Contra Costa Times	Tampa Tribune	Lexington (Ky.) Herald-Leader	San Francisco Examiner
Hartford Courant	Vancouver Province	Louisville (Ky.) Courier-Journal	Seattle Times

Best Sportswriting of 1999

Winners of the Annual Associated Press Sports Editors Contest for best sportswriting in 1999. Eventual winners were chosen from five finalists in each writing division. Selections are made by a committee of APSE members. Note the investigative writing division included all circulation categories.

Circulation over 250,000

Column:	Bill Plaschke, *Los Angeles Times*	**Game story:**	Selena Roberts, *New York Times*
Enterprise:	Paula Bott, *San Diego Union-Tribune*	**News story:**	Paul Harber, *Boston Globe*
Feature:	Mitch Albom, *Detroit Free Press*		

Circulation 100,000-250,000

Column:	Ken Burger, *Charleston Post and Courier*	**Feature:**	Joe Henderson, *Tampa Tribune*
Enterprise:	Fourteen different writers, *Hartford Courant*	**Game story:**	T.J. Quinn, *The Record (Hackensack, N.J.*
		News story:	Steve Dulas, *Contra Costa Times*

All Categories

Investigative: Judy Borger, George Dohrmann, Blake Morrison, Kris Pope, Bob Sansevere, Jeff Seidel, and Dave Shaffer, *St. Paul (Min.) Pioneer Press*

Directory of Organizations

Listing of the major sports organizations, teams and media addresses and officials as of Sept. 1, 2000.

AUTO RACING

CART
(Championship Auto Racing Teams, Inc.)
755 W. Big Beaver Rd., Suite 800, Troy, MI 48084
(248) 362-8800
President-CEO ....Bobby Rahal
Director of Publicity ....Mike Zizzo

IRL
(Indy Racing League)
4565 West 16th St., Indianapolis, IN 46222
(317) 484-6526
Founder ....Tony George
Dir. of Racing Ops. ....Brian Barnhart
Director of Public Relations ....Mai Lindstrom

FIA— Formula One
(Federation Internationale de L'Automobile)
2 Chemin de Blandonnet, 1215 Geneva 15, Switzerland
TEL: 011-41-2254-4400
President ....Max Mosley
Secretary General ....Pierre de Coninck
Director of Public Relations ...Francesco Longanesi-Cattani

NASCAR
(National Assn. for Stock Car Auto Racing)
P.O. Box 2875, Daytona Beach, FL 32120
(904) 253-0611
President ....William C. France
Managing Director of Communications ....John Griffin

NHRA
(National Hot Rod Association)
2035 Financial Way, Glendora, CA 91741
(626) 914-4761
President ....Tom Compton
Executive V.P./General Manager ....Graham Light
V.P. of Communications ....Jerry Archambeault

MAJOR LEAGUE BASEBALL

Office of the Commissioner
245 Park Ave., 31st Floor, New York, NY 10160
(212) 931-7800
Commissioner ....Bud Selig
President-COO ....Paul Beeston
General Counsel ....Thomas Ostertag
Executive Dir. of Public Relations ....Richard Levin

Player Relations Committee
245 Park Ave.
New York, NY 10160
(212) 931-7800
Chief Labor Negotiator ....Frank Coonelly
Associate Counsels ....Jennifer Gefsky
                                       & Derek Jackson

Major League Baseball Players Association
12 East 49th St., 24th Floor
New York, NY 10017
(212) 826-0808
Exec. Director & General Counsel ....Donald Fehr
Associate General Counsel ....Gene Orza

AL

American League Office
245 Park Ave., 28th Floor, New York, NY 10167
(212) 931-7800

Anaheim Angels
P. O. Box 2000, Anaheim, CA 92803
(714) 940-2000
Chairman ....Michael Eisner
Owner ....Walt Disney Co.
President & CEO ....Tony Tavares
V.P. & General Manager ....Bill Stoneman
V.P. of Communications ....Tim Mead

Baltimore Orioles
333 West Camden St., Baltimore, MD 21201
(410) 685-9800
CEO ....Peter Angelos
Vice Chairman, Business & Finance ....Joseph Foss
V.P. of Baseball Operations ....Syd Thrift
Director of Public Relations ....Bill Stetka

Boston Red Sox
Fenway Park, 4 Yawkey Way, Boston, MA 02215
(617) 267-9440
General Partner ....Jean R. Yawkey Trust
CEO ....John Harrington
Exec. V.P./General Manager ....Dan Duquette
Director of Communications ....Kevin Shea

Chicago White Sox
Comiskey Park, 333 W. 35th St., Chicago, IL 60616
(312) 674-1000
Chairman ....Jerry Reinsdorf
Vice Chairman ....Eddie Einhorn
Senior V.P./General Manager ....Ron Schueler
Director of Public Relations ....Scott Reifert

Cleveland Indians
Jacobs Field, 2401 Ontario St., Cleveland, OH 44115
(216) 420-4200
Owner-Chairman-CEO ....Lawrence Dolan
Exec. V.P./General Manager ....John Hart
V.P., Public Relations ....Bob DiBiasio

Detroit Tigers
Comerica Park, 2100 Woodward Ave., Detroit, MI 48201
(313) 962-4000
Owner and Director ....Mike Ilitch
Owner-Secretary-Treasurer ....Marian Ilitch
President/CEO ....John McHale Jr.
V.P. of Baseball Operations ....Randy Smith
Sr. Dir. or Marketing and Communications ....Tyler Barnes

Kansas City Royals
P.O. Box 419969, Kansas City, MO 64141
(816) 921-8000
Owner ....David Glass
Executive V.P./COO ....Herk Robinson
General Manager ....Allard Baird
Director of Media Relations ....TBA

Minnesota Twins
Hubert H. Humphrey Metrodome
34 Kirby Puckett Place, Minneapolis, MN 55415
(612) 375-1366
Owner ....Carl Pohlad
President ....Jerry Bell
V.P./General Manager ....Terry Ryan
Manager of Media Relations ....Sean Harlin

New York Yankees
Yankee Stadium, Bronx, NY 10451
(718) 293-4300
Principal Owner ....George Steinbrenner
General Partners .....Hal Steinbrenner & Stephen Swindal
V.P./General Manager ....Brian Cashman
Dir. of Media Relations/Publicity ....Rick Cerrone

Oakland Athletics
7677 Oakport St., Suite 200
Oakland, CA 94621
(510) 638-4900
Co-Owners ....Steve Schott and Ken Hofmann
President ....Mike Crowley
General Manager ....Billy Beane
Baseball Information Manager ....Mike Selleck

Seattle Mariners
P.O. Box 4100, Seattle, WA 98104
(206) 346-4000
Chairman-CEO ....Howard Lincoln
President-COO ....Chuck Armstrong
Executive V.P./General Manager ....Pat Gillick
Director of Baseball Information ....Tim Hevly

Tampa Bay Devil Rays
Tropicana Field, One Tropicana Dr.
St. Petersburg, FL 33705
(727) 825-3137
Managing General Partner/CEO ....Vincent J. Naimoli
Senior V.P., Baseball Ops./GM ....Chuck Lamar
V.P. of Public Relations ....Rick Vaughn

Texas Rangers
1000 Ballpark Way, Arlington, TX 76011
(817) 273-5222
Owner ....Thomas Hicks
President ....Jim Lites
V.P., General Manager ....Doug Melvin
Senior V.P. of Communications ....John Blake

Toronto Blue Jays
SkyDome, One Blue Jays Way, Suite 3200
Toronto, Ontario M5V 1J1
(416) 341-1000
Majority Owner ....Rogers Communications
Chairman ....Sam Pollock
Pres. Baseball Operations/General Manager ...Gord Ash
V.P. of Media Relations ....Howie Starkman

NL

National League Office
245 Park Ave., 28th Floor, New York, NY 10167
(212) 931-7800

Arizona Diamondbacks
Bank One Ballpark, 401 E.Jefferson St. Phoenix, AZ 85004
(602) 462-6500
Chairman/CEO ....Jerry Colangelo
President ....Richard H. Dozer
V.P./General Manager ....Joe Garagiola Jr.
Direcor of Public Relations ....Mike Swanson

Atlanta Braves
755 Hank Aaron Drive, Atlanta, GA 30315
(404) 522-7630
Owner ....Ted Turner
President ....Stan Kasten
Exec. V.P./General Manager ....John Schuerholz
Director of Public Relations ....Jim Schultz

Chicago Cubs
1060 West Addison St., Chicago, IL 60613
(773) 404-2827
Owner ....The Tribune Company
President-CEO-GM ....Andy MacPhail
Director of Media Relations ....Sharon Pannozzo

Cincinnati Reds
100 Cinergy Field, Cincinnati, OH 45202
(513) 421-4510
Majority Owner ....Carl Lindner
General Manager ....Jim Bowden
Director of Media Relations ....Rob Butcher

Colorado Rockies
Coors Field, 2001 Blake St., Denver, CO 80205
(303) 292-0200
Chairman-President-CEO ....Jerry McMorris
Executive V.P./General Manager ....Dan O'Dowd
V.P. of Business Ops. ....Keli McGregor
Director of Public Relations ....Jay Alves

Florida Marlins
2267 N.W. 199th St., Miami, FL 33056
(305) 626-7400
Owner ....John W. Henry
President/General Manager ....Dave Dombrowski
Director of Media Relations ....Eric Carrington

Houston Astros
Enron Field, P.O. Box 288, Houston, TX 77001
(713) 259-8000
Chairman-CEO ....Drayton McLane Jr.
President ....Tal Smith
General Manager ....Gerry Hunsicker
Director of Media Relations ....Rob Matwick

Los Angeles Dodgers
1000 Elysian Park Ave., Los Angeles, CA 90012
(323) 224-1500
Owner - ....News Corp
President/COO ....Bob Graziano
General Manager ....Kevin Malone
Director of Media Relations ....Julio Sarmiento

Milwaukee Brewers
County Stadium, P.O. Box 3099, Milwaukee, WI 53201
(414) 933-4114
President-CEO ....Wendy Selig-Prieb
Asst. to President ....Sal Bando
General Manager ....Dean Taylor
Director of Media Relations ....Jon Greenberg

Montreal Expos
P.O. Box 500, Station M, Montreal, Quebec H1V 3P2
(514) 253-3434
General Partner-President ....Jeffrey Loria
V.P./General Manager ....Jim Beattie
V.P. of Baseball Operations ....Bill Stoneman
Director of Media Relations ....Peter Loyello

New York Mets
123-01 Roosevelt Ave., Flushing, NY 11368
(718) 507-6387
Chairman ....Nelson Doubleday
President-CEO ....Fred Wilpon
General Manager ....Steve Phillips
Director of Media Relations ....Jay Horwitz

Philadelphia Phillies
P.O. Box 7575, Philadelphia, PA 19101
(215) 463-6000
Managing Gen. Partner/Pres./CEO ...David Montgomery
General Partner/Chairman ....Bill Giles
General Manager ....Ed Wade
V.P. of Public Relations ....Larry Shenk

Pittsburgh Pirates
P.O. Box 7000, Pittsburgh, PA 15212
(412) 323-5000
CEO/Managing General Partner ....Kevin McClatchy
COO ....Richard Freeman
Senior V.P. & General Manager ....Cam Bonifay
Director of Media Relations ....Jim Trdinich

St. Louis Cardinals
250 Stadium Plaza, St. Louis, MO 63102
(314) 421-3060
Owner ....Frederick O. Hanser
President ....Mark Lamping
V.P./General Manager ....Walt Jocketty
Director of Public Relations ....Brian Bartow

San Diego Padres
P.O. Box 122000, San Diego, CA 92112
(619) 881-6500
Chairman . . . . John Moores
President-CEO . . . . Larry Lucchino
V.P., Baseball Operations & G.M . . . . Kevin Towers
Director of Media Relations . . . . Glenn Geffner

San Francisco Giants
Pacific Bell Park, 24 Willie Mays Plaza
San Francisco, CA 94107
(415) 468-3700
President . . . . Peter Magowan
Executive V.P./COO . . . . Laurence Baer
Senior V.P./General Manager . . . . Brian Sabean
V.P. of Communications . . . . Bob Rose

PRO BASKETBALL
NBA

League Office
Olympic Tower, 645 Fifth Ave., New York, NY 10022
(212) 407-8000
Commissioner . . . . David Stern
Senior V.P. of Basketball Ops. . . . . Stuart Jackson
Deputy Commissioner . . . . Russell Granik
Sr. V.P. Sports Media Relations . . . . Brian McIntyre
Executive V.P. Global Media . . . . Heidi Ueberroth

NBA Players Association
1700 Broadway, Suite 1400, New York, NY 10019
(212) 655-0880
Exec. Director . . . . William Hunter
General Counsel . . . . Robert Lanza
President . . . . Patrick Ewing

Atlanta Hawks
One CNN Center, South Tower, Suite 405
Atlanta, GA 30303
(404) 827-3800
Owner . . . . Ted Turner
President . . . . Stan Kasten
General Manager . . . . Pete Babcock
V.P. of Communications . . . . Arthur Triche

Boston Celtics
151 Merrimac St., 4th Floor, Boston, MA 02114
(617) 523-6050
Chairman . . . . Paul Gaston
President & Head Coach . . . . Rick Pitino
General Manager . . . . Chris Wallace
V.P. of Media Relations . . . . Jeff Twiss

Charlotte Hornets
100 Hive Drive, Charlotte, NC 28217
(704) 357-0252
Owners . . . . George Shinn and Ray Wooldridge
Executive V.P., Basketball Operations . . . . Bob Bass
V.P. of Public Relations . . . . Harold Kaufman

Chicago Bulls
United Center, 1901 West Madison St., Chicago, IL 60612
(312) 455-4000
Chairman . . . . Jerry Reinsdorf
V.P., Basketball Operations . . . . Jerry Krause
Director of Media Services . . . . Tim Hallam

Cleveland Cavaliers
Gund Arena, One Centre Court, Cleveland, OH 44115
(216) 420-2000
Owner-Chairman . . . . Gordon Gund
Owner-Vice Chairman . . . . George Gund III
President & COO . . . . TBA
Senior V.P./General Manager . . . . Jim Paxson
Sr. Dir. of Communications and PR . . . . Bob Price

Dallas Mavericks
Reunion Arena, 777 Sports St., Dallas, TX 75207
(214) 748-1808
Owners . . . . Mark Cuban
General Manager . . . . Don Nelson
V.P. Marketing and Communications . . . . Greg Anderson

Denver Nuggets
1000 Chopper Cir., Denver, CO 80204
(303) 405-1100
Owner . . . . Stan Kroenke
General Manager & Head Coach . . . . Dan Issel
Director of Media Services . . . . Tommy Sheppard

Detroit Pistons
The Palace of Auburn Hills
Two Championship Dr., Auburn Hills, MI 48326
(248) 377-0100
Managing Partner . . . . William Davidson
President . . . . Tom Wilson
President of Basketball Operations . . . . Joe Dumars
V.P. of Public Relations . . . . Matt Dobek

Golden State Warriors
1011 Broadway, Oakland, CA 94607
(510) 986-2200
Owner-CEO . . . . Chris Cohan
General Manager . . . . Garry St. Jean
Director of Public Relations . . . . Raymond Ridder

Houston Rockets
2 Greenway Plaza, Suite 400, Houston, TX 77046
(713) 627-3865
Owner . . . . Leslie L. Alexander
COO . . . . George Postolos
Sr. Exec. V.P. of Basketball Affairs . . . . TBA
Manager of Team Communications . . . . Tim Frank

Indiana Pacers
1 Conseco Court, Indianapolis, IN 46204
(317) 917-2500
Owners . . . . Melvin Simon & Herb Simon
President . . . . Donnie Walsh
General Manager . . . . David Kahn
Executive V.P./Head Coach . . . . Isiah Thomas
Director of Media Relations . . . . David Benner

Los Angeles Clippers
Staples Center
1111 S. Figueroa St., Suite 1100
Los Angeles, CA 90015
(213) 745-0400
Owner-Chairman . . . . Donald T. Sterling
Executive V.P. . . . . Andy Roeser
V.P., Basketball Operations . . . . Elgin Baylor
Director of Communications . . . . Rob Raichlen

Los Angeles Lakers
555 N. Nash St., El Segundo, CA 90245
(310) 426-6000
Owner . . . . Jerry Buss
Exec. V.P., Basketball Operations . . . . Mitch Kupchak
General Manager . . . . Mitch Kupchak
Director of Public Relations . . . . John Black

Miami Heat
AmericanAirlines Arena, 601 Biscayne Blvd.
Miami, FL 33132
(786) 777-4328
Managing General Partner . . . . Micky Arison
President & Head Coach . . . . Pat Riley
General Manager . . . . Randy Pfund
Director of Media Relations . . . . Tim Donovan

Milwaukee Bucks
Bradley Center, 1001 N. Fourth St., Milwaukee, WI 53203
(414) 227-0500
President . . . . Sen. Herb Kohl (D., Wisc.)
General Manager . . . . Ernie Grunfeld
Director of Publicity . . . . TBA

Minnesota Timberwolves
Target Center
600 First Ave. North, Minneapolis, MN 55403
(612) 673-1600
Owner ....Glen Taylor
President ....Rob Moor
V.P., Basketball Operations ....Kevin McHale
General Manager & Head Coach ....Flip Saunders
Dir. of Public Relations/Communications ....Kent Wipf

New Jersey Nets
390 Murray Hill Pkwy., East Rutherford, NJ 07073
(201) 935-8888
Co-Chairman/CEO ....Finn Wentworth
Co-Chair/Owner ....Lewis Katz
General Manager ....John Nash
Director of Public Relations ....John Mertz

New York Knickerbockers
Madison Square Garden
2 Penn Plaza, 14th Floor, New York, NY 10121
(212) 465-6000
Owner ....Cablevision Systems Inc.
President (MSG) ....Dave Checketts
General Manager ....Scott Layden
V.P. of Public Relations ....Lori Hamamoto

Orlando Magic
2 Magic Place
8701 Maitland Summit Blvd., Orlando, FL 32810
(407) 916-2400
Owner ....Rich DeVos
President ....Bob Vander Weide
V.P., Basketball Ops. & GM ....John Gabriel
Director of Media Relations ....Joel Glass

Philadelphia 76ers
First Union Center
3601 S. Broad St., Philadelphia, PA 19148
(215) 339-7600
Owner-President ....Pat Croce
General Manager ....Billy King
Player Personnel Director ....Tony DiLeo
Director of Communications ....Karen Frascona

Phoenix Suns
P.O. Box 1369, Phoenix, AZ 85001
(602) 379-7900
Chairman-CEO/Managing Gen. Partner . Jerry Colangelo
President/General Manager ....Bryan Colangelo
Sr. V.P. of Player Personnel ....Dick Van Arsdale
V.P. of Basketball Communications ....Julie Fie

Portland Trail Blazers
One Centre Court, Suite 200, Portland, OR 97227
(503) 234-9291
Owner-Chairman ....Paul Allen
President & General Manager ....Bob Whitsitt
Assistant General Manager ....Mark Wakenstein
Director of Communications ....Sue Carpenter

Sacramento Kings
One Sports Parkway, Sacramento, CA 95834
(916) 928-0000
Controlling Partners ....Joe Maloof and Gavin Maloof
President ....John Thomas
V.P., Basketball Operations ....Geoff Petrie
Director of Media Relations ....Troy Hanson

San Antonio Spurs
The Alamodome
100 Montana St., San Antonio, TX 78203
(210) 554-7700
Chairman ....Peter Holt
GM & Head Coach ....Gregg Popovich
Director of Player Personnel ....Sam Schuler
Director of Media Services ....Tom James

Seattle SuperSonics
351 Elliott Ave. West
Seattle, WA 98119
(206) 281-5800
Owner-Chairman ....Barry Ackerley
President & General Manager ....Wally Walker
Executive V.P. of Basketball Ops. ....Billy McKinney
Director of Media Relations ....Cheri Hanson

Toronto Raptors
40 Bay St., Suite 400
Toronto, Ontario M5J 2X2
(416) 815-5600
Owner ....Steve Stavro
President ....Richard Peddie
Sr. V.P./General Manager ....Glen Grunwald
V.P. of Commications ....John Lashway

Utah Jazz
Delta Center, 301 West South Temple
Salt Lake City, UT 84101
(801) 325-2500
Owner ....Larry Miller
President ....Dennis Haslam
V.P. of Basketball Operations ....Kevin O'Connor
Director of Media Relations ....Kim Turner

Vancouver Grizzlies
General Motors Place, 800 Griffiths Way
Vancouver, B.C. V6B 6G1
(604) 899-7650
Owner ....Michael Heisley
President ....Dick Versace
General Manager ....Billy Knight
Coordinator of Media Relations ....Dianne Schultz

Washington Wizards
MCI Center, 601 F Street NW
Washington, D.C., 20004
(202) 661-5000
Chairman ....Abe Pollin
President ....Susan O'Malley
Director Of Basketball Operations ....Michael Jordan
V.P./General Manager ....Wes Unseld
Director of Public Relations ....Maureen Lewis

Other Men's Pro Leagues

Continental Basketball Association
400 North 5th St., Suite 1425, Phoenix, AZ 85004
(602) 254-6677
President ....Dan Welsh
Dir. of Media Relations ....Deron Filip
   Member teams (9): Connecticut Pride, Ft. Wayne (IN)
Fury, Grand Rapids Hoops, Idaho Stampede, LaCrosse
Bobcats, Quad City (IL) Thunder, Rockford (IL) Lightning,
Sioux Falls (SD) Skyforce and Yakima (WA) Sun Kings.

United States Basketball League
46 Quirk Road, Milford, CT 06460
(203) 877-9508
Commissioner ....Daniel T. Meisenheimer III
Dir. of Public Relations ....Sean Fisher
   Member teams (11): Atlantic City Seagulls, Brooklyn
Kings, Dodge City Legends, Florida Seadragons, Gulf
Coast Sundogs, Kansas Cagerz, Long Island Surf, New
Jersey Shorecats, Oklahoma Storm, Pennsylvania Valley-
dawgs and Washington D.C. Congressionals.

WNBA
Women's National Basketball Association
645 5th Ave., New York, NY 10022
(212) 826–7000
President ....Val Ackerman
Manager, Communications ....Gail Fuller
Director of Media Relations ....Mark Pray

Charlotte Sting
3308 Oak Lace Blvd., Ste. B, Charlotte, NC 28208
(704) 357-0252
Executive V.P. ....Sam Russo
Head Coach ...............................T.R. Dunn
Director of Media Relations ....John Maxwell

Cleveland Rockers
Gund Arena, One Center Court
Cleveland, OH 44115
(216) 420-2000
President ....Jim Boland
Head Coach ....Dan Hughes
General Manager ....Jim Paxson
Director of Media Relations ....Lori Montgomery

Detroit Shock
The Palace at Auburn Hills
Two Championship Dr., Auburn Hills, MI 48326
(248) 377-0100
GM/Head Coach ....Nancy Lieberman-Cline
Dir. of Public Relations ....Dennis Sampier

Houston Comets
Two Greenway Plaza, Suite 400
Houston, TX 77046-3865
(713) 627-9622
Owner/President ....Leslie L. Alexander
GM/Head Coach ....Van Chancellor
Director of Media Relations ....Megan Bonifas

Indiana Fever
125 S. Pennsylvania St., Indianapolis, IN 46204
(317) 917-2500
President ....Donnie Walsh
Head Coach ....Anne Donovan
Director of Media Relations ....Tom Savage

Los Angeles Sparks
Great Western Forum
3900 W.Manchester Blvd., Inglewood, CA 90306
(310) 330-2434
General Manager ....Penny Toler
Head Coach ....Michael Cooper
Interim Dir. of Media Relations ....Chrystal Ship

Miami Sol
601 Biscayne Blvd., Miami, FL 33132
(786) 777-1000
Owner ....Micky Arison
President ....Pat Riley
GM/Head Coach ....Ron Rothstein
Director of Media Relations ....Amanda Ludwig

Minnesota Lynx
Target Center
600 First Ave. N., Minneapolis, MN 55403
(612) 673-1600
Owner ....Glen Taylor
GM/Head Coach ....Brain Agler
Manager of Media Relations ....Kent Wipt

New York Liberty
Madison Square Garden
Two Penn Plaza, New York, NY 10121
(212) 564-9622
General Manager ....Carol Blazejowski
Head Coach ....Richie Adubato
Manager of Public Relations ....Jeff Schwartzenberg

Orlando Miracle
2 Magic Place
8701 Maitland Summit Blvd., Orlando, FL., 32810
(407) 916-2400
President ....Bob Vander Weide
GM/Head Coach ....Carolyn Peck
Media/Community Relations Manager ......Katherine Wu

Phoenix Mercury
America West Arena
201 E. Jefferson St.
Phoenix, AZ 85004
(602) 514-8333
President ....Brian Colangelo
GM/Head Coach ....Cheryl Miller
Director of Communications ....Neda Kia

Portland Fire
One Centre Court, Suite 150
Portland, OR 97227
(503) 234-9291
Owner ....Paul Allen
GM/Head Coach ....Linda Hargrove
Director of Media Relations ....Jill Wiggins

Sacramento Monarchs
ARCO Arena, One Sports Pkwy.
Sacramento, CA 95834
(916) 928-0000
General Manager ....Jerry Reynolds
Head Coach ....Sonny Allen
Director of Communications/Ops. ....Andrea Lepore

Seattle Storm
351 Elliott Ave. W.
Seattle, WA 98119
(206) 281-5800
Owner/President ....Barry and Ginger Ackerly
GM/Head Coach ....Lin Dunn
Director of Media Relations ....Valerie O'Neil

Utah Starzz
Delta Center, 301 West South Temple
Salt Lake City, UT 84101
(801) 325-2500
V.P. of Basketball Operations ....Kevin O'Connor
Head Coach ....Fred Williams
Director of Public/Comm. Relations ....Tami Scott

Washington Mystics
MCI Center, 601 F St. NW
Washington D.C. 20004
(202) 661-5000
V.P./General Manager ....Wes Unseld
Head Coach ....Nancy Darsch
Director of Public Relations ....Jeff Venyon

BOWLING

ABC
(American Bowling Congress)
5301 South 76th St.
Greendale, WI 53129
(414) 421-6400
Executive Director ....Roger Dalken
Director of PR/Marketing ....Michael Deering

BPAA
(Bowling Proprietors' Assn. of America)
P.O. Box 5802
Arlington, TX 76005
(817) 649-5105
CEO ....Jack Kelly
President ....Michael Ducat
Director of Public Relations ....Cary Richmond

PWBA
(Professional Women's Bowling Association)
7171 Cherryvale Blvd.
Rockford, IL 61112
(815) 332-5756
President ....John Falzone
Media Director ....Darlene Priscilla

PBA
(Professional Bowlers Association)
1720 Merriman Road, P.O. Box 5118
Akron, OH 44334
(330) 836-5568
Commissioner . . . . .Mark Gerberich
Public Relations Director . . . . .Dave Schroeder

WIBC
(Women's International Bowling Congress, Inc.)
5301 South 76th St., Greendale, WI 53129
(414) 421-9000
President . . . . Joyce Deitch
Public Relations Manager . . . . .Mark Whitney

BOXING

IBF
(International Boxing Federation)
134 Evergreen Place, 9th Floor
East Orange, NJ 07018
(973) 414-0300
President . . . . .Hiawatha Knight
Executive Secretary . . . . .Marian Muhammad
Ratings Chairman . . . . .Daryl Peoples

WBA
(World Boxing Association)
P.O. Box 377, Maracay 2110–A
Venezuela
TEL: 011-58-44-63-1584
President . . . . .Gilberto Mendoza
General Counsel/U.S. Spokesman . . . . Jimmy Binns
1735 Market St., 39th Floor, Phila., PA 19103
(215) 557-8000
Ratings Chairman . . . . .Bolivar Icaza
P.O. Box 1833, Panama 1, Rep. de Panama
TEL: 011-507-63-5167

WBC
(World Boxing Council)
Genova 33-503, Col. Juarez,
MEXICO, 06600, D.F., Mexico
TEL: 011-525-208-2440
President . . . . Jose Sulaiman
Ratings Chairman . . . . .Frank Quill
Press Information/U.S. Spokesman . . . . John Brister
411 Ballentine St., Bay St. Louis, MS 39520
(228) 467-3304

WBO
(World Boxing Organization)
1st Federal Bldg.
1056 Ave Munoz Revera, Suite 711
San Juan, P.R. 00927
(787) 765-4444
President . . . . .Francisco Paco Valcarcel
Past Pres./Attorney .Luis Batista Salas
Ratings Chairman . . . . .Luis Perez
Public Relations Dir. . . . . .Mario Rivera-Martino

Don King Productions, Inc.
501 Fairway Dr.
Deerfield Beach, FL 33441
(954) 418-5800
President . . . . .Don King
V.P. of Boxing Ops. . . . . .Bob Goodman
Director of Public Relations . . . . .Greg Fritz

Top Rank
3980 Howard Hughes Pkwy. Ste. 580
Las Vegas, NV 89109
(702) 732-2717
Chairman . . . . .Bob Arum
Director of Marketing . . . . .Ben Bee

COLLEGE SPORTS

CCA
(Collegiate Commissioners Association)
2201 Stemmons Freeway, Dallas, TX 75207
(214) 742-1212
President . . . . John Steinbrecher (Mid-Continent)
Exec. V.P. .Michael Slive (Conf. USA)
Secretary-Treasurer . . . . .Britton Banowsky (Big 12)

NAIA
(National Assn. of Intercollegiate Athletics)
6120 South Yale, Suite 1450, Tulsa, OK 74136
(918) 494-8828
President-CEO . . . . .Steve Baker
Public Relations Director .Darin David

NCAA
(National Collegiate Athletic Association)
P.O. Box 6222, Indianapolis, IN 46206
(317) 957-6222
Chief Operating Officer . . . . .Daniel Boggan Jr.
President . . . . .Cedric Dempsey
V.P. of Enforcement . . . . .David Price
Director of Public Relations . . . . .Wallace I. Renfro

WSF
(Women's Sports Foundation)
Eisenhower Park, East Meadow, NY 11554
(516) 542-4700
Executive Director . . . . .Donna Lopiano
President . . . . .Nancy Lieberman-Cline
Public Relations Coordinator . . . . .Kristen Conti

Major NCAA Conferences
See pages 441-449 for basketball coaches, football
coaches, nicknames and colors of all Division I basketball
schools and Division I-A and I-AA football schools.

ATLANTIC COAST CONFERENCE
P.O. Drawer ACC
Greensboro, NC 27417-6724
(336) 854-8787   Founded: 1953
Commissioner . . . . John Swofford
Asst. Commis. of Media Relations . . . . .Brian Morrison
2000-01 members: BASKETBALL & FOOTBALL (9)—
Clemson, Duke, Florida St., Georgia Tech, Maryland,
North Carolina, North Carolina St., Virginia and Wake
Forest.

Clemson University
Clemson, SC 29633   Founded: 1889
SID: (864) 656-2114   Enrollment: 16,685
President . . . . .James F. Barker
Athletic Director . . . . .Bobby Robinson
Sports Information Director . . . . .Tim Baurret

Duke University
Durham, NC 27708   Founded: 1838
SID: (919) 684-2633   Enrollment: 6,207
President . . . . .Nannerl Keohane
Athletic Director . . . . .Joe Alleva
Sports Information Director . . . . .John Jackson

Florida State University
Tallahassee, FL 32316   Founded: 1857
SID: (850) 644-1403   Enrollment: 35,000
President .Talbot (Sandy) D'Alemberte
Athletic Director . . . . .Dave Hart Jr.
Sports Information Director . . . . .Rob Wilson

Georgia Tech
Atlanta, GA 30332   Founded: 1885
SID: (404) 894-5445   Enrollment: 14,000
President . . . . .Wayne Clough
Athletic Director . . . . .Dave Braine
Sports Information Director . . . . .Mike Stamus

University of Maryland
College Park, MD 20741 — Founded: 1807
SID: (301) 314-7064 — Enrollment: 33,006
President . . . . .Dr. Clayton D. Mote Jr.
Athletic Director . . . . .Deborah Yow
Sports Information Director . . . . .Dave Haglund

University of North Carolina
Chapel Hill, NC 27514 — Founded: 1789
SID: (919) 962-2123 — Enrollment: 24,635
Chancellor . . . . .James Moeser
Athletic Director . . . . .Dick Baddour
Sports Information Director . . . . .Steve Kirschner

North Carolina State University
Raleigh, NC 27695 — Founded: 1887
SID: (919) 515-2102 — Enrollment: 28,011
Chancellor . . . . .Mary Anne E. Fox
Athletic Director . . . . .Les Robinson
Sports Information Director . . . . .Annabelle Vaughan

University of Virginia
Charlottesville, VA 22903 — Founded: 1819
SID: (804) 982-5500 — Enrollment: 18,473
President . . . . .John T. Casteen III
Athletic Director . . . . .Terry Holland
Sports Information Director . . . . .Rich Murray

Wake Forest University
Winston-Salem, NC 27109 — Founded: 1834
SID: (336) 758-5640 — Enrollment: 3,850
President . . . . .Thomas K. Hearn Jr.
Athletic Director . . . . .Ron Wellman
Sports Information Director . . . . .Dean Buchan

&a &a &a

BIG EAST CONFERENCE
222 Richmond Street, 1st Floor, Providence, RI 02903
(401) 272-9108 — Founded: 1979
Commissioner . . . . .Mike Tranghese
Assoc. Commissioner/P.R . . . . .John Paquette
   2000-01 members: BASKETBALL (14)— Boston College, Connecticut, Georgetown, Miami-FL, Notre Dame, Pittsburgh, Providence, Rutgers, St. John's, Seton Hall, Syracuse, Villanova, Virginia Tech and West Virginia; FOOTBALL (8)— Boston College, Miami-FL, Pittsburgh, Rutgers, Syracuse, Temple, Virginia Tech and West Virginia.

Boston College
Chestnut Hill, MA 02467 — Founded: 1863
SID: (617) 552-3004 — Enrollment: 9,190
President . . . . .Rev. William P. Leahy, S.J.
Athletic Director . . . . .Gene DeFillippo
Sports Information Director . . . . .Michael Enright

University of Connecticut
Storrs, CT 06269 — Founded: 1881
SID: (860) 486-3531 — Enrollment: 21,901
President . . . . .Philip Austin
Athletic Director . . . . .Lew Perkins
Sports Information Director . . . . .Tim Tolokan

Georgetown University
Washington, DC 20057 — Founded: 1789
SID: (202) 687-2492 — Enrollment: 6,361
President .Rev. Leo J. O'Donovan, S.J.
Athletic Director . . . . .Joseph C. Lang
Sr. Sports Communication Director . . . . .Bill Shapland

University of Miami
Coral Gables, FL 33146 — Founded: 1926
SID: (305) 284-3244 — Enrollment: 13,781
President . . . . .Edward T. Foote II
Athletic Director . . . . .Paul Dee
Asst. Athletic Director/Communications . . . . .Bob Burda

University of Notre Dame
Notre Dame, IN 46556 — Founded: 1842
SID: (219) 631-7516 — Enrollment: 10,301
President . . . . .Rev. Edward (Monk) Malloy
Athletic Director . . . . .Kevin White
Sports Information Director . . . . .John Heisler

University of Pittsburgh
Pittsburgh, PA 15213 — Founded: 1787
SID: (412) 648-8240 — Enrollment: 32,293
Chancellor . . . . .Mark A. Nordenberg
Athletic Director . . . . .Steve Pederson
Sports Information Director . . . . .E.J. Borghetti

Providence College
Providence, RI 02918 — Founded: 1917
SID: (401) 865-2272 — Enrollment: 3,812
President . . . . .Philip A. Smith, OP
Athletic Director . . . . .John Marinatto
Sports Information Director . . . . .Arthur Parks

Rutgers University
New Brunswick, NJ 08903 — Founded: 1766
SID: (732) 445-4200 — Enrollment: 33,500
President . . . . .Francis L. Lawrence
Athletic Director . . . . .Robert E. Mulcahy III
Sports Information Director . . . . .John Wooding

St. John's University
Jamaica, NY 11439 — Founded: 1870
SID: (718) 990-6367 — Enrollment: 17,250
President . . . . .Rev. Donald J. Harrington, CM
Athletic Director . . . . .Edward J. Manetta Jr.
Sports Information Director . . . . .Dominic Scianna

Seton Hall University
South Orange, NJ 07079 — Founded: 1856
SID: (973) 761-9493 — Enrollment: 9,608
President . . . . .Monsignor Robert Sheeran
Athletic Director . . . . .Jeff Fogelson
Sports Information Director . . . . .Marie Wozniak

Syracuse University
Syracuse, NY 13244 — Founded: 1870
SID: (315) 443-2608 — Enrollment: 10,700
Chancellor . . . . .Kenneth Shaw
Athletic Director . . . . .Jake Crouthamel
Sports Information Director . . . . .Sue Edson

Temple University
Philadelphia, PA 19122 — Founded: 1884
SID: (215) 204-7445 — Enrollment: 30,000
President . . . . .Dr. David Adamany
Athletic Director . . . . .David O'Brien
Sports Information Director . . . . .Brian Kirschner

Villanova University
Villanova, PA 19085 — Founded: 1842
SID: (610) 519-4120 — Enrollment: 6,150
President . . . . .Rev. Edmund J. Dobbin, OSA
Athletic Director . . . . .Vince Nicastro
Sports Information Director . . . . .Dean Kenefick

Virginia Tech
Blacksburg, VA 24061 — Founded: 1872
SID: (540) 231-6796 — Enrollment: 25,000
President . . . . .Charles Steger
Athletic Director . . . . .Jim Weaver
Sports Information Director . . . . .Dave Smith

West Virginia University
Morgantown, WV 26507 — Founded: 1867
SID: (304) 293-2821 — Enrollment: 22,300
President . . . . .David Hardesty
Athletic Director . . . . .Ed Pastilong
Sports Information Director . . . . .Shelly Poe

BIG 12 CONFERENCE
2201 Stemmons Fwy., 28th Floor
Dallas, TX 75207
(214) 742-1212   Founded: 1996
Commissioner ....Kevin Weiberg
Media Relations Director ....Bo Carter
    2000-01 members: BASKETBALL & FOOTBALL (12)—
Baylor, Colorado, Iowa St., Kansas, Kansas St., Missouri,
Nebraska, Oklahoma, Oklahoma St., Texas, Texas A&M
and Texas Tech.

Baylor University
Waco, TX 76711   Founded: 1845
SID: (254) 710-2743   Enrollment: 13,334
President ....Robert B. Sloan
Athletic Director ....Tom Stanton
Sports Information Director ....Scott Stricklin

University of Colorado
Boulder, CO 80309   Founded: 1876
SID: (303) 492-5626   Enrollment: 28,373
President ....Dr. Alexander Bracken
Athletic Director ....Dick Tharp
Sports Information Director ....Dave Plati

Iowa State University
Ames, IA 50011   Founded: 1858
SID: (515) 294-3372   Enrollment: 26,110
President ....TBA
Athletic Director ....TBA
Sports Information Director ....Tom Kroeschell

University of Kansas
Lawrence, KS 66045   Founded: 1866
SID: (785) 864-3417   Enrollment: 27,838
Chancellor ....Robert Hemenway
Athletic Director ....Bob Frederick
Asst. Athletic Director/Media Relations ......Doug Vance

Kansas State University
Manhattan, KS 66502   Founded: 1863
SID: (785) 532-6735   Enrollment: 21,345
President ....Jon Wefald
Athletic Director ....Max Urick
Sports Information Director ....Doug Dull

University of Missouri
Columbia, MO 65205   Founded: 1839
SID: (573) 882-3241   Enrollment: 22,898
Chancellor ....Richard Wallace
Athletic Director ....Michael Alden
Interim Sports Information Director ....Chad Moller

University of Nebraska
Lincoln, NE 68588   Founded: 1869
SID: (402) 472-2263   Enrollment: 25,000
Interim Chancellor ....Harvey Perlman
Athletic Director ....Bill Byrne
Sports Information Director ....Chris Anderson

University of Oklahoma
Norman, OK 73019   Founded: 1890
SID: (405) 325-8231   Enrollment: 25,000
President ....David Boren
Athletic Director ....Joe Castiglione
Sports Information Director ....Mike Prusinski

Oklahoma State University
Stillwater, OK 74078   Founded: 1890
SID: (405) 707-7830   Enrollment: 21,216
President ....James Halligan
Athletic Director ....Terry Don Phillips
Sports Information Director ....Steve Buzzard

University of Texas
Austin, TX 78713   Founded: 1883
SID: (512) 471-7437   Enrollment: 46,484
President ....Dr. Larry Faulkner
Athletic Director ....De Loss Dodds
Sports Information Director ....John Bianco

Texas A&M University
College Station, TX 77843   Founded: 1876
SID: (409) 845-5725   Enrollment: 43,442
President ....Ray Bowen
Athletic Director ....Wally Groff
Sports Information Director ....Alan Cannon

Texas Tech University
Lubbock, TX 79409   Founded: 1923
SID: (806) 742-2770   Enrollment: 22,078
Chancellor ....John Montford
Athletic Director ....Gerald Myers
Sports Information Director ....Kent Partridge

        🍂   🍂   🍂

BIG TEN CONFERENCE
1500 West Higgins Road
Park Ridge, IL 60068-6300
(847) 696-1010   Founded: 1895
Commissioner ....Jim Delany
Assisitant Commssioner of Media Relations ......Sue Lister
    2000-01 members: BASKETBALL & FOOTBALL (11)—
Illinois, Indiana, Iowa, Michigan, Michigan St., Minnesota,
Northwestern, Ohio St., Penn St., Purdue and Wisconsin.

University of Illinois
Champaign, IL 61820   Founded: 1867
SID: (217) 333-1390   Enrollment: 36,000
President ....James J. Stukel
Athletic Director ....Ron Guenther
Dir. of Communications ....Kent Brown

Indiana University
Bloomington, IN 47408   Founded: 1820
SID: (812) 855-9399   Enrollment: 36,000
President ....Myles Brand
Athletic Director ....Clarence Doninger
Sports Information Director ....Kit Klingelhoffer

University of Iowa
Iowa City, IA 52242   Founded: 1847
SID: (319) 335-9411   Enrollment: 28,705
President ....Mary Sue Coleman
Athletic Director ....Bob Bowlsby
Sports Information Director ....Phil Haddy

University of Michigan
Ann Arbor, MI 48109   Founded: 1817
SID: (734) 763-1381   Enrollment: 36,450
President ....Lee Bollinger
Interim Athletic Director...................William Martin
Sports Information Director ....Bruce Madej

Michigan State University
East Lansing, MI 48824   Founded: 1855
SID: (517) 355-2271   Enrollment: 43,189
President ....Peter McPherson
Interim Athletic Director ....Clarence Underwood
Sports Information Director ....John Lewandowski

University of Minnesota
Minneapolis, MN 55455   Founded: 1851
SID: (612) 625-4090   Enrollment: 39,595
President ....Mark Yudof
Interim Athletic Director ....Tom Moe
Sports Information Director ....TBA

Northwestern University
Evanston, IL 60208   Founded: 1851
SID: (847) 491-7503   Enrollment: 7,400
President ....Henry S. Bienen
Athletic Director ....Rick Taylor
Asst. Athletic Director/Media Services ....Brad Hurlbut

Ohio State University
Columbus, OH 43210   Founded: 1870
SID: (614) 292-6861   Enrollment: 54,989
President ....William E. Kirwan
Athletic Director ....Andy Geiger
Sports Information Director ....Steve Snapp

Penn State University
University Park, PA 16802   Founded: 1855
SID: (814) 865-1757   Enrollment: 33,147
President ....Graham Spanier
Athletic Director ....Tim Curley
Sports Information Director ....Jeff Nelson

Purdue University
West Lafayette, IN 47907   Founded: 1869
SID: (765) 494-3202   Enrollment: 36,878
President ....Martin C. Jischke
Athletic Director ....Morgan Burke
Sports Information Director ....Tom Schott

University of Wisconsin
Madison, WI 53711   Founded: 1848
SID: (608) 262-1811   Enrollment: 40,610
Chancellor ....David Ward
Athletic Director ....Pat Richter
Sports Information Director ....Steve Malchow

     ❧   ❧   ❧

BIG WEST CONFERENCE
Two Corporate Park, Suite 206
Irvine, CA 92606
(949) 261-2525   Founded: 1969
Commissioner ....Dennis Farrell
Director of Information ....Michael Daniels
2000-01 members: BASKETBALL (9)— Boise St.,
CS-Fullerton, Cal Poly-SLO, Idaho, Long Beach St., Pacific,
UC-Irvine, UC-Santa Barbara, Utah St.; FOOTBALL (6)—
Arkansas St., Boise St., Idaho, New Mexico St., North
Texas, Utah St.

Arkansas State University
State University, AR 72467   Founded: 1909
SID: (870) 972-2541   Enrollment: 10,050
President ....Les Wyatt
Athletic Director ....Joe Hollis
Sports Information Director ....Gina Bowman

Boise State
Boise, ID 83725   Founded: 1932
SID: (208) 426-1515   Enrollment: 16,209
President ....Charles P. Ruch
Athletic Director ....Gene Bleymaier
Sports Information Director ....Max Corbet

Cal State-Fullerton
Fullerton, CA 92834   Founded: 1957
SID: (714) 278-3970   Enrollment: 27,263
President ....Milton A. Gordon
Athletic Director ....John Easterbrook
Sports Information Director ....Mel Franks

Cal Poly SLO
San Luis Obispo, CA 93407   Founded: 1901
SID: (805) 756-6531   Enrollment: 16,700
President ....Dr. Warren J. Baker
Athletic Director ....John McCutcheon
Sports Information Director ....Jason Sullivan

University of Idaho
Moscow, ID 83844   Founded: 1889
SID: (208) 885-0211   Enrollment: 11,305
President ....Bob Hoover
Athletic Director ....Mike Bohn
Sports Information Director ....Becky Paull

Long Beach State
Long Beach, CA 90840   Founded: 1949
SID: (562) 985-7797   Enrollment: 28,000
President ....Robert Maxson
Athletic Director ....Bill Shumard
Sports Information Director ....Steve Janisch

New Mexico State University
Las Cruces, NM 88003   Founded: 1888
SID: (505) 646-3929   Enrollment: 15,449
President ....Dr. Jay Gogue
Athletic Director ....Brian Faison
Asst. Athletic Director/Media Relations .....David Hardee

University of North Texas
Denton, TX 76203   Founded: 1890
SID: (940) 565-2476   Enrollment: 26,500
Chancellor ....Dr. Alfred F. Hurley
Athletic Director ....Craig Helwig
Sports Information Director ....Sean Johnson

University of the Pacific
Stockton, CA 95211   Founded: 1851
SID: (209) 946-2479   Enrollment: 6,000
President ....Donald DeRosa
Athletic Director ....Lynn King
Sports Information Director ....Mike Millerick

University of California, Irvine
Irvine, CA 92697   Founded: 1962
SID: (949) 824-5814   Enrollment: 18,000
Chancellor ....Ralph Cicerone
Athletic Director ....Dan Guerrero
Sports Information Director ....Bob Olson

University of California, Santa Barbara
Santa Barbara, CA 93106   Founded: 1944
SID: (805) 893-3428   Enrollment: 18,400
Chancellor ....Henry Yang
Athletic Director ....Gary Cunningham
Sports Information Director ....Bill Mahoney

Utah State University
Logan, UT 84322   Founded: 1888
SID: (435) 797-1361   Enrollment: 20,808
President ....George Emert
Athletic Director ....Rance Pugmire
Sports Information Director ....Mike Strauss

     ❧   ❧   ❧

CONFERENCE USA
35 East Wacker Drive, Suite 650, Chicago, IL 60601
(312) 553-0483   Founded: 1995
Commissioner ....Mike Slive
Asst. Commissioner ....Brian Teter
2000-01 members: BASKETBALL (12)— UAB, Cincinnati, DePaul, Houston, Louisville, Marquette, Memphis,
UNC-Charlotte, Saint Louis, South Florida, Southern Miss
and Tulane; FOOTBALL (9)— UAB, Army, Cincinnati, East
Carolina, Houston, Louisville, Memphis, Southern Miss and
Tulane.

University of Alabama at Birmingham
Birmingham, AL 35294   Founded: 1969
SID: (205) 934-0722   Enrollment: 16,081
President ....Dr. W. Ann Reynolds
Athletic Director ....Herman Frazier
Sports Information Director ....Grant Shingleton

Army — U.S. Military Academy
West Point, NY 10996 — Founded: 1802
SID: (914) 938-3303 — Enrollment: 4,000
Superintendent ....Lt. Gen. Daniel W. Christman
Athletic Director ....Rick Greenspan
Sports Information Director ....Bob Beretta

University of Cincinnati
Cincinnati, OH 45221 — Founded: 1819
SID: (513) 556-5191 — Enrollment: 34,000
President ....Dr. Joseph A. Steger
Athletic Director ....Bob Goin
Sports Information Director ....Tom Hathaway

DePaul University
Chicago, IL 60614 — Founded: 1898
SID: (773) 325-7525 — Enrollment: 18,565
President ....Rev. John P. Minogue
Athletic Director ....Bill Bradshaw
Sports Information Director ....Scott Reed

East Carolina University
Greenville, NC 27858 — Founded: 1907
SID: (252) 328-4522 — Enrollment: 18,223
Chancellor ....Dr. Richard Eakin
Athletic Director ....Mike Hamrick
Sports Information Director ....Norm Reilly

University of Houston
Houston, TX 77204 — Founded: 1927
SID: (713) 743-9404 — Enrollment: 30,757
President ....Arthur K. Smith
Athletic Director ....Chet Gladchuk
Sports Information Director ....Chris Buckhalter

University of Louisville
Louisville, KY 40292 — Founded: 1798
SID: (502) 852-6581 — Enrollment: 22,000
President ....Dr. John W. Shumaker
Athletic Director ....Tom Jurich
Sports Information Director ....Kenny Klein

Marquette University
Milwaukee, WI 53233 — Founded: 1881
SID: (414) 288-7447 — Enrollment: 10,600
President ....Rev. Robert A. Wild S.J.
Athletic Director ....Bill Cords
Sports Information Director ....John Farina

University of Memphis
Memphis, TN 38152 — Founded: 1912
SID: (901) 678-2337 — Enrollment: 20,100
Interim President ....Ralph Faudree
Athletic Director ..........................R.C. Johnson
Sports Information Director ....Bob Winn

University of North Carolina at Charlotte
Charlotte, NC 28223 — Founded: 1946
SID: (704) 547-4937 — Enrollment: 16,500
Chancellor ....J. H. Woodward
Athletic Director ....Judy Rose
Sports Information Director ....Tom Whitestone

Saint Louis University
St. Louis, MO 63103 — Founded: 1818
SID: (314) 977-2524 — Enrollment: 11,069
President ....Rev. Lawrence Biondi, S.J.
Athletic Director ....Doug Woolard
Sport Information Director ....Doug McIlhagga

University of South Florida
Tampa, FL 33620 — Founded: 1956
SID: (813) 974-4086 — Enrollment: 37,000
President ....Judy Genshaft
Athletic Director ....Paul Griffin
Sports Information Director ....John Gerdes

University of Southern Mississippi
Hattiesburg, MS 39406 — Founded: 1910
SID: (601) 266-4503 — Enrollment: 14,000
President ....Dr. Horace W. Fleming Jr.
Athletic Director ....Rich Giannini
Sports Information Director ....Regiel Napier

Tulane University
New Orleans, LA 70118 — Founded: 1834
SID: (504) 865-5506 — Enrollment: 11,300
President ....Dr. Scott S. Cowen
Athletic Director ....Rick Dickson
Sports Information Director ....Donna Turner

≈ ≈ ≈

MID-AMERICAN CONFERENCE
24 Public Square, 15th Floor, Cleveland, OH 44113
(216) 566-4622 — Founded: 1946
Commissioner ....Rick Chryst
Director of Communications ....Gary Richter
2000-01 members: BASKETBALL & FOOTBALL (13)—
Akron, Ball St., Bowling Green, Buffalo, Central Michigan,
Eastern Michigan, Kent, Marshall, Miami-OH, Northern
Illinois, Ohio University, Toledo and Western Michigan.

University of Akron
Akron, OH 44325 — Founded: 1870
SID: (330) 972-7468 — Enrollment: 23,264
President ....Louis Proenza
Interim Athletic Director ....Mike Rodriguez
Sports Information Director ....Jeff Brewer

Ball State University
Muncie, IN 47306 — Founded: 1918
SID: (765) 285-8242 — Enrollment: 17,529
President ....Dr. Blaine Brownell
Athletic Director ....Andrea Seger
Sports Information Director ....Joe Hernandez

Bowling Green State University
Bowling Green, OH 43403 — Founded: 1910
SID: (419) 372-7075 — Enrollment: 16,900
President ....Sidney Ribeau
Athletic Director ....Paul Krebs
Co-Sports Information Directors ...Mike Cihon & Jeff Weiss

University of Buffalo
Buffalo, NY 14260 — Founded: 1846
SID: (716) 645-6311 — Enrollment: 24,000
President ....William P. Greiner
Athletic Director ....Bob Arkeilpane
Sports Information Director ....Paul Vecchio

Central Michigan University
Mt. Pleasant, MI 48859 — Founded: 1892
SID: (517) 774-3277 — Enrollment: 26,321
President ....Michael Rao
Athletic Director ....Herb Deromedi
Sports Information Director ....Fred Stabley Jr.

Eastern Michigan University
Ypsilanti, MI 48197 — Founded: 1849
SID: (734) 487-0317 — Enrollment: 24,500
President ....Dr. Samuel Kirkpatrick
Athletic Director ....Dr. David Dials
Sports Information Director ....Jim Streeter

Kent State University
Kent, OH 44242 — Founded: 1910
SID: (330) 672-2110 — Enrollment: 30,287
President ....Carol Cartwright
Athletic Director ....Laing Kennedy
Sports Information Director ....Will Roleson

Marshall University

Huntington, WV 25715 — Founded: 1837
SID: (304) 696-4660 — Enrollment: 14,000
President ....Dan Angel
Athletic Director ....Lance West
Sports Information Director ....Ricky Hazel

Miami University

Oxford, OH 45056 — Founded: 1809
SID: (513) 529-4327 — Enrollment: 16,000
President ....James C. Garland
Athletic Director ....Joel Maturi
Sports Information Director ....Mike Wolf

Northen Illinois University

DeKalb, IL 60115 — Founded: 1895
SID: (815) 753-1706 — Enrollment: 22,843
President ....John G. Peters
Athletic Director ....Cary Groth
Sports Information Director ....Michael Korcek

Ohio University

Athens, OH 45701 — Founded: 1804
SID: (740) 593-1299 — Enrollment: 27,605
President ....Robert Glidden
Athletic Director ....Tom Boeh
Sports Information Director ....Heather Czeczok

University of Toledo

Toledo, OH 43606 — Founded: 1872
SID: (419) 530-3790 — Enrollment: 20,786
Interim President ....William Decatur
Athletic Director ....Pete Liske
Sports Information Director ....Paul Helgren

Western Michigan University

Kalamazoo, MI 49008 — Founded: 1903
SID: (616) 387-4138 — Enrollment: 27,744
President ....Dr. Elson Floyd
Athletic Director ....Kathy Beauregard
Sports Information Director ....Dan Jankowski

෴ ෴ ෴

MOUNTAIN WEST CONFERENCE

P.O. Box 35670
Colorado Springs, CO 80935
(719) 533-9500 — Founded: 1999
Commissioner ....Craig Thompson
Media Relations Director ....Amy Turner
 2000-01members: BASKETBALL & FOOTBALL (8)—
Air Force, BYU, Colorado State, UNLV, New Mexico, San
Diego St., Utah, Wyoming.

U.S. Air Force Academy

US Academy, CO 80840 — Founded: 1959
SID: (719) 333-2313 — Enrollment: 4,100
Superintendent ....Lt. Gen. John R. Dallager
Athletic Director ....Col. Randall W. Spetman
Sports Information Director ....Dave Kellogg

Brigham Young University

Provo, UT 84602 — Founded: 1875
SID: (801) 378-4911 — Enrollment: 28,300
President ....Merril J. Bateman
Athletic Director ....Val Hale
Sports Information Director ....Norma Collett

Colorado State University

Fort Collins, CO 80523 — Founded: 1870
SID: (970) 491-5067 — Enrollment: 23,500
President ....Dr. Albert Yates
Athletic Director ....Tim Wieser
Sports Information Director ....Gary Ozzello

University of New Mexico

Albuquerque, NM 87131 — Founded: 1889
SID: (505) 925-5520 — Enrollment: 24,250
President ....Dr. William Gordon
Athletic Director ....Rudy Davalos
Sports Information Director ....Greg Remington

San Diego State University

San Diego, CA 92182 — Founded: 1897
SID: (619) 594-5547 — Enrollment: 29,500
President ....Dr. Stephen L. Weber
Athletic Director ....Rick Bay
Interim Sports Information Director ....Kevin Klintworth

UNLV — University of Nevada, Las Vegas

Las Vegas, NV 89154 — Founded: 1957
SID: (702) 895-3207 — Enrollment: 23,000
President ....Dr. Carol Harter
Athletic Director ....Charles Cavognaro
Sports Information Director .... Jim Gemma

University of Utah

Salt Lake City, UT 84112 — Founded: 1850
SID: (801) 581-3510 — Enrollment: 25,803
President ....Dr. Bernard Machen
Athletic Director ....Dr. Chris Hill
Sports Information Director ....Liz Abel

University of Wyoming

Laramie, WY 82071 — Founded: 1886
SID: (307) 766-2256 — Enrollment: 10,600
President ....Philip Dubois
Athletic Director ....Lee Moon
Sports Information Director ....Kevin McKinney

෴ ෴ ෴

PACIFIC-10 CONFERENCE

800 South Broadway, Suite 400
Walnut Creek, CA 94596
(925) 932-4411 — Founded: 1915
Commissioner ....Thomas Hansen
Asst. Commissioner, Public Relations .....Jim Muldoon
 2000-01 members: BASKETBALL & FOOTBALL (10)—
Arizona, Arizona St., California, Oregon, Oregon St.,
Stanford, UCLA, USC, Washington and Washington St.

University of Arizona

Tucson, AZ 85721 — Founded: 1885
SID: (520) 621-4163 — Enrollment: 35,000
President ....Peter Likins
Athletic Director ....Jim Livengood
Sports Information Director ....Tom Duddleston

Arizona State University

Tempe, AZ 85287 — Founded: 1885
SID: (480) 965-6592 — Enrollment: 43,379
President ....Lattie F. Coor
Athletic Director ....Gene Smith
Sports Information Director ....Mark Brand

University of California

Berkeley, CA 94720 — Founded: 1868
SID: (510) 642-5363 — Enrollment: 31,000
Chancellor ....Robert Berdahl
Athletic Director ....John Kasser
Sports Information Director ....Herb Benenson

University of Oregon

Eugene, OR 97401 — Founded: 1876
SID: (541) 346-5488 — Enrollment: 17,200
President ....David Frohnmeyer
Athletic Director ....Bill Moos
Sports Information Director ....Dave Williford

Oregon State University
Corvallis, OR 97331   Founded: 1868
SID: (541) 737-3720   Enrollment: 17,000
President ....Paul G. Risser
Athletic Director ....Mitch Barnhart
Sports Information Director ....Hal Cowan

Stanford University
Stanford, CA 94305   Founded: 1891
SID: (650) 723-4418   Enrollment: 13,075
President ....John Hennessy
Athletic Director ....Ted Leland
Sports Information Director ....Gary Migdol

UCLA — Univ. of California, Los Angeles
Los Angeles, CA 90024   Founded: 1919
SID: (310) 206-6831   Enrollment: 34,000
Chancellor ....Albert Carnesale
Athletic Director ....Pete Dalis
Sports Information Director ....Marc Dellins

USC — Univ. of Southern California
Los Angeles, CA 90089   Founded: 1880
SID: (213) 740-8480   Enrollment: 29,000
President ....Steven Sample
Athletic Director ....Mike Garrett
Sports Information Director ....Tim Tessalone

University of Washington
Seattle, WA 98195   Founded: 1861
SID: (206) 543-2230   Enrollment: 25,000
President ....Richard McCormick
Athletic Director ....Barbara Hedges
Sports Information Director ....Jim Daves

Washington State University
Pullman, WA 99164   Founded: 1890
SID: (509) 335-2684   Enrollment: 20,500
President ....V. Lane Rawlins
Athletic Director ....Jim Sterk
Sports Information Director ....Rod Commons

ᏋᎾ   ᏋᎾ   ᏋᎾ

SOUTHEASTERN CONFERENCE
2201 Richard Arrington Blvd. North
Birmingham, AL 35203
(205) 458-3000   Founded: 1933
Commissioner ....Roy Kramer
Asst. Commis. of Media Relations ....Charles Bloom
  2000-01 members: BASKETBALL & FOOTBALL (12)—
Alabama, Arkansas, Auburn, Florida, Georgia, Kentucky,
LSU, Mississippi St., Ole Miss, South Carolina, Tennessee
and Vanderbilt.

University of Alabama
Tuscaloosa, AL 35487   Founded: 1831
SID: (205) 348-6084   Enrollment: 19,000
President ....Dr. Andrew Sorensen
Interim Athletic Director ....Mal Moore
Sports Information Director ....Larry White

University of Arkansas
Fayetteville, AR 72701   Founded: 1871
SID: (501) 575-2751   Enrollment: 14,577
Chancellor ....John White
Athletic Director ....Frank Broyles
Women's Athletic Director ....Bev Lewis
Sports Information Director ....Kevin Trainor

Auburn University
Auburn, AL 36831   Founded: 1856
SID: (334) 844-9800   Enrollment: 21,775
President ....William V. Muse
Athletic Director ....David Housel
Sports Information Director ....Meredith Jenkins

University of Florida
Gainesville, FL 32604   Founded: 1853
SID: (352) 375-4683 ext. 6100   Enrollment: 42,000
Interim President ....Charles Young
Athletic Director ....Jeremy Foley
Sports Information Director ....John Humenik

University of Georgia
Athens, GA 30603   Founded: 1785
SID: (706) 542-1621   Enrollment: 30,912
President ....Michael F. Adams
Athletic Director ....Vince Dooley
Sports Information Director ....Claude Felton

University of Kentucky
Lexington, KY 40506   Founded: 1865
SID: (606) 257-3838   Enrollment: 30,006
President ....Charles T. Wethington Jr.
Athletic Director ....Larry Ivy
Asst. Atheltic Director/Media Relations ....Rena Vicini

LSU — Louisiana State University
Baton Rouge, LA 70894   Founded: 1860
SID: (225) 388-8226   Enrollment: 30,977
Chancellor ....Dr. Mark Emmert
Athletic Director ....Joe Dean
Sports Information Director ....Michael Bonnette

Mississippi State University
Starkville, MS 39762   Founded: 1878
SID: (662) 325-2703   Enrollment: 16,047
President ....Dr. Malcolm Portera
Athletic Director ....Larry Templeton
Sports Information Director ....Mike Nemeth

Ole Miss — University of Mississippi
U. of M., MS 38677   Founded: 1848
SID: (662) 232-7522   Enrollment: 13,526
Chancellor ....Dr. Robert C. Khayat
Athletic Director ....John Shafer
Sports Information Director ....Langston Rogers

University of South Carolina
Columbia, SC 29208   Founded: 1801
SID: (803) 777-5204   Enrollment: 22,875
President ....John Palms
Athletic Director ....Mike McGee
Sports Information Director ....Kerry Tharp

University of Tennessee
Knoxville, TN 37996   Founded: 1794
SID: (865) 974-1212   Enrollment: 25,612
President ....J. Wade Gilley
Athletic Director ....Doug Dickey
Women's Athletic Director ....Joan Cronan
Sports Information Director ....Bud Ford

Vanderbilt University
Nashville, TN 37212   Founded: 1873
SID: (615) 322-4121   Enrollment: 5,818
Chancellor ....Gordon Gee
Athletic Director ....Todd Turner
Sports Information Director ....Rod Williamson

ᏋᎾ   ᏋᎾ   ᏋᎾ

WESTERN ATHLETIC CONFERENCE
9250 East Costilla Ave., Suite 300
Englewood, CO 80112
(303) 799-9221   Founded: 1962
Commissioner ....Karl Benson
Directors of Communications .....Dave Chaffin & Lisa Vad
  2000-01 members: BASKETBALL & FOOTBALL (9)—
Fresno St., Hawaii, Nevada, Rice, San Jose St., SMU, TCU,
Tulsa and UTEP.

Fresno State University
Fresno, CA 93740 — Founded: 1911
SID: (559) 278-2509 — Enrollment: 17,800
President ....Dr. John D. Welty
Athletic Director ....Dr. Al Bohl
Sports Information Director ....Steve Weakland

University of Hawaii
Honolulu, HI 96822 — Founded: 1907
SID: (808) 956-7523 — Enrollment: 17,500
President ....Dr. Kenneth Mortimer
Athletic Director ....Hugh Yoshida
Sports Information Director ....Lois Manin

University of Nevada
Reno, NV 89557 — Founded: 1874
SID: (775) 784-6900 — Enrollment: 12,000
President ....Joe Crowley
Athletic Director ....Chris Ault
Sports Information Director ....Jamie Klund

Rice University
Houston, TX 77005 — Founded: 1912
SID: (713) 348-5775 — Enrollment: 2,600
President ....Dr. Malcolm Gillis
Athletic Director ....Bobby May
Sports Information Director ....Bill Cousins

San Jose State University
San Jose, CA 95192 — Founded: 1857
SID: (408) 924-1217 — Enrollment: 27,000
President ....Dr. Robert L. Caret
Athletic Director ....Chuck Bell
Sports Information Director ....Lawrence Fan

SMU — Southern Methodist University
Dallas, TX 75275 — Founded: 1911
SID: (214) 768-2883 — Enrollment: 10,038
President ....Dr. R. Gerald Turner
Athletic Director ....Jim Copeland
Sports Information Director ....Chris Walker

TCU — Texas Christian University
Fort Worth, TX 76129 — Founded: 1873
SID: (817) 257-5394 — Enrollment: 7,200
Chancellor ....Dr. Michael Ferrari
Athletic Director ....Eric Hyman
Sports Information Director ....Steve Fink

University of Tulsa
Tulsa, OK 74104 — Founded: 1894
SID: (918) 631-2395 — Enrollment: 4,200
President ....Dr. Bob Lawless
Athletic Director ....Judy MacLeod
Sports Information Director ....Don Tomkalski

UTEP — University of Texas at El Paso
El Paso, TX 79902 — Founded: 1914
SID: (915) 747-6653 — Enrollment: 14,695
President ....Dr. Diana Natalicio
Athletic Director ....Bob Stull
Sports Information Director ....Jeff Darby

Major Independents
Division I-A football independents in 2000.

University of Central Florida
Orlando, FL 32816 — Founded: 1963
SID: (407) 823-2729 — Enrollment: 33,000
President ....Dr. John C. Hitt
Athletic Director ....Steve Sloan
Sports Information Director ....John Marini

Louisiana Tech University
Ruston, LA 71272 — Founded: 1894
SID: (318) 257-3144 — Enrollment: 10,000
President ....Dan Reneau
Athletic Director ....Jim Oakes
Sports Information Director ....Malcolm Butler

University of Louisiana at Lafayette
Lafayette, LA 70506 — Founded: 1898
SID: (337) 482-6331 — Enrollment: 17,000
President ....Ray Authement
Athletic Director ....Nelson Schexnayder
Sports Information Director ....Dan McDonald

University of Louisiana at Monroe
Monroe, LA 71209 — Founded: 1931
SID: (318) 342-5460 — Enrollment: 10,427
President ....Lawson Swearingen, Jr.
Athletic Director ....Warner Alford
Sports Information Director ....Hank Largin

Navy — U.S. Naval Academy
Annapolis, MD 21402 — Founded: 1845
SID: (410) 268-6226 — Enrollment: 4,000
Superintendent ....Adm. John Ryan
Athletic Director ....Jack Lengyel
Sports Information Director ....Scott Strasemeier

University of Notre Dame
Notre Dame, IN 46556 — Founded: 1842
SID: (219) 631-7516 — Enrollment: 10,301
President ....Rev. Edward (Monk) Malloy
Athletic Director ....Kevin White
Sports Information Director ....John Heisler

Other Major Division I Conferences
Conferences that play either Division I basketball or Division
I-AA football, or both.

America East
10 High St., Suite 860, Boston, MA 02110
(617) 695-6369 — Founded: 1979
Commissioner ....Chris Monasch
Director of Communications ....Matt Bourque
  2000-01 members: BASKETBALL (10)— Boston University, Delaware, Drexel, Hartford, Hofstra, Maine, New Hampshire, Northeastern, Towson and Vermont.

Atlantic 10 Conference
2 Penn Center Plaza
Philadelphia, PA 19102 — Founded: 1976
(215) 751-0500 — A-10 Football founded: 1997
Commissioner ....Linda Bruno
Director of Information ....Ray Cella
  2000-01 members: BASKETBALL (11)— Dayton, Duquesne, Fordham, George Washington, La Salle, Massachusetts, Rhode Island, St. Bonaventure, St. Joseph's-PA, Temple and Xavier-OH. FOOTBALL (10)— Delaware, James Madison, Maine, Massachusetts, New Hampshire, Northeastern, Rhode Island, Richmond, Villanova and William & Mary.

Division I Hockey Conferences
The six Division I hockey conferences are the Eastern Collegiate Athletic Conference (ECAC) in Centerville, Mass., (508) 771-5060; College Hockey America (CHA) in Denver, Colorado, (303) 871-4223, the Central Collegiate Hockey Assn. (CCHA) in Ann Arbor, Mich. (248) 888-0600; Hockey East in Lawrence, Mass., (978) 687-8535; the Metro Atlantic Athletic Assn. in Edison, N.J. (732) 738-5455 and the Western Collegiate Hockey Assn. in Madison, Wisc. (608) 829-0100.

Big Sky Conference
2491 Washington Blvd. Suite 201
Ogden, UT 84401
(801) 392-1978, ext. 2
Commissioner . . . . .Douglas Fullerton
Asst. Commissioner, Media Relations . . . . .Eric Capper

Founded: 1963

2000-01 members: BASKETBALL & FOOTBALL (9)—
Cal St. Northridge, Cal. St. Sacramento, Eastern Washington, Idaho St., Montana, Montana St., Northern Arizona, Portland St. and Weber St.

Big South Conference
6428 Bannington Dr., Ste A
Charlotte, NC 28226
(704) 341-7990
Commissioner . . . . .Kyle Kallander
Director of Media Relations . . . . .Drew Dickerson

Founded: 1983

2000-01 members: BASKETBALL (8)— Charleston
Southern, Coastal Carolina, Elon, High Point, Liberty, NC-Asheville, Radford and Winthrop.

Colonial Athletic Association
8625 Patterson Ave., Richmond, VA 23229
(804) 754-1616
Commissioner . . . . .Thomas E. Yeager
Sports Information Director . . . . .Steve Vehorn

Founded: 1985

2000-01 members: BASKETBALL (9)— American,
East Carolina, George Mason, James Madison, NC-Wilmington, Old Dominion, Richmond, Virginia Commonwealth and William & Mary.

Gateway Football Conference
1818 Chouteau Ave.
St. Louis, MO 63103
(314) 421-2268
Commissioner . . . . .Patty Viverito
Asst. Commissioner . . . . .Mike Kern

Founded: 1985

2000 members: FOOTBALL (7)— Illinois St., Indiana
St., Northern Iowa, Southern Illinois, SW Missouri St., Western Illinois and Youngstown St..

Ivy League
330 Alexander Street
Princeton, NJ 08544
(609) 258-6426
Executive Director . . . . .Jeffrey Orleans
Director of Information .Brett Hoover

Founded: 1954

2000-01 members: BASKETBALL & FOOTBALL (8)—
Brown, Columbia, Cornell, Dartmouth, Harvard, Pennsylvania, Princeton and Yale.

Metro Atlantic Athletic Conference
712 Amboy Avenue
Edison, NJ 08837
(732) 738-5455
Commissioner . . . . .Richard Ensor
Director of Media Relations . . . . .Catherine Hughes

Founded: 1980

2000-01 members: BASKETBALL (10)— Canisius,
Fairfield, Iona, Loyola-MD, Manhattan, Marist, Niagara, Rider, St. Peter's and Siena. FOOTBALL (9)— Canisius, Duquesne, Fairfield, Georgetown, Iona, La Salle, Marist, St. Peter's and Siena.

Mid-Continent Conference
340 West Butterfield Rd., Ste 3D
Elmhurst, IL 60126
(630) 516-0661
Commissioner . . . . .Jon Steinbrecher
Director of Media Relations . . . . .Nancy Smith

Founded: 1982

2000-01 members: BASKETBALL (9)— Chicago St.,
Indiana U-Purdue U Indianapolis, UMKC, Oakland, Oral Roberts, Southern Utah, Valparaiso, Western Illinois, Youngstown St.

Mid-Eastern Athletic Conference
102 North Elm St.
SE Building, Suite 401
Greensboro, NC 27401
(336) 275-9961
Commissioner . . . . .Charles S. Harris
Asst. Commissioner, Media Relations . . .Bradford Evans, Jr.

Founded: 1970

2000-01 members: BASKETBALL (11)— Bethune-
Cookman, Coppin St., Delaware St., Florida A&M, Hampton, Howard, MD-Eastern Shore, Morgan St., Norfolk St., North Carolina A&T and South Carolina St.; FOOTBALL (9)— all but Coppin St. and MD-Eastern Shore.

Midwestern Collegiate Conference
201 South Capitol Ave., Suite 500
Indianapolis, IN 46225
(317) 237-5622
Commissioner . . . . .John LeCrone
Director of Communications . . . . .Josh Lehman

Founded: 1979

2000-01 members: BASKETBALL (8)— Butler, Cleveland St., Detroit Mercy, Illinois-Chicago, Loyola-IL, Wisconsin-Green Bay, Wisconsin-Milwaukee and Wright St.

Missouri Valley Conference
1818 Chouteau Ave.
St. Louis, MO 63103
(314) 421-0339
Commissioner . . . . .Doug Elgin
Asst. Commiss. Media Rel. . . . . Jack Watkins & Mike Kern

Founded: 1907

2000-01 members: BASKETBALL (10)— Bradley,
Creighton, Drake, Evansville, Illinois St., Indiana St., Northern Iowa, Southern Illinois, SW Missouri St., and Wichita St.

Northeast Conference
220 Old New Brunswick Rd.
Piscataway, NJ 08854
(732) 562-0877
Commissioner . . . . .John Iamarino
Asst. Commissioner, Public Relations . . . . .Ron Ratner

Founded: 1981

2000-01 members: BASKETBALL (12)— Cent. Conn.
St., Fairleigh Dickinson, LIU-Brooklyn, Maryland-Baltimore County, Monmouth, Mount St. Mary's, Quinnipiac, Robert Morris, Sacred Heart, St. Francis-NY, St. Francis-PA and Wagner. FOOTBALL (9)—Albany, Cent. Conn. St., Monnouth, Robert Morris, Sacred Heart, St. Francis (PA), St. John's, Stony Brook and Wagner.

Ohio Valley Conference
278 Franklin Road, Suite 103
Brentwood, TN 37027
(615) 371-1698
Commissioner . . . . .Dan Beebe
Asst. Commis., Info. and Champs. . . . . .Rob Washburn

Founded: 1948

2000-01 members: BASKETBALL (9)— Austin Peay
St., Eastern Illinois, Eastern Kentucky, Morehead St., Murray St., SE Missouri St., Tennessee-Martin, Tennessee St. and Tennessee Tech; FOOTBALL (8)— Eastern Illinois, Eastern Kentucky, Murray St., SE Missouri St., Tennessee-Martin, Tennessee St., Tennessee Tech and Western Kentucky

Patriot League
3897 Adler Place
Building C, Suite 310
Bethlehem, PA 18017
(610) 691-2414
Executive Director .Carolyn Femovich
Director of Media Relations . . . . .Tom Byrnes

Founded: 1984

2000-01 members: BASKETBALL (7)— Army, Bucknell, Colgate, Holy Cross, Lafayette, Lehigh and Navy; FOOTBALL (7)— Bucknell, Colgate, Fordham, Holy Cross, Lafayette, Lehigh and Towson.

Pioneer Football League
1818 Chouteau Ave., St. Louis, MO 63103
(314) 421-2268 Founded: 1993
Commissioner ....Patty Viverito
Media Relations ....Cindy Kern
   2000 members: FOOTBALL (5): Butler, Dayton, Drake, San Diego and Valparaiso.

Southern Conference
1 West Pack Square, Suite 1508
Asheville, NC 28801
(828) 255-7872 Founded: 1921
Commissioner ....Alfred B. White
Asst. Commissioner, Public Affairs ....Steve Shutt
   2000-01 members: BASKETBALL (12)— Appalachian St., The Citadel, College of Charleston, Davidson, East Tennessee St., Furman, Georgia Southern, UNC-Greensboro, Tennessee-Chattanooga, VMI, Western Carolina and Wofford; FOOTBALL (9)—all except College of Charleston, Davidson and UNC-Greensboro.

Southland Conference
8150 North Central Expressway, Suite 930
Dallas, TX 75206
(214) 750-7522 Founded: 1963
Commissioner ....Greg Sankey
Director of Media Relations ....Bruce Ludlow
   2000-01 members: BASKETBALL (11)— Lamar, McNeese St., Nicholls St., LA-Monroe, Northwestern St., Sam Houston St., SE Louisiana, Southwest Texas St., Stephen F. Austin St., Texas-Arlington and Texas-San Antonio; FOOTBALL (8)— Jacksonville St., McNeese St., Nicholls St., Northwestern St., Sam Houston St., Southwest Texas St., Stephen F. Austin St. and Troy St.

Southwestern Athletic Conference
1527 Fifth Ave. North
Birmingham, AL 35203
(205) 320-0263 Founded: 1920
Commissioner ....Rudy Washington
Director of Publicity ....Lonza Hardy Jr.
   2000-01 members: BASKETBALL & FOOTBALL (10)— Alabama A&M, Alabama St., Alcorn St., Arkansas-Pine Bluff, Grambling St., Jackson St., Mississippi Valley St., Prairie View A&M, Southern-Baton Rouge and Texas Southern.

Sun Belt Conference
601 Poydras Street, Suite 2355
New Orleans, LA 70130
(504) 299-9066 Founded: 1976
Commissioner ....Wright Waters
Director of Media Services ....Judy Willson
   2000-01 members: BASKETBALL (12)— Arkansas-Little Rock, Arkansas St., Denver, Florida International, LA-Lafayette, Louisiana Tech, Middle Tenn. State, New Mexico State, New Orleans, North Texas, South Alabama and Western Kentucky.

Trans America Athletic Conference
3370 Vineville Ave., Suite 108-B,
Macon, GA 31204
(912) 474-3394 Founded: 1978
Commissioner ....Bill Bibb
Director of Information ....Tom Snyder
   2000-01 members: BASKETBALL (10)— Campbell, Central Florida, Florida Atlantic, Georgia St., Jacksonville, Jacksonville St., Mercer, Samford, Stetson and Troy St.

West Coast Conference
1200 Bayhill Dr., Suite 302, San Bruno, CA 94066
(650) 873-8622 Founded: 1952
Commissioner ....Michael Gilleran
Director of Communication ....Brad Walker
   2000-01 members: BASKETBALL (8)— Gonzaga, Loyola Marymount, Pepperdine, Portland, St. Mary's, San Diego, San Francisco and Santa Clara.

PRO FOOTBALL

National Football League

League Office
280 Park Ave.
New York, NY 10017
(212) 450-2000
Commissioner ....Paul Tagliabue
President ....Neil Austrian
Exec. V.P. & League Counsel ....Jeff Pash
AFC Info. Coordinator ....Dan Masonson
NFC Info. Coordinator ....Chris McCloskey

NFL Management Council
280 Park Ave.
New York, NY 10017
(212) 450-2000
Chairman ....Harold Henderson
V.P. & General Counsel ....Dennis Curran

NFL Players Association
2021 L Street NW, Suite 600
Washington, DC 20036
(202) 463-2200
Executive Director ....Gene Upshaw
Asst. Exec. Director ....Doug Allen
General Counsel ....Richard Berthelsen
Director of Retired Players ....Frank Woschitz

AFC

Baltimore Ravens
11001 Owings Mills Blvd.
Owings Mills, MD 21117
(410) 654-6200
Owner/CEO ....Arthur B. Modell
President/COO ....David Modell
Secretary/General Counsel ....Jim Bailey
V.P. of Communications ....Kevin Byrne

Buffalo Bills
One Bills Drive, Orchard Park, NY 14127
(716) 648-1800
Owner-President ....Ralph C. Wilson Jr.
Exec. V.P./General Manager ....John Butler
V.P. of Communications ....Scott Berchtold

Cincinnati Bengals
One Paul Brown Stadium, Cincinnati, OH 45204
(513) 621-3550
Chairman ....Austin E. Knowlton
President/GM ....Mike Brown
Public Relations Director ....Jack Brennan

Cleveland Browns
76 Lou Groza Blvd., Berea, OH 44017
(440) 891-5000
Owner/Chairman ....Al Lerner
President/CEO ....Carmen Policy
V.P. of Director of Football Ops. ....Dwight Clark
Director of Publicity/Media Relations ....Todd Stewart

Denver Broncos
13655 Broncos Parkway, Englewood, CO 80112
(303) 649-9000
Owner-President-CEO ....Pat Bowlen
General Manager ....Neal Dahlen
Director of Media Relations ....Jim Saccomano

Indianapolis Colts
7001 W 56th St., Indianapolis, IN 46254
(317) 297-2658
Owner-CEO ....Jim Irsay
President ....Bill Polian
Dir. of Football Operations ....Dom Anile
V.P. of Public Relations ....Craig Kelley

Jacksonville Jaguars
One ALLTEL Stadium Place
Jacksonville, FL 32202
(904) 633-6000
Chairman-CEO-President . . . . .Wayne Weaver
Sr. V.P., Football Operations . . . . .Michael Huyghue
Exec. Director of Communications . . . . .Dan Edwards

Kansas City Chiefs
One Arrowhead Drive, Kansas City, MO 64129
(816) 920-9300
Owner-Founder . . . . .Lamar Hunt
Chairman . . . . Jack Steadman
President-CEO-General Manager . . . . .Carl Peterson
Director of Public Relations . . . . .Bob Moore

Miami Dolphins
7500 SW 30th St., Davie, FL 33314
(954) 452-7000
Owner-Chairman . . . . .H. Wayne Huizenga
President & COO . . . . .Eddie Jones
V.P. of Player Personnel . . . . .Rick Spielman
V.P. of Media Relations . . . . .Harvey Greene

New England Patriots
Foxboro Stadium, 60 Washington St., Foxboro, MA 02035
(508) 543-8200
Owner-President-CEO & General Manager . . . . . .Bob Kraft
Asst. Dir. of Player Personnel . . . . .Scott Pioli
Director of Media Relations . . . . .Stacey James

New York Jets
1000 Fulton Ave., Hempstead, NY 11550
(516) 560-8100
Owner-Chairman . . . . .Robert Wood Johnson IV
President . . . . .Steve Gutman
Director of Football Operations . . . . .Bill Parcells
Director of Public Relations . . . . .Frank Ramos

Oakland Raiders
1220 Harbor Bay Parkway, Alameda, CA 94502
(510) 864-5000
Managing General Partner .Al Davis
Executive Assistant . . . . .Al LoCasale
Director of Public Relations . . . . .Mike Taylor

Pittsburgh Steelers
300 Stadium Circle, Pittsburgh, PA 15212
(412) 323-0300
Owner-President . . . . .Dan Rooney
V.P.s . . . . John McGinley, Art Rooney Jr. & Art Rooney II
Communications Coordinator . . . . .Ron Wahl

San Diego Chargers
4020 Murphy Canyon Rd.
San Diego, CA 92123
(838) 874-4500
Owner-Chairman . . . . .Alex Spanos
President-Vice Chairman . . . . .Dean Spanos
V.P. of Football Ops. . . . . .Ed McGuire
Director of Public Relations . . . . .Bill Johnston

Seattle Seahawks
11220 NE 53rd Street, Kirkland, WA 98033
(425) 827-9777
Owner . . . . .Paul Allen
President . . . . .Bob Whitsitt
V.P./GM/Head Coach . . . . .Mike Holmgren
Public Relations Director . . . . .Dave Pearson

Tennessee Titans
460 Great Circle Road, Nashville, TN 37228
(615) 565-4000
Owner . . . . .K.S. (Bud) Adams Jr.
President . . . . .Jeff Diamond
Exec. V.P./General Manager . . . . .Floyd Reese
Director of Media Services . . . . .Tony Wyllie

NFC

Arizona Cardinals
P.O. Box 888, Phoenix, AZ 85001
(602) 379-0101
Owner-President . . . . .Bill Bidwill
Vice President . . . . .Bill Bidwill, Jr.
General Manager . . . . .Bob Ferguson
Public Relations Director . . . . .Paul Jensen

Atlanta Falcons
4400 Falcon Pkwy
Flowery Branch, GA 30542
(770) 945-1111
Owner-President . . . . .Taylor Smith
Exec. V.P. Football Ops./Head Coach . . . . .Dan Reeves
V.P., Football Ops. . . . . .Ron Hill
Director of Public Relations . . . . .Aaron Salkin

Carolina Panthers
800 South Mint St.
Charlotte, NC 28202-1502
(704) 358-7000
Founder-Owner .Jerry Richardson
President . . . . .Mark Richardson
Dir. of Player Personnel . . . . .Jack Bushofsky
Director of Communications . . . . .Charlie Dayton

Chicago Bears
1000 Football Drive, Lake Forest, IL 60045
(847) 295-6600
Owner-Chairman Emeritus . . . . .Edward McCaskey
Chairman of the Board . . . . .Michael McCaskey
President-CEO . . . . .Ted Phillips
Director of Public Relations . . . . .Bryan Harlan

Dallas Cowboys
Cowboys Center
One Cowboys Parkway
Irving, TX 75063
(972) 556-9900
Owner-President-GM . . . . Jerry Jones
V.P./Dir. of Player Personnel . . . . .Stephen Jones
Public Relations Director . . . . .Rich Dalrymple

Detroit Lions
Pontiac Silverdome
1200 Featherstone Rd., Pontiac, MI 48342
(248) 335-4131
Owner-President . . . . .William Clay Ford
Executive V.P. & COO . . . . .Chuck Schmidt
V.P. of Player Personnel . . . . .Ron Hughes
Director of Media Relations . . . . .Steve Reaven

Green Bay Packers
1265 Lombardi Ave.,
Green Bay, WI 54304
(920) 496-5700
President-CEO . . . . .Bob Harlan
Exec. V.P./ General Manager . . . . .Ron Wolf
Exec. Dir. of Public Relations . . . . .Lee Remmel

Minnesota Vikings
9520 Viking Drive, Eden Prairie, MN 55344
(612) 828-6500
Owner . . . . .Red McCombs
President . . . . .Gary Woods
Executive Vice President . . . . .Michael Kelly
Director of Public Relations . . . . .Bob Hagan

New Orleans Saints
5800 Airline Drive, Metairie, LA 70003
(504) 733-0255
Owner . . . . .Tom Benson
General Manager . . . . .Randy Meuller
V.P. of Football Operations . . . . .Charles Bailey
Director of Media/Public Relations . . . . .Greg Bensel

New York Giants

Giants Stadium
East Rutherford, NJ 07073
(201) 935-8111
President/co-CEO .... Wellington Mara
Chairman/co-CEO .... Preston Robert Tisch
V.P. & General Manager .... Ernie Accorsi
V.P. of Communications .... Pat Hanlon

Philadelphia Eagles

Veterans Stadium
3501 S. Broad St.
Philadelphia, PA 19148
(215) 463-2500
Owner .... Jeff Lurie
Executive V.P. & CEO .... Joe Banner
Director of Football Operations .... Tom Modrak
Director of Public Relations .... Ron Howard

St. Louis Rams

One Rams Way, St. Louis, MO 63045
(314) 982-7267
Owner-Chairman .... Georgia Frontiere
Owner-Vice Chairman .... Stan Kroenke
President .... John Shaw
Pres. of Football Operations .... Jay Zygmunt
Director of Public Relations .... Rick Smith

San Francisco 49ers

4949 Centennial Blvd.
Santa Clara, CA 95054
(408) 562-4949
Owners .... Denise DeBartolo-York
V.P./General Manager .... Bill Walsh
Director of Public Relations .... Kirk Reynolds

Tampa Bay Buccaneers

One Buccaneer Place, Tampa, FL 33607
(813) 870-2700
Owner-President .... Malcolm Glazer
General Manager .... Rich McKay
Director of Communications .... Reggie Roberts

Washington Redskins

Redskins Park
P.O. Box 17247, Washington D.C. 20041
(703) 478-8900
Owner .... Daniel M. Snyder
General Manager .... Vinnie Cerrato
Director of Public Relations .... Doug Green

Canadian Football League

League Office

CFL Building, 110 Eglinton Avenue West, 5th Floor
Toronto, Ontario M4R 1A3
(416) 322-9650
Chairman/Acting Commissioner .... John Tory
President/COO .... Jeff Giles
V.P. of Football Operations .... Ed Chalupka
Director of Communications .... Jim Neish

CFL Players Association

467 Speers Rd., Unit 5
Oakville, Ontario L6K 3S4
(905) 844-7852
President .... Dan Ferrone
Legal Counsel .... Ed Molstad

British Columbia Lions

10605 135th St.
Surrey, B.C. V3T 4C8
(604) 930-5466
Owner .... David Braley
President & CEO .... Glen Ringdal
Dir. of Media/Public Relations .... Rob Malich

Calgary Stampeders

McMahon Stadium
1817 Crowchild Trail, NW
Calgary, Alberta T2M 4R6
(403) 289-0205
Owner .... Sig Gutsche
President .... Stan Schwartz
General Manager & Head Coach .... Wally Buono
V.P. of Marketing & Communications .... Ron Rooke

Edmonton Eskimos

9023 111th Ave.
Edmonton, Alberta T5B 0C3
(780) 448-1525
Owner .... Community-owned
President .... Hugh Campbell
General Manager .... Tom Higgins

Hamilton Tiger-Cats

75 Balsam Ave. N
Hamilton, Ontario L8L 8C1
(905) 547-2418
Chairman/Owner .... David M. Macdonald
Vice Chairman/Owner .... George Grant
GM/Dir. of Business Ops. .... Neil Lumsden
Communications Director .... Marty Knack

Montreal Alouettes

1255 University St., Suite 120
Montreal, Quebec H3B 3A9
(514) 252-4600
Owner .... Robert Wetenhall
President & CEO .... Larry Smith
Dir. of Football Ops./GM .... Jim Popp
Dir. of Communications .... Louis-Philippe Dorais

Saskatchewan Roughriders

2940 — 10th Avenue, P.O. Box 1277
Regina, Saskatchewan S4P 3B8
(306) 569-2323
Owner .... Community-owned
President .... Bob Ellard
General Manager and Dir. of Football Ops. ... Roy Shivers
Media Coordinator .... Tony Playter

Toronto Argonauts

1100 Central Pkwy W., Suite 3, Mississauga, Ontario L5C 4E5
(416) 341-5151
Owner/Chairman .... Sherwood Schwarz
Managing Director .... J.I. Albrecht
Director of Public Relations .... Greg Mandziuk

Winnipeg Blue Bombers

1465 Maroons Road, Winnipeg, Manitoba R3G 0L6
(204) 784-2583
Owner .... Community-owned
President .... Robert Miles
Dir. of Football Ops./Head Coach .... Dave Ritchie
Dir. of Media/Public Relations .... Shawn Coates

NFL Europe

President .... Oliver Luck
Director of Public Relations .... David Tossell
Public Relations Assistant .... Michael Signora

League Offices

Frankfurt

Westerbach Str. 47
Frankfurt, Gerammy 60489
011-49-69-978-2790

London

26A Albemarle St.
London, England W1X 3FA
011-44-171-355-1955

New York
280 Park Avenue
New York, NY 10017
(212) 450-2000
    Member teams (6): Amsterdam Admirals, Barcelona
Dragons, Berlin Thunder, Frankfurt Galaxy, Rhein Fire (Dus-
seldorf), Scottish Claymores (Edinburgh).

Arena Football League
75 East Wacker Dr., 10th Floor
Chicago, IL 60601
(312) 332-5510
Commissioner . . . . .C. David Baker
Deputy Commissioner . . . . .Ronald J. Kurpiers II
V.P. of Football Operations . . . . .Jerry Trice
V.P. of Media Services .David Cooper
    Member teams (18): American Conference— Arizona
Rattlers, Detroit Fury, Grand Rapids Rampage, Houston
Thunderbears, Iowa Barnstormers, Los Angeles Avengers,
Milwaukee Mustangs, Oklahoma Wranglers and San Jose
Sabrecats. National Conference— Albany (NY) Firebirds,
Buffalo Destroyers, Carolina Cobras, Florida Bobcats,
Nashville Kats, New Jersey Red Dogs, New England Sea
Wolves, Orlando Predators and Tampa Bay Storm.

GOLF

LPGA Tour
(Ladies' Professional Golf Association)
100 International Golf Drive
Daytona Beach, FL 32124
(904) 274-6200
Commissioner . . . . .Ty Votaw
Deputy Commissioner . . . . .Jim Webb
Director of Communications . . . . .Leslie King

PGA of America
100 Avenue of the Champions
Palm Beach Gardens, FL 33410
(561) 624-8400
President . . . . .Will Mann
CEO . . . . .Jim Awtrey
Director of Communications . . . . .Terry McSweeney

PGA European Tour
Wentworth Drive, Virginia Water
Surrey, England GU25 4LX
TEL: 011-44-1344-842881
Executive Director . . . . .Ken Schofield
Director of Communications . . . . .Mitchell Platts

PGA Tour
112 PGA Tour Blvd.
Ponte Vedra, FL 32082
(904) 285-3700
Commissioner . . . . .Tim Finchem
Senior V.P. of Communications . . . . .Bob Combs

Royal & Ancient Golf Club of St. Andrews
St. Andrews, Fife
Scotland KY16 9JD
TEL: 011-44-1334-472112
Secretary . . . . .Peter Dawson
Press Officer . . . . .Stewart McDougall

USGA
(United States Golf Association)
P.O. Box 708, Liberty Corner Road
Far Hills, NJ 07931
(908) 234-2300
President . . . . .Trey Holland
Executive Director . . . . .David Fay
Sr. Director of Communications . . . . .Marty Parkes

PRO HOCKEY

NHL
National Hockey League
Commissioner . . . . .Gary Bettman
Pres., NHL Enterprises . . . . .TBA
Senior V.P., Dir. of Hockey Ops. . . . . .Colin Campbell
V.P. of Media Relations . . . . .Frank Brown

League Offices

Montreal
1800 McGill College Ave., Suite 2600
Montreal, Quebec H3A 3J6
(514) 288-9220

New York
1251 Sixth Ave., 47th Floor, New York, NY 10020
(212) 789-2000

Toronto
50 Bay St., 11th Floor
Toronto, Ontario M5J 2X8
(416) 981-2777

NHL Players' Association
777 Bay St., Suite 2400
P.O. Box 121
Toronto, Ontario M5G 2C8
(416) 408-4040
Executive Director . . . . .Bob Goodenow
Associate Counsel . . . . .Ian Pulver,
            Jeff Citron, Chris DiFrancesco and Rick Olczyk
Media Relations Mgr. . . . . .Devin Smith

Anaheim, Mighty Ducks of
Arrowhead Pond of Anaheim
2695 Katella Ave.
Anaheim, CA 92806
(714) 940-2900
Owner . . . . .Walt Disney Co.
Anaheim Sports, Inc. Pres. . . . . .Tony Tavares
President/General Manager . . . . .Pierre Gauthier
Dir., Communications and Team Services . . . .Alex Gilchrist

Atlanta Thrashers
1 CNN Center
12th Floor, South Tower
Atlanta, GA 30303
(404) 584-7825
Owner . . . . .Time Warner
President/Governor . . . . .Stan Kasten
Executive V.P. . . . . .Dave Maggard
V.P./General Manager . . . . .Don Waddell
Public Relations Director . . . . .Tom Hughes

Boston Bruins
1 FleetCenter, Suite 250
Boston, MA 02114
(617) 624-1900
Owner . . . . .Jeremy Jacobs
President & General Manager . . . . .Harry Sinden
Director of Media Relations . . . . .Heidi Holland

Buffalo Sabres
HSBC Arena
One Seymour H. Knox III Plaza
Buffalo, NY 14203-3096
(716) 855-4100
CEO . . . . .Timothy Rigas
General Manager . . . . .Darcy Regier
V.P. of Communications . . . . .Michael Gilbert

Calgary Flames
Canadian Airlines Saddledome, P.O. Box 1540 Station M
Calgary, Alberta T2P 3B9
(403) 777-2177
Owners ....Harley Hotchkiss, Grant A. Bartlett, Murray
Edwards, Ronald V. Joyce, Alvin G. Libin, Allan P. Markin,
J.R. McCaig, Byron and Daryl Seamen
President & CEO ....Ron Bremner
Executive V.P./General Manager ....TBA
Director of Communications ....Peter Hanlon

Carolina Hurricanes
The Raleigh Entertainment Sports Arena
1400 Edward Mill Rd., Raleigh, NC 27607
(919) 467-7825
Owner-CEO ....Peter Karmanos Jr.
President & General Manager ....Jim Rutherford
Dir., Media Relations/Team Services ....Chris Brown

Chicago Blackhawks
United Center, 1901 West Madison St.
Chicago, IL 60612
(312) 455-7000
Owner-President ....William Wirtz
General Manager ....Mike Smith
Executive Director of P.R. ....Jim DeMaria

Colorado Avalanche
1000 Chopper Cir., Denver, CO 80204
(303) 405-1100
Owner ....Stan Kroenke
President/GM/Alt. Governor ....Pierre Lacroix
Dir., Media Relations/Team Services .....Jean Martineau

Columbus Blue Jackets
150 E.Wilson Bridge Rd., Columbus, OH 43085
(614) 246-4625
Owner ....John H. McConnell
General Manager ....Doug MacLean
Director of Communications ....Todd Sharrock

Dallas Stars
211 Cowboys Parkway, Irving, TX 75063
(214) 868-2890
Owner ....Thomas O. Hicks
President ....Jim Lites
General Manager ....Bob Gainey
Director of Public Relations ....Larry Kelly

Detroit Red Wings
Joe Louis Arena, 600 Civic Center Drive
Detroit, MI 48226
(313) 396-7544
Owner/President ....Mike Ilitch
Owner/Secretary-Treasurer ....Marian Ilitch
General Manager ....Ken Holland
Director of Media Relations ....John Hahn

Edmonton Oilers
11230 110th St., Edmonton, Alberta, T5G 3H7
(780) 414-4000
Owners ....Edmonton Investors Group, Ltd.
President & CEO ....Patrick LaForge
General Manager ....Kevin Lowe
Director of Public Relations ....Bill Tuele

Florida Panthers
National Car Rental Center
1 Panther Parkway, Sunrise, FL 33323
(954) 835-7000
Owner ....H. Wayne Huizenga
President ....Bill Torrey
General Manager ....Bryan Murray
Dir. of Public & Media Relations ....Mike Hanson

Los Angeles Kings
Staples Center
1111 S. Figueroa, Los Angeles, CA 90017
(310) 419-3160
Majority Owners ....Philip Anschutz and Ed Roski
President ....Tim Leiweke
General Manager ....Dave Taylor
Director of Media Relations ....Mike Altieri

Minnesota Wild
444 Cedar Street, Suite 900
St. Paul, MN 55101
(651) 222-9453
Owner ....Bob Naegele Jr.
Exec. V.P./General Manager ....Doug Risebrough
Director of Media Relations ....Bill Robertson

Montreal Canadiens
Molson Centre, 1260 Gauchetière St. West
Montreal, Quebec H3B 5E8
(514) 932-2582
Owner ....Molson Companies, Ltd.
President ....Pierre Boivin
General Manager ....Rejean Houle
Director of Communications ....Don Beauchamp

Nashville Predators
501 Broadway, Nashville, TN 37203
(615) 770-2300
Chairman and Maj. Owner ....Craig Leipold
President ....Jack Diller
General Manager ....David Poile
Mgr., Team Services/Media Relations .....Frank Buonomo

New Jesey Devils
Continental Airlines Arena, P.O. Box 504
East Rutherford, NJ 07073
(201) 935-6050
Owner ....Puck Holdings LLC
President & GM ....Lou Lamoriello
Director of Public Relations ....Kevin Dessart

New York Islanders
Nassau Veterans' Memorial Coliseum, 1255 Hempstead Tpk,
Uniondale, NY 11553
(516) 794-4100
Owner ....Charles Wang & Sanjay Kumar
General Manager ....Mike Milbury
Director of Media Relations ....Chris Botta

New York Rangers
2 Penn Plaza, 14th Floor
New York, NY 10121
(212) 465-6486
Owner ....Cablevision Systems Inc.
President (MSG) ....Dave Checketts
President & General Manager ....Glen Sather
V.P. of Public Relations ....John Rosasco

Ottawa Senators
1000 Palladium Dr.
Kanata, Ontario, K2V 1A5
(613) 599-0250
Chairman & Gov. ....Rod Bryden
President & CEO ....Roy Mlakar
General Manager ....Marshall Johnston
Director of Media Relations ....Steve Keogh

Philadelphia Flyers
3601 S. Broad St., Philadelphia, PA 19148
(215) 465-4500
Chairman ....Ed Snider
President & General Manager ....Bob Clarke
Director of Media Relations ....Zack Hill

Phoenix Coyotes
Altell Ice Den, 9375 E. Bell Rd., Scottsdale, AZ 85260
(480) 473-5600
Owner ....Steve Ellman
President ....Shawn Hunter
General Manager ....Bobby Smith
Director of Media Relations ....Richard Nairn

Pittsburgh Penguins
Mellon Arena, Chatham Ctr., Suite 400, Pittsburgh, PA 15219
(412) 642-1800
Owner/Chairman ....Mario Lemieux
President & General Manager ....Craig Patrick
V.P. of Communications ....Thomas McMillan

St. Louis Blues
Kiel Center, 1401 Clark Ave.
St. Louis, MO 63103
(314) 622-2500
Owners ....Bill and Nancy Laurie
General Manager ....Larry Pleau
Director of Public Relations ....Jeff Trammel

San Jose Sharks
525 West Santa Clara St., San Jose, CA 95113
(408) 287-7070
Owner-Chairman ....George Gund III
Co-Owner ....Gordon Gund
President-CEO ....Greg Jamison
Exec. V.P.& GM ....Dean Lombardi
Director of Media Relations ....Ken Arnold

Tampa Bay Lightning
401 Channelside Drive, Tampa, FL 33602
(813) 301-6500
Owner ....Palace Sports & Ent.
CEO & Governor ....Tom Wilson
President ....Ron Campbell
V.P./General Manager ....Rick Dudley
Director of Public Relations ....Jay Preble

Toronto Maple Leafs
Air Canada Center
40 Bay Street, Toronto, Ontario M5J 2X2
(416) 815-5500
Owner ....Steve Stavro
President ....Ken Dryden
Coach/G.M. ....Pat Quinn
Manager of Media Relations ....Pat Park

Vancouver Canucks
General Motors Place, 800 Griffiths Way
Vancouver, B.C. V6B 6G1
(604) 899-4600
Owners ....John McCaw
CEO ....David Cobb
President & General Manager ....Brian Burke
Manager of Media Relations ....Chris Brumwell

Washington Capitals
MCI Center, 401 9th St., Suite 7500
Washington, D.C. 20004
(202) 628-3200
Owners ....Ted Leonsis, Jon Ledecky, Dick Patrick
President ....Dick Patrick
V.P./General Manager ....George McPhee
V.P. of Communications ....Andy McGowan

AHL

American Hockey League
One Monarch Place, Springfield, MA 01144
(413) 781-2030
President ....David Andrews
Director of Hockey Ops. ....Jim Mill
Dir. of Media Relations/Communications .....Brett Stothart

IHL

International Hockey League
1395 E. Twelve Mile Rd., Madison Heights, MI 48071
(248) 546-3230
President/CEO ....Doug Moss
Interim Dir. of Public Relations ....Sean Krabach

IIHF

International Ice Hockey Federation
Parkring 11
CH-8002 Zurich, Switzerland
TEL: 011-411-289-8600
President ....Rene Fasel
General Secretary ....Jan-Ake Edvinsson
P.R./Marketing Mgr. ....Kimmo Leinonen

HORSE RACING

Breeders' Cup Limited
PO Box 4230, Lexington, KY 40544–4230
(606) 223-5444
President .............................D.G. Van Clief, Jr.
Director of Marketing ....Damon Thayer

National Museum of Racing and Hall of Fame
191 Union Ave.
Saratoga Springs, NY 12866
(518) 584-0400
Executive Director ....Peter Hammell
Assistant Director ....Catherine Maguire
Communications Officer ....Richard Hamilton

The Jockeys' Guild
P.O. Box 250, Lexington, KY 40588-0250
(606) 259-3211
President ....Pat Day
National Manager ....John Giovanni
Communications ....John Ball

NTRA
(National Thoroughbred Racing Association)
230 Lexington Green Cir., Suite 310
Lexington, KY 40503
(606) 223-0658
CEO-Commissioner ....Tim Smith
Executive Director ....Nick Nicholson
V.P. of Communications ....Chip Tuttle

TRA
(Thoroughbred Racing Associations of N. America, Inc.)
420 Fair Hill Drive, Suite 1
Elkton, MD 21921
(410) 392-9200
President ....Stella Thayer
Executive V.P. ....Christopher N. Scherf

NTRA Communications
(National Thoroughbred Racing Association Communications)
444 Madison Ave., Suite 503
New York, NY 10022
(212) 907-9280
V.P. of Communications ....Chip Tuttle
Director of Media Relations ....Eric Wing

USTA
(United States Trotting Association)
750 Michigan Ave., Columbus, OH 43215
(614) 224-2291
President ....Corwin Nixon
Executive V.P. ....Fred Noe
Director of Public Relations ....John Pawlak

MEDIA

PERIODICALS

ESPN, The Magazine
19 E 34th St., 7th Floor, New York, NY 10016
(212) 515-1000
Editor in Chief .... John Papanek
Executive Editors .... Gary Hoenig, Steve Wulf
Senior V.P./GM .... Michael Rooney
Public Relations Manager .... Kim Shapiro

Sports Illustrated
135 West 50th St., New York, NY 10020
(212) 522-9797
President/CEO .... Mike Klingensmith
Managing Editor .... William Colson
Executive Editors ..... B. Peter Carry, Rob Fleder and David
                                                    Bauer

The Sporting News
10176 Corporate Square Dr., Suite 200
St. Louis, MO 63132
(314) 997-7111
Senior V.P./Editorial Director .... John D. Rawlings
President .... James H. Nuckols

The Sports Business Daily
120 West Morehead St., Ste. 220
Charlotte, NC 28202
(704) 973-1500
President .... Sal Schiliro
Editor .... Abe Madkour
Media Relations Mgr. .... Bill Magrath

USA Today
1000 Wilson Blvd., Arlington, VA 22229
(703) 276-3400
Owner .... Gannett Co.
President-Publisher .... Tom Curley
Managing Editor/Sports .... Monte Lorell

WIRE SERVICES

Associated Press
50 Rockefeller Plaza 5th Floor, New York, NY 10020
(212) 621-1630
Sports Editor .... Terry Taylor
Deputy Sports Editor .... Brian Friedman

United Press International
1510 H Street, Washington, DC 20005
(202) 898-8000
Sports Editor .... Ron Colbert

The Sports Network
95 James Way, Suite 107 & 109
Southampton, PA 18966
(215) 942-7890
President .... Mickey Charles
Director of Operations .... Phil Sokol
Managing Editor .... Jim Gillis

Sportsticker
800 Plaza Two, Harborside Financial Ctr., Jersey City, NJ 07311
(201) 309-1200
Senior V.P./General Manager .... Rick Alessandri
Exec. Director, News .... Jim Morganthaler

TV NETWORKS

ABC Sports
47 West 66th St., 13th Floor, New York, NY 10023
(212) 456-4867
President .... Howard Katz
Senior V.P., Production .... John Filippelli
V.P. of Media Relations .... Mark Mandel

CBC Sports
P.O. Box 500, Station A 5H 100
Toronto, Ontario M5W 1E6
(416) 205-6523
Head of Sports .... Alan Clark
Sr. Executive Producer .... Joel Darling
Publicist .... Susan Procter

CBS Sports
51 West 52nd St., 25th Floor
New York, NY 10019
(212) 975-5230
President .... Sean McManus
Executive Producer .... Terry Ewert
Sr. V.P., Programming/Bus. Affairs .... Mike Aresco
V.P., Communications .... Leslie Ann Wade

ESPN
ESPN Plaza, Bristol, CT 06010
(860) 585-2000
President .... George Bodenheimer
Sr. V.P. of Programming .... John Wildhack
Sr. V.P. & Exec. Editor of Internet .... John Walsh
Sr. V.P. and Managing Editor .... Bob Eaton
Director of Communications .... Mike Soltys

ESPN Classic
ESPN Plaza, Bristol, CT 06010
(860) 585-2000
Executive Producer .... Vince Doria
Communications Coordinator .... Amy Swanson

FOX Sports
10201 W. Pico Blvd., Los Angeles, CA 90035
(310) 369-1000
Chairman-CEO .... David Hill
President .... Ed Goren
V.P. of Media Relations (NYC) .... Vince Wladika

The Golf Channel
7580 Commerce Center Drive
Orlando, FL 32819
(407) 345-4653
President-CEO .... Joe Gibbs
V.P., Production .... Tony Tortorici
Director of Public Relations .... Dan Higgins

HBO Sports
1100 Ave. of the Americas
New York, NY 10036
(212) 512-1987
President-CEO .... Seth Abraham
V.P., Executive Producer .... Ross Greenburg
Sr. V.P., Programming .... Kery Davis
Director of Publicity .... Ray Stallone

MTV Sports
1633 Broadway, 32nd Floor
New York, NY 10019
(212) 654-6177
Producer .... Chris Martello
Publicity Contact .... Greg Baldwin

NBC Sports
30 Rockefeller Plaza, New York, NY 10112
(212) 664-2160
Chairman .... Dick Ebersol
President .... Ken Schanzer
Executive Producer .... Tommy Roy
Director of Public Relations .... Ed Markey

Rainbow Sports
111 Stewart Ave.
Bethpage, NY 11714
(516) 396-3000
President .... Greg Moyer
Vice President of Marketing .... Dan Ronayne

TSN-The Sports Network
2225 Shepherd Ave. East, Suite 100
Willowdale, Ontario, M2J-5C2
(416) 494-1212
Exec. V.P. of Netstar ....Lorne Stephenson
President ....Rick Brace
Communications Manager ....David Rosenbloom

Turner Sports
One CNN Center
13th Floor, Atlanta, GA 30303
(404) 827-1735
President ....Mark Lazarus
Sr. V.P., Programming ....Kevin O'Malley
V.P., Production ....Mike Pearl
V.P. of Public Relations ....Greg Hughes

Univision (Spanish)
9405 NW 41st St., Miami, FL 33178
(305) 477-3412
V.P. of Ops./Sports ....Tony Oquendo
Publicity Coordinator ....Rosalyn Sariol

USA Network
1230 Ave. of the Americas, New York, NY 10020
(212) 408-9100
Sr. V.P., Production in Sports ....Gordon Beck
V.P., Sports Programming ....Kevin Landy
Sports Publicity ....David Schwarz

OLYMPICS

IOC
(International Olympic Committee)
Chateau de Vidy
CH-1007 Lausanne, Switzerland
TEL: 011-41-21-621-6111
President ....Juan Antonio Samaranch
Director General ....Francois Carrard
Secretary General ....Francoise Zweifel
Dir. of International Cooperation ....Fekrou Kidane
Director of Communications/New Media ..Franklin Servan-
Schreiber

2002 WINTER GAMES

Salt Lake Olympic Organizing Committee
299 South Main Street, Suite 1300
Salt Lake City, UT 84111
(801) 212-2002
Chairman ....Robert H. Garff
President & CEO ....W. Mitt Romney
CFO/COO ....Frasier Bullock
Senior V.P., Communications ....Shelly Thomas
(XIXth Olympic Winter Games, Feb. 8-24)

2004 SUMMER GAMES

Athens Olympic Organizing Committee
Zappio, Megaro, Athens, Greece
TEL: 011-30-1-12004
Time difference: 7 hours ahead of New York (EDT)
Chairman ....Stratis Stratigis
Managing Director ....Kostas Bakouris
(XXVIIIth Olympic Summer Games, Aug. 13-29)

COA
(Canadian Olympic Association)
2380 Avenue Pierre Dupuy
Montreal, Quebec H3C-3R4
(514) 861-3371
CEO ....Carol Anne Letheren
President ....Bill Warren
IOC members ......Carol Anne Letheren & Richard Pound
Media Relations .....Lisa Beatty (Tor.) .....Dina Bell (Ott.)

USOC
(United States Olympic Committee)
One Olympic Plaza
Colorado Springs, CO 80909
(719) 632-5551
Chairman ....Bill Hybl
CEO ....Norman T. Blake
IOC members ...Anita DeFrantz, James Easton & Bob Ctvrlik
Managing Director/Media Relations ....Mike Moran

2006 WINTER GAMES

Turin Olympic Organizing Committee
Via Nizza 262/58–10126
Turin, Italy
TEL: 39-011-63-10-511
Exec. President ....Giorgetto Giugiaro
Director General ....Evelina Christillin

U.S. OLYMPICS TRAINING CENTERS

Colorado Springs Training Center
One Olympic Plaza, Colorado Springs, CO 80909
(719) 578-4500
Sr. Dir. of Sport Services ....Benita Fitzgerald-Mosley
Sports Services ....John Smyth

Lake Placid Training Center
421 Old Military Road, Lake Placid, NY 12946
(518) 523-2600
Director ....Jack Favro
Operations Manager ....Tracy Lamb

Arco Olympic Training Center
2800 Olympic Parkway, Chula Vista, CA 91915
(619) 656-1500
Director ....Patrice Milkovich

U.S. OLYMPIC ORGANIZATIONS

National Archery Association
One Olympic Plaza, Colorado Springs, CO 80909
(719) 578-4576
President ....Norm Graham
Executive Director ....George Greenway
Media Contact ....Bill Kellick

U.S. Badminton Association
One Olympic Plaza, Colorado Springs, CO 80909
(719) 578-4808
President ....Don Chew
Executive Director ....Dan Cloppas

USA Baseball
3400 E Camino Camtestre, Tucson, AZ 85716
(520) 327-9700
Executive Director & CEO ....Paul Seiler
Dir. of Media Relations ....David Fannuchi

USA Basketball
5465 Mark Dabling Blvd.
Colorado Springs, CO 80918
(719) 590-4800
President ....Russell Granik
Executive Director ....Warren S. Brown
Director of Public Relations ....Craig Miller

U.S. Biathlon Association
29 Ethan Allen Ave.
Colchester, VT 05446
(802) 654-7833
President ....Lyle Nelson
Exec. Director ....Stephen Sands
Director of Summer Biathlon ....Marc Sheppard
Public Relations Contact ....Mary Grace

U.S. Bobsled and Skeleton Federation
421 Old Military Road
Lake Placid, NY 12946
(518) 523-1842
President . . . . Jim Morris
Executive Director . . . . Matt Roy
Media/P.R. Director . . . . Julie Urbansky

USA Boxing
One Olympic Plaza, Colorado Springs, CO 80909
(719) 578-4506
President . . . . Gary Tony
Executive Director . . . . Paul Montville
Dir. of Media/Public Relations . . . . Shilpa Bakre

U.S. Canoe and Kayak Team
15 Parkside Drive
Lake Placid, NY 12946
(518) 523-1855
Chairman . . . . Howard Turner
Executive Director . . . . Terry Kent
Public Relations Director . . . . Lisa Fish

USA Curling
1100 Center Point Drive, Box 866
Stevens Point, WI 54481
(715) 344-1199
President . . . . Albert Anderson
Executive Director . . . . David Garber
Media Contact . . . . Rick Patzke

USA Cycling
One Olympic Plaza
Colorado Springs, CO 80909
(719) 578-4581
President . . . . Mike Plant
Executive Director & CEO . . . . Lisa Voight
COO . . . . Phil Milburn
Director of Communications . . . . Rich Wanninger

United States Diving, Inc.
Pan American Plaza, Suite 430,
201 South Capitol Avenue, Indianapolis, IN 46225
(317) 237-5252
President . . . . William Walker
Executive Director . . . . Todd Smith
Director of Communications . . . . Seth Pederson

U.S. Equestrian Team
Pottersville Road, Gladstone, NJ 07934
(908) 234-1251
President . . . . Finn M. W. Caspersen
Executive Director . . . . Bob Standish
Director of Public Relations . . . . Marty Bauman
(508) 698-6810

U.S. Fencing Association
One Olympic Plaza, Colorado Springs, CO 80909
(719) 578-4511
President . . . . Stacey Johnson
Executive Director . . . . Michael Massik
Media Relations Contact . . . . Cindy Bent

U.S. Field Hockey Assocation
One Olympic Plaza, Colorado Springs, CO 80909
(719) 578-4567
President . . . . Jenepher Shillingford
Executive Director . . . . Jane Betts
Director of Media/Public Relations . . . . Howard Thomas

U.S. Figure Skating Association
20 First Street, Colorado Springs, CO 80906
(719) 635-5200
President . . . . Phyllis Howard
Executive Director . . . . John Le Fevre
Director of Events . . . . Carrie Wolf

USA Gymnastics (Artistic & Rythmic)
Pan American Plaza, Suite 300
201 South Capitol Avenue, Indianapolis, IN 46225
(317) 237-5050
President-Exec. Director . . . . Robert V. Colarossi
Director of Public Relations . . . . Courtney Caress

USA Hockey, Inc.
1775 Bob Johnson Dr., Colorado Springs, CO 80906
(719) 576-8724
President . . . . Walter Bush Jr.
Executive Director . . . . Doug Palazzari
Dir. of Public and Media Relations . . . . Chuck Menke

United States Judo, Inc.
One Olympic Plaza, Suite 202
Colorado Springs, CO 80909
(719) 578-4730
President . . . . Yosh Uchida
Public Relations Director . . . . John Miller

U.S. Luge Association
35 Church Street, Lake Placid, NY 12946
(518) 523-2071
President . . . . Doug Bateman
Executive Director . . . . Ron Rossi
Public Relations Manager . . . . John Lundin
Communications Manager . . . . Dmitry Feld

USA Pentathlon
7330 San Pedro, Box 10, San Antonio, TX 78216
(210) 528-2999
President . . . . Dr. Risto Hurme
Executive Director . . . . Rob Stull

U.S. Rowing
Pan American Plaza, Suite 400
201 South Capitol Avenue, Indianapolis, IN 46225
(317) 237-5656
President . . . . Monk Terry
Executive Director . . . . Frank Coyle
Media Contact . . . . Brett Johnson

U.S. Sailing Association
P.O. Box 1260, 15 Maritime Drive, Portsmouth, RI 02871
(401) 683-0800
President . . . . James P. Muldoon
Executive Director . . . . Terry D. Harper
Media Liaison . . . . Barby MacGowan (Olympics)
(401) 849-0220
Media Contact . . . . Penny Piva

U.S. Shooting Team
One Olympic Plaza
Colorado Springs, CO 80909
(719) 578-4670
Executive Director . . . . Robert Mitchell
Public Relations Director . . . . Tori Svenningson

U.S. Ski & Snowboard Assoc.
P.O. Box 100, 1500 Kearns Blvd.
Park City, UT 84060
(435) 649-9090
Chairman . . . . Jim McCarthy
CEO/President . . . . Bill Marolt
V.P. of Public Relations . . . . Tom Kelly
Public Information Manager . . . . Juliann Fritz

U.S. Soccer Federation
U.S. Soccer House
1801-1811 South Prairie Ave.
Chicago, IL 60616
(312) 808-1300
President . . . . Dr. S. Robert Contiguglia
Secretary General . . . . Dan Flynn
Director of Communications . . . . Jim Moorhouse

Amateur Softball Association
2801 N.E. 50th Street
Oklahoma City, OK 73111
(405) 424-5266
President ....G. Pat Adkinson
Executive Director ....Ron Radigonda
Director of Communications ....Brian McCall

U.S. Speedskating
P.O. Box 450639, Westlake, OH 44145
(440) 899-0128
President ....Fred Benjamin
Executive Director ....Katie Marquard
Public Relations Director ....Nick Paulenich

U.S.A. Swimming
One Olympic Plaza, Colorado Springs, CO 80909
(719) 578-4578
President ....Dale Neuberger
Executive Director ....Chuck Weilgus
Dir. of Public and Media Relations ....Mary Wagner

U.S. Synchronized Swimming, Inc.
Pan American Plaza, Suite 901
201 South Capitol Avenue
Indianapolis, IN 46225
(317) 237-5700
President ....Laurette Longmire
Executive Director ....Debbie Hesse
Media Relations Director ....Brian Eaton

USA Table Tennis
One Olympic Plaza
Colorado Springs, CO 80909
(719) 578-4583
President ....Sherri Pittman
Executive Director ....Ben Nisbit
Dir. of Public & Media Relations ....Vicki Ulrich

USA Team Handball
1903 Powers Ferry Rd., Ste. 230
Atlanta, GA 30339
(770) 956-7660
President ....Dennis Berkholtz
Executive Director ....Mike Cavanaugh
Director of Sport Programs ....Danette Leininger

U.S. Tennis Association
70 West Red Oak Lane
White Plains, NY 10604
(914) 696-7000
President ....Julia A. Levering
Executive Director ....Richard D. Fermin
Dir. of Communications ....Andrea Jayson

USA Track and Field
1 RCA Dome, Suite 140
Indianapolis, IN 46206
(317) 261-0500
President ....Patricia Rico
CEO ....Craig Masback
Director of Communications ....Jill Geer

USA Triathlon
3595 East Fountain Blvd., Ste. F-1
Colorado Springs, CO 80910
(719) 597-9090
President ....Mike Highfield
Executive Director ....Steven M. Locke
Communications Director ..................B.J. Hoeptner

USA Volleyball
715 S. Circle Dr., 2nd Floor
Colorado Springs, CO 80910
(719) 228-6800
President ....Rebecca Howard
Director of Media Relations ....Gavin Markoutz

United States Water Polo
1685 W. Uintah St., Colorado Springs, CO 80904
(719) 634-0699
President ....Bret B. Bernard
Executive Director ....Bruce Wigo
Dir. of Media/Public Relations ....Eric Velasquez

USA Weightlifting
One Olympic Plaza, Colorado Springs, CO 80909
(719) 578-4508
President ....Brian Derwin
Exec. Dir./Comm. Dir. ....James J. Fox

USA Wrestling
6155 Lehman Drive, Colorado Springs, CO 80918
(719) 598-8181
President ....Bruce Baumgartner
Executive Director ....Jim Scherr
Dir. of Communications ....Gary Abbott

PAN AMERICAN SPORT
ORGANIZATIONS

USA Bowling
5301 South 76th St., Greendale, WI 53129
(414) 421-9008
President ....Kevin Dornberger
Executive Director ....Gerald Koenig

USA National Karate-Do Federation, Inc.
P.O. Box 77083, 8351 15th Ave. NW, Seattle, WA 98117-7083
(206) 440-8386
President ....Julius Thiry
Executive Director ....Brian Lynch
Public/Media Information ....Howard High

United States Raquetball Association
1685 West Uintah, Colorado Springs, CO 80904
(719) 635-5396
President ....Otto Dietrich
Executive Director ....Luke Saint Onge
Associate Exec. Dir./Communications ....Linda Mojer

USA Roller Skating
P.O. Box 6579, Lincoln, NE 68506
(402) 483-7551
President ....Sue Dooley
Executive Director ....TBA
Information Director ....Bill Wolf

U.S. Squash Racquets Association
P.O. Box 1216 (23 Cynwyd Rd.)
Bala Cynwyd, PA 19004
(610) 667-4006
President ....Eben Hardie
Executive Director ....Craig W. Brand

U.S. Taekwondo Union
One Olympic Plaza, Colorado Springs, CO 80909
(719) 578-4632
President ....Dr. Sang Chul Lee
Executive Director ....R. Jay Warwick

USA Water Ski Association
799 Overlook Drive, S.E., Winter Haven, FL 33884
(941) 324-4341
President ....Andrea Plough
Executive Director ....Steve McDermett
Director of Communications ....Scott Atkinson

AFFILIATED ORGANIZATIONS

U.S. Orienteering Federation
P.O. Box 1444, Forest Park, GA 30298
(404) 363-2110
President ....Charles Ferguson
Executive Director ....Robin Shannonhouse
Media Contact ....Jon Nash

USA Rugby
3595 East Fountain Blvd., Ste. M2
Colorado Springs, CO 80910
(719) 637-1022
President ....Anne Barry
Executive V.P. ....Neal Brendel
Communications Director ....Mark Rudolph

U.S. Sports Acrobatics Federation
P.O. Box 41356, Sacramento, CA 95841-0356
(916) 488-9499
President ....Tonya Case-Patterson

Underwater Society of America
P.O. Box 628, Daly City, CA 94080
(650) 583-0614
President/Exec. Director ....Carol Rose

SOCCER
FIFA

(Federation Internationale de Football Assn.)
P.O. Box 85, 8030 Zurich, Switzerland
TEL: 011-41-1-384-9595
President ....Joseph Blatter
General Secretary ....Michael Zen-Russinen
Director of Communications ....Keith Cooper

MLS

Major League Soccer
110 E. 42nd Street, 10th Floor
New York, NY 10017
(212) 450-1200
Founder ....Alan I. Rothenberg
Commissioner ....Don Garber
V.P. of Communications ....Dan Courtemanche
Director of Information ....Bob Prior

Chicago Fire
311 W Superior St., #444
Chicago, IL 60610
(312) 705-7200
Investor/Operator ....Philip F. Anschutz
General Manager ....Peter Wilt
Director of Communications ....Adam Low

Colorado Rapids
555 17th Street, Suite 3350, Denver, CO 80202
(303) 299-1570
Investor/Operator ....Philip F. Anschutz
General Manager ....Dan Counce
Media Relations ....Ben Grossman

Columbus Crew
Columbus Crew Stadium
2121 Velma Ave., Columbus, OH 43211
(614) 447-2739
Investor/Operator ....Lamar Hunt and Family
President/GM ....Jim Smith
Director of Media Relations ....Jeff Wuerth

Dallas Burn
2602 McKinney, Suite 200, Dallas, TX 75204
(214) 979-0303
Investor/Operator ....League-owned
President/GM ....Andy Swift
Director of Media Relations ....Chris Ward

Kansas City Wizards
2 Arrowhead Drive
Kansas City, MO 64129
(816) 920-9300
Investor/Operator ....Lamar Hunt and Family
General Manager ....Curt Johnson
Director of Media Relations ....Rob Thomson

Los Angeles Galaxy
1010 Rose Bowl Dr., Pasadena, CA 91103
(626) 432-1540
Investor/Operator ....Philip F. Anschutz
President ....Tim Leiweke
General Manager ....Time Luse
Director of Media Relations ....Luis Garcia

Miami Fusion
2200 Commercial Blvd., Ste. 104
Ft. Lauderdale, FL 33309
(954) 717-2200
Investor/Operator ....Kenneth Horowitz
V.P./General Manager ....Doug Hamilton
Director of Public Relations ....Gabe Gabor

New England Revolution
Foxboro Stadium, 60 Washington St.
Foxboro, MA 02035
(508) 543-5001
Investor/Operator ....Robert Kraft and Family
COO ....Brian O'Donovan
Director of Media Relations .... Jurgen Mainka

New York/New Jersey MetroStars
One Harmon Plaza, 3rd Floor
Seacaucus, NJ 07094
(201) 583-7000
Investor/Operator .... John Kluge and Stuart Subotnick
General Manager ....Nick Sakiewicz
Media Relations ....John Neves

San Jose Earthquakes
3550 Stevens Creek Blvd., Suite 200
San Jose, CA 95117
(408) 241-9922
Investor/Operator ....Kraft Family Sports Group
General Manager ....Lynne Meterparel
Director of Media Relations ....Roger Horn

Tampa Bay Mutiny
Raymond-James Stadium
4042 N. Himes, Tampa, FL 33607
(813) 386-2000
Investor/Operator ....League-owned
President/GM ....Bill Manning
Director of Media Relations ....Tracey Judd

Washington D.C. United
13832 Redskin Drive, Herndon, VA 20171
(703) 478-6600
Owner ....Washington Soccer, L.P.
President/GM ....Kevin Payne
Director of Communications ....Chris Stockton

Other Soccer

CONCACAF
(Confederation of North, Central American &
Caribbean Association Football)
725 Fifth Ave., 17th Floor
New York, NY 10022
(212) 308-0044
President .... Jack Austin Warner
General Secretary ....Chuck Blazer
Senior Consultant ....Clive Toye
Press Officer ....Rick Lawes

U.S. Soccer
(United States Soccer Federation)
Soccer House, 1801-1811 South Prairie Ave.
Chicago, IL 60616
(312) 808-1300
President ....Dr. S. Robert Contiguglia
Secretary General ....Dan Flynn
Director of Communications .... Jim Moorhouse

NPSL
(National Professional Soccer League)
115 Dewalt Avenue NW, 5th Fl.
Canton, OH 44702
(330) 455-4625
Commissioner . . . . .Steve M. Paxos
Director of Operations . . . . .TBA
Director of Media Relations . . . . .Chuck Murr
   Member teams (15): Baltimore Blast, Buffalo Blizzard, Cleveland Crunch, Detroit Rockers, Edmonton Drillers, Harrisburg Heat, Kansas City Attack, Milwaukee Wave, Montreal Impact, North Carolina TBA, Philadelphia Kixx, St. Louis Ambush, Toronto Thundercats and Wichita Wings.

USL
(United Soccer Leagues)
14497 N. Dale Mabry Hwy., Ste. 201
Tampa, FL 33618
(813) 963-3909
Commissioner . . . . .Francisco Marcos
Administrative Manager . . . . .Beverly Wright
Director of Public Relations . . . . .Scott Creighton

SWIMMING

FINA
(Federation Internationale de Natation Amateur)
9 ave de Beaumont
1012 Lausanne, Switzerland
TEL: 011-4121-312-6602
President . . . . .Mustapha Larfaoui
Honrary Secretary . . . . .Gunnar Werner

TENNIS

ATP Tour
(Association of Tennis Professionals)
201 ATP Tour Blvd.
Ponte Vedra Beach, FL 32082
(904) 285-8000
Chief Executive Officer . . . . Mark Miles
V.P. of Corporate Comm. . . . . .David Higdon
Dir. of Comm., Americas . . . . .Greg Sharko

ITF
(International Tennis Federation)
Palliser Rd., Barons Court
London, England W14 9EN
TEL: 011-44-181-878-6464
President . . . . .Ricci Bitti
Executive V.P. . . . . .Juan Margets
Head of Communications . . . . .Alun James

Dupont World TeamTennis
445 North Wells, Suite 404, Chicago, IL 60610
(312) 245-5300
Director/Co-Founder . . . . .Billie Jean King
Executive Director . . . . .Ilana Kloss
Communications Director . . . . .TBA

USTA
(United States Tennis Association)
70 West Red Oak Lane, White Plains, NY 10604
(914) 696-7000
President . . . . .Juila A. Levering
Executive Director .Richard D. Fermin
Dir. of Communications . . . . .Andrea Jayson

WTA Tour
(Women's Tennis Association)
1266 East Main St. 4th Floor, Stamford, CT 06902
(203) 978-1740
CEO . . . . .Bartlett H. McGuire
COO . . . . .Elizabeth Garger
V.P. of Communications/Development . . . . .Chris De Maria

TRACK & FIELD

IAAF
(International Ameteur Athletics Federation)
17 Rue Princesse Florestine
BP 359, MC-98007, Monaco Cedex
TEL: 377-93-10-8888
President . . . . .Lamine Diack
General Secretariat .Sandrine Steva
Director of Information . . . . .Sandrine Steva

USA Track & Field
P.O. Box 120
Indianapolis, IN 46206
(317) 261-0500
President . . . . .Patricia Rico
CEO . . . . .Craig Masbak
Director of Communications . . . . Jill Geer

MISCELLANEOUS

AAU
(Amateur Athletic Union)
c/o Walt Disney World Resorts
P.O. Box 10000
Lake Buena Vista, FL 32830-1000
(407) 934-7200
President . . . . .Bobby Dodd
Media/Public Relations Director . . . . .Melissa Wilson

American Powerboating Association
P.O. Box 377
Eastpointe, MI 48021
(810) 773-9700
President . . . . .Mike Jones
Executive Administrator . . . . .Gloria Urbin

Association of Surfing Professionals
P.O. Box 1095, Coolangatta
Queensland, Australia 4225
61-07-5599-1550
President/CEO .Wayne Bartholomew
Tour Director . . . . .Peter Whittaker
Tour Supervisor . . . . .Al Hunt

BASS, Inc.
(Bass Anglers Sportsmen Society)
5845 Carmichael Road
Mongomery, AL 36117
(334) 272-9530
CEO . . . . .Helen Sevier
Publicity Director . . . . .George McNeilly

Iditarod Trail Committee
P.O. Box 870800
Wasilla, AK 99687
(907) 376-5155
Executive Director . . . . .Stan Hooley
Race Director . . . . .Joanne Potts

International Game Fish Association
300 Gulf Steam Way
Dania Baech, FL 33004
(954) 927-2628
Chairman . . . . .Michael Levitt
President . . . . .Mike Leach
Editor . . . . .Ray Crawford

Little League Baseball Incorporated
P.O. Box 3485
Williamsport, PA 17701
(570) 326-1921
CEO-President . . . . .Steven Keener
Director of Communications . . . . .TBA
Dir. of Publications/Media Relations . . . . .Lance Van Auken

National Association for Girls and Women in Sport
1900 Association Drive, Reston, VA 20191
(703) 476-3452
Executive Director ....MaryAnn Borysowicz
President ....Dr. Jan Rintala

National Lacrosse League
237 Main St., Ste 1500, Buffalo, NY 14203
(716) 855-1NLL
Commissioner .... John Livsey Jr.
V.P. of Public Relations ....Bruce Wawrzyniak
   Member teams (8): Albany, Baltimore, Buffalo, Long Island (N.Y.), Philadelphia, Rochester (N.Y.), Syracuse (N.Y.) and Toronto.

National Sports Foundation
P.O. Box 888886, Atlanta, GA 30356
(678) 417-0041
Executive Director ....Ed Harris

Professional Rodeo Cowboys Association
101 Pro Rodeo Drive
Colorado Springs, CO 80919
(719) 593-8840
Commissioner ....Steve Hatchell
Director of Communications ....Steve Fleming

Roller Hockey International
650 S. Cherry Creek Dr., Ste. 1025
Denver, CO 80246
(303) 399-0800
Commissioner ....Ralph Backstrom
CEO ....Bernie Mullin
Media Relations ....Mark Ehrhart

Special Olympics
1325 G St. NW Suite 500
Washington, DC 20005
(202) 628-3630
Founder ....Eunice Kennedy Shriver
COB ....Sargent Shriver
COO ....Kim Elliott
Sr. Media Relations Manager ....Charmaine Dittmar

U.S. Association of Blind Athletes
33 N. Institute St.
Colorado Springs, CO 80903
(719) 630-0422
Executive Director ....Charlie Huebner
Asst. Exec. Director ....Mark Lucas

U.S. Polo Association
4059 Iron Works Pkwy., Ste. 1
Lexington, KY 40511
(606) 255-0593
Executive Director ....David Cummings

U.S. Windsurfing
P.O. Box 978
Hood River, OR 97031
(541) 386-8708
President ....Dick Tillman
Executive Director ....Holly Macpherson

Wheelchair Sports USA
3595 East Fountain Blvd., Suite L-1
Colorado Springs, CO 80910
(719) 574-1150
Chairman ....Paul DePace
Executive Director ....Patricia Shepherd

Commissioners and Presidents
Chief Executives of Established Major Sports Organizations since 1876

Major League Baseball

Commissioner	Tenure
Kenesaw Mountain Landis*	1920-44
Albert (Happy) Chandler	1945-51
Ford Frick	1951-65
William Eckert	1965-68
Bowie Kuhn	1969-84
Peter Ueberroth	1984-89
A. Bartlett Giamatti*	1989
Fay Vincent	1989-92
Bud Selig†	1998—

*Died in office.
†Served as interim commissioner from 1992-98.

National League

President	Tenure
Morgan G. Bulkeley	1876
William A. Hulbert*	1877-82
A.G. Mills	1883-84
Nicholas Young	1885-1902
Henry Pulliam*	1903-09
Thomas J. Lynch	1910-13
John K. Tener	1914-18
John A. Heydler	1918-34
Ford Frick	1935-51
Warren Giles	1951-69
Charles (Chub) Feeney	1970-86
A. Bartlett Giamatti	1987-89
Bill White	1989-94
Leonard Coleman	1994-99

*Died in office.
Note: League president jobs were eliminated after the 1999 season.

American League

President	Tenure
Bancroft (Ban) Johnson	1901-27
Ernest Barnard*	1927-31
William Harridge	1931-59
Joe Cronin	1959-73
Lee McPhail	1974-83
Bobby Brown	1984-94
Gene Budig	1994-99

*Died in office.
Note: League president jobs were eliminated after the 1999 season.

NBA

Commissioner	Tenure
Maurice Podoloff	1949-63
Walter Kennedy	1963-75
Larry O'Brien	1975-84
David Stern	1984—

NFL

President	Tenure
Jim Thorpe	1920
Joe Carr	1921-39
Carl Storck	1939-41

Commissioner	
Elmer Layden	1941-46
Bert Bell*	1946-59
Austin Gunsel	1959-60
Pete Rozelle	1960-89
Paul Tagliabue	1989—

*Died in office.

NHL

President	Tenure
Frank Calder*	1917-43
Red Dutton	1943-46
Clarence Campbell	1946-77
John Ziegler	1977-92
Gil Stein	1992-93

Commissioner	
Gary Bettman	1993—

*Died in office.

NCAA

Executive Director	Tenure
Walter Byers	1951-88
Dick Schultz	1988-93
Cedric Dempsey	1993—

IOC

President	Tenure
Demetrius Vikelas, Greece	1894-96
Baron Pierre de Coubertin, France	1896-1925
Count Henri de Baillet-Latour, Belgium	1925-42
Vacant	1942-46
J. Sigfried Edstrom, Sweden	1946-52
Avery Brundage, USA	1952-72
Lord Michael Killanin, Ireland	1972-80
Juan Antonio Samaranch, Spain	1980—

International Sports

Encore

Lance Armstrong gives a repeat performance with another amazing Tour de France victory in 2000.

by

Jack Edwards

All of France—and all the cycling world—looked up to the podium and cheered on a perfect midsummer's day, and the man they were cheering for, Lance Armstrong, did not notice. His body was worn and weary but he felt none of it. He was looking into the eyes of a miracle.

Armstrong won his second consecutive Tour de France in 2000. He proved beyond any rumor-monger's shadow of doubt that he is one of the elite cyclists of all time...for what that is worth. It would be Armstrong himself who could put the value on his achievement.

After all, he beat Jan Ullrich, Marco Pantani and all the would-be contenders who either got scared away by drug testing in 1999 or were hurt or had just backed down from the test.

Jack Edwards has been with ESPN since 1991 as a *Sports-Center* anchor and currently as a play-by-play announcer.

He proved he could win without the luck (the residue of strategic design) that had his team ahead of the pack before 1999's massive crash took out many of his rivals for good. He proved that a topical cream used to treat a saddle sore was not a legitimate story about possible drug use.

Any near-silent whisper that last year was a fluke now was utter balderdash. Lance Armstrong will ride with the all-time greats when the final peloton forms. But that's maybe third on his list of what's really important. I had a few brushes with Armstrong in his up-and-coming days and he seemed to be a no-nonsense guy who occasionally got caught-up in his self-perceived importance.

The results were good enough to win him a place in the sports fan's mind. He won the World Championship road race. He was a big star in cycling. Then came the snowstorm. I've actually held the x-ray of his lungs. It reminded me of a flash picture taken on a stormy winter's night.

the 2000 men's World Cup skiing championship with a record amount of points. It's "The Hermannator's" second overall World Cup championship in the last three years.

5. Moroccan **Khalid Khannouchi**, the men's marathon world-record holder (2:05:42), becomes a U.S. citizen in May, 2000 and is sworn in just in time to participate in the U.S. Olympic Trials. He is met by protests and political wranglings from, among others, the Moroccan Olympic authorities, but he decides to skip the Trials due to injury anyway.

4. The "**speedsuit**," which has been used successfully by speedskaters and track athletes to shave fractions off their times, finally makes its way into the swimming pool in 2000. Some of the world's elite swimmers started using them and the world records began to tumble.

3. Canadian speed skater **Jeremy Wotherspoon** breaks the 500-meter (34.63) and 1000-meter (1:08.49) world records in January at Calgary.

2. **Tiny Tegla Loroupe**, drafting behind three male pacesetters for the first 25 miles, sets the women's world record in the marathon, running 2:20:43 on the swift course of the Berlin Marathon in late 1999.

1. **Lance Armstrong**, one year after becoming only the second American to win the world's biggest cycling race, wins his second-straight Tour de France. ∎

AP/Wide World Photos

The **speedsuit** was one of the most talked-about and controversial technological innovations in swimming. Many observers credit them with (or blame them for) the rash of broken records set in 2000.

AP/Wide World Photos

American figure skater **Michelle Kwan** is all smiles after winning her third career gold medal at the World Figure Skating Championships in 2000.

AMERICANS IN PARIS

In 1999, Lance Armstrong joined Greg LeMond as the only Americans to win cycling's biggest race, the Tour de France. The following year he successfully defended his title as the world's greatest cyclist. Here is a closer look at the two American winners:

	LeMond	Armstrong
Races	8	6
Wins	3	2
Stage Wins	5	7
Top 5 Stage Finishes	5	2
DNF	2	3

TOP SIX UNDER TEN

Maurice Greene, the world record holder and 2000 gold medalist in the 100 meters, leads all runners with 31 performances under 10 seconds. Here is a look at the men with the most times under 10 seconds (as of Sept. 27, 2000).

Maurice Greene, USA	31
Frank Fredericks, Namibia	26
Ato Boldon, Trinidad & Tobago	24
Donovan Bailey, Canada	15
Carl Lewis, USA	15
Dennis Mitchell, USA	12

CLOSE CALLS

It went right down to the wire in Beantown this year. The Boston Marathon saw the closest finishes ever in both the men's and women's races in 2000. Elijah Lagat and Gezahenge Abera both finished in 2:09:47 while two-time winner Moses Tanui was a close third in 2:09:50. On the women's side, Catherine Ndereba (2:26:11) beat Irina Bogacheva and Fatuma Roba who both finished in 2:26:27. Here's a look at the closest finishes in Boston Marathon history.

Men

Year	Margin	First	Second
2000	0 seconds	E. Lagat	G. Abera
1988	1 second	I. Hussein	J. Ikangaa
1978	2 seconds	B. Rodgers	J. Wells
1982	2 seconds	A. Salazar	D. Beardsley
1998	3 seconds	M. Tanui	J. Chebet

Women

Year	Margin	First	Second
2000	16 seconds	C. Ndereba	I. Bogacheva
1973	30 seconds	J. Hansen	N. Kuscsik
1980	40 seconds	J. Gareau	P. Lyons
1978	44 seconds	G. Barron	P. DeMoss
1997	46 seconds	F. Roba	E. Meyer

TRACK & FIELD

2000 IAAF Mobil Grand Prix Final

The final meeting of the International Amateur Athletic Federation's Outdoor Grand Prix season, which includes the world's 10 leading outdoor invitational meets. Athletes earn points throughout the season with the leading point winners invited to the Grand Prix Final. The 2000 final was held Oct. 5, 2000 in Doha, Qatar.

MEN

Event		Time
100 meters	Darren Campbell, GBR	10.25
400 meters	Mark Richardson, GBR	45.20
1500 meters	Noah Ngeny, KEN	3:36.62
3000 meters	Luke Kipkosgei, KEN	7:46.21
400m hurdles	Angelo Taylor, USA	48.14

Event		Hgt/Dist
High Jump	Vyacheslav Voronin, RUS	7-7¼
Pole Vault	Tim Lobinger, GER	18-8¼
Triple Jump	Jonathan Edwards, GBR	56-2
Shot Put	Andy Bloom, USA	71-7¼
Hammer Throw	Andrey Skvaruk, UKR	267-2

WOMEN

Event		Time
100 meters	Marion Jones, USA	11.00
400 meters	Lorraine Graham, JAM	50.21
1500 meters	Violeta Beclea-Szekely, ROM	4:15.63
3000 meters	Sonia O'Sullivan, IRL	8:52.01
100m hurdles	Gail Devers, USA	12.85

Event		Hgt/Dist
Long Jump	Heike Drechsler, GER	23-2½
Discus	Franka Dietzsch, GER	201-6
Javelin	Sonia Bisset, CUB	216-2

Final Top 10 Standings

Overall Men's and Women's winners receive $200,000 (US) each; all ties broken by complex Grand Prix scoring system.

MEN

1. Angelo Taylor, USA (101 points); 2. Yuriy Belonog, UKR (94); 3. Adam Nelson, USA (93); 4. Nick Hysong, USA (86.5); 5. Bernard Lagat, KEN (78); 6. Tim Lobinger, GER (77.5); 7. Maurice Greene, USA and Eric Thomas, USA (77); 9. Luke Kipkosgei, KEN (75) and Samuel Matete, ZAM (75).

WOMEN

1. Trine Hattestad, NOR (110 points); 2. Gail Devers, USA and Marion Jones, USA (104); 4. Violeta Beclea-Szekely, ROM (94); 5. Glory Alozie, NGR (91); 6. Osleidys Menendez, CUB (90); 7. Tatyana Shikolenko, RUS (88); 8. Fiona May, ITA (83); 9. Kutre Dulecha, ETH and Delloreen Ennis-London, JAM (81).

World, Olympic and American Records

As of Oct. 1, 2000

World outdoor records officially recognized by the International Amateur Athletics Federation (IAAF); (p) indicates record is pending ratification.

MEN
Running

Event		Time		Date Set	Location
100 meters:	**World**	9.79	**Maurice Greene**, USA	June 16, 1999	Athens
	Olympic	9.84	Donovan Bailey, Canada	July 27, 1996	Atlanta
	American	9.79	Greene (same as World)	—	—
200 meters:	**World**	19.32	**Michael Johnson**, USA	Aug. 1, 1996	Atlanta
	Olympic	19.32	Johnson (same as World)	—	—
	American	19.32	Johnson (same as World)	—	—
400 meters:	**World**	43.18	**Michael Johnson**, USA	Aug. 26, 1999	Seville
	Olympic	43.49	Michael Johnson, USA	July 29, 1996	Atlanta
	American	43.18	Johnson (same as World)	—	—
800 meters:	**World**	1:41.11	**Wilson Kipketer**, Denmark	Aug. 24, 1997	Cologne
	Olympic	1:42.58	Vebjoern Rodal, Norway	July 31, 1996	Atlanta
	American	1:42.60	Johnny Gray	Aug. 28, 1985	Koblenz, W. Ger.
1000 meters:	**World**	2:11.96	**Noah Ngeny**, Kenya	Sept. 5, 1999	Rieti, ITA
	Olympic		Not an event	—	—
	American	2:13.9	Rick Wohlhuter	July 30, 1974	Oslo
1500 meters:	**World**	3:26.00	**Hicham El Guerrouj**, Morocco	July 14, 1998	Rome
	Olympic	3:32.07	Noah Ngeny, Kenya	Sept. 29, 2000	Sydney
	American	3:29.77	Sydney Maree	Aug. 25, 1985	Cologne

Event		Time		Date Set	Location
Mile:	**World**	.....3:43.13	**Hicham El Guerrouj**, Morocco	July 7, 1999	Rome
	Olympic	....	Not an event	—	—
	American	..3:47.69	Steve Scott	July 7, 1982	Oslo
2000 meters:	**World**	.....4:44.79	**Hicham El Guerrouj**, Morocco	Sept. 7, 1999	Berlin
	Olympic	....	Not an event	—	—
	American	..4:52.44	Jim Spivey	Sept. 15, 1987	Lausanne, SWI
3000 meters:	**World**	....7:20.67	**Daniel Komen**, Kenya	Sept. 1, 1996	Rieti, ITA
	Olympic	....	Not an event	—	—
	American	..7:30.84	Bob Kennedy	Aug. 8, 1998	Monte Carlo
5000 meters:	**World**	..12:39.36	**Haile Gebrselassie**, Ethiopia	June 13, 1998	Helsinki
	Olympic	.13:05.59	Said Aouita, Morocco	Aug. 11, 1984	Los Angeles
	American	.12:58.21	Bob Kennedy	Aug. 14, 1996	Zurich
10,000 meters:	**World**	...26:22.75	**Haile Gebrselassie**, Ethiopia	June 1, 1998	Hengelo, NED
	Olympic	.27:07.34	Haile Gebrselassie, Ethiopia	July 29, 1996	Atlanta
	American	.27:20.56	Mark Nenow	Sept. 5, 1986	Brussels
20,000 meters:	**World**	.....56:55.6	**Arturo Barrios**, Mexico	Mar. 30, 1991	La Fleche, FRA
	Olympic	....	Not an event	—	—
	American	..58:15.0	Bill Rodgers	Aug. 9, 1977	Boston
Marathon:	**World**	.....2:05:42†	**Khalid Khannouchi**, Morocco	Oct. 24, 1999	Chicago
	Olympic	...2:09:21	Carlos Lopes, Portugal	Aug. 12, 1984	Los Angeles
	American	..2:09:32	David Morris	Oct. 24, 1999	Chicago
		2:08:52*	Alberto Salazar	Apr. 19, 1982	Boston

Note: The Mile run is 1,609.344 meters and the Marathon is 42,194.988 meters (26 miles, 385 yards).
†Marathon records are not officially recognized by the IAAF.
*Former American record no longer officially recognized.

Relays

Event		Time		Date Set	Location
4 x 100m:	**World**	.......37.40	**USA** (Marsh, Burrell, Mitchell, C. Lewis)	Aug. 8, 1992	Barcelona
		37.40	**USA** (Drummond, Cason, Mitchell, Burrell)	Aug. 21, 1993	Stuttgart
	Olympic	......37.40	USA (same as World)	—	—
	American	.....37.40	USA (same as World)	—	—
4 x 200m:	**World**	......1:18.68	**USA** (Marsh, Burrell, Heard, C. Lewis)	Apr. 17, 1994	Walnut, Calif.
	Olympic	....	Not an event	—	—
	American	...1:18.68	USA (same as World)	—	—
4 x 400m:	**World**	......2:54.20	**USA** (Young, Pettigrew, Washington, Johnson)	July 22, 1998	Uniondale, N.Y.
	Olympic	....2:55.74	USA (Valmon, Watts, Johnson, S. Lewis)	Aug. 8, 1992	Barcelona
	American	...2:54.20	USA (same as World)	—	—
4 x 800m:	**World**	......7:03.89	**Great Britain** (Elliott, Cook, Cram, Coe)	Aug. 30, 1982	London
	Olympic	....	Not an event	—	—
	American	.....7:06.5	Santa Monica TC (J. Robinson, Mack, E. Jones, Gray)	Apr. 26, 1986	Walnut, Calif.
4 x 1500m:	**World**	......14:38.8	**West Germany** (Wessinghage, Hudak, Lederer, Fleschen)	Aug. 17, 1977	Cologne
	Olympic	....	Not an event	—	—
	American	....14:46.3	USA (Aldredge, Clifford, Harbour, Duits)	June 24, 1979	Bourges, FRA

Hurdles

Event		Time		Date Set	Location
110 meters:	**World**	.......12.91	**Colin Jackson**, Great Britain	Aug. 20, 1993	Stuttgart
	Olympic	......12.95	Allen Johnson, USA	July 29, 1996	Atlanta
	American	....12.92	Roger Kingdom	Aug. 16, 1989	Zurich
		12.92	Allen Johnson	June 23, 1996	Atlanta
400 meters:	**World**	.......46.78	**Kevin Young**, USA	Aug. 6, 1992	Barcelona
	Olympic	......46.78	Young (same as World)	—	—
	American	.....46.78	Young (same as World)	—	—

Note: The 10 hurdles at 110 meters are 3 feet, 6 inches high and those at 400 meters are 3 feet.

Walking

Event		Time		Date Set	Location
20 km:	**World**	....1:17:26	**Bernardo Segura**, Mexico	May 7, 1994	Fana, NOR
	Olympic	....1:18:59	Robert Korzeniowski, Poland	Sept. 22, 2000	Sydney
	American	..1:22:17	Tim Lewis	Sept. 24, 1989	Dearborn, Mich.
50 km:	**World**	...3:37:26p	**Valeriy Spytsyn**, Russia	May 21, 2000	Moscow
	Olympic	...3:38:29	Vyacheslav Ivanenko, USSR	Sept. 30, 1988	Seoul
	American	..3:48:04	Curt Clausen	May. 2, 1999	Deauville, FRA

Steeplechase

Event		Time		Date Set	Location
3000 meters:	**World**	.....7:55.72	**Bernard Barmasai**, Kenya	Aug. 24, 1997	Cologne
	Olympic	....8:05.51	Julius Kariuki, Kenya	Sept. 30, 1988	Seoul
	American	..8:09.17	Henry Marsh	Aug. 28, 1985	Koblenz

Note: A men's steeplechase course consists of 28 hurdles (3 feet high) and seven water jumps (12 feet long).

Field Events

Event		Mark		Date Set	Location
High Jump:	World	8-0½	**Javier Sotomayor**, Cuba	July 27, 1993	Salamanca, SPA
	Olympic	7-10	Charles Austin, USA	July 28, 1996	Atlanta
	American	7-10½	Charles Austin	Aug. 7, 1991	Zurich
Pole Vault:	World	20-1¾	**Sergey Bubka**, Ukraine	July 31, 1994	Sestriere, ITA
	Olympic	19-5¼	Jean Galfione, France	Aug. 2, 1996	Atlanta
		19-5¼	Igor Trandenkov, Russia	Aug. 2, 1996	Atlanta
		19-5¼	Andrei Tiwontschik, Germany	Aug. 2, 1996	Atlanta
	American	19-9¼	Jeff Hartwig	June 14, 2000	Jonesboro, Ark.
Long Jump:	World	29-4¾*	**Ivan Pedroso**, Cuba	July 29, 1995	Sestriere, ITA
		29-4½	**Mike Powell**, USA	Aug. 30, 1991	Tokyo
	Olympic	29-2½	Bob Beamon, USA	Oct. 18, 1968	Mexico City
	American	29-4½	Powell (same as World)	—	—
Triple Jump:	World	60-0¼	**Jonathan Edwards**, GBR	Aug. 7, 1995	Göteborg, SWE
	Olympic	59-4¼	Kenny Harrison, USA	July 27, 1996	Atlanta
	American	59-4¼	Kenny Harrison (same as Olympic)	—	—
Shot Put:	World	75-10¼	**Randy Barnes**, USA	May 20, 1990	Los Angeles
	Olympic	73- 8¾	Ulf Timmermann, East Germany	Sept. 23, 1988	Seoul
	American	75-10¼	Barnes (same as World)	—	—
Discus:	World	243-0	**Jurgen Schult**, East Germany	June 6, 1986	Neubrandenburg
	Olympic	227-8	Lars Riedel, Germany	July 31, 1996	Atlanta
	American	237-4	Ben Plucknett	July 7, 1981	Stockholm
Javelin:	World	323-1	**Jan Zelezny**, Czech Republic	May 25, 1996	Jena, GER
	Olympic	295-10	Jan Zelezny, Czech Republic	Sept. 23, 2000	Sydney
	American	285-10	Tom Pukstys	May 25, 1997	Jena, GER
Hammer:	World	284-7	**Yuriy Sedykh**, USSR	Aug. 30, 1986	Stuttgart
	Olympic	278-2	Sergey Litvinov, USSR	Sept. 26, 1988	Seoul
	American	270-9	Lance Deal	Sept. 7, 1996	Milan

Note: The international weights for men— **Shot** (16 lbs); **Discus** (4 lbs/6.55 oz); **Javelin** (minimum 1 lb/12¼ oz.); **Hammer** (16 lbs).

*Apparent world record disallowed because of interference with wind gauge at altitude.

Decathlon

Event		Points		Date Set	Location
Ten Events:	World	8994	**Tomas Dvorak**, Czech.	July 3-4, 1999	Prague
	Olympic	8847	Daley Thompson, Great Britain	Aug. 8-9, 1984	Los Angeles
	American	8891	Dan O'Brien	Sept. 4-5, 1992	Talence, FRA

Note: Dvorak's WR times and distances, in order over two days— **100m** (10.54); **LJ** (25-11); **Shot** (55-0); **HJ** (6-8¼); **400m** (48.08); **110m H** (13.73); **Discus** (158-6); **PV** (16-0¾); **Jav** (237-3); **1500m** (4:37.20).

WOMEN
Running

Event		Time		Date Set	Location
100 meters:	World	10.49	**Florence Griffith Joyner**, USA	July 16, 1988	Indianapolis
	Olympic	10.62	Florence Griffith Joyner, USA	Sept. 24, 1988	Seoul
	American	10.49	Griffith Joyner (same as World)	—	—
200 meters:	World	21.34	**Florence Griffith Joyner**, USA	Sept. 29, 1988	Seoul
	Olympic	21.34	Griffith Joyner (same as World)	—	—
	American	21.34	Griffith Joyner (same as World)	—	—
400 meters:	World	47.60	**Marita Koch**, East Germany	Oct. 6, 1985	Canberra, AUS
	Olympic	48.25	Marie-Jose Perec, France	July 29, 1996	Atlanta
	American	48.83	Valerie Brisco	Aug. 6, 1984	Los Angeles
800 meters:	World	1:53.28	**Jarmila Kratochvilova**, Czech.	July 26, 1983	Munich
	Olympic	1:53.42	Nadezhda Olizarenko, USSR	July 27, 1980	Moscow
	American	1:56.40	Jearl Miles-Clark	Aug. 11, 1999	Zurich
1000 meters:	World	2:28.98	**Svetlana Masterkova**, Russia	Aug. 23, 1996	Brussels
	Olympic		Not an event	—	—
	American	2:31.80	Regina Jacobs	July 3, 1999	Brunswick, Me.
1500 meters:	World	3:50.46	**Qu Yunxia**, China	Sept. 11, 1993	Beijing
	Olympic	3:53.96	Paula Ivan, Romania	Oct. 1, 1988	Seoul
	American	3:57.12	Mary Slaney	July 26, 1983	Stockholm
Mile:	World	4:12.56	**Svetlana Masterkova**, Russia	Aug. 14, 1996	Zurich
	Olympic		Not an event	—	—
	American	4:16.71	Mary Slaney	Aug. 21, 1985	Zurich
2000 meters:	World	5:25.36	**Sonia O'Sullivan**, Ireland	July 8, 1994	Edinburgh
	Olympic		Not an event	—	—
	American	5:32.7	Mary Slaney	Aug. 3, 1984	Eugene
3000 meters:	World	8:06.11	**Wang Junxia**, China	Sept. 13, 1993	Beijing
	Olympic	8:26.53	Tatyana Samolenko, USSR	Sept. 25, 1988	Seoul
	American	8:25.83	Mary Slaney	Sept. 7, 1985	Rome

Event		Time		Date Set	Location
5000 meters:	**World**	...14:28.09	**Jiang Bo**, China	Oct. 23, 1997	Shanghai
	Olympic	..14:40.79	Gabriela Szabo, Romania	Sept. 25, 2000	Sydney
	American	.14:45.35p	Regina Jacobs	July 27, 2000	Sacramento
10,000 meters:	**World**	...29:31.78	**Wang Junxia**, China	Sept. 8, 1993	Beijing
	Olympic	..30:17.49	Derartu Tulu, Ethiopia	Sept. 30, 2000	Sydney
	American	.31:19.89	Lynn Jennings	Aug. 7, 1992	Barcelona
Marathon:	**World**	....2:20:43†	**Tegla Loroupe**, Kenya	Sept. 26, 1999	Berlin
	Olympic	...2:23:14	Naoko Takahashi, Japan	Sept. 24, 2000	Sydney
	American	..2:21:21	Joan Benoit Samuelson	Oct. 20, 1985	Chicago

Note: The Mile run is 1,609.344 meters and the Marathon is 42,194.988 meters (26 miles, 385 yards).
†Marathon records are not officially recognized by the IAAF.

Relays

Event		Time		Date Set	Location
4 x 100m:	**World**	.......41.37	**East Germany** (Gladisch, Rieger, Auerswald, Gohr)	Oct. 6, 1985	Canberra, AUS
	Olympic	......41.60	East Germany (Muller, Wockel, Auerswald, Gohr)	Aug. 1, 1980	Moscow
	American	.....41.47	USA (Gaines, Jones, Miller, Devers)	Aug. 9, 1997	Athens
4 x 200m:	**World**	.....1:27.46p	**USA** (Jenkins, Colander-Richardson, Perry, Jones)	Apr. 29, 2000	Philadelphia
	Olympic	....	Not an event	—	—
	American	...1:27.46	USA (same as World)	—	—
4 x 400m:	**World**	.....3:15.17	**USSR** (Ledovskaya, Nazarova, Pinigina, Bryzgina)	Oct. 1, 1988	Seoul
	Olympic	...3:15.17	USSR (same as World)	—	—
	American	..3:15.51	USA (Howard, Dixon, Brisco, Griffith Joyner)	Oct. 1, 1988	Seoul
4 x 800m:	**World**	.....7:50.17	**USSR** (Olizarenko, Gurina, Borisova, Podyalovskaya)	Aug. 5, 1984	Moscow
	Olympic	....	Not an event	—	—
	American	...8:17.09	Athletics West (Addison, Arbogast, Decker Slaney, Mullen)	Apr. 24, 1983	Walnut, Calif.

Hurdles

Event		Time		Date Set	Location
100 meters:	**World**	......12.21	**Yordanka Donkova**, Bulgaria	Aug. 20, 1988	Stara Zagora, BUL
	Olympic	.....12.38	Yordanka Donkova, Bulgaria	Sept. 30, 1988	Seoul
	American	...12.33p	Gail Devers	July 23, 2000	Sacramento
400 meters:	**World**	.....52.61	**Kim Batten**, USA	Aug. 11, 1995	Göteborg, SWE
	Olympic	....52.82	Deon Hemmings, Jamaica	July 31, 1996	Atlanta
	American	...52.61	Batten (same as World)	—	—

Note: The 10 hurdles at 110 meters are 3 feet, 6 inches high and those at 400 meters are 3 feet.

Walking

Event		Time		Date Set	Location
20 km:	**World**	......1:25:18p	**Tatyana Gudkova**, Russia	May 19, 2000	Moscow
(road)	Olympic	.....1:29:05	Wang Liping, China	Sept. 28, 2000	Sydney
	American	....1:31:51	Michelle Rohl	May 13, 2000	Kenosha, Wisc.

Steeplechase

Event		Time		Date Set	Location
3000 meters:	**World**	...9:40.20p	**Cristina Iloc-Casandra**, Romania	Aug. 30, 2000	Reims
	Olympic	....	Not an event	—	—
	American	...9:57.20p	Elizabeth Jackson	July 17, 2000	Sacramento

Note: A women's steeplechase course consists of 28 hurdles (30 inches high) and seven water jumps (10 feet long).

Field Events

Event		Mark		Date Set	Location
High Jump:	**World**	......6-10¼	**Stefka Kostadinova**, Bulgaria	Aug. 30, 1987	Rome
	Olympic	......6-8¾	Stefka Kostadinova, Bulgaria	Aug. 3, 1996	Atlanta
	American	6-8	Louise Ritter	July 8, 1988	Austin, Tex.
Pole Vault:	**World**	......15-2¼p	**Stacy Dragila**, USA	July 23, 2000	Sacramento
	Olympic	15-1	Stacy Dragila, USA	Sept. 25, 2000	Sydney
	American	....15-2¼p	Dragila (same as World)	—	—
Long Jump:	**World**	.....24-8¼	**Galina Chistyakova**, USSR	June 11, 1988	Leningrad
	Olympic	....24-3¼	Jackie Joyner-Kersee, USA	Sept. 29, 1988	Seoul
	American	24-7	Jackie Joyner-Kersee	May 22, 1994	New York

Event	Mark		Date Set	Location
Triple Jump:	**World**.....50-10¼	**Inessa Kravets**, Ukraine	Aug. 8, 1995	Göteborg, SWE
	Olympic.....50-3½	Inessa Kravets, Ukraine	July 31, 1996	Atlanta
	American....47-3½	Sheila Hudson	July 8, 1996	Stockholm
Shot Put:	**World**.....74-3	**Natalya Lisovskaya**, USSR	June 7, 1987	Moscow
	Olympic....73-6¼	Ilona Slupianek, E. Germany	July 24, 1980	Moscow
	American....66-2½	Ramona Pagel	June 25, 1988	San Diego
Discus:	**World**.....252-0	**Gabriele Reinsch**, E. Germany	July 9, 1988	Neubrandenburg
	Olympic....237-2½	Martina Hellmann, E. Germany	Sept. 29, 1988	Seoul
	American .216-10	Carol Cady	May 31, 1986	San Jose
Javelin:	**World** ..227-11*	**Trine Hattestad**, Norway	July 28, 2000	Oslo
	Olympic....226-1*	Trine Hattestad, Norway	Sept. 30, 2000	Sydney
	American...192-3*	Lynda Blutriech	July 1, 2000	New Haven, Ct.
Hammer:	**World**....249-7	**Mihaela Melinte**, Romania	Aug. 29, 1999	Rudlingen, SWI
	Olympic... 233-5¾	Kamila Skolimowska, Poland	Sept. 29, 2000	Sydney
	American...231-2p	Dawn Ellerbe	Apr. 29, 2000	Philadelphia

*The IAAF changed the official design and weight for the women's javelin beginning April 1, 1999. The records shown are with the new-style javelins.
Note: The international weights for women— **Shot** (8 lbs/13 oz); **Discus** (2 lbs/3.27 oz); **Javelin** (minimum 1 lb/5.16 oz); **Hammer** (8 lbs/13 oz).

Heptathlon

	Points		Date Set	Location
Seven Events:	**World**.......7291	**Jackie Joyner-Kersee**, USA	Sept. 23-24, 1988	Seoul
	Olympic 7291	Joyner-Kersee (same as World)	—	—
	American 7291	Joyner-Kersee (same as World)	—	—

Note: Joyner-Kersee's WR times and distances, in order over two days— **100m H** (12.69); **HJ** (61¼); **Shot** (51-10); **200m** (22.56); **LJ** (2310¼); **Jav** (149-10); **800m** (2:08.51).

World and American Indoor Records
As of Oct. 1, 2000
World indoor records officially recognized by the International Amateur Athletics Federation (IAAF); (p) indicates record is pending ratification by the IAAF; (a) indicates record was set at an altitude over 1000 meters.

MEN
Running

Event	Time		Date Set	Location
50 meters:	**World**........5.56a	**Donovan Bailey**, Canada	Feb. 9, 1996	Reno, Nev.
	5.56p	**Maurice Greene**, USA	Feb. 13, 1999	Los Angeles
	American......5.56	Greene (same as World)	Feb. 13, 1999	Los Angeles
60 meters:	**World**........6.39	**Maurice Greene**, USA	Feb. 3, 1998	Madrid
	American......6.39	Greene (same as World)	—	—
200 meters:	**World** 19.92	**Frankie Fredericks**, Namibia	Feb. 18, 1996	Lievin, FRA
	American ...20.26	John Capel	Mar. 11, 2000	Fayetteville, Ark.
	20.26	Shawn Crawford	Mar. 11, 2000	Fayetteville, Ark.
400 meters:	**World** 44.63	**Michael Johnson**, USA	Mar. 4, 1995	Atlanta
	American ...44.63	Johnson (same as World)	—	—
800 meters:	**World**.....1:42.67	**Wilson Kipketer**, Denmark	Mar. 9, 1997	Paris
	American...1:45.00	Johnny Gray	Mar. 8, 1992	Sindelfingen, GER
1000 meters:	**World**.....2:14.96	**Wilson Kipketer**, Denmark	Feb. 20, 2000	Birmingham, ENG
	American...2:18.19	Ocky Clark	Feb. 12, 1989	Stuttgart
1500 meters:	**World**....3:31.18	**Hicham El Guerrouj**, Morocco	Feb. 2, 1997	Stuttgart
	American...3:38.12	Jeff Atkinson	Mar. 5, 1989	Budapest
Mile:	**World**....3:48.45	**Hicham El Guerrouj**, Morocco	Feb. 12, 1997	Ghent, BEL
	American...3:51.8	Steve Scott	Feb. 20, 1981	San Diego
3000 meters:	World......7:24.90	**Daniel Komen**, Kenya	Feb. 6, 1998	Budapest
	American...7:39.94	Steve Scott	Feb. 10, 1989	E. Rutherford, N.J.
5000 meters:	**World** ...12:50.38	**Haile Gebrselassie**, Ethiopia	Feb. 14, 1999	Birmingham, ENG
	American .13:20.55	Doug Padilla	Feb. 12, 1982	New York

Note: The Mile run is 1,609.344 meters.

Hurdles

Event	Time		Date Set	Location
50 meters:	**World**........6.25	**Mark McKoy**, Canada	Mar. 5, 1986	Kobe, JPN
	American......6.35	Greg Foster	Jan. 27, 1985	Rosemont, Ill.
	6.35	Greg Foster	Jan. 31, 1987	Ottawa
60 meters:	**World**........7.30	**Colin Jackson**, Britain	Mar. 6, 1994	Sindelfingen, GER
	American......7.36	Greg Foster	Jan. 16, 1987	Los Angeles

Note: The hurdles for both distances are 3 feet, 6 inches high. There are four hurdles in the 50 meters and five in the 60.

Relays

Event		Time		Date Set	Location
4 x 200 meters:	World	1:22.11	Great Britain	Mar. 3, 1991	Glasgow
	American	1:22.71	National Team	Mar. 3, 1991	Glasgow
4 x 400 meters:	World	3:02.83	United States	Mar. 7, 1999	Maebashi, JPN
	American	3:02.83	National Team (same as World)	Mar. 7, 1999	Maebashi, JPN
4 x 800 meters:	World	7:13.94	United States	Feb. 6, 2000	Boston
	American	7:13.94	Global Athletics (same as World)	Feb. 6, 2000	Boston

Field Events

Events		Mark		Date Set	Location
High Jump:	World	7-11½	Javier Sotomayor, Cuba	Mar. 4, 1989	Budapest
	American	7-10½	Hollis Conway	Mar. 10, 1991	Seville
Pole Vault:	World	20-2	Sergey Bubka, Ukraine	Feb. 21, 1993	Donyetsk, UKR
	American	19-6¼	Jeff Hartwig	Mar. 6, 1999	Maebashi, JPN
Long Jump:	World	28-10¼	Carl Lewis, USA	Jan. 27, 1984	New York
	American	28-10¼	Lewis (same as World)	—	—
Triple Jump:	World	58-6	Aliecer Urrutia, Cuba	Mar. 1, 1997	Sindelfingen, GER
	American	58-3¼	Mike Conley	Feb. 27, 1987	New York
Shot Put:	World	74-4¼	Randy Barnes, USA	Jan. 20, 1989	Los Angeles
	American	74-4¼	Barnes (same as World)	—	—

Note: The international shot put weight for men is 16 lbs.

Heptathlon

Seven Events:		Points		Date Set	Location
	World	6476	Dan O'Brien, USA	Mar. 13-14, 1993	Toronto
	American	6476	O'Brien (same as World)	—	—

Note: O'Brien's WR times and distances, in order over two days— **60m** (6.67); **LJ** (25-8¾); **SP** (52-6¾); **HJ** (6-11¾); **60m H** (7.85); **PV** (17-0¾); **1000m** (2:57.96).

WOMEN

Running

Event		Time		Date Set	Location
50 meters:	World	5.96	Irina Privalova, Russia	Feb. 9, 1995	Madrid
	American	6.02	Gail Devers	Feb. 21, 1999	Lievin, FRA
60 meters:	World	6.92	Irina Privalova, Russia	Feb. 11, 1993	Madrid
		6.92	Irina Privalova, Russia	Feb. 9, 1995	Madrid
	American	6.95	Gail Devers	Mar. 12, 1993	Toronto
		6.95	Marion Jones	Mar. 7, 1998	Maebashi, JPN
200 meters:	World	21.87	Merlene Ottey, Jamaica	Feb. 13, 1993	Lievin, FRA
	American	22.33	Gwen Torrence	Mar. 2, 1996	Atlanta
400 meters:	World	49.59	Jarmila Kratochvilova, Czech.	Mar. 7, 1982	Milan
	American	50.64	Diane Dixon	Mar. 10, 1991	Seville
800 meters:	World	1:56.36*	Christine Wachtel, E. Germany	Feb. 13, 1988	Vienna
	American	1:58.9	Mary Slaney	Feb. 22, 1980	San Diego
		1:58.92p	Suzy Hamilton	Feb. 7, 1999	Boston
1000 meters:	World	2:30.94	Maria Mutola, Mozambique	Feb. 25, 1999	Stockholm
	American	2:35.29	Regina Jacobs	Feb. 6, 2000	Boston
1500 meters:	World	4:00.27	Doina Melinte, Romania	Feb. 9, 1990	E. Rutherford, N.J.
	American	4:00.8	Mary Slaney	Feb. 8, 1980	New York
Mile:	World	4:17.14	Doina Melinte, Romania	Feb. 9, 1990	E. Rutherford, N.J.
	American	4:20.5	Mary Slaney	Feb. 19, 1982	San Diego
3000 meters:	World	8:33.82	Elly van Hulst, Holland	Mar. 4, 1989	Budapest
	American	8:39.14	Regina Jacobs	Mar. 7, 1999	Maebashi, JPN
5000 meters:	World	14:47.35	Gabriela Szabo, Romania	Feb. 13, 1999	Dortmund, GER
	American	15:22.64	Lynn Jennings	Jan. 7, 1990	Hanover, N.H.

Note: The Mile run is 1,609.344 meters.
*Maria Mutola's apparent record of 1:56.36 in February 1998 was not ratified by the IAAF because she ran outside of her lane on the final turn.

Hurdles

Event		Time		Date Set	Location
50 meters:	World	6.58	Cornelia Oschkenat, E. Ger.	Feb. 20, 1988	East Berlin
	American	6.67a	Jackie Joyner-Kersee	Feb. 10, 1995	Reno, Nev.
60 meters:	World	7.69	Lyudmila Narozhilenko, USSR	Feb. 4, 1990	Chelyabinsk, USSR
	American	7.81	Jackie Joyner-Kersee	Feb. 5, 1989	Fairfax, Va.

Note: The hurdles for both distances are 2 feet, 9 inches high. There are four hurdles in the 50 meters and five in the 60.

Walking

Event		Time		Date Set	Location
3000 meters:	World	11:40.33	Claudia Iovan, Romania	Jan. 30, 1999	Bucharest
	American	12:20.79	Debbi Lawrence	Mar. 12, 1993	Toronto

Relays

Event		Time		Date Set	Location
4 x 200 meters:	**World**	1:32.55	**West Germany**	Feb. 20, 1988	Dortmund, W. Ger.
		1:32.55	Germany	Feb. 21, 1999	Karlsruhe, GER
	American	1:33.24	National Team	Feb. 12, 1994	Glasgow
4 x 400 meters:	**World**	3:24.25	**Russia**	Mar. 7, 1999	Maebashi, JPN
	American	3:27.59	National Team	Mar. 7, 1999	Maebashi, JPN
4 x 800 meters:	**World**	8:18.71	**Russia**	Feb. 4, 1994	Moscow
	American	8:25.5p	Villanova	Feb. 7, 1987	Gainesville, Fla.

Field Events

Event		Mark		Date Set	Location
High Jump:	**World**	6-9½	**Heike Henkel**, Germany	Feb. 9, 1992	Karlsruhe, GER
	American	6-7	Tisha Waller	Feb. 28, 1998	Atlanta
Pole Vault:	**World**	15-1¾	**Stacy Dragila** USA	Mar. 3 2000	Atlanta
	American	15-1¾	Dragila (same as World)	—	—
Long Jump:	**World**	24-2¼	**Heike Drechsler**, E. Germany	Feb. 13, 1988	Vienna
	American	23-4¾	Jackie Joyner-Kersee	Mar. 5, 1994	Atlanta
Triple Jump:	**World**	49-9	**Ashia Hansen**, Great Britain	Feb. 28, 1998	Valencia, SPA
	American	46-8¼	Sheila Hudson	Mar. 4, 1995	Atlanta
Shot Put:	**World**	73-10	**Helena Fibingerova**, Czech.	Feb. 19, 1977	Jablonec, CZE
	American	65-0¾	Ramona Pagel	Feb. 20, 1987	Inglewood, Calif.

Note: The international shotput weight for women is 8 lbs. and 13 oz.

Pentathlon

Event		Points		Date Set	Location
Five Events:	**World**	4991	**Irina Byelova**, Russia	Feb. 14-15, 1992	Berlin
	American	4753	DeDee Nathan	Mar. 4-5, 1999	Maebashi, JPN

Note: Byelova's WR times and distances, in order over two days– **60m H** (8.22); **HJ** (6-4); **SP** (43-5¾); **LJ** (21-1¾); **800m** (2:10.26).

SWIMMING

World, Olympic and American Records
As of Oct. 1, 2000

World long course records officially recognized by the Federation Internationale de Natation Amateur (FINA). Note that (p) indicates preliminary heat; (r) relay lead-off split; and (s) indicates split time.

MEN
Freestyle

Distance		Time		Date Set	Location
50 meters:	**World**	21.64	**Aleksandr Popov**, Russia	June 16, 2000	Moscow
	Olympic	21.91	Aleksandr Popov, Unified Team	July 30, 1992	Barcelona
	American	21.76	Gary Hall Jr.	Aug. 15, 2000	Indianapolis
100 meters:	**World**	47.84p	**P. van den Hoogenband**, Netherlands	Sept. 19, 2000	Sydney
	Olympic	47.84	P. van den Hoogenband, NED (same as world)	—	—
	American	48.42	Matt Biondi	Aug. 10, 1988	Austin, Tex.
200 meters:	**World**	1:45.35	**P. van den Hoogenband**, Netherlands	Sept. 18, 2000	Sydney
	Olympic	1:45.35	P. van den Hoogenband, NED (same as world)	—	—
	American	1:46.73	Josh Davis	Sept. 18, 2000	Sydney
400 meters:	**World**	3:40.59	**Ian Thorpe**, Australia	Sept. 16, 2000	Sydney
	Olympic	3:40.59	Ian Thorpe, Australia (same as world)	—	—
	American	3:47.00	Klete Keller	Sept. 16, 2000	Sydney
800 meters:	**World**	7:46.00s	**Kieren Perkins**, Australia	Aug. 24, 1994	Victoria, CAN
	Olympic		Not an event	—	—
	American	7:52.45	Sean Killion	July 27, 1987	Clovis, Calif.
1500 meters:	**World**	14:41.66	**Kieren Perkins**, Australia	Aug. 24, 1994	Victoria, CAN
	Olympic	14:43.48	Kieren Perkins, Australia	July 31, 1992	Barcelona
	American	14:56.81	Chris Thompson	Sept. 23, 2000	Sydney

Backstroke

Distance		Time		Date Set	Location
50 meters:	**World**	24.99	**Lenny Krayzelburg**, USA	Aug. 28, 1999	Sydney
	Olympic		Not an event	—	—
	American	24.99	Krayzelburg (same as World)	—	—
100 meters:	**World**	53.60	**Lenny Krayzelburg**, USA	Aug. 24, 1999	Sydney
	Olympic	53.72	Lenny Krayzelburg, USA	Sept. 18, 2000	Sydney
	American	53.60	Krayzelburg (same as World)	—	—

Distance	Time		Date Set	Location
200 meters:	**World** 1:55.87	**Lenny Krayzelburg**, USA	Aug. 27, 1999	Sydney
	Olympic 1:56.76	Lenny Krayzelburg, USA	Sept. 21, 2000	Sydney
	American . . .1:55.87	Krayzelburg (same as World)	—	—

Breaststroke

Distance	Time		Date Set	Location
50 meters:	**World** 27.61	**Alexander Dzhaburiya**, UKR	April 27, 1996	Kharkov, UKR
	Olympic	Not an event	—	—
	American 28.24	Jay Schindler	Apr. 1 1999	Long Island
100 meters:	**World** 1:00.36	**Roman Sloudnov**, Russia	June 15, 2000	Moscow
	Olympic 1:00.46	Domenico Fioravanti, Italy	Sept. 17, 2000	Sydney
	American . . .1:00.73	Ed Moses	Sept. 17, 2000	Sydney
200 meters:	**World** 2:10.16	**Mike Barrowman**, USA	July 29, 1992	Barcelona
	Olympic . . .2:10.16	Barrowman (same as World)	—	—
	American . .2:10.16	Barrowman (same as World)	—	—

Butterfly

Distance	Time		Date Set	Location
50 meters:	**World** 23.60	**Geoffrey Huegill**, Australia	May 14, 2000	Sydney
	Olympic	Not an event	—	—
	American 23.89	Neil Walker	Aug. 12, 1997	Fukuoka, JPN
100 meters:	**World** 51.81	**Michael Klim**, Australia	Dec. 12, 1999	Canberra, AUS
	Olympic 51.96p	Geoffrey Huegill, Australia	Sept. 21, 2000	Sydney
	American 52.44	Ian Crocker	Sept. 22, 2000	Sydney
200 meters:	**World** 1:55.18	**Tom Malchow**, USA	June 17, 2000	Charlotte, N.C.
	Olympic . . .1:55.35	Tom Malchow, USA	Sept. 19, 2000	Sydney
	American . .1:55.18	Tom Malchow (same as world)	—	—

Individual Medley

Distance	Time		Date Set	Location
200 meters:	**World** 1:58.16	**Jani Sievinen**, Finland	Sept. 11, 1994	Rome
	Olympic 1:58.98	Massimiliano Rosolino, ITA	Sept. 21, 2000	Sydney
	American 1:59.77	Tom Dolan	Sept. 21, 2000	Sydney
400 meters:	**World** 4:11.76	**Tom Dolan**, USA	Sept. 17, 2000	Sydney
	Olympic 4:11.76	Dolan (same as World)	—	—
	American 4:11.76	Dolan (same as World)	—	—

Relays

Distance	Time		Date Set	Location
4x100m medley:	**World** 3:33.73	**USA** (Krayzelburg, Moses, Crocker, Hall Jr.)	Sept. 23, 2000	Sydney
	Olympic 3:33.73	USA (same as World)	—	—
	American 3:33.73	USA (same as World)	—	—
4x100m free:	**World** 3:13.67	**Australia** (Klim, Fydler, Callus, Thorpe)	Sept. 16, 2000	Sydney
	Olympic 3:13.67	Australia (same as world)	—	—
	American 3:13.86	USA (Ervin, Walker, Lezak, Hall Jr.)	Sept. 16, 2000	Sydney
4x200m free:	**World** 7:07.05	**Australia** (Thorpe, Klim, Pearson, Kirby)	Sept. 19, 2000	Sydney
	Olympic 7:07.05	Australia (same as world)	—	—
	American 7:12.51	USA (Dalbey, Cetlinski, Gjertsen, Biondi)	Sept. 21, 1988	Seoul

WOMEN
Freestyle

Distance	Time		Date Set	Location
50 meters:	**World** 24.13p	**Inge de Bruijn**, Netherlands	Sept. 22, 2000	Sydney
	Olympic 24.13	de Bruijn (same as world)	—	—
	American 24.63	Dara Torres	Sept. 23, 2000	Sydney
100 meters:	**World** 53.77p	**Inge de Bruijn**, Netherlands	Sept. 20, 2000	Sydney
	Olympic 53.77	de Bruijn (same as world)	—	—
	American 54.07	Jenny Thompson	Aug. 14, 2000	Indianapolis
200 meters:	**World** 1:56.78	**Franziska Van Almsick**, Ger.	Sept. 6, 1994	Rome
	Olympic . . .1:57.65	Heike Friedrich, E. Germany	Sept. 21, 1988	Seoul
	American . .1:57.90	Nicole Haislett	July 27, 1992	Barcelona
400 meters:	**World** 4:03.85	**Janet Evans**, USA	Sept. 22, 1988	Seoul
	Olympic . . .4:03.85	Evans (same as World)	—	—
	American . . .4:03.85	Evans (same as World)	—	—
800 meters:	**World** 8:16.22	**Janet Evans**, USA	Aug. 20, 1989	Tokyo
	Olympic . . .8:19.67	Brooke Bennett, USA	Sept. 22, 2000	Sydney
	American . . .8:16.22	Evans (same as World)	—	—
1500 meters:	**World** . . .15:52.10	**Janet Evans**, USA	Mar. 26, 1988	Orlando
	Olympic	Not an event	—	—
	American .15:52.10	Evans (same as World)	—	—

Backstroke

Distance		Time		Date Set	Location
50 meters:	World	......28.25	**Sandra Volker**, Germany	June 17, 2000	Berlin
	Olympic	....	Not an event	—	—
	American	....29.01	Natalie Coughlin	Aug. 6, 1998	Concord, Calif.
100 meters:	World	....1:00.16r	**He Cihong**, China	Sept. 10, 1994	Rome
	Olympic	....1:00.21	Diana Mocanu, Romania	Sept. 18, 2000	Sydney
	American	..1:00.77p	Lea Maurer	Jan. 14, 1998	Perth, AUS
200 meters:	World	....2:06.62	**Krisztina Egerszegi**, Hungary	Aug. 25, 1991	Athens
	Olympic	....2:07.06	Krisztina Egerszegi, Hungary	July 31, 1992	Barcelona
	American	..2:08.60	Betsy Mitchell	June 27, 1986	Orlando

Breaststroke

Distance		Time		Date Set	Location
50 meters:	World	......30.83	**Penny Heyns**, South Africa	Aug. 28, 1999	Sydney
	Olympic	....	Not an event	—	—
	American	....31.54p	Megan Quann	June 10, 2000	Federal Way, Wash.
100 meters:	World	....1:06.52p	**Penny Heyns**, South Africa	Aug. 23, 1999	Sydney
	Olympic	....1:07.02	Penny Heyns, South Africa	July 21, 1996	Atlanta
	American	..1:07.05	Megan Quann	Sept. 18, 2000	Sydney
200 meters:	World	....2:23.64	**Penny Heyns**, South Africa	Aug. 27, 1999	Sydney
	Olympic	....2:24.03p	Agnes Kovacs, Hungary	Sept. 20, 2000	Sydney
	American	..2:24.56	Kristy Kowal	Sept. 21, 2000	Sydney

Butterfly

Distance		Time		Date Set	Location
50 meters:	World	......25.64	**Inge de Bruijn**, Netherlands	May 26, 2000	Sheffield, GBR
	Olympic	....	Not an event	—	—
	American	....25.64p	Dara Torres	Aug. 9, 2000	Indianapolis
100 meters:	World	......56.61	**Inge de Bruijn**, Netherlands	Sept. 17, 2000	Sydney
	Olympic	......56.61	de Bruijn, NED (same as world)	—	—
	American	....57.58p	Dara Torres	Aug. 9, 2000	Indianapolis
200 meters:	World	....2:05.81	**Susan O'Neill**, Austrailia	May 17, 2000	Sydney
	Olympic	....2:05.88	Misty Hyman, USA	Sept. 20, 2000	Sydney
	American	..2:05.88	Misty Hyman	Sept. 20, 2000	Sydney

Individual Medley

Distance		Time		Date Set	Location
200 meters:	World	.....2:09.72	**Wu Yanyan**, China	Oct. 17, 1997	Shanghai
	Olympic	....2:10.68	Yana Klochkova, Ukraine	Sept. 19, 2000	Sydney
	American	..2:11.91	Summer Sanders	July 30, 1992	Barcelona
400 meters:	World	.....4:33.59	**Yana Klochkova**, Ukraine	Sept. 16, 2000	Sydney
	Olympic	....4:33.59	Klochkova, UKR (same as world)	—	—
	American	...4:37.58	Summer Sanders	July 26, 1992	Barcelona

Relays

Distance		Time		Date Set	Location
4x100m free:	World	.........3:36.61	**USA** (Van Dyken, Torres, Shealy, Thompson)	Sept. 16, 2000	Sydney
	Olympic	........3:36.61	USA (same as world)	—	—
	American	......3:36.61	USA (same as world)	—	—
4x200m free:	World	.........7:55.47	**E. Germany** (Stellmach, Strauss, Mohring, Friedrich)	Aug. 18, 1987	Strasbourg, FRA
	Olympic	.... 7:57.80	USA (Arsenault, Munz, Benko, Thompson)	Sept. 20, 2000	Sydney
	American	........7:57.61	USA (Benko, Stonebraker, Thompson, Teuscher)	Aug. 26, 1999	Sydney
4x100m medley:	World	.........3:58.30	**USA** (Bedford, Quann, Thompson, Torres)	Sept. 23, 2000	Sydney
	Olympic	........3:58.30	USA (same as world)	—	—
	American	........3:58.30	USA (same as world)	—	—

FINA Short Course World Championships

at Athens, Greece, March 16-19.

(WR) indicates world record. Note that short course world records are not included in the list on the previous pages; that list is of long course world records.

Final Medal Standings

		G	S	B	Total				G	S	B	Total
1	United States	9	7	9	25	9	Canada	0	4	1	5
2	Germany	5	6	2	13	10	Slovakia	1	2	1	4
	Great Britain	4	4	5	13		Australia	1	1	2	4
4	Sweden	7	3	1	11	12	Finland	2	1	0	3
5	Ukraine	2	2	3	7		Poland	0	2	1	3
	Russia	2	0	5	7		Italy	0	1	2	3
7	South Africa	2	4	0	6	15	Cuba	0	1	1	2
	China	2	2	2	6	16	Eight countries tied with 1 medal each.				

MEN			WOMEN		
Event		**Time**	**Event**		**Time**
50m free	Mark Foster, GBR	21.58	50m free	Therese Alshammar, SWE	23.59 WR
100m free	Lars Frolander, SWE	46.80	100m free	Therese Alshammar, SWE	52.17 WR
200m free	Bela Szabados, HUN	1:45.27	200m free	Yang Yu, CHN	1:56.06
400m free	Chad Carvin, USA	3:41.13	400m free	Lindsay Benko, USA	4:02.44
1500m free	Jorg Hoffmann, GER	14:47.57	800m free	Chen Hua, CHN	8:17.03
50m back	Neil Walker, USA	23.99* WR	50m back	Antje Buschschulte, GER	27.90
100m back	Neil Walker, USA	50.75 WR	100m back	Sandra Volker, GER	58.66
200m back	Gordan Kozulj, CRO	1:53.31	200m back	Antje Buschschulte, GER	2:07.29
50m breast	Mark Warnecke, GER	27.22	50m breast	Sarah Poewe, RSA	30.66
100m breast	Roman Sloudnov, RUS	58.57* WR	100m breast	Sarah Poewe, RSA	1:06.21
200m breast	Roman Sloudnov, RUS	2:07.59 WR	200m breast	Rebecca Brown, AUS	2:23.41
50m fly	Mark Foster, GBR	23.30* WR	50m fly	Jenny Thompson, USA	26.13
100m fly	Lars Frolander, SWE	50.44 WR	100m fly	Jenny Thompson, USA	57.67* WR
200m fly	James Hickman, GBR	1:53.57	200m fly	Mette Jacobsen, DEN	2:08.10
100m I.M.	Neil Walker, USA	52.79 WR	100m I.M.	Martina Moravcova, SVK	59.71
200m I.M.	Jani Sievinen, FIN	1:56.27	200m I.M.	Yana Klochkova, UKR	2:08.97
400m I.M.	Jani Sievinen, FIN	4:09.54	400m I.M.	Yana Klochkova, UKR	4:32.45
4x100m free	Sweden	3:09.57 WR	4x100m free	Sweden	3:35.54
4x200m free	USA	7:01.33 WR	4x200m free	Great Britain	7:49:11 WR
4x100m medley	USA	3:30.03	4x100m medley	Sweden	3:59.53

*Walker swam a 23.42 in a preliminary heat to set the world record in the 50m backstroke. Sloudnov swam a 58.51 in a preminnary heat to set the world record in the 100m breaststroke. In the 50m butterfly, Frolander set the world record in a preliminary heat with a 23.19.

*Thompson swam a 56.56 in a preliminary heat to set the world record in the 100m butterfly.

2000 FINA World Cup Diving Championships

Major individual event winners in the 12th FINA World Cup Diving Championships at the Sydney International Aquatic Centre in Australia (Jan. 25-29, 2000).

MEN			WOMEN		
Event		**Points**	**Event**		**Points**
1-meter Springboard	Tianling Wang, CHN	417.60	1-meter Springboard	Irina Lashko, RUS	287.76
3-meter Springboard	Dmitriy Sautin, RUS	708.72	3-meter Springboard	Guo Jingjing, CHN	571.68
10-meter Platform	Tian Liang, CHN	679.41	10-meter Platform	Li Na, CHN	552.72
3-meter Springboard (Synchronized)	Xiong Ni & Hailiang Xiao, CHN	353.70	3-meter Springboard (Synchronized)	Vera Ilyina & Yulia Pakhalina, RUS	320.55
10-meter Platform (Synchronized)	Tian Liang & Huang Oiang, CHN	353.34	10-meter Platform (Synchronized)	Li Na & Sang Xue, CHN	309.24

WINTER SPORTS

Alpine Skiing
2000 World Cup Champions

MEN		WOMEN	
Overall	Hermann Maier, Austria	Overall	Renate Goetschl, Austria
Downhill	Hermann Maier, Austria	Downhill	Regina Haeusl, Germany
Slalom	Kjetil Andre Aamodt, Norway	Slalom	Spela Pretnar, Slovenia
Giant Slalom	Hermann Maier, Austria	Giant Slalom	Michaela Dorfmeister, Austria
Super G	Hermann Maier, Austria	Super G	Renate Goetschl, Austria
Combined	Kjetil Andre Aamodt, Norway	Combined	Renate Goetschl, Austria

Top Five Standings

Overall 1. Hermann Maier, AUT (2000 pts); 2. Kjetil Andre Aamodt, NOR (1440); 3. Josef Strobl, AUT (994); 4. Kristian Ghedina, ITA (958); 5. Andreas Schifferer, AUT (905). *Best USA—* Daron Rahlves (20th, 462 pts).

Downhill 1. Hermann Maier, AUT (800 pts); 2. Kristian Ghedina, ITA (677); 3. Josef Strobl, AUT (533); 4. Hannes Trinkl, AUT (507); 5. Stephan Eberharter, AUT (454). *Best USA—* Daron Rahlves (10th, 273 pts).

Slalom 1. Kjetil Andre Aamodt, NOR (598 pts); 2. Ole Christian Furuseth, NOR (544); 3. Matjaz Vrhovnik, SLO (538); 4. Mario Matt, AUT (384); 5. Thomas Stangassinger, AUT (369). *Best USA—* Erik Schlopy (41st, 44 pts).

Giant Slalom 1. Hermann Maier, AUT (520 pts); 2. Christian Mayer, AUT (517); 3. Michael Von Gruenigen, SWI (466); 4. Benjamin Raich, AUT (420); 5. Joel Chenal, FRA (349). *Best USA—* Bode Miller (31st, 39 pts).

Super G 1. Hermann Maier, AUT (540 pts); 2. Werner Franz, AUT (371); 3. Fritz Strobl, AUT (354); 4. Josef Strobl, AUT (305); 5. Andreas Schifferer, AUT (294). *Best USA—* Daron Rahlves (10th, 183 pts).

Combined 1. Kjetil Andre Aamodt, NOR (200 pts); 2. Hermann Maier, AUT (140); 3. Fredrik Nyberg, SWE (102); 4. Paul Accola, SWI (100); 5. Fritz Strobl, AUT (82). *Best USA—* no US competitors.

Top Five Standings

Overall 1. Renate Goetschl, AUT (1631 pts); 2. Michaela Dorfmeister, AUT (1306); 3. Regine Cavagnoud, FRA (1036); 4. Isolde Kostner, ITA (878); 5. Brigitte Obermoser, AUT (806). *Best USA—* Kristina Koznick (19th, 503 pts).

Downhill 1. Regina Haeusl, GER (529 pts); 2. Renate Goetschl, AUT (524); 3. Isolde Kostner, ITA (484); 4. Corinne Rey Bellet, SWI (435); 5. Regine Cavagnoud, FRA (417). *Best USA—* Kirsten L. Clark (27th, 92 pts).

Slalom 1. Spela Pretnar, SLO (645 pts); 2. Christel Saioni, FRA (626); 3. Anja Paerson, SWE (499); 4. Trine Bakke, NOR (434); 5. Kristina Koznick, USA (428).

Giant Slalom 1. Michaela Dorfmeister, AUT (684 pts); 2. Sonja Nef, SWI (602); 3. Anita Wachter, AUT (470); 4. Anna Ottosson, SWE (402); 5. Allison Forsyth, CAN (373). *Best USA—* Sarah Schleper (t-25th, 83 pts).

Super G 1. Renate Goetschl, AUT (554 pts); 2. Melanie Turgeon, CAN (343); 3. Mojca Suhadolc, SLO (341); 4. Regine Cavagnoud, FRA (330); 5. Isolde Kostner, ITA (300). *Best USA—* Kirsten L. Clark (32nd, 41 pts).

Combined 1. Renate Goetschl, AUT (100 pts); 2. Caroline Lalive, USA (80); 3. Andrine Flemmen, NOR (60); 4. Stefanie Schuster, AUT (50); 5. Michaela Dorfmeister, AUT (45). *Best USA—* Jonna Mendes (13th, 20 pts).

2000 U.S. Championships
at Jackson Hole, Wyoming (March 21-29)

MEN

Downhill
1	Chris Puckett	1:07.80
2	Darin McBeath	1:08.12
3	Kevin Wert	1:08.45

Slalom
1	Erik Schlopy	1:30.76
2	Bode Miller	1:31.11
3	Sacha Gros	1:32.41

Giant Slalom
1	Casey Puckett	2:07.40
2	Erik Schlopy	2:07.47
3	Daron Rahlves	2:07.74

Super G
1	Daron Rahlves	1:23.93
2	Casey Puckett	1:24.58
3	Bode Miller	1:24.63

Combined (4 events)
1	Casey Puckett	49.01 pts
2	Bode Miller	57.02 pts
3	Josh Transue	108.51 pts

WOMEN

Downhill
1	Kirsten L. Clark	1:11.25
2	Lindsey Kildow	1:11.93
3	Caroline Lalive	1:12.08

Slalom
1	Caroline Lalive	1:31.86
2	Kristina Koznick	1:32.28
3	Sarah Schleper	1:34.86

Super G
1	Kirsten L. Clark	1:23.50
2	Julia Mancuso	1:24.66
3	Caroline Lalive	1:24.87

Combined (3 events)
1	Caroline Lalive	30.29 pts
2	Julia Mancuso	69.11 pts
3	Mia Cullman	142.73 pts

Note: The Women's Giant Slalom competition was cancelled due to adverse weather conditions.

Freestyle Skiing
World Cup Champions

MEN	**WOMEN**
Aerials......................Nicolas Fontaine, Canada	Aerials......................Jacqui Cooper, Australia
Moguls..........................Janne Lahtela, Finland	Moguls..................Ann Battelle, United States
Dual Moguls...................Janne Lahtela, Finland	Dual Moguls..........................Kari Traa, Norway

2000 U.S. Championships
at Sunday River, Newry, Maine (March 19-26)

MEN

WOMEN

	Acro	Pts		Acro	Pts
1	Ian Edmondson..........................26.50		1	Lara Rosenbaum..........................24.65	
2	Ryan St. Onge..........................24.80		2	Erin Reinhardt..........................24.40	
3	Jeremy April..........................21.75		3	Nori Lupfer..........................20.75	

	Moguls	Pts		Moguls	Pts
1	Evan Dybvig..........................27.40		1	Hannah Hardaway..........................25.96	
2	Garth Hager..........................27.25		2	Justine Van Houte..........................25.32	
3	Ryan Riley..........................26.93		3	Shannon Bahrke..........................25.24	

	Aerials	Pts		Aerials	Pts
1	Eric Bergoust..........................230.01		1	Kelly Hilliman..........................155.44	
2	Joe Pack..........................228.45		2	Brenda Petzold..........................149.80	
3	Britt Swartley..........................200.60		3	Kate Reed..........................142.23	

	Dual Moguls		Dual Moguls
1	Garth Hager	1	Hannah Hardaway
2	William Boyle	2	Erin Resko
3	Donavan Power	3	Ann Battelle

Cross Country Skiing
World Cup Champions

MEN

WOMEN

	Overall	Pts		Overall	Pts
1	Johann Muehlegg, Spain..........................948		1	Bente Martinsen, Norway..........................1176	
2	Jari Isometsa, Finland..........................708		2	Kristina Smigun, Estonia..........................1165	
3	Odd-Bjorn Hjelmeset, Norway..........................586		3	Larissa Lazutina, Russia..........................1008	
4	Per Elofsson, Sweden..........................536		4	Olga Danilova, Russia..........................880	
5	Thomas Alsgaard, Norway..........................461		5	Nina Gavriljuk, Russia..........................857	

2000 U.S. Championships
at Soldier Hollow, Midway, Utah (Jan. 8-15)

MEN

WOMEN

	Sprints		Sprints
1	Marcus Nash	1	Beckie Scott
2	Phil Villeneuve	2	Sarah Renner
3	Justin Wadsworth	3	Jamie Fortier

	10-k Classic			10-k Classic	
1	Marcus Nash..........................22:28.0		1	Beckie Scott..........................41:00.4	
2	Justin Wadsworth..........................22:42.0		2	Nina Kemppel..........................43:00.6	
3	Rob Whitney..........................22:44.0		3	Jaime Fortier..........................43:20.0	

	15-k Classic			15-k Classic	
1	Marcus Nash..........................1:00:03.7		1	Beckie Scott..........................52:21.3	
2	Justin Wadsworth..........................1:00:38.8		2	Nina Kemppel..........................53:53.5	
3	Rob Whitney..........................1:00:40.8		3	Rebecca Dussault..........................54:22.7	

	30-k Classic			5-k Freestyle	
1	Donald Farley..........................1:34:49.1		1	Beckie Scott..........................12:54.0	
2	Joern Frohs..........................1:34:56.5		2	Katerina Hanusova..........................13:31.0	
3	Kris Freeman..........................1:35:29.6		3	Sara Renner..........................13:32.3	

	50-k Freestyle			30-k Freestyle	
1	Carl Swenson..........................1:59:55.0		1	Nina Kemppel..........................1:25:03.3	
2	Marcus Nash..........................1:59:55.2		2	Katerina Hanusova..........................1:27:39.0	
3	Justin Wadsworth..........................1:59:55.5		3	Sarah Konrad..........................1:29:30.8	

Nordic Combined/Ski Jumping

Nordic Combined
World Cup Champions
MEN

	Overall	Pts
1	Samppa Lajunen, Finland	2175
2	Bjarte Engen Vik, Norway	1990
3	Ladislav Rygl, Czech Republic	1274
4	Todd Lodwick, United States	1138
5	Ronny Ackermann, Germany	1100

Ski Jumping
World Cup Champions
MEN

	Overall	Pts
1	Martin Schmitt, Germany	1833
2	Andreas Widholzl, Austria	1452
3	Janne Ahonen, Finland	1437
4	Sven Hannawald, Germany	1065
5	Andreas Goldberger, Austria	1034

2000 U.S. Nordic Combined/Jumping Championships
at Steamboat Springs, Colorado (March 24-26)
Nordic Combined
Men's 90-meter jump/10-k cross country ski

1 Todd Lodwick
2 Bill Demong
3 Carl Van Loan

MEN
Ski Jumping

Normal Hill (88 meters)		Pts
1	Brendan Doran	240.0
2	Vladimir Glyvka	233.5
3	Todd Lodwick	229.0

Large Hill (112 meters)		Pts
1	Clint Jones	243.9
2	Todd Lodwick	243.2
3	Brendan Doran	239.6

WOMEN
Ski Jumping

Normal Hill (88 meters)		Pts
1	Lindsey Van	179.0
2	Karla Keck	176.5
3	Liz Szotyori	125.5

Large Hill (112 meters)		Pts
1	Lindsey Van	138.4
2	Karla Keck	116.8
3	Liz Szotyori	73.2

Snowboarding
World Cup Champions

MEN

Overall	Mathieu Bozzetto, France
Halfpipe	Thomas Johansson, Sweden
Parallel Slalom	Mathieu Bozzetto, France
Giant Slalom	Stefan Kaltschuetz, Austria
Cross	Pontus Stahlkloo, Sweden

WOMEN

Overall	Manuela Riegler, Austria
Halfpipe	Sabine Wehr-Hasler, Germany
Parallel Slalom	Isabelle Blanc, France
Giant Slalom	Margherita Parini, Italy
Cross	Sandra Farmand, Germany

2000 U.S. Championships
at Okemo Mountain, Ludlow, Vermont (March 23-26)

MEN

Halfpipe		Pts
1	Adam Petraska	37.20
2	Elijah Teter	34.40
3	Mark Reilly	34.20

Slalom		Time
1	Anton Pogue	56.09
2	Jasey Jay Anderson	56.75
3	Charles Boivin	57.36

Giant Slalom		Time
1	Jasey Jay Anderson	2:41.77
2	Chris Klug	2:45.97
3	David Vaughan	2:47.17

Snowboard Cross	
1	Seth Wescott
2	Jasey Jay Anderson
3	Brandon Steig

WOMEN

Halfpipe		Pts
1	Kim Stacey	35.80
2	Tricia Byrnes	33.10
3	Gretchen Bleiler	32.80

Slalom		Time
1	Rosey Fletcher	1:00.83
2	Stacia Hookom	1:03.45
3	Paule Bertrand	1:03.81

Giant Slalom		Time
1	Sondra Van Ert	2:58.71
2	Lynn Ott	3:01.37
3	Paule Bertrand	3:04.66

Snowboard Cross	
1	Kelly Clark
2	Candice Drouin
3	Dominique Vallee

Figure Skating

World Championships
at Nice, France (March 26-April 2)

Men's —1. Alexei Yagudin, Russia; 2. Elvis Stojko, Canada; 3. Michael Weiss, USA; 4. Evgeni Plushenko, Russia; 5. Chengjiang Li, China

Women's — 1. Michelle Kwan, USA; 2. Irina Slutskaya, Russia; 3. Maria Butyrskaya, Russia; 4. Vanessa Gusmeroli, France; 5. Sarah Hughes, USA

Pairs — 1. Maria Petrova & Alexei Tikhonov, Russia; 2. Xue Shen & Hongbo Zhao, China; 3. Sarah Abitbol & Stephane Bernadis, France; 4. Jamie Sale & David Pelletier, Canada; 5. Dorota Zagorska & Mariusz Siudek, Poland

Ice Dance — 1. Marina Anissina & Gwendal Peizerat, France; 2. Barbara Fusar-Poli & Maurizio Margaglio, Italy; 3. Margarita Drobiazko & Povilas Vanagas, Lithuania; 4. Irina Lobacheva & Ilia Averbukh, Russia; 5. Galit Chait & Sergei Sakhnovski, Israel

U.S. Championships
at Cleveland, Ohio (Feb. 6-13)

Men's	...........................Michael Weiss
Women's	...........................Michelle Kwan
Pairs	...........................Kyoko Ina
	& John Zimmerman
Ice Dance	...........................Naomi Lang
	& Peter Tchernyshev

European Championships
at Vienna, Austria (Feb. 6-13)

Men's	...........................Evgeni Plushenko, Russia
Women's	...........................Irina Slutskaya, Russia
Pairs	...........................Elena Berezhnaya
	& Anton Sikharulidze, Russia
Ice Dance	...........................Marina Anissina
	& Gwendal Peizerat, France

Speed Skating
World Cup Champions

MEN		WOMEN	
500 meters	Jeremy Wotherspoon, Canada	500 meters	Monique Garbrecht, Germany
1000 meters	Jeremy Wotherspoon, Canada	1000 meters	Monique Garbrecht, Germany
1500 meters	Adne Sondral, Norway	1500 meters	Gunda Niemann-Stirnemann, Germany
5000/10,000 meters	Gianni Romme, Netherlands	3000/5000 meters	Gunda Niemann-Stirnemann, Germany

2000 World Championships
at Milwaukee, Wisconsin (Feb. 4-6)

MEN		WOMEN	
500 meters	Jae-Bong Choi, Korea	500 meters	Edel Therese Hoiseth, Norway
1500 meters	Adne Sondral, Norway	1500 meters	Maki Tabata, Japan
5000 meters	Gianni Romme, Netherlands	3000 meters	Claudia Pechstein, Germany
10,000 meters	Gianni Romme, Netherlands	5000 meters	Gunda Niemann-Stirnemann, Germany
All-Around	Gianni Romme, Netherlands	All-Around	Claudia Pechstein, Germany

2000 World Short Track Championships
at Sheffield, Great Britain (March 10-12)

MEN		WOMEN	
500 meters	Eric Bedard, Canada	500 meters	Evgenia Radanova, Bulgaria
1000 meters	Li Jiajun, China	1500 meters	Yang Yang (A), China
1500 meters	Ryoung Min, Korea	3000 meters	Sang-Mi An, Korea
3000 meters	Ryoung Min, Korea	All-Around	Yang Yang (A), China
All-Around	Ryoung Min, Korea		

Note: There were two Chinese skaters with the name Yang Yang. To differentiate, one goes by Yang Yang (A) and one by Yang Yang (S).

SUMMER SPORTS

Cross Country
IAAF World Championships

The 28th IAAF World Cross Country Championships held at Vilamoura, Portugal (March 18-19).

MEN		WOMEN	
12 km	1. Mohammed Mourhit, Belgium 35:00	8 km	1. Derartu Tulu, Ethiopia 25:42
(7.46 mi)	2. Assefa Mezgebu , Ethiopia 35:01	(4.97 mi)	2. Gete Wami, Ethiopia 25:48
	3. Paul Tergat, Kenya 35:02		3. Susan Chepkemei, Kenya 25:50
	Best USA— Mebrahtom Keflezighi, 26th, 36:45		*Best USA*— Deena Drossin, 12th, 26:59

Cycling
Tour de France

The 87th Tour de France (July 1-23, 2000) ran 20 stages plus a prologue, covering 2,276 miles starting in Futuroscope, France passing through the Alps and Pyrenncs in France and small bits of Switzerland and Germany and finishing on the Avenue des Champs-Elysees in Paris.

American Lance Armstrong, 28, once again impressed the world, with his second straight Tour de France victory in a time of 92 hours, 33 minutes and 8 seconds. His time was six minutes, two seconds ahead of runner-up Jan Ullrich of Germany. Spain's Joseba Beloki took third, completing the course 10 minutes, four seconds behind Armstrong.

Armstrong took home $315,000 for the victory plus more in bonus money. In many ways this victory was even sweeter for Armstrong than last year's when several top riders including Ullrich were absent.

Less than three years before Armstrong rode down the Champs-Elysees for his first Tour de France victory in 1999, he was diagnosed with testicular cancer. The cancer then spread to his lungs and his brain and doctors gave him less than a 40 percent chance of survival. He underwent two operations and extensive chemotherapy and began his comeback in early 1998. He is only the second American to win cycling's premier event.

		Team	Behind			Team	Behind
1	Lance Armstrong, USA	U.S. Postal	—	6	Richard Virenque, FRA	Polti	13:26
2	Jan Ullrich, GER	Deutsche Telekom	6:02	7	Santiago Botero, COL	Kelme	14:18
3	Joseba Beloki, SPA	Festina	10:04	8	Fernando Escartin, SPA	Kelme	17:21
4	Christophe Moreau, FRA	Festina	10:34	9	Francis Mancebo, SPA	Banesto	18:09
5	Roberto Heras, SPA	Kelme	11:50	10	Daniele Nardello, ITA	Mapei	18:25

Other Worldwide Champions

2000 Major UCI (Union Cycliste Internationale) Road Results. Note that in some instances, the date shown below is the final day of that particular race.

MEN

Race	Winner	Race	Winner
Jan. 23: Tour Down Under (AUS)	Gilles Maignan, FRA	Apr. 2: Tour de Flanders (BEL)	Andrei Tschmil, BEL
Feb. 6: Tour de Langwaki (MAS)	Chris Horner, USA	Apr. 5: Ghent-Wevelgem (BEL)	Geert Van Bondt, BEL
Feb. 10: Majorca Challenge (SPA)	Francesca Cabello, SPA	Apr. 7: Tour of the Basque Country (SPA)	Andreas Kloden, GER
Feb. 13: Mediterranean Tour (FRA)	Laurent Jalabert, FRA		
Feb. 17: Ruta del Sol (SPA)	Miguel Angel Pena, SPA	Apr. 9: Paris-Roubaix (FRA)	Johan Museeuw, BEL
Feb. 26: Tour de Valencia (SPA)	Abraham Olano, SPA	Apr. 12: Fleche Wallonne (BEL)	Francesco Casagrande, ITA
Feb. 26: Omloop Het Volk (BEL)	Johan Museeuw, BEL	May 7: Tour de Romandie (SWI)	Paolo Savoldelli, ITA
Mar. 12: Paris-Nice (FRA)	Andreas Kloden, GER	May 7: Four Days of Dunkirk (FRA)	Martin Rittsel, SPA
Mar. 15: Tirreno-Adriatico (ITA)	Abraham Olano, SPA	June 4: Giro d'Italia (ITA)	Stefano Garzelli, ITA
Mar. 18: Milan-San Remo (ITA)	Erik Zabel, GER	June 11: Dauphine Libere (FRA)	Tyler Hamilton, USA
Mar. 24: Setmana Catalana (SPA)	Laurent Jalabert, SPA	June 22: Tour of Switzerland (SWI)	Oscar Camenzind, SWI
Mar. 26: Criterium Int'l (FRA)	Abraham Olano, SPA	Aug. 26: Tour of the Netherlands (NED)	Erik Dekker, NED
Mar. 30: Three Days of de Panne (BEL)	Viatcheslav Ekimov, RUS	Sept. 17: Vuelta a Espana (SPA)	Roberto Heras, SPA

WOMEN

Race	Winner	Race	Winner
Mar. 12: Canberra World Cup (AUS)	Anna Wilson, AUS	June 19: HP Women's Classic (USA)	Anna Wilson, AUS
Mar. 18: Primavera Rosa (ITA)	Diana Ziliute, LIT	July 9: Giro d'Italia Femminile (ITA)	Joane Somarriba, SPA
Apr. 12: Fleche Wallonne (BEL)	Genevieve Jeanson, CAN	Aug. 20: Grande Boucle Feminine (FRA)	Joane Somarriba, SPA
May 14: Tour de L'Aude (FRA)	Hanka Kupfernagel, GER		
May 29: Montreal World Cup (CAN)	Pia Sundstedt, FIN	Aug. 27: Rotterdam Tour (NED)	Chantal Beltman, NED
June 4: Liberty Classic (USA)	Petra Rossner, GER	Sept. 6: Embrach World Cup (SWI)	Pia Sundstedt, FIN

2000 World Road Championships
at Plouay, France (Oct. 10-15)

MEN

Elite Road Race (268.9 km)
Romans Vainsteins, LAT 6:19:29
Under-23 Road Race (169.8 km)
Evgeni Petrov, RUS 3:56:51
Junior Road Race (127.4 km)
Jeremy Yates, NZE 2:59:26

Elite Time Trial (40.4 km)
Sergei Gontchar, UKR 56:21.75
Under-23 Time Trial (35.2 km)
Evgeni Petrov, RUS 43:54.14
Junior Time Trial (24.5 km)
Peter Mazur, POL 30:58.23

WOMEN

Elite Road Race (127.4 km)
Zinaida Stahurskaia, BLR 3:17:39
Junior Road Race (70.8 km)
Nicole Cooke, GBR 1:49:02

Elite Time Trial (24.5 km)
Mari Holden, USA 33:14.62
Junior Time Trial (16.1 km)
Juliette Vandekerckhove, FRA 22:16.03

Mountain Biking
2000 World Championships
at Sierra Nevada, Spain (June 7-11)

MEN			WOMEN		
Cross Country (Elite)		**Time**	**Cross Country (Elite)**		**Time**
1	Miguel Martinez, FRA	2:17.38	1	Marga Fullana, SPA	2:07.42
2	Roland Green, CAN	2:19.90	2	Alison Sydor, CAN	2:10.69
3	Brent Brentjens, NED	2:21.89	3	Paola Pezzo, ITA	2:11.56
Downhill (Elite)		**Time**	**Downhill (Elite)**		**Time**
1	Myles Rockwell, USA	3:55.01	1	Anne-Caroline Chausson, FRA	4:18.13
2	Steve Peat, GBR	3:55.59	2	Katja Repo, FIN	4:19.26
3	Mickael Pascal, FRA	3:55.69	3	Marla Streb, USA	4:20.03
Dual (Elite)			**Dual (Elite)**		
1	Wade Bootes, AUS		1	Anne-Caroline Chausson, FRA	
2	Brian Lopes, USA		2	Tara Llanes, USA	
3	Mickael Deldycke, FRA		3	Sabrina Jonnier, FRA	

2000 UCI World Cup Champions

MEN			WOMEN		
Cross Country		**Pts**	**Cross Country**		**Pts**
1	Miguel Martinez, FRA	1103	1	Barbara Blatter, SWI	1265
2	Bas Van Dooren, NED	993	2	Alison Dunlap, USA	1180
3	Christophe Dupouey, FRA	970	3	Alison Sydor, CAN	1012
Downhill		**Pts**	**Downhill**		**Pts**
1	Nicolas Vouilloz, FRA	1800	1	Anne-Caroline Chausson, FRA	1900
2	Steve Peat, GBR	1330	2	Missy Giove, USA	1540
3	David Vazquez Lopez, SPA	1139	3	Leigh Donovan, USA	1020

Marathons
2000 Boston Marathon

The 104th edition of the Boston Marathon was held Monday, April 17, 2000 and run, as always, from Hopkinton through Ashland, Framingham, Natick, Wellesley, Newton and Brookline to Boston, Mass. Kenya's Elijah Lagat held on to win the closest Boston Marathon in history by outdueling countryman Moses Tanui and Ethiopian Gezahenge Abera with a time of two hours, nine minutes and 47 seconds. Only three seconds separated the top three finishers.

Kenya's Catherine Ndereba ended Ethiopian Fatuma Roba's three year run as the Boston Marathon's women's champion. Ndereba finished the race in two hours, 26 minutes, and 11 seconds to become the first Kenyan woman to win in Boston.

American Jean Driscoll (2:00:52) took home her eighth women's wheelchair race breaking her tie with Clarence DeMar for most wins in one Boston division. Switzerland's Franz Nietlispach (1:33:32) continued his dominance in the men's wheelchair division by winning his fifth race and fourth in a row. Winners in the men's and women's divisions earned $80,000.

Distance: 26.2 miles.

MEN			WOMEN		
		Time			**Time**
1	Elijah Lagat, KEN	2:09:47	1	Catherine Ndereba, KEN	2:26:11
2	Gezahenge Abera, ETH	2:09:47	2	Irina Bogacheva, KYR	2:26:27
3	Moses Tanui, KEN	2:09:50	3	Fatuma Roba, ETH	2:26:27
4	Ondoro Osoro, KEN	2:10:29	4	Anuta Catuna, ROM	2:29:46
5	David Busienei, KEN	2:11:26	5	Lornah Kiplagat, KEN	2:30:12

Best USA: 19th— Fedor Ryjov, Boston, Mass., 2:17:38

Best USA: 18th— Maria Trujillo de Rios, Los Gatos, Calif., 2:42:24

WHEELCHAIR			WHEELCHAIR		
		Time			**Time**
1	Franz Nietlispach, SWI	1:33:32	1	Jean L. Driscoll, USA	2:00:52
2	Heinz Frei, SWI	1:38:43	2	Louise Sauvage, AUS	2:01:16
3	Saul Mendoza, MEX	1:39:37	3	Miriam Nibley, USA	2:14:47

Other 2000 Winners

Tokyo

Feb. 13	Men	Japhet Kosgei, KEN	2:07:15
	(No women's division)		

Los Angeles

Mar. 5	Men	Benson Mbithi, KEN	2:11:55
	Women	Jane Salumae, EST	2:23:33

New York City

Nov. 7	Men	Joseph Chebet, KEN	2:09:14
	Women	Adriana Fernandez, MEX	2:25:06

London

Apr. 16	Men	Antonio Pinto, POR	2:06:36
	Women	Tegla Loroupe, KEN	2:24:33

Rotterdam

Apr. 16	Men	Kenneth Cheruiyot, KEN	2:08:22
	Women	Ana Isabel Alonso, SPA	2:30:12

Late 1999

Tokyo Women's

Nov. 21	Women	Eri Yamaguchi, JPN	2:25:24

Fukuoka

Dec. 5	Men	Gezahenge Abera, ETH	2:07:54
	(No women's division)		

TRACK & FIELD

IAAF World Championships

While the Summer Olympics have served as the unofficial world outdoor championships for track and field throughout the century, a separate World Championship meet was started in 1983 by the International Amateur Athletic Federation (IAAF). The meet was held every four years from 1983-91, but began an every-other-year cycle in 1993. World Championship sites include Helsinki (1983), Rome (1987), Tokyo (1991), Stuttgart (1993), Göteborg, Sweden (1995), Athens (1997) and Seville, Spain (1999). Looking forward, the Championships will be held in Edmonton (2001), Paris (2003) and London (2005). Note that (WR) indicates world record and (CR) indicates championship meet record.

MEN

Multiple gold medals (including relays): Michael Johnson (9); Carl Lewis (8); Sergey Bubka (6); Haile Gebrselassie, Maurice Greene, Lars Riedel and Calvin Smith (4); Donovan Bailey, Greg Foster, Werner Gunthor, Wilson Kipketer, Moses Kiptanui, Noureddine Morceli, Dan O'Brien, Ivan Pedroso, Antonio Pettigrew and Butch Reynolds (3); Andrey Abduvaliyev, Abel Anton, Leroy Burrell, Andre Cason, Maurizio Damilano, Jon Drummond, Tomas Dvorak, Hicham El Guerrouj, John Godina, Colin Jackson, Allen Johnson, Ismael Kirui, Billy Konchellah, Sergey Litvinov, Dennis Mitchell, Edwin Moses, Mike Powell, Javier Sotmayor and Jan Zelezny (2).

100 Meters

Year		Time	
1983	Carl Lewis, USA	10.07	
1987	Carl Lewis, USA	9.93	
1991	Carl Lewis, USA	9.86	**WR**
1993	Linford Christie, GBR	9.87	
1995	Donovan Bailey, CAN	9.97	
1997	Maurice Greene, USA	9.86	
1999	Maurice Greene, USA	9.80	**CR**

Note: Ben Johnson was the original winner in 1987, but was stripped of his title and world record time (9.83) following his 1989 admission of drug taking.

200 Meters

Year		Time	
1983	Calvin Smith, USA	20.14	
1987	Calvin Smith, USA	20.16	
1991	Michael Johnson, USA	20.01	
1993	Frank Fredericks, NAM	19.85	
1995	Michael Johnson, USA	19.79	**CR**
1997	Ato Boldon, USA	20.04	
1999	Maurice Greene, USA	19.90	

400 Meters

Year		Time	
1983	Bert Cameron, JAM	45.05	
1987	Thomas Schonlebe, E. Ger	44.33	
1991	Antonio Pettigrew, USA	44.57	
1993	Michael Johnson, USA	43.65	
1995	Michael Johnson, USA	43.39	
1997	Michael Johnson, USA	44.12	
1999	Michael Johnson, USA	43.18	**WR**

800 Meters

Year		Time	
1983	Willi Wülbeck, W. Ger	1:43.65	
1987	Billy Konchellah, KEN	1:43.06	**CR**
1991	Billy Konchellah, KEN	1:43.99	
1993	Paul Ruto, KEN	1:44.71	
1995	Wilson Kipketer, DEN	1:45.08	
1997	Wilson Kipketer, DEN	1:43.38	
1999	Wilson Kipketer, DEN	1:43.30	

1500 Meters

Year		Time	
1983	Steve Cram, GBR	3:41.59	
1987	Abdi Bile, SOM	3:36.80	
1991	Noureddine Morceli, ALG	3:32.84	
1993	Noureddine Morceli, ALG	3:34.24	
1995	Noureddine Morceli, ALG	3:33.73	
1997	Hicham El Guerrouj, MOR	3:35.83	
1999	Hicham El Guerrouj, MOR	3:27.65	**CR**

5000 Meters

Year		Time	
1983	Eammon Coghlan, IRL	13:28.53	
1987	Said Aouita, MOR	13:26.44	
1991	Yobes Ondieki, KEN	13:14.45	
1993	Ismael Kirui, KEN	13:02.75	
1995	Ismael Kirui, KEN	13:16.77	
1997	Daniel Komen, KEN	13:07.38	
1999	Salah Hissou, MOR	12:58.13	**CR**

10,000 Meters

Year		Time	
1983	Alberto Cova, ITA	28:01.04	
1987	Paul Kipkoech, KEN	27:38.63	
1991	Moses Tanui, KEN	27:38.74	
1993	Haile Gebrselassie, ETH	27:46.02	
1995	Haile Gebrselassie, ETH	27:12.95	**CR**
1997	Haile Gebrselassie, ETH	27:24.58	
1999	Haile Gebrselassie, ETH	27:57.27	

Marathon

Year		Time	
1983	Rob de Castella, AUS	2:10:03	**CR**
1987	Douglas Wakiihuri, KEN	2:11:48	
1991	Hiromi Taniguchi, JPN	2:14:57	
1993	Mark Plaatjes, USA	2:13:57	
1995	Martin Fiz, SPA	2:11:41	
1997	Abel Anton, SPA	2:13:16	
1999	Abel Anton, SPA	2:13:36	

Track & Field (Cont.)

110-Meter Hurdles

Year		Time	
1983	Greg Foster, USA	13.42	
1987	Greg Foster, USA	13.21	
1991	Greg Foster, USA	13.06	
1993	Colin Jackson, GBR	12.91	WR
1995	Allen Johnson, USA	13.00	
1997	Allen Johnson, USA	12.93	
1999	Colin Jackson, GBR	13.04	

400-Meter Hurdles

Year		Time	
1983	Edwin Moses, USA	47.50	
1987	Edwin Moses, USA	47.46	
1991	Samuel Matete, ZAM	47.64	
1993	Kevin Young, USA	47.18	CR
1995	Derrick Adkins, USA	47.98	
1997	Stephane Diagana, FRA	47.70	
1999	Fabrizio Mori, ITA	47.72	

3000-Meter Steeplechase

Year		Time	
1983	Patriz Ilg, W. Ger	8:15.06	
1987	Francesco Panetta, ITA	8:08.57	
1991	Moses Kiptanui, KEN	8:12.59	
1993	Moses Kiptanui, KEN	8:06.36	
1995	Moses Kiptanui, KEN	8:04.16	CR
1997	Wilson B. Kipketer, KEN	8:05.84	
1999	Christopher Koskei, KEN	8:11.76	

4 x 100-Meter Relay

Year		Time	
1983	United States	37.86	WR
1987	United States	37.90	
1991	United States	37.50	WR
1993	United States	37.48	CR
1995	Canada	38.31	
1997	Canada	37.86	
1999	United States	37.59	

4 x 400-Meter Relay

Year		Time	
1983	Soviet Union	3:00.79	
1987	United States	2:57.29	
1991	Great Britain	2:57.53	
1993	United States	2:54.29	WR
1995	United States	2:57.32	
1997	United States	2:56.47	
1999	United States	2:56.45	

20-Kilometer Walk

Year		Time	
1983	Ernesto Canto, MEX	1:20.49	
1987	Maurizio Damilano, ITA	1:20.45	
1991	Maurizio Damilano, ITA	1:19.37	CR
1993	Valentin Massana, SPA	1:22.31	
1995	Michele Didoni, ITA	1:19.59	
1997	Daniel Garcia, MEX	1:21:43	
1999	Ilya Markov, RUS	1:23:34	

50-Kilometer Walk

Year		Time	
1983	Ronald Weigel, E. Ger	3:43:08	
1987	Hartwig Gauder, E. Ger	3:40:53	CR
1991	Aleksandr Potashov, USSR	3:53:09	
1993	Jesus Angel Garcia, SPA	3:41:41	
1995	Valentin Kononen, FIN	3:43:42	
1997	Robert Korzeniowski, POL	3:44:46	
1999	German Skurygin, RUS	3:44:23	

High Jump

Year		Height	
1983	Gennedy Avdeyenko, USSR	7- 7¼	
1987	Patrik Sjoberg, SWE	7- 9¾	
1991	Charles Austin, USA	7- 9¾	
1993	Javier Sotomayor, CUB	7-10½	CR
1995	Troy Kemp, BAH	7- 9¼	
1997	Javier Sotomayor, CUB	7- 9¼	
1999	Vyacheslav Voronin, RUS	7- 9¼	

Pole Vault

Year		Height	
1983	Sergey Bubka, USSR	18- 8¼	
1987	Sergey Bubka, USSR	19- 2¼	
1991	Sergey Bubka, USSR	19- 6¼	CR
1993	Sergey Bubka, UKR	19- 8¼	
1995	Sergey Bubka, UKR	19- 5	
1997	Sergey Bubka, UKR	19- 8½	CR
1999	Maksim Tarasov, RUS	19- 9	CR

Long Jump

Year		Distance	
1983	Carl Lewis, USA	28- 0¾	
1987	Carl Lewis, USA	28- 0¼	
1991	Mike Powell, USA	29- 4½	WR
1993	Mike Powell, USA	28- 2¼	
1995	Ivan Pedroso, CUB	28- 6½	
1997	Ivan Pedroso, CUB	27- 7½	
1999	Ivan Pedroso, CUB	28- 1	

Triple Jump

Year		Distance	
1983	Zdzislaw Hoffmann, POL	57- 2	
1987	Khristo Markov, BUL	58- 9	
1991	Kenny Harrison, USA	58- 4	
1993	Mike Conley, USA	58- 7¼	
1995	Jonathan Edwards, GBR	60- 0¼	WR
1997	Yoelvis Quesada, CUB	58- 6¾	
1999	Charles Michael Friedek, GER	57- 8½	

Shot Put

Year		Distance	
1983	Edward Sarul, POL	70- 2¼	
1987	Werner Günthör, SWI	72-11¼	CR
1991	Werner Günthör, SWI	71- 1¼	
1993	Werner Günthör, SWI	72- 1	
1995	John Godina, USA	70- 5¼	
1997	John Godina, USA	70- 4¼	
1999	C.J. Hunter, USA	71- 6	

Discus

Year		Distance	
1983	Imrich Bugar, CZE	222- 2	
1987	Jurgen Schult, E. Ger	225- 6	
1991	Lars Riedel, GER	217- 2	
1993	Lars Riedel, GER	222- 2	
1995	Lars Riedel, GER	225- 7	CR
1997	Lars Riedel, GER	224- 10	
1999	Anthony Washington, USA	226- 7	CR

Hammer Throw

Year		Distance	
1983	Sergey Litvinov, USSR	271- 3	
1987	Sergey Litvinov, USSR	272- 6	CR
1991	Yuri Sedykh, USSR	268- 0	
1993	Andrey Abduvaliyev, TAJ	267-10	
1995	Andrey Abduvaliyev, TAJ	267- 7	
1997	Heinz Weis, GER	268- 4	
1999	Karsten Kobs, GER	263- 3	

Javelin

Year		Distance	
1983	Detlef Michel, E. Ger	293-7	
1987	Seppo Raty, FIN	274-1	
1991	Kimmo Kinnunen, FIN	297-11	CR
1993	Jan Zelezny, CZE	282-1	
1995	Jan Zelezny, CZE	293-11	
1997	Marius Corbett, S. Afr.	290-0	
1999	Aki Parviainen, FIN	293-8	

Decathlon

Year		Points	
1983	Daley Thompson, GBR	8714	
1987	Torsten Voss, E. Ger	8680	
1991	Dan O'Brien, USA	8812	CR
1993	Dan O'Brien, USA	8817	CR
1995	Dan O'Brien, USA	8695	
1997	Tomas Dvorak, CZE	8837	CR
1999	Tomas Dvorak, CZE	8744	

WOMEN

Multiple gold medals (including relays): Gail Devers (5); Jackie Joyner-Kersee (4); Tatyana Samolenko Dorovskikh, Silke Gladisch, Marion Jones, Marita Koch, Astrid Kumbernuss, Jearl Miles, Merlene Ottey and Gwen Torrence (3); Hassiba Boulmerka, Sabine Braun, Olga Bryzgina, Mary Decker, Heike Daute Drechsler, Cathy Freeman, Chryste Gaines, Trine Hattestad, Martina Optiz Hellmann, Stefka Kostadinova, Katrin Krabbe, Jarmila Kratochvilova, Inger Miller, Marie-José Pérec, Ana Quirot, Gabriela Szabo and Huang Zhihong (2).

100 Meters

Year		Time	
1983	Marlies Gohr, E. Ger	10.97	
1987	Silke Gladisch, E. Ger	10.90	
1991	Katrin Krabbe, GER	10.99	
1993	Gail Devers, USA	10.81	CR
1995	Gwen Torrence, USA	10.85	
1997	Marion Jones, USA	10.83	
1999	Marion Jones, USA	10.70	CR

10,000 Meters

Year		Time	
1983	Not held		
1987	Ingrid Kristiansen, NOR	31:05.85	
1991	Liz McColgan, GBR	31:14.31	
1993	Wang Junxia, CHN	30:49.30	CR
1995	Fernanda Ribeiro, POR	31:04.99	
1997	Sally Barsosio, KEN	31:32.92	
1999	Gete Wami, ETH	30:24.56	CR

200 Meters

Year		Time	
1983	Marita Koch, E. Ger	22.13	
1987	Silke Gladisch, E. Ger	21.74	CR
1991	Katrin Krabbe, GER	22.09	
1993	Merlene Ottey, JAM	21.98	
1995	Merlene Ottey, JAM	22.12	
1997	Zhanna Pintusevich, UKR	22.32	
1999	Inger Miller, USA	21.77	

Marathon

Year		Time	
1983	Grete Waitz, NOR	2:28:09	
1987	Rose Mota, POR	2:25:17	CR
1991	Wanda Panfil, POL	2:29:53	
1993	Junko Asari, JPN	2:30:03	
1995	Manuela Machado, POR	2:25:39	
1997	Hiromi Suzuki, JPN	2:29:48	
1999	Jong Song-Ok, N. Kor	2:26:59	

400 Meters

Year		Time	
1983	Jarmila Kratochvilova, CZE	47.99	WR
1987	Olga Bryzgina, USSR	49.38	
1991	Marie-José Pérec, FRA	49.13	
1993	Jearl Miles, USA	49.82	
1995	Marie-José Pérec, FRA	49.28	
1997	Cathy Freeman, AUS	49.77	
1999	Cathy Freeman, AUS	49.67	

100-Meter Hurdles

Year		Time	
1983	Bettine Jahn, E. Ger	12.35w	
1987	Ginka Zagorcheva, BUL	12.34	CR
1991	Lyudmila Narozhilenko, USSR	12.59	
1993	Gail Devers, USA	12.46	
1995	Gail Devers, USA	12.68	
1997	Ludmila Engquist, SWE	12.50	
1999	Gail Devers, USA	12.37	

w indicates wind-aided.

800 Meters

Year		Time	
1983	Jarmila Kratochvilova, CZE	1:54.68	CR
1987	Sigrun Wodars, E. Ger	1:55.26	
1991	Lilia Nurutdinova, USSR	1:57.50	
1993	Maria Mutola, MOZ	1:55.43	
1995	Ana Quirot, CUB	1:56.11	
1997	Ana Quirot, CUB	1:57.14	
1999	Ludmila Formanova, CZE	1:56.68	

400-Meter Hurdles

Year		Time	
1983	Yekaterina Fesenko, USSR	54.14	
1987	Sabine Busch, E. Ger	53.62	
1991	Tatiana Ledovskaya, USSR	53.11	
1993	Sally Gunnell, GBR	52.74	WR
1995	Kim Batten, USA	52.61	WR
1997	Nezha Bidouane, MOR	52.97	
1999	Daima Pernia, CUB	52.89	

1500 Meters

Year		Time	
1983	Mary Decker, USA	4:00.90	
1987	Tatiana Samolenko, USSR	3:58.56	CR
1991	Hassiba Boulmerka, ALG	4:02.21	
1993	Liu Dong, CHN	4:00.50	
1995	Hassiba Boulmerka, ALG	4:02.42	
1997	Carla Sacramento, POR	4:04.24	
1999	Svetlana Masterkova, RUS	3:59.53	

4 x 100-Meter Relay

Year		Time	
1983	East Germany	41.76	
1987	United States	41.58	
1991	Jamaica	41.94	
1993	Russia	41.49	CR
1995	United States	42.12	
1997	United States	41.47	CR
1999	Bahamas	41.92	

5000 Meters

Held as 3000-meter race from 1983-93

Year		Time	
1983	Mary Decker, USA	8:34.62	
1987	Tatyana Samolenko, USSR	8:38.73	
1991	T. Samolenko Dorovskikh, USSR	8:35.82	
1993	Qu Yunxia, CHN	8:28.71	CR
1995	Sonia O'Sullivan, IRL	14:46.47	CR
1997	Gabriela Szabo, ROM	14:57.68	
1999	Gabriela Szabo, ROM	14:41.82	CR

4 x 400-Meter Relay

Year		Time	
1983	East Germany	3:19.73	
1987	East Germany	3:18.63	
1991	Soviet Union	3:18.43	
1993	United States	3:16.71	CR
1995	United States	3:22.39	
1997	Germany	3:20.92	
1999	Russia	3:21.98	

Track & Field (Cont.)

20-Kilometer Walk

Held as 10-Kilometer race from 1987-97

Year		Time	
1983	Not held		
1987	Irina Strakhova, USSR	44:12	
1991	Alina Ivanova, USSR	42:57	
1993	Sari Essayah, FIN	42:59	
1995	Irina Stankina, RUS	42:13	CR
1997	Anna Sidoti, ITA	42:55	
1999	Hongyu Liu, CHN	1:30:50	CR

High Jump

Year		Height	
1983	Tamara Bykova, USSR	6-7	
1987	Stefka Kostadinova, BUL	6-10¼	WR
1991	Heike Henkel, GER	6-8¾	
1993	Ioamnet Quintero, CUB	6-6¼	
1995	Stefka Kostadinova, BUL	6-7	
1997	Hanne Haugland, NOR	6-6¼	
1999	Inga Babakova, UKR	6-6¼	

Pole Vault

Year		Height	
1999	Stacy Dragila, USA	15-1	=WR

Long Jump

Year		Distance	
1983	Heike Daute, E. Ger	23-10¼ʷ	
1987	Jackie Joyner-Kersee, USA	24-1¾	CR
1991	Jackie Joyner-Kersee, USA	24-0¼	
1993	Heike Drechsler, GER	23-4	
1995	Fiona May, ITA	22-10¾ʷ	
1997	Lyudmila Galkina, RUS	23-1¾	
1999	Niurka Montalvo, SPA	23-2	

ʷ indicates wind-aided.

Triple Jump

Year		Distance	
1993	Ana Biryukova, RUS	46-6¼	WR
1995	Inessa Kravets, UKR	50-10¾	WR
1997	Sarka Kasparkova, CZE	49-10½	
1999	Paraskevi Tsiamita, GRE	48-10	

Shot Put

Year		Distance	
1983	Helena Fibingerova, CZE	69-0	
1987	Natalia Lisovskaya, USSR	69-8	CR
1991	Huang Zhihong, CHN	68-4	
1993	Huang Zhihong, CHN	67-6	
1995	Astrid Kumbernuss, GER	69-7½	
1997	Astrid Kumbernuss, GER	67-11½	
1999	Astrid Kumbernuss, GER	65-1½	

Discus

Year		Distance	
1983	Martina Opitz, E. Ger	226-2	
1987	Martina Opitz Hellmann, E. Ger	235-0	CR
1991	Tsvetanka Khristova, BUL	233-0	
1993	Olga Burova, RUS	221-1	
1995	Ellina Zvereva, BLR	225-2	
1997	Beatrice Faumuina, NZL	219-3	
1999	Franka Dietzsch, GER	223-6	

Hammer Throw

Year		Distance	
1999	Mihaela Melinte, ROM	246-8¾	CR

Javelin

Year		Distance	
1983	Tiina Lillak, FIN	232-4	
1987	Fatima Whitbread, GBR	251-5	CR
1991	Xu Demei, CHN	225-8	
1993	Trine Hattestad, NOR	227-0	
1995	Natalya Shikolenko, BLR	221-8	
1997	Trine Hattestad, NOR	225-8	
1999	Mirela Manjani-Tzelili, GRE	220-1	

Heptathlon

Year		Points	
1983	Ramona Neubert, E. Ger	6770	
1987	Jackie Joyner-Kersee, USA	7128	CR
1991	Sabine Braun, GER	6672	
1993	Jackie Joyner-Kersee, USA	6837	
1995	Ghada Shouaa, SYR	6651	
1997	Sabine Braun, GER	6739	
1999	Eunice Barber, FRA	6861	

World Cross Country Championships

MEN

Multiple winners: John Ngugi and Paul Tergat (5); Carlos Lopes (3); Khalid Skah, William Sigei and Craig Virgin (2).

Year	Winner	Year	Winner	Year	Winner
1973	Pekka Paivarinta, Finland	1983	Bekele Debele, Ehtiopia	1993	William Sigei, Kenya
1974	Eric DeBeck, Belgium	1984	Carlos Lopes, Portugal	1994	William Sigei, Kenya
1975	Ian Stewart, Scotland	1985	Carlos Lopes, Portugal	1995	Paul Tergat, Kenya
1976	Carlos Lopes, Portugal	1986	John Ngugi, Kenya	1996	Paul Tergat, Kenya
1977	Leon Schots, Belgium	1987	John Ngugi, Kenya	1997	Paul Tergat, Kenya
1978	John Treacy, Ireland	1988	John Ngugi, Kenya	1998	Paul Tergat, Kenya
1979	John Treacy, Ireland	1989	John Ngugi, Kenya	1999	Paul Tergat, Kenya
1980	Craig Virgin, USA	1990	Khalid Skah, Morocco	2000	Mohammed Mourhit, Belgium
1981	Craig Virgin, USA	1991	Khalid Skah, Morocco		
1982	Mohammed Kedir, Ethiopia	1992	John Ngugi, Kenya		

WOMEN

Multiple winners: Grete Waitz (5); Lynn Jennings and Derartu Tulu (3); Zola Budd, Paola Cacchi, Maricica Puica, Annette Sergent, Carmen Valero and Gete Wami (2).

Year	Winner	Year	Winner	Year	Winner
1973	Paola Cacchi, Italy	1983	Grete Waitz, Norway	1993	Albertina Dias, Portugal
1974	Paola Cacchi, Italy	1984	Maricica Puica, Romania	1994	Helen Chepngeno, Kenya
1975	Julie Brown, USA	1985	Zola Budd, England	1995	Derartu Tulu, Ethiopia
1976	Carmen Valero, Spain	1986	Zola Budd, England	1996	Gete Wami, Ethiopia
1977	Carmen Valero, Spain	1987	Annette Sergent, France	1997	Derartu Tulu, Ethiopia
1978	Grete Waitz, Norway	1988	Ingrid Kristiansen, Norway	1998	Sonia O'Sullivan, Ireland
1979	Grete Waitz, Norway	1989	Annette Sergent, France	1999	Gete Wami, Ethiopia
1980	Grete Waitz, Norway	1990	Lynn Jennings, USA	2000	Derartu Tulu, Ethiopia
1981	Grete Waitz, Norway	1991	Lynn Jennings, USA		
1982	Maricica Puica, Romania	1992	Lynn Jennings, USA		

Marathons
Boston

America's oldest regularly contested foot race, the Boston Marathon is held on Patriots' Day every April. It has been run at four different distances: 24 miles, 1232 yards (1897-1923); 26 miles, 209 yards (1924-26); 26 miles, 385 yards (1927-52, since 1957); 25 miles, 958 yards (1953-56).

MEN

Multiple winners: Clarence DeMar (7); Gerard Cote and Bill Rodgers (4); Ibrahim Hussein, Cosmas Ndeti and Leslie Pawson (3); Tarzan Brown, Jim Caffrey, John A. Kelley, John Miles, Eino Oksanen, Toshihiko Seko, Geoff Smith, Moses Tanui and Aurele Vandendriessche (2).

Year		Time
1897	John McDermott, New York	2:55:10
1898	Ronald McDonald, Massachusetts	2:42:00
1899	Lawrence Brignolia, Massachusetts	2:54:38
1900	Jim Caffrey, Canada	2:39:44
1901	Jim Caffrey, Canada	2:29:23
1902	Sam Mellor, New York	2:43:12
1903	J.C. Lorden, Massachusetts	2:41:29
1904	Mike Spring, New York	2:38:04
1905	Fred Lorz, New York	2:38:25
1906	Tim Ford, Massachusetts	2:45:45
1907	Tom Longboat, Canada	2:24:24
1908	Tom Morrissey, New York	2:25:43
1909	Henri Renaud, New Hampshire	2:53:36
1910	Fred Cameron, Nova Scotia	2:28:52
1911	Clarence DeMar, Massachusetts	2:21:39
1912	Mike Ryan, Illinois	2:21:18
1913	Fritz Carlson, Minnesota	2:25:14
1914	James Duffy, Canada	2:25:01
1915	Edouard Fabre, Canada	2:31:41
1916	Arthur Roth, Massachusetts	2:27:16
1917	Bill Kennedy, New York	2:28:37
1918	World War relay race	
1919	Carl Linder, Massachusetts	2:29:13
1920	Peter Trivoulidas, New York	2:29:31
1921	Frank Zuna, New Jersey	2:18:57
1922	Clarence DeMar, Massachusetts	2:18:10
1923	Clarence DeMar, Massachusetts	2:23:37
1924	Clarence DeMar, Massachusetts	2:29:40
1925	Charles Mellor, Illinois	2:33:00
1926	John Miles, Nova Scotia	2:25:40
1927	Clarence DeMar, Massachusetts	2:40:22
1928	Clarence DeMar, Massachusetts	2:37:07
1929	John Miles, Nova Scotia	2:33:08
1930	Clarence DeMar, Massachusetts	2:34:48
1931	James Henigan, Massachusetts	2:46:45
1932	Paul deBruyn, Germany	2:33:36
1933	Leslie Pawson, Rhode Island	2:31:01
1934	Dave Komonen, Canada	2:32:53
1935	John A. Kelley, Massachusetts	2:32:07
1936	Ellison (Tarzan) Brown, Rhode Island	2:33:40
1937	Walter Young, Canada	2:33:20
1938	Leslie Pawson, Rhode Island	2:35:34
1939	Ellison (Tarzan) Brown, Rhode Island	2:28:51
1940	Gerard Cote, Canada	2:28:28
1941	Leslie Pawson, Rhode Island	2:30:38
1942	Joe Smith, Massachusetts	2:26:51
1943	Gerard Cote, Canada	2:28:25
1944	Gerard Cote, Canada	2:31:50
1945	John A. Kelley, Massachusetts	2:30:40
1946	Stylianos Kyriakides, Greece	2:29:27
1947	Yun Bok Suh, Korea	2:25:39
1948	Gerard Cote, Canada	2:31:02
1949	Karle Leandersson, Sweden	2:31:50
1950	Kee Yonh Ham, Korea	2:32:39
1951	Shigeki Tanaka, Japan	2:27:45
1952	Doroteo Flores, Guatemala	2:31:53
1953	Keizo Yamada, Japan	2:18:51
1954	Veiko Karvonen, Finland	2:20:39
1955	Hideo Hamamura, Japan	2:18:22
1956	Antti Viskari, Finland	2:14:14
1957	John J. Kelley, Connecticut	2:20:05
1958	Franjo Mihalic, Yugoslavia	2:25:54
1959	Eino Oksanen, Finland	2:22:42
1960	Paavo Kotila, Finland	2:20:54
1961	Eino Oksanen, Finland	2:23:39
1962	Eino Oksanen, Finland	2:23:48
1963	Aurele Vandendriessche, Belgium	2:18:58
1964	Aurele Vandendriessche, Belgium	2:19:59
1965	Morio Shigematsu, Japan	2:16:33
1966	Kenji Kimihara, Japan	2:17:11
1967	David McKenzie, New Zealand	2:15:45
1968	Amby Burfoot, Connecticut	2:22:17
1969	Yoshiaki Unetani, Japan	2:13:49
1970	Ron Hill, England	2:10:30
1971	Alvaro Mejia, Colombia	2:18:45
1972	Olavi Suomalainen, Finland	2:15:39
1973	Jon Anderson, Oregon	2:16:03
1974	Neil Cusack, Ireland	2:13:39
1975	Bill Rodgers, Massachusetts	2:09:55
1976	Jack Fultz, Pennsylvania	2:20:19
1977	Jerome Drayton, Canada	2:14:46
1978	Bill Rodgers, Massachusetts	2:10:13
1979	Bill Rodgers, Massachusetts	2:09:27
1980	Bill Rodgers, Massachusetts	2:12:11
1981	Toshihiko Seko, Japan	2:09:26
1982	Alberto Salazar, Oregon	2:08:52
1983	Greg Meyer, New Jersey	2:09:00
1984	Geoff Smith, England	2:10:34
1985	Geoff Smith, England	2:14:05
1986	Rob de Castella, Australia	2:07:51
1987	Toshihiko Seko, Japan	2:11:50
1988	Ibrahim Hussein, Kenya	2:08:43
1989	Abebe Mekonnen, Ethiopia	2:09:06
1990	Gelindo Bordin, Italy	2:08:19
1991	Ibrahim Hussein, Kenya	2:11:06
1992	Ibrahim Hussein, Kenya	2:08:14
1993	Cosmas Ndeti, Kenya	2:09:33
1994	Cosmas Ndeti, Kenya	2:07:15*
1995	Cosmas Ndeti, Kenya	2:09:22
1996	Moses Tanui, Kenya	2:09:16
1997	Lameck Aguta, Kenya	2:10:34
1998	Moses Tanui, Kenya	2:07:34
1999	Joseph Chebet, Kenya	2:09:52
2000	Elijah Lagat, Kenya	2:09:47

*Course record.

Track & Field (Cont.)
WOMEN

Multiple winners: Rosa Mota, Uta Pippig and Fatuma Roba (3); Joan Benoit, Miki Gorman, Ingrid Kristiansen and Olga Markova (2).

Year		Time	Year		Time
1972	Nina Kuscsik, New York	3:08:58	1987	Rosa Mota, Portugal	2:25:21
1973	Jacqueline Hansen, California	3:05:59	1988	Rosa Mota, Portugal	2:24:30
1974	Miki Gorman, California	2:47:11	1989	Ingrid Kristiansen, Norway	2:24:33
1975	Liane Winter, West Germany	2:42:24	1990	Rosa Mota, Portugal	2:25:23
1976	Kim Merritt, Wisconsin	2:47:10	1991	Wanda Panfil, Poland	2:24:18
1977	Miki Gorman, California	2:48:33	1992	Olga Markova, CIS	2:23:43
1978	Gayle Barron, Georgia	2:44:52	1993	Olga Markova, Russia	2:25:27
1979	Joan Benoit, Maine	2:35:15	1994	Uta Pippig, Germany	2:21:45*
1980	Jacqueline Gareau, Canada	2:34:28	1995	Uta Pippig, Germany	2:25:11
1981	Allison Roe, New Zealand	2:26:46	1996	Uta Pippig, Germany	2:27:12
1982	Charlotte Teske, West Germany	2:29:33	1997	Fatuma Roba, Ethiopia	2:26:23
1983	Joan Benoit, Maine	2:22:43	1998	Fatuma Roba, Ethiopia	2:23:21
1984	Lorraine Moller, New Zealand	2:29:28	1999	Fatuma Roba, Ethiopia	2:23:25
1985	Lisa Larsen Weidenbach, Mass	2:34:06	2000	Catherine Ndereba, Kenya	2:26.11
1986	Ingrid Kristiansen, Norway	2:24:55	*Course record.		

New York City

Started in 1970, the New York City Marathon is run in the fall, usually on the first Sunday in November. The route winds through all of the city's five boroughs and finishes in Central Park.

MEN

Multiple winners: Bill Rodgers (4); Alberto Salazar (3); Tom Fleming, John Kagwe, Orlando Pizzolato and German Silva (2).

Year		Time	Year		Time	Year		Time
1970	Gary Muhrcke, USA	2:31:38	1981	Alberto Salazar, USA	2:08:13	1992	Willie Mtolo, S. Afr.	2:09:29
1971	Norman Higgins, USA	2:22:54	1982	Alberto Salazar, USA	2:09:29	1993	Andres Espinosa, MEX	2:10:04
1972	Sheldon Karlin, USA	2:27:52	1983	Rod Dixon, NZ	2:08:59	1994	German Silva, MEX	2:11:21
1973	Tom Fleming, USA	2:21:54	1984	Orlando Pizzolato, ITA.	2:14:53	1995	German Silva, MEX	2:11:00
1974	Norbert Sander, USA	2:26:30	1985	Orlando Pizzolato, ITA.	2:11:34	1996	Giacomo Leone, ITA	2:09:54
1975	Tom Fleming, USA	2:19:27	1986	Gianni Poli, ITA	2:11:06	1997	John Kagwe, KEN	2:08:12
1976	Bill Rodgers, USA	2:10:09	1987	Ibrahim Hussein, KEN	2:11:01	1998	John Kagwe, KEN	2:08:45
1977	Bill Rodgers, USA	2:11:28	1988	Steve Jones, WAL	2:08:20	1999	Joseph Chebet, KEN	2:09:14
1978	Bill Rodgers, USA	2:12:12	1989	Juma Ikangaa, TAN	2:08:01*	*Course record.		
1979	Bill Rodgers, USA	2:11:42	1990	Douglas Wakiihuri, KEN	2:12:39			
1980	Alberto Salazar, USA	2:09:41	1991	Salvador Garcia, MEX.	2:09:28			

WOMEN

Multiple winners: Grete Waitz (9); Miki Gorman, Nina Kuscsik and Tegla Loroupe (2).

Year		Time	Year		Time	Year		Time
1970	No Finisher		1981	Allison Roe, NZ	2:25:29	1992	Lisa Ondieki, AUS	2:24:40*
1971	Beth Bonner, USA	2:55:22	1982	Grete Waitz, NOR	2:27:14	1993	Uta Pippig, GER	2:26:24
1972	Nina Kuscsik, USA	3:08:41	1983	Grete Waitz, NOR	2:27:00	1994	Tegla Loroupe, KEN	2:27:37
1973	Nina Kuscsik, USA	2:57:07	1984	Grete Waitz, NOR	2:29:30	1995	Tegla Loroupe, KEN	2:28:06
1974	Katherine Switzer, USA	3:07:29	1985	Grete Waitz, NOR	2:28:34	1996	Anuta Catuna, ROM	2:28:18
1975	Kim Merritt, USA	2:46:14	1986	Grete Waitz, NOR	2:28:06	1997	F. Rochat-Moser, SWI	2:28:43
1976	Miki Gorman, USA	2:39:11	1987	Priscilla Welch, GBR	2:30:17	1998	Franca Fiacconi, ITA	2:25:17
1977	Miki Gorman, USA	2:43:10	1988	Grete Waitz, NOR	2:28:07	1999	Adriana Fernandez,	
1978	Grete Waitz, NOR	2:32:30	1989	Ingrid Kristiansen, NOR	2:25:30		MEX	2:25:06
1979	Grete Waitz, NOR	2:27:33	1990	Wanda Panfil, POL	2:30:45	*Course record.		
1980	Grete Waitz, NOR	2:25:41	1991	Liz McColgan, SCO	2:27:23			

Annual Awards
Track & Field News Athletes of the Year

Voted on by an international panel of track and field experts and presented since 1959 for men and 1974 for women.

MEN

Multiple winners: Carl Lewis (3); Sergey Bubka, Sebastian Coe, Haile Gebrselassie, Michael Johnson, Alberto Juantorena, Noureddine Morceli, Jim Ryun and Peter Snell (2).

Year		Event	Year		Event
1959	Martin Lauer, W. Germany	110H/Decathlon	1969	Bill Toomey, USA	Decathlon
1960	Rafer Johnson, USA	Decathlon	1970	Randy Matson, USA	Shot Put
1961	Ralph Boston, USA	Long Jump/110 Hurdles	1971	Rod Milburn, USA	110 Hurdles
1962	Peter Snell, New Zealand	800/1500	1972	Lasse Viren, Finland	5000/10,000
1963	C.K. Yang, Taiwan	Decathlon/Pole Vault	1973	Ben Jipcho, Kenya	1500/5000/Steeplechase
1964	Peter Snell, New Zealand	800/1500	1974	Rick Wohlhuter, USA	800/1500
1965	Ron Clarke, Australia	5000/10,000	1975	John Walker, New Zealand	800/1500
1966	Jim Ryun, USA	800/1500	1976	Alberto Juantorena, Cuba	400/800
1967	Jim Ryun, USA	1500	1977	Alberto Juantorena, Cuba	400/800
1968	Bob Beamon, USA	Long Jump	1978	Henry Rono, Kenya	5000/10,000/Steeplechase

Year		Event
1979	Sebastian Coe, Great Britain	800/1500
1980	Edwin Moses, USA	400 Hurdles
1981	Sebastian Coe, Great Britain	800/1500
1982	Carl Lewis, USA	100/200/Long Jump
1983	Carl Lewis, USA	100/200/Long Jump
1984	Carl Lewis, USA	100/200/Long Jump
1985	Said Aouita, Morocco	1500/5000
1986	Yuri Sedykh, USSR	Hammer Throw
1987	Ben Johnson, Canada	100
1988	Sergey Bubka, USSR	Pole Vault
1989	Roger Kingdom, USA	110 Hurdles

Year		Event
1990	Michael Johnson, USA	200/400
1991	Sergey Bubka, USSR	Pole Vault
1992	Kevin Young, USA	400 Hurdles
1993	Noureddine Morceli, Algeria	Mile/1500/3000
1994	Noureddine Morceli, Algeria	Mile/1500/3000
1995	Haile Gebrselassie, Ethopia	5000/10,000
1996	Michael Johnson, USA	200/400
1997	Wilson Kipketer, Denmark	800
1998	Haile Gebrselassie, Ethopia	3000/5000/10,000
1999	Hicham El Guerrouj, Morocco	Mile/1500

WOMEN

Multiple winners: Marita Koch (4); Jackie Joyner-Kersee (3); Evelyn Ashford and Marion Jones (2).

Year		Event
1974	Irena Szewinska, Poland	100/200/400
1975	Faina Melnik, USSR	Shot Put/Discus
1976	Tatiana Kazankina, USSR	800/1500
1977	Rosemarie Ackermann, E. Germany	High Jump
1978	Marita Koch, E. Germany	100/200/400
1979	Marita Koch, E. Germany	100/200/400
1980	Ilona Briesenick, E. Germany	Shot Put
1981	Evelyn Ashford, USA	100/200
1982	Marita Koch, E. Germany	100/200/400
1983	Jarmila Kratochvilova, Czech	200/400/800
1984	Evelyn Ashford, USA	100
1985	Marita Koch, E. Germany	100/200/400
1986	Jackie Joyner-Kersee, USA	Heptathlon/Long Jump

Year		Event
1987	Jackie Joyner-Kersee, USA	100H/Heptathlon/LJ
1988	Florence Griffith Joyner, USA	100/200
1989	Ana Quirot, Cuba	400/800
1990	Merlene Ottey, Jamaica	100/200
1991	Heike Henkel, Germany	High Jump
1992	Heike Drechsler, Germany	Long Jump
1993	Wang Junxia, China	1500/3000/10,000
1994	Jackie Joyner-Kersee, USA	100H/Heptathlon/LJ
1995	Sonia O'Sullivan, Ireland	1500/3000/5000
1996	Svetlana Masterkova, Russia	800/1500
1997	Marion Jones, USA	100/200
1998	Marion Jones, USA	100/200/LJ
1999	Gabriela Szabo, Romania	3000/5000

SWIMMING & DIVING

FINA World Championships

While the Summer Olympics have served as the unofficial world championships for swimming and diving throughout the century, a separate World Championship meet was started in 1973 by the Federation Internationale de Natation Amateur (FINA). The meet was held three times between 1973-78, then every four years since then. Sites have been Belgrade (1973); Cali, COL (1975); West Berlin (1978); Guayaquil, ECU (1982); Madrid (1986); Perth (1991 & 98) and Rome (1994). Looking forward, the Championships will be held in Fukuoka, JPN (2001) and Barcelona (2003).

MEN

Most gold medals (including relays): Jim Montgomery (7); Matt Biondi (6); Rowdy Gaines (5); Joe Bottom, Tamas Darnyi, Michael Gross, Tom Jager, Michael Klim, David McCagg, Vladimir Salnikov and Tim Shaw (4); Billy Forrester, Andras Hargitay, Roland Matthes, John Murphy, Aleksandr Popov, Jeff Rouse, Norbert Rozsa and David Wilkie (3).

50-Meter Freestyle

Year		Time	
1973-82 Not held			
1986	Tom Jager, USA	22.49	
1991	Tom Jager, USA	22.16	CR
1994	Aleksandr Popov, RUS	22.17	
1998	Bill Pilczuk, USA	22.29	

100-Meter Freestyle

Year		Time
1973	Jim Montgomery, USA	51.70
1975	Tim Shaw, USA	51.25
1978	David McCagg, USA	50.24
1982	Jorg Woithe, E. Ger	50.18
1986	Matt Biondi, USA	48.94
1991	Matt Biondi, USA	49.18
1994	Aleksandr Popov, RUS	49.12
1998	Aleksandr Popov, RUS	48.93 CR

200-Meter Freestyle

Year		Time	
1973	Jim Montgomery, USA	1:53.02	
1975	Tim Shaw, USA	1:52.04	
1978	Billy Forrester, USA	1:51.02	
1982	Michael Gross, W. Ger	1:49.84	
1986	Michael Gross, W. Ger	1:47.92	
1991	Giorgio Lamberti, ITA	1:47.27	
1994	Antti Kasvio, FIN	1:47.32	CR
1998	Michael Klim, AUS	1:47.41	

400-Meter Freestyle

Year		Time	
1973	Rick DeMont, USA	3:58.18	
1975	Tim Shaw, USA	3:54.88	
1978	Vladimir Salnikov, USSR	3:51.94	
1982	Vladimir Salnikov, USSR	3:51.30	
1986	Rainer Henkel, W. Ger	3:50.05	
1991	Jorg Hoffman, GER	3:48.04	
1994	Kieren Perkins, AUS	3:43.80	WR
1998	Ian Thorpe, AUS	3:46.29	

1500-Meter Freestyle

Year		Time	
1973	Stephen Holland, AUS	15:31.85	
1975	Tim Shaw, USA	15:28.92	
1978	Vladimir Salnikov, USSR	15:03.99	
1982	Vladimir Salnikov, USSR	15:01.77	
1986	Rainer Henkel, W. Ger	15:05.31	
1991	Jorg Hoffman, GER	14:50.36	WR
1994	Kieren Perkins, AUS	14:50.52	
1998	Grant Hackett, AUS	14:51.70	

100-Meter Backstroke

Year		Time	
1973	Roland Matthes, E. Ger	57.47	
1975	Roland Matthes, E. Ger	58.15	
1978	Bob Jackson, USA	56.36	
1982	Dirk Richter, E. Ger	55.95	
1986	Igor Polianski, USSR	55.58	
1991	Jeff Rouse, USA	55.23	
1994	Martin Lopez-Zubero, SPA	55.17	CR
1998	Lenny Krayzelburg, USA	55.00	

Swimming & Diving (Cont.)

200-Meter Backstroke

Year		Time	
1973	Roland Matthes, E. Ger	2:01.87	
1975	Zoltan Varraszto, HUN	2:05.05	
1978	Jesse Vassallo, USA	2:02.16	
1982	Rick Carey, USA	2:00.82	
1986	Igor Polianski, USSR	1:58.78	CR
1991	Martin Zubero, SPA	1:59.52	
1994	Vladimir Selkov, RUS	1:57.42	
1998	Lenny Krayzelburg, USA	1:58.84	

100-Meter Breaststroke

Year		Time	
1973	John Hencken, USA	1:04.02	
1975	David Wilkie, GBR	1:04.26	
1978	Walter Kusch, W. Ger	1:03.56	
1982	Steve Lundquist, USA	1:02.75	
1986	Victor Davis, CAN	1:02.71	
1991	Norbert Rozsa, HUN	1:01.45	WR
1994	Norbert Rozsa, HUN	1:01.24	
1998	Frederik deBurghgraeve, BEL	1:01.34	

200-Meter Breaststroke

Year		Time	
1973	David Wilkie, GBR	2:19.28	
1975	David Wilkie, GBR	2:18.23	
1978	Nick Nevid, USA	2:18.37	
1982	Victor Davis, CAN	2:14.77	WR
1986	Jozsef Szabo, HUN	2:14.27	
1991	Mike Barrowman, USA	2:11.23	WR
1994	Norbert Rozsa, HUN	2:12.81	
1998	Kurt Grote, USA	2:13.40	

100-Meter Butterfly

Year		Time	
1973	Bruce Robertson, CAN	.55.69	
1975	Greg Jagenburg, USA	.55.63	
1978	Joe Bottom, USA	.54.30	
1982	Matt Gribble, USA	.53.88	
1986	Pablo Morales, USA	.53.54	
1991	Anthony Nesty, SUR	.53.29	
1994	Rafal Szukala, POL	.53.51	
1998	Michael Klim, AUS	.52.25	CR

200-Meter Butterfly

Year		Time	
1973	Robin Backhaus, USA	2:03.32	
1975	Billy Forrester, USA	2:01.95	
1978	Mike Bruner, USA	1:59.38	
1982	Michael Gross, W. Ger	1:58.85	
1986	Michael Gross, W. Ger	1:56.53	
1991	Melvin Stewart, USA	1:55.69	WR
1994	Denis Pankratov, RUS	1:56.54	
1998	Denys Sylantyev, UKR	1:56.61	

200-Meter Individual Medley

Year		Time	
1973	Gunnar Larsson, SWE	2:08.36	
1975	Andras Hargitay, HUN	2:07.72	
1978	Graham Smith, CAN	2:03.65	WR
1982	Alexander Sidorenko, USSR	2:03.30	
1986	Tamás Darnyi, HUN	2:01.57	
1991	Tamás Darnyi, HUN	1:59.36	WR
1994	Janis Sievinen, FIN	1:58.16	WR
1998	Marcel Wouda, NET	2:01.18	

400-Meter Individual Medley

Year		Time	
1973	Andras Hargitay, HUN	4:31.11	
1975	Andras Hargitay, HUN	4:32.57	
1978	Jesse Vassallo, USA	4:20.05	WR
1982	Ricardo Prado, BRA	4:19.78	WR
1986	Tamás Darnyi, HUN	4:18.98	
1991	Tamás Darnyi, HUN	4:12.36	WR
1994	Tom Dolan, USA	4:12.30	WR
1998	Tom Dolan, USA	4:14.95	

4 x 100-Meter Freestyle Relay

Year		Time	
1973	United States	3:27.18	
1975	United States	3:24.85	
1978	United States	3:19.74	
1982	United States	3:19.26	WR
1986	United States	3:19.98	
1991	United States	3:17.15	
1994	United States	3:16.90	
1998	United States	3:16.69	CR

4 x 200-Meter Freestyle Relay

Year		Time	
1973	United States	7:33.22	WR
1975	West Germany	7:39.44	
1978	United States	7:20.82	
1982	United States	7:21.09	
1986	East Germany	7:15.91	
1991	Germany	7:13.50	CR
1994	Sweden	7:17.34	
1998	Australia	7:12.48	

4 x 100-Meter Medley Relay

Year		Time	
1973	United States	3:49.49	
1975	United States	3:49.00	
1978	United States	3:44.63	
1982	United States	3:40.84	WR
1986	United States	3:41.25	
1991	United States	3:39.66	
1994	United States	3:37.74	CR
1998	Australia	3:37.98	

WOMEN

Most gold medals (including relays): Kornelia Ender (8); Kristin Otto (7); Tracy Caulkins, Heike Friedrich, Le Jingyi, Rosemarie Kother, Ulrike Richter and Jenny Thompson (4); Hannalore Anke, Lu Bin, He Cihong, Janet Evans, Nicole Haislett, Lui Limin, Birgit Meineke, Joan Pennington, Manuela Stellmach, Amy Van Dyken, Renate Vogel and Cynthia Woodhead (3).

50-Meter Freestyle

Year		Time	
1973-82 Not held			
1986	Tamara Costache, ROM	25.28	WR
1991	Zhuang Yong, CHN	25.47	
1994	Le Jingyi, CHN	24.51	WR
1998	Amy Van Dyken, USA	25.15	

100-Meter Freestyle

Year		Time	
1973	Kornelia Ender, E. Ger	.57.54	
1975	Kornelia Ender, E. Ger	.56.50	
1978	Barbara Krause, E. Ger	.55.68	
1982	Birgit Meineke, E. Ger	.55.79	
1986	Kristin Otto, E. Ger	.55.05	
1991	Nicole Haislett, USA	.55.17	
1994	Le Jingyi, CHN	.54.01	WR
1998	Jenny Thompson, USA	.54.95	

200-Meter Freestyle

Year		Time	
1973	Keena Rothhammer, USA	2:04.99	
1975	Shirley Babashoff, USA	2:02.50	
1978	Cynthia Woodhead, USA	1:58.53	WR
1982	Annemarie Verstappen, HOL	1:59.53	
1986	Heike Friedrich, E. Ger	1:58.26	
1991	Hayley Lewis, AUS	2:00.48	

Year		Time	
1994	Franziska Van Almsick, GER	1:56.78	WR
1998	Claudia Poll, CRC	1:58.90	

400-Meter Freestyle

Year		Time	
1973	Heather Greenwood, USA	4:20.28	
1975	Shirley Babashoff, USA	4:22.70	
1978	Tracey Wickham, AUS	4:06.28	WR
1982	Carmela Schmidt. E. Ger	4:08.98	
1986	Heike Friedrich, E. Ger	4:07.45	
1991	Janet Evans, USA	4:08.63	
1994	Yang Aihua, CHN	4:09.64	
1998	Yan Chen, CHN	4:06.72	

800-Meter Freestyle

Year		Time	
1973	Novella Calligaris, ITA	8:52.97	
1975	Jenny Turrall, AUS	8:44.75	
1978	Tracey Wickham, AUS	8:25.94	
1982	Kim Linehan, USA	8:27.48	
1986	Astrid Strauss, E. Ger	8:28.24	
1991	Janet Evans, USA	8:24.05	CR
1994	Janet Evans, USA	8:29.85	
1998	Brooke Bennett, USA	8:28.71	

100-Meter Backstroke

Year		Time	
1973	Ulrike Richter, E. Ger	1:05.42	
1975	Ulrike Richter, E. Ger	1:03.30	
1978	Linda Jezek, USA	1:02.55	
1982	Kristin Otto, E. Ger	1:01.30	
1986	Betsy Mitchell, USA	1:01.74	
1991	Krisztina Egerszegi, HUN	1:01.78	
1994	He Cihong, CHN	1:00.57	WR
1998	Lea Maurer, USA	1:01.16	

200-Meter Backstroke

Year		Time	
1973	Melissa Belote, USA	2:20.52	
1975	Birgit Treiber, E. Ger	2:15.46	WR
1978	Linda Jezek, USA	2:11.93	WR
1982	Cornelia Sirch, E. Ger	2:09.91	WR
1986	Cornelia Sirch, E. Ger	2:11.37	
1991	Krisztina Egerszegi, HUN	2:09.15	
1994	He Cihong, CHN	2:07.40	CR
1998	Roxanna Maracineanu, FRA	2:11.26	

100-Meter Breaststroke

Year		Time	
1973	Renate Vogel, E. Ger	1:13.74	
1975	Hannalore Anke, E. Ger	1:12.72	
1978	Julia Bogdanova, USSR	1:10.31	WR
1982	Ute Geweniger, E. Ger	1:09.14	
1986	Sylvia Gerasch, E. Ger	1:08.11	WR
1991	Linley Frame, AUS	1:08.81	
1994	Samantha Riley, AUS	1:07.69	WR
1998	Kristy Kowal, USA	1:08.42	

200-Meter Breaststroke

Year		Time	
1973	Renate Vogel, E. Ger	2:40.01	
1975	Hannalore Anke, E. Ger	2:37.25	
1978	Lina Kachushite, USSR	2:31.42	WR
1982	Svetlana Varganova, USSR	2:28.82	
1986	Silke Hoerner, E. Ger	2:27.40	WR
1991	Elena Volkova, USSR	2:29.53	
1994	Samantha Riley, AUS	2:26.87	
1998	Agnes Kovacs, HUN	2:25.45	CR

100-Meter Butterfly

Year		Time	
1973	Kornelia Ender, E. Ger	1:02.53	
1975	Kornelia Ender, E. Ger	1:01.24	WR

Year		Time	
1978	Joan Pennington, USA	1:00.20	
1982	Mary T. Meagher, USA	59.41	
1986	Kornelai Gressler, E. Ger	59.51	
1991	Qian Hong, CHN	59.68	
1994	Liu Limin, CHN	58.98	
1998	Jenny Thompson, USA	58.46	CR

200-Meter Butterfly

Year		Time	
1973	Rosemarie Kother, E. Ger	2:13.76	
1975	Rosemarie Kother, E. Ger	2:15.92	
1978	Tracy Caulkins, USA	2:09.78	WR
1982	Ines Geissler, E. Ger	2:08.66	
1986	Mary T. Meagher, USA	2:08.41	
1991	Summer Sanders, USA	2:09.24	
1994	Liu Limin, CHN	2:07.25	CR
1998	Susie O'Neill, AUS	2:07.93	

200-Meter Individual Medley

Year		Time	
1973	Andre Huebner, E. Ger	2:20.51	
1975	Kathy Heddy, USA	2:19.80	
1978	Tracy Caulkins, USA	2:19.80	WR
1982	Petra Schneider, E. Ger	2:11.79	CR
1986	Kristin Otto, E. Ger	2:15.56	
1991	Lin Li, CHN	2:13.40	
1994	Lu Bin, CHN	2:12.34	
1998	Yanyan Wu, CHN	2:10.88	CR

400-Meter Individual Medley

Year		Time	
1973	Gudrun Wegner, E. Ger	4:57.71	
1975	Ulrike Tauber, E. Ger	4:52.76	
1978	Tracy Caulkins, USA	4:40.83	WR
1982	Petra Schneider, E. Ger	4:36.10	WR
1986	Kathleen Nord, E. Ger	4:43.75	
1991	Lin Li, CHN	4:41.45	
1994	Dai Guohong, CHN	4:39.14	
1998	Yan Chen, CHN	4:36.66	

4 x 100-Meter Freestyle Relay

Year		Time	
1973	East Germany	3:52.45	
1975	East Germany	3:49.37	
1978	United States	3:43.43	WR
1982	East Germany	3:43.97	
1986	East Germany	3:40.57	
1991	United States	3:43.26	
1994	China	3:37.91	WR
1998	United States	3:42.11	

4 x 200-Meter Freestyle Relay

Year		Time	
1973-82	Not held		
1986	East Germany	7:59.33	WR
1991	Germany	8:02.56	
1994	China	7:57.96	CR
1998	Germany	8:01.46	

4 x 100-Meter Medley Relay

Year		Time	
1973	East Germany	4:16.84	
1975	East Germany	4:14.74	
1978	United States	4:08.21	
1982	East Germany	4:05.8	WR
1986	East Germany	4:04.82	
1991	United States	4:06.51	
1994	China	4:01.67	CR
1998	United States	4:01.93	

Swimming & Diving (Cont.)
Diving

Multiple Gold Medals: MEN– Greg Louganis (5); Phil Boggs and Dmitry Sautin (3); Klaus Dibiasi and Yu Zhuocheng (2). WOMEN– Irina Kalinina and Gao Min (3); Fu Mingxia (2).

MEN

1-Meter Springboard

Year		Pts
1991	Edwin Jongejans, HOL	588.51
1994	Evan Stewart, ZIM	382.14
1998	Yu Zhuocheng, CHN	417.54

3-Meter Springboard

Year		Pts
1973	Phil Boggs, USA	618.57
1975	Phil Boggs, USA	597.12
1978	Phil Boggs, USA	913.95
1982	Greg Louganis, USA	752.67
1986	Greg Louganis, USA	750.06
1991	Kent Ferguson, USA	650.25
1994	Yu Zhuocheng, CHN	655.44
1998	Dmitry Sautin, RUS	746.79

Platform

Year		Pts
1973	Klaus Dibiasi, ITA	559.53
1975	Klaus Dibiasi, ITA	547.98
1978	Greg Louganis, USA	844.11
1982	Greg Louganis, USA	634.26
1986	Greg Louganis, USA	668.58
1991	Sun Shuwei, CHN	626.79
1994	Dmitry Sautin, RUS	634.71
1998	Dmitry Sautin, RUS	750.99

WOMEN

1-Meter Springboard

Year		Pts
1991	Gao Min, CHN	478.26
1994	Chen Lixia, CHN	279.30
1998	Irina Lashko, RUS	296.07

3-Meter Springboard

Year		Pts
1973	Christa Koehler, E. Ger	442.17
1975	Irina Kalinina, USSR	489.81
1978	Irina Kalinina, USSR	691.43
1982	Megan Neyer, USA	501.03
1986	Gao Min, CHN	582.90
1991	Gao Min, CHN	539.01
1994	Tan Shuping, CHN	548.49
1998	Yulia Pakhalina, RUS	544.52

Platform

Year		Pts
1973	Ulrike Knape, SWE	406.77
1975	Janet Ely, USA	403.89
1978	Irina Kalinina, USSR	412.71
1982	Wendy Wyland, USA	438.79
1986	Chen Lin, CHN	449.67
1991	Fu Mingxia, CHN	426.51
1994	Fu Mingxia, CHN	434.04
1998	Olena Zhupyna	550.41

ALPINE SKIING

World Cup Overall Champions

World Cup Overall Champions (downhill and slalom events combined) since the tour was organized in 1967.

MEN

Multiple winners: Marc Girardelli (5), Gustavo Thoeni and Pirmin Zurbriggen (4); Phil Mahre and Ingemar Stenmark (3); Jean-Claude Killy, Lasse Kjus, Hermann Maier and Karl Schranz (2).

Year		Year		Year	
1967	Jean-Claude Killy, France	1978	Ingemar Stenmark, Sweden	1989	Marc Girardelli, Luxembourg
1968	Jean-Claude Killy, France	1979	Peter Luescher, Switzerland	1990	Pirmin Zurbriggen, Switzerland
1969	Karl Schranz, Austria	1980	Andreas Wenzel, Liechtenstein	1991	Marc Girardelli, Luxembourg
1970	Karl Schranz, Austria	1981	Phil Mahre, USA	1992	Paul Accola, Switzerland
1971	Gustavo Thoeni, Italy	1982	Phil Mahre, USA	1993	Marc Girardelli, Luxembourg
1972	Gustavo Thoeni, Italy	1983	Phil Mahre, USA	1994	Kjetil Andre Aamodt, Norway
1973	Gustavo Thoeni, Italy	1984	Pirmin Zurbriggen, Switzerland	1995	Alberto Tomba, Italy
1974	Piero Gros, Italy	1985	Marc Girardelli, Luxembourg	1996	Lasse Kjus, Norway
1975	Gustavo Thoeni, Italy	1986	Marc Girardelli, Luxembourg	1997	Luc Alphand, France
1976	Ingemar Stenmark, Sweden	1987	Pirmin Zurbriggen, Switzerland	1998	Hermann Maier, Austria
1977	Ingemar Stenmark, Sweden	1988	Pirmin Zurbriggen, Switzerland	1999	Lasse Kjus, Norway
				2000	Hermann Maier, Austria

WOMEN

Multiple winners: Annemarie Moser-Proell (6); Petra Kronberger and Vreni Schneider (3); Michela Figini, Nancy Greene, Erika Hess, Katja Seizinger, Maria Walliser and Hanni Wenzel (2).

Year		Year		Year	
1967	Nancy Greene, Canada	1979	Annemarie Moser-Pröll, Austria	1990	Petra Kronberger, Austria
1968	Nancy Greene, Canada	1980	Hanni Wenzel, Liechtenstein	1991	Petra Kronberger, Austria
1969	Gertrud Gabi, Austria	1981	Marie-Therese Nadig,	1992	Petra Kronberger, Austria
1970	Michele Jacot, France		Switzerland	1993	Anita Wachter, Austria
1971	Annemarie Pröll, Austria	1982	Erika Hess, Switzerland	1994	Vreni Schneider, Switzerland
1972	Annemarie Pröll, Austria	1983	Tamara McKinney, USA	1995	Vreni Schneider, Switzerland
1973	Annemarie Pröll, Austria	1984	Erika Hess, Switzerland	1996	Katja Seizinger, Germany
1974	Annemarie Pröll, Austria	1985	Michela Figini, Switzerland	1997	Pernilla Wiberg, Sweden
1975	Annemarie Moser-Pröll, Austria	1986	Maria Walliser, Switzerland	1998	Katja Seizinger, Germany
1976	Rosi Mittermaier, W. Germany	1987	Maria Walliser, Switzerland	1999	Alexandra Meissnitzer, Austria
1977	Lise-Marie Morerod, Switzerland	1988	Michela Figini, Switzerland	2000	Renate Goetschl, Austria
1978	Hanni Wenzel, Liechtenstein	1989	Vreni Schneider, Switzerland		

World Cup Event Champions

World Cup Champions in each individual event since the tour was organized in 1967.

MEN
Downhill

Multiple winners: Franz Klammer (5); Luc Alphand, Franz Heinzer and Peter Muller (3); Roland Collumbin, Marc Girardelli, Helmut Hoflehner, Bernard Russi, Karl Schranz and Pirmin Zurbriggen (2).

Year	Year	Year
1967 Jean-Claude Killy, France	1978 Franz Klammer, Austria	1989 Marc Girardelli, Luxembourg
1968 Gerhard Nenning, Austria	1979 Peter Muller, Switzerland	1990 Helmut Hoflehner, Austria
1969 Karl Schranz, Austria	1980 Peter Muller, Switzerland	1991 Franz Heinzer, Switzerland
1970 Karl Schranz, Austria	1981 Harti Weirather, Autria	1992 Franz Heinzer, Switzerland
Karl Cordin, Austria	1982 Steve Podborski, Canada	1993 Franz Heinzer, Switzerland
1971 Bernard Russi, Switzerland	Peter Muller, Switzerland	1994 Marc Girardelli, Luxembourg
1972 Bernard Russi, Switzerland	1983 Franz Klammer, Austria	1995 Luc Alphand, France
1973 Roland Collumbin, Switzerland	1984 Urs Raber, Switzerland	1996 Luc Alphand, France
1974 Roland Collumbin, Switzerland	1985 Helmut Hoflehner, Austria	1997 Luc Alphand, France
1975 Franz Klammer, Austria	1986 Peter Wirnsberger, Austria	1998 Andreas Schifferer, Austria
1976 Franz Klammer, Austria	1987 Pirmin Zurbriggen, Switzerland	1999 Lasse Kjus, Norway
1977 Franz Klammer, Austria	1988 Pirmin Zurbriggen, Switzerland	2000 Hermann Maier, Austria

Slalom

Multiple winners: Ingemar Stenmark (8); Alberto Tomba (4); Jean-Noel Augert and Marc Girardelli (3); Armin Bittner, Thomas Sykora and Gustavo Thoeni (2).

Year	Year	Year
1967 Jean-Claude Killy, France	1978 Ingemar Stenmark, Sweden	1990 Armin Bittner, West Germany
1968 Domeng Giovanoli, Switzerland	1979 Ingemar Stenmark, Sweden	1991 Marc Girardelli, Luxembourg
1969 Jean-Noel Augert, France	1980 Ingemar Stenmark, Sweden	1992 Alberto Tomba, Italy
1970 Patrick Russel, France	1981 Ingemar Stenmark, Sweden	1993 Tomas Fogdof, Sweden
Alain Penz, France	1982 Phil Mahre, USA	1994 Alberto Tomba, Italy
1971 Jean-Noel Augert, France	1983 Ingemar Stenmark, Sweden	1995 Alberto Tomba, Italy
1972 Jean-Noel Augert, France	1984 Marc Girardelli, Luxembourg	1996 Sebastien Amiez, France
1973 Gustavo Thoeni, Italy	1985 Marc Girardelli, Luxembourg	1997 Thomas Sykora, Austria
1974 Gustavo Thoeni, Italy	1986 Rok Petrovic, Yugoslavia	1998 Thomas Sykora, Austria
1975 Ingemar Stenmark, Sweden	1987 Bojan Krizaj, Yugoslavia	1999 Thomas Stangassinger, Austria
1976 Ingemar Stenmark, Sweden	1988 Alberto Tomba, Italy	2000 Kjetil Andre Aamodt, Norway
1977 Ingemar Stenmark, Sweden	1989 Armin Bittner, West Germany	

Giant Slalom

Multiple winners: Ingemar Stenmark (8); Alberto Tomba (4); Michael von Gruenigen and Pirmin Zurbriggen (3); Joel Gaspoz, Jean-Claude Killy, Phil Mahre, Hermann Maier and Gustavo Thoeni (2).

Year	Year	Year
1967 Jean-Claude Killy, France	1980 Ingemar Stenmark, Sweden	1991 Alberto Tomba, Italy
1968 Jean-Claude Killy, France	1981 Ingemar Stenmark, Sweden	1992 Alberto Tomba, Italy
1969 Karl Schranz, Austria	1982 Phil Mahre, USA	1993 Kjetil Andre Aamodt, Norway
1970 Gustavo Thoeni, Italy	1983 Phil Mahre, USA	1994 Christian Mayer, Austria
1971 Patrick Russel, France	1984 Ingemar Stenmark, Sweden	1995 Alberto Tomba, Italy
1972 Gustavo Thoeni, Italy	Pirmin Zurbriggen, Switzerland	1996 Michael von Gruenigen,
1973 Hans Hinterseer, Austria	1985 Marc Girardelli, Luxembourg	Switzerland
1974 Piero Gros, Italy	1986 Joel Gaspoz, Switzerland	1997 Michael von Gruenigen,
1975 Ingemar Stenmark, Sweden	1987 Joel Gaspoz, Switzerland	Switzerland
1976 Ingemar Stenmark, Sweden	Pirmin Zurbriggen, Switzerland	1998 Hermann Maier, Austria
1977 Heini Hemmi, Switzerland	1988 Alberto Tomba, Italy	1999 Michael von Gruenigen,
Ingemar Stenmark, Sweden	1989 Pirmin Zurbriggen, Switzerland	Switzerland
1978 Ingemar Stenmark, Sweden	1990 Ole-Cristian Furuseth, Norway	2000 Hermann Maier, Austria
1979 Ingemar Stenmark, Sweden	Gunther Mader, Austria	

Super G

Multiple winners: Pirmin Zurbriggen (4); Hermann Maier (3).

Year	Year	Year
1986 Markus Wasmeier,	1991 Franz Heinzer, Switzerland	1997 Luc Alphand, France
West Germany	1992 Paul Accola, Switzerland	1998 Hermann Maier, Austria
1987 Pirmin Zurbriggen, Switzerland	1993 Kjetil Andre Aamodt, Norway	1999 Hermann Maier, Austria
1988 Pirmin Zurbriggen, Switzerland	1994 Jan Einar Thorsen, Norway	2000 Hermann Maier, Austria
1989 Pirmin Zurbriggen, Switzerland	1995 Peter Runggaldier, Italy	
1990 Pirmin Zurbriggen, Switzerland	1996 Atle Skaardal, Norway	

Combined

Multiple winners: Marc Girardelli and Andreas Wenzel (4); Phil Mahre (3); Kjetil Andre Aamodt and Pirmin Zurbriggen (2).

Year	Year	Year
1979 Andreas Wenzel, Liechtenstein	1986 Markus Wasmeier, West Germany	1992 Paul Accola, Switzerland
1980 Andreas Wenzel, Liechtenstein	1987 Pirmin Zurbriggen, Switzerland	1993 Marc Girardelli, Luxembourg
1981 Phil Mahre, USA	1988 Hubert Strolz, Austria	1994 Kjetil Andre Aamodt, Norway
1982 Phil Mahre, USA	1989 Marc Girardelli, Luxembourg	1995 Marc Girardelli, Luxembourg
1983 Phil Mahre, USA	1990 Pirmin Zurbriggen, Switzerland	1996 Gunther Mader, Austria
1984 Andreas Wenzel, Liechtenstein	1991 Marc Girardelli, Luxembourg	1997-99 Not awarded
1985 Andreas Wenzel, Liechtenstein		2000 Kjetil Andre Aamodt, Norway

WOMEN
Downhill

Multiple winners: Annemarie Moser-Pröll (7), Michela Figini and Katja Seizinger (4); Renate Goetschl, Isabelle Mir, Marie-Therese Nadig, Picabo Street, Bridgitte Totschnig-Habersatter and Maria Walliser (2).

Year	Year	Year
1967 Marielle Goitschel, France	1978 Annemarie Moser-Pröll, Austria	1989 Michela Figini, Switzerland
1968 Isabelle Mir, France	1979 Annemarie Moser-Pröll, Austria	1990 Katrin Gutensohn-Knopf, Germany
Olga Pall, Austria	1980 Marie-Therese Nadig, Switzerland	1991 Chantal Bournissen, Switzerland
1969 Wiltrud Drexel, Austria	1981 Marie-Therese Nadig, Switzerland	1992 Katja Seizinger, Germany
1970 Isabelle Mir, France	1982 Marie-Cecile Gros-Gaudenier, France	1993 Katja Seizinger, Germany
1971 Annemarie Pröll, Austria	1983 Doris De Agostini, Switzerland	1994 Katja Seizinger, Germany
1972 Annemarie Pröll, Austria	1984 Maria Walliser, Switzerland	1995 Picabo Street, USA
1973 Annemarie Pröll, Austria	1985 Michela Figini, Switzerland	1996 Picabo Street, USA
1974 Annemarie Pröll, Austria	1986 Maria Walliser, Switzerland	1997 Renate Goetschl, Austria
1975 Annemarie Moser-Pröll, Austria	1987 Michela Figini, Switzerland	1998 Katja Seizinger, Germany
1976 Bridgitte Totschnig-Habersatter, Austria	1988 Michela Figini, Switzerland	1999 Renate Goetschl, Austria
1977 Bridgitte Totschnig-Habersatter, Austria		2000 Regina Haeusl, Germany

Slalom

Multiple winners: Vreni Schneider (6); Erika Hess (5); Marielle Goitschel, Britt Lafforgue, Lisa-Marie Morerod and Roswitha Steiner (2).

Year	Year	Year
1967 Marielle Goitschel, France	1978 Hanni Wenzel, Liechtenstein	1991 Petra Kronberger, Austria
1968 Marielle Goitschel, France	1979 Regina Sackl, Austria	1992 Vreni Schneider, Switzerland
1969 Gertrud Gabl, Austria	1980 Perrine Pelene, France	1993 Vreni Schneider, Switzerland
1970 Ingrid Lafforgue, France	1981 Erika Hess, Switzerland	1994 Vreni Schneider, Switzerland
1971 Britt Lafforgue, France	1982 Erika Hess, Switzerland	1995 Vreni Schneider, Switzerland
1972 Britt Lafforgue, France	1983 Erika Hess, Switzerland	1996 Elfi Eder, Austria
1973 Patricia Emonet, France	1984 Tamara McKinney, USA	1997 Pernilla Wiberg, Sweden
1974 Christa Zechmeister, West Germany	1985 Erika Hess, Switzerland	1998 Ylva Nowen, Sweden
1975 Lisa-Marie Morerod, Switzerland	1986 Roswitha Steiner, Austria / Erika Hess, Switzerland	1999 Sabine Egger, Austria
1976 Rosi Mittermaier, West Germany	1987 Corrine Schmidhauser, Switzerland	2000 Spela Pretnar, Slovenia
1977 Lisa-Marie Morerod, Switzerland	1988 Roswitha Steiner, Austria	
	1989 Vreni Schneider, Switzerland	
	1990 Vreni Schneider, Switzerland	

Giant Slalom

Multiple winners: Vreni Schneider (5); Lisa-Marie Morerod and Annemarie Moser-Pröll (3); Martina Ertl, Nancy Greene, Carole Merle, Anita Wachter and Hanni Wenzel (2).

Year	Year	Year
1967 Nancy Greene, Canada	1979 Christa Kinshofer, West Germany	1991 Vreni Schneider, Switzerland
1968 Nancy Greene, Canada	1980 Hanni Wenzel, Liechtenstein	1992 Carole Merle, France
1969 Marilyn Cochran, USA	1981 Marie-Therese Nadig, Switzerland	1993 Carole Merle, France
1970 Michele Jacot, France / Francoise Macchi, France	1982 Irene Epple, West Germany	1994 Anita Wachter, Austria
1971 Annemarie Pröll, Austria	1983 Tamara McKinney, USA	1995 Vreni Schneider, Switzerland
1972 Annemarie Pröll, Austria	1984 Erika Hess, Switzerland	1996 Martina Ertl, Germany
1973 Monika Kaserer, Austria	1985 Maria Keihl, West Germany / Michela Figini, Switzerland	1997 Deborah Compagnoni, Italy
1974 Hanni Wenzel, Liechtenstein	1986 Vreni Schneider, Switzerland	1998 Martina Ertl, Germany
1975 Annemarie Moser-Pröll, Austria	1987 Vreni Schneider, Switzerland / Maria Walliser, Switzerland	1999 Alexandra Meissnitzer, Austria
1976 Lisa-Marie Morerod, Switzerland	1988 Mateja Svet, Yugoslavia	2000 Michaela Dorfmeister, Austria
1977 Lisa-Marie Morerod, Switzerland	1989 Vreni Schneider, Switzerland	
1978 Lisa-Marie Morerod, Switzerland	1990 Anita Wachter, Austria	

Super G

Multiple winners: Katja Seizinger (5); Carole Merle (4).

Year		Year		Year	
1986	Maria Kiehl, West Germany	1991	Carole Merle, France	1996	Katja Seizinger, Germany
1987	Maria Walliser, Switzerland	1992	Carole Merle, France	1997	Hilde Gerg, Germany
1988	Michela Figini, Switzerland	1993	Katja Seizinger, Germany	1998	Katja Seizinger, Germany
1989	Carole Merle, France	1994	Katja Seizinger, Germany	1999	Alexandra Meissnitzer, Austria
1990	Carole Merle, France	1995	Katja Seizinger, Germany	2000	Renate Goetschl, Austria

Combined

Multiple winners: Brigitte Oertli (5); Anita Wachter and Hanni Wenzel (3); Sabine Ginther and Pernilla Wiberg (2).

Year		Year		Year	
1979	Annemarie Moser-Pröll, Austria	1985	Brigitte Oertli, Switzerland	1992	Sabine Ginther, Austria
	Hanni Wenzel, Liechtenstein	1986	Maria Walliser, Switzerland	1993	Anita Wachter, Austria
1980	Hanni Wenzel, Liechtenstein	1987	Brigitte Oertli, Switzerland	1994	Pernilla Wiberg, Sweden
1981	Maria-Therese Nadig,	1988	Brigitte Oertli, Switzerland	1995	Pernilla Wiberg, Sweden
	Switzerland	1989	Brigitte Oertli, Switzerland	1996	Anita Wachter, Austria
1982	Irene Epple, West Germany	1989	Brigitte Oertli, Switzerland	1997-99	Not Awarded
1983	Hanni Wenzel, Liechtenstein	1990	Anita Wachter, Austria	2000	Renate Goetschl, Austria
1984	Erika Hess, Switzerland	1991	Sabine Ginther, Austria		

TOUR DE FRANCE

The world's premier cycling event, the Tour de France is staged throughout the country (sometimes passing through neighboring countries) over four weeks. The 1946 Tour, however, the first after World War II, was only a five-day race.

Multiple winners: Jacques Anquetil, Bernard Hinault, Miguel Induráin and Eddy Merckx (5); Louison Bobet, Greg LeMond and Phillippe Thys (3); Lance Armstrong, Gino Bartali Ottavio Bottecchia, Fausto Coppi, Laurent Fignon, Nicholas Frantz, Firmin Lambot, André Leducq, Sylvere Maes, Antonin Magne, Lucien Petit-Breton and Bernard Thevenet (2).

Year		Year		Year	
1903	Maurice Garin, France	1937	Roger Lapebie, France	1973	Luis Ocana, Spain
1904	Henri Cornet, France	1938	Gino Bartali, Italy	1974	Eddy Merckx, Belgium
1905	Louis Trousselier, France	1939	Sylvere Maes, Belgium	1975	Bernard Thevenet, France
1906	René Pottier, France			1976	Lucien van Impe, Belgium
1907	Lucien Petit-Breton, France	1940-45	Not held	1977	Bernard Thevenet, France
1908	Lucien Petit-Breton, France	1946	Jean Lazarides, France	1978	Bernard Hinault, France
1909	Francois Faber, Luxembourg	1947	Jean Robic, France	1979	Bernard Hinault, France
		1948	Gino Bartali, Italy		
1910	Octave Lapize, France	1949	Fausto Coppi, Italy	1980	Joop Zoetemelk, Holland
1911	Gustave Garrigou, France			1981	Bernard Hinault, France
1912	Odile Defraye, Belgium	1950	Ferdinand Kubler, Switzerland	1982	Bernard Hinault, France
1913	Philippe Thys, Belgium	1951	Hugo Koblet, Switzerland	1983	Laurent Fignon, France
1914	Philippe Thys, Belgium	1952	Fausto Coppi, Italy	1984	Laurent Fignon, France
1915-18	Not held	1953	Louison Bobet, France	1985	Bernard Hinault, France
1919	Firmin Lambot, Belgium	1954	Louison Bobet, France	1986	Greg LeMond, USA
		1955	Louison Bobet, France	1987	Stephen Roche, Ireland
1920	Philippe Thys, Belgium	1956	Roger Walkowiak, France	1988	Pedro Delgado, Spain
1921	Léon Scieur, Belgium	1957	Jacques Anquetil, France	1989	Greg LeMond, USA
1922	Firmin Lambot, Belgium	1958	Charly Gaul, Luxembourg		
1923	Henri Pelissier, France	1959	Federico Bahamontes, Spain	1990	Greg LeMond, USA
1924	Ottavio Bottecchia, Italy			1991	Miguel Induráin, Spain
1925	Ottavio Bottecchia, Italy	1960	Gastone Nencini, Italy	1992	Miguel Induráin, Spain
1926	Lucien Buysse, Belgium	1961	Jacques Anquetil, France	1993	Miguel Induráin, Spain
1927	Nicholas Frantz, Luxembourg	1962	Jacques Anquetil, France	1994	Miguel Induráin, Spain
1928	Nicholas Frantz, Luxembourg	1963	Jacques Anquetil, France	1995	Miguel Induráin, Spain
1929	Maurice Dewaele, Belgium	1964	Jacques Anquetil, France	1996	Bjarne Riis, Denmark
		1965	Felice Gimondi, Italy	1997	Jan Ullrich, Germany
1930	André Leducq, France	1966	Lucien Aimar, France	1998	Marco Pantani, Italy
1931	Antonin Magne, France	1967	Roger Pingeon, France	1999	Lance Armstrong, USA
1932	André Leducq, France	1968	Jan Janssen, Holland		
1933	Georges Speicher, France	1969	Eddy Merckx, Belgium	2000	Lance Armstrong, USA
1934	Antonin Magne, France				
1935	Romain Maes, Belgium	1970	Eddy Merckx, Belgium		
1936	Sylvere Maes, Belgium	1971	Eddy Merckx, Belgium		
		1972	Eddy Merckx, Belgium		

FIGURE SKATING

World Champions

Skaters who won World and Olympic championships in the same year are listed in **bold** type.

MEN

Multiple winners: Ulrich Salchow (10); Karl Schafer (7); Dick Button (5); Willy Bockl, Kurt Browning, Scott Hamilton and Hayes Jenkins (4); Emmerich Danzer, Gillis Grafstrom, Gustav Hugel, David Jenkins, Fritz Kachler, Ondrej Nepela, Elvis Stojko and Alexei Yagudin (3); Brian Boitano, Gilbert Fuchs, Jan Hoffmann, Felix Kaspar, Vladimir Kovalev and Tim Wood (2).

Year		Year		Year	
1896	Gilbert Fuchs, Germany	1934	Karl Schafer, Austria	1971	Ondrej Nepela, Czechoslovakia
1897	Gustav Hugel, Austria	1935	Karl Schafer, Austria	1972	**Ondrej Nepela**, Czechoslovakia
1898	Henning Grenander, Sweden	1936	**Karl Schafer**, Austria	1973	Ondrej Nepela, Czechoslovakia
1899	Gustav Hugel, Austria	1937	Felix Kaspar, Austria	1974	Jan Hoffmann, E. Germany
1900	Gustav Hugel, Austria	1938	Felix Kaspar, Austria	1975	Sergie Volkov, USSR
1901	Ulrich Salchow, Sweden	1939	Graham Sharp, Britain	1976	**John Curry**, Britain
1902	Ulrich Salchow, Sweden	1940-46	Not held	1977	Vladimir Kovalev, USSR
1903	Ulrich Salchow, Sweden	1947	Hans Gerschwiler, Switzerland	1978	Charles Tickner, USA
1904	Ulrich Salchow, Sweden	1948	**Dick Button**, USA	1979	Vladimir Kovalev, USSR
1905	Ulrich Salchow, Sweden	1949	Dick Button, USA	1980	Jan Hoffmann, E. Germany
1906	Gilbert Fuchs, Germany	1950	Dick Button, USA	1981	Scott Hamilton, USA
1907	Ulrich Salchow, Sweden	1951	Dick Button, USA	1982	Scott Hamilton, USA
1908	**Ulrich Salchow**, Sweden	1952	**Dick Button**, USA	1983	Scott Hamilton, USA
1909	Ulrich Salchow, Sweden	1953	Hayes Jenkins, USA	1984	**Scott Hamilton**, USA
1910	Ulrich Salchow, Sweden	1954	Hayes Jenkins, USA	1985	Alexander Fadeev, USSR
1911	Ulrich Salchow, Sweden	1955	Hayes Jenkins, USA	1986	Brian Boitano, USA
1912	Fritz Kachler, Austria	1956	**Hayes Jenkins**, USA	1987	Brian Orser, Canada
1913	Fritz Kachler, Austria	1957	David Jenkins, USA	1988	**Brian Boitano**, USA
1914	Gosta Sandhal, Sweden	1958	David Jenkins, USA	1989	Kurt Browning, Canada
1915-21	Not held	1959	David Jenkins, USA	1990	Kurt Browning, Canada
1922	Gillis Grafstrom, Sweden	1960	Alan Giletti, France	1991	Kurt Browning, Canada
1923	Fritz Kachler, Austria	1961	Not held	1992	**Viktor Petrenko**, CIS
1924	Gillis Grafstrom, Sweden	1962	Donald Jackson, Canada	1993	Kurt Browning, Canada
1925	Willy Bockl, Austria	1963	Donald McPherson, Canada	1994	Elvis Stojko, Canada
1926	Willy Bockl, Austria	1964	**Manfred Schnelldorfer**,	1995	Elvis Stojko, Canada
1927	Willy Bockl, Austria		W. Ger	1996	Todd Eldredge, USA
1928	Willy Bockl, Austria	1965	Alain Calmat, France	1997	Elvis Stojko, Canada
1929	Gillis Grafstrom, Sweden	1966	Emmerich Danzer, Austria	1998	Alexei Yagudin, Russia
1930	Karl Schafer, Austria	1967	Emmerich Danzer, Austria	1999	Alexei Yagudin, Russia
1931	Karl Schafer, Austria	1968	Emmerich Danzer, Austria	2000	Alexei Yagudin, Russia
1932	**Karl Schafer**, Austria	1969	Tim Wood, USA		
1933	Karl Schafer, Austria	1970	Tim Wood, USA		

WOMEN

Multiple winners: Sonja Henie (10); Carol Heiss and Herma Planck Szabo (5); Lily Kronberger and Katarina Witt (4); Sjoukje Dijkstra, Peggy Fleming, Meray Horvath and Michelle Kwan (3); Tenley Albright, Linda Fratianne, Anett Poetzsch, Beatrix Schuba, Barbara Ann Scott, Gabriele Seyfert, Megan Taylor, Alena Vrzanova and Kristi Yamaguchi (2).

Year		Year		Year	
1906	Madge Syers, Britain	1934	Sonja Henie, Norway	1962	Sjoukje Dijkstra, Holland
1907	Madge Syers, Britian	1935	Sonja Henie, Norway	1963	Sjoukje Dijkstra, Holland
1908	Lily Kronberger, Hungary	1936	**Sonja Henie**, Norway	1964	**Sjoukje Dijkstra**, Holland
1909	Lily Kronberger, Hungary	1937	Cecilia Colledge, Britain	1965	Petra Burka, Canada
1910	Lily Kronberger, Hungary	1938	Megan Taylor, Britain	1966	Peggy Fleming, USA
1911	Lily Kronberger, Hungary	1939	Megan Taylor, Britain	1967	Peggy Fleming, USA
1912	Meray Horvath, Hungary	1940-46	Not held	1968	**Peggy Fleming**, USA
1913	Meray Horvath, Hungary	1947	Barbara Ann Scott, Canada	1969	Gabriele Seyfert, E. Germany
1914	Meray Horvath, Hungary	1948	**Barbara Ann Scott**,	1970	Gabriele Seyfert, E. Germany
1915-21	Not held		Canada	1971	Beatrix Schuba, Austria
1922	Herma Planck-Szabo, Austria	1949	Alena Vrzanova, Czechoslovakia	1972	**Beatrix Schuba**, Austria
1923	Herma Planck-Szabo, Austria	1950	Alena Vrzanova, Czechoslovakia	1973	Karen Magnussen, Canada
1924	**Herma Planck-Szabo**,	1951	Jeannette Altwegg, Britain	1974	Christine Errath, E. Germany
	Austria	1952	Jacqueline Du Bief, France	1975	Dianne DeLeeuw, Holland
1925	Herma Planck-Szabo, Austria	1953	Tenley Albright, USA	1976	**Dorothy Hamill**, USA
1926	Herma Planck-Szabo, Austria	1954	Gundi Busch, W. Germany	1977	Linda Fratianne, USA
1927	Sonja Henie, Norway	1955	Tenley Albright, USA	1978	Anett Poetzsch, E. Germany
1928	**Sonja Henie**, Norway	1956	Carol Heiss, USA	1979	Linda Fratianne, USA
1929	Sonja Henie, Norway	1957	Carol Heiss, USA	1980	**Anett Poetzsch**, E. Germany
1930	Sonja Henie, Norway	1958	Carol Heiss, USA	1981	Denise Biellmann, Switzerland
1931	Sonja Henie, Norway	1959	Carol Heiss, USA	1982	Elaine Zayak, USA
1932	**Sonja Henie**, Norway	1960	**Carol Heiss**, USA	1983	Rosalyn Sumners, USA
1933	Sonja Henie, Norway	1961	Not held	1984	**Katarina Witt**, E. Germany

Year
1985 Katarina Witt, E. Germany
1986 Debi Thomas, USA
1987 Katarina Witt, E. Germany
1988 **Katarina Witt**, E. Germany
1989 Midori Ito, Japan
1990 Jill Trenary, USA

Year
1991 Kristi Yamaguchi, USA
1992 **Kristi Yamaguchi**, USA
1993 Oksana Baiul, Ukraine
1994 Yuka Sato, Japan
1995 Lu Chen, China
1996 Michelle Kwan, USA

Year
1997 Tara Lipinski, USA
1998 Michelle Kwan, USA
1999 Maria Butyrskaya, Russia

2000 Michelle Kwan, USA

PAIRS

Year
1908 Anna Hubler
& Heinrich Burger, GER
1909 Phyllis Johnson
& James H. Johnson, GBR

1910 Anna Hubler
& Heinrich Burger, GER
1911 Ludowika Eilers, GER
& Walter Jakobsson, FIN
1912 Phyllis Johnson
& James H. Johnson, GBR
1913 Helene Engelmann
& Karl Majstrik, GER
1914 Ludowika Jakobsson-Eilers
& Walter Jakobsson-Eilers, FIN
1915-21 Not held
1922 Helene Engelmann
& Alfred Berger, GER
1923 Ludowika Jakobsson-Eilers
& Walter Jakobsson-Eilers, FIN
1924 Helene Engelmann
& Alfred Berger, GER
1925 Herma Jaross-Szabo
& Ludwig Wrede, AUT
1926 Andree Joly
& Pierre Brunet, FRA
1927 Herma Jaross-Szabo
& Ludwig Wrede, AUT
1928 Andree Joly
& Pierre Brunet, FRA
1929 Lilly Scholz
& Otto Kaiser, AUT

1930 Andree Brunet-Joly
& Pierre Brunet-Joly, FRA
1931 Emilie Rotter
& Laszlo Szollas, HUN
1932 Andree Brunet-Joly
& Pierre Brunet-Joly, FRA
1933 Emilie Rotter
& Laszlo Szollas, HUN
1934 Emilie Rotter
& Laszlo Szollas, HUN
1935 Emilie Rotter
& Laszlo Szollas, HUN
1936 Maxi Herber
& Ernst Bajer, GER
1937 Maxi Herber
& Ernst Bajer, GER
1938 Maxi Herber
& Ernst Bajer, GER
1939 Maxi Herber
& Ernst Bajer, GER

1940-46 Not held
1947 Micheline Lannoy
& Pierre Baugniet, BEL

Year
1948 Micheline Lannoy
& Pierre Baugniet, BEL
1949 Andrea Kekessy
& Ede Kiraly, HUN

1950 Karol Kennedy
& Peter Kennedy, USA
1951 Ria Baran
& Paul Falk, W. Ger
1952 Ria Baran
& Paul Falk, W. Ger
1953 Jennifer Nicks
& John Nicks, GBR
1954 Frances Dafoe
& Norris Bowden, CAN
1955 Frances Dafoe
& Norris Bowden, CAN
1956 Sissy Schwarz
& Kurt Oppelt, AUT
1957 Barbara Wagner
& Robert Paul, CAN
1958 Barbara Wagner
& Robert Paul, CAN
1959 Barbara Wagner
& Robert Paul, CAN

1960 Barbara Wagner
& Robert Paul, CAN
1961 Not held
1962 Maria Jelinek
& Otto Jelinek, CAN
1963 Marika Kilius
& H.J. Baumler, W. Ger
1964 Marika Kilius
& H.J. Baumler, W. Ger
1965 Ljudmila Protopopov
& Oleg Protopopov, USSR
1966 Ljudmila Protopopov
& Oleg Protopopov, USSR
1967 Ljudmila Protopopov
& Oleg Protopopov, USSR
1968 Ljudmila Protopopov
& Oleg Protopopov, USSR
1969 Irina Rodnina
& Alexsei Ulanov, USSR

1970 Irina Rodnina
& Alexsei Ulanov, USSR
1971 Irina Rodnina
& Alexsei Ulanov, USSR
1972 Irina Rodnina
& Alexsei Ulanov, USSR
1973 Irina Rodnina
& Aleksandr Zaitsev, USSR
1974 Irina Rodnina
& Aleksandr Zaitsev, USSR

Year
1975 Irina Rodnina
& Aleksandr Zaitsev, USSR
1976 Irina Rodnina
& Aleksandr Zaitsev, USSR
1977 Irina Rodnina
& Aleksandr Zaitsev, USSR
1978 Irina Rodnina
& Aleksandr Zaitsev, USSR
1979 Tai Babilonia
& Randy Gardner, USA

1980 Maria Cherkasova
& Sergei Shakhrai, USSR
1981 Irina Vorobieva
& Igor Lisovsky, USSR
1982 Sabine Baess
& Tassilio Thierbach, E. Ger
1983 Elena Valova
& Oleg Vasiliev, USSR
1984 Barbara Underhill
& Paul Martini, CAN
1985 Elena Valova
& Oleg Vasiliev, USSR
1986 Ekaterina Gordeeva
& Sergei Grinkov, USSR
1987 Ekaterina Gordeeva
& Sergei Grinkov, USSR
1988 Elena Valova
& Oleg Vasiliev, USSR
1989 Ekaterina Gordeeva
& Sergei Grinkov, USSR

1990 Ekaterina Gordeeva
& Sergei Grinkov, USSR
1991 Natalia Mishkutienok
& Artur Dmitriev, USSR
1992 Natalia Mishkutienok
& Artur Dmitriev, USSR
1993 Isabelle Brasseur
& Lloyd Eisler, CAN
1994 Evgenia Shishkova
& Vadim Naumov, RUS
1995 Radka Kovarikova
& Rene Novotny, CZR
1996 Marina Eltsova
& Andrey Buskhov, RUS
1997 Mandy Wotzel
& Ingo Steuer, GER
1998 Jenni Meno
& Todd Sand, USA
1999 Elena Berrzhnaya
& Anton Sikharulidze, RUS

2000 Maria Petrova
& Alexei Tikhonov, RUS

DANCE

Year		Year		Year	
1950	Lois Waring & Michael McGean, USA	1968	Diane Towler & Bernard Ford, GBR	1985	Natalia Bestemianova & Andrei Bukin, USSR
1951	Jean Westwood & Lawrence Demmy, GBR	1969	Diane Towler & Bernard Ford, GBR	1986	Natalia Bestemianova & Andrei Bukin, USSR
1952	Jean Westwood & Lawrence Demmy, GBR	1970	Ljudmila Pakhomova & Aleksandr Gorshkov, USSR	1987	Natalia Bestemianova & Andrei Bukin, USSR
1953	Jean Westwood & Lawrence Demmy, GBR	1971	Ljudmila Pakhomova & Aleksandr Gorshkov, USSR	1988	Natalia Bestemianova & Andrei Bukin, USSR
1954	Jean Westwood & Lawrence Demmy, GBR	1972	Ljudmila Pakhomova & Aleksandr Gorshkov, USSR	1989	Marina Klimova & Sergei Ponomarenko, USSR
1955	Jean Westwood & Lawrence Demmy, GBR	1973	Ljudmila Pakhomova & Aleksandr Gorshkov, USSR	1990	Marina Klimova & Sergei Ponomarenko, USSR
1956	Pamela Wieght & Paul Thomas, GBR	1974	Ljudmila Pakhomova & Aleksandr Gorshkov, USSR	1991	Isabelle Duchesnay & Paul Duchesnay, FRA
1957	June Markham & Courtney Jones, GBR	1975	Irina Moiseeva & Andreij Minenkov, USSR	1992	Marina Klimova & Sergei Ponomarenko, USSR
1958	June Markham & Courtney Jones, GBR	1976	Ljudmila Pakhomova & Aleksandr Gorshkov, USSR	1993	Renee Roca & Gorsha Sur, USA
1959	Doreen D. Denny & Courtney Jones, GBR	1977	Irina Moiseeva & Andreij Minenkov, USSR	1994	Oksana Grishuk & Evgeny Platov, RUS
1960	Doreen D. Denny & Courtney Jones, GBR	1978	Natalia Linichuk & Gennadi Karponosov, USSR	1995	Oksana Grishuk & Evgeny Platov, RUS
1961	Not held	1979	Natalia Linichuk & Gennadi Karponosov, USSR	1996	Oksana Grishuk & Evgeny Platov, RUS
1962	Eva Romanova & Pavel Roman, CZE	1980	Krisztina Regoeczy & Andras Sallai, HUN	1997	Oksana Grishuk & Evgeny Platov, RUS
1963	Eva Romanova & Pavel Roman, CZE	1981	Jayne Torvill & Christopher Dean, GBR	1998	Anjelika Krylova & Oleg Ovsyannikov, RUS
1964	Eva Romanova & Pavel Roman, CZE	1982	Jayne Torvill & Christopher Dean, GBR	1999	Anjelika Krylova & Oleg Ovsyannikov, RUS
1965	Eva Romanova & Pavel Roman, CZE	1983	Jayne Torvill & Christopher Dean, GBR	2000	Marina Anissina & Gwendal Peizerat, FRA
1966	Diane Towler & Bernard Ford, GBR	1984	Jayne Torvill & Christopher Dean, GBR		
1967	Diane Towler & Bernard Ford, GBR				

U.S. Champions

Skaters who won U.S., World and Olympic championships in same year are in **bold** type.

MEN

Multiple winners: Dick Button and Roger Turner (7); Sherwin Badger, Todd Eldredge and Robin Lee (5); Brian Boitano, Scott Hamilton, David Jenkins, Hayes Jenkins and Charles Tickner (4); Gordon McKellen, Nathaniel Niles and Tim Wood (3); Scott Allen, Christopher Bowman, Scott Davis, Eugene Turner, Gary Visconti and Michael Weiss (2).

Year		Year		Year		Year	
1914	Norman Scott	1938	Robin Lee	1961	Bradley Lord	1983	Scott Hamilton
1915-17	Not held	1939	Robin Lee	1962	Monty Hoyt	1984	**Scott Hamilton**
1918	Nathaniel Niles	1940	Eugene Turner	1963	Thomas Litz	1985	Brian Boitano
1919	Not held	1941	Eugene Turner	1964	Scott Allen	1986	Brian Boitano
1920	Sherwin Badger	1942	Robert Specht	1965	Gary Visconti	1987	Brian Boitano
1921	Sherwin Badger	1943	Arthur Vaughn	1966	Scott Allen	1988	**Brian Boitano**
1922	Sherwin Badger	1944-45	Not held	1967	Gary Visconti	1989	Christopher Bowman
1923	Sherwin Badger	1946	Dick Button	1968	Tim Wood	1990	Todd Eldredge
1924	Sherwin Badger	1947	Dick Button	1969	Tim Wood	1991	Todd Eldredge
1925	Nathaniel Niles	1948	**Dick Button**	1970	Tim Wood	1992	Christopher Bowman
1926	Chris Christenson	1949	Dick Button	1971	John (Misha) Petkevich	1993	Scott Davis
1927	Nathaniel Niles	1950	Dick Button	1972	Ken Shelley	1994	Scott Davis
1928	Roger Turner	1951	Dick Button	1973	Gordon McKellen	1995	Todd Eldredge
1929	Roger Turner	1952	**Dick Button**	1974	Gordon McKellen	1996	Rudy Galindo
1930	Roger Turner	1953	Hayes Jenkins	1975	Gordon McKellen	1997	Todd Eldredge
1931	Roger Turner	1954	Hayes Jenkins	1976	Terry Kubicka	1998	Todd Eldredge
1932	Roger Turner	1955	Hayes Jenkins	1977	Charles Tickner	1999	Michael Weiss
1933	Roger Turner	1956	**Hayes Jenkins**	1978	Charles Tickner	2000	Michael Weiss
1934	Roger Turner	1957	David Jenkins	1979	Charles Tickner		
1935	Robin Lee	1958	David Jenkins	1980	Charles Tickner		
1936	Robin Lee	1959	David Jenkins	1981	Scott Hamilton		
1937	Robin Lee	1960	David Jenkins	1982	Scott Hamilton		

WOMEN

Multiple winners: Maribel Vinson (9); Theresa Weld Blanchard and Gretchen Merrill (6); Tenley Albright, Peggy Fleming, and Janet Lynn (5); Linda Fratianne, Carol Heiss and Michelle Kwan (4); Dorothy Hamill, Beatrix Loughran, Rosalyn Summers, Joan Tozzer and Jill Trenary (3); Yvonne Sherman and Debi Thomas (2).

Year		Year		Year		Year	
1914	Theresa Weld	1937	Maribel Vinson	1958	Carol Heiss	1979	Linda Fratianne
1915-17	Not held	1938	Joan Tozzer	1959	Carol Heiss	1980	Linda Fratianne
1918	Rosemary Beresford	1939	Joan Tozzer	1960	**Carol Heiss**	1981	Elaine Zayak
1919	Not held	1940	Joan Tozzer	1961	Laurence Owen	1982	Rosalyn Sumners
1920	Theresa Weld	1941	Jane Vaughn	1962	Barbara Pursley	1983	Rosalyn Sumners
1921	Theresa Blanchard	1942	Jane Sullivan	1963	Lorraine Hanlon	1984	Rosalyn Sumners
1922	Theresa Blanchard	1943	Gretchen Merrill	1964	Peggy Fleming	1985	Tiffany Chin
1923	Theresa Blanchard	1944	Gretchen Merrill	1965	Peggy Fleming	1986	Debi Thomas
1924	Theresa Blanchard	1945	Gretchen Merrill	1966	Peggy Fleming	1987	Jill Trenary
1925	Beatrix Loughran	1946	Gretchen Merrill	1967	Peggy Fleming	1988	Debi Thomas
1926	Beatrix Loughran	1947	Gretchen Merrill	1968	**Peggy Fleming**	1989	Jill Trenary
1927	Beatrix Loughran	1948	Gretchen Merrill	1969	Janet Lynn	1990	Jill Trenary
1928	Maribel Vinson	1949	Yvonne Sherman	1970	Janet Lynn	1991	Tonya Harding
1929	Maribel Vinson	1950	Yvonne Sherman	1971	Janet Lynn	1992	**Kristi Yamaguchi**
1930	Maribel Vinson	1951	Sonya Klopfer	1972	Janet Lynn	1993	Nancy Kerrigan
1931	Maribel Vinson	1952	Tenley Albright	1973	Janet Lynn	1994	vacated*
1932	Maribel Vinson	1953	Tenley Albright	1974	Dorothy Hamill	1995	Nicole Bobek
1933	Maribel Vinson	1954	Tenley Albright	1975	Dorothy Hamill	1996	Michelle Kwan
1934	Suzanne Davis	1955	Tenley Albright	1976	**Dorothy Hamill**	1997	Tara Lipinski
1935	Maribel Vinson	1956	Tenley Albright	1977	Linda Fratianne	1998	Michelle Kwan
1936	Maribel Vinson	1957	Carol Heiss	1978	Linda Fratianne	1999	Michelle Kwan
						2000	Michelle Kwan

* Tonya Harding was stripped of the 1994 women's title and banned from membership in the U.S. Figure Skating Assn. for life on June 30, 1994 for violating the USFSA Code of Ethics after she pleaded guilty to a charge of conspiracy to hinder the prosecution related to the Jan. 6, 1994 attack on Nancy Kerrigan.

PAIRS

Year		Year		Year	
1914	Jeanne Chevalier & Norman M. Scott	1937	Maribel Vinson & George E.B. Hill	1956	Carole Ann Ormaca & Robin Greiner
1915-17	Not held	1938	Joan Tozzer & M. Bernard Fox	1957	Nancy Rouillard Ludington & Ronald Ludington
1918	Theresa Weld & Nathaniel W. Niles	1939	Joan Tozzer & M. Bernard Fox	1958	Nancy Rouillard Ludington & Ronald Ludington
1919	Not held	1940	Joan Tozzer & M. Bernard Fox	1959	Nancy Rouillard Ludington & Ronald Ludington
1920	Theresa Weld & Nathaniel W. Niles	1941	Donna Atwood & Eugene Turner	1960	Nancy Rouillard Ludington & Ronald Ludington
1921	Theresa Weld Blanchard & Nathaniel W. Niles	1942	Doris Schubach & Walter Noffke	1961	Maribel Y. Owen & Dudley S. Richards
1922	Theresa Weld Blanchard & Nathaniel W. Niles	1943	Doris Schubach & Walter Noffke	1962	Dorothyann Nelson & Pieter Kollen
1923	Theresa Weld Blanchard & Nathaniel W. Niles	1944	Doris Schubach & Walter Noffke	1963	Judianne Fotheringill & Jerry J. Fotheringill
1924	Theresa Weld Blanchard & Nathaniel W. Niles	1945	Donna Jeanne Pospisil & Jean-Pierre Brunet	1964	Judianne Fotheringill & Jerry J. Fotheringill
1925	Theresa Weld Blanchard & Nathaniel W. Niles	1946	Donna Jeanne Pospisil & Jean-Pierre Brunet	1965	Vivian Joseph & Ronald Joseph
1926	Theresa Weld Blanchard & Nathaniel W. Niles	1947	Yvonne Claire Sherman & Robert J. Swenning	1966	Cynthia Kauffman & Ronald Kauffman
1927	Theresa Weld Blanchard & Nathaniel W. Niles	1948	Karol Kennedy & Peter Kennedy	1967	Cynthia Kauffman & Ronald Kauffman
1928	Maribel Vinson & Thornton L. Coolidge	1949	Karol Kennedy & Peter Kennedy	1968	Cynthia Kauffman & Ronald Kauffman
1929	Maribel Vinson & Thornton L. Coolidge	1950	Karol Kennedy & Peter Kennedy	1969	Cynthia Kauffman & Ronald Kauffman
1930	Beatrix Loughran & Sherwin C. Badger	1951	Karol Kennedy & Peter Kennedy	1970	Jo Jo Starbuck & Kenneth Shelley
1931	Beatrix Loughran & Sherwin C. Badger	1952	Karol Kennedy & Peter Kennedy	1971	Jo Jo Starbuck & Kenneth Shelley
1932	Beatrix Loughran & Sherwin C. Badger	1953	Carole Ann Ormaca & Robin Greiner	1972	Jo Jo Starbuck & Kenneth Shelley
1933	Maribel Vinson & George E.B. Hill	1954	Carole Ann Ormaca & Robin Greiner	1973	Melissa Militano & Mark Militano
1934	Grace E. Madden & James L. Madden	1955	Carole Ann Ormaca & Robin Greiner	1974	Melissa Militano & Johnny Johns
1935	Maribel Vinson & George E.B. Hill			1975	Melissa Militano & Johnny Johns
1936	Maribel Vinson & George E.B. Hill			1976	Tai Babilonia & Randy Gardner

Year		Year		Year	
1977	Tai Babilonia & Randy Gardner	1985	Jill Watson & Peter Oppegard	1993	Calla Urbanski & Rocky Marval
1978	Tai Babilonia & Randy Gardner	1986	Gillian Wachsman & Todd Waggoner	1994	Jenni Meno & Todd Sand
1979	Tai Babilonia & Randy Gardner	1987	Jill Watson & Peter Oppegard	1995	Jenni Meno & Todd Sand
1980	Tai Babilonia & Randy Gardner	1988	Jill Watson & Peter Oppegard	1996	Jenni Meno & Todd Sand
1981	Caitlin Carruthers & Peter Carruthers	1989	Kristi Yamaguchi & Rudy Galindo	1997	Kyoko Ina & Jason Dungjen
1982	Caitlin Carruthers & Peter Carruthers	1990	Kristi Yamaguchi & Rudy Galindo	1998	Kyoko Ina & Jason Dungjen
1983	Caitlin Carruthers & Peter Carruthers	1991	Natasha Kuchiki & Todd Sand	1999	Danielle Hartsell & Steve Hartsell
1984	Caitlin Carruthers & Peter Carruthers	1992	Calla Urbanski & Rocky Marval	2000	Kyoko Ina & John Zimmerman

RUGBY

World Cup

The inaugural Rugby World Cup was held in 1987. Like soccer's World Cup, it is held every four years. Sixteen national teams were assembled for the first three tournaments but beginning in 1999, 20 teams played for the William Webb Ellis Cup, named for the game's inventor. The Rugby World Cup is now billed as the world's third largest athletic event, behind the Olympics and the soccer World Cup. Australia and New Zealand will co-host the competition in 2003.

Year	Winner	Score	Runner up	Host Country
1987	New Zealand	29-9	France	Australia & New Zealand
1991	Australia	12-6	England	United Kingdom & France
1995	South Africa	15-12	New Zealand	South Africa
1999	Australia	35-12	France	Wales

Six Nations Tournament

The annual Six Nations rugby tournament, a.k.a. the International Championship, was first contested in 1882 as a match between England and Wales. England, Ireland, Scotland and Wales competed in the early years. France made it five nations by joining the competition in 1910 and played until 1931 when they were expelled because of the sad state of French rugby. France rejoined the tournament in 1947. The Five Nations became the Six Nations in 2000 with the addition of Italy. Each team plays each other once (two points are earned for a win and one for a tie) and the team with the most points is declared the winner. (*) indicates Grand Slam, meaning team won all of its games.

In the 2000 tournament, England won its first four matches against Ireland, France, Wales and Italy to clinch the title. They were then surprisingly upended by Scotland, 19-13, in the final match of the tournament, losing their bid for a Grand Slam. England wound up with eight points (4-1-0), followed by France, Ireland and Wales with six points (all 3-2-0), and Scotland and Italy with two points (1-4-0).

Multiple Winners: Wales and England (33); Scotland (21); France (19); Ireland (18).

Year		Year		Year		Year	
1882	England	1911	Wales*	1940-46	Not held—WW II	1973	Five way tie
1883	England	1912	England & Ireland	1947	Wales & England	1974	Ireland
1884	England	1913	England*	1948	Ireland*	1975	Wales
1885	Not completed	1914	England*	1949	Ireland	1976	Wales*
1886	England & Scotland	1915-19	Not held—WW I	1950	Wales*	1977	France*
1887	Scotland	1920	England, Scotland & Wales	1951	Ireland	1978	Wales*
1888	Not completed			1952	Wales*	1979	Wales
1889	Not completed	1921	England*	1953	England	1980	England*
1890	England & Scotland	1922	Wales	1954	England, France & Wales	1981	France*
1891	Scotland	1923	England*			1982	Ireland
1892	England	1924	England*	1955	France & Wales	1983	France & Ireland
1893	Wales	1925	Scotland*	1956	Wales	1984	Scotland*
1894	Ireland	1926	Scotland & Ireland	1957	England*	1985	Ireland
1895	Scotland	1927	Scotland & Ireland	1958	England	1986	France & Scotland
1896	Ireland	1928	England*	1959	France	1987	France*
1897	Not completed	1929	Scotland	1960	France & England	1988	Wales & France
1898	Not completed	1930	England	1961	France	1989	France
1899	Ireland	1931	Wales	1962	France	1990	Scotland*
1900	Wales	1932	England, Wales & Ireland	1963	England	1991	England*
1901	Scotland			1964	Scotland & Wales	1992	England*
1902	Wales	1933	Scotland	1965	Wales	1993	France
1903	Scotland	1934	England	1966	Wales	1994	Wales
1904	Scotland	1935	Ireland	1967	France	1995	England*
1905	Wales	1936	Wales	1968	France*	1996	England
1906	Ireland & Wales	1937	England	1969	Wales	1997	France*
1907	Scotland	1938	Scotland	1970	France & Wales	1998	France*
1908	Wales*	1939	England, Wales & Ireland	1971	Wales*	1999	Scotland
1909	Wales*			1972	Not completed	2000	England
1910	England						

Olympics

Australian sprinter **Cathy Free-man** *gets the show started in Sydney.*

Australian for Olympics

The first games of the new millennium harkened back to Olympics past with starring performances from familiar faces.

by

Robin Roberts

The 2000 Sydney Olympics were billed as "The Games of the New Millennium" but older athletes were the real stars. The three oldest members of the U.S. women's swim team: 33-year-old Dara Torres, 27-year-old Jenny Thompson and 27-year-old Amy Van Dyken, along with 25-year-old Ashley Tappin took gold in the 4x100 freestyle relay.

I was taken by how Torres, Thompson and Van Dyken, Olympic veterans with nothing to prove, poured their hearts into singing the national anthem. Perhaps they took these types of moments for granted before. But now as women with perspective they seemed to soak in every drop of their victory.

Robin Roberts is host of ABC's *Wide World of Sports* and has been with ESPN since 1990.

The same could be said of Teresa Edwards. In 1984 she began her Olympic career as the youngest member of the first U.S. women's basketball team to win gold. Now 16 years and five Olympic Games later Edwards says she has had enough. Yes, she was the oldest player on this year's squad but not a weak link by any means. Edwards was the team captain, the starting point guard, and a major contributor to Team USA's success. The most decorated Olympic basketball player ever, male or female, began and ended her Olympic career with a gold medal draped around her neck.

Michael Johnson was the toast of the Atlanta Games in 1996. We saw a quieter, gentler Johnson in Sydney. He seemed to enjoy the fact that he only had to concentrate on the 400. At the age of 33, Johnson proved he is still

While she fell short of her well-publicized goal of five gold medals, **Marion Jones** still became the first woman to win five track and field medals in a single games. She won gold in the 100, 200 and 4 x 400 and bronze in the long jump and 4 x 100 all while dealing with her husband's drug scandal.

the best. In his Olympic finale he was never really challenged in becoming the first man to win the 400 in consecutive Olympics.

Two athletes making their Olympic debuts seemed more "old school" than rookies.

Marion Jones arrived in Sydney as the one to watch. But just two days after capturing gold in the 100 meters, Jones found herself in a different sort of spotlight. Her husband, shot putter C.J. Hunter, tested positive for an illegal substance (the steroid nandrolone) and she was by his side to publicly support him. The next day she was back on the track and easily won her second gold, this time in the 200m. When Jones fouled on four of her six attempts in the finals and finished third in the long jump, thereby ending her quest for a historic five gold medals, she didn't make excuses. Later

when the 4 x 100 relay she anchored finished in third place, she didn't complain that the absence of the injured Gail Devers and Inger Miller weakened the team. Despite the intense media scrutiny, on and off the track, Mrs. Jones kept her composure. Can you dig it? I can!

Australia's hopes rested on the broad shoulders of a 17-year-old swimmer who did not disappoint. Ian Thorpe lived up to all the hype and more. His four gold and one silver proved he was a champion. The way he handled the aquatic-crazy Aussies also proved he had class. He didn't strut around the pool and make wild gestures in front of the home folks.

Apparently Thorpe and Jones learned from their elders and they gave us something to look forward to in the new millennium of Olympic Games. ∎

Romanian **Andreea Raducan** was on top of the world after she won gold in the individual all-around. The 4-foot-10 gymnast was knocked from her lofty perch when the IOC stripped her of the gold medal for testing positive for a banned substance...cold medicine.

Robin Roberts' Top Ten Memories of the 2000 Sydney Olympics

10. **Sydney, Australia**. For three spectacular weeks the city with the breath taking harbor views, the famous opera house, the stunning beaches and some of the kindest people you'll ever meet, captivated the world.

9. American diver **Laura Wilkinson winning the 10-meter platform** with a broken foot. She wore a protective boot that she would toss from the platform before she would dive. How gutsy is that?

8. Dad-of-the-Year **Alonzo Mourning, returning home** in the middle of the Olympic basketball tournament (nearly 10,000 miles each way) to Miami for the birth of his daughter, Myka Sydney. I hope 'Zo got to keep those frequent flyer miles.

7. **Australian women winning gold**, again, in field hockey in front of a raucous home crowd. It's just called hockey Down Under and the players are treated like rock stars.

6. **Venus and Serena Williams capturing** the doubles title in women's tennis. What's better than winning a gold medal? Winning a gold medal with your sister.

5. The **U.S. softball team** having their 112 international game-win streak snapped, then immediately losing three in a row and being left

Swimmer **Eric Moussambani** from Equatorial Guinea had an unimpressive time in the pool but inspired plenty of people.

Al Bello/Allsport

The Australian 4 x 100 swim team, with **Michael Klim** on lead air-guitar and **Ian Thorpe** on his left, celebrates their upset victory over the Americans for the gold medal.

with what would have been his fourth Olympic gold medal.

2. When Equatorial Guinea swimmer, **Eric Moussambani**, stood alone at the edge of the pool in a 100 meter heat he looked so small. But when he swam it was absolutely inspiring. I don't remember his time, it doesn't matter. All we need to remember is his determination.

1. The image that will stay with me for a lifetime is that of Australian sprinter **Cathy Freeman in the opening ceremony** holding the world's attention while she held high the flame that would ignite the 2000 Games. Freeman carried not just the hopes of a nation but of a people and ran the 400-meter final with the spirit of both in becoming the first Australian aborigine to win Olympic gold. ∎

for dead. And then coming back to successfully defend their gold medal.

4. The **sound of over 17,500 people** at the Sydney International Aquatic Centre screaming at the top of their lungs when Australia upset the U.S. in the men's 4 x 100 meter freestyle relay on the first night of competition.

3. U.S. Greco-Roman wrestler **Rulon Gardner upsetting** Russian Alexandre Kareline in the super heavyweight gold medal match. Kareline hadn't lost a match in 13 years! So sure he was going to win, IOC President Juan Antonio Samaranch was on hand to personally present the Russian

AP/Wide World Photos

American 17-year-old **Cheryl Hayworth** won a bronze medal in the Olympic debut of women's weightlifting.

AP/Wide World Photos

Wyoming farm boy **Rulon Gardner** beat the unbeatable when he bested Russia's Greco-Roman legend Alexandre Kareline, 1-0, in overtime of the 130 kg gold medal match. It was the first ever international loss of Kareline's glorious career and his first loss of any kind since the 1987 Soviet championships.

inside**the**numbers

POOL SHARKS

The United States usually dominates the pool at Olympic Games, in fact they have lost the swimming medals race just twice since 1948. This year the U.S. was expected to be pushed hard by the Australians. It wasn't as close as you might think, although the Aussies did edge the Americans when it came to setting world records.

Swimming	AUS	USA
Gold Medals	5	14
Total Medals	18	33
World Records Set	5	4

Note: There were 15 swimming world records set or tied at the Sydney Games.

GOLD RUSH

Marion Jones became the first woman to win five track and field medals at a single Olympics at the 2000 Summer Games in Sydney. But Dutch sprinter/hurdler Fanny Blankers-Koen still holds the record she set for most track and field *gold* medals won at a single Games when she took home four golds at the 1948 London Games. Jones won three gold (100m, 200m, 4x400m) and two bronze medals (long jump and 4x100m) in Sydney.

	Year	Golds
Fanny Blankers-Koen, NED	1948	4
Marion Jones, USA	2000	3
Florence Griffith Joyner, USA	1988	3
Valerie Brisco-Hooks, USA	1984	3
Wilma Rudolph, USA	1960	3
Betty Cuthbert, AUS	1956	3

Final Medal Standings

National Medal Standings are not recognized by the IOC. The unofficial point totals are based on three points for every gold medal, two for each silver and one for each bronze.

		G	S	B	Total	Points			G	S	B	Total	Points
1	**United States**	40	24	33	97	201	41	Azerbaijan	2	0	1	3	7
2	Russia	32	28	28	88	180		Belgium	0	2	3	5	7
3	China	28	16	15	59	131		South Africa	0	2	3	5	7
4	Australia	16	25	17	58	115		Uzbekistan	1	1	2	4	7
5	Germany	13	17	26	56	99	45	Argentina	0	2	2	4	6
6	France	13	14	11	38	78		Chinese Taipei	0	1	4	5	6
7	Italy	13	8	13	34	68		Georgia	0	0	6	6	6
8	Cuba	11	11	7	29	62		Latvia	1	1	1	3	6
9	Great Britain	11	10	7	28	60		Morocco	0	1	4	5	6
10	Netherlands	12	9	4	25	58		New Zealand	1	0	3	4	6
11	Romania	11	6	9	26	54		Nigeria	0	3	0	3	6
	South Korea	8	10	10	28	54		Slovenia	2	0	0	2	6
13	Hungary	8	6	3	17	39		Yugoslavia	1	1	1	3	6
	Ukraine	3	10	10	23	39	54	Bahamas	1	1	0	2	5
15	Japan	5	8	5	18	36		Estonia	1	0	2	3	5
16	Poland	6	5	3	14	31		North Korea	0	1	3	4	5
17	Bulgaria	5	6	2	13	29		Thailand	1	0	2	3	5
18	Greece	4	6	3	13	27	58	Croatia	1	0	1	2	4
19	Belarus	3	3	11	17	26	59	Cameroon	1	0	0	1	3
20	Sweden	4	5	3	12	25		Colombia	1	0	0	1	3
21	Canada	3	3	8	14	23		Moldova	0	1	1	2	3
22	Norway	4	3	3	10	21		Mozambique	1	0	0	1	3
23	Spain	3	3	5	11	20		Saudi Arabia	0	1	1	2	3
24	Brazil	0	6	6	12	18		Trinidad and Tobago	0	1	1	2	3
25	Ethiopia	4	1	3	8	17	65	Costa Rica	0	0	2	2	2
	Kazakhstan	3	4	0	7	17		Ireland	0	1	0	1	2
	Switzerland	1	6	2	9	17		Portugal	0	0	2	2	2
28	Czech Republic	2	3	3	8	15		Uruguay	0	1	0	1	2
29	Kenya	2	3	2	7	14		Vietnam	0	1	0	1	2
30	Denmark	2	3	1	6	13	70	Armenia	0	0	1	1	1
31	Indonesia	1	3	2	6	11		Barbados	0	0	1	1	1
	Jamaica	0	4	3	7	11		Chile	0	0	1	1	1
	Turkey	3	0	2	4	11		Iceland	0	0	1	1	1
34	Iran	3	0	1	4	10		India	0	0	1	1	1
	Mexico	1	2	3	6	10		Israel	0	0	1	1	1
	Slovakia	1	3	1	5	10		Kyrgyzstan	0	0	1	1	1
37	Finland	2	1	1	4	9		Kuwait	0	0	1	1	1
	Lithuania	2	0	3	5	9		Macedonia	0	0	1	1	1
39	Algeria	1	1	3	5	8		Qatar	0	0	1	1	1
	Austria	2	1	0	3	8		Sri Lanka	0	0	1	1	1
								TOTALS	**297**	**294**	**325**	**916**	**1804**

Leading Medal Winners

(*) indicates at least one medal earned as preliminary member of eventual medal-winning relay team. USA medalists in **bold** type.

Men

No		Sport	G-S-B	No		Sport	G-S-B
6	Alexei Nemov, RUS	Gymnastics	2-1-3	3	**Lenny Krayzelburg**, USA	Swimming	3-0-0
5	Ian Thorpe, AUS	Swimming	3-2-0	3	Florian Rousseau, FRA	Cycling	2-1-0
4	Michael Klim, AUS	Swimming	2-2-0	3	Massimiliano Rosolino, ITA	Swimming	1-1-1
4	**Gary Hall Jr.**, USA	Swimming	2-1-1	3	Matthew Welsh, AUS	Swimming	0-2-1
4	Pieter van den Hoogenband, NED	Swimming	2-0-2	2	Robert Bartko, GER	Cycling	2-0-0
4	Dmitri Sautin, RUS	Diving	1-1-2	2	Domenico Fioravanti, ITA	Swimming	2-0-0

No		Sport	G-S-B
2	**Maurice Greene**, USA	Track/Field	2-0-0
2*	Grant Hackett, AUS	Swimming	2-0-0
2	Michael Johnson, USA.	Track/Field	2-0-0
2	Robert Korzeniowski, POL	Track/Field	2-0-0
2*	Todd Pearson, AUS	Swimming	2-0-0
2*	**Angelo Taylor**, USA.	Track/Field	2-0-0
2	Li Xiaopeng, CHN	Gymnastics	2-0-0
2	**Anthony Ervin**, USA	Swimming	1-1-0
2	**Alvin Harrison**, USA	Track/Field	1-1-0
2	Andrew Hoy, AUS	Equestrian	1-1-0
2	Jens Lehmann, GER.	Cycling	1-1-0
2*	**Jason Lezak**, USA	Swimming	1-1-0
2	**Ed Moses**, USA	Swimming	1-1-0
2*	Adam Pine, AUS	Swimming	1-1-0
2	Jason Queally, GBR	Cycling	1-1-0
2	Liang Tian, CHN	Diving	1-1-0
2	Jan Ullrich, GER	Cycling	1-1-0
2*	**Neil Walker**, USA	Swimming	1-1-0
2	Wei Yang, CHN	Gymnastics	1-1-0

No		Sport	G-S-B
2	**David O'Connor**, USA	Equestrian	1-0-1
2*	**Josh Davis**, USA	Swimming	0-2-0
2	Mathieu Gourdain, FRA	Fencing	0-2-0
2	Jia Hu, CHN	Diving	0-2-0
2	Wiradech Kothny, GER	Fencing	0-2-0
2	Hugues Obry, FRA	Fencing	0-2-0
2	Igor Basinsky, BLR	Shooting	0-1-1
2	Oleksandr Beresh, UKR	Gymnastics	0-1-1
2	Ato Bolden, TRI	Track/Field	0-1-1
2	Alexey Bondarenko, RUS	Gymnastics	0-1-1
2	Geoff Huegill, AUS	Swimming	0-1-1
2	**Klete Keller**, USA	Swimming	0-1-1
2	Joo-Hyung Lee, S. Kor	Gymnastics	0-1-1
2	Gary Neiwand, AUS	Cycling	0-1-1
2	**Victor Wunderle**, USA	Archery	0-1-1
2	Jens Fiedler, GER		0-0-2
2	Gregory Haughton, JAM	Track/Field	0-0-2
2	Iordan Iovtchev, BUL	Gymnastics	0-0-2
2	Stev Theloke, GER	Swimming	0-0-2

AP/Wide World Photos
Marion Jones

AP/Wide World Photos
Alexei Nemov

AP/Wide World Photos
Inge de Bruijn

AP/Wide World Photos
Ian Thorpe

Women

No		Sport	G-S-B
5	**Marion Jones**, USA	Track/Field	3-0-2
5	**Dara Torres**, USA	Swimming	2-0-3
4	Inge de Bruijn, NED.	Swimming	3-1-0
4	Leontien Zijlaard, NED.	Cycling	3-1-0
4	**Jenny Thompson**, USA	Swimming	3-0-1
4	Susie O'Neill, AUS	Swimming	1-3-0
3	Yana Klochkova, UKR	Swimming	2-1-0
3	Elena Zamolodtchikova, RUS	Gymnastics	2-1-0
3	Simona Amanar, ROM	Gymnastics	2-0-1
3	Svetlana Khorkina, RUS	Gymnastics	1-2-0
3	Liu Xuan, CHN	Gymnastics	1-0-2
3	Therese Alshammer, SWE	Swimming	0-2-1
3	Ekaterina Lobazniouk, RUS	Gymnastics	0-2-1
3	Petria Thomas, AUS	Swimming	0-2-1
2	Felicia Ballanger, FRA	Cycling	2-0-0
2	**Brooke Bennett**, USA	Swimming	2-0-0
2	Olga Brusnikina, RUS	Sync-swimming	2-0-0
2	Maria Kisseleva, RUS	Sync-swimming	2-0-0
2	Diana Mocanu, ROM	Swimming	2-0-0
2	**Megan Quann**, USA	Swimming	2-0-0
2*	**Courtney Shealy**, USA	Swimming	2-0-0
2*	**Ashley Tappin**, USA	Swimming	2-0-0
2*	**Amy van Dyken**, USA	Swimming	2-0-0
2	Valentina Vezzali, ITA	Fencing	2-0-0
2	**Venus Williams**, USA	Tennis	2-0-0
2	Mi-Jin Yun, S. Kor	Archery	2-0-0
2	Pauline Davis-Thompson, BAH	Track/Field	1-1-0
2	Nam-Soon Kim, S. Kor	Archery	1-1-0
2	Na Li, CHN	Diving	1-1-0

No		Sport	G-S-B
2	**Diana Munz**, USA	Swimming	1-1-0
2	Maria Olaru, ROM	Gymnastics	1-1-0
2	Andreea Raducan, ROM	Gymnastics	1-1-0
2	Luna Tao, CHN	Shooting	1-1-0
2	Anky van Grunsven, NED	Equestrian	1-1-0
2	Isabell Werth, GER	Equestrian	1-1-0
2	Soo-Nyung Kim, S. Kor	Archery	1-0-1
2	Irina Privalova, RUS	Track/Field	1-0-1
2	Ulla Salzgeber, GER	Equestrian	1-0-1
2	Gabriela Szabo, ROM	Track/Field	1-0-1
2	Giovanna Trillini, ITA	Fencing	1-0-1
2	Gianna Buerki, SWI	Fencing	0-2-0
2	Lorraine Graham, JAM	Track/Field	0-2-0
2	Deon Hemmings, JAM	Track/Field	0-2-0
2	Leisel Jones, AUS	Swimming	0-2-0
2	Martina Moravcova, SVK	Swimming	0-2-0
2*	Giaan Rooney, AUS	Swimming	0-2-0
2	Miya Tachibana, JPN	Sync-swimming	0-2-0
2	Miho Takeda, JPN	Sync-swimming	0-2-0
2	Beatrice Caslaru, ROM	Swimming	0-1-1
2	Rita Koenig, GER	Fencing	0-1-1
2	Tanya Lawrence, JAM	Track/Field	0-1-1
2	Jie Ling, CHN	Gymnastics	0-1-1
2	Anne Montminy, CAN	Diving	0-1-1
2	Elena Prodounova, RUS	Gymnastics	0-1-1
2	Gete Wami, ETH	Track/Field	0-1-1
2	Claudia Poll, CRC	Swimming	0-0-2
2	Yang Yun, CHN	Gymnastics	0-0-2

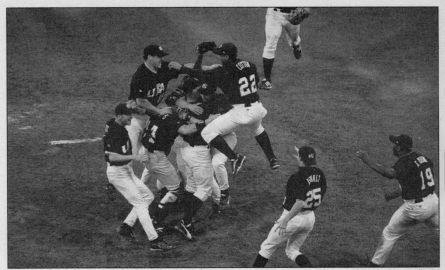

Adam Pretty/AUS /Allsport

United States pitcher **Ben Sheets** is mobbed by his teammates moments after recording the final out in a 4-0 upset of Cuba in the gold medal game.

Medal Sports

Medal winners in individual and team sports contested at Sydney, Australia from Sept. 16-Oct. 1, 2000. (**OR**) indicates a new Olympic record was set; (**WR**) indicates new world record.

ARCHERY

(70 meters)
MEN
Individual: 1. Simon Fairweather, AUS def. **2.** Victor Wunderle, USA (113-106); **3.** Wietse van Alten, NED def. Magnus Petersson, SWE (114-109).

Team: 1. South Korea (Jang Yong-Ho, Kim Chung-Tae and Oh Kyo-Moon) def. **2.** Italy (255-247); **3.** United States def. Russia (239-239; tiebreak 29-26).

WOMEN
Individual: 1. Yun Mi-Jin, S. Kor def. **2.** Kim Nam-Soon, S. Kor (107-106); **3.** Kim Soo-Nyung, S. Kor def. Choe Ok Sil N. Kor (103-101).

Team: 1. South Korea (Kim Nam-Soon, Kim Soo-Nyung and Yun Mi-Jin) def. **2.** Ukraine (251-239); **3.** Germany def. Turkey (240-234).

BADMINTON

MEN
Singles: 1. Ji Xinpeng, CHN def. **2.** Hendrawan, INA (15-4, 15-13); **3.** Xia Xuanze, CHN def. Peter Gade, DEN (15-13, 15-5).

Doubles: 1. Tony Gunawan & Candra Wijaya, INA def. **2.** Lee Dong-Soo & Yoo Yong-Sung, S. Kor (15-10, 9-15, 15-7); **3.** Ha Tae-Kwon & Kim Dong-Moon, S. Kor def. Choong Tan Fook & Lee Wan Wah, MAS (15-2, 15-8).

WOMEN
Singles: 1. Gong Zhichao, CHN def. **2.** Camilla Martin, DEN (13-10, 11-3); **3.** Ye Zhaoying, CHN def. Dai Yun, CHN (8-11, 11-2, 11-6).

Doubles: 1. Ge Fei & Gu Jun, CHN def. **2.** Huang Nan-yan & Yang Wei, CHN (15-5, 15-5); **3.** Gao Ling & Qin Yiyuan, CHN def. Chung Jae Hee & Ra Kyung-Min, S. Kor (15-10, 15-4).

MIXED
Doubles: 1. Zhang Jun & Gao Ling, CHN def. **2.** Tri Kush-aryanto & Minarti Timur, INA, (1-15, 15-13, 15-11); **3.** Simon Archer & Joanne Goode, GBR def. Michael Sogaard & Rikke Olsen, DEN (15-4, 12-15, 17-14).

BASEBALL

Round Robin Standings

Top four teams advance to medal round. Note that RF stands for Runs For and RA stands for Runs Against.

	Gm	W	L	Pct	RF	RA	Medal Round
*Cuba	7	6	1	.857	50	17	1-1
*United States	7	6	1	.857	42	14	2-0
*South Korea	7	4	3	.571	40	26	1-1
*Japan	7	4	3	.571	41	23	0-2
Netherlands	7	3	4	.429	19	29	—
Italy	7	2	5	.286	33	43	—
Australia	7	2	5	.286	30	41	—
South Africa	7	1	6	.143	11	73	—

Semifinals

Cuba 3 .... Japan 0
United States 3 .... South Korea 2

Bronze Medal

South Korea 3 .... Japan 1

Gold Medal

United States 4 .... Cuba 0

Baseball (Cont.)

Team USA Batting

(Min. 10 AB)	Pos	Avg	AB	R	H	HR	RBI
Pat Borders	C	.429	14	0	6	0	2
Doug Mientkiewicz	1B	.414	29	6	12	2	8
Brent Abernathy	2B	.385	39	4	15	0	4
Ernie Young	OF	.385	26	7	10	1	8
Mike Neill	OF	.219	32	9	7	3	5
Brad Wilkerson	OF	.216	37	7	8	1	1
Mike Kinkade	C	.207	29	4	6	0	3
John Cotton	OF	.185	27	3	5	0	6
Marcus Jensen	C	.167	18	2	3	1	5
Adam Everett	3B	.043	23	1	1	0	0
TOTALS		.262	294	49	77	8	44
OPPONENTS		.187	283	16	53	1	15

Team USA Pitching

(Min. 2.0 IP)	ERA	Gm	W-L	SV	IP	BB	SO
Ryan Franklin	0.00	4	3-0	0	8.1	3	8
Todd Williams	0.00	5	1-0	1	5.0	1	6
Chris George	0.00	3	0-0	0	3.2	1	3
Ben Sheets	0.41	3	1-0	0	22.0	1	11
Jon Rauch	0.82	2	1-0	0	11.0	0	21
Roy Oswalt	1.38	2	0-0	0	13.0	3	10
Kurt Ainsworth	1.54	2	2-0	0	11.2	2	6
Shane Heams	7.71	3	0-0	0	2.1	1	1
Rick Krivda	18.00	1	0-1	0	2.0	1	1
TOTALS	1.35	9	8-1	1	80.0	15	68
OPPONENTS	5.07	9	1-8	0	76.1	36	67

BASKETBALL

Round Robin Standings
Top four teams (*) advance to medal round.

MEN

Group A	Gm	W	L	Pts	For	Opp	Medal Round
*United States	5	5	0	10	101.0	71.8	3-0
*Italy	5	3	2	8	66.4	69.8	1-1
*Lithuania	5	3	2	8	74.4	67.8	2-1
*France	5	2	3	7	74.4	74.8	2-1
China	5	2	3	7	73.6	83.8	—
New Zealand	5	0	5	5	61.4	83.2	—

Group B	Gm	W	L	Pts	For	Opp	Medal Round
*Canada	5	4	1	9	86.6	74.6	1-1
*Yugoslavia	5	4	1	9	74.4	67.6	0-2
*Australia	5	3	2	8	81.6	81.4	1-2
*Russia	5	3	2	8	73.4	65.6	0-2
Spain	5	1	4	6	69.8	75.2	—
Angola	5	0	5	5	60.6	82.0	—

Quarterfinals
United States 85 .Russia 70
Lithuania 76 . . . . .Yugoslavia 63
France 68 . . . . .Canada 63
Australia 65 . . . . .Italy 62

Semifinals
United States 85 . . . . .Lithuania 83
France 76 . . . . .Australia 52

Bronze Medal
Lithuania 89 . . . . .Australia 71

Gold Medal
United States 85 .France 75

WOMEN

Group A	Gm	W	L	Pts	For	Opp	Medal Round
*Australia	5	5	0	10	78.8	52.8	2-1
*France	5	4	1	9	67.6	57.4	1-1
*Brazil	5	2	3	7	71.6	46.4	2-1
*Slovakia	5	2	3	7	58.8	58.4	1-1
Canada	5	2	3	7	56.6	63.4	—
Senegal	5	0	5	5	39.8	76.6	—

Group B	Gm	W	L	Pts	For	Opp	Medal Round
*United States	5	5	0	10	87.2	62.4	3-0
*Russia	5	3	2	8	79.6	65.0	0-2
*South Korea	5	3	2	8	76.4	71.4	1-2
*Poland	5	3	2	8	65.4	67.8	0-2
Cuba	5	1	4	6	63.6	71.6	—
New Zealand	5	0	5	5	53.0	87.0	—

Quarterfinals
Australia 76 . . . . .Poland 48
Brazil 68 . . . . .Russia 67
United States 58 . . . . .Slovakia 43
South Korea 68 .France 59

Semifinals
Australia 64 . . . . .Brazil 52
United States 78 . . . . .South Korea 65

Bronze Medal
Brazil 84 . . . . .South Korea 73

Gold Medal
United States 76 . . . . .Australia 54

Men's Team USA Scoring

	Gm	FG%	FT%	Min	Pts	Reb	Ast
Vince Carter	8	.506	.694	22.6	14.8	3.6	1.4
Kevin Garnett	8	.544	.632	22.1	10.8	9.1	2.1
Alonzo Mourning	6	.595	.850	22.8	10.2	4.2	1.3
Ray Allen	8	.538	1.00	15.9	9.8	1.9	1.3
Vin Baker	8	.639	.581	13.8	8.0	3.0	0.8
Allan Houston	7	.474	.800	16.0	8.0	1.9	1.0
Antonio McDyess	8	.675	.467	14.8	7.6	5.9	1.0
S. Abdur-Rahim	8	.548	.810	10.5	6.4	3.3	0.1
Steve Smith	8	.458	.793	15.4	6.1	2.4	1.4
Jason Kidd	8	.516	.800	20.0	6.0	5.3	4.4
Gary Payton	8	.349	.706	20.5	5.5	2.1	3.4
Tim Hardaway	8	.385	.600	13.4	5.5	1.4	1.5
TOTALS	8	.519	.722	320.0	95.0	42.6	19.1
OPPONENTS	8	.390	.682	320.0	73.4	25.0	13.3

Women's Team USA Scoring

	Gm	FG%	FT%	Min	Pts	Reb	Ast
Lisa Leslie	8	.490	.692	26.3	15.8	7.9	1.4
Sheryl Swoopes	8	.517	.692	29.0	13.4	4.6	3.0
Yolanda Griffith	8	.685	.750	21.0	11.5	8.8	0.4
Natalie Williams	8	.564	.680	15.1	7.6	5.9	1.0
Katie Smith	8	.513	.667	19.4	6.8	0.6	1.1
Teresa Edwards	8	.613	.800	22.5	6.1	1.9	3.4
Nikki McCray	8	.400	.800	18.4	5.1	0.9	1.1
R. Bolton-Holifield	8	.326	.500	14.8	5.0	2.0	1.8
DeLisha Milton	8	.500	.500	11.4	4.5	2.6	0.0
Dawn Staley	8	.474	1.000	17.5	4.0	1.3	3.6
Kara Wolters	6	.417	.000	6.3	1.7	2.0	0.0
C. Holdsclaw	8	.000	.000	0.0	0.0	0.0	0.0
TOTALS	8	.508	.706	320.0	81.0	37.6	16.8
OPPONENTS	8	.377	.788	320.0	59.3	22.9	9.8

BOXING

Two bronze medals are awarded in each weight class.

Light Flyweight (106 lbs)**: 1.** Brahim Asloum, FRA dec. **2.** Rafael Munoz Lozano, SPA (23-10); **3.** Kim Un Chol, N. Kor, and Maikro Romero, CUB.

Flyweight (112 lbs)**: 1.** Wijan Ponlid, THA dec. **2.** Bulat Jumadilov, KAZ (19-12); **3.** Jerome Thomas, FRA, and Volodymyr Sydorenko, UKR.

Bantamweight (119 lbs)**: 1.** Guillermo Rigondeaux, CUB dec. **2.** Raimkoul Malakhbekov, RUS (18-12); **3.** Serguey Daniltchenko, UKR, and Clarence Vinson, USA.

Featherweight (125 lbs)**: 1.** Bekzat Sattarkhanov, KAZ dec. **2.** Ricardo Juarez, USA (22-14); **3.** Tahar Amsamani, MOR, and Kamil Djamaloudinov, RUS.

Lightweight (132 lbs)**: 1.** Mario Kindelan, CUB dec. **2.** Andriy Kotelnyk, UKR (14-4); **3.** Alexandre Maletine, RUS, and Cristian Bejarano, MEX.

Light Welterweight (139 lbs)**: 1.** Mahamadkadyz Abdullaev, UZB dec. **2.** Ricardo Williams, USA (27-20); **3.** Diogenes Luna, CUB, and Mohamed Allalou, ALG.

Welterweight (147 lbs)**: 1.** Oleg Saitov, RUS dec. **2.** Sergey Dotsenko, UKR (24-16); **3.** Dorel Simion, ROM, and Vitalie Grusac, MDA.

Light Middleweight (156 lbs)**: 1.** Yermakhan Ibraimov, KAZ dec. **2.** Marin Simion, ROM (25-23); **3.** Pornchai Thongburan, THA, and Jermain Taylor, USA.

Middleweight (165 lbs)**: 1.** Jorge Gutierrez, CUB dec. **2.** Gaidarbek Gaidarbekov, RUS (17-15); **3.** Zsolt Erdei, HUN, and Vugar Alakparov, AZE.

Light Heavyweight (178 lbs)**: 1.** Alexander Lebziak, RUS dec. **2.** Rudolf Kraj, CZR (20-6); **3.** Andriy Fedchuck, UKR, and Sergey Mihaylov, UZB.

Heavyweight (201 lbs)**: 1.** Felix Savon, CUB dec. **2.** Sultanahmed Ibzagimov, RUS (21-13); **3.** Sebastian Koeber, GER, and Vladimer Tchanturia, GEO.

Super Heavyweight (over 201 lbs)**: 1.** Audley Harrison, GBR dec. **2.** Mukhtarkhan Dildabekov, KAZ (30-16); **3.** Rustam Saidov, UZB and Paulo Vidoz, ITA.

CANOE/KAYAK

MEN

Canoe Sprint 500m Singles: 1. Gyorgy Kolonics, HUN (2:24.81); **2.** Maxim Opalev, RUS (2:25.81); **3.** Andreas Dittmer, GER (2:27.59).

Canoe Sprint 1000m Singles: 1. Andreas Dittmer, GER (3:54.38); **2.** Ledys Frank Balceiro, CUB (3:56.07); **3.** Steve Giles, CAN (3:56.44).

Canoe Sprint 500m Doubles: 1. Ferenc Novak & Imre Pulai, HUN (1:51.28); **2.** Daniel Jedraszko & Pawel Baraszkiewicz, POL (1:51.54); **3.** Florin Popescu & Mitica Pricop, ROM (1:54.26).

Canoe Doubles 1000m Doubles: 1. Mitica Pricop & Florin Popescu, ROM (3:37.36); **2.** Ibrahin Rojas & Leobaldo Pereira, CUB (3:38.75); **3.** Stefan Utess & Lars Kober, GER (3:41.13).

Canoe Slalom Singles: 1. Tony Estanguet, FRA (231.87 pts); **2.** Michal Martikan, SVK (233.76); **3.** Juraj Mincik, SVK (234.22).

Canoe Slalom Doubles: 1. Pavol Hochschorner & Peter Hochschorner, SVK (237.74 pts); **2.** Krzysztof Kolomanski & Michal Staniszewski, POL (243.81); **3.** Marek Jiras & Tomas Mader, CZR (249.45).

Kayak Sprint 500m Singles: 1. Knut Holmann, NOR (1:57.85); **2.** Petar Merkov, BUL (1:58.39); **3.** Michael Kolganov, ISR (1:59.56).

Kayak Sprint 1000m Singles: 1. Knut Holmann, NOR (3:33.27); **2.** Petar Merkov, BUL (3:34.65); **3.** Tim Brabants, GBR (3:35.06).

Kayak Sprint 500m Doubles: 1. Zoltan Kammerer & Botond Storcz, HUN (1:47.06); **2.** Andrew Trim & Daniel Collins, AUS (1:47.90); **3.** Ronald Rauhe & Tim Wieskoetter, GER (1:48.77).

Kayak Sprint 1000m Doubles: 1. Antonio Rossi & Beniamino Bonomi, ITA (3:14.46); **2.** Markus Oscarsson & Henrik Nilsson, SWE (3:16.08); **3.** Krisztian Bartfai & Krisztian Vereb, HUN (3:16.36).

Kayak Sprint 1000m Fours: 1. Hungary (2:55.19); **2.** Germany (2:55.70); **3.** Poland (2:57.19).

Kayak Slalom Singles: 1. Thomas Schmidt, GER (217.25 pts); **2.** Paul Ratcliffe, GBR (223.71); **3.** Pierpaolo Ferrazzi, ITA (225.03).

WOMEN

Kayak Sprint 500m Singles: 1. Josefa Idem Guerrini, ITA (2:13.85); **2.** Caroline Brunet, CAN (2:14.65); **3.** Katrin Borchert, AUS (2:15.14).

Kayak Sprint 500m Doubles: 1. Birgit Fischer & Katrin Wagner, GER (1:57.00); **2.** Katalin Kovacs & Szilvia Szabo, HUN (1:58.58); **3.** Beata Sokolowska & Aneta Pastuszka, POL (1:58.78).

Kayak Sprint 500m Fours: 1. Germany (1:34.53); **2.** Hungary (1:34.95); **3.** Romania (1:37.01).

Kayak Slalom Singles: 1. Stepanka Hilgertova, CZR (247.04 pts); **2.** Brigitte Guibal, FRA (251.88); **3.** Anne-Lise Bardet, FRA (254.77).

CYCLING

MEN
Mountain Bike

Cross Country (30.7 miles)**: 1.** Miguel Martinez, FRA (2:09:03); **2.** Filip Meirhaeghe, BEL (2:10:05); **3.** Christoph Sauser, SWI (2:11:20).

Road

Individual Road Race (240 km)**: 1.** Jan Ullrich, GER (5:29:08); **2.** Alexandre Vinokourov, KAZ (5:29:17); **3.** Andreas Kloden, GER (5:29:20).

Individual Time Trial (46.8 km)**: 1.** Viacheslav Ekimov, RUS (57:40); **2.** Jan Ullrich, GER (57:48); **3.** Lance Armstrong, USA (58:14).

Track

Time Trial (1 km)**: 1.** Jason Queally, GBR (1:01.609) **OR**; **2.** Stefan Nimke, GER (1:02.487); **3.** Shane Kelly, AUS (1:02.818).

Individual Match Sprint (3 laps)**: 1.** Marty Nothstein, USA; **2.** Florian Rousseau, FRA **3.** Jens Fiedler, GER.

Individual Points Race (40 km)**: 1.** Juan Llaneras, SPA (14 pts); **2.** Milton Wynants, URU (18); **3.** Alexey Markov, RUS (16).

Individual Pursuit (4 km)**: 1.** Robert Bartko, GER (4:18.515) **OR**; **2.** Jens Lehmann, GER (4:23.824); **3.** Brad McGee, AUS (4:19.250).

Team Pursuit (4 km)**: 1.** Germany (3:59.710) **WR**; **2.** Ukraine (4:04.520); **3.** Great Britain (4:01.979).

Keiren (8 laps)**: 1.** Florian Rousseau, FRA; **2.** Gary Neiwand, AUS; **3.** Jens Fiedler, GER.

Madison (60 km)**: 1.** Brett Aitken & Scott McGrory, AUS (26 pts); **2.** Etienne de Wilde & Matthew Gilmore, BEL (22); **3.** Marco Villa & Silvio Martinello, ITA (15).

Olympic Sprint (3 laps)**: 1.** France (44.233); **2.** Great Britain (44.680); **3.** Australia (45.161).

WOMEN
Mountain Bike

Cross Country (22.2 miles)**: 1.** Paola Pezzo, ITA (1:49:24); **2.** Barbara Blatter, SWI (1:49:51); **3.** Margarita Fullana, SPA (1:49:57).

Road

Individual Road Race (126 km)**: 1.** Leontien Zijlaard, NED (3:06:31); **2.** Hanka Kupfernagel, GER (3:06:31); **3.** Diana Ziliute, LIT (3:06:31).

Individual Time Trial (31.2 km)**: 1.** Leontien Zijlaard, NED (42:00); **2.** Mari Holden, USA (42:37); **3.** Jeannie Longo-Ciprelli, FRA (42:52).

Track

Time Trial (500 m)**: 1.** Felicia Ballanger, FRA (34.140) **OR**; **2.** Michelle Ferris, AUS (34.696); **3.** Cuihua Jiang, CHN (34.768).

Individual Match Sprint (3 laps)**: 1.** Felicia Ballanger, FRA def. **2.** Oxana Grichina, RUS; **3.** Iryna Yanovych, UKR def. Michelle Ferris, AUS.

Individual Pursuit (3 km)**: 1.** Leontien Zijlaard, NED (3:33.360); **2.** Marion Clignet, FRA (3:38.751); **3.** Yvonne McGregor, GBR (3:38.850).

Individual Points Race (25 km)**: 1.** Antonella Bellutti, ITA (19 pts); **2.** Leontien Zijlaard, NED (16); **3.** Olga Slioussareva, RUS (15).

DIVING

MEN

3m Springboard: 1. Xiong Ni, CHN (708.72 pts); **2.** Fernando Platas, MEX (708.42); **3.** Dmitri Sautin, RUS (703.20).

10m Platform: 1. Tian Liang, CHN (724.53 pts); **2.** Hu Jia, CHN (713.55); **3.** Dmitri Sautin, RUS (679.26).

Synchronized 3m Springboard: 1. Xiao Hailiang & Xiong Ni, CHN (365.58 pts); **2.** Alexandre Dobroskok & Dmitri Sautin, RUS (329.97); **3.** Robert Newbery & Dan Pullar, AUS (322.86).

Synchronized 10m Platform: 1. Igor Loukachine & Dmitri Sautin, RUS (365.04 pts); **2.** Hu Jia & Tian Liang, CHN (358.74); **3.** Jan Hempel & Heiko Meyer, GER (338.88).

WOMEN

3m Springboard: 1. Fu Mingxia, CHN (609.42 pts); **2.** Guo Jingjing, CHN (597.81); **3.** Doerte Lindner, GER (574.35).

10m Platform: 1. Laura Wilkinson, USA (543.75 pts); **2.** Li Na, CHN (542.01); **3.** Anne Montminy, CAN (540.15).

Synchronized 3m Springboard: 1. Vera Ilyina & Yulia Pakhalina, RUS (332.64 pts); **2.** Fu Mingxia & Guo Jingjing, CHN (321.60); **3.** Ganna Sorokina & Olena Zhupina, UKR (290.34).

Synchronized 10m Platform: 1. Li Na & Sang Xue, CHN (345.12); **2.** Emilie Heymans & Anne Montminy, CAN (312.03); **3.** Rebecca Gilmore & Loudy Tourky, AUS (301.50).

EQUESTRIAN

Horses in parentheses.

Individual Dressage: 1. Anky van Grunsven (Bonfire) NED (239.18 pts); **2.** Isabell Werth (Gigolo) GER (234.19); **3.** Ulla Salzgeber (Rusty) GER (230.57).

Team Dressage: 1. Germany (5,632 pts); **2.** Netherlands (5,579); **3.** United States (5,166).

Individual Show Jumping: 1. Jeroen Dubbeldam (Sjiem) NED (4.00 pts); **2.** Albert Voorn (Lando) NED (4.00); **3.** Khaled Al Eid (Khashm Al Aan) KSA (4.00).

Team Show Jumping: 1. Germany (15.00 pts); **2.** Switzerland (16.00); **3.** Brazil (24.00).

Individual 3-Day Event: 1. David O'Connor (Custom Made) USA (34.00 pts); **2.** Andrew Hoy (Swizzle In) AUS (39.80); **3.** Mark Todd (Eyespy II) NZE (42.00).

Team 3-Day Event: 1. Australia (146.80); **2.** Great Britain (161.00); **3.** United States (175.80).

USA Team Dressage entry: Robert Dover, Susan Blinks, Guenter Seidel and Christine Traurig.

USA 3-Day entry: Nina Fout, David O'Connor and Karen O'Connor.

FENCING

MEN

Individual Épée: 1. Pavel Kolobkov, RUS def. **2.** Hugues Obry, FRA (15-12); **3.** Lee Sang-Ki, S. Kor. def. Marcel Fischer, SWI (15-14).

Team Epée: 1. Italy def. **2.** France (39-38); **3.** Cuba def. South Korea (45-31).

Individual Foil: 1. Kim Young-Ho, S. Kor def. **2.** Ralf Bissdorf, GER (15-14); **3.** Dmitri Chevtchenko, RUS def. Jean-Noel Ferrari, FRA (15-14).

Team Foil: 1. France def. **2.** China (45-44); **3.** Italy def. Poland (45-38).

Individual Sabre: 1. Mihai Claudiu Covaliu, ROM def. **2.** Mathieu Gourdain, FRA (15-12); **3.** Wiradech Kothny, GER def. Domonkos Ferjancsik, HUN (15-11).

Team Sabre: 1. Russia def. **2.** France (45-32); **3.** Germany def. Romania (45-27).

WOMEN

Individual Epée: 1. Timea Nagy, HUN def. **2.** Gianna Habluetzel-Buerki, SWI (15-11); **3.** Laura Flessel-Colovic, FRA def. Tatiana Logounova, RUS (15-6).

Team Epée: 1. Russia def. **2.** Switzerland (45-35); **3.** China def. Hungary (41-39).

Individual Foil: 1. Valentina Vezzali, ITA def. **2.** Rita Koenig, GER (15-5); **3.** Giovanna Trillini, ITA def. Laura Gabriela Carlescu Badea, ROM (15-9).

Team Foil: 1. Italy def. **2.** Poland (45-36); **3.** Germany def. United States (45-42).

FIELD HOCKEY

Round Robin Standings
Top two teams (*) advance to medal round.

MEN

Group A	Gm	W	L	T	Pts	GF	GA	Medal Round
*Pakistan	5	2	0	3	9	15	6	0-2
*Netherlands	5	2	1	2	8	11	8	2-0
Germany	5	2	1	2	8	7	6	—
Great Britain	5	1	2	2	5	8	16	—
Malaysia	5	0	1	4	4	5	6	—
Canada	5	0	2	3	3	7	11	—

Group B	Gm	W	L	T	Pts	GF	GA	Medal Round
*Australia	5	3	0	2	11	12	6	1-1
*South Korea	5	2	1	2	8	9	7	1-1
India	5	2	1	2	8	9	7	—
Argentina	5	1	2	2	5	13	13	—
Poland	5	1	2	2	5	12	14	—
Spain	5	0	3	2	2	7	15	—

Semifinals
South Korea 1 .... Pakistan 0
Netherlands 5 .... Australia 4

Bronze Medal
Australia 6 .... Pakistan 3

Gold Medal
Netherlands 8 .... South Korea 7

WOMEN
Medal round standings.

	Gm	W	L	T	Pts	GF	GA	Medal Round
*Australia	5	4	1	0	13	17	3	1-0
*Argentina	5	3	0	2	9	13	7	0-1
*Netherlands	5	2	0	3	6	8	14	1-0
*Spain	5	1	3	1	6	5	5	0-1
China	5	1	1	3	4	4	10	—
New Zealand	5	1	1	3	4	8	16	—

Bronze Medal
Netherlands 2 .... Spain 0

Gold Medal
Australia 3 .... Argentina 1

GYMNASTICS

MEN

All-Around

		Points
1	Alexei Nemov, RUS	58.474
2	Yang Wei, CHN	58.361
3	Oleksandr Beresh, UKR	58.212

Top USA: 6th—Blaine Wilson (57.936), 14th—Paul Hamm (57.049).

Floor Exercise

		Points
1	Igors Vihrovs, LAT	9.812
2	Alexei Nemov, RUS	9.800
3	Iordan Iovtchev, BUL	9.787

Top USA: 7th—Morgan Hamm (9.262).

Horizontal Bar

		Points
1	Alexei Nemov, RUS	9.787
2	Benjamin Varonian, FRA	9.787
3	Lee Joo-Hyung, S. Kor	9.775

Parallel Bars

		Points
1	Li Xiaopeng, CHN	9.825
2	Lee Joo-Hyung, S. Kor	9.812
3	Alexei Nemov, RUS	9.800

Pommel Horse

		Points
1	Marius Urzica, ROM	9.862
2	Eric Poujade, FRA	9.825
3	Alexei Nemov, RUS	9.800

Rings

		Points
1	Szilveszter Csollany, HUN	9.850
2	Dimosthenis Tampakos, GRE	9.762
3	Iordan Iovtchev, BUL	9.737

Vault

		Points
1	Gervasio Deferr, SPA	9.712
2	Alexey Bondarenko, RUS	9.587
3	Leszek Blanik, POL	9.475

Top USA: 6th—Blaine Wilson (9.362).

Team

		Points
1	China	231.919
2	Ukraine	230.306
3	Russia	230.019

USA entry: 5th—Morgan Hamm, Paul Hamm, Stephen McCain, John Roethlisberger, Sean Townsend and Blaine Wilson.

Men's Trampoline

		Points
1	Alexandre Moskalenko, RUS	41.70
2	Ji Wallace, AUS	39.30
3	Mathieu Turgeon, CAN	39.10

WOMEN

All-Around

		Points
1	Simona Amanar, ROM*	38.642
2	Maria Olaru, ROM	38.581
3	Liu Xuan, CHN	38.418

*Romania's Andreea Raducan was stripped of her all-around gold medal after testing positive for a banned substance. She was, however, allowed to keep her team gold and the silver medal she won in the vault.

Floor Exercise

		Points
1	Elena Zamolodtchikova, RUS	9.850
2	Svetlana Khorkina, RUS	9.812
3	Simona Amanar, ROM	9.712

Balance Beam

		Points
1	Liu Xuan, CHN	9.825
2	Ekaterina Lobazniouk, RUS	9.787
3	Elena Prodounova, RUS	9.775

Top USA: 8th—Elise Ray (9.387).

Uneven Bars

		Points
1	Svetlana Khorkina, RUS	9.862
2	Ling Jie, CHN	9.837
3	Yang Yun, CHN	9.787

Vault

		Points
1	Elena Zamolodtchikova, RUS	9.731
2	Andreea Raducan, ROM	9.693
3	Ekaterina Lobazniouk, RUS	9.674

Team

		Points
1	Romania	154.608
2	Russia	154.403
3	China	154.008

USA entry: 4th—Amy Chow, Jamie Dantzscher, Dominique Dawes, Kristin Maloney, Ray Elise and Tasha Schwikert-Warren.

Rhythmic All-Around

		Points
1	Yulia Barsukova, RUS	39.632
2	Yulia Raskina, BLR	39.548
3	Alina Kabaeva, RUS	39.466

Rhythmic Team

		Points
1	Russia	39.500
2	Belarus	39.500
3	Greece	39.283

Note: Russia won the tiebreak by posting a higher score in qualifying.

Women's Trampoline

		Points
1	Irina Karavaeva, RUS	38.90
2	Oxana Tsyhuleva, UKR	37.70
3	Karen Cockburn, CAN	37.40

HANDBALL

Top four teams (*) in each group advance to medal round.

MEN

Group A	Gm	W	L	T	Pts	GF	GA	Medal Round
*Russia	5	4	1	0	8	129	121	3-0
*Germany	5	3	1	1	7	128	113	2-1
*Yugoslavia	5	3	2	0	6	130	127	1-2
*Egypt	5	3	2	0	6	122	115	1-2
South Korea	5	1	3	1	3	128	131	—
Cuba	5	0	5	0	0	128	158	—

Group B	Gm	W	L	T	Pts	GF	GA	Medal Round
*Sweden	5	5	0	0	10	155	121	2-1
*France	5	3	1	1	7	120	104	1-2
*Spain	5	3	2	0	6	144	126	2-1
*Slovenia	5	2	2	1	5	137	127	0-3
Tunisia	5	1	4	0	2	111	117	—
Australia	5	0	5	0	0	106	178	—

Quarterfinals

Russia 33 .... Slovenia 22
Yugoslavia 26 .... France 21
Spain 27 .... Germany 26
Sweden 27 .... Egypt 23

Semifinals

Russia 29 .... Yugoslavia 26
Sweden 32 .... Spain 25

Bronze Medal

Spain 26 .... Yugoslavia 22

Gold Medal

Russia 28 .... Sweden 26

WOMEN

Group A	Gm	W	L	T	Pts	GF	GA	Medal Round
*South Korea	4	4	0	0	8	131	100	1-2
*Hungary	4	2	1	1	5	119	106	2-1
*France	4	2	2	0	4	90	93	1-2
*Romania	4	1	2	1	3	99	101	0-3
Angola	4	0	4	0	0	98	137	—

Group B	Gm	W	L	T	Pts	GF	GA	Medal Round
*Norway	4	4	0	0	8	101	72	2-1
*Denmark	4	3	1	0	6	124	83	3-0
*Austria	4	2	2	0	4	131	90	2-1
*Brazil	4	1	3	0	2	100	133	0-3
Australia	4	0	4	0	0	59	137	—

Quarterfinals

South Korea 35 .... Brazil 24
Hungary 28 .... Austria 27
Denmark 28 .... France 26
Norway 28 .... Romania 16

Semifinals

Hungary 28 .... Norway 23
Denmark 31 .... South Korea 29

Bronze Medal

Norway 22 .... South Korea 21

Gold Medal

Denmark 31 .... Hungary 27

JUDO

Two bronze medals are awarded in each weight class.

MEN

Extra Lightweight (132 lbs): **1.** Tadahiro Nomura, JPN def. **2.** Jung Bu-Kyung, S. Kor; **3.** Manolo Poulot, CUB and Aidyn Smagulov, KGZ.

Half-Lightweight (143 lbs): **1.** Huseyin Ozkan, TUR def. **2.** Larbi Benboudaoud, FRA; **3.** Girolamo Giovinazzo, ITA and Giorgi Vazagashvili, GEO.

Lightweight (157 lbs): **1.** Giuseppe Maddaloni, ITA def. **2.** Tiago Camilo, BRA; **3.** Anatoly Laryukov, BLR and Vsevolods Zelonijs, LAT.

Half-Middleweight (172 lbs): **1.** Makoto Takimoto, JPN def. **2.** Cho In-Chul, S. Kor; **3.** Aleksei Budolin, EST and Nuno Delgado, POR.

Middleweight (190 lbs): **1.** Mark Huizinga, NED def. **2.** Carlos Honorato, BRA; **3.** Frederic Demontfaucon, FRA and Ruslan Mashurenko, UKR.

Half-Heavyweight (209 lbs): **1.** Kosei Inoue, JPN def. **2.** Nicolas Gill, CAN; **3.** Iouri Stepkine, RUS and Stephane Traineau, FRA.

Heavyweight (over 209 lbs): **1.** David Douillet, FRA def. **2.** Shinichi Shinohara, JPN; **3.** Indrek Pertelson, EST and Tamerlan Tmenov, RUS.

WOMEN

Extra Lightweight (106 lbs): **1.** Ryoko Tamura, JPN def. **2.** Lioubov Brouletova, RUS; **3.** Anna-Maria Gradante, GER and Ann Simons, BEL.

Half-Lightweight (115 lbs): **1.** Legna Verdecia, CUB def. **2.** Noriko Narazaki, JPN; **3.** Kye Sun Hui, N. Kor and Liu Yuxiang, CHN.

Lightweight (123 lbs): **1.** Isabel Fernandez, SPA def. **2.** Driulys Gonzalez, CUB; **3.** Kie Kusakabe, JPN and Maria Pekli, AUS.

Half-Middleweight (134 lbs): **1.** Severine Vandenhende, FRA def. **2.** Li Shufang, CHN; **3.** Jung Sung-Sook, S Kor and Gella Vandecaveye, BEL.

Middleweight (146 lbs): **1.** Sibelis Veranes, CUB def. **2.** Kate Howey, GBR; **3.** Cho Min-Sun, S. Kor and Ylenia Scapin, ITA.

Half-Heavyweight (159 lbs): **1.** Tang Lin, CHN def. **2.** Celine Lebrun, FRA; **3.** Simona Marcela Richter, ROM and Emanuela Pierantozzi, ITA.

Heavyweight (over 159 lbs): **1.** Yuan Hua, CHN def. **2.** Daima Mayelis Beltran, CUB; **3.** Kim Seon-Young, S. Kor and Mayumi Yamashita, JPN.

MODERN PENTATHLON

Five events in one day—shooting (4.5mm air pistol), fencing (one-touch epée), swimming (200m freestyle), horse riding (450m stadium course with 12 jumps), and running (3,000m cross country).

Men: 1. Dmitry Svatkovsky, RUS (5,376 pts); **2.** Gabor Balogh, HUN (5,353); **3.** Pavel Dovgal, BLR (5,338).

USA entry: 14th—Chad Senior (5,256).

Women: 1. Stephanie Cook, GBR (5,318 pts); **2.** Emily deRiel, USA (5,310); **3.** Kate Allenby, GBR (5,273).

ROWING

(2000-meter course)

MEN

Single Sculls: 1. Rob Waddell, NZE (6:48.90); **2.** Xeno Mueller, SWI (6:50.55); **3.** Marcel Hacker, GER (6:50.83).

Lightweight Double Sculls: 1. Tomasz Kucharski & Robert Sycz, POL (6:21.75); **2.** Elia Luini & Leonardo Pettinari, ITA (6:23.47); **3.** Pascal Touron & Thibaud Chapelle, FRA (6:24.85).

Double Sculls: 1. Luka Spik & Iztok Cop, SLO (6:16.63); **2.** Olaf Tufte & Fredrik Raaen Bekken, NOR (6:17.98); **3.** Giovanni Calabrese & Nicola Sartori, ITA (6:20.49).

Quadruple Sculls: 1. Italy (5:45.56); **2.** Netherlands (5:47.91); **3.** Germany (5:48.64).

Coxless Pairs: 1. Michel Andrieux & Jean-Christophe Rolland, FRA (6:32.97); **2.** Ted Murphy & Sebastian Bea, USA (6:33.80); **3.** Matthew Long & James Tomkins, AUS (6:34.26).

Lightweight Coxless Fours: 1. France (6:01.68); **2.** Australia (6:02.09); **3.** Denmark (6:03.51).

Coxless Fours: 1. Great Britain (5:56.24); **2.** Italy (5:56.62); **3.** Australia (5:57.61).

Coxed Eight: 1. Great Britain (5:33.08); **2.** Australia (5:33.88); **3.** Croatia (5:34.85).

USA entry: 5th—Bryan Volpenhein, Robert Kaehler, Porter Collins, Thomas Welsh, David Simon, Christian Ahrens, Garrett Miller, Jeffrey Klepacki and Pete Cipollone. (5:39.16).

Women

Single Sculls: 1. Ekaterina Karsten, BLR (7:28.14); **2.** Rumyana Neykova, BUL (7:28.15); **3.** Katrin Rutschow-Stomporowski, GER (7:28.99).

Lightweight Double Sculls: 1. Constanta Burcica & Angela Alupei, ROM (7:02.64); **2.** Valerie Viehoff & Claudia Blasberg, GER (7:02.95); **3.** Christine Collins & Sarah Garner, USA (7:06.37).

Double Sculls: 1. Jana Thieme & Kathrin Boron, GER (6:55.44); **2.** Pieta van Dishoeck & Eeke van Nes, NED (7:00.36); **3.** Birute Sakickiene & Kristina Poplavskaja, LIT (7:01.71).

Quadruple Sculls: 1. Germany (6:19.58); **2.** Great Britain (6:21.64); **3.** Russia (6:21.65).

Coxless Pairs: 1. Georgeta Damian & Doina Ignat, ROM (7:11.00); **2.** Rachel Taylor & Kate Slatter, AUS (7:12.56); **3.** Melissa Ryan & Karen Kraft, USA (7:13.00).

Coxed Eights: 1. Romania (6:06.44); **2.** Netherlands (6:09.39); **3.** Canada (6:11.58).

USA entry: 6th—Katherine Maloney, Linda Miller, Amy Martin, Betsy McCagg, Torrey Folk, Amy Fuller, Sarah Jones, Lianne Nelson and Raj Shah.

SAILING

OPEN

Laser: 1. Ben Ainslie, GBR (42 pts); **2.** Robert Scheidt, BRA (44); **3.** Michael Blackburn, AUS (60).

Tornado: 1. Hans Peter Steinacher & Roman Hagara, AUT (16 pts); **2.** John Forbes & Darren Bundock, AUS (25); **3.** Roland Gaebler & Rene Schwall, GER (38).

Star: 1. Mark Reynolds & Magnus Liljedahl, USA (34 pts); **2.** Mark Covell & Ian Walker, GBR (35); **3.** Torben Grael & Marcelo Ferreira, BRA (39).

Soling: 1. Denmark (Jesper Bank, Henrik Blakskjaer, Thomas Jacobsen) def. **2.** Germany (Gunnar Bahr, Ingo Borkowski, Jochen Schuemann), 4-3; **3.** Norway (Paul Davis, Herman Horn Johannessen, Espen Stokkeland) def. Netherlands (Dirk de Ridder, Roy Heiner, Peter van Niekerk), 3-1.

49er: 1. Thomas Johanson & Jyrki Jarvi, FIN (55 pts); **2.** Ian Barker & Simon Hiscocks, GBR (60); **3.** Jonathan McKee & Charlie McKee, USA (64).

MEN

Finn: 1. Iain Percy, GBR (35 pts); **2.** Luca Devoti, ITA (46); **3.** Fredrik Loof, SWE (47).

Mistral: 1. Christoph Sieber, AUT (38 pts); **2.** Carlos Espinola, ARG (43); **3.** Aaron McIntosh, NZE (48).

470: 1. Mark Turnbull & Tom King, AUS (38 pts); **2.** Paul Foerster & Bob Merrick, USA (42); **3.** Javier Conte & Juan de la Fuente, ARG (57).

WOMEN

Europe: 1. Shirley Robertson, GBR (37 pts); **2.** Margriet Matthysse, NED (39); **3.** Serena Amato, ARG (51).

Mistral: 1. Alessandra Sensini, ITA (15 pts); **2.** Amelie Lux, GER (15); **3.** Barbara Kendall, NZE (19).

470: 1. Belinda Stowell & Jenny Armstrong, AUS (33 pts); **2.** J.J. Isler & Pease Glaser, USA (47); **3.** Olena Pakholchyk & Ruslana Taran, UKR (48).

SHOOTING

MEN

50m Free Pistol: 1. Tanyu Kiriakov, BUL (666.0 pts); **2.** Igor Basinsky, BLR (663.3); **3.** Martin Tenk, CZR (662.5).

50m Free Rifle/3 Positions: 1. Rajmond Debevec, SLO (1,275.1 pts) **OR**; **2.** Juha Hirvi, FIN (1,270.5); **3.** Harald Stenvaag, NOR (1,268.6).

50m Free Rifle/Prone: 1. Jonas Edman, SWE (701.3 pts); **2.** Torben Grimmel, DEN (700.4); **3.** Sergei Martynov, BLR (700.3).

25m Rapid Fire Pistol: 1. Serguei Alifirenko, RUS (687.6 pts); **2.** Michel Ansermet, SWI (686.1); **3.** Iulian Raicea, ROM (677.4).

10m Running Game Target: 1. Yang Ling, CHN (681.1 pts); **2.** Oleg Moldovan, MDA (681.0); **3.** Niu Zhiyuan, CHN (677.4).

10m Air Pistol: 1. Franck Dumoulin, FRA (688.9 pts) **OR**; **2.** Wang Yifu, CHN (686.9); **3.** Igor Basinsky, BLR (682.7).

10m Air Rifle: 1. Cai Yalin, CHN (969.4 pts); **2.** Artem Khadjibekov, RUS (695.1); **3.** Evgueni Aleinikov, RUS (693.8).

Trap: 1. Michael Diamond, AUS (147.0 pts); **2.** Ian Peel, GBR (142.0); **3.** Giovanni Pellielo, ITA (140.0).

Double Trap: 1. Richard Faulds, GBR (187.0 pts, won shootoff); **2.** Russell Mark, AUS (187.0); **3.** Fehaid Al Deehani, KUW (186.0).

Skeet: 1. Mykola Milchev, UKR (150.0 pts) **WR**; **2.** Petr Malek, CZR (148.0); **3.** James Graves, USA (147.0).

WOMEN

25m Sport Pistol: 1. Maria Grozdeva, BUL (690.3 pts) **OR**; **2.** Tao Luna, CHN (689.8); **3.** Lolita Evglevskaya, BLR (686.0).

10m Air Pistol: 1. Tao Luna, CHN (488.2 pts); **2.** Jasna Sekaric, YUG (486.5); **3.** Annemarie Forder, AUS (484.0).

50m Rifle/3 Positions: 1. Renata Mauer-Rozanska, POL (684.6 pts); **2.** Tatiana Goldobina, RUS (680.9); **3.** Maria Feklistova, RUS (679.9).

10m Air Rifle: 1. Nancy Johnson, USA (497.7 pts); **2.** Kang Cho-Hyun, S. Kor (497.5); **3.** Gao Jing, CHN (497.2).

Trap: 1. Daina Gudzineviciute, LIT (93.0 pts) **OR**; **2.** Delphine Racinet, FRA (92.0); **3.** Gao E, CHN (90.0).

Double Trap: 1. Pia Hansen, SWE (148.0 pts) **OR**; **2.** Deborah Gelisio, ITA (144.0); **3.** Kimberly Rhode, USA (139.0).

Skeet: 1. Zemfira Meftakhetdinova, AZE (98.0 pts) **OR**; **2.** Svetlana Demina, RUS (95.0); **3.** Diana Igaly, HUN (93.0, won shootoff).

SOCCER

Top two teams (*) advance to medal round.

MEN

Group A	Gm	W	L	T	Pts	GF	GA	Medal Round
*Italy	3	2	0	1	7	5	2	0-1
*Nigeria	3	1	0	2	5	7	6	0-1
Honduras	3	1	1	1	4	6	7	—
Australia	3	0	3	0	0	3	6	—

Group B	Gm	W	L	T	Pts	GF	GA	Medal Round
*Chile	3	2	1	0	6	7	3	2-1
*Spain	3	2	1	0	6	6	3	2-1
South Korea	3	2	1	0	6	2	3	—
Morocco	3	0	3	0	0	1	7	—

Group C	Gm	W	L	T	Pts	GF	GA	Medal Round
*United States	3	1	0	2	5	6	4	1-2
*Cameroon	3	1	0	2	5	5	4	3-0
Kuwait	3	1	2	0	3	6	8	—
Czech Republic	3	0	1	2	2	5	6	—

Group D	Gm	W	L	T	Pts	GF	GA	Medal Round
*Brazil	3	2	1	0	6	5	4	0-1
*Japan	3	2	1	0	6	4	3	0-1
South Africa	3	1	2	0	3	5	5	—
Slovakia	3	1	2	0	3	4	6	—

Quarterfinals

Spain 1 .... Italy 0
United States 2 .... 2 OT .... Japan 2
(U.S. won shootout 5-4)
Chile 4 .... Nigeria 1
Cameroon 2 .... 2 OT .... Brazil 1

Semifinals

Spain 3 .... United States 1
Cameroon 2 .... Chile 1

Bronze Medal

Chile 2 .... United States 0

Gold Medal

Cameroon 2 .... Spain 2
(Cameroon won shootout 7-5)

WOMEN

Group E	Gm	W	L	T	Pts	GF	GA	Medal Round
*Germany	3	3	0	0	9	6	1	1-1
*Brazil	3	2	1	0	6	5	3	0-1
Sweden	3	0	2	1	1	1	4	—
Australia	3	0	2	1	1	2	6	—

Group F	Gm	W	L	T	Pts	GF	GA	Medal Round
*United States	3	2	0	1	7	6	2	1-1
*Norway	3	2	1	0	6	5	4	2-0
China	3	1	1	1	4	5	4	—
Nigeria	3	0	3	0	0	3	9	—

Semifinals

Norway 1 .... Germany 0
United States 1 .... Brazil 0

Bronze Medal

Germany 2 .... Brazil 0

Gold Medal

Norway 3 .... OT .... United States 2

SOFTBALL

Top four teams (*) advance to semifinals.

	Gm	W	L	RF	RA	Medal Round
*Japan	7	7	0	18	7	1-1
*Australia	7	6	1	22	5	0-2
*China	7	5	2	26	4	0-1
*United States	7	4	3	19	6	3-0
Italy	7	2	5	3	27	—
New Zealand	7	2	5	12	22	—
Cuba	7	1	6	6	30	—
Canada	7	1	6	13	18	—

Semifinals

Japan 1 .... Australia 0
United States 3 .... China 0

Bronze Medal
(loser gets medal)

United States 1 .... Australia 0

Gold Medal

United States 2 .... Japan 1

SWIMMING

MEN

50-meter Freestyle

		Time
1	Anthony Ervin, USA	21.98
	Gary Hall Jr., USA	21.98
3	Pieter van den Hoogenband, NED	22.03

100-meter Freestyle

		Time
1	Pieter van den Hoogenband, NED	48.30
2	Aleksandr Popov, RUS	48.69
3	Gary Hall Jr., USA	48.73

Note: van den Hoogenband's time of 47.84 in a preliminary heat established a new world record.

200-meter Freestyle

		Time
1	Pieter van den Hoogenband, NED	1:45.35 WR
2	Ian Thorpe, AUS	1:45.83
3	Massimiliano Rosolino, ITA	1:46.65

400-meter Freestyle

		Time
1	Ian Thorpe, AUS	3:40.59 WR
2	Massimiliano Rosolino, ITA	3:43.40
3	Klete Keller, USA	3:47.00

1500-meter Freestyle

		Time
1	Grant Hackett, AUS	14:48.33
2	Kieren Perkins, AUS	14:53.59
3	Chris Thompson, USA	14:56.81

100-meter Backstroke

		Time
1	Lenny Krayzelburg, USA	53.72 OR
2	Matthew Welsh, AUS	54.07
3	Stev Theloke, GER	54.82

200-meter Backstroke

		Time
1	Lenny Krayzelburg, USA	1:56.76 OR
2	Aaron Peirsol, USA	1:57.35
3	Matthew Welsh, AUS	1:57.59

100-meter Breaststroke

		Time
1	Domenico Fioravanti, ITA	1:00.46 OR
2	Ed Moses, USA	1:00.73
3	Roman Sloudnov, RUS	1:00.91

200-meter Breaststroke

		Time
1	Domenico Fioravanti, ITA	2:10.87
2	Terence Parkin, RSA	2:12.50
3	Davide Rummolo, ITA	2:12.73

100-meter Butterfly

		Time
1	Lars Frolander, SWE	52.00
2	Michael Klim, AUS	52.18
3	Geoff Huegill, AUS	52.22

200-meter Butterfly

		Time	
1	Tom Malchow, USA	1:55.35	OR
2	Denys Sylant'yev, UKR	1:55.76	
3	Justin Norris, AUS	1:56.17	

200-meter Individual Medley

		Time	
1	Massimiliano Rosolino, ITA	1:58.98	OR
2	Tom Dolan, USA	1:59.77	
3	Tom Wilkens, USA	2:00.87	

400-meter Individual Medley

		Time	
1	Tom Dolan, USA	4:11.76	WR
2	Erik Vendt, USA	4:14.23	
3	Curtis Myden, CAN	4:15.33	

4x100-meter Freestyle Relay

		Time	
1	Australia	3:13.67	WR
2	United States	3:13.86	
3	Brazil	3:17.40	

AUS—Michael Klim, Chris Fydler, Ashley Callus, Ian Thorpe; **USA**—Anthony Ervin, Neil Walker, Jason Lezak, Gary Hall Jr.; **BRA**—Fernando Scherer, Gustavo Borges, Carlos Jayme, Edvaldo Silva Filho.

4x200-meter Freestyle Relay

		Time	
1	Australia	7:07.05	WR
2	United States	7:12.64	
3	Netherlands	7:12.70	

AUS—Ian Thorpe, Michael Klim, Todd Pearson, William Kirby; **USA**—Scott Goldblatt, Josh Davis, Jamie Rauch, Klete Keller; **NED**—Martijn Zuijdweg, Johan Kenkhuis, Marcel Wouda, Pieter van den Hoogenband.

4x100-meter Medley Relay

		Time	
1	United States	3:33.73	WR
2	Australia	3:35.27	
3	Germany	3:35.88	

USA—Lenny Krayzelburg, Ed Moses, Ian Crocker, Gary Hall Jr.; **AUS**—Matthew Welsh, Regan Harrison, Geoff Huegill, Michael Klim; **GER**—Stev Theloke, Jens Kruppa, Thomas Rupprath, Torsten Spanneberg.

WOMEN

50-meter Freestyle

		Time
1	Inge de Bruijn, NED	24.32
2	Theresa Alshammar, SWE	24.51
3	Dara Torres, USA	24.63

Note: de Bruijn's time of 24.13 in a preliminary heat established a new world record.

100-meter Freestyle

		Time
1	Inge de Bruijn, NED	53.83
2	Theresa Alshammar, SWE	54.33
3	Dara Torres, USA	54.43
	Jenny Thompson, USA	54.43

Note: de Bruijn's time of 53.77 in a preliminary heat established a new world record.

200-meter Freestyle

		Time
1	Susie O'Neill, AUS	1:58.24
2	Martina Moracova, SVK	1:58.32
3	Claudia Poll, CRC	1:58.81

400-meter Freestyle

		Time
1	Brooke Bennett, USA	4:05.80
2	Diana Munz, USA	4:07.07
3	Claudia Poll, CRC	4:07.83

800-meter Freestyle

		Time	
1	Brooke Bennett, USA	8:19.67	OR
2	Yana Klochkova, UKR	8:22.66	
3	Kaitlin Sandeno, USA	8:24.29	

100-meter Backstroke

		Time	
1	Diana Mocanu, ROM	1:00.21	OR
2	Mai Nakamura, JPN	1:00.55	
3	Nina Zhivanevskaya, SPA	1:00.89	

200-meter Backstroke

		Time
1	Diana Mocanu, ROM	2:08.16
2	Roxana Maracineanu, FRA	2:10.25
3	Miki Nakao, JPN	2:11.05

100-meter Breaststroke

		Time
1	Megan Quann, USA	1:07.05
2	Leisel Jones, AUS	1:07.49
3	Penny Heyns, RSA	1:07.55

200-meter Breaststroke

		Time
1	Agnes Kovacs, HUN	2:24.35
2	Kristy Kowal, USA	2:24.56
3	Amanda Beard, USA	2:25.35

Note: Kovacs' time of 2:24.03 in a preliminary heat established a new Olympic record.

100-meter Butterfly

		Time	
1	Inge de Bruijn, NED	56.61	OR
2	Martina Moravcova, SVK	57.97	
3	Dara Torres, USA	58.70	

200-meter Butterfly

		Time	
1	Misty Hyman, USA	2:05.88	OR
2	Susie O'Neill, AUS	2:06.58	
3	Petria Thomas, AUS	2:07.12	

200-meter Individual Medley

		Time	
1	Yana Klochkova, UKR	2:10.68	OR
2	Beatrice Caslaru, ROM	2:12.57	
3	Cristina Teuscher, USA	2:13.32	

400-meter Individual Medley

		Time	
1	Yana Klochkova, UKR	4:33.59	WR
2	Yasuko Tajima, JPN	4:35.96	
3	Beatrice Caslaru, ROM	4:37.18	

4x 100-meter Freestyle Relay

		Time
1	United States	3:36.61 **WR**
2	Netherlands	3:39.83
3	Sweden	3:40.30

USA—Amy van Dyken, Dara Torres, Courtney Shealy, Jenny Thompson; **NED**—Manon van Rooijen, Wilma van Rijn, Thamar Henneken, Inge de Bruijn; **SWE**—Louise Joehncke, Therese Alshammar, Johanna Sjoeberg, Anna-Karin Kammerling.

4x 200-meter Freestyle Relay

		Time
1	United States	7:57.80 **OR**
2	Australia	7:58.52
3	Germany	7:58.64

USA—Samantha Arsenault, Diana Munz, Lindsay Benko, Jenny Thompson; **AUS**—Susie O'Neill, Giaan Rooney, Kirsten Thomson, Petria Thomas; **GER**—Franziska van Almsick, Antje Buschschulte, Sara Harstick, Kerstin Kielgass.

4x 100-meter Medley Relay

		Time
1	United States	3:58.30 **WR**
2	Australia	4:01.59
3	Japan	4:04.16

USA—B.J. Bedford, Megan Quann, Jenny Thompson, Dara Torres; **AUS**—Dyana Calub, Leisel Jones, Petria Thomas, Susie O'Neill; **JPN**—Mai Nakamura, Masami Tanaka, Junko Onishi, Sumika Minamoto.

Synchronized Swimming

Duet: 1. Olga Brusnikina & Maria Kisseleva, RUS (99.580 pts); **2.** Miya Tachibana & Miho Takeda, JPN (98.650); **3.** Virginie Dedieu & Myriam Lignot, FRA (97.437).

Team: 1. Russia (99.146 pts); **2.** Japan (98.860); **3.** Canada (97.357).

USA entry—5th Carrie Barton, Tammy Cleland-McGregor, Bridget Finn, Anna Kozlova, Kristina Lum, Elicia Marshall, Heather Pease-Olson, Kim Wurzel.

TABLE TENNIS

MEN

Singles: 1. Kong Linghui, CHN def. **2.** Jan-Ove Waldner, SWE (21-16, 21-19, 17-21, 14-21, 21-13); **3.** Liu Guoliang, CHN def. Joergen Persson, SWE (21-18, 19-21, 21-14, 21-13).

Doubles: 1. Wang Ligin & Yan Sen, CHN def. **2.** Kong Linghui & Liu Guoliang, CHN (22-20, 17-21, 21-19, 21-18); **3.** Patrick Chila & Jean-Philippe Gatien, FRA def. Lee Chul-Seung & Yoo Seung-Min, S. Kor (22-20, 21-23, 21-19, 21-10).

WOMEN

Singles: 1. Wang Nan, CHN def. **2.** Li Ju, CHN (21-12, 12-21, 19-21, 21-17, 21-18); **3.** Chen Jing, TPE def. Jing Jun Hong, SIN (18-21, 21-14, 21-15, 21-10).

Doubles: 1. Li Ju & Wang Nan, CHN def. **2.** Sun Jin & Yang Ying, CHN (21-18, 21-11, 21-11); **3.** Kim Moo-Kyo & Ryu Ji-Hye, S. Kor def. Csilla Batorfi & Krisztina Toth, HUN (21-18, 21-19, 22-24, 19-21, 21-19).

TAEKWONDO

MEN

Flyweight (under 128 lbs): **1.** Michail Mouroutsos, GRE def. **2.** Gabriel Esparza, SPA (4-2); **3.** Huang Chih-Hsiung, TPE def. Gabriel Alberto Taraburelli, ARG (3-0).

Featherweight (under 148 lbs): **1.** Steven Lopez, USA def. **2.** Sin Joon-Sik, S. Kor (1-0); **3.** Hadi Saeibonehkohal, IRN def. Tuncay Caliskan, AUT (4-2).

Welterweight (under 176 lbs): **1.** Angel Valodia Matos Fuentes, CUB def. **2.** Faissal Ebnoutalib, GER (3-1); **3.** Victor Manuel Estrada Garibay, MEX def. Roman Livaja, SWE (2-1).

Heavyweight (176+ lbs): **1.** Kim Kyong-Hun, S. Kor def. **2.** Daniel Trenton, AUS (6-2); **3.** Pascal Gentil, FRA def. Khalid Al-Dosari, KSA (won by withdrawal).

WOMEN

Flyweight (under 108 lbs): **1.** Lauren Burns, AUS def. **2.** Urbia Melendez Rodriguez, CUB (4-2); **3.** Chi Shu-Ju, TPE def. Hanne Hoegh Poulsen, DEN (4-0).

Featherweight (under 123 lbs): **1**. Jung Jae-Eun, S. Kor def. **2.** Hieu Ngan Tran, VIE (2-0); **3.** Hamide Bikcin, TUR def. Virginia Lourens, NED (7-5).

Welterweight (under 146 lbs): **1.** Lee Sun-Hee, S. Kor def. **2.** Trude Gundersen, NOR (6-3); **3.** Yoriko Okamoto, JPN def. Sarah Stevenson, GBR (6-5).

Heavyweight (146+ lbs): **1.** Chen Zhong, CHN def. **2.** Natalia Ivanova, RUS (8-3); **3.** Dominique Bosshart, CAN def. Natasa Vezmar, CRO (11-8).

TENNIS

MEN

Singles: 1. Yevgeny Kafelnikov, RUS def. **2.** Tommy Haas, GER 7-6 (7-4), 3-6, 6-2, 4-6, 6-3; **3.** Arnaud Di Pasquale, FRA def. Roger Federer, SWI 7-6 (7-5), 6-7 (7-9), 6-3.

Doubles: 1. Sebastien Lareau & Daniel Nestor, CAN def. **2.** Todd Woodbridge & Mark Woodforde, AUS 5-7, 6-3, 6-4, 7-6 (7-2); **3.** Alex Corretja & Albert Costa, SPA def. David Adams & John-Laffinie De Jager, RSA 2-6, 6-4, 6-3.

WOMEN

Singles: 1. Venus Williams, USA def. **2.** Elena Dementieva, RUS 6-2, 6-4; **3.** Monica Seles, USA def. Jelena Dokic, AUS, 6-1, 6-4.

Doubles: 1. Serena Williams & Venus Williams, USA def. **2.** Kristie Boogert & Miriam Oremans, NED 6-1, 6-1; **3.** Els Callens & Dominique van Roost, BEL def. Olga Barabanshchikova & Natasha Zvereva, BLR 4-6, 6-4, 6-1.

TRIATHLON

1.5 km swim, 40 km bike ride, and 10 km run.

MEN

			Time
1	Simon Whitfield, CAN		1:48:24.02
2	Stephan Vuckovic, GER		1:48:37.58
3	Jan Rehula, CZR		1:48:46.64

WOMEN

			Time
1	Brigitte McMahon, SWI		2:00:40.52
2	Michellie Jones, AUS		2:00:42.55
3	Magali Messmer, SWI		2:01:08.83

TRACK & FIELD

MEN
100 Meters

		Time
1	Maurice Greene, USA	9.87
2	Ato Boldon, TRI	9.99
3	Obadele Thompson, BAR	10.04

200 meters

		Time
1	Konstantinos Kenteris, GRE	20.09
2	Darren Campbell, GBR	20.14
3	Ato Boldon, TRI	20.20

Top USA—7th Coby Miller (20.35); 8th John Capel Jr. (20.49).

400 meters

		Time
1	Michael Johnson, USA	.43.84
2	Alvin Harrison, USA	.44.70
3	Gregory Haughton, JAM	.44.70

Other Top USA—7th Antonio Pettigrew (45.42)

800 meters

		Time
1	Nils Schumann, GER	.1:45.08
2	Wilson Kipketer, DEN	.1:45.14
3	Aissa Djabir Said-Guerni, ALG	.1:45.16

1500 meters

		Time
1	Noah Ngeny, KEN	.3:32.07 **OR**
2	Hicham El Guerrouj, MOR	.3:32.32
3	Bernard Lagat, KEN	.3:32.44

5000 meters

		Time
1	Millon Wolde, ETH	.13:35.49
2	Ali Saidi-Sief, ALG	.13:36.20
3	Brahim Lahlafi, MOR	.13:36.47

10,000 meters

		Time
1	Haile Gebrselassie, ETH	.27:18.20
2	Paul Tergat, KEN	.27:18.29
3	Assefa Mezgebu, ETH	.27:19.75

Marathon

		Time
1	Gezahenge Abera, ETH	.2:10:11
2	Eric Wainaina, KEN	.2:10:31
3	Tesfaye Tola, ETH	.2:11:10

Top USA—69th Rod Dehaven (2:30:46).

4x100-meter Relay

		Time
1	United States	.37.61
2	Brazil	.37.90
3	Cuba	.38.04

USA—Jonathan Drummond, Bernard Williams III, Brian Lewis, Maurice Greene; **BRA**—Vincente Lima, Edson Ribeiro, Andre Silva, Claudinei da Silva; **CUB**—Jose Angel Cesar, Luis Alberto, Ivan Garcia, Freddy Mayola.

4x400-meter Relay

		Time
1	United States	.2:56.35
2	Nigeria	.2:58.68
3	Jamaica	.2:58.78

USA—Alvin Harrison, Antonio Pettigrew, Calvin Harrison, Michael Johnson; **NGR**—Clement Chukwu, Jude Monye, Sunday Bada, Enefiok Udo-Obong; **JAM**—Michael Blackwood, Gregory Haughton, Christopher Williams, Danny McFarlane.

110-meter Hurdles

		Time
1	Anier Garcia, CUB	.13.00
2	Terrence Trammell, USA	.13.16
3	Mark Crear, USA	.13.22

400-meter Hurdles

		Time
1	Angelo Taylor, USA	.47.50
2	Hadi Souan Somayli, KSA	.47.53
3	Llewellyn Herbert, RSA	.47.81

3000-meter Steeplechase

		Time
1	Reuben Kosgei, KEN	.8:21.43
2	Wilson Boit Kipketer, KEN	.8:21.77
3	Ali Ezzine, MOR	.8:22.15

20-kilometer Walk

		Time
1	Robert Korzeniowski, POL	.1:18:59 **OR**
2	Noe Hernandez, MEX	.1:19:03
3	Vladimir Andreyev, RUS	.1:19:27

Top USA—40th Timothy Seamen (1:30:32).

50-kilometer Walk

		Time
1	Robert Korzeniowski, POL	.3:42:22
2	Aigars Fadejevs, LAT	.3:43:40
3	Joel Sanchez, MEX	.3:44:36

Top USA—22nd Curt Clausen (3:58:59); 28th Philip Dunn (4:03.05); 31st Andrew Hermann (4:07:18).

High Jump

		Height
1	Sergey Kliugin, RUS	.7-8½
2	Javier Sotomayor, CUB	.7-7¼
3	Abderrahmane Hammad, ALG	.7-7¼

Pole Vault

		Height
1	Nick Hysong, USA	.19-4¼
2	Lawrence Johnson, USA	.19-4¼
3	Maksim Tarasov, RUS	.19-4¼

Note: Hysong won the tiebreak because he failed fewer heights earlier in the competition.

Long Jump

		Distance
1	Ivan Pedroso, CUB	.28-0¾
2	Jai Taurima, AUS	.27-10¼
3	Roman Schurenko, UKR	.27-3¼

Triple Jump

		Distance
1	Johathan Edwards, GBR	.58-1¼
2	Yoel Garcia, CUB	.57-3¾
3	Denis Kapustin, RUS	.57-3½

Top USA—7th Robert Howard (55-11¼).

Shot Put

		Distance
1	Arsi Harju, FIN	.69-10¼
2	Adam Nelson, USA	.69-7
3	John Godina, USA	.69-6¾

Other Top USA—4th Andrew Bloom (68-5¾).

Discus

		Distance
1	Virgilijus Alekna, LIT	.227-4
2	Lars Riedel, GER	.224-9
3	Frantz Kruger, RSA	.223-8

Hammer Throw

		Distance
1	Szymon Ziolkowski, POL	.262-6
2	Nicola Vizzoni, ITA	.261-3
3	Igor Astapkovich, BLR	.259-9

Javelin

		Distance
1	Jan Zelezny, CZR	.295-10 **OR**
2	Steve Backley, GBR	.294-9
3	Sergey Makarov, RUS	.290-11

Top USA—12th Breaux Greer (262-2).

Decathlon

		Points
1	Erki Nool, EST	.8641
2	Roman Sebrle, CZR	.8606
3	Chris Huffins, USA	.8595

WOMEN

100 meters

		Time
1	Marion Jones, USA	.10.75
2	Ekaterini Thanou, GRE	.11.12
3	Tanya Lawrence, JAM	.11.18

200 meters

		Time
1	Marion Jones, USA	.21.84
2	Pauline Davis-Thompson, BAH	.22.27
3	Susanthika Jayasinghe, SRI	.22.28

400 meters

		Time
1	Cathy Freeman, AUS	.49.11
2	Lorraine Graham, JAM	.49.58
3	Katharine Merry, GBR	.49.72

800 meters

		Time
1	Maria Mutola, MOZ	.1:56.15
2	Stephanie Graf, AUT	.1:56.64
3	Kelly Holmes, GBR	.1:56.80

Top USA—7th Hazel Clark (1:58.75).

1500 meters

		Time
1	Nouria Merah-Benida, ALG	.4:05.10
2	Violeta Szekely, ROM	.4:05.15
3	Gabriela Szabo, ROM	.4:05.27

Top USA—8th Marla Runyan (4:08.30).

5000 meters

		Time	
1	Gabriela Szabo, ROM	.14:40.79	OR
2	Sonia O'Sullivan, IRE	.14:41.02	
3	Gete Wami, ETH	.14:42.23	

10,000 meters

		Time	
1	Derartu Tulu, ETH	.30:17.49	OR
2	Gete Wami, ETH	.30:22.48	
3	Fernanda Ribeiro, POR	.30:22.88	

Marathon

		Time
1	Naoko Takahashi, JPN	.2:23:14
2	Lidia Simon, ROM	.2:23:22
3	Joyce Chepchumba, KEN	.2:24.45

Top USA— 19th Christine Clark (2:31:35).

4x100-meter Relay

		Time
1	Bahamas	.41.95
2	Jamaica	.42.13
3	United States	.42.20

BAH—Sevatheda Fynes, Chandra Sturrup, Pauline Davis-Thompson, Debbie Ferguson; **JAM**—Tanya Lawrence, Veronica Campbell, Beverly McDonald, Merlene Ottey; **USA**—Chryste Gaines, Torri Edwards, Nanceen Perry, Marion Jones.

4x400-meter Relay

		Time
1	United States	.3:22.62
2	Jamaica	.3:23.25
3	Russia	.3:23.46

USA—Jearl Miles-Clark, Monique Hennagan, Marion Jones, La Tasha Colander-Richardson; **JAM**—Sandie Richards, Catherine Scott-Pomales, Deon Hemmings, Lorraine Graham; **RUS**—Yulia Sotnikova, Svetlana Gontcharenko, Olga Kotlyarova, Irina Privalova.

100-meter Hurdles

		Time
1	Olga Shishigina, KAZ	.12.65
2	Glory Alozie, NGR	.12.68
3	Melissa Morrison, USA	.12.76

400-meter Hurdles

		Time
1	Irina Privalova, RUS	.53.02
2	Deon Hemmings, JAM	.53.45
3	Nouzha Bidouane, MOR	.53.57

20-kilometer Walk

		Time	
1	Wang Liping, CHN	.1:29:05	OR
2	Kjersti Plaetzer, NOR	.1:29:33	
3	Maria Vasco, SPA	.1:30:23	

Top USA— 17th Michelle Rohl (1:34:26).

High Jump

		Height
1	Yelena Yelesina, RUS	.6-7
2	Hestrie Cloete, RSA	.6-7
3	Kajsa Bergqvist, SWE	.6-6¼

Long Jump

		Distance
1	Heike Drechsler, GER	.22-11¼
2	Fiona May, ITA	.22-8½
3	Marion Jones, USA	.22-8½

Triple Jump

		Distance
1	Tereza Marinova, BUL	.49-10½
2	Tatyana Lebedeva, RUS	.49-2½
3	Olena Hovorova, UKR	.49-1

Pole Vault

		Height	
1	Stacy Dragila, USA	.15-1	OR
2	Tatiana Grigorieva, AUS	.14-11	
3	Vala Flosadottir, ICE	.14-9	

Shot Put

		Distance
1	Yanina Korolchik, BLR	.67-5½
2	Larisa Peleshenko, RUS	.65-4¼
3	Astrid Kumbernuss, GER	.64-4½

Discus

		Distance
1	Ellina Zvereva, BLR	.224-5
2	Anastasia Kelesidou, GRE	.215-7
3	Irina Yatchenko, BLR	.213-11

Top USA— 10th Seilala Sua (196-4).

Hammer Throw

		Distance	
1	Kamila Skolimowska, POL	.233-5¾	OR
2	Olga Kuzenkova, RUS	.228-11	
3	Kirsten Muenchow, GER	.227-3¾	

Top USA—7th Dawn Ellerbe (219-2); 8th Amy Palmer (217-0½).

Javelin

		Distance	
1	Trine Hattestad, NOR	.226-1	OR
2	Mirella Maniani-Tzelili, GRE	.221-6	
3	Osleidys Menendez, CUB	.217-1	

Heptathlon

		Points
1	Denise Lewis, GBR	.6584
2	Yelena Prokhorova, RUS	.6531
3	Natalya Sazanovich, BLR	.6527

Top USA—9th Dedee Nathan (6150).

VOLLEYBALL

Top four teams (*) advance to quarterfinals. Note that SF stands for Sets For and SA stands for Sets Against.

MEN

Group A	Gm	W	L	Pts	SF	SA	Medal Round
*Brazil	5	5	0	10	15	1	1-2
*Netherlands	5	4	1	9	12	5	2-1
*Cuba	5	3	2	8	9	7	0-2
*Australia	5	2	3	7	6	10	0-2
Spain	5	1	4	6	7	12	—
Egypt	5	0	5	5	1	15	—

Group B	Gm	W	L	Pts	SF	SA	Medal Round
*Italy	5	5	0	10	15	4	2-1
*Russia	5	4	1	9	13	7	2-1
*Yugoslavia	5	3	2	8	12	9	3-0
*Argentina	5	2	3	7	7	11	1-2
South Korea	5	1	4	6	8	14	—
United States	5	0	5	5	5	15	—

Quarterfinals

Argentina 3 . . . . .Brazil 1
    (17-25, 25-21, 25-19, 27-25)
Russia 3 . . . . .Cuba 2
    (21-25, 25-23, 25-19, 19-25, 15-13)
Yugoslavia 3 . . . . .Netherlands 2
    (25-21, 18-25, 25-18, 30-32, 17-15)
Italy 3 . . . . .Australia 1
    (25-14, 22-25, 25-19, 25-15)

Semifinals

Russia 3 . . . . .Argentina 1
    (27-25, 32-30, 21-25, 25-11)
Yugoslavia 3 . . . . .Italy 0
    (27-25, 34-32, 25-14)

Bronze Medal

Italy 3 . . . . .Argentina 0
    (25-16, 25-15, 25-18)

Gold Medal

Yugoslavia 3 . . . . .Russia 0
    (25-22, 25-22, 25-20)

WOMEN

Group A	Gm	W	L	Pts	SF	SA	Medal Round
*Brazil	5	5	0	10	15	1	2-1
*United States	5	4	1	9	13	4	1-2
*Croatia	5	3	2	8	9	9	1-2
*China	5	2	3	7	8	9	2-1
Australia	5	1	4	6	4	13	—
Kenya	5	0	5	5	2	15	—

Group B	Gm	W	L	Pts	SF	SA	Medal Round
*Russia	5	5	0	10	15	5	2-1
*Cuba	5	4	1	9	14	4	3-0
*South Korea	5	3	2	8	9	9	0-3
*Germany	5	2	3	7	8	10	1-2
Italy	5	1	4	6	7	12	—
Peru	5	0	5	5	2	15	—

Quarterfinals

Brazil 3 . . . . .Germany 0
    (25-22, 25-18, 25-17)
Cuba 3 . . . . .Croatia 0
    (25-18, 25-23, 25-21)
United States 3 .South Korea 2
    (26-24, 17-25, 25-23, 25-27, 16-14)
Russia 3 . . . . .China 0
    (27-25, 25-23, 27-25)

Semifinals

Cuba 3 . . . . .Brazil 2
    (27-29, 25-19, 21-25, 25-19, 15-9)
Russia 3 . . . . .United States 2
    (25-15, 23-25, 25-15, 26-28, 15-8)

Bronze Medal

Brazil 3 . . . . .United States 0
    (25-18, 25-22, 25-21)

Gold Medal

Cuba 3 . . . . .Russia 2
    (25-27, 32-34, 25-19, 25-18, 15-7)

Beach Volleyball

Men: 1. Dain Blanton & Eric Fonoimoana, USA def. **2.** Jose Marco Melo & Ricardo Santos, BRA (12-11, 12-9); **3.** Jorg Ahmann & Axel Hager, GER def. Miguel Maia & Joao Brenha, POR (12-9, 12-6).

    Women: 1. Natalie Cook & Kerri Pottharst, AUS def. **2.** Adriana Behar & Shelda Bede, BRA (12-11, 12-10); **3.** Adriana Samuel & Sandra Pires, BRA def. Yukiko Takahashi & Mika Saiki, JPN (12-4, 12-6).

WATER POLO

Round Robin Standings

Top four teams (*) in each group advance to quarterfinals. Note that GF stands for Goals For and GA stands for Goals Against.

MEN

Group A	Gm	W	L	T	Pts	GF	GA	Medal Round
*Russia	5	4	0	1	9	51	28	2-1
*Italy	5	4	0	1	9	43	32	2-1
*Spain	5	2	2	1	5	32	34	1-2
*Australia	5	1	2	2	4	38	36	0-3
Kazakhstan	5	1	3	1	3	41	46	—
Slovakia	5	0	5	0	0	30	59	—

Group B	Gm	W	L	T	Pts	GF	GA	Medal Round
*Yugoslavia	5	4	0	1	9	41	22	2-1
*Croatia	5	4	0	1	9	42	30	1-2
*Hungary	5	3	2	0	6	49	39	3-0
*United States	5	2	3	0	4	42	39	1-2
Netherlands	5	1	4	0	2	34	55	—
Greece	5	0	5	0	0	22	45	—

Quarterfinals

Russia 11 . . . . .United States 10
Spain 9 . . . . .Croatia 8
Hungary 8 . . . . .Italy 5
Yugoslavia 7 . . . . .Australia 3

Semifinal

Russia 8 . . . . .Spain 7
Hungary 8 . . . . .Yugoslavia 7

Bronze Medal

Yugoslavia 8 . . . . .Spain 3

Gold Medal

Hungary 13 . . . . .Russia 6

WOMEN

	Gm	W	L	T	Pts	GF	GA	Medal Round
*Australia	5	4	1	0	8	35	20	2-0
*United States	5	3	1	1	7	36	30	1-1
*Netherlands	5	3	2	0	6	27	26	0-2
*Russia	5	2	2	1	5	36	29	1-1
Canada	5	1	2	2	4	33	34	—
Kazakhstan	5	0	5	0	0	23	51	—

Semifinal

Australia 7 . . . . .Russia 6
United States 6 . . . . .Netherlands 5

Bronze Medal

Russia 4 . . . . .Netherlands 3

Gold Medal

Australia 4 . . . . .United States 3

WEIGHTLIFTING

Weights in the parenthesis are as follows: (snatch-clean & jerk—total weight), all converted to pounds. In the event of a tie, medals are awarded based on body weight from lightest to heaviest.

MEN

123 lbs (56 kg): **1.** Halil Mutlu, TUR (303-369—672 lbs); **2.** Wu Wenxiong, CHN* (275-358—634); **3.** Zhang Xiangxiang, CHN (275-358—634).

137 lbs (62 kg): **1.** Nikolay Pechalov, CRO (331-386—717 lbs); **2.** Leonidas Sabanis, GRE (324-375—699); **3.** Gennady Oleshchuk, BLR† (309-390—699).

152 lbs (69 kg): **1.** Galabin Boevski, BUL (357-430—787 lbs); **OR**; **2.** Georgi Markov, BUL (364-412—776); **3.** Sergei Lavrenov, BLR (346-401—750).

170 lbs (77 kg): **1.** Zhan Xugang, CHN (352-456—810 lbs); **2.** Viktor Mitrou, GRE (364-446—810); **3.** Arsen Melikyan, ARM (369-435—805).

187 lbs (85 kg): **1.** Pyrros Dimas, GRE (386-474—860 lbs); **2.** Marc Huster, GER (391-468—860); **3.** George Asanidze, GEO (397-463—860).

207 lbs (94 kg): **1.** Akakios Kakiasvilis, GRE (408-485—893 lbs); **2.** Szymon Kolecki, POL (401-490—893); **3.** Alexei Petrov, RUS (397-490—886).

231 lbs (105 kg): **1.** Hossein Tavakoli, IRN (419-518—937 lbs); **2.** Alan Tsagaev, BUL (412-518—931); **3.** Said S Asaad, QAT (419-507—926).

Over 231 lbs (105+ kg): **1.** Hossein Rezazadeh, IRN (467-573—1041 lbs) **WR**; **2.** Ronny Weller, GER (463-567—1030); **3.** Andrei Chemerkin, RUS# (446-573—1020).

*Ivan Ivanov, Bulgaria, was stripped of his silver medal for failing a drug test.
†Sevdalin Minchev Alelev, Bulgaria, was stripped of his bronze medal for failing a drug test.
#Ashot Danielyan, Armenia, was stripped of his bronze medal for failing a drug test.

WOMEN

106 lbs (48 kg): **1.** Tara Nott, USA% (181-225—408 lbs); **2.** Raema Lisa Rumbewas, INA (176-232—408); **3.** Sri Indriyani, INA (181-221—401).

117 lbs (53 kg): **1.** Yang Xia, CHN (221-276—496 lbs) **WR**; **2.** Li Feng-Ying, TPE (214-254—467); **3.** Winarni Binti Slamet, INA (198-247—445).

128 lbs (58 kg): **1.** Soraya Jimenez Mendivil, MEX (209-280—490 lbs); **2.** Ri Song Hui, N. Kor (214-269—485); **3.** Khassaraporn Suta, THA (203-258—463).

139 lbs (63 kg): **1.** Chen Xiaomin, CHN (247-287—534 lbs) **WR**; **2.** Valentina Popova, RUS (236-280—518); **3.** Ioanna Chatiioannou, GRE (214-276—490).

152 lbs (69 kg): **1.** Lin Weining, CHN (243-291—534 lbs); **2.** Erzsebet Markus, HUN (247-287—534); **3.** Karnam Malleswari, IND (243-287—529).

165 lbs (75 kg): **1.** Maria Isabel Urrutia, COL (243-298—540); **2.** Ruth Ogbeifo, NGR (232-309—540); **3.** Kuo Yi-Hang, TPE (236-302—540).

Over 165 lbs (75+ kg): **1.** Ding Meiyuan, CHN (298-364—661) **WR**; **2.** Agata Wrobel, POL (292-358—650); **3.** Cheryl Haworth, USA (276-320—595).

%Isabela Dragneva, Bulgaria, was stripped of her gold medal for failing a drug test.

WRESTLING

Freestyle

119 lbs (54 kg): **1.** Namig Abdullayev, AZE def. **2.** Samuel Henson, USA (4-3); **3.** Amiran Karntanov, GRE def. German Kontoev, BLR (5-4).

128 lbs (58 kg): **1.** Alireza Dabir, IRN def. **2.** Yevgen Buslovych, UKR (3-0); **3.** Terry Brands, USA def. Damir Zakhartdinov, UZB (3-2).

139 lbs (63 kg): **1.** Mourad Oumakhanov, RUS def. **2.** Serafim Barzakov, BUL (3-2); **3.** Jang Jae Sung, S. Kor def. Mohammad Talaei, IRN (12-2).

152 lbs (69 kg): **1.** Daniel Igali, CAN def. **2.** Arsen Gitinov, RUS (7-4); **3.** Lincoln McIlravy, USA def. Sergei Demchenko, BLR (3-1).

168 lbs (76 kg): **1.** Brandon Slay, USA* def. **2.** Moon Eui Jae, S. Kor (4-0); **3.** Adem Bereket, TUR (3-0).

187 lbs (85 kg): **1.** Adam Saitiev, RUS def. **2.** Yoel Romero, CUB def. **3.** Mogamed Ibragimov, YRM def. Amirreza Khadem Azghadi, IRN (4-1).

214 lbs (97 kg): **1.** Saghid Mourtasaliyev, RUS def. **2.** Islam Bairamukov, KAZ (6-0); **3.** Eldar Kurtanidze, GEO def. Marek Garmulewicz, POL (4-1).

287 lbs (130 kg): **1.** David Moussoulbes, RUS def. **2.** Artur Taymazov, UZB (5-2); **3.** Alexis Rodriguez, CUB def. Abbas Jadidi, IRN (1-0).

* Alexander Leipold, GER, was stripped of his gold medal for failing a drug test.

Greco-Roman

119 lbs (54 kg): **1.** Sim Kwon Ho, S. Kor def. **2.** Lazaro Rivas, CUB (8-0); **3.** Kang Yong Gyun, N. Kor def. Andriy Kalashnikov, UKR (7-0).

128 lbs (58 kg): **1.** Armen Nazarian, BUL def. **2.** Kim In-Sub, S. Kor (10-3); **3.** Sheng Zetian, CHN def. Rifat Yildiz, GER (2-0).

139 lbs (63 kg): **1.** Varteres Samourgachev, RUS def. **2.** Juan Luis Maren, CUB (3-0); **3.** Akaki Chachua, GEO def. Beat Motzer, SWI (6-2).

152 lbs (69 kg): **1.** Filiberto Azcuy, CUB def. **2.** Katsuhiko Nagata, JPN (11-0); **3.** Alexei Glouchkov, RUS def. Valeri Nikitin, EST (5-0).

168 lbs (76 kg): **1.** Mourat Kardanov, RUS def. **2.** Matt James Lindland, USA (3-0); **3.** Marko Yli-Hannuksela, FIN def. David Manukyan, UKR (4-2).

187 lbs (85 kg): **1.** Hamza Yerlikaya, TUR def. **2.** Sandor Istvan Bardosi, HUN (3-3, ref's decision); **3.** Mukhran Vakhtangadze, GEO def. Fritz Aanes, NOR (4-0).

214 lbs (97 kg): **1.** Mikael Ljungberg, SWE def. **2.** Davyd Saldadze, UKR (2-1); **3.** Garrett Lowney, USA def. Konstantinos Thanos, GRE (3-1).

287 lbs (130 kg): **1.** Rulon Gardner, USA def. **2.** Alexandre Kareline, RUS (1-0); **3.** Dmitry Debelka, BLR def. Juri Yevseychyc, ISR (1-0).

Event-by-Event

Gold medal winners from 1896-2000 in the following events: Baseball, Basketball, Boxing, Diving, Field Hockey, Gymnastics, Soccer, Swimming, Tennis and Track & Field.

BASEBALL

Multiple gold medals: Cuba (2).

Year		Year	
1992	**Cuba**, Taiwan, Japan	2000	**United States**, Cuba, South Korea
1996	**Cuba**, Japan, United States		

BASKETBALL
MEN

Multiple gold medals: USA (12), USSR (2).

Year		Year	
1936	**United States**, Canada, Mexico	1976	**United States**, Yugoslavia, Soviet Union
1948	**United States**, France, Brazil	1980	**Yugoslavia**, Italy, Soviet Union
1952	**United States**, Soviet Union, Uruguay	1984	**United States**, Spain, Yugoslavia
1956	**United States**, Soviet Union, Uruguay	1988	**Soviet Union**, Yugoslavia, United States
1960	**United States**, Soviet Union, Brazil	1992	**United States**, Croatia, Lithuania
1964	**United States**, Soviet Union, Brazil	1996	**United States**, Yugoslavia, Lithuania
1968	**United States**, Yugoslavia, Soviet Union	2000	**United States**, France, Lithuania
1972	**Soviet Union**, United States, Cuba		

U.S. Medal-Winning Men's Basketball Teams

1936 (gold medal): Sam Balter, Ralph Bishop, Joe Fortenberry, Tex Gibbons, Francis Johnson, Carl Knowles, Frank Lubin, Art Mollner, Don Piper, Jack Ragland, Carl Shy, Willard Schmidt, Duane Swanson and William Wheatley. Coach–Jim Needles; Assistant–Gene Johnson. Final: USA over Canada, 19-8.

1948 (gold medal): Cliff Barker, Don Barksdale, Ralph Beard, Louis Beck, Vince Boryla, Gordon Carpenter, Alex Groza, Wallace Jones, Bob Kurland, Ray Lumpp, R.C. Pitts, Jesse Renick, Robert (Jackie) Robinson and Ken Rollins. Coach–Omar Browning; Assistant–Adolph Rupp. Final: USA over France, 65-21.

1952 (gold medal): Ron Bontemps, Mark Freiberger, Wayne Glasgow, Charlie Hoag, Bill Hougland, John Keller, Dean Kelley, Bob Kenney, Bob Kurland, Bill Lienhard, Clyde Lovellette, Frank McCabe, Dan Pippin and Howie Williams. Coach–Warren Womble; Assistant–Forrest (Phog) Allen. Final: USA over USSR, 36-25.

1956 (gold medal): Dick Boushka, Carl Cain, Chuck Darling, Bill Evans, Gib Ford, Burdy Haldorson, Bill Hougland, Bob Jeangerard, K.C. Jones, Bill Russell, Ron Tomsic and Jim Walsh. Coach–Gerald Tucker; Assistant–Bruce Drake. Final: USA over USSR, 89-55.

1960 (gold medal): Jay Arnette, Walt Bellamy, Bob Boozer, Terry Dischinger, Jerry Lucas, Oscar Robertson, Adrian Smith, Burdy Haldorson, Darrall Imhoff, Allen Kelley, Lester Lane and Jerry West. Coach–Pete Newell; Assistant–Warren Womble. Final round: USA defeated USSR (81-57), Italy (112-81) and Brazil (90-63) in round robin.

1964 (gold medal): Jim (Bad News) Barnes, Bill Bradley, Larry Brown, Joe Caldwell, Mel Counts, Dick Davies, Walt Hazzard, Lucious Jackson, Pete McCaffrey, Jeff Mullins, Jerry Shipp and George Wilson. Coach–Hank Iba; Assistant–Henry Vaughn. Final: USA over USSR, 73-59.

1968 (gold medal): Mike Barrett, John Clawson, Don Dee, Cal Fowler, Spencer Haywood, Bill Hosket, Jim King, Glynn Saulters, Charlie Scott, Mike Silliman, Ken Spain, and JoJo White. Coach–Hank Iba; Assistant–Henry Vaughn. Final: USA over Yugoslavia, 65-50.

1972 (silver medal refused): Mike Bantom, Jim Brewer, Tom Burleson, Doug Collins, Kenny Davis, Jim Forbes, Tom Henderson, Bobby Jones, Dwight Jones, Kevin Joyce, Tom McMillen and Ed Ratleff. Coach–Hank Iba; Assistants– John Bach and Don Haskins. Final: USSR over USA, 51-50.

1976 (gold medal): Tate Armstrong, Quinn Buckner, Kenny Carr, Adrian Dantley, Walter Davis, Phil Ford, Ernie Grunfeld, Phil Hubbard, Mitch Kupchak, Tommy LaGarde, Scott May and Steve Sheppard. Coach–Dean Smith; Assistants–Bill Guthridge and John Thompson. Final: USA over Yugoslavia, 95-74.

1980 (no medal): USA boycotted Moscow Games. Final: Yugoslavia over Italy, 86-77.

1984 (gold medal): Steve Alford, Patrick Ewing, Vern Fleming, Michael Jordan, Joe Kleine, Jon Koncak, Chris Mullin, Sam Perkins, Alvin Robertson, Wayman Tisdale, Jeff Turner and Leon Wood. Coach–Bobby Knight; Assistants– Don Donoher and George Raveling. Final: USA over Spain, 96-65.

1988 (bronze medal): Stacey Augmon, Willie Anderson, Bimbo Coles, Jeff Grayer, Hersey Hawkins, Dan Majerle, Danny Manning, Mitch Richmond, J.R. Reid, David Robinson, Charles D. Smith and Charles E. Smith. Coach–John Thompson; Assistants–George Raveling and Mary Fenlon. Final: USSR over Yugoslavia, 76-63.

1992 (gold medal): Charles Barkley, Larry Bird, Clyde Drexler, Patrick Ewing, Magic Johnson, Michael Jordan, Christian Laettner, Karl Malone, Chris Mullin, Scottie Pippen, David Robinson and John Stockton. Coach–Chuck Daly; Assistants–Lenny Wilkens, Mike Krzyzewski and P.J. Carlesimo. Final: USA over Croatia, 117-85.

Basketball (Cont.)

1996 (gold medal): Charles Barkley, Anfernee Hardaway, Grant Hill, Karl Malone, Reggie Miller, Hakeem Olajuwon, Shaquille O'Neal, Gary Payton, Scottie Pippen, David Robinson and John Stockton. Coach–Lenny Wilkens; Assistants–Bobby Cremins, Clem Haskins and Jerry Sloan. Final: USA over Yugoslavia, 95-69.

2000 (gold medal): Shareef Abdur-Rahim, Ray Allen, Vin Baker, Vince Carter, Kevin Garnett, Tim Hardaway, Allan Houston, Jason Kidd, Antonio McDyess, Alonzo Mourning, Gary Payton and Steve Smith. Coach–Rudy Tomjanovich; Assistants–Larry Brown, Gene Keady and Tubby Smith. Final: USA over France, 85-75.

WOMEN

Multiple gold medals: USA (4), USSR/UT (3).

Year		Year	
1976	**Soviet Union**, United States, Bulgaria	1992	**Unified Team**, China, United States
1980	**Soviet Union**, Bulgaria, Yugoslavia	1996	**United States**, Brazil, Australia
1984	**United States**, South Korea, China	2000	**United States**, Australia, Brazil
1988	**United States**, Yugoslavia, Soviet Union		

U.S. Gold Medal-Winning Women's Basketball Teams

1984 (gold medal): Cathy Boswell, Denise Curry, Anne Donovan, Teresa Edwards, Lea Henry, Janice Lawrence, Pamela McGee, Carol Menken-Schaudt, Cheryl Miller, Kim Mulkey, Cindy Noble and Lynette Woodard. Coach–Pat Summitt; Assistant–Kay Yow. Final: USA over South Korea, 85-55.

1988 (gold medal): Cindy Brown, Vicky Bullett, Cynthia Cooper, Anne Donovan, Teresa Edwards, Kamie Ethridge, Jennifer Gillom, Bridgette Gordon, Andrea Lloyd, Katrina McClain, Suzie McConnell and Teresa Weatherspoon. Coach–Kay Yow; Assistants–Sylvia Hatchell and Susan Yow. Final: USA over Yugoslavia, 77-70.

1996 (gold medal): Jennifer Azzi, Ruthie Bolton, Teresa Edwards, Venus Lacy, Lisa Leslie, Rebecca Lobo, Katrina McClain, Nikki McCray, Carla McGee, Dawn Staley, Katy Steding and Sheryl Swoopes. Coach–Tara VanDerveer; Assistants–Ceal Barry, Nancy Darsch and Marian Washington. Final: USA over Brazil, 111-87.

2000 (gold medal): Ruthie Bolton-Holyfield, Teresa Edwards, Yolanda Griffith, Chamique Holdsclaw, Lisa Leslie, Nikki McCray, DeLisha Milton, Katie Smith, Dawn Staley, Sheryl Swoopes, Natalie Williams and Kara Wolters. Coach–Nell Fortner; Assistants–Geno Auriemma and Peggie Gillom. Final: USA over Australia, 76-54.

BOXING

Multiple gold medals: László Papp, Felix Savon and Teófilo Stevenson (3); Ariel Hernandez, Angel Herrera, Oliver Kirk, Jerzy Kulej, Boris Lagutin, Harry Mallin, Oleg Saitor and Hector Vinent (2). All fighters won titles in consecutive Olympics, except Kirk, who won both the bantamweight and featherweight titles in 1904 (he only had to fight once in each division).

Light Flyweight (106 lbs)

Year		Final Match	Year		Final Match
1968	Francisco Rodriguez, VEN	Decision, 3-2	1988	Ivailo Hristov, BUL	Decision, 5-0
1972	György Gedó, HUN	Decision, 5-0	1992	Rogelio Marcelo, CUB	Decision, 24-10
1976	Jorge Hernandez, CUB	Decision, 4-1	1996	Daniel Petrov Bojilov, BUL	Decision, 19-6
1980	Shamil Sabyrov, USSR	Decision, 3-2	2000	Brahim Asloum, FRA	Decision, 23-10
1984	Paul Gonzales, USA	Default			

Flyweight (112 lbs)

Year		Final Match	Year		Final Match
1904	George Finnegan, USA	Stopped, 1st	1964	Fernando Atzori, ITA	Decision, 4-1
1920	Frank Di Gennara, USA	Decision	1968	Ricardo Delgado, MEX	Decision, 5-0
1924	Fidel LaBarba, USA	Decision	1972	Georgi Kostadinov, BUL	Decision, 5-0
1928	Antal Kocsis, HUN	Decision	1976	Leo Randolph, USA	Decision, 3-2
1932	István Énekes, HUN	Decision	1980	Peter Lessov, BUL	Stopped, 2nd
1936	Willi Kaiser, GER	Decision	1984	Steve McCrory, USA	Decision, 4-1
1948	Pascual Perez, ARG	Decision	1988	Kim Kwang-Sun, S. Kor	Decision, 4-1
1952	Nate Brooks, USA	Decision, 3-0	1992	Su Choi-Chol, N. Kor	Decision, 12-2
1956	Terence Spinks, GBR	Decision	1996	Maikro Romero, CUB	Decision, 12-11
1960	Gyula Török, HUN	Decision, 3-2	2000	Wijan Ponlid, THA	Decision, 19-12

Bantamweight (119 lbs)

Year		Final Match	Year		Final Match
1904	Oliver Kirk, USA	Stopped, 3rd	1964	Takao Sakurai, JPN	Stopped, 2nd
1908	Henry Thomas, GBR	Decision	1968	Valery Sokolov, USSR	Stopped, 2nd
1920	Clarence Walker, RSA	Decision	1972	Orlando Martinez, CUB	Decision, 5-0
1924	William Smith, RSA	Decision	1976	Gu Yong-Ju, N. Kor	Decision, 5-0
1928	Vittorio Tamagnini, ITA	Decision	1980	Juan Hernandez, CUB	Decision, 5-0
1932	Horace Gwynne, CAN	Decision	1984	Maurizio Stecca, ITA	Decision, 4-1
1936	Ulderico Sergo, ITA	Decision	1988	Kennedy McKinney, USA	Decision, 5-0
1948	Tibor Csik, HUN	Decision	1992	Joel Casamayor, CUB	Decision, 14-8
1952	Pentti Hämäläinen, FIN	Decision, 2-1	1996	Istvan Kovacs, HUN	Decision, 14-7
1956	Wolfgang Behrendt, GER	Decision	2000	Guillermo Rigondeaux, CUB	Decision, 18-12
1960	Oleg Grigoryev, USSR	Decision			

Featherweight (125 lbs)

Year		Final Match	Year		Final Match
1904	Oliver Kirk, USA	Decision	1964	Stanislav Stepashkin, USSR	Decision, 3-2
1908	Richard Gunn, GBR	Decision	1968	Antonio Roldan, MEX	Won on Disq.
1920	Paul Fritsch, FRA.	Decision	1972	Boris Kousnetsov, USSR.	Decision, 3-2
1924	John Fields, USA	Decision	1976	Angel Herrera, CUB	KO, 2nd
1928	Lambertus van Klaveren, NED	Decision	1980	Rudi Fink, E. Ger	Decision, 4-1
1932	Carmelo Robledo, ARG	Decision	1984	Meldrick Taylor, USA.	Decision, 5-0
1936	Oscar Casanovas, ARG	Decision	1988	Giovanni Parisi, ITA	Stopped, 1st
1948	Ernesto Formenti, ITA.	Decision	1992	Andreas Tews, GER	Decision, 16-7
1952	Jan Zachara, CZE	Decision, 2-1	1996	Somluck Kamsing, THA.	Decision, 8-5
1956	Vladimir Safronov, USSR.	Decision	2000	Bekzat Sattarkhanov, KAZ	Decision, 22-14
1960	Francesco Musso, ITA	Decision, 4-1			

Lightweight (132 lbs)

Year		Final Match	Year		Final Match
1904	Harry Spanger, USA	Decision	1964	Józef Grudzien, POL	Decision
1908	Frederick Grace, GBR	Decision	1968	Ronnie Harris, USA	Decision, 5-0
1920	Samuel Mosberg, USA	Decision	1972	Jan Szczepanski, POL	Decision, 5-0
1924	Hans Nielsen, DEN	Decision	1976	Howard Davis, USA.	Decision, 5-0
1928	Carlo Orlandi, ITA	Decision	1980	Angel Herrera, CUB.	Stopped, 3rd
1932	Lawrence Stevens, RSA	Decision	1984	Pernell Whitaker, USA.	Foe quit, 2nd
1936	Imre Harangi, HUN	Decision	1988	Andreas Zuelow, E. Ger	Decision, 5-0
1948	Gerald Dreyer, RSA	Decision	1992	Oscar De La Hoya, USA	Decision, 7-2
1952	Aureliano Bolognesi, ITA	Decision, 2-1	1996	Hocine Soltani, ALG	Tiebreak, 3-3
1956	Richard McTaggart, GBR.	Decision	2000	Mario Kindelan, CUB.	Decision, 14-4
1960	Kazimierz Pazdzior, POL.	Decision, 4-1			

Light Welterweight (139 lbs)

Year		Final Match	Year		Final Match
1952	Charles Adkins, USA.	Decision, 2-1	1980	Patrizio Oliva, ITA	Decision, 4-1
1956	Vladimir Yengibaryan, USSR	Decision	1984	Jerry Page, USA	Decision, 5-0
1960	Bohumil Nemecek, CZE	Decision, 5-0	1988	Vyacheslav Yanovsky, USSR	Decision, 5-0
1964	Jerzy Kulej, POL	Decision, 5-0	1992	Hector Vinent, CUB	Decision, 11-1
1968	Jerzy Kulej, POL	Decision, 3-2	1996	Hector Vinent, CUB	Decision, 20-13
1972	Ray Seales, USA	Decision, 3-2	2000	Mahamadkadyz Abdullaev, UZB	Decision, 27-20
1976	Ray Leonard, USA	Decision, 5-0			

Welterweight (147 lbs)

Year		Final Match	Year		Final Match
1904	Albert Young, USA.	Decision	1964	Marian Kasprzyk, POL	Decision, 4-1
1920	Bert Schneider, CAN.	Decision	1968	Manfred Wolke, E. Ger	Decision, 4-1
1924	Jean Delarge, BEL	Decision	1972	Emilio Correa, CUB	Decision, 5-0
1928	Edward Morgan, NZE	Decision	1976	Jochen Bachfeld, E. Ger	Decision, 3-2
1932	Edward Flynn, USA	Decision	1980	Andrés Aldama, CUB	Decision, 4-1
1936	Sten Suvio, FIN	Decision	1984	Mark Breland, USA	Decision, 5-0
1948	Julius Torma, CZE	Decision	1988	Robert Wangila, KEN	KO, 2nd
1952	Zygmunt Chychla, POL	Decision, 3-0	1992	Michael Carruth, IRE	Decision, 13-10
1956	Nicolae Linca, ROM	Decision, 3-2	1996	Oleg Saitov, RUS	Decision, 14-9
1960	Nino Benvenuti, ITA	Decision, 4-1	2000	Oleg Saitov, RUS	Decision, 24-16

Light Middleweight (156 lbs)

Year		Final Match	Year		Final Match
1952	László Papp, HUN	Decision, 3-0	1980	Armando Martinez, CUB	Decision, 4-1
1956	László Papp, HUN	Decision	1984	Frank Tate, USA	Decision, 5-0
1960	Skeeter McClure, USA	Decision, 4-1	1988	Park Si-Hun, S. Kor	Decision, 3-2
1964	Boris Lagutin, USSR	Decision, 4-1	1992	Juan Lemus, CUB	Decision, 6-1
1968	Boris Lagutin, USSR	Decision, 5-0	1996	David Reid, USA	KO, 3rd
1972	Dieter Kottysch, W. Ger	Decision, 3-2	2000	Yermakhan Ibraimov, KAZ	Decision, 25-23
1976	Jerzy Rybicki, POL	Decision, 5-0			

Middleweight (165 lbs)

Year		Final Match	Year		Final Match
1904	Charles Mayer, USA	Stopped, 3rd	1964	Valery Popenchenko, USSR	Stopped, 1st
1908	John Douglas, GBR	Decision	1968	Christopher Finnegan, GBR	Decision, 3-2
1920	Harry Mallin, GBR	Decision	1972	Vyacheslav Lemechev, USSR	KO, 1st
1924	Harry Mallin, GBR	Decision	1976	Michael Spinks, USA	Stopped, 3rd
1928	Piero Toscani, ITA	Decision	1980	José Gomez, CUB	Decision, 4-1
1932	Carmen Barth, USA	Decision	1984	Shin Joon-Sup, S. Kor	Decision, 3-2
1936	Jean Despeaux, FRA	Decision	1988	Henry Maske, E. Ger	Decision, 5-0
1948	László Papp, HUN	Decision	1992	Ariel Hernandez, CUB	Decision, 12-7
1952	Floyd Patterson, USA	KO, 1st	1996	Ariel Hernandez, CUB	Decision, 11-3
1956	Gennady Schatkov, USSR	KO, 1st	2000	Jorge Gutierrez, CUB	Decision, 17-15
1960	Eddie Crook, USA	Decision, 3-2			

Boxing (Cont.)

Light Heavyweight (178 lbs)

Year		Final Match	Year		Final Match
1920	Eddie Eagan, USA	Decision	1968	Dan Poznjak, USSR	Default
1924	Harry Mitchell, GBR	Decision	1972	Mate Parlov, YUG	Stopped, 2nd
1928	Victor Avendaño, ARG	Decision	1976	Leon Spinks, USA	Stopped, 3rd
1932	David Carstens, RSA	Decision	1980	Slobodan Kacar, YUG	Decision, 4-1
1936	Roger Michelot, FRA	Decision	1984	Anton Josipovic, YUG	Default
1948	George Hunter, RSA	Decision	1988	Andrew Maynard, USA	Decision, 5-0
1952	Norvel Lee, USA	Decision, 3-0	1992	Torsten May, GER	Decision, 8-3
1956	Jim Boyd, USA	Decision	1996	Vasilii Jirov, KAZ	Decision, 17-4
1960	Cassius Clay, USA	Decision, 5-0	2000	Alexander Lebziak, RUS	Decision, 20-6
1964	Cosimo Pinto, ITA	Decision, 3-2			

Note: Cassius Clay changed his name to Muhammad Ali after winning the world heavyweight championship in 1964.

Heavyweight (201 lbs)

Year		Final Match	Year		Final Match
1984	Henry Tillman, USA	Decision, 5-0	1996	Felix Savon, CUB	Decision, 20-2
1988	Ray Mercer, USA	KO, 1st	2000	Felix Savon, CUB	Decision, 21-13
1992	Felix Savon, CUB	Decision, 14-1			

Super Heavyweight (Unlimited)

Year		Final Match	Year		Final Match
1904	Samuel Berger, USA	Decision	1964	Joe Frazier, USA	Decision, 3-2
1908	Albert Oldham, GBR	KO, 1st	1968	George Foreman, USA	Stopped, 2nd
1920	Ronald Rawson, GBR	Decision	1972	Teófilo Stevenson, CUB	Default
1924	Otto von Porat, NOR	Decision	1976	Teófilo Stevenson, CUB	KO, 3rd
1928	Arturo Rodriguez Jurado, ARG	Stopped, 1st	1980	Teófilo Stevenson, CUB	Decision, 4-1
1932	Santiago Lovell, ARG	Decision	1984	Tyrell Biggs, USA	Decision, 4-1
1936	Herbert Runge, GER	Decision	1988	Lennox Lewis, CAN	Stopped, 2nd
1948	Rafael Iglesias, ARG	KO, 2nd	1992	Roberto Balado, CUB	Decision, 13-2
1952	Ed Sanders, USA	Won on Disq.*	1996	Vladimir Klichko, UKR	Decision, 7-3
1956	Pete Rademacher, USA	Stopped, 1st	2000	Audley Harrison, GBR	Decision, 30-16
1960	Franco De Piccoli, ITA	KO, 1st			

*Sanders' opponent, Ingemar Johansson, was disqualified in 2nd round for not trying.
Note: Called heavyweight through 1980.

DIVING

MEN

Multiple gold medals: Greg Louganis (4); Klaus Dibiasi (3); Pete Desjardins, Sammy Lee, Xiong Ni, Bob Webster and Albert White (2).

Springboard

Year		Points	Year		Points
1908	Albert Zürner, GER	85.5	1964	Ken Sitzberger, USA	159.90
1912	Paul Günther, GER	79.23	1968	Bernie Wrightson, USA	170.15
1920	Louis Kuehn, USA	675.4	1972	Vladimir Vasin, USSR	594.09
1924	Albert White, USA	696.4	1976	Phil Boggs, USA	619.05
1928	Pete Desjardins, USA	185.04	1980	Aleksandr Portnov, USSR	905.03
1932	Michael Galitzen, USA	161.38	1984	Greg Louganis, USA	754.41
1936	Richard Degener, USA	163.57	1988	Greg Louganis, USA	730.80
1948	Bruce Harlan, USA	163.64	1992	Mark Lenzi, USA	676.53
1952	David Browning, USA	205.29	1996	Xiong Ni, CHN	701.46
1956	Bob Clotworthy, USA	159.56	2000	Xiong Ni, CHN	708.72
1960	Gary Tobian, USA	170.00			

Platform

Year		Points	Year		Points
1904	George Sheldon, USA	12.66	1960	Bob Webster, USA	165.56
1906	Gottlob Walz, GER	156.0	1964	Bob Webster, USA	148.58
1908	Hjalmar Johansson, SWE	83.75	1968	Klaus Dibiasi, ITA	164.18
1912	Erik Adlerz, SWE	73.94	1972	Klaus Dibiasi, ITA	504.12
1920	Clarence Pinkston, USA	100.67	1976	Klaus Dibiasi, ITA	600.51
1924	Albert White, USA	97.46	1980	Falk Hoffmann, E. Ger	835.65
1928	Pete Desjardins, USA	98.74	1984	Greg Louganis, USA	710.91
1932	Harold Smith, USA	124.80	1988	Greg Louganis, USA	638.61
1936	Marshall Wayne, USA	113.58	1992	Sun Shuwei, CHN	677.31
1948	Sammy Lee, USA	130.05	1996	Dmitri Sautin, RUS	692.34
1952	Sammy Lee, USA	156.28	2000	Tian Liang, CHN	724.53
1956	Joaquin Capilla, MEX	152.44			

WOMEN

Multiple gold medals: Pat McCormick and Fu Mingxia (4); Ingrid Engel-Krämer (3); Vicki Draves, Dorothy Poynton Hill and Gao Min (2).

Springboard

Year		Points	Year		Points
1920	Aileen Riggin, USA	539.9	1968	Sue Gossick, USA	150.77
1924	Elizabeth Becker, USA	474.5	1972	Micki King, USA	450.03
1928	Helen Meany, USA	78.62	1976	Jennifer Chandler, USA	506.19
1932	Georgia Coleman, USA	87.52	1980	Irina Kalinina, USSR	725.91
1936	Marjorie Gestring, USA	89.27	1984	Sylvie Bernier, CAN	530.70
1948	Vicki Draves, USA	108.74	1988	Gao Min, CHN	580.23
1952	Pat McCormick, USA	147.30	1992	Gao Min, CHN	572.40
1956	Pat McCormick, USA	142.36	1996	Fu Mingxia, CHN	547.68
1960	Ingrid Krämer, GER	155.81	2000	Fu Mingxia, CHN	609.42
1964	Ingrid Engel-Kräamer, GER	145.00			

Platform

Year		Points	Year		Points
1912	Greta Johansson, SWE	39.9	1964	Lesley Bush, USA	99.80
1920	Stefani Fryland-Clausen, DEN	34.6	1968	Milena Duchková, CZE	109.59
1924	Caroline Smith, USA	33.2	1972	Ulrika Knape, SWE	390.00
1928	Elizabeth Becker Pinkston, USA	31.6	1976	Elena Vaytsekhovskaya, USSR	406.59
1932	Dorothy Poynton, USA	40.26	1980	Martina Jäschke, E. Ger	596.25
1936	Dorothy Poynton Hill, USA	33.93	1984	Zhou Jihong, CHN	435.51
1948	Vicki Draves, USA	68.87	1988	Xu Yanmei, CHN	445.20
1952	Pat McCormick, USA	79.37	1992	Fu Mingxia, CHN	461.43
1956	Pat McCormick, USA	84.85	1996	Fu Mingxia, CHN	521.58
1960	Ingrid Krämer, GER	91.28	2000	Laura Wilkinson, USA	543.75

FIELD HOCKEY

MEN

Multiple gold medals: India (8); Great Britain and Pakistan (3); West Germany/Germany and Netherlands (2).

Year		Year	
1908	**Great Britain**, Ireland, Scotland	1968	**Pakistan**, Australia, India
1920	**Great Britain**, Denmark, Belgium	1972	**West Germany**, Pakistan, India
1928	**India**, Netherlands, Germany	1976	**New Zealand**, Australia, Pakistan
1932	**India**, Japan, United States	1980	**India**, Spain, Soviet Union
1936	**India**, Germany, Netherlands	1984	**Pakistan**, West Germany, Great Britain
1948	**India**, Great Britain, Netherlands	1988	**Great Britain**, West Germany, Netherlands
1952	**India**, Netherlands, Great Britain	1992	**Germany**, Australia, Pakistan
1956	**India**, Pakistan, Germany	1996	**Netherlands**, Spain, Australia
1960	**Pakistan**, India, Spain	2000	**Netherlands**, South Korea, Australia
1964	**India**, Pakistan, Australia		

WOMEN

Multiple gold medals: Australia (3).

Year		Year	
1980	**Zimbabwe**, Czechoslovakia, Soviet Union	1992	**Spain**, Germany, Great Britain
1984	**Netherlands**, West Germany, United States	1996	**Australia**, South Korea, Netherlands
1988	**Australia**, South Korea, Netherlands	2000	**Australia**, Argentina, Netherlands

GYMNASTICS

MEN

At least 4 gold medals (including team events): Sawao Kato (8); Nikolai Andrianov, Viktor Chukarin and Boris Shakhlin (7); Akinori Nakayama and Vitaly Scherbo (6); Yukio Endo, Anton Heida, Mitsuo Tsukahara and Takashi Ono (5); Vladimir Artemov, Georges Miez, Valentin Muratov and Alexei Nemov (4).

All-Around

Year		Points	Year		Points
1900	Gustave Sandras, FRA	.302	1960	Boris Shakhlin, USSR	115.95
1904	Julius Lenhart, AUT	69.80	1964	Yukio Endo, JPN	115.95
1906	Pierre Payssé, FRA	97.0	1968	Sawao Kato, JPN	115.9
1908	Alberto Braglia, ITA	317.0	1972	Sawao Kato, JPN	114.650
1912	Alberto Braglia, ITA	135.0	1976	Nikolai Andrianov, USSR	116.65
1920	Giorgio Zampori, ITA	88.35	1980	Aleksandr Dityatin, USSR	118.65
1924	Leon Stukelj, YUG	110.340	1984	Koji Gushiken, JPN	118.7
1928	Georges Miez, SWI	247.500	1988	Vladimir Artemov, USSR	119.125
1932	Romeo Neri, ITA	140.625	1992	Vitaly Scherbo, UT	59.025
1936	Alfred Schwarzmann, GER	113.100	1996	Li Xiaoshuang, CHN	58.423
1948	Veikko Huhtanen, FIN	229.7	2000	Alexei Nemov, RUS	58.474
1952	Viktor Chukarin, USSR	115.7			
1956	Viktor Chukarin, USSR	114.25			

Gymnastics (Cont.)
Horizontal Bar

Year		Points	Year		Points
1896	Hermann Weingärtner, GER	–	1968	(TIE) Akinori Nakayama, JPN	19.55
1904	(TIE) Anton Heida, USA	.40		& Mikhail Voronin, USSR	19.55
	& Edward Hennig, USA	.40	1972	Mitsuo Tsukahara, JPN	19.725
1924	Leon Stukelj, YUG	19.73	1976	Mitsuo Tsukahara, JPN	19.675
1928	Georges Miez, SWI	19.17	1980	Stoyan Deltchev, BUL	19.825
1932	Dallas Bixler, USA	18.33	1984	Shinji Morisue, JPN	20.00
1936	Aleksanteri Saarvala, FIN	19.367	1988	(TIE) Vladimir Artemov, USSR	19.900
1948	Josef Stalder, SWI	19.85		& Valeri Lyukin, USSR	19.900
1952	Jack Günthard, SWI	19.55	1992	Trent Dimas, USA	9.875
1956	Takashi Ono, JPN	19.60	1996	Andreas Wecker, GER	9.850
1960	Takashi Ono, JPN	19.60	2000	Alexei Nemov, RUS	9.787
1964	Boris Shakhlin, USSR	19.625			

Parallel Bars

Year		Points	Year		Points
1896	Alfred Flatow, GER	–	1964	Yukio Endo, JPN	19.675
1904	George Eyser, USA	.44	1968	Akinori Nakayama, JPN	19.475
1924	August Güttinger, SWI	21.63	1972	Sawao Kato, JPN	19.475
1928	Ladislav Vácha, CZE	18.83	1976	Sawao Kato, JPN	19.675
1932	Romeo Neri, ITA	18.97	1980	Aleksandr Tkachyov, USSR	19.775
1936	Konrad Frey, GER	19.067	1984	Bart Conner, USA	19.95
1948	Michael Reusch, SWI	19.75	1988	Vladimir Artemov, USSR	19.925
1952	Hans Eugster, SWI	19.65	1992	Vitaly Scherbo, UT	9.900
1956	Viktor Chukarin, USSR	19.20	1996	Rustam Sharipov, UKR	9.837
1960	Boris Shakhlin, USSR	19.40	2000	Li Xiaopeng, CHN	9.825

Vault

Year		Points	Year		Points
1896	Karl Schumann, GER	–	1960	(TIE) Takashi Ono, JPN	19.35
1904	(TIE) George Eyser, USA	.36		& Boris Shakhlin, USSR	19.35
	& Anton Heida, USA	.36	1964	Haruhiro Yamashita, JPN	19.60
1924	Frank Kriz, USA	9.98	1968	Mikhail Voronin, USSR	19.00
1928	Eugen Mack, SWI	9.58	1972	Klaus Köste, E. Ger	18.85
1932	Savino Guglielmetti, ITA	18.03	1976	Nikolai Andrianov, USSR	19.45
1936	Alfred Schwarzmann, GER	19.20	1980	Nikolai Andrianov, USSR	19.825
1948	Paavo Aaltonen, FIN	19.55	1984	Lou Yun, CHN	19.95
1952	Viktor Chukarin, USSR	19.20	1988	Lou Yun, CHN	19.875
1956	(TIE) Helmut Bantz, GER	18.85	1992	Vitaly Scherbo, UT	9.856
	& Valentin Muratov, USSR	18.85	1996	Alexei Nemov, RUS	9.787
			2000	Gervasio Deferr, SPA	9.712

Pommel Horse

Year		Points	Year		Points
1896	Louis Zutter, SWI	–	1968	Miroslav Cerar, YUG	19.325
1904	Anton Heida, USA	.42	1972	Viktor Klimenko, SOV	19.125
1924	Josef Wilhelm, SWI	21.23	1976	Zoltán Magyar, HUN	19.70
1928	Hermann Hänggi, SWI	19.75	1980	Zoltán Magyar, HUN	19.925
1932	István Pelle, HUN	19.07	1984	(TIE) Li Ning, CHN	19.95
1936	Konrad Frey, GER	19.333		& Peter Vidmar, USA	19.95
1948	(TIE) Paavo Aaltonen, FIN	19.35	1988	(TIE) Dmitri Bilozerchev, USSR,	19.95
	Veikko Huhtanen, FIN	19.35		Zsolt Borkai, HUN	19.95
	& Heikki Savolainen, FIN	19.35		& Lyubomir Geraskov, BUL	19.95
1952	Viktor Chukarin, USSR	19.50	1992	(TIE) Pae Gil-Su, N. Kor	9.925
1956	Boris Shakhlin, USSR	19.25		& Vitaly Scherbo, UT	9.925
1960	(TIE) Eugen Ekman, FIN	19.375	1996	Li Donghua, SWI	9.875
	& Boris Shakhlin, USSR	19.375	2000	Marius Urzica, ROM	9.862
1964	Miroslav Cerar, YUG	19.525			

Rings

Year		Points	Year		Points
1896	Ioannis Mitropoulos, GRE	–	1968	Akinori Nakayama, JPN	19.45
1904	Hermann Glass, USA	.45	1972	Akinori Nakayama, JPN	19.35
1924	Francesco Martino, ITA	21.553	1976	Nikolai Andrianov, USSR	19.65
1928	Leon Stukelj, YUG	19.25	1980	Aleksandr Dityatin, USSR	19.875
1932	George Gulack, USA	18.97	1984	(TIE) Koji Gushiken, JPN	19.85
1936	Alois Hudec, CZE	19.433		& Li Ning, CHN	19.85
1948	Karl Frei, SWI	19.80	1988	(TIE) Holger Behrendt, E. Ger	19.925
1952	Grant Shaginyan, USSR	19.75		& Dmitri Bilozerchev, USSR	19.925
1956	Albert Azaryan, USSR	19.35	1992	Vitaly Scherbo, UT	9.937
1960	Albert Azaryan, USSR	19.725	1996	Yuri Chechi, ITA	9.887
1964	Takuji Haytta, JPN	19.475	2000	Szilveszter Csollany, HUN	9.850

Floor Exercise

Year		Points	Year		Points
1932	Istvan Pelle, HUN	9.60	1972	Nikolai Andrianov, USSR	19.175
1936	Georges Miez, SWI	18.666	1976	Nikolai Andrianov, USSR	19.45
1948	Ferenc Pataki, HUN	19.35	1980	Roland Brückner, E. Ger	19.75
1952	William Thoresson, SWE	19.25	1984	Li Ning, CHN	19.925
1956	Valentin Muratov, USSR	19.20	1988	Sergei Kharkov, USSR	19.925
1960	Nobuyuki Aihara, JPN	19.45	1992	Li Xiaosahuang, CHN	9.925
1964	Franco Menichelli, ITA	19.45	1996	Ioannis Melissanidis, GRE	9.850
1968	Sawao Kato, JPN	19.475	2000	Igors Vihrovs, LAT	9.812

Team Combined Exercises

Year		Points	Year		Points
1904	United States	374.43	1960	Japan	575.20
1906	Norway	19.00	1964	Japan	577.95
1908	Sweden	438	1968	Japan	575.90
1912	Italy	265.75	1972	Japan	571.25
1920	Italy	359.855	1976	Japan	576.85
1924	Italy	839.058	1980	Soviet Union	598.60
1928	Switzerland	1718.625	1984	United States	591.40
1932	Italy	541.850	1988	Soviet Union	593.35
1936	Germany	657.430	1992	Unified Team	585.45
1948	Finland	1358.30	1996	Russia	576.778
1952	Soviet Union	574.40	2000	China	231.919
1956	Soviet Union	568.25			

WOMEN

At least 4 gold medals (including team events): Larissa Latynina (9); Vera Cáslavská (7); Polina Astakhova, Nadia Comaneci, Agnes Keleti and Nelli Kim (5); Olga Korbut, Ecaterina Szabó and Lyudmila Tourischeva (4).

All-Around

Year		Points	Year		Points
1952	Maria Gorokhovskaya, USSR	76.78	1988	Yelena Shushunova, USSR	79.662
1956	Larissa Latynina, USSR	74.933	1992	Tatiana Gutsu, UT	39.737
1960	Larissa Latynina, USSR	77.031	1996	Lilia Podkopayeva, UKR	39.255
1964	Vera Cáslavská, CZE	77.564	2000	Simona Amanar, ROM*	38.642
1968	Vera Cáslavská, CZE	78.25			
1972	Lyudmila Tourischeva, USSR	77.025			
1976	Nadia Comaneci, ROM	79.275			
1980	Yelena Davydova, USSR	79.15			
1984	Mary Lou Retton, USA	79.175			

*Amanar finished second to Andreea Raducan, Romania, who was disqualified for testing positive for pseudoephedrine, a drug banned by the IOC and found in Nurofen—an over-the-counter medicine she purportedly took to treat a cold.

Vault

Year		Points	Year		Points
1952	Yekaterina Kalinchuk, USSR	19.20	1984	Ecaterina Szabó, ROM	19.875
1956	Larissa Latynina, USSR	18.833	1988	Svetlana Boginskaya, USSR	19.905
1960	Margarita Nikolayeva, USSR	19.316	1992	(TIE) Henrietta Onodi, HUN	9.925
1964	Vera Cáslavská, CZE	19.483		& Lavinia Milosovici, ROM	9.925
1968	Vera Cáslavská, CZE	19.775	1996	Simona Amanar, ROM	9.775
1972	Karin Janz, E. Ger	19.525	2000	Elena Zamolodtchikova, RUS	9.731
1976	Nelli Kim, USSR	19.80			
1980	Natalia Shaposhnikova, USSR	19.725			

Uneven Bars

Year		Points	Year		Points
1952	Margit Korondi, HUN	19.40	1980	Maxi Gnauck, E. Ger	19.875
1956	Agnes Keleti, HUN	18.966	1984	(TIE) Julianne McNamara, USA	19.95
1960	Polina Astakhova, USSR	19.616		& Ma Yanhong, CHN	19.95
1964	Polina Astakhova, USSR	19.332	1988	Daniela Silivas, ROM	20.00
1968	Vera Cáslavská, CZE	19.65	1992	Lu Li, CHN	10.00
1972	Karin Janz, E. Ger	19.675	1996	Svetlana Khorkina, RUS	9.850
1976	Nadia Comaneci, ROM	20.00	2000	Svetlana Khorkina, RUS	9.862

Balance Beam

Year		Points	Year		Points
1952	Nina Bocharova, USSR	19.22	1984	(TIE) Simona Pauca, ROM	19.80
1956	Agnes Keleti, HUN	18.80		& Ecaterina Szabó, ROM	19.80
1960	Eva Bosakova, CZE	19.283	1988	Daniela Silivas, ROM	19.924
1964	Vera Cáslavská, CZE	19.449	1992	Tatiana Lyssenko, UT	9.975
1968	Natalya Kuchinskaya, USSR	19.65	1996	Shannon Miller, USA	9.862
1972	Olga Korbut, USSR	19.40	2000	Liu Xuan, CHN	9.825
1976	Nadia Comaneci, ROM	19.95			
1980	Nadia Comaneci, ROM	19.80			

Gymnastics (Cont.)
Floor Exercise

Year	Points	Year	Points
1952 Agnes Keleti, HUN	19.36	1976 Nelli Kim, USSR	19.85
1956 (TIE) Agnes Keleti, HUN	18.733	1980 (TIE) Nadia Comaneci, ROM	19.875
& Larissa Latynina, USSR	18.733	& Nelli Kim, USSR	19.875
1960 Larissa Latynina, USSR	19.583	1984 Ecaterina Szabó, ROM	19.975
1964 Larissa Latynina, USSR	19.599	1988 Daniela Silivas, ROM	19.937
1968 (TIE) Vera Cáslavská, CZE	19.675	1992 Lavinia Milosovici, ROM	10.000
& Larissa Petrik, USSR	19.675	1996 Lilia Podkopayeva, UKR	9.887
1972 Olga Korbut, USSR	19.575	2000 Elena Zamolodtchikova, RUS	9.850

Team Combined Exercises

Year	Points	Year	Points
1928 Netherlands	316.75	1972 Soviet Union	380.50
1936 Germany	506.50	1976 Soviet Union	466.00
1948 Czechoslovakia	445.45	1980 Soviet Union	394.90
1952 Soviet Union	527.03	1984 Romania	392.02
1956 Soviet Union	444.800	1988 Soviet Union	395.475
1960 Soviet Union	382.320	1992 Unified Team	395.666
1964 Soviet Union	280.890	1996 United States	389.225
1968 Soviet Union	382.85	2000 Romania	154.608

SOCCER

MEN

Multiple gold medals: Great Britain and Hungary (3); Uruguay and USSR (2).

Year		Year	
1900	**Great Britain**, France, Belgium	1960	**Yugoslavia**, Denmark, Hungary
1904	**Canada**, USA I, USA II	1964	**Hungary**, Czechoslovakia, Germany
1906	**Denmark**, Smyrna (Int'l entry), Greece	1968	**Hungary**, Bulgaria, Japan
1908	**Great Britain**, Denmark, Netherlands	1972	**Poland**, Hungary, East Germany & Soviet Union
1912	**Great Britain**, Denmark, Netherlands	1976	**East Germany**, Poland, Soviet Union
1920	**Belgium**, Spain, Netherlands	1980	**Czechoslovakia**, East Germany, Soviet Union
1924	**Uruguay**, Switzerland, Sweden	1984	**France**, Brazil, Yugoslavia
1928	**Uruguay**, Argentina, Italy	1988	**Soviet Union**, Brazil, West Germany
1936	**Italy**, Austria, Norway	1992	**Spain**, Poland, Ghana
1948	**Sweden**, Yugoslavia, Denmark	1996	**Nigeria**, Argentina, Brazil
1952	**Hungary**, Yugoslavia, Sweden	2000	**Cameroon**, Spain, Chile
1956	**Soviet Union**, Yugoslavia, Bulgaria		

WOMEN

Year		Year	
1996	**United States**, China, Norway	2000	**Norway**, United States, Germany

SWIMMING

World and Olympic records below that appear to be broken or equaled by winning times in subsequent years, but are not so indicated, were all broken in preliminary heats leading up to the finals. Some events were not held at every Olympics.

MEN

At least 4 gold medals (including relays): Mark Spitz (9); Matt Biondi (8); Charles Daniels, Tom Jager, Don Schollander, and Johnny Weissmuller (5); Tamás Darnyi, Gary Hall Jr., Roland Matthes, John Naber, Aleksandr Popov, Murray Rose, Vladimir Salnikov and Henry Taylor (4).

50-meter Freestyle

Year	Time		Year	Time	
1904 Zoltán Halmay, HUN (50 yds)	28.0		1996 Aleksandr Popov, RUS	22.13	
1906-84 Not held			2000 (TIE) Anthony Ervin, USA	21.98	
1988 Matt Biondi, USA	22.14	**WR**	Gary Hall Jr., USA	21.98	
1992 Aleksandr Popov, UT	21.91	**OR**			

100-meter Freestyle

Year	Time		Year	Time	
1896 Alfréd Hajós, HUN	1:22.2	**OR**	1956 Jon Henricks, AUS	55.4	**OR**
1904 Zoltán Halmay, HUN (100 yds)	1:02.8		1960 John Devitt, AUS	55.2	**OR**
1906 Charles Daniels, USA	1:13.4		1964 Don Schollander, USA	53.4	**OR**
1908 Charles Daniels, USA	1:05.6	**WR**	1968 Michael Wenden, AUS	52.2	**WR**
1912 Duke Kahanamoku, USA	1:03.4		1972 Mark Spitz, USA	51.22	**WR**
1920 Duke Kahanamoku, USA	1:00.4	**WR**	1976 Jim Montgomery, USA	49.99	**WR**
1924 Johnny Weissmuller, USA	59.0	**OR**	1980 Jorg Woithe, E. Ger.	50.40	
1928 Johnny Weissmuller, USA	58.6	**OR**	1984 Rowdy Gaines, USA	49.80	**OR**
1932 Yasuji Miyazaki, JPN	58.2		1988 Matt Biondi, USA	48.63	**OR**
1936 Ferenc Csik, HUN	57.6		1992 Aleksandr Popov, UT	49.02	
1948 Wally Ris, USA	57.3	**OR**	1996 Aleksandr Popov, RUS	48.74	
1952 Clarke Scholes, USA	57.4		2000 Pieter van den Hoogenband, NED	48.30	

200-meter Freestyle

Year		Time		Year		Time	
1900	Frederick Lane, AUS (220 yds)	2:25.2	OR	1984	Michael Gross, W. Ger	1:47.44	WR
1904	Charles Daniels, USA (220 yds)	2:44.2		1988	Duncan Armstrong, AUS	1:47.25	WR
1968	Michael Wenden, AUS	1:55.2	OR	1992	Yevgeny Sadovyi, UT	1:46.70	OR
1972	Mark Spitz, USA	1:52.78	WR	1996	Danyon Loader, NZE	1:47.63	
1976	Bruce Furniss, USA	1:50.29	WR	2000	Pieter van den Hoogenband, NED	1:45.35	WR
1980	Sergei Kopliakov, USSR	1:49.81	OR				

400-meter Freestyle

Year		Time		Year		Time	
1896	Paul Neumann, AUT (550m)	8:12.6		1956	Murray Rose, AUS	4:27.3	OR
1904	Charles Daniels, USA (440 yds)	6:16.2		1960	Murray Rose, AUS	4:18.3	OR
1906	Otto Scheff, AUT	6:23.8		1964	Don Schollander, USA	4:12.2	WR
1908	Henry Taylor, GBR	5:36.8		1968	Mike Burton, USA	4:09.0	OR
1912	George Hodgson, CAN	5:24.4		1972	Bradford Cooper, AUS*	4:00.27	OR
1920	Norman Ross, USA	5:26.8		1976	Brian Goodell, USA	3:51.93	WR
1924	Johnny Weissmuller, USA	5:04.2	OR	1980	Vladimir Salnikov, USSR	3:51.31	OR
1928	Alberto Zorilla, ARG	5:01.6	OR	1984	George DiCarlo, USA	3:51.23	OR
1932	Buster Crabbe, USA	4:48.4	OR	1988	Uwe Dassler, E. Ger	3:46.95	WR
1936	Jack Medica, USA	4:44.5	OR	1992	Yevgeny Sadovyi, UT	3:45.00	WR
1948	Bill Smith, USA	4:41.0	OR	1996	Danyon Loader, NZE	3:47.97	
1952	Jean Boiteux, FRA	4:30.7	OR	2000	Ian Thorpe, AUS	3:40.59	WR

*Cooper finished second to Rick DeMont of the U.S., who was disqualified when he flunked the post-race drug test (his asthma medication was on the IOC's banned list).

1500-meter Freestyle

Year		Time		Year		Time	
1896	Alfréd Hajós, HUN (1200m)	18:22.2	OR	1952	Ford Konno, USA	18:30.3	OR
1900	John Arthur Jarvis, GBR (1000m)	13:40.2		1956	Murray Rose, AUS	17:58.9	
1904	Emil Rausch, GER (1 mile)	27:18.2		1960	Jon Konrads, AUS	17:19.6	OR
1906	Henry Taylor, GBR (1 mile)	28:28.0		1964	Robert Windle, AUS	17:01.7	OR
1908	Henry Taylor, GBR	22:48.4	WR	1968	Mike Burton, USA	16:38.9	OR
1912	George Hodgson, CAN	22:00.0	WR	1972	Mike Burton, USA	15:52.58	WR
1920	Norman Ross, USA	22:23.2		1976	Brian Goodell, USA	15:02.40	WR
1924	Andrew (Boy) Charlton, AUS	20:06.6	WR	1980	Vladimir Salnikov, USSR	14:58.27	WR
1928	Arne Borge, SWE	19:51.8	OR	1984	Mike O'Brien, USA	15:05.20	
1932	Kusuo Kitamura, JPN	19:12.4	OR	1988	Vladimir Salnikov, USSR	15:00.40	
1936	Noboru Terada, JPN	19:13.7		1992	Kieren Perkins, AUS	14:43.48	WR
1948	James McLane, USA	19:18.5		1996	Kieren Perkins, AUS	14:56.40	
				2000	Grant Hackett, AUS	14:48.33	

100-meter Backstroke

Year		Time		Year		Time	
1904	Walter Brack, GER (100 yds)	1:16.8		1960	David Theile, AUS	1:01.9	OR
1908	Arno Bieberstein, GER	1:24.6	WR	1968	Roland Matthes, E. Ger	58.7	OR
1912	Harry Hebner, USA	1:21.2		1972	Roland Matthes, E. Ger	56.58	OR
1920	Warren Kealoha, USA	1:15.2		1976	John Naber, USA	55.49	WR
1924	Warren Kealoha, USA	1:13.2	OR	1980	Bengt Baron, SWE	56.33	
1928	George Kojac, USA	1:08.2	WR	1984	Rick Carey, USA	55.79	
1932	Masaji Kiyokawa, JPN	1:08.6		1988	Daichi Suzuki, JPN	55.05	
1936	Adolf Kiefer, USA	1:05.9	OR	1992	Mark Tewksbury, CAN	53.98	OR
1948	Allen Stack, USA	1:06.4		1996	Jeff Rouse, USA	54.10	
1952	Yoshinobu Oyakawa, USA	1:05.4	OR	2000	Lenny Krayzelburg, USA	53.72	OR
1956	David Theile, AUS	1:02.2	OR				

200-meter Backstroke

Year		Time		Year		Time	
1900	Ernst Hoppenberg, GER	2:47.0		1984	Rick Carey, USA	2:00.23	
1964	Jed Graef, USA	2:10.3	WR	1988	Igor Poliansky, USSR	1:59.37	
1968	Roland Matthes, E. Ger	2:09.6	OR	1992	Martin Lopez-Zubero, SPA	1:58.47	OR
1972	Roland Matthes, E. Ger	2:02.82	=WR	1996	Brad Bridgewater, USA	1:58.54	
1976	John Naber, USA	1:59.19	WR	2000	Lenny Krayzelburg, USA	1:56.76	OR
1980	Sándor Wládár, HUN	2:01.93					

100-meter Breaststroke

Year		Time		Year		Time	
1968	Don McKenzie, USA	1:07.7	OR	1988	Adrian Moorhouse, GBR	1:02.04	
1972	Nobutaka Taguchi, JPN	1:04.94	WR	1992	Nelson Diebel, USA	1:01.50	OR
1976	John Hencken, USA	1:03.11	WR	1996	Fred deBurghgraeve, BEL	1:00.60	
1980	Duncan Goodhew, GBR	1:03.44		2000	Domenico Fioravanti, ITA	1:00.46	OR
1984	Steve Lundquist, USA	1:01.65	WR				

Swimming (Cont.)
200-meter Breaststroke

Year		Time		Year		Time	
1908	Frederick Holman, GBR	3:09.2	WR	1964	Ian O'Brien, AUS	2:27.8	WR
1912	Walter Bathe, GER	3:01.8	OR	1968	Felipe Muñoz, MEX	2:28.7	
1920	Hakan Malmroth, SWE	3:04.4		1972	John Hencken, USA	2:21.55	WR
1924	Robert Skelton, USA	2:56.6		1976	David Wilkie, GBR	2:15.11	WR
1928	Yoshiyuki Tsuruta, JPN	2:48.8	OR	1980	Robertas Zhulpa, USSR	2:15.85	
1932	Yoshiyuki Tsuruta, JPN	2:45.4		1984	Victor Davis, CAN	2:13.34	WR
1936	Tetsuo Hamuro, JPN	2:41.5	OR	1988	József Szabó, HUN	2:13.52	
1948	Joseph Verdeur, USA	2:39.3	OR	1992	Mike Barrowman, USA	2:10.16	WR
1952	John Davies, AUS	2:34.4	OR	1996	Norbert Rozsa, HUN	2:12.57	
1956	Masaru Furukawa, JPN	2:34.7*	OR	2000	Domenico Fioravanti, ITA	2:10.87	
1960	Bill Mulliken, USA	2:37.4					

*In 1956, the butterfly stroke and breaststroke were separated into two different events.

100-meter Butterfly

Year		Time		Year		Time	
1968	Doug Russell, USA	55.9	OR	1988	Anthony Nesty, SUR	53.0	OR
1972	Mark Spitz, USA	54.27	WR	1992	Pablo Morales, USA	53.32	
1976	Matt Vogel, USA	54.35		1996	Dennis Pankratov, RUS	52.27	
1980	Pär Arvidsson, SWE	54.92		2000	Lars Frolander, SWE	52.00	
1984	Michael Gross, W. Ger	53.08	WR				

200-meter Butterfly

Year		Time		Year		Time	
1956	Bill Yorzyk, USA	2:19.3	OR	1980	Sergei Fesenko, USSR	1:59.76	
1960	Mike Troy, USA	2:12.8	WR	1984	Jon Sieben, AUS	1:57.04	WR
1964	Kevin Berry, AUS	2:06.6	WR	1988	Michael Gross, W. Ger	1:56.94	OR
1968	Carl Robie, USA	2:08.7		1992	Melvin Stewart, USA	1:56.26	OR
1972	Mark Spitz, USA	2:00.70	WR	1996	Dennis Pankratov, RUS	1:56.51	
1976	Mike Bruner, USA	1:59.23	WR	2000	Tom Malchow, USA	1:55.35	OR

200-meter Individual Medley

Year		Time		Year		Time	
1968	Charles Hickcox, USA	2:12.0	OR	1992	Tamás Darnyi, HUN	2:00.76	
1972	Gunnar Larsson, SWE	2:07.17	WR	1996	Attila Czene, HUN	1:59.91	
1984	Alex Baumann, CAN	2:01.42	WR	2000	Massimiliano Rosolino, ITA	1:58.98	OR
1988	Tamás Darnyi, HUN	2:00.17	WR				

400-meter Individual Medley

Year		Time		Year		Time	
1964	Richard Roth, USA	4:45.4	WR	1984	Alex Baumann, CAN	4:17.41	WR
1968	Charles Hickcox, USA	4:48.4		1988	Tamás Darnyi, HUN	4:14.75	WR
1972	Gunnar Larsson, SWE	4:31.98	OR	1992	Tamás Darnyi, HUN	4:14.23	OR
1976	Rod Strachan, USA	4:23.68	OR	1996	Tom Dolan, USA	4:14.90	
1980	Aleksandr Sidorenko, USSR	4:22.89	OR	2000	Tom Dolan, USA	4:11.76	WR

4x100-meter Freestyle Relay

Year		Time		Year		Time	
1964	United States	3:32.2	WR	1988	United States	3:16.53	WR
1968	United States	3:31.7	WR	1992	United States	3:16.74	
1972	United States	3:26.42	WR	1996	United States	3:15.41	
1976-80 Not held				2000	Australia	3:13.67	WR
1984	United States	3:19.03	WR				

4x200-meter Freestyle Relay

Year		Time		Year		Time	
1906	Hungary (x250m)	16:52.4		1964	United States	7:52.1	WR
1908	Great Britain	10:55.6	WR	1968	United States	7:52.33	
1912	Australia/New Zealand	10:11.6	WR	1972	United States	7:35.78	WR
1920	United States	10:04.4	WR	1976	United States	7:23.22	WR
1924	United States	9:53.4	WR	1980	Soviet Union	7:23.50	
1928	United States	9:36.2	WR	1984	United States	7:15.69	WR
1932	Japan	8:58.4	WR	1988	United States	7:12.51	WR
1936	Japan	8:51.5	WR	1992	Unified Team	7:11.95	WR
1948	United States	8:46.0	WR	1996	United States	7:14.84	
1952	United States	8:31.1	OR	2000	Australia	7:07.05	WR
1956	Australia	8:23.6	WR				
1960	United States	8:10.2	WR				

4x100-meter Medley Relay

Year		Time		Year		Time	
1960	United States	4:05.4	**WR**	1984	United States	3:39.30	**WR**
1964	United States	3:58.4	**WR**	1988	United States	3:36.93	**WR**
1968	United States	3:54.9	**WR**	1992	United States	3:36.93	**=WR**
1972	United States	3:48.16	**WR**	1996	United States	3:34.84	
1976	United States	3:42.22	**WR**	2000	United States	3:33.73	**WR**
1980	Australia	3:45.70					

WOMEN

At least 4 gold medals (including relays): Jenny Thompson (8); Kristin Otto (6); Krisztina Egerszegi and Amy van Dyken (5), Kornelia Ender, Janet Evans, Dawn Fraser and Dara Torres (4).

50-meter Freestyle

Year		Time		Year		Time	
1988	Kristin Otto, E. Ger	25.49	**OR**	1996	Amy Van Dyken, USA	24.87	
1992	Yang Wenyi, CHN	24.79	**WR**	2000	Inge de Bruijn, NED	24.32	

100-meter Freestyle

Year		Time		Year		Time	
1912	Fanny Durack, AUS	1:22.2		1968	Jan Henne, USA	1:00.0	
1920	Ethelda Bleibtrey, USA	1:13.6	**WR**	1972	Sandra Neilson, USA	58.59	**OR**
1924	Ethel Lackie, USA	1:12.4		1976	Kornelia Ender, E. Ger	55.65	**WR**
1928	Albina Osipowich, USA	1:11.0	**OR**	1980	Barbara Krause, E. Ger	54.79	**WR**
1932	Helene Madison, USA	1:06.8	**OR**	1984	(TIE) Nancy Hogshead, USA	55.92	
1936	Rie Mastenbroek, NED	1:05.9	**OR**		Carrie Steinseifer, USA	55.92	
1948	Greta Andersen, DEN	1:06.3		1988	Kristin Otto, E. Ger	54.93	
1952	Katalin Szöke, HUN	1:06.8		1992	Zhuang Yong, CHN	54.65	**OR**
1956	Dawn Fraser, AUS	1:02.0	**WR**	1996	Le Jingyi, CHN	54.50	
1960	Dawn Fraser, AUS	1:01.2	**OR**	2000	Inge de Bruijn, NED	53.83	
1964	Dawn Fraser, AUS	59.5	**OR**				

200-meter Freestyle

Year		Time		Year		Time	
1968	Debbie Meyer, USA	2:10.5	**OR**	1988	Heike Friedrich, E. Ger	1:57.65	**OR**
1972	Shane Gould, AUS	2:03.56	**WR**	1992	Nicole Haislett, USA	1:57.90	
1976	Kornelia Ender, E. Ger	1:59.26	**WR**	1996	Claudia Poll, CRC	1:58.16	
1980	Barbara Krause, E. Ger	1:58.33	**OR**	2000	Susie O'Neill, AUS	1:58.24	
1984	Mary Wayte, USA	1:59.23					

400-meter Freestyle

Year		Time		Year		Time	
1920	Ethelda Bleibtrey, USA (300m)	4:34.0	**WR**	1968	Debbie Meyer, USA	4:31.8	**OR**
1924	Martha Norelius, USA	6:02.2	**OR**	1972	Shane Gould, AUS	4:19.44	**WR**
1928	Martha Norelius, USA	5:42.8	**WR**	1976	Petra Thümer, E. Ger	4:09.89	**WR**
1932	Helene Madison, USA	5:28.5	**WR**	1980	Ines Diers, E. Ger	4:08.76	**OR**
1936	Rie Mastenbroek, NED	5:26.4	**OR**	1984	Tiffany Cohen, USA	4:07.10	**OR**
1948	Ann Curtis, USA	5:17.8	**OR**	1988	Janet Evans, USA	4:03.85	**WR**
1952	Valéria Gyenge, HUN	5:12.1	**OR**	1992	Dagmar Hase, GER	4:07.18	
1956	Lorraine Crapp, AUS	4:54.6	**OR**	1996	Michelle Smith, IRE	4:07.25	
1960	Chris von Saltza, USA	4:50.6	**OR**	2000	Brooke Bennett, USA	4:05.80	
1964	Ginny Duenkel, USA	4:43.3	**OR**				

800-meter Freestyle

Year		Time		Year		Time	
1968	Debbie Meyer, USA	9:24.0	**OR**	1988	Janet Evans, USA	8:20.20	**OR**
1972	Keena Rothhammer, USA	8:53.68	**WR**	1992	Janet Evans, USA	8:25.52	
1976	Petra Thümer, E. Ger	8:37.14	**WR**	1996	Brooke Bennett, USA	8:27.89	
1980	Michelle Ford, AUS	8:28.90	**OR**	2000	Brooke Bennett, USA	8:19.67	**OR**
1984	Tiffany Cohen, USA	8:24.95	**OR**				

100-meter Backstroke

Year		Time		Year		Time	
1924	Sybil Bauer, USA	1:23.2	**OR**	1972	Melissa Belote, USA	1:05.78	**OR**
1928	Maria Braun, NED	1:22.0		1976	Ulrike Richter, E. Ger	1:01.83	**OR**
1932	Eleanor Holm, USA	1:19.4		1980	Rica Reinisch, E. Ger	1:00.86	**WR**
1936	Dina Senff, NED	1:18.9		1984	Theresa Andrews, USA	1:02.55	
1948	Karen-Margrete Harup, DEN	1:14.4	**OR**	1988	Kristin Otto, E. Ger	1:00.89	
1952	Joan Harrison, S. Afr.	1:14.3		1992	Krisztina Egerszegi, HUN	1:00.68	**OR**
1956	Judy Grinham, GBR	1:12.9	**OR**	1996	Beth Botsford, USA	1:01.19	
1960	Lynn Burke, USA	1:09.3	**OR**	2000	Diana Mocanu, ROM	1:00.21	**OR**
1964	Cathy Ferguson, USA	1:07.7	**WR**				
1968	Kaye Hall, USA	1:06.2	**WR**				

Swimming (Cont.)
200-meter Backstroke

Year		Time		Year		Time	
1968	Pokey Watson, USA	2:24.8	OR	1988	Krisztina Egerszegi, HUN	2:09.29	OR
1972	Melissa Belote, USA	2:19.19	WR	1992	Krisztina Egerszegi, HUN	2:07.06	OR
1976	Ulrike Richter, E. Ger	2:13.43	OR	1996	Krisztina Egerszegi, HUN	2:07.83	
1980	Rica Reinisch, E. Ger	2:11.77	WR	2000	Diana Mocanu, ROM	2:08.16	
1984	Jolanda de Rover, NED	2:12.38					

100-meter Breaststroke

Year		Time		Year		Time	
1968	Djurdjica Bjedov, YUG	1:15.8	OR	1988	Tania Dangalakova, BUL	1:07.95	OR
1972	Cathy Carr, USA	1:13.58	WR	1992	Yelena Rudkovskaya, UT	1:08.00	
1976	Hannelore Anke, E. Ger	1:11.16		1996	Penny Heyns, S. Afr.	1:07.73	
1980	Ute Geweniger, E. Ger	1:10.22		2000	Megan Quann, USA	1:07.05	
1984	Petra van Staveren, NED	1:09.88	OR				

200-meter Breaststroke

Year		Time		Year		Time	
1924	Lucy Morton, GBR	3:33.2	OR	1968	Sharon Wichman, USA	2:44.4	OR
1928	Hilde Schrader, GER	3:12.6		1972	Beverley Whitfield, AUS	2:41.71	OR
1932	Clare Dennis, AUS	3:06.3	OR	1976	Marina Koshevaya, USSR	2:33.35	WR
1936	Hideko Maehata, JPN	3:03.6		1980	Lina Kaciusyte, USSR	2:29.54	OR
1948	Petronella van Vliet, NED	2:57.2		1984	Anne Ottenbrite, CAN.	2:30.38	
1952	Éva Székely, HUN	2:51.7	OR	1988	Silke Hörner, E. Ger.	2:26.71	OR
1956	Ursula Happe, GER	2:53.1	OR	1992	Kyoko Iwasaki, JPN	2:26.65	OR
1960	Anita Lonsbrough, GBR	2:49.5	WR	1996	Penny Heyns, S. Afr.	2:25.41	
1964	Galina Prozumenshikova, USSR	2:46.4	OR	2000	Agnes Kovacs, HUN	2:24.35	

100-meter Butterfly

Year		Time		Year		Time	
1956	Shelly Mann, USA	1:11.0	OR	1980	Caren Metschuck, E. Ger	1:00.42	
1960	Carolyn Schuler, USA.	1:09.5	OR	1984	Mary T. Meagher, USA	59.26	
1964	Sharon Stouder, USA	1:04.7	WR	1988	Kristin Otto, E. Ger	59.00	OR
1968	Lynn McClements, AUS	1:05.5		1992	Qian Hong, CHN	58.62	OR
1972	Mayumi Aoki, JPN	1:03.34	WR	1996	Amy Van Dyken, USA	59.13	
1976	Kornelia Ender, E. Ger.	1:00.13	=WR	2000	Inge de Bruijn, NED	56.61	WR

200-meter Butterfly

Year		Time		Year		Time	
1968	Ada Kok, NED	2:24.7	OR	1988	Kathleen Nord, E. Ger.	2:09.51	
1972	Karen Moe, USA	2:15.57	WR	1992	Summer Sanders, USA.	2:08.67	
1976	Andrea Pollack, E. Ger	2:11.41	WR	1996	Susie O'Neill, AUS	2:07.76	
1980	Ines Geissler, E. Ger	2:10.44	OR	2000	Misty Hyman, USA	2:05.88	OR
1984	Mary T. Meagher, USA	2:06.90	OR				

200-meter Individual Medley

Year		Time		Year		Time	
1968	Claudia Kolb, USA	2:24.7	OR	1992	Lin Li, CHN	2:11.65	WR
1972	Shane Gould, AUS	2:23.07	WR	1996	Michelle Smith, IRE	2:13.93	
1984	Tracy Caulkins, USA	2:12.64	OR	2000	Yana Klochkova, UKR	2:10.68	OR
1988	Daniela Hunger, E. Ger	2:12.59	OR				

400-meter Individual Medley

Year		Time		Year		Time	
1964	Donna de Varona, USA	5:18.7	OR	1984	Tracy Caulkins, USA	4:39.24	
1968	Claudia Kolb, USA	5:08.5	OR	1988	Janet Evans, USA	4:37.76	
1972	Gail Neall, AUS	5:02.97	WR	1992	Krisztina Egerszegi, HUN	4:36.54	
1976	Ulrike Tauber, E. Ger	4:42.77	WR	1996	Michelle Smith, IRE	4:39.18	
1980	Petra Schneider, E. Ger	4:36.29	WR	2000	Yana Klochkova, UKR	4:33.59	WR

4x100-meter Freestyle Relay

Year		Time		Year		Time	
1912	Great Britain	5:52.8	WR	1964	United States	4:03.8	WR
1920	United States	5:11.6	WR	1968	United States	4:02.5	OR
1924	United States	4:58.8	WR	1972	United States	3:55.19	WR
1928	United States	4:47.6	WR	1976	United States	3:44.82	WR
1932	United States	4:38.0	WR	1980	East Germany	3:42.71	WR
1936	Netherlands	4:36.0	OR	1984	United States	3:43.43	
1948	United States	4:29.2	OR	1988	East Germany	3:40.63	OR
1952	Hungary	4:24.4	WR	1992	United States	3:39.46	
1956	Australia	4:17.1	WR	1996	United States	3:39.29	WR
1960	United States	4:08.9	WR	2000	United States	3:36.61	WR

4x200-meter Freestyle Relay

Year		Time	Year		Time	
1996	United States	7:59.87	2000	United States	7:57.80	**OR**

4x100-meter Medley Relay

Year		Time		Year		Time	
1960	United States	4:41.1	**WR**	1984	United States	4:08.34	
1964	United States	4:33.9	**WR**	1988	East Germany	4:03.74	**OR**
1968	United States	4:28.3	**OR**	1992	United States	4:02.54	**WR**
1972	United States	4:20.75	**WR**	1996	United States	4:02.88	
1976	East Germany	4:07.95	**WR**	2000	United States	3:58.30	**WR**
1980	East Germany	4:06.67	**WR**				

TENNIS

MEN

Multiple gold medals (including men's doubles): John Boland, Max Decugis, Laurie Doherty, Reggie Doherty, Arthur Gore, Andre Grobert, Vincent Richards, Charles Winslow and Beals Wright (2).

Singles

Year			Year		
1896	John Boland	Great Britain/Ireland	1920	Louis Raymond	South Africa
1900	Laurie Doherty,	Great Britain	1924	Vincent Richards	United States
1904	Beals Wright	United States	1928-84	Not held	
1906	Max Decugis	France	1988	Miloslav Mecir	Czechoslovakia
1908	Josiah Ritchie	Great Britain	1992	Marc Rosset	Switzerland
	(Indoor) Arthur Gore	Great Britain	1996	Andre Agassi	United States
1912	Charles Winslow	South Africa	2000	Yevgeny Kafelnikov	Russia
	(Indoor) André Gobert	France			

Doubles

Year		Year	
1896	John Boland, IRE & Fritz Traun, GER	1920	Noel Turnbull & Max Woosnam, GBR
1900	Laurie and Reggie Doherty, GBR	1924	Vincent Richards & Frank Hunter, USA
1904	Edgar Leonard & Beals Wright, USA	1928-84	Not held
1906	Max Decugis & Maurice Germot, FRA	1988	Ken Flach & Robert Seguso, USA
1908	George Hillyard & Reggie Doherty, GBR	1992	Boris Becker & Michael Stich, GER
	(Indoor) Arthur Gore & Herbert Barrett, GBR	1996	Todd Woodbridge & Mark Woodforde, AUS
1912	Charles Winslow & Harold Kitson, S. Afr.	2000	Sebastien Lareau & Daniel Nestor, CAN
	(Indoor) Andre Gobert & Maurice Germot, FRA		

WOMEN

Multiple gold medals (including women's doubles): Helen Wills, Gigi Fernandez, Mary Joe Fernandez and Venus Williams (2).

Singles

Year			Year		
1900	Charlotte Cooper	Great Britain	1924	Helen Wills	United States
1906	Esmee Simiriotou	Greece	1928-84	Not held	
1908	Dorothea Chambers	Great Britain	1988	Steffi Graf	West Germany
	(Indoor) Gwen Eastlake-Smith	Great Britain	1992	Jennifer Capriati	United States
1912	Marguerite Broquedis	France	1996	Lindsay Davenport	United States
	(Indoor) Edith Hannam	Great Britain	2000	Venus Williams	United States
1920	Suzanne Lenglen	France			

Doubles

Year		Year	
1920	Winifred McNair & Kitty McKane, GBR	1992	Gigi Fernandez & Mary Joe Fernandez, USA
1924	Hazel Wightman & Helen Wills, USA	1996	Gigi Fernandez & Mary Joe Fernandez, USA
1928-84	Not held	2000	Serena Williams & Venus Williams, USA
1988	Pam Shriver & Zina Garrison, USA		

TRACK & FIELD

World and Olympic records below that appear to be broken or equaled by winning times, heights and distances in subsequent years, but are not so indicated, were all broken in preliminary races and field events leading up to the finals.

MEN

At least 4 gold medals (including relays and discontinued events): Ray Ewry (10); Carl Lewis and Paavo Nurmi (9); Ville Ritola and Martin Sheridan (5); Harrison Dillard, Archie Hahn, Michael Johnson, Hannes Kolehmainen, Alvin Kraenzlein, Eric Lemming, Jim Lightbody, Al Oerter, Jesse Owens, Meyer Prinstein, Mel Sheppard, Lasse Viren and Emil Zátopek (4). Note that all of Ewry's gold medals came before 1912, in the Standing High Jump, Standing Long Jump and Standing Triple Jump.

Track & Field (Cont.)

100 meters

Year		Time		Year		Time	
1896	Tom Burke, USA	12.0		1956	Bobby Morrow, USA	10.5	
1900	Frank Jarvis, USA	11.0		1960	Armin Hary, GER	10.2	OR
1904	Archie Hahn, USA	11.0		1964	Bob Hayes, USA	10.0	=WR
1906	Archie Hahn, USA	11.2		1968	Jim Hines, USA	9.95	WR
1908	Reggie Walker, S. Afr.	10.8	=OR	1972	Valery Borzov, USSR	10.14	
1912	Ralph Craig, USA	10.8		1976	Hasely Crawford, TRI	10.06	
1920	Charley Paddock, USA	10.8		1980	Allan Wells, GBR	10.25	
1924	Harold Abrahams, GBR	10.6	=OR	1984	Carl Lewis, USA	9.99	
1928	Percy Williams, CAN	10.8		1988	Carl Lewis, USA*	9.92	WR
1932	Eddie Tolan, USA	10.3	OR	1992	Linford Christie, GBR	9.96	
1936	Jesse Owens, USA	10.3ʷ		1996	Donovan Bailey, CAN.	9.84	WR
1948	Harrison Dillard, USA	10.3	=OR	2000	Maurice Greene, USA.	9.87	
1952	Lindy Remigino, USA	10.4					

ʷindicates wind-aided.

*Lewis finished second to Ben Johnson of Canada, who set a world record of 9.79 seconds. Two days later, Johnson was stripped of his gold medal and his record when he tested positive for steroid use in a post-race drug test.

200 meters

Year		Time		Year		Time	
1900	John Walter Tewksbury, USA	22.2		1960	Livio Berruti, ITA	20.5	=WR
1904	Archie Hahn, USA	21.6	OR	1964	Henry Carr, USA	20.3	OR
1908	Bobby Kerr, CAN	22.6		1968	Tommie Smith, USA	19.83	WR
1912	Ralph Craig, USA	21.7		1972	Valery Borzov, USSR	20.00	
1920	Allen Woodring, USA	22.0		1976	Donald Quarrie, JAM	20.23	
1924	Jackson Scholz, USA	21.6		1980	Pietro Mennea, ITA	20.19	
1928	Percy Williams, CAN	21.8		1984	Carl Lewis, USA	19.80	OR
1932	Eddie Tolan, USA	21.2	OR	1988	Joe DeLoach, USA	19.75	OR
1936	Jesse Owens, USA	20.7	OR	1992	Mike Marsh, USA	20.01	
1948	Mel Patton, USA	21.1		1996	Michael Johnson, USA	19.32	WR
1952	Andy Stanfield, USA	20.7		2000	Konstantinos Kenteris, GRE.	20.09	
1956	Bobby Morrow, USA	20.6	OR				

400 meters

Year		Time		Year		Time	
1896	Tom Burke, USA	54.2		1956	Charley Jenkins, USA	46.7	
1900	Maxey Long, USA	49.4	OR	1960	Otis Davis, USA	44.9	WR
1904	Harry Hillman, USA	49.2	OR	1964	Mike Larrabee, USA	45.1	
1906	Paul Pilgrim, USA	53.2		1968	Lee Evans, USA	43.86	WR
1908	Wyndham Halswelle, GBR	50.0		1972	Vince Matthews, USA	44.66	
1912	Charlie Reidpath, USA	48.2	OR	1976	Alberto Juantorena, CUB	44.26	
1920	Bevil Rudd, S. Afr.	49.6		1980	Viktor Markin, USSR	44.60	
1924	Eric Liddell, GBR	47.6	OR	1984	Alonzo Babers, USA	44.27	
1928	Ray Barbuti, USA	47.8		1988	Steve Lewis, USA	43.87	
1932	Bill Carr, USA	46.2	WR	1992	Quincy Watts, USA	43.50	OR
1936	Archie Williams, USA	46.5		1996	Michael Johnson, USA	43.49	OR
1948	Arthur Wint, JAM	46.2		2000	Michael Johnson, USA	43.84	
1952	George Rhoden, JAM	45.9	OR				

800 meters

Year		Time		Year		Time	
1896	Teddy Flack, AUS	2:11.0		1956	Tom Courtney, USA	1:47.7	OR
1900	Alfred Tysoe, GBR	2:01.2		1960	Peter Snell, NZE	1:46.3	OR
1904	Jim Lightbody, USA	1:56.0	OR	1964	Peter Snell, NZE	1:45.1	OR
1906	Paul Pilgrim, USA	2:01.5		1968	Ralph Doubell, AUS	1:44.3	=WR
1908	Mel Sheppard, USA	1:52.8	WR	1972	Dave Wottle, USA	1:45.9	
1912	Ted Meredith, USA	1:51.9	WR	1976	Alberto Juantorena, CUB	1:43.50	WR
1920	Albert Hill, GBR	1:53.4		1980	Steve Ovett, GBR	1:45.4	
1924	Douglas Lowe, GBR	1:52.4		1984	Joaquim Cruz, BRA	1:43.00	OR
1928	Douglas Lowe, GBR	1:51.8	OR	1988	Paul Ereng, KEN	1:43.45	
1932	Tommy Hampson, GBR	1:49.7	WR	1992	William Tanui, KEN	1:43.66	
1936	John Woodruff, USA	1:52.9		1996	Vebjoern Rodal, NOR.	1:42.58	OR
1948	Mal Whitfield, USA	1:49.2	OR	2000	Nils Schumann, GER.	1:45.08	
1952	Mal Whitfield, USA	1:49.2	=OR				

1500 meters

Year		Time		Year		Time	
1896	Teddy Flack, AUS	4:33.2		1912	Arnold Jackson, GBR	3:56.8	OR
1900	Charles Bennett, GBR	4:06.2	WR	1920	Albert Hill, GBR	4:01.8	
1904	Jim Lightbody, USA	4:05.4	WR	1924	Paavo Nurmi, FIN	3:53.6	OR
1906	Jim Lightbody, USA	4:12.0		1928	Harry Larva, FIN	3:53.2	OR
1908	Mel Sheppard, USA	4:03.4	OR	1932	Luigi Beccali, ITA	3:51.2	OR

Year		Time		Year		Time	
1936	John Lovelock, NZE	3:47.8	WR	1976	John Walker, NZE	3:39.17	
1948	Henry Eriksson, SWE	3:49.8		1980	Sebastian Coe, GBR	3:38.4	
1952	Josy Barthel, LUX	3:45.1	OR	1984	Sebastian Coe, GBR	3:32.53	OR
1956	Ron Delany, IRE	3:41.2	OR	1988	Peter Rono, KEN	3:35.96	
1960	Herb Elliott, AUS	3:35.6	WR	1992	Fermin Cacho, SPA	3:40.12	
1964	Peter Snell, NZE	3:38.1		1996	Noureddine Morceli, ALG	3:35.78	
1968	Kip Keino, KEN	3:34.9	OR	2000	Noah Ngeny, KEN	3:32.07	OR
1972	Pekka Vasala, FIN	3:36.3					

5000 meters

Year		Time		Year		Time	
1912	Hannes Kolehmainen, FIN	14:36.6	WR	1964	Bob Schul, USA	13:48.8	
1920	Joseph Guillemot, FRA	14:55.6		1968	Mohamed Gammoudi, TUN	14:05.0	
1924	Paavo Nurmi, FIN	14:31.2	OR	1972	Lasse Viren, FIN	13:26.4	OR
1928	Ville Ritola, FIN	14:38.0		1976	Lasse Viren, FIN	13:24.76	
1932	Lauri Lehtinen, FIN	14:30.0	OR	1980	Miruts Yifter, ETH	13:21.0	
1936	Gunnar Höckert, FIN	14:22.2	OR	1984	Said Aouita, MOR	13:05.59	OR
1948	Gaston Reiff, BEL	14:17.6	OR	1988	John Ngugi, KEN	13:11.70	
1952	Emil Zátopek, CZE	14:06.6	OR	1992	Dieter Baumann, GER	13:12.52	
1956	Vladimir Kuts, USSR	13:39.6	OR	1996	Venuste Niyongabo, BUR	13:07.96	
1960	Murray Halberg, NZE	13:43.4		2000	Millon Wolde, ETH	13:35.49	

10,000 meters

Year		Time		Year		Time	
1912	Hannes Kolehmainen, FIN	31:20.8		1964	Billy Mills, USA	28:24.4	OR
1920	Paavo Nurmi, FIN	31:45.8		1968	Naftali Temu, KEN	29:27.4	
1924	Ville Ritola, FIN	30:23.2	WR	1972	Lasse Viren, FIN	27:38.4	WR
1928	Paavo Nurmi, FIN	30:18.8	OR	1976	Lasse Viren, FIN	27:40.38	
1932	Janusz Kusocinski, POL	30:11.4	OR	1980	Miruts Yifter, ETH	27:42.7	
1936	Ilmari Salminen, FIN	30:15.4		1984	Alberto Cova, ITA	27:47.54	
1948	Emil Zátopek, CZE	29:59.6	OR	1988	Brahim Boutaib, MOR	27:21.46	OR
1952	Emil Zátopek, CZE	29:17.0	OR	1992	Khalid Skah, MOR	27:46.70	
1956	Vladimir Kuts, USSR	28:45.6	OR	1996	Haile Gebrselassie, ETH	27:07.34	OR
1960	Pyotr Bolotnikov, USSR	28:32.2	OR	2000	Haile Gebrselassie, ETH	27:18.20	

Marathon

Year		Time		Year		Time	
1896	Spiridon Louis, GRE	2:58:50		1956	Alain Mimoun, FRA	2:25:00.0	
1900	Michel Théato, FRA	2:59:45		1960	Abebe Bikila, ETH	2:15:16.2	WB
1904	Thomas Hicks, USA	3:28:53		1964	Abebe Bikila, ETH	2:12:11.2	WB
1906	Billy Sherring, CAN	2:51:23.6		1968	Mamo Wolde, ETH	2:20:26.4	
1908	Johnny Hayes, USA*	2:55:18.4	OR	1972	Frank Shorter, USA	2:12:19.8	
1912	Kenneth McArthur, S. Afr.	2:36:54.8		1976	Waldemar Cierpinski, E. Ger	2:09:55.0	OR
1920	Hannes Kolehmainen, FIN	2:32:35.8	WB	1980	Waldemar Cierpinski, E. Ger	2:11:03.0	
1924	Albin Stenroos, FIN	2:41:22.6		1984	Carlos Lopes, POR	2:09:21.0	OR
1928	Boughèra El Ouafi, FRA	2:32:57.0		1988	Gelindo Bordin, ITA	2:10:32	
1932	Juan Carlos Zabala, ARG	2:31:36.0	OR	1992	Hwang Young-Cho, S. Kor	2:13:23	
1936	Sohn Kee-Chung, JPN†	2:29:19.2	OR	1996	Josia Thugwane, S. Afr.	2:12:36	
1948	Delfo Cabrera, ARG	2:34:51.6		2000	Gezahenge Abera, ETH	2:10.11	
1952	Emil Zátopek, CZE	2:23:03.2	OR				

*Dorando Pietri of Italy placed first, but was disqualified for being helped across the finish line.

†Sohn was a Korean, but he was forced to compete under the name Kitei Son by Japan, which occupied Korea at the time.

Note: Marathon distances–40,000 meters (1896,1904); 40,260 meters (1900); 41,860 meters (1906); 42,195 meters (1908 and since 1924); 40,200 meters (1912); 42,750 meters (1920). Current distance of 42,195 meters measures 26 miles, 385 yards.

110-meter Hurdles

Year		Time		Year		Time	
1896	Tom Curtis, USA	17.6		1956	Lee Calhoun, USA	13.5	OR
1900	Alvin Kraenzlein, USA	15.4	OR	1960	Lee Calhoun, USA	13.8	
1904	Frederick Schule, USA	16.0		1964	Hayes Jones, USA	13.6	
1906	Robert Leavitt, USA	16.2		1968	Willie Davenport, USA	13.3	OR
1908	Forrest Smithson, USA	15.0	WR	1972	Rod Milburn, USA	13.24	=WR
1912	Frederick Kelly, USA	15.1		1976	Guy Drut, FRA	13.30	
1920	Earl Thomson, CAN	14.8	WR	1980	Thomas Munkelt, E. Ger	13.39	
1924	Daniel Kinsey, USA	15.0		1984	Roger Kingdom, USA	13.20	OR
1928	Syd Atkinson, S. Afr.	14.8		1988	Roger Kingdom, USA	12.98	OR
1932	George Saling, USA	14.6		1992	Mark McKoy, CAN	13.12	
1936	Forrest (Spec) Towns, USA	14.2		1996	Allen Johnson, USA	12.95	OR
1948	William Porter, USA	13.9	OR	2000	Anier Garcia, CUB	13.00	
1952	Harrison Dillard, USA	13.7	OR				

Track & Field (Cont.)
400-meter Hurdles

Year		Time		Year		Time	
1900	John Walter Tewksbury, USA	57.6		1960	Glenn Davis, USA	49.3	OR
1904	Harry Hillman, USA	53.0		1964	Rex Cawley, USA	49.6	
1908	Charley Bacon, USA	55.0	WR	1968	David Hemery, GBR	48.12	WR
1920	Frank Loomis, USA	54.0	WR	1972	John Akii-Bua, UGA	47.82	WR
1924	Morgan Taylor, USA	52.6		1976	Edwin Moses, USA	47.64	WR
1928	David Burghley, GBR	53.4	OR	1980	Volker Beck, E. Ger	48.70	
1932	Bob Tisdall, IRE	51.7		1984	Edwin Moses, USA	47.75	
1936	Glenn Hardin, USA	52.4		1988	Andre Phillips, USA	47.19	OR
1948	Roy Cochran, USA	51.1	OR	1992	Kevin Young, USA	46.78	WR
1952	Charley Moore, USA	50.8	OR	1996	Derrick Adkins, USA	47.54	
1956	Glenn Davis, USA	50.1	=OR	2000	Angelo Taylor, USA	47.50	

3000-meter Steeplechase

Year		Time		Year		Time	
1900	George Orton, CAN	7:34.4		1960	Zdzislaw Krzyszkowiak, POL	8:34.2	OR
1904	Jim Lightbody, USA	7:39.6		1964	Gaston Roelants, BEL	8:30.8	OR
1908	Arthur Russell, GBR	10:47.8		1968	Amos Biwott, KEN	8:51.0	
1920	Percy Hodge, GBR	10:00.4	OR	1972	Kip Keino, KEN	8:23.6	OR
1924	Ville Ritola, FIN	9:33.6	OR	1976	Anders Gärderud, SWE	8:08.2	WR
1928	Toivo Loukola, FIN	9:21.8	WR	1980	Bronislaw Malinowski, POL	8:09.7	
1932	Volmari Iso-Hollo, FIN	10:33.4*		1984	Julius Korir, KEN	8:11.80	
1936	Volmari Iso-Hollo, FIN	9:03.8	WR	1988	Julius Kariuki, KEN	8:05.51	OR
1948	Thore Sjöstrand, SWE	9:04.6		1992	Matthew Birir, KEN	8:08.84	
1952	Horace Ashenfelter, USA	8:45.4	WR	1996	Joseph Keter, KEN	8:07.12	
1956	Chris Brasher, GBR	8:41.2	OR	2000	Reuben Kosgei, KEN	8:21.43	

*Iso-Hollo ran one extra lap due to lap counter's mistake.
Note: Other steeplechase distances– 2500 meters (1900); 2590 meters (1904); 3200 meters (1908) and 3460 meters (1932).

4x100-meter Relay

Year		Time		Year		Time	
1912	Great Britain	42.4		1964	United States	39.0	WR
1920	United States	42.2	WR	1968	United States	38.23	WR
1924	United States	41.0	=WR	1972	United States	38.19	WR
1928	United States	41.0	=WR	1976	United States	38.33	
1932	United States	40.0	WR	1980	Soviet Union	38.26	
1936	United States	39.8	WR	1984	United States	37.83	WR
1948	United States	40.6		1988	Soviet Union	38.19	
1952	United States	40.1		1992	United States	37.40	WR
1956	United States	39.5	WR	1996	Canada	37.69	
1960	Germany	39.5	=WR	2000	United States	37.61	

4x400-meter Relay

Year		Time		Year		Time	
1908	United States	3:29.4		1964	United States	3:00.7	WR
1912	United States	3:16.6	WR	1968	United States	2:56.16	WR
1920	Great Britain	3:22.2		1972	Kenya	2:59.8	
1924	United States	3:16.0	WR	1976	United States	2:58.65	
1928	United States	3:14.2	WR	1980	Soviet Union	3:01.1	
1932	United States	3:08.2	WR	1984	United States	2:57.91	
1936	Great Britain	3:09.0		1988	United States	2:56.16	=WR
1948	United States	3:10.4		1992	United States	2:55.74	WR
1952	Jamaica	3:03.9	WR	1996	United States	2:55.99	
1956	United States	3:04.8		2000	United States	2:56.35	
1960	United States	3:02.2	WR				

20-kilometer Walk

Year		Time		Year		Time	
1956	Leonid Spirin, USSR	1:31:27.4		1980	Maurizio Damilano, ITA	1:23:35.5	OR
1960	Vladimir Golubnichiy, USSR	1:34:07.2		1984	Ernesto Canto, MEX	1:23:13	OR
1964	Ken Matthews, GBR	1:29:34.0	OR	1988	Jozef Pribilinec, CZE	1:19:57	OR
1968	Vladimir Golubnichiy, USSR	1:33:58.4		1992	Daniel Plaza Montero, SPA	1:21:45	
1972	Peter Frenkel, E. Ger	1:26:42.4	OR	1996	Jefferson Perez, ECU	1:20:07	
1976	Daniel Bautista, MEX	1:24:40.6	OR	2000	Robert Korzeniowski, POL	1:18.59	OR

50-kilometer Walk

Year		Time		Year		Time	
1932	Thomas Green, GBR	4:50:10		1960	Don Thompson, GBR	4:25:30.0	OR
1936	Harold Whitlock, GBR	4:30:41.4	OR	1964	Abdon Pamich, ITA	4:11:12.4	OR
1948	John Ljunggren, SWE	4:41:52		1968	Christoph Höhne, E. Ger	4:20:13.6	
1952	Giuseppe Dordoni, ITA	4:28:07.8	OR	1972	Bernd Kannenberg, W. Ger	3:56:11.6	OR
1956	Norman Read, NZE	4:30:42.8		1976	Not held		

Year		Time		Year		Time	
1980	Hartwig Gauder, E. Ger	3:49:24.0	OR	1996	Robert Korzeniowski, POL	3:43:30	
1984	Raul Gonzalez, MEX	3:47:26	OR	2000	Robert Korzeniowski, POL	3:42.22	
1988	Vyacheslav Ivanenko, USSR	3:38:29	OR				
1992	Andrei Perlov, UT	3:50:13					

High Jump

Year		Height		Year		Height	
1896	Ellery Clark, USA	5-11¼		1956	Charley Dumas, USA	6-11½	OR
1900	Irving Baxter, USA	6-2¾	OR	1960	Robert Shavlakadze, USSR	7-1	OR
1904	Sam Jones, USA	5-11		1964	Valery Brumel, USSR	7-1¾	OR
1906	Cornelius Leahy, GBR/IRE	5-10		1968	Dick Fosbury, USA	7-4¼	OR
1908	Harry Porter, USA	6-3	OR	1972	Yuri Tarmak, USSR	7-3¾	
1912	Alma Richards, USA	6-4	OR	1976	Jacek Wszola, POL	7-4½	OR
1920	Richmond Landon, USA	6-4	=OR	1980	Gerd Wessig, E. Ger	7-8¾	WR
1924	Harold Osborn, USA	6-6	OR	1984	Dietmar Mögenburg, W. Ger	7-8½	
1928	Bob King, USA	6-4½		1988	Gennady Avdeyenko, USSR	7-9¾	OR
1932	Duncan McNaughton, CAN	6-5½		1992	Javier Sotomayor, CUB	7-8	
1936	Cornelius Johnson, USA	6-8	OR	1996	Charles Austin, USA	7-10	OR
1948	John Winter, AUS	6-6		2000	Sergey Klugin, RUS	7-8½	
1952	Walt Davis, USA	6-8½	OR				

Pole Vault

Year		Height		Year		Height	
1896	William Hoyt, USA	10-10		1952	Bob Richards, USA	14-11	OR
1900	Irving Baxter, USA	10-10		1956	Bob Richards, USA	14-11½	OR
1904	Charles Dvorak, USA	11-5¾		1960	Don Bragg, USA	15-5	OR
1906	Fernand Gonder, FRA	11-5¾		1964	Fred Hansen, USA	16-8¾	OR
1908	(TIE) Edward Cooke, USA	12-2		1968	Bob Seagren, USA	17-8½	OR
	Alfred Gilbert, USA	12-2	OR	1972	Wolfgang Nordwig, E. Ger	18-0½	OR
1912	Harry Babcock, USA	12-11½		1976	Tadeusz Slusarski, POL	18-0½	=OR
1920	Frank Foss, USA	13-5	WR	1980	Wladyslaw Kozakiewicz, POL	18-11½	WR
1924	Lee Barnes, USA	12-11½		1984	Pierre Quinon, FRA	18-10¼	
1928	Sabin Carr, USA	13-9¼	OR	1988	Sergey Bubka, USSR	19-4¼	OR
1932	Bill Miller, USA	14-1¾	OR	1992	Maksim Tarasov, UT	19-0¼	
1936	Earle Meadows, USA	14-3¼	OR	1996	Jean Galfione, FRA	19-5¼	OR
1948	Guinn Smith, USA	14-1¼		2000	Nick Hysong, USA	19-4¼	

Long Jump

Year		Distance		Year		Distance	
1896	Ellery Clark, USA	20-10		1956	Greg Bell, USA	25-8¼	
1900	Alvin Kraenzlein, USA	23-6¾	OR	1960	Ralph Boston, USA	26-7¾	OR
1904	Meyer Prinstein, USA	24-1	OR	1964	Lynn Davies, GBR	26-5¾	
1906	Meyer Prinstein, USA	23-7½		1968	Bob Beamon, USA	29-2½	WR
1908	Frank Irons, USA	24-6½	OR	1972	Randy Williams, USA	27-0½	
1912	Albert Gutterson, USA	24-11¼	OR	1976	Arnie Robinson, USA	27-4¾	
1920	William Petersson, SWE	23-5½		1980	Lutz Dombrowski, E. Ger	28-0¼	
1924	De Hart Hubbard, USA	24-5		1984	Carl Lewis, USA	28-0¼	
1928	Ed Hamm, USA	25-4½	OR	1988	Carl Lewis, USA	28-7¼	
1932	Ed Gordon, USA	25-0¾		1992	Carl Lewis, USA	28-5½	
1936	Jesse Owens, USA	26-5½	OR	1996	Carl Lewis, USA	27-10¾	
1948	Willie Steele, USA	25-8		2000	Ivan Pedroso, CUB	28-0¾	
1952	Jerome Biffle, USA	24-10					

Triple Jump

Year		Distance		Year		Distance	
1896	James Connolly, USA	44-11¾		1956	Adhemar da Silva, BRA	53-7¾	OR
1900	Meyer Prinstein, USA	47-5¾	OR	1960	Józef Schmidt, POL	55-2	
1904	Meyer Prinstein, USA	47-1		1964	Józef Schmidt, POL	55-3½	OR
1906	Peter O'Connor, GBR/IRE	46-2¼		1968	Viktor Saneyev, USSR	57-0¾	WR
1908	Timothy Ahearne, GBR/IRE	48-11¼	OR	1972	Viktor Saneyev, USSR	56-11¼	
1912	Gustaf Lindblom, SWE	48-5¼		1976	Viktor Saneyev, USSR	56-8¾	
1920	Vilho Tuulos, FIN	47-7		1980	Jaak Uudmäe, USSR	56-11¼	
1924	Nick Winter, AUS	50-11¼	WR	1984	Al Joyner, USA	56-7½	
1928	Mikio Oda, JPN	49-11		1988	Khristo Markov, BUL	57-9¼	OR
1932	Chuhei Nambu, JPN	51-7	WR	1992	Mike Conley, USA	59-7½ ʷ	OR
1936	Naoto Tajima, JPN	52-6	WR	1996	Kenny Harrison, USA	59-4¼	OR
1948	Arne Ahman, SWE	50-6¼		2000	Jonathan Edwards, GBR	58-1¼	
1952	Adhemar da Silva, BRA	53-2¾	WR		ʷindicates wind-aided.		

Track & Field (Cont.)

Shot Put

Year		Distance		Year		Distance	
1896	Bob Garrett, USA	36- 9¾		1956	Parry O'Brien, USA	60-11¼	OR
1900	Richard Sheldon, USA	46- 3¼	OR	1960	Bill Nieder, USA	64- 6¾	OR
1904	Ralph Rose, USA	48- 7	WR	1964	Dallas Long, USA	66- 8½	OR
1906	Martin Sheridan, USA	40- 5¼		1968	Randy Matson, USA	67- 4¾	
1908	Ralph Rose, USA	46- 7½		1972	Wladyslaw Komar, POL	69- 6	OR
1912	Patrick McDonald, USA	50- 4	OR	1976	Udo Beyer, E. Ger	69- 0¾	
1920	Ville Pörhölä, FIN	48- 7¼		1980	Vladimir Kiselyov, USSR	70- 0½	OR
1924	Bud Houser, USA	49- 2¼		1984	Alessandro Andrei, ITA	69- 9	
1928	John Kuck, USA	52- 0¾	WR	1988	Ulf Timmermann, E. Ger	73- 8¾	OR
1932	Leo Sexton, USA	52- 6	OR	1992	Mike Stulce, USA	71- 2½	
1936	Hans Woellke, GER	53- 1¾	OR	1996	Randy Barnes, USA	70-11¼	
1948	Wilbur Thompson, USA	56- 2	OR	2000	Arsi Harju, FIN	69-10¼	
1952	Parry O'Brien, USA	57- 1½	OR				

Discus Throw

Year		Distance		Year		Distance	
1896	Bob Garrett, USA	95- 7½		1956	Al Oerter, USA	184-11	OR
1900	Rudolf Bauer, HUN	118- 3	OR	1960	Al Oerter, USA	194- 2	OR
1904	Martin Sheridan, USA	128-10½	OR	1964	Al Oerter, USA	200- 1	OR
1906	Martin Sheridan, USA	136- 0		1968	Al Oerter, USA	212- 6	OR
1908	Martin Sheridan, USA	134- 2	OR	1972	Ludvik Danek, CZE	211- 3	
1912	Armas Taipale, FIN	148- 3	OR	1976	Mac Wilkins, USA	221- 5	
1920	Elmer Niklander, FIN	146- 7		1980	Viktor Rashchupkin, USSR	218- 8	
1924	Bud Houser, USA	151- 4	OR	1984	Rolf Danneberg, W. Ger	218- 6	
1928	Bud Houser, USA	155- 3	OR	1988	Jürgen Schult, E. Ger	225- 9	OR
1932	John Anderson, USA	162- 4	OR	1992	Romas Ubartas, LIT	213- 8	
1936	Ken Carpenter, USA	165- 7	OR	1996	Lars Riedel, GER	227-8	
1948	Adolfo Consolini, ITA	173- 2	OR	2000	Virgilijus Alekna, LIT	227-4	
1952	Sim Iness, USA	180- 6	OR				

Hammer Throw

Year		Distance		Year		Distance	
1900	John Flanagan, USA	163- 1		1960	Vasily Rudenkov, USSR	220- 2	OR
1904	John Flanagan, USA	168- 1	OR	1964	Romuald Klim, USSR	228-10	OR
1908	John Flanagan, USA	170- 4	OR	1968	Gyula Zsivótzky, HUN	240- 8	OR
1912	Matt McGrath, USA	179- 7	OR	1972	Anatoly Bondarchuk, USSR	247- 8	OR
1920	Pat Ryan, USA	173- 5		1976	Yuri Sedykh, USSR	254- 4	OR
1924	Fred Tootell, USA	174-10		1980	Yuri Sedykh, USSR	268- 4	WR
1928	Pat O'Callaghan, IRE	168- 7		1984	Juha Tiainen, FIN	256- 2	
1932	Pat O'Callaghan, IRE	176-11		1988	Sergey Litvinov, USSR	278- 2	OR
1936	Karl Hein, GER	185- 4	OR	1992	Andrei Abduvaliyev, UT	270- 9	
1948	Imre Németh, HUN	183-11		1996	Balazs Kiss, HUN.	266-6	
1952	József Csérmák, HUN	197-11	WR	2000	Szymon Ziolkowski, POL	262-6	
1956	Harold Connolly, USA	207- 3	OR				

Javelin Throw

Year		Distance		Year		Distance	
1908	Eric Lemming, SWE	179-10	WR	1964	Pauli Nevala, FIN	271- 2	
1912	Eric Lemming, SWE	198-11	WR	1968	Jänis Lüsis, USSR	295- 7	OR
1920	Jonni Myyrä, FIN	215-10	OR	1972	Klaus Wolfermann, W. Ger	296-10	OR
1924	Jonni Myyrä, FIN	206- 7		1976	Miklos Németh, HUN	310- 4	WR
1928	Erik Lundkvist, SWE	218- 6	OR	1980	Dainis Kula, USSR	299- 2	
1932	Matti Järvinen, FIN	238- 6	OR	1984	Arto Härkönen, FIN	284- 8	
1936	Gerhard Stöck, GER	235- 8		1988	Tapio Korjus, FIN	276- 6	
1948	Kai Tapio Rautavaara, FIN	228-10		1992	Jan Zelezny, CZR	294- 2*	OR
1952	Cy Young, USA	242- 1	OR	1996	Jan Zelezny, CZR	289-3	
1956	Egil Danielson, NOR	281- 2	WR	2000	Jan Zelezny, CZR	295-10	OR
1960	Viktor Tsibulenko, USSR	277- 8					

*In 1986 the balance point of the javelin was modified and new records have been kept since.

Decathlon

Year		Points		Year		Points	
1904	Thomas Kiely, IRE	6036		1932	Jim Bausch, USA	8462	WR
1906-08 Not held				1936	Glenn Morris, USA	7900	WR
1912	Jim Thrope, USA	8412	WR	1948	Bob Mathias, USA	7139	
1920	Helge Lövland, NOR	6803		1952	Bob Mathias, USA	7887	WR
1924	Harold Osborn, USA	7711	WR	1956	Milt Campbell, USA	7937	OR
1928	Paavo Yrjölä, FIN	8053	WR	1960	Rafer Johnson, USA	8392	OR

Year		Points		Year		Points	
1964	Willi Holdorf, GER	7887		1988	Christian Schenk, E. Ger	8488	
1968	Bill Toomey, USA	8193	**OR**	1992	Robert Zmelik, CZE	8611	
1972	Nikolai Avilov, USSR	8454	**WR**	1996	Dan O'Brien, USA	8824	
1976	Bruce Jenner, USA	8617	**WR**	2000	Erki Nool, EST	8641	
1980	Daley Thompson, GBR	8495					
1984	Daley Thompson, GBR	8798	**=WR**				

WOMEN

At least 4 gold medals (including relays): Evelyn Ashford, Fanny Blankers-Koen, Betty Cuthbert and Bärbel Eckert Wöckel (4).

100 meters

Year		Time		Year		Time	
1928	Betty Robinson, USA	12.2	**=WR**	1972	Renate Stecher, E. Ger	11.07	
1932	Stella Walsh, POL*	11.9	**=WR**	1976	Annegret Richter, W. Ger	11.08	
1936	Helen Stephens, USA	11.5ʷ		1980	Lyudmila Kondratyeva, USSR	11.06	
1948	Fanny Blankers-Koen, NED	11.9		1984	Evelyn Ashford, USA	10.97	**OR**
1952	Marjorie Jackson, AUS	11.5	**=WR**	1988	Florence Griffith Joyner, USA	10.54ʷ	**OR**
1956	Betty Cuthbert, AUS	11.5		1992	Gail Devers, USA	10.82	**OR**
1960	Wilma Rudolph, USA	11.0 ʷ		1996	Gail Devers, USA	10.94	
1964	Wyomia Tyus, USA	11.4		2000	Marion Jones, USA	10.75	
1968	Wyomia Tyus, USA	11.08	**WR**				

*An autopsy performed after Walsh's death in 1980 revealed that she was a man.
ʷindicates wind-aided.

200 meters

Year		Time		Year		Time	
1948	Fanny Blankers-Koen, NED	24.4		1976	Bärbel Eckert, E. Ger	22.37	**OR**
1952	Marjorie Jackson, AUS	23.7	**OR**	1980	Bärbel Eckert Wockel, E. Ger	22.03	**OR**
1956	Betty Cuthbert, AUS	23.4	**=OR**	1984	Valerie Brisco-Hooks, USA	21.81	**OR**
1960	Wilma Rudolph, USA	24.0		1988	Florence Griffith Joyner, USA	21.34	**WR**
1964	Edith McGuire, USA	23.0	**OR**	1992	Gwen Torrence, USA	21.81	
1968	Irena Szewinska, POL	22.5	**WR**	1996	Marie-Jose Perec, FRA	22.12	
1972	Renate Stecher, E. Ger	22.40	**=WR**	2000	Marion Jones, USA	21.84	

400 meters

Year		Time		Year		Time	
1964	Betty Cuthbert, AUS	52.0		1984	Valerie Brisco-Hooks, USA	48.83	**OR**
1968	Colette Besson, FRA	52.03	**=OR**	1988	Olga Bryzgina, USSR	48.65	**OR**
1972	Monika Zehrt, E. Ger	51.08	**OR**	1992	Marie-Jose Perec, FRA	48.83	
1976	Irena Szewinska, POL	49.29	**WR**	1996	Marie-Jose Perec, FRA	48.25	**OR**
1980	Marita Koch, E. Ger	48.88	**OR**	2000	Cathy Freeman, AUS	49.11	

800 meters

Year		Time		Year		Time	
1928	Lina Radke, GER	2:16.8	**WR**	1980	Nadezhda Olizarenko, USSR	1:53.42	**WR**
1932-56	Not held			1984	Doina Melinte, ROM	1:57.60	
1960	Lyudmila Shevtsova, USSR	2:04.3	**=WR**	1988	Sigrun Wodars, E. Ger	1:56.10	
1964	Ann Packer, GBR	2:01.1	**OR**	1992	Ellen van Langen, NED	1:55.54	
1968	Madeline Manning, USA	2:00.9	**OR**	1996	Svetlana Masterkova, RUS	1:57.73	
1972	Hildegard Falck, W. Ger	1:58.55	**OR**	2000	Maria Mutola, MOZ	1:56.15	
1976	Tatyana Kazankina, USSR	1:54.94	**WR**				

1500 meters

Year		Time		Year		Time	
1972	Lyudmila Bragina, USSR	4:01.4	**WR**	1988	Paula Ivan, ROM	3:53.96	**OR**
1976	Tatyana Kazankina, USSR	4:05.48		1992	Hassiba Boulmerka, ALG	3:55.30	
1980	Tatyana Kazankina, USSR	3:56.6	**OR**	1996	Svetlana Masterkova, RUS	4:00.83	
1984	Gabriella Dorio, ITA	4:03.25		2000	Nouria Merah-Benida, ALG	4:05.10	

5000 meters

Year		Time		Year		Time	
1984	Maricica Puica, ROM	8:35.96		1996	Wang Junxia, CHN	14:59.88	
1988	Tatyana Samolenko, USSR	8:26.53	**OR**	2000	Gabriela Szabo, ROM	14:40.79	**OR**
1992	Elena Romanova, UT	8:46.04			**Note:** Event held over 3000 meters from 1984-92.		

10,000 meters

Year		Time		Year		Time	
1988	Olga Bondarenko, USSR	31:05.21	**OR**	1996	Fernanda Ribeiro, POR	31:01.63	**OR**
1992	Derartu Tulu, ETH	31:06.02		2000	Derartu Tulu, ETH	30:17.49	**OR**

Marathon

Year		Time		Year		Time	
1984	Joan Benoit, USA	2:24:52		1996	Fatuma Roba, ETH	2:26:05	
1988	Rosa Mota, POR	2:25:40		2000	Naoko Takahashi, JPN	2:23:14	
1992	Valentina Yegorova, UT	2:32:41					

Track & Field (Cont.)

100-meter Hurdles

Year		Time		Year		Time	
1932	Babe Didrikson, USA	11.7	WR	1976	Johanna Schaller, E. Ger	12.77	
1936	Trebisonda Valla, ITA	11.7		1980	Vera Komisova, USSR	12.56	OR
1948	Fanny Blankers-Koen, NED	11.2	OR	1984	Benita Fitzgerald-Brown, USA	12.84	
1952	Shirley Strickland, AUS	10.9	WR	1988	Yordanka Donkova, BUL	12.38	OR
1956	Shirley Strickland, AUS	10.7	OR	1992	Paraskevi Patoulidou, GRE	12.64	
1960	Irina Press, USSR	10.8		1996	Ludmila Enquist, SWE	12.58	
1964	Karin Balzer, GER	10.5ʷ		2000	Olga Shishigina, KAZ	12.65	
1968	Maureen Caird, AUS	10.3	OR		ʷindicates wind-aided.		
1972	Annelie Ehrhardt, E. Ger	12.59	WR				

Note: Event held over 80 meters from 1932-68.

400-meter Hurdles

Year		Time		Year		Time	
1984	Nawal El Moutawakel, MOR	54.61	OR	1996	Deon Hemmings, JAM	52.82	OR
1988	Debra Flintoff-King, AUS	53.17	OR	2000	Irina Privalova, RUS	53.02	
1992	Sally Gunnell, GBR	53.23					

4x100-meter Relay

Year		Time		Year		Time	
1928	Canada	48.4	WR	1972	West Germany	42.81	WR
1932	United States	46.9	WR	1976	East Germany	42.55	OR
1936	United States	46.9		1980	East Germany	41.60	WR
1948	Holland	47.5		1984	United States	41.65	
1952	United States	45.9	WR	1988	United States	41.98	
1956	Australia	44.5	WR	1992	United States	42.11	
1960	United States	44.5		1996	United States	41.95	
1964	Poland	43.6		2000	Bahamas	42.20	
1968	United States	42.87	WR				

4x400-meter Relay

Year		Time		Year		Time	
1972	East Germany	3:23.0	WR	1988	Soviet Union	3:15.18	WR
1976	East Germany	3:19.23	WR	1992	Unified Team	3:20.20	
1980	Soviet Union	3:20.2		1996	United States	3:20.91	
1984	United States	3:18.29	OR	2000	United States	3:22.62	

20-kilometer Walk

Year		Time	Year		Time
1992	Chen Yueling, CHN	44:32	2000	Wang Liping, CHN	1:29.05
1996	Yelena Ninikolayeva, RUS	41:49			

Note: Event was held over 10 kilometers from 1992-96.

High Jump

Year		Height		Year		Height	
1928	Ethel Catherwood, CAN	5- 2½		1972	Ulrike Meyfarth, W. Ger	6- 3½	=WR
1932	Jean Shiley, USA	5- 5¼	WR	1976	Rosemarie Ackermann, E. Ger	6- 4	OR
1936	Ibolya Csák, HUN	5- 3		1980	Sara Simeoni, ITA	6- 5½	OR
1948	Alice Coachman, USA	5- 6	OR	1984	Ulrike Meyfarth, W. Ger	6- 7½	OR
1952	Esther Brand, RSA	5- 5¾		1988	Louise Ritter, USA	6- 8	OR
1956	Mildred McDaniel, USA	5- 9¼	WR	1992	Heike Henkel, GER	6- 7½	
1960	Iolanda Balas, ROM	6- 0¾	OR	1996	Stefka Kostadinova, BUL	6-8¾	
1964	Iolanda Balas, ROM	6- 2¾	OR	2000	Yelena Yelesina, RUS	6-7	
1968	Miloslava Rezkova, CZE	5-11½					

Pole Vault

Year		Height	
2000	Stacy Dragila, USA	15-1	OR

Long Jump

Year		Distance		Year		Distance	
1948	Olga Gyarmati, HUN	18- 8¼		1976	Angela Voigt, E. Ger	22- 0¾	
1952	Yvette Williams, NZE	20- 5¾	OR	1980	Tatyana Kolpakova, USSR	23- 2	OR
1956	Elzbieta Krzesinska, POL	20-10	=WR	1984	Anisoara Cusmir-Stanciu, ROM	22-10	
1960	Vyera Krepkina, USSR	20-10¾	OR	1988	Jackie Joyner-Kersee, USA	24- 3¼	OR
1964	Mary Rand, GBR	22- 2¼	WR	1992	Heike Drechsler, GER	23- 5¼	
1968	Viorica Viscopoleanu, ROM	22- 4½	WR	1996	Chioma Ajunwa, NGR	23-4½	
1972	Heidemarie Rosendahl, W. Ger	22- 3		2000	Heike Drechsler, GER	22-11¼	

Triple Jump

Year		Distance	Year		Distance
1996	Inessa Kravets, UKR	50-3½	2000	Tereza Marinova, BUL	49-10½

Shot Put

Year		Distance		Year		Distance	
1948	Micheline Ostermeyer, FRA	45-1½		1976	Ivanka Hristova, BUL	69-5¼	OR
1952	Galina Zybina, USSR	50-1¾	WR	1980	Ilona Slupianek, E. Ger	73-6¼	OR
1956	Tamara Tyshkevich, USSR	54-5	OR	1984	Claudia Losch, W. Ger	67-2¼	
1960	Tamara Press, USSR	56-10	OR	1988	Natalia Lisovskaya, USSR	72-11¾	
1964	Tamara Press, USSR	59-6¼	OR	1992	Svetlana Krivaleva, UT	69-1¼	
1968	Margitta Gummel, E. Ger	64-4	WR	1996	Astrid Kumbernuss, GER	67-5½	
1972	Nadezhda Chizhova, USSR	69-0	WR	2000	Yanina Korolchik, BLR	67-5½	

Discus Throw

Year		Distance		Year		Distance	
1928	Halina Konopacka, POL	129-11¾	WR	1972	Faina Melnik, USSR	218-7	OR
1932	Lillian Copeland, USA	133-2	OR	1976	Evelin Schlaak, E. Ger	226-4	OR
1936	Gisela Mauermayer, GER	156-3	OR	1980	Evelin Schlaak Jahl, E. Ger	229-6	OR
1948	Micheline Ostermeyer, FRA	137-6		1984	Ria Stalman, NED	214-5	
1952	Nina Romaschkova, USSR	168-8	OR	1988	Martina Hellmann, E. Ger	237-2½	OR
1956	Olga Fikotová, CZE	176-1	OR	1992	Maritza Marten, CUB	229-10	
1960	Nina Ponomaryeva, USSR	180-9	OR	1996	Ilke Wyludda, GER	228-6	
1964	Tamara Press, USSR	187-10	OR	2000	Ellina Zvereva, BLR	224-5	
1968	Lia Manoliu, ROM	191-2	OR				

Hammer Throw

Year		Distance	
2000	Kamila Skolimowska, POL	233-5¾	OR

Javelin Throw

Year		Distance		Year		Distance	
1932	Babe Didrikson, USA	143-4		1976	Ruth Fuchs, E. Ger	216-4	OR
1936	Tilly Fleischer, GER	148-3	OR	1980	Maria Colon Rueñes, CUB	224-5	OR
1948	Herma Bauma, AUT	149-6	OR	1984	Tessa Sanderson, GBR	228-2	OR
1952	Dana Zátopková, CZE	165-7	OR	1988	Petra Felke, E. Ger	245-0	OR
1956	Ineze Jaunzeme, USSR	176-8	OR	1992	Silke Renk, GER	224-2	
1960	Elvira Ozolina, USSR	183-8	OR	1996	Heli Rantanen, FIN	222-11	
1964	Mihaela Penes, ROM	198-7	OR	2000	Trine Hattestad, NOR	226-1	OR
1968	Angéla Németh, HUN	198-0					
1972	Ruth Fuchs, E. Ger	209-7	OR				

Heptathlon

Year		Points		Year		Points	
1964	Irina Press, USSR	5246	WR	1984	Glynis Nunn, AUS	6390	OR
1968	Ingrid Becker, W. Ger	5098		1988	Jackie Joyner-Kersee, USA	7291	WR
1972	Mary Peters, GBR	4801	WR	1992	Jackie Joyner-Kersee, USA	7044	
1976	Siegrun Siegl, E. Ger	4745		1996	Ghada Shouaa, SYR	6780	
1980	Nadezhda Tkachenko, USSR	5083	WR	2000	Denise Lewis, GBR	6584	

Note: Seven-event Heptathlon replaced five-event Pentathlon in 1984.

All-Time Leading Medal Winners – Single Games

Athletes who have won the most medals in a single Summer Olympics. Totals include individual, relay and team medals. U.S. athletes are in **bold** type.

MEN

No		Sport	G-S-B	No		Sport	G-S-B
8	Aleksandr Dityatin, USSR (1980)	Gym	3-4-1	6	Viktor Chukarin, USSR (1956)	Gym	4-2-0
7	**Mark Spitz**, USA (1972)	Swim	7-0-0	6	Konrad Frey, GER (1936)	Gym	3-1-2
7	**Willis Lee**, USA (1920)	Shoot	5-1-1	6	Ville Ritola, FIN (1924)	Track	4-2-0
7	**Matt Biondi**, USA (1988)	Swim	5-1-1	6	Hubert Van Innis, BEL (1920)	Arch	4-2-0
7	Boris Shakhlin, USSR (1960)	Gym	4-2-1	6	**Carl Osburn**, USA (1920)	Shoot	4-1-1
7	**Lloyd Spooner**, USA (1920)	Shoot	4-1-2	6	Louis Richardet, SWI (1906)	Shoot	3-3-0
7	Mikhail Voronin, USSR (1968)	Gym	2-4-1	6	**Anton Heida**, USA (1904)	Gym	5-1-0
7	Nikolai Andrianov, USSR (1976)	Gym	2-4-1	6	**George Eyser**, USA (1904)	Gym	3-2-1
6	Vitaly Scherbo, UT (1992)	Gym	6-0-0	6	**Burton Downing**, USA (1904)	Cycle	2-3-1
6	Li Ning, CHN (1984)	Gym	3-2-1	6	Alexei Nemov, RUS (1996)	Gym	2-1-3
6	Akinori Nakayama, JPN (1968)	Gym	4-1-1	6	Alexei Nemov, RUS (2000)	Gym	2-1-3
6	Takashi Ono, JPN (1960)	Gym	3-1-2				

WOMEN

No		Sport	G-S-B	No		Sport	G-S-B
7	Maria Gorokhovskaya, USSR (1952)	Gym	2-5-0	5	Ecaterina Szabó, ROM (1984)	Gym	4-1-0
6	Kristin Otto, E. Ger (1988)	Swim	6-0-0	5	Shane Gould, AUS (1972)	Swim	3-1-1
6	Agnes Keleti, HUN (1956)	Gym	4-2-0	5	Nadia Comaneci, ROM (1976)	Gym	3-1-1
6	Vera Cáslavská, CZE (1968)	Gym	4-2-0	5	Karin Janz, E. Ger (1972)	Gym	2-2-1
6	Larisa Latynina, USSR (1956)	Gym	4-1-1	5	Ines Diers, E. Ger (1980)	Swim	2-2-1
6	Larisa Latynina, USSR (1960)	Gym	3-2-1	5	**Shirley Babashoff**, USA (1976)	Swim	1-4-0
6	Daniela Silivas, ROM (1988)	Gym	3-2-1	5	**Mary Lou Retton**, USA (1984)	Gym	1-2-2
6	Larisa Latynina, USSR (1964)	Gym	2-2-2	5	**Shannon Miller**, USA (1992)	Gym	0-2-3
6	Margit Korondi, HUN, (1956)	Gym	1-1-4	5	**Marion Jones**, USA (2000)	Track	3-0-2
5	Kornelia Ender, E. Ger (1976)	Swim	4-1-0	5	**Dara Torres**, USA (2000)	Swim	2-0-3

All-Time Leading Medal Winners – Career

MEN

No		Sport	G-S-B
15	Nikolai Andrianov, USSR	Gymnastics	7-5-3
13	Boris Shakhlin, USSR	Gymnastics	7-4-2
13	Edoardo Mangiarotti, ITA	Fencing	6-5-2
13	Takashi Ono, JPN	Gymnastics	5-4-4
12	Paavo Nurmi, FIN	Track/Field	9-3-0
12	Sawao Kato, JPN	Gymnastics	8-3-1
12	Alexei Nemov, RUS	Gymnastics	4-2-6
11	**Mark Spitz**, USA	Swimming	9-1-1
11*	**Matt Biondi**, USA	Swimming	8-2-1
11	Viktor Chukarin, USSR	Gymnastics	7-3-1
11	**Carl Osburn**, USA	Shooting	5-4-2
10	**Ray Ewry**, USA	Track/Field	10-0-0
10	**Carl Lewis**, USA	Track/Field	9-1-0
10	Aladár Gerevich, HUN	Fencing	7-1-2
10	Akinori Nakayama, JPN	Gymnastics	6-2-2
10	Aleksandr Dityatin, USSR	Gymnastics	3-6-1
9	Vitaly Scherbo, BLR	Gymnastics	6-0-3
9	**Martin Sheridan**, USA	Track/Field	5-3-1
9	Zoltán Halmay, HUN	Swimming	3-5-1
9	Giulio Gaudini, ITA	Fencing	3-4-2
9	Mikhail Voronin, USSR	Gymnastics	2-6-1
9	Heikki Savolainen, FIN	Gymnastics	2-1-6
9	Yuri Titov, USSR	Gymnastics	1-5-3

*Includes gold medal as preliminary member of 1st-place relay team.

Note: Medals won by Ewry (2-0-0), Sheridan (2-3-0) and Halmay (1-1-0) at the 1906 Intercalated games are not officially recognized by the IOC.

Games Participated In
Andrianov (1972,76,80); **Biondi** (1984,88,92); **Chukarin** (1952,56); **Dityatin** (1976,80); **Ewry** (1900,04,06,08); **Gerevich** (1932,36,48,52,56,60); **Gaudini** (1928,32,36); **Halmay** (1900,04,06,08); **Kato** (1968,72,76); **Lewis** (1984,88,92,96); **Mangiarotti** (1936,48,52,56,60); **Nakayama** (1968,72); **Nemov** (1996,2000) **Nurmi** (1920,24,28); **Ono** (1952,56,60,64); **Osburn** (1912,20, 24); **Savolainen** (1928,32,36,48,52); **Scherbo** (1992,96); **Shakhlin** (1956,60,64); **Sheridan** (1904,06,08); **Spitz** (1968,72); **Titov** (1956,60,64); **Voronin** (1968,72).

WOMEN

No		Sport	G-S-B
18	Larissa Latynina, USSR	Gymnastics	9-5-4
11	Vera Cáslavská, CZE	Gymnastics	7-4-0
10	**Jenny Thompson**, USA	Swimming	8-1-1
10	Agnes Keleti, HUN	Gymnastics	5-3-2
10	Polina Astaknova, USSR	Gymnastics	5-2-3
9	Nadia Comaneci, ROM	Gymnastics	5-3-1
9	Lyudmila Tourischeva, USSR	Gymnastics	4-3-2
9	**Dara Torres**, USA	Swimming	4-1-4
8	Kornelia Ender, E. Ger	Swimming	4-4-0
8	Dawn Fraser, AUS	Swimming	4-4-0
8	**Shirley Babashoff**, USA	Swimming	2-6-0
8	Sofia Muratova, USSR	Gymnastics	2-2-4
7	Krisztina Egerszegi, HUN	Swimming	5-1-1
7	Irena Kirszenstein Szewinska, POL	Track/Field	3-2-2
7	Shirley Strickland, AUS	Track/Field	3-1-3
7	Maria Gorokhovskaya, USSR	Gymnastics	2-5-0
7	Ildikó Ságiné-Ujlaki-Rejtö, HUN	Fencing	2-3-2
7	**Shannon Miller**, USA	Gymnastics	2-2-3
7	Susie O'Neill, AUS	Swimming	2-4-1
7	Merlene Ottey, JAM	Track/Field	0-2-5

Games Participated In
Astaknova (1956,60,64); **Babashoff** (1972,76); **Cáslavská** (1960,64,68); **Comaneci** (1976,80); **Egerszegi** (1988,92,96) **Ender** (1972,76); **Fraser** (1956,60,64); **Gorokhovskaya** (1952); **Keleti** (1952,56); **Latynina** (1956,60,64); **Miller** (1992,96); **Muratova** (1956,60); **O'Neill** (1996,2000) **Ottey** (1980,84,88,92,96) **Ságiné-Ujlaki-Rejtä** (1960,64, 68,72,76); **Strickland** (1948,52,56); **Szewinska** (1964,68,72,76,80); **Thompson** (1992,96,2000) **Torres** (1984,88,92,2000) **Tourischeva** (1968, 72,76).

Most Individual Medals
Not including team competition.

	Sport	G-S-B
Men: 12-Nikolai Andrianov, USSR	Gym	6-3-3
Women: 14-Larissa Latynina, USSR	Gym	7-4-3

Most Gold Medals
MEN

No		Sport	G-S-B
10*	**Ray Ewry**, USA	Track/Field	10-0-0
9	Paavo Nurmi, FIN	Track/Field	9-3-0
9	**Mark Spitz**, USA	Swimming	9-1-1
9	**Carl Lewis**, USA	Track/Field	9-1-0
8	Sawao Kato, JPN	Gymnastics	8-3-1
8†	**Matt Biondi**, USA	Swimming	8-2-1
7	Nikolai Andrianov, USSR	Gymnastics	7-5-3

No		Sport	G-S-B
7	Boris Shakhlin, USSR	Gymnastics	7-4-2
7	Viktor Chukarin, USSR	Gymnastics	7-3-1
7	Aladar Gerevich, HUN	Fencing	7-1-2

*Medals won by Ewry (2-0-0) at the 1906 Intercalated games are not officially recognized by the IOC.
†Includes gold medal as preliminary member of 1st-place relay team.

WOMEN

No		Sport	G-S-B	No		Sport	G-S-B
9	Larissa Latynina, USSR	Gymnastics	9-5-4	4	Dawn Fraser, AUS	Swimming	4-4-0
8	**Jenny Thompson**, USA	Swimming	8-1-1	4	Lyudmila Tourischeva, USSR	Gymnastics	4-3-2
7	Vera Cáslavská, CZE	Gymnastics	7-4-0	4	**Dara Torres**, USA	Swimming	4-1-4
6	Kristin Otto, E. Ger	Swimming	6-0-0	4	**Evelyn Ashford**, USA	Track/Field	4-1-0
6	**Amy Van Dyken**, USA	Swimming	6-0-0	4	**Janet Evans**, USA	Swimming	4-1-0
5	Agnes Keleti, HUN	Gymnastics	5-3-2	4	Fanny Blankers-Koen, NED	Track/Field	4-0-0
5	Nadia Comaneci, ROM	Gymnastics	5-3-1	4	Betty Cuthbert, AUS	Track/Field	4-0-0
5	Polina Astaknova, USSR	Gymnastics	5-2-3	4	**Pat McCormick**, USA	Diving	4-0-0
5	Krisztina Egerszegi, HUN	Swimming	5-1-1	4	Bärbel Eckert Wäckel, E. Ger	Track/Field	4-0-0
4	Kornelia Ender, E. Ger	Swimming	4-4-0				

Most Silver Medals

MEN

No		Sport	G-S-B
6	Alexandr Dityatin, USSR	Gymnastics	3-6-1
6	Mikhail Voronin, USSR	Gymnastics	2-6-1
5	Nikolai Andrianov, USSR	Gymnastics	7-5-3
5	Edoardo Mangiarotti, ITA	Fencing	6-5-2
5	Zoltán Halmay, HUN	Swimming	3-5-1
5	Gustavo Marzi, ITA	Fencing	2-5-0
5	Yuri Titov, USSR	Gymnastics	1-5-3
5	Viktor Lisitsky, USSR	Gymnastics	0-5-0

WOMEN

No		Sport	G-S-B
6	**Shirley Babashoff**, USA	Swimming	2-6-0
5	Larissa Latynina, USSR	Gymnastics	9-5-4
5	Maria Gorokhovskaya, USSR	Gymnastics	2-5-0
4	Vera Cáslavská, CZE	Gymnastics	7-4-0
4	Kornelia Ender, E. Ger	Swimming	4-4-0
4	Dawn Fraser, AUS	Swimming	4-4-0
4	Erica Zuchold, E. Ger	Gymnastics	0-4-1

Most Bronze Medals

MEN

No		Sport	G-S-B
6	Alexei Nemov, RUS	Gymnastics	4-2-6
6	Heikki Savolainen, FIN	Gymnastics	2-1-6
5	Daniel Revenu, FRA	Fencing	1-0-5
5	Philip Edwards, CAN	Track/Field	0-0-5
5	Adrianus Jong, NED	Fencing	0-0-5

WOMEN

No		Sport	G-S-B
5	Merlene Ottey, JAM	Track/Field	0-2-5
4	Larissa Latynina, USSR	Gymnastics	9-5-4
4	**Dara Torres**, USA	Swimming	4-1-4
4	Sofia Muratova, USSR	Gymnastics	2-2-4

All-Time Leading USA Medal Winners
Most Overall Medals
MEN

No		Sport	G-S-B	No		Sport	G-S-B
11	Mark Spitz	Swimming	9-1-1	6	Anton Heida	Gymnastics	5-1-0
11	*Matt Biondi	Swimming	8-2-1	6	Don Schollander	Swimming	5-1-0
11	Carl Osburn	Shooting	5-4-2	6	Johnny Weissmuller	Swim/Water Polo	5-0-1
10	†Ray Ewry	Track/Field	10-0-0	6	Alfred Lane	Shooting	5-0-1
10	Carl Lewis	Track/Field	9-1-0	6	Jim Lightbody	Track/Field	4-2-0
9	†Martin Sheridan	Track/Field	5-3-1	6	George Eyser	Gymnastics	3-2-1
8	Charles Daniels	Swimming	5-1-2	6	Ralph Rose	Track/Field	3-2-1
8	Gary Hall Jr.	Swimming	4-3-1	6	Michael Plumb	Equestrian	2-4-0
7	‡Tom Jager	Swimming	5-1-1	6	Burton Downing	Cycling	2-3-1
7	Willis Lee	Shooting	5-1-1	6	Bob Garrett	Track/Field	2-2-2
7	Lloyd Spooner	Shooting	4-1-2				

*Includes gold medal as prelim. member of 1st-place relay team.

†Medals won by Ewry (2-0-0) and Sheridan (2-3-0) at the 1906 Intercalated games are not officially recognized by the IOC.

‡Includes 3 gold medals as prelim. member of 1st-place relay teams.

Games Participated In

Biondi (1984,88,92); **Daniels** (1904,06,08); **Downing** (1904); **Ewry** (1900,04,06,08); **Eyser** (1904); **Garrett** (1896,1900); **Hall** (1996,2000) **Heida** (1904); **Jager** (1984,88,92); **Lane** (1912,20); **Lee** (1920); **Lewis** (1984,88,92,96); **Lightbody** (1904,06); **Osburn** (1912,20,24); **Plumb** (1960, 64,68,72,76,84); **Rose** (1904,08,12); **Schollander** (1964, 68); **Sheridan** (1904,06,08); **Spitz** (1968,72); **Spooner** (1920); **Weissmuller** (1924,28).

WOMEN

No		Sport	G-S-B	No		Sport	G-S-B
10	Jenny Thompson	Swimming	8-1-1	4	Pat McCormick	Diving	4-0-0
9	Dara Torres	Swimming	4-1-4	4	Valerie Brisco-Hooks	Track/Field	3-1-0
8	Shirley Babashoff	Swimming	2-6-0	4	Nancy Hogshead	Swimming	3-1-0
7	Shannon Miller	Gymnastics	2-2-3	4	Sharon Stouder	Swimming	3-1-0
6	Jenny Thompson	Swimming	5-1-0	4	Wyomia Tyus	Track/Field	3-1-0
6	Amy Van Dyken	Swimming	6-0-0	4	Wilma Rudolph	Track/Field	3-0-1
6	Jackie Joyner-Kersee	Track/Field	3-1-2	4	Chris von Saltza	Swimming	3-1-0
5	Evelyn Ashford	Track/Field	4-1-0	4	Sue Pederson	Swimming	2-2-0
5	Janet Evans	Swimming	4-1-0	4	Jan Henne	Swimming	2-1-1
5	*Mary T. Meagher	Swimming	3-1-1	4	Dorothy Poynton Hill	Diving	2-1-1
5	Florence Griffith Joyner	Track/Field	3-2-0	4	*Summer Sanders	Swimming	2-1-1
5	Marion Jones	Track/Field	3-0-2	4	Kathy Ellis	Swimming	2-0-2
5	Mary Lou Retton	Gymnastics	1-2-2	4	Georgia Coleman	Diving	1-2-1

*Includes silver medal as prelim. member of 2nd-place relay team.

Games Participated In

Ashford (1976,84,88,92); **Babashoff** (1972,76); **Brisco-Hooks** (1984,88); **Coleman** (1928,32); **Ellis** (1964); **Evans** (1988,92); **Griffith Joyner** (1984,88); **Henne** (1968); **Hogshead** (1984); **Jones** (2000) **Joyner-Kersee** (1984,88,92,96); **McCormick** (1952,56); **Meagher** (1984,88); **Miller** (1992, 96); **Pederson** (1968); **Poynton Hill** (1928,32,36); **Retton** (1984); **Rudolph** (1956,60); **Sanders** (1992); **Stouder** (1964); **Thompson** (1988,92,96,2000);**Torres** (1984,88,92,2000); **Tyus** (1964,68); **Van Dyken** (1996,2000); **von Saltza** (1960).

Most Gold Medals

MEN

No		Sport	G-S-B
10*	Raymond Ewry	Track/Field	10-0-0
9	Mark Spitz	Swimming	9-1-1
9	Carl Lewis	Track/Field	9-1-0
8†	Matt Biondi	Swimming	8-2-1
5	Carl Osburn	Shooting	5-4-2
5*	Martin Sheridan	Track/Field	5-3-1
5	Charles Daniels	Swimming	5-1-2
5‡	Tom Jager	Swimming	5-1-1
5	Willis Lee	Shooting	5-1-1
5	Anton Heida	Gymnastics	5-1-0
5	Don Schollander	Swimming	5-1-0
5	Johnny Weissmuller	Swim/Water Polo	5-0-1
5	Alfred Lane	Shooting	5-0-1
5	Morris Fisher	Shooting	5-0-0
4	Gary Hall Jr.	Swimming	4-3-1
4	Jim Lightbody	Track/Field	4-2-0
4	Lloyd Spooner	Shooting	4-1-2
4	Greg Louganis	Diving	4-1-0
4	John Naber	Swimming	4-1-0
4	Meyer Prinstein	Track/Field	4-1-0
4	Mel Sheppard	Track/Field	4-1-0
4	Marcus Hurley	Cycling	4-0-1
4	Harrison Dillard	Track/Field	4-0-0
4	Archie Hahn	Track/Field	4-0-0
4	Alvin Kraenzlein	Track/Field	4-0-0
4	Al Oerter	Track/Field	4-0-0
4	Jesse Owens	Track/Field	4-0-0

*Medals won by Ewry (2-0-0) and Sheridan (2-3-0) at the 1906 Intercalated games are not officially recognized by the IOC.
†Includes gold medal as prelim. member of 1st-place relay team.
‡ Includes 3 gold medals as prelim. member of 1st-place relay teams.

WOMEN

No		Sport	G-S-B
8	Jenny Thompson	Swimming	8-1-1
6*	Amy Van Dyken	Swimming	6-0-0
4	Dara Torres	Swimming	4-1-4
4	Evelyn Ashford	Track/Field	4-1-0
4	Janet Evans	Swimming	4-1-0
4	Pat McCormick	Diving	4-0-0
3	Florence Griffith Joyner	Track/Field	3-2-0
3	Jackie Joyner-Kersee	Track/Field	3-1-2
3*	Mary T. Meagher	Swimming	3-1-1
3	Valerie Brisco-Hooks	Track/Field	3-1-0
3	Nancy Hogshead	Swimming	3-1-0
3	Sharon Stouder	Swimming	3-1-0
3	Wyomia Tyus	Track/Field	3-1-0
3	Chris von Saltza	Swimming	3-1-0
3	Wilma Rudolph	Track/Field	3-0-1
3	Melissa Belote	Swimming	3-0-0
3	Ethelda Bleibtrey	Swimming	3-0-0
3	Tracy Caulkins	Swimming	3-0-0
3*	Nicole Haislett	Swimming	3-0-0
3	Helen Madison	Swimming	3-0-0
3	Debbie Meyer	Swimming	3-0-0
3	Sandra Neilson	Swimming	3-0-0
3	Martha Norelius	Swimming	3-0-0
3*	Carrie Steinseifer	Swimming	3-0-0

*Includes gold medal as prelim. member of 1st-place relay team.

Most Silver Medals

MEN

No		Sport	G-S-B
4	Carl Osburn	Shooting	5-4-2
4	Michael Plumb	Equestrian	2-4-0
3	Martin Sheridan	Track/Field	5-3-1
3	Burton Downing	Cycling	2-3-1
3	Irving Baxter	Track/Field	2-3-0
3	Earl Thomson	Equestrian	2-3-0

WOMEN

No		Sport	G-S-B
6	Shirley Babashoff	Swimming	2-6-0

All-Time Medal Standings, 1896-2000

All-time Summer Games medal standings, according to *The Golden Book of the Olympic Games*. Medal counts include the 1906 Intercalated Games, which are not recognized by the IOC.

		G	S	B	Total			G	S	B	Total
1	**United States**	872	658	586	2116	15	Poland	56	72	113	241
2	USSR (1952-88)	395	319	296	1010	16	Canada	51	81	98	230
3	Great Britain	180	233	225	638	17	China	80	79	64	223
4	France	188	193	217	598	18	Netherlands	61	67	85	213
5	Italy	179	143	157	479	19	Bulgaria	48	82	65	195
6	Sweden	136	156	177	469	20	Switzerland	47	75	61	183
7	East Germany (1968-88)	159	150	136	445	21	Denmark	40	63	58	161
8	Hungary	150	135	158	443	22	Russia (1896-1912, 96-)	58	52	46	156
9	Germany (1896-64,92-)	137	138	160	435	23	South Korea	46	52	56	154
10	Australia	102	110	138	350	24	Czechoslovakia (1924-92)	49	49	44	142
11	West Germany (1968-88)	77	104	120	301	25	Belgium	37	51	52	140
12	Finland	101	81	114	296	26	Cuba	55	44	38	137
	Japan	97	97	102	296	27	Norway	49	44	41	134
14	Romania	74	83	108	265	28	Greece	32	48	46	126

Rank	Country	G	S	B	Total
29	Unified Team (1992)	45	38	29	112
30	Yugoslavia (1924-88, 96-)	28	32	33	93
31	Austria	20	32	34	86
32	Spain	25	28	22	75
33	New Zealand	30	12	32	74
34	Brazil	12	19	35	66
35	Turkey	33	16	15	64
36	South Africa	19	20	24	63
37	Argentina	13	23	18	54
	Kenya	16	20	18	54
39	Mexico	10	15	22	47
40	Iran	8	13	19	40
41	Jamaica	5	20	12	37
42	North Korea	8	7	15	30
43	Estonia	8	6	12	26
44	Ethiopia	12	2	10	24
45	Ukraine	3	10	10	23
46	Great Britain/Ireland	6	11	3	20
	Ireland	8	6	6	20
48	Czech Republic	6	6	7	19
49	Portugal	3	4	10	17
	Belarus	3	3	11	17
	Nigeria	2	8	7	17
52	India	8	3	5	16
	Egypt	6	5	5	16
	Indonesia	4	7	5	16
	Morocco	4	3	9	16
56	Mongolia	0	5	9	14
57	Algeria	4	1	7	12
58	Trinidad & Tobago	1	3	7	11
59	Pakistan	3	3	4	10
	Uruguay	2	2	6	10
	Latvia	1	6	3	10
	Chinese Taipei	0	4	6	10
63	Lithuania	3	0	6	9
	Thailand	2	1	6	9
	Chile	0	6	3	9
	Philippines	0	2	7	9
67	Slovakia	2	4	2	8
	Venezuela	1	2	5	8
	Georgia	0	0	8	8
70	Kazakhstan	3	4	0	7
	Croatia	2	2	3	7
	Colombia	1	2	4	7
73	Bahamas	2	2	2	6
	Slovenia	2	2	2	6
	Uganda	1	3	2	6
	Tunisia	1	2	3	6
	Uzbekistan	1	2	3	6
	Bohemia	0	1	5	6
	Puerto Rico	0	1	5	6
80	Azerbaijan	2	1	1	4
	Peru	1	3	0	4
	Costa Rica	1	1	2	4
	Namibia	0	4	0	4
	Lebanon	0	2	2	4
	Moldova	0	2	2	4
	Ghana	0	1	3	4
	Israel	0	1	3	4
88	Luxembourg	2	1	0	3
	Armenia	1	1	1	3

Rank	Country	G	S	B	Total
	Cameroon	1	1	1	3
	Iceland	0	1	2	3
	Malaysia	0	1	2	3
94	Syria	1	1	0	2
	Japan/Korea	1	0	1	2
	Mozambique	1	0	1	2
	Surinam	1	0	1	2
	Tanzania	0	2	0	2
	Great Britain/USA	0	1	1	2
	Haiti	0	1	1	2
	Russia/Estonia	0	1	1	2
	Saudi Arabia	0	1	1	2
	United Arab Republic	0	1	1	2
	Zambia	0	1	1	2
	The Antilles	0	0	2	2
	Panama	0	0	2	2
	Qatar	0	0	2	2
108	Australia/New Zealand	1	0	0	1
	Burkina Faso	1	0	0	1
	Cuba/USA	1	0	0	1
	Denmark/Sweden	1	0	0	1
	Ecuador	1	0	0	1
	Gr. Britain/Ireland/Germany	1	0	0	1
	Gr. Britain/Ireland/USA	1	0	0	1
	Hong Kong	1	0	0	1
	Ireland/USA	1	0	0	1
	Zimbabwe	1	0	0	1
	Belgium/Greece	0	1	0	1
	Ceylon	0	1	0	1
	France/USA	0	1	0	1
	France/Gr. Britain/Ireland	0	1	0	1
	Ivory Coast	0	1	0	1
	Netherlands Antilles	0	1	0	1
	Senegal	0	1	0	1
	Singapore	0	1	0	1
	Smyrna	0	1	0	1
	Tonga	0	1	0	1
	Vietnam	0	1	0	1
	Virgin Islands	0	1	0	1
	Australia/Great Britain	0	0	1	1
	Barbados	0	0	1	1
	Bermuda	0	0	1	1
	Bohemia/Great Britain	0	0	1	1
	Djibouti	0	0	1	1
	Dominican Republic	0	0	1	1
	France/Great Britain	0	0	1	1
	Guyana	0	0	1	1
	Iraq	0	0	1	1
	Kuwait	0	0	1	1
	Kyrgyzstan	0	0	1	1
	Macedonia	0	0	1	1
	Mexico/Spain	0	0	1	1
	Niger	0	0	1	1
	Scotland	0	0	1	1
	Sri Lanka	0	0	1	1
	Thessalonika	0	0	1	1
	Wales	0	0	1	1

Combined totals:

	G	S	B	Total
USSR/UT/Russia	498	409	371	1278
Germany/E. Ger/W. Ger	374	392	416	1182

Notes: Athletes from the USSR participated in the Summer Games from 1952-88, returned as the Unified Team in 1992 after the breakup of the Soviet Union (in 1991) and have competed as independent republics since the 1994 Winter Games. Croatia and Bosnia-Herzegovina gained independence from Yugoslavia in 1991. Yugoslavia was not invited to the 1992 games (though Serbian and Montenegrin athletes were allowed to compete as independent athletes) but returned in 1996. Czechoslovakia split into Slovakia and the Czech Republic in 1993. Germany was barred from the Olympics in 1924 and 1948 following World Wars I and II. Divided into East and West Germany after WWII, both countries competed together from 1952-64, then separately from 1968-88. Germany was reunified in 1990.

WINTER OLYMPICS
1924-1998 Through the Years

ESPN

information please
SPORTS ALMANAC

PAGE 706

The Winter Olympics

The move toward a winter version of the Olympics began in 1908 when figure skating made an appearance at the Summer Games in London. Ten-time world champion Ulrich Salchow of Sweden, who originated the backwards, one revolution jump that bears his name, and Madge Syers of Britain were the first singles champions. Germans Anna Hubler and Heinrich Berger won the pairs competition.

Organizers of the 1916 Summer Games in Berlin planned to introduce a "Skiing Olympia," featuring nordic events in the Black Forest, but the Games were cancelled after the outbreak of World War I in 1914.

The Games resumed in 1920 at Antwerp, Belgium, where figure skating returned and ice hockey was added as a medal event. Sweden's Gillis Grafstrom and Magda Julin took individual honors, while Ludovika and Walter Jakobsson were the top pair. In hockey, Canada won the gold medal with the United States second and Czechoslovakia third.

Despite the objections of Modern Olympics' founder Baron Pierre de Coubertin and the resistance of the Scandinavian countries, which had staged their own Nordic championships every four or five years from 1901-26 in Sweden, the International Olympic Committee sanctioned an "International Winter Sports Week" at Chamonix, France, in 1924. The 11-day event, which included nordic skiing, speed skating, figure skating, ice hockey and bobsledding, was a huge success and was retroactively called the first Olympic Winter Games.

Seventy years after those first cold weather Games, the 17th edition of the Winter Olympics took place in Lillehammer, Norway, in 1994. The event ended the four-year Olympic cycle of staging both Winter and Summer Games in the same year and began a new schedule that calls for the two Games to alternate every two years.

Year	No	Location	Dates	Nations	Most medals	USA Medals
1924	I	Chamonix, FRA	Jan. 25-Feb. 4	16	Norway (4-7-6–17)	1-2-1– 4 (3rd)
1928	II	St. Moritz, SWI	Feb. 11-19	25	Norway (6-4-5–15)	2-2-2– 6 (2nd)
1932	III	Lake Placid, USA	Feb. 4-15	17	USA (6-4-2–12)	6-4-2–12 (1st)
1936	IV	Garmisch-Partenkirchen, GER ..	Feb. 6-16	28	Norway (7-5-3–15)	1-0-3– 4 (T-5th)
1940-a	–	Sapporo, JPN	Cancelled (WWII)			
1944	–	Cortina d'Ampezzo, ITA	Cancelled (WWII)			
1948	V	St. Moritz, SWI	Jan. 30-Feb. 8	28	Norway (4-3-3–10), Sweden (4-3-3–10) & Switzerland (3-4-3–10)	3-4-2– 9 (4th)
1952-b	VI	Oslo, NOR	Feb. 14-25	30	Norway (7-3-6–16)	4-6-1–11 (2nd)
1956-c	VII	Cortina d'Ampezzo, ITA	Jan. 26-Feb. 5	32	USSR (7-3-6–16)	2-3-2– 7 (T-4th)
1960	VIII	Squaw Valley, USA	Feb. 18-28	30	USSR (7-5-9–21)	3-4-3–10 (2nd)
1964	IX	Innsbruck, AUT	Jan. 29-Feb. 9	36	USSR (11-8-6–25)	1-2-3– 6 (7th)
1968-d	X	Grenoble, FRA	Feb. 6-18	37	Norway (6-6-2–14)	1-5-1– 7 (T-7th)
1972	XI	Sapporo, JPN	Feb. 3-13	35	USSR (8-5-3–16)	3-2-3– 8 (6th)
1976-e	XII	Innsbruck, AUT	Feb. 4-15	37	USSR (13-6-8–27)	3-3-4–10 (T-3rd)
1980	XIII	Lake Placid, USA	Feb. 14-23	37	E. Germany (9-7-7–23)	6-4-2–12 (3rd)
1984	XIV	Sarajevo, YUG	Feb. 7-19	49	USSR (6-10-9–25)	4-4-0– 8 (T-5th)
1988	XV	Calgary, CAN	Feb. 13-28	57	USSR (11-9-9–29)	2-1-3– 6 (T-8th)
1992-f	XVI	Albertville, FRA	Feb. 8-23	63	Germany (10-10-6–26)	5-4-2–11 (6th)
1994-g	XVII	Lillehammer, NOR	Feb. 12-27	67	Norway (10-11-5–26)	6-5-2–13 (T-5th)
1998	XVIII	Nagano, JPN	Feb. 7-22	72	Germany (12-9-8–29)	6-3-4–13 (5th)
2002	XIX	Salt Lake City, USA	Feb. 8-24			
2006	XX	Turin, ITA	Feb. 4-19			

a–The 1940 Winter Games are originally scheduled for Sapporo, but Japan resigns as host in 1937 when the Sino-Japanese war breaks out. St. Moritz is the next choice, but the Swiss feel that ski instructors should not be considered professionals and the IOC withdraws its offer. Finally, Garmisch-Partenkirchen is asked to serve again as host, but the Germans invade Poland in 1939 and the Games are eventually cancelled.

b–Germany and Japan are allowed to rejoin the Olympic community for the first time since World War II. Though a divided country, the Germans send a joint East-West team through 1964.

c–The Soviet Union (USSR) participates in its first Winter Olympics and takes home the most medals, including the gold medal in ice hockey.

d–East Germany and West Germany officially send separate teams for the first time and will continue to do so through 1988.

e–The IOC grants the 1976 Winter Games to Denver in May 1970, but in 1972 Colorado voters reject a $5 million bond issue to finance the undertaking. Denver immediately withdraws as host and the IOC selects Innsbruck, the site of the 1964 Games, to take over.

f–Germany sends a single team after East and West German reunification in 1990 and the USSR competes as the Unified Team after the breakup of the Soviet Union in 1991.

g–The IOC moves the Winter Games' four-year cycle ahead two years in order to separate them from the Summer Games and alternate Olympics every two years.

Event-by-Event

Gold medal winners from 1924-98 in the following events: Alpine Skiing, Biathlon, Bobsled, Cross-country Skiing, Curling, Figure Skating, Ice Hockey, Luge, Nordic Combined, Ski Jumping, Snowboarding and Speed Skating.

ALPINE SKIING

MEN

Multiple gold medals: Jean-Claude Killy, Toni Sailer and Alberto Tomba (3); Hermann Maier, Henri Oreiller, Ingemar Stenmark and Markus Wasmeier (2).

Downhill

Year		Time	Year		Time
1948	Henri Oreiller, FRA	2:55.0	1976	Franz Klammer AUT	1:45.73
1952	Zeno Colò, ITA	2:30.8	1980	Leonhard Stock, AUS	1:45.50
1956	Toni Sailer, AUT	2:52.2	1984	Bill Johnson, USA	1:45.59
1960	Jean Vuarnet, FRA	2:06.0	1988	Pirmin Zurbriggen, SWI	1:59.63
1964	Egon Zimmermann, AUT	2:18.16	1992	Patrick Ortlieb, AUT	1:50.37
1968	Jean-Claude Killy, FRA	1:59.85	1994	Tommy Moe, USA	1:45.75
1972	Bernhard Russi, SWI	1:51.43	1998	Jean-Luc Cretier, FRA.	1:50.11

Slalom

Year		Time	Year		Time
1948	Edi Reinalter, SWI	2:10.3	1976	Piero Gros, ITA	2:03.29
1952	Othmar Schneider, AUT	2:00.0	1980	Ingemar Stenmark, SWE	1:44.26
1956	Toni Sailer, AUT	3:14.7	1984	Phil Mahre, USA	1:39.41
1960	Ernst Hinterseer, AUT	2:08.9	1988	Alberto Tomba, ITA	1:39.47
1964	Pepi Stiegler, AUT	2:11.13	1992	Finn Christian Jagge, NOR	1:44.39
1968	Jean-Claude Killy, FRA	1:39.73	1994	Thomas Stangassinger, AUT	2:02.02
1972	Francisco Ochoa, SPA	1:49.27	1998	Hans-Petter Buraas, NOR	1:49.31

Giant Slalom

Year		Time	Year		Time
1952	Stein Eriksen, NOR	2:25.0	1980	Ingemar Stenmark, SWE	2:40.74
1956	Toni Sailer, AUS	3:00.1	1984	Max Julen, SWI	2:41.18
1960	Roger Staub, SWI	1:48.3	1988	Alberto Tomba, ITA	2:06.37
1964	Francois Bonlieu, FRA	1:46.71	1992	Alberto Tomba, ITA	2:06.98
1968	Jean-Claude Killy, FRA	3:29.28	1994	Markus Wasmeier, GER	2:52.46
1972	Gustav Thöni, ITA	3:09.62	1998	Hermann Maier, AUT	2:38.51
1976	Heini Hemmi, SWI	3:26.97			

Super Giant Slalom

Year		Time	Year		Time
1988	Frank Piccard, FRA	1:39.66	1994	Markus Wasmeier, GER	1:32.53
1992	Kjetil Andre Aamodt, NOR	1:13.04	1998	Hermann Maier, AUT	1:34.82

Alpine Combined

Year		Points	Year		Points
1936	Franz Pfnür, GER	99.25	1992	Josef Polig, ITA	14.58
1948	Henri Oreiller, FRA	3.27	Year		Time
1952-84 Not held			1994	Lasse Kjus, NOR	3:17.53
1988	Hubert Strolz, AUT	36.55	1998	Mario Reiter, AUT	3:08.06

WOMEN

Multiple gold medals: Deborah Compagnoni, Vreni Schneider and Katja Seizinger (3); Marielle Goitschel, Trude Jochum-Beiser, Petra Kronberger, Andrea Mead Lawrence, Rosi Mittermaier, Marie-Theres Nadig, Hanni Wenzel and Pernilla Wiberg (2).

Downhill

Year		Time	Year		Time
1948	Hedy Schlunegger, SWI	2:28.3	1976	Rosi Mittermaier, W. Ger	1:46.16
1952	Trude Jochum-Beiser, AUT	1:47.1	1980	Annemarie Moser-Pröll, AUT	1:37.52
1956	Madeleine Berthod, SWI	1:40.7	1984	Michela Figini, SWI	1:13.36
1960	Heidi Biebl, GER	1:37.6	1988	Marina Kiehl, W. Ger	1:25.86
1964	Christl Haas, AUT	1:55.39	1992	Kerrin Lee-Gartner, CAN	1:52.55
1968	Olga Pall, AUT	1:40.87	1994	Katja Seizinger, GER	1:35.93
1972	Marie-Theres Nadig, SWI	1:36.68	1998	Katja Seizinger, GER	1:28.89

Slalom

Year		Time	Year		Time
1948	Gretchen Fraser, USA	1:57.2	1976	Rosi Mittermaier, W. Ger	1:30.54
1952	Andrea Mead Lawrence, USA	2:10.6	1980	Hanni Wenzel, LIE	1:25.09
1956	Renée Colliard, SWI	1:52.3	1984	Paoletta Magoni, ITA	1:36.47
1960	Anne Heggtveit, CAN	1:49.6	1988	Vreni Schneider, SWI	1:36.69
1964	Christine Goitschel, FRA	1:29.86	1992	Petra Kronberger, AUT	1:32.68
1968	Marielle Goitschel, FRA	1:25.86	1994	Vreni Schneider, SWI	1:56.01
1972	Barbara Cochran, USA	1:31.24	1998	Hilde Gerg, GER	1:32.40

Giant Slalom

Year		Time	Year		Time
1952	Andrea Mead Lawrence, USA	2:06.8	1980	Hanni Wenzel, LIE	2:41.66
1956	Ossi Reichert, GER	1:56.5	1984	Debbie Armstrong, USA	2:20.98
1960	Yvonne Rügg, SWI	1:39.9	1988	Vreni Schneider, SWI	2:06.49
1964	Marielle Goitschel, FRA	1:52.24	1992	Pernilla Wiberg, SWE	2:12.74
1968	Nancy Greene, CAN	1:51.97	1994	Deborah Compagnoni, ITA	2:30.97
1972	Marie-Theres Nadig, SWI	1:29.90	1998	Deborah Compagnoni, ITA	2:50.59
1976	Kathy Kreiner, CAN	1:29.13			

Super Giant Slalom

Year		Time	Year		Time
1988	Sigrid Wolf, AUT	1:19.03	1994	Diann Roffe-Steinrotter, USA	1:22.15
1992	Deborah Compagnoni, ITA	1:21.22	1998	Picabo Street, USA	1:18.02

Alpine Combined

Year		Points	Year		Points
1936	Christl Cranz, GER	97.06	1992	Petra Kronberger, AUT	2.55
1948	Trude Beiser, AUT	6.58	Year		Time
1952-84	Not held		1994	Pernilla Wiberg, SWE	3:05.16
1988	Anita Wachter, AUT	29.25	1998	Katja Seizinger, GER	2:40.74

BIATHLON

MEN

Multiple gold medals (including relays): Aleksandr Tikhonov (4); Mark Kirchner and Ricco Gross (3); Anatoly Alyabyev, Ivan Biakov, Sergei Chepikov, Sven Fischer, Frank Luck, Viktor Mamatov, Frank-Peter Roetsch, Magnar Solberg and Dmitri Vasilyev (2).

10 kilometers

Year		Time	Year		Time
1980	Frank Ullrich, E. Ger.	32:10.69	1992	Mark Kirchner, GER	26:02.3
1984	Erik Kvalfoss, NOR	30:53.8	1994	Sergei Chepikov, RUS.	28:07.0
1988	Frank-Peter Roetsch, E. Ger	25:08.1	1998	Ole Einar Bjoerndalen, NOR.	27:16.2

20 kilometers

Year		Time	Year		Time
1960	Klas Lestander, SWE.	1:33:21.6	1984	Peter Angerer, W. Ger	1:11:52.7
1964	Vladimir Melanin, USSR.	1:20:26.8	1988	Frank-Peter Roetsch, E. Ger	56:33.3
1968	Magnar Solberg, NOR	1:13:45.9	1992	Yevgeny Redkine, UT	57:34.4
1972	Magnar Solberg, NOR	1:15:55.50	1994	Sergei Tarasov, RUS	57:25.3
1976	Nikolai Kruglov, USSR	1:14:12.26	1998	Halvard Hanevold, NOR	56:16.4
1980	Anatoly Alyabyev, USSR	1:08:16.31			

4x7.5-kilometer Relay

Year		Time	Year		Time	Year		Time
1968	Soviet Union	2:13:02.4	1980	Soviet Union	1:34:03.27	1992	Germany	1:24:43.5
1972	Soviet Union	1:51:44.92	1984	Soviet Union	1:38:51.7	1994	Germany	1:30:22.1
1976	Soviet Union	1:57:55.64	1988	Soviet Union	1:22:30.0	1998	Germany	1:21:36.2

WOMEN

Multiple gold medals (including relays): Myriam Bedard and Anfisa Reztsova (2). Note that Reztsova won a third gold medal in 1988 in the Cross-country 4x5-kilometer Relay.

7.5 kilometers

Year		Time	Year		Time
1992	Anfisa Reztsova, UT	24:29.2	1998	Galina Koukleva, RUS	23:08.0
1994	Myriam Bedard, CAN	26:08.8			

15 kilometers

Year		Time	Year		Time
1992	Antje Misersky, GER	51:47.2	1998	Ekaterina Dafovska, BUL	54:52.0
1994	Myriam Bedard, CAN	52:06.6			

4x7.5-kilometer Relay

Year		Time	Year		Time	Year		Time
1992	France	1:15:55.6	1994	Russia	1:47:19.5	1998	Germany	1:40:13.6

Note: Event featured three skiers per team in 1992.

BOBSLED

Only drivers are listed in parentheses.
Multiple gold medals: DRIVERS—Meinhard Nehmer (3); Billy Fiske, Wolfgang Hoppe, Eugenio Monti, Andreas Ostler and Gustav Weder (2). CREW—Bernard Germeshausen (3); Donat Acklin, Luciano De Paolis, Cliff Gray, Lorenz Nieberl and Dietmar Schauerhammer (2).

Two-Man

Year	Time	Year	Time
1932 United States (Hubert Stevens)	8:14.74	1972 West Germany (Wolfgang Zimmerer)	4:57.07
1936 United States (Ivan Brown)	5:29.29	1976 East Germany (Meinhard Nehmer)	3:44.42
1948 Switzerland (Felix Endrich)	5:29.2	1980 Switzerland (Erich Schärer)	4:09.36
1952 Germany (Andreas Ostler)	5:24.54	1984 East Germany (Wolfgang Hoppe)	3:25.56
1956 Italy (Lamberto Dalla Costa)	5:30.14	1988 Soviet Union (Janis Kipurs)	3:54.19
1960 Not held		1992 Switzerland I (Gustav Weder)	4:03.26
1964 Great Britain (Anthony Nash)	4:21.90	1994 Switzerland I (Gustav Weder)	3:30.81
1968 Italy (Eugenio Monti)	4:41.54	1998 Italy I (Guenther Huber)	3:37.24

Four-Man

Year	Time	Year	Time
1924 Switzerland (Eduard Scherrer)	5:45.54	1968 Italy (Eugenio Monti)	2:17.39
1928 United States (Billy Fiske)	3:20.5	1972 Switzerland (Jean Wicki)	4:43.07
1932 United States (Billy Fiske)	7:53.68	1976 East Germany (Meinhard Nehmer)	3:40.43
1936 Switzerland (Pierre Musy)	5:19.85	1980 East Germany (Meinhard Nehmer)	3:59.92
1948 United States (Francis Tyler)	5:20.1	1984 East Germany (Wolfgang Hoppe)	3:20.22
1952 Germany (Andreas Ostler)	5:07.84	1988 Switzerland (Ekkehard Fasser)	3:47.51
1956 Switzerland (Franz Kapus)	5:10.44	1992 Austria I (Ingo Appelt)	3:53.90
1960 Not held		1994 Germany II (Harald Czudaj)	3:27.78
1964 Canada (Vic Emery)	4:14.46	1998 Germany II (Christoph Langen)	2:39.41

Note: Five-man sleds were used in 1928.

CROSS COUNTRY SKIING

There have been two significant changes in men's and women's cross country racing since the end of the 1984 Winter Games in Sarajevo. First, the classical and freestyle (i.e., skating) techniques were designated for specific events beginning in 1988, and the Pursuit race was introduced in 1992.

MEN

Multiple gold medals (including relays): Bjorn Dählie (8); Sixten Jernberg, Gunde Svan, Thomas Wassberg and Nikolai Zimyatov (4); Veikko Hakulinen, Eero Mäntyranta and Vegard Ulvang (3); Hallgeir Brenden, Harald Grönningen, Thorlief Haug, Jan Ottoson, Päl Tyldum and Vyacheslav Vedenine (2).
Multiple gold medals (including Nordic Combined): Johan Gröttumsbråten and Thorlief Haug (3).

10-kilometer Classical

Year	Time	Year	Time
1924-88 Not held		1994 Bjorn Dählie, NOR	24:20.1
1992 Vegard Ulvang, NOR	27:36.0	1998 Bjorn Dählie, NOR	27:24.5

15-kilometer Combined Pursuit

A 15-km Freestyle race in which the starting order is determined by order of finish in the 10-km Classical race. Time given is combined time of both events.

Year	Time	Year	Time
1924-88 Not held		1994 Bjorn Dählie, NOR	1:00.08.8
1992 Bjorn Dählie, NOR	1:05:37.9	1998 Thomas Alsgaard, NOR	1:07:01.7

15-kilometer Classical (Discont.)

Discontinued in 1992 and replaced by the freestyle 15-km Combined Pursuit. Event was held over 18 kilometers from 1924-52.

Year	Time	Year	Time
1924 Thorleif Haug, NOR	1:14:31.0	1964 Eero Mäntyranta, FIN	50:54.1
1928 Johan Gröttumsbråten, NOR	1:37:01.0	1968 Harald Grönningen, NOR	47:54.2
1932 Sven Utterström, SWE	1:23:07.0	1972 Sven-Ake Lundback, SWE	45:28.24
1936 Erik-August Larsson, SWE	1:14:38.0	1976 Nikolai Bazhukov, USSR	43:58.47
1948 Martin Lundström, SWE	1:13:50.0	1980 Thomas Wassberg, SWE	41:57.63
1952 Hallgeir Brenden, NOR	1:01:34.0	1984 Gunde Svan, SWE	41:25.6
1956 Hallgeir Brenden, NOR	49:39.0	1988 Mikhail Devyatyarov, USSR	41:18.9
1960 Hakon Brusveen NOR	51:55.5		

Youngest and Oldest Gold Medalists in an Individual Event

Youngest: MEN— Toni Nieminen, Finland, Large Hill Ski Jumping, 1992 (16 years, 261 days); WOMEN—Tara Lipinski, United States, Figure Skating, 1998 (15 years, 256 days).
Oldest: MEN— Magnar Solberg, NOR, 20-km Biathlon, 1972 (35 years, 4 days); WOMEN— Christina Baas-Kaiser, Holland, 3,000m Speed Skating, 1972 (33 years, 268 days).

30-kilometer Freestyle (Discont.)
Discontinued in 1998 and replaced by the 30-kilometer Classical.

Year	Time	Year	Time
1924-52 Not held		1976 Sergei Saveliev, USSR	1:30:29.38
1956 Veikko Hakulinen, FIN	1:44:06.0	1980 Nikolai Zimyatov, USSR	1:27:02.80
1960 Sixten Jernberg, SWE	1:51:03.9	1984 Nikolai Zimyatov, USSR	1:28:56.3
1964 Eero Mäntyranta, FIN	1:30:50.7	1988 Alexi Prokurorov, USSR	1:24:26.3
1968 Franco Nones, ITA	1:35:39.2	1992 Vegard Ulvang, NOR	1:22:27.8
1972 Vyacheslav Vedenine, USSR	1:36:31.15	1994 Thomas Alsgaard, NOR	1:12:26.4

30-kilometer Classical

Year	Time
1998 Mila Myllylae, FIN	1:33:55.8

50-kilometer Classical (Discont.)
Discontinued in 1998 and replaced by the 50-kilometer Freestyle.

Year	Time	Year	Time
1924 Thorleif Haug, NOR	3:44:32.0	1968 Ole Ellefsaeter, NOR	2:28:45.8
1928 Per Erik Hedlund, SWE	4:52:03.0	1972 Päl Tyldum, NOR	2:43:14.75
1932 Veli Saarinen, FIN	4:28:00.0	1976 Ivar Formo, NOR	2:37:30.05
1936 Elis Wiklund, SWE	3:30:11.0	1980 Nikolai Zimyatov, USSR	2:27:24.60
1948 Nils Karlsson, SWE	3:47:48.0	1984 Thomas Wassberg, SWE	2:15:55.8
1952 Veikko Hakulinen, FIN	3:33:33.0	1988 Gunde Svan, SWE	2:04:30.9
1956 Sixten Jernberg, SWE	2:50:27.0	1992 Bjorn Dählie, NOR	2:03:41.5
1960 Kalevi Hämäläinen, FIN	2:59:06.3	1994 Vladimir Smirnov, KAZ	2:07:20.3
1964 Sixten Jernberg, SWE	2:43:52.6		

50-kilometer Freestyle

Year	Time
1998 Bjorn Dählie, NOR	2:05:08.2

4x10-kilometer Mixed Relay
Two Classical and two Freestyle legs.

Year	Time	Year	Time	Year	Time
1936 Finland	2:41:33.0	1964 Sweden	2:18:34.6	1984 Sweden	1:55:06.3
1948 Sweden	2:32:08.0	1968 Norway	2:08:33.5	1988 Sweden	1:43:58.6
1952 Finland	2:20:16.0	1972 Soviet Union	2:04:47.94	1992 Norway	1:39:26.0
1956 Soviet Union	2:15:30.0	1976 Finland	2:07:59.72	1994 Italy	1:41:15.0
1960 Finland	2:18:45.6	1980 Soviet Union	1:57:03.46	1998 Norway	1:40:55.7

WOMEN

Multiple gold medals (including relays): Lyubov Egorova (6); Galina Kulakova and Raisa Smetanina (4); Claudia Boyarskikh and Marja-Liisa Hämäläinen (3); Manuela Di Centa, Toini Gustafsson, Larisa Lazutina, Barbara Petzold and Elena Valbe (2).

Multiple gold medals (including relays and Biathlon): Anfisa Reztsova (2).

5-kilometer Classical

Year	Time	Year	Time
1964 Claudia Boyarskikh, USSR	17:50.5	1984 Marja-Liisa Hämäläinen, FIN	17:04.0
1968 Toini Gustafsson, SWE	16:45.2	1988 Marjo Matikainen, FIN	15:04.0
1972 Galina Kulakova, USSR	17:00.50	1992 Marjut Lukkarinen, FIN	14:13.8
1976 Helena Takalo, FIN	15:48.69	1994 Lyubov Egorova, RUS	14:08.8
1980 Raisa Smetanina, USSR	15:06.92	1998 Larissa Lazutina, RUS	17:37.9

10-kilometer Combined Pursuit
A 10-km Freestyle race in which the starting order is determined by order of finish in the 5-km Classical race. Time given is combined time of both events.

Year	Time	Year	Time
1952-88 Not held		1994 Lyubov Egorova, RUS	41:38.1
1992 Lyubov Egorova, UT	40:07.7	1998 Larissa Lazutina, RUS	17:37.9

10-kilometer Classical (Discont.)
Discontinued in 1992 and replaced by the freestyle 10-km Combined Pursuit.

Year	Time	Year	Time
1952 Lydia Wideman, FIN	41:40.0	1972 Galina Kulakova, USSR	34:17.82
1956 Lyubov Kosyreva, USSR	38:11.0	1976 Raisa Smetanina, USSR	30:13.41
1960 Maria Gusakova, USSR	39:46.6	1980 Barbara Petzold, E. Ger.	30:31.54
1964 Claudia Boyarskikh, USSR	40:24.3	1984 Marja-Liisa Hämäläinen, FIN	31:44.2
1968 Toini Gustafsson, SWE	36:46.5	1988 Vida Venciene, USSR	30:08.3

15-kilometer Freestyle (Discont.)
Discontinued in 1998 and replaced by the 15-kilometer Classical.

Year	Time	Year	Time
1992 Lyubov Egorova, UT	.42:20.8	1994 Manuela Di Centa, ITA	.39:44.5

15-kilometer Classical

Year	Time
1998 Olga Danilova, RUS	.46:55.4

20-kilometer Classical (Discont.)
Discontinued in 1992 and replaced by the 30-kilometer Freestyle.

Year	Time	Year	Time
1984 Marja-Liisa Hämäläinen, FIN	.1:01:45.0	1988 Tamara Tikhonova, USSR	.55:53.6

30-kilometer Freestyle

Year	Time	Year	Time
1992 Stefania Belmondo, ITA	.1:22:30.1	1998 Julija Tchepalova, RUS	.1:22:01.5
1994 Manuela Di Centa, ITA	.1:25:41.6		

4x5-kilometer Relay
Two Classical and two Freestyle legs since 1992. Event featured three skiers per team from 1956-72.

Year	Time	Year	Time	Year	Time
1956	Finland .1:09:01.0	1972	Soviet Union .48:46.15	1988	Soviet Union .59:51.1
1960	Sweden .1:04:21.4	1976	Soviet Union .1:07:49.75	1992	Unified Team .59:34.8
1964	Soviet Union .59:20.2	1980	East Germany .1:02:11.10	1994	Russia .57:12.5
1968	Norway .57:30.0	1984	Norway .1:06:49.7	1998	Russia .55:13.5

CURLING

MEN

Year	
1998	**Switzerland**, Canada, Norway

WOMEN

Year	
1998	**Canada**, Denmark, Sweden

FIGURE SKATING

MEN
Multiple gold medals: Gillis Grafström (3); Dick Button and Karl Schäfer (2).

Year		Year		Year	
1908	Ulrich Salchow .SWE	1948	Dick Button .USA	1976	John Curry .GBR
1912	Not held	1952	Dick Button .USA	1980	Robin Cousins .GBR
1920	Gillis Grafström .SWE	1956	Hayes Alan Jenkins .USA	1984	Scott Hamilton .USA
1924	Gillis Grafström .SWE	1960	David Jenkins .USA	1988	Brian Boitano .USA
1928	Gillis Grafström .SWE	1964	Manfred Schnelldorfer .GER	1992	Victor Petrenko .UT
1932	Karl Schäfer .AUT	1968	Wolfgang Schwarz .AUT	1994	Alexei Urmanov .RUS
1936	Karl Schäfer .AUT	1972	Ondrej Nepela .CZE	1998	Ilia Kulik .RUS

WOMEN
Multiple gold medals: Sonja Henie (3); Katarina Witt (2).

Year		Year		Year	
1908	Madge Syers .GBR	1948	Barbara Ann Scott .CAN	1976	Dorothy Hamill .USA
1912	Not held	1952	Jeanette Altwegg .GBR	1980	Anett Pötzsch .E. Ger
1920	Magda Julin-Mauroy .SWE	1956	Tenley Albright .USA	1984	Katarina Witt .E. Ger
1924	Herma Planck-Szabö .AUT	1960	Carol Heiss .USA	1988	Katarina Witt .E. Ger
1928	Sonja Henie .NOR	1964	Sjoukje Dijkstra .NED	1992	Kristi Yamaguchi .USA
1932	Sonja Henie .NOR	1968	Peggy Fleming .USA	1994	Oksana Baiul .UKR
1936	Sonja Henie .NOR	1972	Beatrix Schuba .AUT	1998	Tara Lipinski .USA

PAIRS

Multiple gold medals: MEN–Pierre Brunet, Artur Dmitriev, Sergei Grinkov, Oleg Protopopov and Aleksandr Zaitsev (2). WOMEN–Irina Rodnina (3); Ludmila Belousova, Ekaterina Gordeeva and Andree Joly Brunet (2).

Year		
1908	Anna Hübler & Heinrich Burger	Germany
1912	Not held	
1920	Ludovika & Walter Jakobsson	Finland
1924	Helene Engelmann & Alfred Berger	Austria
1928	Andrée Joly & Pierre Brunet	France
1932	Andrée & Pierre Brunet	France
1936	Maxi Herber & Ernst Baier	Germany
1948	Micheline Lannoy & Pierre Baugniet	Belgium
1952	Ria & Paul Falk	Germany
1956	Elisabeth Schwartz & Kurt Oppelt	Austria
1960	Barbara Wagner & Robert Paul	Canada
1964	Ludmila Belousova & Oleg Protopopov	USSR
1968	Ludmila Belousova & Oleg Protopopov	USSR
1972	Irina Rodnina & Aleksei Ulanov	USSR
1976	Irina Rodnina & Aleksandr Zaitsev	USSR
1980	Irina Rodnina & Aleksandr Zaitsev	USSR
1984	Elena Valova & Oleg Vasiliev	USSR
1988	Ekaterina Gordeeva & Sergei Grinkov	USSR
1992	Natalya Mishkutienok & Arthur Dmitriev	UT
1994	Ekaterina Gordeeva & Sergei Grinkov	RUS
1998	Oksana Kazakova & Artur Dmitriev	RUS

Ice Dancing

Multiple gold medals: Yevegny Platov (2).

Year		
1976	Lyudmila Pakhomova & Aleksandr Gorshkov	USSR
1980	Natalia Linichuk & Gennady Karponosov	USSR
1984	Jayne Torvill & Christopher Dean	Great Britain
1988	Natalia Bestemianova & Andrei Bukin	USSR
1992	Marina Klimova & Sergei Ponomarenko	UT
1994	Oksana Gritschuk & Yevgeny Platov	RUS
1998	Pasha Grishuk & Yevgeny Platov	RUS

FREESTYLE SKIING

MEN

Aerials

Year		Points
1994	Andreas Schoebaechler, SWI	234.67
1998	Eric Bergoust, USA	255.6

Moguls

Year		Points
1994	Jean-Luc Brassard, CAN	27.24
1998	Jonny Moseley, USA	26.93

WOMEN

Aerials

Year		Points
1994	Lina Cherjazova, UZB	166.84
1998	Nikki Stone, USA	193.00

Moguls

Year		Points
1994	Stine Lise Hattestad, NOR	25.97
1998	Tae Satoya, JPN	25.06

ICE HOCKEY

MEN

Multiple gold medals: Soviet Union/Unified Team (8); Canada (6); United States (2).

Year	
1920	**Canada**, United States Czechoslovakia
1924	**Canada**, United States, Great Britain
1928	**Canada**, Sweden, Switzerland
1932	**Canada**, United States, Germany
1936	**Great Britain**, Canada, United States
1948	**Canada**, Czechoslovakia, Switzerland
1952	**Canada**, United States, Sweden
1956	**Soviet Union**, United States, Canada
1960	**United States**, Canada, Soviet Union
1964	**Soviet Union**, Sweden, Czechoslovakia
1968	**Soviet Union**, Czechoslovakia, Canada
1972	**Soviet Union**, United States, Czechoslovakia
1976	**Soviet Union**, Czechoslovakia, West Germany
1980	**United States**, Soviet Union, Sweden
1984	**Soviet Union**, Czechoslovakia, Sweden
1988	**Soviet Union**, Finland, Sweden
1992	**Unified Team**, Canada, Czechoslovakia
1994	**Sweden**, Canada, Finland
1998	**Czech Republic**, Russia, Finland

WOMEN

Year	
1998	**United States**, Canada, Finland

U.S. Gold Medal Hockey Teams

1960

Forwards: Billy Christian, Roger Christian, Billy Cleary, Gene Grazia, Paul Johnson, Bob McVey, Dick Meredith, Weldy Olson, Dick Rodenheiser and Tom Williams. **Defensemen:** Bob Cleary, Jack Kirrane (captain), John Mayasich, Bob Owen and Rod Paavola. **Goaltenders:** Jack McCartan and Larry Palmer. **Coach:** Jack Riley.

1980

Forwards: Neal Broten, Steve Christoff, Mike Eruzione (captain), John Harrington, Mark Johnson, Rob McClanahan, Mark Pavelich, Buzz Schneider, Dave Silk, Eric Strobel, Phil Verchota and Mark Wells. **Defensemen:** Bill Baker, Dave Christian, Ken Morrow, Jack O'Callahan, Mike Ramsey and Bob Suter. **Goaltenders:** Jim Craig and Steve Janaszak. **Coach:** Herb Brooks.

1998

Forwards: Laurie Baker, Alana Blahoski, Lisa Brown-Miller, Karen Bye, Tricia Dunn, Cammi Granato, Katie King, Shelley Looney, A.J. Mleczko, Jenny Schmidgall, Gretchen Ulion, Sandra Whyte. **Defensemen:** Chris Bailey, Colleen Coyne, Sue Mertz, Tara Mounsey, Vicki Movessian, Angela Ruggiero. **Goaltenders:** Sarah DeCosta and Sarah Tueting. **Coach:** Ben Smith.

LUGE

MEN

Multiple gold medals: (including doubles): Georg Hackl (3); Norbert Hahn, Paul Hildgartner, Thomas Kohler and Hans Rinn (2).

Singles

Year		Time	Year		Time
1964	Thomas Köhler, GER	3:26.77	1984	Paul Hildgartner, ITA	3:04.258
1968	Manfred Schmid, AUT	2:52.48	1988	Jens Müller, E. Ger	3:05.548
1972	Wolfgang Scheidel, E. Ger	3:27.58	1992	Georg Hackl, GER	3:02.363
1976	Dettlef Günther, E. Ger	3:27.688	1994	Georg Hackl, GER	3:21.571
1980	Bernhard Glass, E. Ger	2:54.796	1998	Georg Hackl, GER	3:18.436

Doubles

Year		Time	Year		Time
1964	Austria	1:41.62	1984	West Germany	1:23.620
1968	East Germany	1:35.85	1988	East Germany	1:31.940
1972	(TIE) East Germany	1:28.35	1992	Germany	1:32.053
	& Italy	1:28.35	1994	Italy	1:36.720
1976	East Germany	1:25.604	1998	Germany	1:41.105
1980	East Germany	1:19.331			

WOMEN

Multiple gold medals: Steffi Martin Walter (2).

Singles

Year		Time	Year		Time
1964	Ortrun Enderlein, GER	3:24.67	1984	Steffi Martin, E. Ger	2:46.570
1968	Erica Lechner, ITA	2:28.66	1988	Steffi Martin Walter, E. Ger	3:03.973
1972	Anna-Maria Müller, E. Ger	2:59.18	1992	Doris Neuner, AUT	3:06.696
1976	Margit Schumann, E. Ger	2:50.621	1994	Gerda Weissensteiner, ITA	3:15.517
1980	Vera Zozulya, USSR	2:36.537	1998	Silke Kraushaar, GER	3:23.779

NORDIC COMBINED

Multiple gold medals: Ulrich Wehling (3); Johan Gröttumsbråten (2).

Individual

Year		Points	Year		Points
1924	Thorleif Haug, NOR	18.906	1972	Ulrich Wehling, E. Ger	413.340
1928	Johan Gröttumsbråten, NOR	17.833	1976	Ulrich Wehling, E. Ger	423.39
1932	Johan Gröttumsbråten, NOR	446.00	1980	Ulrich Wehling, E. Ger	432.200
1936	Oddbjörn Hagen, NOR	430.3	1984	Tom Sandberg, NOR	422.595
1948	Heikki Hasu, FIN	448.80	1988	Hippolyt Kempf, SWI.	432.230
1952	Simon Slattvik, NOR	451.621	1992	Fabrice Guy, FRA.	426.470
1956	Sverre Stenersen, NOR	455.000	1994	Fred Borre Lundberg, NOR.	457.970
1960	Georg Thoma, GER	457.952			**Time**
1964	Tormod Knutsen, NOR.	469.28	1998	Bjarte Engen Vik, NOR.	41:21.1
1968	Franz Keller, W. Ger	449.04			

Team

Year		Points	Year		Points
1924-84	Not held		1994	Japan	1368.320
1988	West Germany	792.08			**Time**
1992	Japan	1247.180	1998	Norway	54:11.5

SKI JUMPING

Multiple gold medals (including team jumping): Matti Nykänen (4); Jens Weissflog (3); Birger Ruud and Toni Nieminen (2).

Normal Hill–90 Meters

Year		Points	Year		Points
1924-60	Not held		1984	Jens Weissflog, E. Ger	215.2
1964	Veikko Kankkonen, FIN	229.9	1988	Matti Nykänen, FIN	229.1
1968	Jiri Raska, CZE	216.5	1992	Ernst Vettori, AUT	222.8
1972	Yukio Kasaya, JPN	244.2	1994	Espen Bredesen, NOR	282.0
1976	Hans-Georg Aschenbach, E. Ger	252.0	1998	Jani Soininen, FIN	234.5
1980	Anton Innauer, AUT	266.3	**Note:** Jump held at 70 meters from 1964-92.		

Large Hill–120 Meters

Year		Points	Year		Points
1924	Jacob Tullin Thams, NOR	18.960	1968	Vladimir Beloussov, USSR	231.3
1928	Alf Andersen, NOR	19.208	1972	Wojciech Fortuna, POL	219.9
1932	Birger Ruud, NOR	228.1	1976	Karl Schäabl, AUT	234.8
1936	Birger Ruud, NOR	232.0	1980	Jouko Törmänen, FIN	271.0
1948	Petter Hugsted, NOR	228.1	1984	Matti Nykänen, FIN	231.2
1952	Arnfinn Bergmann, NOR.	226.0	1988	Matti Nykänen, FIN	224.0
1956	Antti Hyvärinen, FIN	227.0	1992	Toni Nieminen, FIN.	239.5
1960	Helmut Recknagel, GER.	227.2	1994	Jens Weissflog, GER.	274.5
1964	Toralf Engan, NOR.	230.7	1998	Kazuyoshi Funaki, JPN.	272.3

Note: Jump held at various lengths from 1924-56; at 80 meters from 1960-64; and at 90 meters from 1968-88.

Team Large Hill

Year		Points	Year		Points
1924-84	Not held		1994	Germany	970.1
1988	Finland	634.4	1998	Japan	933.0
1992	Finland	644.4			

SNOWBOARDING

MEN
Halfpipe

Year		Points
1998	Gian Simmen, SWI	85.2

WOMEN
Halfpipe

Year		Points
1998	Nicola Thost, GER	74.6

Giant Slalom

Year		Points
1998	Ross Rebagliati, CAN	2:03.96

Giant Slalom

Year		Points
1998	Karine Ruby, FRA	2:17.34

SPEED SKATING

MEN

Multiple gold medals: Eric Heiden and Clas Thunberg (5); Ivar Ballangrud, Yevgeny Grishin and Johann Olav Koss (4); Hjalmar Andersen, Tomas Gustafson, Irving Jaffee and Ard Schenk (3); Gaétan Boucher, Knut Johannesen, Erhard Keller, Uwe-Jens Mey, Gianni Romme and Jack Shea (2). Note that Thunberg's total includes the All-Around, which was contested for the only time in 1924.

500 meters

Year		Time		Year		Time	
1924	Charles Jewtraw, USA	44.0		1968	Erhard Keller, W. Ger.	40.3	
1928	(TIE) Bernt Evensen, NOR.	43.4	OR	1972	Erhard Keller, W. Ger.	39.44	OR
	& Clas Thunberg, FIN	43.4	OR	1976	Yevgeny Kulikov, USSR	39.17	OR
1932	Jack Shea, USA	43.4	=OR	1980	Eric Heiden, USA	38.03	OR
1936	Ivar Ballangrud, NOR.	43.4	=OR	1984	Sergei Fokichev, USSR	38.19	
1948	Finn Helgesen, NOR.	43.1	OR	1988	Uwe-Jens Mey, E. Ger	36.45	WR
1952	Ken Henry, USA	43.2		1992	Uwe-Jens Mey, GER	37.14	
1956	Yevgeny Grishin, USSR.	40.2	=WR	1994	Aleksandr Golubev, RUS	36.33	OR
1960	Yevgeny Grishin, USSR.	40.2	=WR	1998	Hiroyashu Shimizu, JPN.	71.35	OR
1964	Terry McDermott, USA	40.1	OR				

1000 meters

Year		Time		Year		Time	
1924-72	Not held			1988	Nikolai Gulyaev, USSR	1:13.03	OR
1976	Peter Mueller, USA	1:19.32		1992	Olaf Zinke, GER	1:14.85	
1980	Eric Heiden, USA	1:15.18	OR	1994	Dan Jansen, USA	1:12.43	WR
1984	Gaétan Boucher, CAN	1:15.80		1998	Ids Postma, NED	1:10.64	OR

1500 meters

Year		Time		Year		Time	
1924	Clas Thunberg, FIN	2:20.8		1964	Ants Antson, USSR	2:10.3	
1928	Clas Thunberg, FIN	2:21.1		1968	Kees Verkerk, NED	2:03.4	OR
1932	Jack Shea, USA	2:57.5		1972	Ard Schenk, NED	2:02.96	OR
1936	Charles Mathisen, NOR.	2:19.2	OR	1976	Jan Egil Storholt, NOR.	1:59.38	OR
1948	Sverre Farstad, NOR.	2:17.6	OR	1980	Eric Heiden, USA	1:55.44	OR
1952	Hjalmar Andersen, NOR	2:20.4		1984	Gaétan Boucher, CAN	1:58.36	
1956	(TIE) Yevgeny Grishin, USSR	2:08.6	WR	1988	Andre Hoffman, E. Ger	1:52.06	WR
	& Yuri Mikhailov, USSR	2:08.6	WR	1992	Johann Olav Koss, NOR	1:54.81	
1960	(TIE) Roald Aas, NOR	2:10.4		1994	Johann Olav Koss, NOR.	1:51.29	WR
	& Yevgeny Grishin, USSR	2:10.4		1998	Aadne Sondral, NOR	1:47.87	WR

5000 meters

Year		Time		Year		Time	
1924	Clas Thunberg, FIN	8:39.0		1968	Fred Anton Maier, NOR	7:22.4	**WR**
1928	Ivar Ballangrud, NOR	8:50.5		1972	Ard Schenk, NED	7:23.61	
1932	Irving Jaffee, USA	9:40.8		1976	Sten Stensen, NOR	7:24.48	
1936	Ivar Ballangrud, NOR	8:19.6	**OR**	1980	Eric Heiden, USA	7:02.29	**OR**
1948	Reidar Liaklev, NOR	8:29.4		1984	Tomas Gustafson, SWE	7:12.28	
1952	Hjalmar Andersen, NOR	8:10.6	**OR**	1988	Tomas Gustafson, SWE	6:44.63	**WR**
1956	Boris Shilkov, USSR	7:48.7	**OR**	1992	Geir Karlstad, NOR	6:59.97	
1960	Viktor Kosichkin, USSR	7:51.3		1994	Johann Olav Koss, NOR	6:34.96	**WR**
1964	Knut Johannesen, NOR	7:38.4	**OR**	1998	Gianni Romme, NED	6:22.20	**WR**

10,000 meters

Year		Time		Year		Time	
1924	Julius Skutnabb, FIN	18:04.8		1968	Johnny Höglin, SWE	15:23.6	**OR**
1928	Irving Jaffee, USA*	18:36.5		1972	Ard Schenk, NED	15:01.35	**OR**
1932	Irving Jaffee, USA	19:13.6		1976	Piet Kleine, NED	14:50.59	**OR**
1936	Ivar Ballangrud, NOR	17:24.3	**OR**	1980	Eric Heiden, USA	14:28.13	**WR**
1948	Ake Seyffarth, SWE	17:26.3		1984	Igor Malkov, USSR	14:39.90	
1952	Hjalmar Andersen, NOR	16:45.8	**OR**	1988	Tomas Gustafson, SWE	13:48.20	**WR**
1956	Sigvard Ericsson, SWE	16:35.9	**OR**	1992	Bart Veldkamp, NED	14:12.12	
1960	Knut Johannesen, NOR	15:46.6	**WR**	1994	Johann Olav Koss, NOR	13:30.55	**WR**
1964	Jonny Nilsson, SWE	15:50.1		1998	Gianni Romme, NED	13:15.33	**WR**

*Unofficial, according to the IOC. Jaffee recorded the fastest time, but the event was called off in progress due to thawing ice.

WOMEN

Multiple gold medals: Lydia Skoblikova (6); Bonnie Blair (5); Karin Enke, Gunda Niemann-Stirnemann and Yvonne van Gennip (3); Tatiana Averina, Claudia Pechstein and Christa Rothenburger (2).

500 meters

Year		Time		Year		Time	
1960	Helga Haase, GER	45.9		1984	Christa Rothenburger, E. Ger	41.02	**OR**
1964	Lydia Skoblikova, USSR	45.0	**OR**	1988	Bonnie Blair, USA	39.10	**WR**
1968	Lyudmila Titova, USSR	46.1		1992	Bonnie Blair, USA	40.33	
1972	Anne Henning, USA	43.33	**OR**	1994	Bonnie Blair, USA	39.25	
1976	Sheila Young, USA	42.76	**OR**	1998	Catriona Lemay-Doan, CAN	76.60	**OR**
1980	Karin Enke, E. Ger	41.78	**OR**				

1000 meters

Year		Time		Year		Time	
1960	Klara Guseva, USSR	1:34.1		1984	Karin Enke, E. Ger	1:21.61	**OR**
1964	Lydia Skoblikova, USSR	1:33.2	**OR**	1988	Christa Rothenburger, E. Ger	1:17.65	**WR**
1968	Carolina Geijssen, NED	1:32.6	**OR**	1992	Bonnie Blair, USA	1:21.90	
1972	Monika Pflug, W. Ger	1:31.40	**OR**	1994	Bonnie Blair, USA	1:18.74	
1976	Tatiana Averina, USSR	1:28.43	**OR**	1998	Marianne Timmer, NED	1:16.51	**OR**
1980	Natalia Petruseva, USSR	1:24.10	**OR**				

1500 meters

Year		Time		Year		Time	
1960	Lydia Skoblikova, USSR	2:25.2	**WR**	1984	Karin Enke, E. Ger	2:03.42	**WR**
1964	Lydia Skoblikova, USSR	2:22.6	**OR**	1988	Yvonne van Gennip, NED	2:00.68	**OR**
1968	Kaija Mustonen, FIN	2:22.4	**OR**	1992	Jacqueline Börner, GER	2:05.87	
1972	Dianne Holum, USA	2:20.85	**OR**	1994	Emese Hunyady, AUT	2:02.19	
1976	Galina Stepanskaya, USSR	2:16.58	**OR**	1998	Marianne Timmer, NED	1:57.58	**WR**
1980	Annie Borckink, NED	2:10.95	**OR**				

3000 meters

Year		Time		Year		Time	
1960	Lydia Skoblikova, USSR	5:14.3		1984	Andrea Schöne, E. Ger	4:24.79	**OR**
1964	Lydia Skoblikova, USSR	5:14.9		1988	Yvonne van Gennip, NED	4:11.94	**WR**
1968	Johanna Schut, NED	4:56.2	**OR**	1992	Gunda Niemann, GER	4:19.90	
1972	Christina Baas-Kaiser, NED	4:52.14	**OR**	1994	Svetlana Bazhanova, RUS	4:17.43	
1976	Tatiana Averina, USSR	4:45.19	**OR**	1998	Gunda Niemann-Stirnemann, GER	4:07.29	**OR**
1980	Bjorg Eva Jensen, NOR	4:32.13	**OR**				

5000 meters

Year		Time		Year		Time	
1960-84	Not held			1994	Claudia Pechstein, GER	7:14.37	
1988	Yvonne van Gennip, NED	7:14.13	**WR**	1998	Claudia Pechstein, GER	6:59.61	**WR**
1992	Gunda Niemann, GER	7:31.57					

AP/Wide World Photos

Speed Skater **Bonnie Blair** is the most decorated Winter Olympian, male or female, in American history. Winner of five gold medals and six overall, Blair is pictured above in the 500-meter final in the 1994 Games at Lillehammer, Norway. Blair finished the race with a time of 39.25 for her fourth career gold.

All-Time Leading Medal Winners

MEN

No		Sport	G-S-B
12	Bjorn Dählie, NOR	Cross-country	8-4-0
9	Sixten Jernberg, SWE	Cross-country	4-3-2
7	Clas Thunberg, FIN	Speed Skating	5-1-1
7	Ivar Ballangrud, NOR	Speed Skating	4-2-1
7	Veikko Hakulinen, FIN	Cross-country	3-3-1
7	Eero Mäntyranta, FIN	Cross-country	3-2-2
7	Bogdan Musiol, E. Ger/GER	Bobsled	1-5-1
6	Gunde Svan, SWE	Cross-country	4-1-1
6	Vegard Ulvang, NOR	Cross-country	3-2-1
6	Johan Gröttumsbråten, NOR	Nordic	3-1-2
6	Wolfgang Hoppe, E. Ger/GER	Bobsled	2-3-1
6	Eugenio Monti, ITA	Bobsled	2-2-2
6	Vladimir Smirnov, USSR/UT/KAZ	X-country	1-4-1
6	Mika Myllylae, FIN	Cross-country	1-1-4
6	Roald Larsen, NOR	Speed Skating	0-2-4
6	**Eric Heiden, USA**	Speed Skating	5-0-0
5	Yevgeny Grishin, USSR	Speed Skating	4-1-0
5	Johann Olav Koss, NOR	Speed Skating	4-1-0
5	Matti Nykänen, FIN	Ski Jumping	4-1-0
5	Aleksandr Tikhonov, USSR	Biathlon	4-1-0
5	Nikolai Zimyatov, USSR	Cross-country	4-1-0
5	Alberto Tomba, ITA	Alpine	3-2-0
5	Harald Grönningen, NOR	Cross-country	2-3-0
5	Päl Tyldum, NOR	Cross-country	2-3-0
5	Knut Johannesen, NOR	Speed Skating	2-2-1
5	Kjetil André Aamodt, NOR	Alpine	1-2-2
5	Peter Angerer, W. Ger/GER	Biathlon	1-2-2
5	Juha Mieto, FIN	Cross-country	1-2-2
5	Fritz Feierabend, SWI	Bobsled	0-3-2
5	Rintje Ritsma, NED	Speed Skating	0-2-3

WOMEN

No		Sport	G-S-B
10	Raisa Smetanina, USSR/UT	Cross-country	4-5-1
9	Lyubov Egorova, UT/RUS	Cross-country	6-3-0
8	Galina Kulakova, USSR	Cross-country	4-2-2
8	Karin (Enke) Kania, E. Ger	Speed Skating	3-4-1
8	Gunda Neimann-Stirnemann, GER	Speed Skating	3-4-1
7	Larisa Lazutina, UT/RUS	Cross-country	5-1-1
7	Marja-Liisa (Hämäläinen) Kirvesniemi, FIN	Cross-country	3-0-4
7	Elena Valbe, UT/RUS	Cross-country	3-0-4
7	Andrea (Mitscherlich, Schöne) Ehrig, E. Ger	Speed Skating	1-5-1
7	Stefania Belmondo, ITA	Cross-country	1-2-4
6	Lydia Skoblikova, USSR	Speed Skating	6-0-0
6	**Bonnie Blair, USA**	Speed Skating	5-0-1
6	Manuela Di Centa, ITA	Cross-country	2-2-2
5	Lee-Kyung Chun, S. Kor	ST Sp. Skating	4-0-1
5	Anfisa Reztsova, USSR/UT	CC/Biathlon	3-1-1
5	Vreni Schneider, SWI	Alpine	3-1-1
5	Katja Seizinger, GER	Alpine	3-0-2
5	Claudia Pechstein, GER	Speed Skating	2-1-2
5	Helena Takalo, FIN	Cross-country	1-3-1
5	Ursula Disl, GER	Biathlon	1-2-2
5	Alevtina Kolchina, USSR	Cross-country	1-1-3

Games Medaled In

MEN– **Aamodt** (1992,94); **Angerer** (1980,84,88); **Ballangrud** (1928,32,36); **Dählie** (1992,94,98); **Feierabend** (1936,48,52); **Grishin** (1956,60,64); **Gröttumsbråten** (1924,28,32); **Grönningen** (1960,64,68); **Hakulinen** (1952,56,60); **Heiden** (1980); **Hoppe** (1984,88,92,94); **Jernberg** (1956,60,64); **Johannesen** (1956,60,64); **Koss** (1992,94). **Larsen** (1924,28); **Mäntyranta** (1960,64,68); **Mieto** (1976,80,84); **Monti** (1956,60,64,68); **Musiol** (1980,84,88,92); **Myllylae** (1994,98); **Nykänen** (1984,88); **Ritsma** (1994,98); **Smirnov** (1988,92,94,98); **Svan** (1984,88); **Thunberg** (1924,28); **Tikhonov** (1968,72,76,80); **Tomba** (1988,92,94); **Tyldum** (1968,72,76); **Ulvang** (1988,92,94); **Zimyatov** (1980,84).

WOMEN– **Belmondo** (1992,94,98); **Blair** (1988,92,94); **Chun** (1994,98); **Di Centa** (1992,94); **Disl** (1994,98); **Egorova** (1992,94); **Ehrig** (1976,80,84,88); **Kania** (1980,84,88); **Kirvesniemi** (1984,88,94); **Kolchina** (1956,64,68); **Kulakova** (1968,72,76,80); **Lazutina** (1992,94,98); **Niemann-Stirnemann** (1992,94,98); **Pechstein** (1992,94,98); **Reztsova** (1988,92,94); **Schneider** (1988,92,94); **Seizinger** (1992,94,98); **Skoblikova** (1960,64); **Smetanina** (1976,80,84,88,92); **Takalo** (1972,76,80); **Valbe** (1992,94,98).

Most Gold Medals

MEN

No		Sport	G-S-B
8	Bjorn Dählie, NOR	Cross-country	8-4-0
5	Clas Thunberg, FIN	Speed Skating	5-1-1
5	**Eric Heiden, USA**	Speed Skating	5-0-0
4	Sixten Jernberg, SWE	Cross-country	4-3-2
4	Ivar Ballangrud, NOR	Speed Skating	4-2-1
4	Gunde Svan, SWE	Cross-country	4-1-1
4	Yevgeny Grishin, USSR	Speed Skating	4-1-0
4	Johann Olav Koss, NOR	Speed Skating	4-1-0
4	Matti Nykänen, FIN	Ski Jumping	4-1-0
4	Aleksandr Tikhonov, USSR	Biathlon	4-1-0
4	Nikolai Zimyatov, USSR	Cross-country	4-1-0
4	Thomas Wassberg, SWE	Cross-country	4-0-0
3	Veikko Hakulinen, FIN	Cross-country	3-3-1
3	Eero Mäntyranta, FIN	Cross-country	3-2-2
3	Vegard Ulvang, NOR	Cross-country	3-2-1
3	Alberto Tomba, ITA	Alpine	3-2-0
3	Johan Gröttumsbråten, NOR	Nordic	3-1-2
3	Bernhard Germeshausen, E. Ger	Bobsled	3-1-0
3	Gillis Grafström, SWE	Figure Skating	3-1-0
3	Tomas Gustafson, SWE	Speed Skating	3-1-0
3	Vladislav Tretiak, USSR	Ice Hockey	3-1-0
3	Jens Weissflog, E. Ger/GER	Ski Jumping	3-1-0
3	Meinhard Nehmer, E. Ger	Bobsled	3-0-1
3	Hjalmar Andersen, NOR	Speed Skating	3-0-0
3	Vitaly Davydov, USSR	Ice Hockey	3-0-0
3	Anatoly Firsov, USSR	Ice Hockey	3-0-0
3	Thorleif Haug, NOR	Cross-country	3-0-0
3	**Irving Jaffee, USA**	Speed Skating	3-0-0
3	Andrei Khomoutov, USSR/UT	Ice Hockey	3-0-0
3	Jean-Claude Killy, FRA	Alpine	3-0-0
3	Viktor Kuzkin, USSR	Ice Hockey	3-0-0
3	Aleksandr Ragulin, USSR	Ice Hockey	3-0-0
3	Toni Sailer, AUT	Alpine	3-0-0
3	Ard Schenk, NED	Speed Skating	3-0-0
3	Ulrich Wehling, E. Ger	Ski Jumping	3-0-0

WOMEN

No		Sport	G-S-B
6	Lyubov Egorova, UT/RUS	Cross-country	6-3-0
6	Lydia Skoblikova, USSR	Speed Skating	6-0-0
5	Larissa Lazutina, UT/RUS	Cross-country	5-1-1
5	**Bonnie Blair, USA**	Speed Skating	5-0-1
4	Raisa Smetanina, USSR/UT	Cross-country	4-5-1
4	Galina Kulakova, USSR	Cross-country	4-2-2
4	Lee-Kyung Chun, S. Kor.	ST Sp. Skating	4-0-1
3	Karin (Enke) Kania, E. Ger	Speed Skating	3-4-1
3	Gunda Neimann-Stirnemann, GER	Speed Skating	3-4-1
3	Anfisa Reztsova, USSR/UT	CC/Biathlon	3-1-1
3	Vreni Schneider, SWI	Alpine	3-1-1
3	Marja-Liisa (Hämäläinen) Kirvesniemi, FIN	Cross-country	3-0-4
3	Elena Valbe, UT/RUS	Cross-country	3-0-4
3	Katja Seizinger, GER	Alpine	3-0-2
3	Claudia Boyarskikh, USSR	Cross-country	3-0-0
3	Sonja Henie, NOR	Figure Skating	3-0-0
3	Irina Rodnina, USSR	Figure Skating	3-0-0
3	Yvonne van Gennip, NED	Speed Skating	3-0-0

Athletes with Winter and Summer Medals

Only three athletes have won medals in both the Winter and Summer Olympics:

Eddie Eagan, USA– Light Heavyweight Boxing gold (1920) and Four-man Bobsled gold (1932).

Jacob Tullin Thams, Norway– Ski Jumping gold (1924) and 8-meter Yachting silver (1936).

Christa Luding-Rothenburger, East Germany– Speed Skating gold at 500 meters (1984) and 1,000m (1988), silver at 500m (1988) and bronze at 500m (1992) and Match Sprint Cycling silver (1988). Luding- Rothenburger is the only athlete to ever win medals in both Winter and Summer Games in the same year.

All-Time Leading USA Medalists
MEN

No		Sport	G-S-B	No		Sport	G-S-B
5	Eric Heiden	Speed Skating	5-0-0	2	Billy Fiske	Bobsled	2-0-0
3*	Irving Jaffee	Speed Skating	3-0-0	2	Cliff Gray	Bobsled	2-0-0
3	Pat Martin	Bobsled	1-2-0	2	Jack Shea	Speed Skating	2-0-0
3	John Heaton	Bobsled/Cresta	0-2-1	2	Billy Cleary	Ice Hockey	1-1-0
2	Dick Button	Figure Skating	2-0-0	2	Jennison Heaton	Bobsled/Cresta	1-1-0
2†	Eddie Eagan	Boxing/Bobsled	2-0-0	2	John Mayasich	Ice Hockey	1-1-0

No		Sport	G-S-B	No		Sport	G-S-B
2	Terry McDermott............Speed Skating		1-1-0	2	Stan Benham....................Bobsled		0-2-0
2	Dick Meredith.....................Ice Hockey		1-1-0	2	Herb Drury....................Ice Hockey		0-2-0
2	Tommy Moe........................Alpine		1-1-0	2	Eric Flaim...........Sp. Skate/ST Sp. Skate		0-2-0
2	Weldy Olson.....................Ice Hockey		1-1-0	2	Frank Synott...................Ice Hockey		0-2-0
2	Dick Rodenheiser................Ice Hockey		1-1-0	2	John Garrison..................Ice Hockey		0-1-1
2	David Jenkins.............Figure Skating		1-1-0				

*Jaffee is generally given credit for a third gold medal in the 10,000-meter Speed Skating race of 1928. He had the fastest time before the race was cancelled due to thawing ice. The IOC considers the race unofficial.
†Eagan won the Light Heavyweight boxing title at the 1920 Summer Games in Antwerp and the four-man Bobsled at the 1932 Winter Games in Lake Placid. He is the only athlete ever to win gold medals in both the Winter and Summer Olympics.

WOMEN

No		Sport	G-S-B	No		Sport	G-S-B
6	Bonnie Blair.................Speed Skating		5-0-1	2	Carol Heiss.................Figure Skating		1-1-0
4	Cathy Turner ....ST Sp. Skating		2-1-1	2	Picabo Street ....Alpine		1-1-0
4	Dianne Holum................Speed Skating		1-2-1	2	Diann Roffe-Steinrotter.........Alpine		1-1-0
3	Sheila Young................Speed Skating		1-1-1	2	Anne Henning...............Speed Skating		1-0-1
3	Leah Poulos Mueller ....Speed Skating		0-3-0	2	Penny Pitou........................Alpine		0-2-0
3	Beatrix Loughran ....Figure Skating		0-2-1	2	Nancy Kerrigan.............Figure Skating		0-1-1
3	Amy Peterson ....ST Sp. Skating		0-2-1	2	Jean Saubert.....................Alpine		0-1-1
2	Andrea Mead Lawrence ....Alpine		2-0-0	2	Chris Witty....................Sp. Skating		0-1-1
2	Tenley Albright.............Figure Skating		1-1-0	2	Nikki Ziegelmeyer...........ST Sp. Skating		0-1-1
2	Gretchen Fraser ....Alpine		1-1-0				

Notes: The Cresta run is undertaken on a heavy sled ridden head first in the prone position and has only been held at St. Moritz in 1928 and '48. Also, the term ST Sp. Skating refers to Short Track (or pack) Speed Skating.

All-Time Medal Standings, 1924-98

All-time Winter Games medal standings, according to *The Golden Book of the Olympic Games*. Medal counts include figure skating medals (1908 and '20) and hockey medals (1920) awarded at the Summer Games. National medal standings for the Winter and Summer Games are not recognized by the IOC.

		G	S	B	Total			G	S	B	Total
1	Norway 83		87	69	239	22	Liechtenstein..............2		2	5	9
2	Soviet Union (1956-88)......78		57	59	194	23	Hungary....................0		2	4	6
3	**United States**..........59		59	41	159	24	Kazakhstan (1994–)..........1		2	2	5
4	Austria 39		53	53	145		Belgium.....................1		1	3	5
5	Finland 38		49	48	135	26	Poland......................1		1	2	4
6	East Germany (1968-88)......43		39	36	118		Yugoslavia (1924-88)........0		3	1	4
7	Sweden.....................39		28	35	102		Belarus (1994–).............0		2	2	4
8	Switzerland 29		31	32	92	29	Czech Republic (1998–).....1		1	1	3
9	Germany (1928-36, 52-64, 92–)......35		30	25	90		Ukraine (1994–)............1		1	1	3
							Slovenia (1992–)...........0		0	3	3
10	Canada 25		25	29	79	32	Bulgaria....................1		0	1	2
11	Italy.......................27		27	23	77		Spain.......................1		0	1	2
12	Netherlands.................19		23	19	61		Luxembourg.................0		2	0	2
	France.....................18		17	26	61		North Korea................0		1	1	2
14	West Germany (1968-88)....18		20	19	57		Australia...................0		0	2	2
15	Russia (1994–) 21		14	7	42	37	Uzbekistan (1994–)..........1		0	0	1
16	Japan.......................8		9	12	29		Denmark....................0		1	0	1
17	Czechoslovakia (1924-92) ...2		8	16	26		New Zealand...............0		1	0	1
18	Great Britain...............7		4	13	24		Romania....................0		0	1	1
19	Unified Team (1992)..........9		6	8	23						
20	South Korea 9		3	4	16	**Combined totals**		**G**	**S**	**B**	**Total**
21	China 0		10	4	14	Germany/E. Ger/W. Ger 96		89	80	265
						USSR/UT/Russia..............108		77	74	259

Notes: Athletes from the USSR participated in the Winter Games from 1956-88, returned as the Unified Team in 1992 after the breakup of the Soviet Union (in 1991) and then competed for the independent republics of Belarus, Kazakhstan, Russia, Ukraine, Uzbekistan and three others in 1994. Yugoslavia divided into Croatia and Bosnia-Herzegovina in 1992, while Czechoslovakia split into Slovakia and the Czech Republic in 1993.

Germany was barred from the Olympics in 1924 and 1948 as an aggressor nation in both World Wars I and II. Divided into East and West Germany after WWII, both countries competed under one flag from 1952-64, then as separate teams from 1968-88. Germany was reunified in 1990.

Soccer

Kansas City's **Miklos Molnar** *celebrates his game-winning goal in MLS Cup 2000.*

AP/Wide World Photos

Wizards Cast Spell on MLS

Kansas City, led by goaltender Tony Meola, shuts down the rest of the league in what turns out to be a good year for American soccer.

by

Jack Edwards

In spite of a media environment desperate to find the cloud that surrounds the silver lining, the American Soccer Culture continued to nurture its passionate core in 2000.

Only one nation put both men's and women's teams in the Olympic semifinals. It was the United States. The women already had proven that they belonged there, having won the 1996 gold medal and the 1999 World Cup. But the men went further than they ever had, finishing fourth after never previously advancing past group play. The reason was Major League Soccer–the oft-maligned league that

Jack Edwards calls the play-by-play for MLS games among his ESPN assignments. He played Division I college soccer.

seems, in the view of many editors, rarely newsworthy unless its attendance figures are the angle.

On October 11 in Columbus, the U.S. Men's National Team was playing Costa Rica. At stake: the potential to clinch advancement to the CONCACAF Final Qualifying round, which will produce the region's three teams at the 2002 World Cup.

This was no "friendly," no public relations exercise–it was an all-out international game played at furious pace. Late in the game, Costa Rican Coach Gilson Nunes subbed-in Mauricio Solis and William Sunsing. At that juncture, 11 of the 22 players on the field were either current or former MLS players–10 of them active, plus ex-New England Rev Joe Max Moore, who now plays for Everton in England's Premiere League.

AP/Wide World Photos

The **Kansas City Wizards** celebrate their 1-0 victory over the Chicago Fire in MLS Cup 2000. The Wizards went from last place in the division a year ago to the pinnacle of American professional soccer.

Four days later at RFK Stadium in Washington, MLS Cup was as thrilling a 1-0 game as this country has ever hosted. Kansas City midfielder Chris Klein picked the ball off the foot of Chicago's Diego Gutierrez and beat all challengers on a 65-yard run to the right wing corner. He then hammered a low cross that Miklos Molnar would deflect in on a second-chance touch.

Kansas City goalkeeper Tony Meola, who had posted 16 shutouts in 31 starts during the regular season–and four more in the playoffs–then would make the league's best defense stand strong against MLS's top offense.

Chicago emptied its arsenal. Hristo Stoitchkov literally moved the goal with a left-footed cannonball that struck the top of the left post in the first half. Gutierrez had horrible luck when his short volley in traffic slammed off the crossbar in the second. Jesse Marsch attempted a bicycle kick early . . . Lubos Kubik got-off a rocket late. Some of the shots went right at Meola–others, the keeper punched, blocked, or smothered. To add to his raft of awards (comeback player of the year for his 1999 ACL tear, goalkeeper of the year, and regular season MVP), Meola also was named MLS Cup MVP.

MLS is growing. It is to sports what FM was to radio about 30 years ago. Deeper album cuts, a LOT more time between ads (45 minutes uninterrupted, twice), and targeting a niche market on a higher intellectual plane than the old formula AM stations used to.

The soccer culture knows where and when to gather–and as it continues to get more stadiums that are built for its favorite game, controlling dates

Kansas City goaltender **Tony Meola** smothers a shot from the Chicago Fire's Ante Razov in MLS Cup 2000. Meola, the MLS Comeback Player of the Year as well as the regular season MVP, doused the Fire on his way to winning game MVP honors.

and revenue streams, the game will grow in the U.S. The year 2000, on balance, was a pretty good year. ■

Jack Edwards' Highlights of the Year in MLS

10. **MLS makes some rule changes**, abandoning the overtime shootout (thereby allowing ties) and returning control of the official clock to the referee on the field.

9. Defending (and three times out of four) champion **D.C. United gets spanked**, 4-0, by the Los Angeles Galaxy in its season opener and never seems to recover, missing the playoffs altogether and finishing the year in last place with an 8-18-6 record.

8. Tampa Bay Mutiny striker **Mamadou Diallo finishes with 26 goals** on the year, falling just short of Roy Lassiter's MLS single season goal-scoring record.

7. Goalkeeper **Tony Meola comes back** from blowing out his ACL in 1999 to post 16 shutouts in 31 regular season games for the Kansas City Wizards, then notches five more in the playoffs on his way to winning regular season and MLS Cup MVP honors in addition to comeback player of the year.

6. Defender **Carlos Bocanegra skips** his senior season at UCLA, and immediately establishes himself as a tenacious man-marker for

AP/Wide World Photos

Sasha Victorine celebrates his goal in the over-time shootout that gives the U.S. Men's Olympic Soccer team a victory over Japan and their first-ever spot in the medal round.

MetroStars and **Luis Hernandez's failure** to put the projected thousands of fannies in the seats in Los Angeles **give folks reason to re-think** the MLS's expensive efforts to chase international "name" players when up-and-coming American players are looking overseas to make more money.

2. The New York/New Jersey **MetroStars go from having the worst record** in MLS history (7-25) to a division-winning 17-12-3 regular-season mark and a spot in the league semifinals, before getting edged-out by Chicago.

1. The **Kansas City Wizards**, the worst team in the West (8-24) the year before, play great defense, scale the heights and **win MLS Cup 2000**. ∎

the Chicago Fire, winning the MLS Rookie of the Year Award.

5. Kansas City rookie defender **Nick Garcia has an equally sensational season**, leaving Indiana University just a month after winning the 1999 NCAA Championship as a junior. His Wizards give up only 29 goals in 32 games, establishing a new MLS record for fewest goals allowed in a season.

4. Forward **Ante Razov sticks results** in the face of his doubters, delivering his third straight club-leading season for Chicago and shows he can score goals in World Cup Qualifiers as well.

3. Former German Bundesliga Player of the Year **Lothar Matthäus' utter flop** for the

Shaun Botterill/Allsport

Manuel Sanchis of Real Madrid hoists the **UEFA Champions League Cup** that Real Madrid won with their win over Valencia in the all-Spanish final on May 24.

insidethe**numbers**

GLOBAL CHAMPS

Only three nations in international soccer have been reigning World Cup and Olympic champions simultaneously. France, the 1998 World Cup champions, didn't play in the 2000 Olympic Games. The U.S. women could have kept their streak alive but fell to Norway in the gold medal match. Cameroon, winner of the men's gold in Sydney is not one of the favorites for the upcoming 2002 World Cup. Norway, the women's gold medallists will have to wait until 2003 for their chance to add themselves to this list.

Since 1992, the men's Olympic tournament has been limited to players under 23 years old with the exception of three "over-age" players. The women's Olympic tournament, which debuted in 1996, is open to players 16 and over. Also note that West Germany won the 1974 World Cup and then East Germany won the gold medal at the 1976 Olympic Games.

Team	Year	Tournament
United States (women)	1999	World Cup
	1996	Olympics
Italy (men)	1938	World Cup
	1936	Olympics
	1934	World Cup
Uruguay (men)	1930	World Cup
	1928	Olympics

Note: Soccer was not played at the 1932 Olympics.

NO ADMITTANCE

Kansas City Wizards goalkeeper Tony Meola set an MLS record, by a large margin, with 16 shutouts this season. Here's a look at the most shutouts in one season in the MLS:

	Year	Shutouts
Tony Meola, KC	2000	16
Matt Jordan, Dal.	1999	11
Kevin Hartman, LA	1999	11
Tony Meola, NY/NJ	1996	9
Ian Feuer, Col.	1999	8
Zach Thornton, Chi.	1998	8

USA MEN IN OLYMPICS

The USA men's soccer team had their best ever Olympic Games in 2000, advancing to the medal round before finishing fourth out of 16 teams. Here's a look at how previous U.S. Olympic soccer teams have fared since the first non-European teams started playing in 1924.

Year	W-L-T	Result
1924	1-1-0	eliminated in 2nd round by the eventual champions Uruguay
1928	0-1-0	eliminated, 11-2, in 1st round by eventual silver medallist Argentina
1936	0-1-0	eliminated, 1-0, in 1st round by eventual champions Italy
1948	0-1-0	eliminated, 9-0, in 1st round by Italy
1952	0-1-0	eliminated, 8-0, in 1st round by Italy
1956	0-1-0	eliminated, 9-1, in 2nd round by eventual silver medallist Yugoslavia
1960	—	did not qualify
1964	—	did not qualify
1968	—	did not qualify
1972	0-2-1	failed to advance past 1st round
1976	—	did not qualify
1980	—	USA boycotted Games
1984	1-1-1	failed to advance past 1st round
1988	0-1-2	failed to advance past 1st round
1992	1-1-1	failed to advance past 1st round
1996	1-1-1	failed to advance past 1st round
2000	2-2-2	lost bronze medal match to Chile, 2-0

Note: In 1956, the U.S. advanced directly to the 2nd round from qualifying because there was an uneven number of entrants. ∎

SOCCER
1999-2000 Season in Review

ESPN

information please
SPORTS ALMANAC

PAGE 725

2000 European Championship

The UEFA European Football Championship is held every four years to determine the best national team in Europe and in 2000 it was contested for the 11th time since its inception in 1960. Held June 10-July 2 and hosted by Belgium and The Netherlands.

First Round

Round robin; each team played the other three teams in its group once. Note that three points were awarded for a win and one point for a tie. (*) indicates team advanced to second round.

Group A	Gm	W	L	T	Pts	GF	GA
*Portugal	3	3	0	0	9	7	2
*Romania	3	1	1	1	4	4	4
England	3	1	2	0	3	5	6
Germany	3	0	2	1	1	1	5

RESULTS: **June 12**–Germany 1, Romania 1; Portugal 3, England 2; **June 17**–Portugal 1, Romania 0; England 1, Germany 0; **June 20**–Romania 3, England 2; Portugal 3, Germany 0.

Group B	Gm	W	L	T	Pts	GF	GA
*Italy	3	3	0	0	9	6	2
*Turkey	3	1	1	1	4	3	2
Belgium	3	1	2	0	3	2	5
Sweden	3	0	2	1	1	2	4

RESULTS: **June 10**–Belgium 2, Sweden 1; **June 11**–Italy 2, Turkey 1; **June 14**–Italy 2, Belgium 0; **June 15**–Sweden 0, Turkey 0; **June 19**–Turkey 2, Belgium 0; Italy 2, Sweden 1.

Group C	Gm	W	L	T	Pts	GF	GA
*Spain	3	2	1	0	6	6	5
*Yugoslavia	3	1	1	1	4	7	7
Norway	3	1	1	1	4	1	1
Slovenia	3	0	1	2	2	4	5

RESULTS: **June 13**–Norway 1, Spain 0; Slovenia 3, Yugoslavia 3; **June 18**–Spain 2, Slovenia 1; Yugoslavia 1, Norway 0; **June 21**–Norway 0, Slovenia 0; Spain 4, Yugoslavia 3.

Group D	Gm	W	L	T	Pts	GF	GA
Netherlands	3	3	0	0	9	7	2
France	3	2	1	0	6	7	4
Czech Republic	3	1	2	0	3	3	3
Denmark	3	0	3	0	0	0	8

RESULTS: **June 11**–France 3, Denmark 0; Netherlands 1, Czech Republic 0; **June 16**–France 2, Czech Republic 1; Netherlands 3, Denmark 0; **June 21**–Czech Republic 2, Denmark 0; Netherlands 3, France 2.

Quarterfinals

Single elimination with a 30 minute "golden goal" overtime period. If still tied, games are decided by shoot-out.

June 24 Portugal 2 . . . . .Turkey 0
June 24 Italy 2 . . . . .Romania 0
June 25 Netherlands 6 . . . . .Yugoslavia 1
June 25 France 2 . . . . .Spain 1

Semifinals

June 28 France 2 . . . . .OT . . . . .Portugal 1
June 29 Italy 0 . . . . .Netherlands 0
Italy won shoot-out, 3-1

Final

July 2, 2000 in Rotterdam. Attendance: 50,000

France 2 . . . . .OT . . . . .Italy 1
Scoring: France–Sylvain Wiltford 90, David Trezeguet 103; Italy– Marco Delvecchio 55.
Referee: Anders Frisk, Sweden.

Leading Goal Scorers

		Goals
1	Patrick Kluivert, Netherlands	5
	Savo Milosevic, Yugoslavia	5
3	Nuno Gomes, Portugal	4
4	Zlatko Zahovic, Slovenia	3
	Sergio Conceicao, Portugal	3
	Thierry Henry, France	3
7	Fourteen players tied with two goals each.	

1999 FIFA U-17 World Championship

Held Nov. 10-27 in New Zealand for Under-17 national teams.

First Round

Round Robin; each team plays the other teams in its group once. Note that three points are awarded for a win and one for a tie. (*) indicates team advanced to the quarterfinals.

Group A	W	L	T	GA	GA	Pts
*United States	2	0	1	4	2	7
*Uruguay	1	1	1	6	4	4
New Zealand	1	2	0	3	8	3
Poland	0	1	2	3	4	2

RESULTS: **Nov. 10**–United States 2, New Zealand 1; **Nov. 11**–Uruguay 1, Poland 1; **Nov. 13**–Uruguay 2, New Zealand 0; United States 1, Poland 1; **Nov. 16**–New Zealand 2, Poland 1; United States 1, Uruguay 0.

Group B	W	L	T	GF	GA	Pts
*Ghana	2	0	1	12	2	7
*Mexico	2	1	0	5	4	6
Spain	1	1	1	7	2	4
Thailand	0	3	0	1	17	0

RESULTS: **Nov. 11**–Ghana 1, Spain 1; Mexico 4, Thailand 0; **Nov. 13**–Spain 6, Thailand 0; Ghana 4, Mexico 0; **Nov. 16**–Ghana 7, Thailand 1; Mexico 1, Spain 0.

Group C	W	L	T	GF	GA	Pts
*Australia	2	1	0	4	3	6
*Brazil	1	0	2	2	1	5
Germany	0	1	2	1	2	2
Mali	0	1	2	0	1	2

RESULTS: **Nov. 12**–Brazil 2, Australia 1; Mali 0, Germany 0; **Nov. 14**–Australia 2, Germany 1; Brazil 0, Mali 0; **Nov. 17**–Germany 0, Brazil 0; Australia 1, Mali 0.

Group D	W	L	T	GF	GA	Pts
*Paraguay	2	0	1	9	2	7
*Qatar	2	1	0	6	3	6
Burkina Faso	1	1	1	4	4	4
Jamaica	0	3	0	0	10	0

RESULTS: **Nov. 12**–Burkina Faso 1, Jamaica 0; Paraguay 2, Qatar 0; **Nov. 14**–Qatar 2, Burkina Faso 1; Paraguay 5, Jamaica 0; **Nov. 17**–Qatar 4, Jamaica 0; Burkina Faso 2, Paraguay 2.

Quarterfinals

Date	Site	Result
Nov. 20	Auckland	United States 3, Mexico 2
Nov. 20	Napier	Ghana 3, Uruguay 2 (OT)
Nov. 21	Christchurch	Australia 1, Qatar 0
Nov. 21	Dunedin	Brazil 4, Paraguay 1

Third Place

Nov. 27	Auckland	Ghana 2, United States 0

Semifinals

Date	Site	Result
Nov. 24	Christchurch	Australia 2, United States 2
		Australia won shoot-out, 7-6
Nov. 24	Auckland	Brazil 2, Paraguay 2
		Brazil won shoot-out, 4-2

Final

Nov. 27, 1999 in Auckland. Attendance: 22,859

Brazil 0 . . . . Australia 0

Brazil won the shoot-out, 8-7

FIFA Top 50 World Rankings

FIFA announced a new monthly world ranking system on Aug. 13, 1993 designed to "provide a constant international comparison of national team performances." The rankings are based on a mathematical formula that weighs strength of schedule, importance of matches and goals scored for and against. Games considered include World Cup qualifying and final rounds, Continental championship qualifying and final rounds, and friendly matches.

The formula was altered slightly in January 1999. Now the rankings annually take into account a team's seven best matches of the last eight years. Thereby favoring some teams that have been consistent over a long period of time but that may have stumbled just recently. At the end of the year, FIFA designates a Team of the Year. Teams of the Year so far have been Germany (1993) and Brazil (1994-99).

1999

		Points	1998 Rank			Points	1998 Rank			Points	1998 Rank
1	Brazil	839	1	18	Russia	643	40	35	Ireland	576	56
2	Czech Republic	774	8	19	Netherlands	641	11	36	Zambia	571	29
3	France	765	2	20	Scotland	639	38	37	Bulgaria	563	49
4	Spain	753	15	21	Slovakia	626	32	38	Egypt	556	28
5	Germany	739	3	22	USA	620	23		Saudi Arabia	556	30
6	Argentina	721	5	23	Chile	618	16	40	Slovenia	544	88
7	Norway	718	14	24	Morocco	615	13	41	Jamaica	539	33
8	Romania	715	12	25	Colombia	614	34	42	Peru	538	72
9	Croatia	713	4	26	Israel	609	43	43	Iceland	536	64
10	Mexico	706	10		Ukraine	609	47		Trinidad and Tobago	536	51
11	Denmark	697	19	28	Austria	603	22	45	Hungary	533	46
12	England	695	9	29	Turkey	598	57		Uruguay	533	76
13	Yugoslavia	694	6	30	South Africa	597	26	47	Switzerland	531	83
14	Italy	685	7	31	Tunisia	596	21	48	Ghana	525	48
15	Portugal	672	36	32	Poland	589	31		Iran	525	27
16	Sweden	663	18	33	Belgium	588	35	50	Lithuania	524	54
17	Paraguay	648	25	34	Greece	582	53				

2000 (as of Sept. 6)

		Points	1999 Rank			Points	1999 Rank			Points	1999 Rank
1	Brazil	818	1	18	Denmark	652	11	35	Israel	577	26
2	France	807	3	19	USA	646	22	36	Poland	568	31
3	Argentina	752	6	20	Chile	645	23		Slovenia	568	40
4	Czech Republic	746	2	21	Sweden	639	16	38	Ireland	565	35
5	Spain	740	4	22	Scotland	631	20		Jamaica	565	41
6	Italy	725	14		South Africa	631	30		Peru	565	42
7	Portugal	724	15	24	Russia	625	18		Ukraine	565	26
8	Yugoslavia	714	13	25	Belgium	607	33	42	Austria	563	28
9	Germany	712	5	26	Morocco	605	24		South Korea	563	51
10	Netherlands	710	19		Tunisia	605	31	44	Iran	559	48
11	Norway	698	7	28	Slovakia	604	21	45	Zambia	557	36
	Romania	698	8	29	Trinidad and Tobago	597	43	46	Honduras	545	69
13	Mexico	693	10	30	Turkey	588	29	47	Finland	543	56
14	England	682	12	31	Egypt	586	38	48	Ivory Coast	542	53
15	Croatia	675	9	32	Uruguay	583	45	49	Hungary	540	45
16	Paraguay	672	17	33	Greece	581	34	50	Japan	537	57
17	Colombia	668	25	34	Cameroon	580	58				

CONCACAF Gold Cup

Championship for the Confederation of North, Central and Caribbean Association Football (CONCACAF). Contested for every two years since its revival in 1991. Held Feb. 12-27, 2000 in Miami, Los Angeles and San Diego.

First Round

Round Robin; each team plays the other teams in its group once. Note that three points are awarded for a win and one for a tie. (*) indicates team advanced to quarterfinals.

Group A	W	L	T	GF	GA	Pts
*Honduras	2	0	0	4	0	6
*Colombia	1	1	0	1	2	3
Jamaica	0	2	0	0	3	0

RESULTS: **Feb. 12**–Colombia 1, Jamaica 0; **Feb. 14**–Honduras 2, Jamaica 0; **Feb. 16**–Honduras 2, Colombia 0.

Group B	W	L	T	GF	GA	Pts
*United States	2	0	0	4	0	6
*Peru	0	1	1	2	2	1
Haiti	0	1	1	1	4	1

RESULTS: **Feb. 12**–United States 3, Haiti 0; **Feb. 14**–Haiti 1, Peru 1; **Feb. 16**–United States 1, Peru 1.

Group C	W	L	T	GF	GA	Pts
*Mexico	1	0	1	5	1	4
*Trinidad & Tobago	1	1	0	4	6	3
Guatemala	0	1	1	3	5	1

RESULTS: **Feb. 13**–Mexico 4, Trinidad & Tobago 0; **Feb. 15**–Trinidad & Tobago 4, Guatemala 2; **Feb. 17**–Guatemala 1, Mexico 1.

Group D	W	L	T	GF	GA	Pts
*Costa Rica	0	0	2	4	4	2
*Canada	0	0	2	2	2	2
South Korea	0	0	2	2	2	2

RESULTS: **Feb. 13**–Costa Rica 2, Canada 2; **Feb. 15**–Canada 0, South Korea 0; **Feb. 17**–South Korea 2, Costa Rica 2.

Quarterfinals

Date	Result
Feb. 19	Colombia 2, United States 2
	Colombia won shoot-out, 2-1
Feb. 19	Peru 5, Honduras 2
Feb. 20	Trinidad & Tobago 2, Costa Rica 1 (OT)
Feb. 20	Canada 2, Mexico (OT)

Semifinals

Date	Result
Feb. 23	Colombia 2, Peru 1
Feb. 24	Canada 1, Trinidad & Tobago 0

Final

Attendance: 6,197

Date	Site	Result
Feb. 27	Los Angeles	Canada 2, Colombia 0

Scoring: CAN–Jason de Vos 46, Carlo Corazzin 68.

2000 CONCACAF Women's Gold Cup

Held June 23-July 3 in the United States.

First Round

Group A	W	L	T	GF	GA	Pts
*United States	2	0	1	19	0	7
*Brazil	2	0	1	19	0	7
Costa Rica	0	2	1	2	18	1
Trinidad & Tobago	0	2	1	2	24	1

RESULTS: **June 23**–Brazil 8, Costa Rica 0; United States 11, Trinidad & Tobago 0; **June 25**–Brazil 11, Trinidad & Tobago 0; United States 8, Costa Rica 0; **June 27**–Trinidad & Tobago 2, Costa Rica 2; United States 0, Brazil 0.

Group B	W	L	T	GF	GA	Pts
*China	3	0	0	20	2	9
*Canada	2	1	0	18	6	6
Mexico	1	2	0	10	7	3
Guatemala	0	3	0	0	33	0

RESULTS: **June 24**–China 14, Guatemala 0; Canada 4, Mexico 3; **June 26**–Mexico 7, Guatemala 3; China 3, Canada 2; **June 28**–Canada 12, Guatemala 0; China 3, Mexico 0.

Semifinals

July 1		Brazil 3, China 2 (OT)
July 1		United States 4, Canada 1

Third Place

July 3		China 2, Canada 1

Final

July 3, 2000 at Foxboro Stadium, Foxboro, Mass.
Attendance: 20,123.

United States 1	Brazil 0

Scoring: US– Tiffeny Milbrett 44.

U.S. Men's National Team
2000 Schedule and Results

Through Oct. 1, 2000.

Date		Result	USA Goals	Site	Crowd
Jan. 16	Iran	T, 1-1	Armas	Los Angeles	50,181
Jan. 29	Chile	W, 2-1	Lewis, Jones	Coquimbo, Chile	—
Feb. 12	Haiti	W, 3-0	Kirovski, Wynalda, Jones	Miami	49,591
Feb. 16	Peru	W, 1-0	Jones	Miami	36,004
Feb. 19	Colombia	T, 2-2*	McBride, Armas	Miami	32,972
Mar. 12	Tunisia	T, 1-1	Olsen	Birmingham, Ala.	21,637
Apr. 26	Russia	L, 0-2	—	Moscow	—
June 3	South Africa	W, 4-0	Jones (2), Reyna, Stewart	Washington, D.C.	16,570
June 6	Ireland	T, 1-1	Razov	Foxboro, Mass.	16,319
June 11	Mexico	W, 3-0	McBride, Hejduk, Razov	E. Rutherford, N.J.	45,008
July 16	Guatemala	T, 1-1	Razov	Mazatanengo, Guatemala	9,500
July 23	Costa Rica	L, 1-2	Stewart	San Jose, Costa Rica	20,000

Date	Result	USA Goals	Site	Crowd
Aug. 16	Barbados............W, 7-0	Pope, McBride, Moore (2), O'Brien, Ramos, Stewart	Foxboro, Mass.	18,334
Sept. 3	Guatemala ....W, 1-0	McBride	Washington, D.C.	51,996

*Colombia won the shoot-out, 2-1.
Overall record: 7-2-5. **Team scoring:** Goals For–28; Goals Against–11.

2000 U.S. Men's National Team Statistics

Individual records for season through Oct. 1, 2000. Note that the column labeled "Career C/G" refers to career caps and goals.

Forwards	GP	GS	Mins	G	A	Pts	Career C/G
Chris Albright.......1	0	28	0	0	0		2/1
Jason Kreis 5	2	180	0	0	0		14/1
Roy Lassiter 1	0	34	0	0	0		30/4
Brian McBride 10	9	765	4	1	9		45/13
Joe-Max Moore 2	2	180	2	1	5		81/22
Ante Razov 7	4	393	3	1	7		11/3
Earnie Stewart 7	6	515	3	4	10		63/9
Brian West 1	0	2	0	0	0		1/0
Eric Wynalda.......4	4	317	1	2	4		106/34

Defenders	GP	GS	Mins	G	A	Pts	Career C/G
Jeff Agoos...........5	5	480	0	0	0		101/3
Marcelo Balboa 1	1	90	0	0	0		128/13
Gregg Berhalter....6	5	469	0	0	0		15/0
C.J. Brown 3	3	327	0	0	0		14/0
Robin Fraser 5	5	450	0	0	0		27/0
Carlos Llamosa 6	5	444	0	0	0		11/0
Eddie Pope..........6	6	526	1	0	2		35/4
David Regis 8	8	720	0	0	0		15/0
Tony Sanneh........9	8	674	0	0	0		14/1
Greg Vanney 5	4	374	0	0	0		9/0

Midfielders	GP	GS	Mins	G	A	Pts	Career C/G
Chris Armas.......12	12	1020	2	1	5		20/2
Chad Deering 4	1	123	0	0	0		17/1
John Harkes 1	0	45	0	0	0		90/6
Frankie Hejduk......6	3	310	1	0	2		29/5
Cobi Jones 14	11	966	5	8	18		133/13
Jovan Kirovski 8	6	476	1	0	2		35/6
Eddie Lewis 12	10	914	1	3	5		26/2
John O'Brien 5	4	349	1	1	3		6/1
Ben Olsen 9	3	403	1	0	2		17/3
Steve Ralston 2	1	53	0	0	0		7/0
Tab Ramos 2	0	49	1	0	2		80/8
Claudio Reyna.....12	11	1000	1	3	5		78/5
Richie Williams 3	1	159	0	0	0		11/0

Goalkeepers	GP	GS	Mins	W-L-T	SO	GAA	Career Caps
Brad Friedel 6	6	570	3-0-3	3	0.63		66
Kasey Keller 6	6	540	3-2-1	3	0.83		45
Tony Meola.........2	2	180	1-0-1	0	1.00		92

Yellow cards: Agoos, Armas (3), Hejduk (2), Kreis, Lewis (2), McBride, Olsen (2), Regis (2), Sanneh, Stewart (3), Vanney. **Red cards:** Lewis.

Head coach: Bruce Arena; **Assistant coaches:** Bob Bradley and Ivo Wortmann; **Goal coach:** Milutin Soskic; **General manager:** Pam Perkins.

U.S. Women's National Team
2000 Schedule and Results

Through Sept. 1, 2000. For Olympic results see the Olympics Chapter.

Date	Result	USA Goals	Site	Crowd
Jan. 7	Czech Republic..........W, 8-1	Mascaro (2), Kester (2), Bush, Serlenga, Welsh, Zepeda	Melbourne, Australia	1,200
Jan. 10	Sweden.................T, 0-0	—	Melbourne, Australia	2,000
Jan. 13	Australia................W, 3-1	Kester, Slaton, Wagner	Adelaide, Australia	3,500
Feb. 6	Norway ....L, 2-3	Hamm, Lilly	Ft. Lauderdale, Fla.	12,031
Feb. 9	Norway ....L, 1-2	Welsh	Ft. Lauderdale, Fla.	—
Mar. 12	Portugal ....W, 7-0	Parlow (3), MacMillan, Fawcett, Venturini, Foudy	Silves, Portugal	250
Mar. 14	Denmark................W, 2-1	Fair, MacMillan	Faro, Portugal	300
Mar. 16	Sweden ....W, 1-0	Hamm	Lagos, Portugal	350
Mar. 18	Norway ....W, 1-0	Chastain	Loulé, Portugal	850
Apr. 5	Iceland ....W, 8-0	Welsh (3), Wagner, Pearce (2), Hamm, Lilly	Davidson, N.C.	—
Apr. 8	Iceland ....T, 0-0	—	Charlotte, N.C.	10,315
May 5	Mexico ....W, 8-0	MacMillan (2), Lilly, Serlenga, Milbrett, Hamm, Fair, Welsh	Portland, Ore.	6,517
May 7	Canada ....W, 4-0	Foudy, Parlow, Milbrett, Welsh	Portland, Ore.	7,659
May 31	China ....L, 0-1	—	Canberra, Australia	550
June 2	Canada ....W, 9-1	Milbrett (3), MacMillan, Parlow (3), Fair (2)	Sydney, Australia	10,049
June 4	New Zealand ....W, 5-0	Welsh (2), Parlow (3)	Sydney, Australia	3,947
June 8	Japan ....W, 4-1	Parlow, MacMillan, Chastain, Wagner	Newcastle, Australia	1,100
June 11	Australia................W, 1-0	MacMillan	Newcastle, Australia	3,617
June 23	Trinidad & Tobago......W, 11-0	Parlow (3), Fair (2), Milbrett, Hamm (2), MacMillan, Whalen (2)	Hershey, Pa.	10,483
June 25	Costa Rica ....W, 8-0	Serlenga (3), Welsh (2), MacMillan, Bush, Whalen	Louisville, Ky.	7,043
June 27	Brazil...................T, 0-0	—	Foxboro, Mass.	16,386
July 1	Canada ....W, 4-1	MacMillan (2), Milbrett, Hamm	Louisville, Ky.	11,140

Date	Result		USA Goals	Site	Crowd
July 3	Brazil	W, 1-0	Milbrett	Foxboro, Mass.	20,123
July 7	Italy	W, 4-1	Wagner, Whalen, Bush, Putz	Central Islip, N.Y.	6,022
July 16	Norway	W, 1-0	Milbrett	Osnabruck, Germany	2,500
July 19	China	T, 1-1	Hamm	Gottigen, Germany	4,200
July 22	Germany	W, 1-0	Foudy	Braunschweig, Germany	6,050
July 27	Norway	T, 1-1	Serlenga	Tromsø, Norway	3,810
July 30	Norway	L. 1-2	Parlow	Oslo, Norway	15,762
Aug. 13	Russia	W, 7-1	Milbrett (2), Foudy, Hamm, Parlow (2), Akers	Annapolis, Md.	21,278
Aug. 15	Russia	T, 1-1	Fawcett	College Park, Md.	—
Aug. 20	Canada	T, 1-1	Lilly	Kansas City, Mo.	21,246
Sept. 1	Brazil	W, 4-0	Foudy, Fawcett, Hamm (2)	San Jose, Calif.	26,853

Overall record: 22-4-7.
Team Scoring: Goals for– 110; Goals against– 20.
Note: the matches on Feb. 8, April 5 and Aug. 15 were closed door matches.

2000 U.S. Women's National Team Statistics

Individual records through Sept. 1, 2000. Note that the column labeled "Career C/G" refers to career caps and goals.

Forwards	GP	GS	Mins	G	A	Pts	Career C/G
Susan Bush	7	3	366	3	5	11	10/3
Mandy Clemens	3	3	205	0	1	1	3/0
Mia Hamm	25	21	1924	11	11	33	208/125
Sherrill Kester	3	3	180	3	1	7	3/3
Tiffeny Milbrett	27	24	1888	11	9	31	156/79
Cindy Parlow	24	15	1269	17	7	41	91/43
Caroline Putz	1	0	3	1	0	2	1/1
Alyssa Ramsey	3	1	96	0	0	0	3/0
Chrsitie Welsh	15	5	744	11	3	25	15/11
Veronica Zepeda	4	0	109	1	0	2	5/1

Defenders	GP	GS	Mins	G	A	Pts	Career C/G
Heather Aldama	3	0	80	0	1	1	3/0
Thori Bryan	1	1	45	0	0	0	1/0
Brandi Chastain	26	24	1875	2	3	7	132/23
Lorrie Fair	25	21	1765	6	1	13	77/7
Joy Fawcett	24	24	2160	3	3	9	178/24
Michelle French	6	6	540	0	1	1	9/0
Anna Kraus	1	0	22	0	0	0	1/0
Kelly Lindsey	3	3	270	0	0	0	3/0
Carla Overbeck	10	7	424	0	0	0	165/7
Christie Pearce	25	22	1863	2	2	6	79/4
Nandi Pryce	8	7	675	0	1	1	8/0
Catherine Reddick	1	0	17	0	0	0	1/0
Danielle Slaton	23	13	1448	1	3	5	24/1
Kate Sobrero	22	22	1841	0	1	1	55/0
Sara Whalen	21	7	911	4	6	14	63/7

Midfielders	GP	GS	Mins	G	A	Pts	Career C/G
Michelle Akers	7	3	238	1	0	2	153/105
Aleisha Cramer	5	5	382	0	1	1	5/0
Julie Foudy	25	23	1874	5	4	14	191/37
Jena Kluegel	3	2	210	0	1	1	3/0
Kristine Lilly	26	22	1994	4	4	12	217/85
S. MacMillan	27	21	1755	11	9	31	116/33
Jen Mascaro	3	3	195	2	2	6	3/2
M.F. Monroe	2	1	120	0	1	1	2/0
Nikki Serlenga	22	9	1263	6	2	14	22/6
Tisha Venturini	4	4	270	1	1	3	132/44
Aly Wagner	10	6	679	4	2	10	16/5

Goalkeepers	GP	GS	Mins	W-L-T	SO	GAA	Career Caps
Lakeysia Beene	3	3	270	2-0-1	1	0.67	3
Jen Branam	5	5	450	5-0-0	1	0.80	5
Siri Mullinix	21	20	1724	14-3-3	13	0.37	22
Briana Scurry	5	3	301	0-0-3	0	1.20	103
Hope Solo	2	1	135	1-0-0	0	3.00	2
Saskia Webber	1	1	90	0-1-0	1	0.00	1

Yellow Cards: Parlow (3), Foudy (2), MacMillan (2), Chastain, Hamm, Overbeck, Serlenga, Slaton, Whalen.
Red Cards: none.
Head coach: April Heinrichs; **Assistant coach:** John Ellis; **Goalkeeper coach:** David Vanole; **Co-Captains:** Julie Foudy and Carla Overbeck. **General Manager:** Nils Krumins.

U.S. Under-23 Men's National Team

2000 Schedule and Results

Through Sept. 5, 2000. CONCACAF Olympic Qualifying Tournament games are in **bold** type. For Olympic results see Olympics chapter.

Date	Result		USA Goals	Site	Crowd
Jan. 16	Armenia	W, 3-1	Casey, Vagenas, Donovan	Los Angeles, Calif.	50,181
Jan. 25	Portugal	L, 0-1	—	Alverca, Portugal	—
Jan. 27	FC Estoril	L, 0-1	—	Lisbon, Portugal	—
Jan. 30	Offenbach FC (Germany)	W, 3-2	McCarty, Victorine, Beasley	Lagos, Portugal	—
Apr. 12	Miami Fusion (MLS)	L, 2-3	Casey, Donovan	Ft. Lauderdale, Fla.	—
April 15	So. Fla. Future	W, 10-0	Casey (3), Olsen (2), Wolff (2), Albright (2), Donovan Own Goal, Casey, Donovan,	Boca Raton, Fla.	—
April 18	Hershey (A-League)	W, 4-0	Wolff	Annville, Pa.	—
April 21	**Honduras**	W, 3-0	Albright (2), Thorrington	Hershey, Pa.	11,229
April 25	**Canada**	T, 0-0	—	Hershey, Pa.	5,798
April 28	**Guatemala**	W, 4-0	O'Brien, Wolff, Donovan (2)	Hershey, Pa.	12,299
April 30	**Honduras**	L, 1-2	Wolff	Hershey, Pa.	12,126
July 30	Bolton (England)	W, 1-0	Victorine	Indianapolis, Ind.	5,327
Sept. 5	San Diego (A-League)	W, 2-0	Donovan (2)	Chula Vista, Calif.	—

Overall record: 8-4-1. **Team scoring:** Goals For–33; Goals Against–10.

2000 U.S. Under-23 Men's National Team Statistics

Individual records for season through Sept. 5, 2000.

		GP	GS	G	A	Pts
Chris Albright	M/F	13	11	5	4	14
DeMarcus Beasley	M	10	7	1	3	5
Chris Brown	F	2	1	0	0	0
Danny Califf	D	9	4	0	1	1
Conor Casey	F	12	10	6	4	16
Steve Cherundolo	D	8	8	0	1	1
Matt Chulis	D	5	2	0	0	0
Ramiro Corrales	D	13	10	0	2	2
Eric Denton	D	5	1	0	0	0
Joey DiGiamarino	M	1	1	0	0	0
Landon Donovan	F	10	6	8	1	17
Brian Dunseth	D	11	11	0	0	0
Frankie Hejduk	D/M	1	1	0	0	0
Chad McCarty	D	12	11	1	1	3
Matt Napoleon	M	1	1	0	0	0
John O'Brien	M	5	5	1	0	2
Ben Olsen	M	8	7	2	2	6
Antonio Otero	M	1	1	0	0	0

		GP	GS	G	A	Pts
Carlos Parra	M	3	2	0	0	0
John Thorrington	M	9	6	1	3	5
Peter Vagenas	M	10	9	1	2	4
Sasha Victorine	M	4	3	2	0	4
Brian West	F	2	1	0	0	0
Evan Whitfield	D	3	2	0	0	0
Brian Winters	M	6	4	0	0	0
Josh Wolff	F	8	3	5	2	12

Goalkeepers	GP		GS	W-L-T	SO
Adin Brown	6		6	5-1-0	4
Brad Friedel	1		1	1-0-0	0
Tim Howard	6		4	1-2-1	2
Andy Kirk	2		2	1-1-0	0
Matt Napoleon	1		0	1-1-0	0

Yellow cards: Casey, Cherundolo, Chulis, Corrales, McCarty, Thorrington. **Red cards:** Califf, Casey, Dunseth. **Head coach:** Clive Charles; **Assistant coach:** John Ellinger; **Goalkeeper coach:** Peter Mellor.

Club Team Competition
2000 FIFA Club World Championship

Inaugural professional club championships organized by FIFA, not to be confused with the Toyota/Intercontinental Cup which is played annually between the winners of the Liberatadores and European Cup champions. Each of the six FIFA confederations (Africa, Asia, Europe, South America, North/Central America and Oceania) nominated teams for the eight-team tournament. Each confederation could submit a team meeting any of the following criteria: the winner of the confederation club championship or the winner of the confederation cup, the winner of the national league championship of the organizing national association or the winner of the 1998 Intercontinental Cup. Two teams were taken from both Europe and South America, while one team was taken from the four remaining confederations.

The eight teams participating in the first FIFA Club World Championship shared a $28 million purse. The champions received $6 million while the remaining teams received lesser amounts depending on where they finished. This is the first time that FIFA has offered prize money to teams playing in a FIFA competition. In the World Cup finals, each of the 32 national federations receives a fixed sum for each of the matches its team plays, which means that the top four teams all receive the same amount with no win bonus. At the 1998 World Cup in France, each team received approximately $650,000 per match. The 2000 FIFA Club World Championship was played in Brazil from January 5-14, 2000. The top team from each group advances to the championship match while the second-place team from each group meet in the third-place match. Both matches were played Jan. 14 in Rio de Janeiro.

First Round

Round Robin; each team plays the other teams in its group once. Note that three points are awarded for a win and one for a tie. (*) indicates team advanced to the final; (†) indicated team advanced to third-place game.

Group A	W	L	T	GA	GA	Pts
*Corinthians (Brazil)	2	0	1	6	2	7
†Real Madrid (Spain)	2	0	1	8	5	7
Al-Nassr (Saudi Arabia)	1	2	0	5	8	3
Raja Casablanca (Morocco)	0	3	0	5	9	0

RESULTS: **Jan. 5**–Real Madrid 3, Al-Nassr 1; Corinthians 2, Raja Casablanca 0; **Jan. 7**–Real Madrid 2, Corinthians 2; Al-Nassr 4, Raja Casablanca 3; **Jan. 10**–Real Madrid 3, Raja Casablanca 2; Corinthians 2, Al-Nassr 0.
Note: Corinthians advanced to the final on goal differential.

Group B	W	L	T	GF	GA	Pts
*Vasco da Gama (Brazil)	3	0	0	7	2	9
†Necaxa (Mexico)	1	1	1	5	4	4
Man. United (England)	1	1	1	4	4	4
So. Melbourne (Australia)	0	3	0	1	7	0

RESULTS: **Jan. 6**–Manchester United 1, Necaxa 1; Vasco da Gama 2, South Melbourne 0; **Jan. 8**–Vasco da Gama 3, Manchester United 1; Necaxa 3, South Melbourne 1; **Jan. 11**–Manchester United 2, South Melbourne 0; Vasco da Gama 2, Necaxa 1.
Note: Necaxa advanced to the third-place game on goal differential.

Third Place

Necaxa 1 . . . . Real Madrid 1
Necaxa won the shoot-out, 4-3

Final

Jan. 14, 2000 in Rio de Janeiro. Attendance: 73,000

Corinthians 0 . . . . Vasco da Gama 0
Corinthians won the shoot-out, 4-3

1999 Toyota Cup

Also known as the Intercontinental Cup; a year-end match for the World Club Championship between the European Cup and Copa Liberatadores winners. Played on Nov. 30 in front of 53,372 at Tokyo's National Stadium. It's winner is generally recognized as the World Club Champion but with the recent advent of FIFA's World Club Championship that could change.

Final

Manchester United (England) 1 . . . . Palmerias (Brazil) 0
Scoring: Man U–Roy Keane (35).

SOUTH AMERICA

2000 Liberatadores Cup

Contested by the league champions of South America's football union. Two-leg Semifinals and two-leg Final; home teams listed first. Winner Boca Juniors of Argentina plays European Champions League winner Real Madrid in the 2000 Toyota Cup in Tokyo in December.

Final Four: Boca Juniors (Argentina), Club America (Mexico), Corinthians (Brazil), and Palmeiras (Brazil)

Semifinals

Palmeiras vs. Corinthians

Palmeiras 3 . . . . Corinthians 4
Corinthians 2 . . . . Palmeiras 3
    Aggregate tied 6-6, Palmeiras won shootout, 5-4

Boca Juniors vs. Club America

Boca Juniors 4 . . . . Club America 1
Club America 3 . . . . Boca Juniors 1
    Boca Juniors won 5-4 on aggregate

Final

Boca Juniors 2 . . . . Palmeiras 2
Palmeiras 0 . . . . Boca Juniors 0
    Aggregate tied 2-2, Boca Juniors won shootout, 4-2

EUROPE

There are two major European club competitions sanctioned by the Union of European Football Associations (UEFA). The newly devised **Champions League** is a 72-team tournament made up from UEFA member countries. The teams are ranked 1-72 depending on how they finish in their own domestic leagues. UEFA ranks the quality of the 50 European national football associations (from number one Italy to number 50 Bosnia-Herzegovina) and assigns each association a number weighted by their respective ranking (UEFA calls this number a coefficient). Each team's domestic league finish is then multiplied by the coefficient and the teams are finally ranked (countries can enter a maximum of four teams).

The defending champions Manchester United (from the UEFA Champions' Cup) and the other 15 highest-ranked teams form Group 1 and are given a direct entry into the League but the remaining 16 teams are determined by dividing teams 17-72 into three groups–Group 2 (teams 17-34), Group 3 (35-52) and Group 4 (53-72). The 22 teams in the lowest Group (Group 4) play two-leg, total goal elimination series. The 11 survivors advance to the Second Qualifying Phase and join the 17 teams from Group 3 to play 14 two-leg, total goal elimination series. The 14 clubs that survive this phase join the 18 teams from Group 2 to play in the Third Qualifying Phase. The winning clubs from the 16 two-leg, total goal elimination series advance to the Champions League for the right to play against the top-ranked 16 teams in Europe.

The 32 teams are separated into eight groups of four and play a round-robin series of home-and-home matches. The eight group winners and eight group runners-up advance to the next round where they are split up into four groups of four. The four group winners and runners-up then advance to the quarterfinals where home-and-home series are played through the semifinals until ultimately a single championship match for the European club championship is held. Winner Real Madrid plays Libertadores Cup champion Boca Juniors of Argentina in the 2000 Toyota Cup this December in Tokyo.

The updated **UEFA Cup**, which is basically a combination of the what was known as the Cup Winners' Cup (played between national cup champions) and the old UEFA Cup (sort of a "best of the rest" tournament), is single-elimination throughout and features 121 additional teams plus 24 teams that have been already eliminated from the Champions League.

1999-2000 Champions League

Following the first three qualifying phases, the first group phase starts with six-game double round robin in eight four-team groups (Sept. 9-Nov. 3); top two teams in each group advance to second group phase (Nov. 23-Mar. 22) where four four-team groups compete in the same format. Group winners and runners-up advance to the quarterfinals. (*) indicates team advanced to the next round. Note that in results listing under each table that the home team is listed first.

First Group Phase

Group A	W	T	L	GF	GA	Pts
*Lazio (Italy) 4	2	0	13	3	14
*Dynamo Kiev (Ukraine) 2	1	3	8	8	7
Bayer Leverkusen (Germany) . .1	4	1	7	7	7
Maribor (Slovenia) 1	1	4	2	12	4

RESULTS: **Sept. 9**–Bayer Leverkusen 1, Lazio 1; Dynamo Kiev 0, Maribor 1; **Sept. 22**–Lazio 2, Dynamo Kiev 1; Maribor 0, Bayer Leverkusen 2; **Sept. 29**–Bayer Leverkusen 1, Dynamo Kiev 1; Lazio 4, Maribor 0; **Oct. 19**–Dynamo Kiev 4, Bayer Leverkusen 2; Maribor 0, Lazio 4; **Oct. 27**–Lazio 1, Bayer Leverkusen 1; Maribor 1, Dynamo Kiev 2; **Nov. 2**–Bayer Leverkusen 0, Maribor 0; Dynamo Kiev 0, Lazio 1.

Group B	W	T	L	GF	GA	Pts
*Barcelona (Spain) 4	2	0	19	9	14
*Fiorentina (Italy) 2	3	1	9	7	9
Arsenal (England) 2	2	2	9	8	8
A.I.K. (Sweden) 0	1	5	4	16	1

RESULTS: **Sept. 14**–AIK 1, Barcelona 2; Fiorentina 0, Arsenal 0; **Sept. 22**–Arsenal 3, AIK 1; Barcelona 4, Fiorentina 2; **Sept. 29**–AIK 0, Fiorentina 0; Barcelona 1, Arsenal 1; **Oct. 19**–Arsenal 2, Barcelona 4; Fiorentina 3, AIK 0; **Oct. 27**–Arsenal 0, Fiorentina 1; Barcelona 5, AIK 0; **Nov. 2**–AIK 2, Arsenal 3; Fiorentina 3, Barcelona 3.

EUROPE (Cont.)

Group C	W	T	L	GF	GA	Pts
*Rosenborg (Norway)	3	2	1	12	5	11
*Feyenoord (Netherlands)	1	5	0	7	6	8
Borussia Dortmund (Germany)	1	3	2	9	6	6
Boavista (Portugal)	1	2	3	4	10	5

RESULTS: **Sept. 14**–Boavista 0, Rosenborg 3; Feyenoord 1, Borussia Dortmund 1; **Sept. 22**–Borussia Dortmund 3, Boavista 1; Rosenborg 2, Feyenoord 2; **Sept. 29**–Boavista 1, Feyenoord 1; Rosenborg 2, Borussia Dortmund 2; **Oct. 19**–Borussia Dortmund 0, Rosenborg 3; Feyenoord 1, Boavista 1; **Oct. 27**– Borussia Dortmund 1, Feyenoord 1; Rosenborg 2, Boavista 0; **Nov. 2**–Boavista 1; Borussia Dortmund 0; Feyenoord 1, Rosenborg 0.

Group D	W	T	L	GF	GA	Pts
*Manchester United (England)	4	1	1	9	4	13
*Marseille (France)	3	1	2	10	8	10
Sturm Graz (Austria)	2	0	4	5	12	6
Croatia Zagreb	1	2	3	7	7	5

RESULTS: **Sept. 14**–Manchester United 0, Croatia Zagreb 0; Marseille 1, Sturm Graz 0; **Sept. 22**–Croatia Zagreb 1, Marseille 2; Sturm Graz 0, Manchester United 3; **Sept. 29**–Croatia Zagreb 3, Sturm Graz 0; Manchester United 2, Marseille 1; **Oct. 19**–Marseille 1, Manchester United 0; Sturm Graz 1, Croatia Zagreb 0; **Oct. 27**–Croatia Zagreb 1, Manchester United 2; Sturm Graz 3, Marseille 2; **Nov. 2**–Manchester United 2, Sturm Graz 1; Marseille 2, Croatia Zagreb 2.

Group E	W	T	L	GF	GA	Pts
*Real Madrid (Spain)	4	1	1	15	7	13
*FC Porto (Portugal)	4	0	2	9	6	12
Olympiakos (Greece)	2	1	3	9	12	7
Molde (Norway)	1	0	5	6	14	3

RESULTS: **Sept. 15**–Porto 0, Olympiakos 3; Real Madrid 3; **Sept. 21**–Porto 0, Olympiakos 0; Real Madrid 4, Molde 1; **Sept. 28**–Olympiakos 3, Molde 1; Real Madrid 3, Porto 1; **Oct. 20**–Molde 3, Olympiakos 2; Porto 2, Real Madrid 1; **Oct. 26**–Porto 3, Molde 1; Real Madrid 3, Olympiakos 0; **Nov. 3**–Molde 0, Real Madrid 1; Olympiakos 1, Porto 0.

Group F	W	T	L	GF	GA	Pts
*Valencia (Spain)	3	3	0	8	4	12
*Bayern Munich (Germany)	2	3	1	7	6	9
Rangers (Scotland)	2	1	3	7	7	7
PSV Eindhoven (Netherlands)	1	1	4	5	10	4

RESULTS: **Sept. 15**–Bayern Munich 2, PSV Eindhoven 1; Valencia 2, Rangers 0; **Sept. 21**–PSV Eindhoven 1, Valencia 1; Rangers 1, Bayern Munich 1; **Sept. 28**–Bayern Munich 1, Valencia 1; PSV Eindhoven 0, Rangers 1; **Oct. 20**–Rangers 4, PSV Eindhoven 1; Valencia 1, Bayern Munich 1; **Oct. 26**–PSV Eindhoven 0, Bayern Munich 1; Rangers 1, Valencia 2; **Nov. 3**–Bayern Munich 1, Rangers 0; Valencia 1, PSV Eindhoven 0.

Group G	W	T	L	GF	GA	Pts
*Sparta Prague (Czech Rep.)	3	3	0	14	6	12
*Bordeaux (France)	3	3	0	7	4	12
Spartak Moscow (Russia)	1	2	3	9	12	5
Willen II (Netherlands)	0	2	4	7	15	2

RESULTS: **Sept. 15**–Sparta Prague 0, Bordeaux 0; Willem II 1, Spartak Moscow 3; **Sept. 21**–Bordeaux 3, Willem II 2; Spartak Moscow 1, Sparta Prague 1; **Sept. 28**–Bordeaux 2, Spartak Moscow 1; Sparta Prague 4, Willem II 0; **Oct. 20**–Spartak Moscow 2, Sparta Prague 2; Willem II 3, Sparta Prague 4; **Oct. 26**–Bordeaux 0, Sparta Prague 0; Spartak Moscow 0, Willem II 1; **Nov. 3**–Sparta Prague 5, Spartak Moscow 2; Willem II 0, Bordeaux 0.

Group H	W	T	L	GF	GA	Pts
*Chelsea (England)	3	2	1	10	3	11
*Hertha Berlin (Germany)	2	2	2	7	10	8
Galatasaray (Turkey)	2	1	3	10	13	7
AC Milan (Italy)	1	3	2	7	6	6

RESULTS: **Sept. 15**–Chelsea 0, AC Milan 0; Galatasaray 2, Hertha Berlin 2; **Sept. 21**–Hertha Berlin 2, Chelsea 1; AC Milan 2, Galatasaray 2; **Sept. 28**–Chelsea 1, Galatasaray 0; AC Milan 1, Hertha Berlin 1; **Oct. 20**–Galatasaray 0, Chelsea 5; Hertha Berlin 1, AC Milan 0; **Oct. 26**–Hertha Berlin 1, Galatasaray 4; AC Milan 1, Chelsea 1; **Nov. 3**–Chelsea 2, Hertha Berlin 0.

Second Group Phase

Group A	W	T	L	GF	GA	Pts
*Barcelona	5	1	0	17	5	16
*FC Porto	3	1	2	8	8	10
Sparta Prague	1	2	3	5	12	5
Hertha Berlin	0	2	4	3	8	2

RESULTS: **Nov. 23**–Hertha Berlin 1, Barcelona 1; Sparta Prague 0, FC Porto 2; **Dec. 8**–Barcelona 5, Sparta Prague 0; FC Porto 1, Hertha Berlin 0; **Mar. 1**–Barcelona 4, FC Porto 1; Hertha Berlin 1, Sparta Prague 1; **Mar. 7**– FC Porto 0, Barcelona 2; Sparta Prague 1, Hertha Berlin; **Mar. 15**–FC Porto 2, Sparta Prague 2; Barcelona 3, Hertha Berlin 1; **Mar 21**– Hertha Berlin 0, FC Porto 1; Sparta Prague 1, Barcelona 2.

Group B	W	T	L	GF	GA	Pts
*Manchester United	4	1	1	10	4	13
*Valencia	3	1	2	9	5	10
Fiorentina	2	2	2	7	8	8
Bordeaux	0	2	4	5	14	2

RESULTS: **Nov. 23**–Fiorentina 2, Manchester United 0; Valencia 3, Bordeaux 0; **Dec. 8**–Bordeaux 0, Manchester United 3, Valencia 0; **Mar. 1**–Fiorentina 1, Valencia 0; Manchester United 2, Bordeaux 0; **Mar. 7**–Bordeaux 1, Manchester United 2; Valencia 2, Fiorentina 0; **Mar. 15**–Bordeaux 1, Valencia 4; Manchester United 3, Fiorentina 1; **Mar. 21**–Fiorentina 3, Bordeaux 3; Valencia 0, Manchester United 0.

Group C	W	T	L	GF	GA	Pts
*Bayern Munich	4	1	1	13	8	13
*Real Madrid	3	1	2	11	12	10
Dynamo Kiev	3	1	2	10	8	10
Rosenborg	0	1	5	5	11	1

RESULTS: **Nov. 24**–Dynamo Kiev 1, Real Madrid 2; Rosenborg 1, Bayern Munich 1; **Dec. 7**–Bayern Munich 2, Dynamo Kiev 1; Real Madrid 3, Rosenborg 0; **Feb. 29**–Dynamo Kiev 0, Rosenborg 2; Real Madrid 2, Bayern Munich 4; **Mar. 8**–Bayern Munich 4, Real Madrid 1; Rosenborg 1, Dynamo Kiev 0; **Mar. 14**–Bayern Munich 2, Rosenborg 1; Real Madrid 2, Dynamo Kiev 2; **Mar. 22**–Dynamo Kiev 2, Bayern Munich 0; Rosenborg 0, Real Madrid 1.

Group D	W	T	L	GF	GA	Pts
*Lazio	3	2	1	10	4	11
*Chelsea	3	1	2	8	5	10
Feyenoord	2	2	2	7	7	8
Marseille	1	4	2	11	4	4

RESULTS: **Nov. 24**–Chelsea 3, Feyenoord 1; Marseille 0, Lazio 2; **Dec. 7**–Feyenoord 3, Marseille 0; Lazio 0, Chelsea 0; **Feb. 29**–Lazio 2, Feyenoord 2; Marseille 1, Chelsea 0; **Mar. 8**–Chelsea 1, Marseille 0; Feyenoord 0, Lazio 2; **Mar. 14**–Feyenoord 1, Chelsea 3; Lazio 5, Marseille 1; **Mar. 22**–Chelsea 1, Lazio 2; Marseille 0, Feyenoord 0.

Quarterfinals
Two legs, total goals; home team listed first.

FC Porto vs. Bayern Munich
Apr. 4– FC Porto 1..................Bayern Munich 1
Apr. 19– Bayern Munich 2..................FC Porto 1
Bayern Munich win 3-2 on aggregate

Real Madrid vs. Manchester United
Apr. 4– Real Madrid 0 ....Manchester United 0
Apr. 19– Manchester United 2 ....Real Madrid 3
Real Madrid wins 3-2 on aggregate

Chelsea vs. Barcelona
Apr. 5 Chelsea 3 ....Barcelona 1
Apr. 18 Barcelona 5 ....Chelsea 1
Barcelona wins 6-4 on aggregate

Valencia vs. Lazio
Apr. 5 Valencia 5 ....Lazio 2
Apr. 18 Lazio 1 ....Valencia 0
Valencia wins 5-3 on aggregate

Semifinals
Two legs, total goals; home team listed first.

Valencia vs. Barcelona
May 2 Valencia 4 ....Barcelona 1
May 10 Barcelona 2 ....Valencia 1
Valencia wins 5-3 on aggregate

Bayern Munich vs. Real Madrid
May 3 Real Madrid 2 ....Bayern Munich 0
May 9 Bayern Munich 2 ....Real Madrid 1
Real Madrid wins 3-2 on aggregate

Final
May 24 at Stade de France, St. Denis, France.
Attendance: 80,000

Real Madrid 3 ....Valencia 0
Scoring: Real Madrid— Fernando Morientes (39th), Steve McManaman (67th), Raul (75th).

2000 UEFA Cup
Two-leg Quarterfinals and Semifinals, one-game Final; home team listed first.
Final Eight: Arsenal (England), Celta Vigo (Spain), Galatasaray (Turkey), Leed United (England), Racing Lens (France), Real Mallorca (Spain), Slavia Prague (Czech Republic), Werder Bremen (Germany)

Quarterfinals

Arsenal vs. Werder Bremen
Mar. 16 Arsenal 2 ....Werder Bremen 0
Mar. 23 Werder Bremen 2 ....Arsenal 4
Arsenal wins 6-2 on aggregate

Leeds United vs. Slavia Prague
Mar. 16 Leeds United 3 ....Slavia Prague 0
Mar. 23 Slavia Prague 2 ....Leeds United 1
Leeds United wins 4-2 on aggregate

Real Mallorca vs. Galatsaray
Mar. 16 Real Mallorca 1 ....Galatasary 4
Mar. 23 Galatasaray 2 ....Real Mallorca 1
Galatasaray wins 6-2 on aggregate

Celta Vigo vs. Racing Lens
Mar. 16 Celta Vigo 0 ....Lens 0
Mar. 23 Lens 2 ....Celta Vigo 1
Racing Lens wins 2-1 on aggregate

Semifinals
Arsenal vs. Racing Lens
Apr. 6 Arsenal 1 ....Lens 0
Apr. 20 Lens 1 ....Arsenal 2
Arsenal wins 3-1 on aggregate

Galatasaray vs. Leeds United
Apr. 6 Galatasaray 2 ....Leeds United 0
Apr. 20 Leeds United 2 ....Galatasaray 2
Galatasaray wins 4-2 on aggregate

Final
May 17 at Parken Stadium, Copenhagen.
Galatasaray 0................................Arsenal 0
Galatasaray won shoot-out 4-1.

Major League Soccer
2000 Final Regular Season Standings

Conference champions (*) and playoff qualifiers (†) are noted. Teams receive three points for a win. The GF and GA columns refer to Goals For and Goals Against in regulation play. Number of seasons listed after each head coach refers to current tenure with club through the 2000 season.

Eastern Conference

Team	W	L	T	Pts	GF	GA
* NY/NJ Metrostars	17	12	3	54	64	56
† N.E. Revolution	13	13	6	45	47	49
Miami Fusion	12	15	5	41	54	52
D.C. United	8	18	6	30	43	63

Head Coaches: NY/NJ— Octavio Zambrano (1st season); **NE—** Fernando Clavijo (1st); **Mia—** Ivo Wortmann (3rd); **DC—** Thomas Rongen (2nd).

Central Conference

Team	W	L	T	Pts	GF	GA
* Chicago Fire	17	9	6	57	67	50
† Tampa Bay Mutiny	16	12	4	52	62	50
† Dallas Burn	14	14	4	46	54	53
Columbus Crew	11	16	5	38	47	56

Head Coaches: Chi— Bob Bradley (3rd season); **TB—** Tim Hankinson (3rd); **Dal—** David Dir (5th); **Clb—** Tom Fitzgerald (5th).

Western Conference

Team	W	L	T	Pts	GF	GA
* Kansas City Wizards	16	7	9	57	47	29
† Los Angeles Galaxy	14	10	8	50	47	37
† Colorado Rapids	13	15	4	43	44	61
San Jose Earthqaukes	7	17	8	29	35	50

Head Coaches: KC— Bob Gansler (2nd season); **LA—** Sigi Schmid (2nd); **Colo—** Glenn Myernick (4th); **SJ—** Lothar Osiander (2nd).

MLS All-Star Game

West, 6-4

Date: Saturday, July 29, 2000 at Columbus Crew Stadium in Columbus; **Attendance:** 23,495; **Coaches:** Octavio Zambrano, NY/NJ (East) and Bob Gansler, KC (West); **MVP:** Mamadou Diallo, Tampa Bay forward (East) — two goals, one assist.

	1	2	Final
West	4	0	— 4
East	3	6	— 9

Scoring

1st Half: EAST— Clint Mathis (Mark Chung) 2; WEST— Ante Razov (Cobi Jones, Preki) 17; WEST— Mauricio Cienfuegos (Cobi Jones) 19; WEST— Ante Razov (Cobi Jones, Khodadad Azizi) 22; EAST— Jaime Moreno (Mark Chung) 36; EAST— Adolfo Valencia (Jaime Moreno) 39; WEST— Peter Nowak (Cobi Jones, Preki) 44.

2nd Half: EAST— Mark Chung (Brian McBride, Carlos Valderrama) 51; EAST— Mamadou Diallo (Carlos Valderrama) 59; EAST— Mamadou Diallo (Carlos Valderrama) 61; EAST— Jay Heaps (Mamadou Diallo, Brian McBride) 65; EAST— Dante Washington (Mike Petki) 67; EAST— Brian McBride (Dante Washington, Carlos Valderrama) 76.

Goaltenders

Saves: EAST— Scott Garlick 7. Mike Ammann 3; WEST— Tony Meola 4. Zach Thornton 4.

Leading Scorers

Points

	Gm	G	A	Pts
Mamadou Diallo, TB	28	26	43	56
Clint Mathis, NY/NJ	29	16	14	46
Ante Razov, CHI	24	18	6	42
Diego Serna, MIA	31	16	10	42
Adolfo Valencia, NY/NJ	31	16	9	41
Dante Washington, CLB	30	15	9	39
Wolde Harris, NE	31	15	73	37
Jason Kreis, DAL	27	11	13	35
Ariel Graziani, DAL	24	15	3	33
Alex Comas, NY/NJ	25	13	6	32

Goals

	Gm	No
Mamadou Diallo, TB	28	26
Ante Razov, CHI	24	18
Clint Mathis, NY/NJ	29	16
Diego Serna, MIA	31	16
Adolfo Valencia, NY/NJ	31	16
Ariel Graziani, DAL	24	15
Dante Washington, CLB	30	15
Wolde Harris, NE	31	15
Alex Comas, NY/NJ	25	13
Miklos Molnar, KC	17	12

2000 MLS Attendance

Number in parentheses indicates last year's rank.

	Gm	Total	Avg
Los Angeles (2)	16	326,392	20,400
Wash. D.C. (3)	16	297,279	18,580
N.Y./N.J.(7)	16	281,938	17,621
New England (4)	16	247,409	15,463
Columbus (1)	16	247,220	15,451
Chicago (5)	16	214,189	13,387
Dallas (10)	16	209,637	13,102
Colorado (8)	16	201,280	12,580
San Jose (6)	16	199,364	12,460
Tampa Bay (9)	16	151,232	9,452
Kansas City (12)	16	145,793	9,112
Miami (11)	16	119,352	7,460
TOTAL	192	2,641,085	13,756

Assists

	Gm	No
Carlos Valderrama, TB	32	26
Steve Ralston, TB	30	17
Martin Machon, MIA	24	16
Preki, KC	31	15
Peter Nowak, CHI	28	14
Clint Mathis, NY/NJ	29	14
Diego Gutierrez, CHI	24	13
Jason Kreis, DAL	27	13
Robert Warzycha, CLB	30	13

Three players tied with 11 each.

Shots

	Gm	No
Mamadou Diallo, TB.	28	152
Ante Razov, CHI	24	127
Junior Agogo, COL.	23	103
Wolde Harris, NE	31	101
Preki, KC	31	95

Shots on Goal

	Gm	No
Mamadou Diallo, TB.	28	76
Ante Razov, CHI	24	63
Junior Agogo, COL.	23	48
Clint Mathis, NY/NJ.	29	47
Wolde Harris, NE.	31	46
Ariel Graziani, DAL	24	45
Dante Washington, CLB	30	44

Game-Winning Goals

	Gm	GWG
Miklos Molnar, KC	17	6
Ante Razov, CHI	24	6
Mamadou Diallo, TB.	28	6
Clint Mathis, NY/NJ.	29	6
Junior Agogo, COL.	23	5

Hat Trick Leaders

	Gm	Hats
Diego Serna, MIA.	31	3
Mamadou Diallo, TB.	28	2
Ante Razov, CHI	24	1
Jaime Moreno, DC	25	1
Alex Comas, NY/NJ	25	1
Clint Mathis, NY/NJ.	29	1

Fouls Committed

	Gm	No
Diego Serna, MIA.	31	83
Chris Henderson, KC	31	79
Carey Talley. DC	29	76
Matt McKeon, KC	30	75
Mamadou Diallo, TB.	28	74
Chris Martinez, COL	30	70
Josh Keller, TB	31	69
Richie Williams, DC	29	68

Fouls Suffered

	Gm	No
Jason Moore, COL	27	83
Jaime Moreno, DC	25	81
Oscar Pareja, DAL	29	77
Diego Serna, MIA	31	77
Mamadou Diallo, TB.	28	72
Peter Nowak, CHI	28	70
Ante Razov, CHI	24	68

Offsides

	Gm	Offs
Mamadou Diallo, TB.	28	82
Adolfo Valencia, NY/NJ	31	49
Roy Lassiter, MIA.	27	45
Junior Agogo, COL.	23	37
Ariel Graziani, DAL	24	37
Chris Henderson, KC	31	36

Corner Kicks

	Gm	CKs
Marco Etcheverry, DC	22	141
Robert Warzycha, CLB	30	126
Richard Mulrooney, SJ	29	98
John Harkes, NE	28	81
Greg Vanney, LA	27	80

Minutes Played

	Mins
Joseph Addo, TB	2934
Scott Garlick, TB.	2934
Nick Garcia, KC	2916
Peter Vermes, KC.	2916
Carlos Valderrama, TB	2897
Steve Trittschuh, TB.	2878
Matt Jordan, DAL	2830

Leading Goaltenders

Goals Against Avg.

	Gm	Min	Shts	Svs	GAA	W-L
Tony Meola, KC	31	2826	162	129	0.92	15-7
Kevin Hartman, LA	26	2422	126	91	1.00	12-7
Zach Thornton, CHI	25	2319	127	91	1.28	15-4
Joe Cannon, SJ	26	2420	181	137	1.49	6-13
Scott Garlick, TB	32	2934	247	184	1.53	16-12
Jeff Causey, NE	22	1975	110	67	1.55	13-13
Mark Simpson, DC	13	1179	593	38	1.60	4-5
Mike Ammann, NY/NJ	22	1960	162	108	1.61	11-9
David Kramer, COL	20	1804	125	79	1.65	9-8
Matt Jordan, DAL	31	2830	188	124	1.69	13-14

Saves

	Gm	No
Scott Garlick, TB	32	184
Joe Cannon, SJ	26	137
Tony Meola, KC	31	129
Matt Jordan, DAL	31	124
Mark Dougherty, CLB	25	111

Shutouts

	Gm	No
Tony Meola, KC	31	16
Kevin Hartman, LA	26	7
Joe Cannon, SJ	26	7
Matt Jordan, DAL	31	7
Scott Garlick, TB	32	6

Save Percentage

	Svs	SOG	SV Pct
Tony Meola, KC	129	162	.796
Joe Cannon, SJ	137	181	.757
Scott Garlick, TB	184	247	.745
Kevin Hartman, LA	91	126	.722
Zach Thorton, CHI	91	127	.717

Team-by-Team Statistics

At least two games played. Players who played with more than one club during the season are listed with final team.

Eastern Conference

D.C. United

	Pos	Gm	Min	G	A	Pts
Jaime Moreno	F	25	2213	12	71	31
Raul Diaz Arce	F	23	1874	9	2	20
DC		16	1422	5	1	11
TB		7	452	4	1	9
Marco Etcheverry	M	22	1810	4	8	16
A.J. Wood	F	24	1237	3	3	9
Pete Marino	F	15	572	4	0	8
Carey Talley	D	29	2458	3	1	7
Chris Albright	M	25	1823	3	0	6
Geoff Aunger	M	26	2081	1	4	6
Jeff Agoos	D	23	2089	1	3	5
Ben Olsen	M	13	1020	1	3	5
Carlos Llamosa	D	23	1974	2	1	5
Judah Cooks	D	15	601	2	1	5
Bobby Convey	M	22	1614	0	2	2
Eddie Pope	D	21	1740	0	2	2
Richie Williams	M	29	2445	0	2	2
Antonio Otero	M	13	954	0	1	1
Eric Denton	M	16	1114	0	1	1
David Hayes	F	10	414	0	0	0

Goalkeepers	Gm	Min	W-L	Shts	Svs	GAA
Mark Simpson	13	1179	4-5	59	38	1.60
Tom Presthus	20	1741	4-13	127	78	2.17

Miami Fusion

	Pos	Gm	Min	G	A	Pts
Diego Serna	F	31	2236	16	10	42
Roy Lassiter	F	27	1838	8	9	25
Martin Machon	M	24	1952	2	16	20
Jim Rooney	M	30	2429	6	4	16
Jay Heaps	M/D	29	2627	5	6	16
Welton	F	26	1365	4	7	15
Henry Gutierrez	M	27	1994	3	8	14
Andy Williams	F	20	1297	4	4	12
Ivan McKinley	D	23	1918	3	1	7
MIA		10	897	2	0	4
NE		13	1021	1	1	3
Tyrone Marshall	F	23	1780	1	2	4
Nelson Vargas	M	14	893	0	3	3
Brian Kamler	M	28	1977	0	3	3
Kyle Beckerman	M	2	110	1	0	2
Nick Rimando	GK	22	2002	0	2	2
Pablo Mastroeni	M	29	2661	0	1	1
Leo Cullen	D	22	1944	0	1	1
Jeff Bilyk	D	9	613	0	1	1
Tim Sahaydak	D	9	709	0	0	0
Francis Okaroh	D	13	1191	0	0	0
Jeremy Aldrich	D	4	154	0	0	0

Goalkeepers	Gm	Min	W-L	Shts	Svs	GAA
Jeff Cassar	9	773	2-2	41	28	1.16
Garth Lagerwey	2	167	0-2	17	11	2.69

New England Revolution

	Pos	Gm	Min	G	A	Pts
Wolde Harris	F	31	2608	15	7	37
Imad Baba	M	30	2508	9	8	26
Mauricio Ramos	M	21	1677	3	8	14
Ted Chronopoulas	D	25	2205	5	2	12
John Harkes	M	28	2511	2	6	10
Jamar Beasley	F	19	880	3	3	9
Johnny Torres	F	20	1328	1	4	6
Joe Franchino	D	30	2604	2	2	6
William Sunsing	F	26	1263	1	3	5
Eric Wynalda	F	11	679	1	2	4
NE		5	195	0	1	1
MIA		6	484	1	1	3
Leonel Alvarez	M	28	2474	1	2	4
Mauricio Wright	D	26	2404	1	1	3
NE		16	1464	1	1	3
SJ		10	940	0	0	0
Paul Keegan	F	11	83	1	1	3
Jose Luis Morales	F	89	422	1	0	2
Brian Dunseth	D	22	1970	1	0	2
Shaker Asad	M	8	246	0	1	1
Eduardo Hurtado	F	3	161	0	0	0
Rusty Pierce	D	29	2600	0	0	0
Carlos Parra	M	14	438	0	0	0
Adam Eyre	D	10	742	0	0	0

Goalkeepers	Gm	Min	W-L	Shts	Svs	GAA
Juergen Sommer	11	977	5-5	62	40	1.38
Jeff Causey	22	1975	8-8	110	67	1.55

New York/New Jersey MetroStars

	Pos	Gm	Min	G	A	Pts
Clint Mathis	M/F	29	2520	16	14	46
NY/NJ		21	1796	13	13	39
LA		8	724	3	1	7
Adolfo Valencia	F	31	2295	16	9	41
Alex Comas	M	25	1571	13	6	32
Mark Chung	M	30	2539	3	11	17
Peter Villegas	M	29	2341	5	6	16
Tab Ramos	M	20	1660	2	6	10
Roy Myers	M/F	25	1712	1	7	9
NY/NJ		17	1011	1	6	8
LA		8	701	0	1	1
Mike Petke	D	30	2672	3	1	7
Billy Walsh	M	24	1756	3	1	7
Steve Jolley	M/D	28	2496	2	2	6
Lothar Matthaus	D	16	1345	0	3	3
Steve Shak	D	23	1393	1	1	3
Daniel Hernandez	M	17	1351	0	2	2
NY/NJ		15	1344	0	2	2
TB		2	7	0	0	0
Thomas Dooley	D	20	1318	0	2	2
Ramiro Corrales	D	22	1460	0	2	2
Mark Semioli	D	16	715	0	0	0
Orlando Perez	D	15	546	0	0	0
Dahir Mohammed	D	3	208	0	0	0

Goalkeepers	Gm	Min	W-L	Shts	Svs	GAA
Paul Grafer	1	90	1-0	7	6	1.00
Tim Howard	9	794	5-2	63	40	1.59
Mike Ammann	22	1960	11-9	162	108	1.61
Paul Grafer	1	90	0-1	10	6	4.00
Russell Payne	1	8	0-0	5	1	22.50

Central Conference

Chicago Fire

	Pos	Gm	Min	G	A	Pts
Ante Razov	F	24	2145	18	6	42
Hristo Stoitchkov	F	18	987	9	7	25
Dema Kovalenko	F	31	2429	10	5	25
Peter Nowak	M	28	2402	5	14	24
Josh Wolff	F	25	1917	7	5	19
Diego Gutierrez	M	24	1959	2	13	17
Jesse Marsch	M	30	2658	2	8	12
Lubis Kubik	D	13	973	3	6	12
Evan Whitfield	D	25	1278	2	7	11
DaMarcus Beasley	M	18	1805	2	2	6
Chris Armas	M	16	1479	0	5	5
Mike Sorber	M	19	1091	1	3	5
John Wolyniec	F	15	461	1	1	3
Carlos Bocanegra	D	27	2402	1	1	3
Andrew Lewis	D	19	1589	1	0	2
Tom Soehn	D	19	1091	1	0	2
C.J. Brown	D	27	2497	0	1	1
Justin Evans	M/F	2	180	0	1	1

Goalkeepers	Gm	Min	W-L	Shts	Svs	GAA
Zach Thornton	25	2319	15-4	127	91	1.28
Chris Snitko	5	450	2-3	31	20	2.00
Greg Sutton	2	180	0-2	21	12	4.00

Columbus Crew

	Pos	Gm	Min	G	A	Pts
Dante Washington	F	30	2541	15	9	39
Robert Warzycha	M	30	2646	6	13	25
Brian West	F	28	2249	6	6	18
Brian McBride	F	18	1523	6	5	17
Jeff Cunningham	F	29	1755	2	8	12
John Wilmar Perez	M	30	2600	3	3	9
Jason Farrell	M	24	1257	3	2	8
Miles Joseph	M/F	23	942	2	1	5
CLB		20	767	2	0	4
NY/NJ		3	175	0	1	1
Ansil Elock	D	19	1679	1	2	4
Mike Duhaney	D	20	1205	1	2	4
Mike Lapper	D	24	1923	1	1	3
Mike Clark	D	28	2448	0	3	3
Mario Gori	D	25	1656	1	0	2
Roland Aguilera	M	16	445	0	1	1
John DeBrito	D	20	1466	0	1	1
Rob Smith	M	1	39	0	1	1
Steve Armas	M	46	276	0	0	0
Miroslaw Rzepa	M/D	5	352	0	0	0
Dominic Schell	M/D	7	138	0	0	0
Todd Yeagley	M	25	2192	0	0	0
Matt Chulis	D	6	165	0	0	0

Goalkeepers	Gm	Min	W-L	Shts	Svs	GAA
Matt Napoleon	8	671	1-4	38	26	1.61
Mark Dougherty	25	2269	10-12	170	111	1.82

Dallas Burn

	Pos	Gm	Min	G	A	Pts
Jason Kreis	M	27	2409	11	13	35
Ariel Graziani	F	24	2138	15	3	33
Oscar Pareja	M	29	2354	3	10	16
Jorge Rodriguez	M/D	25	2066	4	6	14
Chad Deering	M	29	2195	2	9	13
Aleksey Korol	F	21	1024	5	3	13
Eric Dade	D	31	2666	4	2	10
Lazo Alavanja	M	24	1440	2	5	9
Bobby Rhine	F	23	1384	1	6	8
Ted Eck	M/F	29	1918	3	2	8
Antonio Martinez	M	15	531	2	3	7
Paul Broome	M	20	1112	0	7	7
Mark Santel	M/D	25	1744	1	4	6
Sergi Daniv	M	18	1319	0	2	2
Ricardo Iribarren	D	22	1675	0	2	2
Esmundo Rodriguez	M	8	275	1	0	2
Matt Jordan	GK	31	2830	0	1	1
Richard Farrer	M/D	28	2095	0	1	1
Mike Burke	F	9	331	0	0	0

Goalkeepers	Gm	Min	W-L	Shts	Svs	GAA
Johann Noetzel	1	90	1-0	8	7	1.00
Matt Jordan	31	2830	13-14	188	124	1.69

Tampa Bay Mutiny

	Pos	Gm	Min	G	A	Pts
Mamadou Diallo	F	28	2405	26	4	56
Carlos Valderrama	M	32	2897	1	26	28
Steve Ralston	M	30	2631	5	17	27
Manuel Lagos	M	27	1500	8	7	23
Eric Quill	F	30	2205	5	11	21
Josh Keller	M	31	2775	2	7	11
Dominic Kinnear	M	23	1275	1	8	10
Steve Trittschuh	D	32	2878	4	1	9
Kevin Anderson	M	21	891	3	2	8
TB		17	808	3	2	8
COL		4	83	0	0	0
Ritchie Kotschau	M	32	2707	1	3	5
John Maessner	M	24	1486	1	2	4
TB		14	779	0	1	1
DC		10	707	1	1	3
Chad McCarty	D	22	1830	0	4	4
Kalin Bankov	M	18	890	1	1	3
Joseph Addo	D	32	2934	1	1	3
Manuel Bucuane	F	6	147	0	0	0
Chris Houser	D	3	56	0	0	0

Goalkeepers	Gm	Min	W-L	Shts	Svs	GAA
Scott Garlick	32	2934	16-12	247	184	1.53

Western Conference

Colorado Rapids

	Pos	Gm	Min	G	A	Pts
Junior Agogo	F	23	1993	10	7	27
Paul Bravo	M	27	2009	7	3	17
Jorge Dely Valdes	F	20	1352	7	1	15
Marcelo Balboa	D	28	2495	4	5	13
Anders Limpar	M	18	1116	1	9	11
Matt Okoh	F	21	1039	2	6	10
Henry Zambrano	M	18	1077	2	4	8
Jason Bent	M	21	1897	2	2	6
Scott Vermillion	D	28	2244	2	1	5
Jason Moore	M	27	2385	0	5	5
Joey DiGiamarino	M	18	824	1	3	5
Ross Paule	M	16	807	2	1	5
Wes Hart	M	7	480	2	0	4
Paul Dougherty	M	24	1596	0	3	3
David Vaudreuil	M/D	28	2479	0	3	3
Chris Martinez	D	30	2662	0	2	2
Lance Key	D	20	1850	0	1	1
Adin Brown	GK	13	1146	0	1	1
Keyeno Thomas	M/D	12	592	0	0	0
Jeff DiMaria	F	4	193	0	0	0
Seth Trembly	M/D	4	21	0	0	0
Danny DeVall	M	2	110	0	0	0
Craig Waibel	D	2	62	0	0	0
Tahj Jakins	D	1	57	0	0	0
Alan Woods	D	1	5	0	0	0

Goalkeepers	Gm	Min	W-L	Shts	Svs	GAA
David Kramer	20	1804	9-8	125	79	1.65
Adin Brown	13	1146	4-7	102	72	2.04

Kansas City Wizards

	Pos	Gm	Min	G	A	Pts
Chris Henderson	M	31	2694	9	9	27
Miklos Molnar	F	17	1353	12	1	25
Preki	M	31	2485	3	15	21
Chris Klein	M	27	2205	6	8	20
Matt McKeon	D	30	2631	3	11	17
Mo Johnston	M/F	25	1982	4	7	15
Gary Glasgow	F	11	479	3	2	8
Kerry Zavagnin	D	31	2743	2	3	7
Peter Vermes	D	32	2916	2	3	7
Francisco Gomez	M	14	709	2	1	5
Vicente Figueroa	M	8	322	1	1	3
Brian Johnson	M	18	586	0	2	2
Peter Byaruhanga	F	6	170	0	2	2
Chris Brown	F	22	1116	0	1	1
Tony Meola	GK	31	2826	0	1	1
Alex Bunbury	F	5	259	0	0	0
Brandon Prideaux	D	31	2809	0	0	0
Nick Garcia	D	32	2916	0	0	0
Tahj Jakins	D	2	118	0	0	0
Uche Okafor	D	14	398	0	0	0
John Wilson	D	3	103	0	0	0
Ihor Dotsenko	F	2	90	0	0	0

Goalkeepers	Gm	Min	W-L	Shts	Svs	GAA
Bo Oshoniyi	1	90	1-0	3	2	0.00
Tony Meola	31	2826	15-7	162	129	0.92

San Jose Earthquakes

	Pos	Gm	Min	G	A	Pts
Abdul Thompson Conteh	F	31	2356	8	3	19
Dario Brose	M	28	2088	5	4	14
Khodadad Azizi	F	20	1548	3	4	10
Wojtek Krakowiak	M	24	1282	5	0	10
John Doyle	D	20	1776	4	2	10
Richard Mulrooney	M	29	2646	0	9	9
Ronald Cerritos	F	9	850	4	1	9
Ian Russell	M	28	1917	2	3	7
Harut Karapetyan	F	24	1744	2	2	6
Mauricio Solis	M	18	1565	2	1	5
Mike Burns	D	26	2011	0	2	2
SJ		18	1660	0	2	2
NE		8	351	0	0	0
Jim Conrad	D	26	2377	0	2	2
Joe Cannon	GK	26	2420	0	2	2
Jamie Clark	D	8	501	0	2	2
Giovanni Savarese	F	4	303	0	1	1
Dan Calichman	D	20	1750	0	1	1
Travis Mulraine	M	15	622	0	1	1
Ryan Tinsley	M	25	2048	0	1	1
Scott Bower	M	12	537	0	0	0
Justin Evans	M	13	860	0	0	0

Goalkeepers	Gm	Min	W-L	Shts	Svs	GAA
Joe Cannon	26	2420	6-13	181	137	1.49
Jon Conway	6	550	1-4	43	31	1.64

Los Angeles Galaxy

	Pos	Gm	Min	G	A	Pts
Cobi Jones	M	25	2291	7	6	20
Simon Elliott	M/F	28	2497	5	5	15
Mauricio Cienfuegos	M	28	2612	4	7	15
Luis Hernandez	F	16	1407	4	6	14
Greg Vanney	M	27	2526	6	2	14
Sasha Victorine	M	26	1953	3	6	12
Paul Caligiuri	D	28	2212	3	4	10
Sebastien Vorbe	M	19	915	4	0	8
Peter Vagenas	M	16	1044	3	1	7

	Pos	Gm	Min	G	A	Pts
Ezra Hendrickson	D	22	1867	1	3	5
Zak Ibsen	D	27	1516	0	4	4
Danny Califf	D	18	1518	1	1	3
Danny Pena	D	14	1197	1	0	2
Seth George	F	14	459	1	0	2
Robin Fraser	D	25	2244	0	0	0

Goalkeepers	Gm	Min	W-L	Shts	Svs	GAA
Kevin Hartman	26	2422	12-7	126	91	1.00
Matt Reis	6	559	2-3	31	21	1.61

MLS Playoffs

The format of the MLS Quarterfinal and Semifinals series changed for 2000. Instead of a best-of-three series, each quarterfinal and semifinal will be won by the first team to accumulate five points. Just like in the regular season, three points were awarded for a win and one for a tie. The standard 10-minute, sudden-death overtime are played following each game in the event the score is tied. The winner of the series is the first team to reach or exceed five points within the three games. All three games can not end as draws. Should the series remain even on points following regulation or overtime of the third game (3-3, or 4-4) the two clubs would move directly to an additional 20-minute golden-goal overtime period (two 10-minute halves). If neither team scores during the 20-minute period, the game would be decided on penalty kicks.

Quarterfinals

Date	Result
Sept. 14	Los Angeles 1, at Tampa Bay 0
Sept. 20	at Los Angeles 5, Tampa Bay 2

Los Angeles wins series, 6-0

Date	Result
Sept. 15	at N.Y./N.J. 2, Dallas 1 (OT)
Sept. 20	N.Y./N.J. 2, at Dallas 1

New York/New Jersey wins series, 6-0

Date	Result
Sept. 15	at Chicago 2, New England 1
Sept. 19	at New England 2, Chicago 1
Sept. 22	at Chicago 6, New England 0

Chicago wins series, 6-3

Date	Result
Sept. 16	at Kansas City 1, Colorado 0
Sept. 20	at Colorado 0, Kansas City 0 (OT)
Sept. 24	at Kansas City 3, Colorado 2

Kansas City wins series, 7-1

Semifinals

Date	Result
Sept. 26	at Chicago 3, N.Y./N.J. 1
Sept. 30	at N.Y./N.J. 2, Chicago 0
Oct. 6	at Chicago 3, N.Y./N.J. 2

Chicago wins series, 6-2

Date	Result
Sept. 29	at Kansas City 0, Los Angeles 0 (OT)
Oct. 3	at Los Angeles 2, Kansas City 1 (OT)
Oct. 6	at Kansas City 1, Los Angeles 0

Series tied 4-4, KC wins in golden goal overtime

MLS Cup 2000
Kansas City Wizards, 1-0

Oct. 15 at RFK Stadium, Washington, D.C.
Attendance: 39,159.

	1	2	
Chicago	0	0	— 0
Kansas City	1	0	— 1

First Half: KC– Miklos Molnar (Chris Klein), 11th minute

MVP: Tony Meola, Kansas City, goalkeeper

2000 A-League Final Standings (Outdoor)

The A-League serves as a type of minor league system for Major League Soccer. The division II outdoor league is part of the United Systems of Independent Soccer Leagues (USISL) and is recognized by U.S. Soccer. MLS and the USISL have an agreement where MLS teams can assign players to the A-League and call-up A-League players when desired. Also, the U.S. Pro-40 Select team is made-up of players from the MLS's Project 40 program. Project 40 is a joint venture between MLS and U.S. Soccer aimed at developing young American players, giving them the chance to train with MLS clubs and play games at various professional levels. The U.S. Pro-40 team played all their games on the road. Boston and U.S. Pro-40 received a three-point deduction due to the use of ineligible players

Eastern Conference

Northeast Division	W	L	T	Pts	GF	GA
* Long Island Rough Riders	16	9	3	76	54	36
† Rochester Raging Rhinos	17	9	2	75	42	24
† Toronto Lynx	13	11	4	59	35	30
Motreal Impact	12	13	3	54	34	41
Boston Bulldogs	9	16	3	39	32	41
Connecticut Wolves	1	19	8	13	22	57

Atlantic Division	W	L	T	Pts	GF	GA
* Charleston Battery	18	8	2	87	59	36
† Richmond Kickers	20	7	1	84	42	25
† Hershey Wildcats	15	10	3	70	49	30
† Hampton Roads Mariners	14	12	2	62	44	38
† Raleigh Capital Express	12	12	4	58	48	52
Atlanta Silverbacks	11	14	3	55	51	42
Pittsburgh Riverhounds	10	14	4	49	41	43

Western Conference

Central Division	W	L	T	Pts	GF	GA
* Minnesota Thunder	20	4	4	99	74	30
† Milwaukee Rampage	18	9	1	89	69	47
† Indiana Blast	9	15	4	45	40	57
U.S. Pro-40	8	19	1	33	35	60
Tennessee Rhythm	6	22	0	25	36	103
Cincinnati Riverhawks	2	23	3	13	25	80

Pacific Division	W	L	T	Pts	GF	GA
* Seattle Sounders	18	7	3	85	56	38
† San Diego Flash	16	9	3	75	54	32
† Vancouver 86ers	14	11	3	70	62	41
† El Paso Patriots	12	14	2	57	48	50
† Bay Area Seals	12	13	3	56	42	53
Orange County Waves	12	15	1	55	44	52

Note: Three points are awarded for a victory in regulation or overtime. One point is awarded for a shootout win. Shootouts occur if a game is tied after a 15-minute sudden-death overtime.

Playoffs
Round of 16 (Single elimination)

Sept. 8	Toronto 2, Long Island 1	at Long Island
Sept. 9	Richmond 2, Hampton Roads 1 OT	at Richmond
Sept. 9	Rochester 4, Hershey 2	at Rochester
Sept. 9	Charleston 1, Raleigh 0	at Charleston
Sept. 9	Milwaukee 3, El Paso 2 OT	at Milwaukee
Sept. 9	Vancouver 1, San Diego 1	at San Diego
	Vancouver won shoot-out, 5-4	
Sept. 9	Minnesota 7, Indiana 0	at Minnesota
Sept. 10	Seattle 2, Bay Area 1	at Seattle

Quarterfinals (Total Goals)

Eastern Conference
Richmond vs. Toronto

Sept. 15	Toronto 1, Richmond 0	at Toronto
Sept. 17	Toronto 1, Richmond 0	at Richmond
	Hershey wins on aggregate, 2-0	

Rochester vs. Charleston

Sept. 15	Rochester 2, Charleston 0	at Rochester
Sept. 16	Rochester 1, Charleston 0	at Charleston
	Rochester wins on aggregate, 3-0	

Western Conference
Seattle vs. Milwaukee

Sept. 15	Milwaukee 2, Seattle 1	at Milwaukee
Sept. 17	Milwaukee 2, Seattle 1	at Seattle
	Milwaukee wins on aggregate, 4-2	

Minnesota vs. Vancouver

Sept. 13	Vancouver 3, Minnesota 0	at Vancouver
Sept. 16	Minnesota 4, Vancouver 0 OT	at Minnesota
	Minnesota wins on aggregate, 4-3	

Semifinals (Total Goals)

Eastern Conference
Rochester vs. Toronto

Sept. 22	Rochester 1, Toronto 1	at Toronto
Sept. 24	Rochester 1, Toronto 0	at Rochester
	Rochester wins on aggregate, 2-1	

Western Conference
Minnesota vs. Milwaukee

Sept. 21	Minnesota 4, Milwaukee 3	at Milwaukee
Sept. 23	Minnesota 5, Milwaukee 0	at Minnesota
	Minnesota wins on aggregate, 9-3	

Final

September 30 at Rochester, NY. Attendance: 14,276

	1	2—	F
Minnesota	0	1—	1
Rochester	2	1—	3

Scoring: Rochester–Martin Nash (14th), Yari Allnutt (38th), Onandi Lowe (78th); Minnesota–Chugger Adair (74th).

Colleges

MEN

1999 Final *Soccer America* Top 20

Final 1999 regular season poll including games through Nov. 14. Conducted by the national weekly *Soccer America* and released in the Nov. 29 issue. Listing includes records through conference playoffs as well as NCAA tournament record and team lost to. Teams in **bold** type went on to reach NCAA Final Four. All tournament games decided by penalty kicks are considered ties.

		Nov.15 Record	NCAA Recap
1	Duke	15-0-3	1-1 (Santa Clara
2	**Indiana**	16-3-0	5-0
3	Furman	19-1-1	2-1 (Connecticut)
4	**UCLA**	16-2-0	3-1 (Indiana)
5	SW Missouri	17-0-3	0-1 (UAB)
6	Penn St.	17-3-1	2-1 (Indiana)
7	**Connecticut**	16-4-0	3-1 (Santa Clara)
8	Maryland	14-5-0	0-1 (St. John's)
9	SMU	15-3-0	1-1 (UAB)
10	Washington	14-4-2	1-1 (Indiana)
11	UMBC	19-0-2	0-1 (Duke)
12	Wake Forest	12-2-5	1-1 (Furman)
13	UAB	15-5-0	2-1 (Santa Clara)
14	San Diego	14-3-0	0-1 (UCLA)
15	Stanford	12-4-2	0-0-1 (Santa Clara)
16	Portland	12-4-2	0-1 (Washington)
17	Brown	12-4-0	1-1 (Virginia)
18	Rhode Island	17-3-1	0-1 (Brown)
19	**Santa Clara**	13-3-2	3-1-1 (Indiana)
20	Wm. & Mary	14-6-3	0-1 (Penn St.)

NCAA Division I Tournament
First Round (Nov. 19-21)

Santa Clara 2 .... at Stanford 2
(Santa Clara won shoot-out 6-5)
Yale 1 .... at Rutgers 0
at SMU 2 .... 2 OT .... Creighton 1
at Saint Louis 2 .... Illinois-Chicago 0
at Penn State 1 .... William & Mary 0
at UCLA 4 .... San Diego 0
Washington 3 .... at Portland 0
at UAB 2 .... SW Mo. St. 1
at Indiana 1 .... 2 OT .... Kentucky 0
at Furman 2 .... 2 OT .... North Carolina 1
at Virginia 2 .... 3 OT .... Princeton 1
at Brown 2 .... OT .... Rhode Island 1
at Duke 4 .... OT .... UMBC 3
at Wake Forest 2 .... Va. Commonwealth 1
at Connecticut 2 .... 4 OT .... Hartford 1
St. John's 1 .... at Maryland 0

Second Round (Nov. 27-28)

UAB 2 .... at SMU 0
Santa Clara 4 .... at Duke 2
Furman 4 .... at Wake Forest 2
at Connecticut 3 .... Yale 2
UCLA 2 .... at Saint Louis 0
at Virginia 3 .... Brown 1
at Penn St. 2 .... 3 OT .... St. John's 1
at Indiana 3 .... Washington 0

Quarterfinals (Dec. 4-5)

Santa Clara 3 .... OT .... at UAB 2
at Connecticut 3 .... Furman 2
UCLA 2 .... at Virginia 0
at Indiana 3 .... Penn St. 0

1999 COLLEGE CUP
at Charlotte, N.C. (Dec. 10 & 12)
Semifinals

Santa Clara 2 .... 4 OT .... Connecticut 1
Indiana 3 .... 4 OT .... UCLA 2

Championship

Indiana 1 .... Santa Clara 0
Scoring: IU— Yuri Lavrinenko (Aleksey Karol); 29:50;
Attendance: 15,439
Final records: Indiana (21-3), Santa Clara (16-6-3).
Most Outstanding Offensive Player: Yuri Larinenko, IU; **Most Outstanding Defensive Player:** Nick Garcia, IU
All-Tournament Team: Adam Eyre, Ari Rodopolous and Shawn Percell from Santa Clara; Ryan Mack, Lavrinenko, Garcia and Aleksey Karol from Indiana; Darin Lewis and Brent Rahim from UConn; Sasha Victorine and Pete Vagenas from UCLA.

WOMEN

1999 Final *Soccer America* Top 20

Final 1999 regular season poll including games through Nov. 8. Conducted by the national weekly *Soccer America* and released in the Nov. 22 issue. Listing includes records through conference playoffs as well as NCAA tournament record and team lost to. Teams in **bold** type went on to reach NCAA Final Four. All tournament games decided by penalty kicks are considered ties.

		Nov. 8 Record	NCAA Recap
1	**Santa Clara**	20-0-0	3-1 (Notre Dame)
2	**North Carolina**	19-2-0	5-0
3	Florida	21-1-0	0-1 (Hartford)
4	Nebraska	20-1-1	2-0-1 (Notre Dame)
5	**Notre Dame**	18-3-0	3-1-1 (North Carolina)
6	Harvard	14-1-1	0-1 (Boston College)
7	William & Mary	18-3-0	1-1 (North Carolina)
8	Connecticut	15-7-0	2-1 (Santa Clara)
9	Clemson	13-6-1	1-1-1 (North Carolina)
10	**Penn St.**	18-3-1	3-1 (North Carolina)
11	Wake Forest	15-6-0	1-0-1 (Clemson)
12	Stanford	14-4-1	1-1 (Notre Dame)
13	USC	14-5-0	0-1 (SMU)
14	Kentucky	16-2-2	0-1 (Texas A&M)
15	Virginia	12-8-0	1-1 (Hartford)
16	UCLA	14-4-1	1-1 (Santa Clara)
17	Michigan	16-5-1	0-1 (Wake Forest)
18	Texas A&M	15-4-1	1-1 (Nebraska)
19	SMU	15-5-1	1-1 (Penn St.)
20	Fresno St.	14-5-2	0-1 (Cal Poly)

NCAA Division I Tournament
First Round (Nov. 10)

C. Florida 1 .... at Furman 0
at Duke 3 .... Elon 1
at Michigan 5 .... Wright St. 0
Marquette 3 .... 4 OT .... at Missouri 2
at Maryland 6 .... LIU 0
at SMU 4 .... Baylor 0
at James Madison 1 .... Penn 0
at Hartford 2 .... Princeton 1
at Minnesota 2 .... E. Michigan 0
at Texas A&M 2 .... Montana 1
Cal Poly 2 .... at Fresno St. 1
at Dayton 3 .... Evansville 1
at Boston College 4 .... Fairfield 1
at Dartmouth 6 .... Colgate 0
at San Diego 2 .... San Diego St. 1
at BYU 2 .... California 0

Second Round (Nov. 13-14)

at North Carolina 8 . . . . .C. Florida 0
at William & Mary 3 . . . . .Duke 0
at Clemson 1 . . . . .Marquette 0
at Penn St. 3 . . . . .Maryland 2
SMU 1 . . . . .2 OT . . . . .at USC 0
at Virginia 3 . . . . .James Madison 1
Hartford 1 . . . . .at Florida 0
at Nebraska 5 . . . . .Minnesota 0
Texas A&M 3 . . . . .OT . . . . .at Kentucky 2
at Stanford 3 . . . . .Cal Poly 1
at Notre Dame 5 . . . . .Dayton 1
Boston College 1 . . . . .at Harvard 0
at Connecticut 3 . . . . .Dartmouth 0
at UCLA 2 . . . . .OT . . . . .San Diego 1
at Santa Clara 2 . . . . .BYU 0

Third Round (Nov. 19-21)

at North Carolina 5 . . . . .William & Mary 1
Clemson 0 . . . . .at Wake Forest 0
   (Clemson won shoot-out 3-1)
at Penn St. 5 . . . . .SMU 0
at Hartford 3 . . . . .3 OT . . . . .Virginia 2
at Nebraska 1 . . . . .Texas A&M 0
Notre Dame 1 . . . . .at Stanford 0
at Connecticut 5 . . . . .Boston College 0
at Santa Clara 7 . . . . .UCLA 0

Quarterfinals (Nov. 26-28)

at Penn St. 2 . . . . .Hartford 0
at North Carolina 3 . . . . .Clemson 0
at Santa Clara 3 .Connecticut 0
Notre Dame 1 . . . . .at Nebraska 1
   (Notre Dame won shoot-out 4-3)

1999 COLLEGE CUP
at San Jose, Calif. (Dec. 3 and 5)
Semifinals

North Carolina 2 . . . . .Penn St. 0
Notre Dame 1 . . . . .Santa Clara 0

Championship

North Carolina 2 . . . . .Notre Dame 0
Scoring: UNC— Meredith Florance (Kim Patrick, Susan Bush), 55:11; Beth Sheppard (Raven McDonald, Bush), 79:06.
Attendance: 14,410
Final records: North Carolina (24-2), Notre Dame (21-4-1).
Most Outstanding Offensive Player: Susan Bush, UNC; **Most Outstanding Defensive Player:** Lorrie Fair, UNC.
All Tournament Team: Fair, Bush, Kim Patrick, Anne Remy, Jena Kluege and Meredith Florance from UNC; LaKeysia Beene, Jen Grubb and Jenny Streiffer from Notre Dame; Christi Welsh from Penn St.; Nikki Serelenga and Danielle Slaton from Santa Clara

1999 Annual Awards
Men's Players of the Year

Hermann Trophy . . . . .Ali Curtis, Duke, F
MAC Award/NSCAA . . . . .Sasha Victorine, UCLA, MF
Soccer America . . . . .Aleksey Korol, Indiana, F

Women's Player of the Year

Hermann Trophy . . . . .Mandy Clemens, Santa Clara, F
MAC Award/NSCAA . . . . .Mandy Clemens, Santa Clara, F
Soccer America . . . . .Lorrie Fair, UNC, D

NSCAA Coaches of the Year

Division I: Women's . . . . .Patrick Farmer, Penn St.
         Men's . . . . .Jerry Yeagley, Indiana

Division I All-America Teams
MEN

The 1999 first team All-America selections of the National Soccer Coaches Association of America (NSCAA). Holdovers from the 1998 NSCAA All-America team are in **bold** type.
   GOALKEEPER— **Adin Brown**, William & Mary, Sr.
   DEFENDERS— Eric Denton, Santa Clara, Sr.; David Wright, Indiana, Jr.; **Nick Garcia**, Indiana, So.
   MIDFIELDERS— Daniel Alvarez, Furman, Sr.; Carl Bussey, SMU, So.; Jeff Dimaria, Saint Louis, Sr.; Sasha Victorine, UCLA, Sr.
   FORWARDS— **Aleksey Korol**, Indiana, Sr.; John Barry Nusum, Furman, So.; Mohamed Fahim, SMU, So.; Ricardo Villar, Penn St., Jr.

WOMEN

The 1999 first team All-America selections of the National Soccer Coaches Association of America (NSCAA). Holdovers from the combined 1998 All-America team are in **bold** type.
   GOALKEEPER— Emily Oleksiuk, Penn St., So.
   DEFENDERS— Heather Mitts, Florida, Sr.; Danielle Slaton, Santa Clara, So.; Sharolta Nonen, Nebraska, Sr.
   MIDFIELDERS— **Nikki Serlenga**, Santa Clara, Sr.; **Lorrie Fair**, North Carolina, Sr.; Kaye Brownlee, Furman, So.
   FORWARDS— **Mandy Clemens**, Santa Clara, Sr.; Maren Hendershot, BYU, Sr.; Christie Welch, Penn State, Fr.; Abby Wambach, Florida, So.

Small College Final Fours
MEN
NCAA Division II

at Barry University, Miami Shores, Fla. (Dec. 3-5)
Semifinals: Southern Conn. St. def. Charleston (W. Va.), 1-0; Fort Lewis (Colo.) def. Barry (Fla.), 2-0.
Championship: Southern Conn. St. def. Fort Lewis, 2-1 (OT). Final records: Southern Conn. St. (20-0), Fort Lewis (19-3-2).

NCAA Division III

at Wheaton, Ill. (Nov. 26-27)
Semifinals: St. Lawrence (N.Y.) def. Alma (Mich.), 2-0; Wheaton (Ill.) def. Richard Stockton College (N.J.), 4-0.
Championship: St. Lawrence def. Wheaton, 2-0; Final records: St. Lawrence (21-0), Wheaton (18-3-2).

NAIA

at Albuquerque, N.M. (Nov. 21-23)
Semifinals: Lindsey Wilson (Ky.) def. Birmingham-Southern (Ala.), 3-2; Mobile (Ala.) def. Illinois-Springfield, 2-1 (OT).
Championship: Lindsey Wilson def. Mobile, 2-1; Final records: Lindsey Wilson (24-1-1), Mobile (24-1-1).

WOMEN
NCAA Division II

at Barry University, Miami Shores, Fla. (Dec. 2-4)
Semifinals: Franklin Pierce (NH) def. Northern Kentucky, 2-0; Cal Poly Pomona def. Barry, 2-1 (4 OT).
Championship: Franklin Pierce (N.H.) def. Cal Poly Pomona, 3-1. Final records: Franklin Pierce (20-1), Cal Poly Pomona. (17-6-1).

NCAA Division III

at Williams College, Williamstown, Mass. (Nov. 20-21)
Semifinals: UC-San Diego def. College of New Jersey, 1-0; Macalester def. Williams (Mass.), 1-0.
Championship: UC-San Diego def. Macalester, 1-0. Final records: UC-San Diego (19-1-2), Macalester (20-3)

NAIA

at Miami, Fla. (Nov. 21-23)
Semifinals: Transylvania (Ky.) def. Oklahoma City, 3-2; Westmont (Calif.) def. Azusa Pacific (Calif.), 2-1.
Championship: Westmont def. Transylvania, 3-0; Final records: Westmont (21-2), Transylvania (22-1).

SOCCER
1900-2000 Through the Years

ESPN

PAGE 742

information please
SPORTS ALMANAC

The World Cup

The Federation Internationale de Football Association (FIFA) began the World Cup championship tournament in 1930 with a 13-team field in Uruguay. Sixty-four years later, 138 countries competed in qualifying rounds to fill 24 berths in the 1994 World Cup finals. FIFA increased the World Cup '98 tournament field from 24 to 32 teams, and it will remain at 32 in 2002 including automatic berths for defending champion France and co-hosts Japan and South Korea. The other 29 slots will be allotted by region: Europe (13), Africa (5), South America (4), CONCACAF (3), Asia (2), the two remaining positions will be determined via two home and away playoff series. One will be between the #14 European team and the #3 Asian team and the other will be between the #5 South American team and the champion of Oceania.

Tournaments have now been played three times in North America (Mexico 2 and U.S.), four times in South America (Argentina, Chile, Brazil and Uruguay) and nine times in Europe (France 2, Italy 2, England, Spain, Sweden, Switzerland and West Germany). Following an outcry when Germany was awarded the 2006 World Cup over South Africa, FIFA announced that, starting in 2010, the World Cup will be rotated among six continents.

Brazil retired the first World Cup (called the Jules Rimet Trophy after FIFA's first president) in 1970 after winning it for the third time. The new trophy, first presented in 1974, is known as simply the World Cup.

Multiple winners: Brazil (4); Italy and West Germany (3); Argentina and Uruguay (2).

Year	Champion	Manager	Score	Runner-up	Host Country	Third Place
1930	Uruguay	Alberto Suppici	4-2	Argentina	Uruguay	No game
1934	Italy	Vittório Pozzo	2-1*	Czechoslovakia	Italy	Germany 3, Austria 2
1938	Italy	Vittório Pozzo	4-2	Hungary	France	Brazil 4, Sweden 2
1942-46 Not held						
1950	Uruguay	Juan Lopez	2-1	Brazil	Brazil	No game
1954	West Germany	Sepp Herberger	3-2	Hungary	Switzerland	Austria 3, Uruguay 1
1958	Brazil	Vicente Feola	5-2	Sweden	Sweden	France 6, W. Ger. 3
1962	Brazil	Aimoré Moreira	3-1	Czechoslovakia	Chile	Chile 1, Yugoslavia 0
1966	England	Alf Ramsey	4-2*	W. Germany	England	Portugal 2, USSR 1
1970	Brazil	Mario Zagalo	4-1	Italy	Mexico	W. Ger. 1, Uruguay 0
1974	West Germany	Helmut Schoen	2-1	Holland	W. Germany	Poland 1, Brazil 0
1978	Argentina	Cesar Menotti	3-1*	Holland	Argentina	Brazil 2, Italy 1
1982	Italy	Enzo Bearzot	3-1	W. Germany	Spain	Poland 3, France 2
1986	Argentina	Carlos Bilardo	3-2	W. Germany	Mexico	France 4, Belgium 2*
1990	West Germany	Franz Beckenbauer	1-0	Argentina	Italy	Italy 2, England 1
1994	Brazil	Carlos Parreira	0-0†	Italy	USA	Sweden 4, Bulgaria 0
1998	France	Aimé Jacquet	3-0	Brazil	France	Croatia 2, Holland 1
2002	at Japan/South Korea (May 31-June 30)					
2006	at Germany					

*Winning goals scored in overtime (no sudden death); †Brazil defeated Italy in shootout (3-2) after scoreless overtime period.

All-Time World Cup Leaders
Career Goals

World Cup scoring leaders through 1998. Years listed are years played in World Cup.

	No
Gerd Müller, West Germany (1970, 74)	14
Just Fontaine, France (1958)	13
Pelé, Brazil (1958, 62, 66, 70)	12
Sandor Kocsis, Hungary (1954)	11
Juergen Klinsmann, Germany (1990, 94, 98)	11
Helmut Rahn, West Germany (1954, 58)	10
Teofilo Cubillas, Peru (1970, 78)	10
Gregorz Lato, Poland (1974, 78, 82)	10
Gary Lineker, England (1986, 90)	10

Most Valuable Player

Officially, the Golden Ball Award, the Most Valuable Player of the World Cup tournament has been selected since 1982 by a panel of international soccer journalists.

Year		Year	
1982	Paolo Rossi, Italy	1994	Romario, Brazil
1986	Diego Maradona, Arg.	1998	Ronaldo, Brazil
1990	Toto Schillaci, Italy		

Single Tournament Goals

World Cup tournament scoring leaders through 1998.

Year		Gm	No
1930	Guillermo Stabile, Argentina	4	8
1934	Angelo Schiavio, Italy	3	4
	Oldrich Nejedly, Czechoslovakia	4	4
	& Edmund Conen, Germany	4	4
1938	Leônidas, Brazil	3	8
1950	Ademir, Brazil	6	7
1954	Sandor Kocsis, Hungary	5	11
1958	Just Fontaine, France	6	13
1962	Drazen Jerkovic, Yugoslavia	6	5
1966	Eusébio, Portugal	6	9
1970	Gerd Müller, West Germany	6	10
1974	Grzegorz Lato, Poland	7	7
1978	Mario Kempes, Argentina	7	6
1982	Paolo Rossi, Italy	7	6
1986	Gary Lineker, England	5	6
1990	Toto Schillaci, Italy	7	6
1994	Oleg Salenko, Russia	3	6
	Hristo Stoichkov, Bulgaria	7	6
1998	Davor Suker, Croatia	7	6

All-Time World Cup Ranking Table

Since the first World Cup in 1930, Brazil is the only country to play in all 16 final tournaments. The FIFA all-time table below ranks all nations that have ever qualified for a World Cup final tournament by points earned through 1998. Victories, which earned two points from 1930-90, were awarded three points starting in 1994. Note that Germany's appearances include 10 made by West Germany from 1954-90. Participants in the 1998 World Cup final are in **bold** type.

		App	Gm	W	L	T	Pts	GF	GA
1	**Brazil**	16	80	53	13	14	120	173	78
2	**Germany**	14	78	45	16	17	107	162	103
3	**Italy**	14	66	38	12	16	92	105	62
4	**Argentina**	12	57	29	18	10	68	100	69
5	**England**	10	45	20	12	13	53	62	42
6	**France**	10	41	21	14	6	48	86	58
7	**Spain**	10	40	16	14	10	42	61	48
8	**Yugoslavia**	9	37	16	13	8	40	60	46
9	Uruguay	9	37	15	14	8	38	61	52
	Russia	8	34	16	12	6	38	60	40
11	Sweden	9	38	14	15	9	37	66	60
	Netherlands	7	31	14	9	9	37	56	36
13	Hungary	9	32	15	14	3	33	87	57
14	Poland	5	25	13	7	5	31	39	29
15	Austria	7	29	12	13	4	28	43	47
16	Czech Republic	8	30	11	14	5	27	44	45
17	**Mexico**	11	37	8	19	10	26	39	75
18	Belgium	10	32	9	16	7	25	40	56
19	**Romania**	7	21	8	8	5	21	30	32
20	Chile	7	25	7	12	6	20	31	40
21	**Scotland**	8	23	4	12	7	15	25	41
	Switzerland	7	22	6	13	3	15	33	51
23	**Bulgaria**	7	26	3	15	8	14	22	53
	Paraguay	5	15	4	6	5	14	19	27
25	**Cameroon**	4	14	3	5	6	12	13	26
26	Portugal	2	9	6	3	0	12	19	12
27	Peru	4	15	4	8	3	11	19	31
	No. Ireland	3	13	3	5	5	11	13	23
	Denmark	2	9	5	3	1	11	19	13
30	Croatia	1	7	5	2	0	10	11	5
31	**USA**	6	17	4	12	1	9	18	38
32	**Morocco**	4	13	2	7	4	8	12	18
	Colombia	4	13	3	8	2	8	14	23

		App	Gm	W	L	T	Pts	GF	GA
	Nigeria	2	8	4	4	0	8	13	13
35	Ireland	2	9	1	3	5	7	4	7
	Norway	2	8	2	3	3	7	7	8
37	East Germany	1	6	2	2	2	6	5	5
38	**Saudi Arabia**	2	7	2	4	1	5	7	13
	Algeria	2	6	2	3	1	5	6	10
	Wales	1	5	1	1	3	5	4	4
41	**South Korea**	5	14	0	10	4	4	11	43
	Tunisia	2	6	1	3	2	4	4	6
	Costa Rica	1	4	2	2	0	4	4	6
44	**Iran**	2	6	1	4	1	3	4	12
	North Korea	1	4	1	2	1	3	5	9
	Cuba	1	3	1	1	1	3	5	12
	Jamaica	1	3	1	2	0	3	3	9
48	Egypt	2	4	0	2	2	2	3	6
	Honduras	1	3	0	1	2	2	2	3
	Israel	1	3	0	1	2	2	1	3
	Turkey	1	3	1	2	0	2	10	11
	South Africa	1	3	0	1	2	2	3	6
53	Bolivia	3	6	0	5	1	1	1	20
	Australia	1	3	0	2	1	1	0	5
	Kuwait	1	3	0	2	1	1	2	6
56	El Salvador	2	6	0	6	0	0	1	22
	Canada	1	3	0	3	0	0	0	5
	East Indies	1	1	0	1	0	0	0	6
	Greece	1	3	0	3	0	0	0	10
	Haiti	1	3	0	3	0	0	2	14
	Iraq	1	3	0	3	0	0	1	4
	Japan	1	3	0	3	0	0	1	4
	New Zealand	1	3	0	3	0	0	2	12
	UAE	1	3	0	3	0	0	2	11
	Zaire	1	3	0	3	0	0	0	14

The United States in the World Cup

While the United States has fielded a national team every year of the World Cup, only five of those teams have been able to make it past the preliminary competition and qualify for the final World Cup tournament. The 1994 national team automatically qualified because the U.S. served as host of the event for the first time. The U.S. played in three of the first four World Cups (1930, '34 and '50) and each of the last three (1990, '94 and '98). The Americans have a record of 4-12-1 in 17 World Cup matches, with two victories in 1930, a 1-0 upset of England in 1950, and a 2-1 shocker over Colombia in 1994.

1930

1st Round Matches

United States 3 ....Belgium 0
United States 3 ....Paraguay 0

Semifinals

Argentina 6 ....United States 1
U.S. Scoring—Bert Patenaude (3), Bart McGhee (2), James Brown and Thomas Florie.

1934

1st Round Match

Italy 7 ....United States 1
U.S. Scoring—Buff Donelli (who later became a noted college and NFL football coach).

1950

1st Round Matches

Spain 3 ....United States 1
United States 1 ....England 0
Chile 5 ....United States 2
U.S. Scoring—Joe Gaetjens, Joe Maca, John Souza and Frank Wallace.

1990

1st Round Matches

Czechoslovakia 5 ....United States 1
Italy 1 ....United States 0
Austria 2 ....United States 1
U.S. Scoring—Paul Caligiuri and Bruce Murray.

1994

1st Round Matches

United States 1 ....Switzerland 1
United States 2 ....Colombia 1
Romania 1 ....United States 0

Round of 16

Brazil 1 ....United States 0
Overall U.S. Scoring— Eric Wynalda, Ernie Stewart and own goal (Colombia defender Andres Escobar).

1998

1st Round Matches

Germany 2 ....United States 0
Iran 2 ....United States 1
Yugoslavia 1 ....United States 0
U.S. Scoring— Brian McBride.

World Cup Finals

Brazil and West Germany (now Germany) have played in the most Cup finals with six. Note that a four-team round robin determined the 1950 championship—the deciding game turned out to be the last one of the tournament between Uruguay and Brazil.

1930
Uruguay 4, Argentina 2
(at Montevideo, Uruguay)

		1	2–T
July 30	Uruguay (4-0)	1	3–4
	Argentina (4-1)	2	0–2

Goals: Uruguay–Pablo Dorado (12th minute), Pedro Cea (54th), Santos Iriarte (68th), Castro (89th); Argentina–Carlos Peucelle (20th), Guillermo Stabile (37th).
Uruguay–Ballesteros, Nasazzi, Mascheroni, Andrade, Fernandez, Gestido, Dorado, Scarone, Castro, Cea, Iriarte.
Argentina–Botasso, Della Torre, Paternoster, J. Evaristo, Monti, Suarez, Peucelle, Varallo, Stabile, Ferreira, M. Evaristo.
Attendance: 90,000. **Referee:** Langenus (Belgium).

1934
Italy 2, Czechoslovakia 1 (OT)
(at Rome)

		1	2	OT–T
June 10	Italy (4-0-1)	0	1	1–2
	Czechoslovakia (3-1)	0	1	0–1

Goals: Italy–Raimondo Orsi (80th minute), Angelo Schiavio (95th); Czechoslovakia–Puc (70th).
Italy–Combi, Monzeglio, Allemandi, Ferraris IV, Monti, Bertolini, Guaita, Meazza, Schiavio, Ferrari, Orsi.
Czechoslovakia–Planicka, Zenisek, Ctyroky, Kostalek, Cambal, Krcil, Junek, Svoboda, Sobotka, Nejedly, Puc.
Attendance: 55,000. **Referee:** Eklind (Sweden).

1938
Italy 4, Hungary 2
(at Paris)

		1	2–T
June 19	Italy (4-0)	3	1–4
	Hungary (3-1)	1	1–2

Goals: Italy–Gino Colaussi (5th minute), Silvio Piola (16th), Colassi (35th), Piola (82nd); Hungary–Titkos (7th), Georges Sarosi (70th).
Italy–Olivieri, Foni, Rava, Serantoni, Andreolo, Locatelli, Biavati, Meazza, Piola, Ferrari, Colaussi.
Hungary–Szabo, Polgar, Biro, Szalay, Szucs, Lazar, Sas, Vincze, G. Sarosi, Szengeller, Titkos.
Attendance: 65,000. **Referee:** Capdeville (France).

1950
Uruguay 2, Brazil 1
(at Rio de Janeiro)

		1	2–T
July 16	Uruguay (3-0-1)	0	2–2
	Brazil (4-1-1)	0	1–1

Goals: Uruguay–Juan Schiaffino (66th minute), Chico Ghiggia (79th); Brazil–Friaca (47th).
Uruguay–Maspoli, M. Gonzales, Tejera, Gambetta, Varela, Andrade, Ghiggia, Perez, Miguez, Schiaffino, Moran.
Brazil–Barbosa, Augusto, Juvenal, Bauer, Danilo, Bigode, Friaça, Zizinho, Ademir, Jair, Chico.
Attendance: 199,854. **Referee:** Reader (England).

1954
West Germany 3, Hungary 2
(at Berne, Switzerland)

		1	2–T
July 4	West Germany (4-1)	2	1–3
	Hungary (4-1)	2	0–2

Goals: West Germany–Max Morlock (10th minute), Helmut Rahn (18th), Rahn (84th); Hungary–Ferenc Puskas (4th), Zoltan Czibor (9th).
West Germany–Turek, Posipal, Liebrich, Kohlmeyer, Eckel, Mai, Rahn, Morlock, O. Walter, F. Walter, Schaefer.
Hungary–Grosics, Buzansky, Lorant, Lantos, Bozsik, Zakarias, Czibor, Kocsis, Hidegkuti, Puskas, J. Toth.
Attendance: 60,000. **Referee:** Ling (England).

1958
Brazil 5, Sweden 2
(at Stockholm)

		1	2–T
June 29	Brazil (5-0-1)	2	3–5
	Sweden (4-1-1)	1	1–2

Goals: Brazil–Vava (9th minute), Vava (32nd), Pelé (55th), Mario Zagalo (68th), Pelé (90th); Sweden–Nils Liedholm (3rd), Agne Simonsson (80th).
Brazil–Gilmar, D. Santos, N. Santos, Zito, Bellini, Orlando, Garrincha, Didi, Vava, Pelé, Zagalo.
Sweden–Svensson, Bergmark, Axbom, Boerjesson, Gustavsson, Parling, Hamrin, Gren, Simonsson, Liedholm, Skoglund.
Attendance: 49,737. **Referee:** Guigue (France).

1962
Brazil 3, Czechoslovakia 1
(at Santiago, Chile)

		1	2–T
June 17	Brazil (5-0-1)	1	2–3
	Czechoslovakia (3-2-1)	1	0–1

Goals: Brazil–Amarildo (17th minute), Zito (68th), Vava (77th); Czechoslovakia–Josef Masopust (15th).
Brazil–Gilmar, D. Santos, N. Santos, Zito, Mauro, Zozimo, Garrincha, Didi, Vava, Amarildo, Zagalo.
Czechoslovakia–Schroiff, Tichy, Novak, Pluskal, Popluhar, Masopust, Pospichal, Scherer, Kvasniak, Kadraba, Jelinek.
Attendance: 68,679. **Referee:** Latishev (USSR).

1966
England 4, West Germany 2 (OT)
(at London)

		1	2	OT–T
July 30	England (5-0-1)	1	1	2–4
	West Germany (4-1-1)	1	1	0–2

Goals: England–Geoff Hurst (18th minute), Martin Peters (78th), Hurst (101st), Hurst (120th); West Germany–Helmut Haller (12th), Wolfgang Weber (90th).
England–Banks, Cohen, Wilson, Stiles, J. Charlton, Moore, Ball, Hurst, B. Charlton, Hunt, Peters.
West Germany–Tilkowski, Hottges, Schnellinger, Beckenbauer, Schulz, Weber, Haller, Seeler, Held, Overath, Emmerich.
Attendance: 93,802. **Referee:** Dienst (Switzerland).

1970
Brazil 4, Italy 1
(at Mexico City)

		1	2–T
June 21	Brazil (6-0)	1	3–4
	Italy (3-1-2)	1	0–1

Goals: Brazil–Pelé (18th minute), Gerson (65th), Jairzinho (70th), Carlos Alberto (86th); Italy–Roberto Boninsegna (37th).
Brazil–Felix, C. Alberto, Everaldo, Clodoaldo, Brito, Piazza, Jairzinho, Gerson, Tostão, Pelé, Rivelino.
Italy–Albertosi, Burgnich, Facchetti, Bertini (Juliano, 73rd), Rosato, Cera, Domenghini, Mazzola, Boninsegna (Rivera, 84th), De Sisti, Riva.
Attendance: 107,412. **Referee:** Glockner (E. Germany).

1974
West Germany 2, Holland 1
(at Munich)

		1	2–T
July 7	West Germany (6-1)	2	0–2
	Holland (5-1-1)	1	0–1

Goals: West Germany–Paul Breitner (25th minute, penalty kick), Gerd Müller (43rd); Holland–Johan Neeskens (1st, penalty kick).
West Germany–Maier, Beckenbauer, Vogts, Breitner, Schwarzenbeck, Overath, Bonhof, Hoeness, Grabowski, Muller, Holzenbein.
Holland–Jongbloed, Suurbier, Rijsbergen (De Jong, 58th), Krol, Haan, Jansen, Van Hanegem, Neeskens, Rep, Cruyff, Rensenbrink (R. Van de Kerkhof, 46th).
Attendance: 77,833. **Referee:** Taylor (England).

1978
Argentina 3, Holland 1 (OT)
(at Buenos Aires)

		1	2	OT–T
June 25	Argentina (5-1-1)	1	0	2–3
	Holland (3-2-2)	0	1	0–1

Goals: Argentina–Mario Kempes (37th minute), Kempes (104th), Daniel Bertoni (114th); Holland–Dirk Nanninga (81st).
Argentina–Fillol, Olguin, L. Galvan, Passarella, Tarantini, Ardiles (Larrosa, 65th), Gallego, Kempes, Luque, Bertoni, Ortiz (Houseman, 77th).
Holland–Jongbloed, Jansen (Suurbier, 72nd), Brandts, Krol, Poortvliet, Haan, Neeskens, W. Van de Kerkhof, R. Van de Kerkhof, Rep (Nanninga, 58th), Rensenbrink.
Attendance: 77,260. **Referee:** Gonella (Italy).

1982
Italy 3, West Germany 1
(at Madrid)

		1	2–T
July 11	Italy (4-0-3)	0	3–3
	West Germany (4-2-1)	0	1–1

Goals: Italy–Paolo Rossi (57th minute), Marco Tardelli (68th), Alessandro Altobelli (81st); West Germany–Paul Breitner (83rd).
Italy–Zoff, Scirea, Gentile, Cabrini, Collovati, Bergomi, Tardelli, Oriali, Conti, Rossi, Graziani (Altobelli, 8th, and Causio, 89th).
West Germany–Schumacher, Stielike, Kaltz, Briegel, K.H. Forster, B. Forster, Breitner, Dremmler (Hrubesch, 61st), Littbarski, Fischer, Rummenigge (Muller, 69th).
Attendance: 90,080. **Referee:** Coelho (Brazil).

1986
Argentina 3, West Germany 2
(at Mexico City)

		1	2–T
June 29	Argentina (6-0-1)	1	2–3
	West Germany (4-2-1)	0	2–2

Goals: Argentina–Jose Brown (22nd minute), Jorge Valdano (55th), Jorge Burruchaga (83rd); West Germany–Karl-Heinz Rummenigge (73rd), Rudi Voller (81st).
Argentina–Pumpido, Cuciuffo, Olarticoechea, Ruggeri, Brown, Batista, Burruchaga (Trobbiani, 89th), Giusti, Enrique, Maradona, Valdano.
West Germany–Schumacher, Jakobs, B. Forster, Berthold, Briegel, Eder, Brehme, Matthaus, Rummenigge, Magath (Hoeness, 61st), Allofs (Voller, 46th).
Attendance: 114,590. **Referee:** Filho (Brazil).

1990
West Germany 1, Argentina 0
(at Rome)

		1	2–T
July 8	West Germany (6-0-1)	0	1–1
	Argentina (4-2-1)	0	0–0

Goals: West Germany–Andreas Brehme (85th minute, penalty kick).
West Germany–Illgner, Berthold (Reuter, 73rd), Kohler, Augenthaler, Buchwald, Brehme, Haessler, Matthaus, Littbarski, Klinsmann, Voller.
Argentina–Goycoechea, Ruggeri (Monzon, 46th), Simon, Serrizuela, Lorenzo, Basualdo, Troglio, Burruchaga (Calderon, 53rd), Sensini, Dezotti, Maradona.
Attendance: 73,603. **Referee:** Codesal (Mexico).

1994
Brazil 0, Italy 0 (Shootout)
(at Pasadena, Calif.)

		1	2	OT–T
July 17	Brazil (6-0-1)	0	0	0–0*
	Italy (4-2-1)	0	0	0–0

*Brazil wins shootout, 3-2.
Shootout (five shots each, alternating): ITA–Baresi (miss, 0-0); BRA–Santos (blocked, 0-0); ITA–Albertini (goal, 1-0); BRA–Romario (goal, 1-1); ITA–Evani (goal, 2-1); BRA–Branco (goal, 2-2); ITA–Massaro (blocked, 2-2); BRA–Dunga (goal, 2-3); ITA–R. Baggio (miss, 2-3).
Brazil– Taffarel, Jorginho (Cafu, 21st minute), Branco, Aldair, Santos, Mazinho, Silva, Dunga, Zinho (Viola, 106th), Bebeto, Romario.
Italy– Pagliuca, Mussi (Apolloni, 35th minute), Baresi, Benarrivo, Maldini, Albertini, D. Baggio (Evani, 95th), Berti, Donadoni, R. Baggio, Massaro.
Attendance: 94,194. **Referee:** Puhl (Hungary).

1998
France 3, Brazil 0
(at Paris)

		1	2– T
July 12	Brazil (6-1)	0	0– 0
	France (7-0)	2	1– 3

Goals: France– Zinedine Zidane (27th and 46th minutes), Petit (92).
Brazil– Taffarel, Cafu, Aldair, Baiano, Carlos, Sampaio (Edmundo, 74th minute), Dunga, Rivaldo, Leonardo (Denilson, 46th minute), Bebeto, Ronaldo.
France– Barthez, Lizarazu, Desailly, Thuram, Leboeuf, Djorkaeff (Viera, 75th minute), Deschamps, Zidane, Petit, Karembeu (Boghossian, 57th minute), Guivarc'h, Dugarry.
Attendance: 75,000. **Referee:** Belqola (Morocco).

Year-by-Year Comparisons

How the 16 World Cup tournaments have compared in nations qualifying, matches played, players participating, goals scored, average goals per game, overall attendance and attendance per game.

Year	Host	Continent	Nations	Matches	Players	Goals Scored	Goals Per Game	Attendance Overall	Attendance Per Game
1930	Uruguay	So. America	13	18	189	70	3.8	589,300	32,739
1934	Italy	Europe	16	17	208	70	4.1	361,000	21,235
1938	France	Europe	15	18	210	84	4.7	376,000	20,889
1942-46	Not held								
1950	Brazil	So. America	13	22	192	88	4.0	1,044,763	47,489
1954	Switzerland	Europe	16	26	233	140	5.3	872,000	33,538
1958	Sweden	Europe	16	35	241	126	3.6	819,402	23,411
1962	Chile	So. America	16	32	252	89	2.8	892,812	27,900
1966	England	Europe	16	32	254	89	2.8	1,464,944	45,780
1970	Mexico	No. America	16	32	270	95	3.0	1,690,890	52,840
1974	West Germany	Europe	16	38	264	97	2.6	1,809,953	47,630
1978	Argentina	So. America	16	38	277	102	2.7	1,685,602	44,358
1982	Spain	Europe	24	52	396	146	2.8	2,108,723	40,552
1986	Mexico	No. America	24	52	414	132	2.5	2,393,031	46,020
1990	Italy	Europe	24	52	413	115	2.2	2,516,354	48,391
1994	United States	No. America	24	52	437	140	2.7	3,587,088	68,982
1998	France	Europe	32	64	704	171	2.7	2,775,400	43,366

World Team of the 20th Century

The team, comprised of the century's best players, was voted on by a panel that included 250 international soccer journalists and released on June 10, 1998 in conjunction with the opening of the 1998 World Cup. The panel first selected the European and South American Teams of the Century and then chose the World Team from those two lists.

World Team

Pos		Pos	
GK	Lev Yashin, Soviet Union	MF	Alfredo Di Stefano, Argentina
D	Carlos Alberto, Brazil	MF	Michel Platini, France
D	Franz Beckenbauer, West Germany	F	Pele, Brazil
D	Bobby Moore, England	F	Garrincha, Brazil
D	Nilton Santos, Brazil	F	Diego Maradona, Argentina
MF	Johan Cryuff, Netherlands		

European Team

Pos	
GK	Lev Yashin, Soviet Union
D	Paolo Maldini, Italy
D	Franz Beckenbauer, West Germany
D	Bobby Moore, England
D	Franco Baresi, Italy
MF	Johan Cryuff, Netherlands
MF	Eusebio, Portugal
MF	Michel Platini, France
F	Ferenc Puskas, Hungary
F	Bobby Charlton, England
F	Marco Van Basten, Netherlands

South American Team

Pos	
GK	Ubaldo Fillol, Argentina
D	Carlos Alberto, Brazil
D	Elias Figueroa, Chile
D	Daniel Passarella, Argentina
D	Nilton Santos, Brazil
MF	Didi, Brazil
MF	Alfredo Di Stefano, Argentina
MF	Rivelino, Brazil
F	Pele, Brazil
F	Garrincha, Brazil
F	Diego Maradona, Argentina

World Cup Shootouts

Introduced in 1982; winning sides in **bold** type.

Year	Round		Final	SO	Year	Round		Final	SO
1982	Semi	**W. Germany** vs. France	3-3	(5-4)		Semi	**W. Germany** vs. England	1-1	(4-3)
1986	Quarter	**Belgium** vs. Spain	1-1	(5-4)					
	Quarter	**France** vs. Brazil	1-1	(4-3)	1994	Second	**Bulgaria** vs. Mexico	1-1	(3-1)
	Quarter	**W. Germany** vs. Mexico	0-0	(4-1)		Quarter	**Sweden** vs. Romania	2-2	(5-4)
1990	Second	**Ireland** vs. Romania	0-0	(5-4)		Final	**Brazil** vs. Italy	0-0	(3-2)
	Quarter	**Argentina** vs. Yugoslavia	0-0	(3-2)	1998	Second	**Argentina** vs. England	2-2	(4-3)
	Semi	**Argentina** vs. Italy	1-1	(4-3)		Quarter	**France** vs. Italy	0-0	(4-3)

OTHER WORLDWIDE COMPETITION

The Olympic Games

Held every four years since 1896, except during World War I (1916) and World War II (1940-44). Soccer was not a medal sport in 1896 at Athens or in 1932 at Los Angeles. By agreement between FIFA and the IOC, Olympic soccer competition is currently limited to players 23-years old and under with a few exceptions. See Olympics chapter for 2000 results.

Multiple winners: England and Hungary (3); Soviet Union and Uruguay (2).

MEN

Year		Year	
1900	**England**, France, Belgium	1956	**Soviet Union**, Yugoslavia, Bulgaria
1904	**Canada**, USA I, USA II	1960	**Yugoslavia**, Denmark, Hungary
1906	**Denmark**, Smyrna (Int'l entry), Greece	1964	**Hungary**, Czechoslovakia, East Germany
1908	**England**, Denmark, Holland	1968	**Hungary**, Bulgaria, Japan
1912	**England**, Denmark, Holland	1972	**Poland**, Hungary, East Germany
1920	**Belgium**, Spain, Holland	1976	**East Germany**, Poland, Soviet Union
1924	**Uruguay**, Switzerland, Sweden	1980	**Czechoslovakia**, East Germany, Soviet Union
1928	**Uruguay**, Argentina, Italy	1984	**France**, Brazil, Yugoslavia
1936	**Italy**, Austria, Norway	1988	**Soviet Union**, Brazil, West Germany
1948	**Sweden**, Yugoslavia, Denmark	1992	**Spain**, Poland, Ghana
1952	**Hungary**, Yugoslavia, Sweden	1996	**Nigeria**, Argentina, Brazil

WOMEN

Year	
1996	**USA**, China, Norway

The Under-20 World Cup

Held every two years since 1977. Officially, the World Youth Championship for the FIFA/Coca-Cola Cup.

Multiple winners: Argentina and Brazil (3); Portugal (2).

Year		Year	
1977	Soviet Union	1991	Portugal
1979	Argentina	1993	Brazil
1981	West Germany	1995	Argentina
1983	Brazil	1997	Argentina
1985	Brazil	1999	Spain
1987	Yugoslavia	2001	(at Argentina)
1989	Portugal		

The Under-17 World Cup

Held every two years since 1985. Officially, the U-17 World Tournament for the FIFA/JVC Cup.

Multiple winners: Brazil, Ghana and Nigeria (2).

Year		Year	
1985	Nigeria	1995	Ghana
1987	Soviet Union	1997	Brazil
1989	Saudi Arabia	1999	Brazil
1991	Ghana	2001	(at Trinidad &
1993	Nigeria		Tobago)

Indoor World Championship

First held in 1989. FIFA's only Five-a-Side tournament.

Multiple winners: Brazil (3).

Year		Year	
1989	Brazil	1996	Brazil
1992	Brazil	2000	(at Guatemala)

Women's World Cup

First held in 1991. Officially, the FIFA Women's World Championship.

Multiple winners: United States (2).

Year		Year	
1991	United States	1999	United States
1995	Norway		

Confederations Cup

First held in 1992. Contested by the Continental champions of Africa, Asia, Europe, North America and South America and originally called the Intercontinental Championship for the King Fahd Cup until it was redubbed the FIFA/Confederations Cup for the King Fahd Trophy in 1997.

Year		Year	
1992	Argentina	1997	Brazil
1995	Denmark	1999	Mexico

CONTINENTAL COMPETITION

European Championship

Held every four years since 1960. Officially, the European Football Championship. Winners receive the Henri Delaunay trophy, named for the Frenchman who first proposed the idea of a European Soccer Championship in 1927. The first one would not be played until five years after his death in 1955.

Multiple winners: France and West Germany (2).

Year		Year		Year		Year	
1960	Soviet Union	1972	West Germany	1984	France	1996	Germany
1964	Spain	1976	Czechoslovakia	1988	Holland	2000	France
1968	Italy	1980	West Germany	1992	Denmark		

Copa America

Held irregularly since 1916. Unofficially, the Championship of South America.

Multiple winners: Argentina and Uruguay (14); Brazil (6); Paraguay and Peru (2).

Year	Year	Year	Year	Year
1916 Uruguay	1925 Argentina	1942 Uruguay	1957 Argentina	1987 Uruguay
1917 Uruguay	1926 Uruguay	1945 Argentina	1958 Argentina	1989 Brazil
1919 Brazil	1927 Argentina	1946 Argentina	1959 Uruguay	1991 Argentina
1920 Uruguay	1929 Argentina	1947 Argentina	1963 Bolivia	1993 Argentina
1921 Argentina	1935 Uruguay	1949 Brazil	1967 Uruguay	1995 Uruguay
1922 Brazil	1937 Argentina	1953 Paraguay	1975 Peru	1997 Brazil
1923 Uruguay	1939 Peru	1955 Argentina	1979 Paraguay	1999 Brazil
1924 Uruguay	1941 Argentina	1956 Uruguay	1983 Uruguay	2001 (at Colombia)

African Nations Cup

Contested since 1957 and held every two years since 1968.

Multiple winners: Egypt and Ghana (4); Cameroon and Congo/Zaire (3); Nigeria (2).

Year	Year	Year	Year	Year
1957 Egypt	1968 Zaire	1978 Ghana	1988 Cameroon	1998 Egypt
1959 Egypt	1970 Sudan	1980 Nigeria	1990 Algeria	2000 Cameroon
1962 Ethiopia	1972 Congo	1982 Ghana	1992 Ivory Coast	2002 (at Mali)
1963 Ghana	1974 Zaire	1984 Cameroon	1994 Nigeria	2004 (at Tunisia)
1965 Ghana	1976 Morocco	1986 Egypt	1996 South Africa	

CONCACAF Gold Cup

The Confederation of North, Central American and Caribbean Football Championship. Contested irregularly from 1963-81 and revived as CONCACAF Gold Cup in 1991.

Multiple winners: Mexico (6); Costa Rica (2).

Year	Year	Year	Year	Year
1963 Costa Rica	1969 Costa Rica	1977 Mexico	1993 Mexico	2000 Canada
1965 Mexico	1971 Mexico	1981 Honduras	1996 Mexico	
1967 Guatemala	1973 Haiti	1991 United States	1998 Mexico	

CLUB COMPETITION

Toyota Cup

Also known as the Intercontinental Cup. Contested annually in December between the winners of the European Champions League (formerly European Cup) and South America's Copa Libertadores for the unofficial World Club Championship. Four European Cup winners refused to participate in the championship match in the 1970s and were replaced each time by the European Cup runner-up: Panathinaikos (Greece) for Ajax Amsterdam (Holland) in 1971; Juventus (Italy) for Ajax in 1973; Atlético Madrid (Spain) for Bayern Munich (West Germany) in 1974; and Malmo (Sweden) for Nottingham Forest (England) in 1979. Another European Cup winner, Marseille of France, was prohibited by the Union of European Football Associations (UEFA) from playing for the 1993 Toyota Cup because of its involvement in the match-rigging scandal.

Best-of-three game format from 1960-68, then a two-game/total goals format from 1969-79. Toyota became Cup sponsor in 1980, changed the format to a one-game championship and moved it to Toyko.

Multiple winners: AC Milan, Nacional and Penarol (3); Ajax Amsterdam, Independiente, Inter Milan, Juventus, Real Madrid, Santos and Sao Paulo (2).

Year	Year	Year
1960 Real Madrid (Spain)	1973 Independiente (Argentina)	1986 River Plate (Argentina)
1961 Peñarol (Uruguay)	1974 Atlético Madrid (Spain)	1987 FC Porto (Portugal)
1962 Santos (Brazil)	1975 Not held	1988 Nacional (Uruguay)
1963 Santos (Brazil)	1976 Bayern Munich (W. Germany)	1989 AC Milan (Italy)
1964 Inter Milan (Italy)	1977 Boca Juniors (Argentina)	1990 AC Milan (Italy)
1965 Inter Milan (Italy)	1978 Not held	1991 Red Star (Yugoslavia)
1966 Penarol (Uruguay)	1979 Olimpia (Paraguay)	1992 Sao Paulo (Brazil)
1967 Racing Club (Argentina)	1980 Nacional (Uruguay)	1993 Sao Paulo (Brazil)
1968 Estudiantes (Argentina)	1981 Flamengo (Brazil)	1994 Velez Sarsfield (Argentina)
1969 AC Milan (Italy)	1982 Peñarol (Uruguay)	1995 Ajax Amsterdam (Holland)
1970 Feyenoord (Holland)	1983 Gremio (Brazil)	1996 Juventus (Italy)
1971 Nacional (Uruguay)	1984 Independiente (Argentina)	1997 Borussia Dortmund (Germany)
1972 Ajax Amsterdam (Holland)	1985 Juventus (Italy)	1998 Real Madrid (Spain)
		1999 Manchester United (England)

European Cup/Champions League

Contested annually since the 1955-56 season by the league champions of the member countries of the Union of European Football Associations (UEFA). In 1999, UEFA announced the formation of a new competition called the UEFA Champions League to take the place of the Cup competition. See further explanation on page 731.

Multiple winners: Real Madrid (8); AC Milan (5); Ajax Amsterdam and Liverpool (4); Bayern Munich (3); Benfica, Inter-Milan, Juventus and Nottingham Forest (2).

Year	Year	Year
1956 Real Madrid (Spain)	1958 Real Madrid (Spain)	1960 Real Madrid (Spain)
1957 Real Madrid (Spain)	1959 Real Madrid (Spain)	1961 Benfica (Portugal)

Year	Year	Year
1962 Benfica (Portugal)	1975 Bayern Munich (W. Germany)	1988 PSV Eindhoven (Holland)
1963 AC Milan (Italy)	1976 Bayern Munich (W. Germany)	1989 AC Milan (Italy)
1964 Inter Milan (Italy)	1977 Liverpool (England)	
1965 Inter Milan (Italy)	1978 Liverpool (England)	1990 AC Milan (Italy)
1966 Real Madrid (Spain)	1979 Nottingham Forest (England)	1991 Red Star Belgrade (Yugo.)
1967 Glasgow Celtic (Scotland)		1992 Barcelona (Spain)
1968 Manchester United (England)	1980 Nottingham Forest (England)	1993 Marseille (France)*
1969 AC Milan (Italy)	1981 Liverpool (England)	1994 AC Milan (Italy)
	1982 Aston Villa (England)	1995 Ajax Amsterdam (Holland)
1970 Feyenoord (Holland)	1983 SV Hamburg (W. Germany)	1996 Juventus (Italy)
1971 Ajax Amsterdam (Holland)	1984 Liverpool (England)	1997 Borussia Dortmund (Germany)
1972 Ajax Amsterdam (Holland)	1985 Juventus (Italy)	1998 Real Madrid (Spain)
1973 Ajax Amsterdam (Holland)	1986 Steaua Bucharest (Romania)	1999 Manchester United (England)
1974 Bayern Munich (W. Germany)	1987 FC Porto (Portugal)	
		2000 Real Madrid (Spain)

*title vacated

European Cup Winner's Cup

Contested annually since the 1960-61 season by the cup winners of the member countries of the Union of European Football Associations (UEFA). The Cup Winner's Cup was absorbed by the UEFA Cup in 2000.

Multiple winners: Barcelona (4); AC Milan, RSC Anderlecht, Chelsea and Dinamo Kiev (2).

Year	Year	Year
1961 Fiorentina (Italy)	1975 Dinamo Kiev (USSR)	1989 Barcelona (Spain)
1962 Atletico Madrid (Spain)	1976 RSC Anderlecht (Belgium)	
1963 Tottenham Hotspur (England)	1977 SV Hamburg (W. Germany)	1990 Sampdoria (Italy)
1964 Sporting Lisbon (Portugal)	1978 RSC Anderlecht (Belgium)	1991 Manchester United (England)
1965 West Ham United (England)	1979 Barcelona (Spain)	1992 Werder Bremen (Germany)
1966 Borussia Dortmund (W.Germany)		1993 Parma (Italy)
1967 Bayern Munich (W. Germany)	1980 Valencia (Spain)	1994 Arsenal (England)
1968 AC Milan (Italy)	1981 Dinamo Tbilisi (USSR)	1995 Real Zaragoza (Spain)
1969 Slovan Bratislava (Czech.)	1982 Barcelona (Spain)	1996 Paris St. Germain (France)
	1983 Aberdeen (Scotland)	1997 Barcelona (Spain)
1970 Manchester City (England)	1984 Juventus (Italy)	1998 Chelsea (England)
1971 Chelsea (England)	1985 Everton (England)	1999 Lazio (Italy)
1972 Glasgow Rangers (Scotland)	1986 Dinamo Kiev (USSR)	
1973 AC Milan (Italy)	1987 Ajax Amsterdam (Holland)	2000 discontinued
1974 FC Magdeburg (E. Germany)	1988 Mechelen (Belgium)	

UEFA Cup

Contested annually since the 1957-58 season by teams other than league champions and cup winners of the Union of European Football Associations (UEFA). Teams selected by UEFA based on each country's previous performance in the tournament. Teams from England were banned from UEFA Cup play from 1985-90 for the criminal behavior of their supporters. In 1999, with the formation of the new Champions League, UEFA announced that the UEFA Cup would be expanded and include any teams that would have normally played in the Cup Winner's Cup.

Multiple winners: Barcelona, Inter Milan and Juventus (3); Borussia Mönchengladbach, IFK Göteborg, Leeds United, Liverpool, Parma, Real Madrid, Tottenham Hotspur and Valencia (2).

Year	Year	Year
1958 Barcelona (Spain)	1973 Liverpool (England)	1986 Real Madrid (Spain)
1959 Not held	1974 Feyenoord (Holland)	1987 IFK Göteborg (Sweden)
	1975 Borussia Mönchengladbach (W. Germany)	1988 Bayer Leverkusen (W. Germany)
1960 Barcelona (Spain)		1989 Napoli (Italy)
1961 AS Roma (Italy)	1976 Liverpool (England)	
1962 Valencia (Spain)	1977 Juventus (Italy)	1990 Juventus (Italy)
1963 Valencia (Spain)	1978 PSV Eindhoven (Holland)	1991 Inter Milan (Italy)
1964 Real Zaragoza (Spain)	1979 Borussia Mönchengladbach (W. Germany)	1992 Ajax Amsterdam (Holland)
1965 Ferencvaros (Hungary)		1993 Juventus (Italy)
1966 Barcelona (Spain)	1980 Eintracht Frankfurt (W. Germany)	1994 Inter Milan (Italy)
1967 Dinamo Zagreb (Yugoslavia)	1981 Ipswich Town (England)	1995 Parma (Italy)
1968 Leeds United (England)	1982 IFK Göteborg (Sweden)	1996 Bayern Munich (Germany)
1969 Newcastle United (England)	1983 RSC Anderlecht (Belgium)	1997 Schalke 04 (Germany)
1970 Arsenal (England)	1984 Tottenham Hotspur (England)	1998 Inter Milan (Italy)
1971 Leeds United (England)	1985 Real Madrid (Spain)	1999 Parma (Italy)
1972 Tottenham Hotspur (England)		
		2000 Galatasaray (Turkey)

Copa Libertadores

Contested annually since the 1955-56 season by the league champions of South America's football union.

Multiple winners: Independiente (7); Peñarol (5); Estudiantes and Nacional-Uruguay (3); Boca Juniors, Cruzeiro, Gremio, Olimpia, River Plate, Santos and São Paulo (2).

Year	Year	Year
1960 Peñarol (Uruguay)	1966 Peñarol (Uruguay)	1971 Nacional (Uruguay)
1961 Peñarol (Uruguay)	1967 Racing Club (Argentina)	1972 Independiente (Argentina)
1962 Santos (Brazil)	1968 Estudiantes de la Plata (Argentina)	1973 Independiente (Argentina)
1963 Santos (Brazil)	1969 Estudiantes de la Plata (Argentina)	1974 Independiente (Argentina)
1964 Independiente (Argentina)	1970 Estudiantes de la Plata (Argentina)	1975 Independiente (Argentina)
1965 Independiente (Argentina)		1976 Cruzeiro (Brazil)

Year		Year		Year	
1977	Boca Juniors (Argentina)	1985	Argentinos Jrs. (Argentina)	1993	São Paulo (Brazil)
1978	Boca Juniors (Argentina)	1986	River Plate (Argentina)	1994	Velez Sarsfield (Argentina)
1979	Olimpia (Paraguay)	1987	Peñarol (Uruguay)	1995	Gremio (Brazil)
1980	Nacional (Uruguay)	1988	Nacional (Uruguay)	1996	River Plate (Argentina)
1981	Flamengo (Brazil)	1989	Nacional Medellin (Colombia)	1997	Cruzeiro (Brazil)
1982	Peñarol (Uruguay)			1998	Vasco da Gama (Brazil)
1983	Gremio (Brazil)	1990	Olimpia (Paraguay)	1999	Palmeiras (Brazil)
1984	Independiente (Argentina)	1991	Colo Colo (Chile)		
		1992	São Paulo (Brazil)		

Annual Awards
World Player of the Year

Presented by FIFA, the European Sports Magazine Association (ESM) and Adidas, the sports equipment manufacturer, since 1991. Winners are selected by national team coaches from around the world.

Year		Nat'l Team	Year		Nat'l Team
1991	Lothar Matthäus, Inter Milan	Germany	1996	Ronaldo, Barcelona	Brazil
1992	Marco Van Basten, AC Milan	Holland	1997	Ronaldo, Inter Milan	Brazil
1993	Roberto Baggio, Juventus	Italy	1998	Zinedine Zidane, Juventus	France
1994	Romario, Barcelona	Brazil	1999	Rivaldo, Barcelona	Brazil
1995	George Weah, AC Milan	Liberia			

European Player of the Year

Officially, the "Ballon d'Or" and presented by *France Football* magazine since 1956. Candidates are limited to European players in European leagues and winners are selected by a panel of 49 European soccer journalists.

Multiple winners: Johan Cruyff, Michel Platini and Marco Van Basten (3); Franz Beckenbauer, Alfredo di Stéfano, Kevin Keegan and Karl-Heinz Rummenigge (2).

Year		Nat'l Team	Year		Nat'l Team
1956	Stanley Matthews, Blackpool	England	1978	Kevin Keegan, SV Hamburg	England
1957	Alfredo di Stéfano, Real Madrid	Arg./Spain	1979	Kevin Keegan, SV Hamburg	England
1958	Raymond Kopa, Real Madrid	France	1980	K.H. Rummenigge, Bayern Munich	W. Ger.
1959	Alfredo di Stéfano, Real Madrid	Arg./Spain	1981	K.H. Rummenigge, Bayern Munich	W. Ger.
1960	Luis Suarez, Barcelona	Spain	1982	Paolo Rossi, Juventus	Italy
1961	Enrique Sivori, Juventus	Arg./Italy	1983	Michel Platini, Juventus	France
1962	Josef Masopust, Dukla Prague	Czech.	1984	Michel Platini, Juventus	France
1963	Lev Yashin, Dinamo Moscow	Soviet Union	1985	Michel Platini, Juventus	France
1964	Denis Law, Manchester United	Scotland	1986	Igor Belanov, Dinamo Kiev	Soviet Union
1965	Eusébio, Benfica	Portugal	1987	Ruud Gullit, AC Milan	Holland
1966	Bobby Charlton, Manchester United	England	1988	Marco Van Basten, AC Milan	Holland
1967	Florian Albert, Ferencvaros	Hungary	1989	Marco Van Basten, AC Milan	Holland
1968	George Best, Manchester United	No. Ireland	1990	Lothar Matthäus, Inter Milan	W. Ger.
1969	Gianni Rivera, AC Milan	Italy	1991	Jean-Pierre Papin, Marseille	France
1970	Gerd Müller, Bayern Munich	W. Ger.	1992	Marco Van Basten, AC Milan	Holland
1971	Johan Cruyff, Ajax Amsterdam	Holland	1993	Roberto Baggio, Juventus	Italy
1972	Franz Beckenbauer, Bayern Munich	W. Ger.	1994	Hristo Stoitchkov, Barcelona	Bulgaria
1973	Johan Cruyff, Barcelona	Holland	1995	George Weah, AC Milan	Liberia
1974	Johan Cruyff, Barcelona	Holland	1996	Matthias Sammer, Bor. Dortmund	Germany
1975	Oleg Blokhin, Dinamo Kiev	Soviet Union	1997	Ronaldo, Inter Milan	Brazil
1976	Franz Beckenbauer, Bayern Munich	W. Ger.	1998	Zinedine Zidane, Juventus	France
1977	Allan Simonsen, B. Mönchengladbach	Denmark	1999	Rivaldo, Barcelona	Brazil

South American Player of the Year

Presented by El Pais of Uruguay since 1971. Candidates are limited to South American players in South American leagues and winners are selected by a panel of 80 Latin American sports editors.

Multiple winners: Elias Figueroa and Zico (3); Enzo Francescoli, Diego Maradona and Carlos Valderrama (2).

Year		Nat'l Team	Year		Nat'l Team
1971	Tostao, Cruzeiro	Brazil	1985	Julio Cesar Romero, Fluminense	Paraguay
1972	Teofilo Cubillas, Alianza Lima	Peru	1986	Antonio Alzamendi, River Plate	Uruguay
1973	Pelé, Santos	Brazil	1987	Carlos Valderrama, Deportivo Cali	Colombia
1974	Elias Figueroa, Internacional	Chile	1988	Ruben Paz, Racing Buenos Aires	Uruguay
1975	Elias Figueroa, Internacional	Chile	1989	Bebeto, Vasco da Gama	Brazil
1976	Elias Figueroa, Internacional	Chile	1990	Raul Amarilla, Olimpia	Paraguay
1977	Zico, Flamengo	Brazil	1991	Oscar Ruggeri, Velez Sarsfield	Argentina
1978	Mario Kempes, Valencia	Argentina	1992	Rai, Sao Paulo	Brazil
1979	Diego Maradona, Argentinos Juniors	Argentina	1993	Carlos Valderrama, Atl. Junior	Colombia
1980	Diego Maradona, Boca Juniors	Argentina	1994	Cafu, Sao Paulo	Brazil
1981	Zico, Flamengo	Brazil	1995	Enzo Francescoli, River Plate	Uruguay
1982	Zico, Flamengo	Brazil	1996	Jose Luis Chilavert, Velez Sarsfield	Paraguay
1983	Socrates, Corinthians	Brazil	1997	Marcelo Salas, River Plate	Chile
1984	Enzo Francescoli, River Plate	Uruguay	1998	Martin Palermo, Boca Juniors	Argentina
			1999	Javier Saviola, River Plate	Argentina

African Player of the Year

Officially, the African "Ballon d'Or" and presented by *France Football* magazine from 1970-96. The Arican Player of the Year award has been presented by the CAF (African Football Confederation) since 1997. All African players are eligible for the award.

Multiple winners: George Weah and Abedi Pelé (3); Nwankwo Kanu, Roger Milla and Thomas N'Kono (2).

Year		Year		Year	
1970	Salif Keita, Mali	1980	Jean Manga Onguene, Cameroon	1990	Roger Milla, Cameroon
1971	Ibrahim Sunday, Ghana	1981	Lakhdar Belloumi, Algeria	1991	Abedi Pelé, Ghana
1972	Cherif Souleymane, Guinea	1982	Thomas N'Kono, Cameroon	1992	Abedi Pelé, Ghana
1973	Tshimimu Bwanga, Zaire	1983	Mahmoud Al-Khatib, Egypt	1993	Abedi Pelé, Ghana
1974	Paul Moukila, Congo	1984	Theophile Abega, Cameroon	1994	George Weah, Liberia
1975	Ahmed Faras, Morocco	1985	Mohamed Timoumi, Morocco	1995	George Weah, Liberia
1976	Roger Milla, Cameroon	1986	Badou Zaki, Morocco	1996	Nwankwo Kanu, Nigeria
1977	Dhiab Tarak, Tunisia	1987	Rabah Madjer, Algeria	1997	Victor Ikpeba, Nigeria
1978	Abdul Razak, Ghana	1988	Kalusha Bwalya, Zambia	1998	Mustapha Hadji, Morocco
1979	Thomas N'Kono, Cameroon	1989	George Weah, Liberia	1999	Nwankwo Kanu, Nigeria

U.S. Player of the Year

Presented by Honda and the Spanish-speaking radio show "Futbol de Primera" since 1991. Candidates are limited to American players who have played with the U.S. National Team and winners are selected by a panel of U.S. soccer journalists.

Multiple winner: Eric Wynalda (2).

Year		Year		Year		Year		Year	
1991	Hugo Perez	1993	Thomas Dooley	1995	Alexi Lalas	1997	Eddie Pope	1999	Kasey Keller
1992	Eric Wynalda	1994	Marcelo Balboa	1996	Eric Wynalda	1998	Cobi Jones		

U.S. PRO LEAGUES

OUTDOOR

Major League Soccer

Sanctioned by U.S. Soccer and FIFA, the international soccer federation. MLS was founded on the heels of the successful 1994 World Cup tournament hosted by the United States and it remains the only FIFA-sanctioned division I outdoor league in the United States. The annual MLS title game is known as the MLS Cup.

Multiple Winner: D.C. United (3).

MLS Cup

Year	Winner	Head Coach	Score	Loser	Head Coach	Site
1996	D.C. United	Bruce Arena	3-2	Los Angeles Galaxy	Lothar Osiander	Foxboro, Mass.
1997	D.C. United	Bruce Arena	2-1	Colorado Rapids	Glen Myernick	Washington, D.C.
1998	Chicago Fire	Bob Bradley	2-0	D.C. United	Bruce Arena	Pasadena, Calif.
1999	D.C. United	Thomas Rongen	2-0	Los Angeles Galaxy	Sigi Schmid	Foxboro, Mass.
2000	K.C. Wizards	Bob Gansler	1-0	Chicago Fire	Bob Bradley	Washington, D.C.

MLS Cup '96
D.C. United, 3-2 (OT)
Oct. 20 at Foxboro Stadium, Foxboro, Mass.
Attendance: 34,643

	1	2	OT	
Los Angeles Galaxy	1	1	0	—2
D.C. United	0	2	1	—3

First Half: LA–Eduardo Hurtado (Mauricio Cienfuegos), 5th minute.
Second Half: LA–Chris Armas (unassisted), 56th; DC–Tony Sanneh (Marco Etcheverry), 73rd; DC–Shawn Medved (unassisted), 82nd.
Overtime: DC–Eddie Pope (Etcheverry), 94th.
MVP: Marco Etcheverry, D.C. United, Midfielder

MLS Cup '97
D.C. United, 2-1
Oct. 26 at RFK Stadium, Washington, D.C.
Attendance: 57,431

	1	2	
Colorado Rapids	0	1	—1
D.C. United	1	1	—2

First Half: DC–Jaime Moreno (Tony Sanneh, David Vaudreuil), 37th minute.
Second Half: DC–Sanneh (John Harkes, Richie Williams), 68th; COL–Adrian Paz (David Patino, Matt Kmosko), 75th.
MVP: Jaime Moreno, D.C. United, Forward

MLS Cup '98
Chicago Fire, 2-0
Oct. 25 at the Rose Bowl, Pasadena, Calif.
Attendance: 51,350

	1	2	
D.C. United	0	0	—0
Chicago	2	0	—2

First Half: CHI–Jerzy Podbrozny (Peter Nowak, Ante Razov), 29th minute; CHI–Diego Gutierrez (Nowak), 45th.
MVP: Nowak, Chicago, Midfielder

MLS Cup '99
D.C. United, 2-0
Nov. 21 at Foxboro Stadium, Foxboro, Mass..
Attendance: 44,910

	1	2	
D.C. United	2	0	—2
Los Angeles	0	0	—0

First Half: DC– Jaime Moreno (Roy Lassiter), 19th minute; DC–Ben Olsen (unassisted), 48th
MVP: Olsen, D.C. United, Midfielder

Regular Season

Most Valuable Player		Leading Scorer	G	A	Pts
1996	Carlos Valderrama, Tampa Bay	1996 Roy Lassiter, Tampa Bay	27	4	58
1997	Preki, Kansas City	1997 Preki, Kansas City	12	17	41
1998	Marco Etcheverry, D.C.	1998 Stern John, Columbus	26	5	57
1999	Jason Kreis, Dallas	1999 Jason Kreis, Dallas	18	15	51
2000	Tony Meola, Kansas City	2000 Mamadou Diallo, Tampa Bay	26	4	56

National Professional Soccer League (1967)

Not sanctioned by FIFA, the international soccer federation. The NPSL recruited individual players to fill the rosters of its 10 teams. The league lasted only one season.

	Playoff Final			Regular Season			
Year	Winner	Scores	Loser	Leading Scorer	G	A	Pts
1967	Oakland Clippers	0-1, 4-1	Baltimore Bays	Yanko Daucik, Toronto	20	8	48

United Soccer Association (1967)

Sanctioned by FIFA. Originally called the North American Soccer League, it became the USA to avoid being confused with the National Professional Soccer League (see above). Instead of recruiting individual players, the USA imported 12 entire teams from Europe to represent its 12 franchises. It, too, only lasted a season. The league champion Los Angeles Wolves were actually Wolverhampton of England and the runner-up Washington Whips were Aberdeen of Scotland.

	Playoff Final			Regular Season			
Year	Winner	Score	Loser	Leading Scorer	G	A	Pts
1967	Los Angeles Wolves	6-5 (OT)	Washington Whips	Roberto Boninsegna, Chicago	10	1	21

North American Soccer League (1968-84)

The NPSL and USA merged to form the NASL in 1968 and the new league lasted through 1984. The NASL championship was known as the Soccer Bowl from 1975-84. One game decided the NASL title every year but five. There were no playoffs in 1969; a two-game/aggregate goals format was used in 1968 and '70; and a best-of-three games format was used in 1971 and '84; (*) indicates overtime and (†) indicates game decided by shootout.

Multiple winners: NY Cosmos (5); Chicago (2).

	Playoff Final			Regular Season			
Year	Winner	Score(s)	Loser	Leading Scorer	G	A	Pts
1968	Atlanta Chiefs	0-0,3-0	San Diego Toros	John Kowalik, Chicago	30	9	69
1969	Kansas City Spurs	No game	Atlanta Chiefs	Kaiser Motaung, Atlanta	16	4	36
1970	Rochester Lancers	3-0,1-3	Washington Darts	Kirk Apostolidis, Dallas	16	3	35
1971	Dallas Tornado	1-2*,4-1,2-0	Atlanta Chiefs	Carlos Metidieri, Rochester	19	8	46
1972	New York Cosmos	2-1	St. Louis Stars	Randy Horton, New York	9	4	22
1973	Philadelphia Atoms	2-0	Dallas Tornado	Kyle Rote Jr., Dallas	10	10	30
1974	Los Angeles Aztecs	3-3†	Miami Toros	Paul Child, San Jose	15	6	36
1975	Tampa Bay Rowdies	2-0	Portland Timbers	Steve David, Miami	23	6	52
1976	Toronto Metros	3-0	Minnesota Kicks	Giorgio Chinaglia, New York	19	11	49
1977	New York Cosmos	2-1	Seattle Sounders	Steve David, Los Angeles	26	6	58
1978	New York Cosmos	3-1	Tampa Bay Rowdies	Giorgio Chinaglia, New York	34	11	79
1979	Vancouver Whitecaps	2-1	Tampa Bay Rowdies	Oscar Fabbiani, Tampa Bay	25	8	58
1980	New York Cosmos	3-0	Ft. Laud. Strikers	Giorgio Chinaglia, New York	32	13	77
1981	Chicago Sting	0-0†	New York Cosmos	Giorgio Chinaglia, New York	29	16	74
1982	New York Cosmos	1-0	Seattle Sounders	Giorgio Chinaglia, New York	20	15	55
1983	Tulsa Roughnecks	2-0	Toronto Blizzard	Roberto Cabanas, New York	25	16	66
1984	Chicago Sting	2-1,3-2	Toronto Blizzard	Steve Zungul, Golden Bay	20	10	50

Note: In 1969, Kansas City won the NASL regular season championship with 110 points to 109 for Atlanta. There were no playoffs.

Regular Season MVP

Regular season Most Valuable Player as designated by the NASL.

Multiple winner: Carlos Metidieri (2).

Year		Year		Year	
1967	Rueben Navarro, Phila (NPSL)	1974	Peter Silvester, Baltimore	1981	Giorgio Chinaglia, New York
1968	John Kowalik, Chicago	1975	Steve David, Miami	1982	Peter Ward, Seattle
1969	Cirilio Fernandez, KC	1976	Pelé, New York	1983	Roberto Cabanas, New York
1970	Carlos Metidieri, Rochester	1977	Franz Beckenbauer, New York	1984	Steve Zungul, Golden Bay
1971	Carlos Metidieri, Rochester	1978	Mike Flanagan, New England		
1972	Randy Horton, New York	1979	Johan Cruyff, Los Angeles		
1973	Warren Archibald, Miami	1980	Roger Davies, Seattle		

A-League (American Professional Soccer League)

The American Professional Soccer League was formed in 1990 with the merger of the Western Soccer League and the New American Soccer League. The APSL was officially sanctioned as an outdoor pro league in 1992 and changed its name to the A-League in 1995.

Multiple winners: Colorado and Seattle (2).

Year		Year		Year		Year	
1990	Maryland Bays	1993	Colorado Foxes	1996	Seattle Sounders	1999	Minnesota Thunder
1991	SF Bay Blackhawks	1994	Montreal Impact	1997	Milwaukee Rampage		
1992	Colorado Foxes	1995	Seattle Sounders	1998	Rochester Rhinos		

INDOOR
Major Soccer League (1978-92)

Originally the Major Indoor Soccer League from 1978-79 season through 1989-90. The MISL championship was decided by one game in 1980 and 1981; a best-of-three games series in 1979, best-of-five games in 1982 and 1983; and best-of-seven games since 1984. The MSL folded after the 1991-92 season.

Multiple winners: San Diego (8); New York (4).

	Playoff Final			**Regular Season**			
Year	Winner	Series	Loser	Leading Scorer	G	A	Pts
1979	New York Arrows	2-0 (WW)	Philadelphia	Fred Grgurev, Philadelphia	46	28	74
1980	New York Arrows	7-4 (1 game)	Houston	Steve Zungul, New York	90	46	136
1981	New York Arrows	6-5 (1 game)	St. Louis	Steve Zungul, New York	108	44	152
1982	New York Arrows	3-2 (LWWLW)	St. Louis	Steve Zungul, New York	103	60	163
1983	San Diego Sockers	3-2 (WWLLW)	Baltimore	Steve Zungul, NY/Golden Bay	75	47	122
1984	Baltimore Blast	4-1 (LWWWW)	St. Louis	Stan Stamenkovic, Baltimore	34	63	97
1985	San Diego Sockers	4-1 (WWLWW)	Baltimore	Steve Zungul, San Diego	68	68	136
1986	San Diego Sockers	4-3 (WLLLWWW)	Minnesota	Steve Zungul, Tacoma	55	60	115
1987	Dallas Sidekicks	4-3 (LLWWLWW)	Tacoma	Tatu, Dallas	73	38	111
1988	San Diego Sockers	4-0	Cleveland	Eric Rasmussen, Wichita	55	57	112
1989	San Diego Sockers	4-3 (LWWWLLW)	Baltimore	Preki, Tacoma	51	53	104
1990	San Diego Sockers	4-2 (LWWWLW)	Baltimore	Tatu, Dallas	64	49	113
1991	San Diego Sockers	4-2 (WLWLWW)	Cleveland	Tatu, Dallas	78	66	144
1992	San Diego Sockers	4-2 (WWWLLW)	Dallas	Zoran Karic, Cleveland	39	63	102

Playoff MVPs

MSL playoff Most Valuable Players, selected by a panel of soccer media covering the playoffs.

Multiple winners: Steve Zungul (4); Brian Quinn (2).

Year		Year	
1979	Shep Messing, NY	1986	Brian Quinn, SD
1980	Steve Zungul, NY	1987	Tatu, Dallas
1981	Steve Zungul, NY	1988	Hugo Perez, SD
1982	Steve Zungul, NY	1989	Victor Nogueira, SD
1983	Juli Veee, SD	1990	Brian Quinn, SD
1984	Scott Manning, Bal.	1991	Ben Collins, SD
1985	Steve Zungul, SD	1992	Thompson Usiyan, SD

Regular Season MVPs

MSL regular season Most Valuable Players, selected by a panel of soccer media from every city in the league.

Multiple winners: Steve Zungul (6); Victor Nogueira and Tatu (2).

Year		Year	
1979	Steve Zungul, NY	1986	Steve Zungul, SD/Tac.
1980	Steve Zungul, NY	1987	Tatu, Dallas
1981	Steve Zungul, NY	1988	Erik Rasmussen, Wich.
1982	Steve Zungul, NY & Stan Terlecki, Pit.	1989	Preki, Tacoma
1983	Alan Mayer, SD	1990	Tatu, Dallas
1984	Stan Stamenkovic, Bal.	1991	Victor Nogueira, SD
1985	Steve Zungul, SD	1992	Victor Nogueira, SD

NASL Indoor Champions (1980-84)

The North American Soccer League started an indoor league in the fall of 1979. The indoor NASL, which featured many of the same teams and players who played in the outdoor NASL, crowned champions from 1980-82 before suspending play. It was revived for the 1983-84 indoor season but folded for good in 1984. The NASL held indoor tournaments in 1975 (San Jose Earthquakes won) and 1976 (Tampa Bay Rowdies won) before the indoor league was started.

Multiple winner: San Diego (2).

Year		Year		Year		Year	
1980	Tampa Bay Rowdies	1982	San Diego Sockers	1983	Play suspended	1984	San Diego Sockers
1981	Edmonton Drillers						

National Professional Soccer League

The winter indoor NPSL began as the American Indoor Soccer Association in 1984-85, then changed its name in 1989-90.

Multiple winners: Canton (5); Cleveland (3); Kansas City and Milwaukee (2).

Year		Year		Year		Year	
1985	Canton (OH) Invaders	1989	Canton Invaders	1993	Kansas City Attack	1997	Kansas City Attack
1986	Canton Invaders	1990	Canton Invaders	1994	Cleveland Crunch	1998	Milwaukee Wave
1987	Louisville Thunder	1991	Chicago Power	1995	St. Louis Ambush	1999	Cleveland Crunch
1988	Canton Invaders	1992	Detroit Rockers	1996	Cleveland Crunch	2000	Milwaukee Wave

Continental Indoor Soccer League (1993-97)

The summer indoor CISL played its first season in 1993 and folded following the 1997 season.

Multiple winner: Monterrey (2).

Year		Year		Year	
1993	Dallas Sidekicks	1995	Monterrey La Raza	1997	Seattle Seadogs
1994	Las Vegas Dustdevils	1996	Monterrey La Raza		

U.S. COLLEGES

NCAA Men's Division I Champions

NCAA Division I champions since the first title was contested in 1959. The championship has been shared three times—in 1967, 1968 and 1989. There was a playoff for third place from 1974-81.

Multiple winners: Saint Louis (10); Indiana, San Francisco and Virginia (5); UCLA (3); Clemson, Howard and Michigan St. (2).

Year	Winner	Head Coach	Score	Runner-up	Host/Site	Semifinalists
1959	Saint Louis	Bob Guelker	5-2	Bridgeport	UConn	West Chester, CCNY
1960	Saint Louis	Bob Guelker	3-2	Maryland	Brooklyn	West Chester, UConn
1961	West Chester	Mel Lorback	2-0	Saint Louis	Saint Louis	Bridgeport, Rutgers
1962	Saint Louis	Bob Guelker	4-3	Maryland	Saint Louis	Mich. St., Springfield
1963	Saint Louis	Bob Guelker	3-0	Navy	Rutgers	Army, Maryland
1964	Navy	F.H. Warner	1-0	Michigan St.	Brown	Army, Saint Louis
1965	Saint Louis	Bob Guelker	1-0	Michigan St.	Saint Louis	Army, Navy
1966	San Francisco	Steve Negoesco	5-2	LIU-Brooklyn	California	Army, Mich. St.
1967-a	Michigan St. & Saint Louis	Gene Kenney Harry Keough	0-0	—	Saint Louis	LIU-Bklyn, Navy
1968-b	Michigan St. & Maryland	Gene Kenney Doyle Royal	2-2 (2 OT)	—	Ga. Tech	Brown, San Jose St.
1969	Saint Louis	Harry Keough	4-0	San Francisco	San Jose St.	Harvard, Maryland
1970	Saint Louis	Harry Keough	1-0	UCLA	SIU-Ed'sville	Hartwick, Howard
1971-c	Howard	Lincoln Phillips	3-2	Saint Louis	Miami	Harvard, San Fran.
1972	Saint Louis	Harry Keough	4-2	UCLA	Miami	Cornell, Howard
1973	Saint Louis	Harry Keough	2-1 (OT)	UCLA	Miami	Brown, Clemson

Year	Winner	Head Coach	Score	Runner-up	Host/Site	Third Place
1974	Howard	Lincoln Phillips	2-1 (4OT)	Saint Louis	Saint Louis	Hartwick 3, UCLA 1
1975	San Francisco	Steve Negoesco	4-0	SIU-Ed'sville	SIU-Ed'sville	Brown 2, Howard 0
1976	San Francisco	Steve Negoesco	1-0	Indiana	Penn	Hartwick 4, Clemson 3
1977	Hartwick	Jim Lennox	2-1	San Francisco	California	SIU-Ed'sville 3, Brown 2
1978-d	San Francisco	Steve Negoesco	4-3 (OT)	Indiana	Tampa	Clemson 6, Phi. Textile 2
1979	SIU-Ed'sville	Bob Guelker	3-2	Clemson	Tampa	Penn St. 2, Columbia 1
1980	San Francisco	Steve Negoesco	4-3 (OT)	Indiana	Tampa	Ala. A&M 2, Hartwick 0
1981	Connecticut	Joe Morrone	2-1 (OT)	Alabama A&M	Stanford	East. Ill. 4, Phi. Textile 2

Year	Winner	Head Coach	Score	Runner-up	Host/Site	Semifinalists
1982	Indiana	Jerry Yeagley	2-1 (8 OT)	Duke	Ft. Lauderdale	UConn, SIU-Ed'sville
1983	Indiana	Jerry Yeagley	1-0 (2 OT)	Columbia	Ft. Lauderdale	UConn, Virginia
1984	Clemson	I.M. Ibrahim	2-1	Indiana	Seattle	Hartwick, UCLA
1985	UCLA	Sigi Schmid	1-0 (8 OT)	American	Seattle	Evansville, Hartwick
1986	Duke	John Rennie	1-0	Akron	Tacoma	Fresno St., Harvard
1987	Clemson	I.M. Ibrahim	2-0	San Diego St.	Clemson	Harvard, N. Carolina
1988	Indiana	Jerry Yeagley	1-0	Howard	Indiana	Portland, S. Carolina
1989-e	Santa Clara & Virginia	Steve Sampson Bruce Arena	1-1 (2 OT)	—	Rutgers	Indiana, Rutgers
1990-f	UCLA	Sigi Schmid	0-0 (PKs)	Rutgers	South Fla.	Evansville, N.C. State
1991-g	Virginia	Bruce Arena	0-0 (PKs)	Santa Clara	Tampa	Indiana, Saint Louis
1992	Virginia	Bruce Arena	2-0	San Diego	Davidson	Davidson, Duke
1993	Virginia	Bruce Arena	2-0	South Carolina	Davidson	CS-Fullerton, Princeton
1994	Virginia	Bruce Arena	1-0	Indiana	Davidson	Rutgers, UCLA
1995	Wisconsin	Jim Launder	2-0	Duke	Richmond	Portland, Virginia
1996	St. John's	Dave Masur	4-1	Fla. International	Richmond	Creighton, NC-Charlotte
1997	UCLA	Sigi Schmid	2-0	Virginia	Richmond	Indiana, Saint Louis
1998	Indiana	Jerry Yeagley	3-1	Stanford	Richmond	Maryland, Santa Clara
1999	Indiana	Jerry Yeagley	1-0	Santa Clara	Richmond	Connecticut, UCLA

a–game declared a draw due to inclement weather after regulation time; **b**–game declared a draw after two overtimes; **c**–Howard vacated title for using ineligible player; **d**–San Francisco vacated title for using ineligible player; **e**–game declared a draw due to inclement weather after two overtimes. **f**–UCLA wins on penalty kicks (4-3) after four overtimes; **g**–Virginia wins on penalty kicks (3-1) after four overtimes.

Women's NCAA Division I Champions

NCAA Division I women's champions since the first tournament was contested in 1982.

Multiple winner: North Carolina (15).

Year	Winner	Coach	Score	Runner-up	Host/Site
1982	North Carolina	Anson Dorrance	2-0	Central Florida	Central Florida
1983	North Carolina	Anson Dorrance	4-0	George Mason	Central Florida
1984	North Carolina	Anson Dorrance	2-0	Connecticut	North Carolina
1985	George Mason	Hank Leung	2-0	North Carolina	George Mason
1986	North Carolina	Anson Dorrance	2-0	Colorado College	George Mason
1987	North Carolina	Anson Dorrance	1-0	Massachusetts	Massachusetts
1988	North Carolina	Anson Dorrance	4-1	N.C. State	North Carolina
1989	North Carolina	Anson Dorrance	2-0	Colorado College	N.C. State
1990	North Carolina	Anson Dorrance	6-0	Connecticut	North Carolina
1991	North Carolina	Anson Dorrance	3-1	Wisconsin	North Carolina
1992	North Carolina	Anson Dorrance	9-1	Duke	North Carolina
1993	North Carolina	Anson Dorrance	6-0	George Mason	North Carolina
1994	North Carolina	Anson Dorrance	5-0	Notre Dame	Portland
1995	Notre Dame	Chris Petrucelli	1-0 (3OT)	Portland	North Carolina
1996	North Carolina	Anson Dorrance	1-0 (2OT)	Notre Dame	Santa Clara
1997	North Carolina	Anson Dorrance	2-0	Connecticut	NC-Greensboro
1998	Florida	Becky Burleigh	1-0	North Carolina	NC-Greensboro
1999	North Carolina	Anson Dorrance	2-0	Notre Dame	San Jose, Calif.

Annual Awards
MEN
Hermann Trophy

College Player of the Year. Voted on by Division I college coaches and selected sportswriters and first presented in 1967 in the name of Robert Hermann, one of the founders of the North American Soccer League.

Multiple winners: Mike Fisher, Mike Seerey, Ken Snow and Al Trost (2).

Year	Year	Year
1967 Dov Markus, LIU	1978 Angelo DiBernardo, Indiana	1989 Tony Meola, Virginia
1968 Manuel Hernandez, San Jose St.	1979 Jim Stamatis, Penn St.	1990 Ken Snow, Indiana
1969 Al Trost, Saint Louis	1980 Joe Morrone, Jr. UConn	1991 Alexi Lalas, Rutgers
1970 Al Trost, Saint Louis	1981 Armando Betancourt, Indiana	1992 Brad Friedel, UCLA
1971 Mike Seerey, Saint Louis	1982 Joe Ulrich, Duke	1993 Claudio Reyna, Virginia
1972 Mike Seerey, Saint Louis	1983 Mike Jeffries, Duke	1994 Brian Maisonneuve, Indiana
1973 Dan Counce, Saint Louis	1984 Amr Aly, Columbia	1995 Mike Fisher, Virginia
1974 Farrukh Quraishi, Oneonta St.	1985 Tom Kain, Duke	1996 Mike Fisher, Virginia
1975 Steve Ralbovsky, Brown	1986 John Kerr, Duke	1997 Johnny Torres, Creighton
1976 Glenn Myernick, Hartwick	1987 Bruce Murray, Clemson	1998 Wojtek Krakowiak, Clemson
1977 Billy Gazonas, Hartwick	1988 Ken Snow, Indiana	1999 Ali Curtis, Duke

Missouri Athletic Club Award

College Player of the Year. Voted on by men's team coaches around the country from Division I to junior college level and first presented in 1986 by the Missouri Athletic Club of St. Louis.

Multiple winners: Claudio Reyna and Ken Snow (2).

Year	Year	Year
1986 John Kerr, Duke	1991 Alexi Lalas, Rutgers	1996 Mike Fisher, Virginia
1987 John Harkes, Virginia	1992 Claudio Reyna, Virginia	1997 Johnny Torres, Creighton
1988 Ken Snow, Indiana	1993 Claudio Reyna, Virginia	1998 Jay Heaps, Duke
1989 Tony Meola, Virginia	1994 Todd Yeagley, Indiana	1999 Sasha Victorine, UCLA
1990 Ken Snow, Indiana	1995 Matt McKeon, St. Louis	

Coach of the Year

Men's Coach of the Year. Voted on by the National Soccer Coaches Association of America. From 1973-81 all Senior College coaches were eligible. In 1982, the award was split into several divisions. The Division I Coach of the Year is listed since 1982.

Multiple winner: Jerry Yeagley (5).

Year	Year	Year
1973 Robert Guelker, SIU-Edwardsville	1983 Dieter Ficken, Columbia	1993 Bob Bradley, Princeton
1974 Jack MacKenzie, Quincy College	1984 James Lennox, Hartwick	1994 Jerry Yeagley, Indiana
1975 Paul Reinhardt, Vermont	1985 Peter Mehlert, American	1995 Jim Launder, Wisconsin
1976 Jerry Yeagley, Indiana	1986 Steve Parker, Akron	1996 Dave Masur, St. John's
1977 Klass Deboer, Cleveland St.	1987 Anson Dorrance, N. Carolina	1997 Sigi Schmid, UCLA
1978 Cliff McCrath, Seattle Pacific	1988 Keith Tucker, Howard	1998 Jerry Yeagley, Indiana
1979 Walter Bahr, Penn St.	1989 Steve Sampson, Santa Clara	1999 Jerry Yeagley, Indiana
1980 Jerry Yeagley, Indiana	1990 Bob Reasso, Rutgers	
1981 Schellas Hyndman, E. Illinois	1991 Mitch Murray, Santa Clara	
1982 John Rennie, Duke	1992 Charles Slagle, Davidson	

WOMEN
Hermann Trophy

Women's College Player of the year. Voted on by Division I college coaches and selected sportswriters and first presented in 1988 in the name of Robert Hermann, one of the founders of the North American Soccer League.

Multiple winners: Mia Hamm and Cindy Parlow (2).

Year	Year	Year
1988 Michelle Akers, Central Fla.	1992 Mia Hamm, N. Carolina	1996 Cindy Daws, Notre Dame
1989 Shannon Higgins, N. Carolina	1993 Mia Hamm, N. Carolina	1997 Cindy Parlow, N. Carolina
1990 April Kater, Massachusetts	1994 Tisha Venturini, N. Carolina	1998 Cindy Parlow, N. Carolina
1991 Kristine Lilly, N. Carolina	1995 Shannon McMillan, Portland	1999 Mandy Clemens, Santa Clara

Missouri Athletic Club Award

Women's College Player of the Year. Voted on by women's team coaches around the country from Division I to junior college level and first presented in 1991 by the Missouri Athletic Club of St. Louis.

Multiple winners: Mia Hamm and Cindy Parlow (2).

Year	Year	Year
1991 Kristine Lilly, N. Carolina	1994 Tisha Venturini, N. Carolina	1997 Cindy Parlow, N. Carolina
1992 Mia Hamm, N. Carolina	1995 Shannon McMillan, Portland	1998 Cindy Parlow, N. Carolina
1993 Mia Hamm, N. Carolina	1996 Cindy Daws, Notre Dame	1999 Mandy Clemens, Santa Clara

Coach of the Year

Women's Coach of the Year. Voted on by the National Soccer Coaches Association of America. From 1982-87 all Senior College coaches were eligible. In 1988, the award was split into several divisions. The Division I Coach of the Year is listed since 1988.

Multiple winners: Kalenkeni M. Banda, Anson Dorrance and Chris Petrucelli (2).

Year	Year	Year
1982 Anson Dorrance, N. Carolina	1988 Larry Gross, N.C. State	1994 Chris Petrucelli, Norte Dame
1983 David Lombardo, Keene St.	1989 Austin Daniels, Hartford	1995 Chris Petrucelli, Norte Dame
1984 Phillip Picince, Brown	1990 Lauren Gregg, Virginia	1996 John Walker, Nebraska
1985 Kalenkeni M. Banda, UMass	1991 Greg Ryan, Wisc-Madison	1997 Len Tsantiris, UConn
1986 Anson Dorrance, N. Carolina	1992 Bell Hempen, Duke	1998 Becky Burleigh, Florida
1987 Kalenkeni M. Banda, UMass	1993 Jac Cicala, George Mason	1999 Patrick Farmer, Penn St.

All-Century Teams

Soccer America named their Men's and Women's Collegiate All-Century Teams as well as their Men's Player of the Century (Claudio Reyna) and Women's Player of the Century (Mia Hamm) in their January 17, 2000 issue.

Men

Pos	Player	Years Played
GK	Brad Friedel, UCLA	1990-95
D	Erik Imler, Virginia	1989-92
D	Paul Caligiuri, UCLA	1982-83, 85-86
D	Adubarie Otorubio, Clemson	1981-84
M	Andy Atuegbu, San Francisco	1974-77
M	Claudio Reyna, Virginia	1991-93
M	Mike Fisher, Virginia	1993-96
M	Bruce Murray, Clemson	1984-87
F	Angelo DiBernardo, Indiana	1976-78
F	Ken Snow, Indiana	1987-89
F	Armando Betancourt, Indiana	1979-81

Women

Pos	Player	Years Played
GK	Kim Maslin, George Mason	1983-86
D	Carla Werden, North Carolina	1986-89
D	Debbie Belkin, Massachusetts	1984-87
D	Sara Whalen, Connecticut	1994-97
M	Kristine Lilly, North Carolina	1989-92
M	Shannon Higgins, North Carolina	1986-89
M	Michelle Akers, Central Florida	1984-89
M	Julie Foudy, Stanford	1989-92
F	April Heinrichs, North Carolina	1983-86
F	Carin Jennings, UC-Santa Barbara	1983-86
F	Mia Hamm, North Carolina	1989-90, 92-93

Bowling

Standout **Parker Bohn III** *was inducted into the PBA Hall of Fame in 2000.*

AP/Wide World Photos

Tournament Results

Winners of stepladder finals in all PBA, Seniors and PWBA tournaments from Sept. 19, 1999, through Aug. 9, 2000; major tournaments in **bold** type.

PBA
Late 1999 Fall Tour

Final	Event	Winner	Earnings	Score	Runner-up
Sept. 19	Japan Cup	Parker Bohn III	$50,000	234-233	Norm Duke
Oct. 6	ACDelco Challenge	Mark Mosayebi	31,000	212-138	Jason Couch
Oct. 12	Brunswick ProSource Open	Rick Lawrence	19,000	248-221	Parker Bohn III
Oct. 20	Canandaigua Open	Parker Bohn III	20,000	274-246	Walter Ray Williams Jr.
Oct. 27	Greater Detroit Open	Dave Wodka	15,000	214-206	Steve Hoskins
Nov. 3	Bay City Classic	Jason Couch	15,000	205-159	Tim Criss
Nov. 10	Indianapolis Open	Randy Pederson	15,000	236-206	Eric Forkel
Nov. 17	**Brunswick World TOC**	Jason Couch	100,000	197-193	Chris Barnes

2000 Winter/Spring Tour

Final	Event	Winner	Earnings	Score	Runner-up
Jan. 15	National/Senior Doubles	Dave Husted/ Pete Couture	$15,000	224-233	Robert Smith/ Bob Glass
Jan. 21	The Orleans Casino Open	Ryan Shafer	25,000	211-202	Mike Aulby
Jan. 29	Don Carter PBA Classic	Norm Duke	20,000	267-266	Steve Jaros
Feb. 5	Chattanooga Open	Parker Bohn III	20,000	226-203	John May
Feb. 12	Empire State Open	Pete Weber	15,000	209-198	Brian Himmler
Feb. 19	**PBA National Championship**	Norm Duke	23,000	214-198	Jason Couch
Feb. 22	**Bayer/Brunswick TPC**	Dennis Horan	40,000	266-189	Pete Weber

2000 Summer Tour

Final	Event	Winner	Earnings	Score	Runner-up
June 17	**ABC Masters**	Mika Koivuniemi	$35,000	236-235	Pete Weber
July 1	Wichita Open	Ryan Shafer	15,000	217-205	Bob Learn Jr.
July 8	MSN Open	Norm Duke	20,000	236-228	Chris Barnes
July 15	**BPAA U.S. Open**	Robert Smith	35,000	202-201	Norm Duke

Note: The American Bowling Congress Masters tournament is not a PBA Tour event.

SENIOR PBA
Late 1999 Fall Tour

Final	Event	Winner	Earnings	Score	Runner-up
Sept. 29	Naples Senior Open	Johnny Petraglia	$9,000	245-179	Chuck Pierce
Oct. 7	Villages Senior TOC	Dave Soutar	10,000	267-196	John Hricsina
Oct. 22	Senior National Championship	Steve Neff	20,000	236-224	Bob Glass

2000 Winter Tour

Final	Event	Winner	Earnings	Score	Runner-up
Jan. 9	ABC Senior Masters	Dave Soutar	$18,000	236-192	Donald Breihan
Jan. 15	National/Senior Doubles	Dave Husted/ Pete Couture	15,000	224-233	Robert Smith/ Bob Glass

2000 Spring/Summer Tour

Final	Event	Winner	Earnings	Score	Runner-up
Mar. 31	The Villages Senior World Championship	Roger Workman	$20,000	244-209	Gene Stus
May 18	Central Pennsylvania Open	Bob Glass	8,000	245-215	Pete Couture
June 1	Seattle Open	Butch Soper	8,000	222-210	Norb Wetzel
June 8	Northwest Senior Classic	Al Sanford	9,000	226-224	Norb Wetzel
June 23	The Orleans Casino Open	Dave Davis	18,000	215-187	Dick Baker
July 6	Northern California Senior Classic	Lauri Karppala	8,500	257-199	Larry Laub

PWBA
Late 1999 Fall Tour

Final	Event	Winner	Earnings	Score	Runner-up
Sept. 30	Visionary Bowling Products Classic	Carolyn Dorin-Ballard	$14,400	225-170	Marianne DiRupo
Oct. 7	**AMF Gold Cup**	Dana Miller-Mackie	35,000	236-222	Cara Honeychurch
Oct. 14	Three Rivers Open	Cathy Dorin	11,500	234-212	Michelle Feldman
Oct. 21	Brunswick World Open	Cara Honeychurch	14,400	237-204	Tiffany Stanbrough
Nov. 6	**Sam's Town Invitational**	Wendy Macpherson	14,000	209-195	Marianne DiRupo

2000 Spring/Summer Tour

Final	Event	Winner	Earnings	Score	Runner-up
Apr. 20	New Mexico Open	Kim Adler	$11,000	216-211	Pauliina Aalto
Apr. 28	Bowl for Blindness Classic	Carolyn Dorin-Ballard	11,000	217-189	Michelle Feldman
May 5	Greater San Diego Open	Michelle Feldman	11,000	218-214	Carolyn Dorin-Ballard
May 11	Track Doubles	Robin Mossontte/	10,500	231-207	Maxine Nable/Carol
		Jeanne Naccarato	(each)		Giannotti-Block
May 18	Bowl the Rouge Open	Michelle Feldman	11,000	242-230	Kim Adler
May 26	**WIBC Queens**	Wendy Macpherson	23,000	227-202	Marianne DiRupo
June 2	Omaha Open	Michelle Feldman	11,000	238-212	Lynda Barnes
June 8	St. Clair Classic	Kim Adler	11,000	203-181	Wendy Macpherson
June 15	Clabber Girl Open	Carol Gianotti-Block	11,500	224-193	Kim Adler
July 15	**BPAA U.S. Open**	Tennelle Grijalva	35,000	239-155	Kelly Kulick
July 27	Southern Virginia Open	Wendy Macpherson	11,000	205-182	Carolyn Dorin-Ballard
Aug. 3	Lady Ebonite Classic	Michelle Feldman	14,400	188-173	Leanne Barrette
Aug. 9	Greater Atlanta Open	Aleta Sill	11,000	217-205	Tish Johnson

Note: The Women's International Bowling Congress Queens tournament is not an official PWBA Tour event.

2000 Fall Tour Schedules

PBA: Japan Cup – Tokyo, JPN (Sept. 14-17); Track Canandaigua Open – Canandaigua, N.Y. (Oct. 7-10); Brunswick Johnny Petraglia Open – North Brunswick, N.J. (Oct. 14-17); Flagship Open – Erie, Penn. (Oct. 21-24); Indianapolis Open – Indianapolis, Ind. (Oct. 28-31); **Brunswick World Tournament of Champions** – Lake Zurich, Ill. (Nov. 3-7); Columbia 300 Open – Austin, Texas (Nov. 11-15); Lone Star Open – Pasadena, Texas (Nov. 17-21).

SENIOR PBA: Atlantic City Open – Egg Harbor Township, N.J. (Sept. 17-21); Columbia 300 Open – Naples, Fla. (Sept. 23-27); Gastonia Classic – Gastonia, N.C. (Oct. 1-5); **Brunswick PBA Senior National Championship** – Jackson, Mich. (Oct. 7-13); Hammond Open – Hammond, Ind. (Oct. 16-20).

PWBA: Greater Orlando Classic – Altamonte Springs, Fla. (Sept. 3-7); Paula Carter Classic – Davie, Fla. (Sept. 9-14); The Foundation Games II – Sebring, Fla. (Sept. 16-21); Brunswick Women's World Open – Newman, Ga. (Sept. 24-28); North Myrtle Beach Classic – North Myrtle Beach, S.C. (Oct. 1-5); Columbia 300 Open – Lancaster, Ohio (Oct. 8-12); Three Rivers Open – Pittsburgh, Penn. (Oct. 14-19); Greater Harrisburg Open – Mechanicsburg, Penn. (Oct. 21-26); Hammer Players Championship – Rockford, Ill. (Oct. 28-Nov. 2); **Sam's Town Invitational** – Las Vegas, Nev. (Nov. 4-11); Storm Shootout – Las Vegas, Nev. (Nov. 11).

AMF Bowling World Cup
Oct. 15-21 in Lisbon, Portugal. See Updates chapter for 2000 results.

MEN

1965 Lauri Ajanto	1974 Jairo Ocampo	1983 You-Tien Chu	1992 Paeng Nepomuceno
1966 John Wilcox	1975 Lorenzo Monti	1984 Jack Jurek	1993 Rainer Puisis
1967 Jack Connaughton	1976 Paeng Nepomuceno	1985 Alfonso Rodriguez	1994 Tore Torgersen
1968 Fritz Blum	1977 Arne Stroem	1986 Peter Ljung	1995 Patrick Healey Jr.
1969 Graydon Robinson	1978 Samran Banyan	1987 Remo Fornasari	1996 Paeng Nepomuceno
1970 Klaus Muller	1979 Philippe Dubois	1988 Mohammed Khalifa	1997 Christian Nokel
1971 Roger Dalkin	1980 Paeng Nepomuceno	1989 Salem Al-Monsouri	1998 Cheng-Ming Yang
1972 Ray Mitchell	1981 Bob Worrall	1990 Tom Hahl	1999 Ahmed Shaheen
1973 Bernie Caterer	1982 Arne Stroem	1991 Jon Juneau	

WOMEN

1972 Irma Urrea	1980 Jean Gordon	1988 Linda Kelly	1996 Cara Honeychurch
1973 Kesinee Srivises	1981 Pauline Smith	1989 Patty Ann	1997 Su-Fen Tseng
1974 Birgitte Lund	1982 Jeanette Baker	1990 Linda Graham	1998 Maxine Nable
1975 Cathy Townsend	1983 Jeanette Baker	1991 Asa Larsson	1999 Amanda Bradley
1976 Lucy Giovinco	1984 Eliana Rigato	1992 Martina Beckel	
1977 Rea Rennox	1985 Marjorie McEntee	1993 Pauline (Smith) Buck	
1978 Lita de la Rosa	1986 Annette Hagre	1994 Anne Jacobs	
1979 Bong Coo	1987 Irene Gronert	1995 Gemma Burden	

Tour Leaders

Official standings for 1999 and unofficial standings for 2000. Note that (TB) indicates Tournaments Bowled; (CR) Championship Rounds as Stepladder Finalist; and (1st) Titles Won.

FINAL 1999
PBA
Top 10 Money Winners

		TB	CR	1st	Earnings
1	Parker Bohn III	24	11	5	$232,595
2	Jason Couch	23	10	2	220,990
3	Chris Barnes	26	6	2	123,985
4	Norm Duke	23	4	0	92,930
5	Bob Learn Jr.	23	3	1	92,498
6	Steve Hoskins	21	3	1	91,430
7	Walter Ray Williams Jr.	22	5	1	90,215
8	Ricky Ward	19	6	1	81,820
9	Danny Wiseman	25	6	0	80,625
10	Tim Criss	26	3	1	75,060

Top 10 Averages

		TB	Games	Avg
1	Parker Bohn III	24	844	228.04
2	Jason Couch	23	931	225.18
3	Norm Duke	23	851	224.81
4	Walter Ray Williams Jr.	22	769	224.47
5	Ryan Shafer	24	867	224.26
6	Ricky Ward	19	631	224.08
7	Chris Barnes	26	860	223.86
8	Bob Learn Jr.	23	855	223.31
9	Danny Wiseman	25	901	223.21
10	Amleto Monacelli	20	674	222.84

SENIOR PBA
Top 5 Money Winners

		TB	CR	1st	Earnings
1	Dave Soutar	14	3	1	$137,190
2	Dale Eagle	14	8	4	79,465
3	Steve Neff	11	3	2	40,150
4	Johnny Petraglia	7	3	2	34,320
5	Roger Workman	12	4	1	33,505

Top 5 Averages

		TB	Games	Avg
1	Dale Eagle	14	600	225.28
2	Dave Soutar	14	607	224.98
3	Pete Couture	14	573	224.51
4	Ron Winger	14	577	223.00
5	Mike Durbin	14	507	222.20

PWBA
Top 10 Money Winners

		TB	CR	1st	Earnings
1	Wendy Macpherson	18	9	2	$86,265
2	Kim Adler	18	5	2	83,495
3	Leanne Barrette	18	7	2	78,810
4	Carolyn Dorin-Ballard	18	7	2	70,115
5	Dana Miller-Mackie	18	4	1	63,580
6	Cathy Dorin	18	3	1	56,068
7	Kim Canady	18	5	1	53,880
8	Lisa Bishop	18	3	2	52,915
9	Marianne DiRupo	18	4	0	50,105
10	Cara Honeychurch	4	3	1	48,900

Note: Earnings include WIBC Queens.

Top 5 Averages

		TB	Games	Avg
1	Wendy Macpherson	18	740	218.85
2	Carolyn Dorin-Ballard	18	682	216.56
3	Leanne Barrette	18	660	215.03
4	Kim Canady	18	658	214.56
5	Anne Marie Duggan	18	641	214.10

2000 (through Aug. 9)
PBA
Top 10 Money Winners

		TB	CR	1st	Earnings
1	Norm Duke	10	5	3	$96,800
2	Ryan Shafer	11	6	2	66,510
3	Mika Koivuniemi	11	2	1	56,475
4	Robert Smith	10	2	1	48,100
5	Chris Barnes	11	5	0	46,900
6	Pete Weber	8	3	1	44,950
7	Dennis Horan Jr.	11	1	1	44,450
8	Jason Couch	11	2	0	36,190
9	Parker Bohn III	11	2	1	35,925
10	Paul Fleming	10	2	0	30,520

Top 10 Averages

		TB	Games	Avg
1	Norm Duke	10	416	220.25
2	Chris Barnes	11	446	219.64
3	Ryan Shafer	11	372	219.02
4	Pete Weber	8	276	217.80
5	Eric Forkel	7	245	217.07
6	Patrick Healey Jr.	10	312	216.57
7	Brian Voss	11	367	216.40
8	Walter Ray Williams Jr.	10	365	216.19
9	Tim Criss	9	301	216.10
10	John May	7	233	216.06

SENIOR PBA
Top 5 Money Winners

		TB	CR	1st	Earnings
1	Roger Workman	8	2	1	$128,775
2	Robert Glass	8	5	1	38,200
3	Dave Soutar	8	3	1	29,600
4	Dave Davis	5	2	1	28,575
5	Pete Couture	8	2	1	27,625

Top 5 Averages

		TB	Games	Avg
1	Norb Wetzel	4	162	222.70
2	Robert Glass	8	351	222.57
3	Butch Soper	6	153	218.78
4	Dave Soutar	8	278	218.64
5	Pete Couture	8	272	218.41

PWBA
Top 10 Money Winners

		TB	CR	1st	Earnings
1	Wendy Macpherson	13	8	2	$68,525
2	Michelle Feldman	13	6	3	67,275
3	Kim Adler	13	7	2	54,235
4	Carolyn Dorin-Ballard	13	5	2	53,837
5	Tennelle Grijalva	13	3	1	52,115
6	Carol Gianotti-Block	13	3	1	49,515
7	Marianne DiRupo	13	4	0	37,440
8	Anne Marie Duggan	13	1	0	33,350
9	Leanne Barrette	12	3	0	31,950
10	Kim Terrell	13	3	0	29,280

Note: Earnings include WIBC Queens.

Top 5 Averages

		TB	Games	Avg
1	Michelle Feldman	13	484	215.59
2	Carolyn Dorin-Ballard	13	510	214.22
3	Wendy Macpherson	13	486	214.10
4	Carol Gianotti-Block	13	482	213.36
5	Cara Honeychurch	13	395	212.89

Major Championships
MEN
BPAA U.S. Open

Started in 1941 by the Bowling Proprietors' Association of America, 18 years before the founding of the Professional Bowlers Association. Originally the BPAA All-Star Tournament, it became the U.S. Open in 1971. There were two BPAA All-Star tournaments in 1955, in January and December.

Multiple winners: Don Carter and Dick Weber (4); Dave Husted (3); Del Ballard Jr., Marshall Holman, Junie McMahon, Connie Schwoegler, Andy Varipapa and Pete Weber (2).

Year	Winner	Score	Runner-Up	Location
1942	John Crimmons	265.09-262.33	Joe Norris	Chicago
1943	Connie Schwoegler	n/a	Frank Benkovic	Chicago
1944	Ned Day	315.21-298.21	Paul Krumske	Chicago
1945	Buddy Bomar	304.46-296.16	Joe Wilman	Chicago
1946	Joe Wilman	310.27-305.37	Therman Gibson	Chicago
1947	Andy Varipapa	314.16-308.04	Allie Brandt	Chicago
1948	Andy Varipapa	309.23-309.06	Joe Wilman	Chicago
1949	Connie Schwoegler	312.31-307.27	Andy Varipapa	Chicago
1950	Junie McMahon	318.37-307.17	Ralph Smith	Chicago
1951	Dick Hoover	305.29-304.07	Lee Jouglard	Chicago
1952	Junie McMahon	309.29-305.41	Bill Lillard	Chicago
1953	Don Carter	304.17-297.36	Ed Lubanski	Chicago
1954	Don Carter	308.02-307.25	Bill Lillard	Chicago
1955	Steve Nagy	307.17-303.34	Ed Lubanski	Chicago
1956	Bill Lillard	304.30-304.22	Joe Wilman	Chicago
1957	Don Carter	308.49-305.45	Dick Weber	Chicago
1958	Don Carter	311.03-308.09	Buzz Fazio	Minneapolis
1959	Billy Welu	311.48-310.26	Ray Bluth	Buffalo
1960	Harry Smith	312.24-308.12	Bob Chase	Omaha, Neb.
1961	Bill Tucker	318.49-309.11	Dick Weber	San Bernardino, Calif.
1962	Dick Weber	299.34-297.38	Roy Lown	Miami Beach
1963	Dick Weber	642-591	Billy Welu	Kansas City
1964	Bob Strampe	714-616	Tommy Tuttle	Dallas
1965	Dick Weber	608-586	Jim St. John	Philadelphia
1966	Dick Weber	684-681	Nelson Burton Jr.	Lansing, Mich.
1967	Les Schissler	613-610	Pete Tountas	St. Ann, Mo.
1968	Jim Stefanich	12,401-12,104	Billy Hardwick	Garden City, N.Y.
1969	Billy Hardwick	12,585-11,463	Dick Weber	Miami
1970	Bobby Cooper	12,936-12,307	Billy Hardwick	Northbrook, Ill.
1971	Mike Limongello	397 (2 games)	Teata Semiz	St. Paul, Minn.
1972	Don Johnson	233 (1 game)	George Pappas	New York, N.Y.
1973	Mike McGrath	712 (3 games)	Earl Anthony	New York, N.Y.
1974	Larry Laub	749 (3 games)	Dave Davis	New York, N.Y.
1975	Steve Neff	279 (1 game)	Paul Colwell	Grand Prairie, Tex.
1976	Paul Moser	226 (1 game)	Jim Frazier	Grand Prairie, Tex.
1977	Johnny Petraglia	279 (1 game)	Bill Spigner	Greensboro, N.C.
1978	Nelson Burton Jr.	873 (4 games)	Jeff Mattingly	Greensboro, N.C.
1979	Joe Berardi	445 (2 games)	Earl Anthony	Windsor Locks, Ct.
1980	Steve Martin	930 (3 games)	Earl Anthony	Windsor Locks, Ct.
1981	Marshall Holman	684 (3 games)	Mark Roth	Houston
1982	Dave Husted	1011 (4 games)	Gil Sliker	Houston
1983	Gary Dickinson	214 (1 game)	Steve Neff	Oak Hill, Ill.
1984	Mark Roth	244 (1 game)	Guppy Troup	Oak Hill, Ill.
1985	Marshall Holman	233 (1 game)	Wayne Webb	Venice, Fla.
1986	Steve Cook	467 (2 games)	Frank Ellenburg	Venice, Fla.
1987	Del Ballard Jr.	525 (2 games)	Pete Weber	Tacoma, Wash.
1988	Pete Weber	929 (4 games)	Marshall Holman	Atlantic City

Major Championships (Cont.)

Year	Winner	Score	Runner-Up	Location
1989	Mike Aulby	.429 (2 games)	Jim Pencak	Edmond, Okla.
1990	Ron Palombi Jr.	.269 (1 game)	Amleto Monacelli	Indianapolis
1991	Pete Weber	.956 (4 games)	Mark Thayer	Indianapolis
1992	Robert Lawrence	.667 (3 games)	Scott Devers	Canandaigua, N.Y.
1993	Del Ballard Jr.	.505 (2 games)	Walter Ray Williams Jr.	Canandaigua, N.Y.
1994	Justin Hromek	.267 (1 game)	Parker Bohn III	Troy, Mich.
1995	Dave Husted	.266 (1 game)	Paul Koehler	Troy, Mich.
1996	Dave Husted	.730 (3 games)	George Brooks	Indianapolis
1997	Not held			
1998	Walter Ray Williams Jr.	.466 (2 games)	Tim Criss	Fairfield, Ct.
1999	Bob Learn Jr.	.231 (1 game)	Jason Couch	Uncasville, Ct.
2000	Robert Smith	.202 (1 game)	N. Duke	Phoenix

PBA National Championship

The Professional Bowlers Association was formed in 1958 and its first national championship tournament was held in Memphis in 1960. The tournament has been held in Toledo, Ohio, since 1981.

Multiple winners: Earl Anthony (6); Mike Aulby, Dave Davis, Mike McGrath, Pete Weber and Wayne Zahn (2).

Year	Winner	Score	Runner-Up	Location
1960	Don Carter	6,369 (30 games)	Ronnie Gaudern	Memphis, Tenn.
1961	Dave Soutar	5,792 (27 games)	Morrie Oppenheim	Cleveland
1962	Carmen Salvino	5,369 (25 games)	Don Carter	Philadelphia
1963	Billy Hardwick	13,541 (61 games)	Ray Bluth	Long Island, N.Y.
1964	Bob Strampe	13,979 (61 games)	Ray Bluth	Long Island, N.Y.
1965	Dave Davis	13,895 (61 games)	Jerry McCoy	Detroit
1966	Wayne Zahn	14,006 (60 games)	Nelson Burton Jr.	Long Island, N.Y.
1967	Dave Davis	.421 (2 games)	Pete Tountas	New York, N.Y.
1968	Wayne Zahn	14,182 (60 games)	Nelson Burton Jr.	New York, N.Y.
1969	Mike McGrath	13,670 (60 games)	Bill Allen	Garden City, N.Y.
1970	Mike McGrath	.660 (3 games)	Dave Davis	Garden City, N.Y.
1971	Mike Limongello	.911 (4 games)	Dave Davis	Paramus, N.J.
1972	Johnny Guenther	12,986 (56 games)	Dick Ritger	Rochester, N.Y.
1973	Earl Anthony	.212 (1 game)	Sam Flanagan	Oklahoma City
1974	Earl Anthony	.218 (1 game)	Mark Roth	Downey, Calif.
1975	Earl Anthony	.245 (1 game)	Jim Frazier	Downey, Calif.
1976	Paul Colwell	.191 (1 game)	Dave Davis	Seattle
1977	Tommy Hudson	.206 (1 game)	Jay Robinson	Seattle
1978	Warren Nelson	.453 (2 games)	Joseph Groskind	Reno, Nev.
1979	Mike Aulby	.727 (3 games)	Earl Anthony	Las Vegas
1980	Johnny Petraglia	.235 (1 game)	Gary Dickinson	Sterling Hts., Mich.
1981	Earl Anthony	.242 (1 game)	Ernie Schlegel	Toledo, Ohio
1982	Earl Anthony	.233 (1 game)	Charlie Tapp	Toledo, Ohio
1983	Earl Anthony	.210 (1 game)	Mike Durbin	Toledo, Ohio
1984	Bob Chamberlain	.961 (4 games)	Dan Eberl	Toledo, Ohio
1985	Mike Aulby	.476 (2 games)	Steve Cook	Toledo, Ohio
1986	Tom Crites	.190 (1 game)	Mike Aulby	Toledo, Ohio
1987	Randy Pedersen	.759 (3 games)	Amleto Monacelli	Toledo, Ohio
1988	Brian Voss	.246 (1 game)	Todd Thompson	Toledo, Ohio
1989	Pete Weber	.221 (1 game)	Dave Ferraro	Toledo, Ohio
1990	Jim Pencak	.900 (4 games)	Chris Warren	Toledo, Ohio
1991	Mike Miller	.450 (2 games)	Norm Duke	Toledo, Ohio
1992	Eric Forkel	.833 (4 games)	Bob Vespi	Toledo, Ohio
1993	Ron Palombi Jr.	.237 (1 game)	Eugene McCune	Toledo, Ohio
1994	David Traber	.196 (1 game)	Dale Traber	Toledo, Ohio
1995	Scott Alexander	.246 (1 game)	Wayne Webb	Toledo, Ohio
1996	Butch Soper	.442 (2 games)	Walter Ray Williams Jr.	Toledo, Ohio
1997	Rick Steelsmith	.888 (4 games)	Brian Voss	Toledo, Ohio
1998	Pete Weber	.277 (1 game)	David Ozio	Toledo, Ohio
1999	Tim Criss	.238 (1 game)	Dave Arnold	Toledo, Ohio
2000	Norm Duke	.214 (1 game)	Jason Couch	Toledo, Ohio

Brunswick World Tournament of Champions

Originally the Firestone Tournament of Champions (1965-93), the tournament has also been sponsored by General Tire (1994) and Brunswick Corp. (since 1995). Held in Akron, Ohio in 1965, then Fairlawn, Ohio (1966-94), Lake Zurich, Ill. (1995-96), Reno, N.V. (1997) and Overland Park, Kan.(since 1998).

Multiple winners: Mike Durbin (3); Earl Anthony, Dave Davis, Jim Godman, Marshall Holman and Mark Williams (2).

Year	Winner	Score	Runner-Up	Location
1965	Billy Hardwick	484 (2 games)	Dick Weber	Akron, Ohio
1966	Wayne Zahn	595 (3 games)	Dick Weber	Fairlawn, Ohio
1967	Jim Stefanich	275 (1 game)	Don Johnson	Fairlawn, Ohio
1968	Dave Davis	213 (1 game)	Don Johnson	Fairlawn, Ohio
1969	Jim Godman	266 (1 game)	Jim Stefanich	Fairlawn, Ohio
1970	Don Johnson	299 (1 game)	Dick Ritger	Fairlawn, Ohio
1971	Johnny Petraglia	245 (1 game)	Don Johnson	Fairlawn, Ohio
1972	Mike Durbin	775 (3 games)	Tim Harahan	Fairlawn, Ohio
1973	Jim Godman	451 (2 games)	Barry Asher	Fairlawn, Ohio
1974	Earl Anthony	679 (3 games)	Johnny Petraglia	Fairlawn, Ohio
1975	Dave Davis	448 (2 games)	Barry Asher	Fairlawn, Ohio
1976	Marshall Holman	441 (2 games)	Billy Hardwick	Fairlawn, Ohio
1977	Mike Berlin	434 (2 games)	Mike Durbin	Fairlawn, Ohio
1978	Earl Anthony	237 (1 game)	Teata Semiz	Fairlawn, Ohio
1979	George Pappas	224 (1 game)	Dick Ritger	Fairlawn, Ohio
1980	Wayne Webb	750 (3 games)	Gary Dickinson	Fairlawn, Ohio
1981	Steve Cook	287 (1 game)	Pete Couture	Fairlawn, Ohio
1982	Mike Durbin	448 (2 games)	Steve Cook	Fairlawn, Ohio
1983	Joe Berardi	865 (4 games)	Henry Gonzalez	Fairlawn, Ohio
1984	Mike Durbin	950 (4 games)	Mike Aulby	Fairlawn, Ohio
1985	Mark Williams	616 (3 games)	Bob Handley	Fairlawn, Ohio
1986	Marshall Holman	233 (1 game)	Mark Baker	Fairlawn, Ohio
1987	Pete Weber	928 (4 games)	Jim Murtishaw	Fairlawn, Ohio
1988	Mark Williams	237 (1 game)	Tony Westlake	Fairlawn, Ohio
1989	Del Ballard Jr.	490 (2 games)	Walter Ray Williams Jr.	Fairlawn, Ohio
1990	Dave Ferraro	226 (1 game)	Tony Westlake	Fairlawn, Ohio
1991	David Ozio	476 (2 games)	Amleto Monacelli	Fairlawn, Ohio
1992	Marc McDowell	471 (2 games)	Don Genalo	Fairlawn, Ohio
1993	George Branham III	227 (1 game)	Parker Bohn III	Fairlawn, Ohio
1994	Norm Duke	422 (2 games)	Eric Forkel	Fairlawn, Ohio
1995	Mike Aulby	502 (2 games)	Bob Spaulding	Lake Zurich, Ill.
1996	Dave D'Entremont	971 (4 games)	Dave Arnold	Lake Zurich, Ill.
1997	John Gant	446 (2 games)	Mike Aulby	Reno, Nev.
1998	Bryan Goebel	245 (1 game)	S. Hoskins	Overland Park, Ks.
1999	Jason Couch	197 (1 game)	Chris Barnes	Overland Park, Ks.

ABC Masters Tournament

Sponsored by the American Bowling Congress. The Masters is not a PBA event, but is considered one of the four major tournaments on the men's tour and is open to qualified pros and amateurs.

Multiple winners: Mike Aulby (3); Earl Anthony, Billy Golembiewski, Dick Hoover and Billy Welu (2).

Year	Winner	Score	Runner-Up	Location
1951	Lee Jouglard	201.8	Joe Wilman	St. Paul, Minn.
1952	Willard Taylor	200.32	Andy Varipapa	Milwaukee
1953	Rudy Habetler	200.1	Ed Brosius	Chicago
1954	Red Elkins	205.1	Willard Taylor	Seattle
1955	Buzz Fazio	204.1	Joe Kristof	Ft. Wayne, Ind.
1956	Dick Hoover	209.9	Ray Bluth	Rochester, N.Y.
1957	Dick Hoover	216.3	Bill Lillard	Ft. Worth, Tex.
1958	Tom Hennessey	209.1	Lou Frantz	Syracuse, N.Y.
1959	Ray Bluth	214.2	Billy Golembiewski	St. Louis
1960	Billy Golembiewski	206.1	Steve Nagy	Toledo, Ohio
1961	Don Carter	211.1	Dick Hoover	Detroit
1962	Billy Golembiewski	223.1	Ron Winger	Des Moines, Iowa
1963	Harry Smith	219.3	Bobby Meadows	Buffalo
1964	Billy Welu	227.0	Harry Smith	Oakland, Calif.
1965	Billy Welu	202.1	Don Ellis	St. Paul, Minn.
1966	Bob Strampe	219.8	Al Thompson	Rochester, N.Y.
1967	Lou Scalia	216.9	Bill Johnson	Miami Beach
1968	Pete Tountas	220.1	Buzz Fazio	Cincinnati
1969	Jim Chestney	223.2	Barry Asher	Madison, Wisc.
1970	Don Glover	215.1	Bob Strampe	Knoxville, Tenn.
1971	Jim Godman	229.8	Don Johnson	Detroit
1972	Bill Beach	220.2	Jim Godman	Long Beach, Calif.

Major Championships (Cont.)

Year	Winner	Score	Runner-Up	Location
1973	Dave Soutar	218.6	Dick Ritger	Syracuse, N.Y.
1974	Paul Colwell	234.1	Steve Neff	Indianapolis
1975	Eddie Ressler Jr.	213.5	Sam Flanagan	Dayton, Ohio
1976	Nelson Burton Jr.	220.7	Steve Carson	Oklahoma City
1977	Earl Anthony	218.2	Jim Godman	Reno, Nev.
1978	Frank Ellenburg	200.6	Earl Anthony	St. Louis
1979	Doug Myers	202.9	Bill Spigner	Tampa, Fla.
1980	Neil Burton	206.6	Mark Roth	Louisville, Ky.
1981	Randy Lightfoot	218.2	Skip Tucker	Memphis, Tenn.
1982	Joe Berardi	207.1	Ted Hannahs	Baltimore
1983	Mike Lastowski	212.7	Pete Weber	Niagara Falls, N.Y.
1984	Earl Anthony	212.5	Gil Sliker	Reno, Nev.
1985	Steve Wunderlich	210.4	Tommy Kress	Tulsa, Okla.
1986	Mark Fahy	206.5	Del Ballard Jr.	Las Vegas
1987	Rick Steelsmith	210.7	Brad Snell	Niagara Falls, N.Y.
1988	Del Ballard Jr.	219.1	Keith Smith	Jacksonville, Fla.
1989	Mike Aulby	218.5	Mike Edwards	Wichita, Kan.
1990	Chris Warren	231.6	Dave Ozio	Reno, Nev.
1991	Doug Kent	226.8	George Branham III	Toledo, Ohio
1992	Ken Johnson	234.0	Dave D'Entremont	Corpus Christi, Tex.
1993	Norm Duke	234.7	Patrick Allen	Tulsa, Okla.
1994	Steve Fehr	234.6	Steve Anderson	Greenacres, Fla.
1995	Mike Aulby	232.5	Mark Williams	Reno, Nev.
1996	Ernie Schlegel	234.5	Mike Aulby	Salt Lake City
1997	Jason Queen	233.4	Eric Forkel	Huntsville, Ala.
1998	Mike Aulby	224.0	Parker Bohn III	Reno, Nev.
1999	Brian Boghosian	247.0	Parker Bohn III	Syracuse, N.Y.
2000	Mika Koivuniemi	236.0	Pete Weber	Albuquerque, N.M.

WOMEN
BPAA U.S. Open

Started by the Bowling Proprietors' Association of America in 1949, 11 years before the founding of the Professional Women's Bowling Association. Originally the BPAA Women's All-Star Tournament, it became the U.S. Open in 1971. There were two BPAA All-Star tournaments in 1955, in January and December. Note that (a) indicates amateur.

Multiple winners: Marion Ladewig (8); Donna Adamek, Paula Sperber Carter, Pat Costello, Dotty Fothergill, Dana Miller-Mackie, Aleta Sill and Sylvia Wene (2).

Year	Winner	Score	Runner-Up	Location
1949	Marion Ladewig	113.26-104.26	Catherine Burling	Chicago
1950	Marion Ladewig	151.46-146.06	Stephanie Balogh	Chicago
1951	Marion Ladewig	159.17-148.03	Sylvia Wene	Chicago
1952	Marion Ladewig	154.39-142.05	Shirley Garms	Chicago
1953	Not held			
1954	Marion Ladewig	148.29-143.01	Sylvia Wene	Chicago
1955	Sylvia Wene	142.30-141.11	Sylvia Fanta	Chicago
1955	Anita Cantaline	144.40-144.13	Doris Porter	Chicago
1956	Marion Ladewig	150.16-145.41	Marge Merrick	Chicago
1957	Not held			
1958	Merle Matthews	145.09-143.14	Marion Ladewig	Minneapolis
1959	Marion Ladewig	149.33-143.00	Donna Zimmerman	Buffalo
1960	Sylvia Wene	144.14-143.26	Marion Ladewig	Omaha, Neb.
1961	Phyllis Notaro	144.13-143.12	Hope Riccilli	San Bernardino, Calif.
1962	Shirley Garms	138.44-135.49	Joy Abel	Miami Beach
1963	Marion Ladewig	586-578	Bobbie Shaler	Kansas City
1964	LaVerne Carter	683-609	Evelyn Teal	Dallas
1965	Ann Slattery	597-570	Sandy Hooper	Philadelphia
1966	Joy Abel	593-538	Bette Rockwell	Lansing, Mich.
1967	Gloria Simon	578-516	Shirley Garms	St. Ann, Mo.
1968	Dotty Fothergill	9,000-8,187	Doris Coburn	Garden City, N.Y.
1969	Dotty Fothergill	8,284-8,258	Kayoka Suda	Miami
1970	Mary Baker	8,730-8,465	Judy Cook	Northbrook, Ill.
1971	a-Paula Sperber	5,660-5,650	June Llewellyn	Kansas City
1972	a-Lorrie Koch	5,272-5,189	Mary Baker	Denver
1973	Millie Martorella	5,553-5,294	Patty Costello	Garden City, N.Y.
1974	Patty Costello	219-216	Betty Morris	Irving, Tex.
1975	Paula Sperber Carter	6,500-6,352	Lorrie Nichols	Toledo, Ohio
1976	Patty Costello	11,341-11,281	Betty Morris	Tulsa, Okla.

Year	Winner	Score	Runner-Up	Location
1977	Betty Morris	10,511-10,358	Virginia Norton	Milwaukee
1978	Donna Adamek	236-202	Vesma Grinfelds	Miami
1979	Diana Silva	11,775-11,718	Bev Ortner	Phoenix
1980	Patty Costello	223-199	Shinobu Saitoh	Rockford, Ill.
1981	Donna Adamek	201-190	Nikki Gianulias	Rockford, Ill.
1982	Shinobu Saitoh	12,184-12,028	Robin Romeo	Hendersonville, Tenn.
1983	Dana Miller	247-200	Aleta Sill	St. Louis
1984	Karen Ellingsworth	236-217	Lorrie Nichols	St. Louis
1985	Pat Mercatanti	214-178	Nikki Gianulias	Topeka, Kan.
1986	Wendy Macpherson	265-179	Lisa Wagner	Topeka, Kan.
1987	Carol Norman	206-179	Cindy Coburn	Mentor, Ohio
1988	Lisa Wagner	226-218	Lorrie Nichols	Winston-Salem, N.C.
1989	Robin Romeo	187-163	Michelle Mullen	Addison, Ill.
1990	Dana Miller-Mackie	190-189	Tish Johnson	Dearborn Hts., Mich.
1991	Anne Marie Duggan	196-185	Leanne Barrette	Fountain Valley, Calif.
1992	Tish Johnson	216-213	Aleta Sill	Fountain Valley, Calif.
1993	Dede Davidson	213-194	Dana Miller-Mackie	Garland, Tex.
1994	Aleta Sill	229-170	Anne Marie Duggan	Wichita, Kan.
1995	Cheryl Daniels	235-180	Tish Johnson	Blaine, Minn.
1996	Liz Johnson	265-236	Marianne DiRupo	Indianapolis
1997	Not held			
1998	Aleta Sill	276-151	Tammy Turner	Fairfield, Ct.
1999	Kim Adler	213-195	Lynda Barnes	Uncasville, Ct.
2000	Tennelle Grijalva	239-155	Kelly Kulick	Phoenix

WIBC Queens

Sponsored by the Women's International Bowling Congress, the Queens is a double elimination, match play tournament. It is not a PWBA event, but is open to qualified pros and amateurs. Note that (a) indicates amateur.

Multiple winners: Millie Martorella (3); Donna Adamek, Dotty Fothergill, Wendy Macpherson, Aleta Sill and Katsuko Sugimoto (2).

Year	Winners	Score	Runner-Up	Location
1961	Janet Harman	794-776	Eula Touchette	Fort Wayne, Ind.
1962	Dorothy Wilkinson	799-794	Marion Ladewig	Phoenix
1963	Irene Monterosso	852-803	Georgette DeRosa	Memphis, Tenn.
1964	D.D. Jacobson	740-682	Shirley Garms	Minneapolis
1965	Betty Kuczynski	772-739	LaVerne Carter	Portland, Ore.
1966	Judy Lee	771-742	Nancy Peterson	New Orleans
1967	Millie Martorella	840-809	Phyllis Massey	Rochester, N.Y.
1968	Phyllis Massey	884-853	Marian Spencer	San Antonio
1969	Ann Feigel	832-765	Millie Ignizio	San Diego
1970	Millie Martorella	807-797	Joan Holm	Tulsa, Okla.
1971	Millie Martorella	809-778	Katherine Brown	Atlanta
1972	Dotty Fothergill	890-841	Maureen Harris	Kansas City
1973	Dotty Fothergill	804-791	Judy Soutar	Las Vegas
1974	Judy Soutar	939-705	Betty Morris	Houston
1975	Cindy Powell	758-674	Patty Costello	Indianapolis
1976	Pam Rutherford	214-178	Shirley Sjostrom	Denver
1977	Dana Stewart	175-167	Vesma Grinfelds	Milwaukee
1978	Loa Boxberger	197-176	Cora Fiebig	Miami
1979	Donna Adamek	216-181	Shinobu Saitoh	Tucson, Ari.
1980	Donna Adamek	213-165	Cheryl Robinson	Seattle
1981	Katsuko Sugimoto	166-158	Virginia Norton	Baltimore
1982	Katsuko Sugimoto	160-137	Nikki Gianulias	St. Louis
1983	Aleta Sill	214-188	Dana Miller-Mackie	Las Vegas
1984	Kazue Inahashi	248-222	Aleta Sill	Niagara Falls, N.Y.
1985	Aleta Sill	279-192	Linda Graham	Toledo, Ohio
1986	Cora Fiebig	223-177	Barbara Thorberg	Orange County, Calif.
1987	Cathy Almeida	850-817	Lorrie Nichols	Hartford, Ct.
1988	Wendy Macpherson	213-199	Leanne Barrette	Reno, Nev.
1989	Carol Gianotti	207-177	Sandra Jo Shiery	Bismarck, N.D.
1990	a-Patty Ann	207-173	Vesma Grinfelds	Tampa, Fla.
1991	Dede Davidson	231-159	Jeanne Maiden	Cedar Rapids, Iowa
1992	Cindy Coburn-Carroll	184-170	Dana Miller-Mackie	Lansing, Mich.
1993	Jan Schmidt	201-163	Patty Costello	Baton Rouge, La.
1994	Anne Marie Duggan	224-177	Wendy Macpherson	Salt Lake City
1995	Sandra Postma	226-187	Carolyn Dorin	Tucson, Ari.
1996	Lisa Wagner	231-226	Tammy Turner	Buffalo
1997	Sandra Jo Odom	209-185	Audry Allen	Reno, Nev.

Major Championships (Cont.)

Year	Winners	Score	Runner-Up	Location
1998	Lynda Norry	213-157	Karen Stroud	Davenport, Iowa
1999	Leanne Barrette	256-174	Dede Davidson	Indianapolis
2000	Wendy Macpherson	227-202	Marianne DiRupo	Reno, Nev.

Sam's Town Invitational

Originally held in Milwaukee as the Pabst Tournament of Champions, but discontinued after one year (1981). The event was revived in 1984, moved to Las Vegas and renamed the Sam's Town Tournament of Champions. Since then it has been known as the LPBT Tournament of Champions (1985), the Sam's Town National Pro/Am (1986-88) and the Sam's Town Invitational (since 1989).

Multiple winners: Tish Johnson (3); Aleta Sill (2).

Year	Winners	Score	Runner-Up	Location
1981	Cindy Coburn	n/a	n/a	Milwaukee
1982-83	Not held			
1984	Aleta Sill	238 (1 game)	Cheryl Daniels	Las Vegas
1985	Patty Costello	236 (1 game)	Robin Romeo	Las Vegas
1986	Aleta Sill	238 (1 game)	Dina Wheeler	Las Vegas
1987	Debbie Bennett	880 (4 games)	Lorrie Nichols	Las Vegas
1988	Donna Adamek	634 (3 games)	Robin Romeo	Las Vegas
1989	Tish Johnson	210 (1 game)	Dede Davidson	Las Vegas
1990	Wendy Macpherson	900 (4 games)	Jeanne Maiden	Las Vegas
1991	Lorrie Nichols	469 (2 games)	Dana Miller-Mackie	Las Vegas
1992	Tish Johnson	279 (1 game)	Robin Romeo	Las Vegas
1993	Robin Romeo	194 (1 game)	Tammy Turner	Las Vegas
1994	Tish Johnson	178 (1 game)	Carol Gianotti	Las Vegas
1995	Michelle Mullen	202 (1 game)	Cheryl Daniels	Las Vegas
1996	Carol Gianotti-Block	892 (4 games)	Leanne Barrette	Las Vegas
1997	Kim Adler	953 (4 games)	Wendy Macpherson	Las Vegas
1998	Julie Gardner	268-226	Dede Davidson	Las Vegas
1999	Wendy Macpherson	209-195	Marianne DiRupo	Las Vegas

Annual Leaders
Average
PBA Tour

The George Young Memorial Award, named after the late ABC Hall of Fame bowler. Based on at least 16 national PBA tournaments from 1959-78, and at least 400 games of tour competition since 1979.

Multiple winners: Mark Roth (6); Earl Anthony (5); Walter Ray Williams Jr. (4); Marshall Holman (3); Norm Duke, Billy Hardwick, Don Johnson and Wayne Zahn (2).

Year		Avg	Year		Avg	Year		Avg
1962	Don Carter	212.84	1975	Earl Anthony	219.06	1988	Mark Roth	218.04
1963	Billy Hardwick	210.35	1976	Mark Roth	215.97	1989	Pete Weber	215.43
1964	Ray Bluth	210.51	1977	Mark Roth	218.17	1990	Amleto Monacelli	218.16
1965	Dick Weber	211.90	1978	Mark Roth	219.83	1991	Norm Duke	218.21
1966	Wayne Zahn	208.63	1979	Mark Roth	221.66	1992	Dave Ferraro	219.70
1967	Wayne Zahn	212.14	1980	Earl Anthony	218.54	1993	Walter Ray Williams Jr.	222.98
1968	Jim Stefanich	211.90	1981	Mark Roth	216.70	1994	Norm Duke	222.83
1969	Billy Hardwick	212.96	1982	Marshall Holman	216.15	1995	Mike Aulby	225.49
1970	Nelson Burton Jr.	214.91	1983	Earl Anthony	216.65	1996	Walter Ray Williams Jr.	225.37
1971	Don Johnson	213.98	1984	Marshall Holman	213.91	1997	Walter Ray Williams Jr.	222.00
1972	Don Johnson	215.29	1985	Mark Baker	213.72	1998	Walter Ray Williams Jr.	226.13
1973	Earl Anthony	215.80	1986	John Gant	214.38	1999	Parker Bohn III	228.04
1974	Earl Anthony	219.34	1987	Marshall Holman	216.80			

WPBA National Championship (1960-1980)

The Women's Professional Bowling Association National Championship tournament was discontinued when the WPBA broke up in 1981. The WPBA changed its name from the Professional Women Bowlers Association (PWBA) in 1978.

Multiple winners: Patty Costello (3); Dotty Fothergill (2).

Year		Year		Year		Year	
1960	Marion Ladewig	1966	Judy Lee	1972	Patty Costello	1978	Toni Gillard
1961	Shirley Garms	1967	Betty Mivelaz	1973	Betty Morris	1979	Cindy Coburn
1962	Stephanie Balogh	1968	Dotty Fothergill	1974	Pat Costello	1980	Donna Adamek
1963	Janet Harman	1969	Dotty Fothergill	1975	Pam Buckner		
1964	Betty Kuczynski	1970	Bobbe North	1976	Patty Costello		
1965	Helen Duval	1971	Patty Costello	1977	Vesma Grinfelds		

AP/Wide World Photos

Carol Gianotti-Block smiles after bowling a turkey (three strikes in a row) during the championship game of the Clabber Girl Open on June 15, 2000. The Australia native has won major events at the 1989 WIBC Queens and 1996 Sam's Town Invitational and was the Bowler of the Year in 1998.

PWBA Tour

The Professional Women's Bowling Association (PWBA) went by the name Ladies Professional Bowling Tour (LPBT) from 1981-1997 and the Women's Professional Bowling Association prior to that. This table is based on at least 282 games of tour competition.

Multiple winners: Leanne Barrette, Nikki Gianulias, Wendy Macpherson and Lisa Rathgeber Wagner (3); Anne Marie Duggan and Aleta Sill (2).

Year		Avg	Year		Avg	Year		Avg
1981	Nikki Gianulias	213.71	1988	Lisa Wagner	213.02	1995	Anne Marie Duggan	215.79
1982	Nikki Gianulias	210.63	1989	Lisa Wagner	211.87	1996	Tammy Turner	215.23
1983	Lisa Rathgeber	208.50	1990	Leanne Barrette	211.53	1997	Wendy Macpherson	214.68
1984	Aleta Sill	210.68	1991	Leanne Barrette	211.48	1998	Dede Davidson	217.25
1985	Aleta Sill	211.10	1992	Leanne Barrette	211.36	1999	Wendy Macpherson	218.85
1986	Nikki Gianulias	213.89	1993	Tish Johnson	215.39			
1987	Wendy Macpherson	211.11	1994	Anne Marie Duggan	213.47			

Money Won
PBA Tour

Multiple winners: Earl Anthony (6); Walter Ray Williams Jr. (5); Mark Roth and Dick Weber (4); Mike Aulby (3); Don Carter (2).

Year		Earnings	Year		Earnings	Year		Earnings
1959	Dick Weber	$7,672	1973	Don McCune	$69,000	1987	Pete Weber	$179,516
1960	Don Carter	22,525	1974	Earl Anthony	99,585	1988	Brian Voss	225,485
1961	Dick Weber	26,280	1975	Earl Anthony	107,585	1989	Mike Aulby	298,237
1962	Don Carter	49,972	1976	Earl Anthony	110,833			
1963	Dick Weber	46,333	1977	Mark Roth	105,583	1990	Amleto Monacelli	204,775
1964	Bob Strampe	33,592	1978	Mark Roth	134,500	1991	David Ozio	225,585
1965	Dick Weber	47,675	1979	Mark Roth	12-+,517	1992	Marc McDowell	176,215
1966	Wayne Zahn	54,720				1993	Walter Ray Williams Jr.	296,370
1967	Dave Davis	54,165	1980	Wayne Webb	116,700	1994	Norm Duke	273,752
1968	Jim Stefanich	67,375	1981	Earl Anthony	164,735	1995	Mike Aulby	219,792
1969	Billy Hardwick	64,160	1982	Earl Anthony	134,760	1996	Walter Ray Williams Jr.	244,630
			1983	Earl Anthony	135,605	1997	Walter Ray Williams Jr.	240,544
1970	Mike McGrath	52,049	1984	Mark Roth	158,712	1998	Walter Ray Williams Jr.	238,225
1971	Johnny Petraglia	85,065	1985	Mike Aulby	201,200	1999	Parker Bohn III	232,595
1972	Don Johnson	56,648	1986	Walter Ray Williams Jr.	145,550			

WPBA and PWBA Tours

WPBA leaders through 1980; PWBA leaders since 1981.

Multiple winners: Aleta Sill (6); Donna Adamek (4); Patty Costello, Tish Johnson, Wendy Macpherson and Betty Morris (3); Dotty Fothergill (2).

Year		Earnings	Year		Earnings	Year		Earnings
1965	Betty Kuczynski	$ 3,792	1977	Betty Morris	$23,802	1989	Robin Romeo	$113,750
1966	Joy Abel	5,795	1978	Donna Adamek	31,000	1990	Tish Johnson	94,420
1967	Shirley Garms	4,920	1979	Donna Adamek	26,280	1991	Leanne Barrette	87,618
1968	Dotty Fothergill	16,170				1992	Tish Johnson	96,872
1969	Dotty Fothergill	9,220	1980	Donna Adamek	31,907	1993	Aleta Sill	57,995
			1981	Donna Adamek	41,270	1994	Aleta Sill	126,325
1970	Patty Costello	9,317	1982	Nikki Gianulias	45,875	1995	Tish Johnson	123,440
1971	Vesma Grinfelds	4,925	1983	Aleta Sill	42,525	1996	Wendy Macpherson	107,230
1972	Patty Costello	11,350	1984	Aleta Sill	81,452	1997	Wendy Macpherson	165,425
1973	Judy Cook	11,200	1985	Aleta Sill	52,655	1998	Carol Gianotti-Block	150,350
1974	Betty Morris	30,037	1986	Aleta Sill	36,962	1999	Wendy Macpherson	86,265
1975	Judy Soutar	20,395	1987	Betty Morris	63,735			
1976	Patty Costello	39,585	1988	Lisa Wagner	105,500			

All-Time Leaders

All-time leading money winners on the PBA and PWBA tours, through 1999. PBA figures date back to 1959, while PWBA figures include Women's Pro Bowlers Association (WPBA) earnings through 1980. National tour titles are also listed.

Money Won

PBA Top 20

		Titles	Earnings
1	Walter Ray Williams Jr.	30	$2,403,763
2	Pete Weber	24	2,165,873
3	Mike Aulby	26	1,974,600
4	Parker Bohn III	22	1,828,019
5	Amleto Monacelli	18	1,743,748
6	Brian Voss	20	1,723,820
7	Marshall Holman	22	1,694,515
8	Dave Husted	13	1,540,028
9	Mark Roth	36	1,522,653
10	Norm Duke	16	1,474,406
11	Earl Anthony	41	1,441,061
12	Wayne Webb	20	1,341,318
13	David Ozio	11	1,306,649
14	Gary Dickinson	8	1,256,676
15	Mark Williams	7	1,124,462
16	Tom Baker	9	1,123,070
17	Del Ballard Jr.	12	1,111,247
18	Dave Ferraro	10	1,044,176
19	Johnny Petraglia	14	1,003,650
20	Dave Soutar	17	1,003,508

WPBA-PWBA Top 12

		Titles	Earnings
1	Aleta Sill	30	$1,016,580
2	Tish Johnson	22	920,838
3	Wendy Macpherson	16	874,870
4	Lisa Wagner	32	827,226
5	Anne Marie Duggan	15	789,868
6	Leanne Barrette	21	781,193
7	Carol Gianotti-Block	14	755,999
8	Robin Mossontte	16	669,029
9	Cheryl Daniels	10	664,604
10	Dana Miller-Mackie	16	619,517

Senior PBA Top 5

		Titles	Earnings
1	John Handegard	14	$418,285
2	Gary Dickinson	10	369,608
3	Gene Stus	10	360,545
4	Teata Semiz	8	334,205
5	John Hricsina	7	341,583

Annual Awards
MEN
BWAA Bowler of the Year

Winners selected by Bowling Writers Association of America.

Multiple winners: Earl Anthony and Don Carter (6); Walter Ray Williams Jr. (5); Mark Roth (4); Mike Aulby and Dick Weber (3); Buddy Bomar, Ned Day, Billy Hardwick, Don Johnson, and Steve Nagy (2).

Year		Year		Year		Year	
1942	Johnny Crimmins	1957	Don Carter	1971	Don Johnson	1986	Walter Ray Williams Jr.
1943	Ned Day	1958	Don Carter	1972	Don Johnson	1987	Marshall Holman
1944	Ned Day	1959	Ed Lubanski	1973	Don McCune	1988	Brian Voss
1945	Buddy Bomar			1974	Earl Anthony	1989	Mike Aulby
1946	Joe Wilman	1960	Don Carter	1975	Earl Anthony		
1947	Buddy Bomar	1961	Dick Weber	1976	Earl Anthony	1990	Amleto Monacelli
1948	Andy Varipapa	1962	Don Carter	1977	Mark Roth	1991	David Ozio
1949	Connie Schwoegler	1963	Dick Weber	1978	Mark Roth	1992	Marc McDowell
		1964	Billy Hardwick	1979	Mark Roth	1993	Walter Ray Williams Jr.
1950	Junie McMahon	1965	Dick Weber			1994	Norm Duke
1951	Lee Jouglard	1966	Wayne Zahn	1980	Wayne Webb	1995	Mike Aulby
1952	Steve Nagy	1967	Dave Davis	1981	Earl Anthony	1996	Walter Ray Williams Jr.
1953	Don Carter	1968	Jim Stefanich	1982	Earl Anthony	1997	Walter Ray Williams Jr.
1954	Don Carter	1969	Billy Hardwick	1983	Earl Anthony	1998	Walter Ray Williams Jr.
1955	Steve Nagy			1984	Mark Roth	1999	Parker Bohn III
1956	Bill Lillard	1970	Nelson Burton Jr.	1985	Mike Aulby		

AP/Wide World Photos

Dave Husted shows us the kind of form that made him a three-time winner of the BPAA U.S. Open and a 1996 PBA Hall of Fame inductee. He ranks eighth on the PBA all-time money list through 1999.

PBA Player of the Year

Named after longtime broadcaster Chris Schenkel, winners are selected by members of Professional Bowlers Association. The PBA Player of the Year has differed from the BWAA Bowler of the Year four times—in 1963, '64, '89 and '92.

Multiple winners: Earl Anthony (6); Walter Ray Williams Jr. (5); Mark Roth (4); Mike Aulby, Billy Hardwick, Don Johnson and Amleto Monacelli (2).

Year		Year		Year	
1963	Billy Hardwick	1976	Earl Anthony	1989	Amleto Monacelli
1964	Bob Strampe	1977	Mark Roth	1990	Amleto Monacelli
1965	Dick Weber	1978	Mark Roth	1991	David Ozio
1966	Wayne Zahn	1979	Mark Roth	1992	Dave Ferraro
1967	Dave Davis	1980	Wayne Webb	1993	Walter Ray Williams Jr.
1968	Jim Stefanich	1981	Earl Anthony	1994	Norm Duke
1969	Billy Hardwick	1982	Earl Anthony	1995	Mike Aulby
1970	Nelson Burton Jr.	1983	Earl Anthony	1996	Walter Ray Williams Jr.
1971	Don Johnson	1984	Mark Roth	1997	Walter Ray Williams Jr.
1972	Don Johnson	1985	Mike Aulby	1998	Walter Ray Williams Jr.
1973	Don McCune	1986	Walter Ray Williams Jr.	1999	Parker Bohn III
1974	Earl Anthony	1987	Marshall Holman		
1975	Earl Anthony	1988	Brian Voss		

PBA Rookie of the Year

Named after PBA Hall of Famer Harry Golden, who was the PBA's national tournament director for 30 years. Winners selected by members of Professional Bowlers Association.

Year		Year		Year	
1964	Jerry McCoy	1976	Mike Berlin	1988	Rick Steelsmith
1965	Jim Godman	1977	Steve Martin	1989	Steve Hoskins
1966	Bobby Cooper	1978	Joseph Groskind	1990	Brad Kiszewski
1967	Mike Durbin	1979	Mike Aulby	1991	Ricky Ward
1968	Bob McGregor	1980	Pete Weber	1992	Jason Couch
1969	Larry Lichstein	1981	Mark Fahy	1993	Mark Scroggins
1970	Denny Krick	1982	Mike Steinbach	1994	Tony Ament
1971	Tye Critchlow	1983	Toby Contreras	1995	Billy Myers Jr.
1972	Tommy Hudson	1984	John Gant	1996	C.K. Moore
1973	Steve Neff	1985	Tom Crites	1997	Anthony Lombardo
1974	Cliff McNealy	1986	Marc McDowell	1998	Chris Barnes
1975	Guy Rowbury	1987	Ryan Shafer	1999	Paul Fleming

Annual Awards (Cont.)
WOMEN
BWAA Bowler of the Year
Winners selected by Bowling Writers Association of America.

Multiple winners: Marion Ladewig (9); Donna Adamek and Lisa Rathgeber Wagner (4); Tish Johnson, Wendy Macpherson and Betty Morris (3); Patty Costello, Dotty Forthergill, Shirley Garms, Val Mikiel, Aleta Sill, Judy Soutar and Sylvia Wene (2).

Year		Year		Year	
194L	Val Mikiel	1966	Joy Abel	1984	Aleta Sill
1949	Val Mikiel	1967	Millie Martorella	1985	Aleta Sill
1950	Marion Ladewig	1968	Dotty Fothergill	1986	Lisa Wagner
1951	Marion Ladewig	1969	Dotty Fothergill	1987	Betty Morris
1952	Marion Ladewig	1970	Mary Baker	1988	Lisa Wagner
1953	Marion Ladewig	1971	Paula Sperber	1989	Robin Romeo
1954	Marion Ladewig	1972	Patty Costello	1990	Tish Johnson
1955	Sylvia Wene	1973	Judy Soutar	1991	Leanne Barrette
1956	Anita Cantaline	1974	Betty Morris	1992	Tish Johnson
1957	Marion Ladewig	1975	Judy Soutar	1993	Lisa Wagner
1958	Marion Ladewig	1976	Patty Costello	1994	Anne Marie Duggan
1959	Marion Ladewig	1977	Betty Morris	1995	Tish Johnson
1960	Sylvia Wene	1978	Donna Adamek	1996	Wendy Macpherson
1961	Shirley Garms	1979	Donna Adamek	1997	Wendy Macpherson
1962	Shirley Garms	1980	Donna Adamek	1998	Carol Gianotti-Block
1963	Marion Ladewig	1981	Donna Adamek	1999	Wendy Macpherson
1964	LaVerne Carter	1982	Nikki Gianulias		
1965	Betty Kuczynski	1983	Lisa Rathgeber		

PWBA Player of the Year
Winners selected by members of Professional Women's Bowling Association. The PWBA Player of the Year has differed from the BWAA Bowler of the Year three times—in 1985, '86 and '90.

Multiple winners: Wendy Macpherson and Lisa Rathgeber Wagner (3); Leanne Barrette and Tish Johnson (2).

Year		Year		Year	
1983	Lisa Rathgeber	1989	Robin Romeo	1995	Tish Johnson
1984	Aleta Sill	1990	Leanne Barrette	1996	Wendy Macpherson
1985	Patty Costello	1991	Leanne Barrette	1997	Wendy Macpherson
1986	Jeanne Maiden	1992	Tish Johnson	1998	Carol Gianotti-Block
1987	Betty Morris	1993	Lisa Wagner	1999	Wendy Macpherson
1988	Lisa Wagner	1994	Anne Marie Duggan		

Note: This award was known as the LPBT Player of the Year Award from 1983-97.

WPBA and PWBA Rookie of the Year
Winners selected by members of Women's Professional Bowlers Association (1978-80) and the Professional Women's Bowling Association (since 1981).

Year		Year		Year	
1978	Toni Gillard	1986	Wendy Macpherson	1994	Tammy Turner
1979	Nikki Gianulias	1987	Paula Drake	1995	Krissy Stewart
1980	Lisa Rathgeber	1988	Mary Martha Cerniglia	1996	Liz Johnson
1981	Cindy Mason	1989	Kim Terrell	1997	Lisa Bishop
1982	Carol Norman	1990	Debbie McMullen	1998	Jody Ellis
1983	Anne Marie Pike	1991	Kim Kahrman	1999	Tiffany Stanbrough
1984	Paula Vidad	1992	Marianne DiRupo		
1985	Dede Davidson	1993	Kathy Zielke		

SENIORS
PBA Senior Player of the Year
Winners selected by members of Professional Bowlers Association.

Multiple winners: Gary Dickinson and John Handegard (3).

Year		Year		Year	
1989	Jimmy Certain	1993	Gary Dickinson	1997	Gary Dickinson
1990	John Hricsina	1994	Gary Dickinson	1998	Pete Couture
1991	John Handegard	1995	John Handegard	1999	Dale Eagle
1992	Gene Stus	1996	John Handegard		

Horse Racing

Jockey **Kent Desormeaux** celebrates his Kentucky Derby win with Fusaichi Pegasus in the winner's circle of Churchill Downs.

AP/Wide World Photos

Flying High

Pre-race favorite Fusaichi Pegasus lives up to the hype and storms to victory at the Kentucky Derby.

by

Hank Goldberg

The Triple Crown season in 2000 was one of colossal expectation, mystery, cameos and upset. Derby fever hit the equine world in mid-March when Fusaichi Pegasus, a $4 million purchase by eccentric Japanese businessman Fusao Sekiguchi, overwhelmed the field in the San Felipe Stakes at Santa Anita.

On that same day at Aqueduct, Red Bullet beat a fast-closing Aptitude to the finish line in the Gotham Stakes. These horses would be the major players of the season.

Meanwhile, a feel-good story had emerged at Gulfstream where Hal's Hope, owned and trained by 89-year-old Harold Rose, topped D. Wayne Lukas' High Yield in the Florida Derby.

"Fu-Peg" headed east, passing on the Santa Anita Derby for the Wood Memorial in New York. Again he

Hank Goldberg is an analyst for ESPN's horse racing coverage.

won in enormously impressive fashion under the watchful eye of his trainer, Neil Drysdale.

The stage was set for the first Saturday in May. Rose had the sentimental favorite in Hal's Hope, Jenine Sahadi was seeking to become the first female trainer to win the Run for the Roses with The Deputy, and Drysdale, who would be elected to horse racing's Hall of Fame later in the year, was trying to record his first Derby win with the race's most celebrated entry. Another Hall of Fame trainer, Bobby Frankel, was looking to score with Aptitude.

Breaking out of the 15 hole, Kent Desormeaux bided his time on Fusaichi Pegasus, weaving his way through the usual Derby traffic before a monster inside move down the stretch. Like his mythological namesake, he appeared to fly to victory. Aptitude had to take the outside route and settled for second.

After the race, an unprecedented amount of Triple Crown strategizing

AP/Wide World Photos

Kent Desormeaux, left, hands the Kentucky Derby Trophy to Fusaichi Pegasus owner **Fusao Sekiguchi** after their win in the first jewel of the Triple Crown on May 6.

set in. Because of Aptitude's finishing style, Frankel opted to pass on the Preakness, which is a sixteenth of a mile shorter than the Kentucky Derby distance, and wait for the mile-and-a-half Belmont Stakes.

Enter Frank Stronach's Red Bullet, well rested from his spring New York campaign. The weather in Baltimore for the Preakness was wet and miserable and the track was described as "greasy." While Fusaichi Pegasus found the going too tough, Red Bullet thrived on it, ending the possibility of a Triple Crown winner in 2000.

Red Bullet's handlers decided to skip the Belmont and one week before the race Fusaichi Pegasus withdrew with foot problems. On that blazing hot afternoon, Commendable, owned by Bob and Beverly Lewis and trained by Lukas, found himself in a soft, uncontested pace and prevailed. Again, Aptitude came on too late, running second, while Unshaded, who would be heard from later in the summer, was third.

The $39.60 mutuel was sweet for Commendable's backers and the win was something of a make-good for the Lewis-Lukas combination which was denied a Triple Crown win in 1999 when Charismatic was beaten and injured in the Belmont.

The summer handicap division saw Lemon Drop Kid establish himself as the favorite for the Breeders' Cup Classic at Churchill Downs in November. Trained by Scotty Schulhofer, the 1999 Belmont champ reeled off victories in the $500,000 Suburban on July 4, the $750,000 Whitney on Aug. 6, and the $500,000 Woodward on Sept. 16.

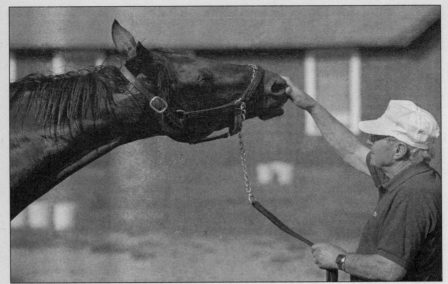

Under the tutelage of trainer **Scotty Schulhofer**, 1999 Belmont Stakes winner **Lemon Drop Kid** continued to shine in 2000, winning five races through September and staking his claim as Horse of the Year.

Frankel was also on a tear, winning the Beverly Hills Handicap in Hollywood with Happyanunoit, the Arlington Million with Chester House, and the $1,000,000 Pacific Classic at Delaware with Skimming, his fifth win in the ten-year history of that race.

Other major stakes winners went to Dixie Union in Monmouth's Haskell, Captain Steve in the Swaps at Hollywood, and Unshaded at Saratoga's Travers.

Unfortunately, Dubai Millennium, the winner of the Dubai World Cup, was knocked out of the Breeders' Cup after being injured in his score in the Prince of Wales at Royal Ascot. Fusaichi Pegasus returned in September to win the seven-furlong Jerome at Belmont and waged a hearty battle with Lemon Drop Kid for Horse of the Year in the Breeders' Cup in Louisville. ■

Hank Goldberg's Top Horse Racing Stories from 1999-00

10. **On the business side,** Chicago's Arlington Park owner Richard Duchossois becomes the largest stockholder in Churchill Downs (with his 25 percent stake) as Churchill assumes ownership of Arlington.

9. **Neil Drysdale,** who trained five Breeders' Cup winners through 1999 as well as 1992 Belmont winner A.P. Indy and 2000 Kentucky Derby winner Fusaichi Pegasus, is inducted into the National Horse Racing Hall of Fame in Saratoga Springs.

8. Joining Drysdale in the Hall of Fame is **Julie Krone**, who won over 3,500 races including the 1993 Belmont with Colonial Affair, making her the only woman

AP/Wide World Photos

Laffit Pincay Jr. became thoroughbred racing's all-time winningest jockey in December, 1999 with his 8,834th win. Pincay won three consecutive Belmont Stakes in the early 80s and was also aboard Kentucky Derby winner Swale in 1984.

to ride a Triple Crown event winner. Also inducted are 1956 Kentucky Derby champion, Needles, Drysdale's A.P. Indy, and Winning Colors, who became the third filly to take the Kentucky Derby, beating Forty Niner in 1988.

7. **Among those who passed on** in 2000 was owner Allen Paulson, who had in his stable the immortal Cigar. Owner Fred Hooper, whose standouts included Precisionist, died at the ripe old age of 102, and trainer Eddie Gregson, whose Gato Del Sol won the 1982 Kentucky Derby, also died in 2000.

6. **A new Breeders' Cup event** makes its debut at Gulfstream in November, 1999 as Jerry Bailey rides Soaring Softly to victory in the inaugural mile-and-three-eighths Filly and Mare Turf.

5. Other **Breeders' Cup winners** from Gulfstream include Cash Run in the Juvenile Fillies, Artax in the Sprint, Beautiful Pleasure in the Distaff, Silic in the Mile, Anees in the Juvenile, Daylami in the one and one-half mile Turf, and in the race of the day, Cat Thief over Budroyale in the Classic.

4. On the strength of his 1999 Kentucky Derby and Preakness victories, D. Wayne Lukas' **Charismatic** is given the Eclipse Award for Horse of the Year.

3. With his 8,834th career victory, **Laffit Pincay Jr.** passes legend Bill Shoemaker as the winningest jockey of all time.

2. After a disappointing 17th-place finish in the Kentucky Derby, **Commendable**, owned by Bob and Beverly Lewis and trained by D. Wayne Lukas, surprises with a win in the Belmont.

1. Finally after 20 years of futility, the pre-race favorite actually wins the Kentucky Derby as **Fusaichi Pegasus** (at 9-5 odds) flies to victory. He is upset, however, in the Preakness by Jerry Bailey and Red Bullet, removing any hopes for a Triple Crown winner in 2000. ■

PREAKNESS UNIQUENESS

Red Bullet became just the fifth horse since 1952 to win the Preakness after not starting the Kentucky Derby. Here is a look at the list of horses who surprised at the Preakness, none of which would go on to win the Belmont Stakes.

Year	Horse
2000	Red Bullet
1983	Deputed Testamony
1980	Codex
1972	Bee Bee Bee
1962	Greek Money

BIG RED STILL THE ONE

Fusaichi Pegasus ran one of the fastest Kentucky Derbies in history in 2000 (2:01⅕), finishing just out of the all-time top five. But Secretariat, on his way to the 1973 Triple Crown, is still the only horse to run under two minutes in horse racing's marquee event. Here's a look at the fastest times in Derby history.

	Time
Secretariat, 1973	1:59 ⅖
Northern Dancer, 1964	2:00
Spend a Buck, 1985	2:00 ⅕
Decidedly, 1962	2:00 ⅖
Proud Clarion, 1967	2:00 ⅗

BELMONT LONGSHOTS

Commendable paid a healthy $18.80 on a one-dollar bet at the 2000 Belmont Stakes. Here's a look at the biggest-paying ponies in Belmont Stakes history.

		To $1
1961	Sherluck	65.05
1980	Temperence Hill	53.40
1971	Pass Catcher	34.50
1999	Lemon Drop Kid	29.75
2000	Commendable	18.80
1944	Bounding Home	16.35

NOT PREAK-PERFORMERS

Fusaichi Pegasus, off his convincing win in the Kentucky Derby, was a big favorite to continue his run at the Triple Crown in 2000. Instead he tied the record for the biggest favorite not to win at the follow up to the Derby.

	Odds	Finish
Fusaichi Pegasus, 2000	.30-1	2nd
Riva Ridge, 1972	.30-1	4th
Gilded Knight, 1939	.45-1	2nd
Linkage, 1982	.50-1	2nd

TRIPLE CROWN TRAINERS

D. Wayne Lukas won the Belmont Stakes with Commendable in 2000 to tie James "Sunny Jim" Fitzsimmons for the most wins by a trainer in Triple Crown races.

	Wins
D. Wayne Lukas	13
James Fitzsimmons	13
Robert Walden	12
James Rowe	10
Ben Jones	9
Max Hirsch	9
	■

Thoroughbred Racing
Major Stakes Races

Winners of major stakes races from Oct. 9, 1999 through Sept. 17, 2000; (T) indicates turf race course; (F) indicates furlongs.

LATE 1999

Date	Race	Track	Miles	Winner	Jockey	Purse
Oct. 9	Hawthorne Gold Cup Handicap	Hawthorne	1 1/16	Supreme Sound	Randall Meier	$500,000
Nov. 6	Breeders Cup - Juv. Fillies	Gulfstream Park	1 1/16	Cash Run	Jerry Bailey	1,000,000
Nov. 6	Breeders Cup - Sprint	Gulfstream Park	6 F	Artax	Jorge Chavez	1,000,000
Nov. 6	Breeders Cup - Distaff	Gulfstream Park	1 1/8	Beautiful Pleasure	Jorge Chavez	2,000,000
Nov. 6	Breeders Cup - Mile	Gulfstream Park	1	Silic	Corey Nakatani	1,000,000
Nov. 6	Breeders Cup - Juvenile	Gulfstream Park	1 1/16	Anees	Gary Stevens	1,000,000
Nov. 6	Breeders Cup - Turf	Gulfstream Park	1 1/2 (T)	Daylami	Frankie Dettori	2,000,000
Nov. 6	Breeders Cup - Filly & Mare Turf	Gulfstream Park	1 3/8 (T)	Soaring Softly	Jerry Bailey	1,000,000
Nov. 6	Breeders Cup - Classic	Gulfstream Park	1 1/4	Cat Thief	Pat Day	4,000,000
Nov. 27	Japan Cup	Tokyo Racecourse	2400 M	Special Week	Yutaka Take	3,424,545
Nov. 29	Matriarch Stakes	Hollywood	1 1/4 (T)	Happyanunoit	Brice Blanc	500,000
Nov. 29	Hollywood Derby	Hollywood	1 1/8 (T)	Super Quercus	Alex Solis	500,000
Dec. 12	Hollywood Turf Cup	Hollywood	1 1/2 (T)	Lazy Lode	Laffit Pincay Jr.	500,000
Dec. 12	Hollywood Futurity	Hollywood	1 1/16	Captain Steve	Robby Albarado	419,000

2000 (through Sept. 16)

Date	Race	Track	Miles	Winner	Jockey	Purse
Jan. 5	Spectacular Bid Stakes*	Gulfstream	6 F	B L's Appeal	Mike Smith	$75,000
Jan. 8	San Miguel Stakes*	Santa Anita	6 F	Swept Overboard	Eddie Delahoussaye	100,000
Jan. 15	Holy Bull Stakes*	Gulfstream	1 1/16	Hal's Hope	Roger Velez	100,000
Jan. 15	Golden Gate Derby	Golden Gate	1 1/16	New Advantage	Alderto Lopez	150,000
Jan. 29	Hutcheson Stakes*	Gulfstream	7 F	Summer Note	Shane Sellers	150,000
Jan. 30	Santa Catalina Stakes*	Santa Anita	1 1/16	The Deputy	Chris McCarron	100,000
Feb. 5	*Donn Handicap*	Gulfstream	1 1/8	Stephen Got Even	Shane Sellers	500,000
Feb. 5	Charles H. Strub Stakes	Santa Anita	1 1/8	General Challenge	Corey Nakatani	500,000
Feb. 5	San Vicente Stakes*	Santa Anita	7 F	Archer City Slew	Kent Desormeaux	150,000
Feb. 19	Fountain of Youth Stakes*	Gulfstream	1 1/16	High Yield	Pat Day	200,000
Feb. 26	Gulfstream Park Handicap	Gulfstream	1 1/4	Behrens	Jorge Chavez	350,000
Feb. 27	Rampart Handicap	Gulfstream	1 1/16	Bella Chiarra	Shane Sellers	200,000
Mar. 4	San Rafael Stakes*	Santa Anita	1	War Chant	Kent Desormeaux	200,000
Mar. 4	The Southwest	Oaklawn	1	Afternoon Affair	Joseph Judice	75,000
Mar. 4	*Santa Anita Handicap*	Santa Anita	1 1/4	General Challenge	Corey Nakatani	1,000,000
Mar. 5	Santa Margarita Handicap	Santa Anita	1 1/8	Riboletta	Corey Nakatani	300,000
Mar. 11	El Camino Real Derby*	Bay Meadows	1 1/16	Remember Sheikh	Frank Alvarado	200,000
Mar. 11	Swale Stakes*	Gulfstream	7 F	Trippi	Jerry Bailey	100,000
Mar. 11	Florida Derby*	Gulfstream	1 1/8	Hal's Hope	Roger Velez	750,000
Mar. 12	Louisiana Derby*	Fairgrounds	1 1/16	Mighty	Shane Sellers	750,000
Mar. 12	Santa Anita Oaks	Santa Anita	1 1/16	Surfside	Pat Day	300,000
Mar. 19	Gotham Stakes*	Aqueduct	1	Red Bullet	Alex Solis	200,000
Mar. 19	Tampa Bay Derby*	Tampa Bay	1 1/16	Wheelaway	Richard Migliore	150,000
Mar. 19	San Felipe Stakes*	Santa Anita	1 1/16	Fusaichi Pegasus	Kent Desormeaux	250,000
Mar. 25	Rebel Stakes*	Oaklawn	1 1/16	Snuck In	Cash Asmussen	100,000
Mar. 25	Spiral Stakes†*	Turfway	1 1/16	Globalize	Francisco Torres	600,000
Mar. 25	Dubai Classic	Nad al-Sheba	1 1/4	Dubai Millennium	Frankie Dettori	6,000,000
Apr. 8	Santa Anita Derby*	Santa Anita	1 1/8	The Deputy	Chris McCarron	1,000,000
Apr. 8	Flamingo Stakes	Hialeah	1 1/8	Trippi	Eibar Coa	250,000
Apr. 8	Ashland Stakes	Keeneland	1 1/16	Rings A Chime	Shane Sellers	500,000
Apr. 8	The Oaklawn Handicap	Oaklawn	1 1/8	K One King	Calvin Borel	600,000
Apr. 9	Apple Blossom Handicap	Oaklawn	1 1/16	Heritage of Gold	Shane Sellers	500,000
Apr. 12	Lafayette Stakes*	Keeneland	7 F	Caller One	Robbie Davis	100,000
Apr. 15	Blue Grass Stakes*	Keeneland	1 1/8	High Yield	Pat Day	750,000

Date	Race	Track	Miles	Winner	Jockey	Purse
Apr. 15	Arkansas Derby*	Oaklawn	1⅛	Graeme Hall	Robby Albarado	$500,000
Apr. 15	Wood Memorial*	Aqueduct	1⅛	Fusaichi Pegasus	Kent Desormeaux	750,000
Apr. 15	Bay Shore Stakes*	Aqueduct	7 F	Precise End	Jorge Chavez	100,000
Apr. 15	California Derby	Golden Gate	1⅛	Bet on Red	Ronnie Warren	250,000
Apr. 22	Federico Tesio Stakes*	Pimlico	1⅛	Runspastum	Robbie Davis	200,000
Apr. 22	San Juan Capistrano Handicap	Santa Anita	1¾	Sunshine Street	Jerry Bailey	400,000
Apr. 22	Lexington Stakes*	Keeneland	1¹/₁₆	Unshaded	Shane Sellers	325,000
Apr. 22	Lone Star Derby*	Lone Star	1¹/₁₆	Tahkodha Hills	Eibar Coa	300,000
Apr. 29	Derby Trial*	Churchill Downs	1	Performing Magic	Pat Day	100,000
Apr. 30	Snow Chief Stakes	Hollywood	1⅛	Grey Memo	Matt Garcia	250,000
May 5	Kentucky Oaks	Churchill Downs	1⅛	Secret Status	Pat Day	500,000
May 6	**Kentucky Derby***	Churchill Downs	1¼	Fusaichi Pegasus	Kent Desormeaux	1,000,000
May 6	Withers Stakes*	Aqueduct	1	Big E E	Herberto Castillo Jr.	150,000
May 13	*Pimlico Special*	Pimlico	1³/₁₆	Golden Missile	Kent Desormeaux	750,000
May 13	Illinois Derby*	Sportsman's Park	1⅛	Performing Magic	Shane Sellers	500,000
May 19	Black-Eyed Susan Stakes	Pimlico	1⅛	Jostle	Kent Desormeaux	200,000
May 20	**Preakness Stakes***	Pimlico	1³/₁₆	Red Bullet	Jerry Bailey	1,000,000
May 27	Peter Pan Stakes*	Belmont	1⅛	Postponed	Edgar Prado	200,000
May 29	Metropolitan Mile	Belmont	1	Yankee Victor	Herberto Castillo	750,000
May 29	Charles Whittgham Handicap	Hollywood Park	1¼ (T)	White Heart	Kent Desormeaux	300,000
June 3	*Massachusetts Handicap*	Suffolk Downs	1⅛	Running Stag	John Velazquez	600,000
June 9	Acorn Stakes	Belmont	1	Finder's Fee	John Velazquez	200,000
June 10	**Belmont Stakes***	Belmont	1½	Commendable	Pat Day	1,000,000
June 10	Riva Ridge Stakes*	Belmont	7 F	Trippi	Jerry Bailey	150,000
June 10	Round Table Stakes*	Arlington	1⅛	Fan the Flame	Eddie Martin Jr.	125,000
June 10	Vodafone English Derby	Epsom Downs	1½ (T)	Sinndar	Johnny Murtagh	1,474,056
June 11	The Californian	Hollywood Park	1⅛	Big Ten	Alex Solis	250,000
June 17	Stephen Foster Handicap	Churchill Downs	1⅛	Golden Missile	Kent Desormeaux	750,000
June 18	Shoemaker BC Mile	Hollywood	1 (T)	Silic	Corey Nakatani	250,000
June 18	Leonard Richards Stakes*	Delaware	1¹/₁₆	Grundlefoot	Travis Dunkelberger	200,000
June 24	Jersey Shore BC*	Monmouth	6 F	Disco Rico	Joe Bravo	100,000
June 25	Vanity Handicap	Hollywood Park	1⅛	Riboletta	Chris McCarron	300,000
June 25	Queen's Plate	Woodbine	1¼	Scatter the Gold	Todd Kabel	1,000,000
July 1	Mother Goose Stakes	Belmont	1⅛	Secret Status	Pat Day	250,000
July 1	Affirmed Handicap*	Hollywood Park	1¹/₁₆	Tiznow	Victor Espinoza	125,000
July 2	Irish Derby	Curragh	1½ (T)	Sinndar	Johnny Murtagh	1,550,000
July 2	Beverly Hills Handicap	Hollywood Park	1¼ (T)	Happyanunoit	Brice Blanc	250,000
July 4	Suburban Handicap	Belmont	1¼	Lemon Drop Kid	Edgar Prado	500,000
July 9	*Hollywood Gold Cup*	Hollywood Park	1¼	Early Pioneer	Victor Espinoza	1,000,000
July 9	Dwyer Stakes*	Belmont	1¹/₁₆	Albert the Great	Richard Migliore	150,000
July 15	Frank J. DeFrancis Memorial	Laurel Park	6 F	Richter Scale	Richard Migliore	300,000
July 15	Ohio Derby*	Thistledown	1⅛	Milwaukee Brew	Michael McCarthy	300,000
July 15	Carry Back Stakes*	Calder	6 F	Caller One	Corey Nakatani	200,000
July 22	Coaching Club Am. Oaks	Belmont	1½	Jostle	Mike Smith	350,000
July 22	Hollywood Oaks	Hollywood Park	1⅛	Kumari Continent	Kent Desormeaux	150,000
July 23	Swaps Stakes*	Hollywood Park	1⅛	Captain Steve	Corey Nakatani	500,000
July 29	K. George VI and Q. Elizabeth Diamond Stakes	Ascot	1½ (T)	Montjeu	Michael Kinane	600,000
July 30	Eddie Read Handicap	Del Mar	1⅛ (T)	Ladies Din	Kent Desormeaux	400,000
July 30	Go for Wand Handicap	Saratoga	1⅛	Heritage of Gold	Shane Sellers	250,000
Aug. 4	Amsterdam Stakes*	Saratoga	6 F	Personal First	Pat Day	100,000
Aug. 5	Jim Dandy Stakes*	Saratoga	1⅛	Graeme Hall	Jerry Bailey	400,000
Aug. 6	*Whitney Handicap*	Saratoga	1⅛	Lemon Drop Kid	Edgar Prado	750,000
Aug. 6	Haskell Invitational*	Monmouth	1⅛	Dixie Union	Alex Solis	1,000,000
Aug. 19	Alabama Stakes	Saratoga	1¼	Jostle	Mike Smith	750,000
Aug. 25	Personal Ensign Handicap	Saratoga	1¼	Beautiful Pleasure	Jorge Chavez	400,000
Aug. 26	King's Bishop Stakes*	Saratoga	7 F	More Than Ready	Pat Day	200,000
Aug. 26	Travers Stakes*	Saratoga	1¼	Unshaded	Shane Sellers	1,000,000
Aug. 26	Pacific Classic	Del Mar	1¼	Skimming	Garrett Gomez	1,000,000
Aug. 27	Philip H. Iselin Handicap	Monmouth	1⅛	Rize	Jose Ferrer	350,000
Aug. 27	Saratoga BC Handicap	Saratoga	1¼	Pleasant Breeze	Jorge Chavez	300,000
Aug. 27	Remington Park Derby	Remington	1¹/₁₆	Performing Magic	Shane Sellers	300,000
Sept. 9	Man o' War Stakes	Belmont	1⅜ (T)	Fantastic Light	Jerry Bailey	500,000
Sept. 10	Atto Mile	Woodbine	1 (T)	Riviera	John Velazquez	1,000,000
Sept. 16	The Woodward Stakes	Belmont	1⅛	Lemon Drop Kid	Edgar Prado	500,000
Sept. 16	Ruffian Handicap	Belmont	1¹/₁₆	Riboletta	Chris McCarron	250,000

* VISA 3-Year-Old Championship Series race (see tables on p. 780).
Races in *italics* make up the Super Series Races of the NTRA Champions on Fox racing series.
† known as GalleryFurniture.com Stakes in 1999.

The 2000 Triple Crown

Thoroughbred racing's Triple Crown for three-year-olds consists of the Kentucky Derby, Preakness Stakes and Belmont Stakes run over six weeks on May 6, May 20 and June 10, respectively.

126th KENTUCKY DERBY

Grade I for three-year-olds; 8th race at Churchill Downs in Louisville. **Date**— May 6, 2000; **Distance**— 1¼ miles; **Stakes Purse**— $1,000,000 ($700,000 to winner; $170,000 for 2nd; $85,000 for 3rd; $45,000 for 4th); **Track**— Fast; **Off**— 5:29 p.m. EDT; **Favorite**— Fusaichi Pegasus (9-5 odds).

Winner— Fusaichi Pegasus; **Field**— 19 horses; **Time**— 2:01⅕; **Start**— Good for all; **Won**— Driving; **Sire**— Mr. Prospector; **Dam**— Angel Fever; **Record** (going into race)— 5 starts, 4 wins, 1 second; **Last start**— 1st in Wood Memorial (Apr. 15); **Breeder**— Arthur B. Hancock III and Stonerside Ltd.

Order of Finish	Jockey	PP	1/4	1/2	3/4	Mile	Stretch	Finish	To $1
Fusaichi Pegasus	Kent Desormeaux	15	15-3½	13½	11½	6-1	1-hd	1-1½	2.30
Aptitude	Alex Solis	2	13½	14-1½	10-hd	8-1	4-3½	2-4	11.80
Impeachment	Craig Perret	14	19	19	17-hd	13-1½	7-hd	3½	6.20
More Than Ready	John Velazquez	9	3-hd	3-hd	3½	4-hd	2-hd	4-nk	11.30
Wheelaway	Richard Migliore	3	6-hd	8½	7-hd	5-1	3½	5-3	20.80
China Visit	Frankie Dettori	11	12-5	11-hd	9-1½	7-hd	6-hd	6-hd	23.70
Curule	Marlon St. Julien	18	14-1	15-1	16-4	9½	8½	7-4½	23.70
Captain Steve	Robby Albarado	7	7-hd	6½	6-1½	1-hd	5-1	8¾	8.10
War Chant	Jerry Bailey	8	11-1	10-1	12½	14-hd	10-2	9-3¾	9.90
Deputy Warlock	Mark Guidry	6	17-1½	17-3	18-2½	18-1½	17-3	10½	20.80
Trippi	Jorge Chavez	5	2-2½	2-1	2-1½	2-hd	9-1	11-1	6.20
Exchange Rate	Calvin Borel	16	5-hd	7-hd	8-hd	12½	12-hd	12¾	59.20
Anees	Corey Nakatani	1	16-1	16-6	15½	11-hd	11-1½	13-2¾	17.10
The Deputy	Chris McCarron	10	9½	12-2½	14½	17-hd	16-hd	14¾	4.60
High Yield	Pat Day	17	8½	5½	5½	10½	15-hd	15-nk	6.20
Hal's Hope	Roger Velez	4	1-hd	1-1	1½	3-1	13-1	16-1¾	22.70
Commendable	Edgar Prado	12	10-hd	9½	13-hd	16-1½	18-1	17-3½	6.20
Ronton	Brice Blanc	19	18-1½	18-1½	19	19	19	18	20.80
Graeme Hall	Shane Sellers	13	4-1	4-1	4-hd	15½	14-1½	19-DNF	46.30

Times— 22⅖; 45⅘; 1:09⅘; 1:35⅗; 2:01⅕.

$2 Mutual Prices— #12 Fusaichi Pegasus ($6.60, $5.60, $4.00); #5 Aptitude ($9.80, $5.80); #1C Impeachment ($4.00). **Exacta**— (12-5) for $66.00; **Trifecta**— (12-5-1) for $435.00; **Superfecta**— (12-5-1-9) for $1,635.40; **Pick Six**— (14-5-8-1-6-3/12) (5-correct) $9,523.80; **Scratched**— Globalize; **Overweights**— none; **Attendance**— 153,204; **TV Rating**— 6.6/17 share (ABC).

Trainers & Owners (by finish): **1**— Neil Drysdale & Fusao Sekiguchi; **2**— Robert Frankel & Juddmonte Farms; **3**— Todd Pletcher & Dogwood Stable; **4**— Todd Pletcher & James Scatuorchio; **5**— John Kimmel & Caesar Kimmel/Philip Solondz; **6**— Saeed bin Suroor & Godolphin Racing Inc.; **7**— Saeed bin Suroor & Godolphin Racing Inc.; **8**— Bob Baffert & Michael Pegram; **9**— Neil Drysdale & Marjorie/Irving Cowan; **10**— Kenneth McPeek & Select Stable; **11**— Todd Pletcher & Dogwood Stable; **12**— D. Wayne Lukas & Padua Stables; **13**— Alex Hassinger Jr. & The Thoroughbred Corp.; **14**— Jenine Sahadi & Team Valor/Gary Barber; **15**— D. Wayne Lukas & Beverly/Robert Lewis/Michael Tabor/John Magnier; **16**— Harold Rose & Rose Family Stables; **17**— D. Wayne Lukas & Beverly/Robert Lewis; **18**— Vladimir Cerin & Jaltipan LLC; **19**— Todd Pletcher & Laura/Eugene Melnyk.

125th PREAKNESS STAKES

Grade I for three-year-olds; 10th race at Pimlico in Baltimore. **Date**— May 20, 2000; **Distance**— $1\frac{3}{16}$ miles; **Stakes Purse**— $1,000,000 ($650,000 to winner; $200,000 for 2nd; $100,000 for 3rd; $50,000 for 4th); **Track**— Good; **Off**— 5:28 p.m. EDT; **Favorite**— Fusaichi Pegasus (3-5).

Winner— Red Bullet; **Field**— 8 horses; **Time**— 1:56; **Start**— Good for all; **Won**— Driving; **Sire**— Unbridled; **Dam**— Cargo; **Record** (going into race)— 4 starts, 3 wins, 1 second; **Last start**— 2nd in Wood Memorial (Apr. 15); **Breeder**— Frank Stronach.

Order of Finish	Jockey	PP	1/4	1/2	3/4	Stretch	Finish	To $1
Red Bullet	Jerry Bailey	4	7-7	7-10	6-1½	1-1	1-3¾	6.20
Fusaichi Pegasus	Kent Desormeaux	7	6-1½	5-1	5-hd	3-hd	2-hd	.30
Impeachment	Craig Perret	3	8	8	8	6-1½	3-nk	19.10
Captain Steve	Robby Albarado	6	5-hd	6-1	7-4	7-12	4-3¼	11.50
Snuck In	Cash Asmussen	2	4-2½	4-3	4½	5-1	5-1	19.60
Hugh Hefner	Victor Espinoza	1	1½	2-1½	1-hd	4½	6½	49.70
High Yield	Pat Day	5	2½	1½	2½	2½	7-30	7.30
Hal's Hope	Roger Velez	8	3-1½	3-hd	3-1	8	8	35.10

Times— 23⅕; 46⅗; 1:11⅕; 1:37; 1:56.

$2 Mutual Prices— #4 Red Bullet ($14.40, $3.20, $2.80); #7 Fusaichi Pegasus ($2.60, $2.20); #3 Impeachment ($3.60).

Exacta— (4-7) for $24.00; **Trifecta**— (4-7-3) for $115.80; **Pick Six**— none; **Scratched**— none; **Overweights**— none; **Attendance**— 98,304; **TV Rating**— 4.6/11 share (ABC).

Trainers & Owners (by finish): **1**— Joe Orseno & Stronach Stable; **2**— Neil Drysdale & Fusao Sekiguchi; **3**— Todd Pletcher & Dogwood Stable; **4**— Bob Baffert & Michael Pegram; **5**— Steve Asmussen & Ackerley Brothers Farm; **6**— Martin Jones & King Edward Racing Stable; **7**— D. Wayne Lukas & Beverly/Robert Lewis, Michael Tabor, John Magnier; **8**— Harold Rose & Rose Family Stables.

132nd BELMONT STAKES

Grade I for three-year-olds; 9th race at Belmont Park in Elmont, N.Y. **Date**— June 10, 2000; **Distance**— 1½ miles; **Stakes Purse**— $1,000,000 ($600,000 to winner; $200,000 for 2nd; $110,000 for 3rd; $60,000 for 4th; $30,000 for 5th); **Track**— Fast; **Off**— 5:28 p.m. EDT; **Favorite**— Aptitude (8-5).

Winner— Commendable; **Field**— 11 horses; **Time**— 2:31⅕; **Start**— Good for all; **Won**— Driving; **Sire**— Gone West; **Dam**— Bought Twice; **Record** (going into race): 7 starts, 1 win; **Last Start**— 17th in Kentucky Derby (May 6); **Breeder**— Edward J. Kelly and Michael M. Kelly.

Order of Finish	Jockey	PP	1/4	1/2	3/4	Mile	Stretch	Finish	To $1
Commendable	Pat Day	3	2-2½	2-5	2-2½	1-1½	1-2½	1-1½	18.80
Aptitude	Alex Solis	5	10-hd	11	10-2½	6-hd	3-1½	2-1	1.75
Unshaded	Shane Sellers	4	8-hd	9-1	11	4½	2-hd	3-6	5.50
Wheelaway	Richard Migliore	9	3-1½	3-hd	3-2½	2-1½	4-5	4-3¼	5.70
Impeachment	Craig Perret	8	11	10-1	7-hd	7-2	5-6	5-6¾	6.40
Appearing Now	Mike Luzzi	1	7-1½	8-1½	8-hd	8-1½	6-1½	6-2¼	63.50
Postponed	Edgar Prado	2	4-hd	7-1½	9-1	10-8	8-hd	7-1¼	13.00
Hugh Hefner	Jorge Chavez	10	1-1½	1½	1-hd	3-1	7-1½	8-1	40.25
Tahkodha Hills	Eibar Coa	11	5-hd	5-hd	6-1	9-1	10	9-nk	48.25
Globalize	Mike Smith	6	9-2½	4-hd	4-2½	5-hd	9½	10	10.60
Curule	Jerry Bailey	7	6½	6½	5-hd	11	11	11-DNF	7.80

Times— 24; 49⅕; 1:14⅕; 1:39; 2:05; 2:31⅕.
$2 Mutual Prices— #3 Commendable ($39.60, $12.80, $6.30); #5 Aptitude ($3.80, $2.80); #4 Unshaded ($4.40).
Exacta— (3-5) for $213.00; **Trifecta**— (3-5-4) for $1,310.00; **Pick Three**— (2-9-3) for $1,773.00; **Scratched**— None; **Overweights**— None; **Attendance**— 67,810; **TV Rating**— 3.4/9 share (ABC).
Trainers & Owners (by finish): **1**— D. Wayne Lukas & Robert/Beverly Lewis; **2**— Robert Frankel & Juddmonte Farms Inc.; **3**— Carl Nafzger & James Tafel; **4**— John Kimmel & Caesar Kimmel/Philip Solondz; **5**— Todd Pletcher & Dogwood Stable; **6**— Juan Ortiz & John Valentino; **7**— Scotty Schulhofer & Jeanne Vance; **8**— Martin Jones & King Edward Racing Stable; **9**— Ralph Ziadie & Centaur Farms Inc.; **10**— Jerry Hollendorfer & George Todaro/Howard Litt/Jerry Hollendorfer; **11**— Saeed bin Suroor & Godolphin Racing Inc.

NTRA National Thoroughbred Poll

The NTRA Thoroughbred Poll conducted by National Thoroughbred Racing Association, covering races through Sept. 18, 2000. Rankings are based on the votes of sports and thoroughbred media representatives on a 10-9-8-7-6-5-4-3-2-1 basis. First place votes are in parentheses.

		Pts	Age	Sex	'00 Record Sts—1-2-3	Owner	Trainer
1	Lemon Drop Kid (15)	159	4	Colt	7—5-0-1	Jeanne G. Vance	Scotty Schulhofer
2	Riboletta	98	5	Mare	9—6-0-2	Aaron and Maria Jones	Eduardo Inda
3	Beautiful Pleasure	93	5	Mare	5—3-1-0	John Oxley	John Ward
4	Heritage of Gold	88	5	Mare	6—5-1-0	Jack Garey	Tom Amoss
5	Behrens	85	6	Horse	6—1-3-2	Rudlein Stable & W. Clifton Jr.	H. James Bond
6	Fusaichi Pegasus (1)	61	3	Colt	6—5-1-0	Fusao Sekiguchi	Neil Drysdale
7	Captain Steve	59	3	Colt	9—3-1-3	Michael Pegram	Bob Baffert
8	Manndar	57	4	Colt	5—2-1-1	Columbine Stable	C. Beau Greely
9	Perfect Sting	43	4	Filly	4—4-0-0	Stronach Stable	Joe Orseno
10	Golden Missile	37	5	Horse	6—2-3-0	Stronach Stable	Joe Orseno

Others receiving votes: 11. Fantastic Light (27 points); **12.** Caller One and Gaviola (12); **14.** City Zip (10); **15.** Bet On Sunshine and Skimming (7); **17.** General Challenge, Gold Mover, Jostle and Raging Fever (5); **21.** Burning Roma and Lisieux Rose (2); **23.** Kona Gold (1).

Final VISA 3-year-old Series Standings

The VISA Championship Series consists of 45 stakes races to determine the VISA 3-Year-Old Champion. Points are awarded to the first, second and third-place finishers as follows: Triple Crown races are scored 20-10-7; Grade I races are scored 10-7-5; Grade II races 7-5-3; and Grade III and ungraded 5-3-1. Top horses and jockeys are listed below.

Horses

		Pts
1	Fusaichi Pegasus	44
2	More Than Ready	34
3	Red Bullet	33
4	High Yield	32
	Unshaded	32
6	Captain Steve	28
7	Aptitude	26
8	Commendable	25
9	Hal's Hope	22
	The Deputy	22
11	Impeachment	20
12	Globalize	15
13	Albert the Great	14
	Graeme Hall	14
	War Chant	14
16	Dixie Union	13
	Performing Magic	13
	Trippi	13
19	Archer City Slew	12
	Milwaukee Brew	12
	Tiznow	12

Jockeys

		Pts
1	Pat Day	77
2	Jerry Bailey	61
3	Kent Desormeaux	60
4	Shane Sellers	58
5	Alex Solis	43
6	Jorge Chavez	33
7	Chris McCarron	30
	Corey Nakatani	30
	John Velazquez	30
10	Richard Migliore	26
11	Roger Velez	25
12	Robby Albarado	18
	Victor Espinoza	18
14	Craig Perret	17
	Mike Smith	17
16	Edgar Prado	14
17	Michael McCarthy	13
18	Francisco Torres	12
19	Robbie Davis	11
20	Cash Asmussen	10
	Herberto Castillo Jr.	10
	Eibar Coa	10

1999-00 Money Leaders

Official Top 10 standings for 1999 and unofficial Top 10 standings for 2000, through Sept. 17, 2000.

2000 (Through Sept. 17)

HORSES	Age	Sts	1-2-3	Earnings
Dubai Millennium	4	1	1-0-0	$3,600,000
Fusaichi Pegasus	3	6	5-1-0	1,897,800
Behrens	6	6	1-3-2	1,764,500
Lemon Drop Kid	4	7	5-0-1	1,548,500
Chester House	5	6	1-1-2	1,408,500
Captain Steve	3	9	3-1-3	1,229,876
Golden Missile	5	7	2-3-0	1,206,700
General Challenge	4	6	2-1-1	1,198,118
Unshaded	3	7	4-1-2	1,055,188
Heritage of Gold	5	6	5-1-0	1,021,907

JOCKEYS	Mts	1st	Earnings
Jerry Bailey	732	206	$13,180,980
Pat Day	947	194	12,702,154
Kent Desormeaux	695	140	11,021,165
Corey Nakatani	663	150	10,736,621
Jorge Chavez	1122	208	10,692,832
Shane Sellers	839	130	9,997,764
Edgar Prado	1231	181	9,432,384
Victor Espinoza	952	178	8,852,521
Alex Solis	685	112	7,757,325
Robby Albarado	972	188	7,493,339

TRAINERS	Sts	1st	Earnings
Robert Frankel	256	70	$8,746,411
Bob Baffert	511	112	8,477,155
D. Wayne Lukas	592	89	6,909,018
Bill Mott	515	122	6,280,180
Todd Pletcher	502	85	5,547,404
Joseph Orseno	183	42	4,600,447
Neil Drysdale	138	34	4,489,269
Saeed bin Suroor	20	3	4,396,179
Steve Asmussen	802	164	4,304,417
Richard Mandella	240	50	4,032,881

FINAL 1999

HORSES	Age	Sts	1-2-3	Earnings
Almutawakel	4	4	1-1-1	$3,290,000
Cat Thief	3	13	2-3-5	3,020,500
Daylami (IRE)	5	2	1-0-0	2,190,000
Charismatic	3	10	4-2-1	2,007,404
Budroyale	6	11	4-5-1	1,735,640
Behrens	5	9	4-4-0	1,735,000
Beautiful Pleasure	4	7	4-2-0	1,716,404
Silverbulletday	3	11	8-1-0	1,707,640
Menifee	3	9	3-4-1	1,695,400
General Challenge	3	11	6-2-0	1,658,100

JOCKEYS	Mts	1st	Earnings
Pat Day	1265	254	$18,092,845
Jerry Bailey	984	244	17,650,705
Jorge Chavez	1595	319	17,013,337
Shane Sellers	1279	245	13,065,825
Alex Solis	1119	200	12,884,862
David Flores	1197	208	11,938,125
John Velazquez	1432	259	11,148,255
Robby Albarado	1421	249	10,793,785
Edgar Prado	1902	402	10,581,436
Corey Nakatani	829	159	10,110,510

TRAINERS	Sts	1st	Earnings
Bob Baffert	735	169	$16,934,607
D. Wayne Lukas	739	126	12,068,460
Elliott Walden	436	105	7,752,758
Robert Frankel	299	58	7,044,738
Richard Mandella	391	67	6,934,363
Bill Mott	521	107	6,337,634
Saeed bin Suroor	29	4	6,333,200
John Kimmel	419	92	5,411,582
Jerry Hollendorfer	952	224	5,326,901
Todd Pletcher	673	110	4,985,810

Harness Racing
1999-2000 Major Stakes Races

Winners of major stakes races from Nov. 10, 1999 through Sept. 21, 2000; all paces and trots cover one mile; (BC) indicates year-end Breeders' Crown series.

LATE 1999

Date	Race	Raceway	Winner	Time	Driver	Purse
Nov. 10	Windy City Pace	Maywood	Looking For Art	1:54⅖	Eric Ledford	$300,000
Nov. 18	Three Diamonds Pace	Garden St.	Art's Virtue	1:53⅖	John Campbell	394,200
Nov. 18	Valley Victory	Garden St.	Fast Photo	1:56⅘	Cat Manzi	396,000
Nov. 18	Governor's Cup	Garden St.	Tyberwood	1:51⅘	Richard Silverman	572,400

2000 (through Sept. 21)

Date	Race	Raceway	Winner	Time	Driver	Purse
May 13	Berry's Creek	Meadowlands	Camotion	1:51	Ron Pierce	$300,000
June 3	New Jersey Classic	Meadowlands	Riverboat King	1:50⅕	Jim Morrill Jr.	500,000
June 24	North America Cup	Woodbine	Gallo Blue Chip	1:50⅕	Daniel Dube	1,000,000
July 14	Del Miller Memorial	Meadowlands	Sammie's Girl	1:56	Donald Dupont	406,000
July 14	Budweiser Beacon Course	Meadowlands	Dreamaster	1:54⅖	Dave Magee	380,000
July 15	Meadowlands Pace	Meadowlands	Gallo Blue Chip	1:50⅘	Daniel Dube	1,150,000
July 29	BC Open Pace	Meadowlands	Western Ideal	1:48	Mike Lachance	440,000
July 29	BC Open Trot	Meadowlands	Magician	1:53⅕	Dave Miller	1,000,000
July 29	BC Mare Pace	Meadowlands	Rons Girl	1:50⅘	Mike Lachance	332,500
Aug. 3	Peter Haughton Memorial	Meadowlands	Yankee Mustang	1:57⅖	Berndt Lindstedt	460,400
Aug. 3	Merrie Annabelle Final	Meadowlands	Spellbound Hanover	1:59	John Campbell	346,000
Aug. 4	Sweetheart Pace	Meadowlands	Hawaiian Jenna	1:53⅘	George Brennan	433,800
Aug. 4	Woodrow Wilson Pace	Meadowlands	Whitefish Falls	1:52	Cat Manzi	703,000
Aug. 5	**Hambletonian**	Meadowlands	Yankee Paco	1:53⅖	Trevor Ritchie	1,000,000
Aug. 5	Hambletonian Oaks	Meadowlands	Marita's Victory	1:54	Berndt Lindstedt	500,000
Aug. 5	Nat Ray	Meadowlands	Moni Maker	1:52⅕	Wally Hennessey	500,000
Aug. 12	Adios Final	Ladbroke	Riverboat King	1:51⅘	Mark Kesmodel	450,000
Aug. 19	Hoosier Cup	Hoosier Park	Aces N' Sevens	1:50⅗	Cat Manzi	500,000
Aug. 20	Confederation Cup XXII	Flamboro	High On Emotion	1:56⅕	Ron Pierce	350,000
Aug. 26	Maple Leaf Trot	Woodbine	Magician	1:52⅗	Dave Miller	550,000

Date	Race	Raceway	Winner	Time	Driver	Purse
Aug. 26	**Yonkers Trot**	Yonkers	Goalfish	1:59	Jacqueline Ingrassia	$350,000
Aug. 26	Metro Pace	Woodbine	Pro Bono Best	1:51	John Campbell	600,000
Sept. 2	World Trotting Derby	Du Quoin	Tejano	1:53⅖	Eric Ledford	525,000
Sept. 4	**Cane Pace**	Freehold	Powerful Toy	1:51⅘	Luc Ouellette	350,000
Sept. 21	**Little Brown Jug**	Delaware	Astreos	1:55⅗	Chris Christoforou	550,000

1999-2000 Money Leaders
Official Top 10 standings for 1999 and unofficial Top 10 standings for 2000 through Sept. 12, 2000.

2000 (Through Sept. 12)

HORSES	Age	Sts	1-2-3	Earnings
Gallo Blue Chip	3pg	17	11-2-1	$1,615,802
Western Ideal	5ph	13	9-3-0	1,210,000
Yankee Paco	3tc	11	8-1-0	1,190,296
Moni Maker	7tm	14	7-4-1	1,173,273
Magician	5tg	15	9-2-2	1,112,550
Dragon Again	5ph	24	13-5-4	891,740
Credit Winner	3tc	8	1-4-1	655,575
Astreos	3pc	10	3-3-0	583,020
Royalflush Hanover	4pg	29	9-5-4	583,020
Big Tom	5ph	25	8-5-5	577,225

DRIVERS	Mts	1st	Earnings
John Campbell	1416	245	$8,437,438
Mike Lachance	1706	208	6,666,880
Luc Ouellette	1867	308	6,425,363
Chris Christoforou	1915	421	5,807,109
David Miller	1862	255	5,400,859
Ron Pierce	1502	185	5,216,917
Randy Waples	1780	293	5,091,954
Daniel Dube	1910	236	4,897,093
George Brennan	1649	241	4,510,592
Eric Ledford	1667	368	4,357,669

FINAL 1999

HORSES	Age	Sts	1-2-3	Earnings
Blissfull Hall	3pc	23	15-3-4	$1,326,819
The Panderosa	3pc	13	5-1-0	1,126,207
Self Possessed	3tc	14	9-2-0	1,065,220
Grinfromeartoear	3pc	26	12-5-3	1,010,834
CR Renegade	3tc	23	9-3-2	900,585
Tyberwood	2pg	13	7-4-2	871,876
Art's Conquest	3pc	23	6-8-3	831,474
Dream of Joy	2tf	10	3-2-2	826,601
Red Bow Tie	5pg	16	9-2-1	818,250
Odies Fame	3pf	21	8-5-2	799,511

DRIVERS	Mts	1st	Earnings
Luc Oullette	2688	528	$10,841,495
John Campbell	1524	273	10,318,997
Mike Lachance	1984	262	9,304,941
Chris Christoforou	3170	642	6,669,192
David Miller	2328	294	6,272,912
Ron Pierce	2437	311	6,155,563
Randall Waples	2387	454	5,110,233
Jack Moiseyev	2114	319	4,997,614
Eric Ledford	2366	529	4,836,738
Steve Condren	1547	229	4,280,509

Hambletonian Society/Breeders Crown Standardbred Poll
Final Poll conducted by Harness Racing Communications as of Sept. 18, 2000 and based on the votes of 35 harness racing media representatives. First place votes are in parentheses. (p-pacer, t-trotter, h-horse, f-filly, m-mare, c-colt, g-gelding)

		Pts	Age/Gait/Sex	'00 Sts—1-2-3	Earnings
1	Western Ideal (25)	338	5ph	13—9-3-0	$1,210,000
2	Gallo Blue Chip (9)	308	3pg	17—11-2-1	1,615,802
3	Yankee Paco (1)	268	3tc	11—8-1-0	1,190,296
4	Moni Maker	244	7tm	14—7-4-1	1,173,273
5	Dragon Again	214	5ph	24—13-5-4	891,740
6	Magician	156	5tg	15—9-2-2	1,112,550
7	Pro Bono Best	147	2pc	9—7-0-2	486,500
8	Rons Girl	115	4pm	14—10-1-0	309,815
9	Spellbound Hanover	41	2tf	9—0-0-0	364,500
10	Space Shuttle	23	4ph	11—6-0-0	271,000

Others receiving votes: 11. DM Dilinger (16 points); **12.** Dex The Balls and Teeth Of The Dog (7); **14.** I Scoot Hanover, Royalflush Hanover and Yankee Mustang (4); **17.** Art's Virtue, Casual Breeze, Dreamaster, French Panicure, Galleria and Rama's Pleasure (3); **23.** Astreos, Earlofmydreams, Eternal Camnation, Powerful Toy, Reimburse and Tejano (1).

Steeplechase Racing
1999-2000 Major Stakes Races
Winners of major steeplechase races from Nov. 21, 1999 through Aug. 24, 2000.

LATE 1999

Date	Race	Location	Miles	Winner	Jockey	Purse
Nov. 21	Colonial Cup	Camden, S.C.	2¾	Ninepins	Arch Kingsley	$100,000

2000 (through Aug. 24)

Date	Race	Location	Miles	Winner	Jockey	Purse
Apr. 15	Atlanta Cup	Kingston, Ga.	2	All Gong	Blythe Miller	$100,000
Apr. 22	Grand National	Butler, Md.	3	Welter Weight	Mike Elmore	30,000
Apr. 29	Maryland Hunt Cup	Glyndon, Md.	4	Swayo	Joe Gillet	65,000
May 6	Virginia Gold Cup	The Plains, Va.	4	Priceless Room	J.W. Delozier	50,000
May 13	Iroquois	Nashville, Tenn.	3	Pinkie Swear	Sean Clancy	100,000
Aug. 24	N.Y. Turf Writers Cup	Saratoga, N.Y.	2⅜	Ninepins	Arch Kingsley	112,100

Thoroughbred Racing
The Triple Crown

The term "Triple Crown" was coined by sportswriter Charles Hatton while covering the 1930 victories of Gallant Fox in the Kentucky Derby, Preakness Stakes and Belmont Stakes. Before then, only Sir Barton (1919) had won all three races in the same year. Since then, nine horses have won the Triple Crown. Two trainers, James (Sunny Jim) Fitzsimmons and Ben A. Jones, have saddled two Triple Crown champions, while Eddie Arcaro is the only jockey to ride two champions.

Year		Jockey	Trainer	Owner	Sire/Dam
1919	**Sir Barton**	Johnny Loftus	H. Guy Bedwell	J.K.L. Ross	Star Shoot/Lady Sterling
1930	**Gallant Fox**	Earl Sande	J.E. Fitzsimmons	Belair Stud	Sir Gallahad III/Marguerite
1935	**Omaha**	Willie Saunders	J.E. Fitzsimmons	Belair Stud	Gallant Fox/Flambino
1937	**War Admiral**	Charley Kurtsinger	George Conway	Samuel Riddle	Man o' War/Brushup
1941	**Whirlaway**	Eddie Arcaro	Ben A. Jones	Calumet Farm	Blenheim II/Dustwhirl
1943	**Count Fleet**	Johnny Longden	Don Cameron	Mrs. J.D. Hertz	Reigh Count/Quickly
1946	**Assault**	Warren Mehrtens	Max Hirsch	King Ranch	Bold Venture/Igual
1948	**Citation**	Eddie Arcaro	Ben A. Jones	Calumet Farm	Bull Lea/Hydroplane II
1973	**Secretariat**	Ron Turcotte	Lucien Laurin	Meadow Stable	Bold Ruler/Somethingroyal
1977	**Seattle Slew**	Jean Cruguet	Billy Turner	Karen Taylor	Bold Reasoning/My Charmer
1978	**Affirmed**	Steve Cauthen	Laz Barrera	Harbor View Farm	Exclusive Native/Won't Tell You

Note: Gallant Fox (1930) is the only Triple Crown winner to sire another Triple Crown winner, Omaha (1935). Wm. Woodward Sr., owner of Belair Stud, was breeder-owner of both horses and both were trained by Sunny Jim Fitzsimmons.

Triple Crown Near Misses

Forty-four horses have won two legs of the Triple Crown. Of those, fifteen won the Kentucky Derby (KD) and Preakness Stakes (PS) only to be beaten in the Belmont Stakes (BS). Two others, Burgoo King (1932) and Bold Venture (1936), won the Derby and Preakness, but were forced out of the Belmont with the same injury—a bowed tendon—that effectively ended their racing careers. In 1978, Alydar finished second to Affirmed in all three races, the only time that has happened. Note that the Preakness preceded the Kentucky Derby in 1922, '23 and '31; (*) indicates won on disqualification.

Year		KD	PS	BS	Year		KD	PS	BS
1877	**Cloverbrook**	DNS	won	won	1961	**Carry Back**	won	won	7th
1878	**Duke of Magenta**	DNS	won	won	1963	**Chateaugay**	won	2nd	won
1880	**Grenada**	DNS	won	won	1964	**Northern Dancer**	won	won	3rd
1881	**Saunterer**	DNS	won	won	1966	**Kauai King**	won	won	4th
					1967	**Damascus**	3rd	won	won
1895	**Belmar**	DNS	won	won	1968	**Forward Pass**	won*	won	2nd
1920	**Man o' War**	DNS	won	won	1969	**Majestic Prince**	won	won	2nd
1922	**Pillory**	DNS	12th	won					
1923	**Zev**	won	12th	won	1971	**Canonero II**	won	won	4th
					1972	**Riva Ridge**	won	4th	won
1931	**Twenty Grand**	won	2nd	won	1974	**Little Current**	5th	won	won
1932	**Burgoo King**	won	won	DNS	1976	**Bold Forbes**	won	3rd	won
1936	**Bold Venture**	won	won	DNS	1979	**Spectacular Bid**	won	won	3rd
1939	**Johnstown**	won	5th	won					
					1981	**Pleasant Colony**	won	won	3rd
1940	**Bimelech**	2nd	won	won	1984	**Swale**	won	7th	won
1942	**Shut Out**	won	5th	won	1987	**Alysheba**	won	won	4th
1944	**Pensive**	won	won	2nd	1988	**Risen Star**	3rd	won	won
1949	**Capot**	2nd	won	won	1989	**Sunday Silence**	won	won	2nd
1950	**Middleground**	won	2nd	won	1991	**Hansel**	10th	won	won
1953	**Native Dancer**	2nd	won	won	1994	**Tabasco Cat**	6th	won	won
1955	**Nashua**	2nd	won	won	1995	**Thunder Gulch**	won	3rd	won
1956	**Needles**	won	2nd	won	1997	**Silver Charm**	won	won	2nd
1958	**Tim Tam**	won	won	2nd	1998	**Real Quiet**	won	won	2nd
					1999	**Charismatic**	won	won	3rd

The Triple Crown Challenge (1987-93)

Seeking to make the Triple Crown more than just a media event and to insure that owners would not be attracted to more lucrative races, officials at Churchill Downs, the Maryland Jockey Club and the New York Racing Association created Triple Crown Productions in 1985 and announced that a $1 million bonus would be given to the horse that performs best in the Kentucky Derby, Preakness Stakes and Belmont Stakes. Furthermore, a bonus of $5 million would be presented to any horse winning all three races.

Revised in 1991, the rules stated that the winning horse must: 1. finish all three races; 2. earn points by finishing first, second, third or fourth in at least one of the three races; and 3. earn the highest number of points based on the following system—10 points to win, five to place, three to show and one to finish fourth. In the event of a tie, the $1 million is distributed equally among the top point-getters. From 1987-90, the system was five points to win, three to place and one to show. The Triple Crown Challenge was discontinued in 1994.

Year		KD	PS	BS	Pts	Year		KD	PS	BS	Pts
1987	1 **Bet Twice**	2nd	2nd	1st —	11	1991	1 **Hansel**	10th	1st	1st —	20
	2 Alysheba	1st	1st	4th —	10		2 Strike the Gold	1st	6th	2nd —	15
	3 Cryptoclearance	4th	3rd	2nd —	4		3 Mane Minister	3rd	3rd	3rd —	9
1988	1 **Risen Star**	3rd	1st	1st —	11	1992	1 **Pine Bluff**	5th	1st	3rd —	13
	2 Winning Colors	1st	3rd	6th —	6		2 Casual Lies	2nd	3rd	5th —	8
	3 Brian's Time	6th	2nd	3rd —	4		(No other horses ran all three races.)					
1989	1 **Sunday Silence**	1st	1st	2nd —	13	1993	1 **Sea Hero**	1st	5th	7th —	10
	2 Easy Goer	2nd	2nd	1st —	11		2 Wild Gale	3rd	8th	3rd —	6
	3 Hawkster	5th	5th	5th —	0		(No other horses ran all three races.)					
1990	1 **Unbridled**	1st	2nd	4th —	8							
	2 Summer Squall	2nd	1st	DNR —	8							
	3 Go and Go	DNR	DNR	1st —	5							
	(Unbridled was only horse to run all three races.)											

Kentucky Derby

For three-year-olds. Held the first Saturday in May at Churchill Downs in Louisville, Ky. Inaugurated in 1875. Originally run at 1½ miles (1875-95), shortened to present 1¼ miles in 1896.

Trainers with most wins: Ben Jones (6); D. Wayne Lukas and Dick Thompson (4); Sunny Jim Fitzsimmons and Max Hirsch (3).

Jockeys with most wins: Eddie Arcaro and Bill Hartack (5); Bill Shoemaker (4); Angel Cordero Jr., Issac Murphy, Earl Sande and Gary Stevens (3).

Winning fillies: Regret (1915), Genuine Risk (1980) and Winning Colors (1988).

Year		Time	Jockey	Trainer	2nd place	3rd place
1875	**Aristides**	2:37¾	Oliver Lewis	Ansel Anderson	Volcano	Verdigris
1876	**Vagrant**	2:38¼	Bobby Swim	James Williams	Creedmore	Harry Hill
1877	**Baden-Baden**	2:38	Billy Walker	Ed Brown	Leonard	King William
1878	**Day Star**	2:37¼	Jimmy Carter	Lee Paul	Himyar	Leveler
1879	**Lord Murphy**	2:37	Charlie Shauer	George Rice	Falsetto	Strathmore
1880	**Fonso**	2:37½	George Lewis	Tice Hutsell	Kimball	Bancroft
1881	**Hindoo**	2:40	Jim McLaughlin	James Rowe Sr.	Lelex	Alfambra
1882	**Apollo**	2:40¼	Babe Hurd	Green Morris	Runnymede	Bengal
1883	**Leonatus**	2:43	Billy Donohue	John McGinty	Drake Carter	Lord Raglan
1884	**Buchanan**	2:40¼	Isaac Murphy	William Bird	Loftin	Audrain
1885	**Joe Cotton**	2:37¼	Babe Henderson	Alex Perry	Bersan	Ten Booker
1886	**Ben Ali**	2:36½	Paul Duffy	Jim Murphy	Blue Wing	Free Knight
1887	**Montrose**	2:39¼	Isaac Lewis	John McGinty	Jim Gore	Jacobin
1888	**MacBeth II**	2:38¼	George Covington	John Campbell	Gallifet	White
1889	**Spokane**	2:34½	Thomas Kiley	John Rodegap	Proctor Knott	Once Again
1890	**Riley**	2:45	Isaac Murphy	Edward Corrigan	Bill Letcher	Robespierre
1891	**Kingman**	2:52¼	Isaac Murphy	Dud Allen	Balgowan	High Tariff
1892	**Azra**	2:41½	Lonnie Clayton	John Morris	Huron	Phil Dwyer
1893	**Lookout**	2:39¼	Eddie Kunze	Wm. McDaniel	Plutus	Boundless
1894	**Chant**	2:41	Frank Goodale	Eugene Leigh	Pearl Song	Sigurd
1895	**Halma**	2:37½	Soup Perkins	Byron McClelland	Basso	Laureate
1896	**Ben Brush**	2:07¾	Willie Simms	Hardy Campbell	Ben Eder	Semper Ego
1897	**Typhoon II**	2:12½	Buttons Garner	J.C. Cahn	Ornament	Dr. Catlett
1898	**Plaudit**	2:09	Willie Simms	John E. Madden	Lieber Karl	Isabey
1899	**Manuel**	2:12	Fred Taral	Robert Walden	Corsini	Mazo
1900	**Lieut. Gibson**	2:06¼	Jimmy Boland	Charles Hughes	Florizar	Thrive
1901	**His Eminence**	2:07¾	Jimmy Winkfield	F.B. Van Meter	Sannazarro	Driscoll
1902	**Alan-a-Dale**	2:08¾	Jimmy Winkfield	T.C. McDowell	Inventor	The Rival
1903	**Judge Himes**	2:09	Hal Booker	J.P. Mayberry	Early	Bourbon
1904	**Elwood**	2:08½	Shorty Prior	C.E. Durnell	Ed Tierney	Brancas
1905	**Agile**	2:10¾	Jack Martin	Robert Tucker	Ram's Horn	Layson
1906	**Sir Huon**	2:08⅘	Roscoe Troxler	Pete Coyne	Lady Navarre	James Reddick
1907	**Pink Star**	2:12⅗	Andy Minder	W.H. Fizer	Zal	Ovelando
1908	**Stone Street**	2:15⅕	Arthur Pickens	J.W. Hall	Sir Cleges	Dunvegan
1909	**Wintergreen**	2:08⅕	Vincent Powers	Charles Mack	Miami	Dr. Barkley

Year		Time	Jockey	Trainer	2nd place	3rd place
1910	**Donau**	2:06⅖	Fred Herbert	George Ham	Joe Morris	Fighting Bob
1911	**Meridian**	2:05	George Archibald	Albert Ewing	Governor Gray	Colston
1912	**Worth**	2:09⅖	C.H. Shilling	Frank Taylor	Duval	Flamma
1913	**Donerail**	2:04⅘	Roscoe Goose	Thomas Hayes	Ten Point	Gowell
1914	**Old Rosebud**	2:03⅖	John McCabe	F.D. Weir	Hodge	Bronzewing
1915	**Regret**	2:05⅖	Joe Notter	James Rowe Sr.	Pebbles	Sharpshooter
1916	**George Smith**	2:04	Johnny Loftus	Hollie Hughes	Star Hawk	Franklin
1917	**Omar Khayyam**	2:04⅗	Charles Borel	C.T. Patterson	Ticket	Midway
1918	**Exterminator**	2:10⅘	William Knapp	Henry McDaniel	Escoba	Viva America
1919	**SIR BARTON**	2:09⅘	Johnny Loftus	H. Guy Bedwell	Billy Kelly	Under Fire
1920	**Paul Jones**	2:09	Ted Rice	Billy Garth	Upset	On Watch
1921	**Behave Yourself**	2:04⅕	Charles Thompson	Dick Thompson	Black Servant	Prudery
1922	**Morvich**	2:04⅗	Albert Johnson	Fred Burlew	Bet Mosie	John Finn
1923	**Zev**	2:05⅖	Earl Sande	David Leary	Martingale	Vigil
1924	**Black Gold**	2:05⅕	John Mooney	Hanly Webb	Chilhowee	Beau Butler
1925	**Flying Ebony**	2:07⅗	Earl Sande	William Duke	Captain Hal	Son of John
1926	**Bubbling Over**	2:03⅘	Albert Johnson	Dick Thompson	Bagenbaggage	Rock Man
1927	**Whiskery**	2:06	Linus McAtee	Fred Hopkins	Osmand	Jock
1928	**Reigh Count**	2:10⅖	Chick Lang	Bert Michell	Misstep	Toro
1929	**Clyde Van Dusen**	2:10⅘	Linus McAtee	Clyde Van Dusen	Naishapur	Panchio
1930	**GALLANT FOX**	2:07⅗	Earl Sande	Jim Fitzsimmons	Gallant Knight	Ned O.
1931	**Twenty Grand**	2:01⅘	Charley Kurtsinger	James Rowe Jr.	Sweep All	Mate
1932	**Burgoo King**	2:05⅕	Eugene James	Dick Thompson	Economic	Stepenfetchit
1933	**Brokers Tip**	2:06⅘	Don Meade	Dick Thompson	Head Play	Charley O.
1934	**Cavalcade**	2:04	Mack Garner	Bob Smith	Discovery	Agrarian
1935	**OMAHA**	2:05	Willie Saunders	Jim Fitzsimmons	Roman Soldier	Whiskolo
1936	**Bold Venture**	2:03⅗	Ira Hanford	Max Hirsch	Brevity	Indian Broom
1937	**WAR ADMIRAL**	2:03⅕	Charley Kurtsinger	George Conway	Pompoon	Reaping Reward
1938	**Lawrin**	2:04⅘	Eddie Arcaro	Ben Jones	Dauber	Can't Wait
1939	**Johnstown**	2:03⅖	James Stout	Jim Fitzsimmons	Challedon	Heather Broom
1940	**Gallahadion**	2:05	Carroll Bierman	Roy Waldron	Bimelech	Dit
1941	**WHIRLAWAY**	2:01⅖	Eddie Arcaro	Ben Jones	Staretor	Market Wise
1942	**Shut Out**	2:04⅖	Wayne Wright	John Gaver	Alsab	Valdina Orphan
1943	**COUNT FLEET**	2:04	Johnny Longden	Don Cameron	Blue Swords	Slide Rule
1944	**Pensive**	2:04⅕	Conn McCreary	Ben Jones	Broadcloth	Stir Up
1945	**Hoop Jr**	2:07	Eddie Arcaro	Ivan Parke	Pot O'Luck	Darby Dieppe
1946	**ASSAULT**	2:06⅗	Warren Mehrtens	Max Hirsch	Spy Song	Hampden
1947	**Jet Pilot**	2:06⅘	Eric Guerin	Tom Smith	Phalanx	Faultless
1948	**CITATION**	2:05⅖	Eddie Arcaro	Ben Jones	Coaltown	My Request
1949	**Ponder**	2:04⅕	Steve Brooks	Ben Jones	Capot	Palestinian
1950	**Middleground**	2:01⅗	William Boland	Max Hirsch	Hill Prince	Mr. Trouble
1951	**Count Turf**	2:02⅗	Conn McCreary	Sol Rutchick	Royal Mustang	Ruhe
1952	**Hill Gail**	2:01⅗	Eddie Arcaro	Ben Jones	Sub Fleet	Blue Man
1953	**Dark Star**	2:02	Hank Moreno	Eddie Hayward	Native Dancer	Invigorator
1954	**Determine**	2:03	Raymond York	Willie Molter	Hasty Road	Hasseyampa
1955	**Swaps**	2:01⅘	Bill Shoemaker	Mesh Tenney	Nashua	Summer Tan
1956	**Needles**	2:03⅖	David Erb	Hugh Fontaine	Fabius	Come On Red
1957	**Iron Liege**	2:02⅕	Bill Hartack	Jimmy Jones	Gallant Man	Round Table
1958	**Tim Tam**	2:05	Ismael Valenzuela	Jimmy Jones	Lincoln Road	Noureddin
1959	**Tomy Lee**	2:02⅕	Bill Shoemaker	Frank Childs	Sword Dancer	First Landing
1960	**Venetian Way**	2:02⅖	Bill Hartack	Victor Sovinski	Bally Ache	Victoria Park
1961	**Carry Back**	2:04	John Sellers	Jack Price	Crozier	Bass Clef
1962	**Decidedly**	2:00⅖	Bill Hartack	Horatio Luro	Roman Line	Ridan
1963	**Chateaugay**	2:01⅘	Braulio Baeza	James Conway	Never Bend	Candy Spots
1964	**Northern Dancer**	2:00	Bill Hartack	Horatio Luro	Hill Rise	The Scoundrel
1965	**Lucky Debonair**	2:01⅕	Bill Shoemaker	Frank Catrone	Dapper Dan	Tom Rolfe
1966	**Kauai King**	2:02	Don Brumfield	Henry Forrest	Advocator	Blue Skyer
1967	**Proud Clarion**	2:00⅗	Bobby Ussery	Loyd Gentry	Barbs Delight	Damascus
1968	**Forward Pass***	—	Ismael Valenzuela	Henry Forrest	Francie's Hat	T.V. Commercial
1969	**Majestic Prince**	2:01⅘	Bill Hartack	Johnny Longden	Arts and Letters	Dike
1970	**Dust Commander**	2:03⅖	Mike Manganello	Don Combs	My Dad George	High Echelon
1971	**Canonero II**	2:03⅕	Gustavo Avila	Juan Arias	Jim French	Bold Reason
1972	**Riva Ridge**	2:01⅘	Ron Turcotte	Lucien Laurin	No Le Hace	Hold Your Peace
1973	**SECRETARIAT**	1:59⅖	Ron Turcotte	Lucien Laurin	Sham	Our Native
1974	**Cannonade**	2:04	Angel Cordero Jr.	Woody Stephens	Hudson County	Agitate
1975	**Foolish Pleasure**	2:02	Jacinto Vasquez	LeRoy Jolley	Avatar	Diabolo
1976	**Bold Forbes**	2:01⅗	Angel Cordero Jr.	Laz Barrera	Honest Pleasure	Elocutionist
1977	**SEATTLE SLEW**	2:02⅕	Jean Cruguet	Billy Turner	Run Dusty Run	Sanhedrin
1978	**AFFIRMED**	2:01⅕	Steve Cauthen	Laz Barrera	Alydar	Believe It

Kentucky Derby (Cont.)

Year	Time	Jockey	Trainer	2nd place	3rd place
1979 **Spectacular Bid**	2:02⅖	Ron Franklin	Bud Delp	General Assembly	Golden Act
1980 **Genuine Risk**	2:02	Jacinto Vasquez	LeRoy Jolley	Rumbo	Jaklin Klugman
1981 **Pleasant Colony**	2:02	Jorge Velasquez	John Campo	Woodchopper	Partez
1982 **Gato Del Sol**	2:02⅖	E. Delahoussaye	Eddie Gregson	Laser Light	Reinvested
1983 **Sunny's Halo**	2:02⅕	E. Delahoussaye	David Cross Jr.	Desert Wine	Caveat
1984 **Swale**	2:02⅖	Laffit Pincay Jr.	Woody Stephens	Coax Me Chad	At The Threshold
1985 **Spend A Buck**	2:00⅕	Angel Cordero Jr.	Cam Gambolati	Stephan's Odyssey	Chief's Crown
1986 **Ferdinand**	2:02⅘	Bill Shoemaker	Chas. Whittingham	Bold Arrangement	Broad Brush
1987 **Alysheba**	2:03⅖	Chris McCarron	Jack Van Berg	Bet Twice	Avies Copy
1988 **Winning Colors**	2:02⅕	Gary Stevens	D. Wayne Lukas	Forty Niner	Risen Star
1989 **Sunday Silence**	2:05	Pat Valenzuela	Chas. Whittingham	Easy Goer	Awe Inspiring
1990 **Unbridled**	2:02	Craig Perret	Carl Nafzger	Summer Squall	Pleasant Tap
1991 **Strike the Gold**	2:03	Chris Antley	Nick Zito	Best Pal	Mane Minister
1992 **Lil E. Tee**	2:03	Pat Day	Lynn Whiting	Casual Lies	Dance Floor
1993 **Sea Hero**	2:02⅖	Jerry Bailey	Mack Miller	Prairie Bayou	Wild Gale
1994 **Go For Gin**	2:03⅗	Chris McCarron	Nick Zito	Strodes Creek	Blumin Affair
1995 **Thunder Gulch**	2:01⅕	Gary Stevens	D. Wayne Lukas	Tejano Run	Timber Country
1996 **Grindstone**	2:01	Jerry Bailey	D. Wayne Lukas	Cavonnier	Prince of Thieves
1997 **Silver Charm**	2:02⅖	Gary Stevens	Bob Baffert	Captain Bodgit	Free House
1998 **Real Quiet**	2:02⅕	Kent Desormeaux	Bob Baffert	Victory Gallop	Indian Charlie
1999 **Charismatic**	2:03⅕	Chris Antley	D. Wayne Lukas	Menifee	Cat Thief
2000 **Fusaichi Pegasus**	2:01⅕	Kent Desormeaux	Neil Drysdale	Aptitude	Impeachment

*Dancer's Image finished first (in 2:02½), but was disqualified after traces of prohibited medication were found in his system.

Preakness Stakes

For three-year-olds. Held two weeks after the Kentucky Derby at Pimlico Race Course in Baltimore. Inaugurated 1873. Originally run at 1½ miles (1873-88), then at 1¼ miles (1889), 1½ miles (1890), $1\frac{1}{16}$ miles (1894-1900), 1 mile & 70 yards (1901-07), $1\frac{1}{16}$ miles (1908), 1 mile (1909-1910), 1⅛ miles (1911-24), and the present $1\frac{3}{16}$ miles since 1925.

Trainers with most wins: Robert W. Walden (7); T.J. Healey and D. Wayne Lukas (5); Sunny Jim Fitzsimmons and Jimmy Jones (4); and J. Whalen (3).

Jockeys with most wins: Eddie Arcaro (6); Pat Day (5); G. Barbee, Bill Hartack and Lloyd Hughes (3).

Winning fillies: Flocarline (1903), Whimsical (1906), Rhine Maiden (1915) and Nellie Morse (1924).

Year	Time	Jockey	Trainer	2nd place	3rd place
1873 **Survivor**	2:43	G. Barbee	A.D. Pryor	John Boulger	Artist
1874 **Culpepper**	2:56½	W. Donohue	H. Gaffney	King Amadeus	Scratch
1875 **Tom Ochiltree**	2:43½	L. Hughes	R.W. Walden	Viator	Bay Final
1876 **Shirley**	2:44¾	G. Barbee	W. Brown	Rappahannock	Compliment
1877 **Cloverbrook**	2:45½	C. Holloway	J. Walden	Bombast	Lucifer
1878 **Duke of Magenta**	2:41¾	C. Holloway	R.W. Walden	Bayard	Albert
1879 **Harold**	2:40½	L. Hughes	R.W. Walden	Jericho	Rochester
1880 **Grenada**	2:40½	L. Hughes	R.W. Walden	Oden	Emily F.
1881 **Saunterer**	2:40½	T. Costello	R.W. Walden	Compensation	Baltic
1882 **Vanguard**	2:44½	T. Costello	R.W. Walden	Heck	Col. Watson
1883 **Jacobus**	2:42½	G. Barbee	R. Dwyer	Parnell	(2-horse race)
1884 **Knight of Ellerslie**	2:39½	S. Fisher	T.B. Doswell	Welcher	(2-horse race)
1885 **Tecumseh**	2:49	Jim McLaughlin	C. Littlefield	Wickham	John C.
1886 **The Bard**	2:45	S. Fisher	J. Huggins	Eurus	Elkwood
1887 **Dunboyne**	2:39½	W. Donohue	W. Jennings	Mahoney	Raymond
1888 **Refund**	2:49	F. Littlefield	R.W. Walden	Bertha B.*	Glendale
1889 **Buddhist**	2:17½	W. Anderson	J. Rogers	Japhet	(2-horse race)
1890 **Montague**	2:36¾	W. Martin	E. Feakes	Philosophy	Barrister
1891-93 Not held					
1894 **Assignee**	1:49¼	F. Taral	W. Lakeland	Potentate	Ed Kearney
1895 **Belmar**	1:50½	F. Taral	E. Feakes	April Fool	Sue Kittie
1896 **Margrave**	1:51	H. Griffin	Byron McClelland	Hamilton II	Intermission
1897 **Paul Kauvar**	1:51¼	T. Thorpe	T.P. Hayes	Elkins	On Deck
1898 **Sly Fox**	1:49¾	W. Simms	H. Campbell	The Huguenot	Nuto
1899 **Half Time**	1:47	R. Clawson	F. McCabe	Filigrane	Lackland
1900 **Hindus**	1:48⅖	H. Spencer	J.H. Morris	Sarmatian	Ten Candles
1901 **The Parader**	1:47⅕	F. Landry	T.J. Healey	Sadie S.	Dr. Barlow
1902 **Old England**	1:45⅘	L. Jackson	G.B. Morris	Maj. Daingerfield	Namtor
1903 **Flocarline**	1:44⅘	W. Gannon	H.C. Riddle	Mackey Dwyer	Rightful
1904 **Bryn Mawr**	1:44⅕	E. Hildebrand	W.F. Presgrave	Wotan	Dolly Spanker
1905 **Cairngorm**	1:45⅘	W. Davis	A.J. Joyner	Kiamesha	Coy Maid
1906 **Whimsical**	1:45	Walter Miller	T.J. Gaynor	Content	Larabie
1907 **Don Enrique**	1:45⅖	G. Mountain	J. Whalen	Ethon	Zambesi
1908 **Royal Tourist**	1:46⅖	Eddie Dugan	A.J. Joyner	Live Wire	Robert Cooper

Year		Time	Jockey	Trainer	2nd place	3rd place
1909	**Effendi**	1:39 4/5	Willie Doyle	F.C. Frisbie	Fashion Plate	Hill Top
1910	**Layminster**	1:40 3/5	R. Estep	J.S. Healy	Dalhousie	Sager
1911	**Watervale**	1:51	Eddie Dugan	J. Whalen	Zeus	The Nigger
1912	**Colonel Holloway**	1:56 3/5	C. Turner	D. Woodford	Bwana Tumbo	Tipsand
1913	**Buskin**	1:53 2/5	James Butwell	J. Whalen	Kleburne	Barnegat
1914	**Holiday**	1:53 4/5	A. Schuttinger	J.S. Healy	Brave Cunarder	Defendum
1915	**Rhine Maiden**	1:58	Douglas Hoffman	F. Devers	Half Rock	Runes
1916	**Damrosch**	1:54 4/5	Linus McAtee	A.G. Weston	Greenwood	Achievement
1917	**Kalitan**	1:54 2/5	E. Haynes	Bill Hurley	Al M. Dick	Kentucky Boy
1918	**War Cloud**	1:53 3/5	Johnny Loftus	W.B. Jennings	Sunny Slope	Lanius
1918	**Jack Hare Jr**	1:53 2/5	Charles Peak	F.D. Weir	The Porter	Kate Bright
1919	**SIR BARTON**	1:53	Johnny Loftus	H. Guy Bedwell	Eternal	Sweep On
1920	**Man o' War**	1:51 3/5	Clarence Kummer	L. Feustel	Upset	Wildair
1921	**Broomspun**	1:54 1/5	F. Coltiletti	James Rowe Sr.	Polly Ann	Jeg
1922	**Pillory**	1:51 3/5	L. Morris	Thomas Healey	Hea	June Grass
1923	**Vigil**	1:53 3/5	B. Marinelli	Thomas Healey	General Thatcher	Rialto
1924	**Nellie Morse**	1:57 1/5	John Merimee	A.B. Gordon	Transmute	Mad Play
1925	**Coventry**	1:59	Clarence Kummer	William Duke	Backbone	Almadel
1926	**Display**	1:59 4/5	John Maiben	Thomas Healey	Blondin	Mars
1927	**Bostonian**	2:01 3/5	Whitey Abel	Fred Hopkins	Sir Harry	Whiskery
1928	**Victorian**	2:00 1/5	Sonny Workman	James Rowe Jr.	Toro	Solace
1929	**Dr. Freeland**	2:01 3/5	Louis Schaefer	Thomas Healey	Minotaur	African
1930	**GALLANT FOX**	2:00 3/5	Earl Sande	Jim Fitzsimmons	Crack Brigade	Snowflake
1931	**Mate**	1:59	George Ellis	J.W. Healy	Twenty Grand	Ladder
1932	**Burgoo King**	1:59 4/5	Eugene James	Dick Thompson	Tick On	Boatswain
1933	**Head Play**	2:02	Charley Kurtsinger	Thomas Hayes	Ladysman	Utopian
1934	**High Quest**	1:58 1/5	Robert Jones	Bob Smith	Cavalcade	Discovery
1935	**OMAHA**	1:58 2/5	Willie Saunders	Jim Fitzsimmons	Firethorn	Psychic Bid
1936	**Bold Venture**	1:59	George Woolf	Max Hirsch	Granville	Jean Bart
1937	**WAR ADMIRAL**	1:58 2/5	Charley Kurtsinger	George Conway	Pompoon	Flying Scot
1938	**Dauber**	1:59 4/5	Maurice Peters	Dick Handlen	Cravat	Menow
1939	**Challedon**	1:59 4/5	George Seabo	Louis Schaefer	Gilded Knight	Volitant
1940	**Bimelech**	1:58 3/5	F.A. Smith	Bill Hurley	Mioland	Gallahadion
1941	**WHIRLAWAY**	1:58 4/5	Eddie Arcaro	Ben Jones	King Cole	Our Boots
1942	**Alsab**	1:57	Basil James	Sarge Swenke	Requested & Sun Again (dead heat)	
1943	**COUNT FLEET**	1:57 2/5	Johnny Longden	Don Cameron	Blue Swords	Vincentive
1944	**Pensive**	1:59 1/5	Conn McCreary	Ben Jones	Platter	Stir Up
1945	**Polynesian**	1:58 4/5	W.D. Wright	Morris Dixon	Hoop Jr.	Darby Dieppe
1946	**ASSAULT**	2:01 2/5	Warren Mehrtens	Max Hirsch	Lord Boswell	Hampden
1947	**Faultless**	1:59	Doug Dodson	Jimmy Jones	On Trust	Phalanx
1948	**CITATION**	2:02 2/5	Eddie Arcaro	Jimmy Jones	Vulcan's Forge	Bovard
1949	**Capot**	1:56	Ted Atkinson	J.M. Gaver	Palestinian	Noble Impulse
1950	**Hill Prince**	1:59 1/5	Eddie Arcaro	Casey Hayes	Middleground	Dooly
1951	**Bold**	1:56 2/5	Eddie Arcaro	Preston Burch	Counterpoint	Alerted
1952	**Blue Man**	1:57 2/5	Conn McCreary	Woody Stephens	Jampol	One Count
1953	**Native Dancer**	1:57 4/5	Eric Guerin	Bill Winfrey	Jamie K.	Royal Bay Gem
1954	**Hasty Road**	1:57 2/5	Johnny Adams	Harry Trotsek	Correlation	Hasseyampa
1955	**Nashua**	1:54 3/5	Eddie Arcaro	Jim Fitzsimmons	Saratoga	Traffic Judge
1956	**Fabius**	1:58 2/5	Bill Hartack	Jimmy Jones	Needles	No Regrets
1957	**Bold Ruler**	1:56 1/5	Eddie Arcaro	Jim Fitzsimmons	Iron Liege	Inside Tract
1958	**Tim Tam**	1:57 1/5	Ismael Valenzuela	Jimmy Jones	Lincoln Road	Gone Fishin'
1959	**Royal Orbit**	1:57	William Harmatz	R. Cornell	Sword Dancer	Dunce
1960	**Bally Ache**	1:57 3/5	Bobby Ussery	Jimmy Pitt	Victoria Park	Celtic Ash
1961	**Carry Back**	1:57 3/5	Johnny Sellers	Jack Price	Globemaster	Crozier
1962	**Greek Money**	1:56 1/5	John Rotz	V.W. Raines	Ridan	Roman Line
1963	**Candy Spots**	1:56 1/5	Bill Shoemaker	Mesh Tenney	Chateaugay	Never Bend
1964	**Northern Dancer**	1:56 4/5	Bill Hartack	Horatio Luro	The Scoundrel	Hill Rise
1965	**Tom Rolfe**	1:56 1/5	Ron Turcotte	Frank Whiteley	Dapper Dan	Hail To All
1966	**Kauai King**	1:55 2/5	Don Brumfield	Henry Forrest	Stupendous	Amberoid
1967	**Damascus**	1:55 1/5	Bill Shoemaker	Frank Whiteley	In Reality	Proud Clarion
1968	**Forward Pass**	1:56 4/5	Ismael Valenzuela	Henry Forrest	Out Of the Way	Nodouble
1969	**Majestic Prince**	1:55 3/5	Bill Hartack	Johnny Longden	Arts and Letters	Jay Ray
1970	**Personality**	1:56 1/5	Eddie Belmonte	John Jacobs	My Dad George	Silent Screen
1971	**Canonero II**	1:54	Gustavo Avila	Juan Arias	Eastern Fleet	Jim French
1972	**Bee Bee Bee**	1:55 3/5	Eldon Nelson	Red Carroll	No Le Hace	Key To The Mint
1973	**SECRETARIAT**	1:54 2/5	Ron Turcotte	Lucien Laurin	Sham	Our Native
1974	**Little Current**	1:54 3/5	Miguel Rivera	Lou Rondinello	Neapolitan Way	Cannonade
1975	**Master Derby**	1:56 2/5	Darrel McHargue	Smiley Adams	Foolish Pleasure	Diabolo
1976	**Elocutionist**	1:55	John Lively	Paul Adwell	Play The Red	Bold Forbes

Preakness Stakes (Cont.)

Year		Time	Jockey	Trainer	2nd place	3rd place
1977	**SEATTLE SLEW**	1:54⅖	Jean Cruguet	Billy Turner	Iron Constitution	Run Dusty Run
1978	**AFFIRMED**	1:54⅖	Steve Cauthen	Laz Barrera	Alydar	Believe It
1979	**Spectacular Bid**	1:54⅕	Ron Franklin	Bud Delp	Golden Act	Screen King
1980	**Codex**	1:54⅕	Angel Cordero Jr.	D. Wayne Lukas	Genuine Risk	Colonel Moran
1981	**Pleasant Colony**	1:54⅗	Jorge Velasquez	John Campo	Bold Ego	Paristo
1982	**Aloma's Ruler**	1:55⅖	Jack Kaenel	John Lenzini Jr.	Linkage	Cut Away
1983	**Deputed Testamony**	1:55⅖	Donald Miller Jr.	Bill Boniface	Desert Wine	High Honors
1984	**Gate Dancer**	1:53⅗	Angel Cordero Jr.	Jack Van Berg	Play On	Fight Over
1985	**Tank's Prospect**	1:53⅖	Pat Day	D. Wayne Lukas	Chief's Crown	Eternal Prince
1986	**Snow Chief**	1:54⅘	Alex Solis	Melvin Stute	Ferdinand	Broad Brush
1987	**Alysheba**	1:55⅘	Chris McCarron	Jack Van Berg	Bet Twice	Cryptoclearance
1988	**Risen Star**	1:56⅕	E. Delahoussaye	Louie Roussel III	Brian's Time	Winning Colors
1989	**Sunday Silence**	1:53⅘	Pat Valenzuela	Chas. Whittingham	Easy Goer	Rock Point
1990	**Summer Squall**	1:53⅗	Pat Day	Neil Howard	Unbridled	Mister Frisky
1991	**Hansel**	1:54	Jerry Bailey	Frank Brothers	Corporate Report	Mane Minister
1992	**Pine Bluff**	1:55⅗	Chris McCarron	Tom Bohannan	Alydeed	Casual Lies
1993	**Prairie Bayou**	1:56⅗	Mike Smith	Tom Bohannan	Cherokee Run	El Bakan
1994	**Tabasco Cat**	1:56⅖	Pat Day	D. Wayne Lukas	Go For Gin	Concern
1995	**Timber Country**	1:54⅖	Pat Day	D. Wayne Lukas	Oliver's Twist	Thunder Gulch
1996	**Louis Quatorze**	1:53⅖	Pat Day	Nick Zito	Skip Away	Editor's Note
1997	**Silver Charm**	1:54⅖	Gary Stevens	Bob Baffert	Free House	Captain Bodgit
1998	**Real Quiet**	1:54⅘	Kent Desormeaux	Bob Baffert	Victory Gallop	Classic Cat
1999	**Charismatic**	1:55⅕	Chris Antley	D. Wayne Lukas	Menifee	Badge
2000	**Red Bullet**	1:56	Jerry Bailey	Joe Orseno	Fusaichi Pegasus	Impeachment

* Later named Judge Murray.

Belmont Stakes

For three-year-olds. Held three weeks after Preakness Stakes at Belmont Park in Elmont, N.Y. Inaugurated in 1867 at Jerome Park, moved to Morris Park in 1890 and then to Belmont Park in 1905.

Originally run at 1 mile and 5 furlongs (1867-89), then 1¼ miles (1890-1905), 1⅜ miles (1906-25), and the present 1½ miles since 1926.

Trainers with most wins: James Rowe Sr. (8); Sam Hildreth (7); Sunny Jim Fitzsimmons (6); Woody Stephens (5); Max Hirsch, D. Wayne Lukas and Robert W. Walden (4); Elliott Burch, Lucien Laurin, F. McCabe and D. McDaniel (3).

Jockeys with most wins: Eddie Arcaro and Jim McLaughlin (6); Earl Sande and Bill Shoemaker (5); Braulio Baeza, Pat Day, Laffit Pincay Jr. and James Stout (3).

Winning fillies: Ruthless (1867) and Tanya (1905).

Year		Time	Jockey	Trainer	2nd place	3rd place
1867	**Ruthless**	3:05	J. Gilpatrick	A.J. Minor	DeCourcey	Rivoli
1868	**General Duke**	3:02	Bobby Swim	A. Thompson	Northumberland	Fanny Ludlow
1869	**Fenian**	3:04¼	C. Miller	J. Pincus	Glenelg	Invercauld
1870	**Kingfisher**	2:59½	W. Dick	R. Colston	Foster	Midday
1871	**Harry Bassett**	2:56	W. Miller	D. McDaniel	Stockwood	By the Sea
1872	**Joe Daniels**	2:58¼	James Roe	D. McDaniel	Meteor	Shylock
1873	**Springbok**	3:01¾	James Roe	D. McDaniel	Count d'Orsay	Strachino
1874	**Saxon**	2:39½	G. Barbee	W. Prior	Grinstead	Aaron Pennington
1875	**Calvin**	2:42¼	Bobby Swim	A. Williams	Aristides	Milner
1876	**Algerine**	2:40½	Billy Donohue	Major Doswell	Fiddlesticks	Barricade
1877	**Cloverbrook**	2:46	C. Holloway	J. Walden	Loiterer	Baden-Baden
1878	**Duke of Magenta**	2:43½	L. Hughes	R.W. Walden	Bramble	Sparta
1879	**Spendthrift**	2:42¾	George Evans	T. Puryear	Monitor	Jericho
1880	**Grenada**	2:47	L. Hughes	R.W. Walden	Ferncliffe	Turenne
1881	**Saunterer**	2:47	T. Costello	R.W. Walden	Eole	Baltic
1882	**Forester**	2:43	Jim McLaughlin	L. Stuart	Babcock	Wyoming
1883	**George Kinney**	2:42½	Jim McLaughlin	James Rowe Sr.	Trombone	Renegade
1884	**Panique**	2:42	Jim McLaughlin	James Rowe Sr.	Knight of Ellerslie	Himalaya
1885	**Tyrant**	2:43	Paul Duffy	W. Claypool	St. Augustine	Tecumseh
1886	**Inspector B**	2:41	Jim McLaughlin	F. McCabe	The Bard	Linden
1887	**Hanover**	2:43½	Jim McLaughlin	F. McCabe	Oneko	(2-horse race)
1888	**Sir Dixon**	2:40¼	Jim McLaughlin	F. McCabe	Prince Royal	(2-horse race)
1889	**Eric**	2:47¼	W. Hayward	J. Huggins	Diablo	Zephyrus
1890	**Burlington**	2:07¾	Pike Barnes	A. Cooper	Devotee	Padishah
1891	**Foxford**	2:08¾	Ed Garrison	M. Donavan	Montana	Laurestan
1892	**Patron**	2:12	W. Hayward	L. Stuart	Shellbark	(2-horse race)
1893	**Commanche**	1:53¼	Willie Simms	G. Hannon	Dr. Rice	Rainbow
1894	**Henry of Navarre**	1:56½	Willie Simms	B. McClelland	Prig	Assignee
1895	**Belmar**	2:11½	Fred Taral	E. Feakes	Counter Tenor	Nanki Poo

Year		Time	Jockey	Trainer	2nd place	3rd place
1896	**Hastings**	2:24½	H. Griffin	J.J. Hyland	Handspring	Hamilton II
1897	**Scottish Chieftain**	2:23¼	J. Scherrer	M. Byrnes	On Deck	Octagon
1898	**Bowling Brook**	2:32	F. Littlefield	R.W. Walden	Previous	Hamburg
1899	**Jean Beraud**	2:23	R. Clawson	Sam Hildreth	Half Time	Glengar
1900	**Ildrim**	2:21¼	Nash Turner	H.E. Leigh	Petruchio	Missionary
1901	**Commando**	2:21	H. Spencer	James Rowe Sr.	The Parader	All Green
1902	**Masterman**	2:22⅗	John Bullman	J.J. Hyland	Renald	King Hanover
1903	**Africander**	2:21¾	John Bullman	R. Miller	Whorler	Red Knight
1904	**Delhi**	2:06⅗	George Odom	James Rowe Sr.	Graziallo	Rapid Water
1905	**Tanya**	2:08	E. Hildebrand	J.W. Rogers	Blandy	Hot Shot
1906	**Burgomaster**	2:20	Lucien Lyne	J.W. Rogers	The Quail	Accountant
1907	**Peter Pan**	N/A	G. Mountain	James Rowe Sr.	Superman	Frank Gill
1908	**Colin**	N/A	Joe Notter	James Rowe Sr.	Fair Play	King James
1909	**Joe Madden**	2:21⅗	E. Dugan	Sam Hildreth	Wise Mason	Donald MacDonald
1910	**Sweep**	2:22	James Butwell	James Rowe Sr.	Duke of Ormonde	(2-horse race)
1911-12	Not held					
1913	**Prince Eugene**	2:18	Roscoe Troxler	James Rowe Sr.	Rock View	Flying Fairy
1914	**Luke McLuke**	2:20	Merritt Buxton	J.F. Schorr	Gainer	Charlestonian
1915	**The Finn**	2:18⅖	George Byrne	E.W. Heffner	Half Rock	Pebbles
1916	**Friar Rock**	2:22	E. Haynes	Sam Hildreth	Spur	Churchill
1917	**Hourless**	2:17⅘	James Butwell	Sam Hildreth	Skeptic	Wonderful
1918	**Johren**	2:20⅖	Frank Robinson	A. Simons	War Cloud	Cum Sah
1919	**SIR BARTON**	2:17⅖	John Loftus	H. Guy Bedwell	Sweep On	Natural Bridge
1920	**Man o' War**	2:14⅕	Clarence Kummer	L. Feustel	Donnacona	(2-horse race)
1921	**Grey Lag**	2:16⅘	Earl Sande	Sam Hildreth	Sporting Blood	Leonardo II
1922	**Pillory**	2:18⅘	C.H. Miller	T.J. Healey	Snob II	Hea
1923	**Zev**	2:19	Earl Sande	Sam Hildreth	Chickvale	Rialto
1924	**Mad Play**	2:18⅘	Earl Sande	Sam Hildreth	Mr. Mutt	Modest
1925	**American Flag**	2:16⅘	Albert Johnson	G.R. Tompkins	Dangerous	Swope
1926	**Crusader**	2:32⅕	Albert Johnson	George Conway	Espino	Haste
1927	**Chance Shot**	2:32⅖	Earl Sande	Pete Coyne	Bois de Rose	Flambino
1928	**Vito**	2:33⅕	Clarence Kummer	Max Hirsch	Genie	Diavolo
1929	**Blue Larkspur**	2:32⅘	Mack Garner	C. Hastings	African	Jack High
1930	**GALLANT FOX**	2:31⅗	Earl Sande	Jim Fitzsimmons	Whichone	Questionnaire
1931	**Twenty Grand**	2:29⅗	Charley Kurtsinger	James Rowe Jr.	Sun Meadow	Jamestown
1932	**Faireno**	2:32⅘	Tom Malley	Jim Fitzsimmons	Osculator	Flag Pole
1933	**Hurryoff**	2:32⅗	Mack Garner	H. McDaniel	Nimbus	Union
1934	**Peace Chance**	2:29⅕	W.D. Wright	Pete Coyne	High Quest	Good Goods
1935	**OMAHA**	2:30⅗	Willie Saunders	Jim Fitzsimmons	Firethorn	Rosemont
1936	**Granville**	2:30	James Stout	Jim Fitzsimmons	Mr. Bones	Hollyrood
1937	**WAR ADMIRAL**	2:28⅗	Charley Kurtsinger	George Conway	Sceneshifter	Vamoose
1938	**Pasteurized**	2:29⅖	James Stout	George Odom	Dauber	Cravat
1939	**Johnstown**	2:29⅗	James Stout	Jim Fitzsimmons	Belay	Gilded Knight
1940	**Bimelech**	2:29⅗	Fred Smith	Bill Hurley	Your Chance	Andy K.
1941	**WHIRLAWAY**	2:31	Eddie Arcaro	Ben Jones	Robert Morris	Yankee Chance
1942	**Shut Out**	2:29⅕	Eddie Arcaro	John Gaver	Alsab	Lochinvar
1943	**COUNT FLEET**	2:28⅕	Johnny Longden	Don Cameron	Fairy Manhurst	Deseronto
1944	**Bounding Home**	2:32⅕	G.L. Smith	Matt Brady	Pensive	Bull Dandy
1945	**Pavot**	2:30⅕	Eddie Arcaro	Oscar White	Wildlife	Jeep
1946	**ASSAULT**	2:30⅘	Warren Mehrtens	Max Hirsch	Natchez	Cable
1947	**Phalanx**	2:29⅖	R. Donoso	Syl Veitch	Tide Rips	Tailspin
1948	**CITATION**	2:28⅕	Eddie Arcaro	Jimmy Jones	Better Self	Escadru
1949	**Capot**	2:30⅕	Ted Atkinson	John Gaver	Ponder	Palestinian
1950	**Middleground**	2:28⅗	William Boland	Max Hirsch	Lights Up	Mr. Trouble
1951	**Counterpoint**	2:29	David Gorman	Syl Veitch	Battlefield	Battle Morn
1952	**One Count**	2:30⅕	Eddie Arcaro	Oscar White	Blue Man	Armageddon
1953	**Native Dancer**	2:28⅗	Eric Guerin	Bill Winfrey	Jamie K.	Royal Bay Gem
1954	**High Gun**	2:30⅘	Eric Guerin	Max Hirsch	Fisherman	Limelight
1955	**Nashua**	2:29	Eddie Arcaro	Jim Fitzsimmons	Blazing Count	Portersville
1956	**Needles**	2:29⅘	David Erb	Hugh Fontaine	Career Boy	Fabius
1957	**Gallant Man**	2:26⅗	Bill Shoemaker	John Nerud	Inside Tract	Bold Ruler
1958	**Cavan**	2:30⅕	Pete Anderson	Tom Barry	Tim Tam	Flamingo
1959	**Sword Dancer**	2:28⅖	Bill Shoemaker	Elliott Burch	Bagdad	Royal Orbit
1960	**Celtic Ash**	2:29⅕	Bill Hartack	Tom Barry	Venetian Way	Disperse
1961	**Sherluck**	2:29⅕	Braulio Baeza	Harold Young	Globemaster	Guadalcanal
1962	**Jaipur**	2:28⅘	Bill Shoemaker	B. Mulholland	Admiral's Voyage	Crimson Satan
1963	**Chateaugay**	2:30⅕	Braulio Baeza	James Conway	Candy Spots	Choker
1964	**Quadrangle**	2:28⅖	Manuel Ycaza	Elliott Burch	Roman Brother	Northern Dancer
1965	**Hail to All**	2:28⅖	John Sellers	Eddie Yowell	Tom Rolfe	First Family

Belmont Stakes (Cont.)

Year	Time	Jockey	Trainer	2nd place	3rd place
1966 **Amberoid**	2:29$^{3}/_{5}$	William Boland	Lucien Laurin	Buffle	Advocator
1967 **Damascus**	2:28$^{4}/_{5}$	Bill Shoemaker	F.Y. Whiteley Jr.	Cool Reception	Gentleman James
1968 **Stage Door Johnny**	2:27$^{1}/_{5}$	Gus Gustines	John Gaver	Forward Pass	Call Me Prince
1969 **Arts and Letters**	2:28$^{4}/_{5}$	Braulio Baeza	Elliott Burch	Majestic Prince	Dike
1970 **High Echelon**	2:34	John Rotz	John Jacobs	Needles N Pens	Naskra
1971 **Pass Catcher**	2:30$^{2}/_{5}$	Walter Blum	Eddie Yowell	Jim French	Bold Reason
1972 **Riva Ridge**	2:28	Ron Turcotte	Lucien Laurin	Ruritania	Cloudy Dawn
1973 **SECRETARIAT**	2:24	Ron Turcotte	Lucien Laurin	Twice A Prince	My Gallant
1974 **Little Current**	2:29$^{1}/_{5}$	Miguel Rivera	Lou Rondinello	Jolly Johu	Cannonade
1975 **Avatar**	2:28$^{1}/_{5}$	Bill Shoemaker	Tommy Doyle	Foolish Pleasure	Master Derby
1976 **Bold Forbes**	2:29	Angel Cordero Jr.	Laz Barrera	McKenzie Bridge	Great Contractor
1977 **SEATTLE SLEW**	2:29$^{3}/_{5}$	Jean Cruguet	Billy Turner	Run Dusty Run	Sanhedrin
1978 **AFFIRMED**	2:26$^{4}/_{5}$	Steve Cauthen	Laz Barrera	Alydar	Darby Creek Road
1979 **Coastal**	2:28$^{3}/_{5}$	Ruben Hernandez	David Whiteley	Golden Act	Spectacular Bid
1980 **Temperence Hill**	2:29$^{4}/_{5}$	Eddie Maple	Joseph Cantey	Genuine Risk	Rockhill Native
1981 **Summing**	2:29	George Martens	Luis Barerra	Highland Blade	Pleasant Colony
1982 **Conquistador Cielo**	2:28$^{1}/_{5}$	Laffit Pincay Jr.	Woody Stephens	Gato Del Sol	Illuminate
1983 **Caveat**	2:27$^{4}/_{5}$	Laffit Pincay Jr.	Woody Stephens	Slew o' Gold	Barberstown
1984 **Swale**	2:27$^{1}/_{5}$	Laffit Pincay Jr.	Woody Stephens	Pine Circle	Morning Bob
1985 **Creme Fraiche**	2:27	Eddie Maple	Woody Stephens	Stephan's Odyssey	Chief's Crown
1986 **Danzig Connection**	2:29$^{4}/_{5}$	Chris McCarron	Woody Stephens	Johns Treasure	Ferdinand
1987 **Bet Twice**	2:28$^{1}/_{5}$	Craig Perret	Jimmy Croll	Cryptoclearance	Gulch
1988 **Risen Star**	2:26$^{2}/_{5}$	E. Delahoussaye	Louie Roussel III	Kingpost	Brian's Time
1989 **Easy Goer**	2:26	Pat Day	Shug McGaughey	Sunday Silence	Le Voyageur
1990 **Go And Go**	2:27$^{1}/_{5}$	Michael Kinane	Dermot Weld	Thirty Six Red	Baron de Vaux
1991 **Hansel**	2:28	Jerry Bailey	Frank Brothers	Strike the Gold	Mane Minister
1992 **A.P. Indy**	2:26	E. Delahoussaye	Neil Drysdale	My Memoirs	Pine Bluff
1993 **Colonial Affair**	2:29$^{4}/_{5}$	Julie Krone	Scotty Schulhofer	Kissin Kris	Wild Gale
1994 **Tabasco Cat**	2:26$^{4}/_{5}$	Pat Day	D. Wayne Lukas	Go For Gin	Strodes Creek
1995 **Thunder Gulch**	2:32	Gary Stevens	D. Wayne Lukas	Star Standard	Citadeed
1996 **Editor's Note**	2:28$^{4}/_{5}$	Rene Douglas	D. Wayne Lukas	Skip Away	My Flag
1997 **Touch Gold**	2:28$^{4}/_{5}$	Chris McCarron	David Hofmans	Silver Charm	Free House
1998 **Victory Gallop**	2:29	Gary Stevens	Elliott Walden	Real Quiet	Thomas Jo
1999 **Lemon Drop Kid**	2:27$^{4}/_{5}$	Jose Santos	Scotty Schulhofer	Vision and Verse	Charismatic
2000 **Commendable**	2:31$^{1}/_{5}$	Pat Day	D. Wayne Lukas	Aptitude	Unshaded

Breeders' Cup Championship

Inaugurated on Nov. 10, 1984, the Breeders' Cup Championship consists of seven races on one track on one day late in the year to determine thoroughbred racing's principle champions.

The Breeders' Cup has been held at the following tracks (in alphabetical order): Aqueduct Racetrack (N.Y.) in 1985; Belmont Park (N.Y.) in 1990 and '95; Churchill Downs (Ky.) in 1988, '91, '94 and '98; Gulfstream Park (Fla.) in 1989, '92 and '99; Hollywood Park (Calif.) in 1984, '87 and '97; Santa Anita Park (Calif.) in 1986 and '93 and Woodbine (Toronto) in 1996.

Trainers with most wins: D. Wayne Lukas (15); Shug McGaughey (7); Neil Drysdale and Bill Mott (5); Ron McAnally (4); Francois Boutin and Patrick Byrne (3).

Jockeys with most wins: Pat Day (11); Jerry Bailey (9); Mike Smith (8); Eddie Delahoussaye, Chris McCarron, Laffit Pincay Jr. and Gary Stevens (7); Jose Santos and Pat Valenzuela (6); Corey Nakatani (5); Angel Cordero and Craig Perret (4); Randy Romero (3).

Juvenile

Distances: one mile (1984-85, 87); 1$^{1}/_{16}$ miles (1986 and since 1988).

Year	Time	Jockey	Trainer	2nd place	3rd place
1984 **Chief's Crown**	1:36$^{1}/_{5}$	Don MacBeth	Roger Laurin	Tank's Prospect	Spend A Buck
1985 **Tasso**	1:36$^{1}/_{5}$	Laffit Pincay Jr.	Neil Drysdale	Storm Cat	Scat Dancer
1986 **Capote**	1:43$^{4}/_{5}$	Laffit Pincay Jr.	D. Wayne Lukas	Qualify	Alysheba
1987 **Success Express**	1:35$^{1}/_{5}$	Jose Santos	D. Wayne Lukas	Regal Classic	Tejano
1988 **Is It True**	1:46$^{3}/_{5}$	Laffit Pincay Jr.	D. Wayne Lukas	Easy Goer	Tagel
1989 **Rhythm**	1:43$^{3}/_{5}$	Craig Perret	Shug McGaughey	Grand Canyon	Slavic
1990 **Fly So Free**	1:43$^{2}/_{5}$	Jose Santos	Scotty Schulhofer	Take Me Out	Lost Mountain
1991 **Arazi**	1:44$^{3}/_{5}$	Pat Valenzuela	Francois Boutin	Bertrando	Snappy Landing
1992 **Gilded Time**	1:43$^{2}/_{5}$	Chris McCarron	Darrell Vienna	It'sali'lknownfact	River Special
1993 **Brocco**	1:42$^{4}/_{5}$	Gary Stevens	Randy Winick	Blumin Affair	Tabasco Cat
1994 **Timber Country**	1:44$^{2}/_{5}$	Pat Day	D. Wayne Lukas	Eltish	Tejano Run
1995 **Unbridled's Song**	1:41$^{3}/_{5}$	Mike Smith	James Ryerson	Hennessy	Editor's Note
1996 **Boston Harbor**	1:43$^{2}/_{5}$	Jerry Bailey	D. Wayne Lukas	Acceptable	Ordway
1997 **Favorite Trick**	1:41$^{2}/_{5}$	Pat Day	Patrick Byrne	Dawson's Legacy	Nationalore
1998 **Answer Lively**	1:44	Jerry Bailey	Bobby Barnett	Aly's Alley	Cat Thief
1999 **Anees**	1:42$^{1}/_{5}$	Gary Stevens	Alex Hassinger Jr.	Chief Seattle	High Yield

Juvenile Fillies

Distances: one mile (1984-85, 87); 1 1/16 miles (1986 and since 1988).

Year		Time	Jockey	Trainer	2nd place	3rd place
1984	**Outstandingly***	1:37⅘	Walter Guerra	Pancho Martin	Dusty Heart	Fine Spirit
1985	**Twilight Ridge**	1:35⅘	Jorge Velasquez	D. Wayne Lukas	Family Style	Steal A Kiss
1986	**Brave Raj**	1:43⅕	Pat Valenzuela	Melvin Stute	Tappiano	Saros Brig
1987	**Epitome**	1:36⅖	Pat Day	Phil Hauswald	Jeanne Jones	Dream Team
1988	**Open Mind**	1:46⅗	Angel Cordero Jr.	D. Wayne Lukas	Darby Shuffle	Lea Lucinda
1989	**Go for Wand**	1:44⅕	Randy Romero	Wm. Badgett, Jr.	Sweet Roberta	Stella Madrid
1990	**Meadow Star**	1:44	Jose Santos	LeRoy Jolley	Private Treasure	Dance Smartly
1991	**Pleasant Stage**	1:46⅖	Eddie Delahoussaye	Chris Speckert	La Spia	Cadillac Women
1992	**Liza**	1:42⅘	Pat Valenzuela	Alex Hassingfer	Educated Risk	Boots 'n Jackie
1993	**Phone Chatter**	1:43	Laffit Pincay Jr.	Richard Mandella	Sardula	Heavenly Prize
1994	**Flanders**	1:45⅕	Pat Day	D. Wayne Lukas	Serena's Song	Stormy Blues
1995	**My Flag**	1:42⅖	Jerry Bailey	Shug McGaughey	Cara Rafaela	Golden Attraction
1996	**Storm Song**	1:43⅗	Craig Perret	Nick Zito	Love That Jazz	Critical Factor
1997	**Countess Diana**	1:42⅕	Shane Sellers	Patrick Byrne	Career Collection	Primaly
1998	**Silverbulletday**	1:43⅗	Gary Stevens	Bob Baffert	Excellent Meeting	Three Ring
1999	**Cash Run**	1:43⅕	Jerry Bailey	D. Wayne Lukas	Chilukki	Surfside

*In 1984, winner Fran's Valentine was disqualified for interference in the stretch and placed 10th.

Sprint

Distance: six furlongs (since 1984).

Year		Time	Jockey	Trainer	2nd place	3rd place
1984	**Eillo**	1:10⅕	Craig Perret	Budd Lepman	Commemorate	Fighting Fit
1985	**Precisionist**	1:08⅖	Chris McCarron	L.R. Fenstermaker	Smile	Mt. Livermore
1986	**Smile**	1:08⅖	Jacinto Vasquez	Scotty Schulhofer	Pine Tree Lane	Bedside Promise
1987	**Very Subtle**	1:08⅘	Pat Valenzuela	Melvin Stute	Groovy	Exclusive Enough
1988	**Gulch**	1:10⅖	Angel Cordero Jr.	D. Wayne Lukas	Play The King	Afleet
1989	**Dancing Spree**	1:09	Angel Cordero Jr.	Shug McGaughey	Safely Kept	Dispersal
1990	**Safely Kept**	1:09⅗	Craig Perret	Alan Goldberg	Dayjur	Black Tie Affair
1991	**Sheikh Albadou**	1:09⅕	Pat Eddery	Alexander Scott	Pleasant Tap	Robyn Dancer
1992	**Thirty Slews**	1:08⅕	Eddie Delahoussaye	Bob Baffert	Meafara	Rubiano
1993	**Cardmania**	1:08⅗	Eddie Delahoussaye	Derek Meredith	Meafara	Gilded Time
1994	**Cherokee Run**	1:09⅖	Mike Smith	Frank Alexander	Soviet Problem	Cardmania
1995	**Desert Stormer**	1:09	Kent Desormeaux	Frank Lyons	Mr. Greeley	Lit de Justice
1996	**Lit de Justice**	1:08⅗	Corey Nakatani	Jenine Sahadi	Paying Dues	Honour and Glory
1997	**Elmhurst**	1:08⅕	Corey Nakatani	Jenine Sahadi	Hesabull	Bet On Sunshine
1998	**Reraise**	1:09	Corey Nakatani	Craig Dollase	Grand Slam	Kona Gold
1999	**Artax**	1:07⅘	Jorge Chavez	Louis Albertrani	Kona Gold	Big Jag

Mile

Year		Time	Jockey	Trainer	2nd place	3rd place
1984	**Royal Heroine**	1:32⅗	Fernando Toro	John Gosden	Star Choice	Cozzene
1985	**Cozzene**	1:35	Walter Guerra	Jan Nerud	Al Mamoon*	Shadeed
1986	**Last Tycoon**	1:35⅕	Yves St.-Martin	Robert Collet	Palace Music	Fred Astaire
1987	**Miesque**	1:32⅘	Freddie Head	Francois Boutin	Show Dancer	Sonic Lady
1988	**Miesque**	1:38⅗	Freddie Head	Francois Boutin	Steinlen	Simply Majestic
1989	**Steinlen**	1:37⅕	Jose Santos	D. Wayne Lukas	Sabona	Most Welcome
1990	**Royal Academy**	1:35⅕	Lester Piggott	M.V. O'Brien	Itsallgreektome	Priolo
1991	**Opening Verse**	1:37⅖	Pat Valenzuela	Dick Lundy	Val des Bois	Star of Cozzene
1992	**Lure**	1:32⅘	Mike Smith	Shug McGaughey	Paradise Creek	Brief Truce
1993	**Lure**	1:33⅖	Mike Smith	Shug McGaughey	Ski Paradise	Fourstars Allstar
1994	**Barathea**	1:34⅖	Frankie Dettori	Luca Cumani	Johann Quatz	Unfinished Symph
1995	**Ridgewood Pearl**	1:43⅗	John Murtagh	John Oxx	Fastness	Sayyedati
1996	**Da Hoss**	1:35⅘	Gary Stevens	Michael Dickinson	Spinning World	Same Old Wish
1997	**Spinning World**	1:32⅗	Cash Asmussen	Jonathan Pease	Geri	Decorated Hero
1998	**Da Hoss**	1:35⅕	John Velazquez	Michael Dickinson	Hawksley Hill	Labeeb
1999	**Silic**	1:34⅕	Corey Nakatani	Julio Canani	Tuzla	Docksider

*In 1985, 2nd place finisher Palace Music was disqualified for interference and placed 9th.

Distaff

Distances: 1¼ miles (1984-87); 1⅛ miles (since 1988).

Year		Time	Jockey	Trainer	2nd place	3rd place
1984	**Princess Rooney**	2:02⅖	Eddie Delahoussaye	Neil Drysdale	Life's Magic	Adored
1985	**Life's Magic**	2:02	Angel Cordero Jr.	D. Wayne Lukas	Lady's Secret	DontstopThemusic
1986	**Lady's Secret**	2:01⅕	Pat Day	D. Wayne Lukas	Fran's Valentine	Outstandingly
1987	**Sacahuista**	2:02⅘	Randy Romero	D. Wayne Lukas	Clabber Girl	Oueee Bebe
1988	**Personal Ensign**	1:52	Randy Romero	Shug McGaughey	Winning Colors	Goodbye Halo
1989	**Bayakoa**	1:47⅖	Laffit Pincay Jr.	Ron McAnally	Gorgeous	Open Mind
1990	**Bayakoa**	1:49⅕	Laffit Pincay Jr.	Ron McAnally	Colonial Waters	Valay Maid
1991	**Dance Smartly**	1:50⅘	Pat Day	Jim Day	Versailles Treaty	Brought to Mind
1992	**Paseana**	1:48	Chris McCarron	Ron McAnally	Versailles Treaty	Magical Maiden
1993	**Hollywood Wildcat**	1:48⅕	Eddie Delahoussaye	Neil Drysdale	Paseana	Re Toss

Breeders' Cup Championship (Cont.)

Year		Time	Jockey	Trainer	2nd place	3rd place
1994	**One Dreamer**	1:50⅗	Gary Stevens	Thomas Proctor	Heavenly Prize	Miss Dominique
1995	**Inside Information**	1:46	Mike Smith	Shug McGaughey	Heavenly Prize	Lakeway
1996	**Jewel Princess**	1:48⅕	Corey Nakatani	Wallace Dollase	Serena's Song	Different
1997	**Ajina**	1:47⅕	Mike Smith	Bill Mott	Sharp Cat	Escena
1998	**Escena**	1:49⅘	Gary Stevens	Bill Mott	Banshee Breeze	Keeper Hill
1999	**Beautiful Pleasure**	1:47⅖	Jorge Chavez	John Ward Jr.	Banshee Breeze	Heritage of Gold

Turf

Distance: 1½ miles (since 1984).

Year		Time	Jockey	Trainer	2nd place	3rd place
1984	**Lashkari**	2:25⅕	Yves St.-Martin	de Royer-Dupre	All Along	Raami
1985	**Pebbles**	2:27	Pat Eddery	Clive Brittain	StrawberryRoad II	Mourjane
1986	**Manila**	2:25⅖	Jose Santos	Leroy Jolley	Theatrical	Estrapade
1987	**Theatrical**	2:24⅖	Pat Day	Bill Mott	Trempolino	Village Star II
1988	**Gt. Communicator**	2:35⅕	Ray Sibille	Thad Ackel	Sunshine Forever	Indian Skimmer
1989	**Prized**	2:28	Eddie Delahoussaye	Neil Drysdale	Sierra Roberta	Star Lift
1990	**In The Wings**	2:29⅗	Gary Stevens	Andre Fabre	With Approval	El Senor
1991	**Miss Alleged**	2:30⅘	Eric Legrix	Pascal Bary	Itsallgreektome	Quest for Fame
1992	**Fraise**	2:24	Pat Valenzuela	Bill Mott	Sky Classic	Quest for Fame
1993	**Kotashaan**	2:25	Kent Desormeaux	Richard Mandella	Bien Bien	Luazur
1994	**Tikkanen**	2:26⅖	Mike Smith	Jonathan Pease	Hatoof	Paradise Creek
1995	**Northern Spur**	2:42	Chris McCarron	Ron McAnally	Freedom Cry	Carnegie
1996	**Pilsudski**	2:30⅕	Walter Swinburn	Michael Stoute	Singspiel	Swain
1997	**Chief Bearhart**	2:24	Jose Santos	Mark Frostad	Borgia	Flag Down
1998	**Buck's Boy**	2:28⅗	Shane Sellers	Noel Hickey	Yagli	Dushyantor
1999	**Daylami**	2:24⅗	Frankie Dettori	Saeed bin Suroor	Royal Anthem	Buck's Boy

Filly & Mare Turf

Distance: 1⅜ miles (since 1999).

Year		Time	Jockey	Trainer	2nd place	3rd place
1999	**Soaring Softly**	2:13⅘	Jerry Bailey	James J. Toner	Coretta	Zomarradah

Classic

Distance: 1¼ miles (since 1984).

Year		Time	Jockey	Trainer	2nd place	3rd place
1984	**Wild Again**	2:03⅖	Pat Day	Vincent Timphony	Slew o' Gold	Gate Dancer*
1985	**Proud Truth**	2:00⅘	Jorge Velasquez	John Veitch	Gate Dancer	Turkoman
1986	**Skywalker**	2:00⅖	Laffit Pincay Jr.	M. Whittingham	Turkoman	Precisionist
1987	**Ferdinand**	2:01⅖	Bill Shoemaker	C. Whittingham	Alysheba	Judge Angelucci
1988	**Alysheba**	2:04⅘	Chris McCarron	Jack Van Berg	Seeking the Gold	Waquoit
1989	**Sunday Silence**	2:00⅕	Chris McCarron	C. Whittingham	Easy Goer	Blushing John
1990	**Unbridled**	2:02⅕	Pat Day	Carl Nafzger	Ibn Bey	Thirty Six Red
1991	**Black Tie Affair**	2:02⅘	Jerry Bailey	Ernie Poulos	Twilight Agenda	Unbridled
1992	**A.P. Indy**	2:00⅕	Eddie Delahoussaye	Neil Drysdale	Pleasant Tap	Jolypha
1993	**Arcangues**	2:00⅘	Jerry Bailey	Andre Fabre	Bertrando	Kissin Kris
1994	**Concern**	2:02⅖	Jerry Bailey	Richard Small	Tabasco Cat	Dramatic Gold
1995	**Cigar**	1:59⅖	Jerry Bailey	Bill Mott	L'Carriere	Unaccounted For
1996	**Alphabet Soup**	2:01	Chris McCarron	David Hofmans	Louis Quatorze	Cigar
1997	**Skip Away**	1:59⅕	Mike Smith	Hubert Hine	Deputy Commander	Dowty
1998	**Awesome Again**	2:02	Pat Day	Patrick Byrne	Silver Charm	Swain
1999	**Cat Thief**	1:59⅖	Pat Day	D. Wayne Lukas	Budroyale	Golden Missile

*In 1984, 2nd place finisher Gate Dancer was disqualified for interference and placed 3rd.

Breeders' Cup Leaders

The all-time money-winning horses and race winning jockeys in the history of the Breeders' Cup through 1999.

Top 10 Horses

		Sts	1-2-3	Earnings
1	Awesome Again	1	1-0-0	$2,662,400
2	Skip Away	2	1-0-0	2,288,000
3	Cat Thief	2	1-0-1	2,200,000
4	Alysheba	3	1-1-1	2,133,000
5	Alphabet Soup	1	1-0-0	2,080,000
6	Cigar	2	1-0-1	2,040,000
7	Unbridled	2	1-0-1	1,710,000
8	Black Tie Affair (IRE)	3	1-0-1	1,668,000
9	A.P. Indy	1	1-0-0	1,560,000
	Arcangues	1	1-0-0	1,560,000
	Concern	1	1-0-0	1,560,000

Top 10 Jockeys

		Sts	1-2-3	Earnings
1	Pat Day	89	11-14-10	$19,853,000
2	Chris McCarron	89	7-11-7	12,760,000
3	Gary Stevens	76	7-14-9	12,030,680
4	Jerry Bailey	59	9-5-6	11,775,400
5	Mike Smith	39	8-3-3	7,860,200
6	Eddie Delahoussaye	64	7-3-6	7,719,000
7	Laffit Pincay Jr.	61	7-4-9	6,811,000
8	Angel Cordero Jr.	48	4-7-7	6,020,000
9	Corey Nakatani	35	5-5-5	5,916,520
10	Jose Santos	48	6-2-4	5,801,000

Annual Money Leaders
Horses

Annual money-leading horses since 1910, according to *The American Racing Manual*.

Multiple leaders: Round Table, Buckpasser, Alysheba and Cigar (2).

Year		Age	Sts	1st	Earnings	Year		Age	Sts	1st	Earnings
1910	Novelty	2	16	11	$ 72,630	1955	Nashua	3	12	10	$752,550
1911	Worth	2	13	10	16,645	1956	Needles	3	8	4	440,850
1912	Star Charter	4	17	6	14,655	1957	Round Table	3	22	15	600,383
1913	Old Rosebud	2	14	12	19,057	1958	Round Table	4	20	14	662,780
1914	Roamer	3	16	12	29,105	1959	Sword Dancer	3	13	8	537,004
1915	Borrow	7	9	4	20,195	1960	Bally Ache	3	15	10	445,045
1916	Campfire	2	9	6	49,735	1961	Carry Back	3	16	9	565,349
1917	Sun Briar	2	9	5	59,505	1962	Never Bend	2	10	7	402,969
1918	Eternal	2	8	6	56,173	1963	Candy Spots	3	12	7	604,481
1919	Sir Barton	3	13	8	88,250	1964	Gun Bow	4	16	8	580,100
1920	Man o' War	3	11	11	166,140	1965	Buckpasser	2	11	9	568,096
1921	Morvich	2	11	11	115,234	1966	Buckpasser	3	14	13	669,078
1922	Pillory	3	7	4	95,654	1967	Damascus	3	16	12	817,941
1923	Zev	3	14	12	272,008	1968	Forward Pass	3	13	7	546,674
1924	Sarzen	3	12	8	95,640	1969	Arts and Letters	3	14	8	555,604
1925	Pompey	2	10	7	121,630	1970	Personality	3	18	8	444,049
1926	Crusader	3	15	9	166,033	1971	Riva Ridge	2	9	7	503,263
1927	Anita Peabody	2	7	6	111,905	1972	Droll Role	4	19	7	471,633
1928	High Strung	2	6	5	153,590	1973	Secretariat	3	12	9	860,404
1929	Blue Larkspur	3	6	4	153,450	1974	Chris Evert	3	8	5	551,063
1930	Gallant Fox	3	10	9	308,275	1975	Foolish Pleasure	3	11	5	716,278
1931	Gallant Flight	2	7	7	219,000	1976	Forego	6	8	6	401,701
1932	Gusto	3	16	4	145,940	1977	Seattle Slew	3	7	6	641,370
1933	Singing Wood	2	9	3	88,050	1978	Affirmed	3	11	8	901,541
1934	Cavalcade	3	7	6	111,235	1979	Spectacular Bid	3	12	10	1,279,334
1935	Omaha	3	9	6	142,255	1980	Temperence Hill	3	17	8	1,130,452
1936	Granville	3	11	7	110,295	1981	John Henry	6	10	8	1,798,030
1937	Seabiscuit	4	15	11	168,580	1982	Perrault (GB)	5	8	4	1,197,400
1938	Stagehand	3	15	8	189,710	1983	All Along (FRA)	4	7	4	2,138,963
1939	Challedon	3	15	9	184,535	1984	Slew o' Gold	4	6	5	2,627,944
1940	Bimelech	3	7	4	110,005	1985	Spend A Buck	3	7	5	3,552,704
1941	Whirlaway	3	20	13	272,386	1986	Snow Chief	3	9	6	1,875,200
1942	Shut Out	3	12	8	238,872	1987	Alysheba	3	10	3	2,511,156
1943	Count Fleet	3	6	6	174,055	1988	Alysheba	4	9	7	3,808,600
1944	Pavot	2	8	8	179,040	1989	Sunday Silence	3	9	7	4,578,454
1945	Busher	3	13	10	273,735	1990	Unbridled	3	11	4	3,718,149
1946	Assault	3	15	8	424,195	1991	Dance Smartly	3	8	8	2,876,821
1947	Armed	6	17	11	376,325	1992	A.P. Indy	3	7	5	2,622,560
1948	Citation	3	20	19	709,470	1993	Kotashaan (FRA)	5	10	6	2,619,014
1949	Ponder	3	21	9	321,825	1994	Paradise Creek	5	11	8	2,610,187
1950	Noor	5	12	7	346,940	1995	Cigar	5	10	10	4,819,800
1951	Counterpoint	3	15	7	250,525	1996	Cigar	6	8	5	4,910,000
1952	Crafty Admiral	4	16	9	277,225	1997	Skip Away	4	11	4	4,089,000
1953	Native Dancer	3	10	9	513,425	1998	Silver Charm	4	9	6	4,696,506
1954	Determine	3	15	10	328,700	1999	Almutawakel	4	4	1	3,290,000

Jockeys

Annual money-leading jockeys since 1910, according to *The American Racing Manual*.

Multiple leaders: Bill Shoemaker (10); Laffit Pincay Jr. (7); Eddie Arcaro (6); Braulio Baeza (5); Chris McCarron and Jose Santos (4); Jerry Bailey, Angel Cordero Jr. and Earl Sande (3); Ted Atkinson, Laverne Fator, Mack Garner, Bill Hartack, Charles Kurtsinger, Johnny Longden, Mike Smith, Gary Stevens, Sonny Workman and Wayne Wright (2).

Year		Mts	Wins	Earnings	Year		Mts	Wins	Earnings
1910	Carroll Shilling	506	172	$176,030	1920	Clarence Kummer	353	87	$292,376
1911	Ted Koerner	813	162	88,308	1921	Earl Sande	340	112	263,043
1912	Jimmy Butwell	684	144	79,843	1922	Albert Johnson	297	43	345,054
1913	Merritt Buxton	887	146	82,552	1923	Earl Sande	430	122	569,394
1914	J. McCahey	824	155	121,845	1924	Ivan Parke	844	205	290,395
1915	Mack Garner	775	151	96,628	1925	Laverne Fator	315	81	305,775
1916	John McTaggart	832	150	155,055	1926	Laverne Fator	511	143	361,435
1917	Frank Robinson	731	147	148,057	1927	Earl Sande	179	49	277,877
1918	Lucien Luke	756	178	201,864	1928	Linus McAtee	235	55	301,295
1919	John Loftus	177	65	252,707	1929	Mack Garner	274	57	314,975

Year	Jockey	Mts	Wins	Earnings
1930	Sonny Workman	.571	152	$420,438
1931	Charley Kurtsinger	.519	93	392,095
1932	Sonny Workman	.378	87	385,070
1933	Robert Jones	.471	63	226,285
1934	Wayne Wright	.919	174	287,185
1935	Silvio Coucci	.749	141	319,760
1936	Wayne Wright	.670	100	264,000
1937	Charley Kurtsinger	.765	120	384,202
1938	Nick Wall	.658	97	385,161
1939	Basil James	.904	191	353,333
1940	Eddie Arcaro	.783	132	343,661
1941	Don Meade	.1164	210	398,627
1942	Eddie Arcaro	.687	123	481,949
1943	Johnny Longden	.871	173	573,276
1944	Ted Atkinson	.1539	287	899,101
1945	Johnny Longden	.778	180	981,977
1946	Ted Atkinson	.1377	233	1,036,825
1947	Douglas Dodson	.646	141	1,429,949
1948	Eddie Arcaro	.726	188	1,686,230
1949	Steve Brooks	.906	209	1,316,817
1950	Eddie Arcaro	.888	195	1,410,160
1951	Bill Shoemaker	.1161	257	1,329,890
1952	Eddie Arcaro	.807	188	1,859,591
1953	Bill Shoemaker	.1683	485	1,784,187
1954	Bill Shoemaker	.1251	380	1,876,760
1955	Eddie Arcaro	.820	158	1,864,796
1956	Bill Hartack	.1387	347	2,343,955
1957	Bill Hartack	.1238	341	3,060,501
1958	Bill Shoemaker	.1133	300	2,961,693
1959	Bill Shoemaker	.1285	347	2,843,133
1960	Bill Shoemaker	.1227	274	2,123,961
1961	Bill Shoemaker	.1256	304	2,690,819
1962	Bill Shoemaker	.1126	311	2,916,844
1963	Bill Shoemaker	.1203	271	2,526,925
1964	Bill Shoemaker	.1056	246	2,649,553
1965	Braulio Baeza	.1245	270	$2,582,702
1966	Braulio Baeza	.1341	298	2,951,022
1967	Braulio Baeza	.1064	256	3,088,888
1968	Braulio Baeza	.1089	201	2,835,108
1969	Jorge Velasquez	.1442	258	2,542,315
1970	Laffit Pincay Jr.	.1328	269	2,626,526
1971	Laffit Pincay Jr.	.1627	380	3,784,377
1972	Laffit Pincay Jr.	.1388	289	3,225,827
1973	Laffit Pincay Jr.	.1444	350	4,093,492
1974	Laffit Pincay Jr.	.1278	341	4,251,060
1975	Braulio Baeza	.1190	196	3,674,398
1976	Angel Cordero Jr.	.1534	274	4,709,500
1977	Steve Cauthen	.2075	487	6,151,750
1978	Darrel McHargue	.1762	375	6,188,353
1979	Laffit Pincay Jr.	.1708	420	8,183,535
1980	Chris McCarron	.1964	405	7,666,100
1981	Chris McCarron	.1494	326	8,397,604
1982	Angel Cordero Jr.	.1838	397	9,702,520
1983	Angel Cordero Jr.	.1792	362	10,116,807
1984	Chris McCarron	.1565	356	12,038,213
1985	Laffit Pincay Jr.	.1409	289	13,415,049
1986	Jose Santos	.1636	329	11,329,297
1987	Jose Santos	.1639	305	12,407,355
1988	Jose Santos	.1867	370	14,877,298
1989	Jose Santos	.1459	285	13,847,003
1990	Gary Stevens	.1504	283	13,881,198
1991	Chris McCarron	.1440	265	14,456,073
1992	Kent Desormeaux	.1568	361	14,193,006
1993	Mike Smith	.1510	343	14,024,815
1994	Mike Smith	.1484	317	15,979,820
1995	Jerry Bailey	.1367	287	16,311,876
1996	Jerry Bailey	.1187	298	19,465,376
1997	Jerry Bailey	.1136	269	18,206,013
1998	Gary Stevens	.869	178	19,358,840
1999	Pat Day	.1265	254	18,092,845

Trainers

Annual money-leading trainers since 1908, according to *The American Racing Manual*.

Multiple Leaders: D. Wayne Lukas (14); Sam Hildreth (9); Charlie Whittingham (7); Sunny Jim Fitzsimmons and Jimmy Jones (5); Laz Barrera, Ben Jones and Willie Molter (4); Hirsch Jacobs, Eddie Neloy and James Rowe Sr. (3); Bob Baffert, H. Guy Bedwell, Jack Gaver, John Schorr, Humming Bob Smith, Silent Tom Smith and Mesh Tenney (2).

Year	Trainer	Wins	Earnings
1908	James Rowe Sr.	50	$284,335
1909	Sam Hildreth	73	123,942
1910	Sam Hildreth	84	148,010
1911	Sam Hildreth	67	49,418
1912	John Schorr	63	58,110
1913	James Rowe Sr.	18	45,936
1914	R.C. Benson	45	59,315
1915	James Rowe Sr.	19	75,596
1916	Sam Hildreth	39	70,950
1917	Sam Hildreth	23	61,698
1918	H. Guy Bedwell	53	80,296
1919	H. Guy Bedwell	63	208,728
1920	Louis Feustel	22	186,087
1921	Sam Hildreth	85	262,768
1922	Sam Hildreth	74	247,014
1923	Sam Hildreth	75	392,124
1924	Sam Hildreth	77	255,608
1925	G.R. Tompkins	30	199,245
1926	Scott Harlan	21	205,681
1927	W.H. Bringloe	63	216,563
1928	John Schorr	65	258,425
1929	James Rowe Jr.	25	314,881
1930	Sunny Jim Fitzsimmons	47	397,355
1931	Big Jim Healy	33	297,300
1932	Sunny Jim Fitzsimmons	68	266,650
1933	Humming Bob Smith	53	$135,720
1934	Humming Bob Smith	43	249,938
1935	Bud Stotler	87	303,005
1936	Sunny Jim Fitzsimmons	42	193,415
1937	Robert McGarvey	46	209,925
1938	Earl Sande	15	226,495
1939	Sunny Jim Fitzsimmons	45	266,205
1940	Silent Tom Smith	14	269,200
1941	Ben Jones	70	475,318
1942	Jack Gaver	48	406,547
1943	Ben Jones	73	267,915
1944	Ben Jones	60	601,660
1945	Silent Tom Smith	52	510,655
1946	Hirsch Jacobs	99	560,077
1947	Jimmy Jones	85	1,334,805
1948	Jimmy Jones	81	1,118,670
1949	Jimmy Jones	76	978,587
1950	Preston Burch	96	637,754
1951	Jack Gaver	42	616,392
1952	Ben Jones	29	662,137
1953	Harry Trotsek	54	1,028,873
1954	Willie Molter	136	1,107,860
1955	Sunny Jim Fitzsimmons	66	1,270,055
1956	Willie Molter	142	1,227,402
1957	Jimmy Jones	70	1,150,910

Year		Wins	Earnings
1958	Willie Molter	.69	$1,116,544
1959	Willie Molter	.71	847,290
1960	Hirsch Jacobs	.97	748,349
1961	Jimmy Jones	.62	759,856
1962	Mesh Tenney	.58	1,099,474

Year		Sts	Wins	Earnings
1963	Mesh Tenney	192	40	$860,703
1964	Bill Winfrey	287	61	1,350,534
1965	Hirsch Jacobs	610	91	1,331,628
1966	Eddie Neloy	282	93	2,456,250
1967	Eddie Neloy	262	72	1,776,089
1968	Eddie Neloy	212	52	1,233,101
1969	Elliott Burch	156	26	1,067,936
1970	Charlie Whittingham	551	82	1,302,354
1971	Charlie Whittingham	393	77	1,737,115
1972	Charlie Whittingham	429	79	1,734,020
1973	Charlie Whittingham	423	85	1,865,385
1974	Pancho Martin	846	166	2,408,419
1975	Charlie Whittingham	487	3	2,437,244
1976	Jack Van Berg	2362	496	2,976,196
1977	Laz Barrera	781	127	2,715,848

Year		Sts	Wins	Earnings
1978	Laz Barrera	592	100	$3,307,164
1979	Laz Barrera	492	98	3,608,517
1980	Laz Barrera	559	99	2,969,151
1981	Charlie Whittingham	376	74	3,993,302
1982	Charlie Whittingham	410	63	4,587,457
1983	D. Wayne Lukas	595	78	4,267,261
1984	D. Wayne Lukas	805	131	5,835,921
1985	D. Wayne Lukas	1140	218	11,155,188
1986	D. Wayne Lukas	1510	259	12,345,180
1987	D. Wayne Lukas	1735	343	17,502,110
1988	D. Wayne Lukas	1500	318	17,842,358
1989	D. Wayne Lukas	1398	305	16,103,998
1990	D. Wayne Lukas	1396	267	14,508,871
1991	D. Wayne Lukas	1497	289	15,942,223
1992	D. Wayne Lukas	1349	230	9,806,436
1993	Bobby Frankel	345	79	8,933,252
1994	D. Wayne Lukas	693	147	9,247,457
1995	D. Wayne Lukas	837	194	12,834,483
1996	D. Wayne Lukas	1006	192	15,966,344
1997	D. Wayne Lukas	824	169	9,993,569
1998	Bob Baffert	538	139	15,000,870
1999	Bob Baffert	735	169	16,934,607

All-Time Leaders

The all-time money-winning horses and race-winning jockeys of North America through 1999, according to the *National Thoroughbred Racing Association* Records include all available information on races in foreign countries.

Top 35 Horses — Money Won

Note that horses who raced in 1999 are in **bold** type.

		Sts	1st	2nd	3rd	Earnings
1	Cigar	33	19	4	5	$9,999,815
2	Skip Away	38	18	10	6	9,616,360
3	**Silver Charm**	24	12	7	2	6,944,369
4	Alysheba	26	11	8	2	6,679,242
5	John Henry	83	39	15	9	6,597,947
6	Singspiel	20	9	8	0	5,950,217
7	Best Pal	47	18	11	4	5,668,245
8	Taiki Blizzard	22	6	8	2	5,544,484
9	Sunday Silence	14	9	5	0	4,968,554
10	Easy Goer	20	14	5	1	4,873,770
11	**Daylami**	21	11	3	4	4,594,647
12	Unbridled	24	8	6	6	4,489,875
13	Pilsudski	22	10	6	2	4,389,167
14	Awesome Again	12	9	0	2	4,374,590
15	Spend A Buck	15	10	3	2	4,220,689
16	Creme Fraiche	64	17	12	13	4,024,727
17	**Seeking the Pearl**	21	8	2	3	4,022,286
18	Devil His Due	41	11	12	3	3,920,405
19	Sandpit	40	14	11	6	3,802,971
20	Ferdinand	29	8	9	6	3,777,978
21	Swain	22	10	4	6	3,777,115
22	**Gentlemen**	24	13	4	2	3,608,598
23	Slew o' Gold	21	12	5	1	3,533,534
24	**Cat Thief**	21	4	7	6	3,517,512
25	**Victory Gallop**	17	9	5	1	3,505,895
26	Precisionist	46	20	10	4	3,485,398
27	Lando	23	10	2	1	3,484,413
28	**Chief Bearhart**	26	12	5	3	3,462,014
29	**Almutawakel**	13	4	3	1	3,459,398
30	Strike the Gold	31	6	8	5	3,457,026
31	Paradise Creek	25	14	7	1	3,386,925
32	Snow Chief	24	13	3	5	3,383,210
33	Cryptoclearance	44	12	10	7	3,376,327
34	Black Tie Affair	45	18	9	6	3,370,694
35	Bet Twice	26	10	6	4	3,308,599

Top 35 Jockeys — Races Won

Note that jockeys active in 1999 are in **bold** type.

		Yrs	Wins	Earnings
1	**Laffit Pincay Jr.**	34	8848	$207,340,991
2	Bill Shoemaker	42	8833	123,375,524
3	**Pat Day**	27	7616	224,020,694
4	David Gall	43	7396	24,972,821
5	**Chris McCarron**	26	7058	233,930,157
6	Angel Cordero Jr.	35	7057	164,561,227
7	**Russell Baze**	26	6809	96,741,224
8	Jorge Velasquez	33	6795	125,534,962
9	Sandy Hawley	31	6449	88,677,062
10	Larry Snyder	35	6388	47,207,289
11	Carl Gambardella	39	6349	29,389,041
12	Earlie Fires	35	6105	75,937,130
13	E. Delahoussaye	32	6088	175,002,193
14	John Longden	41	6032	24,665,800
15	Jacinto Vasquez	37	5231	80,780,712
16	**Ron Ardoin**	27	4940	53,539,768
17	**Rudy Baez**	25	4875	30,474,225
18	Eddie Arcaro	31	4779	30,039,543
19	**Jerry Bailey**	26	4676	181,856,743
20	Don Brumfield	37	4573	43,567,861
21	**Gary Stevens**	21	4511	187,176,371
22	**Rick Wilson**	27	4453	63,067850
23	Steve Brooks	34	4451	18,239,817
24	Eddie Maple	34	4398	104,526,553
25	Walter Blum	22	4382	26,497,189
26	**Randy Romero**	26	4294	75,264,198
27	Bill Hartack	22	4272	26,466,758
28	**Craig Perret**	33	4241	102,039,619
29	**Jeffrey Lloyd**	23	4212	33,234,418
30	**Mario Pino**	22	4205	59,073,414
31	**Anthony Black**	30	4106	38,764,077
32	Avelino Gomez	34	4081	11,777,297
33	Hugo Dittfach	33	4000	13,506,052
34	Phil Grove	30	3991	16,507,393
35	**Ray Sibille**	31	3975	60,250,968

Horse of the Year (1936-70)

In 1971, the *Daily Racing Form*, the Thoroughbred Racing Associations, and the National Turf Writers Assn. joined forces to create the Eclipse Awards. Before then, however, the *Racing Form* (1936-70) and the TRA (1950-70) issued separate selections for Horse of the Year. Their picks differed only four times from 1950-70 and are so noted. Horses listed in CAPITAL letters are Triple Crown winners; (f) indicates female.

Multiple winners: Kelso (5); Challedon, Native Dancer and Whirlaway (2).

Year		Year		Year		Year	
1936	Granville	1946	ASSAULT	1955	Nashua	1964	Kelso
1937	WAR ADMIRAL	1947	Armed	1956	Swaps	1965	Roman Brother (DRF)
1938	Seabiscuit	1948	CITATION	1957	Bold Ruler (DRF)		Moccasin (TRA)
1939	Challedon	1949	Capot		Dedicate (TRA)	1966	Buckpasser
1940	Challedon	1950	Hill Prince	1958	Round Table	1967	Damascus
1941	WHIRLAWAY	1951	Counterpoint	1959	Sword Dancer	1968	Dr. Fager
1942	Whirlaway	1952	One Count (DRF)	1960	Kelso	1969	Arts and Letters
1943	COUNT FLEET		Native Dancer (TRA)	1961	Kelso	1970	Fort Marcy (DRF)
1944	Twilight Tear (f)	1953	Tom Fool	1962	Kelso		Personality (TRA)
1945	Busher (f)	1954	Native Dancer	1963	Kelso		

Eclipse Awards

The Eclipse Awards, honoring the Horse of the Year and other champions of the sport, are sponsored by the National Thoroughbred Racing Association (NTRA), *Daily Racing Form* and the National Turf Writers Assn. In 1998, the NTRA replaced the Thoroughbred Racing Associations of North America as co-sponsor.

The awards are named after the 18th century racehorse and sire, Eclipse, who began racing at age five and was unbeaten in 18 starts (eight wins were walkovers). As a stallion, Eclipse sired winners of 344 races, including three Epsom Derby champions.

Horses listed in CAPITAL letters won the Triple Crown that year. Age of horse in parentheses where necessary.

Multiple winners: (horses): Forego (8); John Henry (7); Affirmed, Lonesome Glory and Secretariat (5); Cigar, Flatterer, Seattle Slew, Skip Away and Spectacular Bid (4); Ack Ack, Susan's Girl and Zaccio (3); All Along, Alysheba, Bayakoa, Black Tie Affair, Cafe Prince, Charismatic, Conquistador Cielo, Desert Vixen, Favorite Trick, Ferdinand, Flawlessly, Go for Wand, Holy Bull, Housebuster, Kotashaan, Lady's Secret, Life's Magic, Miesque, Morley Street, Open Mind, Paseana, Riva Ridge, Silverbulletday, Slew o' Gold and Spend A Buck (2).

Multiple winners: (people): Laffit Pincay Jr. (5); Laz Barrera, Pat Day, John Franks and D. Wayne Lukas (4); Bob Baffert, Jerry Bailey, Steve Cauthen, Harbor View Farm, Fred W. Hooper, Nelson Bunker Hunt, Mr. & Mrs. Gene Klein, Dan Lasater, John & Betty Mabee, Ogden Phipps, Bill Shoemaker, Edward Taylor and Charlie Whittingham (3); Braulio Baeza, C.T. Chenery, Claiborne Farm, Angel Cordero Jr., Kent Desormeaux, William S. Farish, John W. Galbreath, Chris McCarron, Paul Mellon, Bill Mott, Allen Paulson, Mike Smith and Frank Stronach (2).

Horse of the Year

Year		Year		Year		Year	
1971	Ack Ack (5)	1979	Affirmed (4)	1987	Ferdinand (4)	1995	Cigar (5)
1972	SECRETARIAT (2)	1980	Spectacular Bid (4)	1988	Alysheba (4)	1996	Cigar (6)
1973	SECRETARIAT (3)	1981	John Henry (6)	1989	Sunday Silence (3)	1997	Favorite Trick (2)
1974	Forego (4)	1982	Conquistador Cielo (3)	1990	Criminal Type (5)	1998	Skip Away (5)
1975	Forego (5)	1983	All Along (4)	1991	Black Tie Affair (5)	1999	Charismatic (3)
1976	Forego (6)	1984	John Henry (9)	1992	A.P. Indy (3)		
1977	SEATTLE SLEW (3)	1985	Spend A Buck (3)	1993	Kotashaan (5)		
1978	AFFIRMED (3)	1986	Lady's Secret (4)	1994	Holy Bull (3)		

Older Male

Year		Year		Year		Year	
1971	Ack Ack (5)	1979	Affirmed (4)	1987	Ferdinand (4)	1995	Cigar (5)
1972	Autobiography (4)	1980	Spectacular Bid (4)	1988	Alysheba (4)	1996	Cigar (6)
1973	Riva Ridge (4)	1981	John Henry (6)	1989	Blushing John (4)	1997	Skip Away (4)
1974	Forego (4)	1982	Lemhi Gold (4)	1990	Criminal Type (5)	1998	Skip Away (5)
1975	Forego (5)	1983	Bates Motel (4)	1991	Black Tie Affair (5)	1999	Victory Gallop (4)
1976	Forego (6)	1984	Slew o' Gold (4)	1992	Pleasant Tap (5)		
1977	Forego (7)	1985	Vanlandingham (4)	1993	Bertrando (4)		
1978	Seattle Slew (4)	1986	Turkoman (4)	1994	The Wicked North (4)		

Older Filly or Mare

Year		Year		Year		Year	
1971	Shuvee (5)	1979	Waya (5)	1987	North Sider (5)	1995	Inside Information (4)
1972	Typecast (5)	1980	Glorious Song (4)	1988	Personal Ensign (4)	1996	Jewel Princess (4)
1973	Susan's Girl (4)	1981	Relaxing (5)	1989	Bayakoa (5)	1997	Hidden Lake (4)
1974	Desert Vixen (4)	1982	Track Robbery (6)	1990	Bayakoa (6)	1998	Escena (5)
1975	Susan's Girl (6)	1983	Amb. of Luck (4)	1991	Queena (5)	1999	Beautiful Pleasure (4)
1976	Proud Delta (4)	1984	Princess Rooney (4)	1992	Paseana (5)		
1977	Cascapedia (4)	1985	Life's Magic (4)	1993	Paseana (6)		
1978	Late Bloomer (4)	1986	Lady's Secret (4)	1994	Sky Beauty (4)		

3-Year-Old Colt or Gelding

Year		Year		Year		Year	
1971	Canonero II	1979	Spectacular Bid	1987	Alysheba	1995	Thunder Gulch
1972	Key to the Mint	1980	Temperence Hill	1988	Risen Star	1996	Skip Away
1973	SECRETARIAT	1981	Pleasant Colony	1989	Sunday Silence	1997	Silver Charm
1974	Little Current	1982	Conquistador Cielo	1990	Unbridled	1998	Real Quiet
1975	Wajima	1983	Slew o' Gold	1991	Hansel	1999	Charismatic
1976	Bold Forbes	1984	Swale	1992	A.P. Indy		
1977	SEATTLE SLEW	1985	Spend A Buck	1993	Prairie Bayou		
1978	AFFIRMED	1986	Snow Chief	1994	Holy Bull		

3-Year-Old Filly

Year		Year		Year		Year	
1971	Turkish Trousers	1979	Davona Dale	1987	Sacahuista	1995	Serena's Song
1972	Susan's Girl	1980	Genuine Risk	1988	Winning Colors	1996	Yanks Music
1973	Desert Vixen	1981	Wayward Lass	1989	Open Mind	1997	Ajina
1974	Chris Evert	1982	Christmas Past	1990	Go for Wand	1998	Banshee Breeze
1975	Ruffian	1983	Heartlight No. One	1991	Dance Smartly	1999	Silverbulletday
1976	Revidere	1984	Life's Magic	1992	Saratoga Slew		
1977	Our Mims	1985	Mom's Command	1993	Hollywood Wildcat		
1978	Tempest Queen	1986	Tiffany Lass	1994	Heavenly Prize		

2-Year-Old Colt or Gelding

Year		Year		Year		Year	
1971	Riva Ridge	1979	Rockhill Native	1987	Forty Niner	1995	Maria's Mon
1972	Secretariat	1980	Lord Avie	1988	Easy Goer	1996	Boston Harbor
1973	Protagonist	1981	Deputy Minister	1989	Rhythm	1997	Favorite Trick
1974	Foolish Pleasure	1982	Roving Boy	1990	Fly So Free	1998	Answer Lively
1975	Honest Pleasure	1983	Devil's Bag	1991	Arazi	1999	Anees
1976	Seattle Slew	1984	Chief's Crown	1992	Gilded Time		
1977	Affirmed	1985	Tasso	1993	Dehere		
1978	Spectacular Bid	1986	Capote	1994	Timber Country		

2-Year-Old Filly

Year		Year		Year		Year	
1971	Numbered Account	1979	Smart Angle	1988	Open Mind	1997	Countess Diana
1972	La Prevoyante	1980	Heavenly Cause	1989	Go for Wand	1998	Silverbulletday
1973	Talking Picture	1981	Before Dawn	1990	Meadow Star	1999	Chilukki
1974	Ruffian	1982	Landaluce	1991	Pleasant Stage		
1975	Dearly Precious	1983	Althea	1992	Eliza		
1976	Sensational	1984	Outstandingly	1993	Phone Chatter		
1977	Lakeville Miss	1985	Family Style	1994	Flanders		
1978	(tie) Candy Eclair	1986	Brave Raj	1995	Golden Attraction		
	& It's in the Air	1987	Epitome	1996	Storm Song		

Champion Turf Horse

Year		Year		Year		Year	
1971	Run the Gantlet (3)	1973	SECRETARIAT (3)	1975	Snow Knight (4)	1977	Johnny D (3)
1972	Cougar II (6)	1974	Dahlia (4)	1976	Youth (3)	1978	Mac Diarmida (3)

Champion Male Turf Horse

Year		Year		Year		Year	
1979	Bowl Game (5)	1984	John Henry (9)	1989	Steinlen (6)	1994	Paradise Creek (5)
1980	John Henry (5)	1985	Cozzene (4)	1990	Itsallgreektome (3)	1995	Northern Spur (4)
1981	John Henry (6)	1986	Manila (3)	1991	Tight Spot (4)	1996	Singspiel (4)
1982	Perrault (5)	1987	Theatrical (5)	1992	Sky Classic (5)	1997	Chief Bearhart (4)
1983	John Henry (8)	1988	Sunshine Forever (3)	1993	Kotashaan (5)	1998	Buck's Boy (5)
						1999	Daylami (5)

Champion Female Turf Horse

Year		Year		Year		Year	
1979	Trillion (5)	1985	Pebbles (4)	1991	Miss Alleged (4)	1997	Ryafan (3)
1980	Just A Game II (4)	1986	Estrapade (6)	1992	Flawlessly (4)	1998	Fiji (4)
1981	De La Rose (3)	1987	Miesque (3)	1993	Flawlessly (5)	1999	Soaring Softly (4)
1982	April Run (4)	1988	Miesque (4)	1994	Hatoof (5)		
1983	All Along (4)	1989	Brown Bess (7)	1995	Possibly Perfect (5)		
1984	Royal Heroine (4)	1990	Laugh and Be Merry (5)	1996	Wandesta (5)		

Eclipse Awards (Cont.)
Sprinter

Year		Year		Year		Year	
1971	Ack Ack (5)	1979	Star de Naskra (4)	1988	Gulch (4)	1997	Smoke Glacken (3)
1972	Chou Croute (4)	1980	Plugged Nickle (3)	1989	Safely Kept (3)	1998	Reraise (3)
1973	Shecky Greene (3)	1981	Guilty Conscience (5)	1990	Housebuster (3)	1999	Artax (4)
1974	Forego (4)	1982	Gold Beauty (3)	1991	Housebuster (4)		
1975	Gallant Bob (3)	1983	Chinook Pass (4)	1992	Rubiano (5)		
1976	My Juliet (4)	1984	Eillo (4)	1993	Cardmania (7)		
1977	What a Summer (4)	1985	Precisionist (4)	1994	Cherokee Run (4)		
1978	(tie) Dr. Patches (4)	1986	Smile (4)	1995	Not Surprising (4)		
	& J.O. Tobin (4)	1987	Groovy (4)	1996	Lit de Justice (6)		

Steeplechase or Hurdle Horse

Year		Year		Year		Year	
1971	Shadow Brook (7)	1979	Martie's Anger (4)	1987	Inlander (6)	1995	Lonesome Glory (7)
1972	Soothsayer (5)	1980	Zaccio (4)	1988	Jimmy Lorenzo (6)	1996	Correggio (5)
1973	Athenian Idol (5)	1981	Zaccio (5)	1989	Highland Bud (4)	1997	Lonesome Glory (9)
1974	Gran Kan (8)	1982	Zaccio (6)	1990	Morley Street (6)	1998	Flat Top (5)
1975	Life's Illusion (4)	1983	Flatterer (4)	1991	Morley Street (7)	1999	Lonesome Glory (11)
1976	Straight and True (6)	1984	Flatterer (5)	1992	Lonesome Glory (4)		
1977	Cafe Prince (7)	1985	Flatterer (6)	1993	Lonesome Glory (5)		
1978	Cafe Prince (8)	1986	Flatterer (7)	1994	Warm Spell (6)		

Outstanding Jockey

Year		Year		Year		Year	
1971	Laffit Pincay Jr.	1979	Laffit Pincay Jr.	1987	Pat Day	1995	Jerry Bailey
1972	Braulio Baeza	1980	Chris McCarron	1988	Jose Santos	1996	Jerry Bailey
1973	Laffit Pincay Jr.	1981	Bill Shoemaker	1989	Kent Desormeaux	1997	Jerry Bailey
1974	Laffit Pincay Jr.	1982	Angel Cordero Jr.	1990	Craig Perret	1998	Gary Stevens
1975	Braulio Baeza	1983	Angel Cordero Jr.	1991	Pat Day	1999	Jorge Chavez
1976	Sandy Hawley	1984	Pat Day	1992	Kent Desormeaux		
1977	Steve Cauthen	1985	Laffit Pincay Jr.	1993	Mike Smith		
1978	Darrel McHargue	1986	Pat Day	1994	Mike Smith		

Outstanding Apprentice Jockey

Year		Year		Year		Year	
1971	Gene St. Leon	1979	Cash Asmussen	1987	Kent Desormeaux	1995	Ramon B. Perez
1972	Thomas Wallis	1980	Frank Lovato Jr.	1988	Steve Capanas	1996	Neil Poznansky
1973	Steve Valdez	1981	Richard Migliore	1989	Michael Luzzi	1997	Roberto Rosado
1974	Chris McCarron	1982	Alberto Delgado	1990	Mark Johnston		& Philip Teator
1975	Jimmy Edwards	1983	Declan Murphy	1991	Mickey Walls	1998	Shaun Bridgmohan
1976	George Martens	1984	Wesley Ward	1992	Rosemary Homeister	1999	Ariel Smith
1977	Steve Cauthen	1985	Art Madrid Jr.	1993	Juan Umana		
1978	Ron Franklin	1986	Allen Stacy	1994	Dale Beckner		

Outstanding Trainer

Year		Year		Year		Year	
1971	Charlie Whittingham	1979	Laz Barrera	1987	D. Wayne Lukas	1995	Bill Mott
1972	Lucien Laurin	1980	Bud Delp	1988	Shug McGaughey	1996	Bill Mott
1973	H. Allen Jerkens	1981	Ron McAnally	1989	Charlie Whittingham	1997	Bob Baffert
1974	Sherill Ward	1982	Charlie Whittingham	1990	Carl Nafzger	1998	Bob Baffert
1975	Steve DiMauro	1983	Woody Stephens	1991	Ron McAnally	1999	Bob Baffert
1976	Laz Barrera	1984	Jack Van Berg	1992	Ron McAnally		
1977	Laz Barrera	1985	D. Wayne Lukas	1993	Bobby Frankel		
1978	Laz Barrera	1986	D. Wayne Lukas	1994	D. Wayne Lukas		

Outstanding Owner

Year		Year		Year		Year	
1971	Mr. & Mrs. E.E. Fogleson	1979	Harbor View Farm	1986	Mr. & Mrs. Gene Klein	1994	John Franks
1972-73	No award	1980	Mr. & Mrs. Bertram Firestone	1987	Mr. & Mrs. Gene Klein	1995	Allen Paulson
1974	Dan Lasater	1981	Dotsam Stable	1988	Ogden Phipps	1996	Allen Paulson
1975	Dan Lasater	1982	Viola Sommer	1989	Ogden Phipps	1997	Carolyn Hine
1976	Dan Lasater	1983	John Franks	1990	Frances Genter	1998	Frank Stronach
1977	Maxwell Gluck	1984	John Franks	1991	Sam-Son Farms	1999	Frank Stronach
1978	Harbor View Farm	1985	Mr. & Mrs. Gene Klein	1992	Juddmonta Farms		
				1993	John Franks		

Outstanding Breeder

Year		Year		Year		Year	
1971	Paul Mellon	1979	Claiborne Farm	1987	Nelson Bunker Hunt	1995	Juddmonte Farms
1972	C.T. Chenery	1980	Mrs. Henry Paxson	1988	Ogden Phipps	1996	Farnsworth Farms
1973	C.T. Chenery	1981	Golden Chance Farm	1989	North Ridge Farm	1997	John & Betty Mabee
1974	John W. Galbreath	1982	Fred W. Hooper	1990	Calumet Farm	1998	John & Betty Mabee
1975	Fred W. Hooper	1983	Edward P. Taylor	1991	John & Betty Mabee	1999	William S. Farish
1976	Nelson Bunker Hunt	1984	Claiborne Farm	1992	William S. Farish		
1977	Edward P. Taylor	1985	Nelson Bunker Hunt	1993	Allan Paulson		
1978	Harbor View Farm	1986	Paul Mellon	1994	William T. Young		

Outstanding Achievement

Man of the Year

Year		Year		Year		Year	
1971	Charles Engelhard*	1972	Arthur B. Hancock Jr.*	1972	John W. Galbreath	1974	William L. McKnight
				1973	Edward P. Taylor	1975	John A. Morris

*Awarded posthumously.

Award of Merit

Year		Year		Year		Year	
1976	Jack J. Dreyfus	1981	Bill Shoemaker	1988	John Forsythe	1992	Joe Hirsch
1977	Steve Cauthen	1984	John Gaines	1989	Michael Sandler		& Robert P. Strub
1978	Dinny Phipps	1985	Keene Daingerfield	1990	Warner L. Jones	1995	James E. Bassett III
1979	Jimmy Kilroe	1986	Herman Cohen	1991	Fred W. Hooper	1997	Robert & Beverly
1980	John D. Shapiro	1987	J.B. Faulconer				Lewis

Special Award

Year		Year		Year		Year	
1971	Robert J. Kleberg	1980	John T. Landry	1985	Arlington Park	1989	Richard Duchossois
1974	Charles Hatton		& Pierre E. Bellocq	1987	Anheuser-Busch	1995	Russell Baze
1976	Bill Shoemaker	1984	C.V. Whitney	1988	Edward J. DeBartolo Sr.		

HARNESS RACING

Triple Crown Winners
PACERS

Nine three-year-olds have won the Cane Pace, Little Brown Jug and Messenger Stakes in the same year since the Pacing Triple Crown was established in 1956. No trainer or driver has won it more than once.

Year		Driver	Trainer	Owner
1959	**Adios Butler**	Clint Hodgins	Paige West	Paige West & Angelo Pellillo
1965	**Bret Hanover**	Frank Ervin	Frank Ervin	Richard Downing
1966	**Romeo Hanover**	Bill Myer & George Sholty*	Jerry Silverman	Lucky Star Stables & Morton Finder
1968	**Rum Customer**	Billy Haughton	Billy Haughton	Kennilworth Farms & L.C. Mancuso
1970	**Most Happy Fella**	Stanley Dancer	Stanley Dancer	Egyptian Acres Stable
1980	**Niatross**	Clint Galbraith	Clint Galbraith	Niagara Acres, Niatross Stables & Clint Galbraith
1983	**Ralph Hanover**	Ron Waples	Stew Firlotte	Waples Stable, Pointsetta Stable, Grant's Direct Stable & P.J. Baugh
1997	**Western Dreamer**	Mike Lachance	Bill Robinson Stable	Matthew, Daniel and Patrick Daly
1999	**Blissful Hall**	Ron Pierce	Benn Wallace	Daniel Plouffe

*Myer drove Romeo Hanover in the Cane, Sholty in the other two races.

TROTTERS

Six three-year-olds have won the Yonkers Trot, Hambletonian and Kentucky Futurity in the same year since the Trotting Triple Crown was established in 1955. Stanley Dancer is the only driver/trainer to win it twice.

Year		Driver/Trainer	Owner
1955	**Scott Frost**	Joe O'Brien	S.A. Camp Farms
1963	**Speedy Scot**	Ralph Baldwin	Castleton Farms
1964	**Ayres**	John Simpson Sr.	Charlotte Sheppard
1968	**Nevele Pride**	Stanley Dancer	Nevele Acres & Lou Resnick
1969	**Lindy's Pride**	Howard Beissinger	Lindy Farms
1972	**Super Bowl**	Stanley Dancer	Rachel Dancer & Rose Hild Breeding Farm

Triple Crown Near Misses

PACERS

Nine horses have won the first two legs of the Triple Crown, but not the third. The Cane Pace (CP), Little Brown Jug (LBJ), and Messenger Stakes (MS) have not always been run in the same order so numbers after races won indicate sequence for that year.

Year		CP	LBJ	MS
1957	**Torpid**	won, 1	won, 2	DNF*
1960	**Countess Adios**	won, 2	NE	won, 1
1971	**Albatross**	won, 2	2nd*	won, 1
1976	**Keystone Ore**........	won, 1	won, 2	2nd*
1986	**Barberry Spur**	won, 1	won, 2	2nd*
1990	**Jake and Elwood**....	won, 1	NE	won, 2
1992	**Western Hanover**....	won, 1	2nd*	won, 2
1993	**Rijadh**	won, 1	2nd*	won, 2
1998	**Shady Character**	won, 1	won, 2	6th*

*****Winning horses:** Meadow Lands (1957), Nansemond (1971), Windshield Wiper (1976), Amity Chef (1986), Fake Left (1992), Life Sign (1993), Fit for Life (1998).
Note: Torpid (1957) scratched before the final heat; Countess Adios (1960) and Jake and Elwood (1990) not eligible for Little Brown Jug.

TROTTERS

Eight horses have won the first two legs of the Triple Crown—the Yonkers Trot (YT) and the Hambletonian (Ham)—but not the third. The winner of the Ky. Futurity (KF) is listed.

Year		YT	Ham	KF
1962	**A.C.'s Viking**........	won	won	Safe Mission
1976	**Steve Lobell**.........	won	won	Quick Pay
1977	**Green Speed**	won	won	Texas
1978	**Speedy Somolli**	won	won	Doublemint
1987	**Mack Lobell**.........	won	won	Napoletano
1993	**American Winner**....	won	won	Pine Chip
1996	**Continentalvictory** ...	won	won	Running Sea
1998	**Muscles Yankee**.....	won	won	Trade Balance

Note: Green Speed (1977) not eligible for Ky. Futurity; Continentalvictory (1996) was withdrawn from the Ky. Futurity due to a leg injury.

The Hambletonian

For three-year-old trotters. Inaugurated in 1926 and has been held in Syracuse, N.Y.; Lexington, Ky.; Goshen, N.Y.; Yonkers, N.Y.; Du Quoin, Ill.; and since 1981 at The Meadowlands in East Rutherford, N.J.

Run at one mile since 1947. Winning horse must win two heats.

Drivers with most wins: John Campbell (5); Stanley Dancer, Billy Haughton and Ben White (4); Howard Beissinger, Del Cameron, Mike Lachance and Henry Thomas (3).

Year		Driver	Fastest Heat	Year		Driver	Fastest Heat
1926	**Guy McKinney**	Nat Ray	2:04¾	1964	**Ayres**	John Simpson Sr.	1:56⅘
1927	**Iosola's Worthy** ...	Marvin Childs	2:03¾	1965	**Egyptian Candor** ..	Del Cameron	2:03⅘
1928	**Spencer**	W.H. Lessee	2:02½	1966	**Kerry Way**	Frank Ervin	1:58⅘
1929	**Walter Dear**	Walter Cox	2:02¾	1967	**Speedy Streak**	Del Cameron	2:00
1930	**Hanover's Bertha** .	Tom Berry	2:03	1968	**Nevele Pride**	Stanley Dancer	1:59⅖
1931	**Calumet Butler** ..	R.D. McMahon	2:03¼	1969	**Lindy's Pride**	Howard Beissinger	1:57⅗
1932	**The Marchioness** ..	Will Caton	2:01¼	1970	**Timothy T**	John Simpson Jr.	1:58⅖
1933	**Mary Reynolds**	Ben White	2:03¾	1971	**Speedy Crown**	Howard Beissinger	1:57⅖
1934	**Lord Jim**	Doc Parshall	2:02¾	1972	**Super Bowl**	Stanley Dancer	1:56⅖
1935	**Greyhound**	Sep Palin	2:02¼	1973	**Flirth**	Ralph Baldwin	1:57⅕
1936	**Rosalind**	Ben White	2:01¾	1974	**Christopher T**	Billy Haughton	1:58⅗
1937	**Shirley Hanover** ..	Henry Thomas	2:01½	1975	**Bonefish**	Stanley Dancer	1:59
1938	**McLin Hanover**	Henry Tomas	2:02¼	1976	**Steve Lobell**	Billy Haughton	1:56⅖
1939	**Peter Astra**	Doc Parshall	2:04¼	1977	**Green Speed**	Billy Haughton	1:55⅗
1940	**Spencer Scott**	Fred Egan	2:02	1978	**Speedy Somolli** ...	Howard Beissinger	1:55
1941	**Bill Gallon**	Lee Smith	2:05	1979	**Legend Hanover** ..	George Sholty	1:56⅕
1942	**The Ambassador** ..	Ben White	2:04	1980	**Burgomeister**	Billy Haughton	1:56⅗
1943	**Volo Song**	Ben White	2:02½	1981	**Shiavay St. Pat** ...	Ray Remmen	2:01⅕
1944	**Yankee Maid**	Henry Thomas	2:04	1982	**Speed Bowl**	Tommy Haughton	1:56⅘
1945	**Titan Hanover**	Harry Pownall Sr.	2:04	1983	**Duenna**	Stanley Dancer	1:57⅖
1946	**Chestertown**	Thomas Berry	2:02½	1984	**Historic Freight**	Ben Webster	1:56⅖
1947	**Hoot Mon**	Sep Palin	2:00	1985	**Prakas**	Bill O'Donnell	1:54⅗
1948	**Demon Hanover** ..	Harrison Hoyt	2:02	1986	**Nuclear Kosmos** ..	Ulf Thoresen	1:55⅖
1949	**Miss Tilly**	Fred Egan	2:01⅖	1987	**Mack Lobell**	John Campbell	1:53⅖
1950	**Lusty Song**	Del Miller	2:02	1988	**Armbro Goal**	John Campbell	1:54⅖
1951	**Mainliner**	Guy Crippen	2:02⅗	1989	**Park Avenue Joe** ..	Ron Waples	1:54⅗
1952	**Sharp Note**	Bion Shively	2:02⅗		& **Probe** *	Bill Fahy	
1953	**Helicopter**	Harry Harvey	2:01⅗	1990	**Harmonious**	John Campbell	1:54⅕
1954	**Newport Dream** .	Del Cameron	2:02⅘	1991	**Giant Victory**	Jack Moiseyev	1:54⅘
1955	**Scott Frost**	Joe O'Brien	2:00⅗	1992	**Alf Palema**	Mickey McNichol	1:56⅖
1956	**The Intruder**	Ned Bower	2:01⅖	1993	**American Winner** .	Ron Pierce	1:53⅕
1957	**Hickory Smoke** ...	John Simpson Sr.	2:00⅕	1994	**Victory Dream**	Mike Lachance	1:54⅕
1958	**Emily's Pride**	Flave Nipe	1:59⅘	1995	**Tagliabue**	John Campbell	1:54⅘
1959	**Diller Hanover**	Frank Ervin	2:01⅕	1996	**Continentalvictory** .	Mike Lachance	1:52⅘
1960	**Blaze Hanover** ...	Joe O'Brien	1:59⅗	1997	**Malabar Man**......	Mal Burroughs	1:55
1961	**Harlan Dean**	James Arthur	1:58⅖	1998	**Muscles Yankee** ..	John Campbell	1:52⅖
1962	**A.C.'s Viking**	Sanders Russell	1:59⅗	1999	**Self Possessed**	Mike Lachance	1:51⅗
1963	**Speedy Scot**	Ralph Baldwin	1:57⅗	2000	**Yankee Paco**......	Trevor Ritchie	1:53⅖

*In 1989, Park Avenue Joe and Probe finished in a dead heat in the race-off. They were later declared co-winners, but Park Avenue Joe was awarded 1st place money because his three-race summary (2-1-1) was better than Probe's (1-9-1).

The Little Brown Jug

Harness racing's most prestigious race for three-year-old pacers. Inaugurated in 1946 and held annually at the Delaware, Ohio County Fairgrounds. Winning horse must win two heats.

Drivers with most wins: Billy Haughton (5); Stanley Dancer and Mike Lachance (4); John Campbell, Frank Ervin and John Simpson Sr. (3); Adelbert Cameron, Herve Filion, Jack Moiseyev, Joe O'Brien, Bill O'Donnell, Ron Pierce, "Curly" Smart and Ron Waples (2).

Year		Driver	Fastest Heat	Year		Driver	Fastest Heat
1946	Ensign Hanover	"Curly" Smart	2:02	1974	Armbro Omaha	Billy Haughton	1:57
1947	Forbes Chief	Adelbert Cameron	2:05	1975	Seatrain	Ben Webster	1:56⅘
1948	Knight Dream	Frank Safford	2:07	1976	Keystone Ore	Stanley Dancer	1:56⅘
1949	Good Time	Frank Ervin	2:03⅘	1977	Governor Skipper	John Chapman	1:56⅕
				1978	Happy Escort	Bill Popfinger	1:55⅘
1950	Dudley Hanover	Delvin Miller	2:02⅗	1979	Hot Hitter	Herve Filion	1:55⅗
1951	Tar Heel	Adelbert Cameron	2:00				
1952	Meadow Rice	"Curly" Smart	2:01⅘	1980	Niatross	Clint Galbraith	1:54⅘
1953	Keystoner	Frank Ervin	2:02⅕	1981	Fan Hanover (f)	Glen Garnsey	1:56
1954	Adios Harry	Morris MacDonald	2:02⅖	1982	Merger	John Campbell	1:54⅗
1955	Quick Chief	Billy Haughton	2:00	1983	Ralph Hanover	Ron Waples	1:55⅗
1956	Noble Adios	John Simpson, Sr.	2:00⅘	1984	Colt Fortysix	Chris Boring	1:53⅗
1957	Torpid	John Simpson, Sr.	2:00⅘	1985	Nihilator	Bill O'Donnell	1:52⅕
1958	Shadow Wave	Joe O'Brien	2:01	1986	Barberry Spur	Bill O'Donnell	1:52⅘
1959	Adios Butler	Clint Hodgkins	1:59⅖	1987	Jaguar Spur	Dick Stillings	1:54
				1988	B.J. Scoot	Mike Lachance	1:52⅗
1960	Bullet Hanover	John Simpson, Sr.	1:58⅗	1989	Goalie Jeff	Mike Lachance	1:54⅕
1961	Henry T. Adios	Stanley Dancer	1:58⅘				
1962	Lehigh Hanover	Stanley Dancer	1:58⅘	1990	Beach Towel	Ray Remmen	1:53⅗
1963	Overtrick	John Patterson, Sr.	1:57⅕	1991	Precious Bunny	Jack Moiseyev	1:53⅘
1964	Vicar Hanover	Billy Haughton	2:00⅘	1992	Fake Left	Ron Waples	1:53⅗
1965	Bret Hanover	Frank Ervin	1:57	1993	Life Sign	John Campbell	1:52
1966	Romeo Hanover	George Sholty	1:59⅗	1994	Magical Mike	Mike Lachance	1:52⅗
1967	Best Of All	Jim Hackett	1:59	1995	Nick's Fantasy	John Campbell	1:51⅖
1968	Rum Customer	Billy Haughton	1:59⅗	1996	Armbro Operative	Jack Moiseyev	1:52⅗
1969	Laverne Hanover	Billy Haughton	2:00⅖	1997	Western Dreamer	Mike Lachance	1:51⅕
				1998	Shady Character	Ron Pierce	1:52⅘
1970	Most Happy Fella	Stanley Dancer	1:57⅕	1999	Blissfull Hall	Ron Pierce	1:55⅗
1971	Nansemond	Herve Filion	1:57⅖	2000	Astreos	Chris Christoforou	1:55⅗
1972	Strike Out	Keith Waples	1:56⅗				
1973	Melvin's Woe	Joe O'Brien	1:57⅗				

All-Time Leaders

The all-time winning trotters, pacers and drivers through 1999, according to *The Trotting and Pacing Guide*. Purses for horses include races in foreign countries. Earnings and wins for drivers include only races held in North America.

Top 10 Horses — Money Won

		T/P	Sts	1st	Earnings
1	Moni Maker	T	91	60	$4,415,983
2	Peace Corps	T	42	35	4,137,737
3	Ourasi (FRA)	T	N/A	32	4,010,105
4	Mack Lobell	T	86	65	3,917,594
5	Reve d'Udon	T	23	18	3,611,351
6	Zoogin	T	N/A	N/A	3,428,311
7	Nihilator	P	38	35	3,225,653
8	Sea Cove	T	N/A	N/A	3,138,986
9	Artsplace	P	49	37	3,085,083
10	Presidential Ball	P	38	26	3,021,363

Top 10 Drivers — Races Won

		Yrs	1st	Earnings
1	Herve Filion	35	14,783	$85,044,653
2	Walter Case Jr.	22	8,799	34,630,699
3	Mike Lachance	32	8,550	119,635,360
4	Cat Manzi	32	8,388	74,226,197
5	Dave Magee	27	8,363	61,122,410
6	John Campbell	28	8,192	176,466,322
7	Jack Moiseyev	24	7,847	79,847,499
8	Doug Brown	27	7,357	72,390,765
9	Eddie Davis	36	7,223	36,773,650
10	Carmine Abbatiello	43	7,170	50,323,136

Annual Awards

Harness Horse of the Year

Selected since 1947 by U.S. Trotting Association and the U.S. Harness Writers Association; age of winning horse is noted; (t) indicates trotter and (p) indicates pacer. USTA added Trotter and Pacer of the Year awards in 1970.

Multiple winners: Bret Hanover and Nevele Pride (3); Adios Butler, Albatross, Cam Fella, Good Time, Mack Lobell, Moni Maker, Niatross and Scott Frost (2).

Year		Year		Year		Year	
1947	Victory Song (4t)	1951	Pronto Don (6t)	1955	Scott Frost (3t)	1959	Bye Bye Byrd (4p)
1948	Rodney (4t)	1952	Good Time (6t)	1956	Scott Frost (4t)	1960	Adios Butler (4p)
1949	Good Time (3p)	1953	Hi Lo's Forbes (5p)	1957	Torpid (3p)	1961	Adios Butler (5p)
1950	Proximity (8t)	1954	Stenographer (3t)	1958	Emily's Pride (3t)	1962	Su Mac Lad (8t)

Year		Year		Year		Year	
1963	Speedy Scot (3t)	1973	Sir Dalrai (4p)	1983	Cam Fella (4p)	1993	Staying Together (4p)
1964	Bret Hanover (2p)	1974	Delmonica Hanover (5t)	1984	Fancy Crown (3t)	1994	Cam's Card Shark (3p)
1965	Bret Hanover (3p)	1975	Savoir (7t)	1985	Nihilator (3p)	1995	CR Kay Suzie (3t)
1966	Bret Hanover (4p)	1976	Keystone Ore (3p)	1986	Forrest Skipper (4p)	1996	Continentalvictory (3t)
1967	Nevele Pride (2t)	1977	Green Speed (3t)	1987	Mack Lobell (3t)	1997	Malabar Man (3t)
1968	Nevele Pride (3t)	1978	Abercrombie (3p)	1988	Mack Lobell (4t)	1998	Moni Maker (5t)
1969	Nevele Pride (4t)	1979	Niatross (2p)	1989	Matt's Scooter (4p)	1999	Moni Maker (6t)
1970	Fresh Yankee (7t)	1980	Niatross (3p)	1990	Beach Towel (3p)		
1971	Albatross (3p)	1981	Fan Hanover (3p)	1991	Precious Bunny (3p)		
1972	Albatross (4p)	1982	Cam Fella (3p)	1992	Artsplace (4p)		

Driver of the Year

Determined by Universal Driving Rating System (UDR) and presented by the Harness Tracks of America since 1968. Eligible drivers must have at least 1,000 starts for the season.

Multiple winners: Herve Filion (10); John Campbell, Walter Case Jr. and Mike Lachance (3); Tony Morgan, Bill O'Donnell, Luc Ouellette and Ron Waples (2).

Year		Year		Year		Year	
1968	Stanley Dancer	1977	Donald Dancer	1985	Mike Lachance	1994	Dave Magee
1969	Herve Filion	1978	Carmine Abbatiello	1986	Mike Lachance	1995	Luc Ouellette
1970	Herve Filion		& Herve Filion	1987	Mike Lachance	1996	Tony Morgan
1971	Herve Filion	1979	Ron Waples	1988	John Campbell		& Luc Ouellette
1972	Herve Filion	1980	Ron Waples	1989	Herve Filion	1997	Tony Morgan
1973	Herve Filion	1981	Herve Filion	1990	John Campbell	1998	Walter Case Jr.
1974	Herve Filion	1982	Bill O'Donnell	1991	Walter Case Jr.	1999	Dave Palone
1975	Joe O'Brien	1983	John Campbell	1992	Walter Case Jr.		
1976	Herve Filion	1984	Bill O'Donnell	1993	Jack Moiseyev		

STEEPLECHASE RACING

Champion Horses

Annual horse of the year since 1956 based on vote of the National Turf Writers Association and other selected media.
Multiple Winners: Lonesome Glory (5); Flatterer (4); Bon Nouvel and Zaccio (3); Café Prince, Morley Street and Neji (2).

Year		Year		Year		Year	
1956	Shipboard	1968	Bon Nouvel	1979	Martie's Anger	1991	Morley Street
1957	Neji	1969	L'Escargot	1980	Zaccio	1992	Lonesome Glory
1958	Neji	1970	Top Bid	1981	Zaccio	1993	Lonesome Glory
1959	Ancestor	1971	Shadow Brok	1982	Zaccio	1994	Warm Spell
1960	Benguala	1972	Soothsayer	1983	Flatterer	1995	Lonesome Glory
1961	Peal	1973	Athenian Idol	1984	Flatterer	1996	Correggio
1962	Barnaby's Bluff	1974	Gran Kan	1985	Flatterer	1997	Lonesome Glory
1963	Amber Diver	1975	Life's Illusion	1986	Flatterer	1998	Flat Top
1964	Bon Nouvel	1976	Fire Control &	1987	Inlander	1999	Lonesome Glory
1965	Bon Nouvel		Straight and True	1988	Jimmy Lorenzo		
1966	Tuscalee & Mako	1977	Café Prince	1989	Highland Bud		
1967	Quick Pitch	1978	Café Prince	1990	Morley Street		

Champion Jockeys

Annual leading jockeys by races won since 1956, according to the National Steeplechase Association.
Multiple Winners: Joe Aitcheson Jr. (7); Jerry Fishback (5); John Cushman and Alfred P. Smithwick (4); Tom Skiffington and Jeff Teter (3); Ricky Hendriks, Jonathan Kiser, James Lawrence, Blythe Miller, Chip Miller and Thomas Walsh (2).

Year		Year		Year		Year	
1956	Alfred P. Smithwick	1968	Joe Aitcheson Jr.	1980	John Cushman	1992	Craig Thornton
1957	Alfred P. Smithwick	1969	Joe Aitcheson Jr.	1981	John Cushman	1993	James Lawrence
1958	Alfred P. Smithwick	1970	Joe Aitcheson Jr.	1982	John Cushman	1994	Blythe Miller
1959	James Murphy	1971	Jerry Fishback	1983	John Cushman	1995	Blythe Miller
1960	Thomas Walsh	1972	Michael O'Brien	1984	Jeff Teter	1996	Chip Miller
1961	Joe Aitcheson Jr.	1973	Jerry Fishback	1985	Bernie Houghton	1997	Arch Kingsley Jr.
1962	Alfred P. Smithwick	1974	Jerry Fishback	1986	Ricky Hendriks		& Jonathan Kiser
1963	Joe Aitcheson Jr.	1975	Jerry Fishback	1987	Ricky Hendriks	1998	Chip Miller
1964	Joe Aitcheson Jr.	1976	Tom Skiffington	1988	Jonathan Smart		& Sean Clancy
1965	Doug Small Jr.	1977	Jerry Fishback	1989	James Lawrence	1999	Jonathan Kiser
1966	Thomas Walsh	1978	Tom Skiffington	1990	Jeff Teter		
1967	Joe Aitcheson Jr.	1979	Tom Skiffington	1991	Jeff Teter		

Tennis

Venus Williams *won her first two Grand Slam singles titles and was virtually unbeatable for the second half of 2000.*

Lucky Thirteen

Pete Sampras passes Roy Emerson and into history with his victory at Wimbledon.

by

Sal Paolantonio

Two minutes until 9 o'clock in the evening, the sun was disappearing over the western edge of Centre Court in Wimbledon and each time Pete Sampras cracked a serve, flashbulbs sparkled like a hundred little flickering candles.

The flashes of light seemed to blind Australian Patrick Rafter, who now struggled to get his racquet on the ball, which seemed to vanish in the moment.

And then, in the magic dusk of the 2000 Wimbledon finals, Sampras propelled a 130-mile-an-hour serve that Rafter just admired and history was made — Pete Sampras won the 13th Grand Slam singles title of his career, breaking Roy Emerson's three-decades old record of 12.

As the television cameras focused in on Sampras' normally implacable face, the seven-time Wimbledon champion broke down. And for the first time anyone can remember,

Sal Paolantonio covers tennis for ESPN.

the world saw tears in his eyes. He glanced toward the players' box, where his coach, Paul Annacone, and his fiancée, Bridgette Wilson, were overcome with emotion too.

Then, Sampras climbed into the stands to find his parents, Sam and Georgia, who — despite their son's remarkable career on the grasscourts in England — were attending their first match at Wimbledon. Shedding his career-long reluctance to display emotion publicly, Sampras hugged his parents and reveled in his historic achievement.

"It was a very emotional time. My parents were here, so it just kind of hit me at the end," Sampras told me in a Sunday Conversation on *SportsCenter* about two hours after the match. "I grew up watching Wimbledon. I always wanted to play here. I never imagined I would win seven Wimbledons."

Sampras' celebration was in marked contrast to what happened the day before on Centre Court. In the women's final, Venus Williams defeated defending champion Lindsay

For the fourth consecutive year and the seventh out of the last eight, **Pete Sampras** was the one holding the trophy at the end of Wimbledon. This particular win was a little more special as it marked his 13th Grand Slam singles title, giving him more than any other man in history.

Davenport to capture her first Grand Slam singles final.

She was the first African-American woman to win Wimbledon since Althea Gibson. After his daughter's victory, Richard Williams climbed onto the roof of a television broadcast booth and did a jig. Venus understood the history that she, too, had made.

"There is always someone who comes before you that you have to say thank you to," Venus said. "And it's great that Althea is alive to see me and my sister, Serena, accomplish so much. And maybe the best way to say thank you to her is to win Wimbledon."

The Williams family had dominated talk at Wimbledon for nearly a week. On Friday, Venus beat Serena in the semifinals. Remember, it was Serena who had brought the first Grand Slam singles title to the family, winning the 1999 U.S. Open.

So, there was public speculation in the British tabloids that Richard had pre-ordained that Serena would allow Venus to beat her in the Wimbledon semis.

Whatever the truth, the sisters played an erratic match and Serena crumbled under the pressure, losing to her big sister. They exchanged a hug at the net and Venus said to her younger sibling, "Let's get out of here," in a way that clearly suggested they never want to have to go through that again.

After capturing Wimbledon, Venus tore through the summer tournaments

Mary Pierce had a pretty good year in her own right. She entered the French Open a No. 6 seed and left as a champion, defeating Spain's Conchita Martinez in straight sets. It was the second career Grand Slam singles title for Pierce but the first in her home country.

and arrived at the U.S. Open undefeated over the last two months of the women's tour. She cruised through the field at the U.S. Open and beat Davenport in the final for the title.

The next afternoon, Sampras could not win back-to-back slams. He was overwhelmed by the speed and power of 20-year-old Marat Safin, who dispatched a stunned Sampras in three sets. Afterwards, Sampras proclaimed the young Russian as someone who could dominate the men's game for years to come. ■

Sal Paolantonio's Top Ten Tennis Highlights of 2000

10. **Andre Agassi wins** the Australian Open, starting 2000 where he left off in 1999, when he won two Grand Slams.

9. **Mary Pierce prevails**. She grabs her second career Grand Slam title, winning the French Open in her home country over Spaniard Conchita Martinez.

8. **Lindsay Davenport wins** the Australian Open, cementing her claim that she's the queen of hardcourts in the women's game and, at the same time, inspiring Venus Williams to re-evaluate her dedication to being a champion.

7. **Gustavo Kuerten wins** his second French Open title, this time sans the ponytail haircut.

6. **Marat Safin shocks** Pete Sampras in three sets in the U.S. Open final, winning his first Grand Slam

Russian **Marat Safin**, left, greets Pete Sampras at the net after winning the U.S. Open on Sept. 10, 2000, in what could be a sign of things to come. The relatively unknown 20-year-old is unknown no more after whipping Sampras in straight sets, 6-4, 6-3, 6-3.

and establishing himself as the future cover boy of the men's tennis game.

5. **Venus Williams wins** every match of the summer of 2000, from the opening round of Wimbledon to the finals of the U.S. Open.

4. **Venus Williams defeats** her younger sister, Serena, in a dramatic showdown in the semifinals of Wimbledon. Their father, Richard, hearing whispers that he predetermined the outcome to give his oldest daughter a shot at her first Grand Slam title, leaves the premises and takes a long walk in Wimbledon Village until the match is over.

3. **Venus Williams wins Wimbledon**, her first Grand Slam singles title, with a straight-set victory over Lindsay Davenport.

2. **Venus Williams wins the U.S. Open**, defeating Davenport in the second straight all-American Grand Slam final of the year.

1. **Pete Sampras beats** Patrick Rafter in four sets to win his seventh Wimbledon and record 13th career Grand Slam singles title. It is his fourth consecutive Wimbledon championship. As twilight descends on Centre Court, Sampras climbs into the crowd to hug his parents, who made their first sojourn to Wimbledon to see him break Roy Emerson's three-decade old record. ∎

insidethenumbers

	Event	Last title
Pete Sampras	Wimbledon	2000
Bill Tilden	U.S. Open	1929
Bill Larned	U.S. Open	1911
Willie Renshaw	Wimbledon	1889
Richard Sears	U.S. Open	1887

Note: Here is a list of players who have accomplished the equivalent on the women's side. *Australian Open*–Margaret Court Smith (11 singles titles); *French Open*– Chris Evert (7); *Wimbledon*–Martina Navratilova (9), Helen Wills Moody (8), Dorothea Douglass Chambers and Steffi Graf (7); *U.S. Open*–Molla Mallory Bjurstedt (8), Helen Wills Moody (7).

GOOD JOB, YOUNG MAN

The surprising Marat Safin became one of the youngest U.S. Open champions in recent memory with his victory over Pete Sampras in 2000. Sampras himself knows a little bit about winning the Grand Slam event at a young age. Here is a look at the youngest U.S. Open men's champions (and the year they won their first Open) since 1968.

	Age
Pete Sampras, 1990	19 yrs, 0 mos.
John McEnroe, 1979	20 yrs, 6 mos.
Marat Safin, 2000	20 yrs, 7 mos.
Jimmy Connors, 1974	22 yrs, 0 mos.
Boris Becker, 1989	22 yrs, 9 mos.

FIVE FRESH FACES

For the first time ever, Wimbledon had five different women's singles champions in a five-year span. Here's a look at the women who made history.

Year	Final result
2000	Venus Williams def. L. Davenport
1999	Lindsay Davenport def. S. Graf
1998	Jana Novotna def. N. Tauziat
1997	Martina Hingis def. J. Novotna
1996	Steffi Graf def. A.S. Vicario

SEVENTH HEAVEN

With his historic seventh Wimbledon singles title in 2000, Pete Sampras joined an exclusive list of men who have dominated a Grand Slam event thoroughly enough to have won seven singles titles.

GRAND SLAM DUNK

Pete Sampras has the highest final round winning percentage in Grand Slam events of any player with at least 10 Grand Slam singles titles. Here is a look at the players who took care of business best in the biggest matches of their careers.

	Finals W-L	Finals Win Pct.
Pete Sampras	13-3	.813
Roy Emerson	12-3	.800
Bjorn Borg	11-5	.688
Bill Tilden	10-5	.667
Rod Laver	11-6	.647

DOUBLE NO TROUBLE

Only six times in history has Wimbledon and the U.S. Open shared the same women's singles finalists in the same year. Interestingly, the Wimbledon winner went on to win the U.S. Open each time.

Year	Wimbledon and U.S. Open
2000	Venus Williams def. Lindsay Davenport
1989	Steffi Graf def. Martina Navratilova
1987	Steffi Graf def. Martina Navratilova
1984	Martina Navratilova def. Chris Evert Lloyd
1976	Chris Evert def. Evonne Goolagong Cawley
1967	Billie Jean King def. Ann Jones

■

Tournament Results

Winners of men's and women's pro singles championships from Oct. 3, 1999 through Sept. 17, 2000.

Men's ATP Tour

LATE 1999

Finals	Tournament	Winner	Earnings	Runner-Up	Score
Oct. 3	Romanian Open (Bucharest)	Alberto Martin	$46,000	K. Alami	63 62
Oct. 3	Toulouse Open	Nicolas Escude	54,000	D. Vacek	75 61
Oct. 3	Grand Slam Cup (Munich)	Greg Rusedski	1,300,000	T. Haas	63 64 67 76
Oct. 10	Swiss Indoors (Basel)	Karol Kucera	137,000	T. Henman	64 76 46 46 76
Oct. 10	Heineken Open (Shangai)	Magnus Norman	46,000	M. Rios	26 63 75
Oct. 10	Int'l Championship of Sicily	Arnaud Di Pasquale	46,000	A. Berasategui	61 63
Oct. 17	Heineken Open (Singapore)	Marcelo Rios	111,500	M. Tillstrom	62 76
Oct. 17	CA Tennis Trophy (Vienna)	Greg Rusedski	125,400	N. Kiefer	76 26 63 75 64
Oct. 24	Lyon Grand Prix	Nicolas Lapentti	101,500	L. Hewitt	63 62
Oct. 31	Eurocard Open (Stuttgart)	Thomas Enqvist	376,000	R. Krajicek	61 64 57 75
Nov. 7	Paris Open	Andre Agassi	393,000	M. Safin	76 62 46 64
Nov. 14	Kremlin Cup (Moscow)	Yevgeny Kafelnikov	137,000	B. Black	76 64
Nov. 14	Stockholm Open	Thomas Enqvist	112,000	M. Gustafsson	63 64 62
Nov. 21	ATP Doubles Champs (Hartford)	Alex O'Brien/ Sebastien Lareau	170,000	M. Bhupathi/ L. Paes	63 62 62
Nov. 28	ATP Championship (Hannover)	Pete Sampras	1,385,000	A. Agassi	61 75 64

2000

Finals	Tournament	Winner	Earnings	Runner-Up	Score
Jan. 9	Australian Hardcourt Championships	Lleyton Hewitt	$46,000	T. Enqvist	36 63 62
Jan. 9	Qatar Open (Doha)	Fabrice Santoro	137,000	R. Schuttler	36 75 30 ret.
Jan. 9	Gold Flake Open (Chennai)	Jerome Golmard	58,000	M. Hantschk	63 67 63
Jan. 16	Sydney International	Lleyton Hewitt	46,000	J. Stoltenberg	64 60
Jan. 16	Heineken Open (Auckland)	Magnus Norman	46,000	M. Chang	36 63 75
Jan. 30	**Australian Open** (Melbourne)	Andre Agassi	485,000	Y. Kafelnikov	36 63 62 64
Feb. 13	Dubai Open	Nicolas Kiefer	137,000	J.C. Ferrero	75 46 63
Feb. 13	Marseille Open	Marc Rosset	66,400	R. Federer	26 63 76
Feb. 13	Sybase Open (San Jose)	Mark Philippoussis	49,500	M. Tillstrom	75 46 63
Feb. 20	Kroger St. Jude International (Memphis)	Magnus Larsson	120,000	B. Black	62 16 63
Feb. 20	ABN/AMRO World Tennis Tournament (Rotterdam)	Cedric Pioline	139,300	T. Henman	67 64 76
Feb. 27	AXA Cup (London)	Marc Rosset	130,000	Y. Kafelnikov	64 64
Feb. 27	Mexican Open (Mexico City)	Juan Ignacio Chela	130,000	M. Puerta	64 76
Mar. 5	Copenhagen Open	Andreas Vinciguerra	46,000	M. Larsson	63 76
Mar. 5	Citrix Tennis Championships (Delray Beach)	Stefan Koubek	46,000	A. Calatrava	61 46 64
Mar. 5	Chevrolet Cup (Santiago)	Gustavo Kuerten	49,500	M. Puerta	76 63
Mar. 12	Colombia Open (Bogota)	Mariano Puerta	49,500	Y. El Aynaoui	64 76
Mar. 12	Frank Templeton Classic (Scottsdale)	Lleyton Hewitt	49,500	T. Henman	64 76
Mar. 19	TMS—Indian Wells	Alex Corretja	400,000	T. Enqvist	64 64 63
Apr. 2	TMS—The Ericsson Open (Miami)	Pete Sampras	410,000	G. Kuerten	61 67 76 76
Apr. 16	Galleryfurniture.com Tennis Challenge (Atlanta)	Andrew Ilie	49,500	J. Stoltenberg	63 75
Apr. 16	Grand Prix Hassan II (Casablanca)	Fernando Vicente	46,000	S. Grosjean	64 46 76
Apr. 16	Estoril Open	Carlos Moya	84,000	F. Clavet	63 62
Apr. 23	TMS—Monte Carlo Open	Cedric Pioline	400,000	D. Hrbaty	64 76 76
Apr. 30	Open Seat Godo (Barcelona)	Marat Safin	148,000	J.C. Ferrero	63 63 64
May 7	BMW Open (Munich)	Franco Squillari	54,000	T. Haas	64 64
May 7	U.S. Clay Court Championships (Orlando)	Fernando Gonzalez	46,000	N. Massu	62 63
May 7	Mallorca Open	Marat Safin	66,400	M. Tillstrom	64 63
May 14	TMS—Rome	Magnus Norman	400,000	G. Kuerten	63 46 64 64
May 21	TMS—Hamburg	Gustavo Kuerten	400,000	M. Safin	64 57 64 57 76

Tournament Results (Cont.)

Finals	Tournament	Winner	Earnings	Runner-Up	Score
May 27	ATP World Team Championship (Dusseldorf)	Slovakia	$500,000	Russia	3-0
May 27	Int'l Raiffeisen GP at Austria (St. Polten)	Andrei Pavel	57,000	A. Ilie	75 36 62
June 11	**French Open** (Paris)	Gustavo Kuerten	586,112	M. Norman	62 63 26 76
June 18	Gerry Weber Open (Halle)	David Prinosil	137,000	R. Krajicek	63 62
June 18	The Stella Artois Grass Court Champs (London)	Lleyton Hewitt	91,500	P. Sampras	64 64
June 25	Heineken Trophy ('s-Hertogenbosch)	Patrick Rafter	54,000	N. Escude	61 63
June 25	The Nottingham Open	Sebastien Grosjean	49,000	B. Black	76 63
July 9	**Wimbledon** (London)	Pete Sampras	722,201	P. Rafter	67 76 64 62
July 16	Swedish Open (Bastad)	Magnus Norman	49,500	A. Vinciguerra	61 76
July 16	Gstaad Open	Alex Corretja	81,000	M. Puerta	61 63
July 16	Hall of Fame Championships (Newport)	Peter Wessels	49,500	J. Knippschild	76 63
July 23	Mercedes Cup (Stuttgart)	Franco Squillari	167,000	G. Gaudio	62 36 46 64 62
July 23	Dutch Open (Amsterdam)	Magnus Gustafsson	54,000	R. Sluiter	67 63 76 61
July 23	Int'l Championship of Croatia (Umag)	Marcelo Rios	54,000	M. Puerta	76 46 63
July 30	Generali Open (Kitzbuhel)	Alex Corretja	120,000	E. Alvarez	63 61 30 ret.
July 30	Mercedes-Benz Cup (Los Angeles)	Michael Chang	49,500	J. Gambill	67 63 ret.
July 30	Tennis Int'l of San Marino	Alex Calatrava	46,000	S. Bruguera	76 16 64
Aug. 6	TMS—Toronto	Marat Safin	400,000	H. Levy	62 63
Aug. 13	TMS—Cincinnati	Thomas Enqvist	400,000	T. Henman	76 64
Aug. 20	RCA Championships (Indianapolis)	Gustavo Kuerten	115,000	M. Safin	36 76 76
Aug. 20	Legg Mason Classic (Washington)	Alex Corretja	115,000	A. Agassi	62 63
Aug. 27	The Hamlet Cup (Commack)	Magnus Norman	49,500	T. Enqvist	63 57 75
Sept. 10	**U.S. Open** (Flushing)	Marat Safin	800,000	P. Sampras	64 63 63
Sept. 17	Romanian Open (Bucharest)	Juan Balcells	49,500	M. Hantschk	64 36 76
Sept. 17	President's Cup (Tashkent)	Marat Safin	70,000	D. Sanguinetti	63 64

Note: In 2000, the ATP Tour replaced the prestigous Mercedes Super 9 and the ATP Championship tournaments with the Tennis Masters Series and the Tennis Masters Cup (Nov.27–Dec. 3), respectively. Tennis Masters Series tournaments are identified by TMS.

Women's WTA Tour

LATE 1999

Finals	Tournament	Winner	Earnings	Runner-Up	Score
Oct. 3	Grand Slam Cup (Munich)	Serena Williams	$800,000	V. Williams	61 36 63
Oct. 10	Porsche Grand Prix (Filderstadt)	Martina Hingis	80,000	M. Pierce	64 61
Oct. 17	Swisscom Challenge (Zurich)	Venus Williams	150,000	M. Hingis	63 64
Oct. 24	Kremlin Cup (Moscow)	Nathalie Tauziat	150,000	B. Schett	26 64 61
Oct. 24	Slovak Indoor (Bratislava)	Amelie Mauresmo	16,000	K. Clijsters	63 63
Oct. 31	EA Generali Ladies Open (Linz)	Mary Pierce	80,000	S. Testud	76 61
Nov. 7	Bell Challenge (Quebec City)	Jennifer Capriati	27,000	C. Rubin	46 61 62
Nov. 7	Sparkassen Cup (Leipzig)	Nathalie Tauziat	80,000	K. Hrdlickova	61 63
Nov. 14	Advanta Championship (Philadelphia)	Lindsay Davenport	80,000	M. Hingis	63 64
Nov. 14	Wismilak Open (Kuala Lumpur)	Asa Carlsson	27,000	E. De Lone	62 64
Nov. 21	Volvo Women's Open (Pattaya)	Magdalena Maleeva	16,000	A. Kremer	46 61 62
Nov. 21	Chase Championship (New York)	Lindsay Davenport	500,000	M. Hingis	64 62

2000

Finals	Tournament	Winner	Earnings	Runner-Up	Score
Jan. 9	Australian Hardcourt Championships (Gold Coast)	Silvija Talaja	$27,000	C. Martinez	60 06 64
Jan. 9	ASB Bank Classic (Auckland)	Anne Kremer	16,000	C. Black	64 64
Jan. 16	Sydney International	Amelie Mauresmo	75,000	L. Davenport	76 64
Jan. 30	**Australian Open** (Melbourne)	Lindsay Davenport	460,600	M. Hingis	61 75
Feb. 6	Pan Pacific Open (Tokyo)	Martina Hingis	166,000	S. Testud	63 75
Feb. 13	Open Gaz de France (Paris)	Nathalie Tauziat	87,000	S. Williams	75 62
Feb. 13	Copa Colsanitas (Bogota)	Patricia Wartusch	22,000	T. Garbin	46 61 64
Feb. 20	Faber Grand Prix (Hannover)	Serena Williams	87,000	D. Chladkova	61 61
Feb. 20	Brazil Ladies Open (Sao Paulo)	Rita Kuti Kis	22,000	P. Suarez	46 64 75
Feb. 27	IGA Superthrift Classic (Okla. City)	Monica Seles	27,000	N. Dechy	61 76
Mar. 18	TMS—Indian Wells	Lindsay Davenport	330,000	M. Hingis	46 64 60
Apr. 2	Ericsson Open (Miami)	Martina Hingis	350,000	L. Davenport	63 62
Apr. 16	Bausch & Lomb Champs (Amelia Island)	Monica Seles	87,000	C. Martinez	63 62
Apr. 16	Estoril Open	Anke Huber	22,000	N. Dechy	62 16 75
Apr. 23	Family Circle Cup (Hilton Head)	Mary Pierce	116,000	A. Sanchez Vicario	61 60
Apr. 23	Budapest Open	Tathiana Garbin	16,000	K. Boogert	62 76
May 7	Betty Barclay Cup (Hamburg)	Martina Hingis	87,000	A. Sanchez Vicario	63 63
May 7	Croatia Bol Ladies Open	Tina Pisnik	27,000	A. Mauresmo	76 76

Finals	Tournament	Winner	Earnings	Runner-Up	Score
May 14	German Open (Berlin)	Conchita Martinez	$166,900	A. Coetzer	61 62
May 14	Warsaw Cup	Henrieta Nagyova	16,000	A. Hopmans	26 64 75
May 21	TMS—Rome	Monica Seles	166,900	A. Mauresmo	62 76
May 21	Benelux Open (Antwerp)	Amanda Coetzer	22,000	C. Torrens-Valero	46 62 63
May 27	Strasbourg International	Silvija Talaja	27,000	R. Kuti Kis	75 46 63
May 27	Madrid Open	Gala Leon Garcia	27,000	F. Zuluaga	46 62 62
June 11	**French Open** (Paris)	Mary Pierce	593,418	C. Martinez	62 75
June 18	DFS Classic (Birmingham, Eng.)	Lisa Raymond	27,000	T. Tanasugarn	62 67 64
June 18	Tashkent Open	Iroda Tulyaganova	22,000	F. Schiavone	63 26 63
June 25	Direct Line Insurance Champs (Eastbourne)	Julie Halard-Decugis	87,000	D. Van Roost	76 64
June 25	Heineken Trophy ('s-Hertogenbosch)	Martina Hingis	27,000	R. Dragomir	62 30 ret.
July 9	**Wimbledon** (London)	Venus Williams	650,000	L. Davenport	63 76
July 16	International Tournament (Palermo)	Henrieta Nagyova	16,000	P. Nola	63 75
July 16	Uniqa Grand Prix (Klagenfurt)	Barbara Schett	27,000	P. Schnyder	57 64 64
July 23	Polish Open (Sopot)	Anke Huber	27,000	G. Leon Garcia	76 63
July 23	Sanex Trophy (Knokke Heist)	Anna Smashnova	16,000	D. Van Roost	62 75
July 30	Bank of the West Classic (Stanford)	Venus Williams	87,000	L. Davenport	61 64
Aug. 6	Acura Classic (San Diego)	Venus Williams	87,000	M. Seles	60 67 63
Aug. 13	Estyle.com Classic (Los Angeles)	Serena Williams	87,000	L. Davenport	46 64 76
Aug. 20	du Maurier Open (Montreal)	Martina Hingis	166,000	S. Williams	06 63 30 ret.
Aug. 27	Pilot Pen (New Haven)	Venus Williams	87,000	M. Seles	62 64
Sept. 10	**U.S. Open** (Flushing)	Venus Williams	800,000	L. Davenport	64 75

Note: The final match of the State Farm Women's Tennis Classic, scheduled for Mar. 5, was cancelled due to rain. Finalists Martina Hingis and Lindsay Davenport were awarded equal WTA ranking points plus $43,500 each in finalist money and $4,200 apiece as doubles semifinalists.

2000 Grand Slam Tournaments

Australian Open
MEN'S SINGLES

FINAL EIGHT— #1 Andre Agassi; #2 Yevgeny Kafelnikov; #3 Pete Sampras; #4 Nicolas Kiefer; #12 Magnus Norman; plus unseeded Hicham Arazi, Younes El Aynaoui and Chris Woodruff.

Quarterfinals

Agassi def. Arazi	64 64 62
Sampras def. Woodruff	75 63 63
Norman def. Kiefer	36 63 61 76(4)
Kafelnikov def. Aynaoui	60 63 76(4)

Semifinals

Agassi def. Sampras	64 36 67(0) 76(5) 61
Kafelnikov def. Norman	61 62 64

Final

Agassi def. Kafelnikov	36 63 62 64

WOMEN'S SINGLES

FINAL EIGHT— #1 Martina Hingis; #2 Lindsay Davenport; #10 Conchita Martinez; #13 Arantxa Sanchez Vicario; #16 Elena Likhovtseva; plus unseeded Jennifer Capriati, Julie Halard-Decugis and Ai Sugiyama.

Quarterfinals

Hingis def. Sanchez Vicario	61 61
Martinez def. Likhovtseva	63 46 97
Capriati def. Sugiyama	60 62
Davenport def. Halard-Decugis	61 62

Semifinals

Hingis def. Martinez	63 62
Davenport def. Capriati	62 76(4)

Final

Davenport def. Hingis	61 75

DOUBLES FINALS

Men— #5 Ellis Ferreira & Rick Leach def. #8 Wayne Black & Andrew Kratzmann, 6-4, 3-6, 6-3, 3-6, 18-16.

Women— #1 Lisa Raymond & Rennae Stubbs def. #3 Martina Hingis & Mary Pierce, 6-4, 5-7, 6-4.

Mixed— #3 Jared Palmer & Rennae Stubbs def. #4 Todd Woodbridge & Arantxa Sanchez Vicario, 7-5, 7-6 (7-3).

French Open
MEN'S SINGLES

FINAL EIGHT— #3 Magnus Norman; #4 Yevgeny Kafelnikov, #5 Gustavo Kuerten; #10 Alex Corretja; #12 Marat Safin; #16 Juan Carlos Ferrero; plus unseeded Albert Costa, and Franco Squillari.

Quarterfinals

Squillari def. Costa	64 64 26 64
Norman def. Safin	64 63 46 75
Kuerten def. Kafelnikov	63 36 46 64 62
Ferrero def. Corretja	64 64 62

Semifinals

Norman def. Squillari	61 64 63
Kuerten def. Ferrero	75 46 26 64 63

Final

Kuerten def. Norman	62 63 26 76(6)

WOMEN'S SINGLES

FINAL EIGHT— #1 Martina Hingis; #3 Monica Seles; #4 Venus Williams; #5 Conchita Martinez; #6 Mary Pierce; #8 Arantxa Sanchez Vicario; plus unseeded Marta Marrero and Chanda Rubin.

Quarterfinals

Hingis def. Rubin	61 63
Pierce def. Seles	46 63 64
Sanchez Vicario def. V. Williams	60 16 62
Martinez def. Marrero	76(5) 61

Semifinals

Pierce def. Hingis	64 57 62
Martinez def. Sanchez Vicario	61 62

Final

Pierce def. Martinez	62 75

DOUBLES FINALS

Men— #2 Todd Woodbridge & Mark Woodforde def. #3 Paul Haarhuis & Sandon Stolle, 7-6 (9-7), 6-4.

Women— #3 Martina Hingis & Mary Pierce def. #10 Virginia Ruano-Pascua & Paola Suerezl, 6-2, 6-4.

Mixed— #12 Mariaan De Swardt & David Adams def. #1 Rennae Stubbs & Todd Woodbridge, 6-3, 3-6, 6-3.

Wimbledon

MEN'S SINGLES

FINAL EIGHT— #1 Pete Sampras; #2 Andre Agassi; #10 Mark Philippoussis; #12 Patrick Rafter; plus unseeded Byron Black, Jan-Michael Gambill, Alexander Popp and Vladmir Voltchkov.

Quarterfinals

Sampras def. Gambill	.64 67(4) 64 64
Voltchkov def. Black	.76(2) 76(2) 64
Rafter def. Popp	.63 62 76(1)
Agassi def. Philippoussis	.76(4) 63 64

Semifinals

Sampras def. Voltchkov	.76(4) 62 64
Rafter def. Agassi	.75 46 75 46 63

Final

Sampras def. Rafter	.67(10) 76(5) 64 62

WOMEN'S SINGLES

FINAL EIGHT— #1 Martina Hingis; #2 Lindsay Davenport; #5 Venus Williams; #6 Monica Seles; #8 Serena Williams; plus unseeded Jelena Dokic, Lisa Raymond and Magui Serna.

Quarterfinals

V. Williams def. Hingis	.63 46 64
S. Williams def. Raymond	.62 60
Dokic def. Serna	.63 62
Davenport def. Seles	.67(4) 64 60

Semifinals

V. Williams def. S. Williams	.62 76(3)
Davenport def. Dokic	.64 62

Final

V. Williams def. Davenport	.63 76(3)

DOUBLES FINALS

Men— #1 Todd Woodbridge & Mark Woodforde def. #2 Paul Haarhuis & Sandon Stolle 6-3, 6-4, 6-1.

Women— #8 Serena Williams & Venus Williams def. #4 Julie Halard-Decugis & Ai Sugiyama 6-3, 6-2.

Mixed— #8 Donald Johnson & Kimberly Po def. Lleyton Hewitt & Kim Clijsters 6-4, 7-6 (7-3).

U.S. Open

MEN'S SINGLES

FINAL EIGHT— #4 Pete Sampras; #6 Marat Safin; #9 Lleyton Hewitt; #14 Nicolas Kiefer; plus unseeded Arnaud Clement, Thomas Johansson, Richard Krajicek and Todd Martin.

Quarterfinals

Hewitt def. Clement	.62 64 63
Sampras def. Krajicek	.46 76(6) 64 62
Safin def. Kiefer	.75 46 76(5) 63
Martin def. Johansson	.64 64 36 75

Semifinals

Sampras def. Hewitt	.76(7) 64 76(5)
Safin def. Martin	.63 76(4) 76(1)

Final

Safin def. Sampras	.64 63 63

WOMEN'S SINGLES

FINAL EIGHT— #1 Martina Hingis; #2 Lindsay Davenport; #3 Venus Williams; #5 Serena Williams; #6 Monica Seles; #8 Nathalie Tauziat; #10 Anke Huber; plus unseeded Elena Dementieva.

Quarterfinals

Hingis def. Seles	.60 75
V. Williams def. Tauziat	.64 16 61
Dementieva def. Huber	.61 36 63
Davenport def. S. Williams	.64 62

Semifinals

V. Williams def. Hingis	.46 63 75
Davenport def. Dementieva	.62 76(5)

Final

V. Williams def. Davenport	.64 75

DOUBLES FINALS

Men— Lleyton Hewitt & Max Mirnyi def. #4 Ellis Ferreira & Rick Leach 6-4, 5-7, 7-6 (7-5).

Women— #2 Julie Halard-Decugis & Ai Sugiyama def. #10 Cara Black & Elena Likhovtseva 6-0, 1-6, 6-1.

Mixed— #2 Arantxa Sanchez Vicario & Jared Palmer def. #4 Anna Kournikova & Max Mirnyi 6-4, 6-3.

2000 Fed Cup

Originally the Federation Cup and started in 1963 by the International Tennis Federation as the Davis Cup of women's tennis. Played by 32 teams over one week at one site through 1994. Tournament was Davis Cup-style format from 1995-99. In 2000, a new round-robin format was introduced with 12 nations competing in three groups over two weeks. The 1999 winner, the United States, receives a bye from the quarterfinal round and has the right to host the semifinals and final. (*) indicates team advanced to semifinals.

Quarterfinals

(April 27-30)

Group A at Bari, Italy	W-L	Group B at Bratislava, Slovakia	W-L	Group C at Moscow, Russia	W-L
*Spain	3-0	*Czech Republic	3-0	*Belgium	3-0
Germany	2-1	Switzerland	2-1	France	2-1
Italy	1-2	Austria	1-2	Russia	1-2
Croatia	0-3	Slovakia	0-3	Australia	0-3
Germany 2	Italy 1	Austria 2	Slovakia 1	Belgium 3	Russia 0
Spain 2	Germany 1	Czech Republic 2	Slovakia 1	Russia 2	Australia 1
Italy 3	Croatia 0	Switzerland 2	Austria 1	Belgium 2	France 1
Spain 2	Croatia 1	Czech Republic 2	Switzerland 1	France 2	Australia 1
Germany 2	Croatia 1	Czech Republic 2	Austria 1	Belgium 2	Australia 1
Spain 3	Italy 0	Switzerland 2	Slovakia 1	France 3	Russia 0

Semifinals & Final

(Nov. 24-26)
To be held in the United States.

Singles Leaders

Official Top 20 rankings and money leaders of men's and women's tours for 1999 and unofficial rankings and money leaders for 2000 (through Sept. 10), as compiled by the ATP Tour (Association of Tennis Professionals) and WTA (Women's Tennis Association). Note that money lists include doubles earnings.

Final 1999 Computer Rankings and Money Won

Listed are events won and times a finalist and semifinalist (Finish, 1-2-SF), match record (W-L), and earnings for the year.

MEN

		Finish 1-2-SF	W-L	Earnings
1	Andre Agassi	5-3-4	63-14	$4,269,265
2	Yevgeny Kafelnikov	3-2-5	61-32	2,360,498
3	Pete Sampras	5-0-1	40-8	2,816,406
4	Thomas Enqvist	3-1-3	48-28	1,729,056
5	Gustavo Kuerten	2-0-1	50-25	1,762,269
6	Nicolas Kiefer	3-2-4	54-25	1,232,268
7	Todd Martin	1-2-3	42-20	1,185,394
8	Nicolas Lapentti	2-1-4	58-24	1,234,278
9	Marcelo Rios	3-2-1	47-18	1,794,244
10	Richard Krajicek	2-1-1	43-21	1,348,977
11	Tommy Haas	1-3-2	47-26	1,447,308
12	Tim Henman	0-4-1	44-29	1,537,594
13	Cedric Pioline	1-0-3	43-32	723,428
14	Greg Rusedski	2-2-3	48-26	2,122,535
15	Magnus Norman	5-0-1	44-22	609,035
16	Patrick Rafter	1-2-1	38-16	1,254,574
17	Karol Kucera	1-0-2	43-22	870,957
18	Albert Costa	3-0-2	40-22	620,629
19	Mark Philippoussis	2-0-0	35-17	1,019,856
20	Vince Spadea	0-1-0	33-27	605,609

WOMEN

		Finish 1-2-SF	W-L	Earnings
1	Martina Hingis	7-6-4	71-13	$3,291,780
2	Lindsay Davenport	6-1-5	61-10	2,734,205
3	Venus Williams	6-4-3	61-13	2,316,005
4	Serena Williams	5-1-0	41-7	2,605,102
5	Mary Pierce	1-4-3	45-20	996,442
6	Monica Seles	1-2-4	38-13	822,218
7	Nathalie Tauziat	2-2-3	37-25	864,507
8	Barbara Schett	0-1-3	47-25	725,685
9	Julie Halard-Decugis	2-3-1	47-20	514,070
10	Amelie Mauresmo	1-2-2	35-15	582,468
11	Amanda Coetzer	0-2-3	37-25	486,120
12	Anna Kournikova	0-1-3	35-19	748,424
13	Sandrine Testud	1-0-1	35-25	488,496
14	Dominique Van Roost	0-3-1	35-28	450,401
15	Conchita Martinez	1-0-1	38-22	486,392
16	Anke Huber	0-0-2	34-26	411,987
17	Arantxa Sanchez Vicario	1-0-3	24-18	807,921
18	Elena Likhovtseva	0-0-1	37-32	525,307
19	Amy Frazier	1-0-3	31-20	257,686
20	Ruxandra Dragomir	0-1-2	30-23	309,222

2000 Rankings (through Sept. 17)

Listed are tournaments won and times a finalist and semifinalist (Finish, 1-2-SF), match record (W-L), and computer points earned (Pts). The **ATP Champions Race 2000** replaced the men's pro tennis tour's 27-year-old computer ranking system in 2000. Under the new system players start from zero on Jan. 1 and accumulate points during the calendar year with the player accumulating the most points becoming the World No.1. Points are awarded in 18 tournaments, including the nine Tennis Masters Series events, four Grand Slams and five other International Series events.

MEN

Final ATP Tour singles rankings will be based on points earned from 18 tournaments played in 2000. Tournaments, titles and match won-lost records are for 2000 only.

Rank 00	(99)		Finish 1-2-SF	W-L	Pts
1	25	Marat Safin	5-3-1	57-21	639
2	3	Pete Sampras	2-2-1	40-11	637
3	5	Gustavo Kuerten	4-2-2	46-15	623
4	15	Magnus Norman	4-1-3	58-17	586
5	22	Lleyton Hewitt	4-0-4	52-13	435
6	26	Alex Corretja	4-0-2	44-12	422
7	1	Andre Agassi	1-1-2	32-12	418
8	4	Thomas Enqvist	1-3-2	44-18	402
9	2	Yevgeny Kafelnikov	0-3-2	44-28	392
10	12	Tim Henman	0-3-1	41-20	321
11	43	Juan Carlos Ferrero	0-2-2	38-19	310
12	52	Franco Squillari	2-0-2	31-20	296
13	13	Cedric Pioline	2-0-1	29-16	282
14	16	Patrick Rafter	1-1-0	25-13	250
15	19	Mark Philippoussis	1-0-1	29-16	248
16	99	Mariano Puerta	1-4-2	37-17	244
17	53	Wayne Ferreira	0-0-2	34-18	239
18	6	Nicolas Kiefer	1-0-2	25-15	230
19	34	Younes El Aynaoui	0-1-1	34-22	210
20	56	Arnaud Clement	0-0-3	26-22	206

WOMEN

Sanex WTA Tour singles ranking system based on total Round and Quality Points for each tournament played during the last 12 months. Tournaments, titles and match won-lost records, however, are for 2000 only.

Rank 00	(99)		Finish 1-2-SF	W-L	Pts
1	1	Martina Hingis	5-2-5	58-9	5684
2	2	Lindsay Davenport	2-6-0	45-10	5414
3	3	Venus Williams	5-0-0	32-3	4336
4	5	Mary Pierce	2-0-2	29-11	3119
5	6	Monica Seles	3-2-3	46-10	2985
6	15	Conchita Martinez	1-3-3	45-17	2719
7	7	Nathalie Tauziat	1-0-2	25-18	2490
8	4	Serena Williams	2-2-1	33-8	2055
9	17	Arantxa Sanchez Vicario	0-2-3	39-14	1996
10	16	Anke Huber	2-0-1	32-16	1964
11	13	Sandrine Testud	0-1-1	31-20	1897
12	11	Amanda Coetzer	1-1-3	37-18	1704
13	12	Anna Kournikova	0-0-5	35-22	1661
14	14	Dominique Van Roost	0-2-0	21-16	1579
15	10	Amelie Mauresmo	1-2-1	20-9	1560
16	22	Chanda Rubin	0-1-2	32-17	1494
17	62	Elena Dementieva	0-0-3	29-16	1467
18	23	Jennifer Capriati	0-0-2	23-14	1379
19	9	Amy Frazier	0-0-2	22-17	1261
20	9	Julie Halard-Decugis	1-0-1	20-17	1257

Note: Not reflected in the "Finish" column is the State Farm Women's Tennis Classic on March 5. Hingis and Davenport advanced to the final but it was rained out.

2000 Money Winners

Amounts include singles and doubles earnings through Sept. 17.

MEN

	Earnings		Earnings		Earnings
1 Marat Safin	$2,180,869	10 Dominik Hrbaty	$936,637	19 Jiri Novak	$593,243
2 Pete Sampras	1,924,598	11 Cedric Pioline	817,039	20 Max Mirnyi	578,948
3 Gustavo Kuerten	1,846,070	12 Tim Henman	707,923	21 Nicolas Kiefer	537,999
4 Magnus Norman	1,388,029	13 Wayne Ferreira	699,624	22 Nicolas Lapentti	511,655
5 Yevgeny Kafelnikov	1,201,609	14 Patrick Rafter	679,686	23 Fabrice Santoro	503,966
6 Lleyton Hewitt	1,150,172	15 Todd Woodbridge	662,871	24 Mark Philippoussis	484,367
7 Alex Corretja	1,101,325	16 Franco Squillari	660,658	25 Arnaud Clement	474,725
8 Thomas Enqvist	1,073,920	17 Mark Woodforde	647,160		
9 Andre Agassi	987,793	18 Juan Carlos Ferrero	613,676		

WOMEN

	Earnings		Earnings		Earnings
1 Venus Williams	$2,030,650	10 Ai Sugiyama	$620,535	19 Chanda Rubin	$394,145
2 Lindsay Davenport	1,995,484	11 Sandrine Testud	507,384	20 Jelena Dokic	359,430
3 Martina Hingis	1,988,474	12 Nathalie Tauziat	497,161	21 Barbara Schett	358,512
4 Mary Pierce	1,208,018	13 Lisa Raymond	491,574	22 Jennifer Capriati	350,261
5 Conchita Martinez	941,730	14 Anna Kournikova	486,905	23 Rennae Stubbs	300,007
6 Monica Seles	846,850	15 Anke Huber	447,407	24 Amelie Mauresmo	290,424
7 Serena Williams	839,818	16 Amanda Coetzer	447,441	25 Dominique Van Roost	289,654
8 Arantxa Sanchez Vicario	696,639	17 Elena Dementieva	434,277		
9 Julie Halard-Decugis	673,470	18 Elena Likhovtseva	407,464		

Davis Cup

Australia's Mark Philippoussis led his team to a 3-2 victory over France in the 1999 Davis Cup Final. It was the first title since 1986 for Australia and the 27th overall won by an Australian/Australasian team. Here is a recap of the 1999 final, plus a summary of the 2000 Davis Cup tournament.

1999 Final

Australia 3, France 2
at Nice, France (Dec. 3-5)

Day One— Mark Philippoussis (AUS) def. Sebastien Grosjean (FRA) 6-4, 6-2, 6-4; Cedric Pioline (FRA) def. Lleyton Hewitt (AUS) 7-6 (9-7), 7-6 (8-6), 7-5.

Day Two— Mark Woodforde & Todd Woodbridge (AUS) def. Olivier Delaitre & Fabrice Santoro (FRA), 2-6, 7-5, 6-2, 6-2.

Day Three— Philippoussis (AUS) def. Pioline (FRA) 6-3, 5-7, 6-1, 6-2; Grosjean (FRA) def. Hewitt (AUS), 6-4, 6-3.

2000 Early Rounds

FIRST ROUND
(Feb. 4-6)

Winner	Loser
United States 3	at Zimbabwe 2
at Czech Republic 4	Great Britain 1
Spain 4	at Italy 1
Russia 4	at Belgium 1
at Slovak Republic 3	Austria 2
Brazil 4	at France 1
at Germany 4	Netherlands 1
at Australia 3	Switzerland 2

QUARTERFINALS
(Apr. 7-9)

Winner	Loser
United States 3	at Czech Republic 2
Spain 4	at Russia 1
at Brazil 3	Slovak Republic 2
at Australia 3	Germany 2

SEMIFINALS

Spain 5, United States 0
at Santander, Spain (July 21-23)

Day One— Albert Costa (SPA) def. Todd Martin (USA) 6-4, 6-4, 6-4; Alex Corretja (SPA) def. Jan-Michael Gambill (USA) 1-6, 6-3, 6-4, 6-4.

Day Two— Corretja & Juan Balcells (SPA) def. Martin & Chris Woodruff (USA) 7-6 (8-6), 2-6, 6-3, 6-7 (5-7), 6-3.

Day Three— Juan Carlos Ferrero (SPA) def. Vincent Spadea (USA) 4-6, 6-1, 6-4; Balcells (SPA) def. Gambill (USA) 1-6, 7-6 (7-2), 6-4.

Australia 5, Brazil 0
at Brisbane, Australia (July 14-16)

Day One— Patrick Rafter (AUS) def. Gustavo Kuerten (BRA) 6-3, 6-2, 6-3; Lleyton Hewitt (AUS) def. Fernando Meligeni (BRA) 6-4, 6-2, 6-3.

Day Two— Sandon Stolle & Mark Woodforde (AUS) def. Kuerten & Jaime Oncins (BRA) 6-7, (3-7), 6-4, 3-6, 6-3, 6-4.

Day Three— Hewitt (AUS) def. Andre Sa (BRA) 6-4, 6-1; Rafter (AUS) def. Meligeni (BRA) 6-4, 6-3.

FINAL

Spain will host defending champion Australia in the Davis Cup Final Dec. 8-10. This will be the fourth time in event history that these two countries have met. Australia leads the series 3-0. Spain is in search of its first Davis Cup title, while Australia has a chance to win its 28th.

Grand Slam Championships
Australian Open
MEN

Became an Open Championship in 1969. Two tournaments were held in 1977; the first in January, the second in December. Tournament moved back to January in 1987, so no championship was decided in 1986.

Surface: Synpave Rebound Ace (hardcourt surface composed of polyurethane and synthetic rubber).

Multiple winners: Roy Emerson (6); Jack Crawford and Ken Rosewall (4); James Anderson, Rod Laver, Adrian Quist, Mats Wilander and Pat Wood (3); Andre Agassi, Boris Becker, Jack Bromwich, Ashley Cooper, Jim Courier, Stefan Edberg, Rodney Heath, Johan Kriek, Ivan Lendl, John Newcombe, Pete Sampras, Frank Sedgman, Guillermo Vilas and Tony Wilding (2).

Year	Winner	Loser	Score	Year	Winner	Loser	Score
1905	Rodney Heath	A. Curtis	46 63 64 64	1957	Ashley Cooper	N. Fraser	63 9-11 64 62
1906	Tony Wilding	H. Parker	60 64 64	1958	Ashley Cooper	M. Anderson	75 63 64
1907	Horace Rice	H. Parker	63 64 64	1959	Alex Olmedo	N. Fraser	61 62 36 63
1908	Fred Alexander	A. Dunlop	36 36 60 62 63	1960	Rod Laver	N. Fraser	57 36 63 86 86
1909	Tony Wilding	E. Parker	61 75 62	1961	Roy Emerson	R. Laver	16 63 75 64
1910	Rodney Heath	H. Rice	64 63 62	1962	Rod Laver	R. Emerson	86 06 64 64
1911	Norman Brookes	H. Rice	61 62 63	1963	Roy Emerson	K. Fletcher	63 63 61
1912	J. Cecil Parke	A. Beamish	36 63 16 61 75	1964	Roy Emerson	F. Stolle	63 64 62
1913	Ernie Parker	H. Parker	26 61 62 63	1965	Roy Emerson	F. Stolle	79 26 64 75 61
1914	Pat Wood	G. Patterson	64 63 57 61	1966	Roy Emerson	A. Ashe	64 68 62 63
1915	Francis Lowe	H. Rice	46 61 61 64	1967	Roy Emerson	A. Ashe	64 61 61
1916-18	Not held	World War I		1968	Bill Bowrey	J. Gisbert	75 26 97 64
1919	A.R.F. Kingscote	E. Pockley	64 60 63	1969	Rod Laver	A. Gimeno	63 64 75
1920	Pat Wood	R. Thomas	63 46 68 61 63	1970	Arthur Ashe	D. Crealy	64 97 62
1921	Rhys Gemmell	A. Hedeman	75 61 64	1971	Ken Rosewall	A. Ashe	61 75 63
1922	James Anderson	G. Patterson	60 36 63 63 62	1972	Ken Rosewall	M. Anderson	76 63 75
1923	Pat Wood	C.B. St. John	61 61 63	1973	John Newcombe	O. Parun	63 67 75 61
1924	James Anderson	R. Schlesinger	63 64 36 57 63	1974	Jimmy Connors	P. Dent	76 64 46 63
1925	James Anderson	G. Patterson	11-9 26 62 63	1975	John Newcombe	J. Connors	75 36 64 75
1926	John Hawkes	J. Willard	61 63 61	1976	Mark Edmondson	J. Newcombe	67 63 76 61
1927	Gerald Patterson	J. Hawkes	36 64 36 18-16 63	1977	Roscoe Tanner	G. Vilas	63 63 63
1928	Jean Borotra	R.O. Cummings	64 61 46 57 63		Vitas Gerulaitis	J. Lloyd	63 76 57 36 62
1929	John Gregory	R. Schlesinger	62 62 57 75	1978	Guillermo Vilas	J. Marks	64 64 36 63
				1979	Guillermo Vilas	J. Sadri	76 63 62
1930	Gar Moon	H. Hopman	63 61 63	1980	Brian Teacher	K. Warwick	75 76 63
1931	Jack Crawford	H. Hopman	64 62 26 61	1981	Johan Kriek	S. Denton	62 76 67 64
1932	Jack Crawford	H. Hopman	46 63 36 63 61	1982	Johan Kriek	S. Denton	63 63 62
1933	Jack Crawford	K. Gledhill	26 75 63 62	1983	Mats Wilander	I. Lendl	61 64 64
1934	Fred Perry	J. Crawford	63 75 61	1984	Mats Wilander	K. Curren	67 64 76 62
1935	Jack Crawford	F. Perry	26 64 64 64	1985	Stefan Edberg	M. Wilander	64 63 63
1936	Adrian Quist	J. Crawford	62 63 46 36 97	1986	Not held		
1937	Viv McGrath	J. Bromwich	63 16 60 26 61	1987	Stefan Edberg	P. Cash	63 64 36 57 63
1938	Don Budge	J. Bromwich	64 62 61	1988	Mats Wilander	P. Cash	63 67 36 61 86
1939	Jack Bromwich	A. Quist	64 61 63	1989	Ivan Lendl	M. Mecir	62 62 62
1940	Adrian Quist	J. Crawford	63 61 62	1990	Ivan Lendl	S. Edberg	46 76 52 (ret.)
1941-45	Not held	World War II		1991	Boris Becker	I. Lendl	16 64 64 64
1946	Jack Bromwich	D. Pails	57 63 75 36 62	1992	Jim Courier	S. Edberg	63 36 64 62
1947	Dinny Pails	J. Bromwich	46 64 36 75 86	1993	Jim Courier	S. Edberg	62 61 26 75
1948	Adrian Quist	J. Bromwich	64 36 63 26 63	1994	Pete Sampras	T. Martin	76 64 64
1949	Frank Sedgman	J. Bromwich	63 63 62	1995	Andre Agassi	P. Sampras	46 61 76 64
1950	Frank Sedgman	K. McGregor	63 64 46 61	1996	Boris Becker	M. Chang	62 64 26 62
1951	Dick Savitt	K. McGregor	63 26 63 61	1997	Pete Sampras	C. Moya	62 63 63
1952	Ken McGregor	F. Sedgman	75 12-10 26 62	1998	Petr Korda	M. Rios	62 62 62
1953	Ken Rosewall	M. Rose	60 63 64	1999	Yevgeny Kafelnikov	T. Enqvist	46 60 63 76
1954	Mervyn Rose	R. Hartwig	62 06 64 62	2000	Andre Agassi	Y. Kafelnikov	36 63 62 64
1955	Ken Rosewall	L. Hoad	97 64 64				
1956	Lew Hoad	K. Rosewall	64 36 64 75				

WOMEN

Became an Open Championship in 1969. Two tournaments were held in 1977, the first in January, the second in December. Tournament moved back to January in 1987, so no championship was decided in 1986.

Multiple winners: Margaret Smith Court (11); Nancye Wynne Bolton (6); Daphne Akhurst (5); Evonne Goolagong Cawley, Steffi Graf and Monica Seles (4); Jean Hartigan, Martina Hingis and Martina Navratilova (3); Coral Buttsworth, Chris Evert Lloyd, Thelma Long, Hana Mandlikova, Mall Molesworth and Mary Carter Reitano (2).

Year	Winner	Loser	Score	Year	Winner	Loser	Score
1922	Mall Molesworth	E. Boyd	63 10-8	1964	Margaret Smith	L. Turner	63 62
1923	Mall Molesworth	E. Boyd	61 75	1965	Margaret Smith	M. Bueno	57 64 52 (ret)
1924	Sylvia Lance	E. Boyd	63 36 64	1966	Margaret Smith	N. Richey	walkover
1925	Daphne Akhurst	E. Boyd	16 86 64	1967	Nancy Richey	L. Turner	61 64
1926	Daphne Akhurst	E. Boyd	61 63	1968	Billie Jean King	M. Smith	61 62
1927	Esna Boyd	S. Harper	57 61 62	1969	Margaret Court	B.J. King	64 61
1928	Daphne Akhurst	E. Boyd	75 62				
1929	Daphne Akhurst	L. Bickerton	61 57 62	1970	Margaret Court	K. Melville	61 63
				1971	Margaret Court	E. Goolagong	26 76 75
1930	Daphne Akhurst	S. Harper	10-8 26 75	1972	Virginia Wade	E. Goolagong	64 64
1931	Coral Buttsworth	M. Crawford	16 63 64	1973	Margaret Court	E. Goolagong	64 75
1932	Coral Buttsworth	K. Le Messurier	97 64	1974	Evonne Goolagong	C. Evert	76 46 60
1933	Joan Hartigan	C. Buttsworth	64 63	1975	Evonne Goolagong	M. Navratilova	63 62
1934	Joan Hartigan	M. Molesworth	61 64	1976	Evonne Cawley	R. Tomanova	62 62
1935	Dorothy Round	N. Lyle	16 61 63	1977	Kerry Reid	D. Balestrat	75 62
1936	Joan Hartigan	N. Bolton	64 64		Evonne Cawley	H. Gourlay	63 60
1937	Nancye Wynne	E. Westacott	63 57 64	1978	Chris O'Neil	B. Nagelsen	63 76
1938	Dorothy Bundy	D. Stevenson	63 62	1979	Barbara Jordan	S. Walsh	63 63
1939	Emily Westacott	N. Hopman	61 62				
				1980	Hana Mandlikova	W. Turnbull	60 75
1940	Nancye Wynne	T. Coyne	57 64 60	1981	Martina Navratilova	C. Evert Lloyd	67 64 75
1941-45	Not held	World War II		1982	Chris Evert Lloyd	M. Navratilova	63 26 63
1946	Nancye Bolton	J. Fitch	64 64	1983	Martina Navratilova	K. Jordan	62 76
1947	Nancye Bolton	N. Hopman	63 62	1984	Chris Evert Lloyd	H. Sukova	67 61 63
1948	Nancye Bolton	M. Toomey	63 61	1985	Martina Navratilova	C. Evert Lloyd	62 46 62
1949	Doris Hart	N. Bolton	63 64	1986	Not held		
1950	Louise Brough	D. Hart	64 36 64	1987	Hana Mandlikova	M. Navratilova	75 76
1951	Nancye Bolton	T. Long	61 75	1988	Steffi Graf	C. Evert	61 76
1952	Thelma Long	H. Angwin	62 63	1989	Steffi Graf	H. Sukova	64 64
1953	Maureen Connolly	J. Sampson	63 62				
1954	Thelma Long	J. Staley	63 64	1990	Steffi Graf	M.J. Fernandez	63 64
1955	Beryl Penrose	T. Long	64 63	1991	Monica Seles	J. Novotna	57 63 61
1956	Mary Carter	T. Long	36 62 97	1992	Monica Seles	M.J. Fernandez	62 63
1957	Shirley Fry	A. Gibson	63 64	1993	Monica Seles	S. Graf	46 63 62
1958	Angela Mortimer	L. Coghlan	63 64	1994	Steffi Graf	A.S. Vicario	60 62
1959	Mary Reitano	T. Schuurman	62 63	1995	Mary Pierce	A.S. Vicario	63 62
				1996	Monica Seles	A. Huber	64 61
1960	Margaret Smith	J. Lehane	75 62	1997	Martina Hingis	M. Pierce	62 62
1961	Margaret Smith	J. Lehane	61 64	1998	Martina Hingis	C. Martinez	63 63
1962	Margaret Smith	J. Lehane	60 62	1999	Martina Hingis	A. Mauresmo	62 63
1963	Margaret Smith	J. Lehane	62 62	2000	Lindsay Davenport	M. Hingis	61 75

French Open
MEN

Prior to 1925, entry was restricted to members of French clubs. Became an Open Championship in 1968, but closed to contract pros in 1972.

Surface: Red clay.

First year: 1891. **Most wins:** Max Decugis (8).

Multiple winners (since 1925): Bjorn Borg (6); Henri Cochet (4); Rene Lacoste, Ivan Lendl and Mats Wilander (3); Sergi Bruguera, Jim Courier, Jaroslav Drobny, Roy Emerson, Jan Kodes, Gustavo Kuerten, Rod Laver, Frank Parker, Nicola Pietrangeli, Ken Rosewall, Manuel Santana, Tony Trabert and Gottfried von Cramm (2).

Year	Winner	Loser	Score	Year	Winner	Loser	Score
1925	Rene Lacoste	J. Borotra	75 61 64	1938	Don Budge	R. Menzel	63 62 64
1926	Henri Cochet	R. Lacoste	62 64 63	1939	Don McNeill	B. Riggs	75 60 63
1927	Rene Lacoste	B. Tilden	64 46 57 63 11-9				
1928	Henri Cochet	R. Lacoste	57 63 61 63	1941-45	Not held	World War II	
1929	Rene Lacoste	J. Borotra	63 26 60 26 86	1946	Marcel Bernard	J. Drobny	36 26 61 64 63
				1947	Joseph Asboth	E. Sturgess	86 75 64
1930	Henri Cochet	B. Tilden	36 86 63 61	1948	Frank Parker	J. Drobny	64 75 57 86
1931	Jean Borotra	C. Boussus	26 64 75 64	1949	Frank Parker	B. Patty	63 16 61 64
1932	Henri Cochet	G. de Stefani	60 64 46 63	1950	Budge Patty	J. Drobny	61 62 36 57 75
1933	Jack Crawford	H. Cochet	86 61 63	1951	Jaroslav Drobny	E. Sturgess	63 63 63
1934	Gottfried von Cramm	J. Crawford	64 79 36 75 63	1952	Jaroslav Drobny	F. Sedgman	62 60 36 64
1935	Fred Perry	G. von Cramm	63 36 61 63	1953	Ken Rosewall	V. Seixas	63 64 16 62
1936	Gottfried von Cramm	F. Perry	60 26 62 26 60	1954	Tony Trabert	A. Larsen	64 75 61
1937	Henner Henkel	H. Austin	61 64 63	1955	Tony Trabert	S. Davidson	26 61 64 62

Year	Winner	Loser	Score
1956	Lew Hoad	S. Davidson	64 86 63
1957	Sven Davidson	H. Flam	63 64 64
1958	Mervyn Rose	L. Ayala	63 64 64
1959	Nicola Pietrangeli	I. Vermaak	36 63 64 61
1960	Nicola Pietrangeli	L. Ayala	36 63 64 46 63
1961	Manuel Santana	N. Pietrangeli	46 61 36 60 62
1962	Rod Laver	R. Emerson	36 26 63 97 62
1963	Roy Emerson	P. Darmon	36 61 64 64
1964	Manuel Santana	N. Pietrangeli	63 61 46 75
1965	Fred Stolle	T. Roche	36 60 62 63
1966	Tony Roche	I. Gulyas	61 64 75
1967	Roy Emerson	T. Roche	61 64 26 62
1968	Ken Rosewall	R. Laver	63 61 26 62
1969	Rod Laver	K. Rosewall	64 63 64
1970	Jan Kodes	Z. Franulovic	62 64 60
1971	Jan Kodes	I. Nastase	86 62 26 75
1972	Andres Gimeno	P. Proisy	46 63 61 61
1973	Ilie Nastase	N. Pilic	63 63 60
1974	Bjorn Borg	M. Orantes	26 67 60 61 61
1975	Bjorn Borg	G. Vilas	62 63 64
1976	Adriano Panatta	H. Solomon	61 64 46 76
1977	Guillermo Vilas	B. Gottfried	60 63 60
1978	Bjorn Borg	G. Vilas	61 61 63
1979	Bjorn Borg	V. Pecci	63 61 67 64
1980	Bjorn Borg	V. Gerulaitis	64 61 62
1981	Bjorn Borg	I. Lendl	61 46 62 36 61
1982	Mats Wilander	G. Vilas	16 76 60 64
1983	Yannick Noah	M. Wilander	62 75 76
1984	Ivan Lendl	J. McEnroe	36 26 64 75 75
1985	Mats Wilander	I. Lendl	36 64 62 62
1986	Ivan Lendl	M. Pernfors	63 62 64
1987	Ivan Lendl	M. Wilander	75 62 36 76
1988	Mats Wilander	H. Leconte	75 62 61
1989	Michael Chang	S. Edberg	61 36 46 64 62
1990	Andres Gomez	A. Agassi	63 26 64 64
1991	Jim Courier	A. Agassi	36 64 26 61 64
1992	Jim Courier	P. Korda	75 62 61
1993	Sergi Bruguera	J. Courier	64 26 62 36 63
1994	Sergi Bruguera	A. Berasategui	63 75 26 61
1995	Thomas Muster	M. Chang	75 62 64
1996	Yevgeny Kafelnikov	M. Stich	76 75 76
1997	Gustavo Kuerten	S. Bruguera	63 64 62
1998	Carlos Moya	A. Corretja	63 75 63
1999	Andre Agassi	A. Medvedev	16 26 64 63 64
2000	Gustavo Kuerten	M. Norman	62 63 26 76

WOMEN

Prior to 1925, entry was restricted to members of French clubs. Became an Open Championship in 1968, but closed to contract pros in 1972.

First year: 1897. **Most wins:** Chris Evert Lloyd (7); Suzanne Lenglen and Steffi Graf (6).

Multiple winners (since 1925): Chris Evert Lloyd (7); Steffi Graf (6); Margaret Smith Court (5); Helen Wills Moody (4); Arantxa Sanchez Vicario, Monica Seles and Hilde Sperling (3); Maureen Connolly, Margaret Osborne duPont, Doris Hart, Ann Haydon Jones, Suzanne Lenglen, Simone Mathieu, Margaret Scriven, Martina Navratilova and Lesley Turner (2).

Year	Winner	Loser	Score
1925	Suzanne Lenglen	K. McKane	61 62
1926	Suzanne Lenglen	M. Browne	61 60
1927	Kea Bouman	I. Peacock	62 64
1928	Helen Wills	E. Bennett	61 62
1929	Helen Wills	S. Mathieu	63 64
1930	Helen Moody	H. Jacobs	62 61
1931	Cilly Aussem	B. Nuthall	86 61
1932	Helen Moody	S. Mathieu	75 61
1933	Margaret Scriven	S. Mathieu	62 46 64
1934	Margaret Scriven	H. Jacobs	75 46 61
1935	Hilde Sperling	S. Mathieu	62 61
1936	Hilde Sperling	S. Mathieu	63 64
1937	Hilde Sperling	S. Mathieu	62 64
1938	Simone Mathieu	N. Landry	60 63
1939	Simone Mathieu	J. Jedrzejowska	63 86
1940-45	Not held	World War II	
1946	Margaret Osborne	P. Betz	16 86 75
1947	Patricia Todd	D. Hart	63 36 64
1948	Nelly Landry	S. Fry	62 06 60
1949	Margaret duPont	N. Adamson	75 62
1950	Doris Hart	P. Todd	64 46 62
1951	Shirley Fry	D. Hart	63 36 63
1952	Doris Hart	S. Fry	64 64
1953	Maureen Connolly	D. Hart	62 64
1954	Maureen Connolly	G. Bucaille	64 61
1955	Angela Mortimer	D. Knode	26 75 10-8
1956	Althea Gibson	A. Mortimer	60 12-10
1957	Shirley Bloomer	D. Knode	61 63
1958	Susi Kormoczi	S. Bloomer	64 16 62
1959	Christine Truman	S. Kormoczi	64 75
1960	Darlene Hard	Y. Ramirez	63 64
1961	Ann Haydon	Y. Ramirez	62 61
1962	Margaret Smith	L. Turner	63 36 75
1963	Lesley Turner	A. Jones	26 63 75
1964	Margaret Smith	M. Bueno	57 61 62
1965	Lesley Turner	M. Smith	63 64
1966	Ann Jones	N. Richey	63 61
1967	Francoise Durr	L. Turner	46 63 64
1968	Nancy Richey	A. Jones	57 64 61
1969	Margaret Court	A. Jones	61 46 63
1970	Margaret Court	H. Niessen	62 64
1971	Evonne Goolagong	H. Gourlay	63 75
1972	Billie Jean King	E. Goolagong	63 63
1973	Margaret Court	C. Evert	67 76 64
1974	Chris Evert	O. Morozova	61 62
1975	Chris Evert	M. Navratilova	26 62 61
1976	Sue Barker	R. Tomanova	62 06 62
1977	Mima Jausovec	F. Mihai	62 67 61
1978	Virginia Ruzici	M. Jausovec	62 62
1979	Chris Evert Lloyd	W. Turnbull	62 60
1980	Chris Evert Lloyd	V. Ruzici	60 63
1981	Hana Mandlikova	S. Hanika	62 64
1982	Martina Navratilova	A. Jaeger	76 61
1983	Chris Evert Lloyd	M. Jausovec	61 62
1984	Martina Navratilova	C. Evert Lloyd	63 61
1985	Chris Evert Lloyd	M. Navratilova	63 67 75
1986	Chris Evert Lloyd	M. Navratilova	26 63 63
1987	Steffi Graf	M. Navratilova	64 46 86
1988	Steffi Graf	N. Zvereva	60 60
1989	A. Sanchez Vicario	S. Graf	76 36 75
1990	Monica Seles	S. Graf	76 64
1991	Monica Seles	A.S. Vicario	63 64
1992	Monica Seles	S. Graf	62 36 10-8
1993	Steffi Graf	M.J. Fernandez	46 62 64
1994	A. Sanchez Vicario	M. Pierce	64 64
1995	Steffi Graf	A.S. Vicario	76 46 60
1996	Steffi Graf	A.S. Vicario	63 61
1997	Iva Majoli	M. Hingis	64 62
1998	A. Sanchez Vicario	M. Seles	76 06 62
1999	Steffi Graf	M. Hingis	46 75 62
2000	Mary Pierce	C. Martinez	62 75

Wimbledon

MEN

Officially called "The Lawn Tennis Championships" at the All England Club, Wimbledon. Challenge round system (defending champion qualified for following year's final) used from 1877-1921. Became an Open Championship in 1968, but closed to contract pros in 1972.

Surface: Grass.

Multiple winners: Willie Renshaw and Pete Sampras (7); Bjorn Borg and Laurie Doherty (5); Reggie Doherty, Rod Laver and Tony Wilding (4); Wilfred Baddeley, Boris Becker, Arthur Gore, John McEnroe, John Newcombe, Fred Perry and Bill Tilden (3); Jean Borotra, Norman Brookes, Don Budge, Henri Cochet, Jimmy Connors, Stefan Edberg, Roy Emerson, John Hartley, Lew Hoad, Rene Lacoste, Gerald Patterson and Joshua Pim (2).

Year	Winner	Loser	Score	Year	Winner	Loser	Score
1877	Spencer Gore	W. Marshall	61 62 64	1938	Don Budge	H. Austin	61 60 63
1878	Frank Hadow	S. Gore	75 61 97	1939	Bobby Riggs	E. Cooke	26 86 36 63 62
1879	John Hartley	V. St. L. Gould	62 64 62				
1880	John Hartley	H. Lawford	60 62 26 63	1940-45	Not held	World War II	
1881	Willie Renshaw	J. Hartley	60 62 61	1946	Yvon Petra	G. Brown	62 64 79 57 64
1882	Willie Renshaw	E. Renshaw	61 26 46 62 62	1947	Jack Kramer	T. Brown	61 63 62
1883	Willie Renshaw	E. Renshaw	26 63 63 46 63	1948	Bob Falkenburg	J. Bromwich	75 06 62 36 75
1884	Willie Renshaw	H. Lawford	60 64 97	1949	Ted Schroeder	J. Drobny	36 60 63 46 64
1885	Willie Renshaw	H. Lawford	75 62 46 75				
1886	Willie Renshaw	H. Lawford	60 57 63 64	1950	Budge Patty	F. Sedgman	61 8-10 62 63
1887	Herbert Lawford	E. Renshaw	16 63 36 64 64	1951	Dick Savitt	K. McGregor	64 64 64
1888	Ernest Renshaw	H. Lawford	63 75 60	1952	Frank Sedgman	J. Drobny	46 62 63 62
1889	Willie Renshaw	E. Renshaw	64 61 36 60	1953	Vic Seixas	K. Nielsen	97 63 64
				1954	Jaroslav Drobny	K. Rosewall	13-11 46 62 97
1890	William Hamilton	W. Renshaw	68 62 36 61 61	1955	Tony Trabert	K. Nielsen	63 75 61
1891	Wilfred Baddeley	J. Pim	64 16 75 60	1956	Lew Hoad	K. Rosewall	62 46 75 64
1892	Wilfred Baddeley	J. Pim	46 63 63 62	1957	Lew Hoad	A. Cooper	62 61 62
1893	Joshua Pim	W. Baddeley	36 61 63 62	1958	Ashley Cooper	N. Fraser	36 63 64 13-11
1894	Joshua Pim	W. Baddeley	10-8 62 86	1959	Alex Olmedo	R. Laver	64 63 64
1895	Wilfred Baddeley	W. Eaves	46 26 86 62 63				
1896	Harold Mahony	W. Baddeley	62 68 57 86 63	1960	Neale Fraser	R. Laver	64 36 97 75
1897	Reggie Doherty	H. Mahony	64 64 63	1961	Rod Laver	C. McKinley	63 61 64
1898	Reggie Doherty	L. Doherty	63 63 26 57 61	1962	Rod Laver	M. Mulligan	62 62 61
1899	Reggie Doherty	A. Gore	16 46 62 63 63	1963	Chuck McKinley	F. Stolle	97 61 64
				1964	Roy Emerson	F. Stolle	64 12-10 46 63
1900	Reggie Doherty	S. Smith	68 63 61 62	1965	Roy Emerson	F. Stolle	62 64 64
1901	Arthur Gore	R. Doherty	46 75 64 64	1966	Manuel Santana	D. Ralston	64 11-9 64
1902	Laurie Doherty	A. Gore	64 63 36 60	1967	John Newcombe	W. Bungert	63 61 61
1903	Laurie Doherty	F. Riseley	75 63 60	1968	Rod Laver	T. Roche	63 64 62
1904	Laurie Doherty	F. Riseley	61 75 86	1969	Rod Laver	J. Newcombe	64 57 64 64
1905	Laurie Doherty	N. Brookes	86 62 64				
1906	Laurie Doherty	F. Riseley	64 46 62 63	1970	John Newcombe	K. Rosewall	57 63 62 36 61
1907	Norman Brookes	A. Gore	64 62 62	1971	John Newcombe	S. Smith	63 57 26 64 64
1908	Arthur Gore	R. Barrett	63 62 46 36 64	1972	Stan Smith	I. Nastase	46 63 63 46 75
1909	Arthur Gore	M. Ritchie	68 16 62 62 62	1973	Jan Kodes	A. Metreveli	61 98 63
				1974	Jimmy Connors	K. Rosewall	61 61 64
1910	Tony Wilding	A. Gore	64 75 46 62	1975	Arthur Ashe	J. Connors	61 61 57 64
1911	Tony Wilding	R. Barrett	64 46 26 62 (ret)	1976	Bjorn Borg	I. Nastase	64 62 97
1912	Tony Wilding	A. Gore	64 64 46 64	1977	Bjorn Borg	J. Connors	36 62 61 57 64
1913	Tony Wilding	M. McLoughlin	86 63 10-8	1978	Bjorn Borg	J. Connors	62 62 63
1914	Norman Brookes	T. Wilding	64 64 75	1979	Bjorn Borg	R. Tanner	67 61 36 63 64
1915-18	Not held	World War I					
1919	Gerald Patterson	N. Brookes	63 75 62	1980	Bjorn Borg	J. McEnroe	16 75 63 67 86
				1981	John McEnroe	B. Borg	46 76 76 64
1920	Bill Tilden	G. Patterson	26 63 62 64	1982	Jimmy Connors	J. McEnroe	36 63 67 76 64
1921	Bill Tilden	B. Norton	46 26 61 60 75	1983	John McEnroe	C. Lewis	62 62 62
1922	Gerald Patterson	R. Lycett	63 64 62	1984	John McEnroe	J. Connors	61 61 62
1923	Bill Johnston	F. Hunter	60 63 61	1985	Boris Becker	K. Curren	63 67 76 64
1924	Jean Borotra	R. Lacoste	61 36 61 36 64	1986	Boris Becker	I. Lendl	64 63 75
1925	Rene Lacoste	J. Borotra	63 63 46 86	1987	Pat Cash	I. Lendl	76 62 75
1926	Jean Borotra	H. Kinsey	86 61 63	1988	Stefan Edberg	B. Becker	46 76 64 62
1927	Henri Cochet	J. Borotra	46 46 63 64 75	1989	Boris Becker	S. Edberg	60 76 64
1928	Rene Lacoste	H. Cochet	61 46 64 62				
1929	Henri Cochet	J. Borotra	64 63 64	1990	Stefan Edberg	B. Becker	62 62 36 36 64
				1991	Michael Stich	B. Becker	64 76 64
1930	Bill Tilden	W. Allison	63 97 64	1992	Andre Agassi	G. Ivanisevic	67 64 64 16 64
1931	Sidney Wood	F. Shields	walkover	1993	Pete Sampras	J. Courier	76 76 36 63
1932	Ellsworth Vines	H. Austin	64 62 60	1994	Pete Sampras	G. Ivanisevic	76 76 60
1933	Jack Crawford	E. Vines	46 11-9 62 26 64	1995	Pete Sampras	B. Becker	67 62 64 62
1934	Fred Perry	J. Crawford	63 60 75	1996	Richard Krajicek	M. Washington	63 64 63
1935	Fred Perry	G. von Cramm	62 64 64	1997	Pete Sampras	C. Pioline	64 62 64
1936	Fred Perry	G. von Cramm	61 61 60	1998	Pete Sampras	G. Ivanisevic	67 76 64 36 62
1937	Don Budge	G. von Cramm	63 64 62	1999	Pete Sampras	A. Agassi	63 64 75
				2000	Pete Sampras	P. Rafter	67 76 64 62

WOMEN

Officially called "The Lawn Tennis Championships" at the All England Club, Wimbledon. Challenge round system (defending champion qualified for following year's final) used from 1877-1921. Became an Open Championship in 1968, but closed to contract pros in 1972.

Multiple winners: Martina Navratilova (9); Helen Wills Moody (8); Dorothea Douglass Chambers and Steffi Graf (7); Blanche Bingley Hillyard, Billie Jean King and Suzanne Lenglen (6); Lottie Dod and Charlotte Cooper Sterry (5); Louise Brough (4); Maria Bueno, Maureen Connolly, Margaret Smith Court and Chris Evert Lloyd (3); Evonne Goolagong Cawley, Althea Gibson, Dorothy Round, May Sutton and Maud Watson (2).

Year	Winner	Loser	Score	Year	Winner	Loser	Score
1884	Maud Watson	L. Watson	68 63 63	1948	Louise Brough	D. Hart	63 86
1885	Maud Watson	B. Bingley	61 75	1949	Louise Brough	M. duPont	10-8 16 10-8
1886	Blanche Bingley	M. Watson	63 63	1950	Louise Brough	M. duPont	61 36 61
1887	Lottie Dod	B. Bingley	62 60	1951	Doris Hart	S. Fry	61 60
1888	Lottie Dod	B. Hillyard	63 63	1952	Maureen Connolly	L. Brough	75 63
1889	Blanche Hillyard	L. Rice	46 86 64	1953	Maureen Connolly	D. Hart	86 75
1890	Lena Rice	M. Jacks	64 61	1954	Maureen Connolly	L. Brough	62 75
1891	Lottie Dod	B. Hillyard	62 61	1955	Louise Brough	B. Fleitz	75 86
1892	Lottie Dod	B. Hillyard	61 61	1956	Shirley Fry	A. Buxton	63 61
1893	Lottie Dod	B. Hillyard	68 61 64	1957	Althea Gibson	D. Hard	63 62
1894	Blanche Hillyard	E. Austin	61 61	1958	Althea Gibson	A. Mortimer	86 62
1895	Charlotte Cooper	H. Jackson	75 86	1959	Maria Bueno	D. Hard	64 63
1896	Charlotte Cooper	W. Pickering	62 63	1960	Maria Bueno	S. Reynolds	86 60
1897	Blanche Hillyard	C. Cooper	57 75 62	1961	Angela Mortimer	C. Truman	46 64 75
1898	Charlotte Cooper	L. Martin	64 64	1962	Karen Susman	V. Sukova	64 64
1899	Blanche Hillyard	C. Cooper	62 63	1963	Margaret Smith	B.J. Moffitt	63 64
1900	Blanche Hillyard	C. Cooper	46 64 64	1964	Maria Bueno	M. Smith	64 79 63
1901	Charlotte Sterry	B. Hillyard	62 62	1965	Margaret Smith	M. Bueno	64 75
1902	Muriel Robb	C. Sterry	75 61	1966	Billie Jean King	M. Bueno	63 36 61
1903	Dorothea Douglass	E. Thomson	46 64 62	1967	Billie Jean King	A. Jones	63 64
1904	Dorothea Douglass	C. Sterry	60 63	1968	Billie Jean King	J. Tegart	97 75
1905	May Sutton	D. Douglass	63 64	1969	Ann Jones	B.J. King	36 63 62
1906	Dorothea Douglass	M. Sutton	63 97	1970	Margaret Court	B.J. King	14-12 11-9
1907	May Sutton	D. Chambers	61 64	1971	Evonne Goolagong	M. Court	64 61
1908	Charlotte Sterry	A. Morton	64 64	1972	Billie Jean King	E. Goolagong	63 63
1909	Dora Boothby	A. Morton	64 46 86	1973	Billie Jean King	C. Evert	60 75
1910	Dorothea Chambers	D. Boothby	62 62	1974	Chris Evert	O. Morozova	60 64
1911	Dorothea Chambers	D. Boothby	60 60	1975	Billie Jean King	E. Cawley	60 61
1912	Ethel Larcombe	C. Sterry	63 61	1976	Chris Evert	E. Cawley	63 46 86
1913	Dorothea Chambers	R. McNair	60 64	1977	Virginia Wade	B. Stove	46 63 61
1914	Dorothea Chambers	E. Larcombe	75 64	1978	Martina Navratilova	C. Evert	26 64 75
1915-18	Not held	World War I		1979	Martina Navratilova	C. Evert Lloyd	64 64
1919	Suzanne Lenglen	D. Chambers	10-8 46 97	1980	Evonne Cawley	C. Evert Lloyd	61 76
1920	Suzanne Lenglen	D. Chambers	63 60	1981	Chris Evert Lloyd	H. Mandlikova	62 62
1921	Suzanne Lenglen	E. Ryan	62 60	1982	Martina Navratilova	C. Evert Lloyd	61 36 62
1922	Suzanne Lenglen	M. Mallory	62 60	1983	Martina Navratilova	A. Jaeger	60 63
1923	Suzanne Lenglen	K. McKane	62 62	1984	Martina Navratilova	C. Evert Lloyd	76 62
1924	Kathleen McKane	H. Wills	46 64 64	1985	Martina Navratilova	C. Evert Lloyd	46 63 62
1925	Suzanne Lenglen	J. Fry	62 60	1986	Martina Navratilova	H. Mandlikova	76 63
1926	Kathleen Godfree	L. de Alvarez	62 46 63	1987	Martina Navratilova	S. Graf	75 63
1927	Helen Wills	L. de Alvarez	62 64	1988	Steffi Graf	M. Navratilova	57 62 61
1928	Helen Wills	L. de Alvarez	62 63	1989	Steffi Graf	M. Navratilova	62 67 61
1929	Helen Wills	H. Jacobs	61 62	1990	Martina Navratilova	Z. Garrison	64 61
1930	Helen Moody	E. Ryan	62 62	1991	Steffi Graf	G. Sabatini	64 36 86
1931	Cilly Aussem	H. Kranwinkel	62 75	1992	Steffi Graf	M. Seles	62 61
1932	Helen Moody	H. Jacobs	63 61	1993	Steffi Graf	J. Novotna	76 16 64
1933	Helen Moody	D. Round	64 68 63	1994	Conchita Martinez	M. Navratilova	64 36 63
1934	Dorothy Round	H. Jacobs	62 57 63	1995	Steffi Graf	A.S. Vicario	46 61 75
1935	Helen Moody	H. Jacobs	63 36 75	1996	Steffi Graf	A.S. Vicario	63 75
1936	Helen Jacobs	H.K. Sperling	62 46 75	1997	Martina Hingis	J. Novotna	26 63 63
1937	Dorothy Round	J. Jedrzejowska	62 26 75	1998	Jana Novotna	N. Tauziat	64 76
1938	Helen Moody	H. Jacobs	64 60	1999	Lindsay Davenport	S. Graf	64 75
1939	Alice Marble	K. Stammers	62 60	2000	Venus Williams	L. Davenport	63 76
1940-45	Not held	World War II					
1946	Pauline Betz	L. Brough	62 64				
1947	Margaret Osborne	D. Hart	62 64				

U.S. Open

MEN

Challenge round system (defending champion qualified for following year's final) used from 1884-1911. Known as the Patriotic Tournament in 1917 during World War I. Amateur and Open Championships held in 1968 and '69. Became an exclusively Open Championship in 1970.

Surface: Decoturf II (acrylic cement).

Multiple winners: Bill Larned, Richard Sears and Bill Tilden (7); Jimmy Connors (5); John McEnroe, Pete Sampras and Robert Wrenn (4); Oliver Campbell, Ivan Lendl, Fred Perry and Malcolm Whitman (3); Don Budge, Stefan Edberg, Roy Emerson, Neale Fraser, Pancho Gonzales, Bill Johnston, Jack Kramer, Rene Lacoste, Rod Laver, Maurice McLoughlin, Lindley Murray, John Newcombe, Frank Parker, Patrick Rafter, Bobby Riggs, Ken Rosewall, Frank Sedgman, Henry Slocum Jr., Tony Trabert, Ellsworth Vines and Dick Williams (2).

Year	Winner	Loser	Score	Year	Winner	Loser	Score
1881	Richard Sears	W. Glyn	60 63 62	1942	Fred Schroeder	F. Parker	86 75 36 46 62
1882	Richard Sears	C. Clark	61 64 60	1943	Joe Hunt	J. Kramer	63 68 10-8 60
1883	Richard Sears	J. Dwight	62 60 97	1944	Frank Parker	B. Talbert	64 36 63 63
1884	Richard Sears	H. Taylor	60 16 60 62	1945	Frank Parker	B. Talbert	14-12 61 62
1885	Richard Sears	G. Brinley	63 46 60 63	1946	Jack Kramer	T. Brown, Jr.	97 63 60
1886	Richard Sears	R. Beeckman	46 61 63 64	1947	Jack Kramer	F. Parker	46 26 61 60 63
1887	Richard Sears	H. Slocum Jr.	61 63 62	1948	Pancho Gonzales	E. Sturgess	62 63 14-12
1888	Henry Slocum Jr.	H. Taylor	64 61 60	1949	Pancho Gonzales	F. Schroeder	16-18 26 61 62 64
1889	Henry Slocum Jr.	Q. Shaw	63 61 46 62	1950	Arthur Larsen	H. Flam	63 46 57 64 63
1890	Oliver Campbell	H. Slocum Jr.	62 46 63 61	1951	Frank Sedgman	V. Seixas	64 61 61
1891	Oliver Campbell	C. Hobart	26 75 79 61 62	1952	Frank Sedgman	G. Mulloy	61 62 63
1892	Oliver Campbell	F. Hovey	75 36 63 75	1953	Tony Trabert	V. Seixas	63 62 63
1893	Robert Wrenn	F. Hovey	64 36 64 64	1954	Vic Seixas	R. Hartwig	36 62 64 64
1894	Robert Wrenn	M. Goodbody	68 61 64 64	1955	Tony Trabert	K. Rosewall	97 63 63
1895	Fred Hovey	R. Wrenn	63 62 64	1956	Ken Rosewall	L. Hoad	46 62 63 63
1896	Robert Wrenn	F. Hovey	75 36 60 16 61	1957	Mal Anderson	A. Cooper	10-8 75 64
1897	Robert Wrenn	W. Eaves	46 86 63 26 62	1958	Ashley Cooper	M. Anderson	62 36 46 10-8 86
1898	Malcolm Whitman	D. Davis	36 62 62 61	1959	Neale Fraser	A. Olmedo	63 57 62 64
1899	Malcolm Whitman	P. Paret	61 62 36 75	1960	Neale Fraser	R. Laver	64 64 97
1900	Malcolm Whitman	B. Larned	64 16 62 62	1961	Roy Emerson	R. Laver	75 63 62
1901	Bill Larned	B. Wright	62 68 64 64	1962	Rod Laver	R. Emerson	62 64 57 64
1902	Bill Larned	R. Doherty	46 62 64 86	1963	Rafael Osuna	F. Froehling	75 64 62
1903	Laurie Doherty	B. Larned	60 63 10-8	1964	Roy Emerson	F. Stolle	64 62 64
1904	Holcombe Ward	B. Clothier	10-8 64 97	1965	Manuel Santana	C. Drysdale	62 79 75 61
1905	Beals Wright	H. Ward	62 61 11-9	1966	Fred Stolle	J. Newcombe	46 12-10 63 64
1906	Bill Clothier	B. Wright	63 60 64	1967	John Newcombe	C. Graebner	64 64 86
1907	Bill Larned	R. LeRoy	62 62 64	1968	Am-Arthur Ashe	B. Lutz	46 63 8-10 60 64
1908	Bill Larned	B. Wright	61 62 86		Op-Arthur Ashe	T. Okker	14-12 57 63 36 63
1909	Bill Larned	B. Clothier	61 62 57 16 61	1969	Am-Stan Smith	B. Lutz	97 63 61
1910	Bill Larned	T. Bundy	61 57 60 68 61		Op-Rod Laver	T. Roche	79 61 63 62
1911	Bill Larned	M. McLoughlin	64 64 62	1970	Ken Rosewall	T. Roche	26 64 76 63
1912	Maurice McLoughlin	W.F. Johnson	36 26 62 64 62	1971	Stan Smith	J. Kodes	36 63 62 76
1913	Maurice McLoughlin	R. Williams	64 57 63 61	1972	Ilie Nastase	A. Ashe	36 63 67 64 63
1914	Dick Williams	M. McLoughlin	63 86 10-8	1973	John Newcombe	J. Kodes	64 16 46 62 63
1915	Bill Johnston	M. McLoughlin	16 60 75 10-8	1974	Jimmy Connors	K. Rosewall	61 60 61
1916	Dick Williams	B. Johnston	46 64 06 62 64	1975	Manuel Orantes	J. Connors	64 63 63
1917	Lindley Murray	N. Niles	57 86 63 63	1976	Jimmy Connors	B. Borg	64 36 76 64
1918	Lindley Murray	B. Tilden	63 61 75	1977	Guillermo Vilas	J. Connors	26 63 76 60
1919	Bill Johnston	B. Tilden	64 64 63	1978	Jimmy Connors	B. Borg	64 62 62
1920	Bill Tilden	B. Johnston	61 16 75 57 63	1979	John McEnroe	V. Gerulaitis	75 63 63
1921	Bill Tilden	W. Johnson	61 63 61	1980	John McEnroe	B. Borg	76 61 67 57 64
1922	Bill Tilden	B. Johnston	46 36 62 63 64	1981	John McEnroe	B. Borg	46 62 64 63
1923	Bill Tilden	B. Johnston	64 61 64	1982	Jimmy Connors	I. Lendl	63 62 46 64
1924	Bill Tilden	B. Johnston	61 97 62	1983	Jimmy Connors	I. Lendl	63 67 75 60
1925	Bill Tilden	B. Johnston	46 11-9 63 46 63	1984	John McEnroe	I. Lendl	63 64 61
1926	Rene Lacoste	J. Borotra	64 60 64	1985	Ivan Lendl	J. McEnroe	76 63 64
1927	Rene Lacoste	B. Tilden	11-9 63 11-9	1986	Ivan Lendl	M. Mecir	64 62 60
1928	Henri Cochet	F. Hunter	46 64 36 75 63	1987	Ivan Lendl	M. Wilander	67 60 76 64
1929	Bill Tilden	F. Hunter	36 63 46 62 64	1988	Mats Wilander	I. Lendl	64 46 63 57 64
1930	John Doeg	F. Shields	10-8 16 64 16-14	1989	Boris Becker	I. Lendl	76 16 63 76
1931	Ellsworth Vines	G. Lott Jr.	79 63 97 75	1990	Pete Sampras	A. Agassi	64 63 62
1932	Ellsworth Vines	H. Cochet	64 64 64	1991	Stefan Edberg	J. Courier	62 64 60
1933	Fred Perry	J. Crawford	63 11-13 46 60 61	1992	Stefan Edberg	P. Sampras	36 64 76 62
1934	Fred Perry	W. Allison	64 63 16 86	1993	Pete Sampras	C. Pioline	64 64 63
1935	Wilmer Allison	S. Wood	62 62 63	1994	Andre Agassi	M. Stich	61 76 75
1936	Fred Perry	D. Budge	26 62 86 16 10	1995	Pete Sampras	A. Agassi	64 63 46 75
1937	Don Budge	G. von Cramm	61 79 61 36 61	1996	Pete Sampras	M. Chang	61 64 76
1938	Don Budge	G. Mako	63 68 62 61	1997	Patrick Rafter	G. Rusedski	63 62 46 75
1939	Bobby Riggs	S.W. van Horn	64 62 64	1998	Patrick Rafter	M. Philippoussis	63 36 62 60
1940	Don McNeill	B. Riggs	46 68 63 63 75	1999	Andre Agassi	T. Martin	64 67 67 63 62
1941	Bobby Riggs	F. Kovacs	57 61 63 63	2000	Marat Safin	P. Sampras	64 63 63

WOMEN

Challenge round system used from 1887-1918. Five set final played from 1887-1901. Amateur and Open Championships held in 1968 and '69. Became an exclusively Open Championship in 1970.

Multiple winners: Molla Mallory Bjurstedt (8); Helen Wills Moody (7); Chris Evert Lloyd (6); Margaret Smith Court and Steffi Graf (5); Pauline Betz, Mario Bueno, Helen Jacobs, Billie Jean King, Alice Marble, Elisabeth Moore, Martina Navratilova and Hazel Hotchkiss Wightman (4); Juliette Atkinson, Mary Browne, Maureen Connolly and Margaret Osborne duPont (3); Tracy Austin, Mabel Cahill, Sarah Palfrey Cooke, Darlene Hard, Doris Hart, Althea Gibson, Monica Seles and Bertha Townsend (2).

Year	Winner	Loser	Score
1887	Ellen Hansell	L. Knight	61 60
1888	Bertha Townsend	E. Hansell	63 65
1889	Bertha Townsend	L. Voorhes	75 62
1890	Ellen Roosevelt	B. Townsend	62 62
1891	Mabel Cahill	E. Roosevelt	64 61 46 63
1892	Mabel Cahill	E. Moore	57 63 64 46 62
1893	Aline Terry	A. Schultz	61 63
1894	Helen Hellwig	A. Terry	75 36 60 36 63
1895	Juliette Atkinson	H. Hellwig	64 62 61
1896	Elisabeth Moore	J. Atkinson	64 46 62 62
1897	Juliette Atkinson	E. Moore	63 63 46 36 63
1898	Juliette Atkinson	M. Jones	63 57 64 26 75
1899	Marion Jones	M. Banks	61 61 75
1900	Myrtle McAteer	E. Parker	62 62 60
1901	Elizabeth Moore	M. McAteer	64 36 75 26 62
1902	Marion Jones	E. Moore	61 10(ret)
1903	Elizabeth Moore	M. Jones	75 86
1904	May Sutton	E. Moore	61 62
1905	Elizabeth Moore	H. Homans	64 57 61
1906	Helen Homans	M. Barger-Wallach	64 63
1907	Evelyn Sears	C. Neely	63 62
1908	Maud B. Wallach	Ev. Sears	63 16 63
1909	Hazel Hotchkiss	M. Wallach	60 61
1910	Hazel Hotchkiss	L. Hammond	64 62
1911	Hazel Hotchkiss	F. Sutton	8-10 61 97
1912	Mary Browne	E. Sears	64 62
1913	Mary Browne	D. Green	62 75
1914	Mary Browne	M. Wagner	62 16 61
1915	Molla Bjurstedt	H. Wightman	46 62 60
1916	Molla Bjurstedt	L. Raymond	60 61
1917	Molla Bjurstedt	M. Vanderhoef	46 60 62
1918	Molla Bjurstedt	E. Goss	64 63
1919	Hazel Wightman	M. Zinderstein	61 62
1920	Molla Mallory	M. Zinderstein	63 61
1921	Molla Mallory	M. Browne	46 64 62
1922	Molla Mallory	H. Wills	63 61
1923	Helen Wills	M. Mallory	62 61
1924	Helen Wills	M. Mallory	61 63
1925	Helen Wills	K. McKane	36 60 62
1926	Molla Mallory	E. Ryan	46 64 97
1927	Helen Wills	B. Nuthall	61 64
1928	Helen Wills	H. Jacobs	62 61
1929	Helen Wills	P. Watson	64 62
1930	Betty Nuthall	A. Harper	61 64
1931	Helen Moody	E. Whitingstall	64 61
1932	Helen Jacobs	C. Babcock	62 62
1933	Helen Jacobs	H. Moody	86 36 30(ret)
1934	Helen Jacobs	S. Palfrey	61 64
1935	Helen Jacobs	S. Fabyan	62 64
1936	Alice Marble	H. Jacobs	46 63 62
1937	Anita Lizana	J. Jedrzejowska	64 62
1938	Alice Marble	N. Wynne	60 63
1939	Alice Marble	H. Jacobs	60 8-10 64
1940	Alice Marble	H. Jacobs	62 63
1941	Sarah Cooke	P. Betz	75 62
1942	Pauline Betz	L. Brough	46 61 64
1943	Pauline Betz	L. Brough	63 57 63
1944	Pauline Betz	M. Osborne	63 86
1945	Sarah Cooke	P. Betz	36 86 64

Year	Winner	Loser	Score
1946	Pauline Betz	P. Canning	11-9 63
1947	Louise Brough	M. Osborne	86 46 61
1948	Margaret duPont	L. Brough	46 64 15-13
1949	Margaret duPont	D. Hart	64 61
1950	Margaret duPont	D. Hart	64 63
1951	Maureen Connolly	S. Fry	63 16 64
1952	Maureen Connolly	D. Hart	63 75
1953	Maureen Connolly	D. Hart	62 64
1954	Doris Hart	L. Brough	68 61 86
1955	Doris Hart	P. Ward	64 62
1956	Shirley Fry	A. Gibson	63 64
1957	Althea Gibson	L. Brough	63 62
1958	Althea Gibson	D. Hard	36 61 62
1959	Maria Bueno	C. Truman	61 64
1960	Darlene Hard	M. Bueno	64 10-12 64
1961	Darlene Hard	A. Haydon	63 64
1962	Margaret Smith	D. Hard	97 64
1963	Maria Bueno	M. Smith	75 64
1964	Maria Bueno	C. Graebner	61 60
1965	Margaret Smith	B.J. Moffitt	86 75
1966	Maria Bueno	N. Richey	63 61
1967	Billie Jean King	A. Jones	11-9 64
1968	Am-Margaret Court	B.J. King	62 62
	Op-Virginia Wade	B.J. King	64 62
1969	Am-Margaret Court	V. Wade	46 63 60
	Op-Margaret Court	N. Richey	62 62
1970	Margaret Court	R. Casals	62 26 61
1971	Billie Jean King	R. Casals	64 76
1972	Billie Jean King	K. Melville	63 75
1973	Margaret Court	E. Goolagong	76 57 62
1974	Billie Jean King	E. Goolagong	36 63 75
1975	Chris Evert	E. Cawley	57 64 62
1976	Chris Evert	E. Cawley	63 60
1977	Chris Evert	W. Turnbull	76 62
1978	Chris Evert	P. Shriver	75 64
1979	Tracy Austin	C. Evert Lloyd	64 63
1980	Chris Evert Lloyd	H. Mandlikova	57 61 61
1981	Tracy Austin	M. Navratilova	16 76 76
1982	Chris Evert Lloyd	H. Mandlikova	63 61
1983	Martina Navratilova	C. Evert Lloyd	61 63
1984	Martina Navratilova	C. Evert Lloyd	46 64 64
1985	Hana Mandlikova	M. Navratilova	76 16 76
1986	Martina Navratilova	H. Sukova	63 62
1987	Martina Navratilova	S. Graf	76 61
1988	Steffi Graf	G. Sabatini	63 36 61
1989	Steffi Graf	M. Navratilova	36 75 61
1990	Gabriela Sabatini	S. Graf	62 76
1991	Monica Seles	M. Navratilova	76 61
1992	Monica Seles	A.S. Vicario	63 63
1993	Steffi Graf	H. Sukova	63 63
1994	A. Sanchez Vicario	S. Graf	16 76 64
1995	Steffi Graf	M. Seles	76 06 63
1996	Steffi Graf	M. Seles	75 64
1997	Martina Hingis	V. Williams	60 64
1998	Lindsay Davenport	M. Hingis	63 75
1999	Serena Williams	M. Hingis	63 76
2000	Venus Williams	L. Davenport	64 75

Grand Slam Summary

Singles winners of the four Grand Slam tournaments–Australian, French, Wimbledon and United States–since the French was opened to all comers in 1925. Note that there were two Australian Opens in 1977 and none in 1986.

MEN

Three wins in one year: Jack Crawford (1933); Fred Perry (1934); Tony Trabert (1955); Lew Hoad (1956); Ashley Cooper (1958); Roy Emerson (1964); Jimmy Connors (1974); Mats Wilander (1988).

Two wins in one year: Roy Emerson and Pete Sampras (4 times); Bjorn Borg (3 times); Rene Lacoste, Ivan Lendl, John Newcombe and Fred Perry (twice); Andre Agassi, Boris Becker, Don Budge, Henri Cochet, Jimmy Connors, Jim Courier, Neale Fraser, Jack Kramer, John McEnroe, Alex Olmedo, Budge Patty, Bobby Riggs, Ken Rosewall, Dick Savitt, Frank Sedgman and Guillermo Vilas (once).

Year	Australian	French	Wimbledon	U.S.	Year	Australian	French	Wimbledon	U.S.
1925	Anderson	Lacoste	Lacoste	Tilden	1964	Emerson	Santana	Emerson	Emerson
1926	Hawkes	Cochet	Borotra	Lacoste	1965	Emerson	Stolle	Emerson	Santana
1927	Patterson	Lacoste	Cochet	Lacoste	1966	Emerson	Roche	Santana	Stolle
1928	Borotra	Cochet	Lacoste	Cochet	1967	Emerson	Emerson	Newcombe	Newcombe
1929	Gregory	Lacoste	Cochet	Tilden	1968	Bowrey	Rosewall	Laver	Ashe
					1969	**Laver**	**Laver**	**Laver**	**Laver**
1930	Moon	Cochet	Tilden	Doeg	1970	Ashe	Kodes	Newcombe	Rosewall
1931	Crawford	Borotra	Wood	Vines	1971	Rosewall	Kodes	Newcombe	Smith
1932	Crawford	Cochet	Vines	Vines	1972	Rosewall	Gimeno	Smith	Nastase
1933	Crawford	Crawford	Crawford	Perry	1973	Newcombe	Nastase	Kodes	Newcombe
1934	Perry	von Cramm	Perry	Perry	1974	Connors	Borg	Connors	Connors
1935	Crawford	Perry	Perry	Allison	1975	Newcombe	Borg	Ashe	Orantes
1936	Quist	von Cramm	Perry	Perry	1976	Edmondson	Panatta	Borg	Connors
1937	McGrath	Henkel	Budge	Budge	1977	Tanner	Vilas	Borg	Vilas
1938	**Budge**	**Budge**	**Budge**	**Budge**		& Gerulaitis			
1939	Bromwich	McNeill	Riggs	Riggs	1978	Vilas	Borg	Borg	Connors
					1979	Vilas	Borg	Borg	McEnroe
1940	Quist	—	—	McNeill	1980	Teacher	Borg	Borg	McEnroe
1941	—	—	—	Riggs	1981	Kriek	Borg	McEnroe	McEnroe
1942	—	—	—	Schroeder	1982	Kriek	Wilander	Connors	Connors
1943	—	—	—	Hunt	1983	Wilander	Noah	McEnroe	Connors
1944	—	—	—	Parker	1984	Wilander	Lendl	McEnroe	McEnroe
1945	—	—	-	Parker	1985	Edberg	Wilander	Becker	Lendl
1946	Bromwich	Bernard	Petra	Kramer	1986	–	Lendl	Becker	Lendl
1947	Pails	Asboth	Kramer	Kramer	1987	Edberg	Lendl	Cash	Lendl
1948	Quist	Parker	Falkenburg	Gonzales	1988	Wilander	Wilander	Edberg	Wilander
1949	Sedgman	Parker	Schroeder	Gonzales	1989	Lendl	Chang	Becker	Becker
1950	Sedgman	Patty	Patty	Larsen	1990	Lendl	Gomez	Edberg	Sampras
1951	Savitt	Drobny	Savitt	Sedgman	1991	Becker	Courier	Stich	Edberg
1952	McGregor	Drobny	Sedgman	Sedgman	1992	Courier	Courier	Agassi	Edberg
1953	Rosewall	Rosewall	Seixas	Trabert	1993	Courier	Bruguera	Sampras	Sampras
1954	Rose	Trabert	Drobny	Seixas	1994	Sampras	Bruguera	Sampras	Agassi
1955	Rosewall	Trabert	Trabert	Trabert	1995	Agassi	Muster	Sampras	Sampras
1956	Hoad	Hoad	Hoad	Rosewall	1996	Becker	Kafelnikov	Krajicek	Sampras
1957	Cooper	Davidson	Hoad	Anderson	1997	Sampras	Kuerten	Sampras	Rafter
1958	Cooper	Rose	Cooper	Cooper	1998	Korda	Moya	Sampras	Rafter
1959	Olmedo	Pietrangeli	Olmedo	Fraser	1999	Kafelnikov	Agassi	Sampras	Agassi
1960	Laver	Pietrangeli	Fraser	Fraser	2000	Agassi	Kuerten	Sampras	Safin
1961	Emerson	Santana	Laver	Emerson					
1962	**Laver**	**Laver**	**Laver**	**Laver**					
1963	Emerson	Emerson	McKinley	Osuna					

WOMEN

Three in one year: Helen Wills Moody (1928 and '29); Margaret Smith Court (1962, '65, '69 and '73); Billie Jean King (1972); Martina Navratilova (1983 and '84); Steffi Graf (1989, '93, '95 and '96); Monica Seles (1991 and '92); and Martina Hingis (1997).

Two in one year: Chris Evert Lloyd (5 times); Helen Wills Moody and Martina Navratilova (3 times); Maria Bueno, Maureen Connolly, Margaraet Smith Court, Althea Gibson, Billie Jean King (twice); Cilly Aussem, Pauleen Betz, Louise Brough, Evonne Goolagong Cawley, Shirley Fry, Darlene Hard, Margaret Osborne duPont, Suzanne Lenglen, Alice Marble, Arantxa Sanchez Vicario and Venus Williams (once).

Year	Australian	French	Wimbledon	U.S.	Year	Australian	French	Wimbledon	U.S.
1925	Akhurst	Lenglen	Lenglen	Wills	1937	Bolton	Sperling	Round	Lizana
1926	Akhurst	Lenglen	Godfree	Mallory	1938	Bundy	Mathieu	Moody	Marble
1927	Boyd	Bouman	Wills	Wills	1939	Westacott	Mathieu	Marble	Marble
1928	Akhurst	Wills	Wills	Wills	1940	Bolton	—	—	Marble
1929	Akhurst	Wills	Wills	Wills	1941	—	—	—	Cooke
1930	Akhurst	Moody	Moody	Nuthall	1942	—	—	—	Betz
1931	Buttsworth	Aussem	Aussem	Moody	1943	—	—	—	Betz
1932	Buttsworth	Moody	Moody	Jacobs	1944	—	—	—	Betz
1933	Hartigan	Scriven	Moody	Jacobs	1945	—	—	—	Cooke
1934	Hartigan	Scriven	Round	Jacobs	1946	Bolton	Osborne	Betz	Betz
1935	Round	Sperling	Moody	Jacobs	1947	Bolton	Todd	Osborne	Brough
1936	Hartigan	Sperling	Jacobs	Marble	1948	Bolton	Landry	Brough	du Pont

Year	Australian	French	Wimbledon	U.S.
1949	Hart	du Pont	Brough	du Pont
1950	Brough	Hart	Brough	du Pont
1951	Bolton	Fry	Hart	Connolly
1952	Long	Hart	Connolly	Connolly
1953	**Connolly**	**Connolly**	**Connolly**	**Connolly**
1954	Long	Connolly	Connolly	Hart
1955	Penrose	Mortimer	Brough	Hart
1956	Carter	Gibson	Fry	Fry
1957	Fry	Bloomer	Gibson	Gibson
1958	Mortimer	Kormoczi	Gibson	Gibson
1959	Reitano	Truman	Bueno	Bueno
1960	Smith	Hard	Bueno	Hard
1961	Smith	Haydon	Mortimer	Hard
1962	Smith	Smith	Susman	Smith
1963	Smith	Turner	Smith	Bueno
1964	Smith	Smith	Bueno	Bueno
1965	Smith	Turner	Smith	Smith
1966	Smith	Jones	King	Bueno
1967	Richey	Durr	King	King
1968	King	Richey	King	Wade
1969	Court	Court	Jones	Court
1970	**Court**	**Court**	**Court**	**Court**
1971	Court	Goolagong	Goolagong	King
1972	Wade	King	King	King
1973	Court	Court	King	Court
1974	Goolagong	Evert	Evert	King
1975	Goolagong	Evert	King	Evert

Year	Australian	French	Wimbledon	U.S.
1976	Cawley	Barker	Evert	Evert
1977	Reid & Cawley	Jausovec	Wade	Evert
1978	O'Neil	Ruzici	Navratilova	Evert
1979	Jordan	Evert Lloyd	Navratilova	Austin
1980	Mandlikova	Evert Lloyd	Cawley	Evert Lloyd
1981	Navratilova	Mandlikova	Evert Lloyd	Austin
1982	Evert Lloyd	Navratilova	Navratilova	Evert Lloyd
1983	Navratilova	Evert Lloyd	Navratilova	Navratilova
1984	Evert Lloyd	Navratilova	Navratilova	Navratilova
1985	Navratilova	Evert Lloyd	Navratilova	Mandlikova
1986	–	Evert Lloyd	Navratilova	Navratilova
1987	Mandlikova	Graf	Navratilova	Navratilova
1988	**Graf**	**Graf**	**Graf**	**Graf**
1989	Graf	Vicario	Graf	Graf
1990	Graf	Seles	Navratilova	Sabatini
1991	Seles	Seles	Graf	Seles
1992	Seles	Seles	Graf	Seles
1993	Seles	Graf	Graf	Graf
1994	Graf	Vicario	Martinez	Vicario
1995	Pierce	Graf	Graf	Graf
1996	Seles	Graf	Graf	Graf
1997	Hingis	Majoli	Hingis	Hingis
1998	Hingis	Vicario	Novotna	Davenport
1999	Hingis	Graf	Davenport	S. Williams
2000	Davenport	Pierce	V. Williams	V. Williams

Overall Leaders

All-Time Grand Slam titleists including all singles and doubles championships at the four major tournaments. Titles listed under each heading are singles and doubles and mixed doubles. Players active in 2000 are in **bold** type.

MEN

		Career	Australian	French	Wimbledon	U.S.	S-D-M	Total Titles
1	Roy Emerson	1959-71	6-3-0	2-6-0	2-3-0	2-4-0	12-16-0	28
2	John Newcombe	1965-76	2-5-0	0-3-0	3-6-0	2-3-1	7-17-1	25
3	Frank Sedgman	1949-52	2-2-2	0-2-2	1-3-2	2-2-2	5-9-8	22
4	Bill Tilden	1913-30	*	*	3-1-0	7-5-4	10-6-5	21
5	Rod Laver	1959-71	3-4-0	2-1-1	4-1-2	2-0-0	11-6-3	20
6	Jack Bromwich	1938-50	2-8-1	0-0-0	0-2-2	0-3-1	2-13-4	19
7	Ken Rosewall	1953-72	4-3-0	2-2-0	0-2-0	2-2-1	8-9-1	18
	Neale Fraser	1957-62	0-3-1	0-3-0	1-2-0	2-3-3	3-11-4	18
	Jean Borotra	1925-36	1-1-1	1-5-2	2-3-1	0-0-1	4-9-5	18
	Fred Stolle	1962-69	0-3-1	1-2-0	0-2-3	1-3-2	2-10-6	18
11	John McEnroe	1977-93	0-0-0	0-0-1	3-5-0	4-4-0	7-9-1	17
	Jack Crawford	1929-35	4-4-3	1-1-1	1-1-1	0-0-0	6-6-5	17
	Adrian Quist	1936-50	3-10-0	0-1-0	0-2-0	0-1-0	3-14-0	17
14	Laurie Doherty	1897-1906	*	*	5-8-0	1-2-0	6-10-0	16
15	Henri Cochet	1922-32	*	4-3-2	2-2-0	1-0-1	7-5-3	15
	Vic Seixas	1952-56	0-1-0	0-2-1	1-0-4	1-2-3	2-5-8	15
	Bob Hewitt	1961-79	0-2-1	0-1-2	0-5-2	0-1-1	0-9-6	15
	Mark Woodforde	1985–	0-2-2	0-0-1	0-5-1	0-3-1	0-10-5	15

WOMEN

		Career	Australian	French	Wimbledon	U.S.	S-D-M	Total Titles
1	Margaret Court Smith	1960-75	11-8-2	5-4-4	3-2-5	5-5-8	24-19-19	62
2	Martina Navratilova	1974-95	3-8-0	2-7-2	9-7-2	4-9-2	18-31-6	55
3	Billie Jean King	1961-81	1-0-1	1-1-2	6-10-4	4-5-4	12-16-11	39
4	Margaret du Pont	1941-60	*	2-3-0	1-5-1	3-13-9	6-21-10	37
5	Louise Brough	1942-57	1-1-0	0-3-0	4-5-4	1-12-4	6-21-8	35
	Doris Hart	1948-55	1-1-2	2-5-3	1-4-5	2-4-5	6-14-15	35
7	Helen Wills Moody	1923-38	*	4-2-0	8-3-1	7-4-2	19-9-3	31
8	Elizabeth Ryan	1914-34	*	0-4-0	0-12-7	0-1-2	0-17-9	26
9	Suzanne Lenglen	1919-26	*	6-2-2	6-6-3	0-0-0	12-8-5	25
10	Steffi Graf	1982-99	4-0-0	6-0-0	7-1-0	5-0-0	22-1-0	23
11	Pam Shriver	1981-97	0-7-0	0-4-1	0-5-0	0-5-0	0-21-1	22
12	Chris Evert	1974-89	2-0-0	7-2-0	3-1-0	6-0-0	18-3-0	21
	Darlene Hard	1958-69	*	1-3-2	0-4-3	2-6-0	3-13-5	21
14	**Natasha Zvereva**	1989–	0-3-2	0-6-0	0-5-0	0-4-0	0-18-2	20
	Nancye Wynne Bolton	1935-52	6-10-4	0-0-0	0-0-0	0-0-0	6-10-4	20
	Maria Bueno	1958-68	0-1-0	0-1-1	3-5-0	4-5-0	7-12-1	20

Men's, Women's & Mixed Doubles Grand Slam

The tennis Grand Slam has only been accomplished in doubles competition six times in the same calendar year. Here are the doubles teams to accomplish the feat. The two men and three women to win the singles Grand Slam are noted in the Grand Slam Summary tables beginning on page 822.

Men's Doubles

1951 ....Frank Sedgman, Australia
        & Ken McGregor, Australia

Mixed Doubles

1963 ....Ken Fletcher, Australia
       & Margaret Smith, Australia
1967 ....Owen Davidson and two partners*
*Davidson's partners: AUS–Lesley Turner; FR, WIM, U.S.–
Billie Jean King.

Women's Doubles

1960 ....Maria Bueno, Brazil & two partners†
1984....................Martina Navratilova, USA
        & Pam Shriver, USA
1998 ....Martina Hingis, Switzerland & two partners#
†Bueno's partners: AUS–Christine Truman; FR, WIM,
U.S.–Darlene Hard.
#Hingis's partners: AUS–Mirjana Lucic; FR, WIM, U.S.–
Jana Novotna.

All-Time Grand Slam Singles Titles

Men and women with the most singles championships in the Australian, French, Wimbledon and U.S. championships, through 2000. Note that (*) indicates player never played in that particular Grand Slam event; and players active in singles play in 2000 are in **bold** type.

Top 15 Men

		Aus	Fre	Wim	US	Total
1	**Pete Sampras**	2	0	7	4	13
2	Roy Emerson	6	2	2	2	12
3	Bjorn Borg	0	6	5	0	11
	Rod Laver	3	2	4	2	11
5	Bill Tilden	*	0	3	7	10
6	Jimmy Connors	1	0	2	5	8
	Ivan Lendl	2	3	0	3	8
	Fred Perry	1	1	3	3	8
	Ken Rosewall	4	2	0	2	8
10	Henri Cochet	*	4	2	1	7
	Rene Lacoste	*	3	2	2	7
	Bill Larned	*	*	0	7	7
	John McEnroe	0	0	3	4	7
	John Newcombe	2	0	3	2	7
	Willie Renshaw	*	*	7	*	7
	Dick Sears	*	*	0	7	7

Top 15 Women

		Aus	Fre	Wim	US	Total
1	Margaret Smith Court	11	5	3	5	24
2	Steffi Graf	4	6	7	5	22
3	Helen Wills Moody	*	4	8	7	19
4	Chris Evert	2	7	3	6	18
	Martina Navratilova	3	2	9	4	18
6	Billie Jean King	1	1	6	4	12
	Suzanne Lenglen	*	6	6	0	12
8	Maureen Connolly	1	2	3	3	9
	Monica Seles	4	3	0	2	9
10	Molla Bjurstedt Mallory	*	*	0	8	8
11	Maria Bueno	0	0	3	4	7
	Evonne Goolagong	4	1	2	0	7
	Dorothea D. Chambers	*	*	7	0	7
14	Nancy Bolton	6	0	0	0	6
	Louise Brough	1	0	4	1	6
	Margaret du Pont	*	2	1	3	6
	Doris Hart	1	2	1	2	6
	Blanche Bingley Hillyard	*	*	6	*	6

Annual Number One Players

Unofficial world rankings for men and women determined by the *London Daily Telegraph* from 1914-72. Since then, official world rankings computed by men's and women's tours. Rankings included only amateur players from 1914 until the arrival of open (professional) tennis in 1968. No rankings were released during World Wars I and II.

MEN

Multiple winners: Pete Sampras and Bill Tilden (6); Jimmy Connors (5); Henri Cochet, Rod Laver, Ivan Lendl and John McEnroe (4); John Newcombe and Fred Perry (3); Bjorn Borg, Don Budge, Ashley Cooper, Stefan Edberg, Roy Emerson, Neale Fraser, Jack Kramer, Rene Lacoste, Ilie Nastase, Frank Sedgman and Tony Trabert (2).

Year		Year		Year		Year	
1914	Maurice McLoughlin	1937	Don Budge	1962	Rod Laver	1982	John McEnroe
1915-18	No rankings	1938	Don Budge	1963	Rafael Osuna	1983	John McEnroe
1919	Gerald Patterson	1939	Bobby Riggs	1964	Roy Emerson	1984	John McEnroe
1920	Bill Tilden	1940-45	No rankings	1965	Roy Emerson	1985	Ivan Lendl
1921	Bill Tilden	1946	Jack Kramer	1966	Manuel Santana	1986	Ivan Lendl
1922	Bill Tilden	1947	Jack Kramer	1967	John Newcombe	1987	Ivan Lendl
1923	Bill Tilden	1948	Frank Parker	1968	Rod Laver	1988	Mats Wilander
1924	Bill Tilden	1949	Pancho Gonzales	1969	Rod Laver	1989	Ivan Lendl
1925	Bill Tilden	1950	Budge Patty	1970	John Newcombe	1990	Stefan Edberg
1926	Rene Lacoste	1951	Frank Sedgman	1971	John Newcombe	1991	Stefan Edberg
1927	Rene Lacoste	1952	Frank Sedgman	1972	Ilie Nastase	1992	Jim Courier
1928	Henri Cochet	1953	Tony Trabert	1973	Ilie Nastase	1993	Pete Sampras
1929	Henri Cochet	1954	Jaroslav Drobny	1974	Jimmy Connors	1994	Pete Sampras
1930	Henri Cochet	1955	Tony Trabert	1975	Jimmy Connors	1995	Pete Sampras
1931	Henri Cochet	1956	Lew Hoad	1976	Jimmy Connors	1996	Pete Sampras
1932	Ellsworth Vines	1957	Ashley Cooper	1977	Jimmy Connors	1997	Pete Sampras
1933	Jack Crawford	1958	Ashley Cooper	1978	Jimmy Connors	1998	Pete Sampras
1934	Fred Perry	1959	Neale Fraser	1979	Bjorn Borg	1999	Andre Agassi
1935	Fred Perry	1960	Neale Fraser	1980	Bjorn Borg		
1936	Fred Perry	1961	Rod Laver	1981	John McEnroe		

WOMEN

Multiple winners: Helen Wills Moody (9); Steffi Graf (8); Margaret Smith Court and Martina Navratilova (7); Chris Evert Lloyd (5); Margaret Osborne duPont and Billie Jean King (4); Maureen Connolly and Monica Seles (3); Maria Bueno, Althea Gibson, Martina Hingis and Suzanne Lenglen (2).

Year		Year		Year		Year	
1925	Suzanne Lenglen	1948	Margaret duPont	1966	Billie Jean King	1984	Martina Navratilova
1926	Suzanne Lenglen	1949	Margaret duPont	1967	Billie Jean King	1985	Martina Navratilova
1927	Helen Wills	1950	Margaret duPont	1968	Billie Jean King	1986	Martina Navratilova
1928	Helen Wills	1951	Doris Hart	1969	Margaret Court	1987	Steffi Graf
1929	Helen Wills Moody	1952	Maureen Connolly	1970	Margaret Court	1988	Steffi Graf
1930	Helen Wills Moody	1953	Maureen Connolly	1971	Evonne Goolagong	1989	Steffi Graf
1931	Helen Wills Moody	1954	Maureen Connolly	1972	Billie Jean King	1990	Steffi Graf
1932	Helen Wills Moody	1955	Louise Brough	1973	Margaret Court	1991	Monica Seles
1933	Helen Wills Moody	1956	Shirley Fry	1974	Billie Jean King	1992	Monica Seles
1934	Dorothy Round	1957	Althea Gibson	1975	Chris Evert	1993	Steffi Graf
1935	Helen Wills Moody	1958	Althea Gibson	1976	Chris Evert	1994	Steffi Graf
1936	Helen Jacobs	1959	Maria Bueno	1977	Chris Evert	1995	Steffi Graf
1937	Anita Lizana	1960	Maria Bueno	1978	Martina Navratilova		& Monica Seles
1938	Helen Wills Moody	1961	Angela Mortimer	1979	Martina Navratilova	1996	Steffi Graf
1939	Alice Marble	1962	Margaret Smith	1980	Chris Evert Lloyd	1997	Martina Hingis
1940-45	No rankings	1963	Margaret Smith	1981	Chris Evert Lloyd	1998	Lindsay Davenport
1946	Pauline Betz	1964	Margaret Smith	1982	Martina Navratilova	1999	Martina Hingis
1947	Margaret Osborne	1965	Margaret Smith	1983	Martina Navratilova		

Annual Top 10 World Rankings (since 1968)

Year by year Top 10 world computer rankings for Men (ATP Tour) and Women (WTA Tour) since the arrival of open tennis in 1968. Rankings from 1968-72 made by Lance Tingay of the London Daily Telegraph. Since 1973, computerized rankings by ATP Tour (men) and WTA Tour (women).

MEN

1968

1 Rod Laver
2 Arthur Ashe
3 Ken Rosewall
4 Tom Okker
5 Tony Roche
6 John Newcombe
7 Clark Graebner
8 Dennis Ralston
9 Cliff Drysdale
10 Pancho Gonzales

1969

1 Rod Laver
2 Tony Roche
3 John Newcombe
4 Tom Okker
5 Ken Rosewall
6 Arthur Ashe
7 Cliff Drysdale
8 Pancho Gonzales
9 Andres Gimeno
10 Fred Stolle

1970

1 John Newcombe
2 Ken Rosewall
3 Tony Roche
4 Rod Laver
5 Arthur Ashe
6 Ilie Nastase
7 Tom Okker
8 Roger Taylor
9 Jan Kodes
10 Cliff Richey

1971

1 John Newcombe
2 Stan Smith
3 Rod Laver
4 Ken Rosewall
5 Jan Kodes
6 Arthur Ashe
7 Tom Okker
8 Marty Riessen
9 Cliff Drysdale
10 Ilie Nastase

1972

1 Stan Smith
2 Ken Rosewall
3 Ilie Nastase
4 Rod Laver
5 Arthur Ashe
6 John Newcombe
7 Bob Lutz
8 Tom Okker
9 Marty Riessen
10 Andres Gimeno

1973

1 Ilie Nastase
2 John Newcombe
3 Jimmy Connors
4 Tom Okker
5 Stan Smith
6 Ken Rosewall
7 Manuel Orantes
8 Rod Laver
9 Jan Kodes
10 Arthur Ashe

1974

1 Jimmy Connors
2 John Newcombe
3 Bjorn Borg
4 Rod Laver
5 Guillermo Vilas
6 Tom Okker
7 Arthur Ashe
8 Ken Rosewall
9 Stan Smith
10 Ilie Nastase

1975

1 Jimmy Connors
2 Guillermo Vilas
3 Bjorn Borg
4 Arthur Ashe
5 Manuel Orantes
6 Ken Rosewall
7 Ilie Nastase
8 John Alexander
9 Roscoe Tanner
10 Rod Laver

1976

1 Jimmy Connors
2 Bjorn Borg
3 Ilie Nastase
4 Manuel Orantes
5 Raul Ramirez
6 Guillermo Vilas
7 Adriano Panatta
8 Harold Solomon
9 Eddie Dibbs
10 Brian Gottfried

1977

1 Jimmy Connors
2 Guillermo Vilas
3 Bjorn Borg
4 Vitas Gerulaitis
5 Brian Gottfried
6 Eddie Dibbs
7 Manuel Orantes
8 Raul Ramirez
9 Ilie Nastase
10 Dick Stockton

1978

1 Jimmy Connors
2 Bjorn Borg
3 Guillermo Vilas
4 John McEnroe
5 Vitas Gerulaitis
6 Eddie Dibbs
7 Brian Gottfried
8 Raul Ramirez
9 Harold Solomon
10 Corrado Barazzutti

1979

1 Bjorn Borg
2 Jimmy Connors
3 John McEnroe
4 Vitas Gerulaitis
5 Roscoe Tanner
6 Guillermo Vilas
7 Arthur Ashe
8 Harold Solomon
9 Jose Higueras
10 Eddie Dibbs

Annual Top 10 World Rankings (since 1968) (Cont.)
MEN

1980
1. Bjorn Borg
2. John McEnroe
3. Jimmy Connors
4. Gene Mayer
5. Guillermo Vilas
6. Ivan Lendl
7. Harold Solomon
8. Jose-Luis Clerc
9. Vitas Gerulaitis
10. Eliot Teltscher

1981
1. John McEnroe
2. Ivan Lendl
3. Jimmy Connors
4. Bjorn Borg
5. Jose-Luis Clerc
6. Guillermo Vilas
7. Gene Mayer
8. Eliot Teltscher
9. Vitas Gerulaitis
10. Peter McNamara

1982
1. John McEnroe
2. Jimmy Connors
3. Ivan Lendl
4. Guillermo Vilas
5. Vitas Gerulaitis
6. Jose-Luis Clerc
7. Mats Wilander
8. Gene Mayer
9. Yannick Noah
10. Peter McNamara

1983
1. John McEnroe
2. Ivan Lendl
3. Jimmy Connors
4. Mats Wilander
5. Yannick Noah
6. Jimmy Arias
7. Jose Higueras
8. Jose-Luis Clerc
9. Kevin Curren
10. Gene Mayer

1984
1. John McEnroe
2. Jimmy Connors
3. Ivan Lendl
4. Mats Wilander
5. Andres Gomez
6. Anders Jarryd
7. Henrik Sundstrom
8. Pat Cash
9. Eliot Teltscher
10. Yannick Noah

1985
1. Ivan Lendl
2. John McEnroe
3. Mats Wilander
4. Jimmy Connors
5. Stefan Edberg
6. Boris Becker
7. Yannick Noah
8. Anders Jarryd
9. Miloslav Mecir
10. Kevin Curren

1986
1. Ivan Lendl
2. Boris Becker
3. Mats Wilander
4. Yannick Noah
5. Stefan Edberg
6. Henri Leconte
7. Joakim Nystrom
8. Jimmy Connors
9. Miloslav Mecir
10. Andres Gomez

1987
1. Ivan Lendl
2. Stefan Edberg
3. Mats Wilander
4. Jimmy Connors
5. Boris Becker
6. Miloslav Mecir
7. Pat Cash
8. Yannick Noah
9. Tim Mayotte
10. John McEnroe

1988
1. Mats Wilander
2. Ivan Lendl
3. Andre Agassi
4. Boris Becker
5. Stefan Edberg
6. Kent Carlsson
7. Jimmy Connors
8. Jakob Hlasek
9. Henri Leconte
10. Tim Mayotte

1989
1. Ivan Lendl
2. Boris Becker
3. Stefan Edberg
4. John McEnroe
5. Michael Chang
6. Brad Gilbert
7. Andre Agassi
8. Aaron Krickstein
9. Alberto Mancini
10. Jay Berger

1990
1. Stefan Edberg
2. Boris Becker
3. Ivan Lendl
4. Andre Agassi
5. Pete Sampras
6. Andres Gomez
7. Thomas Muster
8. Emilio Sanchez
9. Goran Ivanisevic
10. Brad Gilbert

1991
1. Stefan Edberg
2. Jim Courier
3. Boris Becker
4. Michael Stich
5. Ivan Lendl
6. Pete Sampras
7. Guy Forget
8. Karel Novacek
9. Petr Korda
10. Andre Agassi

1992
1. Jim Courier
2. Stefan Edberg
3. Pete Sampras
4. Goran Ivanisevic
5. Boris Becker
6. Michael Chang
7. Petr Korda
8. Ivan Lendl
9. Andre Agassi
10. Richard Krajicek

1993
1. Pete Sampras
2. Michael Stich
3. Jim Courier
4. Sergi Bruguera
5. Stefan Edberg
6. Andrei Medvedev
7. Goran Ivanisevic
8. Michael Chang
9. Thomas Muster
10. Cedric Pioline

1994
1. Pete Sampras
2. Andre Agassi
3. Boris Becker
4. Sergi Bruguera
5. Goran Ivanisevic
6. Michael Chang
7. Stefan Edberg
8. Alberto Berasategui
9. Michael Stich
10. Todd Martin

1995
1. Pete Sampras
2. Andre Agassi
3. Thomas Muster
4. Boris Becker
5. Michael Chang
6. Yevgeny Kafelnikov
7. Thomas Enqvist
8. Jim Courier
9. Wayne Ferreira
10. Goran Ivanisevic

1996
1. Pete Sampras
2. Michael Chang
3. Yevgeny Kafelnikov
4. Goran Ivanisevic
5. Thomas Muster
6. Boris Becker
7. Richard Krajicek
8. Andre Agassi
9. Thomas Enqvist
10. Wayne Ferreira

1997
1. Pete Sampras
2. Patrick Rafter
3. Michael Chang
4. Jonas Bjorkman
5. Yevgeny Kafelnikov
6. Greg Rusedski
7. Carlos Moya
8. Sergi Bruguera
9. Thomas Muster
10. Marcelo Rios

1998
1. Pete Sampras
2. Marcelo Rios
3. Alex Corretja
4. Patrick Rafter
5. Carlos Moya
6. Andre Agassi
7. Tim Henman
8. Karol Kucera
9. Greg Rusedski
10. Richard Krajicek

1999
1. Andre Agassi
2. Yevgeny Kafelnikov
3. Pete Sampras
4. Thomas Enqvist
5. Gustavo Kuerten
6. Nicolas Kiefer
7. Todd Martin
8. Nicolas Lapentti
9. Marcelo Rios
10. Richard Krajicek

WOMEN

1968
1 Billie Jean King
2 Virginia Wade
3 Nancy Richey
4 Maria Bueno
5 Margaret Court
6 Ann Jones
7 Judy Tegart
8 Annette du Plooy
9 Leslie Bowrey
10 Rosie Casals

1969
1 Margaret Court
2 Ann Jones
3 Billie Jean King
4 Nancy Richey
5 Julie Heldman
6 Rosie Casals
7 Kerry Melville
8 Peaches Bartkowicz
9 Virginia Wade
10 Leslie Bowrey

1970
1 Margaret Court
2 Billie Jean King
3 Rosie Casals
4 Virginia Wade
5 Helga Niessen
6 Kerry Melville
7 Julie Heldman
8 Karen Krantczke
9 Francoise Durr
10 Nancy R. Gunter

1971
1 Evonne Goolagong
2 Billie Jean King
3 Margaret Court
4 Rosie Casals
5 Kerry Melville
6 Virginia Wade
7 Judy Tagert
8 Francoise Durr
9 Helga N. Masthoff
10 Chris Evert

1972
1 Billie Jean King
2 Evonne Goolagong
3 Chris Evert
4 Margaret Court
5 Kerry Melville
6 Virginia Wade
7 Rosie Casals
8 Nancy R. Gunter
9 Francoise Durr
10 Linda Tuero

1973
1 Margaret S. Court
2 Billie Jean King
3 Evonne G. Cawley
4 Chris Evert
5 Rosie Casals
6 Virginia Wade
7 Kerry Reid
8 Nancy Richey
9 Julie Heldman
10 Helga Masthoff

1974
1 Billie Jean King
2 Evonne G. Cawley
3 Chris Evert
4 Virginia Wade
5 Julie Heldman
6 Rosie Casals
7 Kerry Reid
8 Olga Morozova
9 Lesley Hunt
10 Francoise Durr

1975
1 Chris Evert
2 Billie Jean King
3 Evonne G. Cawley
4 Martina Navratilova
5 Virginia Wade
6 Margaret S. Court
7 Olga Morozova
8 Nancy Richey
9 Francoise Durr
10 Rosie Casals

1976
1 Chris Evert
2 Evonne G. Cawley
3 Virginia Wade
4 Martina Navratilova
5 Sue Barker
6 Betty Stove
7 Dianne Balestrat
8 Mima Jausovec
9 Rosie Casals
10 Francoise Durr

1977
1 Chris Evert
2 Billie Jean King
3 Martina Navratilova
4 Virginia Wade
5 Sue Barker
6 Rosie Casals
7 Betty Stove
8 Dianne Balestrat
9 Wendy Turnbull
10 Kerry Reid

1978
1 Martina Navratilova
2 Chris Evert Lloyd
3 Evonne G. Cawley
4 Virginia Wade
5 Billie Jean King
6 Tracy Austin
7 Wendy Turnbull
8 Kerry Reid
9 Betty Stove
10 Dianne Balestrat

1979
1 Martina Navratilova
2 Chris Evert Lloyd
3 Tracy Austin
4 Evonne G. Cawley
5 Billie Jean King
6 Dianne Balestrat
7 Wendy Turnbull
8 Virginia Wade
9 Kerry Reid
10 Sue Barker

1980
1 Chris Evert Lloyd
2 Tracy Austin
3 Martina Navratilova
4 Hana Mandlikova
5 Evonne G. Cawley
6 Billie Jean King
7 Andrea Jaeger
8 Wendy Turnbull
9 Pam Shriver
10 Greer Stevens

1981
1 Chris Evert Lloyd
2 Tracy Austin
3 Martina Navratilova
4 Andrea Jaeger
5 Hana Mandlikova
6 Sylvia Hanika
7 Pam Shriver
8 Wendy Turnbull
9 Bettina Bunge
10 Barbara Potter

1982
1 Martina Navratilova
2 Chris Evert Lloyd
3 Andrea Jaeger
4 Tracy Austin
5 Wendy Turnbull
6 Pam Shriver
7 Hana Mandlikova
8 Barbara Potter
9 Bettina Bunge
10 Sylvia Hanika

1983
1 Martina Navratilova
2 Chris Evert Lloyd
3 Andrea Jaeger
4 Pam Shriver
5 Sylvia Hanika
6 Jo Durie
7 Bettina Bunge
8 Wendy Turnbull
9 Tracy Austin
10 Zina Garrison

1984
1 Martina Navratilova
2 Chris Evert Lloyd
3 Hana Mandlikova
4 Pam Shriver
5 Wendy Turnbull
6 Manuela Maleeva
7 Helena Sukova
8 Claudia Kohde-Kilsch
9 Zina Garrison
10 Kathy Jordan

1985
1 Martina Navratilova
2 Chris Evert Lloyd
3 Hana Mandlikova
4 Pam Shriver
5 Claudia Kohde-Kilsch
6 Steffi Graf
7 Manuela Maleeva
8 Zina Garrison
9 Helena Sukova
10 Bonnie Gadusek

1986
1 Martina Navratilova
2 Chris Evert Lloyd
3 Steffi Graf
4 Hana Mandlikova
5 Helena Sukova
6 Pam Shriver
7 Claudia Kohde-Kilsch
8 M. Maleeva-Fragniere
9 Zina Garrison
10 Gabriela Sabatini

1987
1 Steffi Graf
2 Martina Navratilova
3 Chris Evert
4 Pam Shriver
5 Hana Mandlikova
6 Gabriela Sabatini
7 Helena Sukova
8 M. Maleeva-Fragniere
9 Zina Garrison
10 Claudia Kohde-Kilsch

1988
1 Steffi Graf
2 Martina Navratilova
3 Chris Evert
4 Gabriela Sabatini
5 Pam Shriver
6 M. Maleeva-Fragniere
7 Natalia Zvereva
8 Helena Sukova
9 Zina Garrison
10 Barbara Potter

1989
1 Steffi Graf
2 Martina Navratilova
3 Gabriela Sabatini
4 Z. Garrison-Jackson
5 A. Sanchez Vicario
6 Monica Seles
7 Conchita Martinez
8 Helena Sukova
9 M. Maleeva-Fragniere
10 Chris Evert

1990
1 Steffi Graf
2 Monica Seles
3 Martina Navratilova
4 Mary Joe Fernandez
5 Gabriela Sabatini
6 Katerina Maleeva
7 A. Sanchez Vicario
8 Jennifer Capriati
9 M. Maleeva-Fragniere
10 Z. Garrison-Jackson

1991
1 Monica Seles
2 Steffi Graf
3 Gabriela Sabatini
4 Martina Navratilova
5 A. Sanchez Vicario
6 Jennifer Capriati
7 Jana Novotna
8 Mary Joe Fernandez
9 Conchita Martinez
10 M. Maleeva-Fragniere

Annual Top 10 World Rankings (since 1968) (Cont.)
WOMEN

1992	1994	1996	1998
1 Monica Seles	1 Steffi Graf	1 Steffi Graf	1 Lindsay Davenport
2 Steffi Graf	2 A. Sanchez Vicario	2 Monica Seles	2 Martina Hingis
3 Gabriela Sabatini	3 Conchita Martinez	A. Sanchez Vicario	3 Jana Novotna
4 A. Sanchez Vicario	4 Jana Novotna	3 Jana Novotna	4 A. Sanchez Vicario
5 Martina Navratilova	5 Mary Pierce	4 Martina Hingis	5 Venus Williams
6 Mary Joe Fernandez	6 Lindsay Davenport	5 Conchita Martinez	6 Monica Seles
7 Jennifer Capriati	7 Gabriela Sabatini	6 Anke Huber	7 Mary Pierce
8 Conchita Martinez	8 Martina Navratilova	7 Iva Majoli	8 Conchita Martinez
9 M. Maleeva-Fragniere	9 Kimiko Date	8 Kimiko Date	9 Steffi Graf
10 Jana Novotna	10 Natasha Zvereva	9 Lindsay Davenport	10 Nathalie Tauziat
		10 Barbara Paulus	

1993	1995	1997	1999
1 Steffi Graf	1 Steffi Graf	1 Martina Hingis	1 Martina Hingis
2 A. Sanchez Vicario	Monica Seles	2 Jana Novotna	2 Lindsay Davenport
3 Martina Navratilova	2 Conchita Martinez	3 Lindsay Davenport	3 Venus Williams
4 Conchita Martinez	3 A. Sanchez Vicario	4 Amanda Coetzer	4 Serena Williams
5 Gabriela Sabatini	4 Kimiko Date	5 Monica Seles	5 Mary Pierce
6 Jana Novotna	5 Mary Pierce	6 Iva Majoli	6 Monica Seles
7 Mary Joe Fernandez	6 Magdalena Maleeva	7 Mary Pierce	7 Nathalie Tauziat
8 Monica Seles	7 Gabriela Sabatini	8 Irina Spirlea	8 Barbara Schett
9 Jennifer Capriati	8 Mary Joe Fernandez	9 A. Sanchez Vicario	9 Julie Halard-Decugis
10 Anke Huber	9 Iva Majoli	10 Mary Joe Fernandez	10 Amelie Mauresmo
	10 Anke Huber		

All-Time Singles Leaders
Tournaments Won

All-time tournament wins from the arrival of open tennis in 1968 through 1999. Men's totals include ATP Tour, Grand Prix and WCT tournaments. Players active in singles play in 2000 are in **bold** type.

MEN

		Total			Total			Total
1	Jimmy Connors	109	12	Stefan Edberg	41	22	Jose-Luis Clerc	25
2	Ivan Lendl	94	13	Stan Smith	39		Brian Gottfried	25
3	John McEnroe	77	14	Arthur Ashe	33	24	**Jim Courier**	23
4	Bjorn Borg	62		**Michael Chang**	33		Yannick Noah	23
	Guillermo Vilas	62		Mats Wilander	33	26	Eddie Dibbs	22
6	**Pete Sampras**	61	17	John Newcombe	32		Harold Solomon	22
7	Ilie Nastase	57		Manuel Orantes	32	28	Andres Gomez	21
8	Boris Becker	49		Ken Rosewall	32		**Goran Ivanisevic**	21
9	Rod Laver	47	20	Tom Okker	31	30	Brad Gilbert	20
10	**Andre Agassi**	44	21	Vitas Gerulaitis	27		**Yevgeny Kafelnikov**	20
	Thomas Muster	44						

WOMEN

		Total			Total			Total
1	Martina Navratilova	167	9	**Conchita Martinez**	31	17	Nancy Richey	25
2	Chris Evert	154		Olga Morozova	31	18	**Jana Novotna**	24
3	Steffi Graf	107	11	Tracy Austin	29	19	Kerry Melville Reid	22
4	Margaret Court	92	12	Hana Mandlikova	27	20	Pam Shriver	21
5	Billie Jean King	67		Gabriela Sabatini	27	21	Julie Heldman	20
6	E. Goolagong Cawley	65		**A. Sanchez Vicario**	27	22	M. Maleeva-Fragniere	19
7	Virginia Wade	55	15	**Martina Hingis**	26	23	Virginia Ruzici	17
8	**Monica Seles**	44		**Lindsay Davenport**	26		Regina Marsikova	17
						25	Sue Barker	15

Money Won

All-time money winners from the arrival of open tennis in 1968 through 1999. Totals include doubles earnings.

MEN

		Earnings			Earnings			Earnings
1	Pete Sampras	$38,808,561	11	John McEnroe	$12,539,622	21	Todd Woodbridge	$7,052,171
2	Boris Becker	25,079,186	12	Thomas Muster	12,224,410	22	Jonas Bjorkman	6,960,635
3	Ivan Lendl	21,262,417	13	Sergi Bruguera	11,268,285	23	Wayne Ferreira	6,951,378
4	Stefan Edberg	20,630,941	14	Petr Korda	10,447,665	24	Paul Haarhuis	6,829,416
5	Andre Agassi	19,256,281	15	Richard Krajicek	9,403,940	25	Todd Martin	6,774,749
6	Goran Ivanisevic	18,202,844	16	Jimmy Connors	8,641,040	26	Alex Corretja	6,620,072
7	Michael Chang	18,156,718	17	Patrick Rafter	8,618,133	27	Greg Rusedski	6,616,811
8	Yevgeny Kafelnikov	14,429,047	18	Mats Wilander	7,976,256	28	Andrei Medvedev	6,307,436
9	Jim Courier	13,978,963	19	Marcelo Rios	7,929,847	29	Thomas Enqvist	6,299,318
10	Michael Stich	12,590,152	20	Mark Woodforde	7,674,991	30	Jakob Hlasek	5,892,962

WOMEN

		Earnings			Earnings			Earnings
1	Steffi Graf	$21,895,277	11	Natasha Zvereva	$7,474,720	21	Anke Huber	$3,804,329
2	Mart. Navratilova	20,344,061	12	Helena Sukova	6,391,245	22	Amanda Coetzer	3,659,071
3	A. Sanchez Vicario	14,927,563	13	Pam Shriver	5,460,566	23	Iva Majoli	3,535,486
4	Monica Seles	11,750,858	14	Mary Joe Fernandez	5,257,371	24	Lori McNeil	3,429,510
5	Martina Hingis	11,623,276	15	Mary Pierce	4,961,643	25	Hana Mandlikova	3,340,959
6	Jana Novotna	11,249,134	16	Nathalie Tauziat	4,946,731	26	M. Maleeva-Fragniere	3,244,811
7	Lindsay Davenport	9,489,894	17	Gigi Fernandez	4,681,906	27	Serena Williams	2,968,243
8	Chris Evert	8,896,195	18	Z. Garrison Jackson	4,590,816	28	Wendy Turnbull	2,769,024
9	Gabriela Sabatini	8,785,850	19	Venus Williams	4,582,577	29	B. Schultz-McCarthy	2,562,281
10	Conchita Martinez	8,267,333	20	Larisa Neiland	4,073,194	30	Irina Spirlea	2,559,809

Year-end Tournaments

MEN

Masters/ATP Tour World Championship

The year-end championship of the ATP men's tour since 1970. Contested by the year's top eight players. Originally a round-robin, the Masters was revised in 1972 to include a round-robin to decide the four semifinalists then a single elimination format after that. The tournament switched from December to January in 1977-78, then back to December in 1986. Held at Madison Square Garden in New York from 1978-89. Replaced by ATP Tour World Championship in 1990 and held in Frankfurt, Germany since then.

Multiple Winners: Ivan Lendl and Pete Sampras (5); Ilie Nastase (4); Boris Becker and John McEnroe (3); Bjorn Borg (2).

Year	Winner	Runner-Up	Year	Winner	Loser	Score
1970	Stan Smith (4-1)	Rod Laver (4-1)	1986	Ivan Lendl	B. Becker	62 76 63
1971	Ilie Nastase (6-0)	Stan Smith (4-2)	1986	Ivan Lendl	B. Becker	64 64 64
			1987	Ivan Lendl	M. Wilander	62 62 63

Year	Winner	Loser	Score				
1972	Ilie Nastase	S. Smith	63 62 36 26 63	1988	Boris Becker	I. Lendl	57 76 36 62 76
1973	Ilie Nastase	T. Okker	63 75 46 63	1989	Stefan Edberg	B. Becker	46 76 63 61
1974	Guillermo Vilas	I. Nastase	76 62 36 36 64				
1975	Ilie Nastase	B. Borg	62 62 61	1990	Andre Agassi	S. Edberg	57 76 75 62
1976	Manuel Orantes	W. Fibak	57 62 06 76 61	1991	Pete Sampras	J. Courier	36 76 63 64
1978	Jimmy Connors	B. Borg	64 16 64	1992	Boris Becker	J. Courier	64 63 75
1979	John McEnroe	A. Ashe	67 63 75	1993	Michael Stich	P. Sampras	76 26 76 62
			1994	Pete Sampras	B. Becker	46 63 75 64
1980	Bjorn Borg	V. Gerulaitis	62 62	1995	Boris Becker	M. Chang	76 60 76
1981	Bjorn Borg	I. Lendl	64 62 62	1996	Pete Sampras	B. Becker	36 76 76 67 64
1982	Ivan Lendl	V. Gerulaitis	67 26 76 62 64	1997	Pete Sampras	Y. Kafelnikov	63 62 62
1983	Ivan Lendl	J. McEnroe	64 64 62	1998	Alex Corretja	C. Moya	36 36 75 63 75
1984	John McEnroe	I. Lendl	63 64 64	1999	Pete Sampras	A. Agassi	61 75 64
1985	John McEnroe	I. Lendl	75 60 64				

Note: In 1970, Smith was declared the winner because he beat Laver in their round-robin match (4-6, 6-3, 6-4).

WCT Championship (1971-89)

World Championship Tennis was established in 1967 to promote professional tennis and led the way into the open era. It's major singles and doubles championships were held every May among the top eight regular season finishers on the circuit from 1971 until the WCT folded in 1989.

Multiple winners: John McEnroe (5), Jimmy Connors, Ivan Lendl and Ken Rosewall (2).

Year	Winner	Loser	Score	Year	Winner	Loser	Score
1971	Ken Rosewall	R. Laver	64 16 76 76	1973	Stan Smith	A. Ashe	63 63 46 64
1972	Ken Rosewall	R. Laver	46 60 63 67 76	1974	John Newcombe	B. Borg	46 63 63 62

Year	Winner	Loser	Score	Year	Winner	Loser	Score
1975	Arthur Ashe	B. Borg	36 64 64 60	1983	John McEnroe	I. Lendl	62 46 63 67 76
1976	Bjorn Borg	G. Vilas	16 61 75 61	1984	John McEnroe	J. Connors	61 62 63
1977	Jimmy Connors	D. Stockton	67 61 64 63	1985	Ivan Lendl	T. Mayotte	76 64 61
1978	Vitas Gerulaitis	E. Dibbs	63 62 61	1986	Anders Jarryd	B. Becker	67 61 61 64
1979	John McEnroe	B. Borg	75 46 62 76	1987	Miloslav Mercir	J. McEnroe	60 36 62 62
1980	Jimmy Connors	J. McEnroe	26 76 61 62	1988	Boris Becker	S. Edberg	64 16 75 62
1981	John McEnroe	J. Kriek	61 62 64	1989	John McEnroe	B. Gilbert	63 63 76
1982	Ivan Lendl	J. McEnroe	62 36 63 63				

WOMEN
WTA Tour Championship

Originally the Virginia Slims Championships from 1971-94. The WTA Tour's year-end tournament took place in March from 1972 until 1986 when the WTA decided to adopt a January-to-November playing season. Given the changeover, two championships were held in 1986. Held every year since 1979 at Madison Square Garden in New York.

Multiple winners: Martina Navratilova (8); Steffi Graf (5); Chris Evert (4); Monica Seles (3); Evonne Goolagong and Gabriela Sabatini (2).

Year	Winner	Loser	Score	Year	Winner	Loser	Score
1972	Chris Evert	K. Reid	75 64	1986	M. Navratilova	S. Graf	76 63 62
1973	Chris Evert	N. Richey	63 63	1987	Steffi Graf	G. Sabatini	46 64 60 64
1974	Evonne Goolagong	C. Evert	63 64	1988	Gabriela Sabatini	P. Shriver	75 62 62
1975	Chris Evert	M. Navratilova	64 62	1989	Steffi Graf	M. Navratilova	64 75 26 62
1976	Evonne Goolagong	C. Evert	63 57 63	1990	Monica Seles	G. Sabatini	64 57 36 64 62
1977	Chris Evert	S. Barker	26 61 61	1991	Monica Seles	M. Navratilova	64 36 75 60
1978	M. Navratilova	E. Goolagong	76 64	1992	Monica Seles	M. Navratilova	75 63 61
1979	M. Navratilova	T. Austin	63 36 62	1993	Steffi Graf	A. S. Vicario	61 64 36 61
1980	Tracy Austin	M. Navratilova	62 26 62	1994	Gabriela Sabatini	L. Davenport	63 62 64
1981	Chris Evert	A. Jaeger	63 76	1995	Steffi Graf	A. Huber	61 26 61 46 63
1982	Sylvia Hanika	M. Navratilova	16 63 64	1996	Steffi Graf	M. Hingis	63 46 60 46 60
1983	M. Navratilova	C. Evert	62 60	1997	Jana Novotna	M. Pierce	76 62 63
1984	M. Navratilova	C. Evert	63 75 61	1998	Martina Hingis	L. Davenport	75 64 46 62
1985	M. Navratilova	H. Sukova	63 75 64	1999	Lindsay Davenport	M. Hingis	64 62
1986	M. Navratilova	H. Mandlikova	62 60 36 61	*Two tournaments in 1986 due to change in playing season.			

Davis Cup

Established in 1900 as an annual international tournament by American player Dwight Davis. Originally called the International Lawn Tennis Challenge Trophy. Challenge round system until 1972. Since 1981, the top 16 nations in the world have played a straight knockout tournament over the course of a year. The format is a best-of-five match of two singles, one doubles and two singles over three days. Note that from 1900-24 Australia and New Zealand competed together as Australasia.

Multiple winners: USA (31); Australia (21); France (8); Sweden (7); Australasia (6); British Isles (5); Britain (4); Germany (3).

Challenge Rounds

Year	Winner	Loser	Score	Site	Year	Winner	Loser	Score	Site
1900	USA	British Isles	3-0	Boston	1929	France	USA	3-2	Paris
1901	Not held				1930	France	USA	4-1	Paris
1902	USA	British Isles	3-2	New York	1931	France	Britain	3-2	Paris
1903	British Isles	USA	4-1	Boston	1932	France	USA	3-2	Paris
1904	British Isles	Belgium	5-0	Wimbledon	1933	Britain	France	3-2	Paris
1905	British Isles	USA	5-0	Wimbledon	1934	Britain	USA	4-1	Wimbledon
1906	British Isles	USA	5-0	Wimbledon	1935	Britain	USA	5-0	Wimbledon
1907	Australasia	British Isles	3-2	Wimbledon	1936	Britain	Australia	3-2	Wimbledon
1908	Australasia	USA	3-2	Melbourne	1937	USA	Britain	4-1	Wimbledon
1909	Australasia	USA	5-0	Sydney	1938	USA	Australia	3-2	Philadelphia
1910	Not held				1939	Australia	USA	3-2	Philadelphia
1911	Australasia	USA	5-0	Christchurch, NZ	1940-45	Not held	World War II		
1912	British Isles	Australasia	3-2	Melbourne	1946	USA	Australia	5-0	Melbourne
1913	USA	British Isles	3-2	Wimbledon	1947	USA	Australia	4-1	New York
1914	Australasia	USA	3-2	New York	1948	USA	Australia	5-0	New York
1915-18	Not held	World War I			1949	USA	Australia	4-1	New York
1919	Australasia	British Isles	4-1	Sydney	1950	Australia	USA	4-1	New York
1920	USA	Australasia	5-0	Auckland, NZ	1951	Australia	USA	3-2	Sydney
1921	USA	Japan	5-0	New York	1952	Australia	USA	4-1	Adelaide
1922	USA	Australasia	4-1	New York	1953	Australia	USA	3-2	Melbourne
1923	USA	Australasia	4-1	New York	1954	USA	Australia	3-2	Sydney
1924	USA	Australia	5-0	Philadelphia	1955	Australia	USA	5-0	New York
1925	USA	France	5-0	Philadelphia	1956	Australia	USA	5-0	Adelaide
1926	USA	France	4-1	Philadelphia	1957	Australia	USA	3-2	Melbourne
1927	France	USA	3-2	Philadelphia	1958	USA	Australia	3-2	Brisbane
1928	France	USA	4-1	Paris	1959	Australia	USA	3-2	New York

Year	Winner	Loser	Score	Site	Year	Winner	Loser	Score	Site
1960	Australia	Italy	4-1	Sydney	1964	Australia	USA	3-2	Cleveland
1961	Australia	Italy	5-0	Melbourne	1965	Australia	Spain	4-1	Sydney
1962	Australia	Mexico	5-0	Brisbane	1966	Australia	India	4-1	Melbourne
1963	USA	Australia	3-2	Adelaide	1967	Australia	Spain	4-1	Brisbane

Final Rounds

Year	Winner	Loser	Score	Site	Year	Winner	Loser	Score	Site
1968	USA	Australia	4-1	Adelaide	1984	Sweden	USA	4-1	Göteborg
1969	USA	Romania	5-0	Cleveland	1985	Sweden	W. Germany	3-2	Munich
					1986	Australia	Sweden	3-2	Melbourne
1970	USA	W. Germany	5-0	Cleveland	1987	Sweden	India	5-0	Göteborg
1971	USA	Romania	3-2	Charlotte	1988	W. Germany	Sweden	4-1	Göteborg
1972	USA	Romania	3-2	Bucharest	1989	W. Germany	Sweden	3-2	Stuttgart
1973	Australia	USA	5-0	Cleveland					
1974	So. Africa	India	walkover	Not held	1990	USA	Australia	3-2	St. Petersburg
1975	Sweden	Czech.	3-2	Stockholm	1991	France	USA	3-1	Lyon
1976	Italy	Chile	4-1	Santiago	1992	USA	Switzerland	3-1	Ft. Worth
1977	Australia	Italy	3-1	Sydney	1993	Germany	Australia	4-1	Dusseldorf
1978	USA	Britain	4-1	Palm Springs	1994	Sweden	Russia	4-1	Moscow
1979	USA	Italy	5-0	San Francisco	1995	USA	Russia	3-2	Moscow
					1996	France	Sweden	3-2	Malmo
1980	Czech.	Italy	4-1	Prague	1997	Sweden	USA	5-0	Göteborg
1981	USA	Argentina	3-1	Cincinnati	1998	Sweden	Italy	4-1	Milan
1982	USA	France	4-1	Grenoble	1999	Australia	France	3-2	Nice
1983	Australia	Sweden	3-2	Melbourne					

Note: In 1974, India refused to play the final as a protest against the South African government's policies of apartheid.

Fed Cup

Originally the Federation Cup and started in 1963 by the International Tennis Federation as the Davis Cup of women's tennis. Played by 32 teams over one week at one site through 1994. Tournament changed in 1995 to Davis Cup-style format of four rounds and home site.

Multiple winners: USA (16); Australia (7); Czechoslovakia and Spain (5); Germany (2).

Year	Winner	Loser	Score	Site	Year	Winner	Loser	Score	Site
1963	USA	Australia	2-1	London	1982	USA	W. Germany	3-0	Santa Clara
1964	Australia	USA	2-1	Philadelphia	1983	Czech.	W. Germany	2-1	Zurich
1965	Australia	USA	2-1	Melbourne	1984	Czech.	Australia	2-1	Brazil
1966	USA	W. Germany	3-0	Italy	1985	Czech.	USA	2-1	Japan
1967	USA	Britain	2-0	W. Germany	1986	USA	Czech.	3-0	Prague
1968	Australia	Holland	3-0	Paris	1987	W. Germany	USA	2-1	Vancouver
1969	USA	Australia	2-1	Athens	1988	Czech.	USSR	2-1	Melbourne
					1989	USA	Spain	3-0	Tokyo
1970	Australia	Britain	3-0	W. Germany					
1971	Australia	Britain	3-0	Perth	1990	USA	USSR	2-1	Atlanta
1972	So. Africa	Britain	2-1	Africa	1991	Spain	USA	2-1	Nottingham
1973	Australia	So. Africa	3-0	W. Germany	1992	Germany	Spain	2-1	Frankfurt
1974	Australia	USA	2-1	Italy	1993	Spain	Australia	3-0	Frankfurt
1975	Czech.	Australia	3-0	France	1994	Spain	USA	3-0	Frankfurt
1976	USA	Australia	2-1	Philadelphia	1995	Spain	USA	3-2	Valencia
1977	USA	Australia	2-1	Eastbourne	1996	USA	Spain	5-0	Atlantic City
1978	USA	Australia	2-1	Melbourne	1997	France	Netherlands	4-1	Nice, France
1979	USA	Australia	3-0	Spain	1998	Spain	Switzerland	3-2	Geneva
					1999	USA	Russia	4-1	Palo Alto
1980	USA	Australia	3-0	W. Germany					
1981	USA	Britain	3-0	Tokyo					

COLLEGES

NCAA team titles were not sanctioned until 1946. NCAA women's individual and team championships started in 1982.

Men's NCAA Individual Champions (1883-1945)

Multiple winners: Malcolm Chace and Pancho Segura (3); Edward Chandler, George Church, E.B. Dewhurst, Fred Hovey, Frank Guernsey, W.P. Knapp, Robert LeRoy, P.S. Sears, Cliff Sutter, Ernest Sutter and Richard Williams (2).

Year		Year		Year	
1883	J. Clark, Harvard (spring)	1890	Fred Hovey, Harvard	1898	Leo Ware, Harvard
	H. Taylor, Harvard (fall)	1891	Fred Hovey, Harvard	1899	Dwight Davis, Harvard
1884	W.P. Knapp, Yale	1892	William Larned, Cornell	1900	Ray Little, Princeton
1885	W.P. Knapp, Yale	1893	Malcolm Chace, Brown	1901	Fred Alexander, Princeton
1886	G.M. Brinley, Trinity, CT	1894	Malcolm Chace, Yale	1902	William Clothier, Harvard
1887	P.S. Sears, Harvard	1895	Malcolm Chace, Yale	1903	E.B. Dewhurst, Penn
1888	P.S. Sears, Harvard	1896	Malcolm Whitman, Harvard	1904	Robert LeRoy, Columbia
1889	R.P. Huntington Jr, Yale	1897	S.G. Thompson, Princeton	1905	E.B. Dewhurst, Penn

Year		Year		Year	
1906	Robert LeRoy, Columbia	1920	Lascelles Banks, Yale	1933	Jack Tidball, UCLA
1907	G.P. Gardner Jr, Harvard	1921	Philip Neer, Stanford	1934	Gene Mako, USC
1908	Nat Niles, Harvard	1922	Lucien Williams, Yale	1935	Wilbur Hess, Rice
1909	Wallace Johnson, Penn	1923	Carl Fischer, Phi. Osteo.	1936	Ernest Sutter, Tulane
		1924	Wallace Scott, Wash.	1937	Ernest Sutter, Tulane
1910	R.A. Holden Jr, Yale	1925	Edward Chandler, Calif.	1938	Frank Guernsey, Rice
1911	E.H. Whitney, Harvard	1926	Edward Chandler, Calif.	1939	Frank Guernsey, Rice
1912	George Church, Princeton	1927	Wilmer Allison, Texas		
1913	Richard Williams, Harv.	1928	Julius Seligson, Lehigh	1940	Don McNeill, Kenyon
1914	George Church, Princeton	1929	Berkeley Bell, Texas	1941	Joseph Hunt, Navy
1915	Richard Williams, Harv.			1942	Fred Schroeder, Stanford
1916	G.C. Caner, Harvard	1930	Cliff Sutter, Tulane	1943	Pancho Segura, Miami-FL
1917-1918	Not held	1931	Keith Gledhill, Stanford	1944	Pancho Segura, Miami-FL
1919	Charles Garland, Yale	1932	Cliff Sutter, Tulane	1945	Pancho Segura, Miami-FL

NCAA Men's Division I Champions

Multiple winners (Teams): Stanford (17); UCLA and USC (15); Georgia (3); William & Mary (2). (Players): Alex Olmedo, Mikael Pernfors, Dennis Ralston and Ham Richardson (2).

Year	Team winner	Individual Champion	Year	Team winner	Individual Champion
1946	USC	Bob Falkenburg, USC	1974	Stanford	John Whitlinger, Stanford
1947	Wm. & Mary	Garner Larned, Wm.& Mary	1975	UCLA	Bill Martin, UCLA
1948	Wm. & Mary	Harry Likas, San Francisco	1976	USC & UCLA	Bill Scanlon, Trinity-TX
1949	San Francisco	Jack Tuero, Tulane	1977	Stanford	Matt Mitchell, Stanford
			1978	Stanford	John McEnroe, Stanford
1950	UCLA	Herbert Flam, UCLA	1979	UCLA	Kevin Curren, Texas
1951	USC	Tony Trabert, Cincinnati			
1952	UCLA	Hugh Stewart, USC	1980	Stanford	Robert Van't Hof, USC
1953	UCLA	Ham Richardson, Tulane	1981	Stanford	Tim Mayotte, Stanford
1954	UCLA	Ham Richardson, Tulane	1982	UCLA	Mike Leach, Michigan
1955	USC	Jose Aguero, Tulane	1983	Stanford	Greg Holmes, Utah
1956	UCLA	Alex Olmedo, USC	1984	UCLA	Mikael Pernfors, Georgia
1957	Michigan	Barry MacKay, Michigan	1985	Georgia	Mikael Pernfors, Georgia
1958	USC	Alex Olmedo, USC	1986	Stanford	Dan Goldie, Stanford
1959	Tulane & Notre Dame	Whitney Reed, San Jose St.	1987	Georgia	Andrew Burrow, Miami-FL
			1988	Stanford	Robby Weiss, Pepperdine
1960	UCLA	Larry Nagler, UCLA	1989	Stanford	Donni Leaycraft, LSU
1961	UCLA	Allen Fox, UCLA			
1962	USC	Rafael Osuna, USC	1990	Stanford	Steve Bryan, Texas
1963	USC	Dennis Ralston, USC	1991	USC	Jared Palmer, Stanford
1964	USC	Dennis Ralston, USC	1992	Stanford	Alex O'Brien Stanford
1965	UCLA	Arthur Ashe, UCLA	1993	USC	Chris Woodruff, Tennessee
1966	USC	Charlie Pasarell, UCLA	1994	USC	Mark Merklein, Florida
1967	USC	Bob Lutz, USC	1995	Stanford	Sargis Sargisian, Ariz. St.
1968	USC	Stan Smith, USC	1996	Stanford	Cecil Mamiit, USC
1969	USC	Joaquin Loyo-Mayo, USC	1997	Stanford	Luke Smith, UNLV
1970	UCLA	Jeff Borowiak, UCLA	1998	Stanford	Bob Bryan, Stanford
1971	UCLA	Jimmy Connors, UCLA	1999	Georgia	Jeff Morrison, Florida
1972	Trinity-TX	Dick Stockton, Trinity-TX	2000	Stanford	Alex Kim, Stanford
1973	Stanford	Alex Mayer, Stanford			

NCAA Women's Division I Champions

Multiple winners (Teams): Stanford (10); Florida (3); Georgia, Texas and USC (2). (Players): Sandra Birch, Patty Fendick and Lisa Raymond (2).

Year	Team winner	Individual Champion	Year	Team winner	Individual Champion
1982	Stanford	Alycia Moulton, Stanford	1992	Florida	Lisa Raymond, Florida
1983	USC	Beth Herr, USC	1993	Texas	Lisa Raymond, Florida
1984	Stanford	Lisa Spain, Georgia	1994	Georgia	Angela Lettiere, Georgia
1985	USC	Linda Gates, Stanford	1995	Texas	Keri Phoebus, UCLA
1986	Stanford	Patty Fendick, Stanford	1996	Florida	Jill Craybas, Florida
1987	Stanford	Patty Fendick, Stanford	1997	Stanford	Lilia Osterloh, Stanford
1988	Stanford	Shaun Stafford, Florida	1998	Florida	Vanessa Webb, Duke
1989	Stanford	Sandra Birch, Stanford	1999	Stanford	Zuzana Lesenarova, S. Diego
1990	Stanford	Debbie Graham, Stanford	2000	Georgia	Laura Granville, Stanford
1991	Stanford	Sandra Birch, Stanford			

Golf

With his performance in 2000, **Tiger Woods** *reached legendary status.*

Extraordinary

Tiger Woods leaves the golf world in his wake in 2000, winning three majors in stunning fashion.

by

Karl Ravech

Jack Nicklaus stood in the middle of the 18th fairway at Pebble Beach on Friday at the 100th United States Open. He was some 260-plus yards away from the green on one of the most famous holes in all the world. After consulting with his son Jackie, The Golden Bear decided that if in fact this was his last U.S. Open and it was being played on his favorite course, why not try to get home in two.

A mighty rip of the 3-wood and his ball sailed towards the green. With a huge gallery on his right, the Pacific Ocean to the left and memories of defending champion Payne Stewart, tragically killed in an October plane crash, hanging over head, Nicklaus' shot landed on the green. A huge ovation followed.

Jack three-putted for par. He missed the cut but for

Karl Ravech is an analyst for ESPN's golf coverage.

that instant stood alone under the spotlight. As he walked off the course that day, he and everyone else in the world realized the stage belonged to one man and one man only. Not only did Nicklaus fail to make the cut in what was likely his final U.S. Open, but after 36 holes he was 21 shots behind the leader Tiger Woods.

It was a familiar theme throughout the 2000 season. Nicklaus quietly trudging into the history books, Woods confidently re-writing the record books. Most are aware of the obsession Woods has had with Nicklaus. Since he was a child, it was Jack's records Tiger would strive to break, it was Nicklaus' amazing performances in the majors that served as motivation for Woods. To many, it was much more than just a coincidence that as Nicklaus walked up to the 18th hole at Pebble Beach on Friday, Woods was teeing off on the first hole.

Tiger Woods tees off the ninth hole during the first round at the 100th U.S. Open at Pebble Beach, striking a pose even the most casual golf fan became familiar with in 2000.

The 2000 season began in Hawaii. Tiger came to Kapalua riding a four-event winning streak. After beating Ernie Els, another familiar theme for 2000, Woods had accomplished what no one had since Ben Hogan in 1948 — he'd won five tournaments in a row. Byron Nelson's record of 11 had never seemed so attainable. Woods won the next time he teed it up, at the Pebble Beach Pro-Am, making it six straight. As the tour continued on the West Coast, Woods played the Buick Invitational. He trailed by seven heading into the final round and quickly erased the deficit but his winning streak was halted by Phil Mickelson. Between that defeat and his arrival at Pebble Beach for the Open, Woods would win twice more.

When it came to the majors, Woods' success in 2000 can not be measured in wins. Were it not for a 75 in the opening round of the Masters, he very likely would have won all four. As it is, what he did to the field and the course at Pebble Beach will go down as the most dominating performance in U.S. Open history. Woods was victorious by an unprecedented 15 shots. His competitors were in awe. The next stop and final step towards completing a career Grand Slam at the age of 24 — St. Andrews.

The joke after the U.S. Open was that the millennium edition of the British Open would not be played and that the Claret Jug would just be mailed to Woods in the States. In the end, that would not have been such a bad idea. Understand, St. Andrews is a piece of real estate that has been used for golf for about 600 years. The course plays that way. It is rough. The rough is rough, the greens are rough and the bunkers are a joke — all 112

AP/Wide World Photos

Tiger Shmiger. The LPGA has its own superstar in Australian **Karrie Webb**. Webb, 25, won six tournaments (as of Oct. 8) in 2000, including major victories at the Nabisco Championship and the U.S. Women's Open.

of them, and when Woods walked over the Swilken bridge Sunday with thousands of escorts, he hadn't landed in one of them. Not one all weekend. Grand Slam completed. And for the third time in three majors, Ernie Els finished runner-up. Next stop, Valhalla.

Kentucky in the middle of August can be sweltering and for the first two days it was. In a stroke of brilliance the PGA of America had paired Nicklaus with Woods. On the Wednesday prior to the tournament, during a morning practice round, Nicklaus received a phone call telling him that his mother had passed away. Jack finished his practice, announced he would honor his mother's wishes and play the tournament, and teed it up on Thursday with Woods. After 35 holes, Jack once again found himself need-

ing a miracle to make the cut. The par-5 18th hole played all of the nearly 600 yards it measured. Jack was in the fairway some 60 yards away from the pin, needing to make an eagle three. His wedge shot landed five feet right of the hole and quickly spun its way back towards the cup. The crowd held its breath, Woods watched in amazement. The Golden Bear had one golden moment left, but it was not to be. His major career likely over, Nicklaus paid tribute to Woods, validating his greatness, well aware that his own records likely would fall.

Woods hardly cruised to victory. As it turned out, the PGA Championship may have been the most exciting sporting event of the entire year. Woods battled an unknown golfer named Bob May over 72 holes, then

Last year's champion **Jose Maria Olazabal**, left, fits current champ **Vijay Singh** with his very own green jacket after the Fiji native won the Masters by three strokes at Augusta.

into a three-hole playoff. Woods was victorious by one shot. It was May's day, but Woods' year.

The words used to describe Tiger's 2000 season continue to ring as the calendar sets to turn to 2001. Competitors talk of the "bar" being raised to a new level. Nick Faldo, a great champion in his own right, tells how Woods has encouraged his own young son to be stronger and swing harder, like Tiger. The millions of dollars he's earned on the Tour is gravy to Woods. His endorsement deals off the course are unprecedented in golf — and in any sport for that matter. Tiger Woods has become the most recognizable sports figure in the world. We may think there is nothing left for him to accomplish. Thankfully, he doesn't think the same way. ■

The Top Ten Highlights of the Year in Golf

10. Just when it seemed like no one could beat Tiger, the affable **Spaniard Sergio Garcia** edges him, 1-up, in the made-for-TV "Battle at Bighorn."

9. **Close but no cigar.** Ernie Els becomes the first player in PGA history to finish runner-up in three consecutive major tournaments.

8. **The European women** win the Solheim Cup for the first time since 1992 but not before star Annika Sorenstam is brought to tears after being instructed by the Americans to replay her successful chip shot because she had gone out of turn.

7. **Karrie Webb wins** the second major of her career, taking the Nabisco Championship by ten strokes over defending champion Dottie Pepper. It is the largest winning margin in the tournament's history and prompts the usually stoic Webb to jump into the lake by the 18th hole.

6. On Wednesday before the U.S. Open, **21 golfers** stand beside each other and perform a "21-tee shot salute" into the Pacific Ocean, in memory of their friend and defending Open champion Payne Stewart, who was killed in a plane crash in October 1999.

5. **Vijay Singh dons** the familiar green jacket as Masters champ after his 10-under par, three-stroke victory over runner-up Ernie Els. It is his second major victory but first at Augusta.

4. **Karrie Webb wins her second major** of the year and third in the last 12 months, triumphing at the U.S. Women's Open by five shots. The win gives the 25-year-old enough points for induction into the LPGA Hall of Fame (she won't be eligible for induction until after the 2005 season).

3. **Tiger Woods proves** he can win the close ones too, defeating relative unknown Bob May in a three-hole playoff to win his second consecutive PGA Championship at Valhalla.

2. **Tiger Woods wins** the British Open at historic St. Andrews by eight strokes over Ernie Els and Thomas Bjorn to become the fifth (and youngest) career Grand Slam champion in PGA history.

1. **Tiger Woods leads** wire-to-wire and wins the U.S. Open at Pebble Beach by a ridiculous 15 shots. It is the largest margin of victory ever at a major tournament, one of nine records he either broke or tied at the tournament. ∎

TWO FOR THE AGES

It would be fair to say Tiger Woods played some pretty decent golf at the 2000 U.S. and British Opens. Listed are just some of his combined totals at the two majors.

Under Par	-31
Win Margin	+23
Birdies/Bogeys	43/9
Driving Distance	309.5*
Greens in Regulation	81.3 pct.†

*325.5 on Sunday at the British Open.
†117 of 144 greens

SUDDEN SLAM

Tiger Woods was just 24 when he became the fifth career Grand Slam champion in PGA history. As you might expect, he needed fewer major tournaments (not including those he participated in as an amateur) than the other four to complete the feat.

	Majors
Tiger Woods	15
Jack Nicklaus	19
Gary Player	30
Ben Hogan	33
Gene Sarazen	35

∎

Tournament Results

Schedules and results of PGA, European PGA, PGA Seniors and LPGA tournaments from Oct. 17, 1999 through Oct. 15, 2000.

PGA Tour
LATE 1999

Last Rd	Tournament	Winner	Earnings	Runner-Up
Oct. 17	Las Vegas International	Jim Furyk (331)	$450,000	J. Kaye (332)
Oct. 24	National Car Rental Classic	Tiger Woods (271)	450,000	E. Els (272)
Oct. 31	The Tour Championship	Tiger Woods (269)	900,000	D. Love III (273)
Oct. 31	Southern Farm Bureau Classic	Brian Henniger (202)	360,000	C. DiMarco (205)
Nov. 7	American Express Championship	Tiger Woods (278)*	1,000,000	M. A. Jimenez (278)
Nov. 14@	Shark Shootout	Fred Couples/ David Duval (184)	350,000	S. Hoch/S. McCarron (190)
Nov. 14	Johnnie Walker Classic	Michael Campbell (276)	215,328	G. Ogilvy (277)
Nov. 22@	World Cup of Golf	Tiger Woods (263)	1,000,000	F. Nobilo (272)
Nov. 28@	Skins Game	Fred Couples (11)	635,000	M. O'Meara (5)
Dec. 5@	JCPenny Classic	Laura Davies/ John Daly (260)*	440,000	S.R. Pak/P. Azinger (260)
Dec. 12@	Diners Club Matches	Fred Couples/ Mark Calcavecchia (1-up)	200,000	S. Elkington/J. Maggert

@ Unofficial PGA Tour event.

*Playoffs: American Express– Woods won on 1st hole; **JCPenny–** Davies/Daly won on 3rd hole.

2000

Last Rd	Tournament	Winner	Earnings	Runner-Up
Jan. 2@	Williams World Challenge	Tom Lehman (267)	$1,000,000	D. Duval (270)
Jan. 9	Mercedes Championship	Tiger Woods (276)*	522,000	E. Els (276)
Jan. 16	Sony Open	Paul Azinger (261)	522,000	S. Appleby (268)
Jan. 23	Bob Hope Chrysler Classic	Jesper Parnevik (331)	540,000	R. Sabbatini (332)
Jan. 30	Phoenix Open	Tom Lehman (270)	576,000	R. Allenby & R. Mediate (271)
Feb. 6	Pebble Beach Nat'l Pro-Am	Tiger Woods (273)	720,000	M. Gogel & V. Singh (275)
Feb. 13	Buick Invitational	Phil Mickelson (270)	540,000	S. Maruyama & T. Woods (274)
Feb. 20	Nissan Open	Kirk Triplett (272)	558,000	J. Parnevik (273)
Feb. 27	WGC Anderson Consulting Match Play Champs	Darren Clarke (4&3)	1,000,000	T. Woods
Feb. 27	Tucson Open	Jim Carter (269)	540,000	3-way tie
Mar. 5	Doral-Ryder Open	Jim Furyk (265)	540,000	F. Langham (267)
Mar. 12	Honda Classic	Dudley Hart (269)	522,000	J.P. Hayes & K. Wentworth (270)
Mar. 19	Bay Hill Invitational	Tiger Woods (270)	540,000	D. Love III (274)
Mar. 26	The Players Championship	Hal Sutton (278)	1,008,000	T. Woods (279)
Apr. 2	BellSouth Classic	Phil Mickelson (205)#*	504,000	G. Nicklaus (205)
Apr. 9	**The Masters** (Augusta, Ga.)	Vijay Singh (278)	828,000	E. Els (281)
Apr. 16	MCI Classic–The Heritage of Golf	Stewart Cink (270)	540,000	T. Lehman (272)
Apr. 23	Greater Greensboro Chrysler Classic	Hal Sutton (274)	540,000	A. Magee (277)
Apr. 30	Shell Houston Open	Robert Allenby (275)*	504,000	C. Stadler (275)
May 7	Compaq Classic of New Orleans	Carlos Franco (270)*	612,000	B. McCallister (270)
May 14	GTE Byron Nelson Classic	Jesper Parnevik (269)*	720,000	P. Mickelson & D. Love III (269)
May 21	MasterCard Colonial	Phil Mickelson (268)	594,000	S. Cink & D. Love III (270)
May 28	Memorial Tournament	Tiger Woods (269)	558,000	E. Els & J. Leonard (269)
June 4	Kemper Open	Tom Scherrer (271)	540,000	5-way tie (273)
June 11	Buick Classic	Dennis Paulson (276)*	540,000	D. Duval (276)
June 18	**U.S. Open** (Pebble Beach)	Tiger Woods (272)	800,000	E. Els & M.A. Jimenez (287)
June 25	FedEx St. Jude Classic	Notah Begay III (271)	540,000	C. DiMarco & B. May (272)
July 2	Cannon Greater Hartford Open	Notah Begay III (260)	504,000	M. Calcavecchia (261)
July 9	Advil Western Open	Robert Allenby (274)*	540,000	N. Price (274)
July 16	Greater Milwaukee Open	Loren Roberts (260)	450,000	F. Langham (268)

Tournament Results (Cont.)

Last Rd	Tournament	Winner	Earnings	Runner-Up
July 23	**British Open** (St. Andrews) . . . . . . .Tiger Woods (269)		$759,150	T. Bjorn & E. Els (277)
July 23	B.C. Open. . . . . .Brad Faxon (270)		360,000	E. Toledo (271)
July 30	John Deere Classic. . . . . .Michael Clark II (265)*		468,000	K. Triplett (265)
Aug. 6	The International† . . . . .Ernie Els (48 pts)		630,000	P. Mickelson (44)
Aug. 13	Buick Open. . . . . .Rocco Mediate (268)		486,000	C. Perry (269)
Aug. 20	**PGA Championship** (Louisville) . . .Tiger Woods (270)*		900,000	B. May (270)
Aug. 27	WGC NEC Invitational . . . . .Tiger Woods (259)		1,000,000	J. Leonard & P. Price (270)
Aug. 27	Reno-Tahoe Open . . . . .Scott Verplank* (275)		540,000	J. Van de Velde (275)
Sept. 3	Air Canada Championship . . . . .Rory Sabbatini (268)		540,000	G. Waite (269)
Sept. 10	Bell Canadian Open . . . . .Tiger Woods (266)		594,000	G. Waite (267)
Sept. 17	Pennsylvania Classic . . . . .Chris DiMarco (270)		576,000	5-way tie (276)
Sept. 24	Westin Texas Open . . . . .Justin Leonard (261)		468,000	M. Wiebe (266)
Oct. 1	Buick Challenge . . . . .David Duval (269)		414,000	J. Maggert & N. Price (271)
Oct. 8	Michelob Championship . . . . .David Toms (271)*		540,000	M. Weir (271)
Oct. 15	Invensys Classic . . . . .Billy Andrade (332)		765,000	P. Mickelson (333)

#Weather-shortened.

@ Unofficial PGA Tour money event.

†The scoring for The International is based on a modified Stableford system (8 points for a double eagle, 5 for an eagle, 2 for a birdie, 0 for a par, –1 for a bogey, –3 for double bogey or worse).

*Playoffs: **Mercedes**— Woods won on 2nd hole; **BellSouth**— Mickelson won on 1st hole; **Houston**— Allenby won on 4th hole; **Compaq**— Franco won on 2nd hole; **Byron Nelson**— Parnevik won on 3rd hole; **Buick**— Paulson won on 4th hole; **Western**— Allenby won on 1st hole; **John Deere**— Clark II won on 4th hole; **PGA Championship**— Woods (3-4-5–12) beat May (4-4-5–13) in a three-hole playoff; **Reno-Tahoe**— Verplank won on 4th hole; **Michelob**— Toms won on 1st hole.

Second place ties (3 players or more): 5-WAY—**Kemper** (G. Chalmers, K. Hosokawa, F. Langham, J. Leonard, S. Lowery); **Pennsylvania** (M. Calcavecchia, B. Elder, S. Hoch, J. Kaye, C. Perry); 3-WAY— **Tucson** (C. DeMarco, T. Scherrer, J. Van de Velde).

PGA Majors

The Masters

Edition: 64th   **Dates:** April 6–9
Site: Augusta National GC, Augusta, Ga.
Par: 36-36—72 (6925 yards)   **Purse:** $4,600,000

		1	2	3	4	Tot	Earnings
1	Vijay Singh	72	67	70	69	—278	$828,000
2	Ernie Els	72	67	74	68	—281	496,800
3	Loren Roberts	73	69	71	69	—282	266,800
	David Duval	73	65	74	70	—282	266,800
5	Tiger Woods	75	72	68	69	—284	165,600
6	Tom Lehman	69	72	75	69	—285	154,100
7	Davis Love III	75	72	68	71	—286	133,400
	Phil Mickelson	71	68	76	71	—286	133,400
	Carlos Franco	79	68	70	69	—286	133,400
10	Hal Sutton	72	75	71	69	—287	115,000

Early round leaders: 1st— Dennis Paulson (68); 2nd— Duval (138); 3rd— Singh (209).

Top amateur: none.

U.S. Open

Edition: 100th   **Dates:** June 15–18
Site: Pebble Beach Golf Links, Pebble Beach, Calif.
Par: 35-36—71 (6828 yards)   **Purse:** $4,500,000

		1	2	3	4	Tot	Earnings
1	Tiger Woods	65	69	71	67	—272	$800,000
2	Miguel Angel Jimenez	66	74	76	71	—287	391,150
	Ernie Els	74	73	68	72	—287	391,150
4	John Huston	67	75	76	70	—288	212,779
5	Lee Westwood	71	71	76	71	—289	162,526
	Padraig Harrington	73	71	72	71	—289	162,526
7	Nick Faldo	69	74	76	71	—290	137,203
8	Loren Roberts	68	78	73	72	—291	112,766
	David Duval	75	71	74	71	—291	112,766
	Stewart Cink	77	72	72	70	—291	112,766
	Vijay Singh	70	73	80	68	—291	112,766

Early round leaders: 1st— Woods (65); 2nd— Woods (134); 3rd— Woods (205).

Top amateur: Jeffrey Wilson (304).

PGA Championship

Edition: 82nd   **Dates:** Aug. 17–20
Site: Valhalla Golf Club, Louisville, Ky.
Par: 36-36—72 (7167 yards)   **Purse:** $5,000,000

		1	2	3	4	Tot	Earnings
1	Tiger Woods	66	67	70	67	—270	$900,000
	Bob May	72	66	66	66	—270	540,000
3	Thomas Bjorn	72	68	67	68	—275	340,000
4	Jose Maria Olazabal	76	68	63	69	—276	198,667
	Stuart Appleby	70	69	68	69	—276	198,667
	Greg Chalmers	71	69	66	70	—276	198,667
7	Franklin Langham	72	71	65	69	—277	157,000
8	Notah Begay III	72	66	70	70	—278	145,000
9	Scott Dunlap	66	68	70	75	—279	112,500
	Davis Love III	68	69	72	70	—279	112,500
	Phil Mickelson	70	70	69	70	—279	112,500
	Tom Watson	76	70	65	68	—279	112,500
	Fred Funk	69	68	74	68	—279	112,500

*Woods (3-4-5–12) won a three-hole playoff over May (4-4-5–13).

Early round leaders: 1st— Dunlap and Woods (66); 2nd— Woods (133); 3rd— Woods (203).

Top amateur: none.

British Open

Edition: 129th   **Dates:** July 20–23
Site: Old Course at St. Andrews, Scotland
Par: 36-36—72 (7115 yards)   **Purse:** $4,100,000

		1	2	3	4	Tot	Earnings
1	Tiger Woods	67	66	67	69	—269	$759,150
2	Thomas Bjorn	69	69	68	71	—277	371,984
	Ernie Els	66	72	70	69	—277	371,984
4	Tom Lehman	68	70	70	70	—278	197,379
	David Toms	69	67	71	71	—278	197,379
6	Fred Couples	70	68	72	69	—279	151,830
7	Paul Azinger	69	67	71	71	—280	100,587
	Pierre Fulke	69	72	70	69	—280	100,587
	Loren Roberts	69	68	70	73	—280	100,587
	Darren Clarke	70	69	68	73	—280	100,587

Early round leaders: 1st— Els (66); 2nd— Woods (133); 3rd— Woods (200).

Top amateur: none.

European PGA Tour
Official money won on the 2000 European Tour is presented in euros (E).

LATE 1999

Last Rd	Tournament	Winner	Earnings	Runner-Up
Oct. 24	Belgacom Open	Robert Karlsson (272)	E125,000	J. Spence & R. Goosen (273)
Oct. 31	Volvo Masters	Miguel Angel Jimenez (269)	232,400	3-way tie

Second place ties (3 players or more): 3-WAY—**Volvo Masters** (B. Langer, P. Harrington, R. Goosen).

2000

Last Rd	Tournament	Winner	Earnings	Runner-Up
Jan. 16	Alfred Dunhill Championship	Anthony Wall (204)#	E125,927	P. Price & G. Orr (206)
Jan. 23	Mercedes Benz S.A. Open Championship	Mathias Grönberg (274)	156,784	3-way tie (275)
Jan. 30	Heineken Classic	Michael Campbell (268)	199,613	T. Björn (274)
Feb. 6	Greg Norman Holden Int'l	Lucas Parsons (273)	243,118	P. Senior (277)
Feb. 13	B&H Malaysian Open	Wei-Tze Yeh (278)	136,514	3-way tie (279)
Feb. 20	Algarve Portuguese Open	Gary Orr (275)	166,600	P. Price (276)
Mar. 5	Dubai Desert Classic	Jose Coceres (274)	230,742	P. McGinley & P. Sjöland (276)
Mar. 12	Qatar Masters	Rolf Muntz (280)	129,964	I. Woosnam (285)
Mar. 19	Madeira Island Open	Niclas Fasth (279)	91,630	3-way tie (281)
Apr. 2	Brazil 500 Years Open	Padraig Harrington (270)	128,548	G. Norquist (272)
Apr. 16	Eurobet Seve Ballesteros Trophy	Continental Europe (13½)	150,000 (each)	GB & Ireland (12½)
Apr. 23	Moroccan Open	Jamie Spence (266)	110,509	3-way tie (270)
Apr. 30	Peugeot Open de Espana	Brian Davis (274)	166,660	M. Brier (277)
May 7	Novotel Perrier Open de France	Colin Montgomerie (272)	199,920	J. Lomas (274)
May 14	B&H International Open	Jose Maria Olazabal (275)	284,482	P. Price (278)
May 21	SAP Open TPC of Europe	Lee Westwood (273)	449,820	E. Canonica (276)
May 29	Volvo PGA Championship	Colin Montgomerie (271)	415,130	3-way tie (274)
June 4	The Compass Group English Open	Darren Clarke (275)	208,330	M. James & M. Campbell (276)
June 11	The Wales Open	Steen Tinning (273)	199,838	D. Howell (274)
June 25	Compaq European Grand Prix	Lee Westwood (276)	170,276	F. Jacobson (279)
July 2	Murphy's Irish Open	Patrik Sjoland (270)	267,319	F. Jacobson (272)
July 9	Smurfit European Open	Lee Westwood (276)	396,280	A. Cabrera (277)
July 15	Standard Life Loch Lomond	Ernie Els (273)	292,721	T. Lehman (274)
July 30	TNT Dutch Open	Stephen Leaney (269)	225,000	B. Langer (273)
Aug. 6	Volvo Scandinavian Masters	Lee Westwood (270)	266,660	M. Campbell (273)
Aug. 13	Victor Chandler British Masters	Gary Orr (267)	220,703	P. Johansson (269)
Aug. 20	Buzzgolf.com North West of Ireland Open	Massimo Scarpa (275)	58,330	M. Lundberg (276)
Aug. 27	Scottish PGA Championship	Pierre Fulke (271)	109,495	H. Nystrom (273)
Sept. 3	BMW International Open	Thomas Bjorn (268)	250,000	B. Langer (271)
Sept. 10	Cannon European Masters	Eduardo Romero (261)	250,000	T. Bjorn (271)
Sept. 17	Trophèe Lancome	Retief Goosen (271)	218,461	D. Clarke & M. Campbell (272)
Sept. 24	Belgacom Open	Lee Westwood (266)	166,660	E. Romero (270)
Oct. 1	Linde German Masters	Michael Campbell (197)#	450,000	J. Coceres (198)
Oct. 8@	Cisco World Match Play	Lee Westwood (1-up)	425,957	C. Montgomerie
Oct. 15@	Alfred Dunhill Cup	Spain (2)	146,700 (each)	South Africa (1)

#Weather-shortened

@ Unofficial European Tour money event.

Second place ties (3 players or more): 3-WAY— **S.A. Open** (N. Price, D. Fichardt, R. Gonzalez); **Malaysian** (P. Harrington, C. Hainline, D. Terblanche); **Madeira** (R. Drummond, M. Davis, R. Johnson); **Moroccan** (I. Poulter, T. Levet, S. Delagrange); **Volvo Championship** (D. Clarke, A. Coltart, L. Westwood).

The Official World Golf Ranking

Begun in 1986, the Official World Golf Ranking (formerly the Sony World Ranking) combines the best golfers on the world's leading professional tours—Asian, PGA Tour of Australia, European, European Challenge, Japan Golf Tour, Southern African and U.S. (PGA Tour, Buy.com). Rankings are based on a rolling two-year period and weighted in favor of more recent results. Points are awarded after each worldwide tournament according to finish. Final points-per-tournament averages are determined by dividing a player's total points by the number of tournaments played over that two-year period (through Oct. 8, 2000).

	Avg		Avg		Avg
1 Tiger Woods, USA	29.57	6 Colin Montgomerie, SCO	8.89	11 Darren Clarke, N.IRE	7.01
2 Ernie Els, RSA	11.98	7 Davis Love III, USA	8.55	12 Tom Lehman, USA	6.81
3 David Duval, USA	10.91	8 Hal Sutton, USA	8.24	13 Jim Furyk, USA	6.70
4 Lee Westwood, GBR	9.51	9 Vijay Singh, FIJ	7.39	14 Nick Price, RSA	6.57
5 Phil Mickelson, USA	9.04	10 Jesper Parnevik, SWE	7.26	15 Sergio Garcia, SPA	5.99

Tournament Results (Cont.)
Senior PGA Tour
LATE 1999

Last Rd	Tournament	Winner	Earnings	Runner-Up
Oct. 17	Raley's Gold Rush Classic	David Graham (199)	$165,000	L. Mowry (203)
Oct. 24	Kaanapali Classic	Bruce Fleisher (199)	150,000	A. Doyle (200)
Oct. 31	PacificBell Senior Classic	Joe Inman (199)	180,000	D. Stockton & B. Summerhays (201)
Nov. 7	Senior Tour Championship	Gary McCord (276)	347,000	B. Fleisher & L. Nelson (277)
Nov. 14@	Senior Match Play Challenge	Larry Nelson (3&2)	240,000	T. Jenkins
Dec. 12@	Diner's Club Matches	Tom Watson/Jack Nicklaus (1-up)	200,000	B. Fleisher/D. Graham

2000

Last Rd	Tournament	Winner	Earnings	Runner-Up
Jan. 23	Mastercard Championship	George Archer (207)	$199,000	4-way tie (209)
Jan. 29@	Senior Skins Game	Gary Player (4 skins)	220,000	T. Watson (7 skins)
Feb. 6	Royal Caribbean Classic†	Bruce Fleisher (30 pts)	165,000	V. Fernandez (28)
Feb. 13	ACE Group Classic	Lanny Wadkins (202)*	180,000	3-way tie (202)
Feb. 20	GTE Classic	Bruce Fleisher (202)	195,000	D. Quigley (204)
Feb. 27	LiquidGolf.com Invitational	Tom Wargo (202)*	180,000	G. McCord & J.C. Snead (202)
Mar. 5	Toshiba Senior Classic	Allen Doyle (136)#	195,000	J. Thorpe & H. Twitty (137)
Mar. 12	Audi Senior Classic	Hubert Green (197)	225,000	3-way tie (202)
Mar. 19@	Liberty Mutual Legends of Golf	Jim Colbert/Andy North (191)	322,000	B. Fleisher/D. Graham (192)
Mar. 26	Emerald Coast Classic	Gil Morgan (197)	187,500	L. Nelson (201)
Apr. 2	**The Tradition** (Scottsdale, Ariz.)	Tom Kite (280)*	240,000	L. Nelson & T. Watson (280)
Apr. 17	**PGA Seniors Championship** (Dearborn, Mich.)	Doug Tewell (201)#	324,000	4-way tie (208)
Apr. 23	Las Vegas Senior Classic	Larry Nelson (197)	210,000	B. Fleisher & H. Irwin (202)
Apr. 30	Bruno's Memorial Classic	John Jacobs (203)*	195,000	G. Morgan (203)
May 7	Home Depot Invitational	Bruce Fleisher (203)*	195,000	H. Green (203)
May 14	Nationwide Championship	Hale Irwin (207)	217,500	V. Fernandez & T. Jenkins (208)
May 21	TD Waterhouse Championship	Dana Quigley (198)	195,000	T. Watson (199)
May 28	Boone Valley Classic	Larry Nelson (200)	225,000	T. Watson (203)
June 4	BellSouth Senior Classic at Opryland	Hale Irwin (198)	225,000	G. Morgan (199)
June 11	SBC Senior Open	Tom Kite (207)	210,000	B. Fleisher (209)
June 18	SBC Championship	Doug Tewell (274)	165,000	W. Hall & L. Nelson (275)
June 25	Cadilac NFL Golf Classic	Lee Trevino (202)	165,000	W. Hall (204)
July 2	**U.S. Senior Open** (Bethleham, Pa.)	Hale Irwin (267)	400,000	B. Fleisher (270)
July 9	State Farm Senior Classic	Leonard Thompson (205)*	202,500	I. Aoki (205)
July 16	**Ford Senior Players Championship**	Ray Floyd (273)	345,000	L. Nelson & D. Quigley (274)
July 23	Instinet Classic	Gil Morgan (199)	210,000	B. Fliesher & B. Murphy (203)
July 30	Lightpath Long Island Classic	Bruce Fleisher (198)	225,000	D. Quigley (200)
Aug. 6	Coldwell Banker Burnet Classic	Ed Dougherty (197)	240,000	H. Irwin & G. Morgan (199)
Aug. 13	AT&T Canada Senior Open	Tom Jenkins (274)	217,500	K. Zarley (275)
Aug. 20	Novel Utah Showdown	Doug Tewell (199)	217,500	G. Morgan (201)
Aug. 27	FleetBoston Classic	Larry Nelson (203)	195,000	J. Thorpe (207)
Sept. 3	Foremost Insurance Championship	Larry Nelson (198)	165,000	D. Stockton (201)
Sept. 10	Comfort Classic	Gil Morgan (131)#	187,500	J. Ahern (132)
Sept. 17	Kroger Senior Classic	Hubert Green (200)	210,000	L. Nelson (201)
Sept. 24	Bank One Championship	Larry Nelson (203)	210,000	B. Brask & J. Thorpe (204)
Oct. 1	Vantage Championship	Larry Nelson (198)*	225,000	J. Dent & G. Morgan (198)
Oct. 8	The Transamerica	Jim Thorpe (198)	165,000	B. Fleisher (201)
Oct. 15	Raley's Gold Rush Classic	Jim Thorpe (195)	165,000	E. Dougherty (197)

#Weather-shortened.

@ Unofficial Senior PGA Tour money event.

†The scoring for the Royal Caribbean Classic is based on a modified Stableford system (8 points for a double eagle, 5 for an eagle, 2 for a birdie, 0 for a par, –1 for a bogey, –3 for double bogey or worse).

*Playoffs: **ACE Group**— Wadkins won on 3rd hole; **LiquidGolf.com**— Wargo won on 3rd hole; **Tradition**— Kite won on 6th hole; **Bruno's Memorial**— Jacobs won on 1st hole; **Home Depot**— Fleisher won on 3rd hole; **State Farm**— Thompson won 2nd hole; **Vantage**— Nelson won on 5th hole.

Second place ties (3 players or more): 4-WAY—**Mastercard** (H. Irwin, G. Marsh, D. Quigley, L. Trevino); **Seniors Championship** (H. Irwin, T. Kite, D. Quigley, L. Nelson); 3-WAY—**ACE Group** (T. Watson, W. Hall, J.M. Canizares); **Audi** (J. Colbert, D. Overturf, D. Tewell).

Senior PGA Majors

The Tradition

Edition: 12th   **Dates:** March 30–April 2
Site: Desert Mt. Cochise Course, Scottsdale, Ariz.
Par: 36-36—72 (6959 yards)   **Purse:** $1,600,000

		1 2 3 4	Tot	Earnings
1	Tom Kite	66-71-71-72—280	280	$240,000
	Tom Watson	76-66-70-68—280	280	128,000
	Larry Nelson	68-68-75-69—280	280	128,000
4	Bruce Fleisher	74-70-70-68—282	282	96,000
5	Joe Inman	70-73-70-70—283	283	76,800
6	Gary McCord	70-74-71-69—284	284	60,800
	Andy North	71-72-67-74—284	284	60,800
8	John Jacobs	72-70-74-70—286	286	51,200
9	Jack Nicklaus	73-75-72-67—287	287	37,067
	Mike McCullough	72-71-74-70—287	287	37,067
	Fred Gibson	76-71-70-70—287	287	37,067
	John Bland	73-73-69-72—287	287	37,067
	Ed Dougherty	71-72-70-74—287	287	37,067
	Bruce Summerhays	73-70-71-75—287	287	37,067

Early round leaders: 1st— Jim Ahern (65); 2nd— Nelson (136); 3rd— Kite (208).

PGA Seniors' Championship

Edition: 63rd   **Dates:** April 13–17
Site: PGA National GC, Palm Beach Gardens, Fla.
Par: 36-36—72 (6770 yards)   **Purse:** $1,800,000

		1 2 3	Tot	Earnings
1	Doug Tewell	68-66-67—201	201	$324,000
2	Hale Irwin	70-71-67—208	208	117,300
	Tom Kite	73-66-69—208	208	117,300
	Dana Quigley	69-66-73—208	208	117,300
	Larry Nelson	70-68-70—208	208	117,300
6	Hubert Green	69-72-68—209	209	58,500
	Vicente Fernandez	70-71-68—209	209	58,500
8	John Mahaffey	71-72-68—211	211	50,000
	Jim Ahern	73-68-70—211	211	50,000
10	John Bland	77-66-70—213	213	43,500
	Kermit Zarley	71-71-71—213	213	43,500

Early round leaders: 1st— Seiji Ebihara and Tewell (68); 2nd— Tewell (134).
Note: The tournament was reduced to 54 holes due to rain.

PGA Sr. Players Championship

Edition: 18th   **Dates:** July 13–16
Site: TPC of Michigan, Dearborn, Mich.
Par: 36-36—72 (6966 yards)   **Purse:** $2,300,000

		1 2 3 4	Tot	Earnings
1	Ray Floyd	71-67-69-66—273	273	$345,000
2	Larry Nelson	70-68-69-67—274	274	184,000
	Dana Quigley	71-65-67-71—274	274	184,000
4	Hale Irwin	68-68-73-66—275	275	124,200
	Mike McCullough	68-71-67-69—275	275	124,200
6	Tom Kite	66-68-67-76—277	277	92,000
7	Jose Maria Canizares	70-69-72-68—279	279	78,200
	Tom Jenkins	69-71-70-69—279	279	78,200
9	Jesse Patino	66-71-71-72—280	280	64,400
10	Gil Morgan	68-71-71-71—281	281	57,500
	Jim Thorpe	68-74-68-71—281	281	57,500

Early round leaders: 1st— John Jacobs, Bruce Fleisher and Hugh Baiocchi (65); 2nd— Kite and Baiocchi (134); 3rd— Kite (201).

U.S. Senior Open

Edition: 21st   **Dates:** June 30–July 2
Site: Old Course at Saucon Valley CC, Bethlehem, Penn.
Par: 36-35—71 (6749 yards)   **Purse:** $2,250,000

		1 2 3 4	Tot	Earnings
1	Hale Irwin	66-71-65-65—267	267	$400,000
2	Bruce Fleisher	64-69-67-70—270	270	235,000
3	Tom Kite	72-65-66-69—272	272	153,329
4	Ray Floyd	70-69-68-67—274	274	106,878
5	Hubert Green	65-70-69-72—276	276	86,550
6	Dave Stockton	66-72-70-69—277	277	72,790
	Jim Thorpe	69-65-72-71—277	277	72,790
8	Christy O'Connor	68-72-72-67—279	279	61,060
	Allen Doyle	70-68-67-74—279	279	61,060
10	John Jacobs	69-73-73-66—281	281	47,600
	Tom Jenkins	74-70-68-69—281	281	47,600
	Tom Watson	71-69-71-70—281	281	47,600
	Jim Colbert	71-70-70-70—281	281	47,600
	Jose Maria Canizares	69-69-71-72—281	281	47,600

Early round leaders: 1st— Fleisher (64); 2nd— Fleisher (133); 3rd— Fleisher (200).

LPGA Tour

LATE 1999

Last Rd	Tournament	Winner	Earnings	Runner-Up
Oct. 10	First Union Betsy King	Mi Hyun Kim (280)	$116,250	3-way tie (281)
Oct. 11	Lifetime's AFLAC Tourn. of Champions	Akiko Fukushima (279)	122,000	M. Hjorth & K. Webb (280)
Nov. 7	Mizuno Classic	Maria Hjorth (201)	120,000	4-way tie (206)
Nov. 14	LPGA Tour Championship	Se Ri Pak (276)*	215,000	L. Davies & K. Webb (276)
Dec. 5	JCPenny Classic	Laura Davies/ John Daly (260)*	440,000	S. Pak/P. Azinger (260)
Dec. 12	Diners Club Matches	Juli Inkster/ Dottie Pepper (4&3)	200,000	K. Webb/K. Robbins

***Playoffs: Tour Championship**– Pak won on 1st hole. **JCPenny**– Davies/Daly won on 3rd hole.
Second-place ties (3 players or more): 4-WAY— **Mizuno** (L. Davies, O. Ku, A. Nakano, F. Muraguchi); 3-WAY—**Betsy King**– (B. Daniel, H. Dobson, J. Lidback).

2000

Last Rd	Tournament	Winner	Earnings	Runner-Up
Jan. 16	The Office Depot	Karrie Webb (281)	$112,500	J. Inkster (285)
Jan. 23	Subaru Memorial of Naples	Nancy Scranton (275)*	127,500	M. Hjorth (275)
Feb. 13	Los Angeles Women's Championship	Laura Davies (211)	112,500	3-way tie (214)
Feb. 19	Hawaiian Ladies Open	Betsy King (204)	97,500	B. Burton (206)
Feb. 27	Australian Ladies Masters	Karrie Webb (274)	112,500	L. Kane (275)
Mar. 4	LPGA Takefuji Classic	Karrie Webb (207)*	120,000	A. Sorenstam (207)
Mar. 12	Welch's/Circle K Championship	Annika Sorenstam (269)*	105,000	P. Hurst (269)
Mar. 19	Standard Register Ping	Charlotte Sorenstam (276)	127,500	K. Webb (278)

LPGA Tour (Cont.)

Last Rd	Tournament	Winner	Earnings	Runner-Up
Mar. 26	**Nabisco Championship** (Rancho Mirage, Calif.)	Karrie Webb (274)	$187,500	D. Pepper (284)
Apr. 16	Longs Drugs Challenge	Juli Inkster (275)	105,000	B. Burton (280)
Apr. 30	Chick-fil-A Charity Championship	Sophie Gustafson (206)	135,000	A. Fruhwirth & K. Robbins (207)
May 7	Phillips Invitational	Laura Davies (275)	127,500	D. Pepper (277)
May 14	Electrolux USA Championship	Pat Hurst (275)	120,000	J. Inkster (279)
May 21	Firstar LPGA Classic	Annika Sorenstam (197)	97,500	C. Kerr & K. Webb (198)
May 28	LPGA Corning Classic	Betsy King (276)*	120,000	V. Goetze-Ackerman & K. Kuehne (276)
June 4	Greens.com Classic	Grace Park (274)	112,500	P. Hurst & J. Inkster (275)
June 11	Wegmans Rochester Int'l	Meg Mallon (280)	150,000	W. Doolan (282)
June 17	Evian Masters	Annika Sorenstam (276)*	270,000	K. Webb (276)
June 25	**McDonalds LPGA Championship** (Wilmington, Del.)	Juli Inkster (281)*	210,000	S. Croce (281)
July 2	ShopRite LPGA Classic	Janice Moodie (203)	165,000	P. Hurst & G. Park (205)
July 9	Jamie Farr Kroger Classic	Annika Sorenstam (274)*	150,000	R. Hetherington (274)
July 16	JAL Big Apple Classic	Annika Sorenstam (206)	135,000	R. Jones (207)
July 23	**U.S. Women's Open** (Libertyville, Ill.) . .	Karrie Webb (282)	500,000	C. Kerr & M. Mallon (287)
July 30	Giant Eagle LPGA Classic	Dorothy Delasin (205)*	150,000	P. Hurst (205)
Aug. 6	Michelob Light Classic	Lorie Kane (205)	120,000	K. Albers (208)
Aug. 13	**du Maurier Classic** (Aylmer, CAN)	Meg Mallon (282)	180,000	R. Jones (283)
Aug. 20	Weetabix Women's British Open	Sophie Gustafson (282)	178,800	4-way tie (284)
Aug. 27	Oldsmobile Classic	Karrie Webb (265)	112,500	M. Mallon (267)
Sept. 4	State Farm Rail Classic	Laurel Kean (198)	135,000	D. Ammaccapane & M. Hyun Kim (204)
Sept. 10	First Union Betsy King Classic	Michele Redman (202)	120,000	J. Bartholomew & M. Mallon (205)
Sept. 24	Safeway LPGA Golf Championship	Mi Hyun Kim (215)*	120,000	J. Jang (215)
Oct. 1	New Albany Golf Classic	Lorie Kane (277)*	150,000	M. Hyung Kim (277)
Oct. 8	Solheim Cup	Europe (14½)	none	USA (11½)
Oct. 15	Samsung World Championship of Women's Golf	Juli Inkster (274)	152,000	A. Sorenstam (278)

Weather-shortened

*Playoffs: Memorial of Naples— Scranton won on 2nd hole; **Takefuji—** Webb won on 1st hole; **Welch's/Circle K—** Sorenstam won on 2nd hole; **Corning Classic—** King won on 2nd hole; **Evian—** Sorenstam won on 1st hole; **McDonalds Champs—** Inkster won on 2nd hole; **Jamie Farr—** Sorenstam won on 2nd hole; **Giant Eagle—** Delasin won on 2nd hole. **Safeway—** Hyung Kim won on 2nd hole; **New Albany—** Kane won on 1st hole.

Second place ties (3 players or more): 4-WAY—**British Open** (B. Iverson, M. Mallon, L. Neumann, K. Taylor); 3-WAY— **L.A. Champs** (C. Koch, J. Moodie, M. Redman).

LPGA Majors

Nabisco Championship

Edition: 29th **Dates:** March 23–26
Site: Mission Hills CC, Rancho Mirage, Calif.
Par: 36-36—72 (6460 yards) **Purse:** $1,250,000

		1 2 3 4	Tot	Earnings
1	Karrie Webb	67-70-67-70—274		$187,500
2	Dottie Pepper	68-72-72-72—284		116,366
3	Meg Mallon	75-70-73-67—285		84,916
4	Michele Redman	73-73-69-71—286		59,755
	C.Johnston-Forbes . . .	74-71-71-70—286		59,755
6	Chris Johnson	73-68-73-73—287		40,570
	Helen Dobson	73-74-72-68—287		40,570
8	Kim Saiki	72-77-68-71—288		31,135
	Rosie Jones	74-71-74-69—288		31,135
10	Pat Hurst	72-72-70-75—289		24,170
	A.S. Wongluekiet.	75-70-69-75—289		amateur
	Wendy Doolan	73-73-69-74—289		24,170
	Jenny Lidback	75-72-74-68—289		24,170

Early round leaders: 1st— Webb (67); 2nd— Webb (137); 3rd— Webb (204).
Top amateur: Wongluekiet (289).

LPGA Championship

Edition: 46th **Dates:** June 22–25
Site: DuPont CC, Wilmington, Del.
Par: 35-36—71 (6408 yards) **Purse:** $1,400,000

		1 2 3 4	Tot	Earnings
1	Juli Inkster	72-69-65-75—281		$210,000
	Stefania Croce	72-67-74-68—281		130,330
3	Se Ri Pak	73-69-69-71—282		76,319
	Nancy Scranton	72-70-67-73—282		76,319
	Wendy Ward	69-69-68-76—282		76,319
6	Heather Bowie	74-70-70-69—283		42,503
	Laura Davies	70-66-75-72—283		42,503
	Jane Crafter	72-69-69-73—283		42,503
9	Akiko Fukushima	71-72-71-70—284		29,839
	Karrie Webb	72-70-69-73—284		29,839
	Jan Stephenson	70-69-69-76—284		29,839

Note: Inkster (4-4) def. Croce (4-x) on the 2nd hole of a sudden death playoff.

Early round leaders: 1st— Jane Geddes (66); 2nd— Davies (136); 3rd— Inkster and Ward (206). **Top amateur:** none.

U.S. Women's Open

Edition: 55th **Dates:** July 20–23
Site: Merit Club in Libertyville, Ill.
Par: 36-36—72 (6516 yards) **Purse:** $2,750,000

		1 2 3 4	Tot	Earnings
1	Karrie Webb	69-72-68-73	282	$500,000
2	Cristie Kerr	72-71-74-70	287	240,228
	Meg Mallon	68-72-73-74	287	240,228
4	Rosie Jones	73-71-72-72	288	120,119
	Mi Hyun Kim	74-72-70-72	288	120,119
6	Grace Park	74-72-73-70	289	90,458
	Kelli Kuehne	71-74-72-73	289	90,458
8	Beth Daniel	71-74-72-73	290	79,345
9	Annika Sorenstam	73-75-73-70	291	67,369
	Kelly Robbins	74-73-71-73	291	67,369
	Laura Davies	73-71-72-75	291	67,369

Early round leaders: 1st— Mallon (68); 2nd— Mallon (140); 3rd— Webb (209).
Top amateur: Naree Wongluekiet (300).

du Maurier Classic

Edition: 27th **Dates:** Aug. 10–13
Site: Royal Ottawa GC, Aylmer, Quebec, Canada
Par: 36-36—72 (6403 yards) **Purse:** $1,200,000

		1 2 3 4	Tot	Earnings
1	Meg Mallon	73-68-72-69	282	$180,000
2	Rosie Jones	74-70-71-68	283	111,711
3	Annika Sorenstam	69-69-72-74	284	81,519
4	Diana D'Alessio	67-73-73-72	285	63,404
5	Juli Inkster	72-68-74-72	286	46,797
	Lorie Kane	72-67-71-76	286	46,797
7	Becky Iverson	74-74-71-70	289	30,192
	Karrie Webb	71-72-76-70	289	30,192
	Se Ri Pak	69-76-72-72	289	30,192
	Laura Philo	71-69-77-72	289	30,192

Early round leaders: 1st— D'Alessio (67); 2nd— Sorenstam (138); 3rd— Kane and Sorenstam (210).
Top amateur: none.

2000 Statistics (Through Oct. 8)

Statistical leaders on the PGA, European PGA, Senior PGA and LPGA tours.

PGA

	Scoring	Avg.
1	Tiger Woods	.67.64
2	Ernie Els	.69.37
3	Phil Mickelson	.69.38
4	David Duval	.69.46
5	Jesper Parnevik	.69.65
6	Paul Azinger	.69.67
7	Stewart Cink	.69.79
	Loren Roberts	.69.79
9	Tom Lehman	.69.80
10	Steve Flesch	.69.81

	Greens Hit	Pct.
1	Tiger Woods	.74.8
2	Kenny Perry	.72.1
3	Joe Durant	.72.0
4	David Duval	.70.5
5	Glen Hnatiuk	.70.4
6	Tom Lehman	.70.3
7	Chris Perry	.70.0
8	Vijay Singh	.69.9
9	Fred Couples	.69.8
10	Hal Sutton	.69.6

	Driving Accuracy	Pct.
1	Fred Funk	.80.1
2	Joe Durant	.79.5
3	Loren Roberts	.79.3
4	Scott Verplank	.79.3
5	Olin Browne	.77.5
6	Larry Mize	.77.2
7	Jeff Maggert	.77.0
8	Nick Faldo	.76.8
9	Scott Gump	.76.7
10	Glen Hnatiuk	.76.6

	Putting	Putts
1	Tiger Woods	.1.712
2	Phil Mickelson	.1.726
3	Franklin Langham	.1.728
4	Brad Faxon	.1.730
	Jesper Parnevik	.1.730
6	Paul Azinger	.1.732
7	Sergio Garcia	.1.734
8	Jim McGovern	.1.740
	Rory Sabbatini	.1.740
	Mike Weir	.1.740

	Sand Saves	Pct.
1	Paul Stankowski	.66.7
2	Craig Perks	.66.4
3	Fred Couples	.66.0
4	Peter Jacobsen	.65.1
5	Rocco Mediate	.64.8
6	Stuart Appleby	.64.4
7	Robert Allenby	.63.9
8	Jay Williamson	.63.6
9	Kevin Sutherland	.63.2
10	Michael Bradley	.62.4
	Loren Roberts	.62.4

	Driving Distance	Avg.
1	John Daly	.302.2
2	Tiger Woods	.297.0
3	Casey Martin	.289.2
4	Scott McCarron	.287.8
5	Harrison Frazar	.287.3
6	Stuart Appleby	.286.7
7	Davis Love III	.286.5
8	Phil Mickelson	.286.2
9	Mathew Goggin	.285.7
10	Robert Allenby	.285.0

European PGA

	Scoring	Avg.
1	Ernie Els	.69.67
2	Lee Westwood	.69.74
3	Colin Montgomerie	.70.19
4	Bob May	.70.29
5	Michael Campbell	.70.32
6	Darren Clarke	.70.46
7	Padraig Harrington	.70.55
8	Thomas Bjorn	.70.57
9	Gary Orr	.70.68
10	Jose Coceres	.70.69

	Greens Hit	Pct.
1	Gary Orr	.78.2
2	Colin Montgomerie	.77.5
3	Jose Coceres	.76.0
4	Ian Garbutt	.74.3
5	Greg Owen	.74.0
6	Padraig Harrington	.73.7
	Miguel Angel Jimenez	.73.7
8	John Senden	.73.6
9	Andrew Coltart	.72.8
	Angel Cabrera	.72.8

	Driving Accuracy	Pct.
1	Jose Coceres	.79.0
2	Richard Green	.78.8
3	John Bickerton	.77.9
4	Pierre Fulke	.75.8
5	Gary Orr	.75.8
6	Andrew Oldcorn	.74.3
7	Peter O'Malley	.74.1
8	Miguel Angel Jimenez	.72.6
9	Anders Hansen	.72.5
10	Mark McNulty	.72.0

Putting	Putts
1 Michael Campbell	1.715
2 Lee Westwood	1.721
3 Pierre Fulke	1.735
4 Philip Price	1.740
5 Jamie Spence	1.741
6 Gerry Norquist	1.742
7 Jarmo Sandelin	1.749
8 Brian Davis	1.751
Fredrik Jacobson	1.751
10 Jean Van de Velde	1.752
Paul Lawrie	1.752

Sand Saves	Pct.
1 Tony Johnstone	78.1
2 Mark Mouland	77.8
3 Brett Rumford	76.5
4 Ian Hutchings	75.5
5 John Senden	71.2
6 David Park	70.0
7 Jose Maria Olazabal	70.0
8 Pierre Fulke	69.8
9 Bernhard Langer	68.8
10 Seve Ballesteros	68.6

Driving Distance	Avg.
1 Emanuele Canonica	295.4
2 Adam Scott	292.4
3 Angel Cabrera	291.2
4 Stephen Allan	290.5
5 Alberto Binaghi	290.2
6 Ricardo Gonzalez	290.1
7 Paolo Quirici	287.0
8 Mattias Eliasson	286.0
9 Carl Suneson	285.3
10 Des Terblanche	285.1

Senior PGA

Scoring	Avg.
1 Gil Morgan	68.77
2 Larry Nelson	68.91
3 Bruce Fleisher	68.93
4 Hale Irwin	69.08
5 Tom Watson	69.41
6 Allen Doyle	69.69
7 Tom Kite	69.73
8 Dana Quigley	69.80
9 Jim Thorpe	69.93
10 Doug Tewell	69.97

Greens Hit	Pct.
1 Tom Kite	78.0
2 Gil Morgan	77.2
3 Hale Irwin	75.9
4 Bruce Fleisher	74.5
5 John Mahaffey	74.5
6 Doug Tewell	74.2
Tom Watson	74.2
8 Larry Nelson	72.6
Jim Thorpe	72.6
10 Allen Doyle	72.5

Driving Accuracy	Pct.
1 Calvin Peete	83.9
2 Hubert Green	83.3
3 Hale Irwin	80.6
4 Allen Doyle	79.2
Doug Tewell	79.2
6 Bruce Fleisher	78.8
7 Mike Hill	78.5
8 John Bland	78.3
9 John Mahaffey	77.8
10 Bob Murphy	76.6

Putting	Putts
1 Larry Nelson	1.724
2 Hale Irwin	1.732
3 Bruce Fleisher	1.733
Tom Watson	1.733
5 Gil Morgan	1.740
Bob Murphy	1.740
7 Jim Thorpe	1.755
8 Allen Doyle	1.756
9 Dana Quigley	1.757
Dave Stockton	1.757

Sand Saves	Pct.
1 Ray Floyd	63.6
2 Vicente Fernandez	63.1
3 Bob Eastwood	61.9
4 Bruce Fleisher	60.6
Steven Veriato	60.6
6 Tom Kite	59.2
7 Hubert Green	58.5
8 Stewart Ginn	58.0
9 Dale Douglass	57.4
10 Butch Baird	56.0

Driving Distance	Avg.
1 John Jacobs	285.8
2 Terry Dill	285.7
3 Gil Morgan	284.6
4 Jim Ahern	283.8
5 Dana Quigley	280.5
6 Gary McCord	279.1
7 Jim Dent	278.7
8 Larry Nelson	278.3
9 David Graham	277.8
10 Jim Thorpe	277.0

LPGA

Scoring	Avg.
1 Karrie Webb	69.91
2 Annika Sorenstam	70.51
3 Juli Inkster	70.83
4 Meg Mallon	70.86
5 Dottie Pepper	70.95
Pat Hurst	70.95
7 Rosie Jones	71.08
8 Mi Hyun Kim	71.11
9 Lorie Kane	71.45
10 Se Ri Pak	71.51

Greens Hit	Pct.
1 Annika Sorenstam	74.6
2 Karrie Webb	73.5
3 Pat Hurst	71.3
4 Sherri Steinhauer	71.2
5 Meg Mallon	70.8
6 Heather Bowie	70.2
Julie Inkster	70.2
8 Michele Redman	69.1
9 Beth Daniel	69.0
10 Chris Johnson	68.8

Driving Accuracy	Pct.
1 Nancy Ramsbottom	86.3
2 Kim Augusta	84.7
3 Amy Fruhwirth	82.7
4 Tina Barrett	81.4
5 Jenny Lidback	81.2
6 Carin Koch	80.5
7 Barb Whitehead	80.3
8 Donna Andrews	79.4
9 Annika Sorenstam	78.9
Emilee Klein	78.9

Putting	Putts
1 Lisa Kiggens	28.56
2 Dottie Pepper	28.83
3 Alison Nicholas	28.93
4 Amy Benz	29.07
5 Kim Williams	29.12
6 Kelli Kuehne	29.18
7 Stephanie Brecht	29.23
8 Caroline McMillan	29.26
9 Suzanne Strudwick	29.26
10 Oh-Yeon Kwon	29.26

Note: Putts per round.

Sand Saves	Pct.
1 Alison Nicholas	62.7
2 JoAnne Carner	58.9
3 Mi Hyun Kim	57.0
4 Dottie Pepper	56.1
5 Karen Weiss	53.8
6 Caroline McMillan	53.2
7 V. Goetze-Ackerman	52.7
8 Kelli Kuehne	52.6
9 Lisa Kiggens	51.9
10 Beth Daniel	51.8

Driving Distance	Avg.
1 Caroline Blaylock	270.1
2 Wendy Doolan	264.0
3 Jean Bartholomew	262.6
4 Maria Hjorth	261.3
5 Sally Dee	261.1
6 Sophie Gustafson	258.3
7 Karrie Webb	257.0
8 Pat Hurst	256.8
9 Kelly Robbins	256.6
10 Sherri Turner	255.3
Jean Zedlitz	255.3

Key: Scoring— average strokes per round adjusted to the average score of the field each week. If the field is under par, each player's score is adjusted upward a corresponding amount and vice-versa if the field is over par. This keeps a player from receiving an advantage for playing easier-than-average courses; Putting— average number of putts taken on greens hit in regulation; **Greens Hit**— or Greens in Regulation, percentage based on number of greens reached in regulation out of total holes played. A green is considered hit in regulation if any portion of the ball rests on the putting surface in two shots less than par; **Sand Saves**— percentage of up-and-down efforts from greenside sand traps; **Driving Accuracy**— percentage of fairways hit on par-4 and par-5 holes; **Driving Distance**— average computed by charting exact distances of two tee shots on the most open par four or five holes on both front and back nine.

2000 Solheim Cup
The 6th Solheim Cup tournament, Oct. 6-8, at Loch Lomond Golf Club, Luss, Scotland.

ROSTERS

The 2000 U.S. Team players were chosen on the basis of points awarded for wins and top-10 finishes at official LPGA events. The top 10 finishers on the points list automatically qualified for the 12-member team, and U.S. Captain Pat Bradley selected the final two players—Brandie Burton and Beth Daniel.

The 2000 European Team players were chosen on the basis of points awarded weekly to the top 20 finishers at official Ladies European Tour (LET) events. The top seven players in the LET points standings automatically qualify for the 12-member team, and team captain Dale Reid selected the final five players—Helen Alfredsson, Carin Koch, Janice Moodie, Liselotte Neumann and Catrin Nilsmark. Note that Saturday's four-ball competion was suspended due to rain and completed on Sunday.

United States: Qualifiers— Pat Hurst, Juli Inkster, Becky Iverson, Rosie Jones, Meg Mallon, Dottie Pepper, Michele Redman, Kelly Robbins, Nancy Scranton and Sherri Steinhauer; Captain's Selections—Brandie Burton and Beth Daniel.

Europe: Qualifiers— Raquel Carriedo (Spain), Laura Davies (England), Sophie Gustafson (Sweden), Trish Johnson (England), Patricia Meunier Lebouc (France), Alison Nicholas (England), Annika Sorenstam (Sweden); Captain's Selections—Helen Alfredsson (Sweden), Carin Koch (Sweden), Janice Moodie (Scotland), Liselotte Neumann (Sweden), Catrin Nilsmark (Sweden).

First Day
Foursome Match Results

Winner	Score	Loser
Davies/Nicholas	4&3	Pepper/Inkster
Johnson/Gustafson	3&2	Robbins/Hurst
Nilsmark/Koch	2&1	Burton/Iverson
Sorenstam/Moodie	1-up	Mallon/Daniel

Europe wins morning, 4-0

Four-Ball Match Results

Winner	Score	Loser
Iverson/Jones	6&5	Davies/Nicholas
Inkster/Steinhauer	halved	Johnson/Gustafson
Robbins/Hurst	1-up	Neumann/Alfresson
Moodie/Sorenstam	1-up	Mallon/Daniel

USA wins afternoon, 2½-1½; (Europe leads, 5½-2½)

Second Day
Foursome Match Results

Winner	Score	Loser
Johnson/Gustafson	3&2	Jones/Iverson
Nicholas/Alfredsson	3&2	Inkster/Steinhauer

Europe wins morning, 2-0; (Europe leads, 7½-2½)

Four-Ball Match Results

Winner	Score	Loser
Nilsmark/Koch	2&1	Scrandon/Redman
Neumann/Meunier Lebouc	halved	Pepper/Burton
Davies/Carriedo	halved	Mallon/Daniel
Hurst/Robbins	2&1	Sorenstam/Moodie

Teams tie, 2-2; (Europe leads, 9½-4½)

Third Day
Singles Match Results

Winner	Score	Loser
Inkster	5&4	Sorenstam
Burton	4&3	Gustafson
Alfredsson	4&3	Daniel
Pepper	2&1	Johnson
Robbins	3&2	Davies
Hurst	halved	Neumann
Steinhauer	halved	Nicholas
Mallon	1-up	Meunier Lebouc
Nilsmark	1-up	Jones
Iverson	3&2	Carriedo
Koch	2&1	Redman
Moodie	1-up	Scranton

USA wins day, 7-5
Europe wins Solheim Cup, 14½-11½

Overall Records
Team and Individual match play combined

United States	W-L-H
Kelly Robbins	3-1-0
Pat Hurt	2-1-1
Becky Iverson	2-2-0
Brandie Burton	1-1-1
Dottie Pepper	1-1-1
Julie Inkster	1-2-1
Meg Mallon	1-2-1
Rosie Jones	1-2-0
Sherri Steinhauer	0-1-2
Beth Daniel	0-3-1
Michele Redman	0-2-0
Nancy Scranton	0-2-0

Europe	W-L-H
Carin Koch	3-0-0
Catrin Nilsmark	3-0-0
Janice Moodie	3-1-0
Sophie Gustafson	2-1-1
Trish Johnson	2-1-1
Alison Nicholas	2-1-1
Helen Alfredsson	2-1-0
Annika Sorenstam	2-2-0
Laura Davies	1-2-1
Liselotte Neumann	0-1-2
Raquel Carriedo	0-1-1
Patricia Meunier Lebouc	0-1-1

Battle at Bighorn
Aug. 28 at Bighorn Golf Club, Indio, Calif.

This 18-hole match-play exhibition featured Tiger Woods and Sergio Garcia and was broadcast live during primetime on ABC. Garcia rolled in a 35-foot birdie putt on the 16th hole to take a 1-up lead he didn't relinquish. Each player donated $200,000 of their winnings to charity; **Purse:** $1.5 million ($1.1 million to winner, $400,000 to loser); **Sponsored by:** Lincoln Financial Group; **TV Rating:** 7.6/13 (ABC).

SCORECARD

	Hole	1	2	3	4	5	6	7	8	9		
	Par	4	4	5	4	4	3	5	3	4	36	
	Yards	429	435	531	447	367	183	519	220	449	3503	
Woods		4	4	5	4	4	3	4	3	4	even	
Garcia		5	4	4	4	5	3	4	2	4		

	Hole	10	11	12	13	14	15	16	17	18		
	Par	4	4	5	4	5	5	3	4	4	36	72
	Yards	397	434	550	227	351	538	194	457	355	3580	7083
Woods		3	4	5	3	3	4	3	4	x		
Garcia		3	4	5	3	3	4	2	4	3	1-up	1-up

Money Leaders

Official money leaders of PGA, European PGA, Senior PGA and LPGA tours for 1999 and unofficial money leaders for 2000, as compiled by the PGA, European PGA and LPGA. All European amounts are in Euro dollars (E).

PGA

Arnold Palmer Award standings: listed are tournaments played (TP); cuts made (CM); 1st, 2nd and 3rd place finishes; and earnings for the year.

2000 (Through Oct. 8)

	TP	CM	1-2-3	Earnings
1 Tiger Woods	17	17	9-3-0	$8,286,821
2 Phil Mickelson	21	19	3-2-0	3,387,457
3 Ernie Els	18	18	1-5-1	3,207,739
4 Hal Sutton	23	19	2-0-1	2,976,444
5 Jesper Parnevik	18	15	2-1-1	2,322,345
6 David Duval	18	17	1-1-3	2,282,846
7 Davis Love III	22	19	0-3-1	2,117,604
8 Vijay Singh	23	21	1-1-1	1,987,368
9 Tom Lehman	20	17	1-1-0	1,970,499
10 Jim Furyk	24	23	1-0-1	1,881,019

Final 1999

	TP	CM	1-2-3	Earnings
1 Tiger Woods	21	21	8-1-2	$6,616,585
2 David Duval	21	20	4-1-1	3,641,906
3 Davis Love III	23	21	0-4-2	2,475,328
4 Vijay Singh	29	26	1-1-1	2,283,233
5 Chris Perry	31	30	0-2-1	2,145,707
6 Hal Sutton	25	22	1-1-0	2,127,578
7 Payne Stewart	20	16	2-2-0	2,077,950
8 Justin Leonard	28	26	0-2-2	2,020,991
9 Jeff Maggert	23	20	1-1-1	2,016,469
10 David Toms	32	21	2-1-1	1,959,672

EUROPEAN PGA

Volvo Order of Merit standings: listed are tournaments played (TP); cuts made (CM); 1st, 2nd and 3rd place finishes; and earnings for the year.

2000 (Through Oct. 1)

	TP	CM	1-2-3	Earnings
1 Lee Westwood	20	19	5-1-0	E2,334,758
2 Darren Clarke	19	18	2-2-2	2,218,895
3 Ernie Els	10	10	1-3-1	1,987,064
4 Thomas Bjorn	24	21	1-3-1	1,856,841
5 Michael Campbell	19	16	3-3-0	1,665,588
6 Colin Montgomerie	21	20	2-0-3	1,609,566
7 Philip Price	23	19	0-4-0	1,223,618
8 Jose Maria Olazabal	19	16	1-0-0	975,595
9 Padraig Harrington	21	17	1-2-2	950,530
10 Miguel Angel Jimenez	16	13	0-1-0	902,952

Final 1999

	TP	CM	1-2-3	Earnings
1 Colin Montgomerie	20	20	5-1-1	E1,822,880
2 Lee Westwood	19	19	3-1-0	1,320,804
3 Sergio Garcia	15	15	2-2-0	1,317,693
4 Miguel Angel Jimenez	22	22	2-2-0	1,148,289
5 Retief Goosen	28	28	1-5-0	1,059,984
6 Paul Lawrie	27	27	2-0-0	901,452
7 Padraig Harrington	25	25	0-5-0	855,162
8 Darren Clarke	21	21	1-1-0	731,290
9 Jarmo Sandelin	24	24	2-0-0	629,131
10 Angel Cabrera	22	22	0-2-0	622,852

SENIOR PGA

2000 (Through Oct. 8)

	TP	CM	1-2-3	Earnings
1 Larry Nelson	27	27	6-6-1	$2,496,555
2 Bruce Fleisher	28	28	4-5-3	2,321,606
3 Hale Irwin	21	21	3-4-1	1,925,248
4 Gil Morgan	20	20	3-5-0	1,740,910
5 Dana Quigley	35	35	1-5-2	1,716,573
6 Doug Tewell	24	24	3-1-1	1,332,394
7 Jim Thorpe	33	33	1-3-1	1,304,747
8 Allen Doyle	30	30	1-0-3	1,302,254
9 Tom Jenkins	33	33	1-1-1	1,201,174
10 Hubert Green	25	25	2-1-0	1,197,739

Final 1999

	TP	CM	1-2-3	Earnings
1 Bruce Fleisher	32	30	7-7-1	$2,515,705
2 Hale Irwin	26	26	5-2-3	2,025,232
3 Allen Doyle	31	31	4-4-1	1,911,640
4 Larry Nelson	28	27	2-3-1	1,513,524
5 Gil Morgan	27	26	2-0-6	1,493,282
6 Dana Quigley	38	38	0-2-3	1,327,658
7 Tom Jenkins	29	29	1-0-3	1,167,176
8 Bruce Summerhays	36	36	0-2-2	1,118,377
9 Vicente Fernandez	28	26	1-2-1	1,108,245
10 Jose Maria Canizares	33	33	0-1-3	1,087,284

LPGA

2000 (Through Oct. 1)

	TP	CM	1-2-3	Earnings
1 Karrie Webb	19	19	6-3-1	$1,693,053
2 Annika Sorenstam	20	20	5-2-3	1,242,448
3 Meg Mallon	23	21	2-4-2	1,088,758
4 Juli Inkster	17	17	3-3-2	805,705
5 Mi Hyun Kim	25	24	1-2-1	780,464
6 Pat Hurst	23	22	1-4-2	750,766
7 Lorie Kane	26	22	2-1-1	709,532
8 Rosie Jones	22	19	0-2-1	587,834
9 Cristie Kerr	23	21	0-2-1	516,751
10 Laura Davies	20	20	2-0-1	510,652

Final 1999

	TP	CM	1-2-3	Earnings
1 Karrie Webb	25	23	6-6-4	$1,591,959
2 Juli Inkster	24	23	5-0-3	1,337,253
3 Se Ri Pak	27	23	3-0-0	956,926
4 Annika Sorenstam	22	21	2-4-3	863,816
5 Lorie Kane	30	29	0-3-2	757,844
6 Meg Mallon	25	25	2-1-1	679,929
7 Sherri Steinhauer	30	27	2-2-0	663,356
8 Mi Hyun Kim	30	27	2-0-1	584,246
9 Rosie Jones	24	21	1-1-1	583,796
10 Dottie Pepper	21	20	2-2-0	577,875

Major Golf Championships
MEN
The Masters

The Masters has been played every year (except during World War II) since 1934 at the Augusta National Golf Club in Augusta, Ga. Both the course (6905 yards, par 72) and the tournament were created by Bobby Jones; (*) indicates playoff winner.

Multiple winners: Jack Nicklaus (6); Arnold Palmer (4); Jimmy Demaret, Nick Faldo, Gary Player and Sam Snead (3); Seve Ballesteros, Ben Crenshaw, Ben Hogan, Bernhard Langer, Byron Nelson, Jose Maria Olazabal, Horton Smith and Tom Watson (2).

Year	Winner	Score	Runner-up
1934	Horton Smith	284	Craig Wood (285)
1935	Gene Sarazen*	282	Craig Wood (282)
1936	Horton Smith	285	Harry Cooper (286)
1937	Byron Nelson	283	Ralph Guldahl (285)
1938	Henry Picard	285	Ralph Guldahl & Harry Cooper (287)
1939	Ralph Guldahl	279	Sam Snead (280)
1940	Jimmy Demaret	280	Lloyd Mangrum (284)
1941	Craig Wood	280	Byron Nelson (283)
1942	Byron Nelson*	280	Ben Hogan (280)
1943-45	Not held		World War II
1946	Herman Keiser	282	Ben Hogan (283)
1947	Jimmy Demaret	281	Frank Stranahan & Byron Nelson (283)
1948	Claude Harmon	279	Cary Middlecoff (284)
1949	Sam Snead	282	Lloyd Mangrum & Johnny Bulla (285)
1950	Jimmy Demaret	283	Jim Ferrier (285)
1951	Ben Hogan	280	Skee Riegel (282)
1952	Sam Snead	286	Jack Burke Jr. (290)
1953	Ben Hogan	274	Ed Oliver (279)
1954	Sam Snead*	289	Ben Hogan (289)
1955	Cary Middlecoff	279	Ben Hogan (286)
1956	Jack Burke Jr.	289	Ken Venturi (290)
1957	Doug Ford	283	Sam Snead (286)
1958	Arnold Palmer	284	Doug Ford & Fred Hawkins (285)
1959	Art Wall Jr.	284	Cary Middlecoff (285)
1960	Arnold Palmer	282	Ken Venturi (283)
1961	Gary Player	280	Arnold Palmer & Charles R. Coe (281)
1962	Arnold Palmer*	280	Dow Finsterwald & Gary Player (280)
1963	Jack Nicklaus	286	Tony Lema (287)
1964	Arnold Palmer	276	Jack Nicklaus & Dave Marr (282)
1965	Jack Nicklaus	271	Arnold Palmer & Gary Player (280)
1966	Jack Nicklaus*	288	Gay Brewer Jr. & Tommy Jacobs (288)
1967	Gay Brewer Jr.	280	Bobby Nichols (281)
1968	Bob Goalby	277	Roberto DeVicenzo (278)
1969	George Archer	281	Billy Casper, George Knudson & Tom Weiskopf (282)
1970	Billy Casper*	279	Gene Littler (279)

Year	Winner	Score	Runner-up
1971	Charles Coody	279	Jack Nicklaus & Johnny Miller (281)
1972	Jack Nicklaus	286	Bruce Crampton, Bobby Mitchell & Tom Weiskopf (289)
1973	Tommy Aaron	283	J.C. Snead (284)
1974	Gary Player	278	Tom Weiskopf, & Dave Stockton (280)
1975	Jack Nicklaus	276	Johnny Miller & Tom Weiskopf (277)
1976	Ray Floyd	271	Ben Crenshaw (279)
1977	Tom Watson	276	Jack Nicklaus (278)
1978	Gary Player	277	Hubert Green, Rod Funseth & Tom Watson (278)
1979	Fuzzy Zoeller*	280	Ed Sneed & Tom Watson (280)
1980	Seve Ballesteros	275	Gibby Gilbert & Jack Newton (279)
1981	Tom Watson	280	Jack Nicklaus & Johnny Miller (282)
1982	Craig Stadler*	284	Dan Pohl (284)
1983	Seve Ballesteros	280	Ben Crenshaw & Tom Kite (284)
1984	Ben Crenshaw	277	Tom Watson (279)
1985	Bernhard Langer	282	Curtis Strange, Seve Ballesteros & Ray Floyd (284)
1986	Jack Nicklaus	279	Greg Norman & Tom Kite (280)
1987	Larry Mize*	285	Seve Ballesteros & Greg Norman (285)
1988	Sandy Lyle	281	Mark Calcavecchia (282)
1989	Nick Faldo*	283	Scott Hoch (283)
1990	Nick Faldo*	278	Ray Floyd (278)
1991	Ian Woosnam	277	J.M. Olazabal (278)
1992	Fred Couples	275	Ray Floyd (277)
1993	Bernhard Langer	277	Chip Beck (281)
1994	J.M. Olazabal	279	Tom Lehman (281)
1995	Ben Crenshaw	274	Davis Love III (275)
1996	Nick Faldo	276	Greg Norman (281)
1997	Tiger Woods	270	Tom Kite (282)
1998	Mark O'Meara	279	Fred Couples & David Duval (280)
1999	J.M. Olazabal	280	Davis Love III (282)
2000	Vijay Singh	278	Ernie Els (281)

The Masters (Cont.)

*PLAYOFFS:

1935: Gene Sarazen (144) def. Craig Wood (149) in 36 holes. **1942:** Byron Nelson (69) def. Ben Hogan (70) in 18 holes. **1954:** Sam Snead (70) def. Ben Hogan (71) in 18 holes. **1962:** Arnold Palmer (68) def. Gary Player (71) and Dow Finsterwald (77) in 18 holes. **1966:** Jack Nicklaus (70) def. Tommy Jacobs (72) and Gay Brewer Jr. (78) in 18 holes. **1970:** Billy Casper (69) def. Gene Littler (74) in 18 holes. **1979:** Fuzzy Zoeller (4-3) def. Ed Sneed (4-4) and Tom Watson (4-4) on 2nd hole of sudden death. **1982:** Craig Stadler (4) def. Dan Pohl (5) on 1st hole of sudden death. **1987:** Larry Mize (4-3) def. Greg Norman (4-4) and Seve Ballesteros (5) on 2nd hole of sudden death. **1989:** Nick Faldo (5-3) def. Scott Hoch (5-4) on 2nd hole of sudden death. **1990:** Nick Faldo (4-4) def. Raymond Floyd (4) on second hole of sudden death.

U.S. Open

Played at a different course each year, the U.S. Open was launched by the new U.S. Golf Association in 1895. The Open was a 36-hole event from 1895-97 and has been 72 holes since then. It switched from a 3-day, 36-hole Saturday finish to 4 days of play in 1965. Note that (*) indicates playoff winner and (a) indicates amateur winner.

Multiple winners: Willie Anderson, Ben Hogan, Bobby Jones and Jack Nicklaus (4); Hale Irwin (3); Julius Boros, Billy Casper, Ernie Els, Ralph Guldahl, Walter Hagen, Lee Janzen, John McDermott, Cary Middlecoff, Andy North, Gene Sarazen, Alex Smith, Payne Stewart, Curtis Strange and Lee Trevino (2).

Year	Winner	Score	Runner-up	Course	Location
1895	Horace Rawlins	173	Willie Dunn (175)	Newport GC	Newport, R.I.
1896	James Foulis	152	Horace Rawlins (155)	Shinnecock Hills GC	Southampton, N.Y.
1897	Joe Lloyd	162	Willie Anderson (163)	Chicago GC	Wheaton, Ill.
1898	Fred Herd	328	Alex Smith (335)	Myopia Hunt Club	Hamilton, Mass.
1899	Willie Smith	315	George Low, W.H. Way & Val Fitzjohn (326)	Baltimore CC	Baltimore
1900	Harry Vardon	313	J.H. Taylor (315)	Chicago GC	Wheaton, Ill.
1901	Willie Anderson*	331	Alex Smith (331)	Myopia Hunt Club	Hamilton, Mass.
1902	Laurie Auchterlonie	307	Stewart Gardner (313)	Garden City GC	Garden City, N.Y.
1903	Willie Anderson*	307	David Brown (307)	Baltusrol GC	Springfield, N.J.
1904	Willie Anderson*	303	Gil Nicholls (308)	Glen View Club	Golf, Ill.
1905	Willie Anderson	314	Alex Smith (316)	Myopia Hunt Club	Hamilton, Mass.
1906	Alec Smith	295	Willie Smith (302)	Onwentsia Club	Lake Forest, Ill.
1907	Alec Ross	302	Gil Nicholls (304)	Phila. Cricket Club	Chestnut Hill, Pa.
1908	Fred McLeod*	322	Willie Smith (322)	Myopia Hunt Club	Hamilton, Mass.
1909	George Sargent	290	Tom McNamara (294)	Englewood GC	Englewood, N.J.
1910	Alex Smith*	298	Macdonald Smith & John McDermott (298)	Phila. Cricket Club	Chestnut Hill, Pa.
1911	John McDermott*	307	George Simpson & Mike Brady (307)	Chicago GC	Wheaton, Ill.
1912	John McDermott	294	Tom McNamara (296)	CC of Buffalo	Buffalo
1913	a-Francis Ouimet*	304	Harry Vardon & Ted Ray (304)	The Country Club	Brookline, Mass.
1914	Walter Hagen	290	a-Chick Evans (291)	Midlothian CC	Blue Island, Ill.
1915	a-John Travers	297	Tom McNamara (298)	Baltusrol GC	Springfield, N.J.
1916	a-Chick Evans	286	Jock Hutchinson (288)	Minikahda Club	Minneapolis
1917-18 Not held			World War I		
1919	Walter Hagen*	301	Mike Brady (301)	Brae Burn CC	West Newton, Mass.
1920	Ted Ray	295	Jock Hutchison, Jack Burke, Leo Diegel & Harry Vardon (296)	Inverness Club	Toledo, Ohio
1921	Jim Barnes	289	Walter Hagen & Fred McLeod (298)	Columbia CC	Chevy Chase, Md.
1922	Gene Sarazen	288	a-Bobby Jones & John Black (289)	Skokie CC	Glencoe, Ill.
1923	a-Bobby Jones*	296	Bobby Cruickshank (296)	Inwood CC	Inwood, N.Y.
1924	Cyril Walker	297	a-Bobby Jones (300)	Oakland Hills CC	Birmingham, Mich.
1925	Willie Macfarlane*	291	a-Bobby Jones (291)	Worcester CC	Worcester, Mass.
1926	a-Bobby Jones	293	Joe Turnesa (294)	Scioto CC	Columbus, Ohio
1927	Tommy Armour*	301	Harry Cooper (301)	Oakmont CC	Oakmont, Pa.
1928	Johnny Farrell*	294	a-Bobby Jones (294)	Olympia Fields CC	Matteson, Ill.
1929	a-Bobby Jones*	294	Al Espinosa (294)	Winged Foot CC	Mamaroneck, N.Y.
1930	a-Bobby Jones	287	Macdonald Smith (289)	Interlachen CC	Hopkins, Minn.
1931	Billy Burke*	292	George Von Elm (292)	Inverness Club	Toledo, Ohio
1932	Gene Sarazen	286	Bobby Cruickshank & Phil Perkins (289)	Fresh Meadow CC	Flushing, N.Y.
1933	a-Johnny Goodman	287	Ralph Guldahl (288)	North Shore GC	Glenview, Ill.
1934	Olin Dutra	293	Gene Sarazen (294)	Merion Cricket Club	Ardmore, Pa.
1935	Sam Parks Jr.	299	Jimmy Thomson (301)	Oakmont CC	Oakmont, Pa.
1936	Tony Manero	282	Harry E. Cooper (284)	Baltusrol GC	Springfield, N.J.
1937	Ralph Guldahl	281	Sam Snead (283)	Oakland Hills CC	Birmingham, Mich.
1938	Ralph Guldahl	284	Dick Metz (290)	Cherry Hills CC	Denver
1939	Byron Nelson*	284	Craig Wood & Denny Shute (284)	Philadelphia CC	Philadelphia

Year	Winner	Score	Runner-up	Course	Location
1940	Lawson Little*	287	Gene Sarazen (287)	Canterbury GC	Cleveland
1941	Craig Wood	284	Denny Shute (287)	Colonial Club	Ft. Worth
1942-45	Not held		World War II		
1946	Lloyd Mangrum*	284	Byron Nelson & Vic Ghezzi (284)	Canterbury GC	Cleveland
1947	Lew Worsham*	282	Sam Snead (282)	St. Louis CC	Clayton, Mo.
1948	Ben Hogan	276	Jimmy Demaret (278)	Riviera CC	Los Angeles
1949	Cary Middlecoff	286	Clayton Heafner & Sam Snead (287)	Medinah CC	Medinah, Ill.
1950	Ben Hogan*	287	Lloyd Mangrum & George Fazio (287)	Merion Golf Club	Ardmore, Pa.
1951	Ben Hogan	287	Clayton Heafner (289)	Oakland Hills CC	Birmingham, Mich.
1952	Julius Boros	281	Ed Oliver (285)	Northwood Club	Dallas
1953	Ben Hogan	283	Sam Snead (289)	Oakmont CC	Oakmont, Pa.
1954	Ed Furgol	284	Gene Littler (285)	Baltusrol GC	Springfield, N.J.
1955	Jack Fleck*	287	Ben Hogan (287)	Olympic CC	San Francisco
1956	Cary Middlecoff	281	Ben Hogan & Julius Boros (282)	Oak Hill CC	Rochester, N.Y.
1957	Dick Mayer*	282	Cary Middlecoff (282)	Inverness Club	Toledo, Ohio
1958	Tommy Bolt	283	Gary Player (287)	Southern Hills CC	Tulsa
1959	Billy Casper	282	Bob Rosburg (283)	Winged Foot GC	Marmaroneck, N.Y.
1960	Arnold Palmer	280	Jack Nicklaus (282)	Cherry Hills CC	Denver
1961	Gene Littler	281	Doug Sanders & Bob Goalby (282)	Oakland Hills CC	Birmingham, Mich.
1962	Jack Nicklaus*	283	Arnold Palmer (283)	Oakmont CC	Oakmont, Pa.
1963	Julius Boros*	293	Arnold Palmer & Jacky Cupit (293)	The Country Club	Brookline, Mass.
1964	Ken Venturi	278	Tommy Jacobs (282)	Congressional CC	Bethesda, Md.
1965	Gary Player*	282	Kel Nagle (282)	Bellerive CC	St. Louis
1966	Billy Casper*	278	Arnold Palmer (278)	Olympic CC	San Francisco
1967	Jack Nicklaus	275	Arnold Palmer (279)	Baltusrol GC	Springfield, N.J.
1968	Lee Trevino	275	Jack Nicklaus (279)	Oak Hill CC	Rochester, N.Y.
1969	Orville Moody	281	Al Geiberger, Deane Beman & Bob Rosburg (282)	Champions GC	Houston
1970	Tony Jacklin	281	Dave Hill (288)	Hazeltine National GC	Chaska, Minn.
1971	Lee Trevino*	280	Jack Nicklaus (280)	Merion GC	Ardmore, Pa.
1972	Jack Nicklaus	290	Bruce Crampton (293)	Pebble Beach GL	Pebble Beach, Calif.
1973	Johnny Miller	279	John Schlee (280)	Oakmont CC	Oakmont, Pa.
1974	Hale Irwin	287	Forest Fezler (289)	Winged Foot GC	Mamaroneck, N.Y.
1975	Lou Graham*	287	John Mahaffey (287)	Medinah CC	Medinah, Ill.
1976	Jerry Pate	277	Al Geiberger & Tom Weiskopf (279)	Atlanta AC	Duluth, Ga.
1977	Hubert Green	278	Lou Graham (279)	Southern Hills CC	Tulsa
1978	Andy North	285	Dave Stockton & J.C. Snead (286)	Cherry Hills CC	Denver
1979	Hale Irwin	284	Gary Player & Jerry Pate (286)	Inverness Club	Toledo, Ohio
1980	Jack Nicklaus	272	Isao Aoki (274)	Baltusrol GC	Springfield, N.J.
1981	David Graham	273	George Burns & Bill Rogers (276)	Merion GC	Ardmore, Pa.
1982	Tom Watson	282	Jack Nicklaus (284)	Pebble Beach GL	Pebble Beach, Calif.
1983	Larry Nelson	280	Tom Watson (281)	Oakmont CC	Oakmont, Pa.
1984	Fuzzy Zoeller*	276	Greg Norman (276)	Winged Foot GC	Mamaroneck, N.Y.
1985	Andy North	279	Dave Barr, T.C. Chen & Denis Watson (280)	Oakland Hills CC	Birmingham, Mich.
1986	Ray Floyd	279	Lanny Wadkins & Chip Beck (281)	Shinnecock Hills GC	Southampton, N.Y.
1987	Scott Simpson	277	Tom Watson (278)	Olympic Club	San Francisco
1988	Curtis Strange*	278	Nick Faldo (278)	The Country Club	Brookline, Mass.
1989	Curtis Strange	278	Chip Beck, Ian Woosnam & Mark McCumber (279)	Oak Hill CC	Rochester, N.Y.
1990	Hale Irwin*	280	Mike Donald (280)	Medinah CC	Medinah, Ill.
1991	Payne Stewart*	282	Scott Simpson (282)	Hazeltine National GC	Chaska, Minn.
1992	Tom Kite	285	Jeff Sluman (287)	Pebble Beach GL	Pebble Beach, Calif.
1993	Lee Janzen	272	Payne Stewart (274)	Baltusrol GC	Springfield, N.J.
1994	Ernie Els*	279	Colin Montgomerie (279) & Loren Roberts (279)	Oakmont CC	Oakmont, Pa.
1995	Corey Pavin	280	Greg Norman (282)	Shinnecock Hills GC	Southampton, N.Y.

U.S. Open (Cont.)

Year	Winner	Score	Runner-up	Course	Location
1996	Steve Jones	278	Davis Love III & Tom Lehman (279)	Oakland Hills CC	Bloomfield Hills, Mich.
1997	Ernie Els	276	Colin Montgomerie (277)	Congressional CC	Bethesda, Md.
1998	Lee Janzen	280	Payne Stewart (281)	Olympic Club	San Francisco
1999	Payne Stewart	279	Phil Mickelson (280)	Pinehurst CC	Pinehurst, N.C.
2000	Tiger Woods	272	Miguel Angel Jimenez & Ernie Els (287)	Pebble Beach GL	Pebble Beach, Calif.

*PLAYOFFS:

1901: Willie Anderson (85) def. Alex Smith (86) in 18 holes. **1903:** Willie Anderson (82) def. David Brown (84) in 18 holes. **1908:** Fred McLeod (77) def. Willie Smith (83) in 18 holes. **1910:** Alex Smith (71) def. John McDermott (75) & Macdonald Smith (77) in 18 holes. **1911:** John McDermott (80) def. Mike Brady (82) & George Simpson (85) in 18 holes. **1913:** Francis Ouimet (72) def. Harry Vardon (77) & Edward Ray (78) in 18 holes. **1919:** Walter Hagen (77) def. Mike Brady (78) in 18 holes. **1923:** Bobby Jones (76) def. Bobby Cruickshank (78) in 18 holes. **1925:** Willie Macfarlane (75-72—147) def. Bobby Jones (75-73—148) in 36 holes. **1927:** Tommy Armour (76) def. Harry Cooper (79) in 18 holes. **1928:** Johnny Farrell (70-73—143) def. Bobby Jones (73-71—144) in 36 holes. **1929:** Bobby Jones (141) def. Al Espinosa (164) in 36 holes. **1931:** Billy Burke (149-148) def. George Von Elm (149-149) in 72 holes. **1939:** Byron Nelson (68-70) def. Craig Wood (68-73) and Denny Shute (76) in 36 holes. **1940:** Lawson Little (70) def. Gene Sarazen (73) in 18 holes. **1946:** Lloyd Mangrum (72-72—144) def. Byron Nelson (72-73—145) and Vic Ghezzi (72-73—145) in 36 holes. **1947:** Lew Worsham (69) def. Sam Snead (70) in 18 holes. **1950:** Ben Hogan (69) def. Llyod Mangrum (73) & George Fazio (75) in 18 holes. **1955:** Jack Fleck (69) def. Ben Hogan (72) in 18 holes. **1957:** Dick Mayer (72) def. Cary Middlecoff (79) in 18 holes. **1962:** Jack Nicklaus (71) def. Arnold Palmer (74) in 18 holes. **1963:** Julius Boros (70) def. Jacky Cupit (73) & Arnold Palmer (76) in 18 holes. **1965:** Gary Player (71) def. Kel Nagle (74) in 18 holes. **1966:** Billy Casper (69) def. Arnold Palmer (73) in 18 holes. **1971:** Lee Trevino (68) def. Jack Nicklaus (71) in 18 holes. **1975:** Lou Graham (71) def. John Mahaffey (73) in 18 holes. **1984:** Fuzzy Zoeller (67) def. Greg Norman (75) in 18 holes. **1988:** Curtis Strange (71) def. Nick Faldo (75) in 18 holes. **1990:** Hale Irwin (74-3) def. Mike Donald (74-4) on 1st hole of sudden death after 18 holes. **1991:** Payne Stewart (75) def. Scott Simpson (77) in 18 holes. **1994:** Ernie Els (74-4-4) def. Loren Roberts (74-4-5) and Colin Montgomerie (78) on 2nd hole of sudden death after 18 holes.

British Open

The oldest of the Majors, the Open began in 1860 to determine "the champion golfer of the world." While only professional golfers participated in the first year of the tournament, amateurs have been invited ever since. Competition was extended from 36 to 72 holes in 1892. Conducted by the Royal and Ancient Golf Club of St. Andrews, the Open is rotated among select golf courses in England and Scotland. Note that (*) indicates playoff winner and (a) indicates amateur winner.

Multiple winners: Harry Vardon (6); James Braid, J.H. Taylor, Peter Thomson and Tom Watson (5); Walter Hagen, Bobby Locke, Tom Morris Sr., Tom Morris Jr. and Willie Park (4); Jamie Anderson, Seve Ballesteros, Henry Cotton, Nick Faldo, Bob Ferguson, Bobby Jones, Jack Nicklaus and Gary Player (3); Harold Hilton, Bob Martin, Greg Norman, Arnold Palmer, Willie Park Jr. and Lee Trevino (2).

Year	Winner	Score	Runner-up	Course	Location
1860	Willie Park	174	Tom Morris Sr. (176)	Prestwick Club	Ayrshire, Scotland
1861	Tom Morris Sr.	163	Willie Park (167)	Prestwick Club	Ayrshire, Scotland
1862	Tom Morris Sr.	163	Willie Park (176)	Prestwick Club	Ayrshire, Scotland
1863	Willie Park	168	Tom Morris Sr. (170)	Prestwick Club	Ayrshire, Scotland
1864	Tom Morris Sr.	167	Andrew Strath (169)	Prestwick Club	Ayrshire, Scotland
1865	Andrew Strath	162	Willie Park (164)	Prestwick Club	Ayrshire, Scotland
1866	Willie Park	169	David Park (171)	Prestwick Club	Ayrshire, Scotland
1867	Tom Morris Sr.	170	Willie Park (172)	Prestwick Club	Ayrshire, Scotland
1868	Tom Morris Jr.	157	Robert Andrew (159)	Prestwick Club	Ayrshire, Scotland
1869	Tom Morris Jr.	154	Tom Morris Sr. (157)	Prestwick Club	Ayrshire, Scotland
1870	Tom Morris Jr.	149	Bob Kirk (161)	Prestwick Club	Ayrshire, Scotland
1871	Not held				
1872	Tom Morris Jr.	166	David Strath (169)	Prestwick Club	Ayrshire, Scotland
1873	Tom Kidd	179	Jamie Anderson (180)	St. Andrews	St. Andrews, Scotland
1874	Mungo Park	159	Tom Morris Jr. (161)	Musselburgh	Musselburgh, Scotland
1875	Willie Park	166	Bob Martin (168)	Prestwick Club	Ayrshire, Scotland
1876	Bob Martin*	176	David Strath (176)	St. Andrews	St. Andrews, Scotland
1877	Jamie Anderson	160	Bob Pringle (162)	Musselburgh	Musselburgh, Scotland
1878	Jamie Anderson	157	Bob Kirk (159)	Prestwick Club	Ayrshire, Scotland
1879	Jamie Anderson	169	Andrew Kirkaldy & James Allan (172)	St. Andrews	St. Andrews, Scotland
1880	Bob Ferguson	162	Peter Paxton (167)	Musselburgh	Musselburgh, Scotland
1881	Bob Ferguson	170	Jamie Anderson (173)	Prestwick Club	Ayrshire, Scotland
1882	Bob Ferguson	171	Willie Fernie (174)	St. Andrews	St. Andrews, Scotland
1883	Willie Fernie*	159	Bob Ferguson (159)	Musselburgh	Musselburgh, Scotland
1884	Jack Simpson	160	David Rollan & Willie Fernie (164)	Prestwick Club	Ayrshire, Scotland
1885	Bob Martin	171	Archie Simpson (172)	St. Andrews	St. Andrews, Scotland
1886	David Brown	157	Willie Campbell (159)	Musselburgh	Musselburgh, Scotland
1887	Willie Park Jr.	161	Bob Martin (162)	Prestwick Club	Ayrshire, Scotland
1888	Jack Burns	171	David Anderson & Ben Sayers (172)	St. Andrews	St. Andrews, Scotland
1889	Willie Park Jr.*	155	Andrew Kirkaldy (155)	Musselburgh	Musselburgh, Scotland

Year	Winner	Score	Runner-up	Course	Location
1890	a-John Ball	164	Willie Fernie (167) & A. Simpson (167)	Prestwick Club	Ayrshire, Scotland
1891	Hugh Kirkaldy	166	Andrew Kirkaldy & Willie Fernie (168)	St. Andrews	St. Andrews, Scotland
1892	a-Harold Hilton	305	John Ball, Sandy Herd & Hugh Kirkaldy (308)	Muirfield	Gullane, Scotland
1893	Willie Auchterlonie	322	Johnny Laidlay (324)	Prestwick Club	Ayrshire, Scotland
1894	J.H. Taylor	326	Douglas Rolland (331)	Royal St. George's	Sandwich, England
1895	J.H. Taylor	322	Sandy Herd (326)	St. Andrews	St. Andrews, Scotland
1896	Harry Vardon*	316	J.H. Taylor (316)	Muirfield	Gullane, Scotland
1897	a-Harold Hilton	314	James Braid (315)	Hoylake	Hoylake, England
1898	Harry Vardon	307	Willie Park Jr. (308)	Prestwick Club	Ayrshire, Scotland
1899	Harry Vardon	310	Jack White (315)	Royal St. George's	Sandwich, England
1900	J.H. Taylor	309	Harry Vardon (317)	St. Andrews	St. Andrews, Scotland
1901	James Braid	309	Harry Vardon (312)	Muirfield	Gullane, Scotland
1902	Sandy Herd	307	Harry Vardon (308)	Hoylake	Hoylake, England
1903	Harry Vardon	300	Tom Vardon (306)	Prestwick Club	Ayrshire, Scotland
1904	Jack White	296	James Braid (297)	Royal St. George's	Sandwich, England
1905	James Braid	318	J.H. Taylor (323) & Rolland Jones (323)	St. Andrews	St. Andrews, Scotland
1906	James Braid	300	J.H. Taylor (304)	Muirfield	Gullane, Scotland
1907	Arnaud Massy	312	J.H. Taylor (314)	Hoylake	Hoylake, England
1908	James Braid	291	Tom Ball (299)	Prestwick Club	Ayrshire, Scotland
1909	J.H. Taylor	295	James Braid (299)	Deal	Deal, England
1910	James Braid	299	Sandy Herd (303)	St. Andrews	St. Andrews, Scotland
1911	Harry Vardon*	303	Arnaud Massy (303)	Royal St. George's	Sandwich, England
1912	Ted Ray	295	Harry Vardon (299)	Muirfield	Gullane, Scotland
1913	J.H. Taylor	304	Ted Ray (312)	Hoylake	Hoylake, England
1914	Harry Vardon	306	J.H. Taylor (309)	Prestwick Club	Ayrshire, Scotland
1915-19	Not held		World War I		
1920	George Duncan	303	Sandy Herd (305)	Deal	Deal, England
1921	Jock Hutchison*	296	Roger Wethered (296)	St. Andrews	St. Andrews, Scotland
1922	Walter Hagen	300	George Duncan & Jim Barnes (301)	Royal St. George's	Sandwich, England
1923	Arthur Havers	295	Walter Hagen (296)	Royal Troon	Troon, Scotland
1924	Walter Hagen	301	Ernest Whitcombe (302)	Hoylake	Hoylake, England
1925	Jim Barnes	300	Archie Compston & Ted Ray (301)	Prestwick Club	Ayrshire, Scotland
1926	a-Bobby Jones	291	Al Watrous (293)	Royal Lytham	Lytham, England
1927	a-Bobby Jones	285	Aubrey Boomer (291)	St. Andrews	St. Andrews, Scotland
1928	Walter Hagen	292	Gene Sarazen (294)	Royal St. George's	Sandwich, England
1929	Walter Hagen	292	Johnny Farrell (298)	Muirfield	Gullane, Scotland
1930	a-Bobby Jones	291	Macdonald Smith & Leo Diegel (293)	Hoylake	Hoylake, England
1931	Tommy Armour	296	Jose Jurado (297)	Carnoustie	Carnoustie, Scotland
1932	Gene Sarazen	283	Macdonald Smith (288)	Prince's	Prince's, England
1933	Denny Shute*	292	Craig Wood (292)	St. Andrews	St. Andrews, Scotland
1934	Henry Cotton	283	Sid Brews (288)	Royal St. George's	Sandwich, England
1935	Alf Perry	283	Alf Padgham (287)	Muirfield	Gullane, Scotland
1936	Alf Padgham	287	Jimmy Adams (288)	Hoylake	Hoylake, England
1937	Henry Cotton	290	Reg Whitcombe (292)	Carnoustie	Carnoustie, Scotland
1938	Reg Whitcombe	295	Jimmy Adams (297)	Royal St. George's	Sandwich, England
1939	Dick Burton	290	Johnny Bulla (292)	St. Andrews	St. Andrews, Scotland
1940-45	Not held		World War II		
1946	Sam Snead	290	Bobby Locke (294) & Johnny Bulla (294)	St. Andrews	St. Andrews, Scotland
1947	Fred Daly	293	Frank Stranahan & Reg Horne (294)	Hoylake	Hoylake, England
1948	Henry Cotton	284	Fred Daly (289)	Muirfield	Gullane, Scotland
1949	Bobby Locke*	283	Harry Bradshaw (283)	Royal St. George's	Sandwich, England
1950	Bobby Locke	279	Roberto de Vicenzo (281)	Royal Troon	Troon, Scotland
1951	Max Faulkner	285	Tony Cerda (287)	Royal Portrush	Portrush, Ireland
1952	Bobby Locke	287	Peter Thomson (288)	Royal Lytham	Lytham, England
1953	Ben Hogan	282	Frank Stranahan, Dai Rees, Tony Cerda & Peter Thomson (286)	Carnoustie	Carnoustie, Scotland
1954	Peter Thomson	283	Sid Scott, Dai Rees & Bobby Locke (284)	Royal Birkdale	Southport, England
1955	Peter Thomson	281	Johny Fallon (283)	St. Andrews	St. Andrews, Scotland
1956	Peter Thomson	286	Flory Van Donck (289)	Hoylake	Hoylake, England

British Open (Cont.)

Year	Winner	Score	Runner-up	Course	Location
1957	Bobby Locke	279	Peter Thomson (282)	St. Andrews	St. Andrews, Scotland
1958	Peter Thomson*	278	Dave Thomas (278)	Royal Lytham	Lytham, England
1959	Gary Player	284	Flory Van Donck & Fred Bullock (286)	Muirfield	Gullane, Scotland
1960	Kel Nagle	278	Arnold Palmer (279)	St. Andrews	St. Andrews, Scotland
1961	Arnold Palmer	284	Dai Rees (285)	Royal Birkdale	Southport, England
1962	Arnold Palmer	276	Kel Nagle (282)	Royal Troon	Troon, Scotland
1963	Bob Charles*	277	Phil Rodgers (277)	Royal Lytham	Lytham, England
1964	Tony Lema	279	Jack Nicklaus (284)	St. Andrews	St. Andrews, Scotland
1965	Peter Thomson	285	Christy O'Connor & Brian Huggett (287)	Royal Birkdale	Southport, England
1966	Jack Nicklaus	282	Doug Sanders & Dave Thomas (283)	Muirfield	Gullane, Scotland
1967	Roberto de Vicenzo	278	Jack Nicklaus (280)	Hoylake	Hoylake, England
1968	Gary Player	289	Jack Nicklaus & Bob Charles (291)	Carnoustie	Carnoustie, Scotland
1969	Tony Jacklin	280	Bob Charles (282)	Royal Lytham	Lytham, England
1970	Jack Nicklaus*	283	Doug Sanders (283)	St. Andrews	St. Andrews, Scotland
1971	Lee Trevino	278	Lu Liang Huan (279)	Royal Birkdale	Southport, England
1972	Lee Trevino	278	Jack Nicklaus (279)	Muirfield	Gullane, Scotland
1973	Tom Weiskopf	276	Johnny Miller & Neil Coles (279)	Royal Troon	Troon, Scotland
1974	Gary Player	282	Peter Oosterhuis (286)	Royal Lytham	Lytham, England
1975	Tom Watson*	279	Jack Newton (279)	Carnoustie	Carnoustie, Scotland
1976	Johnny Miller	279	Seve Ballesteros & Jack Nicklaus (285)	Royal Birkdale	Southport, England
1977	Tom Watson	268	Jack Nicklaus (269)	Turnberry	Turnberry, Scotland
1978	Jack Nicklaus	281	Tom Kite, Ray Floyd, Ben Crenshaw & Simon Owen (283)	St. Andrews	St. Andrews, Scotland
1979	Seve Ballesteros	283	Jack Nicklaus & Ben Crenshaw (286)	Royal Lytham	Lytham, England
1980	Tom Watson	271	Lee Trevino (275)	Muirfield	Gullane, Scotland
1981	Bill Rogers	276	Bernhard Langer (280)	Royal St. George's	Sandwich, England
1982	Tom Watson	284	Peter Oosterhuis & Nick Price (285)	Royal Troon	Troon, Scotland
1983	Tom Watson	275	Hale Irwin & Andy Bean (276)	Royal Birkdale	Southport, England
1984	Seve Ballesteros	276	Bernhard Langer & Tom Watson (278)	St. Andrews	St. Andrews, Scotland
1985	Sandy Lyle	282	Payne Stewart (283)	Royal St. George's	Sandwich, England
1986	Greg Norman	280	Gordon J. Brand (285)	Turnberry	Turnberry, Scotland
1987	Nick Faldo	279	Paul Azinger & Rodger Davis (280)	Muirfield	Gullane, Scotland
1988	Seve Ballesteros	273	Nick Price (275)	Royal Lytham	Lytham, England
1989	Mark Calcavecchia*	275	Greg Norman & Wayne Grady (275)	Royal Troon	Troon, Scotland
1990	Nick Faldo	270	Payne Stewart & Mark McNulty (275)	St. Andrews	St. Andrews, Scotland
1991	Ian Baker-Finch	272	Mike Harwood (274)	Royal Birkdale	Southport, England
1992	Nick Faldo	272	John Cook (273)	Muirfield	Gullane, Scotland
1993	Greg Norman	267	Nick Faldo (269)	Royal St. George's	Sandwich, England
1994	Nick Price	268	Jesper Parnevik (269)	Turnberry	Turnberry, Scotland
1995	John Daly*	282	Costantino Rocca (282)	St. Andrews	St. Andrews, Scotland
1996	Tom Lehman	271	Mark McCumber & Ernie Els (273)	Royal Lytham	Lytham, England
1997	Justin Leonard	272	Jesper Parnevik & Darren Clarke (275)	Royal Troon	Troon, Scotland
1998	Mark O'Meara*	280	Brian Watts (280)	Royal Birkdale	Southport, England
1999	Paul Lawrie*	290	Justin Leonard & Jean Van de Velde (290)	Carnoustie	Carnoustie, Scotland
2000	Tiger Woods	269	Thomas Bjorn & Ernie Els (277)	St. Andrews	St. Andrews, Scotland

*PLAYOFFS:
1876: Bob Martin awarded title when David Strath refused playoff. **1883:** Willie Fernie (158) def. Robert Ferguson (159) in 36 holes. **1889:** Willie Park Jr. (158) def. Andrew Kirkaldy (163) in 36 holes. **1896:** Harry Vardon (157) def. John H. Taylor (161) in 36 holes. **1911:** Harry Vardon won when Arnaud Massy conceded at 35th hole. **1921:** Jock Hutchison (150) def. Roger Wethered (159) in 36 holes. **1933:** Denny Shute (149) def. Craig Wood (154) in 36 holes. **1949:** Bobby Locke (135) def. Harry Bradshaw (147) in 36 holes. **1958:** Peter Thomson (139) def. Dave Thomas (143) in 36 holes. **1963:** Bob

Charles (140) def. Phil Rogers (148) in 36 holes. **1970:** Jack Nicklaus (72) def. Doug Sanders (73) in 18 holes. **1975:** Tom Watson (71) def. Jack Newton (72) in 18 holes. **1989:** Mark Calcavecchia (4-3-3-3—13) def. Wayne Grady (4-4-4-4—16) and Greg Norman (3-3-4) in 4 holes. **1995:** John Daly (3-4-4-4—15) def. Costantino Rocca (4-5-7-3—19) in 4 holes. **1998:** Mark O'Meara (4-4-5-4—17) def. Brian Watts (5-4-5-5—19) in 4 holes **1999:** Paul Lawrie (5-4-3-3—15) def. Justin Leonard (5-4-4-5—18) and Jean Van de Velde (6-4-3-5—18) in 4 holes.

PGA Championship

The PGA Championship began in 1916 as a professional golfers match play tournament, but switched to stroke play in 1958. Conducted by the PGA of America, the tournament is played on a different course each year.

Mulitple winners: Walter Hagen and Jack Nicklaus (5); Gene Sarazen and Sam Snead (3); Jim Barnes, Leo Diegel, Ray Floyd, Ben Hogan, Byron Nelson, Larry Nelson, Gary Player, Nick Price, Paul Runyan, Denny Shute, Dave Stockton, Lee Trevino and Tiger Woods (2).

Year	Winner	Score	Runner-up	Course	Location
1916	Jim Barnes	1-up	Jock Hutchison	Siwanoy CC	Bronxville, N.Y.
1917-18	Not held		World War I		
1919	Jim Barnes	6 & 5	Fred McLeod	Engineers CC	Roslyn, N.Y.
1920	Jock Hutchison	1-up	J. Douglas Edgar	Flossmoor CC	Flossmoor, Ill.
1921	Walter Hagen	3 & 2	Jim Barnes	Inwood CC	Inwood, N.Y.
1922	Gene Sarazen	4 & 3	Emmet French	Oakmont CC	Oakmont, Pa.
1923	Gene Sarazen*	1-up/38	Walter Hagen	Pelham CC	Pelham, N.Y.
1924	Walter Hagen	2-up	Jim Barnes	French Lick CC	French Lick, Ind.
1925	Walter Hagen	6 & 5	Bill Mehlhorn	Olympia Fields CC	Matteson, Ill.
1926	Walter Hagen	5 & 3	Leo Diegel	Salisbury CC	Westbury, N.Y.
1927	Walter Hagen	1-up	Joe Turnesa	Cedar Crest CC	Dallas
1928	Leo Diegel	6 & 5	Al Espinosa	Five Farms CC	Baltimore
1929	Leo Diegel	6 & 4	John Farrell	Hillcrest CC	Los Angeles
1930	Tommy Armour	1-up	Gene Sarazen	Fresh Meadow CC	Flushing, N.Y.
1931	Tom Creavy	2 & 1	Denny Shute	Wannamoisett CC	Rumford, R.I.
1932	Olin Dutra	4 & 3	Frank Walsh	Keller GC	St. Paul, Minn.
1933	Gene Sarazen	5 & 4	Willie Goggin	Blue Mound CC	Milwaukee
1934	Paul Runyan*	1-up/38	Craig Wood	Park CC	Williamsville, N.Y.
1935	Johnny Revolta	5 & 4	Tommy Armour	Twin Hills CC	Oklahoma City
1936	Denny Shute	3 & 2	Jimmy Thomson	Pinehurst CC	Pinehurst, N.C.
1937	Denny Shute*	1-up/37	Harold McSpaden	Pittsburgh FC	Aspinwall, Pa.
1938	Paul Runyan	8 & 7	Sam Snead	Shawnee CC	Shawnee-on-Del., Pa.
1939	Henry Picard*	1-up/37	Byron Nelson	Pomonok CC	Flushing, N.Y.
1940	Byron Nelson	1-up	Sam Snead	Hershey CC	Hershey, Pa.
1941	Vic Ghezzi*	1-up/38	Byron Nelson	Cherry Hills CC	Denver
1942	Sam Snead	2 & 1	Jim Turnesa	Seaview CC	Atlantic City, N.J.
1943	Not held		World War II		
1944	Bob Hamilton	1-up	Byron Nelson	Manito G & CC	Spokane, Wash.
1945	Byron Nelson	4 & 3	Sam Byrd	Morraine CC	Dayton, Ohio
1946	Ben Hogan	6 & 4	Porky Oliver	Portland GC	Portland, Ore.
1947	Jim Ferrier	2 & 1	Chick Harbert	Plum Hollow CC	Detroit
1948	Ben Hogan	7 & 6	Mike Turnesa	Norwood Hills CC	St. Louis
1949	Sam Snead	3 & 2	John Palmer	Hermitage CC	Richmond, Va.
1950	Chandler Harper	4 & 3	Henry Williams Jr.	Scioto CC	Columbus, Ohio
1951	Sam Snead	7 & 6	Walter Burkemo	Oakmont CC	Oakmont, Pa.
1952	Jim Turnesa	1-up	Chick Harbert	Big Spring CC	Louisville
1953	Walter Burkemo	2 & 1	Felice Torza	Birmingham CC	Birmingham, Mich.
1954	Chick Harbert	4 & 3	Walter Burkemo	Keller GC	St. Paul, Minn.
1955	Doug Ford	4 & 3	Cary Middlecoff	Meadowbrook CC	Detroit
1956	Jack Burke	3 & 2	Ted Kroll	Blue Hill CC	Boston
1957	Lionel Hebert	2 & 1	Dow Finsterwald	Miami Valley GC	Dayton, Ohio
1958	Dow Finsterwald	276	Billy Casper (278)	Llanerch CC	Havertown, Pa.
1959	Bob Rosburg	277	Jerry Barber & Doug Sanders (278)	Minneapolis GC	St. Louis Park, Minn.
1960	Jay Hebert	281	Jim Ferrier (282)	Firestone CC	Akron, Ohio
1961	Jerry Barber**	277	Don January (277)	Olympia Fields CC	Matteson, Ill.
1962	Gary Player	278	Bob Goalby (279)	Aronimink GC	Newtown Square, Pa.
1963	Jack Nicklaus	279	Dave Ragan (281)	Dallas AC	Dallas
1964	Bobby Nichols	271	Jack Nicklaus & Arnold Palmer (274)	Columbus CC	Columbus, Ohio
1965	Dave Marr	280	Jack Nicklaus & Billy Casper (282)	Laurel Valley GC	Ligonier, Pa.
1966	Al Geiberger	280	Dudley Wysong (284)	Firestone CC	Akron, Ohio
1967	Don January**	281	Don Massengale (281)	Columbine CC	Littleton, Colo.
1968	Julius Boros	281	Arnold Palmer & Bob Charles (282)	Pecan Valley CC	San Antonio
1969	Ray Floyd	276	Gary Player (277)	NCR GC	Dayton, Ohio
1970	Dave Stockton	279	Arnold Palmer & Bob Murphy (281)	Southern Hills CC	Tulsa

PGA Championship (Cont.)

Year	Winner	Score	Runner-up	Course	Location
1971	Jack Nicklaus	281	Billy Casper (283)	PGA National GC	Palm Beach Gardens, Fla.
1972	Gary Player	281	Jim Jamieson & Tommy Aaron (283)	Oakland Hills GC	Birmingham, Mich.
1973	Jack Nicklaus	277	Bruce Crampton (281)	Canterbury GC	Cleveland
1974	Lee Trevino	276	Jack Nicklaus (277)	Tanglewood GC	Winston-Salem, N.C.
1975	Jack Nicklaus	276	Bruce Crampton (278)	Firestone CC	Akron, Ohio
1976	Dave Stockton	281	Don January & Ray Floyd (282)	Congressional CC	Bethesda, Md.
1977	Lanny Wadkins**	282	Gene Littler (282)	Pebble Beach GL	Pebble Beach, Calif.
1978	John Mahaffey**	276	Jerry Pate & Tom Watson (276)	Oakmont CC	Oakmont, Pa.
1979	David Graham**	272	Ben Crenshaw (272)	Oakland Hills CC	Birmingham, Mich.
1980	Jack Nicklaus	274	Andy Bean (281)	Oak Hill CC	Rochester, N.Y.
1981	Larry Nelson	273	Fuzzy Zoeller (277)	Atlanta AC	Duluth, Ga.
1982	Ray Floyd	272	Lanny Wadkins (275)	Southern Hills CC	Tulsa
1983	Hal Sutton	274	Jack Nicklaus (275)	Riviera CC	Los Angeles
1984	Lee Trevino	273	Lanny Wadkins & Gary Player (277)	Shoal Creek	Birmingham, Ala.
1985	Hubert Green	278	Lee Trevino (280)	Cherry Hills CC	Denver
1986	Bob Tway	276	Greg Norman (278)	Inverness Club	Toledo, Ohio
1987	Larry Nelson**	287	Lanny Wadkins (287)	PGA National	Palm Beach Gardens, Fla.
1988	Jeff Sluman	272	Paul Azinger 275)	Oak Tree GC	Edmond, Okla.
1989	Payne Stewart	276	Andy Bean, Mike Reid & Curtis Strange (277)	Kemper Lakes GC	Hawthorn Woods, Ill.
1990	Wayne Grady	282	Fred Couples (285)	Shoal Creek	Birmingham, Ala.
1991	John Daly	276	Bruce Lietzke (279)	Crooked Stick GC	Carmel, Ind.
1992	Nick Price	278	Nick Faldo, John Cook, Jim Gallagher & Gene Sauers (281)	Bellerive CC	St. Louis
1993	Paul Azinger**	272	Greg Norman (272)	Inverness Club	Toledo, Ohio
1994	Nick Price	269	Corey Pavin (275)	Southern Hills CC	Tulsa
1995	Steve Elkington**	267	Colin Montgomerie (267)	Riviera CC	Pacific Palisades, Calif.
1996	Mark Brooks**	277	Kenny Perry (277)	Valhalla GC	Louisville, Ky.
1997	Davis Love III	269	Justin Leonard (274)	Winged Foot GC	Mamaroneck, N.Y.
1998	Vijay Singh	271	Steve Stricker (273)	Sahalee CC	Redmond, Wash.
1999	Tiger Woods	277	Sergio Garcia (278)	Medinah CC	Medinah, Ill.
2000	Tiger Woods**	270	Bob May (270)	Valhalla GC	Louisville, Ky.

*While the PGA Championship was a match play tournament from 1916-57, the two finalists played 36 holes for the title. In the five years that a playoff was necessary, the match was decided on the 37th or 38th hole.

PLAYOFFS:

1961: Jerry Barber (67) def. Don January (68) in 18 holes. **1967:** Don January (69) def. Don Massengale (71) in 18 holes. **1977:** Lanny Wadkins (4-4-4) def. Gene Littler (4-4-5) on 3rd hole of sudden death. **1978:** John Mahaffey (4-3) def. Jerry Pate (4-4) and Tom Watson (4-5) on 2nd hole of sudden death. **1979:** David Graham (4-4-2) def. Ben Crenshaw (4-4-4) on 3rd hole of sudden death. **1987:** Larry Nelson (4) def. Lanny Wadkins (5) on 1st hole of sudden death. **1993:** Paul Azinger (4-4) def. Greg Norman (4-5) on 2nd hole of sudden death. **1995:** Steve Elkington (3) def. Colin Montgomerie (4) on 1st hole of sudden death. **1996:** Mark Brooks (4) def. Kenny Perry (5) on 1st hole of sudden death. **2000:** Tiger Woods (3-4-5–12) won a three-hole playoff over Bob May (4-4-5–13).

Major Championship Leaders
Through 2000; active PGA players in **bold** type.

	US Open	British Open	PGA	Masters	US Am	British Am	Total
Jack Nicklaus	4	3	5	6	2	0	**20**
Bobby Jones	4	3	0	0	5	1	**13**
Walter Hagen	2	4	5	0	0	0	**11**
Ben Hogan	4	1	2	2	0	0	**9**
Gary Player	1	3	2	3	0	0	**9**
John Ball	0	1	0	0	0	8	**9**
Arnold Palmer	1	2	0	4	1	0	**8**
Tom Watson	1	5	0	2	0	0	**8**
Tiger Woods	1	1	2	1	3	0	**8**
Harold Hilton	0	2	0	0	1	4	**7**
Gene Sarazen	2	1	3	1	0	0	**7**
Sam Snead	0	1	3	3	0	0	**7**
Harry Vardon	1	6	0	0	0	0	**7**
Nick Faldo	0	3	0	3	0	0	**6**
Lee Trevino	2	2	2	0	0	0	**6**

Tournaments: U.S. Open, British Open, PGA Championship, Masters, U.S. Amateur and British Amateur.

Grand Slam Summary

The only golfer ever to win a recognized Grand Slam—four major championships in a single season—was Bobby Jones in 1930. That year, Jones won the U.S. and British Opens as well as the U.S. and British Amateurs.

The men's professional Grand Slam—the Masters, U.S. Open, British Open and PGA Championship—did not gain acceptance until 30 years later when Arnold Palmer won the 1960 Masters and U.S. Open. The media wrote that the popular Palmer was chasing the "new" Grand Slam and would have to win the British Open and the PGA to claim it. He did not, but then nobody has before or since.

Three wins in one year: Ben Hogan (1953) and Tiger Woods (2000). **Two wins in one year** (18): Jack Nicklaus (5 times); Ben Hogan, Arnold Palmer and Tom Watson (twice); Nick Faldo, Mark O'Meara, Gary Player, Nick Price, Sam Snead, Lee Trevino, Craig Wood and Tiger Woods (once).

Year	Masters	US Open	Brit. Open	PGA	Year	Masters	US Open	Brit. Open	PGA
1934	H. Smith	Dutra	Cotton	Runyan	1968	Goalby	Trevino	Player	Boros
1935	Sarazen	Parks	Perry	Revolta	1969	Archer	Moody	Jacklin	Floyd
1936	H. Smith	Manero	Padgham	Shute	1970	Casper	Jacklin	Nicklaus	Stockton
1937	B. Nelson	Guldahl	Cotton	Shute	1971	Coody	Trevino	Trevino	Nicklaus
1938	Picard	Guldahl	Whitcombe	Runyan	1972	Nicklaus	Nicklaus	Trevino	Player
1939	Guldahl	B. Nelson	Burton	Picard	1973	Aaron	J. Miller	Weiskopf	Nicklaus
1940	Demaret	Little	—	B. Nelson	1974	Player	Irwin	Player	Trevino
1941	Wood	Wood	—	Ghezzi	1975	Nicklaus	L. Graham	T. Watson	Nicklaus
1942	B. Nelson	—	—	Snead	1976	Floyd	J. Pate	Miller	Stockton
1943	—	—	—	—	1977	T. Watson	H. Green	T. Watson	L. Wadkins
1944	—	—	—	Hamilton	1978	Player	North	Nicklaus	Mahaffey
1945	—	—	—	B. Nelson	1979	Zoeller	Irwin	Ballesteros	D. Graham
1946	Keiser	Mangrum	Snead	Hogan	1980	Ballesteros	Nicklaus	T. Watson	Nicklaus
1947	Demaret	Worsham	F. Daly	Ferrier	1981	T. Watson	D. Graham	Rogers	L. Nelson
1948	Harmon	Hogan	Cotton	Hogan	1982	Stadler	T. Watson	T. Watson	Floyd
1949	Snead	Middlecoff	Locke	Snead	1983	Ballesteros	L. Nelson	T. Watson	Sutton
1950	Demaret	Hogan	Locke	Harper	1984	Crenshaw	Zoeller	Ballesteros	Trevino
1951	Hogan	Hogan	Faulkner	Snead	1985	Langer	North	Lyle	H. Green
1952	Snead	Boros	Locke	Turnesa	1986	Nicklaus	Floyd	Norman	Tway
1953	Hogan	Hogan	Hogan	Burkemo	1987	Mize	S. Simpson	Faldo	L. Nelson
1954	Snead	Furgol	Thomson	Harbert	1988	Lyle	Strange	Ballesteros	Sluman
1955	Middlecoff	Fleck	Thomson	Ford	1989	Faldo	Strange	Calcavecchia	Stewart
1956	Burke	Middlecoff	Thomson	Burke	1990	Faldo	Irwin	Faldo	Grady
1957	Ford	Mayer	Locke	L. Hebert	1991	Woosnam	Stewart	Baker-Finch	J. Daly
1958	Palmer	Bolt	Thomson	Finsterwald	1992	Couples	Kite	Faldo	Price
1959	Wall	Casper	Player	Rosburg	1993	Langer	Janzen	Norman	Azinger
1960	Palmer	Palmer	Nagle	J. Hebert	1994	Olazabal	Els	Price	Price
1961	Player	Littler	Palmer	J. Barber	1995	Crenshaw	Pavin	Daly	Elkington
1962	Palmer	Nicklaus	Palmer	Player	1996	Faldo	S. Jones	Lehman	Brooks
1963	Nicklaus	Boros	Charles	Nicklaus	1997	Woods	Els	Leonard	Love
1964	Palmer	Venturi	Lema	Nichols	1998	O'Meara	Janzen	O'Meara	Singh
1965	Nicklaus	Player	Thomson	Marr	1999	Olazabal	Stewart	Lawrie	Woods
1966	Nicklaus	Casper	Nicklaus	Geiberger	2000	Singh	Woods	Woods	Woods
1967	Brewer Jr.	Nicklaus	De Vicenzo	January					

Vardon Trophy

Awarded since 1937 by the PGA of America to the PGA Tour regular with the lowest adjusted scoring average. The award is named after Harry Vardon, the six-time British Open champion who also won the U.S. Open in 1900. A point system was used from 1937-41.

Multiple winners: Billy Casper and Lee Trevino (5); Arnold Palmer and Sam Snead (4); Ben Hogan, Greg Norman and Tom Watson (3); Fred Couples, Bruce Crampton, Tom Kite, Lloyd Mangrum and Nick Price (2).

Year		Pts	Year		Avg	Year		Avg
1937	Harry Cooper	.500	1960	Billy Casper	69.95	1980	Lee Trevino	69.73
1938	Sam Snead	.520	1961	Arnold Palmer	69.85	1981	Tom Kite	69.80
1939	Byron Nelson	.473	1962	Arnold Palmer	70.27	1982	Tom Kite	70.21
1940	Ben Hogan	.423	1963	Billy Casper	70.58	1983	Ray Floyd	70.61
1941	Ben Hogan	.494	1964	Arnold Palmer	70.01	1984	Calvin Peete	70.56
1942-46	No award		1965	Billy Casper	70.85	1985	Don Pooley	70.36
			1966	Billy Casper	70.27	1986	Scott Hoch	70.08
Year		**Avg**	1967	Arnold Palmer	70.18	1987	Dan Pohl	70.25
1947	Jimmy Demaret	69.90	1968	Billy Casper	69.82	1988	Chip Beck	69.46
1948	Ben Hogan	69.30	1969	Dave Hill	70.34	1989	Greg Norman	69.49
1949	Sam Snead	69.37	1970	Lee Trevino	70.64	1990	Greg Norman	69.10
1950	Sam Snead	69.23	1971	Lee Trevino	70.27	1991	Fred Couples	69.59
1951	Lloyd Mangrum	70.05	1972	Lee Trevino	70.89	1992	Fred Couples	69.38
1952	Jack Burke	70.54	1973	Bruce Crampton	70.57	1993	Nick Price	69.11
1953	Lloyd Mangrum	70.22	1974	Lee Trevino	70.53	1994	Greg Norman	68.81
1954	E.J. Harrison	70.41	1975	Bruce Crampton	70.51	1995	Steve Elkington	69.62
1955	Sam Snead	69.86	1976	Don January	70.56	1996	Tom Lehman	69.32
1956	Cary Middlecoff	70.35	1977	Tom Watson	70.32	1997	Nick Price	68.98
1957	Dow Finsterwald	70.30	1978	Tom Watson	70.16	1998	David Duval	69.13
1958	Bob Rosburg	70.11	1979	Tom Watson	70.27	1999	Tiger Woods	68.43
1959	Art Wall	70.35						

U.S. Amateur

Match play from 1895-64, stroke play from 1965-72, match play 1973-79, 36-hole stroke-play qualifying before match play since 1979.

Multiple winners: Bobby Jones (5); Jerry Travers (4); Walter Travis and Tiger Woods (3); Deane Beman, Charles Coe, Gary Cowan, H. Chandler Egan, Chick Evans, Lawson Little, Jack Nicklaus, Francis Ouimet, Jay Sigel, William Turnesa, Bud Ward, Harvie Ward, and H.J. Whigham (2).

Year		Year		Year		Year	
1895	Charles Macdonald	1922	Jess Sweetser	1951	Billy Maxwell	1977	John Fought
1896	H.J. Whigham	1923	Max Marston	1952	Jack Westland	1978	John Cook
1897	H.J. Whigham	1924	Bobby Jones	1953	Gene Littler	1979	Mark O'Meara
1898	Findlay Douglas	1925	Bobby Jones	1954	Arnold Palmer		
1899	H.M. Harriman	1926	George Von Elm	1955	Harvie Ward	1980	Hal Sutton
		1927	Bobby Jones	1956	Harvie Ward	1981	Nathaniel Crosby
1900	Walter Travis	1928	Bobby Jones	1957	Hillman Robbins	1982	Jay Sigel
1901	Walter Travis	1929	Harrison Johnston	1958	Charles Coe	1983	Jay Sigel
1902	Louis James			1959	Jack Nicklaus	1984	Scott Verplank
1903	Walter Travis	1930	Bobby Jones			1985	Sam Randolph
1904	H. Chandler Egan	1931	Francis Ouimet	1960	Deane Beman	1986	Buddy Alexander
1905	H. Chandler Egan	1932	Ross Somerville	1961	Jack Nicklaus	1987	Billy Mayfair
1906	Eben Byers	1933	George Dunlap	1962	Labron Harris	1988	Eric Meeks
1907	Jerry Travers	1934	Lawson Little	1963	Deane Beman	1989	Chris Patton
1908	Jerry Travers	1935	Lawson Little	1964	Bill Campbell		
1909	Robert Gardner	1936	John Fischer	1965	Bob Murphy	1990	Phil Mickelson
		1937	John Goodman	1966	Gary Cowan	1991	Mitch Voges
1910	W.C. Fownes Jr.	1938	William Turnesa	1967	Bob Dickson	1992	Justin Leonard
1911	Harold Hilton	1939	Bud Ward	1968	Bruce Fleisher	1993	John Harris
1912	Jerry Travers			1969	Steve Melnyk	1994	Tiger Woods
1913	Jerry Travers	1940	Richard Chapman			1995	Tiger Woods
1914	Francis Ouimet	1941	Bud Ward	1970	Lanny Wadkins	1996	Tiger Woods
1915	Robert Gardner	1942-45	Not held	1971	Gary Cowan	1997	Matt Kuchar
1916	Chick Evans	1946	Ted Bishop	1972	Vinny Giles	1998	Hank Kuehne
1917-18	Not held	1947	Skee Riegel	1973	Craig Stadler	1999	David Gossett
1919	Davidson Herron	1948	William Turnesa	1974	Jerry Pate		
		1949	Charles Coe	1975	Fred Ridley	2000	Jeff Quinney
1920	Chick Evans	1950	Sam Urzetta	1976	Bill Sander		
1921	Jesse Guilford						

British Amateur

Match play since 1885.

Multiple winners: John Ball (8); Michael Bonallack (5); Harold Hilton (4); Joe Carr (3); Horace Hutchinson, Ernest Holderness, Trevor Homer, Johnny Laidley, Lawson Little, Peter McEvoy, Dick Siderowf, Frank Stranahan, Freddie Tait and Cyril Tolley (2).

Year		Year		Year		Year	
1885	Allen MacFie	1912	John Ball	1948	Frank Stranahan	1975	Vinny Giles
1886	Horace Hutchinson	1913	Harold Hilton	1949	Samuel McCready	1976	Dick Siderowf
1887	Horace Hutchinson	1914	J.L.C. Jenkins			1977	Peter McEvoy
1888	John Ball	1915-19	Not held	1950	Frank Stranahan	1978	Peter McEvoy
1889	Johnny Laidley			1951	Richard Chapman	1979	Jay Sigel
		1920	Cyril Tolley	1952	Harvie Ward		
1890	John Ball	1921	William Hunter	1953	Joe Carr	1980	Duncan Evans
1891	Johnny Laidley	1922	Ernest Holderness	1954	Douglas Bachli	1981	Phillipe Ploujoux
1892	John Ball	1923	Roger Wethered	1955	Joe Conrad	1982	Martin Thompson
1893	Peter Anderson	1924	Ernest Holderness	1956	John Beharrell	1983	Philip Parkin
1894	John Ball	1925	Robert Harris	1957	Reid Jack	1984	Jose-Maria Olazabal
1895	Leslie Balfour-Melville	1926	Jesse Sweetser	1958	Joe Carr	1985	Garth McGimpsey
1896	Freddie Tait	1927	William Tweddell	1959	Deane Beman	1986	David Curry
1897	Jack Allan	1928	Thomas Perkins			1987	Paul Mayo
1898	Freddie Tait	1929	Cyril Tolley	1960	Joe Carr	1988	Christian Hardin
1899	John Ball			1961	Michael Bonallack	1989	Stephen Dodd
		1930	Bobby Jones	1962	Richard Davies		
1900	Harold Hilton	1931	Eric Smith	1963	Michael Lunt	1990	Rolf Muntz
1901	Harold Hilton	1932	John deForest	1964	Gordon Clark	1991	Gary Wolstenholme
1902	Charles Hutchings	1933	Michael Scott	1965	Michael Bonallack	1992	Stephen Dundas
1903	Robert Maxwell	1934	Lawson Little	1966	Bobby Cole	1993	Ian Pyman
1904	Walter Travis	1935	Lawson Little	1967	Bob Dickson	1994	Lee James
1905	Arthur Barry	1936	Hector Thomson	1968	Michael Bonallack	1995	Gordon Sherry
1906	James Robb	1937	Robert Sweeny Jr.	1969	Michael Bonallack	1996	Warren Bledon
1907	John Ball	1938	Charles Yates			1997	Craig Watson
1908	E.A. Lassen	1939	Alexander Kyle	1970	Michael Bonallack	1998	Sergio Garcia
1909	Robert Maxwell	1940-45	Not held	1971	Steve Melnyk	1999	Graeme Storm
1910	John Ball	1946	James Bruen	1972	Trevor Homer		
1911	Harold Hilton	1947	William Turnesa	1973	Dick Siderowf	2000	Mikko Ilonen
				1974	Trevor Homer		

WOMEN
Nabisco Championship

Formerly known as the Colgate Dinah Shore (1972-81) and the Nabisco Dinah Shore (1982-99), the tournament became the LPGA's fourth designated major championship in 1983. Shore's name, which was dropped from the tournament in 2000, is preserved with the Nabisco Dinah Shore Trophy, which is awarded to the winner. The tourney has been played at Mission Hills CC in Rancho Mirage, Calif., since it began; (*) indicates playoff winner.

Multiple winners: (as a major): Amy Alcott and Betsy King (3); Juli Inkster and Dottie Pepper (2).

Year	Winner	Score	Runner-up	Year	Winner	Score	Runner-up
1972	Jane Blalock	213	Carol Mann	1987	Betsy King*	283	Patty Sheehan (283)
			& Judy Rankin (216)	1988	Amy Alcott	274	Colleen Walker (276)
1973	Mickey Wright	284	Joyce Kazmierski (286)	1989	Juli Inkster	279	Tammie Green
1974	Jo Anne Prentice*	289	Jane Blalock				& JoAnne Carner (284)
			& Sandra Haynie (289)	1990	Betsy King	283	Kathy Postlewait
1975	Sandra Palmer	283	Kathy McMullen (284)				& Shirley Furlong (285)
1976	Judy Rankin	285	Betty Burfeindt (288)	1991	Amy Alcott	273	Dottie Pepper (281)
1977	Kathy Whitworth	289	JoAnne Carner	1992	Dottie Pepper*	279	Juli Inkster (279)
			& Sally Little (290)	1993	Helen Alfredsson	284	Amy Benz
1978	Sandra Post*	283	Penny Pulz (283)				& Tina Barrett (286)
1979	Sandra Post	276	Nancy Lopez (277)	1994	Donna Andrews	276	Laura Davies (277)
1980	Donna Caponi	275	Amy Alcott (277)	1995	Nanci Bowen	285	Susie Redman (286)
1981	Nancy Lopez	277	Carolyn Hill (279)	1996	Patty Sheehan	281	Kelly Robbins,
1982	Sally Little	278	Hollis Stacy				Meg Mallon
			& Sandra Haynie (281)				& Annika Sorenstam
1983	Amy Alcott	282	Beth Daniel				(276)
			& Kathy Whitworth (284)	1997	Betsy King	276	Kris Tschetter (278)
1984	Juli Inkster*	280	Pat Bradley (280)	1998	Pat Hurst	281	Helen Dobson (282)
1985	Alice Miller	275	Jan Stephenson (278)	1999	Dottie Pepper	269	Meg Mallon (275)
1986	Pat Bradley	280	Val Skinner (282)	2000	Karrie Webb	274	Dottie Pepper (284)

*PLAYOFFS:

1974: Jo Ann Prentice def. Jane Blalock in sudden death. **1978:** Sandra Post def. Penny Pulz in sudden death. **1984:** Juli Inkster def. Pat Bradley in sudden death. **1987:** Betsy King def. Patty Sheehan in sudden death. **1992:** Dottie Pepper def. Juli Inkster in sudden death.

LPGA Championship

Officially the McDonald's LPGA Championship since 1994 (Mazda sponsored from 1987-93), the tournament began in 1955 and has had extended stays at the Stardust CC in Las Vegas (1961-66), Pleasant Valley CC in Sutton, Mass. (1967-68, 70-74), the Jack Nicklaus Sports Center at Kings Island, Ohio (1978-89), Bethesda CC in Maryland (1990-93) and DuPont CC in Wilmington, Del. (since 1994); (*) indicates playoff winner and (#) weather-shortened.

Multiple winners: Mickey Wright (4); Nancy Lopez, Patty Sheehan and Kathy Whitworth (3); Donna Caponi, Laura Davies, Sandra Haynie, Juli Inkster, Mary Mills and Betsy Rawls (2).

Year	Winner	Score	Runner-up	Year	Winner	Score	Runner-up
1955	Beverly Hanson	220	Louise Suggs (223)	1980	Sally Little	285	Jane Blalock (288)
1956	Marlene Hagge*	291	Patty Berg (291)	1981	Donna Caponi	280	Jerilyn Britz
1957	Louise Suggs	285	Wiffi Smith (288)				& Pat Meyers (281)
1958	Mickey Wright	288	Fay Crocker (294)	1982	Jan Stephenson	279	JoAnne Carner (281)
1959	Betsy Rawls	288	Patty Berg (289)	1983	Patty Sheehan	279	Sandra Haynie (281)
1960	Mickey Wright	292	Louise Suggs (295)	1984	Patty Sheehan	272	Beth Daniel
1961	Mickey Wright	287	Louise Suggs (296)				& Pat Bradley (282)
1962	Judy Kimball	282	Shirley Spork (286)	1985	Nancy Lopez	273	Alice Miller (281)
1963	Mickey Wright	294	Mary Lena Faulk	1986	Pat Bradley	277	Patty Sheehan (278)
			& Mary Mills (296)	1987	Jane Geddes	275	Betsy King (275)
1964	Mary Mills	278	Mickey Wright (280)	1988	Sherri Turner	281	Amy Alcott (282)
1965	Sandra Haynie	279	Clifford A. Creed (280)	1989	Nancy Lopez	274	Ayako Okamoto (277)
1966	Gloria Ehret	282	Mickey Wright (285)	1990	Beth Daniel	280	Rosie Jones (281)
1967	Kathy Whitworth	284	Shirley Englehorn (285)	1991	Meg Mallon	274	Pat Bradley
1968	Sandra Post	294	Kathy Whitworth (294)				& Ayako Okamoto (275)
1969	Betsy Rawls	293	Susie Berning	1992	Betsy King	267	JoAnne Carner,
			& Carol Mann (297)				Karen Noble
1970	Shirley Englehorn	285	Kathy Whitworth (285)				& Liselotte Neumann
1971	Kathy Whitworth	288	Kathy Ahern (292)				(278)
1972	Kathy Ahern	293	Jane Blalock (299)	1993	Patty Sheehan	275	Lauri Merten (276)
1973	Mary Mills	288	Betty Burfeindt (289)	1994	Laura Davies	279	Alice Ritzman (280)
1974	Sandra Haynie	288	JoAnne Carner (290)	1995	Kelly Robbins	274	Laura Davies (275)
1975	Kathy Whitworth	288	Sandra Haynie (289)	1996	Laura Davies#	213	Julie Piers (214)
1976	Betty Burfeindt	287	Judy Rankin (288)	1997	Chris Johnson*	281	Leta Lindley (281)
1977	Chako Higuchi	279	Pat Bradley, Sandra Post	1998	Se Ri Pak	273	Donna Andrews
			& Judy Rankin (282)				& Lisa Hackney (276)
1978	Nancy Lopez	275	Amy Alcott (281)	1999	Juli Inkster	268	Liselotte Neumann (272)
1979	Donna Caponi	279	Jerilyn Britz (282)	2000	Juli Inkster*	281	Stefania Croce (281)

*PLAYOFFS:

1956: Marlene Hagge def. Patti Berg in sudden death. **1968:** Sandra Post (68) def. Kathy Whitworth (75) in 18 holes.
1970: Shirley Englehorn def. Kathy Whitworth in sudden death. **1997:** Chris Johnson def. Leta Lindley in sudden death.
2000: Juli Inkster def. Stephania Croce in sudden death.

U.S. Women's Open

The U.S. Women's Open began under the direction of the defunct Women's Professional Golfers Assn. in 1946, passed to the LPGA in 1949 and to the USGA in 1953. The tournament used a match play format its first year then switched to stroke play; (*) indicates playoff winner and (a) indicates amateur winner.

Multiple winners: Betsy Rawls and Mickey Wright (4); Susie Maxwell Berning, Hollis Stacy and Babe Zaharis (3); JoAnne Carner, Donna Caponi, Betsy King, Patty Sheehan, Annika Sorenstam and Louise Suggs (2).

Year	Winner	Score	Runner-up	Course	Location
1946	Patty Berg	5&4	Betty Jameson	Spokane CC	Spokane, Wash.
1947	Betty Jameson	295	a-Sally Sessions & a-Rolly Riley (301)	Starmount Forest CC	Greensboro, N.C.
1948	Babe Zaharias	300	Betty Hicks (308)	Atlantic City CC	Northfield, N.J.
1949	Louise Suggs	291	Babe Zaharias (305)	Prince Georges CC	Landover, Md.
1950	Babe Zaharias	291	a-Betsy Rawls (300)	Rolling Hills CC	Wichita, Kan.
1951	Betsy Rawls	293	Louise Suggs (298)	Druid Hills GC	Atlanta, Ga.
1952	Louise Suggs	284	Marlene Hagge (291)	Bala GC	Philadelphia, Penn.
1953	Betsy Rawls*	302	Jackie Pung (302)	CC of Rochester	Rochester, N.Y.
1954	Babe Zaharias	291	Betty Hicks (303)	Salem CC	Peabody, Mass.
1955	Fay Crocker	299	Mary Lena Faulk (303)	Wichita CC	Wichita, Kan.
1956	Kathy Cornelius*	302	Barbara McIntire (302)	Northland CC	Duluth, Minn.
1957	Betsy Rawls	299	Patty Berg (305)	Winged Foot GC	Mamaroneck, N.Y.
1958	Mickey Wright	290	Louise Suggs (295)	Forest Lake CC	Detroit, Mich.
1959	Mickey Wright	287	Louise Suggs (289)	Chuchill Valley CC	Pittsburgh, Penn.
1960	Betsy Rawls	292	Joyce Ziske (293)	Worcester CC	Worcester, Mass.
1961	Mickey Wright	293	Betsy Rawls (299)	Baltusrol GC	Springfield, N.J.
1962	Murle Breer	301	Jo Anne Prentice & Ruth Jessen (303)	Dunes GC	Myrtle Beach, S.C.
1963	Mary Mills	289	Sandra Haynie & Louise Suggs (292)	Kenwood CC	Cincinnati, Ohio
1964	Mickey Wright*	290	Ruth Jessen (290)	San Diego CC	Chula Vista, Calif.
1965	Carol Mann	290	Kathy Cornelius (292)	Atlantic City CC	Northfield, N.J.
1966	Sandra Spuzich	297	Carol Mann (298)	Hazeltine National GC	Chaska, Minn.
1967	a-Catherine LaCoste	294	Susie Berning & Beth Stone (296)	Hot Springs GC	Hot Springs, Va.
1968	Susie Berning	289	Mickey Wright (292)	Moselem Springs GC	Fleetwood, Penn.
1969	Donna Caponi	294	Peggy Wilson (295)	Scenic Hills CC	Pensacola, Fla.
1970	Donna Caponi	287	Sandra Haynie (288)	Muskogee CC	Muskogee, Okla.
1971	JoAnne Carner	288	Kathy Whitworth (295)	Kahkwa CC	Erie, Penn.
1972	Susie Berning	299	Kathy Ahern, Pam Barnett & Judy Rankin (300)	Winged Foot GC	Mamaroneck, N.Y.
1973	Susie Berning	290	Gloria Ehret (295)	CC of Rochester	Rochester, N.Y.
1974	Sandra Haynie	295	Carol Mann & Beth Stone (296)	La Grange CC	La Grange, Ill.
1975	Sandra Palmer	295	JoAnne Carner, a-Nancy Lopez & Sandra Post (299)	Atlantic City CC	Northfield, N.J.
1976	JoAnne Carner*	292	Sandra Palmer (292)	Rolling Green CC	Springfield, Penn.
1977	Hollis Stacy	292	Nancy Lopez (294)	Hazeltine National GC	Chaska, Minn.
1978	Hollis Stacy	289	JoAnne Carner & Sally Little (290)	CC of Indianapolis	Indianapolis, Ind.
1979	Jerilyn Britz	284	Debbie Massey & Sandra Palmer (286)	Brooklawn CC	Fairfield, Conn.
1980	Amy Alcott	280	Hollis Stacy (289)	Richland CC	Nashville, Tenn.
1981	Pat Bradley	279	Beth Daniel (280)	La Grange CC	La Grange, Ill.
1982	Janet Anderson	283	Beth Daniel, Sandra Haynie & Donna White (289)	Del Paso CC	Sacramento, Calif.
1983	Jan Stephenson	290	JoAnne Carner (291)	Cedar Ridge CC	Tulsa, Okla.
1984	Hollis Stacy	290	Rosie Jones (291)	Salem CC	Peabody, Mass.
1985	Kathy Baker	280	Judy Dickenson (283)	Baltusrol GC	Springfield, N.J.
1986	Jane Geddes*	287	Sally Little (287)	NCR GC	Dayton, Ohio
1987	Laura Davies*	285	Ayako Okamoto & JoAnne Carner (285)	Plainfield CC	Plainfield, N.J.
1988	Liselotte Neumann	277	Patty Sheehan (280)	Baltimore CC	Baltimore, Md.
1989	Betsy King	278	Nancy Lopez (282)	Indianwood GC	Lake Orion, Mich.
1990	Betsy King	284	Patty Sheehan (285)	Atlanta Athletic Club	Duluth, Ga.
1991	Meg Mallon	283	Pat Bradley (285)	Colonial CC	Ft. Worth, Texas

Year	Winner	Score	Runner-up	Course	Location
1992	Patty Sheehan*	280	Juli Inkster (280)	Oakmont CC	Oakmont, Penn.
1993	Lauri Merten	280	Donna Andrews & Helen Alfredsson (281)	Crooked Stick GC	Carmel, Ind.
1994	Patty Sheehan	277	Tammie Green (278)	Indianwood CC	Lake Orion, Mich.
1995	Annika Sorenstam	278	Meg Mallon (279)	The Broadmoor	Colorado Springs, Colo.
1996	Annika Sorenstam	272	Kris Tschetter (278)	Pine Needles Lodge & GC	Southern Pines, N.C.
1997	Alison Nicholas	274	Nancy Lopez (275)	Pumpkin Ridge GC	Cornelius, Ore.
1998	Se Ri Pak*	290	a-Jenny Chuasiriporn (290)	Blackwolf Run GC	Kohler, Wis.
1999	Juli Inkster	272	Sherri Turner (277)	Old Waverly GC	West Point, Miss.
2000	Karrie Webb	282	Cristie Kerr & Meg Mallon (287)	Merit Club	Libertyville, Ill.

*PLAYOFFS:

1953: Betsy Rawls (70) def. Jackie Pung (77) in 18 holes. **1956:** Kathy Cornelius (75) def. Barbara McIntire (82) in 18 holes. **1964:** Mickey Wright (70) def. Ruth Jessen (72) in 18 holes. **1976:** JoAnne Carner (76) def. Sandra Palmer (78) in 18 holes. **1986:** Jane Geddes (71) def. Sally Little (73) in 18 holes. **1987:** Laura Davies (71) def. Ayako Okamoto (73) and JoAnne Carner (74) in 18 holes. **1992:** Patty Sheehan (72) def. Juli Inkster (74) in 18 holes. **1998:** Se Ri Pak def. Jenny Chuasiriporn on the second sudden death hole after both players were tied after an 18-hole playoff.

du Maurier Classic

Formerly known as La Canadienne in 1973 and the Peter Jackson Classic from 1974-83, this Canadian stop on the LPGA Tour became the third designated major championship in 1979; (*) indicates playoff winner.

Multiple winners (as a major): Pat Bradley (3); Brandie Burton (2).

Year	Winner	Score	Runner-up	Course	Location
1973	Jocelyne Bourassa*	214	Sandra Hayne & Judy Rankin (214)	Montreal GC	Montreal, Que.
1974	Carole Jo Callison	208	JoAnne Carner (211)	Candiac GC	Montreal, Que.
1975	JoAnne Carner*	214	Carol Mann (214)	St. George's CC	Toronto, Ont.
1976	Donna Caponi*	212	Judy Rankin (212)	Cedar Brae G&CC	Toronto, Ont.
1977	Judy Rankin	214	Pat Meyers & Sandra Palmer (215)	Lachute G&CC	Montreal, Que.
1978	JoAnne Carner	278	Hollis Stacy (286)	St. George's CC	Toronto, Ont.
1979	Amy Alcott	285	Nancy Lopez (288)	Richelieu Valley CC	Montreal, Que.
1980	Pat Bradley	277	JoAnne Carner (278)	St. George's CC	Toronto, Ont.
1981	Jan Stephenson	278	Nancy Lopez & Pat Bradley (279)	Summerlea CC	Dorion, Que.
1982	Sandra Haynie	280	Beth Daniel (281)	St. George's CC	Toronto, Ont.
1983	Hollis Stacy	277	JoAnne Carner & Alice Miller (279)	Beaconsfield GC	Montreal, Que.
1984	Juli Inkster	279	Ayako Okamoto (280)	St. George's G&CC	Toronto, Ont.
1985	Pat Bradley	278	Jane Geddes (279)	Beaconsfield GC	Montreal, Que.
1986	Pat Bradley*	276	Ayako Okamoto (276)	Board of Trade CC	Toronto, Ont.
1987	Jody Rosenthal	272	Ayako Okamoto (274)	Islesmere GC	Laval, Que.
1988	Sally Little	279	Laura Davies (280)	Vancouver GC	Coquitlam, B.C.
1989	Tammie Green	279	Pat Bradley & Betsy King (280)	Beaconsfield GC	Montreal, Que.
1990	Cathy Johnston	276	Patty Sheehan (278)	Westmount G&CC	Kitchener, Ont.
1991	Nancy Scranton	279	Debbie Massey (282)	Vancouver GC	Coquitlam, B.C.
1992	Sherri Steinhauer	277	Judy Dickinson (279)	St. Charles CC	Winnipeg, Man.
1993	Brandie Burton*	277	Betsy King (277)	London Hunt & CC	London, Ont.
1994	Martha Nause	279	Michelle McGann (280)	Ottawa Hunt Club	Ottawa, Ont.
1995	Jenny Lidback	280	Liselotte Neumann (281)	Beaconsfield GC	Pointe-Claire, Que.
1996	Laura Davies	277	Nancy Lopez & Karrie Webb (279)	Edmonton CC	Edmonton, Alb.
1997	Colleen Walker	278	Liselotte Neumann (280)	Glen Abby GC	Oakville, Ont.
1998	Brandie Burton	270	Annika Sorenstam (271)	Essex G&CC	Winssor, Que.
1999	Karrie Webb	277	Laura Davies (279)	Priddis Greens G&CC	Calgary, Alb.
2000	Meg Mallon	282	Rosie Jones (283)	Royal Ottawa GC	Aylmer, Que.

*PLAYOFFS:

1973: Jocelyne Bourassa def. Sandra Haynie & Judy Rankin in sudden death. **1975:** JoAnne Carner def. Carol Mann in sudden death. **1976:** Donna Caponi def. Judy Rankin in sudden death. **1986:** Pat Bradley def. Ayako Okamoto in sudden death. **1993:** Brandie Burton def. Betsy King in sudden death.

Titleholders Championship (1937-72)

The Titleholders was considered a major title on the women's tour until it was discontinued after the 1972 tournament.

Multiple winners: Patty Berg (7); Louise Suggs (4); Babe Zaharias (3); Dorothy Kirby, Marilynn Smith, Kathy Whitworth and Mickey Wright (2).

Year		Year		Year		Year	
1937	Patty Berg	1947	Babe Zaharias	1955	Patty Berg	1963	Marilynn Smith
1938	Patty Berg	1948	Patty Berg	1956	Louise Suggs	1964	Marilynn Smith
1939	Patty Berg	1949	Peggy Kirk	1957	Patty Berg	1965	Kathy Whitworth
				1958	Beverly Hanson	1966	Kathy Whitworth
1940	Betty Hicks	1950	Babe Zaharias	1959	Louise Suggs	1967-71	Not held
1941	Dorothy Kirby	1951	Pat O'Sullivan			1972	Sandra Palmer
1942	Dorothy Kirby	1952	Babe Zaharias	1960	Fay Crocker		
1943-45	Not held	1953	Patty Berg	1961	Mickey Wright		
1946	Louise Suggs	1954	Louise Suggs	1962	Mickey Wright		

Western Open (1930-67)

The Western Open was considered a major title on the women's tour until it was discontinued after the 1967 tournament.

Multiple winners: Patty Berg (7); Louise Suggs and Babe Zaharias (4); Mickey Wright (3); June Beebe, Opal Hill, Betty Jameson and Betsy Rawls (2).

Year		Year		Year		Year	
1930	Mrs. Lee Mida	1940	Babe Zaharias	1950	Babe Zaharias	1960	Joyce Ziske
1931	June Beebe	1941	Patty Berg	1951	Patty Berg	1961	Mary Lena Faulk
1932	Jane Weiller	1942	Betty Jameson	1952	Betsy Rawls	1962	Mickey Wright
1933	June Beebe	1943	Patty Berg	1953	Louise Suggs	1963	Mickey Wright
1934	Marian McDougall	1944	Babe Zaharias	1954	Betty Jameson	1964	Carol Mann
1935	Opal Hill	1945	Babe Zaharias	1955	Patty Berg	1965	Susie Maxwell
1936	Opal Hill	1946	Louise Suggs	1956	Beverly Hanson	1966	Mickey Wright
1937	Betty Hicks	1947	Louise Suggs	1957	Patty Berg	1967	Kathy Whitworth
1938	Bea Barrett	1948	Patty Berg	1958	Patty Berg		
1939	Helen Dettweiler	1949	Louise Suggs	1959	Betsy Rawls		

Grand Slam Summary

From 1955-66, the U.S. Open, LPGA Championship, Western Open and Titleholders tournaments served as the Women's Grand Slam. From 1983-2000, however, the U.S. Open, LPGA, du Maurier Classic in Canada and Nabisco Championship were the major events. In 2001, the Weetabix Women's British Open will replace the du Maurier Classic as the tour's fourth major. No one has won a four-event Grand Slam on the women's tour.

Three wins in one year (3): Babe Zaharias (1950), Mickey Wright (1961) and Pat Bradley (1986).

Two wins in one year (16): Patty Berg and Mickey Wright (3 times); Juli Inkster and Louise Suggs (twice); Laura Davies, Sandra Haynie, Betsy King, Meg Mallon, Se Ri Pak, Betsy Rawls, Karrie Webb and Kathy Whitworth (once).

Year	LPGA	US Open	T'holders	Western
1937	—	—	Berg	Hicks
1938	—	—	Berg	Barrett
1939	—	—	Berg	Dettweiler
1940	—	—	Hicks	Zaharias
1941	—	—	Kirby	Berg
1942	—	—	Kirby	Jameson
1943	—	—	—	Berg
1944	—	—	—	Zaharias
1945	—	—	—	Zaharias
1946	—	Berg	Suggs	Suggs
1947	—	Jameson	Zaharias	Suggs
1948	—	Zaharias	Berg	Berg
1949	—	Suggs	Kirk	Suggs
1950	—	Zaharias	Zaharias	Zaharias
1951	—	Rawls	O'Sullivan	Berg
1952	—	Suggs	Zaharias	Rawls
1953	—	Rawls	Berg	Suggs
1954	—	Zaharias	Suggs	Jameson
1955	Hanson	Crocker	Berg	Berg
1956	Hagge	Cornelius	Suggs	Hanson
1957	Suggs	Rawls	Berg	Berg
1958	Wright	Wright	Hanson	Berg
1959	Rawls	Wright	Suggs	Rawls
1960	Wright	Rawls	Crocker	Ziske
1961	Wright	Wright	Wright	Faulk
1962	Kimball	Lindstrom	Wright	Wright
1963	Wright	Mills	M. Smith	Wright
1964	Mills	Wright	M. Smith	Mann

Year	LPGA	US Open	T'holders	Western
1965	Haynie	Mann	Whitworth	Maxwell
1966	Ehret	Spuzich	Whitworth	Wright
1967	Whitworth	a-LaCoste	—	Whitworth
1968	Post	Berning	—	—
1969	Rawls	Caponi	—	—
1970	Englehorn	Caponi	—	—
1971	Whitworth	Carner	—	—
1972	Ahern	Berning	Palmer	—
1973	Mills	Berning	—	—
1974	Haynie	Haynie	—	—
1975	Whitworth	Palmer	—	—
1976	Burfeindt	Carner	—	—
1977	Higuchi	Stacy	—	—
1978	Lopez	Stacy	—	—

Year	LPGA	US Open	duMaurier	Nabisco
1979	Caponi	Britz	Alcott	—
1980	Little	Alcott	Bradley	—
1981	Caponi	Bradley	Stephenson	—
1982	Stephenson	Anderson	Haynie	—
1983	Sheehan	Stephenson	Stacy	Alcott
1984	Sheehan	Stacy	Inkster	Inkster
1985	Lopez	Baker	Bradley	Miller
1986	Bradley	Geddes	Bradley	Bradley
1987	Geddes	Davies	Rosenthal	King
1988	Turner	Neumann	Little	Alcott
1989	Lopez	King	Green	Inkster
1990	Daniel	King	Johnston	King
1991	Mallon	Mallon	Scranton	Alcott

Year	LPGA	US Open	duMaurier	Nabisco	Year	LPGA	US Open	duMaurier	Nabisco
1992	King	Sheehan	Steinhaur	Pepper	1997	Johnson	Nicholas	Walker	King
1993	Sheehan	Merten	Burton	Alfredsson	1998	Pak	Pak	Burton	Hurst
1994	Davies	Sheehan	Nause	Andrews	1999	Inkster	Inkster	Webb	Pepper
1995	Robbins	Sorenstam	Lidback	Bowen	2000	Inkster	Webb	Mallon	Webb
1996	Davies	Sorenstam	Davies	Sheehan					

Major Championship Leaders
Through 2000; active players in **bold** type.

	US Open	LPGA	duM	Nabisco	Title	Western	US Am	Brit Am	Total
Patty Berg	1	0	0	0	7	7	1	0	**16**
Mickey Wright	4	4	0	0	2	3	0	0	**13**
Louise Suggs	2	1	0	0	4	4	1	1	**13**
Babe Zaharias	3	0	0	0	3	4	1	1	**12**
Juli Inkster	1	2	1	2	0	0	3	0	**9**
Betsy Rawls	4	2	0	0	0	2	0	0	**8**
JoAnne Carner	2	0	0	0	0	0	5	0	**7**
Kathy Whitworth	0	3	0	0	2	1	0	0	**6**
Pat Bradley	1	1	0	1	0	0	0	0	**6**
Betsy King	2	1	0	3	0	0	0	0	**6**
Patty Sheehan	2	3	0	1	0	0	0	0	**6**
Glenna C. Vare	0	0	0	0	0	0	6	0	**6**

Tournaments: U.S. Open, LPGA Championship, du Maurier Classic, Nabisco Championship, Titleholders (1930-72), Western Open (1937-67), U.S. Amateur, and British Amateur.

U.S. Women's Amateur
Stroke play in 1895, match play since 1896.
Multiple winners: Glenna Collett Vare (6); JoAnne Gunderson Carner (5); Margaret Curtis, Beatrix Hoyt, Dorothy Campbell Hurd, Juli Inkster, Alexa Stirling, Virginia Van Wie, Anne Quast Decker Welts (3); Kay Cockerill, Beth Daniel, Vicki Goetze, Katherine Harley, Genevieve Hecker, Betty Jameson, Kelli Kuehne and Barbara McIntire (2).

Year		Year		Year		Year	
1895	Mrs. C.S. Brown	1923	Edith Cummings	1952	Jacqueline Pung	1978	Cathy Sherk
1896	Beatrix Hoyt	1924	Dorothy C. Hurd	1953	Mary Lena Faulk	1979	Carolyn Hill
1897	Beatrix Hoyt	1925	Glenna Collett	1954	Barbara Romack		
1898	Beatrix Hoyt	1926	Helen Stetson	1955	Patricia Lesser	1980	Juli Inkster
1899	Ruth Underhill	1927	Miriam Burns Horn	1956	Marlene Stewart	1981	Juli Inkster
		1928	Glenna Collett	1957	JoAnne Gunderson	1982	Juli Inkster
1900	Frances Griscom	1929	Glenna Collett	1958	Anne Quast	1983	Joanne Pacillo
1901	Genevieve Hecker			1959	Barbara McIntire	1984	Deb Richard
1902	Genevieve Hecker	1930	Glenna Collett			1985	Michiko Hattori
1903	Bessie Anthony	1931	Helen Hicks	1960	JoAnne Gunderson	1986	Kay Cockerill
1904	Georgianna Bishop	1932	Virginia Van Wie	1961	Anne Quast Decker	1987	Kay Cockerill
1905	Pauline Mackay	1933	Virginia Van Wie	1962	JoAnne Gunderson	1988	Pearl Sinn
1906	Harriot Curtis	1934	Virginia Van Wie	1963	Anne Quast Welts	1989	Vicki Goetze
1907	Margaret Curtis	1935	Glenna Collett Vare	1964	Barbara McIntire		
1908	Katherine Harley	1936	Pamela Barton	1965	Jean Ashley	1990	Pat Hurst
1909	Dorothy Campbell	1937	Estelle Lawson	1966	JoAnne G. Carner	1991	Amy Fruhwirth
		1938	Patty Berg	1967	Mary Lou Dill	1992	Vicki Goetze
1910	Dorothy Campbell	1939	Betty Jameson	1968	JoAnne G. Carner	1993	Jill McGill
1911	Margaret Curtis			1969	Catherine Lacoste	1994	Wendy Ward
1912	Margaret Curtis	1940	Betty Jameson			1995	Kelli Kuehne
1913	Gladys Ravenscroft	1941	Elizabeth Hicks	1970	Martha Wilkinson	1996	Kelli Kuehne
1914	Katherine Harley	1942-45	Not held	1971	Laura Baugh	1997	Silvia Cavalleri
1915	Florence Vanderbeck	1946	Babe D. Zaharias	1972	Mary Budke	1998	Grace Park
1916	Alexa Stirling	1947	Louise Suggs	1973	Carol Semple	1999	Dorothy Delasin
1917-18	Not held	1948	Grace Lenczyk	1974	Cynthia Hill		
1919	Alexa Stirling	1949	Dorothy Porter			2000	Marcy Newton
1920	Alexa Stirling			1975	Beth Daniel		
1921	Marion Hollins	1950	Beverly Hanson	1976	Donna Horton		
1922	Glenna Collett	1951	Dorothy Kirby	1977	Beth Daniel		

British Women's Amateur

Match play since 1893.

Multiple winners: Cecil Leitch and Joyce Wethered (4); May Hezlet, Lady Margaret Scott, Brigitte Varangot and Enid Wilson (3); Rhone Adair, Pam Barton, Dorothy Campbell, Elizabeth Chadwick, Helen Holm, Marley Spearman, Frances Stephens, Jessie Valentine and Michelle Walker (2).

Year		Year		Year		Year	
1893	Lady Margaret Scott	1926	Cecil Leitch	1960	Barbara McIntire	1989	Helen Dobson
1894	Lady Margaret Scott	1927	Simone de la Chaume	1961	Marley Spearman	1990	Julie Wade Hall
1895	Lady Maraaret Scott	1928	Nanette le Blan	1962	Marley Spearman	1991	Valerie Michaud
1896	Amy Pascoe	1929	Joyce Wethered	1963	Brigitte Varangot	1992	Bernille Pedersen
1897	Edith Orr	1930	Diana Fishwick	1964	Carol Sorenson	1993	Catriona Lambert
1898	Lena Thomson	1931	Enid Wilson	1965	Brigitte Varangot	1994	Emma Duggleby
1899	May Hezlet	1932	Enid Wilson	1966	Elizabeth Chadwick	1995	Julie Wade Hall
1900	Rhona Adair	1933	Enid Wilson	1967	Elizabeth Chadwick	1996	Kelli Kuehne
1901	Mary Graham	1934	Helen Holm	1968	Brigitte Varangot	1997	Alison Rose
1902	May Hezlet	1935	Wanda Morgan	1969	Catherine Lacoste	1998	Kim Rostron
1903	Rhona Adair	1936	Pam Barton	1970	Dinah Oxley	1999	Marine Monnet
1904	Lottie Dod	1937	Jessie Anderson	1971	Michelle Walker		
1905	Bertha Thompson	1938	Helen Holm	1972	Michelle Walker	2000	Rebecca Hudson
1906	Mrs. W. Kennion	1939	Pam Barton	1973	Ann Irvin		
1907	May Hezlet	1940-45	Not held	1974	Carol Semple		
1908	Maud Titterton	1946	Jean Hetherington	1975	Nancy Roth Syms		
1909	Dorothy Campbell	1947	Babe Zaharias	1976	Cathy Panton		
1910	Elsie Grant-Suttie	1948	Louise Suggs	1977	Angela Uzielli		
1911	Dorothy Campbell	1949	Frances Stephens	1978	Edwina Kennedy		
1912	Gladys Ravenscroft	1950	Lally de St. Sauveur	1979	Maureen Madill		
1913	Muriel Dodd	1951	Catherine MacCann	1980	Anne Quast Sander		
1914	Cecil Leitch	1952	Moira Paterson	1981	Belle Robertson		
1915-19	Not held	1953	Marlene Stewart	1982	Kitrina Douglas		
1920	Cecil Leitch	1954	Frances Stephens	1983	Jill Thornhill		
1921	Cecil Leitch	1955	Jessie Valentine	1984	Jody Rosenthal		
1922	Joyce Wethered	1956	Wiffi Smith	1985	Lillian Behan		
1923	Doris Chambers	1957	Philomena Garvey	1986	Marnie McGuire		
1924	Joyce Wethered	1958	Jessie Valentine	1987	Janet Collingham		
1925	Joyce Wethered	1959	Elizabeth Price	1988	Joanne Furby		

Vare Trophy

The Vare Trophy for best scoring average by a player on the LPGA Tour has been awarded since 1937 by the LPGA. The award is named after Glenna Collett Vare, winner of six U.S. women's amateur titles from 1922-35.

Multiple winners: Kathy Whitworth (7); JoAnne Carner and Mickey Wright (5); Patty Berg, Beth Daniel, Nancy Lopez, Judy Rankin and Annika Sorenstam (3); Pat Bradley, Betsy King and Karrie Webb (2).

Year		Avg	Year		Avg	Year		Avg
1953	Patty Berg	75.00	1969	Kathy Whitworth	72.38	1985	Nancy Lopez	70.73
1954	Babe Zaharias	75.48	1970	Kathy Whitworth	72.26	1986	Pat Bradley	71.10
1955	Patty Berg	74.47	1971	Kathy Whitworth	72.88	1987	Betsy King	71.14
1956	Patty Berg	74.57	1972	Kathy Whitworth	72.38	1988	Colleen Walker	71.26
1957	Louise Suggs	74.64	1973	Judy Rankin	73.08	1989	Beth Daniel	70.38
1958	Beverly Hanson	74.92	1974	JoAnne Carner	72.87			
1959	Betsy Rawls	74.03	1975	JoAnne Carner	72.40	1990	Beth Daniel	70.54
1960	Mickey Wright	73.25	1976	Judy Rankin	72.25	1991	Pat Bradley	70.66
1961	Mickey Wright	73.55	1977	Judy Rankin	72.16	1992	Dottie Pepper	70.80
1962	Mickey Wright	73.67	1978	Nancy Lopez	71.76	1993	Betsy King	70.85
1963	Mickey Wright	72.81	1979	Nancy Lopez	71.20	1994	Beth Daniel	70.90
1964	Mickey Wright	72.46	1980	Amy Alcott	71.51	1995	Annika Sorenstam	71.00
1965	Kathy Whitworth	72.61	1981	JoAnne Carner	71.75	1996	Annika Sorenstam	70.47
1966	Kathy Whitworth	72.60	1982	JoAnne Carner	71.49	1997	Karrie Webb	70.00
1967	Kathy Whitworth	72.74	1983	JoAnne Carner	71.41	1998	Annika Sorenstam	69.99
1968	Carol Mann	72.04	1984	Patty Sheehan	71.40	1999	Karrie Webb	69.43

Senior PGA
PGA Seniors' Championship

First played in 1937. Two championships played in 1979 and 1984.

Multiple winners: Sam Snead (6); Hale Irwin, Gary Player, Al Watrous and Eddie Williams (3); Julius Boros, Jock Hutchison, Don January, Arnold Palmer, Paul Runyan, Gene Sarazen and Lee Trevino (2).

Year		Year		Year		Year	
1937	Jock Hutchison	1954	Gene Sarazen	1970	Sam Snead	1984	Peter Thomson
1938	Fred McLeod*	1955	Mortie Dutra	1971	Julius Boros	1985	Not held
1939	Not held	1956	Pete Burke	1972	Sam Snead	1986	Gary Player
		1957	Al Watrous	1973	Sam Snead	1987	Chi Chi Rodriguez
1940	Otto Hackbarth*	1958	Gene Sarazen	1974	Roberto De Vicenzo	1988	Gary Player
1941	Jack Burke	1959	Willie Goggin	1975	Charlie Sifford*	1989	Larry Mowry
1942	Eddie Williams			1976	Pete Cooper		
1943-44	Not held	1960	Dick Metz	1977	Julius Boros	1990	Gary Player
1945	Eddie Williams	1961	Paul Runyan	1978	Joe Jiminez*	1991	Jack Nicklaus
1946	Eddie Williams*	1962	Paul Runyan	1979	Jack Fleck*	1992	Lee Trevino
1947	Jock Hutchison	1963	Herman Barron	1979	Don January	1993	Tom Wargo*
1948	Charles McKenna	1964	Sam Snead			1994	Lee Trevino
1949	Marshall Crichton	1965	Sam Snead	1980	Arnold Palmer*	1995	Ray Floyd
		1966	Fred Haas	1981	Miller Barber	1996	Hale Irwin
1950	Al Watrous	1967	Sam Snead	1982	Don January	1997	Hale Irwin
1951	Al Watrous*	1968	Chandler Harper	1983	Not held	1998	Hale Irwin
1952	Ernest Newnham	1969	Tommy Bolt	1984	Arnold Palmer	1999	Allen Doyle
1953	Harry Schwab						
						2000	Doug Tewell

*PLAYOFFS:

1938: Fred McLeod def. Otto Hackbarth in 18 holes. **1940:** Otto Hackbarth def. Jock Hutchison in 36 holes. **1946:** Eddie Williams def. Jock Hutchison in 18 holes. **1951:** Al Watrous def. Jock Hutchison in 18 holes. **1975:** Charlie Sifford def. Fred Wampler on 1st extra hole **1978:** Joe Jiminez def. Paul Harney on 1st extra hole. **1979:** Jack Fleck def. Bill Johnston on 1st extra hole. **1980:** Arnold Palmer def. Paul Harney on 1st extra hole. **1993:** Tom Wargo def. Bruce Crampton on 2nd extra hole.

U.S. Senior Open

Established in 1980 for senior players 55 years old and over, the minimum age was dropped to 50 (the PGA Seniors Tour entry age) in 1981. Arnold Palmer, Billy Casper, Hale Irwin, Orville Moody, Jack Nicklaus and Lee Trevino are the only golfers who have won both the U.S. Open and U.S. Senior Open.

Multiple winners: Miller Barber (3); Hale Irwin, Jack Nicklaus and Gary Player (2).

Year		Year		Year		Year	
1980	Roberto De Vicenzo	1986	Dale Douglass	1992	Larry Laoretti	1998	Hale Irwin
1981	Arnold Palmer*	1987	Gary Player	1993	Jack Nicklaus	1999	Dave Eichelberger
1982	Miller Barber	1988	Gary Player*	1994	Simon Hobday	2000	Hale Irwin
1983	Bill Casper*	1989	Orville Moody	1995	Tom Weiskopf		
1984	Miller Barber	1990	Lee Trevino	1996	Dave Stockton		
1985	Miller Barber	1991	Jack Nicklaus*	1997	Graham Marsh		

*PLAYOFFS:

1981: Arnold Palmer (70) def. Bob Stone (74) and Billy Casper (77) in 18 holes. **1983:** Tied at 75 after 18-hole playoff, Casper def. Rod Funseth with a birdie on the 1st extra hole. **1988:** Gary Player (68) def. Bob Charles (70) in 18 holes. **1991:** Jack Nicklaus (65) def. Chi Chi Rodriguez (69) in 18 holes.

Senior Players Championship

First played in 1983 and contested in Cleveland (1983-86), Ponte Vedra, Fla. (1987-89), and Dearborn, Mich. (since 1990).

Multiple winners: Ray Floyd, Arnold Palmer and Dave Stockton (2).

Year		Year		Year		Year	
1983	Miller Barber	1988	Billy Casper	1993	Jim Colbert	1998	Gil Morgan
1984	Arnold Palmer	1989	Orville Moody	1994	Dave Stockton	1999	Hale Irwin
1985	Arnold Palmer	1990	Jack Nicklaus	1995	J.C. Snead*	2000	Ray Floyd
1986	Chi Chi Rodriguez	1991	Jim Albus	1996	Ray Floyd		
1987	Gary Player	1992	Dave Stockton	1997	Larry Gilbert		

*PLAYOFF:

1995: J.C. Snead def. Jack Nicklaus on 1st extra hole.

The Tradition

First played in 1989 and played every year since at the Golf Club at Desert Mountain in Scottsdale, Ariz.

Multiple winners: Jack Nicklaus (4); Gil Morgan (2).

Year		Year		Year		Year	
1989	Don Bies	1992	Lee Trevino	1995	Jack Nicklaus*	1998	Gil Morgan
1990	Jack Nicklaus	1993	Tom Shaw	1996	Jack Nicklaus	1999	Graham Marsh
1991	Jack Nicklaus	1994	Ray Floyd*	1997	Gil Morgan	2000	Tom Kite

*PLAYOFFS:

1994: Ray Floyd def. Dale Douglas on 1st extra hole. **1995:** Jack Nicklaus def. Isao Aoki on 3rd extra hole.

Major Senior Championship Leaders

Through 2000. All players are still active.

		PGA Sr.	US Open	Senior Players	Trad	Total			PGA Sr.	US Open	Senior Players	Trad	Total
1	Jack Nicklaus	1	2	1	4	8	9	Billy Casper	0	1	1	0	2
2	Hale Irwin	3	2	1	0	6		Graham Marsh	0	1	0	1	2
	Gary Player	3	2	1	0	6		Orville Moody	0	1	0	1	2
4	Ray Floyd	1	0	2	1	4		Chi Chi Rodriguez	1	0	1	0	2
	Lee Trevino	2	1	0	1	4		Dave Stockton	0	0	2	0	2
6	Miller Barber	0	2	1	0	3							
	Gil Morgan	0	0	1	2	3							
	Arnold Palmer	1	0	2	0	3							

Grand Slam Summary

The Senior Grand Slam has officially consisted of The Tradition, the PGA Senior Championship, the Senior Players Championship and the U.S. Senior Open since 1990. Jack Nicklaus won three of the four events in 1991, but no one has won all four in one season.

Three wins in one year: Jack Nicklaus (1991). **Two wins in one year:** Gary Player (twice); Hale Irwin, Gil Morgan, Orville Moody, Jack Nicklaus, Arnold Palmer and Lee Trevino (once).

Year	Tradition	PGA Sr.	Players	US Open	Year	Tradition	PGA Sr.	Players	US Open
1983	—	—	M. Barber	Casper	1992	Trevino	Trevino	Stockton	Laoretti
1984	—	Palmer	Palmer	M. Barber	1993	Shaw	Wargo	Colbert	Nicklaus
1985	—	Thomson	Palmer	M. Barber	1994	Floyd	Trevino	Stockton	Hobday
1986	—	Player	Rodriguez	Douglass	1995	Nicklaus	Floyd	Snead	Weiskopf
1987	—	Rodriguez	Player	Player	1996	Nicklaus	Irwin	Floyd	Stockton
1988	—	Player	Casper	Player	1997	Morgan	Irwin	Gilbert	Marsh
1989	Bies	Mowry	Moody	Moody	1998	Morgan	Irwin	Morgan	Irwin
1990	Nicklaus	Player	Nicklaus	Trevino	1999	Marsh	Doyle	Irwin	Eichelberger
1991	Nicklaus	Nicklaus	Albus	Nicklaus	2000	Kite	Tewell	Floyd	Irwin

Annual Money Leaders

Official annual money leaders on the PGA, European PGA, Senior PGA and LPGA tours. European PGA earnings listed in pounds sterling (£).

PGA

Multiple leaders: Jack Nicklaus (8); Ben Hogan and Tom Watson (5); Arnold Palmer (4); Greg Norman, Sam Snead and Curtis Strange (3); Julius Boros, Billy Casper, Tom Kite, Byron Nelson, Nick Price and Tiger Woods (2).

Year		Earnings	Year		Earnings	Year		Earnings
1934	Paul Runyan	$6,767	1956	Ted Kroll	$72,836	1978	Tom Watson	$362,429
1935	Johnny Revolta	9,543	1957	Dick Mayer	65,835	1979	Tom Watson	462,636
1936	Horton Smith	7,682	1958	Arnold Palmer	42,608	1980	Tom Watson	530,808
1937	Harry Cooper	14,139	1959	Art Wall	53,168	1981	Tom Kite	375,699
1938	Sam Snead	19,534	1960	Arnold Palmer	75,263	1982	Craig Stadler	446,462
1939	Henry Picard	10,303	1961	Gary Player	64,540	1983	Hal Sutton	426,668
1940	Ben Hogan	10,655	1962	Arnold Palmer	81,448	1984	Tom Watson	476,260
1941	Ben Hogan	18,358	1963	Arnold Palmer	128,230	1985	Curtis Strange	542,321
1942	Ben Hogan	13,143	1964	Jack Nicklaus	113,285	1986	Greg Norman	653,296
1943	No records kept		1965	Jack Nicklaus	140,752	1987	Curtis Strange	925,941
1944	Byron Nelson	37,968	1966	Billy Casper	121,945	1988	Curtis Strange	1,147,644
1945	Byron Nelson	63,336	1967	Jack Nicklaus	188,998	1989	Tom Kite	1,395,278
1946	Ben Hogan	42,556	1968	Billy Casper	205,169	1990	Greg Norman	1,165,477
1947	Jimmy Demaret	27,937	1969	Frank Beard	164,707	1991	Corey Pavin	979,430
1948	Ben Hogan	32,112	1970	Lee Trevino	157,037	1992	Fred Couples	1,344,188
1949	Sam Snead	31,594	1971	Jack Nicklaus	244,491	1993	Nick Price	1,478,557
1950	Sam Snead	35,759	1972	Jack Nicklaus	320,542	1994	Nick Price	1,499,927
1951	Lloyd Mangrum	26,089	1973	Jack Nicklaus	308,362	1995	Greg Norman	1,654,959
1952	Julius Boros	37,033	1974	Johnny Miller	353,022	1996	Tom Lehman	1,780,159
1953	Lew Worsham	34,002	1975	Jack Nicklaus	298,149	1997	Tiger Woods	2,066,833
1954	Bob Toski	65,820	1976	Jack Nicklaus	266,439	1998	David Duval	2,591,031
1955	Julius Boros	63,122	1977	Tom Watson	310,653	1999	Tiger Woods	6,616,585

Note: In 1944-45, Nelson's winnings were in War Bonds.

Senior PGA

Multiple leaders: Don January (3); Miller Barber, Bob Charles, Jim Colbert, Hale Irwin, Dave Stockton and Lee Trevino (2).

Year		Earnings	Year		Earnings	Year		Earnings
1980	Don January	$44,100	1987	Chi Chi Rodriguez	$509,145	1994	Dave Stockton	$1,402,519
1981	Miller Barber	83,136	1988	Bob Charles	533,929	1995	Jim Colbert	1,444,386
1982	Miller Barber	106,890	1989	Bob Charles	725,887	1996	Jim Colbert	1,627,890
1983	Don January	237,571	1990	Lee Trevino	1,190,518	1997	Hale Irwin	2,343,364
1984	Don January	328,597	1991	Mike Hill	1,065,657	1998	Hale Irwin	2,861,945
1985	Peter Thomson	386,724	1992	Lee Trevino	1,027,002	1999	Bruce Fleisher	2,515,705
1986	Bruce Crampton	454,299	1993	Dave Stockton	1,175,944			

European PGA

Offical money in the Volvo Order of Merit was awarded in British pounds from 1961-98 and euros since 1999.
Multiple leaders: Colin Montgomerie (7); Seve Ballesteros (6); Sandy Lyle (3); Gay Brewer Jr., Nick Faldo, Bernard Hunt, Bernhard Langer, Peter Thomson and Ian Woosnam (2).

Year		Earnings	Year		Earnings	Year		Earnings
1961	Bernard Hunt	£4,492	1974	Peter Oosterhuis	£32,127	1987	Ian Woosnam	£439,075
1962	Peter Thomson	5,764	1975	Dale Hayes	20,507	1988	Seve Ballesteros	502,000
1963	Bernard Hunt	7,209	1976	Seve Ballesteros	39,504	1989	Ronan Rafferty	465,981
1964	Neil Coles	7,890	1977	Seve Ballesteros	46,436	1990	Ian Woosnam	737,977
1965	Peter Thomson	7,011	1978	Seve Ballesteros	54,348	1991	Seve Ballesteros	790,811
1966	Bruce Devlin	13,205	1979	Sandy Lyle	49,233	1992	Nick Faldo	1,220,540
1967	Gay Brewer Jr.	20,235	1980	Greg Norman	74,829	1993	Colin Montgomerie	798,145
1968	Gay Brewer Jr.	23,107	1981	Bernhard Langer	95,991	1994	Colin Montgomerie	920,647
1969	Billy Casper	23,483	1982	Sandy Lyle	86,141	1995	Colin Montgomerie	999,260
1970	Christy O'Connor	31,532	1983	Nick Faldo	140,761	1996	Colin Montgomerie	1,034,752
1971	Gary Player	11,281	1984	Bernhard Langer	160,883	1997	Colin Montgomerie	798,948
1972	Bob Charles	18,538	1985	Sandy Lyle	254,711	1998	Colin Montgomerie	1,082,833
1973	Tony Jacklin	24,839	1986	Seve Ballesteros	259,275	1999	Colin Montgomerie	1,822,880

LPGA

Multiple leaders: Kathy Whitworth (8); Mickey Wright (4); Patty Berg, JoAnne Carner, Beth Daniel, Betsy King, Nancy Lopez and Annika Sorenstam (3); Pat Bradley, Judy Rankin, Betsy Rawls, Louise Suggs, Karrie Webb and Babe Zaharias (2).

Year		Earnings	Year		Earnings	Year		Earnings
1950	Babe Zaharias	$14,800	1967	Kathy Whitworth	$32,937	1984	Betsy King	$266,771
1951	Babe Zaharias	15,087	1968	Kathy Whitworth	48,379	1985	Nancy Lopez	416,472
1952	Betsy Rawls	14,505	1969	Carol Mann	49,152	1986	Pat Bradley	492,021
1953	Louise Suggs	19,816	1970	Kathy Whitworth	30,235	1987	Ayako Okamoto	466,034
1954	Patty Berg	16,011	1971	Kathy Whitworth	41,181	1988	Sherri Turner	350,851
1955	Patty Berg	16,492	1972	Kathy Whitworth	65,063	1989	Betsy King	654,132
1956	Marlene Hagge	20,235	1973	Kathy Whitworth	82,864	1990	Beth Daniel	863,578
1957	Patty Berg	16,272	1974	JoAnne Carner	87,094	1991	Pat Bradley	763,118
1958	Beverly Hanson	12,639	1975	Sandra Palmer	76,374	1992	Dottie Pepper	693,335
1959	Betsy Rawls	26,774	1976	Judy Rankin	150,734	1993	Betsy King	595,992
1960	Louise Suggs	16,892	1977	Judy Rankin	122,890	1994	Laura Davies	687,201
1961	Mickey Wright	22,236	1978	Nancy Lopez	189,814	1995	Annika Sorenstam	666,533
1962	Mickey Wright	21,641	1979	Nancy Lopez	197,489	1996	Karrie Webb	1,002,000
1963	Mickey Wright	31,269	1980	Beth Daniel	231,000	1997	Annika Sorenstam	1,236,789
1964	Mickey Wright	29,800	1981	Beth Daniel	206,998	1998	Annika Sorenstam	1,092,748
1965	Kathy Whitworth	28,658	1982	JoAnne Carner	310,400	1999	Karrie Webb	1,591,959
1966	Kathy Whitworth	33,517	1983	JoAnne Carner	291,404			

All-Time Leaders

PGA, Senior PGA and LPGA leaders through Oct. 8, 2000.

Tournaments Won

PGA

		No			No			No
1	Sam Snead	81	10	Lloyd Mangrum	36	19	Henry Picard	26
2	Jack Nicklaus	70	11	Tom Watson	34	20	Tommy Armour	24
3	Ben Hogan	63	12	Horton Smith	32		Macdonald Smith	24
4	Arnold Palmer	60	13	Harry Cooper	31		Johnny Miller	24
5	Byron Nelson	52		Jimmy Demaret	31		Tiger Woods	24
6	Billy Casper	51	15	Leo Diegel	30			
7	Walter Hagen	40	16	Gene Littler	29			
	Cary Middlecoff	40		Paul Runyan	29			
9	Gene Sarazen	38	18	Lee Trevino	27			

Senior PGA

		No			No			No
1	Lee Trevino	29	8	George Archer	19	15	Jim Dent	12
2	Hale Irwin	28		Jim Colbert	19	16	Dale Douglass	11
3	Miller Barber	24		Gary Player	19		Bruce Fleisher	11
4	Bob Charles	23	11	Mike Hill	18		Orville Moody	11
5	Don January	22		Gil Morgan	18		Bob Murphy	11
	Chi Chi Rodriguez	22	13	Dave Stockton	14		Larry Nelson	11
7	Bruce Crampton	20		Raymond Floyd	14		Peter Thomson	11

All-Time Leaders (Cont.)
LPGA

		No				No				No
1	Kathy Whitworth	88	9	Carol Mann	38		16	Jane Blalock	26
2	Mickey Wright	82	10	Patty Sheehan	35			Judy Rankin	26
3	Patty Berg	57	11	Beth Daniel	32		18	Marlene Hagge	25
4	Betsy Rawls	53	12	Pat Bradley	31		19	Donna Caponi	24
5	Louise Suggs	50		Betsy King	31		20	Juli Inkster	24
6	Nancy Lopez	48		Babe Zaharias	31				
7	JoAnne Carner	42	15	Amy Alcott	29				
	Sandra Haynie	42							

Note: Patty Berg's total includes 13 official pro wins prior to formation of LPGA in 1950.

Money Won
PGA
All-time earnings through Oct. 8, 2000.

		Earnings			Earnings			Earnings
1	Tiger Woods	$19,601,950	10	Scott Hoch	$11,605,057	19	Loren Roberts	$9,199,413
2	Davis Love III	14,605,067	11	Mark O'Meara	11,586,578	20	Corey Pavin	9,077,769
3	Greg Norman	13,087,832	12	Mark Calcavecchia	9,715,456	21	Justin Leonard	8,904,057
4	Nick Price	12,771,503	13	Tom Kite	10,654,707	22	Jim Furyk	8,893,359
5	David Duval	12,330,792	14	Vijay Singh	10,497,157	23	Jeff Sluman	8,626,333
6	Fred Couples	12,194,984	15	Tom Lehman	10,082,736	24	Jeff Maggert	8,470,720
7	Hal Sutton	12,077,000	16	Paul Azinger	9,975,501	25	Steve Elkington	8,333,107
8	Phil Mickelson	12,075,115	17	Tom Watson	9,583,681			
9	Payne Stewart	11,737,008	18	Ernie Els	9,418,512			

Senior PGA
All-time earnings through Oct. 8, 2000.

		Earnings			Earnings			Earnings
1	Hale Irwin	$11,570,733	10	Mike Hall	$7,023,822	19	Tom Wargo	$5,518,941
2	Jim Colbert	9,573,002	11	Isao Aoki	6,881,214	20	Gary Player	5,342,077
3	Lee Trevino	9,185,924	12	Chi Chi Rodriguez	6,509,404	21	Jim Albus	5,321,019
4	Dave Stockton	8,584,730	13	Dale Douglass	6,270,512	22	Al Geiberger	5,124,376
5	Bob Charles	8,276,087	14	Bob Murphy	6,242,549	23	Bruce Summerhays	5,014,988
6	Gil Morgan	7,731,139	15	Jay Sigel	5,864,483	24	Bruce Fleisher	4,837,311
7	George Archer	7,700,466	16	J.C. Snead	5,777,664	25	Bruce Crampton	4,652,684
8	Ray Floyd	7,626,594	17	Larry Nelson	5,765,011			
9	Jim Dent	7,497,054	18	Graham Marsh	5,736,462			

European PGA
All-time earnings through Oct. 1, 2000.

		Earnings			Earnings			Earnings
1	C. Montgomerie	E11,821,248	10	M. A. Jimenez	E5,008,582	19	P-U Johansson	E3,065,160
2	Bernhard Langer	8,354,640	11	Ernie Els	4,863,543	20	Ronan Rafferty	3,057,539
3	Ian Woosnam	7,127,359	12	Mark James	4,372,244	21	Barry Lane	3,056,026
4	Darren Clarke	6,708,890	13	Mark McNulty	4,225,915	22	Padraig Harrington	3,040,520
5	Lee Westwood	6,503,938	14	Eduardo Romero	3,933,150	23	Peter Baker	2,858,976
6	Jose Maria Olazabal	6,369,548	15	Costantino Rocca	3,896,589	24	Phillip Price	2,837,417
7	Nick Faldo	5,949,854	16	Thomas Bjorn	3,843,274	25	Sandy Lyle	2,821,522
8	Seve Ballesteros	5,283,784	17	Retief Goosen	3,843,274			
9	Sam Torrance	5,065,769	18	Gordon Brand Jr.	3,320,084			

LPGA
All-time earnings through Oct. 8, 2000.

		Earnings			Earnings			Earnings
1	Betsy King	$6,811,178	10	Nancy Lopez	$5,292,645	19	Chris Johnson	$3,360,592
2	Annika Sorenstam	6,038,096	11	Laura Davies	5,156,876	20	Brandie Burton	3,136,669
3	Karrie Webb	5,979,095	12	Rosie Jones	4,843,704	21	Jan Stephenson	2,987,515
4	Beth Daniel	5,978,378	13	Liselotte Neumann	4,015,002	22	JoAnne Carner	2,936,725
5	Juli Inkster	5,882,775	14	Kelly Robbins	3,918,328	23	Michelle McGann	2,897,108
6	Pat Bradley	5,734,628	15	Jane Geddes	3,705,450	24	Colleen Walker	2,747,278
7	Dottie Pepper	5,591,631	16	Sherri Steinhauer	3,578,746	25	Ayako Okamoto	2,746,253
8	Patty Sheehan	5,500,983	17	Tammie Green	3,380,028			
9	Meg Mallon	5,408,736	18	Amy Alcott	3,368,340			

Official World Rankings

Begun in 1986, the Official World Golf Ranking (formerly the Sony World Ranking) combines the best golfers on the five PGA men's tours throughout the world. Rankings are based on a rolling two-year period and weighed in favor of more recent results. While annual winners are not announced, certain players reaching No. 1 have dominated each year.

Multiple winners (at year's end): Greg Norman (6); Nick Faldo and Tiger Woods (3); Seve Ballesteros (2).

Year		Year		Year		Year	
1986	Seve Ballesteros	1990	Nick Faldo	1993	Nick Faldo	1998	Tiger Woods
1987	Greg Norman		& Greg Norman	1994	Nick Price	1999	Tiger Woods
1988	Greg Norman	1991	Ian Woosnam	1995	Greg Norman		
1989	Seve Ballesteros	1992	Fred Couples	1996	Greg Norman		
	& Greg Norman		& Nick Faldo	1997	Tiger Woods		

Annual Awards
PGA of America Player of the Year

Awarded by the PGA of America; based on points scale that weighs performance in major tournaments, regular events, money earned and scoring average.

Multiple winners: Tom Watson (6); Jack Nicklaus (5); Ben Hogan (4); Tiger Woods (3); Julius Boros, Billy Casper, Arnold Palmer and Nick Price.

Year		Year		Year		Year	
1948	Ben Hogan	1962	Arnold Palmer	1976	Jack Nicklaus	1990	Nick Faldo
1949	Sam Snead	1963	Julius Boros	1977	Tom Watson	1991	Corey Pavin
1950	Ben Hogan	1964	Ken Venturi	1978	Tom Watson	1992	Fred Couples
1951	Ben Hogan	1965	Dave Marr	1979	Tom Watson	1993	Nick Price
1952	Julius Boros	1966	Billy Casper	1980	Tom Watson	1994	Nick Price
1953	Ben Hogan	1967	Jack Nicklaus	1981	Bill Rogers	1995	Greg Norman
1954	Ed Furgol	1968	No award	1982	Tom Watson	1996	Tom Lehman
1955	Doug Ford	1969	Orville Moody	1983	Hal Sutton	1997	Tiger Woods
1956	Jack Burke	1970	Billy Casper	1984	Tom Watson	1998	Mark O'Meara
1957	Dick Mayer	1971	Lee Trevino	1985	Lanny Wadkins	1999	Tiger Woods
1958	Dow Finsterwald	1972	Jack Nicklaus	1986	Bob Tway	2000	Tiger Woods
1959	Art Wall	1973	Jack Nicklaus	1987	Paul Azinger		
1960	Arnold Palmer	1974	Johnny Miller	1988	Curtis Strange		
1961	Jerry Barber	1975	Jack Nicklaus	1989	Tom Kite		

PGA Tour Player of the Year

Award by the PGA Tour starting in 1990. Winner voted on by tour members from list of nominees. Winner receives the Jack Nicklaus Trophy, which originated in 1997.

Multiple winners: Fred Couples, Nick Price and Tiger Woods (2).

Year		Year		Year		Year	
1990	Wayne Levi	1993	Nick Price	1996	Tom Lehman	1999	Tiger Woods
1991	Fred Couples	1994	Nick Price	1997	Tiger Woods		
1992	Fred Couples	1995	Greg Norman	1998	Mark O'Meara		

PGA Tour Rookie of the Year

Awarded by the PGA Tour in 1990. Winner voted on by tour members from list of first-year nominees.

Year		Year		Year		Year	
1990	Robert Gamez	1993	Vijay Singh	1996	Tiger Woods	1999	Carlos Franco
1991	John Daly	1994	Ernie Els	1997	Stewart Cink		
1992	Mark Carnevale	1995	Woody Austin	1998	Steve Flesch		

PGA Senior Player of the Year

Awarded by th PGA Seniors Tour starting in 1990. Winner voted on by tour members from list of nominees.

Multiple winner: Lee Trevino (3); Jim Colbert and Hale Irwin (2).

Year		Year		Year		Year	
1990	Lee Trevino	1992	Lee Trevino	1995	Jim Colbert	1998	Hale Irwin
1991	George Archer	1993	Dave Stockton	1996	Jim Colbert	1999	Bruce Fleisher
	& Mike Hill	1994	Lee Trevino	1997	Hale Irwin		

PGA Senior Tour Rookie of the Year

Awarded by th PGA Tour starting in 1990. Winner voted on by tour members from list of first-year nominees.

Year		Year		Year		Year	
1990	Lee Trevino	1993	Bob Murphy	1996	John Bland	1999	Bruce Fleisher
1991	Jim Colbert	1994	Jay Sigel	1997	Gil Morgan		
1992	Dave Stockton	1995	Hale Irwin	1998	Joe Inman		

Annual Awards (Cont.)
European Golfer of the Year

Officially, the Johnnie Walker Trophy; voting done by panel of European golf writers and tour members.
Multiple winners: Colin Montgomerie (4); Seve Ballesteros and Nick Faldo (3); Bernhard Langer (2).

Year		Year		Year		Year	
1985	Bernhard Langer	1989	Nick Faldo	1993	Bernhard Langer	1997	Colin Montgomerie
1986	Seve Ballesteros	1990	Nick Faldo	1994	Ernie Els	1998	Lee Westwood
1987	Ian Woosnam	1991	Seve Ballesteros	1995	Colin Montgomerie	1999	Colin Montgomerie
1988	Seve Ballesteros	1992	Nick Faldo	1996	Colin Montgomerie		

LPGA Player of the Year

Awarded by the LPGA; based on performance points accumulated during the year.
Multiple winners: Kathy Whitworth (7); Nancy Lopez (4); JoAnne Carner, Beth Daniel, Betsy King and Annika Sorenstam (3); Pat Bradley and Judy Rankin (2).

Year		Year		Year		Year	
1966	Kathy Whitworth	1975	Sandra Palmer	1984	Betsy King	1993	Betsy King
1967	Kathy Whitworth	1976	Judy Rankin	1985	Nancy Lopez	1994	Beth Daniel
1968	Kathy Whitworth	1977	Judy Rankin	1986	Pat Bradley	1995	Annika Sorenstam
1969	Kathy Whitworth	1978	Nancy Lopez	1987	Ayako Okamoto	1996	Laura Davies
1970	Sandra Haynie	1979	Nancy Lopez	1988	Nancy Lopez	1997	Annika Sorenstam
1971	Kathy Whitworth	1980	Beth Daniel	1989	Betsy King	1998	Annika Sorenstam
1972	Kathy Whitworth	1981	JoAnne Carner	1990	Beth Daniel	1999	Karrie Webb
1973	Kathy Whitworth	1982	JoAnne Carner	1991	Pat Bradley		
1974	JoAnne Carner	1983	Patty Sheehan	1992	Dottie Mochrie		

LPGA Rookie of the Year

Awarded by the LPGA; based on performance points accumulated during the year.

Year		Year		Year		Year	
1962	Mary Mills	1972	Jocelyn Bourassa	1982	Patti Rizzo	1992	Helen Alfredsson
1963	Clifford Ann Creed	1973	Laura Baugh	1983	Stephanie Farwig	1993	Suzanne Strudwick
1964	Susie Berning	1974	Jan Stephenson	1984	Juli Inkster	1994	Annika Sorenstam
1965	Margie Masters	1975	Amy Alcott	1985	Penny Hammel	1995	Pat Hurst
1966	Jan Ferraris	1976	Bonnie Lauer	1986	Jody Rosenthal	1996	Karrie Webb
1967	Sharron Moran	1977	Debbie Massey	1987	Tammie Green	1997	Lisa Hackney
1968	Sandra Post	1978	Nancy Lopez	1988	Liselotte Neumann	1998	Se Ri Pak
1969	Jane Blalock	1979	Beth Daniel	1989	Pamela Wright	1999	Mi Hyun Kim
1970	JoAnne Carner	1980	Myra Van Hoose	1990	Hiromi Kobayashi		
1971	Sally Little	1981	Patty Sheehan	1991	Brandie Burton		

National Team Competition
MEN
Ryder Cup

The Ryder Cup was presented by British seed merchant and businessman Samuel Ryder in 1927 for competition between professional golfers from Great Britain and the United States. The British team was expanded to include Irish players in 1973 and the rest of Europe in 1979. The United States leads the series 24-7-2 after 33 matches.

Year		Year		Year		Year	
1927	USA, 9½-2½	1951	USA, 9½-2½	1969	Draw, 16-16	1987	Europe, 15-13
1929	Britain-Ireland, 7-5	1953	USA, 6½-5½	1971	USA, 18½-13½	1989	Draw, 14-14
1931	USA, 9-3	1955	USA, 8-4	1973	USA, 19-13	1991	USA, 14½-13½
1933	Great Britain, 6½-5½	1957	Britain-Ireland, 7½-4½	1975	USA, 21-11	1993	USA, 15-13
1935	USA, 9-3	1959	USA, 8½-3½	1977	USA, 12½-13½	1995	Europe, 14½-13½
1937	USA, 8-4	1961	USA, 14½-9½	1979	USA, 17-11	1997	Europe, 14½-13½
1939-45	Not held	1963	USA, 23-9	1981	USA, 18½-9½	1999	USA, 14½-13½
1947	USA, 11-1	1965	USA, 19½-12½	1983	USA, 14½-13½		
1949	USA, 7-5	1967	USA, 23½-8½	1985	Europe, 16½-11½		

Playing Sites

1927—Worcester CC (Mass.); **1929**—Moortown, England; **1931**—Scioto CC (Ohio); **1933**—Southport & Ainsdale, England; **1935**—Ridgewood CC (N.J.); **1937**—Southport & Ainsdale, England; **1939-45**—Not held. **1947**—Portland CC (Ore.); **1949**—Ganton GC, England; **1951**—Pinehurst CC (N.C.); **1953**—Wentworth CC, England; **1955**—Thunderbird Ranch &CC (Calif.); **1957**—Lindrick GC, England; **1959**—Eldorado CC (Calif.); **1961**—Royal Lytham & St. Annes, England; **1963**—East Lake CC (Ga.); **1965**—Royal Birkdale, England; **1967**—Champions GC (Tex.); **1969**—Royal Birkdale, England; **1971**—Old Warson CC (Mo.); **1973**—Muirfield, Scotland; **1975**—Laurel Valley GC (Pa.); **1977**—Royal Lytham & St. Annes, England; **1979**—The Greenbrier (W.Va.); **1981**—Walton Heath GC, England; **1983**—PGA National GC (Fla.); **1985**—The Belfry, England; **1987**—Muirfield Village GC (Ohio); **1989**—The Belfry, England; **1991**—Ocean Course (S.C.); **1993**—The Belfry, England; **1995**—Oak Hill CC (N.Y.); **1997**—Valderrama, Costa del Sol, Spain; **1999**—The Country Club (Mass.); **2001**— The Belfry, England; **2003**— Oakland Hills CC (Mich.).

Walker Cup

The Walker Cup was presented by American businessman George Herbert Walker in 1922 for competition between amateur golfers from Great Britain, Ireland and the United States. The U.S. leads the series against the combined Great Britain-Ireland team, 31-5-1, after 37 matches.

Year	Year	Year	Year
1922 USA, 8-4	1940-46 Not held	1965 Draw, 12-12	1985 USA, 13-11
1923 USA, 6½-5½	1947 USA, 8-4	1967 USA, 15-9	1987 USA, 16½-7½
1924 USA, 9-3	1949 USA, 10-2	1969 USA, 13-11	1989 Britain-Ireland,
1926 USA, 6½-5½	1951 USA, 7½-4½	1971 Britain-Ireland, 13-11	12½-11½
1928 USA, 11-1	1953 USA, 9-3	1973 USA, 14-10	1991 USA, 14-10
1930 USA, 10-2	1955 USA, 10-2	1975 USA, 15½-8½	1993 USA, 19-5
1932 USA, 9½-2½	1957 USA, 8½-3½	1977 USA, 16-8	1995 Britain-Ireland, 14-10
1934 USA, 9½-2½	1959 USA, 9-3	1979 USA, 15½-8½	1997 USA, 18-6
1936 USA, 10½-1½	1961 USA, 11-1	1981 USA, 15-9	1999 Britain-Ireland, 15-9
1938 Britain-Ireland, 7½-4½	1963 USA, 14-10	1983 USA, 13½-10½	

Presidents Cup

The Presidents Cup is a biennial event played in non-Ryder Cup years in which the world's best non-European players compete against players from the United States. The U.S. leads the series, 2-1.

Year	Year	Year
1994 USA, 20-12	1998 International, 20½-11½	2000 Oct. 19-22
1996 USA, 16½-15½		(see updates chapter)

WOMEN
Solheim Cup

The Solheim Cup was presented by the Karsten Manufacturing Co. in 1990 for competition between women professional golfers from Europe and the United States. The U.S. leads the series, 4-2.

Year	Year	Year
1990 USA, 11½-4½	1994 USA, 13-7	1998 USA, 16-12
1992 Europe, 11½-6½	1996 USA, 17-11	2000 Europe, 14½-11½

Playing Sites

1990– Lake Nona CC (Fla.); **1992–** Dalmahoy CC, Scotland; **1994–** The Greenbrier (W. Va.); **1996–** Marriott St. Pierre Hotel G&CC, Wales; **1998–** Muirfield Village GC (Ohio); **2000–** Loch Lomond GC, Scotland; **2002–** Interlachen CC (Minn.); **2004–** Barseback G&CC, Sweden.

Curtis Cup

Named after British golfing sisters Harriot and Margaret Curtis, the Curtis Cup was first contested in 1932 between teams of women amateurs from the United States and the British Isles.
Competed for every other year since 1932 (except during WWII). The U.S. leads the series, 22-6-3, after 31 matches.

Year	Year	Year	Year
1932 USA, 5½-3½	1954 USA, 6-3	1970 USA, 11½-6½	1986 British Isles, 13-5
1934 USA, 6½-2½	1956 British Isles, 5-4	1972 USA, 10-8	1988 British Isles, 11-7
1936 Draw, 4½-4½	1958 Draw, 4½-4½	1974 USA, 13-5	1990 USA, 14-4
1938 USA, 5½-3½	1960 USA, 6½-2½	1976 USA, 11½-6½	1992 British Isles, 10-8
1940-46 Not held	1962 USA, 8-1	1978 USA, 12-6	1994 Draw, 9-9
1948 USA, 6½-2½	1964 USA, 10½-7½	1980 USA, 13-5	1996 British Isles, 11½-6½
1950 USA, 7½-1½	1966 USA, 13-5	1982 USA, 14½-3½	1998 USA, 10-8
1952 British Isles, 5-4	1968 USA, 10½-7½	1984 USA, 9½-8½	2000 USA, 10-8

COLLEGES

Men's NCAA Division I Champions

College championships decided by match play from 1897-1964 and stroke play since 1965.
Multiple winners (Teams): Yale (21); Houston (16); Oklahoma St. (9); Stanford (7); Harvard (6); LSU and North Texas (4); Florida and Wake Forest (3); Arizona St., Michigan, Ohio St. and Texas (2).
Multiple winners (Individuals): Ben Crenshaw and Phil Mickelson (3); Dick Crawford, Dexter Cummings, G.T. Dunlop, Fred Lamphrecht and Scott Simpson (2).

Year	Team winner	Individual champion	Year	Team winner	Individual champion
1897	Yale	Louis Bayard, Princeton	1902	Harvard (fall)	Chandler Egan, Harvard
1898	Harvard (spring)	John Reid, Yale	1903	Harvard	F.O. Reinhart, Princeton
1898	Yale (fall)	James Curtis, Harvard	1904	Harvard	A.L. White, Harvard
1899	Harvard	Percy Pyne, Princeton	1905	Yale	Robert Abbott, Yale
1900	Not held		1906	Yale	W.E. Clow Jr., Yale
1901	Harvard	H. Lindsley, Harvard	1907	Yale	Ellis Knowles, Yale
1902	Yale (spring)	Chas. Hitchcock Jr., Yale	1908	Yale	H.H. Wilder, Harvard

Year	Team winner	Individual champion	Year	Team winner	Individual champion
1909	Yale	Albert Seckel, Princeton	1956	Houston	Rick Jones, Ohio St.
1910	Yale	Robert Hunter, Yale	1957	Houston	Rex Baxter Jr., Houston
1911	Yale	George Stanley, Yale	1958	Houston	Phil Rodgers, Houston
1912	Yale	F.C. Davison, Harvard	1959	Houston	Dick Crawford, Houston
1913	Yale	Nathaniel Wheeler, Yale	1960	Houston	Dick Crawford, Houston
1914	Princeton	Edward Allis, Harvard	1961	Purdue	Jack Nicklaus, Ohio St.
1915	Yale	Francis Blossom, Yale	1962	Houston	Kermit Zarley, Houston
1916	Princeton	J.W. Hubbell, Harvard	1963	Oklahoma St.	R.H. Sikes, Arkansas
1917-18	Not held		1964	Houston	Terry Small, San Jose St.
1919	Princeton	A.L. Walker Jr., Columbia	1965	Houston	Marty Fleckman, Houston
1920	Princeton	Jess Sweetster, Yale	1966	Houston	Bob Murphy, Florida
1921	Dartmouth	Simpson Dean, Princeton	1967	Houston	Hale Irwin, Colorado
1922	Princeton	Pollack Boyd, Dartmouth	1968	Florida	Grier Jones, Oklahoma St.
1923	Princeton	Dexter Cummings, Yale	1969	Houston	Bob Clark, Cal St.-LA
1924	Yale	Dexter Cummings, Yale	1970	Houston	John Mahaffey, Houston
1925	Yale	Fred Lamprecht, Tulane	1971	Texas	Ben Crenshaw, Texas
1926	Yale	Fred Lamprecht, Tulane	1972	Texas	Ben Crenshaw, Texas
1927	Princeton	Watts Gunn, Georgia Tech			& Tom Kite, Texas
1928	Princeton	Maurice McCarthy, G'town	1973	Florida	Ben Crenshaw, Texas
1929	Princeton	Tom Aycock, Yale	1974	Wake Forest	Curtis Strange, W.Forest
1930	Princeton	G.T. Dunlap Jr., Princeton	1975	Wake Forest	Jay Haas, Wake Forest
1931	Yale	G.T. Dunlap Jr., Princeton	1976	Oklahoma St.	Scott Simpson, USC
1932	Yale	J.W. Fischer, Michigan	1977	Houston	Scott Simpson, USC
1933	Yale	Walter Emery, Oklahoma	1978	Oklahoma St.	David Edwards, Okla. St.
1934	Michigan	Charles Yates, Ga.Tech	1979	Ohio St.	Gary Hallberg, Wake Forest
1935	Michigan	Ed White, Texas	1980	Oklahoma St.	Jay Don Blake, Utah St.
1936	Yale	Charles Kocsis, Michigan	1981	Brigham Young	Ron Commans, USC
1937	Princeton	Fred Haas Jr., LSU	1982	Houston	Billy Ray Brown, Houston
1938	Stanford	John Burke, Georgetown	1983	Oklahoma St.	Jim Carter, Arizona St.
1939	Stanford	Vincent D'Antoni, Tulane	1984	Houston	John Inman, N.Carolina
1940	Princeton & LSU	Dixon Brooke, Virginia	1985	Houston	Clark Burroughs, Ohio St.
1941	Stanford	Earl Stewart, LSU	1986	Wake Forest	Scott Verplank, Okla. St.
1942	LSU & Stanford	Frank Tatum Jr., Stanford	1987	Oklahoma St.	Brian Watts, Oklahoma St.
1943	Yale	Wallace Ulrich, Carleton	1988	UCLA	E.J. Pfister, Oklahoma St.
1944	Notre Dame	Louis Lick, Minnesota	1989	Oklahoma	Phil Mickelson, Ariz. St.
1945	Ohio State	John Lorms, Ohio St.	1990	Arizona St.	Phil Mickelson, Ariz. St.
1946	Stanford	George Hamer, Georgia	1991	Oklahoma St.	Warren Schuette, UNLV
1947	LSU	Dave Barclay, Michigan	1992	Arizona	Phil Mickelson, Ariz. St.
1948	San Jose St.	Bob Harris, San Jose St.	1993	Florida	Todd Demsey, Ariz. St.
1949	North Texas	Harvie Ward, N.Carolina	1994	Stanford	Justin Leonard, Texas
1950	North Texas	Fred Wampler, Purdue	1995	Oklahoma St.	Chip Spratlin, Auburn
1951	North Texas	Tom Nieporte, Ohio St.	1996	Arizona St.	Tiger Woods, Stanford
1952	North Texas	Jim Vichers, Oklahoma	1997	Pepperdine	Charles Warren, Clemson
1953	Stanford	Earl Moeller, Oklahoma St.	1998	UNLV	James McLean, Minnesota
1954	SMU	Hillman Robbins, Memphis St.	1999	Georgia	Luke Donald, Northwestern
1955	LSU	Joe Campbell, Purdue	2000	Oklahoma St.	Charles Howell, Oklahoma St.

Women's NCAA Division I Champions

College championships decided by stroke play since 1982.
Multiple winners (teams): Arizona St. (6); Arizona, Florida, San Jose St. and Tulsa (2).

Year	Team winner	Individual champion	Year	Team winner	Individual champion
1982	Tulsa	Kathy Baker, Tulsa	1992	San Jose St.	Vicki Goetze, Georgia
1983	TCU	Penny Hammel, Miami	1993	Arizona St.	Charlotta Sorenstam, Ariz. St.
1984	Miami-FL	Cindy Schreyer, Georgia	1994	Arizona St.	Emilee Klein, Ariz. St.
1985	Florida	Danielle Ammaccapane, Ariz.St.	1995	Arizona St.	K. Mourgue d'Algue, Ariz. St.
1986	Florida	Page Dunlap, Florida	1996	Arizona	Marisa Baena, Arizona
1987	San Jose St.	Caroline Keggi, New Mexico	1997	Arizona St.	Heather Bowie, Texas
1988	Tulsa	Melissa McNamara, Tulsa	1998	Arizona St.	Jennifer Rosales, USC
1989	San Jose St.	Pat Hurst, San Jose St.	1999	Duke	Grace Park, Arizona St.
1990	Arizona St.	Susan Slaughter, Arizona	2000	Arizona	Jenna Daniels, Arizona
1991	UCLA	Annika Sorenstam, Arizona			

Auto Racing

Michael Schumacher *gets a lift from his team manager after winning the Formula One driving title.*

AP/Wide World Photos

A Turn for the Worse

A sport mourns as we see more examples of the inherent dangers of auto racing.

by

Rece Davis

Race car drivers know that death or catastrophic injury can always lurk in the next turn. They accept it and summarily dismiss it because they have to.

The news came on Friday afternoon May 12th. Adam Petty had been killed in a practice crash at New Hampshire International Speedway. Eight weeks to the day later, Kenny Irwin died in a similar crash on the same track at nearly the same spot. Those tragedies, the death of burgeoning CART superstar Greg Moore in the 1999 season finale, and the loss of Craftsman Trucks Series driver Tony Roper cast a pall over the 2000 campaign.

I thought about the first time I met Petty. He was 16, driving cars at the *Richard Petty's Driving Experience* and had

Rece Davis is a *SportsCenter* anchor and host of *RPM 2Night* on espn2.

superstar written all over him. The similarities between Adam and his grandfather were striking. The 1000-kilowatt smile beamed even brighter when the talk turned to his Winston Cup dream. Adam fulfilled that when he became the first fourth generation Cup driver by making his debut in Texas just a little over a month before his death.

Irwin was regrouping and harnessing his considerable talent in a fresh start with a new race team. Moore had just cashed in on free agency and was preparing to bring the magic back to Team Penske. Roper was just getting his truck driving career started. It's been said that old men go to death, but death comes to young men. Why did it come to these men and why did it come now? Questions that haunted, but couldn't be answered.

Condolences were expressed. Prayers were offered. Safety improvements were examined. Tributes were

David Leeds/Allsport

A flower was put on the fence at the New Hampshire International Speedway in Loudon, N.H. in honor of NASCAR driver Adam Petty, killed in a crash on May 12. Driver Kenny Irwin was killed less than two months later on the same turn.

organized. All of these things honor the memory of the fallen. None of them eased the heartbreak of their families, friends and competitors. Sometimes when there's really nothing you can do, you simply do what you can. So the racers raced.

Winston Cup

For the second straight season, the reigning Winston Cup champion opened his season by winning the "Super Bowl," the Daytona 500. Dale Jarrett was the latest to turn the trick. But Jarrett didn't win again until mid-October.

In the interim, Bobby Labonte mimicked Jarrett's metronome-like 1999 consistency and had a comfortable 200-point series lead in late October. In the season's first 30 races, Labonte had only two finishes outside the top 20. Consistency was key in a season in which the wealth was spread. There were a record 10 different winners in the first 10 races of the season. Keeping Labonte's rear bumper in sight was Dale Earnhardt. "Capital E" was searching for the opening that he hoped would bring his record eighth championship.

CART

Never has a Vanderbilt Cup been tighter. It's OK. You haven't wandered into a *Victoria's Secret* testimonial. The Vanderbilt Cup is the prize delivered to CART's champion. Heading into the final race of the season, six drivers were separated by 22 points. Fittingly, 22 is the maximum number of points one can win on a race weekend. Perennial juggernaut Team Penske regained its traditional status. Roger Penske's driver Gil de Ferran took the lead to the Fontana,

875

"Little E,"**Dale Earnhardt Jr.**, right, won the first two races of his blossoming career and over $2 million in 2000 (through Oct. 22). Here he gets advice from his dad, a pretty decent driver in his own right.

Calif. finale. Like their Winston Cup brethren, CART's victory lane had an open door policy. Seven different winners in the season's first seven races. Heading to the finale, four first-timers had taken a checkered flag.

IRL

The IRL continued its one-step-forward, two-steps-back existence. The IRL turned in the best race of the season. But as Scott Sharp and Robby McGehee waged a stirring tire-to-tire war on the final lap at Texas Motor Speedway, weather took out the television feed. We at ESPN showed Sharp's win on tape, but even mother nature wouldn't cut the IRL a break. The league was upstaged in its marquee event by a CART interloper. Juan Montoya swooped in and took the Indianapolis 500. Aren't there enough omens that the separate open-wheel factions need to re-unite?

Formula One

The world's greatest drivers returned to the United States for the first time in nearly a decade when F1 hit the Brickyard in Indianapolis. Michael Schumacher won the race and went on to win the driver's championship for the third time in his glorious career. When Schumacher clinched the title in Japan, it triggered a festival in Maranello, Italy, the hometown of Ferrari. Church bells rang and fans waved the automaker's red flag with the prancing stallion in celebration of Ferrari's first title since 1979. ■

Rece Davis' Ten Biggest Auto Racing Stories of 2000

10. **Geoffrey Bodine's wreck.** Bodine catapults down the front stretch at Daytona as his truck disintegrated

876

Craig Jones/Allsport

It was a battle royale at the U.S. 500 in Michigan between **Juan Montoya** and **Michael Andretti**. Montoya, in the Target car, came out on top in one of the closest finishes in CART history.

into a fiery shell. Those of us who saw it expected the worst. Bodine survived with a couple of fractures. Given the tragedy we experienced this year, that's cause for celebration.

9. **Gordon vs. Stewart.** Hoosier blood boils as Jeff Gordon and Tony Stewart wage a spirited verbal exchange outside their haulers at Watkins Glen. *RPM 2Night* cameras were rolling. The duo was sent to neutral corners, but it made for good television.

8. **With the Kiss.** Roberto Moreno wins his first CART race and sets off a kissing frenzy that would have made Morgana the Kissing Bandit proud. If I kept score correctly, the exuberant Brazilian kissed our reporter Marlo Klain and was kissed by Christian Fitti-paldi. That later led to Helio Castro-Neves kissing Marlo in celebration, as did Paul Tracy. It became a tradition. Marlo never kissed back.

7. **Mayfield bumps Earnhardt.** In a move greeted with glee by many in the garage, Jeremy Mayfield does unto the Intimidator as the Intimidator has done unto others and knocks him out of the way on the final lap to win the Pocono 500. Earnhardt takes it in stride saying, "he would've wrecked if I'd hit him that hard."

6. **Coming to America.** The F-1 road show hits Indy in September with the U.S. Grand Prix. The one-time marquee race at the track, the Indianapolis 500, is now relegated to third place on the list of the track's biggest events.

5. **Interloper wins Indy.** It was the IRL's worst nightmare. A CART driver waltzes in and steals the milk at the Indianapolis 500. Reigning CART champion Juan Montoya dominates, leading 167 of the 200 laps.

4. **Texas two-step.** Scott Sharp edges Robby McGehee in a breathless final lap battle at the Casino Magic 500 in Fort Worth in what is arguably the best finish in IRL history.

3. **The Force is still with John.** Nine-time funny car champ John Force passes Bob Glidden for the top spot on the NHRA's all time victory list with 86. He beats Jerry Toliver at the Route 66 Dragway in Illinois to do it.

2. **Little E grabs the torch.** Dale Earnhardt Jr. wins his first race at Texas, then in what might be his most memorable moment, wins a duel with his father at Richmond in May. "Little E" passes "Capital E" to become Winston Cup's first two-time race winner of the season.

1. **Michigan Motoring.** Juan Montoya and Michael Andretti fearlessly battle at speeds of 225 mph over the last 17 laps of the Michigan 500, swapping the lead at least once on each of those laps. The race comes down to the final turn. Montoya barrels down on the lapped car of Tarso Marques, uses a tow and wins in the third-closest finish in CART history. ∎

A DALE OF TWO CAREERS
While all of NASCAR was talking about the meteoric rise of Jeff Gordon, Winston Cup veteran Dale Jarrett was driving up some career numbers of his own. In February, Jarrett followed up his 1999 series title with his third Daytona 500 victory in the last eight years — only Richard Petty and Cale Yarborough have won more. Here's a look at Jarrett's two careers: the one before 1996 and the one since. (Through Oct. 22).

	1984-95	1996-00
Winston Cup seasons	11	5
Wins	4	20
Poles	1	9
Top-5 finishes	34	93
Daytona 500 wins	1	2
Earnings	$5,067,402	$21,897,937

Note: Jarrett did not start any races in 1985.

BEHIND EVERY GREAT DRIVER . . .
. . . there's a great pit crew. Every year since 1967 crews have competed for bragging rights at the Union 76/Rockingham Pit Crew World Championship, the only pit crew competition sanctioned by NASCAR. Jeff Burton's team went home with the title in 2000, setting a new record in the process. Here are the fastest times since 1985 when the competition switched from a two-tire change to four.

Time	Crew Chief	Driver	Year
18.355	Frank Stoddard	Jeff Burton	2000
19.166	Jimmy Makar	Bobby Labonte	1999
19.363	Ray Evernham	Jeff Gordon	1994
20.322	Larry McReynolds	Mike Skinner	1998
20.870	Mike Beam	Bill Elliot	1997

∎

NASCAR RESULTS
Winston Cup Series
Winners of NASCAR Winston Cup races from Oct. 24, 1999 through Oct. 22, 2000.

LATE 1999

Date	Event	Location	Winner (Pos.)	Avg.mph	Earnings	Pole	Qual.mph
Oct. 24	Pop Secret 400	Rockingham	Jeff Burton (6)	131.103	$104,715	M. Martin	157.383
Nov. 7	Dura Lube 500K	Phoenix	Tony Stewart (11)	118.132	168,485	J. Andretti	132.714
Nov. 14	Jiffy Lube Miami 400	Miami	Tony Stewart (7)	140.355	278,265	D. Green	155.759
Nov. 21	NAPA 500	Atlanta	Bobby Labonte (37)	137.942	174,300	K. Lepage	193.731

Winning cars (for entire season): FORD TAURUS (13)— Burton (6), Jarrett (4), Martin (2), Wallace; CHEVY MONTE CARLO (12)— Gordon (7), Earnhardt (3), T. Labonte, Nemechek; PONTIAC GRAND PRIX (9)— B. Labonte (5), Stewart (3), Andretti.

2000 SEASON

Date	Event	Location	Winner (Pos.)	Avg.mph	Earnings	Pole	Qual.mph
Feb. 20	Daytona 500	Daytona	Dale Jarrett (1)	155.669	$2,277,975*+	D. Jarrett	191.091
Feb. 27	Dura Lube/Kmart 400	Rockingham	Bobby Labonte (3)	127.875	131,185	R. Wallace	158.035
Mar. 5	Carsdirect.com 400	Las Vegas	Jeff Burton (11)	119.982	358,925	R. Rudd	172.563
Mar. 12	Cracker Barrell 500	Atlanta	Dale Earnhardt (35)	131.759	123,100	D. Jarrett	192.574
Mar. 19	Mall.com 400	Darlington	Ward Burton (3)	128.076	132,725	J. Gordon	172.662
Mar. 26	Food City 500	Bristol	Rusty Wallace (6)	88.018	87,585	S. Park	126.370
Apr. 2	DirecTV 500	Ft. Worth	Dale Earnhardt (8)	131.152	374,675	T. Labonte	192.137
Apr. 9	Goody's 500	Martinsville	Mark Martin (21)	71.161	104,650	R. Wallace	94.827
Apr. 16	Diehard 500	Talladega	Jeff Gordon (36)	161.157	159,755	J. Mayfield	186.969
Apr. 30	NAPA Auto Parts 500	Fontana	Jeremy Mayfield (24)	149.378	125,925	M. Skinner	186.061
May 6	Pontiac Excitement 400	Richmond	Dale Earnhardt Jr. (5)	99.374	118,850	R. Wallace	124.740
May 20@	The Winston	Charlotte	Dale Earnhardt Jr. (5)	167.035	516,410	B. Elliott	152.928
May 28	Coca-Cola 600	Charlotte	Matt Kenseth (21)	142.640	200,950	D. Earnhardt Jr.	186.034
June 4	MBNA Platinum 400	Dover	Tony Stewart (16)	109.514	152,830	R. Wallace	157.411
June 11	Kmart 400	Brooklyn	Tony Stewart (28)	143.926	123,800	B. Labonte	189.883
June 18	Pocono 500	Long Pond	Jeremy Mayfield (22)	135.741	121,020	R. Wallace	171.625
June 25	Save Mart/Kragen 350K	Sonoma	Jeff Gordon (5)	78.789	143,025	R. Wallace	99.309
July 1	Pepsi 400	Daytona	Jeff Burton (9)	148.576	152,450	D. Jarrett	187.547
July 9	thatlook.com 300	Loudon	Tony Stewart (6)	103.145	164,800	R. Wallace	132.089
July 23	Pennsylvania 500	Long Pond	Rusty Wallace (2)	130.662	125,745	T. Stewart	172.391
Aug. 5	Brickyard 400	Indianapolis	Bobby Labonte (3)	155.912	831,225+	R. Rudd	181.068
Aug. 13	Global Crossing at The Glen	Watkins Glen	Steve Park (18)	91.336	124,870	B. Labonte	—**
Aug. 20	Pepsi 400	Brooklyn	Rusty Wallace (10)	132.586	110,460	D. Earnhardt Jr.	191.149
Aug. 27	Goracing.com 500	Bristol	Rusty Wallace (1)	85.394	107,540	R. Wallace	125.477
Sept. 3	Pepsi Southern 500	Darlington	Bobby Labonte (37)	108.275	198,180+	J. Mayfield	169.444
Sept. 9	Monte Carlo 400	Richmond	Jeff Gordon (13)	99.870	130,220	J. Burton	125.780
Sept. 17	Dura Lube 300	Loudon	Jeff Burton (2)	102.003	195,800	B. Labonte	127.632
Sept. 24	MBNA.com 400	Dover	Tony Stewart (27)	115.191	158,535	J. Mayfield	159.872
Oct. 1	NAPA AutoCare 500	Martinsville	Tony Stewart (1)	73.859	125,875	T. Stewart	95.371
Oct. 8	UAW-GM Quality 500	Charlotte	Bobby Labonte (3)	133.633	220,700+	J. Gordon	185.561
Oct. 15	Winston 500	Talladega	Dale Earnhardt (20)	165.681	135,900	J. Nemechek	190.279
Oct. 22	Pop Secret 400	Rockingham	Dale Jarrett (21)	110.418	125,850	J. Mayfield	157.342

Note: Earnings include bonus money.
@ Non-points exhibition event
*Includes $1 million Winston "No Bull 5" bonus.
**Qualifying for the Global Crossing at The Glen was rained out. The lineup was determined based on owners' points, past champion and qualifying draw.
+Includes carryover Winston Cup leader bonus ($10,000 per race): **Daytona 500**— Jarrett ($10,000); **Brickyard 400**— B. Labonte ($190,000); **Pepsi Southern 500**— B. Labonte ($40,000); **UAW-GM Quality 500**— B. Labonte ($50,000).
Winning cars: FORD TAURUS (13)— Wallace (4), J. Burton (3), Jarrett (2), Mayfield (2), Kenseth, Martin; PONTIAC GRAND PRIX (10)— T. Stewart (5), B. Labonte (4), W. Burton (2); CHEVY MONTE CARLO (9)— Earnhardt Jr. (3), Earnhardt (2), Gordon (3), Park.

2000 Winston Cup Race Locations

February— DAYTONA 500 at Daytona International Speedway in Daytona Beach, Fla.; DURA LUBE/KMART 400 at North Carolina Motor Speedway in Rockingham, N.C.

March— CARSDIRECT.COM 400 at Las Vegas Motor Speedway; CRACKER BARRELL 500 at Atlanta (Ga.) Motor Speedway; MALL.COM 400 at Darlington (S.C.) International Raceway; FOOD CITY 500 at Bristol (Tenn.) Motor Speedway.

April— DIRECTV 500 at Texas Motor Speedway in Ft. Worth, Texas; GOODY'S BODY PAIN 500 at Martinsville (Va.) Speedway; DIEHARD 500 at Talladega (Ala.) Superspeedway; NAPA AUTO PARTS 500 at California Speedway in Fontana, Calif.

May— PONTIAC EXCITEMENT 400 at Richmond (Va.) International Speedway; THE WINSTON at Lowe's Motor Speedway in Charlotte, N.C.; COCA-COLA 600 at Lowe's.

June— MBNA PLATINUM 400 at Dover (Del.) Downs International Speedway; KMART 400 at Michigan Speedway in Brooklyn, Mich.; POCONO 500 at Pocono International Raceway in Long Pond, Pa.; SAVE MART/KRAGEN 350K at Sears Point International Raceway in Sonoma, Calif.

July— PEPSI 400 at Daytona; THATLOOK.COM 300 at New Hampshire International Speedway in Loudon, N.H.; PENNSYLVANIA 500 at Pocono.

August— BRICKYARD 400 at Indianapolis (Ind.) Motor Speedway; GLOBAL CROSSING AT THE GLEN at Watkins Glen (N.Y.) International; PEPSI 400 at Michigan; GORACING.COM 500 at Bristol.

September— PEPSI SOUTHERN 500 at Darlington; CHEVROLET MONTE CARLO 400 at Richmond; DURA LUBE 300 at New Hampshire; MBNA.COM 400 at Dover Downs.

October— NAPA AUTOCARE 500 at Martinsville; UAW-GM QUALITY 500 at Lowe's; WINSTON 500 at Talladega; POP SECRET MICROWAVE POPCORN 400 at North Carolina.

November— CHECKER AUTO PARTS/DURA LUBE 500K at Phoenix (Ariz.) International Raceway; PENNZOIL 400 at Miami-Dade Homestead Motorsports Complex in Homestead, Fla.; NAPA 500 at Atlanta.

2000 Daytona 500

Date— Sunday, Feb. 20, 2000, at Daytona International Speedway. **Distance—** 500 miles; **Course—** 2.5 miles; **Field—** 43 cars; **Average speed—** 155.669 mph; **Margin of victory—** 0.237 seconds; **Time of race—** 3 hours, 55 minutes, 15 seconds; **Caution flags—** 6 for 25 laps; **Lead changes—** 31 among 12 drivers; **Lap leaders—** Jarrett (89), Martin (65), Burton (39), Skinner (3), Little (2), Elliot (1), Rudd (1). **Pole sitter—** Dale Jarrett at 191.091 mph; **Attendance—** 150,000 (estimated). **Rating—** 7.5/18 share (CBS).

Driver (start pos.)	Team	Car	Laps	Ended	Earnings
1 Dale Jarrett (1)	Quality Care/Ford Credit	Ford Taurus	200	Running	$2,277,975
2 Jeff Burton (14)	Exide Batteries	Ford Taurus	200	Running	840,825
3 Bill Elliott (3)	McDonald's	Ford Taurus	200	Running	528,475
4 Rusty Wallace (5)	Miller Lite	Ford Taurus	200	Running	420,775
5 Mark Martin (9)	Valvoline	Ford Taurus	200	Running	326,175
6 Bobby Labonte (13)	Interstate Batteries	Pontiac Grand Prix	200	Running	228,275
7 Terry Labonte (25)	Kellogg's Corn Flakes	Chevrolet Monte Carlo	200	Running	198,625
8 Ward Burton (6)	Caterpillar	Pontiac Grand Prix	200	Running	166,775
9 Ken Schrader (23)	M&M's	Pontiac Grand Prix	200	Running	143,975
10 Matt Kenseth (24)	DeWalt Power Tools	Ford Taurus	200	Running	182,875
11 Jeremy Mayfield (19)	Mobil 1	Ford Taurus	200	Running	129,075
12 Johnny Benson (27)	Lycos.com	Pontiac Grand Prix	200	Running	119,475
13 Dale Earnhardt Jr. (8)	Budweiser	Chevrolet Monte Carlo	200	Running	107,775
14 Kenny Irwin (18)	BellSouth	Chevrolet Monte Carlo	200	Running	120,025
15 Ricky Rudd (2)	Texaco Havoline	Ford Taurus	200	Running	119,475
16 Mike Skinner (4)	Lowe's	Chevrolet Monte Carlo	200	Running	112,225
17 Tony Stewart (7)	The Home Depot	Pontiac Grand Prix	200	Running	118,875
18 Robby Gordon (17)	Turtle Wax/Johns Manville	Ford Taurus	200	Running	99,725
19 Scott Pruett (15)	Tide	Ford Taurus	200	Running	98,475
20 Robert Pressley (32)	Jasper Engines/Federal-Mogul	Ford Taurus	200	Running	102,875
21 Dale Earnhardt (21)	GM Goodwrench Service Plus	Chevrolet Monte Carlo	200	Running	116,075
22 John Andretti (30)	STP	Pontiac Grand Prix	200	Running	113,725
23 Chad Little (21)	John Deere	Ford Taurus	200	Running	105,375
24 Sterling Marlin (38)	Coors Light	Chevrolet Monte Carlo	199	Running	104,325
25 Kyle Petty (42)	Hot Wheels	Pontiac Grand Prix	199	Running	108,175
26 Stacy Compton (33)	Kodiak	Ford Taurus	199	Running	94,225
27 Dave Blaney (31)	Amoco	Pontiac Grand Prix	199	Running	89,625
28 Rick Mast (28)	Big Daddy's	Chevrolet Monte Carlo	199	Running	92,075
29 Kenny Wallace (39)	Square D	Chevrolet Monte Carlo	199	Running	99,275
30 Jimmy Spencer (22)	Big Kmart/Route 66	Ford Taurus	197	Running	99,225
31 Steve Park (36)	Pennzoil	Chevrolet Monte Carlo	197	Running	98,275
32 Darrell Waltrip (43)	Route 66/Big Kmart	Ford Taurus	197	Running	89,325
33 Mike Bliss (35)	Conseco	Pontiac Grand Prix	197	Running	88,875
34 Jeff Gordon (11)	DuPont Auto Finishes	Chevrolet Monte Carlo	195	Running	106,100
35 Jerry Nadeau (20)	Michael Holigan	Chevrolet Monte Carlo	195	Running	93,450
36 Kevin Lepage (41)	Northern Light	Ford Taurus	195	Running	93,000
37 Ed Berrier (26)	Hills Bros.	Ford Taurus	193	Track Bar	84,550
38 Elliott Sadler (40)	Citgo	Ford Taurus	192	Accident	92,100
39 Michael Waltrip (10)	NationsRent	Chevrolet Monte Carlo	192	Accident	91,650
40 Wally Dallenbach (34)	Turner Broadcasting	Ford Taurus	174	Handling	83,200
41 Derrike Cope (12)	Fenley-Moore Motorsports	Ford Taurus	169	Engine	82,750
42 Joe Nemechek (16)	Oakwood Homes	Chevrolet Homes	131	Oil Pressure	90,300
43 Bobby Hamilton (37)	Kodak	Chevrolet Monte Carlo	68	Engine	90,100

Winston Cup Point Standings

Official Top 10 NASCAR Winston Cup point leaders and Top 15 money leaders for 1999 and unofficial Top 10 point leaders and Top 15 money leaders for 2000 (through Oct. 22). Points awarded for all qualifying drivers (winner receives 175) and lap leaders. Earnings include bonuses. Listed are starts (Sts), Top 5 finishes (1-2-3-4-5), poles won (PW) and points (Pts).

FINAL 1999

		Sts	Finishes 1-2-3-4-5	PW	Pts
1	Dale Jarrett	34	4-7-4-5-6	0	5262
2	Bobby Labonte	34	5-7-7-1-4	6	5061
3	Mark Martin	34	2-4-6-5-2	1	4943
4	Tony Stewart	34	3-2-1-4-3	2	4774
5	Jeff Burton	34	7-2-3-5-3	1	4733
6	Jeff Gordon	34	7-4-5-1-1	7	4620
7	Dale Earnhardt	34	4-3-0-0-1	0	4492
8	Rusty Wallace	34	1-0-1-3-2	4	4155
9	Ward Burton	34	0-3-0-2-1	1	4062
10	Mike Skinner	34	0-0-1-4-0	2	4003

2000 (Through Oct. 22)

		Sts	Finishes 1-2-3-4-5	PW	Pts
1	Bobby Labonte	31	4-4-4-1-4	3	4645
2	Dale Earnhardt	31	2-4-4-2-1	0	4444
3	Jeff Burton	31	3-5-2-1-3	1	4394
4	Dale Jarrett	31	2-3-1-5-3	3	4315
5	Ricky Rudd	31	0-1-5-3-3	2	4272
6	Tony Stewart	31	5-2-0-3-1	2	4210
7	Rusty Wallace	31	4-1-1-2-3	8	4115
8	Mark Martin	31	1-1-6-1-3	0	4042
9	Jeff Gordon	31	3-1-1-3-2	2	3904
10	Ward Burton	31	1-0-2-0-0	0	3809

Top 5 Finishing Order + Pole

2000 SEASON

No.	Event	Winner	2nd	3rd	4th	5th	Pole
1	Daytona 500	D. Jarrett	J. Burton	B. Elliott	R. Wallace	M. Martin	D. Jarrett
2	Dura Lube/Kmart 400	B. Labonte	D. Earnhardt	W. Burton	T. Stewart	D. Jarrett	R. Wallace
3	Carsdirect.com 400	J. Burton	T. Stewart	M. Martin	B. Elliot	B. Labonte	R. Rudd
4	Cracker Barrell 500	D. Earnhardt	B. Labonte	M. Martin	S. Park	J. Nemechek	J. Gordon
5	Mall.com 400	W. Burton	D. Jarrett	D. Earnhardt	T. Stewart	J. Burton	J. Gordon
6	Food City 500	R. Wallace	J. Benson	W. Burton	J. Mayfield	T. Labonte	S. Park
7	DirecTV 500	D. Earnhardt Jr.	J. Burton	B. Labonte	R. Wallace	K. Lepage	T. Labonte
8	Goody's Body Pain 500	M. Martin	J. Burton	M. Waltrip	J. Gordon	D. Jarrett	R. Wallace
9	Diehard 500	J. Gordon	M. Skinner	D. Earnhardt	K. Irwin	J. Spencer	J. Mayfield
10	NAPA Auto Parts 500	J. Mayfield	B. Labonte	M. Kenseth	R. Rudd	J. Burton	M. Skinner
11	Pontiac Excitement 400	D. Earnhardt Jr.	T. Labonte	D. Jarrett	R. Rudd	R. Wallace	R. Wallace
12	The Winston	D. Earnhardt Jr.	D. Jarrett	D. Earnhardt	J. Nadeau	J. Burton	B. Elliott
13	Coca-Cola 600	M. Kenseth	B. Labonte	D. Earnhardt	D. Earnhardt Jr.	D. Jarrett	D. Earnhardt Jr.
14	MBNA Platinum 400	T. Stewart	M. Kenseth	B. Labonte	D. Jarrett	R. Rudd	R. Wallace
15	Kmart 400	T. Stewart	D. Earnhardt	B. Labonte	D. Jarrett	R. Pressley	B. Labonte
16	Pocono 500	J. Mayfield	D. Jarrett	R. Rudd	D. Earnhardt	M. Martin	R. Wallace
17	Save Mart/Kragen 350K	J. Gordon	S. Marlin	M. Martin	M. Martin	R. Rudd	R. Wallace
18	Pepsi 400	J. Burton	D. Jarrett	R. Wallace	M. Martin	R. Rudd	D. Jarrett
19	thatlook.com 300	T. Stewart	J. Nemechek	M. Martin	J. Nadeau	J. Gordon	R. Wallace
20	Pennsylvania 500	R. Wallace	J. Burton	J. Gordon	D. Jarrett	M. Kenseth	S. Stewart
21	Brickyard 400	B. Labonte	R. Wallace	B. Elliot	J. Nadeau	T. Stewart	R. Rudd
22	Global Crossing at The Glen	S. Park	M. Martin	J. Burton	R. Gordon	B. Labonte	B. Labonte
23	Pepsi 400	R. Wallace	R. Rudd	B. Labonte	D. Jarrett	J. Bench	D. Earnhardt Jr.
24	Goracing.com 500	R. Wallace	T. Stewart	M. Martin	D. Earnhardt	S. Park	R. Wallace
25	Southern 500	B. Labonte	J. Burton	D. Earnhardt	J. Gordon	D. Jarrett	J. Mayfield
26	Monte Carlo 400	J. Gordon	D. Earnhardt	M. Martin	S. Park	J. Burton	J. Burton
27	Dura Lube 300	J. Burton	B. Labonte	R. Rudd	D. Jarrett	R. Wallace	B. Labonte
28	MBNA.com 400	T. Stewart	J. Benson	R. Rudd	S. Park	B. Labonte	J. Mayfield
29	NAPA AutoCare 500	T. Stewart	D. Earnhardt	J. Burton	R. Rudd	J. Gordon	T. Stewart
30	UAW-GM Quality 500	B. Labonte	J. Mayfield	R. Rudd	T. Stewart	M. Martin	J. Gordon
31	Winston 500	D. Earnhardt	K. Wallace	J. Nemechek	J. Gordon	T. Labonte	J. Nemechek
32	Pop Secret 400	D. Jarrett	J. Gordon	R. Rudd	J. Burton	R. Wallace	J. Mayfield

Money Leaders

FINAL 1999

		Earnings
1	Jeff Gordon	$5,281,361
2	Jeff Burton	5,211,301
3	Dale Jarrett	3,608,829
4	Bobby Labonte	3,550,341
5	Mark Martin	2,783,296
6	Dale Earnhardt	2,712,089
7	Tony Stewart	2,615,226
8	Terry Labonte	2,303,146
9	Mike Skinner	2,222,321
10	Rusty Wallace	2,167,429
11	Ward Burton	2,115,824
12	Kenny Irwin	1,995,821
13	Jeremy Mayfield	1,944,589
14	John Andretti	1,861,706
15	Bobby Hamilton	1,846,454

2000 (Through Oct. 22)

		Earnings
1	Dale Jarrett	$5,002,724
2	Jeff Burton	4,772,609
3	Bobby Labonte	3,735,721
4	Dale Earnhardt	3,471,641
5	Rusty Wallace	2,820,981
6	Tony Stewart	2,788,741
7	Mark Martin	2,466,686
8	Dale Earnhardt Jr.	2,455,436
9	Jeff Gordon	2,449,511
10	Bill Elliot	2,293,338
11	Ricky Rudd	2,202,604
12	Ward Burton	2,170,376
13	Matt Kenseth	1,995,814
14	Terry Labonte	1,872,639
15	Steve Park	1,821,107

CART RESULTS

Schedule and results of CART races from Oct. 31, 1999 through Oct. 15, 2000.

FedEx Championship Series
LATE 1999

Date	Event	Location	Winner (Pos.)	Time	Avg.mph	Pole	Qual.mph
Oct. 31	Marlboro 500	Fontana	Adrian Fernandez (13)	2:57:17.542	171.666	S. Pruett	235.398

Winning cars: (entire season) REYNARD/HONDA (14)— Montoya (7), Franchitti (3), Tracy (2), de Ferran, Kanaan; REYNARD/FORD (5)— Fernandez (2), Andretti, Fittipaldi, Herta; REYNARD/MERCEDES-BENZ (1)— Moore.

2000 SEASON

Date	Event	Location	Winner (Pos.)	Time	Avg.mph	Pole	Qual.mph
Mar. 26	GP of Miami	Homestead	Max Papis (13)	1:22:01.975	164.788	G. de Ferran	208.434
Apr. 16	Toyota GP	Long Beach	Paul Tracy (17)	1:57:11.132	82.626	G. de Ferran	104.969
Apr. 30	Telemar Rio 200	Rio de Janeiro	Adrian Fernandez (16)	1:37:12.490	124.256	A. Tagliani	173.903
May 13	Firestone Firehawk 500	Motegi	Michael Andretti (8)	1:58:52.201	157.154	J. Montoya	212.540
May 27	Bosch Spark Plug GP	Nazareth	Gil de Ferran (5)	2:06:10.334	101.219	J. Montoya	176.868
June 4	Milwaukee Mile 225	West Allis	Juan Montoya (1)	1:37:38.526	142.684	J. Montoya	177.769
June 18	GP of Detroit	Detroit	Helio Castro-Neves (3)	2:01:23.607	97.401	J. Montoya	115.604
June 25	Freightliner/G.I. Joe's 200	Portland	Gil de Ferran (2)	2:00:46.002	109.564	H. Castro-Neves	122.768
July 2	GP of Cleveland	Cleveland	Roberto Moreno (1)	1:52:12.092	112.619	R. Moreno	212.522
July 16	Molson Indy	Toronto	Michael Andretti (3)	2:00:02.313	98.248	H. Castro-Neves	110.455
July 23	Michigan 500	Brooklyn	Juan Montoya (7)	2:48:48.790	177.694	P. Tracy	234.949
July 30	GP of Chicago	Cicero	Cristiano da Matta (5)	2:01:23.727	114.432	J. Montoya	167.567
Aug. 13	Miller Lite 200	Lexington	Helio Castro-Neves (2)	1:44:59.029	106.558	G. de Ferran	124.394
Aug. 20	Motorola 220	Elkhart Lake	Paul Tracy (7)	1:37:53.681	136.457	D. Franchitti	145.924
Sept. 3	Molson Indy	Vancouver	Paul Tracy (2)	1:53:06.024	85.034	D. Franchitti	106.144
Sept. 10	Honda GP/Shell 300	Monterey	Helio Castro-Neves (1)	1:46:11.800	104.949	H. Castro-Neves	118.969
Sept. 17	Motorola 300	Madison	Juan Montoya (1)	1:55:38.003	155.519	J. Montoya	180.334
Oct. 1	GP of Houston	Houston	Jimmy Vasser (3)	1:59:02.000	76.626	G. de Ferran	93.558
Oct. 15	Honda Indy 300	Queensland	Adrian Fernandez (17)	2:00:00.000	81.607	J. Montoya	109.701

Note: CART does not release per race winnings.

Note: The Bosch Spark Plug Grand Prix was originally scheduled for April 9 in Nazareth, Penn. but was canceled due to snow.

Winning cars: REYNARD/HONDA (9)— de Ferran (3), Castro-Neves (3), Tracy (3); REYNARD/FORD (4)— Fernandez (2), Moreno, Papis; LOLA/TOYOTA (4)— Montoya (2), Vasser; LOLA/FORD (3)— Andretti (2); REYNARD/TOYOTA (1)— da Matta.

2000 Michigan 500

Date— Sunday, July 23, 2000, at Michigan International Speedway. **Distance**— 500 miles; **Course**— 2 mile oval; **Field**—24 cars; **Winner's average speed**— 177.694mph. **Margin of victory**— 0.040 seconds; **Time of race**— 2 hours, 48 minutes, 49.790 seconds; **Caution flags**— 5 for 38 laps; **Lead changes**— 52 by 10 drivers; **Lap leaders**— Castroneves (85), Andretti (58), Montoya (39), Brack (18), Fernandez (13), Fittipaldi (13), Papis (9), Tracy (8), Tagliani (5), Servia (2); **Pole Sitter**— Paul Tracy at 234.949 mph; **Attendance**— 50,000 (est.); Note that (r) indicates rookie driver.

	Driver (start pos.)	Country	Car	Laps	Ended
1	Juan Montoya (7)	Colombia	Lola-Toyota	250	Running
2	Michael Andretti (2)	United States	Lola-Ford	250	Running
3	Dario Franchitti (4)	Scotland	Reynard-Honda	250	Running
4	Patrick Carpentier (9)	Canada	Reynard-Ford	250	Running
5	Helio Castro-Neves (13)	Brazil	Reynard-Honda	250	Running
6	Adrian Fernandez (12)	Mexico	Reynard-Ford	250	Running
7	Paul Tracy (1)	Canada	Reynard-Honda	250	Running
8	r-Oriol Servia (15)	Spain	Reynard-Toyota	249	Running
9	Max Papis (11)	Italy	Reynard-Ford	247	Mechanical
10	Memo Gidley (21)	United States	Reynard-Toyota	247	Running
11	Luiz Garcia Jr. (23)	Brazil	Reynard-Mercedes	246	Running
12	Tarso Marques (24)	Brazil	Swift-Ford	246	Electrical
13	Mauricio Gugelmin (20)	Brazil	Reynard-Mercedes	241	Mechanical
14	Christian Fittipaldi (3)	Brazil	Lola-Ford	220	Contact
15	Michel Jourdain Jr. (22)	Mexico	Lola-Mercedes	162	Mechanical
16	r-Alex Tagliani (8)	Canada	Reynard-Ford	160	Contact
17	Cristiano da Matta (14)	Brazil	Reynard-Toyota	142	Pit Incident
18	Gil de Ferran (5)	Brazil	Reynard-Honda	140	Contact
19	Mark Blundell (17)	England	Reynard-Mercedes	131	Mechanical
20	r-Shinji Nakano (19)	Japan	Reynard-Honda	104	Mechanical
21	Jimmy Vasser (6)	United States	Lola-Toyota	102	Mechanical
22	r-Kenny Brack (10)	Sweden	Reynard-Ford	97	Contact
23	Roberto Moreno (16)	Brazil	Reynard-Ford	97	Mechanical
24	Tony Kanaan (18)	Brazil	Reynard-Mercedes	61	Mechanical

Note: CART does not release earnings on a per-race basis.

CART Point Standings

Official Top 10 FedEx Championship Series point leaders and Top 15 money leaders for 1999 and unofficial Top 10 point leaders and Top 15 money leaders for 2000. Points awarded for places 1 to 12, fastest qualifier and overall lap leader. Listed are starts (Sts), Top 5 finishes, poles won (PW) and points (Pts).

FINAL 1999

		Sts	Finishes 1-2-3-4-5	PW	Pts*
1	Juan Montoya	20	7-2-0-1-0	7	212*
2	Dario Franchitti	20	3-3-4-0-1	2	212
3	Paul Tracy	19	1-3-2-2-1	0	161
4	Michael Andretti	20	1-2-1-2-2	1	151
5	Max Papis	20	0-2-1-2-5	1	150
6	Adrian Fernandez	16	2-0-2-2-3	0	140
7	Christian Fittipaldi	15	1-0-4-0-1	1	121
8	Gil de Ferran	20	1-2-1-0-0	2	108
9	Jimmy Vasser	20	0-0-2-3-2	1	104
10	Greg Moore	20	1-1-1-2-0	1	97

*Montoya won the series via his 7-3 advantage in victories over Franchitti.

2000 (Through Oct. 22)

		Sts	Finishes 1-2-3-4-5	PW	Pts
1	Gil de Ferran	19	2-2-2-0-1	4	153
2	Adrian Fernandez	19	2-2-1-0-2	0	148
3	Paul Tracy	19	3-0-3-1-0	1	134
4	Roberto Moreno	19	0-2-2-2-3	0	134
5	Roberto Moreno	19	1-2-2-1-1	1	131
6	Jimmy Vasser	19	1-1-2-1-1	0	131
7	Michael Andretti	19	2-3-0-2-0	0	127
8	Helio Castro-Neves	19	3-1-0-0-2	3	125
9	Juan Montoya	19	3-1-0-1-0	7	123
10	Cristiano da Matta	19	1-0-1-5-1	0	112

Top 5 Finishing Order + Pole
2000 Season

No.	Event	Winner	2nd	3rd	4th	5th	Pole
1	GP of Miami	M. Papis	R. Moreno	P. Tracy	J. Vasser	P. Carpentier	G. de Ferran
2	GP of Long Beach	P. Tracy	H. Castro-Neves	J. Vasser	A. Tagliani	B. Herta	G. de Ferran
3	Rio 200	A. Fernandez	J. Vasser	P. Tracy	C. da Matta	C. Fittipaldi	A. Tagliani
4	Firehawk 500	M. Andretti	D. Franchitti	R. Moreno	C. da Matta	K. Brack	J. Montoya
5	Bosch GP	G. de Ferran	M. Gugelmin	K. Brack	J. Montoya	A. Fernandez	J. Montoya
6	Milwaukee Mile 225	J. Montoya	M. Andretti	P. Carpentier	K. Brack	R. Moreno	J. Montoya
7	GP of Detroit	H. Castro-Neves	M. Papis	O. Servia	D. Franchitti	P. Carpentier	J. Montoya
8	Freightliner/G.I. Joe's 200	G. de Ferran	R. Moreno	C. Fittipaldi	M. Andretti	C. da Matta	H. Castro-Neves
9	GP of Cleveland	R. Moreno	K. Brack	C. da Matta	M. Andretti	P. Carpentier	R. Moreno
10	Molson Indy	M. Andretti	A. Fernandez	P. Tracy	C. da Matta	A. Tagliani	H. Castro-Neves
11	Michigan 500	J. Montoya	M. Andretti	D. Franchitti	P. Charpentier	H. Castro-Neves	P. Tracy
12	GP of Chicago	C. da Matta	M. Andretti	G. de Ferran	K. Brack	A. Fernandez	J. Montoya
13	Miller Lite 200	H. Castro-Neves	G. de Ferran	C. Fittipaldi	M. Papis	K. Brack	G. de Ferran
14	Motorola 220	P. Tracy	A. Fernandez	K. Brack	R. Moreno	J. Vasser	D. Franchitti
15	Molson Indy	P. Tracy	D. Franchitti	A. Fernandez	C. Fittipaldi	G. de Ferran	D. Franchitti
16	GP of Monterey	H. Castro-Neves	G. de Ferran	D. Franchitti	B. Herta	K. Brack	H. Castro-Neves
17	Motorola 300	J. Montoya	P. Carpentier	R. Moreno	C. da Matta	O. Servia	J. Montoya
18	GP of Houston	J. Vasser	J. Montoya	G. de Ferran	P. Tracy	H. Castro-Neves	G. de Ferran
19	Honda Indy 300	A. Fernandez	K. Brack	J. Vasser	C. da Matta	P. Carpentier	J. Montoya

Money Leaders

FINAL 1999

		Earnings
1	Juan Montoya	$1,973,000
2	Dario Franchitti	1,356,750
3	Paul Tracy	978,500
4	Michael Andretti	775,000
5	Adrian Fernandez	706,750
6	Max Papis	675,000
7	Christian Fittipaldi	611,750
8	Gil de Ferran	584,250
9	Greg Moore	553,750
10	Jimmy Vasser	512,500
11	Bryan Herta	377,250
12	Tony Kanaan	357,500
13	Roberto Moreno	277,750
14	Patrick Carpentier	274,250
15	P.J. Jones	253,250

Note: The 1999 totals don't include Performance Award earnings.

2000 (Through Oct. 15)

		Earnings
1	Paul Tracy	$654,750
2	Gil de Ferran	627,000
3	Adrian Fernandez	606,500
4	Michael Andretti	593,500
5	Helio Castro-Neves	561,750
6	Roberto Moreno	547,750
7	Juan Montoya	539,000
8	Jimmy Vasser	508,250
9	Kenny Brack	505,500
10	Cristiano da Matta	465,000
11	Max Papis	399,750
12	Patrick Carpentier	378,250
13	Christian Fittipaldi	373,500
14	Dario Franchitti	366,250
15	Oriol Servia	306,500

INDY RACING LEAGUE RESULTS

Results of Indy Racing League events during the 2000 season.

2000 SEASON

Date	Event	Location	Winner (Pos.)	Time	Avg.mph	Pole	Qual.mph
Jan. 29	Delphi Indy 200	Orlando	Robbie Buhl (22)	1:57:18.676	102.292	G. Ray	—*
Mar. 19	MCI WorldCom Indy 200	Phoenix	Buddy Lazier (26)	1:47:11.029	111.957	G. Ray	176.566
Apr. 22	Vegas Indy 300	Las Vegas	Al Unser Jr. (21)	2:16:57.045	136.691	M. Dinsmore	208.502
May 28	Indy 500	Indianapolis	Juan Montoya (2)	2:58:59.431	167.607	G. Ray	223.471
June 10	Casino Magic 500	Ft. Worth	Scott Sharp (12)	1:47:19.835	169.182	B. Lazier	—†
June 18	Radisson Indy 200	Pikes Peak	Eddie Cheever Jr. (10)	1:28:44.257	135.230	G. Ray	179.874
July 15	Midas 500	Atlanta	Greg Ray (1)	2:02:01.882	153.403	G. Ray	216.104
Aug. 27	Belterra Resort Indy 300	Sparta	Buddy Lazier (7)	1:49:21.309	164.601	S. Goodyear	219.191
Oct. 15	Excite 500	Ft. Worth	Scott Goodyear (2)	1:43:35.926	175.276	G. Ray	215.352

*Qualifying was cancelled due to rain. Starting position was based on final 1999 IRL entrant points which was won by Team Menard with Greg Ray as driver.
†Qualifying was cancelled due to rain. Starting position was based on current Northern Light Cup entrant point standings which was lead by Hemelgarn Racing with Buddy Lazier as driver.
Winning cars: G-FORCE/OLDS AURORA (3)— Buhl, Montoya, Unser Jr.; DALLARA/OLDS AURORA (3)— Goodyear, Ray, Sharp; DALLARA/ INFINITY (1)— Cheever Jr.; RILEY & SCOTT/OLDS AURORA (2)— Lazier (2).

IRL Race Locations

January— DELPHI INDY 200 at Walt Disney World Speedway in Orlando, Fla. **March**— MCI WORLDCOM INDY 200 at Phoenix (Ari.) International Raceway. **April**— LAS VEGAS INDY 300 at Las Vegas (Nev.) Motor Speedway. **May**— INDIANAPOLIS 500 at Indianapolis (Ind.) Motor Speedway. **June**— CASINO MAGIC 500 at Texas Motor Speedway in Fort Worth, Tex.; RADISSON INDY 200 at Pikes Peak International Raceway in Colorado Springs, Colo. **July**—MIDAS 500 at Atlanta Motor Speedway in Hampton, Ga. **August**— BELTERRA RESORT INDY 300 at Kentucky Speedway in Sparta, Ky. **October**— EXCITE 500 at Texas Motor Speedway in Fort Worth, Tex.

84th Indianapolis 500

Date—Sunday, May 28, 2000, at Indianapolis Motor Speedway. **Distance**— 500 miles; **Course**— 2.5 mile oval; **Field**— 33 cars; **Winner's average speed**— 167.607 mph; **Margin of victory**— 7.184 seconds; **Time of race**— 2 hours, 58 minutes, 59.431 seconds; **Caution flags**— 7 for 39 laps; **Lead changes**— 6 by 4 drivers; **Lap leaders**— Montoya (167), Ray (26), Vasser (5), McGehee (2); **Pole Sitter**— Greg Ray at 223.471 mph; **Attendance**— 375,000 (est.); **TV Rating**— 5.4/13 share (ABC). Note that (r) indicates rookie driver.

	Driver (start pos.)	Country	Car	Laps	Ended	Earnings
1	Juan Montoya (2)	Colombia	G/A/F	200	Running	$1,235,690
2	Buddy Lazier (16)	United States	D/A/F	200	Running	567,100
3	Eliseo Salazar (3)	Chile	G/A/F	200	Running	468,900
4	Jeff Ward (6)	United States	G/A/F	200	Running	355,000
5	Eddie Cheever Jr. (10)	United States	D/I/F	200	Running	360,000
6	Robby Gordon (4)	United States	D/A/F	200	Running	214,355
7	Jimmy Vasser (7)	United States	G/A/F	199	Running	207,505
8	Stephan Gregoire (20)	France	G/A/F	199	Running	305,900
9	Scott Goodyear (13)	Canada	D/A/F	199	Running	347,800
10	Scott Sharp (5)	United States	D/A/F	198	Running	312,000
11	Mark Dismore (11)	United States	D/A/F	198	Running	293,500
12	Donnie Beechler (15)	United States	D/A/F	198	Running	283,000
13	Jaques Lazier (26)	United States	D/A/F	198	Running	290,250
14	Jeret Schroeder (29)	United States	D/A/F	198	Running	278,000
15	Billy Boat (31)	United States	G/A/F	198	Running	210,000
16	Raul Boesel (24)	Brazil	G/A/F	197	Running	212,000
17	Jason Leffler (17)	United States	G/A/F	197	Running	169,905
18	Buzz Caulkins (22)	United States	D/A/F	194	Running	169,000
19	Steve Knapp (27)	United States	G/I/F	193	Running	166,000
20	Davey Hamilton (28)	United States	G/A/F	188	Running	165,500
21	Robby McGehee (12)	United States	G/A/F	187	Running	280,400
22	Johnny Unser (30)	United States	G/A/F	186	Running	161,000
23	Stan Wattles (8)	United States	D/A/F	172	Engine	159,000
24	Sam Hornish Jr. (14)	United States	D/A/F	153	Accident	268,250
25	Airton Dare (21)	Brazil	G/A/F	126	Engine	262,250
26	Robbie Buhl (9)	United States	G/A/F	99	Engine	258,500
27	Richie Hearn (23)	United States	D/A/F	97	Electrical	155,000
28	Andy Hillenburg (33)	United States	D/A/F	91	Wheel Bearing	154,250
29	Al Unser Jr. (18)	United States	G/A/F	89	Over Heating	256,000
30	Jimmy Kite (25)	United States	G/A/F	74	Engine	164,000
31	Sarah Fisher (19)	United States	D/A/F	71	Accident	165,750
32	Lyn St. James (32)	United States	G/A/F	69	Accident	152,000
33	Greg Ray (1)	United States	D/A/F	67	Accident	388,700

Car Legend: Chassis/Engine/Tires. D—Dallara; G—G Force (chassis); A—Oldsmobile Aurora V-8; I—Nissan Infiniti V-8 (engine); F—Firestone (tires).

Indy Racing League Point Standings

FINAL 1999

		Finishes			
		Sts	1-2-3-4-5	PW	Pts
1	Greg Ray	10	3-1-1-0-0	4	293
2	Kenny Brack	10	1-1-2-0-0	0	256
3	Mark Dismore	10	1-0-1-0-0	2	240
4	Davey Hamilton	10	0-2-1-0-0	0	237
5	Sam Schmidt	10	1-1-1-0-2	1	233
6	Buddy Lazier	10	0-1-0-1-1	0	224
7	Eddie Cheever Jr.	10	1-0-0-2-0	0	222
8	Scott Sharp	10	1-0-0-2-0	0	220
9	Scott Goodyear	10	2-1-0-0-0	0	217
10	Robby Unser	10	0-1-0-0-0	0	209

FINAL 2000

		Finishes			
		Sts	1-2-3-4-5	PW	Pts
1	Buddy Lazier	9	2-3-0-1-0	1	290
2	Scott Goodyear	9	1-2-0-1-1	1	272
3	Eddie Cheever Jr.	9	1-1-1-1-1	0	257
4	Eliseo Salazar	9	0-0-1-1-2	0	210
5	Mark Dismore	9	0-1-0-1-0	1	202
6	Donnie Beechler	9	0-0-1-0-2	0	202
7	Scott Sharp	9	1-0-1-0-1	0	196
8	Robbie Buhl	9	1-0-0-0-1	0	190
9	Al Unser Jr.	9	1-0-2-0-0	0	188
10	Billy Boat	9	0-0-1-0-0	0	181

Top 5 Finishing Order + Pole

2000 Season

No.	Event	Winner	2nd	3rd	4th	5th	Pole
1	Delphi Indy 200	B. Lazier	B. Lazier	E. Cheever Jr.	S. Goodyear	E. Salazar	G. Ray
2	MCI WorldCom Indy 200	B. Lazier	S. Goodyear	D. Beechler	E. Salazar	S. Sharp	G. Ray
3	Vegas Indy 300	A. Unser Jr.	M. Dismore	S. Hornish Jr.	J. Schroeder	R. Buhl	M. Dismore
4	Indy 500	J. Montoya	B. Lazier	E. Salazar	J. Ward	E. Cheever Jr.	G. Ray
5	Casino Magic 500	S. Sharp	R. McGehee	A. Unser Jr.	B. Calkins	S. Goodyear	B. Lazier
6	Radisson Indy 200	E. Cheever Jr.	A. Dari	S. Sharp	M. Dismore	D. Beechler	G. Ray
7	Atlanta 500	G. Ray	B. Lazier	A. Unser Jr.	R. McGehee	D. Beechler	G. Ray
8	Belterra Resort Indy 300	B. Lazier	S. Goodyear	S. Fisher	E. Cheever Jr.	S. Gregoire	S. Goodyear
9	Excite 500	S. Goodyear	E. Cheever Jr.	B. Boat	B. Lazier	E. Salazar	G. Ray

Money Leaders

FINAL 1999

		Earnings
1	Kenny Brack	$1,933,540
2	Greg Ray	986,800
3	Jeff Ward	981,850
4	Billy Boat	846,000
5	Scott Goodyear	800,450
6	Eddie Cheever Jr.	779,500
7	Mark Dismore	766,650
8	Sam Schmidt	750,900
9	Buddy Lazier	745,150
10	Scott Sharp	720,000

FINAL 2000

		Earnings
1	Juan Montoya	$1,235,690
2	Buddy Lazier	1,168,700
3	Scott Goodyear	884,900
4	Eddie Cheever Jr.	876,200
5	Greg Ray	821,700
6	Eliseo Salazar	820,000
7	Scott Sharp	767,050
8	Al Unser Jr.	730,300
9	Mark Dismore	712,950
10	Robbie Buhl	685,500

FORMULA ONE RESULTS

Results of Formula One Grand Prix races in 2000.

2000 SEASON

Date	Grand Prix	Location	Winner (Pos.)	Time	Avg.mph	Pole	Qual.mph
Mar. 12	Australian	Melbourne	Michael Schumacher (3)	1:34:01.987	121.947	M. Hakkinen	130.996
Mar. 26	Brazilian	Sao Paulo	Michael Schumacher (3)	1:31:35.721	124.525	M. Hakkinen	130.061
Apr. 9	San Marino	Imola	Michael Schumacher (2)	1:31:39.776	124.247	M. Hakkinen	130.259
Apr. 23	British	Silverstone	David Coulthard (4)	1:28:50.108	129.480	R. Barrichello	134.185
May 7	Spanish	Barcelona	Mika Hakkinen (2)	1:33:50.390	122.098	M. Schumacher	130.668
May 21	European	Nurburgring	Michael Schumacher (2)	1:42:00.307	111.520	D. Coulthard	131.454
June 4	Monaco	Monte Carlo	David Coulthard (3)	1:49:28.213	89.469	M. Schumacher	94.854
June 18	Canadian	Montreal	Michael Schumacher (1)	1:41:12.313	112.374	M. Schumacher	126.079
July 2	French	Magny-Course	David Coulthard (2)	1:38:05.538	116.283	M. Schumacher	125.700
July 16	Austrian	Zeltwig	Mika Hakkinen (1)	1:28:15.818	129.765	M. Hakkinen	137.437
July 30	German	Hockenheim	Rubens Barrichello (18)	1:25:34.418	133.834	D. Coulthard	144.442
Aug. 13	Hungarian	Hungaroring	Mika Hakkinen (3)	1:45:33.869	108.096	M. Schumacher	114.713
Aug. 27	Belgian	Francorchamps	Mika Hakkinen (1)	1:28:14.494	129.458	M. Hakkinen	140.872
Sept. 10	Italian	Monza	Michael Schumacher (1)	1:27:31.638	130.654	M. Schumacher	154.692
Sept. 24	U.S.	Indianapolis	Michael Schumacher (1)	1:36:30.883	118.209	M. Schumacher	126.266
Oct. 8	Japan	Suzuka	Michael Schumacher (1)	1:29:53.435	128.820	M. Schumacher	136.890
Oct. 22	Malaysian	Kuala Lumpur	Michael Schumacher (1)	1:35:54.235	120.670	M. Schumacher	127.307

Winning Constructors: FERRARI (10) — M. Schumacher (9), Barrichello; McLAREN-MERCEDES (7) — Hakkinen (4), Coulthard (3).

Formula One Point Standings

Official Top 10 Formula One World Championship point leaders for 1999 and unofficial Top 10 point leaders for 2000. Points awarded for places 1 through 6 only (i.e., 10-6-4-3-2-1). Listed are starts (Sts), Top 6 finishes, poles won (PW) and points (Pts). **Note:** Formula One does not keep Money Leader standings.

FINAL 1999

		Sts	Finishes 1-2-3-4-5-6	PW	Pts
1	Mika Hakkinen	16	6-2-2-0-1-0	11	76
2	Eddie Irvine	16	3-2-3-2-1-2	0	74
3	Heinz-Harald Frentzen	16	2-1-3-6-0-0	1	54
4	David Coulthard	16	2-4-0-0-2-0	0	48
5	Michael Schumacher	10	2-2-1-0-1-0	3	44
6	Ralf Schumacher	16	0-1-2-5-3-0	0	35
7	Rubens Barrichello	16	0-0-4-1-2-0	1	21
8	Johnny Herbert	16	1-1-0-0-1-0	0	15
9	Giancarlo Fisichella	16	0-1-0-1-2-0	0	13
10	Mika Salo	10	0-1-1-0-0-0	0	10

FINAL 2000

		Sts	Finishes 1-2-3-4-5-6	PW	Pts
1	Michael Schumacher	17	9-2-1-0-1-0	9	108
2	Mika Hakkinen	17	4-7-0-2-0-1	5	89
3	David Coulthard	17	3-3-5-1-1-0	2	73
4	Rubens Barrichello	17	1-4-4-4-0-0	1	62
5	Ralf Schumacher	17	0-0-3-2-3-0	0	24
6	Giancarlo Fisichella	17	0-1-2-0-2-0	0	18
7	Jacques Villeneuve	17	0-0-0-4-2-1	0	17
8	Jenson Button	17	0-0-0-1-4-1	0	12
9	Heinz-Harald Frentzen	17	0-0-2-0-0-3	0	11
10	Jarno Trulli	17	0-0-0-1-0-3	0	6
	Mika Salo	17	0-0-0-0-2-2	0	6

Top 5 + Pole Finishing Order

No.	Event	Winner	2nd	3rd	4th	5th	Pole
1	Australian	M. Schumacher	R. Barrichello	R. Schumacher	J. Villeneuve	G. Fisichella	M. Hakkinen
2	Brazilian	M. Schumacher	G. Fisichella	H.H. Frentzen	J. Trulli	R. Schumacher	M. Hakkinen
3	San Marino	M. Schumacher	M. Hakkinen	D. Coulthard	R. Barrichello	J. Villeneuve	M. Hakkinen
4	British	D. Coulthard	M. Hakkinen	M. Schumacher	R. Schumacher	J. Button	R. Barrichello
5	Spanish	M. Hakkinen	D. Coulthard	R. Barrichello	R. Schumacher	M. Schumacher	M. Hakkinen
6	European	M. Hakkinen	M. Schumacher	D. Coulthard	R. Barrichello	G. Fisichella	D. Coulthard
7	Monaco	D. Coulthard	R. Barrichello	G. Fisichella	E. Irvine	M. Salo	M. Schumacher
8	Canadian	M. Schumacher	R. Barrichello	G. Fisichella	M. Hakkinen	J. Verstappen	M. Schumacher
9	French	D. Coulthard	M. Hakkinen	R. Barrichello	J. Villeneuve	R. Schumacher	M. Schumacher
10	Austrian	M. Hakkinen	D. Coulthard	R. Barrichello	J. Villeneuve	J. Button	M. Hakkinen
11	German	R. Barrichello	M. Hakkinen	D. Coulthard	J. Button	M. Salo	D. Coulthard
12	Hungarian	M. Hakkinen	M. Schumacher	D. Coulthard	R. Barrichello	R. Schumacher	M. Schumacher
13	Belgian	M. Hakkinen	M. Schumacher	R. Schumacher	D. Coulthard	J. Button	M. Hakkinen
14	Italian	M. Schumacher	M. Hakkinen	R. Schumacher	J. Verstappen	A. Wurz	M. Schumacher
15	U.S.	M. Schumacher	R. Barrichello	H.H. Frentzen	J. Villeneuve	D. Coulthard	M. Schumacher
16	Japan	M. Schumacher	M. Hakkinen	D. Coulthard	R. Barrichello	J. Button	M. Schumacher
17	Malaysian	M. Schumacher	D. Coulthard	R. Barrichello	M. Hakkinen	J. Villeneuve	M. Schumacher

Major 2000 Endurance Races

24 Hours of Daytona
Feb. 5-6, at Daytona Beach, Fla.

Officially the Rolex 24 at Daytona and first held in 1962 (as a 3-hour race). An IMSA Camel GT race for exotic prototype sports cars and contested over a 3.56-mile road course at Daytona International Speedway. Listed are qualifying position, drivers, chassis, class and laps completed.

1 (21) Olivier Beretta, Karl Wendlinger and Dominique Dupuy; DODGE VIPER GTSR; 723 laps (2,573.88 miles) at 107.207 mph; margin of victory 30.879 seconds.
2 (11) Justin Bell, Ron Fellows and Chris Kneifel; CHEVROLET CORVETTE; 723 laps.
3 (18) Ni Amorim, Jean Philippe Belloc and David Donahue; DODGE VIPER GTSR; 719 laps.
4 (1) Elliot Forbes-Robinson, Max Papis and James Weaver; RILEY & SCOTT-FORD; 717 laps.
5 (17) Tommy Archer, Marc Duez and Vincent Vosse; DODGE VIPER GTSR; 691 laps.
Fastest lap: James Weaver (lap #9), Riley & Scott-Ford; 124.724 mph. **Top qualifier:** James Weaver 126.88 mph. **Weather:** Sunny. **Attendance:** 40,000 (est.).

24 Hours of Le Mans
June 17-18, at Le Mans, France

Officially the Le Mans Grand Prix d'Endurance and first held in 1923. Contested over the 8.451-mile Circuit de la Sarthe in Le Mans, France. Listed are qualifying position, drivers, car, and laps completed.

1 (2) Frank Biela, Tom Kristensen and Emanuele Pirro; AUDI R8; 368 laps (3,109.968 miles) at 128.340.
2 (1) Laurent Aiello, Stephane Ortelli and Allan McNish; AUDI R8; 367 laps.
3 (17) Christian Abt, Michele Alboreto and Rinaldo Capello; AUDI R8; 365 laps.
4 (9) Sebastian Bourdais, Emmanuel Clerico and Oliver Grouillard; COURAGE C52; 344 laps.
5 (8) Hiroki Katoh, Johnny O'Connell and Pierre-Henri Raphanel; PANOZ SPYDER LMP; 342 laps.
Fastest lap: Allan McNish (lap #233); 140.015 mph. **Top qualifier:** Laurent Aiello, Stephane Ortelli and Allan McNish, Audi R8. **Weather:** Sunny. **Attendance:** 200,000 (est.).

NHRA RESULTS

Winners of National Hot Rod Association Drag Racing events in the Top Fuel, Funny Car and Pro Stock divisions through Oct. 8, 2000. All times are based on two cars racing head-to-head from a standing start over a straight line, quarter-mile course. Differences in reaction time account for apparently faster losing times.

2000 Season

Date	Event	Event	Winner	Time	MPH	2nd Place	Time	MPH
Feb. 6	AutoZone Winternationals	Top Fuel	Gary Scelzi	4.163	317.79	T. Schumacher	4.712	309.56
		Funny Car	Jerry Toliver	4.970	309.06	T. Pedregon	4.929	308.35
		Pro Stock	Jeg Coughlin	6.894	199.17	W. Johnson	6.953	197.65
Feb. 27	Kragen Nationals	Top Fuel	Tony Schumacher	5.095	289.57	B. Vandergriff	5.421	243.77
		Funny Car	John Force	4.933	313.88	R. Capps	8.196	101.89
		Pro Stock	Jeg Coughlin	6.961	198.44	M. Pawuk	7.081	195.90
Mar. 19	Gatornationals	Top Fuel	Doug Kalitta	4.614	313.58	T. Schumacher	4.679	314.97
		Funny Car	Jerry Toliver	5.071	296.50	R. Capps	6.185	155.76
		Pro Stock	Warren Johnson	6.900	199.35	T. Coughlin	8.865	106.59
Apr. 9	SummitRacing.com Nationals	Top Fuel	Kenny Bernstein	4.907	282.78	J. Amato	5.213	260.46
		Funny Car	Jim Elper	4.983	302.21	T. Pedregon	5.417	197.02
		Pro Stock	Jeg Coughlin	7.072	195.56	W. Johnson	7.100	195.51
Apr. 16	O'Reilly Nationals	Top Fuel	Larry Dixon	4.665	316.90	T. Schumacher	4.761	309.98
		Funny Car	Bob Gilbertson	5.067	304.25	J. Tolliver	4.934	312.21
		Pro Stock	Jeg Coughlin	6.905	199.29	J. Yates	6.926	199.55
Apr. 30	Moto1.net Nationals	Top Fuel	Larry Dixon	4.674	314.53	K. Bernstein	4.692	306.12
		Funny Car	John Force	5.913	236.01	R. Capps	6.165	133.76
		Pro Stock	Jeg Coughlin	6.861	199.73	J. Yates	6.904	199.73
May 7	Southern Nationals	Top Fuel	Gary Scelzi	4.629	310.70	T. Schumacher	4.697	307.44
		Funny Car	John Force	4.929	289.14	R. Capps	5.023	291.70
		Pro Stock	Jeg Coughlin	6.957	198.12	B. Allen	7.099	195.85
May 28	Castrol Nationals	Top Fuel	Gary Scelzi	4.614	316.67	L. Dixon	4.696	309.59
		Funny Car	John Force	4.9191	313.26	T. Pedregon	9.747	84.38
		Pro Stock	V. Gaines	7.041	196.93	W. Johnson	7.016	197.93
June 4	Fram Route 66 Nationals	Top Fuel	Gary Scelzi	4.642	314.53	L. Dixon	4.702	313.07
		Funny Car	John Force	4.842	318.09	J. Tolliver	4.934	312.64
		Pro Stock	Ron Krisher	6.888	199.43	T. Coughlin	6.924	197.36
June 18	Pontiac Excitement Nationals	Top Fuel	Tony Schumacher	4.648	178.10	J. Amato	5.165	178.10
		Funny Car	Tony Pedregon	4.893	316.08	J. Tolliver	4.876	301.20
		Pro Stock	Mark Pawuk	6.980	197.33	R. Krisher	6.975	197.51
June 24	Sears Craftsman Nationals	Top Fuel	Gary Scelzi	5.892	284.99	K. Bernstein	6.010	307.09
		Funny Car	Jerry Toliver	6.771	186.69	D. Skuza	9.652	88.33
		Pro Stock	Ron Krisher	6.900	198.44	G. Anderson	6.985	196.96
July 8	Winston Showdown*	T.F.-F.C.	Cory McClenathan	4.852	291.32	R. Capps	5.186	275.28
		Pro Stock	Troy Coughlin	7.086	194.10	M. Pawuk	7.100	194.24
July 16	Mile-High Nationals	Top Fuel	Joe Amato	4.837	300.53	T. Schumacher	4.913	281.36
		Funny Car	Whit Bazemore	4.990	301.20	S. Cannon	5.447	273.83
		Pro Stock	Kurt Johnson	7.356	188.04	D. Alderman	7.375	186.28
July 30	Northwest Nationals	Top Fuel	Gary Scelzi	4.711	303.98	D. Kalitta	4.789	291.19
		Funny Car	John Force	4.973	299.60	F. Pedregon	6.530	140.69
		Pro Stock	Richie Stevens	7.018	195.70	J. Coughlin	7.498	146.00
Aug. 6	Autolite Nationals	Top Fuel	Doug Kalitta	5.247	274.33	L. Dixon	5.234	265.33
		Funny Car	John Force	9.055	101.81	T. Pedregon	8.068	101.29
		Pro Stock	Kurt Johnson	6.974	198.61	A. Johnson	7.024	196.67
Aug. 20	Colonel's Truck Accessories Nationals	Top Fuel	Tony Schumacher	4.585	318.69	D. Kalitta	4.655	306.81
		Funny Car	John Force	4.935	309.34	J. Epler	8.889	91.75
		Pro Stock	Kurt Johnson	6.986	196.59	J. Coughlin	6.995	195.85
Sept. 4	U.S. Nationals	Top Fuel	Tony Schumacher	4.644	316.90	G. Clapshaw	10.965	74.25
		Funny Car	Jim Epler	5.017	285.41	W. Bazemore	5.968	197.59
		Pro Stock	Jeg Coughlin	6.968	196.96	R. Krisher	6.927	197.59
Sept. 17	Keystone Nationals	Top Fuel	Joe Amato	4.626	310.27	G. Scelzi	4.639	312.78
		Funny Car	Bruce Sarver	4.993	303.03	R. Capps	5.063	293.73
		Pro Stock	Kurt Johnson	6.885	200.14	W. Johnson	6.914	200.14
Oct. 1	Advance Auto Parts Nationals	Top Fuel	Gary Scelzi	4.672	303.64	D. Kalitta	4.676	303.16
		Funny Car	John Force	4.933	291.82	R. Capps	8.875	91.65
		Pro Stock	Jeg Coughlin	7.022	195.36	D. Alderman	7.083	194.58
Oct. 8	AutoZone Nationals	Top Fuel	Gary Scelzi†	—	—	L. Dixon	—	—
		Funny Car	Ron Capps	4.925	297.22	W. Bazemore	11.125	22.82
		Pro Stock	Jeg Coughlin	6.878	199.64	S. Geoffrion	6.896	199.11

*At the Winston Showdown the Funny Car finalist competes against the Top Fuel finalist in one event.
†Scelzi was awarded the win after Dixon crashed and wreckage from his car crossed the finish line in Scelzi's lane, stopping the clocks. No times (or speeds) were recorded.

NASCAR Circuit
The Crown Jewels

The four biggest races on the NASCAR (National Association for Stock Car Auto Racing) circuit are the Daytona 500, the Winston 500, the Coca-Cola 600 and the Pepsi Southern 500. The Winston Cup Media Guide lists them as the richest (Daytona), the fastest (Winston), the longest (Coca-Cola) and the oldest (Southern). The only drivers to win three of the races in a year are Lee Roy Yarbrough (1969), David Pearson (1976), Bill Elliott (1985) and Jeff Gordon (1997).

Daytona 500

Held early in the NASCAR season; 200 laps around a 2.5-mile high-banked oval at Daytona International Speedway in Daytona Beach, FL. First race in 1959, although stock car racing at Daytona dates back to 1936. Winning drivers who started from pole positions are in **bold** type.

Multiple winners: Richard Petty (7); Cale Yarborough (4); Bobby Allison and Dale Jarrett (3); Bill Elliott, Jeff Gordon and Sterling Marlin (2). **Multiple poles:** Buddy Baker and Cale Yarborough (4); Bill Elliott, Dale Jarrett, Fireball Roberts and Ken Schrader (3); Donnie Allison (2).

Year	Winner	Car	Owner	MPH	Pole Sitter	MPH
1959	Lee Petty	Oldsmobile	Petty Enterprises	135.521	Bob Welborn	140.121
1960	Junior Johnson	Chevrolet	Ray Fox	124.740	Cotton Owens	149.892
1961	Marvin Panch	Pontiac	Smokey Yunick	149.601	Fireball Roberts	155.709
1962	**Fireball Roberts**	Pontiac	Smokey Yunick	152.529	Fireball Roberts	156.999
1963	Tiny Lund	Ford	Wood Brothers	151.566	Fireball Roberts	160.943
1964	Richard Petty	Plymouth	Petty Enterprises	154.334	Paul Goldsmith	174.910
1965-a	Fred Lorenzen	Ford	Holman-Moody	141.539	Darel Dieringer	171.151
1966-b	**Richard Petty**	Plymouth	Petty Enterprises	160.627	Richard Petty	175.165
1967	Mario Andretti	Ford	Holman-Moody	149.926	Curtis Turner	180.831
1968	**Cale Yarborough**	Mercury	Wood Brothers	143.251	Cale Yarborough	189.222
1969	Lee Roy Yarbrough	Ford	Junior Johnson	157.950	Buddy Baker	188.901
1970	Pete Hamilton	Plymouth	Petty Enterprises	149.601	Cale Yarborough	194.015
1971	Richard Petty	Plymouth	Petty Enterprises	144.462	A.J. Foyt	182.744
1972	A.J. Foyt	Mercury	Wood Brothers	161.550	Bobby Isaac	186.632
1973	Richard Petty	Dodge	Petty Enterprises	157.205	Buddy Baker	185.662
1974-c	Richard Petty	Dodge	Petty Enterprises	140.894	David Pearson	185.017
1975	Benny Parsons	Chevrolet	L.G. DeWitt	153.649	Donnie Allison	185.827
1976	David Pearson	Mercury	Wood Brothers	152.181	Ramo Stott	183.456
1977	Cale Yarborough	Chevrolet	Junior Johnson	153.218	Donnie Allison	188.048
1978	Bobby Allison	Ford	Bud Moore	159.730	Cale Yarborough	187.536
1979	Richard Petty	Oldsmobile	Petty Enterprises	143.977	Buddy Baker	196.049
1980	**Buddy Baker**	Oldsmobile	Ranier Racing	177.602*	Buddy Baker	194.099
1981	Richard Petty	Buick	Petty Enterprises	169.651	Bobby Allison	194.624
1982	Bobby Allison	Buick	DiGard Racing	153.991	Benny Parsons	196.317
1983	Cale Yarborough	Pontiac	Ranier Racing	155.979	Ricky Rudd	198.864
1984	**Cale Yarborough**	Chevrolet	Ranier Racing	150.994	Cale Yarborough	201.848
1985	**Bill Elliott**	Ford	Melling Racing	172.265	Bill Elliott	205.114
1986	Geoff Bodine	Chevrolet	Hendrick Motorsports	148.124	Bill Elliott	205.039
1987	**Bill Elliott**	Ford	Melling Racing	176.263	Bill Elliott	210.364†
1988	Bobby Allison	Buick	Stavola Brothers	137.531	Ken Schrader	198.823
1989	Darrell Waltrip	Chevrolet	Hendrick Motorsports	148.466	Ken Schrader	196.996
1990	Derrike Cope	Chevrolet	Bob Whitcomb	165.761	Ken Schrader	196.515
1991	Ernie Irvan	Chevrolet	Morgan-McClure	148.148	Davey Allison	195.955
1992	Davey Allison	Ford	Robert Yates	160.256	Sterling Martin	192.213
1993	Dale Jarrett	Chevrolet	Joe Gibbs Racing	154.972	Kyle Petty	189.426
1994	Sterling Marlin	Chevrolet	Morgan-McClure	156.931	Loy Allen	190.158
1995	Sterling Marlin	Chevrolet	Morgan-McClure	141.710	Dale Jarrett	193.498
1996	Dale Jarrett	Ford	Robert Yates	154.308	Dale Earnhardt	189.510
1997	Jeff Gordon	Chevrolet	Rick Hendrick	148.295	Mike Skinner	189.813
1998	Dale Earnhardt	Chevrolet	Richard Childress	172.712	Bobby Labonte	192.415
1999	**Jeff Gordon**	Chevrolet	Rick Hendrick	161.551	Jeff Gordon	195.067
2000	**Dale Jarrett**	Ford	Robert Yates	155.669	Dale Jarrett	191.091

*Track and race record for winning speed. †Track and race record for qualifying speed.
Notes: a–rain shortened 1965 to 332+ miles; **b**–rain shortened 1966 race to 495 miles; **c**–in 1974, race shortened 50 miles due to energy crisis. **Also:** Pole sitters determined by pole qualifying race (1959-65); by two-lap average (1966-68); by fastest single lap (since 1969).

Winston 500

Held at Talladega (Ala.) Superspeedway. **Multiple winners:** Dale Earnhardt (4); Bobby Allison, Davey Allison, Buddy Baker and David Pearson (3); Mark Martin, Darrell Waltrip and Cale Yarborough (2).

Year		Year		Year		Year	
1970	Pete Hamilton	1978	Cale Yarborough	1986	Bobby Allison	1994	Dale Earnhardt
1971	Donnie Allison	1979	Bobby Allison	1987	Davey Allison	1995	Mark Martin
1972	David Pearson	1980	Buddy Baker	1988	Phil Parsons	1996	Sterling Marlin
1973	David Pearson	1981	Bobby Allison	1989	Davey Allison	1997	Mark Martin
1974	David Pearson	1982	Darrell Waltrip	1990	Dale Earnhardt	1998	Dale Jarrett
1975	Buddy Baker	1983	Richard Petty	1991	Harry Gant	1999	Dale Earnhardt
1976	Buddy Baker	1984	Cale Yarborough	1992	Davey Allison	2000	Dale Earnhardt
1977	Darrell Waltrip	1985	Bill Elliott	1993	Ernie Irvan		

Coca-Cola 600

Held at Charlotte (N.C.) Motor Speedway. **Multiple winners:** Darrell Waltrip (5); Bobby Allison, Buddy Baker, Dale Earnhardt, Jeff Gordon and David Pearson (3); Neil Bonnett, Fred Lorenzen, Jim Paschal and Richard Petty (2).

Year		Year		Year		Year	
1960	Joe Lee Johnson	1971	Bobby Allison	1982	Neil Bonnett	1993	Dale Earnhardt
1961	David Pearson	1972	Buddy Baker	1983	Neil Bonnett	1994	Jeff Gordon
1962	Nelson Stacy	1973	Buddy Baker	1984	Bobby Allison	1995	Bobby Labonte
1963	Fred Lorenzen	1974	David Pearson	1985	Darrell Waltrip	1996	Dale Jarrett
1964	Jim Paschal	1975	Richard Petty	1986	Dale Earnhardt	1997	Jeff Gordon
1965	Fred Lorenzen	1976	David Pearson	1987	Kyle Petty	1998	Jeff Gordon
1966	Marvin Panch	1977	Richard Petty	1988	Darrell Waltrip	1999	Jeff Burton
1967	Jim Paschal	1978	Darrell Waltrip	1989	Darrell Waltrip	2000	Matt Kenseth
1968	Buddy Baker	1979	Darrell Waltrip	1990	Rusty Wallace		
1969	Lee Roy Yarbrough	1980	Benny Parsons	1991	Davey Allison		
1970	Donnie Allison	1981	Bobby Allison	1992	Dale Earnhardt		

Pepsi Southern 500

Held at Darlington (S.C.) International Raceway. **Multiple winners:** Cale Yarborough (5); Bobby Allison and Jeff Gordon (4); Buck Baker, Dale Earnhardt, Bill Elliott, David Pearson and Herb Thomas (3); Harry Gant and Fireball Roberts (2).

Year		Year		Year		Year	
1950	Johnny Mantz	1963	Fireball Roberts	1976	David Pearson	1989	Dale Earnhardt
1951	Herb Thomas	1964	Buck Baker	1977	David Pearson	1990	Dale Earnhardt
1952	Fonty Flock	1965	Ned Jarrett	1978	Cale Yarborough	1991	Harry Gant
1953	Buck Baker	1966	Darel Dieringer	1979	David Pearson	1992	Darrell Waltrip
1954	Herb Thomas	1967	Richard Petty	1980	Terry Labonte	1993	Mark Martin
1955	Herb Thomas	1968	Cale Yarborough	1981	Neil Bonnett	1994	Bill Elliott
1956	Curtis Turner	1969	Lee Roy Yarbrough	1982	Cale Yarborough	1995	Jeff Gordon
1957	Speedy Thompson	1970	Buddy Baker	1983	Bobby Allison	1996	Jeff Gordon
1958	Fireball Roberts	1971	Bobby Allison	1984	Harry Gant	1997	Jeff Gordon
1959	Jim Reed	1972	Bobby Allison	1985	Bill Elliott	1998	Jeff Gordon
1960	Buck Baker	1973	Cale Yarborough	1986	Tim Richmond	1999	Jeff Burton
1961	Nelson Stacy	1974	Cale Yarborough	1987	Dale Earnhardt	2000	Bobby Labonte
1962	Larry Frank	1975	Bobby Allison	1988	Bill Elliott		

All-Time Leaders

NASCAR's all-time Top 20 drivers in victories, pole positions and earnings based on records through 1999. Drivers active in 2000 are in **bold** type.

Victories

1	Richard Petty	200
2	David Pearson	105
3	Bobby Allison	84
	Darrell Waltrip	84
5	Cale Yarborough	83
6	**Dale Earnhardt**	74
7	Lee Petty	55
8	Ned Jarrett	50
	Junior Johnson	50
10	**Rusty Wallace**	49
	Jeff Gordon	49
12	Herb Thomas	48
13	Buck Baker	46
14	**Bill Elliott**	40
	Tim Flock	40
16	Bobby Isaac	37
17	Fireball Roberts	32
18	**Mark Martin**	31
19	Fred Lorenzen	26
	Rex White	26

Pole Positions

1	Richard Petty	126
2	David Pearson	113
3	Cale Yarborough	70
4	**Darrell Waltrip**	59
5	Bobby Allison	57
6	Bobby Isaac	51
7	**Bill Elliott**	49
8	Junior Johnson	47
9	Buck Baker	44
10	Buddy Baker	40
11	Tim Flock	39
	Mark Martin	39
	Herb Thomas	39
14	**Geoff Bodine**	37
15	Ned Jarrett	35
	Rex White	35
	Fireball Roberts	35
18	Fonty Flock	34
19	Fred Lorenzen	33
20	**Jeff Gordon**	30

Earnings

1	**Dale Earnhardt**	$36,492,665
2	**Jeff Gordon**	31,867,679
3	**Mark Martin**	22,269,442
4	**Dale Jarrett**	21,962,615
5	**Terry Labonte**	21,285,075
6	**Rusty Wallace**	21,237,064
7	**Bill Elliott**	21,107,334
8	**Darrell Waltrip**	18,170,338
9	**Ricky Rudd**	16,737,226
10	**Geoff Bodine**	14,043,433
11	**Ken Schrader**	13,994,624
12	**Bobby Labonte**	13,804,859
13	**Sterling Marlin**	13,389,604
14	**Jeff Burton**	12,768,323
15	Ernie Irvan	11,625,817
16	**Kyle Petty**	11,427,738
17	**Michael Waltrip**	9,727,411
18	**Bobby Hamilton**	8,842,974
19	**Brett Bodine**	8,664,268
20	**Morgan Shepherd**	8,498,092

Winston Cup Champions

Originally the Grand National Championship, 1949-70, and based on official NASCAR records.

Multiple winners: Dale Earnhardt and Richard Petty (7); Jeff Gordon, David Pearson, Lee Petty, Darrell Waltrip and Cale Yarborough (3); Buck Baker, Tim Flock, Ned Jarrett, Herb Thomas and Joe Weatherly (2).

Year	Car No.	Driver	Owner	Car	Wins	Poles	Earnings
1949	22	Red Byron	Raymond Parks	Olds	2	1	$5,800
1950	60	Bill Rexford	Julian Buesink	Olds	1	0	6,175
1951	92	Herb Thomas	Herb Thomas	Hudson	7	4	18,200
1952	91	Tim Flock	Ted Chester	Hudson	8	4	20,210
1953	92	Herb Thomas	Herb Thomas	Hudson	11	10	27,300
1954	92	Herb Thomas	Herb Thomas	Hudson	12	8	27,540
1954	42	Lee Petty	Herb Thomas	Chry	7	3	26,706
1955	300	Tim Flock	Carl Kiekhaefer	Chry	18	19	33,750
1956	300B	Buck Baker	Carl Kiekhaefer	Chevy	14	12	29,790
1957	87	Buck Baker	Buck Baker	Chevy	10	5	24,712
1958	42	Lee Petty	Petty Ent.	Olds	7	4	20,600
1959	42	Lee Petty	Petty Ent.	Plym	10	2	45,570
1960	4	Rex White	White-Clements	Chevy	6	3	45,260
1961	11	Ned Jarrett	W.G. Holloway Jr.	Chevy	1	4	27,285
1962	8	Joe Weatherly	Bud Moore	Pont	9	6	56,110
1963	21	Joe Weatherly	Wood Brothers	Ford	3	5	77,636
1963	8	Joe Weatherly	Wood Brothers	Merc	3	6	58,110
1964	43	Richard Petty	Petty Ent.	Plym	9	8	98,810
1965	11	Ned Jarrett	Bondy Long	Ford	13	9	77,960
1966	6	David Pearson	Cotton Owens	Dodge	14	7	59,205
1967	43	Richard Petty	Petty Ent.	Plym	27	18	130,275
1968	17	David Pearson	Holman-Moody	Ford	16	12	118,842
1969	17	David Pearson	Holman-Moody	Ford	11	14	183,700
1970	71	Bobby Isaac	Nord Krauskopf	Dodge	11	13	121,470
1971	43	Richard Petty	Petty Ent.	Plym	21	9	309,225
1972	43	Richard Petty	Petty Ent.	Plym	8	3	227,015
1973	72	Benny Parsons	L.G. DeWitt	Chevy	1	0	114,345
1974	43	Richard Petty	Petty Ent.	Dodge	10	7	299,175
1975	43	Richard Petty	Petty Ent.	Dodge	13	3	378,865
1976	11	Cale Yarborough	Junior Johnson	Chevy	9	2	387,173
1977	11	Cale Yarborough	Junior Johnson	Chevy	9	3	477,499
1978	11	Cale Yarborough	Junior Johnson	Olds	10	8	530,751
1979	43	Richard Petty	Petty Ent.	Chevy	5	1	531,292
1980	2	Dale Earnhardt	Rod Osterlund	Chevy	5	0	588,926
1981	11	Darrell Waltrip	Junior Johnson	Buick	12	11	693,342
1982	11	Darrell Waltrip	Junior Johnson	Buick	12	7	873,118
1983	22	Bobby Allison	Bill Gardner	Buick	6	0	828,355
1984	44	Terry Labonte	Billy Hagan	Chevy	2	2	713,010
1985	11	Darrell Waltrip	Junior Johnson	Chevy	3	4	1,318,735
1986	3	Dale Earnhardt	Richard Childress	Chevy	5	1	1,783,880
1987	3	Dale Earnhardt	Richard Childress	Chevy	11	1	2,099,243
1988	9	Bill Elliott	Harry Meling	Ford	6	6	1,574,639
1989	27	Rusty Wallace	Raymond Beadle	Pont	6	4	2,247,950
1990	3	Dale Earnhardt	Richard Childress	Chevy	9	4	3,083,056
1991	3	Dale Earnhardt	Richard Childress	Chevy	4	0	2,396,685
1992	7	Alan Kulwicki	Alan Kulwicki	Ford	2	6	2,322,561
1993	3	Dale Earnhardt	Richard Childress	Chevy	6	2	3,353,789
1994	3	Dale Earnhardt	Richard Childress	Chevy	4	2	3,400,733
1995	24	Jeff Gordon	Rick Hendrick	Chevy	7	8	4,347,343
1996	5	Terry Labonte	Rick Hendrick	Chevy	2	4	4,030,648
1997	24	Jeff Gordon	Rick Hendrick	Chevy	10	1	6,375,658
1998	24	Jeff Gordon	Rick Hendrick	Chevy	13	7	9,306,584
1999	88	Dale Jarrett	Robert Yates	Ford	4	0	6,649,596

NASCAR Rookie of the Year

Award presented to rookie driver who accumulates the most Winston Cup points based on his best 15 finishes.

Year		Year		Year		Year	
1958	Shorty Rollins	1969	Dick Brooks	1980	Jody Ridley	1991	Bobby Hamilton
1959	Richard Petty	1970	Bill Dennis	1981	Ron Bouchard	1992	Jimmy Hensley
1960	David Pearson	1971	Walter Ballard	1982	Geoff Bodine	1993	Jeff Gordon
1961	Woodie Wilson	1972	Larry Smith	1983	Sterling Marlin	1994	Jeff Burton
1962	Tom Cox	1973	Lennie Pond	1984	Rusty Wallace	1995	Ricky Craven
1963	Billy Wade	1974	Earl Ross	1985	Ken Schrader	1996	Johnny Benson
1964	Doug Cooper	1975	Bruce Hill	1986	Alan Kulwicki	1997	Mike Skinner
1965	Sam McQuagg	1976	Skip Manning	1987	Davey Allison	1998	Kenny Irwin
1966	James Hylton	1977	Ricky Rudd	1988	Ken Bouchard	1999	Tony Stewart
1967	Donnie Allison	1978	Ronnie Thomas	1989	Dick Trickle		
1968	Pete Hamilton	1979	Dale Earnhardt	1990	Rob Moroso		

CART Circuit
FedEx Series Champions

Officially the FedEx Championship Series since 1997. Formerly, AAA (American Automobile Assn., 1909-55), USAC (U.S. Auto Club, 1956-78), CART (Championship Auto Racing Teams, 1979-91). CART was renamed IndyCar in 1992 and then lost use of the name in 1997.

Multiple titles: A.J. Foyt (7); Mario Andretti (4); Jimmy Bryan, Earl Cooper, Ted Horn, Rick Mears, Louie Meyer, Bobby Rahal, Al Unser (3); Tony Bettenhausen, Ralph DePalma, Peter DePaolo, Joe Leonard, Rex Mays, Tommy Milton, Jimmy Murphy, Wilbur Shaw, Tom Sneva, Al Unser Jr., Bobby Unser, Rodger Ward and Alex Zanardi (2).

AAA

Year		Year		Year		Year	
1909	George Robertson	1920	Tommy Milton	1931	Louis Schneider	1942-45	No racing
1910	Ray Harroun	1921	Tommy Milton	1932	Bob Carey	1946	Ted Horn
1911	Ralph Mulford	1922	Jimmy Murphy	1933	Louie Meyer	1947	Ted Horn
1912	Ralph DePalma	1923	Eddie Hearne	1934	Bill Cummings	1948	Ted Horn
1913	Earl Cooper	1924	Jimmy Murphy	1935	Kelly Petillo	1949	Johnnie Parsons
1914	Ralph DePalma	1925	Peter DePaolo	1936	Mauri Rose	1950	Henry Banks
1915	Earl Cooper	1926	Harry Hartz	1937	Wilbur Shaw	1951	Tony Bettenhausen
1916	Dario Resta	1927	Peter DePaolo	1938	Floyd Roberts	1952	Chuck Stevenson
1917	Earl Cooper	1928	Louie Meyer	1939	Wilbur Shaw	1953	Sam Hanks
1918	Ralph Mulford	1929	Louie Meyer	1940	Rex Mays	1954	Jimmy Bryan
1919	Howard Wilcox	1930	Billy Arnold	1941	Rex Mays	1955	Bob Sweikert

USAC

Year		Year		Year		Year	
1956	Jimmy Bryan	1962	Rodger Ward	1968	Bobby Unser	1974	Bobby Unser
1957	Jimmy Bryan	1963	A.J. Foyt	1969	Mario Andretti	1975	A.J. Foyt
1958	Tony Bettenhausen	1964	A.J. Foyt	1970	Al Unser	1976	Gordon Johncock
1959	Rodger Ward	1965	Mario Andretti	1971	Joe Leonard	1977	Tom Sneva
1960	A.J. Foyt	1966	Mario Andretti	1972	Joe Leonard	1978	A.J. Foyt
1961	A.J. Foyt	1967	A.J. Foyt	1973	Roger McCluskey		

CART

Year		Year		Year		Year	
1979	Rick Mears	1985	Al Unser	1991	Michael Andretti	1997	Alex Zanardi
1980	Johnny Rutherford	1986	Bobby Rahal	1992	Bobby Rahal	1998	Alex Zanardi
1981	Rick Mears	1987	Bobby Rahal	1993	Nigel Mansell	1999	Juan Montoya
1982	Rick Mears	1988	Danny Sullivan	1994	Al Unser Jr.		
1983	Al Unser	1989	Emerson Fittipaldi	1995	Jacques Villeneuve		
1984	Mario Andretti	1990	Al Unser Jr.	1996	Jimmy Vasser		

All-Time CART Leaders

CART's all-time Top 20 drivers in victories, pole positions and earnings, based on records through 1999. Drivers active in 2000 are in **bold** type. Totals include victories, poles and earnings before CART was established in 1979.

Victories

1	A.J. Foyt	67
2	Mario Andretti	52
3	Al Unser	39
4	**Michael Andretti**	38
5	Bobby Unser	35
6	Al Unser Jr.	31
7	Rick Mears	29
8	Johnny Rutherford	27
9	Roger Ward	26
10	Gordon Johncock	25
11	Ralph DePalma	24
	Bobby Rahal	24
13	Tommy Milton	23
14	Tony Bettenhausen	22
	Emerson Fittipaldi	22
16	Earl Cooper	20
17	Jimmy Bryan	19
	Jimmy Murphy	19
19	Ralph Mulford	17
	Danny Sullivan	17

Pole Positions

1	Mario Andretti	67
2	A.J. Foyt	53
3	Bobby Unser	49
4	Rick Mears	40
5	**Michael Andretti**	32
6	Al Unser	27
7	Johnny Rutherford	23
8	Gordon Johncock	20
9	Rex Mays	19
	Danny Sullivan	19
11	Bobby Rahal	18
12	Emerson Fittipaldi	17
13	Tony Bettenhausen	14
	Don Branson	14
	Tom Sneva	14
16	Parnelli Jones	12
	Paul Tracy	12
18	Rodger Ward	11
	Danny Ongais	11
20	Johnny Thomson	10
	Dan Gurney	10
	Teo Fabi	10
	Nigel Mansell	10
	Alex Zanardi	10

Earnings

1	**Al Unser Jr.**	$18,828,406
2	Bobby Rahal	16,344,008
3	**Michael Andretti**	16,116,869
4	Emerson Fittipaldi	14,293,625
5	Mario Andretti	11,552,154
6	Rick Mears	11,050,807
7	**Jimmy Vasser**	9,161,744
8	Danny Sullivan	8,884,126
9	Arie Luyendyk	7,732,188
10	**Paul Tracy**	7,206,020
11	Raul Boesel	6,971,887
12	Al Unser	6,740,843
13	Alex Zanardi	5,733,750
14	Scott Pruett	5,440,144
15	A.J. Foyt	5,357,589
16	Teo Fabi	5,045,881
17	**Adrian Fernandez**	4,900,265
18	Scott Brayton	4,807,274
19	Scott Goodyear*	4,579,451
20	Roberto Guerrero*	4,275,163

*Drivers active, but in IRL not CART.

CART Rookie of the Year

Award presented to rookie who accumulates the most FedEx Championship Series points among first year drivers. Originally the CART Rookie of the Year; CART was renamed IndyCar in 1992 and then lost use of the name in 1997.

Year		Year		Year		Year	
1979	Bill Alsup	1985	Arie Luyendyk	1991	Jeff Andretti	1997	Patrick Carpentier
1980	Dennis Firestone	1986	Dominic Dobson	1992	Stefan Johansson	1998	Tony Kanaan
1981	Bob Lazier	1987	Fabrizio Barbazza	1993	Nigel Mansell	1999	Juan Montoya
1982	Bobby Rahal	1988	John Jones	1994	Jacques Villeneuve		
1983	Teo Fabi	1989	Bernard Jourdain	1995	Gil de Ferran		
1984	Roberto Guerrero	1990	Eddie Cheever	1996	Alex Zanardi		

Indy Racing League Circuit
Indianapolis 500

Held every Memorial Day weekend; 200 laps around a 2.5-mile oval at Indianapolis Motor Speedway. First race was held in 1911. The Indy Racing League began in 1996 and made the Indianapolis 500 its cornerstone event. Winning drivers are listed with starting positions. Winners who started from pole position are in **bold** type.

Multiple wins: A.J. Foyt, Rick Mears and Al Unser (4); Louis Meyer, Mauri Rose, Johnny Rutherford, Wilbur Shaw and Bobby Unser (3); Emerson Fittipaldi, Gordon Johncock, Arie Luyendyk, Tommy Milton, Al Unser Jr., Bill Vukovich and Rodger Ward (2).

Multiple poles: Rick Mears (6); Mario Andretti and A.J. Foyt (4); Arie Luyendyk, Rex Mays, Duke Nalon and Tom Sneva (3); Billy Arnold, Bill Cummings, Ralph DePalma, Leon Duray, Walt Faulkner, Parnelli Jones, Jack McGrath, Jimmy Murphy, Johnny Rutherford, Eddie Sachs and Jimmy Snyder (2).

Year	Winner (Pos.)	Car	MPH	Pole Sitter	MPH
1911	Ray Harroun (28)	Marmon Wasp	74.602	Lewis Strang	–
1912	Joe Dawson (7)	National	78.719	Gil Anderson	–
1913	Jules Goux (7)	Peugeot	75.933	Caleb Bragg	–
1914	Rene Thomas (15)	Delage	82.474	Jean Chassagne	–
1915	Ralph DePalma (2)	Mercedes	89.840	Howard Wilcox	98.90
1916-a	Dario Resta (4)	Peugeot	84.001	John Aitken	96.69
1917-18	Not held	World War I			
1919	Howdy Wilcox (2)	Peugeot	88.050	Rene Thomas	104.78
1920	Gaston Chevrolet (6)	Monroe	88.618	Ralph DePalma	99.15
1921	Tommy Milton (20)	Frontenac	89.621	Ralph DePalma	100.75
1922	**Jimmy Murphy** (1)	Murphy Special	94.484	Jimmy Murphy	100.50
1923	**Tommy Milton** (1)	H.C.S. Special	90.954	Tommy Milton	108.17
1924	L.L. Corum & Joe Boyer (21)	Duesenberg Special	98.234	Jimmy Murphy	108.037
1925	Peter DePaolo (2)	Duesenberg Special	101.127	Leon Duray	113.196
1926-b	Frank Lockhart (20)	Miller Special	95.904	Earl Cooper	111.735
1927	George Souders (22)	Duesenberg	97.545	Frank Lockhart	120.100
1928	Louie Meyer (13)	Miller Special	99.482	Leon Duray	122.391
1929	Ray Keech (6)	Simplex Piston Ring Special	97.585	Cliff Woodbury	120.599
1930	**Billy Arnold** (1)	Miller-Hartz Special	100.448	Billy Arnold	113.268
1931	Louis Schneider (13)	Bowes Seal Fast Special	96.629	Russ Snowberger	112.796
1932	Fred Frame (27)	Miller-Hartz Special	104.144	Lou Moore	117.363
1933	Louie Meyer (6)	Tydol Special	104.162	Bill Cummings	118.530
1934	Bill Cummings (10)	Boyle Products Special	104.863	Kelly Petillo	119.329
1935	Kelly Petillo (22)	Gilmore Speedway Special	106.240	Rex Mays	120.736
1936	Louie Meyer (28)	Ring Free Special	109.069	Rex Mays	119.644
1937	Wilbur Shaw (2)	Shaw-Gilmore Special	113.580	Bill Cummings	123.343
1938	**Floyd Roberts** (1)	Burd Piston Ring Special	117.200	Floyd Roberts	125.681
1939	Wilbur Shaw (3)	Boyle Special	115.035	Jimmy Snyder	130.138
1940	Wilbur Shaw (3)	Boyle Special	114.277	Rex Mays	127.850
1941	Floyd Davis & Mauri Rose (17)	Noc-Out Hose Clamp Special	115.117	Mauri Rose	128.691
1942-45	Not held	World War II			
1946	George Robson (15)	Thorne Engineering Special	114.820	Cliff Bergere	126.471
1947	Mauri Rose (3)	Blue Crown Spark Plug Special	116.338	Ted Horn	126.564
1948	Mauri Rose (3)	Blue Crown Spark Plug Special	119.814	Duke Nalon	131.603
1949	Bill Holland (4)	Blue Crown Spark Plug Special	121.327	Duke Nalon	132.939
1950-c	Johnnie Parsons (5)	Wynn's Friction Proofing	124.002	Walt Faulkner	134.343
1951	Lee Wallard (2)	Belanger Special	126.244	Duke Nalon	136.498
1952	Troy Ruttman (7)	Agajanian Special	128.922	Fred Agabashian	138.010
1953	**Bill Vukovich** (1)	Fuel Injection Special	128.740	Bill Vukovich	138.392
1954	Bill Vukovich (19)	Fuel Injection Special	130.840	Jack McGrath	141.033
1955	Bob Sweikert (14)	John Zink Special	128.213	Jerry Hoyt	140.045
1956	**Pat Flaherty** (1)	John Zink Special	128.490	Pat Flaherty	145.596
1957	Sam Hanks (13)	Belond Exhaust Special	135.601	Pat O'Connor	143.948
1958	Jimmy Bryan (7)	Belond AP Special	133.791	Dick Rathmann	145.974
1959	Rodger Ward (6)	Leader Card 500 Roadster	135.857	Johnny Thomson	145.908
1960	Jim Rathmann (2)	Ken-Paul Special	138.767	Eddie Sachs	146.592

Year	Winner (Pos.)	Car	MPH	Pole Sitter	MPH
1961	A.J. Foyt (7)	Bowes Seal Fast Special	139.130	Eddie Sachs	147.481
1962	Rodger Ward (2)	Leader Card 500 Roadster	140.293	Parnelli Jones	150.370
1963	**Parnelli Jones** (1)	Agajanian-Willard Special	143.137	Parnelli Jones	151.153
1964	A.J. Foyt (5)	Sheraton-Thompson Special	147.350	Jim Clark	158.828
1965	Jim Clark (2)	Lotus Ford	150.686	A.J. Foyt	161.233
1966	Graham Hill (15)	American Red Ball Special	144.317	Mario Andretti	165.899
1967-d	A.J. Foyt (4)	Sheraton-Thompson Special	151.207	Mario Andretti	168.982
1968	Bobby Unser (3)	Rislone Special	152.882	Joe Leonard	171.559
1969	Mario Andretti (2)	STP Oil Treatment Special	156.867	A.J. Foyt	170.568
1970	**Al Unser** (1)	Johnny Lightning Special	155.749	Al Unser	170.221
1971	Al Unser (5)	Johnny Lightning Special	157.735	Peter Revson	178.696
1972	Mark Donohue (3)	Sunoco McLaren	162.962	Bobby Unser	195.940
1973-e	Gordon Johncock (11)	STP Double Oil Filters	159.036	Johnny Rutherford	198.413
1974	Johnny Rutherford (25)	McLaren	158.589	A.J. Foyt	191.632
1975-f	Bobby Unser (3)	Jorgensen Eagle	149.213	A.J. Foyt	193.976
1976-g	**Johnny Rutherford** (1)	Hy-Gain McLaren/Goodyear	148.725	Johnny Rutherford	188.957
1977	A.J. Foyt (4)	Gilmore Racing Team	161.331	Tom Sneva	198.884
1978	Al Unser (5)	FNCTC Chaparral Lola	161.363	Tom Sneva	202.156
1979	**Rick Mears** (1)	The Gould Charge	158.899	Rick Mears	193.736
1980	**Johnny Rutherford** (1)	Pennzoil Chaparral	142.862	Johnny Rutherford	192.256
1981-h	**Bobby Unser** (1)	Norton Spirit Penske PC-9B	139.084	Bobby Unser	200.546
1982	Gordon Johncock (5)	STP Oil Treatment	162.029	Rick Mears	207.004
1983	Tom Sneva (4)	Texaco Star	162.117	Teo Fabi	207.395
1984	Rick Mears (3)	Pennzoil Z-7	163.612	Tom Sneva	210.029
1985	Danny Sullivan (8)	Miller American Special	152.982	Pancho Carter	212.583
1986	Bobby Rahal (4)	Budweiser/Truesports/March	170.722	Rick Mears	216.828
1987	Al Unser (20)	Cummins Holset Turbo	162.175	Mario Andretti	215.390
1988	**Rick Mears** (1)	Pennzoil Z-7/Penske Chevy V-8	144.809	Rick Mears	219.198
1989	Emerson Fittipaldi (3)	Marlboro/Penske Chevy V-8	167.581	Rick Mears	223.885
1990	Arie Luyendyk (3)	Domino's Pizza Chevrolet	185.981*	Emerson Fittipaldi	225.301
1991	**Rick Mears** (1)	Marlboro Penske Chevy	176.457	Rick Mears	224.113
1992	Al Unser Jr. (12)	Valvoline Galmer '92	134.477	Roberto Guerrero	232.482
1993	Emerson Fittipaldi (9)	Marlboro Penske Chevy	157.207	Arie Luyendyk	223.967
1994	**Al Unser Jr.** (1)	Marlboro Penske Mercedes	160.872	Al Unser Jr.	228.011
1995	Jacques Villeneuve (5)	Player's Ltd. Reynard Ford	153.616	Scott Brayton	231.604
1996	Buddy Lazier (5)	Reynard Ford	147.956	Tony Stewart	233.100&
1997	**Arie Luyendyk** (1)	G-Force Olds Aurora	145.827	Arie Luyendyk	218.263
1998	Eddie Cheever Jr. (17)	Dallara Olds Aurora	145.155	Billy Boat	223.503
1999	Kenny Brack (8)	Dallara Olds Aurora	153.176	Arie Luyendyk	225.179
2000	Juan Montoya (2)	G-Force Olds Aurora	167.607	Greg Ray	223.471

*Track record for winning time.
& Scott Brayton won the pole position with an avg. mph of 233.718 but was killed in a practice run. Stewart was given pole position with the next fastest speed.
Notes: a–1916 race scheduled for 300 miles; **b**–rain shortened 1926 race to 400 miles; **c**–rain shortened 1950 race to 345 miles; **d**–1967 race postponed due to rain after 18 laps (May 30), resumed next day (May 31); **e**–rain shortened 1973 race to 332.5 miles; **f**–rain shortened 1975 race to 435 miles; **g**–rain shortened 1976 race to 255 miles; **h**–in 1981, runner-up Mario Andretti was awarded 1st place when winner Bobby Unser was penalized a lap after the race was completed for passing cars illegally under the caution flag. Unser and car-owner Roger Penske appealed the race stewards' decision to the U.S. Auto Club. Four months later, USAC overturned the ruling, saying that the penalty was too harsh and Unser should be fined $40,000 rather than stripped of his championship.

Indy 500 Rookie of the Year

Voted on by a panel of auto racing media. Award does not necessarily go to highest-finishing first-year driver. Graham Hill won the race on his first try in 1966, but the rookie award went to Jackie Stewart, who led with 10 laps to go only to lose oil pressure and finish 6th.

Father and son winners: Mario and Michael Andretti (1965 and 1984); Bill and Billy Vukovich III (1968 and 1988).

Year		Year		Year		Year	
1952	Art Cross	1966	Jackie Stewart	1980	Tim Richmond	1993	Nigel Mansell
1953	Jimmy Daywalt	1967	Denis Hulme	1981	Josele Garza	1994	Jacques Villeneuve
1954	Larry Crockett	1968	Bill Vukovich	1982	Jim Hickman	1995	Christian Fittipaldi
1955	Al Herman	1969	Mark Donohue	1983	Teo Fabi	1996	Tony Stewart
1956	Bob Veith	1970	Donnie Allison	1984	Michael Andretti	1997	Jeff Ward
1957	Don Edmunds	1971	Denny Zimmerman		& Roberto Guerrero	1998	Steve Knapp
1958	George Amick	1972	Mike Hiss	1985	Arie Luyendyk	1999	Robby McGehee
1959	Bobby Grim	1973	Graham McRae	1986	Randy Lanier	2000	Juan Montoya
1960	Jim Hurtubise	1974	Pancho Carter	1987	Fabrizio Barbazza		
1961	Parnelli Jones	1975	Bill Puterbaugh	1988	Billy Vukovich III		
	& Bobby Marshman	1976	Vern Schuppan	1989	Bernard Jourdain		
1962	Jimmy McElreath	1977	Jerry Sneva		& Scott Pruett		
1963	Jim Clark	1978	Rick Mears	1990	Eddie Cheever		
1964	Johnny White		& Larry Rice	1991	Jeff Andretti		
1965	Mario Andretti	1979	Howdy Holmes	1992	Lyn St. James		

IRL Champions

Year		Year		Year		Year	
1996	Buzz Calkins	1997	Tony Stewart	1999	Greg Ray	2000	Buddy Lazier
	& Scott Sharp	1998	Kenny Brack				

IRL Rookie of the Year

Officially the Sprint PCS Rookie of the Year. Award presented to rookie driver who accumulates the most points in the IRL standings.

Year		Year		Year		Year	
1996	None	1998	Robby Unser	1999	Scott Harrington	2000	Airton Dare
1997	Jim Guthrie						

Formula One Circuit
United States Grand Prix

There have been 55 official Formula One races held in the United States since 1950, including the Indianapolis 500 from 1950-60. FISA sanctioned two annual U.S. Grand Prix–USA/East and USA/West–from 1976-80 and 1983-84. Phoenix was the site of the U.S. Grand Prix from 1989-91. Indianapolis hosted the U.S. Grand Prix starting in 2000.

Indianapolis 500

Officially sanctioned as Grand Prix race from 1950-60 only. See IRL Circuit for details.

U.S. Grand Prix–East

Held from 1959-80 and 1981-88 at the following locations: Sebring, Fla. (1959); Riverside, Calif. (1960); Watkins Glen, N.Y. (1961-80); and Detroit (1982-88). There was no race in 1981. Race discontinued in 1989.

Multiple winners: Jim Clark, Graham Hill and Ayrton Senna (3); James Hunt, Carlos Reutemann and Jackie Stewart (2).

Year		Car	Year		Car
1959	Bruce McLaren, NZE	Cooper Climax	1974	Carlos Reutemann, ARG	Brabham Ford
1960	Stirling Moss, GBR	Lotus Climax	1975	Niki Lauda, AUT	Ferrari
1961	Innes Ireland, GBR	Lotus Climax	1976	James Hunt, GBR	McLaren Ford
1962	Jim Clark, GBR	Lotus Climax	1977	James Hunt, GBR	McLaren Ford
1963	Graham Hill, GBR	BRM	1978	Carlos Reutemann, ARG	Ferrari
1964	Graham Hill, GBR	BRM	1979	Gilles Villeneuve, CAN	Ferrari
1965	Graham Hill, GBR	BRM	1980	Alan Jones, AUS	Williams Ford
1966	Jim Clark, GBR	Lotus BRM	1981	Not held	
1967	Jim Clark, GBR	Lotus Ford	1982	John Watson, GBR	McLaren Ford
1968	Jackie Stewart, GBR	Matra Ford	1983	Michele Alboreto, ITA	Tyrrell Ford
1969	Jochen Rindt, AUT	Lotus Ford	1984	Nelson Piquet, BRA	Brabham BMW Turbo
1970	Emerson Fittipaldi, BRA	Lotus Ford	1985	Keke Rosberg, FIN	Williams Honda Turbo
1971	Francois Cevert, FRA	Tyrrell Ford	1986	Ayrton Senna, BRA	Lotus Renault Turbo
1972	Jackie Stewart, GBR	Tyrrell Ford	1987	Ayrton Senna, BRA	Lotus Honda Turbo
1973	Ronnie Peterson, SWE	Lotus Ford	1988	Ayrton Senna, BRA	McLaren Honda Turbo

U.S. Grand Prix–West

Held from 1976-83 at Long Beach, Calif. Races also held in Las Vegas (1981-82), Dallas (1984) and Phoenix (1989-91). Race discontinued in 1992.

Multiple winners: Alan Jones and Ayrton Senna (2).

Year		Car	Year		Car
1976	Clay Regazzoni, SWI	Ferrari	1983	John Watson, GBR	McLaren Ford
1977	Mario Andretti, USA	Lotus Ford	1984	Keke Rosberg, FIN	Williams Honda Turbo
1978	Carlos Reutemann, ARG	Ferrari	1985-88	Not held	
1979	Gilles Villeneuve, CAN	Ferrari	1989	Alain Prost, FRA	McLaren Honda
1980	Nelson Piquet, BRA	Brabham Ford	1990	Ayrton Senna, BRA	McLaren Honda
1981	Alan Jones, AUS	Williams Ford	1991	Ayrton Senna, BRA	McLaren Honda
1982	Niki Lauda, AUT	McLaren Ford			

U.S. Grand Prix

New event in 2000. Held at Indianapolis Motor Speedway.

Year		Car
2000	Michael Schumacher, GER	Ferrari

All-Time Leaders

The all-time Top 15 Grand Prix winning drivers, based on records through 1999. Listed are starts (Sts), poles won (Pole), wins (1st), second place finishes (2nd), and third (3rd). Drivers active in 2000 and career victories in **bold** type.

		Sts	Pole	1st	2nd	3rd			Sts	Pole	1st	2nd	3rd
1	Alain Prost	199	33	**51**	35	20	9	Nelson Piquet	204	24	**23**	20	17
2	Ayrton Senna	161	65	**41**	23	16	10	Damon Hill	99	20	**22**	15	5
3	**M. Schumacher**	117	23	**35**	21	14	11	Stirling Moss	66	16	**16**	5	3
4	Nigel Mansell	187	32	**31**	17	11	12	Jack Brabham	126	13	**14**	10	7
5	Jackie Stewart	99	17	**27**	11	5		Emerson Fittipaldi	144	6	**14**	13	8
6	Jim Clark	72	33	**25**	1	6		Graham Hill	176	13	**14**	15	7
	Niki Lauda	171	24	**25**	20	9		**Mika Hakkinen**	129	22	**14**	7	16
8	Juan-Manuel Fangio	51	28	**24**	10	1	16	Alberto Ascari	32	14	**13**	4	0

World Champions

Officially called the World Championship of Drivers and based on Formula One (Grand Prix) records through the 1998 racing season.

Multiple winners: Juan-Manuel Fangio (5); Alain Prost (4); Jack Brabham, Niki Lauda, Nelson Piquet, Ayrton Senna and Jackie Stewart (3); Alberto Ascari, Jim Clark, Emerson Fittipaldi, Mika Hakkinen, Graham Hill and Michael Schumacher (2).

Year		Car	Year		Car
1950	Guiseppe Farina, ITA	Alfa Romeo	1975	Niki Lauda, AUT	Ferrari
1951	Juan-Manuel Fangio, ARG	Alfa Romeo	1976	James Hunt, GBR	McLaren Ford
1952	Alberto Ascari, ITA	Ferrari	1977	Niki Lauda, AUT	Ferrari
1953	Alberto Ascari, ITA	Ferrari	1978	Mario Andretti, USA	Lotus Ford
1954	Juan-Manuel Fangio, ARG	Maserati/Mercedes	1979	Jody Scheckter, SAF	Ferrari
1955	Juan-Manuel Fangio, ARG	Mercedes	1980	Alan Jones, AUS	Williams Ford
1956	Juan-Manuel Fangio, ARG	Ferrari	1981	Nelson Piquet, BRA	Brabham Ford
1957	Juan-Manuel Fangio, ARG	Maserati	1982	Keke Rosberg, FIN	Williams Ford
1958	Mike Hawthorn, GBR	Ferrari	1983	Nelson Piquet, BRA	Brabham BMW Turbo
1959	Jack Brabham, AUS	Cooper Climax	1984	Niki Lauda, AUT	McL. TAG Porsche Turbo
1960	Jack Brabham, AUS	Cooper Climax	1985	Alain Prost, FRA	McL. TAG Porsche Turbo
1961	Phil Hill, USA	Ferrari	1986	Alain Prost, FRA	McL. TAG Porsche Turbo
1962	Graham Hill, GBR	BRM	1987	Nelson Piquet, BRA	Williams Honda Turbo
1963	Jim Clark, GBR	Lotus Climax	1988	Ayrton Senna, BRA	McLaren Honda Turbo
1964	John Surtees, GBR	Ferrari	1989	Alain Prost, FRA	McLaren Honda
1965	Jim Clark, GBR	Lotus Climax	1990	Ayrton Senna, BRA	McLaren Honda
1966	Jack Brabham, AUS	Brabham Repco	1991	Ayrton Senna, BRA	McLaren Honda
1967	Denis Hulme, NZE	Brabham Repco	1992	Nigel Mansell, GBR	Williams-Renault
1968	Graham Hill, GBR	Lotus Ford	1993	Alain Prost, FRA	Williams-Renault
1969	Jackie Stewart,GBR	Matra Ford	1994	Michael Schumacher, GER	Benetton Ford
1970	Jochen Rindt, AUT	Lotus Ford	1995	Michael Schumacher, GER	Benetton Renault
1971	Jackie Stewart, GBR	Tyrrell Ford	1996	Damon Hill, GBR	Williams-Renault
1972	Emerson Fittipaldi, BRA	Lotus Ford	1997	Jacques Villeneuve, CAN	Williams-Renault
1973	Jackie Stewart, GBR	Tyrrell Ford	1998	Mika Hakkinen, FIN	McLaren-Mercedes
1974	Emerson Fittipaldi, BRA	McLaren Ford	1999	Mika Hakkinen, FIN	McLaren-Mercedes

ENDURANCE RACES

The 24 Hours of Le Mans

Officially, the Le Mans Grand Prix d'Endurance. First run May 22-23, 1923, and won by Andre Lagache and Rene Leonard in a 3-litre Chenard & Walcker. All subsequent races have been held in June, except in 1956 (July) and 1968 (September). Originally contested over a 10.73-mile track, the circuit was shortened to its present 8.451-mile distance in 1932. The original start of Le Mans, where drivers raced across the track to their unstarted cars, was discontinued in 1970.

Multiple winners: Jacky Ickx (6); Derek Bell (5); Yannick Dalmas, Oliver Gendebien and Henri Pescarolo (4); Woolf Barnato, Luigi Chinetti, Hurley Haywood, Phil Hill, Al Holbert and Klaus Ludwig (3); Sir Henry Birkin, Ivoe Bueb, Ron Flockhart, Jean-Pierre Jaussaud, Gerard Larrousse, Andre Rossignol, Raymond Sommer, Hans Stuck, Gijs van Lennep and Jean-Pierre Wimille (2).

Year	Drivers	Car	MPH	Year	Drivers	Car	MPH
1923	Andre Lagache & Rene Leonard	Chenard & Walcker	57.21	1937	Jean-Pierre Wimille & Robert Benoist	Bugatti 57G	85.13
1924	John Duff & Francis Clement	Bentley	53.78	1938	Eugene Chaboud & Jean Tremoulet	Delahaye	82.36
1925	Gerard de Courcelles & Andre Rossignol	La Lorraine	57.84	1939	Jean-Pierre Wimille & Pierre Veyron	Bugatti 57G	86.86
1926	Robert Bloch & Andre Rossignol	La Lorraine	66.08	1940-48	Not held		
1927	J.D. Benjafield & Sammy Davis	Bentley	61.35	1949	Luigi Chinetti & Lord Selsdon	Ferrari	82.28
1928	Woolf Barnato & Bernard Rubin	Bentley	69.11	1950	Louis Rosier & Jean-Louis Rosier	Talbot-Lago	89.71
1929	Woolf Barnato & Sir Henry Birkin	Bentley Speed 6	73.63	1951	Peter Walker & Peter Whitehead	Jaguar C	93.50
1930	Woolf Barnato & Glen Kidston	Bentley Speed 6	75.88	1952	Hermann Lang & Fritz Reiss	Mercedes-Benz	96.67
1931	Earl Howe & Sir Henry Birkin	Alfa Romeo	78.13	1953	Tony Rolt & Duncan Hamilton	Jaguar C	98.65
1932	Raymond Sommer & Luigi Chinetti	Alfa Romeo	76.48	1954	Froilan Gonzalez & Maurice Trintignant	Ferrari 375	105.13
1933	Raymond Sommer & Tazio Nuvolari	Alfa Romeo	81.40	1955	Mike Hawthorn & Ivor Bueb	Jaguar D	107.05
1934	Luigi Chinetti & Philippe Etancelin	Alfa Romeo	74.74	1956	Ron Flockhart & Ninian Sanderson	Jaguar D	104.47
1935	John Hindmarsh & Louis Fontes	Lagonda	77.85	1957	Ron Flockhart & Ivor Bueb	Jaguar D	113.83
1936	Not held			1958	Oliver Gendebien & Phil Hill	Ferrari 250	106.18

AP/Wide World Photos

French driver **Maurice Trintignant** rounds the track en route to a sixth-place finish at the 1953 Le Mans Grand Prix d'Endurance. A year later he and Froilan Gonzalez won the race in a Ferrari 375.

Year	Drivers	Car	MPH
1959	Roy Salvadori & Carroll Shelby	Aston Martin	112.55
1960	Oliver Gendebien & Paul Fräre	Ferrari 250	109.17
1961	Oliver Gendebien & Phil Hill	Ferrari 250	115.88
1962	Oliver Gendebien & Phil Hill	Ferrari 250	115.22
1963	Lodovico Scarfiotti & Lorenzo Bandini	Ferrari 250	118.08
1964	Jean Guichel & Nino Vaccarella	Ferrari 275	121.54
1965	Masten Gregory & Jochen Rindt	Ferrari 250	121.07
1966	Bruce McLaren & Chris Amon	Ford Mk. II	125.37
1967	A.J. Foyt & Dan Gurney	Ford Mk. IV	135.46
1968	Pedro Rodriguez & Lucien Bianchi	Ford GT40	115.27
1969	Jacky Ickx & Jackie Oliver	Ford GT40	129.38
1970	Hans Herrmann & Richard Attwood	Porsche 917	119.28
1971	Gijs van Lennep & Helmut Marko	Porsche 917	138.13
1972	Graham Hill & Henri Pescarolo	Matra-Simca	121.45
1973	Henri Pescarolo & Gerard Larrousse	Matra-Simca	125.67
1974	Henri Pescarolo & Gerard Larrousse	Matra-Simca	119.27
1975	Derek Bell & Jacky Ickx	Mirage-Ford	118.98

Year	Drivers	Car	MPH
1976	Jacky Ickx & Gijs van Lennep	Porsche 936	123.49
1977	Jacky Ickx, Jurgen Barth & Hurley Haywood	Porsche 936	120.95
1978	Jean-Pierre Jaussaud & Didier Pironi	Renault-Alpine	130.60
1979	Klaus Ludwig, Bill Wittington & Don Whittington	Porsche 935	108.10
1980	Jean-Pierre Jaussaud & Jean Rondeau	Rondeau-Cosworth	119.23
1981	Jacky Ickx & Derek Bell	Porsche 936	124.94
1982	Jacky Ickx & Derek Bell	Porsche 956	126.85
1983	Vern Schuppan, Hurley Haywood & Al Holbert	Porsche 956	130.70
1984	Klaus Ludwig & Henri Pescarolo	Porsche 956	126.88
1985	Klaus Ludwig, Paolo Barilla & John Winter	Porsche 956	131.75
1986	Derek Bell, Hans Stuck & Al Holbert	Porsche 962	128.75
1987	Derek Bell, Hans Stuck & Al Holbert	Porsche 962	124.06
1988	Jan Lammers, Johnny Dumfries & Andy Wallace	Jaguar XJR	137.75
1989	Jochen Mass, Manuel Reuter & Stanley Dickens	Sauber-Mercedes	136.39
1990	John Nielsen, Price Cobb & Martin Brundle	Jaguar XJR-12	126.71
1991	Volker Weider, Johnny Herbert & Bertrand Gachof	Mazda 787B	127.31
1992	Derek Warwick, Yannick Dalmas & Mark Blundell	Peugeot 905B	123.89
1993	Geoff Brabham, Christophe Bouchut & Eric Helary	Peugeot 905	132.58
1994	Yannick Dalmas, Hurley Haywood & Mauro Baldi	Porsche 962LM	129.82
1995	Yannick Dalmas, J.J. Lehto & Masanori Sekiya	McLaren BMW	105.00
1996	Davy Jones, Manuel Reuter & Alexander Wurz	TWR Porsche	124.65
1997	Michele Alberto, Stefan Johansson & Tom Kristensen	TWR Porsche	126.88
1998	Laurent Aiello, Allan McNish & Stephane Ortelli	Porsche 911 GT1	123.86
1999	Yannick Dalmas, Joachim Winkelhock & Pierluigi Martini	BMW V-12 LMR	129.37
2000	Frank Biela, Tom Kristensen & Emanuele Pirro	Audi R8	128.34

The 24 Hours of Daytona

Officially, the Rolex 24 at Daytona. First run in 1962 as a three-hour race and won by Dan Gurney in a Lotus 19 Ford. Contested over a 3.56-mile course at Daytona (Fla.) International Speedway. There have been several distance changes since 1962: the event was a three-hour race (1962-63); a 2,000-kilometer race (1964-65); a 24-hour race (1966-71); a six-hour race (1972) and a 24-hour race again since 1973. The race was canceled in 1974 due to a national energy crisis.

Multiple winners: Hurley Haywood (5); Peter Gregg, Pedro Rodriguez and Bob Wollek (4); Derek Bell, Butch Leitzinger and Rolf Stommelen (3); A.J. Foyt, Al Holbert, Ken Miles, Brian Redman, Elliott Forbes-Robinson, Lloyd Ruby, Al Unser Jr. and Andy Wallace (2).

Year	Drivers	Car	MPH	Year	Drivers	Car	MPH
1962	Dan Gurney	Lotus 19 Ford	104.101	1986	Al Holbert, Derek Bell & Al Unser Jr	Porsche 962	105.484
1963	Pedro Rodriguez	Ferrari GTO	102.074	1987	Al Holbert, Derek Bell, Chip Robinson & Al Unser Jr	Porsche 962	111.599
1964	Pedro Rodriguez & Phil Hill	Ferrari GTO	98.230	1988	Raul Boesel, Martin Brundle & John Nielsen	Jaguar XJR-9	107.943
1965	Ken Miles & Lloyd Ruby	Ford GT	99.944	1989	John Andretti, Derek Bell & Bob Wollek	Porsche 962	92.009
1966	Ken Miles & Lloyd Ruby	Ford Mk. II	108.020	1990	Davy Jones, Jan Lammers & Andy Wallace	Jaguar XJR-12	112.857
1967	Lorenzo Bandini & Chris Amon	Ferrari 330	105.688	1991	Hurley Haywood, John Winter, Frank Jelinski, Henri Pescarolo & Bob Wollek	Porsche 962-C	106.633
1968	Vic Elford & Jochen Neerpasch	Porsche 907	106.697	1992	Masahiro Hasemi, Kazuyoshi Hoshino & Toshio Suzuki	Nissan R-91	112.897
1969	Mark Donohue & Chuck Parsons	Lola Chevrolet	99.268	1993	P.J. Jones, Mark Dismore & Rocky Moran	Toyota Eagle	103.537
1970	Pedro Rodriguez & Leo Kinnunen	Porsche 917	114.866	1994	Paul Gentilozzi, Scott Pruett, Butch Leitzinger & Steve Millen	Nissan 300 ZXT	104.80
1971	Pedro Rodriguez & Jackie Oliver	Porsche 917K	109.203	1995	Jurgen Lassig, Christophe Bouchut, Giovanni Lavaggi & Marco Werner	Porsche Spyder	102.280
1972	Mario Andretti & Jacky Ickx	Ferrari 312P	122.573	1996	Wayne Taylor, Scott Sharp & Jim Pace	Oldsmobile Arness MK-III	103.32
1973	Peter Gregg & Hurley Haywood	Porsche Carrera	106.225	1997	Rob Dyson, James Weaver, Butch Leitzinger, Andy Wallace, John Paul Jr., Eliot Forbes-Robinson & John Schneider	Ford R&S MK-III	102.29
1974	Not held			1998	Mauro Baldi, Arie Luyendyk & Gianpiero Moretti		
1975	Peter Gregg & Hurley Haywood	Porsche Carrera	108.531	1999	Elliot Forbes-Robinson, Butch Leitzinger & Andy Wallace	Riley & Scott Ford	104.957
1976	Peter Gregg, Brian Redman & John Fitzpatrick	BMW CSL	104.040	2000	Olivier Beretta, Dominique Dupuy & Karl Wendlinger	Dodge Viper	107.207
1977	Hurley Haywood, John Graves & Dave Helmick	Porsche Carrera	108.801				
1978	Peter Gregg, Rolf Stommelen & Antoine Hezemans	Porsche Turbo	108.743				
1979	Hurley Haywood, Ted Field & Danny Ongais	Porsche Turbo	109.249				
1980	Rolf Stommelen, Volkert Merl & Reinhold Joest	Porsche Turbo	114.303				
1981	Bobby Rahal, Brian Redman & Bob Garretson	Porsche Turbo	113.153				
1982	John Paul Sr., John Paul Jr. & Rolf Stommelen	Porsche Turbo	114.794				
1983	A.J. Foyt, Preston Henn, Bob Wollek & Claude Ballot-Lena	Porsche Turbo	98.781				
1984	Sarel van der Merwe, Tony Martin & Graham Duxbury	March Porsche	103.119				
1985	A.J. Foyt, Bob Wollek, Al Unser Sr. & Thierry Boutsen	Porsche 962	104.162				

NHRA Drag Racing
NHRA Winston Champions

Based on points earned during the NHRA Winston Drag Racing series. The series began for Top Fuel, Funny Car and Pro Stock in 1975.

Top Fuel

Multiple winners: Joe Amato (5); Don Garlits and Shirley Muldowney (3); Scott Kalitta and Gary Scelzi (2).

Year		Year		Year		Year	
1975	Don Garlits	1982	Shirley Muldowney	1989	Gary Ormsby	1996	Kenny Bernstein
1976	Richard Tharp	1983	Gary Beck	1990	Joe Amato	1997	Gary Scelzi
1977	Shirley Muldowney	1984	Joe Amato	1991	Joe Amato	1998	Gary Scelzi
1978	Kelly Brown	1985	Don Garlits	1992	Joe Amato	1999	Tony Schumacher
1979	Rob Bruins	1986	Don Garlits	1993	Eddie Hill		
1980	Shirley Muldowney	1987	Dick LaHaie	1994	Scott Kalitta		
1981	Jeb Allen	1988	Joe Amato	1995	Scott Kalitta		

Funny Car

Multiple winners: John Force (9); Don Prudhomme, Kenny Bernstein (4); Raymond Beadle (3); Frank Hawley (2).

Year		Year		Year		Year	
1975	Don Prudhomme	1982	Frank Hawley	1989	Bruce Larson	1996	John Force
1976	Don Prudhomme	1983	Frank Hawley	1990	John Force	1997	John Force
1977	Don Prudhomme	1984	Mark Oswald	1991	John Force	1998	John Force
1978	Don Prudhomme	1985	Kenny Bernstein	1992	Cruz Pedregon	1999	John Force
1979	Raymond Beadle	1986	Kenny Bernstein	1993	John Force		
1980	Raymond Beadle	1987	Kenny Bernstein	1994	John Force		
1981	Raymond Beadle	1988	Kenny Bernstein	1995	John Force		

Pro Stock

Multiple winners: Bob Glidden (9); Warren Johnson (5); Lee Shepherd (4); Darrell Alderman and Jim Yates (2).

Year		Year		Year		Year	
1975	Bob Glidden	1982	Lee Shepherd	1989	Bob Glidden	1996	Jim Yates
1976	Larry Lombardo	1983	Lee Shepherd	1990	John Myers	1997	Jim Yates
1977	Don Nicholson	1984	Lee Shepherd	1991	Darrell Alderman	1998	Warren Johnson
1978	Bob Glidden	1985	Bob Glidden	1992	Warren Johnson	1999	Warren Johnson
1979	Bob Glidden	1986	Bob Glidden	1993	Warren Johnson		
1980	Bob Glidden	1987	Bob Glidden	1994	Darrell Alderman		
1981	Lee Shepherd	1988	Bob Glidden	1995	Warren Johnson		

All-Time Leaders
Career Victories

All-time leaders through 1999. Drivers active in 2000 are in **bold**.

	Top Fuel			Funny Car			Pro Stock	
1	**Joe Amato**	50	1	**John Force**	81	1	Bob Glidden	85
2	Don Garlits	35	2	Don Prudhomme	35	2	**Warren Johnson**	81
3	**Cory McClenathan**	24	3	**Kenny Bernstein**	30	3	**Darrell Alderman**	27
4	**Kenny Bernstein**	21	4	**Cruz Pedregon**	21	4	Lee Shepherd	26
5	Gary Beck	19	5	Mark Oswald	18	5	**Jim Yates**	22

National-Event Victories (pro categories)

1	Bob Glidden	85	8	Don Garlits	35	15	Ed McCulloch	22
2	**John Force**	81	9	John Myers	33		**Jim Yates**	22
3	**Warren Johnson**	79	10	**Darrell Alderman**	27	17	**Cruz Pedregon**	21
4	**Kenny Bernstein**	52	11	Lee Shepherd	26	18	**Mike Dunn**	20
5	**Joe Amato**	50	12	**Cory McClenathan**	24		Mark Oswald	20
6	Don Prudhomme	49		Terry Vance	24	20	Gary Beck	19
7	**Dave Schultz**	43	14	**Matt Hines**	23			

Fastest Mile-Per-Hour Speeds

Fastest performances in NHRA major event history through 1999.

Top Fuel	Funny Car	Pro Stock
MPH	**MPH**	**MPH**
330.23 . . Tony Schumacher, 2/28/99	324.05 . . . . John Force, 3/21/99	202.36 . Warren Johnson, 10/31/99
327.90 . . Tony Schumacher, 10/3/99	324.05 . . . . John Force, 3/21/99	202.33 . Warren Johnson, 10/23/99
327.27 . . Tony Schumacher, 4/25/99	323.89 . . . . John Force, 5/17/98	202.24 . . Warren Johnson, 4/30/99
327.03 . Tony Schumacher, 11/13/99	323.35 . . . . John Force, 5/15/98	202.15 . Warren Johnson, 10/23/99
326.91 . . Tony Schumacher, 10/22/99	322.81 . . . . . . John Force, 10/25/98	202.02 . . . . . Kurt Johnson, 10/23/99
	322.81 . . . . Tony Pedregon, 4/25/99	

Boxing

Andrew Golota *refuses to take the mouthpiece from trainer Al Certo, quitting his fight with Mike Tyson after two rounds.*

Building a Better Tomorrow Today

Several top fighters have constructive years as boxing tries to bounce back from the pitfalls of yesterday.

by

Al Bernstein

After a lackluster 1999, boxing, much like a beleaguered professional sports franchise, needed a "rebuilding" year in 2000. Throughout the year the sport tried to build up both new and old attractions, create "mega-fights" and restore excitement to the sport.

Most of the major matches of the year turned out to be exciting affairs. Shane Mosley's close and thrilling decision win over Oscar De La Hoya played to a packed house at the Staples Center in Los Angeles and a huge pay-per-view audience as well. It proved that Mosley could be a big force as a welterweight and vaulted him into superstar status. For De La Hoya it was his second loss in three

Al Bernstein has been ESPN's boxing analyst since 1980.

fights and his comments after the fight were viewed by many as sour grapes. Then the turmoil continued for him when he initiated a split from his longtime promoter Bob Arum. He filed suit to get out of his contract, setting off a legal battle with Arum.

Joining Mosley in the superstar ranks was Fernando Vargas who won a scintillating showdown with Ike Quartey, en route to a planned December pay-per-view battle with Felix Trinidad. For Trinidad it was another year of winning and another year of beating a U.S. Olympic gold medallist. To go along with his win over De La Hoya in 1999, he added a 2000 victory over David Reid and won the WBA junior middleweight title in the process.

For the best fight of the year we look to the super bantamweight division where Erik Morales and Marco

In perhaps the biggest, and certainly one of the more exciting fights of 2000, **"Sugar" Shane Mosley**, right, edged **Oscar De La Hoya** for the WBA welterweight title in Los Angeles.

Antonio Barrera fought 12 fierce rounds in a title unification match. Morales won a close and disputed decision to take home the WBC and WBO belts. One or both of them could face the box-office king Prince Naseem Hamed in the coming year. Hamed defended his featherweight title twice but looked very vulnerable against inexperienced Augie Sanchez.

The heavyweight division produced its normal share of drama inside and outside the ring. In the ring, following his win over Evander Holyfield in late 1999, Lennox Lewis easily dispatched both Michael Grant and Frans Botha while preparing for a big November date with hard-punching David Tua. In the process Lewis finally started to receive the respect from the boxing community that had previously been withheld from the British champion.

Lewis did lose one of his titles outside the ring when he was stripped of the WBA belt. That belt ended up around a familiar waist—that of Evander Holyfield. He beat number one contender John Ruiz, getting yet another controversial decision win and fighting poorly in the process.

The Mike Tyson circus continued with two wins, one punctuated by both an attack on Lou Savarese well after the referee stopped the fight and a bizarre verbal assault on Lewis during a post-fight television interview. All this set the stage for an Oct. 20 meeting with Andrew Golota, another magnet for controversy. The fight, as might have been expected, ended abruptly, when Golota quit after the second round despite his corner's insistence that he continue with the fight. It turned out that Golota had a

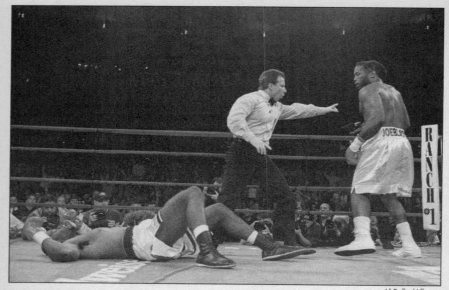

Heavyweight champion **Lennox Lewis** earned some well-deserved respect after demolishing highly regarded contender **Michael Grant** in two rounds in the battle of the giant heavyweights.

concussion, a fractured cheekbone and a herniated disc in his back.

It was a breakthrough year for several young champions like Zab Judah, Acelino Freitas and Diego Corrales, but a disappointing year for 1999 star Floyd Mayweather Jr. He was mostly inactive, had contract difficulties with his promoter and HBO, and had a highly publicized break up with his manager-trainer-father Floyd Mayweather Sr. After his 12-round unanimous decision over Goyo Vargas in March, it wasn't until late October that Mayweather got back to work, stopping Emanuel Burton in the ninth round of their WBC super featherweight bout.

Light heavyweight champ Roy Jones Jr. stayed active, defending his title while waiting (still) for a big challenge that would equate to big pay-per-view money. He hopes that might arrive in 2001 against Felix Trinidad. Jones now has moved down to 168 pounds—a weight Trinidad says he can reach for a showdown with Jones this coming year.

The always colorful Johnny Tapia had an eventful year, moving up to win and then defend the WBO bantamweight title. He also faced more personal demons when he checked into a hospital suffering from depression. But he emerged ready for an October rematch with Paulie Ayala, the man who beat him in a close decision in 1999's Fight of the Year.

As 2000 closed with a slate of big fights scheduled, boxing was indeed culminating the kind of rebuilding year it needed. ∎

Al Bernstein's Top Ten Stories of the Year in Boxing

10. **Clarence "Bones" Adams wins title:** In the surprise of the year the likeable journeyman beats Nestor Garza for the WBA super bantamweight title.

9. **Floyd Mayweather Jr. is largely inactive:** The superstar of 1999 becomes boxing's invisible man in 2000.

8. **Julio Cesar Chavez Retires?** If this decision sticks, it's the end of a long, mostly great career for the Mexican fighter.

7. **Bob Lee acquitted of bribery charges:** The IBF president beats the rap on all but six of 33 counts of bribery, extortion and racketeering in connection with the ratings of boxers over the past 17 years.

6. **Fernando Vargas decisions Ike Quartey:** In a great match Vargas establishes himself as a bona fide star, successfully defending his IBF junior middleweight belt and setting up a meeting with Felix Trinidad.

5. **The WBA strips Lennox Lewis,** the undisputed heavyweight champion of the world, fragmenting the world heavyweight championship once again.

4. **Lennox Lewis knocks out Michael Grant:** Lewis shines at Madison Square Garden and finally gets some of the respect that was overdue, while Grant proves he is not quite ready for prime time.

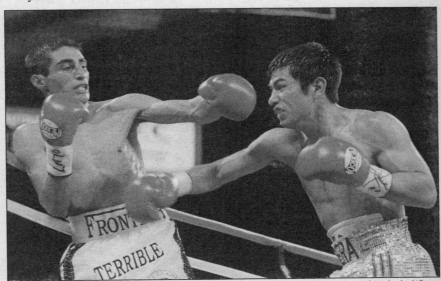

Jed Jacobsohn/Allsport

Erik Morales, left, barely edges **Marco Antonio Barrera** in their war of a WBC-WBO super bantamweight unification bout. The hard-fought battle was widely considered the Fight of the Year.

3. **Oscar De La Hoya splits with Bob Arum:** Boxing's biggest draw bolts from his longtime promoter.

2. **Erik Morales edges Marco Antonio Barrera** in their Feb. 19 WBC-WBO super bantamweight unification bout. In what is certainly the fight of the year, the momentum swings back and forth and despite the official outcome, there is no real loser here.

1. **Shane Mosley beats Oscar De La Hoya**. "Sugar" Shane steps up to welterweight from lightweight, showing he can move up in weight and still be terrific. ∎

insidethenumbers

WELTERWEIGHT TITLE RUNS

Before Felix Trinidad gained weight he put together an amazing run in the welterweight division. With his win over Oscar De La Hoya in their highly-anticipated meeting, Trinidad brought his run of successful title defenses to 15. Here's a look at the most consecutive welterweight title defenses since WWI:

	Years	Fights
Henry Armstrong	1938-40	19
Felix Trinidad	1993-99	15
Pipino Cuevas	1976-80	11
Jose Napoles	1971-75	10
Pernell Whitaker	1993-97	8

IRON EFFICIENCY

Mike Tyson's 38-second demolition of Lou Savarese was tied for the third-quickest knockout of his career. The other four KOs Tyson had under 40 seconds in his career were during his initial rise to the top, including his 30-second disposal of Marvis Frazier in 1986. Tyson also holds two of the five quickest knockouts in heavyweight "title" history with a 91-second KO of Michael Spinks in 1988 and a 93-second ouster of Carl "The Truth" Williams a year later. Here's a look at Iron Mike's quickest KOs:

Date	Opponent, Site	Seconds
1986	Marvis Frazier, Glens Falls, NY	30
1985	Robert Colay, Atlantic City	37
2000	Lou Savarese, Glasgow	38
1985	Rick Spain, Atlantic City	38
1985	Michael Johnson, Atlantic City	39

Note: All were non-title bouts.

HEAVYWEIGHT TITLE RUNS

Entering his Nov. 11 bout with David Tua, Lennox Lewis was 8-0-1 in his last nine heavyweight title fights. That's the longest unbeaten run by any heavyweight since Mike Tyson won 10 straight title bouts in the late 1980's. Lewis' nine-match unbeaten streak in heavyweight championship bouts ranks fifth best among all heavyweights dating back to 1950. Here is a look at the list of heavyweights since 1950 with the longest unbeaten streaks in title bouts.

	Years	Fights
Larry Holmes	1978-85	21
Muhammad Ali	1974-77	11
Mike Tyson	1986-89	10
Muhammad Ali	1964-67	10
Lennox Lewis	1997-00	9
Rocky Marciano	1952-55	7

∎

Current Champions
WBA, WBC and IBF Titleholders (through Oct. 23, 2000)

The champions of professional boxing's 17 principal weight divisions, as recognized by the Word Boxing Association (WBA), World Boxing Council (WBC) and International Boxing Federation (IBF).

	Weight Limit	WBA Champion	WBC Champion	IBF Champion
Heavyweight	—	Evander Holyfield 37-4-1, 25 KOs	Lennox Lewis 37-1-1, 29 KOs	Lennox Lewis 37-1-1, 29 KOs
Cruiserweight	190 lbs	Fabrice Tiozzo 42-1-0, 28 KOs	Juan Carlos Gomez 31-0-0, 25 KOs	Vassily Jirov 26-0-0, 24 KOs
Light Heavyweight	175 lbs	Roy Jones Jr. 43-1-0, 35 KOs	Roy Jones Jr. 43-1-0, 35 KOs	Roy Jones Jr. 43-1-0, 35 KOs
Super Middleweight	168 lbs	Bruno Girard 38-2-1, 5 KOs	Dingaan Thobela 40-7-2, 25 KOs	Sven Ottke 20-0-0, 2 KOs
Middleweight	160 lbs	William Joppy 31-1-1, 23 KOs	Keith Holmes 34-2-0, 23 KOs	Bernard Hopkins 37-2-1, 27 KOs
Jr. Middleweight	154 lbs	Felix Trinidad 38-0-0, 31 KOs	Javier Castillejo 50-4-0, 32 KOs	Fernando Vargas 20-0-0, 18 KOs
Welterweight	147 lbs	Vacant	Shane Mosley 35-0-0, 32 KOs	Vacant
Jr. Welterweight	140 lbs	Sharmba Mitchell 47-2-0, 29 KOs	Kostya Tszyu 25-1-1, 21 KOs	Zab Judah 24-0-0, 18 KOs
Lightweight	135 lbs	Takanori Hatakeyama 23-1-2, 18 KOs	Jose Luis Castillo 41-4-0, 37 KOs	Paul Spadafora 31-0-0, 14 KOs
Jr. Lightweight	130 lbs	Joel Casamayor 23-0-0, 14 KOs	Floyd Mayweather Jr. 23-0-0, 17 KOs	Diego Corrales 33-0-0, 27 KOs
Featherweight	126 lbs	Derrick Gainer 36-5-0, 20 KOs	Guty Espadas* 33-2-0, 21KOs	Paul Ingle 23-1-1, 16 KOs
Jr. Featherweight	122 lbs	Clarence Adams* 40-3-3, 19 KOs	Willie Jorrin 27-0-0, 12 KOs	Lehlohonolo Ledwaba 30-1-1, 20 KOs
Bantamweight	118 lbs	Paulie Ayala 30-1-0, 12 KOs	Veerapol Sahaprom 27-1-0, 18 KOs	Tim Austin 21-0-1, 19 KOs
Jr. Bantamweight	115 lbs	Leo Gamez 33-7-1, 25 KOs	Masanori Tokuyama 22-2-01, 5 KOs	Felix Machado 19-3-1, 10 KOs
Flyweight	112 lbs	Eric Morel 27-0-0, 16 KOs	Malcolm Tunacao 11-0-1, 7 KOs	Irene Pacheco 24-0-0, 19 KOs
Jr. Flyweight	108 lbs	Beibis Mendoza 27-0-0, 23 KOs	Choi Yo-sam 22-1-0, 11 KOs	Ricardo Lopez 48-0-1, 35 KOs
Minimumweight	105 lbs	Joma Gamboa 29-5-1, 20 KOs	Jose Antonio Aguirre 24-1-1, 15 KOs	Zolani Petelo 16-2-2, 9 KOs

Note: The following weight divisions are also known by these names—**Cruiserweight** as Jr. Heavyweight; **Jr. Middleweight** as Super Welterweight; **Jr. Welterweight** as Super Lightweight; **Jr. Lightweight** as Super Featherweight; **Jr. Featherweight** as Super Bantamweight; **Jr. Bantamweight** as Super Flyweight; **Jr. Flyweight** as Light Flyweight; and **Minimum** as Strawweight or Mini-Flyweights.

*Erik Morales (37-0-0, 29 KOs) is currently the interim WBC featherweight champ. Antonio Cermeno (36-3-0, 23 KOs) is currently the interim WBA junior featherweight champ.

Major Bouts, 1999-2000

Division by division, from Oct. 17, 1999 through Oct. 23, 2000.

WBA, WBC and IBF champions are listed in **bold** type. Note the following Result column abbreviations (in alphabetical order): **Disq.** (won by disqualification); **KO** (knockout); **MDraw** (majority draw); **NC** (no contest); **SDraw** (split draw); **TDraw** (technical draw); **TKO** (technical knockout); **TWm** (won by technical majority decision); **TWs** (won by technical split decision); **TWu** (won by technical unanimous decision); **Wm** (won by majority decision); **Ws** (won by split decision) and **Wu** (won by unanimous decision).

Heavyweights

Date	Winner	Loser	Result	Title	Site
Nov. 13	**Lennox Lewis**	**Evander Holyfield**	Wu 12	**WBA-WBC-IBF**	Las Vegas
Dec. 4	Wladimir Klitschko	Lajos Eros	KO 2	—	Hannover, GER
Dec. 11	Vitali Klitschko	Obed Sullivan	TKO 9	WBO	Hamburg, GER
Dec. 12	John Ruiz	Thomas Williams	TKO 2	—	Tunica, Miss.
Jan. 8	Francois Botha	Steve Pannell	TKO 1	—	Albuquerque
Jan. 15	David Izon	Derrick Jefferson	TKO 9	—	New York City
Jan. 19	Chris Byrd	David Washington	TKO 10	—	Mt. Pleasant, Mich.
Jan. 29	Mike Tyson	Julius Francis	TKO 2	—	Manchester, England
Feb. 12	Oliver McCall	Ric Lainhart	TKO 1	—	Pembroke Pines, Fla.
Feb. 22	Henry Akinwande	Christopher Serengo	TKO 1	—	Cape Town, S. Africa
Mar. 1	Hasim Rahman	Moe Wilson	Wu 10	—	Woodlawn, Md.
Mar. 18	Wladimir Klitschko	Paea Wolfgamm	KO 1	—	Hamburg, GER
Apr. 1	Chris Byrd	Vitali Klitschko	TKO 10*	WBO	Berlin
Apr. 1	Obed Sullivan	Jeff Lally	TKO 3	—	Laughlin, Nev.
Apr. 22	Andrew Golota	Marcus Rhode	TKO 3	—	Guangzhou, CHN
Apr. 29	**Lennox Lewis**	Michael Grant	KO 2	**WBA-WBC-IBF**	New York City
May 20	Hasim Rahman	Corrie Sanders	TKO 7	—	Atlantic City
May 20	Oleg Maskaev	Derrick Jefferson	TKO 4	—	Atlantic City
May 25	Larry Donald	Phil Jackson	KO 5	—	Tunica, Miss.
May 25	Henry Akinwande	Russell Chasteen	TKO 5	—	Tunica, Miss.
May 25	Oliver McCall	Markus McIntyre	TKO 3	—	Tunica, Miss.
June 3	David Tua	Obed Sullivan	KO 1	—	Las Vegas
June 11	Lance "Mount" Whitaker	Thomas Williams	TKO 2	—	Conco, Oklahoma
June 16	Andrew Golota	Orlin Norris	Wu 10	—	Las Vegas
June 24	Mike Tyson	Lou Savarese	TKO 1	—	Glasgow
July 8	Tim Witherspoon	David Smith	KO 1	—	Monroe, La.
July 15	**Lennox Lewis**	Francois Botha	TKO 2	**WBC-IBF**	London
July 15	Wladimir Klitschko	Monte Barrett	TKO 7	—	London
July 21	David Tua	Robert Daniels	KO 3	—	Las Vegas
July 21	Lance "Mount" Whitaker	David Dixon	Disq. 1†	—	Las Vegas
Aug. 5	Cliff Couser	Jorge Luis Gonzalez	TKO 3	—	Philadelphia, Pa.
Aug. 5	Hasim Rahman	Frankie Swindell	TKO 7	—	Las Vegas
Aug. 11	Oliver McCall	Sedrick Fields	Ws 10	—	Las Vegas
Aug. 12	Evander Holyfield	John Ruiz	Wu 12	**WBA**	Las Vegas
Oct. 7	Kirk Johnson	Oleg Maskaev	TKO 4	—	Uncasville, Conn.
Oct. 7	Lance "Mount" Whitaker	Robert Davis	TKO 2	—	Uncasville, Conn.
Oct. 14	Wladimir Klitschko	Chris Byrd	Wu 12	WBO	Cologne, GER
Oct. 20	Mike Tyson	Andrew Golota	Wu 12	—	Auburn Hills, Mich.

Note: Lennox Lewis was stripped of the WBA belt when he agreed to fight Michael Grant instead of meeting John Ruiz, the WBA's No. 1 contender at the time. Evander Holyfield beat John Ruiz for the vacant title on Aug. 12.
*Klitschko tore a rotator cuff in his shoulder and did not answer the bell for the tenth round.
†Referee Richard Steele disqualified Dixon for repeated low blows at 2:51 of the first round.

Cruiserweights (190 lbs)
(Jr. Heavyweights)

Date	Winner	Loser	Result	Title	Site
Nov. 6	Johnny Nelson	Christopher Girard	KO 4	WBO	Widnes, ENG
Nov. 13	**Fabrice Tiozzo**	Ken Murphy	TKO 7	**WBA**	Las Vegas
Dec. 11	**Juan Carlos Gomez**	Napoleon Tagoe	KO 9	**WBC**	Hamburg, GER
Feb. 12	**Vassiliy Jirov**	Saul Montana	TKO 9	**IBF**	Boise, Idaho
Feb. 17	Monte Barrett	James Thunder	TKO 7	—	New York City
Feb. 17	Shannon Briggs	Warren Williams	KO 3	—	New York City
Mar. 11	**Juan Carlos Gomez**	Mohamed Siluvangi	TKO 2	**WBC**	Lubeck, GER
Apr. 1	Johnny Nelson	Pietro Aurino	TKO 7	WBO	Berlin
Apr. 8	**Fabrice Tiozzo**	Valery Vikhor	KO 6	**WBA**	Paris
May 6	**Juan Carlos Gomez**	Imamu Mayfield	KO 3	**WBC**	Neuss, GER
May 13	Carl Thompson	Alain Simon	TKO 6	—	Barnsley, ENG
May 19	**Vassiliy Jirov**	Esteban Pizzaro	KO 3	**IBF**	Beverly Hills, Calif.
June 3	Torsten May	Valery Semishkur	TKO 3	—	Karlsruhe, GER
July 29	**Vassiliy Jirov**	Earl Butler	KO 2	**IBF**	Phoenix
Sept. 25	Carl Thompson	Alexei Illin	TKO 2	—	Barnsley, ENG

Light Heavyweights (175 lbs)

Date	Winner	Loser	Result	Title	Site
Jan. 9	Greg Wright............Darrell Spinks		Wm 12	—	Bay St.Louis, Miss.
Jan. 15	**Roy Jones Jr.** ....David Telesco		Wu 12	**WBA-WBC-IBF**	New York City
Apr. 15	Dariuz Michalczewski.....Graciano Rocchigiani		TKO 10*	WBO	Hannover, GER
Apr. 29	Clinton Woods...........Ole Klemetson		TKO 9	—	London
May 13	**Roy Jones Jr.** ....Richard Hall		TKO 11	**WBA-WBC-IBF**	Indianapolis
Sept. 9	**Roy Jones Jr.** ....Eric Harding		TKO 10	**WBA-WBC-IBF**	New Orleans

*Graciano Rocchigiani's corner threw the towel in at the end of the ninth round.

Super Middleweights (168 lbs)

Date	Winner	Loser	Result	Title	Site
Oct. 23	Markus Beyer...........**Richie Woodhall**		Wu 12	**WBC**	London
Nov. 27	**Sven Ottke** ....Glen Johnson		Wu 12	**IBF**	Dusseldorf, GER
Dec. 11	**Byron Mitchell** ....Bruno Girard		Sdraw 12	**WBA**	Tunica, Miss.
Jan. 29	Joe Calzaghe ....David Starie		Wu 12	WBO	Manchester, ENG
Jan. 29	**Markus Beyer** ....Leif Keiski		KO 7	**WBC**	Riesa, GER
Mar. 11	**Sven Ottke** ....Lloyd Bryan		Wu 12	**IBF**	Magdeburg, GER
Apr. 8	Bruno Girard ....**Byron Mitchell**		Wu 12	**WBA**	Paris
May 6	Glenn Catley ....**Markus Beyer**		TKO 12	**WBC**	Frankfurt, GER
May 6	Richie Woodhall.........Errol McDonald		TKO 6	—	Frankfurt, GER
May 26	Thomas Tate ....Anthony Andrews		TKO 5	—	Ledyard, Conn.
June 2	Omar Sheika ....Glen Johnson		Wu 10	—	Philadelphia
June 3	**Sven Ottke** ....Tocker Pudwill		Wu 12	**IBF**	Karlsruhe, GER
June 16	Roberto Duran ....Pat Lawlor		Wu 12	—	Panama City
June 24	Silvio Branco...........Robin Reid		Wu 12	—	Glasgow
Aug. 12	Roberto Duran ....Patrick Goossen		Wu 10	—	Yakima, Wash.
Aug. 12	Joe Calzaghe ....Omar Sheika		TKO 5	WBO	London
Sept. 1	Dingaan Thobela........**Glenn Catley**		TKO 12	**WBC**	Brakpan, S.A.
Sept. 2	**Sven Ottke** ....Charles Brewer		Ws 12	**IBF**	Magdenburg, GER
Sept. 16	Andei Shkalikov.........Frederik Alvarez		TKO 8	—	Loiret Cher, FRA
Sept. 16	**Bruno Girard** ....Manuel Slaca		Wu 12	**WBA**	Chateaubroux, FRA

Middleweights (160 lbs)

Date	Winner	Loser	Result	Title	Site
Dec. 12	**Bernard Hopkins** ......Antwun Echols		Wu 12	**IBF**	Miami
Mar. 3	**William Joppy** ....Fernando Zuniga*		Wu 10	—	Las Vegas
Mar. 11	Armand Krajnc..........Jonathan Com		KO 2	—	Lubeck, GER
Apr. 8	Hacine Cherifi ....Alex Lubo		KO 1	—	Paris
Apr. 29	**Keith Holmes** ....Robert McCracken		TKO 11	**WBC**	London
May 13	**Bernard Hopkins** ......Syd Vanderpool		Wu 12	**IBF**	Indianapolis
May 20	**William Joppy** ....Rito Ruvalcaba		TKO 1	**WBA**	Tunica, Miss.
July 25	Howard Eastman ....Ahmet Dottuev		TKO 4	—	London
Aug. 12	Erland Betare ....Davide Ciarlante		Wu 12	—	St. Marten, FRA
Sept. 16	**William Joppy** ....Hacine Cherifi		Wu 12	**WBA**	Las Vegas

*Zuniga was a last-minute replacement because the No.1 contender, Rito Ruvalcaba, came down with acute tonsillitis and was ruled unfit to challenge. The fight was downgraded to 10-round, non-title belt.

Junior Middleweights (154 lbs)
(Super Welterweights)

Date	Winner	Loser	Result	Title	Site
Dec. 4	**Fernando Vargas** .....Ronald "Winky" Wright		Wm 12	**IBF**	Lincoln City, Ore.
Dec. 12	Tony Ayala ....Tony Menefee Jr.		TKO 8	—	San Antonio, Tex.
Dec. 17	**Javier Castillejo**.......Mikael Rask		TKO 7	**WBC**	Leganes, SPA
Feb. 19	Harry Simon ....Enrique Areco		TKO 11	WBO	Dagenham, ENG
Mar. 3	Felix Trinidad ....**David Reid**		Wu 12	**WBA**	Las Vegas
Apr. 15	**Fernando Vargas** ......Ike Quartey		Wu 12	**IBF**	Las Vegas
Apr. 15	Jose Flores..............Paul Vaden		Wu 12	—	Las Vegas
June 3	Roman Karmazin ....Orhan Delibas		TKO 4	—	Karlsruhe, GER
July 21	**Javier Castillejo**.......Tony Marshall		Wu 12	**WBC**	Leganes, SPA
July 22	**Felix Trinidad** ....Mamadou Thiam		TKO 3	**WBA**	Miami
July 28	Yory Boy Campas ....Tony Ayala		TKO 9	—	San Antonio
Aug. 26	**Fernando Vargas** .....Ross Thompson		TKO 4	**IBF**	Las Vegas
Sept. 4	Anthony Farnell ....Juan Sanchez		Wu 12	—	Manchester, ENG
Sept. 9	Ronald "Winky" Wright ...Bronko McKart		Wu 12	—	Chester, Pa.
Sept. 23	Harry Simon ....Rodney Jones		Wu 12	WBO	Rama, Ontario
Oct. 21	**Javier Castillejo**.......Javier Martinez		KO 4	**WBC**	Mexico City

Welterweights (147 lbs)

Date	Winner	Loser	Result	Title	Site
Jan. 22	Shane Mosley	Willy Wise	KO 3	—	Las Vegas
Jan. 22	Vernon Forrest	Vince Phillips	Wu 10	—	Las Vegas
Feb. 27	Oscar De La Hoya	Derrell Coley	KO 7	—	New York City
May 6	Daniel Santos	Ahmed Kotiev	KO 5	WBO	Neuss, GER
June 13	Antonio Margarito	David Kamau	KO 2	—	Indio, Calif.
June 15	Adrian Stone	Geoff McCreesh	TKO 6	—	London
June 17	Shane Mosley	**Oscar De La Hoya**	Ws 12	**WBC**	Los Angeles
July 1	Alessandro Duran	Jose Eschriche	Wu 12	—	Ferrara, ITA
July 29	Daniel Santos	Giovanni Parisi	KO 4	WBO	Reggio Calabria, ITA
Aug. 26	Vernon Forrest	Raul Frank	NC 3*	IBF†	Las Vegas
Sept. 17	Cory Spinks	Jorge Vaca	KO 7	—	St. Louis

Note: Oscar De La Hoya was awarded the WBC belt he lost to Felix Trinidad after Trinidad relinquished it by moving up to 154 pounds.
*Raul Frank was unable to continue due to a cut from an accidental head butt in the third round.
†The IBF title was vacated when Felix Trinidad moved up to 154 pounds.

Junior Welterweights (140 lbs)
(Super Lightweights)

Date	Winner	Loser	Result	Title	Site
Nov. 6	Hector Camacho Jr.	Juan Rodriguez	KO 3	—	Ventura, Calif.
Nov. 19	**Sharmba Mitchell**	Elio Ortiz	Wu 12	**WBA**	Las Vegas
Dec. 11	Randall Bailey	Hector Lopez	TKO 9	WBO	Tunica, Miss.
Dec. 18	Julio Cesar Chavez	Buck Smith	KO 3	—	Culiacan, MEX
Feb. 6	Hector Camacho Jr.	Harold Warren	KO 1	—	Elgin, Ill.
Feb. 12	**Kostya Tszyu**	Ahmed Santos	TKO 8	**WBC**	Uncasville, Conn.
Feb. 12	Zab Judah	Jan Bergman	TKO 4	IBF†	Uncasville, Conn.
Feb. 26	Arturo Gatti	Joey Gamache	KO 2	—	New York City
Mar. 11	Micky Ward	Shea Neary	TKO 8	—	London
Apr. 8	Randall Bailey	Rocky Martinez	TKO 7	WBO	Paris
Apr. 8	Khalid Rahilou	Josze Kubowsky	TKO 2	—	Paris
Apr. 15	Antonio Diaz	Ivan Robinson	TKO 11	—	Las Vegas
May 16	Ricky Hatton	Ambioris Figuero	TKO 4	—	Warrington, ENG
June 10	Ricky Hatton	Gilbert Quiros	KO 2	—	Detroit
June 13	Antonio Diaz	Omar Weiss	Wu 12	—	Indio, Calif.
June 18	Hector Camacho Jr.	Manard Reed	KO 4	—	Las Vegas
June 24	**Zab Judah**	Junior Witter	Wu 12	IBF	Glasgow
July 22	Ener Julio	Randall Bailey	Ws 12	WBO	Miami
July 29	**Kostya Tszyu**	Julio Cesar Chavez	TKO 6	**WBC**	Phoenix, Ariz
July 29	Hector Camacho Jr.	Phillip Holiday	TWu6*	—	Phoenix, Ariz.
Aug. 5	**Zab Judah**	Terronn Millett	TKO 4	IBF	Uncasville, Conn.
Aug. 11	Vivian Harris	Ivan Robinson	Wm 10	—	Atlantic City
Aug. 19	Antonio Diaz	Mickey Ward	Wu 10	—	Ledyard, Conn.
Sept. 16	Sharmba Mitchell	Felix Flores	Wu 12	WBA	Las Vegas
Sept. 23	Ricky Hatton	Giuseppe Lauri	TKO 5	—	London
Oct. 20	**Zab Judah**	Hector Quiroz	TKO 8	IBF	Auburn Hills, Mich.

†Zab Judah, the interim IBF champ, won the regular belt on Feb. 12 that was left vacant when reigning champion Terronn Millett was stripped of his title. Millett broke his hand in his July 24, 1999 victory over Virgil McClendon and couldn't fight. Millett was named "champion-in-recess."
*Hector Camacho Jr. was awarded the technical decision when Holiday was cut over his left eye and was unable to continue following a collision with Camacho's right elbow.

Lightweights (135 lbs)

Date	Winner	Loser	Result	Title	Site
Nov. 13	Gilberto Serrano	**Stefano Zoff**	TKO 10	**WBA**	Las Vegas
Nov. 29	**Stevie Johnston**	Billy Schwer	Wu 12	**WBC**	London
Dec. 17	**Paul Spadafora**	Renato Cornett	TKO 11	IBF	Pittsburgh
Jan. 7	Juan Lazcano	Julian Wheeler	Ws 10	—	Sacramento, Calif.
Jan. 31	Julien Lorcy	Oscar Garcia-Cano	Wu 12	—	Paris
Feb. 18	Angel Manfredy	Sean Fletcher	KO 4	—	Atlantic City
Mar. 3	**Paul Spadafora**	Victoriano Sosa	Wu 12	IBF	Verona, N.Y.
Mar. 7	Angel Manfredy	Vincent Howard	Wu 10	—	Montreal
Mar. 12	**Gilberto Serrano**	Hiroyuki Sakamoto	TKO 5	**WBA**	Tokyo
Mar. 17	**Stevie Johnston**	Julio Alvarez	TKO 2	**WBC**	Denver, Colo.
Apr. 8	Jean Baptiste Mendy	Pedro Garcia	Wu 10	—	Paris
May 6	**Paul Spadafora**	Mike Griffith	TWm 10	IBF	Pittsburgh
May 12	John John Molina	Emanuel Burton	Wu 10	—	Miami
June 3	Ben Tackie	Roberto Garcia	TKO 10	—	Las Vegas

June 11	Takanori Hatakeyama	**Gilberto Serrano**	TKO 8	**WBA**	Tokyo
June 17	Jose Luis Castillo	**Stevie Johnston**	Wm 12	**WBC**	Bell Gardens, Calif.
June 23	Artur Grigoran	Zoltan Kalocsai	Wu 12	WBO	Budapest, HUN
June 25	Angel Manfredy	Agustin Lorenzo	TKO 1	—	Gary, Ind.
July 15	Leavander Johnson	Larry O'Shields	KO 8 -	—	Biloxi, Miss.
Aug. 5	Juan Lazcano	James Leija	Wu 10	—	Uncasville, Conn.
Sept. 16	Julien Lorcy	Gianni Gelli	KO 3	—	Loriet Cher, FRA
Oct. 11	**Takanori Hatakeyama**	Hiroyuki Sakamoto	KO 10	**WBA**	Yokohama, JPN
Oct. 21	Floyd Mayweather Jr.	Emanuel Burton	TKO 9	—	Detroit

Junior Lightweights (130 lbs)
(Super Featherweights)

Date	Winner	Loser	Result	Title	Site
Oct. 23	Diego Corrales	**Roberto Garcia**	TKO 7	IBF	Las Vegas
Oct. 26	Acelino Freitas	Anthon Martinez	TKO 2	WBO	Salvador Bahia, BRZI
Nov. 7	Baek Jong-Kwon	**Lavka Sim**	Ws 12	**WBA**	Tokyo
Nov. 20	Joel Casamayor	David Santos	Wu 12	WBA†	Miami
Dec. 4	**Diego Corrales**	John Brown	Wu 12	IBF	Lincoln City, Ore.
Jan. 15	Acelino Freitas	Barry Jones	TKO 8	WBO	Doncaster, ENG
Jan. 30	**Baek Jong-Kwon**	Choi Kyu Chul	Mdraw	**WBA**	Pohang, S. Korea
Mar. 5	Robbie Peden	Carlos Rios	Ws 12	—	Las Vegas
Mar. 18	**Diego Corrales**	Derrick Gainer	KO 3	IBF	Las Vegas
Mar. 18	**Floyd Mayweather**	Goyo Vargas	Wu 12	**WBC**	Las Vegas
Mar. 18	Acelino Freitas	Javier Jauregui	KO 1	WBO	Sao Paulo, BRZI
May 21	Joel Casamayor	**Baek Jong-Kwon**	TKO 5	**WBA**	Kansas City, Mo.
June 10	Acelino Freitas	Lamuel Nelson	TKO 2	WBO	Detroit
June 17	**Diego Corrales**	Justin Juuko	TKO 10	IBF	Los Angeles
Sept. 1	Dennis Holbaek	Boris Sinitsin	KO 12	—	Vordingborg, DEN
Sept. 2	**Diego Corrales**	Angel Manfredy	KO 3	IBF	El Paso, Tex.
Sept. 16	**Joel Casamayor**	Radford Beasley	TKO 5	**WBA**	Las Vegas
Sept. 23	Acelino Freitas	Carlos Rios	TKO 9	WBO	Rama, Ontario

†Joel Casamayor defended his interim WBA belt on Nov. 20, 1999 and then beat Baek Jong-Kwon on May 21 for the regular WBA title.

Featherweights (126 lbs)

Date	Winner	Loser	Result	Title	Site
Oct. 22	Naseem Hamed	**Cesar Soto**	Wu 12	**WBC/WBO**	Detroit
Nov. 13	Paul Ingle	**Manuel Medina**	Wu 12	IBF	Hull, ENG
Jan. 30	**Freddie Norwood**	Takashi Koshimoto	KO 9	**WBA**	Nagoya, JPN
Mar. 11	Naseem Hamed	Vuyani Bungu	TKO 4	WBO	London
Apr. 14	Guty Espadas	Luisito Espinosa	TWu 11	WBC†	Merida, MEX
Apr. 29	**Paul Ingle**	Junior Jones	TKO 11	IBF	New York City
May 25	**Freddie Norwood**	Pablo Chacon	Wu 12	**WBA**	Mendoza, ARG
June 17	Erik Morales	Mike Juarez	KO 3	—	Los Angeles
June 23	**Guty Espadas**	Wethya Sakmuangklang	Wu 12	**WBC**	Merida, MEX
July 15	Derrick Gainer	Richard Carrillo	TKO 4	—	Biloxi, Miss.
Aug. 19	Naseem Hamed	Augie Sanchez	TKO 4	WBO	Ledyard, Conn.
Aug. 27	Juan M. Marquez	Daniel Jimenez	TKO 7	—	Las Vegas
Sept. 2	Erik Morales	Kevin Kelley	TKO 7	WBC*	El Paso, Tex.
Sept. 9	Derrick Gainer	**Freddie Norwood**	TKO 11	**WBA**	New Orleans

†Naseem Hamed vacated the WBC title on January 9 after deciding to keep the WBO belt. The WBC only would sanction the Oct. 22, 1999 featherweight title fight between Hamed, the WBO champ, and Cesar Soto, the WBC champ, after both fighters agreed that the winner would keep only one of the belts that was on the line that night.

*Erik Morales won the interim WBC belt that was sanctioned after current WBC featherweight champion Guty Espadas suffered a broken collar bone during training.

Junior Featherweights (122 lbs)
(Super Bantamweights)

Date	Winner	Loser	Result	Title	Site
Oct. 22	**Erik Morales**	Wayne McCullough	Wu 12	**WBC**	Detroit
Nov. 21	**Nestor Garza**	Kozo Ishii	TKO 12	**WBA**	Nagoya, JPN
Jan. 8	Danny Romero	Rodolfo Blanco	KO 1	—	Alburquerque
Feb. 19	**Erik Morales**	Marco Antonio Barrera	Ws 12	**WBC**	Las Vegas
Mar. 4	Clarence Adams	**Nestor Garza**	Wu 12	**WBA**	Las Vegas
Mar. 4	Oba Carr	Yory Boy Campas	TKO 9	—	Las Vegas
Mar. 4	Antonio Cermeno	Arcelino Diaz	TKO 6	WBA*	Coro, VEN
Apr. 7	**Lehlohonolo Ledwaba**	Ernesto Grey	TKO 8	IBF	Bristol, ENG

May 20	Antonio Cermeno........Carlos Rocha	TKO 2	WBA*	Tunica, Miss.
June 17	Marco Antonio Barrera....Luis Carlos Freitas	KO 1	WBO	Mexico City
June 28	Manny Pacquiao.........Seungkon Chae	TKO 1	—	Manila, PHI
July 1	Michael Brodie..........Mustapha Hame	KO 4	—	Manchester, ENG
Aug. 5	**Clarence Adams**.......Andres Fernandez	TKO 6	**WBA**	Madison, Wisc.
Sept. 9	Willie Jorin.............Michael Brodie	Wm 12	**WBC**†	Manchester, ENG
Sept. 9	Marco Antonio Barrera...Jose Luis Valbuena	Wu 12	WBO	New Orleans
Oct. 6	**Lehlohonolo Ledwaba**.Eduardo Alvarez	KO 8	**IBF**	Kent, ENG
Oct. 7	Paulie Ayala............Johnny Tapia	Wu 12	—	Las Vegas

*Interim title.

†The WBC belt was vacated when Erik Morales moved up to 126 pounds.

Bantamweights (118 lbs)

Date	Winner	Loser	Result	Title	Site
Oct. 23	**Paulie Ayala**..........Saohin Srithai Condo	Wu 12	**WBA**	Fort Worth, Tex.
Dec. 18	**Tim Austin**............Bernardo Mendoza	TKO 1	**IBF**	Tunica, Miss.
Jan. 8	Johnny Tapia...........Jorge Eliecer Julio	Wu 12	WBO	Alburquerque
Jan. 9	Mauricio Pastrana.......Ablorh Sowah	Wu 10	—	Bay St. Louis, Miss.
Feb. 16	Jorge Lacierva ....Mauricio Pastrana	Wu 12	—	Miami
Mar. 3	Manny Pacquiao........Arnel Barotillo	KO 4	—	Manila, PHI
Mar. 4	**Paulie Ayala**.........Johnny Bredahl	Wm 12	**WBA**	Las Vegas
Mar. 11	**Veerapol Sahaprom**....Adan Vargas	Wu 12	**WBC**	Sa Kaew, THA
May 6	Johnny Tapia...........Pedro Javier Torres	Wu 12	WBO	Las Cruces, N.M.
June 25	**Veerapol Sahaprom**...Toshiaki Nishioka	Wu 12	**WBC**	Takasago, JPN
July 17	Adan Vargas ....Mauricio Pastrana	Ws 12	—	Las Vegas
Aug. 11	**Tim Austin** ....Arthur Johnson	Wu 12	**IBF**	Las Vegas
Sept. 1	Johnny Bredahl..........Roberto Lopez	Wu 12	—	Vordingborg, DEN
Sept. 4	Mauricio Martinez.......Lester Fuentes	KO 5	WBO*	Manchester, ENG
Sept. 9	Willie Jorran............Michael Brodie	Wm 12	—	Manchester, ENG

*Johnny Tapia vacated his WBO belt to move up in weight.

Junior Bantamweights (115 lbs)
(Super Flyweights)

Date	Winner	Loser	Result	Title	Site
Nov. 7	**Hideki Todaka**........Akihiko Nago	Wu 12	**WBA**	Tokyo
Nov. 19	**Mark Johnson**.........Raul Juarez	NC*	**IBF**	Washington D.C.
Jan. 2	**Cho In-joo** ....Gerry Penalosa	Ws 12	**WBC**	Seoul, S. Korea
Mar. 25	Adonis Rivas............Pedro Morquecho	Twu 12	WBO	Managua, NIC
Apr. 23	**Hideki Todaka**........Yokthai Sith Oar	TKO 11	**WBA**	Nagoya, JPN
May 14	**Cho In-joo** ....Julio Cesar Avila	Wu 12	**WBC**	Seoul, S. Korea
May 20	Julio Gamboa...........Felix Machado	Sdraw	IBF†	Tunica, Miss.
July 1	Samson Sor Isaan ....Raffi Aladi	TKO 8	—	Manchester, ENG
July 22	Felix Machado ....Julio Gamboa	Wu 12	IBF†	Miami
Aug. 27	Masanori Tokuyama .....**Cho In-joo**	Wu 12	**WBC**	Osaka, JPN
Oct. 9	Leo Gamez ....**Hideki Todaka**	KO 7	**WBA**	Nagoya, JPN

*Mark Johnson was unable to continue after getting hit with a low blow.

†Felix Machado and Julio Gamboa fought twice (the first fight ended in a split draw) for the IBF title left vacant when Mark Johnson went to prison following a parole violation.

Flyweights (112 lbs)

Date	Winner	Loser	Result	Title	Site
Dec. 18	Isidro Garcia ....Jose Lopez	Wu 12	WBO	Indio, Calif.
Jan. 14	**Irene Pacheco** ....Pedro Pena	KO 11	**IBF**	El Paso, Tex.
Feb. 25	**Medgoen Singsurat**....Masaki Kawabata	Wu 12	**WBC**	Samut Sakorn, THA
Apr. 8	**S. Kratchingdaeng**.....Gilberto Gonzalez	TKO 5	**WBA**	Bangkok, THA
May 19	Malcolm Tunacao........**Medgoen Singsurat**	TKO 7	**WBC**	Udonthani, THA
June 12	Damaen Kelly...........J.A. Lopez Bueno	Wu 12	—	Detroit
Aug. 5	Eric Morel ....**S. Kratchingdaeng**	Wu 12	**WBA**	Madison, Wisc.
Aug. 19	Isidro Garcia ....Jose Rafael Sosa	TKO 6	WBO	Cordoba, ARG
Aug. 20	**Malcolm Tunacao**......Celes Kobayashi	Sdraw 12	**WBC**	Tokyo, JPN
Sept. 30	Damaen Kelly...........Zoile Mbityi	Wm 12	—	Peterborough, ENG
Oct. 7	**Eric Morel**............Alberto Ontiveros	Wu 12	**WBA**	Las Vegas

Junior Flyweights (108 lbs)
(Light Flyweights)

Date	Winner	Loser	Result	Title	Site
Oct. 17	Choi Yo-Sam	Saman Sorjaturong	Wu 12	WBC	Seoul, S. Korea
Feb. 4	**Pichitnoi Siriwat**	Yang Sang-ik	Wu 12	WBA	Thailand
Feb. 19	Masibulele Makepula	Jacob Matlala	Wu 12	WBO†	Brakspan, S.A.
Mar. 17	Beibis Mendoza	Eduardo Manzano	KO 1	—	Pembroke Pines, Fla.
May 12	Beibis Mendoza	Rafael Orozco	KO 2	—	Pembroke Pines, Fla.
June 17	**Choi Yo-sam**	Chart Kiatpetch	KO 5	WBC	Seoul, S. Korea
July 22	Will Grigsby	Nelson Dieppa	Wu 12	WBO†	Miami
Aug. 12	Beibis Mendoza	Rosendo Alvarez	Disq 7*	WBA‡	Las Vegas

†Masibulele "Hawk" Makepula and Jacob Matlala fought for the WBO title stripped from Michael Carbajal. After winning it, Makepula then vacated the title himself and Will Grigsby beat Nelson Dieppa for the once-again vacant title on July 22.
*Rosendo Alvarez was disqualified in the seventh round for repeated low blows.
‡Beibis Mendoza and Rosendo Alvarez fought for the WBA title that was left vacant after Pichitnoi Siriwat was stripped of the belt for purportedly dodging a match with top-ranked challenger Alvarez.

Minimumweights (105 lbs)
(Strawweights or Mini-Flyweights)

Date	Winner	Loser	Result	Title	Site
Oct. 30	Kermin Guardia	Luis Lazarte	Ws 12	WBO	Mar del Plata, ARG
Dec. 3	**Zolani Petelo**	Juanito Rubilar	Wu 12	IBF	Peterborough, ENG
Dec. 4	Joma Gamboa	Satoru Abe	TKO 6	WBA†	Nagoya, JPN
Feb. 11	Jose Antonio Aguirre	**Wandee Charoen**	Wm 12	WBC	Samut Skaorn, THA
Mar. 4	**Noel Arambulet**	Jose Garcia	Wu 12	WBA	Falcon, VEN
Apr. 9	Joma Gamboa	Atsushi Sai	Wu 12	WBA†	Hachinohe, JPN
June 2	**Zolani Petelo**	Mickey Cantwell	TKO 8	IBF	Kent, ENG
July 7	**Jose Antonio Aguirre**	Jose Luis Zepeda	KO 5	WBC	Villahermosa, MEX
Aug. 20	Joma Gamboa	Noel Arambulet	Ws 12	WBA*	Tokyo
Oct. 21	**Jose Antonio Aguirre**	Erdene Chuluun	KO 4	WBC	Mexico City

†Interim title.
*Noel Arambulet could not defend his title in December 1999 becasue of a viral infection, and Joma Gamboa became the interim champion by beating Satoru Abe to take the vacant interim title. On Aug. 20, Arambulet failed to make weight for his match with Gamboa and even if he had won he would not have kept his title.

Top Fighters Records
The career pro records of Welterweight Oscar De La Hoya, Light Heavyweight Roy Jones Jr. and Heavyweights Evander Holyfield, Lennox Lewis and Mike Tyson, as of Oct. 23, 2000.

Roy Jones Jr.

Born: Jan. 16, 1969   **Pro record:** 43-1-0, 35 KOs
Height: 5'11"   **Weight:** 175
Olympic medal: 1988 Silver as a light middleweight.

No	Date	Opponent, location	Result
1	5/6/89	Ricky Randall, Pensacola, Fla.	KO 2
2	6/11/89	Stephan Johnson, Atlantic City	KO 8
3	9/3/89	Ron Amundsen, Pensacola, Fla.	KO 7
4	11/30/89	Dave McCluskey, Pensacola, Fla.	KO 3
5	1/8/90	Joe Edens, Mobile, Alabama	KO 2
6	2/28/90	Billy Mitchum, Pensacola, Fla.	TKO 2
7	3/28/90	Knox Brown, Pensacola, Fla.	KO 3
8	5/11/90	Ron Johnson, Pensacola, Fla.	KO 2
9	7/14/90	Tony Waddles, Pensacola, Fla.	KO 1
10	9/25/90	Rollin Williams, Pensacola, Fla.	KO 4
11	11/8/90	Reggie Miller, Pensacola, Fla.	KO 5
12	1/31/91	Ricky Stackhouse, Pensacola, Fla.	KO 1
13	4/13/91	Eddie Evans, Pensacola, Fla.	TKO 3
14	8/3/91	Kevin Daigle, Pensacola, Fla.	TKO 2
15	8/31/91	Lester Yarbrough, Pensacola, Fla.	KO 8
16	1/10/92	Jorge Vaca, New York City	KO 1
17	4/3/92	Art Serwano, Reno	KO 1
18	6/30/92	Jorge Castro, Pensacola, Fla.	Wu 12
19	8/28/92	Glenn Thomas, Pensacola, Fla.	KO 8
20	12/5/92	Percy Harris, Atlantic City	KO 4
21	2/13/93	Glenn Wolfe, Las Vegas	KO 1
22	5/22/93	Bernard Hopkins, Washington D.C.	Wu 12
		(won IBF middleweight title)	
23	8/14/93	Thulane Malinga, St. Louis Bay, Miss.	KO 6
24	11/30/93	Fermin Chirino, Pensacola, Fla.	W 10
25	3/22/94	Daniel Garcia, Pensacola, Fla.	KO 6
26	5/27/94	Thomas Tate, Las Vegas	KO 2
27	11/18/94	James Toney, Las Vegas	Wu 12
		(won IBF super middleweight title)	
28	3/18/95	Antoine Byrd, Pensacola, Fla.	TKO 1
29	6/24/95	Vinny Pazienza, Atlantic City	TKO 6
30	9/30/95	Tony Thornton, Pensacola, Fla.	TKO 3
31	1/12/96	Merqui Sosa, New York City	TKO 2
32	6/15/96	Eric Lucas, Jacksonville, Fla.	KO 11
33	8/4/96	Bryant Brannon, New York City	KO 2
34	11/22/96	Mike McCallum, Tampa, Fla.	Wu 12
		(won interim WBC light heavyweight title)	
35	3/21/97	Montel Griffin, Atlantic City	L-DQ 9
		(lost WBC light heavyweight title)	
36	8/21/97	Montel Griffin, Mashantucket, Conn.	KO 1
		(won WBC light heavyweight title)	
37	4/25/98	Virgil Hill, Biloxi, Miss.	KO 4
38	7/18/98	Lou Del Valle, New York City	Wu 12
		(won WBA light heavyweight title)	
39	11/14/98	Otis Grant, Mashantucket, Conn.	TKO 10
40	1/9/99	Richard Frazier, Pensacola, Fla.	TKO 2
41	6/5/99	Reggie Johnson, Biloxi, Miss.	Wu 12
		(won IBF light heavyweight title)	
42	1/15/00	David Telesco, New York City	Wu 12
42	5/13/00	Richard Hall, Indianapolis	TKO 11
43	9/9/00	Eric Harding, New Orleans	TKO 10

Oscar De La Hoya

Born: Feb. 4, 1973   **Pro record:** 32-2, 26 KOs
Height: 5'10½"   **Weight:** 147
Olympic medal: 1992 Gold as a lightweight

No	Date	Opponent, location	Result
1	11/23/92	Lamar Williams, Inglewood, Calif.	KO 1
2	12/12/92	Cliff Hicks, Phoenix	KO 1
3	1/3/93	Paris Alexander, Hollywood	TKO 2
4	2/6/93	Curtis Strong, San Diego	TKO 4
5	3/13/93	Jeff Mayweather, Las Vegas	TKO 4
6	4/6/93	Mike Grable, Rochester, N.Y.	Wu 8
7	5/8/93	Frank Avelar, Lake Tahoe	TKO 4
8	6/7/93	Troy Dorsey, Las Vegas	TKO 1
9	8/14/93	Renaldo Carter, Bay St. Louis, Miss.	KO 6
10	8/27/93	Angelo Nunez, Beverly Hills	TKO 4
11	10/30/93	Narcisco Valenzuela, Phoenix	KO 1
12	3/5/94	Jimmi Bredahl, Los Angeles	TKO 10
13	5/27/94	Giogio Campenella, Las Vegas	KO 3
14	7/29/94	Jorge Paez, Las Vegas	KO 2
15	11/18/94	Carl Griffith, Las Vegas	KO 3
16	12/10/94	John Avila, Los Angeles	TKO 9
17	2/18/95	John John Molina, Las Vegas	Wu 12
18	5/6/95	Rafael Ruelas, Las Vegas	TKO 2
		(won IBF lightweight title)	
19	9/9/95	Genaro Hernandez, Las Vegas	TKO 6
20	12/15/95	James Leija, New York City	TKO 2
21	2/9/96	Darryl Tyson, Las Vegas	KO 2
22	6/7/96	Julio Cesar Chavez, Las Vegas	TKO 4
		(won WBC super lightweight title)	
23	1/18/97	Miguel Angel Gonzalez, Las Vegas	Wu 12
24	4/12/97	Pernell Whitaker, Las Vegas	Wu 12
		(won WBC welterweight title)	
25	6/14/97	David Kamau, San Antonio	KO 2
26	9/13/97	Hector Camacho, Las Vegas	Wu 12
27	12/6/97	Wilfredo Rivera, Atlantic City	TKO 8
28	6/13/98	Patrick Charpentier, El Paso, Texas	TKO 3
29	9/18/98	Julio Cesar Chavez, Las Vegas	TKO 8
30	2/13/99	Ike Quartey, Las Vegas	Ws 12
31	5/22/99	Oba Carr, Las Vegas	TKO 11
32	9/18/99	Felix Trinidad, Las Vegas	Lm 12
		(lost WBC welterweight title)	
33	2/27/00	Derrel Coley, New York City	KO 7
34	6/17/00	Shane Mosley, Los Angeles	Ls 12
		(lost WBC welterweight title)	

Note: Oscar De La Hoya was awarded the WBC belt he lost to Felix Trinidad after Trinidad relinquished it by moving up to 154 pounds.

Evander Holyfield

Born: Oct. 19, 1962   **Pro record:** 37-4-1, 25 KOs
Height: 6' 2½"   **Weight:** 221
Olympic medal: 1984 Bronze as light heavyweight (disqualifed for controversial late knockout punch in semifinal against Kevin Barry of New Zealand)

No	Date	Opponent, location	Result
1	11/15/84	Lionel Byarm, New York	Wu 6
2	1/20/85	Eric Winbush, Atlantic City	Wu 6
3	3/13/85	Freddie Brown, Norfolk	KO 1
4	4/20/85	Mark Rivera, Corpus Christi	KO 2
5	7/20/85	Tyrone Booze, Norfolk	Wu 8
6	8/29/85	Rick Myers, Atlanta	KO 1
7	10/30/85	Jeff Meachem, Atlantic City	KO 5
8	12/21/85	Anthony Davis, Virginia Beach	KO 4
9	3/1/86	Chisanda Mutti, Lancaster, Pa	KO 3
10	4/6/86	Jesse Shelby, Corpus Christi	KO 3
11	5/28/86	Terry Mims, Metairie, LA	KO 5
12	7/20/86	Dwight M. Qawi, Atlanta	Ws 15
		(won WBA cruiserweight title)	
13	12/8/86	Mike Brothers, Paris	KO 3
14	2/14/87	Henry Tillman, Reno	TKO 7
15	5/15/87	Rickey Parkey, Las Vegas	TKO 3
		(won IBF cruiserweight title)	
16	8/15/87	Ossie Ocasio, St.Topez, France	TKO 11
17	12/4/87	Dwight M. Qawi, Atlantic City	TKO 4
18	4/9/88	Carlos DeLeon, Las Vegas	KO 8
		(won WBC cruiserweight title)	
19	7/16/88	James Tillis, Lake Tahoe	KO 5
20	12/9/88	Pinklon Thomas, Atlantic City	TKO 7
21	3/11/89	Michael Dokes, Las Vegas	TKO 10
22	6/1/89	Adilson Rodrigues, Lake Tahoe	KO 2
23	11/4/89	Alex Stewart, Atlantic City	TKO 8
24	6/1/90	Seamus McDonagh, Atlantic City	TKO 4
25	10/25/90	Buster Douglas, Las Vegas	KO 3
		(won undisputed heavyweight title)	
26	4/19/91	George Foreman, Atlantic City	Wu 12
27	11/23/91	Bert Cooper, Atlanta	TKO 7
28	6/19/92	Larry Holmes, Las Vegas	Wu 12
29	11/13/92	Riddick Bowe, Las Vegas	Lu 12
		(lost undisputed heavyweight title)	
30	6/26/93	Alex Stewart, Atlantic City	Wu 12
31	11/6/93	Riddick Bowe, Las Vegas	Wm 12
		(won IBF/WBA heavyweight titles)	
32	4/22/94	Michael Moorer, Las Vegas	Lm 12
		(lost IBF/WBA heavyweight titles)	
33	5/20/95	Ray Mercer, Atlantic City	Wu 10
34	11/4/95	Riddick Bowe, Las Vegas	TKO by 8
35	5/10/96	Bobby Czyz, New York	TKO 5
36	11/9/96	Mike Tyson, Las Vegas	TKO 11
		(won WBC heavyweight title)	
37	6/28/97	Mike Tyson, Las Vegas	W Disq. 3
38	11/8/97	Michael Moorer, Las Vegas	TKO 8
		(won IBF/WBA heavyweight titles)	
39	9/19/98	Vaughn Bean, Atlanta	Wu 12
40	3/13/99	Lennox Lewis, New York City	Draw 12
41	11/13/99	Lennox Lewis, Las Vegas	Lu 12
		(lost IBF/WBA heavyweight titles)	
42	8/12/00	John Ruiz, Las Vegas	Wu 12
		(won vacant WBA heavyweight title)	

Lennox Lewis

Born: Sept. 9, 1965   **Pro record:** 37-1-1, 29 KOs
Height: 6' 5"   **Weight:** 246
Olympic medal: 1988 Gold as super heavyweight for Canada

No	Date	Opponent, location	Result
1	6/27/89	Al Malcolm, London	KO 2
2	7/21/89	Bruce Johnson, Atlantic City	TKO 2
3	9/25/89	Andy Gerrard, London	TKO 4
4	10/10/89	Stever Garber, Hull, ENG	KO 2
5	11/5/89	Melvin Epps, Kensington, ENG	W disq. 2
6	12/18/89	Greg Gorrell, Ontario	TKO 5
7	1/31/90	Noel Quarless, London	KO 2
8	3/22/90	Calvin Jones, Gateshead, ENG	KO 1
9	4/14/90	Mike Simuwelu, London	KO 1
10	5/2/90	Jorge Dascola, London	KO 1
11	5/20/90	Dan Murphy, Sheffield, ENG	TKO 6
12	6/27/90	Ossie Ocasio, Kensington, ENG	Wu 8
13	7/11/90	Mike Acey, Ontario	TKO 2
14	10/31/90	Jean Chanet, London	TKO 6
15	3/6/91	Gary Mason, London	TKO 6
16	7/12/91	Mike Weaver, Stateline, Nev.	KO 6
17	9/30/91	Glenn McCrory, Kensington, ENG	KO 2
18	11/23/91	Tyrell Biggs, Atlanta	TKO 3
19	2/1/92	Levi Billups, Las Vegas	Wu 10
20	4/30/92	Derek Williams, London	KO 3
21	8/11/92	Mike Dixon, Atlantic City	TKO 4
22	10/31/92	Razor Ruddock, London*	KO 2
23	5/8/93	Tony Tucker, Las Vegas	Wu 12
24	10/1/93	Frank Bruno, Cardiff, Wales	TKO 7
25	5/6/94	Phil Jackson, Atlantic City	KO 8
26	9/24/94	Oliver McCall, London (lost WBC heavyweight title)	TKO by 2
27	5/13/95	Lionel Butler, Sacramento	KO 5
28	7/2/95	Justin Fortune, Dublin	TKO 4
29	10/7/95	Tommy Morrison, Atlantic City	TKO 6
30	5/10/96	Ray Mercer, New York City	Wu 12
31	2/7/97	Oliver McCall, Las Vegas (won WBC heavyweight title)	W disq. 5†
32	7/12/97	Henry Akinwande, Lake Tahoe	W disq. 5‡
33	10/4/97	Andrew Golota, Atlantic City	KO 1
34	3/28/98	Shannon Briggs, Atlantic City	TKO 5
35	9/26/98	Zeljko Mavrovic, Uncasville, Conn.	Wu 12
36	3/13/99	Evander Holyfield, New York City	Draw 12
37	11/13/99	Evander Holyfield, Las Vegas (won WBA/IBF heavyweight titles)	Wu 12
38	4/29/00	Michael Grant, New York City	KO 2
39	7/15/00	Frans Botha, London	TKO 2

*Lewis' bout with Ruddock was a title eliminator and Lewis was then awarded the belt when Riddick Bowe surrendered the title in December by dumping it in a London trash can.
†McCall was disqualified in the fifth round after he started crying and refused to put up a fight.
‡Akinwande was disqualified in the fifth round for excessive clutching and grabbing.

Mike Tyson

Born: June 30, 1966   **Pro record:** 49-3-0, 1 NC, 42 KOs
Height: 5'11"   **Weight:** 225

No	Date	Opponent, location	Result
1	3/6/85	Hector Mercedes, Albany, N.Y.	KO 1
2	4/10/85	Trent Singleton, Albany, N.Y.	TKO 1
3	5/23/85	Don Halpin, Albany, N.Y.	KO 4
4	6/20/85	Rick Spain, Atlantic City	KO 1
5	7/11/85	John Anderson, Atlantic City	TKO 2
6	7/19/85	Larry Sims, Poughkeepsie, N.Y.	KO 3
7	8/15/85	Lorenzo Canady, Atlantic City	TKO 1
8	9/5/85	Michael Johnson, Atlantic City	KO 1
9	10/9/85	Donnie Long, Atlantic City	KO 1
10	10/25/85	Robert Colay, Atlantic City	KO 1
11	11/1/85	Sterling Benjamin, Latham, N.Y.	TKO 1
12	11/13/85	Eddie Richardson, Houston	KO 1
13	11/22/85	Conroy Nelson, Latham, N.Y.	KO 2
14	12/6/85	Sammy Scaff, New York City	KO 1
15	12/27/85	Mark Young, Latham, N.Y.	KO 1
16	1/10/86	Dave Jaco, Albany, N.Y.	TKO 1
17	1/24/86	Mike Jameson, Atlantic City	TKO 5
18	2/16/86	Jesse Ferguson, Troy, N.Y.	TKO 6
19	3/10/86	Steve Zouski, Uniondale, N.Y.	KO 3
20	5/3/86	James Tillis, Glens Falls, N.Y.	Wu 10
21	5/20/86	Mitchell Green, New York City	Wu 10
22	6/13/86	Reggie Gross, New York City	TKO 1
23	6/28/86	William Hosea, Troy, N.Y.	KO 1
24	7/11/86	Lorenzo Boyd, Swan Lake, N.Y.	KO 2
25	7/26/86	Marvis Frazier, Glens Falls, N.Y.	KO 1
26	8/17/86	Jose Ribalta, Atlantic City	TKO 10
27	9/6/86	Alfonzo Ratliff, Las Vegas	KO 2
28	11/22/86	Trevor Berbick, Las Vegas (won WBC heavyweight title)	KO 2
29	3/7/87	Bonecrusher Smith, Las Vegas (won WBA heavyweight title)	Wu 12
30	5/30/87	Pinklon Thomas, Las Vegas	TKO 6
31	8/1/87	Tony Tucker, Las Vegas (won IBF heavyweight title)	Wu 12
32	10/16/87	Tyrell Biggs, Atlantic City	TKO 7
33	1/22/88	Larry Holmes, Atlantic City	KO 4
34	3/21/88	Tony Tubbs, Tokyo	TKO 2
35	6/27/88	Michael Spinks, Atlantic City	KO 1
36	2/25/89	Frank Bruno, Las Vegas	TKO 5
37	7/21/89	Carl Williams, Atlantic City	TKO 1
38	2/10/90	Buster Douglas, Tokyo (lost world heavyweight title)	KO by 10
39	6/16/90	Henry Tillman, Las Vegas	KO 1
40	12/8/90	Alex Stewart, Atlantic City	TKO 1
41	3/18/91	Razor Ruddock, Las Vegas	TKO 7
42	6/28/91	Razor Ruddock, Las Vegas	Wu 12
43	8/19/95	Peter McNeeley, Las Vegas (first fight since release from prison)	W disq. 1
44	12/16/95	Buster Mathis Jr., Philadelphia	KO 3
45	3/16/96	Frank Bruno, Las Vegas (won WBC heavyweight title)	TKO 3
46	9/7/96	Bruce Seldon, Las Vegas (won WBA heavyweight title)	TKO 1
47	11/9/96	Evander Holyfield, Las Vegas (lost WBA heavyweight title)	TKO by 11
48	6/28/97	Evander Holyfield, Las Vegas (disqualified for biting Holyfield's ears)	L disq 3
49	1/16/99	Frans Botha, Las Vegas	KO 5
50	10/23/99	Orlin Norris, Las Vegas	NC*
51	1/29/00	Julius Francis, Manchester, ENG	KO 1
52	6/24/00	Lou Savarese, Glasgow, SCOT	TKO 1
53	10/20/00	Andrew Golota, Auburn Hills, MI	TKO 3

*The Tyson-Norris bout was ruled a no-contest after Norris hurt his knee and could not continue following a off-the-clinch-punch from Mike Tyson.

World Heavyweight Championship Fights

Widely accepted world champions in **bold** type. Note following result abbreviations: KO (knockout), TKO (technical knockout), Wu (unanimous decision), Wm (majority decision), Ws (split decision), Ref (referee's decision), ND (no decision), Disq. (won on disqualification).

Year	Date	Winner	Age	Wgt	Loser	Wgt	Result	Location
1892	Sept. 7	James J. Corbett	26	178	John L. Sullivan	212	KO 21	New Orleans
1894	Jan. 25	**James J. Corbett**	27	184	Charley Mitchell	158	KO 3	Jacksonville, Fla.
1897	Mar. 17	Bob Fitzsimmons	34	167	**James J. Corbett**	183	KO 14	Carson City, Nev.
1899	June 9	James J. Jeffries	24	206	**Bob Fitzsimmons**	167	KO 11	Coney Island, N.Y.
1899	Nov. 3	**James J. Jeffries**	24	215	Tom Sharkey	183	Ref 25	Coney Island, N.Y.
1900	Apr. 6	**James J. Jeffries**	24	NA	Jack Finnegan	NA	KO 1	Detroit
1900	May 11	**James J. Jeffries**	25	218	James J. Corbett	188	KO 23	Coney Island, N.Y.
1901	Nov. 15	**James J. Jeffries**	26	211	Gus Ruhlin	194	TKO 6	San Francisco
1902	July 25	**James J. Jeffries**	27	219	Bob Fitzsimmons	172	KO 8	San Francisco
1903	Aug. 14	**James J. Jeffries**	28	220	James J. Corbett	190	KO 10	San Francisco
1904	Aug. 25	**James J. Jeffries***	29	219	Jack Munroe	186	TKO 2	San Francisco
1905	July 3	Marvin Hart	28	190	Jack Root	171	KO 12	Reno, Nev.
1906	Feb. 23	Tommy Burns	24	180	**Marvin Hart**	188	Ref 20	Los Angeles
1906	Oct. 2	**Tommy Burns**	25	NA	Jim Flynn	NA	KO 15	Los Angeles
1906	Nov. 28	**Tommy Burns**	25	172	Phila. Jack O'Brien	163½	Draw 20	Los Angeles
1907	May 8	**Tommy Burns**	25	180	Phila. Jack O'Brien	167	Ref 20	Los Angeles
1907	July 4	**Tommy Burns**	26	181	Bill Squires	180	KO 1	Colma, Calif.
1907	Dec. 2	**Tommy Burns**	26	177	Gunner Moir	204	KO 10	London
1908	Feb. 10	**Tommy Burns**	26	NA	Jack Palmer	NA	KO 4	London
1908	Mar. 17	**Tommy Burns**	26	NA	Jem Roche	NA	KO 1	Dublin
1908	Apr. 18	**Tommy Burns**	26	NA	Jewey Smith	NA	KO 5	Paris
1908	June 13	**Tommy Burns**	26	184	Bill Squires	183	KO 8	Paris
1908	Aug. 24	**Tommy Burns**	27	181	Bill Squires	184	KO 13	Sydney
1908	Sept. 2	**Tommy Burns**	27	183	Bill Lang	187	KO 6	Melbourne
1908	Dec. 26	Jack Johnson	30	192	**Tommy Burns**	168	TKO 14	Sydney
1909	Mar. 10	**Jack Johnson**	30	NA	Victor McLaglen	NA	ND 6	Vancouver
1909	May 19	**Jack Johnson**	31	205	Phila. Jack O'Brien	161	ND 6	Philadelphia
1909	June 30	**Jack Johnson**	31	207	Tony Ross	214	ND 6	Pittsburgh
1909	Sept. 9	**Jack Johnson**	31	209	Al Kaufman	191	ND 10	San Francisco
1909	Oct. 16	**Jack Johnson**	31	205½	Stanley Ketchel	170¼	KO 12	Colma, Calif.
1910	July 4	**Jack Johnson**	32	208	James J. Jeffries	227	KO 15	Reno, Nev.
1912	July 4	**Jack Johnson**	34	195½	Jim Flynn	175	TKO 9	Las Vegas, Nev.
1913	Dec. 19	**Jack Johnson**	35	NA	Jim Johnson	NA	Draw 10	Paris
1914	June 27	**Jack Johnson**	36	221	Frank Moran	203	Ref 20	Paris
1915	Apr. 5	Jess Willard	33	230	**Jack Johnson**	205½	KO 26	Havana
1916	Mar. 25	**Jess Willard**	34	225	Frank Moran	203	ND 10	NYC (Mad. Sq. Garden)
1919	July 4	Jack Dempsey	24	187	**Jess Willard**	245	TKO 4	Toledo, Ohio
1920	Sept. 6	**Jack Dempsey**	25	185	Billy Miske	187	KO 3	Benton Harbor, Mich.
1920	Dec. 14	**Jack Dempsey**	25	188¼	Bill Brennan	197	KO 12	NYC (Mad. Sq. Garden)
1921	July 2	**Jack Dempsey**	26	188	Georges Carpentier	172	KO 4	Jersey City, N.J.
1923	July 4	**Jack Dempsey**	28	188	Tommy Gibbons	175½	Ref 15	Shelby, Mont.
1923	Sept. 14	**Jack Dempsey**	28	192½	Luis Firpo	216½	KO 2	NYC (Polo Grounds)
1926	Sept. 23	Gene Tunney	29	189½	**Jack Dempsey**	190	Wu 10	Philadelphia
1927	Sept. 22	**Gene Tunney**	30	189½	Jack Dempsey	192½	Wu 10	Chicago
1928	July 26	**Gene Tunney****	31	192	Tom Heeney	203	TKO 11	NYC (Yankee Stadium)

*James J. Jeffries retired as champion on May 13, 1905, then came out of retirement to fight Jack Johnson for the title in 1910.
**Gene Tunney retired as champion in 1928.

Year	Date	Winner	Age	Wgt	Loser	Wgt	Result	Location
1930	June 12	Max Schmeling	24	188	Jack Sharkey	197	Disq. 4	NYC (Yankee Stadium)
1931	July 3	**Max Schmeling**	25	189	Young Stribling	186½	TKO 15	Cleveland
1932	June 21	Jack Sharkey	29	205	**Max Schmeling**	188	Ws 15	Long Island City, N.Y.
1933	June 29	Primo Carnera	26	260½	**Jack Sharkey**	201	KO 6	Long Island City, N.Y.
1933	Oct. 22	**Primo Carnera**	26	259½	Paulino Uzcudun	229¼	Wu 15	Rome
1934	Mar. 1	**Primo Carnera**	27	270	Tommy Loughran	184	Wu 15	Miami
1934	June 14	Max Baer	25	209½	**Primo Carnera**	263¼	TKO 11	Long Island City, N.Y.
1935	June 13	James J. Braddock	29	193¾	**Max Baer**	209	Wu 15	Long Island City, N.Y.
1937	June 22	Joe Louis	23	197¼	**James J. Braddock**	197	KO 8	Chicago
1937	Aug. 30	**Joe Louis**	23	197	Tommy Farr	204¼	Wu 15	NYC (Yankee Stadium)
1938	Feb. 23	**Joe Louis**	23	200	Nathan Mann	193½	KO 3	NYC (Mad. Sq. Garden)
1938	Apr. 1	**Joe Louis**	23	202½	Harry Thomas	196	KO 5	Chicago
1938	June 22	**Joe Louis**	24	198¾	Max Schmeling	193	KO 1	NYC (Yankee Stadium)
1939	Jan. 25	**Joe Louis**	24	200¼	John Henry Lewis	180¾	KO 1	NYC (Mad. Sq. Garden)
1939	Apr. 17	**Joe Louis**	24	201¼	Jack Roper	204¾	KO 1	Los Angeles
1939	June 28	**Joe Louis**	25	200¾	Tony Galento	233¾	TKO 4	NYC (Yankee Stadium)
1939	Sept. 20	**Joe Louis**	25	200	Bob Pastor	183	KO 11	Detroit
1940	Feb. 9	**Joe Louis**	25	203	Arturo Godoy	202	Ws 15	NYC (Mad. Sq. Garden)
1940	Mar. 29	**Joe Louis**	25	201½	Johnny Paychek	187½	KO 2	NYC (Mad. Sq. Garden)
1940	June 20	**Joe Louis**	26	199	Arturo Godoy	201¼	TKO 8	NYC (Yankee Stadium)
1940	Dec. 16	**Joe Louis**	26	202¼	Al McCoy	180¾	TKO 6	Boston
1941	Jan. 31	**Joe Louis**	26	202½	Red Burman	188	KO 5	NYC (Mad. Sq. Garden)
1941	Feb. 17	**Joe Louis**	26	203½	Gus Dorazio	193½	KO 2	Philadelphia
1941	Mar. 21	**Joe Louis**	26	202	Abe Simon	254½	TKO 13	Detroit
1941	Apr. 8	**Joe Louis**	26	203½	Tony Musto	199½	TKO 9	St. Louis
1941	May 23	**Joe Louis**	27	201½	Buddy Baer	237½	Disq. 7	Washington, D.C.
1941	June 18	**Joe Louis**	27	199½	Billy Conn	174	KO 13	NYC (Polo Grounds)
1941	Sept. 29	**Joe Louis**	27	202¼	Lou Nova	202½	TKO 6	NYC (Polo Grounds)
1942	Jan. 9	**Joe Louis**	27	206¾	Buddy Baer	250	KO 1	NYC (Mad. Sq. Garden)
1942	Mar. 27	**Joe Louis**	27	207½	Abe Simon	255½	KO 6	NYC (Mad. Sq. Garden)
1942-45 World War II								
1946	June 9	**Joe Louis**	32	207	Billy Conn	187	KO 8	NYC (Yankee Stadium)
1946	Sept. 18	**Joe Louis**	32	211	Tami Mauriello	198½	KO 1	NYC (Yankee Stadium)
1947	Dec. 5	**Joe Louis**	33	211½	Jersey Joe Walcott	194½	Ws 15	NYC (Mad. Sq. Garden)
1948	June 25	**Joe Louis***	34	213½	Jersey Joe Walcott	194¾	KO 11	NYC (Yankee Stadium)
1949	June 22	**Ezzard Charles**	27	181¾	Jersey Joe Walcott	195½	Wu 15	Chicago
1949	Aug. 10	**Ezzard Charles**	28	180	Gus Lesnevich	182	TKO 8	NYC (Yankee Stadium)
1949	Oct. 14	**Ezzard Charles**	28	182	Pat Valentino	188½	KO 8	San Francisco
1950	Aug. 15	**Ezzard Charles**	29	183¼	Freddie Beshore	184½	TKO 14	Buffalo
1950	Sept. 27	**Ezzard Charles**	29	184½	Joe Louis	218	Wu 15	NYC (Yankee Stadium)
1950	Dec. 5	**Ezzard Charles**	29	185	Nick Barone	178½	KO 11	Cincinnati
1951	Jan. 12	**Ezzard Charles**	29	185	Lee Oma	193	TKO 10	NYC (Mad. Sq. Garden)
1951	Mar. 7	**Ezzard Charles**	29	186	Jersey Joe Walcott	193	Wu 15	Detroit
1951	May 30	**Ezzard Charles**	29	182	Joey Maxim	181½	Wu 15	Chicago
1951	July 18	Jersey Joe Walcott	37	194	**Ezzard Charles**	182	KO 7	Pittsburgh
1952	June 5	**Jersey Joe Walcott**	38	196	Ezzard Charles	191½	Wu 15	Philadelphia
1952	Sept. 23	Rocky Marciano	29	184	**Jersey Joe Walcott**	196	KO 13	Philadelphia
1953	May 15	**Rocky Marciano**	29	184½	Jersey Joe Walcott	197¾	KO 1	Chicago
1953	Sept. 24	**Rocky Marciano**	30	185	Roland LaStarza	184¾	TKO 11	NYC (Polo Grounds)
1954	June 17	**Rocky Marciano**	30	187½	Ezzard Charles	185½	Wu 15	NYC (Yankee Stadium)
1954	Sept. 17	**Rocky Marciano**	31	187	Ezzard Charles	192½	KO 8	NYC (Yankee Stadium)
1955	May 16	**Rocky Marciano**	31	189	Don Cockell	205	TKO 9	San Francisco
1955	Sept. 21	**Rocky Marciano****	32	188¼	Archie Moore	188	KO 9	NYC (Yankee Stadium)
1956	Nov. 30	Floyd Patterson	21	182¼	Archie Moore	187¾	KO 5	Chicago
1957	July 29	**Floyd Patterson**	22	184	Tommy Jackson	192½	TKO 10	NYC (Polo Grounds)
1957	Aug. 22	**Floyd Patterson**	22	187¼	Pete Rademacher	202	KO 6	Seattle
1958	Aug. 18	**Floyd Patterson**	23	184½	Roy Harris	194	TKO 13	Los Angeles
1959	May 1	**Floyd Patterson**	24	182½	Brian London	206	KO 11	Indianapolis
1959	June 26	Ingemar Johansson	26	196	**Floyd Patterson**	182	TKO 3	NYC (Yankee Stadium)

*Joe Louis retired as champion on Mar. 1, 1949, then came out of retirement to fight Ezzard Charles for the title in 1950.
**Rocky Marciano retired as undefeated champion on Apr. 27, 1956.

Year	Date	Winner	Age	Wgt	Loser	Wgt	Result	Location
1960	June 20	Floyd Patterson	25	190	**Ingemar Johansson**	194¾	KO 5	NYC (Polo Grounds)
1961	Mar. 13	**Floyd Patterson**	26	194¾	Ingemar Johansson	206½	KO 6	Miami Beach
1961	Dec. 4	**Floyd Patterson**	26	188½	Tom McNeeley	197	KO 4	Toronto
1962	Sept. 25	Sonny Liston	30	214	**Floyd Patterson**	189	KO 1	Chicago
1963	July 22	**Sonny Liston**	31	215	Floyd Patterson	194½	KO 1	Las Vegas
1964	Feb. 25	Cassius Clay**	22	210½	**Sonny Liston**	218	TKO 7	Miami Beach
1965	Mar. 5	Ernie Terrell WBA	25	199	Eddie Machen	192	Wu 15	Chicago
1965	May 25	**Muhammad Ali**	23	206	Sonny Liston	215¼	KO 1	Lewiston, Maine
1965	Nov. 1	Ernie Terrell WBA	26	206	George Chuvalo	209	Wu 15	Toronto
1965	Nov. 22	**Muhammad Ali**	23	210	Floyd Patterson	196¾	TKO 12	Las Vegas
1966	Mar. 29	**Muhammad Ali**	24	214½	George Chuvalo	216	Wu 15	Toronto
1966	May 21	**Muhammad Ali**	24	201½	Henry Cooper	188	TKO 6	London
1966	June 28	Ernie Terrell WBA	27	209½	Doug Jones	187½	Wu 15	Houston
1966	Aug. 6	**Muhammad Ali**	24	209½	Brian London	201½	KO 3	London
1966	Sept. 10	**Muhammad Ali**	24	203½	Karl Mildenberger	194¼	TKO 12	Frankfurt, W. Ger.
1966	Nov. 14	**Muhammad Ali**	24	212¾	Cleveland Williams	210½	TKO 3	Houston
1967	Feb. 6	**Muhammad Ali**	25	212¼	Ernie Terrell WBA	212¼	Wu 15	Houston
1967	Mar. 22	**Muhammad Ali**	25	211½	Zora Folley	202½	KO 7	NYC (Mad. Sq. Garden)
1968	Mar. 4	Joe Frazier	24	204½	Buster Mathis	243½	TKO 11	NYC (Mad. Sq. Garden)
1968	Apr. 27	Jimmy Ellis	28	197	Jerry Quarry	195	Wm 15	Oakland
1968	June 24	Joe Frazier NY	24	203½	Manuel Ramos	208	TKO 2	NYC (Mad. Sq. Garden)
1968	Aug. 14	Jimmy Ellis WBA	28	198	Floyd Patterson	188	Ref 15	Stockholm
1968	Dec. 10	Joe Frazier NY	24	203	Oscar Bonavena	207	Wu 15	Philadelphia
1969	Apr. 22	Joe Frazier NY	25	204½	Dave Zyglewicz	190½	KO 1	Houston
1969	June 23	Joe Frazier NY	25	203½	Jerry Quarry	198½	TKO 8	NYC (Mad. Sq. Garden)
1970	Feb. 16	Joe Frazier NY	26	205	Jimmy Ellis WBA	201	TKO 5	NYC (Mad. Sq. Garden)
1970	Nov. 18	**Joe Frazier**	26	209	Bob Foster	188	KO 2	Detroit
1971	Mar. 8	**Joe Frazier**	27	205½	Muhammad Ali	215	Wu 15	NYC (Mad. Sq. Garden)
1972	Jan. 15	**Joe Frazier**	28	215½	Terry Daniels	195	TKO 4	New Orleans
1972	May 26	**Joe Frazier**	28	217½	Ron Stander	218	TKO 5	Omaha, Neb.
1973	Jan. 22	George Foreman	24	217½	**Joe Frazier**	214	TKO 2	Kingston, Jamaica
1973	Sept. 1	**George Foreman**	24	219½	Jose (King) Roman	196½	KO 1	Tokyo
1974	Mar. 26	George Foreman	25	224¾	Ken Norton	212¾	TKO 2	Caracas, Venezuela
1974	Oct. 30	Muhammad Ali	32	216½	**George Foreman**	220	KO 8	Kinshasa, Zaire
1975	Mar. 24	**Muhammad Ali**	33	223½	Chuck Wepner	225	TKO 15	Cleveland
1975	May 16	**Muhammad Ali**	33	224½	Ron Lyle	219	TKO 11	Las Vegas
1975	July 1	**Muhammad Ali**	33	224½	Joe Bugner	230	Wu 15	Kuala Lumpur, Malaysia
1975	Oct. 1	**Muhammad Ali**	33	224½	Joe Frazier	215	TKO 14	Manila, Philippines
1976	Feb. 20	**Muhammad Ali**	34	226	Jean Pierre Coopman	206	KO 5	San Juan, P.R.
1976	Apr. 30	**Muhammad Ali**	34	230	Jimmy Young	209	Wu 15	Landover, Md.
1976	May 24	**Muhammad Ali**	34	220	Richard Dunn	206½	TKO 5	Munich, W. Ger.
1976	Sept. 28	**Muhammad Ali**	34	221	Ken Norton	217½	Wu 15	NYC (Yankee Stadium)
1977	May 16	**Muhammad Ali**	35	221¼	Alfredo Evangelista	209¼	Wu 15	Landover, Md.
1977	Sept. 29	**Muhammad Ali**	35	225	Earnie Shavers	211¼	Wu 15	NYC (Mad. Sq. Garden)
1978	Feb. 15	Leon Spinks	24	197¼	**Muhammad Ali**	224¼	Ws 15	Las Vegas
1978	June 9	Larry Holmes	28	209	Ken Norton WBC††	220	Ws 15	Las Vegas
1978	Sept. 15	Muhammad Ali†	36	221	**Leon Spinks**	201	Wu 15	New Orleans
1978	Nov. 10	Larry Holmes WBC	29	214	Alfredo Evangelista	208¼	KO 7	Las Vegas
1979	Mar. 24	Larry Holmes WBC	29	214	Osvaldo Ocasio	207	TKO 7	Las Vegas
1979	June 22	Larry Holmes WBC	29	215	Mike Weaver	202	TKO 12	NYC (Mad. Sq. Garden)
1979	Sept. 28	Larry Holmes WBC	29	210	Earnie Shavers	211	TKO 11	Las Vegas
1979	Oct. 20	John Tate	24	240	Gerrie Coetzee	222	Wu 15	Pretoria, S. Africa
1980	Feb. 3	Larry Holmes WBC	30	213½	Lorenzo Zanon	215	TKO 6	Las Vegas
1980	Mar. 31	Mike Weaver	27	232	John Tate WBA	232	KO 15	Knoxville, Tenn.
1980	Mar. 31	Larry Holmes WBC	30	211	Leroy Jones	254½	TKO 8	Las Vegas
1980	July 7	Larry Holmes WBC	30	214¼	Scott LeDoux	226	TKO 7	Minneapolis
1980	Oct. 2	Larry Holmes WBC	30	211½	Muhammad Ali	217½	TKO 11	Las Vegas
1980	Oct. 25	Mike Weaver WBA	28	210	Gerrie Coetzee	226½	KO 13	Sun City, S. Africa

**After defeating Liston, Cassius Clay announced that he had changed his name to Muhammad Ali. He was later stripped of his title by the WBA and most state boxing commissions after refusing induction into the U.S. Army on Apr. 28, 1967.
† Muhammad Ali retired as champion on June 27, 1979, then came out of retirement to fight Larry Holmes for the title in 1980.
†† WBC recognized Ken Norton as world champion when Leon Spinks refused to meet Norton before Spinks' rematch with Muhammad Ali. Norton had scored a 15-round split decision over Jimmy Young on Nov. 5, 1977 in Las Vegas.

Year	Date	Winner	Age	Wgt	Loser	Wgt	Result	Location
1981	Apr. 11	**Larry Holmes**	31	215	Trevor Berbick	215½	Wu 15	Las Vegas
1981	June 12	**Larry Holmes**	31	212½	Leon Spinks	200¼	TKO 3	Detroit
1981	Oct. 3	Mike Weaver WBA	29	215	James (Quick) Tillis	209	Wu 15	Rosemont, Ill.
1981	Nov. 6	**Larry Holmes**	32	213¼	Renaldo Snipes	215¾	TKO 11	Pittsburgh
1982	June 11	**Larry Holmes**	32	212½	Gerry Cooney	225½	TKO 13	Las Vegas
1982	Nov. 26	**Larry Holmes**	33	217½	Randall (Tex) Cobb	234¼	Wu 15	Houston
1982	Dec. 10	Michael Dokes	24	216	Mike Weaver WBA	209¾	TKO 1	Las Vegas
1983	Mar. 27	**Larry Holmes**	33	221	Lucien Rodriguez	209	Wu 12	Scranton, Pa.
1983	May 20	Michael Dokes WBA	24	223	Mike Weaver	218½	Draw 15	Las Vegas
1983	May 20	**Larry Holmes**	33	213	Tim Witherspoon	219½	Ws 12	Las Vegas
1983	Sept. 10	**Larry Holmes**	33	223	Scott Frank	211¼	TKO 5	Atlantic City
1983	Sept. 23	Gerrie Coetzee	28	215	Michael Dokes WBA	217	KO 10	Richfield, Ohio
1983	Nov. 25	**Larry Holmes**	34	219	Marvis Frazier	200	TKO 1	Las Vegas
1984	Mar. 9	Tim Witherspoon*	26	220¼	Greg Page	239½	Wm 12	Las Vegas
1984	Aug. 31	Pinklon Thomas	26	216	Tim Witherspoon WBC	217	Wm 12	Las Vegas
1984	Nov. 9	**Larry Holmes** IBF	35	221½	Bonecrusher Smith	227	TKO 12	Las Vegas
1984	Dec. 1	Greg Page	26	236½	Gerrie Coetzee WBA	218	KO 8	Sun City, S. Africa
1985	Mar. 15	**Larry Holmes** IBF	35	223½	David Bey	233¼	TKO 10	Las Vegas
1985	Apr. 29	Tony Tubbs	26	229	Greg Page WBA	239½	Wu 15	Buffalo
1985	May 20	**Larry Holmes** IBF	35	224¼	Carl Williams	215	Wu 15	Las Vegas
1985	June 15	Pinklon Thomas WBC	27	220¼	Mike Weaver	221¼	KO 8	Las Vegas
1985	Sept. 21	Michael Spinks	29	200	**Larry Holmes** IBF	221½	Wu 15	Las Vegas
1986	Jan. 17	Tim Witherspoon	28	227	Tony Tubbs WBA	229	Wm 15	Atlanta
1986	Mar. 22	Trevor Berbick	33	218½	Pinklon Thomas WBC	222¾	Wu 15	Las Vegas
1986	Apr. 19	**Michael Spinks** IBF	29	205	Larry Holmes	223	Ws 15	Las Vegas
1986	July 19	Tim Witherspoon WBA	28	234¾	Frank Bruno	228	TKO 11	Wembley, England
1986	Sept. 6	**Michael Spinks** IBF	30	201	Steffen Tangstad	214¾	TKO 4	Las Vegas
1986	Nov. 22	Mike Tyson	20	221¼	Trevor Berbick WBC	218½	TKO 2	Las Vegas
1986	Dec. 12	Bonecrusher Smith	33	228½	Tim Witherspoon WBA	233½	TKO 1	NYC (Mad. Sq. Garden)
1987	Mar. 7	Mike Tyson WBC	20	219	Bonecrusher Smith WBA	233	Wu 12	Las Vegas
1987	May 30	Mike Tyson	20	218¾	Pinklon Thomas	217¾	TKO 6	Las Vegas
1987	May 30	Tony Tucker**	28	222¼	Buster Douglas	227¼	TKO 10	Las Vegas
1987	June 15	**Michael Spinks**†	30	208¾	Gerry Cooney	238	TKO 5	Atlantic City
1987	Aug. 1	Mike Tyson	21	221	Tony Tucker IBF	221	Wu 12	Las Vegas
1987	Oct. 16	Mike Tyson	21	216	Tyrell Biggs	228¾	TKO 7	Atlantic City
1988	Jan. 22	Mike Tyson	21	215¾	Larry Holmes	225¾	TKO 4	Atlantic City
1988	Mar. 20	Mike Tyson	21	216¼	Tony Tubbs	238¼	KO 2	Tokyo
1988	June 27	Mike Tyson	21	218¼	**Michael Spinks**	212¼	KO 1	Atlantic City
1989	Feb. 25	**Mike Tyson**	22	218	Frank Bruno	228	TKO 5	Las Vegas
1989	July 21	**Mike Tyson**	23	219¼	Carl Williams	218	TKO 1	Atlantic City
1990	Feb. 10	Buster Douglas	29	231½	**Mike Tyson**	220½	KO 10	Tokyo
1990	Oct. 25	Evander Holyfield	28	208	**Buster Douglas**	246	KO 3	Las Vegas
1991	Apr. 19	**Evander Holyfield**	28	208	George Foreman	257	Wu 12	Atlantic City
1991	Nov. 23	**Evander Holyfield**	29	210	Bert Cooper	215	TKO 7	Atlanta
1992	June 19	**Evander Holyfield**	29	210	Larry Holmes	233	Wu 12	Las Vegas
1992	Nov. 13	Riddick Bowe	25	235	**Evander Holyfield**	205	Wu 12	Las Vegas
1993	Feb. 6	**Riddick Bowe**	25	243	Michael Dokes	244	TKO 1	NYC (Mad. Sq. Garden)
1993	May 8	Lennox Lewis WBC‡	27	235	Tony Tucker	235	Wu 12	Las Vegas
1993	May 22	**Riddick Bowe**	25	244	Jesse Ferguson	224	TKO 2	Washington, D.C.
1993	Oct. 1	Lennox Lewis WBC	28	233	Frank Bruno	238	TKO 7	Cardiff, Wales
1993	Nov. 6	Evander Holyfield	31	217	**Riddick Bowe** WBA/IBF	246	Wm 12	Las Vegas
1994	Apr. 22	Michael Moorer	26	214	**Evander Holyfield**	214	Wm 12	Las Vegas
1994	May 6	Lennox Lewis WBC	28	235	Phil Jackson	218	TKO 8	Atlantic City
1994	Sept. 25	Oliver McCall	29	231¼	**Lennox Lewis** WBC	238	TKO 2	London

*WBC recognized winner of Mar. 9, 1984 fight between Tim Witherspoon and Greg Page as world champion after Larry Holmes relinquished title in dispute. IBF then recognized Holmes.

**IBF recognized winner of May 30, 1987 fight between Tony Tucker and James (Buster) Douglas as world champion after Michael Spinks relinquished title in dispute.

†The July 15, 1987 Spinks-Cooney fight was not an official championship bout because it was not sanctioned by any boxing associations, councils or federations.

‡WBC recognized Lennox Lewis as world champion when Riddick Bowe gave up that portion of his title on Dec. 14, 1992, rather than fight Lewis, the WBC's mandatory challenger.

Year	Date	Winner	Age	Wgt	Loser	Wgt	Result	Location
1994	Nov. 5	George Foreman*	45	250	**Michael Moorer**	222	KO 10	Las Vegas
1995	Apr. 8	Oliver McCall WBC	29	231	Larry Holmes	236	Wu 12	Las Vegas
1995	Apr. 8	Bruce Seldon*	28	236	Tony Tucker	240	TKO 7	Las Vegas
1995	Apr. 22	**George Foreman***	46	256	Axel Schulz	221	Ws 12	Las Vegas
1995	Aug. 19	Bruce Seldon WBA	28	234	Joe Hipp	223	TKO 10	Las Vegas
1995	Sept. 2	Frank Bruno	33	248	Oliver McCall WBC	235	Wu 12	London
1995	Dec. 9	Frans Botha**	27	237	Axel Schulz	222	Wu 12	Stuttgart, GER
1996	Mar. 16	Mike Tyson	29	220	Frank Bruno WBC	247	TKO 3	Las Vegas
1996	June 22	Michael Moorer**	28	222	Axel Schulz	223	Ws 12	Dortmund, GER
1996	Sept. 7	Mike Tyson WBC†	30	219	Bruce Seldon WBA	229	TKO 1	Las Vegas
1996	Nov. 9	Evander Holyfield	34	215	**Mike Tyson** WBA	222	TKO 11	Las Vegas
1997	Feb. 7	Lennox Lewis†	31	251	Oliver McCall	237	TKO 5	Las Vegas
1997	Mar. 29	Michael Moorer IBF	29	212	Vaughn Bean	212	Wm 12	Las Vegas
1997	June 28	**Evander Holyfield** WBA‡	34	218	Mike Tyson	218	Disq. 3	Las Vegas
1997	July 12	Lennox Lewis WBC	31	242	Henry Akinwande	237½	Disq. 5	Stateline, Nev.
1997	Oct. 4	Lennox Lewis WBC	32	244	Andrew Golota	244	TKO 1	Atlantic City
1997	Nov. 8	Evander Holyfield WBA	35	214	Michael Moorer IBF	223	TKO 8	Las Vegas
1998	Mar. 28	Lennox Lewis WBC	32	243	Shannon Briggs	228	TKO 5	Atlantic City
1998	Sept. 19	**Evander Holyfield** WBA/IBF	35	217	Vaughn Bean	231	Wu 12	Atlanta
1998	Sept. 26	Lennox Lewis WBC	33	250	Zeljko Mavrovic	220	Wu 12	Uncasville, Conn.
1999	Mar. 13	Lennox Lewis WBC	33	246	**Evander Holyfield** WBA/IBF	215	Draw 12	NYC (Mad. Sq. Garden)
1999	Nov. 13	Lennox Lewis WBC	34	240	**Evander Holyfield** WBA/IBF	218	Wu 12	Las Vegas
2000	Apr. 29	**Lennox Lewis** WBC/IBF‖	34	247	Michael Grant	250	KO 2	NYC (Mad. Sq. Garden)
2000	July 15	**Lennox Lewis** WBC/IBF	34	250	Frans Botha	237	TKO 2	London
2000	Aug. 12	Evander Holyfield	37	221	John Ruiz	224	Wu 12	Las Vegas

*George Foreman won WBA and IBF championships when he beat Michael Moorer on Nov. 5, 1994. He was stripped of WBA title on Mar. 4, 1995, when he refused to fight No. 1 contender Tony Tucker, and he relinquished IBF title on June 29, 1995, rather than give Axel Schulz a rematch. Tucker lost to Bruce Seldon in their April 8 fight for vacant WBA title.
**Frans Botha won the vacant IBF title with a controversial 12–round decision over Axel Schulz on Dec. 9, 1995, but after legal sparring, was eventually stripped of the IBF belt for using anabolic steroids. Moorer then claimed the revacated title with his June 22, 1996 win over Schulz.
†Mike Tyson won the WBC belt from Frank Bruno on Mar. 16, 1996 and still held it at the time of his Sept. 7, 1996 win over Bruce Seldon (although it was not at risk for that fight) but was forced to relinquish the title after the bout for not fighting mandatory challenge Lennox Lewis. Tyson also paid Lewis $4 million to step aside and allow the Tyson-Seldon bout to take place. Lewis then fought Oliver McCall for the vacant WBC belt. The fight was stopped 55 seconds into round 5 because, inexplicably, McCall was visibly distraught and stopped throwing punches.
‡Holyfield won the bout by disqualification and retained the WBA belt after Tyson spit out his mouthpiece and bit off a piece of Holyfield's ear. Tyson had received a two-point deduction from referee Mills Lane and after a stern warning and a short delay the fight was allowed to continue. Later in round 3, he bit Holyfield's other ear and Tyson was disqualified.
‖Lewis was stripped of the WBA title for choosing to fight Michael Grant instead of John Ruiz, the WBA's #1 challenger. The WBA sanctioned the Evander Holyfield-John Ruiz August 12 bout for its vacant heavyweight belt.

All-Time Heavyweight Upsets

Buster Douglas was a 42-1 underdog when he defeated previously-unbeaten heavyweight champion Mike Tyson on Feb. 10, 1990. That 10th-round knockout ranks as the biggest upset in boxing history. By comparison, 45-year-old George Foreman was only a 3-1 underdog before he unexpectedly won the title from Michael Moorer on Nov. 5, 1994.

Here are the best-known upsets in the annals of the heavyweight division. All fights were for the world championship except the Max Schmeling-Joe Louis bout.

Date	Winner	Loser	Result	KO Time	Location
9/7/1892	James J. Corbett	John L. Sullivan	KO 21	1:30	Olympic Club, New Orleans
4/5/1915	Jess Willard	Jack Johnson	KO 26	1:26	Mariano Race Track, Havana
9/23/26	Gene Tunney	Jack Dempsey	Wu 10	–	Sesquicentennial Stadium, Phila.
6/13/35	James J. Braddock	Max Baer	Wu 15	–	Mad.Sq.Garden Bowl, L.I. City
6/19/36	Max Schmeling	Joe Louis	KO 12	2:29	Yankee Stadium, New York
7/18/51	Jersey Joe Walcott	Ezzard Charles	KO 7	0:55	Forbes Field, Pittsburgh
6/26/59	Ingemar Johansson	Floyd Patterson	TKO 3	2:03	Yankee Stadium, New York
2/25/64	Cassius Clay	Sonny Liston	TKO 7	*	Convention Hall, Miami Beach
10/30/74	Muhammad Ali	George Foreman	KO 8	2:58	20th of May Stadium, Zaire
2/15/78	Leon Spinks	Muhammad Ali	Ws 15	–	Hilton Pavilion, Las Vegas
9/21/85	Michael Spinks	Larry Holmes	Wu 15	–	Riviera Hotel, Las Vegas
2/10/90	Buster Douglas	Mike Tyson	KO 10	1:23	Tokyo Dome, Tokyo
11/5/94	George Foreman	Michael Moorer	KO 10	2:03	MGM Grand, Las Vegas
11/9/96	Evander Holyfield	Mike Tyson	TKO 11	0:37	MGM Grand, Las Vegas

*Liston failed to answer bell for Round 7.

Muhammad Ali's Career Pro Record

Born Cassius Marcellus Clay, Jr. on Jan. 17, 1942, in Louisville; Amateur record of 100-5; won light-heavyweight gold medal at 1960 Olympic Games; Pro record of 56-5 with 37 KOs in 61 fights.

1960

Date	Opponent (location)	Result
Oct. 29	Tunney Hunsaker, Louisville	Wu 6
Dec. 27	Herb Siler, Miami Beach	TKO 4

1961

Date	Opponent (location)	Result
Jan. 17	Tony Esperti, Miami Beach	TKO 3
Feb. 7	Jim Robinson, Miami Beach	TKO 1
Feb. 21	Donnie Fleeman, Miami Beach	TKO 7
Apr. 19	Lamar Clark, Louisville	KO 2
June 26	Duke Sabedong, Las Vegas	Wu 10
July 22	Alonzo Johnson, Louisville	Wu 10
Oct. 7	Alex Miteff, Louisville	TKO 6
Nov. 29	Willi Besmanoff, Louisville	TKO 7

1962

Date	Opponent (location)	Result
Feb. 10	Sonny Banks, New York	TKO 4
Feb. 28	Don Warner, Miami Beach	TKO 4
Apr. 23	George Logan, Los Angeles	TKO 4
May 19	Billy Daniels, Los Angeles	TKO 7
July 20	Alejandro Lavorante, Los Angeles	KO 5
Nov. 15	Archie Moore, Los Angeles	KO 4

1963

Date	Opponent (location)	Result
Jan. 24	Charlie Powell, Pittsburgh	KO 3
Mar. 13	Doug Jones, New York	Wu 10
June 18	Henry Cooper, London	TKO 5

1964

Date	Opponent (location)	Result
Feb. 25	Sonny Liston, Miami Beach	TKO 7

(won World Heavyweight title)

After the fight, Clay announces he is a member of the Black Muslim religious sect and has changed his name to Muhammad Ali.

1965

Date	Opponent (location)	Result
May 25	Sonny Liston, Lewiston, Me	KO 1
Nov. 22	Floyd Patterson, Las Vegas	TKO 12

1966

Date	Opponent (location)	Result
Mar. 29	George Chuvalo, Toronto	Wu 15
May 21	Henry Cooper, London	TKO 6
Aug. 6	Brian London, London	KO 3
Sept.10	Karl Mildenberger, Frankfurt	TKO 12
Nov. 12	Cleveland Williams, Houston	TKO 3

1967

Date	Opponent (location)	Result
Feb. 6	Ernie Terrell, Houston	Wu 15
Mar. 22	Zora Folley, New York	KO 7
Apr. 28	Refuses induction into U.S. Army and is stripped of world title by WBA and most state commissions the next day.	
June 20	Found guilty of draft evasion in Houston; fined $10,000 and sentenced to 5 years; remains free pending appeals, but is barred from the ring.	

1968-69 (Inactive)

1970

Date	Opponent (location)	Result
Feb. 3	Announces retirement.	
Oct. 26	Jerry Quarry, Atlanta	TKO 3
Dec. 7	Oscar Bonavena, New York	TKO 15

1971

Date	Opponent (location)	Result
Mar. 8	Joe Frazier, New York	Lu 15

(for World Heavyweight title)

June 28	U.S. Supreme Court reverses Ali's 1967 conviction saying he had been drafted improperly.	
July 26	Jimmy Ellis, Houston	TKO 12

(won vacant NABF Heavyweight title)

Nov. 17	Buster Mathis, Houston	Wu 12
Dec. 26	Jurgen Blin, Zurich	KO 7

1972

Date	Opponent (location)	Result
Apr. 1	Mac Foster, Tokyo	Wu 15
May 1	George Chuvalo, Vancouver	Wu 12
June 27	Jerry Quarry, Las Vegas	TKO 7
July 19	Al (Blue) Lewis, Dublin, Ire	TKO 11
Sept.20	Floyd Patterson, New York	TKO 7
Nov. 21	Bob Foster, Stateline, Nev	TKO 8

1973

Date	Opponent (location)	Result
Feb. 14	Joe Bugner, Las Vegas	Wu 12
Mar. 31	Ken Norton, San Diego	Ls 12

(lost NABF Heavyweight title)

Sept.10	Ken Norton, Inglewood, Calif	Ws 12

(regained NABF Heavyweight title)

Oct. 20	Rudi Lubbers, Jakarta, Indonesia	Wu 12

1974

Date	Opponent (location)	Result
Jan. 28	Joe Frazier, New York	Wu 12
Oct. 30	George Foreman, Kinshasa, Zaire	KO 8

(regained World Heavyweight title)

1975

Date	Opponent (location)	Result
Mar. 24	Chuck Wepner, Cleveland	TKO 15
May 16	Ron Lyle, Las Vegas	TKO 11
June 30	Joe Bugner, Kuala Lumpur, Malaysia	Wu 15
Oct. 1	Joe Frazier, Manila, Philippines	TKO 14

1976

Date	Opponent (location)	Result
Feb. 20	Jean-Pierre Coopman, San Juan	KO 5
Apr. 30	Jimmy Young, Landover, Md	Wu 15
May 24	Richard Dunn, Munich	TKO 5
Sept.28	Ken Norton, New York	Wu 15

1977

Date	Opponent (location)	Result
May 16	Alfredo Evangelista, Landover	Wu 15
Sept.29	Earnie Shavers, New York	Wu 15

1978

Date	Opponent (location)	Result
Feb. 15	Leon Spinks, Las Vegas	Ls 15

(lost World Heavyweight title)

Sept.15	Leon Spinks, New Orleans	Wu 15

(regained World Heavyweight title)

1979

Date		
June 27	Announces retirement.	

1980

Date	Opponent (location)	Result
Oct. 2	Larry Holmes, Las Vegas	TKO by 11

1981

Date	Opponent (location)	Result
Dec. 11	Trevor Berbick, Nassau	Lu 10

(retires after fight)

Foreman and Frazier

The career pro records of heavyweights George Foreman and Joe Frazier.

George Foreman

Born: Jan. 10, 1949 in Marshall, Tex.

Pro record: 75-5-0, 68 KOs

No	Date	Opponent, location	Result
1	6/23/69	Don Waldhelm, New York	KO 3
2	7/1/69	Fred Ashew, Houston	KO 1
3	7/14/69	Sylvester Dullaire, Wash., D.C.	KO 1
4	8/18/69	Chuck Wepner, New York	TKO 3
5	9/18/69	John Carroll, Seattle	KO 1
6	9/23/69	Cookie Wallace, Houston	KO 2
7	10/7/69	Vernon Clay, Houston	TKO 2
8	10/31/69	Roberto Davila, New York	Wu 8
9	11/5/69	Leo Peterson, Scranton	KO 4
10	11/18/69	Max Martinez, Houston	KO 2
11	12/6/69	Bob Hazelton, Las Vegas	KO 1
12	12/16/69	Levi Forte, Miami Beach	Wu 10
13	12/18/69	Gary Wilder, Seattle	TKO 1
14	1/6/70	Charley Polite, Houston	KO 4
15	1/26/70	Jack O'Halloran, New York	KO 5
16	2/16/70	Gregorio Peralta, New York	Wu 10
17	3/31/70	Rufus Brassell, Houston	KO 1
18	4/17/70	James J. Woody, New York	TKO 3
19	4/29/70	Aaron Easting, Cleveland	TKO 4
20	5/16/70	George Johnson, Inglewood	TKO 7
21	7/20/70	Roger Russell, Philadelphia	TKO 1
22	8/4/70	George Chuvalo, New York	TKO 3
23	11/3/70	Lou Bailey, Oklahoma City	KO 3
24	11/18/70	Boone Kirkman, New York	TKO 2
25	12/19/70	Mel Turnbow, Seattle	TKO 1
26	2/8/71	Charlie Boston, St. Paul, Minn.	KO 1
27	4/3/71	Stanford Harris, Lake Geneva	KO 2
28	5/10/71	Gregorio Peralta, Oakland	TKO 10
29	9/14/91	Vic Scott, El Paso	KO 1
30	9/21/71	Leroy Caldwell, Beaumont, Tex.	KO 2
31	10/7/71	Ollie Wilson, San Antonio	TKO 2
32	10/29/71	Luis F. Pires, New York	TKO 5
33	2/29/72	Murphy Goodwin, Austin, Tex.	KO 2
34	3/7/72	Clarence Boone, Beaumont, Tex.	TKO 2
35	4/10/72	Ted Gullick, Inglewood	KO 2
36	5/11/72	Miguel A. Paez, Oakland	KO 2
37	10/10/72	Terry Sorrels, Salt Lake City	KO 2
38	1/22/73	Joe Frazier, Kingston, Jamaica	TKO 2

(won World Heavyweight title)

No	Date	Opponent, location	Result
39	9/1/73	Jose Roman, Tokyo	KO 1
40	3/26/74	Ken Norton, Caracas, Venezuela	TKO 2
41	10/30/74	Muhammad Ali, Kinshasa, Zaire	KO by 8

(lost World Heavyweight title)

No	Date	Opponent, location	Result
42	1/24/76	Ron Lyle, Las Vegas	KO 5
43	6/15/76	Joe Frazier, Uniondale, N.Y.	TKO 5
44	8/14/76	Scott Le Doux, Utica, N.Y.	KO 3
45	10/15/76	Dino Denis, Hollywood, Fla.	TKO 4
46	1/22/77	Pedro Agosto, Pensacola, Fla.	TKO 4
47	3/17/77	Jimmy Young, Hato Rey, P.R.	Lu 12

(retired after fight)

No	Date	Opponent, location	Result
48	3/9/87	Steve Zouski, Sacramento	TKO 4

(first fight of comeback)

No	Date	Opponent, location	Result
49	7/9/87	Charles Hostetter, Oakland	KO 3
50	9/15/87	Bobby Crabree, Springfield, Mo.	TKO 6
51	11/21/87	Tim Anderson, Orlando	TKO 4
52	12/18/87	Rocky Sekorski, Las Vegas	TKO 3
53	1/23/88	Tom Trimm, Orlando	TKO 1
54	2/5/88	Guido Trane, Las Vegas	TKO 5
55	3/19/88	Dwight Qawi, Las Vegas	TKO 7
56	5/21/88	Frank Williams, Anchorage	KO 3
57	6/26/88	Carlos Hernandez, Atlantic City	TKO 4
58	8/25/88	Ladislao Mijangos, Ft. Myers	TKO 2
59	9/10/88	Bobby Hitz, Auburn Hills, Mich.	KO 1
60	10/27/88	Tony Fulilangi, Marshall, Tex.	TKO 2
61	12/28/88	David Jaco, Bakersfield, Calif.	KO 1

No	Date	Opponent, location	Result
62	1/26/89	Mark Young, Rochester, N.Y.	TKO 7
63	2/16/89	Manuel de Almeida, Orlando	TKO 3
64	4/30/89	J.B. Williamson, Galveston, Tex.	TKO 5
65	6/1/89	Bert Cooper, Phoenix	TKO 3
66	7/20/89	Everett Martin, Tucson	Wu 10
67	1/15/90	Gerry Cooney, Atlantic City	KO 2
68	4/17/90	Mike Jameson, Stateline, Nev.	TKO 4
69	6/16/90	Adilson Rodrigues, Las Vegas	KO 2
70	7/31/90	Ken Lakusta, Edmonton	KO 3
71	9/25/90	Terry Anderson, Millwall, England	KO 1
72	4/19/91	Evander Holyfield, Atlantic City	Lu 12

(for World Heavyweight title)

No	Date	Opponent, location	Result
73	12/7/91	Jimmy Ellis, Reno, Nev.	TKO 3
74	4/11/92	Alex Stewart, Las Vegas	Wm 10
75	1/16/93	Pierre Coetzer, Reno, Nev.	TKO 8
76	6/7/93	Tommy Morrison, Las Vegas	Lu 12
77	11/5/94	Michael Moorer, Las Vegas	KO 10

(won WBA/IBF heavyweight titles)

No	Date	Opponent, location	Result
78	4/22/95	Axel Schulz, Las Vegas	Wm 12
79	11/3/96	Crawford Grimsley, Tokyo	Wu 12
80	11/22/97	Shannon Briggs, Atlantic City	Lm 12

Joe Frazier

Born: Jan. 12, 1944 in Beaufort, S.C.

Pro record: 32-4-1, 27 KOs

No	Date	Opponent	Result
1	8/16/65	Woody Gross	TKO 1
2	9/20/65	Michael Bruce	KO 3
3	9/28/65	Ray Staples	KO 2
4	11/11/65	Abe Davis	KO 1
5	1/17/66	Mel Turnbow	KO 1
6	3/4/66	Dick Wipperman	TKO 5
7	4/4/66	Charley Polite	TKO 2
8	4/28/66	Don Smith	KO 3
9	5/19/66	Chuck Leslie	KO 3
10	5/26/66	Memphis Jones	KO 1
11	7/25/66	Billy Daniels	TKO 6
12	9/21/66	Oscar Bonavena	Wu 10
13	11/21/66	Eddie Machen	TKO 10
14	2/21/67	Doug Jones	KO 5
15	4/11/67	Jeff Davis	KO 5
16	5/4/67	George Johnson	Wu 10
17	7/19/67	George Chuvalo	TKO 4
18	10/17/67	Tony Doyle	TKO 2
19	12/18/67	Marion Connors	KO 3
20	3/4/68	Buster Mathis	KO 11
21	6/24/68	Manuel Ramos	TKO 2
22	12/10/68	Oscar Bonavena	Wu 15
23	4/22/69	Dave Zyglewicz	KO 1
24	6/23/69	Jerry Quarry	TKO 7
25	2/16/70	Jimmy Ellis	TKO 5

(won World Heavyweight title)

No	Date	Opponent	Result
26	11/18/70	Bob Foster	KO 2
27	3/8/71	Muhammad Ali	Wu 15
28	1/15/72	Terry Daniels	TKO 4
29	5/25/72	Ron Stander	TKO 5
30	1/22/73	George Foreman	KO by 2

(lost World Heavyweight title)

No	Date	Opponent	Result
31	7/2/73	Joe Bugner	Wu 12
32	1/28/74	Muhammad Ali	Lu 12
33	6/17/74	Jerry Quarry	TKO 5
34	4/1/75	Jimmy Ellis	TKO 9
35	10/1/75	Muhammad Ali	TKO by 14

(for World Heavyweight title)

No	Date	Opponent	Result
36	6/15/76	George Foreman	KO by 5
37	3/12/81	Floyd Cummings	Draw 10

Major Titleholders

Note the following sanctioning body abbreviations: NBA (National Boxing Association), WBA (World Boxing Association), WBC (World Boxing Council), GBR (Great Britain), IBF (International Boxing Federation), plus other national and state commissions. Fighters who retired as champion are indicated by (*) and champions who abandoned or relinquished their titles are indicated by (†).

Heavyweights

Widely accepted champions in CAPITAL letters. Current champions in **bold** type (as of Oct. 23, 2000).

Note: Muhammad Ali was stripped of his world title in 1967 after refusing induction into the Army (see Muhammad Ali's Career Pro Record). George Foreman was stripped of his WBA and IBF titles in 1995, but remained active as linear champion (see Boxing: Major Bouts 1998-99).

Champion	Held Title	Champion	Held Title
JOHN L. SULLIVAN	1885-92	John Tate (WBA)	1979-80
JAMES J. CORBETT	1892-97	Mike Weaver (WBA)	1980-82
BOB FITZSIMMONS	1897-99	LARRY HOLMES	1980-85
JAMES J. JEFFRIES	1899-1905*	Michael Dokes (WBA)	1982-83
MARVIN HART	1905-06	Gerrie Coetzee (WBA)	1983-84
TOMMY BURNS	1906-08	Tim Witherspoon (WBC)	1984
JACK JOHNSON	1908-15	Pinklon Thomas (WBC)	1984-86
JESS WILLARD	1915-19	Greg Page (WBA)	1984-85
JACK DEMPSEY	1919-26	MICHAEL SPINKS	1985-87
GENE TUNNEY	1926-28*	Tim Witherspoon (WBA)	1986
MAX SCHMELING	1930-32	Trevor Berbick (WBC)	1986
JACK SHARKEY	1932-33	Mike Tyson (WBC)	1986-87
PRIMO CARNERA	1933-34	James (Bonecrusher) Smith (WBA)	1986-87
MAX BAER	1934-35	Tony Tucker (IBF)	1987
JAMES J. BRADDOCK	1935-37	MIKE TYSON (WBC, WBA, IBF)	1987-90
JOE LOUIS	1937-49*	BUSTER DOUGLAS (WBC, WBA, IBF)	1990
EZZARD CHARLES	1949-51	EVANDER HOLYFIELD (WBC, WBA, IBF)	1990-92
JERSEY JOE WALCOTT	1951-52	RIDDICK BOWE (WBA, IBF)	1992-93
ROCKY MARCIANO	1952-56*	Lennox Lewis (WBC)	1992-94
FLOYD PATTERSON	1956-59	EVANDER HOLYFIELD (WBA, IBF)	1993-94
INGEMAR JOHANSSON	1959-60	MICHAEL MOORER (WBA, IBF)	1994
FLOYD PATTERSON	1960-62	Oliver McCall (WBC)	1994-95
SONNY LISTON	1962-64	GEORGE FOREMAN (WBA, IBF)	1994-95
CASSIUS CLAY (MUHAMMAD ALI)	1964-67	Bruce Seldon (WBA)	1995-96
Ernie Terrell (WBA)	1965-67	GEORGE FOREMAN	1995-96
Joe Frazier (NY)	1968-70	Frank Bruno (WBC)	1995-96
Jimmy Ellis (WBA)	1968-70	Mike Tyson (WBC)	1996†
JOE FRAZIER	1970-73	Mike Tyson (WBA)	1996
GEORGE FOREMAN	1973-74	Michael Moorer (IBF)	1996-1997
MUHAMMAD ALI	1974-78	Evander Holyfield (WBA, IBF)	1996-2000
LEON SPINKS	1978	Lennox Lewis (WBC)	1997-2000
Ken Norton (WBC)	1978	LENNOX LEWIS (WBA, WBC, IBF)	2000
Larry Holmes (WBC)	1978-80	**Evander Holyfield** (WBA)	2000–
MUHAMMAD ALI	1978-79*	**LENNOX LEWIS** (WBC, IBF)	2000–

Note: John L. Sullivan held the Bare Knuckle championship from 1882-85.

Cruiserweights

Current champions in **bold** type.

Champion	Held Title	Champion	Held Title
Marvin Camel (WBC)	1980	Glenn McCrory (IBF)	1989-90
Carlos De Leon (WBC)	1980-82	Jeff Lampkin (IBF)	1990
Ossie Ocasio (WBA)	1982-84	Massimiliano Duran (WBC)	1990-91
S.T. Gordon (WBC)	1982-83	Bobby Czyz (WBA)	1991-92†
Carlos De Leon (WBC)	1983-85	Anaclet Wamba (WBC)	1991-95
Marvin Camel (IBF)	1983-84	James Pritchard (IBF)	1991
Lee Roy Murphy (IBF)	1984-86	James Warring (IBF)	1991-92
Piet Crous (WBA)	1984-85	Alfred Cole (IBF)	1992-96
Alfonso Ratliff (WBC)	1985	Orlin Norris (WBA)	1993-95
Dwight Braxton (WBA)	1985-86	Nate Miller (WBA)	1995-97
Bernard Benton (WBC)	1985-86	Marcelo Dominguez (WBC)	1996-98
Carlos De Leon (WBC)	1986-88	Adolpho Washington (IBF)	1996-97
Evander Holyfield (WBA)	1986-88	Uriah Grant (IBF)	1997
Ricky Parkey (IBF)	1986-87	Imamu Mayfield (IBF)	1997-98
Evander Holyfield (WBA/IBF)	1987-88	Arthur Williams (IBF)	1998-99
Evander Holyfield	1988†	**Fabrice Tiozzo** (WBA)	1997—
Toufik Belbouli (WBA)	1989	**Juan Carlos Gomez** (WBC)	1998—
Robert Daniels (WBA)	1989-91	**Vassiliy Jirov** (IBF)	1999—
Carlos De Leon (WBC)	1989-90		

Light Heavyweights
Widely accepted champions in CAPITAL letters. Current champions in **bold** type.

Champion	Held Title	Champion	Held Title
JACK ROOT	1903	Mike Rossman (WBA)	1978-79
GEORGE GARDNER	1903	Marvin Johnson (WBC)	1978-79
BOB FITZSIMMONS	1903-05	Matthew (Franklin) Saad Muhammad (WBC)	1979-81
PHILADELPHIA JACK O'BRIEN	1905-12*	Marvin Johnson (WBA)	1979-80
JACK DILLON	1914-16	Eddie (Gregory)	
BATTLING LEVINSKY	1916-20	Mustapha Muhammad (WBA)	1980-81
GEORGES CARPENTIER	1920-22	Michael Spinks (WBA)	1981-83
BATTLING SIKI	1922-23	Dwight (Braxton) Muhammad Qawi (WBC)	1981-83
MIKE McTIGUE	1923-25	MICHAEL SPINKS	1983-85†
PAUL BERLENBACH	1925-26	J.B.Williamson (WBC)	1985-86
JACK DELANEY	1926-27†	Slobodan Kacar (IBF)	1985-86
Jimmy Slattery (NBA)	1927	Marvin Johnson (WBA)	1986-87
TOMMY LOUGHRAN	1927-29	Dennis Andries (WBC)	1986-87
JIMMY SLATTERY	1930	Bobby Czyz (IBF)	1986-87
MAXIE ROSENBLOOM	1930-34	Leslie Stewart (WBA)	1987
George Nichols (NBA)	1932	Virgil Hill (WBA)	1987-91
Bob Godwin (NBA)	1933	Prince Charles Williams (IBF)	1987-93
BOB OLIN	1934-35	Thomas Hearns (WBC)	1987
JOHN HENRY LEWIS	1935-38	Donny Lalonde (WBC)	1987-88
MELIO BETTINA (NY)	1939	Sugar Ray Leonard (WBC)	1988
Len Harvey (GBR)	1939-42	Dennis Andries (WBC)	1989
BILLY CONN	1939-40†	Jeff Harding (WBC)	1989-90
ANTON CHRISTOFORIDIS (NBA)	1941	Dennis Andries (WBC)	1990-91
GUS LESNEVICH	1941-48	Jeff Harding (WBC)	1991-94
Freddie Mills (GBR)	1942-46	Thomas Hearns (WBA)	1991-92
FREDDIE MILLS	1948-50	Iran Barkley (WBA)	1992†
JOEY MAXIM	1950-52	Virgil Hill (WBA)	1992-97
ARCHIE MOORE	1952-62	Henry Maske (IBF)	1993-96
Harold Johnson (NBA)	1961	Virgil Hill (WBA/IBF)	1996-97
HAROLD JOHNSON	1962-63	Mike McCallum (WBC)	1994-95
WILLIE PASTRANO	1963-65	Fabrice Tiozzo (WBC)	1995-96
Eddie Cotton (Mich.)	1963-64	Roy Jones Jr. (WBC)	1996
JOSE TORRES	1965-66	Montell Griffin (WBC)	1996
DICK TIGER	1966-68	D. Michaelczewski (WBA/IBF)	1997†
BOB FOSTER	1968-74*	William Guthrie (IBF)	1997-98
Vicente Rondon (WBA)	1971-72	Lou Del Valle (WBA)	1997-98
John Conteh (WBC)	1974-77	**ROY JONES JR.** (WBA/WBC)	1997—
Victor Galindez (WBA)	1974-78	Reggie Johnson (IBF)	1998-99
Miguel A. Cuello (WBC)	1977-78	**ROY JONES JR.** (WBA/WBC/IBF)	1999—
Mate Parlov (WBC)	1978		

Super Middleweights
Current champions in **bold** type.

Champion	Held Title	Champion	Held Title
Murray Sutherland (IBF)	1984	Steve Little (WBA)	1994
Chong-Pal Park (IBF)	1984-87	Frank Liles (WBA)	1994-99
Chong-Pal Park (WBA)	1987-88	Roy Jones (IBF)	1994-96
Graziano Rocchigiani (IBF)	1988-89	Thulane Malinga (WBC)	1996
Fugencio Obelmejias (WBA)	1988-89	Vincenzo Nardiello (WBC)	1996
Ray Leonard (WBC)	1988-90†	Robin Reid (WBC)	1996-97
In-Chut Baek (WBA)	1989-90	Charles Brewer (IBF)	1997-98
Lindell Holmes (IBF)	1990-91	**Sven Ottke** (IBF)	1998—
Christophe Tiozzo (WBA)	1990-91	Thulane Malinga (WBC)	1997-98
Mauro Galvano (WBC)	1990-92	Richie Woodhall (WBC)	1998-99
Victor Cordova (WBA)	1991	Byron Mitchell (WBA)	1999-2000
Darrin Van Horn (IBF)	1991-92	Markus Beyer (WBC)	1999-2000
Iran Barkley (WBA)	1992	Glenn Gatley (WBC)	2000
Nigel Benn (WBC)	1992-96	**Dingaan Thobela** (WBC)	2000—
James Toney (IBF)	1992-94	**Bruno Girard** (WBA)	2000—
Michael Nunn (WBA)	1992-94		

Middleweights
Widely accepted champions in CAPITAL letters. Current champions in **bold** type.

Champion	Held Title	Champion	Held Title
JACK (NONPAREIL) DEMPSEY	1884-91	STANLEY KETCHEL	1908
BOB FITZSIMMONS	1891-97	BILLY PAPKE	1908
CHARLES (KID) McCOY	1897-98	STANLEY KETCHEL	1908-10
TOMMY RYAN	1898-1907	FRANK KLAUS	1913

Champion	Held Title
GEORGE CHIP	1913-14
AL McCOY	1914-17
Jeff Smith (AUS)	1914
Mick King (AUS)	1914
Jeff Smith (AUS)	1914-15
Lee Darcy (AUS)	1915-17
MIKE O'DOWD	1917-20
JOHNNY WILSON	1920-23
Wm. Bryan Downey (Ohio)	1921-22
Dave Rosenberg (NY)	1922
Jock Malone (Ohio)	1922-23
Mike O'Dowd (NY)	1922
Lou Bogash (NY)	1923
HARRY GREB	1923-26
TIGER FLOWERS	1926
MICKEY WALKER	1926-31†
GORILLA JONES	1931-32
MARCEL THIL	1932-37
Ben Jeby (NY)	1932-33
Lou Brouillard (NBA, NY)	1933
Vince Dundee (NBA, NY)	1933-34
Teddy Yarosz (NBA, NY)	1934-35
Babe Risko (NBA, NY)	1935-36
Freddie Steele (NBA, NY)	1936-38
FRED APOSTOLI	1937-39
Al Hostak (NBA)	1938
Solly Krieger (NBA)	1938-39
Al Hostak (NBA)	1939-40
CEFERINO GARCIA	1939-40
KEN OVERLIN	1940-41
Tony Zale (NBA)	1940-41
BILLY SOOSE	1941
TONY ZALE	1941-47
ROCKY GRAZIANO	1947-48
TONY ZALE	1948
MARCEL CERDAN	1948-49
JAKE La MOTTA	1949-51
SUGAR RAY ROBINSON	1951
RANDY TURPIN	1951
SUGAR RAY ROBINSON	1951-52*
CARL (BOBO) OLSON	1953-55
SUGAR RAY ROBINSON	1955-57
GENE FULLMER	1957
SUGAR RAY ROBINSON	1957
CARMEN BASILIO	1957-58

Champion	Held Title
SUGAR RAY ROBINSON	1958-60
Gene Fullmer (NBA)	1959-62
PAUL PENDER	1960-61
TERRY DOWNES	1961-62
PAUL PENDER	1962-63
Dick Tiger (WBA)	1962-63
DICK TIGER	1963
JOEY GIARDELLO	1963-65
DICK TIGER	1965-66
EMILE GRIFFITH	1966-67
NINO BENVENUTI	1967
EMILE GRIFFITH	1967-68
NINO BENVENUTI	1968-70
CARLOS MONZON	1970-77*
Rodrigo Valdez (WBC)	1974-76
RODRIGO VALDEZ	1977-78
HUGO CORRO	1978-79
VITO ANTUOFERMO	1979-80
ALAN MINTER	1980
MARVELOUS MARVIN HAGLER	1980-87
SUGAR RAY LEONARD	1987
Frank Tate (IBF)	1987-88
Sumbu Kalambay (WBA)	1987-89
Thomas Hearns (WBC)	1987-88
Iran Barkley (WBC)	1988-89
Michael Nunn (IBF)	1988-91
Roberto Duran (WBC)	1989-90*
Mike McCallum (WBA)	1989-91
Julian Jackson (WBC)	1990-93
James Toney (IBF)	1991-93†
Reggie Johnson (WBA)	1992-93
Roy Jones Jr. (IBF)	1993-94†
Gerald McClellan (WBC)	1993-95†
John David Jackson (WBA)	1993-94
Jorge Castro (WBA)	1994-97
Julian Jackson (WBC)	1995
Bernard Hopkins (IBF)	1995—
Quincy Taylor (WBC)	1995-96
Shinji Takehara (WBA)	1995-96
William Joppy (WBA)	1996-97
Keith Holmes (WBC)	1996-98
Julio Cesar Green (WBA)	1997-98
William Joppy (WBA)	1998—
Hassine Cherifi (WBC)	1998-99
Keith Holmes (WBC)	1999—

Junior Middleweights

Widely accepted champions in CAPITAL letters. Current champions in **bold** type.

Champion	Held Title
ERNILE GRIFFITH (EBU)	1962-63
DENNIS MOYER	1962-63
RALPH DUPAS	1963
SANDRO MAZZINGHI	1963-65
NINO BENVENUTI	1965-66
KI-SOO KIM	1966-68
SANDRO MAZZINGHI	1968
FREDDLIE LITTLE	1969-70
CARMELO BOSSI	1970-71
KOICHI WAJIMA	1971-74
OSCAR ALBARADO	1974-75
KOICHI WAJIMA	1975
Miguel de Oliveira (WBC)	1975-76
JAE-DO YUH	1975-76
Elisha Obed (WBC)	1975-76
KOICHI WAJIMA	1976
JOSE DURAN	1976
Eckhard Dagge (WBC)	1976-77
MIGUEL ANGEL CASTELLINI	1976-77
EDDIE GAZO	1977-78
Rocky Mattioli (WBC)	1977-79
MASASHI KUDO	1978-79

Champion	Held Title
Maurice Hope (WBC)	1979-81
AYUB KALULE	1979-81
Wilfred Benitez (WBC)	1981-82
SUGAR RAY LEONARD	1981-82
Tadashi Mihara (WBA)	1981-82
Davey Moore (WBA)	1982-83
Thomas Hearns (WBC)	1982-84
Roberto Duran (WBA)	1983-84
Mark Medal (IBF)	1984
THOMAS HEARNS	1984-86
Mike McCallum (WBA)	1984-87
Carlos Santos (IBF)	1984-86
Buster Drayton (IBF)	1986-87
Duane Thomas (WBC)	1986-87
Matthew Hilton (IBF)	1987-88
Lupe Aquino (WBC)	1987
Gianfranco Rosi (WBC)	1987-88
Julian Jackson (WBA)	1987-90
Donald Curry (WBC)	1988-89
Robert Hines (IBF)	1988-89
Darrin Van Horn (IBF)	1989
Rene Jacquote (WBC)	1989

Champion	Held Title
John Mugabi (WBC)	1989-90
Gianfranco Rosi (IBF)	1989-94
Terry Norris (WBC)	1990-94
Gilbert Dele (WBA)	1991
Vinny Pazienza (WBA)	1991-92
Julio Cesar Vasquez (WBA)	1992-95
Simon Brown (WBC)	1994
Terry Norris (WBC)	1994
Vincent Pettway (IBF)	1994-95
Paul Vaden (IBF)	1995
Carl Daniels (WBA)	1995

Champion	Held Title
Terry Norris (WBC)	1995-97
Terry Norris (IBF)	1995-96
Laurent Boudouani (WBA)	1996-99
Raul Marquez (IBF)	1997
Keith Mullings (WBC)	1997-99
Yori Boy Campas (IBF)	1997-1998
Fernando Vargas (IBF)	1998—
Javier Castillejo (WBC)	1999—
David Reid (WBA)	1999-00
Felix Trinidad (WBA)	2000—

Welterweights

Widely accepted champions in CAPITAL letters. Current champions in **bold** type.

Champion	Held Title
PADDY DUFFY	1888-90
MYSTERIOUS BILLY SMITH	1892-94
TOMMY RYAN	1894-98
MYSTERIOUS BILLY SMITH	1898-1900
MATTY MATTHEWS	1900
EDDIE CONNOLLY	1900
JAMES (RUBE) FERNS	1900
MATTY MATHEWS	1900-01
JAMES (RUBE) FERNS	1901
JOE WALCOTT	1901-04
THE DIXIE KID	1904-05
HONEY MELLODY	1906-07
Mike (Twin) Sullivan	1907-08†
Harry Lewis	1908-11
Jimmy Gardner	1908
Jimmy Clabby	1910-11
WALDEMAR HOLBERG	1914
TOM McCORMICK	1914
MATT WELLS	1914-15
MIKE GLOVER	1915
JACK BRITTON	1915
TED (KID) LEWIS	1915-16
JACK BRITTON	1916-17
TED (KID) LEWIS	1917-19
JACK BRITTON	1919-22
MICKEY WALKER	1922-26
PETE LATZO	1926-27
JOE DUNDEE	1927-29
JACKIE FIELDS	1929-30
YOUNG JACK THOMPSON	1930
TOMMY FREEMAN	1930-31
YOUNG JACK THOMPSON	1931
LOU BROUILLARD	1931-32
JACKIE FIELDS	1932-33
YOUNG CORBETT III	1933
JIMMY McLARNIN	1933-34
BARNEY ROSS	1934
JIMMY McLARNIN	1934-35
BARNEY ROSS	1935-38
HENRY ARMSTRONG	1938-40
FRITZIE ZIVIC	1940-41
Izzy Jannazzo (Md.)	1940-41
Freddie (Red) Cochrane	1941-46
MARTY SERVO	1946*
SUGAR RAY ROBINSON	1946-51†
Johnny Bratton	1951
KID GAVILAN	1951-54
JOHNNY SAXTON	1954-55
TONY DeMARCO	1955
CARMEN BASILIO	1955-56
JOHNNY SAXTON	1956
CARMEN BASILIO	1956-57†

Champion	Held Title
VIRGIL AKINS	1958
DON JORDAN	1958-60
BENNY (KID) PARET	1960-61
EMILE GRIFFITH	1961
BENNY (KID) PARET	1961-62
EMILE GRIFFITH	1962-63
LUIS RODRIGUEZ	1963
EMILE GRIFFITH	1963-66†
Charlie Shipes (Calif.)	1966-67
CURTIS COKES	1966-69
JOSE NAPOLES	1969-70
BILLY BACKUS	1970-71
JOSE NAPOLES	1971-75
Hedgemon Lewis (NY)	1972-73
Angel Espada (WBA)	1975-76
JOHN H. STRACEY	1975-76
CARLOS PALOMINO	1976-79
Pipino Cuevas (WBA)	1976-80
WILFREDO BENITEZ	1979
SUGAR RAY LEONARD	1979-80
ROBERTO DURAN	1980
Thomas Hearns (WBA)	1980-81
SUGAR RAY LEONARD	1980-82
Donald Curry (WBA)	1983-85
Milton McCrory (WBC)	1983-85
DONALD CURRY	1985-86
LLOYD HONEYGHAN	1986-87
JORGE VACA (WBC)	1987-88
LLOYD HONEYGHAN (WBC)	1988-89
Mark Breland (WBA)	1987
Marlon Starling (WBA)	1987-88
Tomas Molinares (WBA)	1988-89
Simon Brown (IBF)	1988-91
Mark Breland (WBA)	1989-90
MARLON STARLING (WBC)	1989-90
Aaron Davis (WBA)	1990-91
Maurice Blocker (WBC)	1990-91
Meldrick Taylor (WBA)	1991-92
Simon Brown (WBC)	1991
Maurice Blocker (IBF)	1991-93
Buddy McGirt (WBC)	1991-93
Crisanto Espana (WBA)	1992-94
Pernell Whitaker (WBC)	1993-97
Felix Trinidad (IBF)	1993-99
Ike Quartey (WBA)	1994-98†
James Page (WBA)	1998-2000†
Oscar De La Hoya (WBC)	1997-99
Felix Trinidad (WBC/IBF)	1999-2000†
Oscar De La Hoya (WBC)	2000
Shane Mosley (WBC)	2000—

Junior Welterweights

Widely accepted champions in CAPITAL letters. Current champions in **bold** type.

Champion	Held Title	Champion	Held Title
PINKEY MITCHELL	1922-25	Gene Hatcher (WBA)	1984-85
RED HERRING	1925	Ubaldo Sacco (WBA)	1985-86
MUSHY CALLAHAN	1926-30	Lonnie Smith (WBC)	1985-86
JACK (KID) BERG	1930-31	Patrizio Oliva (WBA)	1986-87
TONY CANZONERI	1931-32	Gary Hinton (IBF)	1986
JOHNNY JADICK	1932-33	Rene Arredondo (WBC)	1986
Sammy Fuller	1932-33	Tsuyoshi Hamada (WBC)	1986-87
BATTLING SHAW	1933	Joe Louis Manley (IBF)	1986-87
TONY CANZONERI	1933	Terry Marsh (IBF)	1987
BARNEY ROSS	1933-35	Juan Coggi (WBA)	1987-90
TIPPY LARKIN	1946	Rene Arredondo (WBC)	1987
CARLOS ORTIZ	1959-60	Roger Mayweather (WBC)	1987-89
DUILIO LOI	1960-62	James McGirt (IBF)	1988
EDDIE PERKINS	1962	Meldrick Taylor (IBF)	1988-90
DUILIO LOI	1962-63	Julio Cesar Chavez (WBC)	1989-94
Roberto Cruz	1963	Julio Cesar Chavez (IBF)	1990-91
EDDIE PERKINS	1963-65	Loreto Garza (WBA)	1990-91
CARLOS HERNANDEZ	1965-66	Juan Coggi (WBA)	1991
SANDRO LOPOPOLO	1966-67	Edwin Rosario (WBA)	1991-92
PAUL FUJII	1967-68	Rafael Pineda (IBF)	1991-92
NICOLINO LOCHE	1968-72	Akinobu Hiranaka (WBA)	1992
Pedro Adigue (WBC)	1968-70	Pernell Whitaker (IBF)	1992-93†
Bruno Arcari (WBC)	1970-74	Charles Murray (IBF)	1993-94
ALFONSO FRAZER	1972	Jake Rodriguez (IBF)	1994-95
ANTONIO CERVANTES	1972-76	Juan Coggi (WBA)	1993-94
Perico Fernandez (WBC)	1974-75	Frankie Randall (WBC)	1994
Saensak Muangsurin (WBC)	1975-76	Frankie Randall (WBA)	1994-96
WILFRED BENITEZ	1976-79	Juan Coggi (WBA)	1996
Miguel Velasquez (WBC)	1976	Julio Cesar Chavez (WBC)	1994-96
Saensak Muangsurin (WBC)	1976-78	Kostya Tszyu (IBF)	1995-97
Antonio Cervantes (WBA)	1977-80	Frankie Randall (WBA)	1996-97
Sang-Hyun Kim (WBC)	1978-80	Oscar De La Hoya (WBC)	1996-97†
Saoul Mamby (WBC)	1980-82	Khalid Rahilou (WBA)	1997-98
Aaron Pryor (WBA)	1980-83	**Sharmba Mitchell** (WBA)	1998—
Leroy Haley (WBC)	1982-83	Vincent Phillips (IBF)	1997-99
Aaron Pryor (IBF)	1983-85	Terronn Millet (IBF)	1999-00†
Bruce Curry (WBC)	1983-84	**Kostya Tszyu** (WBC)	1999—
Johnny Bumphus (WBA)	1984	**Zab Judah** (IBF)	2000—
Bill Costello (WBC)	1984-85		

Lightweights

Widely accepted champions in CAPITAL letters. Current champions in **bold** type.

Champion	Held Title	Champion	Held Title
JACK McAULIFFE	1886-94	Slugger White (Md.)	1943
GEORGE (KID) LAVIGNE	1896-99	Bob Montgomery (NY)	1943
FRANK ERNE	1899-02	Sammy Angott (NBA)	1943-44
JOE GANS	1902-04	Beau Jack (NY)	1943-44
JIMMY BRITT	1904-05	Bob Montgomery (NY)	1944-47
BATTLING NELSON	1905-06	Juan Zurita (NBA)	1944-45
JOE GANS	1906-08	IKE WILLIAMS	1947-51
BATTLING NELSON	1908-10	JAMES CARTER	1951-52
AD WOLGAST	1910-12	LAURO SALAS	1952
WILLIE RITCHIE	1912-14	JAMES CARTER	1952-54
FREDDIE WELSH	1915-17	PADDY DeMARCO	1954
BENNY LEONARD	1917-25*	JAMES CARTER	1954-55
JIMMY GOODRICH	1925	WALLACE (BUD) SMITH	1955-56
ROCKY KANSAS	1925-26	JOE BROWN	1956-62
SAMMY MANDELL	1926-30	CARLOS ORTIZ	1962-65
AL SINGER	1930	Kenny Lane (Mich.)	1963-64
TONY CANZONERI	1930-33	ISMAEL LAGUNA	1965
BARNEY ROSS	1933-35†	CARLOS ORTIZ	1965-68
TONY CANZONERI	1935-36	CARLOS TEO CRUZ	1968-69
LOU AMBERS	1936-38	MANDO RAMOS	1969-70
HENRY ARMSTRONG	1938-39	ISMAEL LAGUNA	1970
LOU AMBERS	1939-40	KEN BUCHANAN	1970-72
Sammy Angott (NBA)	1940-41	Pedro Carrasco (WBC)	1971-72
LEW JENKINS	1940-41	Mando Ramos (WBC)	1972
SAMMY ANGOTT	1941-42	ROBERTO DURAN	1972-79†
Beau Jack (NY)	1942-43	Chango Carmona (WBC)	1972

Champion	Held Title
Rodolfo Gonzalez (WBC)	1972-74
Ishimatsu Suzuki (WBC)	1974-76
Esteban De Jesus (WBC)	1976-78
Jim Watt (WBC)	1979-81
Ernesto Espana (WBA)	1979-80
Hilmer Kenty (WBA)	1980-81
Sean O'Grady (WBA, WAA)	1981
Alexis Arguello (WBC)	1981-82
Claude Noel (WBA)	1981
Andrew Ganigan (WAA)	1981-82
Arturo Frias (WBA)	1981-82
Ray Mancini (WBA)	1982-84
ALEXIS ARGUELLO	1982-83
Edwin Rosario (WBC)	1983-84
Choo Choo Brown (IBF)	1984
Livingstone Bramble (WBA)	1984-86
Harry Arroyo (IBF)	1984-85
Jose Luis Ramirez (WBC)	1984-85
Jimmy Paul (IBF)	1985-86
Hector Camacho (WBC)	1985-86
Edwin Rosario (WBA)	1986-87
Greg Haugen (IBF)	1986-87
Julio Cesar Chavez (WBA)	1987-88
Jose Luis Ramirez (WBC)	1987-88
JULIO CESAR CHAVEZ (WBC, WBA)	1988-89
Vinny Pazienza (IBF)	1987-88
Greg Haugen (IBF)	1988-89

Champion	Held Title
Pernell Whitaker (IBF, WBC)	1989-90
Edwin Rosario (WBA)	1989-90
Juan Nazario (WBA)	1990
PERNELL WHITAKER (IBF, WBC, WBA)	1990-92†
Joey Gamache (WBA)	1992
Miguel A. Gonzalez (WBC)	1992-96
Tony Lopez (WBA)	1992-93
Dingaan Thobela (WBA)	1993
Fred Pendleton (IBF)	1993-94
Orzubek Nazarov (WBA)	1993-98
Rafael Ruelas (IBF)	1994-95
Oscar De La Hoya (IBF)	1995†
Phillip Holiday (IBF)	1995-97
Jean-Baptiste Mendy (WBC)	1996-97
Stevie Johnston (WBC)	1997-98
Shane Mosley (IBF)	1997-99†
Cesar Bazan (WBC)	1998-99
Jean-Baptiste Mendy (WBA)	1998-99
Julien Lorcy (WBA)	1999
Stevie Johnston (WBC)	1999-00
Stefano Zoff (WBA)	1999
Israel Cardona (IBF)	1999
Paul Spadafora (IBF)	1999—
Gilberto Serrano (WBA)	1999-00
Takanori Hatakeyama (WBA)	2000—
Jose Luis Castillo (WBC)	2000—

Junior Lightweights

Widely accepted champions in CAPITAL letters. Current champions in **bold** type.

Champion	Held Title
JOHNNY DUNDEE	1921-23
JACK BERNSTEIN	1923
JOHNNY DUNDEE	1923-24
STEVE (KID) SULLIVAN	1924-25
MIKE BALLERINO	1925
TOD MORGAN	1925-29
BENNY BASS	1929-31
KID CHOCOLATE	1931-33
FRANKIE KLICK	1933-34
SANDY SADDLER	1949-50
HAROLD GOMES	1959-60
GABRIEL (FLASH) ELORDE	1960-67
YOSHIAKI NUMATA	1967
HIROSHI KOBAYASHI	1967-71
Rene Barrientos (WBC)	1969-70
Yoshiaki Numata (WBC)	1970-71
ALFREDO MARCANO	1971-72
Ricardo Arredondo (WBC)	1971-74
BEN VILLAFLOR	1972-73
KUNIAKI SHIBATA	1973
BEN VILLAFLOR	1973-76
Kuniaki Shibata (WBC)	1974-75
Alfredo Escalera (WBC)	1975-78
SAMUEL SERRANO	1976-80
Alexis Arguello (WBC)	1978-80
YASUTSUNE UEHARA	1980-81
Rafael Limon (WBC)	1980-81
Cornelius Boza-Edwards (WBC)	1981
SAMUEL SERRANO	1981-83
Rolando Navarrete (WBC)	1981-82
Rafael Limon (WBC)	1982
Bobby Chacon (WBC)	1982-83
ROGER MAYWEATHER	1983-84
Hector Camacho (WBC)	1983-84

Champion	Held Title
ROCKY LOCKRIDGE	1984-85
Hwan-Kil Yuh (IBF)	1984-85
Julio Cesar Chavez (WBC)	1984-87
Lester Ellis (IBF)	1985
WILFREDO GOMEZ	1985-86
Barry Michael (IBF)	1985-87
ALFREDO LAYNE	1986
BRIAN MITCHELL	1986-91
Rocky Lockridge (IBF)	1987-88
Azumah Nelson (WBC)	1988-94
Tony Lopez (IBF)	1988-89
Juan Molina (IBF)	1989-90
Tony Lopez (IBF)	1990-91
Joey Gamache (WBA)	1991
Brian Mitchell (IBF)	1991
Genaro Hernandez (WBA)	1991-95
James Leija (WBC)	1994
Juan Molina (IBF)	1991-95
Gabriel Ruelas (WBC)	1994-95
Eddie Hopson (IBF)	1995
Tracy Patterson (IBF)	1995
Azumah Nelson (WBC)	1995-97
Choi Yong-Soo (WBA)	1995-98
Arturo Gatti (IBF)	1995-98†
Genaro Hernandez (WBC)	1997-98
Floyd Mayweather Jr. (WBC)	1998—
Takanori Hatakeyama (WBA)	1998-99
Roberto Garcia (IBF)	1998-99
Lavka Sim (WBA)	1999
Diego Corrales (IBF)	1999—
Baek Jong-Kwon (WBA)	1999-2000
Joel Casamayor (WBA)	2000—

Featherweights

Widely accepted champions in CAPITAL letters. Current champions in **bold** type.

Champion	Held Title	Champion	Held Title
TORPEDO BILLY MURPHY	1890	Shozo Saijyo (WBA)	1968-71
YOUNG GRIFFO	1890-92	JOHNNY FAMECHON (WBC)	1969-70
GEORGE DIXON	1892-97	VICENTE SALDIVAR (WBC)	1970
SOLLY SMITH	1897-98	KUNIAKI SHIBATA (WBC)	1970-72
Ben Jordan (GBR)	1898-99	Antonio Gomez (WBA)	1971-72
Eddie Santry (GBR)	1899-1900	CLEMENTE SANCHEZ (WBC)	1972
DAVE SULLIVAN	1898	Ernesto Marcel (WBA)	1972-74
GEORGE DIXON	1898-1900	JOSE LEGRA (WBC)	1972-73
TERRY McGOVERN	1900-01	EDER JOFRE (WBC)	1973-74
YOUNG CORBETT II	1901-04	Ruben Olivares (WBA)	1974
JIMMY BRITT	1904	Bobby Chacon (WBC)	1974-75
ABE ATTELL	1904	ALEXIS ARGUELLO (WBA)	1974-76†
BROOKLYN TOMMY SULLIVAN	1904-05	Ruben Olivares (WBA)	1975
ABE ATTELL	1906-12	David (Poison) Kotey (WBC)	1975-76
JOHNNY KILBANE	1912-23	DANNY (LITTLE RED) LOPEZ (WBC)	1976-80
Jem Driscoll (GBR)	1912-13	Rafael Ortega (WBA)	1977
EUGENE CRIQUI	1923	Cecilio Lastra (WBA)	1977-78
JOHNNY DUNDEE	1923-24†	Eusebio Pedroza (WBA)	1978-85
LOUIS (KID) KAPLAN	1925-26†	SALVADOR SANCHEZ (WBC)	1980-82
Dick Finnegan (Mass.)	1926-27	Juan LaPorte (WBC)	1982-84
BENNY BASS	1927-28	Wilfredo Gomez (WBC)	1984
TONY CANZONERI	1928	Min-Keun Oh (IBF)	1984-85
ANDRE ROUTIS	1928-29	Azumah Nelson (WBC)	1984-88
BATTLING BATTALINO	1929-32†	Barry McGuigan (WBA)	1985-86
Tommy Paul (NBA)	1932-33	Ki-Young Chung (IBF)	1985-86
Kid Chocolate (NY)	1932-33	Steve Cruz (WBA)	1986-87
Freddie Miller (NBA)	1933-36	Antonio Rivera (IBF)	1986-88
Baby Arizmendi (MEX)	1935-36	Antonio Esparragoza (WBA)	1987-91
Mike Belloise (NY)	1936-37	Calvin Grove (IBF)	1988
Petey Sarron (NBA)	1936-37	Jorge Paez (IBF)	1988-91†
HENRY ARMSTRONG†	1937-38†	Jeff Fenech (WBC)	1988-90†
Joey Archibald (NY)	1938-39	Marcos Villasana (WBC)	1990-91
Leo Rodak (NBA)	1938-39	Yung-Kyun Park (WBA)	1991-93
JOEY ARCHIBALD	1939-40	Troy Dorsey (IBF)	1991
Petey Scalzo (NBA)	1940-41	Manuel Medina (IBF)	1991-93
Jimmy Perrin (La.)	1940-41	Paul Hodkinson (WBC)	1991-93
HARRY JEFFRA	1940-41	Tom Johnson (IBF)	1993-97
JOEY ARCHIBALD	1941	Goyo Vargas (WBC)	1993
Richie Lemos (NBA)	1941	Kevin Kelley (WBC)	1993-95
CHALKY WRIGHT	1941-42	Eloy Rojas (WBA)	1993-96
Jackie Wilson (NBA)	1941-43	Alejandro Gonzalez (WBC)	1995
WILLIE PEP	1942-48	Manuel Medina (WBC)	1995-96
Jackie Callura (NBA)	1943	Wilfredo Vasquez (WBA)	1996-98†
Phil Terranova (NBA)	1943-44	Luisito Espinosa (WBC)	1995-99
Sal Bartolo (NBA)	1944-46	Naseem Hamed (IBF)	1997†
SANDY SADDLER	1948-49	Hector Lizarraga (IBF)	1997-98
WILLIE PEP	1949-50	Freddie Norwood (WBA)	1998
SANDY SADDLER	1950-57*	Manuel Medina (IBF)	1998-99
HOGAN (KID) BASSEY	1957-59	Antonio Cermeno (WBA)	1998-99
DAVEY MOORE	1959-63	Cesar Soto (WBC)	1999-00
ULTIMINIO (SUGAR) RAMOS	1963-64	**Paul Ingle** (IBF)	1999—
VICENTE SALDIVAR	1964-67*	**Guty Espadas** (WBC)	2000—
Howard Winstone (GBR)	1968	Freddie Norwood (WBA)	1999-00
Raul Rojas (WBA)	1968	**Derrick Gainer** (WBA)	2000—
Jose Legra (WBC)	1968-69		

Junior Featherweights

Current champions in **bold** type.

Champion	Held Title	Champion	Held Title
Jack (Kid) Wolfe	1922-23	Leonardo Cruz (WBA)	1982-84
Carl Duane	1923-24	Jaime Garza (WBC)	1983
Rigoberto Riasco (WBC)	1976	Bobby Berna (IBF)	1983-84
Royal Kobayashi (WBC)	1976	Loris Stecca (WBA)	1984
Dong-Kyun Yum (WBC)	1976-77	Seung-Il Suh (IBF)	1984-85
Wilfredo Gomez (WBC)	1977-83	Victor Callejas (WBA)	1984-85
Soo-Hwan Hong (WBA)	1977-78	Juan (Kid) Meza (WBC)	1984-85
Ricardo Cardona (WBA)	1978-80	Ji-Woo Kim (IBF)	1985-86
Leo Randolph (WBA)	1980	Lupe Pintor (WBC)	1985-86
Sergio Palma (WBA)	1980-82	Samart Payakaroon (WBC)	1986-87

Champion	Held Title	Champion	Held Title
Seung-Hoon Lee (IBF)	1987-88	Daniel Zaragoza (WBC)	1991-92
Louie Espinoza (WBA)	1987	Tracy Patterson (WBC)	1992-94
Jeff French (WBC)	1987	Kennedy McKinney (IBF)	1993-94
Julio Gervacio (WBA)	1987-88	Wilfredo Vasquez (WBA)	1992-95
Daniel Zaragoza (WBC)	1988-90	Vuyani Bungu (IBF)	1994-99†
Jose Sanabria (IBF)	1988-90	Hector Acero Sanchez (WBC)	1994-95
Bernardo Pinango (WBA)	1988	Antonio Cermeno (WBA)	1995-98†
Juan Jose Estrada (WBA)	1988-89	Daniel Zaragoza (WBC)	1995-97
Fabrice Benichou (IBF)	1989-90	Erik Morales (WBC)	1997-00†
Jesus Salud (WBA)	1989-90	Enrique Sanchez (WBA)	1998
Welcome Ncita (IBF)	1990-92	Nestor Garza (WBA)	1998-00
Paul Banke (WBC)	1990	**Lehlohonolo Ledwaba** (IBF)	1999—
Luis Mendoza (WBA)	1990-91	**Clarence Adams** (WBA)	2000—
Raul Perez (WBA)	1992	**Willie Jorrin** (WBC)	2000—
Pedro Decima (WBC)	1990-91		
Kiyoshi Hatanaka (WBC)	1991		

Bantamweights

Widely accepted champions in CAPITAL letters. Current champions in **bold** type.

Champion	Held Title	Champion	Held Title
TOMMY (SPIDER) KELLY	1887	MANUEL ORTIZ	1947-50
HUGHEY BOYLE	1887-88	VIC TOWEEL	1950-52
TOMMY (SPIDER) KELLY	1889	JIMMY CARRUTHERS	1952-54*
CHAPPIE MORAN	1889-90	ROBERT COHEN	1954-56
Tommy (Spider) Kelly	1890-92	Raul Macias (NBA)	1955-57
GEORGE DIXON	1890-91	MARIO D'AGATA	1956-57
Billy Plummer	1892-95	ALPHONSE HALIMI	1957-59
JIMMY BARRY	1894-99	JOE BECERRA	1959-60*
Pedlar Palmer	1895-99	Johnny Caldwell (EBU)	1961-62
TERRY McGOVERN	1899-1900	EDER JOFRE	1961-65
HARRY HARRIS	1901-02	MASAHIKO FIGHTING HARADA	1965-68
DANNY DOUGHERTY	1900-01	LIONEL ROSE	1968-69
HARRY FORBES	1901-03	RUBEN OLIVARES	1969-70
FRANKIE NEIL	1903-04	CHUCHO CASTILLO	1970-71
JOE BOWKER	1904-05	RUBEN OLIVARES	1971-72
JIMMY WALSH	1905-06†	RAFAEL HERRERA	1972
OWEN MORAN	1907-08	ENRIQUE PINDER	1972-73
MONTE ATTELL	1909-10	ROMEO ANAYA	1973
FRANKIE CONLEY	1910-11	Rafael Herrera (WBC)	1973-74
JOHNNY COULON	1911-14	ARNOLD TAYLOR	1973-74
Digger Stanley (GBR)	1910-12	SOO-HWAN HONG	1974-75
Charles Ledoux (GBR)	1912-13	Rodolfo Martinez (WBC)	1974-76
Eddie Campi (GBR)	1913-14	ALFONSO ZAMORA	1975-77
KID WILLIAMS	1914-17	Carlos Zarate (WBC)	1976-79
Johnny Ertle	1915-18	JORGE LUJAN	1977-80
PETE HERMAN	1917-20	Lupe Pintor (WBC)	1979-83
Memphis Pal Moore	1918-19	JULIAN SOLIS	1980
JOE LYNCH	1920-21	JEFF CHANDLER	1980-84
PETE HERMAN	1921	Albert Davila (WBC)	1983-85
JOHNNY BUFF	1921-22	RICHARD SANDOVAL	1984-86
JOE LYNCH	1922-24	Satoshi Shingaki (IBF)	1984-85
ABE GOLDSTEIN	1924	Jeff Fenech (IBF)	1985
CANNONBALL EDDIE MARTIN	1924-25	Daniel Zaragoza (WBC)	1985
PHIL ROSENBERG	1925-27	Miguel (Happy) Lora (WBC)	1985-88
Teddy Baldock (GBR)	1927	GABY CANIZALES	1986
BUD TAYLOR (NBA)	1927-28†	BERNARDO PINANGO	1986-87
Willie Smith (GBR)	1927-28	Wilfredo Vasquez (WBA)	1987-88
Bushy Graham (NY)	1928-29	Kevin Seabrooks (IBF)	1987-88
PANAMA AL BROWN	1929-35	Kaokor Galaxy (WBA)	1988
Sixto Escobar (NBA)	1934-35	Moon Sung-Kil (WBA)	1988-89
BALTAZAR SANGCHILLI	1935-36	Kaokor Galaxy (WBA)	1989
Lou Salica (NBA)	1935	Raul Perez (WBC)	1988-91
Sixto Escobar (NBA)	1935-36	Orlando Canizales (IBF)	1988-94†
TONY MARINO	1936	Luisito Espinosa (WBA)	1989-91
SIXTO ESCOBAR	1936-37	Greg Richardson	1991
HARRY JEFFRA	1937-38	Joichiro Tatsuyoshi (WBC)	1991-92
SIXTO ESCOBAR	1938-39*	Israel Contreras (WBA)	1991-92
Georgie Pace (NBA)	1939-40	Eddie Cook (WBA)	1992
LOU SALICA	1940-42	Victor Rabanales (WBC)	1992-93
MANUEL ORTIZ	1942-47	Jorge Julio (WBA)	1992-93
HAROLD DADE	1947	Jung-Il Byun (WBC)	1993

Champion	Held Title
Junior Jones (WBA)	1993-94
Yasuei Yakushiji (WBC)	1993-95
John M. Johnson (WBA)	1994
Daorung Chuvatana (WBA)	1994-95
Harold Mestre (IBF)	1995
Mbulelo Botile (IBF)	1995-97
Wayne McCullough (WBC)	1995-96
Veeraphol Sahaprom (WBA)	1995-96
Nana Yaw Konadu (WBA)	1996

Champion	Held Title
Daorung Chuvatana (WBA)	1996-97
Nana Yaw Konadu (WBA)	1997-98
Sirimongkol Singmanassak (WBC)	1996-97
Tim Austin (IBF)	1997—
Joichiro Tatsuyoshi (WBC)	1997-98
Johnny Tapia (WBA)	1998-99
Veerapol Sahaprom (WBC)	1998—
Paulie Ayala (WBA)	1999—

Junior Bantamweights

Widely accepted champions in CAPITAL letters. Current champions in **bold** type.

Champion	Held Title
Rafael Orono (WBC)	1980-81
Chul-Ho Kim (WBC)	1981-82
Gustavo Ballas (WBA)	1981
Rafael Pedroza (WBA)	1981-82
Jiro Watanabe (WBA)	1982-84
Rafael Orono (WBA)	1982-83
Payao Poontarat (WBC)	1983-84
Joo-Do Chun (IBF)	1983-85
JIRO WATANABE	1984-86
Kaosai Galaxy (WBA)	1984
Ellyas Pical (IBF)	1985-86
Cesar Polanco (IBF)	1986
GILBERTO ROMAN	1986-87
Ellyas Pical (IBF)	1986
Santos Laciar (WBC)	1987
Tae-Il Chang (IBF)	1987
Sugar Rojas (WBC)	1987-88
Ellyas Pical (IBF)	1987-89
Gilberto Roman (WBC)	1988-89
Juan Polo Perez (IBF)	1989-90
Nana Konadu (WBC)	1989-90
Sung-Kil Moon (WBC)	1990-93

Champion	Held Title
Robert Quiroga (IBF)	1990-93
Julio Borboa (IBF)	1993-94
Katsuya Onizuka (WBA)	1993-94
Lee Hyung-Chul (WBA)	1994-95
Jose Luis Bueno (WBC)	1993-94
Hiroshi Kawashima (WBC)	1994-97
Harold Grey (IBF)	1994-95
Alimi Goitia (WBA)	1995-96
Yokthai Sith-Oar (WBA)	1996-97
Carlos Salazar (IBF)	1995-96
Harold Grey (IBF)	1996
Danny Romero (IBF)	1996-97
Gerry Penalosa (WBC)	1997-98
Johnny Tapia (IBF)	1997-98†
Satoshi Iida (WBA)	1997-98
Cho In-Joo (WBC)	1998-00
Jesus Rojas (WBA)	1998-99
Mark Johnson (IBF)	1999-00†
Hideki Todaka (WBA)	1999-2000
Masanori Tokuyama (WBC)	2000—
Felix Machado (IBF)	2000—
Leo Gamez (WBA)	2000—

Flyweights

Widely accepted champions in CAPITAL letters. Current champions in **bold** type.

Champion	Held Title
Sid Smith (GBR)	1913
Bill Ladbury (GBR)	1913-14
Percy Jones (GBR)	1914
Joe Symonds (GBR)	1914-16
JIMMY WILDE	1916-23
PANCHO VILLA	1923-25
FIDEL LaBARBA	1925-27*
FRENCHY BELANGER (NBA,IBU)	1927-28
Izzy Schwartz (NY)	1927-29
Johnny McCoy (Calif.)	1927-28
Newsboy Brown (Calif.)	1928
FRANKIE GENARO (NBA,IBU)	1928-29
Johnny Hill (GBR)	1928-29
SPIDER PLADNER (NBA,IBU)	1929
FRANKIE GENARO (NBA,IBU)	1929-31
Willie LaMorte (NY)	1929-30
Midget Wolgast (NY)	1930-35
YOUNG PEREZ (NBA,IBU)	1931-32
JACKIE BROWN (NBA,IBU)	1932-35
BENNY LYNCH	1935-38†
Small Montana (NY,Calif.)	1935-37
PETER KANE	1938-43
Little Dado (NBA,Calif.)	1938-40
JACKIE PATERSON	1943-48
RINTY MONAGHAN	1948-50*
TERRY ALLEN	1950
SALVADOR (DADO) MARINO	1950-52
YOSHIO SHIRAI	1953-54
PASCUAL PEREZ	1954-60
PONE KINGPETCH	1960-62
MASAHIKO (FIGHTING) HARADA	1962-63

Champion	Held Title
PONE KINGPETCH	1963
HIROYUKI EBIHARA	1963-64
PONE KINGPETCH	1964-65
SALVATORE BURRINI	1965-66
Horacio Accavallo (WBA)	1966-68
WALTER McGOWAN	1966
CHARTCHAI CHIONOI	1966-69
EFREN TORRES	1969-70
Hiroyuki Ebihara (WBA)	1969
Bernabe Villacampo (WBA)	1969-70
CHARTCHAI CHIONOI	1970
Berkrerk Chartvanchai (WBA)	1970
Masao Ohba (WBA)	1970-73
ERBITO SALAVARRIA	1970-73
Betulio Gonzalez (WBC)	1972
Venice Borkorsor (WBC)	1972-73
VENICE BORKORSOR	1973
Chartchai Chionoi (WBA)	1973-74
Betulio Gonzalez (WBA)	1973-74
Shoji Oguma (WBA)	1974-75
Susumu Hanagata (WBA)	1974-75
Miguel Canto (WBC)	1975-79
Erbito Salavarria (WBA)	1975-76
Alfonso Lopez (WBA)	1976
Guty Espadas (WBA)	1976-78
Betulio Gonzalez (WBA)	1978-79
Chan-Hee Park (WBC)	1979-80
Luis Ibarra (WBA)	1979-80
Tae-Shik Kim (WBA)	1980
Shoji Oguma (WBC)	1980-81
Peter Mathebula (WBA)	1980-81

Champion	Held Title	Champion	Held Title
Santos Laciar (WBA)	1981	Jesus Rojas (WBA)	1989-90
Antonio Avelar (WBC)	1981-82	Yul-Woo Lee (WBA)	1990
Luis Ibarra (WBA)	1981	Leopard Tamakuma (WBA)	1990-91
Juan Herrera (WBA)	1981-82	Muangchai Kittikasem (WBC)	1991-92
Prudencio Cardona (WBC)	1982	Yong-Kang Kim (WBA)	1991-92
Santos Laciar (WBA)	1982-85	Rodolfo Blanco (IBF)	1992
Freddie Castillo (WBC)	1982	Yuri Arbachakov (WBC)	1992-97
Eleoncio Mercedes (WBC)	1982-83	Aquiles Guzman (WBA)	1992
Charlie Magri (WBC)	1983	Phichit Sithbangprachan (IBF)	1992-94†
Frank Cedeno (WBC)	1983-84	David Griman (WBA)	1992-94
Soon-Chun Kwon (IBF)	1983-85	Saen Sor Ploenchit (WBA)	1994-96
Koji Kobayashi (WBC)	1984	Francisco Tejedor (IBF)	1995
Gabriel Bernal (WBC)	1984	Danny Romero (IBF)	1995-96
Sot Chitalada (WBC)	1984-88	Mark Johnson (IBF)	1996-99†
Hilario Zapate (WBA)	1985-87	Jose Bonilla (WBA)	1996-97
Chong-Kwan Chung (IBF)	1985-86	Chatchai Sasakul (WBC)	1997-98
Bi-Won Chung (IBF)	1986	Hugo Soto (WBA)	1998-99
Hi-Sup Shin (IBF)	1986-87	Manny Pacquiao (WBC)	1998-99
Dodie Penalosa (IBF)	1987	**Irene Pacheco** (IBF)	1999—
Fidel Bassa (WBA)	1987-89	Leo Gamez (WBA)	1999
Choi Chang-Ho (IBF)	1987-88	Medgoen Lukchaopormasak (WBC)	1999-00
Rolando Bohol (IBF)	1988	Sornpichai Kratindaenggym (WBA)	1999-00
Yong-Kang Kim (WBC)	1988-89	**Eric Morel** (WBA)	2000—
Duke McKenzie (IBF)	1988-89	**Malcolm Tunacao** (WBC)	2000—
Dave McAuley (IBF)	1989-92		
Sot Chitalada (WBC)	1989-91		

Junior Flyweights
Current champions in **bold** type.

Champion	Held Title	Champion	Held Title
Franco Udella (WBC)	1975	Yul-Woo Lee (WBC)	1989
Jaime Rios (WBA)	1975-76	Muangchai Kittikasem (IBF)	1989-90
Luis Estaba (WBC)	1975-78	Humberto Gonzalez (WBC)	1989-90
Juan Guzman (WBA)	1976	Michael Carbajal (IBF)	1990-94
Yoko Gushiken (WBA)	1976-81	Rolando Pascua (WBC)	1990
Freddy Castillo (WBC)	1978	Melchor Cob Castro (WBC)	1991
Netrnoi Vorasingh (WBC)	1978	Humberto Gonzalez (WBC)	1991-93
Sung-Jun Kim (WBC)	1978-80	Hirokia Ioka (WBA)	1991-92
Shigeo Nakajima (WBC)	1980	Michael Carbajal (WBC)	1993-94
Hilario Zapata (WBC)	1980-82	Myung-Woo Yuh (WBA)	1993
Pedro Flores (WBA)	1981	Leo Gamez (WBA)	1993-95
Hwan-Jin Kim (WBA)	1981	Humberto Gonzalez (WBC/IBF)	1994-95
Katsuo Tokashiki (WBA)	1981-83	Choi Hi-Yong (WBA)	1995-96
Amado Urzua (WBC)	1982	Saman Sor Jaturong (WBC/IBF)	1995-96
Tadashi Tomori (WBC)	1982	Carlos Murillo (WBA)	1996
Hilario Zapata (WBC)	1982-83	Keiji Yamaguchi (WBA)	1996
Jung-Koo Chang (WBC)	1983-88	Michael Carbajal (IBF)	1996-97
Lupe Madera (WBA)	1983-84	Saman Sor Jaturong (WBC)	1995-99
Dodie Penalosa (IBF)	1983-86	Phichit Chor Siriwat (WBA)	1996-00†
Francisco Quiroz (WBA)	1984-85	Mauricio Pastrana (IBF)	1997-98†
Joey Olivo (WBA)	1985	Will Grigsby (IBF)	1999
Myung-Woo Yuh (WBA)	1985-91	**Choi Yo-Sam** (WBC)	1999—
Jum-Hwan Choi (IBF)	1986-88	**Ricardo Lopez** (IBF)	1999—
Tacy Macalos (IBF)	1988-89	**Beibis Mendoza** (WBA)	2000—
German Torres (WBC)	1988-89		

Strawweights
Current champions in **bold** type.

Champion	Held Title	Champion	Held Title
Franco Udella (WBC)	1975	Hwan-Jin Kim (WBA)	1981
Jaime Rios (WBA)	1975-76	Katsuo Tokashiki (WBA)	1981-83
Luis Estraba (WBC)	1975-78	Amado Urzua (WBC)	1982
Juan Guzman (WBA)	1976	Tadashi Tomori (WBC)	1982
Yoko Gushiken (WBA)	1976-81	Hilario Zapata (WBC)	1982-83
Freddy Castillo (WBC)	1978	Jung-Koo Chang (WBC)	1983-88
Netrnoi Vorasingh (WBC)	1978	Lupe Madera (WBA)	1983-84
Sung-Jun Kim (WBC)	1978-80	Dodie Penalosa (IBF)	1983-86
Shigeo Nakajima (WBC)	1980	Francisco Quiroz (WBA)	1984-85
Hilario Zapata (WBC)	1980-82	Joey Olivo (WBA)	1985
Pedro Flores (WBA)	1981	Myung-Woo Yuh (WBA)	1985-93

Champion	Held Title
Jum-Hwan Choi (IBF)	1986-88
Tacy Macalos (IBF)	1988-89
German Torres (WBC)	1988-89
Yul-Woo Lee (WBC)	1989
Muangchai Kittikasem (IBF)	1989-90
Humberto Gonzalez (WBC)	1989-90
Michael Carbajal (IBF)	1990
Rolando Pascua (WBC)	1990
Melchor Cob Castro (WBC)	1991
Ricardo Lopez (WBC)	1990-98

Champion	Held Title
Ratanapol Voraphin (IBF)	1992-97
Chana Porpaoin (WBA)	1993-95
Rosendo Alvarez (WBA)	1995-98
Ricardo Lopez (WBA/WBC)	1998-99†
Zolani Petelo (IBF)	1997—
Wandee Chor Chareon (WBC)	1999-00
Noel Arambulet (WBA)	1999-00†
Joma Gamboa (WBA)	2000—
Jose Antonio Aguirre (WBC)	2000—

Annual Awards
Ring Magazine Fight of the Year

First presented in 1945 by Nat Fleischer, who started *The Ring* magazine in 1922.

Multiple matchups: Muhammad Ali vs. Joe Frazier, Carmen Basilio vs. Sugar Ray Robinson and Rocky Graziano vs. Tony Zale (2).

Multiple fights: Muhammad Ali (6); Carmen Basilio (5); George Foreman and Joe Frazier (4); Rocky Graziano, Rocky Marciano and Tony Zale (3); Nino Benvenuti, Bobby Chacon, Ezzard Charles, Arturo Gatti, Marvin Hagler, Thomas Hearns, Evander Holyfield, Sugar Ray Leonard, Floyd Patterson, Sugar Ray Robinson and Jersey Joe Walcott (2).

Year	Winner	Loser	Result	Year	Winner	Loser	Result
1945	Rocky Graziano	Red Cochrane	KO 10	1973	George Foreman	Joe Frazier	KO 2
1946	Tony Zale	Rocky Graziano	KO 6	1974	Muhammad Ali	George Foreman	KO 8
1947	Rocky Graziano	Tony Zale	KO 6	1975	Muhammad Ali	Joe Frazier	KO 14
1948	Marcel Cerdan	Tony Zale	KO 12	1976	George Foreman	Ron Lyle	KO 4
1949	Willie Pep	Sandy Saddler	W 15	1977	Jimmy Young	George Foreman	W 12
				1978	Leon Spinks	Muhammad Ali	W 15
1950	Jake LaMotta	Laurent Dauthuille	KO 15	1979	Danny Lopez	Mike Ayala	KO 15
1951	Jersey Joe Walcott	Ezzard Charles	KO 7				
1952	Rocky Marciano	Jersey Joe Walcott	KO 13	1980	Saad Muhammad	Yaqui Lopez	KO 14
1953	Rocky Marciano	Roland LaStarza	KO 11	1981	Sugar Ray Leonard	Thomas Hearns	KO 14
1954	Rocky Marciano	Ezzard Charles	KO 8	1982	Bobby Chacon	Rafael Limon	W 15
1955	Carmen Basilio	Tony DeMarco	KO 12	1983	Bobby Chacon	C. Boza-Edwards	W 12
1956	Carmen Basilio	Johnny Saxton	KO 9	1984	Jose Luis Ramirez	Edwin Rosario	KO 4
1957	Carmen Basilio	Sugar Ray Robinson	W 15	1985	Marvin Hagler	Thomas Hearns	KO 3
1958	Sugar Ray Robinson	Carmen Basilio	W 15	1986	Stevie Cruz	Barry McGuigan	W 15
1959	Gene Fullmer	Carmen Basilio	KO 14	1987	Sugar Ray Leonard	Marvin Hagler	W 12
				1988	Tony Lopez	Rocky Lockridge	W 12
1960	Floyd Patterson	Ingemar Johansson	KO 5	1989	Roberto Duran	Iran Barkley	W 12
1961	Joe Brown	Dave Charnley	W 15				
1962	Joey Giardello	Henry Hank	W 10	1990	Julio Cesar Chavez	Meldrick Taylor	KO 12
1963	Cassius Clay	Doug Jones	W 10	1991	Robert Quiroga	Akeem Anifowoshe	W 12
1964	Cassius Clay	Sonny Liston	KO 7	1992	Riddick Bowe	Evander Holyfield	W 12
1965	Floyd Patterson	George Chuvalo	W 12	1993	Michael Carbajal	Humberto Gonzalez	KO 7
1966	Jose Torres	Eddie Cotton	W 15	1994	Jorge Castro	John David Jackson	TKO 9
1967	Nino Benvenuti	Emile Griffith	W 15	1995	Saman Sorjaturong	Chiquita Gonzalez	KO 7
1968	Dick Tiger	Frank DePaula	W 10	1996	Evander Holyfield	Mike Tyson	TKO 11
1969	Joe Frazier	Jerry Quarry	KO 7	1997	Arturo Gatti	Gabriel Ruelas	KO 5
				1998	Ivan Robinson	Arturo Gatti	W 10
1970	Carlos Monzon	Nino Benvenuti	KO 12	1999	Paulie Ayala	Johnny Tapia	W 12
1971	Joe Frazier	Muhammad Ali	W 15				
1972	Bob Foster	Chris Finnegan	KO 14				

Ring Magazine Fighter of the Year

First presented in 1928 by Nat Fleischer, who started *The Ring* magazine in 1922.

Multiple winners: Muhammad Ali (5); Joe Louis (4); Joe Frazier, Evander Holyfield and Rocky Marciano (3); Ezzard Charles, George Foreman, Marvin Hagler, Thomas Hearns, Ingemar Johansson, Sugar Ray Leonard, Tommy Loughran, Floyd Patterson, Sugar Ray Robinson, Barney Ross, Dick Tiger and Mike Tyson (2)

Year		Year		Year		Year	
1928	Gene Tunney	1940	Billy Conn	1953	Carl (Bobo) Olson	1966	No award
1929	Tommy Loughran	1941	Joe Louis	1954	Rocky Marciano	1967	Joe Frazier
		1942	Sugar Ray Robinson	1955	Rocky Marciano	1968	Nino Benvenuti
1930	Max Schmeling	1943	Fred Apostoli	1956	Floyd Patterson	1969	Jose Napoles
1931	Tommy Loughran	1944	Beau Jack	1957	Carmen Basilio		
1932	Jack Sharkey	1945	Willie Pep	1958	Ingemar Johansson	1970	Joe Frazier
1933	No award	1946	Tony Zale	1959	Ingemar Johansson	1971	Joe Frazier
1934	Tony Canzoneri	1947	Gus Lesnevich			1972	Muhammad Ali
	& Barney Ross	1948	Ike Williams	1960	Floyd Patterson		& Carlos Monzon
1935	Barney Ross	1949	Ezzard Charles	1961	Joe Brown	1973	George Foreman
1936	Joe Louis			1962	Dick Tiger	1974	Muhammad Ali
1937	Henry Armstrong	1950	Ezzard Charles	1963	Cassius Clay	1975	Muhammad Ali
1938	Joe Louis	1951	Sugar Ray Robinson	1964	Emile Griffith	1976	George Foreman
1939	Joe Louis	1952	Rocky Marciano	1965	Dick Tiger	1977	Carlos Zarate

Year		Year		Year		Year	
1978	Muhammad Ali	1983	Marvin Hagler	1988	Mike Tyson	1994	Roy Jones Jr.
1979	Sugar Ray Leonard	1984	Thomas Hearns	1989	Pernell Whitaker	1995	Oscar De La Hoya
1980	Thomas Hearns	1985	Donald Curry			1996	Evander Holyfield
1981	Sugar Ray Leonard		& Marvin Hagler	1990	Julio Cesar Chavez	1997	Evander Holyfield
	& Salvador Sanchez	1986	Mike Tyson	1991	James Toney	1998	Floyd Mayweather Jr.
1982	Larry Holmes	1987	Evander Holyfield	1992	Riddick Bowe	1999	Paulie Ayala
				1993	Michael Carbajal		

Note: Cassius Clay changed his name to Muhammad Ali after winning the heavyweight title in 1964.

All-Time Leaders

As compiled by *The Ring Record Book and Encyclopedia.*

Knockouts

		Division	Career	No
1	Archie Moore	Lt. Heavy	1936-63	130
2	Young Stribling	Heavy	1921-33	126
3	Billy Bird	Welter	1920-48	125
4	George Odwel	Welter	1930-45	114
5	Sugar Ray Robinson	Middle	1940-65	110
6	Sandy Saddler	Feather	1944-56	103
7	Sam Langford	Middle	1902-26	102
8	Henry Armstrong	Welter	1931-45	100
9	Jimmy Wilde	Fly	1911-23	98
10	Len Wickwar	Lt. Heavy	1928-47	93

Total Bouts

		Division	Career	No
1	Len Wickwar	Lt. Heavy	1928-47	463
2	Jack Britton	Welter	1905-30	350
3	Johnny Dundee	Feather	1910-32	333
4	Billy Bird	Welter	1920-48	318
5	George Marsden	n/a	1928-46	311
6	Maxie Rosenbloom	Lt. Heavy	1923-39	299
7	Harry Greb	Middle	1913-26	298
8	Young Stribling	Lt. Heavy	1921-33	286
9	Battling Levinsky	Lt. Heavy	1910-29	282
10	Ted (Kid) Lewis	Welter	1909-29	279

Former Champions Who Have Won Back Heavyweight Title

Only 10 times since 1892 has the heavyweight championship been lost by a fighter who was able to win it back. Eight men have done it and Muhammad Ali and Evander Holyfield have done it twice.

	Lost To	Won Back From		Lost To	Won Back From
Floyd Patterson	Johansson (1959)	Johansson (1960)	Mike Tyson	Douglas (1990)	Bruno (1996)
Muhammad Ali	Frazier (1971)	Foreman (1974)	Evander Holyfield	Moorer (1994)	Tyson (1996)
Muhammad Ali	L Spinks (1978)	L Spinks (1978)	Lennox Lewis	McCall (1994)	McCall (1997)
Tim Witherspoon	Thomas (1984)	Tubbs (1986)	Evander Holyfield	Lewis (1999)	Ruiz (2000)*
Evander Holyfield	Bowe (1992)	Bowe (1993)			
George Foreman	Ali (1974)	Moorer (1994)	*Moorer won the vacant IBF title in a fight with Axel		
Michael Moorer	Foreman (1994)	Schulz (1996)*	Schulz. Holyfield won the vacant WBA title in a fight with		
			John Ruiz.		

Triple Champions

Fighters who have won widely-accepted world titles in more than two divisions. Henry Armstrong is the only fighter listed to hold three titles simultaneously. Note that (*) indicates title claimant.

Sugar Ray Leonard (5) WBC Welterweight (1979-80,80-82); WBA Jr. Middleweight (1981); WBC Middleweight (1987); WBC Super Middleweight (1988-90); WBC Light Heavyweight (1988).

Roberto Duran (4) Lightweight (1972-79); WBC Welterweight (1980); WBA Jr. Middleweight (1983-84); WBC Middleweight (1989-90).

Thomas Hearns (4) WBA Welterweight (1980-81); WBC Jr. Middleweight (1982-84); WBC Light Heavyweight (1987); WBA Light Heavyweight (1991); WBC Middleweight (1987-88).

Pernell Whitaker (4) IBF/WBC/WBA Lightweight (1989-92); IBF Jr. Lightweight (1992-93); WBC Welterweight (1993-97); WBC Jr. Middleweight (1995).

Alexis Arguello (3) WBA Featherweight (1974-77); WBC Jr. Lightweight (1978-80); WBC Lightweight (1981-83).

Henry Armstrong (3) Featherweight (1937-38); Welterweight (1938-40); Lightweight (1938-39).

Iran Barkley (3) WBC Middleweight (1988-89); IBF Super Middleweight (1992-93); WBA Light Heavyweight (1992).

Wilfredo Benitez (3) Jr. Welterweight (1976-79); Welterweight (1979); WBC Jr. Middleweight (1981-82).

Tony Canzoneri (3) Featherweight (1928); Lightweight (1930-33); Jr. Welterweight (1931-32,33).

Julio Cesar Chavez (3) WBC Jr. Lightweight (1984-87); WBA/WBC Lightweight (1987-89); WBC/IBF Jr. Welterweight (1989-91); WBC Jr. Welterweight (1991-94, 1994).

Oscar De La Hoya (3) IBF Lightweight (1995-96); WBC Super Lightweight (1996-97); WBC Welterweight (1997-99).

Jeff Fenech (3) IBF Bantamweight (1985); WBC Jr. Featherweight (1986-88); WBC Featherweight (1988-90).

Bob Fitzsimmons (3) Middleweight (1891-97); Light Heavyweight (1903-05); Heavyweight (1897-99).

Wilfredo Gomez (3) WBC Super Bantamweight (1977-83); WBC Featherweight (1984); WBA Jr. Lightweight (1985-86).

Leo Gamez (3) WBA Strawweight (1988-90); WBA Jr. Flyweight (1993-95); WBA Flyweight (1999).

Emile Griffith (3) Welterweight (1961,62-63,63-66); Jr. Middleweight (1962-63); Middleweight (1966-67,67-68).

Roy Jones Jr. (3) IBF Middleweight (1993-94); IBF Super Middleweight (1994-96); WBC Light Heavyweight (1996, 1997-); WBA Light Heavyweight (1998-); IBF Light Heavyweight (1999-).

Mike McCallum (3) WBA Jr. Middleweight (1984-88); WBA Middleweight (1989-91); WBC Light Heavyweight (1994-95).

Terry McGovern (3) Bantamweight (1889-1900); Featherweight (1900-01); Lightweight* (1900-01).

Barney Ross (3) Lightweight (1933-35); Jr. Welterweight (1933-35); Welterweight (1934, 35-38).

Wilfredo Vazquez (3) WBA Bantamweight (1987-88); WBA Jr. Featherweight (1992-95); WBA Featherweight (1996-98).

Miscellaneous Sports

Team New Zealand won the
America's Cup in 2000.

CHESS

World Champions

Garry Kasparov became the youngest man to win the world chess championship when he beat fellow Russian Anatoly Karpov in 1985 at age 22. In 1993, Kasparov and then-No. 1 challenger Nigel Short of England broke away from the established International Chess Federation (FIDE) to form the PCA. FIDE retaliated by stripping Kasparov of their world title and arranging a playoff that was won by Karpov, the former title-holder. Karpov has since successfully defended the FIDE title several times.

In 1999 FIDE sponsored another World Championship tournament, this time at Caesar's Palace in Las Vegas from July 30-Aug. 29. Most of the greatest players in the world were there. However, both Kasparov and Karpov were not. Kasparov was off playing a game on the Internet against the world but Karpov was supposed to be in Las Vegas to defend his FIDE title. He did not show.

The 72 players in the tournament squared off in two- and four-game matches (extra games were held to break ties). The tournament was single elimination and in each round the field was cut in half. Alexander Khalifman was the sole survivor, beating Judith Polgar in the quarterfinals, then Liviu-Dieter Nisipeanu in the semis before facing Vladimir Akopian in the finals. Khalifman beat Akopian 3½-2½ to claim the $660,000 prize and become the new FIDE world champion.

Despite Khalifman's win in Las Vegas, Kasparov is still the world's top-ranked player and continues to be recognized as the world champion. Kasparov was scheduled to defended his crown against world #2 Viswanathan Anand in a 16-game match in late 1999 but the match was cancelled due to lack of sponsorship. Kasparov was set to meet world #3 Vladimir Kramnik for 16 matches in the unofficial world championship from Oct. 8-Nov. 4, 2000 in London.

FIDE was scheduled to host the 2000 World Chess Championships in New Dehli, India and Tehran, Iran from Nov. 27-Dec. 26, 2000.

Years		Years		Years	
1866-94	Wilhelm Steinitz, Austria	1948-57	Mikhail Botvinnik, USSR	1969-72	Boris Spassky, USSR
1894-1921	Emanuel Lasker, Germany	1957-58	Vassily Smyslov, USSR	1972-75	Bobby Fischer, USA*
1921-27	Jose Capablanca, Cuba	1958-59	Mikhail Botvinnik, USSR	1975-85	Anatoly Karpov, USSR
1927-35	Alexander Alekhine, France	1960-61	Mikhail Tal, USSR	1985—	Garry Kasparov, RUS
1935-37	Max Euwe, Holland	1961-63	Mikhail Botvinnik, USSR		*Fischer defaulted the championship
1937-46	Alexander Alekhine, France	1963-69	Tigran Petrosian, USSR		in 1975.

U.S. Champions

After a three-way tie at 6½ points, Joel Benjamin won a three-person playoff with Yasser Seirawan and Alex Shabalov for the championship ring at the 2000 U.S. Chess Championships held Sept. 25-Oct. 6 in Seattle. The three players shared the prize money and the title of U.S. Champions.

Years		Years		Years	
1857-71	Paul Morphy	1954-57	Arthur Bisguier	1986	Yasser Seirawan
1871-76	George Mackenzie	1957-61	Bobby Fischer	1987	Joel Benjamin
1876-80	James Mason	1961-62	Larry Evans		& Nick DeFirmian
1880-89	George Mackenzie	1962-68	Bobby Fischer	1988	Michael Wilder
1889-90	Samuel Lipschutz	1968-69	Larry Evans	1989	Roman Dzindzichashvili,
1890	Jackson Showalter	1969-72	Samuel Reshevsky		Stuart Rachels
1890-91	Max Judd	1972-73	Robert Byrne		& Yasser Seirawan
1891-92	Jackson Showalter	1973-74	Lubomir Kavalek	1990	Lev Alburt
1892-94	Samuel Lipschutz		& John Grefe	1991	Gata Kamsky
1894	Jackson Showalter	1974-77	Walter Browne	1992	Patrick Wolff
1894-95	Albert Hodges	1978-80	Lubomir Kabalek	1993	Alexander Shabalov
1895-97	Jackson Showalter	1980-81	Larry Evans,		& Alex Yermolinsky
1897-1906	Harry Pillsbury		Larry Christiansen	1994	Boris Gulko
1906-09	Vacant		& Walter Browne	1995	Alexander Ivanov
1909-36	Frank Marshall	1981-83	Walter Browne	1996	Alexander Yermolinsky
1936-44	Samuel Reshevsky		& Yasser Seirawan	1997	Joel Benjamin
1944-46	Arnold Denker	1983	Roman Dzindzichashvili,	1998	Nick de Firmian
1946-48	Samuel Reshevsky		Larry Christiansen	1999	Boris Gulko
1948-51	Herman Steiner		& Walter Browne	2000	Joel Benjamin, Yasser Seirawan & Alex Shabalov
1951-54	Larry Evans	1984-85	Lev Alburt		

DOGS

Iditarod Trail Sled Dog Race

Defending champion Doug Swingley became a three-time winner of the Iditarod Trail Sled Dog Race in 2000, passing under the burled arch marking the finish line on Front Street in Nome in a record time of nine days, 58 minutes and six seconds. Swingley, of Lincoln, Mont., still the only non-Alaskan to win the race, beat second place finisher Paul Gebhart by just over five hours.

Swingley broke away from the pack early on before taking the mandatory 24-hour rest, using the same strategy that helped him with the famous race in 1995 and 1999. He earned $60,000 for the win, plus the keys to a new pickup truck (worth $37,000).

Eighty-one teams began the race on March 4 in Anchorage, 68 would finish. Swingley credited good dog breeding and a serious training regimen for his success.

In even-numbered years the trail follows the 1,151-mile Northern Route, while in odd-numbered years, it takes a slightly different 1,161-mile Southern Route.

Multiple winners: Rick Swenson (5); Susan Butcher (4); Martin Buser, Jeff King and Doug Swingley (3); Rick Mackey (2).

Year		Elapsed Time	Year		Elapsed Time
1973	Dick Wilmarth	20 days, 00:49:41	1975	Emmitt Peters	14 days, 14:43:45
1974	Carl Huntington	20 days, 15:02:07	1976	Gerald Riley	18 days, 22:58:17

Year		Elapsed Time	Year		Elapsed Time
1977	Rick Swenson	16 days, 16:27:13	1990	Susan Butcher	11 days, 01:53:23
1978	Dick Mackey	14 days, 18:52:24	1991	Rick Swenson	12 days, 16:34:39
1979	Rick Swenson	15 days, 10:37:47	1992	Martin Buser	10 days, 19:17:00
1980	Joe May	14 days, 07:11:51	1993	Jeff King	10 days, 15:38:15
1981	Rick Swenson	12 days, 08:45:02	1994	Martin Buser	10 days, 13:02:39
1982	Rick Swenson	16 days, 04:40:10	1995	Doug Swingley	9 days, 02:42:19
1983	Rick Mackey	12 days, 14:10:44	1996	Jeff King	9 days, 05:43:13
1984	Dean Osmar	12 days, 15:07:33	1997	Martin Buser	9 days, 08:31:45
1985	Libby Riddles	18 days, 00:20:17	1998	Jeff King	9 days, 05:52:26
1986	Susan Butcher	11 days, 15:06:00	1999	Doug Swingley	9 days, 14:31:07
1987	Susan Butcher	11 days, 02:05:13	2000	Doug Swingley	9 days, 00:58:06*
1988	Susan Butcher	11 days, 11:41:40	*Course record.		
1989	Joe Runyan	11 days, 05:24:34			

Westminster Kennel Club
Best in Show

Ch Salilyn 'N Erin's Shameless, a 42-pound English Springer Spaniel, won Best in Show at the 124th annual Westminster Kennel Club show on Feb. 15 at Madison Square Garden in New York. The 5-year-old bitch, who answers to the name Samantha, was sired by Ch. Salilyn's Condor, who won Best in Show in 1993. Samantha, who was chosen from among 2,500 dogs from 156 breeds, edged presumed favorite Ch. Lakecove That's My Boy, a white standard poodle, and crowd-pleaser Ch. Moonbeam's Astronomer, a basset hound, among others and will now retire to breed.

The Westminster show is the most prestigious dog show in the country, and one of America's oldest annual sporting events.

Multiple winners: Ch. Warren Remedy (3); Ch. Chinoe's Adamant James, Ch. Comejo Wycollar Boy, Ch. Flornell Spicy Piece of Halleston; Ch. Matford Vic, Ch. My Own Brucie, Ch. Pendley Calling of Blarney, Ch. Rancho Dobe's Storm (2).

Year	Breed	Year	Breed
1907 Warren Remedy	Fox Terrier	1954 Carmor's Rise and Shine	Cocker Spaniel
1908 Warren Remedy	Fox Terrier	1955 Kippax Fearnought	Bulldog
1909 Warren Remedy	Fox Terrier	1956 Wilber White Swan	Toy Poodle
1910 Sabine Rarebit	Fox Terrier	1957 Shirkhan of Grandeur	Afghan Hound
1911 Tickle Em Jock	Scottish Terrier	1958 Puttencove Promise	Standard Poodle
1912 Kenmore Sorceress	Airedale	1959 Fontclair Festoon	Miniature Poodle
1913 Strathway Prince Albert	Bulldog	1960 Chick T'Sun of Caversham	Pekingese
1914 Brentwood Hero	Old English Sheepdog	1961 Cappoquin Little Sister	Toy Poodle
1915 Matford Vic	Old English Sheepdog	1962 Elfinbrook Simon	W. Highland Terrier
1916 Matford Vic	Old English Sheepdog	1963 Wakefield's Black Knight	English Springer Spaniel
1917 Comejo Wycollar Boy	Fox Terrier	1964 Courtenay Fleetfoot of Pennyworth	Whippet
1918 Haymarket Faultless	Bull Terrier	1965 Carmichaels Fanfare	Scottish Terrier
1919 Briergate Bright Beauty	Airedale	1966 Zeloy Mooremaides Magic	Fox Terrier
1920 Comejo Wycollar Boy	Fox Terrier	1967 Bardene Bingo	Scottish Terrier
1921 Midkiff Seductive	Cocker Spaniel	1968 Stingray of Derryabah	Lakeland Terrier
1922 Boxwood Barkentine	Airedale	1969 Glamoor Good News	Skye Terrier
1923 No best-in-show award		1970 Arriba's Prima Donna	Boxer
1924 Barberryhill Bootlegger	Sealyham	1971 Chinoe's Adamant James	E.S. Spaniel
1925 Governor Moscow	Pointer	1972 Chinoe's Adamant James	E.S. Spaniel
1926 Signal Circuit	Fox Terrier	1973 Acadia Command Performance	Standard Poodle
1927 Pinegrade Perfection	Sealyham	1974 Gretchenhof Columbia River	German SH Pointer
1928 Talavera Margaret	Fox Terrier	1975 Sir Lancelot of Barvan	Old Eng. Sheepdog
1929 Land Loyalty of Bellhaven	Collie	1976 Jo Ni's Red Baron of Crofton	Lakeland Terrier
1930 Pendley Calling of Blarney	Fox Terrier	1977 Dersade Bobby's Girl	Sealyham
1931 Pendley Calling of Blarney	Fox Terrier	1978 Cede Higgens	Yorkshire Terrier
1932 Nancolleth Markable	Pointer	1979 Oak Tree's Irishtocrat	Irish Water Spaniel
1933 Warland Protector of Shelterock	Airedale	1980 Sierra Cinnar	Siberian Husky
1934 Flornell Spicy Bit of Halleston	Fox Terrier	1981 Dhandy Favorite Woodchuck	Pug
1935 Nunsoe Duc de la Terrace of Blakeen	Stan. Poodle	1982 St. Aubrey Dragonora of Elsdon	Pekingese
1936 St. Margaret Magnificent of Clairedale	Sealyham	1983 Kabik's The Challenger	Afghan Hound
1937 Flornell Spicy Bit of Halleston	Fox Terrier	1984 Seaward's Blackbeard	Newfoundland
1938 Daro of Maridor	English Setter	1985 Braeburn's Close Encounter	Scottish Terrier
1939 Ferry v.Rauhfelsen of Giralda	Doberman	1986 Marjetta National Acclaim	Pointer
1940 My Own Brucie	Cocker Spaniel	1987 Covy Tucker Hill's Manhattan	German Shepherd
1941 My Own Brucie	Cocker Spaniel	1988 Great Elms Prince Charming II	Pomeranian
1942 Wolvey Pattern of Edgerstoune	W. Highland Terrier	1989 Royal Tudor's Wild As The Wind	Doberman
1943 Pitter Patter of Piperscroft	Miniature Poodle	1990 Wendessa Crown Prince	Pekingese
1944 Flornell Rarebit of Twin Ponds	Welsh Terrier	1991 Whisperwind on a Carousel	Stan. Poodle
1945 Shieling's Signature	Scottish Terrier	1992 Lonesome Dove	Fox Terrier
1946 Hetherington Model Rhythm	Fox Terrier	1993 Salilyn's Condor	E.S. Spaniel
1947 Warlord of Mazelaine	Boxer	1994 Chidley Willum	Norwich Terrier
1948 Rock Ridge Night Rocket	Bedling. Terrier	1995 Gaelforce Post Script	Scottish Terrier
1949 Mazelaine's Zazarac Brandy	Boxer	1996 Clussex Country Sunrise	Clumber Spaniel
1950 Walsing Winning Trick of Edgerstoune	Scot. Terrier	1997 Parsifal di Casa Netzer	Standard Schnauzer
1951 Bang Away of Sirrah Crest	Boxer	1998 Fairewood Frolic	Norwich Terrier
1952 Rancho Dobe's Storm	Doberman	1999 Loteki's Supernatural Being	Papillon
1953 Rancho Dobe's Storm	Doberman	2000 Salilyn 'N Erin's Shameless	E.S. Spaniel

FISHING

IGFA All-Tackle World Records

All-tackle records are maintained for the heaviest fish of any species caught on any line up to 130-lb (60 kg) class and certified by the International Game Fish Association. Records logged through Aug. 26, 2000. **Address:** 300 Gulf Stream Way, Dania Beach, Fla. 33004. **Telephone:** 954-927-2628.

FRESHWATER FISH

Species	Lbs-Oz	Where Caught	Date	Angler
Barramundi	83-7	N. Queensland, Australia	Sept. 23, 1999	David Powell
Bass, Guadalupe	3-11	Lake Travis, TX	Sept. 25, 1983	Allen Christenson Jr.
Bass, largemouth	22-4	Montgomery Lake, GA	June 2, 1932	George W. Perry
Bass, redeye	8-12	Apalachicola River, FL	Jan. 28, 1995	Carl W. Davis
Bass, Roanoke	1-5	Nottoway River, VA	Nov. 11, 1991	Tom Elkins
Bass, rock	3-0	York River, Ontario	Aug. 1, 1974	Peter Gulgin
Bass, smallmouth	10-14	Dale Hollow, TN	Apr. 24, 1969	John T. Gorman
Bass, spotted	9-9	Pine Flat Lake, CA	Oct. 12, 1996	Kirk Sakamoto
Bass, striped (landlocked)	67-8	O'Neill Forebay, San Luis, CA	May 7, 1992	Hank Ferguson
Bass, Suwannee	3-14	Suwannee River, FL	Mar. 2, 1985	Ronnie Everett
Bass, white	6-13	Lake Orange, VA	July 31, 1989	Ronald L. Sprouse
Bass, whiterock	27-5	Greers Ferry Lake, AR	Apr. 24, 1997	Jerald C. Shaum
Bass, yellow	2-9	Duck River, TN	Feb. 27, 1998	John T. Campbell
Bass, yellow (hybrid)	3-5	Big Cypress Bayou, TX	Mar. 27, 1991	Patrick Collin Myers
Bluegill	4-12	Ketona Lake, AL	Apr. 9, 1950	T.S. Hudson
Bowfin	21-8	Florence, SC	Jan. 29, 1980	Robert L. Harmon
Buffalo, bigmouth	70-5	Bussey Brake, Bastrop, LA	Apr. 21, 1980	Delbert Sisk
Buffalo, black	63-6	Mississippi River, Iowa	Aug. 14, 1999	Jim Winters
Buffalo, smallmouth	82-3	Athens Lake, AL	June 6, 1993	Randy Collins
Bullhead, black	7-7	Mill Pond, NY	Aug. 25, 1993	Kevin Kelly
Bullhead, brown	6-1	Waterford, NY	Apr. 26, 1998	Bobby Triplett
Bullhead, yellow	4-4	Mormon Lake, AZ	May 11, 1984	Emily Williams
Burbot	18-11	Angenmanelren, Sweden	Oct. 22, 1996	Margit Agren
Carp, bighead	20-0	Mentro, Missouri	July 26, 1999	Rick Hayden
Carp, black	40-12	Chiba, Japan	Apr. 1, 2000	Kenichi Hosoi
Carp, common	75-11	St. Cassien, France	May 21, 1987	Leo van der Gugten
Carp, crucian	5-1	Kalterersee, Italy	July 16, 1997	Jorg Marquand
Catfish, blue	111-0	Wheeler's Reservoir, TN	July 5, 1996	William McKinley
Catfish, channel	58-0	Santee-Cooper Res., SC	July 7, 1964	W.B. Whaley
Catfish, flathead	123-9	Elk City Reservoir, KS	Mar. 14, 1998	Ken Paulie
Catfish, flatwhiskered	9-4	Rio Paraquai, Brazil	Sept. 11, 1996	Cavour Pieranti
Catfish, gilded	85-8	Amazon River, Brazil	Nov. 15, 1986	Gilberto Fernandes
Catfish, redtail	97-7	Amazon River, Brazil	July 16, 1988	Gilberto Fernandes
Catfish, sharptoothed	79-5	Orange River, S. Africa	Dec. 5, 1992	Hennie Moller
Catfish, white	18-14	Inverness, FL	Sept. 21, 1991	Jim Miller
Char, Arctic	32-9	Tree River, Canada	July 30, 1981	Jeffery Ward
Crappie, black	4-8	Kerr Lake, VA	Mar. 1, 1981	L. Carl Herring Jr.
Crappie, white	5-3	Enid Dam, MS	July 31, 1957	Fred L. Bright
Dolly Varden	19-4	Unnamed River, AK	Sept. 4, 1998	Gary D. Ordway
Dorado	51-5	Corrientes, Argentina	Sept. 27, 1984	Armando Giudice
Drum, freshwater	54-8	Nickajack Lake, TN	Apr. 20, 1972	Benny E. Hull
Gar, alligator	279-0	Rio Grande, TX	Dec. 2, 1951	Bill Valverde
Gar, Florida	15-14	Flagler Beach, FL	Oct. 3, 1999	Randy Michael Carmean
Gar, longnose	50-5	Trinity River, TX	July 30, 1954	Townsend Miller
Gar, shortnose	5-12	Rend Lake, Ill.	July 16, 1995	Donna K. Willmart
Gar, spotted	9-12	Lake Mexia, TX	Apr. 7, 1994	Rick Rivard
Goldfish	6-10	Lake Hodges, CA	Apr. 17, 1996	Florentino M. Abena
Grayling, Arctic	5-15	Katseydie River, N.W.T.	Aug. 16, 1967	Jeanne P. Branson
Inconnu	53-0	Pah River, AK	Aug. 20, 1986	Lawrence E. Hudnall
Kokanee	9-6	Okanagan Lake, Brit. Columbia	June 18, 1988	Norm Kuhn
Muskellunge	67-8	Hayward, WI	July 24, 1949	Cal Johnson
Muskellunge, tiger	51-3	Lac Vieux-Desert, WI-MI	July 16, 1919	John A. Knobla
Peacock, butterfly	10-8	Bolivar State, Brazil	Jan. 6, 2000	Antonio Campa G.
Peacock, speckled	27-0	Rio Negro, Brazil	Dec. 4, 1994	Gerald (Doc) Lawson
Perch, Nile	213-0	Lake Nasser, Egypt	Dec. 18, 1997	Adrian Brayshaw
Perch, white	4-12	Messalonskee Lake, ME	June 4, 1949	Mrs. Earl Small
Perch, yellow	4-3	Bordentown, NJ	May, 1865	Dr. C.C. Abbot
Pickerel, chain	9-6	Homerville, GA	Feb. 17, 1961	Baxley McQuaig Jr.
Pickerel, grass	1-0	Dewart Lake, IN	June 9, 1990	Mike Berg
Pickerel, redfin	2-7	St. Pauls, NC	June 27, 1997	Edward C. Davis
Pike, northern	55-1	Lake of Grefeern, Germany	Oct. 16, 1986	Lothar Louis
Redhorse, greater	9-3	Salmon River, Pulaski, NY	May 11, 1985	Jason Wilson

Species	Lbs-Oz	Where Caught	Date	Angler
Redhorse, silver	11-7	Plum Creek, WI	May 29, 1985	Neal D.G. Long
Salmon, Atlantic	79-2	Tana River, Norway	1928	Henrik Henriksen
Salmon, chinook	97-4	Kenai River, AK	May 17, 1985	Les Anderson
Salmon, chum	35-0	Edye Pass, Brit. Columbia	July 11, 1995	Todd Johansson
Salmon, coho	33-4	Salmon River, Pulaski, NY	Sept. 27, 1989	Jerry Lifton
Salmon, pink	13-1	St. Mary's River, Ontario	Sept. 23, 1992	Ray Higaki
Salmon, sockeye	15-3	Kenai River, AK	Aug. 9, 1987	Stan Roach
Sauger	8-12	Lake Sakakawea, ND	Oct. 6, 1971	Mike Fischer
Shad, American	11-4	Conn. River, S. Hadley, MA	May 19, 1986	Bob Thibodo
Shad, gizzard	4-6	Lake Michigan, IN	Mar. 2, 1996	Mike Berg
Sturgeon, lake	168-0	Georgian Bay, Canada	May 29, 1982	Edward Paszkowski
Sturgeon, white	468-0	Benicia, CA	July 9, 1983	Joey Pallotta 3rd
Tigerfish, giant	97-0	Zaire River, Kinshasa, Zaire	July 9, 1988	Raymond Houtmans
Tilapia	6-5	Lake Arenal, Costa Rica	Feb. 10, 1995	Marvin C. Smith
Trout, Apache	5-3	White Mountain, AZ	May 29, 1991	John Baldwin
Trout, brook	14-8	Nipigon River, Ontario	July, 1916	Dr. W.J. Cook
Trout, brown	40-4	Little Red River, AR	May 9, 1992	Rip Collins
Trout, bull	32-0	Lake Pond Orielle, ID	Oct. 27, 1949	N.L. Higgins
Trout, cutthroat	41-0	Pyramid Lake, NV	Dec., 1925	John Skimmerhorn
Trout, golden	11-0	Cooks Lake, WY	Aug. 5, 1948	Charles S. Reed
Trout, lake	72-0	Great Bear Lake, N.W.T.	Aug. 19, 1995	Lloyd E. Bull
Trout, rainbow	42-2	Bell Island, AK	June 22, 1970	David Robert White
Trout, tiger	20-13	Lake Michigan, WI	Aug. 12, 1978	Peter M. Friedland
Walleye	25-0	Old Hickory Lake, TN	Aug. 2, 1960	Mabry Harper
Warmouth	2-7	Guess Lake, Holt, FL	Oct. 19, 1985	Tony D. Dempsey
Whitefish, lake	14-6	Meaford, Ontario	May 21, 1984	Dennis M. Laycock
Whitefish, mountain	5-8	Elbow River, Manitoba	Aug. 1, 1995	Randy G. Woo
Whitefish, round	6-0	Putahow River, Manitoba	June 14, 1984	Allan J. Ristori
Zander	25-2	Trosa, Sweden	June 12, 1986	Harry Lee Tennison

SALTWATER FISH

Species	Lbs-Oz	Where Caught	Date	Angler
Albacore	88-2	Gran Canaria, Canary Islands	Nov. 19, 1977	Siegfried Dickemann
Amberjack, greater	155-12	Challenger Bank, Bermuda	Aug. 16, 1992	Larry Trott
Angelfish, gray	4-0	S.Beach Jetty, Miami, FLA	July 12, 1999	Rene G. de Dios
Barracuda, great	85-0	Christmas Is., Rep. of Kiribati	Apr. 11, 1992	John W. Helfrich
Barracuda, Mexican	21-0	Phantom Island, Costa Rica	Mar. 27, 1987	E. Greg Kent
Barracuda, pickhandle	25-5	Scottburgh, South Africa	July 3, 1996	Demetrios Stamatis
Bass, barred sand	13-3	Huntington Beach, CA	Aug. 29, 1988	Robert Halal
Bass, black sea	10-4	Virginia Beach, VA	Jan. 1, 2000	Allan P. Paschall
Bass, European	20-14	Cap d'Agde, France	Sept. 8, 1999	Robert Mari
Bass, giant sea	563-8	Anacapa Island, CA	Aug. 20, 1968	J.D. McAdam Jr.
Bass, striped	78-8	Atlantic City, NJ	Sept. 21, 1982	Albert R. McReynolds
Bluefish	31-12	Hatteras, NC	Jan. 30, 1972	James M. Hussey
Bonefish	19-0	Zululand, South Africa	May 26, 1962	Brian W. Batchelor
Bonito, Atlantic	18-4	Faial Island, Azores	July 8, 1953	D. Gama Higgs
Bonito, Pacific	21-3	Malibu, CA	July 30, 1978	Gino M. Picciolo
Cabezon	23-0	Juan de Fuca Strait, WA	Aug. 4, 1990	Wesley Hunter
Cobia	135-9	Shark Bay, W. Australia	July 9, 1985	Peter W. Goulding
Cod, Atlantic	98-12	Isle of Shoals, NH	June 8, 1969	Alphonse Bielevich
Cod, Pacific	35-0	Unalaska Bay, Alaska	June 16, 1999	Jim Johnson
Conger	133-4	South Devon, England	June 5, 1995	Vic Evans
Dolphinfish	88-0	Highbourne Cay, Bahamas	May 5, 1998	Richard D. Evans
Drum, black	113-1	Lewes, DE	Sept. 15, 1975	Gerald M. Townsend
Drum, red	94-2	Avon, NC	Nov. 7, 1984	David G. Deuel
Eel, American	9-4	Cape May, NJ	Nov. 9, 1995	Jeff Pennick
Eel, marbled	36-1	Durban, S. Africa	June 10, 1984	Ferdie van Nooten
Flounder, southern	20-9	Nassau Sound, FL	Dec. 23, 1983	Larenza Mungin
Flounder, summer	22-7	Montauk, NY	Sept. 15, 1975	Charles Nappi
Grouper, Warsaw	436-12	Gulf of Mexico, Destin, FL	Dec. 22, 1985	Steve Haeusler
Haddock	14-15	Saltraumen, Germany	Aug. 15, 1997	Heike Neblinger
Halibut, Atlantic	355-6	Valevag, Norway	Oct. 20, 1997	Odd Arve Gunderstad
Halibut, California	58-9	Santa Rosa Island, CA	June 26, 1999	Roger W. Borrell
Halibut, Pacific	459-0	Dutch Harbor, AK	June 11, 1996	Jack Tragis
Jack, almaco (Pacific)	132-0	La Paz, Baja Calif., Mexico	July 21, 1964	Howard H. Hahn
Jack, crevalle	57-14	Southwest Pass, LA	Aug. 15, 1997	Leon D. Richard
Jack, horse-eye	29-8	Ascencion Island, South Atlantic	May 28, 1993	Mike Hanson
Jewfish	680-0	Fernandina Beach, FL	May 20, 1961	Lynn Joyner
Kawakawa	29-0	Clarion Island, Mexico	Dec. 17, 1986	Ronald Nakamura
Lingcod	69-0	Langara Is., Brit. Columbia	June 16, 1992	Murray M. Romer

Species	Lbs-Oz	Where Caught	Date	Angler
Mackerel, cero	17-2	Islamorada, FL	Apr. 5, 1986	G. Michael Mills
Mackerel, king	93-0	San Juan, Puerto Rico	April 18, 1999	Steve Perez Graulau
Mackerel, Spanish	13-0	Ocracoke Inlet, NC	Nov. 4, 1987	Robert Cranton
Marlin, Atlantic blue	1402-2	Vitoria, Brazil	Feb. 29, 1992	Paulo R.A. Amorim
Marlin, black	1560-0	Cabo Blanco, Peru	Aug. 4, 1953	A.C. Glassell Jr.
Marlin, Pacific blue	1376-0	Kaaiwi Point, Kona, HI	May 31, 1982	Jay W. deBeaubien
Marlin, striped	494-0	Tutakaka, New Zealand	Jan. 16, 1986	Bill Boniface
Marlin, white	181-14	Vitoria, Brazil	Dec. 8, 1979	Evandro Luiz Coser
Permit	56-2	Ft. Lauderdale, FL	June 30, 1997	Thomas Sebestyen
Pollock	50-0	Salstraumen, Norway	Nov. 30, 1996	Thor-Magnus Ukang
Pollack, European	27-6	Salcombe, Devon, England	Jan. 16, 1986	Robert S. Milkins
Pompano, African	50-8	Daytona Beach, FL	Apr. 21, 1990	Tom Sargent
Roosterfish	114-0	La Paz, Baja Calif., Mexico	June 1, 1960	Abe Sackheim
Runner, blue	11-2	Dauphin Island, AL	June 28, 1997	Stacey M. Moiren
Runner, rainbow	37-9	Clarion Island, Mexico	Nov. 21, 1991	Tom Pfleger
Sailfish, Atlantic	141-1	Luanda, Angola	Feb. 19, 1994	Alfredo de Sousa Neves
Sailfish, Pacific	221-0	Santa Cruz Is., Ecuador	Feb. 12, 1947	C.W. Stewart
Seabass, white	83-12	San Felipe, Mexico	Mar. 31, 1953	L.C. Baumgardner
Seatrout, spotted	17-7	Ft. Pierce, FL	May 11, 1995	Craig F. Carson
Shark, blue	454-0	Martha's Vineyard, MA	July 19, 1996	Pete Bergin
Shark, great white	2664-0	Ceduna, S. Australia	Apr. 21, 1959	Alfred Dean
Shark, Greenland	1708-9	Trondheimsfjord, Norway	Oct. 18, 1987	Terje Nordtvedt
Shark, hammerhead	991-0	Sarasota, FL	May 30, 1982	Allen Ogle
Shark, shortfin mako	1115-0	Black River, Mauritius	Nov. 16, 1988	Patrick Guillanton
Shark, porbeagle	507-0	Pentland Firth, Scotland	Mar. 9, 1993	Christopher Bennet
Shark, bigeye thresher	802-0	Tutukaka, New Zealand	Feb. 8, 1981	Dianne North
Shark, tiger	1780-0	Cherry Grove, SC	June 14, 1964	Walter Maxwell
Snapper, cubera	121-8	Cameron, LA	July 5, 1982	Mike Hebert
Snapper, red	50-4	Gulf of Mexico, LA	June 23, 1996	Capt. Doc Kennedy
Snook	57-12	Rio Naranjo, Quepos, Costa Rica	Aug. 23, 1991	George Beck
Spearfish, Mediterranean	90-13	Madeira Island, Portugal	June 2, 1980	Joseph Larkin
Swordfish	1182-0	Iquique, Chile	May 7, 1953	Louis Marron
Tarpon	283-4	Sherbro Is., Sierra Leone	Apr. 16, 1991	Yvon Victor Sebag
Tautog	25-0	Ocean City, NJ	Jan. 20, 1998	Anthony R. Monica
Tuna, Atlantic bigeye	392-6	Gran Canaria, Puerto Rico	July 25, 1996	Dieter Vogel
Tuna, blackfin	45-8	Key West, FL	May 4, 1996	Sam J. Burnett
Tuna, bluefin	1496-0	Aulds Cove, Nova Scotia	Oct. 26, 1979	Ken Fraser
Tuna, longtail	79-2	Montague Is., NSW, Australia	Apr. 12, 1982	Tim Simpson
Tuna, Pacific bigeye	435-0	Cabo Blanco, Peru	Apr. 17, 1957	Dr. Russell Lee
Tuna, skipjack	45-4	Flathead Bank, Mexico	Nov. 16, 1996	Brian Evans
Tuna, southern bluefin	348-5	Whakatane, New Zealand	Jan. 16, 1981	Rex Wood
Tuna, yellowfin	388-12	San Benedicto Island, Mexico	Apr. 1, 1977	Curt Wiesenhutter
Tunny, little	35-2	Cape de Garde, Algeria	Dec. 14, 1988	Jean Yves Chatard
Wahoo	158-8	Loreto, Baja Calif., Mexico	June 10, 1996	Keith Winter
Weakfish	19-2	Jones Beach, Long Island, NY	Oct. 11, 1984	Dennis R. Rooney
	19-2	Delaware Bay, DE	May 20, 1989	William E. Thomas

B.A.S.S. Masters Classic

The 15th time was the charm. Woo Daves finally ended his decade and a half drought by winning the 30th annual B.A.S.S. Masters Classic Championship on the waters of Lake Michigan and the Chicago-Calumet river system on July 22. His three-day total of 27 pounds, 13 ounces narrowly defeated California's Mark Rizk (26-11). Daves was crowned champion in Soldier Field in front of over 300 members of the media.

"Winning the Classic is the dream of every bass fisherman in the world," Daves said. "And my dream came true today."

"It means a lot more to me because I'm no spring chicken. I'm 54 years old. My mother keeps asking me if I was ever going to win the Classic before she died. And she's 81."

Daves, a native of Spring Grove, Va., earned a winner's check for $100,000 by using a Zoom tubejig to fish an abandoned seawall under the shadow of the Sears Tower. Daves also fished with a Zoom green pumpkin dipped with chartreuse Spike-it. The 25-year veteran caught a total of 14 fish, but it was the five small mouth bass he corralled in one day that pushed him over the edge.

The B.A.S.S. Masters Classic is fishing's version of the Masters golf tournament. Invitees to the three-day event include the 25 top-ranked pros on the B.A.S.S. tour and the five top-ranked anglers from each BASSMASTER Invitational circuit. Anglers may weigh only seven bass per day and each bass must be at least 12 inches long. Competitors are allowed only seven rods and reels and are limited to the tackle they can pack into two tournament-approved tackleboxes. Only artificial lures are permitted. The first Classic, held at Lake Mead, Nev. in 1971, was a $10,000 winner-take-all event.

Multiple winners: Rick Clunn (4); George Cochran, Bobby Murray and Hank Parker (2).

Year		Weight	Year		Weight
1971	Bobby Murray, Hot Springs, Ark.	43-11	1976	Rick Clunn, Montgomery, Tex	59-15
1972	Don Butler, Tulsa, Okla.	38-11	1977	Rick Clunn, Montgomery, Tex.	27-7
1973	Rayo Breckenridge, Paragould, Ark	52-8	1978	Bobby Murray, Nashville, Tenn	37-9
1974	Tommy Martin, Hemphill, Tex.	33-7	1979	Hank Parker, Clover, S.C	31-0
1975	Jack Hains, Rayne, La.	45-4	1980	Bo Dowden, Natchitoches, La	54-10

Year		Weight	Year		Weight
1981	Stanley Mitchell, Fitzgerald, Ga	.35-2	1991	Ken Cook, Meers, Okla	.33-2
1982	Paul Elias, Laurel, Miss	.32-8	1992	Robert Hamilton Jr., Brandon, Miss	.59-6
1983	Larry Nixon, Hemphill, Tex.	.18-1	1993	David Fritts, Lexington, N.C.	.48-6
1984	Rick Clunn, Montgomery, Tex.	.75-9	1994	Bryan Kerchal, Newtown, Conn	.36-7
1985	Jack Chancellor, Phenix City, Ala	.45-0	1995	Mark Davis, Mount Ida, Ark.	.47-14
1986	Charlie Reed, Broken Bow, Okla.	.23-9	1996	George Cochran, Hot Springs, Ark.	.31-14
1987	George Cochran, N. Little Rock, Ark	.15-5	1997	Dion Hibdon, Stover, Mo.	.34-13
1988	Guido Hibdon, Gravois Mills, Mo.	.28-8	1998	Denny Brauer, Camdenton, Mo.	.46-3
1989	Hank Parker, Denver, N.C.	.31-6	1999	Davy Hite, Prosperity, S.C.	.55-10
1990	Rick Clunn, Montgomery, Tex.	.34-5	2000	Woo Daves, Spring Grove, Va.	.27-13

LITTLE LEAGUE BASEBALL

World Series

Played annually in late August in Williamsport, Penn. at Original Field in Williamsport, Penn. from 1947-1958 and at Howard J. Lamade Stadium since 1959.

Multiple winners: Taiwan (16); California (5); Connecticut, Japan, New Jersey and Pennsylvania (4); Mexico (3); New York, South Korea, Texas and Venezuela (2).

Year	Winner	Score	Loser	Year	Winner	Score	Loser
1947	Williamsport, PA	16-7	Lock Haven, PA	1975	Lakewood, NJ	4-3	*Tampa, FL
1948	Lock Haven, PA	6-5	St. Petersburg, FL	1976	Tokyo, Japan	10-3	Campbell, CA
1949	Hammonton, NJ	5-0	Pensacola, FL	1977	Li-Teh, Taiwan	7-2	El Cajon, CA
1950	Houston, TX	2-1	Bridgeport, CT	1978	Pin-Tung, Taiwan	11-1	Danville, CA
1951	Stamford, CT	3-0	Austin, TX	1979	Hsien, Taiwan	2-1	Campbell, CA
1952	Norwalk, CT	4-3	Monongahela, PA	1980	Hua Lian, Taiwan	4-3	Tampa, FL
1953	Birmingham, AL	1-0	Schenectady, NY	1981	Tai-Chung, Taiwan	4-2	Tampa, FL
1954	Schenectady, NY	7-5	Colton, CA	1982	Kirkland, WA	6-0	Hsien, Taiwan
1955	Morrisville, PA	4-3	Merchantville, NJ	1983	Marietta, GA	3-1	Barahona, D. Rep.
1956	Roswell, NM	3-1	Merchantville, NJ	1984	Seoul, S. Korea	6-2	Altamonte, FL
1957	Monterrey, Mexico	4-0	La Mesa, CA	1985	Seoul, S. Korea	7-1	Mexicali, Mex.
1958	Monterrey, Mexico	10-1	Kankakee, IL	1986	Tainan Park, Taiwan	12-0	Tucson, AZ
1959	Hamtramck, MI	12-0	Auburn, CA	1987	Hua Lian, Taiwan	21-1	Irvine, CA
1960	Levittown, PA	5-0	Ft. Worth, TX	1988	Tai Ping, Taiwan	10-0	Pearl City, HI
1961	El Cajon, CA	4-2	El Campo, TX	1989	Trumbull, CT	5-2	Kaohsiung, Taiwan
1962	San Jose, CA	3-0	Kankakee, IL	1990	Taipei, Taiwan	9-0	Shippensburg, PA
1963	Granada Hills, CA	2-1	Stratford, CT	1991	Taichung, Taiwan	11-0	Danville, CA
1964	Staten Island, NY	4-0	Monterrey, Mex.	1992	Long Beach, CA	6-0	Zamboanga, Phil.
1965	Windsor Locks, CT	3-1	Stoney Creek, Can.	1993	Long Beach, CA	3-2	Panama
1966	Houston, TX	8-2	W. New York, NJ	1994	Maracaibo, Venezuela	4-3	Northridge, CA
1967	West Tokyo, Japan	4-1	Chicago, IL	1995	Tainan, Taiwan	17-3	Spring, TX
1968	Osaka, Japan	1-0	Richmond, VA	1996	Taipei, Taiwan	13-3	Cranston, RI
1969	Taipei, Taiwan	5-0	Santa Clara, CA				(called after 5th inn.)
1970	Wayne, NJ	2-0	Campbell, CA	1997	Guadalupe, Mexico	5-4	Mission Viejo, CA
1971	Tainan, Taiwan	12-3	Gary, IN	1998	Toms River, NJ	12-9	Kashima, Japan
1972	Taipei, Taiwan	6-0	Hammond, IN	1999	Osaka, Japan	5-0	Phenix City, AL
1973	Tainan City, Taiwan	12-0	Tucson, AZ	2000	Maracaibo, Venezuela	3-2	Bellaire, TX
1974	Kao Hsiung, Taiwan	12-1	Red Bluff, CA				

*Foreign teams were banned from the tournament in 1975, but allowed back in the following year.
Note: In 1992, Zamboanga City of the Philippines beat Long Beach, 15-4, but was stripped of the title a month later when it was discovered that the team had used several players from outside the city limits. Long Beach was then awarded the title by forfeit, 6-0 (one run for each inning of the game).

POWER BOAT RACING

APBA Gold Cup

Dave Villwock won the rain-delayed 97th edition of the APBA Gold Cup as he drove *Miss Budweiser* to victory July 9, 2000 on the Detroit River. Villwock and *Miss Budweiser* beat Mark Weber and *Miss DYC* by roughly three roostertails on the 2.5-mile course for his fourth career win in the race.

The American Power Boat Association Gold Cup for unlimited hydroplane racing is the oldest active motorsports trophy in North America. The first Gold Cup was competed for on the Hudson River in New York in June and September of 1904. Since then several cities have hosted the race, led by Detroit (31 times) and Seattle (14). Note that (*) indicates driver was also owner of the winning boat.

Drivers with multiple wins: Chip Hanauer (11); Bill Muncey (8); Gar Wood (5); Dean Chenoweth and Dave Villwock (4); Caleb Bragg, Tom D'Eath, Lou Fageol, Ron Musson, George Reis and J.M. Wainwright (3); Danny Foster, George Henley, Vic Kliesrath, E.J. Schroeder, Bill Schumacher, Zalmon G. Simmons Jr., Joe Taggart, Mark Tate and George Townsend (2).

Year	Boat	Driver	Avg. MPH	Year	Boat	Driver	Avg. MPH
1904	*Standard* (June)	Carl Riotte*	23.160	1906	*Chip II*	J.M. Wainwright*	25.000
1904	*Vingt-Et-Un II* (Sept.)	W. Sharpe Kilmer*	24.900	1907	*Chip II*	J.M. Wainwright*	23.903
				1908	*Dixie II*	E.J. Schroeder*	29.938
1905	*Chip I*	J.M. Wainwright*	15.000	1909	*Dixie II*	E.J. Schroeder*	29.590

Year	Boat	Driver	Avg. MPH	Year	Boat	Driver	Avg. MPH
1910	Dixie III	F.K. Burnham*	32.473	1956	Miss Thriftway	Bill Muncey	96.552
1911	MIT II	J.H. Hayden*	37.000	1957	Miss Thriftway	Bill Muncey	101.787
1912	P.D.Q. II	A.G. Miles*	39.462	1958	Hawaii Kai III	Jack Regas	103.000
1913	Ankle Deep	C.S. Mankowski*	42.779	1959	Maverick	Bill Stead	104.481
1914	Baby Speed Demon II	Jim Blackton & Bob Edgren	48.458	1960	Not held		
1915	Miss Detroit	Johnny Milot & Jack Beebe	37.656	1961	Miss Century 21	Bill Muncey	99.678
				1962	Miss Century 21	Bill Muncey	100.710
1916	Miss Minneapolis	Bernard Smith	48.860	1963	Miss Bardahl	Ron Musson	105.124
1917	Miss Detroit II	Gar Wood*	54.410	1964	Miss Bardahl	Ron Musson	103.433
1918	Miss Detroit II	Gar Wood	51.619	1965	Miss Bardahl	Ron Musson	103.132
1919	Miss Detroit III	Gar Wood*	42.748	1966	Tahoe Miss	Mira Slovak	93.019
				1967	Miss Bardahl	Bill Shumacher	101.484
1920	Miss America I	Gar Wood*	62.022	1968	Miss Bardahl	Bill Shumacher	108.173
1921	Miss America I	Gar Wood*	52.825	1969	Miss Budweiser	Bill Sterett	98.504
1922	Packard Chriscraft	J.G. Vincent*	40.253				
1923	Packard Chriscraft	Caleb Bragg	43.867	1970	Miss Budweiser	Dean Chenoweth	99.562
1924	Baby Bootlegger	Caleb Bragg*	45.302	1971	Miss Madison	Jim McCormick	98.043
1925	Baby Bootlegger	Caleb Bragg*	47.240	1972	Atlas Van Lines	Bill Muncey	104.277
1926	Greenwich Folly	George Townsend*	47.984	1973	Miss Budweiser	Dean Chenoweth	99.043
				1974	Pay 'n Pak	George Henley	104.428
1927	Greenwich Folly	George Townsend*	47.662	1975	Pay 'n Pak	George Henley	108.921
				1976	Miss U.S.	Tom D'Eath	100.412
1928	Not held			1977	Atlas Van Lines	Bill Muncey*	111.822
1929	Imp	Richard Hoyt*	48.662	1978	Atlas Van Lines	Bill Muncey*	100.412
				1979	Atlas Van Lines	Bill Muncey*	100.765
1930	Hotsy Totsy	Vic Kliesrath*	52.673				
1931	Hotsy Totsy	Vic Kliesrath*	53.602	1980	Miss Budweiser	Dean Chenoweth	106.932
1932	Delphine IV	Bill Horn	57.775	1981	Miss Budweiser	Dean Chenoweth	116.387
1933	El Lagarto	George Reis*	56.260	1982	Atlas Van Lines	Chip Hanauer	120.050
1934	El Lagarto	George Reis*	55.000	1983	Atlas Van Lines	Chip Hanauer	118.507
1935	El Lagarto	George Reis*	55.056	1984	Atlas Van Lines	Chip Hanauer	130.175
1936	Impshi	Kaye Don	45.735	1985	Miller American	Chip Hanauer	120.643
1937	Notre Dame	Clell Perry	63.675	1986	Miller American	Chip Hanauer	116.523
1938	Alagi	Theo Rossi*	64.340	1987	Miller American	Chip Hanauer	127.620
1939	My Sin	Z.G. Simmons Jr.*	66.133	1988	Miss Circus Circus	Chip Hanauer & Jim Prevost	123.756
1940	Hotsy Totsy III	Sidney Allen*	48.295				
1941	My Sin	Z.G. Simmons Jr.*	52.509	1989	Miss Budweiser	Tom D'Eath	131.209
1942-45	Not held			1990	Miss Budweiser	Tom D'Eath	143.176
1946	Tempo VI	Guy Lombardo*	68.132	1991	Winston Eagle	Mark Tate	137.771
1947	Miss Peps V	Danny Foster	57.000	1992	Miss Budweiser	Chip Hanauer	136.282
1948	Miss Great Lakes	Danny Foster	46.845	1993	Miss Budweiser	Chip Hanauer	141.296
1949	My Sweetie	Bill Cantrell	73.612	1994	Smokin' Joe's	Mark Tate	145.532
1950	Slo-Mo-Shun IV	Ted Jones	78.216	1995	Miss Budweiser	Chip Hanauer	149.160
1951	Slo-Mo-Shun V	Lou Fageol	90.871	1996	Pico/American Dream	Dave Villwock	149.328
1952	Slo-Mo-Shun IV	Stan Dollar	79.923				
1953	Slo-Mo-Shun IV	Joe Taggart & Lou Fageol	99.108	1997	Miss Budweiser	Dave Villwock	129.366
				1998	Miss Budweiser	Dave Villwock	140.704
1954	Slo-Mo-Shun V	Lou Fageol	92.613	1999	Miss Pico	Chip Hanauer	152.591
1955	Gale V	Lee Schoenith	99.552	2000	Miss Budweiser	Dave Villwock	139.416

PRO RODEO

All-Around Champion Cowboy

Fred Whitfield, of Hockley, Texas, became the first African-American to win the world all-around title at the 41st National Finals Rodeo in Las Vegas Dec. 3-12, 1999. Whitfield, previously a three-time world champ in calf roping, entered the NFR leading the all-around and calf-roping races but watched both leads evaporate as the week progressed. But on the final day he made a solid 9.8-second run, and then watched as reigning calf roping champ Cody Ohl failed to place and leader Blair Burk took a no-time to lift Whitfield to the championship.

The Professional Rodeo Cowboys Association (PRCA) title of All-Around World Champion Cowboy goes to the rodeo athlete who wins the most prize money in a single year in two or more events, earning a minimum of $2,000 in each event. Only prize money earned in sanctioned PRCA rodeos is counted. From 1929-44, All-Around champions were named by the Rodeo Association of America (earnings for those years are not available).

Multiple winners: Ty Murray (7); Tom Ferguson and Larry Mahan (6); Jim Shoulders (5); Lewis Feild and Dean Oliver (3); Joe Beaver, Everett Bowman, Louis Brooks, Clay Carr, Bill Linderman, Phil Lyne, Gerald Roberts, Casey Tibbs and Harry Tompkins (2).

Year		Year		Year		Year	
1929	Earl Thode	1934	Leonard Ward	1939	Paul Carney	1944	Louis Brooks
1930	Clay Carr	1935	Everett Bowman	1940	Fritz Truan	1945-46	No award
1931	John Schneider	1936	John Bowman	1941	Homer Pettigrew		
1932	Donald Nesbit	1937	Everett Bowman	1942	Gerald Roberts		
1933	Clay Carr	1938	Burel Mulkey	1943	Louis Brooks		

Year		Earnings	Year		Earnings	Year		Earnings
1947	Todd Whatley	$18,642	1965	Dean Oliver	$33,163	1983	Roy Cooper	$153,391
1948	Gerald Roberts	21,766	1966	Larry Mahan	40,358	1984	Dee Pickett	122,618
1949	Jim Shoulders	21,495	1967	Larry Mahan	51,996	1985	Lewis Feild	130,347
1950	Bill Linderman	30,715	1968	Larry Mahan	49,129	1986	Lewis Feild	166,042
1951	Casey Tibbs	29,104	1969	Larry Mahan	57,726	1987	Lewis Feild	144,335
1952	Harry Tompkins	30,934				1988	Dave Appleton	121,546
1953	Bill Linderman	33,674	1970	Larry Mahan	41,493	1989	Ty Murray	134,806
1954	Buck Rutherford	40,404	1971	Phil Lyne	49,245			
1955	Casey Tibbs	42,065	1972	Phil Lyne	60,852	1990	Ty Murray	213,772
1956	Jim Shoulders	43,381	1973	Larry Mahan	64,447	1991	Ty Murray	244,231
1957	Jim Shoulders	33,299	1974	Tom Ferguson	66,929	1992	Ty Murray	225,992
1958	Jim Shoulders	32,212	1975	Tom Ferguson	50,300	1993	Ty Murray	297,896
1959	Jim Shoulders	32,905	1976	Tom Ferguson	87,908	1994	Ty Murray	246,170
			1977	Tom Ferguson	65,981	1995	Joe Beaver	141,753
1960	Harry Tompkins	32,522	1978	Tom Ferguson	83,734	1996	Joe Beaver	166,103
1961	Benny Reynolds	31,309	1979	Tom Ferguson	96,272	1997	Dan Mortensen	184,559
1962	Tom Nesmith	32,611				1998	Ty Murray	264,673
1963	Dean Oliver	31,329	1980	Paul Tierney	105,568	1999	Fred Whitfield	217,819
1964	Dean Oliver	31,150	1981	Jimmie Cooper	105,861			
			1982	Chris Lybbert	123,709			

SOAP BOX DERBY

All-American Soap Box Derby

Anderson, Ind. was well represented at the 63rd All-American Soap Box Derby in Akron, Ohio on July 22, 2000 as Anderson natives won two of the three derby divisions. Twelve-year-old Cody Butler, of Anderson, won in the Masters Division with a time of 29.15 seconds and Anderson native Derek Etherington, 11, won the Super Stock division in 29.78 seconds. It was a local girl, 13-year-old Rachel Curran, of nearby Medina, Ohio who won the Stock Division with her time of 29.74, besting Eric Medlock, of Indianapolis and Rachelle Tucker, of Muncie, Ind., in the final heat.

Butler edged Jennifer Bond, of Mooresville, N.C., and Nick Bowers, of Kingman, Ariz., in the Masters finals while Etherington beat out Alyssa Roehrenbeck, of Columbus, Ohio and Melissa Kent of LaCanada, Calif in the Super Stock finals.

Anderson, Ind. is one of only four cities to compete in every Soap Box Derby since the annual race began in 1934. The others are Akron, Cleveland and Indianapolis. Strong winds throughout the day kept racers from approaching any division records. The track record of 27.10 seconds was set in 1974 by Ed Meyers, of Conshohocken, Penn.

The All-American Soap Box Derby is a coasting race for small gravity-powered cars built by their drivers and assembled within strict guidelines on size, weight and cost. The Derby got its name in the 1930s when most cars were built from wooden soap boxes. Held every summer at Derby Downs in Akron, the Soap Box Derby is open to all boys and girls from 9 to 16 years old who qualify.

There are three competitive divisions: 1. Stock (ages 9-16)— made up of generic, prefab racers that come from Derby-approved kits, can be assembled in four hours and don't exceed 200 pounds when driver, car and wheels are weighed together; 2. Super Stock (ages 10-16)— the same as Stock only with a weight limit of 220 pounds; 3. Masters (ages 11-16)— made up of racers designed by the drivers, but constructed with Derby-approved hardware. The racing ramp at Derby Downs is 953.75 feet with an 11 percent grade.

One champion reigned at the All-American Soap Box Derby each year from 1934-75; Junior and Senior division champions from 1976-87; Kit and Masters champions from 1988-91; Stock, Kit and Masters champions from 1992-94; Stock, Super Stock and Masters champions starting in 1995.

Year		Hometown	Age	Year			Hometown	Age
1934	Robert Turner	Muncie, IN	11	1960		Fredric Lake	South Bend, IN	11
1935	Maurice Bale Jr.	Anderson, IN	13	1961		Dick Dawson	Wichita, KS	13
1936	Herbert Muench Jr.	St. Louis	14	1962		David Mann	Gary, IN	14
1937	Robert Ballard	White Plains, NY	12	1963		Harold Conrad	Duluth, MN	12
1938	Robert Berger	Omaha, NE	14	1964		Gregory Schumacher	Tacoma, WA	14
1939	Clifton Hardesty	White Plains, NY	11	1965		Robert Logan	Santa Ana, CA	12
				1966		David Krussow	Tacoma, WA	12
1940	Thomas Fisher	Detroit	12	1967		Kenneth Cline	Lincoln, NE	13
1941	Claude Smith	Akron, OH	14	1968		Branch Lew	Muncie, IN	11
1942-45	Not held			1969		Steve Souter	Midland, TX	12
1946	Gilbert Klecan	San Diego	14					
1947	Kenneth Holmboe	Charleston, WV	14	1970		Samuel Gupton	Durham, NC	13
1948	Donald Strub	Akron, OH	13	1971		Larry Blair	Oroville, CA	13
1949	Fred Derks	Akron, OH	15	1972		Robert Lange Jr.	Boulder, CO	14
				1973		Bret Yarborough	Elk Grove, CA	11
1950	Harold Williamson	Charleston, WV	15	1974		Curt Yarborough	Elk Grove, CA	11
1951	Darwin Cooper	Williamsport, PA	15	1975		Karren Stead	Lower Bucks, PA	11
1952	Joe Lunn	Columbus, GA	11	1976	JR:	Phil Raber	Sugarcreek, OH	11
1953	Fred Mohler	Muncie, IN	14		SR:	Joan Ferdinand	Canton, OH	14
1954	Richard Kemp	Los Angeles	14	1977	JR:	Mark Ferdinand	Canton, OH	10
1955	Richard Rohrer	Rochester, NY	14		SR:	Steve Washburn	Bristol, CT	15
1956	Norman Westfall	Rochester, NY	14	1978	JR:	Darren Hart	Salem, OR	11
1957	Terry Townsend	Anderson, IN	14		SR:	Greg Cardinal	Flint, MI	13
1958	James Miley	Muncie, IN	15	1979	JR:	Russell Yurk	Flint, MI	10
1959	Barney Townsend	Anderson, IN	13		SR:	Craig Kitchen	Akron, OH	14

Year		Hometown	Age	Year		Hometown	Age
1980	JR: Chris Fulton	Indianapolis	11	1993	MAS: Dean Lutton	Delta, OH	14
	SR: Dan Porul	Sherman Oaks, CA	12		KIT: D.M. Del Ferraro	Stow, OH	12
1981	JR: Howie Fraley	Portsmouth, OH	11		STK: Owen Yuda	Boiling Springs, PA	10
	SR: Tonia Schlegel	Hamilton, OH	13	1994	MAS: D.M. Del Ferraro	Akron, OH	13
1982	JR: Carol A. Sullivan	Rochester, NH	10		KIT: Joel Endres	Akron, OH	14
	SR: Matt Wolfgang	Lehigh Val., PA	12		STK: Kristina Damond	Jamestown, NY	13
1983	JR: Tony Carlini	Del Mar, CA	10	1995	MAS: J. Fensterbush	Kingman, AZ	11
	SR: Mike Burdgick	Flint, MI	14		SS: Darcie Davisson	Kingman, AZ	11
1984	JR: Chris Hess	Hamilton, OH	11		STK: Karen Thomas	Jamestown, NY	11
	SR: Anita Jackson	St. Louis	15	1996	MAS: Tim Scrofano	Conneaut, OH	12
1985	JR: Michael Gallo	Danbury, CT	12		SS: Jeremy Phillips	Charlestown, WV	14
	SR: Matt Sheffer	York, PA	14		STK: Matt Perez	No. Canton, OH	12
1986	JR: Marc Behan	Dover, NH	9	1997	MAS: Wade Wallace	Elk Hart, IN	11
	SR: Tami Jo Sullivan	Lancaster, OH	13		SS: Dolline Vance	Salem, OR	13
1987	JR: Matt Margules	Danbury, CT	11		STK: Mark Stephens	Waynesboro, VA	13
	SR: Brian Drinkwater	Bristol, CT	14	1998	MAS: James Marsh	Cleveland, OH	12
1988	KIT: Jason Lamb	Des Moines, IA	10		SS: Stacy Sharp	Kingman, AZ	14
	MAS: David Duffield	Kansas City	13		STK: Hailey Simpson	Salem, OR	10
1989	KIT: David Schiller	Dayton, OH	12	1999	MAS: Allan Endres	Barberton, OH	14
	MAS: Faith Chavarria	Ventura, CA	12		SS: Alisha Ebner	Salem, OR	15
1990	MAS: Sami Jones	Salem, OR	13		STK: Justin Pillow	Deland, FL	12
	KIT: Mark Mihal	Valparaiso, IN	12	2000	MAS: Cody Butler	Anderson, IN	12
1991	MAS: Danny Garland	San Diego, CA	14		SS: Derek Etherington	Anderson, IN	11
	KIT: Paul Greenwald	Saginaw, MI	13		STK: Rachel Curran	Medina, OH	13
1992	MAS: Bonnie Thornton	Redding, CA	12				
	KIT: Carolyn Fox	Sublimity, OR	11				
	STK: Loren Hurst	Hudson, OH	10				

SOFTBALL

Men's and women's national champions since 1933 in Major Fast Pitch, Major Slow Pitch and Super Slow Pitch (men only). Sanctioned by the Amateur Softball Association of America.

MEN
Major Fast Pitch

Multiple winners: Clearwater Bombers (10); Raybestos Cardinals (5); Sealmasters (4); Briggs Beautyware, Decatur Pride, Pay'n Pak and Zollner Pistons (3); Billard Barbell, Hammer Air Field, Kodak Park, Meierhoffer, National Health Care, Penn Corp and Peterbilt Western (2).

Year
1933 J.L. Gill Boosters, Chicago
1934 Ke-Nash-A, Kenosha, WI
1935 Crimson Coaches, Toledo, OH
1936 Kodak Park, Rochester, NY
1937 Briggs Body Team, Detroit
1938 The Pohlers, Cincinnati
1939 Carr's Boosters, Covington, KY

1940 Kodak Park
1941 Bendix Brakes, South Bend, IN
1942 Deep Rock Oilers, Tulsa, OK
1943 Hammer Air Field, Fresno, CA
1944 Hammer Air Field
1945 Zollner Pistons, Ft. Wayne, IN
1946 Zollner Pistons
1947 Zollner Pistons
1948 Briggs Beautyware, Detroit
1949 Tip Top Tailors, Toronto

1950 Clearwater (FL) Bombers
1951 Dow Chemical, Midland, MI
1952 Briggs Beautyware
1953 Briggs Beautyware
1954 Clearwater Bombers
1955 Raybestos Cardinals,
1956 Clearwater Bombers
1957 Clearwater Bombers
1958 Raybestos Cardinals

Year
1959 Sealmasters, Aurora, IL

1960 Clearwater Bombers
1961 Sealmasters
1962 Clearwater Bombers
1963 Clearwater Bombers
1964 Burch Tool, Detroit
1965 Sealmasters
1966 Clearwater Bombers
1967 Sealmasters
1968 Clearwater Bombers
1969 Raybestos Cardinals

1970 Raybestos Cardinals
1971 Welty Way, Cedar Rapids, IA
1972 Raybestos Cardinals
1973 Clearwater Bombers
1974 Gianella Bros., Santa Rosa, CA
1975 Rising Sun Hotel, Reading, PA
1976 Raybestos Cardinals
1977 Billard Barbell, Reading, PA
1978 Billard Barbell
1979 McArdle Pontiac/Cadillac, Midland, MI

1980 Peterbilt Western, Seattle
1981 Archer Daniels Midland, Decatur, IL
1982 Peterbilt Western

Year
1983 Franklin Cardinals, Stratford, CA
1984 California Kings, Merced, CA
1985 Pay'n Pak, Seattle
1986 Pay'n Pak
1987 Pay'n Pak
1988 TransAire, Elkhart, IN
1989 Penn Corp, Sioux City, IA

1990 Penn Corp
1991 Gianella Bros., Rohnert Park, CA
1992 National Health Care, Sioux City, IA
1993 National Health Care
1994 Decatur (IL) Pride
1995 Decatur Pride
1996 Green Bay All-Car, Green Bay, WI
1997 Tampa Bay Smokers, Tampa Bay, FL
1998 Meierhoffer-Fleeman, St. Joseph, MO
1999 Decatur Pride
2000 Meierhoffer

Super Slow Pitch

Multiple winners: Ritch's/Superior (4); Howard's/Western Steer and Steele's Sports (3); Lighthouse/Worth (2).

Year	Year	Year
1981 Howard's/Western Steer, Denver, NC	1988 Starpath, Monticello, KY	1995 Lighthouse/Worth, Stone Mt., GA
1982 Jerry's Catering, Miami	1989 Ritch's Salvage, Harrisburg, NC	1996 Ritch's/Superior
1983 Howard's/Western Steer	1990 Steele's Silver Bullets	1997 Ritch's/Superior
1984 Howard's/Western Steer	1991 Sun Belt/Worth, Atlanta	1998 Lighthouse/Worth
1985 Steele's Sports, Grafton, OH	1992 Ritch's/Superior, Windsor Locks, CT	1999 Team Easton, California
1986 Steele's Sports	1993 Ritch's/Superior	2000 Team TPS, Louisville, KY
1987 Steele's Sports	1994 Bellcorp., Tampa	

Major Slow Pitch

Multiple winners: Gatliff Auto Sales, Riverside Paving and Skip Hogan A.C. (3); Campbell Carpets, Hamilton Tailoring, Howard's Furniture and Long Haul TPS (2).

Year	Year	Year
1953 Shields Construction, Newport, KY	1971 Pile Drivers, Va. Beach, VA	1988 Bell Corp/FAF, Tampa, FL
1954 Waldneck's Tavern, Cincinnati	1972 Jiffy Club, Louisville, KY	1989 Ritch's Salvage, Harrisburg, NC
1955 Lang Pet Shop, Covington, KY	1973 Howard's Furniture, Denver, NC	1990 New Construction, Shelbyville, IN
1956 Gatliff Auto Sales, Newport, KY	1974 Howard's Furniture	1991 Riverside Paving, Louisville
1957 Gatliff Auto Sales	1975 Pyramid Cafe, Lakewood, OH	1992 Vernon's, Jacksonville, FL
1958 East Side Sports, Detroit	1976 Warren Motors, J'ville, FL	1993 Back Porch/Destin (FL) Roofing
1959 Yorkshire Restaurant, Newport, KY	1977 Nelson Painting, Okla. City	1994 Riverside Paving, Louisville
1960 Hamilton Tailoring, Cincinnati	1978 Campbell Carpets, Concord, CA	1995 Riverside Paving
1961 Hamilton Tailoring	1979 Nelco Mfg. Co., Okla. City	1996 Bell II, Orlando, FL
1962 Skip Hogan A.C., Pittsburgh	1980 Campbell Carpets	1997 Long Haul TPS, Albertville, MN
1963 Gatliff Auto Sales	1981 Elite Coating, Gordon, CA	1998 Chase Mortgage/Easton, Wilmington, NC
1964 Skip Hogan A.C.	1982 Triangle Sports, Minneapolis	1999 Gasoline Heaven/Worth, Commack, NY
1965 Skip Hogan A.C.	1983 No.1 Electric & Heating, Gastonia, NC	2000 Long Haul TPS
1966 Michael's Lounge, Detroit	1984 Lilly Air Systems, Chicago	
1967 Jim's Sport Shop, Pittsburgh	1985 Blanton's Fayetteville, NC	
1968 County Sports, Levittown, NY	1986 Non-Ferrous Metals, Cleveland	
1969 Copper Hearth, Milwaukee	1987 Stapath, Monticello, KY	
1970 Little Caesar's, Southgate, MI		

WOMEN

Major Fast Pitch

Multiple winners: Raybestos Brakettes (21); Orange Lionettes (9); Jax Maids (5); California Commotion (4); Arizona Ramblers and Redding Rebels (3); Hi-Ho Brakettes, J.J. Krieg's and National Screw & Manufacturing (2).

Year	Year	Year
1933 Great Northerns, Chicago	1938 J.J. Krieg's, Alameda, CA	1943 Jax Maids
1934 Hart Motors, Chicago	1939 J.J. Krieg's	1944 Lind & Pomeroy, Portland, OR
1935 Bloomer Girls, Cleveland	1940 Arizona Ramblers, Phoenix	1945 Jax Maids
1936 Nat'l Screw & Mfg., Cleveland	1941 Higgins Midgets, Tulsa, OK	1946 Jax Maids
1937 Nat'l Screw & Mfg.	1942 Jax Maids, New Orleans	1947 Jax Maids

Other 2000 Champions

Slow Pitch

MEN

Class A—K&G TPS/Bike/Webbs, North Vernon, IN
Class B—Caraway Steel, Eufala, AL
Major Industrial—Action A's, Belden, MS
Class A Industrial—Worthington Industries, Columbus, OH
35-Over—Thurs Roofing, Brooklyn Park, MN
40-Over—Sun Devils, Orange, CA
45-Over—Maroadi Transfer, Pittsburgh, PA
50-Over Major—Dan Smith Softball, Spokane, WA
55-Over—Sawtre Texas, Garland, TX
60-Over—Florida Crush, Fort Myers, FL
Major Church—Rehobeth Presbyterian, Lilburn, GA
Class A Church—Evangel Temple, Jacksonville, FL

WOMEN

Class A—Shooters/Miken, Orlando, FL
Church—New Testament M.B.C., Columbus, GA

COED

Class A—Advance Door, Cleveland, OH

Fast Pitch

MEN

Class A—All Season Patriot, Breinigsville, PA
Class B—Sharks, Stockton, CA
Class C—McKie Sports, Oswego, NY
40-Over—Decatur Legends, Decatur, IL
45-Over—Nor-Cal Savala Painters, Stockton, CA
23-Under—Don Stram Logging, Pairie du Chein, WI

WOMEN

Class A—San Jose Strikker's, Sunnyvale, CA
Class B—Condors, Tujunga, CA
Class C—Faso Insurance, Williamsville, NY

Modified Pitch

Women's Major—Roger's Renegades, Hookset, NH
Men's Major—L.A. Doughboys, Los Angeles, CA
Men's Class A—Snap-On-Tools/Netspoke, Bow, NH

Year	Year	Year
1948 Arizona Ramblers	1966 Raybestos Brakettes	1985 Hi-Ho Brakettes, Stratford, CT
1949 Arizona Ramblers	1967 Raybestos Brakettes	1986 So. California Invasion
1950 Orange (CA) Lionettes	1968 Raybestos Brakettes	1987 Orange County Majestics,
1951 Orange Lionettes	1969 Orange Lionettes	Anaheim, CA
1952 Orange Lionettes	1970 Orange Lionettes	1988 Hi-Ho Brakettes
1953 Betsy Ross Rockets, Fresno, CA	1971 Raybestos Brakettes	1989 Whittier (CA) Raiders
1954 Leach Motor Rockets, Fresno, CA	1972 Raybestos Brakettes	1990 Raybestos Brakettes
1955 Orange Lionettes	1973 Raybestos Brakettes	1991 Raybestos Brakettes
1956 Orange Lionettes	1974 Raybestos Brakettes	1992 Raybestos Brakettes
1957 Hacienda Rockets, Fresno, CA	1975 Raybestos Brakettes	1993 Redding (CA) Rebels
1958 Raybestos Brakettes,	1976 Raybestos Brakettes	1994 Redding Rebels
Stratford, CT	1977 Raybestos Brakettes	1995 Redding Rebels
1959 Raybestos Brakettes	1978 Raybestos Brakettes	1996 California Commotion,
1960 Raybestos Brakettes	1979 Sun City (AZ) Saints	Woodland Hills
1961 Gold Sox, Whittier, CA	1980 Raybestos Brakettes	1997 California Commotion
1962 Orange Lionettes	1981 Orlando (FL) Rebels	1998 California Commotion
1963 Raybestos Brakettes	1982 Raybestos Brakettes	1999 California Commotion
1964 Erv Lind Florists, Portland, OR	1983 Raybestos Brakettes	2000 Phoenix Storm, Phoenix, AZ
1965 Orange Lionettes	1984 Los Angeles Diamonds	

Major Slow Pitch

Multiple winners: Spooks (5); Dana Gardens (4); Universal Plastics (3); Cannan's Illusions, Bob Hoffman's Dots and Marks Brothers Dots (2).

Year	Year	Year
1959 Pearl Laundry, Richmond, VA	1974 Marks Brothers Dots, Miami	1986 Sur-Way Tomboys, Tifton, GA
	1975 Marks Brothers Dots	1987 Key Ford Mustangs
1960 Carolina Rockets, High Pt., NC	1976 Sorrento's Pizza, Cincinnati	1988 Spooks
1961 Dairy Cottage, Covington, KY	1977 Fox Valley Lassies,	1989 Cannan's Illusions, Houston
1962 Dana Gardens, Cincinnati	St. Charles, IL	
1963 Dana Gardens	1978 Bob Hoffman's Dots, Miami	1990 Spooks
1964 Dana Gardens	1979 Bob Hoffman's Dots	1991 Cannan's Illusions, San Antonio
1965 Art's Acres, Omaha, NE		1992 Universal Plastics, Cookeville, TN
1966 Dana Gardens	1980 Howard's Rubi-Otts,	1993 Universal Plastics
1967 Ridge Maintenance, Cleveland	Graham, NC	1994 Universal Plastics
1968 Escue Pontiac, Cincinnati	1981 Tifton (GA) Tomboys	1995 Armed Forces, Sacramento
1969 Converse Dots, Hialeah, FL	1982 Richmond (VA) Stompers	1996 Spooks
	1983 Spooks, Anoka, MN	1997 Taylor's, Glendale, MD
1970 Rutenschruder Floral, Cincinnati	1984 Spooks	1998 not held
1971 Gators, Ft. Lauderdale, FL	1985 Key Ford Mustangs,	1999 Lakerettes, Conneaut Lake, PA
1972 Riverside Ford, Cincinnati	Pensacola, FL	2000 Premier Sports, Pittsboro, NC
1973 Sweeney Chevrolet, Cincinnati		

TRIATHLON

World Championship

Contested since 1989, the Triathlon World Championship consists of a 1.5-kilometer swim, a 40-kilometer bike ride and a 10-kilometer run. The 2000 championship took place on Apr. 29-30 in Perth, Australia.

Multiple winners: MEN— Simon Lessing (4); Spencer Smith (2). WOMEN— Emma Carney, Michelle Jones and Karen Smyers (2).

MEN

Year		Time
1989	Mark Allen, United States	1:58:46
1990	Greg Welch, Australia	1:51:37
1991	Miles Stewart, Australia	1:48:20
1992	Simon Lessing, Great Britain	1:49:04
1993	Spencer Smith, Great Britain	1:51:20
1994	Spencer Smith, Great Britain	1:51:54
1995	Simon Lessing, Great Britain	1:48:29
1996	Simon Lessing, Great Britain	1:39:50
1997	Chris McCormack, Australia	1:48:29
1998	Simon Lessing, Great Britain	1:55:31
1999	Dimitry Gaag, Kazakhstan	1:45:25
2000	Oliver Marceau, France	1:51:41

WOMEN

Year		Time
1989	Erin Baker, New Zealand	2:10:01
1990	Karen Smyers, United States	2:03:33
1991	Joanne Ritchie, Canada	2:02:04
1992	Michellie Jones, Australia	2:02:08
1993	Michellie Jones, Australia	2:07:41
1994	Emma Carney, Australia	2:03:19
1995	Karen Smyers, USA	2:04:58
1996	Jackie Gallagher, Australia	1:50:52
1997	Emma Carney, Australia	1:59:22
1998	Joanne King, Australia	2:07:25
1999	Loretta Harrop, Australia	1:55:28
2000	Nicole Hackett, Australia	1:54:43

Ironman Championship

Contested in Hawaii since 1978, the Ironman Triathlon Championship consists of a 2.4-mile swim, a 112-mile bike ride and 26.2-mile run. The race begins at 7 a.m. and continues all day until the course is closed at midnight.

MEN

Multiple winners: Mark Allen and Dave Scott (6); Luc Van Lierde, Peter Reid and Scott Tinley (2).

Year	Date	Winner	Time	Runner-up	Margin	Start	Finish	Location
I	2/18/78	Gordon Haller	11:46	John Dunbar	34:00	15	12	Waikiki Beach
II	1/14/79	Tom Warren	11:15:56	John Dunbar	48:00	15	12	Waikiki Beach
III	1/10/80	Dave Scott	9:24:33	Chuck Neumann	1:08	108	95	Ala Moana Park
IV	2/14/81	John Howard	9:38:29	Tom Warren	26:00	326	299	Kailua-Kona
V	2/6/82	Scott Tinley	9:19:41	Dave Scott	17:16	580	541	Kailua-Kona
VI	10/9/82	Dave Scott	9:08:23	Scott Tinley	20:05	850	775	Kailua-Kona
VII	10/22/83	Dave Scott	9:05:57	Scott Tinley	0:33	964	835	Kailua-Kona
VIII	10/6/84	Dave Scott	8:54:20	Scott Tinley	24:25	1036	903	Kailua-Kona
IX	10/25/85	Scott Tinley	8:50:54	Chris Hinshaw	25:46	1018	965	Kailua-Kona
X	10/18/86	Dave Scott	8:28:37	Mark Allen	9:47	1039	951	Kailua-Kona
XI	10/10/87	Dave Scott	8:34:13	Mark Allen	11:06	1380	1284	Kailua-Kona
XII	10/22/88	Scott Molina	8:31:00	Mike Pigg	2:11	1277	1189	Kailua-Kona
XIII	10/15/89	Mark Allen	8:09:15	Dave Scott	0:58	1285	1231	Kailua-Kona
XIV	10/6/90	Mark Allen	8:28:17	Scott Tinley	9:23	1386	1255	Kailua-Kona
XV	10/19/91	Mark Allen	8:18:32	Greg Welch	6:01	1386	1235	Kailua-Kona
XVI	10/10/92	Mark Allen	8:09:08	Cristian Bustos	7:21	1364	1298	Kailua-Kona
XVII	10/30/93	Mark Allen	8:07:45	Paulli Kiuru	6:37	1438	1353	Kailua-Kona
XVIII	10/15/94	Greg Welch	8:20:27	Dave Scott	4:05	1405	1290	Kailua-Kona
XIX	10/7/95	Mark Allen	8:20:34	Thomas Hellriegel	2:25	1487	1323	Kailua-Kona
XX	10/26/96	Luc Van Lierde	8:04:08	Thomas Hellriegel	1:59	1420	1288	Kailua-Kona
XXI	10/18/97	Thomas Hellriegel	8:33:01	Jurgen Zack	6:17	1534	1365	Kailua-Kona
XXII	10/3/98	Peter Reid	8:24:20	Luc Van Lierde	7:37	1487	1379	Kailua-Kona
XXIII	10/23/99	Luc Van Lierde	8:17:17	Peter Reid	5:37	1471	1419	Kailua-Kona
XXIV	10/14/00	Peter Reid	8:21:01	Timothy Deboom	2:09	1525	1426	Kailua-Kona

WOMEN

Multiple winners: Paula Newby-Fraser (8); Natascha Badmann, Erin Baker and Sylviane Puntous (2).

Year	Winner	Time	Runner-up	Year	Winner	Time	Runner-up
1978	No finishers			1989	Paula Newby-Fraser	9:00:56	Sylviane Puntous
1979	Lyn Lemaire	12:55.00	None	1990	Erin Baker	9:13:42	P. Newby-Fraser
1980	Robin Beck	11:21:24	Eve Anderson	1991	Paula Newby-Fraser	9:07:52	Erin Baker
1981	Linda Sweeney	12:00:32	Sally Edwards	1992	Paula Newby-Fraser	8:55:28	Julie Anne White
1982	Kathleen McCartney	11:09:40	Julie Moss	1993	Paula Newby-Fraser	8:58:23	Erin Baker
1982	Julie Leach	10:54:08	Joann Dahlkoetter	1994	Paula Newby-Fraser	9:20:14	Karen Smyers
1983	Sylviane Puntous	10:43:36	Patricia Puntous	1995	Karen Smyers	9:16:46	Isabelle Mouthon
1984	Sylviane Puntous	10:25:13	Patricia Puntous	1996	Paula Newby-Fraser	9:06:49	Natascha Badmann
1985	Joanne Ernst	10:25:22	Liz Bulman	1997	Heather Fuhr	9:31:43	Lori Bowden
1986	Paula Newby-Fraser	9:49:14	Sylviane Puntous	1998	Natascha Badmann	9:24:16	Lori Bowden
1987	Erin Baker	9:35:25	Sylviane Puntous	1999	Lori Bowden	9:13:02	Karen Smyers
1988	Paula Newby-Fraser	9:01:01	Erin Baker	2000	Natascha Badmann	9:26:17	Lori Bowden

X GAMES

The ESPN Extreme Games, orginally envisioned as a biannual showcase for "alternative" sports, were first held June 24-July 1, 1995 in Newport and Providence, R.I. and Mt. Snow, Vt. The success of the inaugural event prompted organizers to make it an annual competition. Newport would again serve as host for the redubbed X Games in 1996 before they moved to San Diego for 1997 and 1998. The X Games has evolved rapidly since its inception. New sports and events are added while others are dropped.

In 1997, the first Winter X Games were held at Snow Summit Mountain Resort in Big Bear Lake, Calif. before moving to Crested Butte, Colo. in 1998.

The 1999 and 2000 Summer X Games were held in San Francisco. The 1999 Winter X Games were again held in Crested Butte, Colo., January 14-17. The 2000 Winter X Games took place Feb. 3-6 at Mt. Snow, Vt. and were scheduled for Feb. 1-4, 2001 at Mt. Snow again.

Summer X Games
Bicycle Stunt

Year	Vert	Year	Dirt	Year	Street/Stunt Park	Year	Flatland
1995	Matt Hoffman	1995	Jay Miron	1996	Dave Mirra	1997	Trevor Meyer
1996	Matt Hoffman	1996	Joey Garcia	1997	Dave Mirra	1998	Trevor Meyer
1997	Dave Mirra	1997	T.J. Lavin	1998	Dave Mirra	1999	Trevor Meyer
1998	Dave Mirra	1998	Brian Foster	1999	Dave Mirra	2000	Martti Kuoppa
1999	Dave Mirra	1999	T.J. Lavin	2000	Dave Mirra		
2000	Jamie Bestwick	2000	Ryan Nyquist				

Big-Air Snowboarding

Year	Men
1997	Peter Line
1998	Kevin Jones
1999	Peter Line
2000	not held

Year	Women
1997	Tina Dixon
1998	Janet Matthews
1999	Barrett Christy
2000	not held

Freestyle Motocross

Year	
1999	Travis Pastrana
2000	Travis Pastrana

Bungee Jumping

Year	
1995	Doug Anderson
1996	Peter Bihun
1997	event discontinued

Street Luge

Year	Dual
1995	Bob Pereyra
1996	Shawn Goular
1997	Biker Sherlock
1998	Biker Sherlock
1999	Dennis Derammelaere
2000	Bob Ozman

Year	Mass
1995	Shawn Gilbert
1996	Biker Sherlock
1997	Biker Sherlock
1998	Rat Sult
1999	event discontinued

Year	Super Mass
1997	Biker Sherlock
1998	Rat Sult
1999	David Rogers
2000	Bob Pereyra

Skysurfing

Year	
1995	Fradet/Zipser
1996	Furrer/Scmid
1997	Hartman/Pappadato
1998	Rozov/Burch
1999	Fradet/Iodice
2000	Klaus/Rogers

Skateboard

Year	Vert Singles
1995	Tony Hawk
1996	Andy Macdonald
1997	Tony Hawk
1998	Andy Macdonald
1999	Bucky Lasek
2000	Bucky Lasek

Year	Vert Doubles
1997	Hawk/Macdonald
1998	Hawk/Macdonald
1999	Hawk/Macdonald
2000	Hawk/Macdonald

Year	Street/Park
1995	Chris Senn
1996	Rodil de Araujo Jr.
1997	Chris Senn
1998	Rodil de Araujo Jr.
1999	Chris Senn
2000	Eric Koston

Year	Best Trick
2000	Bob Burnquist

Sportclimbing

Year	Men's Difficulty
1995	Ian Vickers
1996	Arnaud Petit
1997	Francois Legrand
1998	Christian Core
1999	Chris Sharma
2000	not held

Year	Women's Difficulty
1995	Robyn Erbersfield
1996	Katie Brown
1997	Katie Brown
1998	Katie Brown
1999	Stephanie Bodet
2000	not held

Year	Men's Speed
1995	Hans Florine
1996	Hans Florine
1997	Hans Florine
1998	Vladimir Netsvetaev
1999	Aaron Shamy
2000	Vladimir Zakharov

Year	Women's Speed
1995	Elena Ovtchinnikova
1996	Cecile Le Flem
1997	Elena Ovtchinnikova
1998	Elena Ovtchinnikova
1999	Renata Piszczek
2000	Etti Hendrawati

In-Line Skating

Year	Men's Vert
1995	Tom Fry
1996	Rene Hulgreen
1997	Tim Ward
1998	Cesar Mora
1999	Eito Yasutoko
2000	Eito Yasutoko

Year	Women's Vert
1995	Tash Hodgeson
1996	Fabiola da Silva
1997	Fabiola da Silva
1998	Fabiola da Silva
1999	Ayumi Kawasaki
2000	Fabiola da Silva

Year	Men's Street/Park
1995	Matt Salerno
1996	Arlo Eisenberg
1997	Arron Feinberg
1998	Jonathan Bergeron
1999	Nicky Adams
2000	Sven Boekhorst

Year	Women's Street/Park
1997	Sayaka Yabe
1998	Jenny Curry
1999	Sayaka Yabe
2000	Fabiola da Silva

Year	Vert Triples
1998	Malina/Fogarty/Popa
1999	Khris/Bujanda/Boekhorst
2000	not held

Year	Men's Downhill
1995	Derek Downing
1996	Dante Muse
1997	Derek Downing
1998	Patrick Naylor
1999	not held

Year	Women's Downhill
1995	Julie Brandt
1996	Gypsy Tidwell
1997	Gypsy Tidwell
1998	Julie Brandt
1999	not held

Watersports

Year	Barefoot Waterski Jumping
1995	Justin Seers
1996	Ron Scarpa
1997	Peter Fleck
1998	Peter Fleck
1999	event discontinued

Year	Men's Wakeboarding
1996	Parks Bonifay
1997	Jeremy Kovak
1998	Darin Shapiro
1999	Parks Bonifay
2000	Darin Shapiro

Year	Women's Wakeboarding
1997	Tara Hamilton
1998	Andrea Gaytan
1999	Meaghan Major
2000	Tara Hamilton

X-Venture Race

Year	
1995	Team Threadbo*
1996	Team Kobeer
1997	Team Presidio
1998	event discontinued

*In 1995, Team Threadbo won the Eco-Challenge which was held in conjunction with the ESPN Extreme Games.

CrossOver

Year
1997 Brian Patch
1998 event discontinued

Free Skiing

Year Men's Big Air
1999 J.F. Cusson
2000 Candide Thovex

Year Men's Skier X
1998 Dennis Rey
1999 Enak Gavaggio
2000 Shaun Palmer

Year Women's Skier X
1999 Aleisha Cline
2000 Anik Demers

Ice Climbing

Year Men's Difficulty
1997 Jaren Ogden
1998 Will Gadd
1999 Will Gadd
2000 not held

Year Women's Difficulty
1997 Bird Lew
1998 Kim Csizmazia
1999 Kim Csizmazia
2000 not held

Year Men's Speed
1997 Jared Ogden
1998 Will Gadd
1999 event discontinued

Year Women's Speed
1997 Bird Lew
1998 Kim Csizmazia
1999 event discontinued

Skiboarding

Year
1998 Mike Nick
1999 Chris Hawks
2000 Neal Lyons

Winter X Games

Snowboarding

Year Men's Big Air
1997 Jimmy Halopoff
1998 Jason Borgstede
1999 Kevin Sansalone
2000 Peter Line

Year Women's Big Air
1997 Barrett Christy
1998 Tina Basich
1999 Barrett Christy
2000 Tara Dakides

Year Men's Boarder X
1997 Shaun Palmer
1998 Shaun Palmer
1999 Shaun Palmer
2000 Drew Neilson

Year Women's Boarder X
1997 Jennie Waara
1998 Tina Dixon
1999 Maelle Ricker
2000 Leslee Olson

Year Men's Halfpipe
1997 Todd Richards
1998 Ross Powers
1999 Jimi Scott
2000 Todd Richards

Year Women's Halfpipe
1997 Shannon Dunn
1998 Cara-Beth Burnside
1999 Michele Taggart
2000 S. Brun Kjeldaas

Year Men's Slopestyle
1997 Daniel Franck
1998 Ross Powers
1999 Peter Line
2000 Kevin Jones

Year Women's Slopestyle
1997 Barrett Christy
1998 Jennie Waara
1999 Tara Dakides
2000 Tara Dakides

Super-modified Shovel Racing

Year
1997 Don Adkins
1998 event discontinued

Snow Mountain Bike Racing

Year Men's Downhill
1997 Shaun Palmer
1998 Andrew Shandro
1999 event discontinued

Year Women's Downhill
1997 Missy Giove
1998 Marla Streb
1999 event discontinued

Year Men's Speed
1997 Phil Tintsman
1998 Jurgen Beneke
1999 event discontinued

Year Women's Speed
1997 Cheri Elliott
1998 Elke Brutsaert
1999 event discontinued

Year Men's Biker X
1999 Steve Peat
2000 Myles Rockwell

Year Women's Biker X
1999 Tara Llanes
2000 Katrina Miller

Snocross

Year
1998 Toni Haikonen
1999 Chris Vincent
2000 Tucker Hibbert

Ultracross

Year
2000 McLain/Lind

AP/Wide World Photos

Kirk Hibbert, father and competitor of Snocross winner Tucker Hibbert, catches some air at the 2000 Winter X Games.

YACHTING

The America's Cup

International yacht racing was launched in 1851 when England's Royal Yacht Squadron staged a 60-mile regatta around the Isle of Wight and offered a silver trophy to the winner. The 101-foot schooner *America*, sent over by the New York Yacht Club, won the race and the prize. Originally called the Hundred-Guinea Cup, the trophy was renamed The America's Cup after the winning boat's owners deeded it to the NYYC with instructions to defend it whenever challenged.

From 1870-1980, the NYYC successfully defended the Cup 25 straight times; first in large schooners and J-class boats that measured up to 140 feet in overall length, then in 12-meter boats. A foreign yacht finally won the Cup in 1983 when *Australia II* beat defender *Liberty* in the seventh and deciding race off Newport, R.I. Four years later, the San Diego Yacht Club's *Stars & Stripes* won the Cup back, sweeping the four races of the final series off Fremantle, Australia.

Then in 1988, New Zealand's Mercury Bay Boating Club, unwilling to wait the usual three- to four-year period between Cup defenses, challenged the SDYC to a match race, citing the Cup's 102-year-old Deed of Gift, which clearly stated that every challenge had to be honored. Mercury Bay announced it would race a 133-foot monohull. San Diego countered with a 60-foot catamaran. The resulting best-of-three series (Sept. 7-8) was a mismatch as the SDYC's catamaran *Stars & Stripes* won two straight by margins of better than 18 and 21 minutes. Mercury Bay syndicate leader Michael Fay protested the outcome and took the SDYC to court in New York State (where the Deed of Gift was first filed) claiming San Diego had violated the spirit of the deed by racing a catamaran instead of a monohull. N.Y. State Supreme Court judge Carmen Ciparick agreed and on March 28, 1989, ordered the SDYC to hand the Cup over to Mercury Bay. The SDYC refused, but did consent to the court's appointment of the New York Yacht Club as custodian of the Cup until an appeal was ruled on.

On Sept. 19, 1989, the Appellate Division of the N.Y. Supreme Court overturned Ciparick's decision and awarded the Cup back to the SDYC. An appeal by Mercury Bay was denied by the N.Y. Court of Appeals on April 26, 1990, ending three years of legal wrangling. To avoid the chaos of 1988-90, a new class of boat—75-foot monohulls with 110-foot masts—has been used by all competing countries since 1992. Note that (*) indicates skipper was also owner of the boat.

Schooners And J-Class Boats

Year	Winner	Skipper	Series	Loser	Skipper
1851	*America*	Richard Brown	—	—	
1870	*Magic*	Andrew Comstock	1-0	*Cambria*, GBR	J. Tannock
1871	*Columbia* (2-1) & *Sappho* (2-0)	Nelson Comstock Sam Greenwood	4-0	*Livonia*, GBR	J.R. Woods
1876	*Madeleine*	Josephus Williams	2-0	*Countess of Dufferin*, CAN	J.E. Ellsworth
1881	*Mischief*	Nathanael Clock	2-0	*Atalanta*, CAN	Alexander Cuthbert*
1885	*Puritan*	Aubrey Crocker	2-0	*Genesta*, GBR	John Carter
1886	*Mayflower*	Martin Stone	2-0	*Galatea*, GBR	Dan Bradford
1887	*Volunteer*	Henry Haff	2-0	*Thistle*, GBR	John Barr
1893	*Vigilant*	William Hansen	3-0	*Valkyrie II*, GBR	Wm. Granfield
1895	*Defender*	Henry Haff	3-0	*Valkyrie III*, GBR	Wm. Granfield
1899	*Columbia*	Charles Barr	3-0	*Shamrock I*, GBR	Archie Hogarth
1901	*Columbia*	Charles Barr	3-0	*Shamrock II*, GBR	E.A. Sycamore
1903	*Reliance*	Charles Barr	3-0	*Shamrock III*, GBR	Bob Wringe
1920	*Resolute*	Charles. F. Adams	3-2	*Shamrock IV*, GBR	William Burton
1930	*Enterprise*	Harold Vanderbilt*	4-0	*Shamrock V*, GBR	Ned Heard
1934	*Rainbow*	Harold Vanderbilt*	4-2	*Endeavour*, GBR	T.O.M. Sopwith
1937	*Ranger*	Harold Vanderbilt*	4-0	*Endeavour II*, GBR	T.O.M. Sopwith

12-METER BOATS

Year	Winner	Skipper	Series	Loser	Skipper
1958	*Columbia*	Briggs Cunningham	4-0	*Sceptre*, GBR	Graham Mann
1962	*Weatherly*	Bus Mosbacher	4-1	*Gretel*, AUS	Jock Sturrock
1964	*Constellation*	Bob Bavier & Eric Ridder	4-0	*Sovereign*, AUS	Peter Scott
1967	*Intrepid*	Bus Mosbacher	4-0	*Dame Pattie*, AUS	Jock Sturrock
1970	*Intrepid*	Bill Ficker	4-1	*Gretel II*, AUS	Jim Hardy
1974	*Courageous*	Ted Hood	4-0	*Southern Cross*, AUS	John Cuneo
1977	*Courageous*	Ted Turner	4-0	*Australia*	Noel Robins
1980	*Freedom*	Dennis Conner	4-1	*Australia*	Jim Hardy
1983	*Australia II*	John Bertrand	4-3	*Liberty*, USA	Dennis Conner
1987	*Stars & Stripes*	Dennis Conner	4-0	*Kookaburra III*, AUS	Iain Murray

60-FT CATAMARAN VS 133-FT MONOHULL

Year	Winner	Skipper	Series	Loser	Skipper
1988	*Stars & Stripes*	Dennis Conner	2-0	*New Zealand*, NZE	David Barnes

75-FT INTERNATIONAL AMERICA'S CUP CLASS

Year	Winner	Skipper	Series	Loser	Skipper
1992	*America³*	Bill Koch* & Buddy Melges	4-1	*Il Moro di Venezia*, ITA	Paul Cayard
1995	*Black Magic*, NZE	Russell Coutts	5-0	*Young America*, USA	Dennis Conner & Paul Cayard
2000	*Black Magic*, NZE	Russell Coutts & Dean Barker	5-0	*Luna Rossa*, ITA	Francesco de Angelis

Deaths

There was heartache in the heart-land when Kansas City Chiefs star **Derrick Thomas** died on Feb. 8.

Sid Abel, 81; Hall of Fame player, general manager, coach and broadcaster in the Detroit Red Wings organization; centered the high-scoring "Production Line" between Gordie Howe and Ted Lindsay that helped Detroit win the first four of its league-record seven consecutive regular-season titles and three Stanley Cups; team captain 1942-52; career: 472 points (189 goals, 283 assists); scored a league-high 28 goals in 1948-49 and was named league MVP; left Detroit in 1952 and was player-coach in Chicago for two seasons; returned to Detroit and broadcast games before coaching his former team from 1957-70; also coached St. Louis Blues and Kansas City Scouts (now N.J. Devils); Red Wings radio and TV analyst before 1976-77 season; inducted into Hockey Hall of Fame in 1969; of heart disease; in Farmington Hills, Mich., Feb. 8.

Gary Adams, 56; founder of the Taylor Made Golf Co. in 1979 and golf club innovator known as "the father of the metal wood"; National Golf Foundation Man of the Year in 1984; honored by PGA of America in 1995 for his lifelong impact on the golf industry; of cancer; in Carlsbad, Calif., Jan 2.

Forrest (Forddy) Anderson, 80; former Michigan State men's basketball coach (1954-65); led Spartans to 1957 Final Four; of complications of pneumonia; in Oklahoma City, Oct. 25, 1999.

Hyginus Anugo, 22; Nigerian Olympic 400m runner and reserve for the relay team to compete in Sydney; fiancee of eventual 100m hurdles silver medalist Glory Alozie; struck by a car and killed as he crossed a road a week before the Games; of injuries sustained in the accident; in Sydney, Sept. 7.

Henry (Bunny) Austin, 94; teamed with Fred Perry to help Britain win four Davis Cup finals in a row (1933-36); reached singles finals at Wimbledon in 1932 and 1938 and the 1937 French Open; cause of his death not given; in Coulsdon, England, Aug. 26.

Wayne Bailey, 47; top-fuel drag racing driver who crashed during qualifying at an International Hot Rod Association event at Red River Raceway in Gilliam, La. and died the next morning; ninth in the national standings at the time of his death; of injuries sustained in the crash; in Shreveport, La., Oct. 14.

Greg Barnes, 17; Columbine High School basketball star who committed suicide after a junior year where he averaged 26.2 points per game, earned first-team all-state honors and was actively recruited by Div. I colleges; watched a good friend and teacher die in the 1999 massacre at the school from a science room near the school's library; died after hanging himself; in Littleton, Colo., May 4.

Mike Berticelli, 48; men's soccer coach at Notre Dame who compiled a 104-80-19 record over 10 seasons and led the Irish to NCAA tournament appearances in 1993, 94 and 96; won two Midwestern Collegiate Conference championships and one Big East Tournament title; 1982 NCAA Div. III coach of the year; of a heart attack; in Mission Viejo, Calif., Dec. 20, 1999.

Bold Forbes, 27; oldest-living Kentucky Derby winner; won seven of eight starts in 1975 and in 1976, including the Derby and Belmont; 3-year-old champion in 1976; destroyed due to intestinal problems and kidney failure; in Lexington, Ky., Aug. 9.

Frenchy Bordagaray, 90; third baseman and outfielder on Casey Stengel's Brooklyn Dodgers of the 1930s who showed up to spring training with a mustache hoping to be the first player to sport one in more than 20 years. After a few months the Dodgers told him to shave it off, and facial hair would have to wait until Reggie Jackson arrived at Oakland spring training in 1972; played 11 seasons with five teams; singles hitter who in 1938 hit .452 (20-for-43) as a pinch-hitter with St. Louis; short stint as a minor league manager ended in suspension when he attacked an umpire midway through the 1947 season; cause of death not given; in Ventura, Calif., Apr. 13.

Bill Bowerman, 88; Oregon track coach from 1949-72 who co-founded Nike with his former student Phil Knight; coached 24 NCAA individual champions at Oregon and won four team championships; his most famous student was distance runner Steve Prefontaine; U.S. track coach at the 1972 Olympic Games; his experiments with leather, latex, glue and a waffle iron in the 1960s resulted in the modern running shoe used around the world today; of natural causes; in Fossil, Ore., Dec. 25, 1999.

John Bromwich, 80; two-time Australian Open singles champion and Davis Cup veteran; won two doubles titles and two mixed doubles titles at Wimbledon; three-time U.S. Open doubles champion; was 19-11 in singles and 20-1 in doubles Davis Cup matches from 1937-50; of a heart attack; in Melbourne, Oct. 22, 1999.

Don Budge, 84; tennis champion who used his attacking backhand stroke to sweep all four major tournaments in 1938, becoming the world's first Grand Slam champion; born John Donald Budge; won Wimbledon, U.S. Nationals and led the U.S. to its first Davis Cup title in 11 years in 1937; won six of eight tournaments he played in and had a 92-match, 14-tournament victory streak in 1938; turned pro in 1939; won Sullivan Award in 1937; AP Male Athlete of the Year 1937 and 1938; inducted into the International Tennis Hall of Fame in 1964; Tennis Magazine selected him as one of the 20 greatest players of the 20th century; injured in a car accident in Pennsylvania in December 1999; of cardiac arrest; in Scranton, Penn., Jan. 26.

Philip Burke, 65; New York sports public relations executive in the 1960s who was a publicist at Columbia University and Roosevelt Raceway, then the nation's leading harness racing track, and finally the New York Rangers; of complications following a series of surgeries for brain tumors; in Millville, Del., Aug. 23.

Philippe Chatrier, 72; past president of the French Tennis Federation and the International Tennis Federation; credited with pushing for the sport's "open" format and helped return tennis to the Olympics in 1988; Davis Cup team member for France from 1948-50 and captain from 1969-72; had Alzheimer's disease; cause of his death was not given; in Dinard, France, June 23.

Ellis Clary, 85; longtime baseball scout for the Twins from 1962-84, then the White Sox and Blue Jays; played with Washington and St. Louis; won an A.L. pennant as a reserve infielder with the St. Louis Browns in 1944; managed in the minors and was a coach in the pros from 1955-60; retired in 1993; cause of death not given; in Valdosta, Ga., June 2.

Joe Concannon, 60; sports reporter who covered the Boston Marathon, golf, the Beanpot, college football and the Olympics for the Boston Globe for more than 30 years; retired after covering the Ryder Cup in Brookline, Mass. in 1999; cause of death not given; in Boston, Feb.16.

Harry Cooper, 96; Hall of Fame golfer who won the first Vardon Trophy for the lowest average score and won 32 career PGA Tour titles; arguably the best golfer never to win a major; came close to winning a major several times, including second-place finishes at 1936 Masters and 1927 U.S. Open; nicknamed "Lighthorse" for the speed of his play; longest-serving member of the PGA of America (since 1923); teaching pro at New York's Metropolis CC for 26 years and Westchester CC until he was 93; cause of death not given; in White Plains, N.Y., Oct. 17.

Ward Cornell, 75; host of "Hockey Night in Canada" from 1959-72, when Dave Hodge replaced him; represented the Ontario government as agent general in London until 1978; returned to Canada in 1980 and was Ontario's deputy minister for culture and recreation as well as deputy housing minister; cause of death not given; in Uxbridge, Ontario, Canada, Feb. 5.

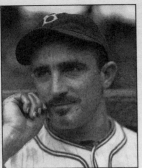

AP/Wide World Photos · NASCAR · Stephen Dunn /Allsport

Frenchy Bordagaray · **Kenny Irwin** · **Tom Landry**

Art Coulter, 92; Hall of Fame defenseman who played 11 NHL seasons with the Blackhawks and Rangers: won Stanley Cups in 1934 and 1940; retired in 1942; cause of death not given; in Mobile, Ala., Oct. 14.

(Aurele) Al Couture, 77; former welterweight boxer who holds the record for fastest knockout in boxing history; dropped Ralph Walton in 10½ seconds on Sept. 24, 1946; fought 296 professional fights and at one time was ranked sixth in the world in his division, ahead of Jake LaMotta; cause of death not given; in Glastonbury, Conn., Aug. 6.

Jim Davis, 103; motorcycling pioneer who was part of the first class inducted into the Motorcycle Hall of Fame in 1998; won more than 70 nationally sanctioned races and six national titles in 1928; a bronze sculpture of Davis sits in the lower atrium of the hall of fame museum; cause of death not given; in Daytona Beach, Fla., Feb. 6.

Mildred (Wiley) Dee, 98; bronze medallist in the high jump at the 1928 Summer Games, the first time women were allowed to compete in track and field events; in Falmouth, Mass., Feb. 7.

Joey Dunlop, 48; five-time motorcycle champion who was awarded an OBE, Officer of the Order of the British Empire, for his charity work and an MBE, or Member of the Order of the British Empire, for his motorcycling exploits; of injuries sustained in a crash during a road race; in Tallinn, Estonia, July 2.

H. Clay Earles, 86; founder, chairman of the board and CEO of Martinsville (Va.) Speedway; after a long illness; in Martinsville, Va., Nov. 16, 1999.

Tom Fears, 76; former Los Angeles Rams wideout (1948-56) whose precise button-hook routes made him one of pro football's best receivers; had 84 catches in 1950; caught three TDs in 1950 division title game; caught 73-yard pass to win 1951 title game; holds NFL record for catches in a game (18), set in 1950; career: 400 catches, 5,397 yards, 38 TDs; enshrined in Pro Football Hall of Fame in 1970; of complications from Alzheimer's disease; in Seminole, Fla., Jan. 4.

Steve Furness, 49; four-time Super Bowl-winning defensive lineman with the Pittsburgh Steelers in the 1970s; served as Steelers' assistant coach in 1992-93; of a heart attack; in Pittsburgh, Feb. 9.

Jack Gardner, 90; legendary college basketball coach who pioneered the fast-break style in the 1950s with Kansas State and then Utah during a time when many teams still relied on set shots; only coach to take two schools to the Final Four two different times (KSU in 1948,51 and Utah in 1961,66); won 486 games over 28 seasons; nicknamed "The Fox"; ranked third among active coaches in career victories when he retired in 1971; elected to Basketball Hall of Fame in 1984; died after a long illness; in Salt Lake City, Apr. 9.

William (Pop) Gates, 82; former player-coach with the Harlem Globetrotters and member of the National Basketball Hall of Fame; played pro basketball in the 1930s and 40s; charter member of NYC Basketball Hall of Fame in 1994; of heart failure; in New York, Dec. 2, 1999.

Colby Goodwin, 32; three-time national finals steer roper champion; died during the National Finals Steer Roping when his horse rolled on him after stepping on slack in his rope; of head injuries sustained in the accident; in Guthrie, Okla., Oct. 30, 1999.

Eddie Gregson, 61; California-based thoroughbred horse trainer who saddled 1982 Kentucky Derby winner Gato Del Sol; of a self-inflicted gunshot wound; in Hollywood Park, Calif., June 4.

Calvin Griffith, 87; baseball owner who moved the Washington Senators to Minnesota and created the Twins franchise; a front-page editorial in *The Minneapolis Star* called for his resignation in 1978 after he made horribly acrimonious remarks about blacks during a speech at a local Rotary meeting; sold the team to Carl Pohlad in 1984, ending 65 years of family ownership; was a Senators bat boy (1924-25), the team for which his uncle and adopted father, Clark, became a Hall of Fame pitcher; of pneumonia; in Melbourne, Fla., Oct. 20, 1999.

James Grogan, 68; U.S. figure skater who won the 1952 Olympic bronze medal and was a four-time silver medallist at consecutive world championships beginning in 1951; director of a skating school in Squaw Valley before coaching in Japan in the 1960s; had coached at Ice Castle International Training Center since 1985, which tutored stars Michelle Kwan, Lu Chen and others; inducted into the U.S. Figure Skating Association Hall of Fame in 1991; of multiple organ failure; in San Bernardino, Calif., July 2.

Jack Haley, 65; surfer who helped lead the sport through its "golden age" from the 1940s to the 1960s; won first U.S. Open of Surfing in 1959; oldest son, Jack Jr., played professional basketball; of cancer; in Seal Beach, Calif., Mar. 25.

Mitch Halpern, 33; renowned boxing referee who officiated some of boxing's biggest matches; began his career in March 1991 and went on to referee 87 championship fights and hundreds of non-title fights around the world; was in the ring when Evander Holyfield knocked out Mike Tyson for the WBA heavyweight title in 1996; was to have refereed the infamous "Bite Fight" rematch but Tyson's camp vehemently opposed and he was replaced by Mills Lane; of a self-inflicted gunshot wound; in Las Vegas, Aug. 20.

Dick Harp, 81; former player, assistant coach and head coach for the University of Kansas men's basketball team; took over for Phog Allen in 1956; had a 121-82 career record over eight seasons; won two conference titles and made two NCAA tournament appearances; one of a handful of men to appear as a player and a head coach in an NCAA championship game and the only one to do it with the same team; coached a Wilt Chamberlain-led Jayhawks team to one of the tournaments most famous final games (a triple-overtime loss to UNC in 1957); cause of death not given; in Lawrence, Kan., Mar. 18.

Molly Hatcher, 21; senior captain of the Kenyon College (Gambier, Ohio) women's swimming team which won its NCAA Div. III 17th straight national title in March 2000; died in a van accident on the way home from a meet in North Carolina; of injuries sustained in the crash; in Coshocton, Ohio, Jan. 13.

(Hubert) Sonny Hine, 69; horse trainer whose 52-year career peaked with Skip Away, horse of the year in 1998; had a knack for turning modestly priced horses like Skip Away, Big Bet, and Skip Trial into major stakes winners; trained 924 winners from 5,593 starters, and earned $28,805,820 in purses; began his training career in 1957; also trained 1981 sprint champion Guilty Conscience, Cojak, Technology, Norquestor, and Dawn Quixote; former investigator for the State Department and a fingerprint specialist for the FBI; of complications of pneumonia but had been battling cancer since 1996; in Miami, Mar. 17.

Fred Hooper, 102; Florida horse owner and breeder who won the 1945 Kentucky Derby and Wood Memorial Stakes with Hoop Jr., the first thoroughbred he ever owned; bred more than 100 stakes winners and stallions at Hooper Farms outside Ocala, Fla.; won Eclipse Award of Merit in 1991 and outstanding breeder awards in 1975 and 1982; cause of death not given; in Miami, Aug. 4.

Chuck Hull, 75; ring announcer for most of the big Las Vegas fights of the 1980s and 1984 Olympic Games; retired in 1995; cause of death not given; in Las Vegas, Feb. 15.

Kenny Irwin, 30; Winston Cup series driver in his third full season; killed during qualifying at New Hampshire International Raceway; in his first season with Felix Sabates' Team SABCO, replacing Joe Nemechek in the No. 42 car; at the time of his death was 28th in points in 2000 with one top-five and one top-10 finish in 17 starts in 2000; best season was 1999 with two top-five finishes, six top-10s and a career-best third place at the Daytona 500; picked to drive the Robert Yates No. 28 Ford in 1998 and won rookie of the year honors; first rookie to top $1 million mark; Craftsman Truck Series rookie of the year in 1997; of multiple injuries sustained in the crash; in Loudon, N.H., July 7.

Stephan Johnson, 31; junior middleweight boxer knocked out by Paul Vaden in the 10th round of a USBA title fight on Nov. 20, 1999; turned professional in 1987 and had a 27-8-1 record; of a brain injury sustained in the ring; in Atlantic City, N.J., Dec. 6, 1999.

(Robert) Trent Jones Sr., 93; innovative golf course architect who designed or remodeled more than 500 courses, including Augusta National, Oakland Hills and Hazeltine National; had a reputation for designing difficult holes and entire courses that frequently drew huge bunkers, creeks, and lakes into play; his courses exist in 45 states and 35 foreign countries and have hosted 79 national championships, including 21 U.S. Opens and 12 PGA Championships; first significant work was his collaboration with Bobby Jones (no relation) to create Peachtree GC in Atlanta in 1948; created putting green at the White House for Dwight Eisenhower and a hole at Camp David, the president's weekend retreat; first architect inducted into the World Golf Hall of Fame in 1987; of a long illness that resulted from a stroke; in Fort Lauderdale, Fla., June 14.

Ted Jones, 90; boat designer whose work revolutionized hydroplane racing; designed six national championship boats, including Slo-Mo-Shun IV; won American Power Boat Association Gold Cup in 1950; race course on Lake Washington is named after him; of pneumonia; in Des Moines, Jan. 10.

Ray Katt, 72; major league catcher with N.Y. Giants and St. Louis Cardinals (1952-59); won World Series title with N.Y. in 1954; coached St. Louis and Cleveland before retiring in 1963; coached Texas Lutheran from 1971-92, compiling a 502-362-2 record; of lymphoma; in New Braunfels, Texas, Oct. 20, 1999.

Glen Keeley, 30; world-class bull rider who was killed after being stepped on by a bull; listed ninth in the Professional Bull Rider's rankings with $33,752 in 2000 earnings at the time of his death; Canadian boys' steer riding champion (1983) and bull-riding champion (1989); of abdominal injuries while undergoing surgery; in Albuquerque, N.M., Mar. 24.

Larry Kelley, 85; second football player to win the Heisman Trophy (1936); All-American end and senior captain at Yale; his 49-yard touchdown reception in 1934 gave Yale a 7-0 victory, snapping Princeton's 15-game winning streak; sold his trophy at auction in 1999 for $328,110 to raise money for his nieces and nephews; elected to the National Football Foundation and College Football Hall of Fame in 1969; of a self-inflicted gunshot wound; in Hightstown, N.J., June 27.

Ron King, 74; former professional cyclist who died minutes after completing his leg of the Olympic torch relay in his hometown northwest of Sydney; of a heart attack; in Muswellbrook, Australia, Aug. 31.

Don Klosterman, 70; pro football executive who helped build the American Football League into a rival of the NFL in the 1960s and 70s; credited with outbidding the NFL for players like Lance Alworth, Jack Kemp (Chargers), Bobby Bell and Buck Buchanan (Chiefs); won Super Bowl as GM with Colts in 1970; was an executive with the Oilers and L.A. Rams; signed BYU quarterback Steve Young to the L.A. Express of the USFL in 1984; joined with Bill Walsh in an unsuccessful bid to bring football back to Los Angeles in 1995; college football's leading passer in 1951 and drafted by the Browns; quarterbacked the CFL's Calgary Stampeders in 1950s; of a heart attack; in Los Angeles, June 7.

Vladimir Kondrashin, 70; coach of the U.S.S.R. men's basketball team that won a disputed gold medal victory over the United States in 1972; won a world championship (1974), European championship (1971) and a bronze medal at the 1976 Olympics; cause of death not given; in St. Petersburg, Russia, Dec. 23, 1999.

(George) Whitey Kurowski, 81; St. Louis Cardinals third baseman whose ninth inning home run in Game 5 of the 1942 World Series beat the Yankees for the first time in nine trips to the series (since 1926) and earned St. Louis its fourth world championship; four-time N.L. All-Star; twice led N.L. third basemen in fielding; of complications from a stroke; in Shillington, Penn., Dec. 9, 1999.

Tom Landry, 75; Dallas Cowboys coach who led "America's Team" to five Super Bowl appearances and is best remembered for pacing the Texas Stadium sidelines in a suit and fedora hat; coached the Cowboys for their first 29 years beginning in 1960 when the team was 0-11-1; had streak of 20 consecutive winning seasons (1966-85); won 13 division titles and two Super Bowl titles (1972,78); at the time of his death Don Shula (347) and George Halas (324) were the only coaches with more than his 270 NFL victories; college star at the University of Texas and defensive back/defensive coach for the N.Y. Giants in the 1950s; his early coaching staffs included future NFL coaches Dan Reeves and Mike Ditka; inducted into Pro Football Hall of Fame in 1990 and the Cowboys' Ring of Honor in 1993; of leukemia; in Dallas, Feb. 12.

Fred Lane, 24; Carolina Panthers all-time leading rusher; won starting running back position in 1997 and led the team in rushing that season and in 1998; traded to Indianapolis in April 2000 for LB Spencer Reid; career: 502 carries, 2,001 yards rushing, 13 TDs; attended Lane College (no relation) in Jackson, Tenn.; finished second for the Division II rushing title as a junior; of gun shot wounds suffered during a domestic dispute with his wife; in Charlotte, N.C., July 6.

Serge Lang, 79; French journalist who created skiing's World Cup circuit in 1967, a format of competition that has since been adopted by countless other sports; of a heart attack; in Sternerberg, France, Nov. 21, 1999.

Henry Laskau, 83; race walker who fled Nazi Germany for United States where he dominated the sport in the 1940s and 50s; a three-time Olympian (1948,52,56); won 42 national titles; during an 11-year span he set five national records and for nine of those years was unbeaten by any American walker; retired in 1957 and served as an official, promoter, coach and national and international committee member; became second walker inducted into National Track & Field Hall of Fame in 1997; suffered from Alzheimer's disease; cause of death not given; in Coconut Creek, Fla., May 7.

Lucien Laurin, 88; Hall of Fame trainer who won five of six Triple Crown races with Riva Ridge and Secretariat in 1972 and 1973; began training in 1942 and had 36 stakes winners; of complications from hip surgery; in Miami, June 26.

Bob Lemon, 79; brilliant all-around baseball player who rose to stardom as a right-handed pitcher with the Cleveland Indians and later managed the N.Y. Yankees to a World Series title; 20-game winner seven times over a nine-year span (1948-56); went 23-7 in 1954 when he combined with Bob Feller, Early Wynn and Mike Garcia to form one of baseball's best rotations ever; pitched no-hitter at Detroit (6/30/48); won two games in 1948 World Series; career: 207-128, 3.23 ERA; remarkable .284 average as a pinch-hitter; hit 37 career HRs; seven-time All-Star; retired in 1958; managed Kansas City and Chicago-AL in the 1970s before taking over the Yankees after Billy Martin resigned on July 25, 1978; beat Boston in one-game playoff in 1978 en route to the A.L. pennant and World Series title; returned to coach Yankees in 1981 and won A.L. pennant; inducted into National Baseball Hall of Fame in 1976; remained on Yankees payroll as a scout and advisor up until his death; cause of death not given; in Long Beach, Calif., Jan. 11.

Donald Liddle, 75; N.Y. Giants pitcher who threw the pitch that Cleveland's Vic Wertz drove 460 feet and Willie Mays turned into his famous over-the-shoulder catch during Game 1 of the 1954 World Series at New York's Polo Grounds; appeared in 117 games with Milwaukee, N.Y. Giants, and St. Louis; retired in 1958; of lung cancer; in Mount Carmel, Ill., June 5.

Alice Lord Landon, 98; swimming and diving pioneer who was an active contributor to the sport; competed in platform diving at 1920 Olympics; Olympic official 1924-36; led American procession at 1984 Summer Games; carried the torch before the 1996 Games; inducted into the International Swimming Hall of Fame in 1993; cause of death not given; in Ormond Beach, Fla., July 13.

Jeff MacNelly, 52; Pulitzer Prize-winning cartoonist whose elaborate comic strips and political cartoons were syndicated nationally; won Pulitzer in 1972, 1978 and 1985; debuted the strip "Shoe" in 1977; joined the Chicago Tribune staff in 1982; his illustrations appeared in the Information Please Sports Almanac from 1991-94; of lymphoma; in Baltimore, June 8.

Sir Stanley Matthews, 85; British soccer star of the 1930s, 40s and 50s who in 1965 became the first in his sport to be knighted; nicknamed "Wizard of Dribble" for his ball-handling skills and "First Gentleman of Soccer" for his sportsmanship; won first European Football Player of the Year Award (1956); set up the last three goals in Blackpool's 4-3 victory over the Bolton Wanderers in the 1953 Football Association Cup final, a game remembered as "The Matthews Final"; made a Commander of the Order of the British Empire (1957); was reprimanded in 1968, while managing, for paying unauthorized signing bonuses to new players and giving them incentive payments for victories; cause of death not given; in Newcastle-Under-Lyme, England, Feb. 23.

Conrad McRae, 29; former Syracuse basketball center (1989-93) who ranked sixth in school history in all-time shot blocking at the time of his death; second-round pick of Washington in 1993; played CBA and later was an all-star on teams in Turkey and Italy; died while practicing with the Orlando Magic's summer league team; cause of death was not given; in Irvine, Calif., July 10.

Percy McRae, 65; retired New York letter carrier who sang the national anthem at the Chicago Cubs game on July 31; suffered a heart attack during the ninth inning and later died; in Chicago, July 31.

Steve McCrory, 36; Olympic boxing gold medalist in the flyweight division at the 1984 Games; brother Milton won welterweight world championship; Detroit native whose success brought fame to the Kronk Gym Boxing team; after a long illness; in Detroit, Aug. 1.

Bobb McKittrick, 64; San Francisco 49ers offensive line coach who worked with five Super Bowl-winning teams over 21 years; coaching career began as an assistant at his alma mater, Oregon St. in 1961; coached with UCLA, L.A. Rams, San Diego Chargers; joined Bill Walsh's 49ers' staff in 1979; tough character known for his military training with players; coached nine Pro Bowl linemen, including Randy Cross and Guy McIntyre; diagnosed with bile duct cancer in January 1999; honored during halftime tribute on Oct. 3, 1999; of cancer; in Stanford, Calif., Mar. 15.

Greg Moore, 24; race car driver from Canada killed during the final CART Fed-Ex Series race of the 1999 season; won five career CART races; became youngest driver to win a CART race in 1997; finished fifth in drivers' standings in 1998; of head injuries sustained in the crash; in Fontana, Calif., Oct. 31, 1999.

Joe Mullaney, 75; former L.A. Lakers and Providence College basketball coach; coached Lakers for two seasons beginning in 1969 and coached the Friars from 1955-69 and 1981-85; led Providence to two NIT championships (1961,63); also coached Norwich University, Brown University and several ABA teams; coached former Georgetown coach John Thompson at Providence; won national championship as a player with Holy Cross in 1947; of cancer; in North Providence, R.I., Mar. 8.

Bill Musselman, 59; Portland Trailblazers assistant coach and former head coach in Cleveland and Minnesota; only man to ever have been a head coach in four U.S. pro basketball leagues (NBA, CBA, ABA and WBA); won four consecutive CBA championships (1985-88); had a 78-180 NBA coaching record over three seasons; won 233 college games at Ashland, Minnesota and South Alabama; of complications from amyloidosis, a disease that affects the liver; in Rochester, Minn., May 5.

George Musso, 90; two-way star for the Chicago Bears in the 1930s and 40s and member of the Pro Football Hall of Fame; nicknamed "Moose"; first player to win all-NFL honors at two positions—tackle (1935) and guard (1937); at Milikin College (Decatur, Ill.) in the 1930s he faced two future U.S. presidents: Eureka College guard Ronald Reagan and Michigan center Gerald Ford; cause of death not given; in Chicago, Sept. 5.

AP/Wide World Photos

Alice Lord Landon

NASCAR

Adam Petty

Charlotte Hornets

Bobby Phills

Primo Nebiolo, 76; president of the International Amateur Athletic Federation (IAAF) since 1981; responsible for creating the world championships and organizing sponsorship and television coverage; no one except IOC president Juan Antonio Samaranch had more influence in the world of international sports at the time of his death; member of the International Olympic Committee; of a heart attack; in Rome, Nov. 7, 1999.

Harry Newman, 90; All-American triple-threat tailback who led Michigan to an undefeated season in 1932 and as a rookie QB led the Giants to the NFL's first title game in 1933; threw the first pass in an NFL title game, but lost to the Bears, 23-21, at Wrigley Field; won NFL title in 1934; lost only one game at Michigan where he ran, passed, kicked and played safety; won the Douglas Fairbanks Trophy (the forerunner of the Heisman Trophy) in 1932; played one season with the Brooklyn Tigers of the AFL and retired in 1937; member of the College Football Hall of Fame; cause of death not given; in Las Vegas, May 2.

Leo Nomellini, 76; two-way lineman who played 14 pro seasons with the San Francisco 49ers and is a member of the Pro Football Hall of Fame; played in 10 Pro Bowl games; two-time All-American at the University of Minnesota; first-ever draft pick of the 49ers in 1950; performed as a pro wrestler during the offseason; of complications of a stroke; in Stanford, Calif., Oct. 17.

Max Patkin, 79; the "Clown Prince of Baseball," whose zany clowning delighted crowds at minor league baseball games for over 50 years; West Philadelphia native and WWII navy veteran; hired as a comic coach by Cleveland owner Bill Veeck who wanted to boost attendance; played himself in 1988 film "Bull Durham"; of an aneurysm; in Paoli, Penn., Oct. 28, 1999.

Allen Paulson, 78; thoroughbred horse owner and breeder whose years of success overseeing Brookside Farm in Kentucky were highlighted by thoroughbred superstar, Cigar; holds Breeders' Cup record for starters (32) and earnings ($7,570,000); other champion horses: Ajina, Arazi, Blushing John, Eliza, Escena, Estrapade, and Theatrical; never won a Triple Crown race; won Eclipse Awards for owner (1995-96), breeder (1993) and the Award of Merit (1996); made his fortune in aerospace design and production; chairman and CEO of Gulfstream Aerospace Corp.; accomplished pilot who set 24 world speed records; named most of his race horses for aeronautical checkpoints; Georgia Southern University's football stadium is named after him; of cancer; in La Jolla, Calif., July 19.

Edie Payne, 94; Australia's oldest living Olympian and the first to represent her country at a track and field event at 1928 Games; cut ribbon to officially open the Olympic Village in Sydney and attended opening ceremonies; cause of her death was not given; in Sydney, Oct. 8.

Walter Payton, 45; NFL's all-time leading rusher with 16,726 yards gained over 13 seasons with the Chicago Bears; nicknamed "Sweetness" for both his kindly demeanor with teammates and fans plus the remarkable grace he maintained for such an explosive tailback; played in a club-record 184 straight games for the Bears from 1975-87; scored 125 career touchdowns (110 rushing); had 77 games of 100 yards or more; gained 1,000 yards or more in 10 seasons; rushed for a then-NFL single-game record 275 yards against Minnesota in 1977; won 1977 and 1985 MVP award; gained 2,034 yards from scrimmage in 1985 en route to a Super Bowl title with Chicago; named to nine Pro Bowls; held seven NFL and 28 Bears records at the time of his death; passed Jim Brown's career rushing mark in 1984; elected to Pro Football Hall of Fame in 1993; member of Bears board of directors, co-owner of CART racing team; minority owner of Walter Payton power equipment and owner of Walter Payton Roundhouse Complex; disclosed he was suffering from a rare liver disease in February 1999; of cancer; in Lake Forest, Ill., Nov. 1, 1999.

Adam Petty, 19; a rising star on the NASCAR Winston Cup circuit who died in a practice-run crash at New Hampshire International Speedway; along with his great-grandfather, Lee, grandfather, Richard, and father, Kyle, represented four generations of NASCAR drivers; was in the midst of his first full season on the Busch Grand National series; made his Winston Cup series debut on April 9; of head trauma sustained in the accident; in Loudon, N.H., May 12.

Lee Petty, 86; stock car racing's first superstar of the 1940s and 50s and patriarch of the first family of NASCAR; won inaugural Daytona 500 in a car bearing his trademark #42; three-time Grand National champion, (now Winston Cup series); never finished lower than sixth in 12 Grand National seasons; compiled 55 career wins, seventh all-time; best season was 1959, where he finished 41 of 49 events, won 12 and amassed an unprecedented $46,000 in earnings; father of Winston Cup great Richard Petty, grandfather of Kyle Petty and great-grandfather of Adam Petty; a serious crash during qualifying at Daytona in 1961 left him with a punctured lung and broken leg; raced occasionally after the crash but retired from racing in 1964; voted mechanic of the year in 1950 and most popular driver in 1953 and 1954; inducted into Motorsports Hall of Fame in 1996; underwent surgery for a stomach aneurysm weeks before his death; cause of death not given; in Greensboro, N.C., Apr. 5.

Bobby Phills, 30; Charlotte Hornets shooting guard/small forward recognized as the team's leader and best defender on the court as well as an active volunteer off it; drafted and released by Milwaukee in 1991; after a stint in CBA, signed a free-agent contract with Cleveland of the NBA and played six seasons with the Cavs; signed free-agent deal with Charlotte before 1997-98 season; career: 11.0 ppg, 3.1 rpg, 2.7 apg; finalist for the NBA's sportsmanship award in 1998; founded the Bobby Phills Educational Foundation; of injuries sustained in a car accident that occurred after he left a team practice; in Charlotte, N.C., Jan. 12.

Denny Price, 62; United States Basketball League co-coach and father of former NBA star Mark and current NBA player Brent; former assistant with the Phoenix Suns; of a heart attack during a pickup game with his sons; in Enid, Okla., July 7.

Nicole Reinhart, 24; two-time U.S. national track cycling champion killed in an accident during the final lap of the BMC Tour of Arlington (Mass.); nine-time junior national champion; won 15 races in 2000 for the Saturn Cycling Team, which is ranked number one in the world; of injuries sustained in the accident; in Cambridge, Mass., Sept. 17.

Maurice (Rocket) Richard, 78; explosive right-winger who won eight Stanley Cups with the Montreal Canadiens and was nothing short of a national hero in his native Canada; blazing speed earned him the nickname "Rocket" when he joined the NHL in 1942; joined C Elmer Lach and LW Toe Blake to form Montreal's "Punch Line" in 1943-44; played all 18 NHL seasons (1942-60) with Montreal; first player to score 500 career goals; first to score 50 goals in a season (in 50 games, 1944-45); eight-time NHL All-Star; league MVP in 1947; led Montreal to five straight Stanley Cups from 1956-60; scored five goals and had three assists, setting a then-NHL record for points in a game (8) against Detroit on Dec. 28, 1944; scored 82 career playoff goals; holds NHL record for career playoff overtime goals (6); caused a riot in Montreal when he was suspended with three games remaining in the 1954-55 season for punching an official; had five-year waiting period waived and elected to Hockey Hall of Fame in 1961; older brother of Henri; of abdominal cancer; in Montreal, May 27.

Aurelio Rodriguez, 52; sure-handed third baseman who played most of his 17-year career with the Detroit Tigers and won a Gold Glove in 1976; played on seven major league teams, beginning with the Angels in 1967; hit .417 in only World Series appearance with Yankees in 1981; played in Mexican league until 1987; Cleveland Indians' minor league coach in 1988; was current Arizona Diamondbacks Rookie League hitting instructor; of injuries sustained when he was struck by a car; in Detroit, Sept. 23.

Tony Roper, 35; Craftsman Truck Series driver killed in a crash during a race at Texas Motor Speedway; made his first start in the truck series during his debut season in 1995; winless in 60 career races; had one top-five finish and eight top-10 efforts; best finish was a second in July 1998 at Indianapolis Raceway Park; father Dean is a former race car driver; of a serious neck injury sustained in the crash; in Ft. Worth, Texas, Oct. 13.

(Matthew) Mack Robinson, 88; silver medallist in the 200-meter race at the 1936 Summer Games and older brother of baseball Hall of Famer Jackie Robinson; lost 200m to Jesse Owens in Berlin by 0.4 seconds; set national junior college records in the 100, 200, and long jump; helped carry the Olympic flag into Los Angeles Memorial Coliseum in 1984; the Pasadena Robinson Memorial, honoring both brothers, was dedicated in 1997; of diabetes complications, kidney failure, and pneumonia; in Pasadena, Calif., Mar. 12.

Tobin Rote, 72; Hall of Fame quarterback who became a star when he replaced Bobby Layne in 1957 and led the Detroit Lions to their last NFL championship; played for Green Bay from 1950-56; led the league in touchdown passes, passing yards, and TDs in 1955; traded to Detroit in 1957 after the Packers drafted Bart Starr in 1956; played for Toronto of the CFL from 1960-62 and broke all of the team's passing records; played for San Diego and Denver of the AFL and retired after the 1966 season; of a heart attack; in Saginaw, Mich., June 27.

Byrum (By) Saam, 85; Philadelphia radio broadcaster who called more than 8,000 baseball games over 38 years for the Phillies and A's; began broadcasting college football in 1937 and baseball a year later; retired in 1975; won Ford Frick Award in 1990; after a stroke; in Philadelphia, Jan. 16.

Fred Saigh Jr., 94; multi-millionaire and former St. Louis Cardinals owner whose decision to sell the team in 1953 to Anheuser-Busch for $3.75 million kept the team in St. Louis; cause of death not given; in St. Louis, Dec. 29, 1999.

Ernest L. (Ernie) Samuel, 69; a giant in the Canadian thoroughbred racing industry who owned Sam-Son Farm and held numerous key positions in the industry; won Eclipse Award as outstanding owner and Sovereign Awards Man of the Year in 1991; longtime vice president on Ontario Jockey Club's board of directors; cause of death not given; in Oakville, Ontario, Canada, May 25.

Sandra Schmirler, 36; curler who helped Canada win a team gold in 1998 Games, the first time it appeared as a medal sport; won three Canadian championships and three world championships in the 1990s; of cancer; in Regina, Saskatchewan, Canada, Mar. 2.

Alfred Schwarzmann, 87; German Olympic gymnast; won three gold medals and two bronze at the 1936 Games and won one a silver 16 years later, at age 40, for West Germany at the Helsinki Games; after a long illness; in Goslar, Germany, Mar. 11.

Malik Sealy, 30; Minnesota Timberwolves guard/forward and former college standout at St. John's who died in an auto accident after leaving teammate Kevin Garnett's birthday party; played eight seasons in the NBA with Indiana, L.A. Clippers, and Detroit before signing with Minnesota in January 1999; first-round draft pick of Indiana in 1992; second-leading career scorer in St. John's history behind Chris Mullin; owned Malik Sealy XXI Inc., a clothing line; father, Sidney, was a bodyguard for Malcolm X; of head and chest injuries sustained in the crash; in St. Louis Park, Minn., May 20.

William Simon, 72; USOC president from 1981-84 and former Treasury secretary and energy expert in President Richard Nixon's administration; USOC vice president and treasurer (1976-80); gave influential speech in support of President Carter's boycott of the 1980 Summer Games; first chairman of the U.S. Olympic Foundation, the financial source for American amateur sports, and a member of the board of trustees until his death; inducted into U.S. Olympic Hall of Fame in 1991; won 1999 Douglas MacArthur Award for his lifetime contributions to the U.S. Olympic movement; headed the Federal Energy Office in 1973; replaced George Shultz as Treasury secretary in 1974; of complications from lung disease; in Santa Barbara, Calif., June 3.

Paul Smith, 54; defensive lineman for the Denver Broncos and member of their famed "Orange Crush" defense; inducted into team's Ring of Fame in 1986; Pro Bowler in 1972 and 1973, posting 11 sacks both seasons; played final two seasons with Washington; of pancreatic cancer; in Aurora, Colo., Mar. 14.

Karsten Solheim, 88; creator of the Ping golf clubs whose popular brand of putters have been used to win more than 1,800 professional events around the world; sponsor of the Solheim Cup, women's golf's answer to the Ryder Cup; won Ernie Sabayrac Award from the PGA of America for his contributions to golf; founder of Karsten Manufacturing Corp. and CEO until 1995; of complications from Parkinson's disease; in Phoenix, Ariz., Feb. 16.

Lido Starelli, 79; San Francisco 49ers No. 1 fan who attended every home game starting Sept. 1, 1946 except for the day his father died; honored in 1998 and rewarded with a trip to the Pro Football Hall of Fame; very superstitious, he always took a city bus to the game, entered the park through the same gate and handed his ticket to the same employee; of cancer; in San Francisco, Mar. 26.

(Aeriwentha) Mae Faggs Starr, 67; Olympic sprinter who participated in three games and won a gold medal as a member of the U.S. women's 400-meter relay team in 1952 Games; competed in London in 1948 as a 16-year-old, won a bronze in 1956; became teacher and administrator in the Cincinnati school system; of cancer; in Cincinnati, Jan. 27.

Clyde Sukeforth, 98; Brooklyn Dodgers scout and manager who scouted and signed baseball's first black player, Jackie Robinson; was the only other person in the room when Dodgers' president Branch Rickey told Robinson of his plans to sign him in Montreal in 1946; managed the Dodgers for two games in 1947, replacing Leo Durocher who was suspended by the league; remained a Dodger coach and in 1951 was in the bullpen when manager Charlie Dressen needed a reliever to face the Giants' Bobby Thomson in the ninth inning of the decisive third game of the N.L. pennant playoff. He passed over Carl Erskine and sent in Ralph Branca, who gave up Thomson's "shot heard 'round the world"; cause of death not given; in Waldoboro, Maine, Sept. 3.

Karl Sweetan, 57; NFL quarterback in the 1960s and 70s who was accused of orchestrating a scheme to sell copies of an L.A. Rams playbook to an opponent in 1972; first-round draft pick of Detroit in 1965; tied NFL record by throwing a 99-yard touchdown pass to Pat Studstill in 1966; also played for New Orleans and Los Angeles; along with his cousin, was charged with wire fraud and interstate transportation of stolen property and arrested by the FBI after Saints coach J.D. Roberts notified the league that Sweetan wanted to sell him a L.A. Rams playbook; indictments were never sought because the value of the playbooks were estimated at less than that would make it a federal crime; of complications of vascular surgery; in Las Vegas, July 2.

Derrick Thomas, 33; nine-time Pro Bowl linebacker for the Kansas City Chiefs who was one of the NFL's most feared pass-rushers and one of the organization's greatest players; ninth on the all-time NFL sack list (126½) at the time of his death; set single game sack record in 1990, sacking Seattle's Dave Krieg seven times; small for his position, Thomas was effective due to a surprisingly quick first step and blazing speed; played 11 seasons in the NFL; had 558 career tackles and 45 forced fumbles; holds team records for sacks, safeties and fumble recoveries; named Chiefs MVP in 1991 and 1994; won league sack title in 1990; received the NFL's two most prestigious humanitarian awards: NFL Man of the Year (1993) and Byron "Whizzer" White Humanitarian Award (1995); consensus defensive player of the year in 1989 after being drafted fourth overall by Kansas City; All-American at Alabama where he set a career records for sacks (52); a car accident on Jan. 23 left him paralyzed from the chest down; of a massive blood clot while in the hospital recovering from surgery; in Miami, Feb. 8.

Duane Thomas, 39; former WBC super welterweight champion; won vacated title by beating John Mugabi; shot to death outside a department store; in Detroit, June 13.

Herb Thomas, 77; NASCAR pioneer who won the Grand National Racing (now Winston Cup) championship in 1951 and 1953; ranks 12th on the career victory list with 48 wins in 230 starts; won Southern 500 three times in the 1950s; inducted in International Motorsports Hall of Fame in 1994; of a heart attack; in Sanford, N.C., Aug. 9.

Eric Turner, 31; Oakland Raiders defensive back who played nine seasons in the NFL following a remarkable college career at UCLA; second pick overall (by Cleveland) in 1991, the highest draft position for a defensive back in league history; played six seasons with Cleveland/Baltimore before signing with Oakland before the 1997 season; tied for league lead in interceptions (9) in 1994; named to Pro Bowl in 1994, 1996; recorded 30 career interceptions and 789 tackles in the NFL; earned All-America honors at UCLA where he ranks fourth in career interceptions and tackles; of complications of abdominal cancer; in Thousand Oaks, Calif., May 28.

Harry Usher, 61; attorney and former executive vice president and general manager of the 1984 Olympic Summer Games; teamed with Peter Ueberroth to successfully raise money and organize the world's first privately funded Olympics; second and last commissioner of the United States Football League; of a heart attack; in Secaucus, N.J., June 22.

Victor Valle, 82; boxing trainer who guided heavyweight Gerry Cooney and others; advocate of boxing safety, he was instrumental in reducing championship fights from 15 to 12 rounds; of heart failure; in New York City, Dec. 24, 1999.

Alfred Gwynne Vanderbilt, 87; owner of four Eclipse Award-winning horses and former chairman of the New York Racing Authority; top-earning U.S. owner in 1935 and 1953; owned Discovery in the 1930s, 1954 Horse of the Year Native Dancer, Bed O' Roses and Next Move; cause of death not given; in Mill Neck, N.Y., Nov. 12, 1999.

Robert Waggenhoffer, 39; world professional figure skating champion and silver medallist in the 1982 U.S. nationals; only U.S. skater to be the junior champion in singles and pairs in the same year; won 33 national and international medals during a 26-year amateur and professional career; of AIDS; in Torrance, Calif., Dec. 13, 1999.

Stan Watts, 88; Hall of Fame men's basketball coach at BYU (1949-72) who led the Cougars to 372 career victories and eight conference championships; finished fourth in the 1951 NCAA tournament, the school's best finish; past president of the National Association of Basketball Coaches; BYU athletic director 1972-76; of heart failure; in Provo, Utah, April 6.

Arnie Weinmeister, 77; outstanding defensive tackle who starred on N.Y. Giants teams of the 1950s; career began with N.Y. Yankees of the All-America Football Conference in 1948; joined the NFL's Giants two years later and appeared in three Pro Bowls from 1950-53; elected to Pro Football Hall of Fame in 1984; director and vice president of the 400,000-member Western Conference of Teamsters in the late 1980s and early 90s; of congestive heart failure; in Seattle, June 28.

Marvin Wood, 71; coach of the Milan High School basketball team that won the 1954 Indiana state championship and inspired the movie "Hoosiers"; coached Milan for just two seasons, reaching the state finals in 1953 and upsetting Muncie Central in the 1954 state title game; actor Gene Hackman played a Wood-inspired character in "Hoosiers"; of bone cancer; in Mishawaka, Ind., Oct. 13, 1999.

RESEARCH MATERIAL

Many sources were used in the gathering of information for this almanac. Day to day material was almost always found in copies of *USA Today*, *The Boston Globe*, and *The New York Times* or online at various World Wide Web addresses (see below).

Several weekly and bi-weekly periodicals were also used in the past year's pursuit of facts and figures, among them— *Baseball America*, *International Boxing Digest*, *ESPN the Magazine*, *FIFA News* (Soccer), *The Hockey News*, *The NCAA News*, *On Track*, *Soccer America*, *Sports Illustrated*, *The Sporting News*, *Street & Smith's Sports Business Journal*,*Track & Field News*, and *USA Today Baseball Weekly*.

In addition, the following books provided background material for one or more chapters of the almanac.

Arenas & Ballparks

The Ballparks, by Bill Shannon and George Kalinsky; Hawthorn Books, Inc. (1975); New York.

Diamonds, by Michael Gershman; Houghton Mifflin Co. (1993); Boston.

Green Cathedrals (Revised Edition), by Philip Lowry; Addison-Wesley Publishing Co. (1992); Reading, Mass.

The NFL's Encyclopedic History of Professional Football, Macmillan Publishing Co. (1977); New York.

Take Me Out to the Ballpark, by Lowell Reidenbaugh; The Sporting News Publishing Co. (1983); St. Louis.

24 Seconds to Shoot (An Informal History of the NBA), by Leonard Koppett; Macmillan Publishing Co. (1968); New York.

Auto Racing

Indy: 75 Years of Racing's Greatest Spectacle, by Rich Taylor; St. Martin's Press (1991); New York.

2000 CART FedEx Championship Series Media Guide; Championship Auto Racing Teams; Troy, Mich.

2000 Pep Boys Indy Racing League Media Guide, by IMS Publications; Indianapolis.

2000 Winston Cup Media Guide, compiled and edited by Sports Marketing Enterprises; NASCAR Winston Cup Series; Winston-Salem, N.C.

Marlboro Grand Prix Guide, 1950-99 (2000 Edition), compiled by Jacques Deschenaux and Claude Michele Deschenaux; Charles Stewart & Company Ltd; Brentford, England.

NASCAR Online, produced by Starwave Corp. and ESPN Inc., http://www.nascar.com

CART Online, maintained by CART and Quokkasports, http://www.cart.com

Baseball

The All-Star Game (A Pictorial History, 1933 to Present), by Donald Honig; The Sporting News Publishing Co. (1987); St. Louis.

2000 American League Red Book, published by The Sporting News Publishing Co.; St. Louis.

The Baseball Chronology, edited by James Charlton; Macmillian Publishing Co. (1991); New York.

The Baseball Encyclopedia (Ninth Edition), editorial director, Rick Wolff; Macmillan Publishing Co. (1993); New York.

The Complete 2000 Baseball Record Book, edited by Craig Carter; The Sporting News Publishing Co.; St. Louis.

2000 National League Green Book, published by The Sporting News Publishing Co.; St. Louis.

The Scrapbook History of Baseball by Jordan Deutsch, Richard Cohen, Roland Johnson and David Neft; Bobbs-Merrill Company, Inc. (1975); Indianapolis/New York.

2000 Sporting News Official Baseball Guide, edited by Craig Carter and Dave Sloan; The Sporting News Publishing Co.; St. Louis.

2000 Sporting News Official Baseball Register, edited by David Walton, John Duxbury and Brendan Roberts; The Sporting News Publishing Co.; St. Louis.

The Sports Encyclopedia: Baseball (1996 Edition), edited by David Neft and Richard Cohen; St. Martin's Press; New York.

Total Baseball (Fourth Edition), edited by John Thorn and Pete Palmer; HarperPerennial (1995); New York.

The Official Site of Major League Baseball, produced by Major League Baseball Properties, Inc., http://www.majorleaguebaseball.com

College Basketball

All the Moves (A History of College Basketball), by Neil D. Issacs; J.B. Lippincott Company (1975); New York.

College Basketball, U.S.A. (Since 1892), by John D. McCallum; Stein and Day (1978); New York.

Collegiate Basketball: Facts and Figures on the Cage Sport, by Edwin C. Caudle; The Paragon Press (1960); Montgomery, Ala.

The Encyclopedia of the NCAA Basketball Tournament, written and compiled by Jim Savage; Dell Publishing (1990); New York.

The Final Four (Reliving America's Basketball Classic), compiled by Billy Reed; Host Communications, Inc. (1988); Lexington, Ky.

2000 NCAA Final Four Records Book, compiled by Gary Johnson; edited by Marty Benson; NCAA Books; Indianapolis, Ind.

The Modern Encyclopedia of Basketball (Second Revised Edition), edited by Zander Hollander; Dolphins Books (1979); Doubleday & Company, Inc.; Garden City, N.Y.

2000 NCAA Men's Records Book, compiled by Gary Johnson and Sean Straziscar; edited by Marty Benson; NCAA Books; Indianapolis, Ind.

2000 NCAA Women's Records Book, compiled by Richard M. Campbell and Jenifer L. Scheibler; edited by Vanessa L. Abell; NCAA Books; Indianapolis, Ind.

NCAA Online, produced by National Collegiate Athletic Association. http://www.ncaa.org

Plus many 1999-2000 NCAA Division I conference guides from America East to the WAC.

Pro Basketball

The Official NBA Basketball Encyclopedia (Second Edition), edited by Alex Sachare; Villard Books (1994); New York.

1999-2000 Sporting News Official NBA Guide, edited by Mark Broussard and Craig Carter; The Sporting News Publishing Co.; St. Louis.

1999-2000 Sporting News Official NBA Register, edited by Mark Bonavita, Mark Broussard and Sean Stewart; The Sporting News Publishing Co.; St. Louis.

NBA Online, produced by NBA Media Ventures, LLC, ESPN Internet Ventures and/or Starwave Corporation. http://www.nba.com

Bowling

1995 Bowlers Journal Annual & Almanac; Luby Publishing; Chicago.

1999 PWBA Guide, Professional Women's Bowling Association; Rockford, Ill.

1999 PBA Media Guide; Professional Bowlers Association; Akron, Ohio.

PBA Online, produced by the Pro Bowlers Association, http://www.pbatour.com

PWBA Online, produced by Professional Women's Bowling Association, http://www.pwba.com

Boxing

The Boxing Record Book (1996), edited by Phill Marder; Fight Fax Inc.; Sicklerville, N.J.

The Ring 1985 Record Book & Boxing Encyclopedia, edited by Herbert G. Goldman; The Ring Publishing Corp.; New York.

The Ring: Boxing, The 20th Century, Steven Farhood, editor-in-chief; BDD Illustrated Books (1993); New York.

College Sports

1994-95 National Collegiate Championships, edited by Ted Breidenthal; NCAA Books; Overland Park, Kan.

1996-97 NAIA Championships History and Records Book; National Assn. of Intercollegiate Athletics; Tulsa, Okla.

1999-2000 National Directory of College Athletics, edited by Kevin Cleary; Collegiate Directories, Inc.; Cleveland.

NCAA Online, produced by National Collegiate Athletic Association, http://www.ncaa.org

College Football

Football: A College History, by Tom Perrin; McFarland & Company, Inc. (1987); Jefferson, N.C.

Football: Facts & Figures, by Dr. L.H. Baker; Farrar & Rinehart, Inc. (1945); New York.

Great College Football Coaches of the Twenties and Thirties, by Tim Cohane; Arlington House (1973); New Rochelle, N.Y.

1999 NCAA College Football Records Book, compiled by Richard M. Campbell, John Painter and Sean Straziscar; edited by Scott Deitch; NCAA Books; Indianapolis, Ind.

Saturday Afternoon, by Richard Whittingham; Workman Publishing Co., Inc. (1985); New York.

Saturday's America, by Dan Jenkins; Sports Illustrated Books; Little, Brown & Company (1970); Boston.

Tournament of Roses, The First 100 Years, by Joe Hendrickson; Knapp Press (1989); Los Angeles.

NCAA Online, produced by National Collegiate Athletic Association, http://www.ncaa.org

Plus numerous college football team and conference guides, especially the 1999 guides compiled by the Atlantic Coast Conference, Big 12 and Southeastern Conference.

Pro Football

1999 Canadian Football League Guide, compiled by the CFL Communications Dept.; Toronto.

The Football Encyclopedia (The Complete History of NFL Football from 1892 to the Present), compiled by David Neft and Richard Cohen; St. Martin's Press (1994); New York.

The Official NFL Encyclopedia, by Beau Riffenburgh; New American Library (1986); New York.

Official NFL 1999 Record and Fact Book, compiled by the NFL Communications Dept. and Seymour Siwoff, Elias Sports Bureau; edited by Chris McCloskey and Matt Marini; produced by NFL Properties, Inc.; Los Angeles.

The Scrapbook History of Pro Football, by Richard Cohen, Jordan Deutsch, Roland Johnson and David Neft; Bobbs-Merrill Company, Inc. (1976); Indianapolis/New York.

1999 Sporting News Football Guide, edited by Craig Carter and Dave Sloan; The Sporting News Publishing Co.; St. Louis.

1999 Sporting News Football Register, edited Brendan Roberts; The Sporting News Publishing Co.; St. Louis.

1995 Sporting News Super Bowl Book, edited by Tom Dienhart, Joe Hoppel and Dave Sloan; The Sporting News Publishing Co.; St. Louis.

NFL.Com, produced by Starwave Corp., http://www.nfl.com

CFL Online, produced by SLAM! Sports, http://www.cfl.ca

Golf

The Encyclopedia of Golf (Revised Edition), compiled by Nevin H. Gibson; A.S. Barnes and Company (1964); New York.

Guinness Golf Records: Facts and Champions, by Donald Steel; Guinness Superlatives Ltd. (1987); Middlesex, England.

The History of the PGA Tour, by Al Barkow; Doubleday (1989); New York.

The Illustrated History of Women's Golf, by Rhonda Glenn, Taylor Publishing Co. (1991); Dallas.

2000 LPGA Player Guide, produced by LPGA Communications Dept.; Ladies Professional Golf Assn. Tour; Daytona Beach, Fla.

2000 PGA Tour Guide, written and edited by Chuck Adams, James Cramer, Nelson Luis and Lee Patterson; Professional Golfers Assn. Tour; Ponte Vedra, Fla.

Official Guide of the PGA Championships; Triumph Books (1994); Chicago.

The PGA World Golf Hall of Fame Book, by Gerald Astor, Prentice Hall Press (1991); New York.

2000 Senior PGA Tour Guide, written and edited by Dave Senko, Phil Stambaugh and Joan Von Thron-Alexander; Professional Golfers Assn. Tour; Ponte Vedra, Fla.

Pro-Golf 2000, PGA European Tour Media Guide, Virginia Water, Surrey, England.

The Random House International Encyclopedia of Golf, by Malcolm Campbell; Random House (1991); New York.

USGA Record Books (1895-1959, 1960-80 and 1981-90); U.S. Golf Association; Far Hills, N.J.

LPGA.com, produced by the LPGA and Black Dog Design Co., http://www.lpga.com

PGA.com, produced by the PGA of America, http://www.pgaonline.com

PGATour.com, produced by PGA Tour Inc., http://www.pgatour.com

Hockey

Canada Cup '87: The Official History, No.1 Publications Ltd.; Toronto.

The Complete Encyclopedia of Hockey; edited by Zander Hollander; Visible Ink Press (1993); Detroit.

The Hockey Encyclopedia, by Stan Fischler and Shirley Walton Fischler; research editor, Bob Duff; Macmillan Publishing Co. (1983); New York.

Hockey Hall of Fame (The Official History of the Game and Its Greatest Stars), by Dan Diamond and Joseph Romain; Doubleday (1988); New York.

The National Hockey League, by Edward F. Dolan Jr.; W H Smith Publishers Inc. (1986); New York.

The Official National Hockey League 75th Anniversary Commemorative Book, edited by Dan Diamond; McClelland & Stewart (1991); Toronto.

1998-99 Official NHL Guide & Record Book, compiled by the NHL Public Relations Dept.; New York/Montreal/Toronto.

1999-2000 Sporting News Hockey Guide, edited by Craig Carter; The Sporting News Publishing Co.; St. Louis.

1999-2000 Sporting News Hockey Register, edited by Brendan Roberts; The Sporting News Publishing Co.; St. Louis.

The Stanley Cup, by Joseph Romain and James Duplacey; Gallery Books (1989); New York.

The Trail of the Stanley Cup (Volumns I-III), by Charles L. Coleman; Progressive Publications Inc. (1969); Sherbrooke, Quebec.

NHL.com, produced by the NHL Interactive Cyber Enterprises, http://www.nhl.com

Horse Racing

1999 NTRA Media Guide, compiled by the National Thoroughbred Racing Association; New York City

1997 American Racing Manual, compiled by the Daily Racing Form; Hightstown, N.J.

1997 Breeders' Cup Statistics; Breeders' Cup Limited; Lexington, Ky.

1996 Directory and Record Book, Thoroughbred Racing Associations of North America Inc.; Elkton, Md.

2000 Trotting and Pacing Guide, compiled and edited by John Pawlak; United States Trotting Association; Columbus, Ohio.

USTA online, produced by the USTA, http://www.ustrotting.com

NTRA online, hosted by Equibase, http://www.ntraracing.com

International Sports

Athletics: A History of Modern Track and Field 1860-1990, Men and Women), by Roberto Quercetani; Vallardi & Associati (1990); Milan, Italy.

1999 International Track & Field Annual, Association of Track & Field Statisticians; edited by Peter Matthews; SportsBooks Ltd.; Surrey, England.

Track & Field News' Little Blue Book; Metric conversion tables; From the editors of Track & Field News 1989); Los Altos, Calif.

US Ski Team online, produced by US Ski Team and Sportsline USA, http://www.usskiteam.com

Miscellaneous

The America's Cup 1851-1987 (Sailing for Supremacy), by Gary Lester and Richard Sleeman; Lester-Townsend Publishing (1986); Sydney, Australia.

The Encyclopedia of Sports (Fifth Revised Edition), by Frank G. Menke; revisions by Suzanne Treat; A.S. Barnes and Co., Inc. (1975); Cranbury, N.J.

ESPN SportsCentury, edited by Michael McCambridge; Hyperion (1999); New York, N.Y.

The Great American Sports Book, by George Gipe; Doubleday & Company, Inc. (1978); Garden City, N.Y.

The 2000 Time/Information Please Almanac, edited by Borgna Brunner; Family Education Network; Boston.

1999 Official PRCA Media Guide, edited by Steve Fleming; Professional Rodeo Cowboys Association; Colorado Springs.

The Sail Magazine Book of Sailing, by Peter Johnson; Alfred A. Knopf (1989); New York.

Ten Years of the Ironman, Triathlete Magazine; October, 1988; Santa Monica, Calif.

The Ultimate Book of Sports Lists, by Mike Meserole; DK Publishing (1999); New York.

Iditarod online, produced by the Iditarod Trail Committtee and GCI, http://www.iditarod.com

PRCA online, produced by the Pro Rodeo Cowboys Association, http://www.prorodeo.com

Olympics

All That Glitters Is Not Gold (An Irreverent Look at the Olympic Games); by William O. Johnson, Jr.; G.P. Putnam's Sons (1972); New York.

Barcelona/Albertville 1992; edited by Lisa H. Albertson; for U.S. Olympic Committee by Commemorative Publications; Salt Lake City.

Chamonix to Lillehammer (The Glory of the Olympic Winter Games); edited by Lisa H. Albertson; for U.S. Olympic Committee by Commemorative Publication (1994); Salt Lake City.

The Complete Book of the Olympics (1992 Edition); by David Wallechinsky; Little, Brown and Co.; Boston.

The Games Must Go On (Avery Brundage and the Olympic Movement), by Allen Guttmann; Columbia University Press (1984); New York.

The Golden Book of the Olympic Games, edited by Erich Kamper and Bill Mallon; Vallardi & Associati (1992); Milan, Italy.

Hitler's Games (The 1936 Olympics), by Duff Hart-Davis; Harper & Row (1986); New York/London.

An Illustrated History of the Olympics (Third Edition); by Dick Schaap; Alfred A. Knopf (1975); New York.

The Nazi Olympics, by Richard D. Mandell; Souvenir Press (1972); London.

The Official USOC Book of the 1984 Olympic Games, by Dick Schaap; Random House/ABC Sports; New York.

The Olympics: A History of the Games, by William Oscar Johnson; Oxmoor House (1992); Birmingham, Ala.

Pursuit of Excellence (The Olympic Story), by The Associated Press and Grolier; Grolier Enterprises Inc. (1979); Danbury, Conn.

The Story of the Olympic Games (776 B.C. to 1948 A.D.), by John Kieran and Arthur Daley; J.B. Lippincott Company (1948); Philadelphia/New York.

United States Olympic Books (Seven Editions): 1936 and 1948-88; U.S. Olympic Association; New York.

The USA and the Olympic Movement, produced by the USOC Information Dept.; edited by Gayle Plant; U.S. Olympic Committee (1988); Colorado Springs.

Soccer

The American Encyclopedia of Soccer, edited by Zander Hollander; Everest House Publishers (1980); New York.

The European Football Yearbook (1994-95 Edition), edited by Mike Hammond; Sports Projects Ltd; West Midlands, England.

The Guinness Book of Soccer Facts & Feats, by Jack Rollin; Guinness Superlatives Ltd. (1978); Middlesex, England.

History of Soccer's World Cup, by Michael Archer; Chartwell Books, Inc. (1978); Secaucus, N.J.

The Simplest Game, by Paul Gardner; Collier Books (1994); New York.

The Story of the World Cup, by Brian Glanville; Faber and Faber Limited (1993); London/Boston.

2000 MLS Official Media Guide, edited by the MLS Communications staff; Los Angeles.

1991-92 MSL Official Guide, Major (Indoor) Soccer League; Overland Park, Kan.

FIFA online, produced by FIFA, http://www.fifa.com

MLSnet, produced by Major League Soccer, http://mlsnet.com

Tennis

Bud Collins' Modern Encyclopedia of Tennis, edited by Bud Collins and Zander Hollander; Visible Ink Press (1994); Detroit.

The Illustrated Encyclopedia of World Tennis, by John Haylett and Richard Evans; Exeter Books (1989); New York.

Official Encyclopedia of Tennis, edited by the staff of the U.S. Lawn Tennis Assn.; Harper & Row (1972); New York.

2000 ATP Tour Player Guide, edited by Greg Sharko; Association of Tennis Professionals Tour Publications; Ponte Vedra Beach, Fla.

2000 Sanex WTA Tour Media Guide, compiled by Sanex WTA Public Relations staff; edited by Mike Broeker and Toni Woods; St. Petersburg, Fla.

ATP Tour online, produced by ATP Tour, Inc., http://www.atptour.com

WTA Tour Site, produced by the WTA Tour, http://www.wtatour.com

Who's Who

The Guiness International Who's Who of Sport, edited by Peter Mathews, Ian Buchanan and Bill Mallon; Guiness Publishing (1993); Middlesex, England.

101 Greatest Athletes of the Century, by Will Grimsley and the Associated Press Sports Staff; Bonanza Books (1987); Crown Publishers, Inc.; New York.

The New York Times Book of Sports Legends, edited by Joseph Vecchione; Simon & Schuster (1991); New York.

Superstars, by Frank Litsky; Vineyard Books, Inc. (1975); Secaucus, N.J.

A Who's Who of Sports Champions (Their Stories and Records), by Ralph Hickok; Houghton Mifflin Co. (1995); Boston.

Other Reference Books/Sites

Facts & Dates of American Sports, by Gorton Carruth & Eugene Ehrlich; Harper & Row, Publishers, Inc. (1988); New York.

Sports Market Place 1997 (January edition), edited by Kevin J. Myers; Franklin Quest Sports; Phoenix, Ariz.

The World Book Encyclopedia (1988 Edition); World Book, Inc.; Chicago.

The World Book Yearbook (Annual Supplements, 1954-95); World Book, Inc.; Chicago.

ESPN.com, produced by ESPN and Starwave Corp., http://ESPN.go.com

CBS SportsLine, produced by CBS and SportsLine USA, http://www.sportsline.com

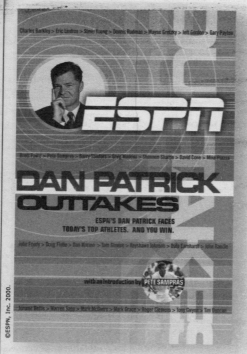